Get connected to the power of the Internet

McDougal Littell's online resources for students and parents provide motivating instruction, practice, and learning support.

Visit classzone.com for eEdition Plus Online purchasing information and a free demo

eEdition Plus ONLINE

This online version of the text encourages students to explore American history through interactive features.

- Animated maps and infographics
- Onscreen notetaking
- Links to online test practice

classzone.com

With a click of the mouse, students gain immediate access to this companion Web site to *The Americans.*

- Links correlated to the text
- Web Research Guide
- Self-scoring quizzes
- Interactive games and activities
- Links to current events
- Test practice

Now it all clicks!™

McDougal Littell

McDougal Littell

The AMERICANS

Reconstruction to the 21st Century

"The genius of America lies in its capacity to forge a single nation from peoples of remarkably diverse racial, religious, and ethnic origins. . . . The American identity will never be fixed and final; it will always be in the making."

Arthur M. Schlesinger, Jr.

MARTIN LUTHER KING, JR., *page 706*
Baptist minister and civil rights leader

MAYA LIN, *page 760*
Designer of the Vietnam Veterans Memorial

BARBARA C. JORDAN
page 802
United States representative from Texas

GERDA WEISSMANN KLEIN
page 542
Holocaust survivor

CÉSAR CHÁVEZ
page 770
Political organizer

KLIN D. ROOSEVELT
9
nd president of
tates

Gerald A. Danzer

J. Jorge Klor de Alva

Larry S. Krieger

Louis E. Wilson

Nancy Woloch

BEN NIGHTHORSE CAMPBELL, *page 771*
United States senator from Colorado

QUEEN LILIUOKALANI, *page 342*
Queen of Hawaii

LYNDON B. JOHNSON
page 687
Thirty-sixth president of the United States

SANDRA DAY O'CONNOR
page 836
United States Supreme Court justice

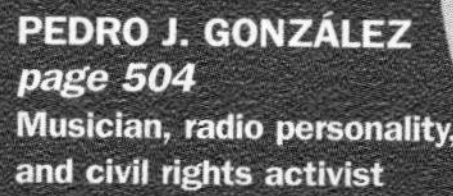

PEDRO J. GONZÁLEZ
page 504
Musician, radio personality, and civil rights activist

Authors and Consultants

Gerald A. Danzer, Ph.D.
Gerald A. Danzer is Professor of History at the University of Illinois at Chicago. He served from 1992 to 1994 as Chair of the Council for Effective Teaching and Learning at UIC and was Director of the Chicago Neighborhood History Project. Dr. Danzer's area of specialization is historical geography, in which he has written *Discovering American History Through Maps and Views* and numerous other publications. Before entering university teaching, Dr. Danzer taught high school history in the Chicago area. Dr. Danzer received his Ph.D. in history from Northwestern University.

J. Jorge Klor de Alva, J.D. and Ph.D.
J. Jorge Klor de Alva is President of Apollo International, Inc., a global education provider. Formerly he was president of the University of Phoenix. Before that he was Class of 1940 Professor of Comparative Ethnic Studies and Anthropology at the University of California at Berkeley and former Professor of Anthropology at Princeton University. Dr. Klor de Alva's interests include interethnic relations, historical ethnography, and educational reform. His publications include *The Aztec Image of Self* and *Society and Interethnic Images: Discourse and Practice in the New World, 1492–1992*, as well as more than ten other books and more than seventy scholarly articles. Dr. Klor de Alva earned his J.D. from the University of California at Berkeley and his Ph.D. in history/anthropology from the University of California at Santa Cruz.

Larry S. Krieger, B.A., M.A., M.A.T.
Larry S. Krieger is the Social Studies Supervisor for Grades K–12 in Montgomery Township Public Schools in New Jersey. For 26 years he has been a world history teacher in public schools. He has also introduced many innovative in-service programs, such as "Putting the Story Back in History," and has co-authored several successful history textbooks. Mr. Krieger earned his B.A. and M.A.T. from the University of North Carolina and his M.A. from Wake Forest University.

Louis E. Wilson, Ph.D.
Louis E. Wilson is Associate Professor and from 1989 through 1998 was the Chair of the Afro-American and African Studies Department at Smith College. In 1999, Dr. Wilson was a Senior Fulbright History Professor at the University of Cape Town, South Africa. Previously Dr. Wilson was on the faculty at the University of Colorado, Boulder, and was a senior Fulbright Scholar at the University of Ghana, Legon. Dr. Wilson is the author of *The Krobo People of Ghana to 1892: A Political, Social, and Economic History* and *Genealogical and Militia Data on Blacks, Indians, and Mustees from Military American Revolutionary War Records.* He is also one of the authors of *Houghton Mifflin Social Studies.* Dr. Wilson is currently writing a book entitled *Forgotten Patriots: African Americans and Native Americans in the American Revolution from Rhode Island.* In 1991, Dr. Wilson received The Blackwell Fellowship and Prize as Outstanding Black New England Scholar. Dr. Wilson received his Ph.D. in history from the University of California at Los Angeles.

Nancy Woloch, Ph.D.
Nancy Woloch teaches history at Barnard College, where she has been on the faculty since 1988. Dr. Woloch's main scholarly interest is the history of women in the United States, and in this area she has published *Women and the American Experience* and *Early American Women: A Documentary History, 1600–1900.* She is also the author of *Muller* v. *Oregon* and the co-author of *The American Century.* Dr. Woloch was the recipient of two National Endowment for the Humanities Fellowships. She received her Ph.D. in history and American studies from Indiana University.

This book contains material written by **John S. Bowes** that originally appeared in *The Americans* © 1985 and © 1991.

Constitution Consultant
Melvin Dubnick
Professor of Political Science
Rutgers University, Trenton
Trenton, New Jersey

Contributing Writer
Miriam Greenblatt
Educational Writer and Consultant
Highland Park, Illinois

Multicultural Advisory Board
The multicultural advisers reviewed the manuscript for appropriateness of content.

Pat A. Brown
Director of the Indianapolis Public Schools Office of African-Centered Multicultural Education
Indianapolis Public Schools
Indianapolis, Indiana

Ogle B. Duff
Associate Professor of English
University of Pittsburgh
Pittsburgh, Pennsylvania

Mary Ellen Maddox
Black Education Commission Director, Los Angeles Unified School District
Los Angeles, California

Jon Reyhner
Associate Professor and Coordinator of the Bilingual Multicultural Education Program
Northern Arizona University
Flagstaff, Arizona

Curtis L. Walker
Executive Officer, Office of Equity and Compliance
Pittsburgh Public Schools
Pittsburgh, Pennsylvania

Ruben Zepeda
Compliance Advisor, Language Acquisition and Curriculum Development
Los Angeles, California

Content Consultants
The content consultants reviewed the manuscript for historical depth and accuracy and for clarity of presentation.

Catherine Clinton
Fellow of the W. E. B. Du Bois Institute
Harvard University
Cambridge, Massachusetts

Theodore Karaminski
Professor of History
Loyola University
Chicago, Illinois

Joseph Kett
Professor of History
University of Virginia
Charlottesville, Virginia

Jack Rakove
Professor of History
Stanford University
Stanford, California

Harvard Sitkoff
Professor of History
University of New Hampshire
Durham, New Hampshire

ISBN-13: 978-0-618-68987-3 ISBN-10: 0-618-68987-7
Printed in the United States of America.
X 2 3 4 5 6 7 8 9—DWO—10 09 08 07 06

Consultants and Reviewers

Teacher Consultants

The following educators contributed ideas and activities for the program.

Edmund Austin
William Tennant High School
Warminster, Pennsylvania

William Brown
Retired,
Northeast High School
Philadelphia, Pennsylvania

Larry Bruno
Denby High School
Detroit, Michigan

Suzanne Cook
Scarborough High School
Houston, Texas

John Devine
Elgin High School
Elgin, Illinois

George Dyche
West Aurora High School
Aurora, Illinois

Steve Ellison
Petaluma High School
Petaluma, California

Betsy Fitzgerald
Erskine Academy
South China, Maine

Michael Fleming
Jupiter High School
Jupiter, Florida

Thomas J. Flynn
Turner High School
Kansas City, Kansas

Dominic Fruscello
West Genesee High School
Camillus, New York

Craig T. Grace
Lanier High School
West Austin, Texas

Cynthia M. Greene
Ridley High School
Folsom, Pennsylvania

Patti Harrold
Edmond Memorial High School
Edmond, Oklahoma

Korri Kinney
Meridian High School
Meridian, Idaho

Don A. Lee
Mira Mesa High School
San Diego, California

Dr. Carol D. McCree
DeBakey Health Prof.
High School
Houston, Texas

Harry McCown
Hazelwood West High School
Hazelwood, Missouri

Lou Morrison
Lake Weir High School
Ocala, Florida

Theresa C. Noonan
West Irondequoit High School
Rochester, New York

Gloria Remijio
Del Valle High School
El Paso, Texas

Diane M. Rodgers
Crooksville High School
Crooksville, Ohio

James Rosenberg
Retired, Crystal Lake South
High School
Crystal Lake, Illinois

John Seeley
Westminster High School
Westminster, California

Brenda G. Smith
Instructional Supervisor,
Social Studies, Colorado
Springs District 11
Colorado Springs, Colorado

Steve Smith
Clayton High School
Clayton, North Carolina

Ruby Thompson
Athens Drive High School
Raleigh, North Carolina

Linda Tillis
South Oak Cliff High School
Dallas, Texas

Mark A. Van Hecke
Anchor Bay High School
New Baltimore, Michigan

Joshua Weiner
Benson High School
Portland, Oregon

Teacher Review Panels

The following educators provided ongoing review during the development of prototypes, the table of contents, and key components of the program.

FLORIDA TEACHER PANEL

David Debs
Mandarin High School
Jacksonville, Florida

Ronald Eckstein
Hudson High School
Hudson, Florida

Sharman Feliciani
Land O'Lakes High School
Land O'Lakes, Florida

Flossie Gautier
Bay High School
Panama City, Florida

Glenn Hallick
Vanguard High School
Ocala, Florida

Mary Kenney
Astronaut High School
Titusville, Florida

Lou Morrison
Lake Weir High School
Ocala, Florida

Brenda Sims Palmer
Lehigh High School
Lehigh Acres, Florida

Marsee Perkins
Maynard Evans High School
Orlando, Florida

Kent Rettig
Pensacola High School
Pensacola, Florida

Jim Sutton
Edgewater High School
Orlando, Florida

ILLINOIS TEACHER PANEL

Rosemary Albright
Conant High School
Hoffman Estates, Illinois

Jeff Anhut
Wheaton Warrenville South
High School
Wheaton, Illinois

James Crider
Downers Grove South
High School
Downers Grove, Illinois

John Devine
Elgin High School
Elgin, Illinois

George Dyche
West Aurora High School
Aurora, Illinois

Diane Ring
St. Charles High School
St. Charles, Illinois

Jim Rosenberg
Crystal Lake South
High School
Crystal Lake, Illinois

Pam Zimmerman
Stevenson High School
Lincolnshire, Illinois

CALIFORNIA TEACHER PANEL

Elaine Deatherage
Hiram Johnson High School
Sacramento, California

Steve Ellison
Petaluma High School
Petaluma, California

Judy Horrigan
Moreno Valley High School
Moreno Valley, California

Don Lee
Mira Mesa High School
San Diego, California

Russom Mesfun
Fremont High School
Oakland, California

Randy Sanford
Hueneme High School
Oxnard, California

John Seeley
Westminster High School
Westminster, California

Kathleen Torosian
Herbert Hoover High School
Fresno, California

Glenda Watanabe
Banning High School
Los Angeles, California

TEXAS TEACHER PANEL

Patricia Brison
Bellaire High School
Houston, Texas

Brian Greeney
Stratford High School
Spring Branch, Texas

Jim Lee
Lamar High School
Arlington, Texas

Janie Maldonado
Lanier High School
Austin, Texas

Leonore Murray
Lubbock High School
Lubbock, Texas

Deborah Pennington
The Woodlands High School
Conroe, Texas

Gloria Remijio
Dell Valley High School
Yselta, Texas

H.V. Stafford
MacArthur High School
Aldine, Texas

Dawn Stapp
Lee Freshman High School
Midland, Texas

Manuscript Reviewers

The educators listed in the next column reviewed the prototype chapter and the manuscript of the entire book.

Arman Afshani
North Tonawanda High School
North Tonawanda, New York

Debra Brown
Eisenhower High School
Houston, Texas

Dianne Bumgarner
Ashbrook High School
Mt. Holly, North Carolina

Sherry Burgin
Garland High School
Garland, Texas

Maurice Bush
South Point High School
Crouse, North Carolina

Bruce Campbell
Bemidji High School
Bemidji, Minnesota

Al Celaya
Robert E. Lee High School
Tyler, Texas

Anne E. Connor
Westridge School
Pasadena, California

James Crider
Downers Grove South
High School
Downers Grove, Illinois

(*continued on R118*)

Student Board

The following students reviewed prototype materials for the book.

John Afordakos
Chantilly High School
Fairfax County, Virginia

Marisha Cook
Rockford East High School
Rockford, Illinois

Matthew Cornejo
New Bedford High School
New Bedford, Massachusetts

Kevin Dodd
Lanier High School
Austin, Texas

Melissa Dugan
Mount Lebanon High School
Mount Lebanon, Pennsylvania

Denise Ford
Douglas Byrd Sr. High School
Cumberland County,
North Carolina

Rebecca Freeman
Foshay Learning Center
Los Angeles, California

(*continued on R118*)

American Beginnings to 1877

Themes in United States History xxviii
Themes in Geography xxx
Strategies for Taking Standardized Tests S1

Review Chapter 1 — Beginnings to 1763

Exploration and the Colonial Era 2

1 The Americas, West Africa, and Europe 4
SCIENCE & TECHNOLOGY *The Caravel* 12
2 Spanish North America 14
3 Early British Colonies 21
4 The Colonies Come of Age 31
DAILY LIFE *Colonial Courtship* 40
Chapter 1 Assessment 42

Review Chapter 2 — 1763–1800

Revolution and the Early Republic 44

1 Colonial Resistance and Rebellion 46
The Declaration of Independence 54
2 The War for Independence 58
TRACING THEMES *Women and Political Power* 64
3 Confederation and the Constitution 66
GEOGRAPHY SPOTLIGHT *The Land Ordinance of 1785* 72
4 Launching the New Nation 74
Chapter 2 Assessment 80

The Living Constitution 82

TRACING THEMES *Voting Rights* 104
The Living Constitution Assessment 106
PROJECTS FOR CITIZENSHIP *Applying the Constitution* 108

Native Americans watch the arrival of a European ship, page 2.

The Battle of Lexington begins the American Revolution, p. 50.

The Supreme Court of the United States, page 93

Review Chapter 3 — 1800–1850

The Growth of a Young Nation — 110

1 The Jeffersonian Era — 112
SUPREME COURT *Marbury* v. *Madison* — 118
2 The Age of Jackson — 120
SCIENCE & TECHNOLOGY *The Cotton Gin* — 121
TRACING THEMES *States' Rights* — 128
3 Manifest Destiny — 130
4 The Market Revolution — 139
5 Reforming American Society — 144
GEOGRAPHY SPOTLIGHT *Mapping the Oregon Trail* — 150
Chapter 3 Assessment — 152

Review Chapter 4 — 1850–1877

The Union in Peril — 154

1 The Divisive Politics of Slavery — 156
SUPREME COURT *Dred Scott* v. *Sandford* — 166
2 The Civil War Begins — 168
3 The North Takes Charge — 175
4 Reconstruction and Its Effects — 184
Chapter 4 Assessment — 190

Thematic Review of Unit 1

Diversity and the National Identity — 192
Immigration and Migration — 193
America in World Affairs — 194
Voting Rights — 194
States' Rights — 195
Women and Political Power — 195
Science and Technology — 196
Civil Rights — 196
Economic Opportunity — 197

VIDEO
Patrick Gass Chronicles the Journey West, page 112

An 1864 Mathew Brady photograph of Civil War soldiers, page 178

Immigrants arrive in New York Harbor, page 193.

Visit the links for Chapters 1–4.

1877–1917

Bridge to the 20th Century

A Sioux man and woman, page 203

The first light bulb, page 248

Coney Island amusement park, page 292

Chapter 5 1877–1900

Changes on the Western Frontier 200
1 Cultures Clash on the Prairie 202
DAILY LIFE *Gold Mining* 212
2 Settling on the Great Plains 214
SCIENCE & TECHNOLOGY *Inventions that Tamed the Prairie* 217
3 Farmers and the Populist Movement 219
AMERICAN LITERATURE *Literature of the West* 224
Chapter 5 Assessment 226

Chapter 6 1877–1900

A New Industrial Age 228
1 The Expansion of Industry 230
GEOGRAPHY SPOTLIGHT *Industry Changes the Environment* 234
2 The Age of the Railroads 236
3 Big Business and Labor 241
Chapter 6 Assessment 250

Chapter 7 1877–1914

Immigrants and Urbanization 252
1 The New Immigrants 254
TRACING THEMES *Diversity and the National Identity* 260
2 The Challenges of Urbanization 262
3 Politics in the Gilded Age 267
Chapter 7 Assessment 272

Chapter 8 1877–1917

Life at the Turn of the 20th Century 274
1 Science and Urban Life 276
SCIENCE & TECHNOLOGY *Aviation Pioneers* 280
2 Expanding Public Education 282
3 Segregation and Discrimination 286
SUPREME COURT *Plessy* v. *Ferguson* 290
4 The Dawn of Mass Culture 292
DAILY LIFE *Going to the Show* 298
Chapter 8 Assessment 300

1890–1920

Modern America Emerges

Chapter 9 **1890–1920**

The Progressive Era 304
1 The Origins of Progressivism 306
2 Women in Public Life 313
3 Teddy Roosevelt's Square Deal 317
AMERICAN LITERATURE *The Muckrakers* 326
4 Progressivism Under Taft 328
5 Wilson's New Freedom 332
Chapter 9 Assessment 338

Chapter 10 **1890–1920**

America Claims an Empire 340
1 Imperialism and America 342
2 The Spanish-American War 346
3 Acquiring New Lands 352
4 America as a World Power 359
SCIENCE & TECHNOLOGY *The Panama Canal* 361
GEOGRAPHY SPOTLIGHT
The Panama Canal: Funnel for Trade 366
Chapter 10 Assessment 368

Chapter 11 **1914–1920**

The First World War 370
1 World War I Begins 372
2 American Power Tips the Balance 381
SCIENCE & TECHNOLOGY *Technology at War* 384
3 The War at Home 388
SUPREME COURT *Schenck* v. *United States* 396
4 Wilson Fights for Peace 398
POINT/COUNTERPOINT *The League of Nations* 401
TRACING THEMES *America in World Affairs* 404
Chapter 11 Assessment 406

Teddy Roosevelt campaigns for president, page 318.

Uncle Sam rides upon two "hemispheres," page 351.

VIDEO
Eddie Rickenbacker and the First World War, page 381

Visit the links for Chapters 5–11.

1919–1940

The 1920s and the Great Depression

Chapter 12 **1919–1929**

Politics of the Roaring Twenties 410
1 Americans Struggle with Postwar Issues 412
2 The Harding Presidency 419
3 The Business of America 422
TRACING THEMES *Economic Opportunity* 428
Chapter 12 Assessment 430

Chapter 13 **1920–1929**

The Roaring Life of the 1920s 432
1 Changing Ways of Life 434
2 The Twenties Woman 440
DAILY LIFE *Youth in the Roaring Twenties* 444
3 Education and Popular Culture 446
4 The Harlem Renaissance 452
AMERICAN LITERATURE *Literature in the Jazz Age* 458
Chapter 13 Assessment 460

Chapter 14 **1929–1933**

The Great Depression Begins 462
1 The Nation's Sick Economy 464
2 Hardship and Suffering During the Depression 472
3 Hoover Struggles with the Depression 478
Chapter 14 Assessment 484

Chapter 15 **1933–1940**

The New Deal 486
1 A New Deal Fights the Depression 488
2 The Second New Deal Takes Hold 495
SUPREME COURT *NLRB* v. *Jones & Laughlin Steel Corp.* 502
3 The New Deal Affects Many Groups 504
4 Culture in the 1930s 510
5 The Impact of the New Deal 515
POINT/COUNTERPOINT *The New Deal* 516
GEOGRAPHY SPOTLIGHT *The Tennessee Valley Authority* 520
Chapter 15 Assessment 522

"Big business" dances with Calvin Coolidge, page 426.

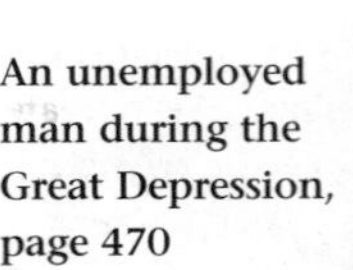

Zora Neale Hurston and the Harlem Renaissance, page 452

An unemployed man during the Great Depression, page 470

1931–1960

World War II and Its Aftermath

Chapter 16 1931–1941

World War Looms 526
1 Dictators Threaten World Peace 528
2 War in Europe 536
3 The Holocaust 542
4 America Moves Toward War 550
POINT/COUNTERPOINT *Isolationism* 552
SCIENCE & TECHNOLOGY *German Wolf Packs* 553
Chapter 16 Assessment 558

Chapter 17 1941–1945

The United States in World War II 560
1 Mobilizing for Defense 562
2 The War for Europe and North Africa 569
3 The War in the Pacific 578
POINT/COUNTERPOINT *Dropping the Atomic Bomb* 585
TRACING THEMES *Science and Technology* 588
4 The Home Front 590
SUPREME COURT *Korematsu* v. *United States* 596
Chapter 17 Assessment 598

Chapter 18 1945–1960

Cold War Conflicts 600
1 Origins of the Cold War 602
2 The Cold War Heats Up 609
3 The Cold War at Home 616
4 Two Nations Live on the Edge 622
AMERICAN LITERATURE *Science Fiction Reflects Cold War Fears* 628
Chapter 18 Assessment 630

Chapter 19 1946–1960

The Postwar Boom 632
1 Postwar America 634
2 The American Dream in the Fifties 641
GEOGRAPHY SPOTLIGHT *The Road to Suburbia* 650
3 Popular Culture 652
DAILY LIFE *The Emergence of the Teenager* 658
4 The Other America 660
Chapter 19 Assessment 664

VIDEO
Kurt Klein and Gerda Weissmann Klein Remember the Holocaust, page 542

The "Tuskegee Airmen" of the 99th Fighter Squadron, page 573

The Cold War creates a climate of fear, page 628.

CLASSZONE.COM *Visit the links for Chapters 12–19.*

UNIT 6

1954–1975
Living with Great Turmoil

Kennedy and Johnson promise active leadership, page 670.

Chapter 20 **1960–1968**

The New Frontier and the Great Society 668
1 Kennedy and the Cold War 670
2 The New Frontier 679
GEOGRAPHY SPOTLIGHT *The Movement of Migrant Workers* 684
3 The Great Society 686
POINT/COUNTERPOINT *The Legacy of the Great Society* 692
SUPREME COURT *Miranda* v. *Arizona* 694
Chapter 20 Assessment 696

Chapter 21 **1954–1968**

Civil Rights 698
1 Taking on Segregation 700
SUPREME COURT *Brown* v. *Board of Education of Topeka* 708
2 The Triumphs of a Crusade 710
3 Challenges and Changes in the Movement 717
TRACING THEMES *Civil Rights* 724
Chapter 21 Assessment 726

VIDEO
Jo Ann Gibson Robinson and the Bus Boycott, page 700

Chapter 22 **1954–1975**

The Vietnam War Years 728
1 Moving Toward Conflict 730
2 U.S. Involvement and Escalation 736
3 A Nation Divided 742
4 1968: A Tumultuous Year 748
5 The End of the War and Its Legacy 754
AMERICAN LITERATURE *Literature of the Vietnam War* 762
Chapter 22 Assessment 764

Chapter 23 **1960–1975**

An Era of Social Change 766
1 Latinos and Native Americans Seek Equality 768
SUPREME COURT *Reynolds* v. *Sims* 774
2 Women Fight for Equality 776
3 Culture and Counterculture 781
DAILY LIFE *Signs of the Sixties* 786
Chapter 23 Assessment 788

Farm workers protest, page 768.

1968–2004
Passage to a New Century

Chapter 24 1968–1980

An Age of Limits 792
1 The Nixon Administration 794
2 Watergate: Nixon's Downfall 802
DAILY LIFE *Television Reflects American Life* 808
3 The Ford and Carter Years 810
SUPREME COURT *Regents* v. *Bakke* 818
4 Environmental Activism 820
SCIENCE & TECHNOLOGY *Three Mile Island* 823
Chapter 24 Assessment 826

Chapter 25 1980–1992

The Conservative Tide 828
1 A Conservative Movement Emerges 830
2 Conservative Policies Under Reagan and Bush 834
3 Social Concerns in the 1980s 839
GEOGRAPHY SPOTLIGHT *Sunbelt, Rustbelt, Ecotopia* 846
4 Foreign Policy After the Cold War 848
POINT/COUNTERPOINT *Intervention Abroad* 853
Chapter 25 Assessment 856

Chapter 26 1992–2004

The United States in Today's World 858
1 The 1990s and the New Millennium 860
2 The New Global Economy 869
AMERICAN LITERATURE *Women Writers Reflect Diversity* 874
3 Technology and Modern Life 876
SCIENCE & TECHNOLOGY *Alternative Cars* 881
4 The Changing Face of America 882
TRACING THEMES *Immigration and Migration* 888
Chapter 26 Assessment 890

Epilogue: Issues for the 21st Century 892

The War on Terrorism 894
Iraq: Confronting a Dictatorship 898
The Debate Over Immigration 900
Crime and Public Safety 902
Issues in Education 904
The Communications Revolution 906
Curing the Health Care System 908
Breaking the Cycle of Poverty 910
Tough Choices About Social Security 912
Women in the Work Force 914
The Conservation Controversy 916

Tape-recorded conversations ensnare the Nixon White House, page 806.

A statue of Saddam Hussein is toppled in Baghdad after the Iraqi dictator is overthrown, page 899.

REFERENCE SECTION

Atlas by RAND McNALLY A1
Skillbuilder Handbook R2
Economics Handbook R38
Facts About the States R48
Presidents of the United States R50
Glossary R53
Spanish Glossary R67
Index R82
Acknowledgments R108

CLASSZONE.COM *Visit the links for Chapters 24–26 and Epilogue.*

Special Features

Marbury v. *Madison* (1803) 118
Dred Scott v. *Sandford* (1857) 166
Plessy v. *Ferguson* (1896) 290
Schenck v. *United States* (1919) 396
NLRB v. *Jones and Laughlin Steel Corp.* (1937) 502
Korematsu v. *United States* (1944) 596
Miranda v. *Arizona* (1966) 694
Brown v. *Board of Education of Topeka* (1954) 708
Reynolds v. *Sims* (1964) 774
Regents of the University of California v. *Bakke* (1978) 818

The Land Ordinance of 1785 72
Mapping the Oregon Trail 150
Industry Changes the Environment 234
The Panama Canal 366
The Tennessee Valley Authority 520
The Road to Suburbia 650
The Movement of Migrant Workers 684
Sunbelt, Rustbelt, Ecotopia 846

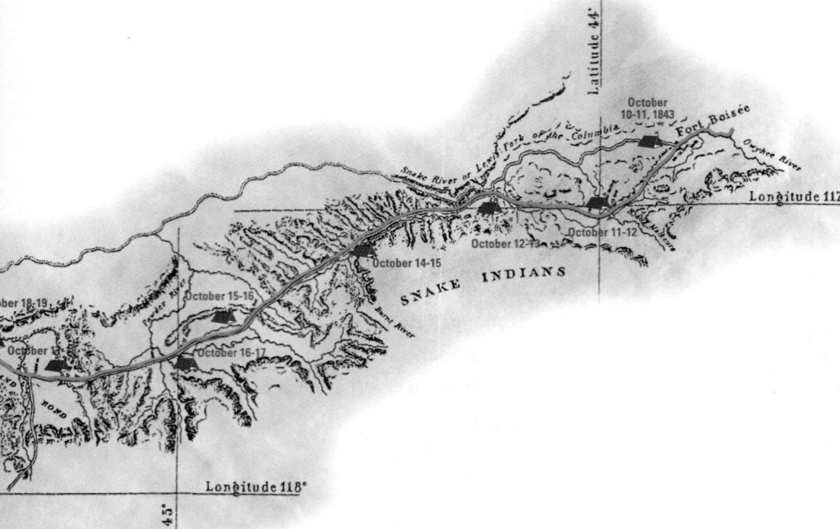

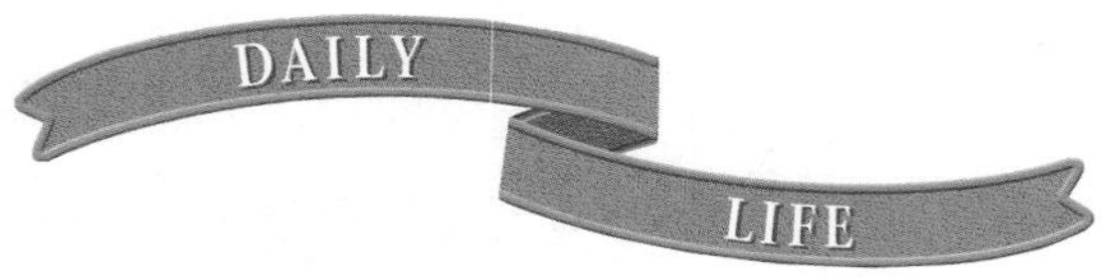

Colonial Courtship 40
Gold Mining 212
Going to the Show 298
Youth in the Roaring Twenties 444
The Emergence of the Teenager 658
Signs of the Sixties 786
Television Reflects American Life 808

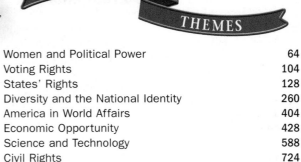

Literature of the West 224
The Muckrakers 326
Literature in the Jazz Age 458
Science Fiction Reflects Cold War Fears 628
Literature of the Vietnam War 762
Women Writers Reflect American Diversity 874

Women and Political Power 64
Voting Rights 104
States' Rights 128
Diversity and the National Identity 260
America in World Affairs 404
Economic Opportunity 428
Science and Technology 588
Civil Rights 724
Immigration and Migration 888

KEY PLAYER

"King Isabella" (1451–1504) 10
Hernándo Cortés (1485–1547) 16
Jonathan Edwards (1703–1758) 36
Benjamin Franklin (1706–1790) 36
John Hancock (1737–1793) 57
George Washington (1732–1799) 60
James Madison (1751–1836) 68
Alexander Hamilton (1755–1804) 75
Thomas Jefferson (1743-1826) 75
Andrew Jackson (1767–1845) 123
Sam Houston (1793—1863) 135
Santa Anna (1795–1876) 135
Elizabeth Cady Stanton (1815–1902) 148
Abraham Lincoln (1809–1865) 172
Jefferson Davis (1808–1889) 172
Ulysses S. Grant (1822–1885) 180
Robert E. Lee (1807–1870) 180
Hiram Revels (1822–1901) 188
Sitting Bull (1831–1890) 204
William Jennings Bryan (1860–1925) 222
John D. Rockefeller (1839–1937) 243
Eugene V. Debs (1855–1926) 248
Mother Jones (1830–1930) 248
Jane Addams (1860–1935) 266
George Eastman (1854–1932) 281
Florence Kelley (1859–1932) 307
Susan B. Anthony (1820–1906) 316
W. E. B. Du Bois (1868–1963) 325
William Howard Taft (1857–1930) 330
Admiral Alfred T. Mahan (1840–1914) 343
José Martí (1853–1895) 347
Theodore Roosevelt (1858–1919) 360
General John J. Pershing (1860–1948) 384
Woodrow Wilson (1856–1924) 399
John Llewellyn Lewis (1880–1969) 418
Calvin Coolidge (1872–1933) 424
F. Scott Fitzgerald (1896–1940) 451
James Weldon Johnson (1871–1938) 453
Duke Ellington (1899–1974) 457
Herbert Hoover (1874–1964) 479
Franklin D. Roosevelt (1882–1945) 489
Eleanor Roosevelt (1884–1962) 489
Frances Perkins (1882–1965) 505
Adolf Hitler (1889–1945) 537
Winston Churchill (1874–1965) 541
Hideki Tojo (1884–1948) 554
Dwight D. "Ike" Eisenhower (1890–1969) 574
Douglas MacArthur (1880–1964) 583
Harry S. Truman (1884–1972) 603
Joseph Stalin (1879–1953) 603
Jonas Salk (1914–1995) 644
John F. Kennedy (1917–1963) 676
Nikita Khrushchev (1894–1971) 676
Lyndon B. Johnson (1908–1973) 687
Thurgood Marshall (1908–1993) 702
Rosa Parks (1913–) 704
Martin Luther King, Jr. (1929–1968) 706
Malcolm X (1925–1965) 719
Ho Chi Minh (1890–1969) 731
General William Westmoreland (1914–) 737
Henry Kissinger (1923–) 758
César Chávez (1927–1993) 770
Gloria Steinem (1934–) 778
Richard M. Nixon (1913–1994) 800
Jimmy Carter (1924–) 812
Rachael Carson (1907–1964) 821
Ronald Reagan (1911–) 832
H. Norman Schwarzkopf (1934–) 855
William Jefferson Clinton (1946–) 861
George W. Bush (1946–) 866

Proposition 13 47
Modern Money 88
Election Reform 98
Congressional Term Limits 102
From Telegraph to Internet 140
Nez Perce in Oregon 208
Inventions That Tamed the Prairie 217
Aviation Pioneers 280
Technology and Schools 284
Catalog Shopping 297
Telephone Operators 314
Meat Inspection 320
Deregulation 333
Puerto Rico 353
Crisis in the Balkans 374
Evolution, Creationism, and Education 438
New York Stock Exchange 468
Social Security 518
Women in the Military 563
The Two Koreas 615
Television: Making News 618
Franchises 642
Southern California and the Automobile 646
Kennedy's Assassination 683
Medicare on the Line 691
Land Mines 739
U.S. Recognition of Vietnam 761
Ben Nighthorse Campbell 771
AIDS Worldwide 840
Affirmative Action 844

History Through...

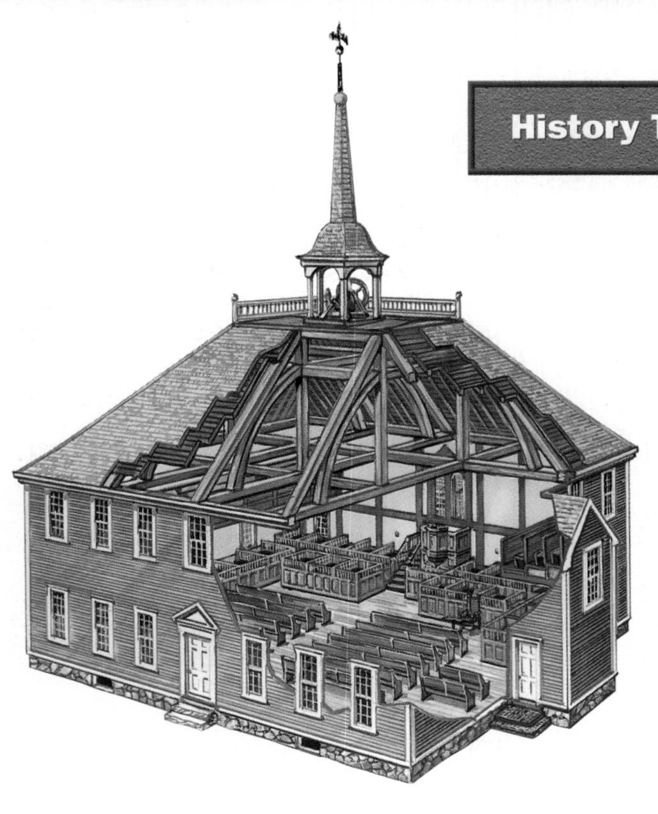

Architecture

Colonial Meetinghouses 27
The Chicago Plan 278
From Splendor to Simplicity 336
Rebuilding the Riverfronts 883

Photojournalism

Mathew Brady's Photographs 178
Images of Child Labor 311
"Migrant Mother": Dorothea Lange 497
Raising the Flag on Iwo Jima 582
Ernest Withers 713
Kent State 757

Art

June, from *Les Très Riches Heures Du Duc De Berry* (c. 1416) by the Limbourg brothers 11
The Boston Massacre (1770) by Paul Revere 48
John Brown Going to His Hanging (1942) by Horace Pippin 164
Stampeded by Lightning (1908) by Frederic Remington 210
The Champion Single Sculls (1871) by Thomas Eakins 295
Zapatistas (1931) by José Orozco 364
The Migration of the Negro, Panel No. 1 (1940–41) by Jacob Lawrence 393

Sacco and Vanzetti (1932) by Ben Shahn 414
Song of the Towers by Aaron Douglas 435
American Gothic (1930) by Grant Wood 513
After the Prom (1957) by Norman Rockwell 645

Film

Echoes of the Great War 402
Hollywood Helps Mobilization 566
Hollywood and Nuclear Fears 824

Music

"Hound Dog"—A Rock 'n' Roll Crossover 656
Protest Songs of the Sixties 784

Analyzing *Political Cartoons*

"The Paris Monster" 78
"The Federal Edifice" 96
"King Andrew the First" 126
Unwelcome Guest 187
The Plight of the Farmers 220
"The Modern Colossus of (Rail) Roads" 240
"The Tammany Tiger Loose" 269
"The Lion-Tamer" 319
"Well, I Hardly Know Which to Take First!" 354
"The World's Constable" 362

The Enemy Within 391
"Yes, Sir, He's My Baby" 426
Day of Wrath 467
Changing Course 493
"It Ain't What It Used to Be" 534
Carving it Up 551
"It's OK—We're Hunting Communists" 620
"Domestic Life" 795
The White House Tapes 806
"The Inflation Stagecoach" 836
"Vacation, 2000" 877

HISTORICAL SPOTLIGHT

Islam 9
Early Representative Government 23
Independence and Slavery 55
John Paul Jones 61
The Supreme Court Boosts National Power 122
Jim Beckwourth 131
Secession and the Border States 165
Boys in War 171
The Wild West Show 211
The Colored Farmers' National Alliance 221
Illuminating the Light Bulb 232
Chinese Immigrants and the Railroad 237
African Americans and the Labor Movement 245
Washington *vs.* Du Bois 288
Anti-Saloon League 308
James S. Hogg, Texas Governor (1891–1895) 310
Yosemite National Park 324
Race Riots 394
Al Capone 437
Hobo Symbols 475
Deportation of Mexican Americans 506
War of the Worlds 511
African Americans Stand by Ethiopians 533
Audie Murphy 576
Navajo Code Talkers 579
Paul Robeson 617
Jackie Robinson 637
TV Quiz Shows 653
Johnson and Mission Control 681
Twenty-fourth Amendment—Barring Poll Taxes 716
Shirley Chisholm 722
"The Ballad of the Green Berets" 745
Vietnam Veterans Memorial: The Wall 760
Desperate Journeys 769
Americans Walk on the Moon 796
The Twenty-sixth Amendment 798
Woodward and Bernstein 804
Private Conservation Groups 825
An Assassination Attempt 837

Special Features

Economic Background

Trade Alliances 377
Roots of Communism 413
Uneven Income Distribution, 1929 466
Deficit Spending 492
War and the Depression 557
What Is a Recession? 680
The 1980s Texas Oil Boom 813
The "Trickle-Down Theory" 835
Greenspan and the Fed 870

Difficult Decisions

Controlling Resources 329
To Prohibit Alcohol or Not? 436
Hoover and Federal Projects 482
Resist the Draft or Serve Your Country? 746
Pardoning President Nixon 811
Sending Money into Space 841

World Stage

The English Civil War and Restoration 26
The Garden City 279
Emmeline Pankhurst 335
The Boxer Protocol 357
Revolution in Russia 380
Global Effects of the Depression 471
Righteous Persons of World War II 548
Taiwan 611
Israel 625
The Berlin Wall, 1961 677
The War in Vietnam 688
Apartheid—Segregation in South Africa 701
The Yom Kippur War 799
Soviet-Afghanistan War 815
Democratic Elections in Russia 849

Another Perspective

"All Men Would Be Tyrants if They Could" 56
On the Wrong Track 238
Intervention in Mexico 363
The Needy 426
An African-American View of the Depression 473
Denmark's Resistance 545
India's Viewpoint 614
Eisenhower's Warning 673

Point Counterpoint

The League of Nations 401
The New Deal 516
Isolationism 552
Dropping the Atomic Bomb 585
The Legacy of the Great Society 692
Intervention Abroad 853

Science Technology

The Caravel 12
The Cotton Gin 121
Inventions that Tamed the Prairie 217
Aviation Pioneers 280
The Panama Canal 361
Technology at War 384
German Wolf Packs 553
The Accident at Three Mile Island 823
Alternative Cars 881

Primary Sources and Personal Voices

CHAPTER 1
Essie Parrish, in *Kashaya Texts,* 4
Al Bakri, in *Africa in the Days of Exploration,* 9
Christopher Columbus, *The Log of Christopher Columbus,* 14
Fray Antonio de Montesinos, in *Reflections, Writing for Columbus,* 18
John Smith, *The General History of Virginia,* 21
Nehemiah Grew, in *The Colonial Period of American History,* 30
Philip Vickers Fithian, *Journal & Letters of Philip Vickers Fithian,* 31
Olaudah Equiano, *The Interesting Narrative of the Life of Olaudah Equiano,* 33
Jonathan Edwards, "Sinners in the Hands of an Angry God," 36
Pontiac, in *Red and White,* 39

CHAPTER 2
John Adams, in *The Black Presence in the Era of the American Revolution,* 46
Thomas Paine, *Common Sense,* 52
The Declaration of Independence, 54
William Franklin, in *A Little Revenge: Benjamin Franklin and His Son,* 58
George Washington, in *Ordeal at Valley Forge,* 60
John Dickinson, in *The Life and Times of John Dickinson, 1732–1808,* 66
James Madison, *The Federalist,* Number 38, 70
George Washington, *The Diaries of George Washington,* 74
8th Resolution, The Virginia and Kentucky Resolutions, 79

CHAPTER 3
Patrick Gass, *A Journal of the Voyages and Travels of a Corps of Discovery,* 112
President James Monroe, Annual Message to Congress, December 2, 1823, 117
Justice John Marshall, *Marbury* v. *Madison* (1803), 118
Robert Fulton, in *Steamboats Come True: American Inventors in Action,* 120
Evan Jones, *Baptist Missionary Magazine,* June 16, 1838, 124
Stephen F. Austin, in *Lone Star: A History of Texas and Texans,* 130
Walter Colton, in *California: A Bicentennial History,* 137
Samuel Young, in *Erie Water West,* 139
Mary Paul, in *Women and the American Experience,* 142
James Forten, in *Forging Freedom: The Formation of Philadelphia's Black Community, 1720–1840,* 144
Sojourner Truth, in *Narrative of Sojourner Truth,* 149

A PERSONAL VOICE
SOJOURNER TRUTH

"Look at me! Look at my arm! I have ploughed, and planted, and gathered into barns, and no man could head me! And ain't I a woman?"

—quoted in *Narrative of Sojourner Truth*

CHAPTER 4
John C. Calhoun, in *The Compromise of 1850,* 156
Stephen A. Douglas, in *The Civil War* by Geoffrey C. Ward, 160
William Tecumseh Sherman, in *None Died in Vain,* 165
Justice Roger Taney, *Dred Scott* v. *Sandford* (1857), 166
Robert Anderson, in *Fifty Basic Civil War Documents,* 168
Abraham Lincoln, The Emancipation Proclamation, 172
Mary Chesnut, in *Mary Chesnut's Civil War,* 175
Abraham Lincoln, "The Gettysburg Address," November 19, 1863, 177
Robert G. Fitzgerald, in *Proud Shoes,* 184
William Beverly Nash, in *The Trouble They Seen: Black People Tell the Story of Reconstruction,* 187

CHAPTER 5
Zitkala-Ša, *The School Days of an Indian Girl,* 202
Gall, a Hunkpapa Sioux, in *Bury My Heart at Wounded Knee,* 206
Black Elk, *Black Elk Speaks,* 208
Esther Clark Hill, in *Pioneer Women,* 214
Frederick Jackson Turner, "The Significance of the Frontier in American History," 216
Mary Elizabeth Lease, in "The Populist Uprising," 219
William Jennings Bryan, Democratic convention speech, Chicago, July 8, 1896, 223
Mark Twain, "The Celebrated Jumping Frog of Calaveras County," 224
Anonymous, "The Ballad of Gregorio Cortez," translated by Américo Paredes, 225
Chief Satanta, *Speech at the Medicine Lodge Creek Council* (1867), 225

CHAPTER 6
Pattillo Higgins, in *Spindeltop,* 230
Richard T. Ely, "Pullman: A Social Study," 236
Andrew Carnegie, *Autobiography of Andrew Carnegie,* 241
Jacob Riis, *How the Other Half Lives,* 245
Hamlin Garland, in *McClure's Magazine,* 247

CHAPTER 7
Lisa See, *On Gold Mountain,* 254
Rosa Cavalleri, in *Rosa: The Life of an Italian Immigrant,* 256
Edward Ferro, in *I Was Dreaming to Come to America,* 257
Jacob Riis, *How the Other Half Lives,* 262
Jack London, *The Story of an Eye-witness,* 265
Mark Twain and Charles Dudley Warner, *The Gilded Age,* 267
James Pendergast, in *The Pendergast Machine,* 268

CHAPTER 8
E. F. Farrington, in *The Great Bridge,* 276
Frederick Law Olmsted, in *Frederick Law Olmsted's New York,* 278
Orville Wright, in *Frontiers of Flight,* 279
William Torrey Harris, in *Public Schools and Moral Education,* 282
anonymous schoolboy, in *The One Best System,* 283
Ida B. Wells, in *Crusade for Justice,* 286
Booker T. Washington, Atlanta Exposition address, (1895), 288
Justice Henry B. Brown, *Plessy* v. *Ferguson* (1896), 290
Bruce Blen, in *Amusing the Million,* 292

CHAPTER 9
Camella Teoli, at congressional hearings, March 1912, 306
Eugene V. Debs, *Debs: His Life, Writings and Speeches,* 308
Susette La Flesche, in *Bright Eyes,* 313
Sophia Smith, in *Alma Mater,* 315
Upton Sinclair, *The Jungle,* 317
W. E. B. Du Bois, *The Souls of Black Folk,* 325
Ida M. Tarbell, "The History of the Standard Oil Company," 326
Lincoln Steffens, *The Shame of the Cities,* 327
Upton Sinclair, *The Jungle,* 327
Gifford Pinchot, *The Fight for Conservation,* 328
Woodrow Wilson, in *The New Freedom,* 331
Carrie Chapman Catt, letter to Maud Wood Park, 332
William Monroe Trotter, address to President Wilson, November 12, 1914, 337

Primary Sources and Personal Voices

CHAPTER 10

Queen Liliuokalani, in *Those Kings and Queens of Old Hawaii,* 342
James Creelman, in *New York World,* May 17, 1896, 346
Luis Muñoz Rivera, in *The Puerto Ricans,* 352
Andrew Carnegie, in *Distant Possessions,* 355
Mark Twain, *To the Person Sitting in Darkness,* 358
Joseph Bucklin Bishop, in *The Impossible Dream: The Building of the Panama Canal,* 359
Pancho Villa, in *New York Times,* January 11, 1915, 364

A PERSONAL VOICE
LUIS MUÑOZ RIVERA

"[G]ive us our independence and you will stand before humanity as . . . a great creator of new nationalities and a great liberator of oppressed peoples."

—quoted in *The Puerto Ricans*

CHAPTER 11

Jeannette Rankin, in *Jeannette Rankin: First Lady in Congress,* 372
Richard Harding Davis, in *Hooray for Peace, Hurrah for War,* 374
Woodrow Wilson, in *American Voices,* 380
Eddie Rickenbacker, *Rickenbacker: An Autobiography,* 381
Joseph Douglas Lawrence, *Fighting Soldier: The AEF in 1918,* 383
Florence Bullard, in *Over There,* 385
John L. Barkley, *No Hard Feelings,* 387
Harriot Stanton Blatch, in *We, the American Women,* 388
Woodrow Wilson, in *Cobb of "The World,"* 391
W. E. B. Du Bois, "Close Ranks," 392
Richard Wright, in *12 Million Black Voices,* 394
Justice Oliver Wendell Holmes, Jr., *Schenck* v. *United States* (1919), 396
Colonel E. M. House, in *Hooray for Peace, Hurrah for War,* 398

CHAPTER 12

Irving Fajans, in *The Jewish Americans,* 412
A. Mitchell Palmer, "The Case Against the Reds," 413
Bartolomeo Vanzetti, in *The National Experience,* 414
Madison Grant, in *United States History: Ideas in Conflict,* 415
Woodrow Wilson, in *Labor in Crisis,* 417
Warren G. Harding, in *The Rise of Warren Gamaliel Harding,* 419
Warren G. Harding, in *Only Yesterday,* 420
a Ford salesman, in *Flappers, Bootleggers, "Typhoid Mary," and the Bomb,* 422
Listerine advertisement, 425
a business owner, in *The Time of Silent Cal,* 427

CHAPTER 13

Billy Sunday, in *How Dry We Were: Prohibition Revisited,* 434
Walter L. George, *Hail Columbia!,* 435
Herbert Asbury, *Gem of the Prairie,* 437
Clarence Darrow and William Jennings Bryan, in *Bryan and Darrow at Dayton,* 439
Zelda Sayre Fitzgerald, "Paint and Powder," *The Smart Set,* May 1929, 440
Helen Wright, in *Wage-Earning Women,* 443
Graham McNamee, in *Time Magazine,* October 3, 1927, 446
F. Scott Fitzgerald, in *The Lawless Decade,* 449
Sinclair Lewis, *Babbit,* 450
Zora Neale Hurston, in *The African American Encyclopedia,* 452
Zora Neale Hurston, *Sorrow's Kitchen: The Life and Folklore of Zora Neale Hurston,* 453
Marcus Garvey, speech at Liberty Hall, New York City, 1922, 453
James Weldon Johnson, "Harlem: The Culture Capital," 454
Louis Armstrong, in *The Negro Almanac,* 456
Alain Locke, *Afro-American Writing: An Anthology of Prose and Poetry,* 457
F. Scott Fitzgerald, *The Great Gatsby,* 458
Edna St. Vincent Millay, "First Fig," from *A Few Figs from Thistles,* 459
Langston Hughes, "Dream Variations," from *The Weary Blues,* 459

CHAPTER 14

Gordon Parks, *A Choice of Weapons,* 464
Frederick Lewis Allen, *Only Yesterday,* 469
Ann Marie Low, *Dust Bowl Diary,* 472
Herman Shumlin, in *Hard Times,* 473
Thomas Wolfe, *You Can't Go Home Again,* 475
Meridel Le Seuer, *America in the Twenties,* 476
Oscar Ameringer, in *The American Spirit,* 478
Herbert Hoover, "Challenge to Liberty," October 1936, 479
A. Everette McIntyre, in *Hard Times,* 483

CHAPTER 15

Hank Oettinger, in *Hard Times,* 488
Franklin Delano Roosevelt, first fireside chat, March 12, 1933, 490
Gardiner C. Means, *The Making of Industrial Policy,* 492
Huey Long, *Record,* 74 Congress, Session 1, 494
Dorothea Lange, in *Restless Spirit: The Life and Work of Dorothea Lange,* 495
John Steinbeck, *The Grapes of Wrath,* 496
Helen Farmer, in *The Great Depression,* 499
Charles Evans Hughes, *NLRB* v. *Jones and Laughlin Steel Corp.* (1937), 502
Pedro J. González, in *Los Angeles Times,* December 9, 1984, 504
Walter White, *A Man Called White,* 506
Jesse Reese, in *The Great Depression,* 508
Don Congdon, *The Thirties: A Time to Remember,* 510
Robert Gwathmey, in *Hard Times,* 513
Woody Guthrie, "Dust Bowl Refugees," 513
George Dobbin, in *These Are Our Lives,* 515
Rexford Tugwell, in *Redeeming the Time,* 516

A PERSONAL VOICE
DOROTHEA LANGE

"The people who are garrulous and wear their heart on their sleeve and tell you everything, that's one kind of person. But the fellow who's hiding behind a tree and hoping you don't see him, is the fellow that you'd better find out why."

—quoted in *Restless Spirit: The Life and Work of Dorothea Lange*

CHAPTER 16

Martha Gellhorn, *The Face of War,* 528
Franklin Delano Roosevelt, "Quarantine Speech," October 5, 1937, 535
William Shirer, *Berlin Diary: The Journal of a Foreign Correspondent, 1934–1941,* 536
Winston Churchill, speech to the House of Commons, in *The Gathering Storm,* 538
Len Jones, in *London at War,* 541
Gerda Weissmann Klein, in the film *One Survivor Remembers,* 542
Liane Reif-Lehrer, in *Failure to Rescue,* 544
Rudolf Reder, in *The Holocaust,* 546
Lilli Kopecky, in *Never Again,* 548
Elie Wiesel, *Night,* 549
Franklin Delano Roosevelt, radio speech, September 3, 1939, 550
John Garcia, in *The Good War,* 555

A PERSONAL VOICE
FRANKLIN DELANO ROOSEVELT

"I have said not once, but many times, that I have seen war and I hate war. . . . As long as it is my power to prevent, there will be no blackout of peace in the U.S."

—radio speech, September 3, 1939

CHAPTER 17

Mrs. Charles Swanson, in *We Pulled Together . . . and Won!,* 562
Sergeant Debs Myers, in *The GI War: 1941–1945,* 563
Alyce Mano Kramer, in *Home Front, U.S.A.,* 565
John Patrick McGrath, *A Cue for Passion,* 569
Ernie Pyle, *Ernie's War: The Best of Ernie Pyle's World War II Dispatches,* 572
Robert T. Johnson, in *Voices: Letters from World War II,* 576
William Manchester, *Goodbye Darkness: A Memoir of the Pacific War,* 578
Ralph G. Martin, *The GI War,* 581
Yamaoka Michiko, in *Japan at War: An Oral History,* 584
Justice Robert Jackson, opening address to the Nuremberg War Crimes Trial, 586
Maya Angelou, *I Know Why the Caged Bird Sings,* 590
Manuel de la Raza, in *A Different Mirror: A History of Multicultural America,* 593
Ted Nakashima, *New Republic Magazine,* June 15, 1942, 595
Justice Hugo Black, *Korematsu* v. *United States* (1944), 596
Frank Murphy, *Korematsu* v. *United States* (1944), 596

CHAPTER 18

Joseph Polowsky, in *The Good War,* 602
Winston Churchill, "Iron Curtain" speech in Fulton, Missouri, 605
Philip Day, Jr., in *The Korean War: Pusan to Chosin,* 609
Beverly Scott, in *No Bugles, No Drums: An Oral History of the Korean War,* 612
Tony Kahn, *The Cold War Comes Home,* 616
Irving Kaufman, in *The Unquiet Death of Julius and Ethel Rosenberg,* 619
Margaret Chase Smith, *Declaration of Conscience,* 620
Annie Dillard, *An American Childhood,* 622
Francis Gary Powers, *Operation Overflight: The U-2 Spy Pilot Tells His Story for the First Time,* 626
Jack Finney, *The Body Snatchers,* 628
Ray Bradbury, *The Martian Chronicles,* 629
Walter M. Miller, Jr., *A Canticle for Leibowitz,* 629

CHAPTER 19

Donald Katz, in *Home Fires,* 634
Harry S. Truman, speech, April 13, 1945, 636
Richard M. Nixon, "Checkers speech," September 23, 1952, 639
Carol Freeman, in *The Fifties: A Women's Oral History,* 641
Ray Kroc, in *The Fifties,* 642
Betty Friedan, *The Feminine Mystique,* 644
Vance Packard, *The Hidden Persuaders,* 649
H. P. Barnum, in *The Rise and Fall of Popular Music,* 652
Newton Minow, speech to the National Association of Broadcasters, Washington, D.C., May 9, 1961, 654
Jack Kerouac, *On the Road,* 655
Thulani Davis, *1959,* 657
James Baldwin, *The Fire Next Time,* 660
Michael Harrington, *The Other America,* 661

CHAPTER 20

John F. Kennedy, "Inaugural Address," 670
Jaqueline Kennedy, in *Life Magazine, John F. Kennedy Memorial Edition,* 672
Robert S. McNamara, *In Retrospect,* 673
C. Douglas Dillon, in *On the Brink,* 676
Alan Shepard, *Moon Shot: The Inside Story of America's Race to the Moon,* 679
President John F. Kennedy, Address on the Nation's Space Effort, 681
Stewart Alsop, "The New President," *Saturday Evening Post,* December 14, 1963, 687
Lyndon B. Johnson, "The Great Society," 689
Chief Justice Earl Warren, *Miranda* v. *Arizona* (1966), 694

CHAPTER 21

Jo Ann Gibson Robinson, in *Voices of Freedom: An Oral History of the Civil Rights Movement,* 700
Martin Luther King, Jr., in *Parting the Waters: America in the King Years, 1954–63,* 705
Chief Justice Earl Warren, *Brown* v. *Board of Education of Topeka* (1954), 708
James Peck, *Freedom Ride,* 710
Martin Luther King, Jr., "Letter from a Birmingham Jail," 712
Martin Luther King, Jr., "I Have a Dream," 714
Fannie Lou Hamer, in *The Civil Rights Movement: An Eyewitness History,* 715
Alice Walker, *In Search of Our Mothers' Gardens,* 717
Malcolm X, in *Eyewitness: The Negro in American History,* 719
Stokely Carmichael, in *The Civil Rights Movement: An Eyewitness History,* 720
Robert F. Kennedy, "A Eulogy for Dr. Martin Luther King, Jr.," 721

A PERSONAL VOICE
MARTIN LUTHER KING, JR.

"We have been repeatedly faced with the cruel irony of watching Negro and white boys on TV screens as they kill and die together for a nation that has been unable to seat them together in the same schools."

—quoted in *America's Vietnam War: A Narrative History*

Primary Sources and Personal Voices

CHAPTER 22

Tim O'Brien, in *A Life in a Year: The American Infantryman in Vietnam,* 736
Dean Rusk, in *In Retrospect,* 737
Salvadore Gonzalez, in *Dear America: Letters Home from Vietnam,* 739
Gerald Coffee, *Beyond Survival,* 740
Stephan Gubar, in *Days of Decision,* 742
Martin Luther King, Jr., in *America's Vietnam War: A Narrative History,* 743
Barry McGuire, "Eve of Destruction," 745
David Harris, in *The War Within,* 746
a firefighter, in *Working-Class War,* 746
Lyndon B. Johnson, in *No Hail, No Farewell,* 747
John Lewis, in *From Camelot to Kent State,* 748
Jack Newfield, in *Nineteen Sixty-Eight,* 751
J. Anthony Lukas, in *Decade of Shocks,* 752
Alfred S. Bradford, in *Some Even Volunteered,* 754

A PERSONAL VOICE
ALFRED S. BRADFORD

"I wanted to be part of that adventure and I believed that it was my duty as an American, both to serve my country and particularly not to stand by while someone else risked his life in my place."

—quoted in *Some Even Volunteered*

Richard M. Nixon, in *The Price of Power,* 755
Lily Jean Lee Adams, in *A Piece of My Heart,* 759
Tim O'Brien, *Going After Cacciato,* 762
Philip Caputo, *A Rumor of War,* 763
Walter Dean Myers, *Fallen Angels,* 763

CHAPTER 23

Jessie Lopez de la Cruz, in *Moving the Mountain: Women Working for Social Change,* 768
Mary Crow Dog, *Lakota Women,* 772
Chief Justice Earl Warren, *Reynolds* v. *Sims* (1964), 774
Betty Freidan, *The Feminine Mystique,* 776
Robin Morgan, *Sisterhood Is Powerful: An Anthology of Writings from the Women's Liberation Movement,* 777
Phyllis Schlafly, in *The Equal Rights Amendment: The History and the Movement,* 779
Alex Forman, in *From Camelot to Kent State,* 781
Tom Mathews, "The Sixties Complex," *Newsweek,* Sept. 5, 1988, 783
Richard M. Nixon, speech at Republican convention, 1968, 785

CHAPTER 24

Henry Kissinger, in *The New Republic,* December 16, 1972, 794
a South Boston mother, in *The School Busing Controversy, 1970–75,* 797
Richard M. Nixon, *The Memoirs of Richard Nixon,* 800
Barbara Jordan, in *Notable Black American Women,* 802
H. R. Haldeman, *The Haldeman Diaries,* 804
James D. Denney, in *Time,* September 23, 1974, 810
Jimmy Carter, in *Keeping Faith,* 812
Justice Lewis Powell, *Regents of the University of California* v. *Bakke* (1978), 818
Lyndon B. Johnson, *1965,* 819
Lois Gibbs, *Love Canal: My Story,* 820
Rachael Carson, *Silent Spring,* 821
anonymous homemaker, in *Accident at Three Mile Island: The Human Dimensions,* 824

CHAPTER 25

Peggy Noonan, *What I Saw at the Revolution: A Political Life in the Reagan Era,* 830
Reverend Jerry Falwell, 832
Ronald Reagan, televised speech to the nation, February 5, 1981, 834
Arthur Laffer, *The Economics of the Tax Revolt: A Reader,* 835
Trevor Ferrell, in *Trevor's Place,* 839
Geraldine Ferraro, in *Vital Speeches of the Day,* 842
Sylvester Monroe, in *The Great Divide,* 843
Colin Powell, *My American Journey,* 848
Ronald Reagan, speech, June 12, 1987, 849
Ronald Reagan, presidential press conference, November 25, 1986, 853

CHAPTER 26

Maya Angelou, "On the Pulse of Morning," 860
Newt Gingrich, *To Renew America,* 864
Ethel Beaudoin, in *Divided We Fall,* 869
Larry Pugh, in *Divided We Fall,* 870
Nikki Giovanni, "Choices," from *Cotton Candy on a Rainy Day,* 874
Amy Tan, *The Joy Luck Club,* 875
Sandra Cisneros, "Four Skinny Trees" from *The House on Mango Street,* 875
Rudy Garcia-Tolson, in *Press-Enterprise,* January 1, 2000, 876
Ellen Ochoa, in *Stanford University School of Engineering Annual Report,* 1997–98, 879
Antonia Hernandez, public statement for *¡Hágase Contar!* Campaign, 2000, 882

A PERSONAL VOICE MAYA ANGELOU

"Lift up your faces, you have a piercing need
For this bright morning dawning for you.
History, despite its wrenching pain,
Cannot be unlived, but if faced
With courage, need not be lived again.

Lift up your eyes
Upon this day breaking for you.
Give birth again
To the dream."

—"On the Pulse of Morning"

Historical and Political Maps

HISTORICAL AND POLITICAL MAPS

North American Cultures in the 1400s 7
European Exploration of the Americas, 1492–1682 17
Site of Jamestown 22
New England Colonies to 1675 25
Middle Colonies to 1700 25
The Thirteen Colonies to the 1700s 29
European Claims in North America, 1754 38
European Claims in North America, 1763 38
Revolutionary War, 1775–1778 59
Revolutionary War, 1778–1781 62
The Land Ordinance of 1785 72
Township #7 73
Lewis and Clark Expedition, 1804–1806 115
U.S. Boundary Settlements, 1803–1819 116
Effects of the Indian Removal Act, 1830s–1840s 125
American Trails West, 1860 132
War for Texas Independence, 1835–1836 134
War with Mexico, 1846–1848 136
Mapping the Oregon Trail 150
The Underground Railroad, 1850–1860 159
Free and Slave States and Territories, 1820–1854 160
Civil War, 1861–1862 170
Battle of Gettysburg, July 1863 176
Vicksburg Campaign, April–July 1863 179
Shrinking Native American Lands, and Battle Sites 205
Cattle Trails and the Railroads, 1870s–1890s 209
Natural Resources and the Birth of a Steel Town, 1886–1906 231
The 14th Ward of Cleveland 234
Major Railroad Lines, 1870–1890 239
U.S. Immigration Patterns, as of 1900 255
New York City, 1910 263
The Chicago Plan 278
Federal Conservation Lands, 1872–1996 323
Election of 1912 331
Alaska, 1867, and Hawaii, 1898 345
The Spanish-American War, 1898 349
U.S. Imperialism, 1867–1906 356
The Panama Canal 366
Europe at the Start of World War I 375
The Western Front, 1914–1916 375
Allied Victories, 1917–1918 386
Europe and the Middle East, 1915 400
Europe and the Middle East, 1919 400
U.S. Patterns of Immigration, 1921–1929 416
Route 66 423
Historic Flights, 1919–1932 449
Harlem in the 1920s 455
The Dust Bowl, 1933–1936 474
The Tennessee Valley Authority 521
The Rise of Nationalism, 1922–1941 530
Japan Invades Manchuria, 1931 532
Italy Invades Ethiopia, 1935–1936 532
German Advances, 1938–1941 538
Japanese Aggression, 1931–1941 556
World War II: Europe and Africa, 1942–1944 572
D-Day, June 6, 1944 575
World War II: The War in the Pacific, 1942–1945 580
African-American Migration, 1940–1950 591
Japanese Relocation Camps, 1942 594
The Iron Curtain, 1949 605
Taiwan 611
The Korean War, 1950–1953 613
The Warsaw Pact and NATO, 1955 624
Israel 625
Presidential Election of 1948 638
Park Forest, Illinois 650
Cuban Missile Crisis, October 1962 675
The Berlin Wall, 1961 677
The Movement of Migrant Workers 685
The War in Vietnam 688
U.S. School Segregation, 1952 701
Indochina, 1959 733
Tet Offensive, Jan. 30–Feb. 24, 1968 749
Presidential Election of 1968 753
Alabama Election Districts, 1901 and 1973 775
Soviet-Afghanistan War 815
Middle East, 1978–1982 816
Presidential Election of 1980 833
Americans on the Move, 1970s 846
Americans on the Move, 1990–2000 847
Central America and the Caribbean, 1981–1992 851
The Persian Gulf War, 1990–1991 854
World Trading Blocs, 2000 872
Changes in U.S. Immigration, 2000 885

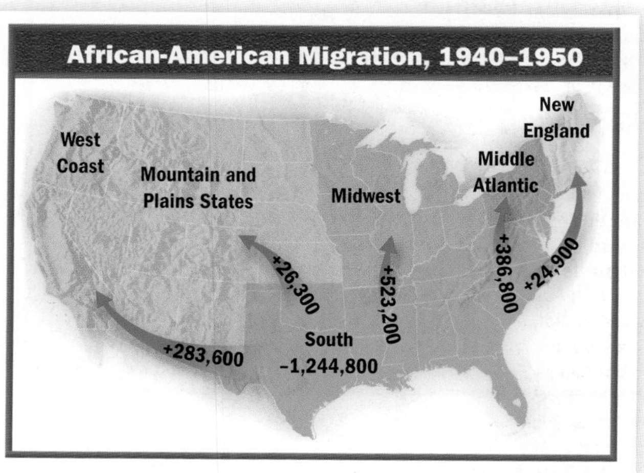

Graphs and Tables

GRAPHS

Voter Turnout, 1998 Federal Elections 105
African Americans in the South, 1860 147
Northern and Southern Resources, 1861 169
The Costs of the Civil War 182
The Growth of Union Membership, 1878–1904 247
U.S. Immigration Patterns, as of 1900 255
Expanding Education/Increasing Literacy 283
Revenue from Individual Federal Income Tax, 1915–1995 334
Hawaii's Changing Population, 1853–1920 344
U.S. Exports to Europe, 1912–1917 377
The War Economy, 1914–1920 389
Immigration to the United States, 1921 and 1929 416
Automobile Registration, 1910–1930 427

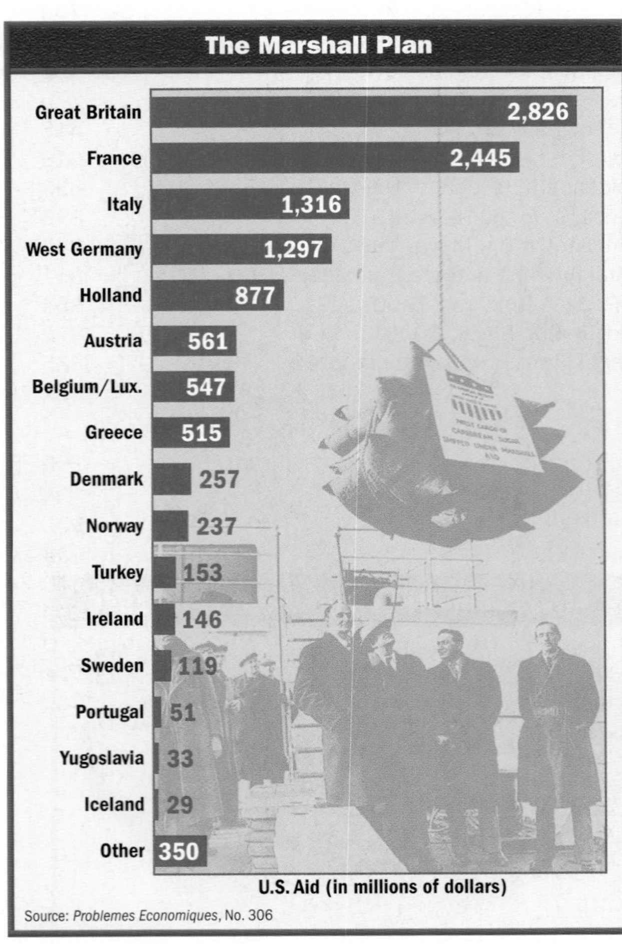

Source: *Problemes Economiques*, No. 306

Women's Changing Employment, 1910–1930 442
High School Enrollment, 1910–1940 447
Uneven Income Distribution, 1929 466
Depression Indicators: Bank Failures, Business Failures, Unemployment, Income and Spending 470
The Growing Labor Movement, 1930–1940 508
Federal Deficit and Unemployment, 1933–1945 517
The Production Miracle 564
The Marshall Plan 606
U.S. Budget, 1940–2000 626
A Dynamic Economy 636
American Birthrate, 1940–1970 643
Glued to the Set 653
U.S. School Enrollments, 1950–1990 659
Teenagers and Employment, 1950–1990 659
Income Gap in America 661
U.S. Space Race Expenditures, 1959–1975 681
Changes in Poverty and Education 723
U.S. Military Personnel in Vietnam 743
U.S. Aerial Bomb Tonnage, 1965-1971 755
Women in the Workplace, 1950–2000 777
Average Weekly Hours of TV Viewing 809
Unemployment and Inflation, 1970–1980 813
Employment in Manufacturing and Service Industries, 1950–2000 814
Regional Internal Migration, 1982–1998 846

TABLES

Average Age at Marriage 41
Who Could Divorce? 41
Early Airplane Engines and Their Weights 280
Changes in the U.S. Workweek 299
Election of 1912 331
Goods and Prices, 1900–1928 425
Estimated Jewish Losses 545
Presidential Election of 1948 638
Election of 1968 753
Presidential Election of 1980 833
Women's and Men's Average Yearly Earnings in Selected Careers, 1982 842
Persons Employed in Three Economic Sectors 871
The Graying of America, 1990–2030 884

Charts and Time Lines

CHARTS

Native American Trade 7
Economic Activities 29
Military Strengths and Weaknesses 59
Weaknesses of the Articles of Confederation 67
Key Conflicts in the Constitutional Convention 69
Contrasting Views of the Federal Government 76
Requirements for Holding Federal Office 84
The Costs of the Civil War: Economic Costs 182
Long Odds 213
Goldbugs and Silverites 222
Alliances During WWI 379
Domestic Consequences of World War I 403
Prohibition, 1920–1933 437
Women's Changing Employment, 1910–1930 442
Slang Expressions 445
Civilian Conservation Corps 491
New Deal Programs 500
The Government Takes Control of the Economy, 1942–1945 567
War Criminals on Trial, 1945–1949 586
Applications of World War II Technology 589
U.S. Aims Versus Soviet Aims in Europe 604
Nationalists Versus Communists, 1945 610
Causes and Effects of McCarthyism 621
Great Society Programs, 1964–1967 690
Civil Rights Acts of the 1950s and 1960s 714
Popular Songs/Popular TV Shows 787
Goals of the Conservative Movement 831

Civilian Conservation Corps

- The CCC provided almost 3 million men aged 18–25 with work and wages between 1933 and 1942.
- The men lived in work camps under a strict regime. The majority of the camps were racially segregated.
- By 1938, the CCC had an 11 percent African-American enrollment.
- Accomplishments of the CCC include planting over 3 billion trees, developing over 800 state parks, and building more than 46,000 bridges.

TIME LINES

British Actions and Colonial Reactions, 1765–1775 48
From Telegraph to Internet 140
The Technological Explosion, 1826–1903 232
Visual Summary: World War Looms 558
World War II: The War in the Pacific and Europe 580
Cuban Missile Crisis, October, 1962 675
Visual Summary: Civil Rights 726
Visual Summary: The Vietnam War Years 764
Native American Legal Victories 773
Signs of the Sixties 787
History of Terrorist Attacks Against the United States 896
History of Saddam Hussein's Regime 898
History of Immigration in the United States 900
History of Crime and Public Safety in the United States 902
History of Education in the United States 904
History of the Communications Revolution 906
History of Health Care in the United States 908
History of the Cycle of Poverty in the United States 910
History of Entitlements in the United States 912
History of Women at Work in the United States 914
History of Conservation in the United States 916

The Technological Explosion, 1826–1903

- **1826** Photography
- **1831** Reaper
- **1837** Telegraph
- **1846** Sewing Machine
- **1860** Internal-Combustion Engine
- **1867** Dynamite; Typewriter
- **1873** Electric Motor
- **1876** Telephone
- **1877** Phonograph
- **1879** Light Bulb
- **1895** Radio; Motion Pictures; X-Ray
- **1903** Airplane

Infographics

INFOGRAPHICS

The Columbian Exchange 15
Spanish Missions in the Southwest 19
Rediscovering Fort James 22
Daily Urban Life in Colonial Times 34
Visual Summary: Exploration and the Colonial Era 42
Visual Summary: Revolution and the Early Republic 80
How a Bill in Congress Becomes a Law 87
Visual Summary: The Living Constitution 106
Southern Plantations 147
Visual Summary: The Growth of a Young Nation 152
Visual Summary: The Union in Peril 190
Importance of the Buffalo 207
Visual Summary: Changes on the Western Frontier 226
Vertical and Horizontal Integration 242
Visual Summary: A New Industrial Age 250
Fire: Enemy of the City 265
Visual Summary: Immigrants and Urbanization 272
Visual Summary: Life at the Turn of the 20th Century 300
Coal Mining in the Early 1900s 321
Visual Summary: The Progressive Era 338
The Panama Canal 361
Visual Summary: America Claims an Empire 368
Trench Warfare 376
World War I Convoy System 383
Visual Summary: The First World War 406
Route 66 423
Visual Summary: Politics of the Roaring Twenties 430
Radio Broadcasts of the 1920s 447
Sports Heroes of the 1920s 448
Harlem in the 1920s 455
Visual Summary: The Roaring Life of the 1920s 460
Visual Summary: The Great Depression Begins 484
The Growing Labor Movement, 1933–1940 508
The Tennessee Valley Authority 520
Visual Summary: The New Deal 522
The Faces of Totalitarianism 531
Visual Summary: The United States in World War II 598
Nationalists Versus Communists, 1945 610
Visual Summary: Cold War Conflicts 630
Americans Hit the Road 647
Visual Summary: The Postwar Boom 664
The Berlin Wall, 1961 677
Visual Summary: The New Frontier and the Great Society 696
Tunnels of the Vietcong 738
Visual Summary: An Era of Social Change 788
The Inner Circle 803
Visual Summary: An Age of Limits 826
Visual Summary: The Conservative Tide 856
Visual Summary: The United States in Today's World 890

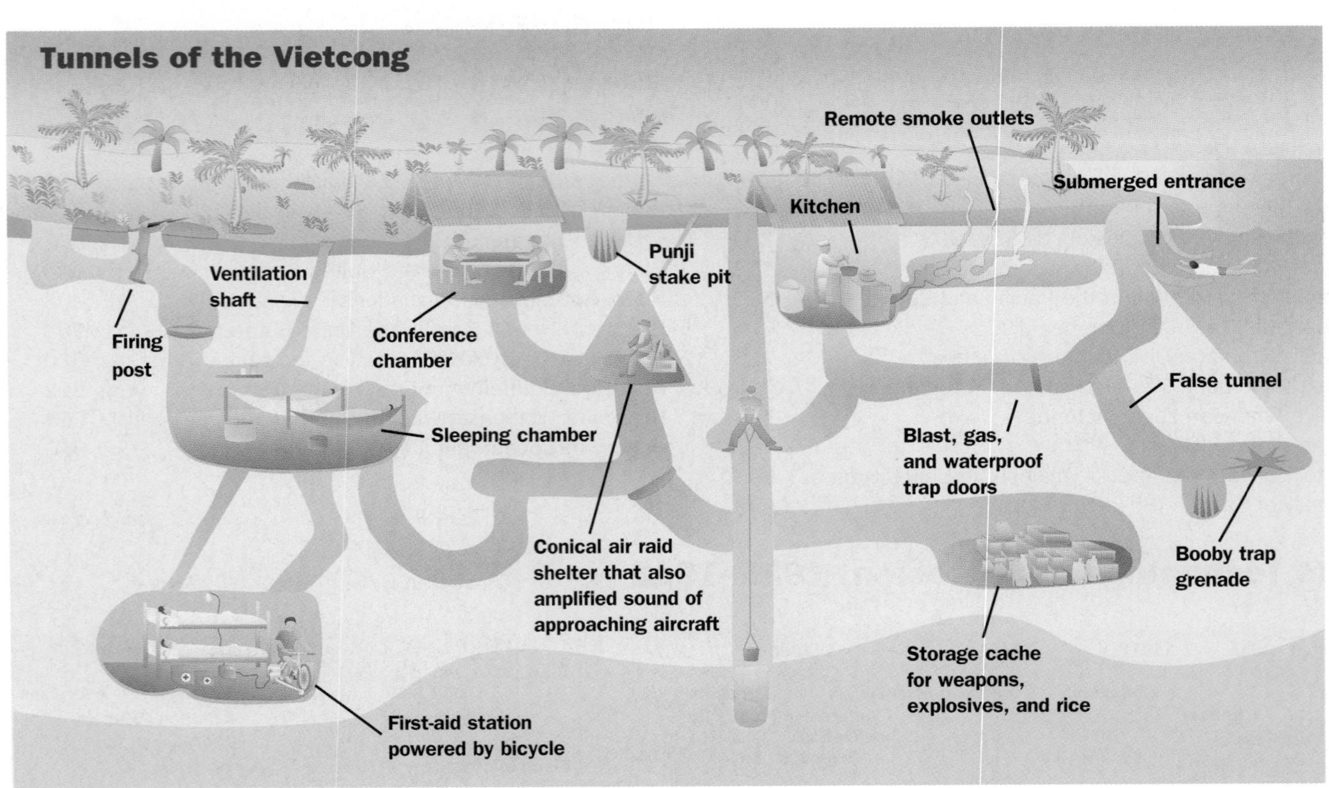

SKILLBUILDER HANDBOOK

1. UNDERSTANDING HISTORICAL READINGS

1.1 Finding Main Ideas R2
1.2 Following Chronological Order R3
1.3 Clarifying; Summarizing R4
1.4 Identifying Problems R5
1.5 Analyzing Motives R6
1.6 Analyzing Causes and Effects R7
1.7 Comparing; Contrasting R8
1.8 Distinguishing Fact from Opinion R9
1.9 Making Inferences R10

2. USING CRITICAL THINKING

2.1 Developing Historical Perspective R11
2.2 Formulating Historical Questions R12
2.3 Hypothesizing R13
2.4 Analyzing Issues R14
2.5 Analyzing Assumptions and Biases R15
2.6 Evaluating Decisions and Courses of Action R16
2.7 Forming Opinions (Evaluating) R17
2.8 Drawing Conclusions R18
2.9 Synthesizing R19
2.10 Making Predictions R20
2.11 Forming Generalizations R21

3. PRINT, VISUAL, AND TECHNOLOGICAL SOURCES

3.1 Primary and Secondary Sources R22
3.2 Visual, Audio, Multimedia Sources R23
3.3 Analyzing Political Cartoons R24
3.4 Interpreting Maps R25
3.5 Interpreting Charts R27
3.6 Interpreting Graphs R28
3.7 Using the Internet R29

4. PRESENTING INFORMATION

4.1 Creating Charts and Graphs R30
4.2 Creating Models R31
4.3 Creating Maps R32
4.4 Creating Databases R33
4.5 Creating Written Presentations R34
4.6 Creating Oral Presentations R36
4.7 Creating Visual Presentations R37

AMERICAN STORIES VIDEO SERIES

American Stories is a powerful video series integrated with the text of *The Americans*. Seventeen fascinating documentaries, each ten to fifteen minutes long, help introduce various sections. Three volumes are available in English and Spanish.

VOLUME 1

PATRIOT FATHER, LOYALIST SON *The Divided House of Benjamin and William Franklin*—Chapter 2

RECRUITED BY LEWIS AND CLARK *Patrick Gass Chronicles the Journey West*—Chapter 3

WAR OUTSIDE MY WINDOW *Mary Chesnut's Diary of the Civil War*—Chapter 4

TEACHER OF A FREED PEOPLE *Robert Fitzgerald and Reconstruction*—Chapter 4

A WALK IN TWO WORLDS *The Education of Zitkala-Ša, a Sioux*—Chapter 5

GUSHER! *Patillo Higgins and the Great Texas Oil Boom*—Chapter 6

VOLUME 2

FROM CHINA TO CHINATOWN *Fong See's American Dream*—Chapter 7

A CHILD ON STRIKE *The Testimony of Camella Teoli, Mill Girl*—Chapter 9

ACE OF ACES *Eddie Rickenbacker and the First World War*—Chapter 11

JUMP AT THE SUN *Zora Neale Hurston and the Harlem Renaissance*—Chapter 13

BROKE, BUT NOT BROKEN *Ann Marie Low Remembers the Dust Bowl*—Chapter 14

A SONG FOR HIS PEOPLE *Pedro J. González and the Fight for Mexican-American Rights*—Chapter 15

VOLUME 3

ESCAPING THE FINAL SOLUTION *Kurt Klein and Gerda Weissmann Klein Remember the Holocaust*—Chapter 16

THE COLD WAR COMES HOME *Hollywood Blacklists the Kahn Family*—Chapter 18

JUSTICE IN MONTGOMERY *Jo Ann Gibson Robinson and the Bus Boycott*—Chapter 21

MATTERS OF CONSCIENCE *Stephan Gubar and the Vietnam War*—Chapter 22

POISONED PLAYGROUND *Lois Gibbs and the Crisis at Love Canal*—Chapter 24

Themes in History

The Americans *focuses on nine themes, described on these pages. As you study U.S. history, you will encounter these and other themes again and again. The Thematic Review on pages 192–197 and the Tracing Themes features organize major events in United States history around these themes. What do you think are the important issues raised by each theme?*

DIVERSITY AND THE NATIONAL IDENTITY

E Pluribus Unum—From the Many, One. Pick up a dollar bill and you'll find this Latin motto on the Great Seal of the United States. From the first settlement, this has been a land of many peoples, cultures, and faiths. This mixing of ethnic, racial, and religious groups has produced a rich and uniquely American culture. It has also led to competition and conflict. Today, the United States is more diverse than ever, yet the nation's motto remains *E Pluribus Unum*. (See **Tracing Themes** on page 260.)

Critical Thinking **How do you think America today is enriched by its diversity?**

AMERICA IN WORLD AFFAIRS

From the earliest colonial times, the United States has been influenced by the events, people, and forms of government in other nations—and America has influenced world affairs. Today, relationships between the United States and other countries are more critical than ever, as modern communications and transportation have drawn the world closer together. As America continues to participate in world affairs, questions of trade, diplomacy, and regional conflict will grow in importance. (See **Tracing Themes** on page 404.)

Critical Thinking **What do you think America's role in the world should be in the 21st century?**

ECONOMIC OPPORTUNITY

America has always been a land of economic opportunity. Blessed with fertile land and abundant resources, this has been a country where anyone who has worked hard has had a chance to prosper. Indeed, American history is full of heartening "rags-to-riches" success stories. Just as inspiring are the heroic struggles of women and minorities who fought to improve their economic prospects. As your generation enters the work force, you and your friends will have the opportunity to write your own success stories. (See **Tracing Themes** on page 428.)

Critical Thinking **What do you think are the most exciting economic opportunities for Americans today?**

SCIENCE AND TECHNOLOGY

Americans have always had a deep respect for the power of science and technology to improve life. In the past two centuries, new inventions, new technologies, and scientific breakthroughs have transformed the United States—and continue to appear at a dizzying pace. Which ones will change your life? You can be sure that some will, and in ways that no one can yet predict. (See **Tracing Themes** on page 588.)

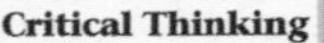

How do you think science and technology will change American life in the 21st century?

WOMEN AND POLITICAL POWER

More than half of all Americans are women, but only recently have their contributions and concerns found their way into history books. American women have helped shape the social and political history of every era. In their private roles as wives and mothers, they have strengthened families and raised America's children. In their more public roles as workers, reformers, and crusaders for equal rights, they have attacked the nation's worst social ills and challenged barriers to women's full participation in American life. (See **Tracing Themes** on page 64.)

Critical Thinking **What do you think is the most important goal for American women today?**

IMMIGRATION AND MIGRATION

Seeking a better life seems to be part of the American character. This nation was first established by and has remained a magnet for immigrants. One out of every ten people living in the United States today was born in another country. Moreover, every year one out of every six Americans moves to a new address. (See **Tracing Themes** on page 888.)

Critical Thinking **Why do you think people continue to have the dream of immigrating to the United States?**

STATES' RIGHTS

The power struggle between states and the federal government has caused controversy since the country's beginning. In 1861 the conflict led to the Civil War, in which Southern states acted upon the belief that they had the right to nullfy acts of the federal government and even to leave the Union if they chose to do so. Throughout the history of this country, state and federal governments have squared off on this and other constitutional issues. (See **Tracing Themes** on page 128.)

Critical Thinking **When do you think a state has the right to challenge a federal law?**

VOTING RIGHTS

When Americans first began their experiment with democracy, only white men with property could vote or hold office. Over the past two centuries, women, African Americans, and other groups have fought for and won the right to vote and participate in government. Today the challenge is getting people to exercise the right to vote. In 2000, only 50.7 percent of eligible voters cast ballots in the presidential election. (See **Tracing Themes** on page 104.)

Critical Thinking **What do you think can be done to bring more Americans into the democratic process?**

CIVIL RIGHTS

The American system of government is based on a simple but revolutionary idea: Every citizen has certain rights and liberties. Among them are the right to participate in government and to exercise such liberties as freedom of speech and worship. Deciding who should have what rights, how these rights should be exercised, and how to protect a person's civil rights is anything but easy. Defining and protecting our civil rights is not likely to get any easier. (See **Tracing Themes** on page 724.)

Critical Thinking **What issue of civil rights do you think is most critical in the United States today?**

Themes in Geography

The history of a nation is shaped as much by geography as by people and events. Paying attention to the following themes of geography can help you recognize when geographic forces are at work in the story of the United States.

LOCATION

Geographers speak of absolute location—the latitude and longitude of an area—and of relative location—where one area is in relation to another. In absolute terms, the city of San Francisco lies at 37°45' North latitude and 122°26' West longitude. This information allows you to pinpoint San Francisco on a map. In relative terms, San Francisco lies at the western edge of North America and looks out across the vast Pacific Ocean. This information helps explain San Francisco's history as a port city where people and ideas have come together.

Critical Thinking **Locate your city or town on both a political and a physical map. How has location influenced the history of your city or town?**

PLACE

Place, in geography, refers to what an area looks like in physical and human terms. An area's landforms, soil, climate, and resources are aspects of place. So are the numbers and cultures of the population. San Francisco's natural harbor has made the city an international port. It is connected to the American River—where gold was discovered in 1848. Its position along a major fault line has subjected it to periodic earthquakes, the most disastrous in 1906. During its history, San Francisco has attracted people from North America, Europe, Asia, and various Pacific islands, making its population one of the most diverse in the United States.

Critical Thinking **What is unique about the place where you live and the people who live there? What past events contributed to its uniqueness?**

REGION

Geographers use the idea of region to show what places in close proximity to one another have in common. As a part of the Pacific Coast region, San Francisco shares with Seattle, Washington, and Portland, Oregon, a mild, rainy climate and an economic interest in international shipping. As a part of California, San Francisco shares economic and environmental concerns of the state as a whole.

Critical Thinking **To what region or regions does your area belong? How have the characteristics and concerns of your region changed over the last generation?**

MOVEMENT

One place or region can influence another through the movement of people, materials, and even ideas. San Francisco has been the site of many important movements of people and cultures. It has been a port of entry for immigrants, many of them Asian. It also lies along the path that Spanish missionaries trod in their quest to convert native peoples.

Critical Thinking **When and by what groups was your area settled? What trends in movement today may shape the future of your area?**

HUMAN-ENVIRONMENT INTERACTION

Wherever people live, they affect the environment in the way they modify their natural surroundings. They build shelters and clear trees. They turn the earth inside out to extract its resources. People in the San Francisco Bay area have built bridges in order to move around more easily. People have also modified the bay itself, reducing its area by about one-third as they filled in tidelands for development.

Critical Thinking **How have people in your area modified their surroundings? What consquences might these modifications have?**

STRATEGIES FOR TAKING STANDARDIZED TESTS

This section of the textbook helps you develop and practice the skills you need to study history and to take standardized tests. Part 1, **Strategies for Studying History,** takes you through the features of the textbook and offers suggestions on how to use these features to improve your reading and study skills.

Part 2, **Test-Taking Strategies and Practice,** offers specific strategies for tackling many of the items you'll find on a standardized test. It gives tips for answering multiple-choice, constructed-response, extended-response, and document-based questions. In addition, it offers guidelines for analyzing primary and secondary sources, maps, political cartoons, charts, graphs, and time lines. Each strategy is followed by a set of questions you can use for practice.

CONTENTS

Part 1: Strategies for Studying History S2

Part 2: Test-Taking Strategies and Practice

- Multiple Choice S6
- Primary Sources S8
- Secondary Sources S10
- Political Cartoons S12
- Charts S14
- Line and Bar Graphs S16
- Pie Graphs S18
- Political Maps S20
- Thematic Maps S22
- Time Lines S24
- Constructed Response S26
- Extended Response S28
- Document-Based Questions S30

Part 1: Strategies for Studying History

Reading is the central skill in the effective study of history or any other subject. You can improve your reading skills by using helpful techniques and by practicing. The better your reading skills, the more you'll remember of what you read. Below you'll find several strategies that involve built-in features of *The Americans*. Careful use of these strategies will help you learn and understand history more effectively.

Preview Chapters Before You Read

Each chapter begins with a two-page chapter opener. Study the chapter opener to help you get ready to read.

1. Read the chapter title. Look for clues that indicate what will be covered in the chapter.
2. Look at the chapter-opening visual. Try to identify the theme or themes of the chapter based on this illustration.
3. Preview the time line. Note the years that the chapter covers and identify the important events that took place in the United States and across the world during this time period.
4. Study the **Interact with History** feature. Examine the major issues discussed in the chapter by answering the questions.

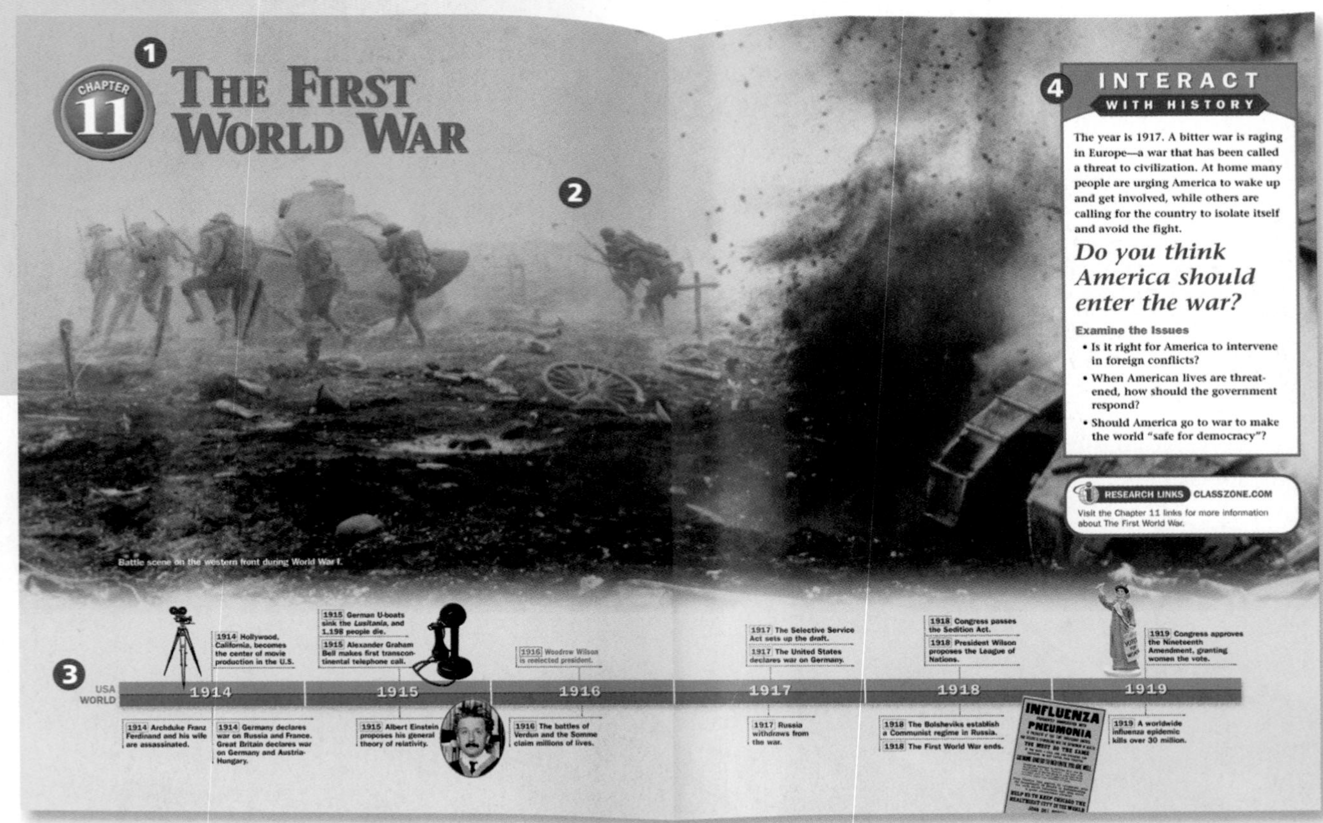

1 CHAPTER 11 THE FIRST WORLD WAR

2

Battle scene on the western front during World War I.

4 INTERACT WITH HISTORY

The year is 1917. A bitter war is raging in Europe—a war that has been called a threat to civilization. At home many people are urging America to wake up and get involved, while others are calling for the country to isolate itself and avoid the fight.

Do you think America should enter the war?

Examine the Issues
- Is it right for America to intervene in foreign conflicts?
- When American lives are threatened, how should the government respond?
- Should America go to war to make the world "safe for democracy"?

RESEARCH LINKS CLASSZONE.COM

Visit the Chapter 11 links for more information about The First World War.

3

USA

1914 Hollywood, California, becomes the center of movie production in the U.S.

1915 German U-boats sink the *Lusitania*, and 1,198 people die.

1915 Alexander Graham Bell makes first transcontinental telephone call.

1916 Woodrow Wilson is reelected president.

1917 The Selective Service Act sets up the draft.

1917 The United States declares war on Germany.

1918 Congress passes the Sedition Act.

1918 President Wilson proposes the League of Nations.

1919 Congress approves the Nineteenth Amendment, granting women the vote.

1914 1915 1916 1917 1918 1919

WORLD

1914 Archduke Franz Ferdinand and his wife are assassinated.

1914 Germany declares war on Russia and France. Great Britain declares war on Germany and Austria-Hungary.

1915 Albert Einstein proposes his general theory of relativity.

1916 The battles of Verdun and the Somme claim millions of lives.

1917 Russia withdraws from the war.

1918 The Bolsheviks establish a Communist regime in Russia.

1918 The First World War ends.

INFLUENZA

PNEUMONIA

1919 A worldwide influenza epidemic kills over 30 million.

Preview Sections Before You Read

Each chapter consists of three, four, or five sections. These sections focus on shorter periods of time or on particular historical themes. Use the section openers to help you prepare to read.

1. Study the sentences under the headings **Main Idea** and **Why It Matters Now.** These tell you what's important in the material that you're about to read.
2. Preview the **Terms & Names** list. This will give you an idea of the issues and personalities you'll encounter in the section.
3. Read **One American's Story** and **A Personal Voice** within it. These provide one individual's view of an important issue of the time.
4. Notice the structure of the section. **Blue** heads label the major topics; **red** subheads signal smaller topics within a major topic. Together, these heads give you a quick outline of the section.

Terms & Names

- nationalism
- militarism
- Allies
- Central Powers
- Archduke Franz Ferdinand
- no man's land
- trench warfare
- *Lusitania*
- Zimmermann note

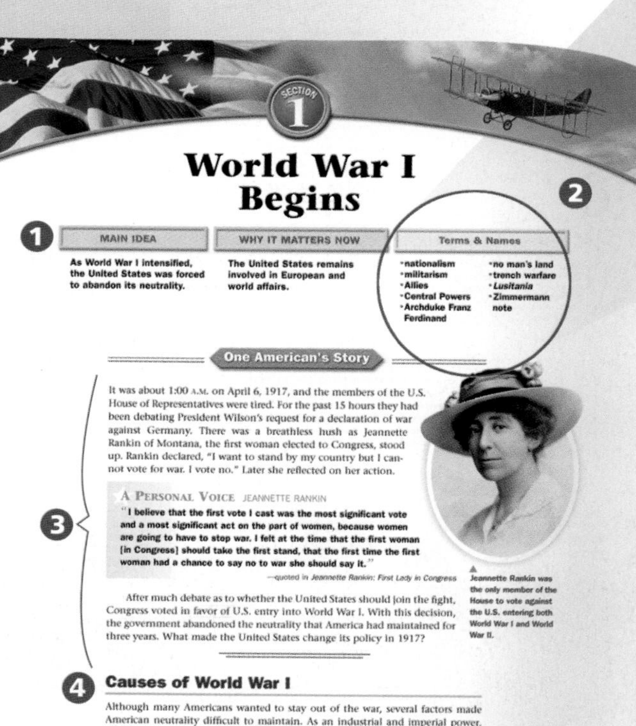

SECTION 1

World War I Begins

2

1

MAIN IDEA

As World War I intensified, the United States was forced to abandon its neutrality.

WHY IT MATTERS NOW

The United States remains involved in European and world affairs.

Terms & Names

- nationalism
- militarism
- Allies
- Central Powers
- Archduke Franz Ferdinand
- no man's land
- trench warfare
- *Lusitania*
- Zimmermann note

One American's Story

3

It was about 1:00 A.M. on April 6, 1917, and the members of the U.S. House of Representatives were tired. For the past 15 hours they had been debating President Wilson's request for a declaration of war against Germany. There was a breathless hush as Jeannette Rankin of Montana, the first woman elected to Congress, stood up. Rankin declared, "I want to stand by my country but I cannot vote for war. I vote no." Later she reflected on her action.

A PERSONAL VOICE JEANNETTE RANKIN

"I believe that the first vote I cast was the most significant vote and a most significant act on the part of women, because women are going to have to stop war. I felt at the time that the first woman [in Congress] should take the first stand, that the first time the first woman had a chance to say no to war she should say it."

—quoted in *Jeannette Rankin: First Lady in Congress*

Jeannette Rankin was the only member of the House to vote against the U.S. entering both World War I and World War II.

After much debate as to whether the United States should join the fight, Congress voted in favor of U.S. entry into World War I. With this decision, the government abandoned the neutrality that America had maintained for three years. What made the United States change its policy in 1917?

4

Causes of World War I

Although many Americans wanted to stay out of the war, several factors made American neutrality difficult to maintain. As an industrial and imperial power, the United States felt many of the same pressures that had led the nations of Europe into devastating warfare. Historians generally cite four long-term causes of the First World War: nationalism, imperialism, militarism, and the formation of a system of alliances.

4

NATIONALISM Throughout the 19th century, politics in the Western world were deeply influenced by the concept of **nationalism**—a devotion to the interests and culture of one's nation. Often, nationalism led to competitive and antagonistic rivalries among nations. In this atmosphere of competition, many feared Germany's growing power in Europe.

In addition, various ethnic groups resented domination by others and longed for their nations to become independent. Many ethnic groups looked to larger nations for protection. Russia regarded itself as the protector of Europe's Slavic peoples, no matter which government they lived under. Among these Slavic peoples were the Serbs. Serbia, located in the Balkans, was an independent nation, but millions of ethnic Serbs lived under the rule of Austria-Hungary. As a result, Russia and Austria-Hungary were rivals for influence over Serbia.

MAIN IDEA

Analyzing Causes

A How did nationalism and imperialism lead to conflict in Europe?

IMPERIALISM For many centuries, European nations had been building empires, slowly extending their economic and political control over various peoples of the world. Colonies supplied the European imperial powers with raw materials and provided markets for manufactured goods. As Germany industrialized, it competed with France and Britain in the contest for colonies. A

MILITARISM Empires were expensive to build and to defend. The growth of nationalism and imperialism led to increased military spending. Because each nation wanted stronger armed forces than those of any potential enemy, the imperial powers followed a policy of **militarism**—the development of armed forces and their use as a tool of diplomacy.

By 1890 the strongest nation on the European continent was Germany, which had set up an army reserve system that drafted and trained young men. Britain was not initially alarmed by Germany's military expansion. As an island nation, Britain had always relied on its navy for defense and protection of its shipping routes—and the British navy was the strongest in the world. However, in 1897, Wilhelm II, Germany's kaiser, or emperor, decided that his nation should also become a major sea power in order to compete more successfully against the British. Soon British and German shipyards competed to build the largest battleships and destroyers. France, Italy, Japan, and the United States quickly joined the naval arms race.

Vocabulary

alliance: a formal agreement or union between nations

ALLIANCE SYSTEM By 1907 there were two major defense alliances in Europe. The Triple Entente, later known as the **Allies,** consisted of France, Britain, and Russia. The Triple Alliance consisted of Germany, Austria-Hungary, and Italy.

German Emperor Wilhelm II *(center)* marches with two of his generals, Hindenburg *(left)* and Ludendorff, during World War I.

Use Active Reading Strategies As You Read

Now you're ready to read the chapter. Read one section at a time, from beginning to end.

1. Try to visualize the people, places, and events you read about. Studying illustrated features, such as **Key Player,** and other visual materials, such as **Science & Technology,** will help you do this.
2. Look for the story behind the events. Read **Background** notes for additional information on particular events.
3. Skim the pages of the section to find key words. Use the **Vocabulary** notes in the margin to find the meaning of unfamiliar terms.
4. Ask and answer questions as you read. Look for the **Main Idea** questions in the margin. Answering these will show whether you understand what you have just read.

MAIN IDEA

Analyzing Effects

D What were the physical and psychological effects of this new kind of warfare?

KEY PLAYER 1

GENERAL JOHN J. PERSHING 1860–1948

When General Pershing, the commander of the American Expeditionary Force (AEF), arrived in France, he found that the Allies intended to use American troops simply as reinforcements. Pershing, however, urged that the AEF operate as an independent fighting force, under American command.

Pershing believed in aggressive combat and felt that three years of trench warfare had made the Allies too defensive. Under Pershing, American forces helped to stop the German advance, capturing important enemy positions. After the war, Pershing was made General of the Armies of the United States—the highest rank given to an officer.

Fighting "Over There"

The **American Expeditionary Force** (AEF), led by **General John J. Pershing,** included men from widely separated parts of the country. American infantrymen were nicknamed doughboys, possibly because of the white belts they wore, which they cleaned with pipe clay, or "dough." Most doughboys had never ventured far from the farms or small towns where they lived, and the sophisticated sights and sounds of Paris made a vivid impression. However, doughboys were also shocked by the unexpected horrors of the battlefield and astonished by the new weapons and tactics of modern warfare.

3

Vocabulary
tactics: the science of using forces on combat

NEW WEAPONS The battlefields of World War I saw the first large-scale use of weapons that would become standard in modern war. Although some of these weapons were new, others, like the machine gun, had been so refined that they changed the nature of warfare. The two most innovative weapons were the tank and the airplane. Together, they heralded mechanized warfare, or warfare that relies on machines powered by gasoline and diesel engines. C

Tanks ran on caterpillar treads and were built of steel so that bullets bounced off. The British first used tanks during the 1916 Battle of the Somme, but not very effectively. By 1917, the British had learned how to drive large numbers of tanks through barbed wire defenses, clearing a path for the infantry.

The early airplanes were so flimsy that at first both sides limited their use to scouting. After a while, the two sides used tanks to fire at enemy planes that were gathering information. Early dogfights, or individual air combats, like the one described by Eddie Rickenbacker, resembled duels. Pilots sat in their open cockpits and shot at each other with pistols. Because it was hard to fly a plane and shoot a pistol at the same time, planes began carrying mounted machine guns. But the planes' propeller blades kept getting in the way of the bullets. Then the Germans introduced an interrupter gear that permitted the stream of bullets to avoid the whirring blades.

2

Meanwhile, airplanes were built to travel faster and ... By 1918 the British had built up a strategic bomber force of 22,000 planes with which to attack German weapons factories and army bases.

Observation balloons were used extensively by both sides in the war in Europe. Balloons were so important strategically that they were often protected by aircraft flying close by, and they became prime targets for Rickenbacker and other ace pilots.

The War Introduces New Hazards

The new weapons and tactics of World War I led to horrific injuries and hazards. The fighting men were surrounded by filth, lice, rats, and polluted water that caused dysentery. They inhaled poison gas and smelled the stench of decaying bodies. They suffered from lack of sleep. Constant bombardments and other experiences often led to battle fatigue and "shell shock," a term coined during World War I to describe a complete emotional collapse from which many never recovered.

4

Physical problems included a disease called trench foot, caused by standing in cold wet trenches for long periods of time without changing into dry socks or boots. First the toes would turn red or blue, then they would become numb, and finally they would start to rot. The only solution was to amputate the toes, and in some cases the entire foot. A painful infection of the gums and throat, called trench mouth, was also common among the soldiers. D

Red Cross ambulances, often staffed by American volunteers, carried the wounded from the battlefield to the hospital. An American nurse named Florence Bullard recounted her experience in a hospital near the front in 1918.

A PERSONAL VOICE FLORENCE BULLARD

"The Army is only twelve miles away from us and only the wounded that are too severely injured to live to be carried a little farther are brought here. . . . Side by side I have Americans, English, Scotch, Irish, and French, and apart in the corners are Boche [Germans]. They have to watch each other die side by side. I am sent for everywhere—in the . . . operating-room, the dressing-room, and back again to the rows of men. . . . The cannon goes day and night and the shells are breaking over and around us. . . . I have had to write many sad letters to American mothers. I wonder if it will ever end."

—quoted in *Over There: The Story of America's First Great Overseas Crusade*

In fact, the end was near, as German forces mounted a final offensive.

1 Science & Technology

TECHNOLOGY AT WAR

Both sides in World War I used new technology to attack more soldiers from greater distances than ever before. Aircraft and long-range guns were even used to fire on civilian targets—libraries, cathedrals, and city districts. The biggest guns could shell a city from 75 miles.

Machine Guns
Firepower increased to 600 rounds per minute.

Airships and Airplanes
One of the most famous WWI planes, the British Sopwith Camel, had a front-mounted machine gun for "dogfights." Planes were also loaded with bombs, as were the floating gas-filled "airships" called zeppelins.

Antiaircraft Gun

Poison Gas
A yellow-green chlorine fog sickened, suffocated, burned, and blinded its victims. Gas masks became standard issue.

Tanks
Tanks, like this French light tank, were used to "mow down" barbed wire and soldiers.

Background

When the U.S. entered the war, its air power was weak. Then, in July 1917, Congress appropriated a hefty $675 million to build an air force.

Review and Summarize What You Have Read

When you finish reading a section, review and summarize what you've read. If necessary, go back and reread information that was not clear the first time through.

1. Look again at the **blue** heads and **red** subheads for a quick summary of the major points covered in the section.
2. Study any **maps** and **charts** in the section. These visual materials usually provide a condensed version of information in the section.
3. Complete all the questions in the **Section Assessment.** This will help you think critically about the material you've just read.

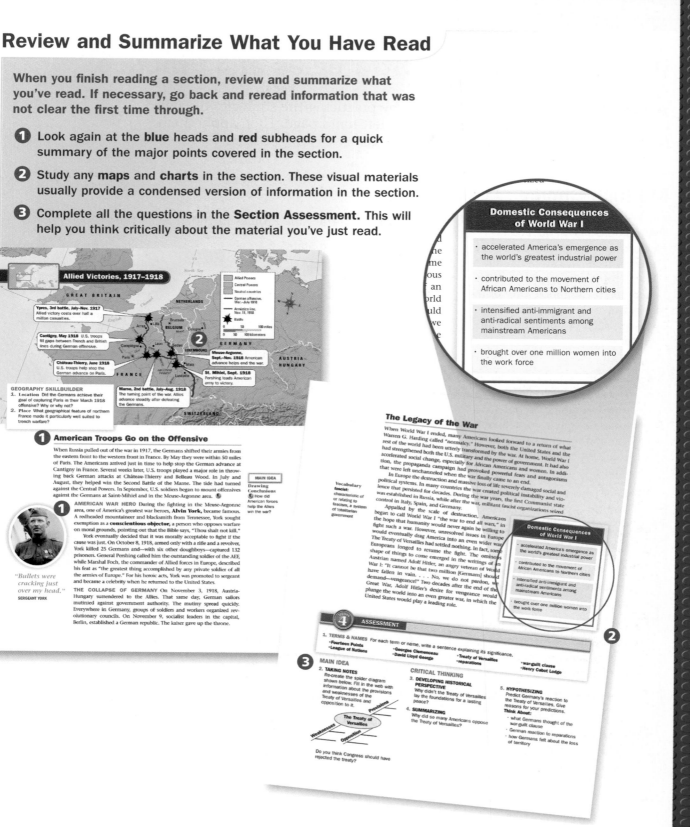

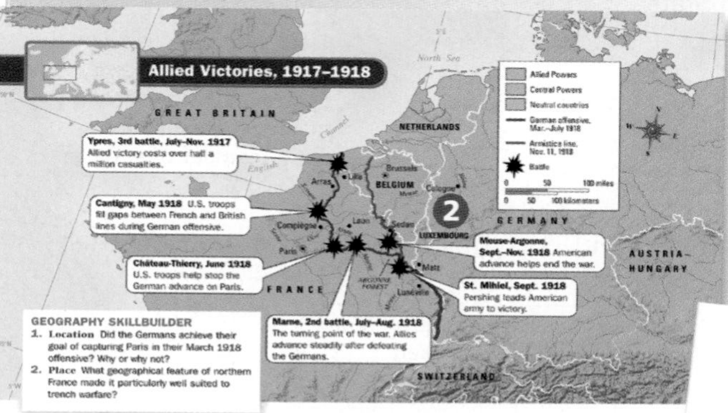

Ypres, 3rd battle, July–Nov. 1917 Allied victory costs over half a million casualties.
Cantigny, May 1918 U.S. troops fill gaps between French and British lines during German offensive.

Marne, 2nd battle, July–Aug. 1918 The turning point of the war. Allies advance steadily after defeating the Germans.
Meuse-Argonne, Sept.–Nov. 1918 American advance helps end the war.
St. Mihiel, Sept. 1918 Pershing leads American army to victory.

GEOGRAPHY SKILLBUILDER
1. Location Did the Germans achieve their goal of capturing Paris in their March 1918 offensive? Why or why not?
2. Place What geographical feature of northern France made it particularly well suited to trench warfare?

American Troops Go on the Offensive

When Russia pulled out of the war in 1917, the Germans shifted their armies from the eastern front to the western front in France. By May they were within 50 miles of Paris. The Americans arrived just in time to help stop the German advance at Cantigny in France. Several weeks later, U.S. troops played a major role in throwing back German attacks at Château-Thierry and Belleau Wood. In July and August, they helped win the Second Battle of the Marne. The tide had turned against the Central Powers. In September, U.S. soldiers began to mount offensives against the Germans at Saint-Mihiel and in the Meuse-Argonne area.

AMERICAN WAR HERO During the fighting in the Meuse-Argonne area, one of America's greatest war heroes, **Alvin York,** became famous. A redheaded mountaineer and blacksmith from Tennessee, York sought exemption as a **conscientious objector,** a person who opposes warfare on moral grounds, pointing out that the Bible says, "Thou shalt not kill."

York eventually decided that it was morally acceptable to fight if the cause was just. On October 8, 1918, armed only with a rifle and a revolver, York killed 25 Germans and—with six other doughboys—captured 132 prisoners. General Pershing called him the outstanding soldier of the AEF, while Marshal Foch, the commander of Allied forces in Europe, described his feat as "the greatest thing accomplished by any private soldier of all the armies of Europe." For his heroic acts, York was promoted to sergeant and became a celebrity when he returned to the United States.

"Bullets were cracking just over my head." SERGEANT YORK

THE COLLAPSE OF GERMANY On November 3, 1918, Austria-Hungary surrendered to the Allies. That same day, German sailors mutinied against government authority. The mutiny spread quickly. Everywhere in Germany, groups of soldiers and workers organized revolutionary councils. On November 9, socialist leaders in the capital, Berlin, established a German republic. The kaiser gave up the throne.

MAIN IDEA
Drawing Conclusions
How did American forces help the Allies win the war?

The Legacy of the War

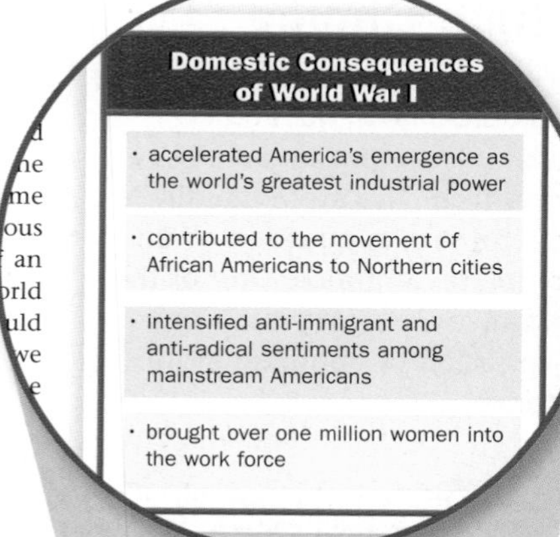

Domestic Consequences of World War I
• accelerated America's emergence as the world's greatest industrial power
• contributed to the movement of African Americans to Northern cities
• intensified anti-immigrant and anti-radical sentiments among mainstream Americans
• brought over one million women into the work force

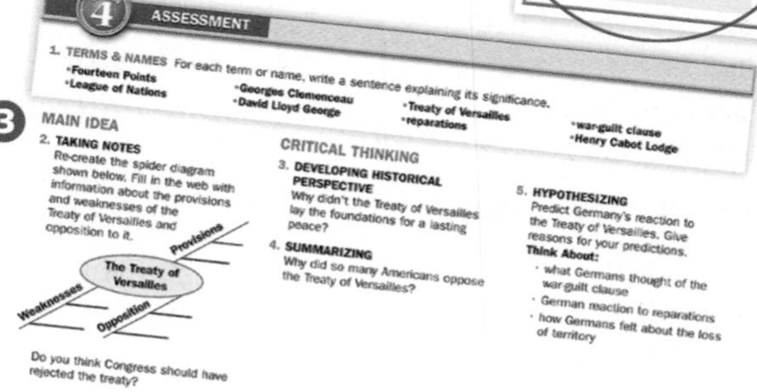

4 ASSESSMENT
1. TERMS & NAMES For each term or name, write a sentence explaining its significance.
•Fourteen Points •League of Nations •Georges Clemenceau •David Lloyd George •Treaty of Versailles •reparations •war-guilt clause •Henry Cabot Lodge
MAIN IDEA
2. TAKING NOTES Re-create the spider diagram shown below. Fill in the web with information about the provisions and weaknesses of the Treaty of Versailles and opposition to it.
The Treaty of Versailles
Provisions
Weaknesses
Opposition
Do you think Congress should have rejected the treaty?
CRITICAL THINKING
3. DEVELOPING HISTORICAL PERSPECTIVE Why didn't the Treaty of Versailles lay the foundations for a lasting peace?
4. SUMMARIZING Why did so many Americans oppose the Treaty of Versailles?
5. HYPOTHESIZING Predict Germany's reaction to the Treaty of Versailles. Give reasons for your predictions.
Think About:
• what Germans thought of the war-guilt clause
• German reaction to reparations
• how Germans felt about the loss of territory
3

Part 2: Test-Taking Strategies and Practice

You can improve your test-taking skills by practicing the strategies discussed in this section. First, read the tips on the left-hand page. Then apply them to the practice items on the right-hand page.

Multiple Choice

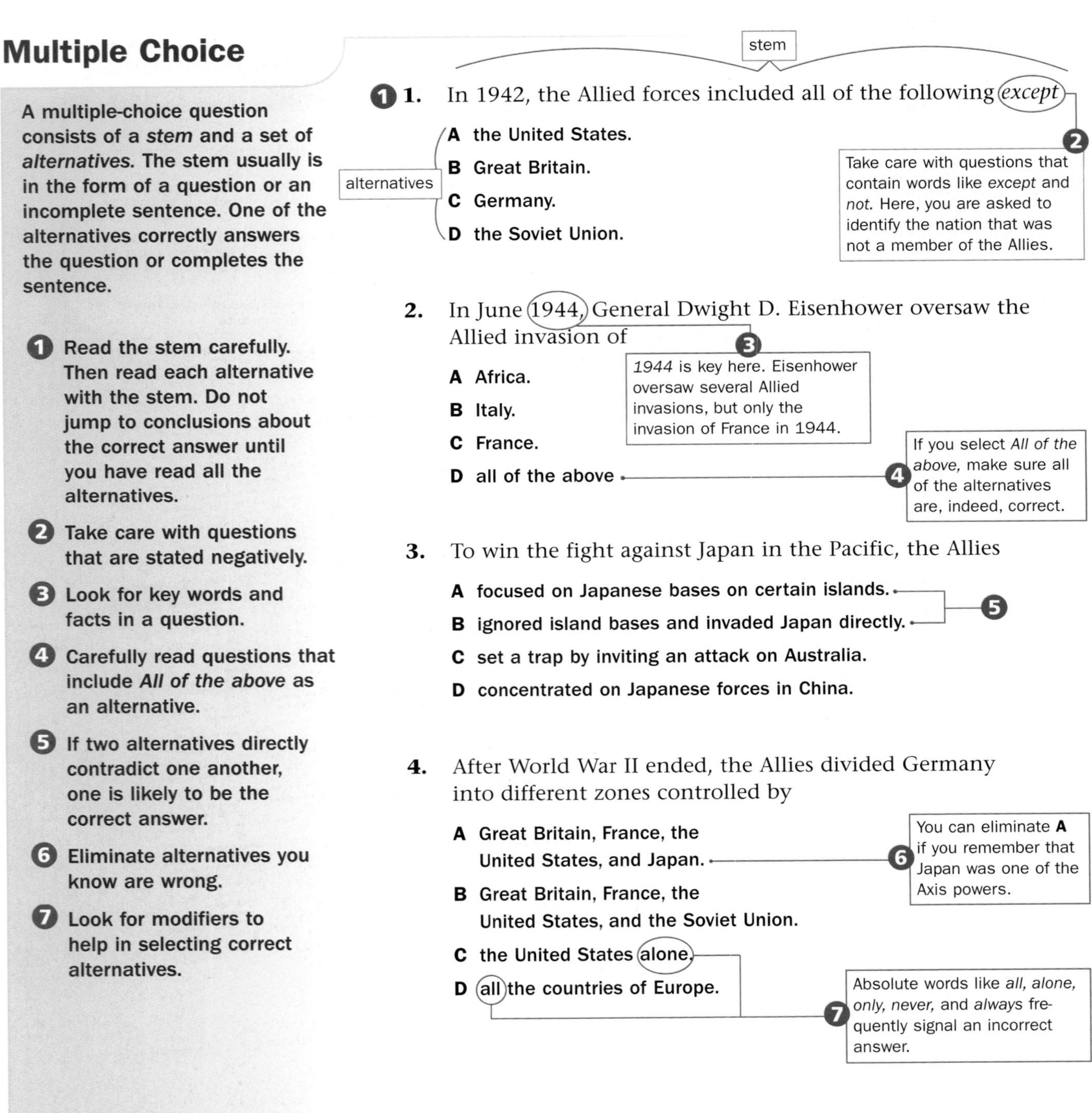

A multiple-choice question consists of a *stem* and a set of *alternatives*. The stem usually is in the form of a question or an incomplete sentence. One of the alternatives correctly answers the question or completes the sentence.

1. Read the stem carefully. Then read each alternative with the stem. Do not jump to conclusions about the correct answer until you have read all the alternatives.
2. Take care with questions that are stated negatively.
3. Look for key words and facts in a question.
4. Carefully read questions that include *All of the above* as an alternative.
5. If two alternatives directly contradict one another, one is likely to be the correct answer.
6. Eliminate alternatives you know are wrong.
7. Look for modifiers to help in selecting correct alternatives.

answers: 1 (C), 2 (C), 3 (A), 4 (B)

1. In 1942, the Allied forces included all of the following *except*

A the United States.
B Great Britain.
C Germany.
D the Soviet Union.

Take care with questions that contain words like *except* and *not*. Here, you are asked to identify the nation that was not a member of the Allies.

2. In June 1944, General Dwight D. Eisenhower oversaw the Allied invasion of

A Africa.
B Italy.
C France.
D all of the above

1944 is key here. Eisenhower oversaw several Allied invasions, but only the invasion of France in 1944.

If you select *All of the above,* make sure all of the alternatives are, indeed, correct.

3. To win the fight against Japan in the Pacific, the Allies

A focused on Japanese bases on certain islands.
B ignored island bases and invaded Japan directly.
C set a trap by inviting an attack on Australia.
D concentrated on Japanese forces in China.

4. After World War II ended, the Allies divided Germany into different zones controlled by

A Great Britain, France, the United States, and Japan.
B Great Britain, France, the United States, and the Soviet Union.
C the United States alone.
D all the countries of Europe.

You can eliminate **A** if you remember that Japan was one of the Axis powers.

Absolute words like *all, alone, only, never,* and *always* frequently signal an incorrect answer.

For more test practice online . . .

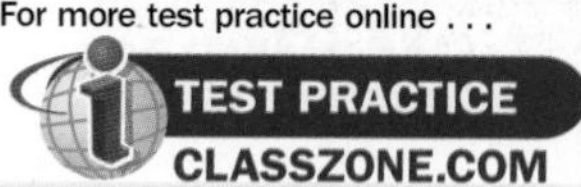

Directions: Read each question carefully and choose the *best* answer from the four alternatives.

1. As a result of the Treaty of Paris of 1898, which ended the Spanish-American War, the United States gained control of

A Panama.

B Hawaii.

C Puerto Rico.

D Cuba.

2. Theodore Roosevelt was known as a trustbuster for his

A attempts to break up huge corporations.

B combat role in the Spanish-American War.

C actions in establishing national parks.

D regulation of meatpacking and food processing.

3. Political reforms urged by Progressives included

A recall, or the power to remove officials from office.

B direct election of senators by popular vote.

C initiative, or the right of people to propose laws.

D all of the above

4. Each of the following was evidence of growing mistrust of foreigners in the 1920s *except* the

A wave of panic known as the Red Scare.

B growth of the Ku Klux Klan.

C rise of the flappers.

D passage of restrictive immigration laws.

Primary Sources

Primary sources are written or made by people who were at a historical event, either as observers or participants. Primary sources include journals, diaries, letters, speeches, newspaper articles, autobiographies, wills, deeds, and financial records.

1. Look at the source line to learn about the document and its author. Consider the reliability of the information in the document.
2. Skim the document to get an idea of what it is about.
3. Use active reading strategies. As you read, ask yourself questions, review sequence, and make predictions. (Here, for example, the first sentences make the sequence of events clear.)
4. As you read, look for the main idea. This is the writer's most important point. Remember that supporting details or arguments will back up this idea.
5. Use context clues to help you understand unfamiliar words. (Here the content of the rest of the paragraph suggests that *enumeration* means "a count" or "a listing.")
6. Before rereading the document, skim the questions. Previewing the questions will help focus your reading.

answers: 1 (B), 2 (C)

The San Francisco Earthquake

On Wednesday morning at a quarter past five came the earthquake. **3** A minute later the flames were leaping upward. In a dozen different quarters south of Market Street, in the working-class ghetto, and in the factories, fires started. There was no opposing the flames. There was no organization, no communication. All the cunning **4** adjustments of a twentieth century city had been smashed by the earthquake. . . . The steel rails were twisted into perpendicular and horizontal angles. The telephone and telegraph systems were disrupted. And the great water mains had burst. All the shrewd contrivances and safeguards of man had been thrown out of gear by thirty seconds' twitching of the earth-crust. . . .

An enumeration of the buildings destroyed would be a **5** directory of San Francisco. An enumeration of the buildings undestroyed would be a line and several addresses. An enumeration of the deeds of heroism would stock a library. . . . The number of the victims of the earthquake will never be known.

—Jack London, "The Story of an Eye-witness." *Collier's The National Weekly,* May 5, 1906

Author Jack London's eyewitness account was published soon after the earthquake.

6 **1.** Based on the information in the passage, which of the following does *not* describe conditions following the 1906 earthquake in San Francisco?

A Fires spread to many parts of the city.

B Communication lines remained intact.

C Municipal water pipes broke.

D Rail lines were disrupted.

Here the key words are *main idea*. Make sure the alternative you select expresses the focus of the passage.

2. Which sentence *best* expresses the main idea of the passage?

A "A minute later the flames were leaping upward."

B "The number of the victims of the earthquake will never be known."

C "All the cunning adjustments of a twentieth-century city had been smashed by the earthquake."

D "The telephone and telegraph systems were disrupted."

For more test practice online . . .
TEST PRACTICE
CLASSZONE.COM

Directions: Use this passage, from an article by women's-rights advocate Amelia Bloomer, and your knowledge of U.S. history to answer questions 1 through 4.

It is objected that it does not belong to woman's sphere to take part in the selection of her rulers, or the enactment of laws to which she is subject.

This is mere matter of opinion. Woman's sphere, like man's sphere, varies according to . . . the circumstances in which she may be placed. A vast majority of the British nation would deny the assumption that Queen Victoria is out of her sphere in reigning over an empire of an hundred and fifty millions of souls! . . .

But, again, one says votes would be unnecessarily multiplied, that women would vote just as the men do, therefore the man's vote will answer for both. Sound logic, truly! But let us apply this rule to men. Votes are unnecessarily multiplied now by so many men voting; a few could do it all, [rather than taking] the mass of men from their business and their families to vote. . . .

Again, another says, "It has always been as now; women never have had equal rights, and that is proof that they should not have." Sound logic again! . . . But whence did man derive this right [to vote], and how long has it been enjoyed? . . .

Must we continue to cling to old laws and customs because they are old? Why then did not [the American] people remain subject to kings?

—Amelia Bloomer, "Woman's Right to the Ballot" (1895)

1. Bloomer's essay was part of the campaign to establish

- **A** temperance.
- **B** woman suffrage.
- **C** urban reform.
- **D** child labor laws.

2. Bloomer uses the example of Queen Victoria to show that

- **A** some countries accept that women can have a role in government.
- **B** the best monarchs are women.
- **C** a monarchy is preferable to democratic government.
- **D** people should follow traditional practices.

3. When Bloomer uses the phrase "sound logic," she is

- **A** agreeing with the argument offered.
- **B** pretending to agree with the argument offered.
- **C** stating her true opinion.
- **D** suggesting that the argument is logical.

4. Bloomer rejects the argument that things should remain the way they have always been by saying that if tradition were so important,

- **A** Victoria would not be queen.
- **B** women would have the vote already.
- **C** women would vote exactly as men do.
- **D** America would still be ruled by kings.

Secondary Sources

Secondary sources are written or made by people who were not at the original events. They often combine information from several primary sources. The most common types of written secondary sources are history books and biographies.

1. Use the title to preview the content of the passage. (The title here signals that the passage is about the courses of action open to President Richard Nixon in Vietnam.)
2. Look at the topic sentences of paragraphs. These, too, indicate what the content will be.
3. Use context clues to help you understand unfamiliar words. (From the discussion of the options, you can tell that *flawed* means that each one had problems.)
4. Read actively by asking yourself questions. (After learning Nixon's four options, you might ask yourself: "How did he overcome these problems?")
5. Look for words like *because*, *since*, or *as a result* that indicate cause-effect relationships.
6. Before rereading the passage, skim the questions to identify the information you need to find.

answers: 1 (B), 2 (A)

1 **President Nixon's Options in Vietnam**

2 When he became president, Richard Nixon had four options regarding the ongoing conflict in Vietnam, each of which was
3 seriously flawed. He could continue to fight an all-out war, but that effort was clearly not working. He could intensify the war by invading the north, but such a step would increase antiwar sentiment at home. He could withdraw American troops, but other countries might see that as a sign of weakness. He could try
4 to negotiate a peace, but North Vietnam was not willing to give up its claim to the south.

Nixon chose not one option but a combination. He announced that American troops would leave Vietnam. However, he made the pullout gradual and increased military aid to South
5 Vietnam. As a result, Nixon continued the war and avoided a show of weakness. He also pursued peace talks with North Vietnam. At the same time, though, he pressured the North to reach an agreement through an intensified bombing campaign and attacks on North Vietnamese bases in Cambodia.

6

1. From the first sentence of the passage, it is clear that the

A war in Vietnam was coming to an end.
B war was being fought when Nixon took office.
C United States was fighting South Vietnam.
D United States was winning in Vietnam.

Some questions focus on specific parts of the passage.

2. Which of the following options was undesirable for domestic political reasons?

A invading North Vietnam
B negotiating a peace
C pulling troops out of Vietnam
D all of the above

Here you are looking for an alternative that would cause Nixon political problems.

Directions: Use the passage and your knowledge of U.S. history to answer questions 1 through 4.

"Fighting Bob" La Follette

Wisconsin's Robert La Follette became a leading Progressive by pushing both economic and political reforms. La Follette served three terms in the House of Representatives as a Republican. Losing reelection in 1890, he returned home to Wisconsin. There he began to build a reform movement within the Republican Party. His goals were to help farmers against the powerful railroads and to clean up politics.

In 1900, La Follette won the first of three terms as governor of Wisconsin. During his time as governor, La Follette won passage of several reforms. One law taxed railroads at higher rates than before, and another set up a government agency to regulate railroads. He also won approval of holding primary elections to choose candidates for state office.

In 1905, La Follette won election to the United States Senate. In Washington, he continued to fight against the power of railroads. He also took on the country's major financial institutions. And he campaigned against American involvement in World War I. In 1924, La Follette ran for president on the Progressive Party ticket. He pulled 5 million votes—about 17 percent of all popular votes cast—but won only his home state in the electoral vote.

1. La Follette held each of the following political offices *except*

A congressman.

B governor.

C senator.

D president.

2. According to the passage, the reforms that La Follette pushed included

A primary elections.

B the Australian ballot.

C higher taxes on banks.

D regulation of oil companies.

3. Which of the following is the *best* explanation of why La Follette was called "Fighting Bob"?

A He fought in World War I.

B He fought for reform.

C He fought in several elections.

D He fought for the railroads.

4. Which of the following is the *best* summary of La Follette's impact as a political leader?

A La Follette was highly respected by the people of Wisconsin, who elected him many times.

B La Follette was a failed politician who never won the presidency.

C La Follette was a reformer who tried to limit the power of big corporations.

D La Follette became a national hero due to his fight for reform.

Political Cartoons

Political cartoons use a combination of words and images to express a point of view on political issues. They are a useful primary source, because they reflect the opinions of the time.

1. Identify the subject of the cartoon. The caption often gives an indication of the subject matter.
2. Try to identify the main characters in the cartoon. (The label in the foreground of the cartoon shows that they are members of the Tammany Ring, New York's Democratic political machine. "Boss" Tweed, the leader, is on the left.)
3. Identify any important symbols—ideas or images that stand for something else.
4. Review labels and any other written information in the cartoon.
5. Analyze the point of view. The use of caricature—the exaggeration of physical features—often signals the cartoonist's attitude.
6. Interpret the cartoonist's message.

The cartoonist uses a diamond stickpin to symbolize Tweed's excesses.
The labels identify other members of the Tweed Ring.
J. W. SMITH
TAMMANY RING
"WHO STOLE THE PEOPLE'S MONEY?" — DO TELL. N.Y. TIMES.
'TWAS HIM.
Tweed's physical appearance is exaggerated, making him look grossly overweight. This suggests that the cartoonist had a low opinion of Tweed and his followers.

The Granger Collection, New York

1. Which sentence *best* summarizes the way members of the Tammany Ring would answer the question in the caption?

A They did not, and would not, steal the people's money.
B They accept responsibility for stealing the people's money.
C They do not know who stole the people's money.
D They each blame someone else for stealing the people's money.

2. Based on the cartoon, what word do you think the cartoonist might use to describe the Tammany Ring?

A lazy
B corrupt
C honest
D hard-working

Since you know that the cartoon is critical of the Tammany Ring, you can eliminate the two positive alternatives—**C** and **D**.

answers: 1 (D), 2 (B)

For more test practice online . . .
TEST PRACTICE
CLASSZONE.COM

Directions: Use the political cartoon and your knowledge of U.S. history to answer questions 1 through 4.

Doug Marlette, *Charlotte Observer*, 1981.

1. According to the cartoon, for every dollar that working men earned, working women earned

A 49 cents.

B 59 cents.

C 69 cents.

D 79 cents.

2. Which of the following *best* summarizes the point of the cartoon?

A Men are happier than women are.

B Working men have bigger offices than working women.

C Working women earn less than working men.

D Working women do the real work in an office.

3. What phrase summarizes feminists' solution to the problem illustrated in the cartoon?

A "We Shall Overcome"

B "Equal Pay for Equal Work"

C "ERA Now"

D "Our Bodies, Ourselves"

4. Today, women make up nearly 50 percent of the workforce. However, they still encounter problems in the workplace, including

A the "glass ceiling."

B lack of quality child care.

C sexual harassment.

D All of the above

Charts

Charts present information in a visual form. The chart most commonly found in standardized tests is the table. This organizes information in columns and rows for easy viewing.

1. Read the title to see the topic and the time period covered by the chart.
2. Examine the column and row headings and other labels to learn more information about the subject addressed in the chart. (Sometimes, terms used in headings are explained in footnotes.)
3. Look for patterns and trends by comparing and contrasting the information from column to column and row to row.
4. Try to make generalizations on, and draw conclusions from, the information in the chart.
5. Study the questions carefully to see if you can eliminate some possible answers.

answers: 1 (D), 2 (B)

1 Place of Residence of Chinese Americans, 1870–1930

2

Year	Living in California	Living in the Rest of the West*	Living Elsewhere in the U.S.
1870	78.0 %	21.4 %	0.6 %
1880	71.2 %	25.6 %	3.2 %
1890	67.4 %	22.7 %	9.9 %
1900	51.5 %	24.4 %	24.6 %
1910	50.7 %	21.9 %	27.4 %
1920	46.7 %	15.9 %	37.4 %
1930	50.1 %	10.0 %	40.1 %

3

* Includes states or territories of Oregon, Washington, Idaho, Montana, Wyoming, Colorado, Utah, Nevada, Arizona, and New Mexico

Source: Roger Daniels, *Coming to America* (1990)

4 One generalization you might make is that a majority of Chinese Americans lived in the West during the time period covered by the chart, although the proportion fell over the years.

1. Between 1870 and 1930, the percentage of Chinese Americans living in California

A increased every decade.

B increased every decade between 1900 and 1930.

C decreased every decade.

D decreased every decade until the period from 1920 to 1930.

5 **A** and **B** are clearly incorrect because the percentage decreased for all decades except 1920 to 1930.

2. Which of the following *best* explains the high percentage of Chinese Americans living in California throughout these years?

A They hoped to join the many Japanese Americans there.

B California, like China, is on the Pacific Ocean.

C California had no laws discriminating against Chinese Americans.

D During all those decades, they worked to build California's railroads.

For more test practice online . . .
TEST PRACTICE
CLASSZONE.COM

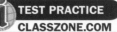

Directions: Use the chart and your knowledge of U.S. history to answer questions 1 through 4.

Ten States with the Largest Population, 1900–2000

1900	1930	1960	2000
1. New York	1. New York	1. New York	1. California
2. Pennsylvania	2. Pennsylvania	2. California	2. Texas
3. Illinois	3. Illinois	3. Pennsylvania	3. New York
4. Ohio	4. Ohio	4. Illinois	4. Florida
5. Missouri	5. Texas	5. Ohio	5. Illinois
6. Texas	6. California	6. Texas	6. Pennsylvania
7. Massachusetts	7. Michigan	7. Michigan	7. Ohio
8. Indiana	8. Massachusetts	8. New Jersey	8. Michigan
9. Michigan	9. New Jersey	9. Massachusetts	9. New Jersey
10. Iowa	10. Missouri	10. Florida	10. Georgia

Source: U.S. Census Bureau

1. In which regions were most of the ten most populous states in 1900?

A Northeast and Midwest
B Northeast and Southeast
C Northeast and Southwest
D Midwest and Southeast

2. Which of the following statements describes a change in the top ten states listing between 1960 and 2000?

A Texas and Florida rose markedly in the standings.
B The Midwestern states fell in the standings.
C Massachusetts fell out of the top ten listing.
D all of the above

3. This chart exemplifies what trend of the late twentieth century?

A The increase in the population of the Northeast
B The decrease in immigration to the United States
C The population shift from the Rustbelt to the Sunbelt
D The population shift from the Sunbelt to the Rustbelt

4. What impact would population changes between 1960 and 2000 have on representation in Congress?

A California and Texas would gain representatives in the House.
B Florida and Georgia would lose representatives in the House.
C California and Georgia would lose members in the Senate.
D Texas and Florida would gain members in the Senate.

Line and Bar Graphs

Graphs, like charts, display information in a visual form. Line graphs show changes and trends over time. Bar graphs allow for comparisons among numbers or sets of numbers.

1. Read the title of the graph to learn what it is about.
2. Study the labels on the vertical and horizontal axes to see the kinds of information presented in the graph. The vertical axis usually shows what is being graphed, while the horizontal axis indicates the time period covered.
3. Study the legend, if there is one. This, too, will provide information on what is being graphed.
4. Review the information in the graph and note any trends or patterns. Look for explanations for these trends or patterns.
5. Carefully read and answer the questions. Note if questions refer to a specific year or time period, or if they focus on trends or historical explanations for trends.

answers: 1 (B), 2 (D)

1 Unemployment Rate, 1930–1960

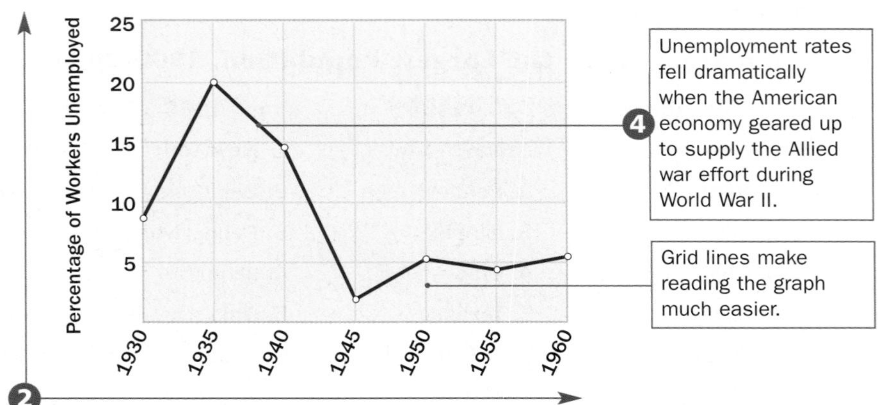
Percentage of Workers Unemployed
25
20
15
10
5
1930
1935
1940
1945
1950
1955
1960
2
4 Unemployment rates fell dramatically when the American economy geared up to supply the Allied war effort during World War II.
Grid lines make reading the graph much easier.

Source: *Statistical Abstract of the United States*

5 **1.** In which year did the unemployment rate hit its peak?

A 1930

B 1935

C 1945

D 1950

1 Percentage of Homes Owned and Rented, 1940–1980

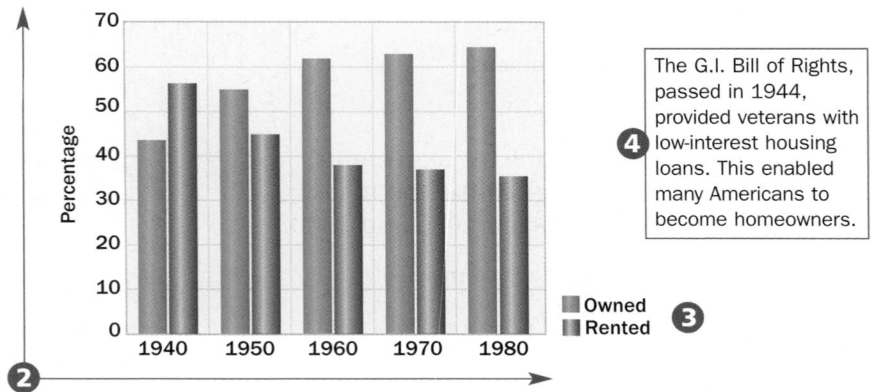
Percentage
70
60
50
40
30
20
10
0
1940
1950
1960
1970
1980
2
Owned
Rented
3
4 The G.I. Bill of Rights, passed in 1944, provided veterans with low-interest housing loans. This enabled many Americans to become homeowners.

Source: *Statistical Abstract of the United States*

5 **2.** Which of the following describes the trend shown in the graph?

A People prefer renting to owning.

B Since 1950, home rentals have steadily increased.

C The number of houses built steadily increased.

D Since 1950, home ownership has steadily increased.

For more test practice online . . .
TEST PRACTICE
CLASSZONE.COM

Directions: Use the graphs and your knowledge of U.S. history to answer questions 1 through 4.

Percentage of Households with Selected Media, 1930–2000

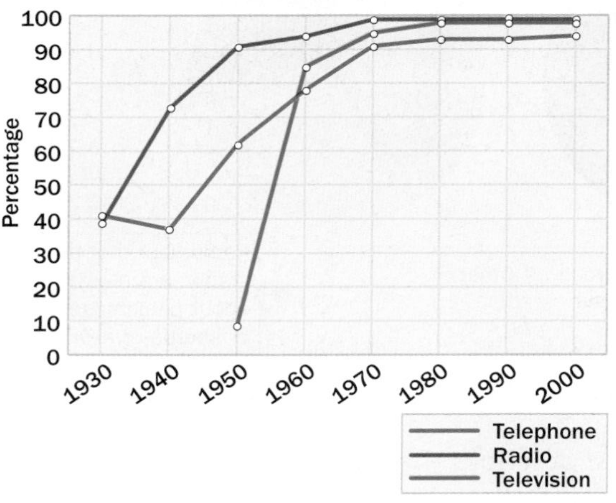

Source: *Statistical Abstract of the United States*

Age Distribution of the Population, 1900–2000

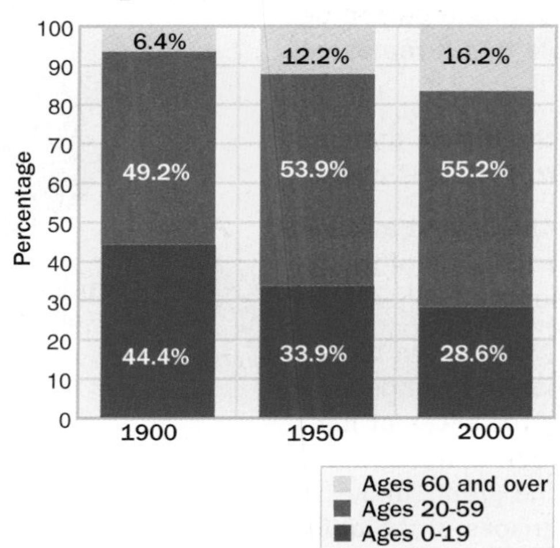

Source: *Historical Statistics of the United States; Statistical Abstract of the United States*

1. The percentage of households with all three media first topped 90 percent in

A 1960.

B 1970.

C 1980.

D 1990.

2. What cultural trend resulted from the rapid spread of radios and televisions into nearly every American home?

A the rise of rock 'n' roll

B the growing influence of popular culture

C the decline in the power of the television networks

D the increase in popularity of newspapers and magazines

3. How did the share of elderly people in the population change from 1900 to 2000?

A It decreased from 44.4 to 28.6 percent.

B It increased from 49.2 to 55.2 percent.

C It increased from 6.4 to 16.2 percent.

D It decreased from 33.9 to 12.2 percent.

4. Which of the following describes changes in the age distribution of the population between 1900 and 2000?

A The percentage of people aged 60 or over grew.

B The percentage of people aged between 20 and 59 increased.

C The percentage of people aged 19 or younger fell.

D all of the above

Pie Graphs

A pie, or circle, graph is useful for showing relationships among the parts of a whole. These parts look like slices of a pie. The size of each slice is proportional to the percentage of the whole that it represents.

1. Read the title of the graph to learn what it is about.
2. Study the legend and note what each slice of the pie represents.
3. Study the data on the graph and make comparisons among the slices of the pie. When there is more than one graph, make comparisons of the different graphs.
4. Try to make generalizations and draw conclusions from your comparisons. (One generalization you might make is that today no one country or region dominates world motor vehicle production.)
5. Read the questions carefully and use key words to reject incorrect alternatives.

answers: 1 (A), 2 (B)

1 World Motor Vehicle Production, 1950 and 2000

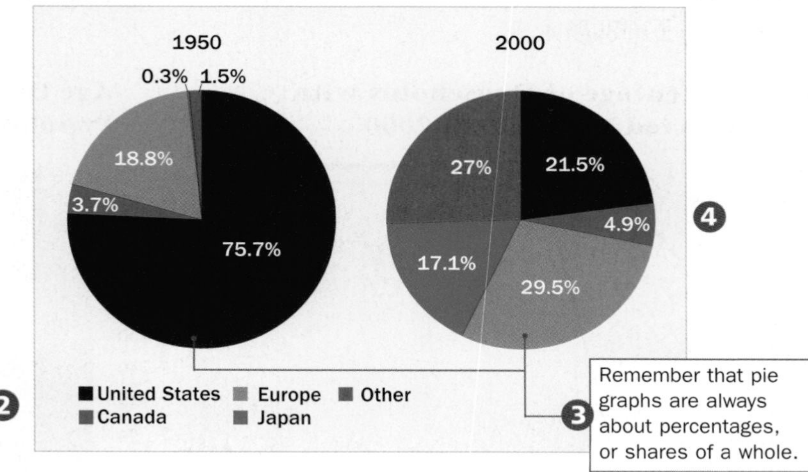

Source: *World Almanac and Book of Facts* (2002)

1. What phrase *best* describes the U.S. share of world motor vehicle production in the years shown?

A It fell dramatically from 1950 to 2000.

B It was less than 75 percent of the total in 1950.

C It was the same as Japan's share in 2000.

D It never exceeded Europe's share.

2. What sentence *best* describes motor vehicle production over the years shown in the two graphs?

A Japan's share of motor vehicle production grew slightly.

B Motor vehicle production became more competitive around the world.

C The United States became the world's top producer of motor vehicles.

D Europe remained the dominant region for motor vehicle production.

5 The key words *slightly*, *became*, and *remained* help you to eliminate alternatives **A**, **C**, and **D**. Japanese production grew markedly, not slightly. The United States fell from its position as the world's top producer of motor vehicles. Finally, Europe never dominated motor vehicle production.

For more test practice online . . .

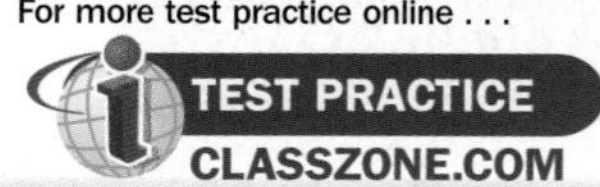

Directions: Use the pie graphs and your knowledge of U.S. history to answer questions 1 through 4.

Energy Consumption in the United States, by Projected Energy Source

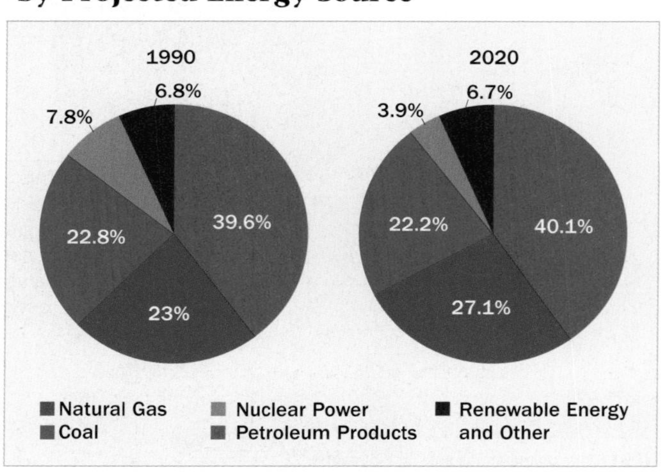

Source: *Statistical Abstract of the United States*

1. Which source of energy is expected to significantly decline in importance?

A Petroleum products
B Natural gas
C Nuclear power
D Renewable energy and other

2. All of the following are considered fossil fuels *except*

A petroleum products.
B natural gas.
C coal.
D nuclear power.

3. Which energy source is least likely to have harmful environmental effects?

A Petroleum products
B Coal
C Nuclear power
D Renewable energy

4. Which of the following most likely predicts energy trends in the United States over the first two decades of the twenty-first century?

A Nuclear power will become a major source of energy.
B Petroleum imports probably will increase as reliance on petroleum increases.
C Coal and natural gas will cease to be important energy sources.
D Renewable energy sources will be exhausted.

Political Maps

Political maps show countries and the political divisions within them—states or provinces, for example. They also show the location of major cities. In addition, political maps often show physical features, such as mountains, oceans, seas, lakes, and rivers.

1. Read the title of the map to identify the area shown and the time period covered.
2. Read the labels on the map. This will reveal more information about the subject and purpose of the map.
3. Note any special features of the map, such as insets.
4. Study the legend to find the meaning of any symbols and colors used on the map.
5. Look at the lines of longitude and latitude. This grid makes locating places much easier.
6. Use the compass rose to determine directions on the map.
7. Use the scale to estimate distances between places shown on the map.
8. Read the questions and then carefully study the map to determine the answers.

answers: 1 (C), 2 (B)

Alaska, 1867, and Hawaii, 1898 1

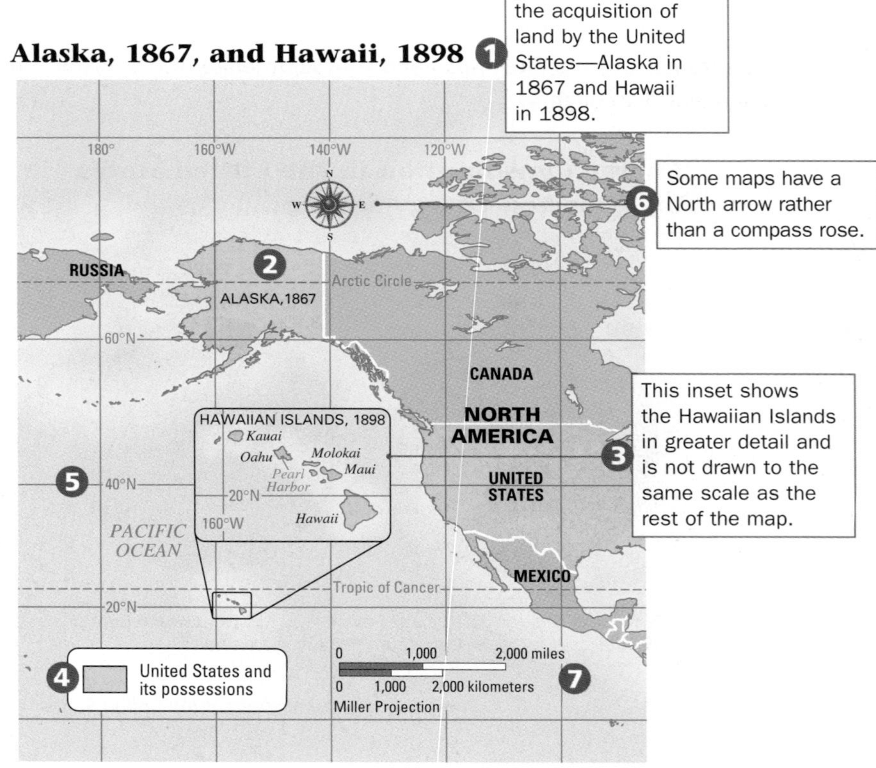

8

1. Which country lies to the west of Alaska?

A Canada

B Mexico

C Russia

D United States

2. About how far are the Hawaiian Islands from the southwest coast of the United States?

A 1,000 miles

B 2,500 miles

C 4,000 miles

D 5,500 miles

For more test practice online . . .
TEST PRACTICE
CLASSZONE.COM

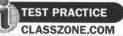

Directions: Use the map and your knowledge of United States history to answer the following questions.

Post-War Germany—Occupation Zones

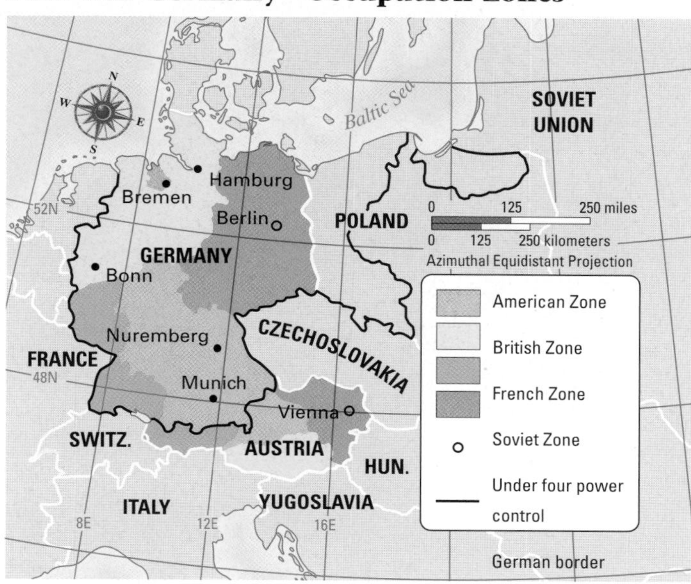

1 Berlin lay entirely in the

A American zone.

B British zone.

C French zone.

D Soviet zone.

2 Which of the following cities lay in the American zone?

A Bremen

B Munich

C Nuremberg

D All of the above

3 Which city is located closest to 48° N 16° E?

A Berlin

B Vienna

C Munich

D Bonn

4 In 1948, France, Great Britain, and the United States combined their zones into one nation—West Germany. The Soviet Union responded by

A blockading Berlin.

B invading Czechoslovakia.

C bombing Berlin.

D invading Hungary.

Thematic Maps

A thematic map, or special-purpose map, focuses on a particular topic. Population density, election results, migration routes, a country's economic activities, international alliances, and major battles in a war are all topics you might see illustrated on a thematic map.

1. Thematic maps show specialized information. Read the title to discover the subject and purpose of the map.
2. Study the labels on the map to find more information about its subject and purpose.
3. Examine the legend to find the meaning of any symbols and colors used on the map.
4. Locate the symbols and colors on the map and try to make generalizations or draw conclusions about the information they convey.
5. Read the questions and carefully study the map to determine the answers.

1 The Panama Canal

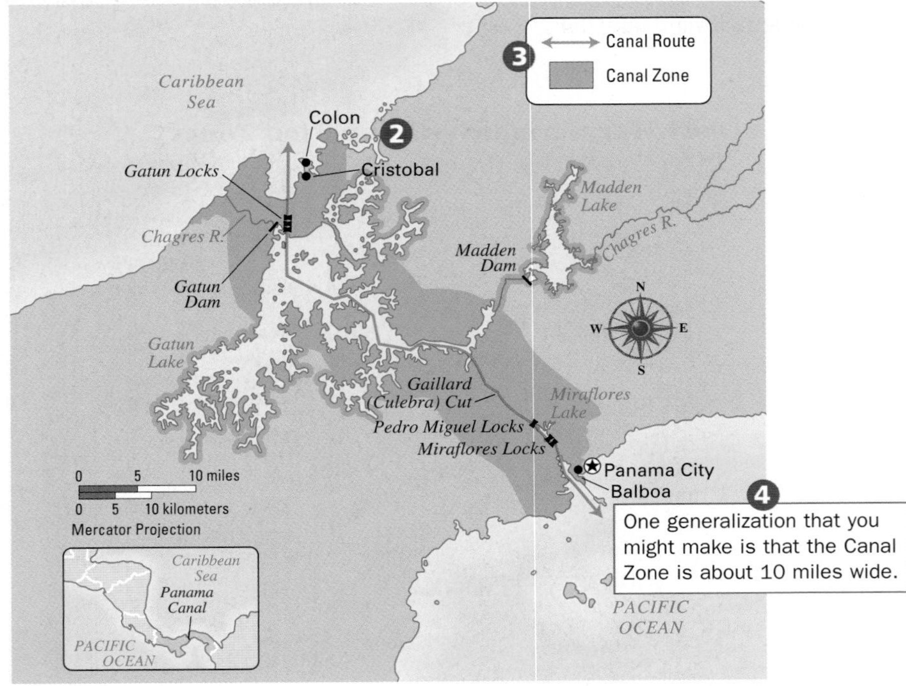

5

1. The longest stretch of land the canal cuts through runs from

Use the scale when answering questions about distance.

A the Atlantic Ocean to Gatun Lake.

B Gatun Lake to Miraflores Lake.

C Madden Lake to Gatun Lake.

D the Pacific Ocean to Miraflores Lake.

2. If a ship were transporting cargo from New York to San Francisco, in which direction would it travel through the Panama Canal?

Use the compass rose when answering questions about direction.

A northeast

B northwest

C southeast

D southwest

answers: 1 (B), 2 (C)

Directions: Use the map and chart and your knowledge of U.S. history to answer questions 1 through 4.

The 2000 Presidential Election

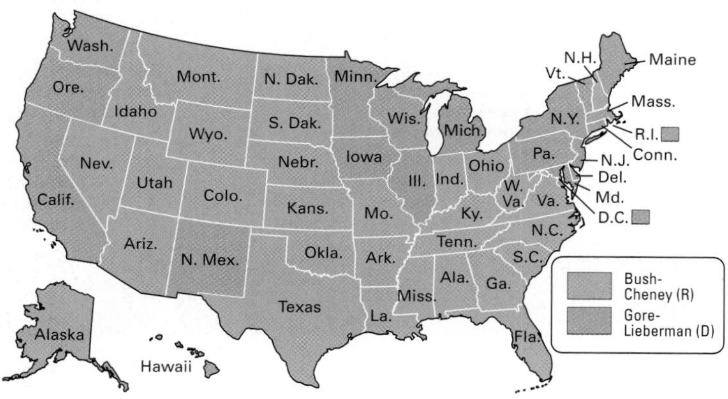

Ticket	Popular Vote	Electoral Vote
Bush-Cheney	50,456,062	271
Gore-Lieberman	50,996,582	266
Nader-LaDuke	2,858,843	0
Buchanan-Foster	438,760	0

Source: *Federal Register*

1. The Gore-Lieberman ticket won all of the New England states *except*

A Maine.
B Massachusetts.
C New Hampshire.
D Rhode Island.

2. The Gore-Lieberman ticket won most of the

A Midwestern states.
B Northeastern states.
C Pacific-coast states.
D all of the above

3. Which areas did the Bush-Cheney ticket win?

A most states in the Northeast and the West
B all of the South and the Midwest
C all of the South and most of the West
D most states in the Northeast and the South

4. Which of the following statements about the 2000 presidential election is true?

A The Bush-Cheney ticket won the electoral vote but not the popular vote.
B The Bush-Cheney ticket won all of the Deep South states.
C The Bush-Cheney ticket won more states than the Gore-Lieberman ticket.
D all of the above

Time Lines

A time line is a type of chart that lists historical events in the order in which they occurred. In other words, time lines are a visual method of showing what happened when.

1. Read the title to discover the subject of the time line.
2. Identify the period of history covered in the time line by noting the first and last dates shown.
3. Read the events in chronological order. Notice the intervals between events.
4. Note how events are related to one another. Look particularly for cause-effect relationships.
5. Make generalizations about the information presented in the time line.
6. Use the information you have gathered from the above strategies to answer the questions.

answers: 1 (C), 2 (D)

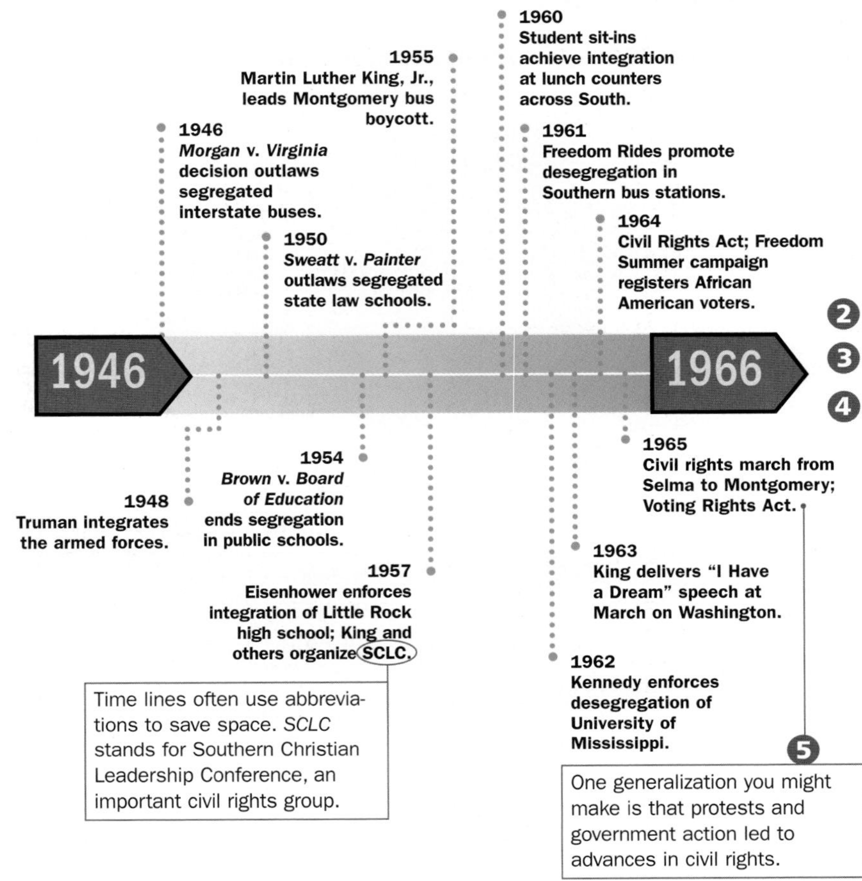

1 The Civil Rights Movement, 1940s–1960s
1946
1966
1946 *Morgan* v. *Virginia* decision outlaws segregated interstate buses.
1948 Truman integrates the armed forces.
1950 *Sweatt* v. *Painter* outlaws segregated state law schools.
1954 *Brown* v. *Board of Education* ends segregation in public schools.
1955 Martin Luther King, Jr., leads Montgomery bus boycott.
1957 Eisenhower enforces integration of Little Rock high school; King and others organize SCLC.
1960 Student sit-ins achieve integration at lunch counters across South.
1961 Freedom Rides promote desegregation in Southern bus stations.
1962 Kennedy enforces desegregation of University of Mississippi.
1963 King delivers "I Have a Dream" speech at March on Washington.
1964 Civil Rights Act; Freedom Summer campaign registers African American voters.
1965 Civil rights march from Selma to Montgomery; Voting Rights Act.
2
3
4
Time lines often use abbreviations to save space. *SCLC* stands for Southern Christian Leadership Conference, an important civil rights group.
5
One generalization you might make is that protests and government action led to advances in civil rights.

6

1 Which was the first major civil rights activity in which Martin Luther King, Jr., was involved?

A "I have a dream" speech
B march from Selma to Montgomery
C Montgomery bus boycott
D organization of the SCLC

2 The success of the civil rights movement resulted from organized protests by African Americans and actions by

A state courts.
B reformed state governments.
C federal courts and Congress.
D all three branches of the federal government.

Recall that southern state governments often resisted civil rights in this period. Therefore, you can eliminate alternatives **A** and **B**.

For more test practice online . . .

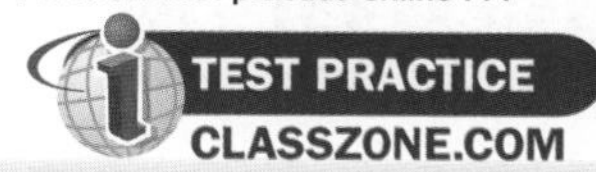

Directions: Use the time line and your knowledge of U.S. history to answer questions 1 through 4.

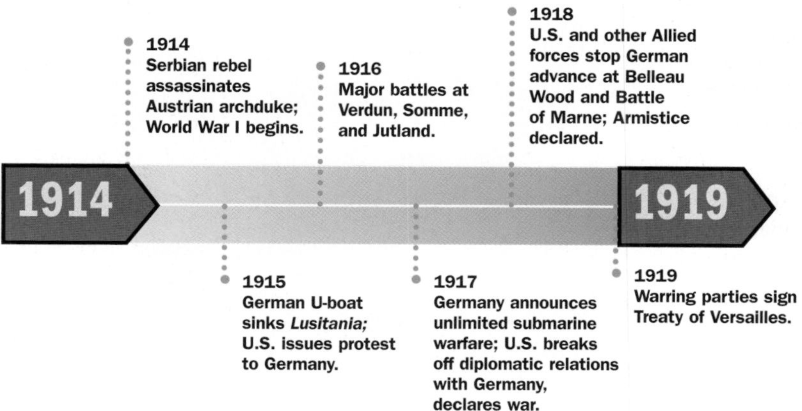

1. What event led the United States to protest German actions in 1915?

A assassination of Austrian archduke
B battle of Jutland
C sinking of *Lusitania*
D battle of Verdun

2. Which of the following actions included U.S. troops?

A Jutland, 1916
B Verdun, 1916
C Somme, 1916
D Marne, 1918

3. The Treaty of Versailles, which officially brought the war to an end, was signed in

A 1917.
B 1918.
C 1919.
D 1920.

4. The Treaty of Versailles called for Germany to

A demilitarize.
B pay war reparations.
C admit sole responsibility for the war.
D all of the above

Constructed Response

Constructed-response questions focus on various kinds of documents. Each document is accompanied by one or more short-answer questions. For the most part, the answers to these questions can be found directly in the document. Some answers, however, require knowledge of the subject or time period addressed in the document.

1. Read the title of the document to discover the subject addressed in the questions.
2. Carefully study the document and take notes on what you see.
3. Read the questions and then study the document again to locate the answers.
4. Carefully write your answers. Unless the directions say otherwise, your answers need not be complete sentences.

1 Japanese-American Internment

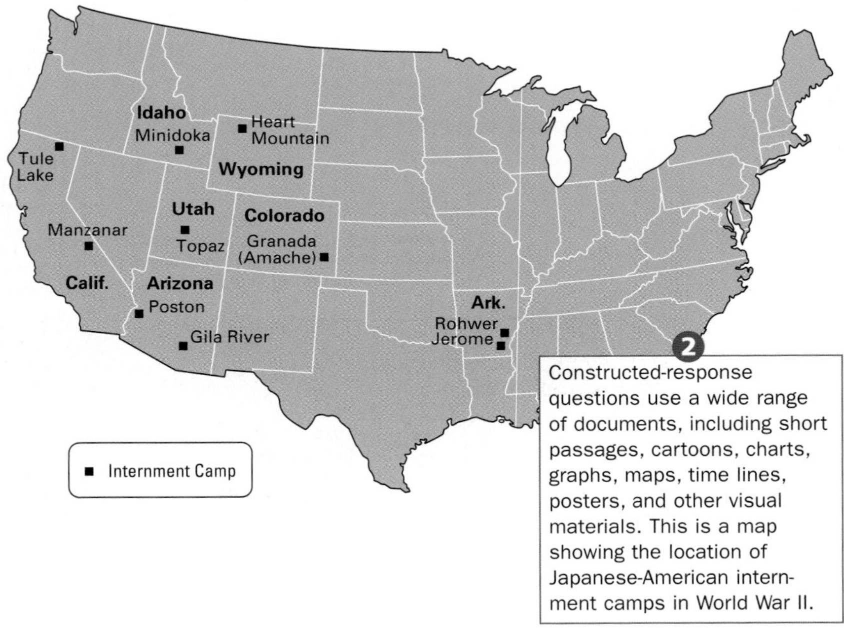

2 Constructed-response questions use a wide range of documents, including short passages, cartoons, charts, graphs, maps, time lines, posters, and other visual materials. This is a map showing the location of Japanese-American internment camps in World War II.

3 **1.** Which states had more than one relocation camp?

4 *Arkansas, Arizona, California*

2. In which region of the country were most relocation camps located?

Southwest

3. What event led to calls for Japanese Americans to be removed from the Pacific Coast?

the Japanese attack on Pearl Harbor

For more test practice online . . .

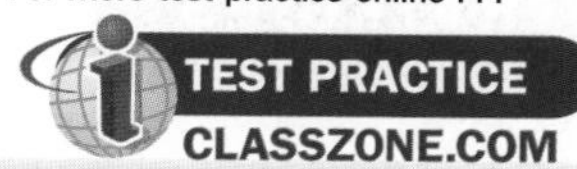

Directions: Use the illustration and your knowledge of U.S. history to answer questions 1 through 3. Your answers need not be complete sentences.

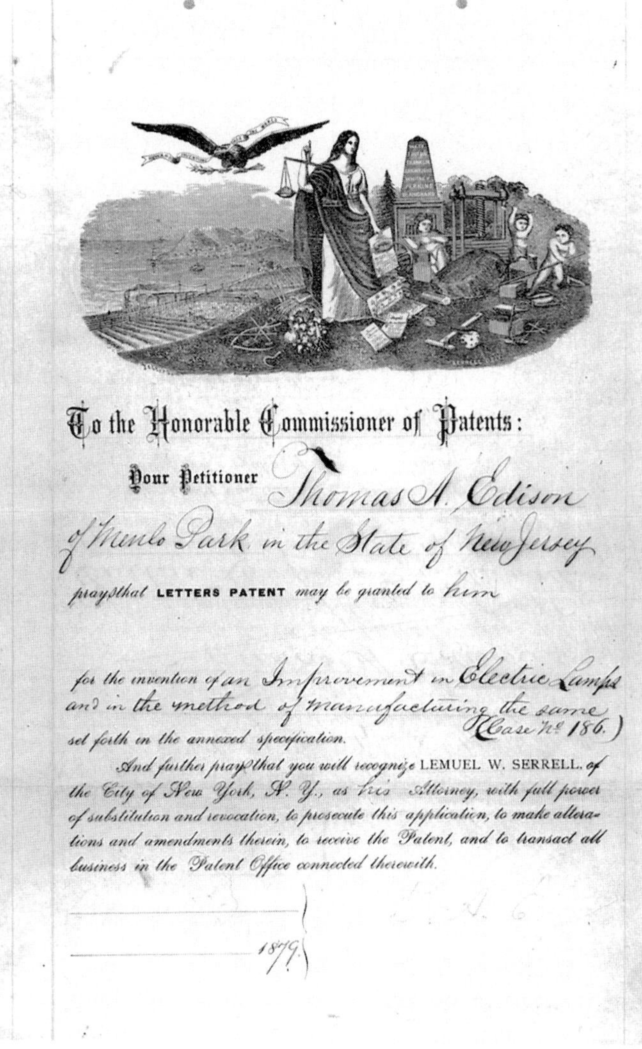

To the Honorable Commissioner of Patents:

Your Petitioner Thomas A. Edison of Menlo Park in the State of New Jersey prays that LETTERS PATENT may be granted to him for the invention of an Improvement in Electric Lamps and in the method of manufacturing the same set forth in the annexed specification. (Case No 186.)

And further pray that you will recognize LEMUEL W. SERRELL, of the City of New York, N. Y., as his Attorney, with full power of substitution and revocation, to prosecute this application, to make alterations and amendments therein, to receive the Patent, and to transact all business in the Patent Office connected therewith.

1879

National Archives and Records Administration

1. Which inventor applied for this patent? What invention was this patent for?

2. When did the inventor apply for this patent?

3. Identify two other developments or inventions for which this inventor is known.

Extended Response

Extended-response questions, like constructed-response questions, usually focus on a document of some kind. However, they are more complex and require more time to complete than short-answer constructed-response questions. Some extended-response questions ask you to present the information in the document in a different form. Others require you to complete a chart, graph, or diagram. Still others ask you to write an essay, a report, or some other extended piece of writing. In most standardized tests, documents have only one extended-response question.

1. Read the title of the document to get an idea of the subject.
2. Carefully read the extended-response questions. (Question 1 asks you to complete a chart. Question 2 assumes that the chart is complete and asks you to write an essay based on information in the chart.)
3. Study and analyze the document.
4. Sometimes the question gives you a partial answer. Analyze that answer to determine what kind of information your answers should contain.
5. If the question requires an essay or other piece of writing, jot down ideas in outline form. Use this outline to write your answer.

❶ **Some Major Events in the Cold War**

Your answers should follow the pattern of this sample entry. ❹

❸

Event	Result
The Hiss, Fuchs, and Rosenberg spy cases give rise to fears of Communist infiltration in the U.S.	Senator Joseph McCarthy rises to prominence by launching an anti-Communist crusade.
John Foster Dulles proposes the policy of brinkmanship—a policy heavily dependent on nuclear weapons and the airplanes that deliver them.	*The U.S. invests heavily in nuclear weapons and increases the size of its air force.*
The Soviet Union threatens to back Egypt's fight for control of the Suez Canal.	*The U.S. warns that it will defend the Middle East against any Communist attack.*
The Soviet Union launches the satellite *Sputnik.*	*The U.S. and the Soviet Union begin a space race for control of outer space.*
The Soviet Union shoots down a U.S. spy plane flying over Soviet territory.	*U.S.-Soviet relations worsen.*
About 3 million Germans flee Communist East Germany for West Berlin.	*The Soviets and East Germans build a wall across Berlin to stem the flow of refugees to the West.*
The Soviet Union installs nuclear missiles in Cuba.	*Soviets remove missiles in exchange for U.S. pledge not to invade Cuba.*

❷

1. In the right-hand column, briefly outline the result of the Cold War event listed in the left-hand column. The first entry has been completed for you.

2. What impact did the Cold War have on international relations?

❺ **Essay Rubric** The best essays will point out that the Cold War led to a division of Europe and much of the rest of the world between countries that sided with the United States and those that allied with the Soviet Union. Increased military spending related to the nuclear arms race made this division potentially very dangerous.

For more test practice online . . .

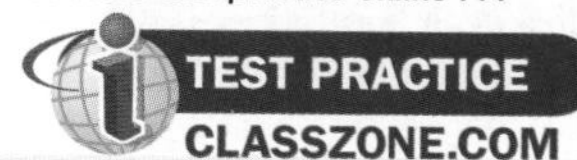
TEST PRACTICE
CLASSZONE.COM

Directions: Use the time line and your knowledge of U.S. history to answer questions 1 and 2.

The Period of Reconstruction

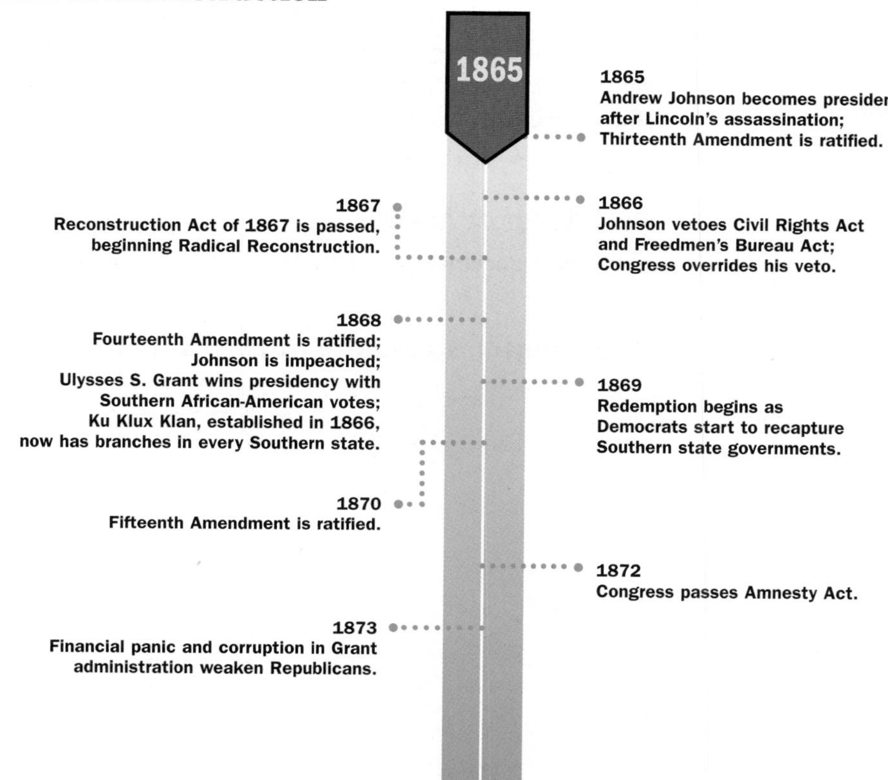
1865
1865
Andrew Johnson becomes president after Lincoln's assassination; Thirteenth Amendment is ratified.
1866
Johnson vetoes Civil Rights Act and Freedmen's Bureau Act; Congress overrides his veto.
1867
Reconstruction Act of 1867 is passed, beginning Radical Reconstruction.
1868
Fourteenth Amendment is ratified; Johnson is impeached; Ulysses S. Grant wins presidency with Southern African-American votes; Ku Klux Klan, established in 1866, now has branches in every Southern state.
1869
Redemption begins as Democrats start to recapture Southern state governments.
1870
Fifteenth Amendment is ratified.
1872
Congress passes Amnesty Act.
1873
Financial panic and corruption in Grant administration weaken Republicans.
1877
Rutherford B. Hayes elected president in disputed election; Reconstruction ends.
1877

1. On a separate sheet of paper make a chart similar to the one below. Then complete the chart by listing the major events of Reconstruction and their significance.

Year	Event	Significance

2. Identify the major turning points of the period of Reconstruction shown on the time line. Write a short essay explaining the impact these events had on the Reconstruction process.

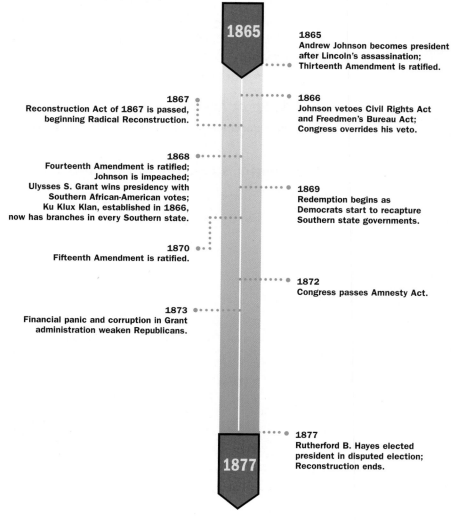

Document-Based Questions

A document-based question focuses on several documents—both visual and written. These documents often are accompanied by short-answer questions. Students use their answers to these questions and information from the documents to write an essay on a specified subject.

1. Carefully read the "Historical Context" section to get an indication of the issue addressed in the question.
2. Note the action words used in the "Task" section. These words will tell you exactly what the essay question requires.
3. Study and analyze each document. Think about how the documents are connected to the essay question. Take notes on your ideas.
4. Read and answer each of the document-specific questions.

Introduction

1 **Historical Context:** Rachel Carson's book *Silent Spring* (1962) awakened Americans to the issue of environmental pollution. Since that time, efforts have been made to protect the environment.

2 **Task:** Trace the progress on the environment made in the United States since the 1960s and consider the environmental challenges still facing the country today.

Part 1: Short Answer

Study each document carefully and answer the questions that follow.

3 **Document 1: Recycling in the United States, 1970–2000**

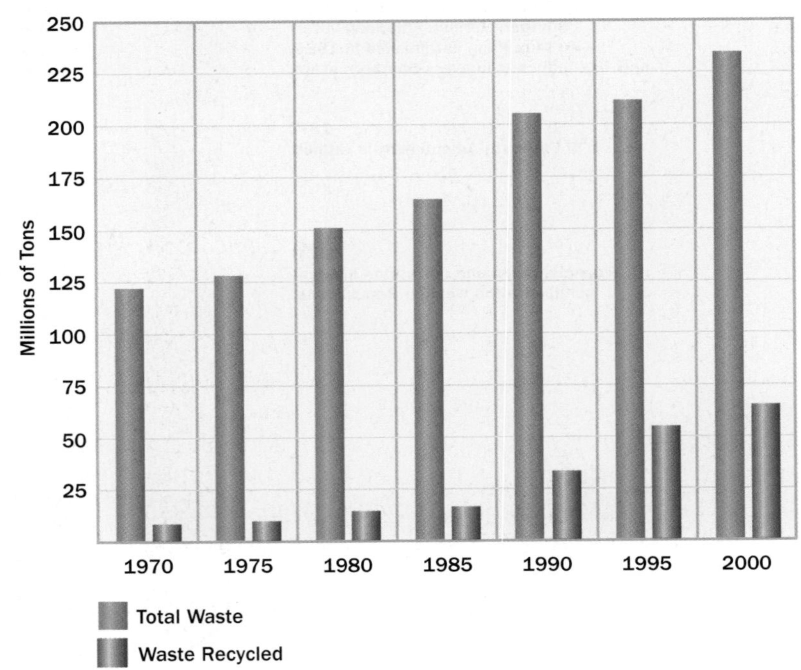

Source: *Historical Statistics of the United States; Statistical Abstract of the United States*

4 **What positive and negative trends does this graph show?**

The amount of waste recycled is increasing, but so, too, is total waste produced.

Document 2: Solar Collectors in the Mojave Desert

What alternative energy source is shown in the photograph? Why has the United States sought alternatives to such traditional energy sources as oil and coal?

solar energy; because supply of fossil fuels is limited and because oil, coal, and nuclear energy all carry a pollution risk

5 Carefully read the essay question. Then, write an outline for your essay.

6 Write your essay. Be sure that it has an introductory paragraph that introduces your argument, main body paragraphs that explain it, and a concluding paragraph that restates your position. In your essay, include extracts or details from specific documents to support your ideas. Add other supporting facts or details that you know from your study of American history.

Document 3: Clean Water

With the enactment of the Clean Water Act in 1972, the nation . . . made a new commitment to restore and maintain the chemical, physical, and biological integrity of [its] waters.

America has honored its commitment to clean water. Since enactment of the Clean Water Act, the number of waters that are safe for fishing and swimming has doubled. National clean water standards stop billions of pounds of industrial pollution from flowing into waters each year. . . . Today, . . . many . . . water bodies that were once severely polluted are well on the way to recovery. . . .

Despite impressive progress, many of the nation's rivers, lakes, and coastal waters do not meet water quality goals. [And] many waters that are now clean face [a] threat . . . from diverse pollution sources.

—Clean Water Action Plan (EPA)

What impact has the Clean Water Act had on America's waterways?

Many bodies of water that once were polluted are clean or well on their way to recovery.

Part 2: Essay

5 Using information from the documents, your answers to the questions in Part 1, and your knowledge of American history, write an essay tracing the progress on the environment made in the United States since the 1960s and considering the environmental challenges that still face the country today. 6

Essay Rubric The best essays will note such progress as cleaner water (Document 3), increased recycling (Document 1), and the search for energy alternatives that neither deplete the country's natural resources nor threaten the environment (Document 2). Essays should refer to such challenges as the increasing amount of waste produced (Document 1) and lingering pollution threats to the water (Document 3).

Introduction

Directions: Read the documents in Part 1 and answer the questions that follow each document. Then, read the directions for Part 2 and write your essay.

Historical Context: From 1929 to 1940, the United States suffered from a severe economic depression. Facing a damaged economy and a shaken public, President Franklin D. Roosevelt took action, creating a new role for the federal government.

Task: Describe how the role of the federal government changed during the Depression and discuss how that change continues to impact life in the United States today.

Part 1: Short Answer

Study each document carefully and answer the questions that follow.

Document 1: Federal Spending, 1925–1940

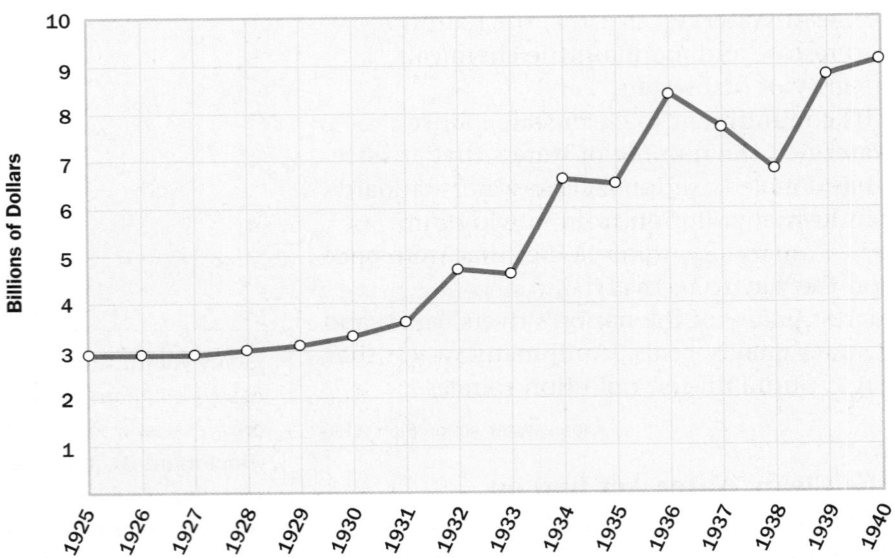

Source: *HIstorical Statistics of the United States*

President Franklin D. Roosevelt began introducing New Deal policies soon after taking office in 1933. What was the overall trend in federal spending in the New Deal years?

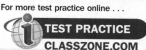

Document 2: The Civilian Conservation Corps

How does the "Old Deal" differ from the "New Deal"?

Document 3: A Policy for Labor (1936)

Among the first items in this growing labor policy of the American government are the following:

1. That the government ought to do everything in its power to establish minimum basic standards for labor, below which competition should not be permitted to force standards of health, wages, or hours.
2. That the government ought to use its influence to bring about arrangements which will make possible peaceful settlements of controversies and relieve labor of the necessity of resorting to strikes to secure equitable conditions and the right to be heard.

—Secretary of Labor Frances Perkins, "A National Labor Policy."

How did the National Labor Relations Act (1935) and the Fair Labor Standards Act (1938) put the New Deal labor policy into practice?

Part 2: Essay

Using information from the documents, your answers to the questions in Part 1, and your knowledge of American history, write an essay in which you describe how the role of the federal government changed during the Depression and discuss how that change continues to impact life in the United States today.

American Beginnings to 1877

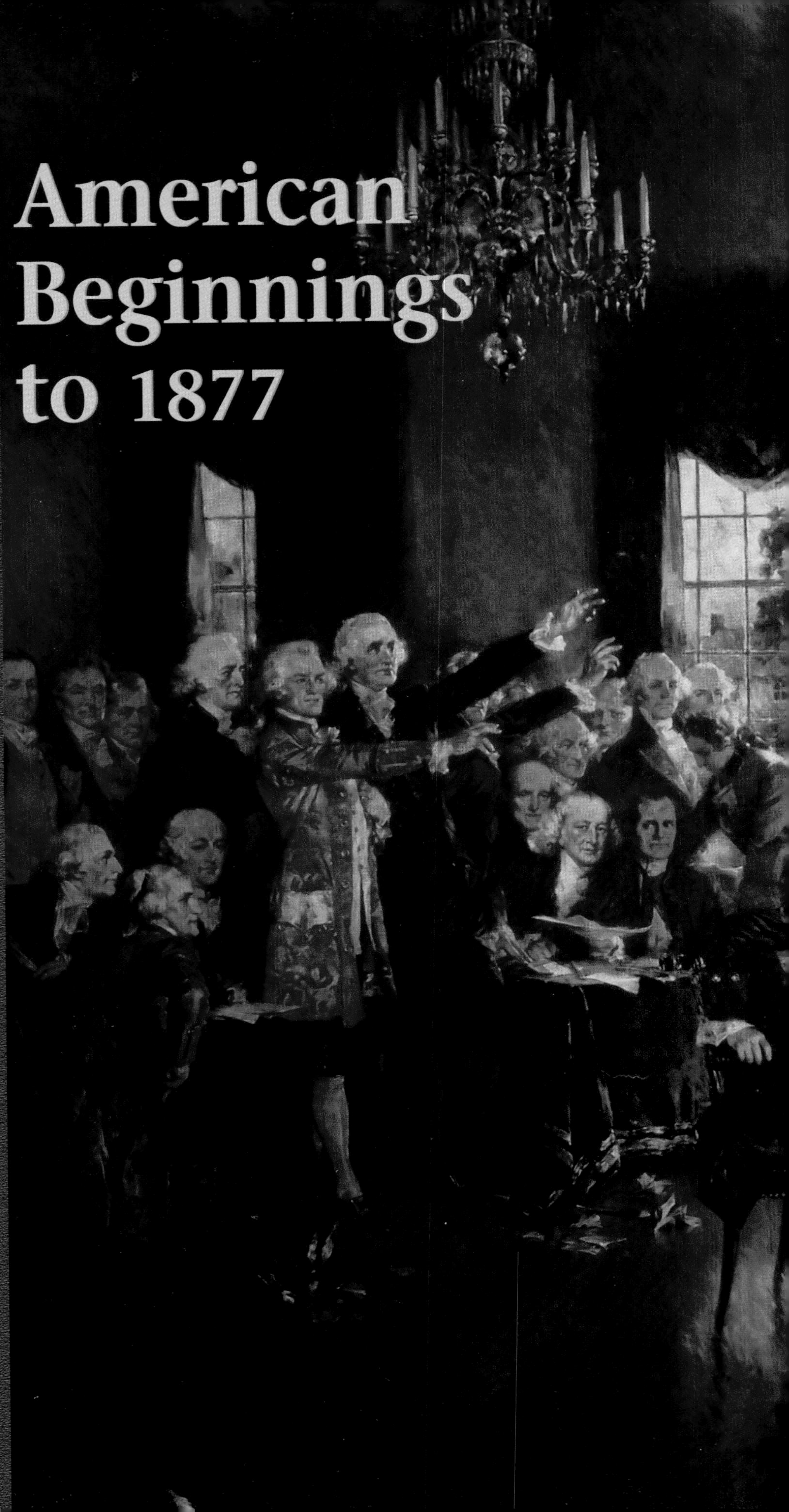

CHAPTER 1
Exploration and the Colonial Era Beginnings to 1763

CHAPTER 2
Revolution and the Early Republic 1763–1800

THE LIVING CONSTITUTION

CHAPTER 3
The Growth of a Young Nation 1800–1850

CHAPTER 4
The Union in Peril 1850–1877

Letter to the Editor

This unit covers the War for Independence and the Civil War. Choose an issue in this unit for which you would be willing to fight. Explain your views in a letter to the editor.

Signing of the Constitution by Howard Chandler Christy

EXPLORATION AND THE COLONIAL ERA

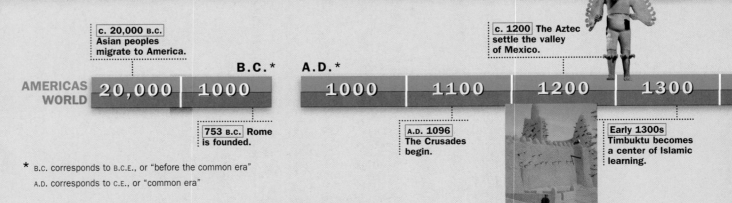

Native Americans observe the arrival of a European ship.

c. 20,000 B.C. Asian peoples migrate to America.

753 B.C. Rome is founded.

A.D. 1096 The Crusades begin.

c. 1200 The Aztec settle the valley of Mexico.

Early 1300s Timbuktu becomes a center of Islamic learning.

AMERICAS / WORLD

B.C.* 20,000 | 1000 — A.D.* 1000 | 1100 | 1200 | 1300

* B.C. corresponds to B.C.E., or "before the common era"
A.D. corresponds to C.E., or "common era"

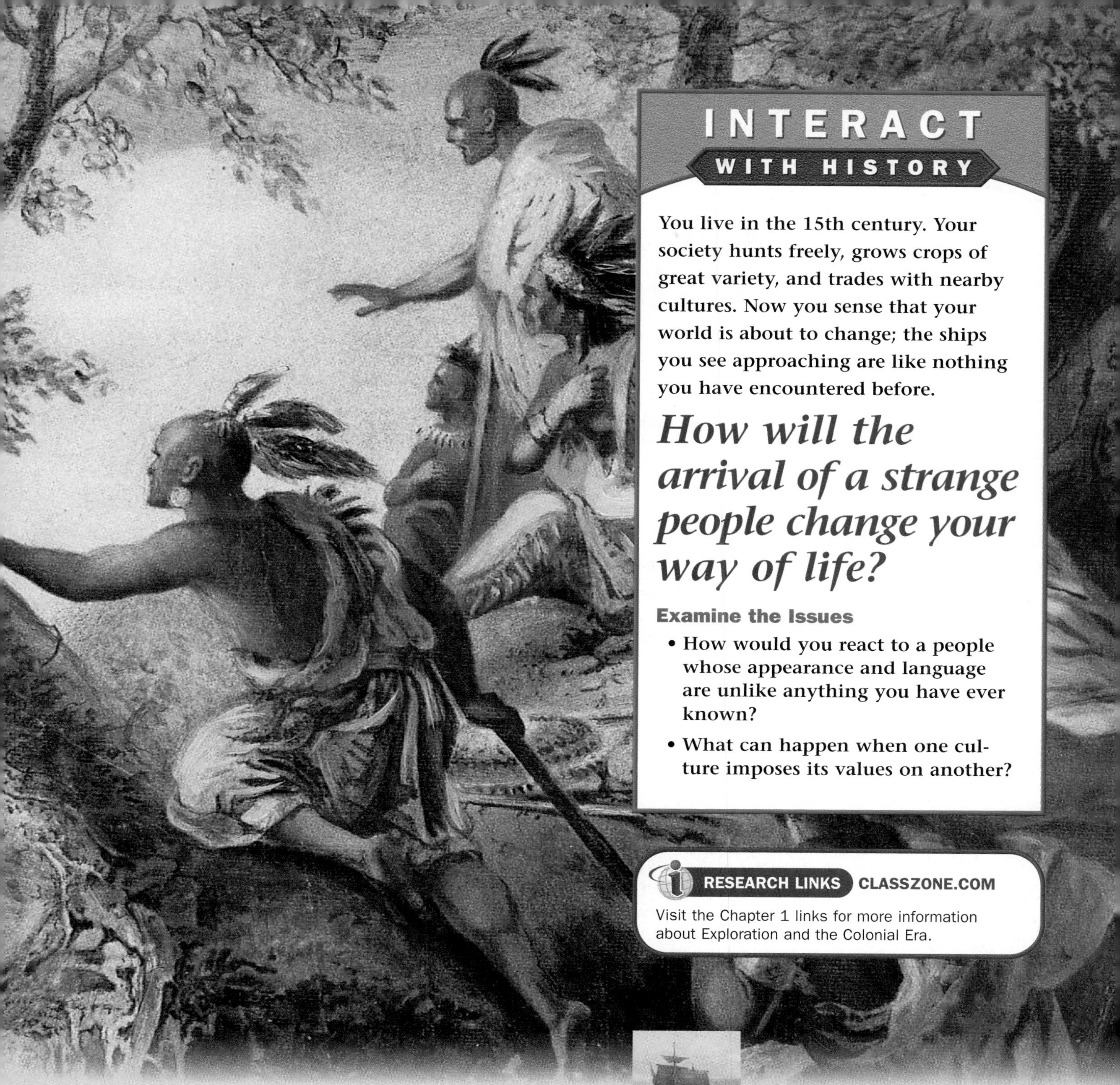

INTERACT
WITH HISTORY

You live in the 15th century. Your society hunts freely, grows crops of great variety, and trades with nearby cultures. Now you sense that your world is about to change; the ships you see approaching are like nothing you have encountered before.

How will the arrival of a strange people change your way of life?

Examine the Issues

- How would you react to a people whose appearance and language are unlike anything you have ever known?
- What can happen when one culture imposes its values on another?

RESEARCH LINKS CLASSZONE.COM

Visit the Chapter 1 links for more information about Exploration and the Colonial Era.

1492 Columbus first reaches North America.

1521 The Spanish destroy the Aztec empire.

1607 Jamestown is founded.

1620 "Pilgrims" settle in Plymouth.

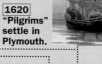

1681 William Penn founds Pennsylvania.

1754 French and Indian War begins.

1400 1500 1600 1700

1440 Johann Gutenberg develops his printing press.

1534 The Reformation begins in England with the Act of Supremacy.

1588 England defeats Spanish Armada.

1642 English Civil War begins between royalist forces and parliamentary forces led by Oliver Cromwell.

1763 With the Treaty of Paris, Britain acquires a vast North American empire.

The Americas, West Africa, and Europe

MAIN IDEA	WHY IT MATTERS NOW	Terms & Names
On the eve of their interaction, Native American, West African, and European peoples lived in complex societies.	The interaction of these cultures helped create the present-day culture of the United States.	• nomadic • Aztec • Anasazi • Pueblo • Iroquois • Benin • Kongo • Islam • Christianity • Reformation • Renaissance

One American's Story

Essie Parrish, a Native American spiritual leader and healer, kept alive stories from a time when her people, the Kashaya Pomo, flourished along the northern California coast. One day in 1958, she invited Robert Oswalt, an anthropologist at the University of California, to time travel with her to the 1540s. As Parrish spoke, the centuries rolled back.

A Personal Voice ESSIE PARRISH

"In the old days, before the white people came up here, there was a boat sailing on the ocean from the south. Because before that . . . [the Kashaya Pomo] had never seen a boat, they said, "Our world must be coming to an end. Couldn't we do something? This big bird floating on the ocean is from somewhere, probably from up high. . . ." [T]hey promised Our Father [a feast,] saying that destruction was upon them. When they had done so, they watched [the ship] sail way up north and disappear. . . . They were saying that nothing had happened to them —the big bird person had sailed northward without doing anything— because of the promise of a feast. . . . Consequently they held a feast and a big dance."

—quoted in *Kashaya Texts*

▲ Dressed for a ceremony in the 1950s, spiritual leader Essie Parrish wears a feathered headdress and holds two bead-covered staffs.

In this chapter, you will learn about three complex societies that met in North America in the late 1400s: the European, the West African, and the Native American. However, it is with the ancient peoples of the Americas that American history actually begins.

Ancient Cultures in the Americas

No one knows for sure when the first Americans arrived, but it may have been as long as 22,000 years ago. At that time, the glaciers of the last Ice Age had frozen vast quantities of the earth's water, lowering sea levels and possibly creating a land bridge between Asia and Alaska across what is now the Bering Strait. Ancient hunters may have trekked across the frozen land, known as Beringia, into North America.

HUNTING AND GATHERING Archaeologists believe that the earliest Americans lived as big-game hunters. That way of life changed around 12,000 to 10,000 years ago when temperatures warmed, glaciers melted, and sea levels rose once again. The land bridge disappeared under the Bering Sea, bringing to an end land travel between the Asian and North American continents. As the climate grew warmer, the large animals no longer thrived. People gradually switched to hunting smaller game and fish and gathering nuts and berries.

▲ Hunters roaming over 10,000 years ago in what is now southern Arizona may have used this spear point to kill large prey.

AGRICULTURE DEVELOPS While many ancient groups settled in North America, others continued south into what is now Mexico and South America. Between 10,000 and 5,000 years ago, an agricultural revolution quietly took place in what is now central Mexico. There, people began to plant crops. Eventually, agricultural techniques spread throughout the Americas.

The introduction of agriculture made it possible for people to settle in one place and to store surplus food. From this agricultural base developed larger communities. However, some Native American cultures never adopted agriculture and remained **nomadic,** moving from place to place in search of food and water. Other tribes mixed nomadic and non-nomadic lifestyles. (A)

Analyzing Effects

(A) What were the effects of agriculture on the hunting and gathering people of the Americas?

MAYA, AZTEC, AND INCA SOCIETIES FLOURISH The first empire of the Americas emerged as early as 1200 B.C. in what is now southern Mexico, where the Olmec people created a thriving civilization. In the wake of the Olmec's mysterious collapse, around 400 B.C., the Maya built a dynamic culture in Guatemala and the Yucatán Peninsula between A.D. 250 and 900. Later, the **Aztec** settled the Valley of Mexico in the 1200s and developed a sophisticated civilization.

In South America, the most prominent empire builders were the Inca. Around A.D. 1400, the Inca created a glittering empire that stretched nearly 2,500 miles along the mountainous western coast of South America.

COMPLEX SOCIETIES ARISE IN NORTH AMERICA In time, several North American groups, including the Hohokam and the **Anasazi** (ä′nə-sä′zē), introduced crops into the arid deserts of the Southwest. Later, between 300 B.C. and A.D. 1400, each group had established its own culture.

Artist's rendering of Tenochtitlán, the Aztec capital in the middle of Lake Texcoco. ▼

To the east and west of the Mississippi River, another series of complex societies developed—the Adena, the Hopewell, and the Mississippian. These societies excelled at trade and at building massive earthen mounds as tombs and as platforms for temples and other buildings. B

These early peoples were the ancestors of the many Native American groups that inhabited North America on the eve of its encounter with the European world.

MAIN IDEA

Summarizing

B In what ways did early Native American societies leave their mark upon the landscape?

Native American Societies of the 1400s

The varied regions of the North American continent provided for many different ways of life. The native groups that populated the continent's coasts, deserts, and forests 500 years ago were as diverse as their surroundings.

DIVERSE PEOPLES The inhabitants of California adapted to the region's varied environments. The Kashaya Pomo lived in marshlands along the central coast, hunting waterfowl with slingshots and nets. To the north of them, the Yurok and Hupa searched the forests for acorns and trapped fish in mountain streams.

The waterways and forests of the Northwest Coast sustained large communities year-round. On a coastline that stretched from what is now southern Alaska to northern California, groups such as the Kwakiutl, Nootka, and Haida collected shellfish from the beaches and hunted the ocean for whales, sea otters, and seals.

In the dry Southwest, the **Pueblo** and Pima tribes, descendants of the Anasazi and Hohokam, lived in multistory houses made of stone or adobe, a sun-dried brick of clay and straw, and grew maize (corn), beans, melons, and squash.

Beneath the forest canopy of the Northeast, members of the **Iroquois** (ĭr′ə-kwoi′) nation hunted fish and game, such as wild turkeys, deer, and bear. In the Northeast, where winters could be long and harsh, Northeast peoples relied heavily on wild animals for clothing and food. In the warmer Southeast, groups lived mainly off the land, growing such crops as maize, squash, and beans.

A Northwest powwow, or multitribal gathering, in Cashmere, Washington state, 1989. Gatherings like these preserve a 500-year cultural tradition. ▼

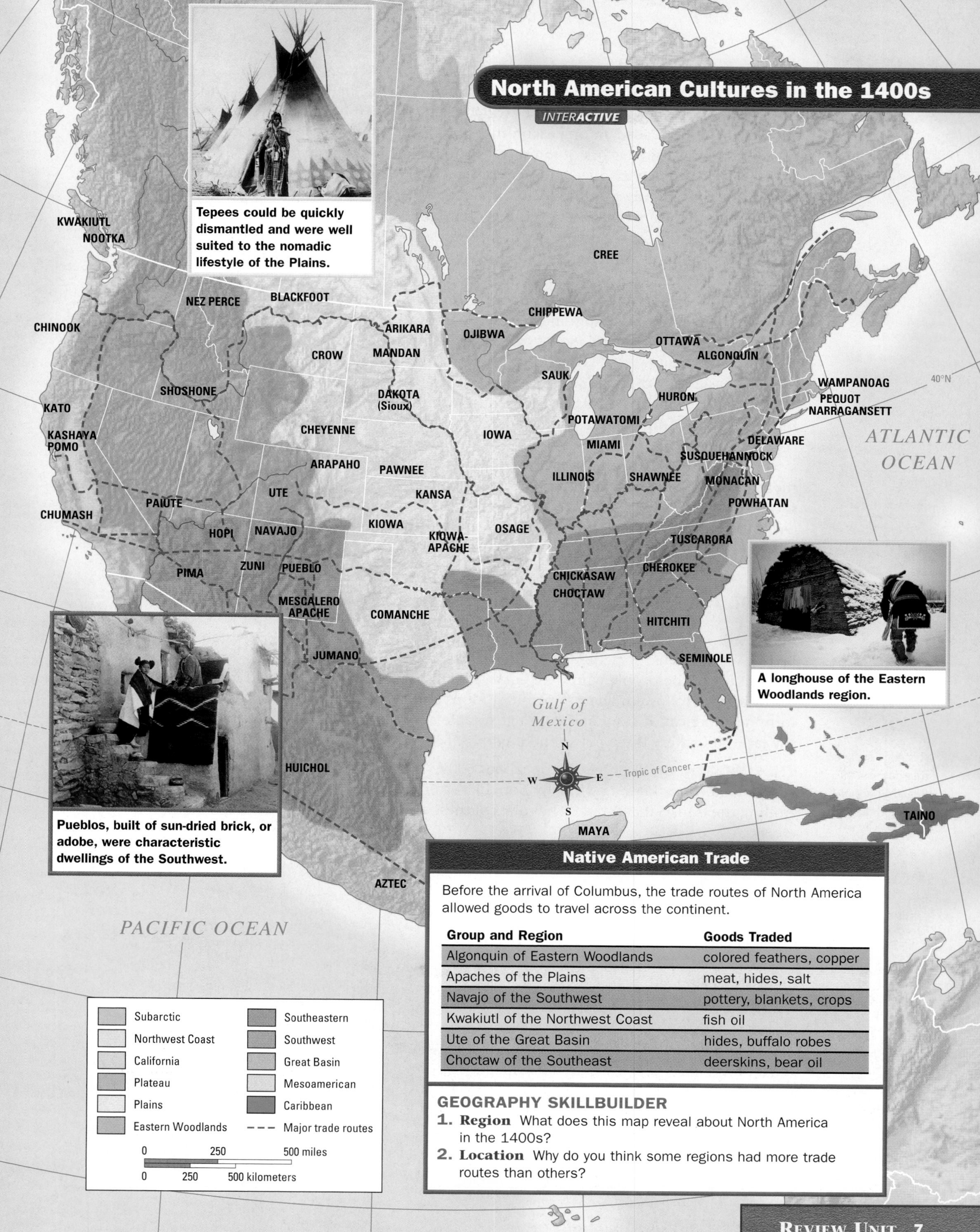

Tepees could be quickly dismantled and were well suited to the nomadic lifestyle of the Plains.

Pueblos, built of sun-dried brick, or adobe, were characteristic dwellings of the Southwest.

A longhouse of the Eastern Woodlands region.

Native American Trade

Before the arrival of Columbus, the trade routes of North America allowed goods to travel across the continent.

Group and Region	Goods Traded
Algonquin of Eastern Woodlands	colored feathers, copper
Apaches of the Plains	meat, hides, salt
Navajo of the Southwest	pottery, blankets, crops
Kwakiutl of the Northwest Coast	fish oil
Ute of the Great Basin	hides, buffalo robes
Choctaw of the Southeast	deerskins, bear oil

GEOGRAPHY SKILLBUILDER

1. **Region** What does this map reveal about North America in the 1400s?
2. **Location** Why do you think some regions had more trade routes than others?

COMMON CHARACTERISTICS Many of the Native American cultures had in common certain patterns of trade, attitudes toward land use, religious beliefs, and social values. As in other parts of the world, trade helped the spread of customs and beliefs. Tribes traded among each other both locally and over long distances. So extensive was the network of forest trails and river roads that an English sailor named David Ingram claimed in 1568 to have walked along Native American trade routes all the way from the Gulf of Mexico to Nova Scotia.

Native Americans traded many things, but land was not one of them. Land was regarded as the source of life, not as a commodity to be sold. "We cannot sell the lives of men and animals," said one Blackfoot chief in the 1800s, "therefore we cannot sell this land." C

MAIN IDEA

Making Inferences

C Why would Native American attitudes toward land ownership lead to conflict with Europeans?

Nearly all Native Americans thought of the natural world as filled with spirits. Every object—both living and nonliving—possessed a voice that might be heard if one listened closely. Some cultures worshiped one supreme being, variously called "Great Spirit," "Great Mystery," or "the Creative Power."

The basic unit of organization among all Native American groups was the family, which included aunts, uncles, cousins, and other relatives. Some tribes further organized the families into clans, or groups of families descended from a common ancestor.

In the late 1400s, on the eve of the first encounter with Europeans, the rhythms of Native American family life were highly developed. All phases of a person's life—birth, marriage, and death—were guided by traditions that often went back hundreds or perhaps thousands of years. On the other side of the Atlantic, in West Africa, customs equally ancient guided another diverse group of people.

West African Societies of the 1400s

Like North America, West Africa in the 1400s was home to a variety of long-established, sophisticated societies. From this region, especially from the coasts, originated most of the people who were enslaved and brought to the Americas in the centuries that followed. Their African traditions and beliefs played a major role in forming American history and culture. Notable among West African societies in the late 1400s were three powerful kingdoms: Songhai, Benin, and Kongo.

THE KINGDOM OF SONGHAI From about 600 to 1600, a succession of empires—first Ghana, then Mali, and finally Songhai—gained power and wealth by controlling the trans-Sahara trade. The rulers of these empires grew rich by taxing the

A desert caravan approaches the fabled Songhai city of Timbuktu. ▼

goods that passed through their realms. In 1067 an Arab geographer in Spain, named Al Bakri, described the duties (import and export taxes) levied in Ghana.

A PERSONAL VOICE AL BAKRI

"For every donkey loaded with salt that enters the country, the king takes a duty of one golden dinar [about one-eighth ounce of gold], and two dinars from every one that leaves. From a load of copper the duty due to the king is five mithquals [also about one-eighth ounce of gold], and from a load of merchandise ten mithquals. . . . The [gold] nuggets found in all the mines . . . are reserved for the king, only gold dust being left for the people."

—quoted in *Africa in the Days of Exploration*

With such wealth, the rulers who controlled the north-south trade routes could raise large armies and conquer new territory. They could also build cities, administer laws, and support the arts and education.

KINGDOMS OF BENIN AND KONGO At its height in the 1500s, Songhai's power extended across much of West Africa. However, it did not control the forest kingdoms along the southern coast. In the 1400s, one of these kingdoms, **Benin,** dominated a large region around the Niger Delta. Leading the expansion was a powerful oba, or ruler, named Ewuare, who developed Benin City.

Within another stretch of rain forest, in West Central Africa, the powerful kingdom of **Kongo** arose on the lower Congo (Zaire) River. In the late 1400s, Kongo consisted of a series of small kingdoms ruled by a single leader called the *manikongo,* who lived in what is today Angola.

WEST AFRICAN CULTURE Most West Africans lived in small villages, where life revolved around family, the community, and tradition. Bonds of kinship—that is, family ties—formed the basis of most aspects of life.

Political leaders claimed authority on the basis of religion. Although West Africans might worship a variety of gods and ancestral spirits, most believed in a single creator.

Throughout West Africa, people supported themselves by farming, herding, hunting, fishing, and by mining and trading. Almost all groups believed in collective ownership of land. Individuals farmed the land, but it reverted to family or village ownership when not in use. D

MAIN IDEA

Comparing
D What did the kingdoms of West Africa have in common?

TRADING PATTERNS WITH THE WIDER WORLD By the 1400s, West Africa had long been connected to the wider world through trade. The city of Timbuktu was the hub of a well-established trading network that connected most of West Africa to the ports of North Africa, and through these ports to markets in Europe and Asia. Along trade routes across the Sahara Desert, merchants carried goods from Mediterranean cities and salt from Saharan mines to exchange for gold, ivory, and dyed cotton cloth.

Along with goods, traders from North Africa also brought across the Sahara the Islamic faith, which increasingly influenced West African cultures. **Islam** is a monotheistic religion—that is, one based on the belief in a single god. The religion of Islam was founded in Arabia in 622 by the prophet Muhammad and spread quickly across the Middle East and North Africa.

HISTORICAL SPOTLIGHT

ISLAM

Islam was founded by the prophet Muhammad (about A.D. 570–632), who worked as a merchant in Mecca, a trading city on the Arabian peninsula. When he was about 40, he believed the angel Gabriel appeared to him and told him to preach a new religion to the Arabs. This religion became known as Islam, which in Arabic means "surrender [to Allah]." (*Allah* is the Arabic word for God.) The followers of Islam are called Muslims, "those who submit to God's will."

The words that Muhammad received from the angel were recorded by his followers in the Qur'an, the holy book of Islam. The Qur'an teaches that "there is no God but Allah, and Muhammad is His Prophet." The Qur'an also sets forth certain duties for righteous Muslims, including a series of daily prayers, the giving of charity, and a pilgrimage to the holy city of Mecca.

THE PORTUGUESE Mariners from Portugal made trading contacts along the West African coast starting in the 1440s. These early contacts with Portuguese traders had two significant consequences for West Africa and the Americas. First, direct trade between the Portuguese and the coastal people of West Africa bypassed the routes across the Sahara and pulled the coastal region into a closer relationship with Europe. Second, the Portuguese began the European trade in enslaved West Africans.

European Societies of the 1400s

In the late 1400s, most Europeans, like most Native Americans and most Africans, lived in small villages, bound to the land and to rhythms of life that had been in place for centuries. For the majority of Europeans, change came slowly.

THE SOCIAL HIERARCHY European communities were based on social hierarchy, that is, they were organized according to rank. At the top of the hierarchy were monarchs and the aristocracy, the landowning elite, who held most of the wealth and power. Members of the clergy also ranked high in the social order. At the bottom were agricultural laborers, or peasants.

Few individuals rose above the social position of their birth. One group that did achieve mobility was the growing number of artisans and merchants, the people who created and traded goods for money. There were relatively few members of this group in the 1400s. However, the profit they earned from trade would eventually make them a valuable source of tax revenue to monarchs seeking to finance costly overseas exploration and expansion. E

MAIN IDEA

Making Inferences
E Why were merchants able to achieve social mobility?

KEY PLAYER

"KING" ISABELLA
1451–1504

Queen Isabella, who played a central role in European exploration by sponsoring Christopher Columbus's voyages to the Americas, made her mark on the Old World as well. As co-ruler of Spain, Isabella actively participated in her country's religious and military affairs.

In championing Spain's Catholicism, the queen often fought openly with the pope to make sure that her candidates were appointed to positions in the Spanish church. In addition, Isabella had tasted battle far more than most rulers, either male or female. The queen rode among her troops in full armor, personally commanding them in Ferdinand's absence. Whenever Isabella appeared on a horse, her troops shouted, "Castile, Castile, for our King Isabella!"

CHRISTIANITY SHAPES THE EUROPEAN OUTLOOK The dominant religion in Western Europe was **Christianity,** a religion based on the life and teachings of Jesus. The leader of the church—the pope—and his bishops held great political as well as spiritual authority.

As the influence of Christianity and Islam spread, the two religions came into conflict. In 1096, Christian armies from all over Western Europe responded to the church's call to force the Muslims out of the Holy Land around Jerusalem. Over the next two centuries, Europeans launched the Crusades, a series of military expeditions to the Middle East in the name of Christianity.

In the end, these bloody Crusades failed to "rescue" the Holy Land, but they resulted in two consequences that encouraged European exploration and expansion. First, the Crusades opened up Asian trade routes, supplying Europeans with luxuries from the East, especially spices such as cinnamon, cloves, nutmeg, and pepper. Second, the Crusades weakened the power of European nobles, many of whom lost their lives or fortunes in the wars. Monarchs eventually took advantage of the nobles' weakened ranks to consolidate their own power.

Background
Spices were important in the Middle Ages when European farmers preserved meat by packing it between layers of salt. Spices helped disguise the bad taste of the meat.

By the early 1500s, many church leaders and ordinary people were eager for reforms. This desire for change led to a movement called the **Reformation,** which criticized church practices and challenged the authority of the pope.

History Through *Art*

JUNE, *FROM* LES TRÈS RICHES HEURES DU DUC DE BERRY

This miniature painting, representing the month of June, is a page from a prayer book calendar begun by the Limbourg brothers around the year 1412. The book was made for a younger son of the French king, and tells us a great deal about the aristocratic view of the European social order.

In the background, the walls of the city of Paris protect a palace and the royal chapel, buildings that represent the two most powerful institutions in medieval European society: church and aristocracy.

In the foreground, peasants mow the fields, in an orderly world of peace and tranquility. However, the image is a fantasy, an idealized vision painted to please the aristocracy. There is no hint of the peasants' grinding poverty or of the violence of the Hundred Years' War that was at that moment devastating northern France.

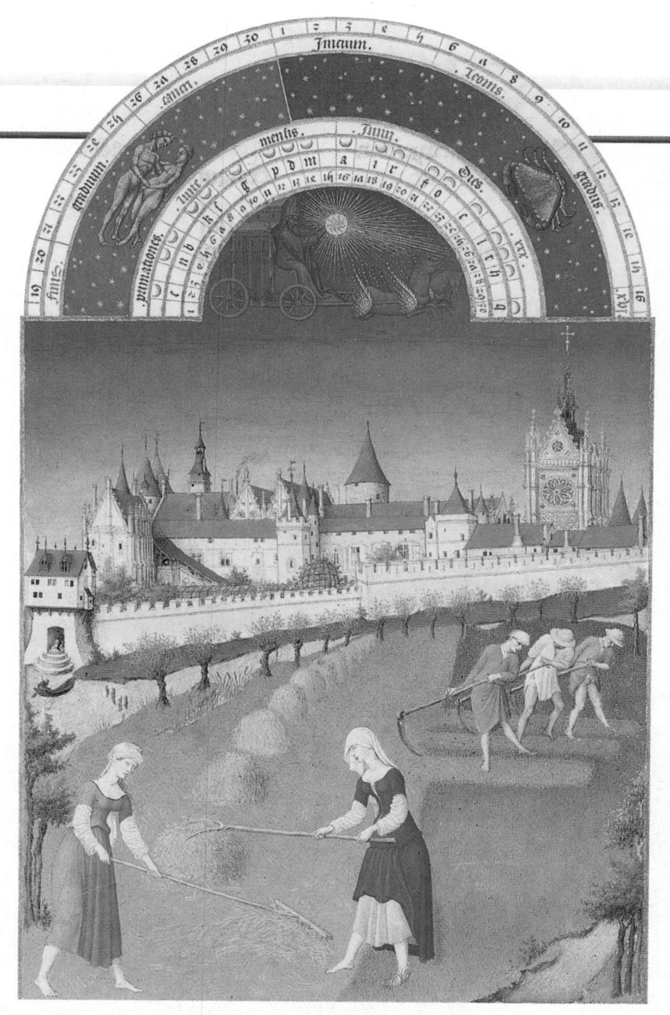

SKILLBUILDER Interpreting Visual Sources

1. What does the painting tell you about the importance of gender in the division of labor during the 1400s?
2. Why might images of poverty have displeased the aristocracy?

SEE SKILLBUILDER HANDBOOK, PAGE R23.

The Reformation led to a religious schism, or split, throughout Europe: those who supported the Reformation became known as Protestants because of their opposition to the established Catholic church. This split deepened the rivalries among European nations during the period of North American colonization a century later and sent some Protestants and some Catholics across the Atlantic to seek religious freedom. (F)

> **MAIN IDEA**
> **Analyzing Causes**
> (F) How did religious events in Europe help spur exploration and settlement of new lands?

EUROPEAN NATIONS TAKE SHAPE During the 1400s, four major nations were taking shape in Europe: Portugal, Spain, France, and England. Ambitious monarchs extended their reach by collecting new taxes, raising professional armies, and forming stronger governments. Among their new allies were the merchants, who paid taxes in exchange for the protection and expansion of trade.

THE RENAISSANCE The 1400s also saw a cultural awakening in Europe, known as the **Renaissance** (rĕn′ĭ-säns′)—a term meaning "rebirth" of the kind of interest in the physical world that had characterized ancient Greece and Rome. In the arts, this meant rejecting the flat, two-dimensional images of medieval painting in favor of the deep perspectives and fully rounded forms of ancient sculpture and painting. Starting in Italy, a region stimulated by commercial contact with Asia and Africa, the Renaissance soon spread throughout Europe. Renaissance artists created works of lasting influence, while European scholars reexamined the texts of ancient philosophers, mathematicians, geographers, and scientists.

> **Vocabulary**
> **medieval**: of or during the Middle Ages, often dated from A.D. 476 to 1453

Although their themes were still often religious in nature, Renaissance artists portrayed their subjects more realistically than had medieval artists, using new

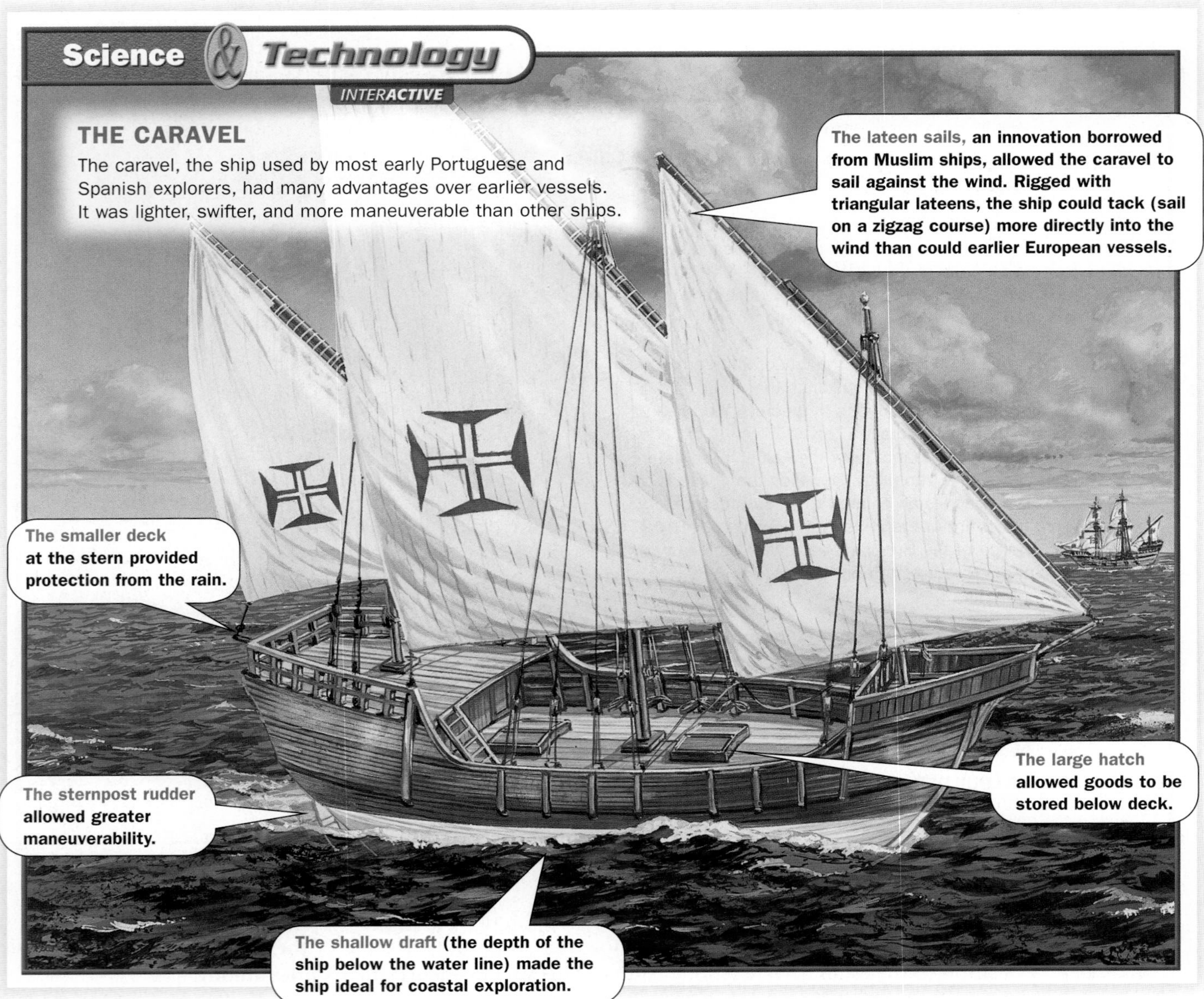

techniques such as perspective. Leonardo da Vinci, investigating how things worked, kept notebooks in which he made detailed drawings of human anatomy and of his inventions, including a flying machine. This energetic spirit of inquiry infused the early explorers and adventurers who, like Christopher Columbus, grew up during the Renaissance.

Science & Technology
INTERACTIVE
THE CARAVEL
The caravel, the ship used by most early Portuguese and Spanish explorers, had many advantages over earlier vessels. It was lighter, swifter, and more maneuverable than other ships.
The lateen sails, an innovation borrowed from Muslim ships, allowed the caravel to sail against the wind. Rigged with triangular lateens, the ship could tack (sail on a zigzag course) more directly into the wind than could earlier European vessels.
The smaller deck at the stern provided protection from the rain.
The large hatch allowed goods to be stored below deck.
The sternpost rudder allowed greater maneuverability.
The shallow draft (the depth of the ship below the water line) made the ship ideal for coastal exploration.

The spread of the Renaissance was advanced by Johann Gutenberg's introduction of printing from movable type in the 1450s. This development made books easier and cheaper to produce, which aided the spread of ideas.

The Renaissance encouraged people to think of themselves as individuals, to have confidence in their capabilities, and to look forward to the fame their achievements might bring. This attitude prompted many to seek glory through adventure, discovery, and conquest. G

> **MAIN IDEA**
> **Developing Historical Perspective**
> G How did Renaissance attitudes encourage the European age of exploration?

EUROPE ENTERS A NEW AGE OF EXPANSION The European interest in overseas expansion probably began in the 1200s with the journey of Marco Polo to China. Later, the publication in 1477 of the first printed edition of Polo's vivid—and sometimes exaggerated—account caused renewed interest in the East. Like other merchants, Polo traveled to Asia by land. The expense and peril involved in such journeys led Europeans to seek alternative routes. In the 1400s, Europeans used the work of Ptolemy, a second-century scholar, along with the work of Arab and

Jewish scholars, to revive the art of cartography, or mapmaking. Although imperfect, the new maps inspired Europeans to start exploring for water routes to Asia.

Vocabulary
bureaucracies: government departments staffed with nonelected officials

European monarchs had powerful motives to finance the search for new lands and trading routes: they needed money to maintain their growing armies and administrative bureaucracies. By the mid-1400s, Europe's gold and silver mines were running low. So the monarchs of Portugal, Spain, France, and England began looking overseas for wealth.

Beginning in the 1300s, monarchs invested some of their tax revenues in new weapons—such as longbows and cannons—which they used to limit the power of the independent nobles. These new weapons, along with the hand-held firearms that were developed in the 1400s, also gave them military advantages over the Africans and Native Americans whom they later encountered. H

MAIN IDEA
Summarizing
H What military advantages did Europeans have over Africans and Native Americans?

SAILING TECHNOLOGY IMPROVES European ship captains in the 1400s experimented with new sailing vessels such as the caravel and navigating tools such as the compass and the astrolabe, which helped sailors plot direction at sea. They also took advantage of sailing innovations, like those that allowed caravels to sail against the wind.

"The best ships that sailed the seas . . ."
ALVISE DA CADAMOSTO, OF THE CARAVEL

One leader in developing and employing these innovations was Prince Henry the Navigator of Portugal, who gathered mariners, geographers, and navigators to his court. According to a contemporary chronicler, Gomes Eanes de Zurara, the prince's driving motivation was the need to know.

For almost 40 years, Prince Henry sent his captains sailing south along the west coast of Africa. Exploration continued after the prince's death. In 1488, Portuguese sailor Bartolomeu Dias rounded the southern tip of Africa; fellow Portuguese explorer Vasco da Gama reached India ten years later. By sailing around Africa to eastern Asia via the Indian Ocean, Portuguese traders were able to cut their costs and increase their profits.

As cartographers redrew their maps to show this eastern route to Asia, an Italian sea captain named Christopher Columbus believed there was an even shorter route—one that headed west across the Atlantic.

ASSESSMENT

1. **TERMS & NAMES** For each term or name, write a sentence explaining its significance.
   - **nomadic**
   - **Aztec**
   - **Anasazi**
   - **Pueblo**
   - **Iroquois**
   - **Benin**
   - **Kongo**
   - **Islam**
   - **Christianity**
   - **Reformation**
   - **Renaissance**

MAIN IDEA

2. **TAKING NOTES**
   For each region and time period shown, write two or three sentences to describe how it was affected by trade and commerce.

   West Africa Before the Portuguese
   Trade and Commerce
   Europe After the Crusades
   America Before Columbus

CRITICAL THINKING

3. **MAKING INFERENCES**
   Why do you think other European nations lagged behind Portugal in overseas exploration? Support your reasons with details from the text.
   Think About:
   - the geography of Portugal
   - the power of monarchs in the 1400s
   - the economic and political situation of European nations during this time

4. **ANALYZING CAUSES**
   What factors do you think contributed to the thriving trade system that flourished in West Africa? Use evidence from the text to support your response.

5. **ANALYZING EFFECTS**
   What effects did Portuguese trade have on West Africa?

SECTION 2

Spanish North America

MAIN IDEA	WHY IT MATTERS NOW	Terms & Names
Beginning with the voyage of Christopher Columbus, the Spanish built a vast colonial empire in the Americas.	**The Spanish left an impact on the cultures of North and South America that helped to shape present-day America.**	• **Christopher Columbus** • **Taino** • **Treaty of Tordesillas** • **Columbian Exchange** • **conquistador** • **Hernándo Cortés** • **Montezuma** • ***mestizo*** • ***encomienda*** • **New Spain** • **New Mexico**

One European's Story

On August 3, 1492, the Genoese mariner **Christopher Columbus** set out on a bold expedition: to find a route to Asia by sailing west across the Atlantic Ocean. It was a journey destined to change the course of world history. A seeker of fame and fortune, Columbus began his travel journal by restating the deal he had struck with the Spanish rulers financing his voyage.

A PERSONAL VOICE CHRISTOPHER COLUMBUS

> **"Based on the information that I had given Your Highnesses about the land of India and about a Prince who is called the Great Khan [of China] . . . Your Highnesses decided to send me . . . to the regions of India, to see . . . the peoples and the lands, and to learn of . . . the measures which could be taken for their conversion to our Holy Faith. . . . I was to go by way of the west, whence until today we do not know with certainty that anyone has gone."**
>
> —*The Log of Christopher Columbus*

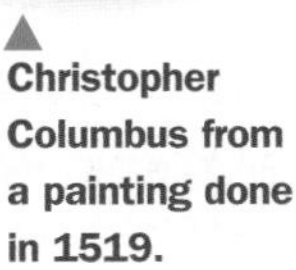

▲ **Christopher Columbus from a painting done in 1519.**

Columbus never reached Asia. He landed on an island he thought was off the coast of Asia but was actually in the Caribbean Sea. Instead of finding the Great Khan, Columbus set in motion a process that brought together the American, European, and African worlds.

Columbus Crosses the Atlantic

In October 1492, roughly two months after leaving Spain, Columbus's small fleet of ships, the *Niña*, the *Pinta*, and the *Santa María*, reached land. Columbus went ashore, where he encountered a group of people who would become known as the **Taino** (tī′nō), from their word for "noble ones." He planted Spanish banners and renamed their island San Salvador ("Holy Savior"), claiming it for Spain. Columbus spent 96 days exploring four coral islands in the Bahamas and the coastlines of two larger Caribbean islands, known today as Cuba and Hispaniola.

Convinced that he had landed on islands off Asia, known to Europeans as the Indies, Columbus called the people he met *los indios*. Thus the name *Indian* came to be mistakenly applied to all the diverse peoples of the Americas. The Spanish monarchs were thrilled with Columbus's discoveries and funded three more of his voyages—this time to colonize the lands he had claimed.

Vocabulary
colonize: to establish settlements under the control of a parent country

THE IMPACT ON NATIVE AMERICANS By the time Columbus set sail for his return to Hispaniola in 1493, Europeans had already developed a pattern for colonization. They had glimpsed the profitability of the plantation system, realized the economic benefits of using native or local peoples for forced labor, and learned to use European weapons to dominate native peoples. These tactics would be used in the Americas.

The arrival of the Europeans devastated Native Americans by another means: disease. The Taino, for example, had not developed any natural immunity to measles, mumps, chickenpox, smallpox, typhus, or other diseases Europeans had unknowingly brought with them. Consequently, the Taino died by the thousands once they were exposed.

THE IMPACT ON AFRICANS With the decline of the native work force the European settlers of the Americas eventually turned to Africa for slaves. The Atlantic slave trade devastated many African societies, particularly in West Africa. Starting in the 1500s, African cultures lost many of their young and more able members. Before the Atlantic slave trade ended in the 1800s, it had drained Africa of at least 10 million people.

THE IMPACT ON EUROPEANS Columbus's voyages had profound effects on Europeans as well. In search of new lives, Europeans began to cross the Atlantic by the thousands in what would become one of the biggest voluntary migrations in world history. Overseas expansion inflamed national rivalries in Europe. In 1494, Spain and Portugal signed the **Treaty of Tordesillas** (tôr′də-sē′əs), in which they agreed to divide the Western Hemisphere between them. (A)

MAIN IDEA
Analyzing Events
(A) What did Spain and Portugal agree to do in the Treaty of Tordesillas?

THE COLUMBIAN EXCHANGE The voyages of Columbus and those after him led to the discovery of plants and animals in the Americas that were new to Europeans and Africans. Ships took items such as corn, potatoes, and tobacco from the Americas to Europe and to Africa. From these countries, they brought back livestock, grains, fruit, and coffee. This global transfer of living things, called the **Columbian Exchange,** began with Columbus's first voyage and continues today.

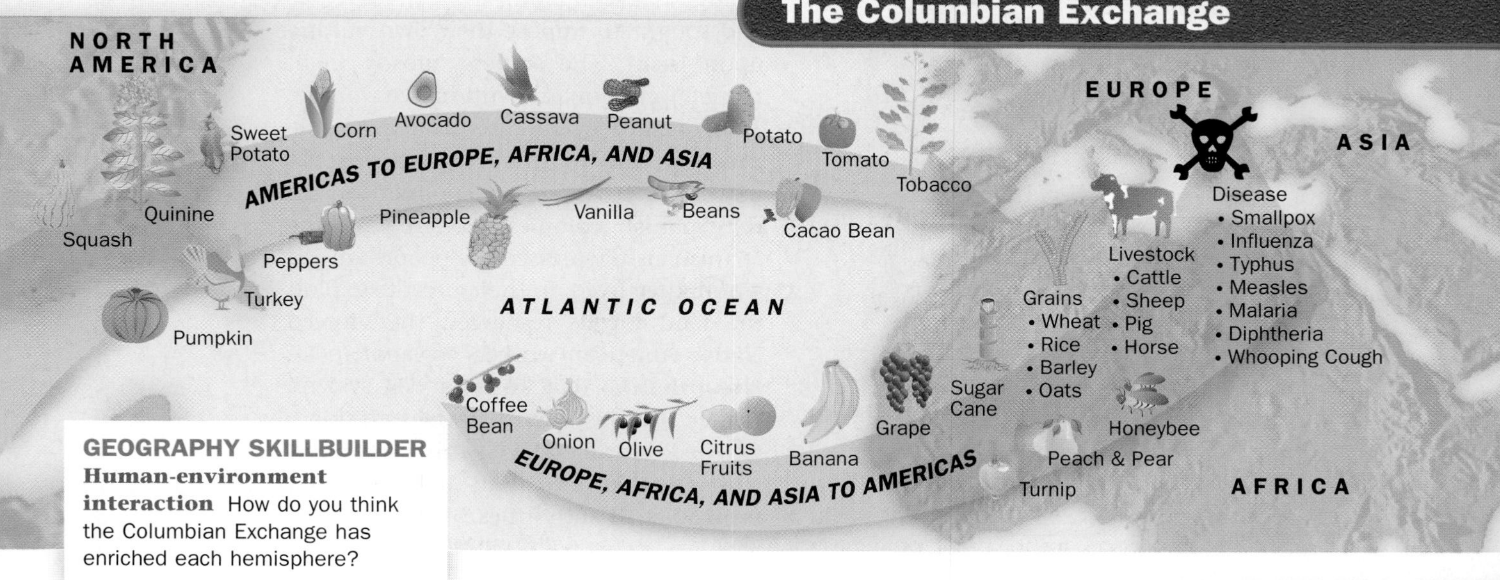

GEOGRAPHY SKILLBUILDER
Human-environment interaction How do you think the Columbian Exchange has enriched each hemisphere?

The Spanish Claim a New Empire

In the wake of Columbus's voyages, Spanish explorers took to the seas to claim new colonies for Spain. These explorers were lured by the prospect of vast lands filled with gold and silver. Known as ***conquistadors*** (kŏng-kē′stə-dôrz′) (conquerors), they conquered much of the Americas.

CORTÉS SUBDUES THE AZTEC Soon after landing in Mexico in 1519, **Hernándo Cortés** learned of the vast and wealthy Aztec empire in the region's interior. With a force of 508 men, 16 horses, 10 cannons, and numerous dogs, the conquistador marched inland.

The Spaniards marveled at Tenochtitlán, the Aztec capital, with its towering temples and elaborate engineering works—including a system that brought fresh water into the city. "We were amazed," one of Cortés's soldiers said of his first glimpse of Tenochtitlán. "Some of our soldiers even asked whether the things we saw were not a dream." While the Aztec city astonished the Spaniards, the capital's glittering gold stock seemed to hypnotize them. "They picked up the gold and fingered it like monkeys," one native witness recalled. "They hungered like pigs for that gold."

The Aztec emperor, **Montezuma,** convinced at first that Cortés was an armor-clad god, agreed to give the Spanish explorer a share of the empire's existing gold supply. The conquistador was not satisfied. Cortés eventually forced the Aztec to mine more gold and silver. In the spring of 1520, the Aztec rebelled against the Spaniards' intrusion. Regarding Montezuma as a traitor, the Aztec are believed to have stoned their ruler to death before driving out Cortés's forces.

While they had successfully repelled the Spanish invaders, the Aztec were falling victim to the diseases that the Spanish had brought with them. By the time Cortés launched a counterattack in 1521, the Spanish and their native allies overran an Aztec force that had been greatly reduced by smallpox and measles. After several months of fighting, the invaders sacked and burned Tenochtitlán, and the Aztec surrendered. **B**

MAIN IDEA

Summarizing

B What factors enabled the Spanish to conquer the Aztec?

KEY PLAYER

HERNÁNDO CORTÉS
1485–1547

Cortés made himself the enemy of thousands of Native Americans, but the daring conquistador did not have many friends among Spaniards. Spanish authorities on Cuba, where Cortés owned land, accused the conquistador of murdering his wife, Catalina Juárez. "There were ugly accusations, but none proved," wrote Juárez's biographer.

In addition, the Cuban governor, Diego Velázquez, who resented Cortés's arrogance, relieved him of the command of a gold-seeking expedition to the mainland. Cortés left Cuba anyway. As he fought his way through Mexico, Cortés had to battle not only the Native Americans but also the Spanish forces that Velázquez sent to arrest him.

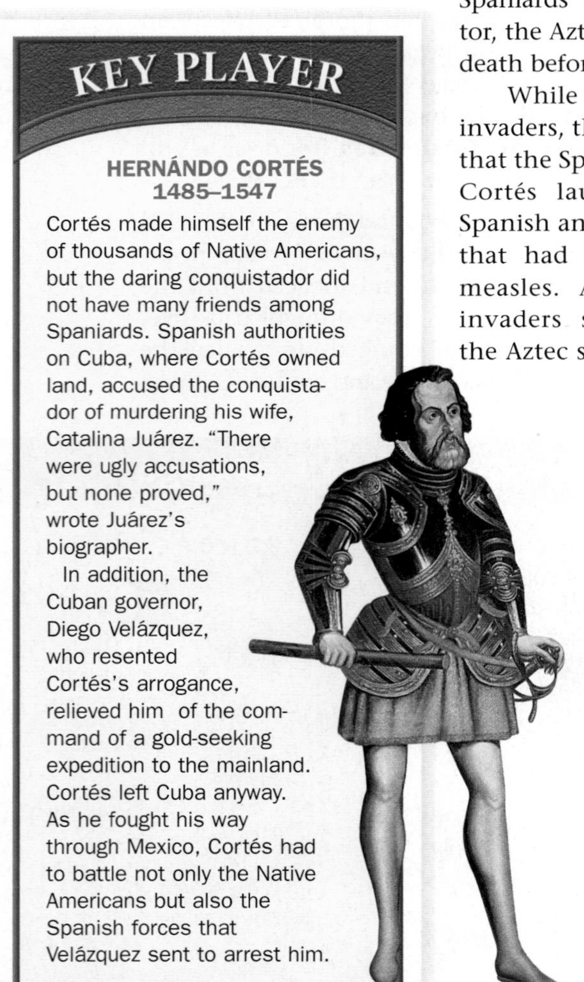

THE SPANISH PATTERN OF CONQUEST In building their American empire, the Spaniards lived among the native people and sought to impose their own culture upon them. The settlers, mostly men, tended to intermarry with native women. This practice eventually created a large ***mestizo*** (mĕs-tē′zō)—or mixed Spanish and Native American—population in the Spanish colonies. Nonetheless, the Spanish also oppressed the people among whom they lived. In their effort to exploit the land for its resources, they forced Native American workers to labor in an ***encomienda*** (ĕng-kô-myĕn′dä) system. Under that system, natives farmed, ranched, or mined for Spanish landlords, who received the rights to their labor from Spanish authorities.

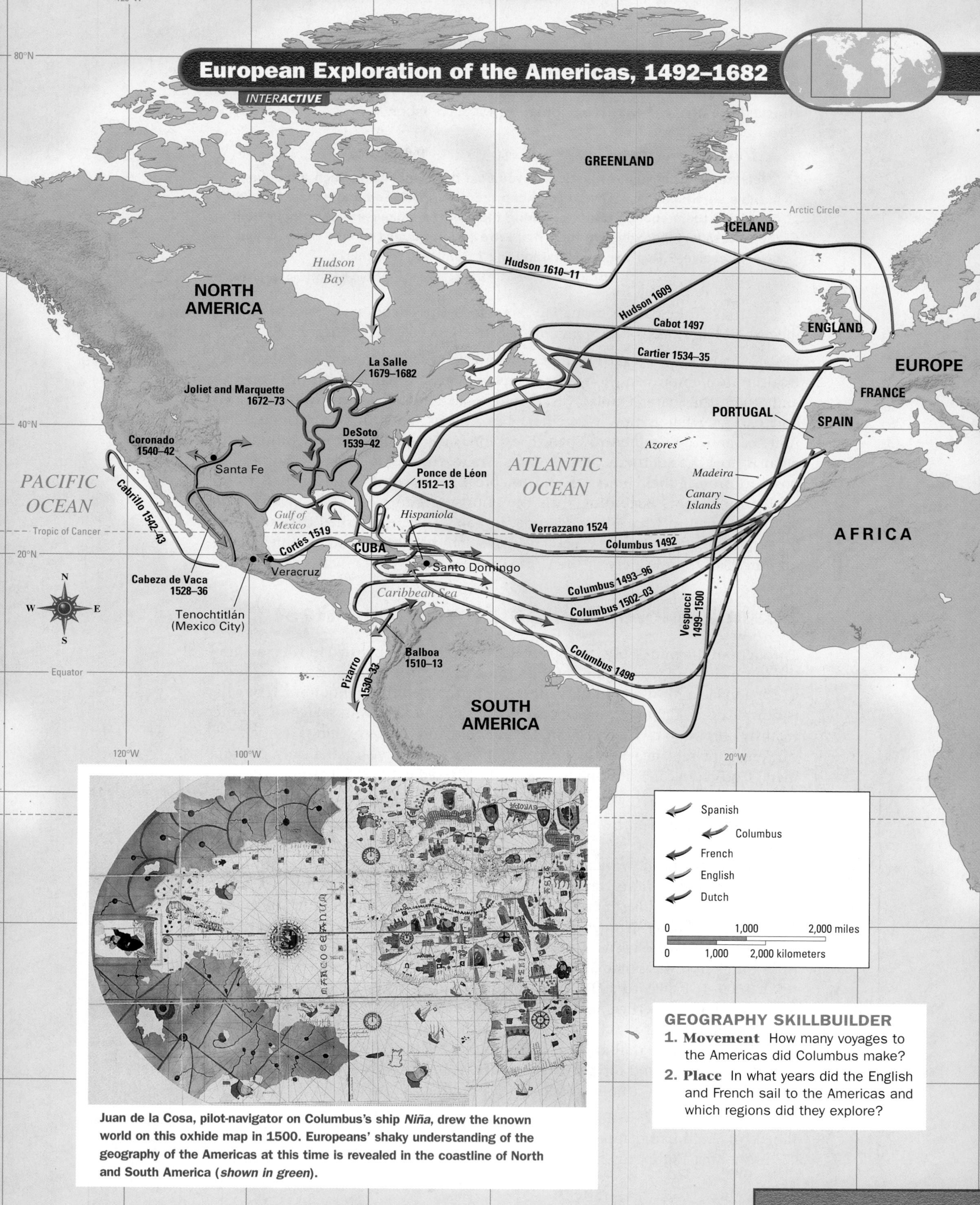

Juan de la Cosa, pilot-navigator on Columbus's ship *Niña*, drew the known world on this oxhide map in 1500. Europeans' shaky understanding of the geography of the Americas at this time is revealed in the coastline of North and South America (*shown in green*).

GEOGRAPHY SKILLBUILDER

1. **Movement** How many voyages to the Americas did Columbus make?
2. **Place** In what years did the English and French sail to the Americas and which regions did they explore?

A number of Spanish priests demanded an end to the harsh encomienda system. In 1511, Fray Antonio de Montesinos delivered a fiery sermon in which he attacked the use of the native population for slave labor.

A PERSONAL VOICE FRAY ANTONIO DE MONTESINOS

"Tell me, by what right or justice do you hold these Indians in such a cruel and horrible servitude? . . . Why do you keep them so oppressed and exhausted, without giving them enough to eat or curing them of the sicknesses they incur from the excessive labor you give them? . . . Are you not bound to love them as you love yourselves? Don't you understand this? Don't you feel this?"

—quoted in *Reflections, Writing for Columbus*

MAIN IDEA

Analyzing Motives

C Why did some Spanish priests demand an end to the encomienda system?

In 1542, the Spanish monarchy abolished the encomienda system, and to meet their labor needs, the Spaniards began to use enslaved Africans. C

SPAIN ENJOYS A GOLDEN AGE In 1532, Francisco Pizarro plundered the wealthy Inca empire on the western coast of South America. With this conquest and others, the Spanish built a vast empire, which included **New Spain** (Mexico, and part of what is now Guatemala), as well as lands in Central and South America and the Caribbean. Spanish explorers also undertook expeditions into what is now the southern United States. There, they established a string of outposts to protect their holdings and to spread their culture and religion to the Native Americans. Beginning with the efforts of Ponce de León in 1513, the Spanish settled in what is now Florida. In 1565, they established the outpost of St. Augustine on the Florida coast. The settlement has survived to become the oldest European-founded city in the United States.

Spain Explores the Southwest and West

Throughout the mid-1500s, the Spanish also explored and settled in what are now the southwest and west regions of the United States. In 1540, Francisco Vásquez de Coronado led a most ambitious venture, as he traveled throughout much of what is now Texas, Oklahoma, Arizona, New Mexico, and Kansas in search of another wealthy empire to conquer. Failing to find gold and other treasures, the dejected conquistador returned home. After wandering for two years, the only precious metal Coronado carried home was his own battered gold-plated armor.

THE SPANISH FOUND NEW MEXICO Some 50 years later, the Spanish returned to the modern-day Southwest—in search not of riches but of Christian converts. In its Royal Orders of New Discoveries of 1573, Spain outlined the duties of these new explorers who now included Roman Catholic priests. When converting the Native Americans, priests were ordered to provide them with "the many . . . essentials of life—bread, silk, linen, horses, cattle, tools, and weapons, and all the rest that Spain has had." Numerous Spanish priests had arrived in the Americas to spread Roman Catholicism. The barren land north of New Spain may have held little gold, but it was home to many Native American souls to convert. In the winter of 1609–1610, Pedro de Peralta, governor of Spain's northern holdings, called **New Mexico,** led settlers to a tributary of the upper Rio Grande. Together they built a capital called Santa Fe, or "Holy Faith." The hooves of pack mules wore down an 1,800-mile trail known as El Camino Real or "the Royal Road," as they carried goods back and forth between Santa Fe and Mexico City. In the next two decades, a string of Catholic missions arose among the Pueblos in the area. D

MAIN IDEA

Analyzing Motives

D What attracted the Spanish to what is now the Southwest?

THE SPANISH OPEN MISSIONS IN TEXAS As early as 1519, Alonso Álvarez de Piñeda of Spain had mapped the coast of what is today Texas. Soon afterward, in 1528, the first Europeans had begun to settle in the interior. Over the next 200

years, using the San Antonio area as their administrative center, the Spanish sent more than 30 expeditions inland to explore and to settle. The land was already sparsely inhabited by Native Americans, including members of the large and diverse Apache group, whom Spanish missionaries sought to convert to Christianity. The first two Spanish missions in Texas were founded in 1682 near what is now El Paso.

Beginning in 1718, a number of missions opened along the San Antonio River. Founded in 1720, Mission San José y San Miguel de Aguayo in San Antonio was by many accounts the most beautiful and successful Texas mission. Its compound included buildings for living, worshipping, storing grain, spinning and weaving cotton and wool, carpentry, iron working, and tailoring.

A STRING OF MISSIONS SPANS CALIFORNIA In 1542 the navigator Juan Rodriguez Cabrillo, exploring the west coast of North America, discovered the harbor that was later named San Diego. In 1769, the Spanish missionary Father Junípero Serra founded the first California mission at San Diego.

By 1823, Spanish Franciscan priests, followers of Saint Francis of Assisi, had founded a string of 21 missions, each one day's walk (about 30 miles) from the next. Many of the missions were protected by forts, called presidios, built nearby. A presidio and a mission founded in 1776 in San Francisco preceded the development of that city. The aims of the missionaries in California, as in Texas, were to convert the Native Americans to Christianity, to educate them in European ways and skills, and to secure the area for Spanish settlement. Many Spanish mis-

Spanish Missions in the Southwest

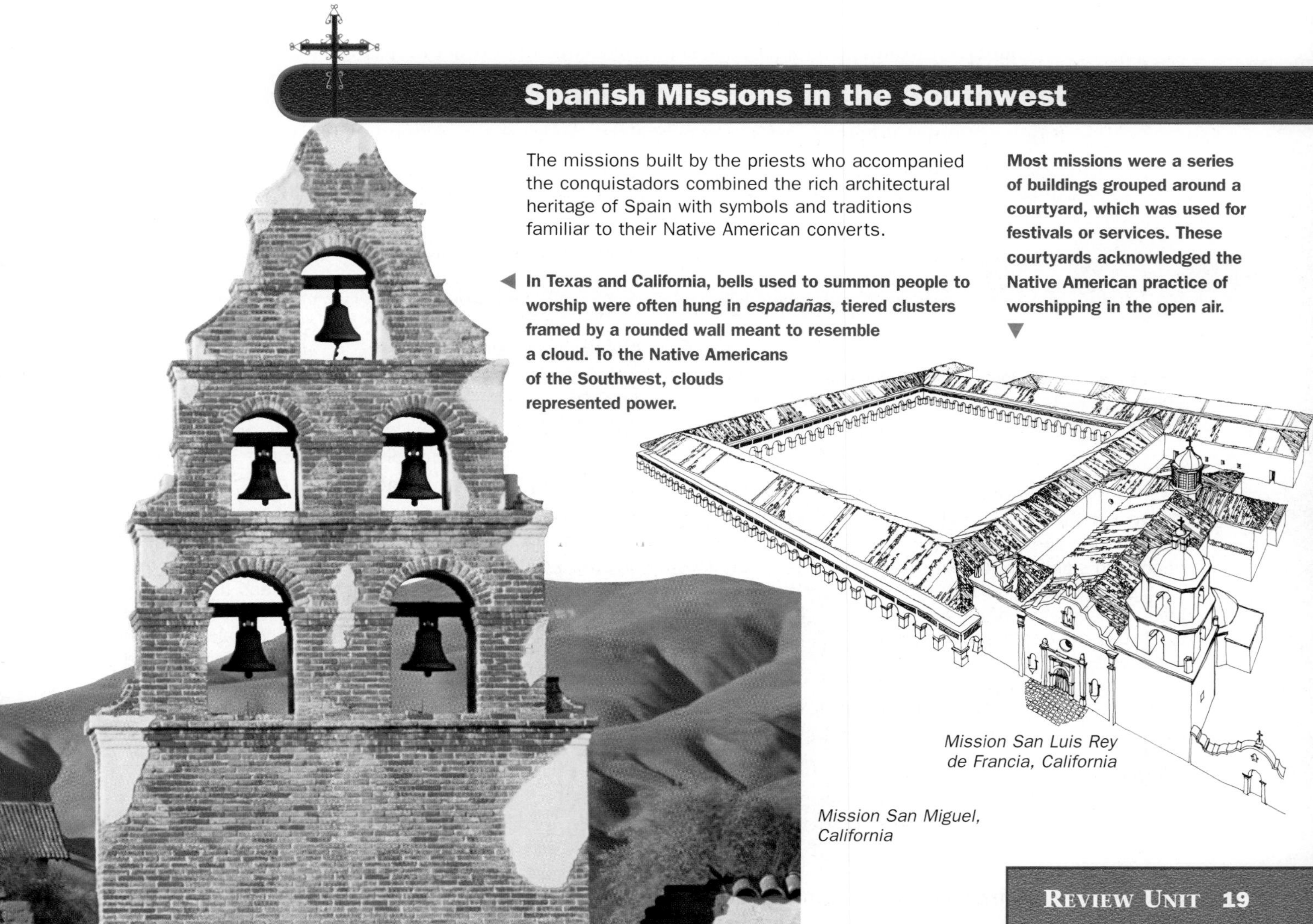

The missions built by the priests who accompanied the conquistadors combined the rich architectural heritage of Spain with symbols and traditions familiar to their Native American converts.

In Texas and California, bells used to summon people to worship were often hung in *espadañas*, tiered clusters framed by a rounded wall meant to resemble a cloud. To the Native Americans of the Southwest, clouds represented power.

Most missions were a series of buildings grouped around a courtyard, which was used for festivals or services. These courtyards acknowledged the Native American practice of worshipping in the open air.

Mission San Luis Rey de Francia, California

Mission San Miguel, California

sions are still standing and some are still in use. They remain as lasting memorials to the great cultures reflected in their architecture.

RESISTANCE TO THE SPANISH The impact of the Spanish missions on Native American cultures has been a subject of much historical controversy. Recent historians assert that the mission system negatively affected many Native American communities in several ways. The Spanish required Native Americans who converted to Christianity to live inside the missions, separating them from their families and cultures. Native Americans who tried to leave were punished. The Spanish also forced Native Americans to provide labor for farming and construction, give up their self-government, and adopt European dress, diet, and living arrangements. During the 1670s, priests and soldiers around Santa Fe began forcing Native Americans to help support the missions by paying a tribute, an offering of either goods or services. The tribute was usually a bushel of maize or a deer hide, but the Spanish also forced Native Americans to work for them and sometimes abused them physically. Native Americans who practiced their native religion or refused to pay a tribute were beaten.

> *"The heathen have concealed a mortal hatred for our holy faith and enmity for the Spanish nation."*
>
> SPANISH OFFICER, WRITING OF POPÉ'S REBELLION

Spanish priests punished the Pueblo religious leader Popé for his worship practices, which they interpreted as witchcraft. In 1680, the angered leader led a well-organized uprising against the Spanish that involved some 17,000 warriors from villages all over New Mexico. The triumphant fighters destroyed Catholic churches, executed priests and settlers, and drove the Spaniards back into New Spain. For the next 12 years—until the Spanish regained control of the area—the southwest region of the future United States once again belonged to its original inhabitants.

But Spain would never again have complete control of the Americas. In 1588, England had defeated the Spanish Armada, a naval fleet assembled to invade England, ending Spain's naval dominance in the Atlantic. In time, England began forging colonies along the eastern shore of North America, thus extending its own empire in the New World. But Spain's influence continues in the people and customs of the Southeast and Southwest.

ASSESSMENT

1. **TERMS & NAMES** For each term or name, write a sentence explaining its significance.
   - **Christopher Columbus**
   - **Taino**
   - **Treaty of Tordesillas**
   - **Columbian Exchange**
   - **conquistador**
   - **Hernándo Cortés**
   - **Montezuma**
   - ***mestizo***
   - ***encomienda***
   - **New Spain**
   - **New Mexico**

MAIN IDEA

2. **TAKING NOTES**
   Create a time line of the major events and significant dates of Columbus's voyages and the Spanish exploration of the New World. Use the dates already plotted on the time line below as a guide.

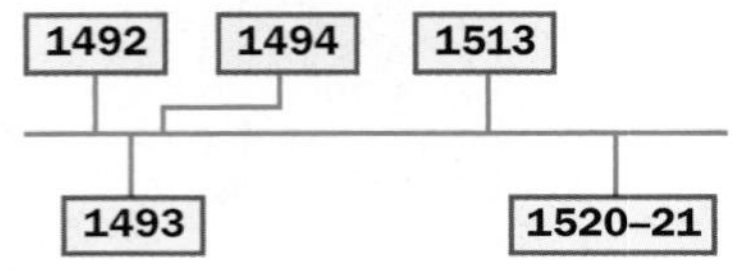

CRITICAL THINKING

3. **ANALYZING EFFECTS**
   What do you think were the most important long-term consequences of Columbus's encounters in the Americas? **Think About:**
   - conquering and claiming land
   - forced labor of Native Americans and Africans
   - the impact on Africa, Europe, and the Americas

4. **DRAWING CONCLUSIONS**
   State three conclusions about Spanish exploration and settlement north of Mexico and the Spaniards' interaction with Native Americans there. Why did the Native Americans of New Mexico revolt against the Spanish settlers?

SECTION 3

Early British Colonies

MAIN IDEA	WHY IT MATTERS NOW	Terms & Names
Beginning in the early 1600s, the English established colonies along the eastern shore of North America.	The original 13 English colonies in North America formed the foundation of what would become the United States of America.	• John Smith • Jamestown • joint-stock companies • indentured servant • Puritan • John Winthrop • King Philip's War • William Penn • Quaker • mercantilism • Navigation Acts

One European's Story

John Smith craved adventure. Smith's father had urged him to be a merchant, but the restless Englishman wanted to see the world. In 1606, he offered his services as a colonist to the Virginia Company, a group of merchants charged with starting an English colony in North America. He later recalled his vision of the opportunities that awaited those who settled the Americas.

A PERSONAL VOICE JOHN SMITH

> **"What man who is poor or who has only his merit to advance his fortunes can desire more contentment than to walk over and plant the land he has obtained by risking his life? . . . Here nature and liberty . . . give us freely that which we lack or have to pay dearly for in England. . . . What pleasure can be greater than to grow tired from . . . planting vines, fruits, or vegetables? . . ."**
>
> —*The General History of Virginia*

▲ John Smith, seen here in a 19th-century painting based on a 1616 engraving, was a self-proclaimed soldier of fortune, sea captain, and poet.

Smith would need all of his abilities to steer the new colony, Jamestown, through what turned out to be a disastrous beginning. In time, however, the colony survived to become England's first permanent settlement in North America.

The English Settle at Jamestown

In April of 1607, nearly four months after the Virginia Company's three ships had left England, they reached the North American shore. Sailing part way up a broad river leading into Chesapeake Bay, the colonists selected a small, defensible peninsula and built Fort James to protect the settlement of **Jamestown,** named for their king.

A DISASTROUS START Unlike Spanish colonies, which were funded by Spanish rulers, the English colonies were originally funded by **joint-stock companies.** Stock companies allowed several investors to pool their wealth in support of a colony that would, they hoped, yield a profit. Investors in the Jamestown colony demanded a quick return on their investment, and the colonists hoped to find gold to satisfy them. Consequently, they neglected farming and soon

Rediscovering Fort James

INTERACTIVE

Erosion turned the Jamestown Peninsula into an island and, for many years, the site of the original Fort James was assumed to be under water. However, in 1996, archaeologists from the Association for the Preservation of Virginia Antiquities discovered artifacts on what they concluded was the original site of the fort.

Since then, archaeologists have discovered armor, weapons, even games used by the first colonists. Archaeologists and historians are constantly learning more and more about this long-buried treasure of American history.

16th-century helmet and breastplate. ▶

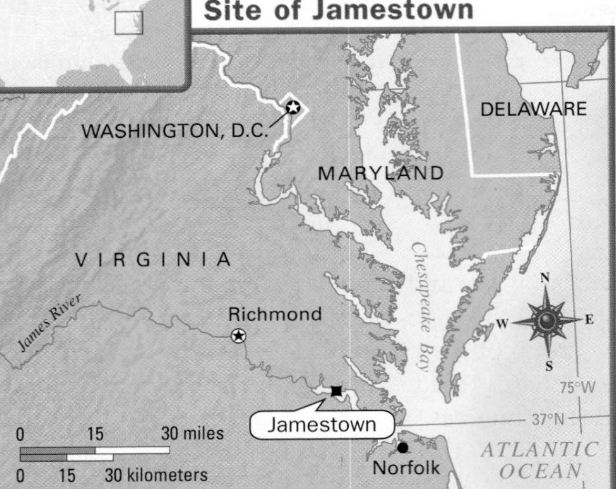

▲ **An archaeologist kneels beside holes left from the original palisade fence of Fort James. Note that the palisades were less than one foot in width.**

Rounded bulwarks, or watch towers, mounted with cannon were located at each corner of the fort. The range of each cannon was approximately one mile.

The walls of the triangular-shaped fort measured 420 feet on the river side and 300 feet on the other two sides.

A barracks or "bawn" stood along the wall.

Colonists' houses were built about ten feet from the fort's walls. Houses measured sixteen by forty feet and several colonists lived in each.

The main gate, located on the long side, faced the James river.

▲ **This illustration re-creates what historians and archaeologists now believe Fort James looked like early in its history.**

MAIN IDEA

Analyzing Causes

A Why was the early settlement at Jamestown a near disaster?

suffered the consequences. Disease from contaminated river water struck them first, followed soon by hunger. After several months, one settler described the terrifying predicament: "Thus we lived for the space of five months in this miserable distress, . . . our men night and day groaning in every corner of the fort, most pitiful to hear." **A**

Smith held the colony together by forcing the colonists to farm and by securing food and support from the native Powhatan peoples. Then Smith was injured and returned to England. Without Smith's leadership, the colony eventually deteriorated to the point of famine. The settlement was saved, however, by the arrival of new colonists and by the development of a highly profitable crop, tobacco.

TOBACCO REQUIRES A SUPPLY OF LABOR In order to grow tobacco, the Virginia Company needed field laborers. Immigration jumped in 1618, when the company introduced the headright system, offering 50 acres of land to "adventurers" who would pay their own or anothers' transportation from England. Many of those who arrived in Virginia, however, came as **indentured servants.** In exchange for passage to North America and food and shelter upon arrival, an indentured servant agreed to a limited term of servitude—usually four to seven years. Indentured servants were mainly from the lower classes of English society and therefore had little to lose by leaving for a new world.

The first enslaved Africans arrived in Virginia aboard a Dutch merchant ship in 1619. After a few years, most of them received land and freedom. It would be several decades before the English colonists in North America began the systematic use of enslaved Africans as laborers.

COLONISTS CLASH WITH NATIVE AMERICANS The colonists' desire for more land—to accommodate their growing population and the demand for more crop space—led to warfare with the original inhabitants of Virginia. Unlike the Spanish, the English followed a pattern of driving away the people they defeated. Their conquest over the native peoples was total and complete, which is one reason a large mestizo-like population never developed in the United States.

ECONOMIC DIFFERENCES SPLIT VIRGINIA The English colonists who migrated to North America in increasing numbers battled not only Native Americans but sometimes each other. By the 1670s, one-quarter of the free white men in Virginia were poor former indentured servants who lived mainly on the western frontier of Virginia, where they constantly fought with Native Americans for land.

Although Virginia's governor, William Berkeley, proposed building forts to protect the settlers, the settlers refused to pay taxes to maintain these forts. The colonists, under the leadership of a young planter named Nathaniel Bacon, marched on Jamestown in September of 1676. Bacon confronted colonial leaders with a number of grievances, including the frontier's lack of representation in Virginia's colonial legislature, or law-making body, the House of Burgesses. Although Bacon's Rebellion ultimately failed, it exposed the restlessness of the colony's former indentured servants. **B**

MAIN IDEA

Analyzing Issues

B Why were Virginia's frontier settlers frustrated with their government?

HISTORICAL SPOTLIGHT

EARLY REPRESENTATIVE GOVERNMENT

As the English settlers colonized North America, they sowed the seeds of the representative style of government that would become the foundation of American democracy.

Virginia's House of Burgesses served as the first representative body in colonial America. The House first met in Jamestown in 1619 and included two citizens, or burgesses, from each of Virginia's eleven districts. The body claimed the authority to raise taxes and pass legislation—subject to veto by the English governor.

The Mayflower Compact, which the Pilgrims crafted as they sailed to North America in 1620, created a civil government and pledged loyalty to the king. It stated that the purpose of their government in America would be to frame "just and equal laws . . . for the general good of the colony."

Created in 1639, the Fundamental Orders of Connecticut extended voting rights to a greater number of white males in that colony. It also declared that the colonial legislature could assemble without a call by the governor.

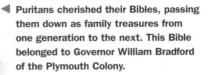

◀ Puritans cherished their Bibles, passing them down as family treasures from one generation to the next. This Bible belonged to Governor William Bradford of the Plymouth Colony.

Puritans Create a "New England"

After King Henry VIII (1491–1547) broke with Roman Catholicism in the 1530s, the Church of England was formed. Although the new church was free of Catholic control, one religious group, the **Puritans,** felt that the church had kept too much Catholic ritual. They wanted to "purify," or reform, the church by eliminating all traces of Catholicism. Some Puritans, called Separatists, wanted to separate from the English Church. They often met in secret to avoid the punishment inflicted upon those who did not follow the Anglican form of worship. C

One congregation of Separatists, known today as the Pilgrims, eventually migrated to America. There, in 1620, this small group of families founded the Plymouth Colony, the second permanent English colony in North America. Their Mayflower Compact, named for the ship on which they sailed to North America, became an important landmark in the development of American democracy.

MAIN IDEA

Analyzing Issues

C Why were the Puritans unhappy with the Church of England?

THE MASSACHUSETTS BAY COLONY Other Puritans who were not Separatists turned their thoughts toward New England in the 1620s. They felt the burden of increasing religious persecution, political repression, and dismal economic conditions. In 1630, a group of Puritans established the Massachusetts Bay Colony along the upper coast of North America. The port town of Boston soon became the colony's thriving capital. Settlers established other towns nearby and eventually incorporated the Plymouth Colony into the Massachusetts Bay Colony.

Vocabulary
repression: the act of putting down by force

The Puritans believed they had a special covenant, or agreement, with God. To fulfill their part, they were to create a moral society that would serve as a beacon for others to follow. Puritan leader **John Winthrop** expressed the sense of mission that bound the Puritans together, in a sermon delivered aboard the flagship *Arbella*: "We [in New England] shall be as a City upon a Hill; the eyes of all people are on us."

Although Puritans made no effort to create a democracy, the Massachusetts Bay Company extended the right to vote to all adult male members of the Puritan church—40 percent of the colony's men. As their system of self-government evolved, so did the close relationship between the government and the Puritan church. The Puritan view dominated Massachusetts society: taxes supported the Puritan church, and laws required church attendance. D

MAIN IDEA

Forming Generalizations

D What type of society did the Puritans want to create?

DISSENT IN THE PURITAN COMMUNITY The Puritans came to America to follow their own form of worship, and they were intolerant of people who had dissenting religious beliefs. One such dissenter was Roger Williams, an extreme Separatist, who expressed two controversial views. First, he declared that the English settlers had no rightful claim to the land unless they purchased it from Native Americans. Second, he argued that every person should be free to worship according to his or her conscience.

MAIN IDEA

Analyzing Issues

E In what principles did the government of Providence differ from that of Massachusetts?

When officials tried to deport Williams back to England, he fled Massachusetts and traveled south. He negotiated with a local Native American group for a plot of land and set up a new colony, which he called Providence. In Providence, later the capital of Rhode Island, Williams guaranteed religious freedom and separation of church and state. **E**

Another dissenter, Anne Hutchinson, taught that worshippers did not need the church or its ministers to interpret the Bible for them. Banished from the colony, Hutchinson, with her family and a band of followers, fled first to Rhode Island and, after her husband died, to New Netherland—which later became part of New York—where she died in a war with Native Americans.

NATIVE AMERICANS RESIST COLONIAL EXPANSION While Williams and his followers were settling Rhode Island, thousands of other white settlers fanned out to western Massachusetts and to new colonies in New Hampshire and Connecticut. From the beginning, Native Americans had helped the colonists, providing them with land and giving them agricultural advice. Soon, however, disputes between the Puritans and Native Americans arose over land and religion. As Native Americans saw their lands taken over by settlers, they feared an end to their way of life. In addition, Native Americans resented the Puritans' efforts to convert them and bristled under Puritan laws such as the prohibition of hunting and fishing on Sunday.

KING PHILIP'S WAR Great tension continued between Native Americans and settlers for nearly 40 years. Eventually, the Wampanoag chief Metacom, whom the English called King Philip, organized his tribe and several others into an alliance to wipe out the invaders. The eruption of **King Philip's War** in the spring of 1675 startled the Puritans with its intensity. Native Americans attacked

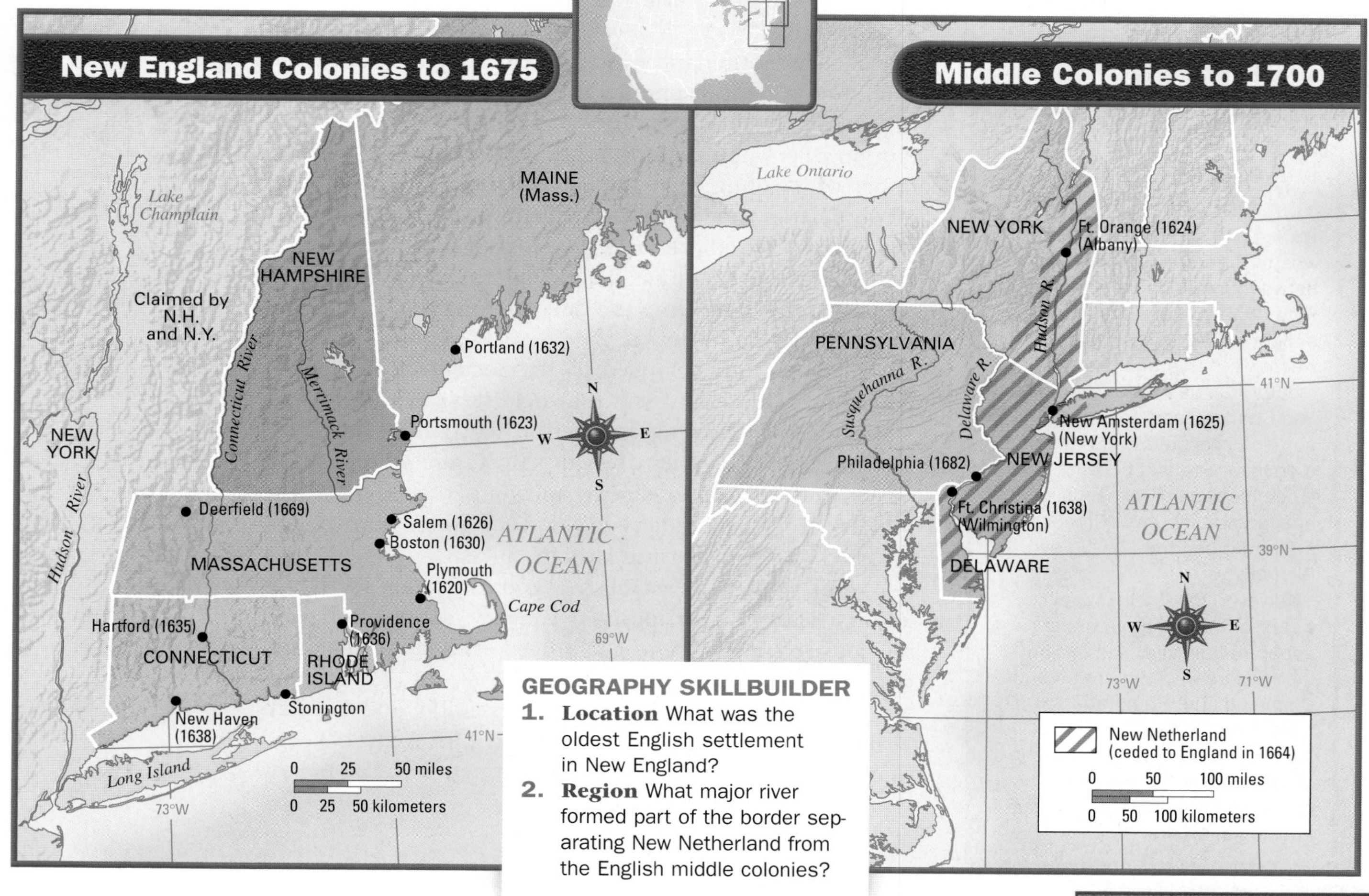

GEOGRAPHY SKILLBUILDER

1. **Location** What was the oldest English settlement in New England?
2. **Region** What major river formed part of the border separating New Netherland from the English middle colonies?

and burned outlying settlements throughout New England. Within months they were striking the outskirts of Boston. The alarmed and angered colonists responded by killing as many Native Americans as they could, even some from friendly tribes. For over a year, the two sides waged a war of mutual brutality and destruction. Finally, food shortages, disease, and heavy casualties wore down the Native Americans' resistance, and they gradually surrendered or fled. F

MAIN IDEA

Predicting Effects

F What long-term effects would you predict followed King Philip's War?

Settlement of the Middle Colonies

While English Puritans were establishing colonies in New England, the Dutch were founding one to the south. As early as 1609, Henry Hudson—an Englishman employed by the Dutch—had sailed up the river that now bears his name. The Dutch soon established a fur trade with the Iroquois and built trading posts on the Hudson River.

THE DUTCH FOUND NEW NETHERLAND In 1621, the Dutch government granted the newly formed Dutch West India Company permission to colonize New Netherland and expand the thriving fur trade. New Amsterdam (now New York City), founded in 1625, became the capital of the colony (see map on page 25). In 1655, the Dutch extended their claims by taking over New Sweden, a tiny colony of Swedish and Finnish settlers that had established a rival fur trade along the Delaware River. To encourage settlers to come and stay, the colony opened its doors to a variety of ethnic and religious groups. G

MAIN IDEA

Analyzing Events

G How did the Dutch create an ethnically diverse colony?

In 1664, the English took over the colony without a fight. The duke of York, the new proprietor, or owner, of the colony, renamed it New York. The duke later gave a portion of this land to two of his friends, naming this territory New Jersey for the British island of Jersey.

THE QUAKERS SETTLE PENNSYLVANIA The acquisition of New Netherland was one step in England's quest to extend its American empire after 1660, when the English monarchy was restored after a period of civil war and Puritan rule. The new king, Charles II, owed a debt to the father of a young man named **William Penn.** As payment, Charles gave the younger Penn a large property that the king insisted be called Pennsylvania, or "Penn's Woods," after the father. Following this, in 1682, Penn acquired more land from the duke of York, the three counties that became Delaware.

William Penn belonged to the Society of Friends, or **Quakers,** a Protestant sect that held services without formal ministers, allowing any person to speak as the spirit moved him or her. They dressed plainly, refused to defer to persons of rank, opposed war, and refused to serve in the military. For their radical views, they were scorned and harassed by Anglicans and Puritans alike.

Penn wanted to establish a good and fair society in keeping with Quaker ideals of equality, cooperation, and religious toleration. Penn guaranteed every adult male settler 50 acres of land and the right to vote. His plan for government called for a representative assembly and freedom of religion. Like Roger Williams before him, Penn believed that the land belonged to the Native Americans, and he saw to it that they were paid for it.

WORLD STAGE

THE ENGLISH CIVIL WAR AND RESTORATION

From 1642 to 1651, England was torn apart by great wars between loyalist supporters of King Charles I, and those who supported Parliament, many of whom were Puritans. The parliamentary armies were victorious, and Charles I was tried for treason and executed in 1649. For a decade, England became a commonwealth, or republic, headed first by Oliver Cromwell, a Puritan, and then by his son Richard.

However, the English grew weary of the rather grim and sober Puritan rule, and in 1660 the monarchy was restored under Charles II. The Restoration would have a profound effect on America, leading to the creation of new colonies and to more direct involvement by the Crown in colonial affairs.

History Through *Architecture*

COLONIAL MEETINGHOUSES

The Puritans of the Northeast, the Quakers of Pennsylvania, and the Anglicans of the Southern colonies held profound but often different convictions about community, social responsibility, and individual freedom. These convictions were expressed in the religious services of each group and in the architecture of the places of worship where these services were held.

MEN'S SEATS

WOMEN'S SEATS

Quaker Meetinghouse

Quaker services, which were called "meetings," relied on the inspiration of the "inner light." Meetings reflected a respect for conscience and freedom of speech.

Men and women entered by separate doors and sat on opposite sides, facing each other. In some meetinghouses, women sat in slightly elevated seats. Both men and women could speak during the meeting.

PULPIT

Puritan Meetinghouse

Puritan services focused on preaching. Sermons, which sometimes lasted for hours, instructed the individual conscience to be mindful of the common good.

The pulpit was the focal point of the meetinghouse. A plain interior reflected a value for austerity and simplicity. Meetinghouses were also used for town meetings.

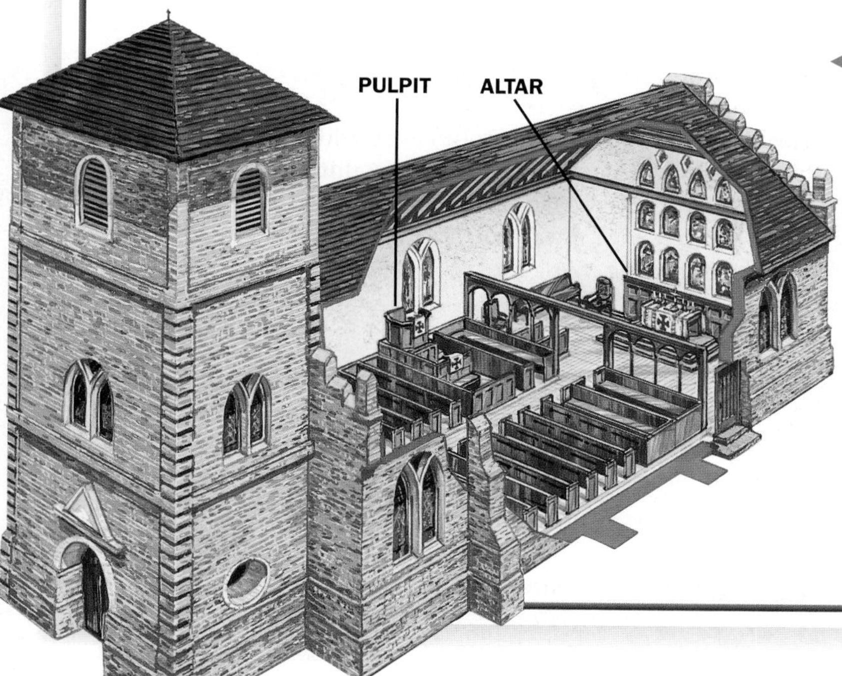

Anglican Church

The head of the Anglican church was the British monarch. Anglican services valued ritual. Their churches stressed the importance of authority and status.

Anglican churches emphasized the altar through ornamentation and elaborate windows. A screen separated the altar from the congregation. Elaborate pews were reserved for wealthy church members.

SKILLBUILDER **Interpreting Visual Sources**

1. In what ways do the Puritan and Quaker meetinghouses resemble each other? In what ways are they different?
2. How does the interior of the Anglican church show respect for hierarchy?

SEE SKILLBUILDER HANDBOOK, PAGE R23.

Penn himself spent only about four years in Pennsylvania. Meanwhile, his idealistic vision had faded but did not disappear. The Quakers became a minority in a colony thickly populated by people from all over western Europe. Slavery was introduced, and, in fact, many prominent Quakers in Pennsylvania owned slaves. However, the principles of equality, cooperation, and religious tolerance on which he had founded his vision would eventually become fundamental values of the new American nation. H

MAIN IDEA

Contrasting
H How did Penn's actions toward Native Americans differ from those of the Puritans in Massachusetts?

England and Its Colonies Prosper

THIRTEEN COLONIES Throughout the 1600s and 1700s, more British colonies in North America were founded, each for very different reasons. In 1632, King Charles I granted land north of Chesapeake Bay to George Calvert, the first Lord Baltimore. Calvert's son Cecil, the second Lord Baltimore, named the colony Maryland, after Queen Henrietta Maria, Charles's wife. In 1663, King Charles II awarded a group of key supporters the land between Virginia and Spanish Florida, a territory that soon became North and South Carolina.

In 1732, an English philanthropist named James Oglethorpe, along with several associates, received a charter for a colony he hoped could be a haven for those imprisoned for debt. Oglethorpe named the colony Georgia, after King George II. Few debtors actually came to Georgia, and the British Crown assumed direct control of the colony in 1752. By that time, the Crown had begun to exercise more and more control over colonial economies and governments.

Vocabulary
charter: A document issued by a monarch or other authority creating a public or private corporation

The thirteen British colonies existed primarily for the benefit of England. The colonies exported to England a rich variety of raw materials, such as lumber and furs, and in return they imported the manufactured goods that England produced. The thirteen colonies that became the original United States were founded over a period of 125 years. Together, the colonies represented a wide variety of people, skills, motives, industries, resources, and agricultural products.

MERCANTILISM AND THE NAVIGATION ACTS Beginning in the 16th century, the nations of Europe competed for wealth and power through a new economic system called **mercantilism** (mûr′kən-tē-lĭz′əm), in which the colonies played a critical role. According to the theory of mercantilism, a nation could increase its wealth and power in two ways: by obtaining as much gold and silver as possible, and by establishing a favorable balance of trade, in which it sold more goods than it bought. A nation's ultimate goal was to become self-sufficient so that it did not have to depend on other countries for goods.

The key to this process was the establishment of colonies. Colonies provided products, especially raw materials, that could not be found in the home country.

In 1651, England's Parliament, the country's legislative body, moved to tighten control of colonial trade by passing a series of measures known as the **Navigation Acts.** These acts enforced the following rules:

- No country could trade with the colonies unless the goods were shipped in either colonial or English ships.
- All vessels had to be operated by crews that were at least three-quarters English or colonial.
- The colonies could export certain products, including tobacco and sugar—and later rice, molasses, and furs—only to England.
- Almost all goods traded between the colonies and Europe first had to pass through an English port.

The system created by the Navigation Acts obviously benefited England. It proved to be good for most colonists as well. By restricting trade to English or colonial

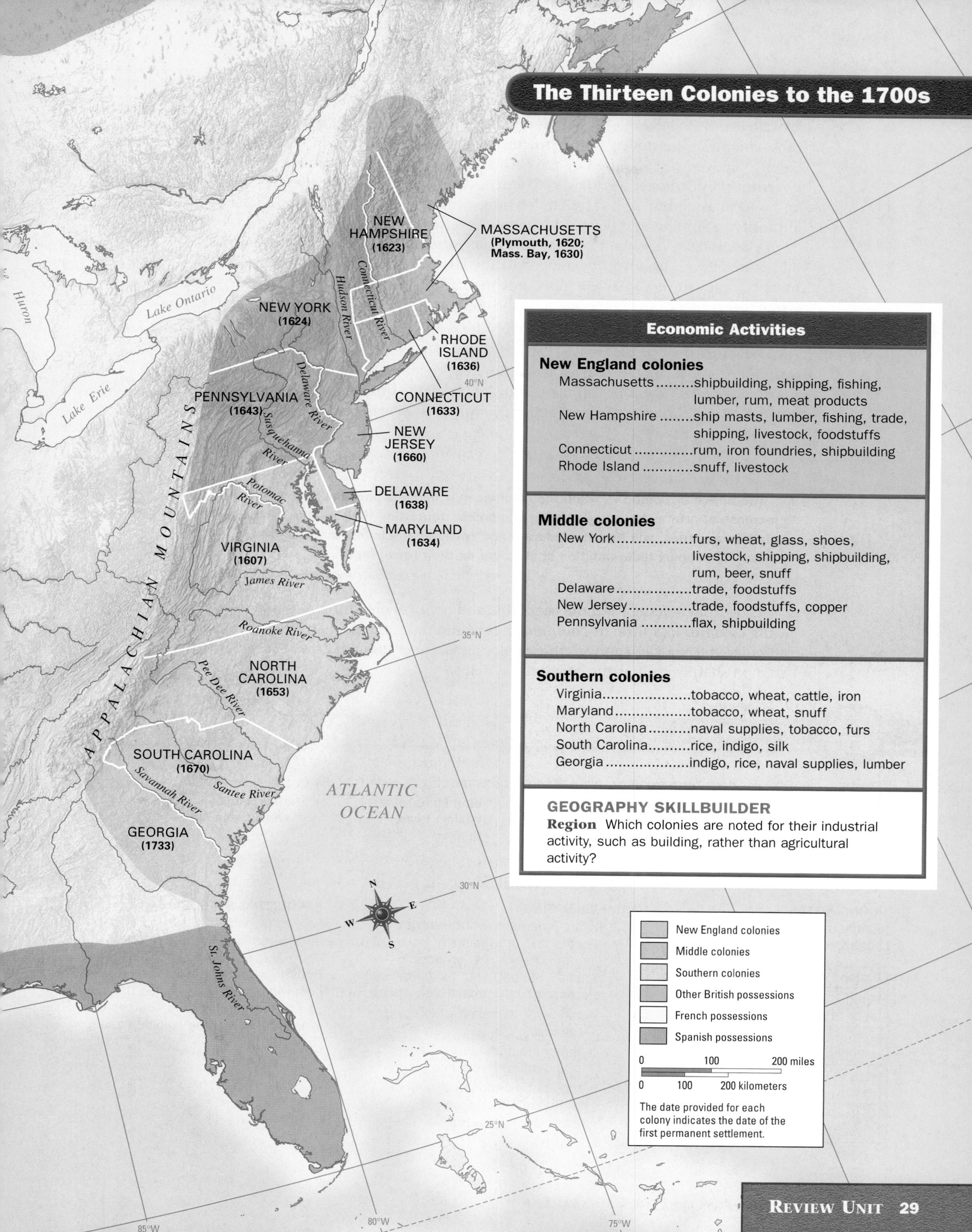

Economic Activities

New England colonies

Massachusetts	shipbuilding, shipping, fishing, lumber, rum, meat products
New Hampshire	ship masts, lumber, fishing, trade, shipping, livestock, foodstuffs
Connecticut	rum, iron foundries, shipbuilding
Rhode Island	snuff, livestock

Middle colonies

New York	furs, wheat, glass, shoes, livestock, shipping, shipbuilding, rum, beer, snuff
Delaware	trade, foodstuffs
New Jersey	trade, foodstuffs, copper
Pennsylvania	flax, shipbuilding

Southern colonies

Virginia	tobacco, wheat, cattle, iron
Maryland	tobacco, wheat, snuff
North Carolina	naval supplies, tobacco, furs
South Carolina	rice, indigo, silk
Georgia	indigo, rice, naval supplies, lumber

GEOGRAPHY SKILLBUILDER

Region Which colonies are noted for their industrial activity, such as building, rather than agricultural activity?

ships, the acts spurred a boom in the colonial shipbuilding industry and helped support the development of numerous other colonial industries. (I)

MAIN IDEA

Analyzing Effects

(I) What effects did the Navigation Acts have on both Britain and its colonies?

COLONIAL GOVERNMENTS Whatever their form of charter, by the mid 1700s, most colonies were similar in the structure of their governments. In nearly every colony, a governor appointed by the Crown served as the highest authority. The governor presided over an advisory council, usually appointed by the governor, and a local assembly elected by landowning white males. The governor had the authority to appoint and dismiss judges and oversee colonial trade.

In addition to raising money through taxes, the colonial assembly initiated and passed laws. The governor could veto any law but did so at a risk—because in most colonies the colonial assembly, not the Crown, paid the governor's salary. Using this power of the purse liberally, the colonists influenced the governor in a variety of ways, from the approval of laws to the appointment of judges.

GROWING SPIRIT OF SELF–DETERMINATION The colonies were developing a taste for self-government that would ultimately create the conditions for rebellion. Nehemiah Grew, a British mercantilist, voiced one of the few early concerns when he warned his compatriots about the colonies' growing self-determination in 1707.

A PERSONAL VOICE NEHEMIAH GREW

"The time may come . . . when the colonies may become populous and with the increase of arts and sciences strong and politic, forgetting their relation to the mother countries, will then confederate and consider nothing further than the means to support their ambition of standing on their [own] legs."

—quoted in *The Colonial Period of American History*

Aside from a desire for more economic and political breathing room, however, the colonies had little in common that would unite them against Britain. In particular, the Northern and Southern colonies were developing distinct societies, based on sharply contrasting economic systems.

SECTION 3 ASSESSMENT

1. **TERMS & NAMES** For each term or name, write a sentence explaining its significance.
   - **John Smith**
   - **Jamestown**
   - **joint-stock companies**
   - **indentured servant**
   - **Puritan**
   - **John Winthrop**
   - **King Philip's War**
   - **William Penn**
   - **Quaker**
   - **mercantilism**
   - **Navigation Acts**

MAIN IDEA

2. **TAKING NOTES**
   Identify the effects of each of the causes listed in the chart below.

Cause	Effect
Virginia colonists need labor to grow tobacco	
Puritans are persecuted in England	
William Penn acquires Pennsylvania	
Parliament passes the Navigation Acts	

CRITICAL THINKING

3. **EVALUATING**
   In your judgment, what were the benefits and drawbacks of using indentured servants for labor in Virginia? Support your judgment with references to the text. **Think About:**
   - the labor demands of growing tobacco
   - the characteristics and cost of indentured servants
   - the causes and consequences of Bacon's Rebellion

4. **PREDICTING EFFECTS**
   Reread Nehemiah Grew's prediction for the colonies in the Personal Voice above. How do you think the British government would respond to his prediction? What issues do you see arising as potential sources of tension between the colonies and Great Britain?

The Colonies Come of Age

MAIN IDEA

Even though both Northern and Southern colonies prospered, many colonists began to question British authority.

WHY IT MATTERS NOW

Regional differences between Northern and Southern colonies have survived in the culture and politics of the modern United States.

Terms & Names

- **triangular trade**
- **middle passage**
- **Enlightenment**
- **Benjamin Franklin**
- **Great Awakening**
- **Jonathan Edwards**
- **French and Indian War**
- **William Pitt**
- **Pontiac**
- **Proclamation of 1763**

One American's Story

In 1773, Philip Vickers Fithian left his home in Princeton, New Jersey, for the unfamiliar world of Virginia. Fithian, a theology student, had agreed to tutor the children of Robert Carter III and his wife at their magnificent brick manor house. In Fithian's journal of his one-year stay there, he recalled an evening walk along the property.

A PERSONAL VOICE PHILIP VICKERS FITHIAN

"We stroll'd down the Pasture quite to the River, admiring the Pleasantness of the evening, & the delightsome Prospect of the River, Hills, Huts on the Summits, low Bottoms, Trees of various Kinds, and Sizes, Cattle & Sheep feeding some near us, & others at a great distance on the green sides of the Hills."

—*Journal & Letters of Philip Vickers Fithian*

Plantations, or large farms, like the Carters' played a dominant role in the South's economy, which had come to rely heavily on agriculture. The development of this plantation economy led to a largely rural society, in which enslaved Africans played an unwilling yet important role.

The Shirley plantation house in Virginia is representative of many old Southern mansions. Built in 1723, it was the birthplace of Ann Hill Carter, the mother of Civil War general Robert E. Lee.

A Plantation Economy Arises in the South

While there were cities in the South, on the whole the region developed as a rural society of self-sufficient plantations. Plantations sprang up along the rivers, making it possible for planters to ship their goods directly to the Northern colonies and Europe without the need for public dock facilities. Because plantation owners produced much of what they needed on their property, they did not often need shops, bakeries, and markets.

Plantations specialized in raising a single cash crop—one grown primarily for sale rather than for livestock feed. In Maryland, Virginia, and North Carolina, planters grew tobacco. Planters in South Carolina and Georgia harvested rice and later indigo (for blue dye) as cash crops.

LIFE IN A DIVERSE SOUTHERN SOCIETY In addition to English settlers, thousands of German immigrants as well as Scots and Scots-Irish settled in the South. Women in Southern society, as in the North, endured second-class citizenship. For the most part they could not vote, preach, or own property.

While small farmers made up the majority of the Southern population, prosperous plantation owners controlled much of the South's economy as well as its political and social institutions.

At the bottom of Southern society were enslaved Africans. In the 18th century, Southerners turned increasingly to slavery to fill the labor needs of their agricultural economy. By 1690, about 13,000 slaves were working in the Southern colonies. By 1750, the number of slaves had increased to more than 200,000. (A)

MAIN IDEA

Summarizing
(A) Describe the social structure of Southern society.

THE MIDDLE PASSAGE During the 17th century, Africans had become part of a transatlantic trading network described as the **triangular trade.** This term refers to a trading process in which goods and enslaved people were exchanged across the Atlantic Ocean. For example, merchants carrying rum and other goods from the New England colonies exchanged their merchandise for enslaved Africans. Africans were then transported to the West Indies where they were sold for sugar and molasses. These goods were then sold to rum producers in New England and the cycle began again.

The voyage that brought Africans to the West Indies and later to North America was known as the **middle passage**, after the middle leg of the transatlantic trade triangle. Extreme cruelty characterized this journey. In the ports of West Africa, European traders branded Africans for identification and packed them into the dark holds of large ships. On board a slave ship, Africans were beaten into submission and often fell victim to diseases that spread rapidly. Some committed suicide by jumping overboard. Nearly 13 percent of the Africans aboard each slave ship perished during the

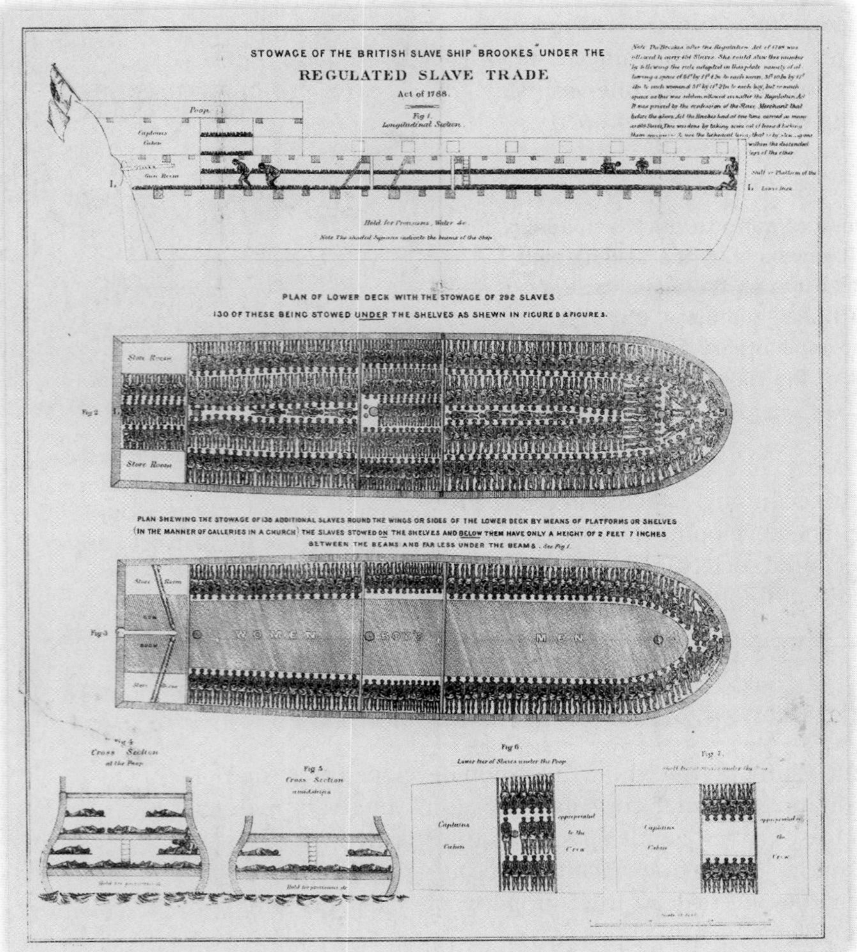

◀ **This plan and section of the British slave ship *Brookes* was published in London around 1790 by a leading British antislavery advocate named Thomas Clarkson. The image effectively conveys the degradation and inhumanity of the slave trade, which reduced human beings to the level of merchandise.**

MAIN IDEA

Making Inferences

B If 13 percent of the enslaved Africans died on the journey to America, why did the merchants treat them so badly?

brutal trip to the New World. One enslaved African, Olaudah Equiano, recalled the inhumane conditions on his trip from West Africa to the West Indies in 1762 when he was 12 years old. **B**

A PERSONAL VOICE OLAUDAH EQUIANO

"**The closeness of the place and the heat of the climate, added to the number in the ship, which was so crowded that each had scarcely room to turn himself, almost suffocated us. This produced copious perspirations, so that the air soon became unfit for respiration from a variety of loathsome smells, and brought on a sickness among the slaves, of which many died. . . .**"

—*The Interesting Narrative of the Life of Olaudah Equiano*

Olaudah Equiano

AFRICANS COPE IN THEIR NEW WORLD Africans who survived the ocean voyage entered an extremely difficult life of bondage in North America. Probably 80 to 90 percent worked in the fields. The other 10 to 20 percent worked as domestic slaves or as artisans. Domestic slaves worked in the houses of their masters, cooking, cleaning, and helping to raise the master's children. Artisans developed skills as carpenters, blacksmiths, and bricklayers and were sometimes loaned out to the master's neighbors.

In the midst of the horrors of slavery, Africans developed a way of life based on their cultural heritage. They kept alive their musical, dance, and storytelling traditions. When a slave owner sold a parent to another plantation, other slaves stepped in to raise the children left behind.

MAIN IDEA

Drawing Conclusions

C How did enslaved Africans maintain their sense of self esteem?

Slaves also resisted their position of subservience. Throughout the colonies, planters reported slaves faking illness, breaking tools, and staging work slowdowns. A number of slaves tried to run away, even though escape attempts brought severe punishment. **C**

Some slaves even pushed their resistance to open revolt. One uprising, the Stono Rebellion, began on a September Sunday in 1739. That morning, about 20 slaves gathered at the Stono River just south of Charles Town (later Charleston), South Carolina. Wielding guns and other weapons, they killed several planter families and marched south, beating drums and inviting other slaves to join them in their plan to flee to Spanish-held Florida. Many slaves died in the fighting that followed. Those captured were executed. Despite the rebellion's failure, it sent a chill through many Southern colonists and led to the tightening of harsh slave laws already in place.

Commerce Grows in the North

The development of thriving commercial cities and diverse economic activities gradually made the North radically different from the South. Grinding wheat, harvesting fish, and sawing lumber became thriving industries. By the 1770s, the colonists had built one-third of all British ships and were producing more iron than England did. Many colonists prospered. In particular, the number of merchants grew. By the mid-1700s, merchants were one of the most powerful groups in the North. In contrast to the South, where Charles Town was the only major port, the North boasted Boston, New York, and Philadelphia.

Vocabulary
tallow: fat from livestock used to make candles and soap

COLONIAL CITIES AND TRADE The expansion of trade caused port cities to grow. Philadelphia became the second largest port in the British empire, after London. Toward the end of the 1700s, Yankee traders were sailing around Cape Horn at the tip of South America to trade with Spanish missionaries as far away as California. There they exchanged manufactured goods for hides, tallow, wine, olive oil, and grain raised with the help of the Native American labor on the missions.

Daily Urban Life in Colonial Times

By the mid-18th century, colonial cities were prosperous and growing. Brick rowhouses were replacing the wooden structures of the 17th century, while large mansions and churches, built of brick or stone, were rising everywhere.

English colonists had brought with them a preference for houses (as opposed to apartments, which were the norm in the cities of other European countries). As in Britain, the size of the house indicated the social position of its occupant.

▲ **In contemporary Philadelphia, Elfreth's Alley preserves the scale and appearance of a mid-18th-century city street. Narrow rowhouses like these were occupied by artisans and shopkeepers. A neighborhood like this could have commercial and residential uses. Many people lived above the shops where they worked.**

◀ **The house known as Cliveden, also in Philadelphia, was completed in 1767. In contrast to the artisan or lower-middle-class housing of Elfreth's Alley, this large freestanding mansion shows the kind of building that the rich could afford.**

The Northern colonies attracted a variety of immigrants. During the 18th century, about 463,000 Europeans migrated to America. Before 1700, most immigrants came as indentured servants from England, but by 1755, over one-half of all European immigrants were from other countries. They included large numbers of Germans and Scots-Irish. Other ethnic groups included the Dutch in New York, Scandinavians in Delaware, and Jews in such cities as Newport and Philadelphia.

FARMING IN THE NORTH Unlike Southern plantations, a farm in New England and the middle colonies typically produced several cash crops rather than a single one. Because growing wheat and corn did not require as much labor as did growing tobacco and rice, Northerners had less need to rely on slave labor. However, slavery did exist in New England and was extensive throughout the middle colonies, as was racial prejudice against blacks—free or enslaved. As in the South, women in the North had extensive work responsibilities but few legal or social rights.

The Enlightenment

During the 1700s, the Enlightenment, an intellectual movement that began in Europe, and the Great Awakening, a colonial religious movement, influenced people's thinking throughout the thirteen colonies.

EUROPEAN IDEAS INSPIRE THE COLONISTS During the Renaissance in Europe, scientists had begun looking beyond religious beliefs and traditional assumptions for answers about how the world worked. Careful observation and reason, or rational thought, led to the discovery of some of the natural laws and principles governing the world and human behavior. The work of Nicolaus Copernicus, Galileo Galilei, and Sir Isaac Newton established that the earth revolved around the sun and not vice versa. This observation, which challenged the traditional assumption that the earth was the center of the universe, was at first fiercely resisted. It was thought to contradict the Bible and other religious teachings. The early scientists also concluded that the world is governed by fixed mathematical laws rather than solely by the will of God. These ideas about nature led to a movement called the **Enlightenment,** in which philosophers valued reason and scientific methods.

Enlightenment ideas spread from Europe to the colonies, where people such as **Benjamin Franklin** embraced the notion of obtaining truth through experimentation and reason. For example, Franklin's most famous experiment—flying a kite in a thunderstorm—demonstrated that lightning is a form of electrical power.

Enlightenment ideas spread quickly through the colonies by means of books and pamphlets. Literacy was particularly high in New England because the Puritans had long supported public education, partly to make it possible for everyone to read the Bible. However, Enlightenment views were disturbing to some people. The Enlightenment suggested that people could use science and logic—rather than the pronouncements of church authorities—to arrive at truths. As the English poet John Donne had written, "[The] new philosophy calls all in doubt."

MAIN IDEA

Analyzing Effects

D What effects did the Enlightenment have on political thought in the colonies?

The Enlightenment also had a profound effect on political thought in the colonies. Colonial leaders such as Thomas Jefferson reasoned that human beings are born with natural rights that governments must respect. Enlightenment principles eventually would lead many colonists to question the authority of the British monarchy. **D**

The Great Awakening

By the early 1700s, the Puritans had lost some of their influence. Under the new Massachusetts charter of 1691, Puritans were required to practice religious tolerance and could no longer limit voting privileges to members of their own church. Furthermore, as Puritan merchants prospered, they developed a taste for fine houses, stylish clothes, and good food and wine. As a result, their interest in maintaining the strict Puritan code declined. A series of religious revivals aimed at restoring the intensity and dedication of the early Puritan church swept through the colonies. These came to be known collectively as the **Great Awakening.**

Vocabulary
revival: a time of reawakened interest in religion

The British minister George Whitefield was a major force behind the Great Awakening. In his seven journeys to the American colonies between 1738 and 1769, Whitefield preached dramatic sermons that brought many listeners to tears.

KEY PLAYERS

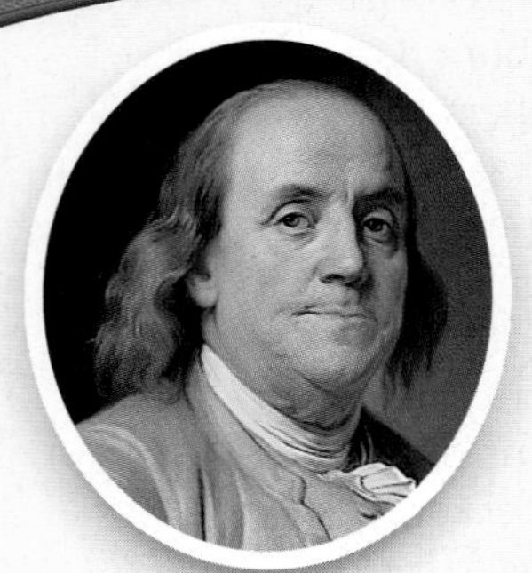

BENJAMIN FRANKLIN
1706–1790

A true student of the Enlightenment, Benjamin Franklin devised an orderly method to develop moral perfection in himself. In his autobiography, he records how he decided on a list of virtues he thought he should have. Then, every night, he reviewed whether his behavior lived up to those standards and recorded his faults in a notebook.

Originally, he concentrated on only 12 virtues until a Quaker friend told him he was too proud. Franklin promptly added a 13th virtue to the list—the virtue of humility, which he felt he never quite achieved.

Franklin took great pleasure in seeing his character improve. He wrote: "I was surpris'd to find myself so much fuller of faults than I had imagined; but I had the satisfaction of seeing them diminish."

JONATHAN EDWARDS
1703–1758

Unlike Benjamin Franklin, Jonathan Edwards did not believe that humans had the power to perfect themselves. Descended from a long line of Puritan ministers, he believed that "however you may have reformed your life in many things," all were sinners who were destined for hell unless they had a "great change of heart."

Edwards was a brilliant thinker who entered Yale College when he was only 13. His preaching was one of the driving forces of the Great Awakening. Ironically, when the religious revival died down, Edwards's own congregation rejected him for being too strict about doctrine. Edwards moved to Stockbridge, Massachusetts, in 1751, where he lived most of his remaining years as a missionary to a Native American settlement.

RELIGIOUS REVIVALS Among those clergy who sought to revive the fervor of the original Puritan vision was **Jonathan Edwards,** of Northampton, Massachusetts. One of the most learned religious scholars of his time, Edwards preached that it was not enough for people simply to come to church. In order to be saved, they must feel their sinfulness and feel God's love for them. In his most famous sermon, delivered in 1741, Edwards vividly described God's mercy toward sinners.

A Personal Voice
JONATHAN EDWARDS

> "**The God that holds you over the pit of Hell, much as one holds a spider, or some loathsome insect over the fire, abhors [hates] you, and is dreadfully provoked: His wrath towards you burns like fire; He looks upon you as worthy of nothing else but to be cast into the fire . . . and yet it is nothing but His hand that holds you from falling into the fire every moment.**"
>
> —"Sinners in the Hands of an Angry God"

While the Great Awakening, which lasted throughout the 1730s and 1750s, restored many colonists' Christian religious faith, the movement also challenged the authority of established churches. Preachers traveled from village to village, attracting thousands to outdoor revival meetings, giving impassioned sermons, and stirring people to rededicate themselves to God. Some colonists abandoned their old Puritan or Anglican congregations, while independent denominations, such as the Baptists and Methodists, gained new members.

EFFECTS OF THE GREAT AWAKENING AND ENLIGHTENMENT Although the Great Awakening emphasized emotionalism and the Enlightenment emphasized reason, the two movements had similar consequences. Both caused people to question traditional authority. Moreover, both stressed the importance of the individual: the Enlightenment by emphasizing human reason, and the Great Awakening by de-emphasizing the role of church authority. Because these movements helped lead the colonists to question Britain's authority over their lives, they were important in creating the intellectual and social atmosphere that eventually led to the American Revolution. E

MAIN IDEA

Analyzing Effects

E What effects did the Great Awakening have on organized religion in the colonies?

The French and Indian War

Background
Hats made from beaver skin were popular in Europe beginning in the late 16th century. Because of the demand for beaver, the fur trade was enormously successful.

As the French empire in North America expanded, it collided with the growing British empire. During the late 17th and first half of the 18th centuries, France and Great Britain had fought three inconclusive wars. Each war had begun in Europe but spread to their overseas colonies. In 1754, after six relatively peaceful years, the French–British conflict reignited. This conflict is known as the **French and Indian War.**

MAIN IDEA

Contrasting
F How was the French colony in North America unlike the British colonies?

RIVALS FOR AN EMPIRE From the start the French colony in North America, called New France, differed from the British colonies. Typical French colonists were young, single men who engaged in the fur trade and Catholic priests who sought to convert Native Americans. The French were more interested in exploiting their territories than in settling them. However, they usually enjoyed better relations with Native Americans, in part because they needed the local people as partners in the fur trade. In fact, several military alliances developed out of the French–Native American trade relationship. F

WAR ERUPTS One major area of contention between France and Great Britain was the rich Ohio River valley just west of Pennsylvania and Virginia. In 1754, the French built Fort Duquesne in the region despite the fact that the Virginia government had already granted 200,000 acres of land in the Ohio country to a group of wealthy planters. In response, the Virginia governor sent militia, a group of ordinary citizens who performed military duties, to evict the French. This was the opening of the French and Indian War, the fourth war between Great Britain and France for control of North America.

In the first battle of the war, the French delivered a crushing defeat to the outnumbered Virginians and their leader, an ambitious 22-year-old officer named George Washington.

A year after his defeat, Washington again headed into battle, this time as an aide to the British general Edward Braddock. Braddock's first task was to relaunch an attack on Fort Duquesne. As Braddock and nearly 1,500 soldiers neared the fort, French soldiers and their Native American allies ambushed them. The startled British soldiers turned and fled.

In this scene from the French and Indian War, the British general Edward Braddock meets defeat and death on his march to Fort Duquesne in July of 1755.

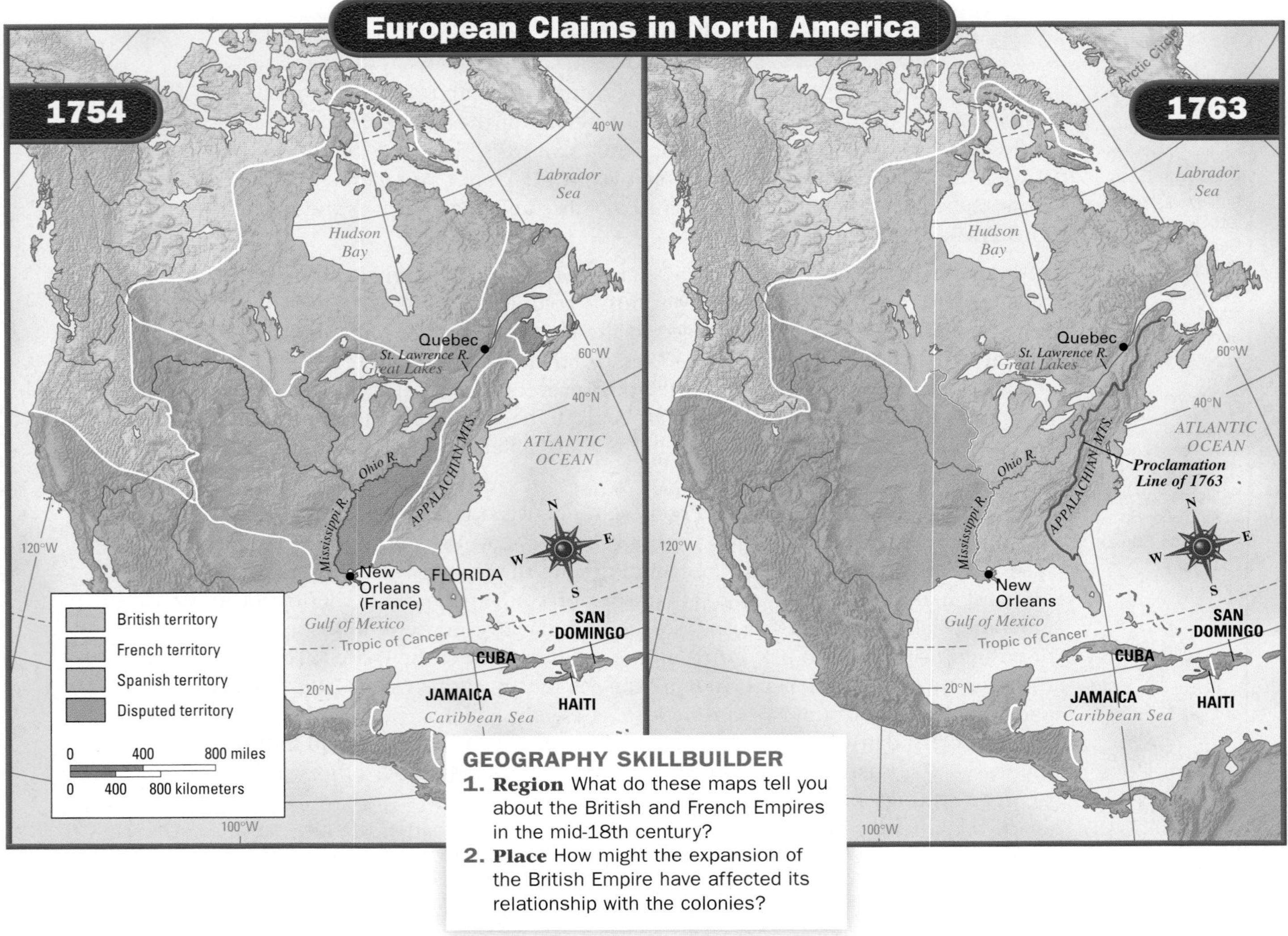

GEOGRAPHY SKILLBUILDER

1. **Region** What do these maps tell you about the British and French Empires in the mid-18th century?
2. **Place** How might the expansion of the British Empire have affected its relationship with the colonies?

The weakness of the British army surprised Washington, who showed great courage. As Washington tried to rally the troops, two horses were shot from under him and four bullets pierced his coat—yet he escaped unharmed. Many other colonists began to question the competence of the British army, which suffered defeat after defeat during 1755 and 1756.

BRITAIN DEFEATS AN OLD ENEMY Angered by French victories, Britain's King George II selected new leaders to run his government in 1757. One of these was **William Pitt** the elder, an energetic, self-confident politician. Under Pitt, the British and colonial troops finally began winning battles. These successes earned Britain the support of the powerful Iroquois, giving Britain some Native American allies to counterbalance those of France.

In September 1759, the war took a dramatic and decisive turn on the Plains of Abraham just outside Quebec. Under cover of night, British troops scaled the high cliffs that protected the city and defeated the French in a surprise attack. The British triumph at Quebec brought them victory in the war.

The war officially ended in 1763 with the signing of the Treaty of Paris. Great Britain claimed Canada and virtually all of North America east of the Mississippi River. Britain also took Florida from Spain, which had allied itself with France. The treaty permitted Spain to keep possession of its lands west of the Mississippi and the city of New Orleans, which it had gained from France in 1762. France retained control of only a few islands and small colonies near Newfoundland, in the West Indies, and elsewhere.

CHANGES FOR NATIVE AMERICANS Others who lost ground in the war were the Native Americans, who found the victorious British harder to bargain with than the French had been. Native Americans resented the growing number of British settlers crossing the Appalachian Mountains and feared the settlers would soon drive away the game they depended on for survival. In the spring of 1763, the Ottawa leader Pontiac recognized that the French loss was a loss for Native Americans. G

MAIN IDEA

Making Inferences

G How did Great Britain's victory over France affect Native Americans?

A PERSONAL VOICE PONTIAC

"When I go to see the English commander and say to him that some of our comrades are dead, instead of bewailing their death, as our French brothers do, he laughs at me and at you. If I ask for anything for our sick, he refuses with the reply that he has no use for us. For all this you can well see that they are seeking our ruin. Therefore, my brothers, we must all swear their destruction and wait no longer."

—quoted in *Red and White*

Led by **Pontiac,** Native Americans captured eight British forts in the Ohio Valley and the Great Lakes area and laid siege to another. In response, British officers deliberately presented blankets contaminated with smallpox to two Delaware chiefs during peace negotiations, and the virus spread rapidly among the Native Americans. Weakened by disease and tired of fighting, most Native American groups negotiated treaties with the British by the summer of 1766.

To avoid further costly conflicts with Native Americans, the British government prohibited colonists from settling west of the Appalachian Mountains. The **Proclamation of 1763** established a Proclamation Line along the Appalachians, which the colonists were not allowed to cross. However, the colonists, eager to expand westward from the increasingly crowded Atlantic seaboard, ignored the proclamation and continued to stream onto Native American lands.

ASSESSMENT

1. **TERMS & NAMES** For each term or name, write a sentence explaining its signficance.
   - **triangular trade**
   - **middle passage**
   - **Enlightenment**
   - **Benjamin Franklin**
   - **Great Awakening**
   - **Jonathan Edwards**
   - **French and Indian War**
   - **William Pitt**
   - **Pontiac**
   - **Proclamation of 1763**

MAIN IDEA

2. **TAKING NOTES**
   Re-create the tree diagram below. Fill in the diagram to show developments that took place in the colonies during the 18th century.

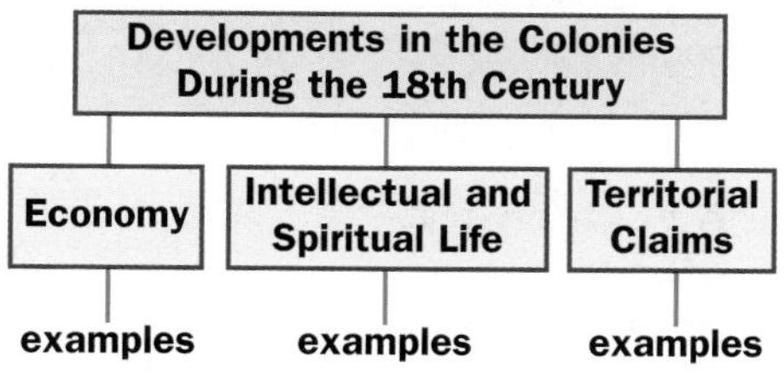

Which events or developments helped prepare the colonies for independence?

CRITICAL THINKING

3. **ANALYZING CAUSES**
   Why did the plantation system come to play such an important role in the Southern economy?
4. **SUMMARIZING**
   How did the Enlightenment affect the colonies?
5. **ANALYZING PRIMARY SOURCES**
   Read the following quotation, written in 1774 by the African-American poet, Phillis Wheatley. How does the quotation express both religious belief and Enlightenment thought?
   "For in every human breast God has implanted a principle, which we call love of freedom."
6. **ANALYZING ISSUES**
   In what ways was slavery a brutal system? Support your statement with examples from the text.
   Think About:
   - how people were taken from Africa
   - the working conditions of enslaved people
   - the attitudes toward enslaved people

DAILY LIFE 1630–1763

Colonial Courtship

The concept of dating among teenagers was nonexistent in colonial times. Young people were considered either children or adults, and as important as marriage was in the colonies, sweethearts were older than one might suspect. The practices of courtship and marriage varied among the different communities.

▼ FRONTIER OR BACKCOUNTRY PEOPLE

Andrew Jackson, depicted with his wife in the painting below, "stole" his wife (she was willing) from her family. Jackson was following a custom of the backcountry people, who lived along the western edge of the colonies.

These colonists, mostly Scots-Irish, based their marriages on the old custom of "abduction"—stealing the bride—often with her consent. Even regular marriages began with the groom and his friends coming to "steal" the bride. Much drinking and dancing accompanied these wild and hilarious weddings.

PURITANS

For Puritans, marriage was a civil contract, not a religious or sacred union. Although adults strictly supervised a couple's courting, parents allowed two unusual practices. One was the use of a courting stick, a long tube into which the couple could whisper while the family was in another room. The other was the practice of "bundling": a young man spent the night in the same bed as his sweetheart, with a large bundling board (shown below) between them.

Before marrying, the couple had to allow for Puritan leaders to voice any objections to the marriage at the meeting house. Passing that, the couple would marry in a very simple civil ceremony and share a quiet dinner.

THE SOUTH ▲

Many African slaves married in a "jumping the broomstick" ceremony, in which the bride and groom jumped over a broomstick to seal their union. Although there is disagreement among African-American scholars, some suggest that the above painting depicts a slave wedding on a South Carolina plantation in the late 1700s.

◀ QUAKERS

Quaker couples intent on marrying needed the consent not only of the parents but also of the whole Quaker community. Quakers who wanted to marry had to go through a 16-step courtship phase before they could wed. Quaker women, however, were known to reject men at the last minute.

VIRGINIA ▶

In Virginia, marriage was a sacred union. Since the marriage often involved a union of properties, and love was not necessary, parents were heavily involved in the negotiations. In this illustration from a dance manual (right), a young upper-class couple work to improve their social graces by practicing an elaborate dance step.

DATA FILE

WHO MARRIED?

Puritans:
- 98% of males and 94% of females married
- Grooms were usually a few years older than brides
- Discouraged marriages between first cousins

Virginians:
- 25% of males never married; most females married
- Grooms nearly 10 years older than brides
- Allowed first-cousin marriages

Quakers:
- 16% of women single at age 50
- forbade first-cousin marriages

Frontier People:
- Almost all women and most men married
- Ages of bride and groom about the same
- Youngest group to marry

Average Age at Marriage

Group	Males	Females
Puritan	26	23
Virginians	26	19
Quakers		
in Delaware	31	29
in Penn. & N.J.	26	22
Philadelphians	26	23
Frontier People	21	19
Modern Americans	25	24

Who Could Divorce?

Puritans:	Yes
Virginians:	No
Quakers:	No

Source: David Hackett Fischer, *Albion's Seed*

THINKING CRITICALLY

CONNECT TO HISTORY

1. **Interpreting Data** What was a common characteristic of courtship among Puritans, Quakers, and Virginians?

 **SEE SKILLBUILDER HANDBOOK, PAGE R22**

CONNECT TO TODAY

2. **Synthesizing** Research modern courtship practices by interviewing your parents or relatives. Write a brief paper comparing and contrasting modern-day and colonial courtship practices.

 **RESEARCH LINKS** CLASSZONE.COM

REVIEW CHAPTER 1 ASSESSMENT

TERMS & NAMES

For each term or name, write a sentence explaining its connection to exploration and the colonial era.

1. nomadic
2. Reformation
3. Christopher Columbus
4. Columbian Exchange
5. indentured servant
6. Puritan
7. Navigation Acts
8. triangular trade
9. Enlightenment
10. French and Indian War

MAIN IDEAS

Use your notes and the information in the chapter to answer the following questions.

The Americas, West Africa, and Europe *(pages 4–13)*

1. What effects did Portuguese trade routes have on West Africa?
2. In what ways did Renaissance ideas and attitudes inspire and motivate European explorers?

Spanish North America *(pages 14–20)*

3. What impact did the Columbian Exchange have on people's lives throughout the world?
4. Why did the Spanish want to colonize the Americas?

Early British Colonies *(pages 21–30)*

5. How did the goals of the Jamestown colonists differ from those of the Puritan colonists in Massachusetts?
6. Why did the English Parliament pass the Navigation Acts? What effects did they have?

The Colonies Come of Age *(pages 31–39)*

7. How did immigration contribute to the ethnic diversity of the American colonies after 1700?
8. How did the differences between the Northern and Southern economies lead to the development of two distinct cultural regions?

CRITICAL THINKING

1. **USING YOUR NOTES** In a chart like the one shown, compare and contrast Spanish and British colonial policies toward Native Americans.

Colonial Policies Toward Native Americans	
Spanish	British

2. **DEVELOPING HISTORICAL PERSPECTIVE** What were some of the cultural characteristics of the ancient civilizations that flourished in the Americas?

3. **INTERPRETING MAPS** Look at the map on page 29. Compare the economic activities of the three regions of British colonies in the Americas—New England, Middle, and Southern.

VISUAL SUMMARY EXPLORATION AND THE COLONIAL ERA

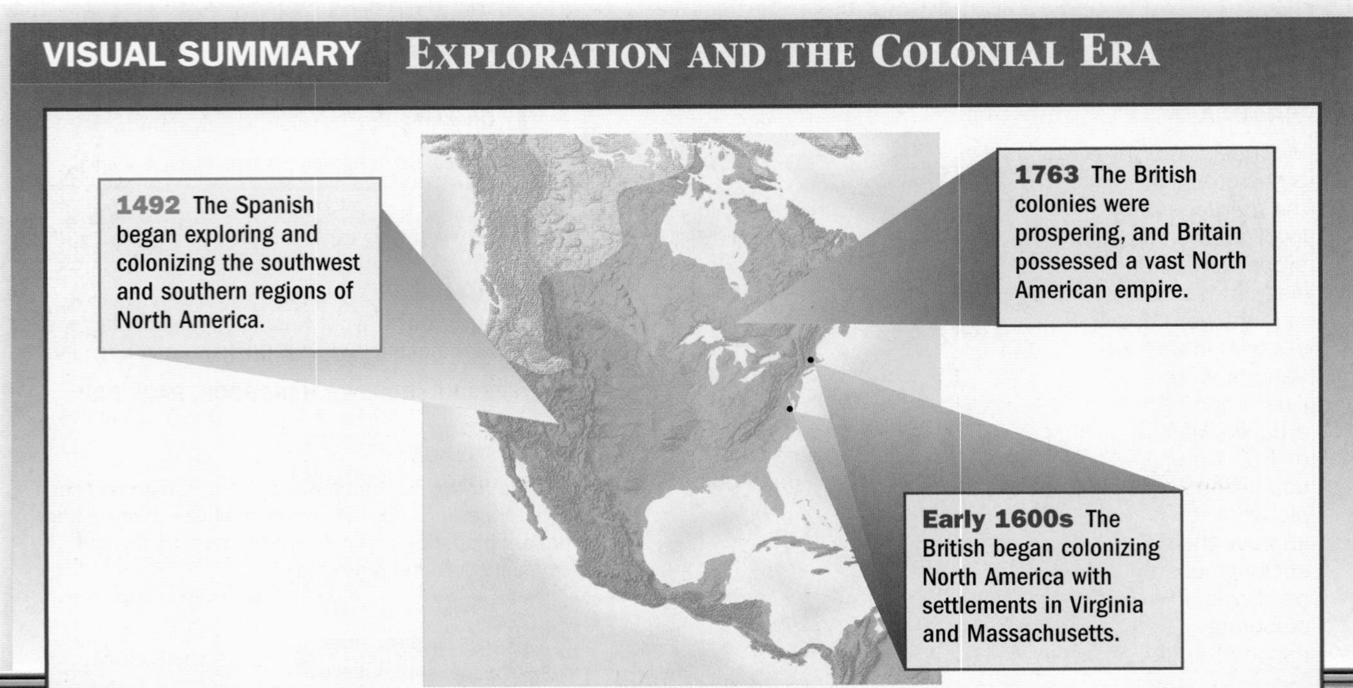

1492 The Spanish began exploring and colonizing the southwest and southern regions of North America.
1763 The British colonies were prospering, and Britain possessed a vast North American empire.
Early 1600s The British began colonizing North America with settlements in Virginia and Massachusetts.

Standardized Test Practice

Use the cartoon below and your knowledge of U.S. history to answer question 1.

1. Benjamin Franklin drew and published this cartoon in 1754, soon after the start of the French and Indian War. The cartoon depicts a snake divided into eight parts representing the eight colonies at the time. What message did Franklin intend?

   A The colonies have been broken apart by the war.

   B The colonies should unite to protect themselves from the French and the Native Americans.

   C The colonies should join with the French to protect themselves from the Native Americans.

   D The colonies should unite to declare independence from Britain.

2. Anne Hutchinson was banished from Massachusetts because she taught that —

   F colonists should remain loyal to the English king.

   G individuals could interpret the Bible for themselves.

   H the colonists should not trade with local Native Americans.

   J the Puritans should break away from the Church of England.

3. In the 1700s an intellectual movement known as the Enlightenment developed in Europe and spread to the colonies. Benjamin Franklin and Thomas Jefferson were among those colonists heavily influenced by Enlightenment ideas. In which of the following ways did the Enlightenment affect the colonists?

   A Enlightenment ideas led people to expand the trade in enslaved persons.

   B Enlightenment ideas stirred people to rededicate themselves to God.

   C Enlightenment ideas persuaded people to establish colonies in order to generate a favorable balance of trade.

   D Enlightenment ideas convinced people of the importance of civil rights.

ADDITIONAL TEST PRACTICE, pages S1–S33.

CLASSZONE.COM

ALTERNATIVE ASSESSMENT

1. INTERACT WITH HISTORY Recall your discussion of the question on page 3:

   How will the arrival of a strange people change your way of life?

   Now that you know how Native Americans' way of life was changed by the arrival of the Europeans, discuss the following question: Would you have resisted or helped the Europeans if you had been a Native American during the days of European colonization?

2. 

LEARNING THROUGH MEDIA How did lawyers defend their clients against some of the colonists' very strict laws?

   Using legal documents from colonial days, find out the legal punishments for infractions of certain laws in specific colonies. Use the CD-ROM *Electronic Library of Primary Sources* and other reference materials to research a specific law and punishment in 17th-century America.

   Cooperative Learning Activity With a group of students, enact a colonial trial. The rest of the class, acting as a colonial jury, must decide the verdict and punishment. Then, have a class discussion about the value of the law and its punishment.

Revolution and the Early Republic

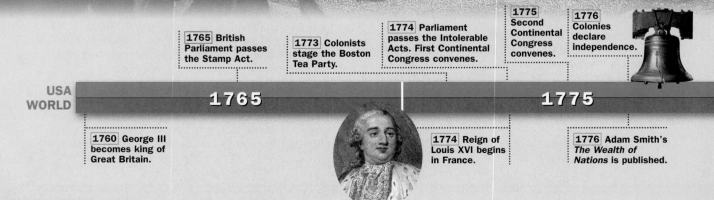

The Sons of Liberty pull down a statue of George III on the Bowling Green, New York, July 9, 1776.

USA

1765 British Parliament passes the Stamp Act.

1773 Colonists stage the Boston Tea Party.

1774 Parliament passes the Intolerable Acts. First Continental Congress convenes.

1775 Second Continental Congress convenes.

1776 Colonies declare independence.

1765 — 1775

WORLD

1760 George III becomes king of Great Britain.

1774 Reign of Louis XVI begins in France.

1776 Adam Smith's *The Wealth of Nations* is published.

INTERACT
WITH HISTORY

The year is 1787. You have recently helped your fellow patriots overthrow decades of oppressive British rule. However, it is easier to destroy an old system of government than to create a new one. In a world of kings and tyrants, your new republic struggles to find its place.

How much power should the national government have?

Examine the Issues

- Which should have more power, the states or the national government?
- How can the new nation avoid a return to tyranny?
- How can the rights of all people be protected?

RESEARCH LINKS CLASSZONE.COM

Visit the Chapter 2 links for more information about Revolution and the Early Republic.

1781 The British surrender at Yorktown.

1786 Daniel Shays leads a rebellion against higher taxes.

1788 The Constitution is ratified.

1789 George Washington is elected president.

1792 George Washington is reelected.

1785 — **1795**

1781 Joseph II allows religious toleration in Austria.

1785 British preacher Edmund Cartwright invents the first power loom.

1787 Sierra Leone in Africa is made a haven for freed American slaves.

1789 The French Revolution starts.

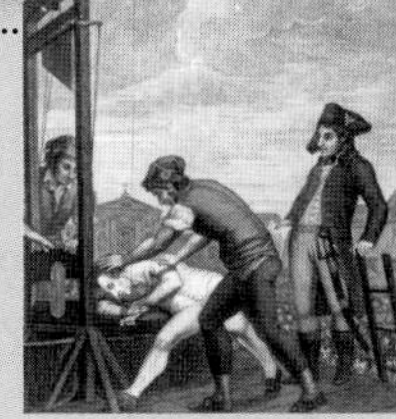

1793 French king Louis XVI is executed.

Colonial Resistance and Rebellion

MAIN IDEA	WHY IT MATTERS NOW	Terms & Names
Conflicts between Great Britain and the American colonies escalated, until the colonists finally declared their independence.	The ideas put forth by the colonists in the Declaration of Independence remain the guiding principles of the United States today.	• King George III • Sugar Act • Stamp Act • Samuel Adams • Boston Massacre • Boston Tea Party • John Locke • *Common Sense* • Thomas Jefferson • Declaration of Independence

One American's Story

Crispus Attucks was a sailor of African and Native-American ancestry. On the night of March 5, 1770, he was part of a large and angry crowd that had gathered at the Boston Customs House to harass the British soldiers stationed there. More soldiers soon arrived, and the mob began hurling stones and snowballs at them. Attucks then stepped forward.

A PERSONAL VOICE JOHN ADAMS

> **"This Attucks . . . appears to have undertaken to be the hero of the night; and to lead this army with banners . . . up to King street with their clubs . . . . This man with his party cried, 'Do not be afraid of them,' . . . He had hardiness enough to fall in upon them, and with one hand took hold of a bayonet, and with the other knocked the man down."**
>
> —quoted in *The Black Presence in the Era of the American Revolution*

▲ Crispus Attucks

Attucks's action ignited the troops. Ignoring orders not to shoot civilians, one soldier and then others fired on the crowd. Five people were killed; several were wounded. Crispus Attucks was, according to a newspaper account, the first to die.

The Colonies Organize to Resist Britain

Because the Proclamation of 1763 sought to halt expansion by the colonists west of the Appalachian Mountains, it convinced the colonists that the British government did not care about their needs. A second result of the French and Indian War—Britain's financial crisis—brought about new laws that reinforced the colonists' opinion.

THE SUGAR ACT Great Britain had borrowed so much money during the war that it nearly doubled its national debt. **King George III,** who had succeeded his grandfather in 1760, hoped to lower that debt. To do so, in 1763 the king chose a financial expert, George Grenville, to serve as prime minister.

By the time Grenville took over, tensions between Britain and one colony, Massachusetts, were on the rise. During the French and Indian War, the British had cracked down on colonial smuggling to ensure that merchants were not doing business in any French-held territories. In 1761, the royal governor of Massachusetts authorized the use of the writs of assistance, a general search warrant that allowed British customs officials to search any colonial ship or building they believed to be holding smuggled goods. Because many merchants worked out of their residences, the writs enabled British officials to enter and search colonial homes whether there was evidence of smuggling or not. The merchants of Boston were outraged.

Grenville's actions, however, soon angered merchants throughout the colonies. The new prime minister noticed that the American customs service, which collected duties, or taxes on imports, was losing money. Grenville concluded that the colonists were smuggling goods into the country without paying duties. In 1764 he prompted Parliament to enact a law known as the Sugar Act.

The **Sugar Act** did three things. It halved the duty on foreign-made molasses in the hopes that colonists would pay a lower tax rather than risk arrest by smuggling. It placed duties on certain imports that had not been taxed before. Most important, it provided that colonists accused of violating the act would be tried in a vice-admiralty court rather than a colonial court. There, each case would be decided by a single judge rather than by a jury of sympathetic colonists.

Colonial merchants complained that the Sugar Act would reduce their profits. Merchants and traders further claimed that Parliament had no right to tax the colonists because the colonists had not elected representatives to the body. The new regulations, however, had little effect on colonists besides merchants and traders. (A)

> **NOW & THEN**
>
> **PROPOSITION 13**
>
> A more recent tax revolt occurred in California on June 6, 1978, when residents voted in a tax reform law known as Proposition 13. By the late 1970s, taxes in California were among the highest in the nation. The property tax alone was fifty-two percent above the national norm.
>
> Proposition 13, initiated by ordinary citizens, limited the tax on real property to one percent of its assessed value in 1975–1976. It passed with sixty-five percent of the vote.
>
> Because of the resulting loss of revenue, many state agencies were scaled down or cut. In 1984, California voters approved a state lottery that provides supplemental funds for education. But Proposition 13 still remains a topic of heated debate, as Californians—like other Americans across the country—struggle with conflicting desires: more government services vs. less taxes.

> **MAIN IDEA**
>
> **Analyzing Issues**
>
> (A) How did the Sugar Act cause tension between the colonists and Britain?

THE STAMP ACT In March 1765 Parliament passed the **Stamp Act**. This act imposed a tax on documents and printed items such as wills, newspapers, and playing cards. A stamp would be placed on the items to prove that the tax had been paid. It was the first tax that affected colonists directly because it was levied on goods and services. Previous taxes had been indirect, involving duties on imports.

In May of 1765, the colonists united to defy the law. Boston shopkeepers, artisans, and laborers organized a secret resistance group called the Sons of Liberty to protest the law. Meanwhile, the colonial assemblies declared that Parliament lacked the power to impose taxes on the colonies because the colonists were not represented in Parliament. In October 1765, merchants in New York, Boston, and Philadelphia agreed to a boycott of British goods until the Stamp Act was repealed. The widespread boycott worked, and in March 1766 Parliament repealed the law.

But on the same day that it repealed the Stamp Act, Parliament passed the Declaratory Act, which asserted Parliament's full right "to bind the colonies and people of America in all cases whatsoever." Then, in 1767, Parliament passed the Townshend Acts, named after Charles Townshend, the leading government minister. The Townshend Acts taxed goods that were imported into the colony from Britain, such as lead, glass, paint, and paper. The Acts also imposed a tax on tea, the most popular drink in the colonies. Led by men such as **Samuel Adams,** one of the founders of the Sons of Liberty, the colonists again boycotted British goods. (B)

> **MAIN IDEA**
>
> **Summarizing**
>
> (B) How did the colonists respond to the Stamp Act and the Townshend Acts?

British Actions and Colonial Reactions, 1765–1775

1765 STAMP ACT

British Action
Britain passes the Stamp Act, a tax law requiring colonists to purchase special stamps to prove payment of tax.

Colonial Reaction
Colonists harass stamp distributors, boycott British goods, and prepare a Declaration of Rights and Grievances.

1767 TOWNSHEND ACTS

British Action
Britain taxes certain colonial imports and stations troops at major colonial ports to protect customs officers.

Colonial Reaction
Colonists protest "taxation without representation" and organize a new boycott of imported goods.

1770 BOSTON MASSACRE

British Action
Taunted by an angry mob, British troops fire into the crowd, killing five colonists.

Colonial Reaction
Colonial agitators label the conflict a massacre and publish a dramatic engraving depicting the violence.

▲ This colonial engraving was meant to warn of the effects of the Stamp Act.

Tension Mounts in Massachusetts

As hostilities between the colonists and the British mounted, the atmosphere in Boston grew increasingly tense. The city soon erupted in bloody clashes and later in a daring tax protest, all of which pushed the colonists and Britain closer to war.

VIOLENCE ERUPTS IN BOSTON On March 5, 1770, a mob gathered in front of the Boston Customs House and taunted the British soldiers standing guard there. Shots were fired and five colonists, including Crispus Attucks, were killed or mortally wounded. Colonial leaders quickly labeled the confrontation the **Boston Massacre**.

Despite strong feelings on both sides, the political atmosphere relaxed somewhat during the next three years. Lord Frederick North, who later followed Grenville as the prime minister, realized that the Townshend Acts were costing more to enforce than they would ever bring in: in their first year, for example, the taxes raised only 295 pounds, while the cost of sending British troops to Boston

Background
Pounds are the basic monetary unit of British currency.

History Through *Art*

THE BOSTON MASSACRE (1770)

Paul Revere was not only a patriot, but a silversmith and an engraver as well. One of the best known of his engravings, depicting the Boston Massacre, is a masterful piece of anti-British propaganda. Widely circulated, Revere's engraving played a key role in rallying revolutionary fervor.

- The sign above the soldiers reads "Butcher's Hall."
- The British commander, Captain Preston (standing at the far right of the engraving) appears to be inciting the troops to fire. In fact, he tried to calm the situation.
- At the center foreground is a small dog, a detail that gave credence to the rumor that, following the shootings, dogs licked the blood of the victims from the street.

SKILLBUILDER Interpreting Visual Sources

1. According to the details of the engraving, what advantages do the soldiers have that the colonists do not? What point does the artist make through this contrast?
2. What do you think is the intended message behind the artist's use of smoke spreading out from the soldiers' rifles?

 SEE SKILLBUILDER HANDBOOK, PAGE R23.

1773 TEA ACT		1774 INTOLERABLE ACTS		1775 LEXINGTON AND CONCORD	
British Action	**Colonial Reaction**	**British Action**	**Colonial Reaction**	**British Action**	**Colonial Reaction**
Britain gives the East India Company special concessions in the colonial tea business and shuts out colonial tea merchants.	Colonists in Boston rebel, dumping 18,000 pounds of East India Company tea into Boston harbor.	King George III tightens control over Massachusetts by closing Boston Harbor and quartering troops.	Colonial leaders form the First Continental Congress and draw up a declaration of colonial rights.	General Gage orders troops to march to Concord, Massachusetts, and seize colonial weapons.	Minutemen intercept the British and engage in battle—first at Lexington, and then at Concord.

SKILLBUILDER Interpreting Charts
In what ways did colonial reaction to British rule intensify between 1765 and 1775?

▲ This bottle contains tea that colonists threw into Boston harbor during the Boston Tea Party.

was over 170,000 pounds. North persuaded Parliament to repeal the Townshend Acts, except for the tax on tea.

Tensions rose again in 1772 when a group of Rhode Island colonists attacked a British customs schooner that patrolled the coast for smugglers. The colonists boarded the vessel, which had accidentally run aground near Providence, and burned it to the waterline. In response, King George named a special commission to seek out the suspects and bring them to England for trial.

The plan to haul Americans to England for trial ignited widespread alarm. The assemblies of Massachusetts and Virginia set up committees of correspondence to communicate with other colonies about this and other threats to American liberties. By 1774, such committees formed a buzzing communication network linking leaders in nearly all the colonies.

THE BOSTON TEA PARTY In 1773, Lord North devised the Tea Act in order to save the nearly bankrupt British East India Company. The act granted the company the right to sell tea to the colonies free of the taxes that colonial tea sellers had to pay. This action would have cut colonial merchants out of the tea trade by enabling the East India Company to sell its tea directly to consumers for less. North hoped the American colonists would simply buy the cheaper tea; instead, they protested dramatically.

On the moonlit evening of December 16, 1773, a large group of Boston rebels disguised themselves as Native Americans and proceeded to take action against three British tea ships anchored in the harbor. In this incident, later known as the **Boston Tea Party,** the "Indians" dumped 18,000 pounds of the East India Company's tea into the waters of Boston harbor.

THE INTOLERABLE ACTS An infuriated King George III pressed Parliament to act. In 1774, Parliament responded by passing a series of measures that colonists called the Intolerable Acts. One law shut down Boston harbor. Another, the Quartering Act, authorized British commanders to house soldiers in vacant private homes and other buildings. In addition to these measures, General Thomas Gage, commander-in-chief of British forces in North America, was appointed the new governor of Massachusetts. To keep the peace, he placed Boston under martial law, or rule imposed by military forces. C

MAIN IDEA

Analyzing Motives
C What do you think King George set out to achieve when he disciplined Massachusetts?

In response to Britain's actions, the committees of correspondence assembled the First Continental Congress. In September 1774, 56 delegates met in Philadelphia and drew up a declaration of colonial rights. They defended the colonies' right to run their own affairs and stated that, if the British used force against the colonies, the colonies should fight back.

▲ **The Battle of Lexington, as depicted in a mid-nineteenth-century painting.**

The Road to Revolution

After the First Continental Congress met, colonists in many eastern New England towns stepped up military preparations. Minutemen—civilian soldiers who pledged to be ready to fight against the British on a minute's notice—quietly stockpiled firearms and gunpowder. General Thomas Gage soon learned about these activities. In the spring of 1775, he ordered troops to march from Boston to nearby Concord, Massachusetts, and to seize illegal weapons. **D**

MAIN IDEA

Evaluating

D Do you think the British underestimated the colonists in 1770–1775?

FIGHTING AT LEXINGTON AND CONCORD Colonists in Boston were watching, and on the night of April 18, 1775, Paul Revere, William Dawes, and Samuel Prescott rode out to spread word that 700 British troops were headed for Concord. The darkened countryside rang with church bells and gunshots—prearranged signals, sent from town to town, that the British were coming.

The king's troops, known as "redcoats" because of their uniforms, reached Lexington, Massachusetts, five miles short of Concord, on the cold, windy dawn of April 19. As they neared the town, they saw 70 minutemen drawn up in lines on the village green. The British commander ordered the minutemen to lay down their arms and leave, and the colonists began to move out without laying down their muskets. Then someone fired, and the British soldiers sent a volley of shots into the departing militia. Eight minutemen were killed and ten more were wounded, but only one British soldier was injured. The Battle of Lexington, the first battle of the Revolutionary War, lasted only 15 minutes.

The British marched on to Concord, where they found an empty arsenal. After a brief skirmish with minutemen, the British soldiers lined up to march back to Boston, but the march quickly became a slaughter. Between 3,000 and 4,000 minutemen had assembled by now, and they fired on the marching troops from behind stone walls and trees. British soldiers fell by the dozen. Bloodied and humiliated, the remaining British soldiers made their way back to Boston that night. Colonists had become enemies of Britain and now held Boston and its encampment of British troops under siege.

THE SECOND CONTINENTAL CONGRESS In May of 1775, colonial leaders called the Second Continental Congress in Philadelphia to debate their next move. The loyalties that divided colonists sparked endless debates at the Second Continental Congress. Some delegates called for independence, while others argued for reconciliation with Great Britain. Despite such differences, the Congress agreed to recognize the colonial militia as the Continental Army and appointed George Washington as its commander.

Vocabulary
reconciliation: the restoration of a former state of harmony or friendship

THE BATTLE OF BUNKER HILL Cooped up in Boston, British general Thomas Gage decided to strike at militiamen on Breed's Hill, north of the city and near Bunker Hill. On June 17, 1775, Gage sent 2,400 British soldiers up the hill. The colonists held their fire until the last minute and then began to mow down the advancing redcoats before finally retreating. By the time the smoke cleared, the colonists had lost 450 men, while the British had suffered over 1,000 casualties. The misnamed Battle of Bunker Hill would prove to be the deadliest battle of the war.

By July, the Second Continental Congress was readying the colonies for war though still hoping for peace. Most of the delegates, like most colonists, felt deep loyalty to George III and blamed the bloodshed on the king's ministers. On July 8, Congress sent the king the so-called Olive Branch Petition, urging a return to "the former harmony" between Britain and the colonies. E

MAIN IDEA
Developing Historical Perspective
E Do you think that the Olive Branch Petition was too little too late?

King George flatly rejected the petition. Furthermore, he issued a proclamation stating that the colonies were in rebellion and urged Parliament to order a naval blockade to isolate a line of ships meant for the American coast.

▲
This painting shows "Bunker's Hill" before the battle, as shells from Boston set nearby Charles Town ablaze. At the battle, the British employed a formation they used throughout the war. They massed together, were visible for miles, and failed to take advantage of ground cover.

The Patriots Declare Independence

Despite the growing crisis, many colonists were uncertain about the idea of independence. Following the Olive Branch Petition, public opinion began to shift.

THE IDEAS BEHIND THE REVOLUTION This shift in public opinion occurred in large part because of the Enlightenment ideas that had spread throughout the colonies in the 1760s and 1770s. One of the key Enlightenment thinkers was English philosopher **John Locke.** Locke maintained that people have natural rights to life, liberty, and property. Furthermore, he contended, every society is based on a social contract—an agreement in which the people consent to choose and obey a government so long as it safeguards their natural rights. If the government violates that social contract by taking away or interfering with those rights, people have the right to resist and even overthrow the government. F

MAIN IDEA

Making Inferences

F Why might the ideals of the Enlightenment appeal to the colonists?

Other influences on colonial leaders who favored independence were religious traditions that supported the cause of liberty. One preacher of the time, Jonathan Mayhew, wrote that he had learned from the holy scriptures that wise, brave, and virtuous men were always friends of liberty. Some ministers even spoke from their pulpits in favor of liberty.

Yet the ideas of limited government and civil rights had been basic to English law since even before A.D. 1215, when the English nobility had forced King John to sign Magna Carta, or the Great Charter. Magna Carta acknowledged certain specific rights of the barons against the king, including some rights to due process, a speedy trial, and trial by a jury of one's peers. Its main significance, though, was to recognize that the sovereign did not have absolute authority, but was subject like all men and women to the rule of law. This principle was reaffirmed by the English Bill of Rights, accepted by King William and Queen Mary in 1689. To the colonists, however, various Acts of Parliament between 1763 and 1775 had clearly violated their rights as Englishmen. In addition to due process, a speedy trial, and trial by a jury of one's peers, those rights included taxation only by consent of property owners, a presumption of innocence, no standing army in peacetime without consent, no quartering of troops in private homes, freedom of travel in peacetime, and the guarantee of regular legislative sessions.

Thomas Paine's pamphlet *Common Sense* helped to overcome many colonists' doubts about separating from Britain.

COMMON SENSE;
ADDRESSED TO THE
INHABITANTS
OF
AMERICA,
On the following interesting
SUBJECTS.
I. Of the Origin and Design of Government in general, with concise Remarks on the English Constitution.
II. Of Monarchy and Hereditary Succession.
III. Thoughts on the present State of American Affairs.
IV. Of the present Ability of America, with some miscellaneous Reflections.
Man knows no Master save creating Heaven,
Or those whom choice and common good ordain.
Thomson.
PHILADELPHIA;
Printed, and Sold, by R. BELL, in Third-Street.
MDCCLXXVI.

THOMAS PAINE'S *COMMON SENSE* Just as important were the ideas of Thomas Paine. In a widely read 50-page pamphlet titled ***Common Sense,*** Paine attacked King George and the monarchy. Paine, a recent immigrant, argued that responsibility for British tyranny lay with "the royal brute of Britain." Paine explained that his own revolt against the king had begun with Lexington and Concord.

A PERSONAL VOICE THOMAS PAINE

> **"No man was a warmer wisher for a reconciliation than myself, before the fatal nineteenth of April, 1775, but the moment the event of that day was made known, I rejected the hardened, sullen tempered Pharaoh of England for ever . . . the wretch, that with the pretended title of Father of his people can unfeelingly hear of their slaughter, and composedly sleep with their blood upon his soul."**
>
> —*Common Sense*

Paine declared that independence would allow America to trade more freely. He also stated that independence would give American colonists the chance to create a better society—one free from tyranny, with equal social and economic opportunities for all. *Common Sense* sold nearly 500,000 copies in 1776 and was widely applauded. In April 1776, George Washington wrote, "I find *Common Sense* is working a powerful change in the minds of many men."

DECLARING INDEPENDENCE By the early summer of 1776, the wavering Continental Congress finally decided to urge each colony to form its own government. On June 7, Virginia delegate Richard Henry Lee moved that "these United Colonies are, and of a right ought to be, free and independent States."

While talks on this fateful motion were under way, the Congress appointed a committee to prepare a formal **Declaration of Independence**. Virginia lawyer **Thomas Jefferson** was chosen to prepare the final draft.

Summarizing
G What reasons did Jefferson give to justify revolt by the colonies?

Drawing on Locke's ideas of natural rights, Jefferson's document declared the rights of "Life, Liberty, and the pursuit of Happiness" to be "unalienable" rights—ones that can never be taken away. Jefferson then asserted that a government's legitimate power can only come from the consent of the governed, and that when a government denies their unalienable rights, the people have the right to "alter or abolish" that government. Jefferson provided a long list of violations committed by the king and Parliament against the colonists' unalienable rights. On that basis, the American colonies declared their independence from Britain. G

The Declaration states flatly that "all men are created equal." When this phrase was written, it expressed the common belief that free citizens were political equals. It did not claim that all people had the same ability or ought to have equal wealth. It was not meant to embrace women, Native Americans, or African-American slaves—a large number of Americans. However, Jefferson's words presented ideals that would later help these groups challenge traditional attitudes. In his first draft, Jefferson included an eloquent attack on the cruelty and injustice of the slave trade. However, South Carolina and Georgia, the two colonies most dependent on slavery, objected. In order to gain the votes of those two states, Jefferson dropped the offending passage.

On July 2, 1776, the delegates voted unanimously that the American colonies were free, and on July 4, 1776, they adopted the Declaration of Independence. The colonists had declared their freedom from Britain. They would now have to fight for it.

SECTION 1 ASSESSMENT

1. **TERMS & NAMES** For each term or name, write a sentence explaining its significance.
   - **King George III**
   - **Sugar Act**
   - **Stamp Act**
   - **Samuel Adams**
   - **Boston Massacre**
   - **Boston Tea Party**
   - **John Locke**
   - ***Common Sense***
   - **Thomas Jefferson**
   - **Declaration of Independence**

MAIN IDEA

2. **TAKING NOTES**
   Create a cluster diagram like the one shown and fill it with events that demonstrate the conflict between Great Britain and the American colonies.

Choose one event to further explain in a paragraph.

CRITICAL THINKING

3. **EVALUATING**
   Explain whether you think the British government acted wisely in its dealings with the colonies between 1765 and 1775. Support your explanation with examples from the text. **Think About:**
   - the reasons for British action
   - the reactions of colonists
   - the results of British actions

4. **ANALYZING EFFECTS**
   While Jefferson borrowed John Locke's ideas, he changed Locke's definition of the rights of men from "life, liberty, and property" to "life, liberty, and the pursuit of happiness." How do you think Jefferson's rewording of Locke's words has affected American life?
   Think About:
   - the experience of immigrants seeking new lives
   - the experience of African Americans and Native Americans
   - the socioeconomic groups living in America

The Declaration of Independence

Thomas Jefferson's Declaration of Independence is one of the most important and influential legal documents of modern times. Although the text frequently refers to eighteenth-century events, its Enlightenment philosophy and politics have continuing relevance today. For more than 200 years the Declaration of Independence has inspired leaders of other independence movements and has remained a crucial document in the struggle for civil rights and human rights.

In Congress, July 4, 1776.

A Declaration by the Representatives of the United States of America, in General Congress assembled.

Jefferson begins the Declaration by attempting to legally and philosophically justify the revolution that was already underway. Here Jefferson is saying that, now that the colonists have begun to separate themselves from British rule, it is time to explain why the colonists have taken this course of action.

When in the Course of human events, it becomes necessary for one people to dissolve the political bands which have connected them with another, and to assume among the powers of the earth, the separate and equal station to which the Laws of Nature and of Nature's God entitle them, a decent respect to the opinions of mankind requires that they should declare the causes which impel them to the separation.

These passages reveal the influence of the English philosopher John Locke. In *Two Treatises of Government* (1690), Locke argued that if a government does not allow its citizens to enjoy certain rights and freedoms, the people have a right to replace that government.

We hold these truths to be self-evident, that all men are created equal, that they are endowed by their Creator with certain unalienable Rights, that among these are Life, Liberty and the pursuit of Happiness; that, to secure these rights, Governments are instituted among Men, deriving their just powers from the consent of the governed; that whenever any Form of Government becomes destructive of these ends, it is the Right of the People to alter or to abolish it, and to institute new Government, laying its foundation on such principles and organizing its powers in such form, as to them shall seem most likely to effect their Safety and Happiness. Prudence, indeed, will dictate that Governments long established should not be changed for light and transient causes; and accordingly all experience hath shewn that mankind are more disposed to suffer, while evils are sufferable, than to right themselves by abolishing the forms to which they are accustomed. But when a long train of abuses and usurpations, pursuing invariably the same Object, evinces a design to reduce them under absolute Despotism, it is their right, it is their duty, to throw off such Government, and to provide new Guards for their future security.

Such has been the patient sufferance of these Colonies; and such is now the necessity which constrains them to alter their former Systems of Government. The history of the present King of Great Britain is a history of repeated injuries and usurpations, all having in direct object the establishment of an absolute Tyranny over these States. To prove this, let facts be submitted to a candid world.

Here begins the section in which Jefferson condemns the behavior of King George, listing the king's many tyrannical actions that have forced his American subjects to rebel.

He has refused his Assent to Laws, the most wholesome and necessary for the public good.

He has forbidden his Governors to pass Laws of immediate and pressing importance, unless suspended in their operation till his assent should be obtained; and, when so suspended, he has utterly neglected to attend to them.

He has refused to pass other Laws for the accommodation of large districts of people, unless those people would relinquish the right of Representation in the Legislature, a right inestimable to them, and formidable to tyrants only.

He has called together legislative bodies at places unusual, uncomfortable, and distant from the depository of their public Records, for the sole purpose of fatiguing them into compliance with his measures.

He has dissolved Representative Houses repeatedly, for opposing with manly firmness his invasions on the rights of the people.

He has refused for a long time, after such dissolutions, to cause others to be elected; whereby the Legislative powers, incapable of Annihilation, have returned to the people at large for their exercise; the State remaining in the mean time exposed to all the dangers of invasions from without, and convulsions within.

He has endeavoured to prevent the population of these States; for that purpose obstructing the Laws for Naturalization of Foreigners; refusing to pass others to encourage their migration hither, and raising the conditions of new Appropriations of Lands.

He has obstructed the Administration of Justice, by refusing his Assent to Laws for establishing Judiciary powers.

He has made Judges dependent on his Will alone, for the tenure of their offices, and the amount and payment of their salaries.

He has erected a multitude of New Offices, and sent hither swarms of Officers to harass our people and eat out their substance.

He has kept among us, in times of peace, Standing Armies, without the Consent of our legislatures.

He has affected to render the Military independent of and superior to the Civil power.

He has combined with others to subject us to a jurisdiction foreign to our constitution and unacknowledged by our laws; giving his Assent to their Acts of pretended Legislation:

For quartering large bodies of armed troops among us;

For protecting them, by a mock Trial, from punishment for any Murders which they should commit on the Inhabitants of these States;

For cutting off our Trade with all parts of the world;

For imposing Taxes on us without our Consent;

For depriving us, in many cases, of the benefits of Trial by Jury;

For transporting us beyond Seas to be tried for pretended offenses;

For abolishing the free System of English Laws in a neighboring Province, establishing therein an Arbitrary government, and enlarging its Boundaries so as to render it at once an example and fit instrument for introducing the same absolute rule into these Colonies;

For taking away our Charters, abolishing our most valuable laws, and altering fundamentally the Forms of our Governments;

For suspending our own Legislatures, and declaring themselves invested with power to legislate for us in all cases whatsoever.

HISTORICAL SPOTLIGHT

INDEPENDENCE AND SLAVERY

The Declaration of Independence went through many revisions before the final draft. Jefferson, a slaveholder himself, regretted having to eliminate one passage in particular—a condemnation of slavery and the slave trade. However, in the face of opposition of delegates from Southern states, the anti-slavery passage was deleted.

This is a reference to the 10,000 troops that the British government stationed in North America after the French and Indian War. Although the British government saw the troops as protection for the colonists, the colonists themselves viewed the troops as a standing army that threatened their freedom.

Here Jefferson condemns both the king and Parliament for passing the Intolerable Acts. Most of these laws were intended to punish the people of Massachusetts for the Boston Tea Party. For example, the Quartering Act of 1765 forced colonists to provide lodging for British troops. Another act allowed British soldiers accused of murder to be sent back to England for trial. The Boston Port Bill closed the port of Boston, "cutting off our Trade with all parts of the world."

Here Jefferson refers to the Quebec Act, which extended the boundaries of the province. He then refers to another act that changed the charter of Massachusetts and restricted town meetings.

ANOTHER
PERSPECTIVE

"ALL MEN WOULD BE TYRANTS IF THEY COULD."

Although the Declaration dealt with issues of equality, justice, and independence, it did not address conditions of inequality within the colonies themselves. Husbands dominated their wives, for example, and slaves lived under complete control of their owners. Speaking on behalf of women, Abigail Adams (above) had this to say to her husband John, who served in the Continental Congress:

> "Remember the Ladies, and be more generous and favourable to them than your ancestors. Do not put such unimited power into the hands of the Husbands. Remember all Men would be tyrants if they could. If particular care . . . is not paid to the Ladies, we are determined to foment a Rebellion."

Here Jefferson turns his attention away from the king and toward the British people. Calling the British the "common kindred" of the colonists, Jefferson reminds them how often the Americans have appealed to their sense of justice. Reluctantly the colonists are now forced to break their political connections with their British kin.

In this passage, the delegates declare independence.

He has abdicated Government here, by declaring us out of his Protection and waging War against us.

He has plundered our seas, ravaged our Coasts, burnt our towns, and destroyed the lives of our people.

He is at this time transporting large Armies of foreign Mercenaries to compleat the works of death, desolation, and tyranny, already begun with circumstances of Cruelty & perfidy scarcely paralleled in the most barbarous ages, and totally unworthy the Head of a civilized nation.

He has constrained our fellow Citizens, taken Captive on the high Seas, to bear Arms against their Country, to become the executioners of their friends and Brethren, or to fall themselves by their Hands.

He has excited domestic insurrections amongst us, and has endeavoured to bring on the inhabitants of our frontiers the merciless Indian Savages, whose known rule of warfare is an undistinguished destruction of all ages, sexes and conditions.

In every stage of these Oppressions We have Petitioned for Redress in the most humble terms; Our repeated Petitions have been answered only by repeated injury. A Prince, whose character is thus marked by every act which may define a Tyrant, is unfit to be the ruler of a free people.

Nor have We been wanting in attentions to our British brethren. We have warned them from time to time of attempts by their legislature to extend an unwarrantable jurisdiction over us. We have reminded them of the circumstances of our emigration and settlement here. We have appealed to their native justice and magnanimity, and we have conjured them by the ties of our common kindred, to disavow these usurpations, which would inevitably interrupt our connections and correspondence. They too have been deaf to the voice of justice and of consanguinity. We must, therefore, acquiesce in the necessity, which denounces our Separation, and hold them, as we hold the rest of mankind, Enemies in War, in Peace Friends.

We, therefore, the Representatives of the United States of America, in General Congress, Assembled, appealing to the Supreme Judge of the world for the rectitude of our intentions, do, in the name, and by the Authority of the good People of these Colonies solemnly publish and declare, That these United Colonies are, and of Right ought to be, Free and Independent States; that they are Absolved from all Allegiance to the British Crown, and that all political connection between them and the State of Great Britain is, and ought to be, totally dissolved; and that as Free and Independent States, they have full Power to levy War, conclude Peace, contract Alliances, establish Commerce, and do all other Acts and Things which Independent States may of right do.

IN CONGRESS, JULY 4, 1776.

The unanimous Declaration of the thirteen united States of America,

And for the support of this Declaration, with a firm reliance on the protection of divine Providence, we mutually pledge to each other our Lives, our Fortunes, and our sacred Honor.

The Declaration ends with the delegates' pledge, or pact. The delegates at the Second Continental Congress knew that, in declaring their independence from Great Britain, they were committing treason—a crime punishable by death. "We must all hang together," Benjamin Franklin reportedly said, as the delegates prepared to sign the Declaration, "or most assuredly we shall all hang separately."

[Signed by]

John Hancock **[President of the Continental Congress]**

[Georgia]
Button Gwinnett
Lyman Hall
George Walton

[Rhode Island]
Stephen Hopkins
William Ellery

[Connecticut]
Roger Sherman
Samuel Huntington
William Williams
Oliver Wolcott

[North Carolina]
William Hooper
Joseph Hewes
John Penn

[South Carolina]
Edward Rutledge
Thomas Heyward, Jr.
Thomas Lynch, Jr.
Arthur Middleton

[Maryland]
Samuel Chase
William Paca
Thomas Stone
Charles Carroll

[Virginia]
George Wythe
Richard Henry Lee
Thomas Jefferson
Benjamin Harrison
Thomas Nelson, Jr.
Francis Lightfoot Lee
Carter Braxton

[Pennsylvania]
Robert Morris
Benjamin Rush
Benjamin Franklin
John Morton
George Clymer
James Smith
George Taylor
James Wilson
George Ross

[Delaware]
Caesar Rodney
George Read
Thomas McKean

[New York]
William Floyd
Philip Livingston
Francis Lewis
Lewis Morris

[New Jersey]
Richard Stockton
John Witherspoon
Francis Hopkinson
John Hart
Abraham Clark

[New Hampshire]
Josiah Bartlett
William Whipple
Matthew Thornton

[Massachusetts]
Samuel Adams
John Adams
Robert Treat Paine
Elbridge Gerry

John Hancock

John Adams

Roger Sherman

Phil. Livingston

Benj. Franklin

KEY PLAYER

JOHN HANCOCK
1737–1793

Born in Braintree, Massachusetts, and raised by a wealthy uncle, John Hancock became one of the richest men in the colonies. He traveled around Boston in a luxurious carriage and dressed only in the finest clothing. "He looked every inch an aristocrat," noted one acquaintance, "from his dress and powdered wig to his smart pumps of grained leather."

Beneath Hancock's refined appearance, however, burned the heart of a patriot. He was only too glad to lead the Second Continental Congress. When the time came to sign the Declaration of Independence, Hancock scrawled his name in big, bold letters. "There," he reportedly said, "I guess King George will be able to read that."

The War for Independence

MAIN IDEA

Key American victories reversed British advances during the American Revolutionary War.

WHY IT MATTERS NOW

The American Revolution is today a national, even international, symbol of the fight for freedom.

Terms & Names

- **Loyalists**
- **Patriots**
- **Saratoga**
- **Valley Forge**
- **inflation**
- **Marquis de Lafayette**
- **Charles Cornwallis**
- **Yorktown**
- **Treaty of Paris**
- **egalitarianism**

One American's Story

Benjamin Franklin, the famous American writer, scientist, statesman, and diplomat, represented the colonies in London throughout the growing feud with Britain. As resistance in the colonies turned to bloodshed, however, Franklin fled London in 1775 and sailed home to Philadelphia.

Ironically, the issue of loyalty versus independence that was dividing the American colonies from their mother country was also dividing Franklin's own family. Franklin's son William, the royal governor of New Jersey, was stubbornly loyal to King George and opposed the rebellious atmosphere in the colonies. In one of his many letters to British authorities regarding the conflict in the colonies, William stated his position and that of others who resisted revolutionary views.

A Personal Voice WILLIAM FRANKLIN

"There is indeed a dread in the minds of many here that some of the leaders of the people are aiming to establish a republic. Rather than submit . . . we have thousands who will risk the loss of their lives in defense of the old Constitution. [They] are ready to declare themselves whenever they see a chance of its being of any avail."

—quoted in *A Little Revenge: Benjamin Franklin and His Son*

William Franklin

Because of William's stand on colonial issues, communication between him and his father virtually ceased. The break between Benjamin Franklin and his son mirrored the chasm that now divided the colonies from Britain. The notion of fighting Britain frightened and horrified some colonists even as it inspired others. Both sides believed that they were fighting for their country and being loyal to what was best for America.

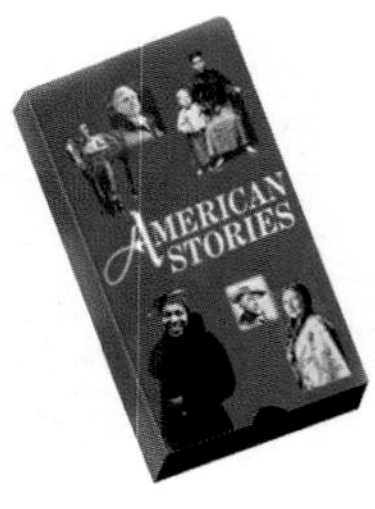

VIDEO

PATRIOT FATHER, LOYALIST SON
The Divided House of Benjamin and William Franklin

The War Begins

As they took on the mighty British Empire, the colonists suffered initial losses in the Middle States, which served as the Revolutionary War's early battleground. In time, however, the colonists would battle their way back.

LOYALISTS AND PATRIOTS As the war began, Americans found themselves on different sides of the conflict. **Loyalists**—those who opposed independence and remained loyal to the British king—included judges and governors, as well as people of more modest means. Many Loyalists thought that the British were going to win and wanted to avoid punishment as rebels. Still others thought that the Crown would protect their rights more effectively than the new colonial governments would.

MAIN IDEA

Forming Generalizations
A How did the thinking of Loyalists differ from that of Patriots?

Patriots—the supporters of independence—drew their numbers from people who saw political and economic opportunity in an independent America. Many Americans remained neutral. **A**

The conflict presented dilemmas for other groups as well. Many African Americans fought on the side of the Patriots, but others joined the Loyalists because the British promised freedom to slaves who would fight for the Crown. Most Native Americans supported the British because they viewed colonial settlers as a greater threat to their lands.

EARLY VICTORIES AND DEFEATS As part of a plan to stop the rebellion by isolating New England, the British quickly attempted to seize New York City. The British sailed into New York harbor in the summer of 1776 with a force of about 32,000 soldiers. They included thousands of German mercenaries, or hired soldiers, known as Hessians because many of them came from the German region of Hesse.

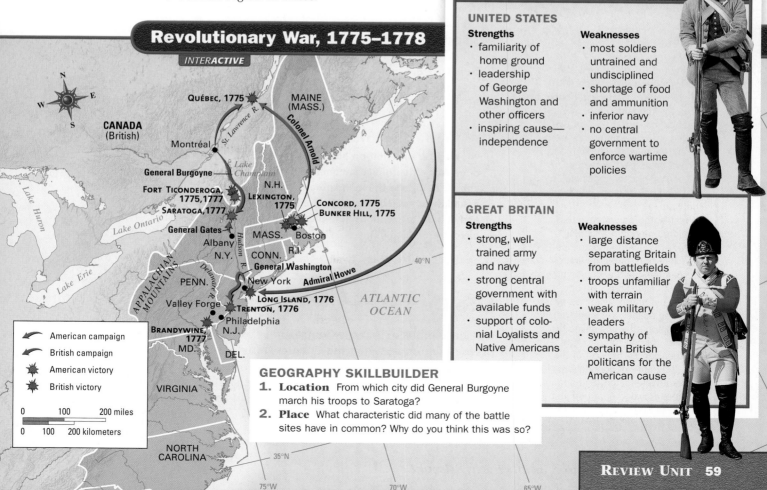

Military Strengths and Weaknesses

UNITED STATES

Strengths	Weaknesses
• familiarity of home ground • leadership of George Washington and other officers • inspiring cause—independence	• most soldiers untrained and undisciplined • shortage of food and ammunition • inferior navy • no central government to enforce wartime policies

GREAT BRITAIN

Strengths	Weaknesses
• strong, well-trained army and navy • strong central government with available funds • support of colonial Loyalists and Native Americans	• large distance separating Britain from battlefields • troops unfamiliar with terrain • weak military leaders • sympathy of certain British politicans for the American cause

Revolutionary War, 1775–1778

INTERACTIVE

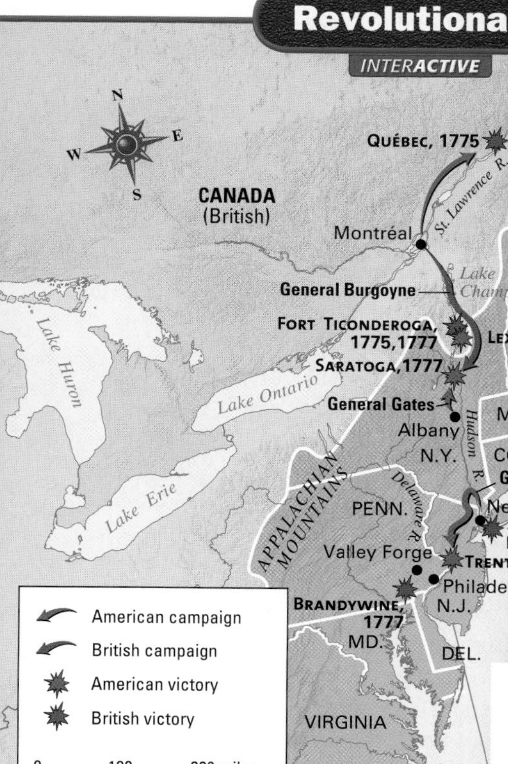

GEOGRAPHY SKILLBUILDER
1. **Location** From which city did General Burgoyne march his troops to Saratoga?
2. **Place** What characteristic did many of the battle sites have in common? Why do you think this was so?

Although the Continental Army attempted to defend New York in late August, the untrained and poorly equipped colonial troops soon retreated. By late fall, the British had pushed Washington's army across the Delaware River into Pennsylvania.

Desperate for an early victory, Washington risked everything on one bold stroke set for Christmas night, 1776. In the face of a fierce storm, he led 2,400 men in small rowboats across the ice-choked Delaware River. They then marched to their objective—Trenton, New Jersey—and defeated a garrison of Hessians in a surprise attack. The British soon regrouped, however, and in September of 1777, they captured the American capital at Philadelphia.

SARATOGA AND VALLEY FORGE In the meantime, one British general was marching straight into the jaws of disaster. In a complex scheme, General John Burgoyne planned to lead an army down a route of lakes from Canada to Albany, where he would meet British troops as they arrived from New York City. The two regiments would then join forces to isolate New England from the rest of the colonies.

As Burgoyne traveled through forested wilderness, militiamen and soldiers from the Continental Army gathered from all over New York and New England. While he was fighting off the colonial troops, Burgoyne didn't realize that his fellow British officers were preoccupied with holding Philadelphia and weren't coming to meet him. American troops finally surrounded Burgoyne at **Saratoga,** where he surrendered on October 17, 1777.

The surrender at Saratoga turned out to be one of the most important events of the war. Although the French had secretly aided the Patriots since early 1776, the Saratoga victory bolstered France's belief that the Americans could win the war. As a result, the French signed an alliance with the Americans in February 1778 and openly joined them in their fight. **B**

MAIN IDEA

Developing Historical Perspective

B Why were these early victories so important to the Continental Army?

While this hopeful turn of events took place in Paris, Washington and his Continental Army—desperately low on food and supplies—fought to stay alive at winter camp in **Valley Forge,** Pennsylvania. More than 2,000 soldiers died, yet the survivors didn't desert. Their endurance and suffering filled Washington's letters to the Congress and his friends.

A Personal Voice GEORGE WASHINGTON

> "**It may be said that no history . . . can furnish an instance of an Army's suffering uncommon hardships as ours have done. . . . To see the men without clothes to cover their nakedness, without blankets to lie upon, without shoes, . . . and submitting without a murmur, is a proof of patience and obedience which in my opinion can scarcely be paralleled.**"
>
> —quoted in *Ordeal at Valley Forge*

KEY PLAYER

GEORGE WASHINGTON
1732–1799

During the Revolutionary War, Commander in Chief George Washington became a national hero. An imposing man, Washington stood six feet two inches tall. He was broad-shouldered, calm, and dignified, and he was an expert horseman. But it was Washington's character that won hearts and, ultimately, the war.

Washington persistently roused dispirited men into a fighting force. At Princeton, he galloped on his white horse into the line of fire, shouting and encouraging his men. At Valley Forge, he bore the same cold and privation as every suffering soldier. Time and again, Washington's tactics saved his smaller, weaker force to fight another day. By the end of the war, the entire nation idolized General Washington, and adoring soldiers crowded near him just to touch his boots when he rode by.

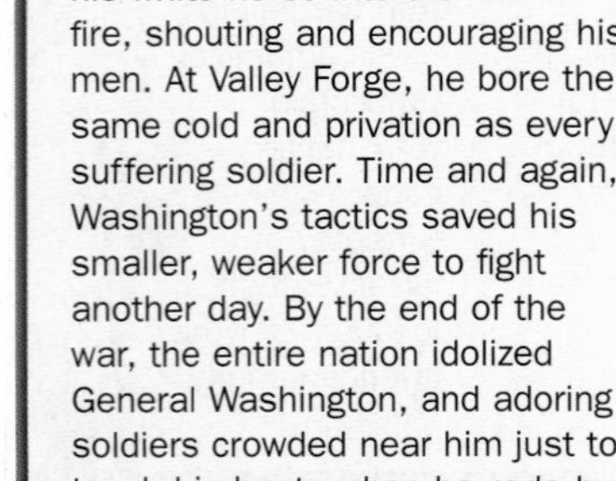

Life During the Revolution

One huge problem that the Continental Congress faced was paying the troops. When the Congress ran out of hard currency—silver and gold—it printed paper money called Continentals (like the Revolutionary soldiers). As Congress printed more and more money, its value plunged, causing rising prices, or **inflation.** The Congress also struggled against great odds to equip the beleaguered army.

Background
See *inflation* on page R42 in the Economics Handbook.

Molly Pitcher was the heroine of the Battle of Monmouth in New Jersey, which was fought in 1778. Afterward, General Washington appointed her as a noncommissioned officer to honor her brave deeds.

In 1781, the Congress appointed a rich Philadelphia merchant named Robert Morris as superintendent of finance. His associate was Haym Salomon, a Jewish political refugee from Poland. Morris and Salomon begged and borrowed on their personal credit to raise money to provide salaries for the Continental Army. They raised funds from Philadelphia's Quakers and Jews. On September 8, 1781, a Continental major wrote in his diary, "This day will be famous in the Annals of History for being the first on which the Troops of the United States received one Month's Pay in Specie [coin]."

The demands of war also affected civilians. When men marched off to fight, many wives stepped into their husbands' shoes, managing farms and businesses as well as households and families. Hundreds of women also followed their husbands to the battlefield, where they washed and cooked for the troops—while some, including Molly Pitcher, even risked their lives in combat. C

MAIN IDEA

Summarizing

C What important contributions did women make in the Revolutionary War?

The war opened some doors for African Americans. Thousands of slaves escaped to freedom in the chaos of war. About 5,000 African Americans served in the Continental Army, where their courage, loyalty, and talent impressed white Americans. Native Americans, however, remained on the fringes of the Revolution, preferring to remain independent and true to their own cultures.

HISTORICAL SPOTLIGHT

JOHN PAUL JONES

As the Revolutionary War raged on land, Britain and the colonies also engaged each other at sea. The newly formed Continental navy was no match for the mighty British fleet. It was only after France and Spain joined the colonists' cause that Britain lost its maritime supremacy.

Nonetheless, the colonists scored several morale-boosting victories over the British navy, due in large part to the heroics of American naval commander John Paul Jones. The Scottish-born Jones captured a number of British vessels, including the *Serapis* in 1779. It was during his epic battle against this ship that Jones rejected the British demand that he surrender by uttering the famous line, "I have not yet begun to fight."

Winning the War

In February 1778, in the midst of the frozen winter at Valley Forge, American troops began an amazing transformation. Friedrich von Steuben, a Prussian captain and talented drillmaster, helped to train the Continental Army. Other foreign military leaders, such as the **Marquis de Lafayette** (mär-kē′ də lăf′ē-ĕt′), also arrived to offer their help. Lafayette lobbied France for French reinforcements in 1779, and led a command in Virginia in the last years of the war. With the help of such European military leaders, the raw Continental Army became an effective fighting force.

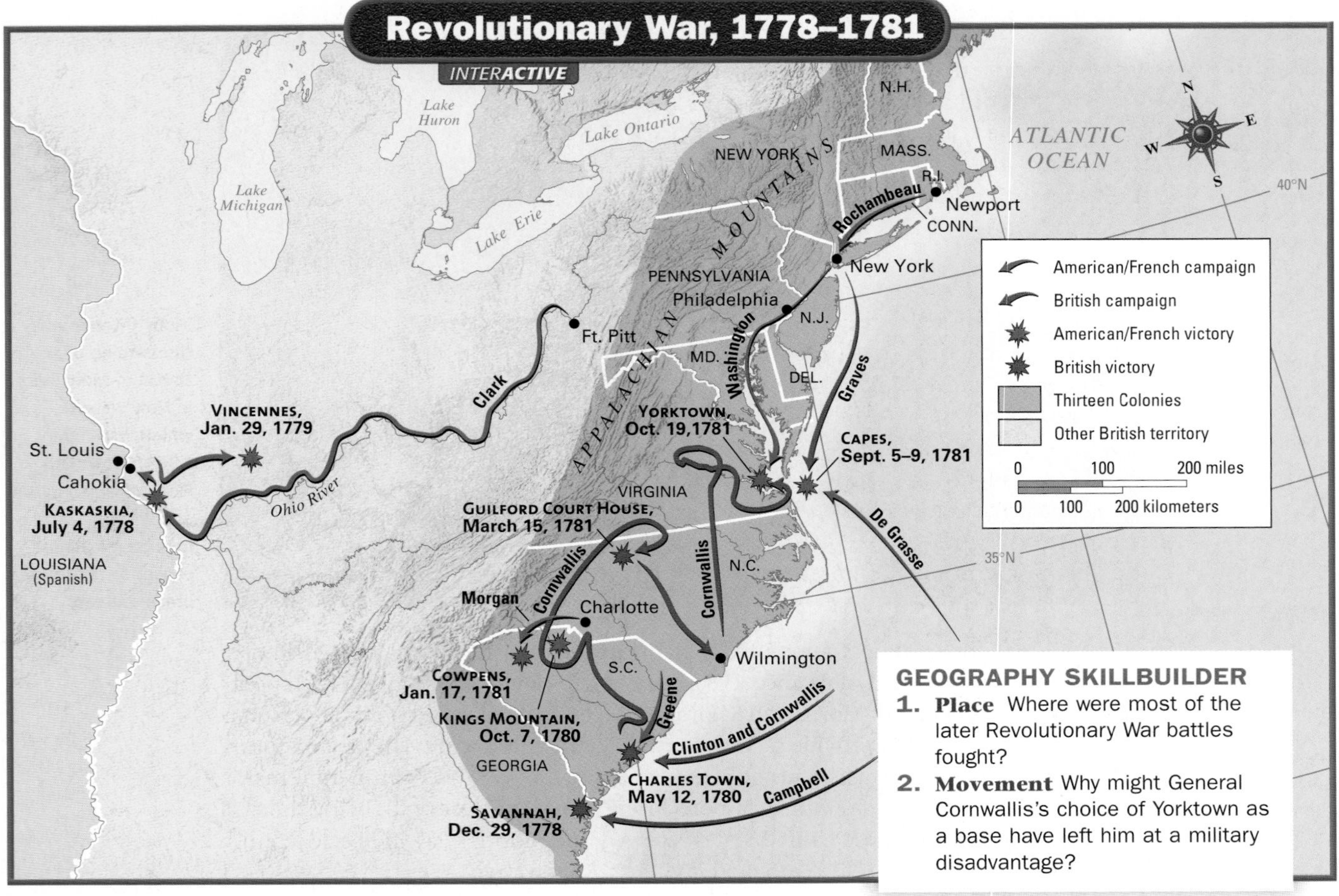

GEOGRAPHY SKILLBUILDER

1. **Place** Where were most of the later Revolutionary War battles fought?
2. **Movement** Why might General Cornwallis's choice of Yorktown as a base have left him at a military disadvantage?

THE BRITISH MOVE SOUTH After their devastating defeat at Saratoga, the British began to shift their operations to the South. At the end of 1778, a British expedition easily took Savannah, Georgia. In their greatest victory of the war, the British under Generals Henry Clinton and **Charles Cornwallis** captured Charles Town, South Carolina, in May 1780. Clinton then left for New York, while Cornwallis continued to conquer land throughout the South.

In early 1781, despite several defeats, the colonists continued to battle Cornwallis—hindering his efforts to take the Carolinas. The British general then chose to move the fight to Virginia. He led his army of 7,500 onto the peninsula between the James and York rivers and camped at **Yorktown.** Cornwallis planned to fortify Yorktown, take Virginia, and then move north to join Clinton's forces.

Vocabulary
peninsula: a piece of land that projects into a body of water

THE BRITISH SURRENDER AT YORKTOWN Shortly after learning of Corwallis's actions, the armies of Lafayette and Washington moved south toward Yorktown. Meanwhile, a French naval force defeated a British fleet and then blocked the entrance to the Chesapeake Bay, thereby obstructing British sea routes to the bay. By late September, about 17,000 French and American troops surrounded the British on the Yorktown peninsula and began bombarding them day and night. Less than a month later, on October 19, 1781, Cornwallis finally surrendered. The Americans had shocked the world and defeated the British.

Peace talks began in Paris in 1782. The American negotiating team included John Adams, John Jay of New York, and Benjamin Franklin. In September 1783, the delegates signed the **Treaty of Paris,** which confirmed U.S. independence and set the boundaries of the new nation. The United States now stretched from the Atlantic Ocean to the Mississippi River and from Canada to the Florida border. D

MAIN IDEA

Evaluating
D What was the most important challenge that faced the new United States?

The War Becomes a Symbol of Liberty

Revolutionary ideals set a new course for American society. During the war, social distinctions had begun to blur as the wealthy wore homespun clothing and as military leaders showed respect for all of their soldiers. Changes like these stimulated the rise of **egalitarianism** (ĭ-găl′ĭ-târ′ē-ə-nĭz′əm)—a belief in the equality of all people. This belief fostered a new attitude: the idea that ability, effort, and virtue, not wealth or family background, defined one's worth.

The egalitarianism of the 1780s, however, applied only to white males. It did not bring any new political rights to women. A few states made it possible for women to divorce, but common law still dictated that a married woman's property belonged to her husband.

Moreover, most African Americans were still enslaved, and even those who were free usually faced discrimination and poverty. However by 1804, many New England and Middle states had taken steps to outlaw slavery.

For Native Americans, the Revolution brought uncertainty. During both the French and Indian War and the Revolution, many Native American communities had been either destroyed or displaced, and the Native American population living east of the Mississippi had declined by about 50 percent. Postwar developments further threatened Native American interests, as settlers began taking tribal lands left unprotected by the Treaty of Paris. E

Analyzing Effects

E How had the American Revolution affected the lives of Native Americans?

In the closing days of the Revolution, the Continental Congress had chosen a quotation from the works of the Roman poet Virgil as a motto for the reverse side of the Great Seal of the United States. The motto, *Novus Ordo Seclorum,* means "a new order of the ages." Establishing a government and resolving internal problems in that new order would be a tremendous challenge for citizens of the newborn United States.

▲ **English potter Josiah Wedgwood designed this anti-slavery cameo and sent copies of it to Benjamin Franklin.**

ASSESSMENT

1. **TERMS & NAMES** For each term or name, write a sentence explaining its significance.
   - **Loyalists**
   - **Patriots**
   - **Saratoga**
   - **Valley Forge**
   - **inflation**
   - **Marquis de Lafayette**
   - **Charles Cornwallis**
   - **Yorktown**
   - **Treaty of Paris**
   - **egalitarianism**

MAIN IDEA

2. **TAKING NOTES**
   On a chart like the one below, list five significant events of the Revolutionary War in the column on the left. Note the significance of each event towards the American cause in the column on the right.

Event	Significance

CRITICAL THINKING

3. **EVALUATING**
   Do you think the colonists could have won their independence without aid from foreigners? Explain.
   Think About:
   - the military needs of the Americans and the strengths of the French
   - the colonists' military efforts in the South
   - the Americans' belief in their fight for independence

4. **ANALYZING EFFECTS**
   What were the effects of the Revolutionary War on the American colonists? **Think About:**
   - political effects
   - economic effects
   - social effects

Women and Political Power

In their families and in the workplace, in speeches and in print, countless American women have worked for justice for all citizens. Throughout the history of the United States, women have played whatever roles they felt were necessary to better this country. They also fought to expand their own political power, a power that throughout much of American history has been denied them.

1770s

PROTEST AGAINST BRITAIN ▶

In the tense years leading up to the Revolution, American women found ways to participate in the protests against the British. Homemakers boycotted tea and British-made clothing. In the painting at right, Sarah Morris Mifflin, shown with her husband Thomas, spins her own thread rather than use British thread. Some business women, such as printer Mary Goddard, who issued the first printed copy of the Declaration of Independence to include the signers' names, took more active roles.

A WOMAN'S DECLARATION

ELIZABETH CAD
the cruel and unju
the office of her fa
child, to find a way
to the abolitionist
ly into the curren
foundation for the
for woman's right
inspiring leader. T
executed the first
Falls, New York, J

1848

SENECA FALLS ▶

As America grew, women became acutely aware of their unequal status in society, particularly their lack of suffrage, or the right to vote.

In 1848, two women—Elizabeth Cady Stanton, shown above, and Lucretia Mott—launched the first woman suffrage movement in the United States at the Seneca Falls Convention in Seneca Falls, N.Y. During the convention, Stanton introduced her Declaration of Sentiments, in which she demanded greater rights for women, including the right to vote.

1920

THE RIGHT TO VOTE ▶

More than a half-century after organizing for the right to vote, women finally won their struggle. In 1920, the United States adopted the Nineteenth Amendment, which granted women the right to vote.

Pictured to the right is one of the many suffrage demonstrations of the early 1900s that helped garner public support for the amendment.

1972–1982

THE EQUAL RIGHTS AMENDMENT MOVEMENT ▶

During the mid-1900s, as more women entered the workforce, many women recognized their continuing unequal status, including the lack of equal pay for equal work. By passing an Equal Rights Amendment, some women hoped to obtain the same social and economic rights as men.

Although millions supported the amendment, many men and women feared the measure would prompt unwanted change. The ERA ultimately failed to be ratified for the Constitution.

2001

WOMEN IN CONGRESS ▲

In spite of the failure of the ERA, many women have achieved strong positions for themselves—politically as well as socially and economically.

In the 107th Congress, 60 women served in the House and 13 served in the Senate. Shown above are Washington's senators Patty Murray (left) and Maria Cantwell in 2000.

THINKING CRITICALLY

CONNECT TO HISTORY

1. **Synthesizing** How did women's political status change from 1770 to 2001?

 **SEE SKILLBUILDER HANDBOOK, PAGE R19.**

CONNECT TO TODAY

2. **Researching and Reporting** Think of a woman who has played an important role in your community. What kinds of things did this woman do? What support did she receive in the community? What problems did she run into? Report your findings to the class.

 **RESEARCH LINKS** CLASSZONE.COM

Confederation and the Constitution

MAIN IDEA	WHY IT MATTERS NOW	Terms & Names
American leaders created the Constitution as a blueprint of government for the United States.	More than 200 years after its creation, the Constitution remains the nation's guiding document for a working government.	• republic • Articles of Confederation • Northwest Ordinance of 1787 • Shays's Rebellion • James Madison • federalism • checks and balances • ratification • Federalists • Antifederalists • Bill of Rights

One American's Story

John Dickinson understood, perhaps better than other delegates to the Continental Congress, the value of compromise. In 1776 Dickinson hoped for reconciliation with Britain and refused to sign the Declaration of Independence. Yet, eight days after the Declaration was adopted, Dickinson presented Congress with the first draft of a plan for setting up a workable government for the new states.

A Personal Voice JOHN DICKINSON

> **"Two rules I have laid down for myself throughout this contest . . . first, on all occasions where I am called upon, as a trustee for my countrymen, to deliberate on questions important to their happiness, disdaining all personal advantages to be derived from a suppression of my real sentiments . . . openly to avow [declare] them; and, secondly, . . . whenever the public resolutions are taken, to regard them though opposite to my opinion, as sacred . . . and to join in supporting them as earnestly as if my voice had been given for them."**
>
> —quoted in *The Life and Times of John Dickinson, 1732–1808*

John Dickinson

Dickinson's two rules became guiding principles for the leaders who faced the formidable task of forming a new nation.

Experimenting with Confederation

As citizens of a new and independent nation, Americans had to create their own political system. Fighting the Revolutionary War gave the states a common goal, but they remained reluctant to unite under a strong central government.

After the Revolution, many Americans favored a **republic**—a government in which citizens rule through their elected representatives. However, many also feared that a democracy—government directly by the people—placed power in the hands of the uneducated masses. These fears and concerns deeply affected the planning of the new government.

THE ARTICLES OF CONFEDERATION The Second Continental Congress set up a new plan of government in a set of laws called the **Articles of Confederation.** The plan established a form of government called a confederation, or alliance, among the thirteen states.

The Articles set up a Congress in which each state would have one vote regardless of population. Powers were divided between the states and the national government. The national government had the power to declare war, make peace, and sign treaties. It could borrow money, set standards for coins and for weights and measures, and establish a postal service. After approval by all thirteen states, the Articles of Confederation went into effect in March 1781.

Weaknesses of the Articles of Confederation
• Congress could not enact and collect taxes.
• Each state had only one vote in Congress, regardless of population.
• Nine out of thirteen states needed to agree to pass important laws.
• Articles could be amended only if all states approved.
• There was no executive branch to enforce laws of Congress.
• There was no national court system to settle legal disputes.
• There were thirteen separate states that lacked national unity.

One of the first issues the Confederation faced had to do with the the Northwest Territory, lands west of the Appalachians, where many people settled after the Revolutionary War. To help govern these lands, Congress passed the Land Ordinance of 1785, which established a plan for surveying the land. (See Geography Spotlight on page 72.) In the **Northwest Ordinance of 1787,** Congress provided a procedure for dividing the land into no fewer than three and no more than five states. The ordinance also set requirements for the admission of new states, which, however, overlooked Native American land claims. A

MAIN IDEA

Contrasting

A What was the difference between the Land Ordinance of 1785 and the Northwest Ordinance of 1787?

The Land Ordinance of 1785 and the Northwest Ordinance of 1787 became the Confederation's most significant achievements. Overshadowing such successes, however, were the Confederation's many problems. The most serious problem was that each state functioned independently by pursuing its own interests rather than considering those of the nation as a whole. The government had no means of raising money or enforcing its laws. Moreover, there was no national court system to settle legal disputes. The Articles of Confederation created a weak central government and little unity among the states.

SHAYS'S REBELLION The need for a stronger central government became obvious in 1786 when many farmers in western Massachusetts rose up in protest over increased state taxes. The farmers' discontent boiled over into mob action in January of 1787 when Daniel Shays, a fellow farmer, led an army of 1,200 farmers toward the arsenal at Springfield, Massachusetts. State officials hurriedly called out the militia to head off the army of farmers, killing four of the rebels and scattering the rest.

Shays's Rebellion, as the farmers' protest came to be called, caused panic and dismay throughout the nation. It was clearly time to talk about a stronger national government. Because the states had placed such severe limits on the government to prevent abuse of power, the government was unable to solve many of the nation's problems. News of the rebellion spread throughout the states. The revolt persuaded twelve states to send delegates to a convention called by Congress in Philadelphia in May of 1787. B

MAIN IDEA

Making Inferences

B Why do you think news of Shays's Rebellion made states eager to participate in the Philadelphia convention?

Creating a New Government

Most of the delegates at the Constitutional Convention recognized the need to strengthen the central government. Within the first five days of the meeting, they gave up the idea of fixing the Articles of Confederation and decided to form an entirely new government that would replace the one created by the Articles.

CONFLICT AND COMPROMISE One major issue that the delegates faced was giving fair representation to both large and small states. **James Madison** proposed the Virginia Plan, which called for a bicameral, or two-house, legislature, with membership based on each state's population. Delegates from the small states vigorously objected to the Virginia Plan because it gave more power to states with large populations. Small states supported William Paterson's New Jersey Plan, which proposed a single-house congress in which each state had an equal vote.

The debate became deadlocked and dragged on through the hot and humid summer days. Eventually, Roger Sherman suggested the Great Compromise, which offered a two-house Congress to satisfy both small and big states. Each state would have equal representation in the Senate, or upper house. The size of the population of each state would determine its representation in the House of Representatives, or lower house. Voters of each state would choose members of the House. The state legislatures would choose members of the Senate.

The Great Compromise settled one major issue but led to conflict over another. Southern delegates, whose states had large numbers of slaves, wanted slaves included in the population count that determined the number of representatives in the House. Northern delegates, whose states had few slaves, disagreed. Not counting the slaves would give the Northern states more representatives than the Southern states in the House of Representatives. The delegates eventually agreed to the Three-Fifths Compromise, which called for three-fifths of a state's slaves to be counted as part of the population. C

MAIN IDEA

Analyzing Issues

C In what ways did the Great Compromise resolve certain problems even as it created new ones?

KEY PLAYER

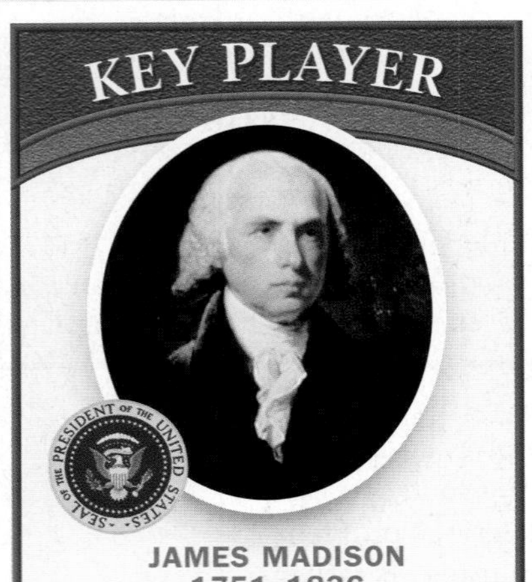

JAMES MADISON
1751–1836

The oldest of 12 children, James Madison grew up in Virginia. He was a sickly child who suffered all his life from physical ailments. Because of a weak speaking voice, he decided not to become a minister and thus entered politics.

Madison's Virginia Plan resulted from extensive research that he had done on political systems before the convention. He asked Edmund Randolph, a fellow delegate from Virginia, to present the plan because his own voice was too weak to be heard throughout the assembly.

Besides providing brilliant political leadership, Madison kept a record of the debates that took place at the convention. Because of his plan and his leadership, Madison is known as the Father of the Constitution.

DIVISION OF POWERS After the delegates reached agreement on the difficult questions of slavery and representation, they dealt with other issues somewhat more easily. They divided power between the states and the national government, and they separated the national government's power into three branches. Thus, they created an entirely new government.

The new system of government that the delegates were building was a form of **federalism,** in which power is divided between a national government and several state governments. The powers granted to the national government by the Constitution are known as delegated powers, or enumerated powers. These include such powers as the control of foreign affairs and regulation of trade between the states. Powers not specifically granted to the national government but kept by the states are called reserved powers. These include powers such as providing for and supervising education. Some powers, such as the right to tax and establish courts, were shared by both the national and the state governments.

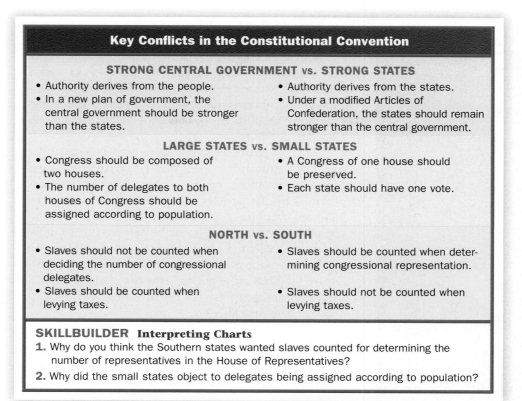

Key Conflicts in the Constitutional Convention	
STRONG CENTRAL GOVERNMENT vs. STRONG STATES	
• Authority derives from the people. • In a new plan of government, the central government should be stronger than the states.	• Authority derives from the states. • Under a modified Articles of Confederation, the states should remain stronger than the central government.
LARGE STATES vs. SMALL STATES	
• Congress should be composed of two houses. • The number of delegates to both houses of Congress should be assigned according to population.	• A Congress of one house should be preserved. • Each state should have one vote.
NORTH vs. SOUTH	
• Slaves should not be counted when deciding the number of congressional delegates. • Slaves should be counted when levying taxes.	• Slaves should be counted when determining congressional representation. • Slaves should not be counted when levying taxes.

SKILLBUILDER Interpreting Charts

1. Why do you think the Southern states wanted slaves counted for determining the number of representatives in the House of Representatives?
2. Why did the small states object to delegates being assigned according to population?

SEPARATION OF POWERS The delegates also limited the authority of the national government. First, they created three branches of government:

- a legislative branch to make laws
- an executive branch to carry out laws
- a judicial branch to interpret the laws and settle disputes

Then the delegates established a system of **checks and balances** to prevent any one branch from dominating the other two. The procedure the delegates established for electing the president reflected their fear of placing too much power in the hands of the people. Instead of choosing the president directly, each state would choose a number of electors equal to the number of senators and representatives that the state had in Congress. This group of electors chosen by the states, known as the electoral college, would then cast ballots for the presidential candidates. D

MAIN IDEA

Making Inferences

D Why did the delegates fear that one branch of the government would gain too much power?

CHANGING THE CONSTITUTION The delegates also provided a means of changing the Constitution through the amendment process. After four months of debate and compromise, the delegates succeeded in creating a Constitution that was an enduring document. In other words, by making the Constitution flexible, the delegates enabled it to pass the test of time.

Ratifying the Constitution

George Washington adjourned the Constitutional Convention on September 17, 1787. The Convention's work was over, but the new government could not become a reality until at least nine states ratified, or approved, the Constitution. Thus, the battle over **ratification** began.

FEDERALISTS AND ANTIFEDERALISTS Supporters of the Constitution called themselves **Federalists,** because they favored the new Constitution's balance of power between the states and the national government. Their opponents became known as **Antifederalists** because they opposed having such a strong central government and thus were against the Constitution.

James Madison

Both sides waged a war of words in the public debate over ratification. *The Federalist,* a series of 85 essays defending the Constitution, appeared in New York newspapers. These were essays written by three influential supporters of ratification: Alexander Hamilton, James Madison, and John Jay.

All three writers felt that there were defects in the new Constitution, but they also felt that its stronger central government was superior to the weak Congress provided by the Articles of Confederation. Using the pen name "Publius," the authors addressed those who argued that ratification should be delayed until a more perfect document could be written. In the following excerpt from one of the essays (now known to be written by Madison), the author asks his readers to compare the admittedly flawed Constitution with its predecessor, the Articles.

A PERSONAL VOICE JAMES MADISON

"It is a matter both of wonder and regret, that those who raise so many objections against the new Constitution should never call to mind the defects of that which is to be exchanged for it [The Articles]. It is not necessary that the former should be perfect; it is sufficient that the latter is more imperfect."

—*The Federalist,* Number 38, 1788

The Antifederalists' main opposition to the new Constitution was that it contained no guarantee that the government would protect the rights of the people or of the states. Antifederalists included such notable figures as Patrick Henry, George Mason, and Richard Henry Lee. *Letters from the Federal Farmer,* most likely written by Lee, was the most widely read Antifederalist publication. Lee listed the rights that Antifederalists believed should be protected, such as freedom of the press and of religion, guarantees against unreasonable searches of people and their homes, and the right to a trial by jury.

The Antifederalists' demand for a bill of rights—a formal summary of citizens' rights and freedoms—stemmed from their fear of a strong central government. All state constitutions guaranteed individual rights, and seven of them included a bill of rights. The states believed they would serve as protectors of the people. Yet in the end, the Federalists yielded to people's overwhelming desire and promised to add a bill of rights if the states would ratify the Constitution. In June 1788, New Hampshire became the ninth state to approve the Constitution, making it the law of the land. (E)

MAIN IDEA

Summarizing

(E) Why did the Antifederalists insist that the Constitution must have a bill of rights?

ADOPTION OF A BILL OF RIGHTS By December 1791, the states also had ratified ten amendments to the Constitution, which became known as the **Bill of Rights.** The first eight amendments spell out the personal liberties the states had requested. The First Amendment guarantees citizens' rights to freedom of religion, speech, the press, and political activity. According to the Second and Third Amendments, the government cannot deny citizens the right to bear arms as members of a militia of citizen-soldiers, nor can the government house troops in private homes in peacetime. The Fourth Amendment prevents the search of citizens' homes without proper warrants. The Fifth through Eighth Amendments guarantee fair treatment for individuals accused of crimes. The Ninth and Tenth Amendments impose general limits on the powers of the federal government.

The protection of rights and freedoms did not apply to all Americans at the time the Bill of Rights was adopted. Native Americans and slaves were excluded. Women were not mentioned in the Constitution. The growing number of free blacks did not receive adequate protection from the Constitution. Although many states permitted free blacks to vote, the Bill of Rights offered them no protection against whites' discrimination and hostility.

Continuing Relevance of the Constitution

The United States Constitution is the oldest written national constitution still in use. It is a "living" document, capable of meeting the changing needs of Americans. One reason for this capability lies in Article I, Section 8, which gives Congress the power "To make all laws which shall be necessary and proper for carrying into execution" the powers that the Constitution enumerates. This clause is referred to as the "elastic clause" because it stretches the power of the government. The framers of the Constitution included these implied powers in order to allow the authority of the government to expand to meet unforeseen circumstances.

The Constitution also can be formally changed when necessary through amendments. The Constitution provides ways for amendments to be proposed and to be ratified. However, the writers made the amendment process difficult in order to avoid arbitrary changes. Through the ratification process, the writers of the Constitution have also ensured that any amendment has the overwhelming support of the people.

MAIN IDEA

Drawing Conclusions
F How did the adoption of the Bill of Rights show the flexibility of the Constitution?

In more than 200 years, only 27 amendments have been added to the Constitution. These amendments have helped the government meet the challenges of a changing world, while still preserving the rights of the American people. F

SECTION 3 ASSESSMENT

1. **TERMS & NAMES** For each term or name, write a sentence explaining its significance.
   - **republic**
   - **Articles of Confederation**
   - **Northwest Ordinance of 1787**
   - **Shays's Rebellion**
   - **James Madison**
   - **federalism**
   - **checks and balances**
   - **ratification**
   - **Federalists**
   - **Antifederalists**
   - **Bill of Rights**

MAIN IDEA

2. **TAKING NOTES**
   Re-create the web below on your paper, and fill it in with specific issues that were debated at the Constitutional Convention.

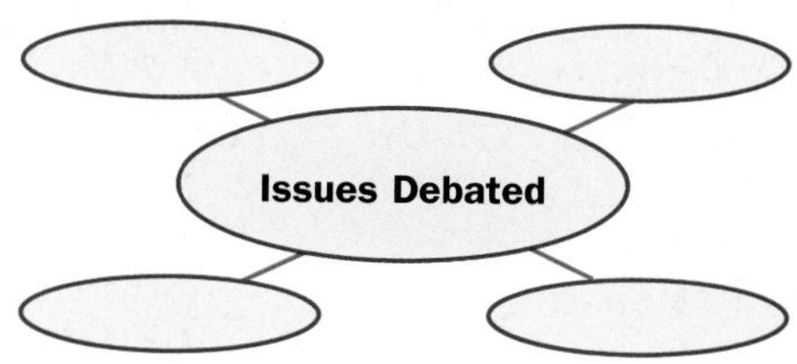

Choose one issue and explain how the delegates resolved that issue.

CRITICAL THINKING

3. **EVALUATING**
   Do you think the Federalists or the Antifederalists had the more valid arguments? Support your opinion with examples from the text. **Think About:**
   - Americans' experience with the Articles of Confederation
   - Americans' experience with Great Britain

4. **ANALYZING ISSUES**
   Several states ratified the Constitution only after being assured that a bill of rights would be added to it. In your opinion, what is the most important value of the Bill of Rights? Why?

5. **ANALYZING VISUAL SOURCES**
   The cartoon above shows a parade held in New York to celebrate the new constitution. Why is Hamilton's name displayed under the "Ship of State" float?

INTERACTIVE

GEOGRAPHY SPOTLIGHT

The Land Ordinance of 1785

▲ **Aerial photograph showing how the Land Ordinance transformed the landscape into a patchwork of farms.**

When states ceded, or gave up, their western lands to the United States, the new nation became "land rich" even though it was "money poor." Government leaders searched for a way to use the land to fund such services as public education.

The fastest and easiest way to raise money would have been to sell the land in huge parcels. However, only the rich would have been able to purchase land. The Land Ordinance of 1785 made the parcels small and affordable.

The Land Ordinance established a plan for dividing the land. The government would first survey the land, dividing it into townships of 36 square miles, as shown on the map below. Then each township would be divided into 36 sections of 1 square mile, or about 640 acres, each. An individual or a family could purchase a section and divide it into farms or smaller units. A typical farm of the period was equal to one-quarter section, or 160 acres. The minimum price per acre was one dollar.

Government leaders hoped the buyers would develop farms and establish communities. In this way settlements would spread across the western territories in an orderly way. Government surveyors repeated the process thousands of times, imposing frontier geometry on the land.

In 1787, the Congress further provided for the orderly development of the Northwest Territory by passing the Northwest Ordinance, which established how states would be created out of the territory.

▼ **The map below shows how an eastern section of Ohio has been subdivided according to the Land Ordinance of 1785.**

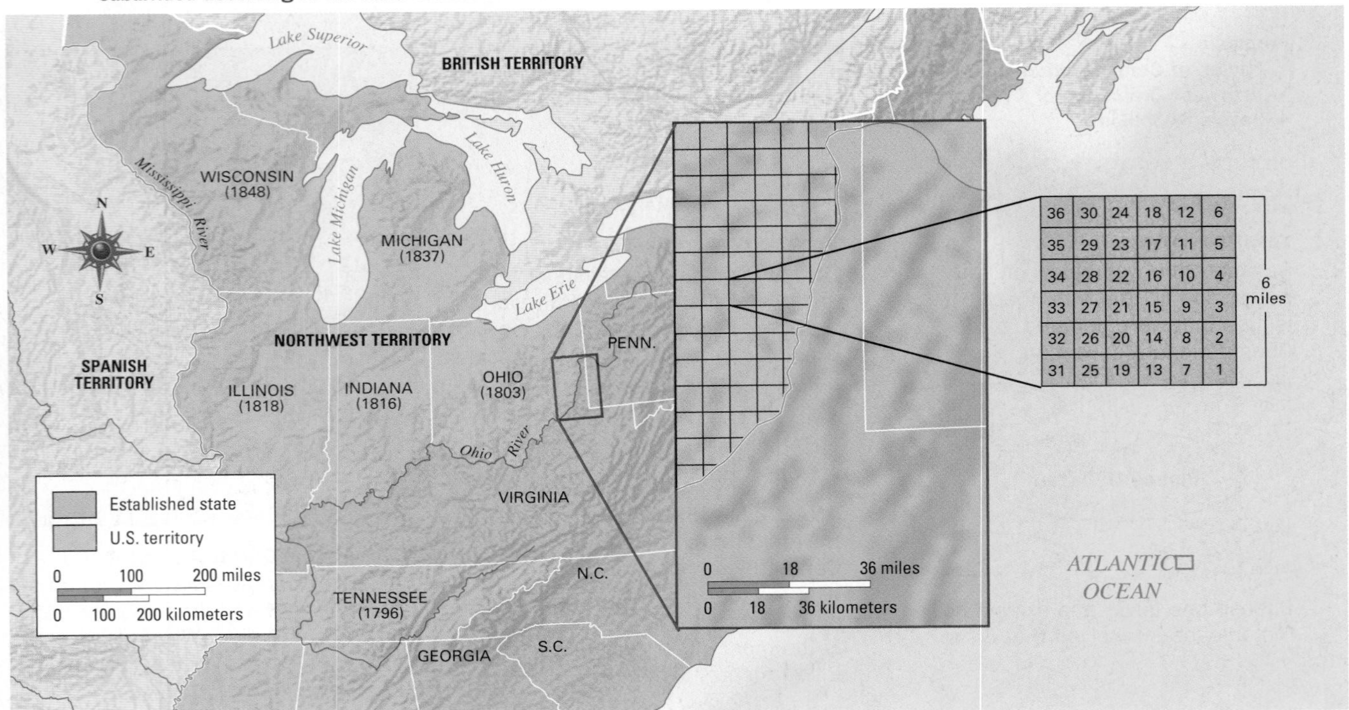

This map shows how a township, now in Meigs County, Ohio, was divided in 1787 into parcels of full square-mile sections and smaller, more affordable plots. The names of the original buyers are written on the full sections.

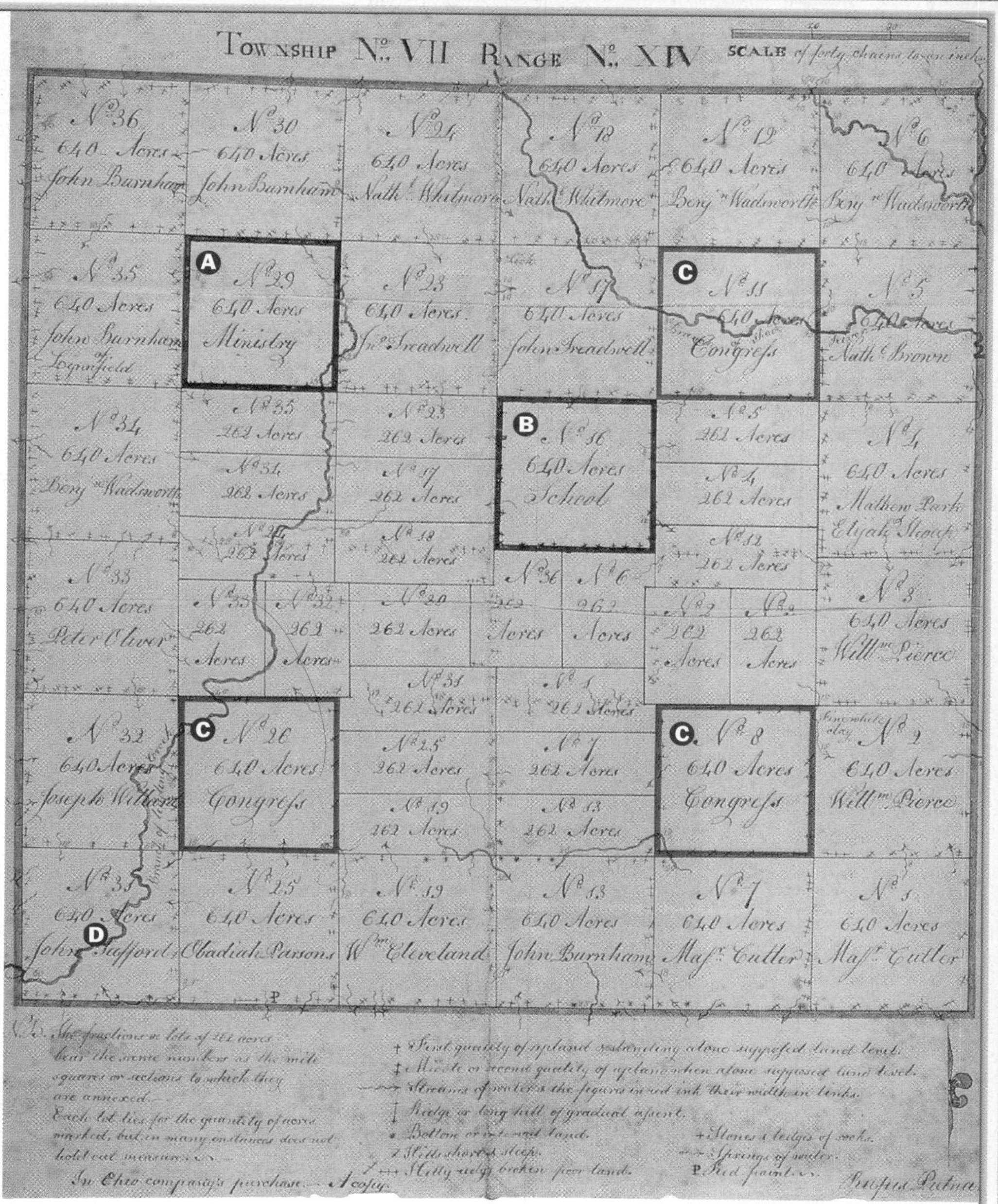

A RELIGION To encourage the growth of religion within the township, the surveyors set aside a full section of land. Most of the land within the section was sold to provide funds for a church and a minister's salary. This practice was dropped after a few years because of concern about the separation of church and state.

B EDUCATION The ordinance encouraged public education by setting aside section 16 of every township for school buildings. Local people used the money raised by the sale of land within this section to build a school and hire a teacher. This section was centrally located so that students could reach it without traveling too far.

C REVENUE Congress reserved two or three sections of each township for sale at a later date. Congress planned to sell the sections then at a tidy profit. The government soon abandoned this practice because of criticism that it should not be involved in land speculation.

D WATER Rivers and streams were very important to early settlers, who used them for transportation. Of most interest, however, was a meandering stream, which indicated flat bottomland that was highly prized for its fertility.

THINKING CRITICALLY

1. **Analyzing Distributions** How did the Land Ordinance of 1785 provide for the orderly development of the Northwest Territory? How did it make land affordable?
2. **Creating a Chart** Create a table that organizes and summarizes the information in the map above. To help you organize your thoughts, pose questions that the map suggests and that a table could help answer.

SEE SKILLBUILDER HANDBOOK, PAGE R30.

CLASSZONE.COM

Launching the New Nation

MAIN IDEA

With George Washington as its first president, the United States began creating a working government for its new nation.

WHY IT MATTERS NOW

The country's early leaders established precedents for organizing government that the United States still follows.

Terms & Names

- **Judiciary Act of 1789**
- **Alexander Hamilton**
- **cabinet**
- **two-party system**
- **Democratic-Republican**
- **protective tariff**
- **XYZ Affair**
- **Alien and Sedition Acts**
- **nullification**

One American's Story

As the hero of the Revolution, George Washington was the unanimous choice in the nation's first presidential election. When the news reached him on April 14, 1789, Washington accepted the call to duty—despite his uncertainty about how to lead the new country. Two days later he set out for New York City to take the oath of office.

A PERSONAL VOICE GEORGE WASHINGTON

"About ten o'clock I bade adieu [farewell] to Mount Vernon, to private life, and to domestic felicity [happiness]; and with a mind oppressed with more anxious and painful sensations than I have words to express, set out for New York . . . with the best dispositions [intentions] to render service to my country in obedience to its call, but with less hope of answering its expectations."

—*The Diaries of George Washington*

When Washington took office as the first president of the United States under the Constitution, he and Congress faced a daunting task to create an entirely new government. The momentous decisions that these early leaders made have resounded through American history.

George Washington

Washington Heads the New Government

Although the Constitution provided a strong foundation, it was not a detailed blueprint for governing. To create a working government, Washington and Congress had to make many practical decisions. Perhaps James Madison put it best: "We are in a wilderness without a single footstep to guide us."

JUDICIARY ACT OF 1789 One of the first tasks Washington and Congress faced was the creation of a judicial system. The **Judiciary Act of 1789** provided for a Supreme Court and federal circuit and district courts. The Judiciary Act allowed state court decisions to be appealed to a federal court when constitutional issues were raised. It also guaranteed that federal laws would remain "the supreme law of the land."

WASHINGTON SHAPES THE EXECUTIVE BRANCH The nation's leaders also faced the task of building an executive branch. To help the president govern, Congress created three executive departments: the Department of State, to deal with foreign affairs; the Department of War, to handle military matters; and the Department of the Treasury, to manage finances.

To head these departments, Washington chose capable leaders—Thomas Jefferson as secretary of state, **Alexander Hamilton** as secretary of the treasury, Henry Knox as secretary of war. These department heads soon became the president's chief advisers, or **cabinet**.

HAMILTON AND JEFFERSON: TWO CONFLICTING VISIONS Hamilton and Jefferson held very different political ideas. Hamilton believed in a strong central government led by a prosperous, educated elite of upper-class citizens. Jefferson distrusted a strong central government and the rich. He favored strong state and local governments rooted in popular participation. Hamilton believed that commerce and industry were the keys to a strong nation; Jefferson favored a society of farmer-citizens. (A)

MAIN IDEA

Contrasting
(A) How did Jefferson's and Hamilton's views of government differ?

HAMILTON'S ECONOMIC PLAN As secretary of the treasury, Hamilton's job was to put the nation's economy on a firm footing. To do this, he called on the nation to pay off its debts, a large amount of which was incurred during the Revolution. He also proposed the establishment of a national bank that would be funded by both the federal government and wealthy private investors. This bank would issue paper money and handle taxes and other government funds.

Opponents of a national bank, such as James Madison, argued that since the Constitution made no provision for such an institution, Congress had no right to authorize it. This argument began the debate between those, like Hamilton, who favored a loose interpretation of the Constitution and those, like Madison, who favored a strict interpretation—a vital debate that has continued throughout U.S. history.

KEY PLAYERS

ALEXANDER HAMILTON
1755–1804

Born into poverty in the British West Indies, Alexander Hamilton was orphaned at age 13 and went to work as a shipping clerk. He later made his way to New York, where he attended King's College (now Columbia University). He joined the army during the Revolution and became an aide to General Washington.

Intensely ambitious, Hamilton quickly moved up in society. Although in his humble origins Hamilton was the opposite of Jefferson, he had little faith in the common citizen and sided with the interests of upper-class Americans. Hamilton said of Jefferson's beloved common people: "Your people, sir, your people is a great beast!"

THOMAS JEFFERSON
1743–1826

The writer of the Declaration of Independence, Thomas Jefferson began his political career at age 26, when he was elected to Virginia's colonial legislature. In 1779 he was elected governor of Virginia, and in 1785 he was appointed minister to France. He served as secretary of state from 1790 to 1793.

A Southern planter, Jefferson was also an accomplished scholar, the architect of Monticello (his Virginia house), an inventor (of, among other things, a machine that made copies of letters), and the founder of the University of Virginia in 1819. Despite his elite background and his ownership of slaves, he was a strong ally of the small farmer and average citizen.

Contrasting Views of the Federal Government	
HAMILTON	**JEFFERSON**
• Concentrating power in federal government	• Sharing power with state and local governments; limited national government
• Fear of mob rule	• Fear of absolute power or ruler
• Republic led by a well-educated elite	• Democracy of virtuous farmers and tradespeople
• Loose interpretation of the Constitution	• Strict interpretation of the Constitution
• National bank constitutional (loose interpretation)	• National bank unconstitutional (strict interpretation)
• Economy based on shipping and manufacturing	• Economy based on farming
• Payment of national and state debts (favoring creditors)	• Payment of only the national debt (favoring debtors)
• Supporters: merchants, manufacturers, landowners, investors, lawyers, clergy	• Supporters: the "plain people" (farmers, tradespeople)

SKILLBUILDER Interpreting Charts

1. Whose view of the federal government was a wealthy person more likely to favor? Why?
2. How do you think Jefferson differed from Hamilton in his view of people and human nature?

THE FIRST POLITICAL PARTIES The differences within Washington's cabinet intensified and soon helped to give rise to a **two-party system.** Those who shared Hamilton's vision of a strong central government (mostly Northerners) called themselves Federalists. Those who supported Jefferson's vision of strong state governments (mostly Southerners) called themselves **Democratic-Republicans.**

THE WHISKEY REBELLION During Washington's second term, an incident occurred that reflected the tension between federal and regional interests. Previously, Congress had passed a **protective tariff,** an import tax on goods produced abroad meant to encourage American production. To generate even more revenue, Secretary Hamilton pushed through an excise tax—a tax on a product's manufacture, sale, or distribution—to be levied on the manufacture of whiskey.

In 1794, furious whiskey producers in western Pennsylvania refused to pay the tax and attacked the tax collectors. The federal government responded by sending some 13,000 militiamen to end the conflict. The Whiskey Rebellion, as it came to be known, marked the first use of armed force to assert federal authority.

Background
In addition to promoting American goods, the Tariff of 1789, as well as tariffs that followed, provided the majority of the federal government's revenue until the 20th century.

French revolutionaries storm the Bastille, an infamous prison in Paris, France, on July 14, 1789. ▼

Challenges at Home and Abroad

At the same time, the new government faced critical problems and challenges overseas as well as at home along the western frontier.

ADDRESSING FOREIGN AFFAIRS In 1789 a stunning revolution in France ended the French monarchy and brought hope for a government based on the will of the people. By 1793, France was engaged in war with Great Britain as well as with other European countries.

In the United States, reaction to the conflict tended to split along party lines. Democratic-Republicans supported France.

Federalists wanted to back the British. President Washington took a middle position. He issued a declaration of neutrality, a statement that the United States would support neither side in the conflict. Washington remained wary of foreign involvement throughout his tenure in office. In his farewell address in 1796, he warned the nation to "steer clear of permanent Alliances with any portion of the foreign World."

In another significant foreign matter, Thomas Pinckney negotiated a treaty with Spain in 1795. According to Pinckney's Treaty, Spain agreed to give up all claims to land east of the Mississippi (except Florida) and recognized the 31st parallel as the northern boundary of Florida. Spain also agreed to open the Mississippi River to American traffic and allow traders to use the port of New Orleans. The treaty was important because it helped pave the way for U.S. expansion west of the Appalachians. B

MAIN IDEA

Developing Historical Perspective
B Why did the United States want access to the Mississippi River?

CHALLENGES IN THE NORTHWEST Meanwhile, Americans faced trouble along their western border, where the British still maintained forts and Native Americans continued to resist white settlers. In 1794, after numerous skirmishes, the U.S. military led by General Anthony Wayne defeated a confederacy of Native Americans at the Battle of Fallen Timbers, near present-day Toledo, Ohio. The victory helped to establish the settlers' supremacy in the region.

JAY'S TREATY At the time of the Battle of Fallen Timbers, John Jay, the chief justice of the Supreme Court, was in London to negotiate a treaty with Great Britain. One of the disputed issues was which nation would control territories west of the Appalachian Mountains. When news of Wayne's victory at Fallen Timbers arrived, the British agreed to evacuate their posts in the Northwest Territory because they did not wish to fight both the United States and the French, with whom they were in conflict, at the same time.

Although Jay's Treaty, signed on November 19, 1794, was a diplomatic victory, the treaty provoked outrage at home. For one thing, it allowed the British to continue their fur trade on the American side of the U.S.-Canadian border. This angered western settlers. Also, the treaty did not resolve a dispute over neutral American trade in the Caribbean. Americans believed that their ships had the right to free passage there. The British, however, had seized a number of these ships, confiscating their crews and cargo. Despite serious opposition, the treaty managed to pass the Senate.

The bitter political fight over Jay's Treaty, along with the growing division between the Federalists and Democratic-Republicans, convinced Washington not to seek a third term.

Adams Provokes Criticism

In the election of 1796, the United States faced a new situation: a contest between opposing parties. The Federalists nominated Vice President John Adams for president, while the Democratic-Republicans chose Thomas Jefferson.

In the election, Adams received 71 electoral votes, while Jefferson received 68. Because the Constitution stated that the runner-up should become vice-president, the country found itself with a Federalist president and a Democratic-Republican vice-president.

The election also underscored the growing danger of sectionalism—placing the interests of one region over those of the nation as a whole. Almost all the electors from the Southern states voted for Jefferson, while all the electors from the Northern states voted for Adams.

▲ **Portrait of a young John Adams by Joseph Badger**

ADAMS TRIES TO AVOID WAR Soon after taking office, President Adams faced his first crisis: a looming war with France. The French government regarded the U.S.-British agreement over the Northwest Territory a violation of the French-American alliance. In retaliation they began to seize American ships bound for Britain. Adams sent a three-man team to Paris to negotiate a solution. (C)

MAIN IDEA

Analyzing Motives

(C) Why did the French begin to seize U.S. ships?

This team, which included future Chief Justice John Marshall, planned to meet with the French foreign minister, Talleyrand. Instead, the French sent three low-level officials, whom Adams in his report to Congress called "X, Y, and Z." The French officials demanded a $250,000 bribe as payment for seeing Talleyrand. News of this insult, which became known as the **XYZ Affair,** provoked a wave of anti-French feeling at home. "Millions for defense, but not one cent for tribute" became the slogan of the day. In 1798, Congress created a navy department and authorized American ships to seize French vessels. For the next two years, an undeclared naval war raged between France and the United States.

The Federalists called for a full-scale war against France, but Adams refused to take that step. Through diplomacy, the two countries eventually smoothed over their differences. Adams damaged his standing among the Federalists, but he kept the United States out of war.

THE ALIEN AND SEDITION ACTS Although Democratic-Republicans cheered Adams for avoiding war with France, they criticized him mercilessly on many other issues. Tensions between Federalists and Democratic-Republicans rose to a fever pitch. Adams regarded Democratic-Republican ideas as dangerous to the welfare of the nation. He and other Federalists accused the Democratic-Republicans of favoring foreign powers.

Many immigrants were active in the Democratic-Republican party. Some of the most vocal critics of the Adams administration were foreign-born. They included French and British radicals as well as recent Irish immigrants who lashed out at anyone who was even faintly pro-British, including the Federalist Adams.

To counter what they saw as a growing threat against the government, the Federalists pushed through Congress in 1798 four measures that became known as the **Alien and Sedition Acts.** Three of these measures, the Alien Acts, raised the residence requirement for American citizenship from 5 years to 14 years and allowed the president to deport or jail any alien considered undesirable.

Vocabulary
alien: belonging to or coming from another country; foreign
sedition: rebellion against one's country; treason

Analyzing *Political Cartoons*

"THE PARIS MONSTER"

"*Cinque-tetes*, or the Paris Monster" is the title of this political cartoon satirizing the XYZ Affair. On the right, the five members of the French Directory, or ruling executive body, are depicted as a five-headed monster demanding money. The three American representatives, Elbridge Gerry, Charles Pinckney, and John Marshall, are on the left, exclaiming "Cease bawling, monster! We will not give you six-pence!"

SKILLBUILDER Analyzing Political Cartoons

1. How would you contrast the cartoon's depiction of the U.S. representatives with its depiction of the French Directory?
2. What other details in the cartoon show the cartoonist's attitude toward the French?

 **SEE SKILLBUILDER HANDBOOK, PAGE R24.**

The fourth measure, the Sedition Act, set fines and jail terms for anyone trying to hinder the operation of the government or expressing "false, scandalous, and malicious statements" against the government. Under the terms of this act, the federal government prosecuted and jailed a number of Democratic-Republican editors, publishers, and politicians. Outraged Democratic-Republicans called the laws a violation of freedom of speech guaranteed by the First Amendment.

VIRGINIA AND KENTUCKY RESOLUTIONS The two main Democratic-Republican leaders, Thomas Jefferson and James Madison, saw the Alien and Sedition Acts as a serious misuse of power on the part of the federal government. They decided to organize opposition to the Alien and Sedition Acts by appealing to the states. Madison drew up a set of resolutions that were adopted by the Virginia Legislature, while Jefferson wrote resolutions that were approved in Kentucky. The resolutions warned of the dangers that the Alien and Sedition Acts posed to a government of checks and balances guaranteed by the Constitution.

A Personal Voice

"Let the honest advocate of confidence [in government] read the alien and sedition acts, and say if the Constitution has not been wise in fixing limits to the government it created, and whether we should be wise in destroying those limits."

—*8th Resolution,* The Virginia and Kentucky Resolutions

MAIN IDEA

Analyzing Issues

D How did the Kentucky Resolutions challenge the authority of the federal government?

The Kentucky Resolutions in particular asserted the principle of **nullification:** the states had the right to nullify, or consider void, any act of Congress that they deemed unconstitutional. Virginia and Kentucky viewed the Alien and Sedition Acts as unconstitutional violations of the First Amendment that deprived citizens of their rights. **D**

The resolutions also called for other states to adopt similar declarations. No other state did so, however, and the issue died out by the next presidential election. Nevertheless, the resolutions showed that the balance of power between the states and the federal government remained a controversial issue. In fact, the election of 1800 between Federalist John Adams and Democratic-Republican Thomas Jefferson would center on this critical debate.

Section 4 ASSESSMENT

1. **TERMS & NAMES** For each term or name, write a sentence explaining its significance.
   - **Judiciary Act of 1789**
   - **Alexander Hamilton**
   - **cabinet**
   - **two-party system**
   - **Democratic-Republican**
   - **protective tariff**
   - **XYZ Affair**
   - **Alien and Sedition Acts**
   - **nullification**

MAIN IDEA

2. **TAKING NOTES**
   In a chart, list the leaders, beliefs, and goals of the country's first political parties.

Federalists	Democratic-Republicans

If you had lived in that time, which party would you have favored? Why?

CRITICAL THINKING

3. **EVALUATING LEADERSHIP**
   How would you judge the leadership qualities of President Washington in his decision to put two such opposed thinkers as Hamilton and Jefferson in his cabinet? Who do you think was the more significant member of the cabinet?

4. **ANALYZING EVENTS**
   Do you agree with the Democratic-Republicans that the Alien and Sedition Acts were a violation of the First Amendment? Were they necessary? Support your opinion with evidence from the text.
   Think About:
   - the intent of the First Amendment
   - what was happening in Europe
   - what was happening in the United States

REVIEW CHAPTER 2 ASSESSMENT

VISUAL SUMMARY

Revolution and the Early Republic

COLONIAL INTERESTS

- To maintain and increase prosperity through trade with Britain and the rest of the world.
- To continue settling new regions by migrating westward over the Appalachian mountains.

BRITISH INTERESTS

- To stop further migration over the Appalachian mountains.
- To tax the colonists in order to raise money to pay for their defense.
- To control colonial trade.

Revolutionary War 1775–1783

The colonies rebel and achieve independence.

U.S.A.

The newly formed United States of America creates a new system of government, with a constitution and a bill of rights.

TERMS & NAMES

For each term or name below, write a sentence explaining its significance.

1. Stamp Act
2. Thomas Jefferson
3. Declaration of Independence
4. Valley Forge
5. Treaty of Paris
6. Articles of Confederation
7. checks and balances
8. Antifederalists
9. cabinet
10. Democratic-Republican

MAIN IDEAS

Use your notes and the information in the chapter to answer the following questions.

Colonial Resistance and Rebellion *(pages 46–53)*

1. How did the first Continental Congress prepare the way for an armed uprising against Britain?
2. Why did Jefferson eliminate criticism of the slave trade from the Declaration of Independence?

The War for Independence *(pages 58–63)*

3. Why did so many colonists remain loyal to Britain during the Revolutionary War?
4. How did the American victory at Saratoga affect the course of the war?

Confederation and the Constitution *(pages 66–71)*

5. What were some of the problems with the kind of government set up by the Articles of Confederation?
6. What was the Great Compromise?

Launching the New Nation *(pages 74–79)*

7. What events after 1789 helped to unify the nation?
8. What issues led to the development of a two-party system?

CRITICAL THINKING

1. **USING YOUR NOTES** In a chart like the one below, show the ideological differences between the two political groups.

Federalists	Antifederalists

2. **DEVELOPING HISTORICAL PERSPECTIVE** In what ways did regional interests assert themselves after the creation of the United States?

3. **EVALUATING** In your view, which compromise during the Constitutional Convention was more important, the Great Compromise or the Three-Fifths Compromise? Explain your choice.

Standardized Test Practice

Use the cartoon and your knowledge of U.S. history to answer question 1.

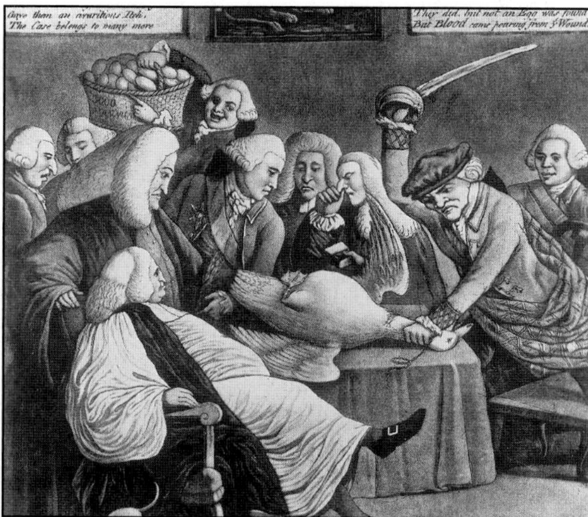

1. This British cartoon was published during the winter of 1775–1776. In it, King George III and his ministers are shown killing the goose that laid the golden egg. The cartoon is criticizing —

   A the killing of British soldiers at Concord and Bunker Hill.
   B British response to the Olive Branch Petition.
   C John Locke's theory of natural rights.
   D Thomas Paine's *Common Sense.*

2. Both Shays's Rebellion and the Boston Tea Party were the result of anger over —

   F religious intolerance.
   G the Boston Massacre.
   H taxes.
   J slavery.

Use the information in the box and your knowledge of U.S. history to answer question 3.

- Declaration of Independence
- Battles of Lexington and Concord
- Second Continental Congress

3. Which of the following lists the events in chronological order from first to last?

   A Declaration of Independence, Battles of Lexington and Concord, Second Continental Congress
   B Battles of Lexington and Concord, Second Continental Congress, Declaration of Independence
   C Second Continental Congress, Battles of Lexington and Concord, Declaration of Independence
   D Second Continental Congress, Declaration of Independence, Battles of Lexington and Concord

ADDITIONAL TEST PRACTICE, pages S1–S33.

TEST PRACTICE CLASSZONE.COM

ALTERNATIVE ASSESSMENT

1. **INTERACT WITH HISTORY** Recall your discussion of the question on page 45:

How much power should the national government have?

Imagine that it is 1787. You have been present at a gathering of your friends who have discussed at length their ideas, concerns, and hopes for the new constitution being written in Philadelphia. Write a journal entry in which you try to record what you heard. Mention some of the conflicts being discussed at the Continental Congress, noting the criticisms as well as the support for the federal government proposed by the Constitution.

2. **VIDEO** **LEARNING FROM MEDIA** View the *American Stories* video, "Patriot Father, Loyalist Son." Discuss the following questions in a small group; then do the activity.

- What political views and concerns did Benjamin Franklin originally share with his son William?
- How did certain events in the American colonies' struggle for independence contribute to the conflict between Benjamin and William Franklin?

Cooperative Learning Activity Both Benjamin and William Franklin had strong opinions about loyalty and patriotism. In your opinion, what makes someone a patriot? Using books, magazines, and newspapers, make a list of people you consider to be patriots. List their names as well as the reasons why you chose them on a chart in your classroom.

The Living Constitution

Table of Contents for the Living Constitution

Preamble	84
Article 1	84
Article 2	90
Article 3	92
Article 4	94
Article 5	94
Article 6	95
Article 7	95
Bill of Rights	96
Amendments 11–27	98
Tracing Themes: Voting Rights	104
Assessment	106
Projects for Citizenship	108

"The Constitution was not made to fit us like a straightjacket. In its elasticity lies its chief greatness."
President Woodrow Wilson

Purposes of the Constitution

The official charge to the delegates who met in Philadelphia in 1787 was to amend the Articles of Confederation. They soon made a fateful decision, however, to ignore the Articles and to write an entirely new constitution. These delegates—the "framers"—set themselves five purposes to fulfill in their effort to create an effective constitution.

1. Establish Legitimacy

First, the framers of the Constitution had to establish the new government's legitimacy—its right to rule. The patriots' theory of government was set out in the Declaration of Independence, which explained why British rule over the colonies was illegitimate. Now the framers had to demonstrate that their new government met the standards of legitimacy referred to in the Declaration.

For the framers of the Constitution, legitimacy had to be based on a compact or contract among those who are to be ruled. This is why the Constitution starts with the words "We the people of the United States . . . do ordain and establish this Constitution."

2. Create Appropriate Structures

The framers' second purpose was to create appropriate structures for the new government. The framers were committed to the principles of representative democracy. They also believed that any new government must include an important role for state governments and ensure that the states retained some legitimacy to rule within their borders.

To achieve their goals, the framers created the Congress, the presidency, and the judiciary to share the powers of the national government. They also created a system of division of powers between the national government and the state governments.

The original manuscript of the Constitution is now kept in the National Archives in Washington, D.C. ▶

We the People of the United States, in Order to form a more perfect Union, establish Justice, insure domestic Tranquility, provide for the common defence, promote the general Welfare, and secure the Blessings of Liberty to ourselves and our Posterity, do ordain and establish this Constitution for the United States of America.

Article. I

Section. 1. All legislative Powers herein granted shall be vested in a Congress of the United States, which shall consist of a Senate and House of Representatives.

3. Describe and Distribute Power

The framers had as their third purpose to describe governmental powers and to distribute them among the structures they created. The powers of the legislative branch, which are those of Congress, are listed in Article 1, Section 8, of the Constitution. Many of the executive powers belonging to the president are listed in Article 2, Sections 2 and 3. The courts are given judicial powers in Article 3. The words of Article 4 imply that the states retain authority over many public matters.

4. Limit Government Powers

The fourth purpose of the framers was to limit the powers of the structures they created. Limits on the Congress's powers are found in Article 1, Section 9. Some of the limits on the powers of state governments are found in Article 1, Section 10. There the framers enumerate functions that are delegated to the national government and so cannot be directed by the states.

5. Allow for Change

The framers' fifth purpose was to include some means for changing the Constitution. Here they faced a dilemma: they wanted to make certain that the government endured by changing with the times, but they did not want to expose the basic rules of government to so many changes that the system would be unstable. So in Article 5 they created a difficult but not impossible means for amending the Constitution.

RESEARCH LINKS CLASSZONE.COM

Visit the Constitution links for more information.

CONSTITUTION PROJECT

RESEARCHING A CONSTITUTIONAL QUESTION

As you study the Constitution, think about a constitutional question that interests you. Here are some possible questions:

- How much, if at all, can the federal government or a state government restrict the sale of firearms?
- Under what conditions does the president have the power to order American troops into battle without congressional approval?
- Under what conditions may a police officer conduct a search of the inside of an automobile?

Once you have chosen a constitutional question, research that question in articles and books on the Constitution. Also check the indexes of well-known newspapers, such as the *New York Times*, for articles that are relevant.

How to Read the Constitution

The Constitution, which appears on pages 84–103, is printed on a beige background, while the explanatory notes next to each article, section, or clause are printed on blue. Each article is divided into sections, and the sections are subdivided into clauses. Headings have been added and the spelling and punctuation modernized for easier reading. Portions of the Constitution no longer in use have been crossed out. The Constitutional Insight questions and answers will help you understand significant issues related to the Constitution.

The Constitution

PREAMBLE. *Purpose of the Constitution*

We the people of the United States, in order to form a more perfect Union, establish justice, insure domestic tranquility, provide for the common defense, promote the general welfare, and secure the blessings of liberty to ourselves and our posterity, do ordain and establish this Constitution for the United States of America.

ARTICLE 1. *The Legislature*

SECTION 1. CONGRESS All legislative powers herein granted shall be vested in a Congress of the United States, which shall consist of a Senate and House of Representatives.

SECTION 2. THE HOUSE OF REPRESENTATIVES

1. **ELECTIONS** The House of Representatives shall be composed of members chosen every second year by the people of the several states, and the electors in each state shall have the qualifications requisite for electors of the most numerous branch of the state legislature.

2. **QUALIFICATIONS** No person shall be a Representative who shall not have attained to the age of twenty-five years, and been seven years a citizen of the United States, and who shall not, when elected, be an inhabitant of that state in which he shall be chosen.

3. **NUMBER OF REPRESENTATIVES** Representatives ~~and direct taxes~~ shall be apportioned among the several states which may be included within this Union, according to their respective numbers, ~~which shall be determined by adding to the whole number of free persons, including those bound to service for a term of years, and excluding Indians not taxed, three fifths of all other persons.~~ The actual enumeration shall be made within three years after the first meeting of the Congress of the United States, and within every subsequent term of ten years, in such manner as they shall by law direct. The number of Representatives shall not exceed one for every thirty thousand, but each state shall have at least one Representative; ~~and until such enumeration shall be made, the state of New Hampshire shall be entitled to choose three, Massachusetts eight, Rhode Island and Providence Plantations one, Connecticut five, New York six, New Jersey four, Pennsylvania eight, Delaware one, Maryland six, Virginia ten, North Carolina five, South Carolina five, and Georgia three.~~

4. **VACANCIES** When vacancies happen in the representation from any state, the executive authority thereof shall issue writs of election to fill such vacancies.

5. **OFFICERS AND IMPEACHMENT** The House of Representatives shall choose their Speaker and other officers; and shall have the sole power of impeachment.

PREAMBLE

Constitutional Insight **Preamble**
Why does the Preamble say "We the people of the United States . . . ordain and establish" the new government? The Articles of Confederation was an agreement among the states. But the framers of the Constitution wanted to be sure its legitimacy came from the American people, not from the states, which might decide to withdraw their support at any time. This is a basic principle of the Constitution.

ARTICLE 1

Constitutional Insight **Section 1**
Why does the first article of the Constitution focus on Congress rather than on the presidency or the courts? The framers were intent on stressing the central role of the legislative branch in the new government because it is the branch that most directly represents the people and is most responsive to them.

A CRITICAL THINKING
Do you think Congress is still the branch of the federal government that is most directly responsible to the people? Why or why not?

Constitutional Insight **Section 2.1**
Why are members of the House of Representatives elected every two years? The House of Representatives was designed to be a truly representative body, with members who reflect the concerns and sentiments of their constituents as closely as possible. The framers achieved this timely representation by establishing two years as a reasonable term for members of the House to serve.

B CRITICAL THINKING
Do you think electing members of the House of Representatives every two years is a good idea? Why or why not?

Requirements for Holding Federal Office

POSITION	MINIMUM AGE	RESIDENCY	CITIZENSHIP
Representative	25	state in which elected	7 years
Senator	30	state in which elected	9 years
President	35	14 years in the United States	natural-born
Supreme Court Justice	none	none	none

SECTION 3. THE SENATE

1. **NUMBERS** The Senate of the United States shall be composed of two Senators from each state, ~~chosen by the legislature thereof,~~ for six years; and each Senator shall have one vote.

2. **CLASSIFYING TERMS** Immediately after they shall be assembled in consequence of the first election, they shall be divided as equally as may be into three classes. The seats of the Senators of the first class shall be vacated at the expiration of the second year, of the second class at the expiration of the fourth year, and of the third class at the expiration of the sixth year, so that one third may be chosen every second year; ~~and if vacancies happen by resignation, or otherwise, during the recess of the legislature of any state, the executive thereof may make temporary appointments until the next meeting of the legislature, which shall then fill such vacancies.~~

3. **Qualifications** No person shall be a Senator who shall not have attained to the age of thirty years, and been nine years a citizen of the United States, and who shall not, when elected, be an inhabitant of that state for which he shall be chosen.

4. **ROLE OF VICE-PRESIDENT** The Vice-President of the United States shall be President of the Senate, but shall have no vote, unless they be equally divided.

5. **OFFICERS** The Senate shall choose their other officers, and also a President pro tempore, in the absence of the Vice-President, or when he shall exercise the office of President of the United States.

6. **IMPEACHMENT TRIALS** The Senate shall have the sole power to try all impeachments. When sitting for that purpose, they shall be on oath or affirmation. When the President of the United States is tried, the Chief Justice shall preside: and no person shall be convicted without the concurrence of two thirds of the members present.

7. **PUNISHMENT FOR IMPEACHMENT** Judgment in cases of impeachment shall not extend further than to removal from office, and disqualification to hold and enjoy any office of honor, trust or profit under the United States; but the party convicted shall nevertheless be liable and subject to indictment, trial, judgment and punishment, according to law.

SECTION 4. CONGRESSIONAL ELECTIONS

1. **REGULATIONS** The times, places and manner of holding elections for Senators and Representatives shall be prescribed in each state by the legislature thereof; but the Congress may at any time by law make or alter such regulations, except as to the places of choosing Senators.

2. **SESSIONS** The Congress shall assemble at least once in every year, ~~and such meeting shall be on the first Monday in December, unless they shall by law appoint a different day.~~

Constitutional Insight **Section 3.1** *Why are members of the Senate elected every six years?* The framers feared the possibility of instability in the government. So they decided that senators should have six-year terms and be elected by the state legislatures rather than directly by the people. The Seventeenth Amendment, as you will see later, changed this. The framers also staggered the terms of the senators so that only one-third of them are replaced at any one time. This stabilizes the Senate still further.

C CRITICAL THINKING

Do you think it is important today for the Senate to have more stability than the House of Representatives? If so, why?

Constitutional Insight **Sections 3.6 and 3.7** *Must an impeached president step down from office?* Not necessarily. An impeachment is the equivalent of a formal accusation of criminal behavor or serious misbehavior. By impeaching the president, the U.S. House of Representatives is officially accusing the nation's chief executive of one or more wrongdoings that warrant possible removal from office. It is then the responsibility of the Senate to conduct a trial to determine whether the president is guilty or not guilty of the charges—and thus whether or not the president must step down. Conviction requires a two-thirds vote of the Senate.

D CRITICAL THINKING

Do you think a president should be put on trial for a crime while he or she is still in office? Explain.

Section 5. Rules and Procedures

1. Quorum Each house shall be the judge of the elections, returns and qualifications of its own members, and a majority of each shall constitute a quorum to do business; but a smaller number may adjourn from day to day, and may be authorized to compel the attendance of absent members, in such manner, and under such penalties, as each house may provide.

2. Rules and Conduct Each house may determine the rules of its proceedings, punish its members for disorderly behavior, and, with the concurrence of two thirds, expel a member.

3. Congressional Records Each house shall keep a journal of its proceedings, and from time to time publish the same, excepting such parts as may in their judgment require secrecy; and the yeas and nays of the members of either house on any question shall, at the desire of one fifth of those present, be entered on the journal.

4. Adjournment Neither house, during the session of Congress, shall, without the consent of the other, adjourn for more than three days, nor to any other place than that in which the two houses shall be sitting.

Section 6. Payment and Privileges

1. Salary The Senators and Representatives shall receive a compensation for their services, to be ascertained by law, and paid out of the treasury of the United States. They shall in all cases, except treason, felony and breach of the peace, be privileged from arrest during their attendance at the session of their respective houses, and in going to and returning from the same; and for any speech or debate in either house, they shall not be questioned in any other place.

2. Restrictions No Senator or Representative shall, during the time for which he was elected, be appointed to any civil office under the authority of the United States, which shall have been created, or the emoluments whereof shall have been increased, during such time; and no person holding any office under the United States shall be a member of either house during his continuance in office.

Section 7. How a Bill Becomes a Law

1. Tax Bills All bills for raising revenue shall originate in the House of Representatives; but the Senate may propose or concur with amendments as on other bills.

2. Lawmaking Process Every bill which shall have passed the House of Representatives and the Senate shall, before it become a law, be presented to the President of the United States; if he approves he shall sign it, but if not he shall return it with his objections to that house in which it shall have originated, who shall enter the objections at large on their journal, and proceed to reconsider it. If after such reconsideration two thirds of that house shall agree to pass the bill, it shall be sent, together with the objections, to the other house, by which it shall likewise be reconsidered, and if approved by two thirds of that house, it shall become a law. But in all such

Constitutional Insight **Section 5.2**
What kinds of rules does Congress make for itself? The Constitution gives each house control over most of its rules of procedure and membership. Rules are important, for they help shape the kinds of laws and policies that pass each body. Senate rules allow a filibuster, whereby a senator holds the floor as long as he or she likes in order to block consideration of a bill he or she dislikes. In recent years, a "cloture" rule has been used to end debate if 60 or more members vote to do so.

In contrast, the House of Representatives has rules to limit debate. A rules committee has the primary task of determining how long a bill on the floor of the House may be discussed and whether any amendments can be offered to the bill. In recent years, the power of the Rules Committee has been limited, but being able to shape the rules remains a powerful tool of members of Congress.

E CRITICAL THINKING
Why do you think the chair of the Rules Committee is in a powerful position?

Constitutional Insight **Section 7.1**
Why must all bills to raise revenue originate in the House? Because its members all stand for election every two years, the House was expected to be more directly responsive to the people. The tradition of restricting the powers of taxation to the people's representatives dates prior to the English Bill of Rights (1689), which granted to Parliament and withheld from the king the right to raise taxes. When colonists protesting the Stamp Act and the Intolerable Acts protested "no taxation without representation," they were appealing to a longstanding right codified in the English Bill of Rights.

Constitutional Insight **Section 7.2**
How often do presidents use the veto, and how often is that action overridden? The use of the veto, which is the refusal to approve a bill, depends on many factors, especially the political conditions of the time. Until 1865, only nine presidents exercised the veto for 36 pieces of legislation, including Andrew Jackson who used it 12 times. Since 1865, every president has used the veto power, some on relatively few occasions, others as frequently as over a hundred times. Usually, Congress is unable to produce the votes (those of two-thirds of the members present in each house) needed to override presidential vetoes.

F CRITICAL THINKING
Do you think it should be easier for Congress to override a president's veto? Why or why not?

cases the votes of both houses shall be determined by yeas and nays, and the names of the persons voting for and against the bill shall be entered on the journal of each house respectively. If any bill shall not be returned by the President within ten days (Sundays excepted) after it shall have been presented to him, the same shall be a law, in like manner as if he had signed it, unless the Congress by their adjournment prevent its return, in which case it shall not be a law.

3. **ROLE OF THE PRESIDENT** Every order, resolution, or vote to which the concurrence of the Senate and House of Representatives may be necessary (except on a question of adjournment) shall be presented to the President of the United States; and before the same shall take effect, shall be approved by him, or being disapproved by him, shall be repassed by two thirds of the Senate and House of Representatives, according to the rules and limitations prescribed in the case of a bill.

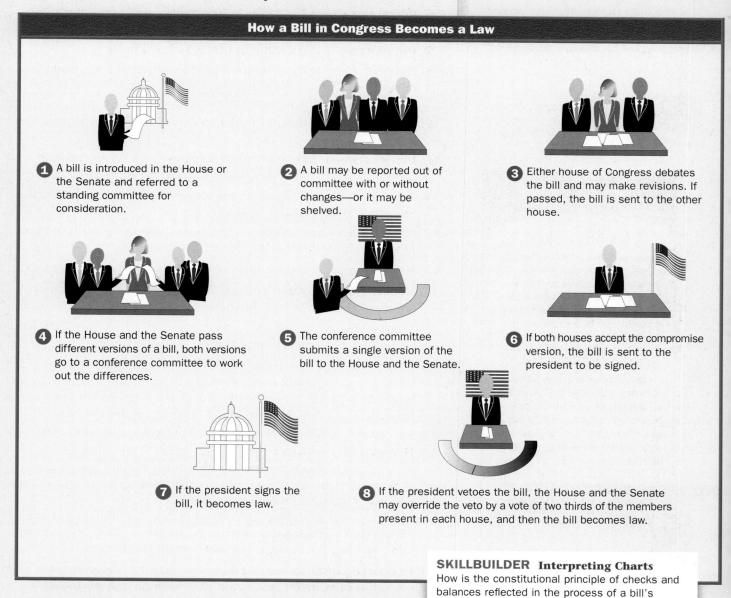

How a Bill in Congress Becomes a Law

1. A bill is introduced in the House or the Senate and referred to a standing committee for consideration.

2. A bill may be reported out of committee with or without changes—or it may be shelved.

3. Either house of Congress debates the bill and may make revisions. If passed, the bill is sent to the other house.

4. If the House and the Senate pass different versions of a bill, both versions go to a conference committee to work out the differences.

5. The conference committee submits a single version of the bill to the House and the Senate.

6. If both houses accept the compromise version, the bill is sent to the president to be signed.

7. If the president signs the bill, it becomes law.

8. If the president vetoes the bill, the House and the Senate may override the veto by a vote of two thirds of the members present in each house, and then the bill becomes law.

SKILLBUILDER Interpreting Charts
How is the constitutional principle of checks and balances reflected in the process of a bill's becoming a law?

Constitutional Insight **Section 8** The powers given to Congress are in Section 8 of Article 1. The first 17 clauses of Section 8 are often called the enumerated powers because they name individually Congress's specific powers. These powers deal with issues ranging from taxation and the national debt to calling out the armed forces of the various states to governing the nation's capital district (Washington, D.C.).

The 18th and final clause is different. It gives Congress the power to do what is "necessary and proper" to carry out the enumurated powers. Thus, the enumerated powers of Congress "to lay and collect taxes," "to borrow money," "to regulate commerce," and "to coin money" imply the power to create a bank in order to execute these powers. Early in the country's history, this elastic clause, as it has been called, was used by Congress to establish the controversial Bank of the United States in 1791 and the Second Bank of the United States in 1816.

G CRITICAL THINKING
Why do you think the elastic clause is still important today?

MODERN MONEY

Because of frequent counterfeiting of U.S. currency, a new design was released for the $100 bill in 1996 and the $50 bill in 1997. To make these bills more difficult to counterfeit, the new design included enlarged, off-center portraits of Benjamin Franklin and Ulysses S. Grant, a security thread, fine-line printing patterns, color-shifting ink, and a watermark to the right of each portrait. Since then, a $20 bill was introduced in 1998, and a $10 and $5 bill were introduced in 2000.

SECTION 8. POWERS GRANTED TO CONGRESS

1. TAXATION The Congress shall have power to lay and collect taxes, duties, imposts and excises, to pay the debts and provide for the common defense and general welfare of the United States; but all duties, imposts and excises shall be uniform throughout the United States;

2. CREDIT To borrow money on the credit of the United States;

3. COMMERCE To regulate commerce with foreign nations, and among the several states, and with the Indian tribes;

4. NATURALIZATION, BANKRUPTCY To establish a uniform rule of naturalization, and uniform laws on the subject of bankruptcies throughout the United States;

5. MONEY To coin money, regulate the value thereof, and of foreign coin, and fix the standard of weights and measures;

6. COUNTERFEITING To provide for the punishment of counterfeiting the securities and current coin of the United States;

7. POST OFFICE To establish post offices and post roads;

8. PATENTS, COPYRIGHTS To promote the progress of science and useful arts, by securing for limited times to authors and inventors the exclusive right to their respective writings and discoveries;

9. FEDERAL COURTS To constitute tribunals inferior to the Supreme Court;

10. INTERNATIONAL LAW To define and punish piracies and felonies committed on the high seas, and offenses against the law of nations;

11. WAR To declare war, grant letters of marque and reprisal, and make rules concerning captures on land and water;

12. ARMY To raise and support armies, but no appropriation of money to that use shall be for a longer term than two years;

13. NAVY To provide and maintain a navy;

14. REGULATION OF ARMED FORCES To make rules for the government and regulation of the land and naval forces;

15. MILITIA To provide for calling forth the militia to execute the laws of the Union, suppress insurrections and repel invasions;

16. REGULATIONS FOR MILITIA To provide for organizing, arming, and disciplining the militia, and for governing such part of them as may be employed in the service of the United States, reserving to the states respectively the appointment of the officers, and the authority of training the militia according to the discipline prescribed by Congress;

17. DISTRICT OF COLUMBIA To exercise exclusive legislation in all cases whatsoever, over such district (not exceeding ten miles square) as may, by cession of particular states, and the acceptance of Congress, become the seat of the government of the United States, and to exercise like authority over all places purchased by the consent of the legislature of the state in which the same shall be, for the erection of forts, magazines, arsenals, dockyards, and other needful buildings;—and

18. ELASTIC CLAUSE To make all laws which shall be necessary and proper for carrying into execution the foregoing powers, and all other powers vested by this Constitution in the government of the United States, or in any department or officer thereof.

Section 9. Powers Denied Congress

~~**1. Slave Trade** The migration or importation of such persons as any of the states now existing shall think proper to admit, shall not be prohibited by the Congress prior to the year one thousand eight hundred and eight, but a tax or duty may be imposed on such importation, not exceeding ten dollars for each person.~~

2. Habeas Corpus The privilege of the writ of habeas corpus shall not be suspended, unless when in cases of rebellion or invasion the public safety may require it.

3. Illegal Punishment No bill of attainder or ex post facto law shall be passed.

4. Direct Taxes No capitation, ~~or other direct, tax~~ shall be laid, ~~unless in proportion to the census or enumeration herein before directed to be taken.~~

5. Export Taxes No tax or duty shall be laid on articles exported from any state.

6. No Favorites No preference shall be given by any regulation of commerce or revenue to the ports of one state over those of another: nor shall vessels bound to, or from, one state be obliged to enter, clear, or pay duties in another.

7. Public Money No money shall be drawn from the treasury, but in consequence of appropriations made by law; and a regular statement and account of the receipts and expenditures of all public money shall be published from time to time.

8. Titles of Nobility No title of nobility shall be granted by the United States: and no person holding any office of profit or trust under them shall, without the consent of the Congress, accept of any present, emolument, office, or title, of any kind whatever, from any king, prince, or foreign state.

Section 10. Powers Denied the States

1. Restrictions No state shall enter into any treaty, alliance, or confederation; grant letters of marque and reprisal; coin money; emit bills of credit; make anything but gold and silver coin a tender in payment of debts; pass any bill of attainder, ex post facto law, or law impairing the obligation of contracts, or grant any title of nobility.

2. Import and Export Taxes No state shall, without the consent of the Congress, lay any imposts or duties on imports or exports, except what may be absolutely necessary for executing its inspection laws; and the net produce of all duties and imposts, laid by any state on imports or exports, shall be for the use of the treasury of the United States; and all such laws shall be subject to the revision and control of the Congress.

Constitutional Insight Section 9

Why didn't the framers include a bill of rights in the original Constitution? Actually, they did. Article 1, Section 9, defines limits on the powers of Congress, just as the first ten amendments (which we call the Bill of Rights) do. While some of the provisions focus on such issues as slavery and taxation, there are three explicit prohibitions dealing with citizens' rights:

- *Writ of habeas corpus.* Section 9, Clause 2 says that, except in time of rebellion or invasion, Congress cannot suspend people's right to a writ of habeas corpus. This means that people cannot be held in prison or jail without being formally charged with a crime.
- *Bill of attainder.* Clause 3 prohibits the passage of any law that convicts or punishes a person directly and without a trial. Any legislative action that would punish someone without recourse to a court of law is called a bill of attainder.
- *Ex post facto law.* The same clause prohibits ex post facto laws. Such a law would punish a person for an act that was legal when it was performed.

The fact that these particular rights were protected by the original document issued by the framers reflects both the framers' experiences during the Revolution and their fear of excessive government power.

H CRITICAL THINKING

Why are American citizens today so intent on having protections against government violations of their rights?

3. **Peacetime and War Restraints** No state shall, without the consent of Congress, lay any duty of tonnage, keep troops or ships of war in time of peace, enter into any agreement or compact with another state, or with a foreign power, or engage in war, unless actually invaded, or in such imminent danger as will not admit of delay.

ARTICLE 2. *The Executive*

ARTICLE 2

Constitutional Insight **Section 1.1**

What exactly is "executive power"? We know the president has it, but nowhere is it explicitly defined. It is most often defined as the power to carry out the laws of the land, but of course no one person can handle such a chore alone. A more appropriate definition is found in Section 3 of this article, which empowers the president to "take care that the laws be faithfully executed." In this sense, the president is the chief administrator.

I CRITICAL THINKING

Why is it important to have an executive who is the chief administrator?

Section 1. The Presidency

1. **Terms of Office** The executive power shall be vested in a President of the United States of America. He shall hold his office during the term of four years and, together with the Vice-President, chosen for the same term, be elected as follows:

2. **Electoral College** Each state shall appoint, in such manner as the legislature thereof may direct, a number of electors, equal to the whole number of Senators and Representatives to which the state may be entitled in the Congress; but no Senator or Representative, or person holding an office of trust or profit under the United States, shall be appointed an elector.

3. ~~**Former Method of Electing President** The electors shall meet in their respective states, and vote by ballot for two persons, of whom one at least shall not be an inhabitant of the same state with themselves. And they shall make a list of all the persons voted for, and of the number of votes for each; which list they shall sign and certify, and transmit sealed to the seat of the government of the United States, directed to the President of the Senate. The President of the Senate shall, in the presence of the Senate and House of Representatives, open all the certificates, and the votes shall then be counted. The person having the greatest number of votes shall be the President, if such number be a majority of the whole number of electors appointed; and if there be more than one who have such majority, and have an equal number of votes, then the House of Representatives shall immediately choose by ballot one of them for President; and if no person have a majority, then from the five highest on the list the said house shall in like manner choose the President. But in choosing the President, the votes shall be taken by states, the representation from each state having one vote; a quorum for this purpose shall consist of a member or members from two thirds of the states, and a majority of all the states shall be necessary to a choice. In every case, after the choice of the President, the person having the greatest number of votes of the electors shall be the Vice-President. But if there should remain two or more who have equal votes, the Senate shall choose from them by ballot the Vice-President.~~

4. **Election Day** The Congress may determine the time of choosing the electors, and the day on which they shall give their votes; which day shall be the same throughout the United States.

5. **Qualifications** No person except a natural-born citizen, ~~or a citizen of the United States at the time of the adoption of this Constitution,~~ shall be eligible to the office of President; neither shall any person be eligible to that office who shall not have attained to the age of thirty-five years, and been fourteen years a resident within the United States.

6. **Succession** In case of the removal of the President from office, or of his death, resignation, or inability to discharge the powers and duties of the said office, the same shall devolve on the Vice-President, and the Congress may by law provide for the case of removal, death, resignation, or inability, both of the President and Vice-President, declaring what officer shall then act as President, and such officer shall act accordingly, until the disability be removed, or a President shall be elected.

7. **Salary** The President shall, at stated times, receive for his services a compensation, which shall neither be increased nor diminished during the period for which he shall have been elected, and he shall not receive within that period any other emolument from the United States, or any of them.

8. **Oath of Office** Before he enter on the execution of his office, he shall take the following oath or affirmation:—"I do solemnly swear (or affirm) that I will faithfully execute the office of President of the United States, and will to the best of my ability, preserve, protect and defend the Constitution of the United States."

Section 2. Powers of the President

1. **Military Powers** The President shall be commander in chief of the army and navy of the United States, and of the militia of the several states, when called into the actual service of the United States; he may require the opinion, in writing, of the principal officer in each of the executive departments, upon any subject relating to the duties of their respective offices, and he shall have power to grant reprieves and pardons for offenses against the United States, except in cases of impeachment.

2. **Treaties, Appointments** He shall have power, by and with the advice and consent of the Senate, to make treaties, provided two thirds of the Senators present concur; and he shall nominate, and by and with the advice and consent of the Senate, shall appoint ambassadors, other public ministers and consuls, judges of the Supreme Court, and all other officers of the United States, whose appointments are not herein otherwise provided for, and which shall be established by law; but the Congress may by law vest the appointment of such inferior officers, as they think proper, in the President alone, in the courts of law, or in the heads of departments.

3. **Vacancies** The President shall have power to fill up all vacancies that may happen during the recess of the Senate, by granting commissions which shall expire at the end of their next session.

Constitutional Insight **Section 1.6**
What happens when the vice-president succeeds a dead or incapacitated president? Section 1.6 provides that the vice-president shall assume the powers and duties of the presidential office. But until the Twenty-fifth Amendment was added to the Constitution in 1967, there was no explicit statement in the document that the vice-president is to become president. That procedure owes its origin to John Tyler, the tenth president of the United States, who in 1841 succeeded William Henry Harrison—the first president to die in office. Tyler decided to take the oath of office and assume the title of president of the United States. Congress voted to go along with his decision, and the practice was repeated after Lincoln was assassinated. It would take another century for the written provisions of the Constitution to catch up with the practice.

J CRITICAL THINKING
Why is it important to know the order of succession if a president dies in office?

Constitutional Insight **Section 2.1**
Just how much authority does the president have as "commander in chief" of the armed forces? The president has the power to give orders to American military forces. There have been several instances in U.S. history when presidents have used that authority in spite of congressional wishes.

President Harry Truman involved the armed forces of the United States in the Korean War from 1950 to 1953 without a congressional declaration of war.

Reacting to criticism of the Vietnam War, Congress in 1973 enacted the War Powers Resolution, making the president more accountable to Congress for any military actions he or she might take. Every president since Richard Nixon has called the resolution unconstitutional. Nevertheless, every president has reported to Congress within 48 hours of sending troops into an international crisis, as is required by the War Powers Resolution.

K CRITICAL THINKING
Why is it important that the commander in chief of the armed forces of the United States be a civilian (the president) rather than a military general?

Constitutional Insight **Section 3**
Is it necessary for the president to deliver a State of the Union address before a joint session of Congress at the start of each legislative year? The Constitution requires only that the president report to Congress on the state of the Union from time to time, and nowhere does it call for an annual address. In 1913, President Woodrow Wilson wanted to influence Congress to take action without delay on some legislation that he thought was important. Wilson revived the tradition—which had been discontinued by Jefferson—of delivering the State of the Union address in person.

L CRITICAL THINKING
How does the president use the State of the Union address today?

Constitutional Insight **Section 4**
Have high-level public officials ever been impeached? In all of American history, the House has impeached two presidents, and neither had to leave office. In 1868, the Senate found President Andrew Johnson not guilty by one vote after the House impeached him, charging him with violating a Congressional Act. In 1999, senators acquitted President Bill Clinton after the House impeached him with charges of lying under oath and obstructing justice in the attempted cover-up of a White House scandal.

The only other president to come close to impeachment was Richard Nixon. In 1974, the House Judiciary Committee, in what is the first step of the impeachment process, recommended three articles of impeachment against Nixon for his role in the infamous Watergate scandal. Before the full House could vote for or against the articles of impeachment, however, Nixon resigned from office.

M CRITICAL THINKING
Why do you think the framers of the Constitution created such an elaborate and seemingly difficult procedure for removing a sitting president?

SECTION 3. PRESIDENTIAL DUTIES He shall from time to time give to the Congress information of the state of the Union, and recommend to their consideration such measures as he shall judge necessary and expedient; he may, on extraordinary occasions, convene both houses, or either of them, and in case of disagreement between them, with respect to the time of adjournment, he may adjourn them to such time as he shall think proper; he shall receive ambassadors and other public ministers; he shall take care that the laws be faithfully executed, and shall commission all the officers of the United States.

SECTION 4. IMPEACHMENT The President, Vice-President and all civil officers of the United States shall be removed from office on impeachment for, and conviction of, treason, bribery, or other high crimes and misdemeanors.

(above) **Rep. Henry Hyde, chairman of the House Judiciary Committee, swears in Independent Counsel Kenneth Starr during the Committee's hearings on impeachment charges against President Bill Clinton in 1998; *(right)* President Andrew Johnson is handed the articles of impeachment before his trial in 1868.**

ARTICLE 3. *The Judiciary*

SECTION 1. FEDERAL COURTS AND JUDGES The judicial power of the United States shall be vested in one Supreme Court, and in such inferior courts as the Congress may from time to time ordain and establish. The judges, both of the Supreme and inferior courts, shall hold their offices during good behavior, and shall, at stated times, receive for their services a compensation, which shall not be diminished during their continuance in office.

Section 2. The Courts' Authority

1. **General Authority** The judicial power shall extend to all cases, in law and equity, arising under this Constitution, the laws of the United States, and treaties made, or which shall be made, under their authority;—to all cases affecting ambassadors, other public ministers and consuls;—to all cases of admiralty and maritime jurisdiction;—to controversies to which the United States shall be a party;—to controversies between two or more states;~~—between a state and citizens of another state;—~~between citizens of different states;—between citizens of the same state claiming lands under grants of different states, ~~and between a state, or the citizens thereof, and foreign states, citizens or subjects.~~

2. **Supreme Court** In all cases affecting ambassadors, other public ministers and consuls, and those in which a state shall be party, the Supreme Court shall have original jurisdiction. In all the other cases before mentioned, the Supreme Court shall have appellate jurisdiction, both as to law and fact, with such exceptions, and under such regulations, as the Congress shall make.

3. **Trial by Jury** The trial of all crimes, except in cases of impeachment, shall be by jury; and such trial shall be held in the state where the said crimes shall have been committed; but when not committed within any state, the trial shall be at such place or places as the Congress may by law have directed.

Section 3. Treason

1. **Definition** Treason against the United States shall consist only in levying war against them, or in adhering to their enemies, giving them aid and comfort. No person shall be convicted of treason unless on the testimony of two witnesses to the same overt act, or on confession in open court.

2. **Punishment** The Congress shall have power to declare the punishment of treason, but no attainder of treason shall work corruption of blood, or forfeiture except during the life of the person attainted.

ARTICLE 3

Constitutional Insight **Section 2.1**
What is judicial review? Is it the same as judicial power? Actually, they are not the same. Judicial power is the authority to hear cases involving disputes over the law or the behavior of people. Judicial review, in contrast, is a court's passing judgment on the constitutionality of a law or government action that is being disputed. Interestingly, nowhere does the Constitution mention judicial review. There are places where it is implied (for example, in Section 2 of Article 6), but the only explicit description of the responsibility of the courts is the reference to judicial power in Section 1 of Article 3. The Supreme Court's power to review laws passed by Congress was explicitly affirmed by the Court itself in *Marbury* v. *Madison*. (See page 118.)

N CRITICAL THINKING
Why is judicial review, although not mentioned in the Constitution, an important activity of the Supreme Court?

The Supreme Court of the United States as of 2001. In the front row (*left to right*) are Associate Justices Antonin Scalia and John Paul Stevens, Chief Justice William H. Rehnquist, and Associate Justices Sandra Day O'Connor and Anthony Kennedy. In the back row are Associate Justices Ruth Bader Ginsburg, David Souter, Clarence Thomas, and Stephen Breyer. ▼

ARTICLE 4. *Relations Among States*

SECTION 1. STATE ACTS AND RECORDS Full faith and credit shall be given in each state to the public acts, records, and judicial proceedings of every other state. And the Congress may by general laws prescribe the manner in which such acts, records, and proceedings shall be proved, and the effect thereof.

SECTION 2. RIGHTS OF CITIZENS

1. **CITIZENSHIP** The citizens of each state shall be entitled to all privileges and immunities of citizens in the several states.
2. **EXTRADITION** A person charged in any state with treason, felony, or other crime, who shall flee from justice, and be found in another state, shall on demand of the executive authority of the state from which he fled, be delivered up, to be removed to the state having jurisdiction of the crime.
3. ~~**Fugitive Slaves** No person held to service or labor in one state, under the laws thereof, escaping into another, shall, in consequence of any law or regulation therein, be discharged from such service or labor, but shall be delivered up on claim of the party to whom such service or labor may be due.~~

SECTION 3. NEW STATES

1. **ADMISSION** New states may be admitted by the Congress into this Union; but no new state shall be formed or erected within the jurisdiction of any other state; nor any state be formed by the junction of two or more states, or parts of states, without the consent of the legislatures of the states concerned as well as of the Congress.
2. **CONGRESSIONAL AUTHORITY** The Congress shall have power to dispose of and make all needful rules and regulations respecting the territory or other property belonging to the United States; and nothing in this Constitution shall be so construed as to prejudice any claims of the United States, or of any particular state.

SECTION 4. GUARANTEES TO THE STATES The United States shall guarantee to every state in this Union a republican form of government, and shall protect each of them against invasion; and on application of the legislature, or of the executive (when the legislature cannot be convened), against domestic violence.

ARTICLE 5. *Amending the Constitution*

The Congress, whenever two thirds of both houses shall deem it necessary, shall propose amendments to this Constitution, or, on the application of the legislatures of two thirds of the several states, shall call a convention for proposing amendments, which, in either case, shall be valid to all intents and purposes, as part of this Constitution, when ratified by the legislatures of three fourths of the several states, or by conventions in three fourths thereof, as the one or the other mode of ratification may be proposed by the Congress; ~~provided that no amendment which may be made prior to the year one thousand eight hundred and eight shall in any manner affect the first and fourth clauses in the ninth section of the first article;~~ and that no state, without its consent, shall be deprived of its equal suffrage in the Senate.

ARTICLE 4

Constitutional Insight **Section 2.1**
Why do college students attending public universities outside their state of residence have to pay higher tuition fees?
The Supreme Court has interpreted the "privileges and immunities" clause to allow higher tuition fees (and fees for hunting permits, etc.) for nonresidents when a state can give a "substantial reason" for the difference. Since state colleges and universities receive some financial support from the states' taxpayers, the difference is regarded as justified in most states. If a student establishes residency in the state, he or she can pay in-state tuition after one year.

O CRITICAL THINKING
Do you think it is fair that a nonresident must pay higher tuition fees at a state college than a resident of the state must pay? Explain.

Constitutional Insight **Section 3.1**
Should there be a West Virginia? The Constitution states that "no new state shall be formed or erected within the jurisdiction of any other state" without the permission of the legislature of the state involved and of the Congress. Vermont, Kentucky, Tennessee, and Maine were created from territory taken from existing states, with the approval of the sitting legislatures.

West Virginia, however, is a different story. During the Civil War, the residents of the westernmost counties of Virginia were angry with their state's decision to secede from the Union. They petitioned Congress to have their counties declared a distinct state. Congress agreed, and so the state of West Virginia was created. After the Civil War, the legislature of Virginia gave its formal approval, perhaps because it was in no position to dispute the matter.

P CRITICAL THINKING
Suppose a section of Texas should decide to become a new state today. Could it do this? Why or why not?

ARTICLE 6. *Supremacy of the National Government*

SECTION 1. VALID DEBTS All debts contracted and engagements entered into, before the adoption of this Constitution, shall be as valid against the United States under this Constitution, as under the Confederation.

SECTION 2. SUPREME LAW This Constitution, and the laws of the United States which shall be made in pursuance thereof; and all treaties made, or which shall be made, under the authority of the United States, shall be the supreme law of the land; and the judges in every state shall be bound thereby, anything in the constitution or laws of any state to the contrary notwithstanding.

SECTION 3. LOYALTY TO CONSTITUTION The Senators and Representatives before mentioned, and the members of the several state legislatures, and all executive and judicial officers, both of the United States and of the several states, shall be bound by oath or affirmation to support this Constitution; but no religious test shall ever be required as a qualification to any office or public trust under the United States.

ARTICLE 7. *Ratification*

The ratification of the conventions of nine states shall be sufficient for the establishment of this Constitution between the states so ratifying the same. Done in convention by the unanimous consent of the states present, the seventeenth day of September in the year of our Lord one thousand seven hundred and eighty-seven and of the independence of the United States of America the twelfth. In witness whereof we have hereunto subscribed our names.

George Washington—President and deputy from Virginia

Delaware: *George Read, Gunning Bedford, Jr., John Dickinson, Richard Bassett, Jacob Broom*

Maryland: *James McHenry, Dan of St. Thomas Jenifer, Daniel Carroll*

Virginia: *John Blair, James Madison, Jr.*

North Carolina: *William Blount, Richard Dobbs Spaight, Hugh Williamson*

South Carolina: *John Rutledge, Charles Cotesworth Pinckney, Charles Pinckney, Pierce Butler*

Georgia: *William Few, Abraham Baldwin*

New Hampshire: *John Langdon, Nicholas Gilman*

Massachusetts: *Nathaniel Gorham, Rufus King*

Connecticut: *William Samuel Johnson, Roger Sherman*

New York: *Alexander Hamilton*

New Jersey: *William Livingston, David Brearley, William Paterson, Jonathan Dayton*

Pennsylvania: *Benjamin Franklin, Thomas Mifflin, Robert Morris, George Clymer, Thomas FitzSimons, Jared Ingersoll, James Wilson, Gouverneur Morris*

ARTICLE 6

Constitutional Insight **Section 2** *Just how "supreme" is the "law of the land"?* The Constitution and all federal laws and treaties are the highest law of the land. (To be supreme, Federal laws must be constitutional.) All state constitutions and laws and all local laws rank below national law and cannot be enforced if they contradict national law. For example, if the United States enters into a treaty protecting migratory Canadian birds, the states must change their laws to fit the provisions of that agreement. That was the decision of the Supreme Court in the case of *Missouri* v. *Holland* (1920). The state of Missouri argued that the national government could not interfere with its power to regulate hunting within its borders, but the Supreme Court concluded that the treaty was a valid exercise of national power and therefore took priority over state and local laws. The states had to adjust their rules and regulations accordingly.

Q CRITICAL THINKING

What would happen if the national law were not supreme?

ARTICLE 7

Constitutional Insight *Why was ratification by only 9 states sufficient to put the Constitution into effect?* In taking such a momentous step as replacing one constitution (the Articles of Confederation) with another, the framers might have been expected to require the agreement of all 13 states. But the framers were political realists. They knew that they would have a difficult time winning approval from all 13 states. But they also knew that they had a good chance of getting 9 or 10 of the states "on board" and that once that happened, the rest would follow. Their strategy worked, but just barely. Although they had the approval of 9 states by the end of June 1788, 2 of the most important states—Virginia and New York—had not yet decided to ratify. Without the approval of these influential states, the new government would have had a difficult time surviving. Finally, by the end of July, both had given their blessing to the new constitution, but not without intense debate.

And then there was the last holdout—Rhode Island. Not only had Rhode Island refused to send delegates to the Constitutional Convention in 1787, but it turned down ratification several times before finally giving its approval in 1790 under a cloud of economic and even military threats from neighboring states.

R CRITICAL THINKING

Do you think all 50 states would ratify the Constitution today? Why or why not?

The Bill of Rights

and Amendments 11–27

Amendments 1–10

Proposed by Congress September 25, 1789. Ratified December 15, 1791.

Amendment 1. Religious and Political Freedom (1791) Congress shall make no law respecting an establishment of religion, or prohibiting the free exercise thereof; or abridging the freedom of speech, or of the press; or the right of the people peaceably to assemble, and to petition the government for a redress of grievances.

Amendment 2. Right to Bear Arms (1791) A well-regulated militia being necessary to the security of a free state, the right of the people to keep and bear arms shall not be infringed.

Amendment 3. Quartering Troops (1791) No soldier shall, in time of peace, be quartered in any house without the consent of the owner, nor in time of war, but in a manner to be prescribed by law.

Amendment 4. Search and Seizure (1791) The right of the people to be secure in their persons, houses, papers, and effects, against unreasonable searches and seizures, shall not be violated, and no warrants shall issue, but upon probable cause, supported by oath or affirmation, and particularly describing the place to be searched, and the persons or things to be seized.

Amendment 5. Rights of Accused Persons (1791) No person shall be held to answer for a capital or otherwise infamous crime, unless on a presentment or indictment of a grand jury, except in cases arising in the land or naval forces, or in the militia, when in actual service in time of war or public danger; nor shall any person be subject for the same offense to be twice put in jeopardy of life or limb; nor shall be compelled in any criminal case to be a witness against himself, nor be deprived of life, liberty, or property, without due process of law; nor shall private property be taken for public use, without just compensation.

BILL OF RIGHTS

Constitutional Insight **Amendment 1**
Do Americans have an absolute right to free speech? The right to free speech is not without limits. In the case of *Schenck* v. *United States* (1919), Justice Oliver Wendell Holmes wrote that this right does "not protect a man in falsely shouting fire in a theatre and causing a panic." Thus, there are some forms of speech that are not protected by the First Amendment, and Congress is allowed to make laws regarding certain types of expression. (See *Schenck* v. *United States* on page 396.)

A CRITICAL THINKING
Why is there controversy over freedom of speech today?

Constitutional Insight **Amendment 4**
Can the police search your car without a court-issued search warrant when they stop you for speeding? The answer, according to Supreme Court decisions, depends on whether they have good reasons—called "probable cause"—for doing so. If a state trooper notices bloody clothing on the back seat of a vehicle she stops for a traffic violation, there might be probable cause for her to insist on searching the vehicle. There is probably not sufficient reason for a search if the trooper is merely suspicious of the driver because of the way he is acting. In such cases, the trooper may make a casual request, such as "Do you mind if I look inside your vehicle?" If the answer is no, then according to the Court, the driver has waived his or her constitutional right against unreasonable searches.

B CRITICAL THINKING
Why do you think the right against unreasonable searches and seizures is highly important to most people?

Constitutional Insight **Amendment 5**
Can you be tried twice for the same offense? The prohibition against "double jeopardy" protects you from having the same charge twice brought against you for the same offense, but you can be tried on different charges related to that offense.

C CRITICAL THINKING
What do you think could happen if a person could be tried twice for the same offense?

Analyzing *Political Cartoons*

"THE FEDERAL EDIFICE"

This 1788 cartoon celebrated the ratification of the Constitution by New York, the 11th state to ratify it. This left only North Carolina and Rhode Island to complete all 13 pillars of the federal structure.

SKILLBUILDER Analyzing Political Cartoons

1. What details in the cartoon convey the unity of the states who have voted for ratification?
2. How does the cartoonist contrast the states who have voted for ratification with those who have not? What message does this convey?

SEE SKILLBUILDER HANDBOOK, PAGE R24.

Amendment 6. Right to a Speedy, Public Trial (1791) In all criminal prosecutions, the accused shall enjoy the right to a speedy and public trial, by an impartial jury of the state and district wherein the crime shall have been committed, which district shall have been previously ascertained by law, and to be informed of the nature and cause of the accusation; to be confronted with the witnesses against him; to have compulsory process for obtaining witnesses in his favor, and to have the assistance of counsel for his defense.

Amendment 7. Trial by Jury in Civil Cases (1791) In suits at common law, where the value in controversy shall exceed twenty dollars, the right of trial by jury shall be preserved, and no fact tried by a jury shall be otherwise reexamined in any court of the United States, than according to the rules of the common law.

Amendment 8. Limits of Fines and Punishments (1791) Excessive bail shall not be required, nor excessive fines imposed, nor cruel and unusual punishments inflicted.

Amendment 9. Rights of People (1791) The enumeration in the Constitution, of certain rights, shall not be construed to deny or disparage others retained by the people.

Amendment 10. Powers of States and People (1791) The powers not delegated to the United States by the Constitution, nor prohibited by it to the states, are reserved to the states respectively, or to the people.

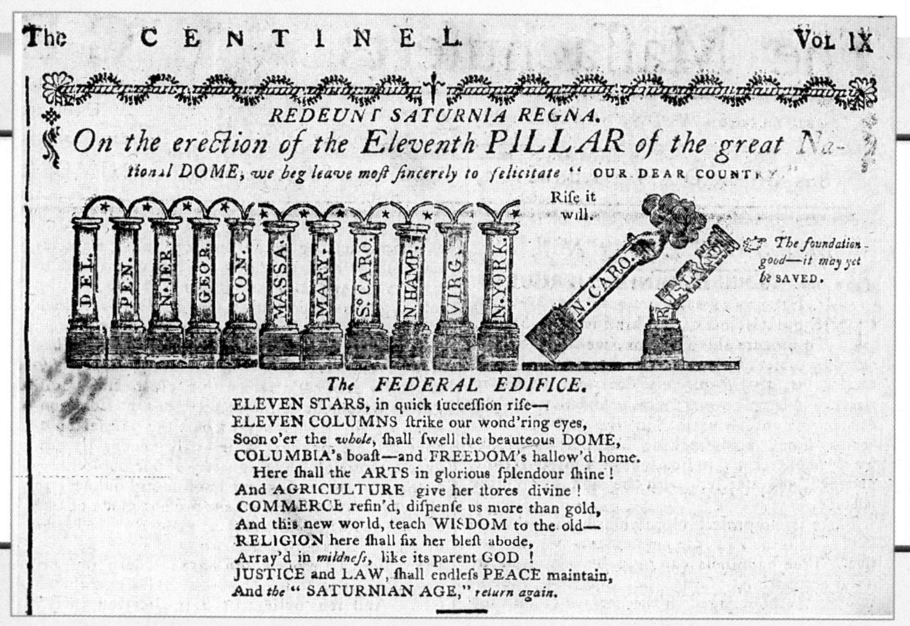

The CENTINEL. Vol IX

REDEUNT SATURNIA REGNA.

On the erection of the Eleventh PILLAR of the great National DOME, we beg leave most sincerely to felicitate "OUR DEAR COUNTRY."

The FEDERAL EDIFICE.

ELEVEN STARS, in quick succession rise—
ELEVEN COLUMNS strike our wond'ring eyes,
Soon o'er the *whole*, shall swell the beauteous DOME,
COLUMBIA's boast—and FREEDOM's hallow'd home.
Here shall the ARTS in glorious splendour shine!
And AGRICULTURE give her stores divine!
COMMERCE refin'd, dispense us more than gold,
And this new world, teach WISDOM to the old—
RELIGION here shall fix her blest abode,
Array'd in *mildness*, like its parent GOD!
JUSTICE and LAW, shall endless PEACE maintain,
And *the* "SATURNIAN AGE," *return again.*

Constitutional Insight **Amendment 6**
What are the Miranda rights? The term comes from the Supreme Court's decision in *Miranda* v. *Arizona* (1966), in which the justices established basic rules that the police must follow when questioning a suspect. If suspected of a crime, you must be told that you have a right to remain silent and that anything you say "can and will" be used against you. You also need to be informed that you have a right to an attorney and that the attorney may be present during questioning. (See *Miranda* v. *Arizona* on page 694.)

D CRITICAL THINKING
How do the Miranda rights protect you?

Constitutional Insight **Amendment 7**
What are the "rules of the common law"? The common law is the body of legal practices and decrees developed in England and English-speaking America from A.D. 1066 through the present. It includes Magna Carta (1215), which acknowledges versions of rights affirmed in the Fifth, Sixth, and Seventh Amendments, as well as the English Bill of Rights (1689), which codified rights asserted in the First, Second, Seventh, and Eighth Amendments. The common law also includes the decisions and published opinions of state and federal appeals courts, including the U.S. Supreme Court.

Constitutional Insight **Amendment 9**
Do you have a right to privacy? Until 1965, no such right had ever been explicitly stated by the courts. That year, in the case of *Griswold* v. *Connecticut*, the Court said there is an implied right of American citizens to make certain personal choices without interference from the government; this case concerned the right to use birth control. Years later, in *Roe* v. *Wade* (1973), the same logic was used to declare unconstitutional a Texas law restricting a woman's right to an abortion in the first stages of pregnancy. Since that decision, both the right to privacy and abortion rights have become the focus of major political controversies.

E CRITICAL THINKING
How do you define the right to privacy?

Amendments 11–27

AMENDMENT 11. LAWSUITS AGAINST STATES (1795) Passed by Congress March 4, 1794. Ratified February 7, 1795.

Note: Article 3, Section 2, of the Constitution was modified by the Eleventh Amendment.

The Judicial power of the United States shall not be construed to extend to any suit in law or equity, commenced or prosecuted against one of the United States by citizens of another state, or by citizens or subjects of any foreign state.

AMENDMENT 12. ELECTION OF EXECUTIVES (1804) Passed by Congress December 9, 1803. Ratified June 15, 1804.

Note: A portion of Article 2, Section 1, of the Constitution was superseded by the Twelfth Amendment.

The electors shall meet in their respective states and vote by ballot for President and Vice-President, one of whom, at least, shall not be an inhabitant of the same state with themselves; they shall name in their ballots the person voted for as President, and in distinct ballots the person voted for as Vice-President, and they shall make distinct lists of all persons voted for as President, and of all persons voted for as Vice-President, and of the number of votes for each, which lists they shall sign and certify, and transmit sealed to the seat of the government of the United States, directed to the President of the Senate;—the President of the Senate shall, in the presence of the Senate and House of Representatives, open all the certificates and the votes shall then be counted;—the person having the greatest number of votes for President shall be the President, if such number be a majority of the whole number of electors appointed; and if no person have such majority, then from the persons having the highest numbers not exceeding three on the list of those voted for as President, the House of Representatives shall choose immediately, by ballot, the President. But in choosing the President, the votes shall be taken by states, the representation from each state having one vote; a quorum for this purpose shall consist of a member or members from two thirds of the states, and a majority of all the states shall be necessary to a choice. And if the House of Representatives shall not choose a President whenever the right of choice shall devolve upon them, ~~before the fourth day of March next following,~~ then the Vice-President shall act as President, as in the case of the death or other constitutional disability of the President. The person having the greatest number of votes as Vice-President shall be the Vice-President, if such number be a majority of the whole number of electors appointed, and if no person have a majority, then from the two highest numbers on the list, the Senate shall choose the Vice-President; a quorum for the purpose shall consist of two thirds of the whole number of Senators, and a majority of the whole number shall be necessary to a choice. But no person constitutionally ineligible to the office of President shall be eligible to that of Vice-President of the United States.

AMENDMENT 13. SLAVERY ABOLISHED (1865) Passed by Congress January 31, 1865. Ratified December 6, 1865.

Note: A portion of Article 4, Section 2, of the Constitution was superseded by the Thirteenth Amendment.

Constitutional Insight **Amendment 12**
How did the election of 1800 lead to the Twelfth Amendment? The election ended in a tie vote between the Republican running mates. The election was decided in Jefferson's favor on the House's 36th ballot. Almost immediately Alexander Hamilton and others designed an amendment that established that the presidential electors would vote for both a presidential and a vice-presidential candidate. This amendment prevents a repeat of the problem experienced in the 1800 election.

F CRITICAL THINKING
Why is the Twelfth Amendment important?

ELECTION REFORM

A new wave of electoral reform efforts was triggered by the controversial presidential election of 2000, in which George W. Bush's narrow victory over Al Gore left many Americans questioning the system in which a candidate can lose the popular vote but win the election.

Eliminating or reworking the electoral college has been historically the most frequently proposed constitutional amendment. Other reform proposals have included improving access to polling places by allowing voting on weekend hours or making Election Day a national holiday. Still other proposals would modernize inaccurate polling and counting machines or replace them with computer stations or online voting.

SECTION 1 Neither slavery nor involuntary servitude, except as a punishment for crime whereof the party shall have been duly convicted, shall exist within the United States, or any place subject to their jurisdiction.

SECTION 2 Congress shall have power to enforce this article by appropriate legislation.

AMENDMENT 14. CIVIL RIGHTS (1868) Passed by Congress June 13, 1866. Ratified July 9, 1868.

Note: Article 1, Section 2, of the Constitution was modified by Section 2 of the Fourteenth Amendment.

SECTION 1 All persons born or naturalized in the United States, and subject to the jurisdiction thereof, are citizens of the United States and of the state wherein they reside. No state shall make or enforce any law which shall abridge the privileges or immunities of citizens of the United States; nor shall any state deprive any person of life, liberty, or property, without due process of law; nor deny to any person within its jurisdiction the equal protection of the laws.

SECTION 2 Representatives shall be apportioned among the several states according to their respective numbers, counting the whole number of persons in each state, excluding Indians not taxed. But when the right to vote at any election for the choice of electors for President and Vice-President of the United States, Representatives in Congress, the executive and judicial officers of a state, or the members of the legislature thereof, is denied to any of the male inhabitants of such state, being twenty-one years of age, and citizens of the United States, or in any way abridged, except for participation in rebellion, or other crime, the basis of representation therein shall be reduced in the proportion which the number of such male citizens shall bear to the whole number of male citizens twenty-one years of age in such state.

SECTION 3 No person shall be a Senator or Representative in Congress, or elector of President and Vice-President, or hold any office, civil or military, under the United States, or under any state, who, having previously taken an oath, as a member of Congress, or as an officer of the United States, or as a member of any state legislature, or as an executive or judicial officer of any state, to support the Constitution of the United States, shall have engaged in insurrection or rebellion against the same, or given aid or comfort to the enemies thereof. But Congress may, by a vote of two thirds of each house, remove such disability.

SECTION 4 The validity of the public debt of the United States, authorized by law, including debts incurred for payment of pensions and bounties for services in suppressing insurrection or rebellion, shall not be questioned. But neither the United States nor any state shall assume or pay any debt or obligation incurred in aid of insurrection or rebellion against the United States, or any claim for the loss or emancipation of any slave; but all such debts, obligations and claims shall be held illegal and void.

SECTION 5 The Congress shall have power to enforce, by appropriate legislation, the provisions of this article.

Constitutional Insight **Amendment 14, Section 1** *Which personal status takes priority—that of a U.S. citizen or that of a state citizen?* The Fourteenth Amendment firmly notes that Americans are citizens of both the nation and the states but that no state can "abridge the privileges or immunities" of U.S. citizens, deprive them "of life, liberty, or property, without due process of law," or deny them "equal protection of the laws."
What does it mean to have "equal protection of the laws"? Equal protection means that the laws are to be applied to all persons in the same way. The legal system may discriminate between persons—treat them differently, or unequally—if there are relevant reasons to do so. For example, a person's income and number of dependents are relevant for how much income tax the person should pay; a person's gender is not. The Supreme Court's 1954 decision in *Brown v. Board of Education of Topeka* (see page 708), which declared segregated public schools unconstitutional, was based on an Equal Protection claim; a child's race is not a relevant reason for the state to assign that child to a particular school.

G CRITICAL THINKING
Do you agree or disagree with the Supreme Court's decision that separate educational facilities are unequal? Explain your position.

The lawyers who successfully challenged segregation in the *Brown* v. *Board of Education* case in 1954 included (*left to right*) George E. C. Hayes, Thurgood Marshall, and James M. Nabrit, Jr.

Constitutional Insight **Amendment 15**
Can you be denied the right to vote? The Fifteenth Amendment prohibits the United States or any state from keeping citizens from voting because of race or color or because they were once slaves. However, a person convicted of a crime can be denied the right to vote, as can someone found to be mentally incompetent.

H CRITICAL THINKING
Why do you think so many people do not exercise the right to vote?

Constitutional Insight **Amendment 16**
How has the ability of Congress to impose taxes been amended? The Sixteenth Amendment permits a federal income tax and in so doing changes Article 1, Section 9, Clause 4, by stating that Congress has the power to levy an income tax—which is a direct tax—without apportioning such a tax among the states according to their populations.

I CRITICAL THINKING
Do you think Congress should have the power to impose an income tax on the people of the nation? Explain your answer.

Constitutional Insight **Amendment 17**
How has the way senators are elected been changed? The Seventeenth Amendment changes Article 1, Section 3, Clause 1, by stating that senators shall be elected by the people of each state rather than by the state legislatures.

J CRITICAL THINKING
Why is the direct election of senators by the people of each state important?

Federal agents enforcing the Eighteenth Amendment prepare to smash containers of illegal whiskey.

AMENDMENT 15. RIGHT TO VOTE (1870) Passed by Congress February 26, 1869. Ratified February 3, 1870.

SECTION 1 The right of citizens of the United States to vote shall not be denied or abridged by the United States or by any state on account of race, color, or previous condition of servitude.

SECTION 2 The Congress shall have power to enforce this article by appropriate legislation.

AMENDMENT 16. INCOME TAX (1913) Passed by Congress July 12, 1909. Ratified February 3, 1913.

Note: Article 1, Section 9, of the Constitution was modified by the Sixteenth Amendment.

The Congress shall have power to lay and collect taxes on incomes, from whatever source derived, without apportionment among the several states, and without regard to any census or enumeration.

AMENDMENT 17. DIRECT ELECTION OF SENATORS (1913) Passed by Congress May 13, 1912. Ratified April 8, 1913.

Note: Article 1, Section 3, of the Constitution was modified by the Seventeenth Amendment.

CLAUSE 1 The Senate of the United States shall be composed of two Senators from each state, elected by the people thereof, for six years; and each Senator shall have one vote. The electors in each state shall have the qualifications requisite for electors of the most numerous branch of the state legislatures.

CLAUSE 2 When vacancies happen in the representation of any state in the Senate, the executive authority of such state shall issue writs of election to fill such vacancies: Provided, that the legislature of any state may empower the executive thereof to make temporary appointments until the people fill the vacancies by election as the legislature may direct.

CLAUSE 3 This amendment shall not be so construed as to affect the election or term of any Senator chosen before it becomes valid as part of the Constitution.

AMENDMENT 18. PROHIBITION (1919) Passed by Congress December 18, 1917. Ratified January 16, 1919. Repealed by Amendment 21.

~~**SECTION 1** After one year from the ratification of this article the manufacture, sale, or transportation of intoxicating liquors within, the importation thereof into, or the exportation thereof from the United States and all territory subject to the jurisdiction thereof for beverage purposes is hereby prohibited.~~

~~**SECTION 2** The Congress and the several states shall have concurrent power to enforce this article by appropriate legislation.~~

~~**SECTION 3** This article shall be inoperative unless it shall have been ratified as an amendment to the Constitution by the legislatures of the several states, as provided in the Constitution, within seven years from the date of the submission hereof to the states by the Congress.~~

Amendment 19. Woman Suffrage (1920) Passed by Congress June 4, 1919. Ratified August 18, 1920.

Clause 1 The right of citizens of the United States to vote shall not be denied or abridged by the United States or by any state on account of sex.

Clause 2 Congress shall have power to enforce this article by appropriate legislation.

Amendment 20. "Lame Duck" Sessions (1933) Passed by Congress March 2, 1932. Ratified January 23, 1933.

Note: Article 1, Section 4, of the Constitution was modified by Section 2 of this amendment. In addition, a portion of the Twelfth Amendment was superseded by Section 3.

Section 1 The terms of the President and Vice-President shall end at noon on the 20th day of January, and the terms of Senators and Representatives at noon on the 3rd day of January, of the years in which such terms would have ended if this article had not been ratified; and the terms of their successors shall then begin.

Section 2 The Congress shall assemble at least once in every year, and such meeting shall begin at noon on the 3rd day of January, unless they shall by law appoint a different day.

Section 3 If, at the time fixed for the beginning of the term of the President, the President elect shall have died, the Vice-President elect shall become President. If a President shall not have been chosen before the time fixed for the beginning of his term, or if the President elect shall have failed to qualify, then the Vice-President elect shall act as President until a President shall have qualified; and the Congress may by law provide for the case wherein neither a President elect nor a Vice-President elect shall have qualified, declaring who shall then act as President, or the manner in which one who is to act shall be selected, and such person shall act accordingly until a President or Vice-President shall have qualified.

Section 4 The Congress may by law provide for the case of the death of any of the persons from whom the House of Representatives may choose a President whenever the right of choice shall have devolved upon them, and for the case of the death of any of the persons from whom the Senate may choose a Vice-President whenever the right of choice shall have devolved upon them.

Section 5 Sections 1 and 2 shall take effect on the 15th day of October following the ratification of this article.

Section 6 This article shall be inoperative unless it shall have been ratified as an amendment to the Constitution by the legislatures of three fourths of the several states within seven years from the date of its submission.

Amendment 21. Repeal of Prohibition (1933) Passed by Congress February 20, 1933. Ratified December 5, 1933.

Section 1 The eighteenth article of amendment to the Constitution of the United States is hereby repealed.

Section 2 The transportation or importation into any state, territory, or possession of the United States for delivery or use therein of intoxicating liquors, in violation of the laws thereof, is hereby prohibited.

Constitutional Insight **Amendment 19**
When did women first get the right to vote in the United States? Women had the right to vote in the state of New Jersey between 1776 and 1807. In the late 19th century, some states and territories began to extend full or limited suffrage to women. Then, in 1920, the Nineteenth Amendment prohibited the United States or any state from denying women the right to vote.

K CRITICAL THINKING
How does the right of women to vote affect politics today?

Constitutional Insight **Amendment 20**
Why is the Twentieth Amendment usually called the "Lame Duck" amendment? A lame duck is a person who continues to hold office after his or her replacement has been elected. Such a person is called a lame duck because he or she no longer has any strong political influence. The Twentieth Amendment reduces the time between the election of a new president and vice-president in November and their assumption of the offices, which it sets at January 20 instead of March 4. It also reduces the time new members of Congress must wait to take their seats from 4 months to about 2 months. They are now seated on January 3 following the November election. As a result, the lame duck period is now quite short.

L CRITICAL THINKING
Why may the framers have specified a longer lame duck period?

Constitutional Insight **Amendment 21**
What is unique about the Twenty-first Amendment? Besides being the only amendment that explicitly repeals another, it was the first, and is so far the only one, to have been ratified by the state convention method outlined in Article 5. Congress, probably fearing that state legislatures would not deal swiftly with the issue of repeal, chose to have each state call a special convention to consider the amendment. The strategy worked well, for the elected delegates to the conventions represented public opinion on the issue and ratified the amendment without delay.

M CRITICAL THINKING
Why is it necessary to pass another amendment to revoke or remove an existing amendment?

Section 3 This article shall be inoperative unless it shall have been ratified as an amendment to the Constitution by conventions in the several states, as provided in the Constitution, within seven years from the date of the submission hereof to the states by the Congress.

Amendment 22. Limit on Presidential Terms (1951) Passed by Congress March 21, 1947. Ratified February 27, 1951.

Section 1 No person shall be elected to the office of the President more than twice, and no person who has held the office of President, or acted as President, for more than two years of a term to which some other person was elected President shall be elected to the office of the President more than once. ~~But this article shall not apply to any person holding the office of President when this article was proposed by the Congress, and shall not prevent any person who may be holding the office of President, or acting as President, during the term within which this article becomes operative from holding the office of President or acting as President during the remainder of such term.~~

Section 2 This article shall be inoperative unless it shall have been ratified as an amendment to the Constitution by the legislatures of three fourths of the several states within seven years from the date of its submission to the states by the Congress.

Amendment 23. Voting in District of Columbia (1961) Passed by Congress June 17, 1960. Ratified March 29, 1961.

Section 1 The district constituting the seat of government of the United States shall appoint in such manner as Congress may direct: a number of electors of President and Vice-President equal to the whole number of Senators and Representatives in Congress to which the district would be entitled if it were a state, but in no event more than the least populous state; they shall be in addition to those appointed by the states, but they shall be considered, for the purposes of the election of President and Vice-President, to be electors appointed by a state; and they shall meet in the district and perform such duties as provided by the twelfth article of amendment.

Section 2 The Congress shall have power to enforce this article by appropriate legislation.

Amendment 24. Abolition of Poll Taxes (1964) Passed by Congress August 27, 1962. Ratified January 23, 1964.

Section 1 The right of citizens of the United States to vote in any primary or other election for President or Vice-President, for electors for President or Vice-President, or for Senator or Representative in Congress, shall not be denied or abridged by the United States or any state by reason of failure to pay any poll tax or other tax.

Section 2 The Congress shall have power to enforce this article by appropriate legislation.

Amendment 25. Presidential Disability, Succession (1967) Passed by Congress July 6, 1965. Ratified February 10, 1967.

Note: Article 2, Section 1, of the Constitution was affected by the Twenty-fifth Amendment.

CONGRESSIONAL TERM LIMITS

In 1995, the Supreme Court struck down all state laws limiting congressional terms, stating that they were unconstitutional. The Court ruled that only a constitutional amendment—such as the Twenty-second, which limits the president to two terms—could impose term limits on members of Congress.

Proposed constitutional amendments for Congressional term limits were defeated in Congress in 1995 and in 1997.

Constitutional Insight **Amendment 23**
Why were residents of the District of Columbia without a vote in presidential elections? First, the district was merely an idea at the time the Constitution was written. Second, no one expected the district to include many residents. Third, the framers designed the electoral college on a state framework. By 1960, however, the fact that nearly 800,000 Americans living in the nation's capital could not vote in presidential elections was an embarrassment. The Twenty-third Amendment gives Washington, D.C., residents the right to vote in presidential elections by assigning them electoral votes.

N CRITICAL THINKING
Do you think the District of Columbia should be made a separate state?

Constitutional Insight **Amendment 24**
Why was the poll tax an issue important enough to require an amendment? The poll tax was used in some places to prevent African-American voters—at least the many who were too poor to pay the tax—from participating in elections. As the civil rights movement gained momentum, the abuse of the poll tax became a major issue, but the national government found it difficult to change the situation because the constitutional provisions in Article 1, Section 4, leave the qualifications of voters in the hands of the states. The Twenty-fourth Amendment changed this by prohibiting the United States or any state from including payment of any tax as a requirement for voting.

O CRITICAL THINKING
What impact do you think the Twenty-fourth Amendment has had on elections?

SECTION 1. In case of the removal of the President from office or of his death or resignation, the Vice-President shall become President.

SECTION 2 Whenever there is a vacancy in the office of the Vice-President, the President shall nominate a Vice-President who shall take office upon confirmation by a majority vote of both houses of Congress.

SECTION 3 Whenever the President transmits to the President pro tempore of the Senate and the Speaker of the House of Representatives his written declaration that he is unable to discharge the powers and duties of his office, and until he transmits to them a written declaration to the contrary, such powers and duties shall be discharged by the Vice-President as Acting President.

SECTION 4 Whenever the Vice-President and a majority of either the principal officers of the executive departments or of such other body as Congress may by law provide, transmit to the President pro tempore of the Senate and the Speaker of the House of Representatives their written declaration that the President is unable to discharge the powers and duties of his office, the Vice-President shall immediately assume the powers and duties of the office as Acting President.

Thereafter, when the President transmits to the President pro tempore of the Senate and the Speaker of the House of Representatives his written declaration that no inability exists, he shall resume the powers and duties of his office unless the Vice-President and a majority of either the principal officers of the executive department[s] or of such other body as Congress may by law provide, transmit within four days to the President pro tempore of the Senate and the Speaker of the House of Representatives their written declaration that the President is unable to discharge the powers and duties of his office. Thereupon Congress shall decide the issue, assembling within forty-eight hours for that purpose if not in session. If the Congress, within twenty-one days after receipt of the latter written declaration, or, if Congress is not in session, within twenty-one days after Congress is required to assemble, determines by two thirds vote of both houses that the President is unable to discharge the powers and duties of his office, the Vice-President shall continue to discharge the same as Acting President; otherwise, the President shall resume the powers and duties of his office.

AMENDMENT 26. 18-YEAR-OLD VOTE (1971) Passed by Congress March 23, 1971. Ratified July 1, 1971.

Note: Amendment 14, Section 2, of the Constitution was modified by Section 1 of the Twenty-sixth Amendment.

SECTION 1 The right of citizens of the United States, who are eighteen years of age or older, to vote shall not be denied or abridged by the United States or by any state on account of age.

SECTION 2 The Congress shall have power to enforce this article by appropriate legislation.

AMENDMENT 27. CONGRESSIONAL PAY (1992) Proposed by Congress September 25, 1789. Ratified May 7, 1992.

No law, varying the compensation for the services of the Senators and Representatives, shall take effect, until an election of Representatives shall have intervened.

Constitutional Insight **Amendment 26**
Why was the Twenty-sixth Amendment passed? Granting 18-year-olds the right to vote became an issue in the 1960s, during the Vietnam War, when people questioned the justice of requiring 18-year-old men to submit to the military draft but refusing them the right to vote. In 1970, Congress passed a voting rights act giving 18-year-olds the right to vote in elections. When the constitutionality of this act was challenged, the Supreme Court decided that states had to honor the 18-year-old vote for congressional and presidential elections but could retain higher age requirements for state and local elections. To avoid confusion at the polls, the Twenty-sixth Amendment was passed. It guarantees 18-year-olds the right to vote in national and state elections.

P CRITICAL THINKING
Do you think 18-year-olds should have the right to vote? Why or why not?

(above) **President Richard M. Nixon signs the Twenty-sixth Amendment to the Constitution, adopted in 1971.**

Constitutional Insight **Amendment 27**
How long did it take to ratify this amendment? Although the Twenty-seventh Amendment was one of the 12 amendments proposed in 1789 as part of the Bill of Rights, it was not ratified until 1992. This amendment, which deals with congressional compensation, allows the members of Congress to increase Congressional pay, but delays the increase until after a new Congress is seated.

Q CRITICAL THINKING
Do you think members of Congress should be able to vote themselves a pay increase? Explain your answer.

TRACING THEMES

Voting Rights

When the American colonists declared their independence from Great Britain in 1776, their struggle to create a representative government was just beginning. The state constitutions that were drafted at that time established voting rights, but only for certain citizens. The Articles of Confederation did not address voting rights; therefore, existing state laws remained intact.

Even the new Constitution that replaced the Articles in 1788 did not extend voting rights to many groups of people living in the new United States. As the Constitution has been amended over the years however, things changed. The right to vote was gradually extended to more and more citizens, enabling them to participate in local and national government.

1789

MALE PROPERTY OWNERS ▶

In the early years of the United States, property qualifications were relaxed in some states (Pennsylvania, Delaware, North Carolina, Georgia, and Vermont) to include all male taxpayers. With few exceptions, women were not allowed to vote. Most state constitutions also required that a voting male be at least 21 years of age.

Those who qualified to vote were generally white, although some states allowed free African Americans to vote.

1870

◀ AFRICAN-AMERICAN MALES

The Fifteenth Amendment to the Constitution attempted to guarantee African-American males the right to vote by stating that the right of U.S. citizens "to vote shall not be denied or abridged [limited] by the United States or by any state on account of race, color, or previous condition of servitude." The picture to the left shows African-American males voting in a state election in 1867. African-American males, however, were often kept from voting through the use of poll taxes, which were finally abolished by the Twenty-fourth Amendment in 1964, and literacy tests, which were suspended by the Voting Rights Act of 1965.

1920

◀ WOMAN SUFFRAGE

In 1920, the Nineteenth Amendment, granting voting rights to women, was finally ratified. Elizabeth Cady Stanton, Susan B. Anthony, and many other women, such as those shown at left marching in a woman suffrage parade in 1919, worked tirelessly for women's voting rights.

Four years after ratification of the Nineteenth Amendment, in 1924, citizenship—including the right to vote—was extended to Native Americans.

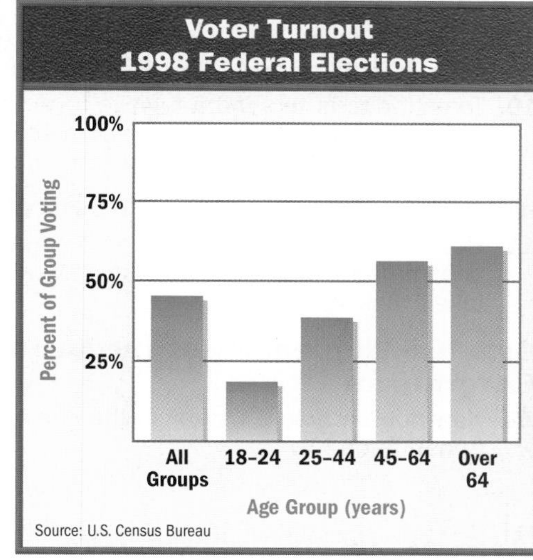

1971

▼ EIGHTEEN-YEAR-OLD VOTE

The Twenty-sixth Amendment, ratified in 1971, granted the right to vote to citizens "eighteen years of age or older." Voting rights for young people had become an issue in the 1960s during the Vietnam War. Many people questioned drafting 18-year-olds to fight but refusing them the right to vote. The picture below shows a young woman exercising her new right to vote.

THINKING CRITICALLY

CONNECT TO HISTORY

1. **Forming Generalizations** What does the information on these pages demonstrate about how voting rights in the United States have changed? How did the Constitution help bring about the changes?

 **SEE SKILLBUILDER HANDBOOK, PAGE R21.**

CONNECT TO TODAY

2. **Interpreting Data** Research voter turnout statistics from a recent election. What age group scored highest? Which scored lowest?

 **RESEARCH LINKS** CLASSZONE.COM

MAIN IDEAS

Article 1. The Legislature

1. Why does the legislative branch of the government represent the people most directly? What is the principal job of this branch?
2. Why are there more members of the House of Representatives than of the Senate?
3. Name four powers Congress has.
4. What powers are denied to Congress? to the states?

Article 2. The Executive

5. What is the main function of the executive branch?
6. Who officially elects the president of the United States? Explain.
7. How can the president lose his or her job before election time?

Article 3. The Judiciary

8. How are Supreme Court justices appointed?
9. What kinds of cases go before the Supreme Court? Why is the Court's decision whether to hear a case important?

Article 4. Relations Among States

10. To extradite is to send a fugitive back to the state in which he or she is accused of committing a crime. How is this an example of relations among states?

Article 5. Amending the Constitution

11. How many states must ratify an amendment for it to become part of the Constitution? Why do you think it takes that many?

Article 6. Supremacy of the National Government

12. How does Article 6 establish the supremacy of the Constitution?

The Amendments

13. Does the First Amendment allow complete freedom of speech—the right to say anything you want at any time, anywhere? Explain your answer.
14. What is the newest amendment? What protection does that amendment give to the American people?

THINKING CRITICALLY

1. **TAKING NOTES** The powers of the federal government are separated among the three branches. Create a chart like the one below that shows how the Constitution's framers used checks and balances to ensure that no one branch of the government could become too much stronger than the others.

Executive	Legislative	Judicial

2. **MAKING INFERENCES** How does the Constitution reflect the fear of too strong a central government?

3. **EVALUATING** The Bill of Rights guarantees a defendant a speedy, public trial. Do you think it is being observed today? Explain.

4. **ANALYZING MOTIVES** Why did the framers make it so difficult to amend the Constitution? Do you agree or disagree with their philosophy? Explain.

5. **DEVELOPING HISTORICAL PERSPECTIVE** The Fifteenth, Nineteenth, and Twenty-sixth amendments give voting rights to specific groups. Why was it necessary for Congress to spell out these groups' rights in amendments?

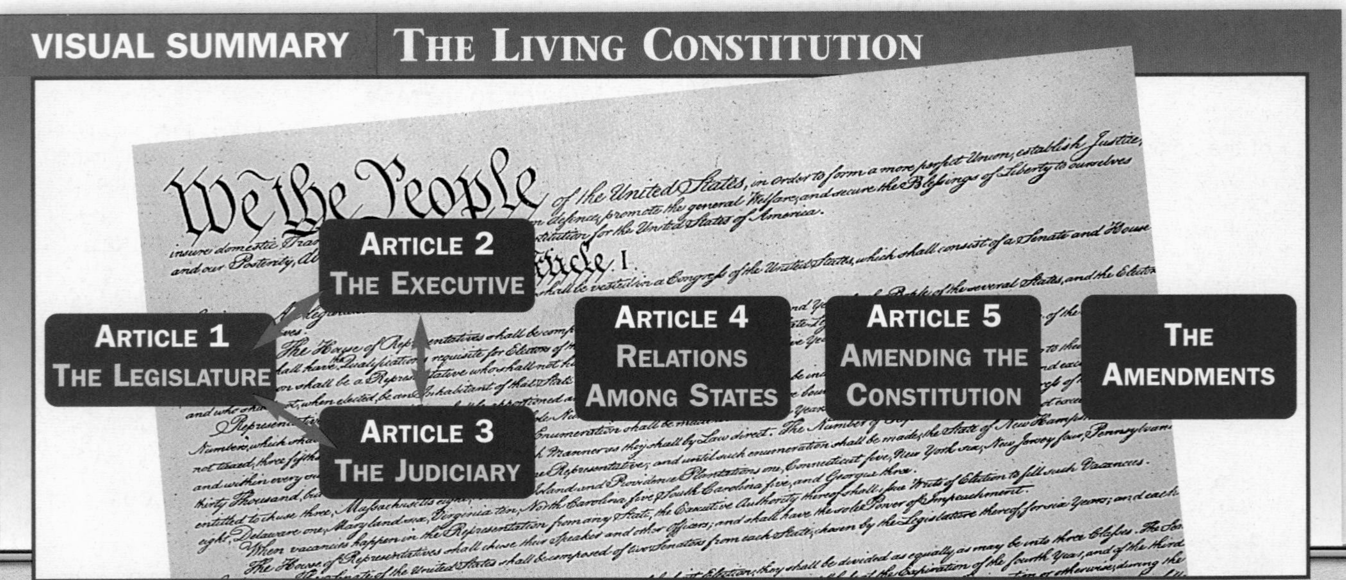

Standardized Test Practice

Use the cartoon and your knowledge of U.S. history to answer question 1.

"It's awful the way they're trying to influence Congress. Why don't they serve cocktails and make campaign contributions like we do?"

1. In the Constitutional Convention, the framers adopted certain principles to be embodied in the Constitution. Which of the following Constitutional principles does the cartoon support?

- **A** The federal government's power should be divided into separate branches.
- **B** The federal government should be stronger than the state governments.
- **C** The federal legislature should be responsive to the will of the people.
- **D** The legislature and the president should check each other's power.

Use the quotation and your knowledge of U.S. history to answer question 2.

> **"[The president] shall have power, by and with the advice and consent of the Senate, to make treaties, provided two thirds of the Senators present concur; and he shall nominate, and by and with the advice and consent of the Senate, shall appoint ambassadors, other public ministers and consuls, judges of the Supreme Court, and all other officers of the United States . . ."**
>
> —U.S. Constitution, Art. 2, Sec. 2, part 2

2. The passage describes checks on the power of—

- **F** the president.
- **G** the Senate.
- **H** the judiciary.
- **J** the states.

3. Which of the following must ratify Constitutional amendments?

- **A** Congress
- **B** the people
- **C** the states
- **D** the president

ADDITIONAL TEST PRACTICE, pages S1–S33.

CLASSZONE.COM

ALTERNATIVE ASSESSMENT

1. *Journal Entry* Imagine that it is 1787, and you are a citizen of one of the original thirteen states. Your vote is necessary to ratify the new Constitution that has been approved by the convention in Philadelphia. You have studied the seven articles and listened to spirited discussions about how you and your state will be affected. Write a journal entry in which you express your views about this document that is so important for the new United States. Make sure you include references to what you have read and heard about the Constitution.

2. **INTERNET ACTIVITY CLASSZONE.COM**

Visit the links for Chapter Assessment to learn more about how bills become law. Because of the process by which bills become laws, problems may occur when the president and a majority of members of Congress are from different political parties. Using the Internet, research bills that were proposed by the president but became stalled in Congress because of party differences. Then divide into groups and do the activity.

Cooperative Learning Activity Have each group research a different bill. Try to follow the debate and see how party differences affected the discussion. Did the bill pass and become law? Present your findings to the class.

Applying the Constitution

The United States Constitution is admired the world over. But a healthy democracy depends on the continuing participation of its citizens—including you. Here are four projects that will help you learn the rewards and challenges of responsible citizenship.

RESEARCH LINKS **CLASSZONE.COM** Visit the links for the Constitution for more information that will help you with these Projects for Citizenship.

PROJECT 1

Becoming an Educated Voter

ENDORSING A CANDIDATE

Choose a campaign for elective office and learn about the issues and the candidates in the campaign. After doing your research, write an endorsement, or a statement in favor, of one of the candidates.

LEARNING ABOUT THE CANDIDATES

✔ **Examine news media and news services.** During campaigns, some services and publications offer endorsements that explain why particular candidates are worthy of support.

✔ **Get information from political parties.** They provide information on the candidates, but their perspective is biased toward their own candidates. The major parties have Internet sites, as do many local groups and individual candidates.

✔ **Contact interest groups,** such as the Sierra Club and the National Association of Manufacturers. They often list candidates' positions on issues and support candidates who share their beliefs.

✔ **Look at databases and voters' guides** published by nonpartisan organizations such as the League of Women Voters and Project Vote Smart.

As you use each source, try to identify any bias. Think about the following questions.

- What does the author of this source stand to gain from supporting a particular candidate?
- Is the information in the source complete and accurate?
- Does the author use loaded or inflammatory language?

PRESENTING YOUR PROJECT

After you have written your endorsement, you might send it to a media outlet, such as a newspaper or a television station, or post it on the Internet. Or you might send it to your local or school newspaper.

PROJECT 2

Expressing Political Opinions

WRITING A LETTER TO THE EDITOR

Identify an issue that concerns you. Then write a letter or send an e-mail message about that issue to the editor of a newspaper or magazine.

WRITING A PERSUASIVE LETTER

✔ **Find an issue** that has been in the news lately and about which you feel strongly.

✔ **Read recent articles,** editorials, and cartoons in newspapers or magazines. Notice how they have addressed this issue.

✔ **Compose a letter** that clearly and concisely explains your views about the issue you have chosen. Your letter should also include reasons and facts that support your opinion on the issue. It might also advocate some specific action to be taken to address the issue.

✔ **Identify the person** to whom you should send your letter, and note any requirements the newspaper or magazine has for writing letters to the editor.

✔ **Edit your letter carefully.** Be sure to use standard grammar, spelling, sentence structure, and punctuation.

PRESENTING YOUR PROJECT

Present the letter you wrote to the rest of the class. When you do, explain why you chose to write about this issue.

A student expresses her political opinions as she addresses an audience.

PROJECT 3

Understanding How to Lobby

PLANNING A LOBBYING CAMPAIGN

Form a committee with other students to organize a lobbying campaign—a campaign to influence legislation or public policy. Create a plan for the campaign that includes materials to be presented to government officials. In creating your plan, keep the following points in mind.

CREATING A LOBBYING PLAN

- ✔ **Establish a clear goal** of what you want to achieve. Make sure all members of the group understand and agree with the established goal.
- ✔ **Identify the appropriate people to lobby**—the people who can best help you to achieve your goal. For example, if your group is planning to lobby to have a bill passed, you would lobby the legislators who will vote on the bill. However, if your group wants to lobby for a local improvement—such as cleaning up an abandoned factory site—you should lobby the local officials who make those decisions.
- ✔ **Gather statistics** and other information that support your case. Explore a variety of resources, including the library, the Internet, and news services. Conduct interviews with appropriate state or local officials. Use the information you gather to develop a brief written report that can be given to the officials you intend to lobby.
- ✔ **Organize public opinion** in favor of your case. Gather signatures on petitions or conduct a letter-writing campaign to encourage people who support your goal to contact government officials. You can also create fliers calling attention to your cause.
- ✔ **Present your case** to government officials firmly but politely. Practice your presentation several times before you actually appear before them.

PRESENTING YOUR PROJECT

Share your lobbying plan with the rest of the class in the form of a written proposal that includes materials, such as petition forms, that you will use in your lobbying effort. If you implement your lobbying plan, describe to the class what response you received from the officials you lobbied.

PROJECT 4

Volunteering in your Community

MAKING AN ORAL REPORT

Identify a local community organization that you might want to help. Find out what kinds of volunteer activities the organization has, such as answering phones in the office, serving food to the homeless, or cleaning vacant lots. Then volunteer to participate in one of those activities. Prepare an oral report to present to the rest of the class about your experiences as a volunteer. Keep the following points in mind as you choose which organization to help.

A group of young volunteers in the Summer of Service project discusses plans with carpenters.

SUGGESTIONS FOR VOLUNTEERING

- ✔ **Decide what kinds of public service projects might interest you.** You might talk to your parents, a teacher, friends, a local church, or a local political organization to learn what kinds of volunteer services are needed in your community.
- ✔ **Call local community organizations** to find out what kinds of volunteer opportunities they offer and decide whether you would like to volunteer for those projects.
- ✔ **Decide what cause you want to support** and identify an organization that addresses that cause.
- ✔ **Decide what type of work you want to do** and work with that organization.

PRESENTING YOUR PROJECT

Deliver an oral report to your class about your experiences as a volunteer. Explain why you chose the specific volunteer activity that you did. Describe the activity you performed. Then explain what effect your volunteering had as well as whether you felt the experience was a good one.

REVIEW CHAPTER 3

The Growth of a Young Nation

The port of New Orleans, Louisiana, was a major center for the cotton trade.

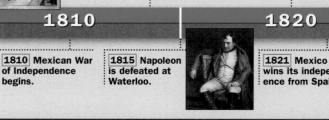

1803 The United States purchases the Louisiana Territory from France.

1814 The Treaty of Ghent is signed, ending the War of 1812.

1820 Congress passes the Missouri Compromise.

USA
WORLD

1800 | 1810 | 1820

1802 Toussaint L'Ouverture defeats French forces sent to recapture Saint Domingue (Haiti).

1810 Mexican War of Independence begins.

1815 Napoleon is defeated at Waterloo.

1821 Mexico wins its independence from Spain.

PRESIDENTS	1800: Thomas Jefferson	1804: Thomas Jefferson	1808: James Madison	1812: James Madison	1816: James Monroe	1820: James Monroe	1824: John Quincy Adams	1828: Andrew Jackson

INTERACT WITH HISTORY

The year is 1828. You are a senator from a Southern state. Congress has just passed a high tax on imported cloth and iron in order to protect Northern industry. The tax will raise the cost of these goods in the South and will cause Britain to buy less cotton. Southern states intend to ignore such federal laws that they consider unfair.

Would you support the federal or your state government?

Examine the Issues

- What might happen if some states enforce laws and others don't?
- How can Congress address the needs of different states?
- What does it mean to be a nation?

RESEARCH LINKS **CLASSZONE.COM**

Visit the Chapter 3 links for more information about The Growth of a Young Nation.

1831 William Lloyd Garrison publishes *The Liberator.*

1836 Texas establishes itself as a republic, with Sam Houston as its first president.

1838–39 Native Americans are relocated in the Trail of Tears.

1844 Samuel Morse sends first telegraph message.

1846 The war with Mexico begins.

1848 Woman's rights convention held at Seneca Falls, New York.

1830 | 1840 | 1850

1833 Great Britain abolishes slavery in the empire.

1837 Victoria becomes queen of England.

1845 The Great Potato Famine begins in Ireland.

1848 Karl Marx's *The Communist Manifesto* is published.

1832: Andrew Jackson | 1836: Martin Van Buren | 1840: William Henry Harrison | 1841: John Tyler (William Henry Harrison dies) | 1844: James K. Polk | 1848: Zachary Taylor | 1850: Millard Filmore (Zachary Taylor dies)

SECTION 1

The Jeffersonian Era

MAIN IDEA

During the presidencies of Thomas Jefferson, James Madison, and James Monroe, the country grew in both size and prestige.

WHY IT MATTERS NOW

Today's Democratic Party traces its roots to Jefferson and the Democratic-Republicans.

Terms & Names

- **Democratic-Republicans**
- **Jeffersonian republicanism**
- ***Marbury* v. *Madison***
- **John Marshall**
- **judicial review**
- **Louisiana Purchase**
- **impressment**
- **James Monroe**
- **Monroe Doctrine**

One American's Story

Patrick Gass was among those who took part in the famous Lewis and Clark expedition. Setting out in 1804, this expedition traveled overland from St. Louis, Missouri, to the Pacific. Along the way, Gass kept a journal in which he took notes on people, places, and the dramatic events he witnessed. Gass described one of those events in his journal entry for May 14, 1805.

A PERSONAL VOICE PATRICK GASS

"This forenoon we passed a large creek on the North side and a small river on the South. About 4 in the afternoon we passed another small river on the South side near the mouth of which some of the men discovered a large brown bear, and six of them went out to kill it. They fired at it; but having only wounded it, it made battle and was near seizing some of them, but they all fortunately escaped, and at length succeeded in dispatching it. These bears are very bold and ferocious; and very large and powerful. The natives say they have killed a number of their brave men."

—*A Journal of the Voyages and Travels of a Corps of Discovery*

VIDEO

RECRUITED BY LEWIS AND CLARK

Patrick Gass Chronicles the Journey West

The journey Gass undertook with Lewis and Clark helped lay the foundations for expansion. The explorers brought back to the new government reports about the vast regions that lay to the west. Meanwhile, other Americans continued to shape the government in their growing nation.

Jefferson's Presidency

The election of 1800 pitted Thomas Jefferson, a leader of the **Democratic-Republicans** (sometimes shortened to "Republicans"), against President John Adams and his Federalist Party.

It was a hard-fought struggle. Each party hurled wild charges at the other.

Democratic-Republicans called Adams a tool of the rich who wanted to turn the executive branch into a British-style monarchy. Federalists protested that Jefferson was a dangerous supporter of revolutionary France and an atheist.

THE ELECTION OF 1800 In the balloting in the electoral college, Jefferson defeated Adams by eight electoral votes. However, since Jefferson's running mate, Aaron Burr, received the same number of votes as Jefferson, the House of Representatives was called upon to break the tie and choose between the two running mates. For six feverish days, the House took one ballot after another—35 ballots in all. Finally, Alexander Hamilton intervened. Although Hamilton opposed Jefferson's philosophy of government, he regarded Burr as unqualified for the presidency. Hamilton persuaded enough Federalists to cast blank votes that Jefferson received a majority of two votes. Burr then became vice-president.

The deadlock revealed a flaw in the electoral process established by the Constitution. As a result, Congress passed the Twelfth Amendment, which called for electors to cast separate ballots for president and vice-president. This system is still in effect today.

In his inaugural address, Jefferson extended the hand of peace to his opponents. "Every difference of opinion is not a difference of principle," he said. "We are all Republicans; we are all Federalists."

SIMPLIFYING THE GOVERNMENT Jefferson's theory of government, often called **Jeffersonian republicanism,** held that the people should control the government and that a simple government best suited the needs of the people. In accord with his belief in decentralized power, Jefferson tried to shrink the government and cut costs wherever possible. He reduced the size of the army, halted a planned expansion of the navy, and lowered expenses for government social functions. He also rolled back Hamilton's economic program by eliminating all internal taxes and reducing the influence of the Bank of the United States. (A)

MAIN IDEA

Making Inferences

(A) How did Jefferson's actions reflect his theory of government?

Jefferson was the first president to take office in the new federal capital, Washington, D.C. Though in appearance the city was a primitive place of dirt roads and few buildings, its location between Virginia and Maryland reflected the growing importance of the South in national politics. In fact, Jefferson and the two presidents who followed him—James Madison and James Monroe—all were from Virginia. This pattern of Southern dominance underscored the declining influence of both New England and the Federalists in national political life at that time.

▲ *John Marshall, Chief Justice of the United States* (about 1832), by William James Hubard.

JOHN MARSHALL AND THE SUPREME COURT Just before leaving office, President Adams had tried to influence future judicial decisions by filling federal judgeships with Federalists. But the signed documents authorizing some of the appointments had not been delivered by the time Adams left office. Jefferson argued that these appointments were invalid and ordered Madison, his secretary of state, not to deliver them.

This argument led to one of the most important Supreme Court decisions of all time in ***Marbury* v. *Madison*** (1803). (See page 118.) The Federalist chief justice **John Marshall** declared that part of Congress's Judiciary Act of 1789, which would have forced Madison to hand over the papers, was unconstitutional. The decision strengthened the Supreme Court by establishing the principle of **judicial review**—the ability of the Supreme Court to declare a law, in this case an act of Congress, unconstitutional. (B)

MAIN IDEA

Evaluating Decisions

(B) Why was the principle of judicial review important for the future of the Supreme Court?

THE LOUISIANA PURCHASE In 1800, Napoleon Bonaparte of France had persuaded Spain to return to France the Louisiana Territory, the land spanning from the Mississippi River west to the Rocky Mountains. France had handed this territory over to Spain in 1762, after the French and Indian War, but Napoleon planned to use it as a "breadbasket" for the colonial empire that he hoped to build in the West Indies. Many Americans were alarmed when they heard of this transfer, as they feared that a strong French presence in North America would force the United States into an alliance with Britain.

Background
Napoleon Bonaparte seized control of the French government in 1799 and expanded French territory until his defeat at Waterloo in Belgium in 1815.

However, by 1803, Napoleon had abandoned his ideas of an American empire and offered to sell the Louisiana Territory to the United States. Jefferson doubted whether the Constitution gave him the power to make such a purchase, but he decided to proceed. At a price of $15 million, the **Louisiana Purchase** more than doubled the size of the United States. Under the direction of President Jefferson, Meriwether Lewis and William Clark organized and led a group, including Patrick Gass, and set off in 1804 to explore the new territory. The explorers brought back valuable information about the West and showed that transcontinental travel was possible.

Madison and the War of 1812

Jefferson easily won reelection in 1804 but a crisis clouded his second administration. Renewed fighting between Britain and France threatened American shipping. The crisis continued into the administration of James Madison, who was elected president in 1808. Some four years later, Madison led the nation into the War of 1812 against Great Britain.

THE CAUSES OF THE WAR Although France and Britain both threatened U.S. ships between 1805 and 1814, Americans focused their anger on the British. One reason was the British policy of **impressment,** the practice of seizing Americans at sea and "impressing," or drafting, them into the British navy. Americans grew even angrier after learning that officials in British Canada were supplying arms to Native Americans in support of their ongoing battle against American settlers. A group of young congressmen from the South and the West, known as the war hawks, demanded war.

THE COURSE OF THE WAR By the spring of 1812, President Madison had decided to commit America to war against Britain, and Congress approved the war declaration in mid-June.

Republican funding cuts and a lack of popular support had left the American military with few volunteers and ill-prepared for war. Britain, however, was too preoccupied with Napoleon in Europe to pay much attention to the Americans. Nonetheless, the British scored a stunning victory in August of 1814, when they brushed aside American troops and sacked Washington, D.C. Madison and other federal officials fled the city as the British burned the Capitol, the Presidential Mansion, and other public buildings. The most impressive American victory occurred at the Battle of New Orleans. There, on January 8, 1815, U.S. troops led by General Andrew Jackson of Tennessee routed a British force. Ironically, British and American diplomats had already signed a peace agreement before the Battle of New Orleans, but news of the pact had not reached Jackson in time. The Treaty of Ghent, signed on Christmas Eve, 1814, declared an armistice, or end to the fighting.

THE CONSEQUENCES OF THE WAR The war had three important consequences. First, it led to the end of the Federalist Party, whose members generally opposed the war. Second, it encouraged the growth of American industries to manufacture products no longer available from Britain because of the war. Third, it confirmed the status of the United States as a free and independent nation. C

MAIN IDEA
Summarizing
C What were the principal consequences of the War of 1812?

Lewis and Clark Expedition, 1804–1806
INTERACTIVE
LIBERTY
IN GOD WE TRUST
2000
This dollar coin honors Sacajawea, a young Shoshone woman who served as interpreter and guide for the expedition.
Mandan Village by Karl Bodmer
5 April 25–26, 1805
In high winds and cold, Lewis searches by land for the Yellowstone River. He rejoins Clark at the junction of the Missouri and Yellowstone rivers.
4 April 7, 1805
A party of 32, including Clark's black servant York, French-Canadian trader Charbonneau, his wife Sacajawea, and their son, depart at 5 P.M. to continue the journey. High northwest wind but otherwise fair weather.
3 November 3, 1804
A hard wind from the northwest sets in as the party makes camp.
December 17, 1804
In minus-45-degree weather, sentries have to be changed every half hour.
BRITISH TERRITORY
Fort Clatsop
Traveler's Rest
Three Forks
Fort Mandan
6 December 8, 1805–March 23, 1806
Lack of provisions forces departure from winter camp.
7 July 3, 1806
The party divides. Lewis takes the direct route to the falls of Missouri. Clark heads toward the Jefferson and Yellowstone rivers.
August 11, 1806
Lewis is accidentally shot by a member of his own party. In pain, he rejoins Clark's party the next day.
2 August 20, 1804
Sergeant Floyd dies, the only fatality of the expedition.
LOUISIANA PURCHASE (1803)
Missouri R.
Mississippi R.
UNITED STATES
1 May 14, 1804
The party departs camp near Saint Louis about 4 P.M. in heavy rain.
Arkansas R.
St. Louis
Page from the journal of Lewis and Clark.
8 September 23, 1806
Taking a shortcut that saves about 580 miles, the party reaches Saint Louis at 12 noon. Total mileage: 7,690.
Red R.
NEW SPAIN
New Orleans
Gulf of Mexico
Compass of Lewis and Clark.
50°N
110°W
90°W
Journey west, 1804–1805
Journey home, 1806
Lewis's route home
Clark's route home
Fort
0 250 500 miles
0 250 500 kilometers
N S E W
PACIFIC OCEAN
GEOGRAPHY SKILLBUILDER
1. Movement About how many miles did the expedition travel on its route to the Pacific Ocean?
2. Movement On average, how many miles per day did they travel from Ft. Clatsop to the place where the party split up on July 3, 1806?

Nationalism Shapes Foreign Policy

As with James Madison, foreign affairs dominated the first term of President **James Monroe,** who was elected in 1816. His secretary of state, John Quincy Adams, established a foreign policy based on nationalism—a belief that national interests should be placed ahead of regional concerns, such as slavery in the South or tariffs in the Northeast.

TERRITORY AND BOUNDARIES High on Adams's list of national interests were the security of the nation and the expansion of its territory. To further these interests, Adams arranged the Convention of 1818, which fixed the U.S. border at the 49th parallel from Michigan west to the Rocky Mountains. Adams also reached a compromise with Britain to jointly occupy the Oregon Territory, the territory west of the Rockies, for ten years. He also convinced Don Luis de Onís, the Spanish minister to the United States, to transfer Florida to the United States. The Adams-Onís Treaty (1819) also established a western boundary for the United States that extended along the Sabine River from the Gulf of Mexico north to the Arkansas River to its source, and then north to the 42nd parallel, and west to the Pacific Ocean. **D**

MAIN IDEA

Summarizing

D What were the major boundary disputes resolved by John Quincy Adams?

THE MONROE DOCTRINE When Napoleon invaded Portugal and Spain in 1807, the two countries did not have the money or military force to both defend themselves and keep control of their overseas territories at the same time. But when Napoleon was defeated in 1815, Portugal and Spain wanted to reclaim their former colonies in Latin America.

Meanwhile, the Russians, who had been in Alaska since 1784, were establishing trading posts in what is now California. In 1821, Czar Alexander I of Russia

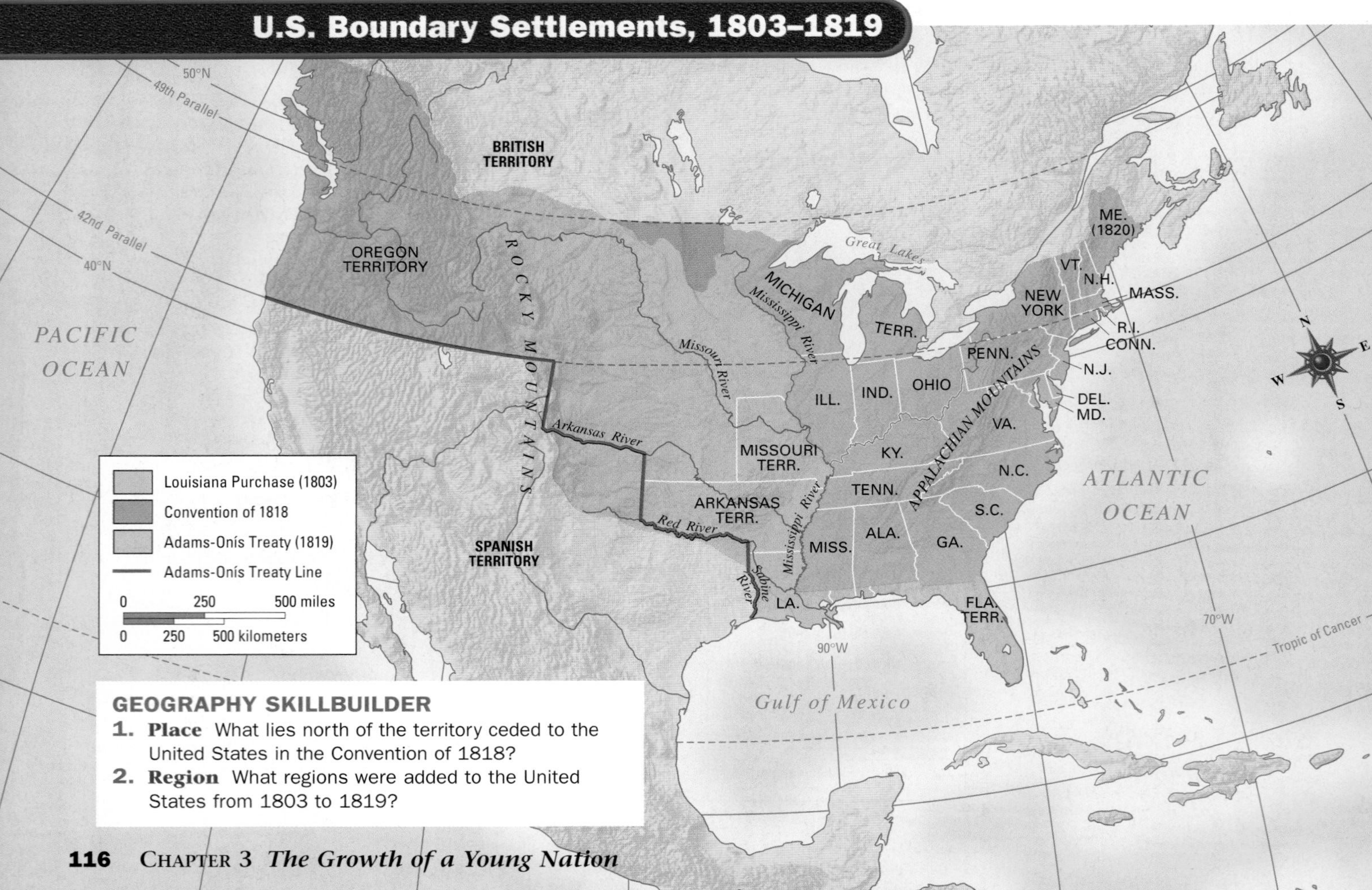

GEOGRAPHY SKILLBUILDER

1. **Place** What lies north of the territory ceded to the United States in the Convention of 1818?
2. **Region** What regions were added to the United States from 1803 to 1819?

claimed that Alaska's southern boundary was the 51st parallel, just north of Vancouver Island. He forbade foreign vessels from using the coast north of this line.

With Spain and Portugal trying to move back into their old colonial areas, and with Russia pushing in from the northwest, the United States knew that it had to do something. Many Americans were interested in acquiring northern Mexico and the Spanish colony of Cuba. Moreover, the Russian action posed a threat to American trade with China, which brought huge profits.

Accordingly, in his 1823 message to Congress, President Monroe warned all European powers not to interfere with affairs in the Western Hemisphere. They should not attempt to create new colonies, he said, or try to overthrow the newly independent republics in the hemisphere. The United States would consider such action "dangerous to our peace and safety." At the same time, the United States would not involve itself in European affairs or interfere with existing colonies in the Western Hemisphere.

A PERSONAL VOICE PRESIDENT JAMES MONROE

"Our policy in regard to Europe . . . is not to interfere in the internal concerns of any of its powers. . . . But in regard to those continents [of the Western Hemisphere], circumstances are eminently and conspicuously different. It is impossible that the allied [European] powers should extend their political system to any portion of either continent without endangering our peace and happiness."

—Annual Message to Congress, December 2, 1823

James Monroe

MAIN IDEA

Predicting Effects

E Do you think that the Monroe Doctrine would be a source of peace or conflict for the United States? Why?

These principles became known as the **Monroe Doctrine.** The doctrine became a foundation for future American policy and represented an important step onto the world stage by the assertive young nation. At home however, sectional differences soon challenged national unity, requiring strong patriotic sentiments and strong leaders like Andrew Jackson to hold the nation together. E

SECTION 1 ASSESSMENT

1. **TERMS & NAMES** For each term or name, write a sentence explaining its significance.
   - **Democratic-Republicans**
   - **Jeffersonian republicanism**
   - ***Marbury* v. *Madison***
   - **John Marshall**
   - **judicial review**
   - **Louisiana Purchase**
   - **impressment**
   - **James Monroe**
   - **Monroe Doctrine**

MAIN IDEA

2. **TAKING NOTES**
   In a chart like the one below, list an event from the administration of each president and note its significance.

Thomas Jefferson
Event
Significance
James Madison
Event
Significance
James Monroe
Event
Significance

CRITICAL THINKING

3. **EVALUATING LEADERSHIP**
   How successful was Thomas Jefferson as president in achieving his goal of simplifying the government? **Think About:**
   - the Louisiana Purchase
   - military spending
   - Jefferson's attitude toward the national bank

4. **EVALUATING**
   Why was the War of 1812 a turning point for the early United States?

5. **DRAWING CONCLUSIONS**
   How did the Monroe Doctrine assert American nationalism?

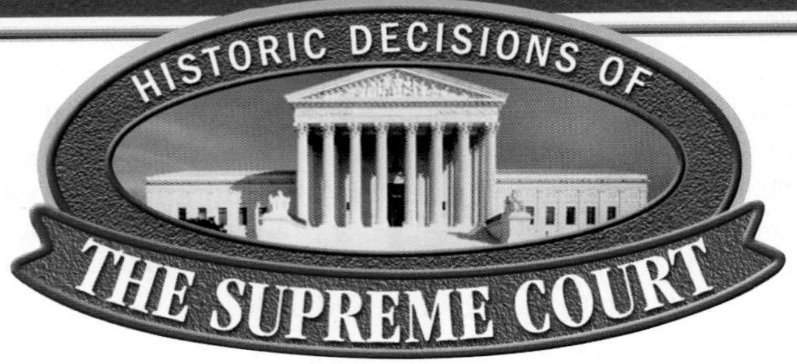

MARBURY v. *MADISON* (1803)

ORIGINS OF THE CASE A few days before Thomas Jefferson's inauguration, outgoing president John Adams appointed William Marbury to be a justice of the peace. But the commission was not delivered to Marbury. Later, Jefferson's new secretary of state, James Madison, refused to give Marbury the commission. Marbury asked the Supreme Court to force Madison to give him his commission.

THE RULING **The Court declared that the law on which Marbury based his claim was unconstitutional, and therefore it refused to order Madison to give Marbury his commission.**

LEGAL REASONING

Writing for the Court, Chief Justice John Marshall decided that Marbury had a right to his commission, and he scolded Madison at length for refusing to deliver it.

However, he then considered Marbury's claim that, under the Judiciary Act of 1789, the Supreme Court should order Madison to deliver the commission. As Marshall pointed out, the powers of the Supreme Court are set by the Constitution, and Congress does not have the authority to alter them. The Judiciary Act attempted to do just that.

Marshall reasoned that, since the Constitution is the "supreme law of the land, no law that goes against the Constitution can be valid."

> **"If . . . the courts are to regard the constitution, and the constitution is superior to any ordinary act of the legislature, the constitution, and not such ordinary act, must govern the case to which they both apply."**

If an act of Congress violates the Constitution, then a judge must uphold the Constitution and declare the act void. In choosing to obey the Constitution, the Supreme Court did declare the Judiciary Act unconstitutional and void, and so refused to grant Marbury's request.

◀ **Chief Justice John Marshall**

LEGAL SOURCES

U.S. CONSTITUTION

U.S. CONSTITUTION, ARTICLE III, SECTION 2 (1788)

"The judicial power shall extend to all cases . . . arising under this Constitution, the laws of the United States, and treaties made . . . under their authority."

U.S. CONSTITUTION, ARTICLE VI, CLAUSE 2 (1788)

"This Constitution, and the laws of the United States which shall be made in pursuance thereof . . . shall be the supreme law of the land; and the judges in every State shall be bound thereby. . . ."

RELATED CASES

***FLETCHER* v. *PECK* (1810)**

The Court ruled a state law unconstitutional for the first time.

***COHENS* v. *VIRGINIA* (1821)**

The Court overturned a state court decision for the first time.

***GIBBONS* v. *OGDEN* (1824)**

The Court ruled that the federal Congress—not the states—had the power under the Constitution to regulate interstate commerce.

◀ William Marbury

WHY IT MATTERED

In 1803, interest in Marbury's commission was primarily about partisan politics. The fight was just one skirmish in the ongoing battle between Federalists, such as Adams, and Democratic-Republicans, led by Jefferson and Madison, which had intensified in the election of 1800.

When Jefferson won the election, Adams made a final effort to hinder Jefferson's promised reforms. Before leaving office, he tried to fill the government with Federalists, including the "midnight" justices such as Marbury. Madison's refusal to deliver Marbury's appointment was part of Jefferson's subsequent effort to rid his administration of Federalists.

Marshall's opinion in *Marbury* might seem like a victory for Jefferson because it denied Marbury his commission. However, by scolding Madison and extending the principle of judicial review—the power of courts to decide whether or not specific laws are valid—the Court sent a message to Jefferson and to the Congress that the judiciary had the power to affect legislation. The Marshall Court, however, never declared another act of Congress unconstitutional.

HISTORICAL IMPACT

In striking down part of the Judiciary Act, an act of Congress, Marshall gave new force to the principle of judicial review. The legacy of John Marshall and of *Marbury* is that judicial review has become a cornerstone of American government. One scholar has called it "America's novel contribution to political theory and the practice of constitutional government." As Justice Marshall recognized, judicial review is an essential component of democratic government; by ensuring that Congress exercises only those powers granted by the Constitution, the courts protect the sovereignty of the people.

Perhaps more importantly, the principle of judicial review plays a vital role in our federal system of checks and balances. With *Marbury,* the judicial branch secured its place as one of three coequal branches of the federal government. The judiciary has no power to make laws or to carry them out. However, judges have an important role in deciding what the law is and how it is carried out.

In *City of Boerne* v. *Flores* (1997), for instance, the Supreme Court declared void the Religious Freedom Restoration Act of 1993. Members of Congress had passed the act in an attempt to change the way federal courts apply the First Amendment's Free Exercise Clause. The Supreme Court ruled that Congress does not have the authority to decide what the First Amendment means—in effect, to define its own powers. The Court, and not Congress, is the interpreter of the Constitution.

Through the 1999–2000 term, the Court had rendered 151 decisions striking down—in whole or part—acts of Congress. It had also voided or restricted the enforcement of state laws 1,130 times. That the entire country has with few exceptions obeyed these decisions, no matter how strongly they disagreed, proves Americans' faith in the Supreme Court as the protector of the rule of law.

THINKING CRITICALLY

CONNECT TO HISTORY

1. **Comparing** Read encyclopedia articles about another Marshall Court decision, such as *Fletcher* v. *Peck*, *Cohens* v. *Virginia*, or *Gibbons* v. *Ogden*. Compare that decision with *Marbury* and consider what the two cases and opinions have in common. Write a paragraph explaining the major similarities between the cases.

 **SEE SKILLBUILDER HANDBOOK, PAGE R8.**

CONNECT TO TODAY

2.  **INTERNET ACTIVITY** **CLASSZONE.COM**

Visit the links for Historic Decisions of the Supreme Court to research a recent Supreme Court decision involving judicial review of an act of Congress. Write a case summary in which you describe the law's purpose, the Court's ruling, and the potential impact of the decision.

The Age of Jackson

MAIN IDEA

During a time of growing sectionalism, Andrew Jackson's election in 1828 ushered in a new era of popular democracy.

WHY IT MATTERS NOW

Jackson's use of presidential powers laid the foundation for the modern presidency.

Terms & Names

- **Henry Clay**
- **American System**
- **John C. Calhoun**
- **Missouri Compromise**
- **Andrew Jackson**
- **John Quincy Adams**
- **Jacksonian democracy**
- **Trail of Tears**
- **John Tyler**

One American's Story

Robert Fulton designed and built the first commercially successful steamboat. In 1807 his *Clermont* made the 150-mile trip up the Hudson River from New York City to Albany in 32 hours. Another one of Fulton's boats, the *Paragon*, was so luxurious that it had a paneled dining room and bedrooms. Fulton even posted regulations on his luxurious steamboats.

▲ Steamboats, like the one pictured here, could move against a river's current or a strong wind.

A PERSONAL VOICE ROBERT FULTON

> **"As the steamboat has been fitted up in an elegant style, order is necessary to keep it so; gentlemen will therefore please to observe cleanliness, and a reasonable attention not to injure the furniture; for this purpose no one must sit on a table under the penalty of half a dollar each time, and every breakage of tables, chairs, sofas, or windows, tearing of curtains, or injury of any kind must be paid for before leaving the boat."**
>
> —quoted in *Steamboats Come True: American Inventors in Action*

Steamboats like the one Fulton described did more than comfortably transport passengers. They also carried freight and played an important role in uniting the nation economically. Although tensions continued to arise between the different sections of the nation, a growing national spirit kept the country together. This spirit was ultimately personified by Andrew Jackson—a self-made man from the growing West who was both confident and dynamic.

Regional Economies Create Differences

In the early decades of the 19th century, the economies of the various regions of the United States developed differently. The Northeast began to industrialize while the South and West continued to be more agricultural.

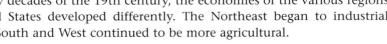

EARLY INDUSTRY IN THE UNITED STATES The Industrial Revolution—large-scale production resulting in massive change in social and economic organization—began in Great Britain in the 18th century and gradually reached the United States.

Industry took off first in New England, whose economy depended on shipping and foreign trade. Agriculture there was not highly profitable, so New Englanders were more ready than other Americans to embrace new forms of manufacturing—and prime among these were mechanized textile, or fabric, mills.

Soon, farmers in the North began to specialize in one or two crops or types of livestock (such as corn and cattle), sell what they produced to urban markets, and then purchase with cash whatever else they needed from stores. Increasingly, these were items made in Northern factories. As a result, a market economy began to develop in which agriculture and manufacturing each supported the growth of the other. (A)

MAIN IDEA

Analyzing Causes

(A) How did agriculture and industry support a market economy in the North?

THE SOUTH REMAINS AGRICULTURAL Meanwhile, the South continued to grow as an agricultural power. Eli Whitney's invention of a cotton gin (short for "engine," or machine) in 1793 made it possible for Southern farmers to produce cotton more profitably. The emergence of a Cotton Kingdom in the South—and

Science & Technology

INTERACTIVE

THE COTTON GIN

In 1794, Eli Whitney was granted a patent for a "new and useful improvement in the mode of Ginning Cotton." Workers who previously could clean only one pound of cotton by hand per day could now clean as much as fifty pounds per day. Because of Whitney's cotton gin, cotton production in the United States increased from three thousand bales in 1790 to more than two million bales in 1850.

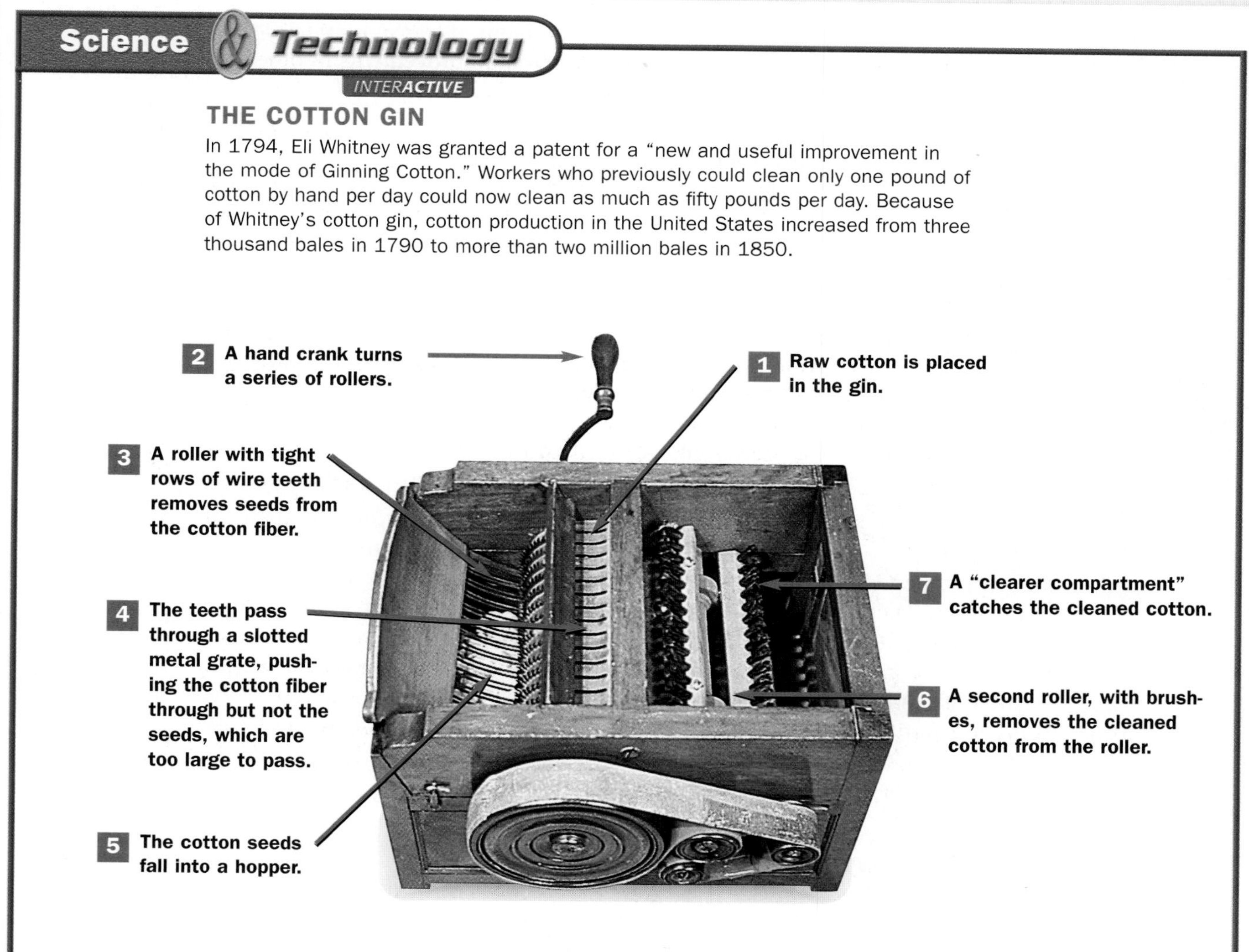
1 Raw cotton is placed in the gin.
2 A hand crank turns a series of rollers.
3 A roller with tight rows of wire teeth removes seeds from the cotton fiber.
4 The teeth pass through a slotted metal grate, pushing the cotton fiber through but not the seeds, which are too large to pass.
5 The cotton seeds fall into a hopper.
6 A second roller, with brushes, removes the cleaned cotton from the roller.
7 A "clearer compartment" catches the cleaned cotton.

thus the need for more field labor—contributed to the expansion of slavery. Between 1790 and 1820, the enslaved population increased from less than 700,000 to over 1.5 million. In the North, things were different. By 1804, states north of Delaware had either abolished slavery or had enacted laws for gradual emancipation. Slavery declined in the North, but some slaves remained there for decades.

Vocabulary
emancipation: the act of freeing from bondage or slavery

Balancing Nationalism and Sectionalism

These economic differences often created political tensions between the different sections of the nation. Throughout the first half of the 19th century, however, American leaders managed to keep the nation together.

THE SUPREME COURT BOOSTS NATIONAL POWER

As Henry Clay promoted the American System in an effort to strengthen nationalism, the Supreme Court also boosted national power with two significant decisions.

In *McCulloch* v. *Maryland* (1819), the high court denied Maryland the right to tax the Bank of the United States, thus strengthening the authority of the national government over state governments.

In *Gibbons* v. *Ogden* (1824), the Court further bolstered federal power by affirming the national government's right to regulate interstate commerce.

CLAY'S AMERICAN SYSTEM As the North, South, and West developed different economies, President Madison developed a plan to move the United States toward economic independence from Britain and other European powers. In 1815 he presented his plan to Congress. It included three major points:

- establishing a protective tariff
- rechartering the national bank
- sponsoring the development of transportation systems and other internal improvements in order to make travel throughout the nation easier

House Speaker **Henry Clay** promoted the plan as the **"American System."** B

Madison and Clay supported tariffs on imports to protect U.S. industry from British competition. Most Northeasterners also welcomed protective tariffs. However, people in the South and West, whose livelihoods did not depend on manufacturing, were not as eager to tax European imports. Nevertheless, Clay, who was from the West (Kentucky), and **John C. Calhoun,** a Southerner (South Carolina), convinced congressmen from their regions to approve the Tariff of 1816. Also in 1816, Congress voted to charter the Second Bank of the United States for a 20-year period and to create a unified currency.

MAIN IDEA
Analyzing Motives
B What was the intention behind the "American System"?

THE MISSOURI COMPROMISE In spite of these efforts to unify the national economy, sectional conflicts remained part of American politics. In 1818 settlers in Missouri requested admission to the Union. Northerners and Southerners disagreed, however, on whether Missouri should be admitted as a free state or a slave state.

Behind the leadership of Henry Clay, Congress passed a series of agreements in 1820–1821 known as the **Missouri Compromise.** Under these agreements, Maine was admitted as a free state and Missouri as a slave state. The rest of the Louisiana Territory was split into two parts. The dividing line was set at 36°30′ north latitude. South of the line, slavery was legal. North of the line—except in Missouri—slavery was banned. C

MAIN IDEA
Summarizing
C What agreements made up the Missouri Compromise?

The Election of Andrew Jackson

Despite these sectional tensions, the story of America in the early 19th century was one of expansion—expanding economies, expanding territory, and expanding democracy. The man who embraced the spirit of that expansion and to many personified it was **Andrew Jackson,** who captured the presidency in 1828.

THE ELECTION OF 1824 In 1824, Andrew Jackson lost his bid for the presidency to **John Quincy Adams.** Jacksonians, or followers of Jackson, accused Adams and Jackson's political enemy, Henry Clay, of stealing the presidency. Then, because Adams appointed Clay secretary of state, the Jacksonians claimed Adams had struck a corrupt bargain. The split between Clay and Jackson tore apart the Democratic-Republican party. While Clay and his faction were called the National Republican Party, the Jacksonians became known as the Democratic Party.

Vocabulary
corrupt: marked by bribery

EXPANDING DEMOCRACY CHANGES POLITICS During John Quincy Adams's presidency, most states had eased property requirements for voting, thereby enlarging the voting population. In the election of 1824, approximately 350,000 white males voted for the presidency. In 1828, over three times that number voted. Many of these new voters were common people who viewed the rugged westerner Jackson as their champion. The support of this new voting bloc gave Jackson victory in the election of 1828.

Jacksonian Democracy

THE SPOILS SYSTEM Jackson's ideal of political power for all classes is often called **Jacksonian democracy.** As part of this philosophy, Jackson sought to give common people a chance to participate in government. He did this through the spoils system, in which new administrations hire their own supporters to replace supporters of the previous administration. Using the spoils system, Jackson gave away huge numbers of jobs to friends and also to political allies.

KEY PLAYER

ANDREW JACKSON
1767–1845

Andrew Jackson thought of himself as a man of the people. He had been born in poverty in the Carolina backcountry, the son of Scots-Irish immigrants. He was the first president since George Washington without a college education.

At the time of his election at the age of 61, however, Jackson was hardly one of the common people. He had built a highly successful career in Tennessee in law, politics, land speculation, cotton planting, and soldiering. His home, the Hermitage, was a mansion, not a log cabin. Anyone who owned more than a hundred slaves, as Jackson did, was very wealthy.

President-elect Andrew Jackson greets well-wishers on his way to Washington, D.C., to be inaugurated president in 1829. ▼

THE INDIAN REMOVAL ACT In 1830 Congress, with the support of Jackson, passed the Indian Removal Act. Under this law, the federal government provided funds to negotiate treaties that would force the Native Americans to move west.

▲ *Trail of Tears,* a 1992 painting by Troy Anderson, a Cherokee artist

Many of the tribes signed removal treaties. However, the Cherokee Nation refused and fought the government in the courts. In 1832, the Supreme Court ruled in *Worcester* v. *Georgia* that the state of Georgia could not regulate the Cherokee Nation by law or invade Cherokee lands. However, Jackson refused to abide by the Supreme Court decision, saying, "John Marshall has made his decision; now let him enforce it." D

MAIN IDEA

Analyzing Events

D How did the federal government initially try to enforce the Indian Removal Act?

THE TRAIL OF TEARS In the years following the Court's ruling, U.S. troops rounded up the Cherokee and drove them into camps to await the journey west. A Baptist missionary described the scene.

A PERSONAL VOICE EVAN JONES

"The Cherokees are nearly all prisoners. They had been dragged from their houses and encamped at the forts and military places, all over the nation. In Georgia especially, multitudes were allowed no time to take anything with them except the clothes they had on. Well-furnished houses were left as prey to plunderers."

—*Baptist Missionary Magazine,* June 16, 1838

Beginning in the fall of 1838, the Cherokee were sent off in groups of about 1,000 each on the 800-mile journey, mostly on foot. As winter came, more and more Cherokee died. The Cherokee buried more than a quarter of their people along the **Trail of Tears,** the forced marches the Cherokee followed from Georgia to the Indian Territory. (See map on page 125.)

Nullification and the Bank War

In 1824 and again in 1828, Congress increased the Tariff of 1816. Jackson's vice-president, John C. Calhoun of South Carolina, called the 1828 tariff a Tariff of Abominations because he blamed it for economic problems in the South.

The South's economy depended on cotton exports. Yet the high tariff on manufactured goods reduced British exports to the United States, and because of this, Britain bought less cotton. With the decline of British goods, the South was now forced to buy the more expensive Northern manufactured goods. From the South's point of view, the North was getting rich at the expense of the South.

THE NULLIFICATION CRISIS To try to free South Carolinians from the tariff, Calhoun developed a theory of nullification. Calhoun's theory held that the U.S. Constitution was based on a compact among the sovereign states. If the Constitution had been established by 13 sovereign states, he reasoned, then the states must still be sovereign, and each would have the right to determine whether acts of Congress were constitutional. If a state found an act to be unconstitutional, the state could declare the offending law nullified, or inoperative, within its borders. E

MAIN IDEA

Making Predictions

E What do you think might be the consequences of Calhoun's nullification theory for federal-state relations?

The Senate debated the tariff question (and the underlying states' rights issue). Senator Daniel Webster of Massachusetts opposed nullification and South Carolina Senator Robert Hayne aired Calhoun's views.

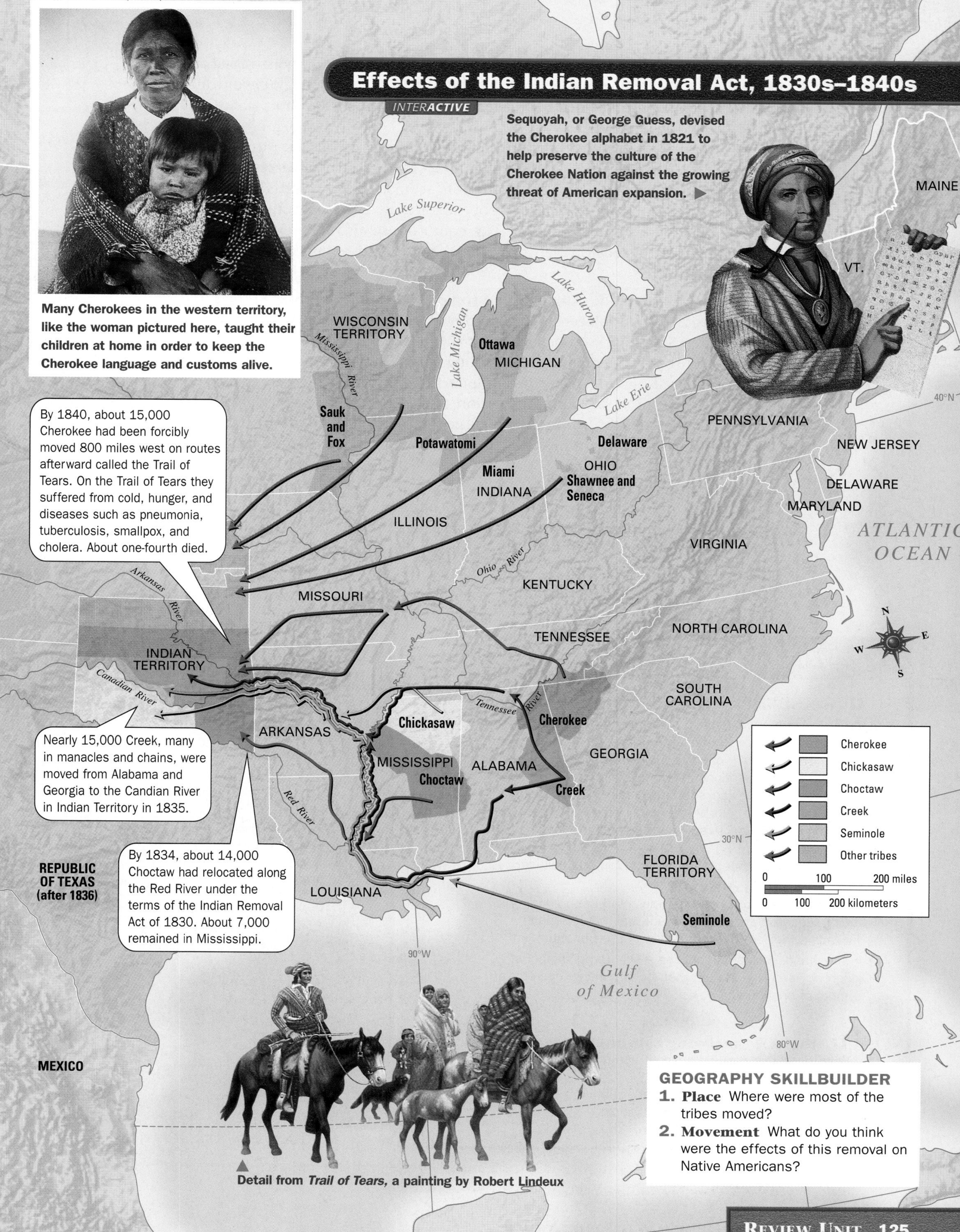

Many Cherokees in the western territory, like the woman pictured here, taught their children at home in order to keep the Cherokee language and customs alive.

Sequoyah, or George Guess, devised the Cherokee alphabet in 1821 to help preserve the culture of the Cherokee Nation against the growing threat of American expansion. ▶

▲ Detail from *Trail of Tears,* a painting by Robert Lindeux

GEOGRAPHY SKILLBUILDER

1. **Place** Where were most of the tribes moved?
2. **Movement** What do you think were the effects of this removal on Native Americans?

In 1832 the issue of states' rights was put to a test when Congress raised tariffs again. South Carolinians declared the tariffs of 1828 and 1832 "null, void, and no law." Then they threatened to secede, or withdraw from the Union, if customs officials tried to collect duties.

In response, an outraged Jackson urged Congress to pass the Force Bill to allow the federal government to use the military if state authorities resisted paying proper duties. A bloody confrontation seemed likely until Henry Clay forged a compromise in 1833. Clay proposed a tariff bill that would gradually lower duties over a ten-year period. The compromise also included passage of the Force Bill. The tension between states' rights and federal authority subsided—temporarily.

JACKSON'S BANK WAR Although Jackson defended federal power in the nullification crisis, he tried to decrease federal power when it came to the Second Bank of the United States. Jackson believed that the national bank was an agent of the wealthy, and that its members cared nothing for the common people.

In 1832 Jackson won reelection despite the efforts of his critics to make a campaign issue out of Jackson's opposition to the bank. After his reelection, he tried to kill the bank by withdrawing all government deposits from the bank's branches and placing them in certain state banks called "pet banks" because of their loyalty to the Democratic Party. As a result, the Bank of the United States became just another bank. F

Jackson won the bank war, but his tactics and policies angered many people. Many accused him of acting more like a king than a president. In 1832, his opponents formed a new political party, which they later called the Whig Party.

MAIN IDEA

Analyzing Motives

F What were some of Jackson's reasons for opposing the Second Bank of the United States?

Analyzing *Political Cartoons*

"KING ANDREW THE FIRST"

Andrew Jackson once justified his tendency to place personal prerogative above constitutional law or national policy by stating that "One man with courage makes a majority." His critics replied with accusations of tyranny. The *New York American* condemned Jackson as a "maniac," who would "trample the rights of our people under his feet." The Whig convention of 1834 declared, "Your president has become your MONARCH."

Both of those sentiments are reflected in this political cartoon that portrays Jackson as a king.

- Ancient portraits of kings often depicted them grinding their conquered enemies beneath their heel. Beneath Jackson's feet are the torn pages of the Constitution.
- In one hand, Jackson is holding a scepter, a symbol of kingly power, while in the other, he is holding the veto, a symbol of presidential power.

SKILLBUILDER Analyzing Political Cartoons

1. What does this cartoon suggest about Jackson's attitude toward the Constitution?
2. How does this cartoon particularly comment on Jackson's use of presidential power?

Successors Deal with Jackson's Legacy

When Jackson announced that he would not run for a third term in 1836, the Democrats chose Vice-President Martin Van Buren as their candidate. The newly formed Whig Party ran three regional candidates against him. With Jackson's support, however, Van Buren easily won the election.

THE PANIC OF 1837 Along with the presidency, however, Van Buren inherited the consequences of Jackson's bank war. Many of the pet banks that accepted federal deposits were wildcat banks that printed bank notes wildly in excess of the gold and silver they had on deposit. Such wildcat banks were doomed to fail when people tried to redeem their currency for gold or silver.

MAIN IDEA

Analyzing Causes

G How did "wildcat banks" contribute to the panic of 1837?

By May 1837, many banks stopped accepting paper currency. In the panic of 1837, bank closings and the collapse of the credit system cost many people their savings, bankrupted hundreds of businesses, and put more than a third of the population out of work. G

HARRISON AND TYLER In 1840 Van Buren ran for reelection against Whig Party candidate William Henry Harrison, who was known as "Tippecanoe" for a battle he won against Native Americans in 1811. The Whigs blamed Van Buren for the weak economy and portrayed Harrison, the old war hero, as a man of the people and Van Buren as an aristocrat.

Harrison won the election, but died just a month after his inauguration. **John Tyler,** Harrison's vice-president, became president. A strong-minded Virginian and former Democrat, Tyler opposed many parts of the Whig program. He halted hopes for significant Whig reforms.

The Democrat and Whig parties went on to dominate national politics until the 1850s. The new politicians appealed more to passion than to reason. They courted popularity in a way that John Quincy Adams and his predecessors never would have. Thus, the style of politics in America had changed drastically since the 1790s. Political speeches became a form of mass entertainment, involving far more Americans in the political process. Also, the West was playing an increasing role in national politics. That trend would continue as more Americans moved to places like Texas and California.

SECTION 2 ASSESSMENT

1. **TERMS & NAMES** For each term or name, write a sentence explaining its significance.
   - **Henry Clay**
   - **American System**
   - **John C. Calhoun**
   - **Missouri Compromise**
   - **Andrew Jackson**
   - **John Quincy Adams**
   - **Jacksonian democracy**
   - **Trail of Tears**
   - **John Tyler**

MAIN IDEA

2. **TAKING NOTES**
   In a chart like the one shown, write newspaper headlines that tell the significance of each date.

Dates	Headlines
1815	
1820	
1828	
1832	
1837	
1838	

CRITICAL THINKING

3. **EVALUATING**
   In what ways do you think the Missouri Compromise and the nullification crisis of 1832 might be considered important milestones in American history? **Think About:**
   - the expansion of slavery into the West
   - Calhoun's nullification theory
   - Jackson's reaction to South Carolina's actions

4. **ANALYZING CAUSES**
   What factors set the stage for the Indian Removal Act of 1830 and the Trail of Tears? **Think About:**
   - U.S. expansion to the west
   - removal treaties
   - Jackson's response to *Worcester* v. *Georgia*

States' Rights

The power struggle between states and the federal government has caused controversy since the country's beginning. At its worst, the conflict resulted in the Civil War. Today, state and federal governments continue to square off on jurisdictional issues.

- In 1996, the Supreme Court ruled that congressional districts in Texas and North Carolina that had been redrawn to increase minority representation were unconstitutional.
- In 2000, the Supreme Court agreed to hear another case in the ongoing—since 1979—dispute between the federal government and the state of Alaska over who has authority to lease offshore land for oil and gas drilling.

Constitutional conflicts between states' rights and federal jurisdiction are pictured here. As you read, see how each issue was resolved.

1787

▼ CONSTITUTIONAL CONVENTION

ISSUE: The Constitution tried to resolve the original debate over states' rights versus federal authority.

At the Constitutional Convention in Philadelphia, delegates wanted to create a federal government that was stronger than the one created by the Articles of Confederation. But delegates disagreed about whether the federal government should have more power than the states. They also disagreed about whether large states should have more power than small states in the national legislature. The convention compromised—the Constitution reserves certain powers for the states, delegates other powers to the federal government, divides some powers between state and federal governments, and tries to balance the differing needs of the states through two houses of Congress.

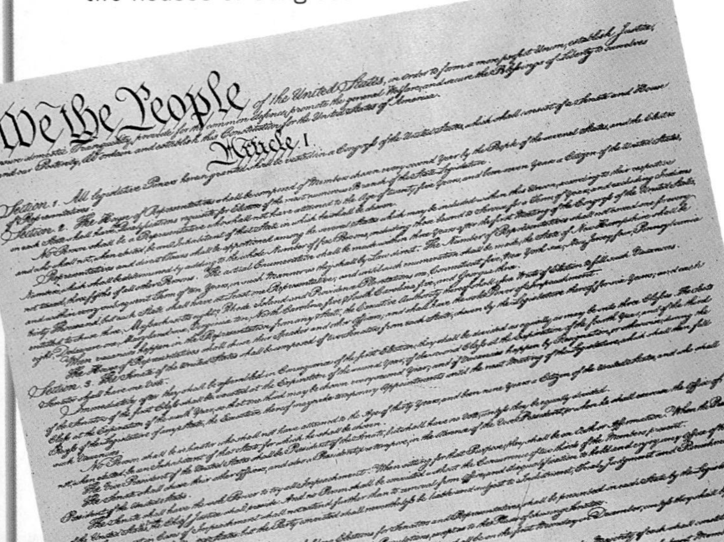

We the People

Article. I.

1832

NULLIFICATION ▲

ISSUE: The state of South Carolina moved to nullify, or declare void, a tariff set by Congress.

In the cartoon above, President Andrew Jackson, right, is playing a game called bragg. One of his opponents, Vice-President John C. Calhoun, is hiding two cards, "Nullification" and "Anti-Tariff," behind him. Jackson is doing poorly in this game, but he eventually won the real nullification dispute. When Congress passed high tariffs on imports in 1832, politicians from South Carolina, led by Calhoun, tried to nullify the tariff law, or declare it void. Jackson threatened to enforce the law with federal troops. Congress reduced the tariff to avoid a confrontation, and Calhoun resigned the vice-presidency.

1860

◄ SOUTH CAROLINA'S SECESSION

ISSUE: The conflict over a state's right to secede, or withdraw, from the Union led to the Civil War.

In December 1860, Southern secessionists cheered "secession" enthusiastically in front of the Mills House (left), a hotel in Charleston, South Carolina. South Carolina seceded after the election of Abraham Lincoln, whom the South perceived as anti-states' rights and antislavery. Lincoln took the position that states did not have the right to secede from the Union. In 1861, he ordered that provisions be sent to the federal troops stationed at Fort Sumter in Charleston harbor. South Carolinians fired on the fort—and the Civil War was under way. The Union's victory in the war ended the most serious challenge to federal authority: states did not have the right to secede from the Union.

1957

LITTLE ROCK CENTRAL HIGH SCHOOL ▲

ISSUE: Some Southern governors refused to obey federal desegregation mandates for schools.

In 1957, President Eisenhower mobilized federal troops in Little Rock, Arkansas, to enforce the Supreme Court's 1954 ruling in the case of *Brown* v. *Board of Education of Topeka.* This ruling made segregation in public schools illegal. The Arkansas National Guard escorted nine African-American students into Little Rock Central High School against the wishes of Governor Orval Faubus, who had tried to prevent the students from entering the school. After this incident, Faubus closed the high schools in Little Rock in 1958 and 1959, thereby avoiding desegregation.

THINKING CRITICALLY

CONNECT TO HISTORY

1. **Creating a Chart** For each incident pictured, create a chart that tells who was on each side of the issue, summarizes each position, and explains how the issue was resolved.

CONNECT TO TODAY

2. **Using Primary and Secondary Sources** Research one of the controversies in the bulleted list in the opening paragraph or another states' rights controversy of the 1990s or 2000s. Decide which side you support. Write a paragraph explaining your position on the issue.

SEE SKILLBUILDER HANDBOOK, PAGE R22.

CLASSZONE.COM

SECTION 3

Manifest Destiny

MAIN IDEA

Through settlement and war, the United States greatly expanded its boundaries during the mid-1800s.

WHY IT MATTERS NOW

The actions Americans took during this period established the current borders of the 48 contiguous states.

Terms & Names

- **manifest destiny**
- **Santa Fe Trail**
- **Oregon Trail**
- **Stephen F. Austin**
- **Texas Revolution**
- **the Alamo**
- **Sam Houston**
- **James K. Polk**
- **Republic of California**
- **Treaty of Guadalupe Hidalgo**

One American's Story

In 1821, Stephen F. Austin led the first of several groups of American settlers to a fertile area along the Brazos River. Drawn by the promise of inexpensive land and economic opportunity, Austin established a colony of American settlers in Tejas, or Texas, then the northernmost province of the Mexican state of Coahuila. However, Austin's plans didn't work out as well as he had hoped; 12 years later, he found himself in a Mexican prison and his new homeland in an uproar. After his release, Austin spoke about the impending crisis between Texas and Mexico.

A PERSONAL VOICE STEPHEN F. AUSTIN

"Texas needs peace, and a local government; its inhabitants are farmers, and they need a calm and quiet life. . . . [But] my efforts to serve Texas involved me in the labyrinth of Mexican politics. I was arrested, and have suffered a long persecution and imprisonment. . . . I fully hoped to have found Texas at peace and in tranquillity, but regret to find it in commotion; all disorganized, all in anarchy, and threatened with immediate hostilities. . . . Can this state of things exist without precipitating the country into a war? I think it cannot."

—quoted in *Lone Star: A History of Texas and Texans*

Stephen F. Austin

Austin's prediction was correct. War did break out in Texas—twice. First, Texans rebelled against the Mexican government. Then, the United States went to war against Mexico over the boundaries of Texas. These conflicts were the climax of decades of competition over the western half of North America—a competition that involved the United States, Mexico, Native Americans, and various European nations. The end result of the competition would be U.S. control over a huge swath of the continent, from the Atlantic to the Pacific.

Settling the Frontier

As various presidents established policies in the early 19th century that expanded U.S. territory, American settlers pushed first into the Northwest Territory and then headed farther west.

AMERICANS PURSUE MANIFEST DESTINY For a quarter century after the War of 1812, only a few Americans explored the West. Then, in the 1840s, expansion fever gripped the country. Many Americans began to believe that their movement westward was predestined by God. The phrase **"manifest destiny"** expressed the belief that the United States was ordained to expand to the Pacific Ocean and into Mexican and Native American territory. Many Americans also believed that this destiny was manifest, or obvious and inevitable.

Most Americans had practical reasons for moving west. For settlers, the abundance of land was the greatest attraction. As the number of western settlers climbed, merchants and manufacturers followed, seeking new markets for their goods. Many Americans also trekked west because of personal economic problems in the East. The panic of 1837, for example, had disastrous consequences and convinced many Americans that they would be better off attempting a fresh start in the West. (A)

MAIN IDEA

Predicting Effects

(A) How might manifest destiny later affect U.S. relations with Native Americans?

TRAILS WEST The settlers and traders who made the trek west used a series of old Native American trails as well as new routes. One of the busiest routes was the **Santa Fe Trail,** which stretched 780 miles from Independence, Missouri, to Santa Fe in the Mexican province of New Mexico. (See map on page 132.) Each spring from 1821 through the 1860s, American traders loaded their covered wagons with goods and set off toward Santa Fe.

For about the first 150 miles, traders traveled individually. After that, fearing attacks by Native Americans, traders banded into organized groups of up to 100 wagons. Cooperation, though, came to an abrupt end when Santa Fe came into view. Traders raced off on their own as each tried to be the first to arrive. After a few days of trading, they loaded their wagons with goods, restocked their animals, and headed back to Missouri.

The **Oregon Trail** stretched from Independence, Missouri, to Oregon City, Oregon. It was blazed in 1836 by two Methodist missionaries named Marcus and Narcissa Whitman. By driving their wagon as far as Fort Boise (near present-day Boise, Idaho), they proved that wagons could travel on the Oregon Trail.

Following the Whitmans' lead, many pioneers migrated west on the Oregon Trail. Some bought "prairie schooners," wooden-wheeled wagons covered with sailcloth and pulled by oxen. Most walked, however, pushing handcarts loaded with a few precious possessions, food, and other supplies. The trip took months, even if all went well.

Background

The Mormon religion was controversial for its belief in polygamy, a practice that allowed a man to have more than one wife.

THE MORMON MIGRATION One group migrated westward along the Oregon Trail to escape persecution. These people were the Mormons, a religious community that would play a major role in the development of the West. Founded by Joseph Smith in upstate New York in 1827, the Mormon community moved to Ohio and then Illinois to escape persecution. After an anti-Mormon mob murdered Smith, a leader named Brigham Young urged the Mormons to move farther west. Thousands of believers walked to Nebraska, across Wyoming to the Rockies, and then southwest. In 1847, the Mormons stopped at the edge of the desert near the Great Salt Lake, in what is now Utah. Young boldly

HISTORICAL SPOTLIGHT

JIM BECKWOURTH 1798–1867?

James Pierson Beckwourth (or Beckwirth) was the toughest kind of pioneer, a mountain man. The son of an African-American woman, he ventured westward with a fur-trading expedition in 1823 and found the place that would become his home for nearly the next quarter century—the Rocky Mountains. He greatly impressed the Crow, who gave him the name "Bloody Arm" because of his skill as a fighter.

Beckwourth served from 1837 until 1848 as an Army scout and trading-post operator. In 1848, he discovered a passage in the Sierra Nevada range that led to California's Sacramento Valley and decided to settle down near the pass and become a rancher. "In the spring of 1852 I established myself in Beckwourth Valley, and finally found myself transformed into a hotel-keeper and chief of a trading-post."

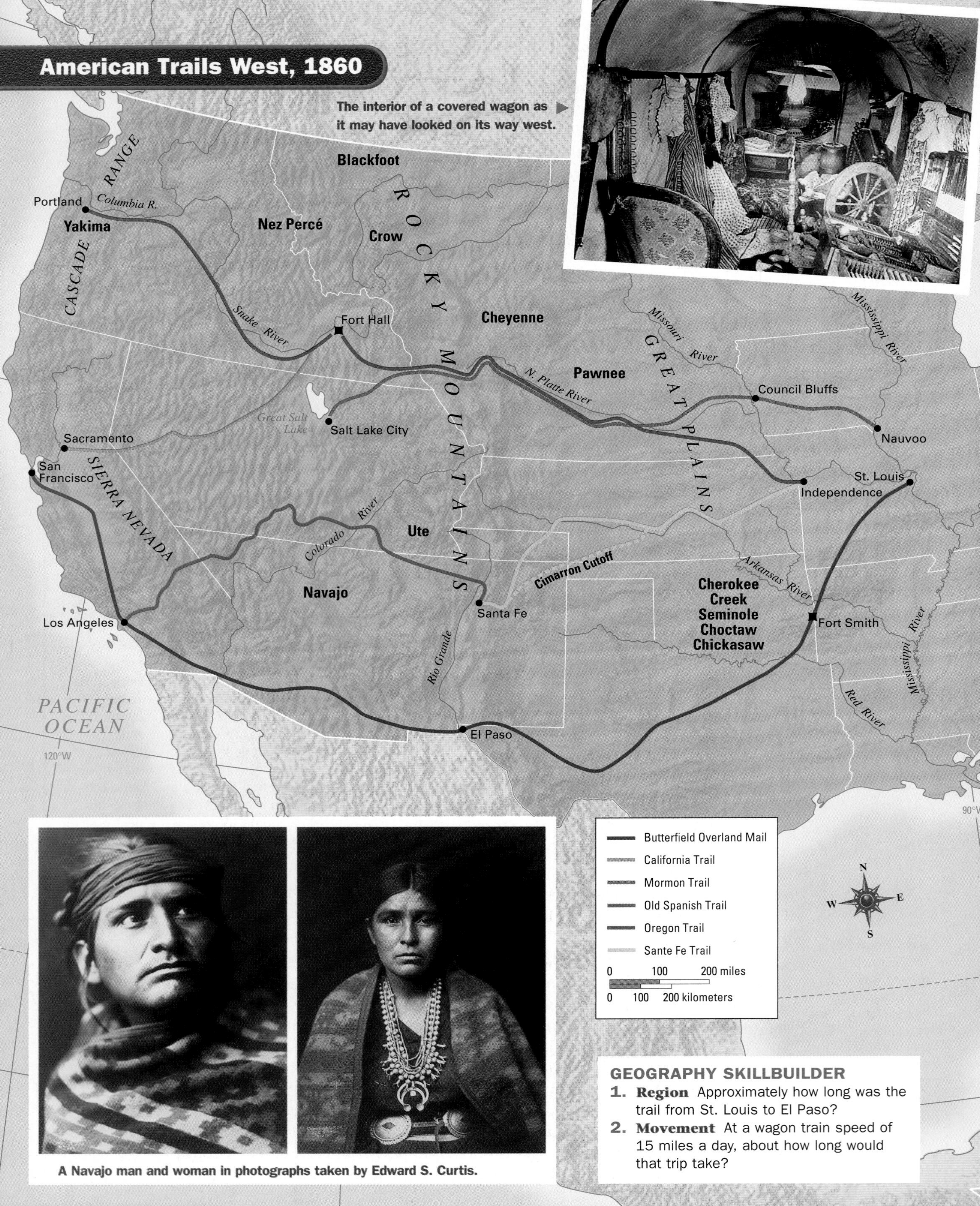

A Navajo man and woman in photographs taken by Edward S. Curtis.

GEOGRAPHY SKILLBUILDER

1. **Region** Approximately how long was the trail from St. Louis to El Paso?
2. **Movement** At a wagon train speed of 15 miles a day, about how long would that trip take?

declared, "This is the place." Soon they had coaxed settlements and farms from the bleak landscape by irrigating their fields. Salt Lake City blossomed out of the land the Mormons called Deseret. B

MAIN IDEA

Analyzing Motives

B Why did the Mormons move farther west in their search for a new home?

SETTING BOUNDARIES In the early 1840s, Great Britain still claimed areas near the Canadian border in parts of what are now Maine and Minnesota. The Webster-Ashburton Treaty of 1842 settled these territorial disputes in the East and the Midwest, but the two nations merely continued the "joint occupation" of the Oregon Territory that they had first established in 1818. In 1846 the two countries agreed to extend the mainland boundary along the 49th parallel westward from the Rocky Mountains to Puget Sound, establishing the current boundary between the United States and Canada. Unfortunately, establishing the boundary in the Southwest with Mexico would not be so peaceful.

Texan Independence

After 300 years of Spanish rule, only a few thousand Mexican settlers had migrated to what is now Texas. After 1820, that changed as Texas became an important region in Mexico and then an independent republic.

MEXICAN INDEPENDENCE AND TEXAN LAND GRANTS The mission system used by Spain declined after Mexico had won independence from Spain in 1821. After freeing the missions from Spanish control, the Mexican government offered the surrounding lands to government officials and ranchers. To make the land more secure and stable, the Mexican government also encouraged Americans to settle in Texas.

Many Americans rushed at the chance to buy inexpensive land in Texas. The population of Anglo, or English-speaking, settlers from the United States soon surpassed the population of Tejanos, or Mexican settlers, who lived in Texas. Among the more prominent leaders of these American settlers was **Stephen F. Austin.** C

MAIN IDEA

Developing Historical Perspective

C Why did many Americans initially settle in Texas?

Austin's father, Moses Austin, had received a land grant from Spain to establish a colony between the Brazos and Colorado rivers but died before he was able to carry out his plans. Stephen obtained permission, first from Spain and then from Mexico after it had won its independence, to carry out his father's project. In 1821 he established a colony where "no drunkard, no gambler, no profane swearer, and no idler" would be allowed.

The main settlement of the colony was named San Felipe de Austin, in Stephen's honor. By 1825, Austin had issued 297 land grants to the group that later became known as Texas's Old Three Hundred. Each family received either 177 very inexpensive acres of farmland, or 4,428 acres for stock grazing, as well as a 10-year exemption from paying taxes. "I am convinced," Austin said, "that I could take on fifteen hundred families as easily as three hundred if permitted to do so." By 1830, there were more than 20,000 Americans in Texas.

THE TEXAS REVOLUTION Despite peaceful cooperation between Anglos and Tejanos, differences over cultural issues intensified between Anglos and the Mexican government. The overwhelmingly Protestant Anglo settlers spoke English instead of Spanish. Furthermore, many of the settlers were Southerners, who had brought slaves with them to Texas. Mexico, which had abolished slavery in 1829, insisted in vain that the Texans free their slaves.

Meanwhile, Mexican politics had become increasingly unstable. Austin had traveled to Mexico City late in 1833 to present petitions to Mexican president Antonio López de Santa Anna for greater self-government for Texas. While Austin was on his way home, Santa Anna had Austin imprisoned for inciting revolution. After Santa Anna suspended local powers in Texas and other

Mexican states, several rebellions broke out, including one that would be known as the **Texas Revolution**.

When Austin returned to Texas in 1835, he was convinced that war was its "only resource." Determined to force Texas to obey Mexican law, Santa Anna marched his army toward San Antonio. At the same time, Austin and his followers issued a call for Texans to arm themselves. D

MAIN IDEA

Analyzing Issues

D What disagreement led to the Texas Revolution?

"REMEMBER THE ALAMO!" The commander of the Anglo troops, Lieutenant Colonel William Travis, moved his men into **the Alamo,** a mission and fort in the center of San Antonio. Travis believed that maintaining control of the Alamo would prevent Santa Anna's movement farther north.

From February 23, 1836, Santa Anna and his troops attacked the rebels holed up in the Alamo. On March 2, 1836, as the battle for the Alamo raged, Texans declared their independence from Mexico and quickly ratified a constitution based on that of the United States. The 13-day siege finally ended on March 6, 1836, when Mexican troops scaled the Alamo's walls. All 187 U.S. defenders and hundreds of Mexicans died.

Later in March, Santa Anna's troops executed 300 rebels at Goliad. The Alamo and the Goliad executions whipped the Texan rebels into a fury. Six weeks after the defeat at the Alamo, the rebels' commander in chief, **Sam Houston,** and 900

War for Texas Independence, 1835–1836

INTERACTIVE

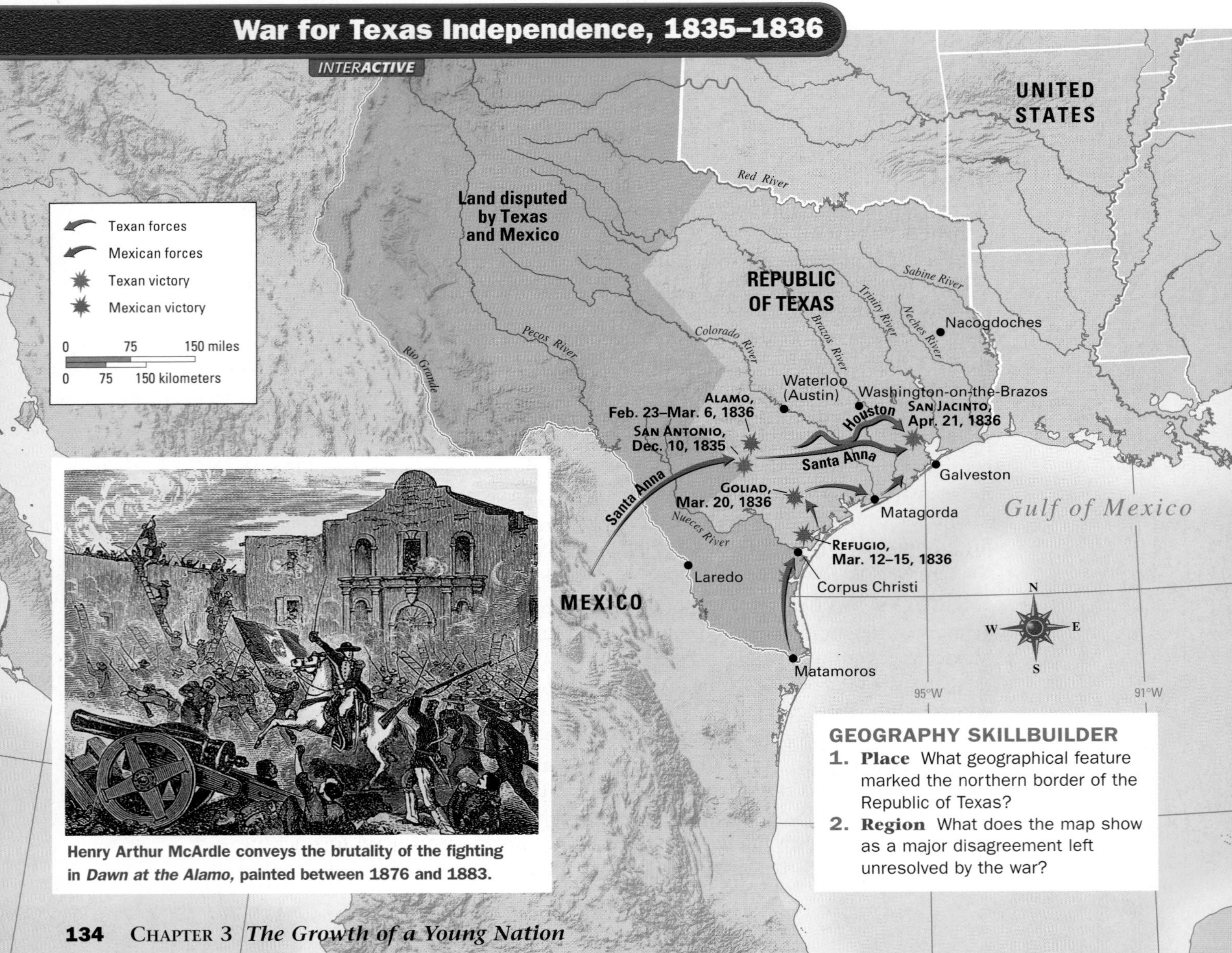

Henry Arthur McArdle conveys the brutality of the fighting in *Dawn at the Alamo*, painted between 1876 and 1883.

GEOGRAPHY SKILLBUILDER

1. **Place** What geographical feature marked the northern border of the Republic of Texas?
2. **Region** What does the map show as a major disagreement left unresolved by the war?

KEY PLAYERS

SAM HOUSTON
1793–1863

Sam Houston ran away from home in Tennessee at about age 15 and lived for three years with the Cherokee. He later fought in the U.S. Army, studied law, was elected to Congress, and became governor of Tennessee.

In his memoirs Houston told of listening in vain for the signal guns indicating that the Alamo still stood. "I listened with an acuteness of sense which no man can understand whose hearing has not been sharpened by the teachings of the dwellers of the forest."

The Republic of Texas chose Houston to be its first president. When Texas became a state, he was elected to the U.S. Senate.

SANTA ANNA
1795–1876

Antonio López de Santa Anna reportedly once said, "If I were God, I would wish to be more." Santa Anna began his career fighting for Spain in the war over Mexican independence. Later, he switched sides to fight for Mexico.

Declaring himself the "Napoleon of the West," Santa Anna took control of the government after Mexico won independence in 1821. He spent the next 35 years alternately serving as president, leading troops into battle, and living in exile. Santa Anna served as president of Mexico 11 times.

Santa Anna was a complex man with much charm. He sacrificed his considerable wealth to return again and again to the battlefield and died in poverty, almost forgotten.

soldiers surprised a group of Mexicans near the San Jacinto River. With shouts of "Remember the Alamo!" the Texans killed 630 of Santa Anna's soldiers in 18 minutes and captured Santa Anna himself. The Texans set Santa Anna free only after he signed the Treaty of Velasco, which granted independence to Texas. In September 1836, Sam Houston was elected president of the new Republic of Texas.

TEXAS MOVES TOWARD THE UNION Most Texans hoped that the United States would annex their republic, but U.S. opinion divided along sectional lines. Southerners wanted Texas in order to extend slavery, which already had been established there. Northerners feared that the annexation of more slave territory would tip the uneasy balance in the Senate in favor of slave states—and prompt war with Mexico. E

MAIN IDEA

Contrasting
E How would you contrast the Northern and Southern positions on the annexation of Texas?

The 1844 U.S. presidential campaign focused on westward expansion. The winner, **James K. Polk,** a slaveholder, firmly favored the annexation of Texas.

The War with Mexico

In March 1845, angered by U.S.-Texas negotiation on annexation, the Mexican government recalled its ambassador from Washington. On December 29, 1845, Texas entered the Union. Events moved quickly toward war.

POLK URGES WAR President Polk believed that war with Mexico would bring not only Texas into the Union, but also New Mexico and California. Hence, the president supported Texan claims in disputes with Mexico over the Texas–Mexico border. While Texas insisted that its southern border extended to the Rio Grande, Mexico maintained that Texas's border stopped at the Nueces River, 100–150 miles northeast of the Rio Grande.

Despite the fact that Mexico had ceased formal diplomatic relations with the U.S., Polk hoped to negotiate secretly the boundary dispute, as well as the sale of California and New Mexico. He dispatched John Slidell, a congressman from Louisiana, to negotiate both matters. The Mexican government refused to receive Slidell. When Polk heard this news, he ordered U.S. troops into the territory between the Rio Grande and the Nueces River that the United States claimed as its own.

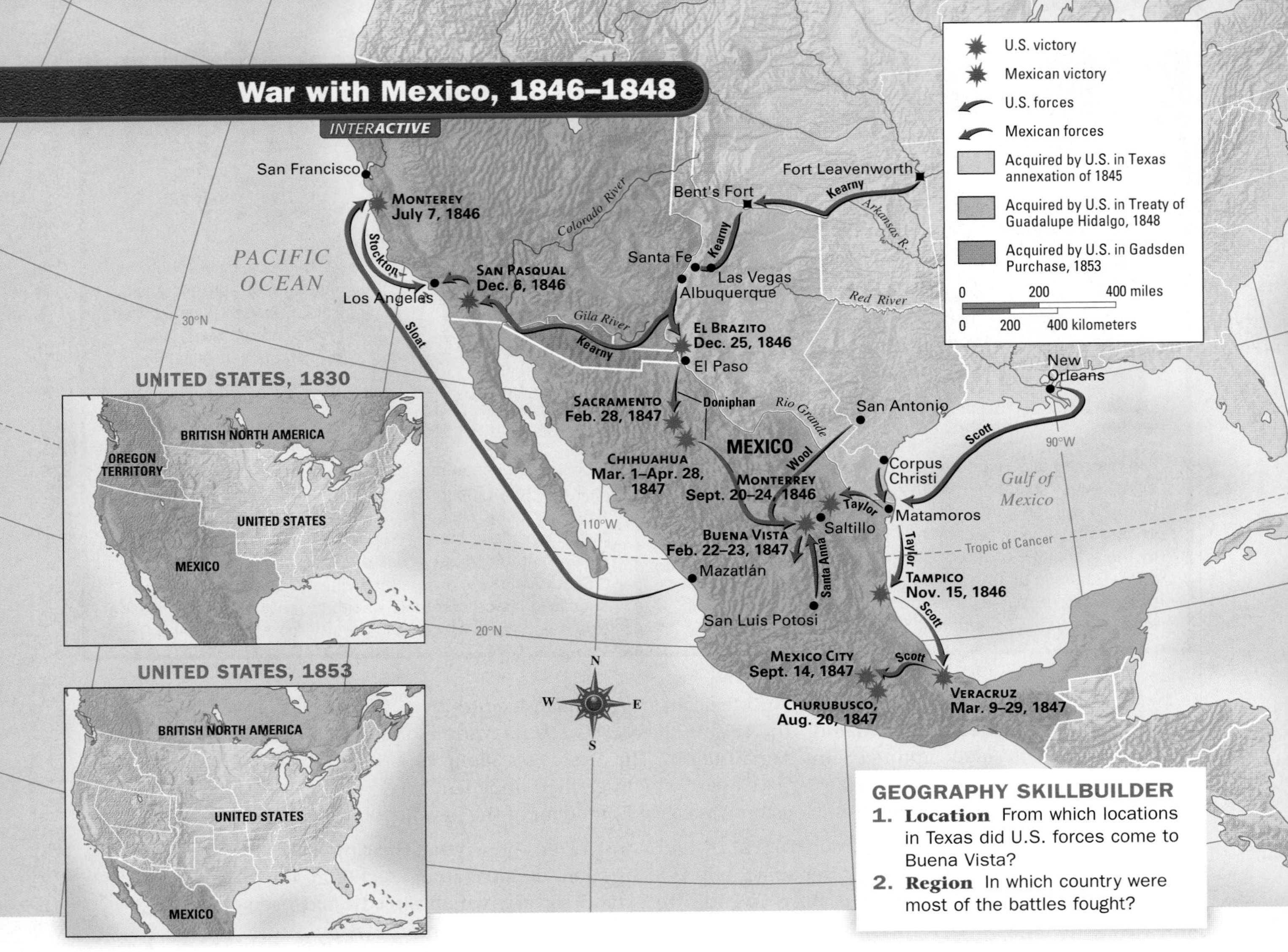

THE WAR BEGINS In 1845, John C. Frémont led an American military exploration party into California, violating Mexico's territorial rights. In response, Mexican troops crossed the Rio Grande. In a skirmish near Matamoros, Mexican soldiers killed 11 U.S. soldiers. Polk immediately called for war and Congress approved. (F)

In 1846, Polk ordered Colonel Stephen Kearny and his troops to march from Fort Leavenworth, Kansas, to Santa Fe, New Mexico. They were met there by a New Mexican contingent that included upper-class Mexicans who wanted to join the United States. New Mexico fell to the United States without a shot.

> **MAIN IDEA**
>
> **Analyzing Issues**
>
> (F) What border dispute affected the war with Mexico?

THE REPUBLIC OF CALIFORNIA In California, a group of American settlers seized the town of Sonoma in June 1846. Hoisting a flag that featured a grizzly bear, the rebels proudly declared their independence from Mexico and proclaimed the nation of the **Republic of California.** Kearny arrived from New Mexico and joined forces with Frémont and an American naval expedition. The Mexican troops quickly gave way, leaving U.S. forces in control of California.

AMERICA WINS THE WAR Meanwhile, American troops in Mexico, led by U.S. generals Zachary Taylor and Winfield Scott, scored one military victory after another. After about a year of fighting, Mexico conceded defeat. On February 2, 1848, the United States and Mexico signed the **Treaty of Guadalupe Hidalgo.** Mexico agreed to the Rio Grande as the border between Texas and Mexico and ceded the New Mexico and California territories to the United States. The United

States agreed to pay $15 million for the Mexican cession, which included present-day California, Nevada, New Mexico, Utah, most of Arizona, and parts of Colorado and Wyoming.

Five years later, in 1853, President Franklin Pierce authorized James Gadsden to pay Mexico an additional $10 million for another piece of territory south of the Gila River in order to secure a southern railroad route to the Pacific Ocean. Along with the settlement of the Oregon boundary and the Treaty of Guadalupe Hidalgo, the Gadsden Purchase established the current borders of the contiguous 48 states.

The California Gold Rush

The United States quickly benefited from its new territories when gold was discovered at Sutter's Mill in the California Sierra Nevada mountains.

THE FORTY-NINERS On the cold clear morning of January 24, 1848, a carpenter named James Marshall discovered a few shiny particles lying near John Sutter's sawmill. Marshall took what he had found to Sutter, who confirmed the carpenter's suspicions: the particles were gold. Soon, more gold was found by other workers at Sutter's mill, and news of the chance discovery began to spread with lightning speed.

When the news reached San Francisco, virtually the whole town hustled to the Sacramento Valley to pan for gold. On June 6, 1848, Monterey's mayor, Walter Colton, sent a scout to report on what was happening. The scout returned on June 14 with news of gold, and the mayor described the scene that followed as news traveled along the town's main street.

▲ **Goldminers at Spanish Flat, California, 1852**

A PERSONAL VOICE WALTER COLTON

> "**The blacksmith dropped his hammer, the carpenter his plane, the mason his trowel, the farmer his sickle, the baker his loaf, and the tapster [bartender] his bottle. All were off for the mines. . . . I have only a community of women left, and a gang of prisoners, with here and there a soldier who will give his captain the slip at first chance. I don't blame the fellow a whit; seven dollars a month, while others [prospectors] are making two or three hundred a day!**"
>
> —quoted in *California: A Bicentennial History*

As gold fever traveled eastward, overland migration to California rose from 400 in 1848 to 44,000 in 1850. By the end of 1849, California's population exceeded 100,000, including Mexicans, free African-American miners, and slaves.

The rest of the world caught the fever as well. Among the so-called forty-niners—the prospectors who flocked to California in 1849 in the California gold rush—were people from Asia, South America, and Europe. In time, the names of

▲ Crowded buildings and a forest of masts stand out in this 1850 photograph of San Francisco.

the mining camps that sprung up in California reflected the diversity of its growing population: French Corral, Irish Creek, Chinese Camp. G

MAIN IDEA

Analyzing Effects

G In what ways did the gold rush change the population of California?

THE GOLDEN ECONOMY The discovery of gold revolutionized California's economy. Gold financed the development of farming, manufacturing, shipping, and banking. By 1855, more newspapers were published in San Francisco than in London, more books were published than in all the rest of the United States west of the Mississippi. Because of its location as a supply center, San Francisco became "a pandemonium of a city." Ships linked California markets to the expanding markets of the rest of the United States.

Mining continued in California throughout the 1850s, but the peak of the gold rush was over by 1853. While most individual efforts yielded little or no profit, those who were able to use more sophisticated methods made fortunes. By 1857, ten years after James Marshall's discovery of a few shiny flakes, the total value of gold production in California approached two billion dollars. H

MAIN IDEA

Analyzing Effects

H How did the discovery of gold affect California's economy?

"GO WEST, YOUNG MAN!" Horace Greeley, editor of the *New York Tribune*, had declared in his paper prior to the gold rush that anyone who made the dangerous journey west was a fool. But when he heard of the discovery in the Sierra Nevadas his curiosity was aroused. Before long, he made the journey west himself and declared California to be "the new El Dorado." "Go west, young man!" Greeley advised. In the spirit of manifest destiny, countless settlers heeded his words in the decades that followed.

SECTION 3 ASSESSMENT

1. **TERMS & NAMES** For each term or name, write a sentence explaining its significance.
   - **manifest destiny**
   - **Santa Fe Trail**
   - **Oregon Trail**
   - **Stephen F. Austin**
   - **Texas Revolution**
   - **the Alamo**
   - **Sam Houston**
   - **James K. Polk**
   - **Republic of California**
   - **Treaty of Guadalupe Hidalgo**

MAIN IDEA

2. **TAKING NOTES**
   Draw a chart like the one below to show how the boundaries of the U.S. mainland were formed from the 1840s to 1853.

Year	Boundary Change
1845	Texas annexed

CRITICAL THINKING

3. **ANALYZING ISSUES**
   What were the benefits and drawbacks of believing in manifest destiny? Use specific references to the section to support your response.
   Think About:
   - the growth of new cities and towns
   - the impact on Native Americans
   - the impact on the nation as a whole

4. **EVALUATING**
   Would you have supported the war with Mexico? Why or why not? Explain your answer, including details from the chapter.

5. **DEVELOPING HISTORICAL PERSPECTIVE**
   How did the California gold rush transform the West in the American imagination?

SECTION 4

The Market Revolution

MAIN IDEA

Inventions and economic developments in the early 19th century helped transform American society.

WHY IT MATTERS NOW

The market revolution and free enterprise system that took hold during this period still drive the nation's economy today.

Terms & Names

- **market revolution**
- **free enterprise**
- **entrepreneurs**
- **Samuel F. B. Morse**
- **Lowell textile mills**
- **strike**
- **immigration**
- **National Trades' Union**
- ***Commonwealth* v. *Hunt***

One American's Story

At sunrise on July 4, 1817, a cannon blast from the United States arsenal in Rome, New York, announced the groundbreaking for the Erie Canal. With visiting dignitaries and local residents in attendance, Samuel Young opened the ceremony.

A PERSONAL VOICE SAMUEL YOUNG

"We have assembled to commence the excavation of the Erie Canal. This work when accomplished will connect our western inland seas with the Atlantic Ocean. . . . By this great highway, unborn millions will easily transport their surplus productions to the shores of the Atlantic, procure their supplies, and hold a useful and profitable intercourse with all the maritime nations of the earth. . . . Let us proceed then to the work, animated by the prospect of its speedy accomplishment, and cheered with the anticipated benedictions of a grateful posterity."

—quoted in *Erie Water West*

▲ **A lock on the Erie Canal in Lockport, New York, shown here in an 1838 engraving, was one of 83 that helped link the Great Lakes with the Northeast.**

When the canal was completed, it stretched 363 miles from Albany, New York, to Lake Erie. The human-made waterway ushered in a new era, in which technology and improved transportation sent new products to markets across the United States.

The Market Revolution

Changes like those brought by the Erie Canal contributed to vast economic changes in the first half of the 19th century in the United States. In this period, known as the **market revolution,** people increasingly bought and sold goods rather than make them for themselves.

U.S. MARKETS EXPAND Over a few decades, buying and selling multiplied while incomes rose. In the 1840s alone, the national economy grew more than it had in the first 40 years of the century. The quickening pace of U.S. economic growth coincided with the growth of **free enterprise**—the freedom of private businesses to operate competitively for profit with little government regulation.

In their pursuit of profit, businessmen called **entrepreneurs,** from a French word that means "to undertake," invested their own money in new industries. In doing this, entrepreneurs risked losing their investment if a venture failed, but they also stood to earn huge profits if it succeeded. (A)

MAIN IDEA

Synthesizing
(A) How did entrepreneurs contribute to the market revolution?

INVENTIONS AND IMPROVEMENTS Inventor-entrepreneurs began to develop goods to make life more comfortable for more people. While some inventions simply made life more enjoyable, others fueled the economic revolution and transformed manufacturing, transportation, and communication.

New communication links began to put people into instant contact with one another. In 1837, **Samuel F. B. Morse,** a New England artist, patented the telegraph, which sent messages in code over a wire in a matter of seconds. Businesses used the new communication device to transmit orders and relay up-to-date information on prices and sales. The new railroads employed the telegraph to keep trains moving regularly and to warn engineers of safety hazards. By 1854, 23,000 miles of telegraph wire crossed the country.

Meanwhile, better transportation systems improved the movement of people and goods. In 1807, Pennsylvanian Robert Fulton had ushered in the steamboat era when his boat, the *Clermont,* made the 150-mile trip up the Hudson River from New York City to Albany in 32 hours, a remarkable speed for that era. By 1830, 200 steamboats traveled the nation's western rivers that flowed into the Mississippi River. Steamboats slashed freight rates as well as voyage times.

Water transport was particularly important in moving raw materials such as lead, copper, and heavy

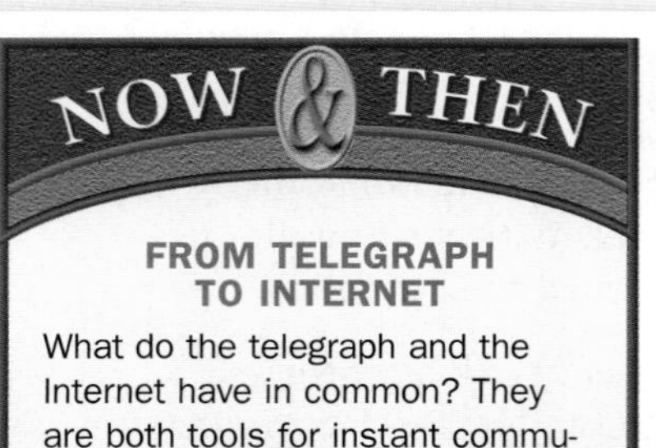

FROM TELEGRAPH TO INTERNET

What do the telegraph and the Internet have in common? They are both tools for instant communication. While the telegraph relied on a network of wires that spanned the country, the Internet—an international network of smaller computer networks—allows any computer user to communicate instantly with any other computer user in the world.

MORSE CODE In 1837 Samuel Morse patents the telegraph, the first instant electronic communicator. Morse taps on a key to send bursts of electricity down a wire to the receiver, where an operator "translates" the coded bursts into understandable language within seconds.

TELEPHONE In 1876 Alexander Graham Bell invents the telephone, which relies on a steady stream of electricity, rather than electrical bursts, to transmit sounds. By 1900, there are over one million telephones in the United States.

MARCONI RADIO In 1895, Guglielmo Marconi, an Italian inventor, sends telegraph code through the air as electromagnetic waves. By the early 1900s, "the wireless" makes voice transmissions possible. Commercial radio stations are broadcasting music and entertainment programs by the 1920s.

machinery. Where waterways didn't exist, Americans made them by building canals. By the 1840s, America boasted more than 3,300 miles of canals.

Canals, however, soon gave way to railroads, which offered the important advantage of speed as well as winter travel. Developed in England in the early 1800s, steam-powered locomotives began operating in the United States in the 1830s. By 1850, over 9,000 miles of track had been laid across the United States.

THE MARKET REVOLUTION TRANSFORMS THE NATION Although most Americans during the early 1800s still lived in rural areas and only 14 percent of workers had manufacturing jobs, these workers produced more and better goods at lower prices than ever before. Many of these goods became affordable for ordinary Americans, and improvements in transportation allowed people to purchase items manufactured in distant places.

By the 1840s, improved transportation and communication also made America's regions more interdependent. Steamboats went up as well as down the Mississippi, linking North to South. The Erie Canal, and eventually railroads and telegraph wires, soon linked the East and the West.

MAIN IDEA

Summarizing

B How did technology influence both the North and the Midwest in the 1840s?

Heavy investment in canals and railroads transformed the Northeast into the center of American commerce. As the Northeast began to industrialize, many people then moved away to farm the fertile soil of the Midwest. They employed new machines, such as the John Deere steel plow, for cultivating the tough prairie sod, and Cyrus McCormick's reaper, for harvesting grain. Meanwhile, most of the South remained agricultural and relied on such crops as cotton, tobacco, and rice. B

Changing Workplaces

The new market economy in the United States did not only affect what people bought and sold, it also changed the ways Americans worked. Moving production from the home to the factory split families, created new communities, and transformed relationships between employers and employees.

By the mid-19th century, new machines allowed unskilled workers to perform tasks that once had taken the effort of trained artisans. To do this work, though, workers needed factories.

TELEVISION In the late 1800s, scientists begin to experiment with transmitting pictures as well as words through the air. In 1923 Vladimir Zworykin, a Russian-born American scientist, files a patent for the iconoscope, the first television camera tube suitable for broadcasting, and in 1924 for the kinescope, the picture tube used in receiving television signals. In 1929, Zworykin demonstrated the first all-electronic television.

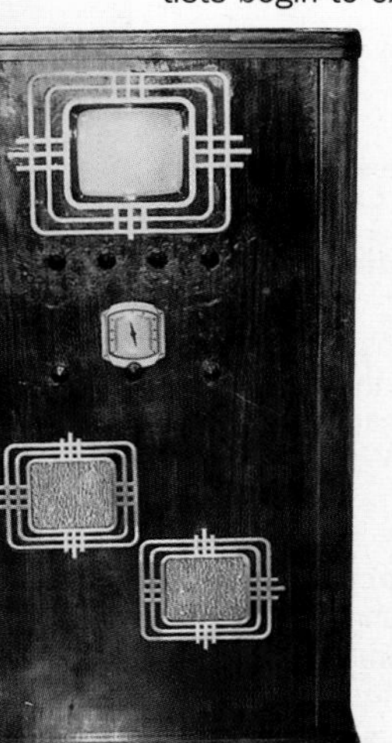

1929

COMPUTERS Scientists develop electronically powered computers during the 1940s. In 1951, UNIVAC I (UNIVersal Advanced Computer) becomes the first commercially available computer. In 1964, IBM initiates System/360, a family of mutually compatible computers that allow several terminals to be attached to one computer system.

1964

INTERNET Today, on the Internet, through e-mail (electronic mail) or online conversation, any two people can have instant dialogue. The Internet becomes the modern tool for instant global communication not only of words but images too. And it is just as amazing now as the telegraph was in its time.

2000

THE LOWELL TEXTILE MILLS In the 1820s, a group of entrepreneurs built several large textile mills in Lowell, Massachusetts. The **Lowell textile mills** soon became booming enterprises. Thousands of people, mostly women, left family farms to find work in Lowell.

Mill owners sought female employees because women provided an abundant source of labor and owners could pay lower wages to women than men. To the girls in the mills, though, textile work offered better pay than their main alternatives: teaching, sewing, and domestic work. In letters written in 1846 to her father in New Hampshire, 16-year-old Mary Paul expressed her satisfaction with her situation at Lowell.

▲ A young mill girl from around 1840. Her swollen hands suggest that she worked as a warper, someone who straightened the strands of cotton or wool as they entered the loom.

A PERSONAL VOICE MARY PAUL

> **"I have a very good boarding place, have enough to eat. . . . The girls are all kind and obliging. . . . I think that the factory is the best place for me and if any girl wants employment, I advise them to come to Lowell."**
>
> —quoted in *Women and the American Experience*

Before long, however, work conditions deteriorated. The workday at Lowell was more than 12 hours long. In addition, mills often were dark, hot, and cramped. Factory owners often showed little sympathy for the plight of workers. In the mid-1840s one mill manager said, "I regard my workpeople just as I regard my machinery. So long as they can do my work for what I choose to pay them, I keep them, getting out of them all I can." (C)

MAIN IDEA

Making Inferences

(C) What was the attitude of many factory owners toward their workers?

Workers Seek Better Conditions

As industry grew, strikes began to break out when workers protested poor working conditions and low wages.

WORKERS STRIKE In 1834, when the Lowell mills announced a 15 percent wage cut, 800 mill girls organized a **strike,** a work stoppage to force an employer to respond to demands. Criticized by the Lowell press and clergy, most of the strikers agreed to return to work at reduced wages. The mill owners fired the strike leader. In 1836, Lowell mill workers struck again, but as in 1834, the company won, and most of the strikers returned to their jobs.

Although only 1 or 2 percent of workers in the United States were organized, the 1830s and 1840s saw dozens of strikes—many for higher wages, but some for shorter hours. Employers defeated most of these strikes because they could easily replace unskilled workers with people recently arrived from Europe who desperately needed jobs. (D)

MAIN IDEA

Summarizing

(D) Why were most labor strikes of the 1880s and 1840s ineffective?

IMMIGRATION INCREASES European **immigration,** leaving one country and settling in another, rose dramatically in the United States between 1830 and 1860. Between 1845 and 1854 alone, nearly 3 million immigrants were added to the population. More than 1 million were Irish immigrants, who fled their homeland after a disease on potatoes caused the Great Potato Famine and led to mass starvation.

Background

During the Great Potato Famine of 1845–1849, about 1,000,000 Irish died of starvation and disease.

Irish immigrants faced prejudice, both because they were Roman Catholic and because they were poor. Frightened by allegations of a Catholic conspiracy to take over the country, Protestant mobs in big cities constantly harassed them. Other workers resented the Irish for their willingness to work as cheap labor, a willingness that made them more desirable to employers.

European immigrants arriving in New York City (from a colored engraving made in 1858)

NATIONAL TRADES' UNION Amid the growing labor unrest in the 1830s, the trade unions in different towns began to join together to expand their power. Journeymen's organizations from several industries united in 1834 to form the **National Trades' Union.** The national trade union movement faced fierce opposition from bankers and owners. In addition, workers' efforts to organize were at first hampered by court decisions declaring strikes illegal. In 1842, however, the Massachusetts Supreme Court supported the workers' right to strike in the case of ***Commonwealth* v. *Hunt*.**

The workplace was not the only area of American life that experienced unrest in the mid-19th century. Indeed, a series of religious and social reform movements went hand in hand with these economic changes.

SECTION 4 ASSESSMENT

1. **TERMS & NAMES** For each term or name, write a sentence explaining its significance.
   - **market revolution**
   - **free enterprise**
   - **entrepreneurs**
   - **Samuel F. B. Morse**
   - **Lowell textile mills**
   - **strike**
   - **immigration**
   - **National Trades' Union**
   - ***Commonwealth* v. *Hunt***

MAIN IDEA

2. **TAKING NOTES**
   Create a time line like the one below on which you label and date important developments in manufacturing during the early 19th century.

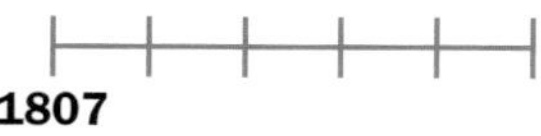

1807

Write a paragraph explaining which development was most important and why.

CRITICAL THINKING

3. **ANALYZING ISSUES**
   Do you think the positive effects of mechanizing the manufacturing process outweighed the negative effects? Why or why not?
   Think About:
   - changes in job opportunities for unskilled laborers
   - changes in employer-employee relationships
   - working conditions in factories
   - the cost of manufactured goods

4. **ANALYZING PRIMARY SOURCES**
   A 20th-century historian said of the 1820s: "It was the miraculous machinery of the times . . . which made it obvious that things were getting better all the time." How do you think the people you have read about in this chapter would have responded to that statement?

Reforming American Society

MAIN IDEA

Throughout the mid-19th century, men and women embarked on a widespread effort to solve problems in American society.

WHY IT MATTERS NOW

A number of achievements from this period, including laws enacted and institutions established, still exist today.

Terms & Names

- abolition
- Unitarians
- Ralph Waldo Emerson
- transcendentalism
- William Lloyd Garrison
- Frederick Douglass
- Nat Turner
- Elizabeth Cady Stanton
- Seneca Falls convention
- Sojourner Truth

One American's Story

James Forten's great-grandfather had been brought from Africa to the American colonies in chains, but James was born free. By the 1830s Forten had become a wealthy sailmaker. A leader of Philadelphia's free black community, Forten took an active role in a variety of political causes. When some people argued that free blacks should return to Africa, Forten disagreed and responded with sarcasm.

James Forten

A PERSONAL VOICE JAMES FORTEN

"Here I have dwelt until I am nearly sixty years of age, and have brought up and educated a family. . . . Yet some ingenious gentlemen have recently discovered that I am still an African; that a continent three thousand miles, and more, from the place where I was born, is my native country. And I am advised to go home. . . . Perhaps if I should only be set on the shore of that distant land, I should recognize all I might see there, and run at once to the old hut where my forefathers lived a hundred years ago."

—quoted in *Forging Freedom: The Formation of Philadelphia's Black Community 1720–1840*

Forten's unwavering belief that he was an American not only led him to oppose colonization—the effort to resettle free blacks in Africa—but also pushed him fervently to oppose slavery. Forten was joined in his opposition to slavery by a growing number of Americans in the 19th century. **Abolition,** the movement to abolish slavery, became the most important of a series of reform movements in America.

A Spiritual Awakening Inspires Reform

Many of these movements had their roots in a spiritual awakening that swept the nation after 1790. People involved in these movements began to emphasize individual responsibility for seeking salvation and insisted that people could improve themselves and society. These religious attitudes were closely linked to the ideas of Jacksonian democracy that stressed the importance and power of the common person.

THE SECOND GREAT AWAKENING The Second Great Awakening was a widespread Christian movement to awaken religious sentiments that lasted from the 1790s to the 1830s. The primary forum for the movement was the revival meeting, where participants attempted to revive religious faith through impassioned preaching. Revival meetings might last for days as participants studied the Bible, reflected on their lives, and heard emotional sermons. Revivalism had a strong impact on the American public. According to one estimate, in 1800 just 1 in 15 Americans belonged to a church, but by 1850 1 in 6 was a member.

UNITARIANS AND TRANSCENDENTALISTS Another growing religious group was the **Unitarians,** who shared with revivalism a faith in the individual. But instead of appealing to emotions, Unitarians emphasized reason as the path to perfection.

As the Second Great Awakening reached its maturity in the 1830s, another kind of awakening led by a writer, philosopher, and former Unitarian minister named **Ralph Waldo Emerson** began in New England. In 1831, Emerson traveled to England, where he discovered romanticism, an artistic and intellectual movement that emphasized nature, human emotions, and the imagination. From these romantic ideals, Emerson, along with other thinkers, developed a philosophy called **transcendentalism,** which emphasized that truth could be discovered intuitively by observing nature and relating it to one's own emotional and spiritual experience.

MAIN IDEA

Evaluating

A How did the existence of separate black churches benefit the African-American community?

THE AFRICAN-AMERICAN CHURCH The urge to reform was growing among African Americans, too. Slaves in the rural South heard the same sermons and sang the same hymns as did their owners, but they often interpreted the stories they heard, especially those describing the exodus from Egypt, as a promise of freedom.

In the North, however, free African Americans were able to form their own churches. These churches often became political, cultural, and social centers for African Americans by providing schools and other services that whites denied free blacks. A

Slavery and Abolition

By the 1820s, abolition—the movement to free African Americans from slavery—had taken hold. More than 100 antislavery societies were advocating that African Americans be resettled in Africa. In 1817, the American Colonization Society had been founded to encourage black emigration. Other abolitionists, however, demanded that African Americans remain in the United States as free citizens.

WILLIAM LLOYD GARRISON The most radical white abolitionist was a young editor named **William Lloyd Garrison.** Active in religious reform movements in Massachusetts, Garrison became the editor of an antislavery paper in 1828. Three years later he established his own paper, *The Liberator,* to deliver an uncompromising demand: immediate emancipation.

THE LIBERATOR.

VOL. I.] WILLIAM LLOYD GARRISON AND ISAAC KNAPP, PUBLISHERS. [NO. 22.

BOSTON, MASSACHUSETTS.] OUR COUNTRY IS THE WORLD—OUR COUNTRYMEN ARE MANKIND. [SATURDAY, MAY 28, 1831.

William Lloyd Garrison's *The Liberator* was published from 1831 to 1865. Its circulation never grew beyond 3,000.

Before Garrison's call for the immediate emancipation of slaves, support for that position had been limited. In the 1830s, however, that position gained support. Whites who opposed abolition hated Garrison. In 1835 a Boston mob paraded him through town at the end of a rope. Nevertheless, Garrison enjoyed widespread black support; three out of four early subscribers to *The Liberator* were African Americans.

"I consider it settled that the black and white people of America ought to share common destiny."

FREDERICK DOUGLASS, 1851

FREDERICK DOUGLASS One of those eager readers was **Frederick Douglass,** who escaped from bondage to become an eloquent and outspoken critic of slavery. Garrison heard him speak and was so impressed that he sponsored Douglass to speak for various anti-slavery organizations. Hoping that abolition could be achieved without violence, Douglass broke with Garrison, who believed that abolition justified whatever means were necessary to achieve it. In 1847, Douglass began his own antislavery newspaper. He named it *The North Star,* after the star that guided runaway slaves to freedom.

LIFE UNDER SLAVERY In the 18th century, most slaves were male, had recently arrived from the Caribbean or Africa, and spoke one of several languages other than English. By 1830, however, the numbers of male and female slaves had become more equal. The majority had been born in America and spoke English. However, two things remained constant in the lives of slaves—hard work and oppression.

The number of slaves owned by individual masters varied widely across the South. Most slaves worked as house servants, farm hands, or in the fields. Some states allowed masters to free their slaves and even allowed slaves to purchase their freedom over time. But these "manumitted" or freed slaves were very few. The vast majority of African Americans in the South were enslaved and endured lives of suffering and constant degradation. (See "Southern Plantations" on page 147.) B

MAIN IDEA

Making Inferences

B How would you describe the lives of enslaved African Americans in the 1830s?

TURNER'S REBELLION Some slaves rebelled against their condition of bondage. One of the most prominent rebellions was led by Virginia slave **Nat Turner.** In August 1831, Turner and more than 50 followers attacked four plantations and killed about 60 whites. Whites eventually captured and executed many members of the group, including Turner.

SLAVE OWNERS OPPOSE ABOLITION The Turner rebellion frightened and outraged slaveholders. In some states, people argued that the only way to prevent slave revolts was through emancipation. Others, however, chose to tighten restrictions on all African Americans to prevent them from plotting insurrections. Some proslavery advocates began to argue that slavery was a benevolent institution. They used the Bible to defend slavery and cited passages that counseled servants to obey their masters.

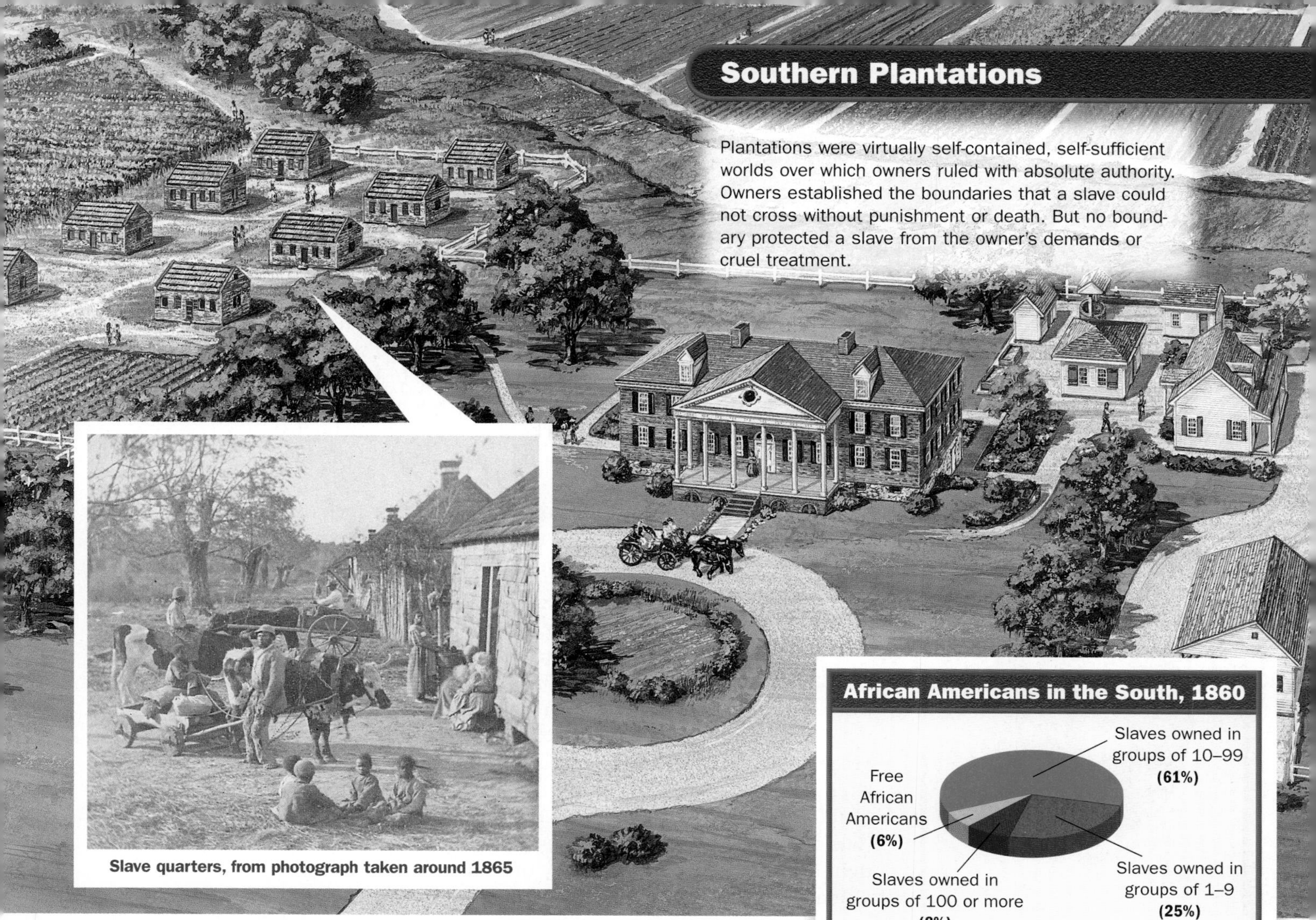

Southern Plantations

Plantations were virtually self-contained, self-sufficient worlds over which owners ruled with absolute authority. Owners established the boundaries that a slave could not cross without punishment or death. But no boundary protected a slave from the owner's demands or cruel treatment.

Slave quarters, from photograph taken around 1865

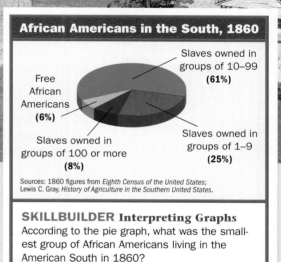

African Americans in the South, 1860

Slaves owned in groups of 10–99 **(61%)**
Free African Americans **(6%)**
Slaves owned in groups of 100 or more **(8%)**
Slaves owned in groups of 1–9 **(25%)**

Sources: 1860 figures from *Eighth Census of the United States*; Lewis C. Gray, *History of Agriculture in the Southern United States.*

SKILLBUILDER Interpreting Graphs
According to the pie graph, what was the smallest group of African Americans living in the American South in 1860?

Nevertheless, opposition to slavery refused to disappear. Much of the strength of the abolition movement came from the efforts of women—many of whom contributed to other reform movements, including a women's rights movement.

Women and Reform

In the early 19th century, women faced limited options. Prevailing customs encouraged women to restrict their activities after marriage to the home and family. As a result, they were denied full participation in the larger community.

WOMEN MOBILIZE FOR REFORM Despite such pressures, women actively participated in all the important reform movements of the 19th century. For many, their efforts to improve society had been inspired by the optimistic message of the Second Great Awakening. From abolition to education, women worked for reform despite the cold reception they got from many men.

MAIN IDEA

Analyzing Issues
C What were some of the areas of society that women worked to reform?

Perhaps the most important reform effort that women participated in was abolition. Women abolitionists raised money, distributed literature, and collected signatures for antislavery petitions to Congress.

Women also played key roles in the temperance movement, the effort to prohibit the drinking of alcohol. Some women, most notably Dorothea Dix, fought to improve treatment for the mentally disabled. Dix also joined others in the effort to reform the nation's harsh and often inhumane prison system. C

EDUCATION FOR WOMEN Work for abolition and temperance accompanied gains in education for women. Until the 1820s, American girls had few educational opportunities beyond elementary school. As Sarah Grimké complained in *Letters on the Equality of the Sexes and the Condition of Woman* (1838), a woman who knew "chemistry enough to keep the pot boiling, and geography enough to know the location of the different rooms in her house" was considered learned enough. Grimké believed that increased education for women was a better alternative.

Background
Sarah Grimké and her sister Angelina were leading voices in the abolition and women's rights movements.

Still, throughout the 1800s, more and more educational institutions for women began to appear. In 1821 Emma Willard opened one of the nation's first academically-oriented schools for girls in Troy, New York. In addition to classes in domestic sciences, the Troy Female Seminary offered classes in math, history, geography, languages, art, music, writing, and literature. The Troy Female Seminary became the model for a new type of women's school. Despite tremendous ridicule—people mocked that "they will be educating cows next"—Willard's school prospered.

In 1833, the first class of Ohio's Oberlin College included four women, thus becoming the nation's first fully coeducational college. In 1837, Mary Lyon surmounted heated resistance to found another important institution of higher learning for women, Mount Holyoke Female Seminary (later Mount Holyoke College) in South Hadley, Massachusetts. **D**

MAIN IDEA

Summarizing
D What improvements in women's education occurred in the 1820s and '30s?

EDUCATION AND WOMEN'S HEALTH Improvement in women's education began to improve women's lives, most notably in health reform. Elizabeth Blackwell, who in 1849 became the first woman to graduate from medical college, later opened the New York Infirmary for Women and Children. In the 1850s, Catharine Beecher, sister of novelist Harriet Beecher Stowe, and a respected educator in her own right, undertook a national survey of women's health. To her dismay, Beecher found three sick women for every healthy one. It was no wonder: women rarely bathed or exercised, and the fashionable women's clothing of the day included corsets so restrictive that breathing sometimes was difficult.

Unfortunately, black women enjoyed even fewer educational opportunities than their white counterparts. In 1831 Prudence Crandall, a white Quaker, opened a school for girls in Canterbury, Connecticut. Two years later she admitted an African-American girl named Sarah Harris. The townspeople protested so vigorously that Crandall decided to enroll only African Americans. This aroused even more opposition, and in 1834 Crandall was forced to close the school and leave town. Only after the Civil War would the severely limited educational opportunities for black women slowly begin to expand.

KEY PLAYER

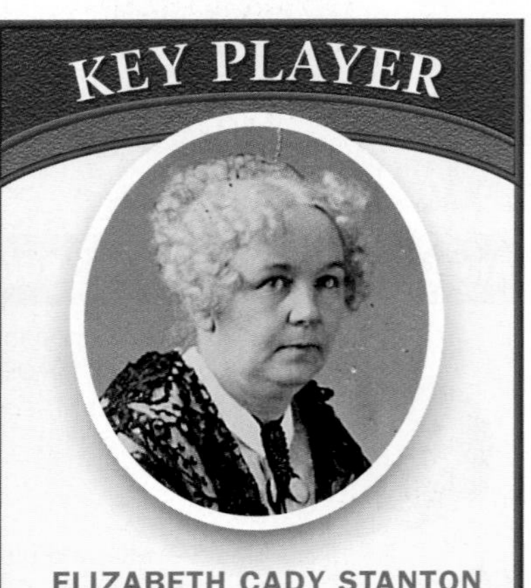

ELIZABETH CADY STANTON 1815–1902

Stanton was an ardent abolitionist, and she timed her marriage in 1840 so that she and her new husband could travel together to London for the World's Anti-Slavery Convention.

She also believed that women deserved the same rights as men and even persuaded the minister to omit the word "obey" from her vow in the marriage ceremony because she felt no need to "obey one with whom I supposed I was entering into an equal relation."

At the antislavery convention, Stanton and the other women delegates were barred from participation in the convention and were forced to sit and listen from a curtained gallery. There she met Lucretia Mott. Stanton and Mott vowed "to hold a convention as soon as we returned home, and form a society to advocate the rights of women." Eight years later, the Seneca Falls convention fulfilled that vow.

WOMEN'S RIGHTS MOVEMENT EMERGES The reform movements of the mid-19th century fed the growth of the women's movement by providing women with increased opportunities to act outside the home. **Elizabeth Cady Stanton** and Lucretia Mott had been ardent abolitionists. Male abolitionists discriminated against them at the World's Anti-Slavery Convention in 1840, so the pair resolved to hold a women's rights convention. In 1848, more than 300 women convened in Seneca Falls, New York. Before the convention started, Stanton and Mott composed an agenda and a detailed statement of grievances.

The participants at the **Seneca Falls convention** approved all parts of the declaration, including a resolution calling for women to have the right to vote. In spite of all the political activity among middle-class white women, African-American women found it difficult to gain recognition of their problems. A former slave named **Sojourner Truth** did not let that stop her, however. At a women's rights convention in 1851, Truth, an outspoken abolitionist, refuted the arguments that because she was a woman she was weak, and because she was black, she was not feminine.

▲ With her dignified bearing and powerful voice, Sojourner Truth made audiences snap to attention. Truth fought for women's rights, abolition, prison reform, and temperance.

A PERSONAL VOICE SOJOURNER TRUTH

"Look at me! Look at my arm! I have ploughed, and planted, and gathered into barns, and no man could head me! And ain't I a woman? I could work as much and eat as much as a man—when I could get it—and bear the lash as well! And ain't I a woman? I have borne thirteen children, and seen most all sold off to slavery, and when I cried out with my mother's grief, none but Jesus heard me! And ain't I a woman?"

—quoted in *Narrative of Sojourner Truth*

Analyzing Issues

E How did Sojourner Truth describe her life as an African-American woman?

As Truth showed, hard work was a fact of life for most women. But she also pointed to the problem of slavery that continued to vex the nation. As abolitionists intensified their attacks, proslavery advocates strengthened their defenses. Before long the issue of slavery threatened to destroy the Union. E

SECTION 5 ASSESSMENT

1. **TERMS & NAMES** For each term or name, write a sentence explaining its significance.
   - **abolition**
   - **Unitarians**
   - **Ralph Waldo Emerson**
   - **transcendentalism**
   - **William Lloyd Garrison**
   - **Frederick Douglass**
   - **Nat Turner**
   - **Elizabeth Cady Stanton**
   - **Seneca Falls convention**
   - **Sojourner Truth**

MAIN IDEA

2. **TAKING NOTES**
   In a diagram similar to the one shown, fill in historical events or key figures related to reforming American society in the 19th century.

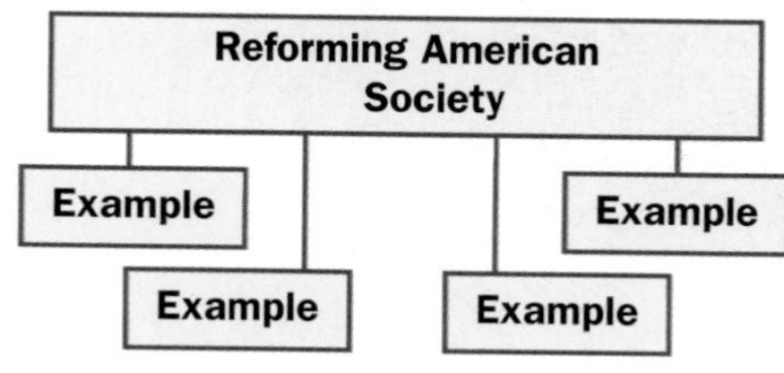

Write a paragraph about one of the examples you chose, explaining its significance.

CRITICAL THINKING

3. **EVALUATING**
   Which do you think was a more effective strategy—violence or nonviolence—for eliminating slavery? Why? **Think About:**
   - Frederick Douglass
   - Nat Turner
   - William Lloyd Garrison
   - Sojourner Truth

4. **MAKING INFERENCES**
   Consider the philosophical and religious ideas expressed during the Second Great Awakening. How did they influence the activities of 19th-century reformers? **Think About:**
   - concepts of individualism and Jacksonian democracy
   - the views of Emerson
   - the activities of Garrison, Douglass, Stanton, and Truth

INTERACTIVE

GEOGRAPHY SPOTLIGHT

Mapping the Oregon Trail

In 1841, Congress appropriated $30,000 for a survey of the Oregon Trail and named John C. Frémont to head the expeditions. Frémont earned his nickname "the Pathfinder" by leading three expeditions—which included artists, scientists, and cartographers, among them the German-born cartographer Charles Preuss—to explore the American West between 1842 and 1848. When Frémont submitted the report of his first expedition, Congress immediately ordered the printing of 10,000 copies, which were widely distributed.

The "Topographical Map of the Road from Missouri to Oregon," drawn by Preuss, appeared in seven sheets. Though settlers first used this route in 1836, it was not until 1846 that Preuss published his map to guide them. The long, narrow map shown here is called a "strip" map, a map that shows a thin strip of the earth's surface—in this case, the last stretch of the trail before reaching Fort Wallah-Wallah.

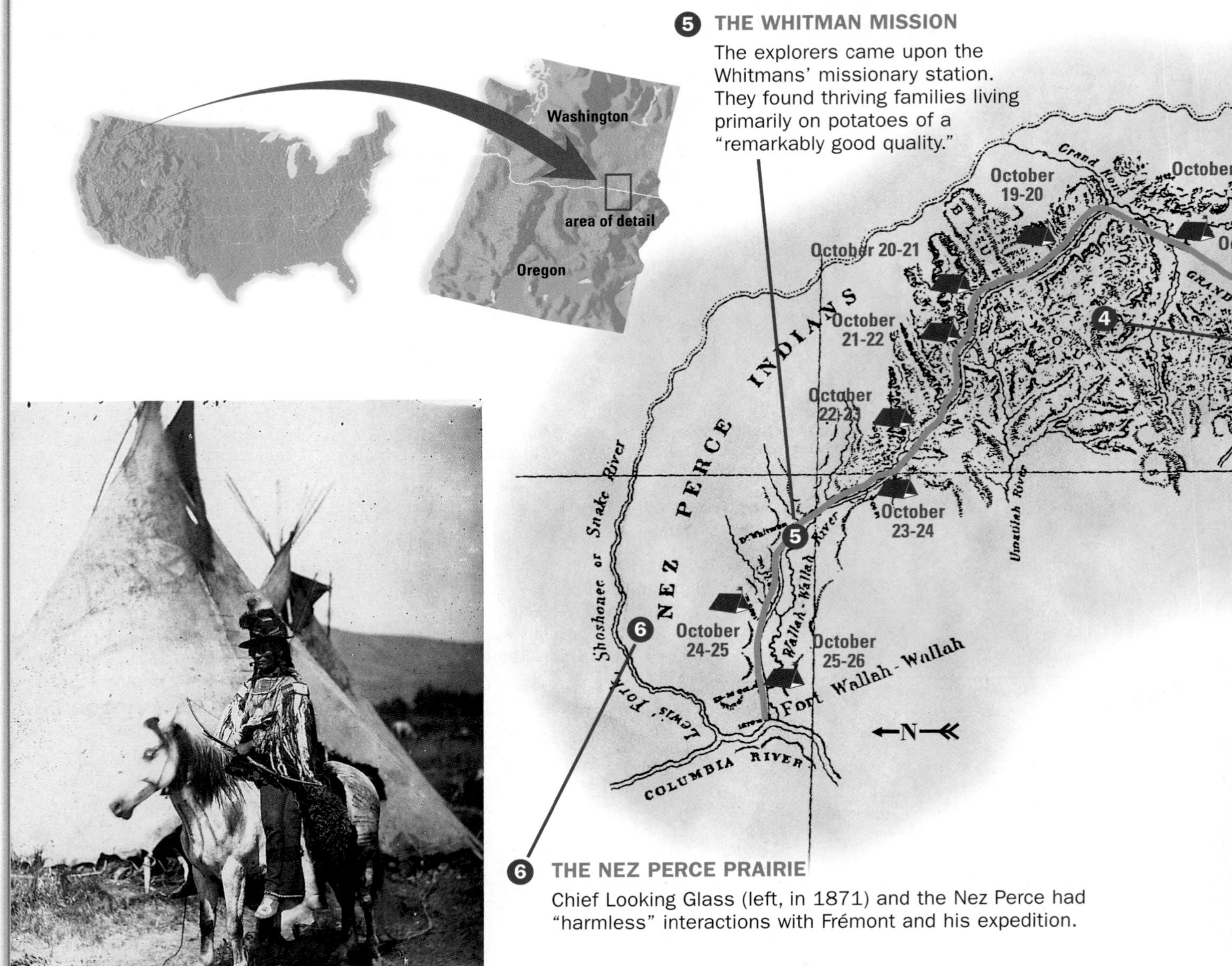

5 THE WHITMAN MISSION

The explorers came upon the Whitmans' missionary station. They found thriving families living primarily on potatoes of a "remarkably good quality."

6 THE NEZ PERCE PRAIRIE

Chief Looking Glass (left, in 1871) and the Nez Perce had "harmless" interactions with Frémont and his expedition.

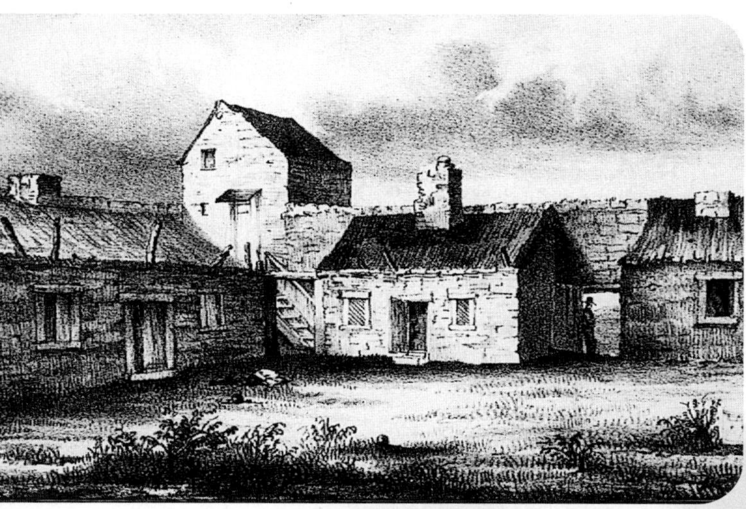

❶ FORT BOISÉE (BOISE)

This post became an important stopping point for settlers along the trail. Though salmon were plentiful in summer, Frémont noted that in the winter Native Americans often were forced to eat "every creeping thing, however loathsome and repulsive," to stay alive.

❷ MAP NOTATION

Preuss recorded dates, distances, temperatures, and geographical features as the expedition progressed along the trail.

❸ RECORDING NATURAL RESOURCES

On October 13, Frémont traveled through a desolate valley of the Columbia River to a region of "arable mountains," where he observed "nutritious grasses" and good soil that would support future flocks and herds.

❹ CROSSING THE MOUNTAINS

Pioneers on the trail cut paths through the Blue Mountains, a wooded range that Frémont believed had been formed by "violent and extensive igneous [volcanic] action."

THINKING CRITICALLY

1. **Analyzing Patterns** Use the map to identify natural obstacles that settlers faced on the Oregon Trail.
2. **Creating a Thematic Map** Do research to find out more about early mapping efforts for other western trails. Then create a settler's map of a small section of one trail. To help you decide what information you should show, pose some questions that a settler might have and that your map will answer. Then, sketch and label your map.

SEE SKILLBUILDER HANDBOOK, PAGE R32.

RESEARCH LINKS CLASSZONE.COM

REVIEW CHAPTER  ASSESSMENT

TERMS & NAMES

For each term or name below, write a sentence explaining its connection to the nation's growth during the early and mid-1800s.

1. Jeffersonian republicanism
2. Monroe Doctrine
3. Missouri Compromise
4. Jacksonian democracy
5. Trail of Tears
6. Stephen F. Austin
7. market revolution
8. Lowell textile mills
9. Frederick Douglass
10. Elizabeth Cady Stanton

MAIN IDEAS

Use your notes and the information in the chapter to answer the following questions.

The Jeffersonian Era *(pages 112–117)*

1. How did the Louisiana Purchase affect the United States?
2. What did the Treaty of Ghent accomplish?

The Age of Jackson *(pages 120–127)*

3. What changes occurred in the voting population and in voting patterns between the presidential elections of 1824 and 1828?
4. Why did Jackson oppose the Bank of the United States?

Manifest Destiny *(pages 130–138)*

5. Why was the concept of manifest destiny such an appealing one to Americans in the 1840s?
6. Describe the battle of the Alamo and explain why it is an important symbol in U.S. history.

The Market Revolution *(pages 139–143)*

7. How did the inventions and innovations of the mid-19th century help fuel the nation's economy?
8. Why did workers go on strike and begin to form trade unions in the 1830s?

Reforming American Society *(pages 144–149)*

9. What new religious ideas set the stage for the reform movements of the mid-19th century?
10. What was the purpose of the Seneca Falls convention?

CRITICAL THINKING

1. **USING YOUR NOTES** What were America's goals and ideals during this period of expansion and economic change? Draw a chart in which you list goals from the period, how they were achieved, and in what ways their effects were positive or negative.

Goal	How Achieved	Positive/Negative Effects

2. **EVALUATING IMPACT** In what ways did the reform movement of the mid-19th century affect the lives of women—both white and black, both free and enslaved? Support your answers with examples from the text.

3. **FORMING GENERALIZATIONS** Westward expansion helped shape the personal identity of Americans in the early 19th century. What values and traits characterized many Western settlers of this era? Think about Jim Beckwourth's life (See the Historical Spotlight on page 131) and the rise of the common person during the Age of Jackson.

VISUAL SUMMARY THE GROWTH OF A YOUNG NATION

TERRITORIES AND EXPLORATION

- National boundaries are extended in the North, West, and South.
- Lewis and Clark expand knowledge of the Louisiana Territory.
- The Oregon and Santa Fe trails extend exploration of and settlement in the Northwest and Southwest.
- The California Gold Rush creates an influx of settlers in the West.

SOCIAL REFORMS

- Voting rights are expanded in many states, although for males only.
- National Trades' Union calls for improved working conditions.
- Women's institutions of higher education are founded.
- Abolitionists call for the end of slavery.

TECHNOLOGY AND COMMERCE

- The telegraph expands the possibilities of communication.
- Textile mills increase manufacturing in the North.
- The cotton gin allows for greater agricultural profits in the South.
- Canals and railroads improve transportation throughout the country.

Standardized Test Practice

Use the image below and your knowledge of U.S history to answer question 1.

1. This print by Robert Cruikshank, entitled *The President's Levee* [reception], or *All Creation Going to the White House*, was issued in 1829. It is satirizing —

A the Louisiana Purchase.
B the California gold rush.
C Jacksonian democracy.
D the Indian Removal Act.

2. The Supreme Court decision *Marbury* v. *Madison* is important for affirming which of the following principles?

F impressment
G the "American System"
H popular sovereignty
J judicial review

3. The main effect of the Missouri Compromise was to —

A admit Missouri as a state.
B resolve disputes over slavery in the territories.
C change the balance of free and slave states.
D incline Southerners toward secession.

4. Between 1830 and 1850, the geographic area of the United States increased by about one third. Most of this land was acquired by —

F war.
G purchase.
H exchange.
J inciting rebellion.

ADDITIONAL TEST PRACTICE, pages S1–S33.

TEST PRACTICE CLASSZONE.COM

ALTERNATIVE ASSESSMENT

1. **INTERACT WITH HISTORY** Recall your discussion of the question on page 111:

Would you support the federal or your state government?

Imagine that you are a visitor to the United States Senate in 1828, listening to senators express their views on a strong federal government versus states' rights. Write a letter to a friend describing what you saw and heard. Include events and issues from U.S. history that senators from the North and South might have used in making their arguments.

2. **VIDEO** **LEARNING FROM MEDIA** View the *American Stories* video, "Recruited by Lewis and Clark: Patrick Gass Chronicles the Journey West." Discuss the following questions in a small group; then do the activity.

- What were some of the roles played by Native Americans in the journey of Lewis and Clark? Provide examples that stand out for you.
- What aspect of the journey do you think that Patrick Gass found most difficult? Why?

Cooperative Learning Activity An explorer can be anyone who discovers important things about living in the world. Who are the explorers of our own day? Using examples you may have read about in books, magazines, or newspapers, or seen on television, choose someone you consider to be an important explorer. Prepare a report and present it to the class.

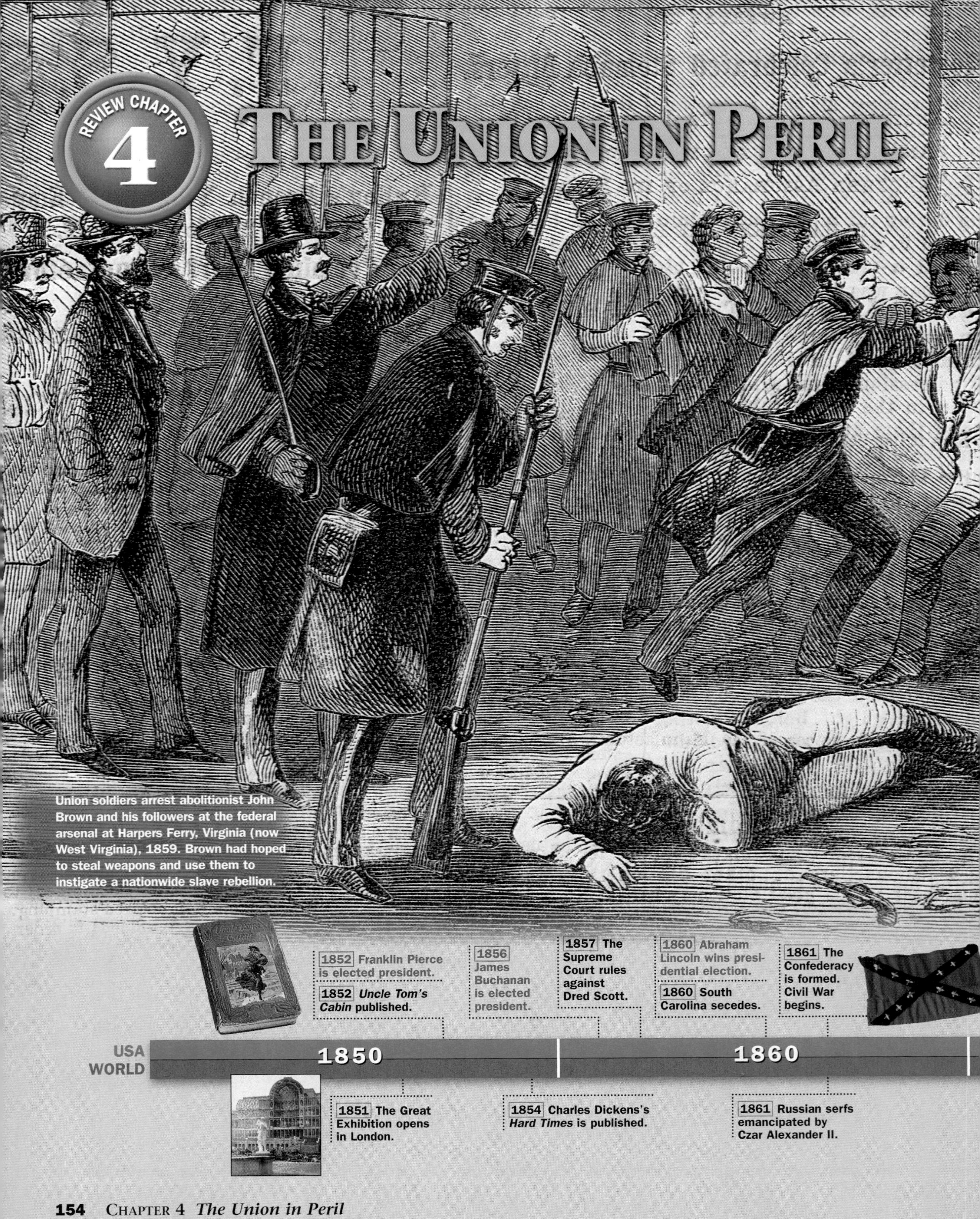

The Union in Peril

Union soldiers arrest abolitionist John Brown and his followers at the federal arsenal at Harpers Ferry, Virginia (now West Virginia), 1859. Brown had hoped to steal weapons and use them to instigate a nationwide slave rebellion.

USA

1852 Franklin Pierce is elected president.

1852 *Uncle Tom's Cabin* published.

1856 James Buchanan is elected president.

1857 The Supreme Court rules against Dred Scott.

1860 Abraham Lincoln wins presidential election.

1860 South Carolina secedes.

1861 The Confederacy is formed. Civil War begins.

1850 — 1860

WORLD

1851 The Great Exhibition opens in London.

1854 Charles Dickens's *Hard Times* is published.

1861 Russian serfs emancipated by Czar Alexander II.

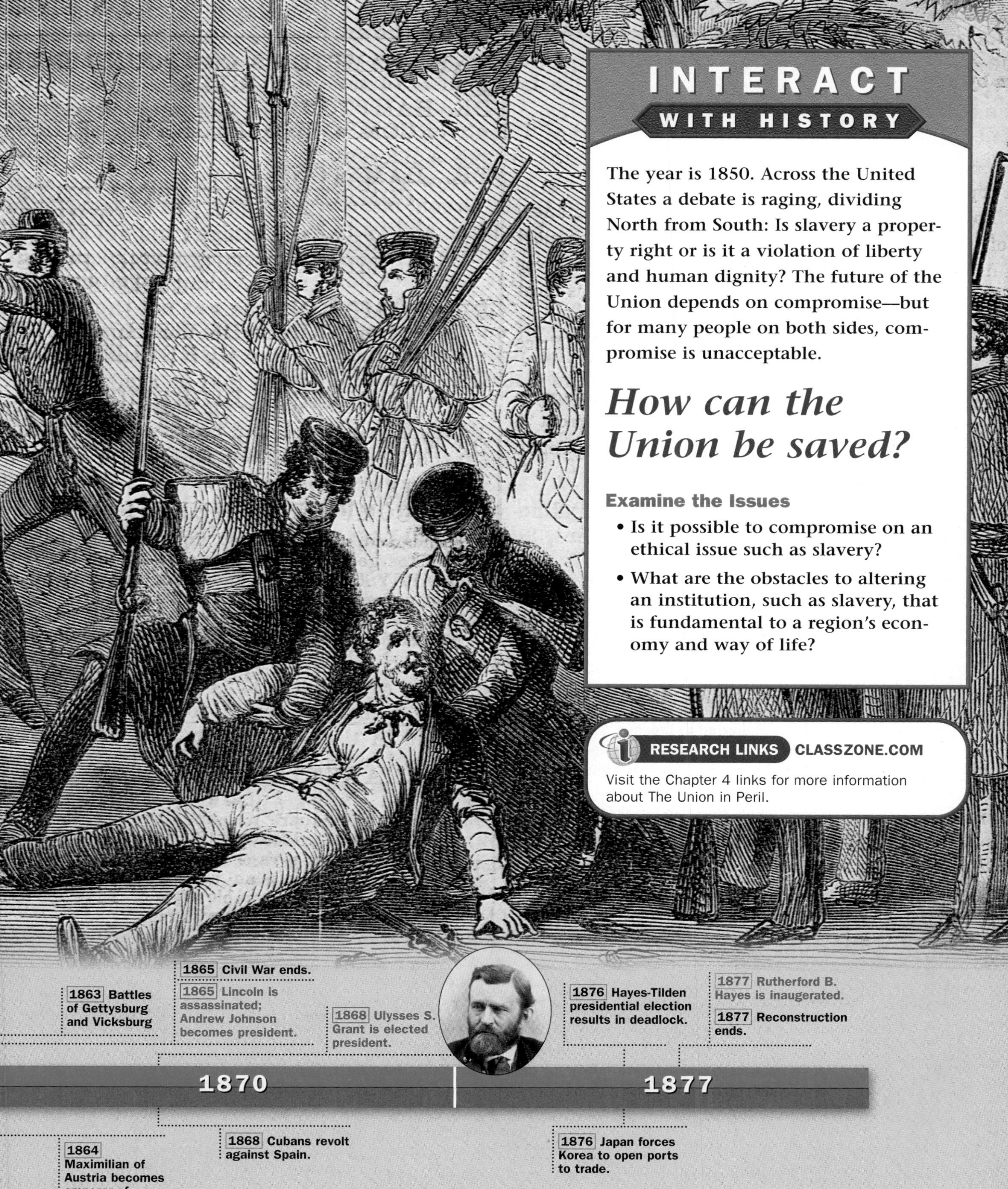

INTERACT WITH HISTORY

The year is 1850. Across the United States a debate is raging, dividing North from South: Is slavery a property right or is it a violation of liberty and human dignity? The future of the Union depends on compromise—but for many people on both sides, compromise is unacceptable.

How can the Union be saved?

Examine the Issues

- Is it possible to compromise on an ethical issue such as slavery?
- What are the obstacles to altering an institution, such as slavery, that is fundamental to a region's economy and way of life?

RESEARCH LINKS **CLASSZONE.COM**

Visit the Chapter 4 links for more information about The Union in Peril.

1863 Battles of Gettysburg and Vicksburg

1865 Civil War ends.

1865 Lincoln is assassinated; Andrew Johnson becomes president.

1868 Ulysses S. Grant is elected president.

1876 Hayes-Tilden presidential election results in deadlock.

1877 Rutherford B. Hayes is inaugurated.

1877 Reconstruction ends.

1870 — 1877

1864 Maximilian of Austria becomes emperor of Mexico.

1868 Cubans revolt against Spain.

1876 Japan forces Korea to open ports to trade.

The Divisive Politics of Slavery

MAIN IDEA

Disagreements over slavery heightened regional tensions and led to the breakup of the Union.

WHY IT MATTERS NOW

The modern Democratic and Republican parties emerged from the political tensions of the mid-19th century.

Terms & Names

- **secession**
- **popular sovereignty**
- **Underground Railroad**
- **Harriet Tubman**
- **Harriet Beecher Stowe**
- **Franklin Pierce**
- **Dred Scott**
- **Stephen Douglas**
- **Abraham Lincoln**
- **Confederacy**
- **Jefferson Davis**

One American's Story

Senator John C. Calhoun was a sick man, too sick to deliver his speech to the Senate. On March 4, 1850, Calhoun asked Senator James M. Mason of Virginia to read his speech for him.

A PERSONAL VOICE JOHN C. CALHOUN

"**I have, Senators, believed from the first that the agitation of the subject of slavery would, if not prevented by some timely and effective measure, end in disunion. . . . The agitation has been permitted to proceed . . . until it has reached a period when it can no longer be disguised or denied that the Union is in danger. You have thus had forced upon you the greatest and the gravest question that can ever come under your consideration: How can the Union be preserved?**"

—quoted in *The Compromise of 1850*

As Senator Calhoun and other Southern legislators demanded the expansion of slavery, Northerners just as vehemently called for its abolition. Once again, the issue of slavery was deepening the gulf between the North and the South.

John C. Calhoun

Differences Between North and South

Over the centuries, the Northern and Southern sections of the United States had developed into two very different cultural and economic regions. The distinction between North and South had its roots in the early 17th century, when British colonists began settling Virginia in the South and Massachusetts in the North. Along with differences in geography and climate, the two regions were noticeably dissimilar in their religious and cultural traditions. However, it was the Southern dependence on the "peculiar institution" of slavery that increased tensions between the regions and that eventually brought them into conflict.

MAIN IDEA

Developing Historical Perspective

A Why did Southerners want to increase the number of slave states?

The South, with its plantation economy, had come to rely on an enslaved labor force. The North, with its diversified industries, was less dependent on slavery. As the North industrialized, Northern opposition to slavery grew more intense. The controversy over slavery only worsened as new territories and states were admitted to the union. Supporters of slavery saw an opportunity to create more slave states, while opponents remained equally determined that slavery should not spread. **A**

Slavery in the Territories

The issue of slavery in California and in the western territories led to heated debates in the halls of Congress, and eventually to a fragile compromise.

STATEHOOD FOR CALIFORNIA Due in large part to the gold rush, California had grown quickly and applied for statehood in December 1850. California's new constitution forbade slavery, a fact that alarmed and angered many Southerners. They had assumed that because most of California lay south of the Missouri Compromise line of 36°30′, the state would be open to slavery. Southerners wanted the 1820 compromise to apply to territories west of the Louisiana Purchase, thus ensuring that California would become a slave state.

THE COMPROMISE OF 1850 As the 31st Congress opened in December 1849, the question of statehood for California topped the agenda. Of equal concern was the border dispute in which the slave state of Texas claimed the eastern half of the New Mexico Territory, where the issue of slavery had not yet been settled. As passions mounted, threats of Southern **secession,** the formal withdrawal of a state from the Union, became more frequent.

Once again, Henry Clay worked to shape a compromise that both the North and the South could accept. After obtaining support of the powerful Massachusetts senator Daniel Webster, Clay presented to the Senate a series of resolutions later called the Compromise of 1850.

Clay's compromise contained provisions to appease Northerners as well as Southerners. To please the North, the compromise provided that California be

1 Daniel Webster strongly supported Clay's compromise. He left the Senate before Stephen Douglas could engineer passage of all the bill's provisions.

2 Henry Clay offered his compromise to the Senate in January 1850. In his efforts to save the Union, Clay earned for himself the name "the Great Compromiser."

3 John C. Calhoun opposed the compromise. He died two months after Clay proposed it.

admitted to the Union as a free state. To please the South, the compromise proposed a new and more effective fugitive slave law. To placate both sides, a provision allowed **popular sovereignty,** the right to vote for or against slavery, for residents of the New Mexico and Utah territories.

Vocabulary
fugitive: running away or fleeing

Despite the efforts of Clay and Webster, the Senate rejected the proposed compromise in July. Tired, ill, and discouraged, Clay withdrew from the fight and left Washington. Senator Stephen A. Douglas of Illinois picked up the pro-compromise reins. Douglas unbundled the package of resolutions and reintroduced them one at a time, hoping to obtain a majority vote for each measure individually. The death of President Taylor aided Douglas's efforts. Taylor's successor, Millard Fillmore, quickly made it clear that he supported the compromise.

At last, in September, after eight months of effort, the Compromise of 1850 became law. For the moment, the crisis over slavery in the territories had passed. However, relief was short-lived. Another crisis loomed on the horizon—enforcement of the new fugitive slave law. B

MAIN IDEA
Summarizing
B What was the compromise that allowed California to be admitted to the Union?

Protest, Resistance, and Violence

The harsh terms of the Fugitive Slave Act surprised many people. Under the law, alleged fugitive slaves were not entitled to a trial by jury. In addition, anyone convicted of helping a fugitive was liable for a fine of $1,000 and imprisonment for up to six months. Infuriated by the Fugitive Slave Act, some Northerners resisted it by organizing "vigilance committees" to send endangered African Americans to safety in Canada. Others resorted to violence to rescue fugitive slaves. Still others worked to help slaves escape from slavery.

Harriet Tubman was called "Moses" by those she helped escape on the Underground Railroad. In her later years, Tubman opened a home for elderly, orphaned, and needy African Americans. ▼

THE UNDERGROUND RAILROAD Attempting to escape from slavery was a dangerous process. It meant traveling on foot at night without any sense of distance or direction, except for the North Star and other natural signs. It meant avoiding patrols of armed men on horseback and struggling through forests and across rivers. Often it meant going without food for days at a time.

As time went on, free African Americans and white abolitionists developed a secret network of people who would, at great risk to themselves, hide fugitive slaves. The system of escape routes they used became known as the **Underground Railroad**. "Conductors" on the routes hid fugitives in secret tunnels and false cupboards, provided them with food and clothing, and escorted or directed them to the next "station." Once fugitives reached the North, many chose to remain there. Others journeyed to Canada to be completely out of reach of their "owners." C

MAIN IDEA
Summarizing
C How did the Underground Railroad operate?

One of the most famous conductors was **Harriet Tubman,** born a slave in Maryland in 1820 or 1821. In 1849, after Tubman's owner died, she heard rumors that she was about to be sold. Fearing this possibility, Tubman decided to make a break for freedom and succeeded in reaching Philadelphia. Shortly after passage of the Fugitive Slave Act, Tubman resolved to become a conductor on the Underground Railroad. In all, she made 19 trips back to the South and is said to have helped 300 slaves—including her own parents—flee to freedom.

UNCLE TOM'S CABIN Meanwhile, another woman brought the horrors of slavery into the homes of a great many Americans. In 1852, **Harriet Beecher Stowe** published her novel *Uncle Tom's Cabin,* which stressed that slavery was not just a political contest, but also a great moral struggle. As a young girl, Stowe had watched boats filled with people on their way to be sold at slave markets. *Uncle Tom's Cabin* expressed her lifetime hatred of slavery. The book stirred Northern abolitionists to increase their protests against the Fugitive Slave Act, while

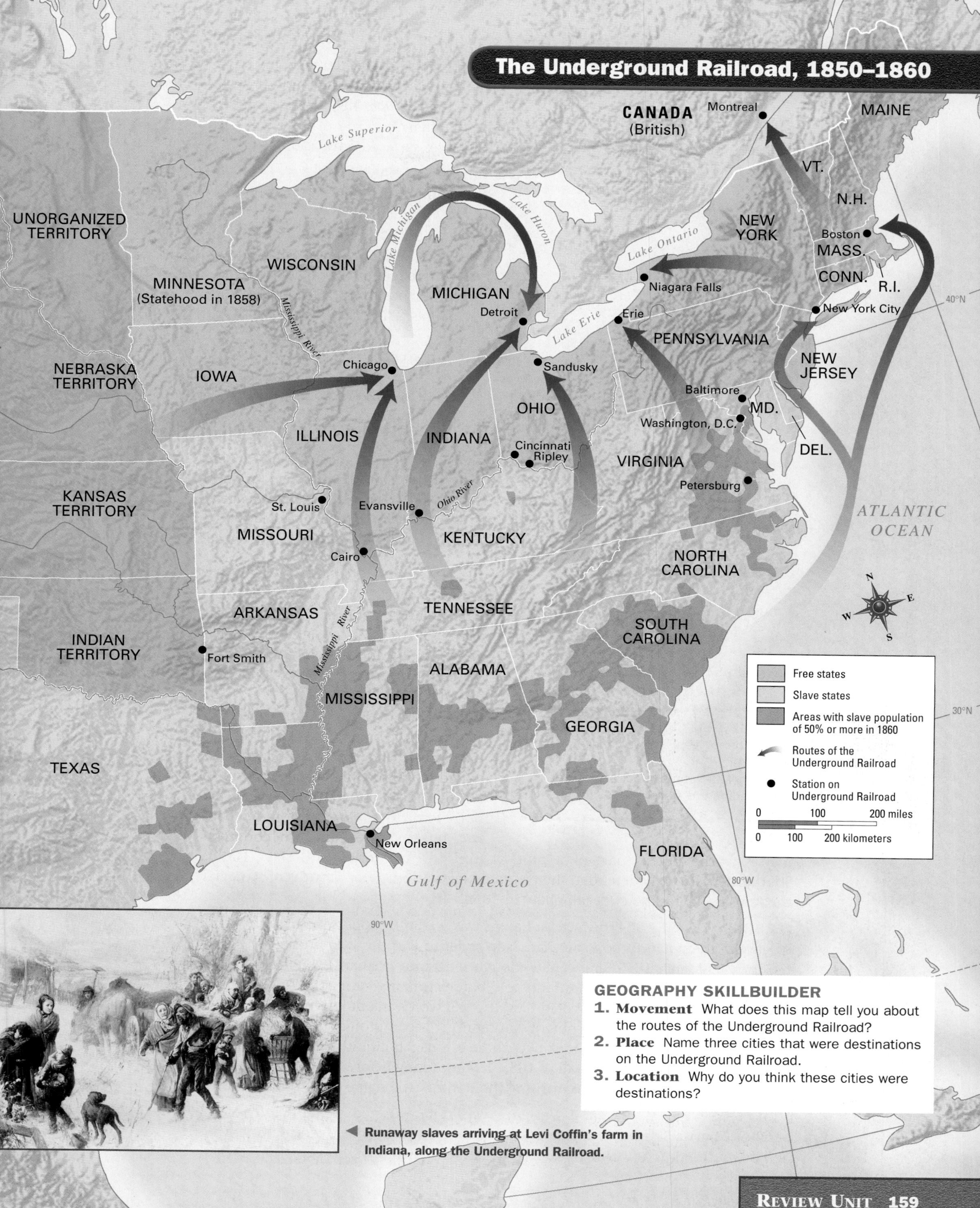

Runaway slaves arriving at Levi Coffin's farm in Indiana, along the Underground Railroad.

GEOGRAPHY SKILLBUILDER

1. **Movement** What does this map tell you about the routes of the Underground Railroad?
2. **Place** Name three cities that were destinations on the Underground Railroad.
3. **Location** Why do you think these cities were destinations?

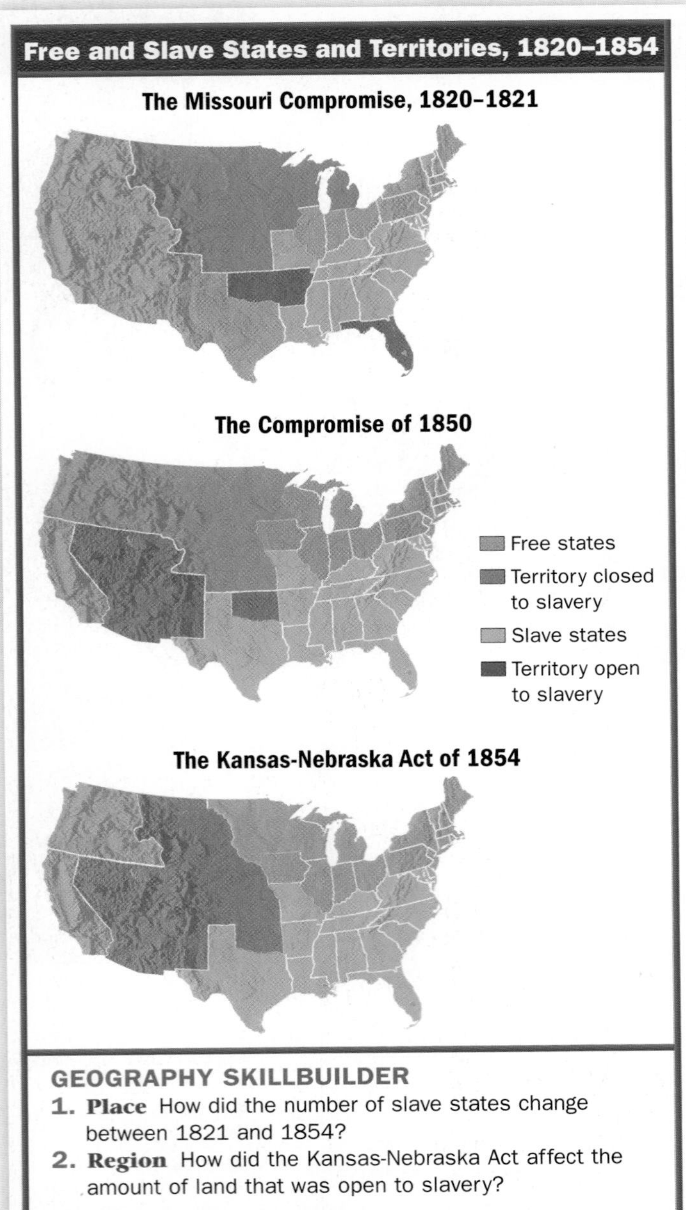

Southerners criticized the book as an attack on the South. The furor over *Uncle Tom's Cabin* had barely begun to settle when the issue of slavery in the territories surfaced once again.

TENSION IN KANSAS AND NEBRASKA The Compromise of 1850 had provided for popular sovereignty in New Mexico and Utah. To Senator Stephen Douglas, popular sovereignty seemed like an excellent way to decide whether slavery would be allowed in the Nebraska Territory.

A Personal Voice
STEPHEN A. DOUGLAS

"If the people of Kansas want a slaveholding state, let them have it, and if they want a free state they have a right to it, and it is not for the people of Illinois, or Missouri, or New York, or Kentucky, to complain, whatever the decision of Kansas may be."

—quoted in *The Civil War* by Geoffrey C. Ward

The only difficulty was that, unlike New Mexico and Utah, the Kansas and Nebraska territory lay north of the Missouri Compromise line of 36°30′ and therefore was legally closed to slavery. Douglas introduced a bill in Congress on January 23, 1854, that would divide the area into two territories: Nebraska in the north and Kansas in the south. If passed, the bill would repeal the Missouri Compromise and establish popular sovereignty for both territories. Congressional debate was bitter. Some Northern congressmen saw the bill as part of a plot to turn the territories into slave states. Southerners strongly defended the proposed legislation. After months of struggle, the Kansas-Nebraska Act became law in 1854. **D**

> **MAIN IDEA**
> **Analyzing Events**
> **D** Why was the debate over the Kansas-Nebraska Act so bitter?

"BLEEDING KANSAS" The race for Kansas was on. Both supporters and opponents of slavery attempted to populate Kansas in order to win the vote on slavery in the territory. By March 1855 Kansas had enough settlers to hold an election for a territorial legislature. However, thousands of "border ruffians" from the slave state of Missouri crossed into Kansas, voted illegally, and won a fraudulent majority for the proslavery candidates. A government was set up at Lecompton and promptly issued a series of proslavery acts. Furious over these events, abolitionists organized a rival government in Topeka in the fall of 1855. It wasn't long before bloody violence surfaced in the struggle for Kansas, earning the territory the name "Bleeding Kansas."

VIOLENCE IN THE SENATE Violence was not restricted to Kansas. In May, Senator Charles Sumner of Massachusetts delivered an impassioned speech in the Senate, entitled "The Crime Against Kansas." For two days he verbally attacked

the South and slavery, singling out Senator Andrew P. Butler of South Carolina for his proslavery beliefs.

Soon after, Butler's nephew, Congressman Preston S. Brooks, walked into the Senate chamber and struck Sumner on the head repeatedly with a cane until the cane broke. Sumner suffered brain damage and did not return to his Senate seat for more than three years.

The widening gulf between the North and the South had far-reaching implications for party politics as well. As the two regions grew further apart, the old national parties ruptured, and new political parties emerged, including a party for antislavery Northerners.

▲ This 1856 cartoon, with its ironic caption, gives the Northern view of Preston Brooks's beating of Charles Sumner.

New Political Parties Emerge

By the end of 1856, the nation's political landscape had a very different appearance than it had exhibited in 1848. The Whig Party had split over the issue of slavery and had lost support in both the North and the South. The Democratic Party, which had survived numerous crises in its history, was still alive, though scarred. A new Republican Party had formed and was moving within striking distance of the presidency. E

MAIN IDEA

Analyzing Effects

E What impact did the slavery issue have on the Democratic and Whig parties?

SLAVERY DIVIDES WHIGS In 1852 the Whig vote in the South fell dramatically, which helped produce a victory for the Democratic candidate, **Franklin Pierce**. In 1854 the Kansas-Nebraska Act completed the demise of the Whigs. Unable to agree on a national platform, the Southern faction splintered as its members looked for a proslavery, pro-Union party to join. At the same time, Whigs in the North sought a political alternative of their own.

One alternative that appeared was the American Party, which soon became known as the Know-Nothing Party, because members were instructed to answer questions about their activities by saying, "I know nothing." The Know-Nothings supported nativism, the favoring of native-born people over immigrants. However, like the Whigs, the Know-Nothings split over the issue of slavery in the territories. Southern Know-Nothings looked for another alternative to the Democrats. Meanwhile, Northern Know-Nothings began to edge toward the Republican Party.

"Free soil, Free speech, Free labor, and Free men"

FREE-SOILERS' CAMPAIGN SLOGAN, 1848

Two antislavery parties had also emerged during the 1840s. The Liberty Party was formed for the purpose of pursuing the cause of abolition by passing new laws, but received only a small percentage of votes in the 1848 presidential election. In that same election, the Free-Soil Party, which opposed the extension of slavery into the territories, received ten percent of the popular vote in the presidential election. From this strong showing, it was clear that many Northerners opposed the extension of slavery in the territories.

THE FREE-SOILERS' VOICE Northern opposition to slavery in the territories was not necessarily based on positive feelings toward African Americans. It was not unusual for Northerners to be Free-Soilers without being abolitionists. Unlike abolitionists, a number of Northern Free-Soilers supported racist laws prohibiting settlement by blacks in their communities and denying them the right to vote.

What Free-Soilers primarily objected to was slavery's competition with free white workers, or a wage-based labor force, upon which the North depended. They feared that such competition would drive down wages. Free-Soilers detected a dangerous pattern in such events as the passage of the Fugitive Slave Act and the repeal of the Missouri Compromise. They were convinced that a conspiracy existed on the part of the "diabolical slave power" to spread slavery throughout the United States. F

MAIN IDEA

Contrasting

F How did Free-Soilers differ from abolitionists?

THE NEW REPUBLICAN PARTY In 1854 opponents of slavery in the territories formed a new political party, the Republican Party. The Republicans were united in opposing the Kansas-Nebraska Act and in keeping slavery out of the territories. Apart from these issues, however, the Republican party embraced a wide range of opinions. As the party grew, it took in Free-Soilers, antislavery Whigs and Democrats, and nativists, mostly from the North. The conservative faction hoped to resurrect the Missouri Compromise. At the opposite extreme were some radical abolitionists.

During the election of 1856 the Republicans chose as their candidate John C. Frémont. The Democrats nominated James Buchanan of Pennsylvania. If Frémont had won, the South might have seceded then and there. However, Buchanan won, and the threat of secession was temporarily averted.

Conflicts Lead to Secession

Political conflicts only intensified after the election of President Buchanan. The first slavery-related controversy arose on March 6, 1857, just two days after he took office.

Dred Scott's lawsuit set off even more controversy over slavery. ▼

THE DRED SCOTT DECISION A major Supreme Court decision was brought about by **Dred Scott,** a slave whose owner took him from the slave state of Missouri to free territory in Illinois and Wisconsin and back to Missouri. Scott appealed to the Supreme Court for his freedom on the grounds that living in a free state—Illinois—and a free territory—Wisconsin—had made him a free man.

The case was in court for years. Finally, on March 6, 1857, the Supreme Court ruled against Dred Scott. According to the ruling, Scott lacked any legal standing to sue in federal court because he was not, and never could be, a citizen. Moreover, the Court ruled that being in free territory did not make a slave free. The Fifth Amendment protected property, including slaves. For territories to exclude slavery would be to deprive slaveholders of their property.

Background

The *Dred Scott* case was only the second one in American history in which the Supreme Court reversed a federal legislative act.

Sectional passions exploded immediately. Many Northerners showered a torrent of abuse upon the Supreme Court, in part because a majority of its justices were Southerners. Warnings about the slave states' influence on the national government spread. Southern slaveholders, on the other hand, were jubilant. In their interpretation, the *Dred Scott* decision not only permitted the extension of slavery but actually guaranteed it. (See *Dred Scott* v. *Sandford* on page 166.)

LINCOLN–DOUGLAS DEBATES Several months after the *Dred Scott* decision, one of Illinois's greatest political contests got underway: the 1858 race for the U.S. Senate between Democratic incumbent **Stephen Douglas** and Republican challenger Congressman **Abraham Lincoln.** To many outsiders it must have seemed like an uneven match. Douglas was a well-known two-term senator with an outstanding record and a large campaign chest, while Lincoln was a self-educated man who had been elected to one term in Congress in 1846. To counteract Douglas, Lincoln challenged the man known as the "Little Giant" to a series of debates on the issue of slavery in the territories. Douglas accepted the challenge, and the stage was set for some of the most celebrated debates in U.S. history.

(left) A Mathew Brady Studio photo of Stephen Douglas from 1860.
(right) A photograph of Abraham Lincoln, also from 1860.

The two men's positions were simple and consistent. Neither wanted slavery in the territories, but they disagreed on how to keep it out. Douglas believed deeply in popular sovereignty. Lincoln, on the other hand, believed that slavery was immoral. However, he did not expect individuals to give up slavery unless Congress abolished slavery with an amendment.

In their second debate, Lincoln asked his opponent a crucial question: Could the settlers of a territory vote to exclude slavery before the territory became a state? Everyone knew that the *Dred Scott* decision said no—that territories could not exclude slavery. Popular sovereignty, Lincoln implied, was thus an empty phrase.

Douglas replied that, if the people of a territory were Free-Soilers, then all they had to do was elect representatives who would not enforce slave property laws in that territory. In other words, people could get around *Dred Scott.*

Douglas won the Senate seat, but his response had widened the split in the Democratic Party. As for Lincoln, his attacks on the "vast moral evil" of slavery drew national attention, and some Republicans began thinking of him as an excellent candidate for the presidency in 1860. G

MAIN IDEA

Comparing
G Compare and contrast Lincoln's and Douglas's views on slavery.

HARPERS FERRY While politicians debated the slavery issue, the abolitionist John Brown was studying the slave uprisings that had occurred in ancient Rome and, more recently, on the French island of Haiti. He believed that the time was ripe for similar uprisings in the United States. Brown secretly obtained financial backing from several prominent Northern abolitionists. On the night of October 16, 1859, he led a band of 21 men, black and white, into Harpers Ferry, Virginia (now West Virginia). His aim was to seize the federal arsenal there and start a general slave uprising.

History Through *Art*

JOHN BROWN GOING TO HIS HANGING

This painting by the African-American artist Horace Pippin shows John Brown being transported by wagon to his execution. The artist has focused our attention on the cruelty of Brown's fate. The abolitionist is shown tied with the rope that will be used to hang him, sitting on the coffin that will receive his body after death. Brown's dark shape is silhouetted by the large white building behind him, a structure that combines the features of both courthouse and prison.

SKILLBUILDER **Interpreting Visual Sources**

1. Why do you think the African-American woman in the right-hand corner is looking away from the scene? How would you describe her expression?
2. How has the artist expressed the hopelessness of the situation?

SEE SKILLBUILDER HANDBOOK, PAGE R23.

No such uprising occurred, however. Instead, troops put down the rebellion. Later, authorities tried Brown and put him to death. Public reaction to Brown's execution was immediate and intense in both sections of the country. In the North, bells tolled, guns fired salutes, and huge crowds gathered to hear fiery speakers denounce the South. The response was equally extreme in the South, where mobs assaulted whites who were suspected of holding antislavery views.

LINCOLN IS ELECTED PRESIDENT As the 1860 presidential election approached, the Republicans nominated Abraham Lincoln. Lincoln appeared to be moderate in his views. Although he pledged to halt the further spread of slavery, he also tried to reassure Southerners that a Republican administration would not "interfere with their slaves, or with them, about their slaves." Nonetheless, many Southerners viewed him as an enemy.

As the campaign developed, three major candidates besides Lincoln vied for office. The Democratic Party finally split over slavery. Northern Democrats rallied behind Douglas and his doctrine of popular sovereignty. Southern Democrats, who supported the *Dred Scott* decision, lined up behind Vice-President John C. Breckinridge of Kentucky. Former Know-Nothings and Whigs from the South organized the Constitutional Union Party and nominated John Bell of Tennessee as their candidate. Lincoln emerged as the winner with less than half the popular vote and with no electoral votes from the South. He did not even appear on the ballot in most of the slave states because of Southern hostility toward him. The outlook for the Union was grim. (H)

> **MAIN IDEA**
>
> **Summarizing**
>
> (H) What happened to the Democratic Party as the 1860 presidential election approached?

SOUTHERN SECESSION Lincoln's victory convinced Southerners—who had viewed the struggle over slavery partly as a conflict between the states' right of self-determination and federal government control—that they had lost their political voice in the national government. Some Southern states decided to act. South Carolina led the way, seceding from the Union on December 20, 1860. When the news reached Northern-born William Tecumseh Sherman, superintendent of the Louisiana State Seminary of Learning and Military Academy (now Louisiana State University), he poured out his fears for the South.

A PERSONAL VOICE WILLIAM TECUMSEH SHERMAN

> **"This country will be drenched in blood. . . . [T]he people of the North . . . are not going to let this country be destroyed without a mighty effort to save it. . . . Besides, where are your men and appliances of war to contend against them? . . . You are rushing into war with one of the most powerful, ingeniously mechanical and determined people on earth—right at your doors. . . . Only in spirit and determination are you prepared for war. In all else you are totally unprepared."**
>
> —quoted in *None Died in Vain*

Mississippi soon followed South Carolina's lead, as did Florida, Alabama, Georgia, Louisiana, and Texas. In February 1861, delegates from the secessionist states met in Montgomery, Alabama, where they formed the Confederate States of America, or **Confederacy.** They also drew up a constitution that closely resembled that of the United States, but with a few notable differences. The most important difference was that it "protected and recognized" slavery in new territories.

The Confederates then unanimously elected former senator **Jefferson Davis** of Mississippi as president. The North had heard threats of secession before. When it finally happened, no one was shocked. But one key question remained in everyone's mind: Would the North allow the South to leave the Union without a fight?

HISTORICAL SPOTLIGHT

SECESSION AND THE BORDER STATES

Four slave states—Maryland, Kentucky, Missouri, and Delaware—were undecided about secession. Lincoln believed that these states would be essential to the success of the Union if war broke out. They had large populations, numerous factories, and strategic access to the Ohio River. Moreover, Maryland nearly surrounded Washington, D.C., the seat of government.

Lincoln faced a choice: free the slaves and make abolitionists happy, or ignore slavery for the moment to keep from alienating the border states. He chose the latter, but that did not prevent violent conflicts between secessionists and Unionists in Maryland, Kentucky, and Missouri. With the intervention of the militia, and some political maneuvering in those states' legislatures, Lincoln kept the four border states in the Union.

ASSESSMENT

1. **TERMS & NAMES** For each term or name, write a sentence explaining its significance.
   - **secession**
   - **popular sovereignty**
   - **Underground Railroad**
   - **Harriet Tubman**
   - **Harriet Beecher Stowe**
   - **Franklin Pierce**
   - **Dred Scott**
   - **Stephen Douglas**
   - **Abraham Lincoln**
   - **Confederacy**
   - **Jefferson Davis**

MAIN IDEA

2. **TAKING NOTES**
   Create a time line like the one below, showing the events that heightened the tensions between the North and the South.

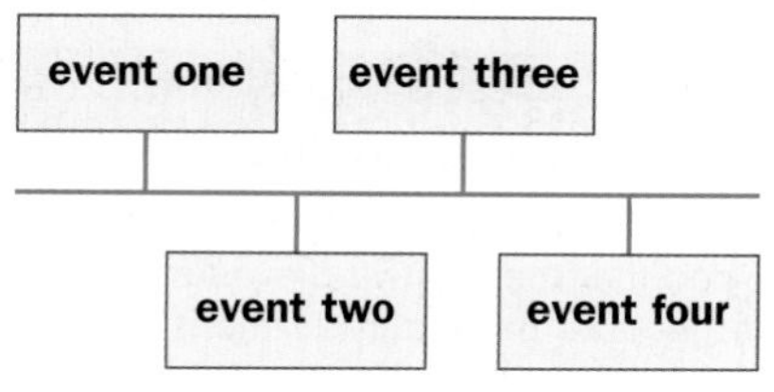

Select one event and explain its significance.

CRITICAL THINKING

3. **HYPOTHESIZING**
   Review issues and events in this section that reflect the growing conflict between the North and the South. Do you think there were any points at which civil war might have been averted? **Think About:**
   - the Compromise of 1850, the Fugitive Slave Act, and the Kansas-Nebraska Act
   - the new political parties
   - the Supreme Court's ruling in the *Dred Scott* decision
   - the election of Abraham Lincoln as president in 1860

4. **EVALUATING LEADERSHIP**
   John Brown, Harriet Tubman, Harriet Beecher Stowe, and Stephen Douglas all opposed slavery. Who do you think had the greatest impact on American history and why?

5. **DEVELOPING HISTORICAL PERSPECTIVE**
   How did the tension between states' rights and national government authority manifest itself in the events leading up to the Civil War?

DRED SCOTT v. *SANDFORD* (1857)

ORIGINS OF THE CASE Dred Scott's slave master had brought him from the slave state of Missouri to live for a time in free territory and in the free state of Illinois. Eventually they returned to Missouri. Scott believed that because he had lived in free territory, he should be free. In 1854 he sued in federal court for his freedom. The court ruled against him, and he appealed to the Supreme Court.

THE RULING **The Supreme Court ruled that African Americans were not and could never be citizens. Thus, Dred Scott had no right even to file a lawsuit and remained enslaved.**

LEGAL REASONING

The Court's decision, conceived and written by Chief Justice Roger Taney, made two key findings. First, it held that because Scott was a slave, he was not a citizen and had no right to sue in a United States court.

> **"We think they [slaves] . . . are not included, and were not intended to be included, under the word 'citizens' in the Constitution, and can therefore claim none of the rights and privileges which that instrument provides for and secures to citizens of the United States."**

This could have been the end of the matter, but Taney went further. He said that by banning slavery, Congress was, in effect, taking away property. Such an action, he wrote, violated the Fifth Amendment, which guarantees the right not to be deprived of property without due process of law (such as a hearing). Thus, all congressional efforts to ban slavery in the territories were prohibited.

Justices John McLean and Benjamin Curtis strongly dissented on both points. They showed that the U.S. Constitution, state constitutions, and other laws had recognized African Americans as citizens. They also pointed to the clause in the Constitution giving Congress the power to "make all needful Rules and Regulations" to govern U.S. territories. In their view, this clause gave Congress the power to prohibit slavery in the territories.

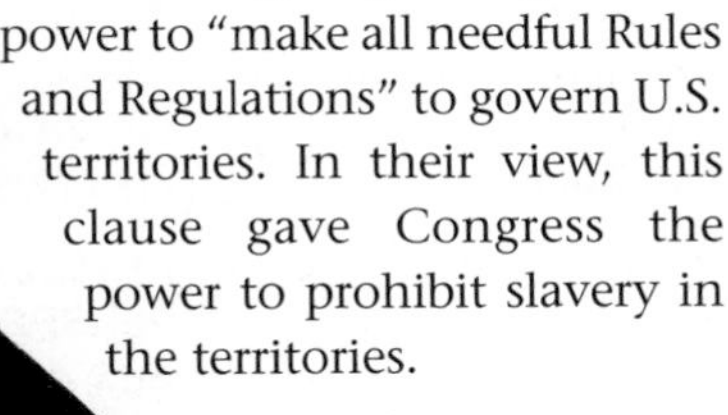

◀ **Chief Justice Roger Taney**

LEGAL SOURCES

U.S. CONSTITUTION

U.S. CONSTITUTION, ARTICLE 4, SECTION 2 (1788)

"No person held to service or labor in one state, . . . escaping into another, shall, in consequence of any law or regulation therein, be discharged from such service or labor. . . ."

U.S. CONSTITUTION, ARTICLE 4, SECTION 3 (1788)

"The Congress shall have Power to dispose of and make all needful Rules and Regulations respecting the Territory or other Property belonging to the United States. . . ."

U.S. CONSTITUTION, FIFTH AMENDMENT (1791)

"No person shall be . . . deprived of life, liberty, or property, without due process of law. . . ."

RELATED CASES

***ABLEMAN* v. *BOOTH* (1858)**

The Court decided that the Fugitive Slave Act was constitutional and that laws passed in Northern states that prohibited the return of fugitive slaves were unconstitutional.

WHY IT MATTERED

Taney's opinion in *Dred Scott* had far-reaching consequences. Legally, the opinion greatly expanded the reach of slavery. Politically, it heightened the sectional tensions that would lead to the Civil War.

Before the Court decided *Dred Scott*, Americans widely accepted the idea that Congress and the states could limit slavery. As the dissenters argued, many previous acts of Congress had limited slavery—for example, the Northwest Ordinance had banned slavery in the Northwest Territory—and no one had claimed that those acts violated property rights.

Taney's opinion in *Dred Scott*, however, was a major change. This expansion of slaveholders' rights cast doubt on whether free states could prevent slave owners from bringing or even selling slaves into free areas.

As a result, *Dred Scott* intensified the slavery debate as no single event had before. In going beyond what was needed to settle the case before him, Taney's ruling became a political act, and threw into question the legitimacy of the Court. Further, Taney's opinion took the extreme proslavery position and installed it as the national law. It not only negated all the compromises made to date by pro- and anti-slavery forces, but it seemed to preclude any possible future compromises.

FRANK LESLIE'S ILLUSTRATED NEWSPAPER

No. 82.—VOL. IV.]

NEW YORK, SATURDAY, JUNE 27, 1857.

[PRICE 6 CENTS.

▲ **Contemporary newspaper article describing the *Dred Scott* case.**

HISTORICAL IMPACT

It took five years of bitter civil war to find out if Taney's opinion would stand as the law of the land. It would not. Immediately after the Civil War, the federal government moved to abolish slavery with the Thirteenth Amendment (1865) and then to extend state and national citizenship with the Fourteenth Amendment (1868) to "[a]ll persons born or naturalized in the United States." The wording of these amendments was expressly intended to nullify *Dred Scott*.

These amendments meant that *Dred Scott* would no longer be used as a precedent—an earlier ruling that can be used to justify a current one. Instead, it is now pointed to as an important lesson on the limits of the Supreme Court's power, as a key step on the road to the Civil War, and as one of the worst decisions ever made by the Supreme Court.

THINKING CRITICALLY

CONNECT TO HISTORY

1. **Developing Historical Perspective** Use the library to find commentaries on *Dred Scott* written at the time the decision was made. Read two of these commentaries and identify which section—North or South—the writer or speaker came from. Explain how each person's region shaped his or her views.

SEE SKILLBUILDER HANDBOOK, PAGE R11.

CONNECT TO TODAY

2. 

CLASSZONE.COM

Visit the links for Historic Decisions of the Supreme Court to research what it means to be a citizen of the United States and what rights that citizenship extends. Research which constitutional amendments, U.S. laws, and Supreme Court decisions guarantee the rights of citizens. Prepare an oral presentation or annotated display to summarize your findings.

The Civil War Begins

MAIN IDEA

Shortly after the nation's Southern states seceded from the Union, war began between the North and South.

WHY IT MATTERS NOW

The nation's identity was forged in part by the Civil War. Sectional divisions remain very strong today.

Terms & Names

- **Fort Sumter**
- **Bull Run**
- **Stonewall Jackson**
- **Ulysses S. Grant**
- **Robert E. Lee**
- **Antietam**
- **Emancipation Proclamation**
- **conscription**
- **Clara Barton**
- **income tax**

One American's Story

On April 18, 1861, Major Robert Anderson was traveling by ship from Charleston, South Carolina, to New York City. That day, Anderson wrote a report to the secretary of war in which he described his most recent command.

A PERSONAL VOICE ROBERT ANDERSON

"Having defended Fort Sumter for thirty-four hours, until the quarters were entirely burned, the main gates destroyed by fire, . . . the magazine surrounded by flames, . . . four barrels and three cartridges of powder only being available, and no provisions but pork remaining, I accepted terms of evacuation . . . and marched out of the fort . . . with colors flying and drums beating . . . and saluting my flag with fifty guns."

—quoted in *Fifty Basic Civil War Documents*

▲ **Major Robert Anderson observes the firing at Fort Sumter in 1861.**

Months earlier, as soon as the Confederacy was formed, Confederate soldiers in each secessionist state began seizing federal installations—especially forts. By the time of Lincoln's inauguration on March 4, 1861, only four Southern forts remained in Union hands. The most important was **Fort Sumter,** on an island in Charleston harbor.

Lincoln decided to neither abandon Fort Sumter nor reinforce it. He would merely send in "food for hungry men." At 4:30 A.M. on April 12, Confederate batteries began thundering away to the cheers of Charleston's citizens. The deadly struggle between North and South was under way.

Union and Confederate Forces Clash

News of Fort Sumter's fall united the North. When Lincoln called for volunteers, the response throughout the Northern states was overwhelming. However, Lincoln's call for troops provoked a very different reaction in the states of the

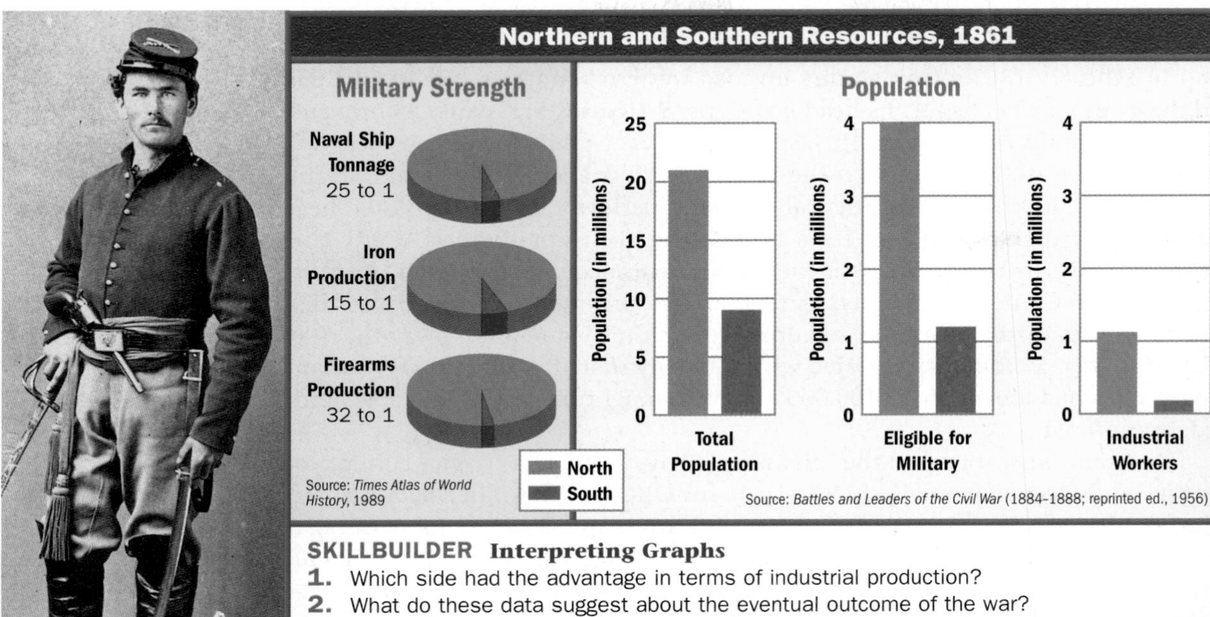

SKILLBUILDER Interpreting Graphs

1. Which side had the advantage in terms of industrial production?
2. What do these data suggest about the eventual outcome of the war?

▲ Most Union troops saw the war as a struggle to preserve the Union.

▲ Most Confederate soldiers fought to protect the South from Northern aggression.

upper South. In April and May, Virginia, Arkansas, North Carolina, and Tennessee seceded, bringing the number of Confederate states to eleven. The western counties of Virginia opposed slavery, so they seceded from Virginia and were admitted into the Union as West Virginia in 1863. The four remaining slave states—Maryland, Delaware, Kentucky, and Missouri—remained in the Union.

STRENGTHS AND STRATEGIES The Union and the Confederacy were unevenly matched. The Union enjoyed enormous advantages in resources over the South—more people, more factories, greater food production, and a more extensive railroad system. The Confederacy's advantages included "King Cotton," first-rate generals, and highly motivated soldiers. (A)

MAIN IDEA

Making Inferences
(A) Why were Northern factories and railroads so advantageous to the Union's war effort?

Both sides adopted military strategies suited to their objectives and resources. The Union, which had to conquer the South to win, devised a three-part plan:

- The navy would blockade Southern ports, so they could neither export cotton nor import much-needed manufactured goods.
- Union riverboats and armies would move down the Mississippi River and split the Confederacy in two.
- Union armies would capture the Confederate capital at Richmond, Virginia.

The Confederacy's strategy was mostly defensive, although Southern leaders encouraged their generals to attack the North if the opportunity arose.

BULL RUN The first bloodshed on the battlefield occurred about three months after Fort Sumter fell, near the little creek of **Bull Run,** just 25 miles from Washington, D.C. The battle was a seesaw affair. In the morning the Union army gained the upper hand, but the Confederates held firm, inspired by General Thomas J. Jackson. "There stands Jackson like a stone wall!" another general shouted, coining the nickname **Stonewall Jackson.** In the afternoon Confederate reinforcements helped win the first Southern victory. Fortunately for the Union, the Confederates were too exhausted to follow up their victory with an attack on Washington. Still, Confederate morale soared. Many Confederate soldiers, confident that the war was over, left the army and went home.

UNION ARMIES IN THE WEST Lincoln responded to the defeat at Bull Run by stepping up enlistments. He also appointed General George McClellan to lead the Union forces encamped near Washington. While McClellan drilled his troops, the Union forces in the west began the fight for control of the Mississippi River.

In February 1862 a Union army invaded western Tennessee. (See the Battles of the West map below.) At its head was General **Ulysses S. Grant,** a brave and decisive military commander. In just eleven days, Grant's forces captured two Confederate forts, Fort Henry on the Tennessee River and Fort Donelson on the Cumberland River. Two months later, Grant narrowly escaped disaster near Shiloh, a small church in Tennessee close to the Mississippi border. After Grant failed to have his troops dig trenches or set out adequate guards and patrols, thousands of Confederate soldiers carried out a surprise attack. Grant averted disaster by reorganizing his troops and driving the Confederate forces away the next day. However, Shiloh demonstrated what a bloody slaughter the war was becoming. Nearly one-fourth of the 100,000 men who fought there were killed, wounded, or captured.

As Grant pushed toward the Mississippi River, David G. Farragut, commanding a Union fleet of about 40 ships, seized New Orleans, the Confederacy's largest city and busiest port. (See the Fall of New Orleans map below.) By June, Farragut had taken control of much of the lower Mississippi. Between Grant and Farragut, the Union had nearly achieved its goal of cutting the Confederacy in two. Only Port Hudson, Louisiana, and Vicksburg, Mississippi, still stood in the way. B

MAIN IDEA

Making Inferences

B Why was control of the Mississippi River so important to the Union?

THE WAR FOR THE CAPITALS In the spring of 1862, while McClellan was leading his army toward Richmond, he met a Confederate army commanded by General Joseph E. Johnston. (See the Battles of the East map on page 171.) After a series of battles, Johnston was wounded, and command of the army passed on to **Robert E. Lee.** Lee was very different from McClellan—modest rather than vain, and willing to go beyond military textbooks in his tactics. Determined to save the Confederate capital, Lee drove McClellan away from Richmond.

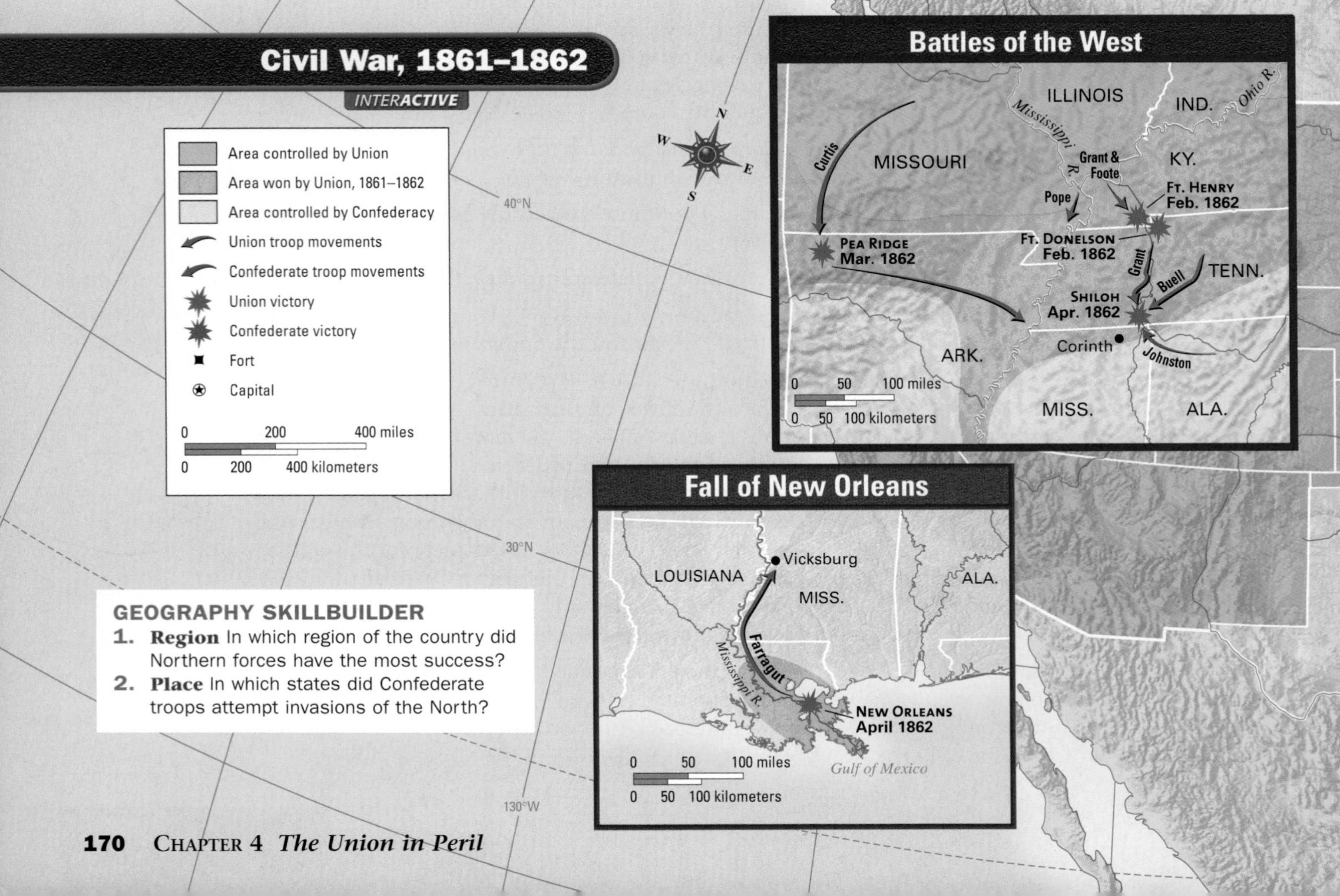

GEOGRAPHY SKILLBUILDER

1. **Region** In which region of the country did Northern forces have the most success?
2. **Place** In which states did Confederate troops attempt invasions of the North?

Now it was Lee's turn to move against Washington. In September his troops crossed the Potomac into the Union state of Maryland. At this point McClellan had an incredible stroke of luck. A Union corporal found a copy of Lee's orders wrapped around some cigars! The plan revealed that Lee's and Stonewall Jackson's armies were separated for the moment.

McClellan ordered his men to pursue Lee, and the two sides fought on September 17 near a creek called the **Antietam** (ăn-tē′təm). The clash proved to be the bloodiest single-day battle in American history, with casualties totaling more than 26,000. The next day, instead of pursuing the battered Confederate army into Virginia and possibly ending the war, McClellan did nothing. As a result, Lincoln removed him from command.

Vocabulary
casualties: those who are injured, killed, captured, or missing in action

The Politics of War

After secession occurred, many Southerners believed that dependence on Southern cotton would force Great Britain to formally recognize the Confederacy as an independent nation. Unfortunately for the South, Britain had accumulated a huge cotton inventory just before the outbreak of war. Instead of importing Southern cotton, the British now needed Northern wheat and corn. Britain decided that neutrality was the best policy. C

MAIN IDEA
Drawing Conclusions
C Why did both the Union and Confederacy care about British neutrality?

HISTORICAL SPOTLIGHT

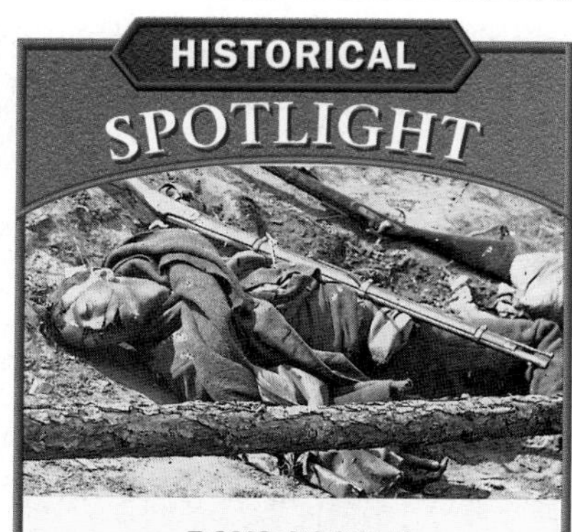

BOYS IN WAR

Both the Union and Confederate armies had soldiers who were under 18 years of age. Examination of some Confederate recruiting lists for 1861–1862 reveals that approximately 5 percent were 17 or younger—with some as young as 13. The percentage of boys in the Union army was lower, perhaps 1.5 percent. These figures, however, do not count the great number of boys who ran away to follow each army without officially enlisting.

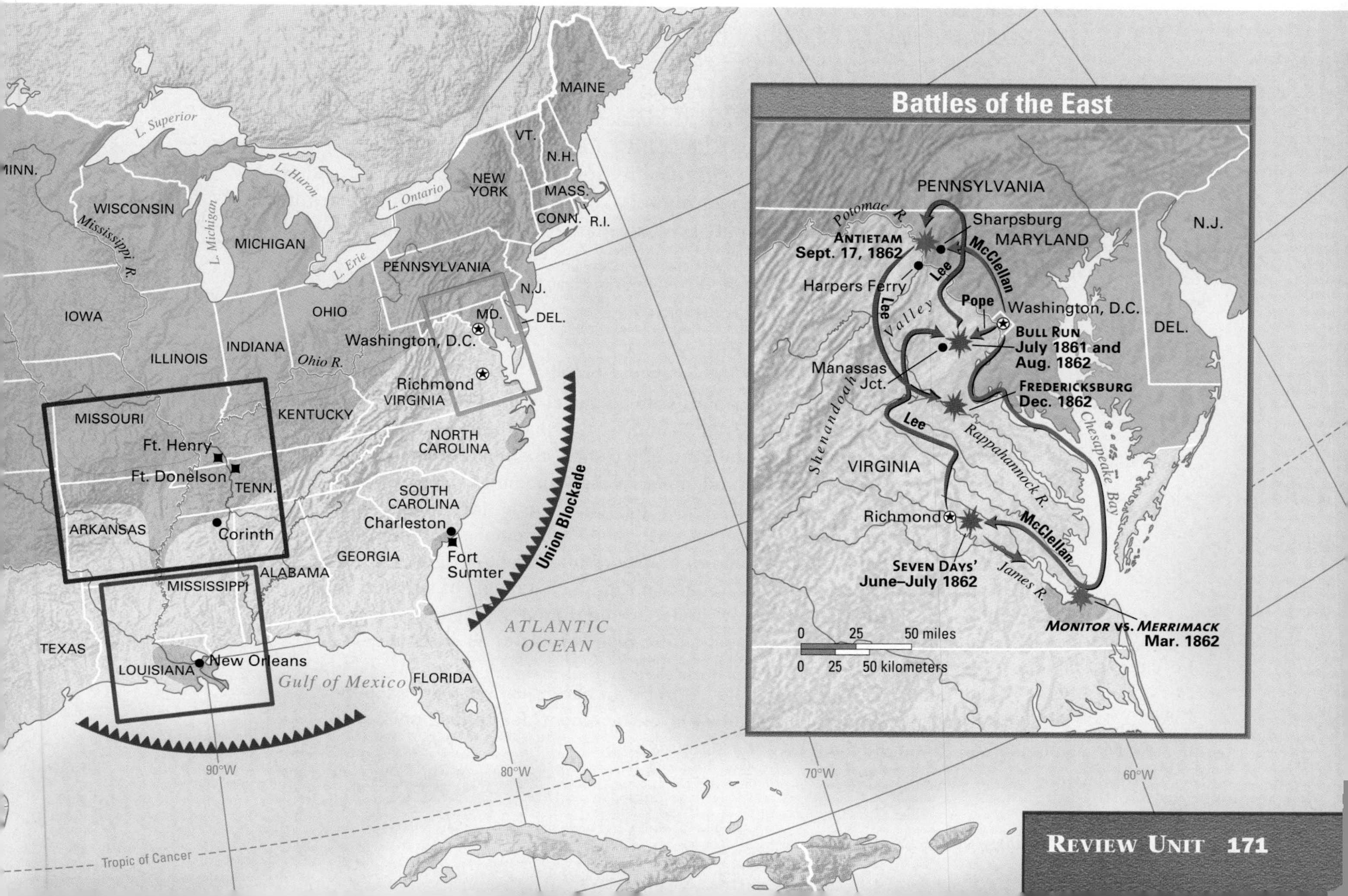

MAINE
VT.
N.H.
MASS.
R.I.
CONN.
NEW YORK
L. Superior
L. Huron
L. Ontario
L. Michigan
L. Erie
MINN.
WISCONSIN
MICHIGAN
Mississippi R.
IOWA
ILLINOIS
INDIANA
OHIO
Ohio R.
PENNSYLVANIA
N.J.
MD.
DEL.
Washington, D.C.
Richmond
VIRGINIA
KENTUCKY
MISSOURI
Ft. Henry
Ft. Donelson
TENN.
NORTH CAROLINA
SOUTH CAROLINA
ARKANSAS
Corinth
Charleston
Fort Sumter
Union Blockade
GEORGIA
ALABAMA
MISSISSIPPI
TEXAS
LOUISIANA
New Orleans
Gulf of Mexico
FLORIDA
ATLANTIC OCEAN
90°W
80°W
70°W
60°W
Tropic of Cancer

Battles of the East

PENNSYLVANIA
Potomac R.
Sharpsburg
MARYLAND
N.J.
ANTIETAM Sept. 17, 1862
McClellan
Lee
Harpers Ferry
Pope
Washington, D.C.
Valley
DEL.
BULL RUN July 1861 and Aug. 1862
Manassas Jct.
FREDERICKSBURG Dec. 1862
Shenandoah
Rappahannock R.
Chesapeake Bay
VIRGINIA
Richmond
SEVEN DAYS' June–July 1862
James R.
MONITOR VS. MERRIMACK Mar. 1862
0 25 50 miles
0 25 50 kilometers

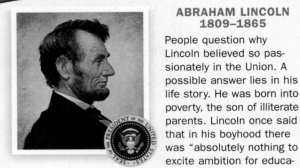

KEY PLAYERS

ABRAHAM LINCOLN
1809–1865

People question why Lincoln believed so passionately in the Union. A possible answer lies in his life story. He was born into poverty, the son of illiterate parents. Lincoln once said that in his boyhood there was "absolutely nothing to excite ambition for education," yet he hungered for knowledge.

Apart from a year's worth of school, Lincoln educated himself and, after working as rail-splitter, flatboatman, storekeeper, and surveyor, he taught himself to be a lawyer. This led to careers in politics and law—and eventually to the White House. Perhaps because of this upward mobility, Lincoln fought passionately to preserve the democracy he described as "the last best hope of earth."

JEFFERSON DAVIS
1808–1889

Davis, who was named after Thomas Jefferson, was born in Kentucky but grew up in Mississippi. After graduating from West Point, he served in the military, then settled down as a planter, before going into politics. He served terms in the U.S. Senate.

His election as president of the Confederacy dismayed him. As his wife Varina wrote, "I thought his genius was military, but as a party manager he would not succeed. He did not know the arts of the politician . . ." Varina was right. Davis fought frequently with other Confederate leaders and was blamed for the refusal of many Southern states to put the Confederacy's welfare above their own.

PROCLAIMING EMANCIPATION As Jefferson Davis's Confederacy struggled in vain to gain foreign recognition, abolitionist feeling grew in the North. Although Lincoln disliked slavery, he did not believe that the federal government had the power to abolish it where it already existed.

As the war progressed, however, Lincoln did find a way to use his constitutional war powers to end slavery. The Confederacy used the labor of slaves to build fortifications and grow food. Lincoln's powers as commander in chief allowed him to order his troops to seize enemy resources. Therefore, he decided that, just as he could order the Union army to take Confederate supplies, he could also authorize the army to emancipate slaves. Emancipation was not just a moral issue; it became a weapon of war.

On January 1, 1863, Lincoln issued his **Emancipation Proclamation.** The following portion captured national attention.

from **THE EMANCIPATION PROCLAMATION** ABRAHAM LINCOLN

"I do order and declare that all persons held as slaves within these said designated States and parts of States are, and henceforward shall be free; and that the Executive Government of the United States, including the military and naval authorities thereof, will recognize and maintain the freedom of said persons.

And I hereby enjoin upon the people so declared to be free to abstain from all violence, unless in necessary self-defense; and I recommend to them, that in all cases, when allowed, they labor faithfully for reasonable wages.

And I further declare and make known that such persons of suitable condition will be received into the armed service of the United States to garrison forts, positions, stations, and other places, and to man vessels of all sorts in said service.

And, upon this, sincerely believed to be an act of justice, warranted by the Constitution, upon military necessity, I invoke the considerate judgment of mankind and the gracious favor of Almighty God."

—from The Emancipation Proclamation, January 1, 1863

MAIN IDEA

Analyzing Motives
D In what way was the Emancipation Proclamation a part of Lincoln's military strategy?

The proclamation did not free any slaves immediately because it applied only to areas behind Confederate lines, outside Union control. Nevertheless, for many, the proclamation gave the war a moral purpose by turning the struggle into a fight to free the slaves. It also ensured that compromise was no longer possible. D

BOTH SIDES FACE POLITICAL DISSENT Neither side in the Civil War was completely unified. The North harbored thousands of Confederate sympathizers, while the South had thousands of Union sympathizers.

Lincoln dealt forcefully with disloyalty and dissent. He suspended the writ of *habeas corpus*, which prevents the government from holding citizens without formally charging them with crimes. Jefferson Davis also adopted this practice.

Life During Wartime

Vocabulary
desertion: the act of abandoning an assigned post or duty

The war led to social upheaval and political unrest in both the North and the South. As the fighting intensified, heavy casualties and widespread desertions led each side to impose **conscription,** a draft that forced men to serve in the army. In the North, conscription led to draft riots, the most violent of which took place in New York City. Sweeping changes occurred in the wartime economies of both sides as well as in the roles played by African Americans and women.

AFRICAN AMERICANS FIGHT FOR FREEDOM Although African Americans made up only 1 percent of the North's population, by war's end about 180,000 African Americans had fought for the Union—about 10 percent of the Northern army. In spite of their dedication, African-American soldiers in the Union army suffered discrimination. They served in separate regiments commanded by white officers and earned lower pay for most of the war.

SOLDIERS SUFFER ON BOTH SIDES Both Union and Confederate soldiers had marched off to war thinking it would be a glorious affair. They were soon disillusioned, not just by heavy battlefield casualties but also by such unhealthy conditions as filthy surroundings, a limited diet, and inadequate medical care. In the 1860s, the technology of killing had outrun the technology of medical care.

Except when fighting or marching, most soldiers lived amid heaps of rubbish and open latrines. As a result, body lice, dysentery, and diarrhea were common.

If conditions in the army camps were bad, those in war prisons were atrocious. The Confederate camps were especially overcrowded and unsanitary. The South's lack of food and tent canvas also contributed to the appalling conditions. Prison camps in the North were only slightly better. Northern prisons provided

Wounded Union troops recuperate after battle near a makeshift field hospital. ▼

more space and adequate amounts of food. However, thousands of Confederate prisoners, housed in quarters with little or no heat, contracted pneumonia and died. Historians estimate that 15 percent of Union prisoners in Southern prisons died, while 12 percent of Confederate prisoners died in Northern prisons.

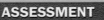

▲ Union nurses, such as Clara Barton *(above)* and Louisa May Alcott, faced the hazards of disease in field hospitals.

WOMEN WORK TO IMPROVE CONDITIONS Although women did not fight, thousands contributed to the war effort. Some 3,000 women served as Union army nurses. One dedicated Union nurse was **Clara Barton,** who went on to found the American Red Cross after the war. Barton cared for the sick and wounded, often at the front lines of battle. Thousands of Southern women also volunteered for nursing duty. Sally Tompkins, for example, performed so heroically in her hospital duties that she eventually was commissioned as a captain.

Background
After the war, Clara Barton became the first woman to head a U.S. government agency, whose employees helped family members to track down missing soldiers.

Both sides benefited because women devoted so much time and energy to nursing. Women's help was desperately needed as a series of battles in the Mississippi Valley and in the East soon sent casualties flooding into Northern and Southern hospitals alike.

THE WAR AFFECTS REGIONAL ECONOMIES In general, the war expanded the North's economy and shattered the South's. The Confederacy soon faced a food shortage due to the drain of manpower into the army, the Union occupation of food-growing areas, and the loss of enslaved field workers. Food prices skyrocketed, and the inflation rate rose 7,000 percent.

Overall, the war's effect on the economy of the North was much more positive. The army's need for supplies supported woolen mills, steel foundries, and many other industries. The economic boom had a dark side, however. Wages did not keep up with prices, and many people's standard of living declined. When white male workers went out on strike, employees hired free blacks, immigrants, and women to replace them for lower wages. As the Northern economy grew, Congress decided to help pay for the war by collecting the nation's first **income tax,** a tax that takes a specified percentage of an individual's income.

SECTION 2 ASSESSMENT

1. **TERMS & NAMES** For each term or name, write a sentence explaining its significance.
   - **Fort Sumter**
   - **Bull Run**
   - **Stonewall Jackson**
   - **Ulysses S. Grant**
   - **Robert E. Lee**
   - **Antietam**
   - **Emancipation Proclamation**
   - **conscription**
   - **Clara Barton**
   - **income tax**

MAIN IDEA

2. **TAKING NOTES**
   Create a chart like the one shown, listing the military actions and social and economic changes of the first two years of the Civil War.

Military Actions	Social & Economic Changes
1.	1.
2.	2.

What changes brought about by the war had the most effect on civilians in both the South and the North?

CRITICAL THINKING

3. **ANALYZING EFFECTS**
   What effects did the Civil War have on women and African Americans?
   Think About:
   - the impact of the Emancipation Proclamation
   - women's role in the war effort

4. **CONTRASTING**
   What advantages did the Union have over the South?

5. **ANALYZING PRIMARY SOURCES**
   This medical kit was used during the Civil War. What difficulties would caregivers and patients have faced during this time?

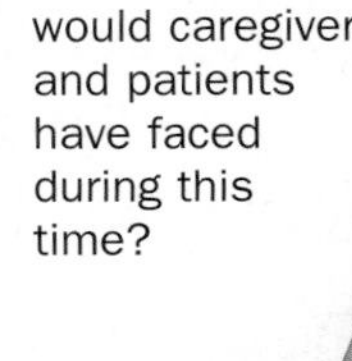

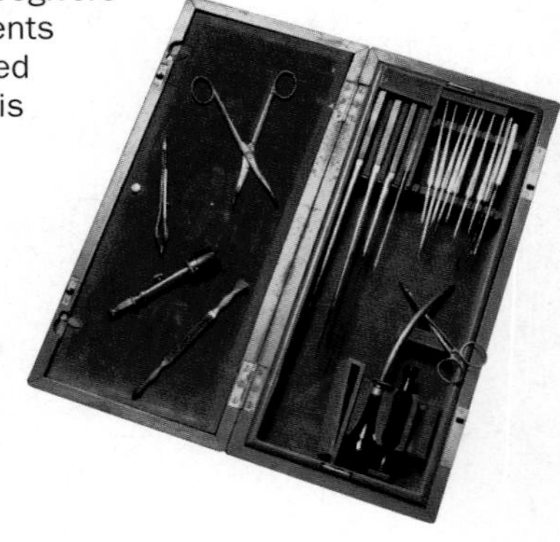

The North Takes Charge

MAIN IDEA

After four years of bloody fighting, the Union wore down the Confederacy and won the war.

WHY IT MATTERS NOW

The Union victory confirmed the authority of the federal government over the states.

Terms & Names

- Gettysburg
- Gettysburg Address
- Vicksburg
- William Tecumseh Sherman
- Appomattox Court House
- Thirteenth Amendment
- John Wilkes Booth

One American's Story

Mary Chesnut was the daughter of a South Carolina governor and the wife of a U.S. senator who resigned his office to serve in the Confederate government. During the war, she recorded her observations and thoughts in a diary. In 1864, Chesnut went to hear Benjamin H. Palmer, a minister and professor, speak about the war. In her diary, she described how Palmer's pessimistic words filled her with foreboding about the future of the Confederacy.

VIDEO

WAR OUTSIDE MY WINDOW
Mary Chesnut's Diary of the Civil War

A Personal Voice MARY CHESNUT

> **"September 21st . . . I did not know before how utterly hopeless was our situation. This man is so eloquent. It was hard to listen and not give way. Despair was his word—and martyrdom. He offered us nothing more in this world than the martyr's crown. . . . He spoke of these times of our agony. And then came the cry: 'Help us, oh God. Vain is the help of man.' And so we came away—shaken to the depths."**
>
> —quoted in *Mary Chesnut's Civil War*

By September 1864, the Northern armies had won several decisive battles. Mary Chesnut must already have had some idea of the threat posed to her way of life, however. In 1863 she wrote that the South, "the only world we cared for," had been "literally kicked to pieces."

The Tide Turns

The year 1863 actually had begun well for the South. In December 1862, Lee's army had defeated the Union Army of the Potomac at Fredericksburg, Virginia. Then, in May, the South defeated the North again at Chancellorsville, Virginia.

The North's only consolation after Chancellorsville came as the result of an accident. As General Stonewall Jackson returned from a patrol on May 2, Confederate guards accidentally shot him in the left arm. A surgeon amputated his arm the following day. When Lee heard the news, he exclaimed, "He has lost his left arm but I have lost my right." The true loss was still to come; Jackson caught pneumonia and died on May 10.

Despite Jackson's death, Lee decided to press his military advantage and invade the North. He needed supplies and he thought that a major Confederate victory on Northern soil might tip the balance of public opinion in the Union to the proslavery politicians. Accordingly, he crossed the Potomac into Maryland and then pushed on into Pennsylvania. (A)

MAIN IDEA

Analyzing Motives

(A) What did Lee hope to gain by invading the North?

THE BATTLE OF GETTYSBURG Near the sleepy town of **Gettysburg,** in southern Pennsylvania, the most decisive battle of the war was fought. The Battle of Gettysburg began on July 1 when Confederate soldiers led by A. P. Hill encountered several brigades of Union cavalry under the command of John Buford, an experienced officer from Illinois.

Buford ordered his men to take defensive positions on the hills and ridges surrounding the town. When Hill's troops marched toward the town from the west, Buford's men were waiting. The shooting attracted more troops and both sides called for reinforcements. By the end of the first day of fighting, 90,000 Union troops under the command of General George Meade had taken the field against 75,000 Confederates, led by General Lee.

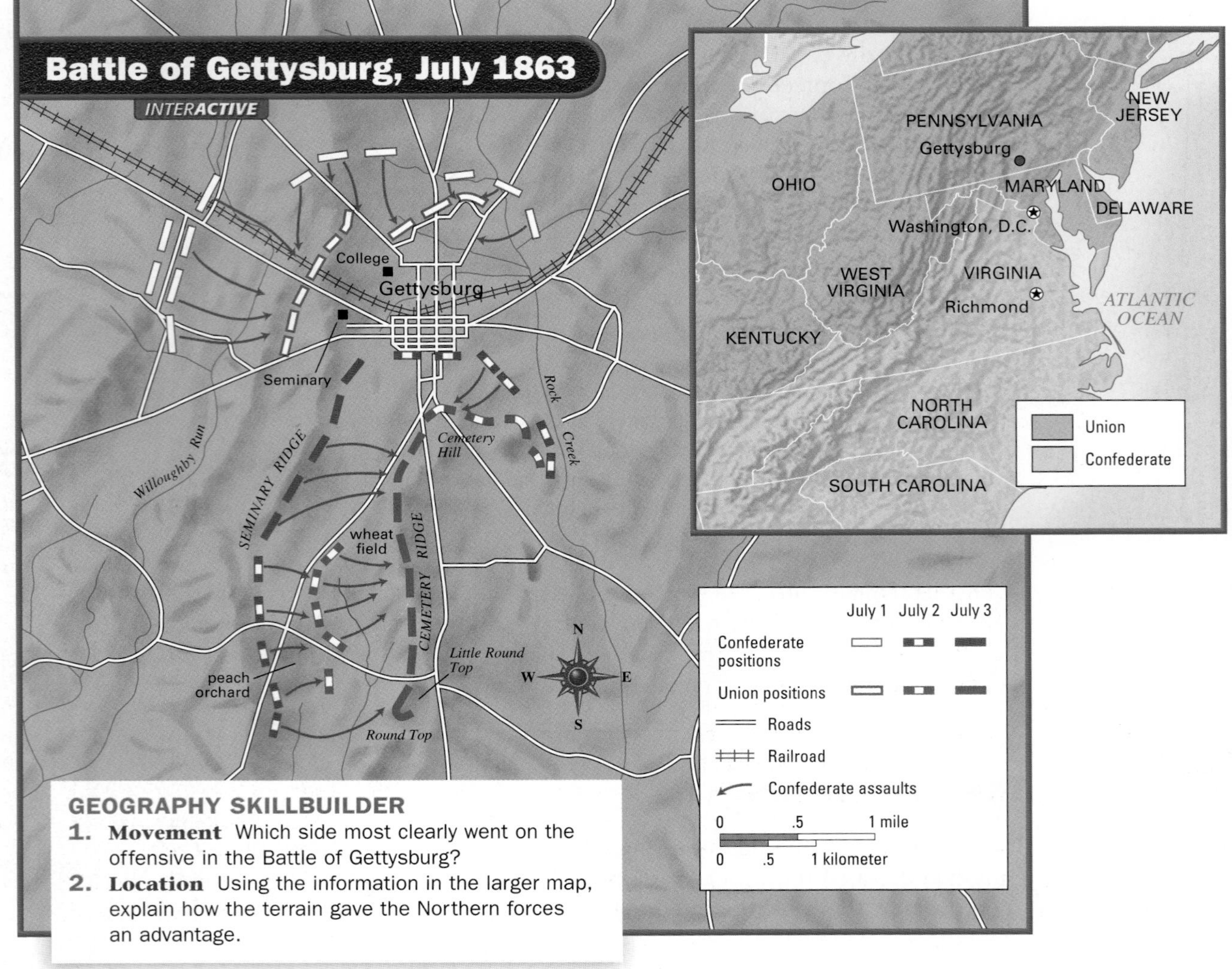

GEOGRAPHY SKILLBUILDER

1. **Movement** Which side most clearly went on the offensive in the Battle of Gettysburg?
2. **Location** Using the information in the larger map, explain how the terrain gave the Northern forces an advantage.

By the second day of battle, the Confederates had driven the Union troops from Gettysburg and had taken control of the town. However, the North still held positions on Cemetery Ridge, the high ground south of Gettysburg. On July 2, Lee ordered General James Longstreet to attack Cemetery Ridge. At about 4:00 P.M., Longstreet's troops advanced from Seminary Ridge, where they were positioned in a peach orchard and wheat field that stood between them and most of the Union army on Cemetery Ridge. The Confederates repeatedly attacked the Union lines. Although the Union troops were forced to concede some territory, their lines withheld the withering Confederate onslaught.

On July 3, Lee ordered an artillery barrage on the center of the Union lines on Cemetery Ridge. For two hours, the two armies fired at one another in a vicious exchange that could be heard in Pittsburgh. Believing they had silenced the Union guns, the Confederates then charged the lines. Confederate forces marched across the farmland between their position and the Union high ground. Suddenly, Northern artillery renewed its barrage, and the infantry fired on the rebels as well. Devastated, the Confederates staggered back to their lines. After the battle, Lee gave up any hopes of invading the North and led his army back to Virginia.

MAIN IDEA

Analyzing Effects

B Why was the Battle of Gettysburg a disaster for the South?

The three-day battle produced staggering losses: 23,000 Union men and 28,000 Confederates were killed or wounded. Total casualties were more than 30 percent. Despite the devastation, Northerners were enthusiastic about breaking "the charm of Robert Lee's invincibility." **B**

THE GETTYSBURG ADDRESS In November 1863, a ceremony was held to dedicate a cemetery in Gettysburg. There, President Lincoln spoke for a little more than two minutes. According to some contemporary historians, Lincoln's **Gettysburg Address** "remade America." Before Lincoln's speech, people said, "The United States are . . ." Afterward, they said, "The United States is . . ." In other words, the speech helped the country to realize that it was not just a collection of individual states; it was one unified nation.

The Gettysburg Address ABRAHAM LINCOLN

Four score and seven years ago our fathers brought forth on this continent a new nation, conceived in Liberty and dedicated to the proposition that all men are created equal.

Now we are engaged in a great civil war, testing whether that nation, or any nation so conceived and so dedicated, can long endure. We are met on a great battle-field of that war. We have come to dedicate a portion of that field, as a final resting-place for those who here gave their lives that that nation might live. It is altogether fitting and proper that we should do this.

But, in a larger sense, we can not dedicate—we can not consecrate—we can not hallow—this ground. The brave men, living and dead, who struggled here, have consecrated it, far above our poor power to add or detract. The world will little note, nor long remember what we say here, but it can never forget what they did here. It is for us the living, rather, to be dedicated here to the unfinished work which they who fought here have thus far so nobly advanced. It is rather for us to be here dedicated to the great task remaining before us—that from these honored dead we take increased devotion to that cause for which they gave the last full measure of devotion—that we here highly resolve that these dead shall not have died in vain—that this nation, under God, shall have a new birth of freedom—and that government of the people, by the people, for the people, shall not perish from the earth. **C**

—"The Gettysburg Address," November 19, 1863

MAIN IDEA

Forming Generalizations

C What ideas about the United States did Lincoln express in the Gettysburg Address?

History Through *Photojournalism*

MATHEW BRADY'S PHOTOGRAPHS

The Civil War marked the first time in United States history that photography, a resource since 1839, played a major role in a military conflict. Hundreds of photographers traveled with the troops, working both privately and for the military. The most famous Civil War photographer was Mathew Brady, who employed about 20 photographers to meet the public demand for pictures from the battlefront. This was the beginning of American news photography, or photojournalism.

Many of Brady's photographs are a mix of realism and artificiality. Due to the primitive level of photographic technology, subjects had to be carefully posed and remain still during the long exposure times.

In this 1864 photograph Brady posed a kneeling soldier, offering a canteen of water, beside a wounded soldier with his arm in a sling. Images like this, showing the wounded or the dead, brought home the harsh reality of war to the civilian population.

"Encampment of the Army of the Potomac" (May 1862). Few photographs of the Civil War are as convincing in their naturalism as this view over a Union encampment. Simply by positioning the camera behind the soldiers, the photographer draws the viewer into the composition. Although we cannot see the soldiers' faces, we are compelled to see through their eyes.

SKILLBUILDER Interpreting Visual Sources

1. What elements in the smaller photograph seem posed or contrived? What elements are more realistic?
2. How do these photographs compare with more heroic imagery of traditional history painting?

SEE SKILLBUILDER HANDBOOK, PAGE R23.

GRANT WINS AT VICKSBURG While Meade's Army of the Potomac was destroying Confederate hopes in Gettysburg, Union general Ulysses S. Grant fought to take **Vicksburg,** one of the two remaining Confederate strongholds on the Mississippi River. Vicksburg itself was particularly important because it rested on bluffs above the river from which guns could control all water traffic. In the winter of 1862–1863, Grant tried several schemes to reach Vicksburg and take it from the Confederates. Nothing seemed to work—until the spring of 1863.

Grant began by weakening the Confederate defenses that protected Vicksburg. He sent Benjamin Grierson to lead his cavalry brigade through the heart of Mississippi. Grierson succeeded in destroying rail lines and distracting Confederate forces from Union infantry working its way toward Vicksburg. Grant was able to land his troops south of Vicksburg on April 30 and immediately sent his men in search of Confederate troops in Mississippi. In 18 days, Union forces had sacked Jackson, the capital of the state.

Their confidence growing with every victory, Grant and his troops rushed to Vicksburg, hoping to take the city while the rebels were reeling from their losses. Grant ordered two frontal attacks on Vicksburg, neither of which succeeded. So, in the last week of May 1863, Grant settled in for a siege. He set up a steady barrage of artillery, shelling the city from both the river and the land for several hours a day, forcing the city's residents into caves that they dug out of the yellow clay hillsides.

MAIN IDEA

Making Inferences

D Why was the Union so intent on gaining control of the Mississippi River?

After food supplies ran so low that people were reduced to eating dogs and mules, the Confederate command of Vicksburg asked Grant for terms of surrender. The city fell on July 4. Five days later Port Hudson, Louisiana, the last Confederate holdout on the Mississippi, also fell. The Union had achieved another of its major military objectives, and the Confederacy was cut in two. D

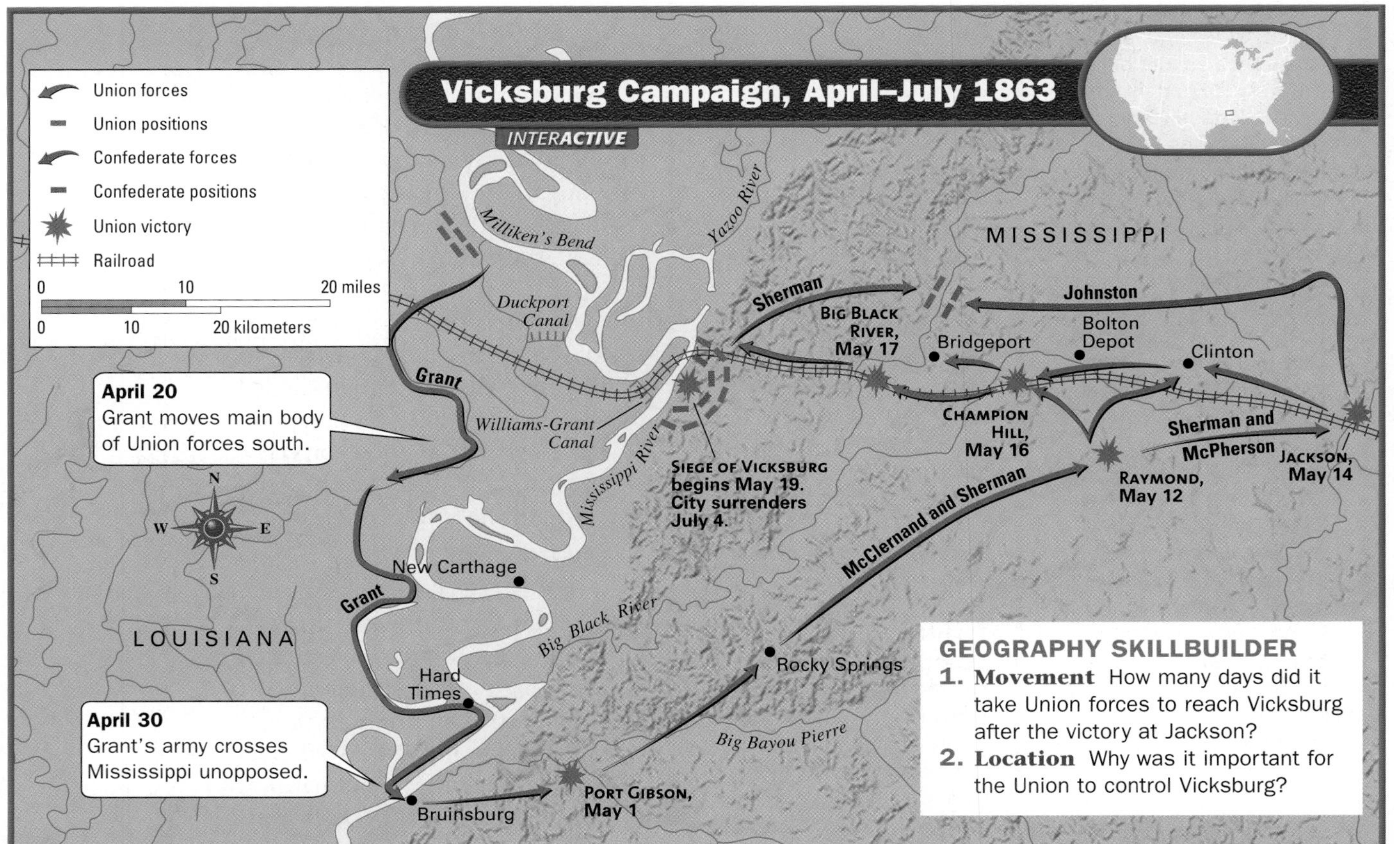

GEOGRAPHY SKILLBUILDER

1. **Movement** How many days did it take Union forces to reach Vicksburg after the victory at Jackson?
2. **Location** Why was it important for the Union to control Vicksburg?

The Confederacy Wears Down

The twin defeats at Gettysburg and Vicksburg cost the South much of its limited manpower. The Confederacy was already low on food, shoes, uniforms, guns, and ammunition. No longer able to attack, it could hope only to hang on long enough to destroy Northern morale and work toward an armistice.

Vocabulary
armistice: truce

That plan proved increasingly unrealistic, however, in part because Southern morale was weakening. Many Confederate soliders had deserted, while newspapers, state legislatures, and individuals throughout the South began to call openly for peace. Worse yet for the Confederacy, Lincoln finally found not just one but two generals who would fight.

KEY PLAYERS

ULYSSES S. GRANT
1822–1885

Born Hiram Ulysses Grant, the future president did not correct a clerk at West Point who recorded his name as Ulysses Simpson Grant. Thereafter, he went by the name U. S. Grant.

Grant once said of himself, "A military life had no charms for me." Yet a military man was what he was destined to be. He fought in the war with Mexico—even though he termed it "wicked"—because he believed his duty was to serve his country. His next post was in the West, where Grant grew so lonely for his family that he resigned.

When the Civil War broke out, the Illinois governor made Grant a colonel of volunteers because George McClellan had been too busy to see him! However, once Grant began fighting in Tennessee, Lincoln was quick to recognize his special strength. When newspapers demanded Grant's dismissal after Shiloh, Lincoln replied firmly, "I can't spare this man. He fights."

ROBERT E. LEE
1807–1870

Lee was an aristocrat, related to some of Virginia's leading families. In fact, his father had been one of George Washington's favorite lieutenants, and his wife, Mary Ann Randolph Custis, was the great-granddaughter of Martha Washington. His sense of family honor may have contributed to his allegiance to his state. As a man who believed slavery was evil, Lee fought for the Confederacy only because of his loyalty to his beloved Virginia. "I did only what my duty demanded. I could have taken no other course without dishonor," he said.

As a general, Lee was tactically brilliant, but he seldom challenged Confederate civilian leaders about their failure to provide his army with adequate food, clothing, or weapons. On the other hand, his soldiers almost worshiped him because he never abused them and always insisted on sharing their hardships. His men called him "Uncle Robert," just as the Union troops called Grant Uncle Sam.

TOTAL WAR In March 1864, President Lincoln appointed Ulysses S. Grant commander of all Union armies. Grant in turn appointed **William Tecumseh Sherman** as commander of the military division of the Mississippi. These two appointments would change the course of the war.

Old friends and comrades in arms, both men believed in waging total war. They reasoned that it was the strength of the people's will that was keeping the war going. If the Union could destroy the Southern population's will to fight, the Confederacy would collapse.

Grant's overall strategy was to decimate Lee's army in Virginia while Sherman raided Georgia. Even if his casualties ran twice as high as those of Lee—and they did—the North could afford it; the South could not. E

MAIN IDEA
Analyzing Motives
E Why did Sherman and Grant want to wage "total war"?

SHERMAN'S MARCH In the spring of 1864, Sherman began his march southeast through Georgia to the sea, creating a wide path of destruction. His army burned almost every house in its path and destroyed livestock and railroads. Sherman was determined to make Southerners

MAIN IDEA

Evaluating
F Do you think that Sherman's destructive march to the sea was necessary? Why or why not?

"so sick of war that generations would pass away before they would again appeal to it." By mid-November he had burned most of Atlanta. After reaching the ocean, Sherman's forces—followed by 25,000 former slaves—turned north to help Grant "wipe out Lee." **F**

THE ELECTION OF 1864 Despite the war, politics in the Union went on as usual. As the 1864 presidential election approached, Lincoln faced heavy opposition from the Democrats and from a faction within his own party. A number of Northerners were dismayed at the war's length and its high casualty rates.

Lincoln was pessimistic about his chances. "I am going to be beaten," he said in August, "and unless some great change takes place, badly beaten." However, some great change did take place. News of General Sherman's victories inspired the North and helped Lincoln win reelection.

THE SURRENDER AT APPOMATTOX On April 3, 1865, Union troops conquered Richmond, the Confederate capital. Southerners had abandoned the city the day before, setting it afire to keep the Northerners from taking it. On April 9, 1865, in a Virginia town called **Appomattox** (ăp′ə-măt′əks) **Court House,** Lee and Grant met at a private home to arrange a Confederate surrender. At Lincoln's request, the terms were generous. Grant paroled Lee's soldiers and sent them home with their possessions and three days' worth of rations. Officers were permitted to keep their side arms. Within a month all remaining Confederate resistance collapsed. After four long years, the Civil War was over.

The War Changes the Nation

The Civil War caused tremendous political, economic, technological, and social change in the United States. It also exacted a high price in terms of human life. Approximately 360,000 Union soldiers and 260,000 Confederates died, nearly as many American combat deaths as in all other American wars combined.

Thomas Lovell's *Surrender at Appomattox* is a modern rendering of Lee's surrender to Grant. This is Lovell's version of the scene—no photographs of the event exist. ▼

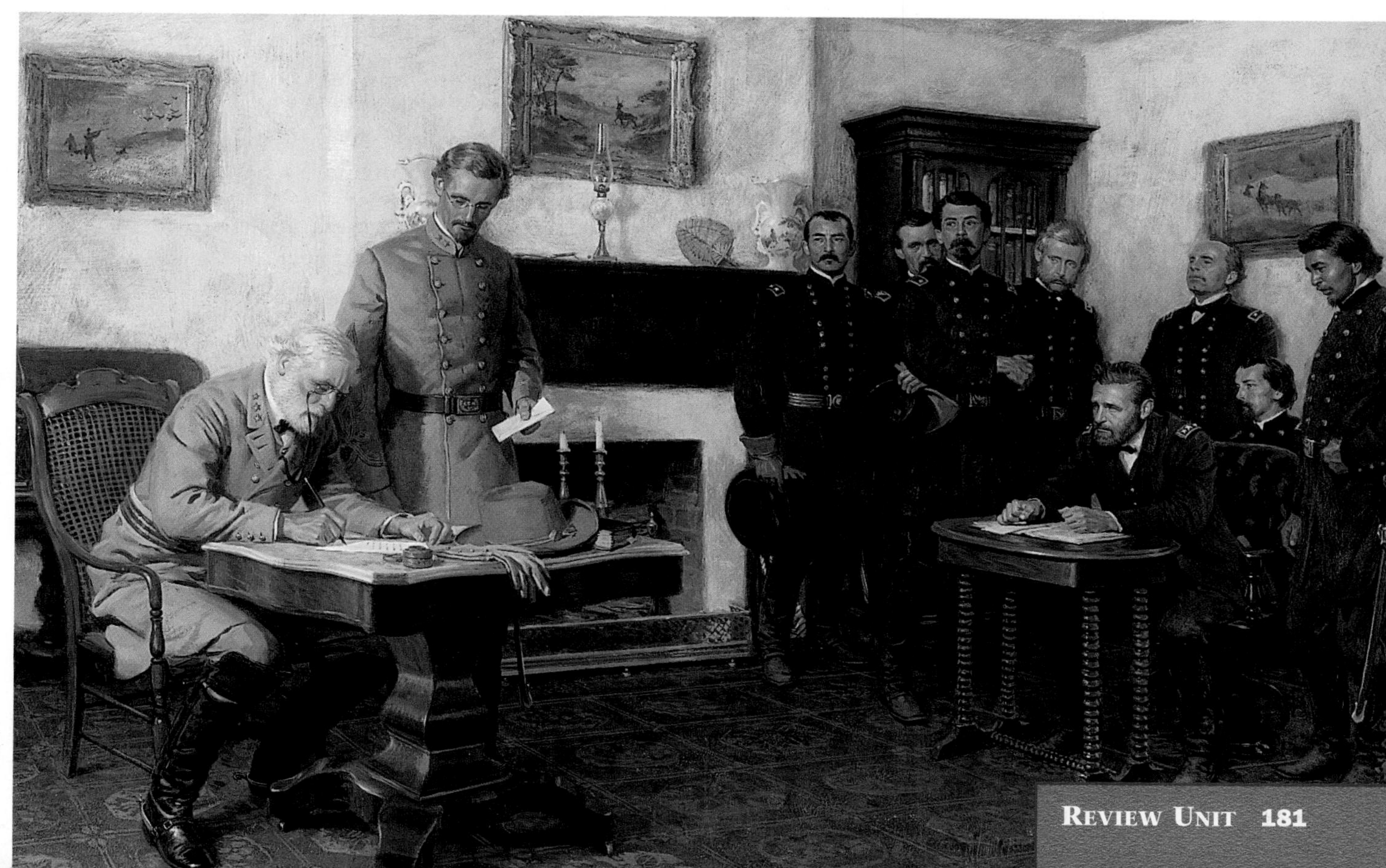

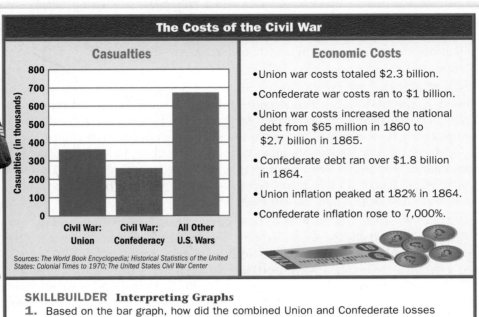

The Costs of the Civil War

Casualties

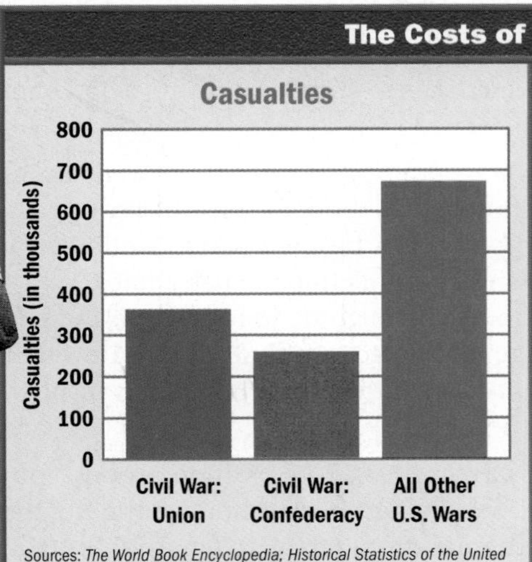

Sources: *The World Book Encyclopedia; Historical Statistics of the United States: Colonial Times to 1970; The United States Civil War Center*

Economic Costs

- Union war costs totaled $2.3 billion.
- Confederate war costs ran to $1 billion.
- Union war costs increased the national debt from $65 million in 1860 to $2.7 billion in 1865.
- Confederate debt ran over $1.8 billion in 1864.
- Union inflation peaked at 182% in 1864.
- Confederate inflation rose to 7,000%.

SKILLBUILDER Interpreting Graphs
1. Based on the bar graph, how did the combined Union and Confederate losses compare with those of other wars?
2. Which side suffered greater inflation?

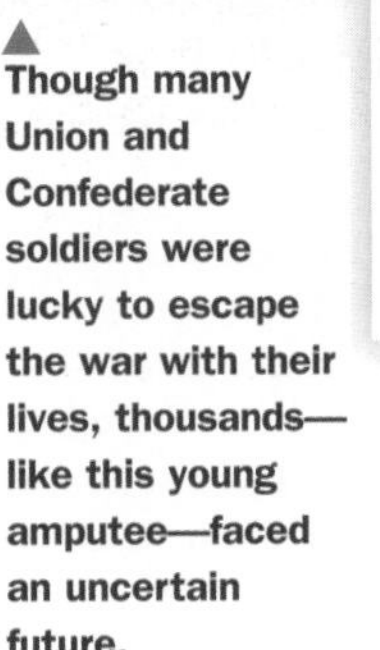

▲ Though many Union and Confederate soldiers were lucky to escape the war with their lives, thousands—like this young amputee—faced an uncertain future.

POLITICAL AND ECONOMIC CHANGES The Civil War greatly increased the federal government's power and authority. During the war, the federal government passed laws, including income tax and conscription laws, that gave it much more control over individual citizens. And after the war, no state ever threatened secession again.

Economically, the Civil War dramatically widened the gap between North and South. During the war, the economy of the Northern states boomed. The Southern economy, on the other hand, was devastated. The war not only marked the end of slavery as a labor system but also wrecked most of the region's industry and farmland. The economic gulf between the regions would not diminish until the 20th century.

Background
Many tycoons of the late 19th century launched their careers during the war. War profiteering helped men like John D. Rockefeller become rich.

A REVOLUTION IN WARFARE Because of developments in technology, the Civil War has been called the last old-fashioned war, or the first modern war. The two deadliest technological improvements were the rifle and the minié ball, a soft lead bullet that was more destructive than earlier bullets. Two other weapons that became more lethal were hand grenades and land mines.

Another technological improvement was the ironclad ship, which could splinter wooden ships by ramming them, withstand cannon fire, and resist burning. On March 9, 1862, every wooden warship in the world became obsolete after the North's ironclad *Monitor* exchanged fire with the South's ironclad *Merrimack*. G

MAIN IDEA
Analyzing Effects
G How did technology affect the Civil War?

The War Changes Lives

The war not only revolutionized weaponry but also changed people's lives. Perhaps the biggest change came for African Americans.

THE THIRTEENTH AMENDMENT The Emancipation Proclamation freed only those slaves who lived in states that were behind Confederate lines, and not yet under Union control. The government had to decide what to do about the border states, where slavery still existed. The president believed that the only solution was a constitutional amendment abolishing slavery.

After some political maneuvering, the **Thirteenth Amendment** was ratified at the end of 1865. The U.S. Constitution now stated, "Neither slavery nor involuntary servitude, except as a punishment for crime whereof the party shall have been duly convicted, shall exist within the United States."

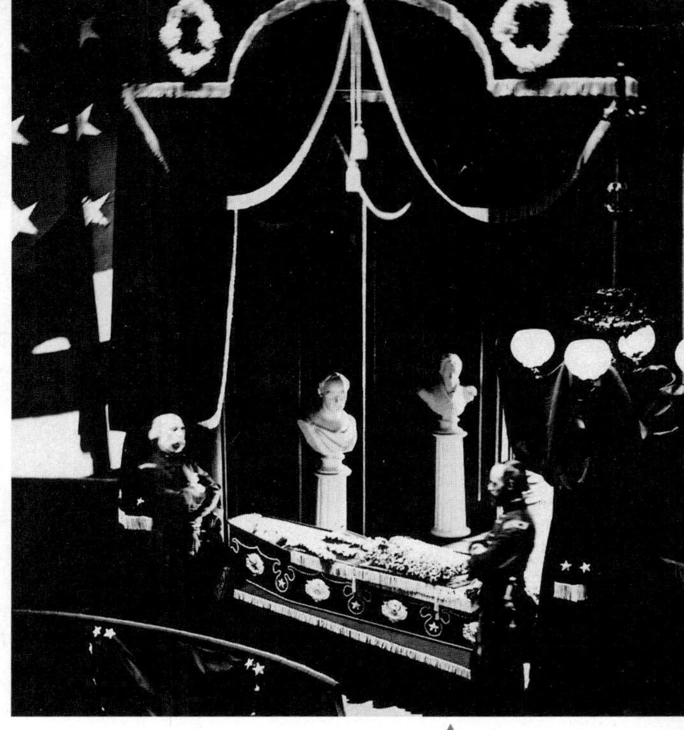

▲ Lincoln's body lies in state in 1865.

LINCOLN IS ASSASSINATED Whatever further plans Lincoln had to reunify the nation after the war, he never got to implement them. On April 14, 1865, five days after Lee surrendered to Grant at Appomattox, Lincoln and his wife went to Ford's Theatre in Washington to see a British comedy, *Our American Cousin.* During its third act, a man crept up behind Lincoln and shot the president in the back of his head.

Lincoln, who never regained consciousness, died on April 15. It was the first time a president of the United States had been assassinated. After the shooting, the assassin, **John Wilkes Booth**—a 26-year-old actor and Southern sympathizer—then leaped down from the presidential box to the stage and escaped. Twelve days later, Union cavalry trapped him in a Virginia tobacco shed and shot him dead.

MAIN IDEA

Developing Historical Perspective

(H) Do you think that the Union would take revenge on the Southern states after the war is over?

The funeral train that carried Lincoln's body from Washington to his hometown of Springfield, Illinois, took 14 days for its journey. Approximately 7 million Americans, or almost one-third of the entire Union population, turned out to mourn publicly their martyred leader.

The Civil War had ended. Slavery and secession were no more. Now the country faced two new problems: how to restore the Southern states to the Union and how to integrate approximately 4 million newly freed African Americans into national life. (H)

SECTION 3 ASSESSMENT

1. **TERMS & NAMES** For each term or name, write a sentence explaining its significance.
   - **Gettysburg**
   - **Gettysburg Address**
   - **Vicksburg**
   - **William Tecumseh Sherman**
   - **Appomattox Court House**
   - **Thirteenth Amendment**
   - **John Wilkes Booth**

MAIN IDEA

2. **TAKING NOTES**
   Copy the multiple-effects chart below on your paper and fill it in with consequences of the Civil War.

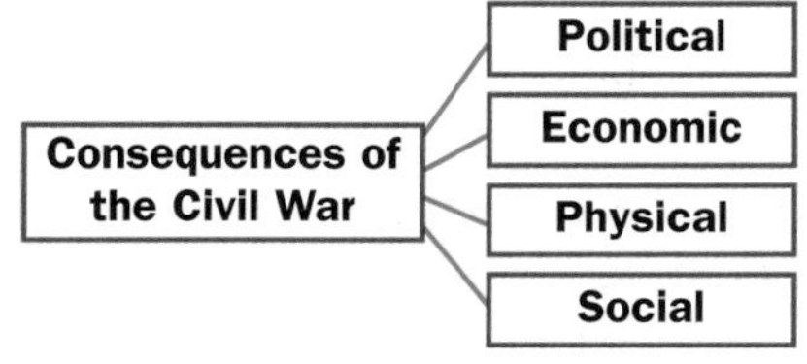

Which consequence of the Civil War do you think has had the most impact on modern life?

CRITICAL THINKING

3. **ANALYZING ISSUES**
   Grant and Sherman used the strategy of total war. Do you think the end justifies the means? That is, did defeating the Confederacy justify harming civilians? Explain.
   Think About:
   - their reasons for targeting the civilian population
   - Sherman's remark about Georgia quoted on page 181
   - Sherman's march through Georgia

4. **SUMMARIZING**
   How did Lincoln abolish slavery in all states?

5. **DRAWING CONCLUSIONS**
   Why did the Union's victory strengthen the power of the national government?

Reconstruction and Its Effects

MAIN IDEA

After the Civil War, the nation embarked on a period known as Reconstruction, during which attempts were made to readmit the South to the Union.

WHY IT MATTERS NOW

The Fourteenth and Fifteenth Amendments, passed as part of Reconstruction, gave civil rights to Americans of all races.

Terms & Names

- **Freedmen's Bureau**
- **Reconstruction**
- **Radical Republicans**
- **Andrew Johnson**
- **Fourteenth Amendment**
- **Fifteenth Amendment**
- **scalawag**
- **carpetbagger**
- **Hiram Revels**
- **sharecropping**
- **Ku Klux Klan (KKK)**

One American's Story

Robert G. Fitzgerald was born a free African American in Delaware in 1840. During the Civil War, he served in both the U.S. Army and the U.S. Navy. In 1866, he taught former slaves in a small Virginia town. A year after his arrival in Virginia, Fitzgerald looked back on what he had accomplished.

A Personal Voice ROBERT G. FITZGERALD

"I came to Virginia one year ago on the 22nd of this month. Erected a school, organized and named the Freedman's Chapel School. Now (June 29th) have about 60 who have been for several months engaged in the study of arithmetic, writing, etc. etc. This morning sent in my report accompanied with compositions from about 12 of my advanced writers instructed from the Alphabet up to their [present] condition, their progress has been surprisingly rapid."

—quoted in *Proud Shoes*

Fitzgerald was working for the **Freedmen's Bureau,** which had been established by Congress to provide food, clothing, hospitals, legal protection, and education for former slaves and poor whites in the South in 1865.

VIDEO

TEACHER OF A FREED PEOPLE
Robert Fitzgerald and Reconstruction

The Politics of Reconstruction

The need to help former slaves was just one of many issues the nation confronted after the war. In addition, the government, led by Andrew Johnson, Lincoln's vice-president and eventual successor, had to determine how to bring the Confederate states back into the Union. **Reconstruction,** the period during which the United States began to rebuild after the Civil War, lasted from 1865 to 1877. The term also refers to the process the federal government used to readmit the defeated Confederate states to the Union. Complicating the process was the fact that Abraham Lincoln, Andrew Johnson, and the members of Congress all had different ideas about how Reconstruction should be handled.

LINCOLN'S PLAN Lincoln made it clear that he favored a lenient Reconstruction policy. In December 1863, Lincoln announced his Proclamation of Amnesty and Reconstruction, also known as the Ten-Percent Plan. Under this plan, the government would pardon all Confederates—except high-ranking officials and those accused of crimes against prisoners of war—who would swear allegiance to the Union. As soon as ten percent of those who had voted in 1860 took this oath of allegiance, a Confederate state could form a new state government and send representatives and senators to Congress. Under Lincoln's terms, four states—Arkansas, Louisiana, Tennessee, and Virginia—moved toward readmission to the Union.

Vocabulary
amnesty: a general pardon by a government, usually for political offenses

▲ Clearing battlefields of human remains was just one of the many tasks facing Reconstruction governments.

However, Lincoln's Reconstruction plan angered a minority of Republicans in Congress, known as **Radical Republicans.** The Radicals, led by Senator Charles Sumner of Massachusetts and Representative Thaddeus Stevens of Pennsylvania, wanted to destroy the political power of former slaveholders. Most of all, they wanted African Americans to be given full citizenship and the right to vote.

JOHNSON'S PLAN FOR RECONSTRUCTION Lincoln was assassinated before he could fully implement his Reconstruction plan. In May 1865, his successor, **Andrew Johnson,** announced his own plan. Johnson's plan differed little from Lincoln's. The major difference was that Johnson tried to break the planters' power by excluding high-ranking Confederates and wealthy Southern landowners from taking the oath needed for voting privileges. However, Johnson also pardoned more than 13,000 former Confederates because he believed that "white men alone must manage the South." (A)

MAIN IDEA
Contrasting
(A) How did the views of Presidents Lincoln and Johnson on Reconstruction differ from the views of the Radical Republicans?

The seven remaining ex-Confederate states quickly agreed to Johnson's terms. In the following months, these states—except for Texas—set up new state governments and elected representatives to Congress. In December 1865, the newly elected Southern legislators arrived in Washington to take their seats. Congress, however, refused to admit the new Southern legislators. At the same time, moderate Republicans pushed for new laws to remedy weaknesses they saw in Johnson's plan. In 1866, Congress voted to enlarge the Freedmen's Bureau and passed the Civil Rights Act of 1866. That law gave African Americans citizenship and forbade states from passing discriminatory laws—black codes—that severely restricted African Americans' lives. Johnson shocked everyone when he vetoed both the Freedmen's Bureau Act and the Civil Rights Act. Congress, Johnson contended, had gone far beyond anything "contemplated by the authors of the Constitution."

CONGRESSIONAL RECONSTRUCTION Angered by Johnson's actions, radical and moderate Republican factions decided to work together to shift the control of the Reconstruction process from the executive branch to the legislature. In mid-1866, they overrode the president's vetoes of the Civil Rights Act and Freedmen's Bureau Act. In addition, Congress drafted the **Fourteenth Amendment,** which prevented states from denying rights and privileges to any U.S. citizen, now defined as "all persons born or naturalized in the United States." This definition was expressly intended to overrule and nullify the *Dred Scott* decision.

In the 1866 elections, moderate and radical Republicans gained control of Congress. They joined together to pass the Reconstruction Act of 1867, which did not recognize state governments—except Tennessee—formed under the Lincoln and Johnson plans.

The act divided the former Confederate states into five military districts. The states were required to grant African-American men the vote and to ratify the Fourteenth Amendment in order to reenter the Union. When Johnson vetoed the Reconstruction legislation, Congress promptly overrode the veto. B

MAIN IDEA

Analyzing Effects

B How did the election of 1866 affect the process of Reconstruction?

"I say, as to the leaders, punishment."

ANDREW JOHNSON

JOHNSON IMPEACHED Because the Radicals thought Johnson was blocking Reconstruction, they looked for grounds on which to impeach him. They found grounds when Johnson removed Secretary of War Edwin Stanton from office in 1868. Johnson's removal of the cabinet member violated the Tenure of Office Act, which stated that a president could not remove cabinet officers during the term of the president who had appointed them without the Senate's approval. The House impeached Johnson, but he remained in office after the Senate voted not to convict.

U. S. GRANT ELECTED In the 1868 presidential election, the Civil War hero Ulysses S. Grant won by a margin of only 306,000 votes out of almost 6 million ballots cast. More than 500,000 Southern African Americans had voted. Of this number, 9 out of 10 voted for Grant. The importance of the African-American vote to the Republican Party was obvious.

After the election, the Radicals introduced the **Fifteenth Amendment**, which states that no one can be kept from voting because of "race, color, or previous condition of servitude." The Fifteenth Amendment, which was ratified by the states in 1870, was an important victory for the Radicals. C

MAIN IDEA

Making Inferences

C Why was the African-American vote so important to the Republicans?

Reconstructing Society

Under the congressional Reconstruction program, state constitutional conventions met and Southern voters elected new, Republican-dominated governments. By 1870, all of the former Confederate states had completed the process. However, even after all the states were back in the Union, the Republicans did not end the process of Reconstruction because they wanted to make economic changes in the South.

CONDITIONS IN THE POSTWAR SOUTH The war had devastated the South economically. Southern planters returned home to find that the value of their property had plummeted. Throughout the South, many small farms were ruined. The region's population was also devastated. Hundreds of thousands of Southern men had died in the war. The Republican governments began public works programs to repair the physical damage and to provide social services.

POLITICS IN THE POSTWAR SOUTH Another difficulty facing the new Republican governments was that the three groups that constituted the Republican Party in the South—scalawags, carpetbaggers, and African Americans—often had conflicting goals.

Scalawags were white Southerners who joined the Republican Party. Many were small farmers who wanted to improve their economic position and did not want the former wealthy planters to regain power. **Carpetbaggers** were Northerners who moved to the South after the war. This negative name came from the misconception that they arrived with so few belongings that they carried everything in small traveling bags made of carpeting.

Analyzing *Political Cartoons*

UNWELCOME GUEST

Of all the political cartoonists of the 19th century, Thomas Nast (1840–1902) had the greatest and most long-lasting influence. Nast created or popularized symbols that have become part of America's visual heritage, symbols that include the Democratic donkey, the Republican elephant, Uncle Sam, and Santa Claus.

This cartoon from a Southern Democratic newspaper depicts Carl Schurz, a liberal Republican who advocated legal equality for African Americans. Schurz is shown as a carpetbagger trudging down a dusty Southern road as a crowd of people watch his arrival.

SKILLBUILDER Analyzing Political Cartoons

1. Is Schurz shown in a positive or negative light? How can you tell?
2. Why do you think the cartoonist chose to place the crowd of onlookers at such a great distance from Schurz?

SEE SKILLBUILDER HANDBOOK, PAGE R24.

a carpet bag

The third and largest group of Southern Republicans—African Americans—gained voting rights as a result of the Fifteenth Amendment. During Reconstruction, African-American men registered to vote for the first time; nine out of ten of them supported the Republican Party. Although many former slaves could neither read nor write and were politically inexperienced, they were eager to exercise their voting rights.

A PERSONAL VOICE WILLIAM BEVERLY NASH

> **"We are not prepared for this suffrage. But we can learn. Give a man tools and let him commence to use them and in time he will earn a trade. So it is with voting. We may not understand it at the start, but in time we shall learn to do our duty."**
>
> —quoted in *The Trouble They Seen: Black People Tell the Story of Reconstruction*

The differing goals of scalawags, carpetbaggers, and African Americans led to a lack of unity in the Republican Party. In particular, few scalawags shared the Republican commitment to civil rights for African Americans.

MAIN IDEA

Contrasting
D Why did scalawags, carpetbaggers, and African Americans support the Radicals?

The new status of African Americans required fundamental changes in the attitudes of most Southern whites. However, many white Southerners refused to accept blacks' new status and resisted the idea of equal rights. D

FORMER SLAVES IMPROVE THEIR LIVES Before the Civil War, African Americans had been denied full membership in many churches. During Reconstruction African Americans founded their own churches, which often became the center of the African American community, and the only institutions that African Americans fully controlled. Many African American ministers emerged as influential community leaders who also played an important role in the broader political life of the country.

With 95% of former slaves illiterate, former slaves required education to become economically self-sufficient. In most of the Southern states, the first public school systems were established by the Reconstruction governments. The new African American churches, aided by missionaries from Northern churches and by $6 million from the Freedmen's Bureau, worked to create and run these and other

KEY PLAYER

HIRAM REVELS
1822–1901

Hiram Revels of Mississippi, pictured above on the far left, was born of free parents in Fayetteville, North Carolina. Because he could not obtain an education in the South, he attended Knox College in Illinois. As an African Methodist Episcopal minister, he recruited African Americans to fight for the Union during the Civil War and also served as an army chaplain.

In 1865, Revels settled in Mississippi, where he helped organize African-American schools and churches. He served on the Natchez city council and then was elected to Mississippi's state senate in 1869. In 1870, Revels became the first African American elected to the U.S. Senate.

schools. Atlanta, Fisk, and Howard Universities, for instance, were all founded by religious groups such as the American Missionary Association.

Thousands of African Americans also took advantage of their new freedom by migrating to reunite with family members or to find jobs in Southern towns and cities.

AFRICAN AMERICANS IN RECONSTRUCTION After the war, African Americans took an active role in the political process. Not only did they vote, but for the first time they held office in local, state, and federal government.

Nevertheless, even though there were almost as many black citizens as white citizens in the South, African-American officeholders remained in the minority. Out of 125 Southerners elected to the U.S. Congress during congressional Reconstruction, only 16 were African Americans. Among these was **Hiram Revels**, the first African-American senator. African Americans also served in political offices on the state and local levels. E

MAIN IDEA

Forming Generalizations
E How did Southern African Americans respond to their new status?

In January 1865, General Sherman had promised the former slaves who followed his army 40 acres per family and the use of army mules. For the most part, however, former slaves received no land. Most Republicans considered private property a basic American right, and thus refused to help redistribute it. As a result, many plantation owners in the South retained their land.

SHARECROPPING AND TENANT FARMING Without their own land, freed African Americans, as well as poor white farmers, could not grow crops to sell or to use to feed their families. Therefore, economic necessity forced many former slaves and impoverished whites to become sharecroppers. In the system of **sharecropping,** landowners divided their land and assigned each head of household a few acres, along with seed and tools. Sharecroppers kept a small share of their crops and gave the rest to the landowners. In theory, "croppers" who saved a little might even rent land for cash and keep all their harvest in a system known as tenant farming.

The Collapse of Reconstruction

Most white Southerners swallowed whatever resentment they felt over African-American suffrage and participation in government. Some whites expressed their feelings by refusing to register to vote. Others were frustrated by their loss of political power and by the South's economic stagnation. These were the people who formed vigilante groups and used violence to intimidate African Americans.

Vocabulary
vigilante: one who takes law enforcement into one's own hands

OPPOSITION TO RECONSTRUCTION The most notorious and widespread of the Southern vigilante groups was the **Ku Klux Klan (KKK).** The Klan's goals were to destroy the Republican Party, to throw out the Reconstruction governments, to aid the planter class, and to prevent African Americans from exercising their political rights. To achieve these goals, the Klan and other groups killed perhaps 20,000 men, women, and children. In addition to violence, some white Southerners refused to hire or do business with African Americans who voted Republican.

To curtail Klan violence and Democratic intimidation, Congress passed a series of Enforcement Acts in 1870 and 1871. One act provided for the federal supervision of elections in Southern states. Another act gave the president the power to use federal troops in areas where the Klan was active.

Although Congress seemed to shore up Republican power with the Enforcement Acts, it soon passed legislation that severely weakened the power of the Republican Party in the South. In May 1872, Congress passed the Amnesty Act, which returned the right to vote and the right to hold federal and state offices to about 150,000 former Confederates. In the same year Congress allowed the Freedmen's Bureau to expire. These actions allowed Southern Democrats to regain political power. F

MAIN IDEA

Summarizing

F How did Southern Democrats regain political power?

SUPPORT FOR RECONSTRUCTION FADES Eventually, support for Reconstruction weakened. The breakdown of Republican unity made it even harder for the Radicals to continue to impose their Reconstruction plan on the South. In addition, a series of bank failures known as the panic of 1873 triggered a five-year depression, which diverted attention in the North away from the South's problems. The Supreme Court also began to undo some of the social and political changes that the Radicals had made. Although political violence continued in the South and African Americans were denied civil and political rights, Republicans slowly retreated from the policies of Reconstruction.

DEMOCRATS "REDEEM" THE SOUTH As the Republicans' hold on the South loosened, Southern Democrats began to regain control of the region. As a result of "redemption"—as the Democrats called their return to power—and a political deal made during the national election of 1876, congressional Reconstruction came to an end.

Background

The Twelfth Amendment (1804) gives the House of Representatives the power to elect the president if no candidate has a majority of electoral votes.

In the election of 1876, Democratic candidate Samuel J. Tilden won the popular vote, but was one vote short of the electoral victory. Southern Democrats in Congress agreed to accept Hayes if federal troops were withdrawn from the South. After Republican leaders agreed to the demands, Hayes was elected, and Reconstruction ended in the South.

Reconstruction ended without much real progress in the battle against discrimination. However, the Thirteenth, Fourteenth, and Fifteenth Amendments remained part of the Constitution. In the 20th century, these amendments provided the necessary constitutional foundation for important civil rights legislation.

SECTION 4 ASSESSMENT

1. **TERMS & NAMES** For each term or name, write a sentence explaining its significance.
   - **Freedmen's Bureau**
   - **Reconstruction**
   - **Radical Republicans**
   - **Andrew Johnson**
   - **Fourteenth Amendment**
   - **Fifteenth Amendment**
   - **scalawag**
   - **carpetbagger**
   - **Hiram Revels**
   - **sharecropping**
   - **Ku Klux Klan (KKK)**

MAIN IDEA

2. **TAKING NOTES**
   Use a table like the one below to list five problems facing the South after the Civil War. Then describe the solution that was attempted for each problem.

Problem	Attempted Solution
1.	
2.	
3.	
4.	
5.	

CRITICAL THINKING

3. **DRAWING CONCLUSIONS**
   Do you think that Reconstruction had positive effects on Southern society? Why or why not?
   Think About:
   - the formation of the Ku Klux Klan
   - the establishment of African American churches and schools
   - why so many African Americans turned to sharecropping

4. **SUMMARIZING**
   How did the Radical Republicans hope to reconstruct the South?

5. **ANALYZING PRIMARY SOURCES**
   This humorous ticket was printed around the time of the Hayes-Tilden presidential election. What does it tell you about popular attitudes toward the candidates?

TILDEN.
HAYES.
OF THE TWO EVILS
CHOOSE THE LEAST.

REVIEW CHAPTER 4 ASSESSMENT

VISUAL SUMMARY

THE UNION IN PERIL

1840s AND 1850s

Tensions between Northern and Southern states intensify over the issues of slavery and Congressional representation. Violence erupts in new territories and states.

1861–1865 CIVIL WAR

Civil War leads to the deaths of hundreds of thousands, the destruction of towns and cities, and the collapse of the Southern economy.

1865–1877

During Reconstruction, the victorious North forces Southern states back into the Union. Congress attempts to rebuild the South and extend civil rights to African Americans. However, Southern Democrats regain control in the South and bring about an end to Reconstruction.

TERMS & NAMES

For each term or name below, write a sentence explaining its significance to the Civil War and Reconstruction.

1. Underground Railroad
2. Harriet Beecher Stowe
3. Dred Scott
4. Bull Run
5. Emancipation Proclamation
6. Clara Barton
7. Gettysburg
8. William Tecumseh Sherman
9. Fifteenth Amendment
10. Ku Klux Klan

MAIN IDEAS

Use your notes and the information in the chapter to answer the following questions.

The Divisive Politics of Slavery *(pages 156–165)*

1. What was the Compromise of 1850?
2. Who supported the Republican Party that was formed in 1854?

The Civil War Begins *(pages 168–174)*

3. What were the military strategies of the North and the South at the onset of the Civil War?
4. What role did African Americans and women play in the Civil War?

The North Takes Charge *(pages 175–183)*

5. Which Northern tactic helped destroy morale in the South after the defeats at Gettysburg and Vicksburg?
6. What effect did the war have on the economies of the North and the South?

Reconstruction and Its Effects *(pages 184–189)*

7. Why did the Radicals want to impeach Andrew Johnson?
8. In what ways did emancipated slaves exercise their freedom?
9. How did Southern whites regain political power during Reconstruction?

CRITICAL THINKING

1. **USING YOUR NOTES** In a chart like the one shown, list the results and the significance of the national elections of 1856, 1860, 1866, 1868, and 1876.

Election Year	Results	Significance
1856		
1860		
1866		
1868		
1876		

2. **DEVELOPING HISTORICAL PERSPECTIVE** How close did African Americans come to gaining full civil rights during Reconstruction? Explain your answer.

3. **INTERPRETING MAPS** Look at the maps on pages 170–171. What was the most important river in the Union's tactic of splitting the Confederacy in two? What city became essential to this goal after the fall of New Orleans?

Standardized Test Practice

Use the information in the passage and your knowledge of U.S. history to answer questions 1 and 2.

> **"In these days men have learned the art of sinning expertly and genteelly, so as not to shock the eyes and senses of respectable society. Human property is high in the market; and is, therefore, well fed, well cleaned, tended, and looked after, that it may come to sale sleek, and strong, and shining."**
>
> —Harriet Beecher Stowe, *Uncle Tom's Cabin*

1. In the mid-19th century, Harriet Beecher Stowe was a leader in the struggle for —

A abolition.
B women's rights.
C better working conditions.
D tax-supported public schools.

2. *Uncle Tom's Cabin* was written in response to —

F the raid on Harpers Ferry.
G the Lincoln-Douglas debates.
H the Fugitive Slave Act.
J the *Dred Scott* decision.

3. Grant's siege of Vicksburg was part of the Union's strategy to —

A destroy Southern morale.
B blockade Southern ports.
C split the Confederacy in two.
D capture the Confederate capital.

4. In the Reconstruction Act of 1867, Congress set requirements for readmission of former Confederate states into the Union. Which of the following problems did the act address?

F Southern states did not allow African Americans to vote.
G Southern states had little money to pay for public works projects.
H Former slaves needed education.
J Confederate bonds and money were worthless.

ADDITIONAL TEST PRACTICE, pages S1–S33.

CLASSZONE.COM

ALTERNATIVE ASSESSMENT

1. INTERACT WITH HISTORY Recall your discussion of the question on page 155:

How can the Union be saved?

Suppose you are a British tourist traveling through the United States in 1860. Write a letter to your friends at home describing the political climate in America. Give your opinion about the possibility of saving the Union.

2. VIDEO **LEARNING FROM MEDIA** View the *American Stories* videos "War Outside My Window" and "Teacher of a Freed People." Discuss the following questions in a group; then do the activity.

- What is your overall impression of Mary Chesnut?
- What, if anything, surprised you about her diary entries?
- Which experiences in Fitzgerald's life helped foster his passion for learning and teaching?
- How did Fitzgerald respond to the difficulties he faced?

Cooperative Learning Activity Imagine that Mary Chesnut and Robert Fitzgerald met to discuss their beliefs. As a group, write a dialogue that might have taken place between the two. Take turns role-playing the pair to establish their personalities and clarify their ideas.

The Changing American Dream: *Beginnings Through Reconstruction*

For two centuries, the American Dream has been the hope that helped America become a great nation. It was the Puritans' desire to find religious freedom and tolerance. It was the patriots' wish to found a new republic that guaranteed the rights of its citizens. It was the reformers' goal of a just society. And it was the guiding beacon for all those who have struggled to make a better life for their families and their compatriots.

To help you make sense of the formative years of the American republic and of the developing American Dream, the next six pages provide a review that is organized around the nine historical themes that are woven into *The Americans*. This Thematic Review will help you focus on the major issues that had emerged in American history by the end of Reconstruction in 1877.

The mission system played a vital role in the development of the Southwest.

Diversity and the National Identity

The United States developed a diverse population, but through continual contact, the diverse groups developed many commonalities. For centuries, Native American groups had followed many different ways of life, each suited to a particular environment. While adopting some aspects of European culture, they passed on parts of their own culture. English settlers did not respect Native American culture, but adopted many native terms and agricultural practices. In the Spanish colonies, settlers and native peoples interacted closely.

As settlers brought different cultures to different regions, continued contact led to the blending of cultures. Nevertheless, the diversity of the populations and the unequal status of the different cultures caused tension. Dutch New Amsterdam and Quaker Pennsylvania showed more tolerance of religious differences than Puritan New England did. German and Scots-Irish immigrants settled from New Netherlands to as far south as the Carolinas. The Southwest and California reflected the culture of the Spanish settlers and the cowboy.

Over time, the Northern and Southern regions of the United States developed distinct cultures. A key feature of Southern culture was slavery. While forced to adapt to slave status in Southern culture, African Americans maintained as best they could their traditions of family relations, dance, music, and crafts. These in turn helped shape Southern culture as Southerners adopted the ways of their captives.

MAIN IDEA

Drawing Conclusions

A What impact did the different cultures in North America have on the United States?

Immigrants arrive in New York harbor in the mid-1800s.

Immigration and Migration

The movement of people has played an important role in shaping American history. Most anthropologists believe that humans began migrating to the Americas about 40,000 years ago, crossing a land bridge that connected Asia to Alaska. Over the centuries, these people spread throughout North and South America.

In 1492, Columbus completed his first voyage to this New World. People from several countries soon started colonies there. The English settled along the Atlantic Coast, in Jamestown (1607), Plymouth Colony (1620), and Massachusetts Bay Colony (1630). The Dutch settled in New Amsterdam (now New York) in 1625. The French established a settlement to the north, in Quebec City.

The Spanish built a fort at St. Augustine, on the Florida coast, and established a capital in the Southwest at Santa Fe, New Mexico. A number of Spanish missions arose in New Mexico and in California.

After centuries of isolation, Native Americans had no defenses against European diseases. They died by the thousands, making it more difficult for them to resist European expansion. Another group that suffered terribly from immigration were the millions of Africans who were forcibly brought to the colonies as enslaved people.

After the colonies won their independence from England, the United States continued to attract new immigrants. Groups already settled in the United States did not always welcome newcomers. But the stream of immigrants—primarily Irish and Germans—continued. By the 1840s, many of these immigrants joined native-born Americans moving west. They drove their long wagon trains as far as the Pacific Coast, where they met thousands of Chinese immigrants who had come to California to work on railroads and in the mines. Americans had spread from coast to coast.

MAIN IDEA

Forming Generalizations

B In what ways did immigration and migration shape the early United States?

The French Revolution was partly inspired by the colonists' revolt against the British in North America.

America in World Affairs

The European settlement of North America began as part of a contest for empire. The British pushed the Dutch out of what is now New York. Then, in 1763, they drove the French from North America. Just 13 years later, though, the British colonies rebelled. The French and Spanish helped them win their independence by supplying money, soldiers, and ships.

England, France, and Spain still held much of the continent, but that changed in the next few decades. First, France sold the United States the Louisiana Territory, doubling the nation's size. Soon, though, conflict with Native Americans and anger over British actions led to the War of 1812, which brought no clear victory but did produce a surge of nationalist feeling. Treaties with Britain and Spain added additional territories.

More confident, the United States began to flex its muscles. With the Monroe Doctrine, the United States warned European powers to stay out of the Western Hemisphere.

After the United States began to act on the idea of "manifest destiny," or the belief that the country should expand to the Pacific coast, Americans in Texas proclaimed a new republic, removing that region from Mexican control. Soon the United States annexed Texas, which led to the War with Mexico. After a swift victory by U.S. forces, the Treaty of Guadalupe Hidalgo gave California and the Southwest to the United States.

In summary, international relations in the nation's early years were marked by two major achievements: establishment of the United States on the world stage and expansion of its territory.

MAIN IDEA

Drawing Conclusions

C What was the most important change in the United States' involvement in foreign affairs from 1789 to 1877?

Voting Rights

The years up to 1877 were critical to the establishment of a stable constitutional democracy in the United States. The Constitution and the Bill of Rights were ratified. The important democratic institutions—Congress, the Presidency, the Supreme Court, and political parties—were firmly established.

During the 1800s, the right to vote was gradually broadened to include more members of society. In the 1820s, state governments enlarged the voter base by easing voter requirements, such as property qualifications. These new voters were critical to the election of Andrew Jackson in 1828 and 1832.

While growing numbers of white males had won the right to vote, women were still denied that right. Elizabeth Cady Stanton led other women to push for this right and other reforms to give women equal status with men. Their efforts were often met with scorn.

Democratic rights were extended to African Americans after the Civil War, when the Fifteenth Amendment gave them the right to vote. Within a few years, though, Southern states instituted harsh new laws against blacks, known as Jim Crow laws. When courts upheld these laws, African Americans lost their rights. Northerners, tired of decades of conflict over slavery and its aftermath, turned their attention toward other matters.

MAIN IDEA

Developing Historical Perspective

D In the period from 1789 until 1877, what were the signs that the United States had developed a stable constitutional democracy?

States' Rights

By the 1770s, the feeling had grown that the colonists' rights would not be secure so long as they remained subject to Great Britain. They fought the Revolutionary War to win their independence.

When the nation's leaders set out to construct a framework for the new government, their first attempt, the Articles of Confederation, leaned too heavily toward protecting states' independence. When a new Constitution was proposed, several leaders expressed alarm at the strong central government that would be created. Only with the promise of passing several amendments that guaranteed individual freedoms—the Bill of Rights—did the framers win approval of the Constitution.

Questions about the relative power of state and national governments still remained. South Carolina threatened to nullify, or disallow, a federal law in the 1830s, but the crisis was defused. The issue of slavery, though, threatened to tear the Union apart. The Civil War was the greatest constitutional crisis the country faced. The war settled the matter of secession, but the balance between states' rights and federal power continued to be an important constitutional issue.

Major Robert Anderson observes the defense of Fort Sumter. South Carolina seceded by firing on Fort Sumter, starting the Civil War.

MAIN IDEA

Identifying Problems

E What difficulties arose from assertions of states' rights against the United States between 1789 and 1877? How were these issues resolved?

Women and Political Power

Beginning in colonial times, women in America confronted many limits, including lack of suffrage. Laws in some colonies prohibited them from owning property. Laws in others said that only single women or widows could run their own businesses.

During the American Revolution, women expanded their roles by filling in for their husbands on the farms and in the shops and, occasionally, taking up arms. In the new nation, however, the concept of republican motherhood emphasized the role of women in preparing the next generation of citizens.

In the early 1800s, many women became more socially active. Reformers such as Elizabeth Cady Stanton and Lucretia Mott pushed for women's rights. Others, like Harriet Beecher Stowe and Sojourner Truth, spoke out against slavery. Women worked to advance the temperance movement against alcohol and to improve health and education.

Women endured much during the Civil War, whether they lived in the North or the South. Many gained strength by meeting new demands placed on them. With hundreds of thousands of men serving in armies and out of the work force, women filled the void by serving as laborers in farms and factories.

Sojourner Truth was a leader in the movement to end slavery.

MAIN IDEA

Comparing and Contrasting

F Compare and contrast women's political activities in the United States in the mid-19th century with those in the Colonial era.

"OUR FIELD IS THE WORLD."
LIGHT DRAFT. SUPERIOR DESIGN.
CLEAN AND RAPID CUTTER.
McCormick Harvesting Machine Co., Chicago.
ESTABLISHED 1831.

Inventions such as McCormick's reaper increased the productivity of laborers.

Science and Technology

During the 1800s, the United States established itself as highly innovative and quick to find commercial applications for technological advances. For instance, the cotton gin—invented by a Northerner, Eli Whitney—speeded up the processing of cotton and spurred a cotton boom. The boom in cotton led, in turn, to the renewed growth of slavery.

The cotton was shipped to the North, where in the mid-19th century entrepreneurs built new factories that turned it into cloth. New shoemaking and sewing machines sped up clothing manufacture. These changes affected Northern society. Skilled artisans gave way to factory workers skilled in the techniques of mass production. Feeling powerless compared with the factory owners, workers tried to organize labor unions.

As the nation expanded, inventors created new technologies that improved transportation and communication. Pioneers traveled over roads and trails to reach the frontier. The Erie Canal brought food from the Midwest to the ports of the east, helping to make New York City a major commercial center. Steamboats sped up and down rivers, increasing trade. Railroads linked cities. With the completion of the transcontinental railroad in 1869, rails stretched from sea to sea. Telegraph lines allowed people to send messages instantly over vast distances.

MAIN IDEA

Analyzing Effects

G What was one innovation that affected how Americans worked and lived? What were the effects of this innovation?

Civil Rights

Racism, labor shortages, and the establishment of plantation agriculture had led to the entrenchment of slavery in the South during the early 19th century. As slaves, African Americans had no civil rights.

Southerners feared that the North would increase its power in Congress and abolish slavery. They pushed to extend the institution to new territories. In the pivotal 1857 *Dred Scott* decision, the Supreme Court declared that slaves were not people, but property, and thus had no rights. Less than ten years later, the North and South fought a bloody civil war.

The Civil War amendments ended slavery (Thirteenth Amendment), recognized African Americans as citizens (Fourteenth Amendment), and banned the denial of voting rights on the basis of race or color (Fifteenth Amendment). African Americans briefly enjoyed full civil rights, but the Supreme Court undermined legal protections. After Southern Democrats regained political power and enacted Jim Crow, Reconstruction ended, leaving African Americans again without civil rights. In the 1950s and the 1960s, however, the Civil War amendments would become powerful tools in the quest for equal rights.

This former slave family welcomed the passage of the Thirteenth Amendment, which abolished slavery.

MAIN IDEA

Analyzing Issues

H What were the successes and failures of the Civil War and Reconstruction in extending civil rights to African Americans?

During the California gold rush of 1849, tens of thousands of people gave up their old lives to go west in hopes of striking it rich.

Economic Opportunity

Europeans were first attracted to the New World by the promise of wealth. Seeing the vast riches that the Spanish had won in conquering native empires, other European nations scrambled to begin their own colonies. Early settlements were created by companies of investors hoping to strike it rich in the new land. The lure of the land and the hope of economic success continued to fuel immigration to the United States—and the movement of people within the country.

Regional differences developed in the American economy during the colonial period. The North focused on farming and some industry. New transportation routes, such as the Erie Canal, brought increased trade among Northern states. As the Industrial Revolution took hold in the early 1800s, factories sprung up throughout the Northern states and farming declined. After this, the rich farmlands of the Midwest became the breadbasket of the nation. The Civil War accelerated economic growth in the North and Midwest. Industry boomed. Farm output grew as well.

A plantation economy geared to raising cash crops for export arose early in the South. At first, planters grew tobacco, rice, and indigo. Beginning in the 1800s, the main crop was cotton. Cotton was called "king," and a small group of large landowners dominated the Southern economy and society. They became wealthy and powerful by exploiting the labor of masses of enslaved African Americans.

With the end of the Civil War, enslaved persons gained their freedom and finally had a chance for economic opportunity. The Congress decided not to redistribute the land, however. Though legally free, many blacks became economically controlled by landowners—mostly whites—through tenant farming or sharecropping.

MAIN IDEA

Analyzing Effects

1 What was one important economic development in the United States between the colonial period and 1877? How did this development affect the everyday lives of Americans?

UNIT 2

Bridge to the 20th Century 1877–1917

CHAPTER 5
Changes on the Western Frontier
1877–1900

CHAPTER 6
A New Industrial Age
1877–1900

CHAPTER 7
Immigrants and Urbanization
1877–1914

CHAPTER 8
Life at the Turn of the 20th Century
1877–1917

Oral Report

This unit describes how the United States transformed itself from a rural, agricultural society to an urban, industrial one. Prepare an oral report that summarizes one or more of the factors that caused this change. Create visuals to accompany your report.

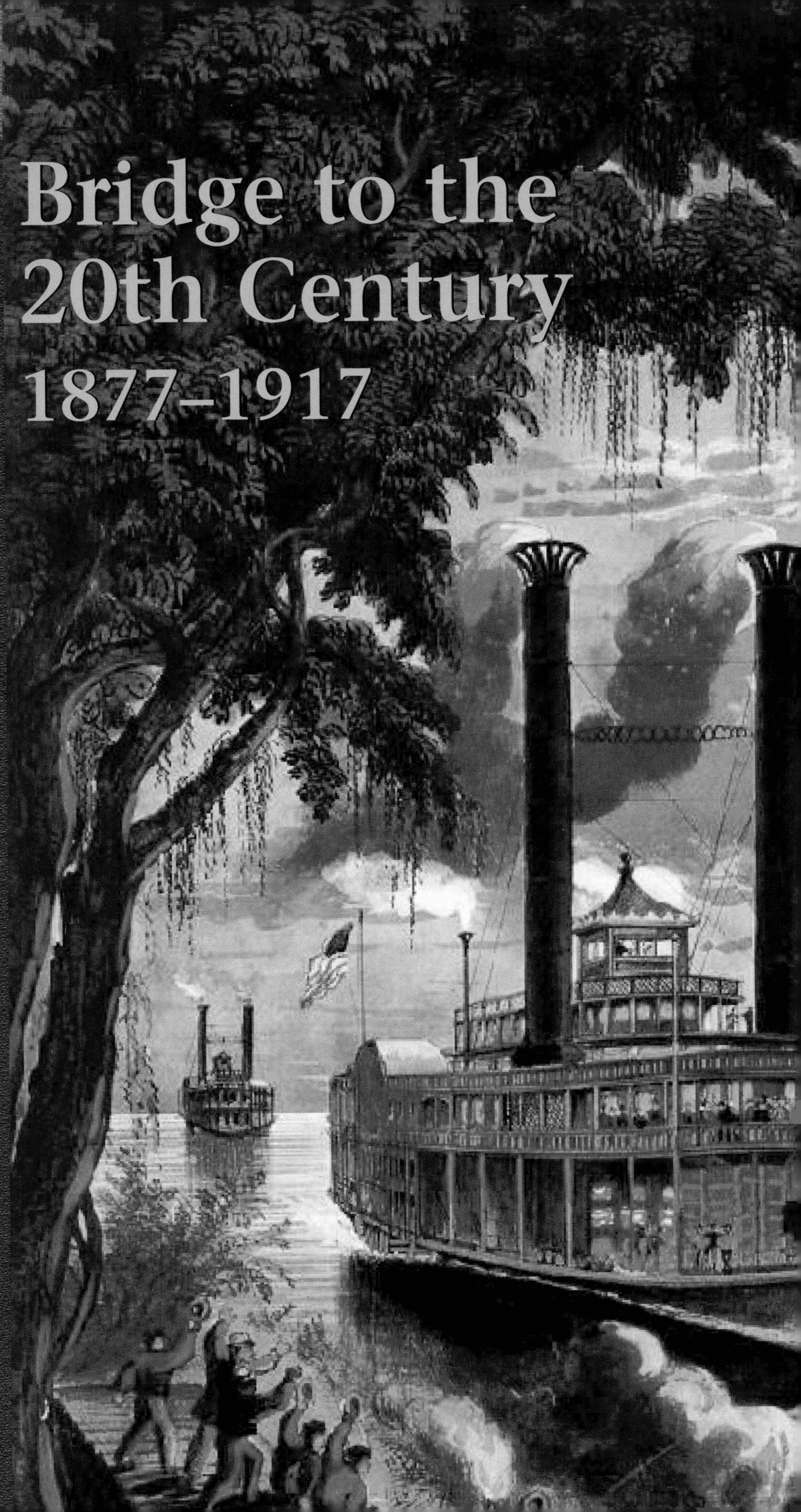

Champions of the Mississippi **by Currier and Ives**

USM
USM
QUEEN OF THE WEST
MORNING STAR

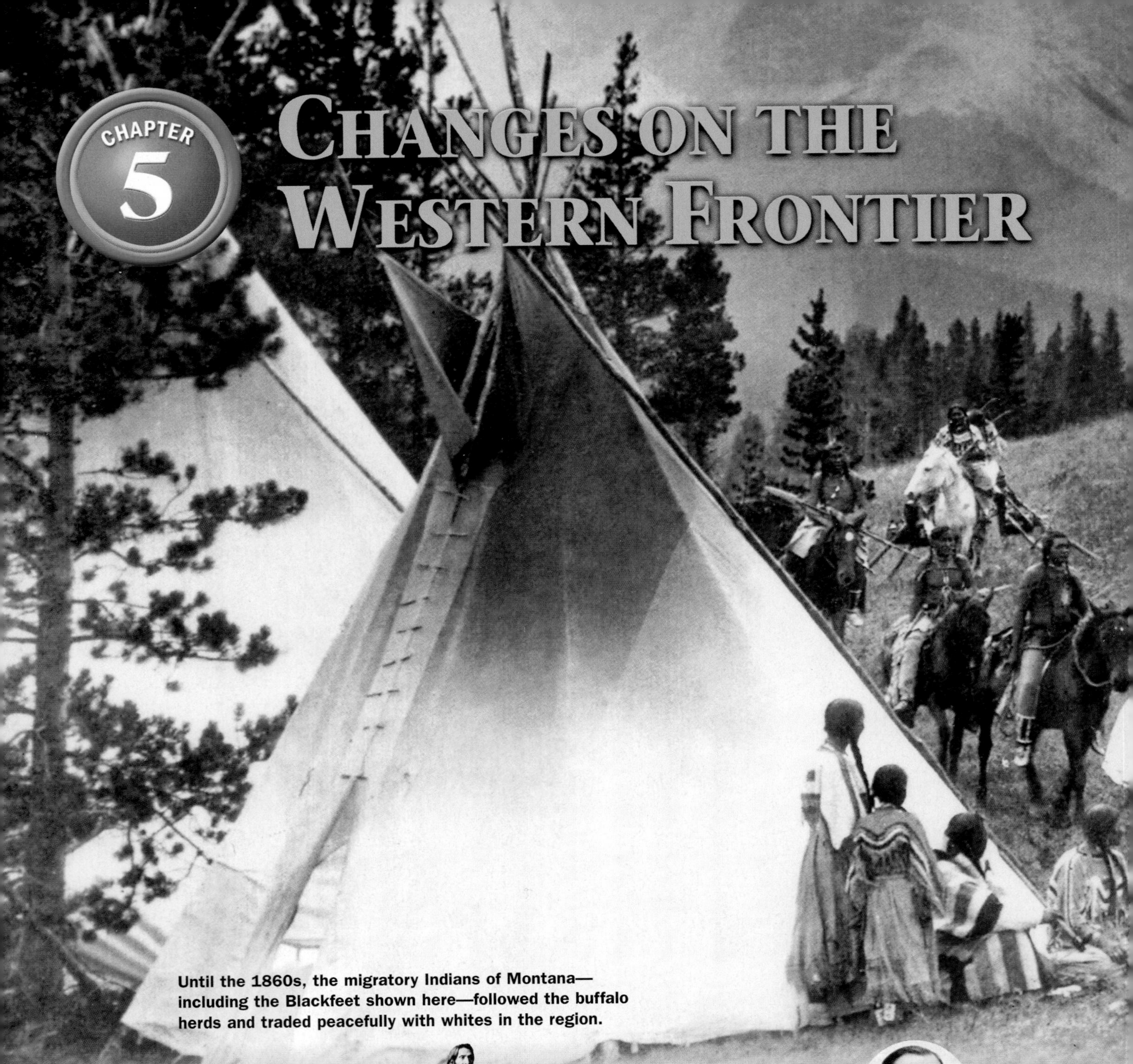

CHAPTER 5 CHANGES ON THE WESTERN FRONTIER

Until the 1860s, the migratory Indians of Montana—including the Blackfeet shown here—followed the buffalo herds and traded peacefully with whites in the region.

USA

1870 Red Cloud, chief of the Oglala Sioux, states his people's case in Washington, D.C.

1880 James Garfield is elected president.

1881 Garfield is assassinated. Chester Arthur becomes president.

1884 Grover Cleveland is elected president.

1870

1880

WORLD

1869 Suez Canal is opened.

1872 Secret ballot is adopted in Britain.

1881 French occupy Tunisia.

INTERACT WITH HISTORY

It is the late 1890s. The American West is the last frontier. Ranchers, cowboys, and miners have changed forever the lives of the Native Americans who hunted on the Western plains. Now westward fever intensifies as "boomers" rush to grab "free" farm land with the government's blessing.

What do you expect to find on settling in the West?

Examine the Issues

- What might be some ways to make a living on the Western frontier?
- If native peoples already live in your intended home, how will you co-exist?
- How might settlers and Native Americans differ regarding use of the land?

RESEARCH LINKS CLASSZONE.COM

Visit the Chapter 5 links for more information about Changes on the Western Frontier.

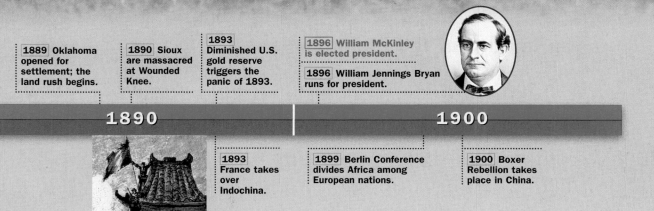

1889 Oklahoma opened for settlement; the land rush begins.

1890 Sioux are massacred at Wounded Knee.

1893 Diminished U.S. gold reserve triggers the panic of 1893.

1896 William McKinley is elected president.

1896 William Jennings Bryan runs for president.

1890

1900

1893 France takes over Indochina.

1899 Berlin Conference divides Africa among European nations.

1900 Boxer Rebellion takes place in China.

Cultures Clash on the Prairie

MAIN IDEA	WHY IT MATTERS NOW	Terms & Names
The cattle industry boomed in the late 1800s, as the culture of the Plains Indians declined.	Today, ranchers and Plains Indians work to preserve their cultural traditions.	• Great Plains • Treaty of Fort Laramie • Sitting Bull • George A. Custer • assimilation • Dawes Act • Battle of Wounded Knee • longhorn • Chisholm Trail • long drive

One American's Story

Zitkala-Ša was born a Sioux in 1876. As she grew up on the Great Plains, she learned the ways of her people. When Zitkala-Ša was eight years old she was sent to a Quaker school in Indiana. Though her mother warned her of the "white men's lies," Zitkala-Ša was not prepared for the loss of dignity and identity she experienced, which was symbolized by the cutting of her hair.

A PERSONAL VOICE ZITKALA-ŠA

> **"I cried aloud . . . and heard them gnaw off one of my thick braids. Then I lost my spirit. Since the day I was taken from my mother I had suffered extreme indignities. . . . And now my long hair was shingled like a coward's! In my anguish I moaned for my mother, but no one came. . . . Now I was only one of many little animals driven by a herder."**
>
> —*The School Days of an Indian Girl*

Zitkala-Ša experienced firsthand the clash of two very different cultures that occurred as ever-growing numbers of white settlers moved onto the Great Plains. In the resulting struggle, the Native American way of life was changed forever.

VIDEO

A WALK IN TWO WORLDS
The Education of Zitkala-Ša, a Sioux

The Culture of the Plains Indians

Zitkala-Ša knew very little about the world east of the Mississippi River. Most Easterners knew equally little about the West, picturing a vast desert occupied by savage tribes. That view could not have been more inaccurate. In fact, distinctive and highly developed Native American ways of life existed on the **Great Plains**, the grassland extending through the west-central portion of the United States. (See map on page 205.)

To the east, near the lower Missouri River, tribes such as the Osage and Iowa had, for more than a century, hunted and planted crops and settled in small villages. Farther west, nomadic tribes such as the Sioux and Cheyenne gathered wild foods and hunted buffalo. Peoples of the Plains, abiding by tribal law, traded and produced beautifully crafted tools and clothing.

THE HORSE AND THE BUFFALO After the Spanish brought horses to New Mexico in 1598, the Native American way of life began to change. As the native peoples acquired horses—and then guns—they were able to travel farther and hunt more efficiently. By the mid-1700s, almost all the tribes on the Great Plains had left their farms to roam the plains and hunt buffalo.

▲ A portrait of a Sioux man and woman in the late 19th century.

Their increased mobility often led to war when hunters in one tribe trespassed on other tribes' hunting grounds. For the young men of a tribe, taking part in war parties and raids was a way to win prestige. A Plains warrior gained honor by killing his enemies, as well as by "counting coup." This practice involved touching a live enemy with a coup stick and escaping unharmed. And sometimes warring tribes would call a truce so that they could trade goods, share news, or enjoy harvest festivals. Native Americans made tepees from buffalo hides and also used the skins for clothing, shoes, and blankets. Buffalo meat was dried into jerky or mixed with berries and fat to make a staple food called pemmican. While the horse gave Native Americans speed and mobility, the buffalo provided many of their basic needs and was central to life on the Plains. (See chart on page 207.) Ⓐ

Vocabulary
coup: a feat of bravery performed in battle

MAIN IDEA
Summarizing
Ⓐ How did the horse influence Native American life on the Great Plains?

FAMILY LIFE Native Americans on the plains usually lived in small extended family groups with ties to other bands that spoke the same language. Young men trained to become hunters and warriors. The women helped butcher the game and prepared the hides that the men brought back to the camp; young women sometimes chose their own husbands.

The Plains Indian tribes believed that powerful spirits controlled events in the natural world. Men or women who showed particular sensitivity to the spirits became medicine men or women, or shamans. Children learned proper behavior and culture through stories and myths, games, and good examples. Despite their communal way of life, however, no individual was allowed to dominate the group. The leaders of a tribe ruled by counsel rather than by force, and land was held in common for the use of the whole tribe.

This Yankton Sioux coup stick was used by warriors. ▼

Settlers Push Westward

The culture of the white settlers differed in many ways from that of the Native Americans on the plains. Unlike Native Americans, who believed that land could not be owned, the settlers believed that owning land, making a mining claim, or starting a business would give them a stake in the country. They argued that the Native Americans had forfeited their rights to the land because they hadn't settled down to "improve" it. Concluding that the plains were "unsettled," migrants streamed westward along railroad and wagon trails to claim the land.

THE LURE OF SILVER AND GOLD The prospect of striking it rich was one powerful attraction of the West. The discovery of gold in Colorado in 1858 drew tens of thousands of miners to the region.

Most mining camps and tiny frontier towns had filthy, ramshackle living quarters. Rows of tents and shacks with dirt "streets" and wooden sidewalks had replaced unspoiled picturesque landscapes. Fortune seekers of every description —including Irish, German, Polish, Chinese, and African-American men—crowded the camps and boomtowns. A few hardy, business-minded women tried their luck too, working as laundresses, freight haulers, or miners. Cities such as Virginia City, Nevada, and Helena, Montana, originated as mining camps on Native American land.

The Government Restricts Native Americans

While allowing more settlers to move westward, the arrival of the railroads also influenced the government's policy toward the Native Americans who lived on the plains. In 1834, the federal government had passed an act that designated the entire Great Plains as one enormous reservation, or land set aside for Native American tribes. In the 1850s, however, the government changed its policy and created treaties that defined specific boundaries for each tribe. Most Native Americans spurned the government treaties and continued to hunt on their traditional lands, clashing with settlers and miners—with tragic results. B

MAIN IDEA

Analyzing Issues

B What was the government's policy toward Native American land?

KEY PLAYER

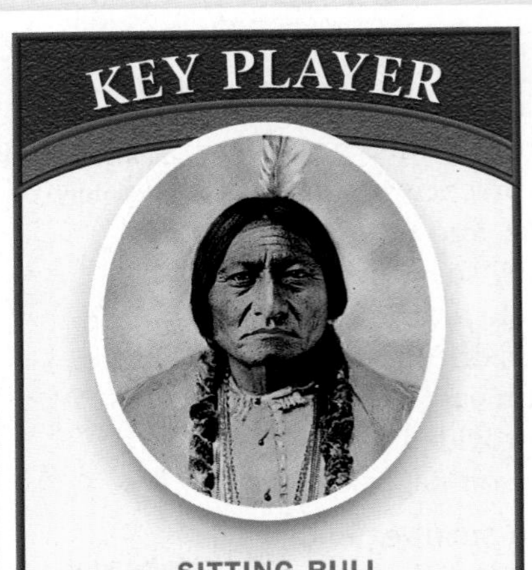

SITTING BULL
1831–1890

As a child, Sitting Bull was known as Hunkesni, or Slow; he earned the name Tatanka Iyotanka (Sitting Bull) after a fight with the Crow, a traditional enemy of the Sioux.

Sitting Bull led his people by the strength of his character and purpose. He was a warrior, spiritual leader, and medicine man, and he was determined that whites should leave Sioux territory. His most famous fight was at the Little Bighorn River. About his opponent, George Armstrong Custer, he said, "They tell me I murdered Custer. It is a lie. . . . He was a fool and rode to his death."

After Sitting Bull's surrender to the federal government in 1881, his dislike of whites did not change. He was killed by Native American police at Standing Rock Reservation in December 1890.

MASSACRE AT SAND CREEK One of the most tragic events occurred in 1864. Most of the Cheyenne, assuming they were under the protection of the U.S. government, had peacefully returned to Colorado's Sand Creek Reserve for the winter. Yet General S. R. Curtis, U.S. Army commander in the West, sent a telegram to militia colonel John Chivington that read, "I want no peace till the Indians suffer more." In response, Chivington and his troops descended on the Cheyenne and Arapaho—about 200 warriors and 500 women and children—camped at Sand Creek. The attack at dawn on November 29, 1864 killed over 150 inhabitants, mostly women and children.

DEATH ON THE BOZEMAN TRAIL The Bozeman Trail ran directly through Sioux hunting grounds in the Bighorn Mountains. The Sioux chief, Red Cloud (Mahpiua Luta), had unsuccessfully appealed to the government to end white settlement on the trail. In December 1866, the warrior Crazy Horse ambushed Captain William J. Fetterman and his company at Lodge Trail Ridge. Over 80 soldiers were killed. Native Americans called this fight the Battle of the Hundred Slain. Whites called it the Fetterman Massacre.

Skirmishes continued until the government agreed to close the Bozeman Trail. In return, the **Treaty of Fort Laramie,** in which the Sioux agreed to live on a reservation along the Missouri River, was forced on the leaders of the Sioux in 1868. **Sitting Bull** (Tatanka Iyotanka), leader of the Hunkpapa Sioux, had never signed it. Although the Ogala and Brule Sioux did sign the treaty, they expected to continue using their traditional hunting grounds.

Shrinking Native American Lands, and Battle Sites

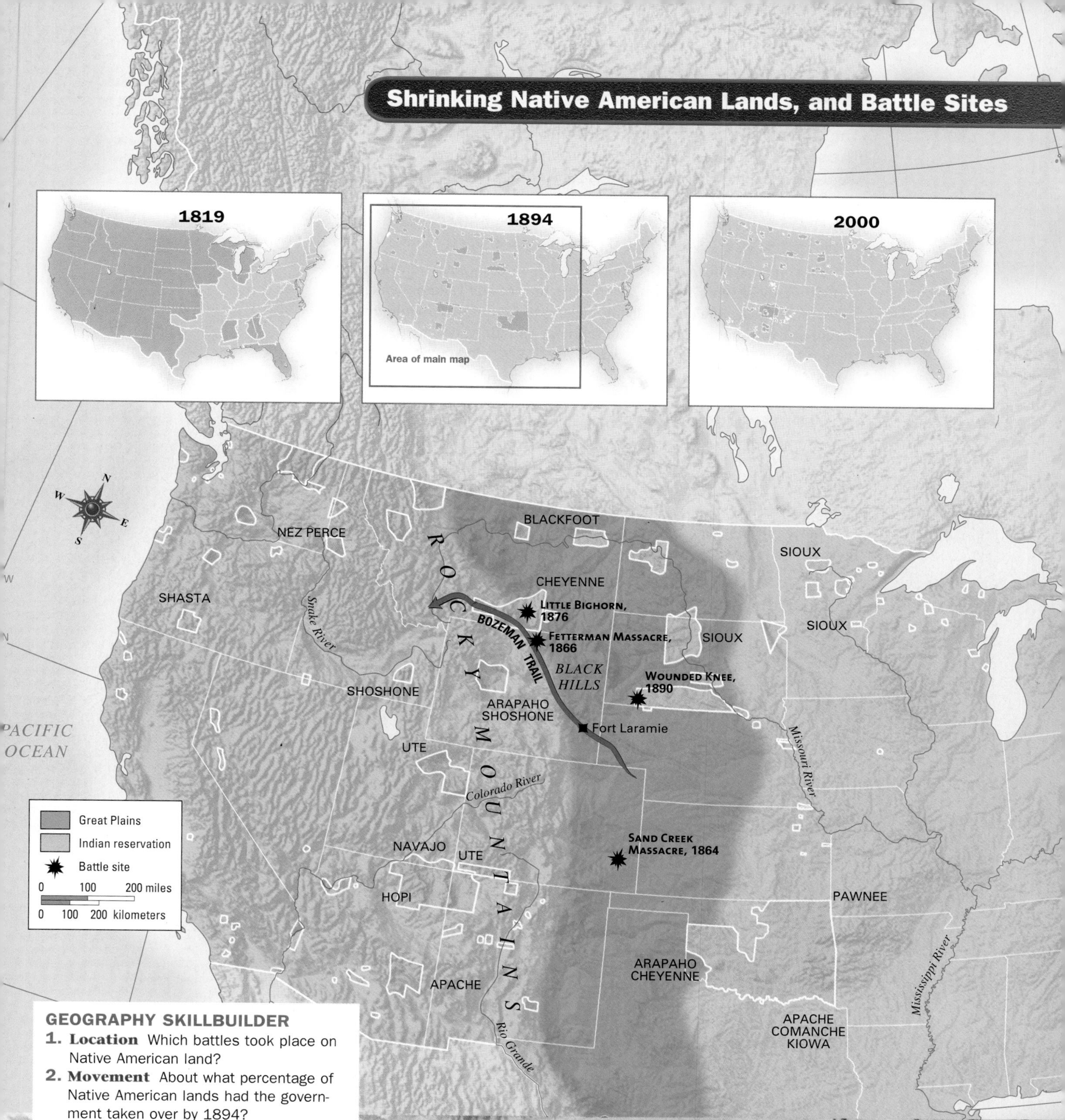

1819

1894

Area of main map

2000

PACIFIC OCEAN

NEZ PERCE

SHASTA

BLACKFOOT

CHEYENNE

SIOUX

SIOUX

SIOUX

SHOSHONE

ARAPAHO SHOSHONE

UTE

NAVAJO

UTE

HOPI

APACHE

PAWNEE

ARAPAHO CHEYENNE

APACHE COMANCHE KIOWA

ROCKY MOUNTAINS

BLACK HILLS

BOZEMAN TRAIL

Fort Laramie

LITTLE BIGHORN, 1876

FETTERMAN MASSACRE, 1866

WOUNDED KNEE, 1890

SAND CREEK MASSACRE, 1864

Snake River

Colorado River

Rio Grande

Missouri River

Mississippi River

N

S

E

W

Great Plains

Indian reservation

Battle site

0 100 200 miles

0 100 200 kilometers

GEOGRAPHY SKILLBUILDER

1. **Location** Which battles took place on Native American land?
2. **Movement** About what percentage of Native American lands had the government taken over by 1894?

A Sioux encampment near the South Dakota-Nebraska border.

Bloody Battles Continue

The Winchester '76 rifle used by government troops, and a Sioux war bow.

The Treaty of Fort Laramie provided only a temporary halt to warfare. The conflict between the two cultures continued as settlers moved westward and Native American nations resisted the restrictions imposed upon them. A Sioux warrior explained why.

A PERSONAL VOICE GALL, A HUNKPAPA SIOUX

> **"[We] have been taught to hunt and live on the game. You tell us that we must learn to farm, live in one house, and take on your ways. Suppose the people living beyond the great sea should come and tell you that you must stop farming, and kill your cattle, and take your houses and lands, what would you do? Would you not fight them?"**
>
> —quoted in *Bury My Heart at Wounded Knee*

RED RIVER WAR In late 1868, war broke out yet again as the Kiowa and Comanche engaged in six years of raiding that finally led to the Red River War of 1874–1875. The U.S. Army responded by herding the people of friendly tribes onto reservations while opening fire on all others. General Philip Sheridan, a Union Army veteran, gave orders "to destroy their villages and ponies, to kill and hang all warriors, and to bring back all women and children." With such tactics, the army crushed resistance on the southern plains.

Colonel George Armstrong Custer, 1865

GOLD RUSH Within four years of the Treaty of Fort Laramie, miners began searching the Black Hills for gold. The Sioux, Cheyenne, and Arapaho protested to no avail. In 1874, when Colonel **George A. Custer** reported that the Black Hills had gold "from the grass roots down," a gold rush was on. Red Cloud and Spotted Tail, another Sioux chief, vainly appealed again to government officials in Washington.

CUSTER'S LAST STAND In early June 1876, the Sioux and Cheyenne held a sun dance, during which Sitting Bull had a vision of soldiers and some Native Americans falling from their horses. When Colonel Custer and his troops reached the Little Bighorn River, the Native Americans were ready for them.

Led by Crazy Horse, Gall, and Sitting Bull, the warriors—with raised spears and rifles—outflanked and crushed Custer's troops. Within an hour, Custer and all of the men of the Seventh Cavalry were dead. By late 1876, however, the Sioux were beaten. Sitting Bull and a few followers took refuge in Canada, where they remained until 1881. Eventually, to prevent his people's starvation, Sitting Bull was forced to surrender. Later, in 1885, he appeared in William F. "Buffalo Bill" Cody's Wild West Show. C

MAIN IDEA

Analyzing Effects
C What were the results of Custer's last stand?

The Government Supports Assimilation

The Native Americans still had supporters in the United States, and debate over the treatment of Native Americans continued. The well-known writer Helen Hunt Jackson, for example, exposed the government's many broken promises in her 1881 book *A Century of Dishonor*. At the same time many sympathizers supported **assimilation,** a plan under which Native Americans would give up their beliefs and way of life and become part of the white culture.

THE DAWES ACT In 1887, Congress passed the **Dawes Act** aiming to "Americanize" the Native Americans. The act broke up the reservations and gave some of the reservation land to individual Native Americans—160 acres to each head of household and 80 acres to each unmarried adult. The government would sell the remainder of the reservations to settlers, and the resulting income would be used by Native Americans to buy farm implements. By 1932, whites had taken about two-thirds of the territory that had been set aside for Native Americans. In the end, the Native Americans received no money from the sale of these lands.

THE DESTRUCTION OF THE BUFFALO Perhaps the most significant blow to tribal life on the plains was the destruction of the buffalo. Tourists and fur traders shot buffalo for sport. U.S. General Sheridan noted with approval that buffalo hunters were destroying the Plains Indians' main source of food, clothing, shelter, and fuel. In 1800, approximately 65 million buffalo roamed the plains; by 1890, fewer than 1000 remained. In 1900, the United States sheltered, in Yellowstone National Park, a single wild herd of buffalo.

The Battle of Wounded Knee

The Sioux continued to suffer poverty and disease. In desperation, they turned to a Paiute prophet who promised that if the Sioux performed a ritual called the Ghost Dance, Native American lands and way of life would be restored.

The Ghost Dance movement spread rapidly among the 25,000 Sioux on the Dakota reservation. Alarmed military leaders ordered the arrest of Sitting Bull. In December 1890, about 40 Native American police were sent to arrest him. Sitting Bull's friend and bodyguard, Catch-the-Bear, shot one of them. The police then killed Sitting Bull. In the aftermath, Chief Big Foot led the fearful Sioux away.

WOUNDED KNEE On December 28, 1890, the Seventh Cavalry—Custer's old regiment—rounded up about 350 starving and freezing Sioux and took them to a camp at Wounded Knee Creek in South Dakota. The next day, the soldiers demanded that the Native Americans give up all their weapons. A shot was fired; from which side, it was not clear. The soldiers opened fire with deadly cannon.

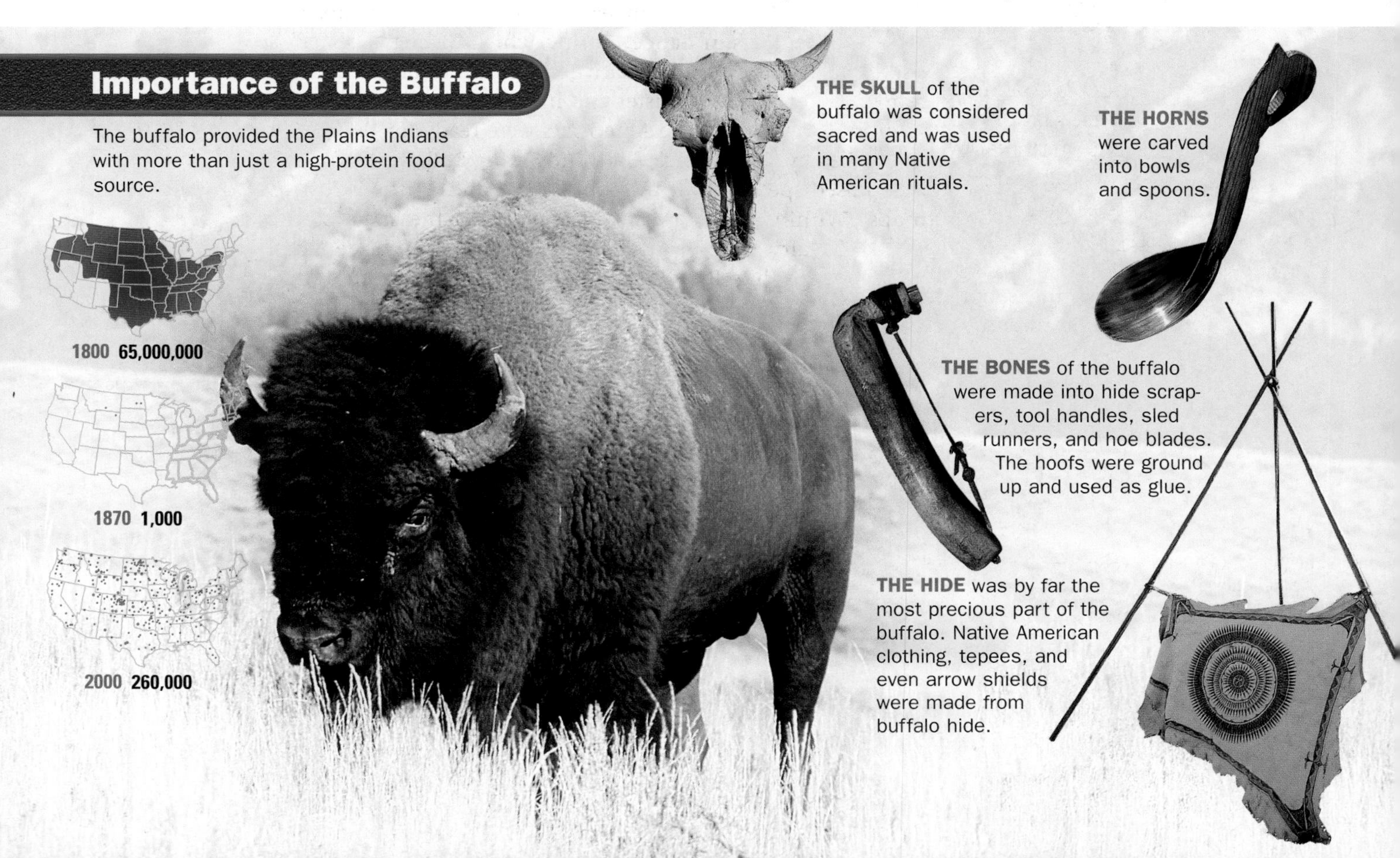

Importance of the Buffalo
The buffalo provided the Plains Indians with more than just a high-protein food source.
1800 65,000,000
1870 1,000
2000 260,000
THE SKULL of the buffalo was considered sacred and was used in many Native American rituals.
THE HORNS were carved into bowls and spoons.
THE BONES of the buffalo were made into hide scrapers, tool handles, sled runners, and hoe blades. The hoofs were ground up and used as glue.
THE HIDE was by far the most precious part of the buffalo. Native American clothing, tepees, and even arrow shields were made from buffalo hide.

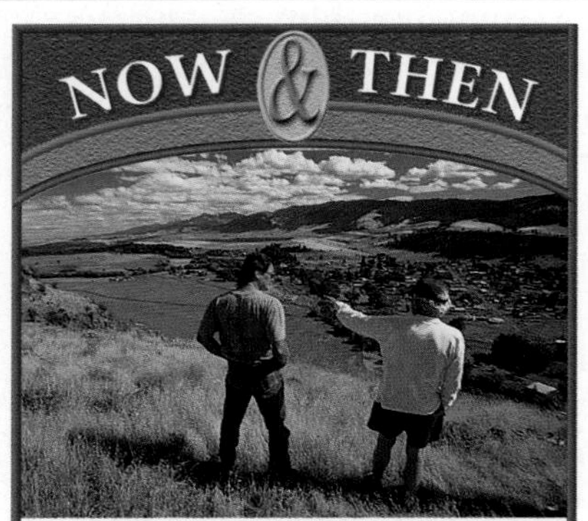

NEZ PERCE IN OREGON

Forced off their tribal lands in Wallowa County, Oregon, in 1877, the Nez Perce are returning almost 120 years later. 1999 figures put the number of Nez Perce in the Oregon area at around 3,000.

In 1997, Wallowa community leaders obtained a grant to develop the Wallowa Band Nez Perce Trail Interpretive Center—a cultural center that hosts powwows and other activities to draw tourists.

"I never thought I'd see the day," said Earl (Taz) Conner, a direct descendant of Chief Joseph, the best known of the Nez Perce. And, in the words of Soy Redthunder, another tribe member, "[We] look at it as homecoming."

Within minutes, the Seventh Cavalry slaughtered as many as 300 mostly unarmed Native Americans, including several children. The soldiers left the corpses to freeze on the ground. This event, the **Battle of Wounded Knee,** brought the Indian wars—and an entire era—to a bitter end. D

MAIN IDEA

Analyzing Causes

D What events led to the Battle of Wounded Knee?

A PERSONAL VOICE BLACK ELK

"I did not know then how much was ended. When I look back . . . I can still see the butchered women and children lying heaped and scattered all along the crooked gulch. . . . And I can see that something else died there in the bloody mud, and was buried in the blizzard. A people's dream died there. It was a beautiful dream."

—*Black Elk Speaks*

Cattle Become Big Business

As the great herds of buffalo disappeared, and Native Americans were forced onto smaller and less desirable reserverations, horses and cattle flourished on the plains. As cattle ranchers opened up the Great Plains to big business, ranching from Texas to Kansas became a profitable investment.

VAQUEROS AND COWBOYS American settlers had never managed large herds on the open range, and they learned from their Mexican neighbors how to round up, rope, brand, and care for the animals. The animals themselves, the Texas **longhorns,** were sturdy, short-tempered breeds accustomed to the dry grasslands of southern Spain. Spanish settlers raised longhorns for food and brought horses to use as work animals and for transportation.

As American as the cowboy seems today, his way of life stemmed directly from that of those first Spanish ranchers in Mexico. The cowboy's clothes, food, and vocabulary were heavily influenced by the Mexican *vaquero,* who was the first to wear spurs, which he attached with straps to his bare feet and used to control his horse. His *chaparreras,* or leather overalls, became known as chaps. He ate *charqui,* or "jerky"—dried strips of meat. The Spanish *bronco caballo,* or "rough horse" that ran wild, became known as a bronco or bronc. The strays, or *mesteños,* were the same mustangs that the American cowboy tamed and prized. The Mexican *rancho* became the American ranch. Finally, the English words *corral* and

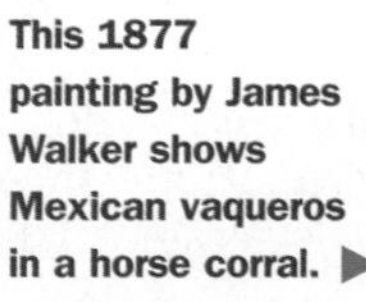

This 1877 painting by James Walker shows Mexican vaqueros in a horse corral. ▶

MAIN IDEA

Drawing Conclusions

E What does the American cowboy tradition owe to the Mexican vaquero?

rodeo were borrowed from Spanish. In his skills, dress, and speech, the Mexican vaquero was the true forerunner of the American "buckaroo" or cowboy. E

Despite the plentiful herds of Western cattle, cowboys were not in great demand until the railroads reached the Great Plains. Before the Civil War, ranchers for the most part didn't stray far from their homesteads with their cattle. There were, of course, some exceptions. During the California gold rush in 1849, some hardy cattlemen on horseback braved a long trek, or drive, through Apache territory and across the desert to collect $25 to $125 a head for their cattle. In 1854, two ranchers drove their cattle 700 miles to Muncie, Indiana, where they put them on stock cars bound for New York City. When the cattle were unloaded in New York, the stampede that followed caused a panic on Third Avenue. Parts of the country were not ready for the mass transportation of animals.

GROWING DEMAND FOR BEEF After the Civil War, the demand for beef skyrocketed, partly due to the rapidly growing cities. The Chicago Union Stock Yards opened in 1865, and by spring 1866, the railroads were running regularly through Sedalia, Missouri. From Sedalia, Texas ranchers could ship their cattle to Chicago and markets throughout the East. They found, however, that the route to Sedalia presented several obstacles: including thunderstorms and rain-swollen rivers. Also, in 1866, farmers angry about trampled crops blockaded cattle in Baxter Springs, Kansas, preventing them from reaching Sedalia. Some herds then had to be sold at cut-rate prices, others died of starvation. F

MAIN IDEA

Summarizing

F What developments led to the rapid growth of the cattle industry?

THE COW TOWN The next year, cattlemen found a more convenient route. Illinois cattle dealer Joseph McCoy approached several Western towns with plans to create a shipping yard where the trails and rail lines came together. The tiny Kansas town of Abilene enthusiastically agreed to the plan. McCoy built cattle pens, a three-story hotel, and helped survey the **Chisholm Trail**—the major cattle route from San Antonio, Texas, through Oklahoma to Kansas. Thirty-five thousand head of cattle were shipped out of the yard in Abilene during its first

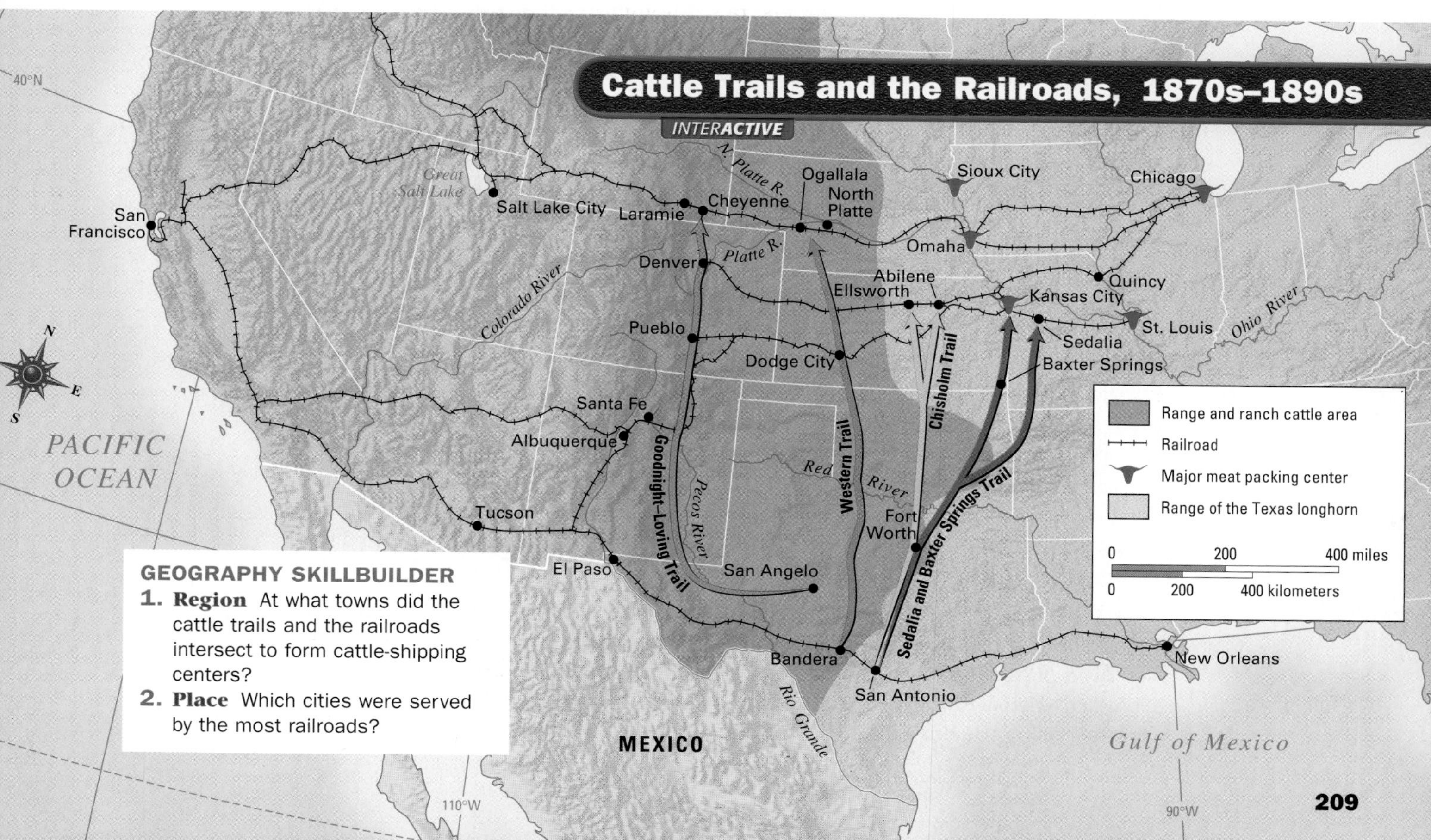

GEOGRAPHY SKILLBUILDER

1. **Region** At what towns did the cattle trails and the railroads intersect to form cattle-shipping centers?
2. **Place** Which cities were served by the most railroads?

History Through Art

STAMPEDED BY LIGHTNING (1908)

Painter and sculptor Frederic Remington is best known for his romantic and spirited depictions of the Western frontier. Remington liked to paint in a single dominant color. Native Americans, cowboys at work, and other familiar Western scenes were all subjects of Remington's work.

What do you learn about the work of the cowboy in this painting?

year in operation. The following year, business more than doubled, to 75,000 head. Soon ranchers were hiring cowboys to drive their cattle to Abilene. Within a few years, the Chisholm Trail had worn wide and deep.

A Day in the Life of a Cowboy

The meeting of the Chisholm Trail and the railroad in Abilene ushered in the heyday of the cowboy. As many as 55,000 worked the plains between 1866 and 1885. Although folklore and postcards depicted the cowboy as Anglo-American, about 25 percent of them were African American, and at least 12 percent were Mexican. The romanticized American cowboy of myth rode the open range, herding cattle and fighting villains. Meanwhile, the real-life cowboy was doing nonstop work.

A DAY'S WORK A cowboy worked 10 to 14 hours a day on a ranch and 14 or more on the trail, alert at all times for dangers that might harm or upset the herds. Some cowboys were as young as 15; most were broken-down by the time they were 40. A cowboy might own his saddle, but his trail horse usually belonged to his boss. He was an expert rider and roper. His gun might be used to protect the herd from wild or diseased animals rather than to hurt or chase outlaws.

ROUNDUP The cowboy's season began with a spring roundup, in which he and other hands from the ranch herded all the longhorns they could find on the open range into a large corral. They kept the herd penned there for several days, until the cattle were so hungry that they preferred grazing to running away. Then the cowboys sorted through the herd, claiming the cattle that were marked with the brand of their ranch and calves that still needed to be branded. After the herd was gathered and branded, the trail boss chose a crew for the long drive.

THE LONG DRIVE This overland transport, or **long drive,** of the animals often lasted about three months. A typical drive included one cowboy for every 250 to 300 head of cattle; a cook who also drove the chuck wagon and set up camp; and a wrangler who cared for the extra horses. A trail boss earned $100 or more a month for supervising the drive and negotiating with settlers and Native Americans.

During the long drive, the cowboy was in the saddle from dawn to dusk. He slept on the ground and bathed in rivers. He risked death and loss every day of the drive, especially at river crossings, where cattle often hesitated and were swept away. Because lightning was a constant danger, cowboys piled their spurs, buckles, and other metal objects at the edge of their camp to avoid attracting lightning bolts. Thunder, or even a sneeze, could cause a stampede. G

MAIN IDEA

Comparing
G How did the cowboy's life differ from the myth about it?

LEGENDS OF THE WEST Legendary figures like James Butler "Wild Bill" Hickok and Martha Jane Burke (Calamity Jane) actually never dealt with cows. Hickok served as a scout and a spy during the Civil War and, later, as a marshal in Abilene, Kansas. He was a violent man who was shot and killed while holding a pair of aces and a pair of eights in a poker game, a hand still known as the "dead man's hand." Calamity Jane was an expert sharpshooter who dressed as a man. She may have been a scout for Colonel George Custer.

HISTORICAL SPOTLIGHT

THE WILD WEST SHOW

In the 1880s, William F. Cody toured the country with a show called Buffalo Bill's Wild West. The show featured trick riding and roping exhibitions. It thrilled audiences with mock battles between cowboys and Indians.

Wild Bill Hickok, Annie Oakley, Calamity Jane (shown here), and even Sitting Bull toured in Wild West shows. Their performances helped make Western life a part of American mythology.

The End of the Open Range

Almost as quickly as cattle herds multiplied and ranching became big business, the cattle frontier met its end. Overgrazing of the land, extended bad weather, and the invention of barbed wire were largely responsible.

Between 1883 and 1887 alternating patterns of dry summers and harsh winters wiped out whole herds. Most ranchers then turned to smaller herds of high-grade stock that would yield more meat per animal. Ranchers fenced the land with barbed wire, invented by Illinois farmer Joseph F. Glidden. It was cheap and easy to use and helped to turn the open plains into a series of fenced-in ranches. The era of the wide-open West was over.

ASSESSMENT

1. **TERMS & NAMES** For each term or name, write a sentence explaining its significance.
   - **Great Plains**
   - **Treaty of Fort Laramie**
   - **Sitting Bull**
   - **George A. Custer**
   - **assimilation**
   - **Dawes Act**
   - **Battle of Wounded Knee**
   - **longhorn**
   - **Chisholm Trail**
   - **long drive**

MAIN IDEA

2. **TAKING NOTES**
Fill in supporting details about the culture of the Plains Indians.

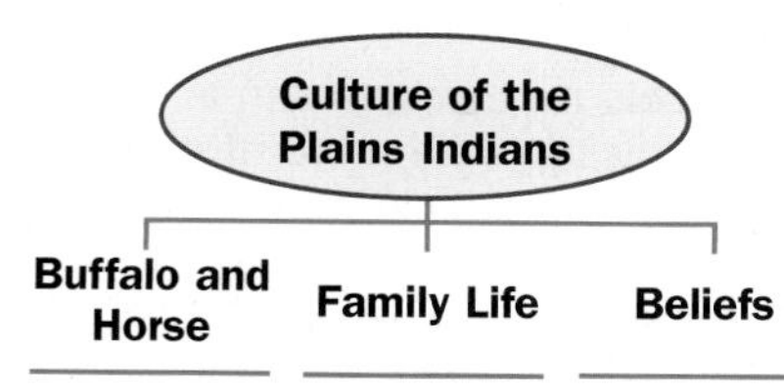

CRITICAL THINKING

3. **MAKING INFERENCES**
Why do you think the assimilation policy of the Dawes Act failed? Support your opinion with information from the text.
Think About:
   - the experience of Native Americans such as Zitkala-Ša
   - the attitudes of many white leaders toward Native Americans
   - the merits of owning property
   - the importance of cultural heritage

4. **ANALYZING CAUSES**
What economic opportunities drew large numbers of people to the Great Plains beginning in the mid-1800s?

5. **DRAWING CONCLUSIONS**
Identify the reasons for the rise and the decline of the cattle industry.

DAILY LIFE 1849–1900

Gold Mining

GOLD! Some struck it rich—some struck out. Between the Civil War and the turn of the century, deposits of the precious yellow metal were discovered in scattered sites from the Black Hills of South Dakota and Cripple Creek, Colorado, to Nome, Alaska. The dream of riches lured hundreds of thousands of prospectors into territories that were previously inhabited only by native peoples. The fortune seekers came from all walks: grizzled veterans from the California gold rush of 1849, youths seeking adventure, middle-class professionals, and even some families.

PANNING FOR GOLD ▶

At the start of a gold rush, prospectors usually looked for easily available gold—particles eroded from rocks and washed downstream. Panning for it was easy—even children could do it. They scooped up mud and water from the streambed in a flat pan and swirled it. The circular motion of the water caused the sand to wash over the side and the remaining minerals to form layers according to weight. Gold, which is heavier than most other minerals, sank to the bottom.

◀SLUICES AND ROCKERS

In 1898, prospectors like this mother and son in Fairbanks, Alaska, found sluicing to be more efficient than panning, since it could extract gold from soil. They would shovel soil into a sluice—a trough through which water flowed—and the water would carry off lightweight materials. The gold sank to the bottom, where it was caught in wooden ridges called cleats. A rocker was a portable sluice that combined the mobility of panning with the efficiency of sluicing.

▼ IN THE BOWELS OF THE EARTH

Although surface gold could be extracted by panning and sluicing, most gold was located in veins in underground rock. Mining these deposits involved digging tunnels along the veins of gold and breaking up tons of ore—hard and dangerous work. Tunnels often collapsed, and miners who weren't killed were trapped in utter darkness for days.

Heat was a problem, too. As miners descended into the earth, the temperature inside the mine soared. At a depth of about 2,000 feet, the temperature of the water that invariably flooded the bottom of a mine could be 160°F.

Cave-ins and hot water weren't the only dangers that miners faced. The pressure in the underground rock sometimes became so intense that it caused deadly explosions.

A FAMILY AFFAIR ▲

This early placer, or surface, mine at Cripple Creek attracted many women and children. It grew out of the vision of a young rancher, Bob Womack. He had found gold particles washed down from higher land and was convinced that the Cripple Creek area was literally a gold mine.

Because Womack was generally disliked, the community ignored him. When a German count struck gold there, however, business boomed. Womack died penniless—but the mines produced a $400 million bonanza.

DATA FILE

BOOM TO BUST

This old signpost from Gleeson, Nevada, illustrates how a gold-rush town that had mushroomed overnight could die just as quickly when the gold ran out.

WELCOME TO
GLEESON 21
POP. 5000 2000 1000 300

LONG ODDS

These statistics for the Klondike gold rush, from 1896 to 1899, show the incredible odds against striking it rich.

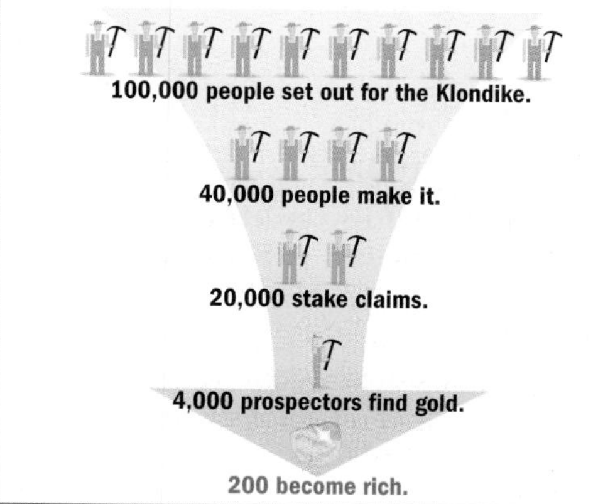
100,000 people set out for the Klondike.
40,000 people make it.
20,000 stake claims.
4,000 prospectors find gold.
200 become rich.

DEADLY DIGGING

An estimated 7,500 people died while digging for gold and silver during the Western gold rushes. That was more than the total number of people who died in the Indian wars.

THINKING CRITICALLY

CONNECT TO HISTORY

1. **Creating Graphs** Use the Data File to create a bar graph that shows the percentage of people who set out for the Klondike who did not get there, got there, staked claims, found gold, and became rich.

 **SEE SKILLBUILDER HANDBOOK, PAGE R30.**

CONNECT TO TODAY

2. **Researching Ghost Towns** Research the history of a ghost town from boom to bust. Present a short report on life in the town and its attempts to survive beyond the gold rush.

RESEARCH LINKS
CLASSZONE.COM

SECTION 2

Settling on the Great Plains

MAIN IDEA

Settlers on the Great Plains transformed the land despite great hardships.

WHY IT MATTERS NOW

The Great Plains region remains the breadbasket of the United States.

Terms & Names

- **Homestead Act**
- **exoduster**
- **soddy**
- **Morrill Act**
- **bonanza farm**

One American's Story

When Esther Clark Hill was a girl on the Kansas prairie in the 1800s, her father often left the family to go on hunting or trading expeditions. His trips left Esther's mother, Allena Clark, alone on the farm.

Esther remembered her mother holding on to the reins of a runaway mule team, "her black hair tumbling out of its pins and over her shoulders, her face set and white, while one small girl clung with chattering teeth to the sides of the rocking wagon." The men in the settlement spoke admiringly about "Leny's nerve," and Esther thought that daily life presented a challenge even greater than driving a runaway team.

▲ Plains settlers, like this woman depicted in Harvey Dunn's painting *Pioneer Woman*, had to be strong and self-reliant.

A PERSONAL VOICE ESTHER CLARK HILL

"I think, as much courage as it took to hang onto the reins that day, it took more to live twenty-four hours at a time, month in and out, on the lonely and lovely prairie, without giving up to the loneliness."

—quoted in *Pioneer Women*

As the railroads penetrated the frontier and the days of the free-ranging cowboy ended, hundreds of thousands of families migrated west, lured by vast tracts of cheap, fertile land. In their effort to establish a new life, they endured extreme hardships and loneliness.

Settlers Move Westward to Farm

It took over 250 years—from the first settlement at Jamestown until 1870—to turn 400 million acres of forests and prairies into flourishing farms. Settling the second 400 million acres took only 30 years, from 1870 to 1900. Federal land policy and the completion of transcontinental railroad lines made this rapid settlement possible.

RAILROADS OPEN THE WEST From 1850 to 1871, the federal government made huge land grants to the railroads—170 million acres, worth half a billion dollars—for laying track in the West. In one grant, both the Union Pacific and the Central Pacific received 10 square miles of public land for every mile of track laid in a state and 20 square miles of land for every mile of track laid in a territory.

In the 1860s, the two companies began a race to lay track. The Central Pacific moved eastward from Sacramento, and the Union Pacific moved westward from Omaha. Civil War veterans, Irish and Chinese immigrants, African Americans, and Mexican Americans did most of the grueling labor. In late 1868, workers for the Union Pacific cut their way through the solid rock of the mountains, laying up to eight miles of track a day. Both companies had reached Utah by the spring of 1869. Fifteen years later, the country boasted five transcontinental railroads. The rails to the East and West Coasts were forever linked.

MAIN IDEA

Analyzing Causes

A How did the railroads help open the West?

The railroad companies sold some of their land to farmers for two to ten dollars an acre. Some companies successfully sent agents to Europe to recruit buyers. By 1880, 44 percent of the settlers in Nebraska and more than 70 percent of those in Minnesota and Wisconsin were immigrants. **A**

GOVERNMENT SUPPORT FOR SETTLEMENT Another powerful attraction of the West was the land itself. In 1862, Congress passed the **Homestead Act**, offering 160 acres of land free to any citizen or intended citizen who was head of the household. From 1862 to 1900, up to 600,000 families took advantage of the government's offer. Several thousand settlers were **exodusters**—African Americans who moved from the post-Reconstruction South to Kansas.

Vocabulary

speculator: a person who buys or sells something that involves a risk on the chance of making a profit

Despite the massive response by homesteaders, or settlers on this free land, private speculators and railroad and state government agents sometimes used the law for their own gain. Cattlemen fenced open lands, while miners and woodcutters claimed national resources. Only about 10 percent of the land was actually settled by the families for whom it was intended. In addition, not all plots of land were of equal value. Although 160 acres could provide a decent living in the fertile soil of Iowa or Minnesota, settlers on drier Western land required larger plots to make farming worthwhile.

Eventually, the government strengthened the Homestead Act and passed more legislation to encourage settlers. In 1889, a major land giveaway in what is now Oklahoma attracted thousands of people. In less than a day, land-hungry settlers claimed 2 million acres in a massive land rush. Some took possession of the land before the government officially declared it open. Because these settlers claimed land sooner than they were supposed to, Oklahoma came to be known as the Sooner State. **B**

MAIN IDEA

Analyzing Effects

B In what ways did government policies encourage settlement of the West?

Posters like the one shown here drew hundreds of thousands of settlers to the West. Among the settlers were thousands of exodusters—freed slaves who had left the South. ▼

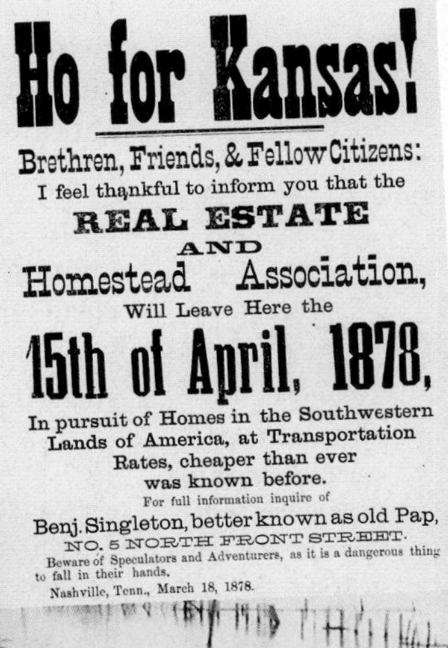

Ho for Kansas!
Brethren, Friends, & Fellow Citizens:
I feel thankful to inform you that the
REAL ESTATE
AND
Homestead Association,
Will Leave Here the
15th of April, 1878,
In pursuit of Homes in the Southwestern Lands of America, at Transportation Rates, cheaper than ever was known before.
For full information inquire of
Benj. Singleton, better known as old Pap,
NO. 5 NORTH FRONT STREET.
Beware of Speculators and Adventurers, as it is a dangerous thing to fall in their hands.
Nashville, Tenn., March 18, 1878.

THE CLOSING OF THE FRONTIER As settlers gobbled up Western land, Henry D. Washburn and fellow explorer Nathaniel P. Langford asked Congress to help protect the wilderness from settlement. In 1870, Washburn, who was surveying land in northwestern Wyoming, described the area's geysers and bubbling springs as: "objects new in experience . . . possessing unlimited grandeur and beauty."

In 1872, the government created Yellowstone National Park. Seven years later, the Department of the Interior forced railroads to give up their claim to Western landholdings that were equal in area to New York, New Jersey, Pennsylvania, Delaware, Maryland, and Virginia combined. Even so, by 1880, individuals had bought more than 19 million acres of government-owned land. Ten years later, the Census Bureau declared that the country no longer had a continuous frontier line—the frontier no longer existed. To many, the frontier was what had made America unique. In an 1893 essay entitled "The Significance of the Frontier in American History," the historian Frederick Jackson Turner agreed.

Background
The U.S. Census Bureau is the permanent collector of timely, relevant data about the people and economy of the United States.

A PERSONAL VOICE FREDERICK JACKSON TURNER

"**American social development has been continually beginning over again on the frontier. This perennial rebirth, this fluidity of American life, this expansion westward with its new opportunities, its continuous touch with the simplicity of primitive society, furnish the forces dominating American character.**"

—"The Significance of the Frontier in American History"

Today many historians question Turner's view. They think he gave too much importance to the frontier in the nation's development and in shaping a special American character. (C)

MAIN IDEA

Summarizing
(C) What was Turner's view of the role of the American frontier in 1893?

Settlers Meet the Challenges of the Plains

The frontier settlers faced extreme hardships—droughts, floods, fires, blizzards, locust plagues, and occasional raids by outlaws and Native Americans. Yet the number of people living west of the Mississippi River grew from 1 percent of the nation's population in 1850 to almost 30 percent by the turn of the century.

Vocabulary
locust: any of numerous grasshoppers that travel in large swarms, often doing great damage to crops

DUGOUTS AND SODDIES Since trees were scarce, most settlers built their homes from the land itself. Many pioneers dug their homes into the sides of ravines or small hills. A stovepipe jutting from the ground was often the only clear sign of such a dugout home.

Those who moved to the broad, flat plains often made freestanding houses by stacking blocks of prairie turf. Like a dugout, a sod home, or **soddy**, was warm in

A pioneer family stands in front of their soddy near Coburg, Nebraska, in 1887. ▶

winter and cool in summer. Soddies were small, however, and offered little light or air. They were havens for snakes, insects, and other pests. Although they were fireproof, they leaked continuously when it rained.

WOMEN'S WORK Virtually alone on the flat, endless prairie, homesteaders had to be almost superhumanly self-sufficient. Women often worked beside the men in the fields, plowing the land and planting and harvesting the predominant crop, wheat. They sheared the sheep and carded wool to make clothes for their families. They hauled water from wells that they had helped to dig, and made soap and candles from tallow. At harvest time, they canned fruits and vegetables. They were skilled in doctoring—from snakebites to crushed limbs. Women also sponsored schools and churches in an effort to build strong communities.

TECHNICAL SUPPORT FOR FARMERS Establishing a homestead was challenging. Once accomplished, it was farming the prairie, year in and year out, that became an overwhelming task. In 1837, John Deere had invented a steel plow that could slice through heavy soil. In 1847, Cyrus McCormick began to mass-produce a reaping machine. But a mass market for these devices didn't fully develop until the late 1800s with the migration of farmers onto the plains.

Other new and improved devices made farm work speedier—the spring-tooth harrow to prepare the soil (1869), the grain drill to plant the seed (1841), barbed wire to fence the land (1874), and the corn binder (1878). Then came a reaper that could cut and thresh wheat in one pass. By 1890, there were more than 900 manufacturers of farm equipment. In 1830, producing a bushel of grain took about 183 minutes. By 1900, with the use of these machines, it took only 10 minutes. These inventions made more grain available for a wider market. D

MAIN IDEA

Summarizing

D How did new inventions change farming in the West?

AGRICULTURAL EDUCATION The federal government supported farmers by financing agricultural education. The **Morrill Act** of 1862 and 1890 gave federal land to the states to help finance agricultural colleges, and the Hatch Act of 1887 established agricultural experiment stations to inform farmers of new developments. Agricultural researchers developed grains for arid soil and techniques for dry farming, which helped the land to retain moisture. These innovations enabled the dry eastern plains to flourish and become "the breadbasket of the nation."

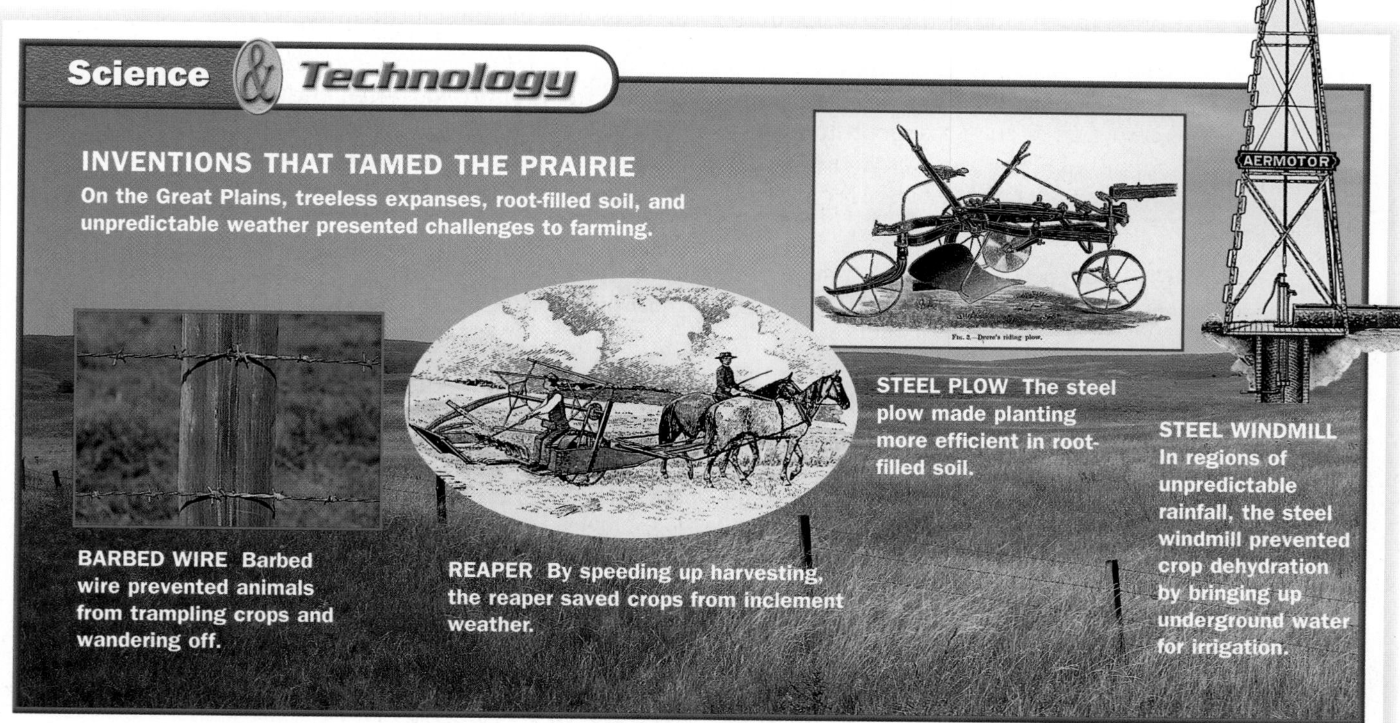

Science & Technology
INVENTIONS THAT TAMED THE PRAIRIE
On the Great Plains, treeless expanses, root-filled soil, and unpredictable weather presented challenges to farming.
AERMOTOR
BARBED WIRE Barbed wire prevented animals from trampling crops and wandering off.
REAPER By speeding up harvesting, the reaper saved crops from inclement weather.
STEEL PLOW The steel plow made planting more efficient in root-filled soil.
STEEL WINDMILL In regions of unpredictable rainfall, the steel windmill prevented crop dehydration by bringing up underground water for irrigation.

Bonanza farms like this one required the labor of hundreds of farm hands and horses.

FARMERS IN DEBT Elaborate machinery was expensive, and farmers often had to borrow money to buy it. When prices for wheat were higher, farmers could usually repay their loans. When wheat prices fell, however, farmers needed to raise more crops to make ends meet. This situation gave rise to a new type of farming in the late 1870s. Railroad companies and investors created **bonanza farms**, enormous single-crop spreads of 15,000–50,000 acres. The Cass-Cheney-Dalrymple farm near Cassleton, North Dakota, for example, covered 24 square miles. By 1900, the average farmer had nearly 150 acres under cultivation. Some farmers mortgaged their land to buy more property, and as farms grew bigger, so did farmers' debts. Between 1885 and 1890, much of the plains experienced drought, and the large single-crop operations couldn't compete with smaller farms, which could be more flexible in the crops they grew. The bonanza farms slowly folded into bankruptcy.

Vocabulary
mortgage: to legally pledge property to a creditor as security for the payment of a loan or debt

Farmers also felt pressure from the rising cost of shipping grain. Railroads charged Western farmers a higher fee than they did farmers in the East. Also, the railroads sometimes charged more for short hauls, for which there was no competing transportation, than for long hauls. The railroads claimed that they were merely doing business, but farmers resented being taken advantage of. "No other system of taxation has borne as heavily on the people as those extortions and inequalities of railroad charges" wrote Henry Demarest Lloyd in an article in the March 1881 edition of *Atlantic Monthly*.

Vocabulary
extortion: illegal use of one's official position or powers to obtain property or funds

Many farmers found themselves growing as much grain as they could grow, on as much land as they could acquire, which resulted in going further into debt. But they were not defeated by these conditions. Instead, these challenging conditions drew farmers together in a common cause.

SECTION 2 ASSESSMENT

1. **TERMS & NAMES** For each term or name, write a sentence explaining its significance.
   - **Homestead Act**
   - **exoduster**
   - **soddy**
   - **Morrill Act**
   - **bonanza farm**

MAIN IDEA

2. **TAKING NOTES**
   Create a time line of four events that shaped the settling of the Great Plains.

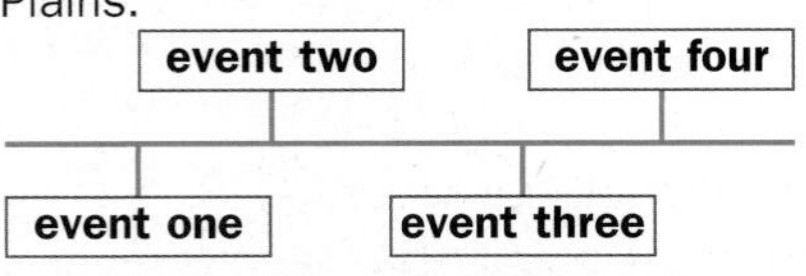

   How might history be different if one of these events hadn't happened?

CRITICAL THINKING

3. **EVALUATING**
   How successful were government efforts to promote settlement of the Great Plains? Give examples to support your answer. **Think About:**
   - the growth in population on the Great Plains
   - the role of railroads in the economy
   - the Homestead Act

4. **DRAWING CONCLUSIONS**
   Review the changes in technology that influenced the life of settlers on the Great Plains in the late 1800s. Explain how you think settlement of the plains would have been different without these inventions.

5. **IDENTIFYING PROBLEMS**
   How did the railroads take advantage of farmers?

Farmers and the Populist Movement

MAIN IDEA	WHY IT MATTERS NOW	Terms & Names
Farmers united to address their economic problems, giving rise to the Populist movement.	**Many of the Populist reform issues, such as income tax and legally protected rights of workers, are now taken for granted.**	**• Oliver Hudson Kelley • Grange • Farmers' Alliances • Populism • bimetallism • gold standard • William McKinley • William Jennings Bryan**

One American's Story

As a young adult in the early 1870s, Mary Elizabeth Lease left home to teach school on the Kansas plains. After marrying farmer Charles Lease, she joined the growing Farmers' Alliance movement and began speaking on issues of concern to farmers. Lease joked that her tongue was "loose at both ends and hung on a swivel," but her golden voice and deep blue eyes hypnotized her listeners.

A PERSONAL VOICE MARY ELIZABETH LEASE

"What you farmers need to do is to raise less corn and more Hell! We want the accursed foreclosure system wiped out. . . . We will stand by our homes and stay by our firesides by force if necessary, and we will not pay our debts to the loan-shark companies until the Government pays its debts to us."

—quoted in "The Populist Uprising"

▲ **Mary Elizabeth Lease, the daughter of Irish immigrants, was a leader of the Populist Party.**

Farmers had endured great hardships in helping to transform the plains from the "Great American Desert" into the "breadbasket of the nation," yet every year they reaped less and less of the bounty they had sowed with their sweat.

Farmers Unite to Address Common Problems

In the late 1800s, many farmers were trapped in a vicious economic cycle. Prices for crops were falling, and farmers often mortgaged their farms so that they could buy more land and produce more crops. Good farming land was becoming scarce, though, and banks were foreclosing on the mortgages of increasing numbers of farmers who couldn't make payments on their loans. Moreover, the railroads were taking advantage of farmers by charging excessive prices for shipping and storage.

Analyzing *Political Cartoons*

THE PLIGHT OF THE FARMERS

Farmers were particularly hard hit in the decades leading to the financial panic of 1893. They regarded big business interests as insurmountable enemies who were bringing them to their knees and leaving them with debts at every turn. This cartoon is a warning of the dangers confronting not only the farmers but the entire nation.

SKILLBUILDER Analyzing Political Cartoons

1. How does this cartoon depict the plight of the farmers?
2. Who does the cartoonist suggest is responsible for the farmers' plight?

SEE SKILLBUILDER HANDBOOK, PAGE R24.

ECONOMIC DISTRESS The troubles of the farmers were part of a larger economic problem affecting the entire nation. During the Civil War, the United States had issued almost $500 million in paper money, called greenbacks. Greenbacks could not be exchanged for silver or gold money. They were worth less than hard money of the same face value. Hard money included both coins and paper money printed in yellow ink that could be exchanged for gold. After the war, the government began to take the greenbacks out of circulation.

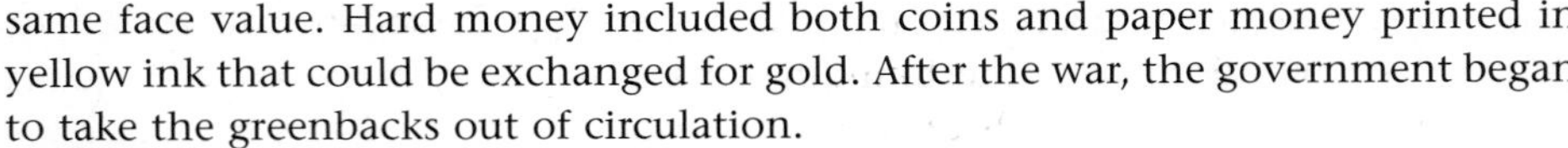

Retiring the greenbacks caused some discontent. It increased the value of the money that stayed in circulation. It meant that farmers who had borrowed money had to pay back their loans in dollars that were worth more than the dollars they had borrowed. At the same time they were receiving less money for their crops. Between 1867 and 1887, for example, the price of a bushel of wheat fell from $2.00 to 68 cents. In effect, farmers lost money at every turn. (A)

> **MAIN IDEA**
> **Analyzing Issues**
> (A) Why did farmers think that an increased money supply would help solve their economic problems?

Throughout the 1870s, the farmers and other debtors pushed the government to issue more money into circulation. Those tactics failed—although the Bland-Allison Act of 1878 required the government to buy and coin at least $2 million to $4 million worth of silver each month. It wasn't enough to support the increase in the money supply that the farmers wanted.

PROBLEMS WITH THE RAILROADS Meanwhile, farmers paid outrageously high prices to transport grain. Lack of competition among the railroads meant that it might cost more to ship grain from the Dakotas to Minneapolis by rail than from Chicago to England by boat. Also, railroads made secret agreements with middlemen—grain brokers and merchants—that allowed the railroads to control grain storage prices and to influence the market price of crops.

Many farmers mortgaged their farms for credit with which to buy seed and supplies. Suppliers charged high rates of interest, sometimes charging more for items bought on credit than they did for cash purchases. Farmers got caught in a cycle of credit that meant longer hours and more debt every year. It was time for reform. (B)

> **MAIN IDEA**
> **Analyzing Causes**
> (B) What were some of the causes of farmers' economic problems?

THE FARMERS' ALLIANCES To push effectively for reforms, however, farmers needed to organize. In 1867, **Oliver Hudson Kelley** started the Patrons of

Husbandry, an organization for farmers that became popularly known as the **Grange**. Its original purpose was to provide a social outlet and an educational forum for isolated farm families. By the 1870s, however, Grange members spent most of their time and energy fighting the railroads. The Grange's battle plan included teaching its members how to organize, how to set up farmers' cooperatives, and how to sponsor state legislation to regulate railroads.

Vocabulary
regulate: to control or direct according to a rule or law

The Grange gave rise to other organizations, such as **Farmers' Alliances.** These groups included many others who sympathized with farmers. Alliances sent lecturers from town to town to educate people about topics such as lower interest rates on loans and government control over railroads and banks. Spellbinding speakers such as Mary Elizabeth Lease helped get the message across.

Background
See *interest rate* on page R42 of the Economics Handbook.

Membership grew to more than 4 million—mostly in the South and the West. The Southern Alliance, including white Southern farmers, was the largest. About 250,000 African Americans belonged to the Colored Farmers' National Alliance. Some alliance members promoted cooperation between black and white alliances, but most members accepted the separation of the organizations.

HISTORICAL SPOTLIGHT

THE COLORED FARMERS' NATIONAL ALLIANCE

A white Baptist missionary, R. M. Humphrey, organized the Colored Farmers' National Alliance in 1886 in Houston, Texas. Like their counterparts in the white alliances, members of the local colored farmers' alliances promoted cooperative buying and selling. Unlike white organizations, however, the black alliances had to work mostly in secret to avoid racially motivated violence at the hands of angry landowners and suppliers.

The Rise and Fall of Populism

Leaders of the alliance movement realized that to make far-reaching changes, they would need to build a base of political power. **Populism**—the movement of the people—was born with the founding of the Populist, or People's, Party, in 1892. On July 2, 1892, a Populist Party convention in Omaha, Nebraska, demanded reforms to lift the burden of debt from farmers and other workers and to give the people a greater voice in their government.

THE POPULIST PARTY PLATFORM The economic reforms proposed by the Populists included an increase in the money supply, which would produce a rise in prices received for goods and services; a graduated income tax; and a federal loan program. The proposed governmental reforms included the election of U.S. senators by popular vote, single terms for the president and the vice-president, and a secret ballot to end vote fraud. Finally, the Populists called for an eight-hour workday and restrictions on immigration.

The proposed changes were so attractive to struggling farmers and desperate laborers that in 1892 the Populist presidential candidate won almost 10 percent of the total vote. In the West, the People's Party elected five senators, three governors, and about 1,500 state legislators. The Populists' programs eventually became the platform of the Democratic Party and kept alive the concept that the government is responsible for reforming social injustices. C

MAIN IDEA

Summarizing
C What was the Populist Party platform?

THE PANIC OF 1893 During the 1880s, farmers were overextended with debts and loans. Railroad construction had expanded faster than markets. In February 1893, the Philadelphia and Reading Railroad went bankrupt, followed by the Erie, the Northern Pacific, the Union Pacific, and the Santa Fe. The government's gold supply had worn thin, partly due to its obligation to purchase silver. People panicked and traded paper money for gold. The panic also spread to Wall Street, where the prices of stocks fell rapidly. The price of silver then plunged, causing silver mines to close. By the end of the year, over 15,000 businesses and 500 banks had collapsed.

Investments declined, and consumer purchases, wages, and prices also fell. Panic deepened into depression as 3 million people lost their jobs. By December 1894, a fifth of the work force was unemployed. Many farm families suffered both hunger and unemployment. D

MAIN IDEA

Analyzing Causes

D What caused the panic of 1893?

KEY PLAYER

WILLIAM JENNINGS BRYAN 1860–1925

William Jennings Bryan might be considered a patron saint of lost causes, largely because he let beliefs, not politics, guide his actions. He resigned his position as secretary of state (1913–1915) under Woodrow Wilson, for example, to protest the president's movement away from neutrality regarding the war in Europe.

Near the end of his life, he went to Tennessee to assist the prosecution in the Scopes "monkey trial," contesting the teaching of evolution in public schools. He is perhaps best characterized by a quote from his own "Cross of Gold" speech: "The humblest citizen in all the land, when clad in the armor of a righteous cause, is stronger than all the hosts of error."

SILVER OR GOLD Populists watched as the two major political parties became deeply divided in a struggle between different regions and economic interests. Business owners and bankers of the industrialized Northeast were Republicans; the farmers and laborers of the agrarian South and West were Democrats.

The central issue of the campaign was which metal would be the basis of the nation's monetary system. On one side were the "silverites," who favored **bimetallism**, a monetary system in which the government would give citizens either gold or silver in exchange for paper currency or checks. On the other side were President Cleveland and the "gold bugs," who favored the **gold standard**—backing dollars solely with gold.

The backing of currency was an important campaign issue because people regarded paper money as worthless if it could not be turned in for gold or silver. Because silver was more plentiful than gold, backing currency with both metals, as the silverites advocated, would make more currency (with less value per dollar) available. Supporters of bimetallism hoped that this measure would stimulate the stagnant economy. Retaining the gold standard would provide a more stable, but expensive, currency.

BRYAN AND THE "CROSS OF GOLD" Stepping into the debate, the Populist Party called for bimetallism and free coinage of silver. Yet their strategy was undecided: should they join forces with sympathetic candidates in the major parties and risk losing their political identity, or should they nominate their own candidates and risk losing the election?

As the 1896 campaign progressed, the Republican Party stated its firm commitment to the gold standard and nominated Ohioan **William McKinley** for president. After much debate, the Democratic Party came out in favor of a combined gold and silver standard, including unlimited coinage of silver. At the Democratic convention, former Nebraska congressman **William Jennings Bryan**, editor of the *Omaha World-Herald,* delivered an impassioned address to the assembled

Gold Bugs and Silverites

	Gold Bugs	Silverites
Who They Were	bankers and businessmen	farmers and laborers
What They Wanted	gold standard less money in circulation	bimetallism more money in circulation
Why	Loans would be repaid in stable money.	Products would be sold at higher prices.
Effects	DEFLATION • Prices fall. • Value of money increases. • Fewer people have money.	INFLATION • Prices rise. • Value of money decreases. • More people have money.

delegates. An excerpt of what has become known as the "Cross of Gold" speech follows.

▲ **William Jennings Bryan's "Cross of Gold" speech inspired many cartoonists.**

A PERSONAL VOICE WILLIAM JENNINGS BRYAN

"Having behind us the producing masses of this nation and the world, supported by the commercial interests, the laboring interests, and the toilers everywhere, we will answer their demand for a gold standard by saying to them: You shall not press down upon the brow of labor this crown of thorns, you shall not crucify mankind upon a cross of gold."

—Democratic convention speech, Chicago, July 8, 1896

Bryan won the Democratic nomination. When the Populist convention met two weeks later, the delegates were both pleased and frustrated. They liked Bryan and the Democratic platform, but they detested the Democratic vice-presidential candidate, Maine banker Arthur Sewall. Nor did they like giving up their identity as a party. They compromised by endorsing Bryan, nominating their own candidate, Thomas Watson of Georgia, for vice-president, and keeping their party organization intact. E

MAIN IDEA

Analyzing Issues

E Why was the metal that backed paper currency such an important issue in the 1896 presidential campaign?

THE END OF POPULISM Bryan faced a difficult campaign. His free-silver stand had led gold bug Democrats to nominate their own candidate. It also weakened his support in cities, where consumers feared inflation because it would make goods more expensive. In addition, Bryan's meager funds could not match the millions backing McKinley. Bryan tried to make up for lack of funds by campaigning in 27 states and sometimes making 20 speeches a day. McKinley, on the other hand, campaigned from his front porch, while thousands of well-known people toured the country speaking on his behalf.

McKinley got approximately 7 million votes and Bryan about 6.5 million. As expected, McKinley carried the East, while Bryan carried the South and the farm vote of the Middle West. The voters of the industrial Middle West, with their fear of inflation, brought McKinley into office.

With McKinley's election, Populism collapsed, burying the hopes of the farmers. The movement left two powerful legacies, however: a message that the downtrodden could organize and have political impact, and an agenda of reforms, many of which would be enacted in the 20th century.

SECTION 3 ASSESSMENT

1. **TERMS & NAMES** For each term or name, write a sentence explaining its significance.
   - **Oliver Hudson Kelley**
   - **Grange**
   - **Farmers' Alliances**
   - **Populism**
   - **bimetallism**
   - **gold standard**
   - **William McKinley**
   - **William Jennings Bryan**

MAIN IDEA

2. **TAKING NOTES**
   Identify the causes of the rise of the Populist Party and the effects the party had.

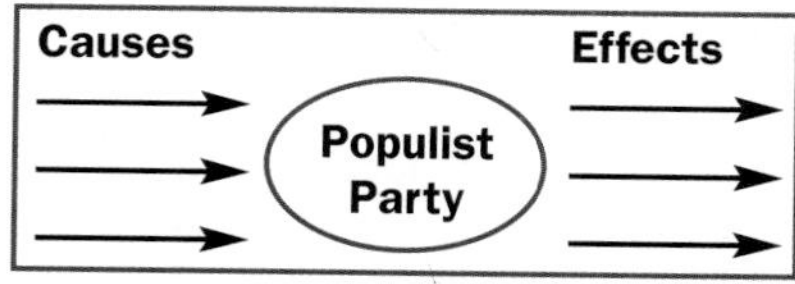

Which effect has the most impact today? Explain.

CRITICAL THINKING

3. **EVALUATING**
   What do you think were the most significant factors in bringing an end to the Populist Party? **Think about:**
   - monetary policy
   - third-party status
   - source of popular support
   - popular participation policy

4. **MAKING INFERENCES**
   How did the Grange and the Farmers' Alliances pave the way for the Populist Party?

Literature of the West

1850–1900 After gold was discovered in California, Americans came to view the West as a region of unlimited possibility. Those who could not venture there in person enjoyed reading about the West in colorful tales by writers such as Mark Twain (Samuel Clemens) and Bret Harte. Dime novels, cheaply bound adventure stories that sold for a dime, were also enormously popular in the second half of the 19th century.

Since much of the West was Spanish-dominated for centuries, Western literature includes legends and songs of Hispanic heroes and villains. It also includes the haunting words of Native Americans whose lands were taken and cultures threatened as white pioneers moved west.

▲ Mark Twain

THE CELEBRATED JUMPING FROG OF CALAVERAS COUNTY

The American humorist Samuel Clemens—better known as Mark Twain—was a would-be gold and silver miner who penned tales of frontier life. "The Celebrated Jumping Frog of Calaveras County" is set in a California mining camp. Most of the tale is told by Simon Wheeler, an old-timer given to exaggeration.

> "Well, Smiley kep' the beast in a little lattice box, and he used to fetch him downtown sometimes and lay for a bet. One day a feller—a stranger in the camp, he was—come acrost him with his box, and says:
>
> "'What might it be that you've got in the box?'
>
> "And Smiley says, sorter indifferent-like, 'It might be a parrot, or it might be a canary, maybe, but it ain't—it's only just a frog.'
>
> "And the feller took it, and looked at it careful, and turned it round this way and that, and says, 'H'm—so 'tis. Well, what's *he* good for?'
>
> "'Well,' Smiley says, easy and careless, 'he's good enough for *one* thing, I should judge—he can outjump any frog in Calaveras County.'
>
> "The feller took the box again, and took another long, particular look, and give it back to Smiley, and says, very deliberate, 'Well,' he says, 'I don't see no p'ints about that frog that's any better'n any other frog.'
>
> "'Maybe you don't,' Smiley says. 'Maybe you understand frogs and maybe you don't understand 'em; maybe you've had experience, and maybe you ain't only a amature, as it were. Anyways, I've got my opinion, and I'll resk forty dollars that he can outjump any frog in Calaveras County.'"

—Mark Twain, "The Celebrated Jumping Frog of Calaveras County" (1865)

THE BALLAD OF GREGORIO CORTEZ

In the border ballads, or *corridos,* of the American Southwest, few figures are as famous as the Mexican vaquero, Gregorio Cortez. This excerpt from a ballad about Cortez deals with a confrontation between Cortez and a group of Texas lawmen. Although he is hotly pursued, Cortez has an amazingly long run before being captured.

> . . . And in the county of Kiansis
> They cornered him after all;
> Though they were more than
> three hundred
> He leaped out of their corral.
>
> Then the Major Sheriff said,
> As if he was going to cry,
> "Cortez, hand over your weapons;
> We want to take you alive."
>
> Then said Gregorio Cortez,
> And his voice was like a bell,
> "You will never get my
> weapons
> Till you put me in a cell."
>
> Then said Gregorio Cortez,
> With his pistol in his hand,
> "Ah, so many mounted Rangers
> Just to take one Mexican!"

—Anonymous, "The Ballad of Gregorio Cortez," translated by Américo Paredes

Vaquero (modeled 1980/cast 1990), *Luis Jiménez.* National Museum of American Art/Art Resource, New York.

▲ **Chief Satanta**

CHIEF SATANTA'S SPEECH AT THE MEDICINE LODGE CREEK COUNCIL

Known as the Orator of the Plains, Chief Satanta represented the Kiowa people in the 1867 Medicine Lodge Creek negotiations with the U.S. government. The speech from which this excerpt is taken was delivered by Satanta in Spanish but was translated into English and widely published in leading newspapers of the day.

> All the land south of the Arkansas belongs to the Kiowas and Comanches, and I don't want to give away any of it. I love the land and the buffalo and will not part with it. I want you to understand well what I say. Write it on paper. Let the Great Father [U.S. president] see it, and let me hear what he has to say. I want you to understand also, that the Kiowas and Comanches don't want to fight, and have not been fighting since we made the treaty. I hear a great deal of good talk from the gentlemen whom the Great Father sends us, but they never do what they say. I don't want any of the medicine lodges [schools and churches] within the country. I want the children raised as I was. When I make peace, it is a long and lasting one—there is no end to it. . . . A long time ago this land belonged to our fathers; but when I go up to the river I see camps of soldiers on its banks. These soldiers cut down my timber; they kill my buffalo; and when I see that, my heart feels like bursting; I feel sorry. I have spoken.

—Chief Satanta, speech at the Medicine Lodge Creek Council (1867)

THINKING CRITICALLY

1. **Comparing and Contrasting** Compare and contrast the views these selections give of the American frontier in the second half of the 19th century. Use details from the selections to help explain your answer.

    **SEE SKILLBUILDER HANDBOOK, PAGE R8.**

2. **INTERNET ACTIVITY CLASSZONE.COM**

   From the gauchos of the Argentine pampas to the workers on Australian sheep stations, many nations have had their own versions of the cowboys of the American West. Use the links for American Literature to research one such nation. Prepare a bulletin-board display that shows the similarities and differences between Western cowboys and their counterparts in that country.

CHAPTER 5 ASSESSMENT

TERMS & NAMES

For each term or name below, write a sentence explaining its connection to changes on the Great Plains.

1. Homestead Act
2. Sitting Bull
3. assimilation
4. Morrill Act
5. exoduster
6. George A. Custer
7. William Jennings Bryan
8. William McKinley
9. Populism
10. Grange

MAIN IDEAS

Use your notes and the information in the chapter to answer the following questions.

Cultures Clash on the Prairie *(pages 202–211)*

1. Identify three differences between the culture of the Native Americans and the culture of the white settlers on the Great Plains.
2. How effective was the Dawes Act in promoting the assimilation of Native Americans into white culture?
3. Why did the cattle industry become a big business in the late 1800s?
4. How did cowboy culture reflect the ethnic diversity of the United States?

Settling on the Great Plains *(pages 214–218)*

5. What measures did the government take to support settlement of the frontier?
6. How did settlers overcome the challenges of living on the Great Plains?

Farmers and the Populist Movement
(pages 219–223)

7. What economic problems confronted American farmers in the 1890s?
8. According to farmers and other supporters of free silver, how would bimetallism help the economy?

CRITICAL THINKING

1. **USING YOUR NOTES** Create a cause/effect diagram identifying the reasons that agricultural output from the Great Plains increased during the late 1800s.

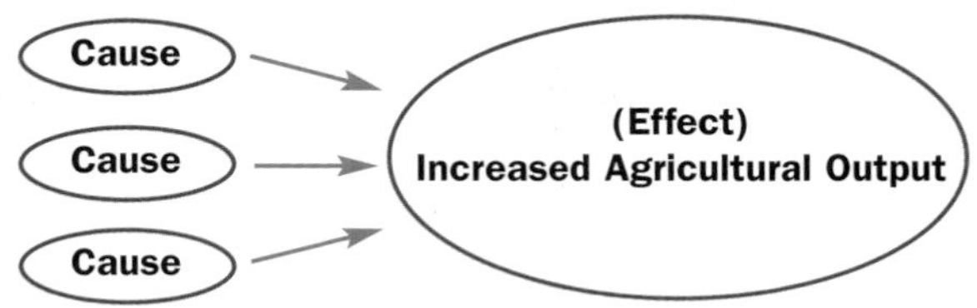

2. **ANALYZING MOTIVES** In 1877, Nez Perce Chief Joseph said, “My people have always been the friends of white men. Why are you in such a hurry?” Why do you think white people hurried to settle the West, with so little regard for Native Americans? Give evidence from the chapter to support your position.

3. **INTERPRETING CHARTS** Look at the chart of Gold Bugs and Silverites on page 222. What would be the result of the policies favored by the gold bugs? by the silverites?

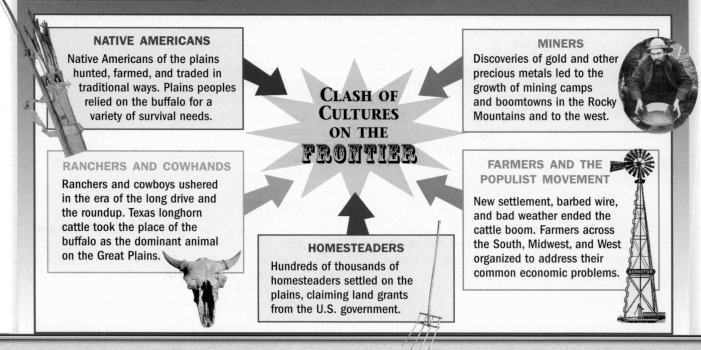

VISUAL SUMMARY CHANGES ON THE WESTERN FRONTIER

CLASH OF CULTURES ON THE FRONTIER

NATIVE AMERICANS
Native Americans of the plains hunted, farmed, and traded in traditional ways. Plains peoples relied on the buffalo for a variety of survival needs.

MINERS
Discoveries of gold and other precious metals led to the growth of mining camps and boomtowns in the Rocky Mountains and to the west.

RANCHERS AND COWHANDS
Ranchers and cowboys ushered in the era of the long drive and the roundup. Texas longhorn cattle took the place of the buffalo as the dominant animal on the Great Plains.

HOMESTEADERS
Hundreds of thousands of homesteaders settled on the plains, claiming land grants from the U.S. government.

FARMERS AND THE POPULIST MOVEMENT
New settlement, barbed wire, and bad weather ended the cattle boom. Farmers across the South, Midwest, and West organized to address their common economic problems.

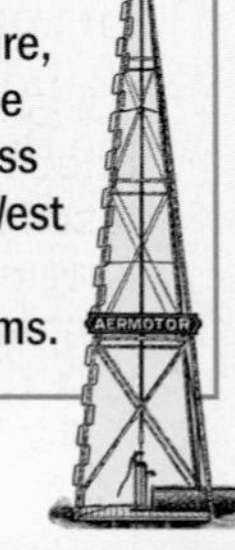

Standardized Test Practice

Use the flowchart and your knowledge of U.S. history to answer question 1.

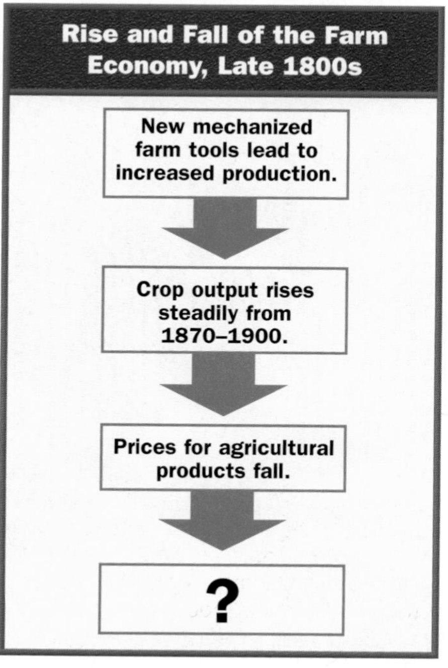

Rise and Fall of the Farm Economy, Late 1800s
New mechanized farm tools lead to increased production.
Crop output rises steadily from 1870–1900.
Prices for agricultural products fall.
?

1. Which effect accurately completes the flowchart?
   - **A** Farmers have less money to repay loans, and many lose their farms.
   - **B** Small farmers live off the land, so are not affected by the economy.
   - **C** Wealthy farmers hoard gold, rather than depend on paper money.
   - **D** The government subsidizes farmers to help them pay their bills.

Use the quotation and your knowledge of U.S. history to answer question 2.

> **"[We] have been taught to hunt and live on the game. You tell us that we must learn to farm, live in one house, and take on your ways. Suppose the people living beyond the great sea should come and tell you that you must stop farming, and kill your cattle, and take your houses and lands, what would you do? Would you not fight them?"**
>
> —Gall, a Hunkpapa Sioux, quoted in *Bury My Heart at Wounded Knee*

2. What was Gall's view of future relations between the Plains Indians and the settlers?
   - **F** peaceful coexistence
   - **G** further conflict
   - **H** mutual respect
   - **J** equality before the law

3. How did the invention of barbed wire change the look of the Western frontier?
   - **A** It endangered wildlife.
   - **B** It ended the cattle frontier.
   - **C** It increased cattle stocks.
   - **D** It enriched the cow towns.

ADDITIONAL TEST PRACTICE, pages S1–S33.

CLASSZONE.COM

ALTERNATIVE ASSESSMENT

1. **INTERACT WITH HISTORY** Recall your discussion of the question on page 201:

   What do you expect to find on settling in the West?

   Suppose you are a frontier settler. Write a letter to the family members you left behind describing your journey west and how you are living now. Perhaps, for example, you and your companions have built a soddy. Use information from Chapter 5 to provide some vivid impressions of life on the frontier.

2. **VIDEO** **LEARNING FROM MEDIA** View the American Stories video, "A Walk in Two Worlds." Discuss the following questions in small groups.
   - How did Zitkala-Ša react to life in the boarding school?
   - What lessons about clashes of cultures did you learn from Zitkala-Ša's experience?
   - How might people make interactions with other cultures a positive, rather than a negative, experience?

   Stage a panel discussion for the class.

CHAPTER 6
A NEW INDUSTRIAL AGE

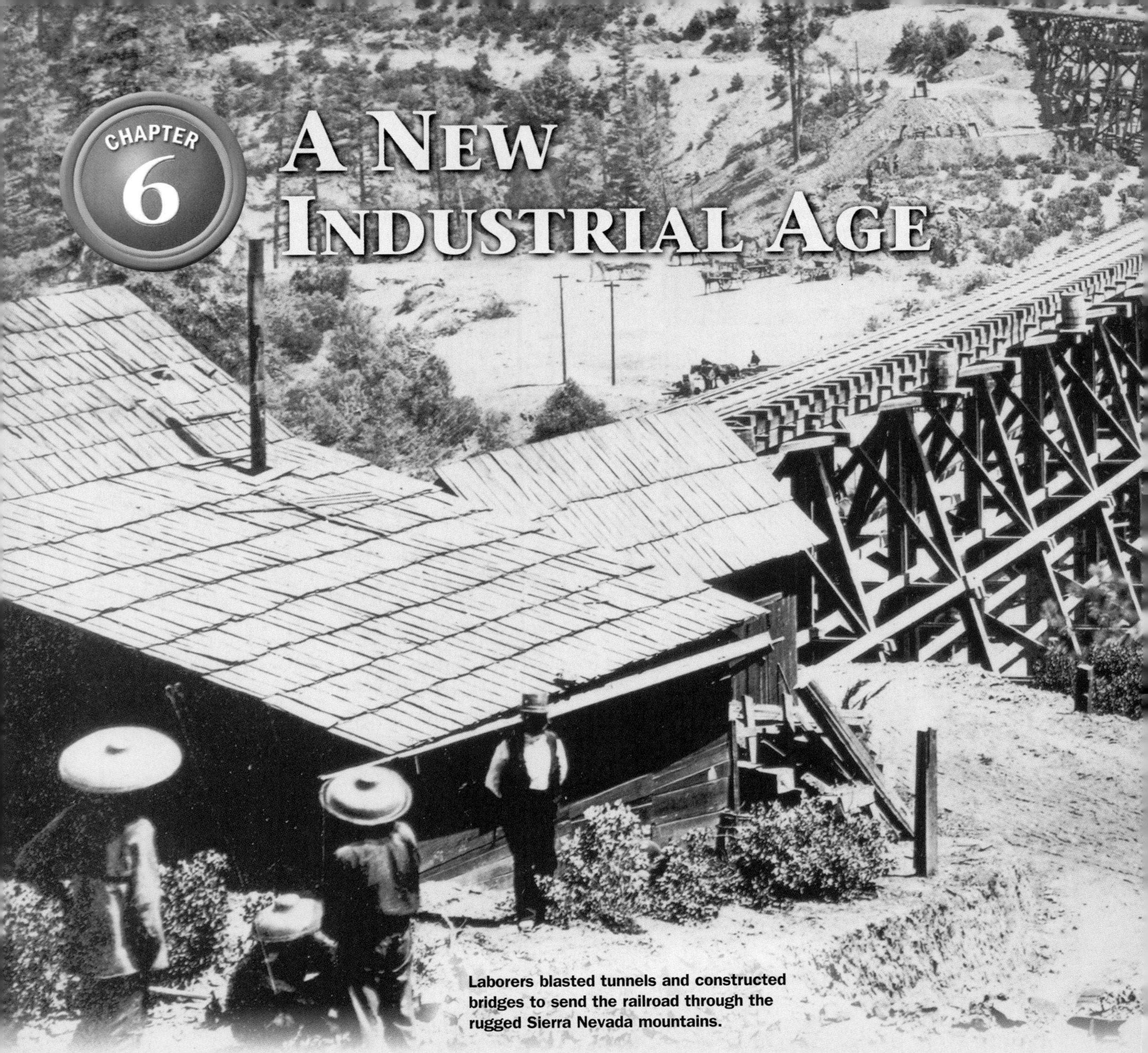

Laborers blasted tunnels and constructed bridges to send the railroad through the rugged Sierra Nevada mountains.

USA

1869 Central Pacific and Union Pacific complete the transcontinental railroad.

1876 Alexander Graham Bell invents the telephone.

1877 *Munn* v. *Illinois* establishes government regulation of railroads.

Mother Jones supports the Great Strike of 1877.

1879 Thomas A. Edison invents a workable light bulb.

1884 Grover Cleveland is elected president.

1870

1880

WORLD

1870 Franco-Prussian War breaks out.

1875 British labor unions win right to strike.

1882 United States restricts Chinese immigration.

1883 Germany becomes the first nation to provide national health insurance.

INTERACT WITH HISTORY

The year is 1863 and railroad construction is booming. In six years, the U.S. will be linked by rail from coast to coast. Central Pacific Railroad employs mainly Chinese immigrants to blast tunnels, lay track, and drive spikes, all for low wages. You are a journalist assigned to describe this monumental construction project for your readers.

What are the pros and cons of railroad expansion?

Examine the Issues

- What dangers do the railroad workers encounter?
- How will businesses and the general public benefit from the transcontinental railroad?
- How might railroad construction affect the environment?

RESEARCH LINKS **CLASSZONE.COM**

Visit the Chapter 6 links for more information about A New Industrial Age.

1886 Haymarket riot turns public sentiment against unions.

1890 Congress passes the Sherman Antitrust Act.

1894 President Cleveland sends federal troops to Illinois to end the Pullman strike.

1896 William McKinley is elected president.

1900 William McKinley is reelected.

1890

1900

1890 Colonization of sub-Saharan Africa peaks.

1893 Women in New Zealand gain voting rights.

1896 First modern Olympic Games are held in Athens, Greece.

SECTION 1

The Expansion of Industry

MAIN IDEA

At the end of the 19th century, natural resources, creative ideas, and growing markets fueled an industrial boom.

WHY IT MATTERS NOW

Technological developments of the late 19th century paved the way for the continued growth of American industry.

Terms & Names

- **Edwin L. Drake**
- **Bessemer process**
- **Thomas Alva Edison**
- **Christopher Sholes**
- **Alexander Graham Bell**

One American's Story

One day, Pattillo Higgins noticed bubbles in the springs around Spindletop, a hill near Beaumont in southeastern Texas. This and other signs convinced him that oil was underground. If Higgins found oil, it could serve as a fuel source around which a vibrant industrial city would develop.

Higgins, who had been a mechanic and a lumber merchant, couldn't convince geologists or investors that oil was present, but he didn't give up. A magazine ad seeking investors got one response—from Captain Anthony F. Lucas, an experienced prospector who also believed that there was oil at Spindletop. When other investors were slow to send money, Higgins kept his faith, not only in Spindletop, but in Lucas.

A PERSONAL VOICE PATTILLO HIGGINS

"**Captain Lucas, . . . these experts come and tell you this or that can't happen because it has never happened before. You believe there is oil here, . . . and I think you are right. I know there is oil here in greater quantities than man has ever found before.**"

—quoted in *Spindletop*

VIDEO

GUSHER!
Pattillo Higgins and the Great Texas Oil Boom

In 1900, the two men found investors, and they began to drill that autumn. After months of difficult, frustrating work, on the morning of January 10, 1901, oil gushed from their well. The Texas oil boom had begun.

Natural Resources Fuel Industrialization

After the Civil War, the United States was still largely an agricultural nation. By the 1920s—a mere 60 years later—it had become the leading industrial power in the world. This immense industrial boom was due to several factors, including: a wealth of natural resources, government support for business, and a growing urban population that provided both cheap labor and markets for new products.

BLACK GOLD Though eastern Native American tribes had made fuel and medicine from crude oil long before Europeans arrived on the continent, early American settlers had little use for oil. In the 1840s, Americans began using kerosene to light lamps after the Canadian geologist Abraham Gesner discovered how to distill the fuel from oil or coal.

It wasn't until 1859, however, when **Edwin L. Drake** successfully used a steam engine to drill for oil near Titusville, Pennsylvania, that removing oil from beneath the earth's surface became practical. This breakthrough started an oil boom that spread to Kentucky, Ohio, Illinois, Indiana, and, later, Texas. Petroleum-refining industries arose in Cleveland and Pittsburgh as entrepreneurs rushed to transform the oil into kerosene. Gasoline, a byproduct of the refining process, originally was thrown away. But after the automobile became popular, gasoline became the most important form of oil.

Vocabulary
entrepreneur: a person who organizes, operates, and assumes the risk for a business venture

BESSEMER STEEL PROCESS Oil was not the only natural resource that was plentiful in the United States. There were also abundant deposits of coal and iron. In 1887, prospectors discovered iron ore deposits more than 100 miles long and up to 3 miles wide in the Mesabi Range of Minnesota. At the same time, coal production skyrocketed—from 33 million tons in 1870 to more than 250 million tons in 1900.

Iron is a dense metal, but it is soft and tends to break and rust. It also usually contains other elements, such as carbon. Removing the carbon from iron produces a lighter, more flexible, and rust-resistant metal—steel. The raw materials needed to make steel were readily available; all that was needed was a cheap and efficient manufacturing process. The **Bessemer process,** developed independently by the British manufacturer Henry Bessemer and American ironmaker William Kelly around 1850, soon became widely used. This technique involved injecting air into molten iron to remove the carbon and other impurities. By 1880, American manufacturers were using the new method to produce more than 90 percent of the nation's steel. In this age of rapid change and innovation, even

Natural Resources and the Birth of a Steel Town, 1886–1906

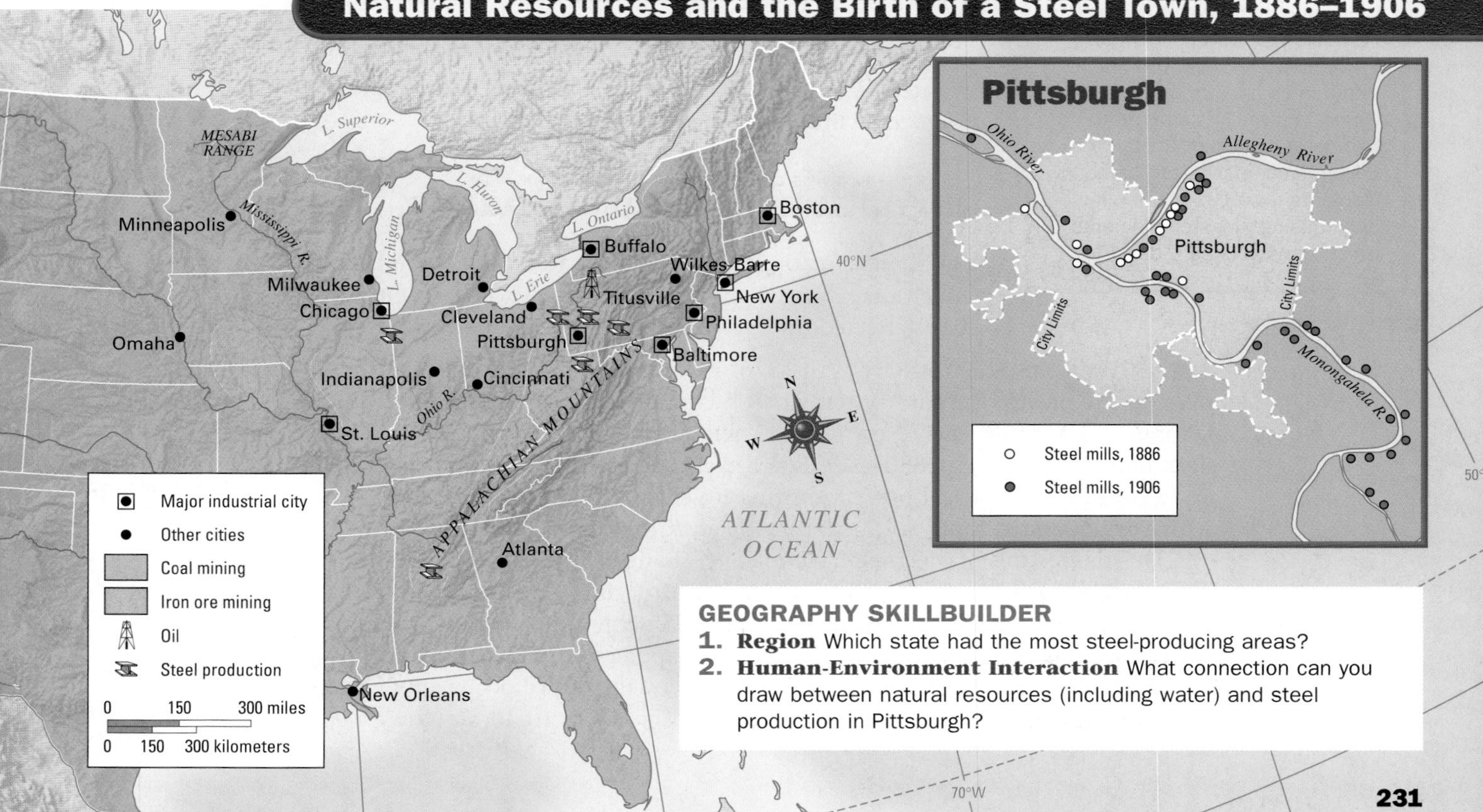

GEOGRAPHY SKILLBUILDER
1. **Region** Which state had the most steel-producing areas?
2. **Human-Environment Interaction** What connection can you draw between natural resources (including water) and steel production in Pittsburgh?

The Technological Explosion, 1826–1903

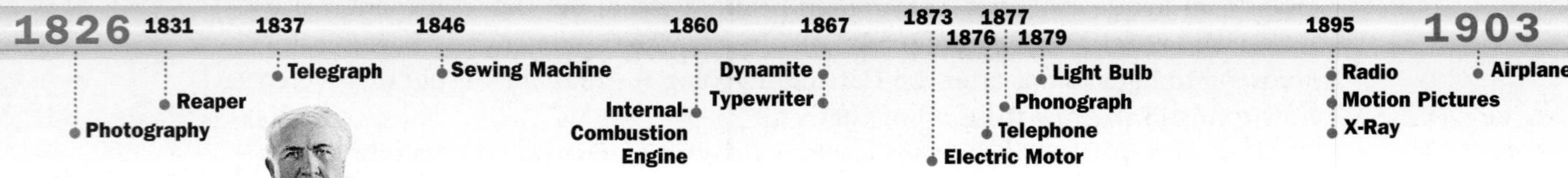

the successful Bessemer process was bettered by the 1860s. It was eventually replaced by the open-hearth process, enabling manufacturers to produce quality steel from scrap metal as well as from raw materials. (A)

MAIN IDEA

Summarizing
(A) What natural resources were most important for industrialization?

NEW USES FOR STEEL The railroads, with thousands of miles of track, became the biggest customers for steel, but inventors soon found additional uses for it. Joseph Glidden's barbed wire and McCormick's and Deere's farm machines helped transform the plains into the food producer of the nation.

Steel changed the face of the nation as well, as it made innovative construction possible. One of the most remarkable structures was the Brooklyn Bridge. Completed in 1883, it spanned 1,595 feet of the East River in New York City. Its steel cables were supported by towers higher than any man-made and weight-bearing structure except the pyramids of Egypt. Like those ancient marvels, the completed bridge was called a wonder of the world.

Around this time, setting the stage for a new era of expansion upward as well as outward, William Le Baron Jenney designed the first skyscraper with a steel frame—the Home Insurance Building in Chicago. Before Jenney had his pioneering idea, the weight of large buildings was supported entirely by their walls or by iron frames, which limited the buildings' height. With a steel frame to support the weight, however, architects could build as high as they wanted. As structures soared into the air, not even the sky seemed to limit what Americans could achieve.

HISTORICAL SPOTLIGHT

ILLUMINATING THE LIGHT BULB

Shortly after moving into a long wooden shed at Menlo Park, Thomas Alva Edison and his associates set to work to develop the perfect incandescent bulb. Arc lamps already lit some city streets and shops, using an electric current passing between two sticks of carbon, but they were glaring and inefficient.

Edison hoped to create a long-lasting lamp with a soft glow, and began searching for a filament that would burn slowly and stay lit. Edison tried wires, sticks, blades of grass, and even hairs from his assistants' beards. Finally, a piece of carbonized bamboo from Japan did the trick. Edison's company used bamboo filaments until 1911, when it began using tungsten filaments, which are still used today.

Inventions Promote Change

By capitalizing on natural resources and their own ingenuity, inventors changed more than the landscape. Their inventions affected the very way people lived and worked.

THE POWER OF ELECTRICITY In 1876, **Thomas Alva Edison** became a pioneer on the new industrial frontier when he established the world's first research laboratory in Menlo Park, New Jersey. There Edison perfected the incandescent light bulb—patented in 1880—and later invented an entire system for producing and distributing electrical power. Another inventor, George Westinghouse, along with Edison, added innovations that made electricity safer and less expensive.

Vocabulary
incandescent: giving off visible light as a result of being heated

The harnessing of electricity completely changed the nature of business in America. By 1890, electric power ran numerous machines, from fans to printing presses. This inexpensive, convenient source of energy soon became available in homes and spurred the invention of time-saving appliances. Electric streetcars made urban travel cheap and efficient and also promoted the outward spread of cities.

More important, electricity allowed manufacturers to locate their plants

MAIN IDEA

Analyzing Effects

B How did electricity change American life?

wherever they wanted—not just near sources of power, such as rivers. This enabled industry to grow as never before. Huge operations, such as the Armour and Swift meatpacking plants, and the efficient processes that they used became the models for new consumer industries. B

INVENTIONS CHANGE LIFESTYLES Edison's light bulb was only one of several revolutionary inventions. **Christopher Sholes** invented the typewriter in 1867 and changed the world of work. Next to the light bulb, however, perhaps the most dramatic invention was the telephone, unveiled by **Alexander Graham Bell** and Thomas Watson in 1876. It opened the way for a worldwide communications network.

▲ The typewriter shown here dates from around 1890.

The typewriter and the telephone particularly affected office work and created new jobs for women. Although women made up less than 5 percent of all office workers in 1870, by 1910 they accounted for nearly 40 percent of the clerical work force. New inventions also had a tremendous impact on factory work, as well as on jobs that traditionally had been done at home. For example, women had previously sewn clothing by hand for their families. With industrialization, clothing could be mass-produced in factories, creating a need for garment workers, many of whom were women.

Industrialization freed some factory workers from backbreaking labor and helped improve workers' standard of living. By 1890, the average workweek had been reduced by about ten hours. However, many laborers felt that the mechanization of so many tasks reduced human workers' worth. As consumers, though, workers regained some of their lost power in the marketplace. The country's expanding urban population provided a vast potential market for the new inventions and products of the late 1800s.

ASSESSMENT

1. **TERMS & NAMES** For each term or name, write a sentence explaining its significance.
   - **Edwin L. Drake**
   - **Bessemer process**
   - **Thomas Alva Edison**
   - **Christopher Sholes**
   - **Alexander Graham Bell**

MAIN IDEA

2. **TAKING NOTES**
   In a chart like the one below, list resources, ideas, and markets that affected the industrial boom of the 19th century. In the second column, note how each item contributed to industrialization.

Resources, Ideas, Markets	Impact

CRITICAL THINKING

3. **MAKING INFERENCES**
   Do you think that consumers gained power as industry expanded in the late 19th century? Why or why not?

4. **HYPOTHESIZING**
   If the U.S. had been poor in natural resources, how would industrialization have been affected?

5. **ANALYZING EFFECTS**
   Which invention or development described in this section had the greatest impact on society? Justify your choice. **Think About:**
   - the applications of inventions
   - the impact of inventions on people's daily lives
   - the effect of inventions on the workplace

GEOGRAPHY SPOTLIGHT

Industry Changes the Environment

By the mid-1870s, new ideas and technology were well on the way to changing almost every aspect of American life. The location of Cleveland, Ohio, on the shores of Lake Erie, gave the city access to raw materials and made it ripe for industrialization. What no one foresaw were the undesirable side effects of rapid development and technological progress.

1 FROM HAYSTACKS TO SMOKESTACKS

In 1874, parts of Cleveland were still rural, with farms like the one pictured dotting the landscape. The smokestacks of the Standard Oil refinery in the distance, however, indicate that industrialization had begun.

2 REFINING THE LANDSCAPE

Industries like the Standard Oil refinery shown in this 1889 photo soon became a source of prosperity for both Cleveland and the entire country. The pollution they belched into the atmosphere, however, was the beginning of an ongoing problem: how to balance industrial production and environmental concerns.

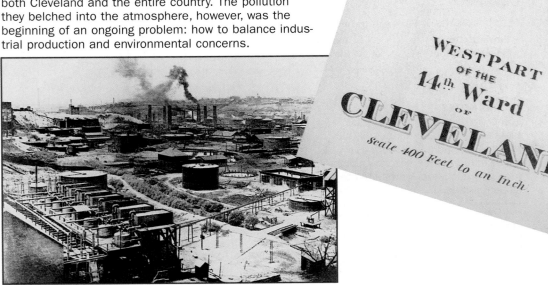

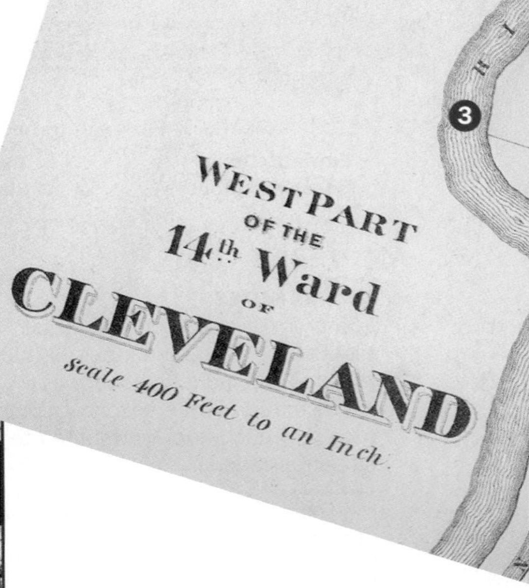

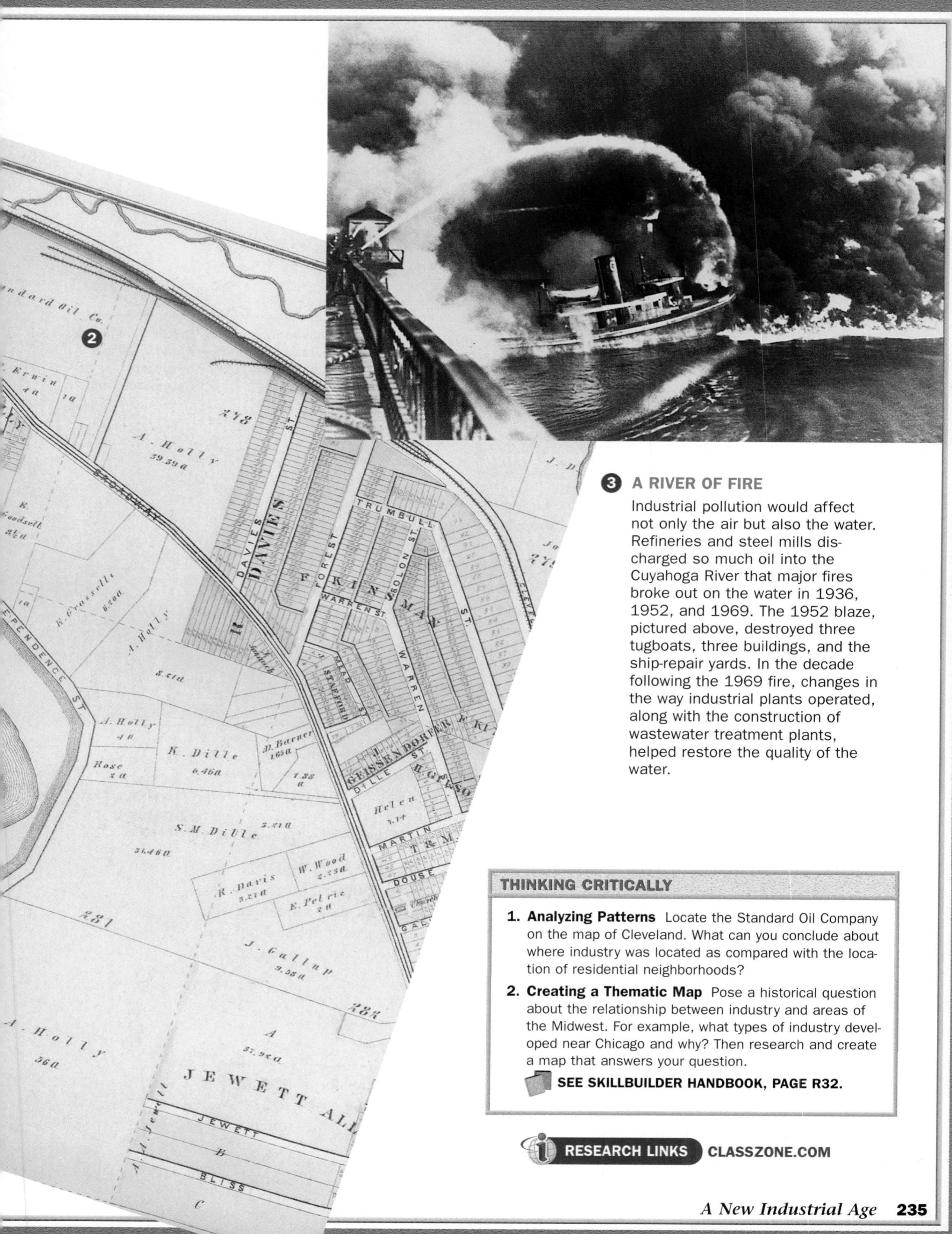

3 A RIVER OF FIRE

Industrial pollution would affect not only the air but also the water. Refineries and steel mills discharged so much oil into the Cuyahoga River that major fires broke out on the water in 1936, 1952, and 1969. The 1952 blaze, pictured above, destroyed three tugboats, three buildings, and the ship-repair yards. In the decade following the 1969 fire, changes in the way industrial plants operated, along with the construction of wastewater treatment plants, helped restore the quality of the water.

THINKING CRITICALLY

1. **Analyzing Patterns** Locate the Standard Oil Company on the map of Cleveland. What can you conclude about where industry was located as compared with the location of residential neighborhoods?
2. **Creating a Thematic Map** Pose a historical question about the relationship between industry and areas of the Midwest. For example, what types of industry developed near Chicago and why? Then research and create a map that answers your question.

SEE SKILLBUILDER HANDBOOK, PAGE R32.

RESEARCH LINKS CLASSZONE.COM

The Age of the Railroads

MAIN IDEA	WHY IT MATTERS NOW	Terms & Names
The growth and consolidation of railroads benefited the nation but also led to corruption and required government regulation.	**Railroads made possible the expansion of industry across the United States.**	**•transcontinental railroad •George M. Pullman •Crédit Mobilier •*Munn* v. *Illinois* •Interstate Commerce Act**

One American's Story

In October 1884, the economist Richard Ely visited the town of Pullman, Illinois, to write about it for *Harper's* magazine. At first, Ely was impressed with the atmosphere of order, planning, and well-being in the town George M. Pullman had designed for the employees of his railroad-car factory. But after talking at length with a dissatisfied company officer, Ely concluded the town had a fatal flaw: it too greatly restricted its residents. Pullman employees were compelled to obey rules in which they had no say. Ely concluded that "the idea of Pullman is un-American."

▲ **The town of Pullman was carefully laid out and strictly controlled.**

A PERSONAL VOICE RICHARD T. ELY

> **"It is benevolent, well-wishing feudalism [a medieval social system], which desires the happiness of the people, but in such way as shall please the authorities. . . . If free American institutions are to be preserved, we want no race of men reared as underlings."**
>
> —"Pullman: A Social Study"

As the railroads grew, they came to influence many facets of American life, including, as in the town of Pullman, the personal lives of the country's citizens. They caused the standard time and time zones to be set and influenced the growth of towns and communities. However, the unchecked power of railroad companies led to widespread abuses that spurred citizens to demand federal regulation of the industry.

Railroads Span Time and Space

Rails made local transit reliable and westward expansion possible for business as well as for people. Realizing how important railroads were for settling the West and developing the country, the government made huge land grants and loans to the railroad companies.

A NATIONAL NETWORK By 1856, the railroads extended west to the Mississippi River, and three years later, they crossed the Missouri. Just over a decade later, crowds across the United States cheered as the Central Pacific and Union Pacific Railroads met at Promontory, Utah, on May 10, 1869. A golden spike marked the spanning of the nation by the first **transcontinental railroad**. Other transcontinental lines followed, and regional lines multiplied as well. At the start of the Civil War, the nation had had about 30,000 miles of track. By 1890, that figure was nearly six times greater.

ROMANCE AND REALITY The railroads brought the dreams of available land, adventure, and a fresh start within the grasp of many Americans. This romance was made possible, however, only by the harsh lives of railroad workers.

The Central Pacific Railroad employed thousands of Chinese immigrants. The Union Pacific hired Irish immigrants and desperate, out-of-work Civil War veterans to lay track across treacherous terrain while enduring attacks by Native Americans. Accidents and diseases disabled and killed thousands of men each year. In 1888, when the first railroad statistics were published, the casualties totaled more than 2,000 employees killed and 20,000 injured.

RAILROAD TIME In spite of these difficult working conditions, the railroad laborers helped to transform the diverse regions of the country into a united nation. Though linked in space, each community still operated on its own time, with noon when the sun was directly overhead. Noon in Boston, for example, was almost 12 minutes later than noon in New York. Travelers riding from Maine to California might reset their watches 20 times.

In 1869, to remedy this problem, Professor C. F. Dowd proposed that the earth's surface be divided into 24 time zones, one for each hour of the day. Under his plan, the United States would contain four zones: the Eastern, Central, Mountain, and Pacific time zones. The railroad companies endorsed Dowd's plan enthusiastically, and many towns followed suit.

Finally, on November 18, 1883, railroad crews and towns across the country synchronized their watches. In 1884, an international conference set worldwide time zones that incorporated railroad time. The U.S. Congress, however, didn't officially adopt railroad time as the standard for the nation until 1918. As strong a unifying force as the railroads were, however, they also opened the way for abuses that led to social and economic unrest. (A)

MAIN IDEA

Analyzing Effects

(A) What were the effects of railroad expansion?

HISTORICAL SPOTLIGHT

CHINESE IMMIGRANTS AND THE RAILROADS

Although the railroads paid all their employees poorly, Asians usually earned less than whites. The average pay for whites working a ten-hour day was $40 to $60 a month plus free meals. Chinese immigrants hired by the Central Pacific performed similar tasks from dawn to dusk for about $35 a month—and they had to supply their own food.

The immigrants' working conditions were miserable, as depicted by artist Jake Lee below. In 1866, for example, the railroad hired them to dig a tunnel through a granite mountain. For five months of that year, the Chinese lived and worked in camps surrounded by banks of snow. The total snowfall reached over 40 feet. Hundreds of the men were buried in avalanches or later found frozen, still clutching their shovels or picks.

Opportunities and Opportunists

The growth of the railroads influenced the industries and businesses in which Americans worked. Iron, coal, steel, lumber, and glass industries grew rapidly as they tried to keep pace with the railroads' demand for materials and parts. The rapid spread of railroad lines also fostered the growth of towns, helped establish new markets, and offered rich opportunities for both visionaries and profiteers.

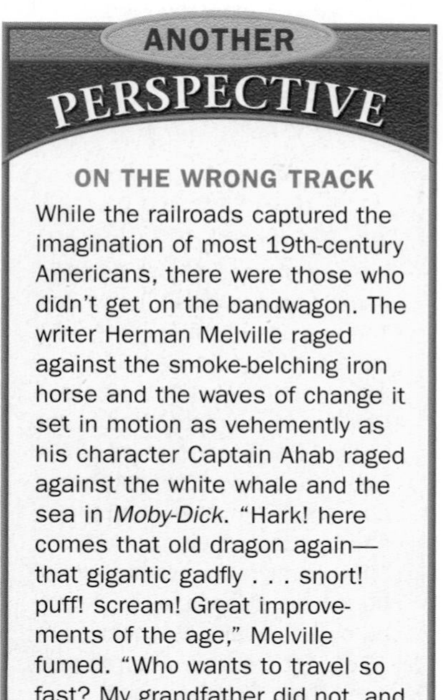

ANOTHER PERSPECTIVE

ON THE WRONG TRACK

While the railroads captured the imagination of most 19th-century Americans, there were those who didn't get on the bandwagon. The writer Herman Melville raged against the smoke-belching iron horse and the waves of change it set in motion as vehemently as his character Captain Ahab raged against the white whale and the sea in *Moby-Dick*. "Hark! here comes that old dragon again—that gigantic gadfly . . . snort! puff! scream! Great improvements of the age," Melville fumed. "Who wants to travel so fast? My grandfather did not, and he was no fool."

NEW TOWNS AND MARKETS By linking previously isolated cities, towns, and settlements, the railroads promoted trade and interdependence. As part of a nationwide network of suppliers and markets, individual towns began to specialize in particular products. Chicago soon became known for its stockyards and Minneapolis for its grain industries. These cities prospered by selling large quantities of their products to the entire country. New towns and communities also grew up along the railroad lines. Cities as diverse as Abilene, Kansas; Flagstaff, Arizona; Denver, Colorado; and Seattle, Washington, owed their prosperity, if not their very existence, to the railroads. (B)

MAIN IDEA

Summarizing
(B) How did the railroads affect cities?

PULLMAN The railroads helped cities not only grow up but branch out. In 1880, for example, **George M. Pullman** built a factory for manufacturing sleepers and other railroad cars on the Illinois prairie. The nearby town that Pullman built for his employees followed in part the models of earlier industrial experiments in Europe. Whereas New England textile manufacturers had traditionally provided housing for their workers, the town of Pullman provided for almost all of workers' basic needs. Pullman residents lived in clean, well-constructed brick houses and apartment buildings with at least one window in every room—a luxury for city dwellers. In addition, the town offered services and facilities such as doctors' offices, shops, and an athletic field.

As Richard Ely observed, however, the town of Pullman remained firmly under company control. Residents were not allowed to loiter on their front steps or to drink alcohol. Pullman hoped that his tightly controlled environment would ensure a stable work force. However, Pullman's refusal to lower rents after cutting his employees' pay led to a violent strike in 1894.

CRÉDIT MOBILIER Pullman created his company town out of the desire for control and profit. In some other railroad magnates, or powerful and influential industrialists, these desires turned into self-serving corruption. In one of the most infamous schemes, stockholders in the Union Pacific Railroad formed, in 1864, a construction company called **Crédit Mobilier** (krĕd′ĭt mō-bēl′yər). The stockholders gave this company a contract to lay track at two to three times the actual cost—and pocketed the profits. They donated shares of stock to about 20 representatives in Congress in 1867.

Pullman cars brought luxury to the rails, as shown in this advertisement from around 1890. ▼

A congressional investigation of the company, spurred by reports in the *New York Sun*, eventually found that the officers of the Union Pacific had taken up to $23 million in stocks, bonds, and cash. Testimony implicated such well-known and respected federal officials as Vice-President Schuyler Colfax and Congressman James Garfield, who later became president. Although these public figures kept their profits and received little more than a slap on the wrist, the reputation of the Republican Party was tarnished. (C)

MAIN IDEA

Summarizing
(C) How did railroad owners use Crédit Mobilier to make huge, undeserved profits?

The Grange and the Railroads

Farmers were especially disturbed by what they viewed as railroad corruption. The Grangers—members of the Grange, a farmers' organization founded in 1867—began demanding governmental control over the railroad industry.

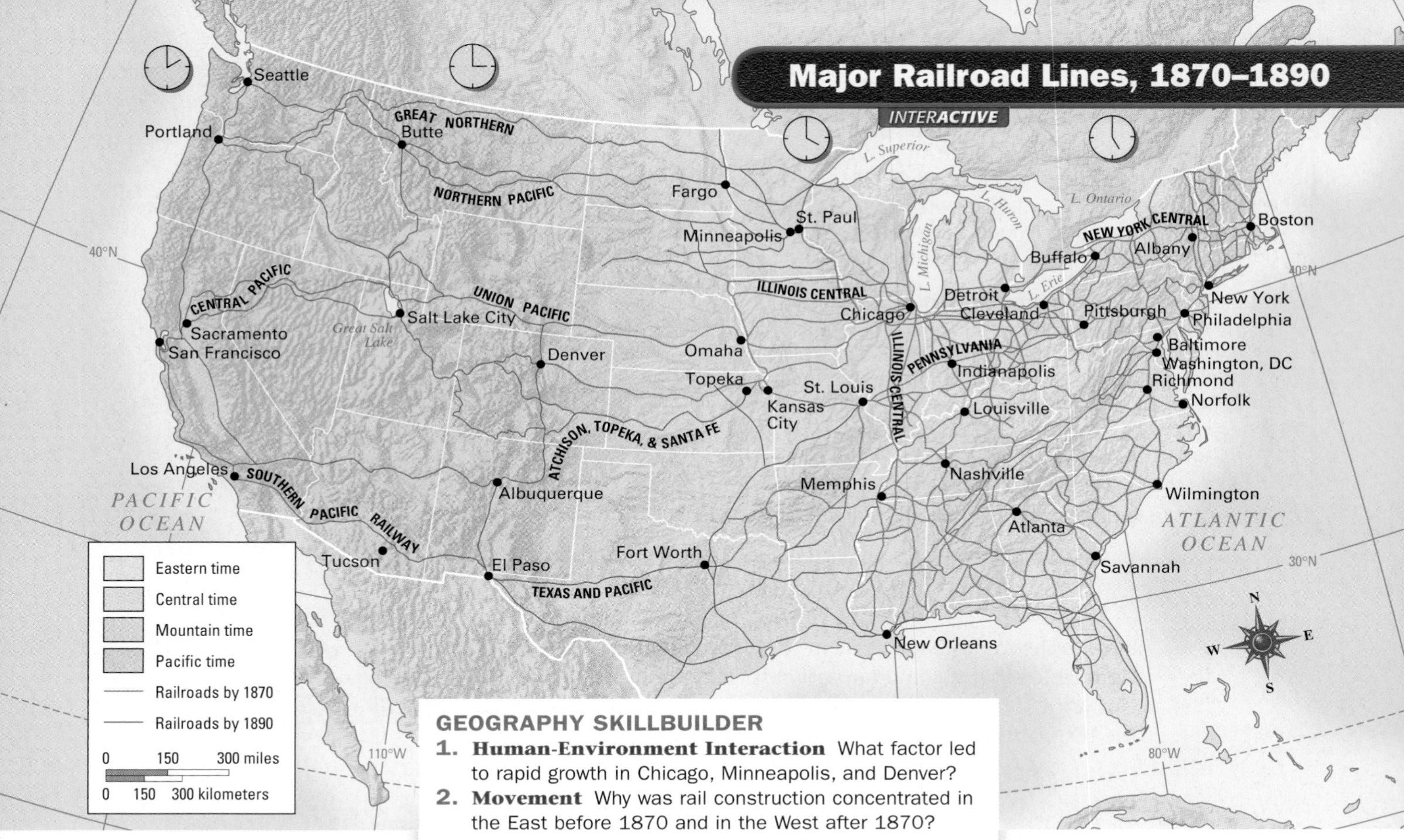

GEOGRAPHY SKILLBUILDER

1. **Human-Environment Interaction** What factor led to rapid growth in Chicago, Minneapolis, and Denver?
2. **Movement** Why was rail construction concentrated in the East before 1870 and in the West after 1870?

Background
Price fixing occurs when companies within an industry all agree to charge the same price for a given service, rather than competing to offer the lowest price.

RAILROAD ABUSES Farmers were angry with railroad companies for a host of reasons. They were upset by misuse of government land grants, which the railroads sold to other businesses rather than to settlers, as the government intended. The railroads also entered into formal agreements to fix prices, which helped keep farmers in their debt. In addition, they charged different customers different rates, often demanding more for short hauls—for which there was no alternative carrier—than they did for long hauls.

GRANGER LAWS In response to these abuses by the railroads, the Grangers took political action. They sponsored state and local political candidates, elected legislators, and successfully pressed for laws to protect their interests. In 1871 Illinois authorized a commission "to establish maximum freight and passenger rates and prohibit discrimination." Grangers throughout the West, Midwest, and Southeast convinced state legislators to pass similar laws, called Granger laws.

The railroads fought back, challenging the constitutionality of the regulatory laws. In 1877, however, in the case of ***Munn* v. *Illinois,*** the Supreme Court upheld the Granger laws by a vote of seven to two. The states thus won the right to regulate the railroads for the benefit of farmers and consumers. The Grangers also helped establish an important principle—the federal government's right to regulate private industry to serve the public interest. D

MAIN IDEA

Analyzing Issues
D How did the Grangers, who were largely poor farmers, do battle with the giant railroad companies?

INTERSTATE COMMERCE ACT The Grangers' triumph was short-lived, however. In 1886, the Supreme Court ruled that a state could not set rates on interstate commerce—railroad traffic that either came from or was going to another state. In response to public outrage, Congress passed the **Interstate Commerce Act** in 1887. This act established the right of the federal government to supervise railroad activities and established a five-member Interstate Commerce Commission (ICC) for that purpose. The ICC had difficulty regulating railroad rates because of a long legal process and resistance from the railroads. The final

Analyzing *Political Cartoons*

"THE MODERN COLOSSUS OF (RAIL) ROADS"

Joseph Keppler drew this cartoon in 1879, featuring the railroad "giants" William Vanderbilt (top), Jay Gould (bottom right), and Cyrus W. Fields (bottom left). The three magnates formed a railroad trust out of their Union Pacific, New York Central, and Lake Shore & Dependence lines.

SKILLBUILDER Analyzing Political Cartoons

1. The title of this cartoon is a pun on the Colossus of Rhodes, a statue erected in 282 B.C. on an island near Greece. According to legend, the 100-foot-tall statue straddled Rhodes's harbor entrance. Do you think the artist means the comparison as a compliment or a criticism? Why?
2. The reins held by the railroad magnates attach not only to the trains but also to the tracks and the railroad station. What does this convey about the magnates' control of the railroads?

 **SEE SKILLBUILDER HANDBOOK, PAGE R24.**

blow to the commission came in 1897, when the Supreme Court ruled that it could not set maximum railroad rates. Not until 1906, under President Theodore Roosevelt, did the ICC gain the power it needed to be effective.

PANIC AND CONSOLIDATION Although the ICC presented few problems for the railroads, corporate abuses, mismanagement, overbuilding, and competition pushed many railroads to the brink of bankruptcy. Their financial problems played a major role in a nationwide economic collapse. The panic of 1893 was the worst depression up to that time: by the end of 1893, around 600 banks and 15,000 businesses had failed, and by 1895, 4 million people had lost their jobs. By the middle of 1894, a quarter of the nation's railroads had been taken over by financial companies. Large investment firms such as J. P. Morgan & Company reorganized the railroads. As the 20th century dawned, seven powerful companies held sway over two-thirds of the nation's railroad tracks.

Vocabulary
consolidation: the act of uniting or combining

SECTION 2 ASSESSMENT

1. **TERMS & NAMES** For each term or name, write a sentence explaining its significance.
   - **transcontinental railroad**
   - **George M. Pullman**
   - **Crédit Mobilier**
   - ***Munn* v. *Illinois***
   - **Interstate Commerce Act**

MAIN IDEA

2. **TAKING NOTES**
   In a chart like the one below, fill in effects of the rapid growth of railroads.

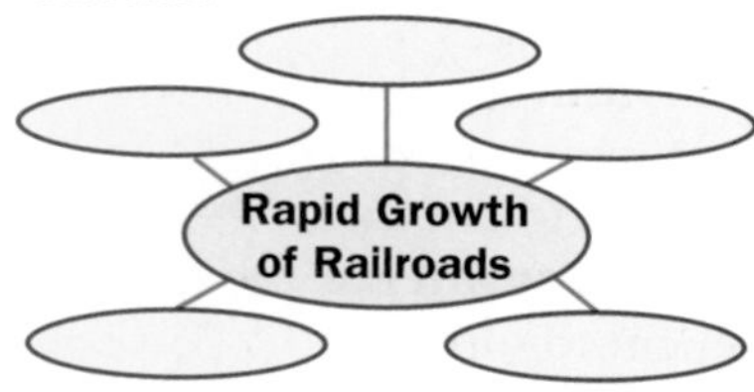

How did the growth of railroads affect people's everyday lives? How did it affect farmers?

CRITICAL THINKING

3. **MAKING INFERENCES**
   Do you think the government and private citizens could have done more to curb the corruption and power of the railroads? Give examples to support your opinion.
   Think About:
   - why the railroads had power
   - the rights of railroad customers and workers
   - the scope of government regulations
4. **SYNTHESIZING**
   The federal government gave land and made loans to the railroad companies. Why was the government so eager to promote the growth of railroads?
5. **ANALYZING MOTIVES**
   Reread "Another Perspective" on railroads (page 238). Why do you think that some Americans disliked this new means of transportation?

SECTION 3

Big Business and Labor

MAIN IDEA

The expansion of industry resulted in the growth of big business and prompted laborers to form unions to better their lives.

WHY IT MATTERS NOW

Many of the strategies used today in industry and in the labor movement, such as consolidation and the strike, have their origins in the late 19th century.

Terms & Names

- **Andrew Carnegie**
- **vertical and horizontal integration**
- **Social Darwinism**
- **John D. Rockefeller**
- **Sherman Antitrust Act**
- **Samuel Gompers**
- **American Federation of Labor (AFL)**
- **Eugene V. Debs**
- **Industrial Workers of the World (IWW)**
- **Mary Harris Jones**

One American's Story

Born in Scotland to penniless parents, **Andrew Carnegie** came to this country in 1848, at age 12. Six years later, he worked his way up to become private secretary to the local superintendent of the Pennsylvania Railroad. One morning, Carnegie single-handedly relayed messages that unsnarled a tangle of freight and passenger trains. His boss, Thomas A. Scott, rewarded Carnegie by giving him a chance to buy stock. Carnegie's mother mortgaged the family home to make the purchase possible. Soon Carnegie received his first dividend.

▲ Nineteenth-century industrialist Andrew Carnegie gave money to build public libraries, hoping to help others write their own rags-to-riches story.

A PERSONAL VOICE ANDREW CARNEGIE

> **"One morning a white envelope was lying upon my desk, addressed in a big John Hancock hand, to 'Andrew Carnegie, Esquire.' . . . All it contained was a check for ten dollars upon the Gold Exchange Bank of New York. I shall remember that check as long as I live. . . . It gave me the first penny of revenue from capital—something that I had not worked for with the sweat of my brow. 'Eureka!' I cried. 'Here's the goose that lays the golden eggs.'"**
>
> —*Autobiography of Andrew Carnegie*

Andrew Carnegie was one of the first industrial moguls to make his own fortune. His rise from rags to riches, along with his passion for supporting charities, made him a model of the American success story.

Carnegie's Innovations

By 1865, Carnegie was so busy managing the money he had earned in dividends that he happily left his job at the Pennsylvania Railroad. He entered the steel business in 1873 after touring a British steel mill and witnessing the awesome spectacle of the Bessemer process in action. By 1899, the Carnegie Steel Company

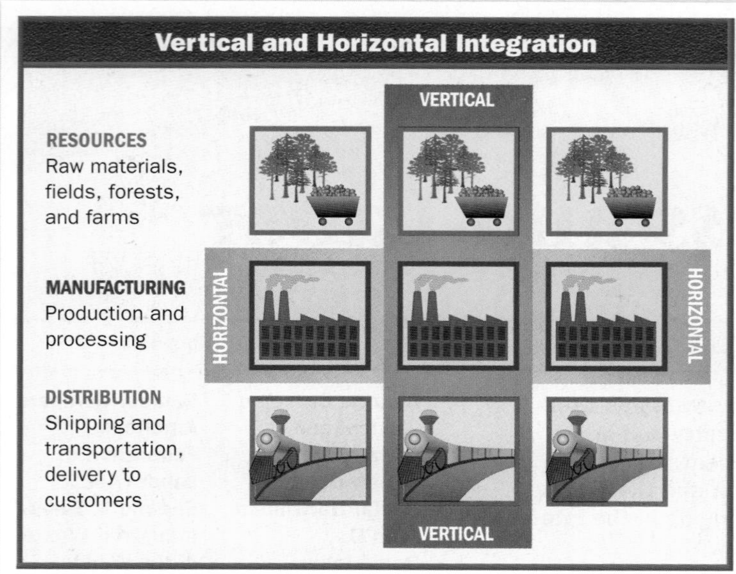

manufactured more steel than all the factories in Great Britain.

NEW BUSINESS STRATEGIES Carnegie's success was due in part to management practices that he initiated and that soon became widespread. First, he continually searched for ways to make better products more cheaply. He incorporated new machinery and techniques, such as accounting systems that enabled him to track precise costs. Second, he attracted talented people by offering them stock in the company, and he encouraged competition among his assistants.

In addition to improving his own manufacturing operation, Carnegie attempted to control as much of the steel industry as he could. He did this mainly by **vertical integration,** a process in which he bought out his suppliers—coal fields and iron mines, ore freighters, and railroad lines—in order to control the raw materials and transportation systems. Carnegie also attempted to buy out competing steel producers. In this process, known as **horizontal integration,** companies producing similar products merge. Having gained control over his suppliers and having limited his competition, Carnegie controlled almost the entire steel industry. By the time he sold his business in 1901, Carnegie's companies produced by far the largest portion of the nation's steel. (A)

MAIN IDEA

Summarizing
(A) What were Andrew Carnegie's management and business strategies?

Social Darwinism and Business

Andrew Carnegie explained his extraordinary success by pointing to his hard work, shrewd investments, and innovative business practices. Late-19th-century social philosophers offered a different explanation for Carnegie's success. They said it could be explained scientifically by a new theory—Social Darwinism.

PRINCIPLES OF SOCIAL DARWINISM The philosophy called **Social Darwinism** grew out of the English naturalist Charles Darwin's theory of biological evolution. In his book *On the Origin of Species*, published in 1859, Darwin described his observations that some individuals of a species flourish and pass their traits along to the next generation, while others do not. He explained that a process of "natural selection" weeded out less-suited individuals and enabled the best-adapted to survive.

The English philosopher Herbert Spencer used Darwin's biological theories to explain the evolution of human society. Soon, economists found in Social Darwinism a way to justify the doctrine of laissez faire (a French term meaning "allow to do"). According to this doctrine, the marketplace should not be regulated. William G. Sumner, a political science professor at Yale University, promoted the theory that success and failure in business were governed by natural law and that no one had the right to intervene.

Popular literature promoted the possibility of rags-to-riches success for anyone who was virtuous and hard-working. ▼

A NEW DEFINITION OF SUCCESS The premise of the survival and success of the most capable naturally made sense to the 4,000 millionaires who had emerged since the Civil War. Because the theory supported the notion of individual responsibility and blame, it also appealed to the Protestant work ethic of many Americans. According to Social Darwinism, riches were a sign of God's favor, and therefore the poor must be lazy or inferior people who deserved their lot in life.

Fewer Control More

Although some business owners endorsed the "natural law" in theory, in practice most entrepreneurs did everything they could to control the competition that threatened the growth of their business empires.

GROWTH AND CONSOLIDATION Many industrialists took the approach "If you can't beat 'em, join 'em." They often pursued horizontal integration in the form of mergers. A merger usually occurred when one corporation bought out the stock of another. A firm that bought out all its competitors could achieve a monopoly, or complete control over its industry's production, wages, and prices.

Background
See *monopoly* on page R43 in the Economics Handbook.

One way to create a monopoly was to set up a holding company, a corporation that did nothing but buy out the stock of other companies. Headed by banker J. P. Morgan, United States Steel was one of the most successful holding companies. In 1901, when it bought the largest manufacturer, Carnegie Steel, it became the world's largest business.

Corporations such as the Standard Oil Company, established by **John D. Rockefeller,** took a different approach to mergers: they joined with competing companies in trust agreements. Participants in a trust turned their stock over to a group of trustees—people who ran the separate companies as one large corporation. In return, the companies were entitled to dividends on profits earned by the trust. Trusts were not legal mergers, however. Rockefeller used a trust to gain total control of the oil industry in America. B

MAIN IDEA
Summarizing
B What strategies enabled big businesses to eliminate competition?

ROCKEFELLER AND THE "ROBBER BARONS" In 1870, Rockefeller's Standard Oil Company of Ohio processed two or three percent of the country's crude oil. Within a decade, it controlled 90 percent of the refining business. Rockefeller reaped huge profits by paying his employees extremely low wages and driving his competitors out of business by selling his oil at a lower price than it cost to produce it. Then, when he controlled the market, he hiked prices far above original levels.

Alarmed at the tactics of industrialists, critics began to call them robber barons. But industrialists were also philanthropists. Although Rockefeller kept most of his assets, he still gave away over $500 million, establishing the Rockefeller Foundation, providing funds to found the University of Chicago, and creating a medical institute that helped find a cure for yellow fever.

KEY PLAYER

JOHN D. ROCKEFELLER
1839–1937

At the height of John Davison Rockefeller's power, an associate noted that he "always sees a little farther than the rest of us—and then he sees around the corner."

Rockefeller's father was a flashy peddler of phony cancer cures with a unique approach to raising children. "I cheat my boys every chance I get. . . . I want to make 'em sharp," he boasted.

It seems that this approach succeeded with the oldest son, John D., who was sharp enough to land a job as an assistant bookkeeper at the age of 16. Rockefeller was very proud of his own son, who succeeded him in the family business. At the end of his life, Rockefeller referred not to his millions but to John D., Jr., as "my greatest fortune."

This 1900 cartoon, captioned "What a funny little government!" is a commentary on the power of the Standard Oil empire. John D. Rockefeller holds the White House in his hand.

Andrew Carnegie donated about 90 percent of the wealth he accumulated during his lifetime; his fortune still supports the arts and learning today. "It will be a great mistake for the community to shoot the millionaires," he said, "for they are the bees that make the most honey, and contribute most to the hive even after they have gorged themselves full." C

SHERMAN ANTITRUST ACT Despite Carnegie's defense of millionaires, the government was concerned that expanding corporations would stifle free competition. In 1890, the **Sherman Antitrust Act** made it illegal to form a trust that interfered with free trade between states or with other countries.

Prosecuting companies under the Sherman act was not easy, however, because the act didn't clearly define terms such as *trust*. In addition, if firms such as Standard Oil felt pressure from the government, they simply reorganized into single corporations. The Supreme Court threw out seven of the eight cases the federal government brought against trusts. Eventually, the government stopped trying to enforce the Sherman act, and the consolidation of businesses continued.

MAIN IDEA

Evaluating

C Do you agree with Carnegie's defense of millionaires? Why or why not?

BUSINESS BOOM BYPASSES THE SOUTH Industrial growth concentrated in the North, where natural and urban resources were plentiful. The South was still trying to recover from the Civil War, hindered by a lack of capital—money for investment. After the war, people were unwilling to invest in risky ventures. Northern businesses already owned 90 percent of the stock in the most profitable Southern enterprise, the railroads, thereby keeping the South in a stranglehold. The South remained mostly agricultural, with farmers at the mercy of railroad rates. Entrepreneurs suffered not only from excessive transportation costs, but also from high tariffs on raw materials and imported goods, and from a lack of skilled workers. The post-Reconstruction South seemed to have no way out of economic stagnation. However, growth in forestry and mining, and in the tobacco, furniture, and textile industries, offered hope. D

MAIN IDEA

Synthesizing

D How did economic factors limit industrialization in the South?

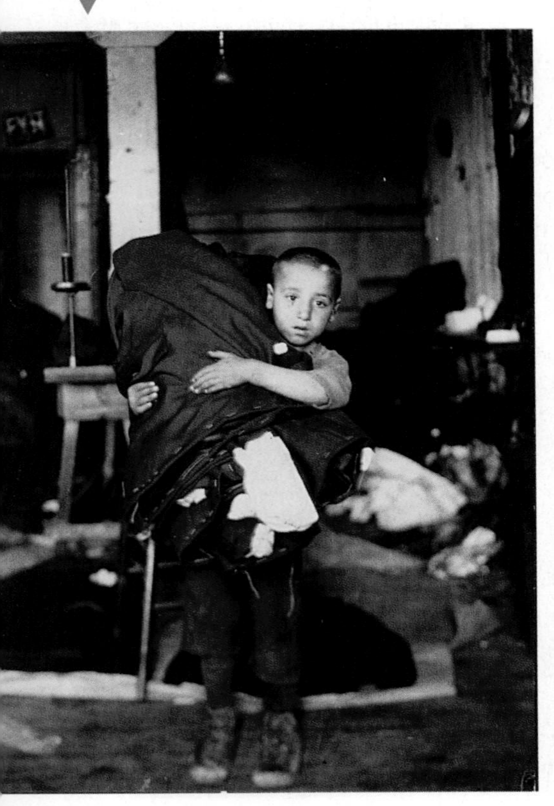

In this photograph, taken by Lewis Hine in 1912, a young sweatshop laborer in New York City carries piecework home.

Labor Unions Emerge

As business leaders merged and consolidated their forces, it seemed necessary for workers to do the same. Although Northern wages were generally higher than Southern wages, exploitation and unsafe working conditions drew workers together across regions in a nationwide labor movement. Laborers—skilled and unskilled, female and male, black and white—joined together in unions to try to improve their lot.

LONG HOURS AND DANGER One of the largest employers, the steel mills, often demanded a seven-day workweek. Seamstresses, like factory workers in most industries, worked 12 or more hours a day, six days a week. Employees were not entitled to vacation, sick leave, unemployment compensation, or reimbursement for injuries suffered on the job.

Yet injuries were common. In dirty, poorly ventilated factories, workers had to perform repetitive, mind-dulling tasks, sometimes with dangerous or faulty equipment. In 1882, an average of 675 laborers were killed in work-related accidents each week. In addition, wages were so low that most families could not survive unless everyone held a job. Between 1890 and 1910, for example, the number of women working for wages doubled, from 4 million to more than 8 million. Twenty percent of the boys and 10 percent of the girls under age 15—some as young as five years old—also held full-time jobs. With little time or energy left for school, child laborers forfeited their futures to help their families make ends meet.

In sweatshops, or workshops in tenements rather than in factories, workers had little choice but to put up with the conditions. Sweatshop employment, which was tedious and required few skills, was often the only avenue open to women and children. Jacob Riis described the conditions faced by "sweaters."

A PERSONAL VOICE JACOB RIIS

"The bulk of the sweater's work is done in the tenements, which the law that regulates factory labor does not reach. . . . In [them] the child works unchallenged from the day he is old enough to pull a thread. There is no such thing as a dinner hour; men and women eat while they work, and the 'day' is lengthened at both ends far into the night."

—*How the Other Half Lives*

Not surprisingly, sweatshop jobs paid the lowest wages—often as little as 27 cents for a child's 14-hour day. In 1899, women earned an average of $267 a year, nearly half of men's average pay of $498. The very next year Andrew Carnegie made $23 million—with no income tax.

EARLY LABOR ORGANIZING Skilled workers had formed small, local unions since the late 1700s. The first large-scale national organization of laborers, the National Labor Union (NLU), was formed in 1866 by ironworker William H. Sylvis. The refusal of some NLU local chapters to admit African Americans led to the creation of the Colored National Labor Union (CNLU). Nevertheless, NLU membership grew to 640,000. In 1868, the NLU persuaded Congress to legalize an eight-hour day for government workers. E

NLU organizers concentrated on linking existing local unions. In 1869, Uriah Stephens focused his attention on individual workers and organized the Noble Order of the Knights of Labor. Its motto was "An injury to one is the concern of all." Membership in the Knights of Labor was officially open to all workers, regardless of race, gender, or degree of skill. Like the NLU, the Knights supported an eight-hour workday and advocated "equal pay for equal work" by men and women. They saw strikes, or refusals to work, as a last resort and instead advocated arbitration. At its height in 1886, the Knights of Labor had about 700,000 members. Although the Knights declined after the failure of a series of strikes, other unions continued to organize.

MAIN IDEA

Analyzing Issues

E How did industrial working conditions contribute to the growth of the labor movement?

Vocabulary

arbitration: a method of settling disputes in which both sides submit their differences to a mutually approved judge

Union Movements Diverge

As labor activism spread, it diversified. Two major types of unions made great gains under forceful leaders.

CRAFT UNIONISM One approach to the organization of labor was craft unionism, which included skilled workers from one or more trades. **Samuel Gompers** led the Cigar Makers' International Union to join with other craft unions in 1886. The **American Federation of Labor (AFL),**

HISTORICAL SPOTLIGHT

AFRICAN AMERICANS AND THE LABOR MOVEMENT

Angered by their exclusion from the NLU, African American laborers formed the Colored National Labor Union (CNLU) in 1869. Led by Isaac Meyers, a caulker from Baltimore, the CNLU emphasized cooperation between management and labor and the importance of political reform.

The CNLU disbanded in the early 1870s, but many African-American laborers found a home in the Knights of Labor, the first union to welcome blacks and whites alike. The Great Strike of 1877 brought whites and African Americans together, but the labor movement remained largely divided along racial lines.

Management often hired African Americans as strikebreakers, which intensified white unions' resistance to accepting blacks. African Americans continued to organize on their own, but discrimination and their small numbers relative to white unions hurt black unions' effectiveness.

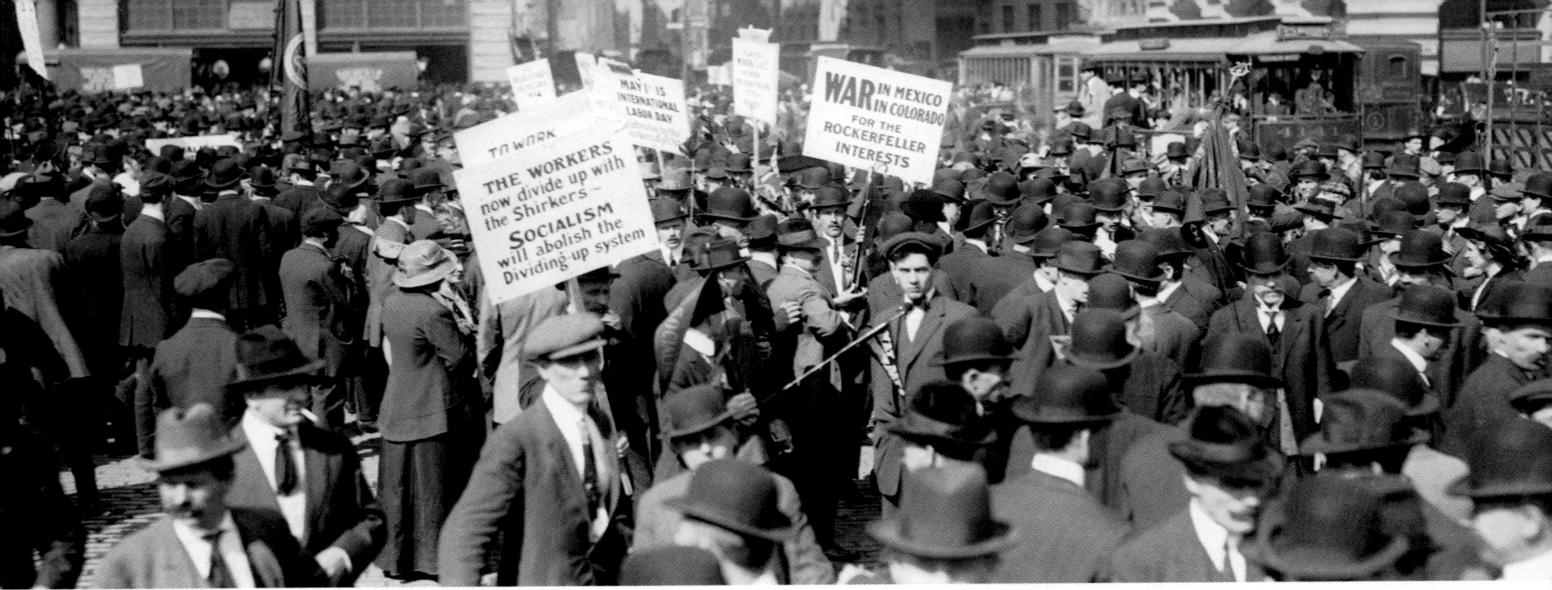

▲ **In New York City's Union Square in 1914, IWW members protest violence against striking coal miners in Colorado.**

with Gompers as its president, focused on collective bargaining, or negotiation between representatives of labor and management, to reach written agreements on wages, hours, and working conditions. Unlike the Knights of Labor, the AFL used strikes as a major tactic. Successful strikes helped the AFL win higher wages and shorter workweeks. Between 1890 and 1915, the average weekly wages in unionized industries rose from $17.50 to $24, and the average workweek fell from almost 54.5 hours to just under 49 hours.

INDUSTRIAL UNIONISM Some labor leaders felt that unions should include all laborers—skilled and unskilled—in a specific industry. This concept captured the imagination of **Eugene V. Debs,** who attempted to form such an industrial union—the American Railway Union (ARU). Most of the new union's members were unskilled and semiskilled laborers, but skilled engineers and firemen joined too. In 1894, the new union won a strike for higher wages. Within two months, its membership climbed to 150,000, dwarfing the 90,000 enrolled in the four skilled railroad brotherhoods. Though the ARU, like the Knights of Labor, never recovered after the failure of a major strike, it added to the momentum of union organizing. F

"The strike is the weapon of the oppressed."
EUGENE V. DEBS

MAIN IDEA

Contrasting
F How did craft unions and industrial unions differ?

Background
See *socialism* on page R44 in the Economics Handbook.

SOCIALISM AND THE IWW In an attempt to solve the problems faced by workers, Eugene Debs and some other labor activists eventually turned to socialism, an economic and political system based on government control of business and property and equal distribution of wealth. Socialism, carried to its extreme form—communism, as advocated by the German philosopher Karl Marx—would result in the overthrow of the capitalist system. Most socialists in late-19th-century America drew back from this goal, however, and worked within the labor movement to achieve better conditions for workers. In 1905, a group of radical unionists and socialists in Chicago organized the **Industrial Workers of the World (IWW),** or the Wobblies. Headed by William "Big Bill" Haywood, the Wobblies included miners, lumberers, and cannery and dock workers. Unlike the ARU, the IWW welcomed African Americans, but membership never topped 100,000. Its only major strike victory occurred in 1912. Yet the Wobblies, like other industrial unions, gave dignity and a sense of solidarity to unskilled workers.

OTHER LABOR ACTIVISM IN THE WEST In April 1903, about 1,000 Japanese and Mexican workers organized a successful strike in the sugar-beet fields of Ventura County, California. They formed the Sugar Beet and Farm Laborers' Union of Oxnard. In Wyoming, the State Federation of Labor supported a union of Chinese and Japanese miners who sought the same wages and treatment as other union miners. These small, independent unions increased both the overall strength of the labor movement and the tension between labor and management.

Strikes Turn Violent

Industry and government responded forcefully to union activity, which they saw as a threat to the entire capitalist system.

THE GREAT STRIKE OF 1877 In July 1877, workers for the Baltimore and Ohio Railroad (B&O) struck to protest their second wage cut in two months. The work stoppage spread to other lines. Most freight and even some passenger traffic, covering over 50,000 miles, was stopped for more than a week. After several state governors asked President Rutherford B. Hayes to intervene, saying that the strikers were impeding interstate commerce, federal troops ended the strike.

THE HAYMARKET AFFAIR Encouraged by the impact of the 1877 strike, labor leaders continued to press for change. On the evening of May 4, 1886, 3,000 people gathered at Chicago's Haymarket Square to protest police brutality—a striker had been killed and several had been wounded at the McCormick Harvester plant the day before. Rain began to fall at about 10 o'clock, and the crowd was dispersing when police arrived. Then someone tossed a bomb into the police line. Police fired on the workers; seven police officers and several workers died in the chaos that followed. No one ever learned who threw the bomb, but the three speakers at the demonstration and five other radicals were charged with inciting a riot. All eight were convicted; four were hanged and one committed suicide in prison. After Haymarket, the public began to turn against the labor movement. G

MAIN IDEA

Analyzing Causes

G How did the 1877 strike and Haymarket cause the public to resent the labor movement?

THE HOMESTEAD STRIKE Despite the violence and rising public anger, workers continued to strike. The writer Hamlin Garland described conditions at the Carnegie Steel Company's Homestead plant in Pennsylvania.

A PERSONAL VOICE HAMLIN GARLAND

> **"Everywhere . . . groups of pale, lean men slouched in faded garments, grimy with the soot and grease of the mills. . . . A roar as of a hundred lions, a thunder as of cannons, . . . jarring clang of falling iron . . . !"**
>
> —quoted in *McClure's Magazine*

The steelworkers finally called a strike on June 29, 1892, after the company president, Henry Clay Frick, announced his plan to cut wages. Frick hired armed

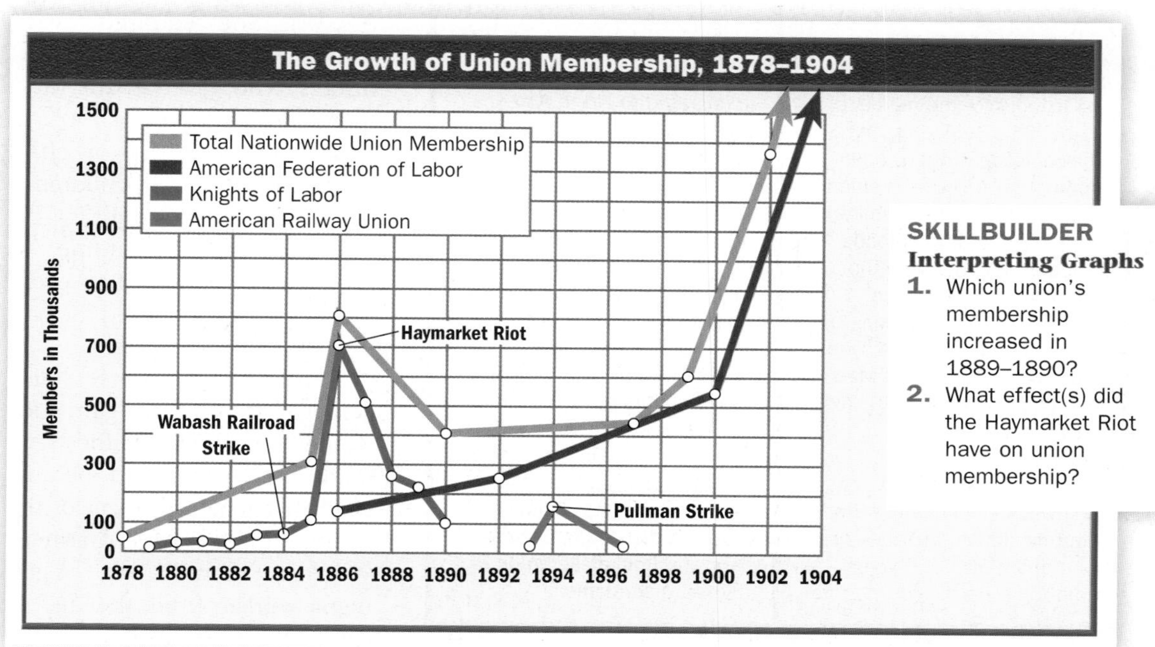

SKILLBUILDER
Interpreting Graphs
1. Which union's membership increased in 1889–1890?
2. What effect(s) did the Haymarket Riot have on union membership?

guards from the Pinkerton Detective Agency to protect the plant so that he could hire scabs, or strikebreakers, to keep it operating. In a pitched battle that left at least three detectives and nine workers dead, the steelworkers forced out the Pinkertons and kept the plant closed until the Pennsylvania National Guard arrived on July 12. The strike continued until November, but by then the union had lost much of its support and gave in to the company. It would take 45 years for steelworkers to mobilize once again.

THE PULLMAN COMPANY STRIKE Strikes continued in other industries, however. During the panic of 1893 and the economic depression that followed, the Pullman company laid off more than 3,000 of its 5,800 employees and cut the wages of the rest by 25 to 50 percent, without cutting the cost of its employee housing. After paying their rent, many workers took home less than $6 a week. A strike was called in the spring of 1894, when the Pullman company failed to restore wages or decrease rents. Eugene Debs asked for arbitration, but Pullman refused to negotiate with the strikers. So the ARU began boycotting Pullman trains.

After Pullman hired strikebreakers, the strike turned violent, and President Grover Cleveland sent in federal troops. In the bitter aftermath, Debs was jailed. Pullman fired most of the strikers, and the railroads blacklisted many others, so they could never again get railroad jobs.

WOMEN ORGANIZE Although women were barred from many unions, they united behind powerful leaders to demand better working conditions, equal pay for equal work, and an end to child labor. Perhaps the most prominent organizer in the women's labor movement was **Mary Harris Jones.** Jones supported the Great Strike of 1877 and later organized for the United Mine Workers of America (UMW). She endured death threats and jail with the coal miners, who gave her the nickname Mother Jones. In 1903, to expose the cruelties of child labor, she led 80 mill children—many with hideous injuries—on a march to the home of President Theodore Roosevelt. Their crusade influenced the passage of child labor laws.

Other organizers also achieved significant gains for women. In 1909, Pauline Newman, just 16 years old, became the first female organizer of the International Ladies' Garment Workers' Union (ILGWU). A garment worker from the age of eight, Newman also supported

KEY PLAYERS

EUGENE V. DEBS
1855–1926

Born in Indiana, Eugene V. Debs left home at the age of 14 to work for the railroads. In 1875 he helped organize a local lodge of the Brotherhood of Locomotive Firemen, and after attempts to unite the local railroad brotherhoods failed, Debs organized the American Railway Union.

While in prison following the Pullman strike in 1894, Debs read the works of Karl Marx and became increasingly disillusioned with capitalism. He became a spokesperson for the Socialist Party of America and was its candidate for president five times. In 1912, he won about 900,000 votes—an amazing 6 percent of the total.

MOTHER JONES
1830–1930

Mary Harris "Mother" Jones was a native of Ireland who immigrated to North America as a child. She became involved in the American labor movement after receiving assistance from the Knights of Labor. According to a reporter who followed "the mother of the laboring class" on her children's march in 1903, "She fights their battles with a Mother's Love." Jones continued fighting until her death at age 100.

Jones was definitely not the kind of woman admired by industrialists. "God almighty made women," she declared, "and the Rockefeller gang of thieves made ladies."

the "Uprising of the 20,000," a 1909 seamstresses' strike that won labor agreements and improved working conditions for some strikers.

The public could no longer ignore conditions in garment factories after a fire broke out at the Triangle Shirtwaist Factory in New York City on March 25, 1911. The fire spread swiftly through the oil-soaked machines and piles of cloth, engulfing the eighth, ninth, and tenth floors. As workers attempted to flee, they discovered that the company had locked all but one of the exit doors to prevent theft. The unlocked door was blocked by fire. The factory had no sprinkler system, and the single fire escape collapsed almost immediately. In all, 146 women died; some were found huddled with their faces raised to a small window. Public outrage flared after a jury acquitted the factory owners of manslaughter. In response, the state of New York set up a task force to study factory working conditions. H

MAIN IDEA

Summarizing

H What factors made the Triangle Shirtwaist fire so lethal?

MANAGEMENT AND GOVERNMENT PRESSURE UNIONS

The more powerful the unions became, the more employers came to fear them. Management refused to recognize unions as representatives of the workers. Many employers forbade union meetings, fired union members, and forced new employees to sign "yellow-dog contracts," swearing that they would not join a union.

Finally, industrial leaders, with the help of the courts, turned the Sherman Antitrust Act against labor. All a company had to do was say that a strike, picket line, or boycott would hurt interstate trade, and the state or federal government would issue an injunction against the labor action. Legal limitations made it more and more difficult for unions to be effective. Despite these pressures, workers—especially those in skilled jobs—continued to view unions as a powerful tool. By 1904, the AFL had about 1,700,000 members in its affiliated unions; by the eve of World War I, AFL membership would climb to over 2 million.

▲ The fire department's ladders reached only to the sixth floor, two floors below the burning Triangle Shirtwaist Company.

SECTION 3 ASSESSMENT

1. **TERMS & NAMES** For each term or name, write a sentence explaining its significance.
   - **Andrew Carnegie**
   - **vertical and horizontal integration**
   - **Social Darwinism**
   - **John D. Rockefeller**
   - **Sherman Antitrust Act**
   - **Samuel Gompers**
   - **American Federation of Labor (AFL)**
   - **Eugene V. Debs**
   - **Industrial Workers of the World (IWW)**
   - **Mary Harris Jones**

MAIN IDEA

2. **TAKING NOTES**
   Make a time line of the notable achievements and setbacks of the labor movement between 1876 and 1911.

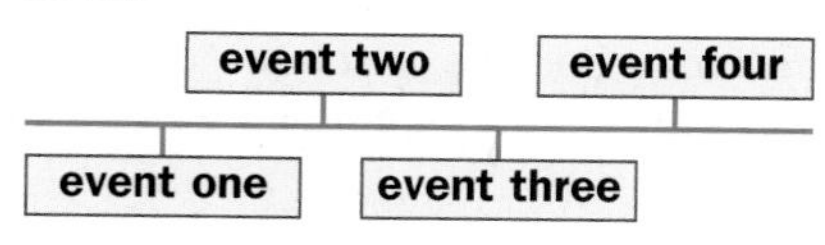

   In what ways did strikes threaten industry?

CRITICAL THINKING

3. **EVALUATING LEADERSHIP**
   Do you think that the tycoons of the late 19th century are best described as ruthless robber barons or as effective captains of industry?
   Think About:
   - their management tactics and business strategies
   - their contributions to the economy
   - their attitude toward competition
4. **DRAWING CONCLUSIONS**
   Does the life of Andrew Carnegie support or counter the philosophy of Social Darwinism? Explain.
5. **HYPOTHESIZING**
   If the government had supported unions instead of management in the late 19th century, how might the lives of workers have been different?

CHAPTER  ASSESSMENT

VISUAL SUMMARY

A New Industrial Age

LONG-TERM CAUSES

- abundant natural resources
- harnessing of early power sources such as water and coal
- invention of the steam engine
- construction of roads, canals, and railroads in early 1800s

IMMEDIATE CAUSES

- expansion of railroads in late 1800s
- cheap labor supply provided by increasing immigration
- burst of technological innovation
- new management techniques and business strategies
- investment capital

BIG BUSINESS BOOMS

1880–1914

IMMEDIATE EFFECTS

- growth of large corporations
- new and plentiful manufactured goods
- poor working conditions in factories and sweatshops
- increased labor activism

LONG-TERM EFFECTS

- regional economies are linked
- labor movement wins shorter workweek

TERMS & NAMES

For each term or name below, write a sentence explaining its connection to the industrialization of the late 19th century.

1. Thomas Alva Edison
2. Alexander Graham Bell
3. George M. Pullman
4. transcontinental railroad
5. Interstate Commerce Act
6. Andrew Carnegie
7. Sherman Antitrust Act
8. Samuel Gompers
9. American Federation of Labor (AFL)
10. Mary Harris Jones

MAIN IDEAS

Use your notes and the information in the chapter to answer the following questions.

The Expansion of Industry *(pages 230–233)*

1. How did the growth of the steel industry influence the development of other industries?
2. How did inventions and developments in the late 19th century change the way people worked?

The Age of the Railroads *(pages 236–240)*

3. Why did people, particularly farmers, demand regulation of the railroads in the late 19th century?
4. Why were attempts at railroad regulation often unsuccessful?

Big Business and Labor *(pages 241–249)*

5. Why were business leaders such as John D. Rockefeller called robber barons?
6. Why did the South industrialize more slowly than the North did?
7. Why did workers form unions in the late 19th century?
8. What factors limited the success of unions?

CRITICAL THINKING

1. **USING YOUR NOTES** In a chart like the one shown, list what you see as the overall costs and benefits of industrialization.

INDUSTRIALIZATION	
Costs	Benefits

2. **RECOGNIZING BIAS** In 1902 George Baer, head of the Philadelphia and Reading Railway Company, said, "The rights and interests of the labor man will be protected and cared for not by the labor agitators but by the Christian men to whom God in his infinite wisdom has given the control of the property interests of the country." What bias does this statement reveal? How does Baer's view reflect Social Darwinism?

3. **IDENTIFYING PROBLEMS** Consider the problems that late-19th-century workers faced and the problems that workers face today. How important do you think unions are for present-day workers? Support your answer.

Standardized Test Practice

Use the quotation below and your knowledge of U.S. history to answer question 1.

> **"No man, however benevolent, liberal, and wise, can use a large fortune so that it will do half as much good in the world as it would if it were divided into moderate sums and in the hands of workmen who had earned it by industry and frugality."**
>
> —Rutherford B. Hayes, from *The Diary and Letters of Rutherford Birchard Hayes*

1. Which of the following people could best be described by Rutherford B. Hayes's words *benevolent*, *liberal*, and *a large fortune?*

   A Thomas Edison
   B Eugene V. Debs
   C Charles Darwin
   D Andrew Carnegie

2. The American Federation of Labor (AFL) differed from the Knights of Labor in that the Knights of Labor focused on —

   F collective bargaining and aggressive use of strikes.
   G organizing only unskilled workers.
   H arbitration and use of strikes as a last resort.
   J winning a shorter workweek.

3. How did the railroads both benefit from and contribute to the industrialization of the United States?

   A The railroads needed government protection, and their development helped government grow.
   B The railroads used new inventions and brought people to see the inventions.
   C The railroads used steel and coal and delivered both to new markets.
   D The railroads needed passengers, and passengers needed to get to new industries.

4. In the 19th century, government attempts to regulate industry in the United States included the Interstate Commerce Act (1887) and the Sherman Antitrust Act (1890). What posed the biggest obstacle to enforcement of these laws?

   F the business tactics of industrialists
   G the use of vertical integration
   H the rulings of the Supreme Court
   J the theory of Social Darwinism

ADDITIONAL TEST PRACTICE, pages S1–S33.

CLASSZONE.COM

ALTERNATIVE ASSESSMENT

1. INTERACT WITH HISTORY Recall your answer to the question on page 229:

What are the pros and cons of railroad expansion?

Consider how your answer might be different based on what you now know about the effects of railroad expansion and business consolidation. Then write a newspaper editorial about the Great Strike of 1877 (see page 247), supporting the position of either the railroad owners or the striking workers.

2. VIDEO **LEARNING FROM MEDIA** View the *American Stories* video, "Gusher! Pattillo Higgins and the Great Texas Oil Boom." Discuss the following questions with a small group; then do the activity.

- What were the effects of the discovery of oil at Spindletop?
- What lessons can people learn from Pattillo Higgins?

Cooperative Learning Activity Make a poster describing Pattillo Higgins's personal qualities and how they helped him to achieve his dream. What present-day figures share Higgins's traits? Add images of these people, with captions, to the poster and display it in your classroom.

IMMIGRANTS AND URBANIZATION

The intersection of Orchard and Hester Streets on New York City's Lower East Side, 1905.

USA

1877 Rutherford B. Hayes is elected president.

1880 James A. Garfield is elected president.

1881 Chester A. Arthur succeeds Garfield after Garfield's assassination.

1884 Grover Cleveland is elected president.

1888 Benjamin Harrison is elected president.

1892 Grover Cleveland is elected to a second term.

1880 | **1890**

WORLD

1876 Porfirio Díaz seizes power in Mexico.

1884 Berlin Conference meets to divide Africa among European nations.

1885 Indian National Congress forms.

1893 France establishes Indochina.

INTERACT
WITH HISTORY

The year is 1880. New York City's swelling population has created a housing crisis. Immigrant families crowd into apartments that lack light, ventilation, and sanitary facilities. Children have nowhere to play except in the streets and are often kept out of school to work and help support their families. You are a reformer who wishes to help immigrants improve their lives.

What would you do to improve conditions?

Examine the Issues

- How can immigrants gain access to the services they need?
- What skills do newcomers need?
- How might immigrants respond to help from an outsider?

RESEARCH LINKS CLASSZONE.COM

Visit the Chapter 7 links for more information about Immigrants and Urbanization.

1896 William McKinley is elected president.

1898 Hawaii is annexed by the United States.

1900 McKinley is reelected.

1901 The Commonwealth of Australia is founded.

1903 The Wright Brothers achieve the first successful airplane flight.

1905 Workers revolt in St. Petersburg, Russia.

1908 Oil is discovered in Persia.

1910 The appearance of Halley's comet causes widespread panic.

1912 Woodrow Wilson is elected president.

1912 Qing dynasty in China is overthrown.

1914 Panama Canal opens.

The New Immigrants

MAIN IDEA

Immigration from Europe, Asia, the Caribbean, and Mexico reached a new high in the late 19th and early 20th centuries.

WHY IT MATTERS NOW

This wave of immigration helped make the United States the diverse society it is today.

Terms & Names

- **Ellis Island**
- **Angel Island**
- **melting pot**
- **nativism**
- **Chinese Exclusion Act**
- **Gentlemen's Agreement**

One American's Story

In 1871, 14-year-old Fong See came from China to "Gold Mountain"—the United States. Fong See stayed, worked at menial jobs, and saved enough money to buy a business. Despite widespread restrictions against the Chinese, he became a very successful importer and was able to sponsor many other Chinese who wanted to enter the United States. Fong See had achieved the American dream. However, as his great-granddaughter Lisa See recalls, he was not satisfied.

VIDEO

FROM CHINA TO CHINATOWN
Fong See's American Dream

A PERSONAL VOICE LISA SEE

"He had been trying to achieve success ever since he had first set foot on the Gold Mountain. His dream was very 'American.' He wanted to make money, have influence, be respected, have a wife and children who loved him. In 1919, when he traveled to China, he could look at his life and say he had achieved his dream. But once in China, he suddenly saw his life in a different context. In America, was he really rich? Could he live where he wanted? . . . Did *Americans* care what he thought? . . . The answers played in his head—no, no, no."

—*On Gold Mountain*

Despite Fong See's success, he could not, upon his death in 1957, be buried next to his Caucasian wife because California cemeteries were still segregated.

Through the "Golden Door"

Millions of immigrants like Fong See entered the United States in the late 19th and early 20th centuries, lured by the promise of a better life. Some of these immigrants sought to escape difficult conditions—such as famine, land shortages, or religious or political persecution. Others, known as "birds of passage," intended to immigrate temporarily to earn money, and then return to their homelands.

Background From 1815 to 1848, a wave of revolutions—mostly sparked by a desire for constitutional governments—shook Europe. In 1830, for example, the Polish people rose up against their Russian rulers.

EUROPEANS Between 1870 and 1920, approximately 20 million Europeans arrived in the United States. Before 1890, most immigrants came from countries in western and northern Europe. Beginning in the 1890s, however, increasing numbers came from southern and eastern Europe. In 1907 alone, about a million people arrived from Italy, Austria-Hungary, and Russia.

Why did so many leave their homelands? Many of these new immigrants left to escape religious persecution. Whole villages of Jews were driven out of Russia by pogroms, organized attacks often encouraged by local authorities. Other Europeans left because of rising population. Between 1800 and 1900, the population in Europe doubled to nearly 400 million, resulting in a scarcity of land for farming. Farmers competed with laborers for too few industrial jobs. In the United States, jobs were supposedly plentiful. In addition, a spirit of reform and revolt had spread across Europe in the 19th century. Influenced by political movements at home, many young European men and women sought independent lives in America.

CHINESE AND JAPANESE While waves of Europeans arrived on the shores of the East Coast, Chinese immigrants came to the West Coast in smaller numbers. Between 1851 and 1883, about 300,000 Chinese arrived. Many came to seek their fortunes after the discovery of gold in 1848 sparked the California gold rush. Chinese immigrants helped build the nation's railroads, including the first transcontinental line. When the railroads were completed, they turned to farming, mining, and domestic service. Some, like Fong See, started businesses. However, Chinese immigration was sharply limited by a congressional act in 1882.

In 1884, the Japanese government allowed Hawaiian planters to recruit Japanese workers, and a Japanese emigration boom began. The United States' annexation of Hawaii in 1898 resulted in increased Japanese immigration to the West Coast. Immigration continued to increase as word of comparatively high American wages spread. The wave peaked in 1907, when 30,000 left Japan for the United States. By 1920, more than 200,000 Japanese lived on the West Coast.

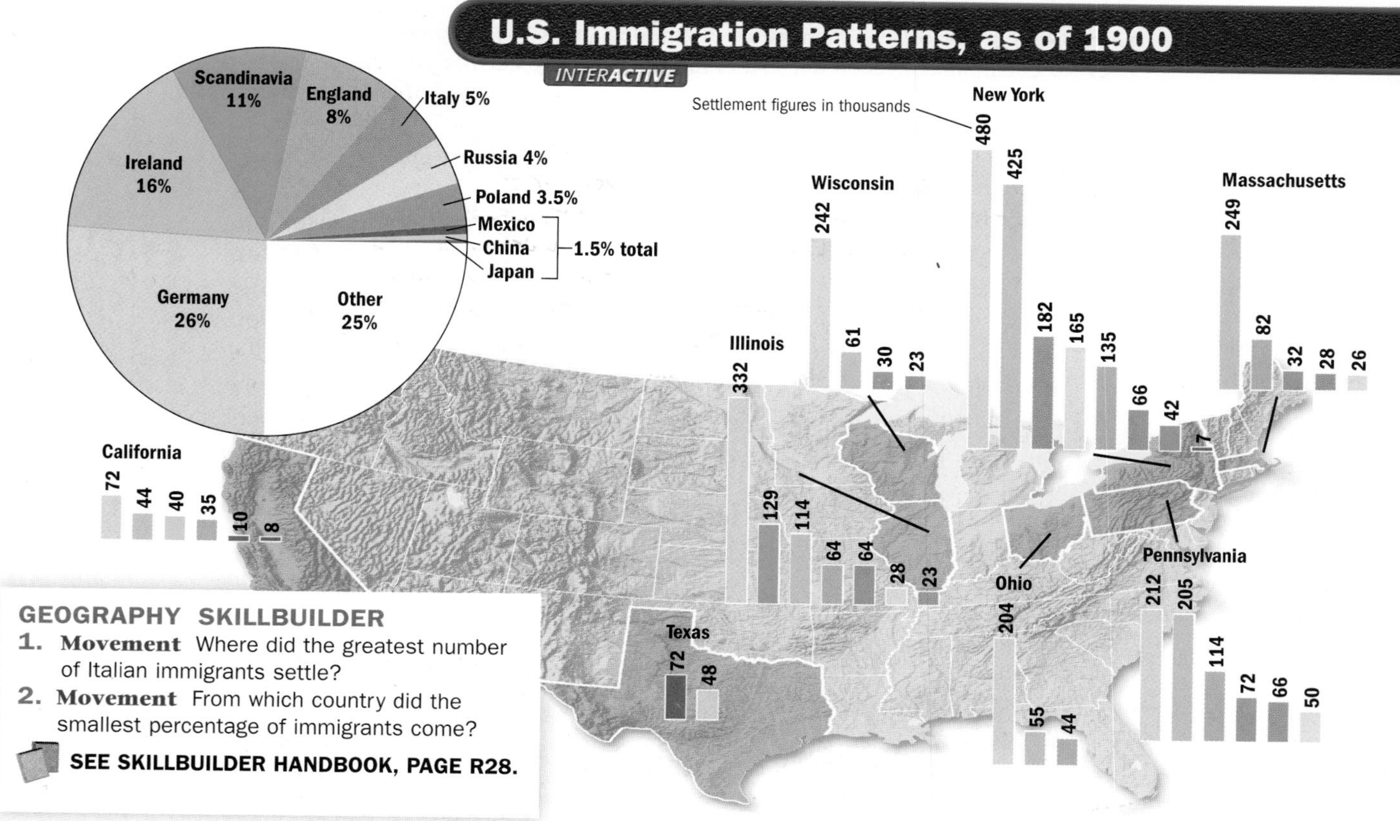

GEOGRAPHY SKILLBUILDER

1. **Movement** Where did the greatest number of Italian immigrants settle?
2. **Movement** From which country did the smallest percentage of immigrants come?

SEE SKILLBUILDER HANDBOOK, PAGE R28.

THE WEST INDIES AND MEXICO Between 1880 and 1920, about 260,000 immigrants arrived in the eastern and southeastern United States from the West Indies. They came from Jamaica, Cuba, Puerto Rico, and other islands. Many West Indians left their homelands because jobs were scarce and the industrial boom in the United States seemed to promise work for everyone.

Mexicans, too, immigrated to the United States to find work, as well as to flee political turmoil. The 1902 National Reclamation Act, which encouraged the irrigation of arid land, created new farmland in Western states and drew Mexican farm workers northward. After 1910, political and social upheavals in Mexico prompted even more immigration. About 700,000 people—7 percent of the population of Mexico at the time—came to the U.S. over the next 20 years. (A)

MAIN IDEA

Analyzing Causes

(A) What reasons did people from other parts of the world have for immigrating to the United States?

Life in the New Land

No matter what part of the globe immigrants came from, they faced many adjustments to an alien—and often unfriendly—culture.

A DIFFICULT JOURNEY By the 1870s, almost all immigrants traveled by steamship. The trip across the Atlantic Ocean from Europe took approximately one week, while the Pacific crossing from Asia took nearly three weeks.

Many immigrants traveled in steerage, the cheapest accommodations in a ship's cargo holds. Rarely allowed on deck, immigrants were crowded together in the gloom, unable to exercise or catch a breath of fresh air. They often had to sleep in louse-infested bunks and share toilets with many other passengers. Under these conditions, disease spread quickly, and some immigrants died before they reached their destination. For those who survived, the first glimpse of America could be breathtaking.

A PERSONAL VOICE ROSA CAVALLERI

"*America!* . . . We were so near it seemed too much to believe. Everyone stood silent—like in prayer. . . . Then we were entering the harbor. The land came so near we could almost reach out and touch it. . . . Everyone was holding their breath. Me too. . . . Some boats had bands playing on their decks and all of them were tooting their horns to us and leaving white trails in the water behind them."

—quoted in *Rosa: The Life of an Italian Immigrant*

ELLIS ISLAND After initial moments of excitement, the immigrants faced the anxiety of not knowing whether they would be admitted to the United States. They had to pass inspection at immigration stations, such as the one at Castle Garden in New York, which was later moved to **Ellis Island** in New York Harbor. About 20 percent of the immigrants at Ellis Island were detained for a day or more before being inspected. However, only about 2 percent of those were denied entry.

The processing of immigrants on Ellis Island was an ordeal that might take five hours or more. First, they had to pass a physical examination by a doctor. Anyone with a serious health problem or a contagious disease, such as tuberculosis, was promptly sent home. Those who passed the medical exam then reported to a government inspector. The inspector checked documents and questioned immigrants

European governments used passports to control the number of professionals and young men of military age who left the country. ▼

Vocabulary
tuberculosis: a bacterial infection, characterized by fever and coughing, that spreads easily

Many immigrants, like these arriving at Ellis Island, were subjected to tests such as the one below. To prove their mental competence, they had to identify the four faces looking left in 14 seconds. Can you do it?

TESTS FOR DETECTION OF DEFECTIVES.

A. B. C. D. E.

FIG. 4.—Moon Section of "V. C." test. The subject should be able to point out the four moons that are looking to the left in fourteen seconds, if he is directed to begin at the upper right hand corner and proceed systematically along each line, left to right.

FIG. 5.—The Key Section of the "V. C." test. The time element has not been worked out for this section, but it is hardly the less valuable. "A" is shown the subject and he is asked to find the nearest like it in Fig. 1, "B" is shown and he is asked to find it in Fig. 3, "C" is shown and he is asked to find it in Fig. 4, "D" is shown and he is asked to find it in Fig. 2, and "E" is shown and he is asked to find it in Fig. 4.

to determine whether they met the legal requirements for entering the United States. The requirements included proving they had never been convicted of a felony, demonstrating that they were able to work, and showing that they had some money (at least $25 after 1909). One inspector, Edward Ferro, an Italian immigrant himself, gave this glimpse of the process.

Vocabulary
felony: any one of the most serious crimes under the law, including murder, rape, and burglary

A PERSONAL VOICE EDWARD FERRO

"The language was a problem of course, but it was overcome by the use of interpreters. . . . It would happen sometimes that these interpreters—some of them—were really softhearted people and hated to see people being deported, and they would, at times, help the aliens by interpreting in such a manner as to benefit the alien and not the government."

—quoted in *I Was Dreaming to Come to America*

From 1892 to 1924, Ellis Island was the chief immigration station in the United States. An estimated 17 million immigrants passed through its noisy, bustling facilities.

ANGEL ISLAND While European immigrants arriving on the East Coast passed through Ellis Island, Asians—primarily Chinese—arriving on the West Coast gained admission at **Angel Island** in San Francisco Bay. Between 1910 and 1940, about 50,000 Chinese immigrants entered the United States through Angel Island. Processing at Angel Island stood in contrast to the procedure at Ellis Island. Immigrants endured harsh questioning and a long detention in filthy, ramshackle buildings while they waited to find out whether they would be admitted or rejected. B

MAIN IDEA
Identifying Problems
B What difficulties did immigrants face in gaining admission to the United States?

COOPERATION FOR SURVIVAL Once admitted to the country, immigrants faced the challenges of finding a place to live, getting a job, and getting along in daily life while trying to understand an unfamiliar language and culture. Many immigrants sought out people who shared their cultural values, practiced their religion, and spoke their native language. The ethnic communities were life rafts for immigrants. People pooled their money to build churches or synagogues. They formed social clubs and aid societies. They founded orphanages and old people's homes, and established cemeteries. They even published newspapers in their own languages.

Vocabulary
synagogue: place of meeting for worship and religious instruction in the Jewish faith

Committed to their own cultures but also trying hard to grow into their new identities, many immigrants came to think of themselves as "hyphenated" Americans. As hard as they tried to fit in, these new Polish- and Italian- and Chinese-Americans felt increasing friction as they rubbed shoulders with people born and raised in the United States. Native-born people often disliked the immigrants' unfamiliar customs and languages, and viewed them as a threat to the American way of life. C

MAIN IDEA

Summarizing
C How did immigrants deal with challenges they faced?

Immigration Restrictions

Many native-born Americans thought of their country as a **melting pot,** a mixture of people of different cultures and races who blended together by abandoning their native languages and customs. Many new immigrants, however, did not wish to give up their cultural identities. As immigration increased, strong anti-immigrant feelings emerged.

THE RISE OF NATIVISM One response to the growth in immigration was **nativism,** or overt favoritism toward native-born Americans. Nativism gave rise to anti-immigrant groups and led to a demand for immigration restrictions.

Many nativists believed that Anglo-Saxons—the Germanic ancestors of the English—were superior to other ethnic groups. These nativists did not object to immigrants from the "right" countries. Prescott F. Hall, a founder in 1894 of the Immigration Restriction League, identified desirable immigrants as "British, German, and Scandinavian stock, historically free, energetic, progressive." Nativists thought that problems were caused by immigrants from the "wrong" countries—"Slav, Latin, and Asiatic races, historically down-trodden . . . and stagnant."

Vocabulary
progressive: favoring advancement toward better conditions or new ideas

Nativists sometimes objected more to immigrants' religious beliefs than to their ethnic backgrounds. Many native-born Americans were Protestants and thought that Roman Catholic and Jewish immigrants would undermine the democratic institutions established by the country's Protestant founders. The American Protective Association, a nativist group founded in 1887, launched vicious anti-Catholic attacks, and many colleges, businesses, and social clubs refused to admit Jews.

In 1897, Congress—influenced by the Immigration Restriction League—passed a bill requiring a literacy test for immigrants. Those who could not read 40 words in English or their native language would be refused entry. Although President Cleveland vetoed the bill, it was a powerful statement of public sentiment. In 1917, a similar bill would be passed into law in spite of President Woodrow Wilson's veto.

Chinese immigrants wait outside the hospital on Angel Island in San Francisco Bay, 1910. ▼

ANTI-ASIAN SENTIMENT Nativism also found a foothold in the labor movement, particularly in the West, where native-born workers feared that jobs would go to Chinese

immigrants, who would accept lower wages. The depression of 1873 intensified anti-Chinese sentiment in California. Work was scarce, and labor groups exerted political pressure on the government to restrict Asian immigration. The founder of the Workingmen's Party, Denis Kearney, headed the anti-Chinese movement in California. He made hundreds of speeches throughout the state, each ending with the message, "The Chinese must go!"

In 1882, Congress slammed the door on Chinese immigration for ten years by passing the **Chinese Exclusion Act.** This act banned entry to all Chinese except students, teachers, merchants, tourists, and government officials. In 1892, Congress extended the law for another ten years. In 1902, Chinese immigration was restricted indefinitely; the law was not repealed until 1943.

▲ Fear and resentment of Chinese immigrants sometimes resulted in mob attacks, like the one shown here.

THE GENTLEMEN'S AGREEMENT The fears that had led to anti-Chinese agitation were extended to Japanese and other Asian people in the early 1900s. In 1906, the local board of education in San Francisco segregated Japanese children by putting them in separate schools. When Japan raised an angry protest at this treatment of its emigrants, President Theodore Roosevelt worked out a deal. Under the **Gentlemen's Agreement** of 1907–1908, Japan's government agreed to limit emigration of unskilled workers to the United States in exchange for the repeal of the San Francisco segregation order.

Although doorways for immigrants had been all but closed to Asians on the West Coast, cities in the East and the Midwest teemed with European immigrants—and with urban opportunities and challenges.

ASSESSMENT

1. **TERMS & NAMES** For each term or name, write a sentence explaining its significance.
   - **Ellis Island**
   - **Angel Island**
   - **melting pot**
   - **nativism**
   - **Chinese Exclusion Act**
   - **Gentlemen's Agreement**

MAIN IDEA

2. **TAKING NOTES**
   Create a diagram such as the one below. List two or more causes of each effect.

Causes ⟶	Effects
1. 2. 3.	Immigrants leave their home countries.
1. 2. 3.	Immigrants face hardships in the United States.
1. 2. 3.	Some nativists want to restrict immigration.

CRITICAL THINKING

3. **IDENTIFYING PROBLEMS**
   Which group of immigrants do you think faced the greatest challenges in the United States? Why?

4. **ANALYZING EFFECTS**
   What were the effects of the massive influx of immigrants to the U.S. in the late 1800s?

5. **EVALUATING**
   What arguments can you make against nativism and anti-immigrant feeling? **Think About:**
   - the personal qualities of immigrants
   - the reasons for anti-immigrant feeling
   - the contributions of immigrants to the United States

Diversity and the National Identity

Before the first Europeans arrived, a variety of cultural groups—coastal fishing societies, desert farmers, plains and woodland hunters—inhabited North America. With the arrival of Europeans and Africans, the cultural mix grew more complex. Although this diversity has often produced tension, it has also been beneficial. As different groups learned from one another about agriculture, technology, and social customs, American culture became a rich blend of cultures from around the world.

1610s–1870s

◀ **SPANISH NORTH AMERICA**

Spanish missionaries in the Southwest tried to impose their culture upon Native Americans. However, many Native Americans retained aspects of their original cultures even as they took on Spanish ways. For example, today many Pueblo Indians of New Mexico perform ancient ceremonies, such as the Corn Dance, in addition to celebrating the feast days of Catholic saints. Later, the first cowboys—descendants of the Spanish—would introduce to white Americans cattle-ranching techniques developed in Mexico.

1776

THE DECLARATION OF INDEPENDENCE ▶

The signers of the Declaration of Independence were descendants of immigrants. The founders' ancestors had come to North America in search of economic opportunity and freedom of religious expression. When the Second Continental Congress declared a "United States" in 1776, they acknowledged that the country would contain diverse regions and interests. Thus the founders placed on the presidential seal the motto *"E Pluribus Unum"*—"out of many, one."

1862–1863

THE EMANCIPATION PROCLAMATION ▲

At the midpoint of the Civil War, President Abraham Lincoln issued the Emancipation Proclamation, freeing all slaves in areas of the Union that were in rebellion. Although the Proclamation could not be enforced immediately, it was a strong statement of opposition to slavery, and it paved the way for African Americans' citizenship.

1886

THE STATUE OF LIBERTY ▶

Poet Emma Lazarus wrote the famous lines inscribed at the foot of the Statue of Liberty, "Give me your tired, your poor,/Your huddled masses yearning to breathe free, . . ." The statue's dedication took place during the most extensive wave of immigration the United States has ever known.

Many native-born Americans felt that the newcomers should fully immerse themselves in their new culture. However, most immigrants combined American language and customs with their traditional ways. As immigrants celebrated Independence Day and Thanksgiving, they introduced into American culture new celebrations, such as Chinese New Year and Cinco de Mayo.

2000

◀ 21ST-CENTURY DIVERSITY

In 1998, three countries (Mexico, China, and India) contributed a third of the total number of immigrants to the United States. The rest of 1998's immigrants came from countries as diverse as Vietnam, Sudan, and Bosnia.

American athletes at the 2000 Olympic Games in Sydney, Australia, reflected the increasing diversity of the U.S., pointing toward a future in which there may no longer be a majority racial or ethnic group.

THINKING CRITICALLY

CONNECT TO HISTORY

1. **Analyzing Motives** Why do you think some groups have tried to suppress the culture of others over the course of history? Why have many groups persisted in retaining their cultural heritage?

SEE SKILLBUILDER HANDBOOK, PAGE R6.

CONNECT TO TODAY

2. **Predicting Effects** Research current U.S. policy on immigration. How might this policy affect cultural diversity? Write a short editorial from one of the following viewpoints:
   - U.S. immigration policy needs to change.
   - U.S. immigration policy should be maintained.

CLASSZONE.COM

The Challenges of Urbanization

MAIN IDEA	WHY IT MATTERS NOW	Terms & Names
The rapid growth of cities forced people to contend with problems of housing, transportation, water, and sanitation.	**Consequently, residents of U.S. cities today enjoy vastly improved living conditions.**	• **urbanization** • **Americanization movement** • **tenement** • **mass transit** • **Social Gospel movement** • **settlement house** • **Jane Addams**

One American's Story

In 1870, at age 21, Jacob Riis left his native Denmark for the United States. Riis found work as a police reporter, a job that took him into some of New York City's worst slums, where he was shocked at the conditions in the overcrowded, airless, filthy tenements. Riis used his talents to expose the hardships of New York City's poor.

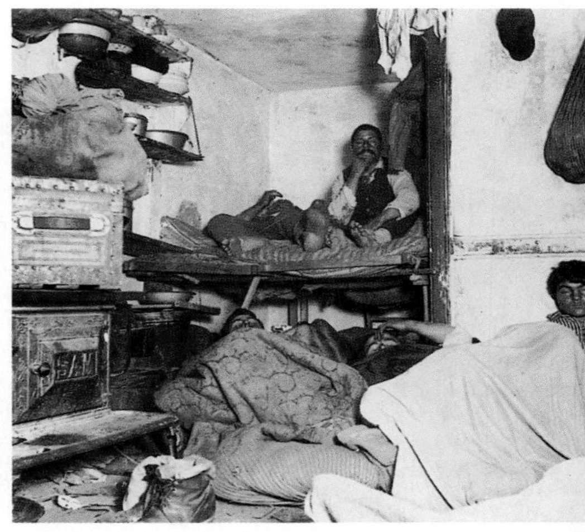

As many as 12 people slept in rooms such as this one in New York City, photographed by Jacob Riis around 1889.

A PERSONAL VOICE JACOB RIIS

"Be a little careful, please! The hall is dark and you might stumble over the children pitching pennies back there. Not that it would hurt them; kicks and cuffs are their daily diet. They have little else. . . . Close [stuffy]? Yes! What would you have? All the fresh air that ever enters these stairs comes from the hall-door that is forever slamming. . . . Here is a door. Listen! That short hacking cough, that tiny, helpless wail—what do they mean? . . . The child is dying with measles. With half a chance it might have lived; but it had none. That dark bedroom killed it."

—*How the Other Half Lives*

Making a living in the late 19th and early 20th centuries was not easy. Natural and economic disasters had hit farmers hard in Europe and in the United States, and the promise of industrial jobs drew millions of people to American cities. The urban population exploded from 10 million to 54 million between 1870 and 1920. This growth revitalized the cities but also created serious problems that, as Riis observed, had a powerful impact on the new urban poor.

Urban Opportunities

The technological boom in the 19th century contributed to the growing industrial strength of the United States. The result was rapid **urbanization,** or growth of cities, mostly in the regions of the Northeast and Midwest.

IMMIGRANTS SETTLE IN CITIES Most of the immigrants who streamed into the United States in the late 19th century became city dwellers because cities were the cheapest and most convenient places to live. Cities also offered unskilled laborers steady jobs in mills and factories. By 1890, there were twice as many Irish residents in New York City as in Dublin, Ireland. By 1910, immigrant families made up more than half the total population of 18 major American cities.

The **Americanization movement** was designed to assimilate people of wide-ranging cultures into the dominant culture. This social campaign was sponsored by the government and by concerned citizens. Schools and voluntary associations provided programs to teach immigrants skills needed for citizenship, such as English literacy and American history and government. Subjects such as cooking and social etiquette were included in the curriculum to help the newcomers learn the ways of native-born Americans. (A)

MAIN IDEA

Analyzing Motives

(A) Why did native-born Americans start the Americanization movement?

Despite these efforts, many immigrants did not wish to abandon their traditions. Ethnic communities provided the social support of other immigrants from the same country. This enabled them to speak their own language and practice their customs and religion. However, these neighborhoods soon became overcrowded, a problem that was intensified by the arrival of new transplants from America's rural areas.

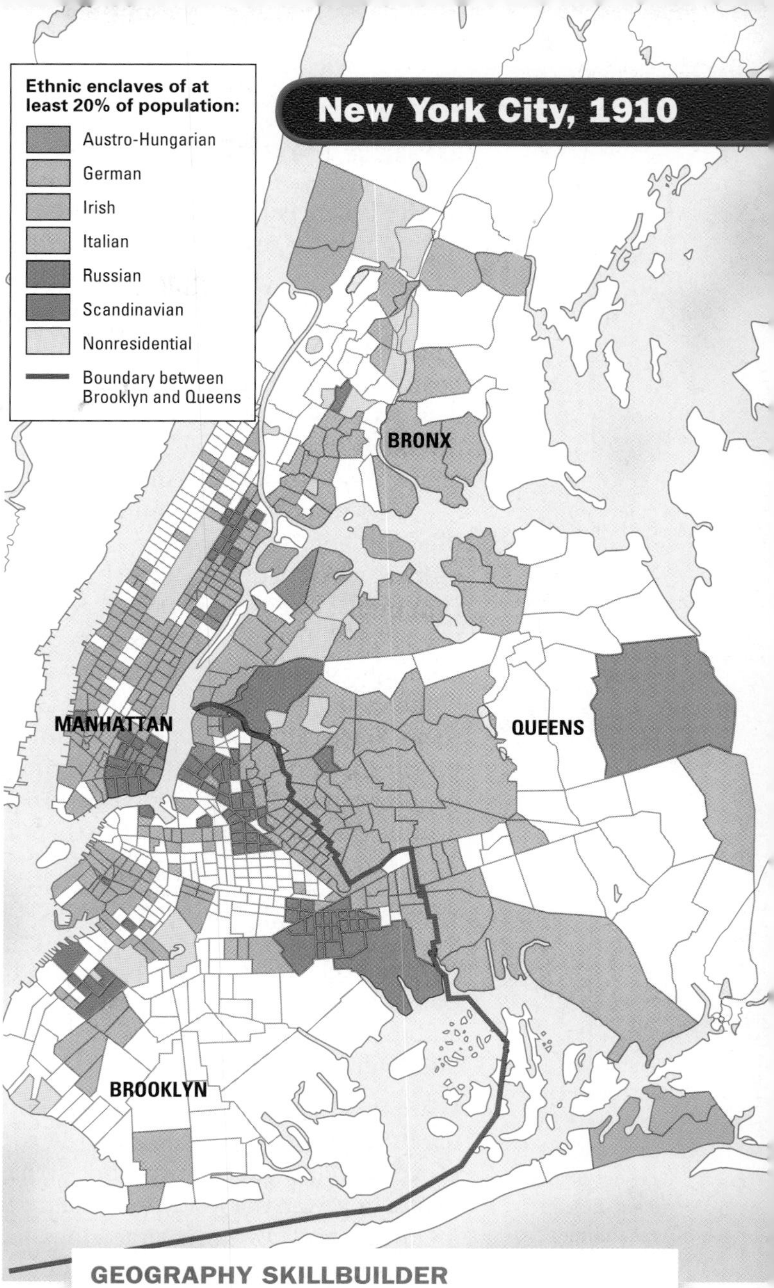

New York City, 1910

GEOGRAPHY SKILLBUILDER

1. **Place** What general pattern of settlement do you notice?
2. **Movement** Which ethnic group settled in the largest area of New York City?

MIGRATION FROM COUNTRY TO CITY Rapid improvements in farming technology during the second half of the 19th century were good news for some farmers but bad news for others. Inventions such as the McCormick reaper and the steel plow made farming more efficient but meant that fewer laborers were needed to work the land. As more and more farms merged, many rural people moved to cities to find whatever work they could.

Many of the Southern farmers who lost their livelihoods were African Americans. Between 1890 and 1910, about 200,000 African Americans moved north and west, to cities such as Chicago and Detroit, in an effort to escape racial violence, economic hardship, and political oppression. Many found conditions only somewhat better than those they had left behind. Segregation and discrimination were often the reality in Northern cities. Job competition between blacks and white immigrants caused further racial tension.

Urban Problems

As the urban population skyrocketed, city governments faced the problems of how to provide residents with needed services and safe living conditions.

HOUSING When the industrial age began, working-class families in cities had two housing options. They could either buy a house on the outskirts of town, where they would face transportation problems, or rent cramped rooms in a boardinghouse in the central city. As the urban population increased, however, new types of housing were designed. For example, row houses—single-family dwellings that shared side walls with other similar houses—packed many single-family residences onto a single block.

After working-class families left the central city, immigrants often took over their old housing, sometimes with two or three families occupying a one-family residence. As Jacob Riis pointed out, these multifamily urban dwellings, called **tenements,** were overcrowded and unsanitary.

In 1879, to improve such slum conditions, New York City passed a law that set minimum standards for plumbing and ventilation in apartments. Landlords began building tenements with air shafts that provided an outside window for each room. Since garbage was picked up infrequently, people sometimes dumped it into the air shafts, where it attracted vermin. To keep out the stench, residents nailed windows shut. Though established with good intent, these new tenements soon became even worse places to live than the converted single-family residences. B

MAIN IDEA

Identifying Problems
B What housing problems did urban working-class families face?

TRANSPORTATION Innovations in **mass transit,** transportation systems designed to move large numbers of people along fixed routes, enabled workers to go to and from jobs more easily. Street cars were introduced in San Francisco in 1873 and electric subways in Boston in 1897. By the early 20th century, mass-transit networks in many urban areas linked city neighborhoods to one another and to outlying communities. Cities struggled to repair old transit systems and to build new ones to meet the demand of expanding populations.

WATER Cities also faced the problem of supplying safe drinking water. As the urban population grew in the 1840s and 1850s, cities such as New York and Cleveland built public waterworks to handle the increasing demand. As late as the 1860s, however, the residents of many cities had grossly inadequate piped water—or none at all. Even in large cities like New York, homes seldom had indoor plumbing, and residents had to collect water in pails from faucets on the street and heat it for bathing. The necessity of improving water quality to control diseases such as cholera and typhoid fever was obvious. To make city water safer, filtration was introduced in the 1870s and chlorination in 1908. However, in the early 20th century, many city dwellers still had no access to safe water.

Vocabulary
chlorination: a method of purifying water by mixing it with the chemical chlorine

Sanitation problems in big cities were overwhelming. It was not unusual to see a dead horse in the street. ▼

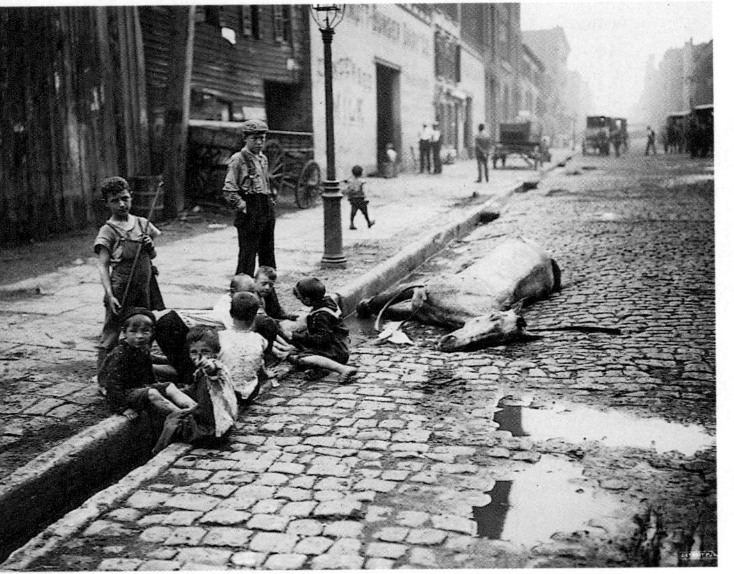

SANITATION As the cities grew, so did the challenge of keeping them clean. Horse manure piled up on the streets, sewage flowed through open gutters, and factories spewed foul smoke into the air. Without dependable trash collection, people dumped their garbage on the streets. Although private contractors called scavengers were hired to sweep the streets, collect garbage, and clean outhouses, they

MAIN IDEA

Analyzing Effects

C How did conditions in cities affect people's health?

often did not do the jobs properly. By 1900, many cities had developed sewer lines and created sanitation departments. However, the task of providing hygienic living conditions was an ongoing challenge for urban leaders. **C**

CRIME As the populations of cities increased, pickpockets and thieves flourished. Although New York City organized the first full-time, salaried police force in 1844, it and most other city law enforcement units were too small to have much impact on crime.

FIRE The limited water supply in many cities contributed to another menace: the spread of fires. Major fires occurred in almost every large American city during the 1870s and 1880s. In addition to lacking water with which to combat blazes, most cities were packed with wooden dwellings, which were like kindling waiting to be ignited. The use of candles and kerosene heaters also posed a fire hazard. In San Francisco, deadly fires often broke out during earthquakes. Jack London described the fires that raged after the San Francisco earthquake of 1906.

A PERSONAL VOICE JACK LONDON

> **"On Wednesday morning at a quarter past five came the earthquake. A minute later the flames were leaping upward. In a dozen different quarters south of Market Street, in the working-class ghetto, and in the factories, fires started. There was no opposing the flames. . . . And the great water-mains had burst. All the shrewd contrivances and safeguards of man had been thrown out of gear by thirty seconds' twitching of the earth-crust."**
>
> —"The Story of an Eye-witness"

At first, most city firefighters were volunteers and not always available when they were needed. Cincinnati, Ohio, tackled this problem when it established the nation's first paid fire department in 1853. By 1900, most cities had full-time professional fire departments. The introduction of a practical automatic fire sprinkler in 1874 and the replacement of wood as a building material with brick, stone, or concrete also made cities safer.

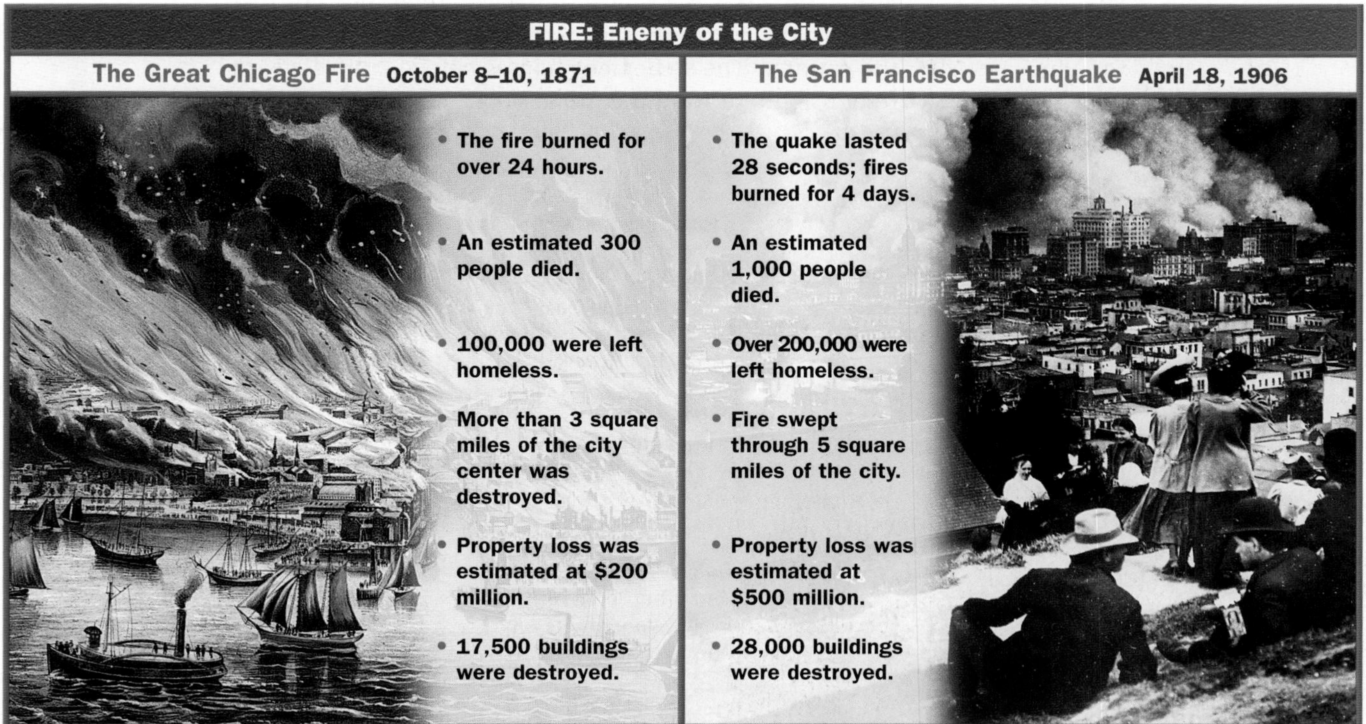

FIRE: Enemy of the City
The Great Chicago Fire October 8–10, 1871
• The fire burned for over 24 hours.
• An estimated 300 people died.
• 100,000 were left homeless.
• More than 3 square miles of the city center was destroyed.
• Property loss was estimated at $200 million.
• 17,500 buildings were destroyed.
The San Francisco Earthquake April 18, 1906
• The quake lasted 28 seconds; fires burned for 4 days.
• An estimated 1,000 people died.
• Over 200,000 were left homeless.
• Fire swept through 5 square miles of the city.
• Property loss was estimated at $500 million.
• 28,000 buildings were destroyed.

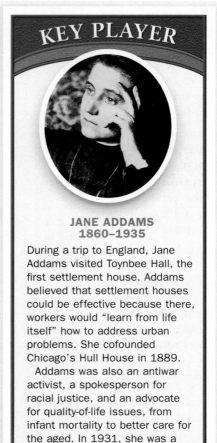

KEY PLAYER

JANE ADDAMS
1860–1935

During a trip to England, Jane Addams visited Toynbee Hall, the first settlement house. Addams believed that settlement houses could be effective because there, workers would "learn from life itself" how to address urban problems. She cofounded Chicago's Hull House in 1889.

Addams was also an antiwar activist, a spokesperson for racial justice, and an advocate for quality-of-life issues, from infant mortality to better care for the aged. In 1931, she was a co-winner of the Nobel Peace Prize.

Until the end of her life, Addams insisted that she was just a "very simple person." But many familiar with her accomplishments consider her a source of inspiration.

Reformers Mobilize

As problems in cities mounted, concerned Americans worked to find solutions. Social welfare reformers targeted their efforts at relieving urban poverty.

THE SETTLEMENT HOUSE MOVEMENT An early reform program, the **Social Gospel movement,** preached salvation through service to the poor. Inspired by the message of the Social Gospel movement, many 19th-century reformers responded to the call to help the urban poor. In the late 1800s, a few reformers established **settlement houses,** community centers in slum neighborhoods that provided assistance to people in the area, especially immigrants. Many settlement workers lived at the houses so that they could learn firsthand about the problems caused by urbanization and help create solutions.

Run largely by middle-class, college-educated women, settlement houses provided educational, cultural, and social services. They provided classes in such subjects as English, health, and painting, and offered college extension courses. Settlement houses also sent visiting nurses into the homes of the sick and provided whatever aid was needed to secure "support for deserted women, insurance for bewildered widows, damages for injured operators, furniture from the clutches of the installment store."

Settlement houses in the United States were founded by Charles Stover and Stanton Coit in New York City in 1886. **Jane Addams**—one of the most influential members of the movement—and Ellen Gates Starr founded Chicago's Hull House in 1889. In 1890, Janie Porter Barrett founded Locust Street Social Settlement in Hampton, Virginia—the first settlement house for African Americans. By 1910, about 400 settlement houses were operating in cities across the country. The settlement houses helped cultivate social responsibility toward the urban poor.

ASSESSMENT

1. **TERMS & NAMES** For each term or name, write a sentence explaining its significance.
   - **urbanization**
   - **Americanization movement**
   - **tenement**
   - **mass transit**
   - **Social Gospel movement**
   - **settlement house**
   - **Jane Addams**

MAIN IDEA

2. **TAKING NOTES**
   Re-create the spider map below on your paper. List urban problems on the vertical lines. Fill in details about attempts that were made to solve each problem.

CRITICAL THINKING

3. **ANALYZING MOTIVES**
   Why did immigrants tend to group together in cities?

4. **EVALUATING**
   Which solution (or attempted solution) to an urban problem discussed in this section do you think had the most impact? Why?

5. **ANALYZING EFFECTS**
   What effects did the migration from rural areas to the cities in the late 19th century have on urban society?
   Think About:
   - why people moved to cities
   - the problems caused by rapid urban growth
   - the differences in the experiences of whites and blacks

Politics in the Gilded Age

MAIN IDEA	WHY IT MATTERS NOW	Terms & Names
Local and national political corruption in the 19th century led to calls for reform.	Political reforms paved the way for a more honest and efficient government in the 20th century and beyond.	• political machine • graft • Boss Tweed • patronage • civil service • Rutherford B. Hayes • James A. Garfield • Chester A. Arthur • Pendleton Civil Service Act • Grover Cleveland • Benjamin Harrison

One American's Story

Mark Twain described the excesses of the late 19th century in a satirical novel, *The Gilded Age,* a collaboration with the writer Charles Dudley Warner. The title of the book has since come to represent the period from the 1870s to the 1890s. Twain mocks the greed and self-indulgence of his characters, including Philip Sterling.

A PERSONAL VOICE
MARK TWAIN AND CHARLES DUDLEY WARNER

"There are many young men like him [Philip Sterling] in American society, of his age, opportunities, education and abilities, who have really been educated for nothing and have let themselves drift, in the hope that they will find somehow, and by some sudden turn of good luck, the golden road to fortune. . . . He saw people, all around him, poor yesterday, rich to-day, who had come into sudden opulence by some means which they could not have classified among any of the regular occupations of life."

—*The Gilded Age*

▲ **A luxurious apartment building rises behind a New York City shantytown in 1889.**

Twain's characters find that getting rich quick is more difficult than they had thought it would be. Investments turn out to be worthless; politicians' bribes eat up their savings. The glittering exterior of the age turns out to hide a corrupt political core and a growing gap between the few rich and the many poor.

The Emergence of Political Machines

In the late 19th century, cities experienced rapid growth under inefficient government. In a climate influenced by dog-eat-dog Social Darwinism, cities were receptive to a new power structure, the political machine, and a new politician, the city boss.

THE POLITICAL MACHINE An organized group that controlled the activities of a political party in a city, the **political machine** also offered services to voters and businesses in exchange for political or financial support. In the decades after the Civil War, political machines gained control of local government in Baltimore, New York, San Francisco, and other major cities.

The machine was organized like a pyramid. At the pyramid's base were local precinct workers and captains, who tried to gain voters' support on a city block or in a neighborhood and who reported to a ward boss. At election time, the ward boss worked to secure the vote in all the precincts in the ward, or electoral district. Ward bosses helped the poor and gained their votes by doing favors or providing services. As Martin Lomasney, elected ward boss of Boston's West End in 1885, explained, "There's got to be in every ward somebody that any bloke can come to . . . and get help. Help, you understand; none of your law and your justice, but help." At the top of the pyramid was the city boss, who controlled the activities of the political party throughout the city. Precinct captains, ward bosses, and the city boss worked together to elect their candidates and guarantee the success of the machine. **A**

MAIN IDEA

Summarizing

A In what way did the structure of the political machine resemble a pyramid?

THE ROLE OF THE POLITICAL BOSS Whether or not the boss officially served as mayor, he controlled access to municipal jobs and business licenses, and influenced the courts and other municipal agencies. Bosses like Roscoe Conkling in New York used their power to build parks, sewer systems, and waterworks, and gave money to schools, hospitals, and orphanages. Bosses could also provide government support for new businesses, a service for which they were often paid extremely well.

It was not only money that motivated city bosses. By solving urban problems, bosses could reinforce voters' loyalty, win additional political support, and extend their influence.

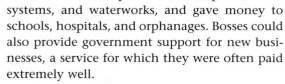

▲ A corrupt 19th-century boss robs the city treasury by easily cutting government red tape, or bureaucracy.

IMMIGRANTS AND THE MACHINE Many precint captains and political bosses were first-generation or second-generation immigrants. Few were educated beyond grammar school. They entered politics early and worked their way up from the bottom. They could speak to immigrants in their own language and understood the challenges that newcomers faced. More important, the bosses were able to provide solutions. The machines helped immigrants with naturalization (attaining full citizenship), housing, and jobs—the newcomers' most pressing needs. In return, the immigrants provided what the political bosses needed—votes. **B**

MAIN IDEA

Analyzing Motives

B Why did immigrants support political machines?

"Big Jim" Pendergast, an Irish-American saloonkeeper, worked his way up from precinct captain to Democratic city boss in Kansas City by aiding Italian, African-American, and Irish voters in his ward. By 1900, he controlled Missouri state politics as well.

A PERSONAL VOICE JAMES PENDERGAST

> **"I've been called a boss. All there is to it is having friends, doing things for people, and then later on they'll do things for you. . . . You can't coerce people into doing things for you—you can't make them vote for you. I never coerced anybody in my life. Wherever you see a man bulldozing anybody he don't last long."**
>
> —quoted in *The Pendergast Machine*

Municipal Graft and Scandal

While the well-oiled political machines provided city dwellers with services, many political bosses fell victim to corruption as their influence grew.

ELECTION FRAUD AND GRAFT When the loyalty of voters was not enough to carry an election, some political machines turned to fraud. Using fake names, party faithfuls cast as many votes as were needed to win.

Once a political machine got its candidates into office, it could take advantage of numerous opportunities for **graft,** the illegal use of political influence for personal gain. For example, by helping a person find work on a construction project for the city, a political machine could ask the worker to bill the city for more than the actual cost of materials and labor. The worker then "kicked back" a portion of the earnings to the machine. Taking these kickbacks, or illegal payments for their services, enriched the political machines—and individual politicians.

Political machines also granted favors to businesses in return for cash and accepted bribes to allow illegal activities, such as gambling, to flourish. Politicians were able to get away with shady dealings because the police rarely interfered. Until about 1890, police forces were hired and fired by political bosses.

THE TWEED RING SCANDAL William M. Tweed, known as **Boss Tweed,** became head of Tammany Hall, New York City's powerful Democratic political machine, in 1868. Between 1869 and 1871, Boss Tweed led the Tweed Ring, a group of corrupt politicians, in defrauding the city.

One scheme, the construction of the New York County Courthouse, involved extravagant graft. The project cost taxpayers $13 million, while the actual construction cost was $3 million. The difference went into the pockets of Tweed and his followers.

Thomas Nast, a political cartoonist, helped arouse public outrage against Tammany Hall's graft, and the Tweed Ring was finally broken in 1871. Tweed was indicted on 120 counts of fraud and extortion and was sentenced to 12 years in jail. His sentence was reduced to one year, but after leaving jail, Tweed was quickly arrested on another charge. While serving a second sentence, Tweed escaped. He was captured in Spain when officials identified him from a Thomas Nast cartoon. By that time, political corruption had become a national issue.

Vocabulary
extortion: illegal use of one's official position to obtain property or funds

▲ **Boss Tweed, head of Tammany Hall.**

Analyzing *Political Cartoons*

"THE TAMMANY TIGER LOOSE"

Political cartoonist Thomas Nast ridiculed Boss Tweed and his machine in the pages of *Harper's Weekly.* Nast's work threatened Tweed, who reportedly said, "I don't care so much what the papers write about me—my constituents can't read; but . . . they can see pictures!"

SKILLBUILDER Analyzing Political Cartoons

1. Under the Tammany tiger's victim is a torn paper that reads "LAW." What is its significance?
2. Boss Tweed and his cronies, portrayed as noblemen, watch from the stands on the left. The cartoon's caption reads "What are you going to do about it?" What effect do you think Nast wanted to have on his audience?

SEE SKILLBUILDER HANDBOOK, PAGE R24.

Civil Service Replaces Patronage

The desire for power and money that made local politics corrupt in the industrial age also infected national politics.

PATRONAGE SPURS REFORM Since the beginning of the 19th century, presidents had complained about the problem of **patronage,** or the giving of government jobs to people who had helped a candidate get elected. In Andrew Jackson's administration, this policy was known as the spoils system. People from cabinet members to workers who scrubbed the steps of the Capitol owed their jobs to political connections. As might be expected, some government employees were not qualified for the positions they filled. Moreover, political appointees, whether qualified or not, sometimes used their positions for personal gain.

Reformers began to press for the elimination of patronage and the adoption of a merit system of hiring. Jobs in **civil service**—government administration—should go to the most qualified persons, reformers believed. It should not matter what political views they held or who recommended them. C

MAIN IDEA

Analyzing Causes

C How did patronage contribute to government incompetence and fraud?

REFORM UNDER HAYES, GARFIELD, AND ARTHUR Civil service reform made gradual progress under Presidents Hayes, Garfield, and Arthur. Republican president **Rutherford B. Hayes,** elected in 1876, could not convince Congress to support reform, so he used other means. Hayes named independents to his cabinet. He also set up a commission to investigate the nation's customhouses, which were notorious centers of patronage. On the basis of the commission's report, Hayes fired two of the top officials of New York City's customhouse, where jobs were controlled by the Republican Party. These firings enraged the Republican New York senator and political boss Roscoe Conkling and his supporters, the Stalwarts.

When Hayes decided not to run for reelection in 1880, a free-for-all broke out at the Republican convention, between the Stalwarts—who opposed changes in the spoils system—and reformers. Since neither Stalwarts nor reformers could win a majority of delegates, the convention settled on an independent presidential candidate, Ohio congressman **James A. Garfield.** To balance out Garfield's ties to reformers, the Republicans nominated for vice-president **Chester A. Arthur,** one of Conkling's supporters. Despite Arthur's inclusion on the ticket, Garfield angered the Stalwarts by giving reformers most of his patronage jobs once he was elected.

On July 2, 1881, as President Garfield walked through the Washington, D.C., train station, he was shot two times by a mentally unbalanced lawyer named Charles Guiteau, whom Garfield had turned down for a job. The would-be assassin announced, "I did it and I will go to jail for it. I am a Stalwart and Arthur is now president." Garfield finally died from his wounds on September 19. Despite his ties to the Stalwarts, Chester Arthur turned reformer when he became president. His first message to Congress urged legislators to pass a civil service law.

The resulting **Pendleton Civil Service Act** of 1883 authorized a bipartisan civil service commission to make

RUTHERFORD B. HAYES (1877–1881)

"Nobody ever left the presidency with less regret . . . than I do."

JAMES A. GARFIELD (1881)

"Assassination can be no more guarded against than death by lightning."

CHESTER A. ARTHUR (1881–1885)

"There doesn't seem to be anything else for an ex-president to do but . . . raise big pumpkins."

appointments to federal jobs through a merit system based on candidates' performance on an examination. By 1901, more than 40 percent of all federal jobs had been classified as civil service positions, but the Pendleton Act had mixed consequences. On the one hand, public administration became more honest and efficient. On the other hand, because officials could no longer pressure employees for campaign contributions, politicians turned to other sources for donations.

Business Buys Influence

MAIN IDEA

Analyzing Effects

D What were the positive and the negative effects of the Pendleton Civil Service Act?

With employees no longer a source of campaign contributions, politicians turned to wealthy business owners. Therefore, the alliance between government and big business became stronger than ever. D

HARRISON, CLEVELAND, AND HIGH TARIFFS Big business hoped the government would preserve, or even raise, the tariffs that protected domestic industries from foreign competition. The Democratic Party, however, opposed high tariffs because they increased prices. In 1884, the Democratic Party won a presidential election for the first time in 28 years with candidate **Grover Cleveland.** As president, Cleveland tried to lower tariff rates, but Congress refused to support him.

In 1888, Cleveland ran for reelection on a low-tariff platform against the former Indiana senator **Benjamin Harrison,** the grandson of President William Henry Harrison. Harrison's campaign was financed by large contributions from companies that wanted tariffs even higher than they were. Although Cleveland won about 100,000 more popular votes than Harrison, Harrison took a majority of the electoral votes and the presidency. He signed the McKinley Tariff Act of 1890, which raised tariffs on manufactured goods to their highest level yet.

In 1892, Cleveland was elected again—the only president to serve two nonconsecutive terms. He supported a bill for lowering the McKinley Tariff but refused to sign it because it also provided for a federal income tax. The Wilson-Gorman Tariff became law in 1894 without the president's signature. In 1897, William McKinley was inaugurated president and raised tariffs once again.

The attempt to reduce the tariff had failed, but the spirit of reform was not dead. New developments in areas ranging from technology to mass culture would help redefine American society as the United States moved into the 20th century.

SECTION 3 ASSESSMENT

1. **TERMS & NAMES** For each term or name, write a sentence explaining its significance.
   - **political machine**
   - **graft**
   - **Boss Tweed**
   - **patronage**
   - **civil service**
   - **Rutherford B. Hayes**
   - **James A. Garfield**
   - **Chester A. Arthur**
   - **Pendleton Civil Service Act**
   - **Grover Cleveland**
   - **Benjamin Harrison**

MAIN IDEA

2. **TAKING NOTES**
   In a chart like the one shown, list examples of corruption in 19th-century politics.

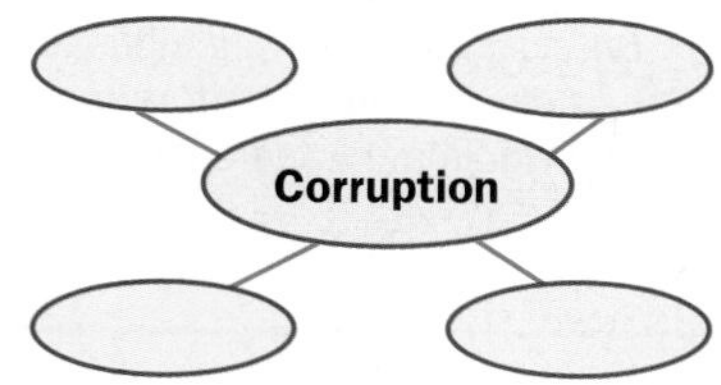

CRITICAL THINKING

3. **EVALUATING LEADERSHIP**
   Reread the quotation from James Pendergast on page 268. Explain whether you agree or disagree that machine politicians did not coerce people.

4. **ANALYZING CAUSES**
   Why do you think tariff reform failed? Support your response with evidence from the chapter.

5. **HYPOTHESIZING**
   How do you think politics in the United States would have been different if the Pendleton Civil Service Act had not been passed?
   Think About:
   - the act's impact on federal workers
   - the act's impact on political fundraising
   - Republican Party conflicts

CHAPTER 7 ASSESSMENT

TERMS & NAMES

For each term or name below, write a sentence explaining its connection to immigration and urbanization.

1. Ellis Island
2. Gentlemen's Agreement
3. Americanization movement
4. Jane Addams
5. political machine
6. graft
7. Boss Tweed
8. patronage
9. Rutherford B. Hayes
10. Pendleton Civil Service Act

MAIN IDEAS

Use your notes and the information in the chapter to answer the following questions.

The New Immigrants *(pages 254–259)*

1. What trends or events in other countries prompted people to move to the United States in the late 19th and early 20th centuries?
2. What difficulties did many of these new immigrants face?

The Challenges of Urbanization *(pages 262–266)*

3. Why did cities in the United States grow rapidly in the decades following the Civil War?
4. What problems did this rapid growth pose for cities?
5. What solutions to urban problems did the settlement-house movement propose?

Politics in the Gilded Age *(pages 267–271)*

6. Why did machine politics become common in big cities in the late 19th century?
7. What government problems arose as a result of patronage?
8. Summarize the views of Grover Cleveland and Benjamin Harrison on tariffs.

CRITICAL THINKING

1. **USING YOUR NOTES** In a diagram like the one below, show one result of and one reaction against (a) the increase in immigration and (b) the increase in machine politics.

		Result		Reaction
Increased Immigration	⟶	______	⟶	______
Increased Machine Politics	⟶	______	⟶	______

2. **EVALUATING** In the 1860s, Horace Greeley—editor of the *New York Tribune*—remarked, "We cannot all live in the cities, yet nearly all seem determined to do so." Why do you think this was true at the end of the 19th century? Do you think it is still true? Why or why not?

3. **COMPARING** How were politicians like Boss Tweed similar to industrial magnates like Carnegie and Rockefeller?

VISUAL SUMMARY IMMIGRANTS AND URBANIZATION

IMMIGRATION AND MIGRATION

- Poverty and persecution cause millions of people to leave Europe, China, Japan, the Caribbean, and Mexico for the United States.
- Immigrants are forced to adapt to a new language and culture.
- Changes in agriculture cause people to migrate from the rural U.S. to the cities in search of work.
- Many immigrants and migrants face discrimination in their efforts to find jobs and housing.

URBANIZATION

- The influx of immigrants and migrants causes a population boom in cities.
- City services, such as housing, transportation, water, and sanitation, are stretched to the limit.
- Reformers try to fix urban problems through education, training, charity, and political action.

POLITICS

- Political machines develop to take advantage of the needs of immigrants and the urban poor.
- City politicians use fraud and graft to maintain political power.
- Corruption in national politics results in the call for civil service jobs to be awarded on the basis of merit.
- Big business's growing influence on politics defeats tariff reform that would aid wage-earners.

Standardized Test Practice

Use the quotation and your knowledge of U.S. history to answer question 1.

> **"The Chinese . . . ask for fair treatment. . . . Since the first restriction law was passed the United States has received as immigrants more than two million Austro-Hungarians, two million Italians and a million and a half Russians and Finns. Each of these totals is from five to seven times the whole amount of Chinese immigration of all classes during thirty years of free immigration. . . . The question is not now of the admission of laborers, but whether other Chinese who are entitled to come under both law and treaty shall receive the same courtesies as people of other nations, and shall be relieved from many harassing regulations. They must no longer be detained, photographed and examined as if they were suspected of crime."**
>
> —Ng Poon Chew, from *The Treatment of the Exempt Classes of Chinese in the United States*

1. The information in the passage supports which *one* of the following points of view?

   A European immigration should be restricted.
   B Chinese laborers should be allowed to immigrate.
   C All immigrants are treated like criminals.
   D Chinese immigrants and European immigrants should be treated the same.

Use the cartoon and your knowledge of U.S. history to answer question 2.

TAMMANY RING
WHO STOLE THE PEOPLE'S MONEY? — DO TELL. N.Y. TIMES.
'TWAS HIM

2. The cartoon suggests that Boss Tweed (the large figure at left) —

   F was solely responsible for stealing the people's money.
   G did not steal the people's money.
   H had help from his associates in stealing the people's money.
   J was loyal to his associates.

ADDITIONAL TEST PRACTICE, pages S1–S33.

CLASSZONE.COM

ALTERNATIVE ASSESSMENT

1. **INTERACT WITH HISTORY** Recall your discussion of the question on page 253:

What would you do to improve conditions?

With what you have learned about the challenges faced by immigrants in the 19th century, consider how you would revise your answer. Discuss the following issue:

- What were the best solutions attempted by government and reformers in the 1800s?

Create a pamphlet promoting the reform, improvement, or government solution you chose.

2. **VIDEO** **LEARNING FROM MEDIA** View the *American Stories* video, "From China to Chinatown: Fong See's American Dream." Discuss the following questions with a small group; then do the activity.

- How did Fong See overcome the difficulties facing Asian immigrants in America during his lifetime?
- What did Lisa See learn about living in a diverse society from her great-grandfather's experience?

Cooperative Learning Activity Share stories of immigration or the experiences of recent immigrants to the U.S. that you have heard or read about. With the group, create a multimedia presentation of these stories. Use pictures, text, and sound to represent the stories.

CHAPTER 8 LIFE AT THE TURN OF THE 20TH CENTURY

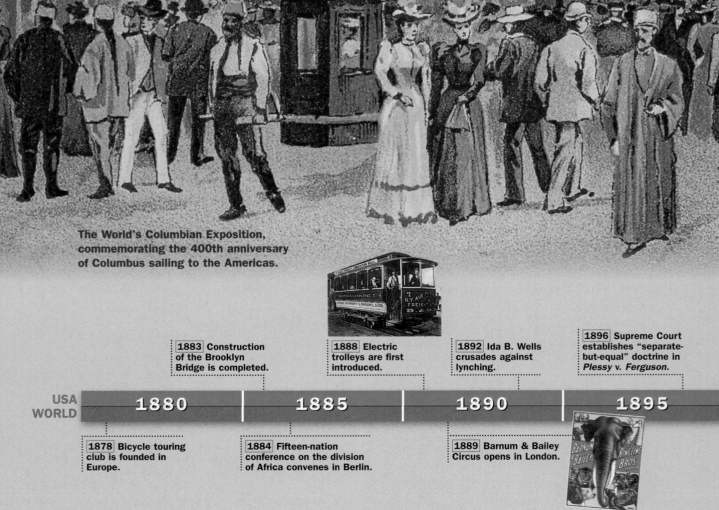

The World's Columbian Exposition, commemorating the 400th anniversary of Columbus sailing to the Americas.

USA

1883 Construction of the Brooklyn Bridge is completed.

1888 Electric trolleys are first introduced.

1892 Ida B. Wells crusades against lynching.

1896 Supreme Court establishes "separate-but-equal" doctrine in *Plessy* v. *Ferguson*.

1880 | 1885 | 1890 | 1895

WORLD

1878 Bicycle touring club is founded in Europe.

1884 Fifteen-nation conference on the division of Africa convenes in Berlin.

1889 Barnum & Bailey Circus opens in London.

INTERACT
WITH HISTORY

It is the summer of 1893. In Chicago, the World's Columbian Exposition is in full swing. Besides Thomas Edison's kinetograph—a camera that records motion, attractions include a towering "Ferris wheel" that lifts trolley cars into the sky and the first hamburgers in America. More than 21 million people will attend the exposition. You will be one of them.

How will the latest technology change your life?

Examine the Issues

- How can technology contribute to new forms of recreation?
- What types of inventions transform communications?
- Why would mass media emerge at this time?

RESEARCH LINKS **CLASSZONE.COM**

Visit the Chapter 8 links for more information about Life at the Turn of the 20th Century.

1900 William McKinley is reelected.

1901 McKinley is assassinated.

1901 Theodore Roosevelt becomes president.

1904 Theodore Roosevelt is elected president.

1908 Henry Ford introduces the Model T.

1908 William H. Taft is elected president.

1912 Woodrow Wilson is elected president.

1916 Woodrow Wilson is reelected.

1900 | 1905 | 1910 | 1915

1899 Austrian psychoanalyst Sigmund Freud publishes *The Interpretation of Dreams.*

1910 Mexican Revolution begins.

1914 World War I begins in Europe.

Science and Urban Life

MAIN IDEA	WHY IT MATTERS NOW	Terms & Names
Advances in science and technology helped solve urban problems, including overcrowding.	American cities continue to depend on the results of scientific and technological research.	•Louis Sullivan •Daniel Burnham •Frederick Law Olmsted •Orville and Wilbur Wright •George Eastman

One American's Story

The Brooklyn Bridge, connecting Brooklyn to the island of Manhattan in New York City, opened in 1883. It took 14 years to build. Each day, laborers descended to work in a caisson, or watertight chamber, that took them deep beneath the East River. E. F. Farrington, a mechanic who worked on the bridge, described the working conditions.

A Personal Voice E. F. FARRINGTON

> **"Inside the caisson everything wore an unreal, weird appearance. There was a confused sensation in the head . . . What with the flaming lights, the deep shadows, the confusing noise of hammers, drills, and chains, the half-naked forms flitting about . . . one might, if of a poetic temperament, get a realizing sense of Dante's Inferno."**
>
> —quoted in *The Great Bridge*

In 1883, New Yorkers celebrated the opening of the world's longest suspension bridge, the 1,595-foot-long Brooklyn Bridge.

Four years later, trains ran across the bridge 24 hours a day and carried more than 30 million travelers each year.

Technology and City Life

Engineering innovations, such as the Brooklyn Bridge, laid the groundwork for modern American life. Cities in every industrial area of the country expanded both outward and upward. In 1870, only 25 American cities had populations of 50,000 or more; by 1890, 58 cities could make that claim. By the turn of the 20th century, due to the increasing number of industrial jobs, four out of ten Americans made their homes in cities.

In response to these changes, technological advances began to meet the nation's needs for communication, transportation, and space. One remedy for more urban space was to build toward the sky.

SKYSCRAPERS Architects were able to design taller buildings because of two factors: the invention of elevators and the development of internal steel skeletons to bear the weight of buildings. In 1890–1891, architect **Louis Sullivan** designed the ten-story Wainwright Building in St. Louis. He called the new breed of skyscraper a "proud and soaring thing." The tall building's appearance was graceful because its steel framework supported both floors and walls.

The skyscraper became America's greatest contribution to architecture, "a new thing under the sun," according to the architect Frank Lloyd Wright, who studied under Sullivan. Skyscrapers solved the practical problem of how to make the best use of limited and expensive space. The unusual form of another skyscraper, the Flatiron Building, seemed perfect for its location at one of New York's busiest intersections. **Daniel Burnham** designed this slender 285-foot tower in 1902. The Flatiron Building and other new buildings served as symbols of a rich and optimistic society. (A)

MAIN IDEA

Analyzing Causes
(A) How did new technologies make the building of skyscrapers practical?

ELECTRIC TRANSIT As skyscrapers expanded upward, changes in transportation allowed cities to spread outward. Before the Civil War, horses had drawn the earliest streetcars over iron rails embedded in city streets. In some cities during the 1870s and 1880s, underground moving cables powered streetcar lines. Electricity, however, transformed urban transportation.

In 1888 Richmond, Virginia, became the first American city to electrify its urban transit. Other cities followed. By the turn of the twentieth century, intricate networks of electric streetcars—also called trolley cars—ran from outlying neighborhoods to downtown offices and department stores.

New railroad lines also fed the growth of suburbs, allowing residents to commute to downtown jobs. New York's northern suburbs alone supplied 100,000 commuters each day to the central business district.

A few large cities moved their streetcars far above street level, creating elevated or "el" trains. Other cities, like New York, built subways by moving their rail lines underground. These streetcars, elevated trains, and subways enabled cities to annex suburban developments that mushroomed along the advancing transportation routes. (B)

MAIN IDEA

Summarizing
(B) How did electric transit impact urban life?

ENGINEERING AND URBAN PLANNING Steel-cable suspension bridges, like the Brooklyn Bridge, also brought cities' sections closer together. Sometimes these bridges provided recreational opportunities. In his design for the Brooklyn Bridge, for example, John Augustus Roebling provided an elevated promenade whose "principal use will be to allow people of leisure, and old and young invalids, to promenade over the bridge on fine days." This need for open spaces in the midst of crowded commercial cities inspired the emerging science of urban planning.

Vocabulary
promenade: a public place for walking

City planners sought to restore a measure of serenity to the environment by designing recreational areas. Landscape architect **Frederick Law Olmsted** spearheaded the movement for planned urban parks.

In 1857 Olmsted, along with English-born architect Calvert Vaux, helped draw up a plan for "Greensward," which was selected to become Central Park, in New York City. Olmsted envisioned the park as a haven in the center of the busy city. The finished park featured boating and

The Flatiron Building, shown here under construction, stands at the intersection of Fifth Avenue and 23rd Street in New York City.

tennis facilities, a zoo, and bicycle paths. Olmsted hoped that the park's beauty would soothe the city's inhabitants and let them enjoy a "natural" setting.

A Personal Voice FREDERICK LAW OLMSTED

"The main object and justification [of the park] is simply to produce a certain influence in the minds of people and through this to make life in the city healthier and happier. The character of this influence . . . is to be produced by means of scenes, through observation of which the mind may be more or less lifted out of moods and habits."

—quoted in *Frederick Law Olmsted's New York*

In the 1870s, Olmsted planned landscaping for Washington, D.C., and St. Louis. He also drew the initial designs for "the Emerald Necklace," Boston's parks system. Boston's Back Bay area, originally a 450-acre swamp, was drained and developed by urban planners into an area of elegant streets and cultural attractions, including Olmstead's parks.

CITY PLANNING By contrast, Chicago, with its explosive growth from 30,000 people in 1850 to 300,000 in 1870, represented a nightmare of unregulated expansion. Fortunately for the city, a local architect, Daniel Burnham, was intrigued

History Through *Architecture*

THE CHICAGO PLAN

This map from Daniel Burnham's original plan of Chicago looks deceptively like an ordinary map today. But at the time, it was almost revolutionary in its vision, and it inspired city planners all over the country.

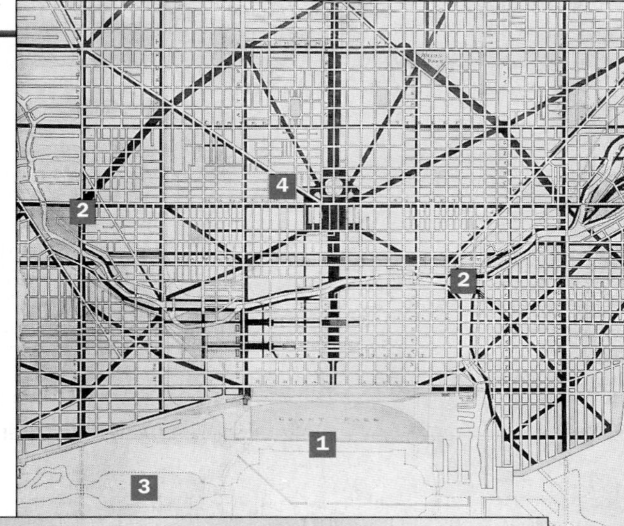

1 **Chicago's Lakefront** First, Burnham designed the "White City" to host the 1893 World's Columbian Exposition. His greatest legacy to Chicago may have been his idea for a lakefront park system, complete with beaches, playing fields, and playgrounds.

2 **Neighborhood Parks** Though not all cities could claim a lakefront vista for recreation, most cities sprinkled neighborhood parks where their residents needed them. Urban planners provided for local parks—such as Lincoln Park in Chicago—so that "the sweet breath of plant life" would be available to everyone.

3 **Harbors For Cities** On the Great Lakes, the shipping business depended on accessible harbors. Burnham saw the advantage of harbors for recreation and commercial purposes, but he advocated moving the harbors away from the central business districts to free space for public use.

4 **The Civic Center** Burnham redesigned the street pattern to create a group of long streets that would converge on a grand plaza, a practice reflected in other American cities. The convergence of major thoroughfares at a city's center helped create a unified city from a host of neighborhoods.

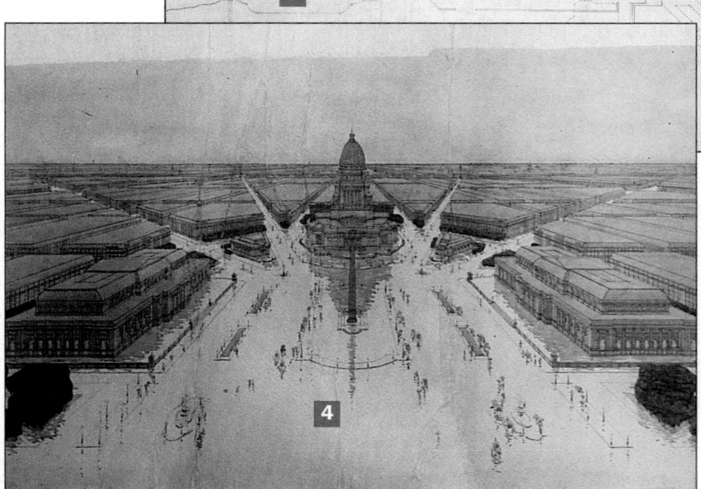

▲ **Unity was the goal of the architect of Chicago's city center.**

SKILLBUILDER Interpreting Visual Sources

1. Why did Chicago's location make it a good choice for urban planning?
2. How was Chicago's importance as a shipping center maintained?

SEE SKILLBUILDER HANDBOOK, PAGE R23.

by the prospect of remaking the city. His motto was "Make no little plans. They have no magic to stir men's blood." He oversaw the transformation of a swampy area near Lake Michigan into a glistening White City for Chicago's 1893 World's Columbian Exposition. Majestic exhibition halls, statues, the first Ferris wheel, and a lagoon greeted more than 21 million visitors who came to the city.

Many urban planners saw in Burnham's White City glorious visions of future cities. Burnham, however, left Chicago an even more important legacy: an overall plan for the city, crowned by elegant parks strung along Lake Michigan. As a result, Chicago's lakefront today features curving banks of grass and sandy beaches instead of a jumbled mass of piers and warehouses. C

MAIN IDEA

Summarizing
C List three major changes in cities near the turn of the century. What effect did each have?

WORLD STAGE

THE GARDEN CITY

Urban planning in the United States had European counterparts. In *Tomorrow: A Peaceful Path to Social Reform* (1898), for example, the British city planner Ebenezer Howard wrote of a planned residential community called a garden city.

Howard wanted to combine the benefits of urban life with easy access to nature. His city plan was based on concentric circles—with a town at the center and a wide circle of rural land on the perimeter. The town center included a garden, concert hall, museum, theater, library, and hospital.

The circle around the town center included a park, a shopping center, a conservatory, a residential area, and industry. Six wide avenues radiated out from the town center. In 1903, Letchworth, England served as the model for Howard's garden city.

New Technologies

New developments in communication brought the nation closer together. In addition to a railroad network that now spanned the nation, advances in printing, aviation, and photography helped to speed the transfer of information.

A REVOLUTION IN PRINTING By 1890, the literacy rate in the United States had risen to nearly 90 percent. Publishers turned out ever-increasing numbers of books, magazines, and newspapers to meet the growing demand of the reading public. A series of technological advances in printing aided their efforts.

American mills began to produce huge quantities of cheap paper from wood pulp. The new paper proved durable enough to withstand high-speed presses. The electrically powered web-perfecting press, for example, printed on both sides of a continuous paper roll, rather than on just one side. It then cut, folded, and counted the pages as they came down the line. Faster production and lower costs made newspapers and magazines more affordable. People could now buy newspapers for a penny a copy.

AIRPLANES In the early 20th century, brothers **Orville and Wilbur Wright**, bicycle manufacturers from Dayton, Ohio, experimented with new engines powerful enough to keep "heavier-than-air" craft aloft. First the Wright brothers built a glider. Then they commissioned a four-cylinder internal combustion engine, chose a propeller, and designed a biplane with a 40∏4© wingspan. Their first successful flight—on December 17, 1903, at Kitty Hawk, North Carolina—covered 120 feet and lasted 12 seconds. Orville later described the take-off.

Vocabulary
internal combustion engine: an engine in which fuel is burned within the engine rather than in an external furnace

A PERSONAL VOICE ORVILLE WRIGHT

> **"After running the motor a few minutes to heat it up, I released the wire that held the machine to the track, and the machine started forward into the wind. Wilbur ran at the side of the machine . . . to balance it. . . . Unlike the start on the 14th, made in a calm, the machine, facing a 27-mile wind, started very slowly. . . . One of the life-saving men snapped the camera for us, taking a picture just as the machine had reached the end of the track and had risen to a height of about two feet."**
>
> —quoted in *Smithsonian Frontiers of Flight*

Orville (*right*) and Wilbur Wright at home in Dayton, Ohio in 1909. ▼

AVIATION PIONEERS

In 1892, Orville and Wilbur Wright opened a bicycle shop in Dayton, Ohio. They used the profits to fund experiments in aeronautics, the construction of aircraft. In 1903, the Wright brothers took a gasoline-powered airplane that they had designed to a sandy hill outside Kitty Hawk, North Carolina.

The airplane was powered by a 4-cylinder 12-horse-power piston engine, designed and constructed by the bicycle shop's mechanic, Charles Taylor. The piston—a solid cylinder fit snugly into a hollow cylinder that moves back and forth under pressure—was standard until jet-propelled aircraft came into service in the 1940s. ▶

The engine is the heaviest component in airplane construction. The design of lighter engines was the most important development in early aviation history. ▶

Early Airplane Engines and Their Weights

Date	Name of Engine	Approximate Weight per Unit of Horsepower
1880s	Otto	440 lbs (200 kg)
1903	Wright	13 lbs (6 kg)
1910	Gnome	3.3 lbs (1.5 kg)
1918	V-12 Liberty	2 lbs (1 kg)
1944	Wright Cyclone	1.1 lbs (0.5 kg)

Source: *The History of Invention,* Trevor I. Williams

◀ **On December 17, Orville Wright made the first successful flight of a powered aircraft in history. The public paid little attention. But within two years, the brothers were making 30-minute flights. By 1908, the pioneer aviators had signed a contract for production of the Wright airplane with the U.S. Army.**

▲ **By 1918, the Postal Service began airmail service, as shown in this preliminary sketch of a DH4-Mail. Convinced of the great potential of flight, the government established the first transcontinental airmail service in 1920.**

Within two years, the Wright brothers had increased their flights to 24 miles. By 1920, convinced of the great potential of flight, the U.S. government had established the first transcontinental airmail service.

PHOTOGRAPHY EXPLOSION Before the 1880s, photography was a professional activity. Because of the time required to take a picture and the weight of the equipment, a photographer could not shoot a moving object. In addition, photographers had to develop their shots immediately.

New techniques eliminated the need to develop pictures right away. **George Eastman** developed a series of more convenient alternatives to the heavy glass plates previously used. Now, instead of carrying their darkrooms around with them, photographers could use flexible film, coated with gelatin emulsions, and could send their film to a studio for processing. When professional photographers were slow to begin using the new film, Eastman decided to aim his product at the masses.

In 1888, Eastman introduced his Kodak camera. The purchase price of $25 included a 100-picture roll of film. After taking the pictures, the photographer would send the camera back to Eastman's Rochester, New York, factory. For $10, the pictures were developed and returned with the camera reloaded. Easily held and operated, the Kodak prompted millions of Americans to become amateur photographers. The camera also helped to create the field of photojournalism. Reporters could now photograph events as they occurred. When the Wright brothers first flew their simple airplane at Kitty Hawk, an amateur photographer captured the first successful flight on film.

KEY PLAYER

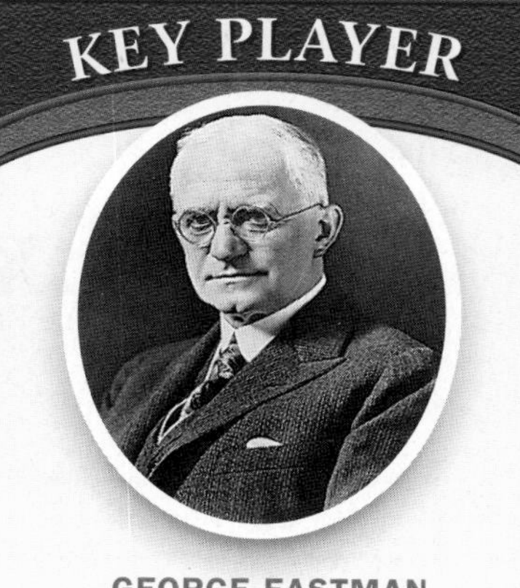

GEORGE EASTMAN
1854–1932

In 1877, when George Eastman took up photography as a hobby, he had to lug more than 100 pounds of equipment for one day's outing. To lighten his load, he replaced heavy glass plates with film that could be rolled onto a spool.

In 1888, Eastman sold his first roll-film camera. Eastman called his new camera (shown at left) the Kodak, because the made-up name was short and memorable. It was popularized by the slogan "You Press the Button, We Do the Rest."

SECTION 1 ASSESSMENT

1. **TERMS & NAMES** For each term or name, write a sentence explaining its significance.
   - **Louis Sullivan**
   - **Daniel Burnham**
   - **Frederick Law Olmsted**
   - **Orville and Wilbur Wright**
   - **George Eastman**

MAIN IDEA

2. **TAKING NOTES**
   Using a three-column chart, such as the one below, list three important changes in city design, communication, and transportation.

City Design	Communication	Transportation
1.	1.	1.
2.	2.	2.
3.	3.	3.

Which change had the greatest impact on urban life? Why?

CRITICAL THINKING

3. **HYPOTHESIZING**
   If you had been an urban planner at the turn of the century, what new ideas would you have included in your plan for the ideal city?
   Think About:
   - Olmsted's plans for Central Park
   - Burnham's ideas for Chicago
   - the concept of the garden city

4. **EVALUATING**
   Which scientific or technological development described in this section had the greatest impact on American culture? Use details from the text to justify your choice.

5. **SUMMARIZING**
   How did bridge building contribute to the growth of cities?

Expanding Public Education

MAIN IDEA

Reforms in public education led to a rise in national literacy and the promotion of public education.

WHY IT MATTERS NOW

The public education system is the foundation of the democratic ideals of American society.

Terms & Names

- **Booker T. Washington**
- **Tuskegee Normal and Industrial Institute**
- **W. E. B. Du Bois**
- **Niagara Movement**

One American's Story

William Torrey Harris was an educational reformer who saw the public schools as a great instrument "to lift all classes of people into . . . civilized life." As U.S. commissioner of education from 1889 to 1906, Harris promoted the ideas of great educators like Horace Mann and John Dewey—particularly the belief that schools exist for the children and not the teachers. Schools, according to Harris, should properly prepare students for full participation in community life.

A PERSONAL VOICE WILLIAM TORREY HARRIS

"Every [educational] method must . . . be looked at from two points of view: first, its capacity to secure the development of rationality or of the true adjustment of the individual to the social whole; and, second, its capacity to strengthen the individuality of the pupil and avoid the danger of obliterating the personality of the child by securing blind obedience in place of intelligent cooperation, and by mechanical memorizing in place of rational insight."

—quoted in *Public Schools and Moral Education*

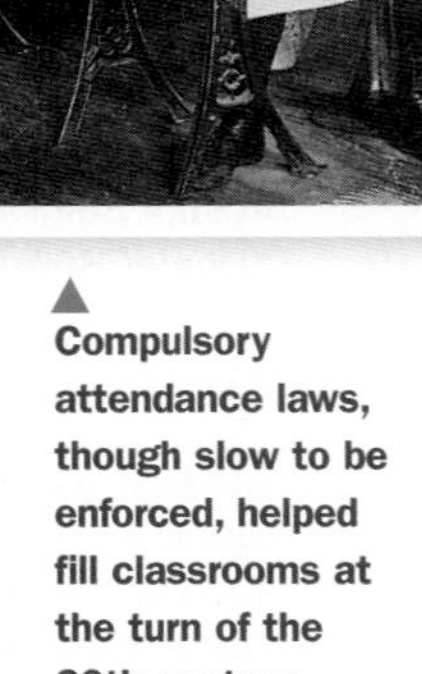

▲ **Compulsory attendance laws, though slow to be enforced, helped fill classrooms at the turn of the 20th century.**

Many other middle-class reformers agreed with Harris and viewed the public schools as training grounds for employment and citizenship. People believed that economic development depended on scientific and technological knowledge. As a result, they viewed education as a key to greater security and social status. Others saw the public schools as the best opportunity to assimilate the millions of immigrants entering American society. Most people also believed that public education was necessary for a stable and prosperous democratic nation.

Expanding Public Education

Although most states had established public schools by the Civil War, many school-age children still received no formal schooling. The majority of students who went to school left within four years, and few went to high school.

SCHOOLS FOR CHILDREN Between 1865 and 1895, states passed laws requiring 12 to 16 weeks annually of school attendance by students between the ages of 8 and 14. The curriculum emphasized reading, writing, and arithmetic. However, the emphasis on rote memorization and the uneven quality of teachers drew criticism. Strict rules and physical punishment made many students miserable.

One 13-year-old boy explained to a Chicago school inspector why he hid in a warehouse basement instead of going to school.

A Personal Voice

"**They hits ye if yer don't learn, and they hits ye if ye whisper, and they hits ye if ye have string in yer pocket, and they hits ye if yer seat squeaks, and they hits ye if ye don't stan' up in time, and they hits ye if yer late, and they hits ye if ye ferget the page.**"

—anonymous schoolboy quoted in *The One Best System*

In spite of such problems, children began attending school at a younger age. Kindergartens, which had been created outside the public school system to offer childcare for employed mothers, became increasingly popular. The number of kindergartens surged from 200 in 1880 to 3,000 in 1900, and, under the guidance of William Torrey Harris, public school systems began to add kindergartens to their programs. (A)

MAIN IDEA

Drawing Conclusions
(A) Why did American children begin attending school at a younger age?

Although the pattern in public education in this era was one of growth, opportunities differed sharply for white and black students. In 1880, about 62 percent of white children attended elementary school, compared to about 34 percent of African-American children. Not until the 1940s would public school education become available to the majority of black children living in the South.

THE GROWTH OF HIGH SCHOOLS In the new industrial age, the economy demanded advanced technical and managerial skills. Moreover, business leaders like Andrew Carnegie pointed out that keeping workers loyal to capitalism required society to "provide ladders upon which the aspiring can rise."

By early 1900, more than half a million students attended high school. The curriculum expanded to include courses in science, civics, and social studies. And new vocational courses prepared male graduates for industrial jobs in drafting, carpentry, and mechanics, and female graduates for office work.

Expanding Education/Increasing Literacy

Year	Students Enrolled	Literacy in English (% of Population age 10 and over)
1871	7.6 million	80%
1880	9.9 million	83%
1890	12.7 million	87%
1900	15.5 million	89%
1910	17.8 million	92%
1920	21.6 million	94%

(icon) =1,000,000 students

Sources: *Statistical Abstract of the United States, 1921; Historical Statistics of the United States.*

SKILLBUILDER
Interpreting Graphs

1. By how much did the illiteracy rate drop from 1870 to 1920?
2. Does the number of immigrants during this period make the reduction more or less impressive? Why?

RACIAL DISCRIMINATION African Americans were mostly excluded from public secondary education. In 1890, fewer than 1 percent of black teenagers attended high school. More than two-thirds of these students went to private schools, which received no government financial support. By 1910, about 3 percent of African Americans between the ages of 15 and 19 attended high school, but a majority of these students still attended private schools.

EDUCATION FOR IMMIGRANTS Unlike African Americans, immigrants were encouraged to go to school. Of the nearly 10 million European immigrants settled in the United States between 1860 and 1890, many were Jewish people fleeing poverty and systematic oppression in eastern Europe. Most immigrants sent their children to America's free public schools, where they quickly became "Americanized." Years after she became a citizen, the Russian Jewish immigrant Mary Antin recalled the large numbers of non-English-speaking immigrant children. By the end of the school year, they could recite "patriotic verses in honor of George Washington and Abraham Lincoln . . . with plenty of enthusiasm."

Some people resented the suppression of their native languages in favor of English. Catholics were especially concerned because many public school systems had mandatory readings from the (Protestant) King James Version of the Bible. Catholic communities often set up parochial schools to give their children a Catholic education.

Vocabulary
parochial school: a school supported by a church parish

Thousands of adult immigrants attended night school to learn English and to qualify for American citizenship. Employers often offered daytime programs to Americanize their workers. At his Model T plant in Highland Park, Michigan, Henry Ford established a "Sociology Department," because "men of many nations must be taught American ways, the English language, and the right way to live." Ford's ideas were not universally accepted. Labor activists often protested that Ford's educational goals were aimed at weakening the trade union movement by teaching workers not to confront management. B

MAIN IDEA
Summarizing
B What institutions encouraged European immigrants to become assimilated?

NOW & THEN

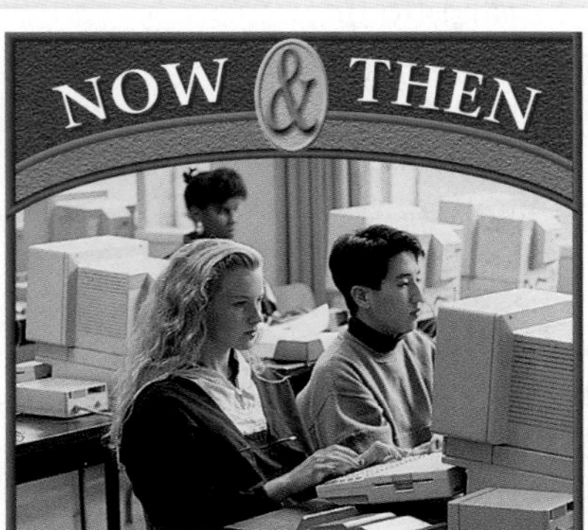

TECHNOLOGY AND SCHOOLS

In 1922, Thomas Alva Edison wrote, "I believe that the motion picture is destined to revolutionize our educational system and that in a few years it will supplant . . . the use of textbooks." Today's high schools show that the brilliant inventor was mistaken.

Recently, some people have predicted that computers will replace traditional classrooms and texts.

Computers allow video course-sharing, in which students in many schools view the same instructors. Students also use computers to access up-to-the-minute scientific data, such as weather information.

Expanding Higher Education

Although the number of students attending high school had increased by the turn of the century, only a minority of Americans had high school diplomas. At the same time, an even smaller minority—only 2.3 percent—of America's young people attended colleges and universities.

CHANGES IN UNIVERSITIES Between 1880 and 1920, college enrollments more than quadrupled. And colleges instituted major changes in curricula and admission policies. Industrial development changed the nation's educational needs. The research university emerged—offering courses in modern languages, the physical sciences, and the new disciplines of psychology and sociology. Professional schools in law and medicine were established. Private colleges and universities required entrance exams, but some state universities began to admit students by using the high school diploma as the entrance requirement.

HIGHER EDUCATION FOR AFRICAN AMERICANS After the Civil War, thousands of freed African Americans pursued higher education, despite their exclusion from white institutions. With the help of the Freedmen's Bureau and other groups, blacks founded Howard, Atlanta, and Fisk Universities, all of which opened between 1865 and 1868. Private donors could not, however, financially support or educate a sufficient number of black college graduates to meet the needs of the segregated communities. By 1900, out of about 9 million African Americans, only 3,880 were in attendance at colleges or professional schools. C

Synthesizing
C Describe the state of higher education for African Americans at the turn of the century.

The prominent African American educator, **Booker T. Washington,** believed that racism would end once blacks acquired useful labor skills and proved their economic value to society. Washington, who was born enslaved, graduated from Virginia's Hampton Institute. By 1881, he headed the **Tuskegee Normal and Industrial Institute,** now called Tuskegee University, in Alabama. Tuskegee aimed to equip African Americans with teaching diplomas and useful skills in agricultural, domestic, or mechanical work."No race," Washington said, "can prosper till it learns that there is as much dignity in tilling a field as in writing a poem."

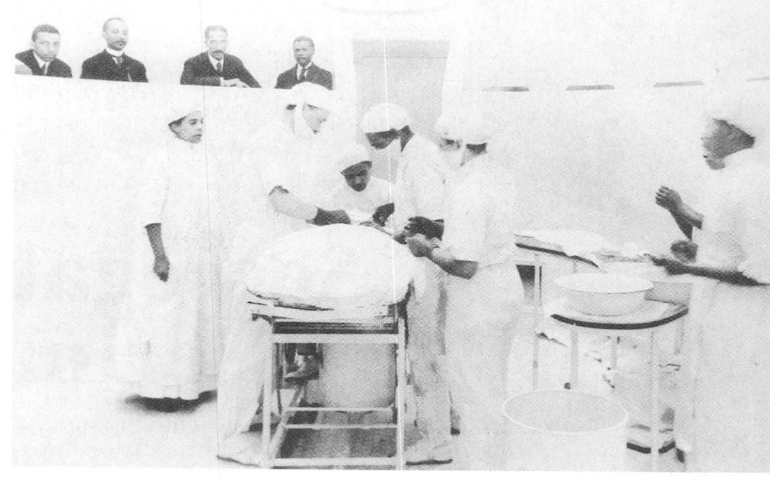

▲ Medical students and their professors work in the operating theater of the Moorland-Spingarn Research Center at Howard University.

By contrast, **W. E. B. Du Bois,** the first African American to receive a doctorate from Harvard (in 1895), strongly disagreed with Washington's gradual approach. In 1905, Dubois founded the **Niagara Movement,** which insisted that blacks should seek a liberal arts education so that the African-American community would have well-educated leaders.

Du Bois proposed that a group of educated blacks, the most "talented tenth" of the community, attempt to achieve immediate inclusion into mainstream American life. "We are Americans, not only by birth and by citizenship," Du Bois argued, "but by our political ideals. . . . And the greatest of those ideals is that ALL MEN ARE CREATED EQUAL."

By the turn of the 20th century, millions of people received the education they needed to cope with a rapidly changing world. At the same time, however, racial discrimination remained a thorn in the flesh of American society.

SECTION 2 ASSESSMENT

1. **TERMS & NAMES** For each term or name, write a sentence explaining its significance.
   - **Booker T. Washington**
   - **Tuskegee Normal and Industrial Institute**
   - **W. E. B. Du Bois**
   - **Niagara Movement**

MAIN IDEA

2. **TAKING NOTES**
   In a chart like the one below, list at least three developments in education at the turn of the 20th century and their major results.

Development	Result
1.	
2.	
3.	

Which educational development do you think was most important? Explain your choice.

CRITICAL THINKING

3. **HYPOTHESIZING**
   How might the economy and culture of the United States have been different without the expansion of public schools? **Think About:**
   - the goals of public schools and whether those goals have been met
   - why people supported expanding public education
   - the impact of public schools on the development of private schools

4. **COMPARING**
   Compare and contrast the views of Booker T. Washington and W. E. B. Du Bois on the subject of the education of African Americans.

Segregation and Discrimination

MAIN IDEA	WHY IT MATTERS NOW	Terms & Names
African Americans led the fight against voting restrictions and Jim Crow laws.	Today, African Americans have the legacy of a century-long battle for civil rights.	• Ida B. Wells • poll tax • grandfather clause • segregation • Jim Crow laws • *Plessy* v. *Ferguson* • debt peonage

One American's Story

Born into slavery shortly before emancipation, **Ida B. Wells** moved to Memphis in the early 1880s to work as a teacher. She later became an editor of a local paper. Racial justice was a persistent theme in Wells's reporting. The events of March 9, 1892 turned that theme into a crusade. Three African-American businessmen, friends of Wells, were lynched—illegally executed without trial. Wells saw lynching for what it was.

A PERSONAL VOICE IDA B. WELLS

"Thomas Moss, Calvin McDowell, and Lee Stewart had been lynched in Memphis . . . [where] no lynching had taken place before. . . . This is what opened my eyes to what lynching really was. An excuse to get rid of Negroes who were acquiring wealth and property and thus keep the race terrorized . . ."

—quoted in *Crusade for Justice*

▲ Ida B. Wells moved north to continue her fight against lynching by writing, lecturing, and organizing for civil rights.

African Americans were not the only group to experience violence and racial discrimination. Native Americans, Mexican residents, and Chinese immigrants also encountered bitter forms of oppression, particularly in the American West.

African Americans Fight Legal Discrimination

As African Americans exercised their newly won political and social rights during Reconstruction, they faced hostile and often violent opposition from whites. African Americans eventually fell victim to laws restricting their civil rights but never stopped fighting for equality. For at least ten years after the end of Reconstruction in 1877, African Americans in the South continued to vote and occasionally to hold political office. By the turn of the 20th century, however, Southern states had adopted a broad system of legal policies of racial discrimination and devised methods to weaken African-American political power.

VOTING RESTRICTIONS All Southern states imposed new voting restrictions and denied legal equality to African Americans. Some states, for example, limited the vote to people who could read, and required registration officials to administer a literacy test to test reading. Blacks trying to vote were often asked more difficult questions than whites, or given a test in a foreign language. Officials could pass or fail applicants as they wished.

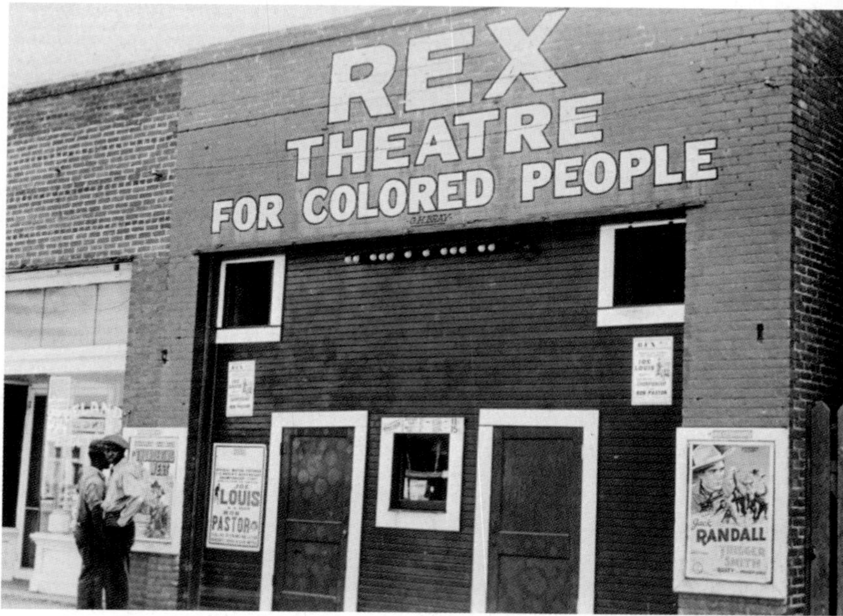

▲ This theater in Leland, Mississippi, was segregated under the Jim Crow laws.

Another requirement was the **poll tax**, an annual tax that had to be paid before qualifying to vote. Black as well as white sharecroppers were often too poor to pay the poll tax. To reinstate white voters who may have failed the literacy test or could not pay the poll tax, several Southern states added the **grandfather clause** to their constitutions. The clause stated that even if a man failed the literacy test or could not afford the poll tax, he was still entitled to vote if he, his father, or his grandfather had been eligible to vote before January 1, 1867. The date is important because before that time, freed slaves did not have the right to vote. The grandfather clause therefore did not allow them to vote.

JIM CROW LAWS During the 1870s and 1880s, the Supreme Court failed to overturn the poll tax or the grandfather clause, even though the laws undermined all federal protections for African Americans' civil rights. At the same time that blacks lost voting rights, Southern states passed racial **segregation** laws to separate white and black people in public and private facilities. These laws came to be known as **Jim Crow laws** after a popular old minstrel song that ended in the words "Jump, Jim Crow." Racial segregation was put into effect in schools, hospitals, parks, and transportation systems throughout the South.

Vocabulary
minstrel: one of a troupe of entertainers in blackface presenting a comic variety show

PLESSY* v. *FERGUSON Eventually a legal case reached the U.S. Supreme Court to test the constitutionality of segregation. In 1896, in ***Plessy* v. *Ferguson***, the Supreme Court ruled that the separation of races in public accommodations was legal and did not violate the Fourteenth Amendment. The decision established the doctrine of "separate but equal," which allowed states to maintain segregated facilities for blacks and whites as long as they provided equal service. The decision permitted legalized racial segregation for almost 60 years. (See *Plessy* v. *Ferguson*, page 290.) Ⓐ

MAIN IDEA
Analyzing Effects
Ⓐ How did the *Plessy* v. *Ferguson* ruling affect the civil rights of African Americans?

Turn-of-the-Century Race Relations

African Americans faced not only formal discrimination but also informal rules and customs, called racial etiquette, that regulated relationships between whites and blacks. Usually, these customs belittled and humiliated African Americans, enforcing their second-class status. For example, blacks and whites never shook hands, since shaking hands would have implied equality. Blacks also had to yield the sidewalk to white pedestrians, and black men always had to remove their hats for whites.

Some moderate reformers, like Booker T. Washington, earned support from whites. Washington suggested that whites and blacks work together for social progress.

A PERSONAL VOICE BOOKER T. WASHINGTON

> **"To those of the white race . . . I would repeat what I say to my own race. . . . Cast down your bucket among these people who have, without strikes and labour wars, tilled your fields, cleared your forests, builded your railroads and cities, and brought forth treasures from the bowels of the earth. . . . In all things that are purely social we can be as separate as the fingers, yet one as the hand in all things essential to mutual progress."**
>
> —Atlanta Exposition address, 1895

Washington hoped that improving the economic skills of African Americans would pave the way for long-term gains. People like Ida B. Wells and W. E. B. Du Bois, however, thought that the problems of inequality were too urgent to postpone. B

HISTORICAL SPOTLIGHT

WASHINGTON *VS.* DU BOIS

Booker T. Washington argued for a gradual approach to racial equality—suggesting that "it is at the bottom of life we must begin, and not at the top."

Ten years later, W. E. B. Du Bois denounced this view of gradual equality. Du Bois demanded full social and economic equality for African Americans, declaring that "persistent manly agitation is the way to liberty."

In 1909 the Niagara Movement, founded by Du Bois in 1905, became the National Association for the Advancement of Colored People (NAACP), with Du Bois as the editor of its journal, *The Crisis*. He wrote, "We refuse to surrender . . . leadership . . . to cowards and trucklers. We are men; we will be treated as men." The NAACP continues the fight for racial equality today.

MAIN IDEA

Summarizing

B What were Booker T. Washington's views about establishing racial equality?

VIOLENCE African Americans and others who did not follow the racial etiquette could face severe punishment or death. All too often, blacks who were accused of violating the etiquette were lynched. Between 1882 and 1892, more than 1,400 African-American men and women were shot, burned, or hanged without trial in the South. Lynching peaked in the 1880s and 1890s but continued well into the 20th century.

DISCRIMINATION IN THE NORTH Most African Americans lived in the segregated South, but by 1900, a number of blacks had moved to Northern cities. Many blacks migrated to Northern cities in search of better-paying jobs and social equality. But after their arrival, African Americans found that there was racial discrimination in the North as well. African Americans found themselves forced into segregated neighborhoods. They also faced discrimination in the workplace. Labor unions often discouraged black membership, and employers hired African-American labor only as a last resort and fired blacks before white employees.

Sometimes the competition between African Americans and working-class whites became violent, as in the New York City race riot of 1900. Violence erupted after a young black man, believing that his wife was being mistreated by a white policeman, killed the policeman. Word of the killing spread, and whites retaliated by attacking blacks. Northern blacks, however, were not alone in facing discrimination. Non-whites in the West also faced oppression. C

MAIN IDEA

Contrasting

C How did conditions for African Americans in the North differ from their circumstances in the South?

Discrimination in the West

Western communities were home to people of many backgrounds working and living side by side. Native Americans still lived in the Western territories claimed by the United States. Asian immigrants went to America's Pacific Coast in search of wealth and work. Mexicans continued to inhabit the American Southwest. African Americans were also present, especially in former slave-holding areas, such as Texas. Still, racial tensions often made life difficult.

MEXICAN WORKERS In the late 1800s, the railroads hired more Mexicans than members of any other ethnic group to construct rail lines in the Southwest.

Mexican track workers for the Southern Pacific railroad posed for this group photo taken sometime between 1910 and 1915.

Mexicans were accustomed to the region's hot, dry climate. But the work was grueling, and the railroads made them work for less money than other ethnic groups.

Mexicans were also vital to the development of mining and agriculture in the Southwest. When the 1902 National Reclamation Act gave government assistance for irrigation projects, many southwest desert areas bloomed. Mexican workers became the major labor force in the agricultural industries of the region.

Vocabulary
peon: a worker bound in servitude to a landlord creditor

Some Mexicans, however, as well as African Americans in the Southwest, were forced into **debt peonage,** a system that bound laborers into slavery in order to work off a debt to the employer. Not until 1911 did the Supreme Court declare involuntary peonage a violation of the Thirteenth Amendment.

EXCLUDING THE CHINESE By 1880, more than 100,000 Chinese immigrants lived in the United States. White people's fear of job competition with the Chinese immigrants often pushed the Chinese into segregated schools and neighborhoods. Strong opposition to Chinese immigration developed, and not only in the West. (See Chinese Exclusion Act, page 259.)

Racial discrimination posed terrible legal and economic problems for nonwhites throughout the United States at the turn of the century. More people, however, whites in particular, had leisure time for new recreational activities, as well as money to spend on a growing arrray of consumer products.

SECTION 3 ASSESSMENT

1. **TERMS & NAMES** For each term or name, write a sentence explaining its significance.
   - **Ida B. Wells**
   - **poll tax**
   - **grandfather clause**
   - **segregation**
   - **Jim Crow laws**
   - ***Plessy* v. *Ferguson***
   - **debt peonage**

MAIN IDEA

2. **TAKING NOTES**
   Review the section, and find five key events to place on a time line as shown.

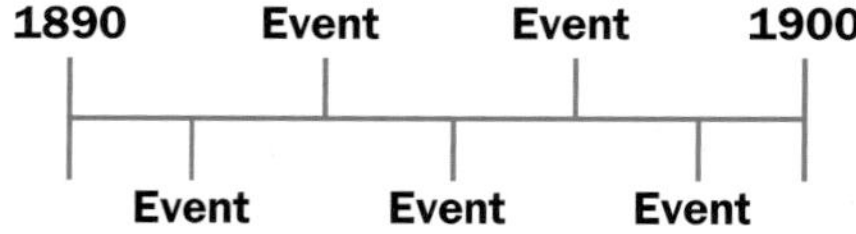

   Which of these events do you think was most important? Why?

CRITICAL THINKING

3. **IDENTIFYING PROBLEMS**
   How did segregation and discrimination affect the lives of African Americans at the turn of the 20th century?
4. **COMPARING**
   What did some African-American leaders do to fight discrimination?
5. **CONTRASTING**
   How did the challenges and opportunities for Mexicans in the United States differ from those for African Americans? **Think About:**
   - the types of work available to each group
   - the effects of government policies on each group
   - the effect of the legal system on each group

PLESSY v. *FERGUSON* (1896)

ORIGINS OF THE CASE In 1892, Homer Plessy took a seat in the "Whites Only" car of a train and refused to move. He was arrested, tried, and convicted in the District Court of New Orleans for breaking Louisiana's segregation law. Plessy appealed, claiming that he had been denied equal protection under the law. The Supreme Court handed down its decision on May 18, 1896.

THE RULING **The Court ruled that separate-but-equal facilities for blacks and whites did not violate the Constitution.**

LEGAL REASONING

Plessy claimed that segregation violated his right to equal protection under the law. Moreover he claimed that, being "of mixed descent," he was entitled to "every recognition, right, privilege and immunity secured to the citizens of the United States of the white race."

Justice Henry B. Brown, writing for the majority, ruled:

> **"The object of the [Fourteenth] amendment was . . . undoubtedly to enforce the absolute equality of the two races before the law, but . . . it could not have been intended to abolish distinctions based upon color, or to enforce social, as distinguished from political equality, or a commingling of the two races upon terms unsatisfactory to either. Laws permitting, and even requiring, their separation in places where they are liable to be brought into contact do not necessarily imply the inferiority of either race to the other."**

In truth, segregation laws did perpetrate an unequal and inferior status for African Americans. Justice John Marshall Harlan understood this fact and dissented from the majority opinion. He wrote, "In respect of civil rights, all citizens are equal before the law." He condemned the majority for letting "the seeds of race hate . . . be planted under the sanction of law." He also warned that "The thin disguise of 'equal' accommodations . . . will not mislead any one, nor atone for the wrong this day done."

Justice John Marshall Harlan

LEGAL SOURCES

LEGISLATION

U.S. CONSTITUTION, FOURTEENTH AMENDMENT (1868)
"No state shall . . . deny to any person within its jurisdiction the equal protection of the laws."

LOUISIANA ACTS 1890, NO. 111
". . . that all railway companies carrying passengers in their coaches in this State, shall provide equal but separate accommodations for the white, and colored races."

RELATED CASES

CIVIL RIGHTS CASES (1883)
The Court ruled that the Fourteenth Amendment could not be used to prevent private citizens from discriminating against others on the basis of race.

***WILLIAMS* v. *MISSISSIPPI* (1898)**
The Court upheld a state literacy requirement for voting that, in effect, kept African Americans from the polls.

***CUMMING* v. *BOARD OF EDUCATION OF RICHMOND COUNTY* (1899)**
The Court ruled that the federal government cannot prevent segregation in local school facilities because education is a local, not federal, issue.

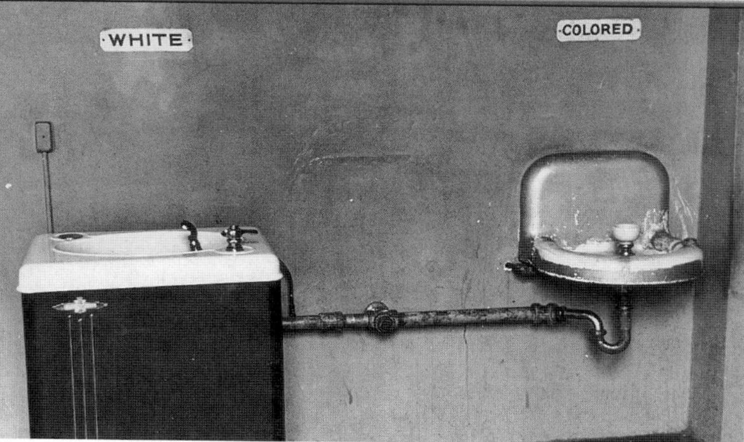

▲ **One result of Jim Crow laws was separate drinking fountains for whites and African Americans.**

WHY IT MATTERED

In the decades following the Civil War [1861–1865], Southern state legislatures passed laws that aimed to limit civil rights for African Americans. The Black Codes of the 1860s, and later Jim Crow laws, were intended to deprive African Americans of their newly won political and social rights granted during Reconstruction.

Plessy was one of several Supreme Court cases brought by African Americans to protect their rights against segregation. In these cases, the Court regularly ignored the Fourteenth Amendment and upheld state laws that denied blacks their rights. *Plessy* was the most important of these cases because the Court used it to establish the separate-but-equal doctrine.

As a result, city and state governments across the South—and in some other states—maintained their segregation laws for more than half of the 20th century. These laws limited African Americans' access to most public facilities, including restaurants, schools, and hospitals. Without exception, the facilities reserved for whites were superior to those reserved for nonwhites. Signs reading "Colored Only" and "Whites Only" served as constant reminders that facilities in segregated societies were separate but not equal.

HISTORICAL IMPACT

It took many decades to abolish legal segregation. During the first half of the 20th century, the National Association for the Advancement of Colored People (NAACP) led the legal fight to overturn *Plessy*. Although they won a few cases over the years, it was not until 1954 in *Brown* v. *Board of Education* that the Court overturned any part of *Plessy*. In that case, the Supreme Court said that separate-but-equal was unconstitutional in public education, but it did not completely overturn the separate-but-equal doctrine.

In later years, the Court did overturn the separate-but-equal doctrine, and it used the *Brown* decision to do so. For example, in 1955, Rosa Parks was convicted for violating a Montgomery, Alabama, law for segregated seating on buses. A federal court overturned the conviction, finding such segregation unconstitutional. The case was appealed to the Supreme Court, which upheld without comment the lower court's decision. In doing so in this and similar cases, the Court signaled that the reasoning behind *Plessy* no longer applied.

▲ **As secretary of the Montgomery chapter of the NAACP, Rosa Parks had protested segregation through everyday acts long before Sepember 1955.**

THINKING CRITICALLY

CONNECT TO TODAY

1. **Analyzing Primary Sources** Read the part of the Fourteenth Amendment reprinted in this feature. Write a paragraph explaining what you think "equal protection of the laws" means. Use evidence to support your ideas.

 **SEE SKILLBUILDER HANDBOOK, PAGE R22.**

CONNECT TO HISTORY

2. **INTERNET ACTIVITY** **CLASSZONE.COM**

Visit the links for Historic Decisions of the Supreme Court to research and read Justice Harlan's entire dissent in *Plessy* v. *Ferguson*. Based on his position, what view might Harlan have taken toward laws that denied African Americans the right to vote? Write a paragraph or two expressing what Harlan would say about those laws.

The Dawn of Mass Culture

MAIN IDEA

As Americans had more time for leisure activities, a modern mass culture emerged.

WHY IT MATTERS NOW

Today, the United States has a worldwide impact on mass culture.

Terms & Names

- **Joseph Pulitzer**
- **William Randolph Hearst**
- **Ashcan school**
- **Mark Twain**
- **rural free delivery (RFD)**

One American's Story

Along the Brooklyn seashore, on a narrow sandbar just nine miles from busy Manhattan, rose the most famous urban amusement center, Coney Island. In 1886, its main developer, George Tilyou, bragged, "If Paris is France, then Coney Island . . . is the world." Indeed, tens of thousands of visitors mobbed Coney Island after work each evening and on Sundays and holidays. When Luna Park, a spectacular amusement park on Coney Island, opened in May 1903, a reporter described the scene.

A Personal Voice BRUCE BLEN

"[Inside the park was] an enchanted, storybook land of trellises, columns, domes, minarets, lagoons, and lofty aerial flights. And everywhere was life—a pageant of happy people; and everywhere was color—a wide harmony of orange and white and gold. . . . It was a world removed—shut away from the sordid clatter and turmoil of the streets."

—quoted in *Amusing the Million*

Coney Island offered Americans a few hours of escape from the hard work week. A schoolteacher who walked fully dressed into the ocean explained her unusual behavior by saying, "It has been a hard year at school, and when I saw the big crowd here, everyone with the brakes off, the spirit of the place got the better of me." The end of the 19th century saw the rise of a "mass culture" in the United States.

▲ **The sprawling amusement center at Coney Island became a model for urban amusement parks.**

American Leisure

Middle-class Americans from all over the country shared experiences as new leisure activities, nationwide advertising campaigns, and the rise of a consumer culture began to level regional differences. As the 19th century drew to a close, many Americans fought off city congestion and dull industrial work by enjoying amusement parks, bicycling, new forms of theater, and spectator sports.

"Eight hours for work, eight hours for rest, eight hours for what we will"

THE CARPENTERS' UNION, WORCESTER, MASSACHUSETTS

AMUSEMENT PARKS To meet the recreational needs of city dwellers, Chicago, New York City, and other cities began setting aside precious green space for outdoor enjoyment. Many cities built small playgrounds and playing fields throughout their neighborhoods for their citizens' enjoyment.

Some amusement parks were constructed on the outskirts of cities. Often built by trolley-car companies that sought more passengers, these parks boasted picnic grounds and a variety of rides. The roller coaster drew daredevil customers to Coney Island in 1884, and the first Ferris wheel drew enthusiastic crowds to the World's Columbian Exposition in Chicago in 1893. Clearly, many Americans were ready for new and innovative forms of entertainment—and a whole panorama of recreational activities soon became available.

BICYCLING AND TENNIS With their huge front wheels and solid rubber tires, the first American bicycles challenged their riders. Because a bump might toss the cyclist over the handlebars, bicycling began as a male-only sport. However, the 1885 manufacture of the first commercially successful "safety bicycle," with its smaller wheels and air-filled tires, made the activity more popular. And the Victor safety bicycle, with a dropped frame and no crossbar, held special appeal to women.

Abandoning their tight corsets, women bicyclists donned shirtwaists (tailored blouses) and "split" skirts in order to cycle more comfortably. This attire soon became popular for daily wear. The bicycle also freed women from the scrutiny of the ever-present chaperone. The suffragist Susan B. Anthony declared, "I think [bicycling] has done more to emancipate women than anything else in the world. . . . It gives women a feeling of freedom and self-reliance." Fifty thousand men and women had taken to cycles by 1888. Two years later 312 American firms turned out 10 million bikes in one year. (A)

MAIN IDEA

Making Inferences

(A) How did the mass production of bicycles change women's lives?

Americans took up the sport of tennis as enthusiastically as they had taken up cycling. The modern version of this sport originated in North Wales in 1873. A year later, the United States saw its first tennis match. The socialite Florence Harriman recalled that in the 1880s her father returned from England with one of New York's first tennis sets. At first, neighbors thought the elder Harriman had installed the nets to catch birds.

Hungry or thirsty after tennis or cycling? Turn-of-the-century enthusiasts turned to new snacks with recognizable brand names. They could munch on a Hershey chocolate bar, first sold in 1900, and wash down the chocolate with a Coca-Cola®. An Atlanta pharmacist originally formulated the drink as a cure for headaches in 1886. The ingredients included extracts from Peruvian coca leaves as well as African cola nuts.

Bicycling and other new sports became fads in the late 1800s. ▼

The Negro Leagues were first formed in 1920.

SPECTATOR SPORTS Americans not only participated in new sports, but became avid fans of spectator sports, especially boxing and baseball. Though these two sports had begun as popular informal activities, by the turn of the 20th century they had become profitable businesses. Fans who couldn't attend an important boxing match jammed barbershops and hotel lobbies to listen to telegraphed transmissions of the contest's highlights.

BASEBALL New rules transformed baseball into a professional sport. In 1845, Alexander J. Cartwright, an amateur player, organized a club in New York City and set down regulations that used aspects of an English sport called rounders. Five years later, 50 baseball clubs had sprung up in the United States, and New York alone boasted 12 clubs in the mid-1860s.

In 1869, a professional team named the Cincinnati Red Stockings toured the country. Other clubs soon took to the road, which led to the formation of the National League in 1876 and the American League in 1900. In the first World Series, held in 1903, the Boston Pilgrims beat the Pittsburgh Pirates. African-American baseball players, who were excluded from both leagues because of racial discrimination, formed their own clubs and two leagues—the Negro National League and the Negro American League.

MAIN IDEA

Drawing Conclusions

B Why do you think sports were so popular among Americans at the turn of the century?

The novelist Mark Twain called baseball "the very symbol . . . and visible expression of the drive and push and rush and struggle of the raging, tearing, booming nineteenth century." By the 1890s, baseball had a published game schedule, official rules, and a standard-sized diamond. **B**

The Spread of Mass Culture

As increasing numbers of Americans attended school and learned to read, the cultural vistas of ordinary Americans expanded. Art galleries, libraries, books, and museums brought new cultural opportunities to more people. Other advances fostered mass entertainment. New media technology led to the release of hundreds of motion pictures. Mass-production printing techniques gave birth to thousands of books, magazines, and newspapers.

MASS CIRCULATION NEWSPAPERS Looking for ways to captivate readers' attention, American newspapers began using sensational headlines. For example, to introduce its story about the horrors of the Johnstown, Pennsylvania flood of 1889, in which more than 2,000 people died, one newspaper used the headline "THE VALLEY OF DEATH."

Joseph Pulitzer, a Hungarian immigrant who had bought the *New York World* in 1883, pioneered popular innovations, such as a large Sunday edition, comics, sports coverage, and women's news. Pulitzer's paper emphasized "sin, sex, and sensation" in an attempt to surpass his main competitor, the wealthy **William Randolph Hearst**, who had purchased the New York *Morning Journal* in 1895. Hearst, who already owned the San Francisco *Examiner*, sought to outdo Pulitzer by filling the *Journal* with exaggerated tales of personal scandals, cruelty, hypnotism, and even an imaginary conquest of Mars. C

MAIN IDEA

Drawing Conclusions

C How did the *World* and the *Journal* attract readers?

The escalation of their circulation war drove both papers to even more sensational news coverage. By 1898, the circulation of each paper had reached more than one million copies a day.

PROMOTING FINE ARTS By 1900, at least one art gallery graced every large city. Some American artists, including Philadelphian Thomas Eakins, began to embrace realism, an artistic school that attempted to portray life as it is really lived. Eakins had studied anatomy with medical students and used painstaking geometric perspective in his work. By the 1880s, Eakins was also using photography to make realistic studies of people and animals.

In the early 20th century, the **Ashcan school** of American art, led by Eakins's student Robert Henri, painted urban life and working people with gritty realism and no frills. Both Eakins and the Ashcan school, however, soon were challenged by the European development known as abstract art, a direction that most people found difficult to understand.

In many cities, inhabitants could walk from a new art gallery to a new public library, sometimes called "the poor man's university." By 1900, free circulating libraries in America numbered in the thousands.

History Through Art

THE CHAMPION SINGLE SCULLS (MAX SCHMITT IN A SINGLE SCULL) (1871)

This painting by Thomas Eakins is an example of the realist movement—an artistic school that aimed at portraying people and environments as they really are.

What realistic details do you see portrayed in this painting?

▲ **Highly popular dime novels often featured adventure stories.**

POPULAR FICTION As literacy rates rose, scholars debated the role of literature in society. Some felt that literature should uplift America's literary tastes, which tended toward crime tales and Western adventures.

Most people preferred to read light fiction. Such books sold for a mere ten cents, hence their name, "dime novels." Dime novels typically told glorified adventure tales of the West and featured heroes like Edward Wheeler's *Deadwood Dick*. Wheeler published his first Deadwood Dick novel in 1877 and in less than a decade produced over 30 more. **D**

MAIN IDEA

Analyzing Causes

D What factors contributed to the popularity of dime novels?

Some readers wanted a more realistic portrayal of American life. Successful writers of the era included Sarah Orne Jewett, Theodore Dreiser, Stephen Crane, Jack London, and Willa Cather. Most portrayed characters less polished than the upper-class men and women of Henry James's and Edith Wharton's novels. Samuel Langhorne Clemens, the novelist and humorist better known as **Mark Twain,** inspired a host of other young authors when he declared his independence of "literature and all that bosh." Yet, some of his books have become classics of American literature. *The Adventures of Huckleberry Finn*, for example, remains famed for its rendering of life along the Mississippi River.

Although art galleries and libraries attempted to raise cultural standards, many Americans had scant interest in high culture—and others did not have access to it. African Americans, for example, were excluded from visiting many museums and other white-controlled cultural institutions.

New Ways to Sell Goods

Along with enjoying new leisure activities, Americans also changed the way they shopped. Americans at the turn of the 20th century witnessed the beginnings of the shopping center, the development of department and chain stores, and the birth of modern advertising.

URBAN SHOPPING Growing city populations made promising targets for enterprising merchants. The nation's earliest form of a shopping center opened in Cleveland, Ohio, in 1890. The glass-topped arcade contained four levels of jewelry, leather goods, and stationery shops. The arcade also provided band music on Sundays so that Cleveland residents could spend their Sunday afternoons strolling through the elegant environment and gazing at the window displays.

Retail shopping districts formed where public transportation could easily bring shoppers from outlying areas. To anchor these retail shopping districts, ambitious merchants started something quite new, the modern department store.

THE DEPARTMENT STORE Marshall Field of Chicago first brought the department store concept to America. While working as a store clerk, Field found that paying close attention to women customers could increase sales considerably. In 1865, Field opened his own store, featuring several floors of specialized departments. Field's motto was "Give the lady what she wants." Field also pioneered the bargain basement, selling bargain goods that were "less expensive but reliable."

THE CHAIN STORE Department stores prided themselves on offering a variety of personal services. New chain stores—retail stores offering the same merchandise under the same ownership—sold goods for less by buying in quantity and limiting personal service. In the 1870s, F. W. Woolworth found that if he offered an item at a very low price, "the consumer would purchase it on the spur of the

Vocabulary
consumer: a person who purchases goods or services for direct use or ownership

moment" because "it was only a nickel." By 1911, the Woolworth chain boasted 596 stores and sold more than a million dollars in goods a week.

ADVERTISING An explosion in advertising also heralded modern consumerism. Expenditures for advertising were under $10 million a year in 1865 but increased tenfold, to $95 million, by 1900. Patent medicines grabbed the largest number of advertising lines, followed by soaps and baking powders. In addition to newspapers and magazines, advertisers used ingenious methods to push products. Passengers riding the train between New York and Philadelphia in the 1870s might see signs for Dr. Drake's Plantation Bitters on barns, houses, billboards, and even rocks.

CATALOGS AND RFD Montgomery Ward and Sears Roebuck brought retail merchandise to small towns. Ward's catalog, launched in 1872, grew from a single sheet the first year to a booklet with ordering instructions in ten languages. Richard Sears started his company in 1886. Early Sears catalogs stated that the company received "hundreds of orders every day from young and old who never [before] sent away for goods." By 1910, about 10 million Americans shopped by mail. The United States Post Office boosted mail-order businesses. In 1896 the Post Office introduced a **rural free delivery (RFD)** system that brought packages directly to every home.

The turn of the 20th century saw prosperity that caused big changes in Americans' daily lives. At the same time, the nation's growing industrial sector faced problems that called for reform.

CATALOG SHOPPING

Catalogs were a novelty when Sears and Montgomery Ward arrived on the scene. However, by the mid-1990s, more than 13 billion catalogs filled the mailboxes of Americans.

Today, the world of mail-order business is changing. After over 100 years of operation, Montgomery Ward filed for bankruptcy on December 28, 2000.

Online shopping threatens to dominate mail-order commerce today. Online retail sales have grown from $500 million in 1995 to $7.8 billion in 1998. What do catalog shoppers order? Clothing ranks first, electronics second. Online book sales also lead—in 1998, book sales had risen over 300% to total $650 million.

ASSESSMENT

1. **TERMS & NAMES** For each term or name, write a sentence explaining its significance.
   - **Joseph Pulitzer**
   - **William Randolph Hearst**
   - **Ashcan school**
   - **Mark Twain**
   - **rural free delivery (RFD)**

MAIN IDEA

2. **TAKING NOTES**
   Re-create the spider diagram below. Add examples to each category.

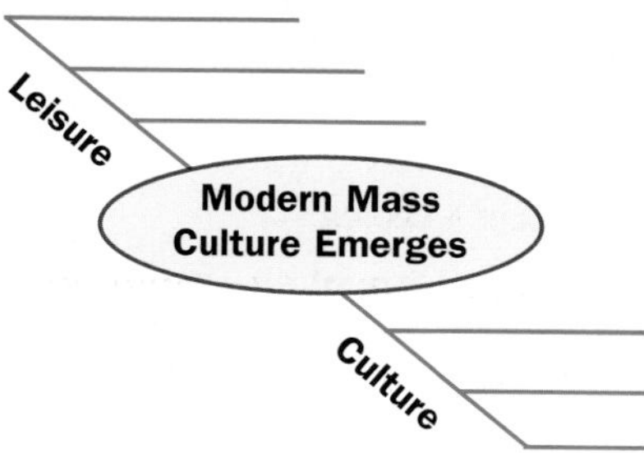

   Why is mass culture often described as a democratic phenomenon?

CRITICAL THINKING

3. **SUMMARIZING**
   How did American methods of selling goods change at the turn of the 20th century?
   Think About:
   - how city people did their shopping
   - how rural residents bought goods
   - how merchants advertised their products

4. **ANALYZING VISUAL SOURCES**
   This cartoon shows the masters of the "new journalism." According to the cartoonist, where were Pulitzer and Hearst leading American journalism?

Going to the Show

As Americans moved from rural areas to cities, they looked for new ways to spend their weekend and evening leisure time. Live theatrical performances brought pleasure to cities and small towns alike. Stars, popular performers who could attract large audiences, compensated for the less-talented supporting actors. Audiences could choose from a wide range of music, drama, circus, and the latest in entertainment—moving pictures.

◀ **VAUDEVILLE THEATER**

Performances that included song, dance, juggling, slapstick comedy, and sometimes chorus lines of female performers were characteristic of vaudeville. Promoters sought large audiences with varied backgrounds. Writing in *Scribner's Magazine* in October 1899, actor Edwin Milton Royle hailed vaudeville theater as "an American invention" that offered something to attract nearly everyone.

Until the 1890s, African-American performers filled roles mainly in minstrel shows that featured exaggerated imitations of African-American music and dance and reinforced racist stereotypes of blacks. By the turn of the century, however, minstrel shows had largely been replaced by more sophisticated musicals, and many black performers entertained in vaudeville.

▲ **THE CIRCUS**

The biggest spectacle of all was often the annual visit of the Barnum & Bailey Circus, which its founders, P. T. Barnum and Anthony Bailey, touted as "The Greatest Show on Earth." Established in 1871, the circus arrived by railroad and staged a parade through town to advertise the show.

Bill "Bojangles" Robinson was a popular tap dancer.

▲ THE SILVER SCREEN

The first films, one-reel, ten minute sequences, consisted mostly of vaudeville skits or faked newsreels. In 1903, the first modern film—an eight minute silent feature called *The Great Train Robbery*—debuted in five-cent theaters called nickelodeons. By showing a film as often as 16 times a day, entrepreneurs could generate greater profits than by a costly stage production. By 1907, an estimated 3,000 nickelodeons dotted the country.

◄ RAGTIME MUSIC

A blend of African-American spirituals and European musical forms, ragtime originated in the 1880s in the saloons of the South. African-American pianist and composer Scott Joplin's ragtime compositions made him famous in the first decade of the 1900s. Ragtime led later to jazz, rhythm and blues, and rock 'n' roll. These forms of popular American culture spread worldwide, creating new dances and fashions that emulated the image of "loud, loose, American rebel."

DATA FILE

A LOOK AT THE FACTS

A shorter workweek allowed many Americans more time for leisure activities, and they certainly took advantage of it.

- In 1890, an average of 60,000 fans attended professional baseball games daily.
- In 1893, a crowd of 50,000 attended the Princeton-Yale football game.
- *A Trip to Chinatown,* one of the popular new musical comedies, ran for an amazing 650 performances in the 1890s.
- In 1900, 3 million phonograph records of Broadway-produced musical comedies were sold.
- The love of the popular musicals contributed to the sale of $42 million worth of musical instruments in 1900.
- By 1900, almost 500 men's social clubs existed. Nine hundred college fraternity and sorority chapters had over 150,000 members.

Changes in the U.S. Workweek

Year	Hours per week
1860	66
1890	60
1920	51

Source: *Historical Statistics of the United States*

THINKING CRITICALLY

CONNECT TO HISTORY

1. **Interpreting Data** Study the statistics in the Data File. What summary statements about the culture and attitudes of this time period can you make? Is this a time in history when you would like to have lived? Why or why not?

 **SEE SKILLBUILDER HANDBOOK, PAGE R27.**

CONNECT TO TODAY

2. **Chronological Order** Trace the development and impact on the rest of the world of one area—music, theater, or film—of popular American culture. Use a time line from the turn of the 20th to the 21st century with "United States developments" on one side and "world impacts" on the other.

CLASSZONE.COM

CHAPTER 8 ASSESSMENT

TERMS & NAMES

For each term or name, write a sentence explaining its connection to late 19th-century American life.

1. Louis Sullivan
2. Orville and Wilbur Wright
3. Booker T. Washington
4. W. E. B. Du Bois
5. Niagara Movement
6. Ida B. Wells
7. Jim Crow laws
8. *Plessy* v. *Ferguson*
9. debt peonage
10. rural free delivery

MAIN IDEAS

Use your notes and the information in the chapter to answer the following questions.

Science and Urban Life *(pages 276–281)*

1. How did new technology promote urban growth around the turn of the century?
2. In what ways did methods of communication improve in the late 19th and early 20th centuries?

Expanding Public Education *(pages 282–285)*

3. How did late 19th century public schools change?
4. Why did some immigrants oppose sending their children to public schools?

Segregation and Discrimination *(pages 286–289)*

5. In what ways was racial discrimination reinforced by the federal government's actions and policies?
6. How did Mexicans help make the Southwest prosperous in the late 19th century?

Dawn of Mass Culture *(pages 292–297)*

7. What leisure activities flourished at the turn of the 20th century?
8. What innovations in retail methods changed the way Americans shopped during this time period?

CRITICAL THINKING

1. **USING YOUR NOTES** Create a table similar to the one shown, listing at least six important trends at the turn of the century, along with a major impact of each.

Trend	Impact
1.	
2.	
3.	
4.	
5.	
6.	

2. **DRAWING CONCLUSIONS** How had changes in technology affected urban life by the turn of the 20th century?

3. **INTERPRETING GRAPHS** Look at the graph of Expanding Education/Increasing Literacy on page 283. Which year reported the greatest gain in the literacy rate? What do you think were the implications on society of a more literate population?

VISUAL SUMMARY Life at the Turn of the 20th Century

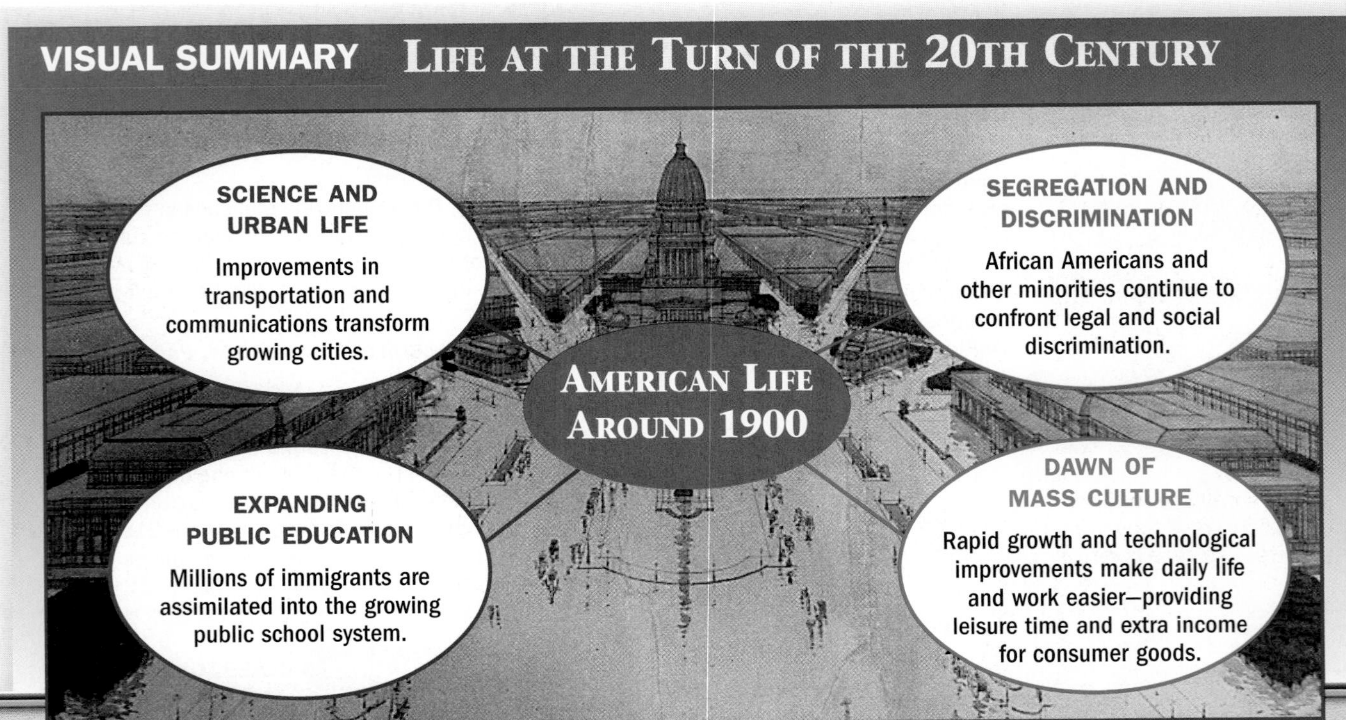

SCIENCE AND URBAN LIFE
Improvements in transportation and communications transform growing cities.
SEGREGATION AND DISCRIMINATION
African Americans and other minorities continue to confront legal and social discrimination.
AMERICAN LIFE AROUND 1900
EXPANDING PUBLIC EDUCATION
Millions of immigrants are assimilated into the growing public school system.
DAWN OF MASS CULTURE
Rapid growth and technological improvements make daily life and work easier—providing leisure time and extra income for consumer goods.

Standardized Test Practice

Use the quotation below and your knowledge of U.S. history to answer question 1.

> **"We boast of the freedom enjoyed by our people above all other peoples. But it is difficult to reconcile that boast with a state of the law which, practically, puts the brand of servitude and degradation upon a large class of our fellow-citizens, our equals before the law."**
>
> —Justice John Marshall Harlan in the dissenting opinion in *Plessy* v. *Ferguson*

1. Justice Harlan used this reasoning for what purpose?

- **A** to celebrate American democracy
- **B** to justify segregation
- **C** to denounce the "separate-but-equal" argument
- **D** to demonstrate that equality before the law is not practical

2. Which of the following was *not* an outcome of expanding public education in the early 20th century?

- **F** the establishment of public high schools and colleges
- **G** the growth of equal education for all
- **H** a rise in the literacy rate
- **J** the founding of kindergartens

3. The turn of the 20th century brought shorter work hours and more leisure time to many urban Americans. Which of the following bar graphs correctly reflects these factors?

A

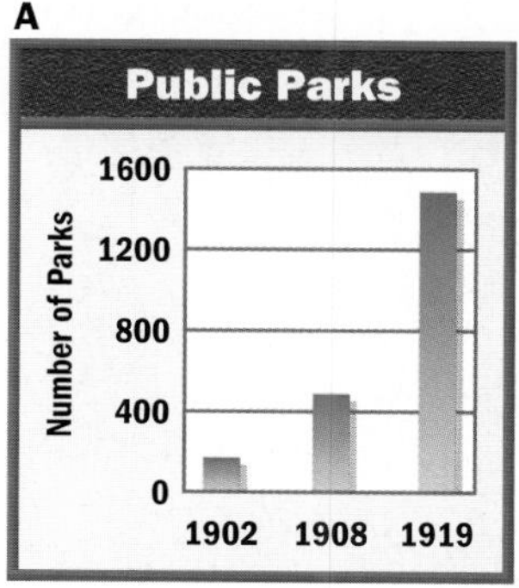

B

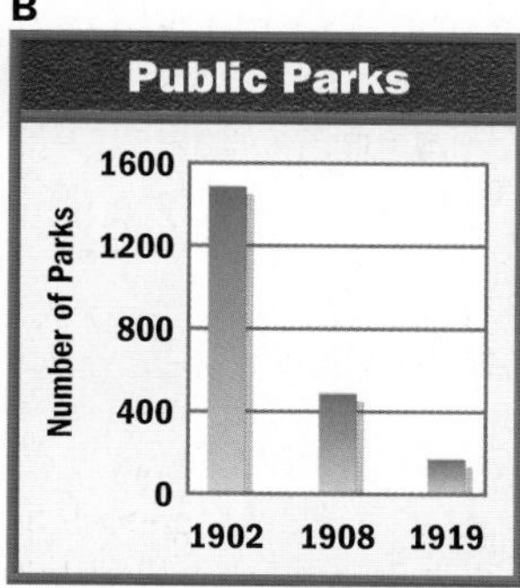

C

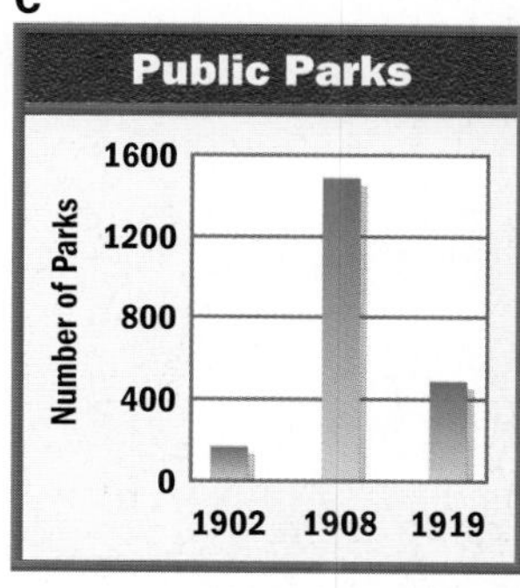

D

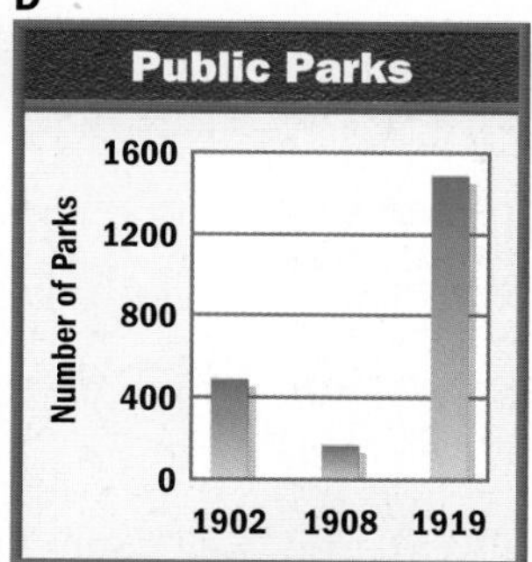

ADDITIONAL TEST PRACTICE, pages S1–S33.

CLASSZONE.COM

ALTERNATIVE ASSESSMENT

1. **INTERACT WITH HISTORY** Recall your discussion of the question on page 275:

How will the latest technology change your life?

Now that you know more about the role of technology in people's lives, would you change any of your responses? Discuss your ideas with a small group. Then make a cause-and-effect chart about one technological innovation of the era and its lasting impacts on society.

2. **INTERNET ACTIVITY** **CLASSZONE.COM**

Visit the links for Chapter Assessment to find out more about the World's Columbian Exposition held in Chicago in 1893.

In a small group, make a list of the "famous firsts," such as the first elevated railway, introduced at the exposition. Illustrate your list, adding pictures and informative captions, on a colorful poster for display in the classroom.

UNIT

3

Modern America Emerges 1890–1920

CHAPTER 9
The Progressive Era
1890–1920

CHAPTER 10
America Claims an Empire
1890–1920

CHAPTER 11
The First World War
1914–1920

News Story

As you read Unit 3, identify a person, issue, or event that interests you. Plan and write an illustrated news story about the subject you have chosen. Use your text as well as information that you research in the library and on the Internet.

The Statue of Liberty by Francis Hopkinson Smith

CHAPTER 9

THE PROGRESSIVE ERA

A 1916 suffrage parade.

USA
WORLD

1890

1900

1896 William McKinley is elected president.

1900 William McKinley is reelected.

1901 McKinley is assassinated; Theodore Roosevelt becomes president.

1904 Theodore Roosevelt is elected president.

1889 Eiffel Tower opens for visitors.

1898 Marie Curie discovers radium.

1899 Boer War in South Africa begins.

1901 Commonwealth of Australia is created.

INTERACT WITH HISTORY

It is the dawn of the 20th century, and the reform movement is growing. Moral reformers are trying to ban alcoholic beverages. Political reformers work toward fair government and business practices. Women fight for equal wages and the right to vote. Throughout society, social and economic issues take center stage.

What kinds of actions can bring about social change?

Examine the Issues

- What types of actions might pressure big business to change?
- How can individuals bring about change in their government?
- How might reformers recruit others?

RESEARCH LINKS **CLASSZONE.COM**

Visit the Chapter 9 links for more information about The Progressive Era.

1908 William H. Taft is elected president.

1909 W. E. B. Du Bois helps found the National Association for the Advancement of Colored People (NAACP).

1910 Mexican revolution begins.

1912 Woodrow Wilson is elected president.

1912 China's Qin dynasty topples.

1914 World War I begins in Europe.

1916 Woodrow Wilson is reelected.

1919 Eighteenth Amendment outlaws alcoholic beverages.

1919 Mohandas Gandhi becomes leader of the independence movement in India.

1920 Nineteenth Amendment grants women the right to vote.

1910

1920

The Origins of Progressivism

MAIN IDEA	WHY IT MATTERS NOW	Terms & Names
Political, economic, and social change in late 19th century America led to broad progressive reforms.	**Progressive reforms in areas such as labor and voting rights reinforced democratic principles that continue to exist today.**	**•progressive movement •Florence Kelley •prohibition •muckraker •scientific management •Robert M. La Follette •initiative •referendum •recall •Seventeenth Amendment**

One American's Story

Camella Teoli was just 12 years old when she began working in a Lawrence, Massachusetts, textile mill to help support her family. Soon after she started, a machine used for twisting cotton into thread tore off part of her scalp. The young Italian immigrant spent seven months in the hospital and was scarred for life.

Three years later, when 20,000 Lawrence mill workers went on strike for higher wages, Camella was selected to testify before a congressional committee investigating labor conditions such as workplace safety and underage workers. When asked why she had gone on strike, Camella answered simply, "Because I didn't get enough to eat at home." She explained how she had gone to work before reaching the legal age of 14.

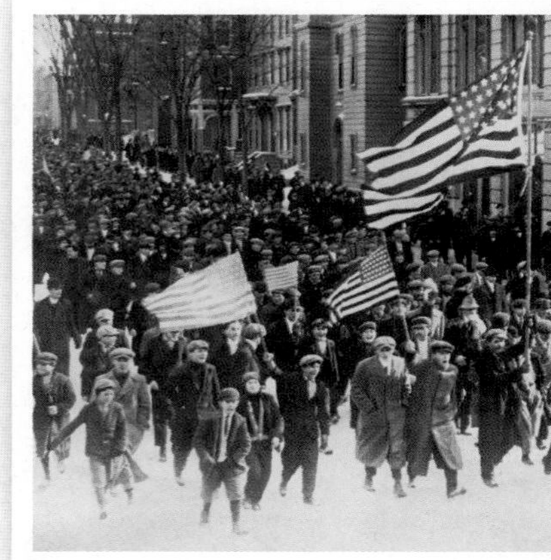

▲ Mill workers on strike in 1912 in Lawrence, Massachusetts

A PERSONAL VOICE CAMELLA TEOLI

"I used to go to school, and then a man came up to my house and asked my father why I didn't go to work, so my father says I don't know whether she is 13 or 14 years old. So, the man say You give me $4 and I will make the papers come from the old country [Italy] saying [that] you are 14. So, my father gave him the $4, and in one month came the papers that I was 14. I went to work, and about two weeks [later] got hurt in my head."

—at congressional hearings, March 1912

VIDEO

A CHILD ON STRIKE

The Testimony of Camella Teoli, Mill Girl

After nine weeks of striking, the mill workers won the sympathy of the nation as well as five to ten percent pay raises. Stories like Camella's set off a national investigation of labor conditions, and reformers across the country organized to address the problems of industrialization.

Four Goals of Progressivism

At the dawn of the new century, middle-class reformers addressed many of the problems that had contributed to the social upheavals of the 1890s. Journalists and writers exposed the unsafe conditions often faced by factory workers, including women and children. Intellectuals questioned the dominant role of large corporations in American society. Political reformers struggled to make government more responsive to the people. Together, these reform efforts formed the **progressive movement,** which aimed to restore economic opportunities and correct injustices in American life.

Even though reformers never completely agreed on the problems or the solutions, each of their progressive efforts shared at least one of the following goals:

- protecting social welfare
- promoting moral improvement
- creating economic reform
- fostering efficiency

KEY PLAYER

FLORENCE KELLEY
1859–1932

The daughter of an antislavery Republican congressman from Pennsylvania, Florence Kelley became a social reformer whose sympathies lay with the powerless, especially working women and children. During a long career, Kelley pushed the government to solve America's social problems.

In 1899, Kelley became general secretary of the National Consumers' League, where she lobbied to improve factory conditions. "Why," Kelley pointedly asked while campaigning for a federal child-labor law, "are seals, bears, reindeer, fish, wild game in the national parks, buffalo, [and] migratory birds all found suitable for federal protection, but not children?"

PROTECTING SOCIAL WELFARE Many social welfare reformers worked to soften some of the harsh conditions of industrialization. The Social Gospel and settlement house movements of the late 1800s, which aimed to help the poor through community centers, churches, and social services, continued during the Progressive Era and inspired even more reform activities.

The Young Men's Christian Association (YMCA), for example, opened libraries, sponsored classes, and built swimming pools and handball courts. The Salvation Army fed poor people in soup kitchens, cared for children in nurseries, and sent "slum brigades" to instruct poor immigrants in middle-class values of hard work and temperance.

Vocabulary
temperance: refraining from alcohol consumption

In addition, many women were inspired by the settlement houses to take action. **Florence Kelley** became an advocate for improving the lives of women and children. She was appointed chief inspector of factories for Illinois after she had helped to win passage of the Illinois Factory Act in 1893. The act, which prohibited child labor and limited women's working hours, soon became a model for other states.

PROMOTING MORAL IMPROVEMENT Other reformers felt that morality, not the workplace, held the key to improving the lives of poor people. These reformers wanted immigrants and poor city dwellers to uplift themselves by improving their personal behavior. **Prohibition,** the banning of alcoholic beverages, was one such program.

Prohibitionist groups feared that alcohol was undermining American morals. Founded in Cleveland in 1874, the Woman's Christian Temperance Union (WCTU) spearheaded the crusade for prohibition. Members advanced their cause by entering saloons, singing, praying, and urging saloonkeepers to stop selling alcohol. As momentum grew, the Union was transformed by Frances Willard from a small midwestern religious group in 1879 to a national organization. Boasting 245,000 members by 1911, the WCTU became the largest women's group in the nation's history. (A)

MAIN IDEA

Analyzing Motives
(A) Why did the prohibition movement appeal to so many women?

WCTU members followed Willard's "do everything" slogan and began opening kindergartens for immigrants, visiting

◄ In the 1890s, Carry Nation worked for prohibition by walking into saloons, scolding the customers, and using her hatchet to destroy bottles of liquor.

HISTORICAL SPOTLIGHT

ANTI–SALOON LEAGUE

Quietly founded by progressive women in 1895, the Anti-Saloon League called itself "the Church in action against the saloon." Whereas early temperance efforts had asked individuals to change their ways, the Anti-Saloon League worked to pass laws to force people to change and to punish those who drank.

The Anti-Saloon League endorsed politicians who opposed "Demon Rum," no matter which party they belonged to or where they stood on other issues. It also organized statewide referendums to ban alcohol. Between 1900 and 1917, voters in nearly half of the states—mostly in the South and the West—prohibited the sale, production, and use of alcohol. Individual towns, city wards, and rural areas also voted themselves "dry."

inmates in prisons and asylums, and working for suffrage. The WCTU reform activities, like those of the settlement-house movement, provided women with expanded public roles, which they used to justify giving women voting rights.

Sometimes efforts at prohibition led to trouble with immigrant groups. Such was the case with the Anti-Saloon League, founded in 1895. As members sought to close saloons to cure society's problems, tension arose between them and many immigrants, whose customs often included the consumption of alcohol. Additionally, saloons filled a number of roles within the immigrant community such as cashing paychecks and serving meals.

CREATING ECONOMIC REFORM As moral reformers sought to change individual behavior, a severe economic panic in 1893 prompted some Americans to question the capitalist economic system. As a result, some Americans, especially workers, embraced socialism. Labor leader Eugene V. Debs, who helped organize the American Socialist Party in 1901, commented on the uneven balance among big business, government, and ordinary people under the free-market system of capitalism.

Background
See *capitalism* and *socialism* on pages R38 and R44 in the Economics Handbook.

A PERSONAL VOICE EUGENE V. DEBS

"**Competition was natural enough at one time, but do you think you are competing today? Many of you think you are competing. Against whom? Against [oil magnate John D.] Rockefeller? About as I would if I had a wheelbarrow and competed with the Santa Fe [railroad] from here to Kansas City.**"

—*Debs: His Life, Writings and Speeches*

Though most progressives distanced themselves from socialism, they saw the truth of many of Debs's criticisms. Big business often received favorable treatment from government officials and politicians and could use its economic power to limit competition.

Journalists who wrote about the corrupt side of business and public life in mass circulation magazines during the early 20th century became known as **muckrakers** (mŭk′rāk′r). (The term refers to John Bunyan's "Pilgrim's Progress," in which a character is so busy using a rake to clean up the muck of this world that he does not raise his eyes to heaven.) In her "History of the Standard Oil Company," a monthly serial in *McClure's Magazine*, the writer Ida M. Tarbell described the company's cutthroat methods of eliminating competition. "Mr. Rockefeller has systematically played with loaded dice," Tarbell charged, "and it is doubtful if there has been a time since 1872 when he has run a race with a competitor and started fair." B

MAIN IDEA

Evaluating
B What contribution did muckrakers make to the reform movement?

FOSTERING EFFICIENCY Many progressive leaders put their faith in experts and scientific principles to make society and the workplace more efficient. In defending an Oregon law that limited women factory and laundry workers to a ten-hour day, lawyer Louis D. Brandeis paid little attention to legal argument. Instead, he focused on data produced by social scientists documenting the high costs of long working hours for both the individual and society. This type of argument—the "Brandeis brief"—would become a model for later reform litigation.

Within industry, Frederick Winslow Taylor began using time and motion studies to improve efficiency by breaking manufacturing tasks into simpler parts. "Taylorism" became a management fad, as industry reformers applied these **scientific management** studies to see just how quickly each task could be performed.

◀ **Workers at the Ford flywheel factory cope with the demanding pace of the assembly line to earn five dollars a day—a good wage in 1914.**

However, not all workers could work at the same rate, and although the introduction of the assembly lines did speed up production, the system required people to work like machines. This caused a high worker turnover, often due to injuries suffered by fatigued workers. To keep automobile workers happy and to prevent strikes, Henry Ford reduced the workday to eight hours and paid workers five dollars a day. This incentive attracted thousands of workers, but they exhausted themselves. As one homemaker complained in a letter to Henry Ford in 1914, "That $5 is a blessing—a bigger one than you know but oh they earn it."

Such efforts at improving efficiency, an important part of progressivism, targeted not only industry, but government as well. C

MAIN IDEA

Contrasting

C Contrast the goals of scientific management with other progressive reforms.

"Everybody will be able to afford [a car], and about everyone will have one."

HENRY FORD, 1909

Cleaning Up Local Government

Cities faced some of the most obvious social problems of the new industrial age. In many large cities, political bosses rewarded their supporters with jobs and kickbacks and openly bought votes with favors and bribes. Efforts to reform city politics stemmed in part from the desire to make government more efficient and more responsive to its constituents. But those efforts also grew from distrust of immigrants' participation in politics.

REFORMING LOCAL GOVERNMENT Natural disasters sometimes played an important role in prompting reform of city governments. In 1900, a hurricane and tidal wave almost demolished Galveston, Texas. The politicians on the city council botched the huge relief and rebuilding job so badly that the Texas legislature appointed a five-member commission of experts to take over. Each expert took charge of a different city department, and soon Galveston was rebuilt. This success prompted the city to adopt the commission idea as a form of government, and by 1917, 500 cities had followed Galveston's example.

Another natural disaster—a flood in Dayton, Ohio, in 1913—led to the widespread adoption of the council-manager form of government. Staunton, Virginia, had already pioneered this system, in which people elected a city council to make laws. The council in turn appointed a manager, typically a person with training and experience in public administration, to run the city's departments. By 1925, managers were administering nearly 250 cities.

REFORM MAYORS In some cities, mayors such as Hazen Pingree of Detroit, Michigan (1890–1897), and Tom Johnson of Cleveland, Ohio (1901–1909), introduced progressive reforms without changing how government was organized.

Concentrating on economics, Pingree instituted a fairer tax structure, lowered fares for public transportation, rooted out corruption, and set up a system of work relief for the unemployed. Detroit city workers built schools, parks, and a municipal lighting plant.

Johnson was only one of 19 socialist mayors who worked to institute progressive reforms in America's cities. In general, these mayors focused on dismissing corrupt and greedy private owners of utilities—such as gasworks, waterworks, and transit lines—and converting the utilities to publicly owned enterprises. Johnson believed that citizens should play a more active role in city government. He held meetings in a large circus tent and invited them to question officials about how the city was managed. D

MAIN IDEA

Summarizing

D How did city government change during the Progressive Era?

Reform at the State Level

Local reforms coincided with progressive efforts at the state level. Spurred by progressive governors, many states passed laws to regulate railroads, mines, mills, telephone companies, and other large businesses.

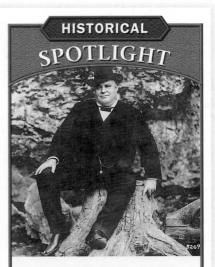

HISTORICAL SPOTLIGHT

JAMES S. HOGG, TEXAS GOVERNOR (1891–1895)

Among the most colorful of the reform governors was James S. Hogg of Texas. Hogg helped to drive illegal insurance companies from the state and championed antitrust legislation. His chief interest, however, was in regulating the railroads. He pointed out abuses in rates—noting, for example, that it cost more to ship lumber from East Texas to Dallas than to ship it all the way to Nebraska. A railroad commission, established largely as a result of his efforts, helped increase milling and manufacturing in Texas by lowering freight rates.

REFORM GOVERNORS Under the progressive Republican leadership of **Robert M. La Follette,** Wisconsin led the way in regulating big business. "Fighting Bob" La Follette served three terms as governor before he entered the U.S. Senate in 1906. He explained that, as governor, he did not mean to "smash corporations, but merely to drive them out of politics, and then to treat them exactly the same as other people are treated."

La Follette's major target was the railroad industry. He taxed railroad property at the same rate as other business property, set up a commission to regulate rates, and forbade railroads to issue free passes to state officials. Other reform governors who attacked big business interests included Charles B. Aycock of North Carolina and James S. Hogg of Texas.

PROTECTING WORKING CHILDREN As the number of child workers rose dramatically, reformers worked to protect workers and to end child labor. Businesses hired children because they performed unskilled jobs for lower wages and because children's small hands made them more adept at handling small parts and tools. Immigrants and rural migrants often sent their children to work because they viewed their children as part of the family economy. Often wages were so low for adults that every family member needed to work to pull the family out of poverty.

In industrial settings, however, children were more prone to accidents caused by fatigue. Many developed serious health problems and suffered from stunted growth. E

MAIN IDEA

Analyzing Causes

E Why did reformers seek to end child labor?

Formed in 1904, the National Child Labor Committee sent investigators to gather evidence of children working in harsh conditions. They then organized exhibitions with photographs and statistics to dramatize the children's plight. They were joined by labor union members who argued that child labor lowered wages for all workers. These groups pressured

History Through *Photojournalism*

IMAGES OF CHILD LABOR

In 1908, Lewis Hine quit his teaching job to document child labor practices. Hine's photographs and descriptions of young laborers—some only three years old—were widely distributed and displayed in exhibits. His compelling images of exploitation helped to convince the public of the need for child labor regulations.

Hine devised a host of clever tactics to gain access to his subjects, such as learning shop managers' schedules and arriving during their lunch breaks. While talking casually with the children, he secretly scribbled notes on paper hidden in his pocket.

Because of their small size, spindle boys and girls *(top)* were forced to climb atop moving machinery to replace parts. For four-year-old Mary *(left)*, shucking two pots of oysters was a typical day's work.

SKILLBUILDER Interpreting Visual Sources

1. Lewis Hine believed in the power of photography to move people to action. What elements of these photographs do you find most striking?
2. Why do you think Hine was a successful photographer?

SEE SKILLBUILDER HANDBOOK, PAGE R23.

national politicians to pass the Keating-Owen Act in 1916. The act prohibited the transportation across state lines of goods produced with child labor.

Two years later the Supreme Court declared the act unconstitutional due to interference with states' rights to regulate labor. Reformers did, however, succeed in nearly every state by effecting legislation that banned child labor and set maximum hours.

EFFORTS TO LIMIT WORKING HOURS The Supreme Court sometimes took a more sympathetic view of the plight of workers. In the 1908 case of *Muller* v. *Oregon*, Louis D. Brandeis—assisted by Florence Kelley and Josephine Goldmark—persuasively argued that poor working women were much more economically insecure than large corporations. Asserting that women required the state's protection against powerful employers, Brandeis convinced the Court to uphold an Oregon law limiting women to a ten-hour workday. Other states responded by enacting or strengthening laws to reduce women's hours of work. A similar Brandeis brief in *Bunting* v. *Oregon* in 1917 persuaded the Court to uphold a ten-hour workday for men.

Progressives also succeeded in winning workers' compensation to aid the families of workers who were hurt or killed on the job. Beginning with Maryland in 1902, one state after another passed legislation requiring employers to pay benefits in death cases.

REFORMING ELECTIONS In some cases, ordinary citizens won state reforms. William S. U'Ren prompted his state of Oregon to adopt the secret ballot (also called the Australian ballot), the initiative, the referendum, and the recall. The initiative and referendum gave citizens the power to create laws. Citizens could petition to place an **initiative**—a bill originated by the people rather than lawmakers—on the ballot. Then voters, instead of the legislature, accepted or rejected the initiative by **referendum,** a vote on the initiative. The **recall** enabled voters to remove public officials from elected positions by forcing them to face another election before the end of their term if enough voters asked for it. By 1920, 20 states had adopted at least one of these procedures. F

MAIN IDEA

Summarizing

F Summarize the impact of the direct election of senators.

In 1899, Minnesota passed the first mandatory statewide primary system. This enabled voters, instead of political machines, to choose candidates for public office through a special popular election. About two-thirds of the states had adopted some form of direct primary by 1915.

DIRECT ELECTION OF SENATORS It was the success of the direct primary that paved the way for the **Seventeenth Amendment** to the Constitution. Before 1913, each state's legislature had chosen its own United States senators, which put even more power in the hands of party bosses and wealthy corporation heads. To force senators to be more responsive to the public, progressives pushed for the popular election of senators. At first, the Senate refused to go along with the idea, but gradually more and more states began allowing voters to nominate senatorial candidates in direct primaries. As a result, Congress approved the Seventeenth Amendment in 1912. Its ratification in 1913 made direct election of senators the law of the land.

Government reform—including efforts to give Americans more of a voice in electing their legislators and creating laws—drew increased numbers of women into public life. It also focused renewed attention on the issue of woman suffrage.

ASSESSMENT

1. **TERMS & NAMES** For each term or name, write a sentence explaining its significance.
   - **progressive movement**
   - **Florence Kelley**
   - **prohibition**
   - **muckraker**
   - **scientific management**
   - **Robert M. La Follette**
   - **initiative**
   - **referendum**
   - **recall**
   - **Seventeenth Amendment**

MAIN IDEA

2. **TAKING NOTES**
   Copy the web below on your paper. Fill it in with examples of organizations that worked for reform in the areas named.

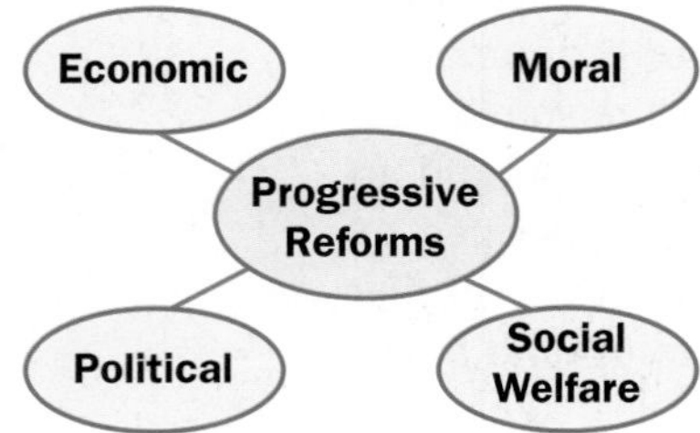

   Which group was most successful and why?

CRITICAL THINKING

3. **FORMING GENERALIZATIONS**
   In what ways might Illinois, Wisconsin, and Oregon all be considered trailblazers in progressive reform? Support your answers. **Think About:**
   - legislative and electoral reforms at the state level
   - the leadership of William U'Ren and Robert La Follette
   - Florence Kelley's appointment as chief inspector of factories for Illinois

4. **INTERPRETING VISUAL SOURCES**
   This cartoon shows Carry Nation inside a saloon that she has attacked. Do you think the cartoonist had a favorable or unfavorable opinion of this prohibitionist? Explain.

Women in Public Life

MAIN IDEA

As a result of social and economic change, many women entered public life as workers and reformers.

WHY IT MATTERS NOW

Women won new opportunities in labor and education that are enjoyed today.

Terms & Names

- **NACW**
- **suffrage**
- **Susan B. Anthony**
- **NAWSA**

One American's Story

In 1879, Susette La Flesche, a young Omaha woman, traveled east to translate into English the sad words of Chief Standing Bear, whose Ponca people had been forcibly removed from their homeland in Nebraska. Later, she was invited with Chief Standing Bear to go on a lecture tour to draw attention to the Ponca's situation.

A PERSONAL VOICE SUSETTE LA FLESCHE

"We are thinking men and women. . . . We have a right to be heard in whatever concerns us. Your government has driven us hither and thither like cattle. . . . Your government has no right to say to us, Go here, or Go there, and if we show any reluctance, to force us to do its will at the point of the bayonet. . . . Do you wonder that the Indian feels outraged by such treatment and retaliates, although it will end in death to himself?"

—quoted in *Bright Eyes*

▲ Susette La Flesche

La Flesche testified before congressional committees and helped win passage of the Dawes Act of 1887, which allowed individual Native Americans to claim reservation land and citizenship rights. Her activism was an example of a new role for American women, who were expanding their participation in public life.

Women in the Work Force

Before the Civil War, married middle-class women were generally expected to devote their time to the care of their homes and families. By the late 19th century, however, only middle-class and upper-class women could afford to do so. Poorer women usually had no choice but to work for wages outside the home.

FARM WOMEN On farms in the South and the Midwest, women's roles had not changed substantially since the previous century. In addition to household tasks such as cooking, making clothes, and laundering, farm women handled a host of other chores such as raising livestock. Often the women had to help plow and plant the fields and harvest the crops.

WOMEN IN INDUSTRY As better-paying opportunities became available in towns, and especially cities, women had new options for finding jobs, even though men's labor unions excluded them from membership. At the turn of the century,

Telephone operators manually connect phone calls in 1915.

NOW & THEN

TELEPHONE OPERATORS

Today, when Americans use the telephone, an automated voice often greets them with instructions about which buttons to press. In the 19th century, every telephone call had to be handled by a telephone operator, a person who connected wires through a switchboard.

Young men, the first telephone operators, proved unsatisfactory. Patrons complained that the male operators used profane language and talked back to callers. Women soon largely replaced men as telephone operators, and were willing to accept the ten-dollar weekly wage.

Department stores advertised shopping by telephone as a convenience. One ad in the Chicago telephone book of 1904 declared, "Every [telephone] order, inquiry, or request will be quickly and intelligently cared for." The ad pictured a line of female telephone operators.

one out of five American women held jobs; 25 percent of them worked in manufacturing.

The garment trade claimed about half of all women industrial workers. They typically held the least skilled positions, however, and received only about half as much money as their male counterparts or less. Many of these women were single and were assumed to be supporting only themselves, while men were assumed to be supporting families.

Women also began to fill new jobs in offices, stores, and classrooms. These jobs required a high school education, and by 1890, women high school graduates outnumbered men. Moreover, new business schools were preparing bookkeepers and stenographers, as well as training female typists to operate the new machines. (A)

MAIN IDEA

Analyzing Causes

(A) What kinds of job opportunities prompted more women to complete high school?

DOMESTIC WORKERS Many women without formal education or industrial skills contributed to the economic survival of their families by doing domestic work, such as cleaning for other families. After almost 2 million African-American women were freed from slavery, poverty quickly drove nearly half of them into the work force. They worked on farms and as domestic workers, and migrated by the thousands to big cities for jobs as cooks, laundresses, scrubwomen, and maids. Altogether, roughly 70 percent of women employed in 1870 were servants.

Unmarried immigrant women also did domestic labor, especially when they first arrived in the United States. Many married immigrant women contributed to the family income by taking in piecework or caring for boarders at home.

Women Lead Reform

Dangerous conditions, low wages, and long hours led many female industrial workers to push for reforms. Their ranks grew after 146 workers, mostly young women, died in a 1911 fire in the Triangle Shirtwaist Factory in New York City. Middle- and upper-class women also entered the public sphere. By 1910, women's clubs, at which these women discussed art or literature, were nearly half a million strong. These clubs sometimes grew into reform groups that addressed issues such as temperance or child labor.

WOMEN IN HIGHER EDUCATION Many of the women who became active in public life in the late 19th century had attended the new women's colleges. Vassar

College—with a faculty of 8 men and 22 women—accepted its first students in 1865. Smith and Wellesley Colleges followed in 1875. Though Columbia, Brown, and Harvard Colleges refused to admit women, each university established a separate college for women.

Although women were still expected to fulfill traditional domestic roles, women's colleges sought to grant women an excellent education. In her will, Smith College's founder, Sophia Smith, made her goals clear.

A PERSONAL VOICE SOPHIA SMITH

"[It is my desire] to furnish for my own sex means and facilities for education equal to those which are afforded now in our College to young men. . . . It is not my design to render my sex any the less feminine, but to develop as fully as may be the powers of womanhood & furnish women with means of usefulness, happiness, & honor now withheld from them."

—quoted in *Alma Mater*

MAIN IDEA

Analyzing Effects

B What social and economic effects did higher education have on women?

By the late 19th century, marriage was no longer a woman's only alternative. Many women entered the work force or sought higher education. In fact, almost half of college-educated women in the late 19th century never married, retaining their own independence. Many of these educated women began to apply their skills to needed social reforms. B

WOMEN AND REFORM Uneducated laborers started efforts to reform workplace health and safety. The participation of educated women often strengthened existing reform groups and provided leadership for new ones. Because women were not allowed to vote or run for office, women reformers strove to improve conditions at work and home. Their "social housekeeping" targeted workplace reform, housing reform, educational improvement, and food and drug laws.

In 1896, African-American women founded the National Association of Colored Women, or **NACW,** by merging two earlier organizations. Josephine Ruffin identified the mission of the African-American women's club movement as "the moral education of the race with which we are identified." The NACW managed nurseries, reading rooms, and kindergartens.

After the Seneca Falls convention of 1848, women split over the Fourteenth and Fifteenth Amendments, which granted equal rights including the right to vote to African American men, but excluded women. **Susan B. Anthony,** a leading proponent of woman **suffrage,** the right to vote, said "[I] would sooner cut off my right hand than ask the ballot for the black man and not for women." In 1869 Anthony and Elizabeth Cady Stanton had founded the National Women Suffrage Association (NWSA), which united with another group in 1890 to

Suffragists recruit supporters for a march. ▼

KEY PLAYER

SUSAN B. ANTHONY
1820–1906

Born to a strict Quaker family, Susan B. Anthony was not allowed to enjoy typical childhood entertainment such as music, games, and toys. Her father insisted on self-discipline, education, and a strong belief system for all of his eight children. At an early age, Anthony developed a positive view of womanhood from a teacher named Mary Perkins who educated the children in their home.

After voting illegally in the presidential election of 1872, Anthony was fined $100 at her trial. "Not a penny shall go to this unjust claim," she defiantly declared. She never paid the fine.

become the National American Woman Suffrage Association, or **NAWSA.** Other prominent leaders included Lucy Stone and Julia Ward Howe, the author of "The Battle Hymn of the Republic."

Woman suffrage faced constant opposition. The liquor industry feared that women would vote in support of prohibition, while the textile industry worried that women would vote for restrictions on child labor. Many men simply feared the changing role of women in society.

A THREE-PART STRATEGY FOR SUFFRAGE Suffragist leaders tried three approaches to achieve their objective. First, they tried to convince state legislatures to grant women the right to vote. They achieved a victory in the territory of Wyoming in 1869, and by the 1890s Utah, Colorado, and Idaho had also granted voting rights to women. After 1896, efforts in other states failed.

Second, women pursued court cases to test the Fourteenth Amendment, which declared that states denying their male citizens the right to vote would lose congressional representation. Weren't women citizens, too? In 1871 and 1872, Susan B. Anthony and other women tested that question by attempting to vote at least 150 times in ten states and the District of Columbia. The Supreme Court ruled in 1875 that women were indeed citizens—but then denied that citizenship automatically conferred the right to vote.

Third, women pushed for a national constitutional amendment to grant women the vote. Stanton succeeded in having the amendment introduced in California, but it was killed later. For the next 41 years, women lobbied to have it reintroduced, only to see it continually voted down. C

> **MAIN IDEA**
> **Making Inferences**
> C Why did suffragist leaders employ a three-part strategy for gaining the right to vote?

Before the turn of the century, the campaign for suffrage achieved only modest success. Later, however, women's reform efforts paid off in improvements in the treatment of workers and in safer food and drug products—all of which President Theodore Roosevelt supported, along with his own plans for reforming business, labor, and the environment.

SECTION 2 ASSESSMENT

1. **TERMS & NAMES** For each term or name, write a sentence explaining its significance.
   - **NACW**
   - **suffrage**
   - **Susan B. Anthony**
   - **NAWSA**

MAIN IDEA

2. **TAKING NOTES**
   In a chart like the one below, fill in details about working women in the late 1800s.

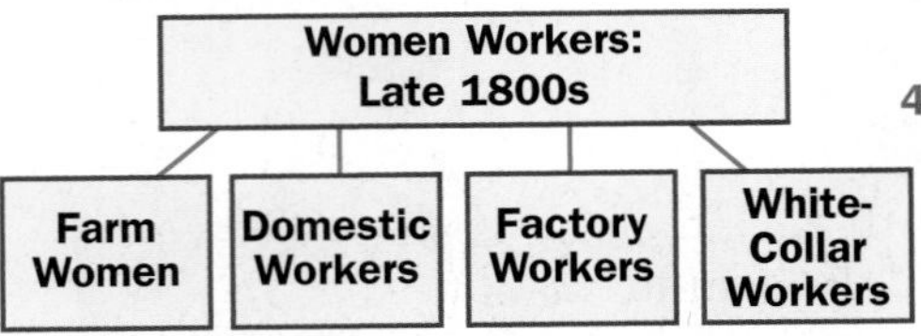

   What generalizations can you make about women workers at this time?

CRITICAL THINKING

3. **SYNTHESIZING**
   What women and movements during the Progressive Era helped dispel the stereotype that women were submissive and nonpolitical?

4. **MAKING INFERENCES**
   Why do you think some colleges refused to accept women in the late 19th century?

5. **ANALYZING ISSUES**
   Imagine you are a woman during the Progressive Era. Explain how you might recruit other women to support the following causes: improving education, housing reform, food and drug laws, the right to vote. **Think About:**
   - the problems that each movement was trying to remedy
   - how women benefited from each cause

Teddy Roosevelt's Square Deal

MAIN IDEA

As president, Theodore Roosevelt worked to give citizens a Square Deal through progressive reforms.

WHY IT MATTERS NOW

As part of his Square Deal, Roosevelt's conservation efforts made a permanent impact on environmental resources.

Terms & Names

- **Upton Sinclair**
- ***The Jungle***
- **Theodore Roosevelt**
- **Square Deal**
- **Meat Inspection Act**
- **Pure Food and Drug Act**
- **conservation**
- **NAACP**

One American's Story

When muckraking journalist **Upton Sinclair** began research for a novel in 1904, his focus was the human condition in the stockyards of Chicago. Sinclair intended his novel to reveal "the breaking of human hearts by a system [that] exploits the labor of men and women for profits." What most shocked readers in Sinclair's book ***The Jungle*** (1906), however, was the sickening conditions of the meatpacking industry.

A PERSONAL VOICE UPTON SINCLAIR

"There would be meat that had tumbled out on the floor, in the dirt and sawdust, where the workers had tramped and spit uncounted billions of consumption [tuberculosis] germs. There would be meat stored in great piles in rooms; . . . and thousands of rats would race about on it. . . . A man could run his hand over these piles of meat and sweep off handfuls of the dried dung of rats. These rats were nuisances, and the packers would put poisoned bread out for them; they would die, and then rats, bread, and meat would go into the hoppers together."

—*The Jungle*

▲ **Upton Sinclair poses with his son at the time of the writing of *The Jungle*.**

President **Theodore Roosevelt,** like many other readers, was nauseated by Sinclair's account. The president invited the author to visit him at the White House, where Roosevelt promised that "the specific evils you point out shall, if their existence be proved, and if I have the power, be eradicated."

A Rough-Riding President

Theodore Roosevelt was not supposed to be president. In 1900, the young governor from New York was urged to run as McKinley's vice-president by the state's political bosses, who found Roosevelt impossible to control. The plot to nominate Roosevelt worked, taking him out of state office. However, as vice-president,

▲ When the president spared a bear cub on a hunting expedition, a toymaker marketed a popular new product, the teddy bear.

Roosevelt stood a heartbeat away from becoming president. Indeed, President McKinley had served barely six months of his second term before he was assassinated, making Roosevelt the most powerful person in the government.

ROOSEVELT'S RISE Theodore Roosevelt was born into a wealthy New York family in 1858. An asthma sufferer during his childhood, young Teddy drove himself to accomplish demanding physical feats. As a teenager, he mastered marksmanship and horseback riding. At Harvard College, Roosevelt boxed and wrestled.

At an early age, the ambitious Roosevelt became a leader in New York politics. After serving three terms in the New York State Assembly, he became New York City's police commissioner and then assistant secretary of the U.S. Navy. The aspiring politician grabbed national attention, advocating war against Spain in 1898. His volunteer cavalry brigade, the Rough Riders, won public acclaim for its role in the battle at San Juan Hill in Cuba. Roosevelt returned a hero and was soon elected governor of New York and then later won the vice-presidency.

THE MODERN PRESIDENCY When Roosevelt was thrust into the presidency in 1901, he became the youngest president ever at 42 years old. Unlike previous presidents, Roosevelt soon dominated the news with his many exploits. While in office, Roosevelt enjoyed boxing, although one of his opponents blinded him in the left eye. On another day, he galloped 100 miles on horseback, merely to prove the feat possible.

In politics, as in sports, Roosevelt acted boldly, using his personality and popularity to advance his programs. His leadership and publicity campaigns helped create the modern presidency, making him a model by which all future presidents would be measured. Citing federal responsibility for the national welfare, Roosevelt thought the government should assume control whenever states proved incapable of dealing with problems. He explained, "It is the duty of the president to act upon the theory that he is the steward of the people, and . . . to assume that he has the legal right to do whatever the needs of the people demand, unless the Constitution or the laws explicitly forbid him to do it."

Teddy Roosevelt enjoyed an active lifestyle, as this 1902 photo reveals. ▶

MAIN IDEA

Synthesizing

A What actions and characteristics of Teddy Roosevelt contributed to his reputation as the first modern president?

Roosevelt saw the presidency as a "bully pulpit," from which he could influence the news media and shape legislation. If big business victimized workers, then President Roosevelt would see to it that the common people received what he called a **Square Deal.** This term was used to describe the various progressive reforms sponsored by the Roosevelt administration. **A**

Using Federal Power

Roosevelt's study of history—he published the first of his 44 books at the age of 24—convinced him that modern America required a powerful federal government. "A simple and poor society can exist as a democracy on the basis of sheer individualism," Roosevelt declared, "but a rich and complex industrial society cannot so exist . . . ." The young president soon met several challenges to his assertion of federal power.

Background

See *trust* on page R47 in the Economics Handbook.

TRUSTBUSTING By 1900, trusts—legal bodies created to hold stock in many companies—controlled about four-fifths of the industries in the United States. Some trusts, like Standard Oil, had earned poor reputations with the public by the use of unfair business practices. Many trusts lowered their prices to drive competitors out of the market and then took advantage of the lack of competition to jack prices up even higher. Although Congress had passed the Sherman Antitrust Act in 1890, the act's vague language made enforcement difficult. As a result, nearly all the suits filed against the trusts under the Sherman Act were ineffective.

President Roosevelt did not believe that all trusts were harmful, but he sought to curb the actions of those that hurt the public interest. The president concentrated his efforts on filing suits under the Sherman Antitrust Act. In 1902, Roosevelt made newspaper headlines as a trustbuster when he ordered the Justice Department to sue the Northern Securities Company, which had established a monopoly over northwestern railroads. In 1904, the Supreme Court dissolved the company. Although the Roosevelt administration filed 44 antitrust suits, winning a number of them and breaking up some of the trusts, it was unable to slow the merger movement in business.

Analyzing *Political Cartoons*

"THE LION-TAMER"

As part of his Square Deal, President Roosevelt aggressively used the Sherman Antitrust Act of 1890 to attack big businesses engaging in unfair practices. His victory over his first target, the Northern Securities Company, earned him a reputation as a hard-hitting trustbuster committed to protecting the public interest. This cartoon shows Roosevelt trying to tame the wild lions that symbolize the great and powerful companies of 1904.

SKILLBUILDER Analyzing Political Cartoons

1. What do the lions stand for?
2. Why are all the lions coming out of a door labeled "Wall St."?
3. What do you think the cartoonist thinks about trustbusting? Cite details from the cartoon that support your interpretation.

SEE SKILLBUILDER HANDBOOK, PAGE R24.

THE LION-TAMER

1902 COAL STRIKE When 140,000 coal miners in Pennsylvania went on strike and demanded a 20 percent raise, a nine-hour workday, and the right to organize a union, the mine operators refused to bargain. Five months into the strike, coal reserves ran low. Roosevelt, seeing the need to intervene, called both sides to the White House to talk, and eventually settled the strike. Irked by the "extraordinary stupidity and bad temper" of the mine operators, he later confessed that only the dignity of the presidency had kept him from taking one owner "by the seat of the breeches" and tossing him out of the window.

Faced with Roosevelt's threat to take over the mines, the opposing sides finally agreed to submit their differences to an arbitration commission—a third party that would work with both sides to mediate the dispute. In 1903, the commission issued its compromise settlement. The miners won a 10 percent pay hike and a shorter, nine-hour workday. With this, however, they had to give up their demand for a closed shop—in which all workers must belong to the union—and their right to strike during the next three years.

> *"In life, as in a football game, the principle . . . is: Hit the line hard."*
> THEODORE ROOSEVELT

President Roosevelt's actions had demonstrated a new principle. From then on, when a strike threatened the public welfare, the federal government was expected to intervene. In addition, Roosevelt's actions reflected the progressive belief that disputes could be settled in an orderly way with the help of experts, such as those on the arbitration commission. B

MAIN IDEA

Analyzing Effects

B What was significant about the way the 1902 coal strike was settled?

RAILROAD REGULATION Roosevelt's real goal was federal regulation. In 1887, Congress had passed the Interstate Commerce Act, which prohibited wealthy railroad owners from colluding to fix high prices by dividing the business in a given area. The Interstate Commerce Commission (ICC) was set up to enforce the new law but had little power. With Roosevelt's urging, Congress passed the Elkins Act in 1903, which made it illegal for railroad officials to give, and shippers to receive, rebates for using particular railroads. The act also specified that railroads could not change set rates without notifying the public.

Vocabulary

collude: to act together secretly to achieve an illegal or deceitful purpose

The Hepburn Act of 1906 strictly limited the distribution of free railroad passes, a common form of bribery. It also gave the ICC power to set maximum railroad rates. Although Roosevelt had to compromise with conservative senators who opposed the act, its passage boosted the government's power to regulate the railroads.

NOW & THEN

MEAT INSPECTION

During the Progressive Era, people worried about the kinds of things that might fall—or walk—into a batch of meat being processed. Today, Americans worry more about contamination by unseen dangers, such as E. coli bacteria, mad cow disease, and antibiotics or other chemicals that may pose long-range health risks to people.

In July 1996, Congress passed the most extensive changes in standards for meat inspection since the Meat Inspection Act of 1906. The costs of the new, more scientific inspections amount to about a tenth of a penny per pound of meat. The FDA has also adopted restrictions on importation of feed and livestock from other countries to prevent the spread of disease.

Health and the Environment

President Roosevelt's enthusiasm and his considerable skill at compromise led to laws and policies that benefited both public health and the environment. He wrote, "We recognize and are bound to war against the evils of today. The remedies are partly economic and partly spiritual, partly to be obtained by laws, and in greater part to be obtained by individual and associated effort."

REGULATING FOODS AND DRUGS After reading *The Jungle* by Upton Sinclair, Roosevelt responded to the public's clamor for action. He appointed a commission of experts to investigate the meatpacking industry. The commission issued a scathing report backing up Sinclair's account of the disgusting conditions in the industry. True to his word, in 1906 Roosevelt pushed for passage of the **Meat Inspection Act,**

Coal Mining in the Early 1900s

INTERACTIVE

Coal played a key role in America's industrial boom around the turn of the century, providing the United States with about 90 percent of its energy. Miners often had to dig for coal hundreds of feet below the earth's surface. The work in these mines was among the hardest and most dangerous in the world. Progressive Era reforms helped improve conditions for miners, as many won wage increases and shorter work hours.

The coal mines employed thousands of children, like this boy pictured in 1909. In 1916, progressives helped secure passage of a child labor law that forbade interstate commerce of goods produced by children under the age of 14. ▶

Most underground mines had two shafts—an elevator shaft (shown here) for transporting workers and coal, and an air shaft for ventilation.

◀ Like these men working in 1908, miners typically spent their days in dark, cramped spaces underground.

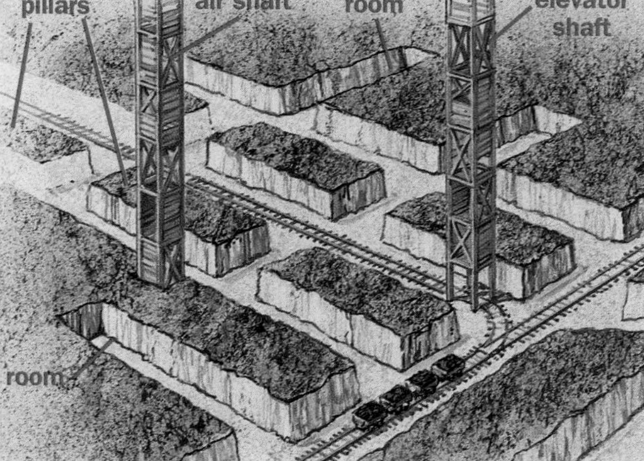

Most mines used a room-and-pillar method for extracting coal. This entailed digging out "rooms" of coal off a series of tunnels, leaving enough coal behind to form a pillar that prevented the room from collapsing.

The miners' main tool was the pick. Many also used drilling machines.

Donkeys or mules pulled the coal cars to the elevators, which transported the coal to the surface.

Government workers inspect meat as it moves through the packinghouse. ▶

which dictated strict cleanliness requirements for meatpackers and created the program of federal meat inspection that was in use until it was replaced by more sophisticated techniques in the 1990s.

The compromise that won the act's passage, however, left the government paying for the inspections and did not require companies to label their canned goods with date-of-processing information. The compromise also granted meatpackers the right to appeal negative decisions in court.

PURE FOOD AND DRUG ACT Before any federal regulations were established for advertising food and drugs, manufacturers had claimed that their products accomplished everything from curing cancer to growing hair. In addition, popular children's medicines often contained opium, cocaine, or alcohol. In a series of lectures across the country, Dr. Harvey Washington Wiley, chief chemist at the Department of Agriculture, criticized manufacturers for adding harmful preservatives to food and brought needed attention to this issue.

A typical late-19th-century product advertisement. ▼

HALL'S
VEGETABLE SICILIAN
HAIR
RENEWER
THICKENS THE GROWTH OF THE HAIR,
PREVENTS BALDNESS,
CURES DANDRUFF,
AND RESTORES GRAY HAIR TO ITS ORIGINAL COLOR AND BEAUTY.
R.P. HALL & CO. PROPRIETORS. NASHUA, N.H.

In 1906, Congress passed the **Pure Food and Drug Act,** which halted the sale of contaminated foods and medicines and called for truth in labeling. Although this act did not ban harmful products outright, its requirement of truthful labels reflected the progressive belief that given accurate information, people would act wisely. C

MAIN IDEA

Comparing

C What similarities did the Meat Inspection Act and Pure Food and Drug Act share?

CONSERVATION AND NATURAL RESOURCES Before Roosevelt's presidency, the federal government had paid very little attention to the nation's natural resources. Despite the establishment of the U.S. Forest Bureau in 1887 and the subsequent withdrawal from public sale of 45 million acres of timberlands for a national forest reserve, the government stood by while private interests gobbled up the shrinking wilderness.

In the late 19th century Americans had shortsightedly exploited their natural environment. Pioneer farmers leveled the forests and plowed up the prairies. Ranchers allowed their cattle to overgraze the Great Plains. Coal companies cluttered the land with refuse from mines. Lumber companies ignored the effect of their logging operations on flood control and neglected to plant trees to replace those they had cut down. Cities dumped untreated sewage and industrial wastes into rivers, poisoning the streams and creating health hazards.

CONSERVATION MEASURES Roosevelt condemned the view that America's resources were endless and made conservation a primary concern. John Muir, a naturalist and writer with whom Roosevelt camped in California's Yosemite National Park in 1903, persuaded the president to set aside 148 million acres of forest reserves. Roosevelt also set aside 1.5 million acres of water-power sites and another 80 million acres of land that experts from the U.S. Geological Survey would explore for mineral and water resources. Roosevelt also established more than 50 wildlife sanctuaries and several national parks.

True to the Progressive belief in using experts, in 1905 the president named Gifford Pinchot as head of the U.S. Forest Service. A professional conservationist, Pinchot had administrative skill as well as the latest scientific and technical information. He advised Roosevelt to conserve forest and grazing lands by keeping large tracts of federal land exempt from private sale.

Conservationists like Roosevelt and Pinchot, however, did not share the views of Muir, who advocated complete preservation of the wilderness. Instead, **conservation** to them meant that some wilderness areas would be preserved while others would be developed for the common good. Indeed, Roosevelt's federal water projects transformed some dry wilderness areas to make agriculture possible. Under the National Reclamation Act of 1902, known as the Newlands

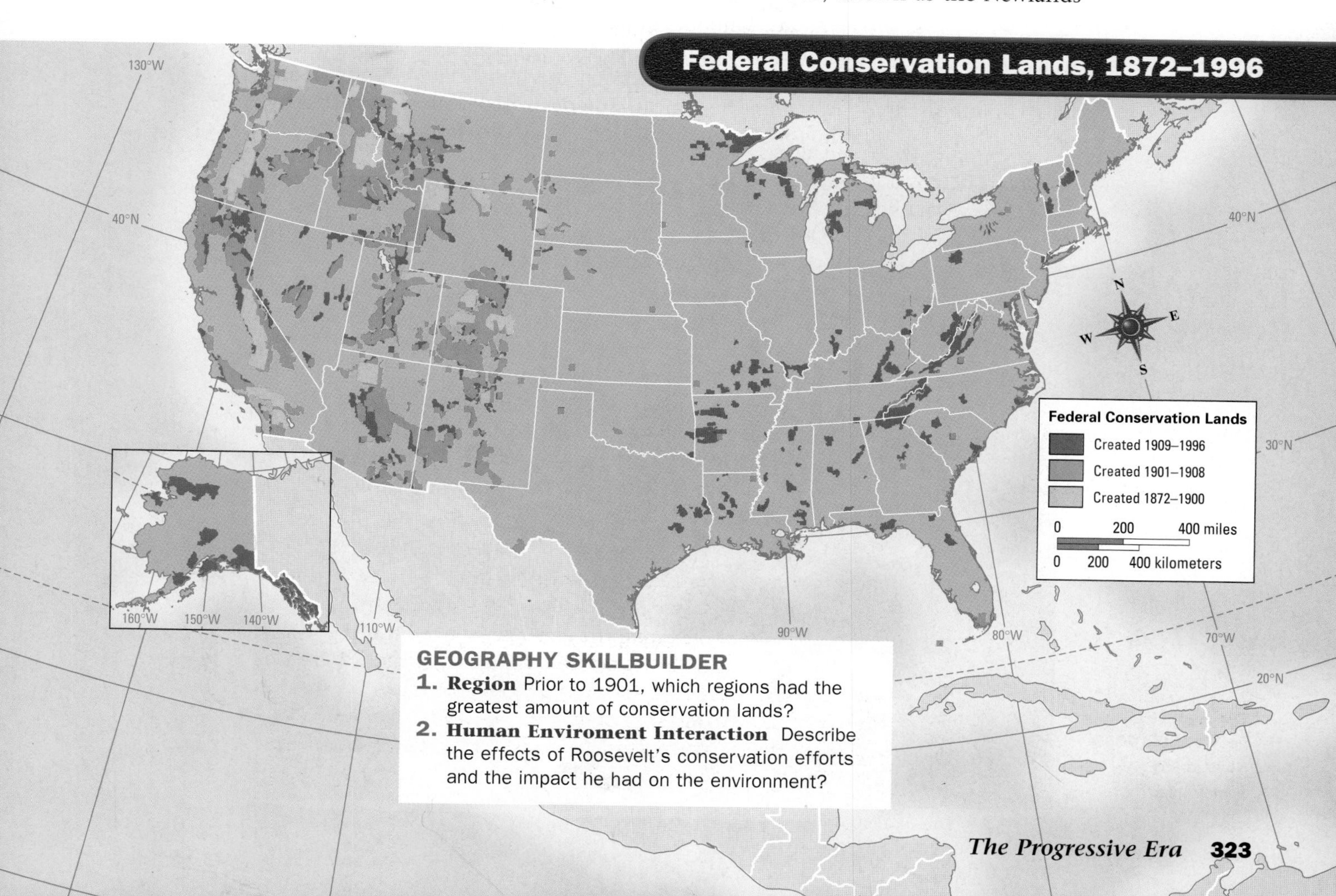

GEOGRAPHY SKILLBUILDER

1. **Region** Prior to 1901, which regions had the greatest amount of conservation lands?
2. **Human Enviroment Interaction** Describe the effects of Roosevelt's conservation efforts and the impact he had on the environment?

HISTORICAL SPOTLIGHT

YOSEMITE NATIONAL PARK

The naturalist John Muir visited the Yosemite region of central California in 1868 and made it his home base for a period of six years while he traveled throughout the West.

Muir was the first to suggest that Yosemite's spectacular land formations had been shaped by glaciers. Today the park's impressive cliffs, waterfalls, lakes, and meadows draw sports enthusiasts and tourists in all seasons.

Act, money from the sale of public lands in the West funded large-scale irrigation projects, such as the Roosevelt Dam in Arizona and the Shoshone Dam in Wyoming. The Newlands Act established the precedent that the federal government would manage the precious water resources of the West. D

MAIN IDEA

Summarizing
D Summarize Roosevelt's approach to environmental problems.

Roosevelt and Civil Rights

Roosevelt's concern for the land and its inhabitants was not matched in the area of civil rights. Though Roosevelt's father had supported the North, his mother, Martha, may well have been the model for the Southern belle Scarlet O'Hara in Margaret Mitchell's famous novel, *Gone with the Wind.* In almost two terms as president, Roosevelt—like most other progressives—failed to support civil rights for African Americans. He did, however, support a few individual African Americans.

Despite opposition from whites, Roosevelt appointed an African American as head of the Charleston, South Carolina, customhouse. In another instance, when some whites in Mississippi refused to accept the black postmistress he had appointed, he chose to close the station rather than give in. In 1906, however, Roosevelt angered many African Americans when he dismissed without question an entire regiment of African-American soldiers accused of conspiracy in protecting others charged with murder in Brownsville, Texas.

As a symbolic gesture, Roosevelt invited Booker T. Washington to dinner at the White House. Washington—head of the Tuskegee Normal and Industrial Institute, an all-black training school—was then the African-American leader most respected by powerful whites. Washington faced opposition, however, from other African

Civil rights leaders gather at the 1905 Niagara Falls conference. ▶

Vocabulary
accommodation: adapting or making adjustments in order to satisfy someone else

Americans, such as W. E. B. Du Bois, for his accommodation of segregationists and for blaming black poverty on blacks and urging them to accept discrimination.

Persistent in his criticism of Washington's ideas, Du Bois renewed his demands for immediate social and economic equality for African Americans. In his 1903 book *The Souls of Black Folk,* Du Bois wrote of his opposition to Washington's position.

A PERSONAL VOICE W. E. B. DU BOIS

"So far as Mr. Washington preaches Thrift, Patience, and Industrial Training for the masses, we must hold up his hands and strive with him. . . . But so far as Mr. Washington apologizes for injustice, North or South, does not rightly value the privilege and duty of voting, belittles the emasculating effects of caste distinctions, and opposes the higher training and ambition of our brighter minds,—so far as he, the South, or the Nation, does this,—we must unceasingly and firmly oppose them."

—*The Souls of Black Folk*

Background
The Niagara Movement was comprised of 29 black intellectuals. They met secretly in 1905 to compose a civil rights manifesto.

Du Bois and other advocates of equality for African Americans were deeply upset by the apparent progressive indifference to racial injustice. In 1905 they held a civil rights conference in Niagara Falls, and in 1909 a number of African Americans joined with prominent white reformers in New York to found the **NAACP**—the National Association for the Advancement of Colored People. The NAACP, which had over 6,000 members by 1914, aimed for nothing less than full equality among the races. That goal, however, found little support in the Progressive Movement, which focused on the needs of middle-class whites. The two presidents who followed Roosevelt also did little to advance the goal of racial equality.

KEY PLAYER

W. E. B. DU BOIS
1868–1963

In 1909, W. E. B. Du Bois helped to establish the NAACP and entered into the forefront of the early U.S. civil rights movement. However, in the 1920s, he faced a power struggle with the NAACP's executive secretary, Walter White.

Ironically, Du Bois had retreated to a position others saw as dangerously close to that of Booker T. Washington. Arguing for a separate economy for African Americans, Du Bois made a distinction, which White rejected, between enforced and voluntary segregation. By mid-century, Du Bois was outside the mainstream of the civil rights movement. His work remained largely ignored until after his death in 1963.

SECTION 3 ASSESSMENT

1. TERMS & NAMES For each term or name, write a sentence explaining its significance.

- **Upton Sinclair**
- ***The Jungle***
- **Theodore Roosevelt**
- **Square Deal**
- **Meat Inspection Act**
- **Pure Food and Drug Act**
- **conservation**
- **NAACP**

MAIN IDEA

2. TAKING NOTES
Create five problem-solution diagrams like the one below to show how the following problems were addressed during Roosevelt's presidency: (a) 1902 coal strike, (b) Northern Securities Company monopoly, (c) unsafe meat processing, (d) exploitation of the environment, and (e) racial injustice.

Problems → **Solutions**

Write headlines announcing the solutions.

CRITICAL THINKING

3. FORMING GENERALIZATIONS
In what ways do you think the progressive belief in using experts played a role in shaping Roosevelt's reforms? Refer to details from the text. **Think About:**

- Roosevelt's use of experts to help him tackle political, economic, and environmental problems
- how experts' findings affected legislative actions

4. EVALUATING
Research the coal strike of 1902. Do you think Roosevelt's intervention was in favor of the strikers or of the mine operators? Why?

5. ANALYZING ISSUES
Why did W. E. B. Du Bois oppose Booker T. Washington's views on racial discrimination?

AMERICAN LITERATURE

The Muckrakers

1902–1917 The tradition of the investigative reporter uncovering corruption was established early in the 20th century by the writers known as muckrakers. Coined by President Theodore Roosevelt, the term *muckraker* alludes to the English author John Bunyan's famous 17th-century religious allegory *The Pilgrim's Progress,* which features a character too busy raking up the muck to see a heavenly crown held over him. The originally negative term soon was applied to many writers whose reform efforts Roosevelt himself supported. The muckraking movement spilled over from journalism as writers such as Upton Sinclair made use of the greater dramatic effects of fiction.

◀ **IDA M. TARBELL**

Ida M. Tarbell's "The History of the Standard Oil Company" exposed the ruthlessness with which John D. Rockefeller had turned his oil business into an all-powerful monopoly. Her writing added force to the trustbusting reforms of the early 20th century. Here Tarbell describes how Standard Oil used lower transportation rates to drive out smaller refineries, such as Hanna, Baslington and Company.

> Mr. Hanna had been refining since July, 1869. . . . Some time in February, 1872, the Standard Oil Company asked [for] an interview with him and his associates. They wanted to buy his works, they said. "But we don't want to sell," objected Mr. Hanna. "You can never make any more money, in my judgment," said Mr. Rockefeller. "You can't compete with the Standard. We have all the large refineries now. If you refuse to sell, it will end in your being crushed." Hanna and Baslington were not satisfied. They went to see . . . General Devereux, manager of the Lake Shore road. They were told that the Standard had special rates; that it was useless to try to compete with them. General Devereux explained to the gentlemen that the privileges granted the Standard were the legitimate and necessary advantage of the larger shipper over the smaller. . . . General Devereux says they "recognised the propriety" of his excuse. They certainly recognised its authority. They say that they were satisfied they could no longer get rates to and from Cleveland which would enable them to live, and "reluctantly" sold out. It must have been reluctantly, for they had paid $75,000 for their works, and had made thirty per cent. a year on an average on their investment, and the Standard appraiser allowed them $45,000.

—Ida M. Tarbell, "The History of the Standard Oil Company" (1904)

LINCOLN STEFFENS ▶

Lincoln Steffens is usually named as a leading figure of the muckraking movement. He published exposés of business and government corruption in *McClure's Magazine* and other magazines. These articles were then collected in two books: *The Shame of the Cities* and *The Struggle for Self-Government*. Below is a section from an article Steffens wrote to expose voter fraud in Philadelphia.

> The police are forbidden by law to stand within thirty feet of the polls, but they are at the box and they are there to see that the [Republican political] machine's orders are obeyed and that repeaters whom they help to furnish are permitted to vote without "intimidation" on the names they, the police, have supplied. The editor of an anti-machine paper who was looking about for himself once told me that a ward leader who knew him well asked him into a polling place. "I'll show you how it's done," he said, and he had the repeaters go round and round voting again and again on the names handed them on slips. . . . The business proceeds with very few hitches; there is more jesting than fighting. Violence in the past has had its effect; and is not often necessary nowadays, but if it is needed the police are there to apply it.

—Lincoln Steffens, *The Shame of the Cities (1904)*

UPTON SINCLAIR

Upton Sinclair's chief aim in writing *The Jungle* was to expose the shocking conditions that immigrant workers endured. The public, however, reacted even more strongly to the novel's revelations of unsanitary conditions in the meatpacking industry. Serialized in 1905 and published in book form one year later, *The Jungle* prompted a federal investigation that resulted in passage of the Meat Inspection Act in 1906.

> Jonas had told them how the meat that was taken out of pickle would often be found sour, and how they would rub it up with [baking] soda to take away the smell, and sell it to be eaten on free-lunch counters; also of all the miracles of chemistry which they performed, giving to any sort of meat, fresh or salted, whole or chopped, any color and any flavor and any odor they chose. . . .
>
> It was only when the whole ham was spoiled that it came into the department of Elzbieta. Cut up by the two-thousand-revolutions-a-minute flyers, and mixed with half a ton of other meat, no odor that ever was in a ham could make any difference. There was never the least attention paid to what was cut up for sausage; there would come all the way back from Europe old sausage that had been rejected, and that was moldy and white—it would be dosed with borax and glycerine, and dumped into the hoppers, and made over again for home consumption.

—Upton Sinclair, *The Jungle (1906)*

THINKING CRITICALLY

1. **Comparing and Contrasting** State the main idea of each of these selections. What role do details play in making the passages convincing?

 **SEE SKILLBUILDER HANDBOOK, PAGE R8.**

2.  **INTERNET ACTIVITY CLASSZONE.COM**

Visit the links for American Literature: The Muckrakers to learn more about the muckrakers. What topics did they investigate? How did they affect public opinion? What legal changes did they help to bring about? Write a summary of the muckrakers' impact on society.

Progressivism Under Taft

MAIN IDEA

Taft's ambivalent approach to progressive reform led to a split in the Republican Party and the loss of the presidency to the Democrats.

WHY IT MATTERS NOW

Third-party candidates continue to wrestle with how to become viable candidates.

Terms & Names

- **Gifford Pinchot**
- **William Howard Taft**
- **Payne-Aldrich Tariff**
- **Bull Moose Party**
- **Woodrow Wilson**

One American's Story

Early in the 20th century, Americans' interest in the preservation of the country's wilderness areas intensified. Writers proclaimed the beauty of the landscape, and new groups like the Girl Scouts gave city children the chance to experience a different environment. The desire for preservation clashed with business interests that favored unrestricted development. **Gifford Pinchot** (pĭn′shō′), head of the U.S. Forest Service under President Roosevelt, took a middle ground. He believed that wilderness areas could be scientifically managed to yield public enjoyment while allowing private development.

▲ Gifford Pinchot

A PERSONAL VOICE GIFFORD PINCHOT

"The American people have evidently made up their minds that our natural resources must be conserved. That is good. But it settles only half the question. For whose benefit shall they be conserved—for the benefit of the many, or for the use and profit of the few? . . . There is no other question before us that begins to be so important, or that will be so difficult to straddle, as the great question between special interest and equal opportunity, between the privileges of the few and the rights of the many, between government by men for human welfare and government by money for profit."

—The Fight for Conservation

President Roosevelt, a fellow conservationist, favored Pinchot's multi-use land program. However, when he left office in 1909, this approach came under increasing pressure from business people who favored unrestricted commercial development.

Taft Becomes President

After winning the election in 1904, Roosevelt pledged not to run for reelection in 1908. He handpicked his secretary of war, **William Howard Taft,** to run against William Jennings Bryan, who had been nominated by the Democrats for the third time. Under the slogan "Vote for Taft this time, You can vote for Bryan any time," Taft and the Republicans won an easy victory.

TAFT STUMBLES As president, Taft pursued a cautiously progressive agenda, seeking to consolidate rather than to expand Roosevelt's reforms. He received little credit for his accomplishments, however. His legal victories, such as busting 90 trusts in a four-year term, did not bolster his popularity. Indeed, the new president confessed in a letter to Roosevelt that he never felt like the president. "When I am addressed as 'Mr. President,'" Taft wrote, "I turn to see whether you are not at my elbow."

The cautious Taft hesitated to use the presidential bully pulpit to arouse public opinion. Nor could he subdue troublesome members of his own party. Tariffs and conservation posed his first problems.

Background
See *tariff* on page R46 in the Economics Handbook.

THE PAYNE–ALDRICH TARIFF Taft had campaigned on a platform of lowering tariffs, a staple of the progressive agenda. When the House passed the Payne Bill, which lowered rates on imported manufactured goods, the Senate proposed an alternative bill, the Aldrich Bill, which made fewer cuts and increased many rates. Amid cries of betrayal from the progressive wing of his party, Taft signed the **Payne-Aldrich Tariff,** a compromise that only moderated the high rates of the Aldrich Bill. This angered progressives who believed Taft had abandoned progressivism. The president made his difficulties worse by clumsily attempting to defend the tariff, calling it "the best [tariff] bill the Republican party ever passed."

DIFFICULT DECISIONS

CONTROLLING RESOURCES

Historically, conservationists such as Gifford Pinchot have stood for the balanced use of natural resources, preserving some and using others for private industry. Free-market advocates like Richard Ballinger pressed for the private development of wilderness areas. Preservationists such as John Muir advocated preserving all remaining wilderness.

1. Examine the pros and cons of each position. With which do you agree? What factors do you think should influence decisions about America's wilderness areas?
2. If you'd been asked in 1902 to decide whether to develop or preserve America's wilderness areas, what would you have decided? Why?

DISPUTING PUBLIC LANDS Next, Taft angered conservationists by appointing as his secretary of the interior Richard A. Ballinger, a wealthy lawyer from Seattle. Ballinger, who disapproved of conservationist controls on western lands, removed 1 million acres of forest and mining lands from the reserved list and returned it to the public domain.

MAIN IDEA

Analyzing Issues
A How did Taft's appointee Richard Ballinger anger conservationists?

When a Department of the Interior official was fired for protesting Ballinger's actions, the fired worker published a muckraking article against Ballinger in *Collier's Weekly* magazine. Pinchot added his voice. In congressional testimony he accused Ballinger of letting commercial interests exploit the natural resources that rightfully belonged to the public. President Taft sided with Ballinger and fired Pinchot from the U.S. Forest Service. **A**

The Republican Party Splits

Taft's cautious nature made it impossible for him to hold together the two wings of the Republican Party: progressives who sought change and conservatives who did not. The Republican Party began to fragment.

PROBLEMS WITHIN THE PARTY Republican conservatives and progressives split over Taft's support of the political boss Joseph Cannon, House Speaker from Illinois. A rough-talking, tobacco-chewing politician, "Uncle Joe" often disregarded seniority in filling committee slots. As chairman of the House Rules Committee, which decides what bills Congress considers, Cannon often weakened or ignored progressive bills.

Reform-minded Republicans decided that their only alternative was to strip Cannon of his power. With the help of Democrats, they succeeded in March 1910 with a resolution that called for the entire House to elect the Committee on Rules and excluded the Speaker from membership in the committee.

William Howard Taft

KEY PLAYER

WILLIAM HOWARD TAFT
1857–1930

William Howard Taft never wanted to be president. After serving one term, Taft left the White House, which he called "the lonesomest place in the world," and taught constitutional law at Yale for eight years.

In 1921, President Harding named Taft chief justice of the Supreme Court. The man whose family had nicknamed him "Big Lub" called this appointment the highest honor he had ever received. As chief justice, Taft wrote that "in my present life I don't remember that I ever was President."

However, Americans remember Taft for, among many other things, initiating in 1910 the popular presidential custom of throwing out the first ball of the major league baseball season.

By the midterm elections of 1910, however, the Republican Party was in shambles, with the progressives on one side and the "old guard" on the other. Voters voiced concern over the rising cost of living, which they blamed on the Payne-Aldrich Tariff. They also believed Taft to be against conservation. When the Republicans lost the election, the Democrats gained control of the House of Representatives for the first time in 18 years.

Vocabulary
"old guard": conservative members of a group

THE BULL MOOSE PARTY After leaving office, Roosevelt headed to Africa to shoot big game. He returned in 1910 to a hero's welcome, and responded with a rousing speech proposing a "New Nationalism," under which the federal government would exert its power for "the welfare of the people."

By 1912, Roosevelt had decided to run for a third term as president. The primary elections showed that Republicans wanted Roosevelt, but Taft had the advantage of being the incumbent—that is, the holder of the office. At the Republican convention in June 1912, Taft supporters maneuvered to replace Roosevelt delegates with Taft delegates in a number of delegations. Republican progressives refused to vote and formed a new third party, the Progressive Party. They nominated Roosevelt for president.

The Progressive Party became known as the **Bull Moose Party**, after Roosevelt's boast that he was "as strong as a bull moose." The party's platform called for the direct election of senators and the adoption in all states of the initiative, referendum, and recall. It also advocated woman suffrage, workmen's compensation, an eight-hour workday, a minimum wage for women, a federal law against child labor, and a federal trade commission to regulate business. **B**

MAIN IDEA
Contrasting
B What were the differences between Taft's and Roosevelt's campaign platforms?

The split in the Republican ranks handed the Democrats their first real chance at the White House since the election of Grover Cleveland in 1892. In the 1912 presidential election, they put forward as their candidate a reform governor of New Jersey named **Woodrow Wilson**.

Democrats Win in 1912

Under Governor Woodrow Wilson's leadership, the previously conservative New Jersey legislature had passed a host of reform measures. Now, as the Democratic presidential nominee, Wilson endorsed a progressive platform called the New Freedom. It demanded even stronger antitrust legislation, banking reform, and reduced tariffs.

The split between Taft and Roosevelt, former Republican allies, turned nasty during the fall campaign. Taft labeled Roosevelt a "dangerous egotist," while Roosevelt branded Taft a "fathead" with the brain of a "guinea pig." Wilson distanced himself, quietly gloating, "Don't interfere when your enemy is destroying himself."

The election offered voters several choices: Wilson's New Freedom, Taft's conservatism, Roosevelt's progressivism, or the Socialist Party policies of Eugene V. Debs. Both Roosevelt and Wilson supported a stronger government role in economic affairs but differed over strategies. Roosevelt supported government action to supervise big business but did not oppose all business monopolies, while Debs called for an end to capitalism. Wilson supported small business and free-market competition and characterized all business monopolies as evil. In a speech, Wilson explained why he felt that all business monopolies were a threat.

A Personal Voice
WOODROW WILSON

"If the government is to tell big business men how to run their business, then don't you see that big business men have to get closer to the government even than they are now? Don't you see that they must capture the government, in order not to be restrained too much by it? . . . I don't care how benevolent the master is going to be, I will not live under a master. That is not what America was created for. America was created in order that every man should have the same chance as every other man to exercise mastery over his own fortunes."

—quoted in *The New Freedom*

Presidential Election of 1912

Party	Candidate	Electoral votes	Popular vote
Democratic	Woodrow Wilson	435	6,296,547
Progressive	Theodore Roosevelt	88	4,118,571
Republican	William H. Taft	8	3,486,720
Socialist	Eugene V. Debs	0	900,672

Roosevelt, 11
Wilson, 2

MAIN IDEA

Predicting Effects

C What might be one of Wilson's first issues to address as president?

Although Wilson captured only 42 percent of the popular vote, he won an overwhelming electoral victory and a Democratic majority in Congress. As a third-party candidate, Roosevelt defeated Taft in both popular and electoral votes. But reform claimed the real victory, with more than 75 percent of the vote going to the reform candidates—Wilson, Roosevelt, and Debs. In victory, Wilson could claim a mandate to break up trusts and to expand the government's role in social reform. **C**

ASSESSMENT

1. **TERMS & NAMES** For each term or name, write a sentence explaining its significance.
   - **Gifford Pinchot**
   - **William Howard Taft**
   - **Payne-Aldrich Tariff**
   - **Bull Moose Party**
   - **Woodrow Wilson**

MAIN IDEA

2. **TAKING NOTES**
   Re-create the chart below on your paper. Then fill in the causes Taft supported that made people question his leadership.

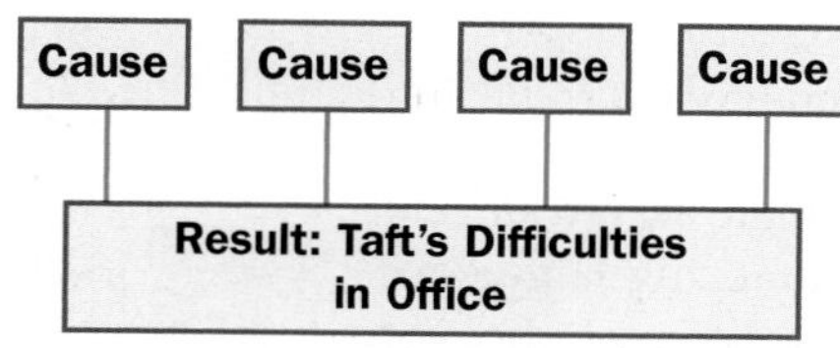

Which causes do you think would upset most people today? Explain.

CRITICAL THINKING

3. **HYPOTHESIZING**
   What if Roosevelt had won another term in office in 1912? Speculate on how this might have affected the future of progressive reforms. Support your answer. **Think About:**
   - Roosevelt's policies that Taft did not support
   - the power struggles within the Republican Party
   - Roosevelt's perception of what is required of a president

4. **EVALUATING**
   Both Roosevelt and Taft resorted to mudslinging during the 1912 presidential campaign. Do you approve or disapprove of negative campaign tactics? Support your opinion.

SECTION 5

Wilson's New Freedom

MAIN IDEA

Woodrow Wilson established a strong reform agenda as a progressive leader.

WHY IT MATTERS NOW

The passage of the Nineteenth Amendment during Wilson's administration granted women the right to vote.

Terms & Names

- **Carrie Chapman Catt**
- **Clayton Antitrust Act**
- **Federal Trade Commission (FTC)**
- **Federal Reserve System**
- **Nineteenth Amendment**

One American's Story

Carrie Chapman Catt

On March 4, 1913, the day of Woodrow Wilson's inauguration, 5,000 woman suffragists marched through hostile crowds in Washington, D.C. Alice Paul and Lucy Burns, the parade's organizers, were members of the National American Woman Suffrage Association (NAWSA). As police failed to restrain the rowdy gathering and congressmen demanded an investigation, Paul and Burns could see the momentum building for suffrage.

By the time Wilson began his campaign for a second term in 1916, the NAWSA's president, **Carrie Chapman Catt**, saw victory on the horizon. Catt expressed her optimism in a letter to her friend Maud Wood Park.

A PERSONAL VOICE CARRIE CHAPMAN CATT

> **"I do feel keenly that the turn of the road has come. . . . I really believe that we might pull off a campaign which would mean the vote within the next six years if we could secure a Board of officers who would have sufficient momentum, confidence and working power in them. . . . Come! My dear Mrs. Park, gird on your armor once more."**
>
> —letter to Maud Wood Park

Catt called an emergency suffrage convention in September 1916, and invited President Wilson, who cautiously supported suffrage. He told the convention, "There has been a force behind you that will . . . be triumphant and for which you can afford. . . . to wait." They did have to wait, but within four years, the passage of the suffrage amendment became the capstone of the progressive movement.

Wilson Wins Financial Reforms

Like Theodore Roosevelt, Woodrow Wilson claimed progressive ideals, but he had a different idea for the federal government. He believed in attacking large concentrations of power to give greater freedom to average citizens. The prejudices of his Southern background, however, prevented him from using federal power to fight off attacks directed at the civil rights of African Americans.

WILSON'S BACKGROUND Wilson spent his youth in the South during the Civil War and Reconstruction. The son, grandson, and nephew of Presbyterian ministers, he received a strict upbringing. Before entering politics, Wilson worked as a lawyer, a history professor, and later as president of Princeton University. In 1910, Wilson became the governor of New Jersey. As governor, he supported progressive legislation programs such as a direct primary, worker's compensation, and the regulation of public utilities and railroads.

As America's newly elected president, Wilson moved to enact his program, the "New Freedom," and planned his attack on what he called the triple wall of privilege: the trusts, tariffs, and high finance.

TWO KEY ANTITRUST MEASURES "Without the watchful . . . resolute interference of the government," Wilson said, "there can be no fair play between individuals and such powerful institutions as the trusts. Freedom today is something more than being let alone." During Wilson's administration, Congress enacted two key antitrust measures. The first, the **Clayton Antitrust Act** of 1914, sought to strengthen the Sherman Antitrust Act of 1890. The Clayton Act prohibited corporations from acquiring the stock of another if doing so would create a monopoly; if a company violated the law, its officers could be prosecuted.

The Clayton Act also specified that labor unions and farm organizations not only had a right to exist but also would no longer be subject to antitrust laws. Therefore, strikes, peaceful picketing, boycotts, and the collection of strike benefits became legal. In addition, injunctions against strikers were prohibited unless the strikers threatened damage that could not be remedied. Samuel Gompers, president of the American Federation of Labor (AFL), saw great value to workers in the Clayton Act. He called it a Magna Carta for labor, referring to the English document, signed in 1215, in which the English king recognized that he was bound by the law and that the law granted rights to his subjects.

Vocabulary
injunction: a court order prohibiting a party from a specific course of action

The second major antitrust measure, the Federal Trade Commission Act of 1914, set up the **Federal Trade Commission (FTC).** This "watchdog" agency was given the power to investigate possible violations of regulatory statutes, to require periodic reports from corporations, and to put an end to a number of unfair business practices. Under Wilson, the FTC administered almost 400 cease-and-desist orders to companies engaged in illegal activity. (A)

MAIN IDEA
Summarizing
(A) What was the impact of the two antitrust measures?

A NEW TAX SYSTEM In an effort to curb the power of big business, Wilson worked to lower tariff rates, knowing that supporters of big business hadn't allowed such a reduction under Taft.

Wilson lobbied hard in 1913 for the Underwood Act, which would substantially reduce tariff rates for the first time since the Civil War. He summoned Congress to a special session to plead his case, and established a precedent of delivering the State of the Union message in person. Businesses lobbied too, looking to block tariff reductions. When manufacturing lobbyists—people hired by manufacturers to present their case to government officials—descended on the capital to urge senators to vote no, passage seemed unlikely. Wilson denounced the lobbyists and urged voters to monitor their senators' votes. Because of the new president's use of the bully pulpit, the Senate voted to cut tariff rates even more deeply than the House had done.

DEREGULATION

In recent years the railroad, airline, and telecommunications industries have all been deregulated, or permitted to compete without government control. It is hoped that this will improve their efficiency and lower prices.

During the Progressive Era, reformers viewed regulation as a necessary role of government to ensure safety and fairness for consumers as well as industrial competitors. Opponents of regulation, however, believed that government regulation caused inefficiency and high prices.

Modern critics of deregulation argue that deregulated businesses may skimp on safety. They may also neglect hard-to-serve populations, such as elderly, poor, or disabled people, while competing for more profitable customers.

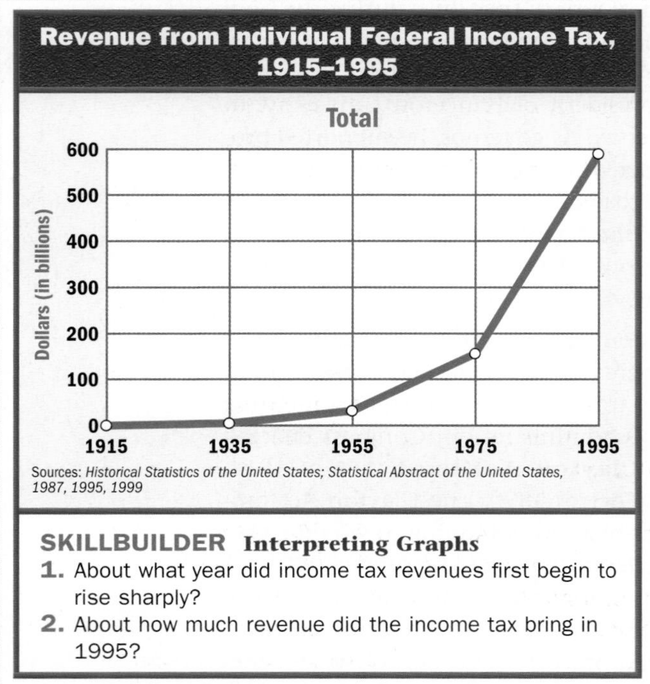

Sources: *Historical Statistics of the United States; Statistical Abstract of the United States, 1987, 1995, 1999*

SKILLBUILDER Interpreting Graphs
1. About what year did income tax revenues first begin to rise sharply?
2. About how much revenue did the income tax bring in 1995?

FEDERAL INCOME TAX With lower tariff rates, the federal government had to replace the revenue that tariffs had previously supplied. Ratified in 1913, the Sixteenth Amendment legalized a federal income tax, which provided revenue by taxing individual earnings and corporate profits.

Under this graduated tax, larger incomes were taxed at higher rates than smaller incomes. The tax began with a modest tax on family incomes over $4,000, and ranged from 1 percent to a maximum of 6 percent on incomes over $500,000. Initially, few congressmen realized the potential of the income tax, but by 1917, the government was receiving more money on the income tax than it had ever gained from tariffs. Today, income taxes on corporations and individuals represent the federal government's main source of revenue.

Background
See *taxation* on page R46 in the Economics Handbook.

FEDERAL RESERVE SYSTEM Next, Wilson turned his attention to financial reform. The nation needed a way to strengthen the ways in which banks were run, as well as a way to quickly adjust the amount of money in circulation. Both credit availability and money supply had to keep pace with the economy.

Wilson's solution was to establish a decentralized private banking system under federal control. The Federal Reserve Act of 1913 divided the nation into 12 districts and established a regional central bank in each district. These "banker's banks" then served the other banks within the district.

The federal reserve banks could issue new paper currency in emergency situations, and member banks could use the new currency to make loans to their customers. Federal reserve banks could transfer funds to member banks in trouble, saving the banks from closing and protecting customers' savings. By 1923, roughly 70 percent of the nation's banking resources were part of the **Federal Reserve System**. One of Wilson's most enduring achievements, this system still serves as the basis of the nation's banking system. B

MAIN IDEA
Evaluating
B Why were tariff reform and the Federal Reserve System important?

Women Win Suffrage

While Wilson pushed hard for reform of trusts, tariffs, and banking, determined women intensified their push for the vote. The educated, native-born, middle-class women who had been active in progressive movements had grown increasingly impatient about not being allowed to vote. As of 1910, women had federal voting rights only in Wyoming, Utah, Colorado, Washington, and Idaho.

Determined suffragists pushed on, however. They finally saw success come within reach as a result of three developments: the increased activism of local groups, the use of bold new strategies to build enthusiasm for the movement, and the rebirth of the national movement under Carrie Chapman Catt.

LOCAL SUFFRAGE BATTLES The suffrage movement was given new strength by growing numbers of college-educated women. Two Massachusetts organizations, the Boston Equal Suffrage Association for Good Government and the College Equal Suffrage League, used door-to-door campaigns to reach potential supporters. Founded by Radcliffe graduate Maud Wood Park, the Boston group spread the message of suffrage to poor and working-class women. Members also took trolley tours where, at each stop, crowds would gather to watch the unusual sight of a woman speaking in public.

Many wealthy young women who visited Europe as part of their education became involved in the suffrage movement in Britain. Led by Emmeline Pankhurst, British suffragists used increasingly bold tactics, such as heckling government officials, to advance their cause. Inspired by their activism, American women returned to the United States armed with similar approaches in their own campaigns for suffrage.

CATT AND THE NATIONAL MOVEMENT Susan B. Anthony's successor as president of NAWSA was Carrie Chapman Catt, who served from 1900 to 1904 and resumed the presidency in 1915. When Catt returned to NAWSA after organizing New York's Women Suffrage Party, she concentrated on five tactics: (1) painstaking organization; (2) close ties between local, state, and national workers; (3) establishing a wide base of support; (4) cautious lobbying; and (5) gracious, ladylike behavior.

Although suffragists saw victories, the greater number of failures led some suffragists to try more radical tactics. Lucy Burns and Alice Paul formed their own more radical organization, the Congressional Union, and its successor, the National Woman's Party. They pressured the federal government to pass a suffrage amendment, and by 1917 Paul had organized her followers to mount a round-the-clock picket line around the White House. Some of the picketers were arrested, jailed, and even force-fed when they attempted a hunger strike.

These efforts, and America's involvement in World War I, finally made suffrage inevitable. Patriotic American women who headed committees, knitted socks for soldiers, and sold liberty bonds now claimed their overdue reward for supporting the war effort. In 1919, Congress passed the **Nineteenth Amendment,** granting women the right to vote. The amendment won final ratification in August 1920—72 years after women had first convened and demanded the vote at the Seneca Falls convention in 1848. C

MAIN IDEA

Analyzing Events

C Why do you think women won the right to vote in 1920, after earlier efforts had failed?

WORLD STAGE

EMMELINE PANKHURST

American women struggling for suffrage received valuable tutoring from their English counterparts, whose bold maneuvers had captured media coverage.

The noted British suffragist Emmeline Pankhurst, who helped found the National Women's Social and Political Union, often engaged in radical tactics. Pankhurst and other suffragists staged parades, organized protest meetings, endured hunger strikes, heckled candidates for Parliament, and spat on policemen who tried to quiet them. They were often imprisoned for their activities, before Parliament granted them the right to vote in 1928.

The Limits of Progressivism

Despite Wilson's economic and political reforms, he disappointed Progressives who favored social reform. In particular, on racial matters Wilson appeased conservative Southern Democratic voters but disappointed his Northern white and black supporters. He placed segregationists in charge of federal agencies, thereby expanding racial segregation in the federal government, the military, and Washington, D.C.

Vocabulary
appease: pacify by granting concessions

WILSON AND CIVIL RIGHTS Like Roosevelt and Taft, Wilson retreated on civil rights once in office. During the presidential campaign of 1912, he won the support of the NAACP's black intellectuals and white liberals by promising to treat blacks equally and to speak out against lynching.

History Through *Architecture*

FROM SPLENDOR TO SIMPLICITY

The progressive movement, which influenced numerous aspects of society, also impacted the world of American architecture. One of the most prominent architects of the time was Frank Lloyd Wright, who studied under the renowned designer Louis Sullivan. In the spirit of progressivism, Wright sought to design buildings that were orderly, efficient, and in harmony with the world around them.

▲ Architecture of the Gilded Age featured ornate decoration and detail, as seen here in this Victorian-style house built between 1884 and 1886. Wright rejected these showy and decorative styles in favor of more simplistic designs.

▲ Wright's "prairie style" design features a low, horizontal, and well-defined structure made predominantly of wood, concrete, brick, and other simple materials. Shown here is the Robie House (1909), one of Wright's most famous prairie-style structures, which incorporates these architectural qualities.

SKILLBUILDER Interpreting Visual Sources

1. What are the most striking differences between the two houses? Cite examples that contrast the two buildings.
2. How does Wright's style reflect the progressive spirit?

SEE SKILLBUILDER HANDBOOK, PAGE R23.

As president, however, Wilson opposed federal antilynching legislation, arguing that these crimes fell under state jurisdiction. In addition, the Capitol and the federal offices in Washington, D.C., which had been desegregated during Reconstruction, resumed the practice of segregation shortly after Wilson's election.

Wilson appointed to his cabinet fellow white Southerners who extended segregation. Secretary of the Navy Josephus Daniels, for example, proposed at a cabinet meeting to do away with common drinking fountains and towels in his department. According to an entry in Daniel's diary, President Wilson agreed because he had "made no promises in particular to negroes, except to do them justice." Segregated facilities, in the president's mind, were just.

African Americans and their liberal white supporters in the NAACP felt betrayed. Oswald Garrison Villard, a grandson of the abolitionist William Lloyd Garrison, wrote to Wilson in dismay, "The colored men who voted and worked for you in the belief that their status as American citizens was safe in your hands are deeply cast down." Wilson's response—that he had acted "in the interest of the negroes" and "with the approval of some of the most influential negroes I know"—only widened the rift between the president and some of his former supporters.

On November 12, 1914, the president's reception of an African-American delegation brought the confrontation to a bitter climax. William Monroe Trotter, editor-in-chief of the *Guardian*, an African-American Boston newspaper, led the delegation. Trotter complained that African Americans from 38 states had asked the president to reverse the segregation of government employees, but that segregation had since increased. Trotter then commented on Wilson's inaction.

A PERSONAL VOICE WILLIAM MONROE TROTTER

"Only two years ago you were heralded as perhaps the second Lincoln, and now the Afro-American leaders who supported you are hounded as false leaders and traitors to their race. . . . As equal citizens and by virtue of your public promises we are entitled at your hands to freedom from discrimination, restriction, imputation, and insult in government employ. Have you a 'new freedom' for white Americans and a new slavery for your 'Afro-American fellow citizens'? God forbid!"

—address to President Wilson, November 12, 1914

Wilson found Trotter's tone infuriating. After an angry Trotter shook his finger at the president to emphasize a point, the furious Wilson demanded that the delegation leave. Wilson's refusal to extend civil rights to African Americans pointed to the limits of progressivism under his administration. America's involvement in the war raging in Europe would soon reveal other weaknesses. D

Analyzing Effects

D What actions of Wilson disappointed civil rights advocates?

THE TWILIGHT OF PROGRESSIVISM After taking office in 1913, Wilson had said, "There's no chance of progress and reform in an administration in which war plays the principal part." Yet he found that the outbreak of World War I in Europe in 1914 demanded America's involvement. Meanwhile, distracted Americans and their legislators allowed reform efforts to stall. As the pacifist and reformer Jane Addams mournfully reflected, "The spirit of fighting burns away all those impulses . . . which foster the will to justice."

International conflict was destined to be part of Wilson's presidency. During the early years of his administration, Wilson had dealt with issues of imperialism that had roots in the late 19th century. However, World War I dominated most of his second term as president. The Progressive Era had come to an end.

SECTION 5 ASSESSMENT

1. **TERMS & NAMES** For each term or name, write a sentence explaining its significance.
   - **Carrie Chapman Catt**
   - **Clayton Antitrust Act**
   - **Federal Trade Commission (FTC)**
   - **Federal Reserve System**
   - **Nineteenth Amendment**

MAIN IDEA

2. **TAKING NOTES**
   Create a time line of key events relating to Progressivism during Wilson's first term. Use the dates already plotted on the time line below as a guide.

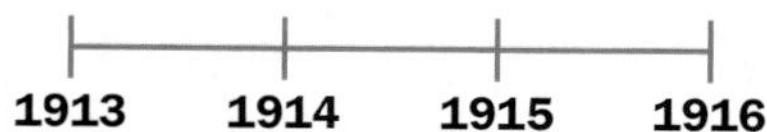

   Write a paragraph explaining which event you think best demonstrates progressive reform.

CRITICAL THINKING

3. **ANALYZING PRIMARY SOURCES**
   Wilson said, "Without the watchful . . . resolute interference of the government, there can be no fair play between individuals and . . . the trusts." How does this statement reflect Wilson's approach to reform? Support your answer. **Think About:**
   - the government's responsibility to the public
   - the passage of two key antitrust measures

4. **ANALYZING MOTIVES**
   Why do you think Wilson failed to push for equality for African Americans, despite his progressive reforms? **Think About:**
   - progressive presidents before Wilson
   - Wilson's background
   - the primary group of people progressive reforms targeted

CHAPTER 9 ASSESSMENT

TERMS & NAMES

For each term or name below, write a sentence explaining its connection to the Progressive Era.

1. progressive movement
2. muckraker
3. suffrage
4. Susan B. Anthony
5. Theodore Roosevelt
6. NAACP
7. Gifford Pinchot
8. Woodrow Wilson
9. Clayton Antitrust Act
10. Federal Reserve System

MAIN IDEAS

Use your notes and the information in the chapter to answer the following questions.

The Origins of Progressivism *(pages 306–312)*

1. What were the four goals that various progressive reform movements struggled to achieve?
2. What kind of state labor laws resulted from progressives' lobbying to protect workers?
3. How did government change during the Progressive Era? How were these changes important?

Women in Public Life *(pages 313–316)*

4. In the late 1890s, what job opportunities were available to uneducated women without industrial skills?
5. Give two examples of national women's organizations committed to social activism. Briefly describe their progressive missions.

Teddy Roosevelt's Square Deal *(pages 317–325)*

6. What scandalous practices did Upton Sinclair expose in his novel *The Jungle*? How did the American public, Roosevelt, and Congress respond?
7. How did Roosevelt earn his reputation as a trust-buster?

Progressivism Under Taft *(pages 328–331)*

8. As a progressive, how did Taft compare with Roosevelt?
9. Why did the Republican Party split during Taft's administration?

Wilson's New Freedom *(pages 332–337)*

10. How did the Clayton Antitrust Act benefit labor?
11. Cite two examples of social welfare legislation that Wilson opposed during his presidency and the arguments he used to defend his position.

CRITICAL THINKING

1. **USING YOUR NOTES** Create a Venn diagram to show some of the similarities and differences between Roosevelt's Square Deal and Wilson's New Freedom.

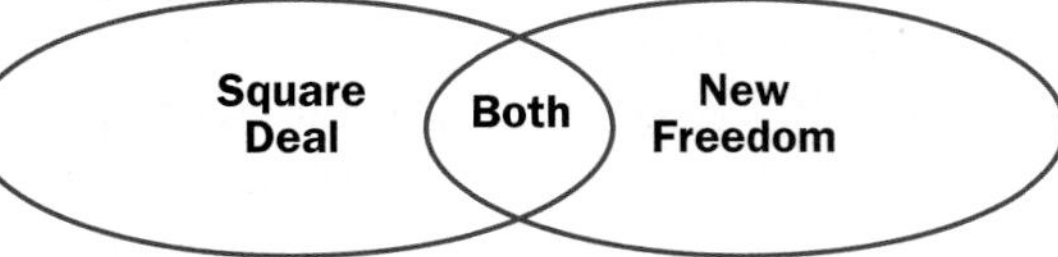

2. **DEVELOPING HISTORICAL PERSPECTIVE** What social, political, and economic trends in American life do you think caused the reform impulse during the Progressive Era? Support your answer with details from the text.

VISUAL SUMMARY THE PROGRESSIVE ERA

PROGRESSIVISM

ECONOMIC
- Roosevelt establishes a Square Deal
- new tax system is instituted
- Roosevelt breaks up trusts

SOCIAL & MORAL
- women fight for the right to vote
- Eighteenth Amendment bans alcoholic beverages
- Social services for women, children, and the poor

POLITICAL
- elections are reformed
- citizens given greater voice in government: recall, initiative, referendum

INDUSTRY
- National Child Labor Committee organizes to end child labor
- reformers improve workplace conditions and set maximum working hours

HEALTH & ENVIRONMENT
- conservationists establish wilderness conservation areas and preserve natural resources
- Pure Food and Drug Act protects consumers

Standardized Test Practice

Use the quotation and your knowledge of U.S. history to answer question 1.

> **"Labor began to organize itself in Trade Unions and to confront the industrialists with a stiff bargaining power. These developments were to lead to a period of protest and reform in the early twentieth century. The gains conferred by large-scale industry were great and lasting, but the wrongs that had accompanied their making were only gradually righted."**
>
> —Winston Churchill, *The Great Republic: A History of America*

1. In the passage, Winston Churchill attempts to explain what prompted Progressive Era reformers. The passage explains the actions of which of the following labor reform leaders?

   A Maria Mitchell
   B Carry Nation
   C Susan B. Anthony
   D Florence Kelley

2. The muckrakers served Progressivism by —

   F informing people about abuses so that they could protest.
   G enacting legislation to prevent political corruption.
   H cleaning up unhealthy meat processing plants.
   J filing and prosecuting antitrust lawsuits.

3. In the presidential election of 1912, three candidates attempted to win the liberal, progressive vote. Which candidate for president in 1912 ran on a conservative platform?

   A Woodrow Wilson
   B William Taft
   C Theodore Roosevelt
   D Eugene V. Debs

ADDITIONAL TEST PRACTICE, pages S1–S33.

CLASSZONE.COM

ALTERNATIVE ASSESSMENT

1. **INTERACT WITH HISTORY** Recall your discussion of the question on page 305:

   What kinds of actions can bring about social change?

   Now that you have read Chapter 9, use your knowledge of the Progressive Era to answer these questions:

   - How did Progressive Era reformers recruit others?
   - How did progressive reformers bring about changes in government?
   - What did progressives do to bring about changes in business?
   - What else might Progressive Era reformers have done to be more effective?

   Explain your answers with examples.

2. **VIDEO** **LEARNING FROM MEDIA** View the *American Stories* video, "A Child on Strike." Discuss the following questions in a group; then do the activity.

   - What was your reaction to Camella Teoli's accident?
   - What labor practices are taken for granted today that were not afforded to people living in 1910?

   Cooperative Learning Activity In your group, imagine you are reporters covering the congressional hearing. Write two articles—one that objectively reports on the findings of the hearings, and one that shows bias in favor of the mill. Share the articles with the class and analyze how language can affect the reporting of information.

CHAPTER 10

AMERICA CLAIMS AN EMPIRE

This lithograph of Roosevelt leading the Rough Riders at San Juan Hill shows the men on horseback, although they actually fought on foot.

1893 Business groups, aided by U.S. marines, overthrow Hawaii's Queen Liliuokalani.

1898 *U.S.S. Maine* explodes and sinks. The Spanish-American War begins.

1901 Theodore Roosevelt becomes president after McKinley is assassinated.

USA
WORLD

1890

1900

1895 Guglielmo Marconi develops the technology that led to modern radio.

1898 Marie Curie discovers radium.

1900 In China, the Boxers rebel.

1903 Panama declares its independence from Colombia.

INTERACT
WITH HISTORY

In the late 1890s, American newspapers are running sensational stories about Spain's harsh rule of Cuba. Such articles anger Americans. Among those willing to fight for Cuba's freedom are a group of volunteers, the Rough Riders. Led by future president Theodore Roosevelt, the Rough Riders become a model for others to follow.

Does the U.S. have a duty to fight for freedom in neighboring countries?

Examine the Issues

- When should the U.S. intervene in the affairs of another country?
- In what ways do dramatic headlines influence American opinion?

RESEARCH LINKS **CLASSZONE.COM**

Visit the Chapter 10 links for more information related to America Claims an Empire.

1908 William Howard Taft is elected president.

1912 Woodrow Wilson is elected president.

1914 The Panama Canal opens.

1917 Puerto Ricans become U.S. citizens.

1917 The United States enters World War I.

1910 | **1920**

1910 The Mexican Revolution begins.

1914 World War I begins in Europe.

CIVILIZATION CALLS
EVERY MAN WOMAN AND CHILD!

1917 Mexico revises and adopts its constitution.

SECTION 1

Imperialism and America

MAIN IDEA	WHY IT MATTERS NOW	Terms & Names
Beginning in 1867 and continuing through the century, global competition caused the United States to expand.	**During this time period, the United States acquired Hawaii and Alaska, both of which became states in 1959.**	•**Queen Liliuokalani** •**imperialism** •**Alfred T. Mahan** •**William Seward** •**Pearl Harbor** •**Sanford B. Dole**

One American's Story

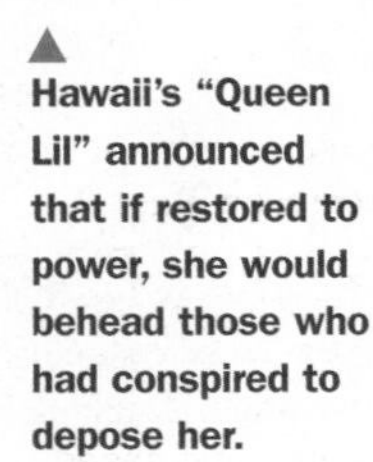

▲ **Hawaii's "Queen Lil" announced that if restored to power, she would behead those who had conspired to depose her.**

In 1893 **Queen Liliuokalani** (lə-lē′ə-ō-kə-lä′nē) realized that her reign in Hawaii had come to an end. More than 160 U.S. sailors and marines stood ready to aid the *haoles* (white foreigners) who planned to overthrow the Hawaiian monarchy. In an eloquent statement of protest, the proud monarch surrendered to the superior force of the United States.

A PERSONAL VOICE QUEEN LILIUOKALANI

"I, Liliuokalani, . . . do hereby solemnly protest against any and all acts done against myself and the constitutional government of the Hawaiian Kingdom. . . . Now, to avoid any collision of armed forces and perhaps the loss of life, I do under this protest . . . yield my authority until such time as the Government of the United States shall . . . undo the action of its representatives and reinstate me in the authority which I claim as the constitutional sovereign of the Hawaiian Islands."

—quoted in *Those Kings and Queens of Old Hawaii*

U.S. ambassador to Hawaii John L. Stevens informed the State Department, "The Hawaiian pear is now fully ripe, and this is the golden hour for the United States to pluck it." The annexation of Hawaii was only one of the goals of America's empire builders in the late 19th century.

American Expansionism

Americans had always sought to expand the size of their nation, and throughout the 19th century they extended their control toward the Pacific Ocean. However, by the 1880s, many American leaders had become convinced that the United States should join the imperialist powers of Europe and establish colonies overseas. **Imperialism**—the policy in which stronger nations extend their economic, political, or military control over weaker territories—was already a trend around the world.

GLOBAL COMPETITION European nations had been establishing colonies for centuries. In the late 19th century Africa had emerged as a prime target of European expansionism. By the early 20th century, only two countries in all of Africa—Ethiopia and Liberia—remained independent. (A)

MAIN IDEA

Analyzing Effects
(A) How did European imperialism affect Africa?

Imperialists also competed for territory in Asia, especially in China. In its late-19th-century reform era, Japan replaced its old feudal order with a strong central government. Hoping that military strength would bolster industrialization, Japan joined European nations in competition for China in the 1890s.

Most Americans gradually warmed to the idea of expansion overseas. With a belief in manifest destiny, they already had pushed the U.S. border to the Pacific Ocean. Three factors fueled the new American imperialism:

- desire for military strength
- thirst for new markets
- belief in cultural superiority

DESIRE FOR MILITARY STRENGTH Seeing that other nations were establishing a global military presence, American leaders advised that the United States build up its own military strength. One such leader was Admiral **Alfred T. Mahan** of the U.S. Navy. Mahan urged government officials to build up American naval power in order to compete with other powerful nations. As a result of the urging of Mahan and others, the United States built nine steel-hulled cruisers between 1883 and 1890. The construction of modern battleships such as the *Maine* and the *Oregon* transformed the country into the world's third largest naval power.

KEY PLAYER

ADMIRAL ALFRED T. MAHAN
1840–1914

Alfred T. Mahan joined the U.S. Navy in the late 1850s and served for nearly forty years. In 1886, he became president of the newly established Naval War College in Newport, Rhode Island.

Throughout his lifetime, Mahan was one of the most outspoken advocates of American military expansion. In his book *The Influence of Sea Power upon History, 1660–1783* (published in 1890), Mahan called for the United States to develop a modern fleet capable of protecting American business and shipping interests around the world. He also urged the United States to establish naval bases in the Caribbean, to construct a canal across the Isthmus of Panama, and to acquire Hawaii and other Pacific islands.

THIRST FOR NEW MARKETS In the late 19th century, advances in technology enabled American farms and factories to produce far more than American citizens could consume. Now the United States needed raw materials for its factories and new markets for its agricultural and manufactured goods. Imperialists viewed foreign trade as the solution to American overproduction and the related problems of unemployment and economic depression.

Background
In the late 1800s, new farm machinery greatly improved grain production. For example, plows, harrows, threshing machines, and reapers increased corn production by 264 percent and the wheat harvest by 252 percent.

In the early 1900s, the Navy's Great White Fleet, so named because its ships were painted white, was a sign of America's growing military power. ▶

BELIEF IN CULTURAL SUPERIORITY Cultural factors also were used to justify imperialism. Some Americans combined the philosophy of Social Darwinism—a belief that free-market competition would lead to the survival of the fittest—with a belief in the racial superiority of Anglo-Saxons. They argued that the United States had a responsibility to spread Christianity and "civilization" to the world's "inferior peoples." This viewpoint narrowly defined "civilization" according to the standards of only one culture.

The United States Acquires Alaska

An early supporter of American expansion was **William Seward,** Secretary of State under presidents Abraham Lincoln and Andrew Johnson. In 1867, Seward arranged for the U.S. to buy Alaska from the Russians for $7.2 million. Seward had some trouble persuading the House of Representatives to approve funding for the purchase. Some people thought it was silly to buy what they called "Seward's Icebox" or "Seward's folly." Time showed how wrong they were. In 1959, Alaska became a state. For about two cents an acre, the United States had acquired a land rich in timber, minerals, and, as it turned out, oil. B

MAIN IDEA

Developing Historical Perspective

B How did time prove that the purchase of Alaska was not an act of folly?

The United States Takes Hawaii

In 1867, the same year in which Alaska was purchased, the United States took over the Midway Islands, which lie in the Pacific Ocean about 1300 miles north of Hawaii. No one lived on the islands, so the event did not attract much attention.

Hawaii was another question. The Hawaiian Islands had been economically important to the United States for nearly a century. Since the 1790s, American merchants had stopped there on their way to China and East India. In the 1820s, Yankee missionaries founded Christian schools and churches on the islands. Their children and grandchildren became sugar planters who sold most of their crop to the United States.

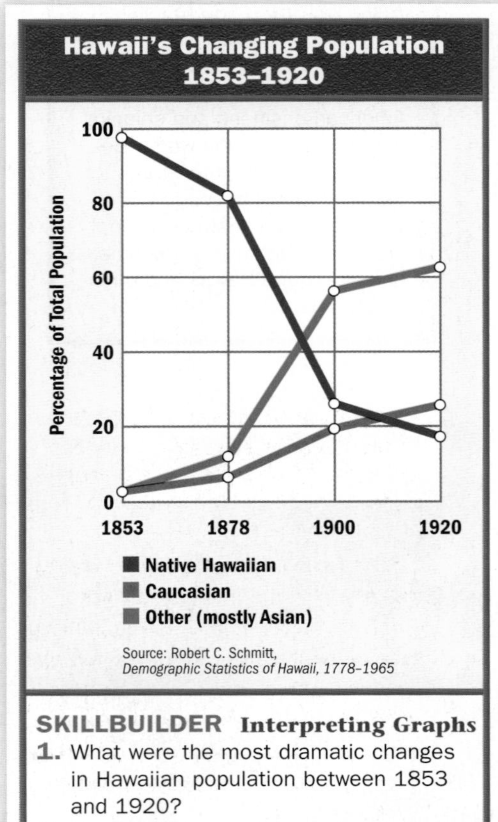

Source: Robert C. Schmitt, *Demographic Statistics of Hawaii, 1778–1965*

SKILLBUILDER Interpreting Graphs

1. What were the most dramatic changes in Hawaiian population between 1853 and 1920?
2. How might these changes have affected the political climate there?

THE CRY FOR ANNEXATION In the mid-19th century, American-owned sugar plantations accounted for about three-quarters of the islands' wealth. Plantation owners imported thousands of laborers from Japan, Portugal, and China. By 1900, foreigners and immigrant laborers outnumbered native Hawaiians about three to one.

White planters profited from close ties with the United States. In 1875, the United States agreed to import Hawaiian sugar duty-free. Over the next 15 years, Hawaiian sugar production increased nine times. Then the McKinley Tariff of 1890 provoked a crisis by eliminating the duty-free status of Hawaiian sugar. As a result, Hawaiian sugar growers faced competition in the American market. American planters in Hawaii called for the United States to annex the islands so they wouldn't have to pay the duty.

Vocabulary
annex: to incorporate territory into an existing country or state

U.S. military and economic leaders already understood the value of the islands. In 1887, they pressured Hawaii to allow the United States to build a naval base at **Pearl Harbor,** the kingdom's best port. The base became a refueling station for American ships.

THE END OF A MONARCHY Also in that year, Hawaii's King Kalakaua had been strong-armed by white business leaders. They forced him to amend Hawaii's constitution, effectively limiting voting rights to only wealthy landowners. But when Kalakaua died in 1891, his sister Queen Liliuokalani came to power with a "Hawaii for Hawaiians" agenda. She proposed removing the property-owning qualifications for voting. To prevent this from happening, business groups—encouraged by Ambassador John L. Stevens—organized a revolution. With the help of marines, they overthrew the queen and set up a government headed by **Sanford B. Dole.**

President Cleveland directed that the queen be restored to her throne. When Dole refused to surrender power, Cleveland formally recognized the Republic of Hawaii. But he refused to consider annexation unless a majority of Hawaiians favored it.

In 1897, William McKinley, who favored annexation, succeeded Cleveland as president. On August 12, 1898, Congress proclaimed Hawaii an American territory, although Hawaiians had never had the chance to vote. In 1959, Hawaii became the 50th state of the United States. (C)

Analyzing Events
(C) What factors led to the annexation of Hawaii in 1898?

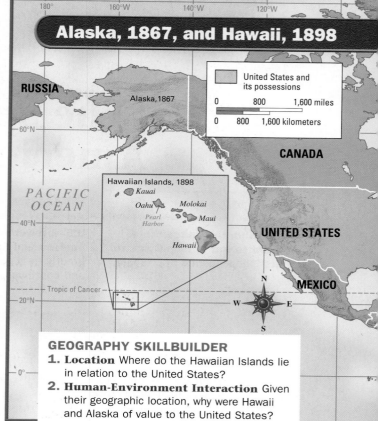

Alaska, 1867, and Hawaii, 1898

United States and its possessions

0 800 1,600 miles
0 800 1,600 kilometers

RUSSIA
Alaska, 1867
CANADA
PACIFIC OCEAN
Hawaiian Islands, 1898
Kauai
Oahu
Pearl Harbor
Molokai
Maui
Hawaii
UNITED STATES
MEXICO
Tropic of Cancer

GEOGRAPHY SKILLBUILDER

1. **Location** Where do the Hawaiian Islands lie in relation to the United States?
2. **Human-Environment Interaction** Given their geographic location, why were Hawaii and Alaska of value to the United States?

SECTION 1 ASSESSMENT

1. **TERMS & NAMES** For each term or name, write a sentence explaining its significance.
   - **Queen Liliuokalani**
   - **imperialism**
   - **Alfred T. Mahan**
   - **William Seward**
   - **Pearl Harbor**
   - **Sanford B. Dole**

MAIN IDEA

2. **TAKING NOTES**
   Copy this web on your paper and fill it in with events and concepts that illustrate the roots of imperialism.

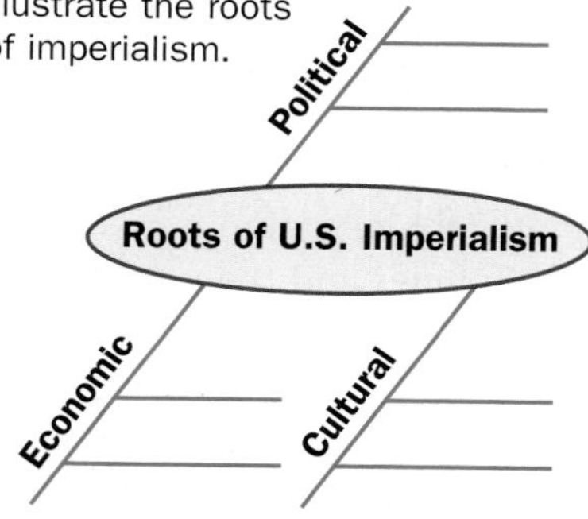

Choose one event to explain further in a paragraph.

CRITICAL THINKING

3. **DRAWING CONCLUSIONS**
   Manifest destiny greatly influenced American policy during the first half of the 19th century. How do you think manifest destiny set the stage for American imperialism at the end of the century?

4. **EVALUATING**
   In your opinion, did Sanford B. Dole and other American planters have the right to stage a revolt in Hawaii in 1893? **Think About:**
   - American business interests in Hawaii
   - the rights of native Hawaiians

5. **ANALYZING PRIMARY SOURCES**
   In the following passage, how does Indiana Senator Albert J. Beveridge explain the need for the U.S. to acquire new territories?

   > **"Fate has written our policy for us; the trade of the world must and shall be ours. . . . We will establish trading posts throughout the world as distributing points for American products. . . Great colonies governing themselves, flying our flag and trading with us, will grow about our posts of trade."**
   >
   > —quoted in *Beveridge and the Progressive Era*

The Spanish-American War

MAIN IDEA	WHY IT MATTERS NOW	Terms & Names
In 1898, the United States went to war to help Cuba win its independence from Spain.	U.S. involvement in Latin America and Asia increased greatly as a result of the war and continues today.	• José Martí • Valeriano Weyler • yellow journalism • *U.S.S. Maine* • George Dewey • Rough Riders • San Juan Hill • Treaty of Paris

One American's Story

Early in 1896, James Creelman traveled to Cuba as a *New York World* reporter, covering the second Cuban war for independence from Spain. While in Havana, he wrote columns about his observations of the war. His descriptions of Spanish atrocities aroused American sympathy for Cubans.

A PERSONAL VOICE JAMES CREELMAN

> **"No man's life, no man's property is safe [in Cuba]. American citizens are imprisoned or slain without cause. American property is destroyed on all sides. . . . Wounded soldiers can be found begging in the streets of Havana. . . . The horrors of a barbarous struggle for the extermination of the native population are witnessed in all parts of the country. Blood on the roadsides, blood in the fields, blood on the doorsteps, blood, blood, blood! . . . Is there no nation wise enough, brave enough to aid this blood-smitten land?"**
>
> —*New York World*, May 17, 1896

Newspapers during that period often exaggerated stories like Creelman's to boost their sales as well as to provoke American intervention in Cuba.

▲ Cuban rebels burn the town of Jaruco in March 1896.

Cubans Rebel Against Spain

By the end of the 19th century, Spain—once the most powerful colonial nation on earth—had lost most of its colonies. It retained only the Philippines and the island of Guam in the Pacific, a few outposts in Africa, and the Caribbean islands of Cuba and Puerto Rico in the Americas.

AMERICAN INTEREST IN CUBA The United States had long held an interest in Cuba, which lies only 90 miles south of Florida. In 1854, diplomats recommended to President Franklin Pierce that the United States buy Cuba from Spain. The Spanish responded by saying that they would rather see Cuba sunk in the ocean.

But American interest in Cuba continued. When the Cubans rebelled against Spain between 1868 and 1878, American sympathies went out to the Cuban people.

The Cuban revolt against Spain was not successful, but in 1886 the Cuban people did force Spain to abolish slavery. After the emancipation of Cuba's slaves, American capitalists began investing millions of dollars in large sugar cane plantations on the island.

THE SECOND WAR FOR INDEPENDENCE Anti-Spanish sentiment in Cuba soon erupted into a second war for independence. **José Martí,** a Cuban poet and journalist in exile in New York, launched a revolution in 1895. Martí organized Cuban resistance against Spain, using an active guerrilla campaign and deliberately destroying property, especially American-owned sugar mills and plantations. Martí counted on provoking U.S. intervention to help the rebels achieve *Cuba Libre!*—a free Cuba.

Vocabulary
guerrilla: a member of a military force that harasses the enemy

Public opinion in the United States was split. Many business people wanted the government to support Spain in order to protect their investments. Other Americans, however, were enthusiastic about the rebel cause. The cry "Cuba Libre!" was, after all, similar in sentiment to Patrick Henry's "Give me liberty or give me death!" (A)

MAIN IDEA
Analyzing Motives
(A) Why did José Martí encourage Cuban rebels to destroy sugar mills and plantations?

KEY PLAYER

JOSÉ MARTÍ
1853–1895

The Cuban political activist José Martí dedicated his life to achieving independence for Cuba. Expelled from Cuba at the age of 16 because of his revolutionary activities, Martí earned a master's degree and a law degree. He eventually settled in the United States.

Wary of the U.S. role in the Cuban struggle against the Spanish, Martí warned, "I know the Monster, because I have lived in its lair." His fears of U.S. imperialism turned out to have been well-founded. U.S. troops occupied Cuba on and off from 1906 until 1922.

Martí died fighting for Cuban independence in 1895. He is revered today in Cuba as a hero and martyr.

War Fever Escalates

In 1896, Spain responded to the Cuban revolt by sending General **Valeriano Weyler** to Cuba to restore order. Weyler tried to crush the rebellion by herding the entire rural population of central and western Cuba into barbed-wire concentration camps. Here civilians could not give aid to rebels. An estimated 300,000 Cubans filled these camps, where thousands died from hunger and disease.

HEADLINE WARS Weyler's actions fueled a war over newspaper circulation that had developed between the American newspaper tycoons William Randolph Hearst and Joseph Pulitzer. To lure readers, Hearst's *New York Journal* and Pulitzer's *New York World* printed exaggerated accounts—by reporters such as James Creelman—of "Butcher" Weyler's brutality. Stories of poisoned wells and of children being thrown to the sharks deepened American sympathy for the rebels. This sensational style of writing, which exaggerates the news to lure and enrage readers, became known as **yellow journalism.**

Hearst and Pulitzer fanned war fever. When Hearst sent the gifted artist Frederic Remington to Cuba to draw sketches of reporters' stories, Remington informed the publisher that a war between the United States and Spain seemed very unlikely. Hearst reportedly replied, "You furnish the pictures and I'll furnish the war."

THE DE LÔME LETTER American sympathy for "Cuba Libre!" grew with each day's headlines. When President William McKinley took office in 1897, demands for American intervention in Cuba were on the rise. Preferring to avoid war with Spain, McKinley tried diplomatic means to resolve the crisis. At first, his efforts appeared to succeed. Spain recalled General Weyler, modified the policy regarding concentration camps, and offered Cuba limited self-government.

In February 1898, however, the *New York Journal* published a private letter written by Enrique Dupuy de Lôme, the Spanish minister to the United States. A Cuban rebel had stolen the letter from a Havana post office and leaked it to the newspaper, which was thirsty for scandal. The de Lôme letter criticized President McKinley, calling him "weak" and "a bidder for the admiration of the crowd." The embarrassed Spanish government apologized, and the minister resigned. Still, Americans were angry over the insult to their president.

THE *U.S.S. MAINE* EXPLODES Only a few days after the publication of the de Lôme letter, American resentment toward Spain turned to outrage. Early in 1898, President McKinley had ordered the ***U.S.S. Maine*** to Cuba to bring home American citizens in danger from the fighting and to protect American property. On February 15, 1898, the ship blew up in the harbor of Havana. More than 260 men were killed.

At the time, no one really knew why the ship exploded. In 1898, however, American newspapers claimed the Spanish had blown up the ship. The *Journal*'s headline read "The warship *Maine* was split in two by an enemy's secret infernal machine." Hearst's paper offered a reward of $50,000 for the capture of the Spaniards who supposedly had committed the outrage. B

MAIN IDEA

Summarizing

B What events increased the tension between the United States and Spain?

War with Spain Erupts

Now there was no holding back the forces that wanted war. "Remember the *Maine!*" became the rallying cry for U.S. intervention in Cuba. It made no difference that the Spanish government agreed, on April 9, to almost everything the United States demanded, including a six-month cease-fire.

▲ **When the *U.S.S. Maine* exploded in the harbor of Havana, newspapers like the *New York Journal* were quick to place the blame on Spain.**

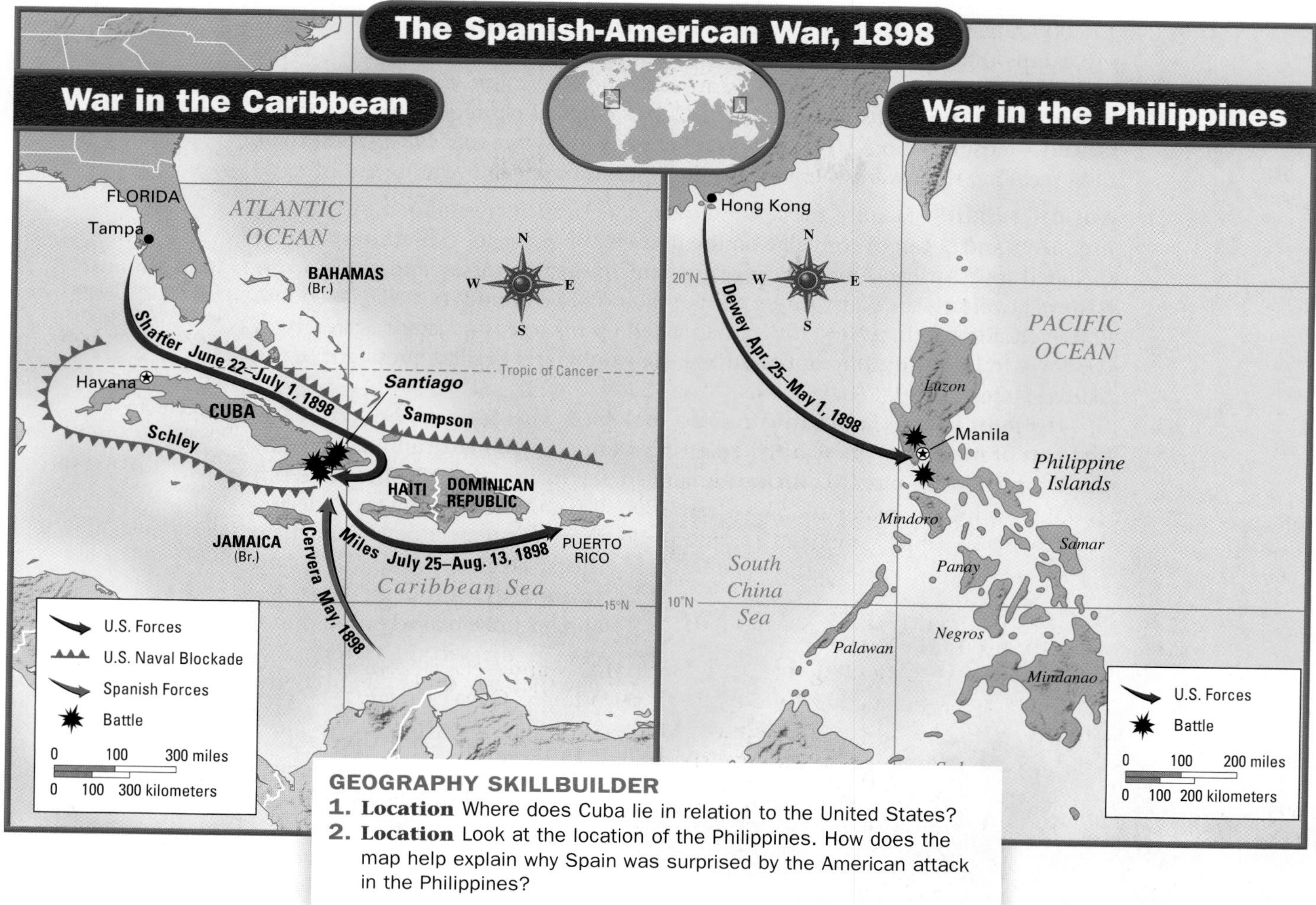

GEOGRAPHY SKILLBUILDER

1. **Location** Where does Cuba lie in relation to the United States?
2. **Location** Look at the location of the Philippines. How does the map help explain why Spain was surprised by the American attack in the Philippines?

MAIN IDEA

Analyzing Events

C How did the Spanish try to avoid war with the United States?

Despite the Spanish concessions, public opinion favored war. On April 11, McKinley asked Congress for authority to use force against Spain. After a week of debate, Congress agreed, and on April 20 the United States declared war. **C**

THE WAR IN THE PHILIPPINES The Spanish thought the Americans would invade Cuba. But the first battle of the war took place in a Spanish colony on the other side of the world—the Philippine Islands.

On April 30, the American fleet in the Pacific steamed to the Philippines. The next morning, Commodore **George Dewey** gave the command to open fire on the Spanish fleet at Manila, the Philippine capital. Within hours, Dewey's men had destroyed every Spanish ship there. Dewey's victory allowed U.S. troops to land in the Philippines.

Dewey had the support of the Filipinos who, like the Cubans, also wanted freedom from Spain. Over the next two months, 11,000 Americans joined forces with Filipino rebels led by Emilio Aguinaldo. In August, Spanish troops in Manila surrendered to the United States.

THE WAR IN THE CARIBBEAN In the Caribbean, hostilities began with a naval blockade of Cuba. Admiral William T. Sampson effectively sealed up the Spanish fleet in the harbor of Santiago de Cuba.

Dewey's victory at Manila had demonstrated the superiority of United States naval forces. In contrast, the army maintained only a small professional force, supplemented by a larger inexperienced and ill-prepared volunteer force. About

125,000 Americans had volunteered to fight. The new soldiers were sent to training camps that lacked adequate supplies and effective leaders. Moreover, there were not enough modern guns to go around, and the troops were outfitted with heavy woolen uniforms unsuitable for Cuba's tropical climate. In addition, the officers—most of whom were Civil War veterans—had a tendency to spend their time recalling their war experiences rather than training the volunteers.

ROUGH RIDERS Despite these handicaps, American forces landed in Cuba in June 1898 and began to converge on the port city of Santiago. The army of 17,000 included four African-American regiments of the regular army and the **Rough Riders,** a volunteer cavalry under the command of Leonard Wood and Theodore Roosevelt. Roosevelt, a New Yorker, had given up his job as Assistant Secretary of the Navy to lead the group of volunteers. He would later become president of the United States.

Background
The Rough Riders trained as cavalry but fought on foot because their horses didn't reach Cuba in time.

The most famous land battle in Cuba took place near Santiago on July 1. The first part of the battle, on nearby Kettle Hill, featured a dramatic uphill charge by the Rough Riders and two African-American regiments, the Ninth and Tenth Cavalries. Their victory cleared the way for an infantry attack on the strategically important **San Juan Hill.** Although Roosevelt and his units played only a minor role in the second victory, U.S. newspapers declared him the hero of San Juan Hill.

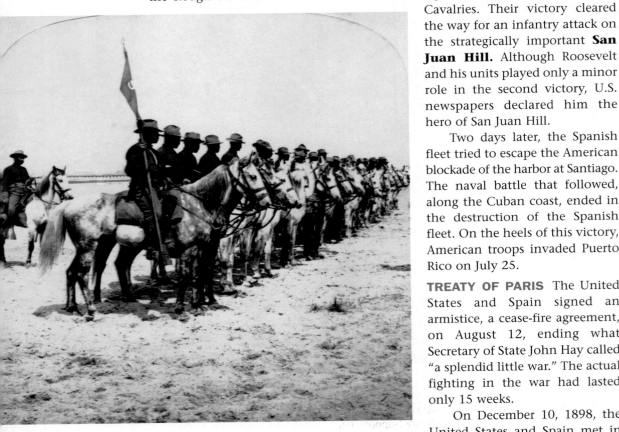

▲ **These African-American troops prepare for battle during the Spanish-American War.**

Two days later, the Spanish fleet tried to escape the American blockade of the harbor at Santiago. The naval battle that followed, along the Cuban coast, ended in the destruction of the Spanish fleet. On the heels of this victory, American troops invaded Puerto Rico on July 25.

TREATY OF PARIS The United States and Spain signed an armistice, a cease-fire agreement, on August 12, ending what Secretary of State John Hay called "a splendid little war." The actual fighting in the war had lasted only 15 weeks.

On December 10, 1898, the United States and Spain met in Paris to agree on a treaty. At the peace talks, Spain freed Cuba and turned over the islands of Guam in the Pacific and Puerto Rico in the West Indies to the United States. Spain also sold the Philippines to the United States for $20 million. D

MAIN IDEA
Summarizing
D What were the terms of the Treaty of Paris?

DEBATE OVER THE TREATY The **Treaty of Paris** touched off a great debate in the United States. Arguments centered on whether or not the United States had the right to annex the Philippines, but imperialism was the real issue. President McKinley told a group of Methodist ministers that he had prayed for guidance on Philippine annexation and had concluded "that there was nothing left for us to do but to take them all [the Philippine Islands], and to educate the Filipinos, and uplift and Christianize them." McKinley's need to justify imperialism may have clouded his memory—most Filipinos had been Christian for centuries.

Other prominent Americans presented a variety of arguments—political, moral, and economic—against annexation. Some felt that the treaty violated the Declaration of Independence by denying self-government to the newly acquired territories. The African-American educator Booker T. Washington argued that the United States should settle race-related issues at home before taking on social problems elsewhere. The labor leader Samuel Gompers feared that Filipino immigrants would compete for American jobs.

On February 6, 1899, the annexation question was settled with the Senate's approval of the Treaty of Paris. The United States now had an empire that included Guam, Puerto Rico, and the Philippines. The next question Americans faced was how and when the United States would add to its dominion.

▲ **This lithograph criticizes American foreign policy in 1898. In the cartoon, Uncle Sam is riding a bicycle with wheels labeled "western hemisphere" and "eastern hemisphere." He has abandoned his horse, on whose saddle appears "Monroe Doctrine," because the horse is too slow.**

ASSESSMENT

1. **TERMS & NAMES** For each term or name, write a sentence explaining its significance.
   - **José Martí**
   - **Valeriano Weyler**
   - **yellow journalism**
   - ***U.S.S. Maine***
   - **George Dewey**
   - **Rough Riders**
   - **San Juan Hill**
   - **Treaty of Paris**

MAIN IDEA

2. **TAKING NOTES**
   In 1898, a debate raged in the United States over whether the U.S. had the right to annex the Philippines. Use a graphic organizer like the one below to summarize the pros and cons of this debate.

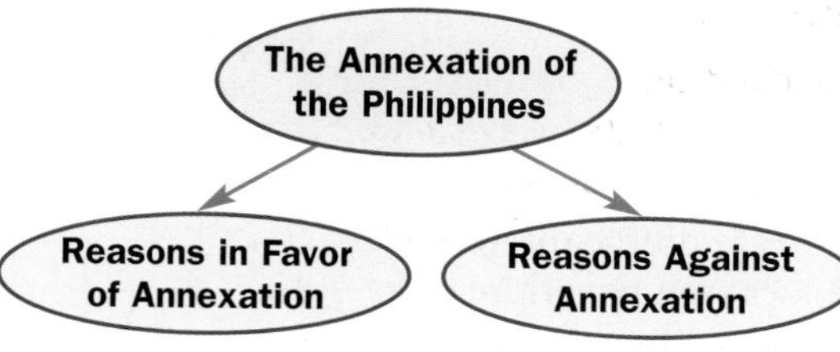

Which side do you support? Why?

CRITICAL THINKING

3. **MAKING INFERENCES**
   What do you think were the unstated editorial policies of yellow journalism? Support your answer with evidence from the text.
   Think About:
   - James Creelman's account of Spanish atrocities against Cubans (page 346)
   - Hearst's remark to Remington
   - the *Journal* headline about the explosion of the battleship *Maine*

4. **ANALYZING EFFECTS**
   Many anti-imperialists worried that imperialism might threaten the American democratic system. How might this happen?

5. **DRAWING CONCLUSIONS**
   In 1898 Theodore Roosevelt resigned his post as Assistant Secretary of the Navy to organize the Rough Riders. Why do you think Roosevelt was willing to take this risk? How do you think this decision affected his political career?

Acquiring New Lands

MAIN IDEA	WHY IT MATTERS NOW	Terms & Names
In the early 1900s, the United States engaged in conflicts in Puerto Rico, Cuba, and the Philippines.	**Today, the United States maintains a strong military and political presence in strategic worldwide locations.**	**• Foraker Act • Platt Amendment • protectorate • Emilio Aguinaldo • John Hay • Open Door notes • Boxer Rebellion**

One American's Story

When Puerto Rico became part of the United States after the Spanish-American War, many Puerto Ricans feared that the United States would not give them the measure of self-rule that they had gained under the Spanish. Puerto Rican statesman and publisher Luis Muñoz Rivera was one of the most vocal advocates of Puerto Rican self-rule. Between 1900 and 1916, he lived primarily in the United States and continually worked for the independence of his homeland. Finally, in 1916, the U.S. Congress, facing possible war in Europe and wishing to settle the issue of Puerto Rico, invited Muñoz Rivera to speak. On May 5, 1916, Muñoz Rivera stood before the U.S. House of Representatives to discuss the future of Puerto Rico.

▲ Luis Muñoz Rivera

A Personal Voice LUIS MUÑOZ RIVERA

"You, citizens of a free fatherland, with its own laws, its own institutions, and its own flag, can appreciate the unhappiness of the small and solitary people that must await its laws from your authority. . . . when you acquire the certainty that you can found in Puerto Rico a republic like that founded in Cuba and Panama . . . give us our independence and you will stand before humanity as . . . a great creator of new nationalities and a great liberator of oppressed peoples."

—quoted in *The Puerto Ricans*

Muñoz Rivera returned to Puerto Rico where he died in November 1916. Three months later, the United States made Puerto Ricans U.S. citizens.

Ruling Puerto Rico

Not all Puerto Ricans wanted independence, as Muñoz Rivera did. Some wanted statehood, while still others hoped for some measure of local self-government as an American territory. As a result, the United States gave Puerto Ricans no promises regarding independence after the Spanish-American War.

MILITARY RULE During the Spanish-American War, United States forces, under General Nelson A. Miles, occupied the island. As his soldiers took control, General Miles issued a statement assuring Puerto Ricans that the Americans were there to "bring you protection, not only to yourselves but to your property, to promote your prosperity, and to bestow upon you the immunities and blessings of the liberal institutions of our government." For the time being, Puerto Rico would be controlled by the military until Congress decided otherwise.

RETURN TO CIVIL GOVERNMENT Although many Puerto Ricans had dreams of independence or statehood, the United States had different plans for the island's future. Puerto Rico was strategically important to the United States, both for maintaining a U.S. presence in the Caribbean and for protecting a future canal that American leaders wanted to build across the Isthmus of Panama. In 1900, Congress passed the **Foraker Act,** which ended military rule and set up a civil government. The act gave the president of the United States the power to appoint Puerto Rico's governor and members of the upper house of its legislature. Puerto Ricans could elect only the members of the legislature's lower house. (A)

In 1901, in the Insular Cases, the U.S. Supreme Court ruled that the Constitution did not automatically apply to people in acquired territories. Congress, however, retained the right to extend U.S. citizenship, and it granted that right to Puerto Ricans in 1917. It also gave them the right to elect both houses of their legislature.

MAIN IDEA

Analyzing Issues
(A) Why was Puerto Rico important to the United States?

NOW & THEN

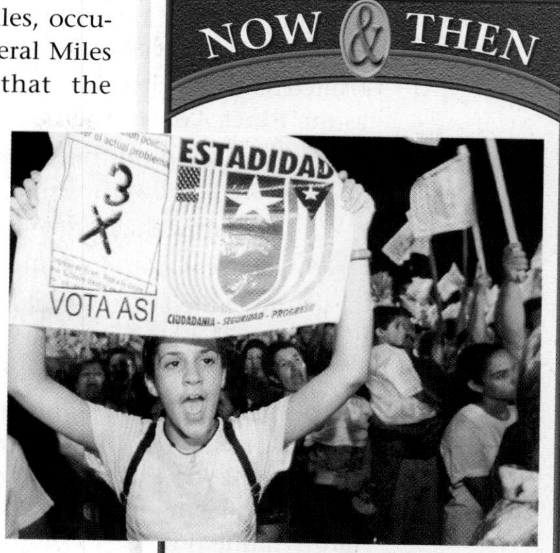

PUERTO RICO

Ever since their transfer under the Treaty of Paris from Spain to the United States, Puerto Ricans have debated their status, as shown above. In 1967, 1993, and 1998, Puerto Ricans rejected both statehood and independence in favor of commonwealth, a status given the island in 1952.

As members of a commonwealth, Puerto Ricans are U.S. citizens. They can move freely between the island and the mainland and are subjected to the military draft but cannot vote in U.S. presidential elections. A majority of Puerto Ricans have rejected statehood because they fear it would mean giving up their Latino culture.

Cuba and the United States

When the United States declared war against Spain in 1898, it recognized Cuba's independence from Spain. It also passed the Teller Amendment, which stated that the United States had no intention of taking over any part of Cuba. The Treaty of Paris, which ended the war, further guaranteed Cuba the independence that its nationalist leaders had been demanding for years.

AMERICAN SOLDIERS Though officially independent, Cuba was occupied by American troops when the war ended. José Martí, the Cuban patriot who had led the movement for independence from Spain, had feared that the United States would merely replace Spain and dominate Cuban politics. In some ways, Martí's prediction came true. Under American occupation, the same officials who had served Spain remained in office. Cubans who protested this policy were imprisoned or exiled.

On the other hand, the American military government provided food and clothing for thousands of families, helped farmers put land back into cultivation, and organized elementary schools. Through improvement of sanitation and medical research, the military government helped eliminate yellow fever, a disease that had killed hundreds of Cubans each year.

Background
Yellow fever damages many body parts, especially the liver. Dr. Carlos Finlay discovered that the disease is carried by mosquitoes. Clearing out the mosquitos' breeding places helped eliminate the disease in Cuba.

PLATT AMENDMENT In 1900 the newly formed Cuban government wrote a constitution for an independent Cuba. The constitution, however, did not specify the relationship between Cuba and the United States. Consequently, in 1901, the United States insisted that Cuba add to its constitution several provisions, known as the **Platt Amendment,** stating that

- Cuba could not make treaties that might limit its independence or permit a foreign power to control any part of its territory
- the United States reserved the right to intervene in Cuba
- Cuba was not to go into debt that its government could not repay
- the United States could buy or lease land on the island for naval stations and refueling stations

The United States made it clear that its army would not withdraw until Cuba adopted the Platt Amendment. In response, a torchlight procession marched on the residence of Governor-General Leonard Wood in protest. Some protestors even called for a return to arms to defend their national honor against this American insult. The U.S. government stood firm, though, and Cubans reluctantly ratified the new constitution. In 1903, the Platt Amendment became part of a treaty between the two nations, and it remained in effect for 31 years. Under the terms of the treaty, Cuba became a U.S. **protectorate,** a country whose affairs are partially controlled by a stronger power.

Vocabulary
ratify: to make valid by approving

PROTECTING AMERICAN BUSINESS INTERESTS The most important reason for the United States to maintain a strong political presence in Cuba was to protect American businesses that had invested in the island's sugar, tobacco, and mining industries, as well as in its railroads and public utilities.

Analyzing *Political Cartoons*

"WELL, I HARDLY KNOW WHICH TO TAKE FIRST!"

Throughout the early 1900s, the United States intervened in the affairs of its Latin American neighbors several times. American troops withdrew from Cuba in 1902 but later returned three times to quell popular uprisings against conservative leaders. The U.S. also intervened in Nicaragua and Haiti. Not surprisingly, few Latin Americans welcomed United States intervention. As the cartoon shows, the United States had a different point of view.

WELL, I HARDLY KNOW WHICH TO TAKE FIRST!

SKILLBUILDER
Analyzing Political Cartoons

1. What is on the bill of fare, or menu, in this restaurant?
2. Which president does the waiter portray?
3. What seems to be Uncle Sam's attitude toward the offerings on the menu?

SEE SKILLBUILDER HANDBOOK, PAGE R24.

Although many businesspeople were convinced that annexing and imposing colonial rule on new territories was necessary to protect American business interests, some were concerned about colonial entanglements. The industrialist Andrew Carnegie argued against the taking of nations as colonies.

A PERSONAL VOICE ANDREW CARNEGIE

"The exports of the United States this year [1898] are greater than those of any other nation in the world. Even Britain's exports are less, yet Britain 'possesses' . . . a hundred 'colonies' . . . scattered all over the world. The fact that the United States has none does not prevent her products and manufactures from invading . . . all parts of the world in competition with those of Britain."

—quoted in *Distant Possessions*

Despite such concerns, the U.S. state department continued to push for control of its Latin American neighbors. In the years to come, the United States would intervene time and again in the affairs of other nations in the Western Hemisphere.

Filipinos Rebel

In the Philippines, Filipinos reacted with outrage to the Treaty of Paris, which called for American annexation of the Philippines. The rebel leader **Emilio Aguinaldo** (ĕ-mēl′yō ä′gē-näl′dō) believed that the United States had promised independence. When he and his followers learned the terms of the treaty, they vowed to fight for freedom.

PHILIPPINE–AMERICAN WAR In February 1899, the Filipinos, led by Aguinaldo, rose in revolt. The United States assumed almost the same role that Spain had played, imposing its authority on a colony that was fighting for freedom. When Aguinaldo turned to guerrilla tactics, the United States forced Filipinos to live in designated zones, where poor sanitation, starvation, and disease killed thousands. This was the very same practice that Americans had condemned Spain for using in Cuba.

▲ U.S. military action in the Philippines resulted in suffering for Filipino civilians. About 200,000 people died as a result of malnutrition, disease, and such guerrilla tactics as the burning of villages.

During the occupation, white American soldiers looked on the Filipinos as inferiors. However, many of the 70,000 U.S. troops sent to the Philippines were African Americans. When African-American newspapers questioned why blacks were helping to spread racial prejudice to the Philippines, some African-American soldiers deserted to the Filipino side and developed bonds of friendship with the Filipinos.

It took the Americans nearly three years to put down the rebellion. About 20,000 Filipino rebels died fighting for independence. The war claimed 4,000 American lives and cost $400 million—20 times the price the United States had paid to purchase the islands. **B**

MAIN IDEA

Contrasting
B What were the aims of the Filipinos? of the Americans?

AFTERMATH OF THE WAR After suppressing the rebellion, the United States set up a government similar to the one it had established for Puerto Rico. The U.S. president would appoint a governor, who would then appoint the upper house of the legislature. Filipinos would elect the lower house. Under American rule, the Philippines moved gradually toward independence and finally became an independent republic on July 4, 1946.

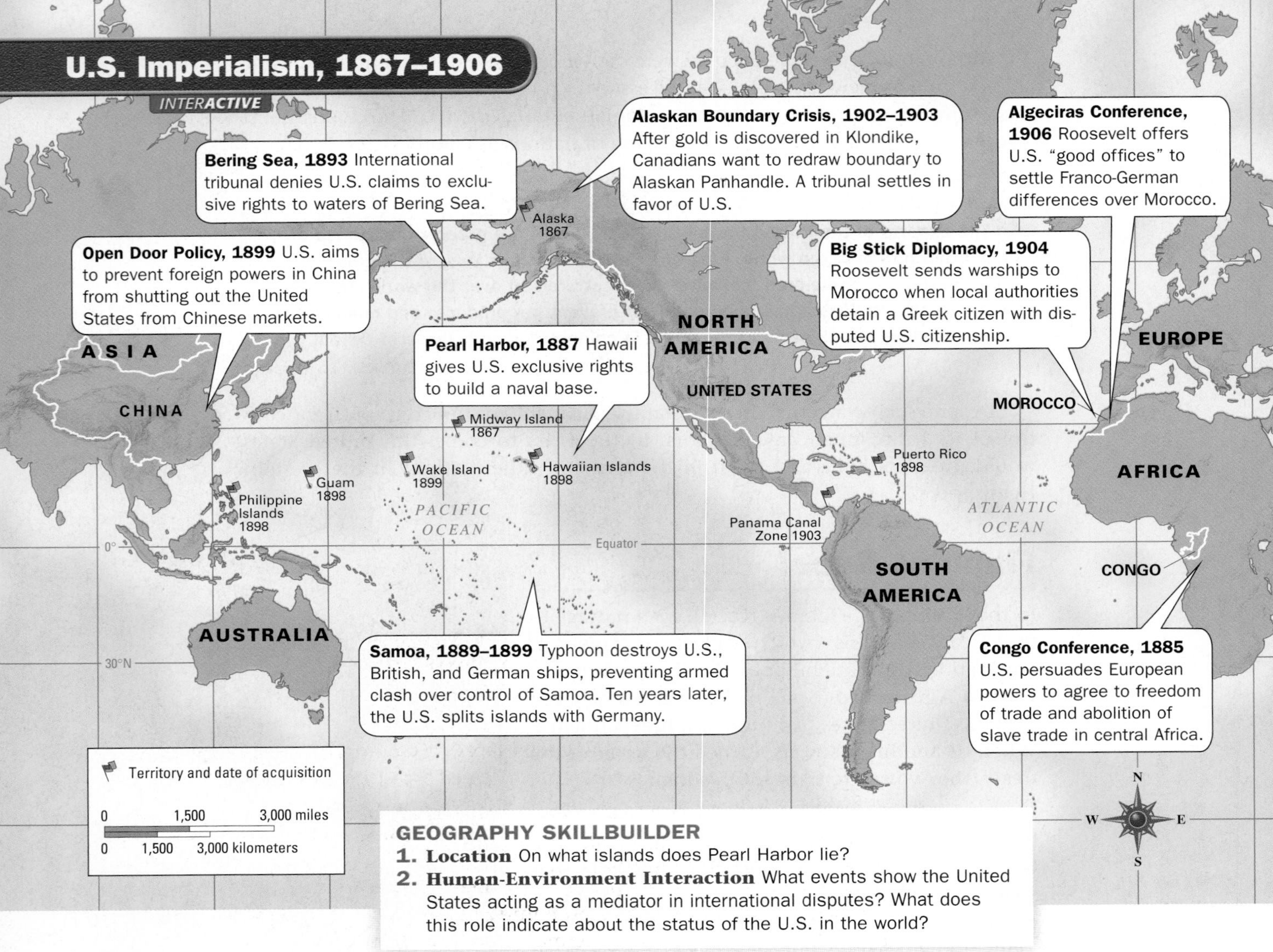

U.S. Imperialism, 1867–1906
INTERACTIVE
Bering Sea, 1893 International tribunal denies U.S. claims to exclusive rights to waters of Bering Sea.
Alaskan Boundary Crisis, 1902–1903 After gold is discovered in Klondike, Canadians want to redraw boundary to Alaskan Panhandle. A tribunal settles in favor of U.S.
Algeciras Conference, 1906 Roosevelt offers U.S. "good offices" to settle Franco-German differences over Morocco.
Open Door Policy, 1899 U.S. aims to prevent foreign powers in China from shutting out the United States from Chinese markets.
Alaska 1867
Big Stick Diplomacy, 1904 Roosevelt sends warships to Morocco when local authorities detain a Greek citizen with disputed U.S. citizenship.
ASIA
CHINA
Pearl Harbor, 1887 Hawaii gives U.S. exclusive rights to build a naval base.
NORTH AMERICA
UNITED STATES
EUROPE
MOROCCO
Midway Island 1867
Wake Island 1899
Hawaiian Islands 1898
Puerto Rico 1898
AFRICA
Guam 1898
Philippine Islands 1898
PACIFIC OCEAN
ATLANTIC OCEAN
Panama Canal Zone 1903
Equator
0°
SOUTH AMERICA
CONGO
AUSTRALIA
30°N
Samoa, 1889–1899 Typhoon destroys U.S., British, and German ships, preventing armed clash over control of Samoa. Ten years later, the U.S. splits islands with Germany.
Congo Conference, 1885 U.S. persuades European powers to agree to freedom of trade and abolition of slave trade in central Africa.
Territory and date of acquisition
0 1,500 3,000 miles
0 1,500 3,000 kilometers
N
W
E
S

GEOGRAPHY SKILLBUILDER

1. **Location** On what islands does Pearl Harbor lie?
2. **Human-Environment Interaction** What events show the United States acting as a mediator in international disputes? What does this role indicate about the status of the U.S. in the world?

Foreign Influence in China

U.S. imperialists saw the Philippines as a gateway to the rest of Asia, particularly to China. China was seen as a vast potential market for American products. It also presented American investors with new opportunities for large-scale railroad construction.

Weakened by war and foreign intervention, China had become known as the "sick man of Asia." France, Germany, Britain, Japan, and Russia had established prosperous settlements along the coast of China. They also had carved out spheres of influence, areas where each nation claimed special rights and economic privileges.

JOHN HAY'S OPEN DOOR NOTES The United States began to fear that China would be carved into colonies and American traders would be shut out. To protect American interests, U.S. Secretary of State **John Hay** issued, in 1899, a series of policy statements called the **Open Door notes.** The notes were letters addressed to the leaders of imperialist nations proposing that the nations share their trading rights with the United States, thus creating an open door. This meant that no single nation would have a monopoly on trade with any part of China. The other imperialist powers reluctantly accepted this policy. C

MAIN IDEA

Analyzing Causes

C Why did Secretary of State John Hay issue the policy statements known as the Open Door notes?

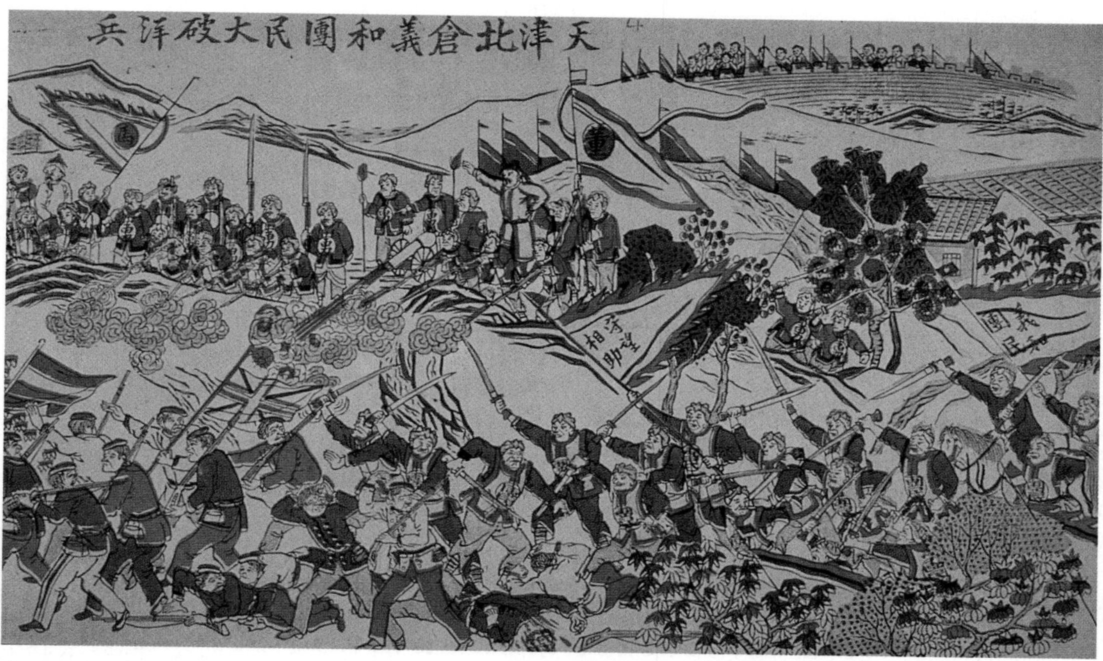

▲ **During the Boxer Rebellion, shown here in this Chinese print, Chinese patriots demanded that all foreigners be expelled from the country. The Boxers surrounded the European section of Beijing and kept it under siege for several months.**

THE BOXER REBELLION IN CHINA Although China kept its freedom, Europeans dominated most of China's large cities. Resentment simmered beneath the surface as some Chinese formed secret societies pledged to rid the country of "foreign devils." The most famous of these secret groups were the Boxers, so named by Westerners because members practiced martial arts.

Vocabulary
martial arts: combat or self defense arts that originated in East Asia, such as judo or karate

The Boxers killed hundreds of missionaries and other foreigners, as well as Chinese converts to Christianity. In August 1900, troops from Britain, France, Germany, and Japan joined about 2,500 American soldiers and marched on the Chinese capital. Within two months, the international forces put down the **Boxer Rebellion.** Thousands of Chinese people died during the fighting.

PROTECTING AMERICAN RIGHTS After the Boxer Rebellion, the United States feared that European nations would use their victory to take even greater control of China. To prevent this, John Hay issued a second series of Open Door notes, announcing that the United States would "safeguard for the world the principle of equal and impartial trade with all parts of the Chinese Empire." This policy paved the way for greater American influence in Asia.

The Open Door policy reflected three deeply held American beliefs about the United States industrial capitalist economy. First, Americans believed that the growth of the U.S. economy depended on exports. Second, they felt the United States had a right to intervene abroad to keep foreign markets open. Third, they feared that the closing of an area to American products, citizens, or ideas threatened U.S. survival. These beliefs became the bedrock of American foreign policy.

WORLD STAGE

THE BOXER PROTOCOL

On September 7, 1901, China and 11 other nations signed the Boxer Protocol—a final settlement of the Boxer Rebellion.

The Qing government agreed to execute some Chinese officials, to punish others, and to pay about $332 million in damages. The United States was awarded a settlement of $24.5 million. It used about $4 million to pay American citizens for actual losses incurred during the rebellion. In 1908, the U.S. government returned the rest of the money to China to be used for the purpose of educating Chinese students in their own country and in the United States.

The Impact of U.S. Territorial Gains

In 1900, Republican William McKinley, a reluctant but confirmed imperialist, was elected to a second term against Democrat William Jennings Bryan, who staunchly opposed imperialism. McKinley's reelection confirmed that a majority of Americans favored his policies. Under McKinley, the United States had gained an empire.

Yet even before McKinley was reelected, an Anti-Imperialist League had sprung into being. The league included some of the most prominent people in America, such as former president Grover Cleveland, industrial leader Andrew Carnegie, the social worker Jane Addams, and many leading writers. Anti-imperialists had different and sometimes conflicting reasons for their opposition, but all agreed that it was wrong for the United States to rule other people without their consent. The novelist Mark Twain questioned the motives for imperialism in a satirical piece written in 1901.

A PERSONAL VOICE MARK TWAIN

"Shall we go on conferring our Civilization upon the peoples that sit in darkness, or shall we give those poor things a rest? . . . Extending the Blessings of Civilization to our Brother who Sits in Darkness has been a good trade and has paid well, on the whole; and there is money in it yet . . . but not enough, in my judgment, to make any considerable risk advisable."

—quoted in *To the Person Sitting in Darkness*

▲ **Mark Twain**

As a novelist, Twain had great influence on American culture but little influence on foreign policy. In the early 20th century, the United States under President Theodore Roosevelt and President Woodrow Wilson would continue to exert its power around the globe.

ASSESSMENT

1. **TERMS & NAMES** For each term or name, write a sentence explaining its significance.
   - **Foraker Act**
   - **Platt Amendment**
   - **protectorate**
   - **Emilio Aguinaldo**
   - **John Hay**
   - **Open Door notes**
   - **Boxer Rebellion**

MAIN IDEA

2. **TAKING NOTES**
   Create a time line of key events relating to U.S. relations with Cuba, Puerto Rico, and the Philippines. Use the dates already plotted on the time line below as a guide.

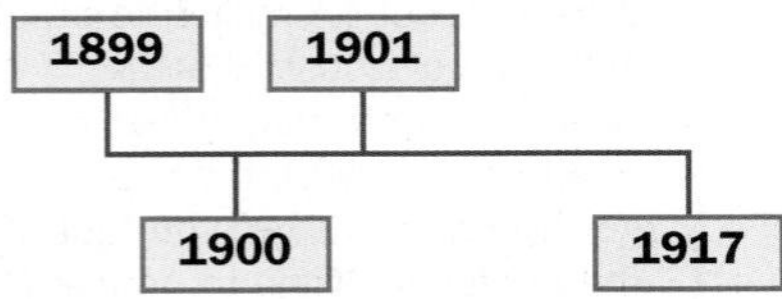

   Which event do you think was most significant? Why?

CRITICAL THINKING

3. **EVALUATING**
   How did American rule of Puerto Rico harm Puerto Ricans? How did it help Puerto Ricans? Do you think the benefits outweighed the harmful effects? Why or why not?

4. **COMPARING**
   How was U.S. policy toward China different from U.S. policy toward the Philippines? To what can you attribute the difference?

5. **ANALYZING ISSUES**
   How did U.S. foreign policy at the turn of the century affect actions taken by the United States toward China? **Think About:**
   - why the United States wanted access to China's markets
   - the purpose of the Open Door notes
   - the U.S. response to the Boxer Rebellion

America as a World Power

MAIN IDEA	WHY IT MATTERS NOW	Terms & Names
The Russo-Japanese War, the Panama Canal, and the Mexican Revolution added to America's military and economic power.	American involvement in conflicts around 1900 led to involvement in World War I and later to a peacekeeper role in today's world.	• Panama Canal • Roosevelt Corollary • dollar diplomacy • Francisco "Pancho" Villa • Emiliano Zapata • John J. Pershing

One American's Story

Joseph Bucklin Bishop played an important role in the building of the Panama Canal as the policy advisor to the canal's chief engineer. As editor of the *Canal Record*, a weekly newspaper that provided Americans with updates on the project, Bishop described a frustrating problem that the workers encountered.

A PERSONAL VOICE JOSEPH BUCKLIN BISHOP

> **"The Canal Zone was a land of the fantastic and the unexpected. No one could say when the sun went down what the condition of the Cut would be when [the sun] rose. For the work of months or even years might be blotted out by an avalanche of earth or the toppling over of a mountain of rock. It was a task to try men's souls; but it was also one to kindle in them a joy of combat . . . and a faith in ultimate victory which no disaster could shake."**
>
> —quoted in *The Impossible Dream: The Building of the Panama Canal*

▲ Workers digging the Panama Canal faced hazardous landslides and death from disease.

The building of the Panama Canal reflected America's new role as a world power. As a technological accomplishment, the canal represented a confident nation's refusal to let any physical obstacle stand in its way.

Teddy Roosevelt and the World

The assassination of William McKinley in 1901 thrust Vice-President Theodore Roosevelt into the role of a world leader. Roosevelt was unwilling to allow the imperial powers of Europe to control the world's political and economic destiny. In 1905, building on the Open Door notes to increase American influence in East Asia, Roosevelt mediated a settlement in a war between Russia and Japan.

ROOSEVELT THE PEACEMAKER In 1904, Russia and Japan, Russia's neighbor in East Asia, were both imperialist powers, and they were competing for control of Korea. The Japanese took the first action in what would become the Russo-Japanese War with a sudden attack on the Russian Pacific fleet. To everyone's surprise, Japan destroyed it. Japan then proceeded to destroy a second fleet sent as reinforcement. Japan also won a series of land battles, securing Korea and Manchuria.

KEY PLAYER

THEODORE ROOSEVELT
1858–1919

Rimless glasses, a bushy mustache, and prominent teeth made Roosevelt easy for cartoonists to caricature. His great enthusiasm for physical activity—boxing, tennis, swimming, horseback riding, and hunting—provided cartoonists with additional material. Some cartoons portrayed Roosevelt with the toy teddy bear that he inspired.

Roosevelt had six children, who became notorious for their rowdy antics. Their father once sent a message through the War Department, ordering them to call off their "attack" on the White House. Roosevelt thrived on the challenges of the presidency. He wrote, "I do not believe that anyone else has ever enjoyed the White House as much as I have."

As a result of these battles, Japan began to run out of men and money, a fact that it did not want to reveal to Russia. Instead, Japanese officials approached President Roosevelt in secret and asked him to mediate peace negotiations. Roosevelt agreed, and in 1905, Russian and Japanese delegates convened in Portsmouth, New Hampshire.

The first meeting took place on the presidential yacht. Roosevelt had a charming way of greeting people with a grasp of the hand, a broad grin, and a hearty "Dee-lighted." Soon the opposing delegates began to relax and cordially shook hands.

The Japanese wanted Sakhalin Island, off the coast of Siberia, and a large sum of money from Russia. Russia refused. Roosevelt persuaded Japan to accept half the island and forgo the cash payment. In exchange, Russia agreed to let Japan take over Russian interests in Manchuria and Korea. The successful efforts in negotiating the Treaty of Portsmouth won Roosevelt the 1906 Nobel Peace Prize.

As U.S. and Japanese interests expanded in East Asia, the two nations continued diplomatic talks. In later agreements, they pledged to respect each other's possessions and interests in East Asia and the Pacific. (A)

MAIN IDEA

Analyzing Effects
(A) What were the results of Roosevelt's negotiations with the Japanese and Russians?

PANAMA CANAL By the time Roosevelt became president, many Americans, including Roosevelt, felt that the United States needed a canal cutting across Central America. Such a canal would greatly reduce travel time for commercial and military ships by providing a shortcut between the Atlantic and Pacific oceans. (See Geography Spotlight, page 366.) As early as 1850, the United States and Britain had agreed to share the rights to such a canal. In the Hay-Pauncefote Treaty of 1901, however, Britain gave the United States exclusive rights to build and control a canal through Central America.

Engineers identified two possible routes for the proposed canal. One, through Nicaragua, posed fewer obstacles because much of it crossed a large lake. The other route crossed through Panama (then a province of Colombia) and was shorter and filled with mountains and swamps. In the late 1800s, a French company had tried to build a canal in Panama. After ten years, the company gave up. It sent an agent, Philippe Bunau-Varilla, to Washington to convince the United States to buy its claim. In 1903, the president and Congress decided to use the Panama route and agreed to buy the French company's route for $40 million.

Before beginning work on the **Panama Canal,** the United States had to get permission from Colombia, which then ruled Panama. When these negotiations broke down, Bunau-Varilla helped organize a Panamanian rebellion against Colombia. On November 3, 1903, nearly a dozen U.S. warships were present as Panama declared its independence. Fifteen days later, Panama and the United

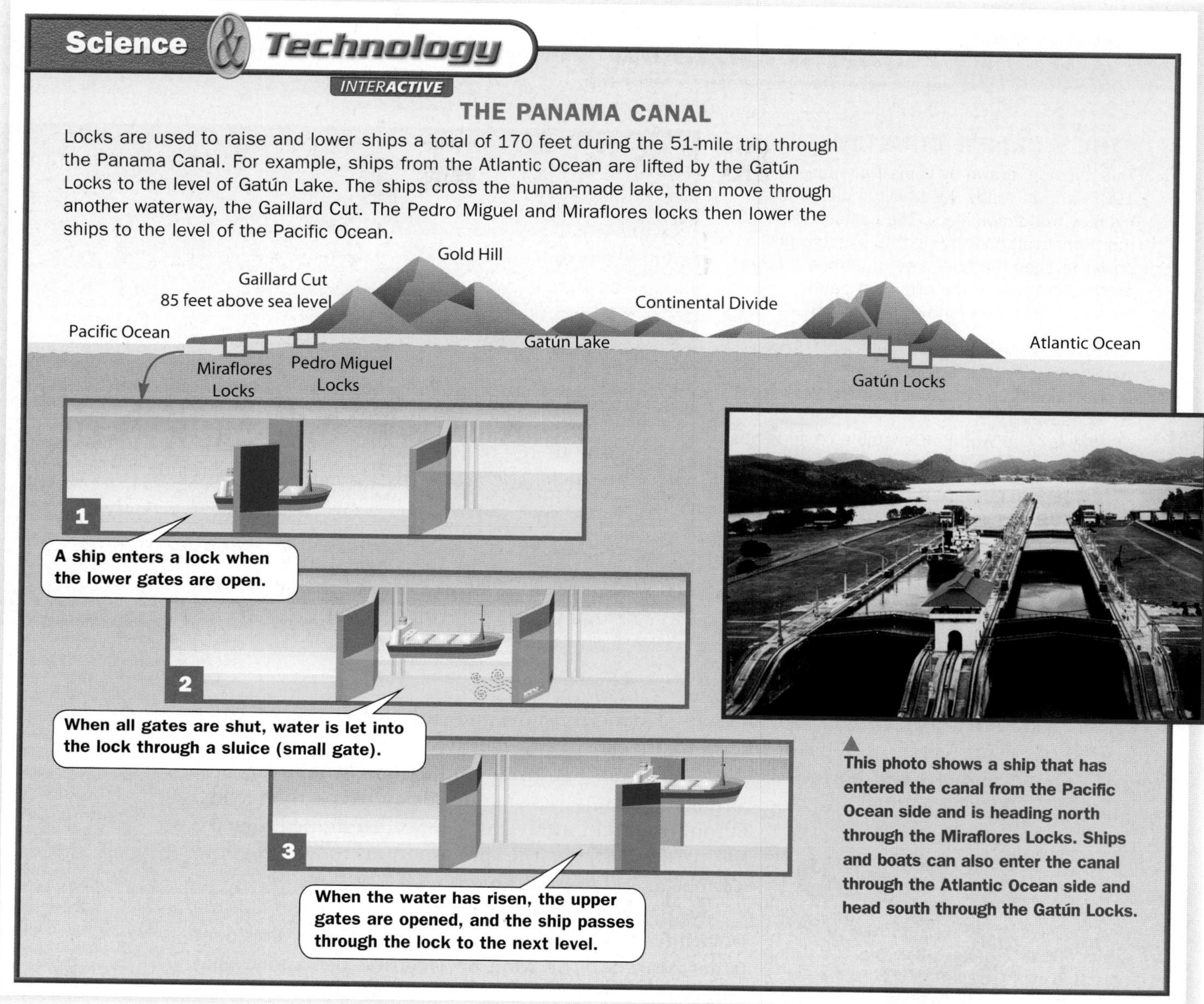

Science & Technology
INTERACTIVE
THE PANAMA CANAL
Locks are used to raise and lower ships a total of 170 feet during the 51-mile trip through the Panama Canal. For example, ships from the Atlantic Ocean are lifted by the Gatún Locks to the level of Gatún Lake. The ships cross the human-made lake, then move through another waterway, the Gaillard Cut. The Pedro Miguel and Miraflores locks then lower the ships to the level of the Pacific Ocean.
Gold Hill
Gaillard Cut
85 feet above sea level
Continental Divide
Pacific Ocean
Gatún Lake
Atlantic Ocean
Miraflores Locks
Pedro Miguel Locks
Gatún Locks
1
A ship enters a lock when the lower gates are open.
2
When all gates are shut, water is let into the lock through a sluice (small gate).
3
When the water has risen, the upper gates are opened, and the ship passes through the lock to the next level.

▲ This photo shows a ship that has entered the canal from the Pacific Ocean side and is heading north through the Miraflores Locks. Ships and boats can also enter the canal through the Atlantic Ocean side and head south through the Gatún Locks.

States signed a treaty in which the United States agreed to pay Panama $10 million plus an annual rent of $250,000 for an area of land across Panama, called the Canal Zone. The payments were to begin in 1913.

CONSTRUCTING THE CANAL Construction of the Panama Canal ranks as one of the world's greatest engineering feats. Builders fought diseases, such as yellow fever and malaria, and soft volcanic soil that proved difficult to remove from where it lay. Work began in 1904 with the clearing of brush and draining of swamps. By 1913, the height of the construction, more than 43,400 workers were employed. Some had come from Italy and Spain; three-quarters were blacks from the British West Indies. More than 5,600 workers on the canal died from accidents or disease. The total cost to the United States was about $380 million. B

MAIN IDEA

Identifying Problems

B What problems did canal workers encounter in constructing the canal?

On August 15, 1914, the canal opened for business, and more than 1,000 merchant ships passed through during its first year. U.S.-Latin American relations, however, had been damaged by American support of the rebellion in Panama. The resulting ill will lasted for decades, despite Congress's paying Colombia $25 million in 1921 to compensate the country for its lost territory.

Analyzing *Political Cartoons*

"THE WORLD'S CONSTABLE"

This cartoon, drawn by Louis Dalrymple in 1905, shows Teddy Roosevelt implementing his new world diplomacy. The cartoon implies that Roosevelt has the right to execute police power to keep the countries of Europe (shown on the right) out of the affairs of Latin American countries (shown on the left).

SKILLBUILDER

Analyzing Political Cartoons

1. How does the cartoonist portray President Roosevelt?
2. Why is "The World's Constable" a good title for this cartoon?

SEE SKILLBUILDER HANDBOOK, PAGE R24.

THE ROOSEVELT COROLLARY Financial factors drew the United States further into Latin American affairs. In the late 19th century, many Latin American nations had borrowed huge sums from European banks to build railroads and develop industries. Roosevelt feared that if these nations defaulted on their loans, Europeans might intervene. He was determined to make the United States the predominant power in the Caribbean and Central America.

"Speak softly and carry a big stick; you will go far."
THEODORE ROOSEVELT

Roosevelt reminded European powers of the Monroe Doctrine, which had been issued in 1823 by President James Monroe. The Monroe Doctrine demanded that European countries stay out of the affairs of Latin American nations. Roosevelt based his Latin America policy on a West African proverb that said, "Speak softly and carry a big stick." In his December 1904 message to Congress, Roosevelt added the **Roosevelt Corollary** to the Monroe Doctrine. He warned that disorder in Latin America might "force the United States . . . to the exercise of an international police power." In effect, the corollary said that the United States would now use force to protect its economic interests in Latin America.

Vocabulary
corollary: an additional statement that follows logically from the first one

DOLLAR DIPLOMACY During the next decade, the United States exercised its police power on several occasions. For example, when a 1911 rebellion in Nicaragua left the nation near bankruptcy, President William H. Taft, Roosevelt's successor, arranged for American bankers to loan Nicaragua enough money to pay its debts. In return, the bankers were given the right to recover their money by collecting Nicaragua's customs duties. The U.S. bankers also gained control of Nicaragua's state-owned railroad system and its national bank. When Nicaraguan citizens heard about this deal, they revolted against President Adolfo Díaz. To prop up

Díaz's government, some 2,000 marines were sent to Nicaragua. The revolt was put down, but some marine detachments remained in the country until 1933.

The Taft administration followed the policy of using the U.S. government to guarantee loans made to foreign countries by American businesspeople. This policy was called **dollar diplomacy** by its critics and was often used to justify keeping European powers out of the Caribbean.

Woodrow Wilson's Missionary Diplomacy

The Monroe Doctrine, issued by President James Monroe in 1823, had warned other nations against expanding their influence in Latin America. The Roosevelt Corollary asserted, in 1904, that the United States had a right to exercise international police power in the Western Hemisphere. In 1913, President Woodrow Wilson gave the Monroe Doctrine a moral tone.

According to Wilson's "missionary diplomacy," the United States had a moral responsibility to deny recognition to any Latin American government it viewed as oppressive, undemocratic, or hostile to U.S. interests. Prior to this policy, the United States recognized any government that controlled a nation, regardless of that nation's policies or how it had come to power. Wilson's policy pressured nations in the Western Hemisphere to establish democratic governments. Almost immediately, the Mexican Revolution put Wilson's policy to the test.

THE MEXICAN REVOLUTION Mexico had been ruled for more than three decades by a military dictator, Porfirio Díaz. A friend of the United States, Díaz had long encouraged foreign investments in his country. As a result, foreigners, mostly Americans, owned a large share of Mexican oil wells, mines, railroads, and ranches. While foreign investors and some Mexican landowners and politicians had grown rich, the common people of the country were desperately poor.

In 1911, Mexican peasants and workers led by Francisco Madero overthrew Díaz. Madero promised democratic reforms, but he proved unable to satisfy the conflicting demands of landowners, peasants, factory workers, and the urban middle class. After two years, General Victoriano Huerta took over the government. Within days Madero was murdered. Wilson refused to recognize the government that Huerta formed. He called it "a government of butchers." C

MAIN IDEA

Analyzing Motives
C Why did President Wilson refuse to recognize Huerta's government?

INTERVENTION IN MEXICO Wilson adopted a plan of "watchful waiting," looking for an opportunity to act against Huerta. The opportunity came in April 1914, when one of Huerta's officers arrested a small group of American sailors in Tampico, on Mexico's eastern shore. The Mexicans quickly released them and apologized, but Wilson used the incident as an excuse to intervene in Mexico and ordered U.S. Marines to occupy Veracruz, an important Mexican port. Eighteen Americans and at least 200 Mexicans died during the invasion.

The incident brought the United States and Mexico close to war. Argentina, Brazil, and Chile stepped in to mediate the conflict. They proposed that Huerta step down and that U.S. troops withdraw without paying Mexico for damages. Mexico rejected the plan, and Wilson refused to recognize a government that had come to power as a result of violence. The Huerta regime soon collapsed, however, and Venustiano Carranza, a nationalist leader, became president in 1915. Wilson withdrew the troops and formally recognized the Carranza government.

ANOTHER PERSPECTIVE

INTERVENTION IN MEXICO

Most U.S. citizens supported American intervention in Mexico. Edith O'Shaughnessy, wife of an American diplomat in Mexico City, had another perspective. After touring Veracruz, O'Shaughnessy wrote to her mother:

> "I think we have done a great wrong to these people; instead of cutting out the sores with a clean, strong knife of war . . . and occupation, . . . we have only put our fingers in each festering wound and inflamed it further."

History Through Art

ZAPATISTAS (1931)

José Orozco, one of Mexico's foremost artists, painted these Zapatistas (followers of Zapata), to honor the peasant men and women who fought in the Mexican revolution. Orozco did many paintings in support of the revolution. **What aspects of the image does the artist use to convey strength and unity?**

REBELLION IN MEXICO Carranza was in charge, but like others before him, he did not have the support of all Mexicans. Rebels under the leadership of **Francisco "Pancho" Villa** (vē′ə) and **Emiliano Zapata** (ĕ-mēl-yä′nō zə-pä′tə) opposed Carranza's provisional government. Zapata—son of a mestizo peasant—was dedicated to land reform. "It is better to die on your feet than live on your knees," Zapata told the peasants who joined him. Villa, a fierce nationalist, had frequently courted the support and aid of the United States.

A PERSONAL VOICE PANCHO VILLA

> **"[A]s long as I have anything to do with the affairs in Mexico there will be no further friction between my country and my friends of the North . . . To President Wilson, the greatest American, I stand pledged to do what I can to keep the faith he has in my people, and if there is anything he may wish I will gladly do it, for I know it will be for the good of my country."**
>
> —*New York Times*, January 11, 1915

Despite Villa's talk of friendship, when President Wilson recognized Carranza's government, Villa threatened reprisals against the United States. In January 1916, Carranza invited American engineers to operate mines in northern Mexico. Before they reached the mines, however, Villa's men took the Americans off a train and shot them. Two months later, some of Villa's followers raided Columbus, New Mexico, and killed 17 Americans. Americans held Villa responsible.

CHASING VILLA With the American public demanding revenge, President Wilson ordered Brigadier General **John J. Pershing** and an expeditionary force of about 15,000 soldiers into Mexico to capture Villa dead or alive. For almost a year, Villa eluded Pershing's forces. Wilson then called out 150,000 National Guardsmen and stationed them along the Mexican border. In the meantime,

Mexicans grew angrier over the U.S. invasion of their land. In June 1916, U.S. troops clashed with Carranza's army, resulting in deaths on both sides.

Carranza demanded the withdrawal of U.S. troops, but Wilson refused. War seemed imminent. However, in the end, both sides backed down. The United States, facing war in Europe, needed peace on its southern border. In February 1917, Wilson ordered Pershing to return home. Later that year, Mexico adopted a constitution that gave the government control of the nation's oil and mineral resources and placed strict regulations on foreign investors.

▲ **Pancho Villa directs a column of his troops through northern Mexico in 1914.**

Although Carranza had called for the constitution of 1917, he failed to carry out its measures. Instead, he ruled oppressively until 1920 when a moderate named Alvaro Obregón came to power. Obregón's presidency marked the end of civil war and the beginning of reform.

U.S. intervention in Mexican affairs provided a clear model of American imperialist attitudes in the early years of the 20th century. Americans believed in the superiority of free-enterprise democracy, and the American government attempted to extend the reach of this economic and political system, even through armed intervention.

The United States pursued and achieved several foreign policy goals in the early 20th century. First, it expanded its access to foreign markets in order to ensure the continued growth of the domestic economy. Second, the United States built a modern navy to protect its interests abroad. Third, the United States exercised its international police power to ensure dominance in Latin America.

SECTION 4 ASSESSMENT

1. **TERMS & NAMES** For each term or name below, write a sentence explaining its significance.
   - **Panama Canal**
   - **Roosevelt Corollary**
   - **dollar diplomacy**
   - **Francisco "Pancho" Villa**
   - **Emiliano Zapata**
   - **John J. Pershing**

SUMMARIZING

2. **TAKING NOTES**
   In a two-column chart, list ways Teddy Roosevelt and Woodrow Wilson used American power around the world during their presidencies.

Using American Power	
Roosevelt	**Wilson**

Choose one example and discuss its impact with your classmates.

CRITICAL THINKING

3. **COMPARING AND CONTRASTING**
   What do you think were the similarities and differences between Roosevelt's Big Stick policy and Wilson's missionary diplomacy? Use evidence from the text to support your response. **Think About:**
   - the goal of each of these foreign policies
   - how the policies defined the role of U.S. intervention in international affairs
   - how the policies were applied

4. **EVALUATING DECISIONS**
   In your opinion, should the United States have become involved in the affairs of Colombia, Nicaragua, and Mexico during the early 1900s? Support your answer with details. **Think About:**
   - the effect of the Roosevelt Corollary
   - the results of dollar diplomacy
   - the implication of Wilson's missionary diplomacy

GEOGRAPHY SPOTLIGHT

The Panama Canal: Funnel for Trade

By the late 19th century, the U.S. position in global trade was firmly established. A glance at a world map during that time revealed the trade advantages of cutting through the world's great landmasses at two strategic points. The first cut, through the Isthmus of Suez in Egypt, was completed in 1869 and was a spectacular success. A second cut, this one through Panama, in Central America, would be especially advantageous to the United States. Such a cut, or canal, would substantially reduce the sailing time between the nation's Atlantic and Pacific ports.

It took the United States ten years, from 1904 to 1914, to build the Panama Canal. By 1999, more than 700,000 vessels, flying the flags of about 70 nations, had passed through its locks. In the year 2000, Panama assumed full control of the canal.

INTERCOASTAL TRADE ▲

The first boat through the canal heralded the arrival of increased trade between the Atlantic and Pacific ports of the United States.

San Francisco

to Asia

NUMBERS TELL THE STORY ▶

A ship sailing from New York to San Francisco by going around South America travels 13,000 miles; the canal shortens the journey to 5,200 miles.

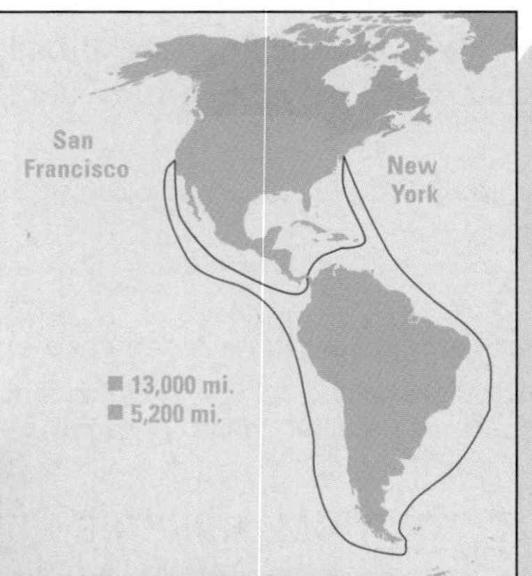

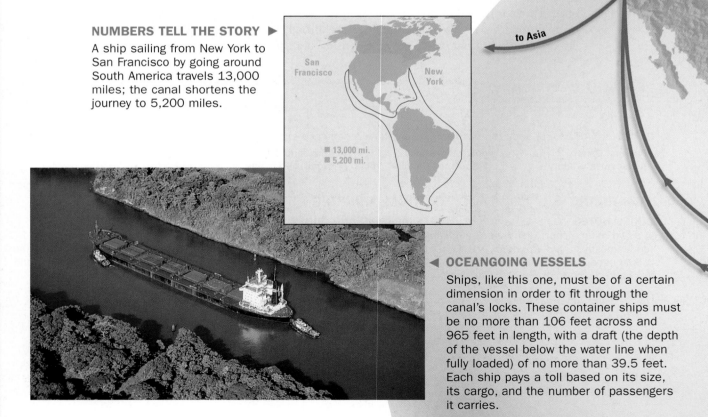

◀ OCEANGOING VESSELS

Ships, like this one, must be of a certain dimension in order to fit through the canal's locks. These container ships must be no more than 106 feet across and 965 feet in length, with a draft (the depth of the vessel below the water line when fully loaded) of no more than 39.5 feet. Each ship pays a toll based on its size, its cargo, and the number of passengers it carries.

◀ **NEW YORK CITY**

New York City and other U.S. Atlantic ports accounted for about 60 percent of the traffic using the Panama Canal in the early decades of its existence.

NEW ORLEANS ▲

Since its founding in 1718, New Orleans has served as a major port for the products of the areas along the Mississippi River. In 1914, the Panama Canal brought Pacific markets into its orbit.

New York
to Europe
to Africa
New Orleans
Panama Canal
to South America

Panama is a narrow stretch of land—or isthmus —that connects North and South America. In building the canal, engineers took advantage of natural waterways. Moving ships through the mountains of the Continental Divide required the use of massive locks. Locks allow a section of the canal to be closed off so that the water level can be raised or lowered.

THINKING CRITICALLY

1. **Analyzing Patterns** On a world map, identify the route that ships took to get from New York City to San Francisco before the Panama Canal opened. How did this route change after the opening of the canal?
2. **Creating a Model** Use clay to shape a model of a cross-section of the Panama Canal as shown in the Science and Technology feature on page 361. For the locks, use styrofoam blocks or pieces of wood which you have glued together. Paint the model, and then label each part of the canal.

SEE SKILLBUILDER HANDBOOK, PAGE R31.

RESEARCH LINKS CLASSZONE.COM

VISUAL SUMMARY

America Claims an Empire

CAUSES

- Economic competition among industrial nations
- Political and military competition, including the creation of a strong naval force
- A belief in Anglo-Saxon superiority

American Imperialism

EFFECTS

- The U.S. purchased Alaska in 1867.
- The U.S. annexed Hawaii in 1898.

- In 1898, the U.S. helped Cuba win independence from Spain.
- In the Treaty of Paris, the U.S. gained Puerto Rico, Guam, and the Philippine Islands.

- Following the Spanish-American War, the U.S.
  —reorganized the government of Puerto Rico
  —established a protectorate over Cuba
  —crushed a revolt in Philippines
- In 1899, the Open Door policy established U.S. trading rights in China.

- In the early 1900s, President Roosevelt initiated plans for the Panama Canal and asserted the right of the U.S. to exercise police power in the Western Hemisphere.
- President Wilson pressured Mexico and other countries in the Western Hemisphere to establish democratic governments.

TERMS & NAMES

For each term or name below, write a sentence explaining its significance to U.S. foreign policy between 1890 and 1920.

1. Queen Liliuokalani
2. imperialism
3. José Martí
4. yellow journalism
5. *U.S.S. Maine*
6. protectorate
7. Open Door notes
8. Boxer Rebellion
9. Panama Canal
10. Roosevelt Corollary

MAIN IDEAS

Use your notes and the information in the chapter to answer the following questions.

Imperialism and America *(pages 342–345)*

1. What three factors spurred American imperialism?
2. How did Queen Liliuokalani's main goal conflict with American imperialists' goals?

The Spanish-American War *(pages 346–351)*

3. Why was American opinion about Cuban independence divided?
4. Briefly describe the terms of the Treaty of Paris of 1898.

Acquiring New Lands *(pages 352–358)*

5. Why was the U.S. interested in events in Puerto Rico?
6. What sparked the Boxer Rebellion in 1900, and how was it crushed?
7. What three key beliefs about America's industrial capitalist economy were reflected in the Open Door policy?

America as a World Power *(pages 359–365)*

8. What conflict triggered the war between Russia and Japan?
9. Why is the construction of the Panama Canal considered one of the world's greatest engineering feats?
10. Explain the key difference between Woodrow Wilson's moral diplomacy and Teddy Roosevelt's "big stick" diplomacy.

CRITICAL THINKING

1. **USING YOUR NOTES** Create a Venn diagram like the one below to show the similarities and differences between José Martí of Cuba and Emilio Aguinaldo of the Philippines.

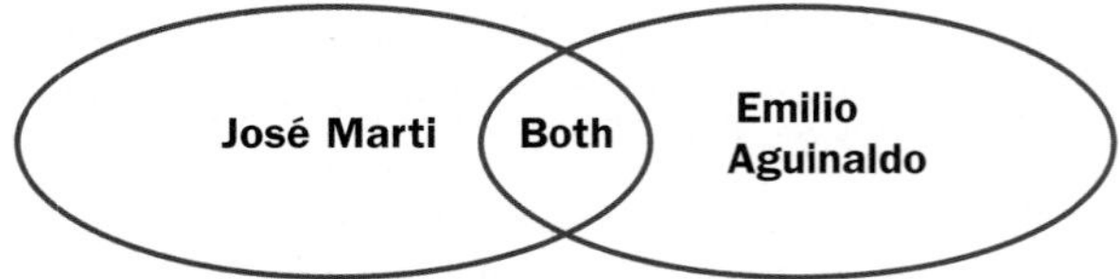

2. **HYPOTHESIZING** Would Cuba have won its independence in the late 19th century if the United States had not intervened there? Support your opinion with details from the text.

3. **INTERPRETING MAPS** Look carefully at the Caribbean map on page 349 and the world map on page 356. Why do you think American naval bases in the Caribbean and the Pacific were beneficial to the United States?

Standardized Test Practice

Use the cartoon and your knowledge of U.S. history to answer question 1.

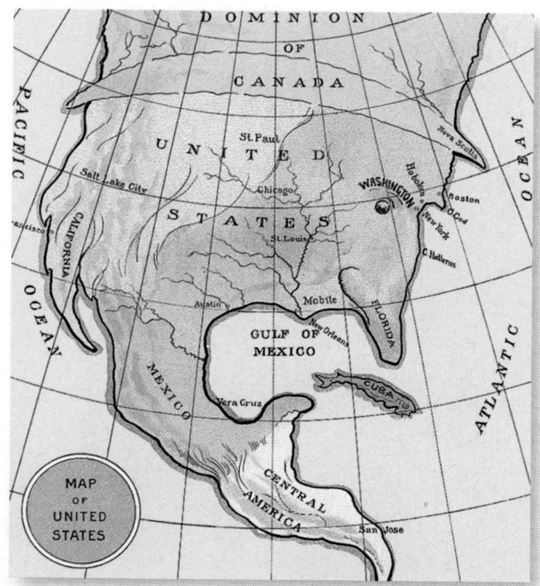

1. What is the cartoonist's point of view concerning the relationship between the United States and Cuba?
   - **A** The United States wishes to be friends with Cuba.
   - **B** The United States will devour Cuba.
   - **C** The United States is wasting its time fighting over such a small area.
   - **D** The United States has no interest in Cuba.

Use the map and your knowledge of U.S. history to answer question 2.

2. How did the building of the Panama Canal support United States efforts to become a world power?
   - **F** It gave the United States a colony in Central America.
   - **G** It prevented Japan and China from attacking Hawaii.
   - **H** It opened up a new avenue for trade with China.
   - **J** By providing a shortcut between the Atlantic Ocean and Pacific Ocean, it opened up new trading opportunities.

ADDITIONAL TEST PRACTICE, pages S1–S33.

TEST PRACTICE **CLASSZONE.COM**

ALTERNATIVE ASSESSMENT

1. **INTERACT WITH HISTORY** Recall your discussion of the question on page 341:

Does the U.S. have a duty to fight for freedom in neighboring countries?

Suppose you are a journalist at the end of the Spanish-American War. You work for William Randolph Hearst's the *New York Journal*. Write a newspaper editorial that presents your point of view about whether or not the Senate should ratify the Treaty of Paris, thus annexing the Philippines.

2. CD-ROM **LEARNING FROM MEDIA** Use the CD-ROM *Electronic Library of Primary Sources* and other resources to research opinions on imperialism between 1895 and 1920.

- Choose a document, incident, or piece of writing about imperialism. Decide if you support it or disagree with it.
- Write a speech that presents your point of view. Decide how you will make your arguments clear and convincing while also addressing opposing concerns.
- Practice your speech aloud and then present it to the class.

THE FIRST WORLD WAR

Battle scene on the western front during World War I.

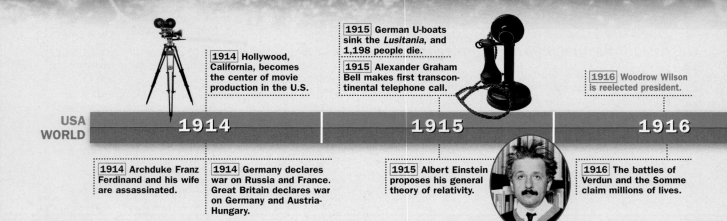

USA

1914 Hollywood, California, becomes the center of movie production in the U.S.

1915 German U-boats sink the *Lusitania*, and 1,198 people die.

1915 Alexander Graham Bell makes first transcontinental telephone call.

1916 Woodrow Wilson is reelected president.

1914 | 1915 | 1916

WORLD

1914 Archduke Franz Ferdinand and his wife are assassinated.

1914 Germany declares war on Russia and France. Great Britain declares war on Germany and Austria-Hungary.

1915 Albert Einstein proposes his general theory of relativity.

1916 The battles of Verdun and the Somme claim millions of lives.

INTERACT WITH HISTORY

The year is 1917. A bitter war is raging in Europe—a war that has been called a threat to civilization. At home many people are urging America to wake up and get involved, while others are calling for the country to isolate itself and avoid the fight.

Do you think America should enter the war?

Examine the Issues

- Is it right for America to intervene in foreign conflicts?
- When American lives are threatened, how should the government respond?
- Should America go to war to make the world "safe for democracy"?

RESEARCH LINKS **CLASSZONE.COM**

Visit the Chapter 11 links for more information about The First World War.

1917 The Selective Service Act sets up the draft.

1917 The United States declares war on Germany.

1917 Russia withdraws from the war.

1918 Congress passes the Sedition Act.

1918 President Wilson proposes the League of Nations.

1918 The Bolsheviks establish a Communist regime in Russia.

1918 The First World War ends.

1919 Congress approves the Nineteenth Amendment, granting women the vote.

1919 A worldwide influenza epidemic kills over 30 million.

World War I Begins

MAIN IDEA

As World War I intensified, the United States was forced to abandon its neutrality.

WHY IT MATTERS NOW

The United States remains involved in European and world affairs.

Terms & Names

- **nationalism**
- **militarism**
- **Allies**
- **Central Powers**
- **Archduke Franz Ferdinand**
- **no man's land**
- **trench warfare**
- ***Lusitania***
- **Zimmermann note**

One American's Story

It was about 1:00 A.M. on April 6, 1917, and the members of the U.S. House of Representatives were tired. For the past 15 hours they had been debating President Wilson's request for a declaration of war against Germany. There was a breathless hush as Jeannette Rankin of Montana, the first woman elected to Congress, stood up. Rankin declared, "I want to stand by my country but I cannot vote for war. I vote no." Later she reflected on her action.

A PERSONAL VOICE JEANNETTE RANKIN

> **"I believe that the first vote I cast was the most significant vote and a most significant act on the part of women, because women are going to have to stop war. I felt at the time that the first woman [in Congress] should take the first stand, that the first time the first woman had a chance to say no to war she should say it."**
>
> —quoted in *Jeannette Rankin: First Lady in Congress*

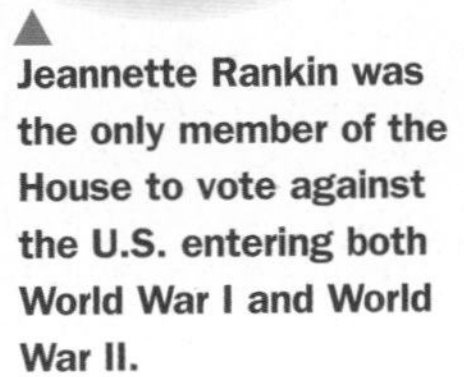

▲ Jeannette Rankin was the only member of the House to vote against the U.S. entering both World War I and World War II.

After much debate as to whether the United States should join the fight, Congress voted in favor of U.S. entry into World War I. With this decision, the government abandoned the neutrality that America had maintained for three years. What made the United States change its policy in 1917?

Causes of World War I

Although many Americans wanted to stay out of the war, several factors made American neutrality difficult to maintain. As an industrial and imperial power, the United States felt many of the same pressures that had led the nations of Europe into devastating warfare. Historians generally cite four long-term causes of the First World War: nationalism, imperialism, militarism, and the formation of a system of alliances.

NATIONALISM Throughout the 19th century, politics in the Western world were deeply influenced by the concept of **nationalism**—a devotion to the interests and culture of one's nation. Often, nationalism led to competitive and antagonistic rivalries among nations. In this atmosphere of competition, many feared Germany's growing power in Europe.

In addition, various ethnic groups resented domination by others and longed for their nations to become independent. Many ethnic groups looked to larger nations for protection. Russia regarded itself as the protector of Europe's Slavic peoples, no matter which government they lived under. Among these Slavic peoples were the Serbs. Serbia, located in the Balkans, was an independent nation, but millions of ethnic Serbs lived under the rule of Austria-Hungary. As a result, Russia and Austria-Hungary were rivals for influence over Serbia.

MAIN IDEA

Analyzing Causes
A How did nationalism and imperialism lead to conflict in Europe?

IMPERIALISM For many centuries, European nations had been building empires, slowly extending their economic and political control over various peoples of the world. Colonies supplied the European imperial powers with raw materials and provided markets for manufactured goods. As Germany industrialized, it competed with France and Britain in the contest for colonies. A

MILITARISM Empires were expensive to build and to defend. The growth of nationalism and imperialism led to increased military spending. Because each nation wanted stronger armed forces than those of any potential enemy, the imperial powers followed a policy of **militarism**—the development of armed forces and their use as a tool of diplomacy.

By 1890 the strongest nation on the European continent was Germany, which had set up an army reserve system that drafted and trained young men. Britain was not initially alarmed by Germany's military expansion. As an island nation, Britain had always relied on its navy for defense and protection of its shipping routes—and the British navy was the strongest in the world. However, in 1897, Wilhelm II, Germany's kaiser, or emperor, decided that his nation should also become a major sea power in order to compete more successfully against the British. Soon British and German shipyards competed to build the largest battleships and destroyers. France, Italy, Japan, and the United States quickly joined the naval arms race.

Vocabulary
alliance: a formal agreement or union between nations

ALLIANCE SYSTEM By 1907 there were two major defense alliances in Europe. The Triple Entente, later known as the **Allies,** consisted of France, Britain, and Russia. The Triple Alliance consisted of Germany, Austria-Hungary, and Italy.

◀ German Emperor Wilhelm II *(center)* marches with two of his generals, Hindenburg *(left)* and Ludendorff, during World War I.

Germany and Austria-Hungary, together with the Ottoman Empire—an empire of mostly Middle Eastern lands controlled by the Turks—were later known as the **Central Powers.** The alliances provided a measure of international security because nations were reluctant to disturb the balance of power. As it turned out, a spark set off a major conflict.

An Assassination Leads to War

That spark flared in the Balkan Peninsula, which was known as "the powder keg of Europe." In addition to the ethnic rivalries among the Balkan peoples, Europe's leading powers had interests there. Russia wanted access to the Mediterranean Sea. Germany wanted a rail link to the Ottoman Empire. Austria-Hungary, which had taken control of Bosnia in 1878, accused Serbia of subverting its rule over Bosnia. The "powder keg" was ready to explode.

In June 1914, **Archduke Franz Ferdinand,** heir to the Austrian throne, visited the Bosnian capital Sarajevo. As the royal entourage drove through the city, Serbian nationalist Gavrilo Princip stepped from the crowd and shot the Archduke and his wife Sophie. Princip was a member of the Black Hand, an organization promoting Serbian nationalism. The assassinations touched off a diplomatic crisis. On July 28, Austria-Hungary declared what was expected to be a short war against Serbia.

The alliance system pulled one nation after another into the conflict. On August 1, Germany, obligated by treaty to support Austria-Hungary, declared war on Russia. On August 3, Germany declared war on Russia's ally France. After Germany invaded Belgium, Britain declared war on Germany and Austria-Hungary. The Great War had begun. **B**

MAIN IDEA

Analyzing Effects

B Why were so many European nations pulled into the conflict?

NOW & THEN

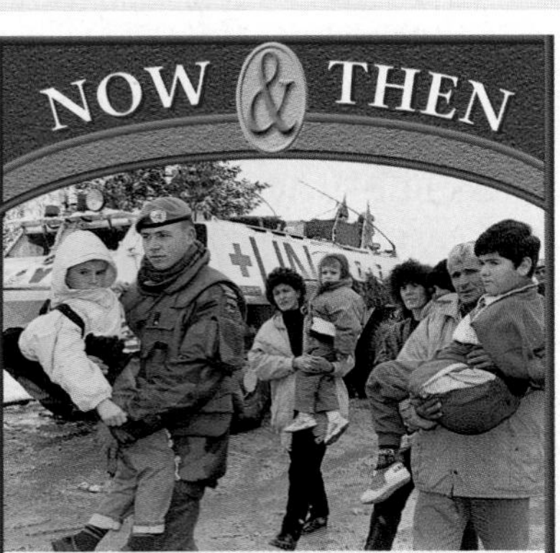

CRISIS IN THE BALKANS

After World War I, Bosnia became part of a country that eventually became known as Yugoslavia. Although Yugoslavia included various religious and ethnic groups, the government was dominated by Serbs.

In 1991, Yugoslavia broke apart, and Bosnia declared independence in 1992. However, Serbs wanted Bosnia to remain part of Serbian-controlled Yugoslavia.

A bloody civil war broke out. This war became notorious for the mass murder and deportation of Bosnian Muslims, a process known as "ethnic cleansing." In 1995, the United States helped negotiate a cease-fire.

But peace in the Balkans did not last. In the late 1990s, Albanians in the province of Kosovo also tried to break away from Serbia. Serbia's violent response, which included the "ethnic cleansing" of Albanians, prompted NATO to intervene. Today, peacekeepers in the Balkans struggle to control the continuing ethnic violence.

The Fighting Starts

On August 3, 1914, Germany invaded Belgium, following a strategy known as the Schlieffen Plan. This plan called for a holding action against Russia, combined with a quick drive through Belgium to Paris; after France had fallen, the two German armies would defeat Russia. As German troops swept across Belgium, thousands of civilians fled in terror. In Brussels, the Belgian capital, an American war correspondent described the first major refugee crisis of the 20th century.

Vocabulary

refugee: a person who flees in search of protection or shelter, as in times of war or religious persecution

A PERSONAL VOICE RICHARD HARDING DAVIS

"[We] found the side streets blocked with their carts. Into these they had thrown mattresses, or bundles of grain, and heaped upon them were families of three generations. Old men in blue smocks, white-haired and bent, old women in caps, the daughters dressed in their one best frock and hat, and clasping in their hands all that was left to them, all that they could stuff into a pillow-case or flour-sack. . . . Heart-broken, weary, hungry, they passed in an unending caravan."

—from *Hooray for Peace, Hurrah for War*

GEOGRAPHY SKILLBUILDER

1. **Location** About how many miles separated the city of Paris from German forces at the point of their closest approach?
2. **Place** Consider the geographical location of the Allies in relation to the Central Powers. What advantage might the Allies have had?

Unable to save Belgium, the Allies retreated to the Marne River in France, where they halted the German advance in September 1914. After struggling to outflank each other's armies, both sides dug in for a long siege. By the spring of 1915, two parallel systems of deep, rat-infested trenches crossed France from the Belgian coast to the Swiss Alps. German soldiers occupied one set of trenches, Allied soldiers the other. There were three main kinds of trenches—front line, support, and reserve. Soldiers spent a period of time in each kind of trench. Dugouts, or underground rooms, were used as officers' quarters and command posts. Between the trench complexes lay **"no man's land"**—a barren expanse of mud pockmarked with shell craters and filled with barbed wire. Periodically, the soldiers charged enemy lines, only to be mowed down by machine gun fire. C

MAIN IDEA

Drawing Conclusions

C Why do you think soldiers were rotated in the trenches?

The scale of slaughter was horrific. During the First Battle of the Somme—which began on July 1, 1916, and lasted until mid-November—the British suffered 60,000 casualties the first day alone. Final casualties totaled about 1.2 million, yet only about seven miles of ground changed hands. This bloody **trench warfare,** in which armies fought for mere yards of ground, continued for over three years. Elsewhere, the fighting was just as devastating and inconclusive.

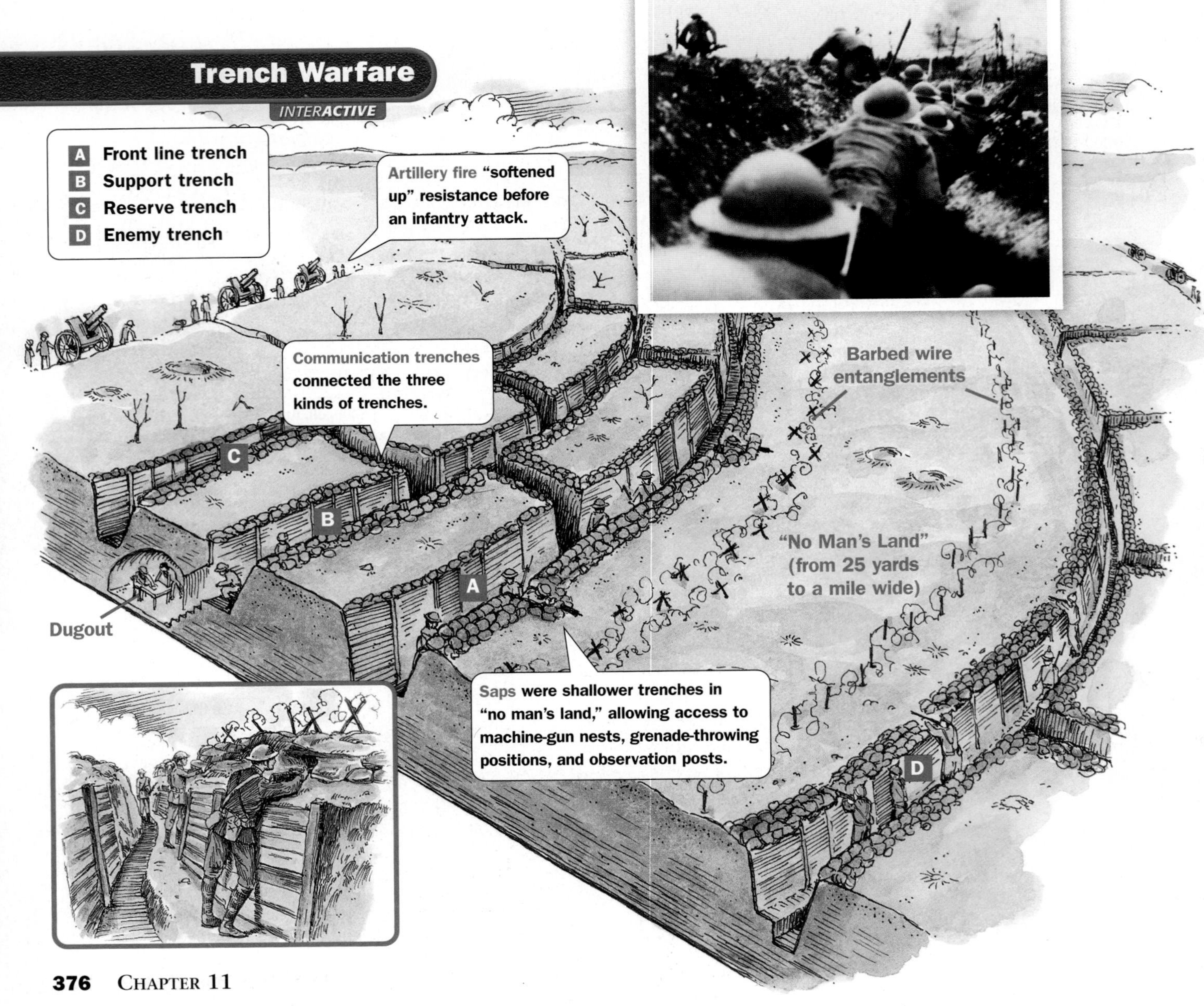
Trench Warfare
INTERACTIVE
A Front line trench
B Support trench
C Reserve trench
D Enemy trench
Artillery fire "softened up" resistance before an infantry attack.
Communication trenches connected the three kinds of trenches.
Barbed wire entanglements
"No Man's Land" (from 25 yards to a mile wide)
Dugout
Saps were shallower trenches in "no man's land," allowing access to machine-gun nests, grenade-throwing positions, and observation posts.
A
B
C
D

Americans Question Neutrality

In 1914, most Americans saw no reason to join a struggle 3,000 miles away. The war did not threaten American lives or property. This does not mean, however, that individual Americans were indifferent to who would win the war. Public opinion was strong—but divided.

DIVIDED LOYALTIES Socialists criticized the war as a capitalist and imperialist struggle between Germany and England to control markets and colonies in China, Africa, and the Middle East. Pacifists, such as lawyer and politician William Jennings Bryan, believed that war was evil and that the United States should set an example of peace to the world.

Many Americans simply did not want their sons to experience the horrors of warfare, as a hit song of 1915 conveyed.

> "I didn't raise my boy to be a soldier,
> I brought him up to be my pride and joy.
> Who dares to place a musket on his shoulder,
> To shoot some other mother's darling boy?"

Millions of naturalized U.S. citizens followed the war closely because they still had ties to the nations from which they had emigrated. For example, many Americans of German descent sympathized with Germany. Americans of Irish descent remembered the centuries of British oppression in Ireland and saw the war as a chance for Ireland to gain its independence.

Vocabulary
emigrate: to leave one's country or region to settle in another; to move

On the other hand, many Americans felt close to Britain because of a common ancestry and language as well as similar democratic institutions and legal systems. Germany's aggressive sweep through Belgium increased American sympathy for the Allies. The Germans attacked civilians, destroying villages, cathedrals, libraries, and even hospitals. Some atrocity stories—spread by British propaganda—later proved to be false, but enough proved true that one American magazine referred to Germany as "the bully of Europe."

More important, America's economic ties with the Allies were far stronger than its ties with the Central Powers. Before the war, American trade with Britain and France was more than double its trade with Germany. During the first two years of the war, America's transatlantic trade became even more lopsided, as the Allies flooded American manufacturers with orders for all sorts of war supplies, including dynamite, cannon powder, submarines, copper wire and tubing, and armored cars. The United States shipped millions of dollars of war supplies to the Allies, but requests kept coming. By 1915, the United States was experiencing a labor shortage. D

MAIN IDEA

Analyzing Motives
D Why did the United States begin to favor Britain and France?

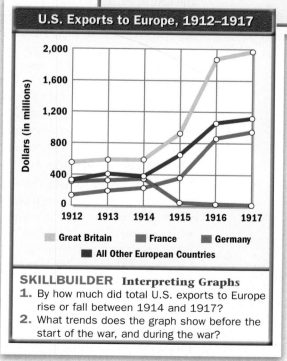

ECONOMIC BACKGROUND

TRADE ALLIANCES

Maintaining neutrality proved difficult for American businesses. Trade with Germany became increasingly risky. Shipments were often stopped by the British blockade. In addition, President Wilson and others spoke out against German atrocities and warned of the threat that the German Empire posed to democracy.

From 1912 to 1917, U.S. trade relationships with European countries shifted dramatically. From 1914 on, trade with the Allies quadrupled, while trade with Germany fell to near zero.

Also, by 1917, American banks had loaned $2.3 billion to the Allies, but only $27 million to the Central Powers. Many U.S. leaders, including Treasury Secretary William McAdoo, felt that American prosperity depended upon an Allied victory. (See *trade* on page R47 in the Economics Handbook.)

U.S. Exports to Europe, 1912–1917

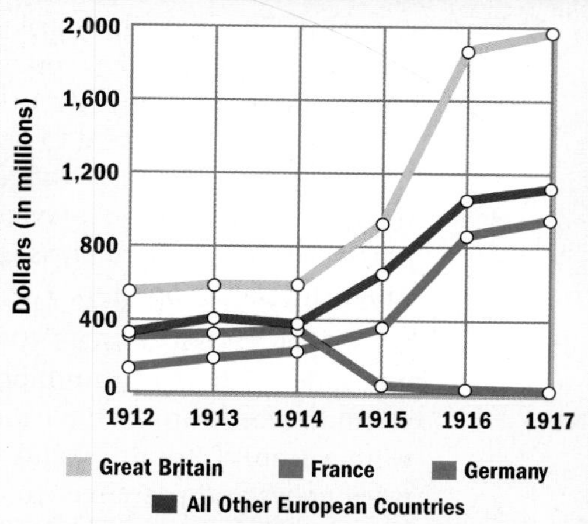

SKILLBUILDER Interpreting Graphs

1. By how much did total U.S. exports to Europe rise or fall between 1914 and 1917?
2. What trends does the graph show before the start of the war, and during the war?

This image of a U-boat crew machine-gunning helpless survivors of the *Lusitania* was clearly meant as propaganda. In fact, U-boats seldom lingered after an attack.

The War Hits Home

Although the majority of Americans favored victory for the Allies rather than the Central Powers, they did not want to join the Allies' fight. By 1917, however, America had mobilized for war against the Central Powers for two reasons: to ensure Allied repayment of debts to the United States and to prevent the Germans from threatening U.S. shipping.

THE BRITISH BLOCKADE As fighting on land continued, Britain began to make more use of its naval strength. It blockaded the German coast to prevent weapons and other military supplies from getting through. However, the British expanded the definition of contraband to include food. They also extended the blockade to neutral ports and mined the entire North Sea.

The results were two fold. First, American ships carrying goods for Germany refused to challenge the blockade and seldom reached their destination. Second, Germany found it increasingly difficult to import foodstuffs and fertilizers for crops. By 1917, famine stalked the country. An estimated 750,000 Germans starved to death as a result of the British blockade.

Americans had been angry at Britain's blockade, which threatened freedom of the seas and prevented American goods from reaching German ports. However, Germany's response to the blockade soon outraged American public opinion.

OCEAN STEAMSHIPS.

CUNARD

EUROPE VIA LIVERPOOL

LUSITANIA

Fastest and Largest Steamer now in Atlantic Service Sails SATURDAY, MAY 1, 10 A. M.

Transylvania, Fri., May 7, 5 P.M.
Orduna, - - Tues., May 18, 10 A.M.
Tuscania, - - Fri., May 21, 5 P.M.
LUSITANIA, Sat., May 29, 10 A.M.
Transylvania, Fri., June 4, 5 P.M.

Gibraltar–Genoa–Naples–Piraeus
S.S. Carpathia, Thur., May 13, Noon

ROUND THE WORLD TOURS
Through bookings to all principal Ports of the World.
Company's Office, 21-24 State St., N. Y.

NOTICE!

TRAVELLERS intending to embark on the Atlantic voyage are reminded that a state of war exists between Germany and her allies and Great Britain and her allies; that the zone of war includes the waters adjacent to the British Isles; that, in accordance with formal notice given by the Imperial German Government, vessels flying the flag of Great Britain, or of any of her allies, are liable to destruction in those waters and that travellers sailing in the war zone on ships of Great Britain or her allies do so at their own risk.

IMPERIAL GERMAN EMBASSY

WASHINGTON, D. C., APRIL 22, 1915.

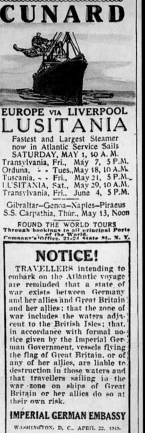

A newspaper ad for the *Lusitania* included a warning from the German Embassy.

GERMAN U–BOAT RESPONSE Germany responded to the British blockade with a counterblockade by U-boats (from *Unterseeboot*, the German word for a submarine). Any British or Allied ship found in the waters around Britain would be sunk—and it would not always be possible to warn crews and passengers of an attack.

One of the worst disasters occurred on May 7, 1915, when a U-boat sank the British liner ***Lusitania*** (lo͞o′sĭ-tā′nē-ə) off the southern coast of Ireland. Of the 1,198 persons lost, 128 were Americans. The Germans defended their action on the grounds that the liner carried ammunition. Despite Germany's explanation, Americans became outraged with Germany because of the loss of life. American public opinion turned against Germany and the Central Powers.

Despite this provocation, President Wilson ruled out a military response in favor of a sharp protest to Germany. Three months later, in August 1915, a U-boat sank another British liner, the *Arabic*, drowning two Americans. Again the United States protested, and this time Germany agreed not to sink any more passenger ships. But in March 1916 Germany broke its promise and torpedoed an unarmed French passenger steamer, the *Sussex*. The *Sussex* sank, and about 80 passengers, including Americans, were killed or injured. Once again the United States warned that it would break off diplomatic relations unless Germany changed its tactics. Again Germany agreed, but there was a condition: if the United States could not persuade Britain to lift its blockade against food and fertilizers, Germany would consider renewing unrestricted submarine warfare. E

MAIN IDEA

Analyzing Effects
E How did the German U-boat campaign affect U.S. public opinion?

THE 1916 ELECTION In November 1916 came the U.S. presidential election. The Democrats renominated Wilson, and the Republicans nominated Supreme Court Justice Charles Evans Hughes. Wilson campaigned on the slogan "He Kept Us Out of War." Hughes pledged to uphold America's right to freedom of the seas but also promised not to be too severe on Germany.

The election returns shifted from hour to hour. In fact, Hughes went to bed believing he had been elected. When a reporter tried to reach him with the news of Wilson's victory, an aide said, "The president can't be disturbed." "Well," replied the reporter, "when he wakes up, tell him he's no longer president."

▲ **Wilson campaign button**

The United States Declares War

After the election, Wilson tried to mediate between the warring alliances. The attempt failed. In a speech before the Senate in January 1917, the president called for "a peace without victory. . . . a peace between equals," in which neither side would impose harsh terms on the other. Wilson hoped that all nations would join in a "league for peace" that would work to extend democracy, maintain freedom of the seas, and reduce armaments.

GERMAN PROVOCATION The Germans ignored Wilson's calls for peace. Germany's leaders hoped to defeat Britain by resuming unrestricted submarine warfare. On January 31 the kaiser announced that U-boats would sink all ships in British waters—hostile or neutral—on sight. Wilson was stunned. The German decision meant that the United States would have to go to war. However, the president held back, saying that he would wait for "actual overt acts" before declaring war.

The overt acts came. First was the **Zimmermann note,** a telegram from the German foreign minister to the German ambassador in Mexico that was intercepted by British agents. The telegram proposed an alliance between Mexico and Germany and promised that if war with the United States broke out, Germany would support Mexico in recovering "lost territory in Texas, New Mexico, and Arizona." Next came the sinking of four unarmed American merchant ships, with a loss of 36 lives. F

Finally, events in Russia removed the last significant obstacle to direct U.S. involvement in the war. In March, the oppressive Russian monarchy was

MAIN IDEA

Making Inferences
F Why did the Zimmermann note alarm the U.S. government?

Alliances During WWI

Allies		Central Powers
Australia	India	Austria-Hungary
Belgium	Italy	Bulgaria
British Colonies	Japan	Germany
Canada & Newfoundland	Montenegro	Ottoman Empire
France	New Zealand	
French North Africa & French Colonies	Portugal	
Great Britain	Romania	
Greece	Russia	
	Serbia	
	South Africa	
	United States	

Although not all of the countries listed above sent troops into the war, they all joined the war on the Allied side at various times.

WORLD STAGE

REVOLUTION IN RUSSIA

At first, the Russians surprised the Germans by mobilizing rapidly. Russian troops advanced quickly into German territory but were turned back at the Battle of Tannenberg in August 1914.

Throughout 1915, the Russians endured defeats and continued to retreat. By the end of 1915 they had suffered about 2.5 million casualties. The war also caused massive bread shortages in Russia.

Revolutionaries ousted the czar in March 1917 and established a provisional government. In November, the Bolsheviks, led by Lenin and Trotsky, overthrew the provisional government. They set up a Communist state and sought peace with the Central Powers.

replaced with a representative government. Now supporters of American entry into the war could claim that this was a war of democracies against brutal monarchies.

AMERICA ACTS A light drizzle fell on Washington on April 2, 1917, as senators, representatives, ambassadors, members of the Supreme Court, and other guests crowded into the Capitol building to hear President Wilson deliver his war resolution.

A PERSONAL VOICE WOODROW WILSON

"Property can be paid for; the lives of peaceful and innocent people cannot be. The present German submarine warfare against commerce is a warfare against mankind. . . . We are glad . . . to fight . . . for the ultimate peace of the world and for the liberation of its peoples. . . . The world must be made safe for democracy. . . . We have no selfish ends to serve. We desire no conquest, no dominion. We seek no indemnities. . . . It is a fearful thing to lead this great peaceful people into war. . . . But the right is more precious than peace."

—quoted in *American Voices*

Congress passed the resolution a few days later. With the hope of neutrality finally shattered, U.S. troops would follow the stream of American money and munitions that had been heading to the Allies throughout the war. But Wilson's plea to make the world "safe for democracy" wasn't just political posturing. Indeed, Wilson and many Americans truly believed that the United States had to join the war to pave the way for a future order of peace and freedom. A resolved but anxious nation held its breath as the United States prepared for war.

ASSESSMENT

1. **TERMS & NAMES** For each term or name, write a sentence explaining its significance.
   - **nationalism**
   - **militarism**
   - **Allies**
   - **Central Powers**
   - **Archduke Franz Ferdinand**
   - **no man's land**
   - **trench warfare**
   - ***Lusitania***
   - **Zimmermann note**

MAIN IDEA

2. **TAKING NOTES**
   In a chart like the one shown, list the causes for the outbreak of World War I.

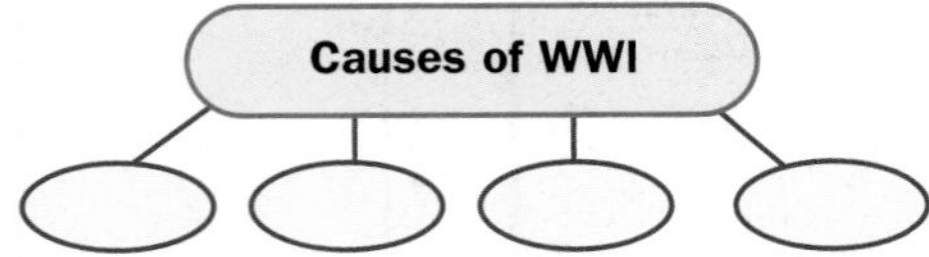

Which was the most significant cause? Explain your answer.

CRITICAL THINKING

3. **SYNTHESIZING**
   Describe some ways in which World War I threatened the lives of civilians on both sides of the Atlantic.

4. **SUMMARIZING**
   Why were America's ties with the Allies stronger than its ties with the Central Powers?

5. **ANALYZING ISSUES**
   Why do you think Germany escalated its U-boat attacks in 1917? **Think About:**
   - Germany's military buildup
   - the effects of the British blockade
   - Germany's reason for using submarine warfare

American Power Tips the Balance

MAIN IDEA

The United States mobilized a large army and navy to help the Allies achieve victory.

WHY IT MATTERS NOW

During World War I, the United States military evolved into the powerful fighting force that it remains today.

Terms & Names

- **Eddie Rickenbacker**
- **Selective Service Act**
- **convoy system**
- **American Expeditionary Force**
- **General John J. Pershing**
- **Alvin York**
- **conscientious objector**
- **armistice**

One American's Story

Eddie Rickenbacker, famous fighter pilot of World War I, was well known as a racecar driver before the war. He went to France as a driver but transferred to the aviation division. He learned to fly on his own time and eventually joined the U.S. Army Air Service. Rickenbacker repeatedly fought the dreaded Flying Circus—a German air squadron led by the "Red Baron," Manfred von Richthofen.

A Personal Voice EDDIE RICKENBACKER

"I put in six or seven hours of flying time each day. . . . My narrowest escape came at a time when I was fretting over the lack of action. . . . Guns began barking behind me, and sizzling tracers zipped by my head. . . . At least two planes were on my tail. . . .

They would expect me to dive. Instead I twisted upward in a corkscrew path called a 'chandelle.' I guessed right. As I went up, my two attackers came down, near enough for me to see their faces. I also saw the red noses on those Fokkers [German planes]. I was up against the Flying Circus again."

—*Rickenbacker: An Autobiography*

VIDEO

ACE OF ACES
Eddie Rickenbacker and the First World War

After engaging in 134 air battles and downing 26 enemy aircraft, Rickenbacker won fame as the Allied pilot with the most victories—"American ace of aces."

America Mobilizes

The United States was not prepared for war. Only 200,000 men were in service when war was declared, and few officers had combat experience. Drastic measures were needed to build an army large and modern enough to make an impact in Europe.

◀ Drafted men line up for service at Camp Travis in San Antonio, Texas, around 1917.

▲ James Montgomery Flagg's portrayal of Uncle Sam became the most famous recruiting poster in American history.

RAISING AN ARMY To meet the government's need for more fighting power, Congress passed the **Selective Service Act** in May 1917. The act required men to register with the government in order to be randomly selected for military service. By the end of 1918, 24 million men had registered under the act. Of this number, almost 3 million were called up. About 2 million troops reached Europe before the truce was signed, and three-fourths of them saw actual combat. Most of the inductees had not attended high school, and about one in five was foreign-born.

About 400,000 African Americans served in the armed forces. More than half of them served in France. African American soldiers served in segregated units and were excluded from the navy and marines. Most African Americans were assigned to noncombat duties, although there were exceptions. The all-black 369th Infantry Regiment saw more continuous duty on the front lines than any other American regiment. Two soldiers of the 369th, Henry Johnson and Needham Roberts, were the first Americans to receive France's highest military honor, the Croix de Guerre—the "cross of war."

Vocabulary
segregated: separated or isolated from others

The eight-month training period took place partly in the United States and partly in Europe. During this time the men put in 17-hour days on target practice, bayonet drill, kitchen duty, and cleaning up the grounds. Since real weapons were in short supply, soldiers often drilled with fake weapons—rocks instead of hand grenades, or wooden poles instead of rifles.

Although women were not allowed to enlist, the army reluctantly accepted women in the Army Corps of Nurses, but denied them army rank, pay, and benefits. Meanwhile, some 13,000 women accepted noncombat positions in the navy and marines, where they served as nurses, secretaries, and telephone operators, with full military rank. (A)

MAIN IDEA
Summarizing
(A) How did the United States raise an army for the war?

MASS PRODUCTION In addition to the vast army that had to be created and trained, the United States had to find a way to transport men, food, and equipment over thousands of miles of ocean. It was an immense task, made more difficult by German submarine activity, which by early 1917 had sunk twice as much ship tonnage as the Allies had built. In order to expand its fleet, the U.S. government took four crucial steps.

First, the government exempted many shipyard workers from the draft and gave others a "deferred" classification, delaying their participation in the draft. Second, the U.S. Chamber of Commerce joined in a public relations campaign to emphasize the importance of shipyard work. They distributed service flags to families of shipyard workers, just like the flags given to families of soldiers and sailors. They also urged automobile owners to give shipyard employees rides to and from work, since streetcars were so crowded. Third, shipyards used fabrication techniques. Instead of building an entire ship in the yard, standardized parts were built elsewhere and then assembled at the yard. This method reduced construction time substantially. As a result, on just one day—July 4, 1918—the United States launched 95 ships. Fourth, the government took over commercial and private ships and converted them for transatlantic war use. **B**

MAIN IDEA

Summarizing

B How did the United States expand its navy so quickly?

America Turns the Tide

German U-boat attacks on merchant ships in the Atlantic were a serious threat to the Allied war effort. American Vice Admiral William S. Sims convinced the British to try the **convoy system,** in which a heavy guard of destroyers escorted merchant ships back and forth across the Atlantic in groups. By fall of 1917, shipping losses had been cut in half.

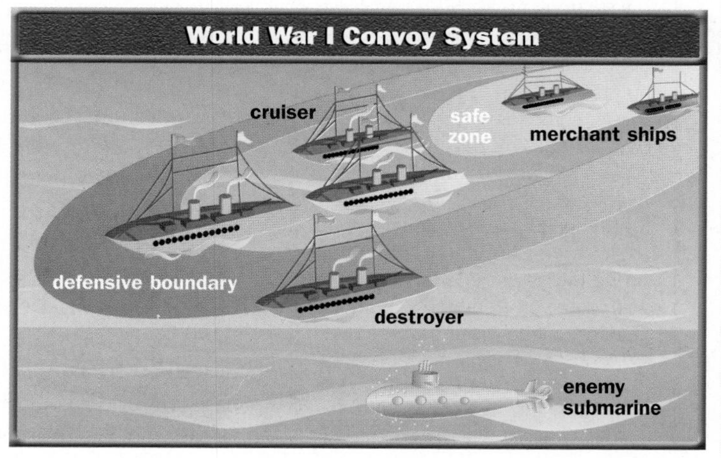

The U.S. Navy also helped lay a 230-mile barrier of mines across the North Sea from Scotland to Norway. The barrier was designed to bottle up the U-boats that sailed from German ports and keep them out of the Atlantic Ocean.

By early 1918 the Germans found it increasingly difficult to replace their losses and to staff their fleet with trained submariners. Of the almost 2 million Americans who sailed to Europe during the war, only 637 were lost to U-boat attacks.

FIGHTING IN EUROPE After two and a half years of fighting, the Allied forces were exhausted and demoralized. One of the main contributions that American troops made to the Allied war effort, apart from their numbers, was their freshness and enthusiasm. They were determined to hit the Germans hard. Twenty-two-year-old Joseph Douglas Lawrence, a U.S. Army lieutenant, remarked on the importance of American enthusiasm when he described his first impression of the trenches.

A PERSONAL VOICE JOSEPH DOUGLAS LAWRENCE

"I have never seen or heard of such an elaborate, complete line of defense as the British had built at this point. There was a trench with dugouts every three hundred yards from the front line in Ypres back four miles to and including Dirty Bucket. Everything was fronted with barbed wire and other entanglements. Artillery was concealed everywhere. Railroad tracks, narrow and standard gauge, reached from the trenches back into the zone of supply. Nothing had been neglected to hold this line, save only one important thing, enthusiasm among the troops, and that was the purpose of our presence."

—*Fighting Soldier: The AEF in 1918*

Lieutenant Joseph D. Lawrence

KEY PLAYER

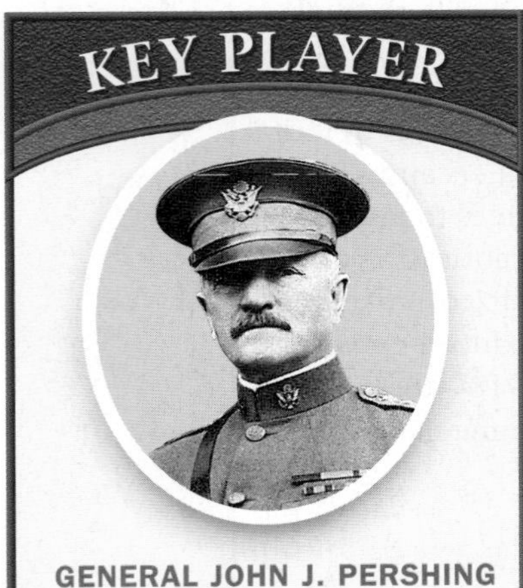

GENERAL JOHN J. PERSHING
1860–1948

When General Pershing, the commander of the American Expeditionary Force (AEF), arrived in France, he found that the Allies intended to use American troops simply as reinforcements. Pershing, however, urged that the AEF operate as an independent fighting force, under American command.

Pershing believed in aggressive combat and felt that three years of trench warfare had made the Allies too defensive. Under Pershing, American forces helped to stop the German advance, capturing important enemy positions. After the war, Pershing was made General of the Armies of the United States—the highest rank given to an officer.

Fighting "Over There"

The **American Expeditionary Force** (AEF), led by **General John J. Pershing,** included men from widely separated parts of the country. American infantrymen were nicknamed doughboys, possibly because of the white belts they wore, which they cleaned with pipe clay, or "dough." Most doughboys had never ventured far from the farms or small towns where they lived, and the sophisticated sights and sounds of Paris made a vivid impression. However, doughboys were also shocked by the unexpected horrors of the battlefield and astonished by the new weapons and tactics of modern warfare.

NEW WEAPONS The battlefields of World War I saw the first large-scale use of weapons that would become standard in modern war. Although some of these weapons were new, others, like the machine gun, had been so refined that they changed the nature of warfare. The two most innovative weapons were the tank and the airplane. Together, they heralded mechanized warfare, or warfare that relies on machines powered by gasoline and diesel engines. C

> **MAIN IDEA**
> **Forming Generalizations**
> C How did World War I change the nature of warfare?

Tanks ran on caterpillar treads and were built of steel so that bullets bounced off. The British first used tanks during the 1916 Battle of the Somme, but not very effectively. By 1917, the British had learned how to drive large numbers of tanks through barbed wire defenses, clearing a path for the infantry.

> **Background**
> When the U.S. entered the war, its air power was weak. Then, in July 1917, Congress appropriated a hefty $675 million to build an air force.

The early airplanes were so flimsy that at first both sides limited their use to scouting. After a while, the two sides used tanks to fire at enemy planes that were gathering information. Early dogfights, or individual air combats, like the one described by Eddie Rickenbacker, resembled duels. Pilots sat in their open cockpits and shot at each other with pistols. Because it was hard to fly a plane and shoot a pistol at the same time, planes began carrying mounted machine guns. But the planes' propeller blades kept getting in the way of the bullets. Then the Germans introduced an interrupter gear that permitted the stream of bullets to avoid the whirring blades.

TECHNOLOGY AT WAR

Both sides in World War I used new technology to attack more soldiers from greater distances than ever before. Aircraft and long-range guns were even used to fire on civilian targets—libraries, cathedrals, and city districts. The biggest guns could shell a city from 75 miles.

Machine Guns
Firepower increased to 600 rounds per minute.

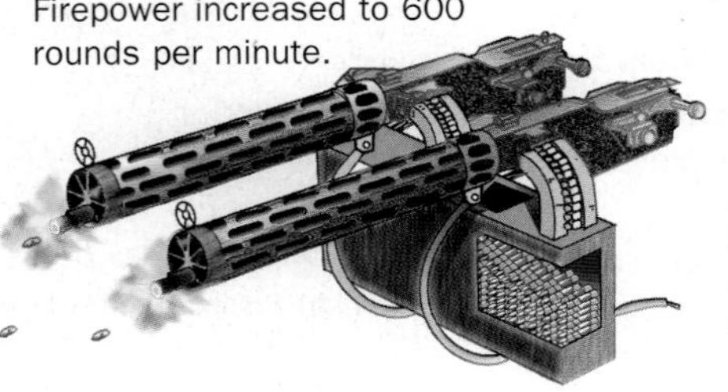

Airships and Airplanes
One of the most famous WWI planes, the British Sopwith Camel, had a front-mounted machine gun for "dogfights." Planes were also loaded with bombs, as were the floating gas-filled "airships" called zeppelins.

Meanwhile, airplanes were built to travel faster and carry heavy bomb loads. By 1918 the British had built up a strategic bomber force of 22,000 planes with which to attack German weapons factories and army bases.

Observation balloons were used extensively by both sides in the war in Europe. Balloons were so important strategically that they were often protected by aircraft flying close by, and they became prime targets for Rickenbacker and other ace pilots.

The War Introduces New Hazards

The new weapons and tactics of World War I led to horrific injuries and hazards. The fighting men were surrounded by filth, lice, rats, and polluted water that caused dysentery. They inhaled poison gas and smelled the stench of decaying bodies. They suffered from lack of sleep. Constant bombardments and other experiences often led to battle fatigue and "shell shock," a term coined during World War I to describe a complete emotional collapse from which many never recovered.

Physical problems included a disease called trench foot, caused by standing in cold wet trenches for long periods of time without changing into dry socks or boots. First the toes would turn red or blue, then they would become numb, and finally they would start to rot. The only solution was to amputate the toes, and in some cases the entire foot. A painful infection of the gums and throat, called trench mouth, was also common among the soldiers. **D**

MAIN IDEA

Analyzing Effects
D What were the physical and psychological effects of this new kind of warfare?

Red Cross ambulances, often staffed by American volunteers, carried the wounded from the battlefield to the hospital. An American nurse named Florence Bullard recounted her experience in a hospital near the front in 1918.

A PERSONAL VOICE FLORENCE BULLARD

"The Army is only twelve miles away from us and only the wounded that are too severely injured to live to be carried a little farther are brought here. . . . Side by side I have Americans, English, Scotch, Irish, and French, and apart in the corners are Boche [Germans]. They have to watch each other die side by side. I am sent for everywhere—in the . . . operating-room, the dressing-room, and back again to the rows of men. . . . The cannon goes day and night and the shells are breaking over and around us. . . . I have had to write many sad letters to American mothers. I wonder if it will ever end."

—quoted in *Over There: The Story of America's First Great Overseas Crusade*

In fact, the end was near, as German forces mounted a final offensive.

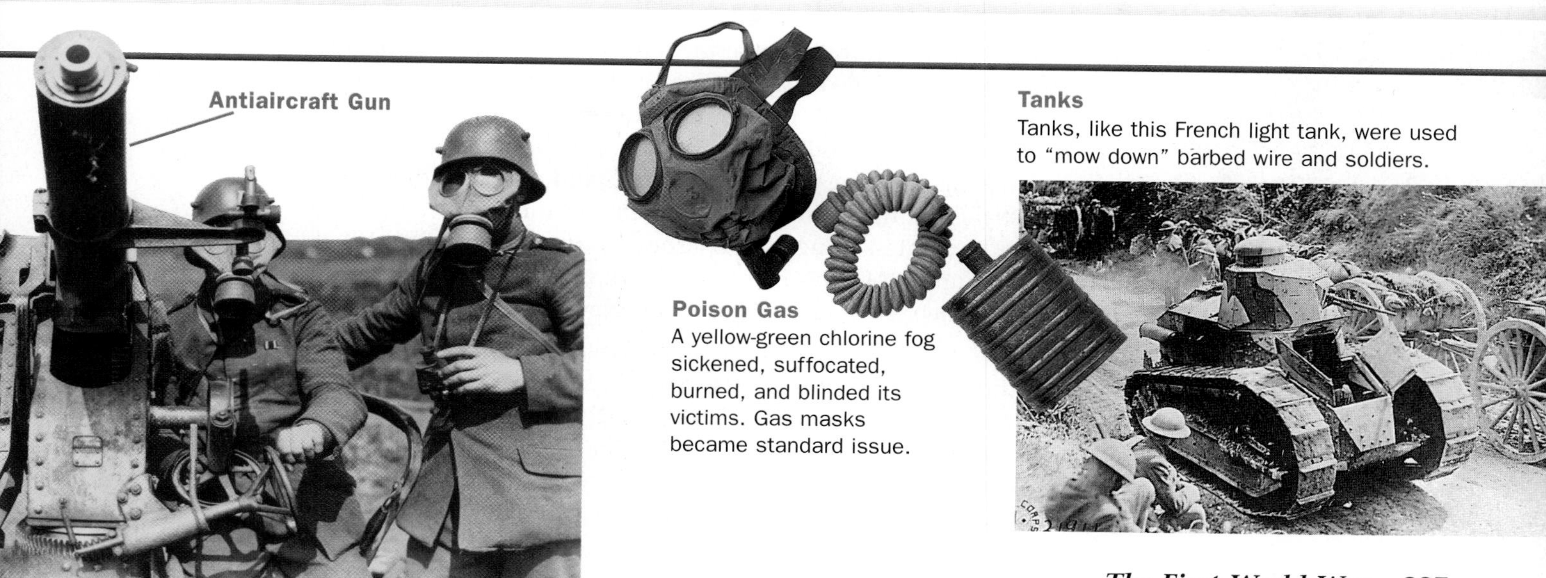

Poison Gas
A yellow-green chlorine fog sickened, suffocated, burned, and blinded its victims. Gas masks became standard issue.

Tanks
Tanks, like this French light tank, were used to "mow down" barbed wire and soldiers.

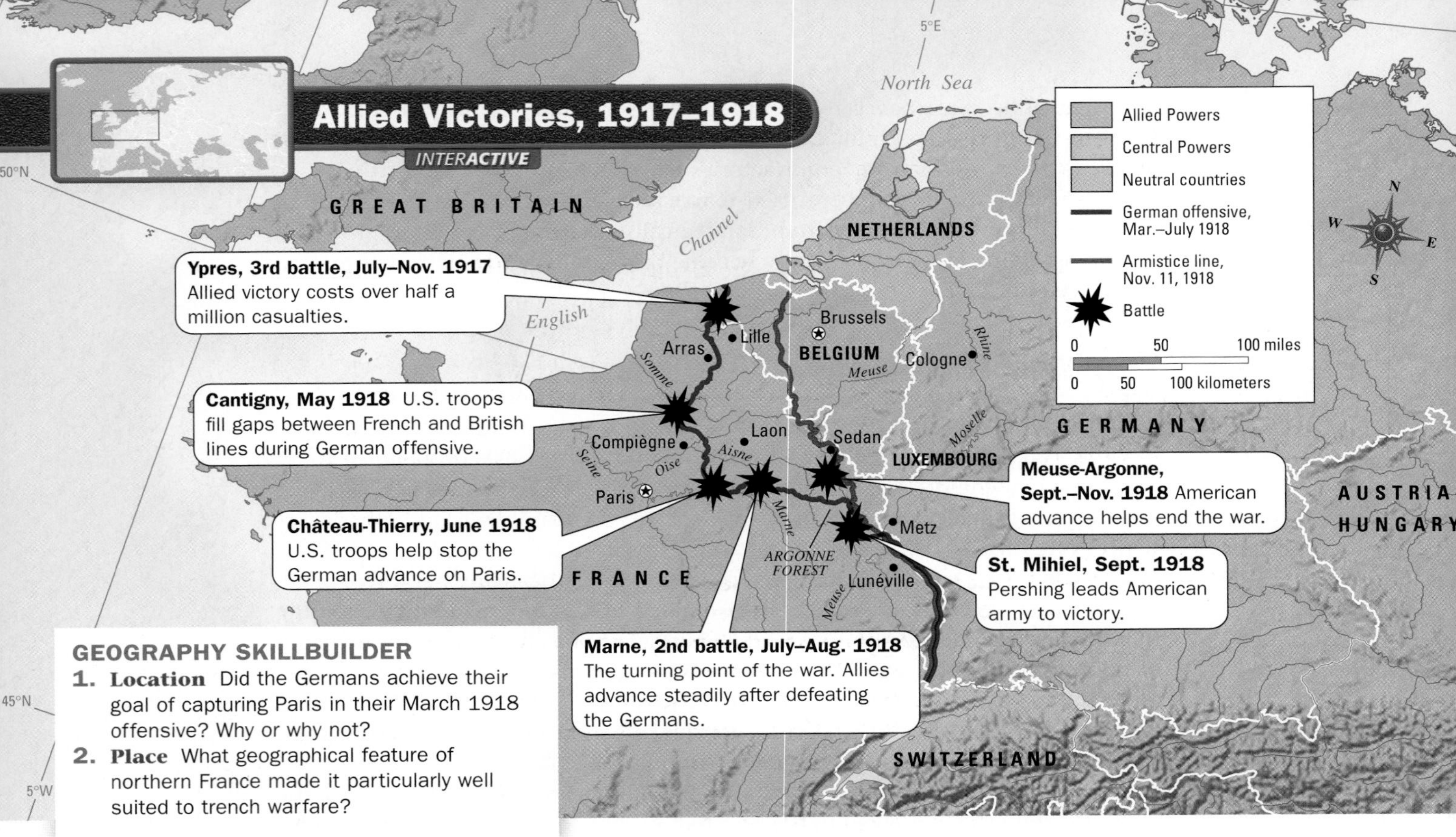

GEOGRAPHY SKILLBUILDER

1. **Location** Did the Germans achieve their goal of capturing Paris in their March 1918 offensive? Why or why not?
2. **Place** What geographical feature of northern France made it particularly well suited to trench warfare?

American Troops Go on the Offensive

When Russia pulled out of the war in 1917, the Germans shifted their armies from the eastern front to the western front in France. By May they were within 50 miles of Paris. The Americans arrived just in time to help stop the German advance at Cantigny in France. Several weeks later, U.S. troops played a major role in throwing back German attacks at Château-Thierry and Belleau Wood. In July and August, they helped win the Second Battle of the Marne. The tide had turned against the Central Powers. In September, U.S. soldiers began to mount offensives against the Germans at Saint-Mihiel and in the Meuse-Argonne area. E

MAIN IDEA

Drawing Conclusions
E How did American forces help the Allies win the war?

AMERICAN WAR HERO During the fighting in the Meuse-Argonne area, one of America's greatest war heroes, **Alvin York,** became famous. A redheaded mountaineer and blacksmith from Tennessee, York sought exemption as a **conscientious objector,** a person who opposes warfare on moral grounds, pointing out that the Bible says, "Thou shalt not kill."

York eventually decided that it was morally acceptable to fight if the cause was just. On October 8, 1918, armed only with a rifle and a revolver, York killed 25 Germans and—with six other doughboys—captured 132 prisoners. General Pershing called him the outstanding soldier of the AEF, while Marshal Foch, the commander of Allied forces in Europe, described his feat as "the greatest thing accomplished by any private soldier of all the armies of Europe." For his heroic acts, York was promoted to sergeant and became a celebrity when he returned to the United States.

"Bullets were cracking just over my head."
SERGEANT YORK

THE COLLAPSE OF GERMANY On November 3, 1918, Austria-Hungary surrendered to the Allies. That same day, German sailors mutinied against government authority. The mutiny spread quickly. Everywhere in Germany, groups of soldiers and workers organized revolutionary councils. On November 9, socialist leaders in the capital, Berlin, established a German republic. The kaiser gave up the throne.

Although there were no Allied soldiers on German territory and no truly decisive battle had been fought, the Germans were too exhausted to continue fighting. So at the eleventh hour, on the eleventh day, in the eleventh month of 1918, Germany agreed to a cease-fire and signed the **armistice,** or truce, that ended the war.

THE FINAL TOLL World War I was the bloodiest war in history up to that time. Deaths numbered about 22 million, more than half of them civilians. In addition, 20 million people were wounded, and 10 million more became refugees. The direct economic costs of the war may have been about $338 billion. The United States lost 48,000 men in battle, with another 62,000 dying of disease. More than 200,000 Americans were wounded.

For the Allies, news of the armistice brought great relief. Private John Barkley described the reaction to the news.

A PERSONAL VOICE JOHN L. BARKLEY

"About 9 o'clock in the evening we heard wild commotion in the little town. The French people, old and young, were running through the streets. Old men and women we'd seen sitting around their houses too feeble to move, were out in the streets yelling, 'Vive la France! Vive la France! Vive l'America!'. . . .

Down the street came a soldier. He was telling everybody the armistice had been signed. I said, 'What's an armistice?' It sounded like some kind of machine to me. The other boys around there didn't know what it meant either.

When the official word came through that it meant peace, we couldn't believe it. Finally Jesse said, 'Well kid, I guess it really does mean the war is over.'

I said, 'I just can't believe it's true.'

But it was."

—*No Hard Feelings*

Across the Atlantic, Americans also rejoiced at the news. Many now expected life to return to normal. However, people found their lives at home changed almost as much as the lives of those who had fought in Europe.

ASSESSMENT

1. **TERMS & NAMES** For each term or name, write a sentence explaining its significance.
   - **Eddie Rickenbacker**
   - **Selective Service Act**
   - **convoy system**
   - **American Expeditionary Force**
   - **General John J. Pershing**
   - **Alvin York**
   - **conscientious objector**
   - **armistice**

MAIN IDEA

2. **TAKING NOTES** Fill in a web like the one below to show how Americans responded to the war.

Why was the entire population affected by America's entry into World War I?

CRITICAL THINKING

3. **DRAWING CONCLUSIONS** In what ways did WWI represent a frightening new kind of warfare? **Think About:**
   - the casualty figures
   - new military technology
   - shell shock

4. **ANALYZING VISUAL SOURCES** This World War I poster shows the role of non-combatants overseas. What is the message in this propaganda poster?

SECTION 3

The War at Home

MAIN IDEA

World War I spurred social, political, and economic change in the United States.

WHY IT MATTERS NOW

Such changes increased government powers and expanded economic opportunities.

Terms & Names

- War Industries Board
- Bernard M. Baruch
- propaganda
- George Creel
- Espionage and Sedition Acts
- Great Migration

One American's Story

▲ Harriot Stanton Blatch followed in the footsteps of her famous mother, Elizabeth Cady Stanton.

The suffragist Harriot Stanton Blatch visited a munitions plant in New Jersey during World War I and proudly described women at work.

A PERSONAL VOICE HARRIOT STANTON BLATCH

"**The day I visited the place, in one of the largest shops women had only just been put on the work, but it was expected that in less than a month they would be found handling all of the twelve hundred machines under that one roof alone. The skill of the women staggers one. After a week or two they master the operations on the 'turret,' gauging and routing machines. The best worker on the 'facing' machine is a woman. She is a piece worker, as many of the women are. . . . This woman earned, the day I saw her, five dollars and forty cents. She tossed about the fuse parts, and played with that machine, as I would with a baby.**"

—quoted in *We, the American Women*

Before World War I, women had been excluded from many jobs. However, the wartime need for labor brought over a million more women into the work force. For women, as for the rest of society, World War I brought about far-reaching changes.

Congress Gives Power to Wilson

Winning the war was not a job for American soldiers alone. As Secretary of War Newton Baker said, "War is no longer Samson with his shield and spear and sword, and David with his sling. It is the conflict of smokestacks now, the combat of the driving wheel and the engine." Because World War I was such an immense conflict, the entire economy had to be refocused on the war effort. The shift from producing consumer goods to producing war supplies was too complicated and important a job for private industry to handle on its own, so business and government collaborated in the effort. In the process, the power of government was greatly expanded. Congress gave President Wilson direct control over much of the economy, including the power to fix prices and to regulate—even to nationalize—certain war-related industries.

WAR INDUSTRIES BOARD The main regulatory body was the **War Industries Board** (WIB). It was established in 1917 and reorganized in 1918 under the leadership of **Bernard M. Baruch** (bə-ro͞ok′), a prosperous businessman. The board encouraged companies to use mass-production techniques to increase efficiency. It also urged them to eliminate waste by standardizing products—for instance, by making only 5 colors of typewriter ribbons instead of 150. The WIB set production quotas and allocated raw materials.

Background
In 1913 Henry Ford speeded up factory production with a constantly moving assembly line. Wartime production spread this technique throughout the country.

Under the WIB, industrial production in the United States increased by about 20 percent. However, the WIB applied price controls only at the wholesale level. As a result, retail prices soared, and in 1918 they were almost double what they had been before the war. Corporate profits soared as well, especially in such industries as chemicals, meatpacking, oil, and steel.

The WIB was not the only federal agency to regulate the economy during the war. The Railroad Administration controlled the railroads, and the Fuel Administration monitored coal supplies and rationed gasoline and heating oil. In addition, many people adopted "gasless Sundays" and "lightless nights" to conserve fuel. In March 1918, the Fuel Administration introduced another conservation measure: daylight-saving time, which had first been proposed by Benjamin Franklin in the 1770s as a way to take advantage of the longer days of summer.

WAR ECONOMY Wages in most industries rose during the war years. Hourly wages for blue-collar workers—those in the metal trades, shipbuilding, and meatpacking, for example—rose by about 20 percent. A household's income, however, was largely undercut by rising food prices and housing costs.

By contrast, stockholders in large corporations saw enormous profits. One industrial manufacturer, the DuPont Company, saw its stock multiply in value 1,600 percent between 1914 and 1918. By that time the company was earning a $68-million yearly profit. As a result of the uneven pay between labor and management, increasing work hours, child labor, and dangerously "sped-up" conditions, unions boomed. Union membership climbed from about 2.5 million in 1916 to more than 4 million in 1919. More than 6,000 strikes broke out during the war months.

To deal with disputes between management and labor, President Wilson established the National War Labor Board in 1918. Workers who refused to obey board decisions could lose their draft exemptions. "Work or fight," the board told them. However, the board also worked to improve factory conditions. It pushed for an eight-hour workday, promoted safety inspections, and enforced the child labor ban. **A**

MAIN IDEA
Making Inferences
A Why would labor disputes affect the war effort?

FOOD ADMINISTRATION To help produce and conserve food, Wilson set up the Food Administration under Herbert Hoover. Instead of rationing food, he called on people to follow the "gospel of the clean plate." He declared one day a week "meatless," another "sweetless," two days "wheatless," and two other days "porkless." Restaurants removed sugar bowls from the table and served bread only after the first course.

The War Economy, 1914–1920

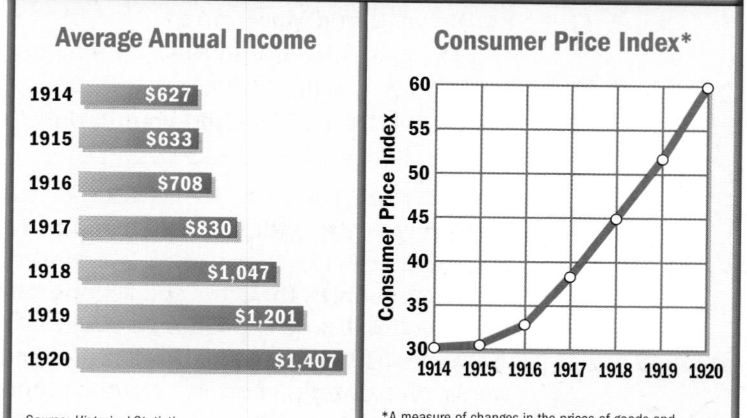

Average Annual Income

Year	Income
1914	$627
1915	$633
1916	$708
1917	$830
1918	$1,047
1919	$1,201
1920	$1,407

Source: *Historical Statistics of the United States*

Consumer Price Index*

Consumer Price Index
60
55
50
45
40
35
30
1914 1915 1916 1917 1918 1919 1920

*A measure of changes in the prices of goods and services commonly bought by consumers; see Economics Handbook, page R39.

SKILLBUILDER Interpreting Graphs

1. How did the rise in average annual income compare with the rise in prices from 1914 to 1920?
2. How might the combined change in wages and prices affect a working family?

A Japanese-American family tends a victory garden in New York City in 1917.

Food *is*
Ammunition-
Don't waste it.

A wartime poster encourages Americans to conserve resources.

Homeowners planted "victory gardens" in their yards. Schoolchildren spent their after-school hours growing tomatoes and cucumbers in public parks. As a result of these and similar efforts, American food shipments to the Allies tripled. Hoover also set a high government price on wheat and other staples. Farmers responded by putting an additional 40 million acres into production. In the process, they increased their income by almost 30 percent.

Selling the War

Once the government had extended its control over the economy, it was faced with two major tasks: raising money and convincing the public to support the war.

WAR FINANCING The United States spent about $35.5 billion on the war effort. The government raised about one-third of this amount through taxes, including a progressive income tax (which taxed high incomes at a higher rate than low incomes), a war-profits tax, and higher excise taxes on tobacco, liquor, and luxury goods. It raised the rest through public borrowing by selling "Liberty Loan" and "Victory Loan" bonds.

The government sold bonds through tens of thousands of volunteers. Movie stars spoke at rallies in factories, in schools, and on street corners. As Treasury Secretary William G. McAdoo put it, only "a friend of Germany" would refuse to buy war bonds. B

MAIN IDEA

Summarizing

B How did the government raise money for the war effort?

COMMITTEE ON PUBLIC INFORMATION To popularize the war, the government set up the nation's first **propaganda** agency, the Committee on Public Information (CPI). Propaganda is a kind of biased communication designed to influence people's thoughts and actions. The head of the CPI was a former muckraking journalist named **George Creel.**

Creel persuaded the nation's artists and advertising agencies to create thousands of paintings, posters, cartoons, and sculptures promoting the war. He recruited some 75,000 men to serve as "Four-Minute Men," who spoke about everything relating to the war: the draft, rationing, bond drives, victory gardens, and topics such as "Why We Are Fighting" and "The Meaning of America."

Nor did Creel neglect the written word. He ordered a printing of almost 25 million copies of "How the War Came to America"—which included Wilson's war message—in English and other languages. He distributed some 75 million pamphlets, booklets, and leaflets, many with the enthusiastic help of the Boy

Scouts. Creel's propaganda campaign was highly effective. However, while the campaign promoted patriotism, it also inflamed hatred and violations of the civil liberties of certain ethnic groups and opponents of the war.

Attacks on Civil Liberties Increase

Early in 1917, President Wilson expressed his fears about the consequences of war hysteria.

> **A PERSONAL VOICE** WOODROW WILSON
>
> **"Once lead this people into war and they'll forget there ever was such a thing as tolerance. To fight you must be brutal and ruthless, and the spirit of ruthless brutality will enter into the very fiber of our national life, infecting Congress, the courts, the policeman on the beat, the man in the street. Conformity would be the only virtue, and every man who refused to conform would have to pay the penalty."**
>
> —quoted in *Cobb of "The World"*

The president's prediction came true. As soon as war was declared, conformity indeed became the order of the day. Attacks on civil liberties, both unofficial and official, erupted.

MAIN IDEA

Developing Historical Perspective
C What effect did the war have on the lives of recent immigrants?

ANTI-IMMIGRANT HYSTERIA The main targets of these attacks were Americans who had emigrated from other nations, especially those from Germany and Austria-Hungary. The most bitter attacks were directed against the nearly 2 million Americans who had been born in Germany, but other foreign-born persons and Americans of German descent suffered as well. **C**

Many Americans with German names lost their jobs. Orchestras refused to play the music of Mozart, Bach, Beethoven, and Brahms. Some towns with German names changed them. Schools stopped teaching the German language, and librarians removed books by German authors from the shelves. People even resorted to violence against German Americans, flogging them or smearing them

Analyzing *Political Cartoons*

THE ENEMY WITHIN

After the United States entered the war, government propaganda helped inflame prejudice against recent immigrants. In the suspicious atmosphere of the time, conspiracy theories flourished, and foreign spies were believed to be everywhere. This cartoon reveals the hysteria that gripped the country in 1917.

SKILLBUILDER Analyzing Political Cartoons

1. What is happening in this cartoon?
2. What does the cartoonist suggest will happen to "enemy aliens"?

SEE SKILLBUILDER HANDBOOK, PAGE R24.

with tar and feathers. A mob in Collinsville, Illinois, wrapped a German flag around a German-born miner named Robert Prager and lynched him. A jury cleared the mob's leader.

Finally, in a burst of anti-German fervor, Americans changed the name of German measles to "liberty measles." Hamburger—named after the German city of Hamburg—became "Salisbury steak" or "liberty sandwich," depending on whether you were buying it in a store or eating it in a restaurant. Sauerkraut was renamed "liberty cabbage," and dachshunds turned into "liberty pups."

ESPIONAGE AND SEDITION ACTS In June 1917 Congress passed the Espionage Act, and in May 1918 it passed the Sedition Act. Under the **Espionage and Sedition Acts** a person could be fined up to $10,000 and sentenced to 20 years in jail for interfering with the war effort or for saying anything disloyal, profane, or abusive about the government or the war effort.

Vocabulary
sedition: rebellion against one's government; treason

Like the Alien and Sedition Acts of 1798, these laws clearly violated the spirit of the First Amendment. Their passage led to over 2,000 prosecutions for loosely defined antiwar activities; of these, over half resulted in convictions. Newspapers and magazines that opposed the war or criticized any of the Allies lost their mailing privileges. The House of Representatives refused to seat Victor Berger, a socialist congressman from Wisconsin, because of his antiwar views. Columbia University fired a distinguished psychologist because he opposed the war. A colleague who supported the war thereupon resigned in protest, saying, "If we have to suppress everything we don't like to hear, this country is resting on a pretty wobbly basis."

The Espionage and Sedition Acts targeted socialists and labor leaders. Eugene V. Debs was handed a ten-year prison sentence for speaking out against the war and the draft. The anarchist Emma Goldman received a two-year prison sentence and a $10,000 fine for organizing the No Conscription League. When she left jail, the authorities deported her to Russia. "Big Bill" Haywood and other leaders of the Industrial Workers of the World (IWW) were accused of sabotaging the war effort because they urged workers to strike for better conditions and higher pay. Haywood was sentenced to a long prison term. (He later skipped bail and fled to Russia.) Under such federal pressure, the IWW faded away. D

MAIN IDEA

Analyzing Effects
D What impact did the Espionage and Sedition Acts have on free speech?

▲ **This Industrial Workers of the World (IWW) sticker encourages workers to join the union.**

The War Encourages Social Change

Wars often unleash powerful social forces. The period of World War I was no exception; important changes transformed the lives of African Americans and women.

AFRICAN AMERICANS AND THE WAR Black public opinion about the war was divided. On one side were people like W. E. B. Du Bois, who believed that blacks should support the war effort.

A PERSONAL VOICE W. E. B. DU BOIS

"That which the German power represents today spells death to the aspirations of Negroes and all darker races for equality, freedom and democracy. . . . Let us, while this war lasts, forget our special grievances and close our ranks shoulder to shoulder with our own white fellow citizens and the allied nations that are fighting for democracy."

—"Close Ranks"

W. E. B. Du Bois ▶

Du Bois believed that African-American support for the war would strengthen calls for racial justice. In contrast, William Monroe Trotter, founder of the *Boston Guardian*, believed that victims of racism should not support a racist government. Trotter condemned Du Bois's accommodationist approach and favored protest instead. Nevertheless, despite grievances over continued racial inequality in the United States, most African Americans backed the war.

THE GREAT MIGRATION In concrete terms, the greatest effect of the First World War on African Americans' lives was that it accelerated the **Great Migration,** the large-scale movement of hundreds of thousands of Southern blacks to cities in the North. This great population shift had already begun before the war in the late 19th century, when African Americans trickled northward to escape the Jim Crow South—but after the turn of the century, the trickle became a tidal wave.

Several factors contributed to the tremendous increase in black migration. First, many African Americans sought to escape racial discrimination in the South, which made it hard to make a living and often threatened their lives. Also, a boll weevil infestation, aided by floods and droughts, had ruined much of the South's cotton fields. In the North, there were more job opportunities. For example, Henry Ford opened his automobile assembly line to black workers in 1914. The outbreak of World War I and the drop in European immigration increased job opportunities for African Americans in steel mills, munitions plants, and stockyards. Northern manufacturers sent recruiting agents to distribute free railroad passes through the South. In addition, the publisher of the black-owned newspaper *Chicago Defender* bombarded Southern blacks with articles contrasting Dixieland lynchings with the prosperity of African Americans in the North. E

MAIN IDEA

Making Inferences

E How did the war open opportunities for African Americans?

History Through **Art**

THE MIGRATION OF THE NEGRO, PANEL NO. 1 (1940–41)

This painting by Jacob Lawrence shows three of the most common destinations for African Americans leaving the South. **Why do you think the artist has not shown any individual facial features?**

HISTORICAL SPOTLIGHT

RACE RIOTS

Racial prejudice against African Americans in the North sometimes took violent forms. In July 1917, a race riot exploded in East St. Louis, Illinois. White workers, furious over the hiring of African Americans as strikebreakers at a munitions plant, rampaged through the streets. Forty blacks and nine whites died.

Another riot erupted in July 1919 in Chicago when a 17-year-old African American swam from the water off a "black beach" to the water off a "white beach." There, white bathers threw rocks at him until he drowned.

African Americans retaliated, and several riots broke out in the city. Order was restored after several days of violence that involved about 10,000 people.

However, racial prejudice against African Americans also existed in the North. The press of new migrants to Northern cities caused overcrowding and intensified racial tensions.

Nevertheless, between 1910 and 1930, hundreds of thousands of African Americans migrated to such cities as Chicago, New York, and Philadelphia. Author Richard Wright described the great exodus.

A PERSONAL VOICE RICHARD WRIGHT

"We are bitter no more; we are leaving! We are leaving our homes, pulling up stakes to move on. We look up at the high southern sky and remember all the sunshine and all the rain and we feel a sense of loss, but we are leaving. We look out at the wide green fields which our eyes saw when we first came into the world and we feel full of regret, but we are leaving. We scan the kind black faces we have looked upon since we first saw the light of day, and, though pain is in our hearts, we are leaving. We take one last furtive look over our shoulders to the Big House—high upon a hill beyond the railroad tracks—where the Lord of the Land lives, and we feel glad, for we are leaving."

—quoted in *12 Million Black Voices*

WOMEN IN THE WAR While African Americans began new lives, women moved into jobs that had been held exclusively by men. They became railroad workers, cooks, dockworkers, and bricklayers. They mined coal and took part in shipbuilding. At the same time, women continued to fill more traditional jobs as nurses, clerks, and teachers. Many women worked as volunteers, serving at Red Cross facilities and encouraging the sale of bonds and the planting of victory gardens. Other women, such as Jane Addams, were active in the peace movement. Addams helped found the Women's Peace Party in 1915 and remained a pacifist even after the United States entered the war. (F)

MAIN IDEA

Analyzing Effects

(F) What effect did the war have on women's lives?

President Wilson acknowledged, "The services of women during the supreme crisis have been of the most signal usefulness and distinction; it is high time that part of our debt should be acknowledged." While acknowledgment of that debt did not include equal pay for equal work, it did help bolster public support for woman suffrage. In 1919, Congress finally passed the Nineteenth Amendment, granting women the right to vote. In 1920 the amendment was ratified by the states.

Women worked in a variety of jobs during the war. Here, women assemble an aircraft wing.

THE FLU EPIDEMIC In the fall of 1918, the United States suffered a home-front crisis when an international flu epidemic affected about one-quarter of the U.S. population. The effect of the epidemic on the economy was devastating. Mines shut down, telephone service was cut in half, and factories and offices staggered working hours to avoid contagion. Cities ran short of coffins, and the corpses of poor people lay unburied for as long as a week. The mysterious illness seemed to strike people who were otherwise in the best of health, and death could come in a matter of days. Doctors did not know what to do, other than to recommend cleanliness and quarantine. One epidemic survivor recalled that "so many people died from the flu they just rang the bells; they didn't dare take [corpses] into the church."

New York City street cleaners wore masks to avoid catching influenza. ▼

In the army, where living conditions allowed contagious illnesses to spread rapidly, more than a quarter of the soldiers caught the disease. In some AEF units, one-third of the troops died. Germans fell victim in even larger numbers than the Allies. Possibly spread around the world by soldiers, the epidemic killed about 500,000 Americans before it disappeared in 1919. Historians believe that the influenza virus killed as many as 30 million people worldwide. G

MAIN IDEA

Making Inferences

G How did wartime conditions help spread the flu?

World War I brought death and disease to millions but, like the flu epidemic, the war also came to a sudden end. After four years of slaughter and destruction, the time had come to forge a peace settlement. Americans hoped that this "war to end all wars" would do just that. Leaders of the victorious nations gathered at Versailles outside Paris to work out the terms of peace, and President Wilson traveled to Europe to ensure it.

SECTION 3 ASSESSMENT

1. **TERMS & NAMES** For each term or name, write a sentence explaining its significance.
   - **War Industries Board**
   - **Bernard M. Baruch**
   - **propaganda**
   - **George Creel**
   - **Espionage and Sedition Acts**
   - **Great Migration**

MAIN IDEA

2. **TAKING NOTES**
   In a chart like the one shown, list some of the changes that the war brought about for each group.

Changes Brought About by the War	
African Americans	
Women	
Immigrants	

Explain how each group benefited from or was disadvantaged by these changes.

CRITICAL THINKING

3. **DRAWING CONCLUSIONS**
   How did the war affect government power? **Think About:**
   - how private business worked with government
   - how much control the president gained over the economy
   - the Espionage and Sedition Acts

4. **MAKING INFERENCES**
   Why do you think the flu spread so quickly among the troops?

5. **EVALUATING**
   Do you think that the war had a positive or a negative effect on American society? **Think About:**
   - how the propaganda campaign influenced people's behavior
   - the new job opportunities for African Americans and women
   - how the government controlled industry

SCHENCK v. *UNITED STATES* (1919)

ORIGINS OF THE CASE Charles Schenck, an official of the U.S. Socialist Party, distributed leaflets that called the draft a "deed against humanity" and compared conscription to slavery, urging conscripts to "assert your rights." Schenck was convicted of sedition and sentenced to prison, but he argued that the conviction, punishment, and even the law itself violated his right to free speech. The Supreme Court agreed to hear his appeal.

THE RULING **A unanimous court upheld Schenck's conviction, stating that under wartime conditions, the words in the leaflets were not protected by the right to free speech.**

LEGAL REASONING

The Supreme Court's opinion in the *Schenck* case, written by Justice Oliver Wendell Holmes, Jr., has become famous as a guide for how the First Amendment defines the right of free speech. Holmes wrote:

> **"The question in every case is whether the words used are used in such circumstances and are of such a nature as to create a clear and present danger that they will bring about the substantive evils that Congress has a right to prevent."**

Justice Holmes noted that "in ordinary times" the First Amendment might have protected Schenck, but "[w]hen a nation is at war many things that might be said in time of peace . . . will not be endured."

The analogy that Holmes used to explain why Schenck could be punished for his words has become probably the best-known observation ever made about free speech:

> **"Protection of free speech would not protect a man in falsely shouting 'Fire!' in a theatre and causing a panic."**

Writing for the Court, Holmes implied that during wartime, Schenck's leaflet was just that dangerous.

Oliver Wendell Holmes, Jr., Supreme Court Justice 1902–1932 ▶

LEGAL SOURCES

LEGISLATION

U.S. CONSTITUTION, FIRST AMENDMENT (1791)
"Congress shall make no law . . . abridging the freedom of speech, or of the press."

THE SEDITION ACT (1918)
"(W)hoever . . . shall willfully utter, print, write or publish any disloyal, profane, scurrilous, or abusive language about the form of government, . . . Constitution, . . . military or naval forces, . . . flag, . . . or the uniform of the Army or Navy of the United States . . . shall be punished by a fine of not more than $10,000 or imprisonment for not more than twenty years, or both."

RELATED CASES

***DEBS* v. *UNITED STATES* (MARCH, 1919)**
The conviction against Eugene Debs for speaking against the war and the draft is upheld.

***FROHWERK* v. *UNITED STATES* (MARCH, 1919)**
The publisher of a newspaper that had criticized the war is sentenced with a fine and ten years in prison.

***ABRAMS* v. *UNITED STATES* (NOV., 1919)**
Leaflets criticizing the U.S. expeditionary force in Russia are found to be unprotected by the First Amendment. Holmes writes a dissenting opinion calling for the "free trade of ideas."

WHY IT MATTERED

During the course of World War I, the federal government brought approximately 2,000 prosecutions for violations of the Espionage Act of 1917 or the Sedition Act of 1918, the same laws under which it convicted Schenck, Debs, and Frohwerk.

By the fall of 1919, however, Holmes had changed his mind. The case of *Abrams* v. *United States* concerned leaflets that criticized President Wilson's "capitalistic" government for sending troops to put down the Russian Revolution. Justice Holmes, joined by Justice Louis Brandeis, dissented from the majority of the Court, which upheld the conviction. In his dissent, Holmes emphasized the importance of a free exchange of ideas so that truth will win out in the intellectual marketplace. His reasoning won him acclaim as a protector of free speech.

The belief that truth will eventually win out in the marketplace of ideas has become important legal justification for promoting freedom of speech.

HISTORICAL IMPACT

Disagreements about what kinds of speech are "free" under the First Amendment continue. During the 1950s, when people were jailed for supporting Communism, and during the Vietnam War, when war protestors supported draft resistance, these issues again reached the Supreme Court.

The Court has also been asked to decide if young people in schools have the same First Amendment rights as adults. In *Tinker* v. *Des Moines School District* (1969), the Court ordered a school to readmit students who had been suspended for wearing black arm bands in protest of the war in Vietnam.

This so-called symbolic speech, such as wearing an armband or burning a draft card or a flag to express an opinion, has sparked heated debate. In *Texas* v. *Johnson* (1989), the Court, by a narrow five to four vote, invalidated a law under which a man who burned an American flag to protest Reagan administration policies had been convicted. The decision so outraged some people that members of Congress considered amending the Constitution to prohibit any "physical desecration" of the flag. The amendment did not pass. Our freedoms of expression continue to depend upon the words in the first article of the Bill of Rights, written more than 200 years ago.

▲ **Eugene Debs was arrested for antiwar speeches like the one he gave at this 1916 presidential campaign stop.**

◀ **In 1965 Mary Beth Tinker and her brother, John, were suspended from school for wearing armbands that symbolically criticized the Vietnam War.**

THINKING CRITICALLY

CONNECT TO HISTORY

1. **Analyzing Primary Sources** Read Justice Holmes's dissent in *Abrams* v. *United States*. Compare it with the opinion he wrote in *Schenck* v. *United States*. Explain the major difference or similarity in the two opinions.

SEE SKILLBUILDER HANDBOOK, PAGE R22.

CONNECT TO TODAY

2. **INTERNET ACTIVITY** **CLASSZONE.COM**

Visit the links for Historic Decisions of the Supreme Court to research articles about free speech issues. Select several of these issues—such as whether hate groups have a right to march—to discuss with other students in your class. Choose one issue and, as a group, write down as many arguments as you can on both sides of the issue. Then present a debate to the class.

Wilson Fights for Peace

MAIN IDEA

European leaders opposed most of Wilson's peace plan, and the U.S. Senate failed to ratify the peace treaty.

WHY IT MATTERS NOW

Many of the nationalist issues left unresolved after World War I continue to trouble the world today.

Terms & Names

- **Fourteen Points**
- **League of Nations**
- **Georges Clemenceau**
- **David Lloyd George**
- **Treaty of Versailles**
- **reparations**
- **war-guilt clause**
- **Henry Cabot Lodge**

One American's Story

In January 1919, at the magnificent Palace of Versailles outside Paris, President Wilson tried to persuade the Allies to construct a just and lasting peace and to establish a League of Nations. Colonel E. M. House, a native of Texas and a member of the American delegation to Versailles, later wrote about the conference.

A PERSONAL VOICE COLONEL E. M. HOUSE

"How splendid it would have been had we blazed a new and better trail! . . . It may be that Wilson might have had the power and influence if he had remained in Washington and kept clear of the Conference. When he stepped from his lofty pedestal and wrangled with representatives of other states, upon equal terms, he became as common clay. . . . To those who are saying that the Treaty is bad and should never have been made and that it will involve Europe in infinite difficulties in its enforcement, I feel like admitting it. But I would also say in reply that empires cannot be shattered and new states raised upon their ruins without disturbance."

—quoted in *Hooray for Peace, Hurrah for War*

House saw what happened when Wilson's idealism ran up against practical politics. The Allied victors, vengeful toward Germany after four years of warfare, rejected most of Wilson's peace program.

▲ **Colonel Edward M. House was a friend and advisor to President Woodrow Wilson.**

Wilson Presents His Plan

Rejection was probably the last thing Wilson expected when he arrived in Europe. Everywhere he went, people gave him a hero's welcome. Italians displayed his picture in their windows; Parisians strewed the street with flowers. Representatives of one group after another, including Armenians, Jews, Ukrainians, and Poles, appealed to him for help in setting up independent nations for themselves.

FOURTEEN POINTS Even before the war was over, Wilson presented his plan for world peace. On January 18, 1918, he delivered his now famous **Fourteen Points** speech before Congress. The points were divided into three groups. The first five points were issues that Wilson believed had to be addressed to prevent another war:

1. There should be no secret treaties among nations.
2. Freedom of the seas should be maintained for all.
3. Tariffs and other economic barriers among nations should be lowered or abolished in order to foster free trade.
4. Arms should be reduced "to the lowest point consistent with domestic safety, thus lessening the possibility of military responses" during diplomatic crises.
5. Colonial policies should consider the interests of the colonial peoples as well as the interests of the imperialist powers.

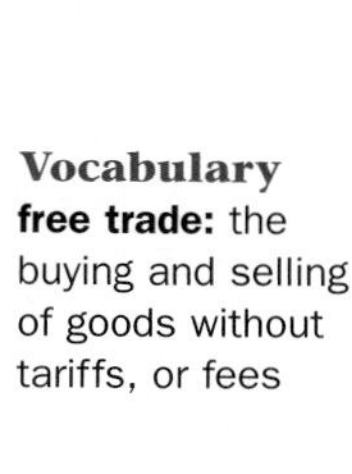

Vocabulary
free trade: the buying and selling of goods without tariffs, or fees

The next eight points dealt with boundary changes. Wilson based these provisions on the principle of self-determination "along historically established lines of nationality." In other words, groups that claimed distinct ethnic identities were to form their own nation-states or decide for themselves to what nations they would belong.

The fourteenth point called for the creation of an international organization to address diplomatic crises like those that had sparked the war. This **League of Nations** would provide a forum for nations to discuss and settle their grievances without having to resort to war.

KEY PLAYER

WOODROW WILSON
1856–1924

At the end of the war, President Wilson wanted the United States to become more involved in international affairs. He believed the nation had a moral obligation to help maintain peace in the world. Wilson's sense of moral purpose had a lasting influence on American foreign policy.

THE ALLIES REJECT WILSON'S PLAN Wilson's naiveté about the political aspects of securing a peace treaty showed itself in his failure to grasp the anger felt by the Allied leaders. The French premier, **Georges Clemenceau** (klĕm′ən-sō′), had lived through two German invasions of France and was determined to prevent future invasions. **David Lloyd George,** the British prime minister, had just won reelection on the slogan "Make Germany Pay." The Italian prime minister, Vittorio Orlando, wanted control of Austrian-held territory. **A**

MAIN IDEA

Developing Historical Perspective
A Why did the Allies reject Wilson's plan?

Contrary to custom, the peace conference did not include the defeated Central Powers. Nor did it include Russia, which was now under the control of a Communist government, or the smaller Allied nations. Instead, the "Big Four"—Wilson, Clemenceau, Lloyd George, and Orlando—worked out the treaty's details among themselves. Wilson conceded on most of his Fourteen Points in return for the establishment of the League of Nations.

(left to right) **David Lloyd George, Georges Clemenceau, and Woodrow Wilson in Paris in 1919.** ▶

GEOGRAPHY SKILLBUILDER

1. **Region** What had happened to German territory in the east by 1920?
2. **Location** Which new nation absorbed Serbia and Montenegro by 1920?

Debating the Treaty of Versailles

On June 28, 1919, the Big Four and the leaders of the defeated nations gathered in the Hall of Mirrors of the Palace of Versailles to sign the peace treaty. After four years of devastating warfare, everyone hoped that the treaty would create stability for a rebuilt Europe. Instead, anger held sway.

PROVISIONS OF THE TREATY The **Treaty of Versailles** (vər-sī′) established nine new nations—including Poland, Czechoslovakia, and Yugoslavia—and shifted the boundaries of other nations. It carved five areas out of the Ottoman Empire and gave them to France and Great Britain as mandates, or temporary colonies. Those two Allies were to administer their respective mandates until the areas were ready for self-rule and then independence.

The treaty barred Germany from maintaining an army. It also required Germany to return the region of Alsace-Lorraine to France and to pay **reparations,** or war damages, amounting to $33 billion to the Allies.

THE TREATY'S WEAKNESSES This treatment of Germany weakened the ability of the Treaty of Versailles to provide a lasting peace in Europe. Several basic flaws in the treaty sowed the seeds of postwar international problems that eventually would lead to the Second World War.

First, the treaty humiliated Germany. It contained a **war-guilt clause** forcing Germany to admit sole responsibility for starting World War I. Although German militarism had played a major role in igniting the war, other European nations had been guilty of provoking diplomatic crises before the war. Furthermore, there was no way Germany could pay the huge financial reparations. Germany was stripped of its colonial possessions in the Pacific, which might have helped it pay its reparations bill. B

MAIN IDEA

Summarizing

B How did the Treaty of Versailles affect Germany?

In addition, for three years the Russians had fought on the side of the Allies, suffering higher casualties than any other nation. However, because Russia was excluded from the peace conference, it lost more territory than Germany did. The Union of Soviet Socialist Republics (or Soviet Union), as Russia was officially called after 1922, became determined to regain its former territory.

Finally, the treaty ignored claims of colonized people for self-determination, as in the case of Southeast Asia, where the Vietnamese people were beginning to demand the same political rights enjoyed by people in Western nations.

OPPOSITION TO THE TREATY When Wilson returned to the United States, he faced strong opposition to the treaty. Some people, including Herbert Hoover, believed it was too harsh. Hoover noted, "The economic consequences alone will pull down all Europe and thus injure the United States." Others considered the treaty a sell-out to imperialism because it simply exchanged one set of colonial rulers for another. Some ethnic groups objected to the treaty because the new national boundaries it established did not satisfy their particular demands for self-determination. For example, before the war many Poles had been under German rule. Now many Germans were under Polish rule.

DEBATE OVER THE LEAGUE OF NATIONS The main domestic opposition, however, centered on the issue of the League of Nations. A few opponents believed that the League threatened the U.S. foreign policy of isolationism. Conservative senators, headed by **Henry Cabot Lodge,** were suspicious of the provision for joint economic and military action against aggression, even though it was voluntary. They wanted the constitutional right of Congress to declare war included in the treaty.

POINT

"The League of Nations was the world's best hope for lasting peace."

President Wilson campaigned for the League of Nations as "necessary to meet the differing and unexpected contingencies" that could threaten world peace. Wilson believed that the League would create a forum where nations could talk through their disagreements. He also hoped it would provide collective security, in which nations would "respect and preserve as against external aggression the territorial integrity and existing political independence of all members of the League," and thereby prevent devastating warfare.

Critics complained that membership in the League would limit American independence in international affairs. However, Wilson argued that League membership included "a moral, not a legal, obligation" that would leave Congress free to decide its own course of action. Wilson tried to assure Congress as well as the general public that the League was "not a straitjacket, but a vehicle of life." It was also a definite guaranty . . . against the things that have just come near bringing the whole structure of civilization into ruin."

COUNTERPOINT

"The League of Nations posed a threat to U.S. self-determination."

Senator William Borah was one of the foremost critics of the Treaty of Versailles because he objected to U.S. membership in the League of Nations. Borah feared that membership in the League "would draw America away from her isolation and into the internal affairs and concerns of Europe" and involve the United States in foreign wars. "Once having surrendered and become a part of the European concerns," Borah wondered, "where, my friends, are you going to stop?"

Many opponents also feared that the League would nullify the Monroe Doctrine by limiting "the right of our people to govern themselves free from all restraint, legal or moral, of foreign powers."

Although Wilson argued that the League of Nations would have no such power of restraint, Borah was unconvinced. He responded to Wilson's argument by asking, "What will your League amount to if it does not contain powers that no one dreams of giving it?"

THINKING CRITICALLY

1. **CONNECT TO HISTORY** **Summarizing** Both supporters and opponents of the League hoped to preserve peace. How did each group propose to secure peace for the United States?

 **SEE SKILLBUILDER HANDBOOK, PAGE R4.**

2. **CONNECT TO TODAY** **Identifying Problems** What are some contemporary arguments against United States participation in international organizations such as the United Nations or the World Court?

History Through *Film*

ECHOES OF THE GREAT WAR

In the 1920s and 1930s, a number of Hollywood horror films were influenced by memories of the Great War. *The Hunchback of Notre Dame* and *The Phantom of the Opera* featured men who, like many veterans, were forced to live with shameful disfigurements.

Other films recalled the war's bleak landscapes. For example, parts of the movie *Frankenstein* were filmed on the same sets as *All Quiet on the Western Front*, the famous war film. James Whale, who directed *Frankenstein*, was a veteran of the war. Like many of his generation, he remained profoundly disturbed by the horrors the war had unleashed.

Lon Chaney in *The Phantom of the Opera* (1925) ▶

Chaney in *The Hunchback of Notre Dame* (1923) ▲

***(top) All Quiet on the Western Front* (1930) ▲**
***(bottom) Frankenstein* (1931)**

SKILLBUILDER Interpreting Visual Sources

1. Why might the theme of human disfigurement be especially powerful to the generation that lived through World War I?
2. How do horror films of your time reflect specific fears and anxieties of the current generation?

SEE SKILLBUILDER HANDBOOK, PAGE R23.

WILSON REFUSES TO COMPROMISE Wilson unwisely ignored the Republican majority in the Senate when he chose the members of the American delegation. If he had been more willing to accept a compromise on the League, it would have been more likely that the Senate would have approved the treaty. Wilson, however, was exhausted from his efforts at Versailles.

Despite ill health, Wilson set out in September 1919 on an 8,000-mile tour. He delivered 34 speeches in about 3 weeks, explaining why the United States should join the League of Nations. On October 2, Wilson suffered a stroke (a ruptured blood vessel to the brain) and lay partially paralyzed for more than two months, unable to even meet with his cabinet. His once-powerful voice was no more than a thick whisper.

When the treaty came up for a vote in the Senate in November 1919, Senator Lodge introduced a number of amendments, the most important of which qualified the terms under which the United States would enter the League of Nations. It was feared that U.S. membership in the League would force the United States to form its foreign policy in accord with the League. Although the Senate rejected the amendments, it also failed to ratify the treaty.

Wilson refused to compromise. "I will not play for position," he proclaimed. "This is not a time for tactics. It is a time to stand square. I can stand defeat; I cannot stand retreat from conscientious duty." The treaty again came up for a vote in March 1920. The Senate again rejected the Lodge amendments—and again failed to muster enough votes for ratification.

The United States finally signed a separate treaty with Germany in 1921, after Wilson was no longer president. The United States never joined the League of Nations, but it maintained an unofficial observer at League meetings. (C)

MAIN IDEA

Making Inferences

(C) Why were some people afraid of the treaty's influence over American foreign policy?

The Legacy of the War

When World War I ended, many Americans looked forward to a return of what Warren G. Harding called "normalcy." However, both the United States and the rest of the world had been utterly transformed by the war. At home, World War I had strengthened both the U.S. military and the power of government. It had also accelerated social change, especially for African Americans and women. In addition, the propaganda campaign had provoked powerful fears and antagonisms that were left unchanneled when the war finally came to an end.

In Europe the destruction and massive loss of life severely damaged social and political systems. In many countries the war created political instability and violence that persisted for decades. During the war years, the first Communist state was established in Russia, while after the war, militant fascist organizations seized control in Italy, Spain, and Germany.

Vocabulary
fascist: characteristic of or relating to fascism, a system of totalitarian government

Appalled by the scale of destruction, Americans began to call World War I "the war to end all wars," in the hope that humanity would never again be willing to fight such a war. However, unresolved issues in Europe would eventually drag America into an even wider war. The Treaty of Versailles had settled nothing. In fact, some Europeans longed to resume the fight. The ominous shape of things to come emerged in the writings of an Austrian named Adolf Hitler, an angry veteran of World War I: "It cannot be that two million [Germans] should have fallen in vain. . . . No, we do not pardon, we demand—vengeance!" Two decades after the end of the Great War, Adolf Hitler's desire for vengeance would plunge the world into an even greater war, in which the United States would play a leading role.

Domestic Consequences of World War I

- accelerated America's emergence as the world's greatest industrial power
- contributed to the movement of African Americans to Northern cities
- intensified anti-immigrant and anti-radical sentiments among mainstream Americans
- brought over one million women into the work force

ASSESSMENT

1. **TERMS & NAMES** For each term or name, write a sentence explaining its significance.
   - **Fourteen Points**
   - **League of Nations**
   - **Georges Clemenceau**
   - **David Lloyd George**
   - **Treaty of Versailles**
   - **reparations**
   - **war-guilt clause**
   - **Henry Cabot Lodge**

MAIN IDEA

2. **TAKING NOTES**
   Re-create the spider diagram shown below. Fill in the web with information about the provisions and weaknesses of the Treaty of Versailles and opposition to it.

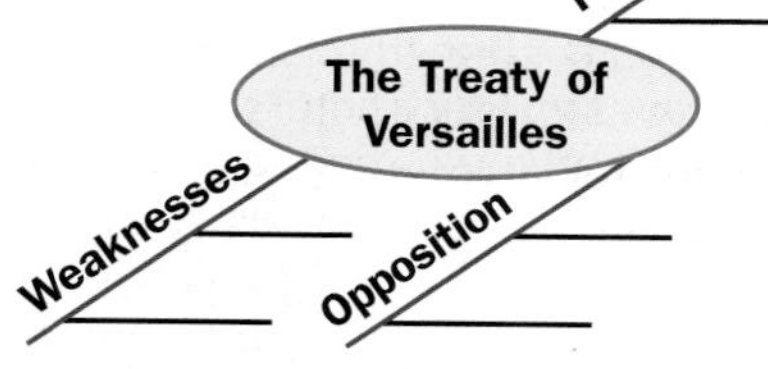

Do you think Congress should have rejected the treaty?

CRITICAL THINKING

3. **DEVELOPING HISTORICAL PERSPECTIVE**
   Why didn't the Treaty of Versailles lay the foundations for a lasting peace?

4. **SUMMARIZING**
   Why did so many Americans oppose the Treaty of Versailles?

5. **HYPOTHESIZING**
   Predict Germany's reaction to the Treaty of Versailles. Give reasons for your predictions.
   Think About:
   - what Germans thought of the war-guilt clause
   - German reaction to reparations
   - how Germans felt about the loss of territory

TRACING
THEMES

America in World Affairs

The United States has not always been as involved in world affairs as it is today. Throughout its history, the nation's foreign policy has swung back and forth between a commitment to involvement with the world and the desire for isolation. "Steer clear of permanent alliances," George Washington cautioned Americans in his Farewell Address of 1796. Washington's warning to the young nation became a theme of government policy for the next hundred years, as domestic issues dominated Americans' attention.

In the late 1800s, however, Americans began to look outward to the larger world. The country had reached the limits of its continental expansion and stretched from ocean to ocean. As its economic power grew stronger, the United States became more involved in the affairs of its neighbors in the Western Hemisphere.

1823–1898

THE UNITED STATES AND LATIN AMERICA ▶

Throughout the 19th century, the United States expanded its influence in the Western Hemisphere. The Monroe Doctrine was intended to diminish European interference. After the Civil War, American trade with Latin America, including the Spanish colony of Cuba, grew. In fact, the United States traded more heavily with Cuba than Spain did.

When the Cubans rebelled against Spain, Americans sympathized with the rebels. After the battleship U.S.S. *Maine* sank in the Cuban harbor of Havana, Americans blamed the Spanish, and Congress declared war. After defeating the Spanish, the United States extended its influence in territories such as Puerto Rico, Panama, and Mexico. A new expansionist era had begun.

DESTRUCTION OF THE U.S BATTLESHIP MAINE

The Only Way We Can Save Her
" STAY OUT! STAY OUT FOR MY SAKE, AS WELL AS YOUR OWN! "
WAR MAD EUROPE
DEMOCRACY
AMERICA THE LAST REFUGE OF DEMOCRACY

1917–1939

◀ INVOLVEMENT AND ISOLATIONISM

Before World War I, the United States had generally limited its military involvement to the Western Hemisphere. As the war in Europe progressed, this position became impossible to maintain, as German U-boats increasingly threatened American lives. In spite of fierce opposition from isolationists, the United States joined World War I in 1917. U.S. involvement in the conflict greatly strengthened its armed forces and revealed the nation's military potential.

After the war, the United States returned to a policy of isolationism. A decade later, as European dictators began menacing other European countries, American public opinion was sharply divided. Many argued that the best way to preserve American democracy was to stay out of war in Europe. It took Japan's attack on Pearl Harbor, Hawaii, in 1941 to force the United States into World War II.

This statue of Lenin, the leader of the 1917 Russian Revolution, was toppled by Latvian citizens in 1991.

U.S. forces in Vietnam in 1968

1945–1991

▲ THE COLD WAR

After World War II, tensions between the United States and Communist countries like the Soviet Union and China developed into a nonmilitary conflict known as the Cold War. During the Cold War, which lasted for nearly 50 years, the United States and the Soviet Union competed to extend their political and economic influence. In some parts of the world, such as Korea and Vietnam, the Cold War led to prolonged military warfare.

The great costs of these conflicts—both in money and in lives—led to renewed calls for isolationism. Nevertheless, the U.S. remained actively involved in the Cold War throughout the 1980s.

1939–1945

INVOLVEMENT IN EUROPE ▼

When the fascist threat to democracy became too great to ignore, the United States joined the Allies in fighting the Axis Powers during World War II. The United States and the Soviet Union emerged from the war as the two strongest military powers in the world. It was now impossible for the nation to return to isolationism. The United States took an active role in rebuilding Europe through programs like the Marshall Plan and was instrumental in establishing the United Nations. The United States also stayed involved with Europe militarily during the Cold War as a member of the North Atlantic Treaty Organization (NATO).

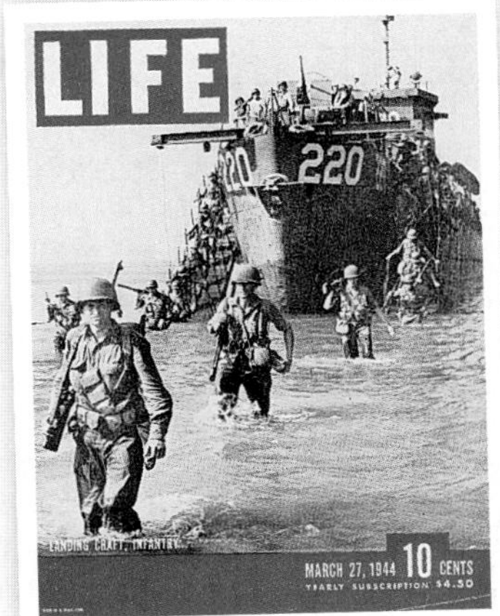

THINKING CRITICALLY

CONNECT TO TODAY

1. **Analyzing Motives** What were America's motives for getting involved in each of the wars described on these two pages? Do you think these motives would be valid today?

SEE SKILLBUILDER HANDBOOK, PAGE R6.

CONNECT TO HISTORY

2. **Writing About Wartime Experience** Imagine that you are a reporter writing at the time about one of the wars in the 20th century. Interview someone you know—or look for information in the library or on the Internet—to find out how a soldier, nurse, cook, sailor, or pilot spent each day as part of the war effort. Write a feature article for a local newspaper, quoting that person.

RESEARCH LINKS **CLASSZONE.COM**

CHAPTER  ASSESSMENT

VISUAL SUMMARY

THE FIRST WORLD WAR

LONG-TERM CAUSES

- Nationalist tensions in Europe
- Competition for colonies
- Arms races and militarism
- Formation of defense alliances

IMMEDIATE CAUSES

- Assassination of Franz Ferdinand
- Austria-Hungary's retaliation against Serbia
- Declarations of war between rival alliances
- Germany's invasion of Belgium

WORLD WAR I

IMMEDIATE EFFECTS

- Destruction and immense loss of life
- Revolution in Russia
- Social change in United States
- Allied victory over Central Powers
- Treaty of Versailles
- Formation of mandates (temporary colonies)
- League of Nations

LONG-TERM EFFECTS

- Breakup of empires
- U.S. policy of isolationism
- United States' emergence as global economic giant
- Rise of militant extremist parties in Europe
- Eruption of World War II

TERMS & NAMES

For each term or name below, write a sentence explaining its connection to World War I.

1. nationalism
2. trench warfare
3. Zimmermann note
4. Selective Service Act
5. General John J. Pershing
6. armistice
7. Espionage and Sedition Acts
8. Great Migration
9. Fourteen Points
10. Treaty of Versailles

MAIN IDEAS

Use your notes and the information in the chapter to answer the following questions.

World War I Begins *(pages 372–380)*

1. What were the main reasons for U.S. involvement in the war?
2. Where did Germany begin its war offensive, and what happened there?

American Power Tips the Balance *(pages 381–387)*

3. How did the United States mobilize a strong military during World War I?
4. What new weapons made fighting in World War I deadlier than fighting in previous wars?

The War at Home *(pages 388–395)*

5. What methods did the U.S. government use to sell the war to the nation?
6. What events during the war undermined civil liberties?

Wilson Fights for Peace *(pages 398–403)*

7. What were the major effects of the Treaty of Versailles?
8. How did Wilson's support for the League of Nations stand in the way of Senate support for the Treaty of Versailles?

CRITICAL THINKING

1. **USING YOUR NOTES** In a chart like the one shown, provide causes for the listed effects of World War I.

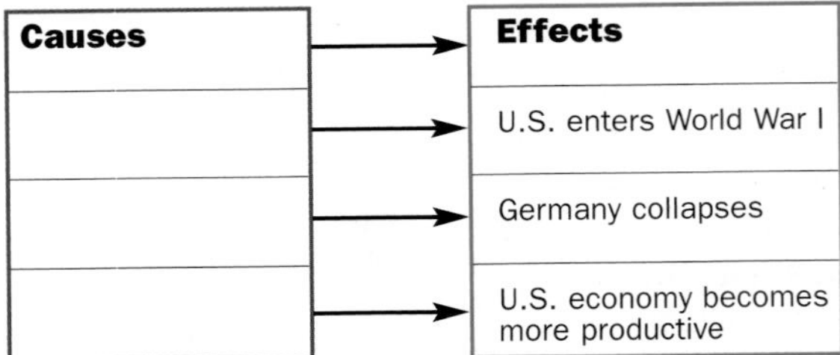

Causes	Effects
	U.S. enters World War I
	Germany collapses
	U.S. economy becomes more productive

2. **DEVELOPING HISTORICAL PERSPECTIVE** Between 1914 and 1920, Americans debated the role their country should have in world affairs. From the events of World War I, what might Americans have learned about intervention in the affairs of other nations?

3. **INTERPRETING MAPS** Look at the maps of Europe before and after World War I (page 400). Describe the changes in national boundaries after the Versailles peace settlement.

Standardized Test Practice

Use the map and your knowledge of United States history to answer question 1.

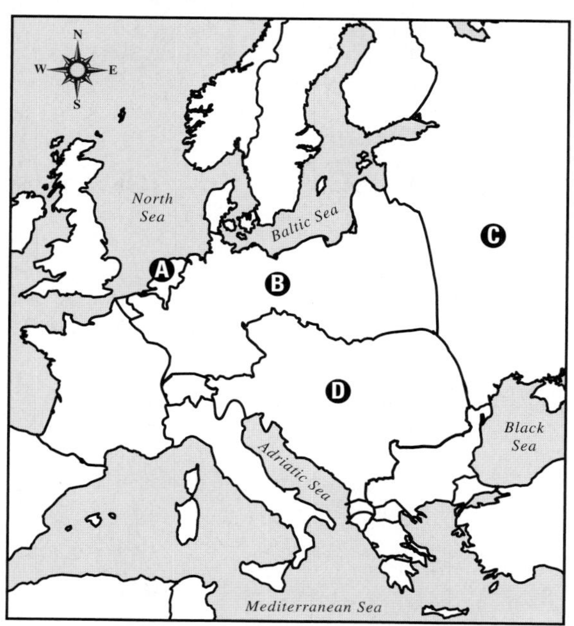

1. Which country was an ally of the United States during World War I?
   A country A
   B country B
   C country C
   D country D

Use the graph and your knowledge of United States history to answer question 2.

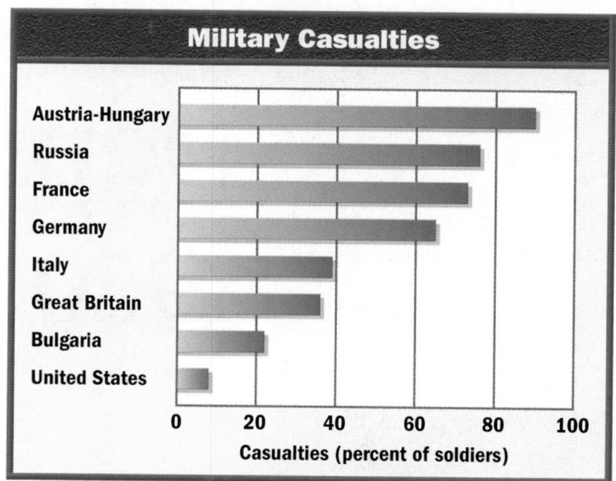

2. The countries with the greatest percentage of military casualties were—
   F members of the Allied Powers.
   G members of the Central Powers.
   H located far from the battlefront.
   J neighboring states.

ADDITIONAL TEST PRACTICE, pages S1–S33.

CLASSZONE.COM

ALTERNATIVE ASSESSMENT

1. INTERACT WITH HISTORY Recall your discussion of the question on page 371:

Do you think America should enter the war?

Write a speech, arguing for or against American involvement in World War I. Use information from the chapter to support your argument. Give your speech to the class.

2. VIDEO **LEARNING FROM MEDIA** View the *American Stories* video "Ace of Aces: Eddie Rickenbacker and the First World War." Discuss the following questions in a group; then do the activity.

- What is your impression of Eddie Rickenbacker?
- How did Rickenbacker adapt his skills and talents to wartime?

Cooperative Learning Activity Rickenbacker's bravery and aviation skills made him a hero. What qualities make people heroes? Using stories and images from magazines and newspapers, make a list of current heroes on a chart for display in your classroom.

The 1920s and the Great Depression 1920–1940

CHAPTER 12
Politics of the Roaring Twenties
1920–1929

CHAPTER 13
The Roaring Life of the 1920s
1920–1929

CHAPTER 14
The Great Depression Begins
1929–1933

CHAPTER 15
The New Deal
1933–1940

Multi-Media Presentation

Create a multi-media presentation that reflects popular culture in the 1920s. Gather a wide variety of sources including excerpts from vintage radio broadcasts and selections of literature. Use sound, visuals, and text in your presentation.

Drouth Stricken Area by Alexandre Hogue

CHAPTER 12 POLITICS OF THE ROARING TWENTIES

Angry mill workers riot after walking off the job during a strike of Tennessee textile plants.

1919–1920 Palmer Raids

1920 Warren G. Harding is elected president.

1921 Sacco and Vanzetti are convicted.

1921 Federal-Aid Road Act funds a national highway system.

1923 President Harding dies and Calvin Coolidge becomes president.

USA
WORLD

1919 | 1921 | 1923

1921 Chinese Communist Party is founded in Shanghai.

1922 Benito Mussolini is appointed prime minister of Italy.

1923 German economic crisis.

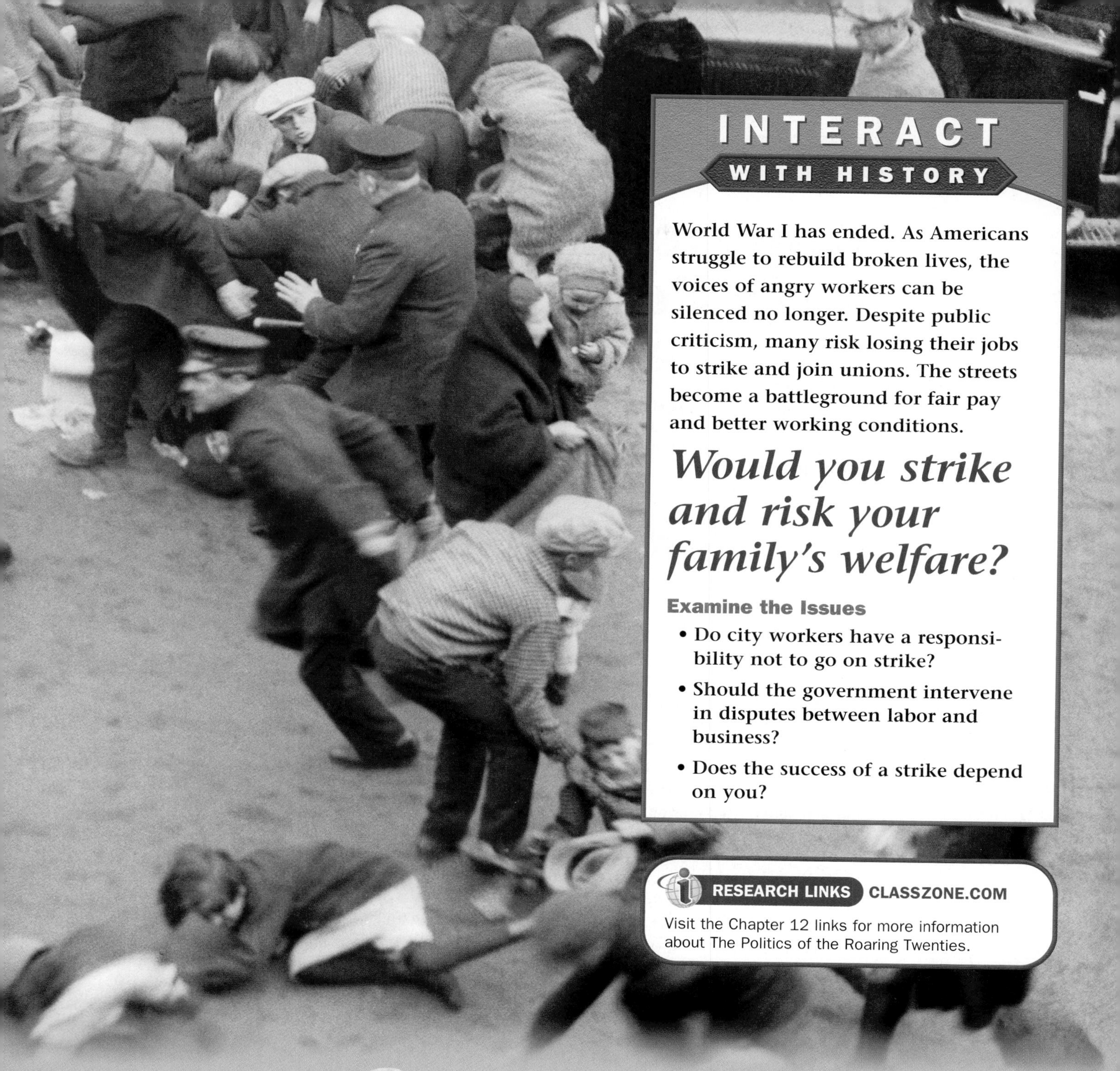

INTERACT WITH HISTORY

World War I has ended. As Americans struggle to rebuild broken lives, the voices of angry workers can be silenced no longer. Despite public criticism, many risk losing their jobs to strike and join unions. The streets become a battleground for fair pay and better working conditions.

Would you strike and risk your family's welfare?

Examine the Issues

- Do city workers have a responsibility not to go on strike?
- Should the government intervene in disputes between labor and business?
- Does the success of a strike depend on you?

RESEARCH LINKS CLASSZONE.COM

Visit the Chapter 12 links for more information about The Politics of the Roaring Twenties.

1924 Calvin Coolidge is elected president.

1925 A. Philip Randolph organizes the Brotherhood of Sleeping Car Porters.

1927 Henry Ford introduces the Model A.

1928 Herbert Hoover is elected president.

1925 **1927** **1929**

1924 Vladimir Ilich Lenin, founder of the Soviet Union, dies.

1926 British laborers declare a general strike.

1926 Hirohito becomes emperor of Japan.

1928 Joseph Stalin launches the first of his Five-Year-Plans in the USSR.

1929 National Revolutionary Party is organized in Mexico.

Americans Struggle with Postwar Issues

MAIN IDEA

A desire for normality after the war and a fear of communism and "foreigners" led to postwar isolationism.

WHY IT MATTERS NOW

Americans today continue to debate political isolationism and immigration policy.

Terms & Names

- nativism
- isolationism
- communism
- anarchists
- Sacco and Vanzetti
- quota system
- John L. Lewis

One American's Story

During the 1920s and 1930s, Irving Fajans, a department store sales clerk in New York City, tried to persuade fellow workers to join the Department Store Employees Union. He described some of the techniques union organizers used.

A PERSONAL VOICE IRVING FAJANS

"If you were caught distributing . . . union literature around the job you were instantly fired. We thought up ways of passing leaflets without the boss being able to pin anybody down. . . . We . . . swiped the key to the toilet paper dispensers in the washroom, took out the paper and substituted printed slips of just the right size! We got a lot of new members that way—It appealed to their sense of humor."

—quoted in *The Jewish Americans*

▲ **Irving Fajans organized department store workers in their efforts to gain better pay and working conditions during the 1920s.**

During the war, workers' rights had been suppressed. In 1919, workers began to cry out for fair pay and better working conditions. Tensions arose between labor and management, and a rash of labor strikes broke out across the country. The public, however, was not supportive of striking workers. Many citizens longed to get back to normal, peaceful living—they felt resentful of anyone who caused unrest.

Postwar Trends

World War I had left much of the American public exhausted. The debate over the League of Nations had deeply divided America. Further, the Progressive Era had caused numerous wrenching changes in American life. The economy, too, was in a difficult state of adjustment. Returning soldiers faced unemployment or took their old jobs away from women and minorities. Also, the cost of living had doubled. Farmers and factory workers suffered as wartime orders diminished.

Many Americans responded to the stressful conditions by becoming fearful of outsiders. A wave of **nativism**, or prejudice against foreign-born people, swept the nation. So, too, did a belief in **isolationism**, a policy of pulling away from involvement in world affairs.

Fear of Communism

One perceived threat to American life was the spread of **communism**, an economic and political system based on a single-party government ruled by a dictatorship. In order to equalize wealth and power, Communists would put an end to private property, substituting government ownership of factories, railroads, and other businesses.

THE RED SCARE The panic in the United States began in 1919, after revolutionaries in Russia overthrew the czarist regime. Vladimir I. Lenin and his followers, or Bolsheviks ("the majority"), established a new Communist state. Waving their symbolic red flag, Communists, or "Reds," cried out for a worldwide revolution that would abolish capitalism everywhere.

A Communist Party formed in the United States. Seventy-thousand radicals joined, including some from the Industrial Workers of the World (IWW). When several dozen bombs were mailed to government and business leaders, the public grew fearful that the Communists were taking over. U.S. Attorney General A. Mitchell Palmer took action to combat this "Red Scare."

A PERSONAL VOICE A. MITCHELL PALMER

"The blaze of revolution was sweeping over every American institution of law and order . . . . eating its way into the homes of the American workman, its sharp tongues of revolutionary heat . . . licking the altars of the churches, leaping into the belfry of the school bell, crawling into the sacred corners of American homes, . . . burning up the foundations of society."

—"The Case Against the Reds"

ECONOMIC BACKGROUND

ROOTS OF COMMUNISM

The first Communist government in Russia was based on the teachings of Karl Marx and Friedrich Engels. In 1848, these two had published *The Communist Manifesto*, which outlined a theory of class struggle. It said that a class that had economic power also had social and political power.

It also said that two classes, the "haves" and the "have-nots," have struggled for control throughout history. During the Industrial Revolution, Communists believed, the struggle was between the capitalists, who owned capital—land, money, and machinery— and workers, who owned only their labor. Marx and Engels urged workers to seize political power and the means of production. Ultimately, they believed, laborers would overthrow capitalism in all industrialized nations.

THE PALMER RAIDS In August 1919, Palmer appointed J. Edgar Hoover as his special assistant. Palmer, Hoover, and their agents hunted down suspected Communists, socialists, and **anarchists**—people who opposed any form of government. They trampled people's civil rights, invading private homes and offices and jailing suspects without allowing them legal counsel. Hundreds of foreign-born radicals were deported without trials.

But Palmer's raids failed to turn up evidence of a revolutionary conspiracy—or even explosives. Many thought Palmer was just looking for a campaign issue to gain support for his presidential aspirations. Soon, the public decided that Palmer didn't know what he was talking about. (A)

MAIN IDEA

Analyzing Motives

(A) Why did Attorney General A. Mitchell Palmer launch a series of raids against suspected Communists?

SACCO AND VANZETTI Although short-lived, the Red Scare fed people's suspicions of foreigners and immigrants. This nativist attitude led to ruined reputations and wrecked lives. The two most famous victims of this attitude were Nicola Sacco and Bartolomeo Vanzetti, a shoemaker and a fish peddler. Both were Italian immigrants and anarchists; both had evaded the draft during World War I.

In May 1920, **Sacco and Vanzetti** were arrested and charged with the robbery and murder of a factory paymaster and his guard in South Braintree, Massachusetts. Witnesses had said the criminals appeared to be Italians. The accused asserted their innocence and provided alibis; the evidence against them was circumstantial; and the presiding judge made prejudicial remarks. Nevertheless, the jury still found them guilty and sentenced them to death.

History Through Art

SACCO AND VANZETTI (1932)

The painting by Ben Shahn shows (*right to left*) Nicola Sacco, Bartolomeo Vanzetti, a miniature Governor Fuller, and a group of Sacco and Vanzetti supporters. **Why do you think Shahn depicts Sacco and Vanzetti as so much larger than Governor Fuller?**

Protests rang out in the United States, Europe, and Latin America. Many people thought Sacco and Vanzetti were mistreated because of their radical beliefs; others asserted it was because they were immigrants. The poet Edna St. Vincent Millay donated proceeds from her poem "Justice Denied in Massachusetts" to their defense. She personally appealed to Governor Fuller of Massachusetts for their lives. However, after reviewing the case and interviewing Vanzetti, the governor decided to let the executions go forward. The two men died in the electric chair on August 23, 1927. Before he was executed, Vanzetti made a statement.

A PERSONAL VOICE BARTOLOMEO VANZETTI

"In all my life I have never stole, never killed, never spilled blood. . . . We were tried during a time . . . when there was hysteria of resentment and hate against the people of our principles, against the foreigner. . . . I am suffering because I am a radical and indeed I am a radical; I have suffered because I was an Italian and indeed I am an Italian. . . . If you could execute me two times, and if I could be reborn two other times, I would live again to do what I have done already." B

—quoted in *The National Experience*

MAIN IDEA

Analyzing Events

B According to Vanzetti, what were the reasons for his imprisonment?

In 1961, new ballistics tests showed that the pistol found on Sacco was in fact the one used to murder the guard. However, there was no proof that Sacco had actually pulled the trigger.

Background

On August 23, 1977, exactly 50 years after the executions, Massachusetts governor Michael Dukakis declared that Sacco and Vanzetti had not been given a fair trial.

Limiting Immigration

During the wave of nativist sentiment, "Keep America for Americans" became the prevailing attitude. Anti-immigrant attitudes had been growing in the United States ever since the 1880s, when new immigrants began arriving from southern and eastern Europe. Many of these immigrants were willing to work for low wages in industries such as coal mining, steel production, and textiles. But after World War I, the need for unskilled labor in the United States decreased. Nativists believed that because the United States now had fewer unskilled jobs available, fewer immigrants should be let into the country. Nativist feelings were fueled by the fact that some of the people involved in postwar labor disputes were immigrant anarchists and socialists, who many Americans believed were actually Communists. Racist ideas like those expressed by Madison Grant, an anthropologist at the American Museum of Natural History in New York City, fed people's attitudes.

A PERSONAL VOICE MADISON GRANT

"The result of unlimited immigration is showing plainly in the rapid decline in the birth rate of native Americans . . . [who] will not bring children into the world to compete in the labor market with the Slovak, the Italian, the Syrian and the Jew. The native American is too proud to mix socially with them."

—quoted in *United States History: Ideas in Conflict*

Vocabulary
bigot: a person who is intolerant of any creed, race, religion, or political belief that differs from his own

THE KLAN RISES AGAIN As a result of the Red Scare and anti-immigrant feelings, different groups of bigots used anti-communism as an excuse to harass any group unlike themselves. One such group was the Ku Klux Klan (KKK). The KKK was devoted to "100 percent Americanism." By 1924, KKK membership reached 4.5 million "white male persons, native-born gentile citizens." The Klan also believed in keeping blacks "in their place," destroying saloons, opposing unions, and driving Roman Catholics, Jews, and foreign-born people out of the country. KKK members were paid to recruit new members into their world of secret rituals and racial violence. Though the Klan dominated state politics in many states, by the end of the decade its criminal activity led to a decrease in power. C

MAIN IDEA

Analyzing Issues
C What were the main goals of the Ku Klux Klan at this time?

▲ **In 1925, nearly 60,000 Ku Klux Klan members marched along Pennsylvania Avenue in Washington, D.C.**

THE QUOTA SYSTEM From 1919 to 1921, the number of immigrants had grown almost 600 percent—from 141,000 to 805,000 people. Congress, in response to nativist pressure, decided to limit immigration from certain countries, namely those in southern and eastern Europe.

The Emergency Quota Act of 1921 set up a **quota system**. This system established the maximum number of people who could enter the United States from each foreign country. The goal of the quota system was to cut sharply European immigration to the United States. As the charts on page 416 show, the system achieved that goal.

As amended in 1924, the law limited immigration from each European nation to 2 percent of the number of its nationals living in the United States in 1890. This provision discriminated against people from eastern and southern Europe—mostly Roman Catholics and Jews—who had not started coming to the United States in large numbers until after 1890. Later, the base year was shifted to 1920. In 1927, the law reduced the total number of persons to be admitted in any one year to 150,000.

In addition, the law prohibited Japanese immigration, causing much ill will between the two nations. Japan—which had faithfully kept the Gentlemen's Agreement to limit emigration to the United States, negotiated by Theodore Roosevelt in 1907—expressed anger over the insult.

U.S. Patterns of Immigration, 1921–1929

The map and graph below show the change in immigration patterns resulting from the Emergency Quota Act, among other factors. Hundreds of thousands of people were affected. For example, while the number of immigrants from Mexico rose from 30,758 in 1921 to 40,154 in 1929, the number of Italian immigrants dropped drastically from 222,260 in 1921 to 18,008 in 1929.

Ellis Island in Upper New York Harbor was the port of entry for most European immigrants.

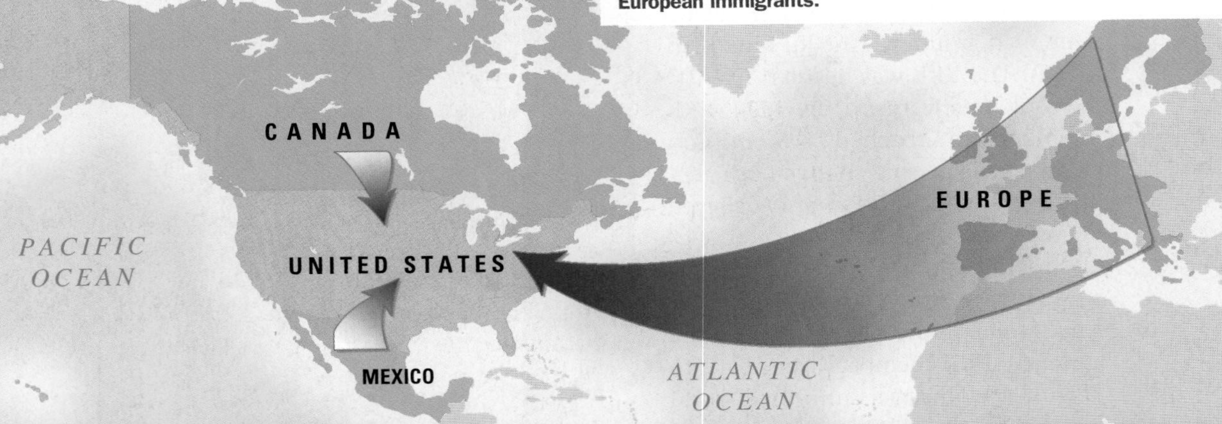

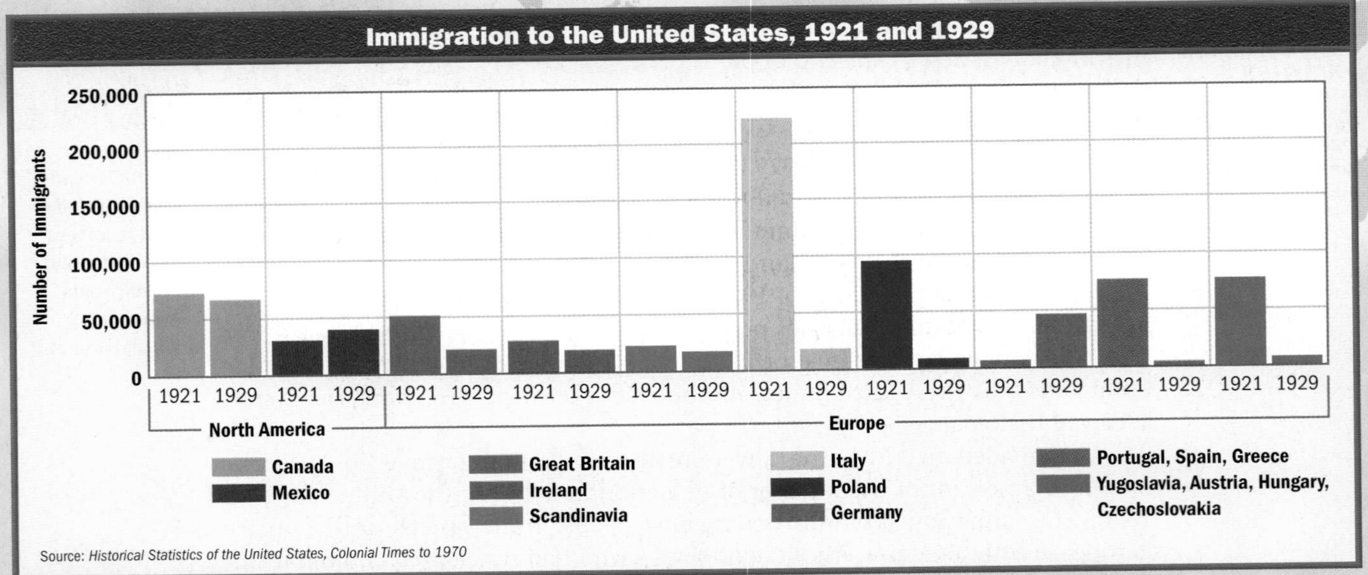

Source: *Historical Statistics of the United States, Colonial Times to 1970*

SKILLBUILDER Interpreting Graphs

1. Which geographical areas show the sharpest decline in immigration to the U.S. between 1921 and 1929? What are the only areas to register an increase in immigration to the U.S.?
2. How did the quota system affect where immigrants came from?

SEE SKILLBUILDER HANDBOOK, PAGE R28.

MAIN IDEA

Developing Historical Perspective

D Why did Congress make changes in immigration laws during the 1920s?

The national origins quota system did not apply to immigrants from the Western Hemisphere, however. During the 1920s, about a million Canadians and almost 500,000 Mexicans crossed the nation's borders. **D**

A Time of Labor Unrest

▲ **Strikers included working women tailors who fought for improved working conditions.**

Another severe postwar conflict formed between labor and management. During the war, the government wouldn't allow workers to strike because nothing could interfere with the war effort. The American Federation of Labor (AFL) pledged to avoid strikes.

However, 1919 saw more than 3,000 strikes during which some 4 million workers walked off the job. Employers didn't want to give raises, nor did they want employees to join unions. Some employers, either out of a sincere belief or because they saw a way to keep wages down, attempted to show that union members were planning a revolution. Employers labeled striking workers as Communists. Newspapers screamed, "Plots to Establish Communism." Three strikes in particular grabbed public attention.

THE BOSTON POLICE STRIKE The Boston police had not been given a raise since the beginning of World War I. Among their many grievances was that they had been denied the right to unionize. When representatives asked for a raise and were fired, the remaining policemen decided to strike. Massachusetts governor Calvin Coolidge called out the National Guard. He said, "There is no right to strike against the public safety by anybody, anywhere, any time." The strike ended but members weren't allowed to return to work; new policemen were hired instead. People praised Coolidge for saving Boston, if not the nation, from communism and anarchy. In the 1920 election he became Warren G. Harding's vice-presidential running mate.

THE STEEL MILL STRIKE Workers in the steel mills wanted the right to negotiate for shorter working hours and a living wage. They also wanted union recognition and collective bargaining rights. In September 1919, the U.S. Steel Corporation refused to meet with union representatives. In response, over 300,000 workers walked off their jobs. Steel companies hired strikebreakers—employees who agreed to work during the strike—and used force. Striking workers were beaten by police, federal troops, and state militias. Then the companies instituted a propaganda campaign, linking the strikers to Communists. In October 1919, negotiations between labor and management produced a deadlock. President Woodrow Wilson made a written plea to the combative "negotiators."

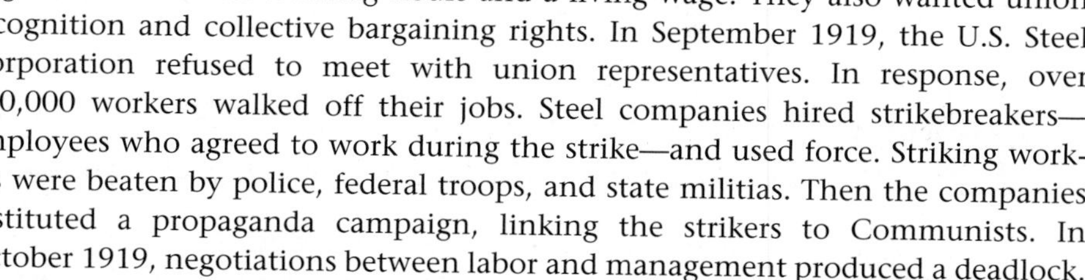

A PERSONAL VOICE WOODROW WILSON

"At a time when the nations of the world are endeavoring to find a way of avoiding international war, are we to confess that there is no method to be found for carrying on industry except . . . the very method of war? . . . Are our industrial leaders and our industrial workers to live together without faith in each other?"

—quoted in *Labor in Crisis*

MAIN IDEA

Comparing

E Compare the results of the Boston police strike and the steel strike.

The steel strike ended in January 1920. In 1923, a report on the harsh working conditions in steel mills shocked the public. The steel companies agreed to an eight-hour day, but the steelworkers remained without a union. **E**

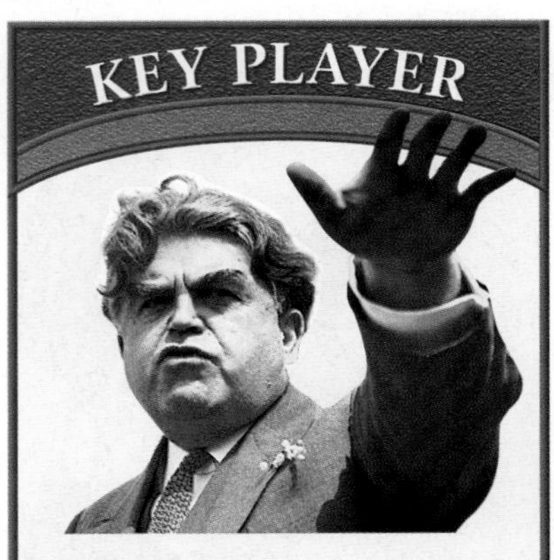

JOHN LLEWELLYN LEWIS
1880–1969

John L. Lewis was born in the little mining town of Lucas, Iowa. His family had traditionally been concerned with labor rights and benefits.

Lewis grew up with a fierce determination to fight for what he believed companies owed their employees: decent working conditions and a fair salary. As he said years later,

> "I have pleaded your case not in the tones of a feeble mendicant [beggar] asking alms but in the thundering voice of the captain of a mighty host, demanding the rights to which free men are entitled."

THE COAL MINERS' STRIKE Unionism was more successful in America's coalfields. In 1919, the United Mine Workers of America, organized since 1890, got a new leader—**John L. Lewis**. In protest of low wages and long workdays, Lewis called his union's members out on strike on November 1, 1919. Attorney General Palmer obtained a court order sending the miners back to work. Lewis then declared it over, but he quietly gave the word for it to continue. In defiance of the court order, the mines stayed closed another month. Then President Wilson appointed an arbitrator, or judge, to put an end to the dispute. The coal miners received a 27 percent wage increase, and John L. Lewis became a national hero. The miners, however, did not achieve a shorter workday and a five-day workweek until the 1930s.

LABOR MOVEMENT LOSES APPEAL In spite of limited gains, the 1920s hurt the labor movement badly. Over the decade, union membership dropped from more than 5 million to around 3.5 million. Membership declined for several reasons:

- much of the work force consisted of immigrants willing to work in poor conditions,
- since immigrants spoke a multitude of languages, unions had difficulty organizing them,
- farmers who had migrated to cities to find factory jobs were used to relying on themselves, and
- most unions excluded African Americans.

By 1929, about 82,000 African Americans—or less than 1 percent of their population—held union memberships. By contrast, just over 3 percent of all whites were union members. However, African Americans joined some unions like the mine workers', longshoremen's, and railroad porters' unions. In 1925, A. Philip Randolph founded the Brotherhood of Sleeping Car Porters to help African Americans gain a fair wage.

While America's attitude toward unions was changing, so, too, was its faith in the presidency.

ASSESSMENT

1. **TERMS & NAMES** For each term or name, write a sentence explaining its significance.
   - **nativism**
   - **isolationism**
   - **communism**
   - **anarchists**
   - **Sacco and Vanzetti**
   - **quota system**
   - **John L. Lewis**

MAIN IDEA

2. **TAKING NOTES**
   In a cause-and-effect chart like the one shown, list examples of the aftereffects of World War I.

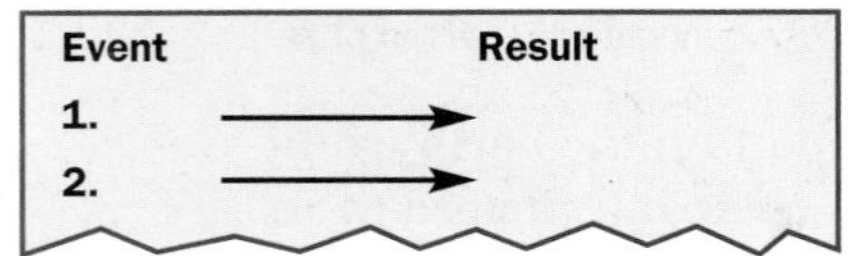

What event do you think was the most significant? Explain your choice.

CRITICAL THINKING

3. **EVALUATING**
   Do you think Americans were justified in their fear of radicals and foreigners in the decade following World War I? Explain your answer.
   Think About:
   - the goals of the leaders of the Russian Revolution
   - the challenges facing the United States

4. **ANALYZING ISSUES**
   In the various fights between management and union members, what did each side believe?

5. **DRAWING CONCLUSIONS**
   What do you think the Sacco and Vanzetti case shows about America in the 1920s?

The Harding Presidency

MAIN IDEA

The Harding administration appealed to America's desire for calm and peace after the war, but resulted in scandal.

WHY IT MATTERS NOW

The government must guard against scandal and corruption to merit public trust.

Terms & Names

- **Warren G. Harding**
- **Charles Evans Hughes**
- **Fordney-McCumber Tariff**
- **Ohio gang**
- **Teapot Dome scandal**
- **Albert B. Fall**

One American's Story

Warren G. Harding was described as a good-natured man who "looked like a president ought to look." When the silver-haired Ohio senator assumed the presidency in 1921, the public yearned for what Harding described as "normalcy," or the simpler days before the Progressive Era and the Great War. His words of peace and calm comforted the healing nation.

A Personal Voice WARREN G. HARDING

"**America's present need is not heroics, but healing; not nostrums, but normalcy; not revolution, but restoration; not agitation, but adjustment; not surgery, but serenity; not the dramatic, but the dispassionate; . . . not submergence in internationality, but sustainment in triumphant nationality.**"

—quoted in *The Rise of Warren Gamaliel Harding*

Despite Harding's soothing speeches, his judgment turned out to be poor. The discord among the major world powers and the conduct within his own cabinet would test his politics and his character.

▲ Warren G. Harding, shown here in 1923, looked presidential, but he is considered one of the least successful presidents.

Harding Struggles for Peace

After World War I, problems surfaced relating to arms control, war debts, and the reconstruction of war-torn countries. In 1921, President Harding invited several major powers to the Washington Naval Conference. Russia was left out because of its Communist government. At the conference, Secretary of State **Charles Evans Hughes** urged that no more warships be built for ten years. He suggested that the five major naval powers—the United States, Great Britain, Japan, France, and Italy—scrap many of their largest warships.

Conference delegates cheered, wept, and threw their hats into the air. For the first time in history, powerful nations agreed to disarm. Later, in 1928, fifteen

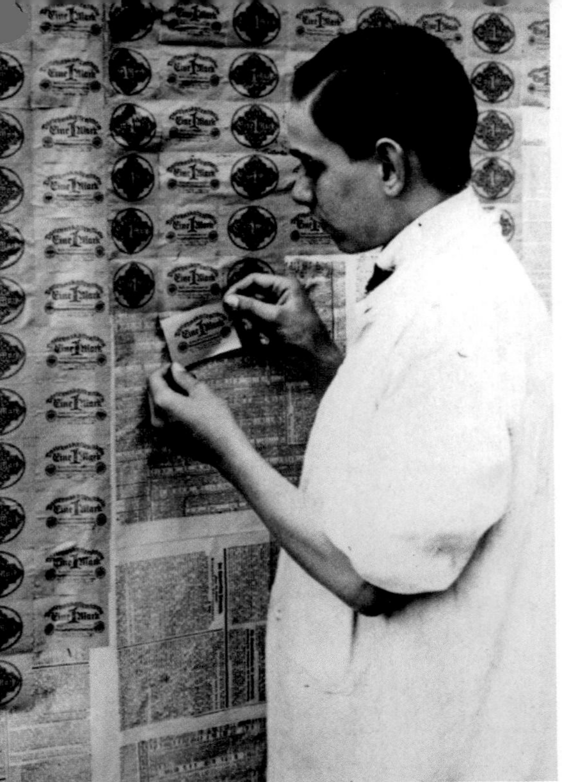

▲ In 1923, a German man papers his walls with money made nearly worthless by high inflation following World War I.

countries signed the Kellogg-Briand Pact, which renounced war as a national policy. However, the pact was futile, as it provided no means of enforcement.

HIGH TARIFFS AND REPARATIONS New conflicts arose when it came time for Britain and France to pay back the $10 billion they had borrowed from America. They could do this in two ways: by selling goods to the United States or by collecting reparations from Germany. However, in 1922, America adopted the **Fordney-McCumber Tariff,** which raised taxes on some U.S. imports to 60 percent—the highest level ever. The tax protected U.S. businesses—especially in the chemical and metals industries—from foreign competition, but made it impossible for Britain and France to sell enough goods in the U.S. to repay debts. (A)

Vocabulary
reparations: payments demanded from a defeated enemy

MAIN IDEA
Summarizing
(A) What were the reasons European countries were not paying their war debts?

The two countries looked to Germany, which was experiencing terrible inflation. When Germany defaulted on (failed to make) payment, French troops marched in. To avoid another war, American banker Charles G. Dawes was sent to negotiate loans. Through what came to be known as the Dawes Plan, American investors loaned Germany $2.5 billion to pay back Britain and France with annual payments on a fixed scale. Those countries then paid the United States. Thus, the United States arranged to be repaid with its own money.

The solution caused resentment all around. Britain and France considered the United States a miser for not paying a fair share of the costs of World War I. Further, the U.S. had benefited from the defeat of Germany, while Europeans had paid for the victory with millions of lives. At the same time, the United States considered Britain and France financially irresponsible.

Scandal Hits Harding's Administration

On domestic issues, Harding favored a limited role for government in business affairs and in social reform. Still, he did set up the Bureau of the Budget to help run the government more efficiently, and he urged U.S. Steel to abandon the 12-hour day.

HARDING'S CABINET Harding appointed Charles Evans Hughes as secretary of state. Hughes later went on to become chief justice of the Supreme Court. The president made Herbert Hoover the secretary of commerce. Hoover had done a masterful job of handling food distribution and refugee problems during World War I. Andrew Mellon, one of the country's wealthiest men, became secretary of the treasury and set about drastically cutting taxes and reducing the national debt. However, the cabinet also included the so-called **Ohio gang,** the president's poker-playing cronies, who would soon cause a great deal of embarrassment. (B)

MAIN IDEA
Evaluating Leadership
(B) What do Harding's appointments indicate about his judgment?

SCANDAL PLAGUES HARDING The president's main problem was that he didn't understand many of the issues. He admitted as much to a secretary.

A PERSONAL VOICE WARREN G. HARDING

"John, I can't make a . . . thing out of this tax problem. I listen to one side and they seem right, and then . . . I talk to the other side and they seem just as right. . . . I know somewhere there is an economist who knows the truth, but I don't know where to find him and haven't the sense to know him and trust him when I find him. . . . What a job!"

—quoted in *Only Yesterday*

Harding's administration began to unravel as his corrupt friends used their offices to become wealthy through graft. Charles R. Forbes, the head of the Veterans Bureau, was caught illegally selling government and hospital supplies to private companies. Colonel Thomas W. Miller, the head of the Office of Alien Property, was caught taking a bribe.

THE TEAPOT DOME SCANDAL The most spectacular example of corruption was the **Teapot Dome scandal**. The government had set aside oil-rich public lands at Teapot Dome, Wyoming, and Elk Hills, California, for use by the U.S. Navy. Secretary of the Interior **Albert B. Fall,** a close friend of various oil executives, managed to get the oil reserves transferred from the navy to the Interior Department. Then, Fall secretly leased the land to two private oil companies, including Henry Sinclair's Mammoth Oil Company at Teapot Dome. Although Fall claimed that these contracts were in the government's interest, he suddenly received more than $400,000 in "loans, bonds, and cash." He was later found guilty of bribery and became the first American to be convicted of a felony while holding a cabinet post. C

In the summer of 1923, Harding declared, "I have no trouble with my enemies. . . . But my. . . friends, they're the ones that keep me walking the floor nights!" Shortly thereafter, on August 2, 1923, he died suddenly, probably from a heart attack or stroke.

Americans sincerely mourned their good-natured president. The crimes of the Harding administration were coming to light just as Vice-President Calvin Coolidge assumed the presidency. Coolidge, a respected man of integrity, helped to restore people's faith in their government and in the Republican Party. The next year, Coolidge was elected president.

MAIN IDEA

Making Inferences

C How did the scandals of the Harding administration hurt the country economically?

The elephant, shaped like a teapot here, is the symbol of the Republican Party (Grand Old Party). The cartoonist implies that Republicans were responsible for the Teapot Dome scandal.

SECTION 2 ASSESSMENT

1. **TERMS & NAMES** For each term or name, write a sentence explaining its significance.
   - **Warren G. Harding**
   - **Charles Evans Hughes**
   - **Fordney-McCumber Tariff**
   - **Ohio gang**
   - **Teapot Dome scandal**
   - **Albert B. Fall**

MAIN IDEA

2. **TAKING NOTES**
   List five significant events from this section and their effects, using a table like the one shown.

Event	Effects
1.	
2.	

Which event benefited the country the most? Why?

CRITICAL THINKING

3. **MAKING INFERENCES**
   How do you think the Harding administration viewed the role of America in world affairs? Support your response with examples from the text.

4. **EVALUATING**
   How successful was Harding in fulfilling his campaign pledge of returning the country to "normalcy"? Support your opinion with specific examples.

5. **ANALYZING EFFECTS**
   How do you think the postwar feelings in America influenced the election of 1920? **Think About:**
   - the desire for normalcy
   - Harding's image
   - the issues Americans wanted to focus on

SECTION 3

The Business of America

MAIN IDEA

Consumer goods fueled the business boom of the 1920s as America's standard of living soared.

WHY IT MATTERS NOW

Business, technological, and social developments of the 1920s launched the era of modern consumerism.

Terms & Names

- **Calvin Coolidge**
- **urban sprawl**
- **installment plan**

One American's Story

In 1927, the last Model T Ford—number 15,077,033—rolled off the assembly line. On December 2, some 1 million New Yorkers mobbed show rooms to view the new Model A. One striking difference between the two models was that customers could order the Model A in such colors as "Arabian Sand" and "Niagara Blue"; the old Model T had come only in black. A Ford spokesman explained some additional advantages of the new automobile.

▲ The Model A was a more luxurious car than the Model T. It was introduced at $495. Model T's were selling for $290.

A PERSONAL VOICE

"Good-looking as that car is, its performance is better than its appearance. We don't brag about it, but it has done seventy-one miles an hour. It will ride along a railroad track without bouncing. . . . It's the smoothest thing you ever rode in."

—a Ford salesman quoted in *Flappers, Bootleggers, "Typhoid Mary," and the Bomb*

The automobile became the backbone of the American economy in the 1920s (and remained such until the 1970s). It profoundly altered the American landscape and American society, but it was only one of several factors in the country's business boom of the 1920s.

American Industries Flourish

The new president, **Calvin Coolidge**, fit into the pro-business spirit of the 1920s very well. It was he who said, "the chief business of the American people is business. . . . The man who builds a factory builds a temple—the man who works there worships there." Both Coolidge and his Republican successor, Herbert Hoover, favored government policies that would keep taxes down and business profits up, and give businesses more available credit in order to expand. Their goal was to keep government interference in business to a minimum and to allow private enterprise to flourish. For most of the 1920s, this approach seemed to work. Coolidge's administration continued to place high tariffs on foreign imports, which helped American manufacturers. At the same time, wages were rising because of new technology, and so was productivity.

THE IMPACT OF THE AUTOMOBILE The automobile literally changed the American landscape. Its most visible effect was the construction of paved roads suitable for driving in all weather. One such road was the legendary Route 66, which provided a route for people trekking west from Chicago to California. Many, however, settled in towns along the route. In addition to the changing landscape, architectural styles also changed, as new houses typically came equipped with a garage or carport and a driveway—and a smaller lawn as a result. The automobile also launched the rapid construction of gasoline stations, repair shops, public garages, motels, tourist camps, and shopping centers. The first automatic traffic signals began blinking in Detroit in the early 1920s. The Holland Tunnel, the first underwater tunnel designed specifically for motor vehicles, opened in 1927 to connect New York City and Jersey City, New Jersey. The Woodbridge Cloverleaf, the first cloverleaf intersection, was built in New Jersey in 1929. **A**

MAIN IDEA

Analyzing Effects

A What was the impact of the automobile?

Gas for cars was cheap and plentiful. Gas stations sprung up on Route 66 charging 25¢ per gallon. ▼

The automobile liberated the isolated rural family, who could now travel to the city for shopping and entertainment. It also gave families the opportunity to vacation in new and faraway places. It allowed both women and young people to become more independent through increased mobility. It allowed workers to live

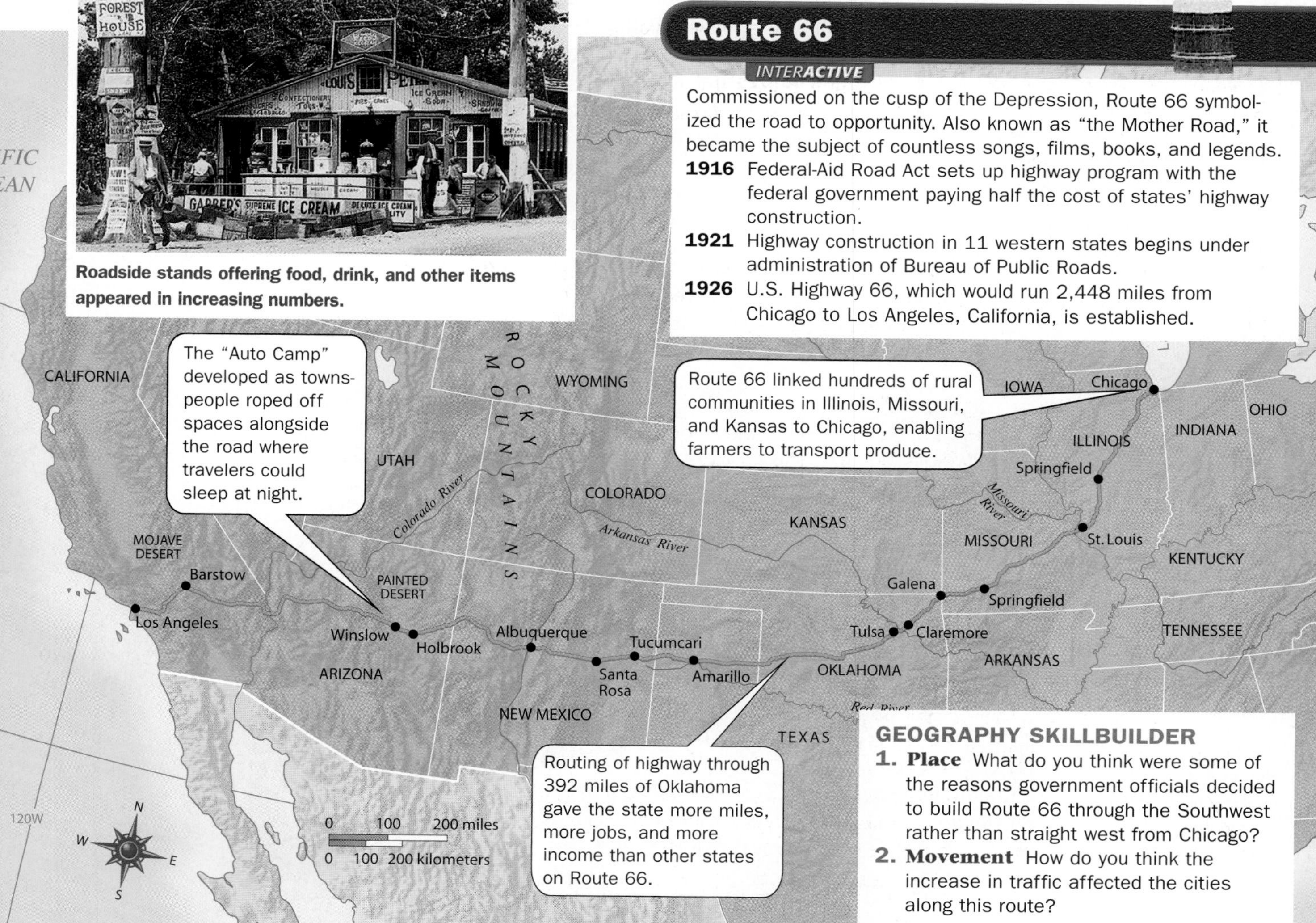

Roadside stands offering food, drink, and other items appeared in increasing numbers.

Route 66

INTERACTIVE

Commissioned on the cusp of the Depression, Route 66 symbolized the road to opportunity. Also known as "the Mother Road," it became the subject of countless songs, films, books, and legends.

1916 Federal-Aid Road Act sets up highway program with the federal government paying half the cost of states' highway construction.

1921 Highway construction in 11 western states begins under administration of Bureau of Public Roads.

1926 U.S. Highway 66, which would run 2,448 miles from Chicago to Los Angeles, California, is established.

GEOGRAPHY SKILLBUILDER

1. **Place** What do you think were some of the reasons government officials decided to build Route 66 through the Southwest rather than straight west from Chicago?
2. **Movement** How do you think the increase in traffic affected the cities along this route?

CALVIN COOLIDGE
1872–1933

Stepping into office in 1923, the tightlipped Vermonter was respected for his solemnity and wisdom. Coolidge supported American business and favored what he called "a constructive economy."

Known for his strength of character, Coolidge forced the resignation of Attorney General Daugherty and other high officials who had created scandal in office.

Shortly after Coolidge was elected, his son died of blood poisoning. Coolidge later wrote, "The power and the glory of the presidency went with him." When he decided not to seek reelection in 1928, Coolidge stumped the nation. Keeping in character, he said, "Goodby, I have had a very enjoyable time in Washington."

miles from their jobs, resulting in **urban sprawl** as cities spread in all directions. The automobile industry also provided an economic base for such cities as Akron in Ohio, and Detroit, Dearborn, Flint, and Pontiac in Michigan. The industry drew people to such oil-producing states as California and Texas. The automobile even became a status symbol—both for individual families and to the rest of the world. In their work *Middletown*, the social scientists Robert and Helen Lynd noted one woman's comment: "I'll go without food before I'll see us give up the car."

Vocabulary
status symbol: a possession believed to enhance the owner's social standing

The auto industry symbolized the success of the free enterprise system and the Coolidge era. Nowhere else in the world could people with little money own their own automobile. By the late 1920s, around 80 percent of all registered motor vehicles in the world were in the United States—about one automobile for every five people. The humorist Will Rogers remarked to Henry Ford, "It will take a hundred years to tell whether you helped us or hurt us, but you certainly didn't leave us where you found us." **B**

MAIN IDEA
Analyzing Effects
B How did the widespread use of the automobile affect the environment and the lives of Americans?

THE YOUNG AIRPLANE INDUSTRY Automobiles weren't the only form of transportation taking off. The airplane industry began as a mail carrying service for the U.S. Post Office. Although the first flight in 1918 was a disaster, a number of successful flights soon established the airplane as a peacetime means of transportation. With the development of weather forecasting, planes began carrying radios and navigational instruments. Henry Ford made a trimotor airplane in 1926. Transatlantic flights by Charles Lindbergh and Amelia Earhart helped to promote cargo and commercial airlines. In 1927, the Lockheed Company produced a single-engine plane, the Vega. It was one of the most popular transport airplanes of the late 1920s. Founded in 1927, Pan American Airways inaugurated the first transatlantic passenger flights.

Flight attendants train for an early United Airlines flight. When commercial airline flights began, all flight attendants were female and white. ▶

America's Standard of Living Soars

The years from 1920 to 1929 were prosperous ones for the United States. Americans owned around 40 percent of the world's wealth, and that wealth changed the way most Americans lived. The average annual income rose more than 35 percent during the period—from $522 to $705. People found it easy to spend all that extra income and then some.

ELECTRICAL CONVENIENCES Gasoline powered much of the economic boom of the 1920s, but the use of electricity also transformed the nation. American factories used electricity to run their machines. Also, the development of an alternating electrical current made it possible to distribute electric power efficiently over longer distances. Now electricity was no longer restricted to central cities but could be transmitted to suburbs. The number of electrified households grew, although most farms still lacked power.

By the end of the 1920s, more and more homes had electric irons, while well-to-do families used electric refrigerators, cooking ranges, and toasters. Eunice Fuller Barnard listed prices for electrical appliances in a 1928 magazine article:

Goods and Prices, 1900 and 1928

1900		1928	
wringer and washboard	$ 5	washing machine	$150
brushes and brooms	$ 5	vacuum cleaner	$ 50
sewing machine (mechanical)	$25	sewing machine (electric)	$ 60

▲ American consumers in the 1920s could purchase the latest household electrical appliances, such as a refrigerator, for as little as a dollar down and a dollar a week.

MAIN IDEA

Forming Generalizations
C How did the use of electricity affect Americans' lifestyle?

These electrical appliances made the lives of housewives easier, freed them for other community and leisure activities, and coincided with a growing trend of women working outside the home. C

THE DAWN OF MODERN ADVERTISING With new goods flooding the market, advertising agencies no longer just informed the public about products and prices. Now they hired psychologists to study how to appeal to people's desire for youthfulness, beauty, health, and wealth. Results were impressive. The slogan "Say it with flowers" doubled florists' business between 1912 and 1924. "Reach for a Lucky instead of a sweet" lured weight-conscious Americans to cigarettes and away from candy. Brand names became familiar from coast to coast, and luxury items now seemed like necessities.

One of those "necessities" was mouthwash. A 1923 Listerine advertisement aimed to convince readers that without Listerine a person ran the risk of having halitosis—bad breath—and that the results could be a disaster.

A Personal Voice

"She was a beautiful girl and talented too. She had the advantages of education and better clothes than most girls of her set. She possessed that culture and poise that travel brings. Yet in the one pursuit that stands foremost in the mind of every girl and woman—marriage—she was a failure."

—Listerine Advertisement

Businesspeople applied the power of advertising to other areas of American life. Across the land, they met for lunch with fellow members of such service organizations as Rotary, Kiwanis, and the Lions. As one observer noted, they sang

ANOTHER
PERSPECTIVE

THE NEEDY

While income rose for many Americans in the 1920s, it did not rise for everyone. Industries such as textile and steel manufacturing made very little profit. Mining and farming actually suffered losses. Farmers were deeply in debt because they had borrowed money to buy land and machinery so that they could produce more crops during World War I. When European agriculture bounced back after the war, the demand for U.S. crops fell, as did prices. Before long there were U.S. farm surpluses.

Many American farmers could not make their loan and mortgage payments. They lost their purchasing power, their equipment, and their farms. As one South Dakota state senator remarked, "There's a saying: 'Depressions are farm led and farm fed.'"

songs, raised money for charities, and boosted the image of the businessman "as a builder, a doer of great things, yes, and a dreamer whose imagination was ever seeking out new ways of serving humanity." Many Americans idolized business during these prosperous times.

A Superficial Prosperity

During the 1920s, most Americans believed prosperity would go on forever—the average factory worker was producing 50 percent more at the end of the decade than at its start. Hadn't national income grown from $64 billion in 1921 to $87 billion in 1929? Weren't most major corporations making fortunes? Wasn't the stock market reaching new heights?

PRODUCING GREAT QUANTITIES OF GOODS As productivity increased, businesses expanded. There were numerous mergers of companies that manufactured automobiles, steel, and electrical equipment, as well as mergers of companies that provided public utilities. Chain stores sprouted, selling groceries, drugs, shoes, and clothes. Five-and-dime stores like Woolworth's also spread rapidly. Congress passed a law that allowed national banks to branch within cities of their main office. But as the number of businesses grew, so did the income gap between workers and managers. There were a number of other clouds in the blue sky of prosperity. The iron and railroad industries, among others, weren't very prosperous, and farms nationwide suffered losses—with new machinery, they were producing more food than was needed and this drove down food prices.

Background
See *productivity* on page R44 in the Economics Handbook.

BUYING GOODS ON CREDIT In addition to advertising, industry provided another solution to the problem of luring consumers to purchase the mountain of goods produced each year: easy credit, or "a dollar down and a dollar forever." The **installment plan**, as it was then called, enabled people to buy goods over

Analyzing ***Political Cartoons***

"YES, SIR, HE'S MY BABY"

This cartoon depicts Calvin Coolidge playing a saxophone labeled "Praise" while a woman representing "Big Business" dances up a storm.

SKILLBUILDER Analyzing Political Cartoons

1. The dancing woman is a 1920s "flapper"—independent, confident, and assertive. In what ways was big business in the 1920s comparable to the flappers?
2. What do you think the cartoonist suggests about Coolidge's relationship with big business?

SEE SKILLBUILDER HANDBOOK, PAGE R24.

MAIN IDEA

Analyzing Issues

D What were the main advantage and disadvantage of buying on credit?

an extended period, without having to put down much money at the time of purchase. Banks provided the money at low interest rates. Advertisers pushed the "installment plan" idea with such slogans as "You furnish the girl, we'll furnish the home" and "Enjoy while you pay."

Some economists and business owners worried that installment buying might be getting out of hand and that it was really a sign of fundamental weaknesses of a superficial economic prosperity. One business owner even wrote to President Coolidge and related a conversation he had overheard on a train. **D**

A Personal Voice

"Have you an automobile yet?"
"No, I talked it over with John and he felt we could not afford one."
"Mr. Budge who lives in your town has one and they are not as well off as you are."
"Yes, I know. Their second installment came due, and they had no money to pay it."
"What did they do? Lose the car?"
"No, they got the money and paid the installment."
"How did they get the money?"
"They sold the cook-stove."
"How could they get along without a cook-stove?"
"They didn't. They bought another on the installment plan."

—a business owner quoted in *In the Time of Silent Cal*

MAIN IDEA

Predicting Effects

E How do you think the changes in spending will affect the economy?

Still, most Americans focused their attention on the present, with little concern for the future. What could possibly go wrong with the nation's economy? The decade of the 1920s had brought about many technological and economic changes. And yet the Coolidge era was built on paradox—the president stood for economy and a frugal way of life, but he was favored by a public who had thrown all care to the wind. Life definitely seemed easier and more enjoyable for hundreds of thousands of Americans. From the look of things, there was little warning of what was to come. **E**

ASSESSMENT

1. **TERMS & NAMES** For each term or name, write a sentence explaining its significance.
   - **Calvin Coolidge**
   - **urban sprawl**
   - **installment plan**

MAIN IDEA

2. **TAKING NOTES**
   Re-create the web below on your paper and fill it in with events that illustrate the central idea.

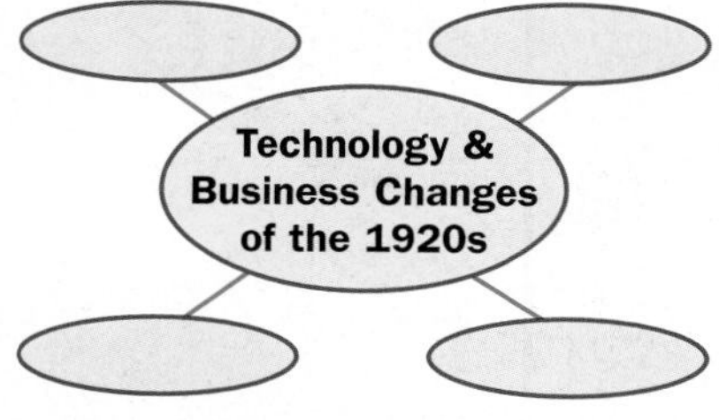

   Choose one event from the web and explain its significance in the 1920s.

CRITICAL THINKING

3. **EVALUATING**
   Do you agree with President Coolidge's statement "The man who builds a factory builds a temple—the man who works there worships there"? Explain your answer. **Think About:**
   - the goals of business and of religion
   - the American idolization of business
   - the difference between workers and management

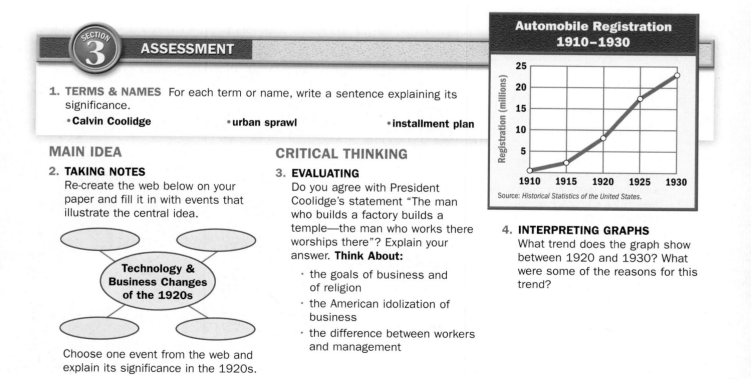

Automobile Registration 1910–1930

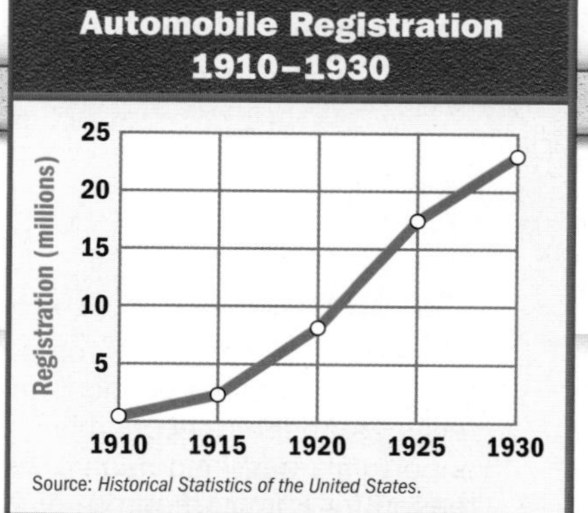

Source: *Historical Statistics of the United States.*

4. **INTERPRETING GRAPHS**
   What trend does the graph show between 1920 and 1930? What were some of the reasons for this trend?

Economic Opportunity

The courage to take risks, the confidence to rely on one's self, the strength to stand in the face of despair, and the resourcefulness to make the most of opportunity—these are all qualities often considered distinctly American. Freedom requires individuals to discover or create opportunities for themselves. However, the government has also played a key role in distributing and creating economic opportunities.

CARAVAN OF EMIGRANTS FOR CALIFORNIA.
(Crossing the Great American Desert in Nebraska.)

1830s–1860s

◀ HOMESTEADING

Even before 1763, Americans looked toward the untamed west in search of greater wealth and freedom. In the 1830s, the Mormons went west to escape religious as well as economic persecution. The government helped to expand economic opportunities for whites by first clearing the land of its native inhabitants, relocating them to reservations or killing them.

As the nation claimed ownership of the land, it also gave it away. The Homestead Act of 1862 provided free of charge 160 acres of public land to anyone 21 years of age or older or the head of a family who had inhabited the land for five years and had improved it. This provided Americans a chance to be independent and self-sufficient if they would work hard. From 1862 until 1900, between 400,000 and 600,000 families were provided homesteads.

1900s

IMMIGRATION ▶

While many people have come to the U.S. seeking political and religious freedom, economic opportunity has also been a key reason for immigration. In 1905, for instance, almost half a million people from southern and eastern Europe migrated to the United States in search of economic freedom and opportunity, as well as to escape religious persecution. Many found work at menial jobs for low pay but still were able to save enough money to eventually open their own businesses.

1960s–1970s

EQUALITY OF OPPORTUNITY AND AFFIRMATIVE ACTION ▶

In the 1960s and 1970s, groups pressed for changes in the law to remove barriers to economic opportunity. A religious-based group, the Southern Christian Leadership Conference, was at the forefront of this movement. Laws such as the Civil Rights Act of 1964 were passed to prevent discrimination against women and racial and ethnic minorities in order to provide equity in educational and business opportunities.

Later, affirmative action programs—a term first used by Lyndon B. Johnson in 1965—opened work and educational opportunities to members of historically disadvantaged groups. Some have labeled affirmative action "reverse discrimination," while others view it as a means to counterbalance continued discrimination that the law has been unable to prevent.

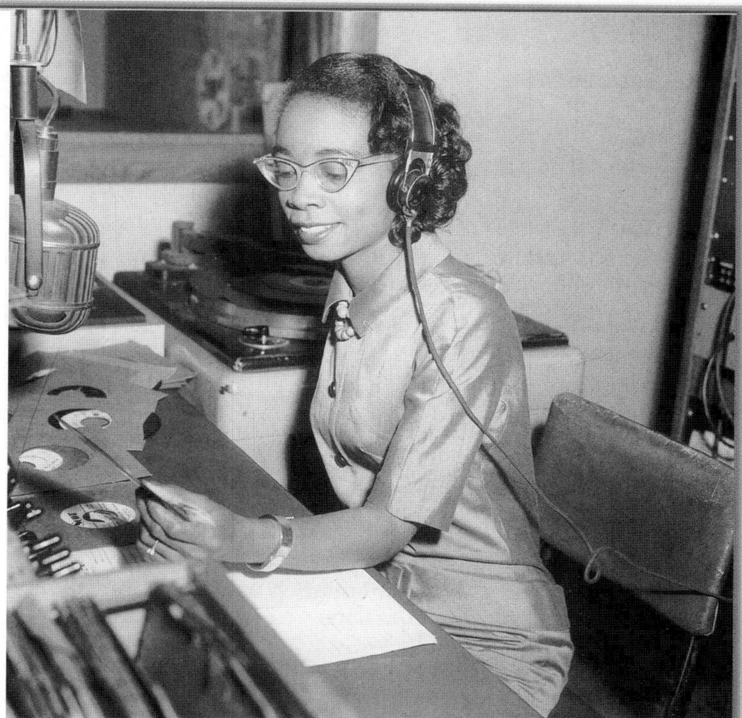

2000s

▼ COMPUTERS AND INTERNET STARTUPS

In recent years, many of the brightest college students have chosen to study computer science in hopes of landing a high-paying job. Alternatively, independent-minded computer experts might become entrepreneurs—people who start and run their own businesses. For an initial period of several months to several years, an entrepreneur may work upwards of 70 or 80 hours each week, yet the business will have no income.

Since the late 1990s, both groups have increasingly looked to the Internet for opportunities. Entrepreneurs seek money-making opportunities as they develop ways to expand the capabilities of this new technology. In turn, the growth of Internet-based businesses creates jobs for people who have specialized computer skills.

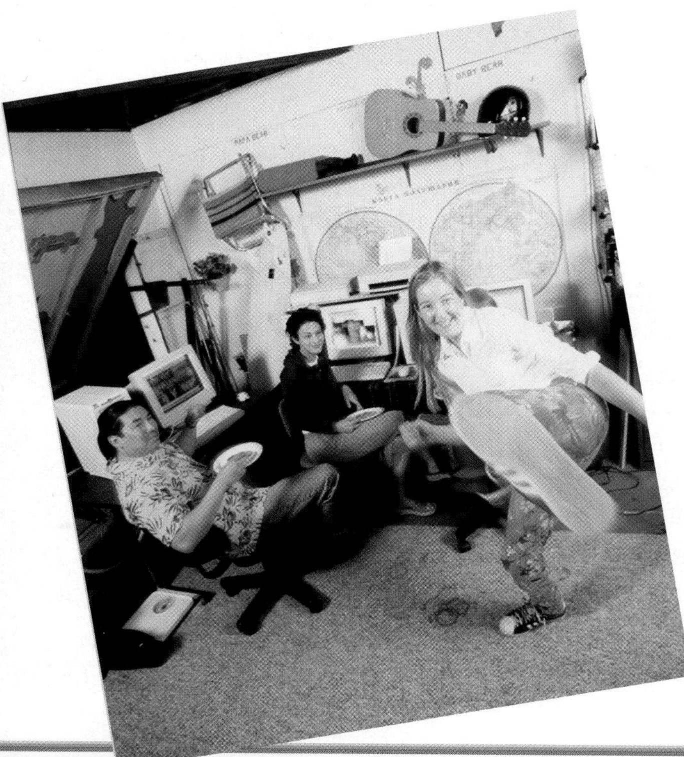

THINKING CRITICALLY

CONNECT TO HISTORY

1. **Identifying Problems** What were some obstacles to achieving equal opportunity in each of the cases described on these two pages? Choose one of the time periods discussed and write a paragraph describing how these obstacles were overcome.

 **SEE SKILLBUILDER HANDBOOK, PAGE R5.**

CONNECT TO TODAY

2. **Evaluating a Business Opportunity** What economic opportunities available to you seem most promising? Discuss with your family and teachers or guidance counselor what jobs and business opportunities they think you might be suited for, then choose one and investigate it. Summarize your research by making a chart listing the pros and cons of the opportunity.

 **RESEARCH LINKS** CLASSZONE.COM

CHAPTER 12 ASSESSMENT

TERMS & NAMES

For each term or name below, write a sentence explaining its connection to the decade following World War I.

1. communism
2. Sacco and Vanzetti
3. Calvin Coolidge
4. John L. Lewis
5. Warren G. Harding
6. Fordney-McCumber Tariff
7. isolationism
8. quota system
9. Teapot Dome scandal
10. installment plan

MAIN IDEAS

Use your notes and the information in the chapter to answer the following questions.

Americans Struggle with Postwar Issues *(pages 412–418)*

1. Explain how the Red Scare, the Sacco and Vanzetti case, and the rise of the Ku Klux Klan reflected concerns held by many Americans.
2. Describe the primary goal of the immigration quota system established in 1921.

The Harding Presidency *(pages 419–421)*

3. What did Harding want to do to return America to "normalcy"?
4. Summarize the Teapot Dome scandal.

The Business of America *(pages 422–427)*

5. How did changes in technology in the 1920s influence American life?
6. What evidence suggests that the prosperity of the 1920s was not on a firm foundation?

CRITICAL THINKING

1. **USING YOUR NOTES** Create a cause-and-effect web, similar to the one shown, in which you give several causes for the declining power of labor unions in the 1920s and give examples of the unions' decline.

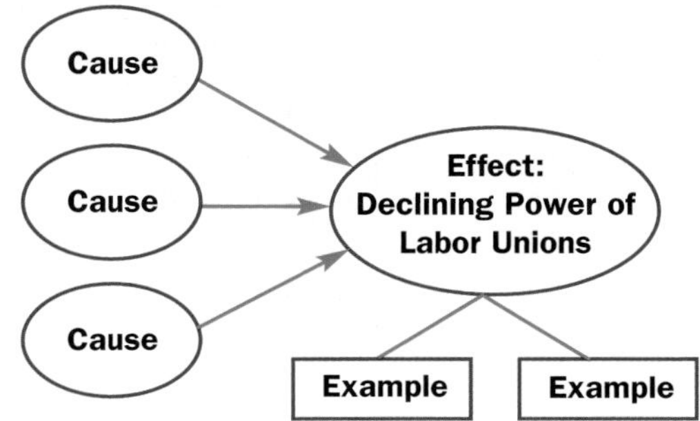

2. **HISTORICAL PERSPECTIVE** Calvin Coolidge said, "After all, the chief business of the American people is business." What events and trends of the 1920s support Coolidge's statement?
3. **INTERPRETING MAPS** Look at the path of Route 66 in the map on page 423. What factors may have influenced where and why the highway was built? Explain your answer.

VISUAL SUMMARY — POLITICS OF THE ROARING TWENTIES

LIFE IN POSTWAR AMERICA

ECONOMIC
- a superficial prosperity ensued
- increased production of consumer goods
- buying on credit
- increased standard of living and consumer spending

GOVERNMENTAL
- election of pro-business presidents Harding and Coolidge
- isolationist philosophy
- immigration quotas
- tariffs on imports to discourage foreign business competition
- corruption in Harding's administration

SOCIETAL/SOCIAL
- a perceived threat of communism
- fear and distrust of immigrants
- fear of the labor movement and faith in business
- strikes and worker unrest

TECHNOLOGY/INDUSTRY
- growth of automobile industry
- introduction of airlines as transportation
- widespread use of electricity
- advertising gains popularity

Standardized Test Practice

Use the cartoon and your knowledge of United States history to answer question 1.

WHAT A FRIEND WE HAVE IN COOLIDGE!
THE CASH REGISTER CHORUS.

1. The cartoon criticizes President Coolidge by suggesting that —

   A Coolidge's policies benefited wealthy business owners.

   B Coolidge was known as "Silent Cal" because he had no economic policy.

   C Coolidge provided cash assistance to struggling industries.

   D Coolidge had supported the Immigration Act.

2. After World War I ended, workers in many industries went on strike for wage increases and better working conditions. But in the decade that followed, public support of labor unions declined, as did union membership. Which of the following helps to explain this decline in labor union popularity?

   F Wages and working conditions in most industries had already improved before the mid-1920s.

   G Most labor unions actively opposed isolationist policies.

   H Most labor unions had large immigrant memberships.

   J Few labor unions would allow unskilled veterans returning from the war to join.

3. Which of the following beliefs did *not* result from America's desire for "normalcy" after World War I?

   A isolationism

   B conservatism

   C nativism

   D anarchism

ADDITIONAL TEST PRACTICE, pages S1–S33.

CLASSZONE.COM

ALTERNATIVE ASSESSMENT

1. **INTERACT WITH HISTORY** Recall your discussion of the question on page 411:

   ### *Would you strike and risk your family's welfare?*

   Suppose you are a reporter covering the Boston police strike. Write a column for your newspaper that explains why people acted as they did. Also describe the mood and tension created by the strike. Invent realistic quotations from workers, union members, strikebreakers, and management.

2. 

   Visit the links for Chapter Assessment to research incomes, prices, employment levels, divorce rates, or other statistics that show how people were affected by the events of the 1920s.

   - Decide the main purpose of your graph. What statistics will you show?
   - Choose the type of graph that would best show your data. Consider using a pie chart, bar or line graph, or circle graph.
   - Clearly label the parts of the graph.
   - Share your graph with the class.

The Roaring Life of the 1920s

Blues singer Gertrude “Ma” Rainey performs with her Georgia Jazz Band in Chicago, Illinois, 1923.

1920 Nineteenth Amendment gives women the right to vote.

1922 Louis Armstrong plays for King Oliver's Creole Jazz Band in Chicago.

1923 *Time* magazine begins publication.

1924 Calvin Coolidge is elected president.

USA
WORLD

1920 | 1922 | 1924

1921 China's Communist Party is founded.

1922 King Tut's tomb is discovered in Egypt.

1923 Mustafa Kemal becomes first president of new Republic of Turkey.

INTERACT
WITH HISTORY

The year is 1920. The World War has just ended. Boosted by the growth of the wartime industry, the U.S. economy is flourishing. Americans live life to the fullest as new social and cultural trends sweep the nation.

How might the new prosperity affect your everyday life?

Examine the Issues

- As Americans leave farms and small towns to take jobs in the cities, how might their lives change?
- How will economic prosperity affect married and unmarried women?
- How might rural and urban areas change as more and more families acquire automobiles?

RESEARCH LINKS **CLASSZONE.COM**

Visit the Chapter 13 links for more information about The Roaring Life of the 1920s.

1925 **The Scopes trial takes place in Tennessee.**

1927 **Charles Lindbergh makes the first nonstop solo transatlantic flight.**

1928 **Herbert Hoover is elected president.**

1926 — 1928 — 1930

1926 **Hirohito becomes emperor of Japan.**

1928 **President Álvaro Obregón of Mexico is assassinated.**

Changing Ways of Life

MAIN IDEA

Americans experienced cultural conflicts as customs and values changed in the 1920s.

WHY IT MATTERS NOW

The way in which different groups react to change continues to cause conflict today.

Terms & Names

- **Prohibition**
- **speakeasy**
- **bootlegger**
- **fundamentalism**
- **Clarence Darrow**
- **Scopes trial**

One American's Story

As the 1920s dawned, social reformers who hoped to ban alcohol—and the evils associated with it—rejoiced. The Eighteenth Amendment to the Constitution, banning the manufacture, sale, and transportation of alcohol, took effect in January of 1920. Billy Sunday, an evangelist who preached against the evils of drinking, predicted a new age of virtue and religion.

A PERSONAL VOICE BILLY SUNDAY

"The reign of tears is over! The slums will soon be only a memory. We will turn our prisons into factories and our jails into storehouses and corncribs. Men will walk upright now, women will smile and the children will laugh. Hell will be forever for rent!"

—quoted in *How Dry We Were: Prohibition Revisited*

Sunday's dream was not to be realized in the 1920s, as the law proved unenforceable. The failure of Prohibition was a sign of cultural conflicts most evident in the nation's cities. Lured by jobs and by the challenge and freedom that the city represented, millions of people rode excitedly out of America's rural past and into its urban future.

▲ 1920s evangelist Billy Sunday

Rural and Urban Differences

America changed dramatically in the years before 1920, as was revealed in the 1920 census. According to figures that year, 51.2 percent of Americans lived in communities with populations of 2,500 to more than 1 million. Between 1922 and 1929, migration to the cities accelerated, with nearly 2 million people leaving farms and towns each year. "Cities were the place to be, not to get away from," said one historian. The agricultural world that millions of Americans left behind was largely unchanged from the 19th century—that world was one of small towns and farms bound together by conservative moral values and close social relationships. Yet small-town attitudes began to lose their hold on the American mind as the city rose to prominence.

THE NEW URBAN SCENE At the beginning of the 1920s, New York, with a population of 5.6 million people, topped the list of big cities. Next came Chicago, with nearly 3 million, and Philadelphia, with nearly 2 million. Another 65 cities claimed populations of 100,000 or more, and they grew more crowded by the day. Life in these booming cities was far different from the slow-paced, intimate life in America's small towns. Chicago, for instance, was an industrial powerhouse, home to native-born whites and African Americans, immigrant Poles, Irish, Russians, Italians, Swedes, Arabs, French, and Chinese. Each day, an estimated 300,000 workers, 150,000 cars and buses, and 20,000 trolleys filled the pulsing downtown. At night people crowded into ornate movie theaters and vaudeville houses offering live variety shows.

"How ya gonna keep 'em down on the farm, after they've seen Paree?"

POPULAR SONG OF THE 1920s

For small-town migrants, adapting to the urban environment demanded changes in thinking as well as in everyday living. The city was a world of competition and change. City dwellers read and argued about current scientific and social ideas. They judged one another by accomplishment more often than by background. City dwellers also tolerated drinking, gambling, and casual dating—worldly behaviors considered shocking and sinful in small towns. (A)

MAIN IDEA

Contrasting

(A) How did small-town life and city life differ?

For all its color and challenge, though, the city could be impersonal and frightening. Streets were filled with strangers, not friends and neighbors. Life was fast-paced, not leisurely. The city demanded endurance, as a foreign visitor to Chicago observed.

A PERSONAL VOICE WALTER L. GEORGE

"It is not for nothing that the predominating color of Chicago is orange. It is as if the city, in its taxicabs, in its shop fronts, in the wrappings of its parcels, chose the color of flame that goes with the smoky black of its factories. It is not for nothing that it has repelled the geometric street arrangement of New York and substituted . . . great ways with names that a stranger must learn if he can. . . . He is in a [crowded] city, and if he has business there, he tells himself, 'If I weaken I shan't last long.'"

—*Hail Columbia!*

History Through *Art*

SONG OF THE TOWERS

This mural by Aaron Douglas is part of a series he painted inside the 135th Street Branch of the New York Public Library to symbolize different aspects of African-American life during the 1920s. In this panel, *Song of the Towers*, he depicts figures before a city backdrop. As seen here, much of Douglas's style was influenced by jazz music and geometric shapes.

SKILLBUILDER **Analyzing Visual Sources**

1. What is the focal point of this panel?
2. What parts of this painting might be symbolic of African Americans' move north?
3. How does Douglas represent new freedoms in this mural? Support your answer with examples.

 **SEE SKILLBUILDER HANDBOOK, PAGE R23.**

DIFFICULT DECISIONS

TO PROHIBIT ALCOHOL OR NOT?

The question of whether to outlaw alcohol divided Americans. Many believed the government should make alcohol illegal to protect the public, while others believed it was a personal decision, and not morally wrong.

1. Examine the pros and cons of each position. Which do you agree with? What other factors, if any, do you think would influence your position?
2. If you had been a legislator asked to vote for the Eighteenth Amendment, what would you have said? Explain.
3. What happens when the government legislates moral values? Give contemporary examples to support your answer.

In the city, lonely migrants from the country often ached for home. Throughout the 1920s, Americans found themselves caught between rural and urban cultures—a tug that pitted what seemed to be a safe, small-town world of close ties, hard work, and strict morals against a big-city world of anonymous crowds, moneymakers, and pleasure seekers.

THE PROHIBITION EXPERIMENT One vigorous clash between small-town and big-city Americans began in earnest in January 1920, when the Eighteenth Amendment went into effect. This amendment launched the era known as **Prohibition,** during which the manufacture, sale, and transportation of alcoholic beverages were legally prohibited.

Reformers had long considered liquor a prime cause of corruption. They thought that too much drinking led to crime, wife and child abuse, accidents on the job, and other serious social problems. Support for Prohibition came largely from the rural South and West, areas with large populations of native-born Protestants. The church-affiliated Anti-Saloon League had led the drive to pass the Prohibition amendment. The Woman's Christian Temperance Union, which considered drinking a sin, had helped push the measure through.

At first, saloons closed their doors, and arrests for drunkenness declined. But in the aftermath of World War I, many Americans were tired of making sacrifices; they wanted to enjoy life. Most immigrant groups did not consider drinking a sin but a natural part of socializing, and they resented government meddling.

Eventually, Prohibition's fate was sealed by the government, which failed to budget enough money to enforce the law. The Volstead Act established a Prohibition Bureau in the Treasury Department in 1919, but the agency was underfunded. The job of enforcement involved patrolling 18,700 miles of coastline as well as inland borders, tracking down illegal stills (equipment for distilling liquor), monitoring highways for truckloads of illegal alcohol, and overseeing all the industries that legally used alcohol to be sure none was siphoned off for illegal purposes. The task fell to approximately 1,500 poorly paid federal agents and local police—clearly an impossible job.

SPEAKEASIES AND BOOTLEGGERS To obtain liquor illegally, drinkers went underground to hidden saloons and nightclubs known as **speakeasies**—so called because when inside, one spoke quietly, or "easily," to avoid detection. Speakeasies could be found everywhere—in penthouses, cellars, office buildings, rooming houses, tenements, hardware stores, and tearooms. To be admitted to a speakeasy, one had to present a card or use a password. Inside, one would find a mix of fashionable middle-class and upper-middle-class men and women.

Before long, people grew bolder in getting around the law. They learned to distill alcohol and built their own stills. Since alcohol was allowed for medicinal and religious purposes, prescriptions

◀ A young woman demonstrates one of the means used to conceal alcohol—hiding it in containers strapped to one's legs. ▶

for alcohol and sales of sacramental wine (intended for church services) skyrocketed. People also bought liquor from **bootleggers** (named for a smuggler's practice of carrying liquor in the legs of boots), who smuggled it in from Canada, Cuba, and the West Indies. "The business of evading [the law] and making a mock of it has ceased to wear any aspects of crime and has become a sort of national sport," wrote the journalist H. L. Mencken. B

MAIN IDEA

Developing Historical Perspective
B Why do you think the Eighteenth Amendment failed to eliminate alcohol consumption?

ORGANIZED CRIME Prohibition not only generated disrespect for the law, it also contributed to organized crime in nearly every major city. Chicago became notorious as the home of Al Capone, a gangster whose bootlegging empire netted over $60 million a year. Capone took control of the Chicago liquor business by killing off his competition. During the 1920s, headlines reported 522 bloody gang killings and made the image of flashy Al Capone part of the folklore of the period. In 1940, the writer Herbert Asbury recalled the Capone era in Chicago.

HISTORICAL SPOTLIGHT

AL CAPONE

By age 26, Al Capone headed a criminal empire in Chicago, which he controlled through the use of bribes and violence. From 1925 to 1931, Capone bootlegged whiskey from Canada, operated illegal breweries in Chicago, and ran a network of 10,000 speakeasies. In 1927, the "Big Fellow," as he liked to be called, was worth an estimated $100 million.

The end came quickly for Capone, though. In 1931, the gangster chief was arrested for tax evasion and went to jail. That was the only crime of which the authorities were ever able to convict him. Capone was later released from jail, but he died several years later at age 48.

A Personal Voice HERBERT ASBURY

"The famous seven-ton armored car, with the pudgy gangster lolling on silken cushions in its darkened recesses, a big cigar in his fat face, and a $50,000 diamond ring blazing from his left hand, was one of the sights of the city; the average tourist felt that his trip to Chicago was a failure unless it included a view of Capone out for a spin. The mere whisper: 'Here comes Al,' was sufficient to stop traffic and to set thousands of curious citizens craning their necks along the curbing."

—*Gem of the Prairie*

By the mid-1920s, only 19 percent of Americans supported Prohibition. The rest, who wanted the amendment changed or repealed, believed that Prohibition caused worse effects than the initial problem. Rural Protestant Americans, however, defended a law that they felt strengthened moral values. The Eighteenth Amendment remained in force until 1933, when it was repealed by the Twenty-first Amendment. C

MAIN IDEA

Analyzing Effects
C How did criminals take advantage of Prohibition?

Prohibition, 1920–1933

Causes	Effects
• Various religious groups thought drinking alcohol was sinful. • Reformers believed that the government should protect the public's health. • Reformers believed that alcohol led to crime, wife and child abuse, and accidents on the job. • During World War I, native-born Americans developed a hostility to German-American brewers and toward other immigrant groups that used alcohol.	• Consumption of alcohol declined. • Disrespect for the law developed. • An increase in lawlessness, such as smuggling and bootlegging, was evident. • Criminals found a new source of income. • Organized crime grew.

Science and Religion Clash

Another bitter controversy highlighted the growing rift between traditional and modern ideas during the 1920s. This battle raged between fundamentalist religious groups and secular thinkers over the validity of certain scientific discoveries.

▲ The evangelist Aimee Semple McPherson in 1922

AMERICAN FUNDAMENTALISM The Protestant movement grounded in a literal, or nonsymbolic, interpretation of the Bible was known as **fundamentalism**. Fundamentalists were skeptical of some scientific discoveries and theories; they argued that all important knowledge could be found in the Bible. They believed that the Bible was inspired by God, and that therefore its stories in all their details were true.

Their beliefs led fundamentalists to reject the theory of evolution advanced by Charles Darwin in the 19th century—a theory stating that plant and animal species had developed and changed over millions of years. The claim they found most unbelievable was that humans had evolved from apes. They pointed instead to the Bible's account of creation, in which God made the world and all its life forms, including humans, in six days.

Fundamentalism expressed itself in several ways. In the South and West, preachers led religious revivals based on the authority of the Scriptures. One of the most powerful revivalists was Billy Sunday, a baseball player turned preacher who staged emotional meetings across the South. In Los Angeles, Aimee Semple McPherson used Hollywood showmanship to preach the word to homesick Midwestern migrants and devoted followers of her radio broadcasts. In the 1920s, fundamentalism gained followers who began to call for laws prohibiting the teaching of evolution. **D**

MAIN IDEA

Summarizing

D Summarize the beliefs of fundamentalism.

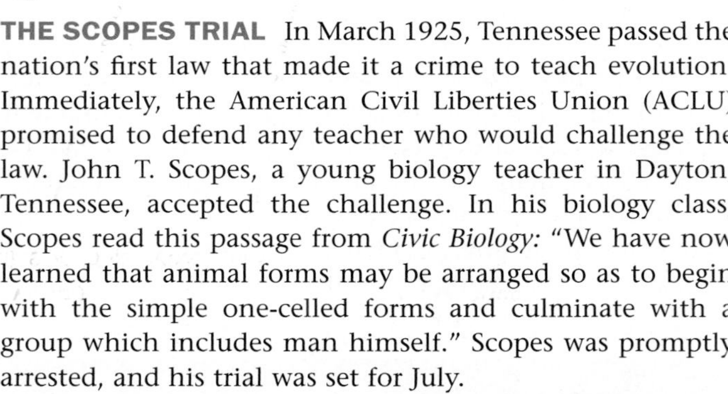

THE SCOPES TRIAL In March 1925, Tennessee passed the nation's first law that made it a crime to teach evolution. Immediately, the American Civil Liberties Union (ACLU) promised to defend any teacher who would challenge the law. John T. Scopes, a young biology teacher in Dayton, Tennessee, accepted the challenge. In his biology class, Scopes read this passage from *Civic Biology:* "We have now learned that animal forms may be arranged so as to begin with the simple one-celled forms and culminate with a group which includes man himself." Scopes was promptly arrested, and his trial was set for July.

Vocabulary
culminate: to come to completion; end

The ACLU hired **Clarence Darrow,** the most famous trial lawyer of the day, to defend Scopes. William Jennings Bryan, three-time Democratic candidate for president and a devout fundamentalist, served as a special prosecutor. There was no real question of guilt or innocence: Scopes was honest about his action. The **Scopes trial** was a fight over evolution and the role of science and religion in public schools and in American society.

The trial opened on July 10, 1925, and almost overnight became a national sensation. Darrow called Bryan as an expert on the Bible—the contest that everyone had been waiting for. To handle the throngs of Bryan supporters, Judge Raulston moved the court outside, to a platform built under the maple trees. There, before a crowd of several

EVOLUTION, CREATIONISM, AND EDUCATION

There is still great controversy today over the teaching of evolution in the public schools. Some people believe that creation theory should be taught as a theory of the origin of life, along with evolution. As recently as 1999, the Kansas State School Board voted to eliminate the teaching of evolution from the curriculum.

The issue of what should be taught about the origin of life—and who should decide this issue—continues to stir up debate. Some have suggested that science and religion are not necessarily incompatible. They believe that a theory of the origin of life can accommodate both the scientific theory of evolution and religious beliefs.

thousand, Darrow relentlessly questioned Bryan about his beliefs. Bryan stood firm, a smile on his face.

A Personal Voice
CLARENCE DARROW AND WILLIAM JENNINGS BRYAN

Mr. Darrow—"You claim that everything in the Bible should be literally interpreted?"

Mr. Bryan—"I believe everything in the Bible should be accepted as it is given there. Some of the Bible is given illustratively. For instance: 'Ye are the salt of the earth.' I would not insist that man was actually salt, or that he had flesh of salt, but it is used in the sense of salt as saving God's people."

—quoted in *Bryan and Darrow at Dayton*

"When Shall We Three Meet Again?"

▲ **A 1925 newspaper cartoon portrays Bryan (*left*) and Darrow (*right*) at the close of the Scopes "monkey" trial on the teaching of evolution, so-called because of a theory of evolution that humans evolved from apes.**

Darrow asked Bryan if he agreed with Bishop James Ussher's calculation that, according to the Bible, Creation happened in 4004 B.C. Had every living thing on earth appeared since that time? Did Bryan know that ancient civilizations had thrived before 4004 B.C.? Did he know the age of the earth? Bryan grew edgy but stuck to his guns. Finally, Darrow asked Bryan, "Do you think the earth was made in six days?" Bryan answered, "Not six days of 24 hours." People sitting on the lawn gasped. (E)

Analyzing Issues
(E) What was the conflict between fundamentalists and those who accepted evolution?

With this answer, Bryan admitted that the Bible might be interpreted in different ways. But in spite of this admission, Scopes was found guilty and fined $100. The Tennessee Supreme Court later changed the verdict on a technicality, but the law outlawing the teaching of evolution remained in effect.

This clash over evolution, the Prohibition experiment, and the emerging urban scene all were evidence of the changes and conflicts occurring during the 1920s. During that period, women also experienced conflict as they redefined their roles and pursued new lifestyles.

ASSESSMENT

1. **TERMS & NAMES** For each term or name, write a sentence explaining its significance.
   - **Prohibition**
   - **speakeasy**
   - **bootlegger**
   - **fundamentalism**
   - **Clarence Darrow**
   - **Scopes trial**

MAIN IDEA

2. **TAKING NOTES**
   Create two diagrams like the one below. Show how government attempted to deal with (a) problems thought to stem from alcohol use and (b) the teaching of evolution.

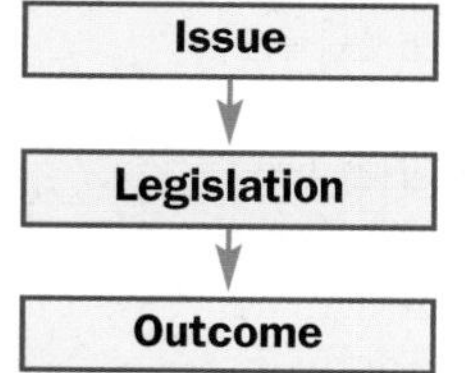

Was the legislation effective? Explain.

CRITICAL THINKING

3. **ANALYZING ISSUES**
   How might the overall atmosphere of the 1920s have contributed to the failure of Prohibition?

4. **ANALYZING CAUSES**
   Why do you think organized crime spread so quickly through the cities during the 1920s? Explain your answer.

5. **EVALUATING**
   Do you think the passage of the Volstead Act and the ruling in the Scopes trial represented genuine triumphs for traditional values?
   Think About:
   - changes in urban life in the 1920s
   - the effects of Prohibition
   - the legacy of the Scopes trial

SECTION 2

The Twenties Woman

MAIN IDEA

American women pursued new lifestyles and assumed new jobs and different roles in society during the 1920s.

WHY IT MATTERS NOW

Workplace opportunities and trends in family life are still major issues for women today.

Terms & Names

- **flapper**
- **double standard**

One American's Story

When Zelda Sayre broke off her engagement with would-be writer F. Scott Fitzgerald in 1919, she told him that he would have to become successful on his own. Later, she wrote about how a woman can achieve greatness.

A PERSONAL VOICE ZELDA SAYRE FITZGERALD

> **"Rouge means that women want to choose their man—not take what lives in the next house. . . . Look back over the pages of history and see how the loveliness of women has always stirred men—and nations—on to great achievement! There have been women who were not pretty, who have swayed hearts and empires, but these women . . . did not disdain that thing for which paint and powder stands. They wanted to choose their destinies—to be successful competitors in the great game of life."**
>
> —"Paint and Powder," *The Smart Set*, May 1929

Zelda Sayre Fitzgerald

Zelda Sayre and F. Scott Fitzgerald married one week after Scott published his first novel, and Zelda continued to be the model for Scott's independent, unconventional, ambitious female characters. He even copied from her letters and other writings. Ironically, Zelda's devotion to her marriage and to motherhood stifled her career ambitions. Nevertheless, she became a model for a generation of young American women who wanted to break away from traditions and forget the hardships of the war years.

Young Women Change the Rules

By the 1920s, the experiences of World War I, the pull of cities, and changing attitudes had opened up a new world for many young Americans. These "wild young people," wrote John F. Carter, Jr., in a 1920 issue of *Atlantic Monthly*, were experiencing a world unknown to their parents: "We have seen man at his lowest, woman at her lightest, in the terrible moral chaos of Europe. We have been forced to question, and in many cases to discard, the religion of our fathers. . . .We have been forced to live in an atmosphere of 'tomorrow we die,' and so, naturally, we drank and were merry." In the rebellious, pleasure-loving atmosphere of the twenties, many women began to assert their independence, reject the values of the 19th century, and demand the same freedoms as men.

▲ Flappers compete in a Charleston dance competition in 1926.

THE FLAPPER During the twenties, a new ideal emerged for some women: the **flapper,** an emancipated young woman who embraced the new fashions and urban attitudes of the day. Close-fitting felt hats, bright waistless dresses an inch above the knees, skin-toned silk stockings, sleek pumps, and strings of beads replaced the dark and prim ankle-length dresses, whalebone corsets, and petticoats of Victorian days. Young women clipped their long hair into boyish bobs and dyed it jet black.

Many young women became more assertive. In their bid for equal status with men, some began smoking cigarettes, drinking in public, and talking openly about sex—actions that would have ruined their reputations not many years before. They danced the fox trot, camel walk, tango, Charleston, and shimmy with abandon.

MAIN IDEA

Evaluating

A How was the flapper like and unlike women of today?

Attitudes toward marriage changed as well. Many middle-class men and women began to view marriage as more of an equal partnership, although both agreed that housework and child-rearing remained a woman's job. A

THE DOUBLE STANDARD Magazines, newspapers, and advertisements promoted the image of the flapper, and young people openly discussed courtship and relationships in ways that scandalized their elders. Although many young women donned the new outfits and flouted tradition, the flapper was more an image of rebellious youth than a widespread reality; it did not reflect the attitudes and values of many young people. During the 1920s, morals loosened only so far. Traditionalists in churches and schools protested the new casual dances and women's acceptance of smoking and drinking.

In the years before World War I, when men "courted" women, they pursued only women they intended to marry. In the 1920s, however, casual dating became increasingly accepted. Even so, a **double standard**—a set of principles granting greater sexual freedom to men than to women—required women to observe stricter standards of behavior than men did. As a result, many women were pulled back and forth between the old standards and the new.

Women Shed Old Roles at Home and at Work

The fast-changing world of the 1920s produced new roles for women in the workplace and new trends in family life. A booming industrial economy opened new work opportunities for women in offices, factories, stores, and professions. The same economy churned out time-saving appliances and products that reshaped the roles of housewives and mothers.

▲ A young woman works as a typesetter in a publishing house in 1920.

NEW WORK OPPORTUNITIES Although women had worked successfully during the war, afterwards employers who believed that men had the responsibility to support their families financially often replaced female workers with men. Women continued to seek paid employment, but their opportunities changed. Many female college graduates turned to "women's professions" and became teachers, nurses, and librarians. Big businesses required extensive correspondence and record keeping, creating a huge demand for clerical workers such as typists, filing clerks, secretaries, stenographers, and office-machine operators. Others became clerks in stores or held jobs on assembly lines. A handful of women broke the old stereotypes by doing work once reserved for men, such as flying airplanes, driving taxis, and drilling oil wells. B

MAIN IDEA

Analyzing Effects

B How did the growth of business and industry affect women?

By 1930, 10 million women were earning wages; however, few rose to managerial jobs, and wherever they worked, women earned less than men. Fearing competition for jobs, men argued that women were just temporary workers whose real job was at home. Between 1900 and 1930, the patterns of discrimination and inequality for women in the business world were established.

THE CHANGING FAMILY Widespread social and economic changes reshaped the family. The birthrate had been declining for several decades, and it dropped at a slightly faster rate in the 1920s. This decline was due in part to the wider availability of birth-control information. Margaret Sanger, who had opened the first birth-control clinic in the United States in 1916, founded the American Birth Control League in 1921 and fought for the legal rights of physicians to give birth-control information to their patients.

At the same time, social and technological innovations simplified household labor and family life. Stores overflowed with ready-made clothes, sliced bread, and canned foods. Public agencies provided services for the elderly, public health clinics served the sick, and workers' compensation assisted those who could no longer work. These innovations and institutions had the effect of freeing homemakers from some of their traditional family responsibilities. Many middle-class housewives, the main shoppers and money managers, focused their attention on their homes, husbands, children, and pastimes. "I consider time for reading clubs and my children more important than . . . careful housework and I just don't do it," said an Indiana woman in the 1920s.

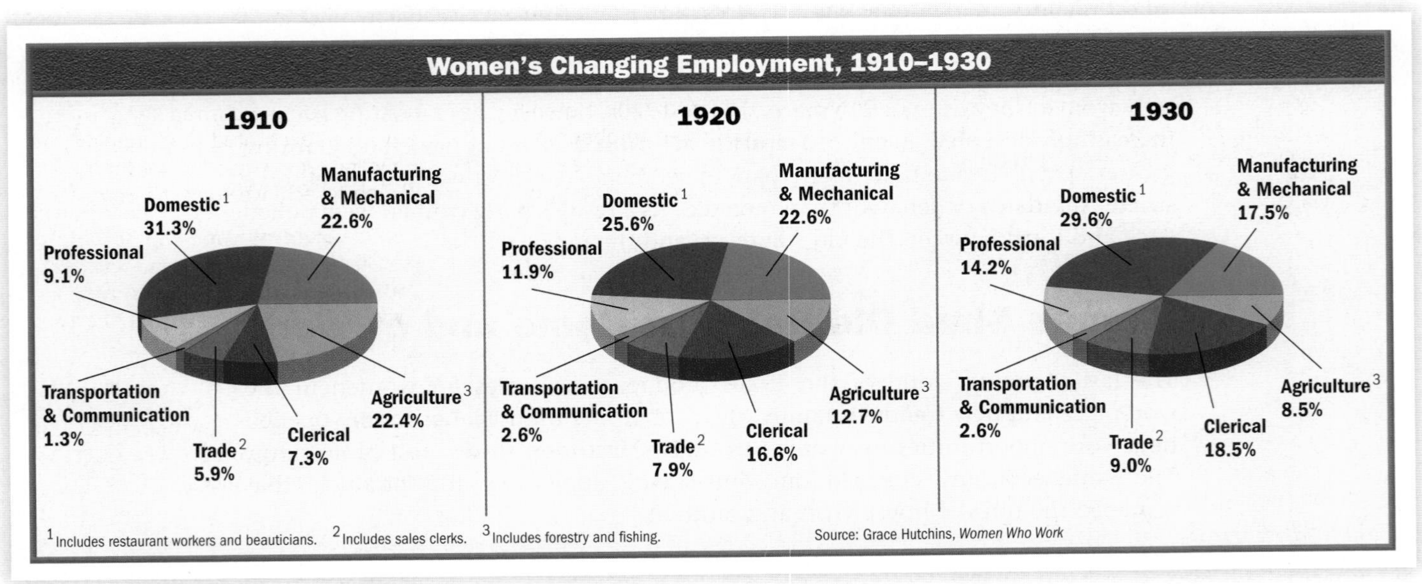

As their spheres of activity and influence expanded, women experienced greater equality in marriage. Marriages were based increasingly on romantic love and companionship. Children, no longer thrown together with adults in factory work, farm labor, and apprenticeships, spent most of their days at school and in organized activities with others their own age. At the same time, parents began to rely more heavily on manuals of child care and the advice of experts.

Working-class and college-educated women quickly discovered the pressure of juggling work and family, but the strain on working-class women was more severe. Helen Wright, who worked for the Women's Bureau in Chicago, recorded the struggle of an Irish mother of two.

A Personal Voice HELEN WRIGHT

"She worked in one of the meat-packing companies, pasting labels from 7 a.m. to 3:30 p.m. She had entered the eldest child at school but sent her to the nursery for lunch and after school. The youngest was in the nursery all day. She kept her house 'immaculately clean and in perfect order,' but to do so worked until eleven o'clock every night in the week and on Saturday night she worked until five o'clock in the morning. She described her schedule as follows: on Tuesday, Wednesday, Thursday, and Friday she cleaned one room each night; Saturday afternoon she finished the cleaning and put the house in order; Saturday night she washed; Sunday she baked; Monday night she ironed."

—quoted in *Wage-Earning Women*

MAIN IDEA

Summarizing

C What changes affected families in the 1920s?

As women adjusted to changing roles, some also struggled with rebellious adolescents, who put an unprecedented strain on families. Teens in the 1920s studied and socialized with other teens and spent less time with their families. As peer pressure intensified, some adolescents resisted parental control, much as the flappers resisted societal control. **C**

This theme of adolescent rebelliousness can be seen in much of the popular culture of the 1920s. Education and entertainment reflected the conflict between traditional attitudes and modern ways of thinking.

SECTION 2 ASSESSMENT

1. **TERMS & NAMES** For each term or name, write a sentence explaining its significance.
   - **flapper**
   - **double standard**

MAIN IDEA

2. **TAKING NOTES**
   Copy the concept web shown below and add to it examples that illustrate how women's lives changed in the 1920s.

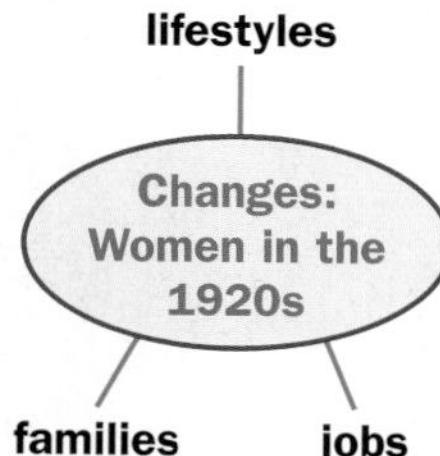

   Write a paragraph explaining how you think women's lives changed most dramatically in the 1920s.

CRITICAL THINKING

3. **EVALUATING**
   During the 1920s, a double standard required women to observe stricter codes of behavior than men. Do you think that some women of this decade made real progress towards equality? Support your answer with examples. **Think About:**
   - the flapper's style and image
   - changing views of marriage

4. **ANALYZING PRIMARY SOURCES**
   In 1920, veteran suffragist Anna Howard Shaw stated that equality in the workplace would be harder for women to achieve than the vote.

   "You younger women will have a harder task than ours. You will want equality in business, and it will be even harder to get than the vote."

   —Anna Howard Shaw

   Why do you think Shaw held this belief? Support your answer with evidence from the text.

DAILY LIFE

1920–1929

Youth in the Roaring Twenties

The decade known as the Roaring Twenties was a celebration of youth and its culture. Crazy and frenetic dances, silly songs, and radically new styles of clothing captured the public's fancy.

During this period of relative prosperity, many people questioned the values of the past and were willing to experiment with new values and behavior as well as with new fashions. This was an especially liberating period for women, who received the right to vote in 1920. Many women also opted for a liberating change of fashion—short skirts and short hair—as well as the freedom to smoke and drink in public.

▼ **FLAGPOLE SITTING**

One of the more bizarre fads of the 1920s began in 1924 as a publicity stunt to attract viewers to movie theaters. The most famous flagpole sitter was "Shipwreck" Kelly (right, waving from high above a movie theater in Union City, New Jersey). In 1929, for a total of 145 days, Kelly took up residence atop various flagpoles throughout the country. Imitators, of course, followed. At one point that year, Baltimore had at least 17 boys and 3 girls sitting atop 18-foot hickory poles, with their friends and families cheering them on.

BESSIE SMITH ▶

Bessie Smith was "Empress of the Blues." In 1923, she sold a million recordings of "Down Hearted Blues."

◀ **BOBBED HAIR**

In keeping with the liberating influence of their new clothing, women bobbed their hair—that is, they had it cut much shorter—freeing themselves of the long tresses that had been fashionable for years. The woman shown is having her hair cut at a barber shop.

◀ **DANCE FADS**

The Charleston was the dance craze of the 1920s. An energetic dance that involved wild, flailing movements of the arms and legs, it demanded an appropriate costume for the woman dancer—a short, straight dress without a waistline.

Another craze was the dance marathon, a contest in which couples would dance continuously for days—taking a 15-minute break every hour—with each alternately holding up the other as he or she slept. Needless to say, dancers dropped from exhaustion.

▼ **GENTLEMEN'S FASHIONS**

Gentlemen enjoyed some outrageous fashions of their own. This young man, with the aid of two flappers, displays the latest fashion in trousers, sometimes called Oxford bags. He also sports "patent-leather hair," parted on the side or in the middle and slicked down close to the head.

DATA FILE

SCHOOL DAYS, SCHOOL DAYS

During the 1920s, children studied reading, writing, and arithmetic in elementary school. In high school, students also studied history and literature and had vocational training. Girls learned cooking and sewing, and boys learned woodworking.

Slang Expressions	
crush	an infatuation
gatecrasher	someone who attends an event uninvited or without paying
keen	attractive or appealing
ritzy	elegant
scram	to leave in a hurry
screwy	crazy
bee's knees	a superb person or thing

RADIO

- KDKA, Pittsburgh, the first commercial radio station, went on the air on November 2, 1920. It was owned by Westinghouse.
- In 1922, 500 radio stations were in operation in the United States.
- In 1924, over 3 million radios were in use throughout the United States. By the end of the 1920s, over 10 million radios were in use. Popular radio shows included *Amos 'n' Andy* and *Jones and Hare*.

SONG TITLES

"Baby Face"
"Barney Google"
"Blue Skies"
"Bye Bye Blackbird"
"Charleston"
"Crazy Rhythm"
"I Want to Be Happy"
"Let A Smile Be Your Umbrella"
"Makin' Whoopie"
"My Blue Heaven"
"My Heart Stood Still"
"Singin' in the Rain"

THINKING CRITICALLY

CONNECT TO TODAY

1. **Comparing** With a small group, listen to several of the songs listed above or to others from the period. Discuss their lyrics and melodies, and compare them with those of popular songs today. What commonalities can you find? How does the music from each period reflect its times? Report your findings to the class.

SEE SKILLBUILDER HANDBOOK, PAGE R8.

CONNECT TO HISTORY

2. **Researching Clothing Styles** Find out more about the clothing styles just before the flapper era. How severe were the changes in fashion in the 1920s? How do you think parents of flappers reacted to these changes? If you had lived at this time, would you have chosen to wear the new styles? Why or why not?

CLASSZONE.COM

Education and Popular Culture

MAIN IDEA	WHY IT MATTERS NOW	Terms & Names
The mass media, movies, and spectator sports played important roles in creating the popular culture of the 1920s—a culture that many artists and writers criticized.	**Much of today's popular culture can trace its roots to the popular culture of the 1920s.**	**•Charles A. Lindbergh •George Gershwin •Georgia O'Keeffe •Sinclair Lewis •F. Scott Fitzgerald •Edna St. Vincent Millay •Ernest Hemingway**

One American's Story

On September 22, 1927, approximately 50 million Americans sat listening to their radios as Graham McNamee, radio's most popular announcer, breathlessly called the boxing match between the former heavyweight champ Jack Dempsey and the current titleholder, Gene Tunney.

A PERSONAL VOICE GRAHAM MCNAMEE

"Good evening, Ladies & Gentlemen of the Radio Audience. This is a big night. Three million dollars' worth of boxing bugs are gathering around a ring at Soldiers' Field, Chicago. . . .

Here comes Jack Dempsey, climbing through the ropes . . . white flannels, long bathrobe. . . . Here comes Tunney. . . . The announcer shouting in the ring . . . trying to quiet 150,000 people. . . . Robes are off."

—*Time* magazine, October 3, 1927

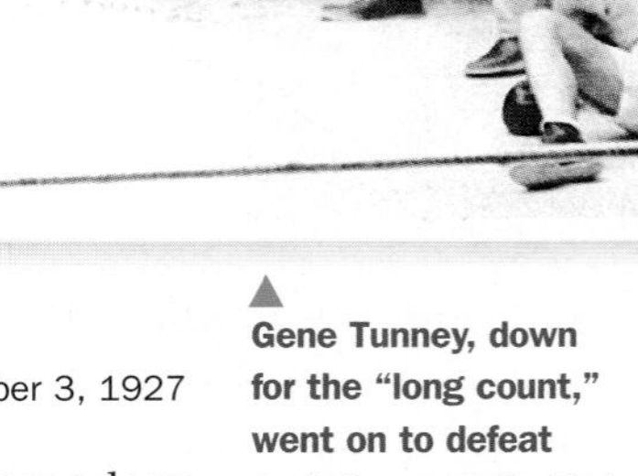

▲ **Gene Tunney, down for the "long count," went on to defeat Jack Dempsey in their epic 1927 battle.**

After punches flew for ten rounds, Tunney defeated the legendary Dempsey. So suspenseful was the brutal match that a number of radio listeners died of heart failure. The "fight of the century" was just one of a host of spectacles and events that transformed American popular culture in the 1920s.

Schools and the Mass Media Shape Culture

During the 1920s, developments in education and mass media had a powerful impact on the nation.

SCHOOL ENROLLMENTS In 1914, approximately 1 million American students attended high school. By 1926, that number had risen to nearly 4 million, an increase sparked by prosperous times and higher educational standards for industry jobs.

Prior to the 1920s, high schools had catered to college-bound students. In contrast, high schools of the 1920s began offering a broad range of courses such as vocational training for those interested in industrial jobs.

The public schools met another challenge in the 1920s—teaching the children of new immigrant families. The years before World War I had seen the largest stream of immigrants in the nation's history—close to 1 million a year. Unlike the earlier English and Irish immigrants, many of the new immigrants spoke no English. By the 1920s their children filled city classrooms. Determined teachers met the challenge and created a large pool of literate Americans. (A)

> **MAIN IDEA**
> **Summarizing**
> (A) How did schools change during the 1920s?

Taxes to finance the schools increased as well. School costs doubled between 1913 and 1920, then doubled again by 1926. The total cost of American education in the mid-1920s amounted to $2.7 billion a year.

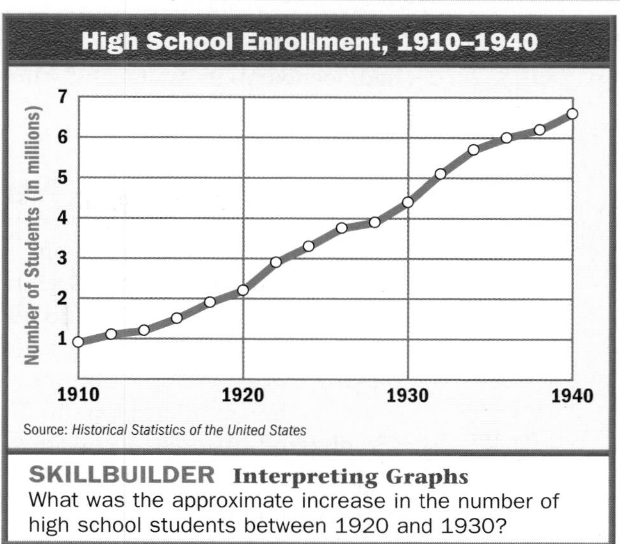

SKILLBUILDER Interpreting Graphs
What was the approximate increase in the number of high school students between 1920 and 1930?

EXPANDING NEWS COVERAGE Widespread education increased literacy in America, but it was the growing mass media that shaped a mass culture. Newspaper circulation rose as writers and editors learned how to hook readers by imitating the sensational stories in the tabloids. By 1914, about 600 local papers had shut down and 230 had been swallowed up by huge national chains, giving readers more expansive coverage from the big cities. Mass-circulation magazines also flourished during the 1920s. Many of these magazines summarized the week's news, both foreign and domestic. By the end of the 1920s, ten American magazines—including *Reader's Digest* (founded in 1922) and *Time* (founded in 1923)—boasted a circulation of over 2 million each.

RADIO COMES OF AGE Although major magazines and newspapers reached big audiences, radio was the most powerful communications medium to emerge in the 1920s. Americans added terms such as "airwaves," "radio audience," and "tune in" to their everyday speech. By the end of the

Radio Broadcasts of the 1920s

Prior to the 1920s, radio broadcasts were used primarily for transmitting important messages and speeches regarding World War I. After the first commercial radio station—KDKA Pittsburgh—made its debut on the airwaves in 1920, the radio industry changed forever. Listeners tuned in for news, entertainment, and advertisements.

▲ Radio dance parties were common in the 1920s.

◀ In the 1920s, radio was a formal affair. Announcers and musicians dressed in their finest attire, even without a live audience.

▲ By 1930, 40 percent of U.S. households had radios, like this 1927 Cosser three-valve Melody Maker.

decade, the radio networks had created something new in the United States—the shared national experience of hearing the news as it happened. The wider world had opened up to Americans, who could hear the voice of their president or listen to the World Series live. B

MAIN IDEA

Analyzing Effects

B Why did radio become so popular?

America Chases New Heroes and Old Dreams

During the 1920s, many people had money and the leisure time to enjoy it. In 1929, Americans spent $4.5 billion on entertainment, much of it on ever-changing fads. Early in the decade, Americans engaged in new leisure pastimes such as working crossword puzzles and playing mahjong, a Chinese game whose playing pieces resemble dominoes. In 1922, after explorers opened the dazzling tomb of the Egyptian pharaoh Tutankhamen, consumers mobbed stores for pharaoh-inspired accessories, jewelry, and furniture. In the mid-1920s, people turned to flagpole sitting and dance marathons. They also flooded athletic stadiums to see sports stars, who were glorified as superheroes by the mass media.

Sports Heroes of the 1920s

Although the media glorified sports heroes, the Golden Age of Sports reflected common aspirations. Athletes set new records, inspiring ordinary Americans. When poor, unknown athletes rose to national fame and fortune, they restored Americans' belief in the power of the individual to improve his or her life.

Gertude Ederle ▶

In 1926, at the age of 19, Gertrude Ederle became the first woman to swim the English Channel. Here, an assistant applies heavy grease to help ward off the effects of the cold Channel waters.

Babe Ruth ▲

New York Yankees slugger Babe Ruth smashed home run after home run during the 1920s. When this legendary star hit a record 60 home runs in 1927, Americans went wild.

◀ Andrew "Rube" Foster

A celebrated pitcher and team manager, Andrew "Rube" Foster made his greatest contribution to black baseball in 1920 when he founded the Negro National League. Although previous attempts to establish a league for black players had failed, Foster led the league to success, earning him the title "The Father of Black Baseball."

Helen Wills ▶

Helen Wills dominated women's tennis, winning the singles title at the U.S. Open seven times and the Wimbledon title eight times. Her nickname was "Little Miss Poker Face."

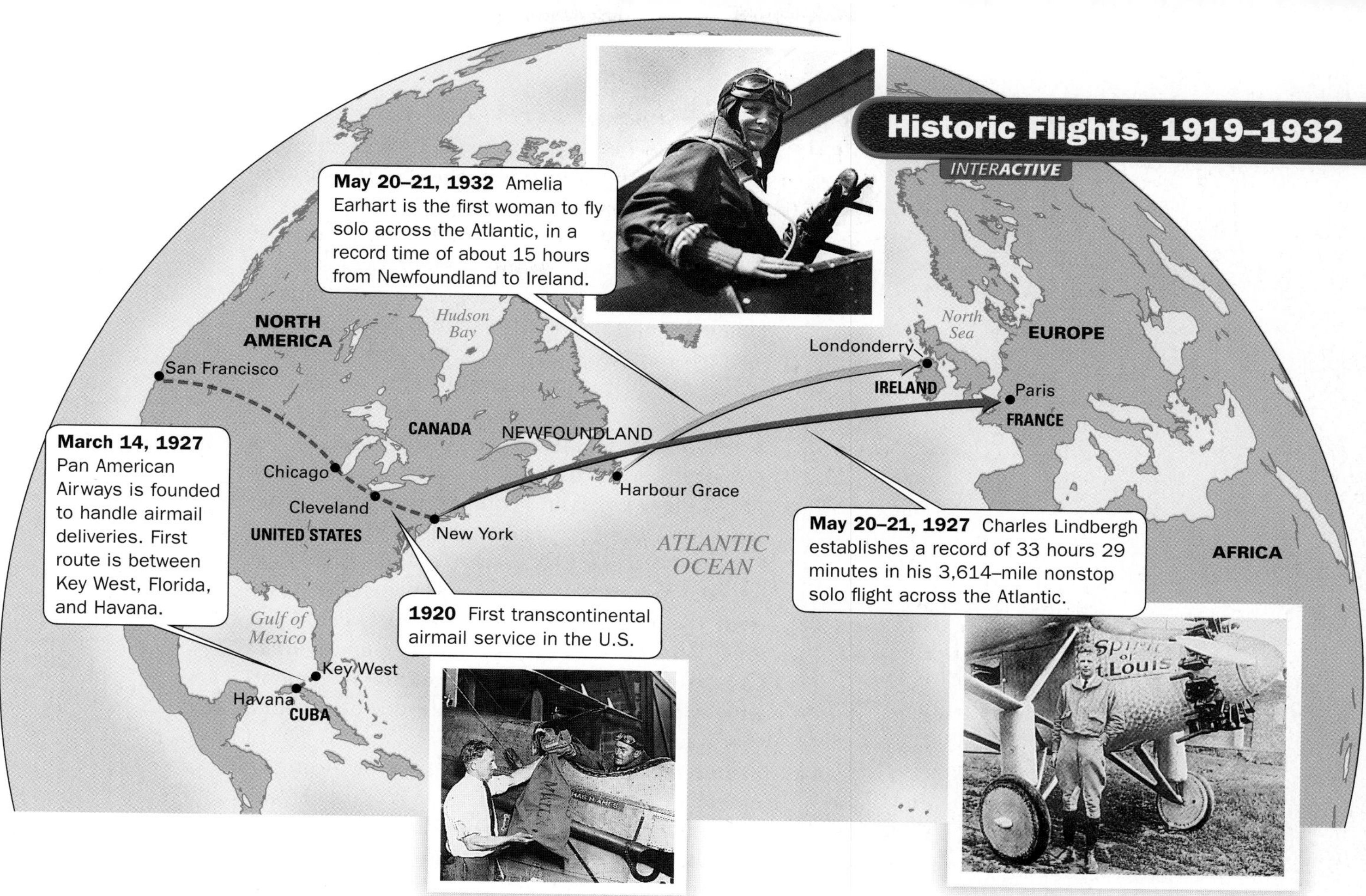
Historic Flights, 1919–1932
INTERACTIVE
May 20–21, 1932 Amelia Earhart is the first woman to fly solo across the Atlantic, in a record time of about 15 hours from Newfoundland to Ireland.
NORTH AMERICA
Hudson Bay
San Francisco
March 14, 1927 Pan American Airways is founded to handle airmail deliveries. First route is between Key West, Florida, and Havana.
CANADA
NEWFOUNDLAND
Chicago
Cleveland
UNITED STATES
New York
Harbour Grace
ATLANTIC OCEAN
1920 First transcontinental airmail service in the U.S.
Gulf of Mexico
Key West
Havana
CUBA
North Sea
EUROPE
Londonderry
IRELAND
Paris
FRANCE
May 20–21, 1927 Charles Lindbergh establishes a record of 33 hours 29 minutes in his 3,614-mile nonstop solo flight across the Atlantic.
AFRICA

LINDBERGH'S FLIGHT America's most beloved hero of the time wasn't an athlete but a small-town pilot named **Charles A. Lindbergh,** who made the first nonstop solo flight across the Atlantic. A handsome, modest Minnesotan, Lindbergh decided to go after a $25,000 prize offered for the first nonstop solo transatlantic flight. On May 20, 1927, he took off near New York City in the *Spirit of St. Louis*, flew up the coast to Newfoundland, and headed over the Atlantic. The weather was so bad, Lindbergh recalled, that "the average altitude for the whole . . . second 1,000 miles of the [Atlantic] flight was less than 100 feet." After 33 hours and 29 minutes, Lindbergh set down at Le Bourget airfield outside of Paris, France, amid beacons, searchlights, and mobs of enthusiastic people.

Paris threw a huge party. On his return to the U.S., New York showered Lindbergh with ticker tape, the president received him at the White House, and America made him its idol. In an age of sensationalism, excess, and crime, Lindbergh stood for the honesty and bravery the nation seemed to have lost. The novelist F. Scott Fitzgerald, a fellow Minnesotan, caught the essence of Lindbergh's fame.

A PERSONAL VOICE F. SCOTT FITZGERALD

"In the spring of 1927, something bright and alien flashed across the sky. A young Minnesotan who seemed to have nothing to do with his generation did a heroic thing, and for a moment people set down their glasses in country clubs and speakeasies and thought of their old best dreams."

—quoted in *The Lawless Decade*

Lindbergh's accomplishment paved the way for others. In the next decade, Amelia Earhart was to undertake many brave aerial exploits, inspired by Lindbergh's example.

In *Radiator Building—Night, New York* (1927), Georgia O'Keeffe showed the dark buildings of New York City thrusting into the night sky.

ENTERTAINMENT AND THE ARTS Despite the feats of real-life heroes, America's thirst for entertainment in the arts and on the screen and stage seemed unquenchable in the 1920s.

Even before the introduction of sound, movies became a national pastime, offering viewers a means of escape through romance and comedy. The first major movie with sound, *The Jazz Singer*, was released in 1927. Walt Disney's *Steamboat Willie,* the first animated film with sound, was released in 1928. By 1930, the new "talkies" had doubled movie attendance, with millions of Americans going to the movies every week. C

MAIN IDEA

Making Inferences

C Why were Americans so delighted by movies in the 1920s?

Both playwrights and composers of music broke away from the European traditions of the 1920s. Eugene O'Neill's plays, such as *The Hairy Ape*, forced Americans to reflect upon modern isolation, confusion, and family conflict. Fame was given to concert music composer **George Gershwin** when he merged traditional elements with American jazz, thus creating a new sound that was identifiably American.

Painters appealed to Americans by recording an America of realities and dreams. Edward Hopper caught the loneliness of American life in his canvases of empty streets and solitary people, while **Georgia O'Keeffe** produced intensely colored canvases that captured the grandeur of New York.

WRITERS OF THE 1920s The 1920s also brought an outpouring of fresh and insightful writing, making it one of the richest eras in the country's literary history.

Sinclair Lewis, the first American to win a Nobel Prize in literature, was among the era's most outspoken critics. In his novel *Babbitt*, Lewis used the main character of George F. Babbitt to ridicule Americans for their conformity and materialism.

A PERSONAL VOICE SINCLAIR LEWIS

"A sensational event was changing from the brown suit to the gray the contents of his pockets. He was earnest about these objects. They were of eternal importance, like baseball or the Republican Party. They included a fountain pen and a silver pencil . . . which belonged in the righthand upper vest pocket. Without them he would have felt naked. On his watch-chain were a gold penknife, silver cigar-cutter, seven keys . . . and incidentally a good watch. . . . Last, he stuck in his lapel the Boosters' Club button. With the conciseness of great art the button displayed two words: 'Boosters—Pep!'"

—*Babbitt*

It was **F. Scott Fitzgerald** who coined the term "Jazz Age" to describe the 1920s. In *This Side of Paradise* and *The Great Gatsby,* he revealed the negative side of the period's gaiety and freedom, portraying wealthy and attractive people leading imperiled lives in gilded surroundings. In New York City, a brilliant group of writers routinely lunched together at the Algonquin Hotel's "Round Table." Among the best known of them was Dorothy Parker, a short story writer, poet, and essayist. Parker was famous for her wisecracking wit, expressed in such lines as "I was the toast of two continents—Greenland and Australia."

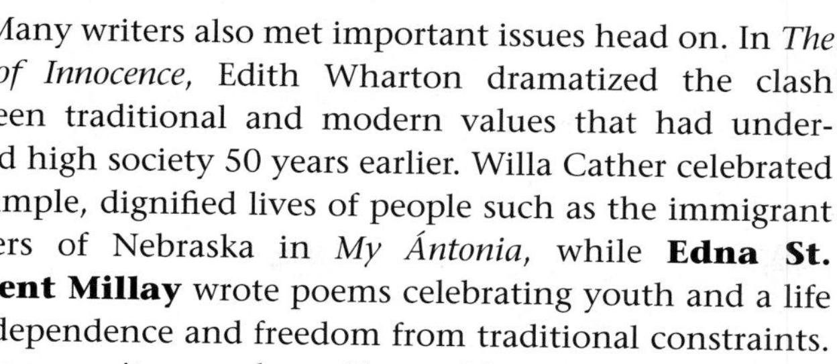

Many writers also met important issues head on. In *The Age of Innocence,* Edith Wharton dramatized the clash between traditional and modern values that had undermined high society 50 years earlier. Willa Cather celebrated the simple, dignified lives of people such as the immigrant farmers of Nebraska in *My Ántonia,* while **Edna St. Vincent Millay** wrote poems celebrating youth and a life of independence and freedom from traditional constraints.

Some writers such as Fitzgerald, Ernest Hemingway, and John Dos Passos were so soured by American culture that they chose to settle in Europe, mainly in Paris. Socializing in the city's cafes, they formed a group that the writer Gertrude Stein called the Lost Generation. They joined other American writers already in Europe such as the poets Ezra Pound and T. S. Eliot, whose poem *The Waste Land* presented an agonized view of a society that seemed stripped of humanity. **D**

MAIN IDEA

Analyzing Causes

D Why did some writers reject American culture and values?

Several writers saw action in World War I, and their early books denounced war. Dos Passos's novel *Three Soldiers* attacked war as a machine designed to crush human freedom. Later, he turned to social and political themes, using modern techniques to capture the mood of city life and the losses that came with success. **Ernest Hemingway,** wounded in World War I, became the best-known expatriate author. In his novels *The Sun Also Rises* and *A Farewell to Arms,* he criticized the glorification of war. He also introduced a tough, simplified style of writing that set a new literary standard, using sentences a *Time* reporter compared to "round stones polished by rain and wind."

Vocabulary
expatriate: a person who has taken up residence in a foreign country

During this rich literary era, vital developments were also taking place in African-American society. Black Americans of the 1920s began to voice pride in their heritage, and black artists and writers revealed the richness of African-American culture.

KEY PLAYER

F. SCOTT FITZGERALD 1896–1940

F. Scott Fitzgerald married vivacious Zelda Sayre in 1920 after his novel *This Side of Paradise* became an instant hit. He said of this time in his life:

> "Riding in a taxi one afternoon between very tall buildings under a mauve and rosy sky,
> I began to bawl because I had everything I wanted and knew I would never be so happy again."

Flush with money, the couple plunged into a wild social whirl and outspent their incomes. The years following were difficult. Zelda suffered from repeated mental breakdowns, and Scott's battle with alcoholism took its toll.

ASSESSMENT

1. **TERMS & NAMES** For each of the following names, write a sentence explaining his or her significance.
   - **Charles A. Lindbergh**
   - **George Gershwin**
   - **Georgia O'Keeffe**
   - **Sinclair Lewis**
   - **F. Scott Fitzgerald**
   - **Edna St. Vincent Millay**
   - **Ernest Hemingway**

MAIN IDEA

2. **TAKING NOTES**
   Create a time line of key events relating to 1920s popular culture. Use the dates below as a guide.

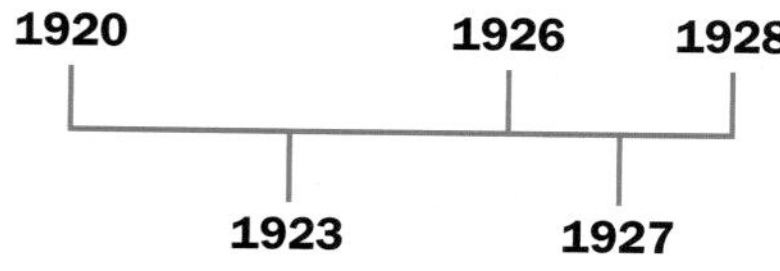

In a sentence or two, explain which of these events interests you the most and why.

CRITICAL THINKING

3. **SYNTHESIZING**
   In what ways do you think the mass media and mass culture helped Americans create a sense of national community in the 1920s? Support your answer with details from the text. **Think About:**
   - the content and readership of newspapers and magazines
   - attendance at sports events and movie theaters
   - the scope of radio broadcasts

4. **EVALUATING**
   Do you think the popular heroes of the 1920s were heroes in a real sense? Why or why not?

5. **SUMMARIZING**
   In two or three sentences, summarize the effects of education and mass media on society in the 1920s.

The Harlem Renaissance

MAIN IDEA

African-American ideas, politics, art, literature, and music flourished in Harlem and elsewhere in the United States.

WHY IT MATTERS NOW

The Harlem Renaissance provided a foundation of African-American intellectualism to which African-American writers, artists, and musicians contribute today.

Terms & Names

- **Zora Neale Hurston**
- **James Weldon Johnson**
- **Marcus Garvey**
- **Harlem Renaissance**
- **Claude McKay**
- **Langston Hughes**
- **Paul Robeson**
- **Louis Armstrong**
- **Duke Ellington**
- **Bessie Smith**

One American's Story

When the spirited **Zora Neale Hurston** was a girl in Eatonville, Florida, in the early 1900s, she loved to read adventure stories and myths. The powerful tales struck a chord with the young, talented Hurston and made her yearn for a wider world.

A PERSONAL VOICE ZORA NEALE HURSTON

> **"My soul was with the gods and my body in the village. People just would not act like gods. . . . Raking back yards and carrying out chamber-pots, were not the tasks of Thor. I wanted to be away from drabness and to stretch my limbs in some mighty struggle."**
>
> —quoted in *The African American Encyclopedia*

After spending time with a traveling theater company and attending Howard University, Hurston ended up in New York where she struggled to the top of African-American literary society by hard work, flamboyance, and, above all, grit. "I have seen that the world is to the strong regardless of a little pigmentation more or less," Hurston wrote later. "I do not weep at [being Negro]—I am too busy sharpening my oyster knife." Hurston was on the move, like millions of others. And, like them, she went after the pearl in the oyster—the good life in America.

VIDEO

JUMP AT THE SUN: **Zora Neale Hurston and the Harlem Renaissance**

African-American Voices in the 1920s

During the 1920s, African Americans set new goals for themselves as they moved north to the nation's cities. Their migration was an expression of their changing attitude toward themselves—an attitude perhaps best captured in a phrase first used around this time, "Black is beautiful."

THE MOVE NORTH Between 1910 and 1920, in a movement known as the Great Migration, hundreds of thousands of African Americans had uprooted themselves from their homes in the South and moved north to the big cities in search of jobs. By the end of the decade, 5.2 million of the nation's 12 million African Americans—over 40 percent—lived in cities. Zora Neale Hurston documented the departure of some of these African Americans.

A PERSONAL VOICE ZORA NEALE HURSTON

> **"Some said goodbye cheerfully . . . others fearfully, with terrors of unknown dangers in their mouths . . . others in their eagerness for distance said nothing. The daybreak found them gone. The wind said North."**
>
> —quoted in *Sorrow's Kitchen: The Life and Folklore of Zora Neale Hurston*

MAIN IDEA

Analyzing Effects

A) How did the influx of African Americans change Northern cities?

However, Northern cities in general had not welcomed the massive influx of African Americans. Tensions had escalated in the years prior to 1920, culminating, in the summer of 1919, in approximately 25 urban race riots. A

AFRICAN-AMERICAN GOALS Founded in 1909, The National Association for the Advancement of Colored People (NAACP) urged African Americans to protest racial violence. W. E. B. Du Bois, a founding member of the NAACP, led a parade of 10,000 African-American men in New York to protest such violence. Du Bois also used the NAACP's magazine, *The Crisis*, as a platform for leading a struggle for civil rights.

Under the leadership of **James Weldon Johnson**—poet, lawyer, and NAACP executive secretary—the organization fought for legislation to protect African-American rights. It made antilynching laws one of its main priorities. In 1919, three antilynching bills were introduced in Congress, although none was passed. The NAACP continued its campaign through antilynching organizations that had been established in 1892 by Ida B. Wells. Gradually, the number of lynchings dropped. The NAACP represented the new, more militant voice of African Americans.

MARCUS GARVEY AND THE UNIA Although many African Americans found their voice in the NAACP, they still faced daily threats and discrimination. **Marcus Garvey,** an immigrant from Jamaica, believed that African Americans should build a separate society. His different, more radical message of black pride aroused the hopes of many.

In 1914, Garvey founded the Universal Negro Improvement Association (UNIA). In 1918, he moved the UNIA to New York City and opened offices in urban ghettos in order to recruit followers. By the mid-1920s, Garvey claimed he had a million followers. He appealed to African Americans with a combination of spellbinding oratory, mass meetings, parades, and a message of pride.

Vocabulary
oratory: the art of public speaking

A PERSONAL VOICE MARCUS GARVEY

> **"In view of the fact that the black man of Africa has contributed as much to the world as the white man of Europe, and the brown man and yellow man of Asia, we of the Universal Negro Improvement Association demand that the white, yellow, and brown races give to the black man his place in the civilization of the world. We ask for nothing more than the rights of 400 million Negroes."**
>
> —speech at Liberty Hall, New York City, 1922

KEY PLAYER

JAMES WELDON JOHNSON
1871–1938

James Weldon Johnson worked as a school principal, newspaper editor, and lawyer in Florida. In 1900, he wrote the lyrics for "Lift Every Voice and Sing," the song that became known as the black national anthem. The first stanza begins as follows:

"Lift every voice and sing
Till earth and heaven ring,
Ring with the harmonies of
Liberty;
Let our rejoicing rise
High as the listening skies,
Let it resound loud as the
rolling sea."

In the 1920s, Johnson straddled the worlds of politics and art. He served as executive secretary of the NAACP, spearheading the fight against lynching. In addition, he wrote well-known works, such as *God's Trombones*, a series of sermon-like poems, and *Black Manhattan*, a look at black cultural life in New York during the Roaring Twenties.

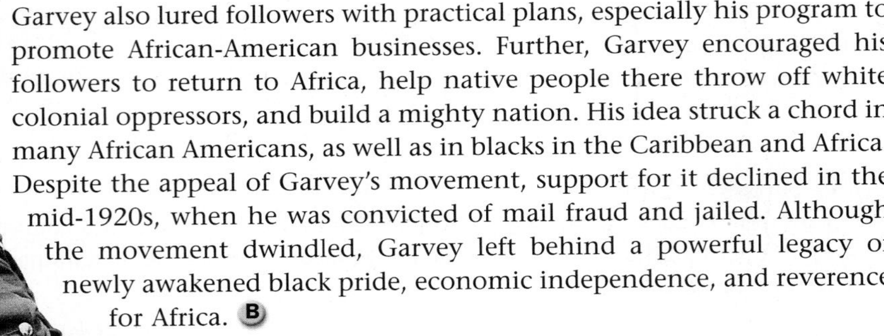

Garvey also lured followers with practical plans, especially his program to promote African-American businesses. Further, Garvey encouraged his followers to return to Africa, help native people there throw off white colonial oppressors, and build a mighty nation. His idea struck a chord in many African Americans, as well as in blacks in the Caribbean and Africa. Despite the appeal of Garvey's movement, support for it declined in the mid-1920s, when he was convicted of mail fraud and jailed. Although the movement dwindled, Garvey left behind a powerful legacy of newly awakened black pride, economic independence, and reverence for Africa. B

MAIN IDEA

Summarizing
B What approach to race relations did Marcus Garvey promote?

▲ Marcus Garvey designed this uniform of purple and gold, complete with feathered hat, for his role as "Provisional President of Africa."

The Harlem Renaissance Flowers in New York

Many African Americans who migrated north moved to Harlem, a neighborhood on the Upper West Side of New York's Manhattan Island. In the 1920s, Harlem became the world's largest black urban community, with residents from the South, the West Indies, Cuba, Puerto Rico, and Haiti. James Weldon Johnson described Harlem as the capital of black America.

A PERSONAL VOICE JAMES WELDON JOHNSON

"Harlem is not merely a Negro colony or community, it is a city within a city, the greatest Negro city in the world. It is not a slum or a fringe, it is located in the heart of Manhattan and occupies one of the most beautiful . . . sections of the city. . . . It has its own churches, social and civic centers, shops, theaters, and other places of amusement. And it contains more Negroes to the square mile than any other spot on earth."

—"Harlem: The Culture Capital"

Like many other urban neighborhoods, Harlem suffered from overcrowding, unemployment, and poverty. But its problems in the 1920s were eclipsed by a flowering of creativity called the **Harlem Renaissance,** a literary and artistic movement celebrating African-American culture.

AFRICAN-AMERICAN WRITERS Above all, the Harlem Renaissance was a literary movement led by well-educated, middle-class African Americans who expressed a new pride in the African-American experience. They celebrated their heritage and wrote with defiance and poignancy about the trials of being black in a white world. W. E. B. Du Bois and James Weldon Johnson helped these young talents along, as did the Harvard-educated former Rhodes scholar Alain Locke. In 1925, Locke published *The New Negro,* a landmark collection of literary works by many promising young African-American writers.

Claude McKay, a novelist, poet, and Jamaican immigrant, was a major figure whose militant verses urged African Americans to resist prejudice and discrimination. His poems also expressed the pain of life in the black ghettos and the strain of being black in a world dominated by whites. Another gifted writer of the time was Jean Toomer. His experimental book *Cane*—a mix of poems and sketches about blacks in the North and the South—was among the first full-length literary publications of the Harlem Renaissance.

Missouri-born **Langston Hughes** was the movement's best-known poet. Many of Hughes's 1920s poems described the difficult lives of working-class African Americans. Some of his poems moved to the tempo of jazz and the blues. (See Literature in the Jazz Age on page 458.)

Harlem in the 1920s

At the turn of the century, New York's Harlem neighborhood was overbuilt with new apartment houses. Enterprising African-American realtors began buying and leasing property to other African Americans who were eager to move into the prosperous neighborhood. As the number of blacks in Harlem increased, many whites began moving out. Harlem quickly grew to become the center of black America and the birthplace of the political, social, and cultural movement known as the Harlem Renaissance.

The Fletcher Henderson Orchestra became one of the most influential jazz bands during the Harlem Renaissance. Here, Henderson, the band's founder, sits at the piano, with Louis Armstrong on trumpet (rear, center).

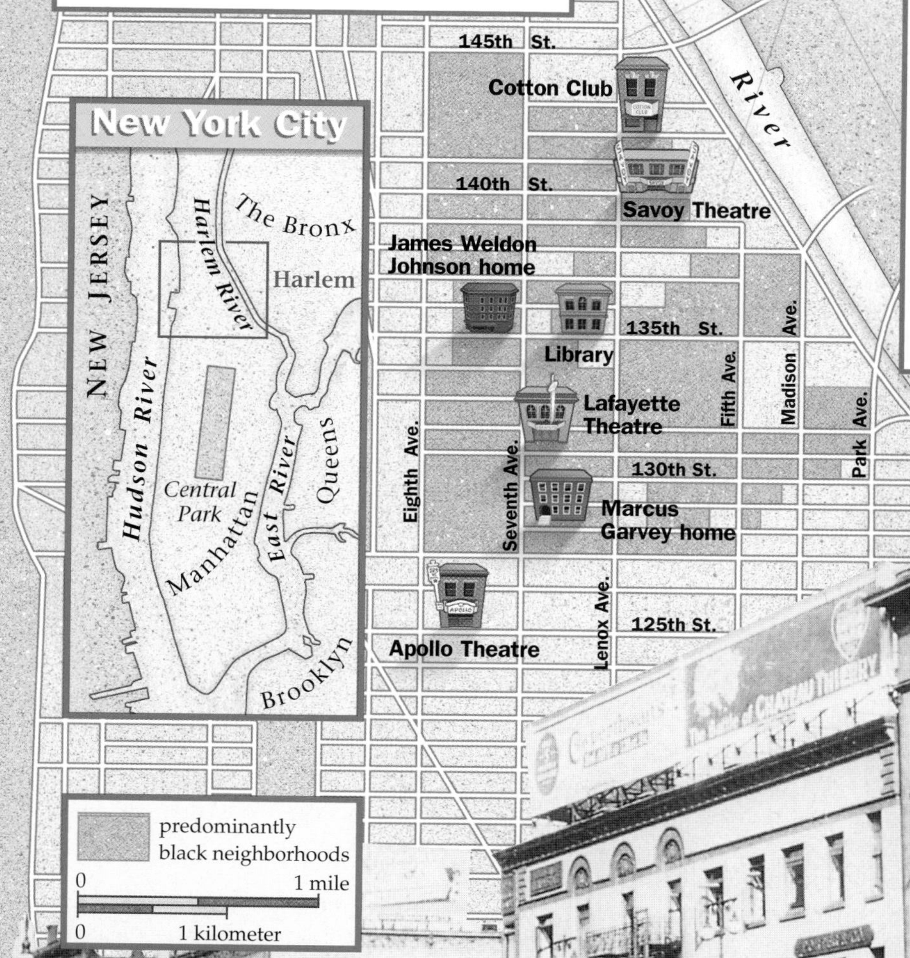

In the mid 1920s, the Cotton Club was one of a number of fashionable entertainment clubs in Harlem. Although many venues like the Cotton Club were segregated, white audiences packed the clubs to hear the new music styles of black performers such as Duke Ellington and Bessie Smith.

In 1927, Harlem was a bustling neighborhood.

In many of her novels, short stories, poems, and books of folklore, Zora Neale Hurston portrayed the lives of poor, unschooled Southern blacks—in her words, "the greatest cultural wealth of the continent." Much of her work celebrated what she called the common person's art form—the simple folkways and values of people who had survived slavery through their ingenuity and strength. C

MAIN IDEA

Synthesizing
C In what ways did writers of the Harlem Renaissance celebrate a "rebirth"?

AFRICAN–AMERICAN PERFORMERS The spirit and talent of the Harlem Renaissance reached far beyond the world of African-American writers and intellectuals. Some observers, including Langston Hughes, thought the movement was launched with *Shuffle Along*, a black musical comedy popular in 1921. "It gave just the proper push . . . to that Negro vogue of the '20s," he wrote. Several songs in *Shuffle Along*, including "Love Will Find a Way," won popularity among white audiences. The show also spotlighted the talents of several black performers, including the singers Florence Mills, Josephine Baker, and Mabel Mercer.

During the 1920s, African Americans in the performing arts won large followings. The tenor Roland Hayes rose to stardom as a concert singer, and the singer and actress Ethel Waters debuted on Broadway in the musical *Africana*. **Paul Robeson,** the son of a one-time slave, became a major dramatic actor. His performance in Shakespeare's *Othello*, first in London and later in New York City, was widely acclaimed. Subsequently, Robeson struggled with the racism he experienced in the United States and the indignities inflicted upon him because of his support of the Soviet Union and the Communist Party. He took up residence abroad, living for a time in England and the Soviet Union.

Background
See Historical Spotlight on page 617.

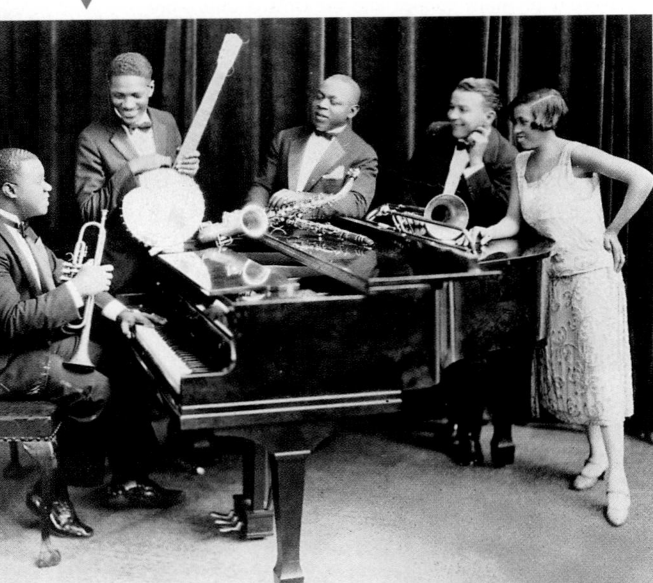

The Hot Five included (*from left*) Louis Armstrong, Johnny St. Cyr, Johnny Dodds, Kid Ory, and Lil Hardin Armstrong.

AFRICAN AMERICANS AND JAZZ Jazz was born in the early 20th century in New Orleans, where musicians blended instrumental ragtime and vocal blues into an exuberant new sound. In 1918, Joe "King" Oliver and his Creole Jazz Band traveled north to Chicago, carrying jazz with them. In 1922, a young trumpet player named **Louis Armstrong** joined Oliver's group, which became known as the Creole Jazz Band. His talent rocketed him to stardom in the jazz world.

Famous for his astounding sense of rhythm and his ability to improvise, Armstrong made personal expression a key part of jazz. After two years in Chicago, in 1924 he joined Fletcher Henderson's band, then the most important big jazz band in New York City. Armstrong went on to become perhaps the most important and influential musician in the history of jazz. He often talked about his anticipated funeral.

A PERSONAL VOICE LOUIS ARMSTRONG

"They're going to blow over me. Cats will be coming from everywhere to play. I had a beautiful life. When I get to the Pearly Gates I'll play a duet with Gabriel. We'll play 'Sleepy Time Down South.' He wants to be remembered for his music just like I do."

—quoted in *The Negro Almanac*

Jazz quickly spread to such cities as Kansas City, Memphis, and New York City, and it became the most popular music for dancing. During the 1920s, Harlem pulsed to the sounds of jazz, which lured throngs of whites to the showy, exotic nightclubs there, including the famed Cotton Club. In the late 1920s, **Edward Kennedy "Duke" Ellington,** a jazz pianist and composer, led his ten-piece orchestra at the Cotton Club. In a 1925 essay titled "The Negro Spirituals," Alain Locke seemed almost to predict the career of the talented Ellington.

A PERSONAL VOICE ALAIN LOCKE

> "Up to the present, the resources of Negro music have been tentatively exploited in only one direction at a time—melodically here, rhythmically there, harmonically in a third direction. A genius that would organize its distinctive elements in a formal way would be the musical giant of his age."
>
> —quoted in *Afro-American Writing: An Anthology of Prose and Poetry*

Through the 1920s and 1930s, Ellington won renown as one of America's greatest composers, with pieces such as "Mood Indigo" and "Sophisticated Lady."

Cab Calloway, a talented drummer, saxophonist, and singer, formed another important jazz orchestra, which played at Harlem's Savoy Ballroom and the Cotton Club, alternating with Duke Ellington. Along with Louis Armstrong, Calloway popularized "scat," or improvised jazz singing using sounds instead of words.

Bessie Smith, a female blues singer, was perhaps the outstanding vocalist of the decade. She recorded on black-oriented labels produced by the major record companies. She achieved enormous popularity and in 1927 became the highest-paid black artist in the world. D

MAIN IDEA

Summarizing

D Besides literary accomplishments, in what areas did African Americans achieve remarkable results?

The Harlem Renaissance represented a portion of the great social and cultural changes that swept America in the 1920s. The period was characterized by economic prosperity, new ideas, changing values, and personal freedom, as well as important developments in art, literature, and music. Most of the social changes were lasting. The economic boom, however, was short-lived.

KEY PLAYER

DUKE ELLINGTON
1899–1974

Edward Kennedy "Duke" Ellington, one of the greatest composers of the 20th century, was largely a self-taught musician. He developed his skills by playing at family socials. He wrote his first song, "Soda Fountain Rag," at age 15 and started his first band at 22.

During the five years Ellington played at Harlem's glittering Cotton Club, he set a new standard, playing mainly his own stylish compositions. Through radio and the film short *Black and Tan,* the Duke Ellington Orchestra was able to reach nationwide audiences. Billy Strayhorn, Ellington's long-time arranger and collaborator, said, "Ellington plays the piano, but his real instrument is his band."

SECTION 4 ASSESSMENT

1. **TERMS & NAMES** For each term or name, write a sentence explaining its significance.
   - **Zora Neale Hurston**
   - **James Weldon Johnson**
   - **Marcus Garvey**
   - **Harlem Renaissance**
   - **Claude McKay**
   - **Langston Hughes**
   - **Paul Robeson**
   - **Louis Armstrong**
   - **Duke Ellington**
   - **Bessie Smith**

MAIN IDEA

2. **TAKING NOTES**
   In a tree diagram, identify three areas of artistic achievement in the Harlem Renaissance. For each, name two outstanding African Americans.

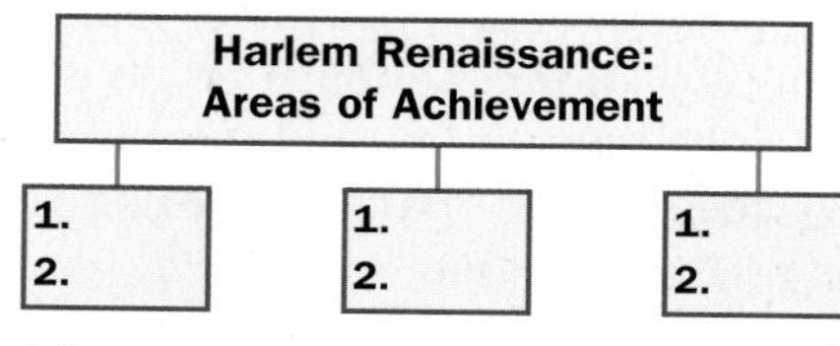

Write a paragraph explaining the impact of these achievements.

CRITICAL THINKING

3. **ANALYZING CAUSES**
   Speculate on why an African-American renaissance flowered during the 1920s. Support your answer. **Think About:**
   - racial discrimination in the South
   - campaigns for equality in the North
   - Harlem's diverse cultures
   - the changing culture of all Americans

4. **FORMING GENERALIZATIONS**
   How did popular culture in America change as a result of the Great Migration?

5. **DRAWING CONCLUSIONS**
   What did the Harlem Renaissance contribute to both black and general American history?

Literature in the Jazz Age

1920–1929 After World War I, American literature—like American jazz—moved to the vanguard of the international artistic scene. Many American writers remained in Europe after the war, some settling in London but many more joining the expatriate community on the Left Bank of the Seine River in Paris, where they could live cheaply.

Back in the United States, such cities as Chicago and New York were magnets for America's young artistic talents. New York City gave birth to the Harlem Renaissance, a blossoming of African-American culture named for the New York City neighborhood where many African-American writers and artists settled. Further downtown, the artistic community of Greenwich Village drew literary talents such as the poets Edna St. Vincent Millay and E. E. Cummings and the playwright Eugene O'Neill.

F. SCOTT FITZGERALD

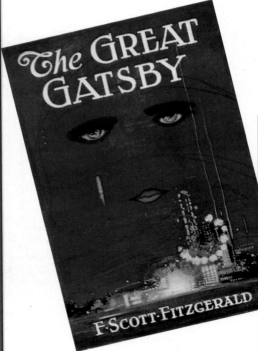

The foremost chronicler of the Jazz Age was the Minnesota-born writer F. Scott Fitzgerald, who in Paris, New York, and later Hollywood rubbed elbows with other leading American writers of the day. In the following passage from Fitzgerald's novel *The Great Gatsby*, the narrator describes a fashionable 1920s party thrown by the title character at his Long Island estate.

> By seven o'clock the orchestra has arrived, no thin five-piece affair, but a whole pitful of oboes and trombones and saxophones and viols and cornets and piccolos, and low and high drums. The last swimmers have come in from the beach now and are dressing up-stairs; the cars from New York are parked five deep in the drive, and already the halls and salons and verandas are gaudy with primary colors, and hair shorn in strange new ways, and shawls beyond the dreams of Castile. The bar is in full swing, and floating rounds of cocktails permeate the garden outside, until the air is alive with chatter and laughter, and casual innuendo and introductions forgotten on the spot, and enthusiastic meetings between women who never knew each other's names.
>
> The lights grow brighter as the earth lurches away from the sun, and now the orchestra is playing yellow cocktail music, and the opera of voices pitches a key higher. Laughter is easier minute by minute, spilled with prodigality, tipped out at a cheerful word. The groups change more swiftly, swell with new arrivals, dissolve and form in the same breath; already there are wanderers, confident girls who weave here and there among the stouter and more stable, become for a sharp, joyous moment the center of a group, and then, excited with triumph, glide on through the sea-change of faces and voices and color under the constantly changing light.
>
> Suddenly one of these gypsies, in trembling opal, seizes a cocktail out of the air, dumps it down for courage and, moving her hands like Frisco, dances out alone on the canvas platform. A momentary hush; the orchestra leader varies his rhythm obligingly for her, and there is a burst of chatter as the erroneous news goes around that she is Gilda Gray's understudy from the Follies. The party has begun.

—F. Scott Fitzgerald, *The Great Gatsby* (1925)

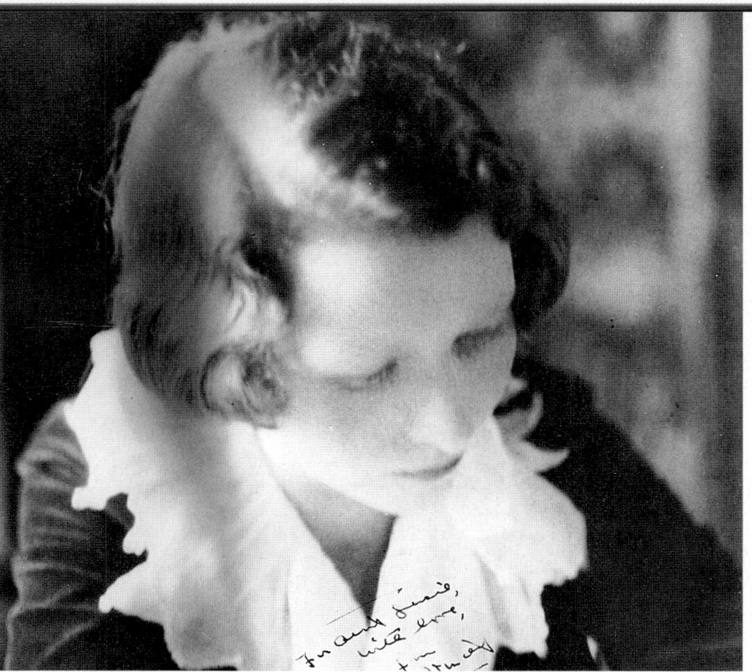

◀ **EDNA ST. VINCENT MILLAY**

In the 1920s, Edna St. Vincent Millay was the quintessential modern young woman, a celebrated poet living a bohemian life in New York's Greenwich Village. The following quatrain memorably proclaims the exuberant philosophy of the young and fashionable in the Roaring Twenties.

> My candle burns at both ends;
> It will not last the night;
> But ah, my foes, and oh, my friends—
> It gives a lovely light!

—Edna St. Vincent Millay, "First Fig,"
from *A Few Figs from Thistles* (1920)

LANGSTON HUGHES ▶

A towering figure of the Harlem Renaissance, Langston Hughes often imbued his poetry with the rhythms of jazz and blues. In the poem "Dream Variations," for example, the two stanzas resemble improvised passages played and varied by a jazz musician. The dream of freedom and equality is a recurring symbol in Hughes's verse and has appeared frequently in African-American literature since the 1920s, when Hughes penned this famous poem.

> To fling my arms wide
> In some place of the sun,
> To whirl and to dance
> Till the white day is done.
> Then rest at cool evening
> Beneath a tall tree
> While night comes on gently,
> Dark like me—
> That is my dream!
>
> To fling my arms wide
> In the face of the sun,
> Dance! Whirl! Whirl!
> Till the quick day is done.
> Rest at pale evening . . .
> A tall, slim tree . . .
> Night coming tenderly
> Black like me.

—Langston Hughes, "Dream Variations,"
from *The Weary Blues* (1926)

THINKING CRITICALLY

1. **Comparing** What connections can you make between the literary and music scenes during the Jazz Age?

 **SEE SKILLBUILDER HANDBOOK, PAGE R8.**

2.  **INTERNET ACTIVITY** **CLASSZONE.COM**

Visit the links for American Literature to research writers of the Jazz Age. Then, create a short report on one writer's life. Include titles of published works and an example of his or her writing style.

CHAPTER  ASSESSMENT

VISUAL SUMMARY

THE ROARING LIFE OF THE 1920s

NEW FORMS OF ENTERTAINMENT

- Movies become a national pastime.
- Radio is a prime source of news and entertainment.
- Americans celebrate sports heroes.

NEW MOVEMENTS IN THE ARTS

- Composers create distinctly American music.
- Writers explore new topics.
- Artists depict life in the 1920s.
- Harlem Renaissance flourishes.

PROBLEMS OF URBANIZATION

- Industrialization leads to growth of big cities.
- African Americans continue to move North.
- Cities struggle with prohibition and organized crime.

NEW ATTITUDES AND FASHION

- Changing attitudes toward women allow them greater freedoms.
- Americans adopt radical new fashions and style.
- Traditional and modern ideals collide.

TERMS & NAMES

For each term or name below, write a sentence explaining its historical significance or contribution to the 1920s.

1. bootlegger
2. fundamentalism
3. flapper
4. double standard
5. Charles A. Lindbergh
6. George Gershwin
7. F. Scott Fitzgerald
8. Zora Neale Hurston
9. Harlem Renaissance
10. Paul Robeson

MAIN IDEAS

Use your notes and the information in the chapter to answer the following questions.

Changing Ways of Life *(pages 434–439)*

1. Why was heavy funding needed to enforce the Volstead Act?
2. Explain the circumstances and outcome of the trial of the biology teacher John Scopes.

The Twenties Woman *(pages 440–443)*

3. In what ways did flappers rebel against the earlier styles and attitudes of the Victorian age?
4. What key social, economic, and technological changes of the 1920s affected women's marriages and family life?

Education and Popular Culture *(pages 446–451)*

5. How did high schools change in the 1920s?
6. Cite examples of the flaws of American society that some famous 1920s authors attacked in their writing.

The Harlem Renaissance *(pages 452–457)*

7. What do the Great Migration and the growth of the NAACP and UNIA reveal about the African-American experience in this period?
8. What were some of the important themes treated by African-American writers in the Harlem Renaissance?

CRITICAL THINKING

1. **USING YOUR NOTES** Create a concept web like the one below, and fill it in with trends in popular culture that emerged in the 1920s and continue to influence American society today.

2. **EVALUATING** In "Literature in the Jazz Age," on pages 458–459, you read excerpts from works written in the 1920s by F. Scott Fitzgerald, Edna St. Vincent Millay, and Langston Hughes. How might a phrase current at the time—"flaming youth"—be an appropriate and accurate phrase to describe the young people and voices in these excerpts?

Standardized Test Practice

Use the visual below and your knowledge of United States history to answer question 1.

1. The woman shown on this magazine cover represents a lifestyle championed by which of the following 1920s figures?

   A Zelda Sayre Fitzgerald
   B Edna St. Vincent Millay
   C Anna Howard Shaw
   D Aimee Semple McPherson

2. The great flowering of African-American artistic activity in the 1920s is known as —

   F the Jazz Age
   G the speakeasy
   H the Harlem Renaissance
   J American fundamentalism

Use the quotation and your knowledge of U.S. history to answer question 3.

> **"No more fear, no more cringing, no more sycophantic begging and pleading; but the Negro must strike straight from the shoulder for manhood rights and for full liberty. Africa calls now more than ever."**

3. The quotation supports the "Back to Africa" movement. One important leader of this movement in the 1920s was —

   A Marcus Garvey
   B James Weldon Johnson
   C Zora Neale Hurston
   D Paul Robeson

ADDITIONAL TEST PRACTICE, pages S1–S33.

CLASSZONE.COM

ALTERNATIVE ASSESSMENT

1. **INTERACT WITH HISTORY** Recall your discussion of the question on page 433:

   How might the new prosperity affect your everyday life?

   Now that you have read about life in the 1920s, what do you think was the most significant cultural development during this time? Write a paragraph describing how this change impacted society and how it evolved. Share your paragraph with your class.

2. **VIDEO** **LEARNING FROM MEDIA** View the *American Stories* video "Jump at the Sun." Discuss the following questions in a group; then do the activity.

   - What effect did World War I have on the attitudes of African Americans?
   - What effect might growing up in Eatonville, Florida, have had on Zora Neale Hurston?
   - How did Hurston connect the study of anthropology with the world of her youth?

   Cooperative Learning Activity With your group, think of visuals that represent Zora Neale Hurston's dramatic life. Search through books, magazines, and encyclopedias for pictures that seem to capture her spirit and life experiences. Make copies of the pictures and assemble them in a collage.

The Great Depression Begins

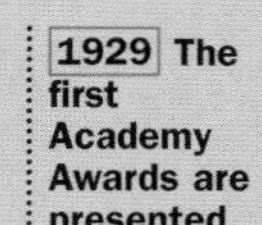

1929 The first Academy Awards are presented.

1929 The stock market crashes.

1930-1933 More than 40% of the nation's banks fail.

1931 Jane Addams shares the Nobel Peace Prize.

1931 8.02 million Americans are unemployed.

USA
WORLD

1929 | 1930 | 1931

1930 Army officers led by José Uriburu seize control of the government of Argentina.

1931 Japan invades Manchuria.

INTERACT
WITH HISTORY

The year is 1929. The U.S. economy has collapsed. Farms, businesses, and banks nationwide are failing, causing massive unemployment and poverty. You are out of work with little prospect of finding a job.

What would you do to feed your family?

Examine the Issues

- What groups of people will be most hurt by the economic crash?
- What can you do to find a paying job?
- What can unemployed and impoverished people do to help each other?

RESEARCH LINKS CLASSZONE.COM

Visit the Chapter 14 links for more information related to The Great Depression Begins.

Women serve soup and slices of bread to unemployed men in an outdoor breadline in Los Angeles, California during the Great Depression.

1932 The Bonus Army arrives in Washington, D.C.

1932 Franklin Delano Roosevelt is elected president.

1933 "Century of Progress Exposition" begins.

1933 The Twenty-first Amendment ends Prohibition.

1933 More than 13 million Americans are unemployed.

1932 | 1933 | 1934

1932 Ibn Sa'ud becomes king of newly-united Saudi Arabia.

1932 From prison, Mohandas K. Gandhi leads a protest against British policies in India.

1933 Adolf Hitler takes power in Germany.

1933 Japan withdraws from the League of Nations.

The Nation's Sick Economy

MAIN IDEA	WHY IT MATTERS NOW	Terms & Names
As the prosperity of the 1920s ended, severe economic problems gripped the nation.	The Great Depression has had lasting effects on how Americans view themselves and their government.	•price support •credit •Alfred E. Smith •Dow Jones Industrial Average •speculation •buying on margin •Black Tuesday •Great Depression •Hawley-Smoot Tariff Act

One American's Story

Gordon Parks, now a well-known photographer, author, and filmmaker, was a 16-year-old high school student in the fall of 1929. He supported himself as a busboy at the exclusive Minnesota Club, where prosperous club members spoke confidently about the economy. Parks, too, looked forward to a bright future. Then came the stock market crash of October 1929. In his autobiography, Parks recalled his feelings at the time.

▲ Gordon Parks, shown here in 1968 discussing the movie version of his autobiographical novel, *The Learning Tree.*

A PERSONAL VOICE GORDON PARKS

"I couldn't imagine such financial disaster touching my small world; it surely concerned only the rich. But by the first week of November . . . I was without a job. All that next week I searched for any kind of work that would prevent my leaving school. Again it was, 'We're firing, not hiring.'. . . I went to school and cleaned out my locker, knowing it was impossible to stay on. A piercing chill was in the air as I walked back to the rooming house."

—*A Choice of Weapons*

The crash of 1929, and the depression that followed, dealt a crushing blow to the hopes and dreams of millions of Americans. The high-flying prosperity of the 1920s was over. Hard times had begun.

Economic Troubles on the Horizon

As the 1920s advanced, serious problems threatened economic prosperity. Though some Americans became wealthy, many more could not earn a decent living. Important industries struggled, and farmers grew more crops and raised more livestock than they could sell at a profit. Both consumers and farmers were steadily going deeper into debt. As the decade drew to a close, these slippages in the economy signaled the end of an era.

INDUSTRIES IN TROUBLE The superficial prosperity of the late 1920s shrouded weaknesses that would signal the onset of the Great Depression. Key basic industries, such as railroads, textiles, and steel had barely made a profit. Railroads lost business to new forms of transportation (trucks, buses, and private automobiles, for instance).

Mining and lumbering, which had expanded during wartime, were no longer in high demand. Coal mining was especially hard-hit, in part due to stiff competition from new forms of energy, including hydroelectric power, fuel oil, and natural gas. By the early 1930s, these sources supplied more than half the energy that had once come from coal. Even the boom industries of the 1920s—automobiles, construction, and consumer goods—weakened. One important economic indicator that declined during this time was housing starts—the number of new dwellings being built. When housing starts fall, so do jobs in many related industries, such as furniture manufacturing and lumbering. (A)

MAIN IDEA

Identifying Problems

(A) What industrial weakness signaled a declining economy in the 1920s?

FARMERS NEED A LIFT Perhaps agriculture suffered the most. During World War I, prices rose and international demand for crops such as wheat and corn soared. Farmers had planted more and taken out loans for land and equipment. However, demand fell after the war, and crop prices declined by 40 percent or more.

Farmers boosted production in the hopes of selling more crops, but this only depressed prices further. Between 1919 and 1921 annual farm income declined from $10 billion to just over $4 billion. Farmers who had gone into debt had difficulty in paying off their loans. Many lost their farms when banks foreclosed and seized the property as payment for the debt. As farmers began to default on their loans, many rural banks began to fail. Auctions were held to recoup some of the banks' losses.

Congress tried to help out farmers with a piece of legislation called the McNary-Haugen bill. This called for federal **price-supports** for key products such as wheat, corn, cotton, and tobacco. The government would buy surplus crops at guaranteed prices and sell them on the world market.

President Coolidge vetoed the bill twice. He commented, "Farmers have never made money. I don't believe we can do much about it."

CONSUMERS HAVE LESS MONEY TO SPEND As farmers' incomes fell, they bought fewer goods and services, but the problem was larger. By the late 1920s,

Farm equipment is auctioned off in Hastings, Nebraska. ▼

Americans were buying less—mainly because of rising prices, stagnant wages, unbalanced distribution of income, and overbuying on credit in the preceding years. Production had also expanded much faster than wages, resulting in an ever-widening gap between the rich and the poor.

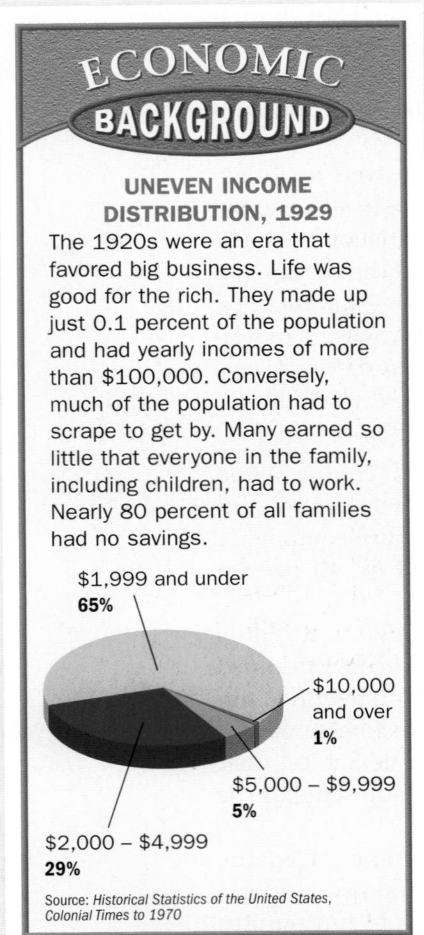

ECONOMIC BACKGROUND

UNEVEN INCOME DISTRIBUTION, 1929

The 1920s were an era that favored big business. Life was good for the rich. They made up just 0.1 percent of the population and had yearly incomes of more than $100,000. Conversely, much of the population had to scrape to get by. Many earned so little that everyone in the family, including children, had to work. Nearly 80 percent of all families had no savings.

Source: *Historical Statistics of the United States, Colonial Times to 1970*

LIVING ON CREDIT Although many Americans appeared to be prosperous during the 1920s, in fact they were living beyond their means. They often bought goods on **credit**—an arrangement in which consumers agreed to buy now and pay later for purchases. This was often in the form of an installment plan (usually in monthly payments) that included interest charges.

By making credit easily available, businesses encouraged Americans to pile up a large consumer debt. Many people then had trouble paying off their growing debts. Faced with debt, consumers cut back on spending.

UNEVEN DISTRIBUTION OF INCOME During the 1920s, the rich got richer, and the poor got poorer. Between 1920 and 1929, the income of the wealthiest 1 percent of the population rose by 75 percent, compared with a 9 percent increase for Americans as a whole.

More than 70 percent of the nation's families earned less than $2,500 per year, then considered the minimum amount needed for a decent standard of living. Even families earning twice that much could not afford many of the household products that manufacturers produced. Economists estimate that the average man or woman bought a new outfit of clothes only once a year. Scarcely half the homes in many cities had electric lights or a furnace for heat. Only one city home in ten had an electric refrigerator.

This unequal distribution of income meant that most Americans could not participate fully in the economic advances of the 1920s. Many people did not have the money to purchase the flood of goods that factories produced. The prosperity of the era rested on a fragile foundation. B

MAIN IDEA

Forming Generalizations

B What did the experience of farmers and consumers at this time suggest about the health of the economy?

Hoover Takes the Nation

"We in America are nearer to the final triumph over poverty than ever before."

HERBERT HOOVER

Although economic disaster was around the corner, the election of 1928 took place in a mood of apparent national prosperity. This election pitted Republican candidate Herbert Hoover against Democrat **Alfred E. Smith.**

THE ELECTION OF 1928 Hoover, the secretary of commerce under Harding and Coolidge, was a mining engineer from Iowa who had never run for public office. Smith was a career politician who had served four terms as governor of New York. He was personable and enjoyed being in the limelight, unlike the quiet and reserved Hoover. Still, Hoover had one major advantage: he could point to years of prosperity under Republican administrations since 1920. Many Americans believed him when he declared, "We in America are nearer to the final triumph over poverty than ever before."

It was an overwhelming victory for Hoover. The message was clear: most Americans were happy with Republican leadership.

DREAMS OF RICHES IN THE STOCK MARKET By 1929, some economists had warned of weaknesses in the economy, but most Americans

Vocabulary
stock: a share of ownership in a company

maintained the utmost confidence in the nation's economic health. In increasing numbers, those who could afford to invested in the stock market. The stock market had become the most visible symbol of a prosperous American economy. Then, as now, the **Dow Jones Industrial Average** was the most widely used barometer of the stock market's health. The Dow is a measure based on the stock prices of 30 representative large firms trading on the New York Stock Exchange.

Through most of the 1920s, stock prices rose steadily. The Dow had reached a high of 381 points, nearly 300 points higher than it had been five years earlier. Eager to take advantage of this "bull market"—a period of rising stock prices—Americans rushed to buy stocks and bonds. One observer wrote, "It seemed as if all economic law had been suspended and a new era opened up in which success and prosperity could be had without knowledge or industry." By 1929, about 4 million Americans—or 3 percent of the nation's population—owned stocks. Many of these investors were already wealthy, but others were average Americans who hoped to strike it rich.

MAIN IDEA

Analyzing Events
C How did speculation and margin buying cause stock prices to rise?

However, the seeds of trouble were taking root. People were engaging in **speculation**—that is, they bought stocks and bonds on the chance of a quick profit, while ignoring the risks. Many began **buying on margin**—paying a small percentage of a stock's price as a down payment and borrowing the rest. With easy money available to investors, the unrestrained buying and selling fueled the market's upward spiral. The government did little to discourage such buying or to regulate the market. In reality, these rising prices did not reflect companies' worth. Worse, if the value of stocks declined, people who had bought on margin had no way to pay off the loans. C

The Stock Market Crashes

In early September 1929, stock prices peaked and then fell. Confidence in the market started to waver, and some investors quickly sold their stocks and pulled out. On October 24, the market took a plunge. Panicked investors unloaded their shares. But the worst was yet to come.

Analyzing *Political Cartoons*

DAY OF WRATH

After the apparent prosperity of the 1920s, virtually few were prepared for the devastating effects of the stock market crash. This cartoon by James N. Rosenberg, which shows Wall Street crumbling on October 29, 1929, is titled *Dies Irae*, Latin for "day of wrath."

SKILLBUILDER Analyzing Political Cartoons

1. What does the cartoonist suggest will happen to individuals because of the crash?
2. How does the cartoonist convey the sense of fear and shock?
3. What do the looks on people's faces indicate about the impact of the crash?

SEE SKILLBUILDER HANDBOOK, PAGE R24.

BLACK TUESDAY On October 29—now known as **Black Tuesday**—the bottom fell out of the market and the nation's confidence. Shareholders frantically tried to sell before prices plunged even lower. The number of shares dumped that day was a record 16.4 million. Additional millions of shares could not find buyers. People who had bought stocks on credit were stuck with huge debts as the prices plummeted, while others lost most of their savings.

NOW & THEN

NEW YORK STOCK EXCHANGE

In the twenty-first century, the New York Stock Exchange (NYSE) remains at its core what it has been since it opened its doors in 1792: the nation's premier marketplace for the buying and selling of stocks. There, stockbrokers known as "members" take orders from their customers to buy and sell shares of stock in any one of more than 3,000 companies.

To execute their customers' orders, the members offer and receive bids in what resembles a loud and fast-paced auction. In general, customers submit two types of orders. A limit order tells the broker to buy or sell only if the stock reaches a certain price. A market order tells the broker to execute a transaction immediately, no matter what the price.

Despite remaining close to its roots, the NYSE is today undergoing perhaps the most significant changes in its long history, in large part due to the growth of computers and the Internet.

A Pen and Paper Operation

In the 1920s, orders to buy or sell a stock arrived at brokers' telephone booths located around the edge of the trading floor. They were then carried by hand or sent by pneumatic tube to the trading post where that stock would be traded.

NYSE employees called reporters had to record every transaction. For each new sale, they wrote out a slip of paper containing the stock's abbreviation, the number of shares, and the price, and then transmitted it to the ticker room. Market information was typed into a keyboard that converted the keystrokes into electrical impulses that drove the clattering print wheels in ticker machines along the network. People would read the current display at the trading posts.

The trading floor in 1914. ▲

Technological Changes

While still centered around human interaction, the exchange has incorporated a number of computer technologies to keep up with the times. For example, members now receive stock bids and offers through an electronic delivery system known as SuperDot, which enables them to make a trade in less than 12 seconds. Electronic communications networks now allow individuals to buy and sell stocks themselves over the Internet at a fraction of what it would cost to use a specialist. Such innovation has prompted some to insist that all future trading will be done via computers, thus eliminating the need for physical exchanges such as the NYSE.

The trading floor in 2000. ▼

SKILLBUILDER

1. **Hypothesizing** What scenarios can you imagine that might prompt someone to submit a market order on a certain stock?
2. **Comparing** How has technology on the trading floor changed since the 1920s?

By mid-November, investors had lost about $30 billion, an amount equal to how much America spent in World War I. The stock market bubble had finally burst. One eyewitness to these events, Frederick Lewis Allen, described the resulting situation.

A PERSONAL VOICE FREDERICK LEWIS ALLEN

"The Big Bull Market was dead. Billions of dollars' worth of profits—and paper profits—had disappeared. The grocer, the window cleaner, and the seamstress had lost their capital [savings]. In every town there were families which had suddenly dropped from showy affluence into debt. . . . With the Big Bull Market gone and prosperity going, Americans were soon to find themselves living in an altered world which called for new adjustments, new ideas, new habits of thought, and a new order of values."

—*Only Yesterday*

Financial Collapse

The stock market crash signaled the beginning of the **Great Depression**—the period from 1929 to 1940 in which the economy plummeted and unemployment skyrocketed. The crash alone did not cause the Great Depression, but it hastened the collapse of the economy and made the depression more severe.

BANK AND BUSINESS FAILURES After the crash, many people panicked and withdrew their money from banks. But some couldn't get their money because the banks had invested it in the stock market. In 1929, 600 banks closed. By 1933, 11,000 of the nation's 25,000 banks had failed. Because the government did not protect or insure bank accounts, millions of people lost their savings accounts.

The Great Depression hit other businesses, too. Between 1929 and 1932, the gross national product—the nation's total output of goods and services—was cut nearly in half, from $104 billion to $59 billion. Approximately 90,000 businesses went bankrupt. Among these failed enterprises were once-prosperous automobile and railroad companies.

As the economy plunged into a tailspin, millions of workers lost their jobs. Unemployment leaped from 3 percent (1.6 million workers) in 1929 to 25 percent (13 million workers) in 1933. One out of every four workers was out of a job. Those who kept their jobs faced pay cuts and reduced hours.

Not everyone fared so badly, of course. Before the crash, some speculators had sold off their stocks and made money. Joseph P. Kennedy, the father of future president John F. Kennedy, was one who did. Most, however, were not so lucky or shrewd. D

MAIN IDEA

Analyzing Effects

D What happened to ordinary workers during the Great Depression?

This British ▲ election poster shows that the Great Depression was a global event.

WORLDWIDE SHOCK WAVES The United States was not the only country gripped by the Great Depression. Much of Europe, for example, had suffered throughout the 1920s. European countries trying to recover from the ravages of World War I faced high war debts. In addition, Germany had to pay war reparations—payments to compensate the Allies for the damages Germany had caused. The Great Depression compounded these problems by limiting America's ability to import European goods. This made it difficult to sell American farm products and manufactured goods abroad.

Depression Indicators

Economic indicators are measures that signal trends in a nation's economy. During the Great Depression several trends were apparent. Those indicated at the right are linked—the conditions of one can affect another. For instance, when banks fail **1**, some businesses may have to close down **2**, which can cause unemployment to rise **3**. Thus, people have less money and spending declines **4**.

SKILLBUILDER Interpreting Graphs

1. In what year did the biggest jump in bank failures occur?
2. What measure on the graphs seems to indicate an improvement in the U.S. economy during the Depression? What might explain this?

1

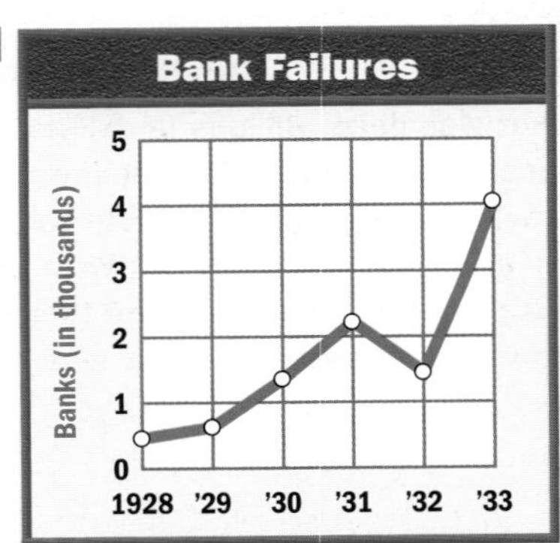

2

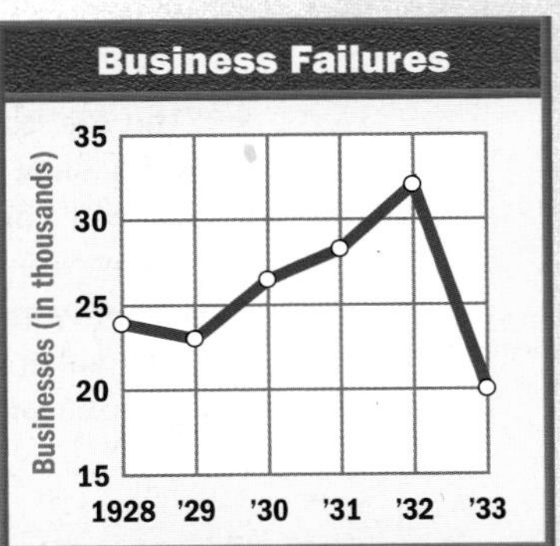

3

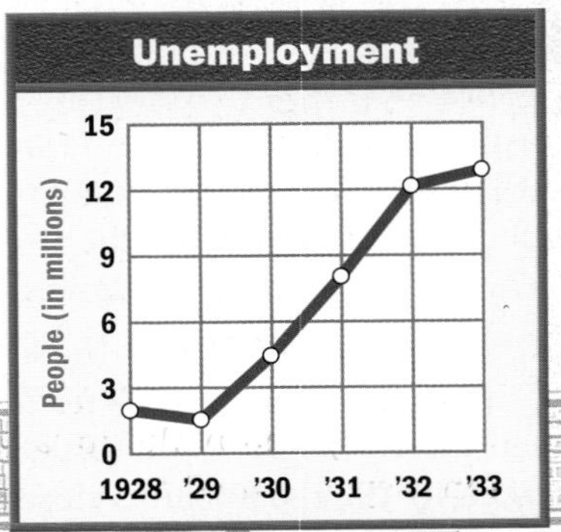

4

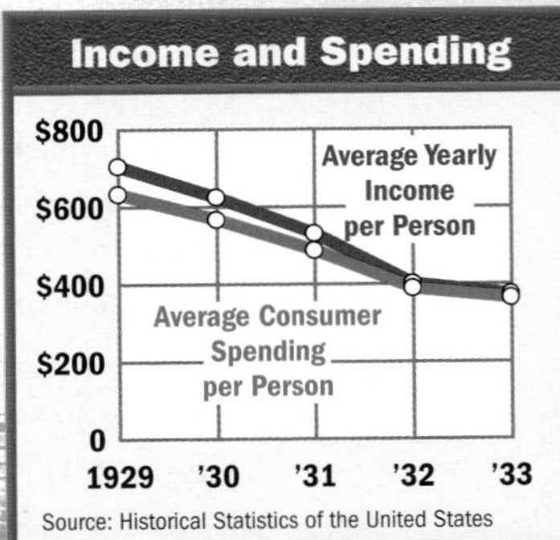

Source: Historical Statistics of the United States

Distraught men try to withdraw their savings from a failing bank.

In 1930, Congress passed the **Hawley-Smoot Tariff Act,** which established the highest protective tariff in United States history. It was designed to protect American farmers and manufacturers from foreign competition. Yet it had the opposite effect. By reducing the flow of goods into the United States, the tariff prevented other countries from earning American currency to buy American goods. The tariff made unemployment worse in industries that could no longer export goods to Europe. Many countries retaliated by raising their own tariffs. Within a few years, world trade had fallen more than 40 percent. E

MAIN IDEA

Summarizing
E How did the Great Depression affect the world economy?

CAUSES OF THE GREAT DEPRESSION Although historians and economists differ on the main causes of the Great Depression, most cite a common set of factors, among them:

- tariffs and war debt policies that cut down the foreign market for American goods
- a crisis in the farm sector
- the availability of easy credit
- an unequal distribution of income

These factors led to falling demand for consumer goods, even as newly mechanized factories produced more products. The federal government contributed to the crisis by keeping interest rates low, thereby allowing companies and individuals to borrow easily and build up large debts. Some of this borrowed money was used to buy the stocks that later led to the crash.

At first people found it hard to believe that economic disaster had struck. In November 1929, President Hoover encouraged Americans to remain confident about the economy. Yet, the most severe depression in American history was well on its way.

WORLD STAGE

GLOBAL EFFECTS OF THE DEPRESSION

As the American economy collapsed, so too did Europe's. The world's nations had become interdependent; international trade was important to most countries. However, when the U.S. economy failed, American investors withdrew their money from European markets.

To keep U.S. dollars in America, the government raised tariffs on goods imported from other countries. World trade dropped. Unemployment rates around the world soared. Germany and Austria were particularly hard hit. In 1931 Austria's largest bank failed. In Asia, both farmers and urban workers suffered as the value of exports fell by half between 1929 and 1931. The crash was felt in Latin America as well. As U.S. and European demand for Latin American products like sugar, beef, and copper dropped, prices collapsed.

ASSESSMENT

1. **TERMS & NAMES** For each term or name, write a sentence explaining its significance.
   - **price support**
   - **credit**
   - **Alfred E. Smith**
   - **Dow Jones Industrial Average**
   - **speculation**
   - **buying on margin**
   - **Black Tuesday**
   - **Great Depression**
   - **Hawley-Smoot Tariff Act**

MAIN IDEA

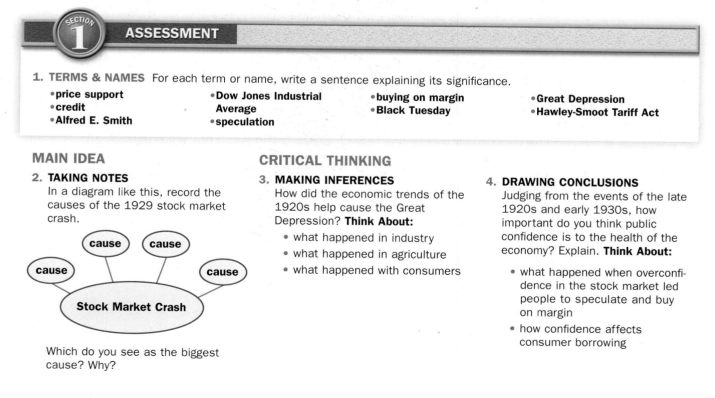

2. **TAKING NOTES**
   In a diagram like this, record the causes of the 1929 stock market crash.

Which do you see as the biggest cause? Why?

CRITICAL THINKING

3. **MAKING INFERENCES**
   How did the economic trends of the 1920s help cause the Great Depression? **Think About:**
   - what happened in industry
   - what happened in agriculture
   - what happened with consumers

4. **DRAWING CONCLUSIONS**
   Judging from the events of the late 1920s and early 1930s, how important do you think public confidence is to the health of the economy? Explain. **Think About:**
   - what happened when overconfidence in the stock market led people to speculate and buy on margin
   - how confidence affects consumer borrowing

Hardship and Suffering During the Depression

MAIN IDEA	WHY IT MATTERS NOW	Terms & Names
During the Great Depression Americans did what they had to do to survive.	Since the Great Depression, many Americans have been more cautious about saving, investing, and borrowing.	•shantytown •soup kitchen •bread line •Dust Bowl •direct relief

One American's Story

Ann Marie Low lived on her parents' North Dakota farm when the stock market crashed in 1929 and the Great Depression hit. Hard times were familiar to Ann's family. But the worst was yet to come. In the early 1930s, a ravenous drought hit the Great Plains, destroying crops and leaving the earth dry and cracked. Then came the deadly dust storms. On April 25, 1934, Ann wrote an account in her diary.

A PERSONAL VOICE ANN MARIE LOW

"[T]he air is just full of dirt coming, literally, for hundreds of miles. It sifts into everything. After we wash the dishes and put them away, so much dust sifts into the cupboards we must wash them again before the next meal. . . . Newspapers say the deaths of many babies and old people are attributed to breathing in so much dirt."

—*Dust Bowl Diary*

The drought and winds lasted for more than seven years. The dust storms in Kansas, Colorado, New Mexico, Nebraska, the Dakotas, Oklahoma, and Texas were a great hardship—but only one of many—that Americans faced during the Great Depression.

BROKE, BUT NOT BROKEN
Ann Marie Low Remembers the Dust Bowl

The Depression Devastates People's Lives

Statistics such as the unemployment rate tell only part of the story of the Great Depression. More important was the impact that it had on people's lives: the Depression brought hardship, homelessness, and hunger to millions.

THE DEPRESSION IN THE CITIES In cities across the country, people lost their jobs, were evicted from their homes and ended up in the streets. Some slept in parks or sewer pipes, wrapping themselves in newspapers to fend off the cold.

Others built makeshift shacks out of scrap materials. Before long, numerous **shantytowns**—little towns consisting of shacks—sprang up. An observer recalled one such settlement in Oklahoma City: "Here were all these people living in old, rusted-out car bodies. . . . There were people living in shacks made of orange crates. One family with a whole lot of kids were living in a piano box. . . . People were living in whatever they could junk together."

▲ Unemployed people built shacks in a shantytown in New York City in 1932.

Background
Relief programs largely discriminated against African Americans. However, some black organizations, like the National Urban League, were able to give private help.

Every day the poor dug through garbage cans or begged. **Soup kitchens** offering free or low-cost food and **bread lines,** or lines of people waiting to receive food provided by charitable organizations or public agencies, became a common sight. One man described a bread line in New York City.

A Personal Voice HERMAN SHUMLIN

"Two or three blocks along Times Square, you'd see these men, silent, shuffling along in a line. Getting this handout of coffee and doughnuts, dealt out from great trucks. . . . I'd see that flat, opaque, expressionless look which spelled, for me, human disaster. Men . . . who had responsible positions. Who had lost their jobs, lost their homes, lost their families . . . They were destroyed men."

—quoted in *Hard Times*

Conditions for African Americans and Latinos were especially difficult. Their unemployment rates were higher, and they were the lowest paid. They also dealt with increasing racial violence from unemployed whites competing for the same jobs. Twenty-four African Americans died by lynching in 1933.

Latinos—mainly Mexicans and Mexican Americans living in the Southwest—were also targets. Whites demanded that Latinos be deported, or expelled from the country, even though many had been born in America. By the late 1930s, hundreds of thousands of people of Mexican descent relocated to Mexico. Some left voluntarily; others were deported by the federal government. (A)

MAIN IDEA
Summarizing
(A) How did the Great Depression affect minorities?

THE DEPRESSION IN RURAL AREAS Life in rural areas was hard, but it did have one advantage over city life: most farmers could grow food for their families. With falling prices and rising debt, though, thousands of farmers lost their land. Between 1929 and 1932, about 400,000 farms were lost through foreclosure—the process by which a mortgage holder takes back property if an occupant has not made payments. Many farmers turned to tenant farming and barely scraped out a living.

ANOTHER PERSPECTIVE

AN AFRICAN-AMERICAN VIEW OF THE DEPRESSION

Although the suffering of the 1930s was severe for many people, it was especially grim for African Americans. Hard times were already a fact of life for many blacks, as one African-American man noted:

> "The Negro was born in depression. It didn't mean too much to him, The Great American Depression. . . . The best he could be is a janitor or a porter or shoeshine boy. It only became official when it hit the white man."

Nonetheless, the African-American community was very hard hit by the Great Depression. In 1932, the unemployment rate among African Americans stood at over 50 percent, while the overall unemployment rate was approximately 25 percent.

The Dust Bowl, 1933–1936

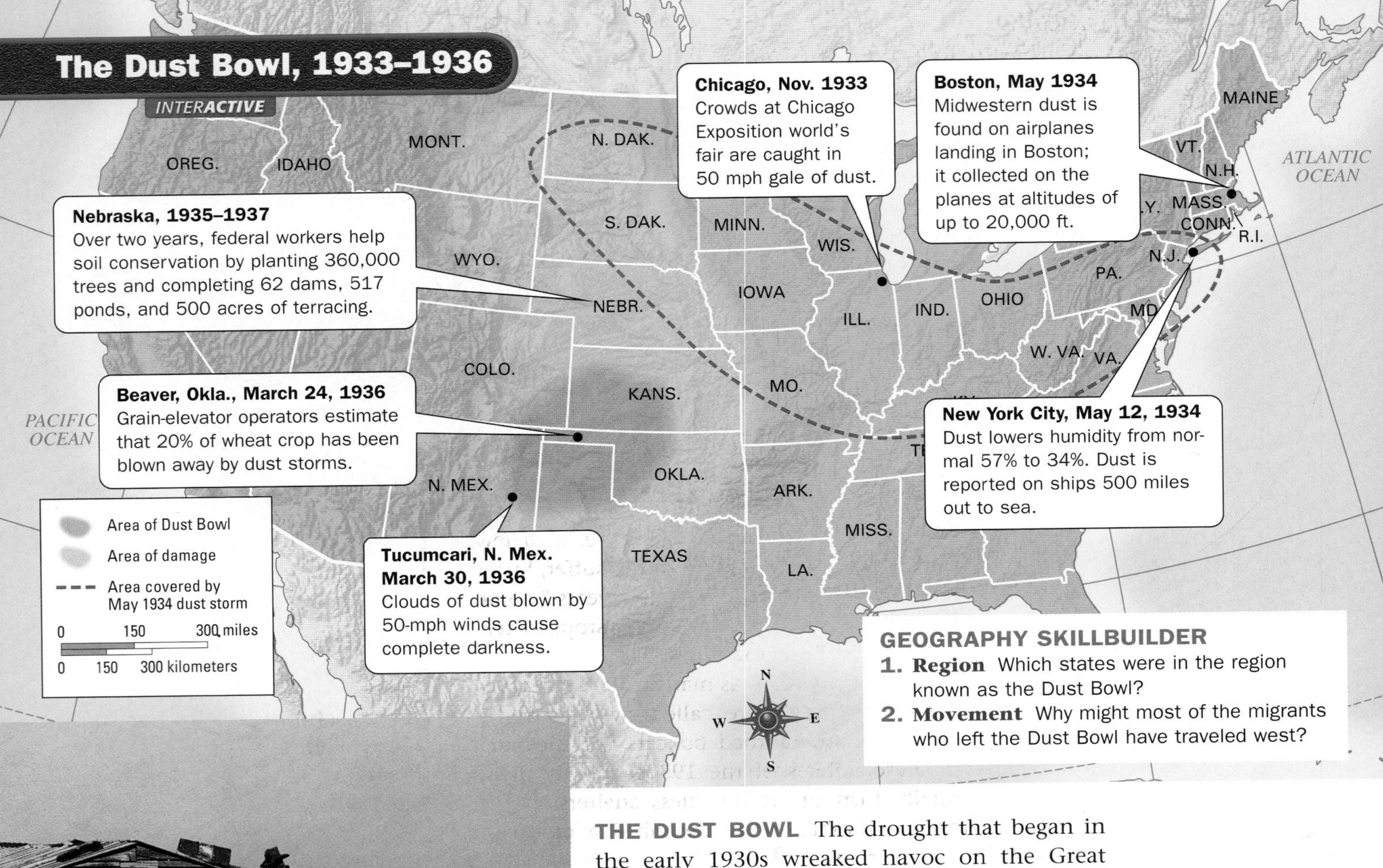

INTERACTIVE
Chicago, Nov. 1933
Crowds at Chicago Exposition world's fair are caught in 50 mph gale of dust.
Boston, May 1934
Midwestern dust is found on airplanes landing in Boston; it collected on the planes at altitudes of up to 20,000 ft.
Nebraska, 1935–1937
Over two years, federal workers help soil conservation by planting 360,000 trees and completing 62 dams, 517 ponds, and 500 acres of terracing.
Beaver, Okla., March 24, 1936
Grain-elevator operators estimate that 20% of wheat crop has been blown away by dust storms.
New York City, May 12, 1934
Dust lowers humidity from normal 57% to 34%. Dust is reported on ships 500 miles out to sea.
Tucumcari, N. Mex. March 30, 1936
Clouds of dust blown by 50-mph winds cause complete darkness.
Area of Dust Bowl
Area of damage
Area covered by May 1934 dust storm
0 150 300 miles
0 150 300 kilometers
OREG.
IDAHO
MONT.
N. DAK.
S. DAK.
MINN.
WIS.
WYO.
NEBR.
IOWA
ILL.
IND.
OHIO
PA.
COLO.
KANS.
MO.
W. VA.
VA.
MD
N.J.
N. MEX.
OKLA.
ARK.
TEXAS
LA.
MISS.
MAINE
VT.
N.H.
MASS
CONN.
R.I.
ATLANTIC OCEAN
PACIFIC OCEAN
N
S
E
W

GEOGRAPHY SKILLBUILDER
1. **Region** Which states were in the region known as the Dust Bowl?
2. **Movement** Why might most of the migrants who left the Dust Bowl have traveled west?

▲ A farmer and his sons brave a dust storm in 1936.

THE DUST BOWL The drought that began in the early 1930s wreaked havoc on the Great Plains. During the previous decade, farmers from Texas to North Dakota had used tractors to break up the grasslands and plant millions of acres of new farmland. Plowing had removed the thick protective layer of prairie grasses. Farmers had then exhausted the land through overproduction of crops, and the grasslands became unsuitable for farming. When the drought and winds began in the early 1930s, little grass and few trees were left to hold the soil down. Wind scattered the topsoil, exposing sand and grit underneath. The dust traveled hundreds of miles. One windstorm in 1934 picked up millions of tons of dust from the plains and carried it to East Coast cities.

The region that was the hardest hit, including parts of Kansas, Oklahoma, Texas, New Mexico, and Colorado, came to be known as the **Dust Bowl.** Plagued by dust storms and evictions, thousands of farmers and sharecroppers left their land behind. They packed up their families and few belongings and headed west, following Route 66 to California. Some of these migrants—known as Okies (a term that originally referred to Oklahomans but came to be used negatively for all migrants)—found work as farmhands. But others continued to wander in search of work. By the end of the 1930s, hundreds of thousands of farm families had migrated to California and other Pacific Coast states.

Background
The most severe storms were called "black blizzards." They were said to have darkened the sky in New York City and Washington, D.C.

Effects on the American Family

In the face of the suffering caused by the Great Depression, the family stood as a source of strength for most Americans. Although some people feared that hard times would undermine moral values, those fears were largely unfounded. In general, Americans believed in traditional values and emphasized the importance of family unity. At a time when money was tight, many families entertained themselves by staying at home and playing board games, such as Monopoly (invented in 1933), and listening to the radio. Nevertheless, the economic difficulties of the Great Depression put severe pressure on family life. Making ends meet was a daily struggle, and, in some cases, families broke apart under the strain.

MEN IN THE STREETS Many men had difficulty coping with unemployment because they were accustomed to working and supporting their families. Every day, they would set out to walk the streets in search of jobs. As Frederick Lewis Allen noted in *Since Yesterday*, "Men who have been sturdy and self-respecting workers can take unemployment without flinching for a few weeks, a few months, even if they have to see their families suffer; but it is different after a year . . . two years . . . three years." Some men became so discouraged that they simply stopped trying. Some even abandoned their families.

During the Great Depression, as many as 300,000 transients—or "hoboes" as they were called—wandered the country, hitching rides on railroad boxcars and sleeping under bridges. These hoboes of the 1930s, mainly men, would occasionally turn up at homeless shelters in big cities. The novelist Thomas Wolfe described a group of these men in New York City. **B**

MAIN IDEA

Analyzing Causes

B Why did so many men leave their homes during the Depression?

HISTORICAL SPOTLIGHT

HOBO SYMBOLS

Hoboes shared a hidden language that helped them meet the challenges of the road. Over time a set of symbols developed for hoboes to alert each other as to where they could get food or work or a place to sleep, and what houses to avoid. They often marked the symbols, such as those shown below, on the sides of houses and fences near railroad yards.

Sit down meal

Only bread given here

Good place for a handout

Sleep in barn

Good water

Danger

A Personal Voice THOMAS WOLFE

"These were the wanderers from town to town, the riders of freight trains, the thumbers of rides on highways, the uprooted, unwanted male population of America. They . . . gathered in the big cities when winter came, hungry, defeated, empty, hopeless, restless . . . always on the move, looking everywhere for work, for the bare crumbs to support their miserable lives, and finding neither work nor crumbs."

—*You Can't Go Home Again*

During the early years of the Great Depression, there was no federal system of **direct relief**—cash payments or food provided by the government to the poor. Some cities and charity services did offer relief to those who needed it, but the benefits were meager. In New York City, for example, the weekly payment was just $2.39 per family. This was the most generous relief offered by any city, but it was still well below the amount needed to feed a family.

WOMEN STRUGGLE TO SURVIVE Women worked hard to help their families survive adversity during the Great Depression. Many women canned food and sewed clothes. They also carefully managed household budgets. Jeane Westin, the author of *Making Do: How Women Survived the '30s*, recalled, "Those days you did everything to save a penny. . . . My next door neighbor and I used to shop together. You could get two pounds of hamburger for a quarter, so we'd buy two pounds and split it—then one week she'd pay the extra penny and the next week I'd pay."

Many women also worked outside the home, though they usually received less money than men did. As the Depression wore on, however, working women became the targets of enormous resentment. Many people believed that women, especially married women, had no right to work when there were men who were unemployed.

In the early 1930s, some cities refused to hire married women as schoolteachers.

Many Americans assumed that women were having an easier time than men during the Great Depression because few were seen begging or standing in bread lines. As a matter of fact, many women were starving to death in cold attics and rooming houses. As one writer pointed out, women were often too ashamed to reveal their hardship.

A PERSONAL VOICE MERIDEL LE SEUER

"I've lived in cities for many months, broke, without help, too timid to get in bread lines. I've known many women to live like this until they simply faint in the street. . . . A woman will shut herself up in a room until it is taken away from her, and eat a cracker a day and be as quiet as a mouse. . . . [She] will go for weeks verging on starvation, . . . going through the streets ashamed, sitting in libraries, parks, going for days without speaking to a living soul, shut up in the terror of her own misery."

—*America in the Twenties*

CHILDREN SUFFER HARDSHIPS Children also suffered during the 1930s. Poor diets and a lack of money for health care led to serious health problems. Milk consumption declined across the country, and clinics and hospitals reported a dramatic rise in malnutrition and diet-related diseases, such as rickets. At the same time, child-welfare programs were slashed as cities and states cut their budgets in the face of dwindling resources.

Background
Rickets is caused by a vitamin D deficiency and results in defective bone growth.

Falling tax revenues also caused school boards to shorten the school year and even close schools. By 1933, some 2,600 schools across the nation had shut down, leaving more than 300,000 students out of school. Thousands of children went to work instead; they often labored in sweatshops under horrendous conditions. C

MAIN IDEA

Analyzing Effects
C How did the Great Depression affect women and children?

"If I leave my mother, it will mean one less mouth to feed."
EUGENE WILLIAMS, AGE 13

Many teenagers looked for a way out of the suffering. Hundreds of thousands of teenage boys and some girls hopped aboard America's freight trains to zigzag the country in search of work, adventure, and an escape from poverty. These "wild boys" came from every section of the United States, from every corner of society. They were the sons of poor farmers, and out-of-work miners, and wealthy parents who had lost everything. "Hoover tourists," as they were called, were eager to tour America for free.

From the age of eleven until seventeen, George Phillips rode the rails, first catching local freights out of his home town of Princeton, Missouri.

"There is no feeling in the world like sitting in a side-door Pullman and watching the world go by, listening to the clickety-clack of the wheels, hearing that old steam whistle blowing for crossings and towns."

While exciting, the road could also be deadly. Many riders were beaten or jailed by "bulls"—armed freight yard patrolmen. Often riders had to sleep standing up in a constant deafening rumble. Some were accidentally locked in ice cars for days on end. Others fell prey to murderous criminals. From 1929 to 1939, 24,647 trespassers were killed and 27,171 injured on railroad property.

◀ Two young boys, ages 15 and 16, walk beside freight cars in the San Joaquin Valley.

SOCIAL AND PSYCHOLOGICAL EFFECTS The hardships of the Great Depression had a tremendous social and psychological impact. Some people were so demoralized by hard times that they lost their will to survive. Between 1928 and 1932, the suicide rate rose more than 30 percent. Three times as many people were admitted to state mental hospitals as in normal times.

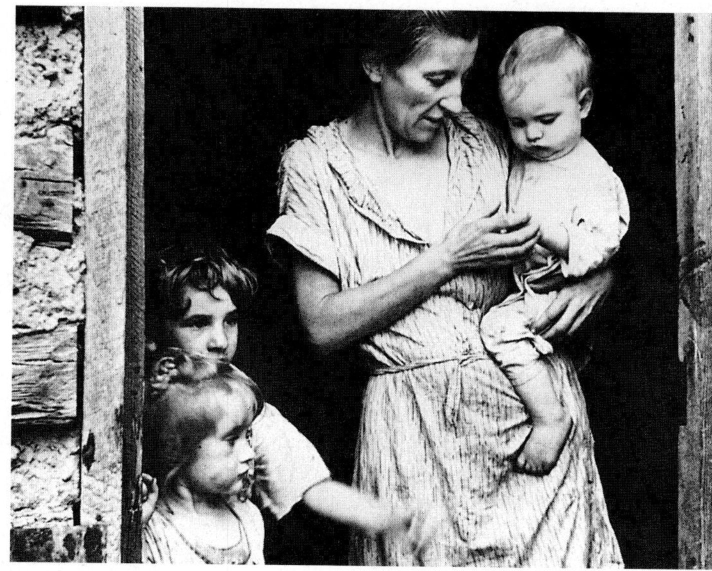

▲ This Ozark sharecropper family was photographed in Arkansas during the 1930s by the artist Ben Shahn.

The economic problems forced many Americans to accept compromises and make sacrifices that affected them for the rest of their lives. Adults stopped going to the doctor or dentist because they couldn't afford it. Young people gave up their dreams of going to college. Others put off getting married, raising large families, or having children at all.

Vocabulary
stigma: a mark or indication of disgrace

For many people, the stigma of poverty and of having to scrimp and save never disappeared completely. For some, achieving financial security became the primary focus in life. As one woman recalled, "Ever since I was twelve years old there was one major goal in my life . . . one thing . . . and that was to never be poor again."

During the Great Depression many people showed great kindness to strangers who were down on their luck. People often gave food, clothing, and a place to stay to the needy. Families helped other families and shared resources and strengthened the bonds within their communities. In addition, many people developed habits of saving and thriftiness—habits they would need to see themselves through the dark days ahead as the nation and President Hoover struggled with the Great Depression. These habits shaped a whole generation of Americans.

SECTION 2 ASSESSMENT

1. **TERMS & NAMES** For each term or name, write a sentence explaining its significance.
   - **shantytown**
   - **soup kitchen**
   - **bread line**
   - **Dust Bowl**
   - **direct relief**

MAIN IDEA

2. **TAKING NOTES**
   In a Venn diagram, list the effects that the Great Depression had on farmers and city dwellers. Find the differences and the similarities.

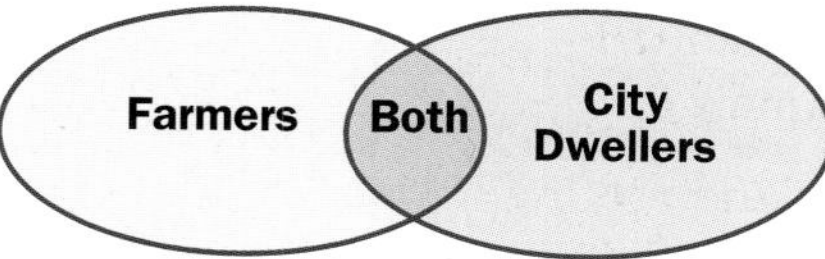

   Which group do you think suffered less?

CRITICAL THINKING

3. **CONTRASTING**
   How was what happened to men during the Great Depression different from what happened to women? children? **Think About:**
   - each group's role in their families
   - the changes each group had to make
   - what help was available to them
4. **ANALYZING EFFECTS**
   How did Dust Bowl conditions in the Great Plains affect the entire country?
5. **DRAWING CONCLUSIONS**
   In what ways did the Great Depression affect people's outlook?

SECTION 3

Hoover Struggles with the Depression

MAIN IDEA

President Hoover's conservative response to the Great Depression drew criticism from many Americans.

WHY IT MATTERS NOW

Worsening conditions in the country caused the government to become more involved in the health and wealth of the people.

Terms & Names

- **Herbert Hoover**
- **Boulder Dam**
- **Federal Home Loan Bank Act**
- **Reconstruction Finance Corporation**
- **Bonus Army**

One American's Story

Oscar Ameringer was a newspaper editor in Oklahoma City during the Great Depression. In 1932, he traveled around the country collecting information on economic and social conditions. Testifying in unemployment hearings that same year, Ameringer described desperate people who were losing patience with the government. "Unless something is done for them and done soon you will have a revolution on hand." Ameringer told the following story.

▲ A Depression-era family from Arkansas walks through Texas, looking for work in the cotton fields along the Rio Grande.

A PERSONAL VOICE OSCAR AMERINGER

"The roads of the West and Southwest teem with hungry hitchhikers. . . . Between Clarksville and Russellville, Ark., I picked up a family. The woman was hugging a dead chicken under a ragged coat. When I asked her where she had procured the fowl, first she told me she had found it dead in the road, and then added in grim humor, 'They promised me a chicken in the pot, and now I got mine.'"

—quoted in *The American Spirit*

The woman was recalling President Hoover's empty 1928 campaign pledge: "A chicken in every pot and a car in every garage." Now many Americans were disillusioned. They demanded that the government help them.

Hoover Tries to Reassure the Nation

After the stock market crash of October 1929, President **Herbert Hoover** tried to reassure Americans that the nation's economy was on a sound footing. "Any lack of confidence in the economic future . . . is foolish," he declared. In his view, the important thing was for Americans to remain optimistic and to go about their business as usual. Americans believed depressions were a normal part of the business cycle. According to this theory, periods of rapid economic growth were naturally followed by periods of depression. The best course in a slump, many experts believed, was to do nothing and let the economy fix itself. Hoover took a slightly different position. He felt that government could play a limited role in helping to solve problems.

HOOVER'S PHILOSOPHY Herbert Hoover had been an engineer, and he put great faith in the power of reason. He was also a humanitarian, as he made clear in one of his last speeches as president.

A PERSONAL VOICE HERBERT HOOVER

> "**Our first objective must be to provide security from poverty and want. . . . We want to see a nation built of home owners and farm owners. We want to see their savings protected. We want to see them in steady jobs. We want to see more and more of them insured against death and accident, unemployment and old age. We want them all secure.**"
>
> —"Challenge to Liberty," October 1936

Like many Americans of the time, Hoover believed that one of government's chief functions was to foster cooperation between competing groups and interests in society. If business and labor were in a conflict, for example, government should step in and help them find a solution that served their mutual interests. This cooperation must be voluntary rather than forced, he said. Government's role was to encourage and facilitate cooperation, not to control it.

On the other hand, Americans also valued "rugged individualism"—the idea that people should succeed through their own efforts. They should take care of themselves and their families, rather than depend on the government to bail them out. Thus, Hoover opposed any form of federal welfare, or direct relief to the needy. He believed that handouts would weaken people's self-respect and "moral fiber." His answer to the needy was that individuals, charities, and local organizations should pitch in to help care for the less fortunate. The federal government should direct relief measures, but not through a vast federal bureaucracy. Such a bureaucracy, he said, would be too expensive and would stifle individual liberties. (A)

MAIN IDEA

Summarizing
(A) What were some of Hoover's key convictions about government?

However, when the Depression took hold, moral fiber wasn't what people were worried about. Hoover's response shocked and frustrated suffering Americans.

HOOVER TAKES CAUTIOUS STEPS Hoover's political philosophy caused him to take a cautious approach to the depression. Soon after the stock market crash, he called together key leaders in the fields of business, banking, and labor. He urged them to work together to find solutions to the nation's economic woes and to act in ways that would not make a bad situation worse. For example, he asked employers not to cut wages or lay off workers, and he asked labor leaders not to demand higher wages or go on strike. He also created a special organization to help private charities generate contributions for the poor.

None of these steps made much of a difference. A year after the crash, the economy was still shrinking, and unemployment was still rising. More companies went out of business, soup kitchens became a common sight, and general misery continued to grow. Shantytowns arose in every city, and hoboes continued to roam.

HERBERT HOOVER
1874–1964

Born to a Quaker family in Iowa, Herbert Hoover was orphaned at an early age. His life was a rags-to-riches story. He worked his way through Stanford University and later made a fortune as a mining engineer and consultant in China, Australia, Europe, and Africa. During and after World War I, he coordinated U.S. relief efforts in Europe, earning a reputation for efficiency and humanitarian ideals.

As president, Hoover asserted, "Every time we find solutions outside of government, we have not only strengthened character, but we have preserved our sense of real government."

LOOKING DOWNSTREAM, COLORADO RIVER
SHOWING THE IMMENSE CONCRETE FORMS OF BOULDER DAM
OAKES PHOTO
4A305

▲ This 1930s postcard, displaying a hand-colored photograph, shows the mammoth scale of Boulder Canyon and Boulder Dam.

BOULDER DAM One project that Hoover approved did make a difference. Years earlier, when Hoover served as secretary of commerce, one of his earliest proposed initiatives was the construction of a dam on the Colorado River. Aiming to minimize federal intervention, Hoover proposed to finance the dam's construction by using profits from sales of the electric power that the dam would generate. He also helped to arrange an agreement on water rights among the seven states of the Colorado River basin—Arizona, California, Colorado, Nevada, New Mexico, Utah, and Wyoming.

By the time the massive project won congressional approval in 1928, as part of a $700 million public works program, Hoover had been elected to the White House. In the fall of 1929, nearly one year into his presidency, Hoover was finally able to authorize construction of **Boulder Dam** (later called Hoover Dam). At 726 ft. high and 1,244 ft. long it would be the world's tallest dam and the second largest. In addition to providing electricity and flood control, the dam also provided a regular water supply, which enabled the growth of California's massive agricultural economy. Today, the dam also helps to provide water for cities such as Los Angeles and Las Vegas.

DEMOCRATS WIN IN 1930 CONGRESSIONAL ELECTIONS As the country's economic difficulties increased, the political tide turned against Hoover and the Republicans. In the 1930 congressional elections, the Democrats took advantage of anti-Hoover sentiments to win more seats in Congress. As a result of that election, the Republicans lost control of the House of Representatives and saw their majority in the Senate dwindle to one vote.

As Americans grew more and more frustrated by the Depression, they expressed their anger in a number of ways. Farmers stung by low crop prices burned their corn and wheat and dumped their milk on highways rather than sell it at a loss. Some farmers even declared a "farm holiday" and refused to work their fields. A number blocked roads to prevent food from getting to market, hoping that food shortages would raise prices. Some farmers also used force to prevent authorities from foreclosing on farms.

By 1930, people were calling the shantytowns in American cities "Hoovervilles"—a direct slap at the president's policies. Homeless people called the newspapers they wrapped themselves in "Hoover blankets." Empty pockets turned inside out were "Hoover flags." Many Americans who had hailed Hoover as a great humanitarian a few years earlier now saw him as a cold and heartless leader.

Despite public criticism, Hoover continued to hold firm to his principles. He refused to support direct relief or other forms of federal welfare. Some Americans were going hungry, and many blamed Hoover for their plight. Criticism of the president and his policies continued to grow. An anonymous ditty of the time was widely repeated. B

MAIN IDEA

Making Inferences

B Why do you think people blamed Hoover for the nation's difficulties?

"Mellon pulled the whistle
Hoover rang the bell
Wall Street gave the signal
And the country went to hell."

In this cartoon, Americans point their fingers at a beleaguered President Hoover.

Hoover Takes Action

As time went on and the depression deepened, President Hoover gradually softened his position on government intervention in the economy and took a more activist approach to the nation's economic troubles.

HOOVER BACKS COOPERATIVES In Hoover's view, Boulder Dam was a model of how the federal government could encourage cooperation. His attempts to relieve the depression involved negotiating agreements among private entities, again reflecting his belief in small government. For example, he backed the creation of the Federal Farm Board, an organization of farm cooperatives. The Farm Board was intended to raise crop prices by helping members to buy crops and keep them off the market temporarily until prices rose.

In addition, Hoover tried to prop up the banking system by persuading the nation's largest banks to establish the National Credit Corporation. This organization loaned money to smaller banks, which helped them stave off bankruptcy.

DIRECT INTERVENTION By late 1931, however, many people could see that these measures had failed to turn the economy around. With a presidential election looming, Hoover appealed to Congress to pass a series of measures to reform banking, provide mortgage relief, and funnel more federal money into business investment. In 1932, Hoover signed into law the **Federal Home Loan Bank Act,** which lowered mortgage rates for homeowners and allowed farmers to refinance their farm loans and avoid foreclosure. It was not until Hoover's time in office was over that Congress passed the Glass-Steagall Banking Act, which separated investment from commercial banking and would, Congress hoped, prevent another crash.

Vocabulary
refinance: to provide new financing; to discharge a mortgage with a new mortgage obtained at a lower interest rate

Hoover's most ambitious economic measure, however, was the **Reconstruction Finance Corporation** (RFC), approved by Congress in January 1932. It authorized up to $2 billion for emergency financing for banks, life insurance companies, railroads, and other large businesses. Hoover believed that the money would trickle down to the average citizen through job growth and higher wages. Many critics questioned this approach; they argued that the program would benefit only corporations and that the poor still needed direct relief. Hungry people could not wait for the benefits to trickle down to their tables.

MAIN IDEA

Evaluating Decisions

C What were some of the projects proposed by Hoover, and how effective were they?

In its first five months of operation, the RFC loaned more than $805 million to large corporations, but business failures continued. The RFC was an unprecedented example of federal involvement in a peacetime economy, but in the end it was too little, too late. C

DIFFICULT
DECISIONS

HOOVER AND FEDERAL PROJECTS

On the one hand, President Hoover opposed federal welfare and intervention in the economy. On the other, he felt that government had a duty to help solve problems and ease suffering. The question was, What kind of assistance would be proper and effective?

1. Consider the pros and cons of Hoover's actions during the Depression. Did he do enough to try to end the Depression? Why or why not?
2. If you had been president during the Great Depression, what policies would you have supported? Explain the approach you would have taken.

Gassing the Bonus Army

In 1932, an incident further damaged Hoover's image and public morale. That spring, between 10,000 and 20,000 World War I veterans and their families arrived in Washington, D.C., from various parts of the country. They called themselves the Bonus Expeditionary Force, or the **Bonus Army**.

THE PATMAN BILL DENIED Led by Walter Waters, an unemployed cannery worker from Oregon, the Bonus Army came to the nation's capital to support a bill under debate in Congress. The Patman Bill authorized the government to pay a bonus to World War I veterans who had not been compensated adequately for their wartime service. This bonus, which Congress had approved in 1924, was supposed to be paid out in 1945 in the form of cash and a life insurance policy, but Congressman Wright Patman believed that the money—an average of $500 per soldier—should be paid immediately.

Hoover thought that the Bonus Marchers were "communists and persons with criminal records" rather than veterans. He opposed the legislation, but he respected the marchers' right to peaceful assembly. He even provided food and supplies so that they could erect a shantytown within sight of the Capitol. On June 17, however, the Senate voted down the Patman Bill. Hoover then called on

In 1932, these veterans from Muncie, Indiana, decided to remain in the capital until their bonus was paid to them. ▼

MAIN IDEA

Summarizing

D What did the Bonus Army want?

the Bonus Army marchers to leave. Most did, but approximately 2,000, still hoping to meet with the president, refused to budge. **D**

HOOVER DISBANDS THE BONUS ARMY Nervous that the angry group could become violent, President Hoover decided that the Bonus Army should be disbanded. On July 28, a force of 1,000 soldiers under the command of General Douglas MacArthur and his aide, Major Dwight D. Eisenhower, came to roust the veterans. A government official watching from a nearby office recalled what happened next.

A Personal Voice A. EVERETTE MCINTYRE

> **"The 12th infantry was in full battle dress. Each had a gas mask and his belt was full of tear gas bombs. . . . At orders, they brought their bayonets at thrust and moved in. The bayonets were used to jab people, to make them move. Soon, almost everybody disappeared from view, because tear gas bombs exploded. The entire block was covered by tear gas. Flames were coming up, where the soldiers had set fire to the buildings to drive these people out. . . . Through the whole afternoon, they took one camp after another."**
>
> —quoted in *Hard Times*

In the course of the operation, the infantry gassed more than 1,000 people, including an 11-month-old baby, who died, and an 8-year-old boy, who was partially blinded. Two people were shot and many were injured. Most Americans were stunned and outraged at the government's treatment of the veterans.

Once again, President Hoover's image suffered, and now an election was nearing. In November, Hoover would face a formidable opponent, the Democratic candidate Franklin Delano Roosevelt. When Roosevelt heard about the attack on the Bonus Army, he said to his friend Felix Frankfurter, "Well, Felix, this will elect me." The downturn in the economy and Hoover's inability to deal effectively with the Depression had sealed his political fate.

ASSESSMENT

1. **TERMS & NAMES** For each term or name, write a sentence explaining its significance.
   - **Herbert Hoover**
   - **Boulder Dam**
   - **Federal Home Loan Bank Act**
   - **Reconstruction Finance Corporation**
   - **Bonus Army**

MAIN IDEA

2. **TAKING NOTES**
   In a cluster diagram, record what Hoover said and did in response to the Great Depression.

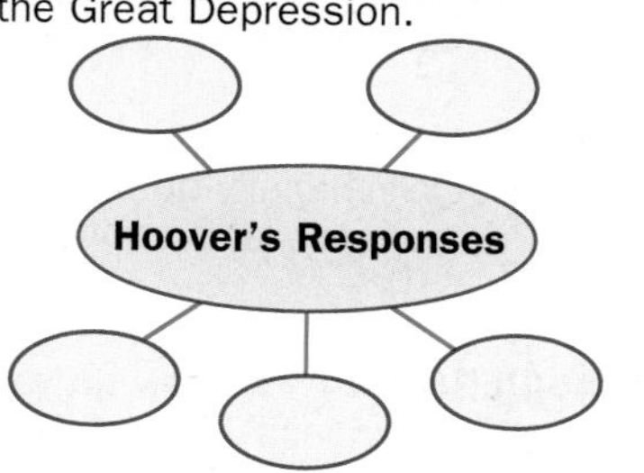

Which response was most helpful? Explain your choice.

CRITICAL THINKING

3. **ANALYZING ISSUES**
   How did Hoover's belief in "rugged individualism" shape his policies during the Great Depression?
   Think About:
   - what his belief implies about his view of people
   - how that translates into the role of government
   - Hoover's policies

4. **DRAWING CONCLUSIONS**
   When Franklin Delano Roosevelt heard about the attack on the Bonus Army, why was he so certain that he would defeat Hoover?
   Think About:
   - the American public's impression of Hoover
   - Hoover's actions to alleviate the Great Depression
   - how people judged Hoover after the attack

CHAPTER 14 ASSESSMENT

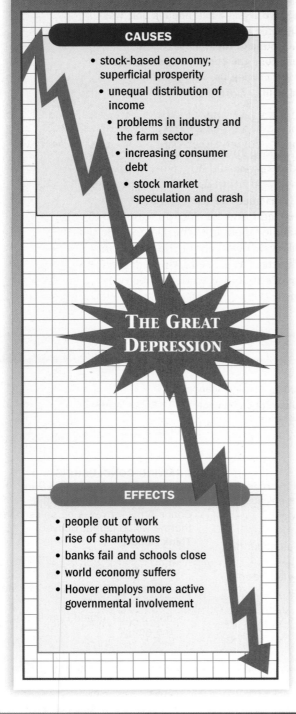

VISUAL SUMMARY

THE GREAT DEPRESSION BEGINS

CAUSES

- stock-based economy; superficial prosperity
- unequal distribution of income
- problems in industry and the farm sector
- increasing consumer debt
- stock market speculation and crash

THE GREAT DEPRESSION

EFFECTS

- people out of work
- rise of shantytowns
- banks fail and schools close
- world economy suffers
- Hoover employs more active governmental involvement

TERMS & NAMES

For each term below, write a sentence explaining its connection to the period 1929–1933. For the person below, explain his role in the events of the period.

1. credit
2. speculation
3. buying on margin
4. Black Tuesday
5. Dow Jones Industrial Average
6. Great Depression
7. Dust Bowl
8. direct relief
9. Herbert Hoover
10. Bonus Army

MAIN IDEAS

Use your notes and the information in the chapter to answer the following questions.

The Nation's Sick Economy *(pages 464–471)*

1. How did what happened to farmers during the 1920s foreshadow events of the Great Depression?
2. What were some of the effects of the stock market crash in October 1929?

Hardship and Suffering During the Depression *(pages 472–477)*

3. How were shantytowns, soup kitchens, and bread lines a response to the Depression?
4. Why did minorities often experience an increase in discrimination during the Great Depression?
5. What pressures did the American family experience during the Depression?

Hoover Struggles with the Depression *(pages 478–483)*

6. How did Hoover's treatment of the Bonus Army affect his standing with the public?
7. In what ways did Hoover try to use the government to relieve the Depression?

CRITICAL THINKING

1. **USING YOUR NOTES** In a chart like the one shown below, show Hoover's responses to the Great Depression. Indicate how his philosophy changed and the reasons for that change.

Herbert Hoover's Philosophy

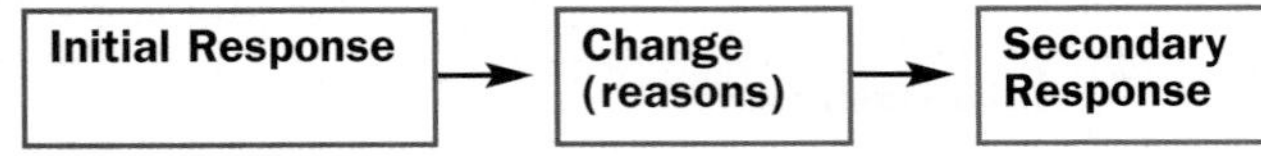

2. **ECONOMIC OPPORTUNITY** Do you think it would have been difficult for individuals to recover financially during the Depression without the entire economy recovering? Why or why not?

3. **DEVELOPING HISTORICAL PERSPECTIVE** How do you think the Great Depression changed Americans' view of themselves? Consider the roles of men, women, and children in society and in the family.

Standardized Test Practice

Use the cartoon and your knowledge of U.S. history to answer question 1.

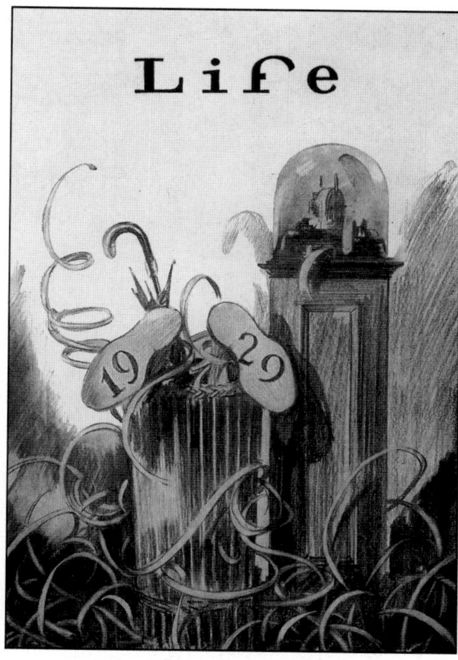

1. The cartoon illustrates which event leading to the Great Depression?

   A bank failures
   B Black Tuesday
   C Bonus March
   D the election of Herbert Hoover

2. In the 1930s, some areas of the country suffered from especially harsh environmental conditions. Thousands of farmers and sharecroppers were forced to abandon their land and look for other work. In which of the following areas were these conditions worst?

   F parts of Idaho, Wyoming, and Oregon
   G parts of Missouri, Illinois, and Iowa
   H parts of Florida, Alabama, and Georgia
   J parts of Kansas, Texas, and Oklahoma

3. How did World War I contribute to causing the Great Depression?

   A Soldiers returning from the war were unskilled and so had difficulty finding employment.
   B Foreign countries had borrowed heavily to pay for the war and so could not afford to buy American goods.
   C Americans had spent their money on war bonds and so had little savings.
   D American industry was geared for producing weapons and could not retool to produce consumer goods.

ADDITIONAL TEST PRACTICE, pages S1–S33.

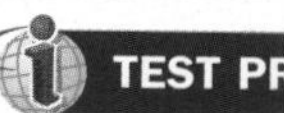

CLASSZONE.COM

ALTERNATIVE ASSESSMENT

1. **INTERACT WITH HISTORY** Recall your discussion of the question on page 463:

   What would you do to feed your family?

   Suppose the year is 1930 and you are the head of your household. Write a letter to a relative overseas in which you describe your family's situation and how you handled the crisis. Discuss the challenges created by the Great Depression and what you've learned as a result of enduring such hardships.

2. **VIDEO** **LEARNING FROM MEDIA** View the American Stories video *Broke, but Not Broken.* Discuss the following questions in a small group:

   - What choices did Ann Marie Low's family make during the Depression? Do you agree with their choices?
   - What did you learn about the relationship between the government and the farmers?
   - What did the older Ann Marie Low's comments add to your understanding of the Great Depression?
   - Share your conclusions with the rest of the class.

CHAPTER 15 THE NEW DEAL

The Civilian Conservation Corps put unemployed young men to work during the Great Depression.

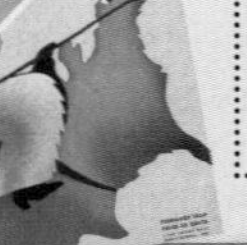

USA

- **1933** Franklin Delano Roosevelt is inaugurated.
- **1934** Congress creates the SEC to regulate the stock market.
- **1934** Indian Reorganization Act is passed.
- **1935** Congress passes the Social Security Act.
- **1936** President Roosevelt is reelected.

1933 | 1934 | 1935 | 1936

WORLD

- **1933** Hitler and the Nazi party come to power in Germany.
- **1935** Mussolini leads Italian invasion of Ethiopia.
- **1935** British Parliament passes the Government of India Act.
- **1936** Civil war begins in Spain.

INTERACT
WITH HISTORY

It is 1933, the height of the Great Depression. Thousands of banks and businesses have failed, and a quarter of the adult population is out of work. Now a new president takes office, promising to bring relief to the ailing economy.

How would you begin to revive the economy?

Examine the Issues

- How can the government help failing industries?
- What can be done to ease unemployment?
- What would you do to restore public confidence and economic security?
- How would you get money to pay for your proposed recovery programs?

RESEARCH LINKS CLASSZONE.COM

Visit the Chapter 15 links for more information about The New Deal.

1937 Labor unions begin using sit-down strikes.

1938 Route 66 is completed, linking Chicago, Illinois, to Los Angeles, California.

1939 *The Wizard of Oz* is released in movie theaters.

1940 President Roosevelt is elected a third time.

1937 | 1938 | 1939 | 1940

1937 Japan invades Northern China.

1937 *Hindenburg* disaster

1939 Germany invades Poland.

SECTION 1

A New Deal Fights the Depression

MAIN IDEA	WHY IT MATTERS NOW	Terms & Names
After becoming president, Franklin Delano Roosevelt used government programs to combat the Depression.	Americans still benefit from programs begun in the New Deal, such as bank and stock market regulations and the Tennessee Valley Authority.	•Franklin Delano Roosevelt •New Deal •Glass-Steagall Act •Federal Securities Act •Agricultural Adjustment Act (AAA) •Civilian Conservation Corps (CCC) •National Industrial Recovery Act (NIRA) •deficit spending •Huey Long

One American's Story

Hank Oettinger was working as a printing press operator in a small town in Wisconsin when the Great Depression began. He lost his job in 1931 and was unemployed for the next two years. In 1933, however, President Roosevelt began creating work programs. Through one of these programs, the Civil Works Administration (CWA), Oettinger went back to work in 1933. As he later recalled, the CWA was cause for great celebration in his town.

A Personal Voice HANK OETTINGER

"**I can remember the first week of the CWA checks. It was on a Friday. That night everybody had gotten his check. The first check a lot of them had in three years. . . . I never saw such a change of attitude. Instead of walking around feeling dreary and looking sorrowful, everybody was joyous. Like a feast day. They were toasting each other. They had money in their pockets for the first time.**"

—quoted in *Hard Times*

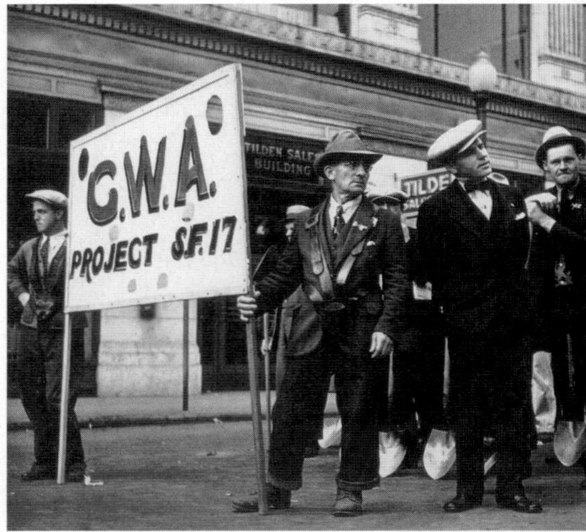

▲ **Civil Works Administration workers prepare for a parade for workers in San Francisco in 1934.**

Programs like the CWA raised the hopes of the American people and sparked great enthusiasm for the new president. To many Americans, it appeared as if the country had turned a corner and was beginning to emerge from the nightmare of the Great Depression.

Americans Get a New Deal

The 1932 presidential election showed that Americans were clearly ready for a change. Because of the depression, people were suffering from a lack of work, food, and hope.

ELECTING FRANKLIN DELANO ROOSEVELT Although the Republicans renominated President Hoover as their candidate, they recognized he had little chance of winning. Too many Americans blamed Hoover for doing too little about the depression and wanted a new president. The Democrats pinned their hopes on **Franklin Delano Roosevelt,** known popularly as FDR, the two-term governor of New York and a distant cousin of former president Theodore Roosevelt.

As governor, FDR had proved to be an effective, reform-minded leader, working to combat the problems of unemployment and poverty. Unlike Hoover, Roosevelt possessed a "can-do" attitude and projected an air of friendliness and confidence that attracted voters.

Indeed, Roosevelt won an overwhelming victory, capturing nearly 23 million votes to Hoover's nearly 16 million. In the Senate, Democrats claimed a nearly two-thirds majority. In the House, they won almost three-fourths of the seats, their greatest victory since before the Civil War.

WAITING FOR ROOSEVELT TO TAKE OVER Four months would elapse between Roosevelt's victory in the November election and his inauguration as president in March 1933. The 20th Amendment, which moved presidential inaugurations to January, was not ratified until February 1933 and did not apply to the 1932 election.

FDR was not idle during this waiting period, however. He worked with his team of carefully picked advisers—a select group of professors, lawyers, and journalists that came to be known as the "Brain Trust." Roosevelt began to formulate a set of policies for his new administration. This program, designed to alleviate the problems of the Great Depression, became known as the **New Deal,** a phrase taken from a campaign speech in which Roosevelt had promised "a new deal for the American people." New Deal policies focused on three general goals: relief for the needy, economic recovery, and financial reform. (A)

MAIN IDEA

Summarizing

(A) What plans did Roosevelt make in the four months while he waited to take office?

THE HUNDRED DAYS On taking office, the Roosevelt administration launched a period of intense activity known as the Hundred Days, lasting from March 9 to June 16, 1933. During this period, Congress passed more than 15 major pieces of New Deal legislation. These laws, and others that followed, significantly expanded the federal government's role in the nation's economy.

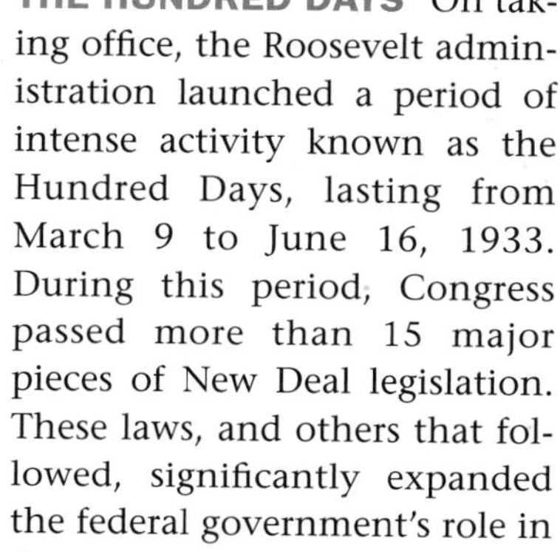

KEY PLAYERS

FRANKLIN D. ROOSEVELT
1882–1945

Born into an old, wealthy New York family, Franklin Delano Roosevelt entered politics as a state senator in 1910 and later became assistant secretary of the navy. In 1921, he was stricken with polio and became partially paralyzed from the waist down. He struggled to regain the use of his legs, and he eventually learned to stand with the help of leg braces.

Roosevelt became governor of New York in 1928, and because he "would not allow bodily disability to defeat his will," he went on to the White House in 1933. Always interested in people, Roosevelt gained greater compassion for others as a result of his own physical disability.

ELEANOR ROOSEVELT
1884–1962

A niece of Theodore Roosevelt and a distant cousin of her husband, Franklin, Eleanor Roosevelt lost her parents at an early age. She was raised by a strict grandmother.

As first lady, she often urged the president to take stands on controversial issues. A popular public speaker, Eleanor was particularly interested in child welfare, housing reform, and equal rights for women and minorities. In presenting a booklet on human rights to the United Nations in 1958, she said, "Where, after all, do human rights begin? . . . [In] the world of the individual person: the neighborhood . . . the school . . . the factory, farm or office where he works."

Roosevelt's first step as president was to carry out reforms in banking and finance. By 1933, widespread bank failures had caused most Americans to lose faith in the banking system. On March 5, one day after taking office, Roosevelt declared a bank holiday and closed all banks to prevent further withdrawals. He persuaded Congress to pass the Emergency Banking Relief Act, which authorized the Treasury Department to inspect the country's banks. Those that were sound could reopen at once; those that were insolvent—unable to pay their debts—would remain closed. Those that needed help could receive loans. This measure revived public confidence in banks, since customers now had greater faith that the open banks were in good financial shape.

AN IMPORTANT FIRESIDE CHAT On March 12, the day before the first banks were to reopen, President Roosevelt gave the first of his many fireside chats—radio talks about issues of public concern, explaining in clear, simple language his New Deal measures. These informal talks made Americans feel as if the president were talking directly to them. In his first chat, President Roosevelt explained why the nation's welfare depended on public support of the government and the banking system. "We have provided the machinery to restore our financial system," he said, "and it is up to you to support and make it work." He explained the banking system to listeners.

"The only thing we have to fear is fear itself."
FRANKLIN DELANO ROOSEVELT

A PERSONAL VOICE FRANKLIN DELANO ROOSEVELT

"When you deposit money in a bank the bank does not put the money into a safe deposit vault. It invests your money. . . . A comparatively small part of the money that you put into the bank is kept in currency—an amount which in normal times is wholly sufficient to cover the cash needs of the average citizen."

The president then explained that when too many people demanded their savings in cash, banks would fail. This was not because banks were weak but because even strong banks could not meet such heavy demands. Over the next few weeks, many Americans returned their savings to banks. **B**

MAIN IDEA

Evaluating Leadership
B How successful was FDR's fireside chat?

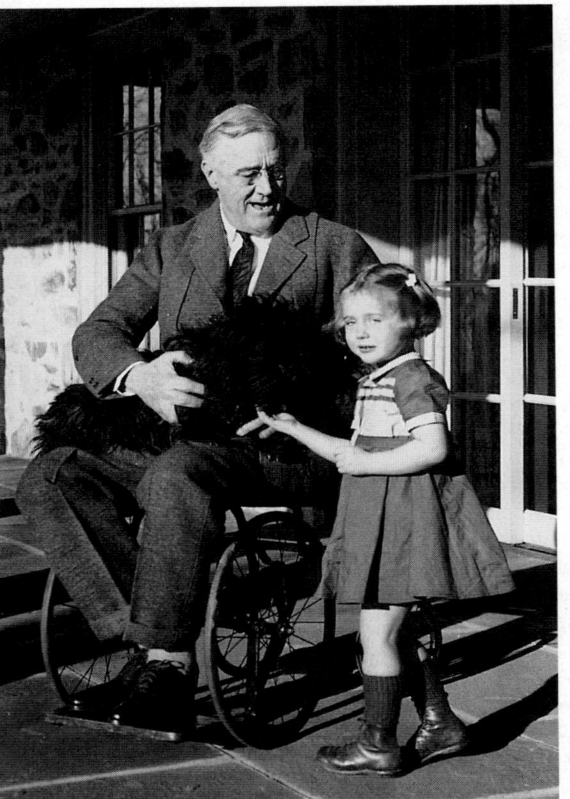

Franklin D. Roosevelt holds his dog Fala and talks to a young family friend. ▼

REGULATING BANKING AND FINANCE Congress took another step to reorganize the banking system by passing the **Glass-Steagall Act** of 1933, which established the Federal Deposit Insurance Corporation (FDIC). The FDIC provided federal insurance for individual bank accounts of up to $5,000, reassuring millions of bank customers that their money was safe. It also required banks to act cautiously with their customers' money.

Congress and the president also worked to regulate the stock market, in which people had lost faith because of the crash of 1929. The **Federal Securities Act,** passed in May 1933, required corporations to provide complete information on all stock offerings and made them liable for any misrepresentations. In June of 1934, Congress created the Securities and Exchange Commission (SEC) to regulate the stock market. One goal of this commission was to prevent people with inside information about companies from "rigging" the stock market for their own profit.

In addition, Roosevelt persuaded Congress to approve a bill allowing the manufacture and sale of some alcoholic beverages. The bill's main purpose was to raise government revenues by taxing alcohol. By the end of 1933, the passage of the 21st Amendment had repealed prohibition altogether.

Helping the American People

While working on banking and financial matters, the Roosevelt administration also implemented programs to provide relief to farmers, perhaps the hardest hit by the depression. It also aided other workers and attempted to stimulate economic recovery.

Background
See *supply and demand* on page R46 in the Economics Handbook.

RURAL ASSISTANCE The **Agricultural Adjustment Act (AAA)** sought to raise crop prices by lowering production, which the government achieved by paying farmers to leave a certain amount of every acre of land unseeded. The theory was that reduced supply would boost prices. In some cases, crops were too far advanced for the acreage reduction to take effect. As a result, the government paid cotton growers $200 million to plow under 10 million acres of their crop. It also paid hog farmers to slaughter 6 million pigs. This policy upset many Americans, who protested the destruction of food when many people were going hungry. It did, however, help raise farm prices and put more money in farmers' pockets.

An especially ambitious program of regional development was the Tennessee Valley Authority (TVA), established on May 18, 1933. (See Geography Spotlight on page 520.) Focusing on the badly depressed Tennessee River Valley, the TVA renovated five existing dams and constructed 20 new ones, created thousands of jobs, and provided flood control, hydroelectric power, and other benefits to an impoverished region.

PROVIDING WORK PROJECTS The administration also established programs to provide relief through work projects and cash payments. One important program, the **Civilian Conservation Corps (CCC),** put young men aged 18 to 25 to work building roads, developing parks, planting trees, and helping in soil-erosion and flood-control projects. By the time the program ended in 1942, almost 3 million young men had passed through the CCC. The CCC paid a small wage, $30 a month, of which $25 was automatically sent home to the worker's family. It also supplied free food and uniforms and lodging in work camps. Many of the camps were located on the Great Plains, where, within a period of eight years, the men of the CCC planted more than 200 million trees. This tremendous reforestation program was aimed at preventing another Dust Bowl.

Civilian Conservation Corps

- The CCC provided almost 3 million men aged 18–25 with work and wages between 1933 and 1942.
- The men lived in work camps under a strict regime. The majority of the camps were racially segregated.
- By 1938, the CCC had an 11 percent African-American enrollment.
- Accomplishments of the CCC include planting over 3 billion trees, developing over 800 state parks, and building more than 46,000 bridges.

The Public Works Administration (PWA), created in June 1933 as part of the **National Industrial Recovery Act (NIRA),** provided money to states to create jobs chiefly in the construction of schools and other community buildings. When these programs failed to make a sufficient dent in unemployment, President Roosevelt established the Civil Works Administration in November 1933. It provided 4 million immediate jobs during the winter of 1933–1934. Although some critics of the CWA claimed that the programs were "make-work" projects and a waste of money, the CWA built 40,000 schools and paid the salaries of more than 50,000 schoolteachers in America's rural areas. It also built more than half a million miles of roads. (C)

MAIN IDEA

Analyzing Effects
(C) How did New Deal programs affect various regions of the United States?

PROMOTING FAIR PRACTICES The NIRA also sought to promote industrial growth by establishing codes of fair practice for individual industries. It created the National Recovery Administration (NRA), which set prices of many products and established standards. The aim of the NRA was to promote recovery by interrupting the trend of wage cuts, falling prices, and layoffs. The economist Gardiner C. Means attempted to justify the NRA by stating the goal of industrial planning.

A PERSONAL VOICE GARDINER C. MEANS

"The National Recovery Administration [was] created in response to an overwhelming demand from many quarters that certain elements in the making of industrial policy . . . should no longer be left to the market place and the price mechanism but should be placed in the hands of administrative bodies."

—*The Making of Industrial Policy*

The codes of fair practice had been drafted in joint meetings of businesses and representatives of workers and consumers. These codes both limited production and established prices. Because businesses were given new concessions, workers made demands. Congress met their demands by passing a section of the NIRA guaranteeing workers' right to unionize and to bargain collectively. D

MAIN IDEA

Evaluating

D How did the New Deal support labor organizations?

Many businesses and politicians were critical of the NRA. Charges arose that the codes served large business interests. There were also charges of increasing code violations.

ECONOMIC BACKGROUND

DEFICIT SPENDING

John Maynard Keynes, an influential British economist, promoted the idea of deficit spending to stimulate economic recovery. In his view, a country should spend its way out of a depression by putting money into the hands of consumers. This would make it possible for them to buy goods and services and thus fuel economic growth. Therefore, even if a government has to go deeply into debt, it should spend great amounts of money to help get the economy growing again. (See *deficit spending* on page R39 and *Keynesian economics* on page R42 in the Economics Handbook.)

FOOD, CLOTHING, AND SHELTER A number of New Deal programs concerned housing and home mortgage problems. The Home Owners Loan Corporation (HOLC) provided government loans to homeowners who faced foreclosure because they couldn't meet their loan payments. In addition, the 1934 National Housing Act created the Federal Housing Administration (FHA). This agency continues to furnish loans for home mortgages and repairs today.

Another program, the Federal Emergency Relief Administration (FERA), was funded with $500 million to provide direct relief for the needy. Half of the money was given to the states as direct grants-in-aid to help furnish food and clothing to the unemployed, the aged, and the ill. The rest was distributed to states to support work relief programs—for every $3 within the state program, FERA donated $1. Harry Hopkins, who headed this program, believed that, whereas money helped people buy food, it was meaningful work that enabled them to gain confidence and self-respect.

The New Deal Comes Under Attack

By the end of the Hundred Days, millions of Americans had benefited from the New Deal programs. As well, the public's confidence in the nation's future had rebounded. Although President Roosevelt agreed to a policy of **deficit spending**—spending more money than the government receives in revenue—he did so with great reluctance. He regarded deficit spending as a necessary evil to be used only at a time of great economic crisis. Nevertheless, the New Deal did not end the depression, and opposition grew among some parts of the population.

Analyzing *Political Cartoons*

CHANGING COURSE

With hopes of lessening opposition to his programs, Roosevelt proposed a court reform bill that would essentially have allowed him to "pack" the Court with judges supportive of the New Deal. This cartoon shows Roosevelt as a sea captain ordering a shocked Congress to change course.

SKILLBUILDER Analyzing Political Cartoons

1. What "compass" did Roosevelt want to change? Explain.
2. How does the cartoonist portray FDR's attitude regarding his power as president?

 **SEE SKILLBUILDER HANDBOOK, PAGE R24.**

THAT COMPASS DOESN'T POINT THE WAY I WANT TO GO. CHANGE IT. NOW!
FDR
SUPREME COURT
CONGRESS

Liberal critics argued that the New Deal did not go far enough to help the poor and to reform the nation's economic system. Conservative critics argued that Roosevelt spent too much on direct relief and used New Deal policies to control business and socialize the economy. Conservatives were particularly angered by laws such as the Agricultural Adjustment Act and the National Industrial Recovery Act, which they believed gave the federal government too much control over agriculture and industry. Many critics believed the New Deal interfered with the workings of a free-market economy. (E)

MAIN IDEA

Contrasting
(E) How did liberal and conservative critics differ in their opposition to the New Deal?

THE SUPREME COURT REACTS By the mid-1930s, conservative opposition to the New Deal had received a boost from two Supreme Court decisions. In 1935, the Court struck down the NIRA as unconstitutional. It declared that the law gave legislative powers to the executive branch and that the enforcement of industry codes within states went beyond the federal government's constitutional powers to regulate interstate commerce. The next year, the Supreme Court struck down the AAA on the grounds that agriculture is a local matter and should be regulated by the states rather than by the federal government.

Fearing that further Court decisions might dismantle the New Deal, President Roosevelt proposed in February 1937 that Congress enact a court-reform bill to reorganize the federal judiciary and allow him to appoint six new Supreme Court justices. This "Court-packing bill" aroused a storm of protest in Congress and the press. Many people believed that the president was violating principles of judicial independence and the separation of powers. As it turned out, the president got his way without reorganizing the judiciary. In 1937, an elderly justice retired, and Roosevelt appointed the liberal Hugo S. Black, shifting the balance of the Court. Rulings of the Court began to favor the New Deal. (See *NLRB* v. *Jones and Laughlin Steel Corp.* on page 502.) Over the next four years, because of further resignations, Roosevelt was able to appoint seven new justices.

THREE FIERY CRITICS In 1934, some of the strongest conservative opponents of the New Deal banded together to form an organization called the American Liberty League. The American Liberty League opposed New Deal measures that it believed violated respect for the rights of individuals and property. Three of the toughest critics the president faced, however, were three men who expressed views that appealed to poor Americans: Charles Coughlin, Dr. Francis Townsend, and Huey Long.

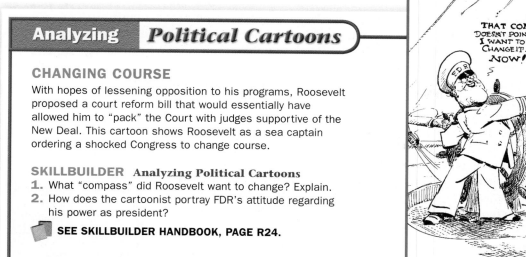

Father Charles Coughlin speaks to a radio audience in 1935. ▼

Every Sunday, Father Charles Coughlin, a Roman Catholic priest from a suburb of Detroit, broadcast radio sermons that combined economic, political, and religious ideas. Initially a supporter of the New Deal, Coughlin soon turned against Roosevelt. He favored a guaranteed annual income and the nationalization of banks. At the height of his popularity, Father Coughlin claimed a radio audience of as many as 40–45 million people, but his increasingly anti-Semitic (anti-Jewish) views eventually cost him support.

Vocabulary
nationalization: conversion from private to governmental ownership

Another critic of New Deal policies was Dr. Francis Townsend, a physician and health officer in Long Beach, California. He believed that Roosevelt wasn't doing enough to help the poor and elderly, so he devised a pension plan that would provide monthly benefits to the aged. The plan found strong backing among the elderly, thus undermining their support for Roosevelt.

Perhaps the most serious challenge to the New Deal came from Senator **Huey Long** of Louisiana. Like Coughlin, Long was an early supporter of the New Deal, but he, too, turned against Roosevelt. Eager to win the presidency for himself, Long proposed a nationwide social program called Share-Our-Wealth. Under the banner "Every Man a King," he promised something for everyone.

Huey Long

A Personal Voice HUEY LONG

> **"We owe debts in America today, public and private, amounting to $252 billion. That means that every child is born with a $2,000 debt tied around his neck. . . . We propose that children shall be born in a land of opportunity, guaranteed a home, food, clothes, and the other things that make for living, including the right to education."**
>
> —*Record,* 74 Congress, Session 1

Long's program was so popular that by 1935 he boasted of having perhaps as many as 27,000 Share-Our-Wealth clubs and 7.5 million members. That same year, however, at the height of his popularity, Long was assassinated by a lone gunman.

As the initial impetus of the New Deal began to wane, President Roosevelt started to look ahead. He knew that much more needed to be done to help the people and to solve the nation's economic problems.

SECTION 1 ASSESSMENT

1. **TERMS & NAMES** For each of the terms and names below, write a sentence explaining its significance.

- **Franklin Delano Roosevelt**
- **New Deal**
- **Glass-Steagall Act**
- **Federal Securities Act**
- **Agricultural Adjustment Act (AAA)**
- **Civilian Conservation Corps (CCC)**
- **National Industrial Recovery Act (NIRA)**
- **deficit spending**
- **Huey Long**

MAIN IDEA

2. **TAKING NOTES**
In a two-column chart, list problems that President Roosevelt confronted and how he tried to solve them.

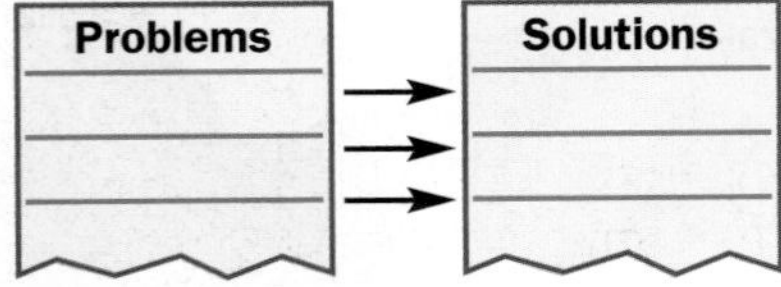

Write a paragraph telling which solution had the greatest impact, and why.

CRITICAL THINKING

3. **EVALUATING**
Of the New Deal programs discussed in this section, which do you consider the most important? Explain your choice. **Think About:**
   - the type of assistance offered by each program
   - the scope of each program
   - the impact of each program

4. **EVALUATING LEADERSHIP**
Do you think Roosevelt was wrong to try to "pack" the Supreme Court with those in favor of the New Deal? Explain your answer.

5. **DEVELOPING HISTORICAL PERSPECTIVE**
The New Deal has often been referred to as a turning point in American history. Cite examples to explain why.

The Second New Deal Takes Hold

MAIN IDEA	WHY IT MATTERS NOW	Terms & Names
The Second New Deal included new programs to extend federal aid and stimulate the nation's economy.	**Second New Deal programs continue to assist homebuyers, farmers, workers, and the elderly in the 2000s.**	**•Eleanor Roosevelt •Works Progress Administration (WPA) •National Youth Administration •Wagner Act •Social Security Act**

One American's Story

Dorothea Lange was a photographer who documented American life during the Great Depression and the era of the New Deal. Lange spent considerable time getting to know her subjects—destitute migrant workers—before she and her assistant set up their cameras.

A PERSONAL VOICE DOROTHEA LANGE

> **"So often it's just sticking around and remaining there, not swooping in and swooping out in a cloud of dust. . . . We found our way in . . . not too far away from the people we were working with. . . . The people who are garrulous and wear their heart on their sleeve and tell you everything, that's one kind of person. But the fellow who's hiding behind a tree and hoping you don't see him, is the fellow that you'd better find out why."**
>
> —quoted in *Restless Spirit: The Life and Work of Dorothea Lange*

▲ **Dorothea Lange taking photographs on the Texas plains in 1934.**

Lange also believed that her distinct limp, the result of a childhood case of polio, worked to her advantage. Seeing that Lange, too, had suffered, people were kind to her and more at ease.

Much of Lange's work was funded by federal agencies, such as the Farm Security Administration, which was established to alleviate rural poverty. Her photographs of migrant workers helped draw attention to the desperate conditions in rural America and helped to underscore the need for direct relief.

The Second Hundred Days

By 1935, the Roosevelt administration was seeking ways to build on the programs established during the Hundred Days. Although the economy had improved during FDR's first two years in office, the gains were not as great as he had expected. Unemployment remained high despite government work programs, and production still lagged behind the levels of the 1920s.

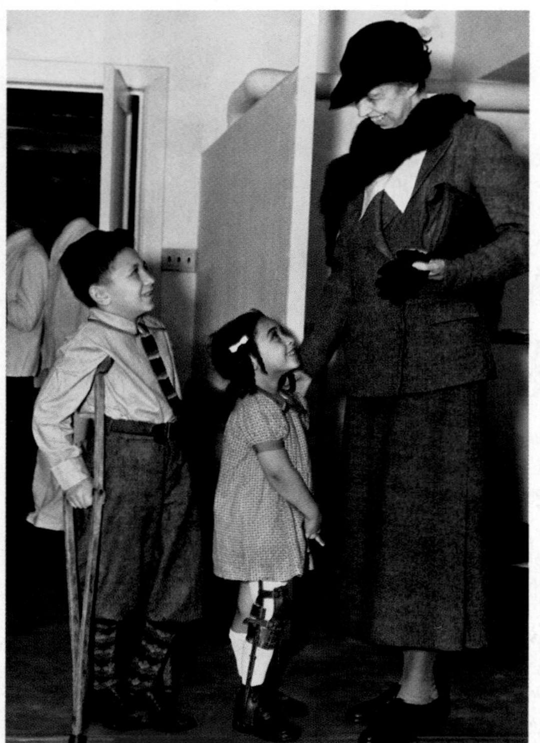

▲ Eleanor Roosevelt visits a children's hospital in 1937.

Nevertheless, the New Deal enjoyed widespread popularity, and President Roosevelt launched a second burst of activity, often called the Second New Deal or the Second Hundred Days. During this phase, the president called on Congress to provide more extensive relief for both farmers and workers.

The president was prodded in this direction by his wife, **Eleanor Roosevelt,** a social reformer who combined her deep humanitarian impulses with great political skills. Eleanor Roosevelt traveled the country, observing social conditions and reminding the president about the suffering of the nation's people. She also urged him to appoint women to government positions. (A)

MAIN IDEA

Summarizing
(A) Why did Roosevelt launch the Second Hundred Days?

REELECTING FDR The Second New Deal was under way by the time of the 1936 presidential election. The Republicans nominated Alfred Landon, the governor of Kansas, while the Democrats, of course, nominated President Roosevelt for a second term. The election resulted in an overwhelming victory for the Democrats, who won the presidency and large majorities in both houses. The election marked the first time that most African Americans had voted Democratic rather than Republican, and the first time that labor unions gave united support to a presidential candidate. The 1936 election was a vote of confidence in FDR and the New Deal.

Helping Farmers

In the mid-1930s, two of every five farms in the United States were mortgaged, and thousands of small farmers lost their farms. The novelist John Steinbeck described the experience of one tenant farmer and his family.

▲ A poster promotes the movie adaption of John Steinbeck's novel *The Grapes of Wrath.*

A Personal Voice JOHN STEINBECK

"Across the dooryard the tractor cut, and the hard, foot-beaten ground was seeded field, and the tractor cut through again; the uncut space was ten feet wide. And back he came. The iron guard bit into the house-corner, crumbled the wall, and wrenched the little house from its foundation so that it fell sideways, crushed like a bug. . . . The tractor cut a straight line on, and the air and the ground vibrated with its thunder. The tenant man stared after it, his rifle in his hand. His wife was beside him, and the quiet children behind. And all of them stared after the tractor."

—*The Grapes of Wrath*

FOCUSING ON FARMS When the Supreme Court struck down the AAA early in 1936, Congress passed another law to replace it: the Soil Conservation and Domestic Allotment Act. This act paid farmers for cutting production of soil-depleting crops and rewarded farmers for practicing good soil conservation methods. Two years later, in 1938, Congress approved a second Agricultural Adjustment Act that brought back many features of the first AAA. The second AAA did not include a processing tax to pay for farm subsidies, a provision of the first AAA that the Supreme Court had declared unconstitutional.

History Through *Photojournalism*

"MIGRANT MOTHER" (1936), DOROTHEA LANGE

In February 1936, Dorothea Lange visited a camp in Nipomo, California, where some 2,500 destitute pea pickers lived in tents or, like this mother of seven children, in lean-tos. Lange talked briefly to the woman and then took five pictures, successively moving closer to her subjects and directing more emphasis on the mother. The last photo, "Migrant Mother" (at right), was published in the *San Francisco News* March 10, 1936.

"Migrant Mother" became one of the most recognizable symbols of the Depression and perhaps the strongest argument in support of New Deal relief programs. Roy Stryker, who hired Lange to document the harsh living conditions of the time, described the mother: "She has all the suffering of mankind in her, but all the perseverance too. A restraint and a strange courage."

Lange reflected upon her assignment. "I saw and approached the hungry and desperate mother, as if drawn by a magnet. . . . She said that they had been living on frozen vegetables from the surrounding fields, and birds that the children killed. She had just sold the tires from her car to buy food."

SKILLBUILDER Interpreting Visual Sources

1. What might the woman be thinking about? Why do you think so?
2. Why do you think "Migrant Mother" was effective in persuading people to support FDR's relief programs?

SEE SKILLBUILDER HANDBOOK, PAGE R23.

The Second New Deal also attempted to help sharecroppers, migrant workers, and many other poor farmers. The Resettlement Administration, created by executive order in 1935, provided monetary loans to small farmers to buy land. In 1937, the agency was replaced by the Farm Security Administration (FSA), which loaned more than $1 billion to help tenant farmers become landholders and established camps for migrant farm workers, who had traditionally lived in squalid housing.

The FSA hired photographers such as Dorothea Lange, Ben Shahn, Walker Evans, Arthur Rothstein, and Carl Mydans to take many pictures of rural towns and farms and their inhabitants. The agency used their photographs to create a pictorial record of the difficult situation in rural America.

Roosevelt Extends Relief

As part of the Second New Deal, the Roosevelt administration and Congress set up a series of programs to help youths, professionals, and other workers. One of the largest was the **Works Progress Administration (WPA),** headed by Harry Hopkins, the former chief of the Federal Emergency Relief Administration.

The WPA set out to create as many jobs as possible as quickly as possible. Between 1935 and 1943, it spent $11 billion to give jobs to more than 8 million workers, most of them unskilled. These workers built 850 airports throughout the country, constructed or repaired 651,000 miles of roads and streets, and put up more than 125,000 public buildings. Women workers in sewing groups made 300 million garments for the needy. Although criticized by some as a make-work project, the WPA produced public works of lasting value to the nation and gave working people a sense of hope and purpose. As one man recalled, "It was really great. You worked, you got a paycheck and you had some dignity. Even when a man raked leaves, he got paid, he had some dignity."

In addition, the WPA employed many professionals who wrote guides to cities, collected historical slave narratives, painted murals on the walls of schools

This photograph by Margaret Bourke-White shows people waiting for food in a Kentucky bread line in 1937.

and other public buildings, and performed in theater troupes around the country. At the urging of Eleanor Roosevelt, the WPA made special efforts to help women, minorities, and young people. B

MAIN IDEA

Evaluating

B Do you think work programs like the WPA were a valid use of federal money? Why or why not?

Another program, the **National Youth Administration** (NYA), was created specifically to provide education, jobs, counseling, and recreation for young people. The NYA provided student aid to high school, college, and graduate students. In exchange, students worked in part-time positions at their schools. One participant later described her experience.

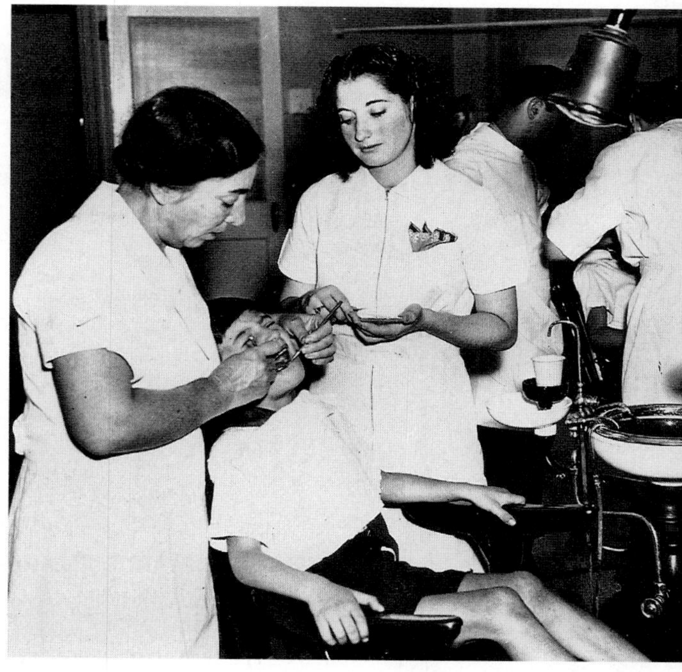

The NYA helped young people, such as this dental assistant (*third from left*), receive training and job opportunities.

A PERSONAL VOICE HELEN FARMER

"**I lugged . . . drafts and reams of paper home, night after night. . . . Sometimes I typed almost all night and had to deliver it to school the next morning. . . . This was a good program. It got necessary work done. It gave teenagers a chance to work for pay. Mine bought me clothes and shoes, school supplies, some movies and mad money. Candy bars, and big pickles out of a barrel. It gave my mother relief from my necessary demands for money.**"

—quoted in *The Great Depression*

For graduates unable to find jobs, or youth who had dropped out of school, the NYA provided part-time jobs, such as working on highways, parks, and the grounds of public buildings.

Improving Labor and Other Reforms

In a speech to Congress in January 1935, the president declared, "When a man is convalescing from an illness, wisdom dictates not only cure of the symptoms but also removal of their cause." During the Second New Deal, Roosevelt, with the help of Congress, brought about important reforms in the areas of labor relations and economic security for retired workers. (See the chart on page 500.)

IMPROVING LABOR CONDITIONS In 1935, the Supreme Court declared the NIRA unconstitutional, citing that the federal government had violated legislative authority reserved for individual states. One of the first reforms of the Second New Deal was passage of the National Labor Relations Act. More commonly called the **Wagner Act,** after its sponsor, Senator Robert F. Wagner of New York, the act reestablished the NIRA provision of collective bargaining. The federal government again protected the right of workers to join unions and engage in collective bargaining with employers.

The Wagner Act also prohibited unfair labor practices such as threatening workers, firing union members, and interfering with union organizing. The act set up the National Labor Relations Board (NLRB) to hear testimony about unfair practices and to hold elections to find out if workers wanted union representation. C

MAIN IDEA

Analyzing Issues

C Why was the Wagner Act significant?

In 1938, Congress passed the Fair Labor Standards Act, which set maximum hours at 44 hours per week, decreasing to 40 hours after two years. It also set minimum wages at 25 cents an hour, increasing to 40 cents an hour by 1945. In addition, the act set rules for the employment of workers under 16 and banned hazardous work for those under 18.

New Deal Programs

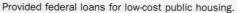

EMPLOYMENT PROJECTS		PURPOSE
1933	**Civilian Conservation Corps (CCC)**	Provided jobs for single males on conservation projects.
1933	**Federal Emergency Relief Administration (FERA)**	Helped states to provide aid for the unemployed.
1933	**Public Works Administration (PWA)**	Created jobs on government projects.
1933	**Civil Works Administration (CWA)**	Provided work in federal jobs.
1935	**Works Progress Administration (WPA)**	Quickly created as many jobs as possible—from construction jobs to positions in symphony orchestras.
1935	**National Youth Administration (NYA)**	Provided job training for unemployed young people and part-time jobs for needy students.
BUSINESS ASSISTANCE AND REFORM		
1933	**Emergency Banking Relief Act (EBRA)**	Banks were inspected by Treasury Department and those stable could reopen.
1933	**Federal Deposit Insurance Corporation (FDIC)**	Protected bank deposits up to $5,000. (Today, accounts are protected up to $100,000.)
1933	**National Recovery Administration (NRA)**	Established codes of fair competition.
1934	**Securities and Exchange Commission (SEC)**	Supervised the stock market and eliminated dishonest practices.
1935	**Banking Act of 1935**	Created seven-member board to regulate the nation's money supply and the interest rates on loans.
1938	**Food, Drug and Cosmetic Act (FDC)**	Required manufacturers to list ingredients in foods, drugs, and cosmetic products.
FARM RELIEF AND RURAL DEVELOPMENT		
1933	**Agricultural Adjustment Administration (AAA)**	Aided farmers and regulated crop production.
1933	**Tennessee Valley Authority (TVA)**	Developed the resources of the Tennessee Valley.
1935	**Rural Electrification Administration (REA)**	Provided affordable electricity for isolated rural areas.
HOUSING		
1933	**Home Owners Loan Corporation (HOLC)**	Loaned money at low interest to homeowners who could not meet mortgage payments.
1934	**Federal Housing Administration (FHA)**	Insured loans for building and repairing homes.
1937	**United States Housing Authority (USHA)**	Provided federal loans for low-cost public housing.
LABOR RELATIONS		
1935	**National Labor Relations Board (Wagner Act)**	Defined unfair labor practices and established the National Labor Relations Board (NLRB) to settle disputes between employers and employees.
1938	**Fair Labor Standards Act**	Established a minimum hourly wage and a maximum number of hours in the workweek for the entire country. Set rules for the employment of workers under 16 and banned hazardous factory work for those under 18.
RETIREMENT		
1935	**Social Security Administration**	Provided a pension for retired workers and their spouses and aided people with disabilities.

THE SOCIAL SECURITY ACT One of the most important achievements of the New Deal was creating the Social Security system. The **Social Security Act,** passed in 1935, was created by a committee chaired by Secretary of Labor Frances Perkins. The act had three major parts:

- *Old-age insurance for retirees 65 or older and their spouses.* The insurance was a supplemental retirement plan. Half of the funds came from the worker and half from the employer. Although some groups were excluded from the system, it helped to make retirement comfortable for millions of people.
- *Unemployment compensation system.* The unemployment system was funded by a federal tax on employers. It was administered at the state level. The initial payments ranged from $15 to $18 per week.
- *Aid to families with dependent children and the disabled.* The aid was paid for by federal funds made available to the states.

MAIN IDEA

Drawing Conclusions

D Whom did Social Security help?

Although the Social Security Act was not a total pension system or a complete welfare system, it did provide substantial benefits to millions of Americans. D

EXPANDING AND REGULATING UTILITIES The Second New Deal also included laws to promote rural electrification and to regulate public utilities. In 1935, only 12.6 percent of American farms had electricity. Roosevelt established under executive order the Rural Electrification Administration (REA), which financed and worked with electrical cooperatives to bring electricity to isolated areas. By 1945, 48 percent of America's farms and rural homes had electricity. That figure rose to 90 percent by 1949.

The Public Utility Holding Company Act of 1935 took aim at financial corruption in the public utility industry. It outlawed the ownership of utilities by multiple holding companies—a practice known as the pyramiding of holding companies. Lobbyists for the holding companies fought the law fiercely, and it proved extremely difficult to enforce.

As the New Deal struggled to help farmers and other workers overcome the Great Depression, it assisted many different groups in the nation, including women, African Americans, and Native Americans.

SECTION 2 ASSESSMENT

1. **TERMS & NAMES** For each term or name, write a sentence explaining its significance.
   - **Eleanor Roosevelt**
   - **Works Progress Administration (WPA)**
   - **National Youth Administration**
   - **Wagner Act**
   - **Social Security Act**

MAIN IDEA

2. **TAKING NOTES**
   Create a chart similar to the one below to show how groups such as farmers, the unemployed, youth, and retirees were helped by Second New Deal programs.

Second New Deal	
Group	How Helped

Which group do you think benefited the most from the Second New Deal? Explain.

CRITICAL THINKING

3. **EVALUATING DECISIONS**
   Why might the Social Security Act be considered the most important achievement of the New Deal?
   Think About:
   - the types of relief needed in the 1930s
   - alternatives to government assistance to the elderly, the unemployed, and the disabled
   - the scope of the act

4. **INTERPRETING VISUAL SOURCES**
   Many WPA posters were created to promote New Deal programs—in this case the Rural Electrification Administration. How does this poster's simplistic design convey the program's goal?

NLRB v. *JONES AND LAUGHLIN STEEL CORP.* (1937)

ORIGINS OF THE CASE In 1936, the Jones and Laughlin Steel Corporation was charged with intimidating union organizers and firing several union members. The National Labor Relations Board (NLRB) found the company guilty of "unfair labor practices" and ordered it to rehire the workers with back pay.

THE RULING **The Supreme Court ruled that Congress had the power to regulate labor relations and confirmed the authority of the NLRB.**

LEGAL REASONING

In the 1935 National Labor Relations Act, or Wagner Act, Congress claimed that its authority to regulate labor relations came from the commerce clause of the Constitution. Jones and Laughlin Steel argued that its manufacturing business did not involve interstate commerce—it operated a plant and hired people locally.

The Court disagreed. Although production itself may occur within one state, it said, production is a part of the interstate "flow of commerce." If labor unrest at a steel mill would create "burdens and obstructions" to interstate commerce, then Congress has the power to prevent labor unrest at the steel mill.

The Court also explained that the act went "no further than to safeguard the right of employees to self-organization and to select representatives . . . for collective bargaining." Departing from earlier decisions, the Court affirmed that these are "fundamental" rights.

> **"Long ago we . . . said . . . that a single employee was helpless in dealing with an employer; that he was dependent . . . on his daily wage for the maintenance of himself and family; that, if the employer refused to pay him the wages that he thought fair, he was . . . unable to leave the employ and resist arbitrary and unfair treatment; that union was essential to give laborers opportunity to deal on an equality with their employer."**

As a result, the Wagner Act was allowed to stand.

Chief Justice Charles Evans Hughes ▶

LEGAL SOURCES

LEGISLATION

U.S. CONSTITUTION, ARTICLE 1, SECTION 8
(COMMERCE CLAUSE)

"The Congress shall have Power . . . To regulate Commerce with foreign Nations and among the several States."

NATIONAL LABOR RELATIONS ACT (1935)

"The term 'affecting commerce' means . . . tending to lead to a labor dispute burdening or obstructing commerce or the free flow of commerce."

"It shall be an unfair labor practice for an employer . . . to interfere with, restrain, or coerce employees in the exercise of the rights [to organize unions]."

RELATED CASES

***SCHECHTER POULTRY CORP.* v. *UNITED STATES* (1935)**

The Court struck down the National Industrial Recovery Act, a key piece of New Deal legislation.

◀ Choosing to work despite the strike, a storekeeper at the Jones and Laughlin Steel Corporation tries to pass through picket lines.

WHY IT MATTERED

The 1935 Wagner Act was one of the most important pieces of New Deal legislation. Conservative justices on the Supreme Court, however, thought New Deal legislation increased the power of the federal government beyond what the Constitution allowed. By the time the Jones and Laughlin case reached the Court in 1937, the Court had already struck down numerous New Deal laws. It appeared to many as if the Wagner Act was doomed.

In February 1937, Roosevelt announced a plan to appoint enough justices to build a Court majority in favor of the New Deal. Critics immediately accused Roosevelt of trying to pack the Supreme Court, thus crippling the Constitution's system of checks and balances.

Two months later, the Court delivered its opinion in *Jones and Laughlin* and at about the same time upheld other New Deal legislation as well. Most historians agree that the Court's switch was not a response to Roosevelt's "Court-packing" plan, which already seemed destined for failure. Nevertheless, the decision resolved a potential crisis.

HISTORICAL IMPACT

The protection that labor unions gained by the Wagner Act helped them to grow quickly. Union membership among non-farm workers grew from around 12 percent in 1930 to around 31 percent by 1950. This increase helped improve the economic standing of many working-class Americans in the years following World War II.

Most significantly, *Jones and Laughlin* greatly broadened Congress's power. Previously, neither the federal nor the state governments were thought to have sufficient power to control the large corporations and holding companies doing business in many states. Now, far beyond the power to regulate interstate commerce, Congress had the power to regulate anything "essential or appropriate" to that function. For example, federal laws barring discrimination in hotels and restaurants rest on the Court's allowing Congress to decide what is an "essential or appropriate" subject of regulation.

More recently, the Court has placed tighter limits on Congress's power to regulate interstate commerce. In *United States* v. *Lopez* (1995), the Court struck down a law that banned people from having handguns near a school. The Court said Congress was not justified in basing this law on its power to regulate interstate commerce.

THINKING CRITICALLY

CONNECT TO HISTORY

1. **Developing Historical Perspective** Lawyers for Jones and Laughlin said that the Wagner Act violated the Tenth Amendment. Chief Justice Hughes said that since the act fell within the scope of the commerce clause, the Tenth Amendment did not apply. Read the Tenth Amendment and then write a paragraph defending Hughes's position.

 **SEE SKILLBUILDER HANDBOOK, PAGE R11.**

CONNECT TO TODAY

2. 

CLASSZONE.COM

Visit the links for Historic Decisions of the Supreme Court and read the opening sections of *United States* v. *Lopez.* There, Chief Justice Rehnquist offers a summary of the Court's interpretation of the commerce clause over the years. Summarize in your own words Rehnquist's description of the current meaning of the commerce clause.

SECTION 3

The New Deal Affects Many Groups

MAIN IDEA

New Deal policies and actions affected various social and ethnic groups.

WHY IT MATTERS NOW

The New Deal made a lasting impact on increasing the government's role in the struggle for equal rights.

Terms & Names

- **Frances Perkins**
- **Mary McLeod Bethune**
- **John Collier**
- **New Deal Coalition**
- **Congress of Industrial Organizations (CIO)**

One American's Story

Pedro J. González came to this country from Mexico in the early 1920s and later became a United States citizen. As the first Spanish-language disc jockey in Los Angeles, González used his radio program to condemn discrimination against Mexicans and Mexican Americans, who were often made scapegoats for social and economic problems during the Depression. For his efforts, González was arrested, jailed, and deported on trumped-up charges. Later in life, he reflected on his experiences.

A PERSONAL VOICE PEDRO J. GONZÁLEZ

"Seeing how badly they treated Mexicans back in the days of my youth I could have started a rebellion. But now there could be a cultural understanding so that without firing one bullet, we might understand each other. We [Mexicans] were here before they [Anglos] were, and we are not, as they still say, 'undesirables' or 'wetbacks.' They say we come to this land and it's not our home. Actually, it's the other way around."

—quoted in the *Los Angeles Times*, December 9, 1984

Pedro J. González became a hero to many Mexican Americans and a symbol of Mexican cultural pride. His life reflected some of the difficulties faced by Mexicans and other minority groups in the United States during the New Deal era.

A SONG FOR HIS PEOPLE
Pedro J. González and the Fight for Mexican-American Rights

The New Deal Brings New Opportunities

In some ways, the New Deal represented an important opportunity for minorities and women, but what these groups gained was limited. Long-standing patterns of prejudice and discrimination continued to plague them and to prevent their full and equal participation in national life.

WOMEN MAKE THEIR MARK One of the most notable changes during the New Deal was the naming of several women to important government positions. **Frances Perkins** became America's first female cabinet member. As secretary of labor, she played a major role in creating the Social Security system and supervised labor legislation. President Roosevelt, encouraged by his wife Eleanor and seeking the support of women voters, also appointed two female diplomats and a female federal judge.

However, women continued to face discrimination in the workplace from male workers who believed that working women took jobs away from men. A Gallup poll taken in 1936 reported that 82 percent of Americans said that a wife should not work if her husband had a job.

Additionally, New Deal laws yielded mixed results. The National Recovery Administration, for example, set wage codes, some of which set lower minimum wages for women. The Federal Emergency Relief Administration and the Civil Works Administration hired far fewer women than men, and the Civilian Conservation Corps hired only men.

In spite of these barriers, women continued their movement into the workplace. Although the overall percentage of women working for wages increased only slightly during the 1930s, the percentage of married women in the workplace grew from 11.7 percent in 1930 to 15.6 percent in 1940. In short, widespread criticism of working women did not halt the long-term trend of women working outside the home.

KEY PLAYER

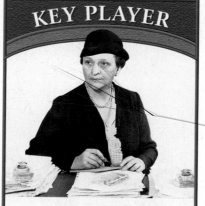

FRANCES PERKINS
1882–1965

As a student at Mount Holyoke College, Frances Perkins attended lectures that introduced her to social reform efforts. Her initial work in the settlement house movement sparked her interest in pursuing the emerging social service organizations. After witnessing the Triangle Shirtwaist Factory fire in 1911 (see Chapter 6, page 249), Perkins pledged to fight for labor reforms, especially those for women. A pioneer for labor and women's issues, she changed her name from Fannie to Frances, believing she would be taken more seriously in her work.

African-American Activism

The 1930s witnessed a growth of activism by African Americans. One notable figure was A. Philip Randolph, who organized the country's first all-black trade union, the Brotherhood of Sleeping Car Porters. His work and that of others laid the groundwork for what would become the civil rights movement.

AFRICAN AMERICANS TAKE LEADERSHIP ROLES During the New Deal, Roosevelt appointed more than 100 African Americans to key positions in the government. **Mary McLeod Bethune**—an educator who dedicated herself to promoting opportunities for young African Americans—was one such appointee. Hired by the president to head the Division of Negro Affairs of the National Youth Administration, Bethune worked to ensure that the NYA hired African-American administrators and provided job training and other benefits to minority students.

Bethune also helped organize a "Black Cabinet" of influential African Americans to advise the Roosevelt administration on racial issues. Among these figures were William H. Hastie and Robert C. Weaver, both appointees to Roosevelt's Department of Interior. Never before had so many African Americans had a voice in the White House. (A)

MAIN IDEA

Synthesizing
(A) Why was the "Black Cabinet" important to the Roosevelt administration?

Eleanor Roosevelt played a key role in opening doors for African Americans in government. She was also instrumental in bringing about one of the most dramatic cultural events of the

◀ Mary McLeod Bethune, a close friend of Eleanor Roosevelt, was a strong supporter of the New Deal.

▲ Marian Anderson sang from the steps of the Lincoln Memorial on April 9, 1939.

period: a performance by the African-American singer Marian Anderson in 1939. When the Daughters of the American Revolution chose not to allow Anderson to perform in their concert hall in Washington, D.C., because of her race, Eleanor Roosevelt resigned from the organization. She then arranged for Anderson to perform at the Lincoln Memorial on Easter Sunday. At the concert, Walter White, an official of the NAACP, noticed one girl in the crowd.

A PERSONAL VOICE WALTER WHITE

> **"Her hands were particularly noticeable as she thrust them forward and upward, trying desperately . . . to touch the singer. They were hands which despite their youth had known only the dreary work of manual labor. Tears streamed down the girl's dark face. Her hat was askew, but in her eyes flamed hope bordering on ecstasy. . . . If Marian Anderson could do it, the girl's eyes seemed to say, then I can, too."**
>
> —*A Man Called White*

THE PRESIDENT FAILS TO SUPPORT CIVIL RIGHTS Despite efforts to promote racial equality, Roosevelt was never committed to full civil rights for African Americans. He was afraid of upsetting white Democratic voters in the South, an important segment of his supporters. He refused to approve a federal antilynching law and an end to the poll tax, two key goals of the civil rights movement. Further, a number of New Deal agencies clearly discriminated against African Americans, including the NRA, the CCC, and the TVA. These programs gave lower wages to African Americans and favored whites.

African Americans recognized the need to fight for their rights and to improve conditions in areas that the New Deal ignored. In 1934, they helped organize the Southern Tenant Farmers Union, which sought to protect the rights of tenant farmers and sharecroppers, both white and black. In the North, the union created tenants' groups and launched campaigns to increase job opportunities.

In general, however, African Americans supported the Roosevelt administration and the New Deal, generally seeing them as their best hope for the future. As one man recalled, "Roosevelt touched the temper of the black community. You did not look upon him as being white, black, blue or green. He was President Roosevelt." B

MAIN IDEA

Evaluating
B Evaluate the actions and policies of the Roosevelt administration on civil rights.

HISTORICAL SPOTLIGHT

DEPORTATION OF MEXICAN AMERICANS

Many Mexican Americans were long-time residents or citizens of the United States. Others came during the 1920s to work on farms in Texas, California, and Arizona. Valued for their low-cost labor during the good times, these migrant workers became the target of hostility during the Great Depression. Many returned to Mexico willingly, while others were deported by the United States government. During the 1930s, as many as 400,000 persons of Mexican descent, many of them U.S. citizens, were deported to Mexico.

Mexican-American Fortunes

Mexican Americans also tended to support the New Deal, even though they received even fewer benefits than African Americans did. Large numbers of Mexican Americans had come to the United States during the 1920s, settling mainly in the Southwest. Most found work laboring on farms, an occupation that was essentially unprotected by state and federal laws. During the Depression, farm wages fell to as little as nine cents an hour. Farm workers who tried to unionize

MAIN IDEA

Identifying Problems
C Why was life difficult for farm laborers during the Depression?

often met with violence from employers and government authorities. Although the CCC and WPA helped some Mexican Americans, these agencies also discriminated against them by disqualifying from their programs migrant workers who had no permanent address. C

Native Americans Gain Support

Native Americans received strong government support from the New Deal. In 1924, Native Americans had received full citizenship by law. In 1933, President Roosevelt appointed **John Collier** as commissioner of Indian affairs. Collier helped create the Indian Reorganization Act of 1934. This act was an extreme change in government policy. It moved away from assimilation and toward Native American autonomy. It also helped to restore some reservation lands to tribal ownership. The act mandated changes in three areas:

- *economic*—Native American lands would belong to an entire tribe. This provision strengthened Native American land claims by prohibiting the government from taking over unclaimed reservation lands and selling them to people other than Native Americans.
- *cultural*—The number of boarding schools for Native American children was reduced, and children could attend school on the reservations.
- *political*—Tribes were given permission to elect tribal councils to govern their reservations.

John Collier talks with Chief Richard, one of several Native American chiefs attending the Four Nation Celebration held at Niagara Falls, New York, in September 1934.

MAIN IDEA

Summarizing
D What changes occurred for Native Americans as a result of the New Deal?

Some Native Americans who valued their tribal traditions hailed the act as an important step forward. Others who had become more "Americanized" as individual landowners under the previous Dawes Act objected, because they were tired of white people telling them what was good for them. D

FDR Creates the New Deal Coalition

Although New Deal policies had mixed results for minorities, these groups generally backed President Roosevelt. In fact, one of FDR's great achievements was to create the **New Deal Coalition**—an alignment of diverse groups dedicated to supporting the Democratic Party. The coalition included Southern whites, various urban groups, African Americans, and unionized industrial workers. As a result, Democrats dominated national politics throughout the 1930s and 1940s.

LABOR UNIONS FLOURISH As a result of the Wagner Act and other prolabor legislation passed during the New Deal, union members enjoyed better working conditions and increased bargaining power. In their eyes, President Roosevelt was a "friend of labor." Labor unions donated money to Roosevelt's reelection campaigns, and union workers pledged their votes to him.

Between 1933 and 1941, union membership grew from less than 3 million to more than 10 million. Unionization especially affected coal miners and workers in mass-production industries, such as the automobile, rubber, and electrical industries. It was in these industries, too, that a struggle for dominance within the labor movement began to develop.

The Growing Labor Movement, 1933–1940

Robert F. Wagner
A Democratic senator from New York (1927–1949), Robert F. Wagner was especially interested in workers' welfare. Wagner introduced the National Labor Relations Act in Congress in 1935. ▼

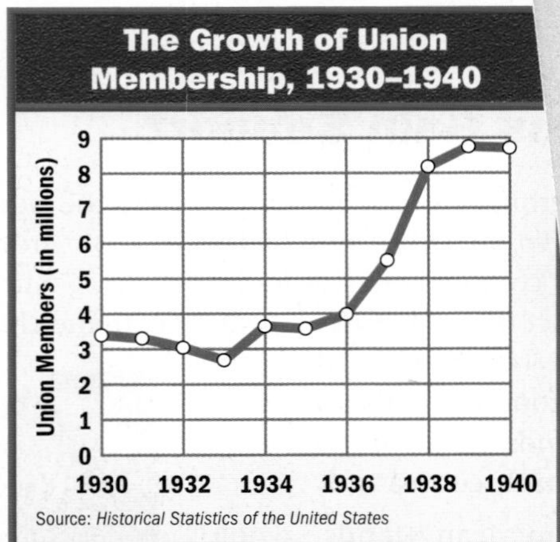

◀ **Union membership soars**
A Ben Shahn poster from the late 1930s boasted of the rise in union membership.

Sit-down strikes ▶
Union workers—such as these CIO strikers at the Fisher automobile plant in Flint, Michigan, in 1937—found the sit-down strike an extremely effective method for getting their demands met.

The American Federation of Labor (AFL) had traditionally been restricted to the craft unions, such as carpenters and electricians. Most of the AFL leaders opposed industrywide unions that represented all the workers in a given industry, such as automobile manufacturing. (E)

MAIN IDEA

Analyzing Effects
(E) How did New Deal policies affect organized labor?

Frustrated by this position, several key labor leaders, including John L. Lewis of the United Mine Workers of America and David Dubinsky of the International Ladies Garment Workers, formed the Committee for Industrial Organization to organize industrial unions. The committee rapidly signed up unskilled and semiskilled workers, and within two years it succeeded in gaining union recognition in the steel and automobile industries. By 1938, after all the unions that made up the group had been expelled from the AFL, the committee changed its name to the **Congress of Industrial Organizations (CIO).** This split lasted until 1955.

LABOR DISPUTES One of the main bargaining tactics of the labor movement in the 1930s was the sit-down strike. Instead of walking off their jobs, workers remained inside their plants, but they did not work. This prevented the factory owners from carrying on production with strikebreakers, or scabs. Some Americans disapproved of the sit-down strike, calling it a violation of private property. Nonetheless, it proved to be an effective bargaining tool.

Background
See *strike* on page R45 in the Economics Handbook.

Not all labor disputes in the 1930s were peaceful. Perhaps the most dramatic incident was the clash at the Republic Steel plant in Chicago on Memorial Day, 1937. Police attacked striking steelworkers outside the plant. One striker, an African-American man, recalled the experience.

A PERSONAL VOICE JESSE REESE

"I began to see people drop. There was a Mexican on my side, and he fell; and there was a black man on my side and he fell. Down I went. I crawled around in the grass and saw that people were getting beat. I'd never seen police beat women, not white women. I'd seen them beat black women, but this was the first time in my life I'd seen them beat white women—with sticks."

—quoted in *The Great Depression*

Ten people were killed and 84 wounded in this incident, which became known as the Memorial Day Massacre. Shortly afterward, the National Labor Relations Board stepped in and required the head of Republic Steel, Tom Girdler, to negotiate with the union. This and other actions helped labor gain strength during the 1930s.

▲ Chicago police attack strikers at what would become known as the Memorial Day Massacre (1937).

FDR WINS IN 1936 Urban voters were another important component of the New Deal coalition. Support for the Democratic Party surged, especially in large Northern cities, such as New York, Boston, Philadelphia, and Chicago. These and other cities had powerful city political organizations that provided services, such as jobs, in exchange for votes. In the 1936 election, President Roosevelt carried the nation's 12 largest cities.

Support for President Roosevelt came from various religious and ethnic groups—Roman Catholics, Jews, Italians, Irish, and Polish and other Slavic peoples—as well as from African Americans. His appeal to these groups was based on New Deal labor laws and work-relief programs, which aided the urban poor. The president also made direct and persuasive appeals to urban voters at election time. To reinforce his support, he also appointed many officials of urban-immigrant backgrounds, particularly Roman Catholics and Jews, to important government positions.

Women, African Americans, Mexican Americans, Native Americans, and workers from all walks of life were greatly affected by the New Deal. It also had a tremendous influence on American society and culture.

ASSESSMENT

1. **TERMS & NAMES** For each of the following terms and names, write a sentence explaining its significance.
   - **Frances Perkins**
   - **Mary McLeod Bethune**
   - **John Collier**
   - **New Deal coalition**
   - **Congress of Industrial Organizations (CIO)**

MAIN IDEA

2. **TAKING NOTES**
   Using a web diagram like the partial one shown here, note the effects of New Deal policies on American women, African Americans, Mexican Americans, Native Americans, unionized workers, and urban Americans.

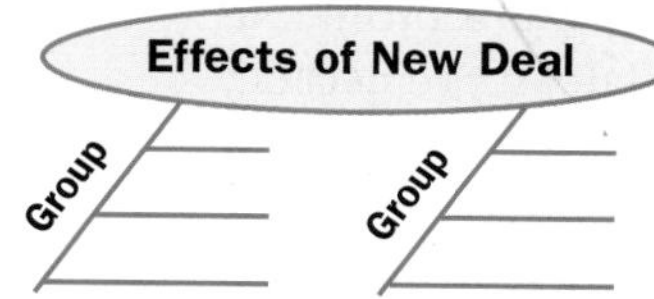

   Write a paragraph explaining the effects of the New Deal on one of the groups.

CRITICAL THINKING

3. **SUMMARIZING**
   What steps did women take toward equality during the 1930s?
   Think About:
   - the role of women in government
   - hiring practices in federal programs
   - women's opportunities in business and industry

4. **EVALUATING**
   In your opinion, did organized labor become too powerful in the 1930s? Explain your answer. **Think About:**
   - why workers joined unions
   - how unions organized workers
   - the role of unions in politics

5. **ANALYZING MOTIVES**
   Why did urban voters support President Roosevelt?

Culture in the 1930s

MAIN IDEA	WHY IT MATTERS NOW	Terms & Names
Motion pictures, radio, art, and literature blossomed during the New Deal.	**The films, music, art, and literature of the 1930s still captivate today's public.**	• ***Gone With the Wind*** • **Orson Welles** • **Grant Wood** • **Richard Wright** • ***The Grapes of Wrath***

One American's Story

Don Congdon, editor of the book *The Thirties: A Time to Remember*, was a high school student when the New Deal began. While many writers and artists in the 1930s produced works that reflected the important issues of the day, it was the movies and radio that most clearly captured the public imagination. Congdon remembers the role movies played at the time.

A Personal Voice DON CONGDON

"Lots of us enjoyed our leisure at the movies. The experience of going was like an insidious [tempting] candy we could never get quite enough of; the visit to the dark theater was an escape from the drab realities of Depression living, and we were entranced by the never-ending variety of stories. Hollywood, like Scheherazade [the storyteller] in *The Thousand and One Nights*, supplied more the next night, and the next night after that."

—*The Thirties: A Time to Remember*

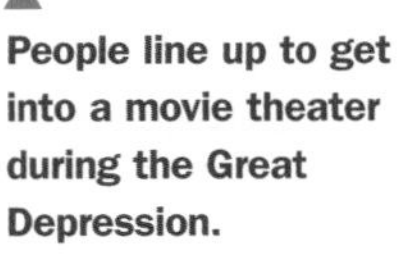

▲ **People line up to get into a movie theater during the Great Depression.**

During the Great Depression, movies provided a window on a different, more exciting world. Despite economic hardship, many people gladly paid the 25 cents it cost to go to the movies. Along with radio, motion pictures became an increasingly dominant feature of American life.

The Lure of Motion Pictures and Radio

Although the 1930s were a difficult time for many Americans, it was a profitable and golden age for the motion-picture and radio industries. By late in the decade, approximately 65 percent of the population was attending the movies once a week. The nation boasted over 15,000 movie theaters, more than the number of banks and double the number of hotels. Sales of radios also greatly increased during the 1930s, from just over 13 million in 1930 to 28 million by 1940. Nearly 90 percent of American households owned a radio. Clearly, movies and radio had taken the country by storm.

▲ Clark Gable and Vivien Leigh starred in *Gone With the Wind*, a sweeping drama about life among Southern plantation owners during the Civil War.

MOVIES ARE A HIT Wacky comedies, lavish musicals, love stories, and gangster films all vied for the attention of the moviegoing public during the New Deal years. Following the end of silent films and the rise of "talking" pictures, new stars such as Clark Gable, Marlene Dietrich, and James Cagney rose from Hollywood, the center of the film industry. These stars helped launch a new era of glamour and sophistication in Hollywood.

Some films made during the 1930s offered pure escape from the hard realities of the Depression by presenting visions of wealth, romance, and good times. Perhaps the most famous film of the era, and one of the most popular of all time, was ***Gone With the Wind*** (1939). Another film, *Flying Down to Rio* (1933), was a light romantic comedy featuring Fred Astaire and Ginger Rogers, who went on to make many movies together, becoming America's favorite dance partners. Other notable movies made during the 1930s include *The Wizard of Oz* (1939) and *Snow White and the Seven Dwarfs* (1937), which showcased the dazzling animation of Walt Disney.

Comedies—such as *Monkey Business* (1931) and *Duck Soup* (1931), starring the zany Marx Brothers—became especially popular. So did films that combined escapist appeal with more realistic plots and settings. Americans flocked to see gangster films that presented images of the dark, gritty streets and looming skyscrapers of urban America. These movies featured hard-bitten characters struggling to succeed in a harsh environment where they faced difficulties that Depression-era audiences could easily understand. Notable films in this genre include *Little Caesar* (1930) and *The Public Enemy* (1931).

Some commentators believed that several films, such as *Mr. Deeds Goes to Town* (1936) by director Frank Capra, presented the social and political accomplishments of the New Deal in a positive light. These films portrayed honest, kindhearted people winning out over those with greedy special interests. In much the same way, the New Deal seemed to represent the interests of average Americans. (A)

MAIN IDEA

Developing Historical Perspective

(A) Why do you think movies were so popular during the Depression?

RADIO ENTERTAINS Even more than movies, radio embodied the democratic spirit of the times. Families typically spent several hours a day gathered together, listening to their favorite programs. It was no accident that President Roosevelt chose radio as the medium for his "fireside chats." It was the most direct means of access to the American people.

Like movies, radio programs offered a range of entertainment. In the evening, radio networks offered excellent dramas and variety programs. **Orson Welles,** an actor, director, producer, and writer, created one of the most renowned radio broadcasts of all time, "The War of the Worlds." Later he directed movie classics such as *Citizen Kane* (1941) and *Touch of Evil* (1958). After making their reputation in

HISTORICAL SPOTLIGHT

WAR OF THE WORLDS

On October 30, 1938, radio listeners were stunned by a special announcement: Martians had invaded Earth! Panic set in as many Americans became convinced that the world was coming to an end. Of course, the story wasn't true: it was a radio drama based on H. G. Wells's novel *The War of the Worlds.*

In his book, Wells describes the canisters of gas fired by the Martians as releasing "an enormous volume of heavy, inky vapour. . . . And the touch of that vapour, the inhaling of its pungent wisps, was death to all that breathes." The broadcast, narrated by Orson Welles (at left), revealed the power of radio at a time when Americans received fast-breaking news over the airwaves.

▲ The comedy couple George Burns and Gracie Allen delighted radio audiences for years, and their popularity continued on television.

radio, comedians Bob Hope, Jack Benny, and the duo Burns and Allen moved on to work in television and movies. Soap operas—so named because they were usually sponsored by soap companies—tended to play late morning to early afternoon for homemakers, while children's programs, such *The Lone Ranger*, generally aired later in the afternoon, when children were home from school.

One of the first worldwide radio broadcasts described for listeners the horrific crash of the *Hindenburg*, a German zeppelin (rigid airship), in New Jersey on May 6, 1937. Such immediate news coverage became a staple in society.

The Arts in Depression America

In contrast to many radio and movie productions of the 1930s, much of the art, music, and literature of the time was sober and serious. Despite grim artistic tones, however, much of this artistic work conveyed a more uplifting message about the strength of character and the democratic values of the American people. A number of artists and writers embraced the spirit of social and political change fostered by the New Deal. In fact, many received direct support through New Deal work programs from government officials who believed that art played an important role in national life. Also, as Harry Hopkins, the head of the WPA, put it, "They've got to eat just like other people." **B**

MAIN IDEA

Analyzing Causes

B Why did the New Deal fund art projects?

ARTISTS DECORATE AMERICA The Federal Art Project, a branch of the WPA, paid artists a living wage to produce public art. It also aimed to increase public appreciation of art and to promote positive images of American society. Project artists created posters, taught art in the schools, and painted murals on the walls of public buildings. These murals, inspired in part by the revolutionary work of

This detail is from the mural *Industries of California*, painted in 1934 by Ralph Stackpole. It decorates San Francisco's Coit Tower, one of the best preserved sites of WPA mural projects. ▶

History Through Art

AMERICAN GOTHIC (1930)

Grant Wood's 1930 painting, *American Gothic,* became one of the most famous portrayals of life in the Midwest during the Great Depression. Painted in the style known as Regionalism, Wood painted familiar subjects in realistic ways. The house in the background was discovered by Wood in Eldon, Iowa, while he was looking for subjects to paint. He returned home with a sketch and a photograph, and used his sister and his dentist as models for the farmer and daughter in the painting's foreground.

SKILLBUILDER Interpreting Visual Sources

1. What is the message Wood portrays in this painting? Explain your answer.
2. Do you think this painting is representative of the Great Depression? Why or why not?

SEE SKILLBUILDER HANDBOOK, PAGE R23.

Mexican muralists such as Diego Rivera, typically portrayed the dignity of ordinary Americans at work. One artist, Robert Gwathmey, recalled these efforts.

A PERSONAL VOICE ROBERT GWATHMEY

"The director of the Federal Arts Project was Edward Bruce. He was a friend of the Roosevelts—from a polite family—who was a painter. He was a man of real broad vision. He insisted there be no restrictions. You were a painter: Do your work. You were a sculptor: Do your work. . . . That was a very free and happy period."

—quoted in *Hard Times*

During the New Deal era, outstanding works of art were produced by a number of American painters, such as Edward Hopper, Thomas Hart Benton, and Iowa's **Grant Wood,** whose work includes the famous painting *American Gothic.*

The WPA's Federal Theater Project hired actors to perform plays and artists to provide stage sets and props for theater productions that played around the country. It subsidized the work of important American playwrights, including Clifford Odets, whose play *Waiting for Lefty* (1935) dramatized the labor struggles of the 1930s. (C)

MAIN IDEA

Summarizing

(C) In what ways did the New Deal deliver art to the public?

WOODY GUTHRIE SINGS OF AMERICA Experiencing firsthand the tragedies of the Depression, singer and songwriter Woody Guthrie used music to capture the hardships of America. Along with thousands of people who were forced by the Dust Bowl to seek a better life, Guthrie traveled the country in search of brighter opportunities, and told of his troubles in his songs.

A PERSONAL VOICE WOODY GUTHRIE

"Yes we ramble and we roam
And the highway, that's our home.
It's a never-ending highway
For a dust bowl refugee

Yes, we wander and we work
In your crops and in your fruit,
Like the whirlwinds on the desert,
That's the dust bowl refugees."

—"Dust Bowl Refugees"

Woody Guthrie

Guthrie wrote many songs about the plight of Americans during the Depression. His honest lyrics appealed to those who suffered similar hardships.

Walker Evans took this photograph of a sharecropper for the influential book *Let Us Now Praise Famous Men.*

DIVERSE WRITERS DEPICT AMERICAN LIFE Many writers received support through yet another WPA program, the Federal Writers' Project. This project gave the future Pulitzer and Nobel Prize winner Saul Bellow his first writing job. It also helped **Richard Wright,** an African-American author, complete his acclaimed novel *Native Son* (1940), about a young man trying to survive in a racist world. Zora Neale Hurston wrote a stirring novel with FWP assistance—*Their Eyes Were Watching God* (1937), about a young woman growing up in rural Florida.

John Steinbeck, one of this country's most famous authors, received assistance from the Federal Writers' Project. He was able to publish his epic novel ***The Grapes of Wrath*** (1939), which reveals the lives of Oklahomans who left the Dust Bowl and ended up in California, where their hardships continued. Before his success, however, Steinbeck had endured the difficulties of the Depression like most other writers. D

Analyzing Issues

D How did the literature of the time reflect issues of the Depression?

Other books and authors examined the difficulties of life during the 1930s. James T. Farrell's *Studs Lonigan* trilogy (1932–1935) provides a bleak picture of working-class life in an Irish neighborhood of Chicago, while Jack Conroy's novel *The Disinherited* (1933) portrays the violence and poverty of the Missouri coalfields, where Conroy's own father and brother died in a mine disaster.

Nevertheless, other writers found hope in the positive values of American culture. The writer James Agee and the photographer Walker Evans collaborated on a book about Alabama sharecroppers, *Let Us Now Praise Famous Men* (1941). Though it deals with the difficult lives of poor farmers, it portrays the dignity and strength of character in the people it presents. Thornton Wilder's play *Our Town* (1938) captures the beauty of small-town life in New England.

Although artists and writers recognized America's flaws, they contributed positively to the New Deal legacy. These intellectuals praised the virtues of American life and took pride in the country's traditions and accomplishments.

SECTION 4 ASSESSMENT

1. **TERMS & NAMES** For each term or name below, write a sentence explaining its significance.
   - ***Gone With the Wind***
   - **Grant Wood**
   - **Richard Wright**
   - ***The Grapes of Wrath***
   - **Orson Welles**

MAIN IDEA

2. **TAKING NOTES**
   Create a web like the one below, filling in the names of those who contributed to each aspect of American culture in the 1930s.

Cultural Figures of the 1930s

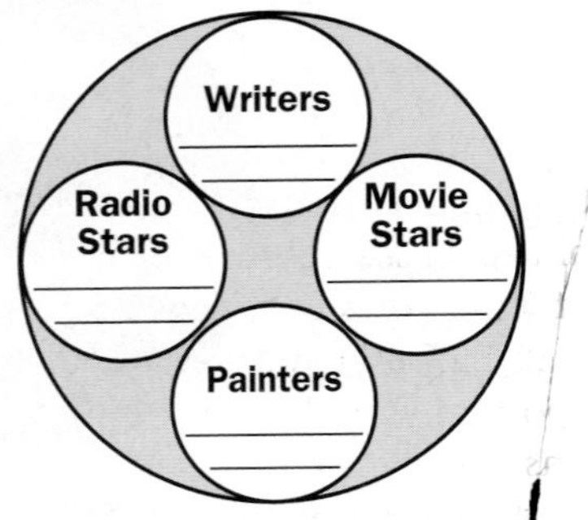

What contribution did each group make?

CRITICAL THINKING

3. **HYPOTHESIZING**
   What type of movies do you think might have been produced if the government had supported moviemaking as part of the New Deal? Use evidence from the chapter to support your response.

4. **ANALYZING EFFECTS**
   How did the entertainment industry affect the economy?

5. **DRAWING CONCLUSIONS**
   In your opinion, what were the main benefits of government support for art and literature in the 1930s? Support your response with details from the text. **Think About:**
   - the experiences of Americans in the Great Depression
   - the writers who got their start through the FWP
   - the subject matter of WPA murals and other New Deal-sponsored art

The Impact of the New Deal

MAIN IDEA

The New Deal affected American society not only in the 1930s but also in the decades that followed.

WHY IT MATTERS NOW

Americans still debate over how large a role government should play in American life.

Terms & Names

- **Federal Deposit Insurance Corporation (FDIC)**
- **Securities and Exchange Commission (SEC)**
- **National Labor Relations Board (NLRB)**
- **parity**
- **Tennessee Valley Authority (TVA)**

One American's Story

George Dobbin, a 67-year-old cotton-mill worker, staunchly supported Franklin Delano Roosevelt and his New Deal policies. In an interview for a book entitled *These Are Our Lives,* compiled by the Federal Writers' Project, Dobbin explained his feelings about the president.

A PERSONAL VOICE GEORGE DOBBIN

"I do think that Roosevelt is the biggest-hearted man we ever had in the White House. . . . It's the first time in my recollection that a President ever got up and said, 'I'm interested in and aim to do somethin' for the workin' man.' Just knowin' that for once . . . [there] was a man to stand up and speak for him, a man that could make what he felt so plain nobody could doubt he meant it, has made a lot of us feel a sight [lot] better even when [there] wasn't much to eat in our homes."

—quoted in *These Are Our Lives*

A coal miner, Zeno Santinello, shakes hands with Franklin D. Roosevelt as he campaigns in Elm Grove, West Virginia, in 1932.

FDR was extremely popular among working-class Americans. Far more important than his personal popularity, however, was the impact of the policies he initiated. Even today, reforms begun under the New Deal continue to influence American politics and society.

New Deal Reforms Endure

During his second term in office, President Roosevelt hinted at plans to launch a Third New Deal. In his inaugural address, the president exclaimed, "I see millions of families trying to live on incomes so meager that the pall of family disaster hangs over them day by day. . . . I see one third of a nation ill-housed, ill-clad, ill-nourished."

However, FDR did not favor deficit spending. More importantly, by 1937 the economy had improved enough to convince many Americans that the Depression was finally ending. Although economic troubles still plagued the nation, President

Roosevelt faced rising pressure from Congress to scale back New Deal programs, which he did. As a result, industrial production dropped again, and the number of unemployed increased from 7.7 million in 1937 to 10.4 million in 1938. By 1939, the New Deal was effectively over, and Roosevelt was increasingly concerned with events in Europe, particularly Hitler's rise to power in Germany. (A)

MAIN IDEA

Analyzing Issues

(A) Why did industrial production drop and unemployment go up again in 1938?

SUPPORTERS AND CRITICS OF THE NEW DEAL Over time, opinions about the New Deal have ranged from harsh criticism to high praise. Most conservatives think President Roosevelt's policies made the federal government too large and too powerful. They believe that the government stifled free enterprise and individual initiative. Liberal critics, in contrast, argue that President Roosevelt didn't do enough to socialize the economy and to eliminate social and economic inequalities. Supporters of the New Deal contend, however, that the president struck a reasonable balance between two extremes—unregulated capitalism and overregulated socialism—and helped the country recover from its economic difficulties. One of Roosevelt's top advisers made this assessment of the president's goals.

A PERSONAL VOICE REXFORD TUGWELL

"He had in mind a comprehensive welfare concept, infused with a stiff tincture of morality. . . . He wanted all Americans to grow up healthy and vigorous and to be practically educated. He wanted business men to work within a set of understood rules. Beyond this he wanted people free to vote, to worship, to behave as they wished so long as a moral code was respected; and he wanted officials to behave as though office were a public trust."

—quoted in *Redeeming the Time*

POINT

"The New Deal transformed the way American government works."

Supporters of the New Deal believe that it was successful. Many historians and journalists make this judgment by using the economic criterion of creating jobs. *The New Republic*, for example, argued that the shortcomings of the WPA "are insignificant beside the gigantic fact that it has given jobs and sustenance to a minimum of 1,400,000 and a maximum of 3,300,000 persons for five years."

Some historians stress that the New Deal was more than a temporary solution to a crisis. Professor A. A. Berle stated that, "human beings cannot indefinitely be sacrificed by millions to the operation of economic forces."

According to the historian William E. Luechtenburg, "It is hard to think of another period in the whole history of the republic that was so fruitful or of a crisis that was met with as much imagination."

To Pulitzer Prize-winning historian Allan Nevins, the New Deal was a turning point in which the U.S. government assumed a greater responsibility for the economic welfare of its citizens.

COUNTERPOINT

"Many more problems have been created than solved by the New Deal."

Critics of the New Deal believe that it failed to reach its goals. The historian Barton J. Bernstein accepted the goals of the New Deal but declared that they were never met. To him, the New Deal "failed to raise the impoverished, it failed to redistribute income, [and] it failed to extend equality."

In Senator Robert A. Taft's opinion, "many more problems have been created than solved" by the New Deal. He maintained, "Whatever else has resulted from the great increase in government activity . . . it has certainly had the effect of checking private enterprise completely. This country was built up by the constant establishment of new business and the expansion of old businesses. . . . In the last six years this process has come to an end because of government regulation and the development of a tax system which penalizes hard work and success." Senator Taft claimed that "The government should gradually withdraw from the business of lending money and leave that function to private capital under proper regulation."

THINKING CRITICALLY

CONNECT TO HISTORY

1. **Comparing and Contrasting** How did the New Deal succeed? How did it fail? Write a paragraph that summarizes the main points.

SEE SKILLBUILDER HANDBOOK, PAGE R8.

CONNECT TO TODAY

2. **Draft a Proposal** Research the programs of the WPA and draft a proposal for a WPA-type program that would benefit your community.

EXPANDING GOVERNMENT'S ROLE IN THE ECONOMY The Roosevelt administration expanded the power of the federal government, giving it—and particularly the president—a more active role in shaping the economy. It did this by infusing the nation's economy with millions of dollars, by creating federal jobs, by attempting to regulate supply and demand, and by increasing the government's active participation in settling labor and management disputes. The federal government also established agencies, such as the **Federal Deposit Insurance Corporation (FDIC)** and the **Securities and Exchange Commission (SEC),** to regulate banking and investment activities. Although the New Deal did not end the Great Depression, it did help reduce the suffering of thousands of men, women, and children by providing them with jobs, food, and money. It also gave people hope and helped them to regain a sense of dignity.

▲ **Unemployed workers sit on a street in a 1936 photograph by Dorothea Lange.**

The federal government had to go deeply into debt to provide jobs and aid to the American people. The federal deficit increased to $2.9 billion in fiscal year 1934. As a result of the cutbacks in federal spending made in 1937–1938, the deficit dropped to $100 million. But the next year it rose again, to $2.9 billion. What really ended the Depression, however, was the massive amount of spending by the federal government for guns, tanks, ships, airplanes, and all the other equipment and supplies the country needed for the World War II effort. During the war, the deficit reached a high of about $54.5 billion in 1943.

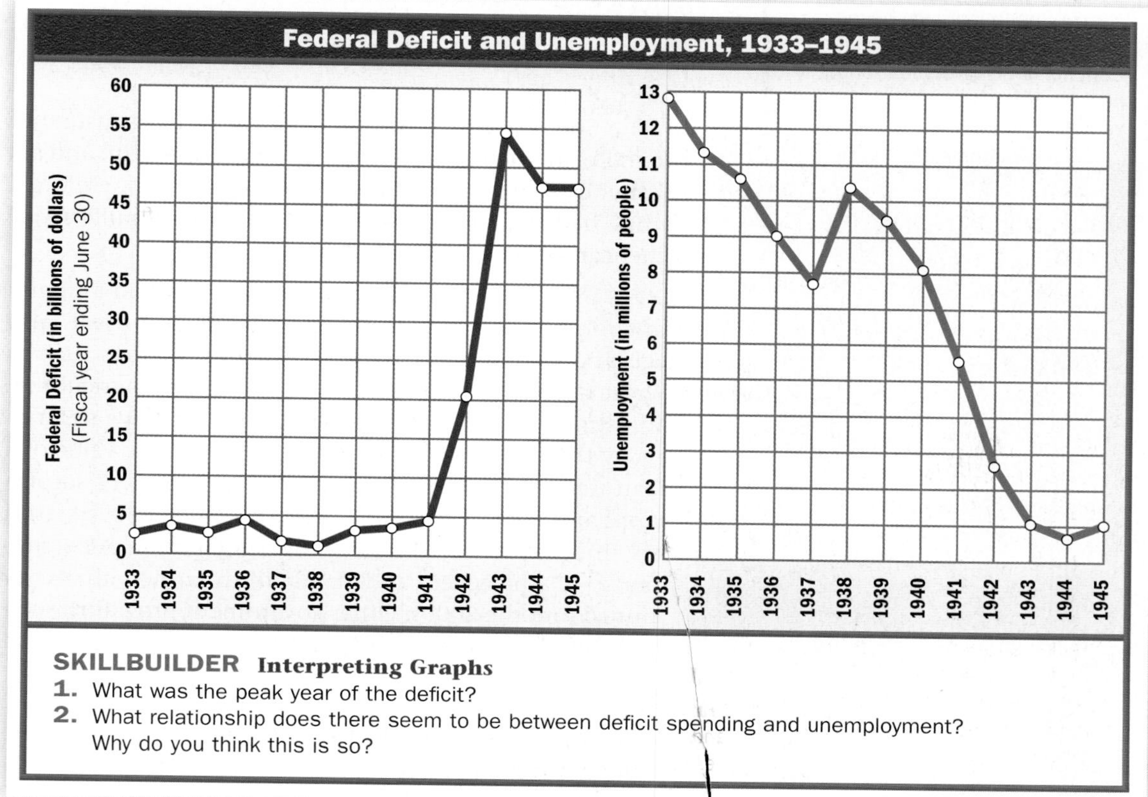

SKILLBUILDER Interpreting Graphs

1. What was the peak year of the deficit?
2. What relationship does there seem to be between deficit spending and unemployment? Why do you think this is so?

PROTECTING WORKERS' RIGHTS One of the areas in which New Deal policies have had a lasting effect is the protection of workers' rights. New Deal legislation, such as the Wagner Act and the Fair Labor Standards Act, set standards for wages and hours, banned child labor, and ensured the right of workers to organize and to bargain collectively with employers. Today, the **National Labor Relations Board (NLRB),** created under the Wagner Act, continues to act as a mediator in labor disputes between unions and employers.

BANKING AND FINANCE New Deal programs established new policies in the area of banking and finance. The Securities and Exchange Commission (SEC), created in 1934, continues to monitor the stock market and enforce laws regarding the sale of stocks and bonds. The Federal Deposit Insurance Corporation (FDIC), created by the Glass-Steagall Act of 1933, has shored up the banking system by reassuring individual depositors that their savings are protected against loss in the event of a bank failure. Today, individual accounts in United States federal banks are insured by the Federal Deposit Insurance Corporation for up to $100,000.

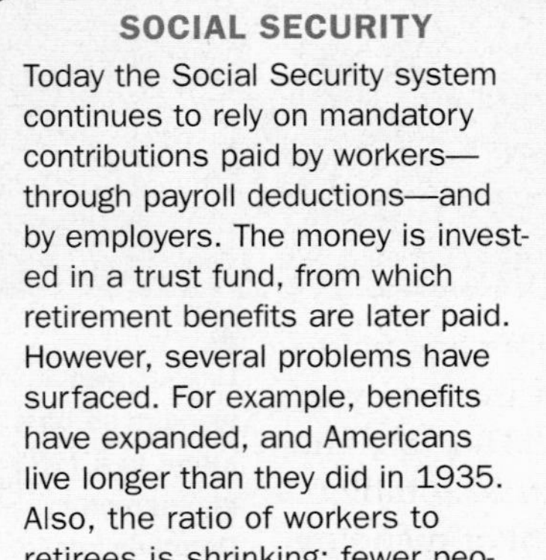

SOCIAL SECURITY

Today the Social Security system continues to rely on mandatory contributions paid by workers—through payroll deductions—and by employers. The money is invested in a trust fund, from which retirement benefits are later paid. However, several problems have surfaced. For example, benefits have expanded, and Americans live longer than they did in 1935. Also, the ratio of workers to retirees is shrinking: fewer people are contributing to the system relative to the number who are eligible to receive benefits.

The long-range payment of benefits may be in jeopardy because of the large number of recipients. Continuing disagreement about how to address the costs has prevented legislative action.

Social and Environmental Effects

New Deal economic and financial reforms, including the creation of the FDIC, the SEC, and Social Security, have helped to stabilize the nation's finances and economy. Although the nation still experiences economic downturns, known as recessions, people's savings are insured, and they can receive unemployment compensation if they lose their jobs.

SOCIAL SECURITY One of the most important legacies of the New Deal has been that the federal government has assumed some responsibility for the social welfare of its citizens. Under President Roosevelt, the government undertook the creation of a Social Security system that would help a large number of needy Americans receive some assistance.

The Social Security Act provides an old-age insurance program, an unemployment compensation system, and aid to the disabled and families with dependent children. It has had a major impact on the lives of millions of Americans since its founding in 1935. **B**

MAIN IDEA

Developing Historical Perspective

B Why was the establishment of the Social Security system such an important part of the New Deal?

THE RURAL SCENE New Deal policies also had a significant impact on the nation's agriculture. New Deal farm legislation set quotas on the production of crops such as wheat to control surpluses. Under the second Agricultural Adjustment Act, passed in 1938, loans were made to farmers by the Commodity Credit Corporation. The value of a loan was determined by the amount of a farmer's surplus crops and the **parity** price, a price intended to keep farmers' income steady. Establishing agricultural price supports set a precedent of federal aid to farmers that continued into the 2000s. Other government programs, such as rural electrification, helped to improve conditions in rural America.

◀ A Social Security poster proclaims the benefits of the system for those who are 65 or older.

THE ENVIRONMENT Americans also continue to benefit from New Deal efforts to protect the environment. President Roosevelt was highly committed to conservation and promoted policies designed to protect the nation's natural resources. The Civilian Conservation Corps planted trees, created hiking trails, and built fire lookout towers. The Soil Conservation Service taught farmers how to conserve the soil through contour plowing, terracing, and crop rotation. Congress also passed the Taylor Grazing Act in 1934 to help reduce grazing on public lands. Such grazing had contributed to the erosion that brought about the dust storms of the 1930s.

▲ **This 1933 cartoon depicts Roosevelt exhausting Congress with his many reform policies.**

The **Tennessee Valley Authority (TVA)** harnessed water power to generate electricity and to help prevent disastrous floods in the Tennessee Valley. The government also added to the national park system in the 1930s, established new wildlife refuges and set aside large wilderness areas. On the other hand, government-sponsored stripmining and coal burning caused air, land, and water pollution. **C**

MAIN IDEA

Recognizing Effects

C How did New Deal programs benefit and harm the environment?

The New Deal legacy has many dimensions. It brought hope and gratitude from some people for the benefits and protections they received. It also brought anger and criticism from those who believed that it took more of their money in taxes and curtailed their freedom through increased government regulations. The deficit spending necessary to fund New Deal programs grew immensely as the nation entered World War II.

SECTION 5 ASSESSMENT

1. **TERMS & NAMES** For each term or name, write a sentence explaining its significance.
   - **Federal Deposit Insurance Corporation (FDIC)**
   - **Securities and Exchange Commission (SEC)**
   - **National Labor Relations Board (NLRB)**
   - **parity**
   - **Tennessee Valley Authority (TVA)**

MAIN IDEA

2. **TAKING NOTES**
   In a cluster diagram like the one below, show long-term effects of the New Deal.

Which long-term benefit do you think has had the most impact? Why?

CRITICAL THINKING

3. **MAKING GENERALIZATIONS**
   Some critics have charged that the New Deal was antibusiness and anti–free enterprise. Explain why you agree or disagree with this charge.
   Think About:
   - the expanded power of the federal government
   - the New Deal's effect on the economy
   - the New Deal's effect on the American people

4. **EVALUATING LEADERSHIP**
   How successful do you think Franklin Roosevelt was as a president? Support your answer with details from the text.

5. **INTERPRETING VISUAL SOURCES**
   Look at the political cartoon above. What does it suggest about Roosevelt's leadership and the role of Congress? Explain.

INTERACTIVE

GEOGRAPHY SPOTLIGHT

The Tennessee Valley Authority

The Tennessee Valley Authority (TVA) is a federal agency that was established in 1933 to construct dams and power plants along the Tennessee River and its tributaries. The Tennessee River basin is one of the largest river basins in the United States, and people who live in this area have a number of common concerns. The TVA has helped the region in various ways: through flood and navigation control, the conservation of natural resources, and the generation of electric power, as well as through agricultural and industrial development.

The Tennessee Valley covers parts of seven states. Thus, the TVA became an enormous undertaking, eventually comprising dozens of major dams, each with associated power plants, recreational facilities, and navigation aids.

MISSOURI

ARKANSAS

HYDROELECTRIC DAM

A hydroelectric dam uses water power to create electricity. The deeper the reservoir, the greater is the force pushing water through the dam.

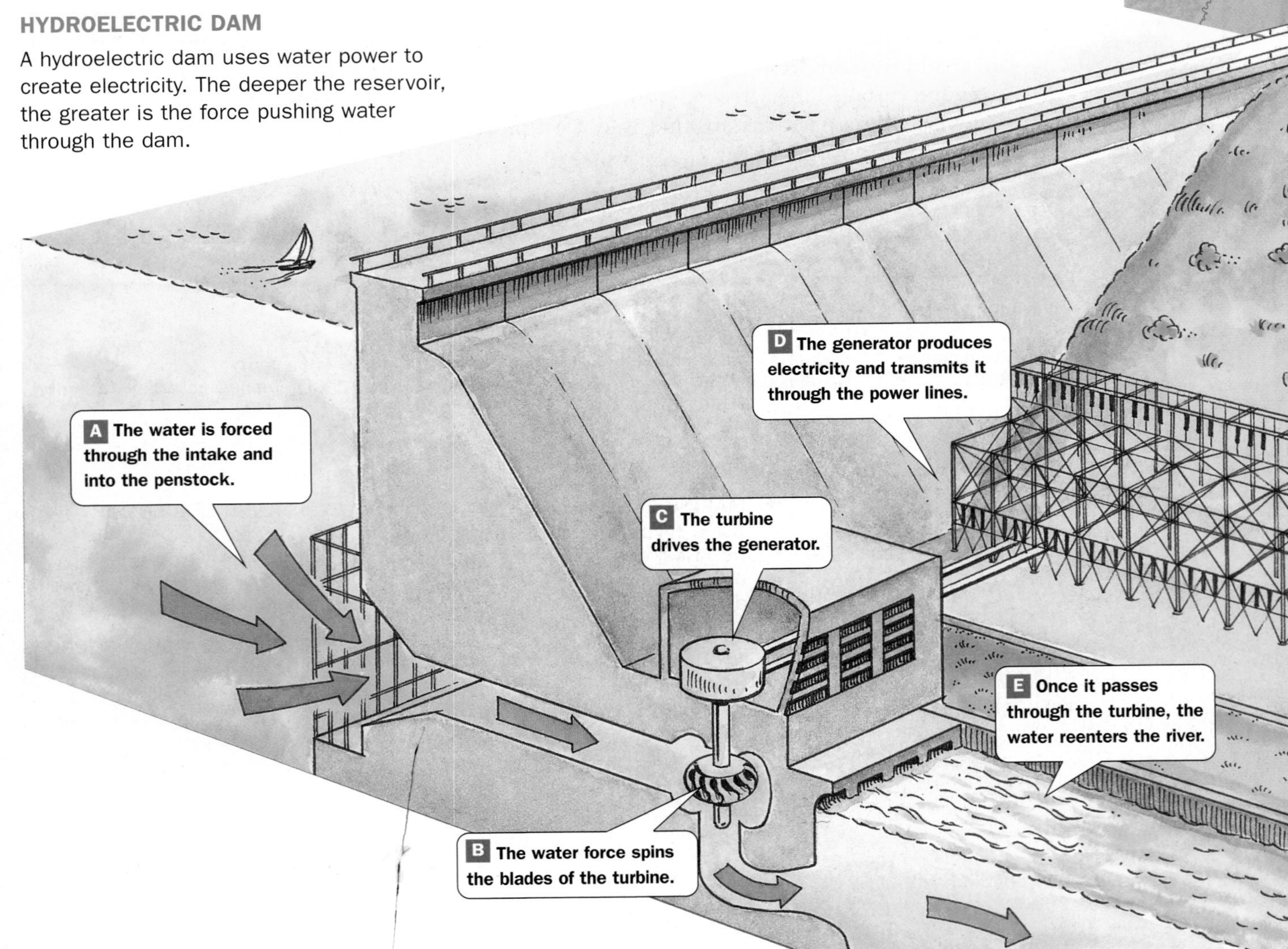
A The water is forced through the intake and into the penstock.
B The water force spins the blades of the turbine.
C The turbine drives the generator.
D The generator produces electricity and transmits it through the power lines.
E Once it passes through the turbine, the water reenters the river.

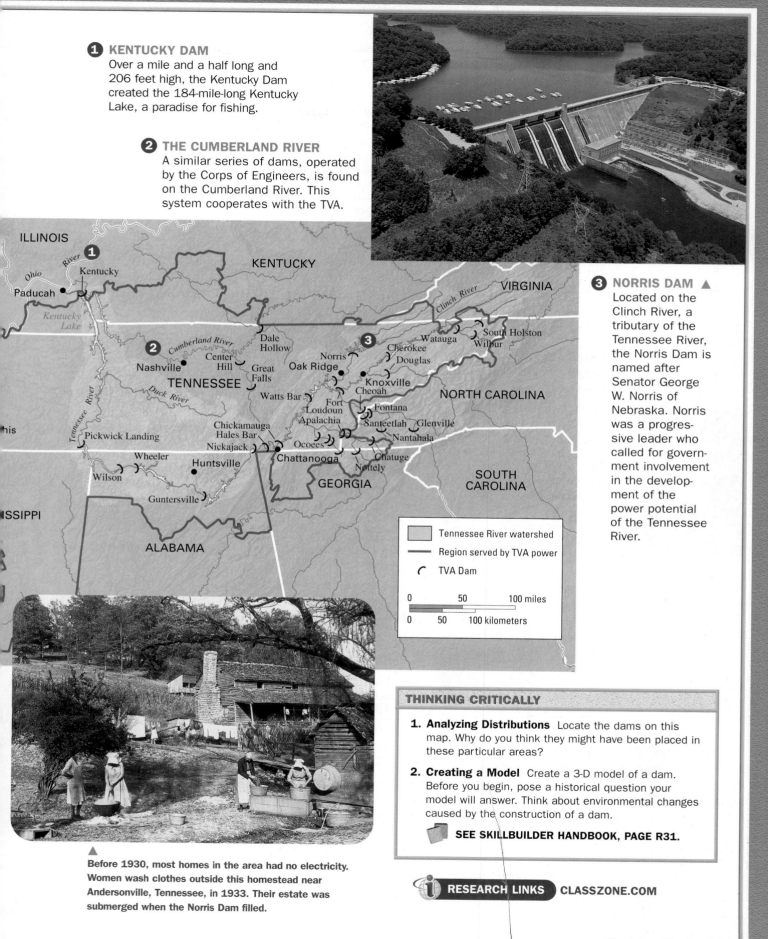

❶ KENTUCKY DAM
Over a mile and a half long and 206 feet high, the Kentucky Dam created the 184-mile-long Kentucky Lake, a paradise for fishing.

❷ THE CUMBERLAND RIVER
A similar series of dams, operated by the Corps of Engineers, is found on the Cumberland River. This system cooperates with the TVA.

❸ NORRIS DAM ▲
Located on the Clinch River, a tributary of the Tennessee River, the Norris Dam is named after Senator George W. Norris of Nebraska. Norris was a progressive leader who called for government involvement in the development of the power potential of the Tennessee River.

▲ **Before 1930, most homes in the area had no electricity. Women wash clothes outside this homestead near Andersonville, Tennessee, in 1933. Their estate was submerged when the Norris Dam filled.**

THINKING CRITICALLY

1. **Analyzing Distributions** Locate the dams on this map. Why do you think they might have been placed in these particular areas?
2. **Creating a Model** Create a 3-D model of a dam. Before you begin, pose a historical question your model will answer. Think about environmental changes caused by the construction of a dam.

SEE SKILLBUILDER HANDBOOK, PAGE R31.

RESEARCH LINKS CLASSZONE.COM

CHAPTER  ASSESSMENT

VISUAL SUMMARY

THE NEW DEAL

PROBLEMS

- Industries and farms failed.
- U.S. stock market crashed and banks closed.
- Bankrupt businesses
- Unemployment
- Homelessness

SOLUTIONS

- Work projects help the unemployed.
- Money given to farmers, sharecroppers, and migrant workers
- New opportunities for women and minorities
- Social Security Act allocates money to the elderly, the unemployed, and the disabled.
- NLRB protects workers' rights.
- SEC monitors stock market.
- FDIC protects individuals' deposits in banks.
- Fireside chats increase public confidence.

CONTINUING EFFECTS

- Banking and finance are reformed.
- Government takes a more active role in the economy.
- Workers benefit from labor standards.
- Social Security system continues to provide for the needy.
- Conservation efforts continue to preserve the environment.

TERMS & NAMES

For each term or name below, write a sentence explaining its historical significance or contribution to the New Deal.

1. Franklin Delano Roosevelt
2. New Deal
3. Eleanor Roosevelt
4. Works Progress Administration (WPA)
5. Social Security Act
6. Mary McCloud Bethune
7. Congress of Industrial Organizations (CIO)
8. Orson Welles
9. Richard Wright
10. Tennessee Valley Authority (TVA)

MAIN IDEAS

Use your notes and the information in the chapter to answer the following questions.

A New Deal Fights the Depression *(pages 488–494)*

1. How did Franklin Roosevelt change the role of the federal government during his first Hundred Days?
2. Summarize the reasons why some people opposed the New Deal.

The Second New Deal Takes Hold *(pages 495–501)*

3. In what ways did the New Deal programs extend federal aid?
4. How did the Wagner Act help working people?

The New Deal Affects Many Groups *(pages 504–509)*

5. Summarize the impact the New Deal had on various ethnic groups.
6. Why did many urban voters support Roosevelt and the Democratic party?

Culture in the 1930s *(pages 510–514)*

7. What purpose did movies and radio serve during the Great Depression?
8. Explain how the New Deal programs supported artists and writers in the 1930s.

The Impact of the New Deal *(pages 515–519)*

9. List five New Deal agencies that are still in place today.
10. What benefits did the Tennessee Valley Authority provide? What negative impact did it have?

THINKING CRITICALLY

1. **USING YOUR NOTES** Copy the web below and fill it in with actions that Americans took to end the economic crisis of the 1930s.

2. **DEVELOPING HISTORICAL PERSPECTIVE** What federal programs instituted in the 1930s and later discontinued might be of use to the nation today? Explain and support your opinion in a paragraph or two.

Standardized Test Practice

Use the information on the time line and your knowledge of U.S. history to answer question 1.

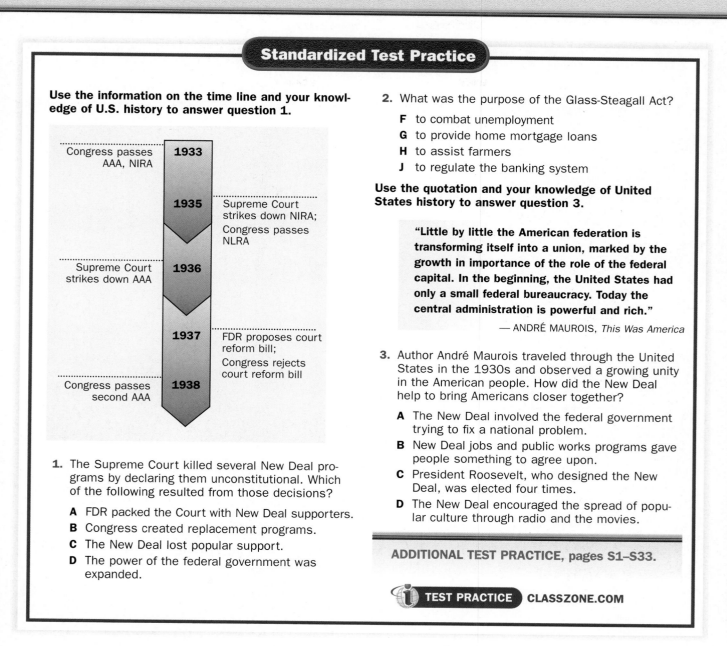

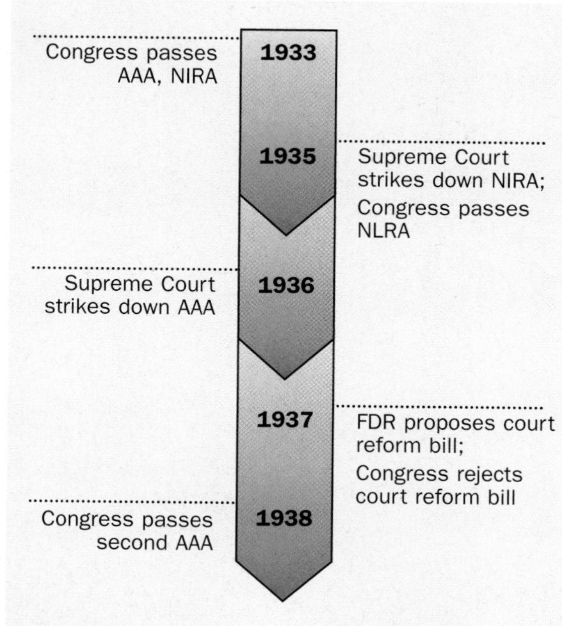

1. The Supreme Court killed several New Deal programs by declaring them unconstitutional. Which of the following resulted from those decisions?
   - **A** FDR packed the Court with New Deal supporters.
   - **B** Congress created replacement programs.
   - **C** The New Deal lost popular support.
   - **D** The power of the federal government was expanded.

2. What was the purpose of the Glass-Steagall Act?
   - **F** to combat unemployment
   - **G** to provide home mortgage loans
   - **H** to assist farmers
   - **J** to regulate the banking system

Use the quotation and your knowledge of United States history to answer question 3.

> **"Little by little the American federation is transforming itself into a union, marked by the growth in importance of the role of the federal capital. In the beginning, the United States had only a small federal bureaucracy. Today the central administration is powerful and rich."**
>
> — ANDRÉ MAUROIS, *This Was America*

3. Author André Maurois traveled through the United States in the 1930s and observed a growing unity in the American people. How did the New Deal help to bring Americans closer together?
   - **A** The New Deal involved the federal government trying to fix a national problem.
   - **B** New Deal jobs and public works programs gave people something to agree upon.
   - **C** President Roosevelt, who designed the New Deal, was elected four times.
   - **D** The New Deal encouraged the spread of popular culture through radio and the movies.

ADDITIONAL TEST PRACTICE, pages S1–S33.

TEST PRACTICE **CLASSZONE.COM**

ALTERNATIVE ASSESSMENT

1. **INTERACT WITH HISTORY** Recall your discussion of the question on page 487:

   ### *How would you begin to revive the economy?*

   Now that you have read the chapter, do you think President Roosevelt adequately addressed the needs of the ailing economy? Do you think his New Deal policies extended far enough to restore public confidence? Support your opinions with examples.

2.  **LEARNING FROM MEDIA** View the *American Stories* video "A Song for His People." Discuss the following questions in a group, then do the activity.
   - Why were thousands of Mexican Americans sent back to Mexico in the 1930s?
   - Why did Pedro J. González become a hero to many Mexican Americans?

   Cooperative Learning Activity Write and present a short broadcast, such as González might have given, in which you comment on the New Deal's effects on immigrants and minorities.

World War II and Its Aftermath 1931–1960

CHAPTER 16
World War Looms
1931–1941

CHAPTER 17
The United States in World War II
1941–1945

CHAPTER 18
Cold War Conflicts
1945–1960

CHAPTER 19
The Postwar Boom
1946–1960

Debate

As you read Unit 5, pay attention to arguments on either side of a political issue. Work with a group to stage a debate. Write a proposition, such as "Resolved: The U.S. has a responsibility to end its isolationism and enter World War II." Choose teams to argue either for or against the resolution.

Dawn Patrol Launching by Paul Sample

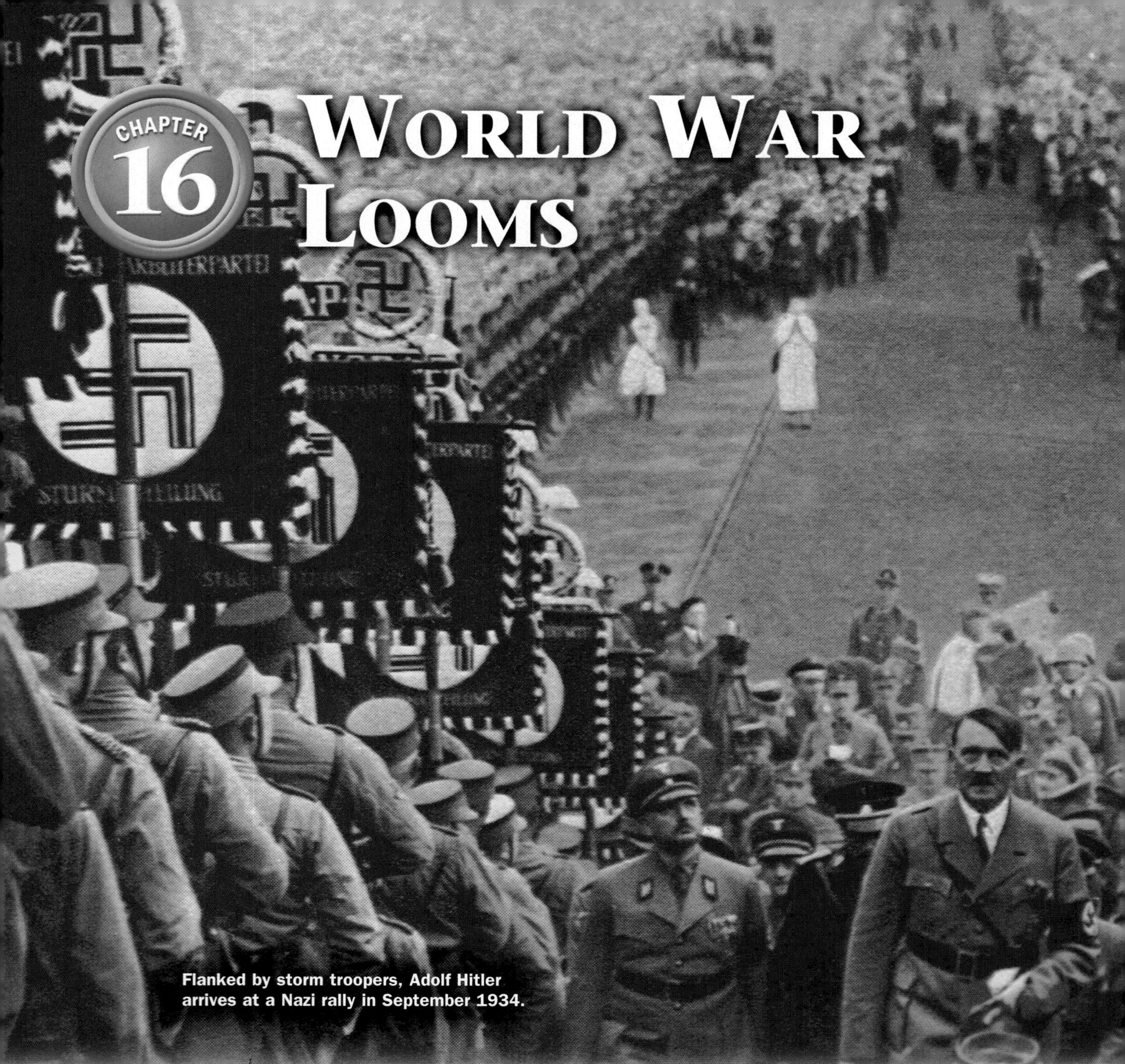

CHAPTER 16

WORLD WAR LOOMS

Flanked by storm troopers, Adolf Hitler arrives at a Nazi rally in September 1934.

USA

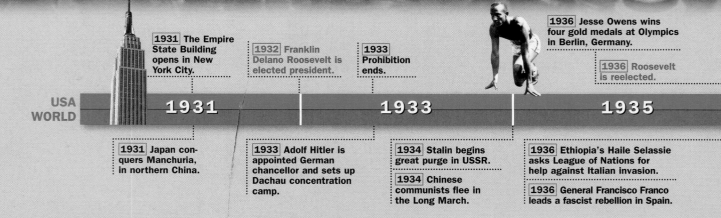

1931 The Empire State Building opens in New York City.

1932 Franklin Delano Roosevelt is elected president.

1933 Prohibition ends.

1936 Jesse Owens wins four gold medals at Olympics in Berlin, Germany.

1936 Roosevelt is reelected.

1931 | 1933 | 1935

WORLD

1931 Japan conquers Manchuria, in northern China.

1933 Adolf Hitler is appointed German chancellor and sets up Dachau concentration camp.

1934 Stalin begins great purge in USSR.

1934 Chinese communists flee in the Long March.

1936 Ethiopia's Haile Selassie asks League of Nations for help against Italian invasion.

1936 General Francisco Franco leads a fascist rebellion in Spain.

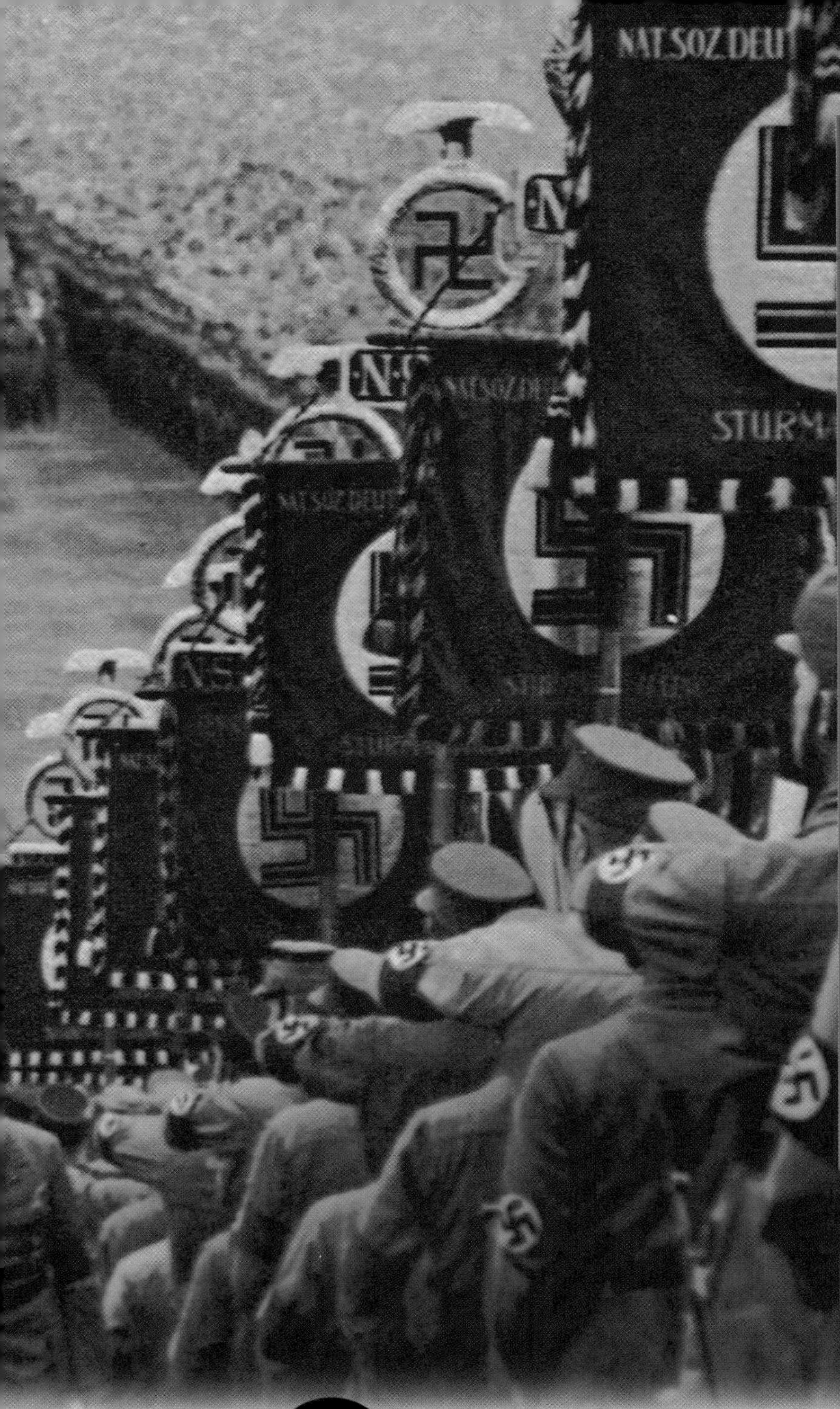

INTERACT

WITH HISTORY

In the summer of 1939, President Franklin Roosevelt addresses an anxious nation in response to atrocities in Europe committed by Hitler's Nazi Germany. Roosevelt declares in his broadcast that the United States "will remain a neutral nation." He acknowledges, however, that he "cannot ask that every American remain neutral in thought."

Why might the United States try to remain neutral?

Examine the Issues

- How might involvement in a large scale war influence the United States?
- How can neutral countries participate in the affairs of warring countries?

RESEARCH LINKS **CLASSZONE.COM**

Visit the Chapter 16 links for more information related to World War Looms.

1937 Amelia Earhart mysteriously disappears attempting solo round-the-world flight.

1938 Orson Welles broadcasts *The War of the Worlds*, a fictional alien invasion.

1940 Roosevelt is elected to a third term.

1941 United States enters World War II.

1937 **1939** **1941**

1938 *Kristallnacht*—Nazis riot, destroying Jewish neighborhoods.

1939 Germany invades Poland. Britain and France declare war.

Evening Standard

GERMANS INVADE AND BOMB POLAND
BRITAIN MOBILISES

Warsaw, Cracow, Nine Other Towns Bombed: Danzig is "Annexed"

FRANCE DECLARES "STATE OF SIEGE"

1941 Japan bombs Pearl Harbor.

Dictators Threaten World Peace

MAIN IDEA

The rise of rulers with total power in Europe and Asia led to World War II.

WHY IT MATTERS NOW

Dictators of the 1930s and 1940s changed the course of history, making world leaders especially watchful for the actions of dictators today.

Terms & Names

- **Joseph Stalin**
- **totalitarian**
- **Benito Mussolini**
- **fascism**
- **Adolf Hitler**
- **Nazism**
- **Francisco Franco**
- **Neutrality Acts**

One American's Story

Martha Gellhorn arrived in Madrid in 1937 to cover the brutal civil war that had broken out in Spain the year before. Hired as a special correspondent for *Collier's Weekly*, she had come with very little money and no special protection. On assignment there, she met the writer Ernest Hemingway, whom she later married. To Gellhorn, a young American writer, the Spanish Civil War was a deadly struggle between tyranny and democracy. For the people of Madrid, it was also a daily struggle for survival.

▲ **Martha Gellhorn, one of the first women war correspondents, began her career during the Spanish Civil War.**

A PERSONAL VOICE MARTHA GELLHORN

"You would be walking down a street, hearing only the city noises of streetcars and automobiles and people calling to one another, and suddenly, crushing it all out, would be the huge stony deep booming of a falling shell, at the corner. There was no place to run, because how did you know that the next shell would not be behind you, or ahead, or to the left or right?"

—*The Face of War*

Less than two decades after the end of World War I—"the war to end all wars"—fighting erupted again in Europe and in Asia. As Americans read about distant battles, they hoped the conflicts would remain on the other side of the world.

Nationalism Grips Europe and Asia

The seeds of new conflicts had been sown in World War I. For many nations, peace had brought not prosperity but revolution fueled by economic depression and struggle. The postwar years also brought the rise of powerful dictators driven by the belief in nationalism—loyalty to one's country above all else—and dreams of territorial expansion.

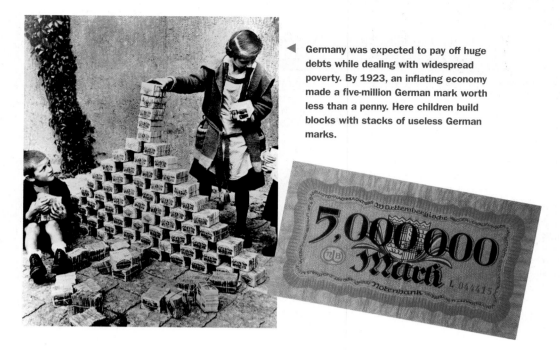

Germany was expected to pay off huge debts while dealing with widespread poverty. By 1923, an inflating economy made a five-million German mark worth less than a penny. Here children build blocks with stacks of useless German marks.

FAILURES OF THE WORLD WAR I PEACE SETTLEMENT Instead of securing a "just and secure peace," the Treaty of Versailles caused anger and resentment. Germans saw nothing fair in a treaty that blamed them for starting the war. Nor did they find security in a settlement that stripped them of their overseas colonies and border territories. These problems overwhelmed the Weimar Republic, the democratic government set up in Germany after World War I. Similarly, the Soviets resented the carving up of parts of Russia. (See map, Chapter 11, p. 400.)

The peace settlement had not fulfilled President Wilson's hope of a world "safe for democracy." New democratic governments that emerged in Europe after the war floundered. Without a democratic tradition, people turned to authoritarian leaders to solve their economic and social problems. The new democracies collapsed, and dictators were able to seize power. Some had great ambitions. (A)

MAIN IDEA

Identifying Problems

(A) Why did the new democracies set up after World War I fail?

JOSEPH STALIN TRANSFORMS THE SOVIET UNION In Russia, hopes for democracy gave way to civil war, resulting in the establishment of a communist state, officially called the Soviet Union, in 1922. After V. I. Lenin died in 1924, **Joseph Stalin,** whose last name means "man of steel," took control of the country. Stalin focused on creating a model communist state. In so doing, he made both agricultural and industrial growth the prime economic goals of the Soviet Union. Stalin abolished all privately owned farms and replaced them with collectives—large government-owned farms, each worked by hundreds of families.

Stalin moved to transform the Soviet Union from a backward rural nation into a great industrial power. In 1928, the Soviet dictator outlined the first of several "five-year plans," to direct the industrialization. All economic activity was placed under state management. By 1937, the Soviet Union had become the world's second-largest industrial power, surpassed in overall production only by the United States. The human costs of this transformation, however, were enormous.

In his drive to purge, or eliminate, anyone who threatened his power, Stalin did not spare even his most faithful supporters. While the final toll will never be known, historians estimate that Stalin was responsible for the deaths of 8 million to 13 million people. Millions more died in famines caused by the restructuring of Soviet society.

By 1939, Stalin had firmly established a **totalitarian** government that tried to exert complete control over its citizens. In a totalitarian state, individuals have no rights, and the government suppresses all opposition. (B)

MAIN IDEA

Summarizing

(B) What are the characteristics of a totalitarian state?

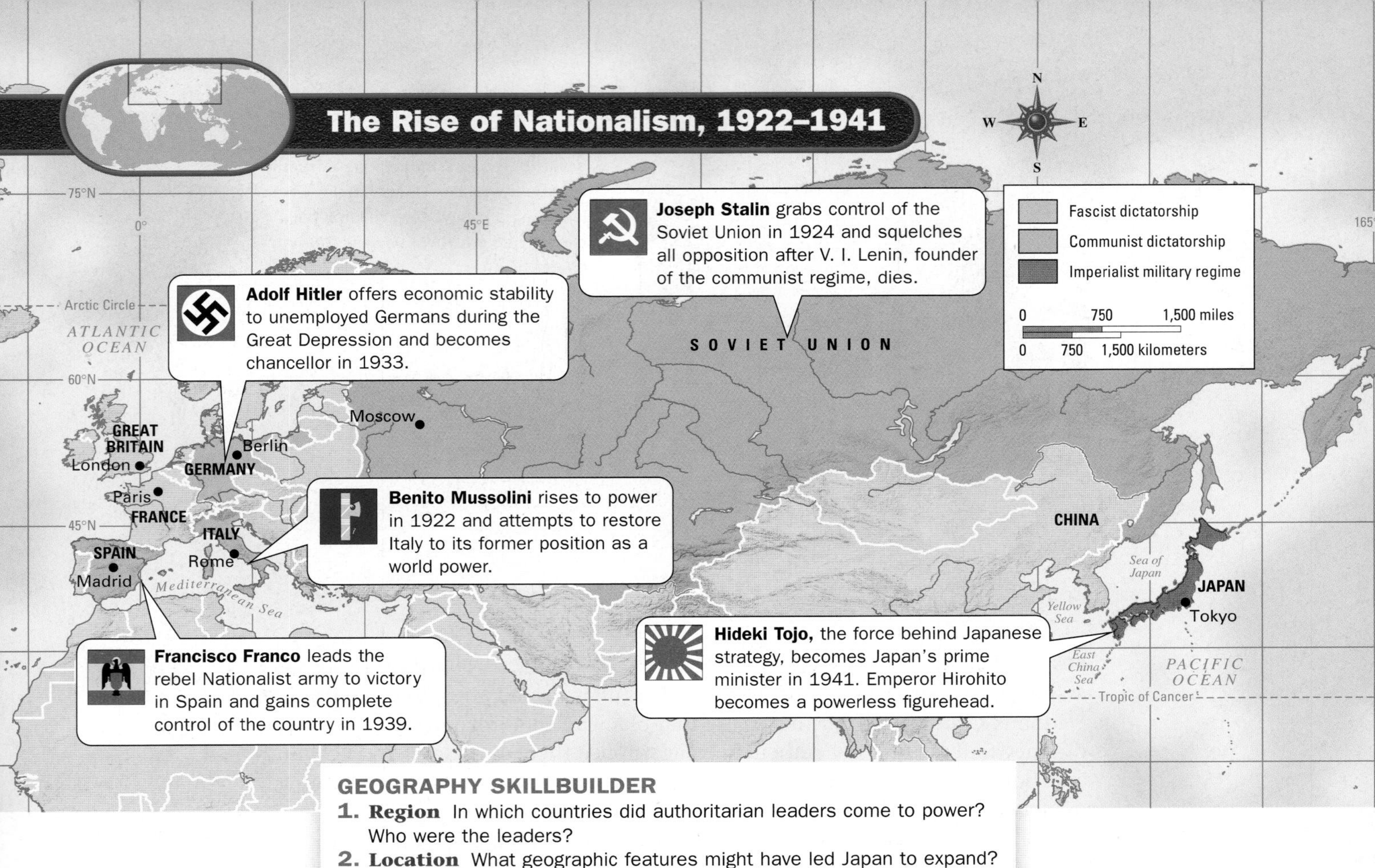
The Rise of Nationalism, 1922–1941
Joseph Stalin grabs control of the Soviet Union in 1924 and squelches all opposition after V. I. Lenin, founder of the communist regime, dies.
Adolf Hitler offers economic stability to unemployed Germans during the Great Depression and becomes chancellor in 1933.
Benito Mussolini rises to power in 1922 and attempts to restore Italy to its former position as a world power.
Francisco Franco leads the rebel Nationalist army to victory in Spain and gains complete control of the country in 1939.
Hideki Tojo, the force behind Japanese strategy, becomes Japan's prime minister in 1941. Emperor Hirohito becomes a powerless figurehead.
Fascist dictatorship
Communist dictatorship
Imperialist military regime
0 750 1,500 miles
0 750 1,500 kilometers
N
S
E
W
75°N
60°N
45°N
0°
45°E
165°E
Arctic Circle
ATLANTIC OCEAN
SOVIET UNION
Moscow
GREAT BRITAIN
London
Berlin
GERMANY
Paris
FRANCE
ITALY
Rome
SPAIN
Madrid
Mediterranean Sea
CHINA
Sea of Japan
JAPAN
Tokyo
Yellow Sea
East China Sea
PACIFIC OCEAN
Tropic of Cancer

GEOGRAPHY SKILLBUILDER

1. **Region** In which countries did authoritarian leaders come to power? Who were the leaders?
2. **Location** What geographic features might have led Japan to expand?

THE RISE OF FASCISM IN ITALY While Stalin was consolidating his power in the Soviet Union, **Benito Mussolini** was establishing a totalitarian regime in Italy, where unemployment and inflation produced bitter strikes, some communist-led. Alarmed by these threats, the middle and upper classes demanded stronger leadership. Mussolini took advantage of this situation. A powerful speaker, Mussolini knew how to appeal to Italy's wounded national pride. He played on the fears of economic collapse and communism. In this way, he won the support of many discontented Italians.

> *"Italy wants peace, work, and calm. I will give these things with love if possible, with force if necessary."*
> **BENITO MUSSOLINI**

By 1921, Mussolini had established the Fascist Party. **Fascism** (făsh′ĭz′əm) stressed nationalism and placed the interests of the state above those of individuals. To strengthen the nation, Fascists argued, power must rest with a single strong leader and a small group of devoted party members. (The Latin *fasces*—a bundle of rods tied around an ax handle—had been a symbol of unity and authority in ancient Rome.)

In October 1922, Mussolini marched on Rome with thousands of his followers, whose black uniforms gave them the name "Black Shirts." When important government officials, the army, and the police sided with the Fascists, the Italian king appointed Mussolini head of the government.

Calling himself *Il Duce*, or "the leader," Mussolini gradually extended Fascist control to every aspect of Italian life. Tourists marveled that *Il Duce* had even "made the trains run on time." Mussolini achieved this efficiency, however, by crushing all opposition and by making Italy a totalitarian state. C

MAIN IDEA
Analyzing Causes
C What factors led to the rise of Fascism in Italy?

The Faces of Totalitarianism

Fascist Italy	Nazi Germany	Communist Soviet Union

• Extreme nationalism • Militaristic expansionism • Charismatic leader • Private property with strong government controls • Anticommunist	• Extreme nationalism and racism • Militaristic expansionism • Forceful leader • Private property with strong government controls • Anticommunist	• Create a sound communist state and wait for world revolution • Revolution by workers • Eventual rule by working class • State ownership of property

▲ **Left to right: Benito Mussolini, Adolf Hitler, Joseph Stalin**

THE NAZIS TAKE OVER GERMANY In Germany, **Adolf Hitler** had followed a path to power similar to Mussolini's. At the end of World War I, Hitler had been a jobless soldier drifting around Germany. In 1919, he joined a struggling group called the National Socialist German Workers' Party, better known as the Nazi Party. Despite its name, this party had no ties to socialism.

Hitler proved to be such a powerful public speaker and organizer that he quickly became the party's leader. Calling himself *Der Führer*—"the Leader"—he promised to bring Germany out of chaos.

In his book *Mein Kampf* [My Struggle], Hitler set forth the basic beliefs of Nazism that became the plan of action for the Nazi Party. **Nazism** (nät′sĭz′əm), the German brand of fascism, was based on extreme nationalism. Hitler, who had been born in Austria, dreamed of uniting all German-speaking people in a great German empire.

Hitler also wanted to enforce racial "purification" at home. In his view, Germans—especially blue-eyed, blond-haired "Aryans"—formed a "master race" that was destined to rule the world. "Inferior races," such as Jews, Slavs, and all nonwhites, were deemed fit only to serve the Aryans.

MAIN IDEA

Summarizing
D What were the key ideas and goals that Hitler presented in *Mein Kampf*?

A third element of Nazism was national expansion. Hitler believed that for Germany to thrive, it needed more *lebensraum*, or living space. One of the Nazis' aims, as Hitler wrote in *Mein Kampf*, was "to secure for the German people the land and soil to which they are entitled on this earth," even if this could be accomplished only by "the might of a victorious sword." D

Background
According to Hitler there were three German empires: the Holy Roman Empire; The German Empire of 1871–1918; and The Third Reich.

The Great Depression helped the Nazis come to power. Because of war debts and dependence on American loans and investments, Germany's economy was hit hard. By 1932, some 6 million Germans were unemployed. Many men who were out of work joined Hitler's private army, the *storm troopers* (or *Brown Shirts*). The German people were desperate and turned to Hitler as their last hope.

By mid 1932, the Nazis had become the strongest political party in Germany. In January 1933, Hitler was appointed chancellor (prime minister). Once in power, Hitler quickly dismantled Germany's democratic Weimar Republic. In its place he established the *Third Reich*, or Third German Empire. According to Hitler, the Third Reich would be a "Thousand-Year Reich"—it would last for a thousand years.

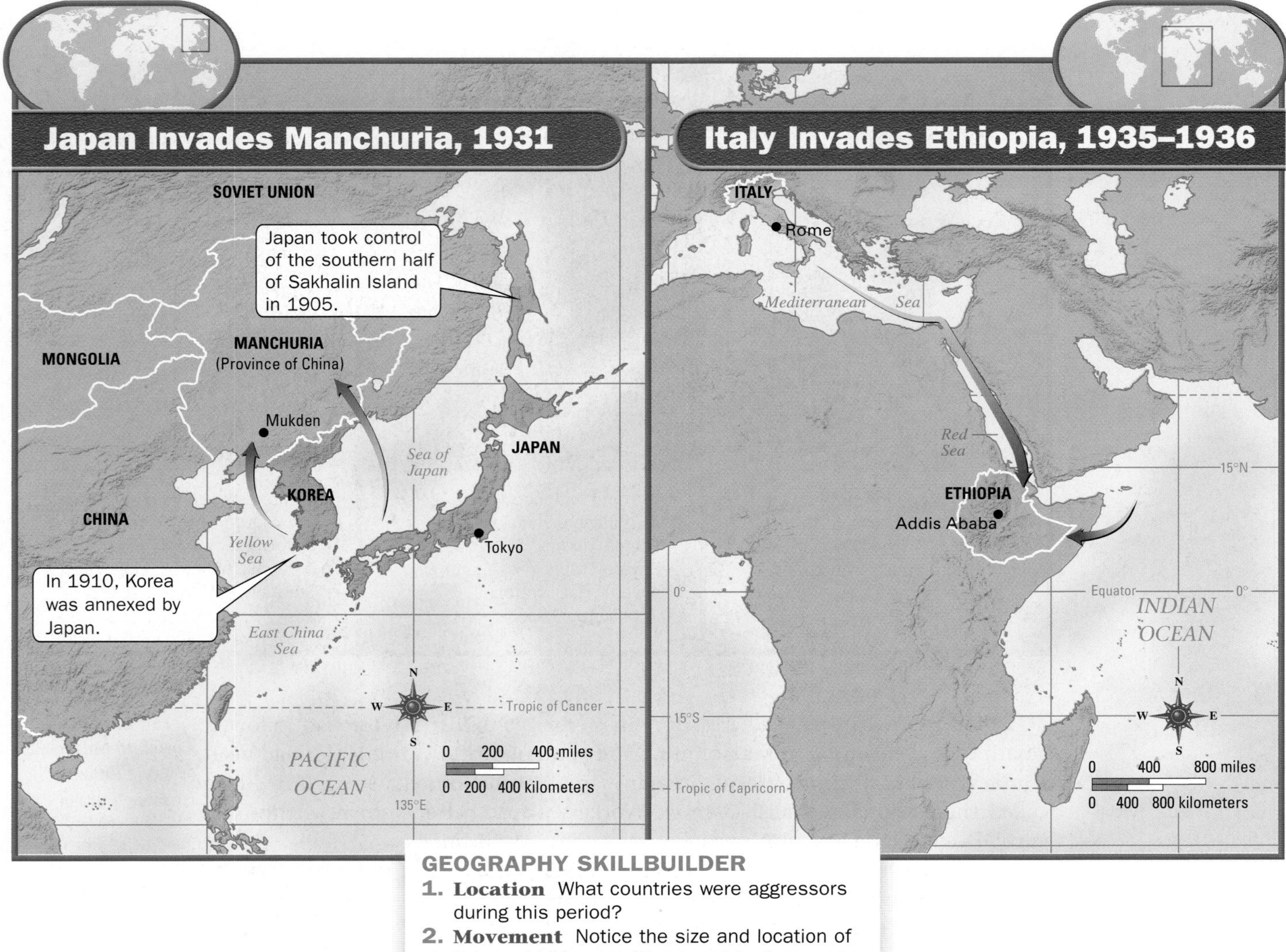

GEOGRAPHY SKILLBUILDER

1. **Location** What countries were aggressors during this period?
2. **Movement** Notice the size and location of Italy and of Japan with respect to the country each invaded. What similarities do you see?

MILITARISTS GAIN CONTROL IN JAPAN Halfway around the world, nationalistic military leaders were trying to take control of the imperial government of Japan. These leaders shared in common with Hitler a belief in the need for more living space for a growing population. Ignoring the protests of more moderate Japanese officials, the militarists launched a surprise attack and seized control of the Chinese province of Manchuria in 1931. Within several months, Japanese troops controlled the entire province, a large region about twice the size of Texas, that was rich in natural resources. E

The watchful League of Nations had been established after World War I to prevent just such aggressive acts. In this greatest test of the League's power, representatives were sent to Manchuria to investigate the situation. Their report condemned Japan, who in turn simply quit the League. Meanwhile, the success of the Manchurian invasion put the militarists firmly in control of Japan's government.

AGGRESSION IN EUROPE AND AFRICA The failure of the League of Nations to take action against Japan did not escape the notice of Europe's dictators. In 1933, Hitler pulled Germany out of the League. In 1935, he began a military buildup in violation of the Treaty of Versailles. A year later, he sent troops into the Rhineland, a German region bordering France and Belgium that was demilitarized as a result of the Treaty of Versailles. The League did nothing to stop Hitler.

MAIN IDEA

Analyzing Motives

E Why did Japan invade Manchuria?

Background

Military government had centuries-old roots in Japan. The shogun lords of the Middle Ages had been military leaders.

Meanwhile, Mussolini began building his new Roman Empire. His first target was Ethiopia, one of Africa's few remaining independent countries. By the fall of 1935, tens of thousands of Italian soldiers stood ready to advance on Ethiopia. The League of Nations reacted with brave talk of "collective resistance to all acts of unprovoked aggression."

When the invasion began, however, the League's response was an ineffective economic boycott—little more than a slap on Italy's wrist. By May 1936, Ethiopia had fallen. In desperation, Haile Selassie, the ousted Ethiopian emperor, appealed to the League for assistance. Nothing was done. "It is us today," he told them. "It will be you tomorrow."

CIVIL WAR BREAKS OUT IN SPAIN In 1936, a group of Spanish army officers led by General **Francisco Franco**, rebelled against the Spanish republic. Revolts broke out all over Spain, and the Spanish Civil War began. The war aroused passions not only in Spain but throughout the world. About 3,000 Americans formed the Abraham Lincoln Battalion and traveled to Spain to fight against Franco. "We knew, we just knew," recalled Martha Gellhorn, "that Spain was the place to stop fascism." Among the volunteers were African Americans still bitter about Mussolini's invasion of Ethiopia the year before.

Such limited aid was not sufficient to stop the spread of fascism, however. The Western democracies remained neutral. Although the Soviet Union sent equipment and advisers, Hitler and Mussolini backed Franco's forces with troops, weapons, tanks, and fighter planes. The war forged a close relationship between the German and Italian dictators, who signed a formal alliance known as the Rome-Berlin Axis. After a loss of almost 500,000 lives, Franco's victory in 1939 established him as Spain's fascist dictator. Once again a totalitarian government ruled in Europe. F

MAIN IDEA

Summarizing

F What foreign countries were involved in the Spanish Civil War?

HISTORICAL SPOTLIGHT

AFRICAN AMERICANS STAND BY ETHIOPIANS

When Mussolini invaded Ethiopia, many Europeans and Americans—especially African Americans—were outraged. Almost overnight, African Americans organized to raise money for medical supplies, and a few went to fight in Ethiopia. Years later, the Ethiopian emperor Haile Selassie (shown above) said of these efforts,

> "We can never forget the help Ethiopia received from Negro Americans during the terrible crisis. . . . It moved me to know that Americans of African descent did not abandon their embattled brothers, but stood by us."

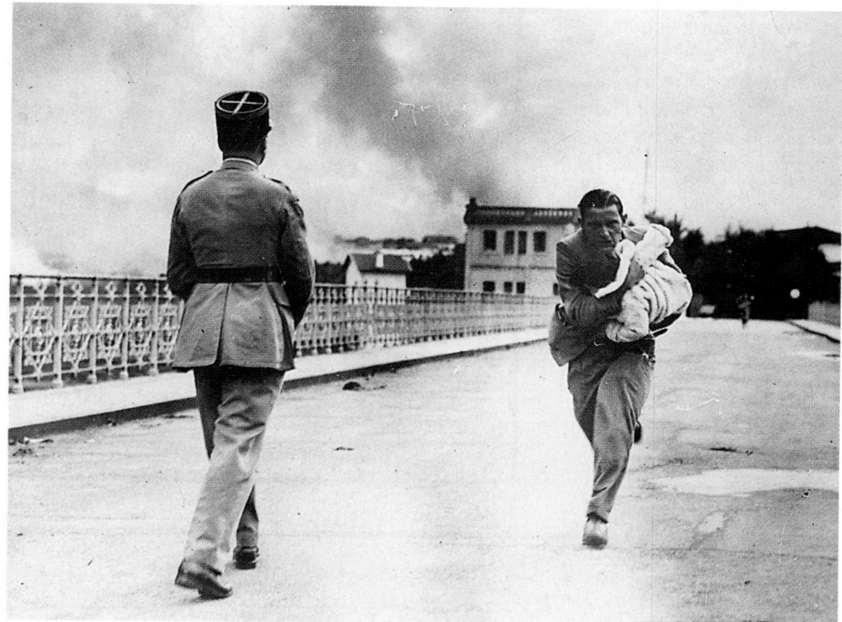

A French journalist escapes from Spain to France with a child he rescued from a street battle. Fighting would soon engulf not only France but the rest of Europe and parts of Asia.

The United States Responds Cautiously

Most Americans were alarmed by the international conflicts of the mid-1930s but believed that the United States should not get involved. In 1928, the United States had signed the Kellogg-Briand Pact. The treaty was signed by 62 countries and declared that war would not be used "as an instrument of national policy." Yet it did not include a plan to deal with countries that broke their pledge. The Pact was, therefore, only a small step toward peace.

AMERICANS CLING TO ISOLATIONISM In the early 1930s, a flood of books argued that the United States had been dragged into World War I by greedy bankers and arms dealers. Public outrage led to the creation of a congressional committee, chaired by North Dakota Senator Gerald Nye, that held hearings on these charges. The Nye committee fueled the controversy by documenting the large profits that banks and manufacturers made during the war. As the furor grew over these "merchants of death," Americans became more determined than ever to avoid war. Antiwar feeling was so strong that the Girl Scouts of America changed the color of its uniforms from khaki to green to appear less militaristic. G

MAIN IDEA

Analyzing Causes
G What factors contributed to Americans' growing isolationism?

Americans' growing isolationism eventually had an impact on President Roosevelt's foreign policy. When he had first taken office in 1933, Roosevelt felt comfortable reaching out to the world in several ways. He officially recognized the Soviet Union in 1933 and agreed to exchange ambassadors with Moscow. He continued the policy of nonintervention in Latin America—begun by Presidents Coolidge and Hoover—with his Good Neighbor Policy and withdrew armed forces stationed there. In 1934, Roosevelt pushed the Reciprocal Trade Agreement Act through Congress. This act lowered trade barriers by giving the president the power to make trade agreements with other nations and was aimed at reducing

Analyzing *Political Cartoons*

"IT AIN'T WHAT IT USED TO BE"

During the late 1930s, Americans were divided about becoming involved in "Europe's quarrels." Some people felt that the United States should be more involved in the economic and political problems occurring across the Atlantic. Isolationists—people who believed the United States should stay completely out of other nations' affairs except in the defense of the United States—strictly opposed intervening. The idea that America and Europe were two separate worlds divided by an ocean that could guarantee safety was quickly eroding.

SKILLBUILDER

Analyzing Political Cartoons

1. What does Uncle Sam's turning his back on Europe show about American attitudes in the late 1930s?
2. What U.S. policy does the cartoon imply?
3. Why might the Atlantic Ocean have appeared to shrink in the late 1930s?

SEE SKILLBUILDER HANDBOOK, PAGE R24.

tariffs by as much as 50 percent. In an effort to keep the United States out of future wars, beginning in 1935, Congress passed a series of **Neutrality Acts**. The first two acts outlawed arms sales or loans to nations at war. The third act was passed in response to the fighting in Spain. This act extended the ban on arms sales and loans to nations engaged in civil wars.

NEUTRALITY BREAKS DOWN Despite congressional efforts to legislate neutrality, Roosevelt found it impossible to remain neutral. When Japan launched a new attack on China in July 1937, Roosevelt found a way around the Neutrality Acts. Because Japan had not formally declared war against China, the president claimed there was no need to enforce the Neutrality Acts. The United States continued sending arms and supplies to China. A few months later, Roosevelt spoke out strongly against isolationism in a speech delivered in Chicago. He called on peace-loving nations to "quarantine," or isolate, aggressor nations in order to stop the spread of war.

A PERSONAL VOICE FRANLKIN DELANO ROOSEVELT

> **"The peace, the freedom, and the security of 90 percent of the population of the world is being jeopardized by the remaining 10 percent who are threatening a breakdown of all international order and law. Surely the 90 percent who want to live in peace under law and in accordance with moral standards that have received almost universal acceptance through the centuries, can and must find some way . . . to preserve peace."**
>
> —"Quarantine Speech," October 5, 1937

At last Roosevelt seemed ready to take a stand against aggression—that is, until isolationist newspapers exploded in protest, accusing the president of leading the nation into war. Roosevelt backed off in the face of criticism, but his speech did begin to shift the debate. For the moment the conflicts remained "over there."

ASSESSMENT

1. **TERMS & NAMES** For each term or name, write a sentence explaining its significance.
   - **Joseph Stalin**
   - **totalitarian**
   - **Benito Mussolini**
   - **fascism**
   - **Adolf Hitler**
   - **Nazism**
   - **Francisco Franco**
   - **Neutrality Acts**

MAIN IDEA

2. **TAKING NOTES**
   Using a web diagram like the one below, fill it in with the main ambition of each dictator.

What ambitions did the dictators have in common?

CRITICAL THINKING

3. **ANALYZING CAUSES**
   How did the Treaty of Versailles sow the seeds of instability in Europe?
   Think About:
   - effects of the treaty on Germany and the Soviet Union
   - effects of the treaty on national pride
   - the economic legacy of the war

4. **DRAWING CONCLUSIONS**
   Why do you think Hitler found widespread support among the German people? Support your answer with details from the text.

5. **FORMING GENERALIZATIONS**
   Would powerful nations or weak nations be more likely to follow an isolationist policy? Explain.

SECTION 2

War in Europe

MAIN IDEA

Using the sudden mass attack called *blitzkrieg*, Germany invaded and quickly conquered many European countries.

WHY IT MATTERS NOW

Hitler's actions started World War II and still serve as a warning to be vigilant about totalitarian government.

Terms & Names

- **Neville Chamberlain**
- **Winston Churchill**
- **appeasement**
- **nonaggression pact**
- ***blitzkrieg***
- **Charles de Gaulle**

One American's Story

▲ **William Shirer, a journalist and historian, became well known for his radio broadcasts from Berlin at the beginning of World War II.**

In 1940, CBS correspondent William Shirer stood in the forest near Compiègne, where 22 years earlier defeated German generals had signed the armistice ending World War I. Shirer was now waiting for Adolf Hitler to deliver his armistice terms to a defeated France. He watched as Hitler walked up to the monument and slowly read the inscription: "Here on the eleventh of November 1918 succumbed the criminal pride of the German empire . . . vanquished by the free peoples which it tried to enslave." Later that day, Shirer wrote a diary entry describing the führer's reaction.

A PERSONAL VOICE WILLIAM SHIRER

"I have seen that face many times at the great moments of his life. But today! It is afire with scorn, anger, hate, revenge, triumph. He steps off the monument and contrives to make even this gesture a masterpiece of contempt. . . . He glances slowly around the clearing, and now, as his eyes meet ours, you grasp the depth of his hatred. But there is triumph there too—revengeful, triumphant hate."

—*Berlin Diary: The Journal of a Foreign Correspondent, 1934–1941*

Again and again Shirer had heard Hitler proclaim that "Germany needs peace. . . . Germany wants peace." The hatred and vengefulness that drove the dictator's every action, however, drew Germany ever closer to war.

Austria and Czechoslovakia Fall

On November 5, 1937, Hitler met secretly with his top military advisers. He boldly declared that to grow and prosper Germany needed the land of its neighbors. His plan was to absorb Austria and Czechoslovakia into the Third Reich. When one of his advisors protested that annexing those countries could provoke war, Hitler replied, "'The German Question' can be solved only by means of force, and this is never without risk."

KEY PLAYER

ADOLF HITLER
1889–1945

"All great world-shaking events have been brought about not by written matter, but by the spoken word!" declared Adolf Hitler. A shy and awkward speaker at first, Hitler rehearsed carefully. He even had photographs (shown above) taken of his favorite gestures so he could study them and make changes to produce exactly the desired effect.

Hitler's extraordinary power as a speaker, wrote Otto Strasser, stemmed from an intuitive ability to sense "the vibration of the human heart . . . telling it what it most wants to hear."

UNION WITH AUSTRIA Austria was Hitler's first target. The Paris Peace Conference following World War I had created the relatively small nation of Austria out of what was left of the Austro-Hungarian Empire. The majority of Austria's 6 million people were Germans who favored unification with Germany. On March 12, 1938, German troops marched into Austria unopposed. A day later, Germany announced that its *Anschluss*, or "union," with Austria was complete. The United States and the rest of the world did nothing.

BARGAINING FOR THE SUDETENLAND Hitler then turned to Czechoslovakia. About 3 million German-speaking people lived in the western border regions of Czechoslovakia called the Sudetenland. The mountainous region formed Czechoslovakia's main defense against German attack. (See map, p. 538.) Hitler wanted to annex Czechoslovakia in order to provide more living space for Germany as well as to control its important natural resources.

Hitler charged that the Czechs were abusing the Sudeten Germans, and he began massing troops on the Czech border. The U.S. correspondent William Shirer, then stationed in Berlin, wrote in his diary: "The Nazi press [is] full of hysterical headlines. All lies. Some examples: 'Women and Children Mowed Down by Czech Armored Cars,' or 'Bloody Regime—New Czech Murders of Germans.'"

Early in the crisis, both France and Great Britain promised to protect Czechoslovakia. Then, just when war seemed inevitable, Hitler invited French premier Édouard Daladier and British prime minister **Neville Chamberlain** to meet with him in Munich. When they arrived, the führer declared that the annexation of the Sudetenland would be his "last territorial demand." In their eagerness to avoid war, Daladier and Chamberlain chose to believe him. On September 30, 1938, they signed the Munich Agreement, which turned the Sudetenland over to Germany without a single shot being fired. (A)

MAIN IDEA

Summarizing
(A) What moves did Germany make in its quest for *lebensraum*?

Chamberlain returned home and proclaimed: "My friends, there has come back from Germany peace with honor. I believe it is peace in our time."

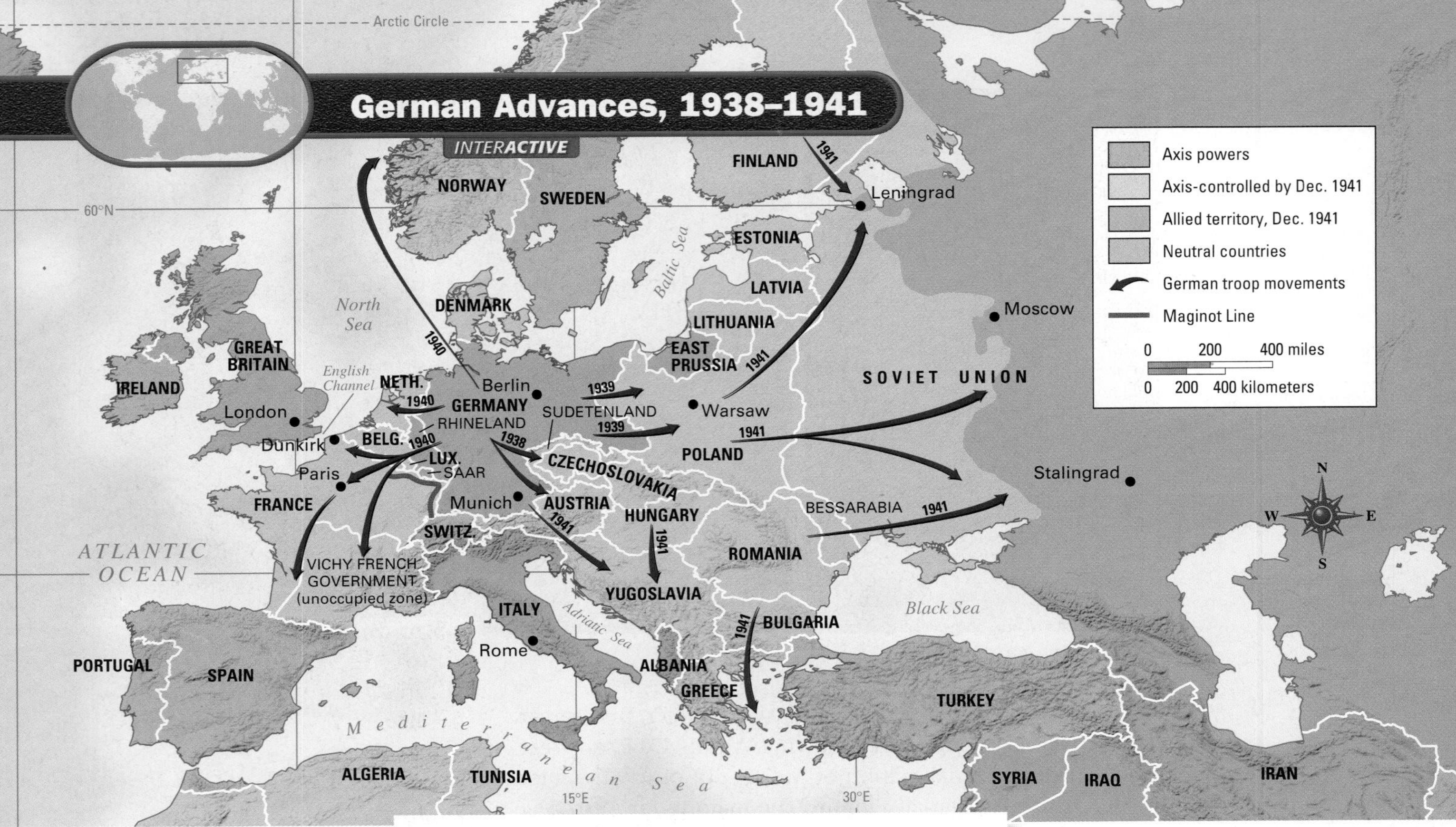

GEOGRAPHY SKILLBUILDER

1. **Region** Which European countries did Germany invade?
2. **Location** How was Germany's geographic location an advantage?

Chamberlain's satisfaction was not shared by **Winston Churchill,** Chamberlain's political rival in Great Britain. In Churchill's view, by signing the Munich Agreement, Daladier and Chamberlain had adopted a shameful policy of **appeasement**—or giving up principles to pacify an aggressor. As Churchill bluntly put it, "Britain and France had to choose between war and dishonor. They chose dishonor. They will have war." Nonetheless, the House of Commons approved Chamberlain's policy toward Germany and Churchill responded with a warning.

A PERSONAL VOICE WINSTON CHURCHILL

"[W]e have passed an awful milestone in our history. . . . And do not suppose that this is the end. . . . This is only the first sip, the first foretaste of a bitter cup which will be proffered to us year by year unless, by a supreme recovery of moral health and martial vigor, we arise again and take our stand for freedom as in the olden time." B

—speech to the House of Commons, quoted in *The Gathering Storm*

MAIN IDEA

Analyzing Motives

B What was appeasement, and why did Churchill oppose it so strongly?

The German Offensive Begins

As Churchill had warned, Hitler was not finished expanding the Third Reich. As dawn broke on March 15, 1939, German troops poured into what remained of Czechoslovakia. At nightfall Hitler gloated, "Czechoslovakia has ceased to exist." After that, the German dictator turned his land-hungry gaze toward Germany's eastern neighbor, Poland.

THE SOVIET UNION DECLARES NEUTRALITY Like Czechoslovakia, Poland had a sizable German-speaking population. In the spring of 1939, Hitler began his familiar routine, charging that Germans in Poland were mistreated by the Poles and needed his protection. Some people thought that this time Hitler must be bluffing. After all, an attack on Poland might bring Germany into conflict with the Soviet Union, Poland's eastern neighbor. At the same time, such an attack would most likely provoke a declaration of war from France and Britain—both of whom had promised military aid to Poland. The result would be a two-front war. Fighting on two fronts had exhausted Germany in World War I. Surely, many thought, Hitler would not be foolish enough to repeat that mistake.

As tensions rose over Poland, Stalin surprised everyone by signing a **nonaggression pact** with Hitler. Once bitter enemies, on August 23, 1939 fascist Germany and communist Russia now committed never to attack each other. Germany and the Soviet Union also signed a second, secret pact, agreeing to divide Poland between them. With the danger of a two-front war eliminated, the fate of Poland was sealed.

Background
Luftwaffe in German means "air weapon."

MAIN IDEA
Evaluating
C How did German blitzkrieg tactics rely on new military technology?

BLITZKRIEG* IN POLAND** As day broke on September 1, 1939, the German *Luftwaffe*, or German air force, roared over Poland, raining bombs on military bases, airfields, railroads, and cities. At the same time, German tanks raced across the Polish countryside, spreading terror and confusion. This invasion was the first test of Germany's newest military strategy, the ***blitzkrieg, or lightning war. Blitzkrieg made use of advances in military technology—such as fast tanks and more powerful aircraft—to take the enemy by surprise and then quickly crush all opposition with overwhelming force. On September 3, two days following the terror in Poland, Britain and France declared war on Germany. **C**

The blitzkrieg tactics worked perfectly. Major fighting was over in three weeks, long before France, Britain, and their allies could mount a defense. In the last week of fighting, the Soviet Union attacked Poland from the east, grabbing some of its territory. The portion Germany annexed in western Poland contained almost two-thirds of Poland's population. By the end of the month, Poland had ceased to exist—and World War II had begun.

▲ German Junkers JU-87 dive-bombers, commonly known as Stukas, were a mainstay of Germany's blitzkrieg style of attack.

◄ A German tank unit in Western Poland in 1939.

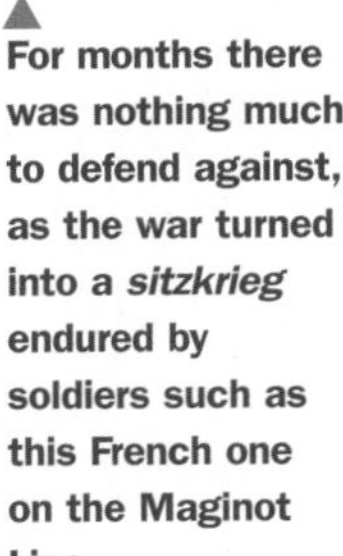

▲ **For months there was nothing much to defend against, as the war turned into a *sitzkrieg* endured by soldiers such as this French one on the Maginot Line.**

THE PHONY WAR For the next several months after the fall of Poland, French and British troops on the Maginot Line, a system of fortifications built along France's eastern border (see map on p. 538), sat staring into Germany, waiting for something to happen. On the Siegfried Line a few miles away German troops stared back. The blitzkrieg had given way to what the Germans called the *sitzkrieg* ("sitting war"), and what some newspapers referred to as the phony war.

After occupying eastern Poland, Stalin began annexing the Baltic states of Estonia, Latvia, and Lithuania. Late in 1939, Stalin sent his Soviet army into Finland. After three months of fighting, the outnumbered Finns surrendered.

Suddenly, on April 9, 1940, Hitler launched a surprise invasion of Denmark and Norway in order "to protect [those countries'] freedom and independence." But in truth, Hitler planned to build bases along the coasts to strike at Great Britain. Next, Hitler turned against the Netherlands, Belgium, and Luxembourg, which were overrun by the end of May. The phony war had ended. D

MAIN IDEA

Analyzing Motives

D How did Hitler rationalize the German invasion of Denmark and Norway?

France and Britain Fight On

France's Maginot Line proved to be ineffective; the German army threatened to bypass the line during its invasion of Belgium. Hitler's generals sent their tanks through the Ardennes, a region of wooded ravines in northeast France, thereby avoiding British and French troops who thought the Ardennes were impassable. The Germans continued to march toward Paris.

THE FALL OF FRANCE The German offensive trapped almost 400,000 British and French soldiers as they fled to the beaches of Dunkirk on the French side of the English Channel. In less than a week, a makeshift fleet of fishing trawlers, tugboats, river barges, pleasure craft—more than 800 vessels in all—ferried about 330,000 British, French, and Belgian troops to safety across the Channel.

A few days later, Italy entered the war on the side of Germany and invaded France from the south as the Germans closed in on Paris from the north. On June 22, 1940, at Compiègne, as William Shirer and the rest of the world watched, Hitler handed French officers his terms of surrender. Germans would occupy the northern part of France, and a Nazi-controlled puppet government, headed by Marshal Philippe Pétain, would be set up at Vichy, in southern France.

Background

Hitler demanded that the surrender take place in the same railroad car where the French had dictated terms to the Germans in World War I.

After France fell, a French general named **Charles de Gaulle** fled to England, where he set up a government-in-exile. De Gaulle proclaimed defiantly, "France has lost a battle, but France has not lost the war."

THE BATTLE OF BRITAIN In the summer of 1940, the Germans began to assemble an invasion fleet along the French coast. Because its naval power could not compete with that of Britain, Germany also launched an air war at the same time. The Luftwaffe began making bombing

◀ **Children watch with wonder and fear as the battling British and German air forces set the skies of London aflame.**

runs over Britain. Its goal was to gain total control of the skies by destroying Britain's Royal Air Force (RAF). Hitler had 2,600 planes at his disposal. On a single day—August 15—approximately 2,000 German planes ranged over Britain. Every night for two solid months, bombers pounded London.

The Battle of Britain raged on through the summer and fall. Night after night, German planes pounded British targets. At first the Luftwaffe concentrated on airfields and aircraft. Next it targeted cities. Londoner Len Jones was just 18 years old when bombs fell on his East End neighborhood.

A PERSONAL VOICE LEN JONES

"After an explosion of a nearby bomb, you could actually feel your eyeballs being sucked out. I was holding my eyes to try and stop them going. And the suction was so vast, it ripped my shirt away, and ripped my trousers. Then I couldn't get my breath, the smoke was like acid and everything round me was black and yellow."

—quoted in *London at War*

The RAF fought back brilliantly. With the help of a new technological device called radar, British pilots accurately plotted the flight paths of German planes, even in darkness. On September 15, 1940 the RAF shot down over 185 German planes; at the same time, they lost only 26 aircraft. Six weeks later, Hitler called off the invasion of Britain indefinitely. "Never in the field of human conflict," said Churchill in praise of the RAF pilots, "was so much owed by so many to so few."

Still, German bombers continued to pound Britain's cities trying to disrupt production and break civilian morale. British pilots also bombed German cities. Civilians in both countries unrelentingly carried on.

KEY PLAYER

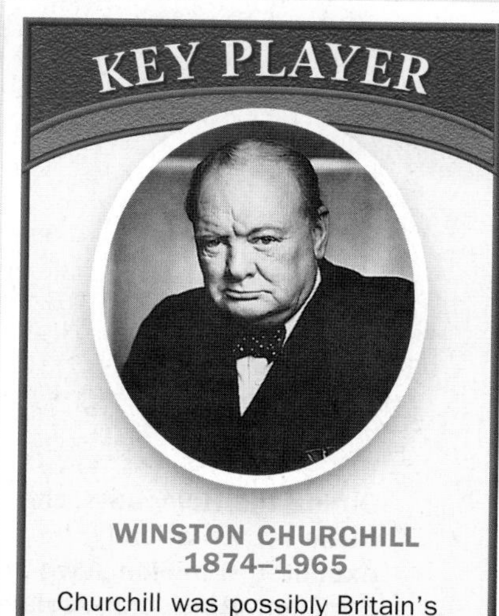

WINSTON CHURCHILL 1874–1965

Churchill was possibly Britain's greatest weapon as that nation faced the Nazis. A born fighter, Churchill became prime minister in May 1940 and used his gift as a speaker to arouse Britons and unite them:

> "[W]e shall defend our island, whatever the cost may be, we shall fight on the beaches, we shall fight on the landing-grounds, we shall fight in the fields and in the streets, we shall fight in the hills; we shall never surrender."

SECTION 2 ASSESSMENT

1. **TERMS & NAMES** For each term or name, write a sentence explaining its significance.
   - **Neville Chamberlain**
   - **Winston Churchill**
   - **appeasement**
   - **nonaggression pact**
   - ***blitzkrieg***
   - **Charles de Gaulle**

MAIN IDEA

2. **TAKING NOTES** Trace the movement of German expansion from 1937 to the end of 1940 by supplying events to follow the dates shown on the time line.

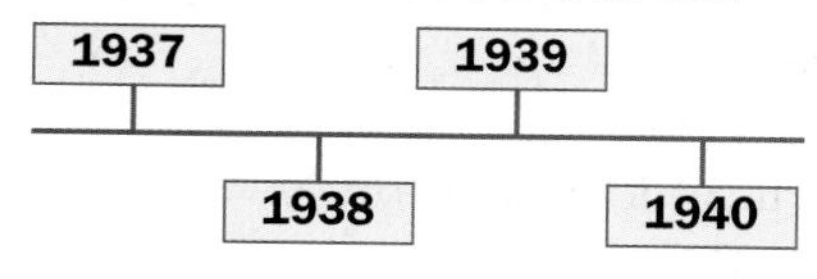

What event was the most significant? Why?

CRITICAL THINKING

3. **ANALYZING MOTIVES** To what extent do you think lies and deception played a role in Hitler's tactics? Support your answer with examples. **Think About:**
   - William Shirer's diary entry about headlines in the Nazi newspapers
   - Soviet-German relations
   - Hitler's justifications for military aggression

4. **EVALUATING DECISIONS** If you had been a member of the British House of Commons in 1938, would you have voted for or against the Munich Agreement? Support your decision.

5. **DRAWING CONCLUSIONS** Review Germany's aggressive actions between 1938 and 1945. At what point do you think Hitler concluded that he could take any territory without being stopped? Why?

SECTION 3

The Holocaust

MAIN IDEA

During the Holocaust, the Nazis systematically executed 6 million Jews and 5 million other "non-Aryans."

WHY IT MATTERS NOW

After the atrocities of the Holocaust, agencies formed to publicize human rights. These agencies have remained a force in today's world.

Terms & Names

- **Holocaust**
- ***Kristallnacht***
- **genocide**
- **ghetto**
- **concentration camp**

One American's Story

Gerda Weissmann was a carefree girl of 15 when, in September 1939, invading German troops shattered her world. Because the Weissmanns were Jews, they were forced to give up their home to a German family. In 1942, Gerda, her parents, and most of Poland's 3,000,000 Jews were sent to labor camps. Gerda recalls when members of Hitler's elite *Schutzstaffel*, or "security squadron" (SS), came to round up the Jews.

A PERSONAL VOICE GERDA WEISSMANN KLEIN

"We had to form a line and an SS man stood there with a little stick. I was holding hands with my mother and . . . he looked at me and said, 'How old?' And I said, 'eighteen,' and he sort of pushed me to one side and my mother to the other side. . . . And shortly thereafter, some trucks arrived . . . and we were loaded onto the trucks. I heard my mother's voice from very far off ask, 'Where to?' and I shouted back, 'I don't know.'"

—quoted in the film *One Survivor Remembers*

VIDEO

ESCAPING THE FINAL SOLUTION
Kurt Klein and Gerda Weissmann Klein Remember the Holocaust

When the American lieutenant Kurt Klein, who would later become Gerda's husband, liberated her from the Nazis in 1945—just one day before her 21st birthday—she weighed 68 pounds and her hair had turned white. Even so, of all her family and friends, she alone had survived the Nazis' campaign to exterminate Europe's Jews.

The Persecution Begins

On April 7, 1933, shortly after Hitler took power in Germany, he ordered all "non-Aryans" to be removed from government jobs. This order was one of the first moves in a campaign for racial purity that eventually led to the **Holocaust**—the systematic murder of 11 million people across Europe, more than half of whom were Jews.

On November 17, 1938, two passersby examine the shattered window of a Jewish-owned store in the aftermath of *Kristallnacht*.

Jewish men holding a "star of David" are rounded up and marched through the streets on their way to a concentration camp.

Vocabulary
scapegoat: someone who is made to bear the blame of others

JEWS TARGETED Although Jews were not the only victims of the Holocaust, they were the center of the Nazis' targets. Anti-Semitism, or hatred of the Jews, had a long history in many European countries. For decades many Germans looking for a scapegoat had blamed the Jews as the cause of their failures. Hitler found that a majority of Germans were willing to support his belief that Jews were responsible for Germany's economic problems and defeat in World War I.

As the Nazis tightened their hold on Germany, their persecution of the Jews increased. In 1935, the Nuremberg Laws stripped Jews of their German citizenship, jobs, and property. To make it easier for the Nazis to identify them, Jews had to wear a bright yellow Star of David attached to their clothing. Worse was yet to come.

MAIN IDEA
Analyzing Issues
A What problems did German Jews face in Nazi Germany from 1935 to 1938?

KRISTALLNACHT November 9–10, 1938, became known as ***Kristallnacht*** (krĭs′täl′nächt′), or "Night of Broken Glass." Nazi storm troopers attacked Jewish homes, businesses, and synagogues across Germany. An American who witnessed the violence wrote, "Jewish shop windows by the hundreds were systematically and wantonly smashed. . . . The main streets of the city were a positive litter of shattered plate glass." Around 100 Jews were killed, and hundreds more were injured. Some 30,000 Jews were arrested and hundreds of synagogues were burned. Afterward, the Nazis blamed the Jews for the destruction. **A**

A FLOOD OF JEWISH REFUGEES Kristallnacht marked a step-up in the Nazi policy of Jewish persecution. Nazis tried to speed Jewish emigration but encountered difficulty. Jews fleeing Germany had trouble finding nations that would accept them. France already had 40,000 Jewish refugees and did not want more. The British worried about fueling anti-Semitism and refused to admit more than 80,000 Jewish refugees. They also controlled Palestine (later Israel) and allowed 30,000 refugees to settle there. Late in 1938, Germany's foreign minister, Joachim von Ribbentrop, observed, "We all want to get rid of our Jews. The difficulty is that no country wishes to receive them."

Muralist Ben Shahn ▶ depicts the 1933 emigration of Albert Einstein and thousands of other Jews to America to escape Nazi terrorism.

Although the average Jew had little chance of reaching the United States, "persons of exceptional merit," including physicist Albert Einstein, author Thomas Mann, architect Walter Gropius, and theologian Paul Tillich were among 100,000 refugees the United States accepted. Many Americans wanted the door closed. Americans were concerned that letting in more refugees during the Great Depression would deny U.S. citizens jobs and threaten economic recovery. Among Americans, there was widespread anti-Semitism and fear that "enemy agents" would be allowed to enter the country. President Roosevelt said that while he sympathized with the Jews, he would not "do anything which would conceivably hurt the future of present American citizens." B

MAIN IDEA

Analyzing Effects

B How did the United States respond to Jewish refugees?

THE PLIGHT OF THE *ST. LOUIS* Official indifference to the plight of Germany's Jews was in evidence in the case of the ship *St. Louis*. This German ocean liner passed Miami in 1939. Although 740 of the liner's 943 passengers had U.S. immigration papers, the Coast Guard followed the ship to prevent anyone from disembarking in America. The ship was forced to return to Europe. "The cruise of the St. Louis," wrote the New York Times, "cries to high heaven of man's inhumanity to man." Passenger Liane Reif-Lehrer recalls her childhood experiences.

A PERSONAL VOICE LIANE REIF-LEHRER

"**My mother and brother and I were among the passengers who survived. . . . We were sent back to Europe and given haven in France, only to find the Nazis on our doorstep again a few months later.**"

—Liane Reif-Lehrer

More than half of the passengers were later killed in the Holocaust.

Hitler's "Final Solution"

By 1939 only about a quarter million Jews remained in Germany. But other nations that Hitler occupied had millions more. Obsessed with a desire to rid Europe of its Jews, Hitler imposed what he called the "Final Solution"—a policy of **genocide,** the deliberate and systematic killing of an entire population.

Background
The first person to use the term Final Solution was General George Custer. He was referring to the execution of Native Americans.

THE CONDEMNED Hitler's Final Solution rested on the belief that Aryans were a superior people and that the strength and purity of this "master race" must be preserved. To accomplish this, the Nazis condemned to slavery and death not only the Jews but other groups that they viewed as inferior or unworthy or as "enemies of the state."

After taking power in 1933, the Nazis had concentrated on silencing their political opponents—communists, socialists, liberals, and anyone else who spoke out against the government. Once the Nazis had eliminated these enemies, they turned against other groups in Germany. In addition to Jews, these groups included the following:

- *Gypsies*—whom the Nazis believed to be an "inferior race"
- *Freemasons*—whom the Nazis charged as supporters of the "Jewish conspiracy" to rule the world
- *Jehovah's Witnesses*—who refused to join the army or salute Hitler

ANOTHER PERSPECTIVE

DENMARK'S RESISTANCE

King Christian X became an important symbol of Danish resistance in World War II. In 1942, he rejected the Nazis' demand to enforce the Nuremberg Laws against the Jews in occupied Denmark. In August 1943, the king spoke out against the German occupying forces, an act that led to his imprisonment for the remainder of the war.

The Nazis also targeted other Germans whom they found unfit to be part of the "master race." Such victims included homosexuals, the mentally deficient, the mentally ill, the physically disabled, and the incurably ill.

Hitler began implementing his Final Solution in Poland with special Nazi death squads. Hitler's elite Nazi "security squadrons" (or SS), rounded up Jews—men, women, children, and babies—and shot them on the spot.

FORCED RELOCATION Jews also were ordered into dismal, overcrowded **ghettos,** segregated Jewish areas in certain Polish cities. The Nazis sealed off the ghettos with barbed wire and stone walls.

Life inside the ghetto was miserable. The bodies of victims piled up in the streets faster than they could be removed. Factories were built alongside ghettos where people were forced to work for German industry. In spite of the impossible living conditions, the Jews hung on. While some formed resistance movements inside the ghettos, others resisted by other means. They published and distributed underground newspapers. Secret schools were set up to educate Jewish children. Even theater and music groups continued to operate.

Estimated Jewish Losses

	Pre-Holocaust Population	Number Killed: Low Estimate	Number Killed: High Estimate
Austria	191,000	50,000	65,500
Belgium	60,000	25,000	29,000
Bohemia/Moravia	92,000	77,000	78,300
Denmark	8,000	60	116
Estonia	4,600	1,500	2,000
France	260,000	75,000	77,000
Germany	566,000	135,000	142,000
Greece	73,000	59,000	67,000
Hungary	725,000	502,000	569,000
Italy	48,000	6,500	9,000
Latvia	95,000	70,000	72,000
Lithuania	155,000	130,000	143,000
Luxembourg	3,500	1,000	2,000
Netherlands	112,000	100,000	105,000
Norway	1,700	800	800
Poland	3,250,000	2,700,000	3,000,000
Romania	441,000	121,000	287,000
Slovakia	89,000	60,000	71,000
USSR	2,825,000	700,000	1,100,000
Yugoslavia	68,000	56,000	65,000
TOTALS	9,067,800	4,869,860	5,894,716

Source: Columbia Guide to the Holocaust

SKILLBUILDER Interpreting Charts
Approximately what percentage of the total Jewish population in Europe was killed during the Holocaust?

On May 9, 1945, inmates at the Ebensee concentration camp in Austria were liberated by U.S. soldiers.

CONCENTRATION CAMPS Finally, Jews in communities not reached by the killing squads were dragged from their homes and herded onto trains or trucks for shipment to **concentration camps,** or labor camps. Families were often separated, sometimes—like the Weissmanns—forever.

Nazi concentration camps were originally set up to imprison political opponents and protesters. The camps were later turned over to the SS, who expanded the concentration camp and used it to warehouse other "undesirables." Life in the camps was a cycle of hunger, humiliation, and work that almost always ended in death.

The prisoners were crammed into crude wooden barracks that held up to a thousand people each. They shared their crowded quarters, as well as their meager meals, with hordes of rats and fleas. Hunger was so intense, recalled one survivor, "that if a bit of soup spilled over, prisoners would converge on the spot, dig their spoons into the mud and stuff the mess into their mouths."

Inmates in the camps worked from dawn to dusk, seven days a week, until they collapsed. Those too weak to work were killed. Some, like Rudolf Reder, endured. He was one of only two Jews to survive the camp at Belzec, Poland.

After stripping their victims of life and dignity, the Nazis hoarded whatever articles of value the victims had possessed, such as wedding rings and gold fillings from teeth.

A PERSONAL VOICE RUDOLF REDER

"The brute Schmidt was our guard; he beat and kicked us if he thought we were not working fast enough. He ordered his victims to lie down and gave them 25 lashes with a whip, ordering them to count out loud. If the victim made a mistake, he was given 50 lashes. . . . Thirty or 40 of us were shot every day. A doctor usually prepared a daily list of the weakest men. During the lunch break they were taken to a nearby grave and shot. They were replaced the following morning by new arrivals from the transport of the day. . . . It was a miracle if anyone survived for five or six months in Belzec."

—quoted in *The Holocaust*

The Final Stage

The Final Solution reached its final stage in early 1942. At a meeting held in Wannsee, a lakeside suburb near Berlin, Hitler's top officials agreed to begin a new phase of the mass murder of Jews. To mass slaughter and starvation they would add a third method of killing—murder by poison gas. C

MAIN IDEA

Summarizing
C What was the goal of the Nazis' Final Solution, and how was that goal nearly achieved?

MASS EXTERMINATIONS As deadly as overwork, starvation, beatings, and bullets were, they did not kill fast enough to satisfy the Nazis. The Germans built six death camps in Poland. The first, Chelmno, began operating in 1941—before the meeting at Wannsee. Each camp had several huge gas chambers in which as many as 12,000 people could be killed a day.

When prisoners arrived at Auschwitz, the largest of the death camps, they had to parade by several SS doctors. With a wave of the hand, the doctors separated those strong enough to work from those who would die that day. Both groups were told to leave all their belongings behind, with a promise that they would be returned later. Those destined to die were then led into a room outside the gas chamber and were told to undress for a shower. To complete the deception, the prisoners were even

▲
Prisoners were required to wear color-coded triangles on their uniforms. The categories of prisoners include communists, socialists, criminals, emigrants, Jehovah's Witnesses, homosexuals, Germans "shy of work," and other nationalities "shy of work." The vertical categories show a variation. One for repeat offenders, one for prisoners assigned to punish other prisoners, and double triangles for Jews. Letters on top of a patch indicate nationality.

Children taken from Eastern Europe and imprisoned in Auschwitz look out from behind the barbed-wire fence in July 1944.

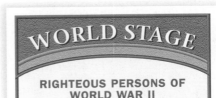

given pieces of soap. Finally, they were led into the chamber and poisoned with cyanide gas that spewed from vents in the walls. This orderly mass extermination was sometimes carried out to the accompaniment of cheerful music played by an orchestra of camp inmates who had temporarily been spared execution.

At first the bodies were buried in huge pits. At Belzec, Rudolf Reder was part of a 500-man death brigade that labored all day, he said, "either at grave digging or emptying the gas chambers." But the decaying corpses gave off a stench that could be smelled for miles around. Worse yet, mass graves left evidence of the mass murder. Lilli Kopecky recalls her arrival at Auschwitz.

A PERSONAL VOICE LILLI KOPECKY

> **"When we came to Auschwitz, we smelt the sweet smell. They said to us: 'There the people are gassed, three kilometers over there.' We didn't believe it."**
>
> —quoted in *Never Again*

At some camps, to try to cover up the evidence of their slaughter, the Nazis installed huge crematoriums, or ovens, in which to burn the dead. At other camps, the bodies were simply thrown into a pit and set on fire.

Gassing was not the only method of extermination used in the camps. Prisoners were also shot, hanged, or injected with poison.

Still others died as a result of horrible medical experiments carried out by camp doctors. Some of these victims were injected with deadly germs in order to study the effect of disease on different groups of people. Many more were used to test methods of sterilization, a subject of great interest to some Nazi doctors in their search for ways to improve the "master race."

WORLD STAGE

RIGHTEOUS PERSONS OF WORLD WAR II

In the midst of the world's overall indifference to the plight of Jewish refugees, thousands of non-Jews risked—and in many cases lost—their own lives to save Jews from the Nazis. In recognition of such heroic efforts, the Israeli Parliament, the Knesset, bestowed on these individuals the title of Righteous Gentiles (or Righteous Persons). As of the year 2001 more than 18,269 individuals were recognized for their courage and morality.

Aristides de Sousa Mendes, a Portuguese diplomat stationed in France, defied his government's orders and issued some 10,000 visas to Jews seeking entry to his country. The Swedish diplomat Raoul Wallenberg issued "protective passports" that allowed thousands of Hungarian Jews to escape the Nazi death camps. Even citizens of Germany lent a hand. And Sempo Sugihara, Japanese consul in Lithuania, helped over 6,000 Jews to escape the Nazis' clutches, an act that cost him his career.

THE SURVIVORS An estimated six million Jews died in the death camps and in the Nazi massacres. But some miraculously escaped the worst of the Holocaust. Many had help from ordinary people who were appalled by the Nazis' treatment of Jews. Some Jews even survived the horrors of the concentration camps.

"Survival is both an exalted privilege and a painful burden."
GERDA WEISSMANN KLEIN

In Gerda Weissmann Klein's view, survival depended as much on one's spirit as on getting enough to eat. "I do believe that if you were blessed with imagination, you could work through it," she wrote. "If, unfortunately, you were a person that faced reality, I think you didn't have much of a chance." Those who did come out of the camps alive were forever changed by what they had witnessed. For survivor Elie Wiesel, who entered Auschwitz in 1944 at the age of 14, the sun had set forever.

A PERSONAL VOICE ELIE WIESEL

> **"Never shall I forget that night, the first night in the camp, which has turned my life into one long night. . . . Never shall I forget the little faces of the children, whose bodies I saw turned into wreaths of smoke beneath a silent blue sky. Never shall I forget those flames which consumed my faith forever. Never shall I forget that nocturnal silence which deprived me, for all eternity, of the desire to live. Never shall I forget those moments which murdered my God and my soul and turned my dreams to dust. Never shall I forget these things, even if I am condemned to live as long as God Himself. Never."**
>
> —*Night*

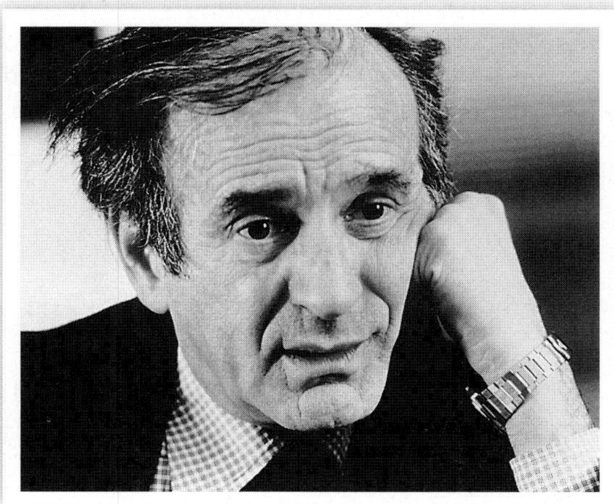

Elie Wiesel, 1986

ASSESSMENT

1. **TERMS & NAMES** For each term or name, write a sentence explaining its significance.
   - **Holocaust**
   - ***Kristallnacht***
   - **genocide**
   - **ghetto**
   - **concentration camp**

MAIN IDEA

2. **TAKING NOTES**
   List at least four events that led to the Holocaust.

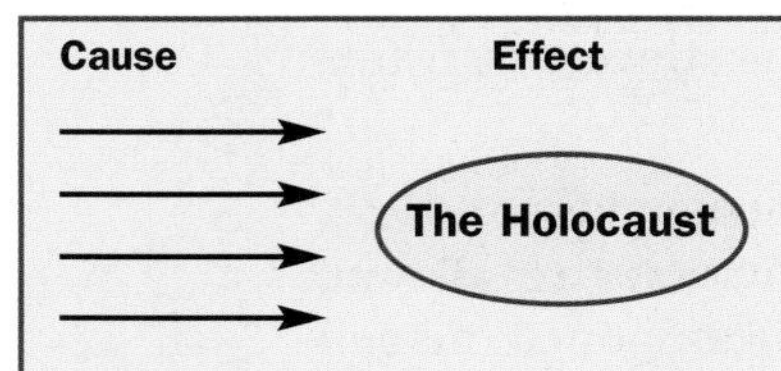

Write a paragraph summarizing one of the events that you listed.

CRITICAL THINKING

3. **EVALUATING DECISIONS**
   Do you think that the United States was justified in not allowing more Jewish refugees to emigrate? Why or why not? **Think About:**
   - the views of isolationists in the United States
   - some Americans' prejudices and fears
   - the incident on the German luxury liner *St. Louis*

4. **DEVELOPING HISTORICAL PERSPECTIVE**
   Why do you think the Nazi system of systematic genocide was so brutally effective? Support your answer with details from the text.

5. **ANALYZING MOTIVES**
   How might concentration camp doctors and guards have justified to themselves the death and suffering they caused other human beings?

America Moves Toward War

MAIN IDEA

In response to the fighting in Europe, the United States provided economic and military aid to help the Allies achieve victory.

WHY IT MATTERS NOW

The military capability of the U. S. became a deciding factor in World War II and in world affairs ever since.

Terms & Names

- **Axis powers**
- **Lend-Lease Act**
- **Atlantic Charter**
- **Allies**
- **Hideki Tojo**

One American's Story

Two days after Hitler invaded Poland, President Roosevelt spoke reassuringly to Americans about the outbreak of war in Europe.

Franklin D. Roosevelt

A PERSONAL VOICE FRANKLIN DELANO ROOSEVELT

"This nation will remain a neutral nation, but I cannot ask that every American remain neutral in thought as well. . . . Even a neutral cannot be asked to close his mind or his conscience. . . . I have said not once, but many times, that I have seen war and I hate war. . . . As long as it is my power to prevent, there will be no blackout of peace in the U.S."

—radio speech, September 3, 1939

Although Roosevelt knew that Americans were still deeply committed to staying out of war, he also believed that there could be no peace in a world controlled by dictators.

The United States Musters Its Forces

As German tanks thundered across Poland, Roosevelt revised the Neutrality Act of 1935. At the same time, he began to prepare the nation for the struggle he feared lay just ahead.

MOVING CAUTIOUSLY AWAY FROM NEUTRALITY In September of 1939, Roosevelt persuaded Congress to pass a "cash-and-carry" provision that allowed warring nations to buy U.S. arms as long as they paid cash and transported them in their own ships. Providing the arms, Roosevelt argued, would help France and Britain defeat Hitler and keep the United States out of the war. Isolationists attacked Roosevelt for his actions. However, after six weeks of heated debate, Congress passed the Neutrality Act of 1939, and a cash-and-carry policy went into effect.

Analyzing Political Cartoons

CARVING IT UP

The three Axis nations—Germany, Italy, and Japan—were a threat to the entire world. They believed they were superior and more powerful than other nations, especially democracies. By signing a mutual defense pact, the Axis powers believed the United States would never risk involvement in a two-ocean war. This cartoon shows the Axis powers' obsession with global domination.

SKILLBUILDER Analyzing Political Cartoons

1. What are the Axis leaders—Hitler, Mussolini, and Tojo—greedily carving up?
2. What do you think the artist means by showing Hitler doing the carving?

SEE SKILLBUILDER HANDBOOK, PAGE R24.

THE AXIS THREAT The United States cash-and-carry policy began to look like too little too late. By summer 1940, France had fallen and Britain was under siege. Roosevelt scrambled to provide the British with "all aid short of war." By June he had sent Britain 500,000 rifles and 80,000 machine guns, and in early September the United States traded 50 old destroyers for leases on British military bases in the Caribbean and Newfoundland. British prime minister Winston Churchill would later recall this move with affection as "a decidedly unneutral act."

On September 27 Americans were jolted by the news that Germany, Italy, and Japan had signed a mutual defense treaty, the Tripartite Pact. The three nations became known as the **Axis Powers.**

The Tripartite Pact was aimed at keeping the United States out of the war. Under the treaty, each Axis nation agreed to come to the defense of the others in case of attack. This meant that if the United States were to declare war on any one of the Axis powers, it would face its worst military nightmare—a two-ocean war, with fighting in both the Atlantic and the Pacific.

BUILDING U.S DEFENSES Meanwhile, Roosevelt asked Congress to increase spending for national defense. In spite of years of isolationism, Nazi victories in 1940 changed U.S. thinking, and Congress boosted defense spending. Congress also passed the nation's first peacetime military draft—the Selective Training and Service Act. Under this law 16 million men between the ages of 21 and 35 were registered. Of these, 1 million were to be drafted for one year but were only allowed to serve in the Western Hemisphere. Roosevelt himself drew the first draft numbers as he told a national radio audience, "This is a most solemn ceremony." (A)

> **MAIN IDEA**
> **Analyzing Effects**
> (A) What impact did the outbreak of war in Europe have on U.S. foreign and defense policy?

ROOSEVELT RUNS FOR A THIRD TERM That same year, Roosevelt decided to break the tradition of a two-term presidency, begun by George Washington, and run for reelection. To the great disappointment of isolationists, Roosevelt's Republican opponent, a public utilities executive named Wendell Willkie, supported Roosevelt's policy of aiding Britain. At the same time, both Willkie and Roosevelt promised to keep the nation out of war. Because there was so little difference between the candidates, the majority of voters chose the one they knew best. Roosevelt was reelected with nearly 55 percent of the votes cast.

"The Great Arsenal of Democracy"

Not long after the election, President Roosevelt told his radio audience during a fireside chat that it would be impossible to negotiate a peace with Hitler. "No man can tame a tiger into a kitten by stroking it." He warned that if Britain fell, the Axis powers would be left unchallenged to conquer the world, at which point, he said, "all of us in all the Americas would be living at the point of a gun." To prevent such a situation, the United States had to help defeat the Axis threat by turning itself into what Roosevelt called "the great arsenal of democracy."

THE LEND-LEASE PLAN By late 1940, however, Britain had no more cash to spend in the arsenal of democracy. Roosevelt tried to help by suggesting a new plan that he called a lend-lease policy. Under this plan, the president would lend or lease arms and other supplies to "any country whose defense was vital to the United States."

Vocabulary
lease: to grant use or occupation of under the terms of a contract

Roosevelt compared his plan to lending a garden hose to a neighbor whose house was on fire. He asserted that this was the only sensible thing to do to prevent the fire from spreading to your own property. Isolationists argued bitterly against the plan, but most Americans favored it, and Congress passed the **Lend-Lease Act** in March 1941.

POINT

"The United States should not become involved in European wars."

Still recovering from World War I and struggling with the Great Depression, many Americans believed their country should remain strictly neutral in the war in Europe.

Representative James F. O'Connor voiced the country's reservations when he asked, "Dare we set America up and commit her as the financial and military blood bank of the rest of the world?" O'Connor maintained that the United States could not "right every wrong" or "police [the] world."

The aviator Charles Lindbergh stated his hope that "the future of America . . . not be tied to these eternal wars in Europe." Lindbergh asserted that "Americans [should] fight anybody and everybody who attempts to interfere with our hemisphere." However, he went on to say, "Our safety does not lie in fighting European wars. It lies in our own internal strength, in the character of the American people and American institutions." Like many isolationists, Lindbergh believed that democracy would not be saved "by the forceful imposition of our ideals abroad, but by example of their successful operation at home."

COUNTERPOINT

"The United States must protect democracies throughout the world."

As the conflict in Europe deepened, interventionists embraced President Franklin D. Roosevelt's declaration that "when peace has been broken anywhere, peace of all countries everywhere is in danger." Roosevelt emphasized the global character of 20th-century commerce and communication by noting, "Every word that comes through the air, every ship that sails the sea, every battle that is fought does affect the American future."

Roosevelt and other political leaders also appealed to the nation's conscience. Secretary of State Cordell Hull noted that the world was "face to face . . . with an organized, ruthless, and implacable movement of steadily expanding conquest." In the same vein, Undersecretary of State Sumner Welles called Hitler "a sinister and pitiless conqueror [who] has reduced more than half of Europe to abject serfdom."

After the war expanded into the Atlantic, Roosevelt declared, "It is time for all Americans . . . to stop being deluded by the romantic notion that the Americas can go on living happily and peacefully in a Nazi-dominated world." He added, "Let us not ask ourselves whether the Americas should begin to defend themselves after the first attack . . . or the twentieth attack. The time for active defense is now."

THINKING CRITICALLY

1. **CONNECT TO TODAY** **Making Inferences** After World War I, many Americans became isolationists. Do you recommend that the United States practice isolationism today? Why or why not?
2. **CONNECT TO HISTORY** **Researching and Reporting** Do research to find out more about Charles Lindbergh's antiwar activities. Present yor findings in an editorial.

SEE SKILLBUILDER HANDBOOK, PAGE R34.

SUPPORTING STALIN Britain was not the only nation to receive lend-lease aid. In June 1941, Hitler broke the agreement he had made in 1939 with Stalin not to go to war and invaded the Soviet Union. Acting on the principle that "the enemy of my enemy is my friend," Roosevelt began sending lend-lease supplies to the Soviet Union. Some Americans opposed providing aid to Stalin; Roosevelt, however, agreed with Winston Churchill, who had said "if Hitler invaded Hell," the British would be prepared to work with the devil himself. B

MAIN IDEA

Drawing Conclusions

B Why did Roosevelt take one "unneutral" step after another to assist Britain and the Soviet Union in 1941?

GERMAN WOLF PACKS Providing lend-lease aid was one thing, but to ensure the safe delivery of goods to Britain and to the Soviet Union, supply lines had to be kept open across the Atlantic Ocean. To prevent delivery of lend-lease shipments, Hitler deployed hundreds of German submarines—U-boats—to attack supply ships.

From the spring through the fall of 1941, individual surface attacks by individual U-boats gave way to what became known as the wolf pack attack. At night groups of up to 40 submarines patrolled areas in the North Atlantic where convoys could be expected. Wolf packs were successful in sinking as much as 350,000 tons of shipments in a single month. In September 1941, President Roosevelt granted the navy permission for U.S. warships to attack German U-boats in self-defense. By late 1943, the submarine menace was contained by electronic detection techniques (especially radar), and by airborne antisubmarine patrols operating from small escort aircraft carriers.

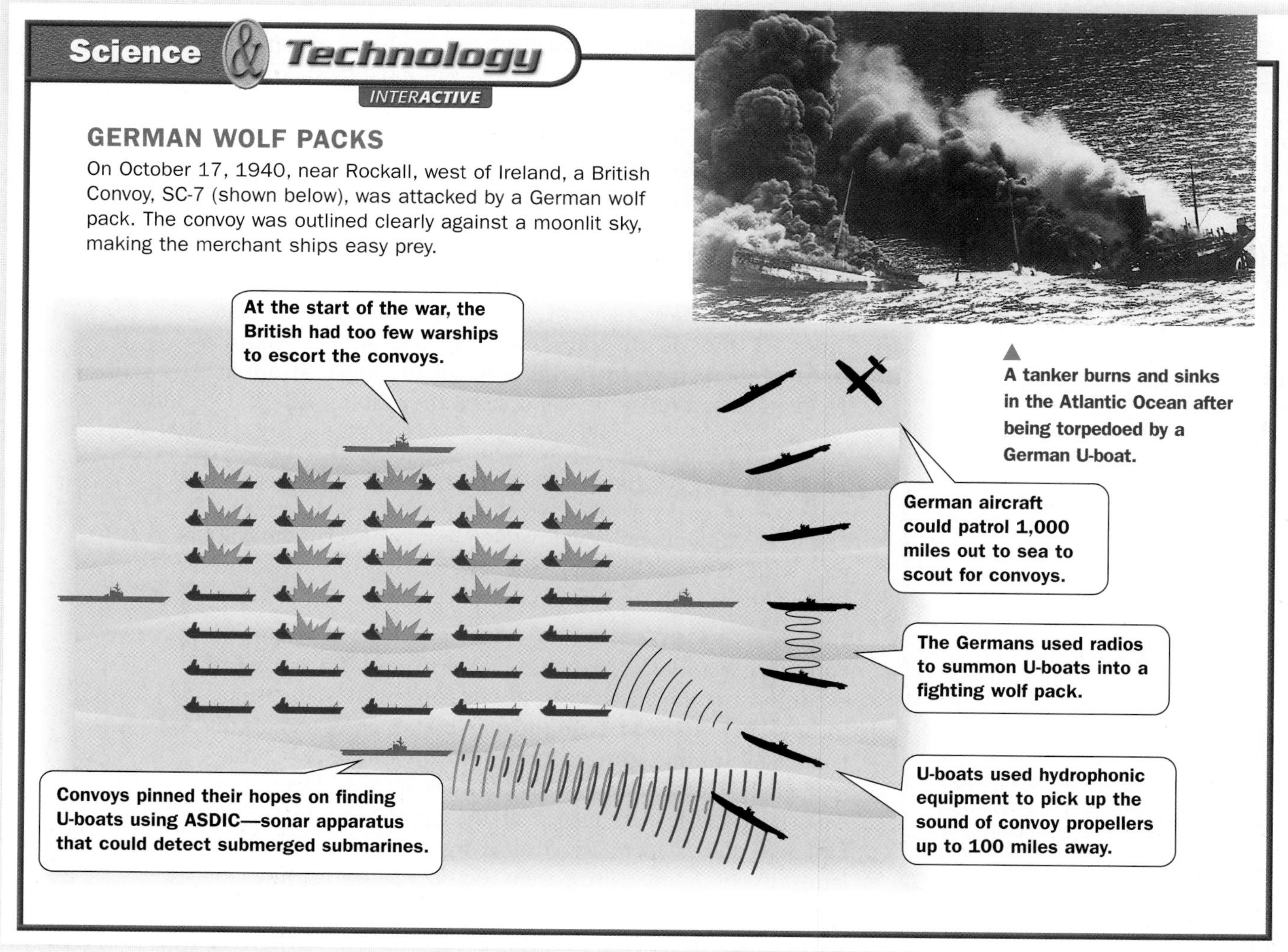
Science & Technology
INTERACTIVE
At the start of the war, the British had too few warships to escort the convoys.
German aircraft could patrol 1,000 miles out to sea to scout for convoys.
The Germans used radios to summon U-boats into a fighting wolf pack.
U-boats used hydrophonic equipment to pick up the sound of convoy propellers up to 100 miles away.
Convoys pinned their hopes on finding U-boats using ASDIC—sonar apparatus that could detect submerged submarines.

GERMAN WOLF PACKS

On October 17, 1940, near Rockall, west of Ireland, a British Convoy, SC-7 (shown below), was attacked by a German wolf pack. The convoy was outlined clearly against a moonlit sky, making the merchant ships easy prey.

▲ A tanker burns and sinks in the Atlantic Ocean after being torpedoed by a German U-boat.

FDR Plans for War

Although Roosevelt was popular, his foreign policy was under constant attack. American forces were seriously underarmed. Roosevelt's August 1941 proposal to extend the term of draftees passed in the House of Representatives by only one vote. With the army provided for, Roosevelt began planning for the war he was certain would come.

THE ATLANTIC CHARTER While Congress voted on the extension of the draft, Roosevelt and Churchill met secretly at a summit aboard the battleship USS *Augusta*. Although Churchill hoped for a military commitment, he settled for a joint declaration of war aims, called the **Atlantic Charter.** Both countries pledged the following: collective security, disarmament, self-determination, economic cooperation, and freedom of the seas. Roosevelt disclosed to Churchill that he couldn't ask Congress for a declaration of war against Germany, but "he would wage war" and do "everything" to "force an incident."

The Atlantic Charter became the basis of a new document called "A Declaration of the United Nations." The term *United Nations* was suggested by Roosevelt to express the common purpose of the **Allies**, those nations that had fought the Axis powers. The declaration was signed by 26 nations, "four-fifths of the human race" observed Churchill. C

Summarizing
C Why was the Atlantic Charter important?

HIDEKI TOJO
1884–1948

U.S. newspapers described Hideki Tojo as "smart, hard-boiled, resourceful, [and] contemptuous of theories, sentiments, and negotiations."

The Nazi press in Germany praised Tojo as "a man charged with energy, thinking clearly and with a single purpose." To a British paper, Tojo was "the son of Satan" whose single purpose was "unleashing all hell on the Far East." In Japan, however, Tojo was looked up to as a man whose "decisive leadership was a signal for the nation to rise and administer a great shock to the anti-Axis powers."

SHOOT ON SIGHT After a German submarine fired on the U.S. destroyer *Greer* in the Atlantic on September 4, 1941, Roosevelt ordered navy commanders to respond. "When you see a rattlesnake poised to strike," the president explained, "you crush him." Roosevelt ordered the navy to shoot the German submarines on sight.

Two weeks later, the *Pink Star*, an American merchant ship, was sunk off Greenland. In mid-October, a U-boat torpedoed the U.S. destroyer *Kearny*, and 11 lives were lost.

Days later, German U-boats sank the U.S. destroyer *Reuben James*, killing more than 100 sailors. "America has been attacked," Roosevelt announced grimly. "The shooting has started. And history has recorded who fired the first shot." As the death toll mounted, the Senate finally repealed the ban against arming merchant ships. A formal declaration of a full-scale war seemed inevitable. D

MAIN IDEA

Analyzing Causes
D Why did the United States enter into an undeclared shooting war with Germany in fall 1941?

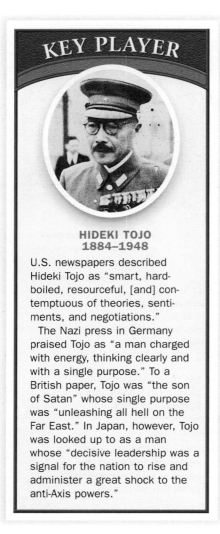

Japan Attacks the United States

The United States was now involved in an undeclared naval war with Hitler. However, the attack that brought the United States into the war came from Japan.

JAPAN'S AMBITIONS IN THE PACIFIC Germany's European victories created new opportunities for Japanese expansionists. Japan was already in control of Manchuria. In July 1937, **Hideki Tojo** (hē′d-kē tō′jō′), chief of staff of Japan's Kwantung Army, launched the invasion into China. As French, Dutch, and British colonies lay unprotected in Asia, Japanese leaders leaped at the opportunity to unite East Asia under Japanese control by seizing the colonial lands. By 1941, the British were too busy fighting Hitler to block Japanese expansion. Only the U.S. and its Pacific islands remained in Japan's way.

The Japanese began their southward push in July 1941 by taking over French military bases in Indochina (now Vietnam, Cambodia, and Laos). The United States protested this new act of aggression by cutting off trade with Japan. The embargoed goods included one Japan could not live without—oil to fuel its war machine. Japanese military leaders warned that without oil, Japan could be defeated without its enemies ever striking a blow. The leaders declared that Japan must either persuade the United States to end its oil embargo or seize the oil fields in the Dutch East Indies. This would mean war. (E)

MAIN IDEA

Analyzing Issues

(E) How was oil a source of conflict between Japan and the United States?

PEACE TALKS ARE QUESTIONED Shortly after becoming the prime minister of Japan, Hideki Tojo met with emperor Hirohito. Tojo promised the emperor that the Japanese government would attempt to preserve peace with the Americans. But on November 5, 1941, Tojo ordered the Japanese navy to prepare for an attack on the United States.

The U.S. military had broken Japan's secret communication codes and learned that Japan was preparing for a strike. What it didn't know was where the attack would come. Late in November, Roosevelt sent out a "war warning" to military commanders in Hawaii, Guam, and the Philippines. If war could not be avoided, the warning said, "the United States desires that Japan commit the first overt act." And the nation waited.

The peace talks went on for a month. Then on December 6, 1941, Roosevelt received a decoded message that instructed Japan's peace envoy to reject all American peace proposals. "This means war," Roosevelt declared.

THE ATTACK ON PEARL HARBOR Early the next morning, a Japanese dive-bomber swooped low over Pearl Harbor—the largest U.S. naval base in the Pacific. The bomber was followed by more than 180 Japanese warplanes launched from six aircraft carriers. As the first Japanese bombs found their targets, a radio operator flashed this message: "Air raid on Pearl Harbor. This is not a drill."

For an hour and a half, the Japanese planes were barely disturbed by U.S. antiaircraft guns and blasted target after target. By the time the last plane soared off around 9:30 A.M., the devastation was appalling. John Garcia, a pipe fitter's apprentice, was there.

Honolulu Star-Bulletin 1st EXTRA

WAR!

(Associated Press by Transpacific Telephone)

SAN FRANCISCO, Dec. 7.—President Roosevelt announced this morning that Japanese planes had attacked Manila and Pearl Harbor.

OAHU BOMBED BY JAPANESE PLANES

▲ Newspaper headlines announce the surprise Japanese attack.

A PERSONAL VOICE JOHN GARCIA

"It was a mess. I was working on the U.S.S. *Shaw.* It was on a floating dry dock. It was in flames. I started to go down into the pipe fitter's shop to get my toolbox when another wave of Japanese came in. I got under a set of concrete steps at the dry dock where the battleship *Pennsylvania* was. An officer came by and asked me to go into the *Pennsylvania* and try to get the fires out. A bomb had penetrated the marine deck, and . . . three decks below. Under that was the magazines: ammunition, powder, shells. I said "There ain't no way I'm gonna go down there." It could blow up any minute. I was young and 16, not stupid."

—quoted in *The Good War*

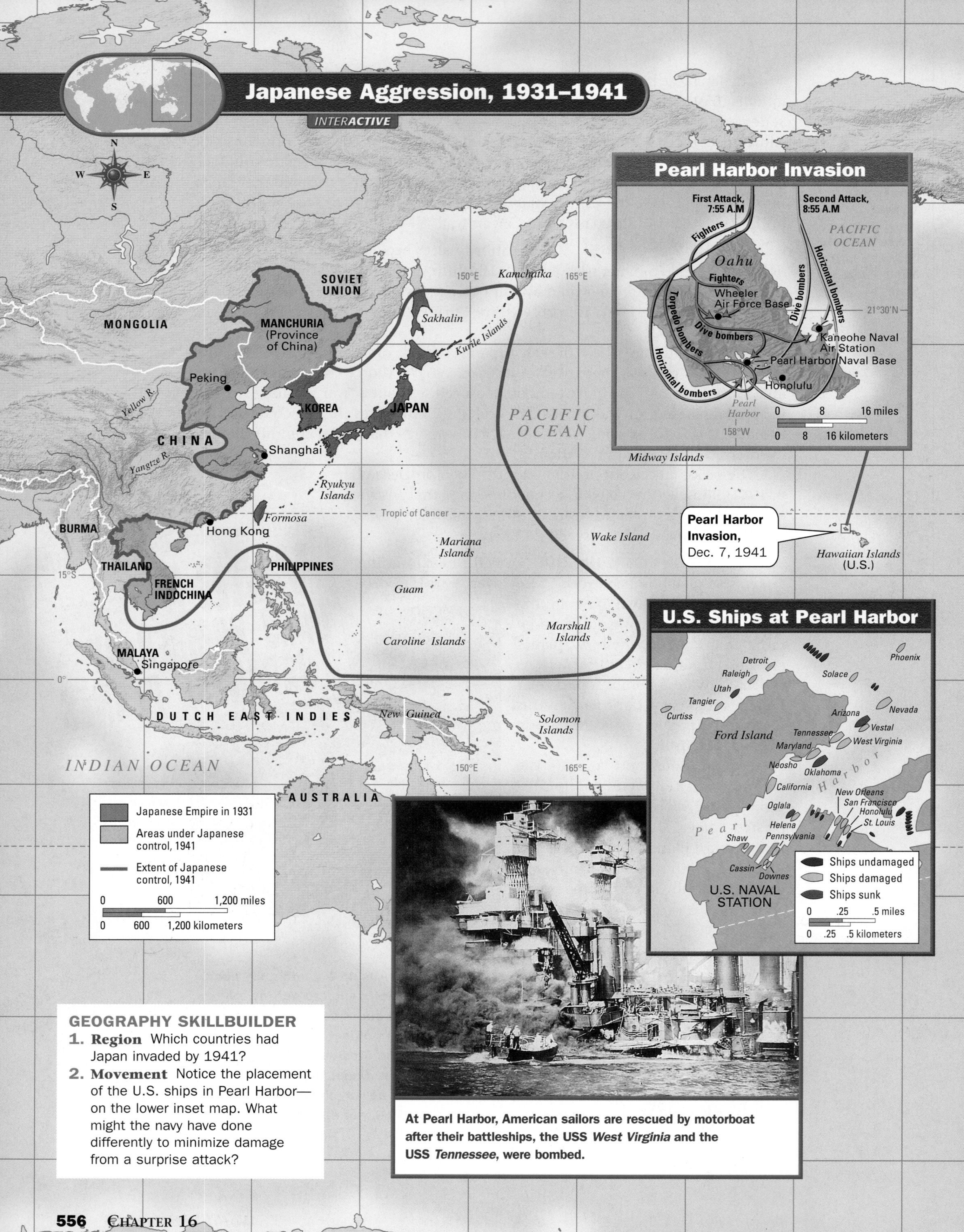

At Pearl Harbor, American sailors are rescued by motorboat after their battleships, the USS *West Virginia* and the USS *Tennessee*, were bombed.

GEOGRAPHY SKILLBUILDER

1. **Region** Which countries had Japan invaded by 1941?
2. **Movement** Notice the placement of the U.S. ships in Pearl Harbor—on the lower inset map. What might the navy have done differently to minimize damage from a surprise attack?

In less than two hours, the Japanese had killed 2,403 Americans and wounded 1,178 more. The surprise raid had sunk or damaged 21 ships, including 8 battleships—nearly the whole U.S. Pacific fleet. More than 300 aircraft were severely damaged or destroyed. These losses constituted greater damage than the U.S. Navy had suffered in all of World War I. By chance, three aircraft carriers at sea escaped the disaster. Their survival would prove crucial to the war's outcome.

REACTION TO PEARL HARBOR In Washington, the mood ranged from outrage to panic. At the White House, Eleanor Roosevelt watched closely as her husband absorbed the news from Hawaii, "each report more terrible than the last." Beneath the president's calm, Eleanor could see how worried he was. "I never wanted to have to fight this war on two fronts," Roosevelt told his wife. "We haven't the Navy to fight in both the Atlantic and the Pacific . . . so we will have to build up the Navy and the Air Force and that will mean that we will have to take a good many defeats before we can have a victory."

The next day, President Roosevelt addressed Congress. "Yesterday, December 7, 1941, a date which will live in infamy," he said, "[the Japanese launched] an unprovoked and dastardly attack." Congress quickly approved Roosevelt's request for a declaration of war against Japan. Three days later, Germany and Italy declared war on the United States.

Vocabulary
infamy: evil fame or reputation

For all the damage done at Pearl Harbor, perhaps the greatest was to the cause of isolationism. Many who had been former isolationists now supported an all-out American effort. After the surprise attack, isolationist senator Burton Wheeler proclaimed, "The only thing now to do is to lick the hell out of them."

ECONOMIC BACKGROUND

WAR AND THE DEPRESSION

The approach of war did what all the programs of the New Deal could not do—end the Great Depression. As defense spending skyrocketed in 1940, long-idle factories came back to life. A merry-go-round company began producing gun mounts; a stove factory made lifeboats; a famous New York toy maker made compasses; a pinball-machine company made armor-piercing shells.

With factories hiring again, the nation's unemployment rolls began shrinking rapidly—by 400,000 in August 1940 and by another 500,000 in September. By the time the Japanese attacked Pearl Harbor, America was heading back to work. (See *Keynesian Economics* on page R42 in the Economics Handbook.)

SECTION 4 ASSESSMENT

1. **TERMS & NAMES** For each term or name, write a sentence explaining its significance.
   - **Axis powers**
   - **Lend-Lease Act**
   - **Atlantic Charter**
   - **Allies**
   - **Hideki Tojo**

MAIN IDEA

2. **TAKING NOTES**
   Create a time line of key events leading to America's entry into World War II. Use the dates below as a guide.

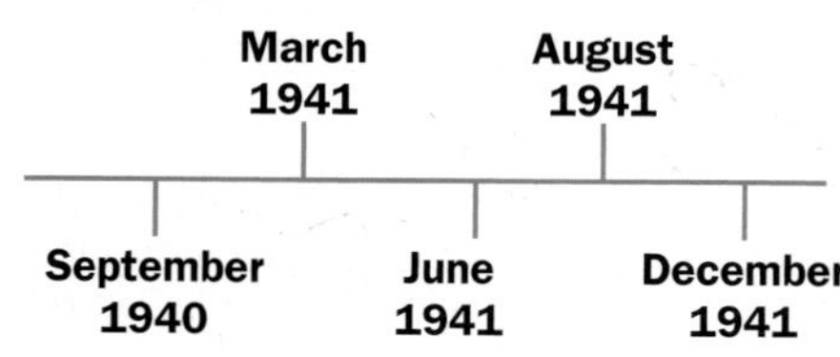

   Which of the events that you listed was most influential in bringing the United States into the war? Why?

CRITICAL THINKING

3. **EVALUATING DECISIONS**
   Do you think that the United States should have waited to be attacked before declaring war? **Think About:**
   - the reputation of the United States
   - the influence of isolationists
   - the events at Pearl Harbor

4. **PREDICTING EFFECTS**
   What problem would the Japanese attack on Pearl Harbor solve for Roosevelt? What new problems would it create?

5. **ANALYZING PRIMARY SOURCES**
   Although the U.S. Congress was still unwilling to declare war early in 1941, Churchill told his war cabinet,

   > **"We must have patience and trust to the tide which is flowing our way, and to events."**

   What do you think Churchill meant by this remark? Support your answer.

CHAPTER 16 ASSESSMENT

VISUAL SUMMARY

WORLD WAR LOOMS

1931
1931 Japan invades Manchuria.

1932
1932 Nazi Party becomes the most powerful in Germany.

1933
Mar. 1933 First concentration camp opens at Oranienburg. Adolf Hitler becomes dictator of Germany.

1934

1935
Sept. 1935 Nuremberg Laws instituted against Jews in Germany.
Oct. 1935 Italian troops invade Ethiopia.

1936
Mar. 1936 Germany occupies Rhineland.
Jul. 1936 Spanish Civil War begins.
Oct. 1936 Germany and Italy form Axis.

1937
1937 Japan invades China.

1938
Nov. 1938 *Kristallnacht,* Night of Broken Glass, Nazis destroy property and arrest over 20,000 Jews.

1939
Mar. 1939 Germany seizes all of Czechoslovakia.
Sept. 1939 Germany invades Poland. Britain and France declare war on Germany and World War II begins.

1940
June 1940 France surrenders.
Sept. 1940 Japan signs tripartite pact with Germany and Italy.

1941
Mar. 1941 Roosevelt signs the Lend-Lease Act.
Jun. 1941 Nazis begin mass murder of the Jews.
Dec. 1941 Pearl Harbor is bombed. U.S. declares war.

TERMS & NAMES

For each term or name below, write a sentence explaining its significance in U.S. foreign affairs between 1931 and 1941.

1. fascism
2. Adolf Hitler
3. Nazism
4. Winston Churchill
5. appeasement
6. Charles de Gaulle
7. Holocaust
8. genocide
9. Axis powers
10. Allies

MAIN IDEAS

Use your notes and the information in the chapter to answer the following questions about the early years of World War II.

Dictators Threaten World Peace *(pages 528–535)*

1. What were Stalin's goals and what steps did he take to achieve them?
2. How did Germany's and Italy's involvement affect the outcome of the Spanish Civil War?

War in Europe *(pages 536–541)*

3. Why was the blitzkrieg effective?
4. What terms of surrender did Hitler demand of the French after the fall of France in 1940? What was General Charles de Gaulle's reaction?

The Holocaust *(pages 542–549)*

5. What groups did Nazis deem unfit to belong to the Aryan "master race"?
6. How did some Europeans show their resistance to Nazi persecution of the Jews?

America Moves Toward War *(pages 550–557)*

7. What congressional measures paved the way for the U.S. entry into World War II?
8. Why did the United States enter World War II?

CRITICAL THINKING

1. **USING YOUR NOTES** In a chart like the one shown, identify the effects of each of these early events of World War II.

Cause	Effect
First blitzkrieg	
Allies stranded at Dunkirk	
British radar detects German aircraft	
Lend-Lease Act	

2. **COMPARING** Compare the ways in which Hitler, Churchill, and Roosevelt used their powers as gifted speakers to accomplish their political aims during World War II. Use details from the chapter text.

3. **INTERPRETING MAPS** Look at the map of German advances on page 538. How might Poland's location have influenced the secret pact that Germany and the Soviet Union signed on August 23, 1939?

Standardized Test Practice

Use the cartoon and your knowledge of U.S. history to answer questions 1 and 2.

I HOPE YOU HAVE BETTER LUCK THAN I DID
WILSON
U.S. NEUTRALI
F.D.R.

1. All of the following are true of F.D.R.'s neutrality policy *except* —
   - **A** Roosevelt found it hard to keep the United States neutral.
   - **B** Roosevelt did not always enforce the Neutrality Acts.
   - **C** Roosevelt promoted the Neutrality Policy of the United States throughout the war.
   - **D** Roosevelt spoke out against isolationism.

2. President Wilson's image rises above President Roosevelt to wish him luck for —
   - **F** helping to pass the bill he is signing.
   - **G** keeping the United States out of a war.
   - **H** winning the next presidential election.
   - **J** gaining greater revenues from Europe.

Use the quotation and your knowledge of U.S. history to answer question 3.

"In the future days, which we seek to make secure, we look forward to a world founded upon four essential human freedoms. The first is freedom of speech and expression. —everywhere in the world. The second is freedom of every person to worship God in his own way. —everywhere in the world. The third is freedom from want. . . . The fourth is freedom from fear."

—Franklin Roosevelt, Address to Congress, 1941

3. The "four freedoms" speech helped gain widespread support in the United States for —
   - **A** increasing aid to the Allies.
   - **B** decreasing immigration.
   - **C** a military and arms buildup.
   - **D** a presidential election.

ADDITIONAL TEST PRACTICE, pages S1–S33.

TEST PRACTICE

CLASSZONE.COM

ALTERNATIVE ASSESSMENT

1. **INTERACT WITH HISTORY** Recall your discussion of the question on page 527:

Why might the United States try to remain neutral?

As a political cartoonist for a major newspaper, your work is seen by millions of Americans. Draw a political cartoon that supports or opposes the policy of neutrality.

2. **VIDEO** **LEARNING FROM MEDIA** View the *American Stories* video, "Escaping the Final Solution: Kurt Klein and Gerda Weissmann Klein Remember the Holocaust."

- What conditions that Gerda faced would be most difficult for you to endure?

Cooperative Learning Activity It has been said, "Those who cannot remember the past are condemned to repeat it."

As a group, collect quotations and historical data about the Holocaust. Then write a book introduction about the Holocaust that incorporates quotations and the importance of the first-person accounts of survivors, such as the Kleins.

The United States in World War II

The raid on Pearl Harbor disabled the bulk of the U.S. fleet, including *(left to right)* the *West Virginia, Tennessee,* and *Arizona.*

USA

1941 The Japanese bomb Pearl Harbor.

1941 A. Philip Randolph demands that war industries hire African Americans.

1942 Roosevelt creates the War Production Board to coordinate mobilization.

1942 Japanese Americans are sent to relocation centers.

1941 | **1942**

WORLD

1941 Hitler invades the Soviet Union.

1942 In the Pacific, the Battle of Midway turns the tide in favor of the Allies.

1942 Nazis develop the "final solution" for exterminating Jews.

INTERACT WITH HISTORY

It is December of 1941. After Japan's attack on Pearl Harbor, the U.S. has entered the war. As a citizen, you and millions like you must mobilize a depressed peacetime country for war. The United States must produce the workers, soldiers, weapons, and equipment that will help to win the war.

How can the United States use its resources to achieve victory?

Examine the Issues

- How can the government encourage businesses to convert to wartime production?
- What sacrifices will you and your family be willing to make?
- How can the military attract recruits?

RESEARCH LINKS CLASSZONE.COM

Visit the Chapter 17 links for more information about The United States in World War II.

1943 Zoot-suit riots rock Los Angeles.

1944 GI Bill of Rights is passed.

1944 President Roosevelt is elected to a fourth term.

1945 U.S. Marines take Iwo Jima.

1945 Harry S. Truman becomes president when Roosevelt dies.

1943 | **1944** | **1945**

1943 Rommel's forces surrender in North Africa.

1944 On June 6, the Allies launch a massive invasion of Europe.

1945 Nazi retreat begins after the Battle of the Bulge.

1945 Japan surrenders after atomic bombing of Hiroshima and Nagasaki.

Mobilizing for Defense

MAIN IDEA

Following the attack on Pearl Harbor, the United States mobilized for war.

WHY IT MATTERS NOW

Military industries in the United States today are a major part of the American economy.

Terms & Names

- **George Marshall**
- **Women's Auxiliary Army Corp (WAAC)**
- **A. Philip Randolph**
- **Manhattan Project**
- **Office of Price Administration (OPA)**
- **War Production Board (WPB)**
- **rationing**

One American's Story

Charles Swanson looked all over his army base for a tape recorder on which to play the tape his wife had sent him for Christmas. "In desperation," he later recalled, "I had it played over the public-address system. It was a little embarrassing to have the whole company hear it, but it made everyone long for home."

A PERSONAL VOICE MRS. CHARLES SWANSON

"Merry Christmas, honey. Surprised? I'm so glad I have a chance to say hello to you this way on our first Christmas apart. . . . About our little girl. . . . She is just big enough to fill my heart and strong enough to help Mommy bear this ache of loneliness. . . . Her dearest treasure is her daddy's picture. It's all marked with tiny handprints, and the glass is always cloudy from so much loving and kissing. I'm hoping you'll be listening to this on Christmas Eve, somewhere over there, your heart full of hope, faith and courage, knowing each day will bring that next Christmas together one day nearer."

—quoted in *We Pulled Together . . . and Won!*

▲ **Mrs. Charles Swanson and her daughter, Lynne, with a picture of her husband.**

As the United States began to mobilize for war, the Swansons, like most Americans, had few illusions as to what lay ahead. It would be a time filled with hard work, hope, sacrifice, and sorrow.

Americans Join the War Effort

The Japanese had attacked Pearl Harbor with the expectation that once Americans had experienced Japan's power, they would shrink from further conflict. The day after the raid, the *Japan Times* boasted that the United States, now reduced to a third-rate power, was "trembling in her shoes." But if Americans were trembling, it was with rage, not fear. Uniting under the battle cry "Remember Pearl Harbor!" they set out to prove Japan wrong.

SELECTIVE SERVICE AND THE GI After Pearl Harbor, eager young Americans jammed recruiting offices. "I wanted to be a hero, let's face it," admitted Roger Tuttrup. "I was havin' trouble in school. . . . The war'd been goin' on for two years. I didn't wanna miss it. . . . I was an American. I was seventeen."

Even the 5 million who volunteered for military service, however, were not enough to face the challenge of an all-out war on two global fronts—Europe and the Pacific. The Selective Service System expanded the draft and eventually provided another 10 million soldiers to meet the armed forces' needs.

Background
The initials *GI* originally stood for "galvanized iron" but were later reinterpreted as "government issue," meaning uniforms and supplies. In time, the abbreviation came to stand for American soldiers.

▲ **In March 1941, a group of African-American men in New York City enlisted in the United States Army Air Corps. This was the first time the Army Air Corps opened its enlistment to African Americans.**

The volunteers and draftees reported to military bases around the country for eight weeks of basic training. In this short period, seasoned sergeants did their best to turn raw recruits into disciplined, battle-ready GIs.

According to Sergeant Debs Myers, however, there was more to basic training than teaching a recruit how to stand at attention, march in step, handle a rifle, and follow orders.

A PERSONAL VOICE SERGEANT DEBS MYERS

"**The civilian went before the Army doctors, took off his clothes, feeling silly; jigged, stooped, squatted, wet into a bottle; became a soldier. He learned how to sleep in the mud, tie a knot, kill a man. He learned the ache of loneliness, the ache of exhaustion, the kinship of misery. He learned that men make the same queasy noises in the morning, feel the same longings at night; that every man is alike and that each man is different.**"

—quoted in *The GI War: 1941–1945*

EXPANDING THE MILITARY The military's work force needs were so great that Army Chief of Staff General **George Marshall** pushed for the formation of a **Women's Auxiliary Army Corps (WAAC).** "There are innumerable duties now being performed by soldiers that can be done better by women," Marshall said in support of a bill to establish the Women's Auxiliary Army Corps. Under this bill, women volunteers would serve in noncombat positions.

Despite opposition from some members of Congress who scorned the bill as "the silliest piece of legislation" they had ever seen, the bill establishing the WAAC became law on May 15, 1942. The law gave the WAACs an official status and salary but few of the benefits granted to male soldiers. In July 1943, after thousands of women had enlisted, the U.S. Army dropped the "auxiliary" status, and granted WACs full U.S. Army benefits. WACs worked as nurses, ambulance drivers, radio operators, electricians, and pilots—nearly every duty not involving direct combat.

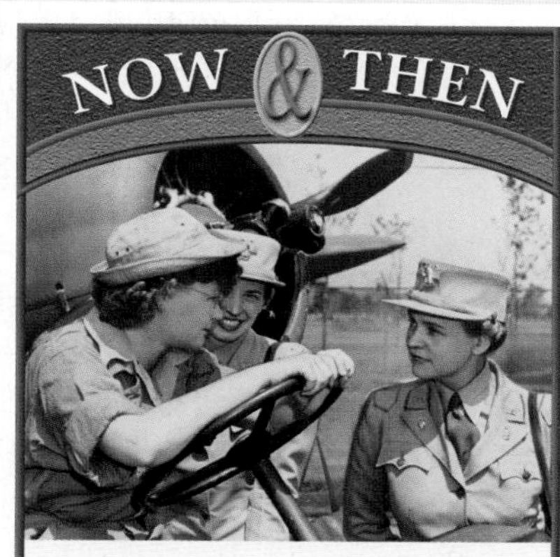

WOMEN IN THE MILITARY

A few weeks after the bill to establish the Women's Auxiliary Army Corps (WAAC) had become law, Oveta Culp Hobby *(shown, far right)*, a Texas newspaper executive and the first director of the WAAC, put out a call for recruits. More than 13,000 women applied on the first day. In all, some 350,000 women served in this and other auxiliary branches during the war.

The WAC remained a separate unit of the army until 1978 when male and female forces were integrated. In 2001, almost 200,000 women served in the United States armed forces.

RECRUITING AND DISCRIMINATION For many minority groups—especially African Americans, Native Americans, Mexican Americans, and Asian Americans—the war created new dilemmas. Restricted to racially segregated neighborhoods and reservations and denied basic citizenship rights, some members of these groups questioned whether this was their war to fight. "Why die for democracy for some foreign country when we don't even have it here?" asked an editorial in an African-American newspaper. On receiving his draft notice, an African American responded unhappily, "Just carve on my tombstone, 'Here lies a black man killed fighting a yellow man for the protection of a white man.'"

DRAMATIC CONTRIBUTIONS Despite discrimination in the military, more than 300,000 Mexican Americans joined the armed forces. While Mexican Americans in Los Angeles made up only a tenth of the city's population, they suffered a fifth of the city's wartime casualties.

About one million African Americans also served in the military. African-American soldiers lived and worked in segregated units and were limited mostly to noncombat roles. After much protest, African Americans did finally see combat beginning in April 1943.

Asian Americans took part in the struggle as well. More than 13,000 Chinese Americans, or about one of every five adult males, joined the armed forces. In addition, 33,000 Japanese Americans put on uniforms. Of these, several thousand volunteered to serve as spies and interpreters in the Pacific war. "During battles," wrote an admiring officer, "they crawled up close enough to be able to hear [Japanese] officers' commands and to make verbal translations to our soldiers."

Some 25,000 Native Americans enlisted in the armed services, too, including 800 women. Their willingness to serve led *The Saturday Evening Post* to comment, "We would not need the Selective Service if all volunteered like Indians." (A)

MAIN IDEA

Contrasting
(A) How did the American response to the Japanese raid on Pearl Harbor differ from Japanese expectations?

A Production Miracle

Early in February 1942, American newspapers reported the end of automobile production for private use. The last car to roll off an automaker's assembly line was a gray sedan with "victory trim,"—that is, without chrome-plated parts. This was just one more sign that the war would affect almost every aspect of life.

THE INDUSTRIAL RESPONSE Within weeks of the shutdown in production, the nation's automobile plants had been retooled to produce tanks, planes, boats, and

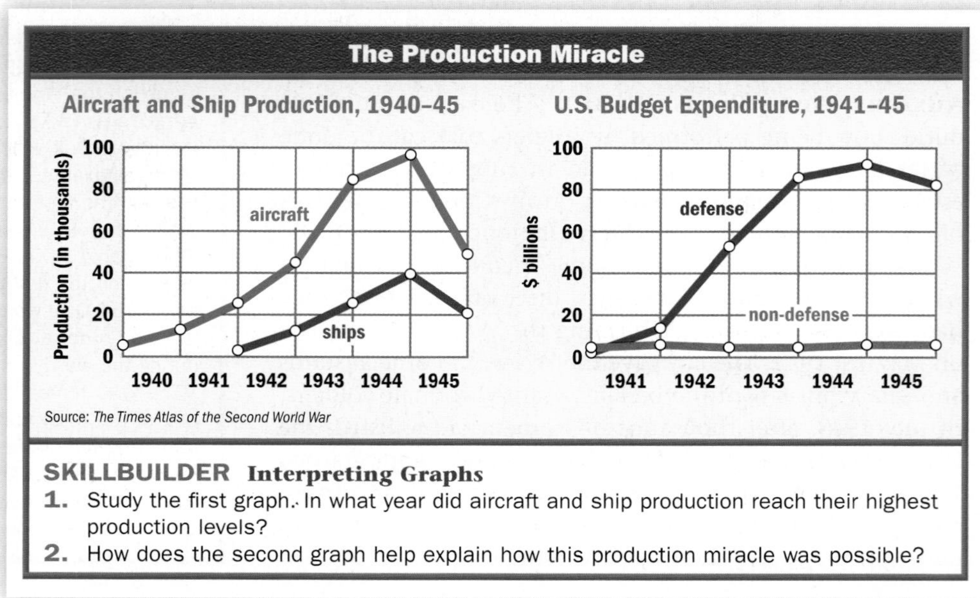

SKILLBUILDER Interpreting Graphs
1. Study the first graph. In what year did aircraft and ship production reach their highest production levels?
2. How does the second graph help explain how this production miracle was possible?

command cars. They were not alone. Across the nation, factories were quickly converted to war production. A maker of mechanical pencils turned out bomb parts. A bedspread manufacturer made mosquito netting. A soft-drink company converted from filling bottles with liquid to filling shells with explosives.

Meanwhile, shipyards and defense plants expanded with dizzying speed. By the end of 1942, industrialist Henry J. Kaiser had built seven massive new shipyards that turned out Liberty ships (cargo carriers), tankers, troop transports, and "baby" aircraft carriers at an astonishing rate. Late that year, Kaiser invited reporters to Way One in his Richmond, California, shipyard to watch as his workers assembled *Hull 440*, a Liberty ship, in a record-breaking four days. Writer Alyce Mano Kramer described the first day and night of construction.

A PERSONAL VOICE ALYCE MANO KRAMER

"At the stroke of 12, Way One exploded into life. Crews of workers, like a champion football team, swarmed into their places in the line. Within 60 seconds, the keel was swinging into position. . . . *Hull 440* was going up. The speed of [production] was unbelievable. At midnight, Saturday, an empty way—at midnight Sunday, a full-grown hull met the eyes of graveyard workers as they came on shift."

—quoted in *Home Front, U.S.A.*

Before the fourth day was up, 25,000 amazed spectators watched as *Hull 440* slid into the water. How could such a ship be built so fast? Kaiser used prefabricated, or factory-made, parts that could be quickly assembled at his shipyards. Equally important were his workers, who worked at record speeds.

LABOR'S CONTRIBUTION When the war began, defense contractors warned the Selective Service System that the nation did not have enough workers to meet both its military and its industrial needs. They were wrong. By 1944, despite the draft, nearly 18 million workers were laboring in war industries, three times as many as in 1941.

More than 6 million of these new workers were women. At first, war industries feared that most women lacked the necessary stamina for factory work and were reluctant to hire them. But once women proved they could operate welding torches or riveting guns as well as men, employers could not hire enough of them—especially since women earned only about 60 percent as much as men doing the same jobs.

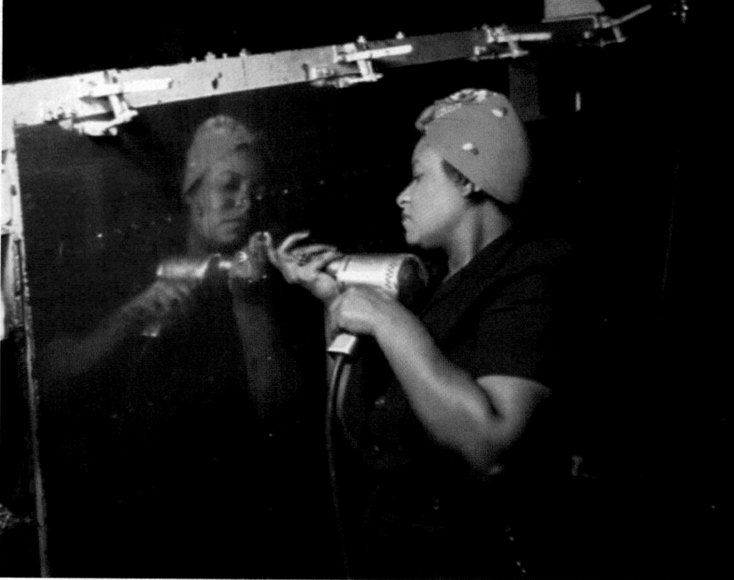

▲ During the war, women took many jobs previously held by men. In this 1943 photo, a young woman is seen operating a hand drill in Nashville, Tennessee.

Defense plants also hired more than 2 million minority workers during the war years. Like women, minorities faced strong prejudice at first. Before the war, 75 percent of defense contractors simply refused to hire African Americans, while another 15 percent employed them only in menial jobs. "Negroes will be considered only as janitors," declared the general manager of North American Aviation. "It is the company policy not to employ them as mechanics and aircraft workers." B

MAIN IDEA

Forming Generalizations

B What difficulties did women and minorities face in the wartime work force?

To protest such discrimination both in the military and in industry, **A. Philip Randolph,** president and founder of the Brotherhood of Sleeping Car Porters and the nation's most respected African-American labor leader, organized a march on Washington. Randolph called on African Americans everywhere to come to the capital on July 1, 1941, and to march under the banner "We Loyal Colored Americans Demand the Right to Work and Fight for Our Country."

Fearing that the march might provoke white resentment or violence, President Roosevelt called Randolph to the White House and asked him to back down. "I'm sorry Mr. President," the labor leader said, "the march cannot be called off." Roosevelt then asked, "How many people do you plan to bring?" Randolph replied, "One hundred thousand, Mr. President." Roosevelt was stunned. Even half that number of African-American protesters would be far more than Washington—still a very segregated city—could feed, house, and transport.

▲ **A. Philip Randolph in 1942.**

In the end it was Roosevelt, not Randolph, who backed down. In return for Randolph's promise to cancel the march, the president issued an executive order calling on employers and labor unions "to provide for the full and equitable participation of all workers in defense industries, without discrimination because of race, creed, color, or national origin."

History Through *Film*

HOLLYWOOD HELPS MOBILIZATION

In the aftermath of Pearl Harbor, Hollywood churned out war-oriented propaganda films. Heroic movies like *Mission to Moscow* and *Song of Russia* glorified America's new wartime ally, the Soviet Union. On the other hand, "hiss-and-boo" films stirred up hatred against the Nazis. In this way, movies energized people to join the war effort.

As the war dragged on, people grew tired of propaganda and war themes. Hollywood responded with musicals, romances, and other escapist fare designed to take filmgoers away from the grim realities of war, if only for an hour or two.

▲ **Moviemakers also turned out informational films. The most important of these films—the *Why We Fight* series—were made by the great director Frank Capra. Capra is shown (*right*) consulting with Colonel Hugh Stewart (commander of the British Army film unit) in a joint effort in the making of *Tunisian Victory*, the first official film record of the campaign that expelled Germany from North Africa.**

▲ ***Hitler, Beast of Berlin*, produced in 1939, was one of the most popular hiss-and-boo films. Viewing audiences watched in rage as the Nazis conducted one horrible act after another.**

SKILLBUILDER Interpeting Visual Sources

1. How does the image from *Hitler, Beast of Berlin* portray the Nazis?
2. How might audiences have responded to propaganda films?

SEE SKILLBUILDER HANDBOOK, PAGE R23.

MOBILIZATION OF SCIENTISTS That same year, in 1941, Roosevelt created the Office of Scientific Research and Development (OSRD) to bring scientists into the war effort. The OSRD spurred improvements in radar and sonar, new technologies for locating submarines underwater. It encouraged the use of pesticides like DDT to fight insects. As a result, U.S. soldiers were probably the first in history to be relatively free from body lice. The OSRD also pushed the development of "miracle drugs," such as penicillin, that saved countless lives on and off the battlefield.

The most significant achievement of the OSRD, however, was the secret development of a new weapon, the atomic bomb. Interest in such a weapon began in 1939, after German scientists succeeded in splitting uranium atoms, releasing an enormous amount of energy. This news prompted physicist and German refugee Albert Einstein to write a letter to President Roosevelt, warning that the Germans could use their discovery to construct a weapon of enormous destructive power.

MAIN IDEA

Summarizing
C Why did President Roosevelt create the OSRD, and what did it do?

Roosevelt responded by creating an Advisory Committee on Uranium to study the new discovery. In 1941, the committee reported that it would take from three to five years to build an atomic bomb. Hoping to shorten that time, the OSRD set up an intensive program in 1942 to develop a bomb as quickly as possible. Because much of the early research was performed at Columbia University in Manhattan, the **Manhattan Project** became the code name for research work that extended across the country. **C**

The Federal Government Takes Control

As war production increased, there were fewer consumer products available for purchase. Much factory production was earmarked for the war. With demand increasing and supplies dropping, prices seemed likely to shoot upwards.

ECONOMIC CONTROLS Roosevelt responded to this threat by creating the **Office of Price Administration (OPA).** The OPA fought inflation by freezing prices on most goods. Congress also raised income tax rates and extended the tax to millions of people who had never paid it before. The higher taxes reduced consumer demand on scarce goods by leaving workers with less to spend. In addition,

The Government Takes Control of the Economy, 1942–1945

Agencies and Laws	What the Regulations Did
Office of Price Administration (OPA)	• Fought inflation by freezing wages, prices, and rents • Rationed foods, such as meat, butter, cheese, vegetables, sugar, and coffee
National War Labor Board (NWLB)	• Limited wage increases • Allowed negotiated benefits, such as paid vacation, pensions, and medical insurance • Kept unions stable by forbidding workers to change unions
War Production Board (WPB)	• Rationed fuel and materials vital to the war effort, such as gasoline, heating oil, metals, rubber, and plastics
Department of the Treasury	• Issued war bonds to raise money for the war effort and to fight inflation
Revenue Act of 1942	• Raised the top personal-income tax rate to 88% • Added lower- and middle-income Americans to the income-tax rolls
Smith-Connally Anti-Strike Act (1943)	• Limited the right to strike in industries crucial to the war effort • Gave the president power to take over striking plants

▲ Boys using pots and pans as helmets and drums encourage New Yorkers to donate aluminum to the war effort

the government encouraged Americans to use their extra cash to buy war bonds. As a result of these measures, inflation remained below 30 percent—about half that of World War I—for the entire period of World War II.

Besides controlling inflation, the government needed to ensure that the armed forces and war industries received the resources they needed to win the war. The **War Production Board (WPB)** assumed that responsibility. The WPB decided which companies would convert from peacetime to wartime production and allocated raw materials to key industries. The WPB also organized nationwide drives to collect scrap iron, tin cans, paper, rags, and cooking fat for recycling into war goods. Across America, children scoured attics, cellars, garages, vacant lots, and back alleys, looking for useful junk. During one five-month-long paper drive in Chicago, schoolchildren collected 36 million pounds of old paper—about 65 pounds per child. D

MAIN IDEA

Identifying Problems

D What basic problems were the OPA and WPB created to solve?

RATIONING In addition, the OPA set up a system for **rationing,** or establishing fixed allotments of goods deemed essential for the military. Under this system, households received ration books with coupons to be used for buying such scarce goods as meat, shoes, sugar, coffee, and gasoline. Gas rationing was particularly hard on those who lived in western regions, where driving was the only way to get around. First Lady Eleanor Roosevelt sympathized with their complaints. "To tell the people in the West not to use their cars," she observed, "means that these people may never see another soul for weeks and weeks nor have a way of getting a sick person to a doctor."

Most Americans accepted rationing as a personal contribution to the war effort. Workers carpooled or rode bicycles. Families coped with shortages of everything from tires to toys. Inevitably, some cheated by hoarding scarce goods or by purchasing them through the "black market," where rationed items could be bought illegally without coupons at inflated prices.

While people tightened their belts at home, millions of other Americans put their lives on the line in air, sea, and land battles on the other side of the world.

SECTION 1 ASSESSMENT

1. **TERMS & NAMES** For each term or name, write a sentence explaining its significance.
   - **George Marshall**
   - **Women's Auxiliary Army Corp (WAAC)**
   - **A. Philip Randolph**
   - **Manhattan Project**
   - **Office of Price Administration (OPA)**
   - **War Production Board (WPB)**
   - **rationing**

MAIN IDEA

2. **TAKING NOTES**
   Re-create the web below on your paper, and fill in ways that America prepared for war.

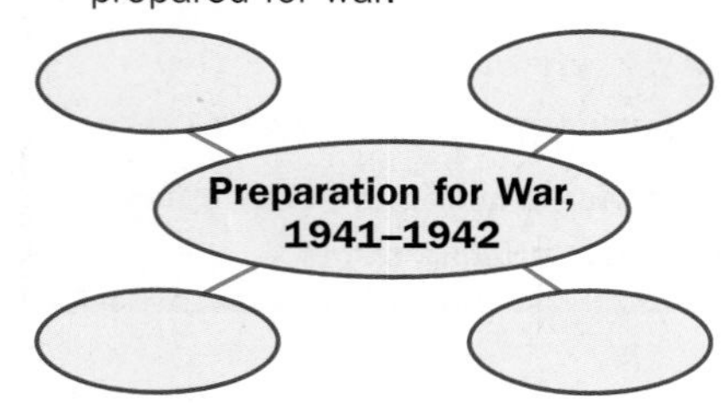

CRITICAL THINKING

3. **ANALYZING EVENTS**
   How did government regulations impact the lives of civilians?

4. **ANALYZING VISUAL SOURCES**
   What is the message of the World War II poster to the right? Why was this message important?

When you ride ALONE you ride with Hitler!
Join a Car-Sharing Club TODAY!

The War for Europe and North Africa

MAIN IDEA

Allied forces, led by the United States and Great Britain, battled Axis powers for control of Europe and North Africa.

WHY IT MATTERS NOW

During World War II, the United States assumed a leading role in world affairs that continues today.

Terms & Names

- **Dwight D. Eisenhower**
- **D-Day**
- **Omar Bradley**
- **George Patton**
- **Battle of the Bulge**
- **V-E Day**
- **Harry S. Truman**

One American's Story

It was 1951, and John Patrick McGrath was just finishing his second year in drama school. For an acting class, his final exam was to be a performance of a death scene. McGrath knew his lines perfectly. But as he began the final farewell, he broke out in a sweat and bolted off the stage. Suddenly he had a flashback to a frozen meadow in Belgium during the Battle of the Bulge in 1945. Three German tanks were spraying his platoon with machine-gun fire.

A PERSONAL VOICE JOHN PATRICK MCGRATH

"Only a few feet away, one of the men in my platoon falls. . . . He calls out to me. 'Don't leave me. Don't. . . .' The tanks advance, one straight for me. I grab my buddy by the wrist and pull him across the snow. . . . The tank nearest to us is on a track to run us down. . . . When the German tank is but 15 yards away, I grab my buddy by the wrist and feign a lurch to my right. The tank follows the move. Then I lurch back to my left. The German tank clamors by, only inches away. . . . In their wake the meadow is strewn with casualties. I turn to tend my fallen comrade. He is dead."

—*A Cue for Passion*

Private John P. McGrath carried this bullet-riddled letter in a pack that saved his life. In 1990, he visited Anzio, where members of his company were buried.

Like countless other soldiers, McGrath would never forget both the heroism and the horrors he witnessed while fighting to free Europe.

The United States and Britain Join Forces

"Now that we are, as you say, 'in the same boat,'" British Prime Minister Winston Churchill wired President Roosevelt two days after the Pearl Harbor attack, "would it not be wise for us to have another conference . . . . and the sooner the better." Roosevelt responded with an invitation for Churchill to come at once. So began a remarkable alliance between the two nations.

WAR PLANS Prime Minister Churchill arrived at the White House on December 22, 1941, and spent the next three weeks working out war plans with President Roosevelt and his advisors. Believing that Germany and Italy posed a greater threat than Japan, Churchill convinced Roosevelt to strike first against Hitler. Once the Allies had gained an upper hand in Europe, they could pour more resources into the Pacific War.

By the end of their meeting, Roosevelt and Churchill had formed, in Churchill's words, "a very strong affection, which grew with our years of comradeship." When Churchill reached London, he found a message from the president waiting for him. "It is fun," Roosevelt wrote in the message, "to be in the same decade with you."

THE BATTLE OF THE ATLANTIC After the attack on Pearl Harbor, Hitler ordered submarine raids against ships along America's east coast. The German aim in the Battle of the Atlantic was to prevent food and war materials from reaching Great Britain and the Soviet Union. Britain depended on supplies from the sea. The 3,000-mile-long shipping lanes from North America were her lifeline. Hitler knew that if he cut that lifeline, Britain would be starved into submission.

▲ A convoy of British and American ships ride at anchor in the harbor of Hvalfjord, Iceland.

For a long time, it looked as though Hitler might succeed in his mission. Unprotected American ships proved to be easy targets for the Germans. In the first four months of 1942, the Germans sank 87 ships off the Atlantic shore. Seven months into the year, German wolf packs had destroyed a total of 681 Allied ships in the Atlantic. Something had to be done or the war at sea would be lost.

The Allies responded by organizing their cargo ships into convoys. Convoys were groups of ships traveling together for mutual protection, as they had done in the First World War. The convoys were escorted across the Atlantic by destroyers equipped with sonar for detecting submarines underwater. They were also accompanied by airplanes that used radar to spot U-boats on the ocean's surface. With this improved tracking, the Allies were able to find and destroy German U-boats faster than the Germans could build them. In late spring of 1943, Admiral Karl Doenitz, the commander of the German U-boat offensive, reported that his losses had "reached an unbearable height."

At the same time, the United States launched a crash shipbuilding program. By early 1943, 140 Liberty ships were produced each month. Launchings of Allied ships began to outnumber sinkings.

By mid-1943, the tide of the Battle of the Atlantic had turned. A happy Churchill reported to the House of Commons that June "was the best month [at sea] from every point of view we have ever known in the whole 46 months of the war." (A)

MAIN IDEA

Analyzing Causes

(A) Why had the tide turned in the Battle of the Atlantic by mid-1943?

The Eastern Front and the Mediterranean

By the winter of 1943, the Allies began to see victories on land as well as sea. The first great turning point came in the Battle of Stalingrad.

THE BATTLE OF STALINGRAD The Germans had been fighting in the Soviet Union since June 1941. In November 1941, the bitter cold had stopped them in their tracks outside the Soviet cities of Moscow and Leningrad. When spring came, the German tanks were ready to roll.

In the summer of 1942, the Germans took the offensive in the southern Soviet Union. Hitler hoped to capture Soviet oil fields in the Caucasus Mountains. He also wanted to wipe out Stalingrad, a major industrial center on the Volga River. (See map, page 572.)

The German army confidently approached Stalingrad in August 1942. "To reach the Volga and take Stalingrad is not so difficult for us," one German soldier wrote home. "Victory is not far away." The Luftwaffe—the German air force—prepared the way with nightly bombing raids over the city. Nearly every wooden building in Stalingrad was set ablaze. The situation looked so desperate that Soviet officers in Stalingrad recommended blowing up the city's factories and abandoning the city. A furious Stalin ordered them to defend his namesake city no matter what the cost.

For weeks the Germans pressed in on Stalingrad, conquering it house by house in brutal hand-to-hand combat. By the end of September, they controlled nine-tenths of the city—or what was left of it. Then another winter set in. The Soviets saw the cold as an opportunity to roll fresh tanks across the frozen landscape and begin a massive counterattack. The Soviet army closed around Stalingrad, trapping the Germans in and around the city and cutting off their supplies. The Germans' situation was hopeless, but Hitler's orders came: "Stay and fight! I won't go back from the Volga."

The fighting continued as winter turned Stalingrad into a frozen wasteland. "We just lay in our holes and froze, knowing that 24 hours later and 48 hours later we should be shivering precisely as we were now," wrote a German soldier, Benno Zieser. "But there was now no hope whatsoever of relief, and that was the worst thing of all." The German commander surrendered on January 31, 1943. Two days later, his starving troops also surrendered.

MAIN IDEA

Synthesizing

B What two key decisions determined the final outcome at Stalingrad?

In defending Stalingrad, the Soviets lost a total of 1,100,000 soldiers—more than all American deaths during the entire war. Despite the staggering death toll, the Soviet victory marked a turning point in the war. From that point on, the Soviet army began to move westward toward Germany. **B**

Dazed, starved, and freezing, these German soldiers were taken prisoner after months of struggle. But they were the lucky ones. More than 230,000 of their comrades died in the Battle of Stalingrad. ▼

THE NORTH AFRICAN FRONT While the Battle of Stalingrad raged, Stalin pressured Britain and America to open a "second front" in Western Europe. He argued that an invasion across the English Channel would force Hitler to divert troops from the Soviet front. Churchill and Roosevelt didn't think the Allies had enough troops to attempt an invasion on European soil. Instead, they launched Operation Torch, an invasion of Axis-controlled North Africa, commanded by American General **Dwight D. Eisenhower.**

In November 1942, some 107,000 Allied troops, the great majority of them Americans, landed in Casablanca, Oran, and Algiers in North Africa. From there they sped eastward, chasing the Afrika Korps led by General Erwin Rommel, the legendary Desert Fox. After months of heavy fighting, the last of the Afrika Korps surrendered in May 1943. British general Harold Alexander sent a message to Churchill, reporting that "All enemy resistance has ceased. We are masters of the North African shores." American war correspondent Ernie Pyle caught the mood of the victorious troops. C

MAIN IDEA

Summarizing

C What was the outcome of the North African campaign?

American journalist Ernie Pyle, shown here in 1944, was one of the most famous war correspondents of World War II. ▼

A PERSONAL VOICE ERNIE PYLE

"This colossal German surrender has done more for American morale here than anything that could possibly have happened. Winning in battle is like winning at poker or catching lots of fish. . . . As a result, the hundreds of thousands of Americans in North Africa now are happy men."

—*Ernie's War: The Best of Ernie Pyle's World War II Dispatches*

World War II: Europe and Africa, 1942–1944

INTERACTIVE

Axis and Axis controlled
Allies
Neutral countries
Axis forces
Allied forces
Soviet forces
Major battles

November 8, 1942
Operation Torch

November 1942
Farthest Axis advance

May 13, 1943
Axis surrender of North Africa

GEOGRAPHY SKILLBUILDER

1. **Place** Which countries were neutral in 1942?
2. **Movement** What was the name of the invasion that the Allies launched in North Africa?

THE ITALIAN CAMPAIGN Even before the battle in North Africa was won, Roosevelt, Churchill, and their commanders met in Casablanca. At this meeting, the two leaders agreed to accept only the unconditional surrender of the Axis powers. That is, enemy nations would have to accept whatever terms of peace the Allies dictated. The two leaders also discussed where to strike next. The Americans argued that the best approach to victory was to assemble a massive invasion fleet in Britain and to launch it across the English Channel, through France, and into the heart of Germany. Churchill, however, thought it would be safer to first attack Italy.

The Italian campaign got off to a good start with the capture of Sicily in the summer of 1943. Stunned by their army's collapse in Sicily, the Italian government forced dictator Benito Mussolini to resign. On July 25, 1943, King Victor Emmanuel III summoned *Il Duce* (Italian for "the leader") to his palace, stripped him of power, and had him arrested. "At this moment," the king told Mussolini, "you are the most hated man in Italy." Italians began celebrating the end of the war.

Their cheers were premature. Hitler was determined to stop the Allies in Italy rather than fight on German soil. One of the hardest battles the Allies encountered in Europe was fought less than 40 miles from Rome. This battle, "Bloody Anzio," lasted four months—until the end of May 1944—and left about 25,000 Allied and 30,000 Axis casualties. During the year after Anzio, German armies continued to put up strong resistance. The effort to free Italy did not succeed until 1945, when Germany itself was close to collapse. D

MAIN IDEA

Analyzing Effects

D What were the results of the Italian campaign?

HEROES IN COMBAT Among the brave men who fought in Italy were pilots of the all-black 99th Pursuit Squadron—the Tuskegee Airmen. In Sicily, the squadron registered its first victory against an enemy aircraft and went on to more impressive strategic strikes against the German forces throughout Italy. The Tuskegee Airmen won two Distinguished Unit Citations (the military's highest commendation) for their outstanding aerial combat against the German Luftwaffe.

On May 31, 1943, the 99th Pursuit Squadron, the first group of African-American pilots trained at the Tuskegee Institute, arrived in North Africa. ▼

Another African-American unit to distinguish itself was the famous 92nd Infantry Division, nicknamed the Buffaloes. In just six months of fighting in Europe, the Buffaloes won 7 Legion of Merit awards, 65 Silver Stars, and 162 Bronze Stars for courage under fire.

Like African Americans, most Mexican Americans served in segregated units. Seventeen Mexican-American soldiers were awarded the Congressional Medal of Honor. An all-Mexican-American unit—Company E of the 141st Regiment, 36th Division—became one of the most decorated of the war.

Japanese Americans also served in Italy and North Africa. At the urging of General Delos Emmons, the army created the 100th Battalion, which consisted of 1,300 Hawaiian Nisei. (The word *Nisei* refers to American citizens whose parents had emigrated from Japan.) The 100th saw brutal combat and became known as the Purple Heart Battalion. Later the 100th was merged into the all-Nisei 442nd Regimental Combat Team. It became the most decorated unit in U.S. history.

The Allies Liberate Europe

Even as the Allies were battling for Italy in 1943, they had begun work on a dramatic plan to invade France and free Western Europe from the Nazis. The task of commanding Operation Overlord, as it was called, fell to American General Dwight D. ("Ike") Eisenhower.

D-DAY Under Eisenhower's direction in England, the Allies gathered a force of nearly 3 million British, American, and Canadian troops, together with mountains of military equipment and supplies. Eisenhower planned to attack Normandy in northern France. To keep their plans secret, the Allies set up a huge phantom army with its own headquarters and equipment. In radio messages they knew the Germans could read, Allied commanders sent orders to this make-believe army to attack the French port of Calais—150 miles away—where the English Channel is narrowest. As a result, Hitler ordered his generals to keep a large army at Calais.

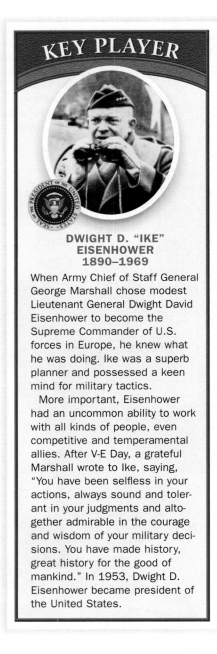

The Allied invasion, code-named Operation Overlord, was originally set for June 5, but bad weather forced a delay. Banking on a forecast for clearing skies, Eisenhower gave the go-ahead for **D-Day**—June 6, 1944, the first day of the invasion. Shortly after midnight, three divisions parachuted down behind German lines. They were followed in the early morning hours by thousands upon thousands of seaborne soldiers—the largest land-sea-air operation in army history.

Despite the massive air and sea bombardment by the Allies, German retaliation was brutal, particularly at Omaha Beach. "People were yelling, screaming, dying, running on the beach, equipment was flying everywhere, men were bleeding to death, crawling, lying everywhere, firing coming from all directions," soldier Felix Branham wrote of the scene there. "We dropped down behind anything that was the size of a golf ball."

THE ALLIES GAIN GROUND Despite heavy casualties, the Allies held the beachheads. After seven days of fighting, the Allies held an 80-mile strip of France. Within a month, they had landed a million troops, 567,000 tons of supplies, and 170,000 vehicles in France. On July 25, General **Omar Bradley** unleashed massive air and land bombardment against the enemy at St. Lô, providing a gap in the German line of defense through which General **George Patton** and his Third Army could advance. On August 23, Patton and the Third Army reached the Seine River south of Paris. Two days later, French resistance forces and American troops liberated the French capital from four years of German occupation. Parisians were delirious with joy. Patton announced this joyous event to his commander in a message that read, "Dear Ike: Today I spat in the Seine."

By September 1944, the Allies had freed France, Belgium, and Luxembourg. This good news—and the American people's desire not to "change horses in midstream"—helped elect Franklin Roosevelt to an unprecedented fourth term in November, along with his running mate, Senator Harry S. Truman. (E)

KEY PLAYER

DWIGHT D. "IKE" EISENHOWER 1890–1969

When Army Chief of Staff General George Marshall chose modest Lieutenant General Dwight David Eisenhower to become the Supreme Commander of U.S. forces in Europe, he knew what he was doing. Ike was a superb planner and possessed a keen mind for military tactics.

More important, Eisenhower had an uncommon ability to work with all kinds of people, even competitive and temperamental allies. After V-E Day, a grateful Marshall wrote to Ike, saying, "You have been selfless in your actions, always sound and tolerant in your judgments and altogether admirable in the courage and wisdom of your military decisions. You have made history, great history for the good of mankind." In 1953, Dwight D. Eisenhower became president of the United States.

Background
American paratroopers on D-Day carried a simple signaling device to help them find one another in the dark. Each had a metal toy cricket to click. No German radio operators could intercept these messages.

MAIN IDEA

Evaluating
(E) Was the Allied invasion of Europe successful? Explain your answer.

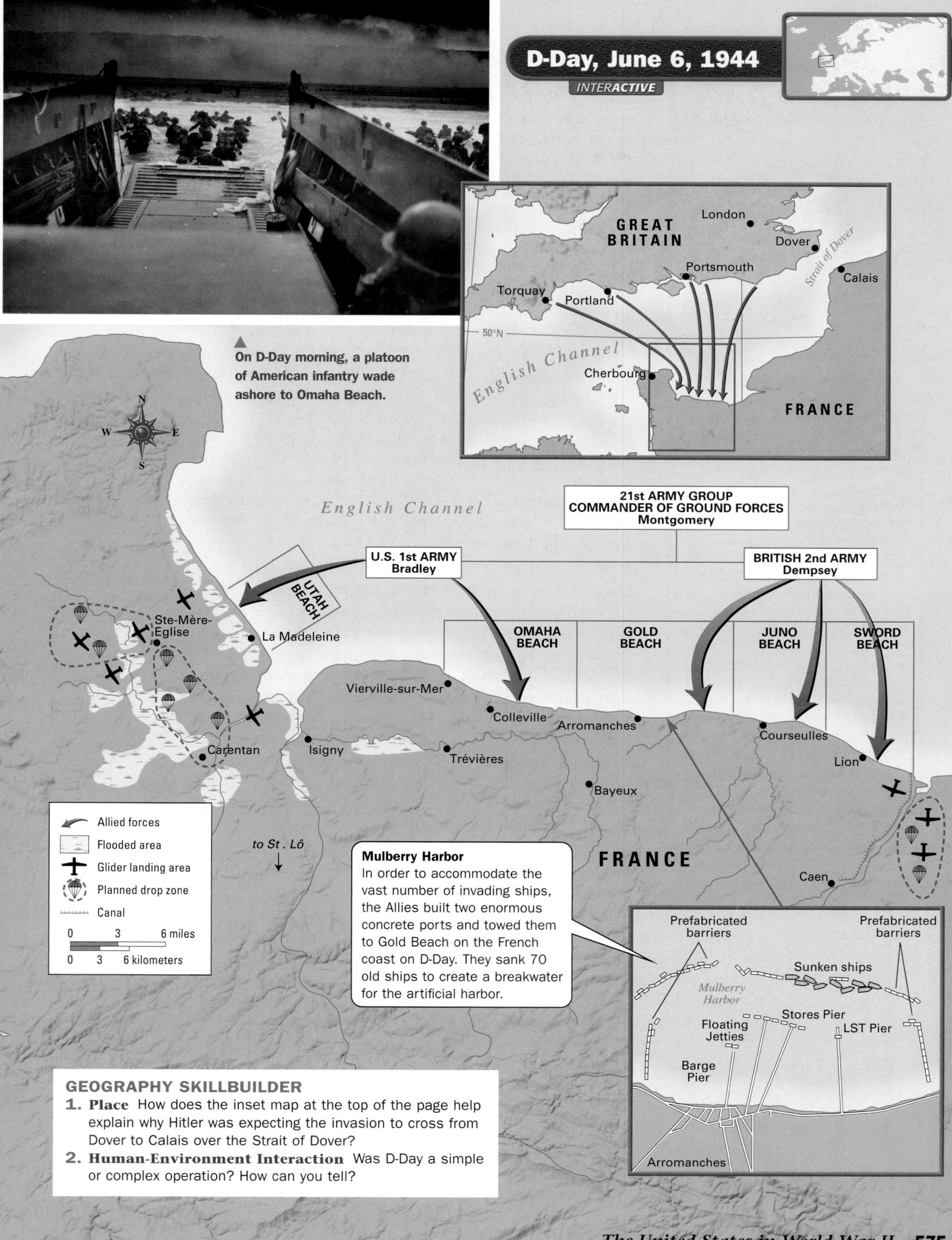

On D-Day morning, a platoon of American infantry wade ashore to Omaha Beach.

GEOGRAPHY SKILLBUILDER

1. **Place** How does the inset map at the top of the page help explain why Hitler was expecting the invasion to cross from Dover to Calais over the Strait of Dover?
2. **Human-Environment Interaction** Was D-Day a simple or complex operation? How can you tell?

HISTORICAL SPOTLIGHT

AUDIE MURPHY

Near the end of the Second World War, Audie Murphy became famous as the most decorated American soldier of the war. He received 24 medals from the United States—including the Congressional Medal of Honor. He was also awarded three medals by France and one more by Belgium.

Born in Kingston, Texas, Murphy enlisted in the army in 1942. He served in North Africa and Europe, and in 1944 he rose to the rank of second lieutenant. His most impressive act of bravery occurred in January 1945 near Colmar, France, when in the midst of a furious German attack, he jumped onto a burning tank destroyer and killed about 50 Axis troops with his machine gun. Although wounded in the leg, he rallied his troops to retake the ground the Germans had gained earlier in the day.

THE BATTLE OF THE BULGE In October 1944, Americans captured their first German town, Aachen. Hitler responded with a desperate last-gasp offensive. He ordered his troops to break through the Allied lines and to recapture the Belgian port of Antwerp. This bold move, the Führer hoped, would disrupt the enemy's supply lines and demoralize the Allies.

On December 16, under cover of dense fog, eight German tank divisions broke through weak American defenses along an 80-mile front. Hitler hoped that a victory would split American and British forces and break up Allied supply lines. Tanks drove 60 miles into Allied territory, creating a bulge in the lines that gave this desperate last-ditch offensive its name, the **Battle of the Bulge.** As the Germans swept westward, they captured 120 American GIs near Malmédy. Elite German troops—the SS troopers—herded the prisoners into a large field and mowed them down with machine guns and pistols.

Vocabulary
elite: a small and privileged group

The battle raged for a month. When it was over, the Germans had been pushed back, and little seemed to have changed. But, in fact, events had taken a decisive turn. The Germans had lost 120,000 troops, 600 tanks and assault guns, and 1,600 planes in the Battle of the Bulge—soldiers and weapons they could not replace. From that point on, the Nazis could do little but retreat. (F)

MAIN IDEA

Analyzing Effects
(F) Why was the Battle of the Bulge important?

LIBERATION OF THE DEATH CAMPS Meanwhile, Allied troops pressed eastward into the German heartland, and the Soviet army pushed westward across Poland toward Berlin. Soviet troops were the first to come upon one of the Nazi death camps, in July 1944. As the Soviets drew near a camp called Majdanek in Poland, SS guards worked feverishly to bury and burn all evidence of their hideous crimes. But they ran out of time. When the Soviets entered Majdanek, they found a thousand starving prisoners barely alive, the world's largest crematorium, and a storehouse containing 800,000 shoes. "This is not a concentration camp," reported a stunned Soviet war correspondent, "it is a gigantic murder plant." The Americans who later liberated Nazi death camps in Germany were equally horrified.

A PERSONAL VOICE ROBERT T. JOHNSON

"We started smelling a terrible odor and suddenly we were at the concentration camp at Landsberg. Forced the gate and faced hundreds of starving prisoners. . . . We saw emaciated men whose thighs were smaller than wrists, many had bones sticking out thru their skin. . . . Also we saw hundreds of burned and naked bodies. . . . That evening I wrote my wife that 'For the first time I truly realized the evil of Hitler and why this war had to be waged.'"

—quoted in *Voices: Letters from World War II*

UNCONDITIONAL SURRENDER By April 25, 1945, the Soviet army had stormed Berlin. As Soviet shells burst overhead, the city panicked. "Hordes of soldiers stationed in Berlin deserted and were shot on the spot or hanged from the nearest tree," wrote Claus Fuhrmann, a Berlin clerk. "On their chests they had placards reading, 'We betrayed the Führer.'"

In his underground headquarters in Berlin, Hitler prepared for the end. On April 29, he married Eva Braun, his longtime companion. The same day, he wrote out his last address to the German people. In it he blamed the Jews for starting the war and his generals for losing it. "I die with a happy heart aware of the immeasurable deeds of our soldiers at the front. I myself and my wife choose to die in order to escape the disgrace of . . . capitulation," he said. The next day Hitler shot himself while his new wife swallowed poison. In accordance with Hitler's orders, the two bodies were carried outside, soaked with gasoline, and burned.

Vocabulary
capitulation: surrender

▲ **New Yorkers celebrate V-E Day with a massive party that began in Times Square and went on for days at sites throughout the city.**

A week later, General Eisenhower accepted the unconditional surrender of the Third Reich. On May 8, 1945, the Allies celebrated **V-E Day**—Victory in Europe Day. The war in Europe was finally over.

ROOSEVELT'S DEATH President Roosevelt did not live to see V-E Day. On April 12, 1945, while posing for a portrait in Warm Springs, Georgia, the president had a stroke and died. That night, Vice President **Harry S. Truman** became the nation's 33rd president.

SECTION 2 ASSESSMENT

1. **TERMS & NAMES** For each term or name, write a sentence explaining its significance.
   - **Dwight D. Eisenhower**
   - **D-Day**
   - **Omar Bradley**
   - **George Patton**
   - **Battle of the Bulge**
   - **V-E Day**
   - **Harry S. Truman**

MAIN IDEA

2. **TAKING NOTES**
   Create a time line of the major events influencing the fighting in Europe and North Africa.

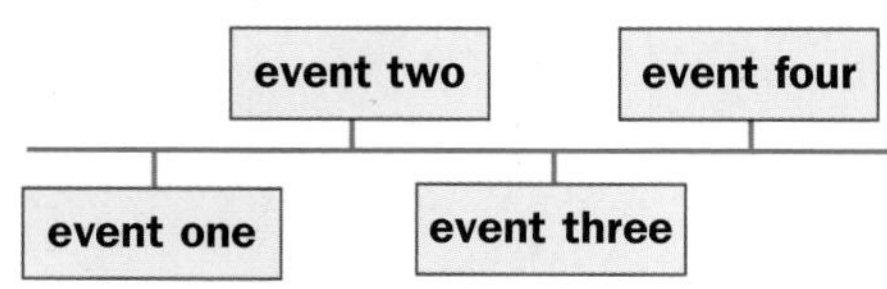

   Write a paragraph indicating how any two of these events are related.

CRITICAL THINKING

3. **EVALUATING DECISIONS**
   Do you agree with the decision made by Roosevelt and Churchill to require unconditional surrender by the Axis powers? Why or why not?
   Think About:
   - the advantages of defeating a foe decisively
   - the advantages of ending a war quickly
   - how other conflicts, such as the Civil War and World War I, ended

4. **ANALYZING PRIMARY SOURCES**
   When President Roosevelt's body was brought by train to Washington, Betty Conrad was among the servicewomen who escorted his casket.

   > **"The body in the casket was not only our leader but the bodies of all the men and women who had given their lives for freedom. They must not and will not have died in vain."**

   What did Roosevelt's body symbolize to Betty Conrad?

The War in the Pacific

MAIN IDEA

In order to defeat Japan and end the war in the Pacific, the United States unleashed a terrible new weapon, the atomic bomb.

WHY IT MATTERS NOW

Countries of the modern world struggle to find ways to prevent the use of nuclear weapons.

Terms & Names

- **Douglas MacArthur**
- **Chester Nimitz**
- **Battle of Midway**
- **kamikaze**
- **J. Robert Oppenheimer**
- **Hiroshima**
- **Nagasaki**
- **Nuremberg trials**

One American's Story

The writer William Manchester left college after Pearl Harbor to join the marines. Manchester says that, as a child, his "horror of violence had been so deep-seated that I had been unable to trade punches with other boys." On a Pacific island, he would have to confront that horror the first time he killed a man in face-to-face combat. Manchester's target was a Japanese sniper firing on Manchester's buddies from a fisherman's shack.

▲ American soldiers on Leyte in the Philippine Islands in late 1944.

A PERSONAL VOICE WILLIAM MANCHESTER

> "**My mouth was dry, my legs quaking, and my eyes out of focus. Then my vision cleared. I . . . kicked the door with my right foot, and leapt inside. . . . I . . . saw him as a blur to my right. . . . My first shot missed him, embedding itself in the straw wall, but the second caught him dead-on . . . . A wave of blood gushed from the wound. . . . He dipped a hand in it and listlessly smeared his cheek red. . . . Almost immediately a fly landed on his left eyeball. . . . A feeling of disgust and self-hatred clotted darkly in my throat, gagging me.**"
>
> —from *Goodbye Darkness: A Memoir of the Pacific War*

The Pacific War was a savage conflict fought with raw courage. Few who took part in that fearsome struggle would return home unchanged.

The Allies Stem the Japanese Tide

While the Allies agreed that the defeat of the Nazis was their first priority, the United States did not wait until V-E Day to move against Japan. Fortunately, the Japanese attack on Pearl Harbor in 1941 had missed the Pacific Fleet's submarines. Even more importantly, the attack had missed the fleet's aircraft carriers, which were out at sea at the time.

JAPANESE ADVANCES In the first six months after Pearl Harbor, the Japanese conquered an empire that dwarfed Hitler's Third Reich. On the Asian mainland, Japanese troops overran Hong Kong, French Indochina, Malaya, Burma, Thailand, and much of China. They also swept south and east across the Pacific, conquering the Dutch East Indies, Guam, Wake Island, the Solomon Islands, and countless other outposts in the ocean, including two islands in the Aleutian chain, which were part of Alaska.

In the Philippines, 80,000 American and Filipino troops battled the Japanese for control. At the time of the Japanese invasion in December 1941, General **Douglas MacArthur** was in command of Allied forces on the islands. When American and Filipino forces found themselves with their backs to the wall on Bataan, President Roosevelt ordered MacArthur to leave. On March 11, 1942, MacArthur left the Philippines with his wife, his son, and his staff. As he left, he pledged to the many thousands of men who did not make it out, "I shall return."

Background
Allied forces held out against 200,000 invading Japanese troops for four months on the Bataan Peninsula. Hunger, disease, and bombardments killed 14,000 Allied troops and wounded 48,000.

DOOLITTLE'S RAID In the spring of 1942, the Allies began to turn the tide against the Japanese. The push began on April 18 with a daring raid on Tokyo and other Japanese cities. Lieutenant Colonel James Doolittle led 16 bombers in the attack. The next day, Americans awoke to headlines that read "Tokyo Bombed! Doolittle Do'od It." Pulling off a Pearl Harbor–style air raid over Japan lifted America's sunken spirits. At the same time, it dampened spirits in Japan.

BATTLE OF THE CORAL SEA The main Allied forces in the Pacific were Americans and Australians. In May 1942 they succeeded in stopping the Japanese drive toward Australia in the five-day Battle of the Coral Sea. During this battle, the fighting was done by airplanes that took off from enormous aircraft carriers. Not a single shot was fired by surface ships. For the first time since Pearl Harbor, a Japanese invasion had been stopped and turned back.

THE BATTLE OF MIDWAY Japan's next thrust was toward Midway, a strategic island which lies northwest of Hawaii. Here again the Allies succeeded in stopping the Japanese. Americans had broken the Japanese code and knew that Midway was to be their next target.

Admiral **Chester Nimitz,** the commander of American naval forces in the Pacific, moved to defend the island. On June 3, 1942, his scout planes found the Japanese fleet. The Americans sent torpedo planes and dive bombers to the attack. The Japanese were caught with their planes still on the decks of their carriers. The results were devastating. By the end of the Battle of Midway, the Japanese had lost four aircraft carriers, a cruiser, and 250 planes. In the words of a Japanese official, at Midway the Americans had "avenged Pearl Harbor." (A)

The **Battle of Midway** was a turning point in the Pacific War. Soon the Allies began "island hopping." Island by island they won territory back from the Japanese. With each island, Allied forces moved closer to Japan.

MAIN IDEA

Comparing
(A) In what ways were the American victory at Midway and the Japanese triumph at Pearl Harbor alike?

HISTORICAL SPOTLIGHT

NAVAJO CODE TALKERS

On each of the Pacific islands that American troops stormed in World War II, the Japanese heard a "strange language gurgling" in their radio headsets. The code seemed to have Asian overtones, but it baffled everyone who heard it. In fact, the language was Navajo, which was spoken only in the American Southwest and traditionally had no alphabet or other written symbols. Its "hiddenness" made it a perfect candidate for a code language.

Though the Navajo had no words for combat terms, they developed terms such as *chicken hawk* for *divebomber* and *war chief* for *commanding general.* Throughout the Pacific campaign—from Midway to Iwo Jima—the code talkers were considered indispensable to the war effort. They finally received national recognition in 1969.

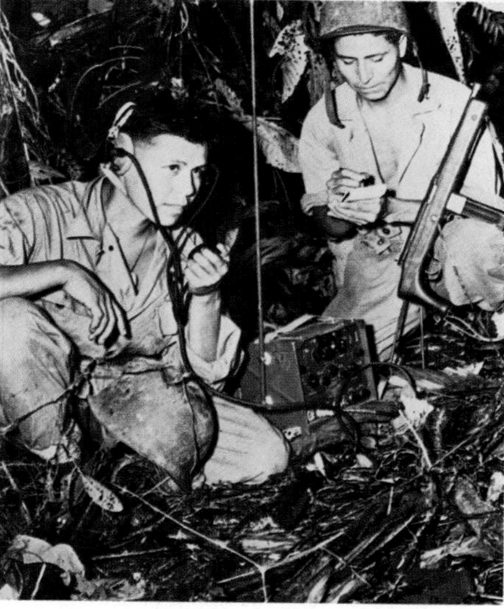

Four hundred Navajo were recruited into the Marine Corps as code talkers. Their primary duty was transmitting telephone and radio messages.

War in the Pacific and in Europe

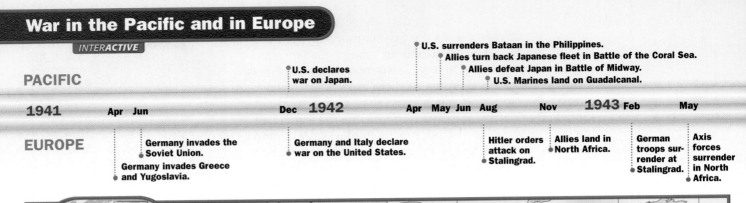

INTERACTIVE

PACIFIC

- Dec 1941: U.S. declares war on Japan.
- Apr 1942: U.S. surrenders Bataan in the Philippines.
- May 1942: Allies turn back Japanese fleet in Battle of the Coral Sea.
- Jun 1942: Allies defeat Japan in Battle of Midway.
- Aug 1942: U.S. Marines land on Guadalcanal.

1941 Apr Jun Dec **1942** Apr May Jun Aug Nov **1943** Feb May

EUROPE

- Apr 1941: Germany invades Greece and Yugoslavia.
- Jun 1941: Germany invades the Soviet Union.
- Dec 1941: Germany and Italy declare war on the United States.
- Aug 1942: Hitler orders attack on Stalingrad.
- Nov 1942: Allies land in North Africa.
- Feb 1943: German troops surrender at Stalingrad.
- May 1943: Axis forces surrender in North Africa.

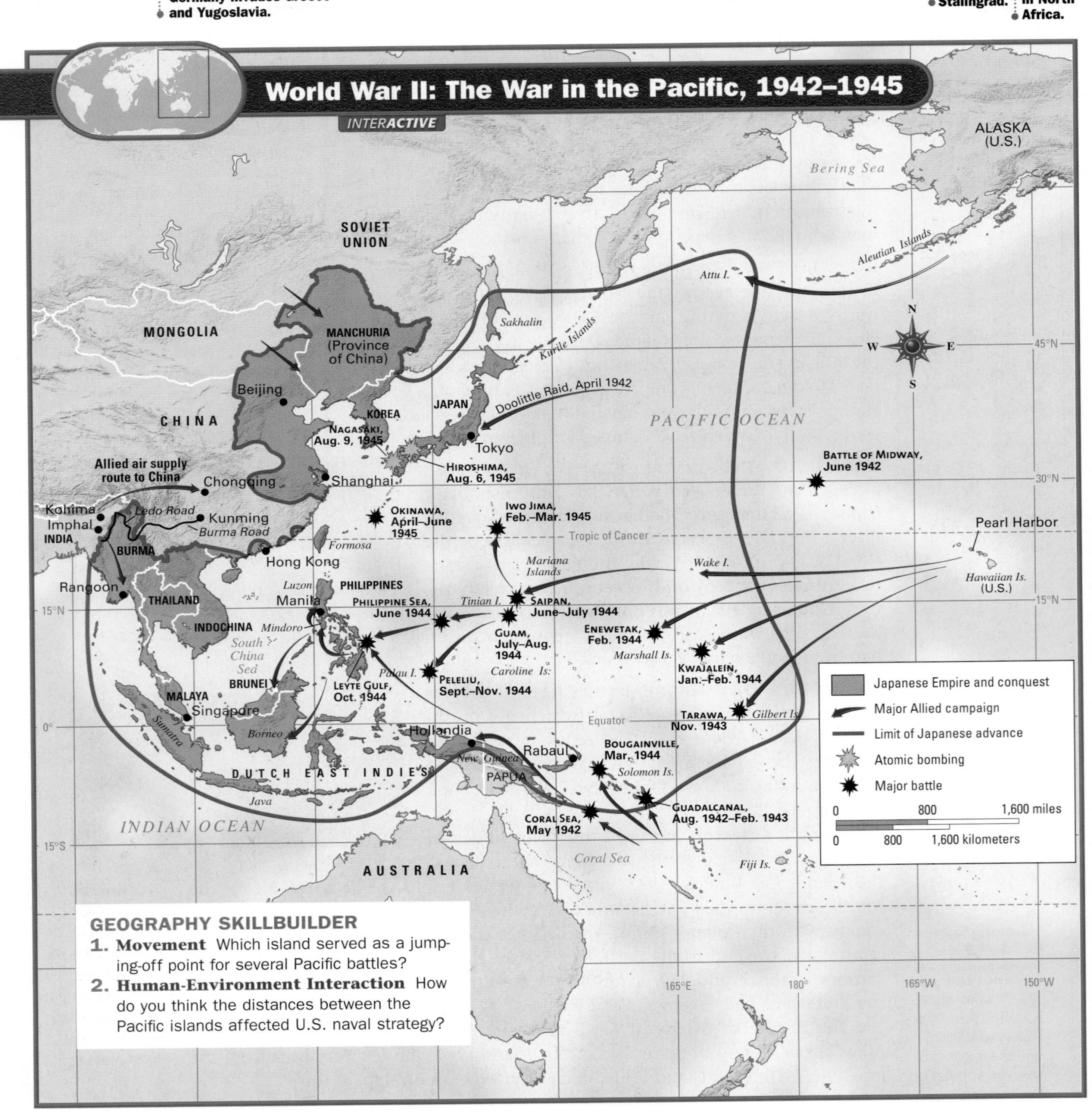

GEOGRAPHY SKILLBUILDER

1. **Movement** Which island served as a jumping-off point for several Pacific battles?
2. **Human-Environment Interaction** How do you think the distances between the Pacific islands affected U.S. naval strategy?

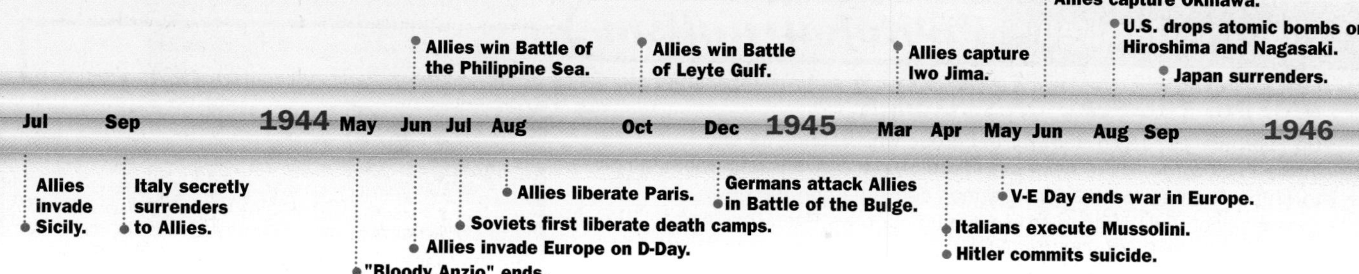
Allies capture Okinawa.
U.S. drops atomic bombs on Hiroshima and Nagasaki.
Japan surrenders.
Allies win Battle of the Philippine Sea.
Allies win Battle of Leyte Gulf.
Allies capture Iwo Jima.
Jul
Sep
1944
May
Jun
Jul
Aug
Oct
Dec
1945
Mar
Apr
May
Jun
Aug
Sep
1946
Allies invade Sicily.
Italy secretly surrenders to Allies.
Allies liberate Paris.
Germans attack Allies in Battle of the Bulge.
V-E Day ends war in Europe.
Soviets first liberate death camps.
Allies invade Europe on D-Day.
"Bloody Anzio" ends.
Italians execute Mussolini.
Hitler commits suicide.

The Allies Go on the Offensive

The first Allied offensive began in August 1942 when 19,000 troops stormed Guadalcanal in the Solomon Islands. By the time the Japanese abandoned Guadalcanal six months later, they called it the Island of Death. To war correspondent Ralph Martin and the troops who fought there, it was simply "hell."

A PERSONAL VOICE RALPH G. MARTIN

> **"Hell was red furry spiders as big as your fist, giant lizards as long as your leg, leeches falling from trees to suck blood, armies of white ants with a bite of fire, scurrying scorpions inflaming any flesh they touched, enormous rats and bats everywhere, and rivers with waiting crocodiles. Hell was the sour, foul smell of the squishy jungle, humidity that rotted a body within hours, . . . stinking wet heat of dripping rain forests that sapped the strength of any man."**
>
> —*The GI War*

Guadalcanal marked Japan's first defeat on land, but not its last. The Americans continued leapfrogging across the Pacific toward Japan, and in October 1944, some 178,000 Allied troops and 738 ships converged on Leyte Island in the Philippines. General MacArthur, who had left the Philippines two years earlier, waded ashore and announced, "People of the Philippines: I have returned."

THE JAPANESE DEFENSE The Japanese threw their entire fleet into the Battle of Leyte Gulf. They also tested a new tactic, the **kamikaze** (kä′mĭ-kä′zē), or suicide-plane, attack in which Japanese pilots crashed their bomb-laden planes into Allied ships. (*Kamikaze* means "divine wind" and refers to a legendary typhoon that saved Japan in 1281 by destroying a Mongol invasion.) In the Philippines, 424 kamikaze pilots embarked on suicide missions, sinking 16 ships and damaging another 80.

Japanese kamikaze pilots receive a briefing on the mission that would be their last.

Americans watched these terrifying attacks with "a strange mixture of respect and pity" according to Vice Admiral Charles Brown. "You have to admire the devotion to country demonstrated by those pilots," recalled Seaman George Marse. "Yet, when they were shot down, rescued and brought aboard our ship, we were surprised to find the pilots looked like ordinary, scared young men, not the wide-eyed fanatical 'devils' we imagined them to be."

MAIN IDEA

Drawing Conclusions

B Why was the Battle of Leyte Gulf so crucial to the Allies?

Despite the damage done by the kamikazes, the Battle of Leyte Gulf was a disaster for Japan. In three days of battle, it lost 3 battleships, 4 aircraft carriers, 13 cruisers, and almost 500 planes. From then on, the Imperial Navy played only a minor role in the defense of Japan. **B**

History Through *Photojournalism*

RAISING THE FLAG ON IWO JIMA

On February 19, 1945, the war in Europe was nearing its end, but in the Pacific one of the fiercest battles of World War II was about to erupt. On that day, 70,000 marines converged on the tiny, Japanese-controlled island of Iwo Jima. Four days later, they had captured Mount Suribachi, the island's highest point, but the battle for Iwo Jima would rage on for four more weeks.

Photographer Lou Lowery documented the men of "Easy Company" hoisting an American flag on a makeshift pole atop Mount Suribachi. But the original flag was soon taken down to be kept as a souvenir by the commanding officer. ▶

▲ **Six marines were sent to replace the flag with an even larger one. Joe Rosenthal, a wire-service photographer, saw the second flag raising, grabbed his camera, and clicked off a frame without even looking through his viewfinder. Rosenthal's photo appeared the next morning on the front pages of American newspapers. In the minds of Americans, it immediately replaced the gloomy, blurred images of Pearl Harbor going up in flames.**

SKILLBUILDER **Interpeting Visual Sources**

1. One of the Mount Suribachi images became one of the most recognized, most reproduced images of World War II. Study the details and point of view in each photo. Explain why you think Rosenthal's image, rather than Lowery's, became important.
2. What human qualities or events do you think Rosenthal's photograph symbolizes?

SEE SKILLBUILDER HANDBOOK, PAGE R23.

IWO JIMA After retaking much of the Philippines and liberating the American prisoners of war there, the Allies turned to Iwo Jima, an island that writer William Manchester later described as "an ugly, smelly glob of cold lava squatting in a surly ocean." Iwo Jima (which means "sulfur island" in Japanese) was critical to the United States as a base from which heavily loaded bombers might reach Japan. It was also perhaps the most heavily defended spot on earth, with 20,700 Japanese troops entrenched in tunnels and caves. More than 6,000 marines died taking this desolate island, the greatest number in any battle in the Pacific to that point. Only 200 Japanese survived. Just one obstacle now stood between the Allies and a final assault on Japan—the island of Okinawa.

THE BATTLE FOR OKINAWA In April 1945, U.S. Marines invaded Okinawa. The Japanese unleashed more than 1,900 kamikaze attacks on the Allies during the Okinawa campaign, sinking 30 ships, damaging more than 300 more, and killing almost 5,000 seamen.

Once ashore, the Allies faced even fiercer opposition than on Iwo Jima. By the time the fighting ended on June 21, 1945, more than 7,600 Americans had died. But the Japanese paid an even ghastlier price—110,000 lives—in defending Okinawa. This total included two generals who chose ritual suicide over the shame of surrender. A witness to this ceremony described their end: "A simultaneous shout and a flash of the sword . . . and both generals had nobly accomplished their last duty to their Emperor."

The Battle for Okinawa was a chilling foretaste of what the Allies imagined the invasion of Japan's home islands would be. Churchill predicted the cost would be a million American lives and half that number of British lives. C

MAIN IDEA

Drawing Conclusions

C Why was Okinawa a significant island in the war in the Pacific?

KEY PLAYER

DOUGLAS MACARTHUR 1880–1964

Douglas MacArthur was too arrogant and prickly to be considered a "regular guy" by his troops. But he was arguably the most brilliant Allied strategist of World War II. For every American soldier killed in his campaigns, the Japanese lost ten.

He was considered a real hero of the war, both by the military and by the prisoners on the Philippines, whom he freed. "MacArthur took more territory with less loss of life," observed journalist John Gunther, "than any military commander since Darius the Great [king of Persia, 522–486 B.C.]."

The Atomic Bomb Ends the War

The taking of Iwo Jima and Okinawa opened the way for an invasion of Japan. However, Allied leaders knew that such an invasion would become a desperate struggle. Japan still had a huge army that would defend every inch of homeland. President Truman saw only one way to avoid an invasion of Japan. He decided to use a powerful new weapon that had been developed by scientists working on the Manhattan Project—the atomic bomb.

THE MANHATTAN PROJECT Led by General Leslie Groves with research directed by American scientist **J. Robert Oppenheimer,** the development of the atomic bomb was not only the most ambitious scientific enterprise in history, it was also the best-kept secret of the war. At its peak, more than 600,000 Americans were involved in the project, although few knew its purpose. Even Truman did not learn about it until he became president.

The first test of the new bomb took place on the morning of July 16, 1945, in an empty expanse of desert near Alamogordo, New Mexico. A blinding flash, which was visible 180 miles away, was followed by a deafening roar as a tremendous shock wave rolled across the trembling desert. Otto Frisch, a scientist on the project, described the huge mushroom cloud that rose over the desert as "a red-hot elephant standing balanced on its trunk." The bomb worked!

President Truman now faced a difficult decision. Should the Allies use the bomb to bring an end to the war? Truman did not hesitate. On July 25, 1945, he ordered the military to make final plans for dropping two atomic bombs on Japanese targets. A day later, the United States warned Japan that it faced "prompt and utter destruction" unless it surrendered at once. Japan refused. Truman later wrote, "The final decision of where and when to use the atomic bomb was up to me. Let there be no mistake about it. I regarded the bomb as a military weapon and never had any doubt that it should be used."

HIROSHIMA AND NAGASAKI On August 6, a B-29 bomber named *Enola Gay* released an atomic bomb, code-named Little Boy, over **Hiroshima,** an important Japanese military center. Forty-three seconds later, almost every building in the city collapsed into dust from the force of the blast. Hiroshima had ceased to exist. Still, Japan's leaders hesitated to surrender. Three days later, a second bomb, code-named Fat Man, was dropped on **Nagasaki,** leveling half the city. By the end of the year, an estimated 200,000 people had died as a result of injuries and radiation poisoning caused by the atomic blasts. Yamaoka Michiko was 15 years old and living near the center of Hiroshima when the first bomb hit.

A PERSONAL VOICE YAMAOKA MICHIKO

> **"They say temperatures of 7,000 degrees centigrade hit me. . . . Nobody there looked like human beings. . . . Humans had lost the ability to speak. People couldn't scream, 'It hurts!' even when they were on fire. . . . People with their legs wrenched off. Without heads. Or with faces burned and swollen out of shape. The scene I saw was a living hell."**
>
> —quoted in *Japan at War: An Oral History*

Emperor Hirohito was horrified by the destruction wrought by the bomb. "I cannot bear to see my innocent people suffer any longer," he told Japan's leaders tearfully. Then he ordered them to draw up papers "to end the war." On September 2, formal surrender ceremonies took place on the U.S. battleship *Missouri* in Tokyo Bay. "Today the guns are silent," said General MacArthur in a speech marking this historic moment. "The skies no longer rain death—the seas bear only commerce—men everywhere walk upright in the sunlight. The entire world is quietly at peace."

Hiroshima in ruins following the atomic bomb blast on August 6, 1945 ▶

POINT

"The only way to end the war against Japan was to bomb the Japanese mainland."

Many advisors to President Truman, including Secretary of War Henry Stimson, had this point of view. They felt the bomb would end the war and save American lives. Stimson said, "The face of war is the face of death."

Some scientists working on the bomb agreed—even more so as the casualty figures from Iwo Jima and Okinawa sank in. "Are we to go on shedding American blood when we have available a means to a steady victory?" they petitioned. "No! If we can save even a handful of American lives, then let us use this weapon—now!"

Two other concerns pushed Americans to use the bomb. Some people feared that if the bomb were not dropped, the project might be viewed as a gigantic waste of money.

The second consideration involved the Soviet Union. Tension and distrust were already developing between the Western Allies and the Soviets. Some American officials believed that a successful use of the atomic bomb would give the United States a powerful advantage over the Soviets in shaping the postwar world.

COUNTERPOINT

"Japan's staggering losses were enough to force Japan's surrender."

Many of the scientists who had worked on the bomb, as well as military leaders and civilian policymakers, had doubts about using it. Dr. Leo Szilard, a Hungarian-born physicist who had helped President Roosevelt launch the project and who had a major role in developing the bomb, was a key figure opposing its use.

A petition drawn up by Szilard and signed by 70 other scientists argued that it would be immoral to drop an atomic bomb on Japan without fair warning. Many supported staging a demonstration of the bomb for Japanese leaders, perhaps by exploding one on a deserted island near Japan, to convince the Japanese to surrender.

Supreme Allied Commander General Dwight D. Eisenhower agreed. He maintained that "dropping the bomb was completely unnecessary" to save American lives and that Japan was already defeated. Ike told Secretary of War Henry Stimson, "I was against it [the bomb] on two counts. First the Japanese were ready to surrender and it wasn't necessary to hit them with that awful thing. Second, I hated to see our country be the first to use such a weapon."

THINKING CRITICALLY

1. **CONNECT TO HISTORY** **Summarizing** What were the main arguments for and against dropping the atomic bomb on Japan?

SEE SKILLBUILDER HANDBOOK, PAGE R4.

2. **CONNECT TO TODAY** **Evaluating Decisions** Do you think the United States was justified in using the bomb against the Japanese? In a paragraph, explain why or why not.

Rebuilding Begins

With Japan's surrender, the Allies turned to the challenge of rebuilding war-torn nations. Even before the last guns fell silent, they began thinking about principles that would govern the postwar world.

THE YALTA CONFERENCE In February 1945, as the Allies pushed toward victory in Europe, an ailing Roosevelt had met with Churchill and Stalin at the Black Sea resort city of Yalta in the Soviet Union. Stalin graciously welcomed the president and the prime minister, and the Big Three, as they were called, toasted the defeat of Germany that now seemed certain.

For eight grueling days, the three leaders discussed the fate of Germany and the postwar world. Stalin, his country devastated by German forces, favored a harsh approach. He wanted to keep Germany divided into occupation zones—areas controlled by Allied military forces—so that Germany would never again threaten the Soviet Union.

> **MAIN IDEA**
> **Analyzing Motives**
> D Why was Roosevelt anxious to make concessions to Stalin concerning the fate of postwar Germany?

When Churchill strongly disagreed, Roosevelt acted as a mediator. He was prepared to make concessions to Stalin for two reasons. First, he hoped that the Soviet Union would stand by its commitments to join the war against Japan that was still waging in the Pacific. (The first test of the atom bomb was still five months away.) Second, Roosevelt wanted Stalin's support for a new world peace-keeping organization, to be named the United Nations. D

The historic meeting at Yalta produced a series of compromises. To pacify Stalin, Roosevelt convinced Churchill to agree to a temporary division of Germany into four zones, one each for the Americans, the British, the Soviets, and the French. Churchill and Roosevelt assumed that, in time, all the zones would be brought together in a reunited Germany. For his part, Stalin promised "free and unfettered elections" in Poland and other Soviet-occupied Eastern European countries.

Stalin also agreed to join in the war against Japan. That struggle was expected to continue for another year or more. In addition, he agreed to participate in an international conference to take place in April in San Francisco. There, Roosevelt's dream of a United Nations (UN) would become a reality. **E**

MAIN IDEA

Summarizing
E What decisions did Roosevelt, Churchill, and Stalin make at the Yalta Conference?

THE NUREMBERG WAR TRIALS Besides geographic division, Germany had another price to pay for its part in the war. The discovery of Hitler's death camps led the Allies to put 24 surviving Nazi leaders on trial for crimes against humanity, crimes against the peace, and war crimes. The trials were held in the southern German town of Nuremberg.

At the **Nuremberg trials,** the defendants included Hitler's most trusted party officials, government ministers, military leaders, and powerful industrialists. As the trial began, U.S. Supreme Court Justice Robert Jackson explained the significance of the event.

A Personal Voice ROBERT JACKSON

> **"The wrongs which we seek to condemn and punish have been so calculated, so malignant and so devastating, that civilization cannot tolerate their being ignored because it cannot survive their being repeated. . . . It is hard now to perceive in these miserable men . . . the power by which as Nazi leaders they once dominated much of the world and terrified most of it. Merely as individuals, their fate is of little consequence to the world. What makes this inquest significant is that these prisoners represent sinister influences that will lurk in the world long after their bodies have returned to dust. They are living symbols of racial hatreds, of terrorism and violence, and of the arrogance and cruelty of power. . . . Civilization can afford no compromise with the social forces which would gain renewed strength if we deal ambiguously or indecisively with the men in whom those forces now precariously survive."**
>
> —quoted in opening address to the Nuremberg War Crimes Trial

War Criminals on Trial, 1945–1949

Each defendant at the Nuremberg trials was accused of one or more of the following crimes:

- **Crimes Against the Peace**—planning and waging an aggressive war
- **War Crimes**—acts against the customs of warfare, such as the killing of hostages and prisoners, the plundering of private property, and the destruction of towns and cities
- **Crimes Against Humanity**—the murder, extermination, deportation, or enslavement of civilians

In the end, 12 of the 24 defendants were sentenced to death, and most of the remaining were sent to prison. In later trials of lesser leaders, nearly 200 more Nazis were found guilty of war crimes. Still, many people have argued that the trials did not go far enough in seeking out and punishing war criminals. Many Nazis who took part in the Holocaust did indeed go free.

Yet no matter how imperfect the trials might have been, they did establish an important principle—the idea that individuals are responsible for their own actions, even in times of war. Nazi executioners could not escape punishment by claiming that they were merely "following orders." The principle of individual responsibility was now firmly entrenched in international law.

> *"I was only following orders."*
>
> DEFENDANTS AT THE NUREMBERG TRIALS

THE OCCUPATION OF JAPAN Japan was occupied by U.S. forces under the command of General Douglas MacArthur. In the early years of the occupation, more than 1,100 Japanese, from former Prime Minister Hideki Tojo to lowly prison guards, were arrested and put on trial. Seven, including Tojo, were sentenced to death. In the Philippines, in China, and in other Asian battlegrounds, additional Japanese officials were tried for atrocities against civilians or prisoners of war.

During the seven-year American occupation, MacArthur reshaped Japan's economy by introducing free-market practices that led to a remarkable economic recovery. MacArthur also worked to transform Japan's government. He called for a new constitution that would provide for woman suffrage and guarantee basic freedoms. In the United States, Americans followed these changes with interest. The *New York Times* reported that "General MacArthur . . . has swept away an autocratic regime by a warrior god and installed in its place a democratic government presided over by a very human emperor and based on the will of the people as expressed in free elections." The Japanese apparently agreed. To this day, their constitution is known as the MacArthur Constitution.

ASSESSMENT

1. **TERMS & NAMES** For each term or name, write a sentence explaining its significance.
   - **Douglas MacArthur**
   - **Chester Nimitz**
   - **Battle of Midway**
   - **kamikaze**
   - **J. Robert Oppenheimer**
   - **Hiroshima**
   - **Nagasaki**
   - **Nuremberg trials**

MAIN IDEA

2. **TAKING NOTES**
   Using a chart such as the one below, describe the significance of key military actions in the Pacific during World War II.

Military Action	Significance
1.	
2.	
3.	
4.	
5.	

Which military action was a turning point for the Allies?

CRITICAL THINKING

3. **DEVELOPING HISTORICAL PERSPECTIVE**
   At the trials, many Nazis defended themselves by saying they were only following orders. What does this rationale tell you about the German military? Why was it important to negate this justification?

4. **DRAWING CONCLUSIONS**
   Explain how the United States was able to defeat the Japanese in the Pacific.

5. **EVALUATING DECISIONS**
   Is it legitimate to hold people accountable for crimes committed during wartime? Why or why not?
   Think About:
   - the laws that govern society
   - the likelihood of conducting a fair trial
   - the behavior of soldiers, politicians, and civilians during war

Science and Technology

Radar, guided missiles, nuclear submarines, reconnaissance satellites, atomic bombs—the inventions of the 20th century seem intended mainly for war, with the usual dreaded results. But these technological developments have also had far-reaching applications in peacetime. Because the innovations were originally intended for the battlefield, they were developed quickly and with a narrow purpose. However, their applications during peacetime have led to life-enhancing benefits that will extend far into the 21st century.

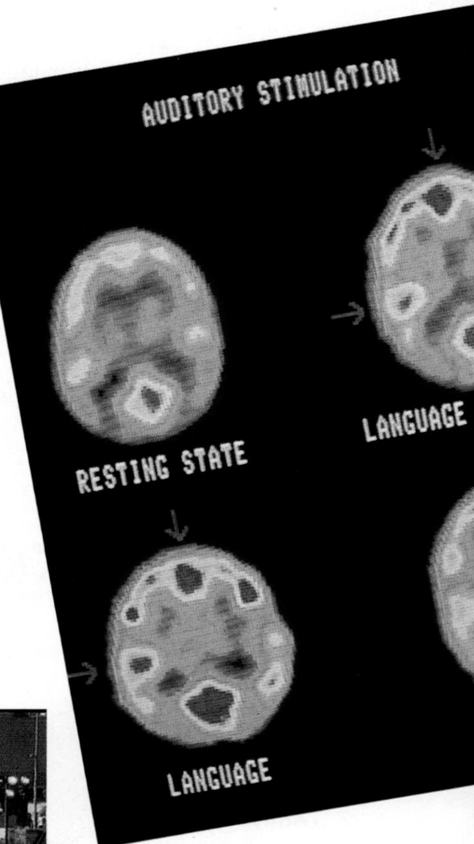

1914–1918 WORLD WAR I

FIGHTER PLANES TO COMMUTER FLIGHTS ▼

Airplanes were first used to gather military information but were soon put to work as fighters and bombers. The *Sopwith Camel* (*shown at right*), was one of the most successful British fighter planes, bringing down almost 1,300 enemy aircraft during World War I. The development of flight technology eventually led to sophisticated supersonic aircraft. Today, non-military aircraft are primarily used for travel and cargo transport. Jumbo jets carry hundreds of passengers with each takeoff.

1939–1945 WORLD WAR II

▼ ATOM BOMBS TO BRAIN SCANS

Faced with alarming rumors of work on a German atomic bomb, America mobilized some of the finest scientific minds in the world to create its own atomic bomb. The energy released by its nuclear reaction was enough to kill hundreds of thousands of people, as evidenced by the destruction of Hiroshima and Nagasaki. But the resulting ability to harness the atom's energy also led to new technologies for diagnosing and treating human diseases. Techniques such as positron emission tomography (PET) now reveal the inner workings of the human brain itself.

Applications of World War II Technology

TECHNOLOGY	MILITARY USE	PEACETIME USE
Semiconductors	Navigation	Transistors, radios, electronics
Computers	Code breaking	Software programs, video games
Freeze-dried food	Soldiers' rations	TV dinners, space-shuttle rations
Synthetic materials	Parachutes, weapons parts, tires	Telephones, automobile fenders, pacemakers
Radar	Tracking and surveillance	Weather tracking, air traffic control, archaeological digs

▼ SATELLITES TO CELLULAR PHONES

The Soviet Union launched *Sputnik*, the first successful artificial space satellite, in 1957. As the United States raced to catch up with the Soviets in space, both countries eventually produced satellites that have improved life for people around the world. Satellites not only track weather patterns and control air traffic but also link the continents in a vast communications network.

THINKING CRITICALLY

CONNECT TO HISTORY

1. **Hypothesizing** Do you think that peacetime technologies would have been developed without the stimulus provided by war? Support your answer.

 **SEE SKILLBUILDER HANDBOOK, PAGE R13.**

CONNECT TO TODAY

2. **Evaluating Technological Impact** What invention or technological breakthrough do you think has had the greatest impact on American society? Write a paragraph to explain your answer. Stage a debate with your classmates in which you defend your choice.

CLASSZONE.COM

SECTION 4

The Home Front

MAIN IDEA

After World War II, Americans adjusted to new economic opportunities and harsh social tensions.

WHY IT MATTERS NOW

Economic opportunities afforded by World War II led to a more diverse middle class in the United States.

Terms & Names

- **GI Bill of Rights**
- **James Farmer**
- **Congress of Racial Equality (CORE)**
- **internment**
- **Japanese American Citizens League (JACL)**

One American's Story

The writer and poet Maya Angelou was a teenager living in San Francisco when the United States got involved in World War II. The first change she noticed was the disappearance of the city's Japanese population. The second change was an influx of workers, including many African Americans, from the South. San Franciscans, she noted, maintained that there was no racism in their city by the bay. But Angelou knew differently.

A PERSONAL VOICE MAYA ANGELOU

"A story went the rounds about a San Franciscan white matron who refused to sit beside a Negro civilian on the streetcar, even after he made room for her on the seat. Her explanation was that she would not sit beside a draft dodger who was a Negro as well. She added that the least he could do was fight for his country the way her son was fighting on Iwo Jima. The story said that the man pulled his body away from the window to show an armless sleeve. He said quietly and with great dignity, 'Then ask your son to look around for my arm, which I left over there.'"

—*I Know Why the Caged Bird Sings*

TWICE A PATRIOT

EX-PRIVATE OBIE BARTLETT LOST LEFT ARM—PEARL HARBOR RELEASED: DEC., 1941—NOW AT WORK WELDING IN A WEST COAST SHIPYARD . . .

▲ **Like many minority veterans, Obie Bartlett was twice a patriot—and was still regarded as a second-class citizen.**

At the end of the war, returning veterans—even those who weren't disabled—had to begin dealing with the very real issues of reentry and adjustment to a society that offered many opportunities but still had many unsolved problems.

Opportunity and Adjustment

In contrast to the Great Depression, World War II was a time of opportunity for millions of Americans. Jobs abounded, and despite rationing and shortages, people had money to spend. At the end of World War II, the nation emerged as the world's dominant economic and military power.

ECONOMIC GAINS The war years were good ones for working people. As defense industries boomed, unemployment fell to a low of 1.2 percent in 1944. Even with price and wage controls, average weekly pay (adjusted for inflation) rose 10 percent during the war. And although workers still protested long hours, overtime, and night shifts, they were able to save money for the future. Some workers invested up to half their paychecks in war bonds.

Farmers also prospered during the war. Unlike the depression years, when farmers had battled dust storms and floods, the early 1940s had good weather for growing crops. Farmers benefited from improvements in farm machinery and fertilizers and reaped the profits from rising crop prices. As a result, crop production increased by 50 percent, and farm income tripled. Before the war ended, many farmers could pay off their mortgages.

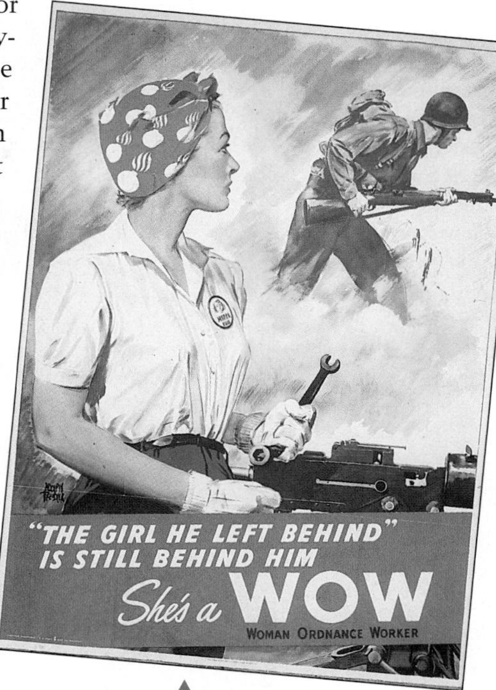

"THE GIRL HE LEFT BEHIND"
IS STILL BEHIND HIM
She's a WOW
WOMAN ORDNANCE WORKER

▲ The war gave women the chance to prove they could be just as productive as men. But their pay usually did not reflect their productivity.

Women also enjoyed employment gains during the war, although many lost their jobs when the war ended. Over 6 million women had entered the work force for the first time, boosting the percentage of women in the total work force to 35 percent. A third of those jobs were in defense plants, which offered women more challenging work and better pay than jobs traditionally associated with women, such as as waitressing, clerking, and domestic service. With men away at war, many women also took advantage of openings in journalism and other professions. "The war really created opportunities for women," said Winona Espinosa, a wife and mother who became a riveter and bus driver during the war. "It was the first time we got a chance to show that we could do a lot of things that only men had done before."

Vocabulary
migration: the act of moving from one country or region to another

POPULATION SHIFTS In addition to revamping the economy, the war triggered one of the greatest mass migrations in American history. Americans whose families had lived for decades in one place suddenly uprooted themselves to seek work elsewhere. More than a million newcomers poured into California between 1941 and 1944. Towns with defense industries saw their populations double and even triple, sometimes almost overnight. As shown in the map to the right, African Americans left the South for cities in the North in record numbers. **A**

MAIN IDEA

Analyzing Causes
A How did World War II cause the U.S. population to shift?

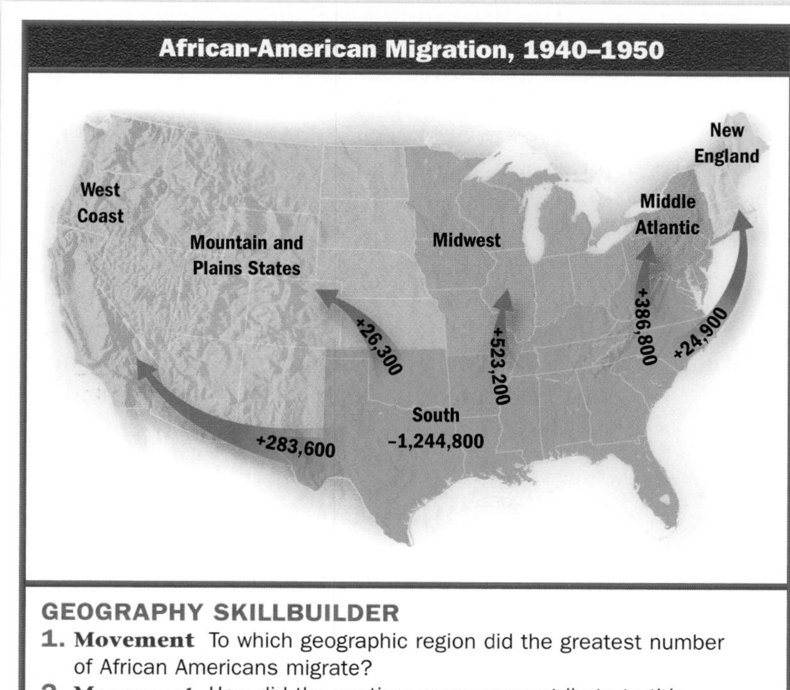

GEOGRAPHY SKILLBUILDER
1. **Movement** To which geographic region did the greatest number of African Americans migrate?
2. **Movement** How did the wartime economy contribute to this mass migration?

Attending Pennsylvania State College under the GI Bill of Rights, William Oskay, Jr., paid $28 a month for the trailer home in which you see him working. ▶

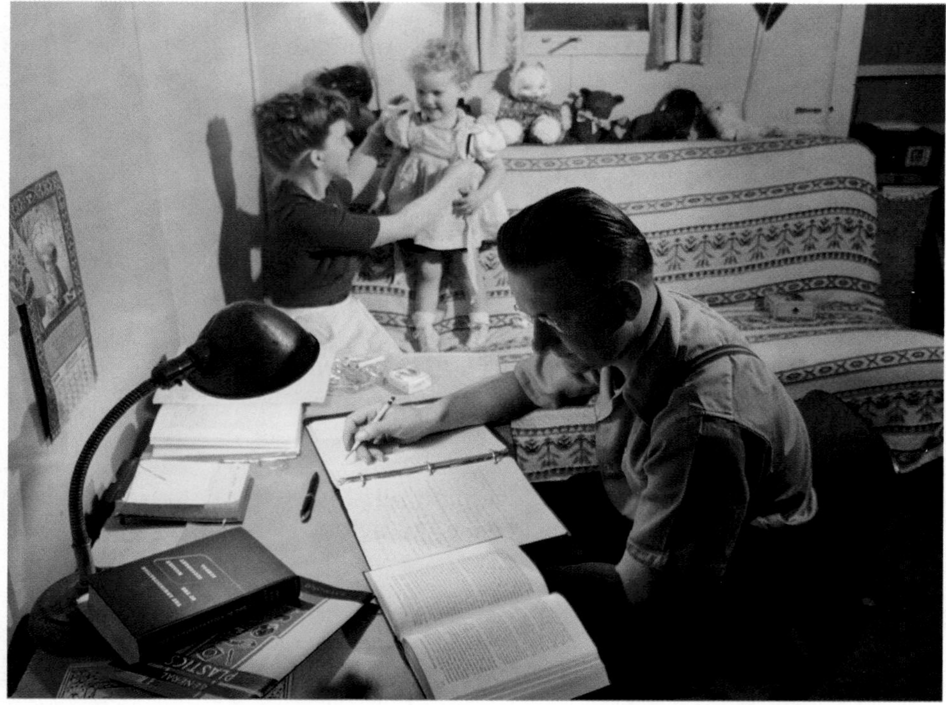

SOCIAL ADJUSTMENTS Families adjusted to the changes brought on by war as best they could. With millions of fathers in the armed forces, mothers struggled to rear their children alone. Many young children got used to being left with neighbors or relatives or in child-care centers as more and more mothers went to work. Teenagers left at home without parents sometimes drifted into juvenile delinquency. And when fathers finally did come home, there was often a painful period of readjustment as family members got to know one another again.

The war helped create new families, too. Longtime sweethearts—as well as couples who barely knew each other—rushed to marry before the soldier or sailor was shipped overseas. In booming towns like Seattle, the number of marriage licenses issued went up by as much as 300 percent early in the war. A New Yorker observed in 1943, "On Fridays and Saturdays, the City Hall area is blurred with running soldiers, sailors, and girls hunting the license bureau, floral shops, ministers, blood-testing laboratories, and the Legal Aid Society."

In 1944, to help ease the transition of returning servicemen to civilian life, Congress passed the Servicemen's Readjustment Act, better known as the **GI Bill of Rights.** This bill provided education and training for veterans, paid for by the federal government. Just over half the returning soldiers, or about 7.8 million veterans, attended colleges and technical schools under the GI Bill. The act also provided federal loan guarantees to veterans buying homes or farms or starting new businesses. B

MAIN IDEA

Analyzing Effects

B How did the war affect families and personal lives?

Discrimination and Reaction

Despite the opportunities that opened up for women and minorities during the war, old prejudices and policies persisted, both in the military and at home.

CIVIL RIGHTS PROTESTS African Americans made some progress on the home front. During the war, thousands of African Americans left the South. The majority moved to the Midwest, where better jobs could be found. Between 1940 and 1944, the percentage of African Americans working in skilled or semiskilled jobs rose from 16 to 30 percent.

Wherever African Americans moved, however, discrimination presented tough hurdles. In 1942, civil rights leader **James Farmer** founded an interracial organization called the **Congress of Racial Equality (CORE)** to confront urban segregation in the North. That same year, CORE staged its first sit-in at a segregated Chicago restaurant.

As African-American migrants moved into already overcrowded cities, tensions rose. In 1943, a tidal wave of racial violence swept across the country. The worst conflict erupted in Detroit on a hot Sunday afternoon in June. What started as a tussle between blacks and whites at a beach on the Detroit River mushroomed into a riot when white sailors stationed nearby joined the fray. The fighting raged for three days, fueled by false rumors that whites had murdered a black woman and her child and that black rioters had killed 17 whites. By the time President Roosevelt sent federal troops to restore order, 9 whites and 25 blacks lay dead or dying.

MAIN IDEA

Analyzing Causes

C What caused the race riots in the 1940s?

The violence of 1943 revealed to many Americans—black and white alike—just how serious racial tensions had become in the United States. By 1945, more than 400 committees had been established by American communities to improve race relations. Progress was slow, but African Americans were determined not to give up the gains they had made. **C**

TENSION IN LOS ANGELES Mexican Americans also experienced prejudice during the war years. In the violent summer of 1943, Los Angeles exploded in anti-Mexican "zoot-suit" riots. The zoot suit was a style of dress adopted by Mexican-American youths as a symbol of their rebellion against tradition. It consisted of a long jacket and pleated pants. Broad-brimmed hats were often worn with the suits.

▲ These Mexican Americans, involved in the 1943 Los Angeles riots, are seen here leaving jail to make court appearances.

The riots began when 11 sailors in Los Angeles reported that they had been attacked by zoot-suit-wearing Mexican Americans. This charge triggered violence involving thousands of servicemen and civilians. Mobs poured into Mexican neighborhoods and grabbed any zoot-suiters they could find. The attackers ripped off their victims' clothes and beat them senseless. The riots lasted almost a week and resulted in the beating of hundreds of Mexican-American youth and other minorities.

Despite such unhappy experiences with racism, many Mexican Americans believed that their sacrifices during wartime would lead to a better future.

A PERSONAL VOICE MANUEL DE LA RAZA

"This war . . . is doing what we in our Mexican-American movement had planned to do in one generation. . . . It has shown those 'across the tracks' that we all share the same problems. It has shown them what the Mexican American will do, what responsibility he will take and what leadership qualities he will demonstrate. After this struggle, the status of the Mexican Americans will be different."

—quoted in *A Different Mirror: A History of Multicultural America*

Japanese Relocation Camps, 1942

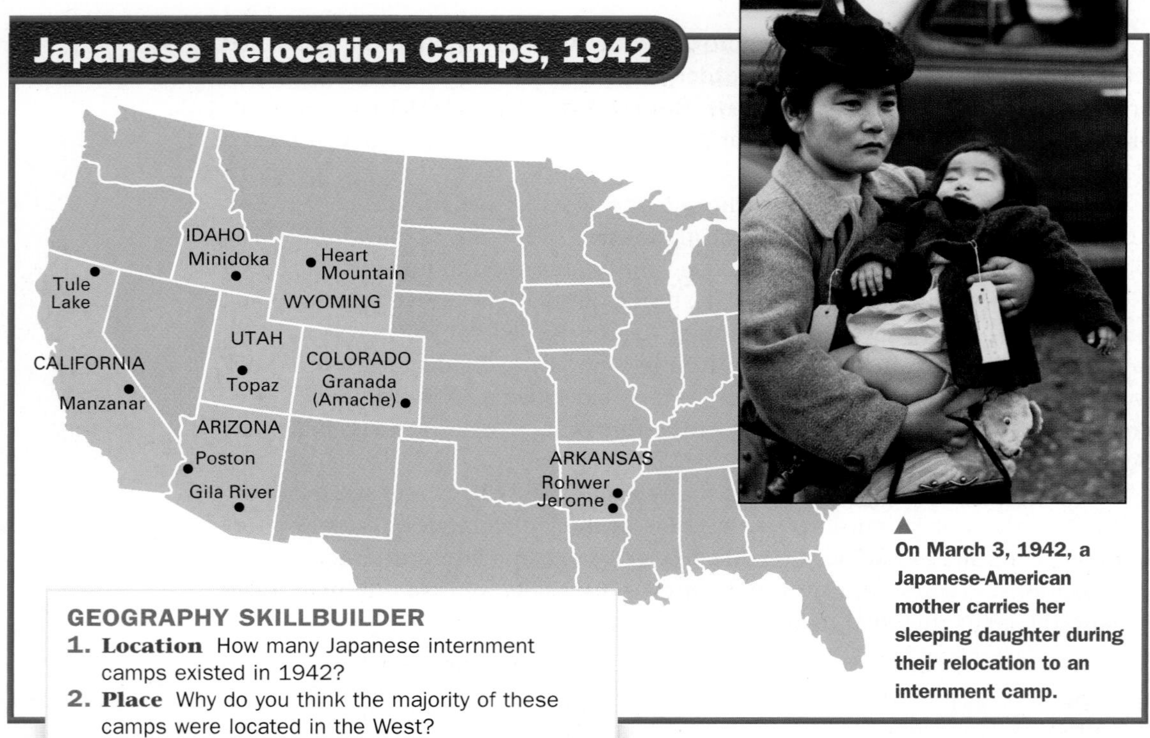

▲ On March 3, 1942, a Japanese-American mother carries her sleeping daughter during their relocation to an internment camp.

GEOGRAPHY SKILLBUILDER

1. **Location** How many Japanese internment camps existed in 1942?
2. **Place** Why do you think the majority of these camps were located in the West?

Internment of Japanese Americans

While Mexican Americans and African Americans struggled with racial tension, the war produced tragic results for Japanese Americans. When the war began, 120,000 Japanese Americans lived in the United States. Most of them were citizens living on the West Coast.

The surprise Japanese attack on Pearl Harbor in Hawaii had stunned the nation. After the bombing, panic-stricken citizens feared that the Japanese would soon attack the United States. Frightened people believed false rumors that Japanese Americans were committing sabotage by mining coastal harbors and poisoning vegetables.

This sense of fear and uncertainty caused a wave of prejudice against Japanese Americans. Early in 1942, the War Department called for the mass evacuation of all Japanese Americans from Hawaii. General Delos Emmons, the military governor of Hawaii, resisted the order because 37 percent of the people in Hawaii were Japanese Americans. To remove them would have destroyed the islands' economy and hindered U.S. military operations there. However, he was eventually forced to order the **internment,** or confinement, of 1,444 Japanese Americans, 1 percent of Hawaii's Japanese-American population.

On the West Coast, however, panic and prejudice ruled the day. In California, only 1 percent of the people were Japanese, but they constituted a minority large enough to stimulate the prejudice of many whites, without being large enough to effectively resist internment. Newspapers whipped up anti-Japanese sentiment by running ugly stories attacking Japanese Americans.

On February 19, 1942, President Roosevelt signed an order requiring the removal of people of Japanese ancestry from California and parts of Washington, Oregon, and Arizona. Based on strong recommendations from the military, he justified this step as necessary for national security. In the following weeks, the army rounded up some 110,000 Japanese Americans and shipped them to ten hastily constructed remote "relocation centers," euphemisms for prison camps.

MAIN IDEA

Analyzing Motives

D Why did President Roosevelt order the internment of Japanese Americans?

About two-thirds were Nisei, or Japanese people born in this country of parents who emigrated from Japan. Thousands of Nisei had already joined the armed forces, and to Ted Nakashima, an architectural draftsman from Seattle, the evacuation seemed utterly senseless. D

A PERSONAL VOICE TED NAKASHIMA

"[There are] electricians, plumbers, draftsmen, mechanics, carpenters, painters, farmers—every trade—men who are able and willing to do all they can to lick the Axis. . . . We're on this side and we want to help. Why won't America let us?"

—from *New Republic* magazine, June 15, 1942

No specific charges were ever filed against Japanese Americans, and no evidence of subversion was ever found. Faced with expulsion, terrified families were forced to sell their homes, businesses, and all their belongings for less than their true value.

Japanese Americans fought for justice, both in the courts and in Congress. The initial results were discouraging. In 1944, the Supreme Court decided, in *Korematsu* v. *United States*, that the government's policy of evacuating Japanese Americans to camps was justified on the basis of "military necessity." (See pages 596–597.) After the war, however, the **Japanese American Citizens League (JACL)** pushed the government to compensate those sent to the camps for their lost property. In 1965, Congress authorized the spending of $38 million for that purpose—less than a tenth of Japanese Americans' actual losses.

The JACL did not give up its quest for justice. In 1978, it called for the payment of reparations, or restitution, to each individual that suffered internment. A decade later, Congress passed, and President Ronald Reagan signed, a bill that promised $20,000 to every Japanese American sent to a relocation camp. When the checks were sent in 1990, a letter from President George Bush accompanied them, in which he stated, "We can never fully right the wrongs of the past. But we can take a clear stand for justice and recognize that serious injustices were done to Japanese Americans during World War II."

ASSESSMENT

1. **TERMS & NAMES** For each term or name, write a sentence explaining its significance.
   - **GI Bill of Rights**
   - **James Farmer**
   - **Congress of Racial Equality (CORE)**
   - **internment**
   - **Japanese American Citizens League (JACL)**

MAIN IDEA

2. **TAKING NOTES**
   List the advances and problems in the economy and in civil rights during World War II.

	Advances	Problems
Economy		
Civil Rights		

Which of these advances and problems do you think had the most far-reaching effect? Explain your answer.

CRITICAL THINKING

3. **COMPARING**
   How were the experiences of African Americans, Mexican Americans, and Japanese Americans similar during World War II? How were they different?

4. **DEVELOPING HISTORICAL PERSPECTIVE**
   Do you think that the government's policy of evacuating Japanese Americans to camps was justified on the basis of "military necessity"? Explain your answer.

5. **ANALYZING EFFECTS**
   What effect did World War II have on American families? **Think About:**
   - the role of women in families and the economy
   - the relationship between the races
   - the impact of the federal government on society

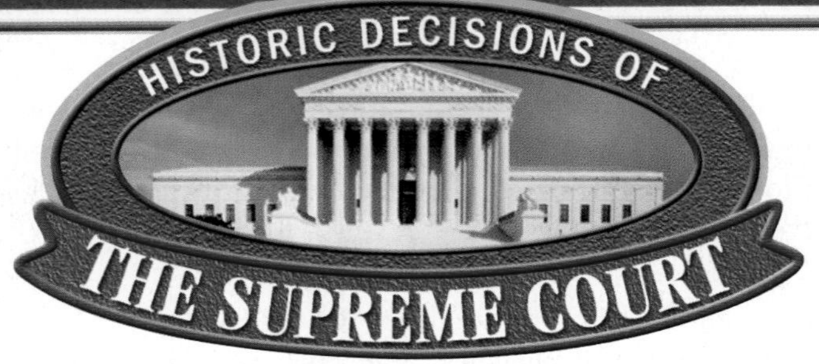

KOREMATSU v. *UNITED STATES* (1944)

ORIGINS OF THE CASE Following the Japanese attack on Pearl Harbor on December 7, 1941, U.S. military officials argued that Japanese Americans posed a threat to the nation's security. Based on recommendations from the military, President Franklin Roosevelt issued Executive Order 9066, which gave military officials the power to limit the civil rights of Japanese Americans. Military authorities began by setting a curfew for Japanese Americans. Later, they forced Japanese Americans from their homes and moved them into detention camps. Fred Korematsu was convicted of defying the military order to leave his home. At the urging of the American Civil Liberties Union (ACLU), Korematsu appealed that conviction.

THE RULING **The Court upheld Korematsu's conviction and argued that military necessity made internment constitutional.**

LEGAL REASONING

Executive Order 9066 was clearly aimed at one group of people—Japanese Americans. Korematsu argued that this order was unconstitutional because it was based on race. Writing for the Court majority, Justice Hugo Black agreed "that all legal restrictions which curtail the civil rights of a single racial group are immediately suspect." However, in this case, he said, the restrictions were based on "a military imperative" and not "group punishment based on antagonism to those of Japanese origin." As such, Justice Black stated that the restrictions were constitutional.

> **"Compulsory exclusion of large groups, . . . except under circumstances of direct emergency and peril, is inconsistent with our basic governmental institutions. But when under conditions of modern warfare our shores are threatened by hostile forces, the power to protect must be commensurate with the threatened danger."**

Justice Frank Murphy, however, dissented—he opposed the majority. He believed that military necessity was merely an excuse that could not conceal the racism at the heart of the restrictions.

> **"This exclusion . . . ought not to be approved. Such exclusion goes over 'the very brink of constitutional power' and falls into the ugly abyss of racism."**

Two other justices also dissented, but Korematsu's conviction stood.

LEGAL SOURCES

LEGISLATION

U.S. CONSTITUTION, FIFTH AMENDMENT (1791)
"No person shall . . . be deprived of life, liberty, or property, without due process of law."

EXECUTIVE ORDER 9066 (1942)
"I hereby authorize and direct the Secretary of War . . . to prescribe military areas in such places and of such extent as he . . . may determine, from which any or all persons may be excluded."

RELATED CASES

***HIRABAYASHI* v. *UNITED STATES* (JUNE 1943)**
The Court upheld the conviction of a Japanese-American man for breaking curfew. The Court argued that the curfew was within congressional and presidential authority.

***EX PARTE ENDO* (DECEMBER 1944)**
The Court ruled that a Japanese-American girl, whose loyalty had been clearly established, could not be held in an internment camp.

President Clinton presents Fred Korematsu with a Presidential Medal of Freedom during a ceremony at the White House on January 15, 1998.

WHY IT MATTERED

About 110,000 Japanese Americans were forced into internment camps, as shown above, during World War II. Many had to sell their businesses and homes at great loss. Thousands were forced to give up their possessions. In the internment camps, Japanese Americans lived in a prison-like setting under constant guard.

The Court ruled that these government actions did not violate people's rights because the restrictions were based on military necessity rather than on race. But the government treated German Americans and Italian Americans much differently. In those instances, the government identified potentially disloyal people but did not harass the people it believed to be loyal. By contrast, the government refused to make distinctions between loyal and potentially disloyal Japanese Americans.

HISTORICAL IMPACT

In the end, the internment of Japanese Americans became a national embarrassment. In 1976, President Gerald R. Ford repealed Executive Order 9066.

Similarly, the Court's decision in *Korematsu* became an embarrassing example of court-sanctioned racism often compared to the decisions on *Dred Scott* (1857) and *Plessy* v. *Ferguson* (1896). In the early 1980s, a scholar conducting research obtained copies of government documents related to the *Hirabayashi* and *Korematsu* cases. The documents showed that the army had lied to the Court in the 1940s. Japanese Americans had not posed any security threat. Korematsu's conviction was overturned in 1984. Hirabayashi's conviction was overturned in 1986. In 1988, Congress passed a law ordering reparations payments to surviving Japanese Americans who had been detained in the camps.

THINKING CRITICALLY

CONNECT TO HISTORY

1. **Hypothesizing** The internment of Japanese Americans during World War II disrupted lives and ripped apart families. What do you think can be done today to address this terrible mistake? How can the government make amends?

SEE SKILLBUILDER HANDBOOK, PAGE R13.

CONNECT TO TODAY

2. 

CLASSZONE.COM

Visit the links for Historic Decisions of the Supreme Court to locate the three dissenting opinions in *Korematsu* written by Justices Frank Murphy, Robert Jackson, and Owen Roberts. Read one of these opinions, and then write a summary that states its main idea. What constitutional principle, if any, does the opinion use?

CHAPTER  ASSESSMENT

VISUAL SUMMARY

THE UNITED STATES IN WORLD WAR II

LONG-TERM CAUSES

- Discontent about Treaty of Versailles
- Economic instability in Europe
- Rise of totalitarian governments

IMMEDIATE CAUSES

- Expansion of Germany, Italy, and Japan
- Failure of appeasement
- German invasion of Poland
- Japanese attack on Pearl Harbor

IMMEDIATE EFFECTS

- Defeat of Axis powers
- Destruction and immense loss of life
- Recognition of Holocaust
- Founding of United Nations

LONG-TERM EFFECTS

- Rise of United States and Soviet Union as superpowers
- Cold War
- Soviet control of Eastern Europe
- Divided Germany
- Development of nuclear capability

TERMS & NAMES

For each term or name below, write a sentence explaining its connection to World War II.

1. A. Philip Randolph
2. Manhattan Project
3. rationing
4. Dwight D. Eisenhower
5. D-Day
6. V-E Day
7. Douglas MacArthur
8. Hiroshima
9. GI Bill of Rights
10. Congress of Racial Equality (CORE)

MAIN IDEAS

Use your notes and the information in the chapter to answer the following questions.

Mobilizing for Defense *(pages 562–568)*

1. How did the U.S. military reflect the diversity of American society during World War II?
2. How did the federal government's actions influence civilian life during World War II?
3. What role did the media play in helping the country mobilize?

The War for Europe and North Africa *(pages 569–577)*

4. How did the Allies win control of the Atlantic Ocean between 1941 and 1943?
5. What was the significance of the Battle of Stalingrad?
6. How did the Battle of the Bulge signal the beginning of the end of World War II in Europe?

The War in the Pacific *(pages 578–587)*

7. Briefly describe the island war in the Pacific.
8. Why did President Truman decide to use atomic weapons?

The Home Front *(pages 590–595)*

9. How did the U.S. economy change during World War II?
10. What events show the persistence of racial tensions?

CRITICAL THINKING

1. **USING YOUR NOTES** In a chart like the one shown, provide causes for the listed effects of World War II.

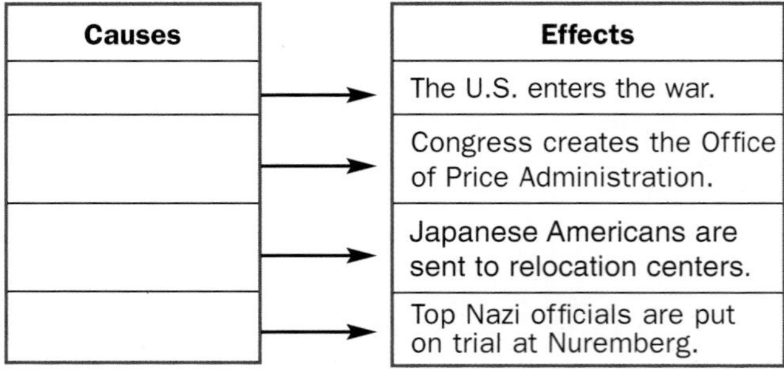

Causes		Effects
	→	The U.S. enters the war.
	→	Congress creates the Office of Price Administration.
	→	Japanese Americans are sent to relocation centers.
	→	Top Nazi officials are put on trial at Nuremberg.

2. **ANALYZING ISSUES** Would you support the use of nuclear weapons today, and if so, under what circumstances?

3. **INTERPRETING MAPS** Judging from the map on page 572, why was a victory in North Africa essential to an invasion of southern Europe?

Standardized Test Practice

Use the map and your knowledge of U.S. history to answer question 1.

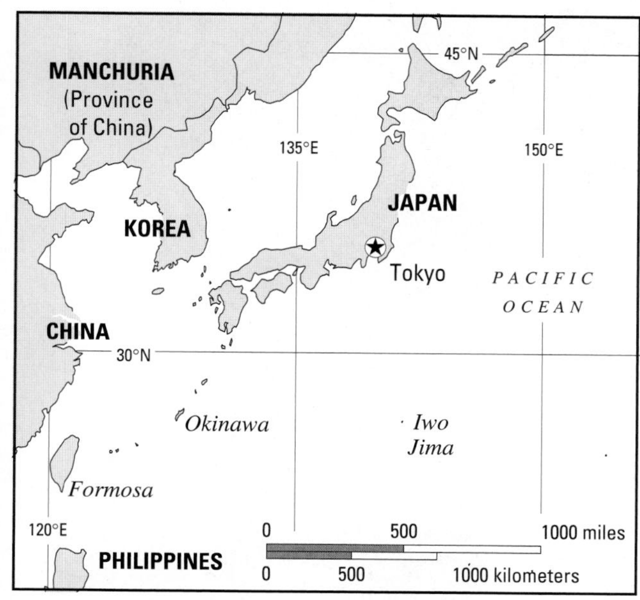

1. Why was it critical for the Allies to take the Japanese-held islands of Iwo Jima and Okinawa?
   - **A** The islands were highly populated areas with little military protection.
   - **B** The islands were critical as bases from which Allied bombers could reach Japan.
   - **C** The islands were centers for Japanese development of a nuclear bomb.
   - **D** The Allies intended to drop atomic bombs on the islands.

2. How did World War II lead to one of the largest population shifts in U.S. history?
   - **F** Service men and women were forced to leave their homes for Europe.
   - **G** The loss of loved ones led people to move in with their families.
   - **H** People moved to states with military bases and factories for better jobs.
   - **J** People moved to the middle of the country to escape wars on both coasts.

3. How did natural geography contribute to Germany's defeat in World War II?
   - **A** Large bodies of water stood between Germany and its enemies.
   - **B** Germany had to fight a war on three fronts: North Africa, Western Europe, and Eastern Europe and the Soviet Union.
   - **C** There were too few rivers to be used for German supplies.
   - **D** Switzerland pledged to remain neutral throughout the war.

ADDITIONAL TEST PRACTICE, pages S1–S33.

TEST PRACTICE CLASSZONE.COM

ALTERNATIVE ASSESSMENT

1. **INTERACT WITH HISTORY** Recall your discussion of the question on page 561:

How can the United States use its resources to achieve victory?

Write a newspaper article in which you describe the ways in which the United States used its resources during World War II. Include information about rationing and about the various offices that the federal government established to monitor inflation and convert a peacetime economy into a wartime economy.

2. 
INTERNET ACTIVITY CLASSZONE.COM

Visit the links for Chapter Assessment to find out more about A. Philip Randolph. Write a brief biography of Randolph in which you describe his lifelong contributions as a labor leader. Here are some questions to consider:

- What did he do during his youth that prepared him for his life's work?
- What role did he play in ending discrimination in the armed services?
- What union did he organize?
- What role did he play in the march on Washington in 1963?

CHAPTER 18 COLD WAR CONFLICTS

Senator Joseph McCarthy, shown here, charged that Communists had infiltrated many areas of American life.

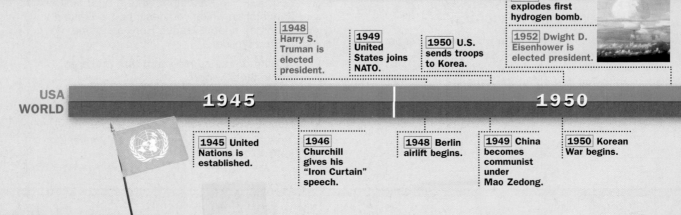

1948 Harry S. Truman is elected president.

1949 United States joins NATO.

1950 U.S. sends troops to Korea.

1952 U.S. explodes first hydrogen bomb.

1952 Dwight D. Eisenhower is elected president.

USA

WORLD

1945

1950

1945 United Nations is established.

1946 Churchill gives his "Iron Curtain" speech.

1948 Berlin airlift begins.

1949 China becomes communist under Mao Zedong.

1950 Korean War begins.

INTERACT WITH HISTORY

At the end of World War II, Americans begin to be haunted by a new fear. The Soviets have embraced a tightly controlled political system called communism. Many believe it threatens the American way of life. Throughout the nation, suspected communists are called before a House subcommittee for questioning. Anyone accused of un-American activity faces public humiliation and professional ruin.

What do you do when a friend is accused?

Examine the issues

- Do Americans with communist beliefs pose a threat to the nation?
- What can individual citizens do to protect the rights of all people?
- Should citizens speak out to preserve the rights of others?

RESEARCH LINKS **CLASSZONE.COM**

Visit the Chapter 18 links for more information about Cold War Conflicts.

1953 Julius and Ethel Rosenberg are executed as spies.

1954 Senator Joseph McCarthy alleges Communist involvement in U.S. Army.

1960 Francis Gary Powers's U-2 spy plane is shot down by the Soviets.

1960 John F. Kennedy is elected president.

1955 **1960**

1953 Participants in Korean War agree on cease-fire.

1954 French are defeated in Vietnam.

1957 Soviets launch *Sputnik.*

1959 Fidel Castro comes to power in Cuba.

SECTION 1

Origins of the Cold War

MAIN IDEA

The United States and the Soviet Union emerged from World War II as two "superpowers" with vastly different political and economic systems.

WHY IT MATTERS NOW

After World War II, differences between the United States and the Soviet Union led to a Cold War that lasted almost to the 21st century.

Terms & Names

- **United Nations (UN)**
- **satellite nation**
- **containment**
- **iron curtain**
- **Cold War**
- **Truman Doctrine**
- **Marshall Plan**
- **Berlin airlift**
- **North Atlantic Treaty Organization (NATO)**

One American's Story

Seventy miles south of Berlin, Joseph Polowsky and a patrol of American soldiers were scouting for signs of the Soviet army advancing from the east. As the soldiers neared the Elbe River, they saw lilacs in bloom. Polowsky later said the sight of the flowers filled them with joy.

Across the Elbe, the Americans spotted Soviet soldiers, who signaled for them to cross over. When the Americans reached the opposite bank, their joy turned to shock. They saw to their horror that the bank was covered with dead civilians, victims of bombing raids.

A PERSONAL VOICE JOSEPH POLOWSKY

"Here we are, tremendously exhilarated, and there's a sea of dead. . . . [The platoon leader] was much moved. . . . He said, 'Joe, let's make a resolution with these Russians here and also the ones on the bank: this would be an important day in the lives of the two countries.' . . . It was a solemn moment. There were tears in the eyes of most of us. . . . We embraced. We swore never to forget."

—quoted in *The Good War*

American and Soviet soldiers meet *(top)* at the Elbe River in Germany near the end of World War II. A 1996 postage stamp *(above)* commemorates the historic meeting.

The Soviet and U.S. soldiers believed that their encounter would serve as a symbol of peace. Unfortunately, such hopes were soon dashed. After World War II, the United States and the Soviet Union emerged as rival superpowers, each strong enough to greatly influence world events.

Former Allies Clash

The United States and the Soviet Union had very different ambitions for the future. These differences created a climate of icy tension that plunged the two countries into a bitter rivalry.

Background
See *communism* on page R39 and *capitalism* on page R38 in the Economics Handbook.

Under Soviet communism, the state controlled all property and economic activity, while in the capitalistic American system, private citizens controlled almost all economic activity. In the American system, voting by the people elected a president and a congress from competing political parties; in the Soviet Union, the Communist Party established a totalitarian government with no opposing parties.

The United States was well aware that Joseph Stalin—the leader of the Soviet Union—had been an ally of Hitler for a time. Stalin had supported the Allies only after Hitler invaded the Soviet Union in June 1941. In some ways, the Americans and Soviets became more suspicious of each other during the war. Stalin resented the Western Allies' delay in attacking the Germans in Europe. Such an attack, he thought, would draw part of the German army away from the Soviet Union. Relations worsened after Stalin learned that the United States had tried to keep its development of the atomic bomb secret. (A)

MAIN IDEA

Analyzing Causes
(A) What caused the tension between the Soviet Union and the United States after the war?

KEY PLAYERS

HARRY S. TRUMAN
1884–1972

Harry S. Truman, the son of a Missouri livestock trader and his wife, did not seem destined for greatness. When he graduated from high school in 1901, he drifted from job to job. After WWI, he invested in a men's clothing store, but the business failed.

Discouraged by his business failure, Truman sought a career in politics. As a politician, his blunt and outspoken style won both loyal friends and bitter enemies. As president, his decisiveness and willingness to accept responsibility for his decisions ("The Buck Stops Here" read a sign on his desk) earned him respect that has grown over the years.

JOSEPH STALIN
1879–1953

As a young revolutionary, Iosif Vissarionovich Dzhugashvili took the name *Stalin*, which means "man of steel" in Russian.

His father was a failed shoemaker and an alcoholic. His mother helped support the family as a washerwoman.

Stalin is credited with turning the Soviet Union into a world power but at a terrible cost to its citizens. He ruled with terror and brutality and saw "enemies" everywhere, even among friends and supporters. He subdued the population with the use of secret police and labor camps, and he is believed to have been responsible for the murder of millions of Soviets.

THE UNITED NATIONS In spite of these problems, hopes for world peace were high at the end of the war. The most visible symbol of these hopes was the **United Nations (UN).** On April 25, 1945, the representatives of 50 nations met in San Francisco to establish this new peacekeeping body. After two months of debate, on June 26, 1945, the delegates signed the charter establishing the UN.

Ironically, even though the UN was intended to promote peace, it soon became an arena in which the two superpowers competed. Both the United States and the Soviet Union used the UN as a forum to spread their influence over others.

TRUMAN BECOMES PRESIDENT For the United States, the key figure in the early years of conflict with the Soviets was President Harry S. Truman. On April 12, 1945, Truman had suddenly become president when Franklin Roosevelt died. This former Missouri senator had been picked as Roosevelt's running mate in 1944. He had served as vice-president for just a few months before Roosevelt's death. During his term as vice-president, Truman had not been included in top policy decisions. He had not even known that the United States was developing an atomic bomb. Many Americans doubted Truman's ability to serve as president. But Truman was honest and had a willingness to make tough decisions—qualities that he would need desperately during his presidency.

THE POTSDAM CONFERENCE Truman's test as a diplomat came in July 1945 when the Big Three—the United States, Great Britain, and the Soviet Union—met at the final wartime conference at Potsdam near Berlin. The countries that participated were the same ones that had been present at Yalta in February 1945. Stalin still represented the Soviet Union. Clement Attlee replaced Churchill as Britain's representative mid-conference, because Churchill's party lost a general election. And Harry Truman took Roosevelt's place.

At Yalta, Stalin had promised Roosevelt that he would allow free elections—that is, a vote by secret ballot in a multiparty system—in Poland and other parts of Eastern Europe that the Soviets occupied at the end of the war. By July 1945, however, it was clear that Stalin would not keep this promise. The Soviets prevented free elections in Poland and banned democratic parties. B

MAIN IDEA

Analyzing Causes

B What did Stalin do to make President Truman distrust him?

Tension Mounts

Stalin's refusal to allow free elections in Poland convinced Truman that U.S. and Soviet aims were deeply at odds. Truman's goal in demanding free elections was to spread democracy to nations that had been under Nazi rule. He wanted to create a new world order in which all nations had the right of self-determination.

BARGAINING AT POTSDAM At the Yalta conference, the Soviets had wanted to take reparations from Germany to help repay Soviet wartime losses. Now, at Potsdam, Truman objected to that. After hard bargaining, it was agreed that the Soviets, British, Americans, and French would take reparations mainly from their own occupation zones.

Truman also felt that the United States had a large economic stake in spreading democracy and free trade across the globe. U.S. industry boomed during the war, making the United States the economic leader of the world. To continue growing, American businesses wanted access to raw materials in Eastern Europe, and they wanted to be able to sell goods to Eastern European countries.

SOVIETS TIGHTEN THEIR GRIP ON EASTERN EUROPE The Soviet Union had also emerged from the war as a nation of enormous economic and military strength. However, unlike the United States, the Soviet Union had suffered heavy devastation on its own soil. Soviet deaths from the war have been estimated at 20 million, half of whom were civilians. As a result, the Soviets felt justified in their claim to Eastern Europe. By dominating this region, the Soviets felt they could stop future invasions from the west.

U.S. Aims Versus Soviet Aims in Europe

The United States wanted to . . .	The Soviets wanted to . . .
• Create a new world order in which all nations had the right of self-determination • Gain access to raw materials and markets for its industries • Rebuild European governments to ensure stability and to create new markets for American goods • Reunite Germany, believing that Europe would be more secure if Germany were productive	• Encourage communism in other countries as part of the worldwide struggle between workers and the wealthy • Rebuild its war-ravaged economy using Eastern Europe's industrial equipment and raw materials • Control Eastern Europe to balance U.S. influence in Western Europe • Keep Germany divided and weak so that it would never again threaten the Soviet Union

SKILLBUILDER Interpreting Charts

1. Which aims involved economic growth of the United States?
2. Which Soviet aims involved self-protection?

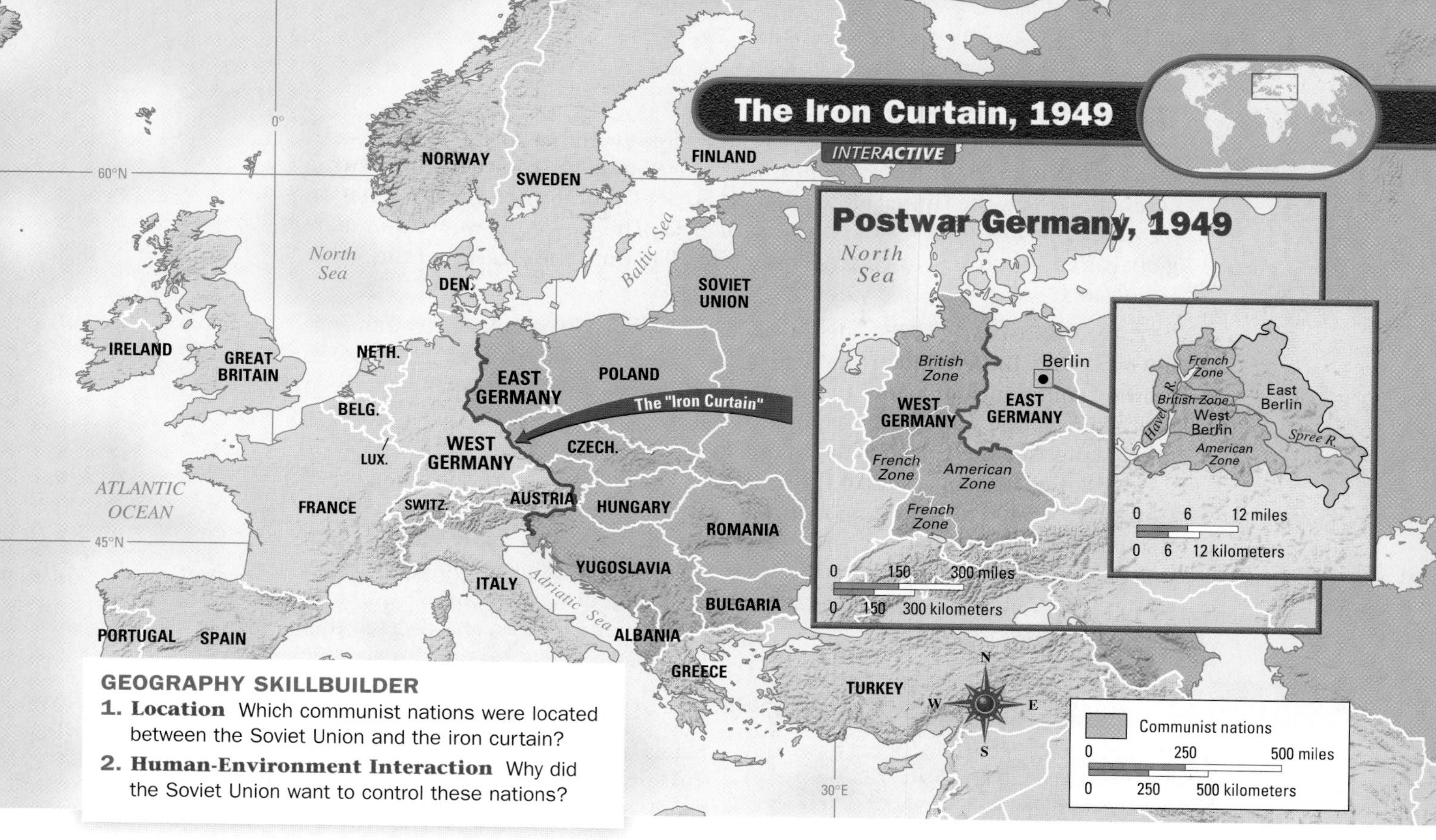

GEOGRAPHY SKILLBUILDER

1. **Location** Which communist nations were located between the Soviet Union and the iron curtain?
2. **Human-Environment Interaction** Why did the Soviet Union want to control these nations?

Stalin installed communist governments in Albania, Bulgaria, Czechoslovakia, Hungary, Romania, and Poland. These countries became known as **satellite nations,** countries dominated by the Soviet Union. In early 1946, Stalin gave a speech announcing that communism and capitalism were incompatible—and that another war was inevitable.

UNITED STATES ESTABLISHES A POLICY OF CONTAINMENT Faced with the Soviet threat, American officials decided it was time, in Truman's words, to stop "babying the Soviets." In February 1946, George F. Kennan, an American diplomat in Moscow, proposed a policy of **containment.** By containment he meant taking measures to prevent any extension of communist rule to other countries. This policy began to guide the Truman administration's foreign policy. C

MAIN IDEA

Analyzing Motives

C What were Truman's goals in establishing the policy of containment?

Europe was now divided into two political regions, a mostly democratic Western Europe and a communist Eastern Europe. In March 1946, Winston Churchill traveled to the United States and gave a speech that described the situation in Europe.

A PERSONAL VOICE WINSTON CHURCHILL

"A shadow has fallen upon the scenes so lately lighted by the Allied victory. . . . From Stettin in the Baltic to Trieste in the Adriatic, an iron curtain has descended across the Continent. Behind that line lie all the capitals of the ancient states of Central and Eastern Europe. . . . All these famous cities and the populations around them lie in . . . the Soviet sphere, and all are subject in one form or another, not only to Soviet influence but to a very high and . . . increasing measure of control from Moscow."

—"Iron Curtain" speech in Fulton, Missouri

Winston Churchill, Prime Minister of Great Britain

The phrase **"iron curtain"** came to stand for the division of Europe. When Stalin heard about the speech, he declared in no uncertain terms that Churchill's words were a "call to war."

Cold War in Europe

The conflicting U.S. and Soviet aims in Eastern Europe led to the **Cold War,** a conflict between the United States and the Soviet Union in which neither nation directly confronted the other on the battlefield. The Cold War would dominate global affairs—and U.S. foreign policy—from 1945 until the breakup of the Soviet Union in 1991.

THE TRUMAN DOCTRINE The United States first tried to contain Soviet influence in Greece and Turkey. Britain was financially supporting both nations' resistance to growing communist influence in the region. However, Britain's economy had been badly hurt by the war, and the formerly wealthy nation could no longer afford to give aid. It asked the United States to take over the responsibility.

President Truman accepted the challenge. On March 12, 1947, Truman asked Congress for $400 million in economic and military aid for Greece and Turkey. In a statement that became known as the **Truman Doctrine,** he declared that "it must be the policy of the United States to support free peoples who are resisting attempted subjugation by armed minorities or by outside pressures." Congress agreed with Truman and decided that the doctrine was essential to keeping Soviet influence from spreading. Between 1947 and 1950, the United States sent $400 million in aid to Turkey and Greece, greatly reducing the danger of communist takeover in those nations.

Vocabulary
subjugation: bringing under control

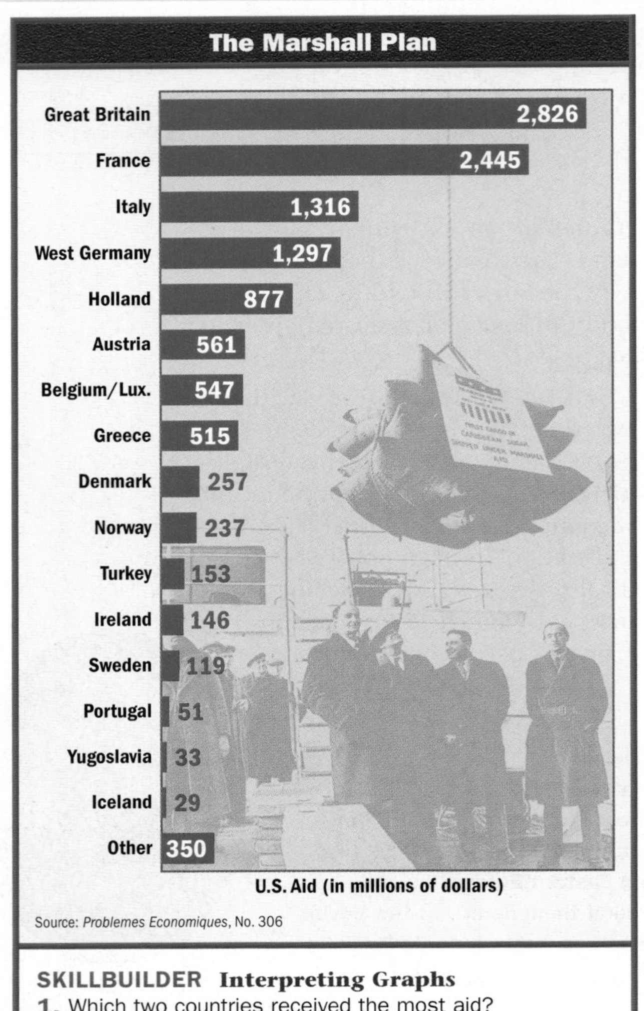

SKILLBUILDER Interpreting Graphs
1. Which two countries received the most aid?
2. Why do you think these countries received so much aid?

THE MARSHALL PLAN Like post-war Greece, Western Europe was in chaos. Most of its factories had been bombed or looted. Millions of people were living in refugee camps while European governments tried to figure out where to resettle them. To make matters worse, the winter of 1946–1947 was the bitterest in several centuries. The weather severely damaged crops and froze rivers, cutting off water transportation and causing a fuel shortage.

In June 1947, Secretary of State George Marshall proposed that the United States provide aid to all European nations that needed it, saying that this move was directed "not against any country or doctrine but against hunger, poverty, desperation, and chaos."

The **Marshall Plan** revived European hopes. Over the next four years, 16 countries received some $13 billion in aid. By 1952, Western Europe was flourishing, and the Communist party had lost much of its appeal to voters.

Background
The Marshall Plan also benefited the United States. To supply Europe with goods, American farms and factories raised production levels. As a result, the American economy continued its wartime boom.

Superpowers Struggle over Germany

As Europe began to get back on its feet, the United States and its allies clashed with the Soviet Union over the issue of German reunification. At the end of World War II, Germany was divided into four zones occupied by the United States, Great Britain, and France in the west and the Soviet Union in the east. In 1948, Britain, France, and the United States decided to combine their three zones into one nation. The western part of Berlin, which had been occupied by the French, British, and Americans, was surrounded by Soviet-occupied territory. (See map, page 605.)

Although the three nations had intended to unify their zones, they had no written agreement with the Soviets guaranteeing free access to Berlin by road or rail. Stalin saw this loophole as an opportunity. If he moved quickly, he might be able to take over the part of Berlin held by the three Western powers. In June 1948, Stalin closed all highway and rail routes into West Berlin. As a result, no food or fuel could reach that part of the city. The 2.1 million residents of the city had only enough food to last for approximately five weeks.

THE BERLIN AIRLIFT The resulting situation was dire. In an attempt to break the blockade, American and British officials started the **Berlin airlift** to fly food and supplies into West Berlin. For 327 days, planes took off and landed every few minutes, around the clock. In 277,000 flights, they brought in 2.3 million tons of supplies—everything from food, fuel, and medicine to Christmas presents that the planes' crews bought with their own money.

West Berlin survived because of the airlift. In addition, the mission to aid Berlin boosted American prestige around the world. By May 1949, the Soviet Union realized it was beaten and lifted the blockade. D

MAIN IDEA

Analyzing Effects

D What were the effects of the Berlin airlift?

Beginning in June 1948, planes bringing tons of food and other supplies to West Berlin landed every few minutes.

In the same month, the western part of Germany officially became a new nation, the Federal Republic of Germany, also called West Germany. It included West Berlin. A few months later, from its occupation zone, the Soviet Union created the German Democratic Republic, called East Germany. It included East Berlin.

▲ **This cartoon depicts the nations that signed the North Atlantic Pact, which created NATO in 1949. The nations, shown as hats, are arranged in a pyramid to show the bigger countries on the bottom supporting the smaller, weaker nations on top.**

THE NATO ALLIANCE The Berlin blockade increased Western European fear of Soviet aggression. As a result, ten Western European nations—Belgium, Denmark, France, Great Britain, Iceland, Italy, Luxembourg, the Netherlands, Norway, and Portugal—joined with the United States and Canada on April 4, 1949, to form a defensive military alliance called the **North Atlantic Treaty Organization (NATO).** (See map, page 624.) The 12 members of NATO pledged military support to one another in case any member was attacked. For the first time in its history, the United States had entered into a military alliance with other nations during peacetime. The Cold War had ended any hope of a return to U.S. isolationism. Greece and Turkey joined NATO in 1952, and West Germany joined in 1955. By then, NATO kept a standing military force of more than 500,000 troops as well as thousands of planes, tanks, and other equipment.

SECTION 1 ASSESSMENT

1. **TERMS & NAMES** For each term or name, write a sentence explaining its significance.
   - **United Nations (UN)**
   - **satellite nation**
   - **containment**
   - **iron curtain**
   - **Cold War**
   - **Truman Doctrine**
   - **Marshall Plan**
   - **Berlin airlift**
   - **North Atlantic Treaty Organization (NATO)**

MAIN IDEA

2. **TAKING NOTES**
   Use a graphic organizer like the one below to describe the U.S. actions and the Soviet actions that contributed most to the Cold War.

U.S. Actions	Soviet Actions

   Write a paragraph explaining which country was more responsible and why you think so.

CRITICAL THINKING

3. **EVALUATING LEADERSHIP**
   People who had served as aides to President Franklin Roosevelt worried that Truman was not qualified to handle world leadership. Considering what you learned in this section, evaluate Truman as a world leader.
   Think About:
   - his behavior toward Stalin
   - his economic support of European nations
   - his support of West Berlin

4. **MAKING INFERENCES**
   Which of the two superpowers do you think was more successful in achieving its aims during the period 1945–1949? Support your answer by referring to historical events.

5. **ANALYZING MOTIVES**
   What were Stalin's motives in supporting Communist governments in Eastern Europe?

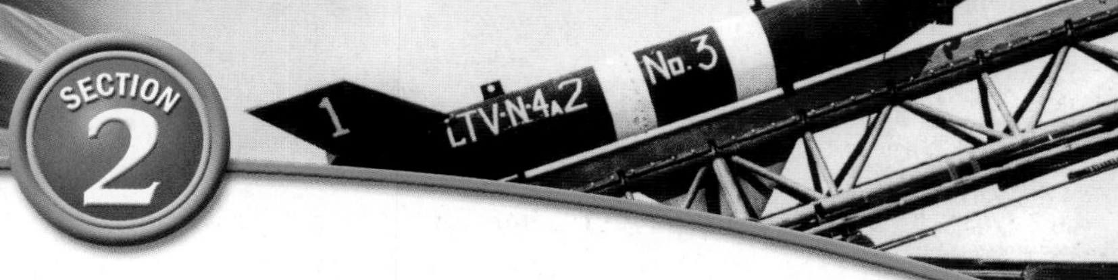

SECTION 2

The Cold War Heats Up

MAIN IDEA

After World War II, China became a communist nation and Korea was split into a communist north and a democratic south.

WHY IT MATTERS NOW

Ongoing tensions with China and North Korea continue to involve the United States.

Terms & Names

- **Chiang Kai-shek**
- **Mao Zedong**
- **Taiwan**
- **38th parallel**
- **Korean War**

One American's Story

First Lieutenant Philip Day, Jr., vividly remembers his first taste of battle in Korea. On the morning of July 5, 1950, Philip Day spotted a column of eight enemy tanks moving toward his company.

A PERSONAL VOICE PHILIP DAY, JR.

"I was with a 75-mm recoilless-rifle team. 'Let's see,' I shouted, 'if we can get one of those tanks.' We picked up the gun and moved it to where we could get a clean shot. I don't know if we were poorly trained, . . . but we set the gun on the forward slope of the hill. When we fired, the recoilless blast blew a hole in the hill which instantly covered us in mud and dirt. . . . When we were ready again, we moved the gun to a better position and began banging away. I swear we had some hits, but the tanks never slowed down. . . . In a little less than two hours, 30 North Korean tanks rolled through the position we were supposed to block as if we hadn't been there."

—quoted in *The Korean War: Pusan to Chosin*

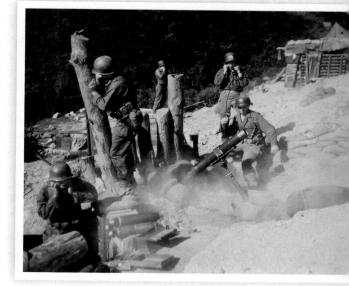

▲ **American soldiers fire mortars at communist strongholds near Mundung-ni in Korea.**

Only five years after World War II ended, the United States became embroiled in a war in Korea. The policy of containment had led the United States into battle to halt communist expansion. In this conflict, however, the enemy was not the Soviet Union, but North Korea and China.

China Becomes a Communist Country

For two decades, Chinese Communists had struggled against the nationalist government of **Chiang Kai-shek** (chăng′ kī′shĕk′). The United States supported Chiang. Between 1945 and 1949, the American government sent the Nationalists approximately $3 billion in aid.

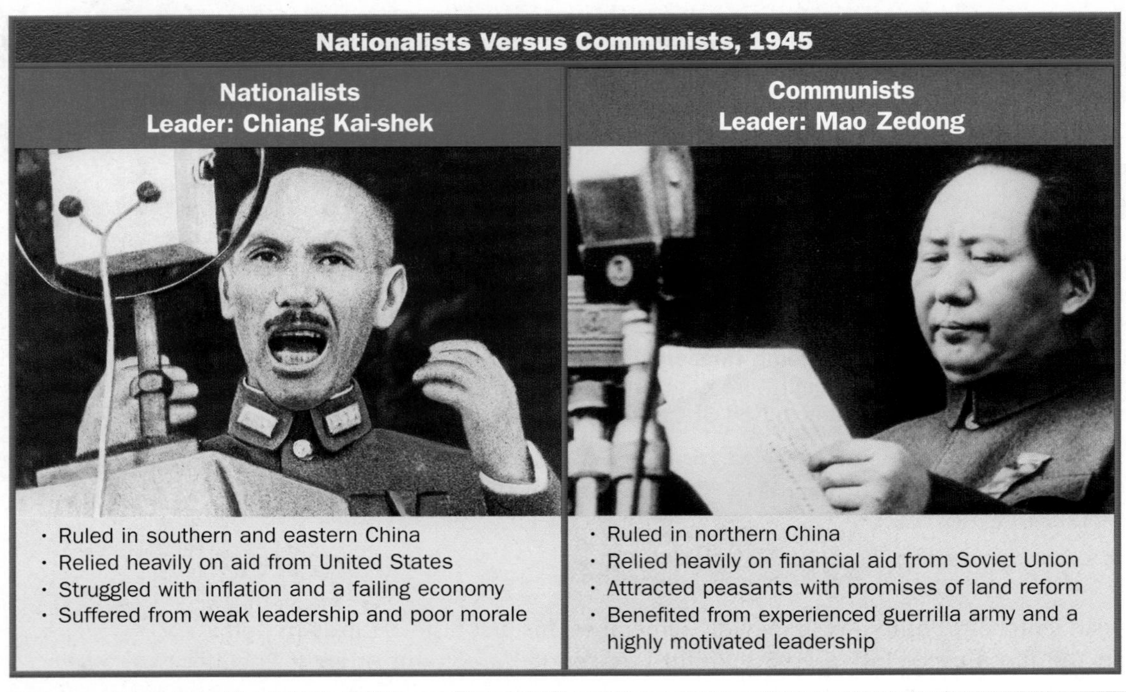

Nationalists Versus Communists, 1945
Nationalists
Leader: Chiang Kai-shek
Communists
Leader: Mao Zedong
• Ruled in southern and eastern China
• Relied heavily on aid from United States
• Struggled with inflation and a failing economy
• Suffered from weak leadership and poor morale
• Ruled in northern China
• Relied heavily on financial aid from Soviet Union
• Attracted peasants with promises of land reform
• Benefited from experienced guerrilla army and a highly motivated leadership

Many Americans were impressed by Chiang Kai-shek and admired the courage and determination that the Chinese Nationalists showed in resisting the Japanese during the war. However, U.S. officials who dealt with Chiang held a different view. They found his government inefficient and hopelessly corrupt.

Furthermore, the policies of Chiang's government undermined Nationalist support. For example, the Nationalists collected a grain tax from farmers even during the famine of 1944. When city dwellers demonstrated against a 10,000 percent increase in the price of rice, Chiang's secret police opened fire on them.

In contrast, the Communists, led by **Mao Zedong** (mou′dzŭ′dŏng′), gained strength throughout the country. In the areas they controlled, Communists worked to win peasant support. They encouraged peasants to learn to read, and they helped to improve food production. As a result, more and more recruits flocked to the Communists' Red Army. By 1945, much of northern China was under communist control.

RENEWED CIVIL WAR As soon as the defeated Japanese left China at the end of World War II, cooperation between the Nationalists and the Communists ceased. Civil war erupted again between the two groups. In spite of the problems in the Nationalist regime, American policy favored the Nationalists because they opposed communism.

From 1944 to 1947, the United States played peacemaker between the two groups while still supporting the Nationalists. However, U.S. officials repeatedly failed to negotiate peace. Truman refused to commit American soldiers to back up the Nationalists, although the United States did send $2 billion worth of military equipment and supplies.

The aid wasn't enough to save the Nationalists, whose weak military leadership and corrupt, abusive practices drove the peasants to the Communist side. In May 1949, Chiang and the remnants of his demoralized government fled to the island of **Taiwan,** which Westerners called Formosa. After more than 20 years of struggle, the Communists ruled all of mainland China. They established a new government, the People's Republic of China, which the United States refused to accept as China's true government. (A)

MAIN IDEA

Analyzing Causes

(A) What factors led to the Communist takeover in China?

AMERICA REACTS TO COMMUNIST TAKEOVER The American public was stunned that China had become Communist. Containment had failed! In Congress, conservative Republicans and Democrats attacked the Truman administration for supplying only limited aid to Chiang. If containing communism was important in Europe, they asked, why was it not equally important in Asia?

The State Department replied by saying that what had happened in China was a result of internal forces. The United States had failed in its attempts to influence these forces, such as Chiang's inability to retain the support of his people. Trying to do more would only have started a war in Asia—a war that the United States wasn't prepared to fight.

Some conservatives in Congress rejected this argument as a lame excuse. They claimed that the American government was riddled with Communist agents. Like wildfire, American fear of communism began to burn out of control, and the flames were fanned even further by events in Korea the following year.

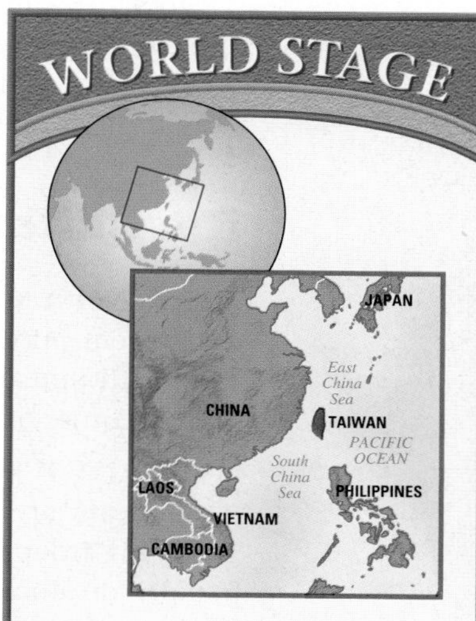

TAIWAN

In 1949, Chiang Kai-shek and other Nationalist leaders retreated to the island of Taiwan, which lies about 100 miles off the southeast coast of the Chinese mainland. There the United States helped set up a Nationalist government—the Republic of China. From 1949 through the 1960s, the United States poured millions of dollars of aid into the Taiwanese economy.

During the 1970s, a number of nations, including the United States, decided to end diplomatic relations with Taiwan and established ties with Communist China. With the collapse of Soviet communism in the early 1990s, relations between Taiwan and the United States improved. In 2001, the United States sold weapons to Taiwan to bolster the island nation's defense system.

The Korean War

Japan had annexed Korea in 1910 and ruled it until August 1945. As World War II ended, Japanese troops north of the **38th parallel** (38° North latitude) surrendered to the Soviets. Japanese troops south of the parallel surrendered to the Americans. As in Germany, two nations developed, one communist and one democratic.

In 1948, the Republic of Korea, usually called South Korea, was established in the zone that had been occupied by the United States. Its government, headed by Syngman Rhee, was based in Seoul, Korea's traditional capital. Simultaneously, the Communists formed the Democratic People's Republic of Korea in the north. Kim Il Sung led its government, which was based in Pyongyang. (See map, page 613.) B

MAIN IDEA

Analyzing Events

B How did Korea become a divided nation after World War II?

Soon after World War II, the United States had cut back its armed forces in South Korea. As a result, by June of 1949 there were only 500 American troops there. The Soviets concluded that the United States would not fight to defend South Korea. They prepared to back North Korea with tanks, airplanes, and money in an attempt to take over the entire peninsula.

NORTH KOREA ATTACKS SOUTH KOREA On June 25, 1950, North Korean forces swept across the 38th parallel in a surprise attack on South Korea. The conflict that followed became known as the **Korean War.**

Within a few days, North Korean troops had penetrated deep into South Korea. South Korea called on the United Nations to stop the North Korean invasion. When the matter came to a vote in the UN Security Council, the Soviet Union was not there. The Soviets were boycotting the council in protest over the presence of Nationalist China (Taiwan). Thus, the Soviets could not veto the UN's plan of military action. The vote passed.

On June 27, in a show of military strength, President Truman ordered troops stationed in Japan to support the South Koreans. He also sent an American fleet into the waters between Taiwan and China.

In all, 16 nations sent some 520,000 troops to aid South Korea. Over 90 percent of these troops were American. South Korean troops numbered an additional 590,000. The combined forces were placed under the command of General Douglas MacArthur, former World War II hero in the Pacific.

The United States Fights in Korea

At first, North Korea seemed unstoppable. Driving steadily south, its troops captured Seoul. After a month of bitter combat, the North Koreans had forced UN and South Korean troops into a small defensive zone around Pusan in the southeastern corner of the peninsula.

MACARTHUR'S COUNTERATTACK MacArthur launched a counterattack with tanks, heavy artillery, and fresh troops from the United States. On September 15, 1950, his troops made a surprise amphibious landing behind enemy lines at Inchon, on Korea's west coast. Other troops moved north from Pusan. Trapped between the two attacking forces, about half of the North Korean troops surrendered; the rest fled back across the 38th parallel. MacArthur's plan had saved his army from almost certain defeat.

Vocabulary
amphibious: capable of traveling both on land and on water

The UN army chased the retreating North Korean troops across the 38th parallel into North Korea. In late November, UN troops approached the Yalu River, the border between North Korea and China. It seemed as if Korea was about to become a single country again.

THE CHINESE FIGHT BACK The Chinese, however, had other ideas. Communist China's foreign minister, Zhou En-lai, warned that his country would not stand idly by and "let the Americans come to the border"—meaning the Yalu River. In late November 1950, 300,000 Chinese troops joined the war on the side of North Korea. The Chinese wanted North Korea as a Communist buffer state to protect their northeastern provinces that made up Manchuria. They also felt threatened by the American fleet that lay off their coast. The fight between North Korea and South Korea had escalated into a war in which the main opponents were the Chinese communists and the Americans.

By sheer force of numbers, the Chinese drove the UN troops southward. At some points along the battlefront, the Chinese outnumbered UN forces ten to one. By early January 1951, all UN and South Korean troops had been pushed out of North Korea. The Chinese advanced to the south, capturing the South Korean capital, Seoul. "We face an entirely new war," declared MacArthur. C

Analyzing Causes
C How did the involvement of communist China affect the Korean War?

For two years, the two sides fought bitterly to obtain strategic positions in the Korean hills, but neither side was able to make important advances. One officer remembered the standoff.

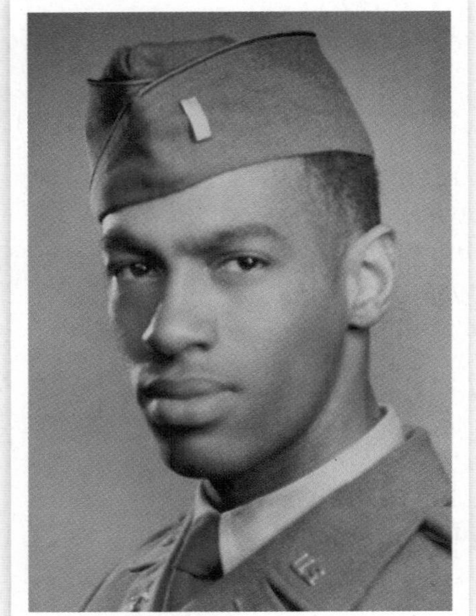

Beverly Scott

A PERSONAL VOICE BEVERLY SCOTT

"Our trenches . . . were only about 20 meters in front of theirs. We were eyeball to eyeball. . . . We couldn't move at all in the daytime without getting shot at. Machine-gun fire would come in, grenades, small-arms fire, all from within spitting distance. It was like World War I. We lived in a maze of bunkers and deep trenches. . . . There were bodies strewn all over the place. Hundreds of bodies frozen in the snow."

—quoted in *No Bugles, No Drums: An Oral History of the Korean War*

The Korean War, 1950–1953

INTER*ACTIVE*

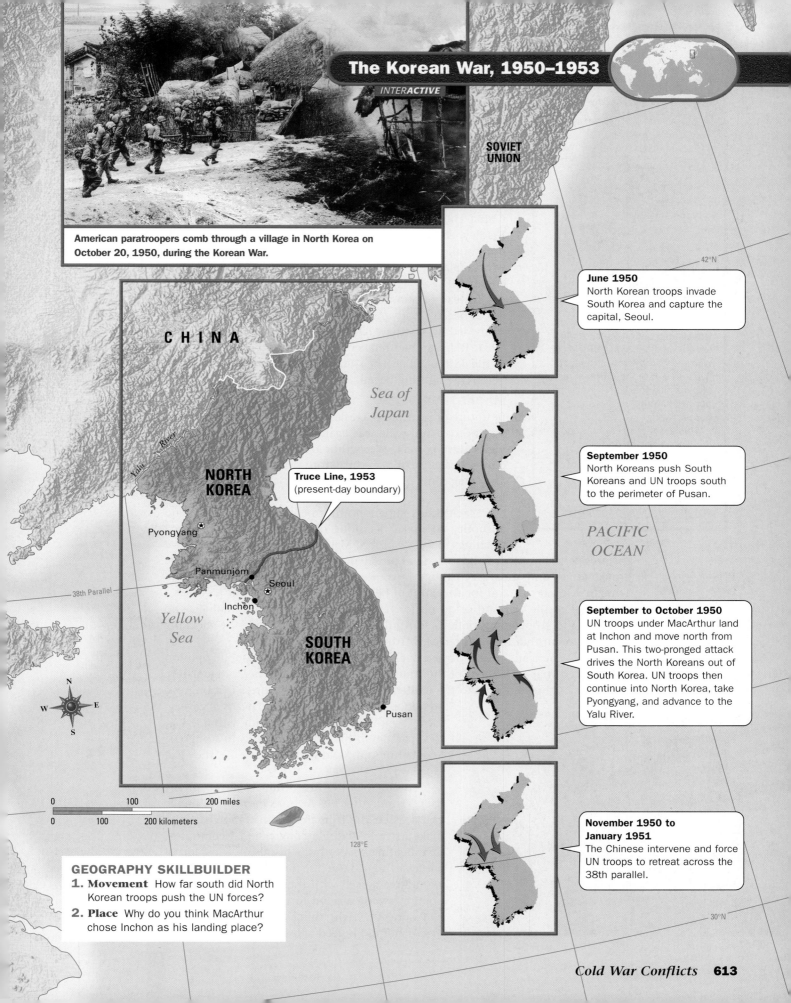

American paratroopers comb through a village in North Korea on October 20, 1950, during the Korean War.

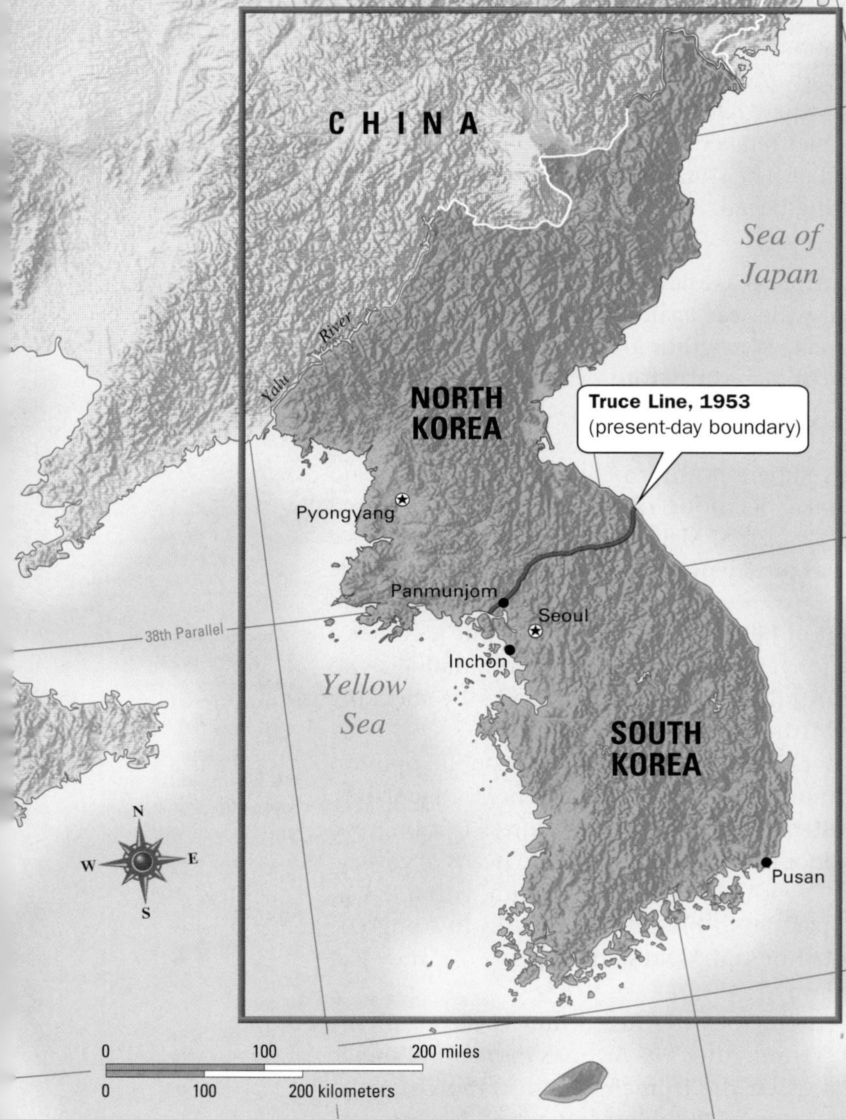

SOVIET UNION

CHINA

Sea of Japan

Yalu River

NORTH KOREA

Truce Line, 1953
(present-day boundary)

Pyongyang

Panmunjom

Seoul

38th Parallel

Inchon

Yellow Sea

SOUTH KOREA

Pusan

N E S W

0 100 200 miles

0 100 200 kilometers

128°E

42°N

30°N

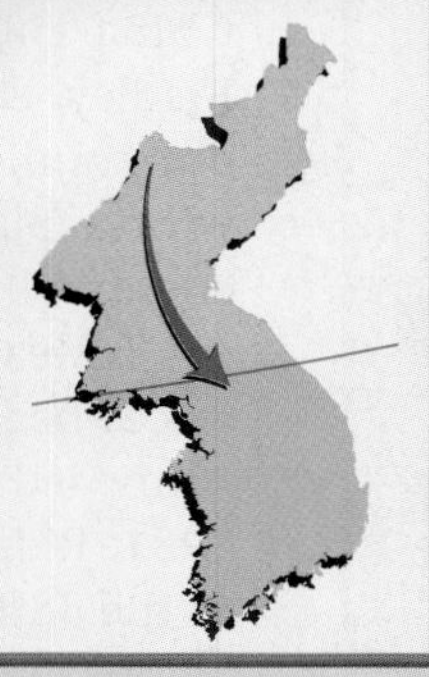

June 1950
North Korean troops invade South Korea and capture the capital, Seoul.

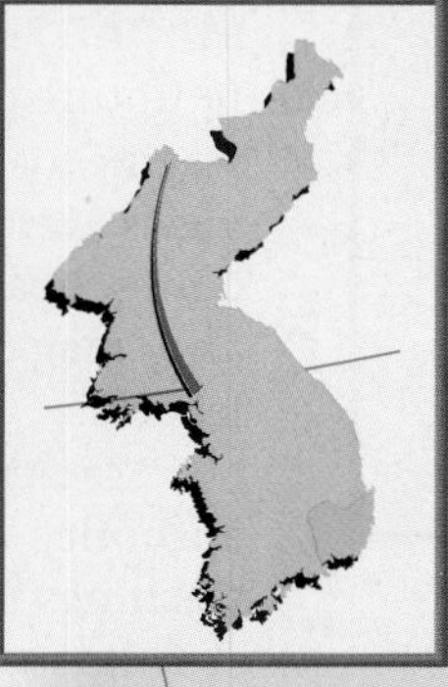

September 1950
North Koreans push South Koreans and UN troops south to the perimeter of Pusan.

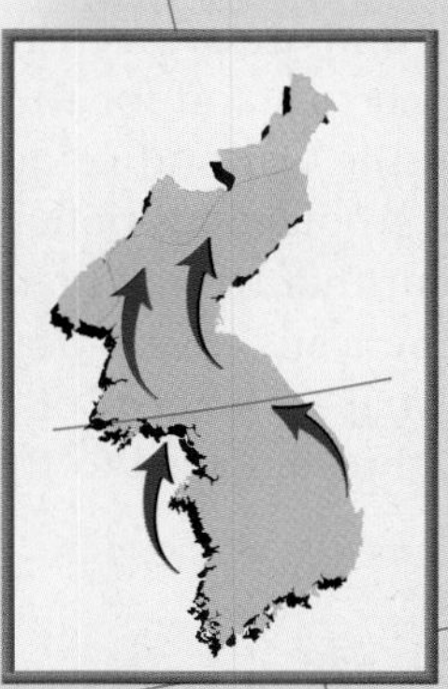

September to October 1950
UN troops under MacArthur land at Inchon and move north from Pusan. This two-pronged attack drives the North Koreans out of South Korea. UN troops then continue into North Korea, take Pyongyang, and advance to the Yalu River.

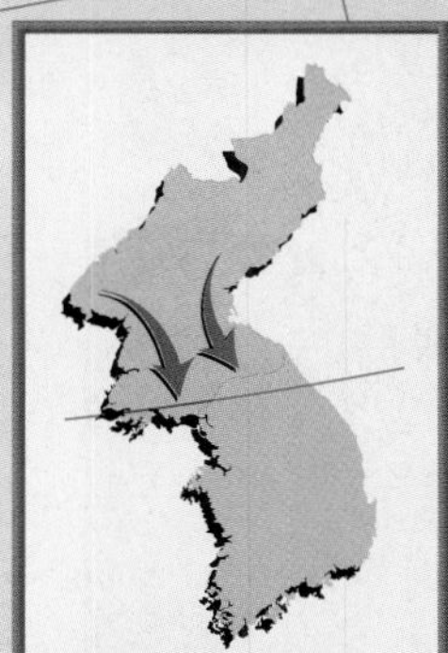

November 1950 to January 1951
The Chinese intervene and force UN troops to retreat across the 38th parallel.

GEOGRAPHY SKILLBUILDER

1. **Movement** How far south did North Korean troops push the UN forces?
2. **Place** Why do you think MacArthur chose Inchon as his landing place?

INDIA'S VIEWPOINT

Nonaligned nations such as India were on neither side of the Cold War and had their own perspectives. In 1951, the prime minister of India, Jawaharlal Nehru *(shown above)*, had this to say about the Korean War:

"This great struggle between the United States and Soviet Russia is hardly the proper role in this world for those great powers. . . . Their role should be to function in their own territories and not be a threat to others."

MACARTHUR RECOMMENDS ATTACKING CHINA To halt the bloody stalemate, in early 1951, MacArthur called for an extension of the war into China. Convinced that Korea was the place "where the Communist conspirators have elected to make their play for global conquest," MacArthur called for the use of nuclear weapons against Chinese cities.

Vocabulary
conspirator: a person who takes part in secretly planning something unlawful

Truman rejected MacArthur's request. The Soviet Union had a mutual-assistance pact with China. Attacking China could set off World War III. As General Omar N. Bradley, chairman of the Joint Chiefs of Staff, said, an all-out conflict with China would be "the wrong war, at the wrong place, at the wrong time, and with the wrong enemy."

Instead of attacking China, the UN and South Korean forces began to advance once more, using the U.S. Eighth Army, led by Matthew B. Ridgway, as a spearhead. By April 1951, Ridgway had retaken Seoul and had moved back up to the 38th parallel. The situation was just what it had been before the fighting began.

MACARTHUR VERSUS TRUMAN Not satisfied with the recapture of South Korea, MacArthur continued to urge the waging of a full-scale war against China. Certain that his views were correct, MacArthur tried to go over the president's head. He spoke and wrote privately to newspaper and magazine publishers and, especially, to Republican leaders.

MacArthur's superiors informed him that he had no authority to make decisions of policy. Despite repeated warnings to follow orders, MacArthur continued to criticize the president. President Truman, who as president was commander-in-chief of the armed forces and thus MacArthur's boss, was just as stubborn as MacArthur. Truman refused to stand for this kind of behavior. He wanted to put together a settlement of the war and could no longer tolerate a military commander who was trying to sabotage his policy. On April 11, 1951, Truman made the shocking announcement that he had fired MacArthur. D

MAIN IDEA
Comparing
D How did Truman and MacArthur differ over strategy in the Korean War?

Many Americans were outraged over their hero's downfall. A public opinion poll showed that 69 percent of the American public backed General MacArthur. When MacArthur returned to the United States, he gave an address to Congress, an honor usually awarded only to heads of government. New York City honored him with a ticker-tape parade. In his closing remarks to Congress, MacArthur said, "Old soldiers never die, they just fade away."

General Douglas MacArthur *(left)* and President Truman *(right)* strongly disagreed about how best to proceed in the Korean War.

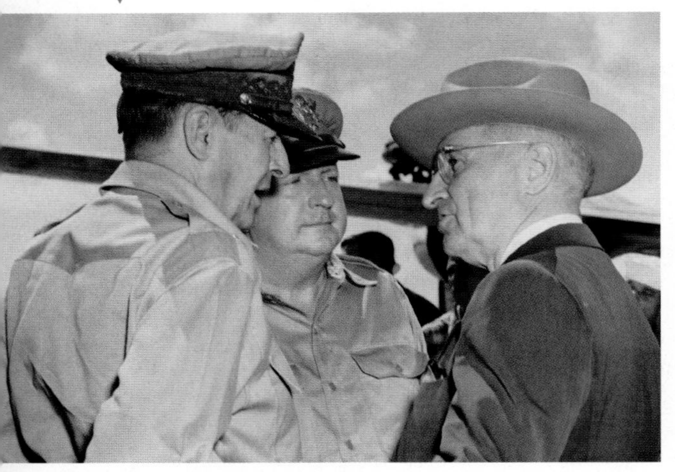

Throughout the fuss, Truman stayed in the background. After MacArthur's moment of public glory passed, the Truman administration began to make its case. Before a congressional committee investigating MacArthur's dismissal, a parade of witnesses argued the case for limiting the war. The committee agreed with them. As a result, public opinion swung around to the view that Truman had done the right thing. As a political figure, MacArthur did indeed fade away.

SETTLING FOR STALEMATE As the MacArthur controversy died down, the Soviet Union unexpectedly suggested a cease-fire on June 23, 1951. Truce talks began in July 1951. The opposing sides reached agreement on two points: the location of the cease-fire line at the existing battle line and the establishment of a demilitarized zone between the opposing sides. Negotiators spent another year wrangling over the exchange of prisoners. Finally, in July 1953, the two sides signed an armistice ending the war.

Vocabulary
demilitarize: to ban military forces in an area or region

At best, the agreement was a stalemate. On the one hand, the North Korean invaders had been pushed back, and communism had been contained without the use of atomic weapons. On the other hand, Korea was still two nations rather than one.

On the home front, the war had affected the lives of ordinary Americans in many ways. It had cost 54,000 American lives and $67 billion in expenditures. The high cost of this unsuccessful war was one of many factors leading Americans to reject the Democratic Party in 1952 and to elect a Republican administration under World War II hero Dwight D. Eisenhower. In addition, the Korean War increased fear of communist aggression and prompted a hunt for Americans who might be blamed for the communist gains.

NOW & THEN

THE TWO KOREAS

Korea is still split into North Korea and South Korea, even after 50 years. South Korea is booming economically, while North Korea, still communist, struggles with severe shortages of food and energy.

Periodically, discussions about reuniting the two countries resume. In 2000, South Korean President Kim Dae-jung won the Nobel Peace Prize for his efforts to improve ties with North Korea. The two nations met in North Korea for the first time since the nations were established in 1948. Although economic and political differences continue to keep the two countries apart, there is renewed hope that one day Korea will become a united nation.

◀ South Korean President Kim Dae-jung waves to cheering North Koreans on June 13, 2000.

SECTION 2 ASSESSMENT

1. **TERMS & NAMES** For each term or name, write a sentence explaining its significance.
   - **Chiang Kai-shek**
   - **Mao Zedong**
   - **Taiwan**
   - **38th parallel**
   - **Korean War**

MAIN IDEA

2. **TAKING NOTES**
   On a time line such as the one shown below, list the major events of the Korean War.

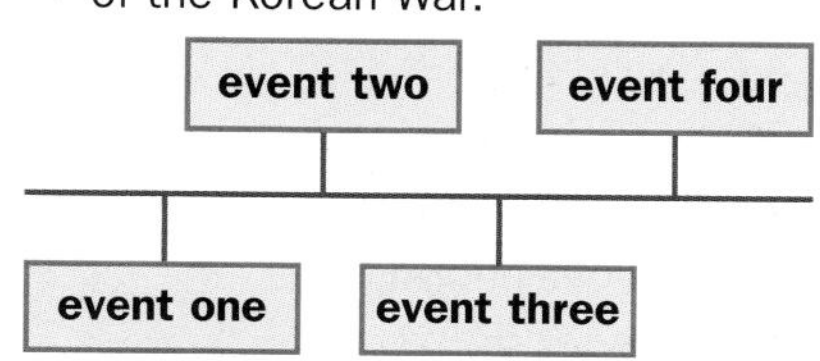

Choose two events and explain how one event led to the other.

CRITICAL THINKING

3. **HYPOTHESIZING**
   What might have happened if MacArthur had convinced Truman to expand the fighting into China? How might today's world be different?

4. **ANALYZING EVENTS**
   Many Americans have questioned whether fighting the Korean War was worthwhile. What is your opinion? Why? **Think About:**
   - the loss of American lives
   - the fear of communism that enveloped the country at the time
   - the stalemate that ended the war

5. **EVALUATING DECISIONS**
   At the end of China's civil war, the United States refused to accept the communist People's Republic of China as China's true government. What were the advantages of such a policy? What were the disadvantages? Do you agree with this decision? Why or why not?

SECTION 3

The Cold War at Home

MAIN IDEA	WHY IT MATTERS NOW	Terms & Names
During the late 1940s and early 1950s, fear of communism led to reckless charges against innocent citizens.	**Americans today remain vigilant about unfounded accusations.**	**•HUAC •Hollywood Ten •blacklist •Alger Hiss •Ethel and Julius Rosenberg •Joseph McCarthy •McCarthyism**

One American's Story

Tony Kahn made the neighbors uncomfortable because they thought his father, Gordon Kahn, was a Communist. In 1947, Gordon Kahn was a successful screenwriter. However, when a congressional committee began to investigate Communists in Hollywood, Kahn was blacklisted—named as unfit to hire. Later, in 1951, he was scheduled to testify before the committee himself.

To save himself, Gordon Kahn simply had to name others as Communists, but he refused. Rather than face the congressional committee, he fled to Mexico. Tony Kahn remembers how the Cold War hurt him and his family.

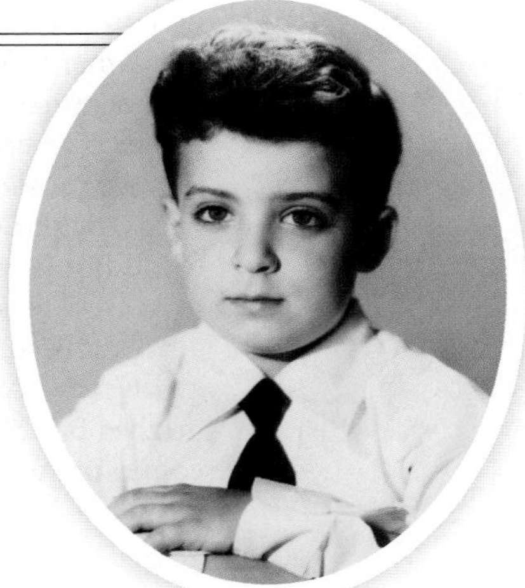

Tony Kahn

A PERSONAL VOICE TONY KAHN

"**The first time I was called a Communist, I was four years old. . . . I'll never forget the look in our neighbors' eyes when I walked by. I thought it was hate. I was too young to realize it was fear.**"

—from *The Cold War Comes Home*

VIDEO

THE COLD WAR COMES HOME
Hollywood Blacklists the Kahn Family

The members of the Kahn family were among thousands of victims of the anti-Communist hysteria that gripped this country in the late 1940s and early 1950s. By the end of the period, no one was immune from accusations.

Fear of Communist Influence

In the early years of the Cold War, many Americans believed that there was good reason to be concerned about the security of the United States. The Soviet domination of Eastern Europe and the Communist takeover of China shocked the American public, fueling a fear that communism would spread around the world. In addition, at the height of World War II, about 100,000 Americans claimed membership in the Communist Party. Some people feared that the first loyalty of these American Communists was to the Soviet Union.

LOYALTY REVIEW BOARD Strongly anti-Communist Republicans began to accuse Truman of being soft on communism. Consequently, in March 1947, President Truman issued an executive order setting up the Federal Employee Loyalty Program, which included the Loyalty Review Board. Its purpose was to investigate government employees and to dismiss those who were found to be disloyal to the U.S. government. The U.S. attorney general drew up a list of 91 "subversive" organizations; membership in any of these groups was grounds for suspicion.

From 1947 to 1951, government loyalty boards investigated 3.2 million employees and dismissed 212 as security risks. Another 2,900 resigned because they did not want to be investigated or felt that the investigation violated their constitutional rights. Individuals under investigation were not allowed to see the evidence against them. (A)

MAIN IDEA

Drawing Conclusions

(A) How did the Loyalty Review Board pose a threat to civil liberties?

THE HOUSE UN-AMERICAN ACTIVITIES COMMITTEE Other agencies investigated possible Communist influence, both inside and outside the U.S. government. The most famous of these was the **House Un-American Activities Committee (HUAC).** HUAC first made headlines in 1947, when it began to investigate Communist influence in the movie industry. The committee believed that Communists were sneaking propaganda into films. The committee pointed to the pro-Soviet films made during World War II when the Soviet Union had been a United States ally.

HUAC subpoenaed 43 witnesses from the Hollywood film industry in September 1947. Many of the witnesses were "friendly," supporting the accusation that Communists had infiltrated the film industry. For example, the movie star Gary Cooper said he had "turned down quite a few scripts because I thought they were tinged with Communistic ideas." However, when asked which scripts he meant, Cooper couldn't remember their titles.

Ten "unfriendly" witnesses were called to testify but refused. These men, known as the **Hollywood Ten,** decided not to cooperate because they believed that the hearings were unconstitutional. Because the Hollywood Ten refused to answer questions, they were sent to prison.

HISTORICAL SPOTLIGHT

PAUL ROBESON

Paul Robeson was an all-American football player and Phi Beta Kappa member at Rutgers University. After earning a law degree in 1923, he began a distinguished international career as a singer and actor. He was a vocal civil rights activist, and he was sympathetic to the Soviet culture and political philosophy.

In 1950, when he refused to sign an affidavit indicating whether he had ever been a member of the Communist Party, the State Department revoked his passport for eight years. During that time, he was unable to perform abroad and was blacklisted at home. His income fell from $150,000 a year to $3,000 a year.

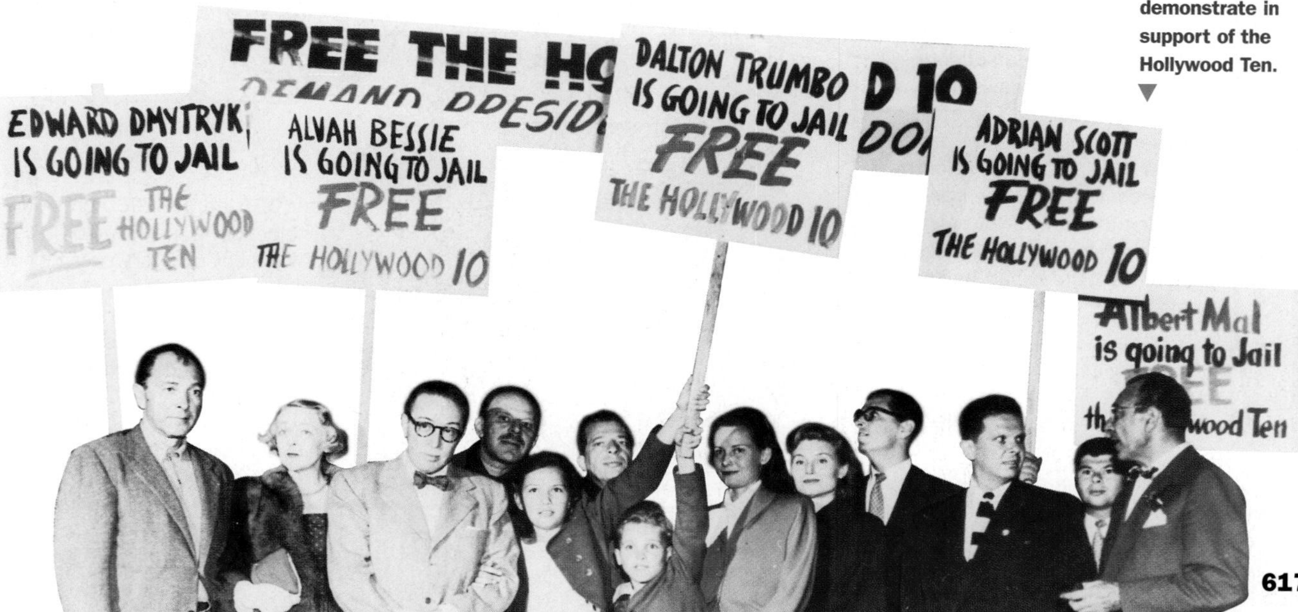

Protesters demonstrate in support of the Hollywood Ten.

In response to the hearings, Hollywood executives instituted a **blacklist,** a list of people whom they condemned for having a Communist background. People who were blacklisted—approximately 500 actors, writers, producers, and directors—had their careers ruined because they could no longer work. B

MAIN IDEA

Analyzing Causes

B Why was Hollywood a target of anti-Communist investigations by Congress?

THE MCCARRAN ACT As Hollywood tried to rid itself of Communists, Congress decided that Truman's Loyalty Review Board did not go far enough. In 1950, Congress passed the McCarran Internal Security Act. This made it unlawful to plan any action that might lead to the establishment of a totalitarian dictatorship in the United States. Truman vetoed the bill, saying, "In a free country, we punish men for the crimes they commit, but never for the opinions they have." But Congress enacted the law over Truman's veto.

Spy Cases Stun the Nation

Two spy cases added to fear that was spreading like an epidemic across the country. One case involved a former State Department official named Alger Hiss.

ALGER HISS In 1948, a former Communist spy named Whittaker Chambers accused **Alger Hiss** of spying for the Soviet Union. To support his charges, Chambers produced microfilm of government documents that he claimed had been typed on Hiss's typewriter. Too many years had passed for government prosecutors to charge Hiss with espionage, but a jury convicted him of perjury—for lying about passing the documents—and sent him to jail. A young conservative Republican congressman named Richard Nixon gained fame for pursuing the charges against Hiss. Within four years of the highly publicized case, Nixon was elected vice president of the United States.

Hiss claimed that he was innocent and that Chambers had forged the documents used against him. However, in the 1990s, Soviet cables released by the National Security Agency seemed to prove Hiss's guilt.

TELEVISION: MAKING NEWS

Historians of popular culture believe that the early 1950s were the best years of television. Most programs were filmed live and had a fresh, unrehearsed look. Along with variety shows, early television presented some of the best serious drama of the age.

Since the 1950s, television has also become a major vehicle for reporting the news. Not only does television report the news, it also has increasingly helped to shape it.

1954 In 1954, the Communist-hunting senator Joseph McCarthy, in U.S. Senate hearings that were televised live, accused the U.S. Army of "coddling Communists." As many as 20 million Americans watched the combative senator malign people who had no chance to defend themselves.

1960 In the 1960 presidential election, a major factor in John Kennedy's victory over Richard Nixon was a series of four televised debates, the first televised presidential debates in history. An estimated 85 million to 120 million Americans watched one or more of the debates, which turned the tide in favor of Kennedy.

THE ROSENBERGS Another spy case rocked the nation even more than the Hiss case, partially because of international events occurring about the same time. On September 3, 1949, Americans learned that the Soviet Union had exploded an atomic bomb. Most American experts had predicted that it would take the Soviets three to five more years to make the bomb. People began to wonder if Communist supporters in the United States had leaked the secret of the bomb.

This second spy case seemed to confirm that suspicion. In 1950, the German-born physicist Klaus Fuchs admitted giving the Soviet Union information about America's atomic bomb. The information probably enabled Soviet scientists to develop their own atomic bomb years earlier than they would have otherwise. Implicated in the Fuchs case were **Ethel and Julius Rosenberg,** minor activists in the American Communist Party.

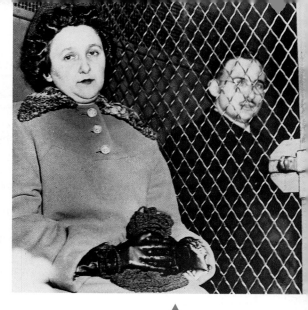

▲ Ethel and Julius Rosenberg were executed in June 1953 despite numerous pleas to spare their lives.

MAIN IDEA

Analyzing Causes

C Why did the cases of Alger Hiss and the Rosenbergs heighten the anti-Communist mood of Americans?

When asked if they were Communists, the Rosenbergs denied the charges against them and pleaded the Fifth Amendment, choosing not to incriminate themselves. They claimed they were being persecuted both for being Jewish and for holding radical beliefs. The Rosenbergs were found guilty of espionage and sentenced to death. In pronouncing their sentence, Judge Irving Kaufman declared their crime "worse than murder." To him, they were directly responsible for one of the deadliest clashes of the Cold War. C

A PERSONAL VOICE IRVING KAUFMAN

"I believe your conduct in putting into the hands of the Russians the A-bomb years before our best scientists predicted Russia would perfect the bomb has already caused, in my opinion, the Communist aggression in Korea . . . ."

—quoted in *The Unquiet Death of Julius and Ethel Rosenberg*

1967 By 1967, American support for the Vietnam War had plummeted as millions of TV viewers witnessed the horrors of war on the nightly news.

2000 During the 2000 presidential election, the TV networks first projected that Al Gore would win Florida. Later, George W. Bush was declared the winner of Florida, a declaration that led Al Gore to concede. Then, when the Florida vote became too close to call, Gore retracted his concession. That "election muddle" blurred even further the already indistinct line between reporting the news and making it.

1974 The Watergate scandal that toppled Richard Nixon's presidency in 1974 played to a rapt TV audience. During the Senate hearings in 1973, the televised testimony of John Dean, the president's counsel, had convinced two out of three Americans that the president had committed a crime.

Analyzing Political Cartoons

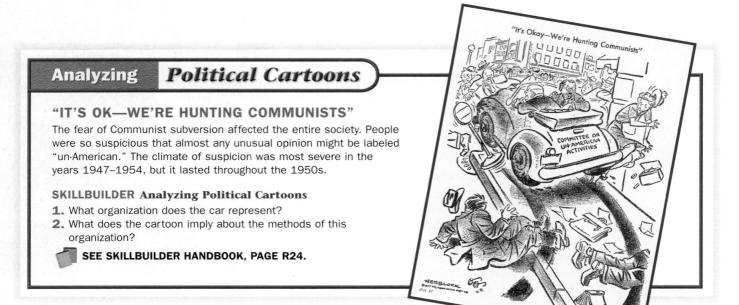

"IT'S OK—WE'RE HUNTING COMMUNISTS"

The fear of Communist subversion affected the entire society. People were so suspicious that almost any unusual opinion might be labeled "un-American." The climate of suspicion was most severe in the years 1947–1954, but it lasted throughout the 1950s.

SKILLBUILDER Analyzing Political Cartoons

1. What organization does the car represent?
2. What does the cartoon imply about the methods of this organization?

SEE SKILLBUILDER HANDBOOK, PAGE R24.

People from all over the world appealed for clemency for the Rosenbergs. Many considered the evidence and the testimony too weak to warrant the death sentence. The case was appealed to the U.S. Supreme Court, but the Court refused to overturn the conviction. Julius and Ethel Rosenberg died in the electric chair in June 1953, leaving behind two sons. They became the first U.S. civilians executed for espionage.

McCarthy Launches His "Witch Hunt"

The most famous anti-Communist activist was Senator **Joseph McCarthy,** a Republican from Wisconsin. During his first three years in the Senate, he had acquired a reputation for being an ineffective legislator. By January 1950, he realized that he was going to need a winning issue in order to be reelected in 1952. Looking for such an issue, McCarthy charged that Communists were taking over the government.

MCCARTHY'S TACTICS Taking advantage of people's concerns about communism, McCarthy made one unsupported accusation after another. These attacks on suspected Communists in the early 1950s became known as **McCarthyism.** Since that time, McCarthyism has referred to the unfair tactic of accusing people of disloyalty without providing evidence. At various times McCarthy claimed to have in his hands the names of 57, 81, and 205 Communists in the State Department. (He never actually produced a single name.) He also charged that the Democratic Party was guilty of "20 years of treason" for allowing Communist infiltration into the government. He was always careful to do his name-calling only in the Senate, where he had legal immunity that protected him from being sued for slander.

Vocabulary
infiltration: the act of penetrating a group or organization without being noticed for purposes such as spying

The Republicans did little to stop McCarthy's attacks because they believed they would win the 1952 presidential election if the public saw them purging the nation of Communists. But one small group of six senators, led by Senator Margaret Chase Smith of Maine, did speak out.

A PERSONAL VOICE MARGARET CHASE SMITH

> **"I speak as a Republican. I speak as a woman. I speak as a United States senator. I speak as an American. . . . I am not proud of the way in which the Senate has been made a publicity platform for irresponsible sensationalism. I am not proud of the reckless abandon in which unproved charges have been hurled from this side of the aisle."**
>
> —*Declaration of Conscience*

MCCARTHY'S DOWNFALL Finally, in 1954, McCarthy made accusations against the U.S. Army, which resulted in a nationally televised Senate investigation. McCarthy's bullying of witnesses alienated the audience and cost him public support. The Senate condemned him for improper conduct that "tended to bring the Senate into dishonor and disrepute." Three years later, Joseph McCarthy, suffering from alcoholism, died a broken man.

OTHER ANTI-COMMUNIST MEASURES Others besides Joseph McCarthy made it their mission to root communism out of American society. By 1953, 39 states had passed laws making it illegal to advocate the violent overthrow of the government. Across the nation, cities and towns passed similar laws. (Later it was ruled that such laws violated the constitutional right of free speech.)

Causes and Effects of McCarthyism

Causes

- Soviets successfully establish Communist regimes in Eastern Europe after World War II.
- Soviets develop the atomic bomb more quickly than expected.
- Korean War ends in a stalemate.
- Republicans gain politically by accusing Truman and Democrats of being soft on communism.

Effects

- Millions of Americans are forced to take loyalty oaths and undergo loyalty investigations.
- Activism by labor unions goes into decline.
- Many people are afraid to speak out on public issues.
- Anti-communism continues to drive U.S. foreign policy.

SKILLBUILDER Interpreting Charts
1. How did world events help lead to McCarthyism?
2. How did McCarthyism affect the behavior of individual Americans?

At times, the fear of communism seemed to have no limits. In Indiana, professional wrestlers had to take a loyalty oath. In experiments run by newspapers, pedestrians on the street refused to sign petitions that quoted the Declaration of Independence because they were afraid the ideas were communist. The government investigated union leaders, librarians, newspaper reporters, and scientists. It seemed that no profession was safe from the hunt for Communists.

ASSESSMENT

1. **TERMS & NAMES** For each term or name, write a sentence explaining its significance.
   - **HUAC**
   - **Hollywood Ten**
   - **blacklist**
   - **Alger Hiss**
   - **Ethel and Julius Rosenberg**
   - **Joseph McCarthy**
   - **McCarthyism**

MAIN IDEA

2. **TAKING NOTES**
   Re-create the web below on your paper and fill in events that illustrate the main idea in the center.

Which event had the greatest impact on the country?

CRITICAL THINKING

3. **HYPOTHESIZING**
   If you had lived in this period and had been accused of being a Communist, what would you have done? **Think About:**
   - the Hollywood Ten, who refused to answer questions
   - the Rosenbergs, who pleaded the Fifth Amendment

4. **ANALYZING MOTIVES**
   Choose one of the following roles: Harry Truman, a member of HUAC, Judge Irving Kaufman, or Joseph McCarthy. As the person you have chosen, explain your motivation for opposing communism.

5. **ANALYZING VISUAL SOURCES**
   What does this cartoon suggest about McCarthy's downfall?

SECTION 4

Two Nations Live on the Edge

MAIN IDEA

During the 1950s, the United States and the Soviet Union came to the brink of nuclear war.

WHY IT MATTERS NOW

The Cold War continued into the following decades, affecting U.S. policies in Cuba, Central America, Southeast Asia, and the Middle East.

Terms & Names

- **H-bomb**
- **Dwight D. Eisenhower**
- **John Foster Dulles**
- **brinkmanship**
- **Central Intelligence Agency (CIA)**
- **Warsaw Pact**
- **Eisenhower Doctrine**
- **Nikita Khrushchev**
- **Francis Gary Powers**
- **U-2 incident**

One American's Story

Writer Annie Dillard was one of thousands of children who grew up in the 1950s with the chilling knowledge that nuclear war could obliterate their world in an instant. Dillard recalls practicing what to do in case of a nuclear attack.

A PERSONAL VOICE ANNIE DILLARD

"At school we had air-raid drills. We took the drills seriously; surely Pittsburgh, which had the nation's steel, coke, and aluminum, would be the enemy's first target. . . . When the air-raid siren sounded, our teachers stopped talking and led us to the school basement. There the gym teachers lined us up against the cement walls and steel lockers, and showed us how to lean in and fold our arms over our heads. . . . The teachers stood in the middle of the room, not talking to each other. We tucked against the walls and lockers. . . . We folded our skinny arms over our heads, and raised to the enemy a clatter of gold scarab bracelets and gold bangle bracelets."

—An American Childhood

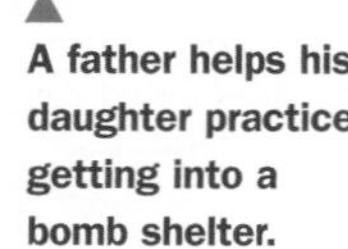

A father helps his daughter practice getting into a bomb shelter.

The fear of nuclear attack was a direct result of the Cold War. After the Soviet Union developed its atomic bomb, the two superpowers embarked on an arms race that enormously increased both the number and the destructive power of weapons.

Brinkmanship Rules U.S. Policy

Although air-raid drills were not common until the Eisenhower years (1953–1961), the nuclear arms race began during Truman's presidency. When the Soviet Union exploded its first atomic bomb in 1949, President Truman had to make a terrible decision—whether to develop an even more horrifying weapon.

RACE FOR THE H-BOMB The scientists who developed the atomic bomb had suspected since 1942 that it was possible to create an even more destructive thermonuclear weapon—the hydrogen bomb, or **H-bomb.** They estimated that such a bomb would have the force of 1 million tons of TNT (67 times the power of the bomb dropped on Hiroshima). But they argued vehemently about the morality of creating such a destructive weapon.

Despite such concerns, the United States entered into a deadly race with the Soviet Union to see which country would be the first to produce an H-bomb. On November 1, 1952, the United States won the race when it exploded the first H-bomb. However, the American advantage lasted less than a year. In August 1953, the Soviets exploded their own thermonuclear weapon. (A)

MAIN IDEA

Analyzing Causes

(A) How did the U.S. and the Soviet Union start the arms race?

▲ A dramatic civil defense poster shows the fear of nuclear attack.

THE POLICY OF BRINKMANSHIP By the time both countries had the H-bomb, **Dwight D. Eisenhower** was president. His secretary of state, **John Foster Dulles,** was staunchly anti-Communist. For Dulles, the Cold War was a moral crusade against communism. Dulles proposed that the United States could prevent the spread of communism by promising to use all of its force, including nuclear weapons, against any aggressor nation. The willingness of the United States, under President Eisenhower, to go to the edge of all-out war became known as **brinkmanship.** Under this policy, the United States trimmed its army and navy and expanded its air force (which would deliver the bombs) and its buildup of nuclear weapons. The Soviet Union followed suit.

The threat of nuclear attack was unlike any the American people had ever faced. Even if only a few bombs reached their targets, millions of civilians would die. Schoolchildren like Annie Dillard practiced air-raid procedures, and some families built underground fallout shelters in their back yards. Fear of nuclear war became a constant in American life for the next 30 years.

The Cold War Spreads Around the World

As the nation shifted to a dependence on nuclear arms, the Eisenhower administration began to rely heavily on the recently formed **Central Intelligence Agency (CIA)** for information. The CIA used spies to gather information abroad. The CIA also began to carry out covert, or secret, operations to weaken or overthrow governments unfriendly to the United States.

Background

From ancient times until 1935, Iran was known as Persia. Persia once ruled a great empire that stretched from the Mediterranean Sea to India's Indus River.

COVERT ACTIONS IN THE MIDDLE EAST AND LATIN AMERICA One of the CIA's first covert actions took place in the Middle East. In 1951, Iran's prime minister, Mohammed Mossadegh, nationalized Iran's oil fields; that is, he placed the formerly private industries (owned mostly by Great Britain) under Iranian control. To protest, the British stopped buying Iranian oil. As the Iranian economy

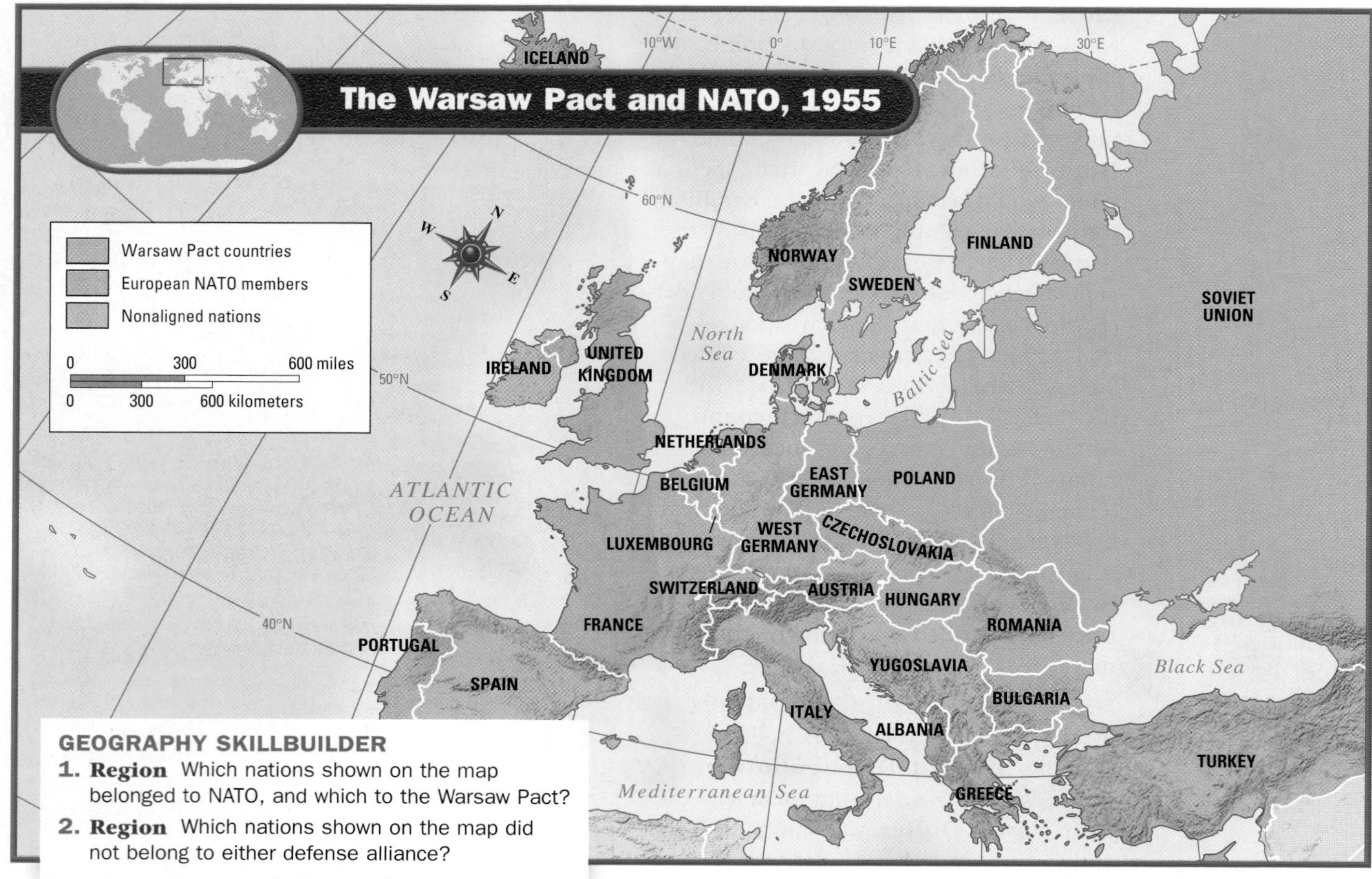

GEOGRAPHY SKILLBUILDER

1. **Region** Which nations shown on the map belonged to NATO, and which to the Warsaw Pact?
2. **Region** Which nations shown on the map did not belong to either defense alliance?

faltered, the United States feared that Mossadegh might turn to the Soviets for help. In 1953, the CIA gave several million dollars to anti-Mossadegh supporters. The CIA wanted the pro-American Shah of Iran, who had recently been forced to flee, to return to power. The plan worked. The Shah returned to power and turned over control of Iranian oil fields to Western companies.

In 1954, the CIA also took covert actions in Guatemala, a Central American country just south of Mexico. Eisenhower believed that Guatemala's government had Communist sympathies because it had given more than 200,000 acres of American-owned land to peasants. In response, the CIA trained an army, which invaded Guatemala. The Guatemalan army refused to defend the president, and he resigned. The army's leader then became dictator of the country. (B)

MAIN IDEA

Summarizing
(B) What was the role of the CIA in the Cold War?

THE WARSAW PACT In spite of the growing tension between the superpowers, U.S.-Soviet relations seemed to thaw following the death of Joseph Stalin in 1953. The Soviets recognized West Germany and concluded peace treaties with Austria and Japan. However, in 1955, when West Germany was allowed to rearm and join NATO, the Soviet Union grew fearful. It formed its own military alliance, known as the **Warsaw Pact.** The Warsaw Pact linked the Soviet Union with seven Eastern European countries.

A SUMMIT IN GENEVA In July 1955, Eisenhower traveled to Geneva, Switzerland, to meet with Soviet leaders. There Eisenhower put forth an "open skies" proposal. The United States and the Soviet Union would allow flights over each other's territory to guard against surprise nuclear attacks. Although the Soviet Union rejected this proposal, the world hailed the "spirit of Geneva" as a step toward peace.

THE SUEZ WAR In 1955, the same year in which the Geneva Summit took place, Great Britain and the United States agreed to help Egypt finance construction of a dam at Aswan on the Nile River. However, Gamal Abdel-Nasser, Egypt's head of government, tried to play the Soviets and the Americans against each other, by improving relations with each one in order to get more aid. In 1956, after learning that Nasser was making deals with the Soviets, Dulles withdrew his offer of a loan. Angered, Nasser responded by nationalizing the Suez Canal, the Egyptian waterway that was owned by France and Great Britain. The French and the British were outraged.

Egyptian control of the canal also affected Israel. Nasser refused to let ships bound for Israel pass through the canal, even though the canal was supposed to be open to all nations. Israel responded by sending troops. So did Great Britain and France. The three countries seized the Mediterranean end of the canal. The UN quickly stepped in to stop the fighting. It persuaded Great Britain, France, and Israel to withdraw. However, it allowed Egypt to keep control of the canal. C

MAIN IDEA

Analyzing Effects
C What were the results of the Suez War?

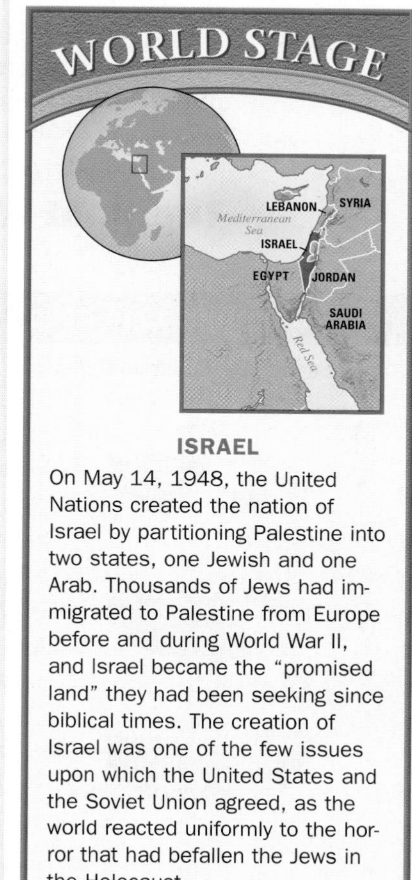

ISRAEL
On May 14, 1948, the United Nations created the nation of Israel by partitioning Palestine into two states, one Jewish and one Arab. Thousands of Jews had immigrated to Palestine from Europe before and during World War II, and Israel became the "promised land" they had been seeking since biblical times. The creation of Israel was one of the few issues upon which the United States and the Soviet Union agreed, as the world reacted uniformly to the horror that had befallen the Jews in the Holocaust.

THE EISENHOWER DOCTRINE The Soviet Union's prestige in the Middle East rose because of its support for Egypt. To counterbalance this development, President Eisenhower issued a warning in January 1957. This warning, known as the **Eisenhower Doctrine,** said that the United States would defend the Middle East against an attack by any communist country. In March, Congress officially approved the doctrine.

THE HUNGARIAN UPRISING Even as fighting was raging in the Middle East, a revolt began in Hungary. Dominated by the Soviet Union since the end of World War II, the Hungarian people rose in revolt in 1956. They called for a democratic government.

Imre Nagy, the most popular and liberal Hungarian Communist leader, formed a new government. He promised free elections, denounced the Warsaw Pact, and demanded that all Soviet troops leave Hungary.

The Soviet response was swift and brutal. In November 1956, Soviet tanks rolled into Hungary and killed approximately 30,000 Hungarians. Armed with only pistols and bottles, thousands of Hungarian freedom fighters threw up barricades in the streets and fought the invaders to no avail. The Soviets overthrew the Nagy government and replaced it with pro-Soviet leaders. Nagy himself was executed. Some 200,000 Hungarians fled to the west.

Although the Truman Doctrine had promised to support free peoples who resisted communism, the United States did nothing to help Hungary break free of Soviet control. Many

Crowds surround a captured Russian tank during the anti-Communist revolution in Hungary. ▼

Hungarians were bitterly disappointed. The American policy of containment did not extend to driving the Soviet Union out of its satellites.

No help came to Hungary from the United Nations either. Although the UN passed one resolution after another condemning the Soviet Union, the Soviet veto in the Security Council stopped the UN from taking any action.

The Cold War Takes to the Skies

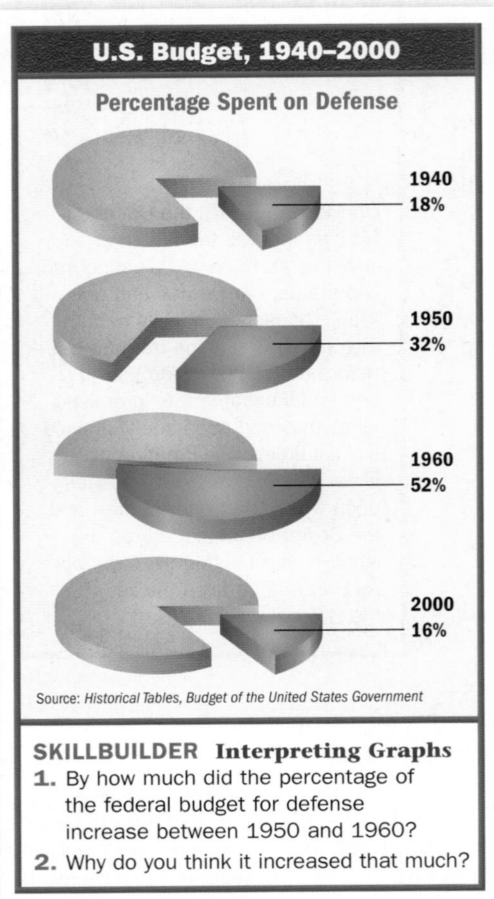

SKILLBUILDER Interpreting Graphs
1. By how much did the percentage of the federal budget for defense increase between 1950 and 1960?
2. Why do you think it increased that much?

After Stalin's death in 1953, the Soviet Union had no well-defined way for one leader to succeed another. For the first few years, a group of leaders shared power. As time went by, however, one man did gain power. That man was **Nikita Khrushchev** (kro͝osh′chĕf). Like Stalin, Khrushchev believed that communism would take over the world, but Khrushchev thought it could triumph peacefully. He favored a policy of peaceful coexistence in which two powers would compete economically and scientifically. D

MAIN IDEA

Comparing
D Compare Joseph Stalin with Nikita Khrushchev. How were they alike? How were they different?

THE SPACE RACE In the competition for international prestige, the Soviets leaped to an early lead in what came to be known as the space race. On October 4, 1957, they launched *Sputnik*, the world's first artificial satellite. *Sputnik* traveled around the earth at 18,000 miles per hour, circling the globe every 96 minutes. Its launch was a triumph of Soviet technology.

Americans were shocked at being beaten and promptly poured money into their own space program. U.S. scientists worked frantically to catch up to the Soviets. The first attempt at an American satellite launch was a humiliating failure, with the rocket toppling to the ground. However, on January 31, 1958, the United States successfully launched its first satellite.

A U-2 IS SHOT DOWN Following the rejection of Eisenhower's "open skies" proposal at the 1955 Geneva summit conference, the CIA began making secret high-altitude flights over Soviet territory. The plane used for these missions was the U-2, which could fly at high altitudes without detection. As a U-2 passed over the Soviet Union, its infrared cameras took detailed photographs of troop movement and missile sites.

By 1960, however, many U.S. officials were nervous about the U-2 program for two reasons. First, the existence and purpose of the U-2 was an open secret among some members of the American press. Second, the Soviets had been aware of the flights since 1958, as **Francis Gary Powers,** a U-2 pilot, explained.

A PERSONAL VOICE FRANCIS GARY POWERS

"**We . . . knew that the Russians were radar-tracking at least some of our flights. . . . We also knew that SAMs [surface-to-air missiles] were being fired at us, that some were uncomfortably close to our altitude. But we knew too that the Russians had a control problem in their guidance system. . . . We were concerned, but not greatly.**"

—*Operation Overflight: The U-2 Spy Pilot Tells His Story for the First Time*

Finally, Eisenhower himself wanted the flights discontinued. He and Khrushchev were going to hold another summit conference on the arms race on May 15, 1960. "If one of these aircraft were lost when we were engaged in apparently sincere deliberations, it could . . . ruin my effectiveness," he told an aide. However, Dulles persuaded him to authorize one last flight.

That flight took place on May 1, and the pilot was Francis Gary Powers. Four hours after Powers entered Soviet airspace, a Soviet pilot shot down his plane, and Powers was forced to parachute into Soviet-controlled territory. The Soviets sentenced Powers to ten years in prison.

◀ Francis Gary Powers's military identification card

Francis Gary Powers at a Senate committee hearing following his release by the Soviets ▼

Background
After 18 months, Francis Gary Powers was released from the Soviet Union in exchange for Soviet agent Rudolf Abel, who had been convicted of spying in the United States.

RENEWED CONFRONTATION At first, Eisenhower denied that the U-2 had been spying. The Soviets had evidence, however, and Eisenhower finally had to admit it. Khrushchev demanded an apology for the flights and a promise to halt them. Eisenhower agreed to stop the U-2 flights, but he would not apologize.

Khrushchev angrily called off the summit. He also withdrew his invitation to Eisenhower to visit the Soviet Union. Because of the **U-2 incident,** the 1960s opened with tension between the two superpowers as great as ever.

ASSESSMENT

1. **TERMS & NAMES** For each term or name, write a sentence explaining its significance.
   - **H-bomb**
   - **Dwight D. Eisenhower**
   - **John Foster Dulles**
   - **brinkmanship**
   - **Central Intelligence Agency (CIA)**
   - **Warsaw Pact**
   - **Eisenhower Doctrine**
   - **Nikita Khrushchev**
   - **Francis Gary Powers**
   - **U-2 incident**

MAIN IDEA

2. **TAKING NOTES**
   List Cold War trouble spots in Iran, Guatemala, Egypt, and Hungary. For each, write a newspaper headline that summarizes the U.S. role and the outcome of the situation.

Trouble Spot	Headline

Choose one headline and write a paragraph about that trouble spot.

CRITICAL THINKING

3. **HYPOTHESIZING**
   How might the Cold War have progressed if the U-2 incident had never occurred? **Think About:**
   - the mutual distrust between the Soviet Union and the United States
   - the outcome of the incident

4. **EVALUATING**
   Which of the two superpowers do you think contributed more to Cold War tensions during the 1950s?

5. **FORMING GENERALIZATIONS**
   Should one nation have the right to remove another nation's head of government from power? If so, when? If not, why?

AMERICAN LITERATURE

Science Fiction Reflects Cold War Fears

1950–1959 Many writers of science fiction draw on the scientific and social trends of the present to describe future societies that might arise if those trends were to continue. Nuclear proliferation, the space race, early computer technology, and the pervasive fear of known and unknown dangers during the Cold War were the realities that prompted a boom in science fiction during the 1950s and 1960s.

THE BODY SNATCHERS

Published in 1955 at the height of the Great Fear, Jack Finney's *The Body Snatchers* (on which the movie *Invasion of the Body Snatchers* was based) tells of giant seed pods from outer space that descend on the inhabitants of a California town. The pods create perfect physical duplicates of the townspeople and lack only one thing—human souls.

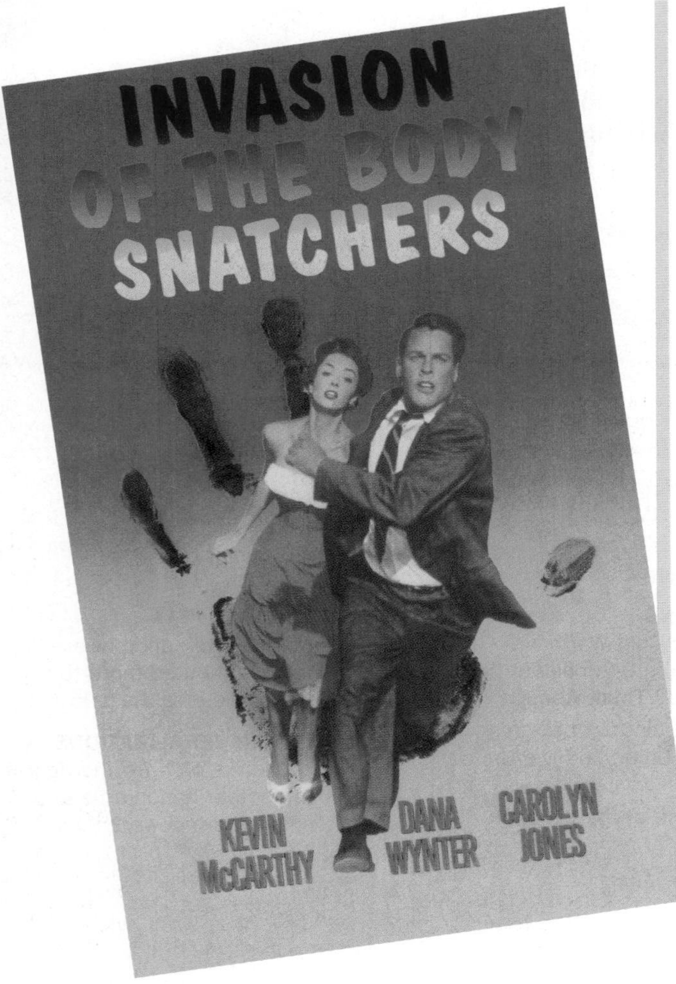

"Miles, he looks, sounds, acts, and remembers exactly like Ira. On the outside. But *inside* he's different. His responses"—she stopped, hunting for the word—"aren't *emotionally* right, if I can explain that. He remembers the past, in detail, and he'll smile and say 'You were sure a cute youngster, Willy. Bright one, too,' just the way Uncle Ira did. But there's something *missing,* and the same thing is true of Aunt Aleda, lately." Wilma stopped, staring at nothing again, face intent, wrapped up in this, then she continued. "Uncle Ira was a father to me, from infancy, and when he talked about my childhood, Miles, there was—always—a special look in his eyes that meant he was remembering the wonderful quality of those days for him. Miles, that look, 'way in back of the eyes, is gone. With this—*this* Uncle Ira, or whoever or whatever he is, I have the feeling, the absolutely certain *knowledge,* Miles, that he's talking by rote. That the facts of Uncle Ira's memories are all in his mind in every last detail, ready to recall. But the emotions are not. There *is* no emotion—none—only the pretense of it. The words, the gestures, the tones of voice, everything else—but not the feeling."

Her voice was suddenly firm and commanding: "Miles, memories or not, appearances or not, possible or impossible, that is not my Uncle Ira."

—Jack Finney, *The Body Snatchers* (1955)

THE MARTIAN CHRONICLES

In *The Martian Chronicles*, Ray Bradbury describes how earthlings who have colonized Mars watch helplessly as their former planet is destroyed by nuclear warfare.

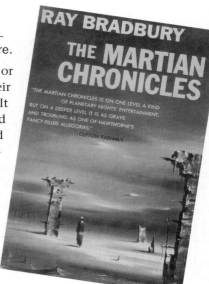

> They all came out and looked at the sky that night. They left their suppers or their washing up or their dressing for the show and they came out upon their now-not-quite-as-new porches and watched the green star of Earth there. It was a move without conscious effort; they all did it, to help them understand the news they had heard on the radio a moment before. There was Earth and there the coming war, and there hundreds of thousands of mothers or grandmothers or fathers or brothers or aunts or uncles or cousins. They stood on the porches and tried to believe in the existence of Earth, much as they had once tried to believe in the existence of Mars; it was a problem reversed. To all intents and purposes, Earth now was dead; they had been away from it for three or four years. Space was an anesthetic; seventy million miles of space numbed you, put memory to sleep, depopulated Earth, erased the past, and allowed these people here to go on with their work. But now, tonight, the dead were risen, Earth was reinhabited, memory awoke, a million names were spoken: What was so-and-so doing tonight on Earth? What about this one and that one? The people on the porches glanced sidewise at each other's faces.
>
> At nine o'clock Earth seemed to explode, catch fire, and burn.
>
> The people on the porches put up their hands as if to beat the fire out.
>
> They waited.

—Ray Bradbury, *The Martian Chronicles* (1950)

A CANTICLE FOR LEIBOWITZ

In *A Canticle for Leibowitz*, Walter M. Miller, Jr., portrays the centuries after a nuclear holocaust as a new "Dark Age" for humanity on earth.

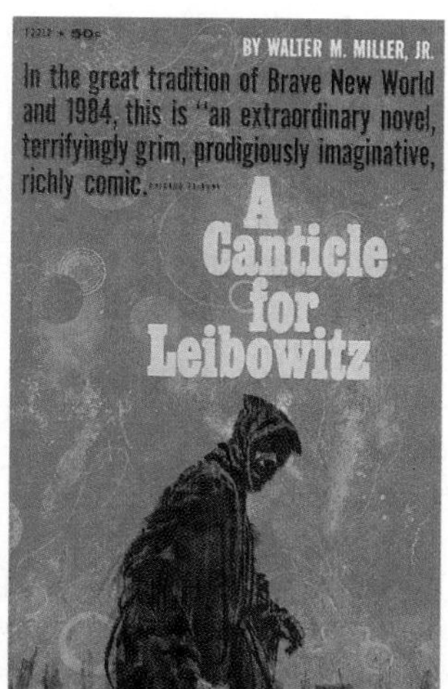

> He had been wandering for a long time. The search seemed endless, but there was always the promise of finding what he sought across the next rise or beyond the bend in the trail. When he had finished fanning himself, he clapped the hat back on his head and scratched at his bushy beard while blinking around at the landscape. There was a patch of unburned forest on the hillside just ahead. It offered welcome shade, but still the wanderer sat there in the sunlight and watched the curious buzzards. . . .
>
> Pickings were good for a while in the region of the Red River; but then out of the carnage, a city-state arose. For rising city-states, the buzzards had no fondness, although they approved of their eventual fall. They shied away from Texarkana and ranged far over the plain to the west. After the manner of all living things, they replenished the Earth many times with their kind.
>
> Eventually it was the Year of Our Lord 3174.
>
> There were rumors of war.

—Walter M. Miller, Jr., *A Canticle for Leibowitz* (1959)

THINKING CRITICALLY

1. **Comparing** What themes, or general messages about life or humanity, do you think these three books convey? How might readers' interpretations of these messages today differ from readers' interpretations during the Cold War?

 **SEE SKILLBUILDER HANDBOOK, PAGE R8.**

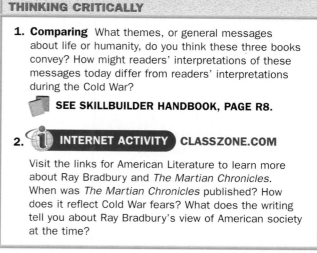

2. 

CLASSZONE.COM

Visit the links for American Literature to learn more about Ray Bradbury and *The Martian Chronicles*. When was *The Martian Chronicles* published? How does it reflect Cold War fears? What does the writing tell you about Ray Bradbury's view of American society at the time?

VISUAL SUMMARY

COLD WAR CONFLICTS

CAUSES

- Soviet domination of Eastern Europe
- Communist victory in China
- Mutual suspicion between United States and Soviet Union

IMMEDIATE EFFECTS

- Truman Doctrine and Marshall Plan
- East-West tensions over Berlin
- Establishment of NATO and Warsaw Pact
- McCarthyism

LONG-TERM EFFECTS

- Arms race between superpowers
- Superpower rivalry for world power

TERMS & NAMES

For each term or name below, write a sentence explaining its significance to the Cold War.

1. containment
2. North Atlantic Treaty Organization (NATO)
3. Mao Zedong
4. Korean War
5. McCarthyism
6. John Foster Dulles
7. brinkmanship
8. Central Intelligence Agency (CIA)
9. Nikita Khrushchev
10. U-2 incident

MAIN IDEAS

Use your notes and the information in the chapter to answer the following questions.

Origins of the Cold War *(pages 602–608)*

1. What were the goals of U.S. foreign policy in the Cold War?
2. Describe the Truman Doctrine and how America reacted to it.
3. What was the purpose of the NATO alliance?

The Cold War Heats Up *(pages 609–615)*

4. What global events led to U.S. involvement in Korea?
5. What issue between General Douglas MacArthur and President Truman eventually cost MacArthur his job?

The Cold War at Home *(pages 616–621)*

6. What actions of Joseph McCarthy worsened the national hysteria about communism?
7. How did the Rosenberg case fuel anti-communist feeling?

Two Nations Live on the Edge *(pages 622–627)*

8. How did the U.S., including the CIA, wage the Cold War in the 1950s?

CRITICAL THINKING

1. **USING YOUR NOTES** Create a cause-and-effect diagram like the one shown for each of these events: (a) the United States' adoption of a policy of containment, and (b) the beginning of the nuclear arms race between the United States and the Soviet Union.

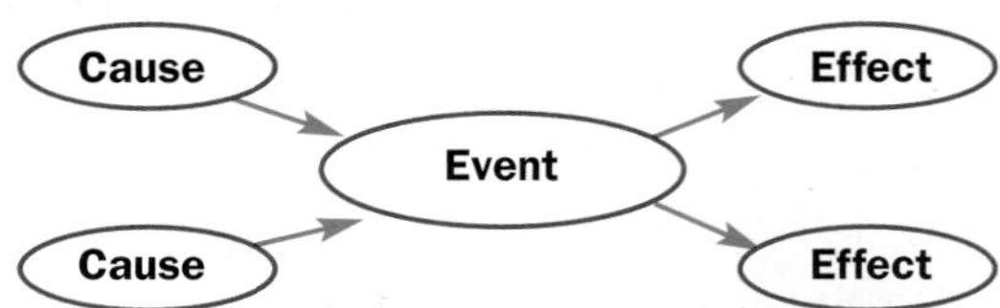

2. **ANALYZING EVENTS** What government actions during the Communist scare conflicted with the Bill of Rights? Explain.

3. **INTERPRETING MAPS** Look carefully at the map on page 605. How did the absence of a natural barrier on the western border of the Soviet Union affect post-World War II Soviet foreign policy? Explain your answer.

Standardized Test Practice

Use the quotation below and your knowledge of U.S. history to answer question 1.

> **"In 1945 I had ordered the A Bomb dropped on Japan at two places devoted almost exclusively to war production. We were at war. We were trying to end it in order to save the lives of our soldiers and sailors. . . . We stopped the war and saved thousands of casualties on both sides.**
>
> **In Korea we were fighting a police action with sixteen allied nations to support the World Organization which had set up the Republic of Korea. We had held the Chinese after defeating the North Koreans and whipping the Russian Air Force. I just could not make the order for a Third World War. I know I was *right.*"**
>
> —*Off the Record: The Private Papers of Harry S. Truman*

1. According to President Truman, what was the main difference between using the atomic bomb on Japan in 1945 and the possibility of using it on China in 1951?

A Japan was more of a military power in 1945 than China was in 1951.

B In 1945 we had many allies, but in 1951 we had only two.

C In 1945 the bomb ended a world war, but in 1951 it would have started one.

D The Japanese were much fiercer fighters than the Chinese were.

Use the cartoon below and your knowledge of U.S. history to answer question 2.

2. What point of view about the arms race does this 1950 cartoon *best* support?

F The arms race between "Russia" and the United States is as dangerous as a war.

G Communism uncontained will spread.

H The bombs of the United States only threaten countries other than the United States.

J The United States needs to build up its arsenal in order to compete with "Russia."

ADDITIONAL TEST PRACTICE, pages S1–S33.

CLASSZONE.COM

ALTERNATIVE ASSESSMENT

1. **INTERACT WITH HISTORY** Recall your discussion of the question on page 601:

What do you do when a friend is accused?

Suppose your best friend has been accused of being a Communist. You have been called to serve as a character witness for him or her.

Write a speech that you will present to the House Un-American Activities Committee (HUAC). In your speech explain why you feel that your friend's constitutional rights are being violated.

2. **VIDEO** **LEARNING FROM MEDIA** View the *American Stories* video, "The Cold War Comes Home: Hollywood Blacklists the Kahn Family." Discuss the following questions, and then do the activity:

- How was Gordon Kahn caught up in events beyond his control?
- What alternatives did Gordon have? Do you think he chose the right path? Explain your opinion.

Cooperative Learning Activity With a small group, create a step-by-step flowchart to show how Gordon Kahn's life, reputation, and career were ruined by blacklisting.

CHAPTER 19 THE POSTWAR BOOM

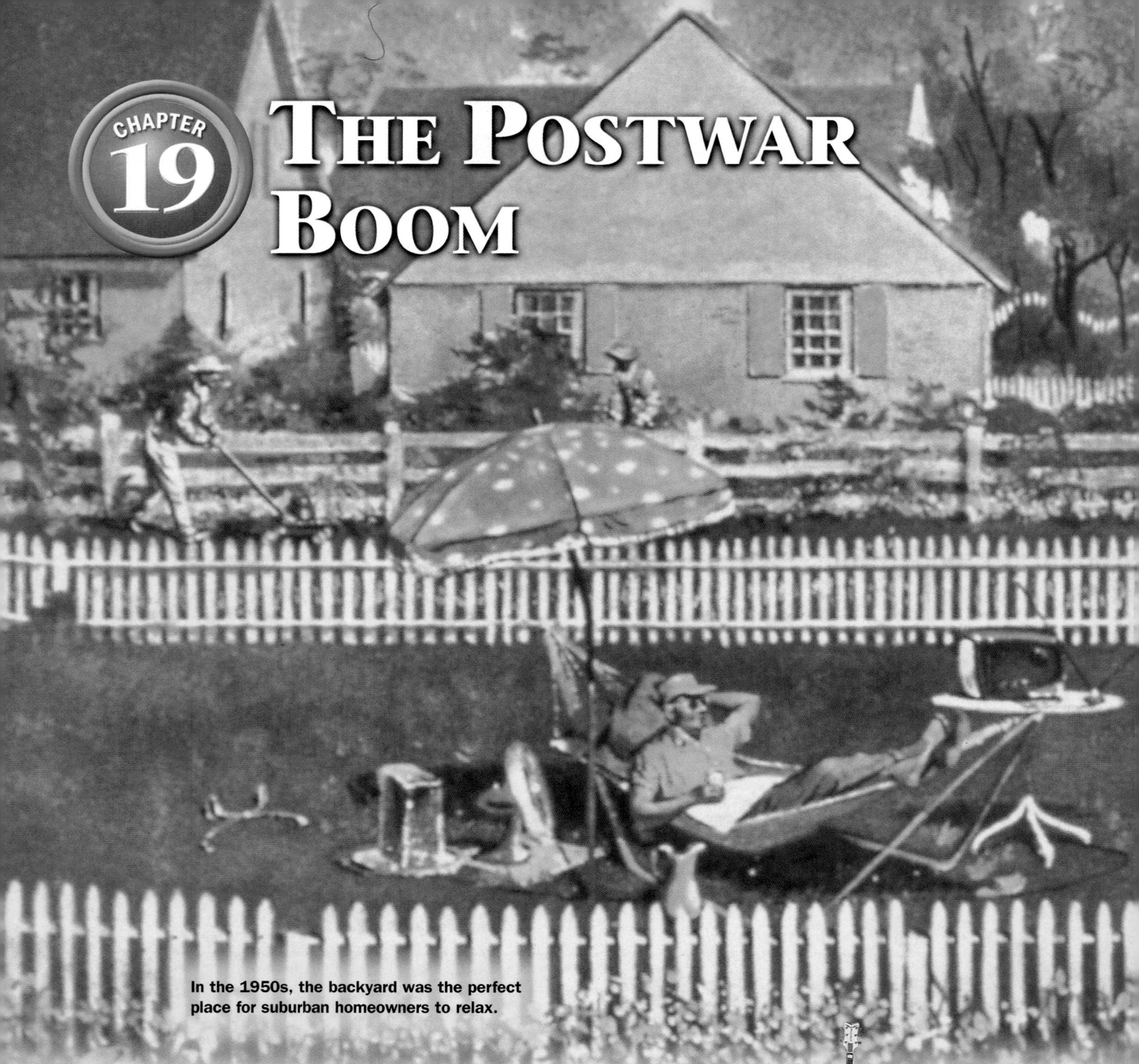

In the 1950s, the backyard was the perfect place for suburban homeowners to relax.

USA

1946 Baby boom begins.

1947 Jackie Robinson integrates major league baseball.

1948 Harry S. Truman is elected president.

1950's Disc jockey Alan Freed is the first to use the term "rock 'n' roll" on the air.

1952 Dwight D. Eisenhower is elected president.

1946 | 1948 | 1950 | 1952

WORLD

1949 Mao Zedong's Communist forces gain control of China.

1950 Korean War begins.

INTERACT WITH HISTORY

You have returned home from serving in World War II to find that your country is changing. The cities have swelled. Outlying suburbs are being built up with almost identical homes. America produces more and cheaper goods. In a booming economy, couples marry and start families in record numbers. As you watch clever ads on TV for the newest labor-saving gadgets, you feel nostalgia for a simpler time.

What is the American dream of the 1950s?

Examine the Issues

- How does pressure to conform affect the American dream?
- Who might be excluded from the new prosperity?
- How does advertising promote certain lifestyles and ideals?

RESEARCH LINKS **CLASSZONE.COM**

Visit the Chapter 19 links for more information about The Postwar Boom.

1953 Korean War cease-fire is signed.

1954 *Brown* v. *Board of Education of Topeka* outlaws school segregation.

1954 USSR opens the first small nuclear power plant.

1956 Eisenhower is reelected.

1956 Soviets crush uprising in Hungary.

1957 Soviets launch *Sputnik I.*

1958 NASA—the National Aeronautics and Space Administration—is established.

1959 Alaska and Hawaii become the 49th and 50th states.

1959 Fidel Castro comes to power in Cuba.

1960 John F. Kennedy is elected president.

1954 1956 1958 1960

SECTION 1

Postwar America

MAIN IDEA

The Truman and Eisenhower administrations led the nation to make social, economic, and political adjustments following World War II.

WHY IT MATTERS NOW

In the years after World War II, the United States became the economic and military power that it still is today.

Terms & Names

- **GI Bill of Rights**
- **suburb**
- **Harry S. Truman**
- **Dixiecrat**
- **Fair Deal**

One American's Story

Sam Gordon had been married less than a year when he was shipped overseas in July 1943. As a sergeant in the United States Army, he fought in Belgium and France during World War II. Arriving back home in November 1945, Sam nervously anticipated a reunion with his family. A friend, Donald Katz, described Sam's reactions.

A PERSONAL VOICE DONALD KATZ

"Sam bulled through the crowd and hailed a taxi. The cab motored north through the warm autumn day as he groped for feelings appropriate to being back home alive from a terrible war. . . . [He was] nearly panting under the weight of fear. . . . *Back home alive . . . married to a girl I haven't seen since 1943 . . . father of a child I've never seen at all.*"

— *Home Fires*

GIs returned home to their families after World War II with new hope, but also with new problems.

Sam Gordon met his daughter, Susan, for the first time the day he returned home from the war, and he went to work the next morning. Like many other young couples, the Gordons began to put the nightmare of the war behind them and to return to normality.

Readjustment and Recovery

By the summer of 1946, about 10 million men and women had been released from the armed forces. Veterans like Sam Gordon—along with the rest of American society—settled down to rebuild their lives.

THE IMPACT OF THE GI BILL To help ease veterans' return to civilian life, Congress passed the Servicemen's Readjustment Act, or the **GI Bill of Rights,** in 1944. In addition to encouraging veterans to get an education by paying part of their tuition, the GI Bill guaranteed them a year's worth of unemployment benefits while job hunting. It also offered low-interest, federally guaranteed loans. Millions of young families used these benefits to buy homes and farms or to establish businesses.

▲ The suburbs were a mass phenomenon, even on moving day.

HOUSING CRISIS In 1945 and 1946, returning veterans faced a severe housing shortage. Many families lived in cramped apartments or moved in with relatives. In response to this housing crisis, developers like William Levitt and Henry Kaiser used efficient, assembly-line methods to mass-produce houses. Levitt, who bragged that his company could build a house in 16 minutes, offered homes in small residential communities surrounding cities, called **suburbs,** for less than $7,000.

Levitt's first postwar development—rows of standardized homes built on treeless lots—was located on New York's Long Island and named Levittown. These homes looked exactly alike, and certain zoning laws ensured that they would stay the same. Despite their rigid conformity, Americans loved the openness and small-town feel to the planned suburbs. With the help of the GI Bill, many veterans and their families moved in and cultivated a new lifestyle.

REDEFINING THE FAMILY Tension created by changes in men's and women's roles after the war contributed to a rising divorce rate. Traditionally, men were the breadwinners and heads of households, while women were expected to stay home and care for the family. During the war, however, about 8 million women, 75 percent of whom were married, entered the paid work force. These women supported their families and made important household decisions. Many were reluctant to give up their newfound independence when their husbands returned. Although most women did leave their jobs, by 1950 more than a million war marriages had ended in divorce.

ECONOMIC READJUSTMENT After World War II, the United States converted from a wartime to a peacetime economy. The U.S. government immediately canceled war contracts totaling $35 billion. Within ten days of Japan's surrender, more than a million defense workers were laid off. Unemployment increased as veterans joined laid-off defense workers in the search for jobs. At the peak of postwar unemployment, in March 1946, nearly 3 million people were seeking work.

Background
See *unemployment rate* on page R47 in the Economics Handbook.

Rising unemployment was not the nation's only postwar economic problem, however. During the war, the Office of Price Administration (OPA) had halted inflation by imposing maximum prices on goods. When these controls ended on June 30, 1946, prices skyrocketed. In the next two weeks, the cost of consumer products soared 25 percent, double the increase of the previous three years. In some cities, consumers stood in long lines, hoping to buy scarce items, such as sugar, coffee, and beans. Prices continued to rise for the next two years until the supply of goods caught up with the demand.

MAIN IDEA

Identifying Problems
A What problems did Americans face after World War II?

While prices spiraled upward, many American workers also earned less than they had earned during the war. To halt runaway inflation and to help the nation convert to a peacetime economy, Congress eventually reestablished controls similar to the wartime controls on prices, wages, and rents. **A**

REMARKABLE RECOVERY Most economists who had forecast a postwar depression were proved wrong because they had failed to consider consumers' pent-up accumulation of needs and wants. People had gone without many goods for so long that by the late 1940s, with more than $135 billion in savings from defense work, service pay, and investments in war bonds, Americans suddenly had money to spend. They snatched up everything from automobiles to houses. After a brief period of postwar economic readjustment, the American economy boomed. The demand for goods and services outstripped the supply and increased production, which created new jobs. Judging from the graphs (shown left), many Americans prospered in the 1950s in what the economist John Kenneth Galbraith called "the affluent society."

The Cold War also contributed to economic growth. Concern over Soviet expansion kept American defense spending high and people employed. Foreign-aid programs, such as the Marshall Plan, provided another boost to the American economy. By helping nations in Western Europe recover from the war, the United States helped itself by creating strong foreign markets for its exports. B

MAIN IDEA

Analyzing Causes

B What factors contributed to the American postwar economic boom?

A Dynamic Economy

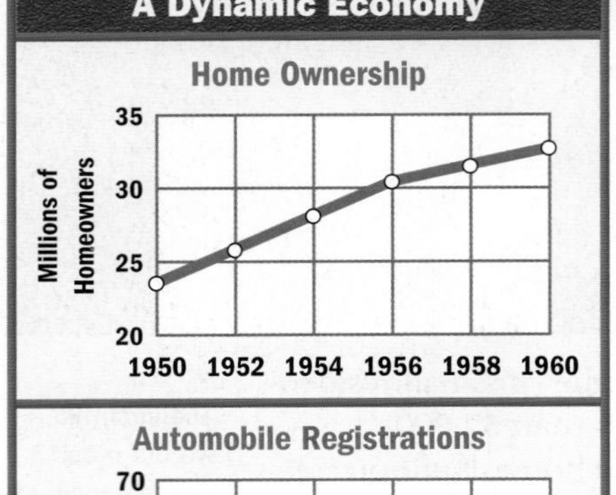

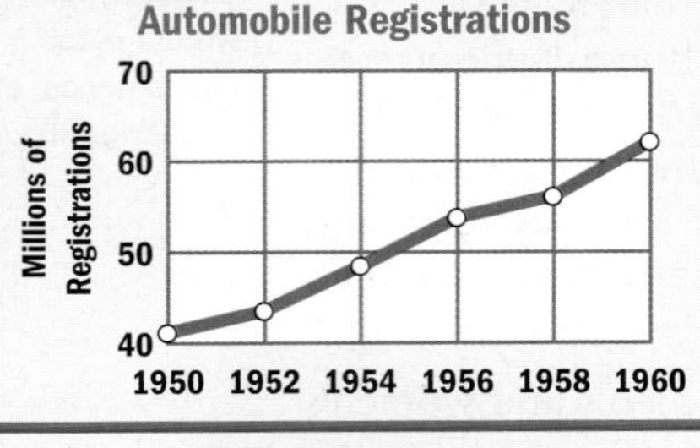

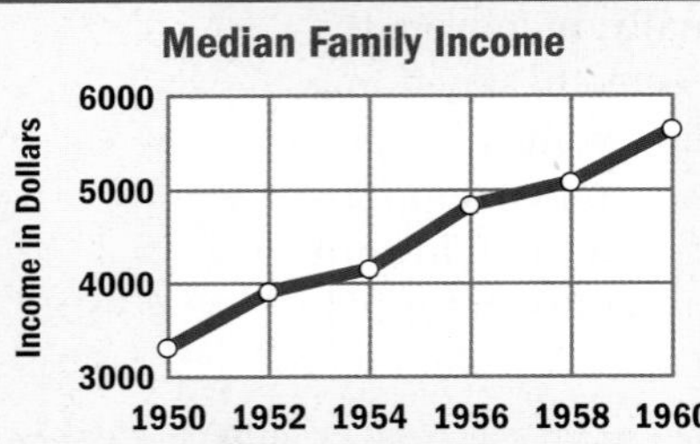

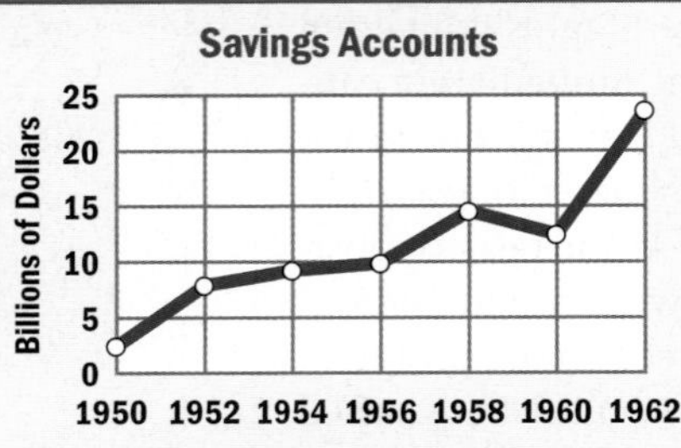

Source: *Historical Statistics of the United States, Colonial times to 1970*

SKILLBUILDER

Interpreting Graphs

1. From 1950 to 1960, by what percentage did each of the economic indicators shown above increase?
2. Which years show the biggest increases for each of the graphs above?

Meeting Economic Challenges

Despite an impressive recovery, Americans faced a number of economic problems. Their lives had been in turmoil throughout the war, and a desire for stability made the country more conservative.

PRESIDENT TRUMAN'S INHERITANCE When **Harry S. Truman** suddenly became president after Franklin D. Roosevelt's death in 1945, he asked Roosevelt's widow, Eleanor, whether there was anything he could do for her. She replied, "Is there anything we can do for you? For you are the one in trouble now." In many ways, President Truman was in trouble.

A PERSONAL VOICE HARRY S. TRUMAN

> **"I don't know whether you fellows ever had a load of hay fall on you, but when they told me yesterday what had happened [Roosevelt's death], I felt like the moon, the stars, and all the planets had fallen on me."**
>
> —excerpt from a speech, April 13, 1945

Despite his lack of preparation for the job, Truman was widely viewed as honorable, down-to-earth, and self-confident. Most important of all, he had the ability to make difficult decisions and to accept full responsibility for their consequences. As the plaque on his White House desk read, "The Buck Stops Here." Truman faced two huge challenges: dealing with the rising threat of communism, as discussed in Chapter 18, and restoring the American economy to a strong footing after the war's end.

TRUMAN FACES STRIKES One economic problem that Truman had to address was strikes. Facing higher prices and lower wages, 4.5 million discontented workers, including steelworkers, coal miners, and railroad workers, went on strike in 1946. Although he generally supported organized labor, Truman refused to let strikes cripple the nation. He threatened to draft the striking workers and to order them as soldiers to stay on the job. He authorized the federal government to seize the mines, and he threatened to take control of the railroads as well. Truman appeared before Congress and asked for the authority to draft the striking railroad workers into the army. Before he could finish his speech, the unions gave in. C

MAIN IDEA

Summarizing
C What actions did President Truman take to avert labor strikes?

"HAD ENOUGH?" Disgusted by shortages of goods, rising inflation, and labor strikes, Americans were ready for a change. The Republicans asked the public, "Had enough?" Voters gave their answer at the polls: in the 1946 congressional elections, the Republican Party won control of both the Senate and the House of Representatives for the first time since 1928. The new 80th Congress ignored Truman's domestic proposals. In 1947, Congress passed the Taft-Hartley Act over Truman's veto. This bill overturned many rights won by the unions under the New Deal.

HISTORICAL SPOTLIGHT

JACKIE ROBINSON

Jackie Robinson took a brave step when he turned the Brooklyn Dodgers into an integrated baseball team in 1947. But he—and the country—had a long way to go.

Unhappy fans hurled insults at Robinson from the stands. Some players on opposing teams tried to hit him with pitches or to injure him with the spikes on their shoes. He even received death threats. But he endured this with poise and restraint, saying,

> "Plenty of times, I wanted to haul off when somebody insulted me for the color of my skin but I had to hold to myself. I knew I was kind of an experiment."

In 1949, Robinson was voted the National League's most valuable player. He later became the first African American to be inducted into the Baseball Hall of Fame.

Social Unrest Persists

Problems arose not only in the economy but in the very fabric of society. After World War II, a wave of racial violence erupted in the South. Many African Americans, particularly those who had served in the armed forces during the war, demanded their rights as citizens.

TRUMAN SUPPORTS CIVIL RIGHTS Truman put his presidency on the line for civil rights. "I am asking for equality of opportunity for all human beings," he said, ". . . and if that ends up in my failure to be reelected, that failure will be in a good cause." In 1946, Truman created a President's Commission on Civil Rights. Following the group's recommendations, Truman asked Congress for several measures including a federal antilynching law, a ban on the poll tax as a voting requirement, and a permanent civil rights commission.

Congress refused to pass these measures, or a measure to integrate the armed forces. As a result, Truman himself took action. In July 1948, he issued an executive order for integration of the armed forces, calling for "equality of treatment and opportunity in the armed forces without regard to race, color, religion, or national origin." In addition, he ordered an end to discrimination in the hiring of government employees. The Supreme Court also ruled that the lower courts could not bar

Vocabulary
discrimination: treatment based on class or category rather than individual merit

In 1947, Jackie Robinson joined the Brooklyn Dodgers, angering some fans but winning the hearts, and respect, of many others.

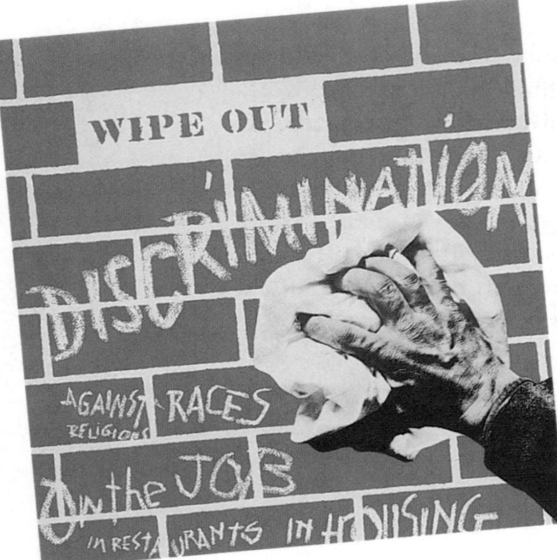

▲ ***Wipe Out Discrimination*** **(1949), a poster by Milton Ackoff, depicts the civil rights consciousness that angered the Dixiecrats.**

African Americans from residential neighborhoods. These actions represented the beginnings of a federal commitment to dealing with racial issues. **D**

MAIN IDEA

Summarizing
D How did Truman use his executive power to advance civil rights?

THE 1948 ELECTION Although many Americans blamed Truman for the nation's inflation and labor unrest, the Democrats nominated him for president in 1948. To protest Truman's emphasis on civil rights, a number of Southern Democrats—who became known as **Dixiecrats**—formed the States' Rights Democratic Party, and nominated their own presidential candidate, Governor J. Strom Thurmond of South Carolina. Discontent reigned at the far left of the Democratic spectrum as well. The former vice-president Henry A. Wallace led his supporters out of mainstream Democratic ranks to form a more liberal Progressive Party.

As the election approached, opinion polls gave the Republican candidate, New York Governor Thomas E. Dewey, a comfortable lead. Refusing to believe the polls, Truman poured his energy into the campaign. First, he called the Republican-dominated Congress into a special session. He challenged it to pass laws supporting such elements of the Democratic Party platform as public housing, federal aid to education, a higher minimum wage, and extended Social Security coverage. Not one of these laws was passed. Then he took his campaign to the people. He traveled from one end of the country to the other by train, speaking from the rear platform in a sweeping "whistlestop campaign." Day after day, people heard the president denounce the "do-nothing, 80th Congress."

STUNNING UPSET Truman's "Give 'em hell, Harry" campaign worked. He won the election in a close political upset. The Democrats gained control of Congress as well, even though they suffered losses in the South, which had been solidly Democratic since Reconstruction.

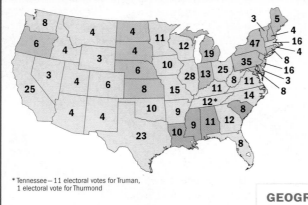

Truman surprised the newspapers by winning the 1948 election. ▶

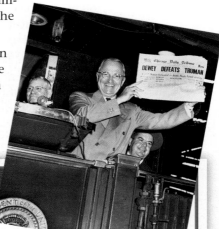

Presidential Election of 1948

Party	Candidate	Electoral Votes	Popular Votes
Democratic	Harry S. Truman	303	24,179,000
Republican	Thomas E. Dewey	189	21,991,000
States' Rights	J. Strom Thurmond	39	1,176,000
Progressive	Henry A. Wallace	—	1,157,000

* Tennessee – 11 electoral votes for Truman, 1 electoral vote for Thurmond

GEOGRAPHY SKILLBUILDER

1. **Region** In which regions of the country did Truman carry states? Dewey? Thurmond?
2. **Region** In which regions was support for Truman the weakest?

THE FAIR DEAL After his victory, Truman continued proposing an ambitious economic program. Truman's **Fair Deal,** an extension of Roosevelt's New Deal, included proposals for a nationwide system of compulsory health insurance and a crop-subsidy system to provide a steady income for farmers. In Congress, some Northern Democrats joined Dixiecrats and Republicans in defeating both measures.

MAIN IDEA

Evaluating Leadership

E What were some of Truman's achievements as president?

In other instances, however, Truman's ideas prevailed. Congress raised the hourly minimum wage from 40 cents to 75 cents, extended Social Security coverage to about 10 million more people, and initiated flood control and irrigation projects. Congress also provided financial support for cities to clear out slums and build 810,000 housing units for low-income families. E

Republicans Take the Middle Road

Despite these social and economic victories, Truman's approval rating sank to an all-time low of 23 percent in 1951. The stalemate in the Korean War and the rising tide of McCarthyism, which cast doubt on the loyalty of some federal employees, became overwhelming issues. Truman decided not to run for reelection. The Democrats nominated the intellectual and articulate governor Adlai Stevenson of Illinois to run against the Republican candidate, General Dwight D. Eisenhower, known popularly as "Ike."

I LIKE IKE! During the campaign, the Republicans accused the Democrats of "plunder at home and blunder abroad." To fan the anti-Communist hysteria that was sweeping over the country, Republicans raised the specter of the rise of communism in China and Eastern Europe. They also criticized the growing power of the federal government and the alleged bribery and corruption among Truman's political allies.

◀ Campaign accessories expressed Ike's popularity and voters' desire for a positive political change.

Eisenhower's campaign hit a snag, however, when newspapers accused his running mate, California Senator Richard M. Nixon, of profiting from a secret slush fund set up by wealthy supporters. Nixon decided to reply to the charges. In an emotional speech to an audience of 58 million, now known as the "Checkers speech," he exhibited masterful use of a new medium—television. Nixon denied any wrongdoing, but he did admit to accepting one gift from a political supporter.

Vocabulary
slush fund: a fund often designated for corrupt practices, such as bribery

A PERSONAL VOICE RICHARD M. NIXON

"**You know what it was? It was a little cocker spaniel dog in a crate, that he'd [the political supporter] sent all the way from Texas. Black and white spotted. And our little girl—Tricia, the six-year-old—named it Checkers. And you know the kids, like all kids, love the dog and I just want to say this right now, that regardless of what they say about it, we're going to keep it.**"

—"Checkers speech," September 23, 1952

▲ **Countering slush fund charges, Richard Nixon speaks to TV viewers about his daughters and their dog, Checkers.**

Nixon's speech saved his place on the Republican ticket. In November 1952, Eisenhower won 55 percent of the popular vote and a majority of the electoral college votes, while the Republicans narrowly captured Congress.

WALKING THE MIDDLE OF THE ROAD President Eisenhower's style of governing differed from that of the Democrats. His approach, which he called "dynamic conservatism," was also known as "Modern Republicanism." He called for government to be "conservative when it comes to money and liberal when it comes to human beings."

Eisenhower followed a middle-of-the-road course and avoided many controversial issues, but he could not completely sidestep a persistent domestic issue—civil rights—that gained national attention due to court rulings and acts of civil disobedience in the mid-1950s. The most significant judicial action occurred in 1954, when the Supreme Court ruled in *Brown* v. *Board of Education of Topeka* that public schools must be racially integrated. (See page 708.) In a landmark act of civil disobedience a year later, a black seamstress named Rosa Parks refused to give up her seat on a bus to a white man. Her arrest sparked a boycott of the entire Montgomery, Alabama, bus system. The civil rights movement had entered a new era.

Although Eisenhower did not assume leadership on civil rights issues, he accomplished much on the domestic scene. Shortly after becoming president, Eisenhower pressed hard for programs that would bring around a balanced budget and a cut in taxes. During his two terms, Ike's administration raised the minimum wage, extended Social Security and unemployment benefits, increased funding for public housing, and backed the creation of interstate highways and the Department of Health, Education, and Welfare. His popularity soared, and he won reelection in 1956.

ASSESSMENT

1. **TERMS & NAMES** For each term or name, write a sentence explaining its significance.
   - **GI Bill of Rights**
   - **Harry S. Truman**
   - **Dixiecrat**
   - **Fair Deal**
   - **suburb**

MAIN IDEA

2. **TAKING NOTES**
   Create a time line of key events relating to postwar America. Use the dates below as a guide.

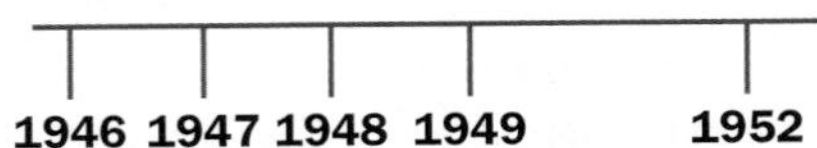

   Write a paragraph describing the effects of one of these events.

CRITICAL THINKING

3. **DRAWING CONCLUSIONS**
   Do you think Eisenhower's actions reflected his philosophy of dynamic conservatism? Why or why not?
   Think About:
   - the definition of dynamic conservatism
   - Eisenhower's actions on civil rights policies
   - Eisenhower's accomplishments on other domestic issues

4. **EVALUATING LEADERSHIP**
   Why do you think most Americans went along with Eisenhower's conservative approach to domestic policy?

5. **CONTRASTING**
   How did Presidents Truman and Eisenhower differ regarding civil rights?

The American Dream in the Fifties

MAIN IDEA	WHY IT MATTERS NOW	Terms & Names
During the 1950s, the economy boomed, and many Americans enjoyed material comfort.	The "American dream," a notion that was largely shaped by the 1950s, is still pursued today.	• conglomerate • franchise • baby boom • Dr. Jonas Salk • consumerism • planned obsolescence

One American's Story

Settled into her brand new house near San Diego, California, Carol Freeman felt very fortunate. Her husband Mark had his own law practice, and when their first baby was born, she became a full-time homemaker. She was living the American dream, yet Carol felt dissatisfied—as if there were "something wrong" with her because she was not happy.

A Personal Voice CAROL FREEMAN

"As dissatisfied as I was, and as restless, I remember so well this feeling [we] had at the time that the world was going to be your oyster. You were going to make money, your kids were going to go to good schools, everything was possible if you just did what you were supposed to do. The future was rosy. There was a tremendous feeling of optimism. . . . Much as I say it was hateful, it was also hopeful. It was an innocent time."

—quoted in *The Fifties: A Women's Oral History*

▲ The dream woman of the 1950s was depicted in advertising and on TV as doing constant housework, but always with a smile.

After World War II ended, Americans turned their attention to their families and jobs. The economy prospered. New technologies and business ideas created fresh opportunities for many, and by the end of the decade Americans were enjoying the highest standard of living in the world. The American dream of a happy and successful life seemed within the reach of many people.

The Organization and the Organization Man

During the 1950s, businesses expanded rapidly. By 1956, the majority of Americans no longer held blue-collar, or industrial, jobs. Instead, more people worked in higher-paid, white-collar positions—clerical, managerial, or professional occupations. Unlike blue-collar workers, who manufactured goods for sale, white-collar workers tended to perform services in fields like sales, advertising, insurance, and communications.

CONGLOMERATES Many white-collar workers performed their services in large corporations or government agencies. Some of these corporations continued expanding by forming **conglomerates**. (A conglomerate is a major corporation that includes a number of smaller companies in unrelated industries.) For example, one conglomerate, International Telephone and Telegraph (ITT), whose original business was communications, bought car-rental companies, insurance companies, and hotel and motel chains. Through this diversification, or investment in various areas of the economy, ITT tried to protect itself from declines in individual industries. Other huge parent companies included American Telephone and Telegraph, Xerox, and General Electric.

NOW & THEN

FRANCHISES

In the decades since Ray Kroc opened his first McDonald's (shown below), franchising has become all but a way of life in the United States. Today, there are nearly 3,000 franchised companies operating over 500,000 businesses throughout the country. Officials estimate that franchises account for nearly one-third of all U.S. retail sales. American franchises today provide a wide array of goods and services, from car maintenance, to tax services, to hair care.

In an attempt to tap into the international market, hundreds of U.S. companies have established overseas franchises. The franchise with perhaps the greatest global reach is the one that started it all. In addition to its more than 10,000 U.S. franchises, McDonald's now operates over 14,000 franchises in dozens of countries around the world.

FRANCHISES In addition to diversifying, another strategy for business expansion—franchising—developed at this time. A **franchise** is a company that offers similar products or services in many locations. (*Franchise* is also used to refer to the right, sold to an individual, to do business using the parent company's name and the system that the parent company developed.) A

MAIN IDEA

Comparing
A How were conglomerates and franchises alike and how were they different?

Fast-food restaurants developed some of the first and most successful franchises. McDonald's, for example, had its start when the McDonald brothers developed unusually efficient service, based on assembly-line methods, at their small drive-in restaurant in San Bernardino, California. They simplified the menu, featured 15-cent hamburgers, and mechanized their kitchen.

Salesman Ray Kroc paid the McDonalds $2.7 million for the franchise rights to their hamburger drive-in. In April 1955, he opened his first McDonald's in Des Plaines, Illinois, where he further improved the assembly-line process and introduced the golden arches that are now familiar all over the world.

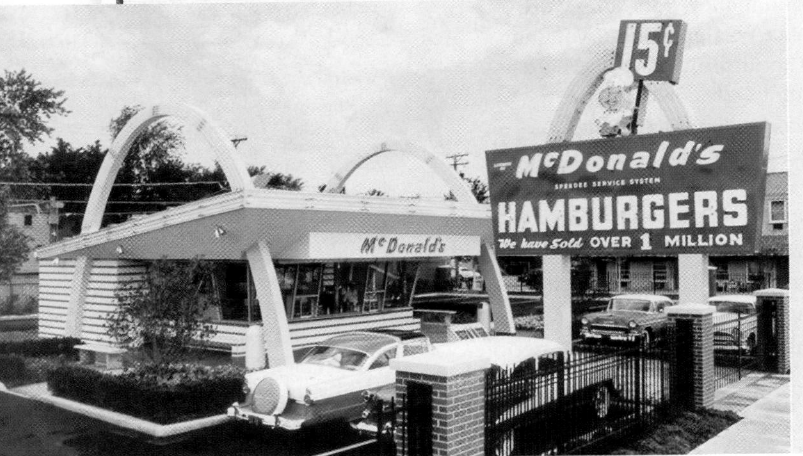

A PERSONAL VOICE RAY KROC

"**It requires a certain kind of mind to see the beauty in a hamburger bun. Yet is it any more unusual to find grace in the texture and softly curved silhouette of a bun than to reflect lovingly on the . . . arrangements and textures and colors in a butterfly's wings? . . . Not if you view the bun as an essential material in the art of serving a great many meals fast.**"

—quoted in *The Fifties*

SOCIAL CONFORMITY While franchises like McDonald's helped standardize what people ate, some American workers found themselves becoming standardized as well. Employees who were well paid and held secure jobs in thriving companies sometimes paid a price for economic advancement: a loss of their individuality. In general, businesses did not want creative thinkers, rebels, or anyone who would rock the corporate boat.

In *The Organization Man*, a book based on a classic 1956 study of suburban Park Forest, Illinois, and other communities, William H. Whyte described how the new, large organizations created "company people." Companies would give personality tests to people applying for jobs to make sure they would "fit in" the corporate culture. Companies rewarded employees for teamwork, cooperation, and loyalty and so contributed to the growth of conformity, which Whyte called "belongingness." Despite their success, a number of workers questioned whether pursuing the American dream exacted too high a price, as conformity replaced individuality. **B**

MAIN IDEA

Analyzing Effects

B What effects did the climate in many corporations have on some workers?

▲ **The "organization man" had to step lively to keep up with the Joneses.**

The Suburban Lifestyle

Though achieving job security did take a psychological toll on some Americans who resented having to repress their own personalities, it also enabled people to provide their families with the so-called good things in life. Most Americans worked in cities, but fewer and fewer of them lived there. New highways and the availability and affordability of automobiles and gasoline made commuting possible. By the early 1960s, every large city in the United States was surrounded by suburbs. Of the 13 million new homes built in the 1950s, 85 percent were built in the suburbs. For many people, the suburbs embodied the American dream of an affordable single-family house, good schools, a safe, healthy environment for children, and congenial neighbors just like themselves.

THE BABY BOOM As soldiers returned from World War II and settled into family life, they contributed to an unprecedented population explosion known as the **baby boom.** During the late 1940s and through the early 1960s, the birthrate (number of live births per 1,000 people) in the United States soared. At the height of the baby boom, in 1957, one American infant was born every seven seconds—a total of 4,308,000 that year. The result was the largest generation in the nation's history.

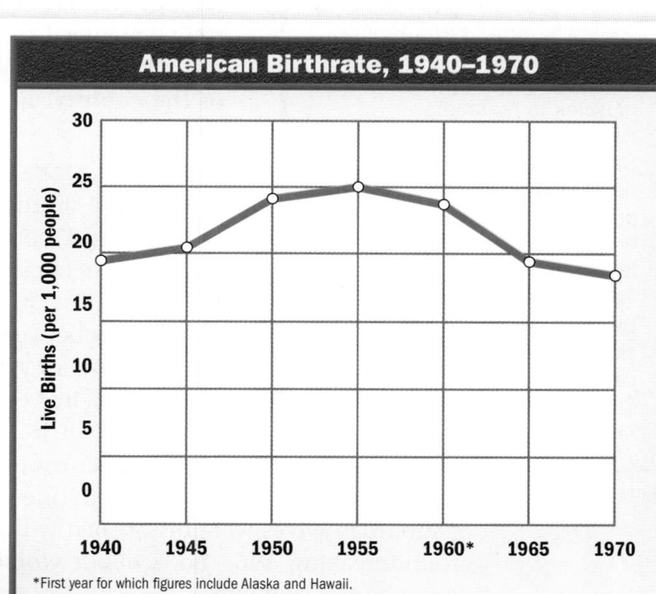

SKILLBUILDER Interpreting Graphs

1. What was the overall trend in the birthrate at the start of World War II, and after the war ended?
2. What was the difference in the birthrate between 1960 and 1970?

◄ **Some of the 40 million new Americans who were born during the baby boom.**

KEY PLAYER

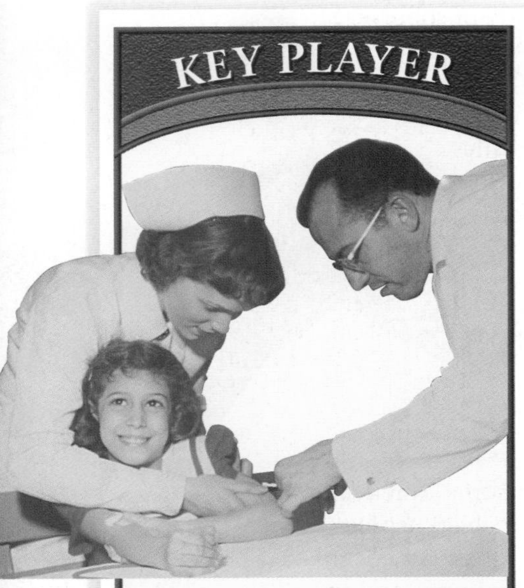

JONAS SALK 1914–1995

One of the most feared diseases in the 1950s was polio, the disease that had partially paralyzed President Franklin D. Roosevelt. Polio afflicted 58,000 American children in 1952, killing some and making others reliant on crutches, wheelchairs, or iron lungs (machines that helped people with paralyzed chest muscles to breathe).

In the early 1950s, Dr. Jonas Salk (at right in photo above) developed an effective vaccine to prevent the disease, and the government sponsored a free inoculation program for children. The vaccine was extremely effective. By 1974, thanks to Salk's vaccine and a new oral vaccine developed by Dr. Albert Sabin, only seven new polio cases were reported in the country.

Contributing to the size of the baby-boom generation were many factors, including: reunion of husbands and wives after the war, decreasing marriage age, desirability of large families, confidence in continued economic prosperity, and advances in medicine.

ADVANCES IN MEDICINE AND CHILDCARE Among the medical advances that saved hundreds of thousands of children's lives was the discovery of drugs to fight and prevent childhood diseases, such as typhoid fever. Another breakthrough came when **Dr. Jonas Salk** developed a vaccine for the crippling disease poliomyelitis—polio.

Many parents raised their children according to guidelines devised by the author and pediatrician Dr. Benjamin Spock. His *Common Sense Book of Baby and Child Care,* published in 1946, sold nearly 10 million copies during the 1950s. In it, he advised parents not to spank or scold their children. He also encouraged families to hold meetings in which children could express themselves. He considered it so important for mothers to be at home with their children that he proposed having the government pay mothers to stay home.

The baby boom had a tremendous impact not only on child care but on the American economy and the educational system as well. In 1958, toy sales alone reached $1.25 billion. During the decade, 10 million new students entered the elementary schools. The sharp increase in enrollment caused overcrowding and teacher shortages in many parts of the country. In California, a new school opened every seven days. (C)

MAIN IDEA

Analyzing Effects

(C) How did the baby boom affect American life in the 1950s?

WOMEN'S ROLES During the 1950s, the role of homemaker and mother was glorified in popular magazines, movies, and TV programs such as *Father Knows Best* and *The Adventures of Ozzie and Harriet. Time* magazine described the homemaker as "the key figure in all suburbia, the thread that weaves between family and community—the keeper of the suburban dream." In contrast to the ideal portrayed in the media, however, some women, like Carol Freeman, who spoke of her discontentment, were not happy with their roles; they felt isolated, bored, and unfulfilled. According to one survey in the 1950s, more than one-fifth of suburban wives were dissatisfied with their lives. Betty Friedan, author of the groundbreaking 1963 book about women and society, *The Feminine Mystique,* described the problem.

Background

The percentage of women college students in the 1950s was smaller than in the 1920s.

A PERSONAL VOICE BETTY FRIEDAN

"For the first time in their history, women are becoming aware of an identity crisis in their own lives, a crisis which . . . has grown worse with each succeeding generation. . . . I think this is the crisis of women growing up—a turning point from an immaturity that has been called femininity to full human identity."

—*The Feminine Mystique*

The number of women working outside the home rose steadily during the decade. By 1960, almost 40 percent of mothers with children between ages 6 and 17 held paying jobs.

But having a job didn't necessarily contribute to a woman's happiness. A woman's career opportunities tended to be limited to fields such as nursing, teaching, and office support, which paid less than other professional and business positions did. Women also earned less than men for comparable work. Although increasing numbers of women attended four-year colleges, they generally received little financial, academic, or psychological encouragement to pursue their goals. D

MAIN IDEA

Contrasting
D How did women's roles and opportunities in the 1950s differ from women's roles today?

LEISURE IN THE FIFTIES Most Americans of the 1950s had more leisure time than ever before. Employees worked a 40-hour week and earned several weeks' vacation per year. People owned more labor-saving devices, such as washing machines, clothes dryers, dishwashers, and power lawn mowers, which allowed more time for leisure activities. *Fortune* magazine reported that, in 1953, Americans spent more than $30 billion on leisure goods and activities.

Americans also enjoyed a wide variety of recreational pursuits—both active and passive. Millions of people participated in such sports as fishing, bowling, hunting, boating, and golf. More fans than ever attended baseball, basketball, and football games; others watched professional sports on television.

Americans also became avid readers. They devoured books about cooking, religion, do-it-yourself projects, and homemaking. They also read mysteries, romance novels, and fiction by popular writers such as Ernest Hemingway, John Steinbeck, Daphne du Maurier, and J. D. Salinger. Book sales doubled, due in part to a thriving paperback market. The circulation of popular magazines like *Reader's Digest* and *Sports Illustrated* steadily rose, from about 148 million to more than 190 million readers. Sales of comic books also reached a peak in the mid-1950s.

History Through Art

AFTER THE PROM (1957)
The artist, Norman Rockwell, chose an innocent junior-high couple to illustrate the easy emotions and the ordinary events of postwar America. **What does this painting convey about life in the 1950s?**

3-D comics and 3-D movies were two of the many fads that mesmerized the nation in the 1950s. ▶

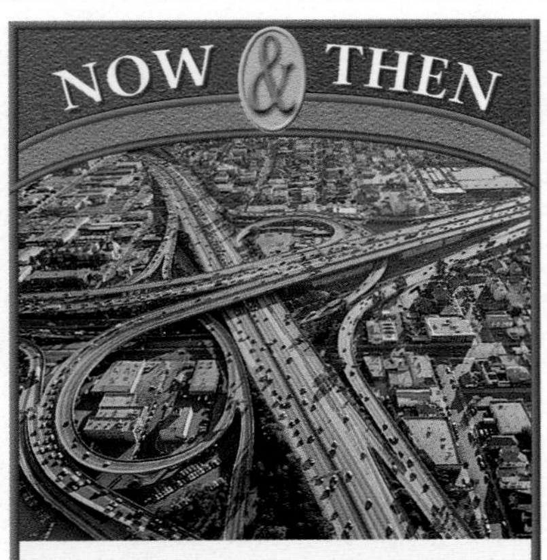

SOUTHERN CALIFORNIA AND THE AUTOMOBILE

No state has exemplified automania in the U.S. more than California. By the late 1990s, Californians owned more cars, held more driver's licenses, and traveled more miles on their roads than the people of any other state. The center of this automobile culture is the metropolitan area of Los Angeles.

Contributing to the importance of the automobile is Southern California's suburban lifestyle. This dependence on cars has contributed to problems of air pollution and traffic jams. But, California is addressing these problems by reviving public transportation systems and promoting the use of electric cars that produce no pollution.

The Automobile Culture

During World War II, the U.S. government had rationed gasoline to curb inflation and conserve supplies. After the war, however, an abundance of both imported and domestically produced petroleum—the raw material from which gasoline is made—led to inexpensive, plentiful fuel for consumers. Easy credit terms and extensive advertising persuaded Americans to buy cars in record numbers. In response, new car sales rose from 6.7 million in 1950 to 7.9 million in 1955. The total number of private cars on the road jumped from 40 million in 1950 to over 60 million in 1960.

AUTOMANIA Suburban living made owning a car a necessity. Most of the new suburbs, built in formerly rural areas, did not offer public transportation, and people had to drive to their jobs in the cities. In addition, many of the schools, stores, synagogues, churches, and doctors' and dentists' offices were not within walking distance of suburban homes. (E)

MAIN IDEA

Analyzing Causes

(E) Why did auto sales surge in the 1950s?

THE INTERSTATE HIGHWAY SYSTEM The more cars there were, the more roads were needed. "Automania" spurred local and state governments to construct roads linking the major cities while connecting schools, shopping centers, and workplaces to residential suburbs. The Interstate Highway Act, which President Eisenhower signed in 1956, authorized the building of a nationwide highway network—41,000 miles of expressways. The new roads, in turn, encouraged the development of new suburbs farther from the cities.

Interstate highways also made high-speed, long-haul trucking possible, which contributed to a decline in the commercial use of railroads. Towns along the new highways prospered, while towns along the older, smaller roads experienced hard times. The system of highways also helped unify and homogenize the nation. As John Keats observed in his 1958 book, *The Insolent Chariots*, "Our new roads, with their ancillaries, the motels, filling stations, and restaurants advertising Eats, have made it possible for you to drive from Brooklyn to Los Angeles without a change of diet, scenery, or culture." With access to cars, affordable gas, and new highways, more and more Americans hit the road. They flocked to mountains, lakes, national parks, historic sites, and amusement parks for family vacations. Disneyland, which opened in California in July 1955, attracted 3 million visitors the next year.

Vocabulary

homogenize: to make the same or similar

MOBILITY TAKES ITS TOLL As the automobile industry boomed, it stimulated production and provided jobs in other areas, such as drive-in movies, restaurants, and shopping malls. Yet cars also created new problems for both society and the environment. Noise and exhaust polluted the air. Automobile accidents claimed more lives every year. Traffic jams raised people's stress levels, and heavy use damaged the roads. Because cars made it possible for Americans to live in suburbs, many upper-class and middle-class whites left the crowded cities. Jobs and businesses eventually followed them to the suburbs. Public transportation declined, and poor people in the inner cities were often left without jobs and vital services. As a result, the economic gulf between suburban and urban dwellers and between the middle class and the poor widened. (F)

MAIN IDEA

Analyzing Effects

(F) What positive and negative effects did the mass availability of the automobile have on American life in the 1950s?

Americans Hit the Road

In the 1950s Americans loved their cars—big, powerful, and flashy. Some car owners spent their leisure time maintaining their automobiles for the daily commute to work or for the annual family vacation on any one of the nation's 22 new interstate highways.

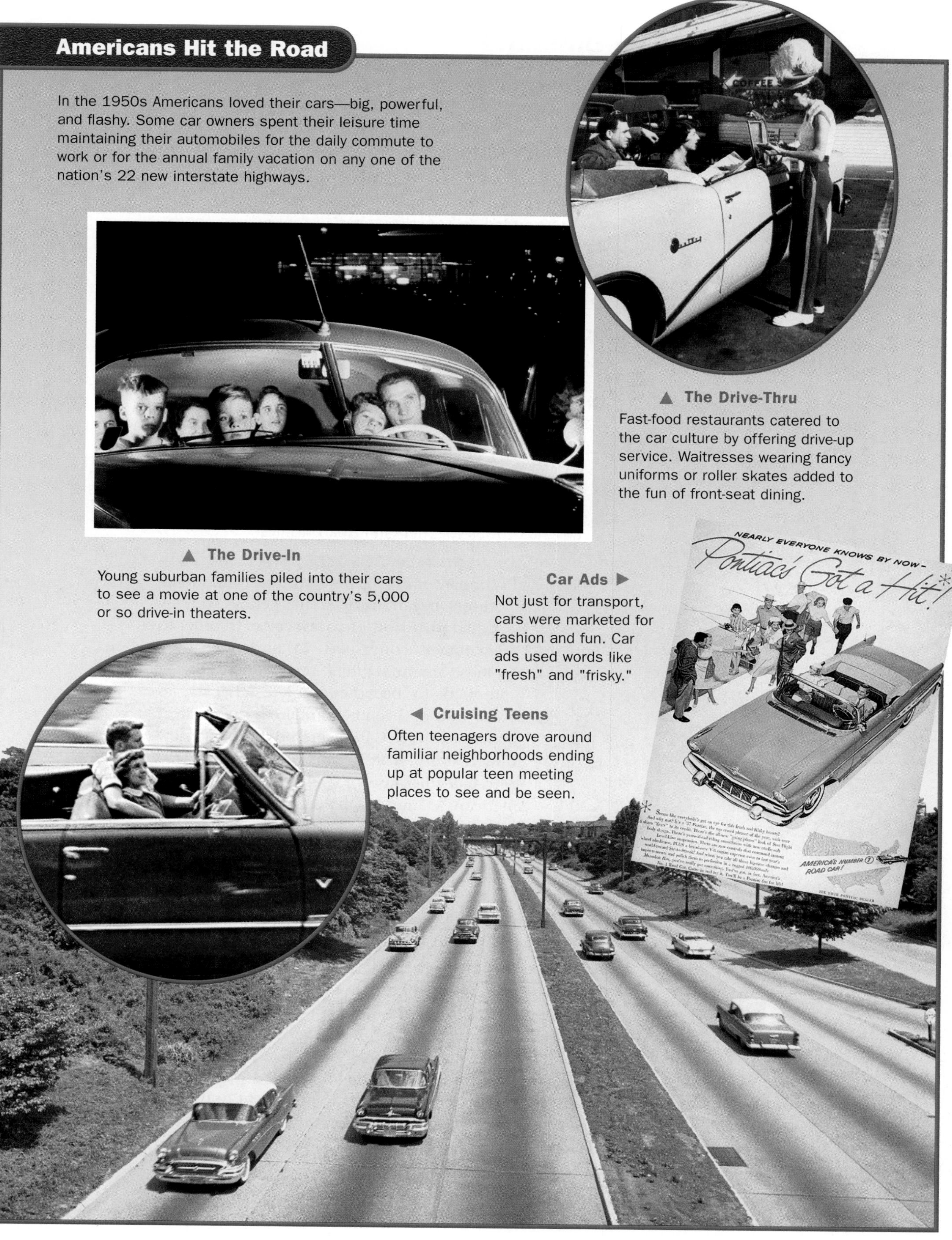

COFFEE
NEARLY EVERYONE KNOWS BY NOW—
Pontiac's Got a Hit!*
AMERICA'S NUMBER 1 ROAD CAR!

▲ **The Drive-Thru**
Fast-food restaurants catered to the car culture by offering drive-up service. Waitresses wearing fancy uniforms or roller skates added to the fun of front-seat dining.

▲ **The Drive-In**
Young suburban families piled into their cars to see a movie at one of the country's 5,000 or so drive-in theaters.

Car Ads ▶
Not just for transport, cars were marketed for fashion and fun. Car ads used words like "fresh" and "frisky."

◀ **Cruising Teens**
Often teenagers drove around familiar neighborhoods ending up at popular teen meeting places to see and be seen.

Consumerism Unbound

By the mid-1950s, nearly 60 percent of Americans were members of the middle class, about twice as many as before World War II. They wanted, and had the money to buy, increasing numbers of products. **Consumerism,** buying material goods, came to be equated with success.

Now! In a full console at only $299.95*, Zenith's revolutionary
Top Tuning
How does your kitchen rate on the electrical living scale?
Just wonderful!
Enjoyable!
Bearable!
Roughing it!
LIVE BETTER
...Electrically

▲ In the 1950s, advertisers made "keeping up with the Joneses" a way of life for consumers.

NEW PRODUCTS One new product after another appeared in the marketplace, as various industries responded to consumer demand. *Newsweek* magazine reported in 1956 that "hundreds of brand-new goods have become commonplace overnight." Consumers purchased electric household appliances—such as washing machines, dryers, blenders, freezers, and dishwashers—in record numbers.

With more and more leisure time to fill, people invested in recreational items. They bought televisions, tape recorders, and the new hi-fi (high-fidelity) record players. They bought casual clothing to suit their suburban lifestyles and power lawn mowers, barbecue grills, swimming pools, and lawn decorations for their suburban homes.

PLANNED OBSOLESCENCE In addition to creating new products, manufacturers began using a marketing strategy called **planned obsolescence.** In order to encourage consumers to purchase more goods, manufacturers purposely designed products to become obsolete—that is, to wear out or become outdated—in a short period of time. Carmakers brought out new models every year, urging consumers to stay up-to-date. Because of planned obsolescence, Americans came to expect new and better products, and they began to discard items that were sometimes barely used. Some observers commented that American culture was on its way to becoming a "throwaway society." G

MAIN IDEA

Analyzing Causes

G How did manufacturers influence Americans to become a "throwaway society"?

BUY NOW, PAY LATER Many consumers made their purchases on credit and therefore did not have to pay for them right away. The Diner's Club issued the first credit card in 1950, and the American Express card was introduced in 1958. In addition, people bought large items on the installment plan and made regular payments over a fixed time. Home mortgages (loans for buying a house) and automobile loans worked the same way. During the decade, the total private debt grew from $73 billion to $179 billion. Instead of saving money, Americans were spending it, confident that prosperity would continue.

THE ADVERTISING AGE The advertising industry capitalized on this runaway consumerism by encouraging even more spending. Ads were everywhere—in newspapers and magazines, on radio and television, and on billboards along the highways—prompting people to buy goods that ranged from cars to cereals to cigarettes. Advertisers spent about $6 billion in 1950; by 1955, the figure was up to $9 billion. Since most Americans had satisfied their basic needs, advertisers tried to convince them to buy things they really didn't need.

A Personal Voice VANCE PACKARD

"On May 18, 1956, *The New York Times* printed a remarkable interview with a young man named Gerald Stahl, executive vice-president of the Package Designers Council. He stated: 'Psychiatrists say that people have so much to choose from that they want help—they will like the package that hypnotizes them into picking it.' He urged food packers to put more hypnosis into their package designing, so that the housewife will stick out her hand for it rather than one of many rivals.

Mr. Stahl has found that it takes the average woman exactly twenty seconds to cover an aisle in a supermarket if she doesn't tarry; so a good package design should hypnotize the woman like a flashlight waved in front of her eyes."

—*The Hidden Persuaders*

More and more, ad executives and designers turned to psychology to create new strategies for selling. Advertisers appealed to people's desire for status and "belongingness" and strived to associate their products with those values.

Television became a powerful new advertising tool. The first one-minute TV commercial was produced in 1941 at a cost of $9. In 1960, advertisers spent a total of $1.6 billion for television ads. By 2001, a 30-second commercial during the Superbowl cost an advertiser $2.2 million. Television had become not only the medium for mass transmission of cultural values, but a symbol of popular culture itself.

ASSESSMENT

1. **TERMS & NAMES** For each term or name, write a sentence explaining its significance.
   - **conglomerate**
   - **franchise**
   - **baby boom**
   - **Dr. Jonas Salk**
   - **consumerism**
   - **planned obsolescence**

MAIN IDEA

2. **TAKING NOTES**
   In a graphic organizer like the one below, list examples of specific goals that characterized the American dream for suburbanites in the 1950s.

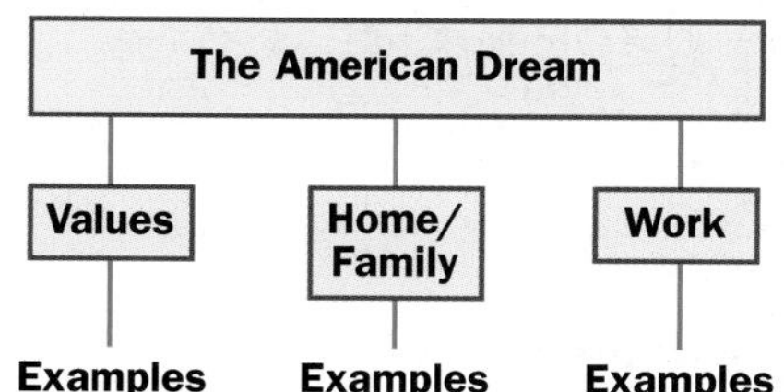

   What do you think the most important goal was?

CRITICAL THINKING

3. **ANALYZING EFFECTS**
   In what ways do you think current environmental consciousness is related to the "throwaway society" of the 1950s? Support your answer.
   Think About:
   - the purchasing habits of 1950s consumers
   - the effects of planned obsolescence
   - today's emphasis on recycling

4. **EVALUATING**
   Do you think that the life of a typical suburban homemaker during the 1950s was fulfilling or not? Support your answer.

5. **INTERPRETING VISUAL SOURCES**
   This ad is typical of how the advertising industry portrayed housewives in the 1950s. What message about women is conveyed by this ad?

The Road to Suburbia

"Come out to Park Forest where small-town friendships grow—and you still live so close to a big city." Advertisements like this one for a scientifically planned Chicago suburb captured the lure of the suburbs for thousands of growing families in the 1950s. The publicity promised affordable housing, congenial neighbors, fresh air and open spaces, good schools, and easy access to urban jobs and culture. Good transportation was the lifeline of suburban growth a half century ago, and it continues to spur expansion today.

PROPOSED PLAN ... VILLAGE OF PARK FOREST, ILLINOIS

AMERICAN COMMUNITY BUILDERS INC.

PARK FOREST HOMES INC.

CHICAGO LOOP

Lake Michigan

TOWN SITE

Chicagoland's COMPLETELY PLANNED *Suburb*

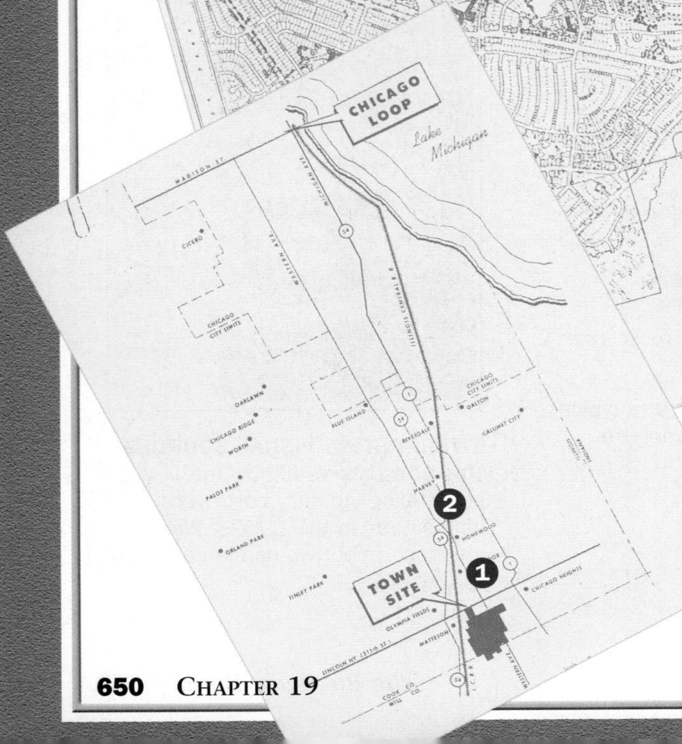

SHARED PRIVACY ► By 1952, development in Park Forest, Illinois had expanded to include both low-cost rental units and single-family homes. All the streets were curved to slow traffic, present a pleasing sweep of space, and give residents maximum privacy and space for yards.

1 WHERE THE 'BURBS ARE

Park Forest was planned from its conception in 1945 to be a "complete community for middle-income families with children." The setting was rural—amidst cornfields and forest preserves about 30 miles south of Chicago. But it was convenient to commuter lines, like the Illinois Central (IC) Railroad, and to major roads, such as Western Avenue.

❷ THE COMMUTER CRUSH

Men commuted to work on the IC railroad, while their wives usually stayed home to take care of the children, who thrived in Park Forest's safe, wholesome family environment.

❸ SHOPPING CENTERS

Consumerism became a driving force in the 1950s, and Park Forest kept up with the trend. The central shopping center served the community well until the late 1960s. When Interstate 57 was built, a mammoth mall, built just off the highway, caused the original shopping area to decline. Park Forest is still struggling to revive its central shopping area.

THINKING CRITICALLY

1. **Analyzing Patterns** How did the availability of transportation influence the creation and ongoing development of Park Forest?
2. **Creating a Database** Pose a historical question about a suburb near you. Collect statistics about changes in population, living patterns, income, and economic development in that suburb. Use those statistics to create a database that will help answer your questions.

SEE SKILLBUILDER HANDBOOK, PAGE R33.

RESEARCH LINKS CLASSZONE.COM

SECTION 3

Popular Culture

MAIN IDEA

Mainstream Americans, as well as the nation's subcultures, embraced new forms of entertainment during the 1950s.

WHY IT MATTERS NOW

Television and rock 'n' roll, integral parts of the nation's culture today, emerged during the postwar era.

Terms & Names

- **mass media**
- **Federal Communications Commission (FCC)**
- **beat movement**
- **rock 'n' roll**
- **jazz**

One American's Story

H. B. Barnum, a 14-year-old saxophone player who later became a music producer, was one of many teenagers in the 1950s drawn to a new style of music that featured hard-driving African-American rhythm and blues. Barnum described the first time he saw the rhythm-and-blues performer Richard Wayne Penniman, better known as Little Richard.

A PERSONAL VOICE H. B. BARNUM

"He'd just burst onto the stage from anywhere, and you wouldn't be able to hear anything but the roar of the audience. . . . He'd be on the stage, he'd be off the stage, he'd be jumping and yelling, screaming, whipping the audience on. . . . Then when he finally did hit the piano and just went into di-di-di-di-di-di-di, you know, well nobody can do that as fast as Richard. It just took everybody by surprise."

—quoted in *The Rise and Fall of Popular Music*

Born poor, Little Richard wore flashy clothes on stage, curled his hair, and shouted the lyrics to his songs. As one writer observed, "In two minutes [he] used as much energy as an all-night party." The music he and others performed became a prominent part of the American culture in the 1950s, a time when both mainstream America and those outside it embraced new and innovative forms of entertainment.

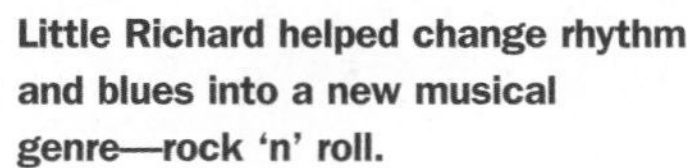

▲ **Little Richard helped change rhythm and blues into a new musical genre—rock 'n' roll.**

New Era of the Mass Media

Compared with other **mass media**—means of communication that reach large audiences—television developed with lightning speed. First widely available in 1948, television had reached 9 percent of American homes by 1950 and 55 percent of homes by 1954. In 1960, almost 90 percent—45 million—of American homes had television sets. Clearly, TV was the entertainment and information marvel of the postwar years.

THE RISE OF TELEVISION Early television sets were small boxes with round screens. Programming was meager, and broadcasts were in black and white. The first regular broadcasts, beginning in 1949, reached only a small part of the East Coast and offered only two hours of programs per week. Post–World War II innovations such as microwave relays, which could transmit television waves over long distances, sent the television industry soaring. By 1956, the **Federal Communications Commission (FCC)**—the government agency that regulates and licenses television, telephone, telegraph, radio, and other communications industries—had allowed 500 new stations to broadcast.

This period of rapid expansion was the "golden age" of television entertainment—and entertainment in the 1950s often meant comedy. Milton Berle attracted huge audiences with *The Texaco Star Theater,* and Lucille Ball and Desi Arnaz's early situation comedy, *I Love Lucy*, began its enormously popular run in 1951.

At the same time, veteran radio broadcaster Edward R. Murrow introduced two innovations: on-the-scene news reporting, with his program, *See It Now* (1951–1958), and interviewing, with *Person to Person* (1953–1960). Westerns, sports events, and original dramas shown on *Playhouse 90* and *Studio One* offered entertainment variety. Children's programs, such as *The Mickey Mouse Club* and *The Howdy Doody Show,* attracted loyal young fans.

American businesses took advantage of the opportunities offered by the new television industry. Advertising expenditures on TV, which were $170 million in 1950, reached nearly $2 billion in 1960.

Sales of *TV Guide,* introduced in 1953, quickly outpaced sales of other magazines. In 1954, the food industry introduced a new convenience item, the frozen TV dinner. Complete, ready-to-heat individual meals on disposable aluminum trays, TV dinners made it easy for people to eat without missing their favorite shows. (A)

MAIN IDEA

Analyzing Effects

(A) How did the emergence of television affect American culture in the 1950s?

HISTORICAL SPOTLIGHT

TV QUIZ SHOWS

Beginning with *The $64,000 Question* in 1955, television created hit quiz shows by adopting a popular format from radio and adding big cash prizes.

The quiz show *Twenty-One* made a star of a shy English professor named Charles Van Doren. He rode a wave of fame and fortune until 1958, when a former contestant revealed that, to heighten the dramatic impact, producers had been giving some of the contestants the right answers.

A scandal followed when a congressional subcommittee confirmed the charges. Most of the quiz shows soon left the air.

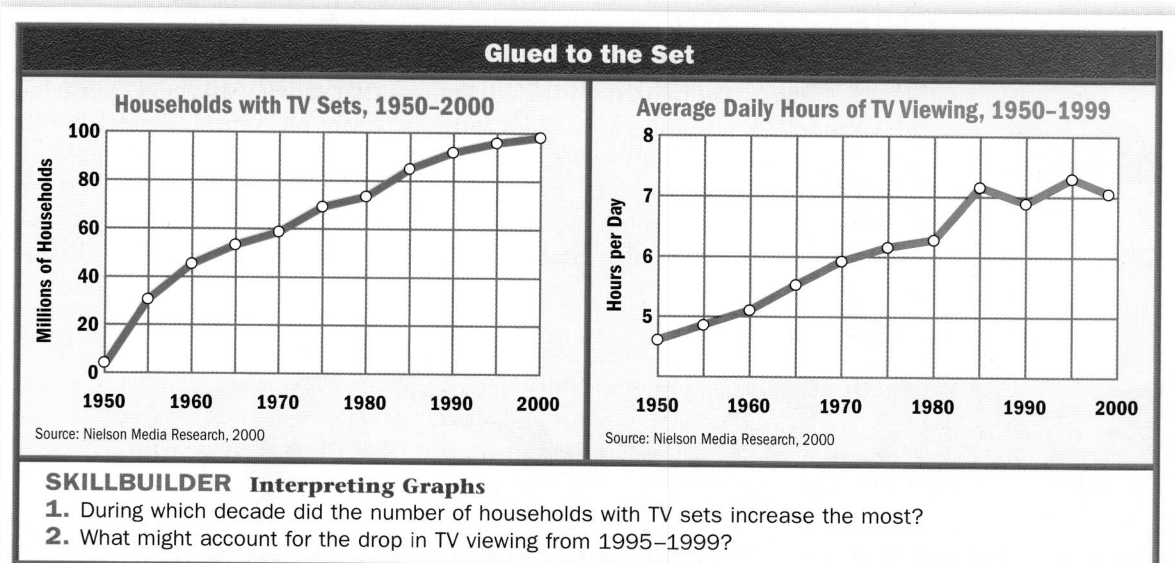

SKILLBUILDER Interpreting Graphs

1. During which decade did the number of households with TV sets increase the most?
2. What might account for the drop in TV viewing from 1995–1999?

▲ **Lucille Ball had to fight to have real-life husband, Cuban-born Desi Arnaz, cast in the popular TV series *I Love Lucy*.**

STEREOTYPES AND GUNSLINGERS Not everyone was thrilled with television, though. Critics objected to its effects on children and its stereotypical portrayal of women and minorities. Women did, in fact, appear in stereotypical roles, such as the ideal mothers of *Father Knows Best* and *The Adventures of Ozzie and Harriet.* Male characters outnumbered women characters three to one. African Americans and Latinos rarely appeared in television programs at all.

Vocabulary
stereotypical: conventional, formulaic, and oversimplified

Television in the 1950s portrayed an idealized white America. For the most part, it omitted references to poverty, diversity, and contemporary conflicts, such as the struggle of the civil rights movement against racial discrimination. Instead, it glorified the historical conflicts of the Western frontier in hit shows such as *Gunsmoke* and *Have Gun Will Travel.* The level of violence in these popular shows led to ongoing concerns about the effect of television on children. In 1961, Federal Communications Commission chairman Newton Minow voiced this concern to the leaders of the television industry.

A PERSONAL VOICE NEWTON MINOW

> **"When television is bad, nothing is worse. I invite you to sit down in front of your television set when your station goes on the air . . . and keep your eyes glued to that set until the station signs off. I can assure you that you will observe a vast wasteland."** (B)
>
> —speech to the National Association of Broadcasters, Washington, D.C., May 9, 1961

MAIN IDEA
Evaluating
(B) Do you think the rise of television had a positive or a negative effect on Americans? Explain.

RADIO AND MOVIES Although TV turned out to be wildly popular, radio and movies survived. But instead of competing with television's mass market for drama and variety shows, radio stations turned to local programming of news, weather, music, and community issues. The strategy paid off. During the decade, radio advertising rose by 35 percent, and the number of radio stations increased by 50 percent.

From the beginning, television cut into the profitable movie market. In 1948, 18,500 movie theaters had drawn nearly 90 million paid admissions per week. As more people stayed home to watch TV, the number of moviegoers decreased by nearly half. As early as 1951, producer David Selznick worried about Hollywood: "It'll never come back. It'll just keep on crumbling until finally the wind blows the last studio prop across the sands."

But Hollywood did not crumble and blow away. Instead, it capitalized on the advantages that movies still held over television—size, color, and stereophonic sound. Stereophonic sound, which surrounded the viewer, was introduced in 1952. By 1954, more than 50 percent of movies were in color. By contrast, color television, which became available that year, did not become widespread until the

James Dean, seen here in the movie *Giant*, had a self-confident indifference that made him the idol of teenagers. He died in a car accident at age 24. ▼

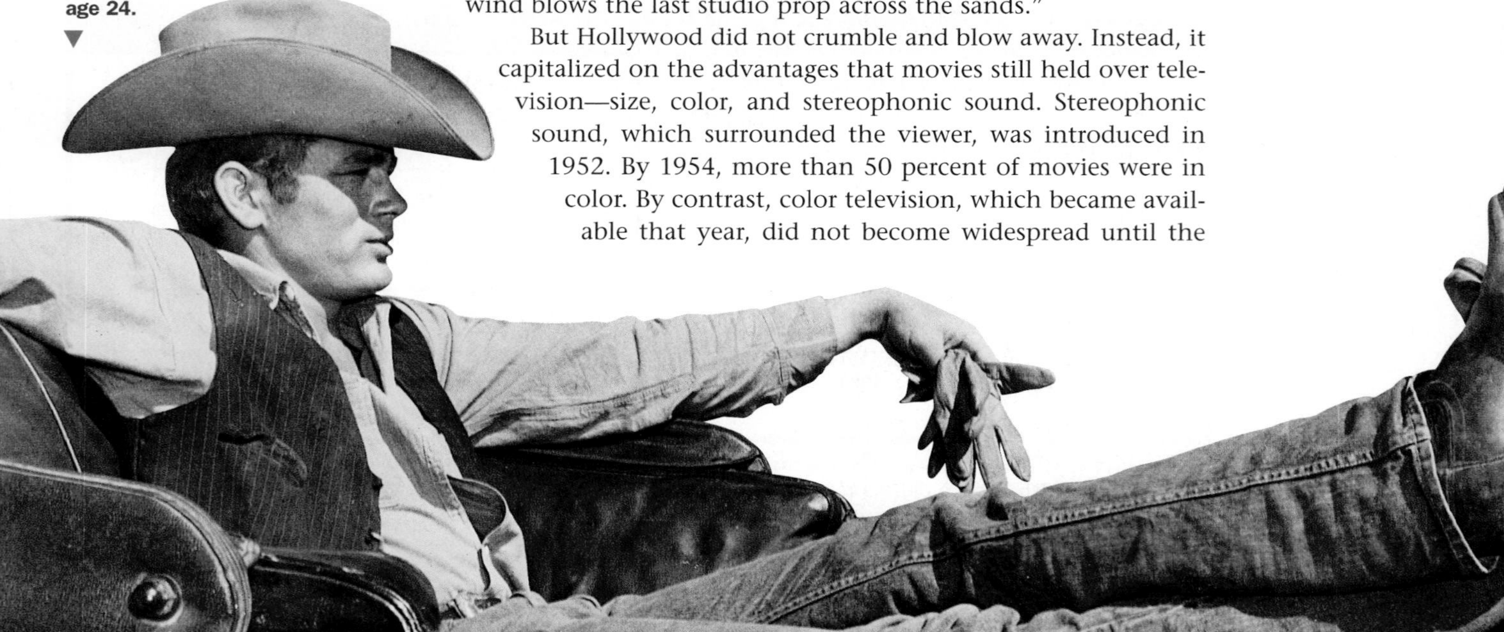

MAIN IDEA

Summarizing
C How did radio and movies maintain their appeal in the 1950s?

next decade. In 1953, 20th Century Fox introduced CinemaScope, which projected a wide-angle image on a broad screen. The industry also tried novelty features: Smell-O-Vision and Aroma-Rama piped smells into the theaters to coincide with events shown on the screen. Three-dimensional images, viewed through special glasses supplied by the theaters, appeared to leap into the audience. **C**

A Subculture Emerges

Although the mass media found a wide audience for their portrayals of mostly white popular culture, dissenting voices rang out throughout the 1950s. The messages of the beat movement in literature, and of rock 'n' roll in music, clashed with the tidy suburban view of life and set the stage for the counterculture that would burst forth in the late 1960s.

THE BEAT MOVEMENT Centered in San Francisco, Los Angeles, and New York City's Greenwich Village, the **beat movement** expressed the social and literary nonconformity of artists, poets, and writers. The word *beat* originally meant "weary" but came to refer as well to a musical beat.

Followers of this movement, called beats or beatniks, lived nonconformist lives. They tended to shun regular work and sought a higher consciousness through Zen Buddhism, music, and, sometimes, drugs.

Many beat poets and writers believed in imposing as little structure as possible on their artistic works, which often had a free, open form. They read their poetry aloud in coffeehouses and other gathering places. Works that capture the essence of this era include Allen Ginsberg's long, free-verse poem, *Howl*, published in 1956, and Jack Kerouac's novel of the movement, *On the Road*, published in 1957. This novel describes a nomadic search across America for authentic experiences, people, and values.

▲ Novelist Jack Kerouac's ***On the Road***, published in 1957, sold over 500,000 copies.

A PERSONAL VOICE JACK KEROUAC

"[T]he only people for me are the mad ones, the ones who are mad to live, mad to talk, mad to be saved . . . the ones who never yawn or say a commonplace thing, but burn, burn, burn like fabulous yellow roman candles exploding like spiders across the stars."

—*On the Road*

MAIN IDEA

Analyzing Causes
D Why do you think many young Americans were attracted to the beat movement?

Many mainstream Americans found this lifestyle less enchanting. *Look* magazine proclaimed, "There's nothing really new about the beat philosophy. It consists merely of the average American's value scale—turned inside out. The goals of the Beat are *not* watching TV, *not* wearing gray flannel, *not* owning a home in the suburbs, and especially—*not* working." Nonetheless, the beatnik attitudes, way of life, and literature attracted the attention of the media and fired the imaginations of many college students. **D**

African Americans and Rock 'n' Roll

While beats expressed themselves in unstructured literature, musicians in the 1950s added electronic instruments to traditional blues music, creating rhythm and blues. In 1951, a Cleveland, Ohio, radio disc jockey named Alan Freed was among the first to play the music. This audience was mostly white but the music usually was produced by African-American musicians. Freed's listeners responded enthusiastically, and Freed began promoting the new music that grew out of rhythm and blues and country and pop. He called the music **rock 'n' roll,** a name that has come to mean music that's both black and white—music that is American.

▲ Chuck Berry is as much known for his "duck walk" as for his electric guitar-playing heard on hit records including "Johnny B. Goode" and "Maybellene."

ROCK 'N' ROLL In the early and mid-1950s, Richard Penniman, Chuck Berry, Bill Haley and His Comets, and especially Elvis Presley brought rock 'n' roll to a frantic pitch of popularity among the newly affluent teens who bought their records. The music's heavy rhythm, simple melodies, and lyrics—featuring love, cars, and the problems of being young—captivated teenagers across the country.

Elvis Presley, the unofficial "King of Rock 'n' Roll," first developed his musical style by singing in church and listening to gospel, country, and blues music on the radio in Memphis, Tennessee. When he was a young boy, his mother gave him a guitar, and years later he paid four dollars of his own money to record two songs in 1953. Sam Phillips, a rhythm-and-blues producer, discovered Presley and produced his first records. In 1955, Phillips sold Presley's contract to RCA for $35,000.

Presley's live appearances were immensely popular, and 45 of his records sold over a million copies, including "Heartbreak Hotel," "Hound Dog," "All Shook Up," "Don't Be Cruel," and "Burning Love." Although *Look* magazine dismissed him as "a wild troubadour who wails rock 'n' roll tunes, flails erratically at a guitar, and wriggles like a peep-show dancer," Presley's rebellious style captivated young audiences. Girls screamed and fainted when he performed, and boys tried to imitate him. E

MAIN IDEA

Making Inferences

E Based on Elvis Presley's song titles, what do you think were teenagers' concerns in the 1950s?

Not surprisingly, many adults condemned rock 'n' roll. They believed that the new music would lead to teenage delinquency and immorality. In a few cities, rock 'n' roll concerts were banned. But despite this controversy, television and radio exposure helped bring rock 'n' roll into the mainstream, and it became more acceptable by the end of the decade. Record sales, which were 189 million in 1950, grew with the popularity of rock 'n' roll, reaching 600 million in 1960.

History Through *Music*

"HOUND DOG"— A ROCK 'N' ROLL CROSSOVER

Few examples highlight the influence African Americans had on rock 'n' roll—and the lack of credit and compensation they received for their efforts—more than the story of Willie Mae "Big Mama" Thornton.

In 1953, she recorded and released the song "Hound Dog" to little fanfare. She received a mere $500 in royalties. Only three years later, Elvis Presley recorded a version of the tune, which sold millions of records. Despite her contributions, Thornton reaped few rewards and struggled her entire career to make ends meet.

▲ Willie Mae "Big Mama" Thornton is remembered as the first artist to record "Hound Dog."

Elvis Presley recorded "Hound Dog" in 1956—making it a popular hit. ▶

SKILLBUILDER

Developing Historical Perspective

1. Why might black musicians have been commercially less successful than white musicians in the 1950s? Explain.
2. What concerns of the current generation are reflected in today's popular music?

SEE SKILLBUILDER HANDBOOK, PAGE R11.

THE RACIAL GAP African-American music had inspired the birth of rock 'n' roll, and many of the genre's greatest performers were—like Berry and Penniman—African Americans. In other musical genres, singers Nat "King" Cole and Lena Horne, singer and actor Harry Belafonte, and many others paved the way for minority representation in the entertainment fields. Musicians like Miles Davis, Sonny Rollins, Charlie Parker, Dizzy Gillespie, and Thelonius Monk played a style of music characterized by the use of improvisation, called **jazz.** These artists entertained audiences of all races.

But throughout the 1950s, African-American shows were mostly broadcast on separate stations. By 1954, there were 250 radio stations nationwide aimed specifically at African-American listeners. African-American stations were part of radio's attempt to counter the mass popularity of television by targeting specific audiences. These stations also served advertisers who wanted to reach a large African-American audience. But it was the black listeners—who had fewer television sets than whites and did not find themselves reflected in mainstream programming—who appreciated the stations most. Thulani Davis, a poet, journalist, and playwright, expressed the feelings of one listener about African-American radio (or "race radio" as the character called it) in her novel *1959*.

▲ Innovative American jazz trumpeter and composer Miles Davis, shown during a recording session in 1959, continued to blaze musical trails throughout his career.

A PERSONAL VOICE THULANI DAVIS

"Billie Holiday died and I turned twelve on the same hot July day. The saddest singing in the world was coming out of the radio, race radio that is, the radio of the race. The white stations were on the usual relentless rounds of Pat Boone, Teresa Brewer, and anybody else who couldn't sing but liked to cover songs that were once colored. . . . White radio was at least honest—they knew anybody in the South could tell Negro voices from white ones, and so they didn't play our stuff."

—1959

At the end of the 1950s, African Americans were still largely segregated from the dominant culture. This ongoing segregation—and the racial tensions it fed—would become a powerful force for change in the turbulent 1960s.

SECTION 3 ASSESSMENT

1. **TERMS & NAMES** For each term, write a sentence explaining its significance.
   - **mass media**
   - **Federal Communications Commission (FCC)**
   - **beat movement**
   - **rock 'n' roll**
   - **jazz**

MAIN IDEA

2. **SUMMARIZING**
   Create a "Who's Who" chart of popular culture idols of the 1950s. Identify the art form and major achievements associated with each person.

Person	Art Form	Achievements

Why do you think they appealed to the young people of the 1950s?

CRITICAL THINKING

3. **EVALUATING**
   Do you agree with Newton Minow's statement, on page 654, that TV was "a vast wasteland"? Support your answer with details from the text.

4. **ANALYZING EFFECTS**
   How did radio, TV, and the movies contribute to the success of rock 'n' roll?

5. **COMPARING AND CONTRASTING**
   In what ways were the rock 'n' roll musicians and the beat poets of the 1950s similar and different? Support your answer with details from the text. **Think About:**
   - the values the musicians and poets believed in
   - people's reactions to the musicians, poets, and writers

DAILY LIFE 1950–1960

The Emergence of the Teenager

Life after World War II brought changes in the family. For the first time, the teenage years were recognized as an important and unique developmental stage between childhood and adulthood. The booming postwar economy made it possible for teenagers to stay in school instead of working to help support their families, and allowed their parents to give them generous allowances. American business, particularly the music and movie industries, rushed to court this new consumer group.

▲ **TEENS AS CONSUMERS** Comic books, pimple creams, and soft drinks were just a few of the products aimed at teenagers with money to spend.

THE TEEN MOVIE SCENE ▲

Teenagers with money in their pockets often found themselves at the movies. Hollywood responded by producing films especially for teens. *Rebel Without a Cause* (1955) told the story of a troubled youth driven by anger and fear. It starred teen heart-throbs James Dean and Natalie Wood.

◀ ROCKING TO A NEW BEAT

Teenagers seeking a collective identity found it in rock 'n' roll, a fresh form of music that delighted teenagers and enraged their parents. Dick Clark's *American Bandstand* (shown at left) showcased young performers playing music ranging from doo-wop (shown above) to hard-driving rhythm and blues. The songs they sang underscored themes of alienation and heartbreak.

DATA FILE

TEENAGE TIDBITS

- A *Life* magazine survey showed that, during the 1950s, teens spent $20 million on lipstick alone.
- In 1956, a total of 42,000 drive-in movie theaters—heavily frequented by teenagers—took in one-quarter of the year's total box-office receipts.
- College enrollments more than doubled between 1946 and 1960.
- A weekly credit payment for a record player was $1.

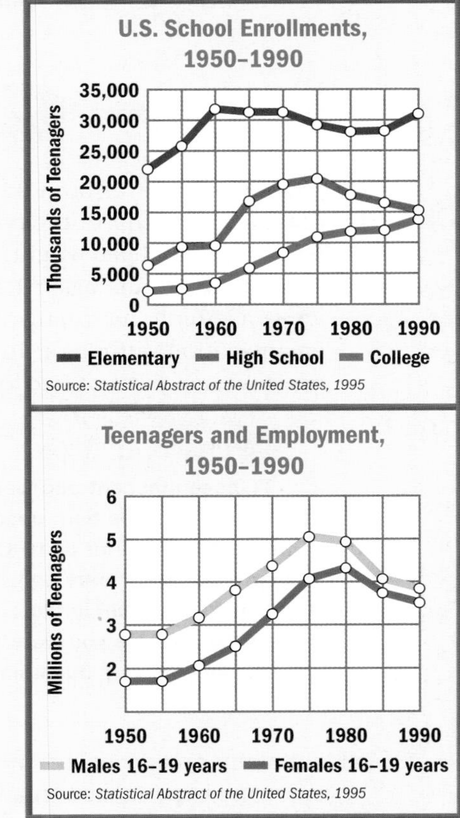

THINKING CRITICALLY

CONNECT TO HISTORY

1. **Interpreting Data** What were some causes of the booming teenage market in the 1950s? To answer the question, review the entire feature, including the Data File.

 **SEE SKILLBUILDER HANDBOOK, PAGE R28.**

CONNECT TO TODAY

2. **Analyzing Movies Today** What types of movies do American studios make for the teenage market today? How do these movies differ from those of the 1950s?

 **RESEARCH LINKS** **CLASSZONE.COM**

The Other America

MAIN IDEA	WHY IT MATTERS NOW	Terms & Names
Amidst the prosperity of the 1950s, millions of Americans lived in poverty.	**America today continues to experience a marked income gap between affluent and nonaffluent people.**	**•urban renewal •bracero •termination policy**

One American's Story

James Baldwin was born in New York City, the eldest of nine children, and grew up in the poverty of the Harlem ghetto. As a novelist, essayist, and playwright, he eloquently portrayed the struggles of African Americans against racial injustice and discrimination. He wrote a letter to his young nephew to mark the 100th anniversary of emancipation, although, in his words, "the country is celebrating one hundred years of freedom one hundred years too soon."

James Baldwin

A PERSONAL VOICE JAMES BALDWIN

"[T]hese innocent and well-meaning people, your countrymen, have caused you to be born under conditions not very far removed from those described for us by Charles Dickens in the London of more than a hundred years ago. . . . This innocent country set you down in a ghetto in which, in fact, it intended that you should perish. . . . You were born where you were born and faced the future that you faced because you were black and *for no other reason.*"

—*The Fire Next Time*

For many Americans, the 1950s were a time of unprecedented prosperity. But not everyone experienced this financial well-being. In the "other" America, about 40 million people lived in poverty, untouched by the economic boom.

The Urban Poor

Despite the portrait painted by popular culture, life in postwar America did not live up to the "American dream." In 1962, nearly one out of every four Americans was living below the poverty level. Many of these poor were elderly people, single women and their children, or members of minority groups, including African Americans, Latinos, and Native Americans.

WHITE FLIGHT In the 1950s, millions of middle-class white Americans left the cities for the suburbs, taking with them precious economic resources and isolating themselves from other races and classes. At the same time, the rural poor migrated to the inner cities. Between the end of World War II and 1960, nearly 5 million African Americans moved from the rural South to urban areas.

The urban crisis prompted by the "white flight" had a direct impact on poor whites and nonwhites. The cities lost not only people and businesses but also the property they owned and income taxes they had paid. City governments could no longer afford to properly maintain or improve schools, public transportation, and police and fire departments—and the urban poor suffered.

THE INNER CITIES While poverty grew rapidly in the decaying inner cities, many suburban Americans remained unaware of it. Some even refused to believe that poverty could exist in the richest, most powerful nation on earth. Each year, the federal government calculates the minimum amount of income needed to survive—the poverty line. In 1959, the poverty line for a family of four was $2,973. In 2000, it was $17,601. (A)

> **MAIN IDEA**
> **Analyzing Effects**
> (A) What effect did white flight have on America's cities?

> **Background**
> See *poverty* on page R43 in the Economics Handbook.

After living among the nation's poor across America, Michael Harrington published a shocking account that starkly illuminated the issue of poverty. In *The Other America: Poverty in the United States* (1962), he not only confirmed that widespread poverty existed but also exposed its brutal reality.

A PERSONAL VOICE MICHAEL HARRINGTON

> **"The poor get sick more than anyone else in the society. . . . When they become sick, they are sick longer than any other group in the society. Because they are sick more often and longer than anyone else, they lose wages and work, and find it difficult to hold a steady job. And because of this, they cannot pay for good housing, for a nutritious diet, for doctors."**
>
> —*The Other America*

URBAN RENEWAL Most African Americans, Native Americans, and Latinos in the cities had to live in dirty, crowded slums. One proposed solution to the housing problem in inner cities was **urban renewal.** The National Housing Act of 1949 was passed to provide "a decent home and a suitable living environment for every American family." This act called for tearing down rundown neighborhoods and constructing low-income housing. Later, the nation's leaders would create a new cabinet position, Housing and Urban Development (HUD), to aid in improving conditions in the inner city.

Although dilapidated areas were razed, parking lots, shopping centers, highways, parks, and factories were constructed on some of the cleared land, and there was seldom enough new housing built to accommodate all the displaced people. For example, a *barrio* in Los Angeles was torn down to make way for Dodger Stadium, and poor people who were displaced from their homes simply moved from one ghetto to another. Some critics of urban renewal claimed that it had merely become urban *removal*. (B)

> **MAIN IDEA**
> **Analyzing Effects**
> (B) Why were attempts at urban renewal viewed as less than successful?

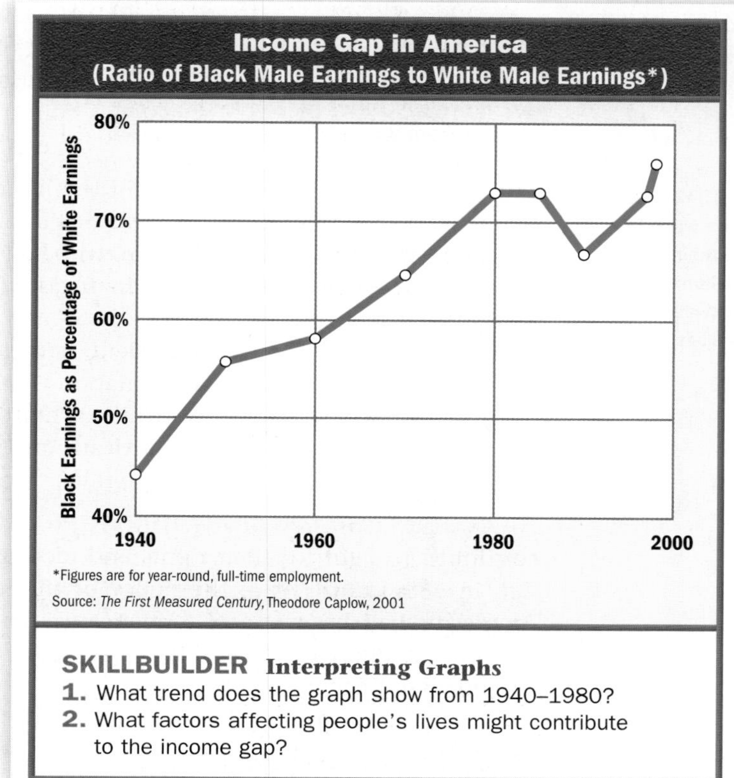

SKILLBUILDER Interpreting Graphs
1. What trend does the graph show from 1940–1980?
2. What factors affecting people's lives might contribute to the income gap?

Poverty Leads to Activism

Despite ongoing poverty, during the 1950s, African Americans began to make significant strides toward the reduction of racial discrimination and segregation. Inspired by the African-American civil rights movement, other minorities also began to develop a deeper political awareness and a voice. Mexican-American activism gathered steam after veterans returned from World War II, and a major change in government policy under Eisenhower's administration fueled Native American protest.

▲ In 1942, Mexican farm workers on their way to California bid farewell to their families.

MEXICANS SEEK EMPLOYMENT Many Mexicans had become U.S. citizens during the 19th century, when the United States had annexed the Southwest after the War with Mexico. Large numbers of Mexicans had also crossed the border to work in the United States during and after World War I.

When the United States entered World War II, the shortage of agricultural laborers spurred the federal government to initiate, in 1942, a program in which Mexican ***braceros*** (brə-sâr′ōs), or hired hands, were allowed into the United States to harvest crops. Hundreds of thousands of braceros entered the United States on a short-term basis between 1942 and 1947. When their employment was ended, the braceros were expected to return to Mexico. However, many remained in the United States illegally. In addition, hundreds of thousands of Mexicans entered the country illegally to escape poor economic conditions in Mexico.

Background
In 1954, the U.S. launched a program designed to find and return undocumented immigrants to Mexico. Between 1953 and 1955, the U.S. deported more than 2 million illegal Mexican immigrants.

THE LONGORIA INCIDENT One of the more notorious instances of prejudice against Mexican Americans involved the burial of Felix Longoria. Longoria was a Mexican-American World War II hero who had been killed in the Philippines. The only undertaker in his hometown in Texas refused to provide Longoria's family with funeral services.

In the wake of the Longoria incident, outraged Mexican Americans stepped up their efforts to stamp out discrimination. In 1948, Mexican-American veterans organized the G.I. Forum. Meanwhile, activist Ignacio Lopez founded the Unity League of California to register Mexican-American voters and to promote candidates who would represent their interests. C

MAIN IDEA
Analyzing Issues
C How did the Longoria incident motivate Mexican Americans to increase their political and social activism?

NATIVE AMERICANS CONTINUE THEIR STRUGGLE Native Americans also continued to fight for their rights and identity. From the passage of the Dawes Act, in 1887, until 1934, the policy of the federal government toward Native Americans had been one of "Americanization" and assimilation. In 1924, the Snyder Act granted citizenship to all Native Americans, but they remained second-class citizens.

In 1934, the Indian Reorganization Act moved official policy away from assimilation and toward Native American autonomy. Its passage signaled a change in federal policy. In addition, because the government was reeling from

Vocabulary
subsidizing: financial assistance given by a government to a person or group to support an undertaking regarded as being in the public interest

the Great Depression, it wanted to stop subsidizing the Native Americans. Native Americans also took the initiative to improve their lives. In 1944, they established the National Congress of American Indians. The congress had two main goals: (1) to ensure for Native Americans the same civil rights that white Americans had, and (2) to enable Native Americans on reservations to retain their own customs.

During World War II, over 65,000 Native Americans left their reservations for military service and war work. As a result, they became very aware of discrimination. When the war ended, Native Americans stopped receiving family allotments and wages. Outsiders also grabbed control of tribal lands, primarily to exploit their deposits of minerals, oil, and timber.

▲ Native Americans like the man above received job training from the Bureau of Indian Affairs to help them settle in urban areas.

THE TERMINATION POLICY In 1953, the federal government announced that it would give up its responsibility for Native American tribes. This new approach, known as the **termination policy,** eliminated federal economic support, discontinued the reservation system, and distributed tribal lands among individual Native Americans. In response to the termination policy, the Bureau of Indian Affairs began a voluntary relocation program to help Native Americans resettle in cities.

The termination policy was a dismal failure, however. Although the Bureau of Indian Affairs helped relocate 35,000 Native Americans to urban areas during the 1950s, they were often unable to find jobs in their new locations because of poor training and racial prejudice. They were also left without access to medical care when federal programs were abolished. In 1963, the termination policy was abandoned.

ASSESSMENT

1. **TERMS & NAMES** For each term, write a sentence explaining its significance.
   - **urban renewal**
   - **bracero**
   - **termination policy**

MAIN IDEA

2. **TAKING NOTES**
   In overlapping circles like the ones below, fill in the common problems that African Americans, Mexican Americans, and Native Americans faced during the 1950s.

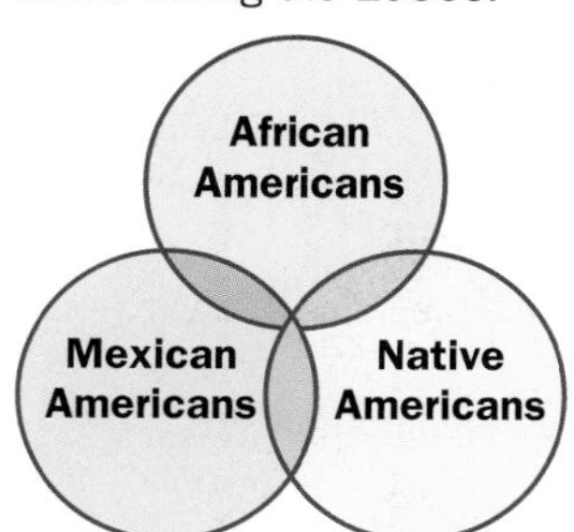

   What do these problems illustrate about life in the 1950s?

CRITICAL THINKING

3. **EVALUATING**
   Do you think that urban renewal was an effective approach to the housing problem in inner cities? Why or why not? **Think About:**
   - the goals of the National Housing Act of 1949
   - the claims made by some critics of urban renewal
   - the residents' best interest

4. **ANALYZING ISSUES**
   How did Native Americans work to increase their participation in the U.S. political process?

5. **DRAWING CONCLUSIONS**
   Which major population shift—"white flight," migration from Mexico, or relocation of Native Americans—do you think had the greatest impact on U.S. society? Why? **Think About:**
   - the impact of "white flight"
   - the influx of "braceros"
   - the effects of the termination policy

CHAPTER 19 ASSESSMENT

TERMS & NAMES

For each item below, write a sentence explaining its historical significance in the 1950s.

1. suburb
2. Dixiecrat
3. Fair Deal
4. conglomerate
5. baby boom
6. mass media
7. beat movement
8. rock 'n' roll
9. urban renewal
10. *bracero*

MAIN IDEAS

Use your notes and the information in the chapter to answer the following questions.

Postwar America *(pages 634–640)*

1. How did the GI Bill of Rights help World War II veterans?
2. What domestic and foreign issues concerned voters during the 1952 presidential election?

The American Dream in the Fifties *(pages 641–649)*

3. What shift in employment trends had occurred by the mid-1950s?
4. How did life in the suburbs provide the model for the American dream?

Popular Culture *(pages 652–657)*

5. What strategies did radio stations use to counteract the mass popularity of television?
6. How did African-American performers influence American popular culture in the 1950s?

The Other America *(pages 660–663)*

7. How did many major cities change in the 1950s?
8. What obstacles to improving their lives did Native Americans face in the 1950s?

CRITICAL THINKING

1. **USING YOUR NOTES** In a web like the one below, show the postwar technological advances you consider most influential.

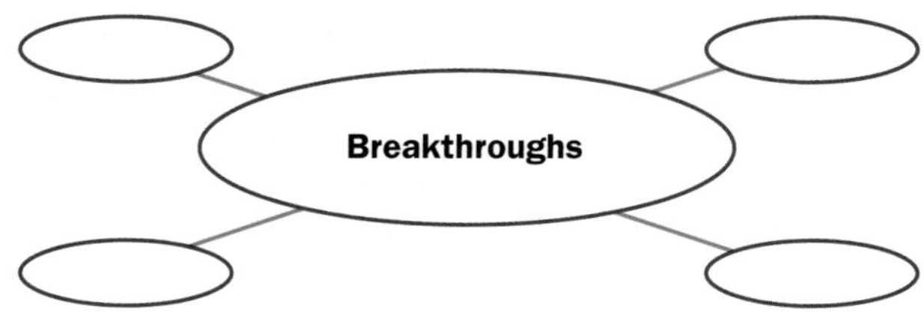

2. **HYPOTHESIZING** During America's first two centuries, the national character was marked by individualism. Why do you think conformity became the norm in the 1950s?

3. **ANALYZING PRIMARY SOURCES** Do you agree or disagree with the following quotation from *Life* magazine on American culture in 1954: "Never before so much for so few"? Support your answer with evidence.

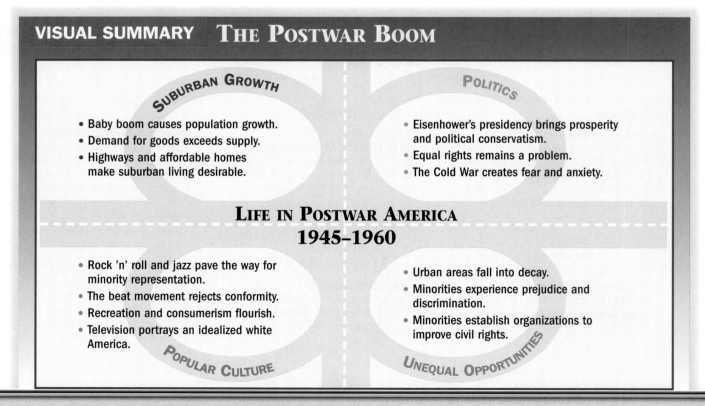

VISUAL SUMMARY THE POSTWAR BOOM

- Baby boom causes population growth.
- Demand for goods exceeds supply.
- Highways and affordable homes make suburban living desirable.

POLITICS

- Eisenhower's presidency brings prosperity and political conservatism.
- Equal rights remains a problem.
- The Cold War creates fear and anxiety.

LIFE IN POSTWAR AMERICA 1945–1960

POPULAR CULTURE

- Rock 'n' roll and jazz pave the way for minority representation.
- The beat movement rejects conformity.
- Recreation and consumerism flourish.
- Television portrays an idealized white America.

UNEQUAL OPPORTUNITIES

- Urban areas fall into decay.
- Minorities experience prejudice and discrimination.
- Minorities establish organizations to improve civil rights.

Standardized Test Practice

Use the chart and your knowledge of U.S. history to answer questions 1 and 2.

Geographic Distribution of U.S. Population, 1930–1970

Year	Central Cities	Suburbs	Rural Areas and Small Towns
1930	31.8%	18.0%	50.2%
1940	31.6%	19.5%	48.9%
1950	32.3%	23.8%	43.9%
1960	32.6%	30.7%	36.7%
1970	31.4%	37.6%	31.0%

Source: Adapated from U.S. Bureau of the Census, *Decennial Censuses, 1930–1970*

1. Which of the following statements supports the information in the chart?
   - **A** From 1940–1960, more people lived in cities than in rural areas.
   - **B** In 1960, twice as many people lived in cities as in suburbs.
   - **C** By 1960, suburbs had surpassed cities in total population.
   - **D** From 1930–1970, the precentage of U.S. population in rural areas decreased every decade.

2. From 1940–1970 the distribution doubled —
   - **F** in cities and suburbs.
   - **G** only in suburbs.
   - **H** only in cities.
   - **J** only in rural areas.

Use the song lyric below and your knowledge of U.S. history to answer question 3.

> **"Little Boxes"**
> **Little boxes on the hillside,**
> **Little boxes made of ticky-tacky,**
> **Little boxes on the hillside,**
> **Little boxes all the same.**
> **There's a pink one and a green one**
> **And a blue one and a yellow one,**
> **And they're all made out of ticky-tacky**
> **And they all look just the same.**
>
> —Malvina Reynolds

3. This popular song of the era describes —
   - **A** planned obsolescence.
   - **B** urban renewal.
   - **C** suburban communities.
   - **D** beatnik life style.

ADDITIONAL TEST PRACTICE, pages S1–S33.

CLASSZONE.COM

ALTERNATIVE ASSESSMENT

1. **INTERACT WITH HISTORY** Recall your discussion of the question on page 633:

What is the American dream of the 1950s?

Suppose you are a beat poet and have been asked to write an original poem entitled *A Postwar American Dream.* Use information from Chapter 19 and your knowledge of American history to support your poem. Remember to include a wide range of lifestyles in your poem.

2. **INTERNET ACTIVITY** **CLASSZONE.COM**

Visit the links for Chapter Assessment to plan and prepare a Web page about one aspect of popular culture—music, television, fashion, or the movies—from the 1950s. Include particular events and personalities of that period.

Cooperative Learning Activity Talk to other students in your class to identify those who chose a topic that was different from yours. Then work with those students to plan an electronic presentation that includes all elements of popular culture. Present your complete guide to 1950s popular culture to the class.

UNIT 6

Living with Great Turmoil
1954–1975

CHAPTER 20
The New Frontier and the Great Society
1960–1968

CHAPTER 21
Civil Rights
1954–1968

CHAPTER 22
The Vietnam War Years
1954–1975

CHAPTER 23
An Era of Social Change
1960–1975

Lobbying Campaign

This unit covers years of great social and political turmoil. Imagine that you have decided to lobby for—convince government officials to support—a cause or issue that is important to you. Create a plan for lobbying in which you encourage others to support your point of view.

Civil Rights March, 1965 by James Karales

CHAPTER 20 THE NEW FRONTIER AND THE GREAT SOCIETY

Scientific and technological advances in the early 1960s made possible the first American spacewalk during the *Gemini 6* mission on June 3, 1965.

USA

1960 John F. Kennedy is elected president.

1961 U.S. launches the Bay of Pigs invasion.

1962 John Glenn becomes the first American to orbit the earth.

1962 U.S. and USSR face off in the Cuban missile crisis.

1963 President Kennedy is assassinated; Lyndon B. Johnson becomes president.

1960 | 1961 | 1962 | 1963

WORLD

1960 Seventeen African countries gain independence.

1961 Soviet cosmonaut Yuri Gagarin becomes the first human in outer space.

1962 The drug thalidomide is pulled from the market after it is found responsible for thousands of birth defects in Europe.

INTERACT
WITH HISTORY

Against the backdrop of an intense space race between America and the Soviet Union, the 1960 presidential election approaches. The leading candidates are a young, charismatic senator and the ambitious, experienced vice-president. The new president will face tremendous responsibilities. Abroad, the Soviet Union is stockpiling nuclear weapons. At home, millions suffer from poverty and discrimination.

What are the qualities of effective leaders?

Examine the Issues

- How can a leader motivate and influence the public?
- What skills are needed to persuade legislators?
- What enables a leader to respond to crises?

RESEARCH LINKS **CLASSZONE.COM**

Visit the Chapter 20 links for more information about The New Frontier and the Great Society.

1964 Lyndon B. Johnson is elected president.

1964 Congress passes the Economic Opportunity Act and Civil Rights Act.

1965 U.S. troops enter Vietnam.

1965 Ferdinand Marcos becomes president of the Philippines.

1966 Indira Gandhi becomes prime minister of India.

1967 Thurgood Marshall becomes the first African-American justice of the Supreme Court.

1967 Israel wins Arab territories in the Six Day War.

1968 Richard M. Nixon is elected president.

1968 Warsaw Pact troops invade Czechoslovakia.

1964 | 1965 | 1966 | 1967

SECTION 1

Kennedy and the Cold War

MAIN IDEA	WHY IT MATTERS NOW	Terms & Names
The Kennedy administration faced some of the most dangerous Soviet confrontations in American history.	America's response to Soviet threats developed the United States as a military superpower.	• John F. Kennedy • flexible response • Fidel Castro • Berlin Wall • hot line • Limited Test Ban Treaty

One American's Story

John F. Kennedy became the 35th president of the United States on a crisp and sparkling day in January 1961. Appearing without a coat in freezing weather, he issued a challenge to the American people. He said that the world was in "its hour of maximum danger," as Cold War tensions ran high. Rather than shrinking from the danger, the United States should confront the "iron tyranny" of communism.

A PERSONAL VOICE JOHN F. KENNEDY

"Let the word go forth from this time and place, to friend and foe alike, that the torch has been passed to a new generation of Americans, born in this century, tempered by war, disciplined by a hard and bitter peace, proud of our ancient heritage, and unwilling to witness or permit the slow undoing of those human rights to which this nation has always been committed. . . .

Let every nation know, whether it wishes us well or ill, that we shall pay any price, bear any burden, meet any hardship, support any friend, oppose any . . . foe, in order to assure . . . the survival and the success of liberty."

—Inaugural Address, January 20, 1961

The young president won praise for his well-crafted speech. However, his words were put to the test when several Cold War crises tried his leadership.

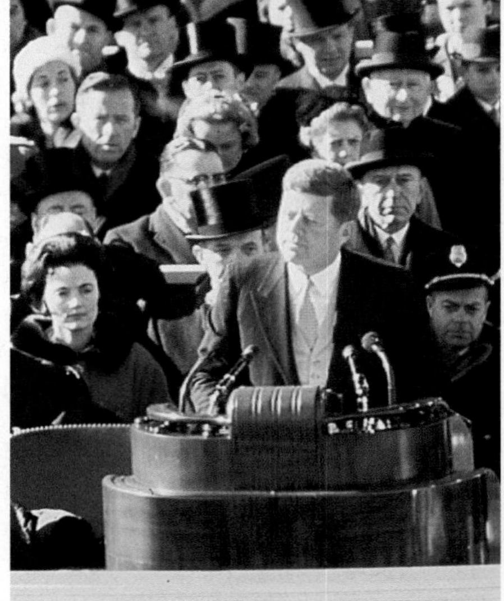

▲ John F. Kennedy delivers his inaugural address on January 20, 1961.

The Election of 1960

In 1960, as President Eisenhower's second term drew to a close, a mood of restlessness arose among voters. The economy was in a recession. The USSR's launch of *Sputnik I* in 1957 and its development of long-range missiles had sparked fears that the American military was falling behind that of the Soviets. Further setbacks including the U-2 incident and the alignment of Cuba with the Soviet Union had Americans questioning whether the United States was losing the Cold War.

◀ John F. Kennedy (*right*) appeared confident and at ease during a televised debate with his opponent Richard M. Nixon.

The Democratic nominee for president, Massachusetts senator John Kennedy, promised active leadership "to get America moving again." His Republican opponent, Vice President Richard M. Nixon, hoped to win by riding on the coattails of Eisenhower's popularity. Both candidates had similar positions on policy issues. Two factors helped put Kennedy over the top: television and the civil rights issue.

Vocabulary
charismatic: possessing personal charm that attracts devoted followers

THE TELEVISED DEBATE AFFECTS VOTES Kennedy had a well-organized campaign and the backing of his wealthy family, and was handsome and charismatic. Yet many felt that, at 43, he was too inexperienced. If elected, he would be the second-youngest president in the nation's history.

Americans also worried that having a Roman Catholic in the White House would lead either to influence of the pope on American policies or to closer ties between church and state. Kennedy was able to allay worries by discussing the issue openly.

MAIN IDEA
Predicting Effects
A What effect do you think the televised debate would have on American politics?

"That night, image replaced the printed word as the natural language of politics."
RUSSELL BAKER

One event in the fall determined the course of the election. Kennedy and Nixon took part in the first televised debate between presidential candidates. On September 26, 1960, 70 million TV viewers watched the two articulate and knowledgeable candidates debating issues. Nixon, an expert on foreign policy, had agreed to the forum in hopes of exposing Kennedy's inexperience. However, Kennedy had been coached by television producers, and he looked and spoke better than Nixon. **A**

Kennedy's success in the debate launched a new era in American politics: the television age. As journalist Russell Baker, who covered the Nixon campaign, said, "That night, image replaced the printed word as the natural language of politics."

KENNEDY AND CIVIL RIGHTS A second major event of the campaign took place in October. Police in Atlanta, Georgia, arrested the Reverend Martin Luther King, Jr., and 33 other African-American demonstrators for sitting at a segregated lunch counter. Although the other demonstrators were released, King was sentenced to months of hard labor—officially for a minor traffic violation. The Eisenhower administration refused to intervene, and Nixon took no public position.

When Kennedy heard of the arrest and sentencing, he telephoned King's wife, Coretta Scott King, to express his sympathy. Meanwhile, Robert Kennedy, his brother and campaign manager, persuaded the judge who had sentenced King to release the civil rights leader on bail, pending appeal. News of the incident captured the immediate attention of the African-American community, whose votes would help Kennedy carry key states in the Midwest and South.

The Camelot Years

President and Mrs. Kennedy enjoy time with their children, Caroline and John, Jr., while vacationing in Hyannis Port, Massachusetts. ▼

The election in November 1960 was the closest since 1884; Kennedy won by fewer than 119,000 votes. His inauguration set the tone for a new era at the White House: one of grace, elegance, and wit. On the podium sat over 100 writers, artists, and scientists that the Kennedys had invited, including opera singer Marian Anderson, who had once been barred from singing at Constitution Hall because she was African American. Kennedy's inspiring speech called for hope, commitment, and sacrifice. "And so, my fellow Americans," he proclaimed, "ask not what your country can do for you—ask what you can do for your country."

During his term, the president and his beautiful young wife, Jacqueline, invited many artists and celebrities to the White House. In addition, Kennedy often appeared on television. The press loved his charm and wit and helped to bolster his image.

THE KENNEDY MYSTIQUE Critics of Kennedy's presidency argued that his smooth style lacked substance. But the new first family fascinated the public. For example, after learning that JFK could read 1,600 words a minute, thousands of people enrolled in speed-reading courses. The first lady, too, captivated the nation with her eye for fashion and culture. It seemed the nation could not get enough of the first family. Newspapers and magazines filled their pages with pictures and stories about the president's young daughter Caroline and his infant son John.

Background
The fictional King Arthur was based on a real fifth- or sixth-century Celt. In literature, Arthur's romantic world is marked by chivalry and magic.

With JFK's youthful glamour and his talented advisers, the Kennedy White House reminded many of a modern-day Camelot, the mythical court of King Arthur. Coincidentally, the musical *Camelot* had opened on Broadway in 1960. Years later, Jackie recalled her husband and the vision of Camelot.

A PERSONAL VOICE JACQUELINE KENNEDY

"At night, before we'd go to sleep, Jack liked to play some records and the song he loved most came at the very end of [the *Camelot*] record. The lines he loved to hear were: 'Don't let it be forgot, that once there was a spot, for one brief shining moment that was known as Camelot.' There'll be great presidents again . . . but there'll never be another Camelot again." B

—quoted in *Life magazine, John F. Kennedy Memorial Edition*

MAIN IDEA

Developing Historical Perspective
B What factors help explain the public's fascination with the Kennedys?

THE BEST AND THE BRIGHTEST Kennedy surrounded himself with a team of advisers that one journalist called "the best and the brightest." They included McGeorge Bundy, a Harvard University dean, as national security adviser; Robert McNamara, president of Ford Motor Company, as secretary of defense; and Dean Rusk, president of the Rockefeller Foundation, as secretary of state. Of all the advisers who filled Kennedy's inner circle, he relied most heavily on his 35-year-old brother Robert, whom he appointed attorney general.

A New Military Policy

From the beginning, Kennedy focused on the Cold War. He thought the Eisenhower administration had not done enough about the Soviet threat. The Soviets, he concluded, were gaining loyalties in the economically less-developed third-world countries of Asia, Africa, and Latin America. He blasted the Republicans for allowing communism to develop in Cuba, at America's doorstep.

Vocabulary
third world: during the Cold War, the developing nations not allied with either the United States or the Soviet Union

DEFINING A MILITARY STRATEGY Kennedy believed his most urgent task was to redefine the nation's nuclear strategy. The Eisenhower administration had relied on the policy of massive retaliation to deter Soviet aggression and imperialism. However, threatening to use nuclear arms over a minor conflict was not a risk Kennedy wished to take. Instead, his team developed a policy of **flexible response.** Kennedy's secretary of defense, Robert McNamara, explained the policy.

A Personal Voice ROBERT S. MCNAMARA

"**The Kennedy administration worried that [the] reliance on nuclear weapons gave us no way to respond to large non-nuclear attacks without committing suicide. . . . We decided to broaden the range of options by strengthening and modernizing the military's ability to fight a nonnuclear war.**"

—*In Retrospect*

ANOTHER PERSPECTIVE

EISENHOWER'S WARNING

The increase in defense spending in the 1960s continued the trend in which Defense Department suppliers were becoming more dominant in the American economy. Before leaving office, President Eisenhower warned against the dangers of what he called the "military-industrial complex." He included in his parting speech the following comments:

"This conjunction of an immense military establishment and a large arms industry is new in the American experience. The total influence—economic, political, even spiritual—is felt in every city, every statehouse, every office of the federal government. We recognize the imperative need for this development. Yet we must not fail to comprehend its grave implications. . . . The potential for the disastrous rise of misplaced power exists and will persist."

Kennedy increased defense spending in order to boost conventional military forces—nonnuclear forces such as troops, ships, and artillery—and to create an elite branch of the army called the Special Forces, or Green Berets. He also tripled the overall nuclear capabilities of the United States. These changes enabled the United States to fight limited wars around the world while maintaining a balance of nuclear power with the Soviet Union. However, even as Kennedy hoped to reduce the risk of nuclear war, the world came perilously close to nuclear war under his command as a crisis arose over the island of Cuba. C

MAIN IDEA
Summarizing
C What was the goal of the doctrine of flexible response?

Crises over Cuba

The first test of Kennedy's foreign policy came in Cuba, just 90 miles off the coast of Florida. About two weeks before Kennedy took office, on January 3, 1961, President Eisenhower had cut off diplomatic relations with Cuba because of a revolutionary leader named **Fidel Castro.** Castro openly declared himself a communist and welcomed aid from the Soviet Union.

THE CUBAN DILEMMA Castro gained power with the promise of democracy. From 1956 to 1959, he led a guerrilla movement to topple dictator Fulgencio Batista. He won control in 1959 and later told reporters, "Revolutionaries are not born, they are made by poverty, inequality, and dictatorship." He then promised to eliminate these conditions from Cuba.

Vocabulary
guerrilla: a soldier who travels in a small group, harassing and undermining the enemy

The United States was suspicious of Castro's intentions but nevertheless recognized the new government. However, when Castro seized three American and British oil refineries, relations between the United States and Cuba worsened. Castro also broke up commercial farms into communes that would be worked by formerly landless peasants. American sugar companies,

▲
(top) **Castro celebrates after gaining power in Cuba.**
(above) **The Bay of Pigs mission was said to have blown up in Kennedy's face.**

which controlled 75 percent of the crop land in Cuba, appealed to the U.S. government for help. In response, Congress erected trade barriers against Cuban sugar.

Castro relied increasingly on Soviet aid—and on the political repression of those who did not agree with him. While some Cubans were taken by his charisma and his willingness to stand up to the United States, others saw Castro as a tyrant who had replaced one dictatorship with another. About 10 percent of Cuba's population went into exile, mostly to the United States. Within the large exile community of Miami, Florida, a counterrevolutionary movement took shape.

Vocabulary
political repression: government intimidation of those with different political views

THE BAY OF PIGS In March 1960, President Eisenhower gave the CIA permission to secretly train Cuban exiles for an invasion of Cuba. The CIA and the exiles hoped it would trigger a mass uprising that would overthrow Castro. Kennedy learned of the plan only nine days after his election. Although he had doubts, he approved it.

On the night of April 17, 1961, some 1,300 to 1,500 Cuban exiles supported by the U.S. military landed on the island's southern coast at Bahia de Cochinos, the Bay of Pigs. Nothing went as planned. An air strike had failed to knock out the Cuban air force, although the CIA reported that it had succeeded. A small advance group sent to distract Castro's forces never reached shore. When the main unit landed, it lacked American air support as it faced 25,000 Cuban troops backed up by Soviet tanks and jets. Some of the invading exiles were killed, others imprisoned.

The Cuban media sensationalized the defeat of "North American mercenaries." One United States commentator observed that Americans "look like fools to our friends, rascals to our enemies, and incompetents to the rest." The disaster left Kennedy embarrassed. Publicly, he accepted blame for the fiasco. Privately, he asked, "How could that crowd at the CIA and the Pentagon be this wrong." **D**

MAIN IDEA
Analyzing Effects
D What were the consequences of the failed invasion for the United States?

Kennedy negotiated with Castro for the release of surviving commandos and paid a ransom of $53 million in food and medical supplies. In a speech in Miami, he promised exiles that they would one day return to a "free Havana." Although Kennedy warned that he would resist further Communist expansion in the Western Hemisphere, Castro defiantly welcomed further Soviet aid.

THE CUBAN MISSILE CRISIS Castro had a powerful ally in Moscow: Soviet Premier Nikita Khrushchev, who promised to defend Cuba with Soviet arms. During the summer of 1962, the flow to Cuba of Soviet weapons—including nuclear missiles—increased greatly. President Kennedy responded with a warning that America would not tolerate offensive nuclear weapons in Cuba. Then, on October 14, photographs taken by American planes revealed Soviet missile bases in Cuba—and some contained missiles ready to launch. They could reach U.S. cities in minutes.

On October 22, Kennedy informed an anxious nation of the existence of Soviet missile sites in Cuba and of his plans to remove them. He made it clear that any missile attack from Cuba would trigger an all-out attack on the Soviet Union.

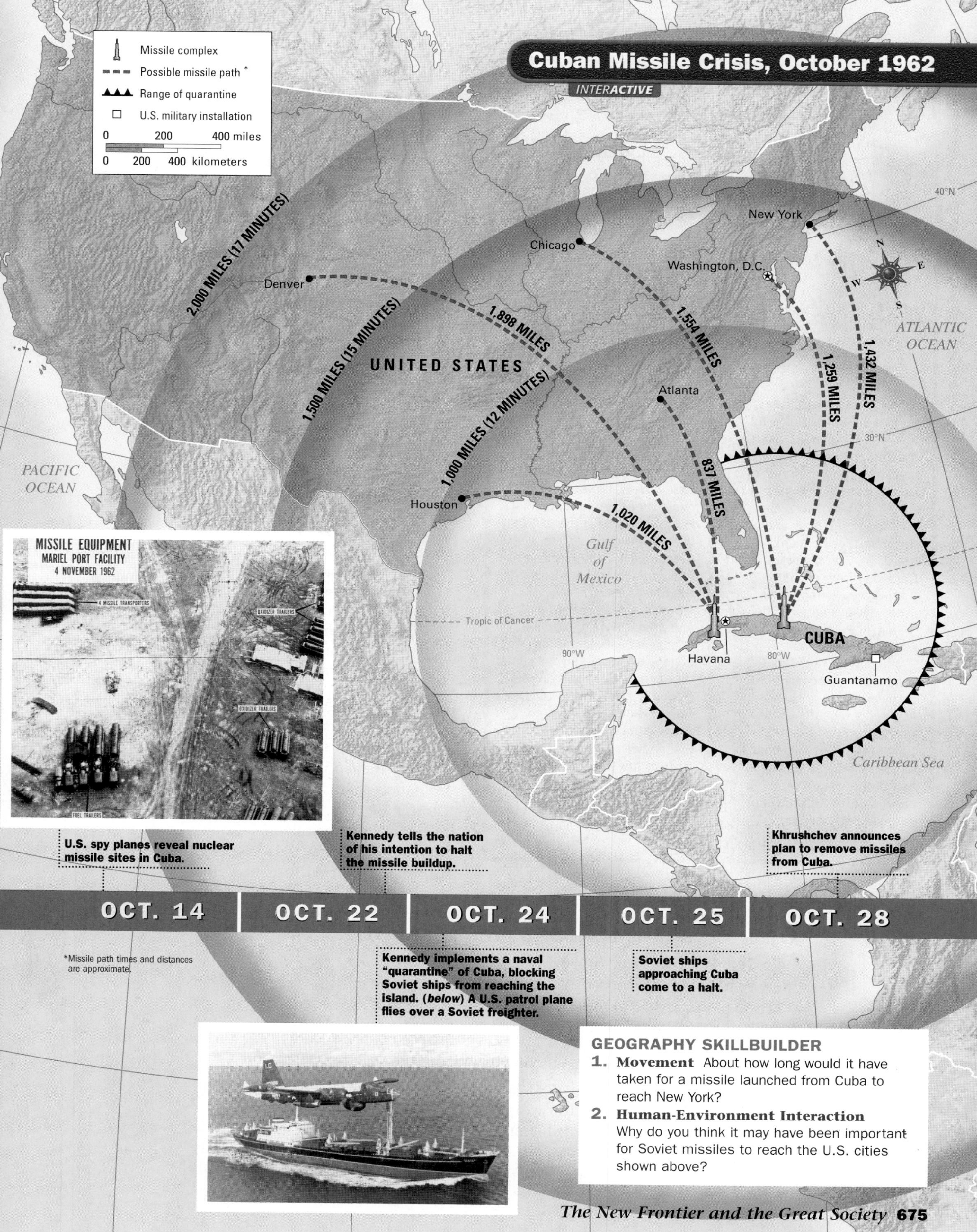

*Missile path times and distances are approximate.

GEOGRAPHY SKILLBUILDER

1. **Movement** About how long would it have taken for a missile launched from Cuba to reach New York?
2. **Human-Environment Interaction** Why do you think it may have been important for Soviet missiles to reach the U.S. cities shown above?

KEY PLAYERS

JOHN F. KENNEDY
1917–1963

John F. "Jack" Kennedy grew up in a politically powerful family that helped make his dreams possible. His parents instilled in him the drive to accomplish great things.

During World War II he enlisted in the navy and was decorated for heroism. In 1946, he won his first seat in Congress from a Boston district where he had never lived. While a senator, he won a Pulitzer Prize for his book *Profiles in Courage*.

Although he radiated self-confidence, Kennedy suffered many ailments, including Addison's disease—a debilitating condition that he treated with daily injections of cortisone. "At least one half of the days that he spent on this earth were days of intense physical pain," recalled his brother Robert.

NIKITA KHRUSHCHEV
1894–1971

"No matter how humble a man's beginnings," boasted Nikita Khrushchev, "he achieves the stature of the office to which he is elected." Khrushchev, the son of a miner, became a Communist Party organizer in the 1920s. Within four years of Stalin's death in 1953, Khrushchev had consolidated his power in the Soviet Union.

During his regime, which ended in 1964, Khrushchev kept American nerves on edge with alternately conciliatory and aggressive behavior. During a 1959 trip to the United States, he met for friendly talks with President Eisenhower. The next year, in front of the UN General Assembly, he took off his shoe and angrily pounded it on a desk to protest the U-2 incident.

For the next six days, the world faced the terrifying possibility of nuclear war. In the Atlantic Ocean, Soviet ships—presumably carrying more missiles—headed toward Cuba, while the U.S. Navy prepared to quarantine Cuba and prevent the ships from coming within 500 miles of it. In Florida, 100,000 troops waited—the largest invasion force ever assembled in the United States. C. Douglas Dillon, Kennedy's secretary of the treasury and a veteran of nuclear diplomacy, recalled those tension-filled days of October.

A Personal Voice
C. DOUGLAS DILLON

"The only time I felt a fear of nuclear war or a use of nuclear weapons was on the very first day, when we'd decided that we had to do whatever was necessary to get the missiles out. There was always some background fear of what would eventually happen, and I think this is what was expressed when people said they feared they would never see another Saturday."

—quoted in *On the Brink*

The first break in the crisis occurred when the Soviet ships stopped suddenly to avoid a confrontation at sea. Secretary of State Dean Rusk said, "We are eyeball to eyeball, and the other fellow just blinked." A few days later, Khrushchev offered to remove the missiles in return for an American pledge not to invade Cuba. The United States also secretly agreed to remove missiles from Turkey. The leaders agreed, and the crisis ended. "For a moment, the world had stood still," Robert Kennedy wrote years later, "and now it was going around again."

KENNEDY AND KHRUSHCHEV TAKE THE HEAT The crisis severely damaged Khrushchev's prestige in the Soviet Union and the world. Kennedy did not escape criticism either. Some people criticized Kennedy for practicing brinkmanship when private talks might have resolved the crisis without the threat of nuclear war. Others believed he had passed up an ideal chance to invade Cuba and oust Castro. (It was learned in the 1990s that the CIA had underestimated the numbers of Soviet troops and nuclear weapons on the island.)

The effects of the crisis lasted long after the missiles had been removed. Many Cuban exiles blamed the Democrats for "losing Cuba" (a charge that Kennedy had earlier leveled at the Republicans) and switched their allegiance to the GOP.

MAIN IDEA

Analyzing Effects
E What were the results of the Cuban missile crisis?

Meanwhile, Castro closed Cuba's doors to the exiles in November 1962 by banning all flights to and from Miami. Three years later, hundreds of thousands of people took advantage of an agreement that allowed Cubans to join relatives in the United States. By the time Castro sharply cut down on exit permits in 1973, the Cuban population in Miami had increased to about 300,000. **E**

Crisis over Berlin

One goal that had guided Kennedy through the Cuban missile crisis was that of proving to Khruschev his determination to contain communism. All the while, Kennedy was thinking of their recent confrontation over Berlin, which had led to the construction of the **Berlin Wall,** a concrete wall topped with barbed wire that severed the city in two.

THE BERLIN CRISIS In 1961, Berlin was a city in great turmoil. In the 11 years since the Berlin Airlift, almost 3 million East Germans—20 percent of that country's population—had fled into West Berlin because it was free from Communist rule. These refugees advertised the failure of East Germany's Communist government. Their departure also dangerously weakened that country's economy.

WORLD STAGE

THE BERLIN WALL, 1961

In 1961, Nikita Khrushchev, the Soviet premier, ordered the Berlin Wall built to stop the flow of refugees from East to West Berlin. Most were seeking freedom from Communist rule.

The wall isolated West Berlin from a hostile German Democratic Republic (GDR). Passing from East to West was almost impossible without the Communist government's permission.

During the 28 years the wall was standing, approximately 5,000 people succeeded in fleeing. Almost 200 people died in the attempt; most were shot by the GDR border guards. In 1989, East Germany opened the Berlin Wall to cheering crowds. Today the rubbled concrete is a reminder of the Cold War tensions between East and West.

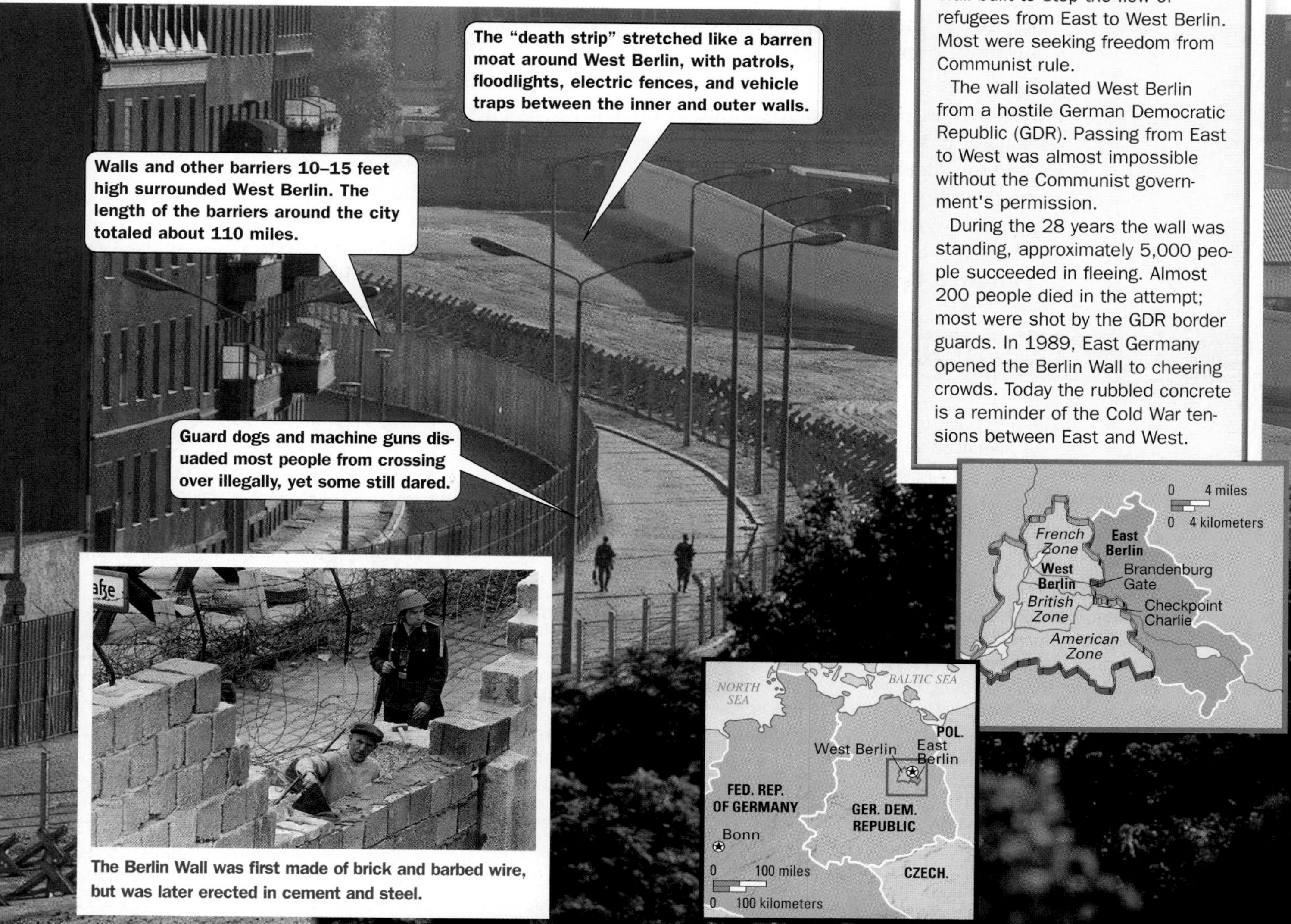
The "death strip" stretched like a barren moat around West Berlin, with patrols, floodlights, electric fences, and vehicle traps between the inner and outer walls.
Walls and other barriers 10–15 feet high surrounded West Berlin. The length of the barriers around the city totaled about 110 miles.
Guard dogs and machine guns dissuaded most people from crossing over illegally, yet some still dared.
0 4 miles
0 4 kilometers
French Zone
East Berlin
West Berlin
Brandenburg Gate
British Zone
Checkpoint Charlie
American Zone
NORTH SEA
BALTIC SEA
POL.
West Berlin
East Berlin
FED. REP. OF GERMANY
GER. DEM. REPUBLIC
Bonn
0 100 miles
0 100 kilometers
CZECH.

The Berlin Wall was first made of brick and barbed wire, but was later erected in cement and steel.

> *"I want peace. But, if you want war, that is your problem."*
>
> **SOVIET PREMIER NIKITA KHRUSHCHEV**

Khrushchev realized that this problem had to be solved. At a summit meeting in Vienna, Austria, in June 1961, he threatened to sign a treaty with East Germany that would enable that country to close all the access roads to West Berlin. When Kennedy refused to give up U.S. access to West Berlin, Khrushchev furiously declared, "I want peace. But, if you want war, that is your problem."

After returning home, Kennedy told the nation in a televised address that Berlin was "the great testing place of Western courage and will." He pledged "[W]e cannot and will not permit the Communists to drive us out of Berlin."

▲ Reading from this note card during a speech in West Berlin, Kennedy proclaimed "Ich bin ein Berliner" ("I am a Berliner").

Kennedy's determination and America's superior nuclear striking power prevented Khrushchev from closing the air and land routes between West Berlin and West Germany. Instead, the Soviet premier surprised the world with a shocking decision. Just after midnight on August 13, 1961, East German troops began to unload concrete posts and rolls of barbed wire along the border. Within days, the Berlin Wall was erected, separating East Germany from West Germany.

The construction of the Berlin Wall ended the Berlin crisis but further aggravated Cold War tensions. The wall and its armed guards successfully reduced the flow of East German refugees to a tiny trickle, thus solving Khrushchev's main problem. At the same time, however, the wall became an ugly symbol of Communist oppression. (F)

MAIN IDEA

Analyzing Motives

(F) What led Khrushchev to erect the Berlin Wall?

SEARCHING FOR WAYS TO EASE TENSIONS Showdowns between Kennedy and Khrushchev made both leaders aware of the gravity of split-second decisions that separated Cold War peace from nuclear disaster. Kennedy, in particular, searched for ways to tone down his hard-line stance. In 1963, he announced that the two nations had established a **hot line** between the White House and the Kremlin. This dedicated phone enabled the leaders of the two countries to communicate at once should another crisis arise. Later that year, the United States and Soviet Union also agreed to a **Limited Test Ban Treaty** that barred nuclear testing in the atmosphere.

ASSESSMENT

1. **TERMS & NAMES** For each term or name, write a sentence explaining its significance.
   - **John F. Kennedy**
   - **flexible response**
   - **Fidel Castro**
   - **Berlin Wall**
   - **hot line**
   - **Limited Test Ban Treaty**

MAIN IDEA

2. **TAKING NOTES**
   Using diagrams such as the one below, list two outcomes for each of these events: first Kennedy-Nixon debate, Bay of Pigs invasion, Cuban missile crisis, and construction of the Berlin Wall.

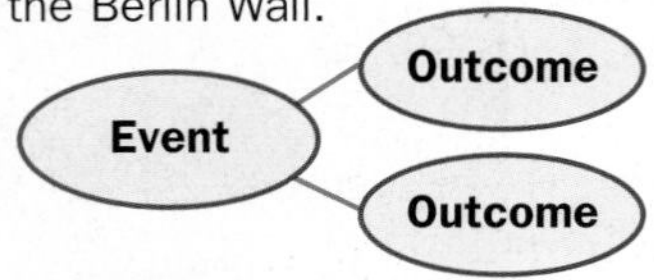

   Which of these outcomes led directly to other events listed here or described in this section?

CRITICAL THINKING

3. **EVALUATING DECISIONS**
   How well do you think President Kennedy handled the Cuban missile crisis? Justify your opinion with specific examples from the text.
   Think About:
   - Kennedy's decision to impose a naval "quarantine" of Cuba
   - the nuclear showdown between the superpowers
   - Kennedy's decision not to invade Cuba

4. **ANALYZING VISUAL SOURCES**
   Examine the cartoon above of Kennedy (*left*) facing off with Khrushchev and Castro. What do you think the cartoonist was trying to convey?
5. **DRAWING CONCLUSIONS**
   What kind of political statement was made by the United States' support of West Berlin?

SECTION 2

The New Frontier

MAIN IDEA

While Kennedy had trouble getting his ideas for a New Frontier passed, several goals were achieved.

WHY IT MATTERS NOW

Kennedy's space program continues to generate scientific and engineering advances that benefit Americans.

Terms & Names

- **New Frontier**
- **mandate**
- **Peace Corps**
- **Alliance for Progress**
- **Warren Commission**

One American's Story

On May 5, 1961, American astronaut Alan Shepard climbed into *Freedom 7*, a tiny capsule on top of a huge rocket booster. The capsule left the earth's atmosphere in a ball of fire and returned the same way, and Shepard became the first American to travel into space. Years later, he recalled his emotions when a naval crew fished him out of the Atlantic.

A Personal Voice ALAN SHEPARD

"Until the moment I stepped out of the flight deck . . . I hadn't realized the intensity of the emotions and feelings that so many people had for me, for the other astronauts, and for the whole manned space program. . . . I was very close to tears as I thought, it's no longer just our fight to get 'out there.' The struggle belongs to everyone in America. . . . From now on there was no turning back."

—*Moon Shot: The Inside Story of America's Race to the Moon*

Astronaut Alan Shepard (*inset*) prepares to enter the space capsule for his *Mercury* flight.

The entire trip—which took only 15 minutes from liftoff to splashdown—reaffirmed the belief in American ingenuity. John F. Kennedy inspired many Americans with the same kind of belief.

The Promise of Progress

Kennedy set out to transform his broad vision of progress into what he called the **New Frontier.** "We stand today on the edge of a New Frontier," Kennedy had announced upon accepting the nomination for president. He called on Americans to be "new pioneers" and explore "uncharted areas of science and space, . . . unconquered pockets of ignorance and prejudice, unanswered questions of poverty and surplus."

Kennedy had difficulty turning his vision into reality, however. He offered Congress proposals to provide medical care for the aged, rebuild blighted urban areas, and aid education, but he couldn't gather enough votes. Kennedy faced the same conservative coalition of Republicans and Southern Democrats that had

ECONOMIC BACKGROUND

WHAT IS A RECESSION?

A recession is, in a general sense, a moderate slowdown of the economy marked by increased unemployment and reduced personal consumption. In 1961, the nation's jobless rate climbed from just under 6 percent to nearly 7 percent. Personal consumption of several major items declined that year, as people worried about job security and spent less money.

Car sales, for example, dropped by more than $1 billion from the previous year, while fewer people took overseas vacations. Perhaps the surest sign that the country had entered a recession was the admission by government officials of how bleak things were. "We are in a full-fledged recession," Labor Secretary Arthur Goldberg declared in February of 1961. (See *recession* on page R44 in the Economics Handbook.)

blocked Truman's Fair Deal, and he showed little skill in pushing his domestic reform measures through Congress. Since Kennedy had been elected by the slimmest of margins, he lacked a popular **mandate**—a clear indication that voters approved of his plans. As a result, he often tried to play it safe politically. Nevertheless, Kennedy did persuade Congress to enact measures to boost the economy, build the national defense, provide international aid, and fund a massive space program. (A)

MAIN IDEA

Identifying Problems

(A) Why did Kennedy have difficulty achieving many of his New Frontier goals?

STIMULATING THE ECONOMY One domestic problem the Kennedy team tackled was the economy. By 1960 America was in a recession. Unemployment hovered around 6 percent, one of the highest levels since World War II. During the campaign, Kennedy had criticized the Eisenhower administration for failing to stimulate growth. The American economy, he said, was lagging behind those of other Western democracies and the Soviet Union.

Kennedy's advisers pushed for the use of deficit spending, which had been the basis for Roosevelt's New Deal. They said that stimulating economic growth depended on increased government spending and lower taxes, even if it meant that the government spent more than it took in.

Background

See *deficit spending* on page R39 in the Economics Handbook.

Accordingly, the proposals Kennedy sent to Congress in 1961 called for increased spending. The Department of Defense received a nearly 20 percent budget increase for new nuclear missiles, nuclear submarines, and an expansion of the armed services. Congress also approved a package that increased the minimum wage to $1.25 an hour, extended unemployment insurance, and provided assistance to cities with high unemployment.

ADDRESSING POVERTY ABROAD One of the first campaign promises Kennedy fulfilled was the creation of the **Peace Corps,** a program of volunteer assistance to the developing nations of Asia, Africa, and Latin America. Critics in the United States called the program "Kennedy's Kiddie Korps" because many volunteers were just out of college. Some foreign observers questioned whether Americans could understand other cultures.

A Peace Corps volunteer gives a ride to a Nigerian girl.

Despite these reservations, the Peace Corps became a huge success. People of all ages and backgrounds signed up to work as agricultural advisers, teachers, or health aides or to do whatever work the host country needed. By 1968, more than 35,000 volunteers had served in 60 nations around the world.

A second foreign aid program, the **Alliance for Progress,** offered economic and technical assistance to Latin American countries. Between 1961 and 1969, the United States invested almost

MAIN IDEA

Analyzing Motives

B Why did Kennedy want to invest in foreign aid?

$12 billion in Latin America, in part to deter these countries from picking up Fidel Castro's revolutionary ideas. While the money brought some development to the region, it didn't bring fundamental reforms. **B**

RACE TO THE MOON On April 12, 1961, Soviet cosmonaut Yuri A. Gagarin became the first human in space. Kennedy saw this as a challenge and decided that America would surpass the Soviets by sending a man to the moon.

In less than a month the United States had duplicated the Soviet feat. Later that year, a communications satellite called Telstar relayed live television pictures across the Atlantic Ocean from Maine to Europe. Meanwhile, America's National Aeronautics and Space Administration (NASA) had begun to construct new launch facilities at Cape Canaveral, Florida, and a mission control center in Houston, Texas. America's pride and prestige were restored. Speaking before a crowd at Houston's Rice University, Kennedy expressed the spirit of "the space race."

HISTORICAL SPOTLIGHT

JOHNSON AND MISSION CONTROL

President Kennedy appointed Vice President Johnson as chairman of the National Aeronautics and Space Council shortly after they assumed office in 1961. The chairman's duties were vague, but Johnson spelled them out: "He is to advise the president of what this nation's space policy ought to be." And Johnson's advice was to land a man on the moon.

A new home for the moon program's Manned Spacecraft Center was created. Some NASA administrators had wanted to consolidate the center and the launch site in Florida. However, when Johnson's friends at Humble Oil donated land to Rice University, which sold 600 acres to NASA and donated the rest, the debate was over. Houston became the center of the new space program.

A PERSONAL VOICE PRESIDENT JOHN F. KENNEDY

"**We choose to go to the moon in this decade and do the other things, not because they are easy, but because they are hard, because that goal will serve to organize and measure the best of our energies and skills, because that challenge is one that we are willing to accept, one we are unwilling to postpone, and one which we intend to win, and the others, too.**"

—Address on the Nation's Space Effort, September 12, 1962

MAIN IDEA

Analyzing Effects

C What effect did the space program have on other areas of American life?

Seven years later, on July 20, 1969, the U.S. would achieve its goal. An excited nation watched with bated breath as U.S. astronaut Neil Armstrong took his first steps on the moon.

As a result of the space program, universities expanded their science programs. The huge federal funding for research and development gave rise to new industries and new technologies, many of which could be used in business and industry and also in new consumer goods. Space- and defense-related industries sprang up in the Southern and Western states, which grew rapidly. **C**

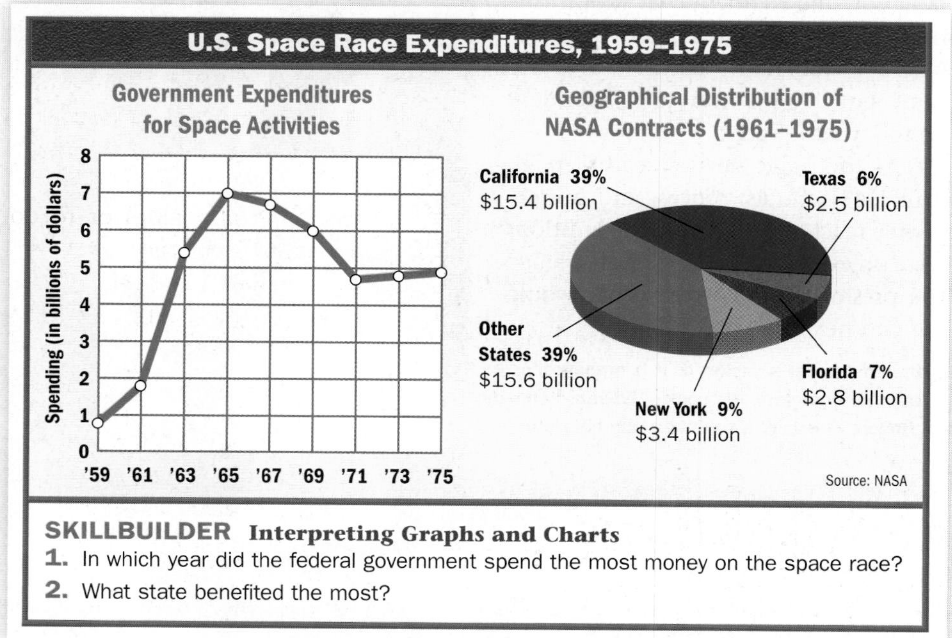

SKILLBUILDER Interpreting Graphs and Charts

1. In which year did the federal government spend the most money on the space race?
2. What state benefited the most?

ADDRESSING DOMESTIC PROBLEMS While progress was being made on the new frontiers of space exploration and international aid, many Americans suffered at home. In 1962, the problem of poverty in America was brought to national attention in Michael Harrington's book *The Other America*. Harrington profiled the 50 million people in America who scraped by each year on less than $1,000 per person. The number of poor shocked many Americans.

While Harrington awakened the nation to the nightmare of poverty, the fight against segregation took hold. Throughout the South, demonstrators raised their voices in what would become some of the most controversial civil rights battles of the 1960s. (See Chapter 21.) Kennedy had not pushed aggressively for legislation on the issues of poverty and civil rights, although he effected changes by executive action. However, now he felt that it was time to live up to a campaign promise.

In 1963, Kennedy began to focus more closely on the issues at home. He called for a "national assault on the causes of poverty." He also ordered Robert Kennedy's Justice Department to investigate racial injustices in the South. Finally, he presented Congress with a sweeping civil rights bill and a proposal to cut taxes by over $10 billion. **D**

MAIN IDEA

Making Inferences

D In what directions did President Kennedy seem to be taking his administration in 1963?

Tragedy in Dallas

In the fall of 1963, public opinion polls showed that Kennedy was losing popularity because of his advocacy of civil rights. Yet most still supported their beloved president. No one could foresee the terrible national tragedy just ahead.

FOUR DAYS IN NOVEMBER On the sunny morning of November 22, 1963, *Air Force One,* the presidential aircraft, landed in Dallas, Texas. President and Mrs. Kennedy had come to Texas to mend political fences with members of the state's Democratic Party. Kennedy had expected a cool reception from the conservative state, but he basked instead in warm waves of applause from crowds that lined the streets of downtown Dallas.

Jacqueline and her husband sat in the back seat of an open-air limousine. In front of them sat Texas Governor John Connally and his wife, Nellie. As the car approached a state building known as the Texas School Book Depository, Nellie Connally turned to Kennedy and said, "You can't say that Dallas isn't friendly to you today." A few seconds later, rifle shots rang out, and Kennedy was shot in the head. His car raced to a nearby hospital, where doctors frantically tried to revive him, but it was too late. President Kennedy was dead.

As the tragic news spread through America's schools, offices, and homes, people reacted with disbelief. Questions were on everyone's lips: Who had killed the president, and why? What would happen next?

John Kennedy, Jr., salutes his father's casket as it is prepared for the trip to Arlington National Cemetery. His uncles, Edward Kennedy and Attorney General Robert Kennedy; his mother; and his sister look on. ▶

"All the News That's Fit to Print"

The New York Times.

LATE CITY EDITION

VOL. CXIII...No. 38,654 — NEW YORK, SATURDAY, NOVEMBER 23, 1963. — TEN CENTS

KENNEDY IS KILLED BY SNIPER AS HE RIDES IN CAR IN DALLAS; JOHNSON SWORN IN ON PLANE

During the next four days, television became "the window of the world." A photograph of a somber Lyndon Johnson taking the oath of office aboard the presidential airplane was broadcast. Soon, audiences watched as Dallas police charged Lee Harvey Oswald with the murder. His palm print had been found on the rifle used to kill John F. Kennedy.

The 24-year-old ex-Marine had a suspicious past. After receiving a dishonorable discharge, Oswald had briefly lived in the Soviet Union, and he supported Castro. On Sunday, November 24, as millions watched live television coverage of Oswald being transferred between jails, a nightclub owner named Jack Ruby broke through the crowd and shot and killed Oswald.

The next day, all work stopped for Kennedy's funeral as America mourned its fallen leader. The assassination and televised funeral became a historic event. Americans who were alive then can still recall what they were doing when they first heard about the shooting of their president.

KENNEDY'S ASSASSINATION

From the beginning, people have questioned the Warren Commission report. Amateur investigators have led to increasing public pressure on the government to tell all it knows about the assassination.

In response, Congress passed the JFK Records Act in 1992, which created a panel to review government and private files and decide which should be part of the public record.

Since the law was enacted, newly declassified information has added some weight to a body of evidence that JFK was shot from the front (the Warren Commission had concluded that a single bullet struck the president from behind) and that Oswald, thus, could not have acted alone. While such evidence challenges the Warren Commission's report, no information has yet surfaced that conclusively disproves its findings.

Vocabulary
conspiracy: an agreement by two or more persons to take illegal political action

UNANSWERED QUESTIONS The bizarre chain of events made some people wonder if Oswald was part of a conspiracy. In 1963, the **Warren Commission** investigated and concluded that Oswald had shot the president while acting on his own. Later, in 1979, a reinvestigation concluded that Oswald was part of a conspiracy. Investigators also said that two persons may have fired at the president. Numerous other people have made investigations. Their explanations have ranged from a plot by anti-Castro Cubans, to a Communist-sponsored attack, to a conspiracy by the CIA. E

MAIN IDEA
Contrasting
E How did the Warren Commission's findings differ from other theories?

What Americans did learn from the Kennedy assassination was that their system of government is remarkably sturdy. A crisis that would have crippled a dictatorship did not prevent a smooth transition to the presidency of Lyndon Johnson. In a speech to Congress, Johnson expressed his hope that "from the brutal loss of our leader we will derive not weakness but strength." Not long after, Johnson drove through Congress the most ambitious domestic legislative package since the New Deal.

SECTION 2 ASSESSMENT

1. **TERMS & NAMES** For each term or name, write a sentence explaining its significance.
   - **New Frontier**
   - **mandate**
   - **Peace Corps**
   - **Alliance for Progress**
   - **Warren Commission**

MAIN IDEA

2. **TAKING NOTES**
   Re-create the web shown and fill it in with programs of the New Frontier.

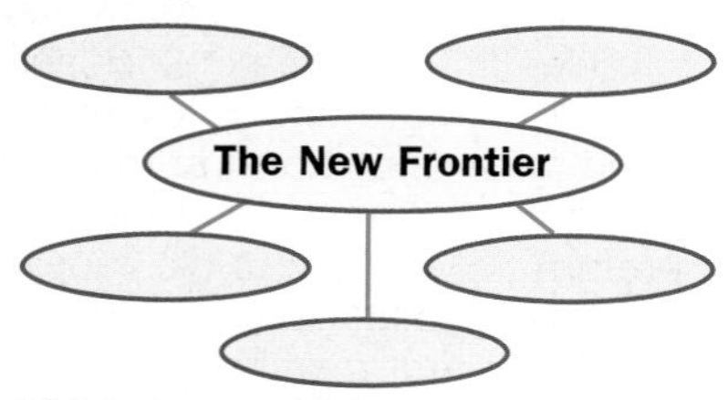

Which do you think was most successful? Why?

CRITICAL THINKING

3. **ANALYZING MOTIVES**
   Why do you think Congress was so enthusiastic about allocating funds for the space program but rejected spending in education, social services, and other pressing needs?
4. **MAKING INFERENCES**
   Why do you think Kennedy lost popularity for supporting civil rights?
5. **EVALUATING LEADERSHIP**
   Do you think President Kennedy was a successful leader? Explain your viewpoint. **Think About:**
   - the reasons for his popularity
   - the goals he expressed
   - his foreign policy
   - his legislative record

The Movement of Migrant Workers

The nation's 3 million farm workers are responsible for harvesting much of the fruit and vegetables that families eat each day. Most field workers on United States farms remain in one place most of the year. Others are migrant workers, who move with their entire family from one region to the next as the growing seasons change. Nationally, migrant workers make up around 10 percent of hired farm workers, depending on the season and other factors.

As the map shows, there were three major streams of migrant worker movements in the 1960s: the Pacific Coast, the Midwest, and the Atlantic Coast. While these paths may have changed slightly since then, the movement of migrant workers into nearly every region of the nation continues today.

▼ THE PACIFIC COAST

The Pacific Coast region's moderate climate allows for year-round harvesting. Most of California's migrant farm workers work on large fruit farms for much of the year. More than 62,000 workers make their way up to Washington each year to pick cherries, apples, and other crops.

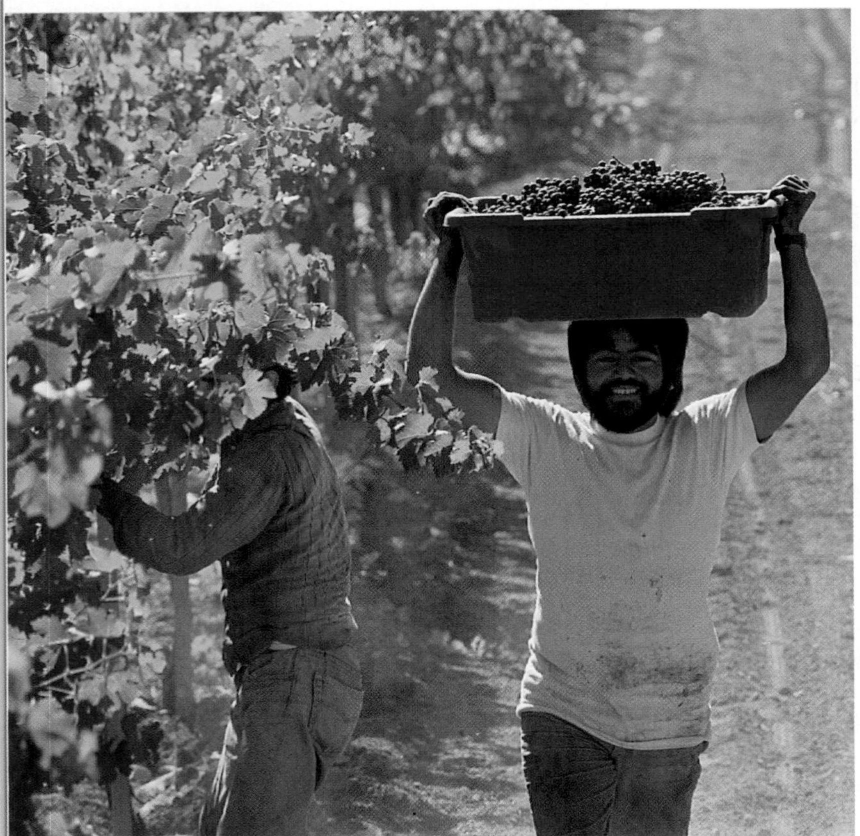

▲ THE MIDWEST

Workers along the Midwest and East Coast streams, where crops are smaller, must keep moving in order to find work. These workers picking strawberries in Michigan will soon move on. For example, one family may travel to Ohio for the tomato harvest and then return to Michigan to pick apples before heading back to Texas for the winter months.

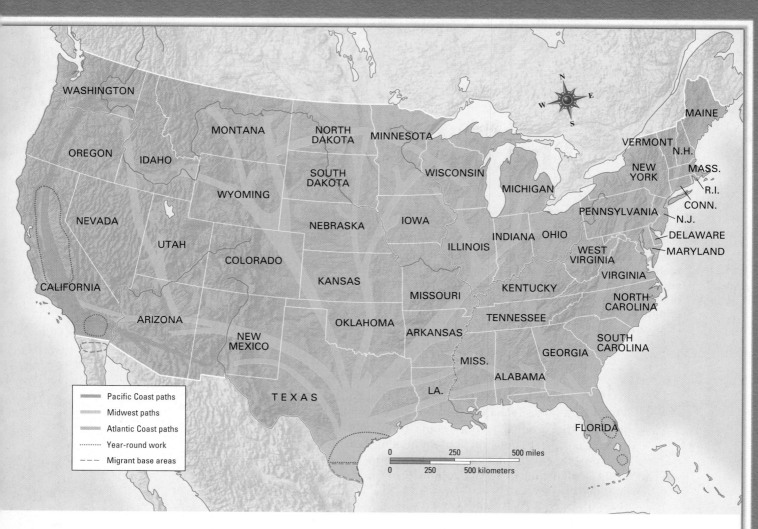

WASHINGTON
OREGON
IDAHO
MONTANA
NORTH DAKOTA
MINNESOTA
SOUTH DAKOTA
WYOMING
WISCONSIN
MICHIGAN
NEVADA
UTAH
COLORADO
NEBRASKA
IOWA
ILLINOIS
INDIANA
OHIO
PENNSYLVANIA
NEW YORK
VERMONT
N.H.
MAINE
MASS.
R.I.
CONN.
N.J.
DELAWARE
MARYLAND
WEST VIRGINIA
VIRGINIA
CALIFORNIA
KANSAS
MISSOURI
KENTUCKY
NORTH CAROLINA
ARIZONA
NEW MEXICO
OKLAHOMA
ARKANSAS
TENNESSEE
SOUTH CAROLINA
GEORGIA
MISS.
ALABAMA
LA.
TEXAS
FLORIDA
N
S
E
W

Pacific Coast paths
Midwest paths
Atlantic Coast paths
Year-round work
Migrant base areas

0 250 500 miles
0 250 500 kilometers

▲ The map above shows the three major streams of migrant worker movements in the 1960s.

▲ THE ATLANTIC COAST

While some workers along the Atlantic Coast stream remain in Florida, like the workers shown here picking beans, others travel as far north as New Hampshire and New York. There, they work from March through September. Due to the winters, migrant workers in most of the Midwest and Atlantic regions can find work for only six months out of the year.

THINKING CRITICALLY

CONNECT TO HISTORY

1. **Analyzing Patterns** Retrace the movement of migrant workers in the three regions. Why do you think migrant workers have to keep moving?

CONNECT TO TODAY

2. **Creating a Database** Pose a historical question about the relationship between crops and planting seasons. For example, what types of crops are harvested in Michigan during the fall? Then research and create a database that answers this and other such questions.

SEE SKILLBUILDER HANDBOOK, PAGE R33

RESEARCH LINKS **CLASSZONE.COM**

Section 3

The Great Society

MAIN IDEA

The demand for reform helped create a new awareness of social problems, especially on matters of civil rights and the effects of poverty.

WHY IT MATTERS NOW

Reforms made in the 1960s have had a lasting effect on the American justice system by increasing the rights of minorities.

Terms & Names

- **Lyndon Baines Johnson**
- **Economic Opportunity Act**
- **Great Society**
- **Medicare and Medicaid**
- **Immigration Act of 1965**
- **Warren Court**
- **reapportionment**

One American's Story

In 1966, family finances forced Larry Alfred to drop out of high school in Mobile, Alabama. He turned to the Job Corps, a federal program that trained young people from poor backgrounds. He learned to operate construction equipment, but his dream was to help people. On the advice of his Job Corps counselor, he joined VISTA—Volunteers in Service to America—often called the "domestic Peace Corps."

Both the Job Corps and VISTA sprang into being in 1964, when President Lyndon B. Johnson signed the Economic Opportunity Act. This law was the main offensive of Johnson's "war on poverty" and a cornerstone of the Great Society.

VISTA assigned Alfred to work with a community of poor farm laborers in Robstown, Texas, near the Mexican border. There he found a number of children with mental and physical disabilities who had no special assistance, education, or training. So he established the Robstown Association for Retarded People, started a parents education program, sought state funds, and created a rehabilitation center. At age 20, Larry Alfred was a high school dropout, Job Corps graduate, VISTA volunteer, and in Robstown, an authority on people with disabilities. Alfred embodied Johnson's Great Society in two ways: its programs helped him turn his life around, and he made a difference in people's lives.

▲ **VISTA volunteers worked in a variety of capacities. This woman is teaching art to young pupils.**

LBJ's Path to Power

By the time **Lyndon Baines Johnson,** or LBJ, as he was called, succeeded to the presidency, his ambition and drive had become legendary. In explaining his frenetic energy, Johnson once remarked, "That's the way I've been all my life. My daddy used to wake me up at dawn and shake my leg and say, 'Lyndon, every boy in town's got an hour's head start on you.'"

FROM THE TEXAS HILLS TO CAPITOL HILL A fourth-generation Texan, Johnson grew up in the dry Texas hill country of Blanco County. The Johnsons never knew great wealth, but they also never missed a meal.

LBJ entered politics in 1937 when he won a special election to fill a vacant seat in the U.S. House of Representatives. Johnson styled himself as a "New Dealer" and spokesperson for the small ranchers and struggling farmers of his district. He caught the eye of President Franklin Roosevelt, who took Johnson under his wing. Roosevelt helped him secure key committee assignments in Congress and steer much-needed electrification and water projects to his Texas district. Johnson, in turn, idolized FDR and imitated his leadership style.

Once in the House, Johnson eagerly eyed a seat in the Senate. In 1948, after an exhausting, bitterly fought campaign, he won the Democratic primary election for the Senate by a margin of only 87 votes out of 988,000.

A MASTER POLITICIAN Johnson proved himself a master of party politics and behind-the-scenes maneuvering, and he rose to the position of Senate majority leader in 1955. People called his legendary ability to persuade senators to support his bills the "LBJ treatment." As a reporter for the *Saturday Evening Post* explained, Johnson also used this treatment to win over reporters.

A PERSONAL VOICE STEWART ALSOP

"The Majority Leader [Johnson] was, it seemed, in a relaxed, friendly, reminiscent mood. But by gradual stages this mood gave way to something rather like a human hurricane. Johnson was up, striding about his office, talking without pause, occasionally leaning over, his nose almost touching the reporter's, to shake the reporter's shoulder or grab his knee. . . . Appeals were made, to the Almighty, to the shades of the departed great, to the reporter's finer instincts and better nature, while the reporter, unable to get a word in edgewise, sat collapsed upon a leather sofa, eyes glazed, mouth half open."

—"The New President," *Saturday Evening Post,* December 14, 1963

Johnson's deft handling of Congress led to the passage of the Civil Rights Act of 1957, a voting rights measure that was the first civil rights legislation since Reconstruction. Johnson's knack for achieving legislative results had captured John F. Kennedy's attention, too, during Kennedy's run for the White House. To Kennedy, Johnson's congressional connections and his Southern Protestant background compensated for his own drawbacks as a candidate, so he asked Johnson to be his running mate. Johnson's presence on the ticket helped Kennedy win key states in the South, especially Texas, which went Democratic by 47,000 votes. (A)

KEY PLAYER

LYNDON B. JOHNSON 1908–1973

LBJ received his teaching degree from Southwest Texas State Teachers College in 1930. To finance his own education, Johnson took a year off from college to work at a Mexican-American school in Cotulla, Texas. He later taught public speaking and debate at the Sam Houston High School in Houston. At age 26, he became the state director of the National Youth Administration, a New Deal agency.

As president, Johnson pushed hard for the passage of the Elementary and Secondary Education Act. In 1965, he signed the act at the one-room schoolhouse near Stonewall, Texas, where his own education had begun. Johnson later wrote,

"My education had begun with what I learned in that schoolroom. Now what I had learned and experienced since that time had brought me back to fulfill a dream."

MAIN IDEA

Analyzing Motives

(A) Why did Kennedy choose Johnson to be his running mate?

Johnson's Domestic Agenda

In the wake of Kennedy's assassination, President Johnson addressed a joint session of Congress. It was the fifth day of his administration. "All I have I would have given gladly not to be standing here today," he began. Kennedy had inspired Americans to begin to solve national and world problems. Johnson urged Congress to pass the civil rights and tax-cut bills that Kennedy had sent to Capitol Hill.

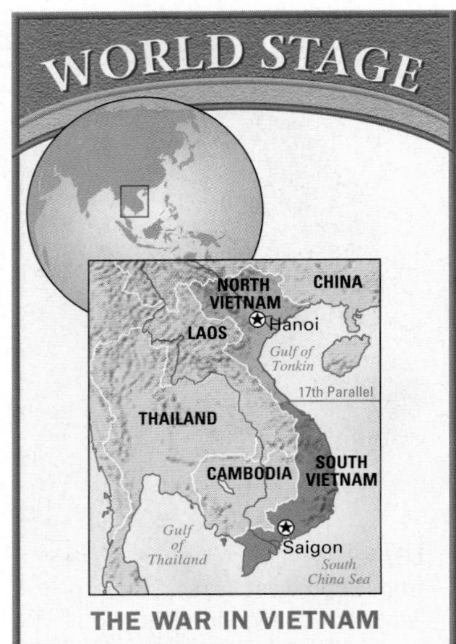

THE WAR IN VIETNAM

As LBJ pushed through his domestic programs, the U.S. grew more interested in halting the spread of communism around the world. In Vietnam, anti-Communist nationalists controlled South Vietnam while Communist leader Ho Chi Minh had taken over North Vietnam. The Geneva Accords had temporarily provided peace, dividing Vietnam along the 17th parallel into two distinct political regions. Despite this treaty, the North was supporting Communist rebels who were trying to take over the South.

Though Presidents Eisenhower and Kennedy had provided economic and military aid to South Vietnam, soon the U.S. would be directly involved in fighting the war.

In February 1964 Congress passed a tax reduction of over $10 billion into law. As the Democrats had hoped, the tax cut spurred economic growth. People spent more, which meant profits for businesses, which increased tax revenues and lowered the federal budget deficit from $6 billion in 1964 to $4 billion in 1966.

Then in July, Johnson pushed the Civil Rights Act of 1964 through Congress, persuading Southern senators to stop blocking its passage. It prohibited discrimination based on race, religion, national origin, and sex and granted the federal government new powers to enforce its provisions.

THE WAR ON POVERTY Following these successes, LBJ pressed on with his own agenda—to alleviate poverty. Early in 1964, he had declared "unconditional war on poverty in America" and proposed sweeping legislation designed to help Americans "on the outskirts of hope."

Background
See *poverty* on page R43 in the Economics Handbook.

In August 1964, Congress enacted the **Economic Opportunity Act** (EOA), approving nearly $1 billion for youth programs, antipoverty measures, small-business loans, and job training. The EOA legislation created:

- the Job Corps Youth Training Program
- VISTA (Volunteers in Service to America)
- Project Head Start, an education program for underprivileged preschoolers
- the Community Action Program, which encouraged poor people to participate in public-works programs. **B**

MAIN IDEA

Identifying Problems
B What problems in American society did the Economic Opportunity Act seek to address?

THE 1964 ELECTION In 1964, the Republicans nominated conservative senator Barry Goldwater of Arizona to oppose Johnson. Goldwater believed the federal government had no business trying to right social and economic wrongs such as poverty, discrimination, and lack of opportunity. He attacked such long-established federal programs as Social Security, which he wanted to make voluntary, and the Tennessee Valley Authority, which he wanted to sell.

In 1964, most American people were in tune with Johnson—they believed that government could and should help solve the nation's problems. Moreover, Goldwater had frightened many Americans by suggesting that he might use nuclear weapons on Cuba and North Vietnam. Johnson's campaign capitalized on this fear. It produced a chilling television commercial in which a picture of a little girl counting the petals on a daisy dissolved into a mushroom cloud created by an atomic bomb. Where Goldwater advocated intervention in Vietnam, Johnson assured the American people that sending U.S. troops there "would offer no solution at all to the real problem of Vietnam."

LBJ won the election by a landslide, winning 61 percent of the popular vote and 486 electoral votes, while Senator Goldwater won only 52. The Democrats also increased their majority in Congress. For the first time since 1938, a Democratic president did not need the votes of conservative Southern Democrats in order to get laws passed. Now Johnson could launch his reform program in earnest.

Campaign ▶ buttons like this one capitalized on the nation's growing liberal democratic sentiments.

▲ These preschoolers in a Head Start classroom are among the millions of Americans whose daily lives have been affected by Great Society programs.

Building the Great Society

In May 1964, Johnson had summed up his vision for America in a phrase: the **Great Society.** In a speech at the University of Michigan, Johnson outlined a legislative program that would end poverty and racial injustice. But, he told an enthusiastic crowd, that was "just the beginning." Johnson envisioned a legislative program that would create not only a higher standard of living and equal opportunity, but also promote a richer quality of life for all.

A PERSONAL VOICE LYNDON B. JOHNSON

> **"The Great Society is a place where every child can find knowledge to enrich his mind and to enlarge his talents. It is a place where leisure is a welcome chance to build and reflect, not a feared cause of boredom and restlessness. It is a place where the city of man serves not only the needs of the body and the demands of commerce but the desire for beauty and the hunger for community. It is a place where man can renew contact with nature. It is a place which honors creation for its own sake and for what it adds to the understanding of the race."**
>
> —"The Great Society," May 22, 1964

Like his idol FDR, LBJ wanted to change America. By the time Johnson left the White House in 1969, Congress had passed 206 of his measures. The president personally led the battle to get most of them passed.

EDUCATION During 1965 and 1966, the LBJ administration introduced a flurry of bills to Congress. Johnson considered education "the key which can unlock the door to the Great Society." The Elementary and Secondary Education Act of 1965 provided more than $1 billion in federal aid to help public and parochial schools purchase textbooks and new library materials. This was one of the earliest federal aid packages for education in the nation's history.

Great Society Programs, 1964–1967

POVERTY	
1964 Tax Reduction Act cut corporate and individual taxes to stimulate growth.	**1965 Medicare Act** established Medicare and Medicaid programs.
1964 Economic Opportunity Act created Job Corps, VISTA, Project Head Start, and other programs to fight the "war on poverty."	**1965 Appalachian Regional Development Act** targeted aid for highways, health centers, and resource development in that economically depressed area.
CITIES	
1965 Omnibus Housing Act provided money for low-income housing.	**1966 Demonstration Cities and Metropolitan Area Redevelopment Act** funded slum rebuilding, mass transit, and other improvements for selected "model cities."
1965 Department of Housing and Urban Development was formed to administer federal housing programs.	
EDUCATION	
1965 Elementary and Secondary Education Act directed money to schools for textbooks, library materials, and special education.	**1965 National Foundation on the Arts and the Humanities** was created to financially assist painters, musicians, actors, and other artists.
1965 Higher Education Act funded scholarships and low-interest loans for college students.	**1967 Corporation for Public Broadcasting** was formed to fund educational TV and radio broadcasting.
DISCRIMINATION	
1964 Civil Rights Act outlawed discrimination in public accommodations, housing, and jobs; increased federal power to prosecute civil rights abuses.	**1965 Voting Rights Act** ended the practice of requiring voters to pass literacy tests and permitted the federal government to monitor voter registration.
1964 Twenty-Fourth Amendment abolished the poll tax in federal elections.	**1965 Immigration Act** ended national-origins quotas established in 1924.
ENVIRONMENT	
1965 Wilderness Preservation Act set aside over 9 million acres for national forest lands.	**1965 Clean Air Act Amendment** directed the federal government to establish emission standards for new motor vehicles.
1965 Water Quality Act required states to clean up their rivers.	**1967 Air Quality Act** set federal air pollution guidelines and extended federal enforcement power.
CONSUMER ADVOCACY	
1966 Truth in Packaging Act set standards for labeling consumer products.	**1966 Highway Safety Act** required states to set up highway safety programs.
1966 National Traffic and Motor Vehicle Safety Act set federal safety standards for the auto and tire industries.	**1966 Department of Transportation** was created to deal with national air, rail, and highway transportation.

SKILLBUILDER Interpreting Charts
What did the Great Society programs indicate about the federal government's changing role?

HEALTHCARE LBJ and Congress changed Social Security by establishing Medicare and Medicaid. **Medicare** provided hospital insurance and low-cost medical insurance for almost every American age 65 or older. **Medicaid** extended health insurance to welfare recipients. C

MAIN IDEA
Comparing
C How are Medicare and Medicaid similar?

HOUSING Congress also made several important decisions that shifted the nation's political power from rural to urban areas. These decisions included: appropriating money to build some 240,000 units of low-rent public housing and helping low- and moderate-income families pay for better private housing; establishing the Department of Housing and Urban Development (HUD); and appointing Robert Weaver, the first African-American cabinet member in American history, as Secretary of HUD.

IMMIGRATION The Great Society also brought profound changes to the nation's immigration laws. The Immigration Act of 1924 and the National Origins Act of 1924 had established immigration quotas that discriminated strongly against people from outside Western Europe. The Act set a quota of about 150,000 people annually. It discriminated against southern and eastern Europeans and barred Asians completely. The **Immigration Act of 1965** opened the door for many non-European immigrants to settle in the United States by ending quotas based on nationality. D

MAIN IDEA

Analyzing Effects

D How did the Immigration Act of 1965 change the nation's immigration system?

THE ENVIRONMENT In 1962, *Silent Spring*, a book by Rachel Carson, had exposed a hidden danger: the effects of pesticides on the environment. Carson's book and the public's outcry resulted in the Water Quality Act of 1965, which required states to clean up rivers. Johnson also ordered the government to search out the worst chemical polluters. "There is no excuse . . . for chemical companies and oil refineries using our major rivers as pipelines for toxic wastes." Such words and actions helped trigger the environmental movement in the United States. (See Chapter 24.)

CONSUMER PROTECTION Consumer advocates also made headway. They convinced Congress to pass major safety laws, including a truth-in-packaging law that set standards for labeling consumer goods. Ralph Nader, a young lawyer, wrote a book, *Unsafe at Any Speed*, that sharply criticized the U.S. automobile industry for ignoring safety concerns. His testimony helped persuade Congress to establish safety standards for automobiles and tires. Precautions extended to food, too. Congress passed the Wholesome Meat Act of 1967. "Americans can feel a little safer now in their homes, on the road, at the supermarket, and in the department store," said Johnson.

NOW & THEN

MEDICARE ON THE LINE

When President Johnson signed the Medicare bill in 1965, only half of the nation's elderly had health insurance. Today, thanks largely to Medicare, nearly all persons 65 years or older are eligible.

In 2000, federal spending on Medicare was about $224 billion. In recent years, experts have debated over whether Medicare can be sustained in the face of changing trends: (1) people are living longer, (2) health care continues to become more expensive, and (3) the large baby boomer generation is moving toward retirement age. Though most Americans are not in favor of cutbacks to Medicare, the Balanced Budget Act of 1997 reduced federal spending on Medicare from 1998 through 2002 by $112 billion.

Reforms of the Warren Court

The wave of liberal reform that characterized the Great Society also swept through the Supreme Court of the 1960s. Beginning with the 1954 landmark decision *Brown* v. *Board of Education*, which ruled school segregation unconstitutional, the Court under Chief Justice Earl Warren took an activist stance on the leading issues of the day.

Several major court decisions in the 1960s affected American society. The **Warren Court** banned state–sanctioned prayer in public schools and declared state-required loyalty oaths unconstitutional. It limited the power of communities to censor books and films and said that free speech included the wearing of black armbands to school by antiwar students. Furthermore, the Court brought about change in federal and state reapportionment and the criminal justice system.

Chief Justice Earl Warren

CONGRESSIONAL REAPPORTIONMENT In a key series of decisions, the Warren Court addressed the issue of **reapportionment,** or the way in which states redraw election districts based on the changing number of people in them. By 1960, about 80 percent of Americans lived in cities and suburbs. However, many states had failed to change their congressional districts to reflect this development; instead, rural districts might have fewer than 200,000 people, while some urban districts had more than 600,000. Thus the voters in rural areas had more representation—and also more power—than those in urban areas.

Baker v. *Carr* (1962) was the first of several decisions that established the principle of "one person, one vote." The Court asserted that the federal courts had the right to tell states to reapportion—redivide—their districts for more equal representation. In later decisions, the Court ruled that congressional district boundaries should be redrawn so that districts would be equal in population, and in *Reynolds* v. *Sims* (1964), it extended the principle of "one person, one vote" to state legislative districts. (See *Reynolds* v. *Sims,* page 774.) These decisions led to a shift of political power throughout the nation from rural to urban areas.

RIGHTS OF THE ACCUSED Other Warren Court decisions greatly expanded the rights of people accused of crimes. In *Mapp* v. *Ohio* (1961), the Court ruled that evidence seized illegally could not be used in state courts. This is called the exclusionary rule. In *Gideon* v. *Wainwright* (1963), the justices required criminal courts to provide free legal counsel to those who could not afford it. In *Escobedo* v. *Illinois* (1964), the justices ruled that an accused person has a right to have a lawyer present during police questioning. In 1966, the Court went one step further in *Miranda* v. *Arizona,* where it ruled that all suspects must be read their rights before questioning. (See *Miranda* v. *Arizona,* page 694.)

These rulings greatly divided public opinion. Liberals praised the decisions, arguing that they placed necessary limits on police power and protected the right of all citizens to a fair trial. Conservatives, however, bitterly criticized the Court. They claimed that *Mapp* and *Miranda* benefited criminal suspects and severely limited the power of the police to investigate crimes. During the late 1960s and 1970s, Republican candidates for office seized on the "crime issue," portraying liberals and Democrats as being soft on crime and citing the decisions of the Warren Court as major obstacles to fighting crime. (E)

MAIN IDEA

Contrasting

(E) What were the differing reactions to the Warren Court decisions on the rights of the accused?

POINT

"The Great Society succeeded in prompting far-reaching social change."

Defenders of the Great Society contend that it bettered the lives of millions of Americans. Historian John Morton Blum notes, "The Great Society initiated policies that by 1985 had had profound consequences: Blacks now voted at about the same rate as whites, and nearly 6,000 blacks held public offices; almost every elderly citizen had medical insurance, and the aged were no poorer than Americans as a whole; a large majority of small children attended preschool programs."

Attorney Margaret Burnham argues that the civil rights gains alone justify the Great Society: "For tens of thousands of human beings . . . giving promise of a better life was significant . . . . What the Great Society affirmed was the responsibility of the federal government to take measures necessary to bring into the social and economic mainstream any segment of the people [who had been] historically excluded."

COUNTERPOINT

"Failures of the Great Society prove that government-sponsored programs do not work."

The major attack on the Great Society is that it created "big government": an oversized bureaucracy, too many regulations, waste and fraud, and rising budget deficits. As journalist David Alpern writes, this comes from the notion that government could solve all the nation's problems: "The Great Society created unwieldy new mechanisms like the Office of Economic Opportunity and began 'throwing dollars at problems. . . .' Spawned in the process were vast new constituencies of government bureaucrats and beneficiaries whose political clout made it difficult to kill programs off."

Conservatives say the Great Society's social welfare programs created a culture of dependency. Economist Paul Craig Roberts argues that "The Great Society . . . reflected our lack of confidence in the institutions of a free society. We came to the view that it is government spending and not business innovation that creates jobs and that it is society's fault if anyone is poor."

THINKING CRITICALLY

CONNECT TO HISTORY

1. **Evaluating** Do you think the Great Society was a success or a failure? Explain.

 **SEE SKILLBUILDER HANDBOOK, PAGE R17.**

CONNECT TO TODAY

2. **Analyzing Social Problems** Research the most pressing problems in your own neighborhood or precinct. Then propose a social program you think would address at least one of those problems while avoiding the pitfalls of the Great Society programs.

Impact of the Great Society

The Great Society and the Warren Court changed the United States. People disagree on whether these changes left the nation better or worse, but most agree on one point: no president in the post–World War II era extended the power and reach of the federal government more than Lyndon Johnson. The optimism of the Johnson presidency fueled an activist era in all three branches of government, for at least the first few years.

The "war on poverty" did help. The number of poor people fell from 21 percent of the population in 1962 to 11 percent in 1973. However, many of Johnson's proposals, though well intended, were hastily conceived and proved difficult to accomplish.

Johnson's massive tax cut spurred the economy. But funding the Great Society contributed to a growing budget deficit—a problem that continued for decades. Questions about government finances, as well as debates over the effectiveness of these programs and the role of the federal government, left a number of people disillusioned. A conservative backlash began to take shape as a new group of Republican leaders rose to power. In 1966, for example, a conservative Hollywood actor named Ronald Reagan swept to victory in the race for governor of California over the Democratic incumbent.

Publishers Newspaper Syndicate, 1967
"SUNRISE....ALL THE FOREIGN TROUBLE MAKERS GOIN' TO SLEEP AN' ALL THE DOMESTIC ONES WAKIN' UP"

As this cartoon points out, President Johnson had much to deal with at home and abroad. This autographed copy was presented to President Johnson by the cartoonist.

Thousands of miles away, the increase of Communist forces in Vietnam also began to overshadow the goals of the Great Society. The fear of communism was deeply rooted in the minds of Americans from the Cold War era. Four years after initiating the Great Society, Johnson, a peace candidate in 1964, would be labeled a "hawk"—a supporter of one of the most divisive wars in recent U.S. history. F

MAIN IDEA

Identifying Problems

F What events and problems may have affected the success of the Great Society?

SECTION 3 ASSESSMENT

1. **TERMS & NAMES** For each term or name, write a sentence explaining its significance.
   - **Lyndon Baines Johnson**
   - **Economic Opportunity Act**
   - **Great Society**
   - **Medicare and Medicaid**
   - **Immigration Act of 1965**
   - **Warren Court**
   - **reapportionment**

MAIN IDEA

2. **TAKING NOTES**
   List four or more Great Society programs and Warren Court rulings.

Great Society Programs	Warren Court Rulings
1.	1.
2.	2.
3.	3.
4.	4.

Choose one item and describe its lasting effects.

CRITICAL THINKING

3. **EVALUATING LEADERSHIP**
   Explain how Lyndon Johnson's personal and political experiences might have influenced his actions as president. **Think About:**
   - his family's background and education
   - his relationship with Franklin Roosevelt
   - his powers of persuasion

4. **ANALYZING VISUAL SOURCES**
   Look at the political cartoon above. What do you think the artist was trying to convey about the Johnson administration?

MIRANDA v. *ARIZONA* (1966)

ORIGINS OF THE CASE In 1963, Ernesto Miranda was arrested at his home in Phoenix, Arizona, on charges of kidnapping and rape. After two hours of questioning by police, he signed a confession and was later convicted, largely based on the confession. Miranda appealed. He claimed that his confession was invalid because it was coerced and because the police never advised him of his right to an attorney or his right to avoid self-incrimination.

THE RULING **The Court overturned Miranda's conviction, holding that the police must inform criminal suspects of their legal rights at the time of arrest and may not interrogate suspects who invoke their rights.**

LEGAL REASONING

Chief Justice Earl Warren wrote the majority opinion in *Miranda* v. *Arizona*. He based his argument on the Fifth Amendment, which guarantees that an accused person cannot be forced "to be a witness against himself" or herself. Warren stressed that when suspects are interrogated in police custody, the situation is "inherently intimidating." Such a situation, he argued, undermines any evidence it produces because "no statement obtained from the defendant [while in custody] can truly be the product of his free choice."

For this reason, the Court majority found that Miranda's confession could not be used as evidence. In the opinion, Chief Justice Warren responded to the argument that police officials might find this requirement difficult to meet.

> **"Not only does the use of the third degree [harassment or torture used to obtain a confession] involve a flagrant violation of law by the officers of the law, but it involves also the dangers of false confessions, and it tends to make police and prosecutors less zealous in the search for objective evidence."**

▲ **Ernesto Miranda (*at right*) converses with attorney John J. Flynn in February 1967.**

LEGAL SOURCES

U.S. CONSTITUTION

U.S. CONSTITUTION, FIFTH AMENDMENT (1791)

"No person . . . shall be compelled in any criminal case to be a witness against himself, nor be deprived of life, liberty, or property, without due process of law."

RELATED CASES

***MAPP* v. *OHIO* (1961)**

The Court ruled that prosecutors may not use evidence obtained in illegal searches (exclusionary rule).

***GIDEON* v. *WAINWRIGHT* (1963)**

The Court said that a defendant accused of a felony has the right to an attorney, which the government must supply if the defendant cannot afford one.

***ESCOBEDO* v. *ILLINOIS* (1964)**

The Court held that a suspect has the right to an attorney when being questioned by police.

WHY IT MATTERED

Miranda was one of four key criminal justice cases decided by the Warren Court (see Related Cases). In each case, the decision reflected the chief justice's strong belief that all persons deserve to be treated with respect by their government. In *Miranda,* the Court directed police to inform every suspect of his or her rights at the time of arrest and even gave the police detailed instructions about what to say.

The rights of accused people need to be protected in order to ensure that innocent people are not punished. These protections also ensure that federal, state, or local authorities will not harass people for political reasons—as often happened to civil rights activists in the South in the 1950s and 1960s, for example.

Critics of the Warren Court claimed that *Miranda* would lead to more crime because it would become more difficult to convict criminals. Police departments, however, adapted to the decision. They placed the list of suspects' rights mentioned in *Miranda* on cards for police officers to read to suspects. The statement of these rights became known as the Miranda warning and quickly became familiar to anyone who watched a police show on television.

As for the defendant, Ernesto Miranda, he was retried and convicted on the basis of other evidence.

HISTORICAL IMPACT

The *Miranda* decision was highly controversial. Critics complained that the opinion would protect the rights of criminals at the expense of public safety.

Since *Miranda,* the Court has continued to try to strike a balance between public safety and the rights of the accused. Several cases in the 1970s and 1980s softened the *Miranda* ruling and gave law enforcement officers more power to gather evidence without informing suspects of their rights. Even so, conservatives still hoped to overturn the *Miranda* decision.

In 2000, however, the Supreme Court affirmed *Miranda* by a 7-to-2 majority in *Dickerson* v. *United States.* Writing for the majority, Chief Justice William Rehnquist argued, "There is no such justification here for overruling *Miranda*. *Miranda* has become embedded in routine police practice to the point where warnings have become part of our national culture."

MIRANDA WARNING
CUSTODIAL INTERROGATION
JUVENILE & ADULT

The officer must determine whether the suspect understands the warning and waives his rights.

1. You have the right to remain silent.
2. Anything you say can be used as evidence against you.
3. You have a right to consult with an attorney before questioning and to have him with you during questioning.
4. If you can not afford an attorney, one will be appointed to represent you free of charge.
5. Knowing these rights, do you want to talk to me without having a lawyer present? You may stop talking to me at any time and you may also demand a lawyer at any time.

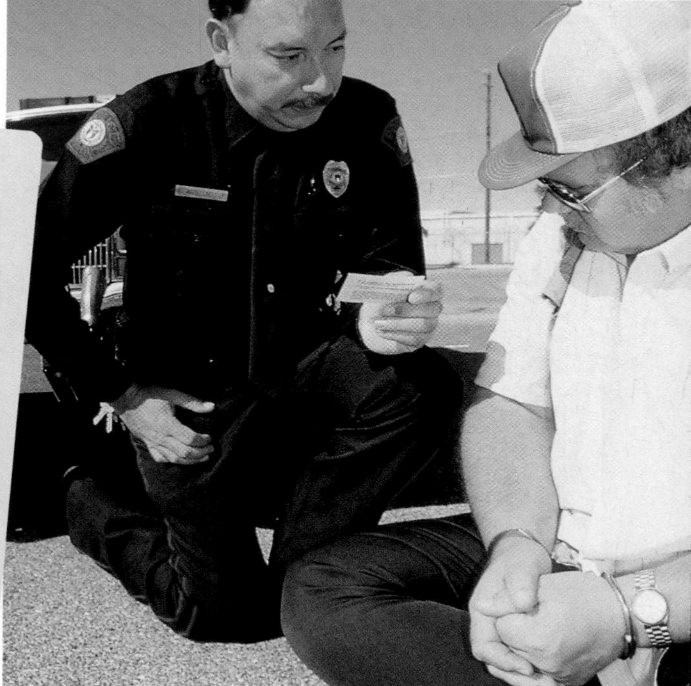

(right) **This card is carried by police officers in order to read suspects their rights.** ***(far right)*** **An officer reads a suspect his rights.**

THINKING CRITICALLY

CONNECT TO HISTORY

1. **Drawing Conclusions** Critics charged that *Miranda* incorrectly used the Fifth Amendment. The right to avoid self-incrimination, they said, should only apply to trials, not to police questioning. Do you agree or disagree? Why?

 **SEE SKILLBUILDER HANDBOOK, PAGE R18.**

CONNECT TO TODAY

2.  **INTERNET ACTIVITY CLASSZONE.COM**

Visit the links for Historic Decisions of the Supreme Court to research laws and other court decisions related to *Mapp* and *Miranda*. Then, prepare a debate on whether courts should or should not set a guilty person free if the government broke the law in establishing that person's guilt.

CHAPTER 20 ASSESSMENT

TERMS & NAMES

For each term or name below, write a sentence explaining its connection to the Kennedy and Johnson administrations.

1. John F. Kennedy
2. Fidel Castro
3. Berlin Wall
4. hot line
5. New Frontier
6. Peace Corps
7. Warren Commission
8. Great Society
9. Medicare and Medicaid
10. Warren Court

MAIN IDEAS

Use your notes and the information in the chapter to answer the following questions.

Kennedy and the Cold War *(pages 670–678)*

1. Explain the factors that led to Kennedy's victory over Nixon in the 1960 presidential campaign.
2. What were the most significant results of the Cuban missile crisis?

The New Frontier *(pages 679–683)*

3. What was Kennedy's New Frontier? Why did he have trouble getting his New Frontier legislation through Congress?
4. What two international aid programs were launched during the Kennedy administration?
5. How did Kennedy's assassination affect the public?

The Great Society *(pages 686–693)*

6. Describe ways that Great Society programs addressed the problem of poverty.
7. How did the courts increase the political power of people in urban areas and those accused of crimes?

CRITICAL THINKING

1. **USING YOUR NOTES** Use a Venn diagram to show the major legislative programs of the New Frontier and the Great Society.

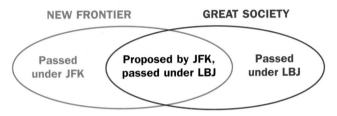

NEW FRONTIER | GREAT SOCIETY

Passed under JFK | Proposed by JFK, passed under LBJ | Passed under LBJ

2. **MAKING GENERALIZATIONS** John F. Kennedy said, "[M]y fellow Americans, ask not what your country can do for you—ask what you can do for your country." Do you agree with his view about the relationship between individuals and the country? Explain your opinion.
3. **EVALUATING** Do you think the Great Society helped people achieve their hopes of making life better for themselves and their children? Explain.

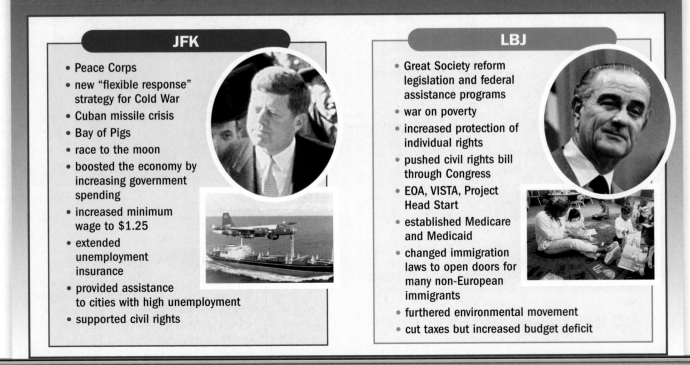

VISUAL SUMMARY THE NEW FRONTIER AND THE GREAT SOCIETY

JFK

- Peace Corps
- new "flexible response" strategy for Cold War
- Cuban missile crisis
- Bay of Pigs
- race to the moon
- boosted the economy by increasing government spending
- increased minimum wage to $1.25
- extended unemployment insurance
- provided assistance to cities with high unemployment
- supported civil rights

LBJ

- Great Society reform legislation and federal assistance programs
- war on poverty
- increased protection of individual rights
- pushed civil rights bill through Congress
- EOA, VISTA, Project Head Start
- established Medicare and Medicaid
- changed immigration laws to open doors for many non-European immigrants
- furthered environmental movement
- cut taxes but increased budget deficit

Standardized Test Practice

Use the quotation and your knowledge of United States history to answer questions 1 and 2.

> **"It is our purpose to win the Cold War, not merely wage it in the hope of attaining a standoff. . . . [I]t is really astounding that our government has never stated its purpose to be that of complete victory over the tyrannical forces of international communism. . . . We need a declaration that our intention is victory. . . . And we need an official act, such as the resumption of nuclear testing, to show our own peoples and the other freedom-loving peoples of the world that we mean business."**
>
> —Senator Barry Goldwater, address to the U.S. Senate, July 14, 1961

1. Based on the quotation, it is reasonable to infer that Senator Goldwater probably opposed —
   - **A** the space race.
   - **B** the Bay of Pigs invasion.
   - **C** the Tax Reduction Act.
   - **D** the Limited Test Ban Treaty.

2. Lyndon Johnson helped to bring about all of the following except —
   - **F** the Voting Rights Act.
   - **G** Head Start.
   - **H** Social Security.
   - **J** Medicare.

Use the graph as well as your knowledge of United States history to answer question 3.

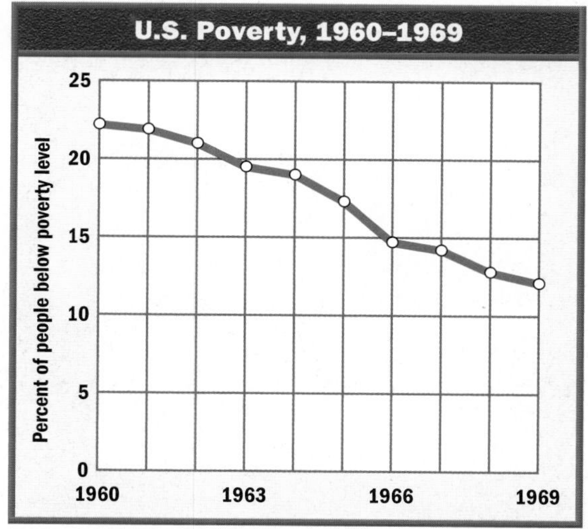

3. Which of the following is true about the graph?
   - **A** Johnson's war on poverty failed.
   - **B** Poverty began to rise again after 1969.
   - **C** Poverty decreased throughout the 1960s.
   - **D** In 1960, the poverty level was about 12%.

ADDITIONAL TEST PRACTICE, pages S1–S33.

TEST PRACTICE CLASSZONE.COM

ALTERNATIVE ASSESSMENT

1. **INTERACT WITH HISTORY** Recall your discussion of the question on p. 669:

What are the qualities of effective leaders?

Write a job description for "U.S. President." Include sections on "Responsibilities" and "Requirements" that list necessary traits and experience.

Think About:

- Kennedy's and Johnson's (and Nixon's) background and style
- the role of the media
- the challenges each leader faced and how he dealt with them
- the American public's tastes and preferences

2. 

LEARNING FROM MEDIA Use the CD-ROM *Electronic Library of Primary Sources* and other resources for Chapter 20. Discuss the following questions in a small group.

- Consider key events such as the Bay of Pigs Invasion, the Cuban missile crisis, and the Berlin crisis. What are the dangers of nuclear armament?
- What are the constitutional responsibilities of the federal government to defend and protect the people of the United States?

Cooperative Learning Activity It is June 1963, and President Kennedy announces his intention to negotiate with the Soviets to limit or halt nuclear testing. What is your reaction to this plan—do you approve or disapprove? Working with a partner, design and create a poster that supports or criticizes President Kennedy's proposal.

CHAPTER 21 CIVIL RIGHTS

Civil Rights activists lead the 1965 voting rights march from Selma to Montgomery, Alabama.

WAITING ROOM FOR COLORED ONLY BY ORDER POLICE DEPT.

1954 *Brown* v. *Board of Education* decision orders the desegregation of public schools.

1955 Montgomery bus boycott begins.

1956 Dwight D. Eisenhower is reelected.

1957 School desegregation crisis occurs in Little Rock, Arkansas.

1960 John F. Kennedy is elected president.

USA
WORLD

1955

1960

1956 Suez Canal crisis occurs in Egypt.

1957 African nation of Ghana wins independence.

1959 Fidel Castro assumes power in Cuba.

INTERACT WITH HISTORY

The year is 1960, and segregation divides the nation's people. African Americans are denied access to jobs and housing and are refused service at restaurants and stores. But the voices of the oppressed rise up in the churches and in the streets, demanding civil rights for all Americans.

What rights are worth fighting for?

Examine the Issues

- Are all Americans entitled to the same civil rights?
- What are the risks of demanding rights?
- Why might some people fight against equal rights?

RESEARCH LINKS **CLASSZONE.COM**

Visit the Chapter 21 links for more information about Civil Rights.

1962 South African civil rights leader Nelson Mandela is imprisoned.

1963 Lyndon B. Johnson becomes president upon John F. Kennedy's assassination.

1964 Lyndon B. Johnson is elected president.

1964 Congress passes the Civil Rights Act.

1965

1966 Cultural Revolution begins in China.

1967 Race riots occur in major U.S. cities.

1968 Richard M. Nixon is elected president.

1968 Martin Luther King, Jr., is assassinated.

1968 Tet offensive begins in Vietnam.

1969 U.S. astronauts walk on the moon.

1970

1970 President Nasser of Egypt dies.

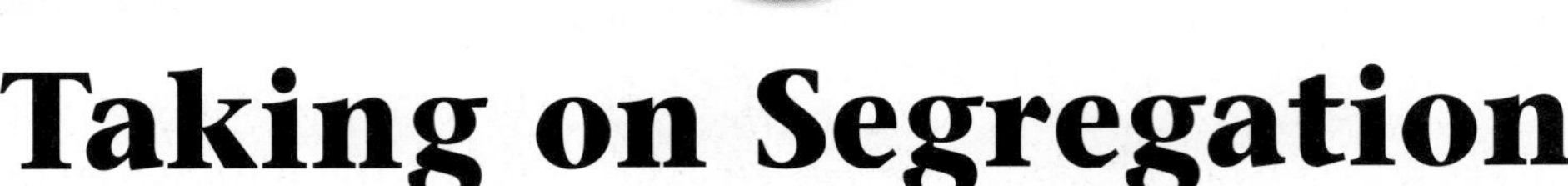

SECTION 1

Taking on Segregation

MAIN IDEA

Activism and a series of Supreme Court decisions advanced equal rights for African Americans in the 1950s and 1960s.

WHY IT MATTERS NOW

Landmark Supreme Court decisions beginning in 1954 have guaranteed civil rights for Americans today.

Terms & Names

- **Thurgood Marshall**
- ***Brown* v. *Board of Education of Topeka***
- **Rosa Parks**
- **Martin Luther King, Jr.**
- **Southern Christian Leadership Conference (SCLC)**
- **Student Nonviolent Coordinating Committee (SNCC)**
- **sit-in**

One American's Story

Jo Ann Gibson Robinson drew back in self-defense as the white bus driver raised his hand as if to strike her. "Get up from there!" he shouted. Robinson, laden with Christmas packages, had forgotten the rules and sat down in the front of the bus, which was reserved for whites.

Humiliating incidents were not new to the African Americans who rode the segregated buses of Montgomery, Alabama, in the mid-1950s. The bus company required them to pay at the front and then exit and reboard at the rear. "I felt like a dog," Robinson later said. A professor at the all-black Alabama State College, Robinson was also president of the Women's Political Council, a group of professional African-American women determined to increase black political power.

A PERSONAL VOICE JO ANN GIBSON ROBINSON

"We had members in every elementary, junior high, and senior high school, and in federal, state, and local jobs. Wherever there were more than ten blacks employed, we had a member there. We were prepared to the point that we knew that in a matter of hours, we could corral the whole city."

—quoted in *Voices of Freedom: An Oral History of the Civil Rights Movement*

On December 1, 1955, police arrested an African-American woman for refusing to give up her seat on a bus. Robinson promptly sent out a call for all African Americans to boycott Montgomery buses.

VIDEO

JUSTICE IN MONTGOMERY

Jo Ann Gibson Robinson and the Bus Boycott

The Segregation System

Segregated buses might never have rolled through the streets of Montgomery if the Civil Rights Act of 1875 had remained in force. This act outlawed segregation in public facilities by decreeing that "all persons . . . shall be entitled to the full and equal enjoyment of the accommodations . . . of inns, public conveyances on land or water, theaters, and other places of public amusement." In 1883, however, the all-white Supreme Court declared the act unconstitutional.

PLESSY V. FERGUSON During the 1890s, a number of other court decisions and state laws severely limited African-American rights. In 1890, Louisiana passed a law requiring railroads to provide "equal but separate accommodations for the white and colored races." In the *Plessy* v. *Ferguson* case of 1896, the Supreme Court ruled that this "separate but equal" law did not violate the Fourteenth Amendment, which guarantees all Americans equal treatment under the law.

Background
See *Plessy* v. *Ferguson* on page 290.

Armed with the *Plessy* decision, states throughout the nation, but especially in the South, passed what were known as Jim Crow laws, aimed at separating the races. These laws forbade marriage between blacks and whites and established many other restrictions on social and religious contact between the races. There were separate schools as well as separate streetcars, waiting rooms, railroad coaches, elevators, witness stands, and public restrooms. The facilities provided for blacks were always inferior to those for whites. Nearly every day, African Americans faced humiliating signs that read: "Colored Water"; "No Blacks Allowed"; "Whites Only!" (A)

MAIN IDEA

Analyzing Effects
(A) What were the effects of the Supreme Court decision *Plessy* v. *Ferguson*?

SEGREGATION CONTINUES INTO THE 20TH CENTURY After the Civil War, some African Americans tried to escape Southern racism by moving north. This migration of Southern African Americans speeded up greatly during World War I, as many African-American sharecroppers abandoned farms for the promise of industrial jobs in Northern cities. However, they discovered racial prejudice and segregation there, too. Most could find housing only in all-black neighborhoods. Many white workers also resented the competition for jobs. This sometimes led to violence.

WORLD STAGE

APARTHEID—SEGREGATION IN SOUTH AFRICA

In 1948, the white government of South Africa passed laws to ensure that whites would stay in control of the country. Those laws established a system called apartheid, which means "apartness." The system divided South Africans into four segregated racial groups—whites, blacks, coloreds of mixed race, and Asians. It restricted what jobs nonwhites could hold, where they could live, and what rights they could exercise. Because of apartheid, the black African majority were denied the right to vote.

In response to worldwide criticism, the South African government gradually repealed the apartheid laws, starting in the late 1970s. In 1994, South Africa held its first all-race election and elected as president Nelson Mandela, a black anti-apartheid leader whom the white government had imprisoned for nearly 30 years.

These photos of the public schools for white children *(top)* and for black children *(above)* in a Southern town in the 1930s show that separate facilities were often unequal in the segregation era.

U.S. School Segregation, 1952

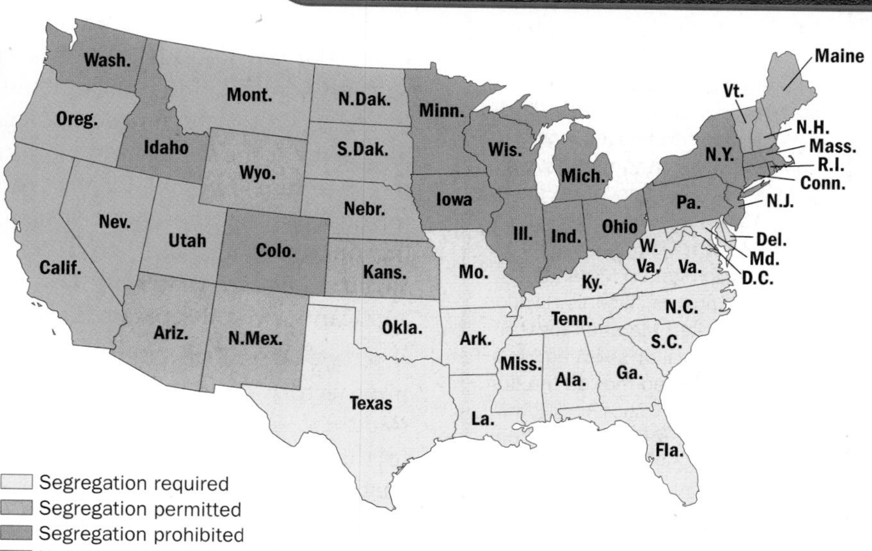

GEOGRAPHY SKILLBUILDER
Region In which regions were schools segregated by law? In which were segregation expressly prohibited?

A DEVELOPING CIVIL RIGHTS MOVEMENT In many ways, the events of World War II set the stage for the civil rights movement. First, the demand for soldiers in the early 1940s created a shortage of white male laborers. That labor shortage opened up new job opportunities for African Americans, Latinos, and white women.

Second, nearly one million African Americans served in the armed forces, which needed so many fighting men that they had to end their discriminatory policies. Such policies had previously kept African Americans from serving in fighting units. Many African-American soldiers returned from the war determined to fight for their own freedom now that they had helped defeat fascist regimes overseas.

Third, during the war, civil rights organizations actively campaigned for African-American voting rights and challenged Jim Crow laws. In response to protests, President Roosevelt issued a presidential directive prohibiting racial discrimination by federal agencies and all companies that were engaged in war work. The groundwork was laid for more organized campaigns to end segregation throughout the United States. B

MAIN IDEA

Developing Historical Perspective

B How did events during World War II lay the groundwork for African Americans to fight for civil rights in the 1950s?

Challenging Segregation in Court

The desegregation campaign was led largely by the NAACP, which had fought since 1909 to end segregation. One influential figure in this campaign was Charles Hamilton Houston, a brilliant Howard University law professor who also served as chief legal counsel for the NAACP from 1934 to 1938.

THE NAACP LEGAL STRATEGY In deciding the NAACP's legal strategy, Houston focused on the inequality between the separate schools that many states provided. At that time, the nation spent ten times as much money educating a white child as an African-American child. Thus, Houston focused the organization's limited resources on challenging the most glaring inequalities of segregated public education.

In 1938, he placed a team of his best law students under the direction of **Thurgood Marshall.** Over the next 23 years, Marshall and his NAACP lawyers would win 29 out of 32 cases argued before the Supreme Court.

Several of the cases became legal milestones, each chipping away at the segregation platform of *Plessy* v. *Ferguson*. In the 1946 case *Morgan* v. *Virginia*, the Supreme Court declared unconstitutional those state laws mandating segregated seating on interstate buses. In 1950, the high court ruled in *Sweatt* v. *Painter* that state law schools must admit black applicants, even if separate black schools exist.

BROWN* V. *BOARD OF EDUCATION Marshall's most stunning victory came on May 17, 1954, in the case known as ***Brown* v. *Board of Education of Topeka*.** (See page 708). In this case, the father of eight-year-old Linda Brown had charged the board of education of Topeka, Kansas, with violating Linda's rights by denying her admission to an all-white elementary school four blocks from her house. The nearest all-black elementary school was 21 blocks away.

In a landmark verdict, the Supreme Court unanimously struck down segregation in schooling as an unconstitutional violation of the Fourteenth Amendment's Equal Protection

KEY PLAYER

THURGOOD MARSHALL
1908–1993

Thurgood Marshall dedicated his life to fighting racism. His father had labored as a steward at an all-white country club, his mother as a teacher at an all-black school. Marshall himself was denied admission to the University of Maryland Law School because of his race.

In 1961, President John F. Kennedy nominated Marshall to the U.S. Court of Appeals. Lyndon Johnson picked Marshall for U.S. solicitor general in 1965 and two years later named him as the first African-American Supreme Court justice. In that role, he remained a strong advocate of civil rights until he retired in 1991.

After Marshall died in 1993, a copy of the *Brown* v. *Board of Education* decision was placed beside his casket. On it, an admirer wrote: "You shall always be remembered."

MAIN IDEA

Making Inferences

C How did the *Brown* decision affect schools outside of Topeka?

Clause. Chief Justice Earl Warren wrote that, "[I]n the field of public education, the doctrine of separate but equal has no place." The *Brown* decision was relevant for some 12 million schoolchildren in 21 states. **C**

Reaction to the *Brown* Decision

Official reaction to the ruling was mixed. In Kansas and Oklahoma, state officials said they expected segregation to end with little trouble. In Texas, the governor warned that plans might "take years" to work out. He actively prevented desegregation by calling in the Texas Rangers. In Mississippi and Georgia, officials vowed total resistance. Governor Herman Talmadge of Georgia said "The people of Georgia will not comply with the decision of the court. . . . We're going to do whatever is necessary in Georgia to keep white children in white schools and colored children in colored schools."

RESISTANCE TO SCHOOL DESEGREGATION Within a year, more than 500 school districts had desegregated their classrooms. In Baltimore, St. Louis, and Washington, D.C., black and white students sat side by side for the first time in history. However, in many areas where African Americans were a majority, whites resisted desegregation. In some places, the Ku Klux Klan reappeared and White Citizens Councils boycotted businesses that supported desegregation.

To speed things up, in 1955 the Supreme Court handed down a second ruling, known as *Brown II,* that ordered school desegregation implemented "with all deliberate speed." Initially President Eisenhower refused to enforce compliance. "The fellow who tries to tell me that you can do these things by force is just plain nuts," he said. Events in Little Rock, Arkansas, would soon force Eisenhower to go against his personal beliefs.

CRISIS IN LITTLE ROCK In 1948, Arkansas had become the first Southern state to admit African Americans to state universities without being required by a court order. By the 1950s, some scout troops and labor unions in Arkansas had quietly ended their Jim Crow practices. Little Rock citizens had elected two men to the school board who publicly backed desegregation—and the school superintendent, Virgil Blossom, began planning for desegregation soon after *Brown.*

However, Governor Orval Faubus publicly showed support for segregation. In September 1957, he ordered the National Guard to turn away the "Little Rock Nine"—nine African-American students who had volunteered to integrate Little Rock's Central High School as the first step in Blossom's plan. A federal judge ordered Faubus to let the students into school.

NAACP members called eight of the students and arranged to drive them to school. They could not reach the ninth student, Elizabeth Eckford, who did not have a phone, and she set out alone. Outside Central High, Eckford faced an abusive crowd. Terrified, the 15-year-old made it to a bus stop where two friendly whites stayed with her. **D**

Analyzing Causes

D Why weren't schools in all regions desegregated immediately after the *Brown II* decision?

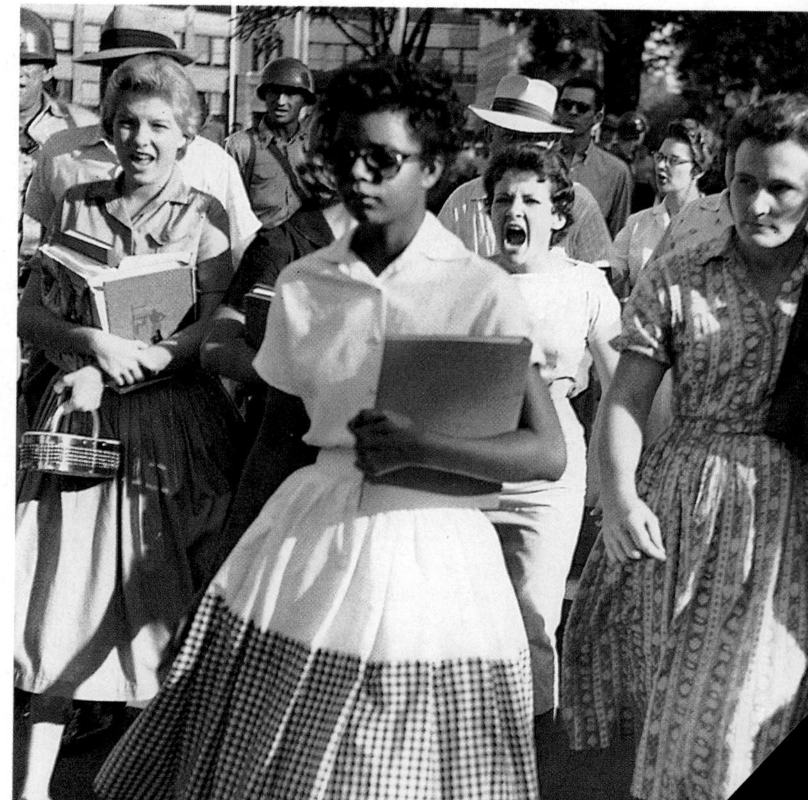

As white students jeer her and Arkansas National Guards look on, Elizabeth Eckford enters Little Rock Central High School in 1957. ▼

The crisis in Little Rock forced Eisenhower to act. He placed the Arkansas National Guard under federal control and ordered a thousand paratroopers into Little Rock. The nation watched the televised coverage of the event. Under the watch of soldiers, the nine African-American teenagers attended class.

But even these soldiers could not protect the students from troublemakers who confronted them in stairways, in the halls, and in the cafeteria. Throughout the year African-American students were regularly harassed by other students. At the end of the year, Faubus shut down Central High rather than let integration continue.

On September 9, 1957, Congress passed the Civil Rights Act of 1957, the first civil rights law since Reconstruction. Shepherded by Senator Lyndon B. Johnson of Texas, the law gave the attorney general greater power over school desegregation. It also gave the federal government jurisdiction—or authority—over violations of African-American voting rights. E

MAIN IDEA

Making Inferences

E What effect do you think television coverage of the Little Rock incident had on the nation?

The Montgomery Bus Boycott

ROSA PARKS
1913–

Long before December 1955, Rosa Parks (shown being finger printed) had protested segregation through everyday acts. She refused to use drinking fountains labeled "Colored Only." When possible, she shunned segregated elevators and climbed stairs instead.

Parks joined the Montgomery chapter of the NAACP in 1943 and became the organization's secretary. A turning point came for her in the summer of 1955, when she attended a workshop designed to promote integration by giving the students the experience of interracial living.

Returning to Montgomery, Parks was even more determined to fight segregation. As it happened, her act of protest against injustice on the buses inspired a whole community to join her cause.

The face-to-face confrontation at Central High School was not the only showdown over segregation in the mid-1950s. Impatient with the slow pace of change in the courts, African-American activists had begun taking direct action to win the rights promised to them by the Fourteenth and Fifteenth Amendments to the Constitution. Among those on the frontline of change was Jo Ann Robinson.

BOYCOTTING SEGREGATION Four days after the *Brown* decision in May 1954, Robinson wrote a letter to the mayor of Montgomery, Alabama, asking that bus drivers no longer be allowed to force riders in the "colored" section to yield their seats to whites. The mayor refused. Little did he know that in about 18 months another African-American woman from Alabama would be at the center of this controversy, and that her name and her words would far outlast segregation.

On December 1, 1955, **Rosa Parks,** a seamstress and an NAACP officer, took a seat in the front row of the "colored" section of a Montgomery bus. As the bus filled up, the driver ordered Parks and three other African-American passengers to empty the row they were occupying so that a white man could sit down without having to sit next to any African Americans. "It was time for someone to stand up—or in my case, sit down," recalled Parks. "I refused to move."

As Parks stared out the window, the bus driver said, "If you don't stand up, I'm going to call the police and have you arrested." The soft-spoken Parks replied, "You may do that."

News of Parks's arrest spread rapidly. Jo Ann Robinson and NAACP leader E. D. Nixon, who had helped to plan Parks's action, suggested a bus boycott. The leaders of the African-American community, including many ministers, formed the Montgomery Improvement Association to organize the boycott. They elected the pastor of the Dexter Avenue Baptist Church, 26-year-old **Martin Luther King, Jr.,** to lead the group. An ordained minister since 1948, King had just earned a Ph.D. degree in theology from Boston University. "Well, I'm not sure I'm the best person for the position," King confided to Nixon, "but if no one else is going to serve, I'd be glad to try."

◀ During the bus boycott, Montgomery's black citizens relied on an efficient car pool system that ferried people between more than forty pickup stations like the one shown.

WALKING FOR JUSTICE On the night of December 5, 1955, Dr. King made the following declaration to an estimated crowd of between 5,000 and 15,000 people.

A PERSONAL VOICE MARTIN LUTHER KING, JR.

"**There comes a time when people get tired of being trampled over by the iron feet of oppression. . . . I want it to be known—that we're going to work with grim and bold determination—to gain justice on buses in this city. And we are not wrong. . . . If we are wrong—the Supreme Court of this nation is wrong. If we are wrong—God Almighty is wrong. . . . If we are wrong—justice is a lie.**"

—quoted in *Parting the Waters: America in the King Years, 1954–63*

King's passionate and eloquent speech brought people to their feet and filled the audience with a sense of mission. African Americans filed a lawsuit and for 381 days refused to ride the buses in Montgomery. In most cases they had to find other means of transportation by organizing car pools or walking long distances. Support came from within the black community—workers donated one-fifth of their weekly salaries—as well as from outside groups like the NAACP, the United Auto Workers, Montgomery's Jewish community, and sympathetic white southerners. The boycotters remained nonviolent even after a bomb ripped apart King's home (no one was injured). Finally, in 1956, the Supreme Court outlawed bus segregation. F

MAIN IDEA

Synthesizing
F Why was Rosa Parks's action on December 1, 1955, significant?

Martin Luther King and the SCLC

The Montgomery bus boycott proved to the world that the African-American community could unite and organize a successful protest movement. It also proved the power of nonviolent resistance, the peaceful refusal to obey unjust laws. Despite threats to his life and family, King urged his followers, "Don't ever let anyone pull you so low as to hate them."

CHANGING THE WORLD WITH SOUL FORCE King called his brand of nonviolent resistance "soul force." He based his ideas on the teachings of several people. From Jesus, he learned to love one's enemies. From writer Henry David Thoreau he took the concept of civil disobedience—the refusal to obey an unjust law. From labor organizer A. Philip Randolph he learned to organize massive demonstrations. From Mohandas Gandhi, the leader who helped India throw off British rule, he learned to resist oppression without violence. G

MAIN IDEA

Summarizing
G What were the central points of Dr. King's philosophy?

"We will not hate you," King said to white racists, "but we cannot . . . obey your unjust laws. . . . We will soon wear you down by our capacity to suffer. And in winning our freedom, we will so appeal to your heart and conscience that we will win you in the process."

King held steadfast to his philosophy, even when a wave of racial violence swept through the South after the *Brown* decision. The violence included the 1955 murder of Emmett Till—a 14-year-old African-American boy who had allegedly flirted with a white woman. There were also shootings and beatings, some fatal, of civil rights workers.

FROM THE GRASSROOTS UP After the bus boycott ended, King joined with ministers and civil rights leaders in 1957 to found the **Southern Christian Leadership Conference (SCLC).** Its purpose was "to carry on nonviolent crusades against the evils of second-class citizenship." Using African-American churches as a base, the SCLC planned to stage protests and demonstrations throughout the South. The leaders hoped to build a movement from the grassroots up and to win the support of ordinary African Americans of all ages. King, president of the SCLC, used the power of his voice and ideas to fuel the movement's momentum.

The nuts and bolts of organizing the SCLC was handled by its first director, Ella Baker, the granddaughter of slaves. While with the NAACP, Baker had served as national field secretary, traveling over 16,000 miles throughout the South. From 1957 to 1960, Baker used her contacts to set up branches of the SCLC in Southern cities. In April 1960, Baker helped students at Shaw University, an African-American university in Raleigh, North Carolina, to organize a national protest group, the **Student Nonviolent Coordinating Committee,** or **SNCC,** pronounced "snick" for short.

It had been six years since the *Brown* decision, and many college students viewed the pace of change as too slow. Although these students risked a great deal—losing college scholarships, being expelled from college, being physically harmed—they were determined to challenge the system. SNCC hoped to harness the energy of these student protesters; it would soon create one of the most important student activist movements in the nation's history. H

Evaluating
H What was the role of the SCLC?

MARTIN LUTHER KING, JR.
1929–1968

Born Michael Luther King, Jr., King had to adjust to a new name in 1934. In that year, his father—Rev. Michael King, Sr.—returned home from a trip to Europe, where he had toured the site where Martin Luther had begun the Protestant Reformation. Upon his return home, the elder King changed his and his son's names to Martin.

Like Luther, the younger King became a reformer. In 1964, he won the Nobel peace prize. Yet there was a side of King unknown to most people—his inner battle to overcome his hatred of the white bigots. As a youth, he had once vowed "to hate all white people." As leader of the civil rights movement, King said all Americans had to be freed: "Negroes from the bonds of segregation and shame, whites from the bonds of bigotry and fear."

The Movement Spreads

Although SNCC adopted King's ideas in part, its members had ideas of their own. Many people called for a more confrontational strategy and set out to reshape the civil rights movement.

DEMONSTRATING FOR FREEDOM The founders of SNCC had models to build on. In 1942 in Chicago, the Congress of Racial Equality (CORE) had staged the first **sit-ins,** in which African-American protesters sat down at segregated lunch counters and refused to leave until they were served. In February 1960, African-American students from North Carolina's Agricultural and Technical College staged a sit-in at a whites-only lunch counter at a Woolworth's store in Greensboro. This time, television crews brought coverage of the protest into homes throughout the United States. There was no denying the ugly face of racism. Day after day, news reporters captured the scenes of whites beating, jeering at, and pouring food over students who refused to strike back. The coverage sparked many other sit-ins across the South. Store managers called

Sit-in demonstrators, such as these at a Jackson, Mississippi, lunch counter in 1963, faced intimidation and humiliation from white segregationists.

in the police, raised the price of food, and removed counter seats. But the movement continued and spread to the North. There, students formed picket lines around national chain stores that maintained segregated lunch counters in the South.

By late 1960, students had descended on and desegregated lunch counters in some 48 cities in 11 states. They endured arrests, beatings, suspension from college, and tear gas and fire hoses, but the army of nonviolent students refused to back down. "My mother has always told me that I'm equal to other people," said Ezell Blair, Jr., one of the students who led the first SNCC sit-in in 1960. For the rest of the 1960s, many Americans worked to convince the rest of the country that blacks and whites deserved equal treatment.

SECTION 1 ASSESSMENT

1. **TERMS & NAMES** For each term or name, write a sentence explaining its significance.
   - **Thurgood Marshall**
   - ***Brown* v. *Board of Education of Topeka***
   - **Rosa Parks**
   - **Martin Luther King, Jr.**
   - **Southern Christian Leadership Conference (SCLC)**
   - **Student Nonviolent Coordinating Committee (SNCC)**
   - **sit-in**

MAIN IDEA

2. **TAKING NOTES**
   Fill in a spider diagram like the one below with examples of tactics, organizations, leaders, and Supreme Court decisions of the civil rights movement up to 1960.

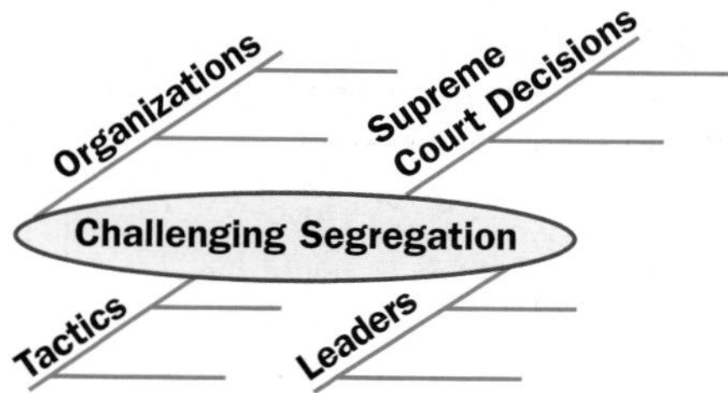

CRITICAL THINKING

3. **EVALUATING**
   Do you think the nonviolence used by civil rights activists was a good tactic? Explain. **Think About:**
   - the Montgomery bus boycott
   - television coverage of events
   - sit-ins

4. **CONTRASTING**
   How did the tactics of the student protesters from SNCC differ from those of the boycotters in Montgomery?

5. **DRAWING CONCLUSIONS**
   After the *Brown* v. *Board of Education of Topeka* ruling, what do you think was the most significant event of the civil rights movement prior to 1960? Why? **Think About:**
   - the role of civil rights leaders
   - the results of confrontations and boycotts
   - the role of grassroots organizations

BROWN v. *BOARD OF EDUCATION OF TOPEKA* (1954)

ORIGINS OF THE CASE In the early 1950s, the school system of Topeka, Kansas, like many other school systems, operated separate schools for "the two races"—blacks and whites. Reverend Oliver Brown protested that this was unfair to his eight-year-old daughter Linda. Although the Browns lived near a "white" school, Linda was forced to take a long bus ride to her "black" school across town.

THE RULING **The Court ruled that segregated public schools were "inherently" unequal and therefore unconstitutional.**

Linda Brown's name headed a list of five school desegregation cases heard by the Supreme Court. ▶

LEGAL REASONING

While the correctness of the *Brown* ruling—which actually involved five segregation cases from across the nation—seems obvious today, some justices had difficulty agreeing to it. One reason was the force of legal precedent. Normally, judges follow a policy of *stare decisis,* "let the decision stand." The *Plessy* v. *Ferguson* decision endorsing segregation had stood for over 50 years. It clearly stated that "separate but equal" facilities did not violate the Fourteenth Amendment.

Thurgood Marshall, the NAACP lawyer who argued *Brown,* spent years laying the groundwork to chip away at Jim Crow—the local laws that required segregated facilities. Marshall had recently won two Supreme Court decisions in 1950 (*Mclaurin* and *Sweatt;* see Legal Sources at right) that challenged segregation at graduate schools. Then in 1952, the Supreme Court agreed to hear the Browns' case. The Court deliberated for two years deciding how to interpret the Fourteenth Amendment.

In the end, Chief Justice Earl Warren carefully sidestepped *Plessy,* claiming that segregated schools were not and never could be equal. On Monday, May 17, 1954, Warren read the unanimous decision:

> "**Does segregation of children in public schools . . . deprive children of . . . equal opportunities? We believe it does. . . . To separate them . . . solely because of their race generates a feeling of inferiority . . . that may affect their hearts and minds in a way unlikely ever to be undone.**"
>
> —*Brown v. Board of Education of Topeka*

LEGAL SOURCES

U.S. CONSTITUTION

FOURTEENTH AMENDMENT, EQUAL PROTECTION CLAUSE (1868)

"No state shall . . . deny to any person within its jurisdiction the equal protection of the laws."

RELATED CASES

***PLESSY* v. *FERGUSON* (1896)**

- Upheld Louisiana's laws requiring that train passengers be segregated by race.
- Established the doctrine of "separate but equal."

***MCLAURIN* v. *OKLAHOMA STATE* (1950)**

Ruled that Oklahoma State University violated the Constitution by keeping its one "Negro" student in the back of the class and the cafeteria.

***SWEATT* v. *PAINTER* (1950)**

Required the University of Texas to admit an African-American student to its previously all-white law school.

WHY IT MATTERED

The Court's decision in *Brown* had an immediate impact on pending rulings. In a series of cases after *Brown,* the Supreme Court prohibited segregation in housing, at public beaches, at recreation facilities, and in restaurants. Later decisions extended equal access to other groups, including women and resident aliens.

The decision encountered fierce resistance, however. It awakened the old battle cry of states' rights. Directly following *Brown,* some Congress members circulated the "Southern Manifesto," claiming the right of the states to ignore the ruling. In taking a stand on a social issue, they said, the Court had taken a step away from simply interpreting legal precedents. Critics charged that the Warren Court had acted as legislators and even as sociologists.

The *Brown* case strengthened the Civil Rights movement, however, and paved the way for the end of Jim Crow. The NAACP had fought and won the legal battle and had gained prestige and momentum. Americans got the strong message that the federal government now took civil rights seriously.

HISTORICAL IMPACT

Three of the parties involved in *Brown*—Delaware, Kansas, and the District of Columbia—began to integrate schools in 1954. Topeka County informed the Court that 123 black students were already attending formerly all-white schools. Even so, the Supreme Court was well aware that its decision would be difficult to enforce. In a follow-up ruling, *Brown II* (1955), the Court required that integration take place with "all deliberate speed." To some this meant quickly. Others interpreted *deliberate* to mean slowly.

Only two Southern states even began to integrate classrooms in 1954: Texas and Arkansas opened one and two districts, respectively. By 1960, less than one percent of the South's students attended integrated schools. Many school districts were ordered to use aggressive means to achieve racial balance. Courts spent decades supervising forced busing, a practice that often pitted community against community.

Still, despite the resistance and the practical difficulties of implementation, *Brown* stands today as a watershed, the single point at which breaking the "color barrier" officially became a federal priority.

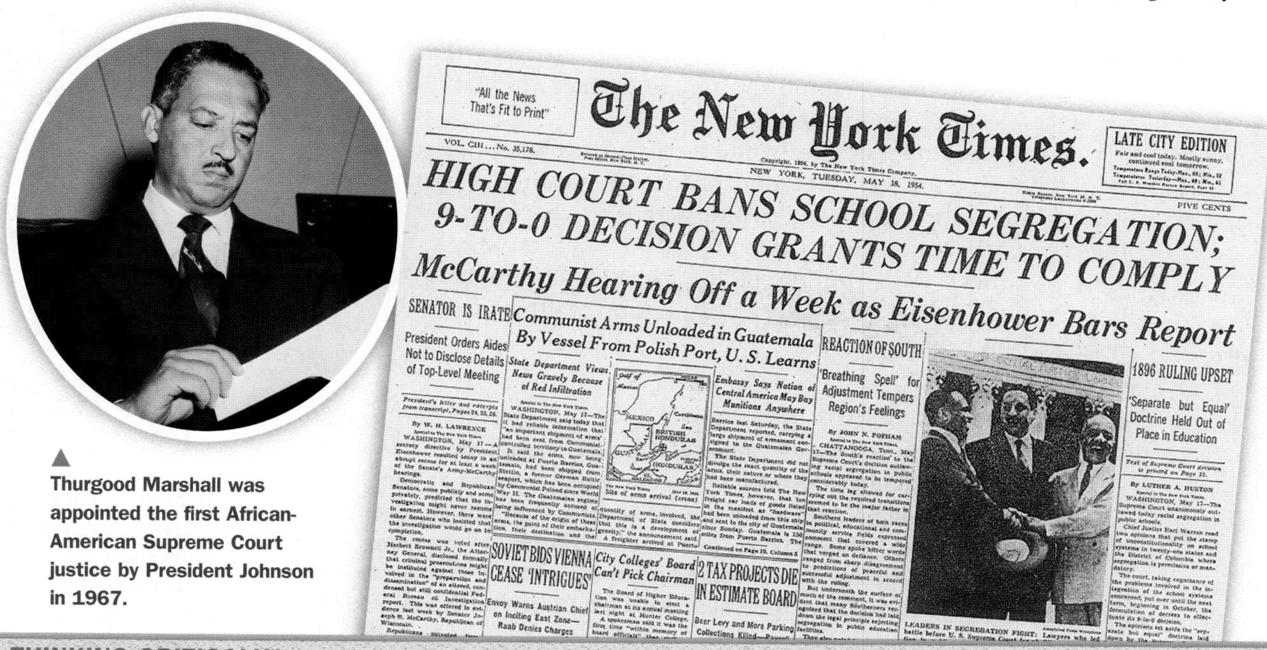

"All the News That's Fit to Print"

The New York Times.

LATE CITY EDITION

VOL. CIII...No. 35,178. NEW YORK, TUESDAY, MAY 18, 1954. FIVE CENTS

HIGH COURT BANS SCHOOL SEGREGATION; 9-TO-0 DECISION GRANTS TIME TO COMPLY

McCarthy Hearing Off a Week as Eisenhower Bars Report

SENATOR IS IRATE

President Orders Aides Not to Disclose Details of Top-Level Meeting

Communist Arms Unloaded in Guatemala By Vessel From Polish Port, U.S. Learns

State Department Views News Gravely Because of Red Infiltration

Embassy Says Nation of Central America May Buy Munitions Anywhere

REACTION OF SOUTH

'Breathing Spell' for Adjustment Tempers Region's Feelings

1896 RULING UPSET

'Separate but Equal' Doctrine Held Out of Place in Education

SOVIET BIDS VIENNA CEASE 'INTRIGUES'

City Colleges' Board Can't Pick Chairman

2 TAX PROJECTS DIE IN ESTIMATE BOARD

LEADERS IN SEGREGATION FIGHT

▲ **Thurgood Marshall was appointed the first African-American Supreme Court justice by President Johnson in 1967.**

THINKING CRITICALLY

CONNECT TO HISTORY

1. **Analyzing Primary Sources** Legal precedents are set not only by rulings but also by dissenting opinions, in which justices explain why they disagree with the majority. Justice John Marshall Harlan was the one dissenting voice in *Plessy* v. *Ferguson.* Read his opinion and comment on how it might apply to *Brown.*

 **SEE SKILLBUILDER HANDBOOK, PAGE R22.**

CONNECT TO TODAY

2.  **INTERNET ACTIVITY CLASSZONE.COM**

Visit the links for Historic Decisions of the Supreme Court to research the Supreme Court's changing opinions on civil rights. Compile a chart or time line to present the facts—date, plaintiff, defendant, major issue, and outcome—of several major cases. Then give an oral presentation explaining the Supreme Court's role in civil rights.

The Triumphs of a Crusade

MAIN IDEA	WHY IT MATTERS NOW	Terms & Names
Civil rights activists broke through racial barriers. Their activism prompted landmark legislation.	**Activism pushed the federal government to end segregation and ensure voting rights for African Americans.**	**• freedom riders • James Meredith • Civil Rights Act of 1964 • Freedom Summer • Fannie Lou Hamer • Voting Rights Act of 1965**

One American's Story

In 1961, James Peck, a white civil rights activist, joined other CORE members on a historic bus trip across the South. The two-bus trip would test the Supreme Court decisions banning segregated seating on interstate bus routes and segregated facilities in bus terminals. Peck and other **freedom riders** hoped to provoke a violent reaction that would convince the Kennedy administration to enforce the law. The violence was not long in coming.

At the Alabama state line, white racists got on Bus One carrying chains, brass knuckles, and pistols. They brutally beat African-American riders and white activists who tried to intervene. Still the riders managed to go on. Then on May 4, 1961—Mother's Day—the bus pulled into the Birmingham bus terminal. James Peck saw a hostile mob waiting, some holding iron bars.

A PERSONAL VOICE JAMES PECK

"I looked at them and then I looked at Charles Person, who had been designated as my team mate. . . . When I looked at him, he responded by saying simply, 'Let's go.' As we entered the white waiting room, . . . we were grabbed bodily and pushed toward the alleyway . . . and out of sight of onlookers in the waiting room, six of them started swinging at me with fists and pipes. Five others attacked Person a few feet ahead."

—*Freedom Ride*

▲ Three days after being beaten unconscious in Birmingham, freedom rider James Peck demonstrates in New York City to pressure national bus companies to support desegregation.

The ride of Bus One had ended, but Bus Two continued southward on a journey that would shock the Kennedy administration into action.

Riding for Freedom

In Anniston, Alabama, about 200 angry whites attacked Bus Two. The mob followed the activists out of town. When one of the tires blew, they smashed a window and tossed in a fire bomb. The freedom riders spilled out just before the bus exploded.

NEW VOLUNTEERS The bus companies refused to carry the CORE freedom riders any farther. Even though the determined volunteers did not want to give up, they ended their ride. However, CORE director James Farmer announced that a group of SNCC volunteers in Nashville were ready to pick up where the others had left off.

When a new band of freedom riders rode into Birmingham, policemen pulled them from the bus, beat them, and drove them into Tennessee. Defiantly, they returned to the Birmingham bus terminal. Their bus driver, however, feared for his life and refused to transport them. In protest, they occupied the whites-only waiting room at the terminal for eighteen hours until a solution was reached. After an angry phone call from U.S. Attorney General Robert Kennedy, bus company officials convinced the driver to proceed. The riders set out for Montgomery on May 20.

▲ **In May 1961, a mob firebombed this bus of freedom riders outside Anniston, Alabama, and attacked passengers as they tried to escape.**

ARRIVAL OF FEDERAL MARSHALS Although Alabama officials had promised Kennedy that the riders would be protected, a mob of whites—many carrying bats and lead pipes—fell upon the riders when they arrived in Montgomery. John Doer, a Justice Department official on the scene, called the attorney general to report what was happening. "A bunch of men led by a guy with a bleeding face are beating [the passengers]. There are no cops. It's terrible. There's not a cop in sight. People are yelling. 'Get 'em, get 'em.' It's awful."

"We will continue our journey one way or another. . . . We are prepared to die."
JIM ZWERG, FREEDOM RIDER

The violence provoked exactly the response the freedom riders wanted. Newspapers throughout the nation and abroad denounced the beatings.

MAIN IDEA
Analyzing Issues
A What did the freedom riders hope to achieve?

President Kennedy arranged to give the freedom riders direct support. The Justice Department sent 400 U.S. marshals to protect the riders on the last part of their journey to Jackson, Mississippi. In addition, the attorney general and the Interstate Commerce Commission banned segregation in all interstate travel facilities, including waiting rooms, restrooms, and lunch counters. **A**

Standing Firm

With the integration of interstate travel facilities under way, some civil rights workers turned their attention to integrating some Southern schools and pushing the movement into additional Southern towns. At each turn they encountered opposition and often violence.

INTEGRATING OLE MISS In September 1962, Air Force veteran **James Meredith** won a federal court case that allowed him to enroll in the all-white University of Mississippi, nicknamed Ole Miss. But when Meredith arrived on campus, he faced Governor Ross Barnett, who refused to let him register as a student.

President Kennedy ordered federal marshals to escort Meredith to the registrar's office. Barnett responded with a heated radio appeal: "I call on every Mississippian to keep his faith and courage. We will never surrender." The broadcast turned out white demonstrators by the thousands.

On the night of September 30, riots broke out on campus, resulting in two deaths. It took thousands of soldiers, 200 arrests, and 15 hours to stop the rioters. In the months that followed, federal officials accompanied Meredith to class and protected his parents from nightriders who shot up their house.

News photos and television coverage of police dogs in Birmingham attacking African Americans shocked the nation.

HEADING INTO BIRMINGHAM The trouble continued in Alabama. Birmingham, a city known for its strict enforcement of total segregation in public life, also had a reputation for racial violence, including 18 bombings from 1957 to 1963.

Reverend Fred Shuttlesworth, head of the Alabama Christian Movement for Human Rights and secretary of the SCLC, decided something had to be done about Birmingham and that it would be the ideal place to test the power of nonviolence. He invited Martin Luther King, Jr., and the SCLC to help desegregate the city. On April 3, 1963, King flew into Birmingham to hold a planning meeting with members of the African-American community. "This is the most segregated city in America," he said. "We have to stick together if we ever want to change its ways."

After days of demonstrations led by Shuttlesworth and others, King and a small band of marchers were finally arrested during a demonstration on Good Friday, April 12th. While in jail, King wrote an open letter to white religious leaders who felt he was pushing too fast.

A PERSONAL VOICE MARTIN LUTHER KING, JR.

"I guess it is easy for those who have never felt the stinging darts of segregation to say, 'Wait.' But when you have seen vicious mobs lynch your mothers and fathers at whim; when you have seen hate-filled policemen curse, kick, brutalize and even kill your black brothers and sisters; . . . when you see the vast majority of your twenty million Negro brothers smothering in the air-tight cage of poverty; . . . when you have to concoct an answer for a five-year-old son asking: . . . 'Daddy, why do white people treat colored people so mean?' . . . then you will understand why we find it difficult to wait."

—"Letter from a Birmingham Jail"

On April 20, King posted bail and began planning more demonstrations. On May 2, more than a thousand African-American children marched in Birmingham; Police commissioner Eugene "Bull" Connor's men arrested 959 of them. On May 3, a second "children's crusade" came face to face with a helmeted police force. Police swept the marchers off their feet with high-pressure fire hoses, set attack dogs on them, and clubbed those who fell. TV cameras captured all of it, and millions of viewers heard the children screaming.

Continued protests, an economic boycott, and negative media coverage finally convinced Birmingham officials to end segregation. This stunning civil rights victory inspired African Americans across the nation. It also convinced President Kennedy that only a new civil rights act could end racial violence and satisfy the demands of African Americans—and many whites—for racial justice. B

MAIN IDEA

Chronological Order

B What events led to desegregation in Birmingham?

History Through *Photojournalism*

ERNEST WITHERS

Born in Memphis in 1922, photographer Ernest Withers believed that if the struggle for equality could be shown to people, things would change. Armed with only a camera, he braved violent crowds to capture the heated racism during the Montgomery bus boycott, the desegregation of Central High in Little Rock, and the 1968 Memphis sanitation workers strike (below) led by Martin Luther King, Jr. The night before the Memphis march, Withers had helped make some of the signs he photographed.

> **"G. C. Brown printed those 'I AM A MAN' signs right over there. . . . I had a car and it was snowing, so we went and rented the saw and came back that night and cut the sticks."**

▲ **Withers in 1950**

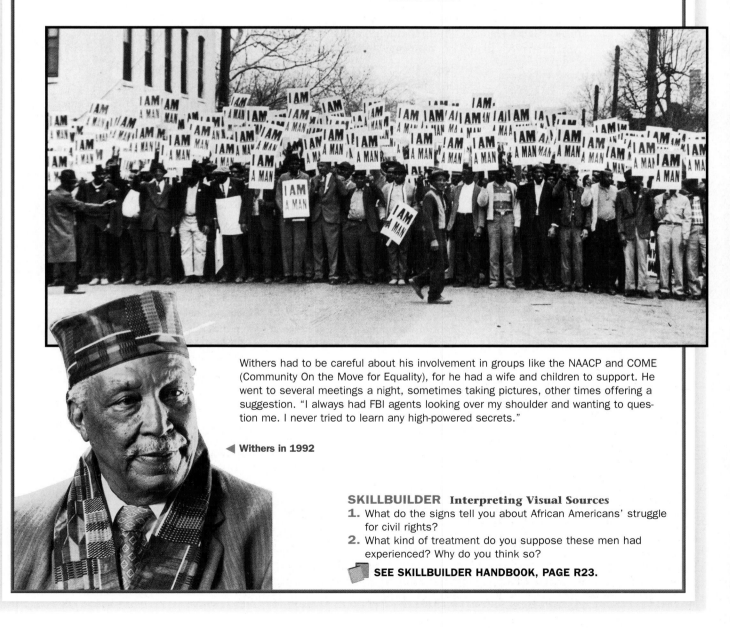

Withers had to be careful about his involvement in groups like the NAACP and COME (Community On the Move for Equality), for he had a wife and children to support. He went to several meetings a night, sometimes taking pictures, other times offering a suggestion. "I always had FBI agents looking over my shoulder and wanting to question me. I never tried to learn any high-powered secrets."

◀ **Withers in 1992**

SKILLBUILDER Interpreting Visual Sources

1. What do the signs tell you about African Americans' struggle for civil rights?
2. What kind of treatment do you suppose these men had experienced? Why do you think so?

SEE SKILLBUILDER HANDBOOK, PAGE R23.

"I say, Segregation now! Segregation tomorrow! Segregation forever!"

GEORGE WALLACE, ALABAMA GOVERNOR, 1963

KENNEDY TAKES A STAND On June 11, 1963, the president sent troops to force Governor George Wallace to honor a court order desegregating the University of Alabama. That evening, Kennedy asked the nation: "Are we to say to the world—and much more importantly, to each other—that this is the land of the free, except for the Negroes?" He demanded that Congress pass a civil rights bill.

A tragic event just hours after Kennedy's speech highlighted the racial tension in much of the South. Shortly after midnight, a sniper murdered Medgar Evers, NAACP field secretary and World War II veteran. Police soon arrested a white supremacist, Byron de la Beckwith, but he was released after two trials resulted in hung juries. His release brought a new militancy to African Americans. Many demanded, "Freedom now!"

Background
Beckwith was finally convicted in 1994, after the case was reopened based on new evidence.

Marching to Washington

The civil rights bill that President Kennedy sent to Congress guaranteed equal access to all public accommodations and gave the U.S. attorney general the power to file school desegregation suits. To persuade Congress to pass the bill, two veteran organizers—labor leader A. Philip Randolph and Bayard Rustin of the SCLC—summoned Americans to a march on Washington, D.C.

Civil Rights Acts of the 1950s and 1960s

CIVIL RIGHTS ACT OF 1957
- Established federal Commission on Civil Rights
- Established a Civil Rights Division in the Justice Department to enforce civil rights laws
- Enlarged federal power to protect voting rights

CIVIL RIGHTS ACT OF 1964
- Banned most discrimination in employment and in public accommodations
- Enlarged federal power to protect voting rights and speed up school desegregation
- Established Equal Employment Opportunity Commission to ensure fair treatment in employment

VOTING RIGHTS ACT OF 1965
- Eliminated voter literacy tests
- Enabled federal examiners to register voters

CIVIL RIGHTS ACT OF 1968
- Prohibited discrimination in the sale or rental of most housing
- Strengthened antilynching laws
- Made it a crime to harm civil rights workers

SKILLBUILDER
Interpreting Charts
Which law do you think benefited the most people? Explain your choice.

THE DREAM OF EQUALITY On August 28, 1963, more than 250,000 people—including about 75,000 whites—converged on the nation's capital. They assembled on the grassy lawn of the Washington Monument and marched to the Lincoln Memorial. There, people listened to speakers demand the immediate passage of the civil rights bill. (C)

When Dr. Martin Luther King, Jr., appeared, the crowd exploded in applause. In his now famous speech, "I Have a Dream," he appealed for peace and racial harmony.

MAIN IDEA
Analyzing Events
(C) Why did civil rights organizers ask their supporters to march on Washington?

A PERSONAL VOICE MARTIN LUTHER KING, JR.

"I have a dream that one day this nation will rise up and live out the true meaning of its creed: 'We hold these truths to be self-evident; that all men are created equal.' . . . I have a dream that my four little children will one day live in a nation where they will not be judged by the color of their skin but by the content of their character. . . . I have a dream that one day the state of Alabama . . . will be transformed into a situation where little black boys and black girls will be able to join hands with little white boys and white girls and walk together as sisters and brothers."

—"I Have a Dream"

MORE VIOLENCE Two weeks after King's historic speech, four young Birmingham girls were killed when a rider in a car hurled a bomb through their church window. Two more African Americans died in the unrest that followed.

Two months later, an assassin shot and killed John F. Kennedy. His successor, President Lyndon B. Johnson, pledged to carry on Kennedy's work. On July 2, 1964, Johnson signed the **Civil Rights Act of 1964,** which prohibited discrimination because of race, religion, national origin, and gender. It gave all citizens the right to enter libraries, parks, washrooms, restaurants, theaters, and other public accommodations.

In the summer of 1964, college students volunteered to go to Mississippi to help register that state's African-American voters.

Fighting for Voting Rights

Meanwhile, the right of all African Americans to vote remained elusive. In 1964, CORE and SNCC workers in the South began registering as many African Americans as they could to vote. They hoped their campaign would receive national publicity, which would in turn influence Congress to pass a voting rights act. Focused in Mississippi, the project became known as **Freedom Summer.**

FREEDOM SUMMER To fortify the project, civil rights groups recruited college students and trained them in nonviolent resistance. Thousands of student volunteers—mostly white, about one-third female—went into Mississippi to help register voters. For some, the job proved deadly. In June of 1964, three civil rights workers disappeared in Neshoba County, Mississippi. Investigators later learned that Klansmen and local police had murdered the men, two of whom were white. Through the summer the racial beatings and murders continued, along with the burning of businesses, homes, and churches. D

MAIN IDEA

Analyzing Motives

D Why did civil rights groups organize Freedom Summer?

A NEW POLITICAL PARTY African Americans needed a voice in the political arena if sweeping change was to occur. In order to gain a seat in Mississippi's all-white Democratic Party, SNCC organized the Mississippi Freedom Democratic Party (MFDP). **Fannie Lou Hamer,** the daughter of Mississippi sharecroppers, would be their voice at the 1964 Democratic National Convention. In a televised speech that shocked the convention and viewers nationwide, Hamer described how she was jailed for registering to vote in 1962, and how police forced other prisoners to beat her.

A Personal Voice FANNIE LOU HAMER

"The first [prisoner] began to beat [me], and I was beat by the first until he was exhausted. . . . The second [prisoner] began to beat. . . . I began to scream and one white man got up and began to beat me in my head and tell me to 'hush.' . . . All of this on account we want to register, to become first-class citizens, and if the Freedom Democratic Party is not seated now, I question America."

—quoted in *The Civil Rights Movement: An Eyewitness History*

MAIN IDEA

Developing Historical Perspective

E Why did young people in SNCC and the MFDP feel betrayed by some civil rights leaders?

In response to Hamer's speech, telegrams and telephone calls poured in to the convention in support of seating the MFDP delegates. President Johnson feared losing the Southern white vote if the Democrats sided with the MFDP, so his administration pressured civil rights leaders to convince the MFDP to accept a compromise. The Democrats would give 2 of Mississippi's 68 seats to the MFDP, with a promise to ban discrimination at the 1968 convention.

When Hamer learned of the compromise, she said, "We didn't come all this way for no two seats." The MFDP and supporters in SNCC felt that the leaders had betrayed them. E

HISTORICAL SPOTLIGHT

TWENTY-FOURTH AMENDMENT—BARRING POLL TAXES

On January 24, 1964, South Dakota became the 38th state to ratify the Twenty-fourth Amendment to the Constitution. The key clause in the amendment reads: "The right of citizens of the United States to vote in any primary or other election . . . shall not be denied or abridged by the United States or any State by reason of failure to pay any poll tax or other tax."

Poll taxes were often used to keep poor African Americans from voting. Although most states had already abolished their poll taxes by 1964, five Southern states—Alabama, Arkansas, Mississippi, Texas, and Virginia—still had such laws on the books. By making these laws unconstitutional, the Twenty-fourth Amendment gave the vote to millions who had been disqualified because of poverty.

THE SELMA CAMPAIGN At the start of 1965, the SCLC conducted a major voting rights campaign in Selma, Alabama, where SNCC had been working for two years to register voters. By the end of 1965, more than 2,000 African Americans had been arrested in SCLC demonstrations. After a demonstrator named Jimmy Lee Jackson was shot and killed, King responded by announcing a 50-mile protest march from Selma to Montgomery, the state capital. On March 7, 1965, about 600 protesters set out for Montgomery.

That night, mayhem broke out. Television cameras captured the scene. The rest of the nation watched in horror as police swung whips and clubs, and clouds of tear gas swirled around fallen marchers. Demonstrators poured into Selma by the hundreds. Ten days later, President Johnson presented Congress with a new voting rights act and asked for its swift passage.

On March 21, 3,000 marchers again set out for Montgomery, this time with federal protection. Soon the number grew to an army of 25,000. F

MAIN IDEA

Comparing

F In what ways was the civil rights campaign in Selma similar to the one in Birmingham?

VOTING RIGHTS ACT OF 1965 That summer, Congress finally passed Johnson's **Voting Rights Act of 1965.** The act eliminated the so-called literacy tests that had disqualified many voters. It also stated that federal examiners could enroll voters who had been denied suffrage by local officials. In Selma, the proportion of African Americans registered to vote rose from 10 percent in 1964 to 60 percent in 1968. Overall the percentage of registered African-American voters in the South tripled.

Although the Voting Rights Act marked a major civil rights victory, some felt that the law did not go far enough. Centuries of discrimination had produced social and economic inequalities. Anger over these inequalities led to a series of violent disturbances in the cities of the North.

SECTION 2 ASSESSMENT

1. **TERMS & NAMES** For each term or name, write a sentence explaining its significance.
   - **freedom riders**
   - **James Meredith**
   - **Civil Rights Act of 1964**
   - **Freedom Summer**
   - **Fannie Lou Hamer**
   - **Voting Rights Act of 1965**

MAIN IDEA

2. **TAKING NOTES**
   In a graphic like the one shown, list the steps that African Americans took to desegregate buses and schools from 1962 to 1965.

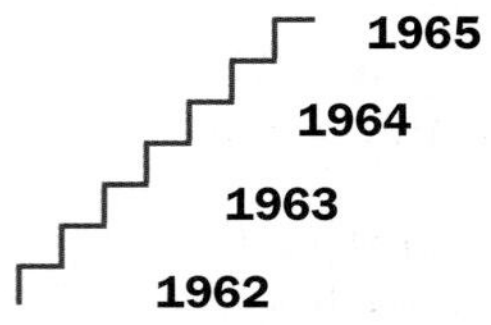

CRITICAL THINKING

3. **ANALYZING ISSUES**
   What assumptions and beliefs do you think guided the fierce opposition to the civil rights movement in the South? Support your answer with evidence from the text. **Think About:**
   - the social and political structure of the South
   - Mississippi governor Ross Barnett's comment during his radio address
   - the actions of police and some white Southerners

4. **ANALYZING PRIMARY SOURCES**
   Just after the Civil Rights Act of 1964 was passed, white Alabama governor George Wallace said,

   > **"It is ironical that this event occurs as we approach the celebration of Independence Day. On that day we won our freedom. On this day we have largely lost it."**

   What do you think Wallace meant by his statement?

Challenges and Changes in the Movement

MAIN IDEA

Disagreements among civil rights groups and the rise of black nationalism created a violent period in the fight for civil rights.

WHY IT MATTERS NOW

From the fight for equality came a resurgence of racial pride for African Americans, a legacy that influences today's generations.

Terms & Names

- **de facto segregation**
- **de jure segregation**
- **Malcolm X**
- **Nation of Islam**
- **Stokely Carmichael**
- **Black Power**
- **Black Panthers**
- **Kerner Commission**
- **Civil Rights Act of 1968**
- **affirmative action**

One American's Story

Alice Walker, the prize-winning novelist, became aware of the civil rights movement in 1960, when she was 16. Her mother had recently scraped together enough money to purchase a television.

▲ Alice Walker during an interview in New York's Central Park in August 1970

A PERSONAL VOICE ALICE WALKER

"Like a good omen for the future, the face of Dr. Martin Luther King, Jr., was the first black face I saw on our new television screen. And, as in a fairy tale, my soul was stirred by the meaning for me of his mission—at the time he was being rather ignominiously dumped into a police van for having led a protest march in Alabama—and I fell in love with the sober and determined face of the Movement."

—*In Search of Our Mothers' Gardens*

The next year, Walker attended the all-black Spelman College. In 1963, Walker took part in the March on Washington and then traveled to Africa to discover her spiritual roots. After returning home in 1964, she worked on voter registration, taught African American history and writing, and wrote poetry and fiction.

Walker's interest in her heritage was part of a growing trend among African Americans in the mid-1960s. But millions of African Americans were still living in poverty. Angry and frustrated over the difficulty in finding jobs and decent housing, some participated in riots that broke out between 1964 and 1966.

African Americans Seek Greater Equality

What civil rights groups had in common in the early 1960s were their calls for a newfound pride in black identity and a commitment to change the social and economic structures that kept people in a life of poverty. However, by 1965, the leading civil rights groups began to drift apart. New leaders emerged as the movement turned its attention to the North, where African Americans faced not legal segregation but deeply entrenched and oppressive racial prejudice.

NORTHERN SEGREGATION The problem facing African Americans in the North was **de facto segregation**—segregation that exists by practice and custom. De facto segregation can be harder to fight than **de jure** (dē jŏŏr′ē) **segregation,** or segregation by law, because eliminating it requires changing people's attitudes rather than repealing laws. Activists in the mid-1960s would find it much more difficult to convince whites to share economic and social power with African Americans than to convince them to share lunch counters and bus seats. (A)

MAIN IDEA

Comparing

(A) How were civil rights problems in Northern cities similar to those in the South?

De facto segregation intensified after African Americans migrated to Northern cities during and after World War II. This began a "white flight," in which great numbers of whites moved out of the cities to the nearby suburbs. By the mid-1960s, most urban African Americans lived in decaying slums, paying rent to landlords who didn't comply with housing and health ordinances. The schools for African-American children deteriorated along with their neighborhoods. Unemployment rates were more than twice as high as those among whites.

In addition, many blacks were angry at the sometimes brutal treatment they received from the mostly white police forces in their communities. In 1966, King spearheaded a campaign in Chicago to end de facto segregation there and create an "open city." On July 10, he led about 30,000 African Americans in a march on City Hall.

In late July, when King led demonstrators through a Chicago neighborhood, angry whites threw rocks and bottles. On August 5, hostile whites stoned King as he led 600 marchers. King left Chicago without accomplishing what he wanted, yet pledging to return.

URBAN VIOLENCE ERUPTS In the mid 1960s, clashes between white authority and black civilians spread like wildfire. In New York City in July 1964, an encounter between white police and African-American teenagers ended in the death of a 15-year-old student. This sparked a race riot in central Harlem. On August 11, 1965, only five days after President Johnson signed the Voting

Between 1964 and 1968, more than 100 race riots erupted in major American cities. The worst included Watts in Los Angeles in 1965 *(top)* and Detroit in 1967 *(right)*. In Detroit, 43 people were killed and property damage topped $40 million.

Rights Act into law, one of the worst race riots in the nation's history raged through the streets of Watts, a predominantly African-American neighborhood in Los Angeles. Thirty-four people were killed, and hundreds of millions of dollars worth of property was destroyed. The next year, 1966, saw even more racial disturbances, and in 1967 alone, riots and violent clashes took place in more than 100 cities.

The African-American rage baffled many whites. "Why would blacks turn to violence after winning so many victories in the South?" they wondered. Some realized that what African Americans wanted and needed was economic equality of opportunity in jobs, housing, and education. (B)

MAIN IDEA

Analyzing Causes

(B) What were some of the causes of urban rioting in the 1960s?

Even before the riots in 1964, President Johnson had announced his War on Poverty, a program to help impoverished Americans. But the flow of money needed to fund Johnson's Great Society was soon redirected to fund the war in Vietnam. In 1967, Dr. King proclaimed, "The Great Society has been shot down on the battlefields of Vietnam."

KEY PLAYER

MALCOLM X
1925–1965

Malcolm X's early life left him alienated from white society. His father was allegedly killed by white racists, and his mother had an emotional collapse, leaving Malcolm and his siblings in the care of the state. At the end of eighth grade, Malcolm quit school and was later jailed for criminal behavior. In 1946, while in prison, Malcolm joined the Nation of Islam. He developed a philosophy of black superiority and separatism from whites.

In the later years of his life, he urged African Americans to identify with Africa and to work with world organizations and even progressive whites to attain equality. Although silenced by gunmen, Malcolm X is a continuing inspiration for many Americans.

New Leaders Voice Discontent

The anger that sent rioters into the streets stemmed in part from African-American leaders who urged their followers to take complete control of their communities, livelihoods, and culture. One such leader, **Malcolm X,** declared to a Harlem audience, "If you think we are here to tell you to love the white man, you have come to the wrong place."

AFRICAN-AMERICAN SOLIDARITY Malcolm X, born Malcolm Little, went to jail at age 20 for burglary. While in prison, he studied the teachings of Elijah Muhammad, the head of the **Nation of Islam**, or the Black Muslims. Malcolm changed his name to Malcolm X (dropping what he called his "slave name") and, after his release from prison in 1952, became an Islamic minister. As he gained a following, the brilliant thinker and engaging speaker openly preached Elijah Muhammad's views that whites were the cause of the black condition and that blacks should separate from white society.

Background

See "Islam" on page 9.

Malcolm's message appealed to many African Americans and their growing racial pride. At a New York press conference in March 1964, he also advocated armed self-defense.

A PERSONAL VOICE MALCOLM X

"**Concerning nonviolence: it is criminal to teach a man not to defend himself when he is the constant victim of brutal attacks. It is legal and lawful to own a shotgun or a rifle. We believe in obeying the law. . . . [T]he time has come for the American Negro to fight back in self-defense whenever and wherever he is being unjustly and unlawfully attacked.**"

—quoted in *Eyewitness: The Negro in American History*

MAIN IDEA

Synthesizing

(C) Why did some Americans find Malcolm X's views alarming?

The press gave a great deal of publicity to Malcolm X because his controversial statements made dramatic news stories. This had two effects. First, his call for armed self-defense frightened most whites and many moderate African Americans. Second, reports of the attention Malcolm received awakened resentment in some other members of the Nation of Islam. (C)

BALLOTS OR BULLETS? In March 1964, Malcolm broke with Elijah Muhammad over differences in strategy and doctrine and formed another Muslim organization. One month later, he embarked on a pilgrimage to Mecca, in Saudi Arabia, a trip required of followers of orthodox Islam. In Mecca, he learned that orthodox Islam preached racial equality, and he worshiped alongside people from many countries. Wrote Malcolm, "I have [prayed] . . . with fellow Muslims whose eyes were the bluest of blue, whose hair was the blondest of blond, and whose skin was the whitest of white." When he returned to the United States, his attitude toward whites had changed radically. He explained his new slogan, "Ballots or bullets," to a follower: "Well, if you and I don't use the ballot, we're going to be forced to use the bullet. So let us try the ballot."

Because of his split with the Black Muslims, Malcolm believed his life might be in danger. "No one can get out without trouble," he confided. On February 21, 1965, while giving a speech in Harlem, the 39-year-old Malcolm X was shot and killed.

BLACK POWER In early June of 1966, tensions that had been building between SNCC and the other civil rights groups finally erupted in Mississippi. Here, James Meredith, the man who had integrated the University of Mississippi, set out on a 225-mile "walk against fear." Meredith planned to walk all the way from the Tennessee border to Jackson, but he was shot by a white racist and was too injured to continue.

Martin Luther King, Jr., of the SCLC, Floyd McKissick of CORE, and **Stokely Carmichael** of SNCC decided to lead their followers in a march to finish what Meredith had started. But it soon became apparent that SNCC and CORE members were quite militant, as they began to shout slogans similar to those of the black separatists who had followed Malcolm X. When King tried to rally the marchers with the refrain of "We Shall Overcome," many SNCC workers—bitter over the violence they'd suffered during Freedom Summer—began singing, "We shall overrun."

Police in Greenwood, Mississippi, arrested Carmichael for setting up a tent on the grounds of an all-black high school. When Carmichael showed up at a rally later, his face swollen from a beating, he electrified the crowd.

A PERSONAL VOICE STOKELY CARMICHAEL

"This is the twenty-seventh time I have been arrested—and I ain't going to jail no more! . . . We been saying freedom for six years—and we ain't got nothin'. What we're gonna start saying now is BLACK POWER."

—quoted in *The Civil Rights Movement: An Eyewitness History*

Stokely Carmichael (1968). The slogan "Black Power" became the battle-cry of militant civil rights activists. ▼

Black Power, Carmichael said, was a "call for black people to begin to define their own goals . . . [and] to lead their own organizations." King urged him to stop using the phrase because he believed it would provoke African Americans to violence and antagonize whites. Carmichael refused and urged SNCC to stop recruiting whites and to focus on developing African-American pride. D

MAIN IDEA

Analyzing Motives

D Why did some leaders of SCLC disagree with SNCC tactics?

BLACK PANTHERS Later that year, another development demonstrated the growing radicalism of some segments of the African-American community. In Oakland, California, in October 1966, Huey Newton and Bobby Seale founded a political party known as the **Black Panthers** to fight police brutality in the ghetto. The party advocated self-sufficiency for African-American communities, as well as full employment and decent housing. Members maintained that African Americans should be exempt from military service because an unfair number of black youths had been drafted to serve in Vietnam.

MAIN IDEA

Making Inferences
E) Why was the public reaction to the Black Panthers mixed?

Dressed in black leather jackets, black berets, and sunglasses, the Panthers preached self-defense and sold copies of the writings of Mao Zedong, leader of the Chinese Communist revolution. Several police shootouts occurred between the Panthers and police, and the FBI conducted numerous investigations of group members (sometimes using illegal tactics). Even so, many of the Panthers' activities—the establishment of daycare centers, free breakfast programs, free medical clinics, assistance to the homeless, and other services—won support in the ghettos. E)

1968—A Turning Point in Civil Rights

Martin Luther King, Jr., objected to the Black Power movement. He believed that preaching violence could only end in grief. King was planning to lead a Poor People's March on Washington, D.C. However, this time the people would have to march without him.

KING'S DEATH Dr. King seemed to sense that death was near. On April 3, 1968, he addressed a crowd in Memphis, where he had gone to support the city's striking garbage workers. "I may not get there with you but . . . we as a people will get to the Promised Land." He added, "I'm not fearing any man. Mine eyes have seen the glory of the coming of the Lord." The next day as King stood on his hotel balcony, James Earl Ray thrust a high-powered rifle out of a window and squeezed the trigger. King crumpled to the floor.

REACTIONS TO KING'S DEATH The night King died, Robert F. Kennedy was campaigning for the Democratic presidential nomination. Fearful that King's death would spark riots, Kennedy's advisers told him to cancel his appearance in an African-American neighborhood in Indianapolis. However, Kennedy attended anyway, making an impassioned plea for nonviolence.

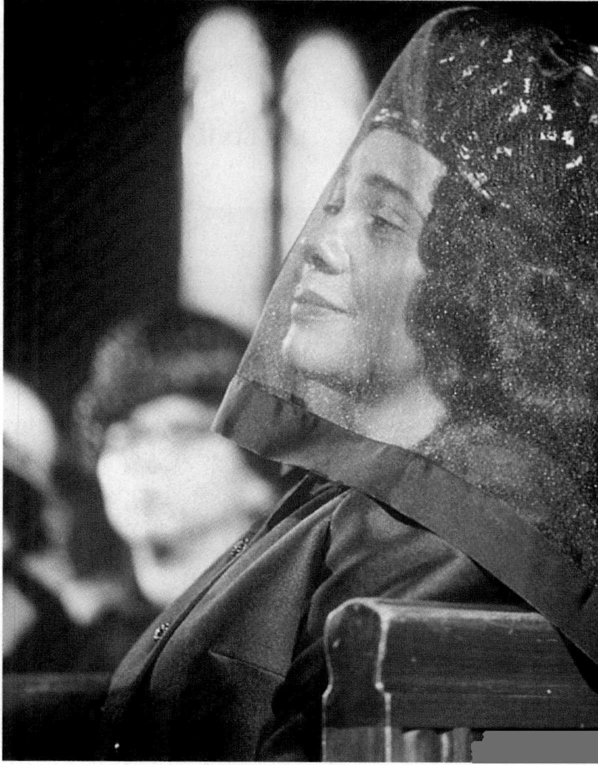

(above) **Coretta Scott King mourns her husband at his funeral service.** *(below)* **Robert F. Kennedy**

A PERSONAL VOICE ROBERT F. KENNEDY

"For those of you who are black—considering the evidence . . . that there were white people who were responsible—you can be filled with bitterness, with hatred, and a desire for revenge. We can move in that direction as a country, in great polarization—black people amongst black, white people amongst white, filled with hatred toward one another.

Or we can make an effort, as Martin Luther King did, to understand and comprehend, and to replace that violence, that stain of bloodshed that has spread across our land, with an effort to understand [with] compassion and love."

—"A Eulogy for Dr. Martin Luther King, Jr."

Vocabulary
polarization: separation into opposite camps

Despite Kennedy's plea, rage over King's death led to the worst urban rioting in United States history. Over 100 cities exploded in flames. The hardest-hit cities included Baltimore, Chicago, Kansas City, and Washington, D.C. Then in June 1968, Robert Kennedy himself was assassinated by a Jordanian immigrant who was angry over Kennedy's support of Israel.

Legacy of the Civil Rights Movement

On March 1, 1968, the **Kerner Commission,** which President Johnson had appointed to study the causes of urban violence, issued its 200,000-word report. In it, the panel named one main cause: white racism. Said the report: "This is our basic conclusion: Our nation is moving toward two societies, one black, one white—separate and unequal." The report called for the nation to create new jobs, construct new housing, and end de facto segregation in order to wipe out the destructive ghetto environment. However, the Johnson administration ignored many of the recommendations because of white opposition to such sweeping changes. So what had the civil rights movement accomplished?

CIVIL RIGHTS GAINS The civil rights movement ended de jure segregation by bringing about legal protection for the civil rights of all Americans. Congress passed the most important civil rights legislation since Reconstruction, including the **Civil Rights Act of 1968,** which ended discrimination in housing. After school segregation ended, the numbers of African Americans who finished high school and who went to college increased significantly. This in turn led to better jobs and business opportunities.

HISTORICAL SPOTLIGHT

SHIRLEY CHISHOLM

African-American women such as Shirley Chisholm exemplified the advances won in the civil rights movement. In 1968, Chisholm became the first African-American woman in the United States House of Representatives.

In the mid-1960s, Chisholm served in the New York state assembly, representing a district in New York City. While there, she supported programs to establish public day-care centers and provide unemployment insurance to domestic workers.

In 1972, Chisholm gained national prominence by running for the Democratic presidential nomination. Despite the fact that she never won more than 10% of the vote in the primaries, she controlled 152 delegates at the Democratic convention in Miami.

Another accomplishment of the civil rights movement was to give African Americans greater pride in their racial identity. Many African Americans adopted African-influenced styles and proudly displayed symbols of African history and culture. College students demanded new Black Studies programs so they could study African-American history and literature. In the entertainment world, the "color bar" was lowered as African Americans began to appear more frequently in movies and on television shows and commercials.

In addition, African Americans made substantial political gains. By 1970, an estimated two-thirds of eligible African Americans were registered to vote, and a significant increase in African-American elected officials resulted. The number of African Americans holding elected office grew from fewer than 100 in 1965 to more than 7,000 in 1992. Many civil rights activists went on to become political leaders, among them Reverend Jesse Jackson, who sought the Democratic nomination for president in 1984 and 1988; Vernon Jordan, who led voter-registration drives that enrolled about 2 million African Americans; and Andrew Young, who has served as UN ambassador and Atlanta's mayor. F

MAIN IDEA

Evaluating

F What were some accomplishments of the civil rights movement?

UNFINISHED WORK The civil rights movement was successful in changing many discriminatory laws. Yet as the 1960s turned to the 1970s, the challenges for the movement changed. The issues it confronted—housing and job discrimination, educational inequality, poverty, and racism—involved the difficult task of changing people's attitudes and behavior. Some of the proposed solutions, such as more tax monies spent in the inner cities and the forced busing of schoolchildren, angered some whites, who resisted further changes. Public support for the civil rights movement declined because some whites were frightened by the urban riots and the Black Panthers.

By 1990, the trend of whites fleeing the cities for the suburbs had reversed much of the progress toward school integration. In 1996–1997, 28 percent of blacks in the South and 50 percent of blacks in the Northeast were attending schools with fewer than 10 percent whites. Lack of jobs also remained a serious problem for African Americans, who had a poverty rate three times that of whites.

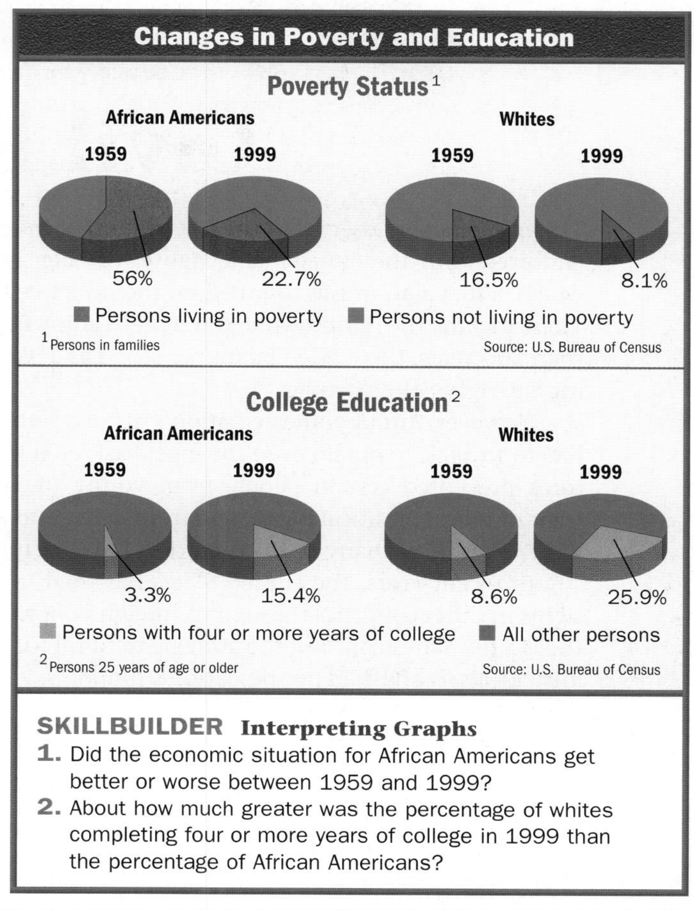

SKILLBUILDER Interpreting Graphs

1. Did the economic situation for African Americans get better or worse between 1959 and 1999?
2. About how much greater was the percentage of whites completing four or more years of college in 1999 than the percentage of African Americans?

To help equalize education and job opportunities, the government in the 1960s began to promote **affirmative action.** Affirmative-action programs involve making special efforts to hire or enroll groups that have suffered discrimination. Many colleges and almost all companies that do business with the federal government adopted such programs. But in the late 1970s, some people began to criticize affirmative-action programs as "reverse discrimination" that set minority hiring or enrollment quotas and deprived whites of opportunities. In the 1980s, Republican administrations eased affirmative-action requirements for some government contractors. The fate of affirmative action is still to be decided.

Vocabulary
quota: requirement that a certain number of positions are filled by minorities

Today, African Americans and whites interact in ways that could have only been imagined before the civil rights movement. In many respects, Dr. King's dream has been realized—yet much remains to be done.

SECTION 3 ASSESSMENT

1. **TERMS & NAMES** For each term or name, write a sentence explaining its significance.

- **de facto segregation**
- **de jure segregation**
- **Malcolm X**
- **Nation of Islam**
- **Stokely Carmichael**
- **Black Power**
- **Black Panthers**
- **Kerner Commission**
- **Civil Rights Act of 1968**
- **affirmative action**

MAIN IDEA

2. **TAKING NOTES**
Create a timeline of key events of the civil rights movement.

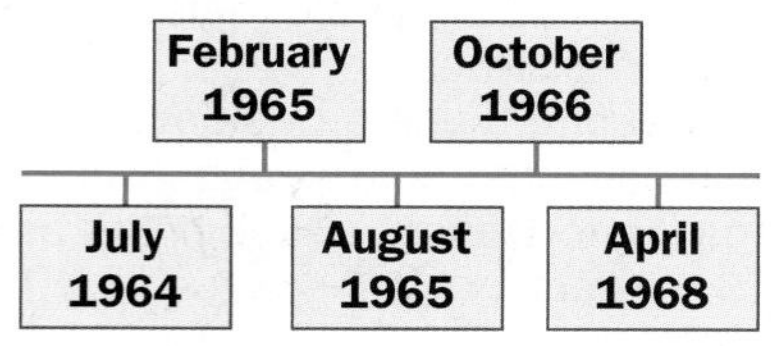

In your opinion, which event was most significant? Why?

CRITICAL THINKING

3. **ANALYZING ISSUES**
What factors contributed to the outbreak of violence in the fight for civil rights? **Think About:**
   - different leaders' approach to civil rights issues
   - living conditions in urban areas
   - de facto and de jure segregation

4. **COMPARING AND CONTRASTING**
Compare and contrast the civil rights strategies of Malcolm X and Martin Luther King, Jr. Whose strategies do you think were more effective? Explain and support your response.

Civil Rights

Thomas Jefferson asserted in the Declaration of Independence that "all men are created equal" and are endowed with the "unalienable rights" of "life, liberty, and the pursuit of happiness." With these words, a new nation was founded on the principle that citizens have certain fundamental civil rights. These include the right to vote, the right to enjoy freedom of speech and religion, and others. For more than 200 years, the United States has stood as a worldwide example of a country committed to securing the rights of its people.

However, throughout the nation's history, some Americans have had to struggle to obtain even the most basic civil rights. Laws or customs prevented certain people from voting freely, from speaking their minds on political issues, and from living and going where they wish. Over time, many of these barriers have been torn down.

In recent years, the United States has tried to promote human rights in other countries through its foreign policy. Even as it does so, the United States continues to struggle to fulfill for all Americans the lofty ideals established by the nation's founders.

1791

▼ BILL OF RIGHTS

During the Constitutional Convention, the question of a bill of rights arose, but none was included. During the process of ratification, many people argued that the Constitution needed to list the basic civil rights and liberties that the federal government could not take away from the people.

Accordingly, the nation ratified ten amendments to the Constitution—the Bill of Rights. It establishes such rights as freedom of speech, religion, and assembly, freedom of the press, and the right to a trial by jury. While these rights have been subject to interpretation over the nation's history, the Bill of Rights serves as the cornerstone of American democracy.

1868

THE FOURTEENTH AMENDMENT ▲

In the engraving above, a crowd of black and white Americans celebrates the passage of the Civil Rights Act of 1866. This act recognized the citizenship of African Americans and granted the same civil rights to all people born in the United States except Native Americans.

The Fourteenth Amendment, ratified two years later, made these changes part of the Constitution. The Amendment declared that states cannot deny anyone "equal protection of the laws" and bolstered the voting rights of all 21-year-old males, including former slaves.

Despite these provisions, African Americans and other groups would still struggle to claim their full rights as U.S. citizens.

1950s & 1960s

THE CIVIL RIGHTS MOVEMENT ▶

Despite the Fourteenth Amendment and later the Fifteenth Amendment, which forbade states from denying anyone the right to vote on account of race, African Americans continued to live as second-class citizens, especially in the South.

During the 1950s and 1960s, African Americans and other Americans led a powerful movement to fight for racial equality. The movement often met with strong resistance, such as in Birmingham, Alabama, where police sprayed demonstrators with high-pressure fire hoses *(right)*. Nevertheless, it succeeded in securing for African Americans the civil rights promised by the Constitution and the Declaration of Independence. The civil rights movement has also been the basis for other groups gaining equal rights, including other minorities, women, and people with disabilities.

1970s

HUMAN RIGHTS ▶

President Jimmy Carter considered human rights an important foreign policy issue. Human rights are what Americans think of as their civil rights, including the right to vote and to receive a fair trial. The Carter administration tried to encourage greater freedom abroad by taking such steps as cutting off military aid to countries with poor human rights records.

While these efforts met with mixed results, the issue of human rights has continued to influence U.S. foreign policy. In the 1990s, for example, the U.S. government tried to push China toward increasing human rights while keeping alive its trade ties with that country.

As a private citizen, Jimmy Carter has also continued to champion human rights causes. In 1982, he and his wife, Rosalynn, founded the Carter Center, whose programs seek to end human rights abuses and promote democracy worldwide.

THINKING CRITICALLY

CONNECT TO HISTORY

1. **Analyzing Issues** The Fourteenth and Fifteenth Amendments both provided for the voting rights of African Americans. Based on what you have read in the chapter, how were these rights denied African Americans? How were they finally secured?

SEE SKILLBUILDER HANDBOOK, PAGE R14.

CONNECT TO TODAY

2. **Writing About Rights** Have you or anyone you've known had their civil rights denied them in any way? Research a current-day instance of an alleged civil rights injustice. Write an account of the issue and share it with your class.

CLASSZONE.COM

CHAPTER 21 ASSESSMENT

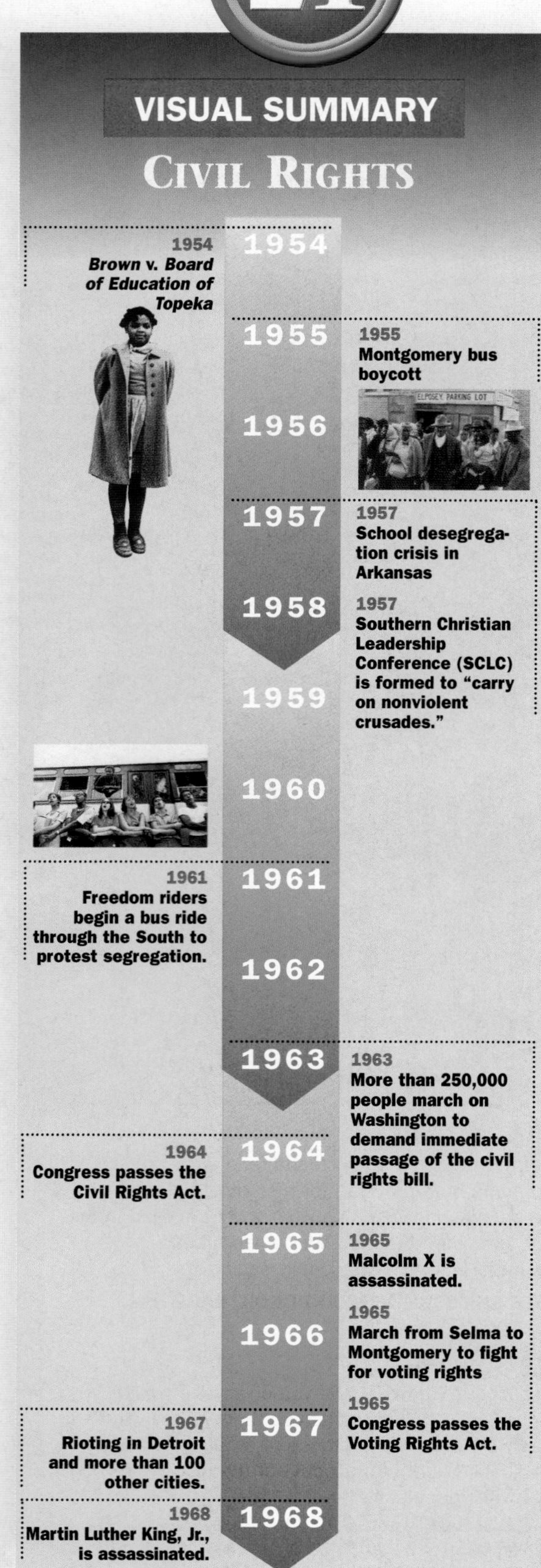
VISUAL SUMMARY
CIVIL RIGHTS
1954
1954
Brown v. Board of Education of Topeka
1955
1955
Montgomery bus boycott
1956
1957
1957
School desegregation crisis in Arkansas
1958
1957
Southern Christian Leadership Conference (SCLC) is formed to "carry on nonviolent crusades."
1959
1960
1961
1961
Freedom riders begin a bus ride through the South to protest segregation.
1962
1963
1963
More than 250,000 people march on Washington to demand immediate passage of the civil rights bill.
1964
1964
Congress passes the Civil Rights Act.
1965
1965
Malcolm X is assassinated.
1966
1965
March from Selma to Montgomery to fight for voting rights
1965
Congress passes the Voting Rights Act.
1967
1967
Rioting in Detroit and more than 100 other cities.
1968
1968
Martin Luther King, Jr., is assassinated.

TERMS & NAMES

For each term or name below, write a sentence explaining its connection to the civil rights movement.

1. *Brown* v. *Board of Education of Topeka*
2. Rosa Parks
3. Martin Luther King, Jr.
4. Student Nonviolent Coordinating Committee
5. freedom rider
6. Civil Rights Act of 1964
7. Fannie Lou Hamer
8. de facto segregation
9. Malcolm X
10. Black Power

MAIN IDEAS

Use your notes and the information in the chapter to answer the following questions.

Taking on Segregation *(pages 700–707)*

1. What were Jim Crow laws and how were they applied?
2. What were the roots of Martin Luther King, Jr.'s beliefs in nonviolent resistance?

The Triumphs of a Crusade *(pages 710–716)*

3. What was the significance of the federal court case won by James Meredith in 1962?
4. Cite three examples of violence committed between 1962 and 1964 against African Americans and civil rights activists.

Challenges and Changes in the Movement *(pages 717–723)*

5. What were some of the key beliefs advocated by Malcolm X?
6. Why did some civil rights leaders urge Stokely Carmichael to stop using the slogan "Black Power"?

THINKING CRITICALLY

1. **USING YOUR NOTES** On your own paper, draw a cluster diagram like the one shown below. Then, fill it in with four events from the civil rights movement that were broadcast on nationwide television and that you find the most compelling.

example:
example:
TV Coverage of Civil Rights Movement
example:
example:

2. **HISTORICAL PERSPECTIVE** Overall, would you characterize the civil rights struggle as a unified or disunified movement? Explain.

3. **INTERPRETING MAPS** Look carefully at the map of U.S. school segregation on page 701. What regional differences do you think spurred civil rights activists to target the South before the North?

Standardized Test Practice

Use the diagram and your knowledge of United States history to answer question 1.

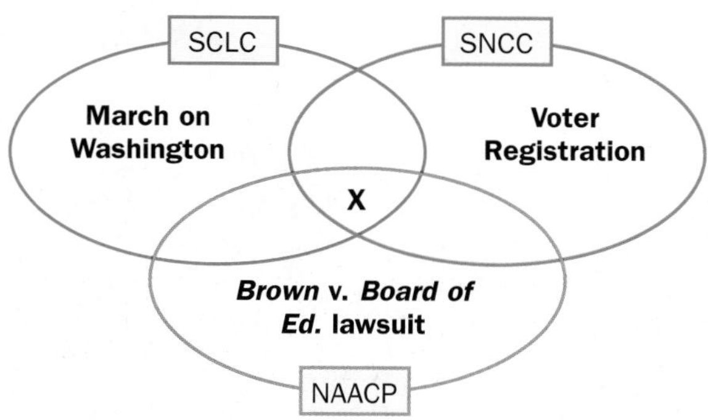

1. The Venn diagram is partially filled in with the strategies of various civil rights groups in the 1960s. Which of the following could be added to the area of the diagram labeled **X**?

   A provide social services to the needy

   B boycotts

   C nonviolent demonstrations

   D armed self-defense

Use the quotation as well as your knowledge of United States history to answer question 2.

> **"An illegal attack, an unjust attack, and an immoral attack can be made against you by any one. Just because a person has on a [police] uniform does not give him the right to come and shoot up your neighborhood. No, this is not right, and my suggestion would be that as long as the police department doesn't use those methods in white neighborhoods, they shouldn't come . . . and use them in our neighborhood. . . ."**
>
> —MALCOLM X, "Prospects for Freedom in 1965"

2. Which of the following events justifies Malcolm X's concerns about police brutality?

   F the Rosa Parks incident in 1955

   G the 1963 Birmingham demonstrations

   H the desegregation of Little Rock's Central High in 1957

   J the first sit-ins in 1942

ADDITIONAL TEST PRACTICE, pages S1–S33.

CLASSZONE.COM

ALTERNATIVE ASSESSMENT

1. **INTERACT WITH HISTORY** Recall your discussion of the question on page 699:

What rights are worth fighting for?

Choose one participant in the civil rights movement. From that person's perspective, write a speech in which you evaluate your role in the movement. Consider these questions:

- What civil rights did you work for?
- Why are these rights important?
- How successful were you?
- What were the costs of your struggle?

2. **VIDEO** **LEARNING FROM MEDIA** View the *American Stories* video, "Justice in Montgomery." Discuss the following questions with a small group of classmates. Then do the activity.

- What role did Jo Ann Gibson Robinson and the African-American women of Montgomery play in the boycott?
- What responsibilities do you think individuals have to stop injustice?

Cooperative Learning Activity You have just seen an account of the Montgomery bus boycott through the eyes of one person, Jo Ann Gibson Robinson. With your group, decide how you would teach people about the boycott—from what perspective and with what materials. Create a multimedia presentation to give to the class.

CHAPTER 22 THE VIETNAM WAR YEARS

U.S. troops on patrol with helicopter support in Vietnam, 1965.

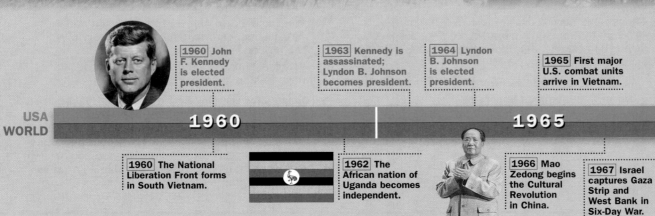

1960 John F. Kennedy is elected president.

1963 Kennedy is assassinated; Lyndon B. Johnson becomes president.

1964 Lyndon B. Johnson is elected president.

1965 First major U.S. combat units arrive in Vietnam.

USA / WORLD — 1960 — 1965

1960 The National Liberation Front forms in South Vietnam.

1962 The African nation of Uganda becomes independent.

1966 Mao Zedong begins the Cultural Revolution in China.

1967 Israel captures Gaza Strip and West Bank in Six-Day War.

INTERACT WITH HISTORY

In 1965, America's fight against communism has spread to Southeast Asia, where the United States is becoming increasingly involved in another country's civil war. Unable to claim victory, U.S. generals call for an increase in the number of combat troops. Facing a shortage of volunteers, the president expands the draft.

Who should be exempt from the draft?

Examine the Issues

- Should people who believe the war is wrong be forced to fight?
- Should people with special skills be exempt?
- How can a draft be made fair?

RESEARCH LINKS CLASSZONE.COM

Visit the Chapter 22 links for more information about The Vietnam War Years.

1968 Martin Luther King, Jr., and Robert Kennedy are assassinated.

1968 Richard M. Nixon is elected president.

1969 U.S. troops begin their withdrawal from Vietnam.

1970 Ohio National Guard kills four students at Kent State University.

1972 Richard M. Nixon is reelected.

1973 United States signs cease-fire with North Vietnam and Vietcong.

1974 Gerald R. Ford becomes president after Richard M. Nixon resigns.

1970

1975

1972 Ferdinand Marcos declares martial law in the Philippines.

1975 Communists capture Saigon; South Vietnam surrenders.

Moving Toward Conflict

MAIN IDEA

To stop the spread of communism in Southeast Asia, the United States used its military to support South Vietnam.

WHY IT MATTERS NOW

The United States' support role in Vietnam began what would become America's longest and most controversial war in its history.

Terms & Names

- **Ho Chi Minh**
- **Vietminh**
- **domino theory**
- **Dien Bien Phu**
- **Geneva Accords**
- **Ngo Dinh Diem**
- **Vietcong**
- **Ho Chi Minh Trail**
- **Tonkin Gulf Resolution**

One American's Story

▲ Lieutenant Colonel A. Peter Dewey

On the morning of September 26, 1945, Lieutenant Colonel A. Peter Dewey was on his way to the Saigon airport in Vietnam. Only 28, Dewey served in the Office of Strategic Services, the chief intelligence-gathering body of the U.S. military and forerunner of the Central Intelligence Agency. Dewey was sent to assess what was becoming an explosive situation in Vietnam, a Southeast Asian country that had recently been freed from Japanese rule as a result of the allied victory in World War II. (See map on page 733.)

Before the war, France had ruled Vietnam and the surrounding countries; now it sought—with British aid—to regain control of the region. The Vietnamese had resisted Japanese occupation; now they were preparing to fight the French. Dewey saw nothing but disaster in France's plan. "Cochinchina [southern Vietnam] is burning," he reported, "the French and British are finished here, and we [the United States] ought to clear out of Southeast Asia."

On his way to the airport, Dewey encountered a roadblock staffed by Vietnamese soldiers and shouted at them in French. Presumably mistaking him for a French soldier, the guards shot him in the head. Thus, A. Peter Dewey, whose body was never recovered, was the first American to die in Vietnam.

Unfortunately, Dewey would not be the last. As Vietnam's independence effort came under communist influence, the United States grew increasingly concerned about the small country's future. Eventually, America would fight a war to halt the spread of communism in Vietnam. The war would claim the lives of almost 60,000 Americans and more than 2 million Vietnamese. It also would divide the American nation as no other event since the Civil War.

America Supports France in Vietnam

America's involvement in Vietnam began in 1950, during the French Indochina War, the name given to France's attempt to reestablish its rule in Vietnam after World War II. Seeking to strengthen its ties with France and to help fight the spread of communism, the United States provided the French with massive economic and military support.

Vocabulary
peasant: a member of the class of agricultural laborers

FRENCH RULE IN VIETNAM From the late 1800s until World War II, France ruled most of Indochina, including Vietnam, Laos, and Cambodia. French colonists, who built plantations on peasant land and extracted rice and rubber for their own profit, encountered growing unrest among the Vietnamese peasants. French rulers reacted harshly by restricting freedom of speech and assembly and by jailing many Vietnamese nationalists. These measures failed to curb all dissent, and opposition continued to grow.

Many Vietnamese revolutionaries fled to China, where in 1924 they began to be organized under the leadership of **Ho Chi Minh.** In 1930 Ho helped to create the Indochinese Communist Party, and throughout the 1930s Ho continued to orchestrate Vietnam's growing independence movement from exile in the Soviet Union and China.

In 1940 the Japanese took control of Vietnam. The next year, Ho Chi Minh returned home and helped form the **Vietminh,** an organization whose goal it was to win Vietnam's independence from foreign rule. When the Allied defeat of Japan in August 1945 forced the Japanese to leave Vietnam, that goal suddenly seemed a reality. On September 2, 1945, Ho Chi Minh stood in the middle of a huge crowd in the northern city of Hanoi and declared Vietnam an independent nation.

KEY PLAYER

HO CHI MINH
1890–1969

Born Nguyen Tat Thanh to a poor Vietnamese family, Ho Chi Minh (which means "He Who Enlightens") found work as a cook on a French steamship. This allowed him to visit such cities as Boston and New York.

Ho Chi Minh based the phrasing of the Vietnamese Declaration of Independence on the U.S. Declaration of Independence. His admiration for the United States turned to disappointment, however, after the government chose to support France rather than his nationalist movement.

The Communist ruler's name lived on after his death in 1969. In 1975, the North Vietnamese Army conquered South Vietnam and changed the name of the South's capital from Saigon to Ho Chi Minh City.

FRANCE BATTLES THE VIETMINH France, however, had no intention of relinquishing its former colony. French troops moved back into Vietnam by the end of 1945, eventually regaining control of the cities and the country's southern half. Ho Chi Minh vowed to fight from the North to liberate the South from French control. "If ever the tiger pauses," Ho had said, referring to the Vietminh, "the elephant [France] will impale him on his mighty tusks. But the tiger will not pause, and the elephant will die of exhaustion and loss of blood."

In 1950, the United States entered the Vietnam struggle—despite A. Peter Dewey's warnings. That year, President Truman sent nearly $15 million in economic aid to France. Over the next four years, the United States paid for much of France's war, pumping nearly $1 billion into the effort to defeat a man America had once supported. Ironically, during World War II, the United States had forged an alliance with Ho Chi Minh, supplying him with aid to resist the Japanese. But by 1950, the United States had come to view its one-time ally as a communist aggressor. **A**

MAIN IDEA
Synthesizing
A How and why did the United States support France's Vietnam War efforts?

THE VIETMINH DRIVE OUT THE FRENCH Upon entering the White House in 1953, President Eisenhower continued the policy of supplying aid to the French war effort. By this time, the United States had settled for a stalemate with the communists in Korea, which only stiffened America's resolve to halt the spread of communism elsewhere. During a news conference in 1954, Eisenhower explained the **domino theory,** in which he likened the countries on the brink of communism to a row of dominoes waiting to fall one after the other. "You have a row of dominoes set up," the president said. "You knock over the first one, and what will happen to the last one is the certainty that it will go over very quickly."

Despite massive U.S. aid, however, the French could not retake Vietnam. They were forced to surrender in May of 1954, when the Vietminh overran the French outpost at **Dien Bien Phu,** in northwestern Vietnam.

From May through July 1954, the countries of France, Great Britain, the Soviet Union, the United States, China, Laos, and Cambodia met in Geneva, Switzerland, with the Vietminh and with South Vietnam's anticommunist nationalists to hammer out a peace agreement. The **Geneva Accords** temporarily divided Vietnam along the 17th parallel. The Communists and their leader, Ho Chi Minh, controlled North Vietnam from the capital of Hanoi. The anticommunist nationalists controlled South Vietnam from the capital and southern port city of Saigon. An election to unify the country was called for in 1956.

The United States Steps In

In the wake of France's retreat, the United States took a more active role in halting the spread of communism in Vietnam. Wading deeper into the country's affairs, the Eisenhower and the Kennedy administrations provided economic and military aid to South Vietnam's non-Communist regime.

DIEM CANCELS ELECTIONS Although he directed a brutal and repressive regime, Ho Chi Minh won popular support in the North by breaking up large estates and redistributing land to peasants. Moreover, his years of fighting the Japanese and French had made him a national hero. Recognizing Ho Chi Minh's widespread popularity, South Vietnam's president, **Ngo Dinh Diem** (ngō′ dĭn′ dē-ĕm′), a strong anti-Communist, refused to take part in the countrywide election of 1956. The United States also sensed that a countrywide election might spell victory for Ho Chi Minh and supported canceling elections. The Eisenhower administration promised military aid and training to Diem in return for a stable reform government in the South. B

MAIN IDEA

Analyzing Motives

B Why did the United States support canceling elections?

Diem, however, failed to hold up his end of the bargain. He ushered in a corrupt government that suppressed opposition of any kind and offered little or no land distribution to peasants. In addition, Diem, a devout Catholic, angered the country's majority Buddhist population by restricting Buddhist practices.

Background

The Buddhist religion is based on the teachings of Siddhartha Gautama, also known as Shakyamuni, an Indian mystic who believed that spiritual enlightenment could be obtained through right conduct, meditation, and wisdom.

By 1957, a Communist opposition group in the South, known as the **Vietcong,** had begun attacks on the Diem government, assassinating thousands of South Vietnamese government officials. Although the political arm of the group would later be called the National Liberation Front (NLF), the United States continued to refer to the fighters as the Vietcong.

The Vietcong saw the United States and South Vietnam as oppressors. This Vietcong propaganda poster reads, "Better death than slavery."

Ho Chi Minh supported the group, and in 1959 began supplying arms to the Vietcong via a network of paths along the borders of Vietnam, Laos, and Cambodia that became known as the **Ho Chi Minh Trail.** (See map on page 733.) As the fighters stepped up their surprise attacks, or guerrilla tactics, South Vietnam grew more unstable. The Eisenhower administration took little action, however, deciding to "sink or swim with Ngo Dinh Diem."

KENNEDY AND VIETNAM The Kennedy administration, which entered the White House in 1961, also chose initially to "swim" with Diem. Wary of accusations that Democrats were "soft" on communism, President Kennedy increased financial aid to Diem's teetering regime and sent thousands of military advisers to help train South Vietnamese troops. By the end of 1963, 16,000 U.S. military personnel were in South Vietnam.

Meanwhile, Diem's popularity plummeted because of ongoing corruption and his failure to respond to calls for land reform. To combat the growing Vietcong presence in the South's countryside, the Diem administration initiated the strategic hamlet program, which meant moving all villagers to protected areas.

After parachuting into the mountains north of Dien Bien Phu, South Vietnamese troops await orders from French officers in 1953.

Rivers serve as places to bathe and wash clothing.

The swampy terrain of South Vietnam made for difficult and dangerous fighting. This 1961 photograph shows South Vietnamese Army troops in combat operations against Vietcong guerrillas.

GEOGRAPHY SKILLBUILDER

1. **Movement** Through which countries did the Ho Chi Minh Trail pass?
2. **Location** How might North Vietnam's location have enabled it to get aid from its ally, China?

A Buddhist monk sets himself on fire in a busy Saigon intersection in 1963 as a protest against the Diem regime. ▶

Many Vietnamese deeply resented being moved from their home villages where they had lived for generations and where ancestors were buried.

Diem also intensified his attack on Buddhism. Fed up with continuing Buddhist demonstrations, the South Vietnamese ruler imprisoned and killed hundreds of Buddhist clerics and destroyed their temples. To protest, several Buddhist monks and nuns publicly burned themselves to death. Horrified, American officials urged Diem to stop the persecutions, but Diem refused. **C**

It had become clear that for South Vietnam to remain stable, Diem would have to go. On November 1, 1963, a U.S.-supported military coup toppled Diem's regime. Against Kennedy's wishes, Diem was assassinated. A few weeks later, Kennedy, too, fell to an assassin's bullet. The United States presidency—along with the growing crisis in Vietnam—now belonged to Lyndon B. Johnson.

MAIN IDEA

Forming Generalizations

C Why was the Diem regime unpopular?

Vocabulary

coup: a sudden appropriation of leadership; a takeover

President Johnson Expands the Conflict

Shortly before his death, Kennedy had announced his intent to withdraw U.S. forces from South Vietnam. "In the final analysis, it's their war," he declared. Whether Kennedy would have withdrawn from Vietnam remains a matter of debate. However, Lyndon Johnson escalated the nation's role in Vietnam and eventually began what would become America's longest war.

THE SOUTH GROWS MORE UNSTABLE Diem's death brought more chaos to South Vietnam. A string of military leaders attempted to lead the country, but each regime was more unstable and inefficient than Diem's had been. Meanwhile, the Vietcong's influence in the countryside steadily grew.

President Johnson believed that a communist takeover of South Vietnam would be disastrous. Johnson, like Kennedy, was particularly sensitive to being perceived as "soft" on communism. "If I . . . let the communists take over South Vietnam," Johnson said, "then . . . my nation would be seen as an appeaser and we would . . . find it impossible to accomplish anything . . . anywhere on the entire globe."

THE TONKIN GULF RESOLUTION On August 2, 1964, a North Vietnamese patrol boat fired a torpedo at an American destroyer, the USS *Maddox*, which was patrolling in the Gulf of Tonkin off the North Vietnamese coast. The torpedo missed its target, but the *Maddox* returned fire and inflicted heavy damage on the patrol boat.

"All the News That's Fit to Print"

The New York Times.

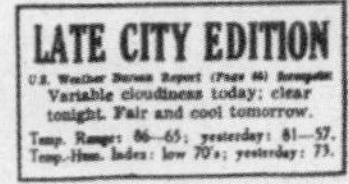
LATE CITY EDITION

VOL. CXIII—No. 38,910. NEW YORK, WEDNESDAY, AUGUST 5, 1964. TEN CENTS

U.S. PLANES ATTACK NORTH VIETNAM BASES; PRESIDENT ORDERS 'LIMITED' RETALIATION AFTER COMMUNISTS' PT BOATS RENEW RAIDS

▲ **A 1964 newspaper headline announces the U.S. military's reaction to the Gulf of Tonkin incident.**

Two days later, the *Maddox* and another destroyer were again off the North Vietnamese coast. In spite of bad weather that could affect visibility, the crew reported enemy torpedoes, and the American destroyers began firing. The crew of the *Maddox* later declared, however, that they had neither seen nor heard hostile gunfire.

The alleged attack on the U.S. ships prompted President Johnson to launch bombing strikes on North Vietnam. He asked Congress for powers to take "all necessary measures to repel any armed attack against the forces of the United States and to prevent further aggression." Congress approved Johnson's request, with only two senators voting against it, and adopted the **Tonkin Gulf Resolution** on August 7. While not a declaration of war, it granted Johnson broad military powers in Vietnam.

Johnson did not tell Congress or the American people that the United States had been leading secret raids against North Vietnam. The *Maddox* had been in the Gulf of Tonkin to collect information for these raids. Furthermore, Johnson had prepared the resolution months beforehand and was only waiting for the chance to push it through Congress.

In February of 1965, President Johnson used his newly granted powers. In response to a Vietcong attack that killed eight Americans, Johnson unleashed "Operation Rolling Thunder," the first sustained bombing of North Vietnam. In March of that year the first American combat troops began arriving in South Vietnam. By June, more than 50,000 U.S. soldiers were battling the Vietcong. The Vietnam War had become Americanized. D

MAIN IDEA

Developing Historical Perspective

D How did the Tonkin Gulf Resolution lead to greater U.S. involvement in the Vietnam War?

SECTION 1 ASSESSMENT

1. **TERMS & NAMES** For each term or name, write a sentence explaining its significance.
   - **Ho Chi Minh**
   - **Vietminh**
   - **domino theory**
   - **Dien Bien Phu**
   - **Geneva Accords**
   - **Ngo Dinh Diem**
   - **Vietcong**
   - **Ho Chi Minh Trail**
   - **Tonkin Gulf Resolution**

MAIN IDEA

2. **TAKING NOTES**
   In a chart like the one below, cite the Vietnam policy for each of the following presidents: Truman, Eisenhower, Kennedy, and Johnson.

President	Vietnam Policy

Choose one of the four presidents and explain his goals in Vietnam.

CRITICAL THINKING

3. **MAKING INFERENCES**
   How did the United States become more involved in the war? Explain your answer in a short paragraph.

4. **SYNTHESIZING**
   In what ways was America's support of the Diem government a conflict of interests? Cite examples to support your answer.

5. **EVALUATING**
   Do you think Congress was justified in passing the Tonkin Gulf Resolution? Use details from the text to support your response.
   Think About:
   - the questionable report of torpedo attacks on two U.S. destroyers
   - the powers that the resolution would give the president
   - the fact that the resolution was not a declaration of war

U.S. Involvement and Escalation

MAIN IDEA	WHY IT MATTERS NOW	Terms & Names
The United States sent troops to fight in Vietnam, but the war quickly turned into a stalemate.	**Since Vietnam, Americans are more aware of the positive and negative effects of using U.S. troops in foreign conflicts.**	**•Robert McNamara •Dean Rusk •William Westmoreland •Army of the Republic of Vietnam (ARVN) •napalm •Agent Orange •search-and-destroy mission •credibility gap**

One American's Story

Tim O'Brien is a novelist who has written several books about his experience in Vietnam and its lasting effects. Drafted at the age of 21, O'Brien was sent to Vietnam in August 1968. He spent the first seven months of his nearly two-year duty patrolling the fields outside of Chu Lai, a seacoast city in South Vietnam. O'Brien described one of the more nerve-racking experiences of the war: walking through the fields and jungles, many of which were filled with land mines and booby traps.

▲ Vietnam's terrain was often treacherous, such as the thick jungles and rivers these U.S. soldiers encountered in 1966.

A PERSONAL VOICE TIM O'BRIEN

"You do some thinking. You hallucinate. You look ahead a few paces and wonder what your legs will resemble if there is more to the earth in that spot than silicates and nitrogen. Will the pain be unbearable? Will you scream and fall silent? Will you be afraid to look at your own body, afraid of the sight of your own red flesh and white bone? . . .

It is not easy to fight this sort of self-defeating fear, but you try. You decide to be ultra-careful—the hard-nosed realistic approach. You try to second-guess the mine. Should you put your foot to that flat rock or the clump of weeds to its rear? Paddy dike or water? You wish you were Tarzan, able to swing on the vines. You trace the footprints of the men to your front. You give up when he curses you for following too closely; better one man dead than two."

—quoted in *A Life in a Year: The American Infantryman in Vietnam 1965–1972*

Deadly traps were just some of the obstacles that U.S. troops faced. As the infiltration of American ground troops into Vietnam failed to score a quick victory, a mostly supportive U.S. population began to question its government's war policy.

Johnson Increases U.S. Involvement

Much of the nation supported Lyndon Johnson's determination to contain communism in Vietnam. In the years following 1965, President Johnson began sending large numbers of American troops to fight alongside the South Vietnamese.

STRONG SUPPORT FOR CONTAINMENT Even after Congress had approved the Tonkin Gulf Resolution, President Johnson opposed sending U.S. ground troops to Vietnam. Johnson's victory in the 1964 presidential election was due in part to charges that his Republican opponent, Barry Goldwater, was an anti-Communist who might push the United States into war with the Soviet Union. In contrast to Goldwater's heated, warlike language, Johnson's speeches were more moderate, yet he spoke determinedly about containing communism. He declared he was "not about to send American boys 9 or 10,000 miles away from home to do what Asian boys ought to be doing for themselves."

However, in March of 1965, that is precisely what the president did. Working closely with his foreign-policy advisers, particularly Secretary of Defense **Robert McNamara** and Secretary of State **Dean Rusk,** President Johnson began dispatching tens of thousands of U.S. soldiers to fight in Vietnam. Some Americans viewed Johnson's decision as contradictory to his position during the presidential campaign. However, most saw the president as following an established and popular policy of confronting communism anywhere in the world. Congress, as well as the American public, strongly supported Johnson's strategy. A 1965 poll showed that 61 percent of Americans supported the U.S. policy in Vietnam, while only 24 percent opposed.

There were dissenters within the Johnson administration, too. In October of 1964, Undersecretary of State George Ball had argued against escalation, warning that "once on the tiger's back, we cannot be sure of picking the place to dismount." However, the president's closest advisers strongly urged escalation, believing the defeat of communism in Vietnam to be of vital importance to the future of America and the world. Dean Rusk stressed this view in a 1965 memo to President Johnson. **A**

MAIN IDEA

Contrasting

A What differing opinions did Johnson's advisers have about Vietnam?

A PERSONAL VOICE DEAN RUSK

"The integrity of the U.S. commitment is the principal pillar of peace throughout the world. If that commitment becomes unreliable, the communist world would draw conclusions that would lead to our ruin and *almost certainly to a catastrophic war.* So long as the South Vietnamese are prepared to fight for themselves, we cannot abandon them without disaster to peace and to our interests throughout the world."

—quoted in *In Retrospect*

THE TROOP BUILDUP ACCELERATES By the end of 1965, the U.S. government had sent more than 180,000 Americans to Vietnam. The American commander in South Vietnam, General **William Westmoreland,** continued to request more troops. Westmoreland, a West Point graduate who had served in World War II and Korea, was less than impressed with the fighting ability of the South Vietnamese Army, or the **Army of the Republic of Vietnam (ARVN).** The ARVN "cannot stand up to this pressure without substantial U.S. combat support on the ground," the general reported. "The only possible response is the aggressive deployment of U.S. troops." Throughout the early years of the war, the Johnson administration complied with Westmoreland's requests; by 1967, the number of U.S. troops in Vietnam had climbed to about 500,000.

KEY PLAYER

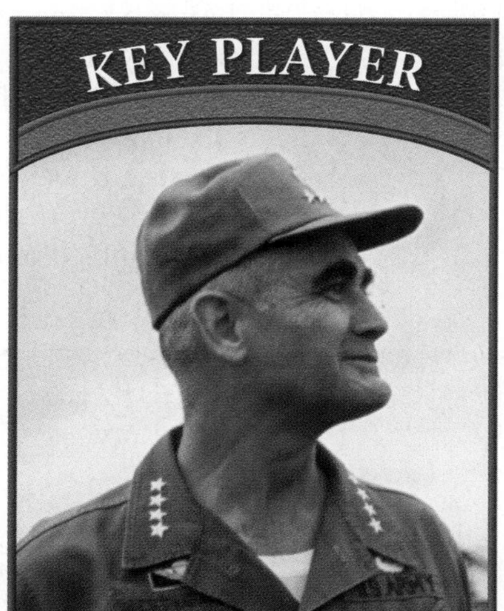

GENERAL WILLIAM WESTMORELAND (1914–2005)

General Westmoreland retired from the military in 1972, but even in retirement, he could not escape the Vietnam War.

In 1982, CBS-TV aired a documentary entitled *The Uncounted Enemy: A Vietnam Deception.* The report, viewed by millions, asserted that Westmoreland and the Pentagon had deceived the U.S. government about the enemy's size and strength during 1967 and 1968 to make it appear that U.S. forces were winning the war.

Westmoreland, claiming he was the victim of "distorted, false, and specious information . . . derived by sinister deception," filed a $120 million libel suit against CBS. The suit was eventually settled, with both parties issuing statements pledging mutual respect. CBS, however, stood by its story.

Fighting in the Jungle

The United States entered the war in Vietnam believing that its superior weaponry would lead it to victory over the Vietcong. However, the jungle terrain and the enemy's guerrilla tactics soon turned the war into a frustrating stalemate.

AN ELUSIVE ENEMY Because the Vietcong lacked the high-powered weaponry of the American forces, they used hit-and-run and ambush tactics, as well as a keen knowledge of the jungle terrain, to their advantage. Moving secretly in and out of the general population, the Vietcong destroyed the notion of a traditional front line by attacking U.S. troops in both the cities and the countryside. Because some of the enemy lived amidst the civilian population, it was difficult for U.S. troops to discern friend from foe. A woman selling soft drinks to U.S. soldiers might be a Vietcong spy. A boy standing on the corner might be ready to throw a grenade.

Adding to the Vietcong's elusiveness was a network of elaborate tunnels that allowed them to withstand airstrikes and to launch surprise attacks and then disappear quickly. Connecting villages throughout the countryside, the tunnels became home to many guerrilla fighters. "The more the Americans tried to drive us away from our land, the more we burrowed into it," recalled Major Nguyen Quot of the Vietcong Army.

In addition, the terrain was laced with countless booby traps and land mines. Because the exact location of the Vietcong was often unknown, U.S. troops laid land mines throughout the jungle. The Vietcong also laid their own traps, and disassembled and reused U.S. mines. American soldiers marching through South

Tunnels of the Vietcong

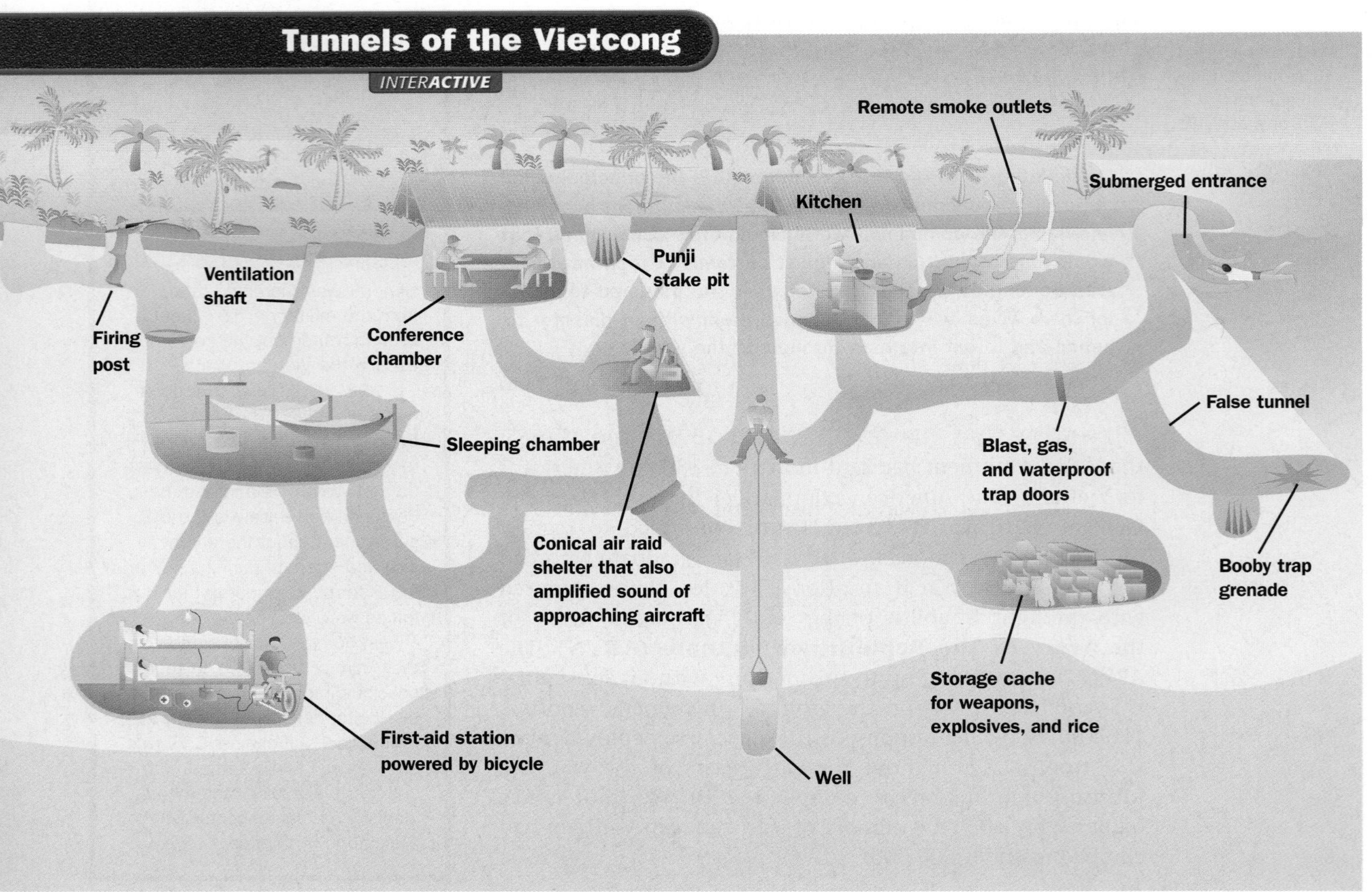

Vietnam's jungles and rice paddies not only dealt with sweltering heat and leeches but also had to be cautious of every step. In a 1969 letter to his sister, Specialist Fourth Class Salvador Gonzalez described the tragic result from an unexploded U.S. bomb that the North Vietnamese Army had rigged. B

MAIN IDEA

Drawing Conclusions
B Why did the U.S. forces have difficulty fighting the Vietcong?

A PERSONAL VOICE SALVADOR GONZALEZ

"Two days ago 4 guys got killed and about 15 wounded from the first platoon. Our platoon was 200 yards away on top of a hill. One guy was from Floral Park [in New York City]. He had five days left to go [before being sent home]. He was standing on a 250-lb. bomb that a plane had dropped and didn't explode. So the NVA [North Vietnamese Army] wired it up. Well, all they found was a piece of his wallet."

—quoted in *Dear America: Letters Home from Vietnam*

A FRUSTRATING WAR OF ATTRITION Westmoreland's strategy for defeating the Vietcong was to destroy their morale through a war of attrition, or the gradual wearing down of the enemy by continuous harassment. Introducing the concept of the body count, or the tracking of Vietcong killed in battle, the general believed that as the number of Vietcong dead rose, the guerrillas would inevitably surrender.

However, the Vietcong had no intention of quitting their fight. Despite the growing number of casualties and the relentless pounding from U.S. bombers, the Vietcong—who received supplies from China and the Soviet Union—remained defiant. Defense Secretary McNamara confessed his frustration to a reporter in 1966: "If I had thought they would take this punishment and fight this well, . . . I would have thought differently at the start."

LAND MINES

Around 3.5 million armed mines remain in Vietnam, causing 160 civilian casualties each month. Worldwide, more than 25,000 civilians are killed or maimed by land mines each year.

The 1997 Mine Ban Treaty bans production and use of antipersonnel mines worldwide. As of 2000, 139 nations had agreed to the treaty, with the notable exceptions of the United States, Russia, and China. In 1998, President Clinton declared that the United States would sign the treaty by 2006, if "suitable alternatives" to land mines had been developed, and asked the military to begin working toward this goal.

The United States has been a big financial contributor to humanitarian land mine clearance. Contributions in 2003–2004 are expected to reach $105 million.

General Westmoreland would say later that the United States never lost a battle in Vietnam. Whether or not the general's words were true, they underscored the degree to which America misunderstood its foe. The United States viewed the war strictly as a military struggle; the Vietcong saw it as a battle for their very existence, and they were ready to pay any price for victory. C

MAIN IDEA

Making Inferences
C In what way did the United States underestimate the Vietcong?

THE BATTLE FOR "HEARTS AND MINDS" Another key part of the American strategy was to keep the Vietcong from winning the support of South Vietnam's rural population. Edward G. Lansdale, who helped found the fighting unit known as the U.S. Army Special Forces, or Green Berets, stressed the plan's importance. "Just remember this. Communist guerrillas hide among the people. If you win the people over to your side, the communist guerrillas have no place to hide."

The campaign to win the "hearts and minds" of the South Vietnamese villagers proved more difficult than imagined. For instance, in their attempt to expose Vietcong tunnels and hideouts, U.S. planes dropped **napalm,** a gasoline-based bomb that set fire to the jungle. They also sprayed **Agent Orange,** a leaf-killing toxic chemical. The saturation use of these weapons often wounded civilians and left villages and their surroundings in ruins. Years later, many would blame Agent Orange for cancers in Vietnamese civilians and American veterans.

U.S. soldiers conducted **search-and-destroy missions,** uprooting civilians with suspected ties to the Vietcong, killing their livestock, and burning villages. Many villagers fled into the cities or refugee camps, creating by 1967 more than 3 million refugees in the South. The irony of the strategy was summed up in February 1968 by a U.S. major whose forces had just leveled the town of Ben Tre: "We had to destroy the town in order to save it."

▲ A soldier with the 61st Infantry Division wears symbols of both war and peace on his chest.

SINKING MORALE The frustrations of guerrilla warfare, the brutal jungle conditions, and the failure to make substantial headway against the enemy took their toll on the U.S. troops' morale. Philip Caputo, a marine lieutenant in Vietnam who later wrote several books about the war, summarized the soldiers' growing disillusionment: "When we marched into the rice paddies . . . we carried, along with our packs and rifles, the implicit convictions that the Vietcong could be quickly beaten. We kept the packs and rifles; the convictions, we lost."

As the war continued, American morale dropped steadily. Many soldiers, required by law to fight a war they did not support, turned to alcohol, marijuana, and other drugs. Low morale even led a few soldiers to murder their superior officers. Morale would worsen during the later years of the war when soldiers realized they were fighting even as their government was negotiating a withdrawal. **D**

MAIN IDEA

Analyzing Causes

D What factors led to the low morale of U.S. troops?

Another obstacle was the continuing corruption and instability of the South Vietnamese government. Nguyen Cao Ky, a flamboyant air marshal, led the government from 1965 to 1967. Ky ignored U.S. pleas to retire in favor of an elected civilian government. Mass demonstrations began, and by May of 1966, Buddhist monks and nuns were once again burning themselves in protest against the South Vietnamese government. South Vietnam was fighting a civil war within a civil war, leaving U.S. officials confused and angry.

FULFILLING A DUTY Most American soldiers, however, firmly believed in their cause—to halt the spread of communism. They took patriotic pride in fulfilling their duty, just as their fathers had done in World War II.

Most American soldiers fought courageously. Particularly heroic were the thousands of soldiers who endured years of torture and confinement as prisoners of war. In 1966, navy pilot Gerald Coffee's plane was shot down over North Vietnam. Coffee spent the next seven years—until he was released in 1973 as part of a cease-fire agreement—struggling to stay alive in an enemy prison camp.

A PERSONAL VOICE GERALD COFFEE

"My clothes were filthy and ragged. . . . With no boots, my socks—which I'd been able to salvage—were barely recognizable. . . . Only a few threads around my toes kept them spread over my feet; some protection, at least, as I shivered through the cold nights curled up tightly on my morguelike slab. . . . My conditions and predicament were so foreign to me, so stifling, so overwhelming. I'd never been so hungry, so grimy, and in such pain."

—*Beyond Survival*

The Early War at Home

The Johnson administration thought the war would end quickly. As it dragged on, support began to waver, and Johnson's domestic programs began to unravel.

THE GREAT SOCIETY SUFFERS As the number of U.S. troops in Vietnam continued to mount, the war grew more costly, and the nation's economy began to suffer. The inflation rate, which was less than 2 percent through most of the early 1960s, more than tripled to 5.5 percent by 1969. In August of 1967, President Johnson asked for a tax increase to help fund the war and to keep inflation in check. Congressional conservatives agreed, but only after demanding and receiving a $6 billion reduction in funding for Great Society programs. Vietnam was slowly claiming an early casualty: Johnson's grand vision of domestic reform.

THE LIVING-ROOM WAR Through the media, specifically television, Vietnam became America's first "living-room war." The combat footage that appeared nightly on the news in millions of homes showed stark pictures that seemed to contradict the administration's optimistic war scenario.

Quoting body-count statistics that showed large numbers of communists dying in battle, General Westmoreland continually reported that a Vietcong surrender was imminent. Defense Secretary McNamara backed up the general, saying that he could see "the light at the end of the tunnel."

The repeated television images of Americans in body bags told a different story, though. While communists may have been dying, so too were Americans—over 16,000 between 1961 and 1967. Critics charged that a **credibility gap** was growing between what the Johnson administration reported and what was really happening.

▲ First used in World War I, dog tags were stamped with personal identification information and worn by U.S. military personnel.

One critic was Senator J. William Fulbright, chairman of the powerful Senate Foreign Relations Committee. Fulbright, a former Johnson ally, charged the president with a "lack of candor" in portraying the war effort. In early 1966, the senator conducted a series of televised committee hearings in which he asked members of the Johnson administration to defend their Vietnam policies. The Fulbright hearings delivered few major revelations, but they did contribute to the growing doubts about the war. One woman appeared to capture the mood of Middle America when she told an interviewer, "I want to get out, but I don't want to give in." E

MAIN IDEA

Analyzing Effects

E What led to the growing concern in America about the Vietnam War?

By 1967, Americans were evenly split over supporting and opposing the war. However, a small force outside of mainstream America, mainly from the ranks of the nation's youth, already had begun actively protesting the war. Their voices would grow louder and capture the attention of the entire nation.

SECTION 2 ASSESSMENT

1. **TERMS & NAMES** For each term or name, write a sentence explaining its significance.
   - **Robert McNamara**
   - **Dean Rusk**
   - **William Westmoreland**
   - **Army of the Republic of Vietnam (ARVN)**
   - **napalm**
   - **Agent Orange**
   - **search-and-destroy mission**
   - **credibility gap**

MAIN IDEA

2. **TAKING NOTES**
   Re-create the chart below. Then, show key military tactics and weapons of the Vietcong and Americans.

	Vietcong	U.S.
Tactics		
Weapons		

   Which weapons and tactics do you think were most successful? Explain.

CRITICAL THINKING

3. **DRAWING CONCLUSIONS**
   Why did Americans fail to win the "hearts and minds" of the Vietnamese?
4. **CONTRASTING**
   In a paragraph, contrast the morale of the U.S. troops with that of the Vietcong. Use evidence from the text to support your response.
5. **FORMING GENERALIZATIONS**
   What were the effects of the nightly TV coverage of the Vietnam War? Support your answer with examples from the text. **Think About:**
   - television images of Americans in body bags
   - the Johnson administration's credibility gap

SECTION 3

A Nation Divided

MAIN IDEA

An antiwar movement in the U.S. pitted supporters of the government's war policy against those who opposed it.

WHY IT MATTERS NOW

The painful process of healing a divided nation continues today.

Terms & Names

- **draft**
- **New Left**
- **Students for a Democratic Society (SDS)**
- **Free Speech Movement**
- **dove**
- **hawk**

One American's Story

In 1969, Stephan Gubar was told to report for possible military service in Vietnam. Gubar, 22, a participant in the civil rights movement, had filed as a conscientious objector (CO), or someone who opposed war on the basis of religious or moral beliefs. He was granted 1-A-O status, which meant that while he would not be forced to carry a weapon, he still qualified for noncombatant military duty. That year, Gubar was drafted—called for military service.

As did many other conscientious objectors, Gubar received special training as a medic. He described the memorable day his training ended.

A PERSONAL VOICE STEPHAN GUBAR

"The thing that stands out most was . . . being really scared, being in formation and listening to the names and assignments being called. The majority of COs I knew had orders cut for Vietnam. And even though I could hear that happening, even though I could hear that every time a CO's name came up, the orders were cut for Vietnam, I still thought there was a possibility I might not go. Then, when they called my name and said 'Vietnam,'. . . I went to a phone and I called my wife. It was a tremendous shock."

—quoted in *Days of Decision*

While many young Americans proudly went off to war, some found ways to avoid the draft, and others simply refused to go. The growing protest movement sharply divided the country between supporters and opponents of the government's policy in Vietnam.

VIDEO

MATTERS OF CONSCIENCE
Stephan Gubar and the Vietnam War

The Working Class Goes to War

The idea of fighting a war in a faraway place for what they believed was a questionable cause prompted a number of young Americans to resist going to Vietnam.

A "MANIPULATABLE" DRAFT Most soldiers who fought in Vietnam were called into combat under the country's Selective Service System, or **draft,** which had been established during World War I. Under this system, all males had to register with their local draft boards when they turned 18. All registrants were screened, and unless they were excluded—such as for medical reasons—in the event of war, men between the ages of 18 and 26 would be called into military service.

As Americans' doubts about the war grew, thousands of men attempted to find ways around the draft, which one man characterized as a "very manipulatable system." Some men sought out sympathetic doctors to grant medical exemptions, while others changed residences in order to stand before a more lenient draft board. Some Americans even joined the National Guard or Coast Guard, which often secured a deferment from service in Vietnam.

Vocabulary
deferment: the act or instance of delaying

One of the most common ways to avoid the draft was to receive a college deferment, by which a young man enrolled in a university could put off his military service. Because university students during the 1960s tended to be white and financially well-off, many of the men who fought in Vietnam were lower-class whites or minorities who were less privileged economically. With almost 80 percent of American soldiers coming from lower economic levels, Vietnam was a working-class war.

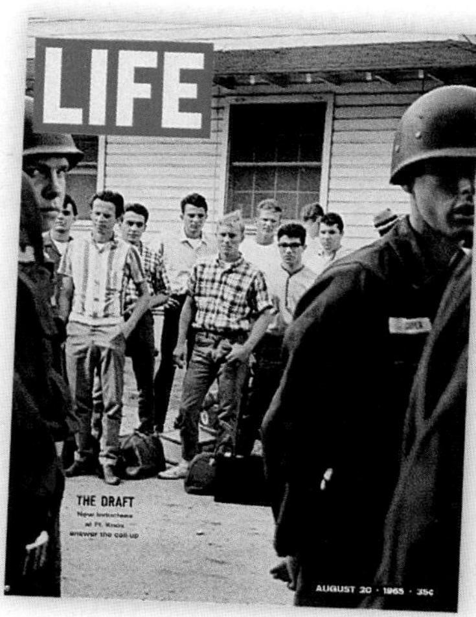

▲ A *Life* magazine cover shows new draft inductees arriving for training at Fort Knox, Kentucky.

AFRICAN AMERICANS IN VIETNAM African Americans served in disproportionate numbers as ground combat troops. During the first several years of the war, blacks accounted for more than 20 percent of American combat deaths despite representing only about 10 percent of the U.S. population. The Defense Department took steps to correct that imbalance by instituting a draft lottery system in 1969.

Martin Luther King, Jr., had refrained from speaking out against the war for fear that it would divert attention from the civil rights movement. But he could not maintain that stance for long. In 1967 he lashed out against what he called the "cruel irony" of American blacks dying for a country that still treated them as second-class citizens.

A Personal Voice DR. MARTIN LUTHER KING, JR.

"We were taking the young black men who had been crippled by our society and sending them eight thousand miles away to guarantee liberties in Southeast Asia which they had not found in Southwest Georgia and East Harlem. . . . We have been repeatedly faced with the cruel irony of watching Negro and white boys on TV screens as they kill and die together for a nation that has been unable to seat them together in the same schools."

—quoted in *America's Vietnam War: A Narrative History*

MAIN IDEA
Synthesizing
A Why did King call African Americans' fighting in Vietnam an "irony"?

Racial tension ran high in many platoons, and in some cases, the hostility led to violence. The racism that gripped many military units was yet another factor that led to low troop morale in Vietnam. **A**

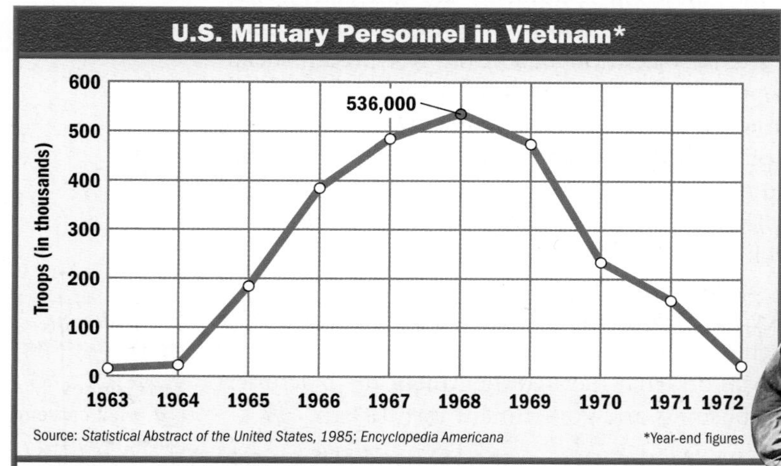

SKILLBUILDER Interpreting Graphs
What years signaled a rapid increase in the deployment of U.S. troops?

Despite racial tensions, black and white soldiers fought side by side in Vietnam. ▼

Two U.S. nurses rest at Cam Ranh Bay, the major entry point in South Vietnam for American supplies and troops.

WOMEN JOIN THE RANKS While the U.S. military in the 1960s did not allow females to serve in combat, 10,000 women served in Vietnam—most of them as military nurses. Thousands more volunteered their services in Vietnam to the American Red Cross and the United Services Organization (USO), which delivered hospitality and entertainment to the troops.

As the military marched off to Vietnam to fight against communist guerrillas, some of the men at home, as well as many women, waged a battle of their own. Tensions flared across the country as many of the nation's youths began to voice their opposition to the war.

The Roots of Opposition

Even before 1965, students were becoming more active socially and politically. Some participated in the civil rights struggle, while others pursued public service. As America became more involved in the war in Vietnam, college students across the country became a powerful and vocal group of protesters.

THE NEW LEFT The growing youth movement of the 1960s became known as the **New Left.** The movement was "new" in relation to the "old left" of the 1930s, which had generally tried to move the nation toward socialism, and, in some cases, communism. While the New Left movement did not preach socialism, its followers demanded sweeping changes in American society.

Voicing these demands was one of the better-known New Left organizations, **Students for a Democratic Society (SDS),** founded in 1960 by Tom Hayden and Al Haber. The group charged that corporations and large government institutions had taken over America. The SDS called for a restoration of "participatory democracy" and greater individual freedom.

In 1964, the **Free Speech Movement** (FSM) gained prominence at the University of California at Berkeley. The FSM grew out of a clash between students and administrators over free speech on campus. Led by Mario Savio, a philosophy student, the FSM focused its criticism on what it called the American "machine," the nation's faceless and powerful business and government institutions. B

MAIN IDEA

Making Inferences

B What concerns about American democratic society did the New Left voice?

CAMPUS ACTIVISM Across the country the ideas of the FSM and SDS quickly spread to college campuses. Students addressed mostly campus issues, such as dress codes, curfews, dormitory regulations, and mandatory Reserved Officer

Training Corps (ROTC) programs. At Fairleigh Dickinson University in New Jersey, students marched merely as "an expression of general student discontent."

With the onset of the Vietnam War, students across the country found a galvanizing issue and joined together in protest. By the mid-sixties, many youths believed the nation to be in need of fundamental change.

The Protest Movement Emerges

Throughout the spring of 1965, groups at a number of colleges began to host "teach-ins" to protest the war. At the University of Michigan, where only a year before President Johnson had announced his sweeping Great Society Program, teachers and students now assailed his war policy. "This is no longer a casual form of campus spring fever," journalist James Reston noted about the growing demonstrations. As the war continued, the protests grew and divided the country.

THE MOVEMENT GROWS In April of 1965, SDS helped organize a march on Washington, D.C., by some 20,000 protesters. By November of that year, a protest rally in Washington drew more than 30,000. Then, in February of 1966, the Johnson administration changed deferments for college students, requiring students to be in good academic standing in order to be granted a deferment. Campuses around the country erupted in protest. SDS called for civil disobedience at Selective Service Centers and openly counseled students to flee to Canada or Sweden. By the end of 1969, SDS had chapters on nearly 400 campuses.

Youths opposing the war did so for several reasons. The most common was the belief that the conflict in Vietnam was basically a civil war and that the U.S. military had no business there. Some said that the oppressive South Vietnamese regime was no better than the Communist regime it was fighting. Others argued that the United States could not police the entire globe and that war was draining American strength in other important parts of the world. Still others saw war simply as morally unjust. C

MAIN IDEA

Summarizing
C For what reasons did the protesters oppose the Vietnam War?

The antiwar movement grew beyond college campuses. Small numbers of returning veterans began to protest the war, and folk singers such as the trio Peter, Paul, and Mary, and Joan Baez used music as a popular protest vehicle. The number one song in September 1965 was "Eve of Destruction," in which singer Barry McGuire stressed the ironic fact that in the 1960s an American male could be drafted at age 18 but had to be 21 to vote:

> **The Eastern world, it is explodin',**
> **Violence flaring, bullets loadin',**
> **You're old enough to kill, but not for votin',**
> **You don't believe in war, but what's that gun you're totin'?**

FROM PROTEST TO RESISTANCE By 1967, the antiwar movement had intensified, with no sign of slowing down. "We were having no effect on U.S. policy," recalled one protest leader, "so we thought we had to up the ante." In the spring of 1967, nearly half a million protesters of all ages gathered in New York's Central Park. Shouting "Burn cards, not people!" and "Hell, no, we won't go!" hundreds tossed their draft cards into a bonfire. A woman from New Jersey told a reporter, "So many of us are frustrated. We want to criticize this war because we think it's wrong, but we want to do it in the framework of loyalty."

HISTORICAL SPOTLIGHT

"THE BALLAD OF THE GREEN BERETS"

Not every Vietnam-era pop song about war was an antiwar song. At the top of the charts for five weeks in 1966 was "The Ballad of the Green Berets" by Staff Sergeant Barry Sadler of the U.S. Army Special Forces, known as the Green Berets:

> Fighting soldiers from the sky,
> Fearless men who jump and die,
> Men who mean just what they say,
> The brave men of the Green Beret.

The recording sold over a million copies in its first two weeks of release and was *Billboard* magazine's song of the year.

DIFFICULT DECISIONS

RESIST THE DRAFT OR SERVE YOUR COUNTRY?

As the fighting in Vietnam intensified, young men of draft age who opposed the war found themselves considering one of two options: register with the draft board and risk heading off to war, or find a way to avoid military service. Ways to avoid service included medical and educational deferments. But a great many men did not qualify for these. The choices that remained, such as fleeing the country, going to jail, or giving in and joining the ranks, came with a high price. Once a decision was made, there was no turning back.

1. Imagine you oppose the war and are called to serve in Vietnam. What decision would you make? Would you feel guilty if you avoided the draft? If you chose to serve, how would you view those who did not serve your country?
2. Do you think more young men would have been willing to serve had this been a different war? Explain.

Others were more radical in their view. David Harris, who would spend 20 months in jail for refusing to serve in Vietnam, explained his motives.

A PERSONAL VOICE DAVID HARRIS

"Theoretically, I can accept the notion that there are circumstances in which you have to kill people. I could not accept the notion that Vietnam was one of those circumstances. And to me that left the option of either sitting by and watching what was an enormous injustice . . . or [finding] some way to commit myself against it. And the position that I felt comfortable with in committing myself against it was total noncooperation—I was not going to be part of the machine."

—quoted in *The War Within*

Draft resistance continued from 1967 until President Nixon phased out the draft in the early 1970s. During these years, the U.S. government accused more than 200,000 men of draft offenses and imprisoned nearly 4,000 draft resisters. (Although some were imprisoned for four or five years, most won parole after 6 to 12 months.) Throughout these years, about 10,000 Americans fled, many to Canada. D

MAIN IDEA

Evaluating

D Do you think it was right for the government to imprison draft resisters? Explain.

In October of 1967, a demonstration at Washington's Lincoln Memorial drew about 75,000 protesters. After listening to speeches, approximately 30,000 demonstrators locked arms for a march on the Pentagon in order "to disrupt the center of the American war machine," as one organizer explained. As hundreds of protesters broke past the military police and mounted the Pentagon steps, they were met by tear gas and clubs. About 1,500 demonstrators were injured and at least 700 arrested.

WAR DIVIDES THE NATION By 1967, Americans increasingly found themselves divided into two camps regarding the war. Those who strongly opposed the war and believed the United States should withdraw were known as **doves.** Feeling just as strongly that America should unleash much of its greater military force to win the war were the **hawks.**

Despite the visibility of the antiwar protesters, a majority of American citizens in 1967 still remained committed to the war. Others, while less certain about the proper U.S. role in Vietnam, were shocked to see protesters publicly criticize a war in which their fellow Americans were fighting and dying. A poll taken in December of 1967 showed that 70 percent of Americans believed the war protests were "acts of disloyalty." A firefighter who lost his son in Vietnam articulated the bitter feelings a number of Americans felt toward the antiwar movement.

This sign reflects the view of many Americans that the antiwar protests undermined the war effort in Vietnam. ▶

A PERSONAL VOICE

"I'm bitter. . . . It's people like us who give up our sons for the country. . . . The college types, the professors, they go to Washington and tell the government what to do. . . . But their sons, they don't end up in the swamps over there, in Vietnam. No sir. They're deferred, because they're in school. Or they get sent to safe places. . . . What bothers me about the peace crowd is that you can tell from their attitude, the way they look and what they say, that they don't really love this country."

—a firefighter quoted in *Working-Class War*

MAIN IDEA

Evaluating

E What were the key issues that divided America?

Responding to antiwar posters, Americans who supported the government's Vietnam policy developed their own slogans: "Support our men in Vietnam" and "America—love it or leave it." E

JOHNSON REMAINS DETERMINED Throughout the turmoil and division that engulfed the country during the early years of the war, President Johnson remained firm. Attacked by doves for not withdrawing and by hawks for not increasing military power rapidly enough, Johnson was dismissive of both groups and their motives. He continued his policy of slow escalation.

A PERSONAL VOICE LYNDON B. JOHNSON

"There has always been confusion, frustration, and difference of opinion in this country when there is a war going on. . . . You know what President Roosevelt went through, and President Wilson in World War I. He had some senators from certain areas . . . that gave him serious problems until victory was assured. . . . We are going to have these differences. No one likes war. All people love peace. But you can't have freedom without defending it."

—quoted in *No Hail, No Farewell*

However, by the end of 1967, Johnson's policy—and the continuing stalemate—had begun to create turmoil within his own administration. In November, Defense Secretary Robert McNamara, a key architect of U.S. escalation in Vietnam, quietly announced he was resigning to become head of the World Bank. "It didn't add up," McNamara recalled later. "What I was trying to find out was how . . . the war went on year after year when we stopped the infiltration [from North Vietnam] or shrunk it and when we had a very high body count and so on. It just didn't make sense."

As it happened, McNamara's resignation came on the threshold of the most tumultuous year of the sixties. In 1968 the war—and Johnson's presidency—would take a drastic turn for the worse.

ASSESSMENT

1. **TERMS & NAMES** For each of the following, write a sentence explaining its significance.

- **draft**
- **New Left**
- **Students for a Democratic Society (SDS)**
- **Free Speech Movement**
- **dove**
- **hawk**

MAIN IDEA

2. **TAKING NOTES** Re-create the tree diagram below on your paper. Then fill it in with examples of student organizations, issues, and demonstrations of the New Left.

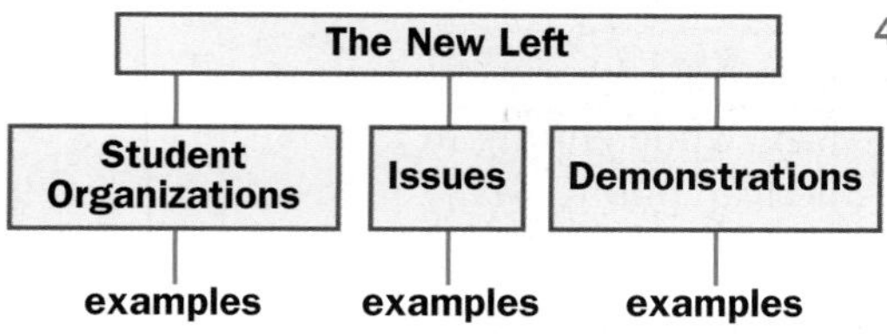

CRITICAL THINKING

3. **DEVELOPING HISTORICAL PERSPECTIVE** Imagine it is 1967. Do you think you would ally yourself with the hawks or the doves? Give reasons that support your position.

4. **EVALUATING** Do you agree that antiwar protests were "acts of disloyalty"? Why or why not?

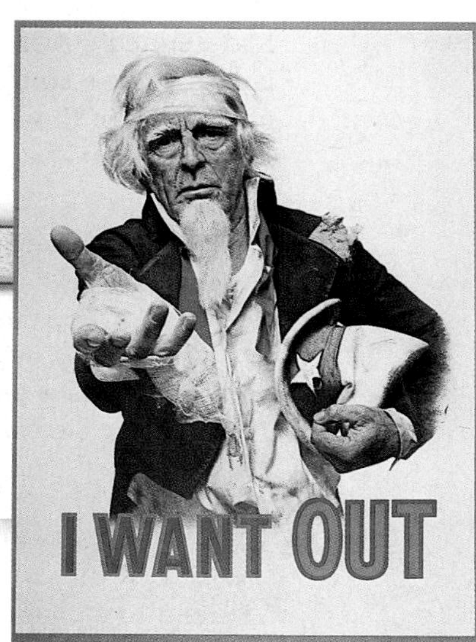

5. **ANALYZING VISUAL SOURCES** This antiwar poster is a parody of the World War I Uncle Sam poster (shown on page 382), which states, "I want you for the U.S. Army." Why might the artist have chosen this American character to express the antiwar message?

1968: A Tumultuous Year

MAIN IDEA

An enemy attack in Vietnam, two assassinations, and a chaotic political convention made 1968 an explosive year.

WHY IT MATTERS NOW

Disturbing events in 1968 accentuated the nation's divisions, which are still healing in the 21st century.

Terms & Names

- **Tet offensive**
- **Clark Clifford**
- **Robert Kennedy**
- **Eugene McCarthy**
- **Hubert Humphrey**
- **George Wallace**

One American's Story

On June 5, 1968, John Lewis, the first chairman of the Student Nonviolent Coordinating Committee, fell to the floor and wept. Robert F. Kennedy, a leading Democratic candidate for president, had just been fatally shot. Two months earlier, when Martin Luther King, Jr., had fallen victim to an assassin's bullet, Lewis had told himself he still had Kennedy. And now they both were gone. Lewis, who later became a congressman from Georgia, recalled the lasting impact of these assassinations.

John Lewis

A Personal Voice JOHN LEWIS

"There are people today who are afraid, in a sense, to hope or to have hope again, because of what happened in . . . 1968. Something was taken from us. The type of leadership that we had in a sense invested in, that we had helped to make and to nourish, was taken from us. . . . Something died in all of us with those assassinations."

—quoted in *From Camelot to Kent State*

These violent deaths were but two of the traumatic events that rocked the nation in 1968. From a shocking setback in Vietnam to a chaotic Democratic National Convention in Chicago, the events of 1968 made it the most tumultuous year of a turbulent decade.

The Tet Offensive Turns the War

The year 1968 began with a daring surprise attack by the Vietcong and the North Vietnamese army on numerous cities. The simultaneous strikes, while ending in military defeat for the Communist guerrillas, stunned the American public. Many people with moderate views began to turn against the war.

A SURPRISE ATTACK January 30 was the Vietnamese equivalent of New Year's Eve, the beginning of the lunar new year festivities known in Vietnam as Tet.

Throughout that day in 1968, villagers—taking advantage of a week-long truce proclaimed for Tet—streamed into cities across South Vietnam to celebrate their new year. At the same time, many funerals were being held for war victims. Accompanying the funerals were the traditional firecrackers, flutes, and, of course, coffins.

The coffins, however, contained weapons, and many of the villagers were Vietcong agents. That night the Vietcong launched an overwhelming attack on over 100 towns and cities in South Vietnam, as well as 12 U.S. air bases. They even attacked the U.S. embassy in Saigon, killing five Americans. The **Tet offensive** continued for about a month before U.S. and South Vietnamese forces regained control of the cities.

General Westmoreland declared the attacks an overwhelming defeat for the Vietcong, whose "well-laid plans went afoul." From a purely military standpoint, Westmoreland was right. The Vietcong lost about 32,000 soldiers during the month-long battle, while the American and ARVN forces lost little more than 3,000.

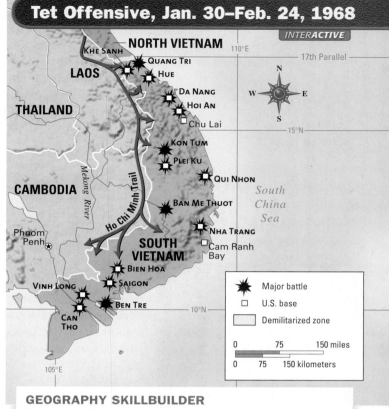

Tet Offensive, Jan. 30–Feb. 24, 1968

INTERACTIVE

NORTH VIETNAM
LAOS
THAILAND
CAMBODIA
SOUTH VIETNAM
Khe Sanh
Quang Tri
Hue
Da Nang
Hoi An
Chu Lai
Kon Tum
Plei Ku
Qui Nhon
Ban Me Thuot
Nha Trang
Cam Ranh Bay
Bien Hoa
Saigon
Ben Tre
Vinh Long
Can Tho
Phnom Penh
Mekong River
Ho Chi Minh Trail
South China Sea
17th Parallel

Major battle
U.S. base
Demilitarized zone
0 75 150 miles
0 75 150 kilometers

GEOGRAPHY SKILLBUILDER
Location What were the geographical destinations of the Tet offensive attacks? What does this suggest about the Vietcong forces?

However, from a psychological—and political—standpoint, Westmoreland's claim could not have been more wrong. The Tet offensive greatly shook the American public, which had been told repeatedly and had come to believe that the enemy was close to defeat. The Johnson administration's credibility gap suddenly widened to a point from which it would never recover. Daily, Americans saw the shocking images of attacks by an enemy that seemed to be everywhere.

TET CHANGES PUBLIC OPINION In a matter of weeks, the Tet offensive changed millions of minds about the war. Despite the years of antiwar protest, a poll taken just before Tet showed that only 28 percent of Americans called themselves doves, while 56 percent claimed to be hawks. After Tet, both sides tallied 40 percent. The mainstream media, which had reported the war in a skeptical but generally balanced way, now openly criticized the war. One of the nation's most respected journalists, Walter Cronkite, told his viewers that it now seemed "more certain than ever that the bloody experience of Vietnam is to end in a stalemate." (A)

MAIN IDEA
Analyzing Issues
(A) Why did American support for the war change after the Tet offensive?

Minds were also changing at the White House. To fill the defense secretary position left vacant by Robert McNamara's resignation, Johnson picked **Clark Clifford,** a friend and supporter of the president's Vietnam policy. However, after settling in and studying the situation, Clifford concluded that the war was unwinnable. "We seem to have a sinkhole," Clifford said. "We put in more—they match it. I see more and more fighting with more and more casualties on the U.S. side and no end in sight to the action."

A *Life* magazine cover shows the capture of a Vietcong guerrilla during the Tet offensive.

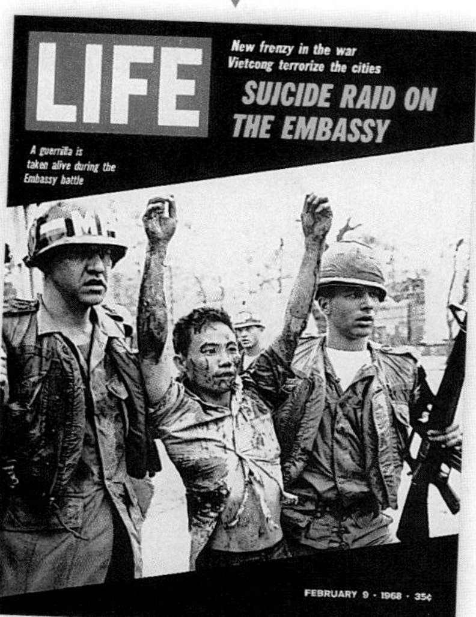

Following the Tet offensive, Johnson's popularity plummeted. In public opinion polls taken at the end of February 1968, nearly 60 percent of Americans disapproved of his handling of the war. Nearly half of the country now felt it had been a mistake to send American troops to Vietnam.

"If I've lost Walter [Cronkite], then it's over. I've lost Mr. Average Citizen."
LYNDON B. JOHNSON

War weariness eventually set in, and 1968 was the watershed year. Johnson recognized the change, too. Upon learning of Cronkite's pessimistic analysis of the war, the president lamented, "If I've lost Walter, then it's over. I've lost Mr. Average Citizen."

Days of Loss and Rage

The growing division over Vietnam led to a shocking political development in the spring of 1968, a season in which Americans also endured two assassinations, a series of urban riots, and a surge in college campus protests.

▲ The Vietnam War and the divisiveness it caused took its toll on President Johnson.

JOHNSON WITHDRAWS Well before the Tet offensive, an antiwar coalition within the Democratic Party had sought a Democratic candidate to challenge Johnson in the 1968 primary elections. **Robert Kennedy,** John F. Kennedy's brother and a senator from New York, decided not to run, citing party loyalty. However, in November of 1967, Minnesota senator **Eugene McCarthy** answered the group's call, declaring that he would run against Johnson on a platform to end the war in Vietnam.

McCarthy's early campaign attracted little notice, but in the weeks following Tet it picked up steam. In the New Hampshire Democratic primary in March 1968, the little-known senator captured 42 percent of the vote. While Johnson won the primary with 48 percent of the vote, the slim margin of victory was viewed as a defeat for the president. Influenced by Johnson's perceived weakness at the polls, Robert Kennedy declared his candidacy for president. The Democratic Party had become a house divided.

In a televised address on March 31, 1968, Johnson announced a dramatic change in his Vietnam policy—the United States would seek negotiations to end the war. In the meantime, the policy of U.S. escalation would end, the bombing would eventually cease, and steps would be taken to ensure that the South Vietnamese played a larger role in the war.

The president paused and then ended his speech with a statement that shocked the nation. Declaring that he did not want the presidency to become "involved in the partisan divisions that are developing in this political year," Lyndon Johnson announced, "Accordingly, I shall not seek, and I will not accept, the nomination of my party for another term as your president." The president was stepping down from national politics, his grand plan for domestic reform done in by a costly and divisive war. "That . . . war," Johnson later admitted, "killed the lady I really loved—the Great Society." B

MAIN IDEA

Analyzing Motives

B Why did President Johnson decide not to run again?

VIOLENCE AND PROTEST GRIP THE NATION The Democrats—as well as the nation—were in for more shock in 1968. On April 4, America was rocked by the assassination of Martin Luther King, Jr. Violence ripped through more than 100 U.S. cities as enraged followers of the slain civil rights leader burned buildings and destroyed neighborhoods.

Just two months later, a bullet cut down yet another popular national figure. Robert Kennedy had become a strong candidate in the Democratic primary, drawing support from minorities and urban Democratic voters. On June 4, Kennedy won the crucial California primary. Just after midnight of June 5, he gave a victory speech at a Los Angeles hotel. On his way out he passed through the hotel's kitchen, where a young Palestinian immigrant, Sirhan Sirhan, was hiding with a gun. Sirhan, who later said he was angered by Kennedy's support of Israel, fatally shot the senator.

Jack Newfield, a speechwriter for Kennedy, described the anguish he and many Americans felt over the loss of two of the nation's leaders.

A PERSONAL VOICE JACK NEWFIELD

> **"Things were not really getting better . . . we shall not overcome. . . . We had already glimpsed the most compassionate leaders our nation could produce, and they had all been assassinated. And from this time forward, things would get worse: Our best political leaders were part of memory now, not hope."**
>
> —quoted in *Nineteen Sixty-Eight*

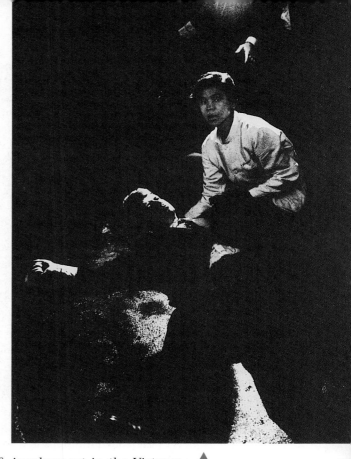

Meanwhile, the nation's college campuses continued to protest. During the first six months of 1968, almost 40,000 students on more than 100 campuses took part in more than 200 major demonstrations. While many of the demonstrations continued to target U.S. involvement in the Vietnam War, students also clashed with university officials over campus and social issues. A massive student protest at Columbia University in New York City held the nation's attention for a week in April. There, students protesting the university's community policies took over several buildings. Police eventually restored order and arrested nearly 900 protesters.

Recalling the violence and turmoil that plagued the nation in 1968, the journalist and historian Garry Wills wrote, "There was a sense everywhere . . . that things were giving way. That [people] had not only lost control of [their] history, but might never regain it." (C)

▲ **Hotel busboy Juan Romero was the first person to reach Robert Kennedy after he was shot June 5, 1968. Kennedy had just won the California Democratic primary.**

MAIN IDEA

Analyzing Issues

(C) Why was 1968 characterized as a year of "lost control" in America?

A Turbulent Race for President

The chaos and violence of 1968 climaxed in August, when thousands of antiwar demonstrators converged on the city of Chicago to protest at the Democratic National Convention. The convention, which featured a bloody riot between protesters and police, fractured the Democratic Party and thus helped a nearly forgotten Republican win the White House.

TURMOIL IN CHICAGO With Lyndon Johnson stepping down and Robert Kennedy gone, the 1968 Democratic presidential primary race pitted Eugene McCarthy against **Hubert Humphrey,** Johnson's vice-president. McCarthy, while still popular with the nation's antiwar segment, had little chance of defeating Humphrey, a loyal party man who had President Johnson's support. During the last week of August, the Democrats met at their convention in Chicago, supposedly to choose a candidate. In reality, Humphrey's nomination had already been determined, a decision that upset many antiwar activists.

As the delegates arrived in Chicago, so too did nearly 10,000 protesters. Led by men such as SDS veteran Tom Hayden, many demonstrators sought to pressure the Democrats into adopting an antiwar platform. Others came to voice their

Vocabulary
platform: a formal declaration of the principles on which a political party makes its appeal to the public

Chicago police attempt to disperse antiwar demonstrators at the 1968 Democratic convention. Protesters shouted, "The whole world is watching!" ▶

displeasure with Humphrey's nomination. Still others, known as Yippies (members of the Youth International Party), had come hoping to provoke violence that might discredit the Democratic Party. Chicago's mayor, Richard J. Daley, was determined to keep the protesters under control. With memories of the nationwide riots after King's death still fresh, Daley mobilized 12,000 Chicago police officers and over 5,000 National Guard. "As long as I am mayor," Daley vowed, "there will be law and order."

Order, however, soon collapsed. On August 28, as delegates cast votes for Humphrey, protesters were gathering in a downtown park to march on the convention. With television cameras focused on them, police moved into the crowd, sprayed the protesters with Mace, and beat them with nightsticks. Many protesters tried to flee, while others retaliated, pelting the riot-helmeted police with rocks and bottles. "The whole world is watching!" protesters shouted, as police attacked demonstrators and bystanders alike. **D**

MAIN IDEA

Summarizing
D What were the reasons protesters demonstrated in Chicago?

The rioting soon spilled out of the park and into the downtown streets. One nearby hotel, observed a *New York Times* reporter, became a makeshift aid station.

A Personal Voice J. ANTHONY LUKAS

"Demonstrators, reporters, McCarthy workers, doctors, all began to stagger into the [hotel] lobby, blood streaming from face and head wounds. The lobby smelled from tear gas, and stink bombs dropped by the Yippies. A few people began to direct the wounded to a makeshift hospital on the fifteenth floor, the McCarthy staff headquarters."

—quoted in *Decade of Shocks*

Disorder of a different kind reigned inside the convention hall, where delegates bitterly debated an antiwar plank in the party platform. When word of the riot filtered into the hall, delegates angrily shouted at Mayor Daley, who was present as a delegate himself. Daley returned their shouts with equal vigor. The whole world indeed was watching—on their televisions. The images of the Democrats—both inside and outside the convention hall—as a party of disorder became etched in the minds of millions of Americans.

NIXON TRIUMPHS One beneficiary of this turmoil was Republican presidential candidate Richard M. Nixon, who by 1968 had achieved one of the greatest political comebacks in American politics. After his loss to Kennedy in the presidential race of 1960, Nixon tasted defeat again in 1962 when he ran for governor of California. His political career all but dead, Nixon joined a New York law firm, but he never strayed far from politics. In 1966, Nixon campaigned for Republican candidates in congressional elections, helping them to win back 47 House seats and 3 Senate seats from Democrats. In 1968, Nixon announced his candidacy for president and won the party's nomination.

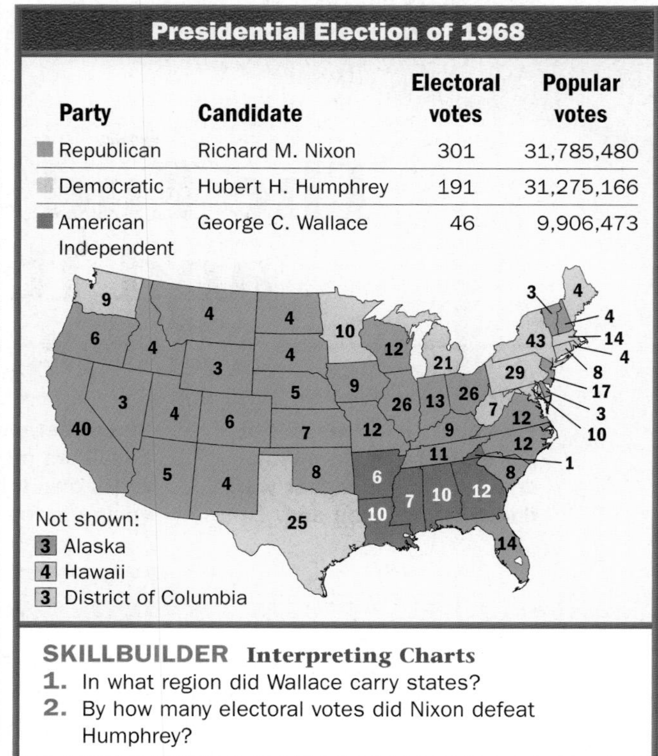

Presidential Election of 1968

Party	Candidate	Electoral votes	Popular votes
Republican	Richard M. Nixon	301	31,785,480
Democratic	Hubert H. Humphrey	191	31,275,166
American Independent	George C. Wallace	46	9,906,473

SKILLBUILDER Interpreting Charts
1. In what region did Wallace carry states?
2. By how many electoral votes did Nixon defeat Humphrey?

During the presidential race, Nixon campaigned on a promise to restore law and order, which appealed to many middle-class Americans tired of years of riots and protests. He also promised, in vague but appealing terms, to end the war in Vietnam. Nixon's candidacy was helped by the entry of former Alabama governor **George Wallace** into the race as a third-party candidate. Wallace, a Democrat running on the American Independent Party ticket, was a longtime champion of school segregation and states' rights. Labeled the "white backlash" candidate, Wallace captured five Southern states. In addition, he attracted a high number of Northern white working-class voters disgusted with inner-city riots and antiwar protests.

In the end, Nixon defeated Humphrey and inherited the quagmire in Vietnam. He eventually would end America's involvement in Vietnam, but not before his war policies created even more protest and uproar within the country.

SECTION 4 ASSESSMENT

1. **TERMS & NAMES** For each term or name, write a sentence explaining its significance.
   - **Tet offensive**
   - **Clark Clifford**
   - **Robert Kennedy**
   - **Eugene McCarthy**
   - **Hubert Humphrey**
   - **George Wallace**

MAIN IDEA

2. **TAKING NOTES**
Create a time line of major events that occurred in 1968. Use the months already plotted on the time line below as a guide.

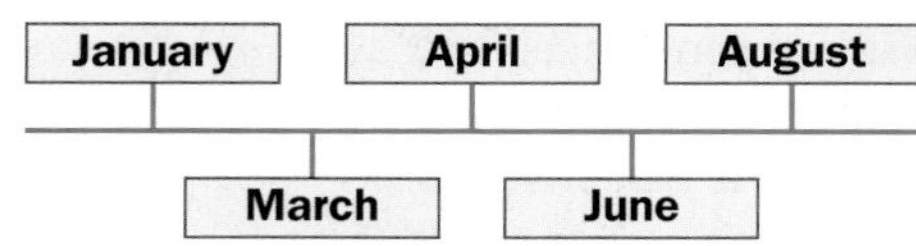

Which event do you think was most significant? Explain.

CRITICAL THINKING

3. **ANALYZING EVENTS**
Why do you think the Tet offensive turned so many Americans against the war? Support your answer with reasons.

4. **MAKING INFERENCES**
Refer to President Johnson's quote on page 750. What do you think he meant when he said "If I've lost Walter [Cronkite], then it's over. I've lost Mr. Average Citizen"? Explain.

5. **MAKING INFERENCES**
Do you think there might have been a relationship between the violence of the Vietnam War and the growing climate of violence in the United States during 1968? Why or why not?

The End of the War and Its Legacy

MAIN IDEA	WHY IT MATTERS NOW	Terms & Names
President Nixon instituted his Vietnamization policy, and America's longest war finally came to an end.	**Since Vietnam, the United States considers more carefully the risks to its own interests before intervening in foreign affairs.**	**•Richard Nixon •Henry Kissinger •Vietnamization •silent majority •My Lai •Kent State University •Pentagon Papers •War Powers Act**

One American's Story

Alfred S. Bradford served in Vietnam from September 1968 to August 1969. A member of the 25th Infantry Division, he was awarded several medals, including the Purple Heart, given to soldiers wounded in battle. One day, Bradford's eight-year-old daughter, Elizabeth, inquired about his experience in Vietnam. "Daddy, why did you do it?" she asked. Bradford recalled what he had told himself.

A PERSONAL VOICE ALFRED S. BRADFORD

"Vietnam was my generation's adventure. I wanted to be part of that adventure and I believed that it was my duty as an American, both to serve my country and particularly not to stand by while someone else risked his life in my place. I do not regret my decision to go, but I learned in Vietnam not to confuse America with the politicians elected to administer America, even when they claim they are speaking for America, and I learned that I have a duty to myself and to my country to exercise my own judgment based upon my own conscience."

—quoted in *Some Even Volunteered*

▲ **A U.S. soldier sits near Quang Tri, Vietnam, during a break in the fighting.**

The legacy of the war was profound; it dramatically affected the way Americans viewed their government and the world. Richard Nixon had promised in 1968 to end the war, but it would take nearly five more years—and over 20,000 more American deaths—to end the nation's involvement in Vietnam.

President Nixon and Vietnamization

In the summer of 1969, newly elected president **Richard Nixon** announced the first U.S. troop withdrawals from Vietnam. "We have to get rid of the nightmares we inherited," Nixon later told reporters. "One of the nightmares is war without end." However, as Nixon pulled out the troops, he continued the war against North Vietnam, a policy that some critics would charge prolonged the "war without end" for several more bloody years.

THE PULLOUT BEGINS As President Nixon settled into the White House in January of 1969, negotiations to end the war in Vietnam were going nowhere. The United States and South Vietnam insisted that all North Vietnamese forces withdraw from the South and that the government of Nguyen Van Thieu, then South Vietnam's ruler, remain in power. The North Vietnamese and Vietcong demanded that U.S. troops withdraw from South Vietnam and that the Thieu government step aside for a coalition government that would include the Vietcong.

In the midst of the stalled negotiations, Nixon conferred with National Security Adviser **Henry Kissinger** on a plan to end America's involvement in Vietnam. Kissinger, a German immigrant who had earned three degrees from Harvard, was an expert on international relations. Their plan, known as **Vietnamization,** called for the gradual withdrawal of U.S. troops in order for the South Vietnamese to take on a more active combat role in the war. By August of 1969, the first 25,000 U.S. troops had returned home from Vietnam. Over the next three years, the number of American troops in Vietnam dropped from more than 500,000 to less than 25,000. (A)

> **MAIN IDEA**
> **Synthesizing**
> (A) What was the impact of Vietnamization on the United States?

"PEACE WITH HONOR" Part of Nixon and Kissinger's Vietnamization policy was aimed at establishing what the president called a "peace with honor." Nixon intended to maintain U.S. dignity in the face of its withdrawal from war. A further goal was to preserve U.S. clout at the negotiation table, as Nixon still demanded that the South Vietnamese government remain intact. With this objective—and even as the pullout had begun—Nixon secretly ordered a massive bombing campaign against supply routes and bases in North Vietnam. The president also ordered that bombs be dropped on the neighboring countries of Laos and Cambodia, which held a number of Vietcong sanctuaries. Nixon told his aide H. R. Haldeman that he wanted the enemy to believe he was capable of anything.

A Personal Voice RICHARD M. NIXON

> **"I call it the madman theory, Bob. . . . I want the North Vietnamese to believe I've reached the point where I might do anything to stop the war. We'll just slip the word to them that 'for God's sake, you know Nixon is obsessed about Communists. We can't restrain him when he's angry—and he has his hand on the nuclear button' —and Ho Chi Minh himself will be in Paris in two days begging for peace."**
>
> —quoted in *The Price of Power*

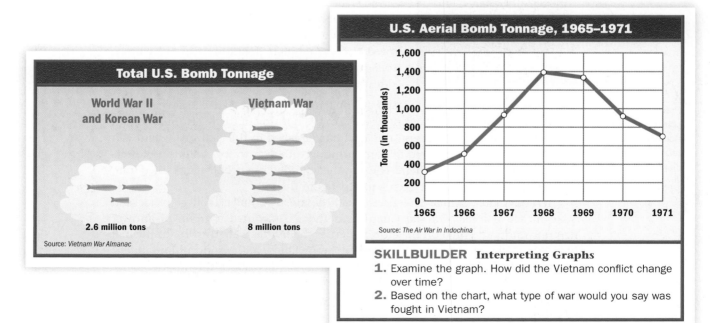

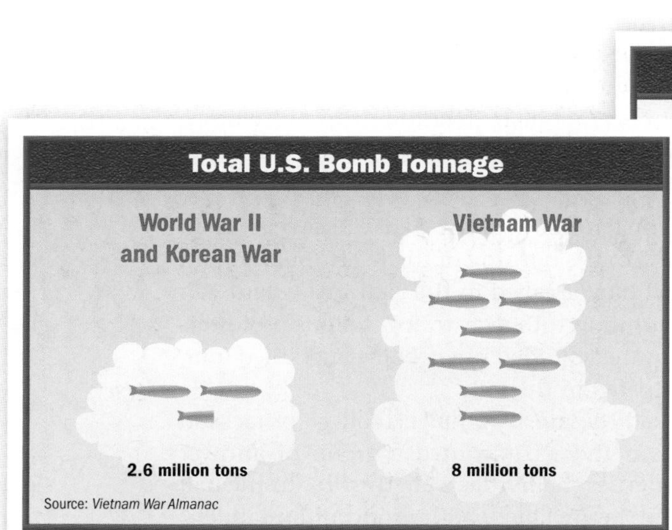

U.S. Aerial Bomb Tonnage, 1965–1971

Tons (in thousands): 0, 200, 400, 600, 800, 1,000, 1,200, 1,400, 1,600

1965 1966 1967 1968 1969 1970 1971

Source: *The Air War in Indochina*

SKILLBUILDER Interpreting Graphs

1. Examine the graph. How did the Vietnam conflict change over time?
2. Based on the chart, what type of war would you say was fought in Vietnam?

Trouble Continues on the Home Front

Seeking to win support for his war policies, Richard Nixon appealed to what he called the **silent majority**—moderate, mainstream Americans who quietly supported the U.S. efforts in Vietnam. While many average Americans did support the president, the events of the war continued to divide the country.

THE MY LAI MASSACRE In November of 1969, Americans learned of a shocking event. That month, *New York Times* correspondent Seymour Hersh reported that on March 16, 1968, a U.S. platoon under the command of Lieutenant William Calley, Jr., had massacred innocent civilians in the small village of **My Lai** (mē′ lī′) in northern South Vietnam. Calley was searching for Vietcong rebels. Finding no sign of the enemy, the troops rounded up the villagers and shot more than 200 innocent Vietnamese—mostly women, children, and elderly men. "We all huddled them up," recalled 22-year-old Private Paul Meadlo. "I poured about four clips into the group. . . . The mothers was hugging their children. . . . Well, we kept right on firing."

The troops insisted that they were not responsible for the shootings because they were only following Lieutenant Calley's orders. When asked what his directive had been, one soldier answered, "Kill anything that breathed." Twenty-five army officers were charged with some degree of responsibility, but only Calley was convicted and imprisoned.

Background
Calley was imprisoned only a short time before President Nixon granted him house arrest. Calley was paroled in 1974, having served three years.

THE INVASION OF CAMBODIA Despite the shock over My Lai, the country's mood by 1970 seemed to be less explosive. American troops were on their way home, and it appeared that the war was finally winding down.

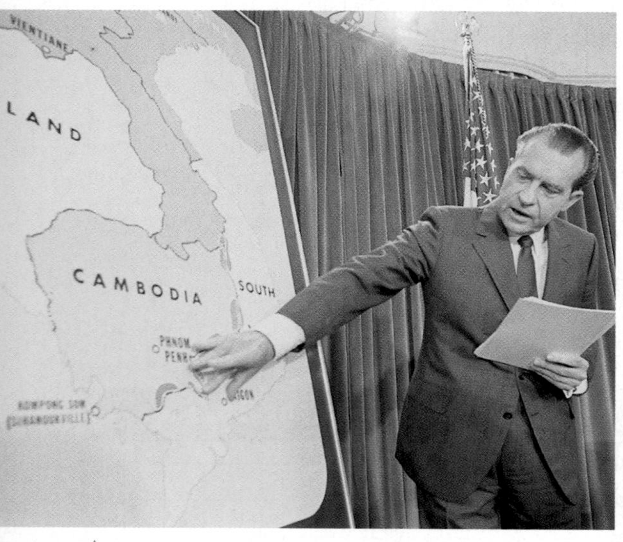

▲ President Nixon points to a map of Cambodia during a televised speech on April 30, 1970.

On April 30, 1970, President Nixon announced that U.S. troops had invaded Cambodia to clear out North Vietnamese and Vietcong supply centers. The president defended his action: "If when the chips are down, the world's most powerful nation acts like a pitiful, helpless giant, the forces of totalitarianism and anarchy will threaten free nations . . . throughout the world."

Upon hearing of the invasion, college students across the country burst out in protest. In what became the first general student strike in the nation's history, more than 1.5 million students closed down some 1,200 campuses. The president of Columbia University called the month that followed the Cambodian invasion "the most disastrous month of May in the history of . . . higher education."

VIOLENCE ON CAMPUS Disaster struck hardest at **Kent State University** in Ohio, where a massive student protest led to the burning of the ROTC building. In response to the growing unrest, the local mayor called in the National Guard. On May 4, 1970, the Guards fired live ammunition into a crowd of campus protesters who were hurling rocks at them. The gunfire wounded nine people and killed four, including two who had not even participated in the rally.

Ten days later, similar violence rocked the mostly all-black college of Jackson State in Mississippi. National Guardsmen there confronted a group of antiwar demonstrators and fired on the crowd after several bottles were thrown. In the hail of bullets, 12 students were wounded and 2 were killed, both innocent bystanders.

In a sign that America still remained sharply divided about the war, the country hotly debated the campus shootings. Polls indicated that many Americans supported the National Guard; respondents claimed that the students "got what

History Through *Photojournalism*

KENT STATE

Photographer John Filo was a senior at Kent State University when antiwar demonstrations rocked the campus. When the National Guard began firing at student protesters, Filo began shooting pictures, narrowly escaping a bullet himself.

As he continued to document the horrific scene, a girl running to the side of a fallen student caught his eye. Just as she dropped to her knees and screamed, Filo snapped a photograph that would later win the Pulitzer Prize and become one of the most memorable images of the decade.

Mary Ann Vecchio grieves over the body of Jeffrey Glenn Miller, a student shot by National Guard troops at Kent State. In the original photograph, a fence post appeared behind the woman's head. It is believed that someone manipulated the image in the early 1970s to make it more visually appealing. ▶

SKILLBUILDER Analyzing Visual Sources

1. Why do you think this photograph remains a symbol of the Vietnam War era today? Explain your answer with specific details of the photograph.
2. What do you think is the most striking element of this photograph? Why?

SEE SKILLBUILDER HANDBOOK, PAGE R23.

MAIN IDEA

Analyzing Issues

B How did the campus shootings demonstrate the continued divisions within the country?

they were asking for." The weeks following the campus turmoil brought new attention to a group known as "hardhats," construction workers and other blue-collar Americans who supported the U.S. government's war policies. In May of 1970, nearly 100,000 members of the Building and Construction Trades Council of New York held a rally outside city hall to support the government. 

THE PENTAGON PAPERS Nixon and Kissinger's Cambodia policy, however, cost Nixon significant political support. By first bombing and then invading Cambodia without even notifying Congress, the president stirred anger on Capitol Hill. On December 31, 1970, Congress repealed the Tonkin Gulf Resolution, which had given the president near independence in conducting policy in Vietnam.

Support for the war eroded even further when in June of 1971 former Defense Department worker Daniel Ellsberg leaked what became known as the **Pentagon Papers.** The 7,000-page document, written for Defense Secretary Robert McNamara in 1967–1968, revealed among other things that the government had drawn up plans for entering the war even as President Lyndon Johnson promised that he would not send American troops to Vietnam. Furthermore, the papers showed that there was never any plan to end the war as long as the North Vietnamese persisted.

For many Americans, the Pentagon Papers confirmed their belief that the government had not been honest about its war intentions. The document, while not particularly damaging to the Nixon administration, supported what opponents of the war had been saying.

KEY PLAYER

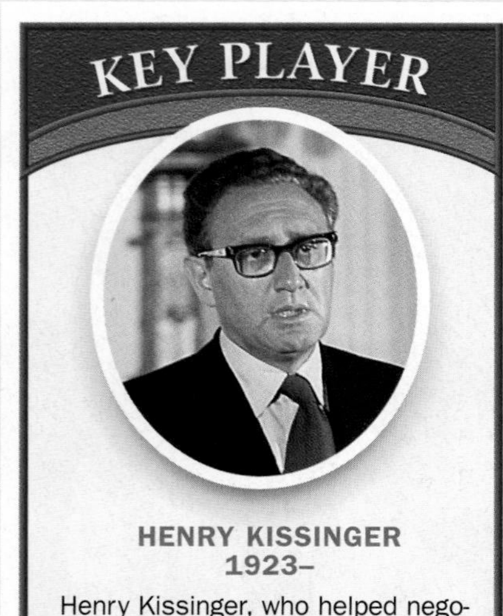

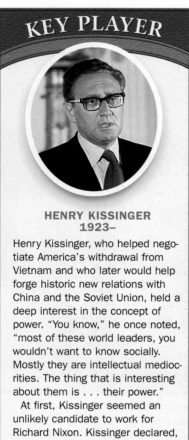

HENRY KISSINGER
1923–

Henry Kissinger, who helped negotiate America's withdrawal from Vietnam and who later would help forge historic new relations with China and the Soviet Union, held a deep interest in the concept of power. "You know," he once noted, "most of these world leaders, you wouldn't want to know socially. Mostly they are intellectual mediocrities. The thing that is interesting about them is . . . their power."

At first, Kissinger seemed an unlikely candidate to work for Richard Nixon. Kissinger declared, "That man Nixon is not fit to be president." However, the two became trusted colleagues.

America's Longest War Ends

In March of 1972, the North Vietnamese launched their largest attack on South Vietnam since the Tet offensive in 1968. President Nixon responded by ordering a massive bombing campaign against North Vietnamese cities. He also ordered that mines be laid in Haiphong harbor, the North's largest harbor, into which Soviet and Chinese ships brought supplies. The Communists "have never been bombed like they are going to be bombed this time," Nixon vowed. The bombings halted the North Vietnamese attack, but the grueling stalemate continued. It was after this that the Nixon administration took steps to finally end America's involvement in Vietnam.

"PEACE IS AT HAND" By the middle of 1972, the country's growing social division and the looming presidential election prompted the Nixon administration to change its negotiating policy. Polls showed that more than 60 percent of Americans in 1971 thought that the United States should withdraw all troops from Vietnam by the end of the year.

Henry Kissinger, the president's adviser for national security affairs, served as Nixon's top negotiator in Vietnam. Since 1969, Kissinger had been meeting privately with North Vietnam's chief negotiator, Le Duc Tho. Eventually, Kissinger dropped his insistence that North Vietnam withdraw all its troops from the South before the complete withdrawal of American troops. On October 26, 1972, days before the presidential election, Kissinger announced, "Peace is at hand."

THE FINAL PUSH President Nixon won reelection, but the promised peace proved to be elusive. The Thieu regime, alarmed at the prospect of North Vietnamese troops stationed in South Vietnam, rejected Kissinger's plan. Talks broke off on December 16. Two days later, the president unleashed a ferocious bombing campaign against Hanoi and Haiphong, the two largest cities in North Vietnam. In what became known as the "Christmas bombings," U.S. planes dropped 100,000 bombs over the course of eleven straight days, pausing only on Christmas Day.

At this point, calls to end the war resounded from the halls of Congress as well as from Beijing and Moscow. Everyone, it seemed, had finally grown weary of the war. The warring parties returned to the peace table, and on January 27, 1973, the United States signed an "Agreement on Ending the War and Restoring Peace in Vietnam." Under the agreement, North Vietnamese troops would remain in South Vietnam. However, Nixon promised to respond "with full force" to any violation of the peace agreement. On March 29, 1973, the last U.S. combat troops left for home. For America, the Vietnam War had ended. C

MAIN IDEA

Chronological Order

C Summarize what led to the agreement to end the war in Vietnam.

THE FALL OF SAIGON The war itself, however, raged on. Within months of the United States' departure, the cease-fire agreement between North and South Vietnam collapsed. In March of 1975, after several years of fighting, the North Vietnamese launched a full-scale invasion against the South. Thieu appealed to the United States for help. America provided economic aid but refused to send troops. Soon thereafter, President Gerald Ford—who assumed the presidency after the Watergate scandal forced President Nixon to resign—gave a speech in which he captured the nation's attitude toward the war:

MAIN IDEA

Evaluating Decisions

D Why might the United States have refused to reenter the war?

"America can regain its sense of pride that existed before Vietnam. But it cannot be achieved by refighting a war that is finished as far as America is concerned." On April 30, 1975, North Vietnamese tanks rolled into Saigon and captured the city. Soon after, South Vietnam surrendered to North Vietnam. D

The War Leaves a Painful Legacy

The Vietnam War exacted a terrible price from its participants. In all, 58,000 Americans were killed and some 303,000 were wounded. North and South Vietnamese deaths topped 2 million. In addition, the war left Southeast Asia highly unstable, which led to further war in Cambodia. In America, a divided nation attempted to come to grips with an unsuccessful war. In the end, the conflict in Vietnam left many Americans with a more cautious outlook on foreign affairs and a more cynical attitude toward their government.

AMERICAN VETERANS COPE BACK HOME While families welcomed home their sons and daughters, the nation as a whole extended a cold hand to its returning Vietnam veterans. There were no brass bands, no victory parades, no cheering crowds. Instead, many veterans faced indifference or even hostility from an America still torn and bitter about the war. Lily Jean Lee Adams, who served as an army nurse in Vietnam, recalled arriving in America in 1970 while still in uniform.

A PERSONAL VOICE LILY JEAN LEE ADAMS

"In the bus terminal, people were staring at me and giving me dirty looks. I expected the people to smile, like, 'Wow, she was in Vietnam, doing something for her country—wonderful.' I felt like I had walked into another country, not my country. So I went into the ladies' room and changed."

—quoted in *A Piece of My Heart*

Many Vietnam veterans readjusted successfully to civilian life. However, about 15 percent of the 3.3 million soldiers who served developed post-traumatic stress disorder. Some had recurring nightmares about their war experiences, while many suffered from severe headaches and memory lapses. Other veterans became

◀ Lieutenant Colonel Robert Stirm, a returning POW, receives a warm welcome from his family in 1973. The longest-held Vietnam POW was Lieutenant Everett Alvarez, Jr., of California. He was imprisoned for more than eight years.

▲ Each year, over two million people visit the Vietnam Veterans Memorial. Many leave remembrances that are collected nightly by park rangers and stored in a museum. Inscribed on the memorial are over 58,000 names of Americans who died in the war or were then still listed as missing in action.

highly apathetic or began abusing drugs or alcohol. Several thousand even committed suicide.

In an effort to honor the men and women who served in Vietnam, the U.S. government unveiled the Vietnam Veterans Memorial in Washington, D.C., in 1982. Many Vietnam veterans, as well as their loved ones, have found visiting the memorial a deeply moving, even healing, experience.

FURTHER TURMOIL IN SOUTHEAST ASIA The end of the Vietnam War ushered in a new period of violence and chaos in Southeast Asia. In unifying Vietnam, the victorious Communists initially held out a conciliatory hand to the South Vietnamese. "You have nothing to fear," declared Colonel Bui Tin of the North Vietnamese Army.

However, the Communists soon imprisoned more than 400,000 South Vietnamese in harsh "reeducation," or labor, camps. As the Communists imposed their rule throughout the land, nearly 1.5 million people fled Vietnam. They included citizens who had supported the U.S. war effort, as well as business owners, whom the Communists expelled when they began nationalizing the country's business sector.

Also fleeing the country was a large group of poor Vietnamese, known as boat people because they left on anything from freighters to barges to rowboats. Their efforts to reach safety across the South China Sea often met with tragedy; nearly 50,000 perished on the high seas due to exposure, drowning, illness, or piracy.

The people of Cambodia also suffered greatly after the war. The U.S. invasion of Cambodia had unleashed a brutal civil war in which a communist group known as the Khmer Rouge, led by Pol Pot, seized power in 1975. In an effort to transform the country into a peasant society, the Khmer Rouge executed professionals and anyone with an education or foreign ties. During its reign of terror, the Khmer Rouge is believed to have killed at least 1 million Cambodians.

HISTORICAL SPOTLIGHT

VIETNAM VETERANS MEMORIAL: THE WALL

In 1981, a national competition was held to determine the Vietnam memorial's design. Maya Ying Lin, above, a 21-year-old architecture student of Chinese descent, submitted the winning design—two long, black granite walls on which are etched the names of the men and women who died or are missing in action.

"I didn't want a static object that people would just look at," Lin said, "but something they could relate to as on a journey, or passage, that would bring each to his own conclusions." Lin's design became known simply as "the Wall."

THE LEGACY OF VIETNAM Even after it ended, the Vietnam War remained a subject of great controversy for Americans. Many hawks continued to insist that the war could have been won if the United States had employed more military power. They also blamed the antiwar movement at home for destroying American morale. Doves countered that the North Vietnamese had displayed incredible resiliency and that an increase in U.S. military force would have resulted only in a continuing stalemate. In addition, doves argued that an unrestrained war against North Vietnam might have prompted a military reaction from China or the Soviet Union. E

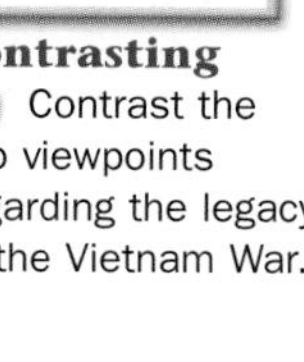

MAIN IDEA

Contrasting

E Contrast the two viewpoints regarding the legacy of the Vietnam War.

The war resulted in several major U.S. policy changes. First, the government abolished the draft, which had stirred so much antiwar sentiment. The country also took steps to curb the president's war-making powers. In November 1973, Congress passed the **War Powers Act,** which stipulated that a president must inform Congress within 48 hours of sending forces into a hostile area without a declaration of war. In addition, the troops may remain there no longer than 90 days unless Congress approves the president's actions or declares war.

In a broader sense, the Vietnam War significantly altered America's views on foreign policy. In what has been labeled the Vietnam syndrome, Americans now pause and consider possible risks to their own interests before deciding whether to intervene in the affairs of other nations.

Finally, the war contributed to an overall cynicism among Americans about their government and political leaders that persists today. Americans grew suspicious of a government that could provide as much misleading information or conceal as many activities as the Johnson and Nixon administrations had done. Coupled with the Watergate scandal of the mid-1970s, the war diminished the optimism and faith in government that Americans felt during the Eisenhower and Kennedy years.

U.S. RECOGNITION OF VIETNAM

In July of 1995, more than 20 years after the Vietnam War ended, the United States extended full diplomatic relations to Vietnam. In announcing the resumption of ties with Vietnam, President Bill Clinton declared, "Let this moment . . . be a time to heal and a time to build." Demonstrating how the war still divides Americans, the president's decision drew both praise and criticism from members of Congress and veterans' groups.

In an ironic twist, Clinton nominated as ambassador to Vietnam a former prisoner of war from the Vietnam War, Douglas Peterson, a congress member from Florida. Peterson, a former air force pilot, was shot down over North Vietnam in 1966 and spent six and a half years in a Hanoi prison.

ASSESSMENT

1. **TERMS & NAMES** For each term or name, write a sentence explaining its significance.
   - **Richard Nixon**
   - **Henry Kissinger**
   - **Vietnamization**
   - **silent majority**
   - **My Lai**
   - **Kent State University**
   - **Pentagon Papers**
   - **War Powers Act**

MAIN IDEA

2. **TAKING NOTES**
   In a web like the one shown, list the effects of the Vietnam War on America.

Choose one effect to further explain in a paragraph.

CRITICAL THINKING

3. **ANALYZING EFFECTS**
   In your opinion, what was the main effect of the U.S. government's deception about its policies and military conduct in Vietnam? Support your answer with evidence from the text. **Think About:**
   - the contents of the Pentagon Papers
   - Nixon's secrecy in authorizing military maneuvers

4. **MAKING INFERENCES**
   How would you account for the cold homecoming American soldiers received when they returned from Vietnam? Support your answer with reasons.

5. **SYNTHESIZING**
   In the end, do you think the United States' withdrawal from Vietnam was a victory for the United States or a defeat? Explain your answer.

AMERICAN LITERATURE

Literature of the Vietnam War

Throughout history, soldiers as well as citizens have written about the traumatic and moving experiences of war. The Vietnam War, which left a deep impression on America's soldiers and citizens alike, has produced its share of literature. From the surreal fantasy of *Going After Cacciato* to the grim realism of *A Rumor of War,* much of this literature reflects the nation's lingering disillusionment with its involvement in the Vietnam War.

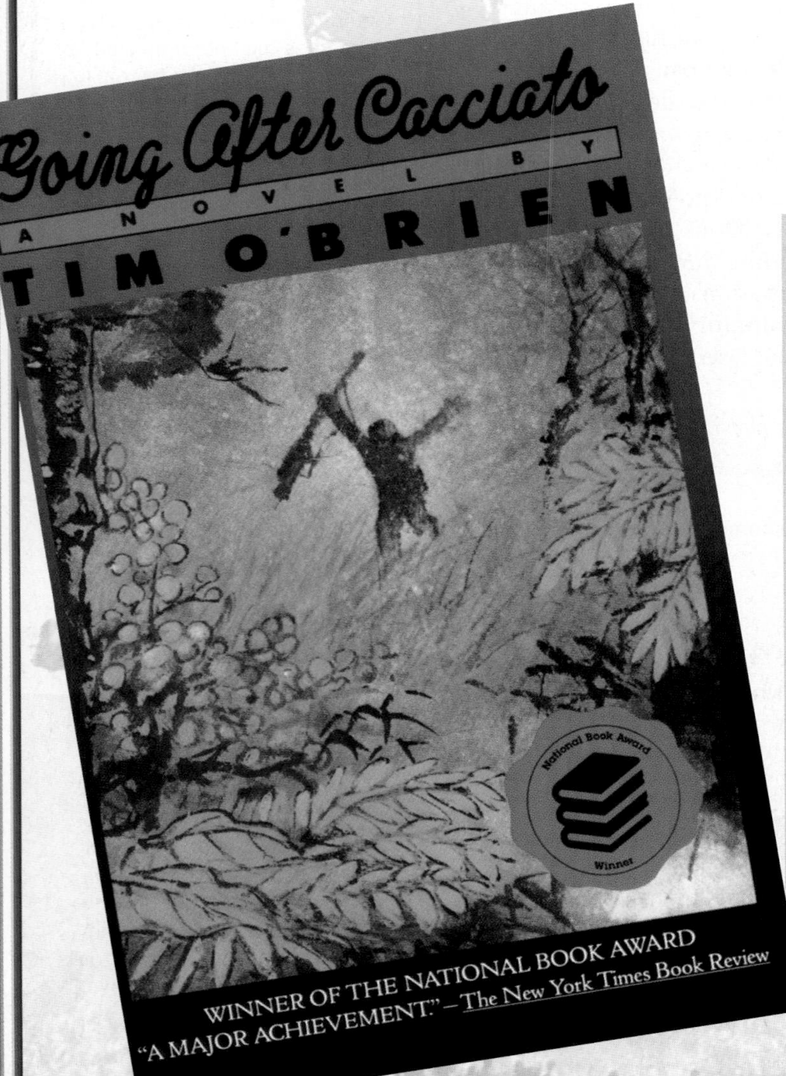

GOING AFTER CACCIATO

In *Going After Cacciato,* Vietnam veteran Tim O'Brien tells the story of Paul Berlin, a newcomer to Vietnam who fantasizes that his squad goes all the way to Paris, France, in pursuit of an AWOL soldier.

"How many days you been at the war?" asked Alpha's [Alpha Company's] mail clerk, and Paul Berlin answered that he'd been at the war seven days now.

The clerk laughed. "Wrong," he said. "Tomorrow, man, that's your first day at the war."

And in the morning PFC [Private First Class] Paul Berlin boarded a resupply chopper that took him fast over charred pocked mangled country, hopeless country, green skies and speed and tangled grasslands and paddies and places he might die, a million possibilities. He couldn't watch. He watched his hands. He made fists of them, opening and closing the fists. His hands, he thought, not quite believing. *His* hands.

Very quickly, the helicopter banked and turned and went down.

"How long you been at the war?" asked the first man he saw, a wiry soldier with ringworm in his hair.

PFC Paul Berlin smiled. "This is it," he said. "My first day."

—Tim O'Brien, *Going After Cacciato* (1978)

A RUMOR OF WAR

In *A Rumor of War,* considered to be among the best nonfiction accounts of the war, former marine Philip Caputo reflects on his years as a soldier in Vietnam.

> At the age of twenty-four, I was more prepared for death than I was for life. . . . I knew how to face death and how to cause it, with everything on the evolutionary scale of weapons from the knife to the 3.5-inch rocket launcher. The simplest repairs on an automobile engine were beyond me, but I was able to field-strip and assemble an M-14 rifle blindfolded. I could call in artillery, set up an ambush, rig a booby trap, lead a night raid.
>
> Simply by speaking a few words into a two-way radio, I had performed magical feats of destruction. Summoned by my voice, jet fighters appeared in the sky to loose their lethal droppings on villages and men. High-explosive bombs blasted houses to fragments, napalm sucked air from lungs and turned human flesh to ashes. All this just by saying a few words into a radio transmitter. Like magic.

—Philip Caputo,
A Rumor of War (1977)

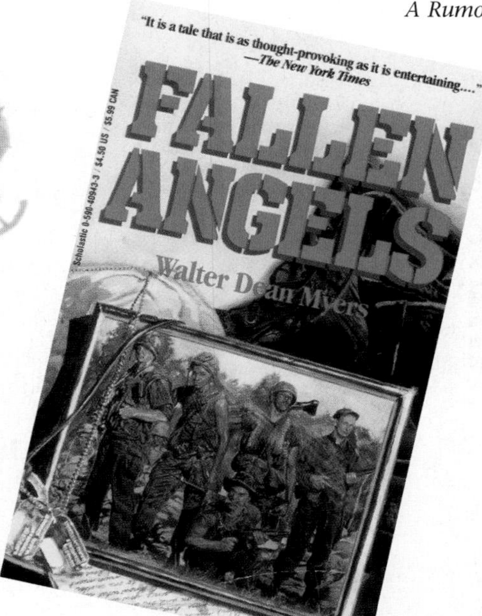

FALLEN ANGELS

Richie Perry, a 17-year-old Harlem youth, describes his harrowing tour of duty in Vietnam in Walter Dean Myers's novel *Fallen Angels.*

> The war was about us killing people and about people killing us, and I couldn't see much more to it. Maybe there were times when it was right. I had thought that this war was right, but it was only right from a distance. Maybe when we all got back to the World and everybody thought we were heroes for winning it, then it would seem right from there. . . . But when the killing started, there was no right or wrong except in the way you did your job, except in the way that you were part of the killing.
>
> What you thought about, what filled you up more than anything, was the being scared and hearing your heart thumping in your temples and all the noises, the terrible noises, the screeches and the booms and the guys crying for their mothers or for their wives.

—Walter Dean Myers,
Fallen Angels (1988)

THINKING CRITICALLY

1. **Comparing** What similar views about war do you think these books convey?

    **SEE SKILLBUILDER HANDBOOK, PAGE R8.**

2.  **INTERNET ACTIVITY CLASSZONE.COM**

   Visit the links for American Literature to research personal accounts of the Vietnam War, such as interviews, letters, and essays. Copy several excerpts you find particularly interesting or moving and assemble them in a book. Write an introduction to your collection explaining why you chose them. Share your book with the class.

CHAPTER 22 ASSESSMENT

VISUAL SUMMARY

THE VIETNAM WAR YEARS

1964 — **1964** Congress passes the Tonkin Gulf Resolution, giving the president broad military powers in Vietnam.

1965 — **1965** First major U.S. combat troops arrive in Vietnam to fight the Vietcong and North Vietnamese Army.

1966

1967 — **1967** Antiwar protests in the United States intensify.

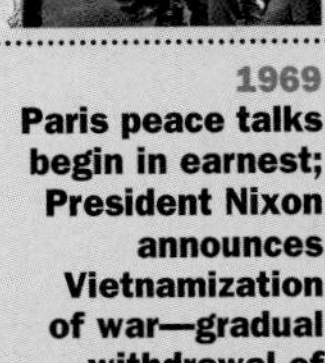

1968 — **1968** Vietcong launch massive Tet offensive on numerous South Vietnamese cities.

1969 — **1969** Paris peace talks begin in earnest; President Nixon announces Vietnamization of war—gradual withdrawal of U.S. troops.

1970 — **1970** President Nixon orders invasion of Cambodia to destroy enemy supply bases; American college campuses erupt in protest.

1971

1972 — **1972** Nixon unleashes "Christmas bombings" on North Vietnamese cities after peace talks break off.

1973 — **1973** United States and North Vietnam sign a truce; the U.S. withdraws the last of its troops from Vietnam.

1974

1975

TERMS AND NAMES

For each term or name below, write a sentence explaining its connection to the Vietnam War years.

1. Ho Chi Minh
2. Ngo Dinh Diem
3. Vietcong
4. William Westmoreland
5. napalm
6. Tet offensive
7. Robert Kennedy
8. Henry Kissinger
9. Vietnamization
10. Pentagon Papers

MAIN IDEAS

Use your notes and the information in the chapter to answer the following questions.

Moving Toward Conflict *(pages 730–735)*

1. How did the Tonkin Gulf Resolution lead to greater U.S. involvement in Vietnam?
2. What was President Eisenhower's explanation of the domino theory?

U.S. Involvement and Escalation *(pages 736–741)*

3. Why did so much of the American public and many in the Johnson administration support U.S. escalation in Vietnam?
4. Why did the war begin to lose support at home? What contributed to the sinking morale of the U.S. troops?

A Nation Divided *(pages 742–747)*

5. What race-related problems existed for African-American soldiers who served in the Vietnam War?
6. Summarize the ways in which the United States was sharply divided between hawks and doves.

1968: A Tumultuous Year *(pages 748–753)*

7. What circumstances set the stage for President Johnson's public announcement that he would not seek another term as president?
8. What acts of violence occurred in the United States during 1968 that dramatically altered the mood of the country?

The End of the War and Its Legacy *(pages 754–761)*

9. Briefly describe the military conflict in Vietnam soon after the last U.S. combat troops departed in 1973.
10. List the immediate effects and the more lasting legacies of America's involvement in the Vietnam War.

CRITICAL THINKING

1. **USING YOUR NOTES** Create a cause-and-effect diagram like the one below for each of these congressional measures: **a.** Tonkin Gulf Resolution (1964), **b.** repeal of the Tonkin Gulf Resolution (1970), **c.** War Powers Act (1973).

2. **DEVELOPING HISTORICAL PERSPECTIVE** Why do you think so many young Americans became so vocal in their condemnation of the Vietnam War?

Standardized Test Practice

Use the cartoon and your knowledge of U.S. history to answer question 1.

REDUCED STRIKE ZONE

1. Which of the following was a reason the U.S. had difficulty winning the war in Vietnam?
   - **A** The Vietcong hid in small villages throughout the country and were difficult to find.
   - **B** Vietcong troops outnumbered U.S. troops.
   - **C** The U.S. had to fight two enemy armies at the same time: the South Vietnamese and the North Vietnamese.
   - **D** The U.S. could not use its tanks because they could not be transported across the Pacific.

Use the quotation and your knowledge of U.S. history to answer question 2.

> **"Perhaps the place to start looking for a credibility gap is not in the offices of the government in Washington, but in the studios of the networks in New York."**
>
> —Spiro T. Agnew

2. During the Vietnam War, the term "credibility gap" referred to the American people's lack of trust in —
   - **F** Presidents Johnson and Nixon.
   - **G** television news reporters.
   - **H** antiwar protesters.
   - **J** Ho Chi Minh.

3. What happened to Vietnam after the U.S. pullout in 1973?
   - **A** The North and South remained divided and at peace.
   - **B** The North and South remained enemies, separated by a United Nations-controlled demilitarized zone.
   - **C** The North became a Chinese puppet state; the South experienced continual violent rebellions.
   - **D** The North defeated the South and incorporated it under a communist government.

ADDITIONAL TEST PRACTICE, pages S1–S33.

CLASSZONE.COM

ALTERNATIVE ASSESSMENT

1. INTERACT WITH HISTORY Recall your discussion of the question on page 729:

Who should be exempt from the draft?

What lessons do you think can be learned from the ways in which Americans reacted to the draft? Write a paragraph expressing and giving reasons for your judgments. Think About:

- how the draft affected Americans' views on the Vietnam War
- how the draft affected Americans' participation in the Vietnam War
- how draft protests affected other Americans

2. VIDEO **LEARNING FROM MEDIA** View the *American Stories* video "Matters of Conscience." Discuss the following questions in a group; then do the activity.

- What different views about the Vietnam War were expressed in the video?
- Why does Gubar say he feels guilt about having served in the war?

Cooperative Learning Activity Organize two teams for debate. One team should argue for the side of the hawks, and the other team should argue on behalf of the doves. Research the arguments put forth by both sides and debate the issue before the class.

CHAPTER 23 AN ERA OF SOCIAL CHANGE

Hippies gather in El Rito, New Mexico, at a Fourth of July parade in 1969.

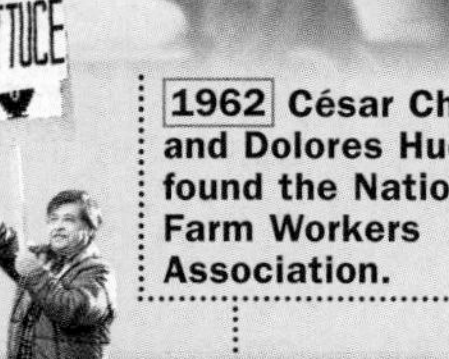

1962 César Chávez and Dolores Huerta found the National Farm Workers Association.

1964 Lyndon B. Johnson is elected president.

1966 National Organization for Women (NOW) is formed.

USA
WORLD

1960 1962 1964 1966

1962 Chinese forces invade India.

1963 Civil war breaks out between Greeks and Turks on Cyprus.

1967 Six-Day War between Israel and Arab nations.

INTERACT
WITH HISTORY

In the late 1960s, a new breed of youth known as the counterculture rejects the fashions, traditions, and morals of American society. Minority groups assert their equal rights, demanding changes to long-standing practices and prejudices. Women protest forms of oppression and male privileges that have "always," it seems, been taken for granted. Many Americans begin to feel as if the whole nation has been turned on its side.

How much can a society change?

Examine the Issues

- Does every individual have a responsibility to follow the unwritten rules of society?
- What are the positive and negative aspects of change?

RESEARCH LINKS **CLASSZONE.COM**

Visit the Chapter 23 links for more information about An Era of Social Change.

1968 Richard M. Nixon is elected president.

1969 President Charles de Gaulle of France resigns.

1970 Political party La Raza Unida is formed.

1970 Grape boycott forces growers to sign contracts with United Farm Workers.

1970 Anwar el-Sadat becomes president of Egypt.

1972 Richard M. Nixon is reelected.

1972 Earthquake kills 10,000 in Nicaragua.

1973 Native Americans stage protest at Wounded Knee, South Dakota.

1968 | 1970 | 1972 | 1974

Section 1

Latinos and Native Americans Seek Equality

MAIN IDEA

Latinos and Native Americans confronted injustices in the 1960s.

WHY IT MATTERS NOW

Campaigns for civil rights and economic justice won better representation and opportunity for Latinos and Native Americans.

Terms & Names

- **César Chávez**
- **United Farm Workers Organizing Committee**
- **La Raza Unida**
- **American Indian Movement (AIM)**

One American's Story

Jessie Lopez de la Cruz's life changed one night in 1962, when **César Chávez** came to her home. Chávez, a Mexican-American farm worker, was trying to organize a union for California's mostly Spanish-speaking farm workers. Chávez said, "The women have to be involved. They're the ones working out in the fields with their husbands." Soon Jessie was in the fields, talking to farm workers about the union.

A PERSONAL VOICE JESSIE LOPEZ DE LA CRUZ

"Wherever I went to speak . . . I told them about . . . how we had no benefits, no minimum wage, nothing out in the fields—no restrooms, nothing. . . . I said, 'Well! Do you think we should be putting up with this in this modern age? . . . We can stand up! We can talk back! . . . This country is very rich, and we want a share of the money those growers make [off] our sweat and our work by exploiting us and our children!'"

—quoted in *Moving the Mountain: Women Working for Social Change*

▲ **Carrying signs that say "Strike" (*huelga*), Mexican-American farm workers protest poor working conditions.**

The efforts of Jessie Lopez de la Cruz were just part of a larger rights movement during the turbulent and revolutionary 1960s. As African Americans were fighting for civil rights, Latinos and Native Americans rose up to assert their own rights and improve their lives.

The Latino Presence Grows

Latinos, or Americans of Latin American descent, are a large and diverse group. During the 1960s, the Latino population in the United States grew from 3 million to more than 9 million. Today the Latino population includes people from several different areas, primarily Mexico, Puerto Rico, Cuba, the Dominican Republic, Central America, and South America. Each of these groups has its own history, its

◀ In the 1920s, thousands of Mexican people came to the U.S. and settled in *barrios*. Shown here, Hispanic men gather in a park in California.

own pattern of settlement in the United States, and its own set of economic, social, cultural, and political concerns.

LATINOS OF VARIED ORIGINS Mexican Americans, the largest Latino group, have lived mostly in the Southwest and California. This group includes descendants of the nearly 100,000 Mexicans who had lived in territories ceded by Mexico to the United States in 1848. Another million or so Mexicans came to the United States in the 1910s, following Mexico's revolution. Still others came as *braceros*, or temporary laborers, during the 1940s and 1950s. In the 1960s close to half a million Mexicans immigrated, most in search of better paying jobs.

Puerto Ricans began immigrating to the United States after the U.S. occupation of Puerto Rico in 1898. As of 1960, almost 900,000 Puerto Ricans were living in the continental United States, including almost half a million on New York City's West Side.

Large Cuban communities also formed in New York City and in Miami and New Jersey. This is because hundreds of thousands of Cubans, many of whom were academics and professionals, fled to the United States in 1959 to escape Fidel Castro's Communist rule. In addition, tens of thousands of Salvadorans, Guatemalans, Nicaraguans, and Colombians immigrated to the United States after the 1960s to escape civil war and chronic poverty.

Wherever they had settled, during the 1960s many Latinos encountered ethnic prejudice and discrimination in jobs and housing. Most lived in segregated *barrios*, or Spanish-speaking neighborhoods. The Latino jobless rate was nearly 50 percent higher than that of whites, as was the percentage of Latino families living in poverty. (A)

MAIN IDEA

Identifying Problems

(A) What problems did different groups of Latino immigrants share?

Latinos Fight for Change

As the presence of Latinos in the United States grew, so too did their demand for greater representation and better treatment. During the 1960s, Latinos demanded not only equal opportunity, but also a respect for their culture and heritage.

HISTORICAL SPOTLIGHT

DESPERATE JOURNEYS

In the 1960s and 1970s, thousands of poor Mexicans illegally crossed the 2,000-mile border between the United States and Mexico each year. The journey these illegal aliens undertook was often made more difficult by "coyotes," guides who charged large amounts of money to help them cross the border, but who often didn't deliver on their promises.

Illegal immigrants' problems didn't end when they entered the United States, where they were denied many social services, including unemployment insurance and food stamps. In addition, the Immigration and Naturalization Service urged businesses to refrain from hiring them. As a result, some owners stopped employing people with Latino names, including legal immigrants.

THE FARM WORKER MOVEMENT As Jessie Lopez de la Cruz explained, thousands working on California's fruit and vegetable farms did backbreaking work for little pay and few benefits. César Chávez believed that farm workers had to unionize, that their strength would come from bargaining as a group. In 1962, Chávez and Dolores Huerta established the National Farm Workers Association. Four years later, this group merged with a Filipino agricultural union (also founded by Huerta) to form the **United Farm Workers Organizing Committee** (UFWOC).

"To us, the boycott of grapes was the most near-perfect of nonviolent struggles."
CÉSAR CHÁVEZ

Chávez and his fellow organizers insisted that California's large fruit and vegetable companies accept their union as the bargaining agent for the farm workers. In 1965, when California's grape growers refused to recognize the union, Chávez launched a nationwide boycott of the companies' grapes. Chávez, like Martin Luther King, Jr., believed in using nonviolence to reach his goal. The union sent farm workers across the country to convince supermarkets and shoppers not to buy California grapes. Chávez then went on a three-week fast in which he lost 35 pounds. He ended his fast by attending Mass with Senator Robert F. Kennedy. The efforts of the farm workers eventually paid off. In 1970, Huerta negotiated a contract between the grape growers and the UFWOC. Union workers would finally be guaranteed higher wages and other benefits long denied them. B

MAIN IDEA
Analyzing Effects
B What impact did the grape boycott have?

KEY PLAYER

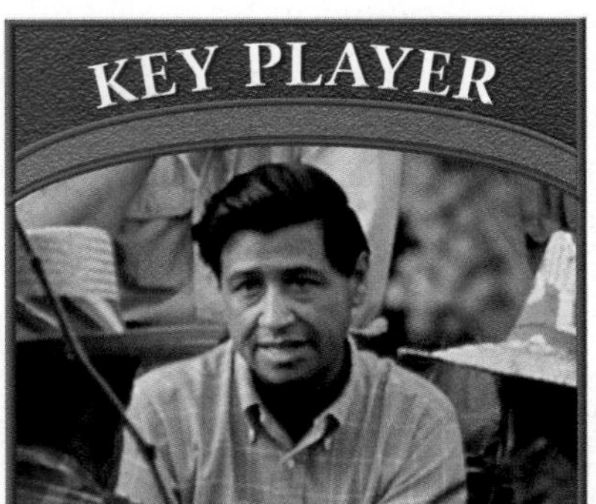

CÉSAR CHÁVEZ 1927–1993

César Chávez spoke from experience when he said, "Many things in farm labor are terrible."

As a teenager, Chávez moved with his family from farm to farm, picking such crops as grapes, apricots, and olives. "The worst crop was the olives," Chávez recalled. "The olives are so small you can never fill the bucket."

The seeds of protest grew early in Chávez. As a teenager, he once went to see a movie, only to find that the theater was segregated—whites on one side of the aisle and Mexicans on the other side. "I really hadn't thought much about what I was going to do, but I had to do something," Chávez recalled. The future union leader sat down in the whites-only section and stayed there until the police arrived and arrested him.

CULTURAL PRIDE The activities of the California farm workers helped to inspire other Latino "brown power" movements across the country. In New York, members of the Puerto Rican population began to demand that schools offer Spanish-speaking children classes taught in their own language as well as programs about their culture. In 1968, Congress enacted the Bilingual Education Act, which provided funds for schools to develop bilingual and cultural heritage programs for non-English-speaking children.

Young Mexican Americans started to call themselves Chicanos or Chicanas—a shortened version of "Mexicanos" that expressed pride in their ethnic heritage. A Chicano community action group called the Brown Berets formed under the leadership of David Sanchez. In 1968, the Brown Berets organized walkouts in East Los Angeles high schools. About 15,000 Chicano students walked out of class demanding smaller classes, more Chicano teachers and administrators, and programs designed to reduce the high Latino dropout rate. Militant Mexican-American students also won the establishment of Chicano studies programs at colleges and universities.

POLITICAL POWER Latinos also began organizing politically during the 1960s. Some worked within the two-party system. For example, the Mexican American Political Association (MAPA) helped elect Los Angeles politician Edward Roybal to the House of Representatives. During the 1960s, eight Hispanic Americans served in the House, and one Hispanic senator was elected—Joseph Montoya of New Mexico.

Background
Prior to 1960, 32 Hispanics had been elected to Congress, beginning with Joseph Hernandez in 1822.

Others, like Texan José Angel Gutiérrez, sought to create an independent Latino political movement. In 1970, he established **La Raza Unida** (The People United). In the 1970s, La Raza Unida ran Latino candidates in five states and won races for mayor, as well as other local positions on school boards and city councils.

Still other Latinos took on a more confrontational tone. In 1963, one-time evangelical preacher Reies Tijerina founded the Alianza Federal de Mercedes (Federal Alliance of Land Grants) to help reclaim U.S. land taken from Mexican landholders in the 19th century. He and his followers raided the Rio Arriba County Courthouse in Tierra Amarilla, New Mexico, in order to force authorities to recognize the plight of New Mexican small farmers. They were later arrested.

Native Americans Struggle for Equality

Vocabulary
homogeneous: uniform or similar throughout

As are Latinos, Native Americans are sometimes viewed as a single homogeneous group, despite the hundreds of distinct Native American tribes and nations in the United States. One thing that these diverse tribes and nations have shared is a mostly bleak existence in the United States and a lack of autonomy, or ability to control and govern their own lives. Through the years, many Native Americans have clung to their heritage, refusing to assimilate, or blend, into mainstream society. Native American nationalist Vine Deloria, Jr., expressed the view that mainstream society was nothing more than "ice cream bars and heart trouble and . . . getting up at six o'clock in the morning to mow your lawn in the suburbs."

NATIVE AMERICANS SEEK GREATER AUTONOMY Despite their cultural diversity, Native Americans as a group have been the poorest of Americans and have suffered from the highest unemployment rate. They have also been more likely than any other group to suffer from tuberculosis and alcoholism. Although the Native American population rose during the 1960s, the death rate among Native American infants was nearly twice the national average, while life expectancy was several years less than for other Americans.

In 1954, the Eisenhower administration enacted a "termination" policy to deal with these problems, but it did not respect Native American culture. Native Americans were relocated from isolated reservations into mainstream urban American life. The plan failed miserably. Most who moved to the cities remained desperately poor.

In 1961, representatives from 61 Native American groups met in Chicago and drafted the Declaration of Indian Purpose, which stressed the determination of Native Americans to "choose our own way of life." The declaration called for an end to the termination program in favor of new policies designed to create economic opportunities for Native Americans on their reservations. In 1968, President Lyndon Johnson established the National Council on Indian Opportunity to "ensure that programs reflect the needs and desires of the Indian people." C

MAIN IDEA
Analyzing Motives
C Why did Native Americans resist assimilation?

VOICES OF PROTEST Many young Native Americans were dissatisfied with the slow pace of reform. Their discontent fueled the growth of the **American Indian Movement (AIM),** an often militant Native American rights organization. While AIM began in 1968 largely as a self-defense group against police brutality, it soon branched out to include protecting the rights of large Native American populations in northern and western states.

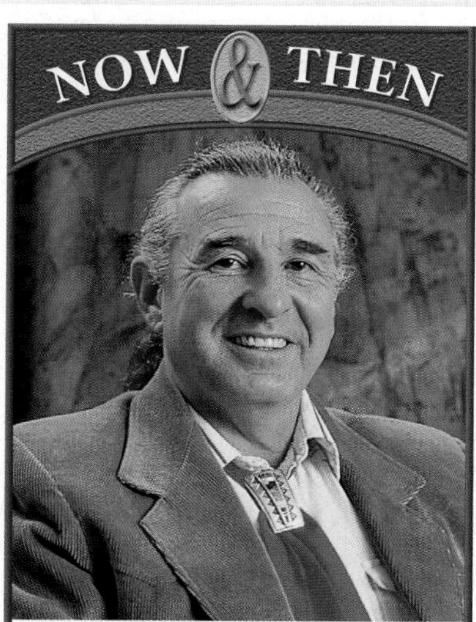

BEN NIGHTHORSE CAMPBELL

Whereas many Native Americans rejected assimilation, Ben Nighthorse Campbell has chosen to work within the system to improve the lives of Native Americans. Campbell's father was a North Cheyenne, and his great-grandfather, Black Horse, fought in the 1876 Battle of the Little Bighorn—in which the Cheyenne and the Sioux defeated Lieutenant Colonel George Custer.

In 1992, Campbell was elected to the U.S. Senate from Colorado, marking the first time since 1929 that a Native American had served in the Senate. Campbell stated that while his new job covered the entire nation, the needs of Native Americans would always remain a high priority.

AIM leader Dennis ▶ Banks speaks at the foot of Mount Rushmore, in South Dakota, during a 1970s rally.

For some, this new activism meant demanding that Native American lands, burial grounds, and fishing and timber rights be restored. Others wanted a new respect for their culture. Mary Crow Dog, a Lakota Sioux, described AIM's impact.

A PERSONAL VOICE MARY CROW DOG

"My first encounter with AIM was at a pow-wow held in 1971. . . . One man, a Chippewa, stood up and made a speech. I had never heard anybody talk like that. He spoke about genocide and sovereignty, about tribal leaders selling out. . . . He had himself wrapped up in an upside-down American flag, telling us that every star in this flag represented a state stolen from the Indians. . . . Some people wept. An old man turned to me and said, 'These are the words I always wanted to speak, but had kept shut up within me.'"

—*Lakota Women*

CONFRONTING THE GOVERNMENT In its early years, AIM, as well as other groups, actively—and sometimes violently—confronted the government. In 1972, AIM leader Russell Means organized the "Trail of Broken Treaties" march in Washington, D.C., to protest the U.S. government's treaty violations throughout history. Native Americans from across the country joined the march. They sought the restoration of 110 million acres of land. They also pushed for the abolition of the Bureau of Indian Affairs (BIA), which many believed was corrupt. The marchers temporarily occupied the BIA building, destroyed records, and caused $2 million in property damage.

"If the government doesn't start living up to its obligations, armed resistance . . . will have to become a regular thing."
CHIPPEWA PROTESTER

A year later, AIM led nearly 200 Sioux to the tiny village of Wounded Knee, South Dakota, where the U.S. cavalry had massacred a Sioux village in 1890. In protest against both tribal leadership and federal policies, the Sioux seized the town, taking hostages. After tense negotiations with the FBI and a shootout that left two Native Americans dead and others wounded, the confrontation ended with a government promise to reexamine Native American treaty rights. D

MAIN IDEA

Summarizing
D What tactics did AIM use in its attempts to gain reforms?

NATIVE AMERICAN VICTORIES Congress and the federal courts did make some reforms on behalf of Native Americans. In 1972, Congress passed the Indian Education Act. In 1975, it passed the Indian Self-Determination and Education

Native American Legal Victories

1970
Taos of New Mexico regain possession of Blue Lake as well as surrounding forestland.

1971
Alaska Native Claims Settlement Act gives Alaskan natives 44 million acres and more than $962 million.

1979
Maine Implementing Act provides $81.5 million for native tribes, including Penobscot and Passamaquoddy, to buy back land.

1980
U.S. awards Sioux $106 million for illegally taken land in South Dakota.

1988
U.S. awards Puyallup tribe $162 million for land claims in Washington.

Assistance Act. These laws gave tribes greater control over their own affairs and over their children's education.

Armed with copies of old land treaties that the U.S. government had broken, Native Americans went to federal court and regained some of their rights to land. In 1970, the Taos of New Mexico regained possession of their sacred Blue Lake, as well as a portion of its surrounding forestland. Land claims by natives of Alaska resulted in the Alaska Native Claims Settlement Act of 1971. This act gave more than 40 million acres to native peoples and paid out more than $962 million in cash. Throughout the 1970s and 1980s, Native Americans won settlements that provided legal recognition of their tribal lands as well as financial compensation.

While the 1960s and the early 1970s saw a wave of activism from the nation's minority groups, another group of Americans also pushed for changes. Women, while not a minority group, were in many ways treated like second-class citizens, and many joined together to demand equal treatment in society.

ASSESSMENT

1. **TERMS & NAMES** For each term or name, write a sentence explaining its significance.
   - **César Chávez**
   - **United Farm Workers Organizing Committee**
   - **La Raza Unida**
   - **American Indian Movement (AIM)**

MAIN IDEA

2. **TAKING NOTES**
   Create a Venn diagram like the one below to show the broad similarities between the issues faced by Latinos and Native Americans during the 1960s, as well as the unique concerns of the two groups.

   Issues Faced by Latinos and Native Americans

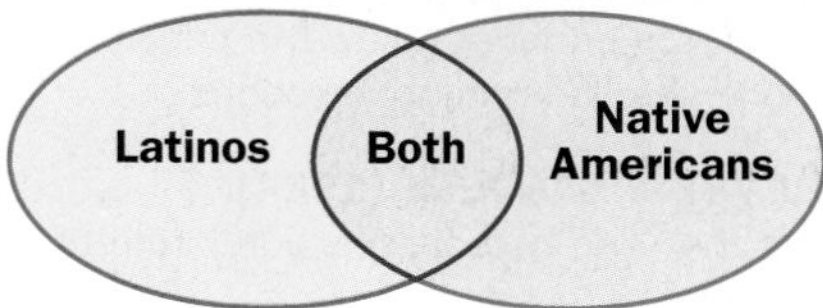

   Which group do you think had more to gain by fighting for what they wanted?

CRITICAL THINKING

3. **EVALUATING**
   How would you judge whether an activist organization was effective? List criteria you would use, and justify your criteria. **Think About:**
   - UFWOC, MAPA, and La Raza Unida
   - AIM
   - the leaders and activities of these organizations

4. **ANALYZING EFFECTS**
   In what ways did the Latino campaign for economic and social equality affect non-Latino Americans?

5. **ANALYZING PRIMARY SOURCES**
   Vine Deloria, Jr., said,

   > **"When you get far enough away from the reservation, you can see it's the urban man who has no identity."**

   What do you think he meant by this?

REYNOLDS v. *SIMS* (1964)

ORIGINS OF THE CASE In 1901, seats in the Alabama state legislature were apportioned, or assigned to districts, based on population. By the early 1960s, each Alabama county still had the same number of representatives as it did in 1901, even though the populations of the counties had changed. A group of voters sued to make representation proportional to the changed populations. When the suit succeeded, state legislators who were threatened with losing their seats appealed to the Supreme Court.

THE RULING **The Supreme Court upheld the principle of "one person, one vote" and ruled that the equal protection clause required representation in state legislatures to be based on population.**

LEGAL REASONING

Prior to *Reynolds*, the Court had already applied the "one person, one vote" principle to federal congressional elections (see Legal Sources). In *Reynolds*, Chief Justice Earl Warren extended this principle to state legislatures. He argued that when representation does not reflect population, some people's votes are worth more than others'.

> **"The fundamental principle of representative government in this country is one of equal representation for equal numbers of people, without regard to . . . place of residence within a State. . . . Legislators represent people, not trees or acres. Legislators are elected by voters, not farms or cities or economic interests."**

Warren concluded that Alabama's apportionment scheme discriminated against people because of where they live.

For these reasons, the Court ruled that any acceptable apportionment plan must provide an equal number of legislative seats for equally populated areas. A plan that does not is unconstitutional because it denies some voters the equal protection of the laws.

LEGAL SOURCES

U.S. CONSTITUTION

U.S. CONSTITUTION, FOURTEENTH AMENDMENT (1868)

"No state shall . . . deprive any person of life, liberty, or property, without due process of law; nor deny to any person within its jurisdiction the equal protection of the laws."

RELATED CASES

***BAKER* v. *CARR* (1962)**

The Court decided that federal courts could settle issues of apportionment. Previously, federal courts had refused to address such issues on the grounds that they were political issues.

***GRAY* v. *SANDERS* (1963)**

The Court ruled that states must follow the principle of "one person, one vote" in primary elections.

***WESBERRY* v. *SANDERS* (1964)**

The Court applied the "one person, one vote" rule to congressional districts.

◀ **Chief Justice Warren *(front, center)* and members of the 1964 Supreme Court.**

WHY IT MATTERED

The voters who initiated the suit against Alabama's apportionment were part of America's tremendous urban growth in the 20th century. During and after World War II, tens of thousands of Americans—including large numbers of African Americans—moved from rural areas to cities and suburbs. Voters in Alabama's more urban areas found that they were underrepresented. Likewise, before *Reynolds*, urban residents as a whole paid far more in taxes than they received in benefits. A great deal was at stake.

The "one person, one vote" principle increased the influence of urban residents by forcing legislatures to create new election districts in the cities to reflect their large populations. As more legislators representing urban and suburban needs were elected, they were able to change funding formulas, funneling more money into their districts. In addition, minorities, immigrants, and professionals, who tend to make up a large proportion of urban populations, gained better representation.

On the other hand, the power of farmers was eroded as election districts in rural areas were combined and incumbents had to campaign against each other for a single seat.

HISTORICAL IMPACT

The Warren Court's reapportionment decisions in *Baker* v. *Carr*, *Gray* v. *Sanders*, *Wesberry* v. *Sanders*, and *Reynolds* were a revolution in U.S. politics. The lawsuit that culminated in the *Reynolds* decision was also part of a broader movement in the 1960s to protect voting rights. Largely because of the Voting Rights Act of 1965, voter registration among African Americans in Mississippi, for instance, climbed from 6.7 percent to 59.8 percent. Viewed together, the combination of increased protection of voting rights and acceptance of the "one person, one vote" principle brought the United States several steps closer to fulfilling its democratic ideals.

In the 1990s, the Court revisited reapportionment. A 1982 act of Congress had required states to create districts with "minority majorities" in order to increase the number of nonwhite representatives. As a result, following the 1990 census, a record number of African Americans were elected to Congress. But opponents contended that defining districts by race violated equal protection and "one person, one vote." In a series of decisions, the Court agreed and abolished minority districting.

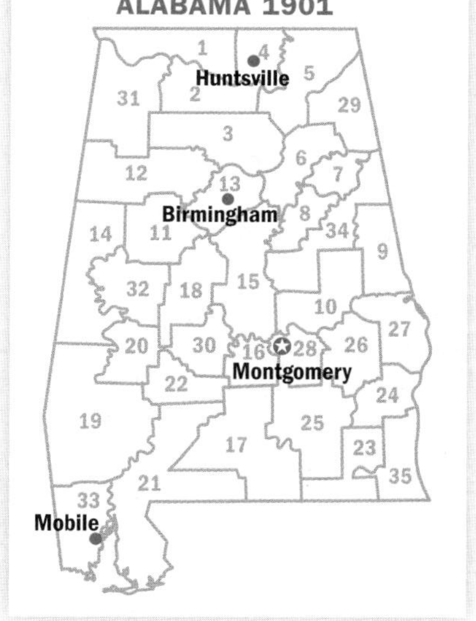

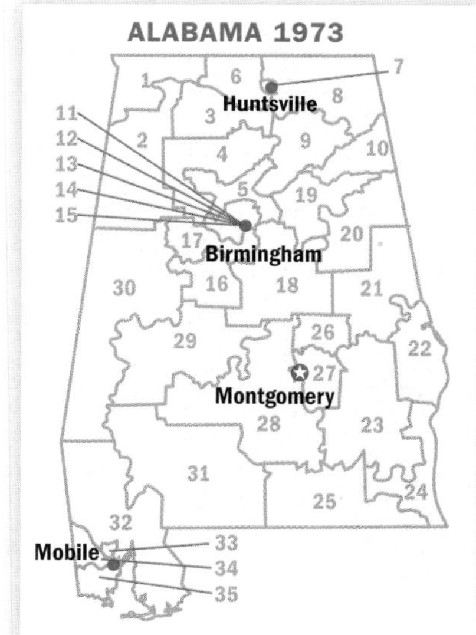

These two apportionment maps show Alabama's 35 state senatorial districts in 1901 *(left)* and 1973 *(right)*. The 1973 map shows how the districts were redrawn after the *Reynolds* decision, based on the 1970 census. Notice how the 1973 map reflects the growth of Alabama cities.

THINKING CRITICALLY

CONNECT TO TODAY

1. **Analyzing Maps** Obtain a map of the state legislative districts in your state. Then compare the map created following the 2000 census with the map based on the 1990 census. Study the differences in the size and location of the districts. Write a paragraph explaining which regions of the state gained representatives and which lost representatives.

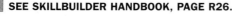

 **SEE SKILLBUILDER HANDBOOK, PAGE R26.**

CONNECT TO HISTORY

2. 

CLASSZONE.COM

Visit the links for Historic Decisions of the Supreme Court to research minority redistricting decisions such as *Shaw* v. *Hunt* (1996). Write a summary of the rulings and how they have affected elections.

SECTION 2

Women Fight for Equality

MAIN IDEA

Through protests and marches, women confronted social and economic barriers in American society.

WHY IT MATTERS NOW

The rise of the women's movement during the 1960s advanced women's place in the work force and in society.

Terms & Names

- **Betty Friedan**
- **feminism**
- **National Organization for Women (NOW)**
- **Gloria Steinem**
- **Equal Rights Amendment (ERA)**
- **Phyllis Schlafly**

One American's Story

During the 1950s, writer **Betty Friedan** seemed to be living the American dream. She had a loving husband, healthy children, and a house in the suburbs. According to the experts—doctors, psychologists, and women's magazines—that was all a woman needed to be fulfilled. Why, then, wasn't she happy? In 1957, after conducting a survey of her Smith College classmates 15 years after graduation, she found she was not alone. Friedan eventually wrote a book, *The Feminine Mystique,* in which she addressed this "problem that has no name."

A PERSONAL VOICE BETTY FRIEDAN

"The problem lay buried, unspoken. . . . It was a strange stirring, a sense of dissatisfaction, a yearning that women suffered in the middle of the twentieth century in the United States. Each suburban wife struggled with it alone. As she made the beds, shopped for groceries, matched slipcover material, ate peanut butter sandwiches with her children, chauffeured Cub Scouts and Brownies, lay beside her husband at night—she was afraid to ask even of herself the silent question—'Is this all?'"

—*The Feminine Mystique*

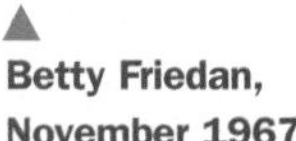

▲ Betty Friedan, November 1967

During the 1960s, women answered Friedan's question with a resounding "no." In increasing numbers they joined the nation's African Americans, Latinos, and Native Americans in the fight for greater civil rights and equality in society.

A New Women's Movement Arises

The theory behind the women's movement of the 1960s was **feminism,** the belief that women should have economic, political, and social equality with men. Feminist beliefs had gained momentum during the mid-1800s and in 1920 won women the right to vote. While the women's movement declined after this achievement, it reawakened during the 1960s, spurred by the political activism of the times.

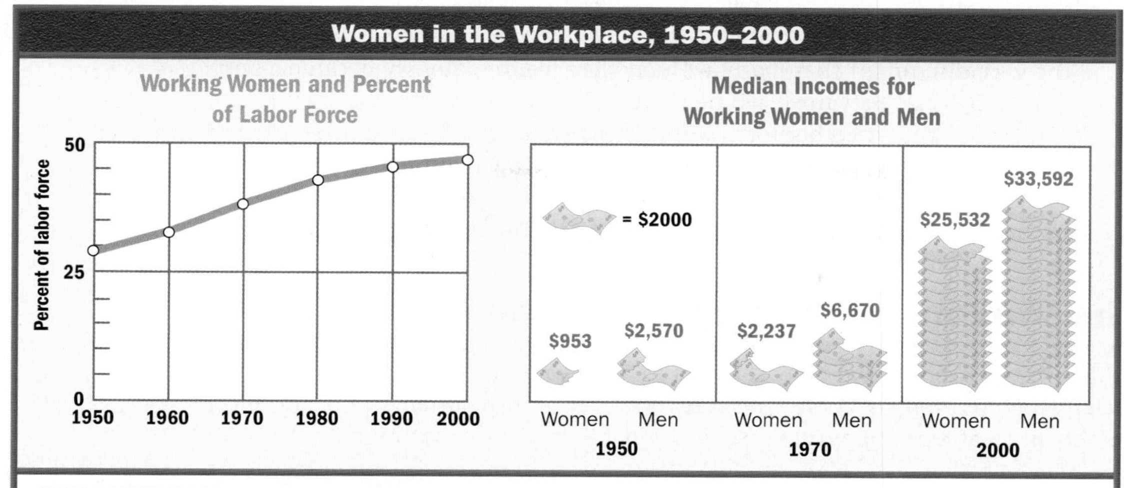

SKILLBUILDER Interpreting Graphs

1. For each year shown, what percentage of men's income did women make?
2. About how many more women were working in 1990 than in 1960?

SEE SKILLBUILDER HANDBOOK, PAGE R28.

This 1960s pin displays a slogan used by Betty Friedan at the National Women's Political Caucus.

WOMEN MAKE POLICY NOT COFFEE

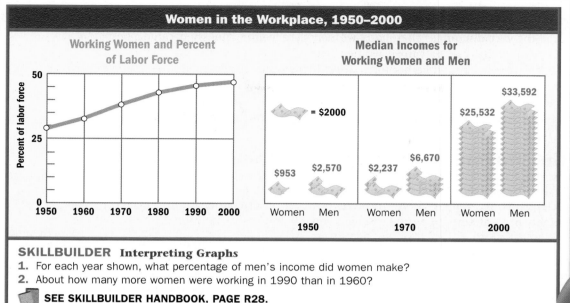

WOMEN IN THE WORKPLACE In 1950, only one out of three women worked for wages. By 1960, that number had increased to about 40 percent. Still, during this time, certain jobs were considered "men's work" and women were shut out. The jobs available to women—mostly clerical work, domestic service, retail sales, social work, teaching, and nursing—paid poorly.

The country largely ignored this discrimination until President Kennedy appointed the Presidential Commission on the Status of Women in 1961. In 1963, the commission reported that women were paid far less than men, even when doing the same jobs. Furthermore, women were seldom promoted to management positions, regardless of their education, experience, and ability. These newly publicized facts awakened many women to their unequal status in society.

WOMEN AND ACTIVISM Ironically, many women felt the sting of discrimination when they became involved in the civil rights and antiwar movements—movements that toted the ideological banner of protecting people's rights. Within some of these organizations, such as SNCC and SDS, men led most of the activities, while women were assigned lesser roles. When women protested this arrangement, the men usually brushed them aside.

> *"Move on little girl; we have more important issues to talk about here than women's liberation."*
>
> A MALE ANTIWAR ACTIVIST

Vocabulary
ideological: concerned with a certain set of ideas

Such experiences led some women to organize small groups to discuss their concerns. During these discussions, or "consciousness-raising" sessions, women shared their lives with each other and discovered that their experiences were not unique. Rather, they reflected a much larger pattern of sexism, or discrimination based on gender. Author Robin Morgan delineated this pattern. (A)

MAIN IDEA

Analyzing Effects
(A) What effects did the civil rights and the antiwar movements have on many women?

A Personal Voice ROBIN MORGAN

> **"It makes you very sensitive—raw, even, this consciousness. Everything, from the verbal assault on the street, to a 'well-meant' sexist joke your husband tells, to the lower pay you get at work (for doing the same job a man would be paid more for), to television commercials, to rock-song lyrics, to the pink or blue blanket they put on your infant in the hospital nursery, to speeches by male 'revolutionaries' that reek of male supremacy—everything seems to barrage your aching brain. . . . You begin to see how all-pervasive a thing is sexism."**
>
> —quoted in *Sisterhood Is Powerful: An Anthology of Writings from the Women's Liberation Movement*

THE WOMEN'S MOVEMENT EMERGES *The Feminine Mystique,* which captured the very discontent that many women were feeling, quickly became a best-seller and helped to galvanize women across the country. By the late 1960s, women were working together for change. "This is not a movement one 'joins,'" observed Robin Morgan. "The Women's Liberation Movement exists where three or four friends or neighbors decide to meet regularly . . . on the welfare lines, in the supermarket, the factory, the convent, the farm, the maternity ward."

The Movement Experiences Gains and Losses

As the women's movement grew, it achieved remarkable and enduring political and social gains for women. Along the way, however, it also suffered setbacks, most notably in its attempt to ensure women's equality in the Constitution.

THE CREATION OF NOW The women's movement gained strength with the passage of the Civil Rights Act of 1964, which prohibited discrimination based on race, religion, national origin, and gender and created the Equal Employment Opportunity Commission (EEOC) to handle discrimination claims. By 1966, however, some women argued that the EEOC didn't adequately address women's grievances. That year, 28 women, including Betty Friedan, created the **National Organization for Women (NOW)** to pursue women's goals. "The time has come," the founders of NOW declared, "to confront with concrete action the conditions which now prevent women from enjoying the equality of opportunity . . . which is their right as individual Americans and as human beings." B

MAIN IDEA

Analyzing Causes

B What prompted women to establish NOW?

NOW members pushed for the creation of child-care facilities that would enable mothers to pursue jobs and education. NOW also pressured the EEOC to enforce more vigorously the ban on gender discrimination in hiring. NOW's efforts prompted the EEOC to declare sex-segregated job ads illegal and to issue guidelines to employers, stating that they could no longer refuse to hire women for traditionally male jobs.

KEY PLAYER

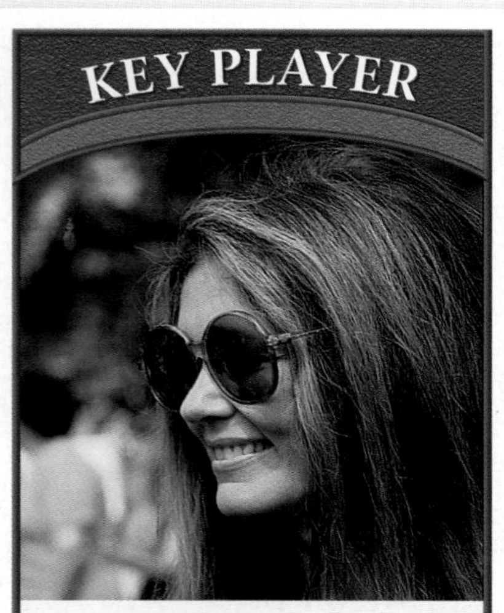

GLORIA STEINEM
1934–

Gloria Steinem became one of the more prominent figures of the women's movement after she and several other women founded *Ms.* magazine in 1972. The magazine soon became a major voice of the women's movement.

Steinem said that she decided to start the feminist magazine after editors in the mainstream media continually rejected her stories about the women's movement:

> "Editors who had assumed I had some valuable biological insight into food, male movie stars, and textured stockings now questioned whether I or other women writers were biologically capable of writing objectively about feminism. That was the beginning."

A DIVERSE MOVEMENT In its first three years, NOW's ranks swelled to 175,000 members. A number of other women's groups sprang up around the country, too. In 1968, a militant group known as the New York Radical Women staged a well-publicized demonstration at the annual Miss America Pageant. The women threw bras, girdles, wigs, and other "women's garbage" into a "Freedom Trash Can." They then crowned a sheep "Miss America." Around this time, **Gloria Steinem,** a journalist, political activist, and ardent supporter of the women's liberation movement, made her voice heard on the subjects of feminism and equality. Steinem's grandmother had served as president of the Ohio Woman's Suffrage Association from 1908 to 1911; Steinem had inherited her passion and conviction. In 1971, Steinem helped found the National Women's Political Caucus, a moderate group that encouraged women to seek political office. In 1972, she and other women created a new women's magazine, *Ms.*, designed to treat contemporary issues from a feminist perspective.

LEGAL AND SOCIAL GAINS As the women's movement progressed, women began to question all sorts of gender-based distinctions. People protested that a woman's physical

Thousands of women march through the streets of New York City during the summer of 1970 to promote women's equality.

appearance was often considered a job qualification. Girls' exclusion from sports such as baseball and football came into question. Some women began using the title Ms., instead of the standard Miss or Mrs., and refused to adopt their husband's last name upon marriage.

These changes in attitude were paralleled by numerous legal changes. In 1972, Congress passed a ban on gender discrimination in "any education program or activity receiving federal financial assistance," as part of the Higher Education Act. As a result, several all-male colleges opened their doors to women. That same year, Congress expanded the powers of the EEOC and gave working parents a tax break for child-care expenses. (C)

MAIN IDEA

Making Generalizations

(C) What sort of gains did the women's movement make by the early 1970s?

ROE* v. *WADE One of the more controversial positions that NOW and other feminist groups supported was a woman's right to have an abortion. In 1973, the Supreme Court ruled in *Roe* v. *Wade* that women do have the right to choose an abortion during the first three months of pregnancy. Some thought the ruling might "bring to an end the emotional and divisive public argument." However, the issue still divides Americans today.

THE EQUAL RIGHTS AMENDMENT (ERA) In what seemed at first to be another triumph for the women's movement, Congress passed the **Equal Rights Amendment (ERA)** in 1972. The amendment then needed ratification by 38 states to become part of the Constitution. First introduced to Congress in 1923, the ERA would guarantee that both men and women would enjoy the same rights and protections under the law. It was, many supporters said, a matter of "simple justice."

The amendment scared many people, and a Stop-ERA campaign was launched in 1972. Conservative **Phyllis Schlafly,** along with conservative religious groups, political organizations, and many anti-feminists, felt that the ERA would lead to "a parade of horribles," such as the drafting of women, the end of laws protecting homemakers, the end of a husband's responsibility to provide for his family, and same-sex marriages. Schlafly said that radical feminists "hate men, marriage, and children" and were oppressed "only in their distorted minds."

A PERSONAL VOICE PHYLLIS SCHLAFLY

"The U.S. Constitution is not the place for symbols or slogans, it is not the proper device to alleviate psychological problems of personal inferiority. Symbols and slogans belong on bumper strips—not in the Constitution. It would be a tragic mistake for our nation to succumb to the tirades and demands of a few women who are seeking a constitutional cure for their personal problems."

— quoted in *The Equal Rights Amendment: The History and the Movement*

Phyllis Schlafly

THE NEW RIGHT EMERGES In order to combat the ERA and the pro-abortion supporters, conservatives built what they called a new "pro-family" movement. In the 1970s, this coalition—which focused on social, cultural, and moral problems—came to be known as the New Right. The New Right and the women's movement debated family-centered issues such as whether the government should pay for daycare, which the New Right opposed. Throughout the 1970s, the New Right built grassroots support for social conservatism. It would later play a key role in the election of Ronald Reagan to the presidency in 1980. (D)

MAIN IDEA

Analyzing Motives

(D) What concerns motivated those who opposed the ERA?

The Movement's Legacy

The New Right and the women's movement clashed most dramatically over the ERA. By 1977 it had won approval from 35 of the 38 states needed for ratification, but the New Right gained strength. By June of 1982—the deadline for ratification—not enough states had approved the amendment. The ERA went down in defeat.

Despite ERA's defeat, the women's movement altered society in countless ways, such as by transforming women's conventional roles and their attitudes toward career and family. Interviews with women graduates at Stanford University reflect the change. Of graduates in 1965, 70 percent planned not to work at all when their children were of preschool age. When the class of 1972 was surveyed, only 7 percent said they would stop working to raise children.

As this poster shows, women have made significant political strides by being elected to the U.S. Congress.

The women's movement also succeeded in expanding career opportunities for women. For instance, as of 1970, 8 percent of all medical school graduates and 5 percent of all law school graduates were women. By 1998, those proportions had risen to 42 and 44 percent, respectively. Yet many women ran into a "glass ceiling"—an invisible, but very real, resistance to promoting women into top positions.

By 1983 women held 13.5 percent of elected state offices as well as 24 seats in the U.S. Congress. More importantly, as historian Sara Evans has noted, by 1980 "feminist concerns were firmly on the national political agenda and clearly there to stay." Most of all, the women's movement helped countless women open their lives to new possibilities. "For we have lived the second American revolution," wrote Betty Friedan in 1976, "and our very anger said a 'new YES' to life."

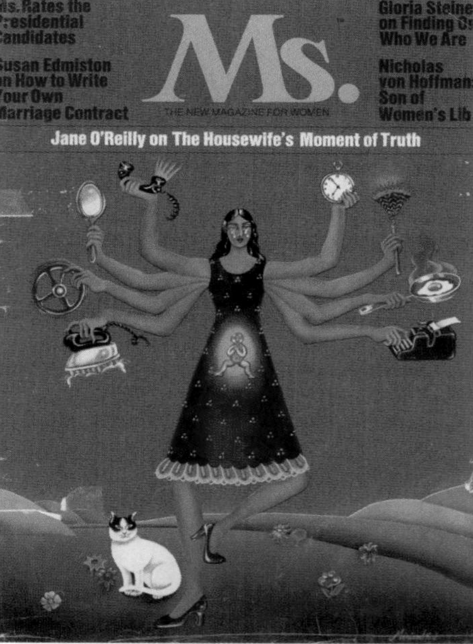

Ms.
THE NEW MAGAZINE FOR WOMEN
Ms. Rates the Presidential Candidates
Susan Edmiston on How to Write Your Own Marriage Contract
Nicholas von Hoffman: Son of Women's Lib
Jane O'Reilly on The Housewife's Moment of Truth

SECTION 2 ASSESSMENT

1. **TERMS & NAMES** For each term or name, write a sentence explaining its significance.
   - **Betty Friedan**
   - **feminism**
   - **National Organization for Women (NOW)**
   - **Gloria Steinem**
   - **Equal Rights Amendment (ERA)**
   - **Phyllis Schlafly**

MAIN IDEA

2. **TAKING NOTES**
   Create a time line of key events relating to the women's movement.

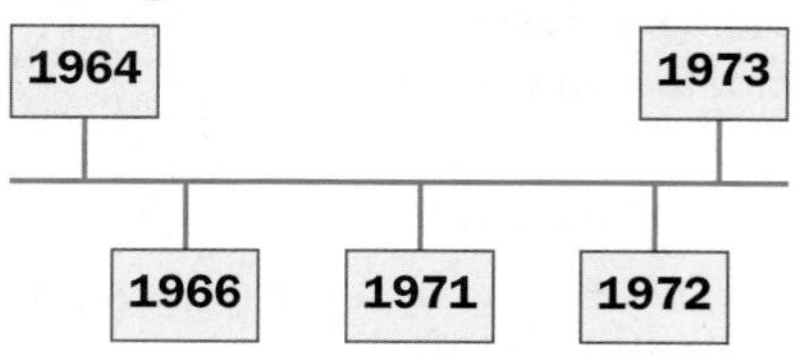

   Explain which event you think best demonstrates progressive reform.

CRITICAL THINKING

3. **HYPOTHESIZING**
   What if the Equal Rights Amendment had been ratified? Speculate on how women's lives might have been different. Use reasons to support your answer.
   Think About:
   - rights addressed by the amendment
   - legal support that the amendment might have provided
   - possible reactions from groups opposing the amendment

4. **ANALYZING VISUAL SOURCES**
   Examine the drawing on this 1972 cover of *Ms.* The woman shown has eight arms and is holding a different object in each hand. What do you think these objects symbolize in terms of women's roles? What do you think this drawing says about women in the 1960s? Explain.

SECTION 3

Culture and Counterculture

MAIN IDEA	WHY IT MATTERS NOW	Terms & Names
The ideals and lifestyle of the counterculture challenged the traditional views of Americans.	**The music, art, and politics of the counterculture have left enduring marks on American society.**	**•counterculture •Haight-Ashbury •the Beatles •Woodstock**

One American's Story

In 1966, Alex Forman left his conventional life in mainstream America and headed to San Francisco. Arriving there with little else but a guitar, he joined thousands of others who were determined to live in a more peaceful and carefree environment. He recalled his early days in San Francisco's Haight-Ashbury district, the hub of hippie life.

A PERSONAL VOICE ALEX FORMAN

"It was like paradise there. Everybody was in love with life and in love with their fellow human beings to the point where they were just sharing in incredible ways with everybody. Taking people in off the street and letting them stay in their homes. . . . You could walk down almost any street in Haight-Ashbury where I was living, and someone would smile at you and just go, 'Hey, it's beautiful, isn't it?'. . . It was a very special time."

—quoted in *From Camelot to Kent State*

Members of the counterculture relax in a California park.

Forman was part of the **counterculture**—a movement made up mostly of white, middle-class college youths who had grown disillusioned with the war in Vietnam and injustices in America during the 1960s. Instead of challenging the system, they turned their backs on traditional America and tried to establish a whole new society based on peace and love. Although their heyday was short-lived, their legacy remains.

The Counterculture

In the late 1960s, the historian Theodore Roszak deemed these idealistic youths the counterculture. It was a culture, he said, so different from the mainstream "that it scarcely looks to many as a culture at all, but takes on the alarming appearance of a barbarian intrusion."

"TUNE IN, TURN ON, DROP OUT" Members of the counterculture, known as hippies, shared some of the beliefs of the New Left movement. Specifically, they felt that American society—and its materialism, technology, and war—had grown hollow. Influenced by the nonconformist beat movement of the 1950s, hippies embraced the credo of Harvard psychology professor and counterculture philosopher Timothy Leary: "Tune in, turn on, drop out." Throughout the mid- and late 1960s, tens of thousands of idealistic youths left school, work, or home to create what they hoped would be an idyllic community of peace, love, and harmony.

"How does it feel to be without a home . . . like a rolling stone?"
BOB DYLAN

HIPPIE CULTURE The hippie era, sometimes known as the Age of Aquarius, was marked by rock 'n' roll music, outrageous clothing, sexual license, and illegal drugs—in particular, marijuana and a new hallucinogenic drug called LSD, or acid. Timothy Leary, an early experimenter with the drug, promoted the use of LSD as a "mind-expanding" aid for self-awareness. Hippies also turned to Eastern religions such as Zen Buddhism, which professed that one could attain enlightenment through meditation rather than the reading of scriptures.

Hippies donned ragged jeans, tie-dyed T-shirts, military garments, love beads, and Native American ornaments. Thousands grew their hair out, despite the fact that their more conservative elders saw this as an act of disrespect. Signs across the country said, "Make America beautiful—give a hippie a haircut."

Hippies also rejected conventional home life. Many joined communes, in which the members renounced private property to live communally. By the mid-sixties, **Haight-Ashbury** in San Francisco was known as the hippie capital, mainly because California did not outlaw hallucinogenic drugs until 1966.

DECLINE OF THE MOVEMENT After only a few years, the counterculture's peace and harmony gave way to violence and disillusionment. The urban communes eventually turned seedy and dangerous. Alex Forman recalled, "There were ripoffs, violence . . . people living on the street with no place to stay." Having dispensed with society's conventions and rules, the hippies had to rely on each other. Many discovered that the philosophy of "do your own thing" did not provide enough guidance for how to live. "We were together at the level of peace and love," said one disillusioned hippie. "We fell apart over who would cook and wash dishes and pay the bills." By 1970, many had fallen victim to the drugs they used, experiencing drug addiction and mental breakdowns. The rock singer Janis Joplin and the legendary guitarist Jimi Hendrix both died of drug overdoses in 1970.

As the mystique of the 1960s wore off, thousands of hippies lined up at government offices to collect welfare and food stamps—dependent on the very society they had once rejected. (A)

MAIN IDEA

Analyzing Causes

(A) What events and other factors hastened the decline of the counterculture movement?

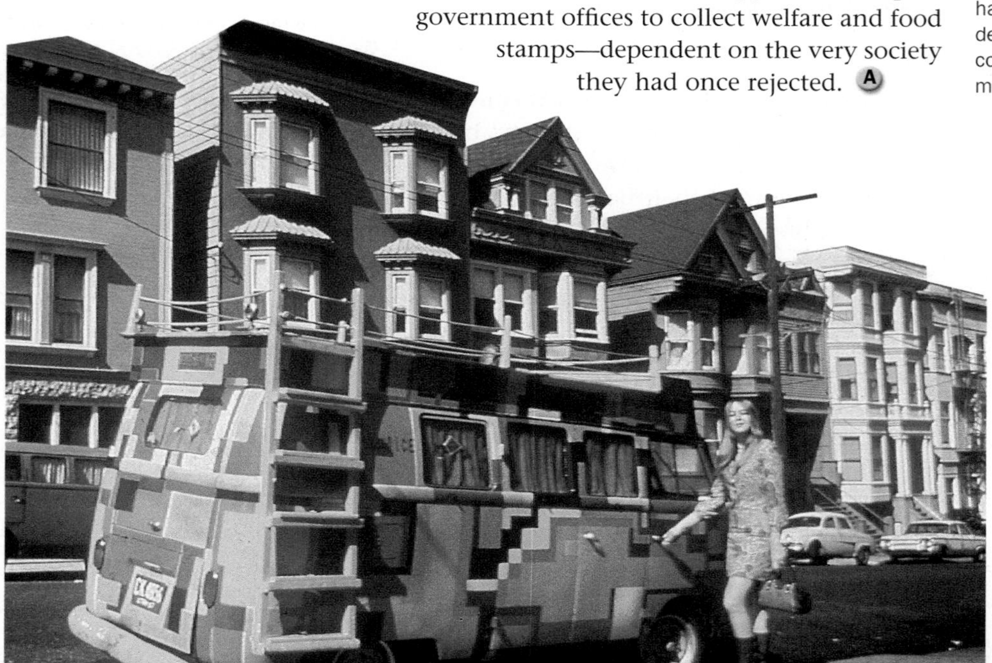

A prominent symbol of the counterculture movement was bright colors. ▶

A Changing Culture

Although short-lived, some aspects of the counterculture—namely, its fine arts and social attitudes—left a more lasting imprint on the world.

ART The counterculture's rebellious style left its mark on the art world. The 1960s saw the rise of pop art (popular art). Pop artists, led by Andy Warhol, attempted to bring art into the mainstream. Pop art was characterized by bright, simple, commercial-looking images often depicting everyday life. For instance, Warhol became famous for his bright silk-screen portraits of soup cans, Marilyn Monroe, and other icons of mass culture. These images were repeated to look mass-produced and impersonal, a criticism of the times implying that individual freedoms had been lost to a more conventional, "cookie-cutter" lifestyle.

MAIN IDEA

Making Inferences

B What did rock 'n' roll symbolize for American youth?

ROCK MUSIC During the 1960s, the counterculture movement embraced rock 'n' roll as its loud and biting anthem of protest. The music was an offshoot of African-American rhythm and blues music that had captivated so many teenagers during the 1950s. **B**

The band that, perhaps more than any other, helped propel rock music into mainstream America was **the Beatles.** The British band, made up of four youths from working-class Liverpool, England, arrived in America in 1964 and immediately took the country by storm. By the time the Beatles broke up in 1970, the four "lads" had inspired a countless number of other bands and had won over millions of Americans to rock 'n' roll.

▲ The Beatles, shown here in 1967, influenced fashion with their long hair and psychedelic clothing.

One example of rock 'n' roll's popularity occurred in August 1969 on a farm in upstate New York. More than 400,000 showed up for a music festival called "**Woodstock** Music and Art Fair." This festival represented, as one songwriter put it, "the '60s movement of peace and love and some higher cultural cause." For three days, the most popular bands and musicians performed, including Jimi Hendrix, Janis Joplin, Joe Cocker, Joan Baez, the Grateful Dead, and Jefferson Airplane. Despite the huge crowd, Woodstock was peaceful and well organized. However, Tom Mathews, a writer who attended the Woodstock festival, recalled his experience there as less than blissful.

A PERSONAL VOICE TOM MATHEWS

"The last night of the concert I was standing in a narrow pit at the foot of the stage. I made the mistake of looking over the board fence separating the pit from Max Yasgur's hillside. When I peered up I saw 400,000 . . . people wrapped in wet, dirty ponchos, sleeping bags and assorted, tie-dyed mufti slowly slipping toward the stage. It looked like a human mud slide. . . . After that night I couldn't get out of there fast enough."

—"The Sixties Complex," *Newsweek*, Sept. 5, 1988

CHANGING ATTITUDES While the counterculture movement faded, its casual "do your own thing" philosophy left its mark. American attitudes toward sexual behavior became more casual and permissive, leading to what became known as the sexual revolution. During the 1960s and 1970s, mass culture—including TV, books,

History Through *Music*

PROTEST SONGS OF THE SIXTIES

During the turbulent climate of the sixties, hippies and other activists used music as a vehicle for political expression. In bus terminals, in the streets, and on the White House lawn, thousands united in song, expressing their rejection of mainstream society, their demand for civil rights, and their outrage over the Vietnam War. Musicians like Bob Dylan stirred up antiwar sentiment in songs like "The Times They Are A-Changin'," while Joan Baez and Pete Seeger popularized the great African-American spiritual "We Shall Overcome," which became the anthem of the Civil Rights Movement.

We Shall Overcome (African-American Spiritual)

We shall overcome,
We shall overcome,
We shall overcome some day.
(*Chorus*) Oh, deep in my heart
I do believe:
We shall overcome some day.
We'll walk hand in hand. . . .
We shall all be free. . . .
We are not afraid. . . .
We are not alone. . . .
The whole wide world around. . . .
We shall overcome. . . .

▲ **Joined in harmony, African-American students in Selma, Alabama, gather on the steps of the Tabernacle Baptist Church to sing "We Shall Overcome." (1963)**

Joan Baez, 1965

Bob Dylan, 1966 ▶

from **The Times They Are A-Changin' (Bob Dylan, 1962)**

Come senators, congressmen
Please heed the call
Don't stand in the doorway
Don't block up the hall
For he that gets hurt
Will be he who has stalled
There's a battle outside
And it is ragin'.
It'll soon shake your windows
And rattle your walls
For the times they are a-changin'.

Come mothers and fathers
Throughout the land
And don't criticize
What you can't understand
Your sons and your daughters
Are beyond your command
Your old road is
Rapidly agin'.
Please get out of the new one
If you can't lend your hand
For the times they are a-changin'.

magazines, music, and movies—began to address subjects that had once been prohibited, particularly sexual behavior and explicit violence.

While some hailed the increasing permissiveness as liberating, others attacked it as a sign of moral decay. For millions of Americans, the new tolerance was merely an uncivilized lack of respect for established social norms. Eventually, the counterculture movement would lead a great many Americans to more liberal attitudes about dress and appearance, lifestyle, and social behavior; yet in the short run, it produced largely the opposite effect.

The Conservative Response

In the late 1960s, many believed that the country was losing its sense of right and wrong. Increasingly, conservative voices began to express people's anger. At the 1968 Republican convention in Miami, candidate Richard M. Nixon expressed that anger.

A PERSONAL VOICE RICHARD NIXON

"**As we look at America, we see cities enveloped in smoke and flame. We hear sirens in the night. . . . We see Americans hating each other . . . at home. . . . Did we come all this way for this? . . . die in Normandy and Korea and in Valley Forge for this?**"

—Speech at Republican Convention, 1968

▲ **In contrast to the 1968 Democratic Convention in Chicago, the Republican convention was orderly and united—particularly in the delegates' opposition to the counterculture.**

CONSERVATIVES ATTACK THE COUNTERCULTURE Nixon was not the only conservative voice expressing alarm. FBI Director J. Edgar Hoover issued a warning that "revolutionary terrorism" was a threat on campuses and in cities. Other conservative critics warned that campus rebels posed a danger to traditional values and threatened to plunge American society into anarchy. Conservatives also attacked the counterculture for what they saw as its decadent values. In the view of psychiatrist Bruno Bettelheim, student rebels and members of the counterculture had been pampered in childhood; as young adults, they did not have the ability for delayed gratification. According to some conservative commentators, the counterculture had abandoned rational thought in favor of the senses and uninhibited self-expression. (C)

MAIN IDEA

Forming Generalizations

(C) Why were conservatives angry about the counterculture?

The angry response of mainstream Americans caused a profound change in the political landscape of the United States. By the end of the 1960s, conservatives were presenting their own solutions on such issues as lawlessness and crime, the size of the federal government, and welfare. This growing conservative movement would propel Nixon into the White House—and set the nation on a more conservative course.

SECTION 3 ASSESSMENT

1. **TERMS & NAMES** For each term or name, write a sentence explaining its significance.
   - **counterculture**
   - **Haight-Ashbury**
   - **the Beatles**
   - **Woodstock**

MAIN IDEA

2. **TAKING NOTES**
   Re-create the tree diagram below on your paper. Then fill in examples that illustrate the topics in the second row of boxes.

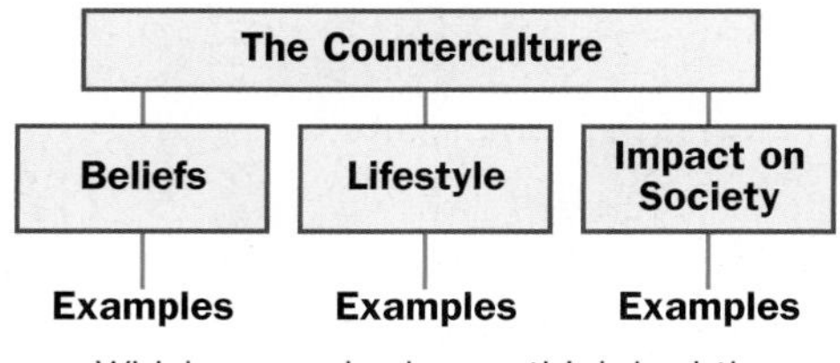

   Which example do you think had the biggest impact on society? Why?

CRITICAL THINKING

3. **DEVELOPING HISTORICAL PERSPECTIVE**
   A stereotype is a generalization made about a group. What stereotype do you think hippies might have formed about mainstream Americans? What stereotype do you think mainstream Americans might have formed about hippies? Why? **Think About:**
   - Alex Forman's comments in "A Personal Voice" (page 781)
   - hippies' values and lifestyle
   - mainstream Americans' values and lifestyle

4. **MAKING INFERENCES**
   In your opinion, why didn't the hippies succeed?

5. **ANALYZING ISSUES**
   What role did the counterculture and antiwar movement play in helping Richard Nixon win the presidency?

DAILY LIFE 1960–1970

Signs of the Sixties

The wave of social change that swept across America during the 1960s affected everyone, but especially the nation's teenagers. Abandoning the conservative and "clean-cut" look of the 1950s, many teens experimented with new and different appearances. In a declaration of their individuality and desire for more freedom, they also embraced a variety of new music and films during the 1960s.

FASHION: A NEW LOOK ▶

During the 1960s, many youths wore a wide range of unconventional clothing. While most Americans did not adopt the outlandish look of hippies, many came out of the sixties wearing longer hair and blue jeans, which became a staple in nearly every wardrobe. Bright colors and psychedelic patterns also became wildly popular.

◀ THE RISE OF SOUL MUSIC

Rock 'n' roll's popularity continued to soar as teenagers listened to a wider variety of sounds in the 1960s. African-American soul artists, whose music had inspired the more popular white rock 'n' roll performers of the 1950s, grew widely popular themselves during the 1960s. During this decade, Detroit's Motown label produced the most popular and successful African-American artists, including Marvin Gaye, Stevie Wonder, and the Supremes (left).

A DIVERSE MUSIC SCENE ▶

Scores of teenagers also tuned to surf music, a harmonic, light sound made popular by a California band, the Beach Boys. Other teens listened to the poetic and socially conscious lyrics of folk rock. Heavy, or psychedelic, rock, sung by bands such as the Doors (whose 1967 concert advertisement appears to the right), also found its way into many album collections. In the later part of the decade, musicians like Jimi Hendrix (far right) took rock 'n' roll in a new direction.

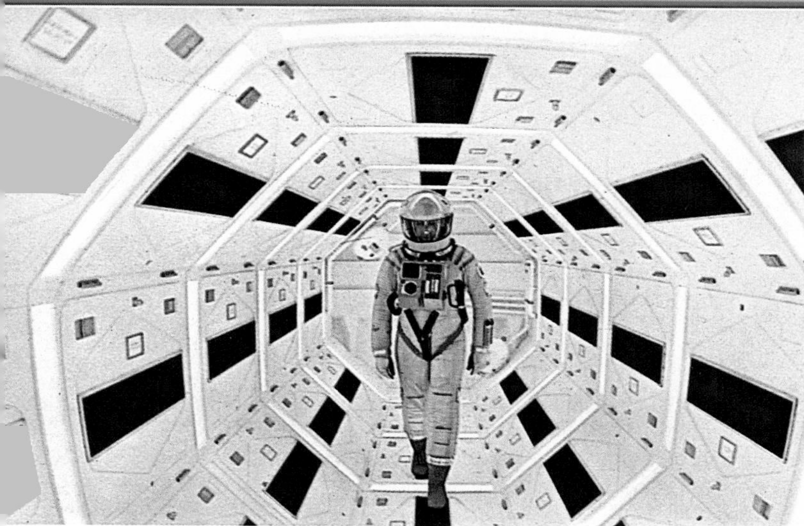

GOING TO THE SHOW ▲

As the nation's movie industry grew, more and more teenagers flocked to the cinema. Teens took in such diverse films as the counterculture classic *Easy Rider* and the science fiction classic *2001: A Space Odyssey* (above), which tells the story of HAL, a spaceship computer that develops a mind of its own.

POP ART ▲

Andy Warhol created this image of movie actress and popular icon Marilyn Monroe. A leader of the pop art movement, Warhol attempted to criticize the conventional lifestyle of the mass culture through commercial-looking images that depicted the loss of individuality.

DATA FILE

POPULAR SONGS

- "Blowin' in the Wind" (1962)
- "Surfin' USA" (1963)
- "Where Did Our Love Go?" (1964)
- "California Dreamin'" (1966)
- "Light My Fire" (1967)
- "Mrs. Robinson" (1967)
- "Aquarius/Let the Sunshine In" (1968)
- "Come Together" (1969)
- "Everyday People" (1968)

POPULAR TV SHOWS

- *The Dick Van Dyke Show* (1962–1966)
- *The Beverly Hillbillies* (1962–1971)
- *Green Acres* (1965–1971)
- *The Addams Family* (1964–1966)
- *The Man from U.N.C.L.E.* (1964–1968)
- *Mission: Impossible* (1966–1973)
- *Laugh-In* (1968–1973)
- *Bonanza* (1959–1973)

1960: Alfred Hitchcock's *Psycho* terrifies movie audiences across the nation.

1962: Wilt Chamberlain scores 100 points in a basketball game.

1963: The movie *Cleopatra*, produced for $37 million, is the most expensive film to date.

1963: Graphic Artist Harvey Ball invents the smiley face for an ad campaign aimed at boosting workers' morale.

1964: The Beatles arrive in America.

1965: The miniskirt is introduced.

1966: The National Association of Broadcasters instructs disc jockeys to screen records for obscene or hidden meanings.

1967: The Green Bay Packers defeat the Kansas City Chiefs in the first Super Bowl.

1968: The government mandates that all new cars must be equipped with seat belts.

1969: Pantsuits become acceptable for everyday wear by women.

THINKING CRITICALLY

CONNECT TO HISTORY

1. **Drawing Conclusions** What conclusions can you draw about teenagers in the 1960s from the images and information in this feature?

 **SEE SKILLBUILDER HANDBOOK, PAGE R18.**

CONNECT TO TODAY

2. **The Role of Culture** Do the arts merely *reflect* social change, or can art, music, fashion, etc. help to *bring about* social change? Think about how music and fashions affect your actions and opinions. Discuss your thoughts with a small group of classmates.

 **RESEARCH LINKS CLASSZONE.COM**

CHAPTER 23 ASSESSMENT

TERMS & NAMES

For each term or name below, write a sentence explaining its connection to the 1960s.

1. César Chávez
2. La Raza Unida
3. American Indian Movement (AIM)
4. feminism
5. Betty Friedan
6. Equal Rights Amendment (ERA)
7. Phyllis Schlafly
8. counterculture
9. Haight-Ashbury
10. Woodstock

MAIN IDEAS

Use your notes and the information in the chapter to answer the following questions.

Latinos and Native Americans Seek Equality *(pages 768–773)*

1. What strategies did both César Chávez and the UFWOC use to achieve their goals? How did they successfully apply these tactics?
2. What were the demands of the American Indian Movement (AIM) organizers who staged "The Trail of Broken Treaties" march on Washington in 1972?

Women Fight for Equality *(pages 776–780)*

3. Name three changes that members of the National Organization of Women (NOW) advocated.
4. What was the Supreme Court's decision in the *Roe* v. *Wade* case?

Culture and Counterculture *(pages 781–785)*

5. Briefly explain the role Timothy Leary played in the counterculture movement.
6. What unintended impact did the counterculture have on many mainstream Americans?

CRITICAL THINKING

1. **USING YOUR NOTES** Re-create the diagram shown below. Then fill in the appropriate areas with key individual and shared achievements of Latinos, Native Americans, and feminists.

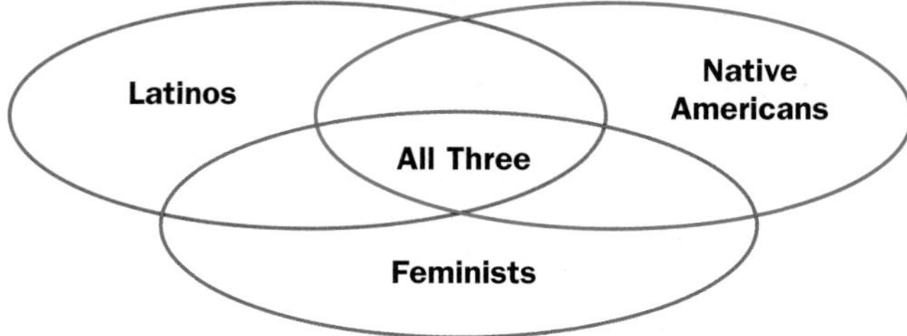

2. **DEVELOPING HISTORICAL PERSPECTIVE** Consider the organizations that Latinos, Native Americans, and women formed during the 1960s. Which do you think was the most influential? Why?

3. **ANALYZING PRIMARY SOURCES** Reread the song lyrics of Bob Dylan's "The Times They Are A-Changin'" on page 784. How do you think this song captured the main message of the counterculture movement?

VISUAL SUMMARY AN ERA OF SOCIAL CHANGE

CHANGES BROUGHT ABOUT BY THE COUNTERCULTURE

POLITICAL
- protests against Vietnam War
- NOW fuels feminism
- the New Right emerges
- ERA defeated
- *Roe* v. *Wade*
- more women in the work force
- AIM wins reforms and land rights
- La Raza Unida and MAPA fight for more rights for Latinos
- bilingual education
- Latino farm workers unionize

SOCIAL
- hippies reject mainstream society
- more communal living
- new fashion trends reflect freedom of expression
- traditional forms of worship rejected in favor of Eastern religious teachings
- more drug use
- women and minorities seek equality
- more permissive sexual behavior
- books, magazines, and movies show explicit violence

MUSIC
- music as political expression
- Motown label produces African-American artists
- rock music; the Beatles; Woodstock festival

ART AND FASHION
- pop art movement
- long hair as rebellion
- hippies popularize bright, colorful clothing, beads, and blue jeans

Standardized Test Practice

Use the flowchart and your knowledge of U.S. history to answer question 1.

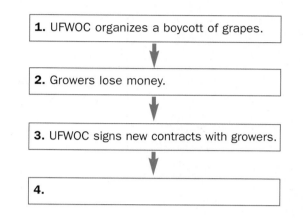

1. UFWOC organizes a boycott of grapes.

↓

2. Growers lose money.

↓

3. UFWOC signs new contracts with growers.

↓

4.

1. Which event accurately completes the cause-and-effect chain?

   A EEOC rules that unhealthful working conditions amount to illegal discrimination.
   B UFWOC disbands.
   C Grape boycott is extended to apricots and olives.
   D Working conditions for migrant farm workers are improved.

2. In the 1960s, women fought in Congress, in the courts, and in their everyday lives for treatment as political and social equals. Today, job discrimination against women is illegal because of —

   F the Fourteenth Amendment.
   G the ERA.
   H the Civil Rights Act of 1964.
   J the *Roe* v. *Wade* decision.

3. Which of the following statements is a fact?

   A Hippies believed that everyone should love each other.
   B Hippies spoiled the Woodstock festival.
   C The hippie movement failed because the hippies' beliefs were too radical.
   D Hippies invented rock music in Liverpool, England.

4. The women's rights movement largely grew out of—

   F the counterculture movement.
   G the civil rights movement.
   H the movement to organize farm workers.
   J reaction to the Warren Court decisions.

ADDITIONAL TEST PRACTICE, pages S1–S33.

CLASSZONE.COM

ALTERNATIVE ASSESSMENT

1. INTERACT WITH HISTORY Recall your discussion of the question on page 767:

How much can a society change?

Write a script in which five people debate the question: a Native American activist, a Latino activist, a feminine activist, a hippie, and a conservative politician who wants to preserve the status quo in 1964. If you work in a group, be sure that each group member considers several points of view.

2. INTERNET ACTIVITIY **CLASSZONE.COM**

Visit the links for Chapter Assessment to find examples of 1960s culture, such as songs, paintings, posters, clothing, cars, and so on. Prepare a paper or electronic museum exhibit of several artifacts that display a trend or theme discussed in the chapter. Write captions for the artifacts explaining their historical context and relating them to your chosen theme.

UNIT

Passage to a New Century 1968–2001

CHAPTER 24
An Age of Limits
1968–1980

CHAPTER 25
The Conservative Tide
1980–1992

CHAPTER 26
The United States in Today's World
1992–2001

EPILOGUE
Issues for the 21st Century

Campaign Scrapbook

As you read this unit, choose a candidate for political office whom you think you would have supported. Create a fictional but realistic scrapbook that recounts your experiences on the campaign trail.

Exhibit at the Ellis Island Immigration Museum, design by MetaForm; portraits in flag by Pablo Delano

CHAPTER 24
AN AGE OF LIMITS

Richard Nixon leaves the White House after resigning as president on Friday, August 9, 1974.

1968 Richard M. Nixon is elected president.

1969 Astronaut Neil Armstrong becomes the first person to walk on the moon.

1970 America celebrates the first Earth Day.

1972 Nixon visits China and the Soviet Union.

1972 Nixon is reelected.

1973 Energy crisis begins, and gasoline prices soar.

USA
WORLD

1968 | 1969 | 1970 | 1971 | 1972 | 1973

1972 China gives the U.S. two pandas.

1972 Terrorists kill eleven Israeli athletes at the XX Olympiad in Munich.

1973 War breaks out in the Middle East when seven Arab states attack Israel on Yom Kippur.

INTERACT
WITH HISTORY

The date is August 9, 1974. You are serving your country as an honor guard at the White House. As a member of the military, you've always felt patriotic pride in your government. Now the highest officer of that government, President Richard M. Nixon, is stepping down in disgrace. The trust you once placed in your leaders has been broken.

In what ways can a president misuse power?

Examine the Issues

- What are some powers granted to the president?
- What systems exist to protect against abuse of power?
- How can a president lose or restore the nation's trust?

RESEARCH LINKS **CLASSZONE.COM**

Visit the Chapter 24 links for more information related to An Age of Limits.

1974 Vice-President Gerald R. Ford becomes president after the Watergate scandal forces President Nixon to resign.

1976 President Jimmy Carter is elected president.

1976 Americans celebrate the nation's bicentennial.

1977 The movie *Saturday Night Fever* inspires disco fashion.

1979 A nuclear power accident occurs at Three Mile Island in Pennsylvania.

1974 | 1975 | 1976 | 1977 | 1978 | 1979

1978 Egyptian and Israeli leaders meet and sign the Camp David Accords with President Carter.

1979 Ayatollah Khomeini seizes power in Iran.

SECTION 1

The Nixon Administration

MAIN IDEA	WHY IT MATTERS NOW	Terms & Names
President Richard M. Nixon tried to steer the country in a conservative direction and away from federal control.	**American leaders of the early 1970s laid the foundations for the broad conservative base that exists today.**	• Richard M. Nixon • New Federalism • revenue sharing • Family Assistance Plan • Southern strategy • stagflation • OPEC (Organization of Petroleum Exporting Countries) • realpolitik • détente • SALT I Treaty

One American's Story

In November of 1968, **Richard M. Nixon** had just been elected president of the United States. He chose Henry Kissinger to be his special adviser on foreign affairs. During Nixon's second term in 1972, as the United States struggled to achieve an acceptable peace in Vietnam, Kissinger reflected on his relationship with Nixon.

A Personal Voice HENRY KISSINGER

"I . . . am not at all so sure I could have done what I've done with him with another president. . . . I don't know many leaders who would entrust to their aide the task of negotiating with the North Vietnamese, informing only a tiny group of people of the initiative."

—quoted in *The New Republic*, December 16, 1972

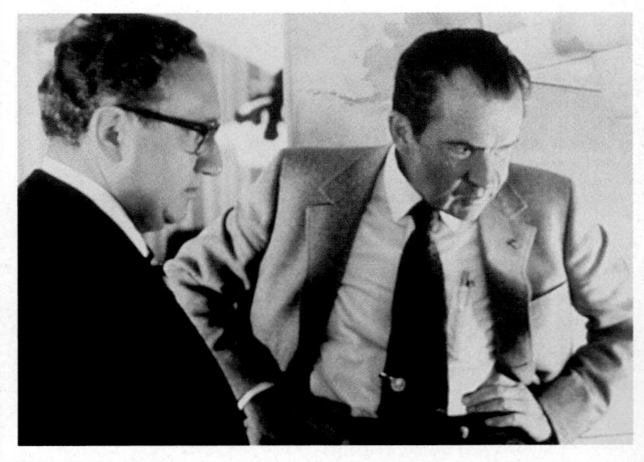

▲ **President Nixon *(right)* confers with Henry Kissinger.**

Nixon and Kissinger ended America's involvement in Vietnam, but as the war wound down, the nation seemed to enter an era of limits. The economic prosperity that had followed World War II was ending. President Nixon wanted to limit the federal government to reduce its power and to reverse some of Johnson's liberal policies. At the same time, he would seek to restore America's prestige and influence on the world stage—prestige that had been hit hard by the Vietnam experience.

Nixon's New Conservatism

President Richard M. Nixon entered office in 1969 determined to turn America in a more conservative direction. Toward that end, he tried to instill a sense of order into a nation still divided over the continuing Vietnam War.

Analyzing Political Cartoons

"DOMESTIC LIFE"

Pulitzer Prize–winning cartoonist Paul Szep frequently used Nixon as the subject of his cartoons. Although President Nixon focused his domestic policy on dismantling a number of Great Society social programs, his chief interest was foreign policy.

SKILLBUILDER

Analyzing Political Cartoons

1. What does the cartoonist suggest about Nixon by showing him leaving with his bags packed?
2. Whom do the children represent in this cartoon?

SEE SKILLBUILDER HANDBOOK, PAGE R24.

NEW FEDERALISM One of the main items on President Nixon's agenda was to decrease the size and influence of the federal government. Nixon believed that Lyndon Johnson's Great Society programs, by promoting greater federal involvement with social problems, had given the federal government too much responsibility. Nixon's plan, known as **New Federalism,** was to distribute a portion of federal power to state and local governments. (A)

MAIN IDEA

Summarizing

(A) What was the goal of Nixon's New Federalism?

To implement this program, Nixon proposed a plan to give more financial freedom to local governments. Normally, the federal government told state and local governments how to spend their federal money. Under **revenue sharing,** state and local governments could spend their federal dollars however they saw fit within certain limitations. In 1972, the revenue-sharing bill, known as the State and Local Fiscal Assistance Act, became law.

WELFARE REFORM Nixon was not as successful, however, in his attempt to overhaul welfare, which he believed had grown cumbersome and inefficient. In 1969, the president advocated the so-called **Family Assistance Plan (FAP).** Under the FAP, every family of four with no outside income would receive a basic federal payment of $1,600 a year, with a provision to earn up to $4,000 a year in supplemental income. Unemployed participants, excluding mothers of preschool children, would have to take job training and accept any reasonable work offered them.

Nixon presented the plan in conservative terms—as a program that would reduce the supervisory role of the federal government and make welfare recipients responsible for their own lives. The House approved the plan in 1970. However, when the bill reached the Senate, lawmakers from both parties attacked it. Liberal legislators considered the minimum payments too low and the work requirement too stiff, while conservatives objected to the notion of guaranteed income. The bill went down in defeat.

NEW FEDERALISM WEARS TWO FACES In the end, Nixon's New Federalism enhanced several key federal programs as it dismantled others. To win backing for his New Federalism program from a Democrat-controlled Congress, Nixon supported a number of congressional measures to increase federal spending for some social programs. Without fanfare, the Nixon administration increased Social

HISTORICAL SPOTLIGHT

AMERICANS WALK ON THE MOON

Not all was political war during the Nixon administration. On July 20, 1969, one of America's long-held dreams became a reality.

Nearly ten years after John F. Kennedy challenged America to put a person on the moon, astronaut Neil Armstrong climbed down the ladder of his lunar module and stepped onto the surface of the moon. "That's one small step for man," Armstrong said, "one giant leap for mankind."

Americans swelled with pride and accomplishment as they watched the historic moon landing on their televisions. Speaking to the astronauts from the White House, President Nixon said, "For every American, this has to be the proudest day of our lives."

▲ Neil Armstrong's photograph of Buzz Aldrin on the moon

Security, Medicare, and Medicaid payments and made food stamps more accessible.

However, the president also worked to dismantle some of the nation's social programs. Throughout his term, Nixon tried unsuccessfully to eliminate the Job Corps program that provided job training for the unemployed and in 1970 he vetoed a bill to provide additional funding for Housing and Urban Development. Confronted by laws that he opposed, Nixon also turned to a little-used presidential practice called impoundment. Nixon impounded, or withheld, necessary funds for programs, thus holding up their implementation. By 1973, it was believed that Nixon had impounded almost $15 billion, affecting more than 100 federal programs, including those for health, housing, and education.

The federal courts eventually ordered the release of the impounded funds. They ruled that presidential impoundment was unconstitutional and that only Congress had the authority to decide how federal funds should be spent. Nixon did use his presidential authority to abolish the Office of Economic Opportunity, a cornerstone of Johnson's antipoverty program. **B**

MAIN IDEA

Analyzing Issues

B In what ways did Nixon both strengthen and weaken federal programs?

LAW AND ORDER POLITICS As President Nixon fought with both houses of Congress, he also battled the more liberal elements of society, including the antiwar movement. Nixon had been elected in 1968 on a dual promise to end the war in Vietnam and mend the divisiveness within America that the war had created. Throughout his first term, Nixon aggressively moved to fulfill both pledges. The president de-escalated America's involvement in Vietnam and oversaw peace negotiations with North Vietnam. At the same time, he began the "law and order" policies that he had promised his "silent majority"—those middle-class Americans who wanted order restored to a country beset by urban riots and antiwar demonstrations.

To accomplish this, Nixon used the full resources of his office—sometimes illegally. Nixon and members of his staff ordered wiretaps of many left-wing individuals and the Democratic Party offices at the Watergate office building in Washington, D.C. The CIA also investigated and compiled documents on thousands of American dissidents—people who objected to the government's policies. The administration even used the Internal Revenue Service to audit the tax returns of antiwar and civil rights activists. Nixon began building a personal "enemies list" of prominent Americans whom the administration would harass.

Nixon also enlisted the help of his combative vice-president, Spiro T. Agnew, to denounce the opposition. The vice-president confronted the antiwar protesters and then turned his scorn on those who controlled the media, whom he viewed as liberal cheerleaders for the antiwar movement. Known for his colorful quotes, Agnew lashed out at the media and liberals as "an effete [weak] corps of impudent snobs" and "nattering nabobs of negativism."

Nixon's Southern Strategy

Even as President Nixon worked to steer the country along a more conservative course, he had his eyes on the 1972 presidential election. Nixon had won a slim majority in 1968—less than one percent of the popular vote. As president, he began working to forge a new conservative coalition to build on his support. In one approach, known as the **Southern strategy,** Nixon tried to attract Southern conservative Democrats by appealing to their unhappiness with federal desegregation policies and a liberal Supreme Court. He also promised to name a Southerner to the Supreme Court.

A NEW SOUTH Since Reconstruction, the South had been a Democratic stronghold. But by 1968 many white Southern Democrats had grown disillusioned with their party. In their eyes, the party—champion of the Great Society and civil rights—had grown too liberal. This conservative backlash first surfaced in the 1968 election, when thousands of Southern Democrats helped former Alabama governor George Wallace, a conservative segregationist running as an independent, carry five Southern states and capture 13 percent of the popular vote.

Nixon wanted these voters. By winning over the Wallace voters and other discontented Democrats, the president and his fellow Republicans hoped not only to keep the White House but also to recapture a majority in Congress. C

MAIN IDEA

Forming Generalizations

C Why had many Democratic voters in the South become potential Republican supporters by 1968?

NIXON SLOWS INTEGRATION To attract white voters in the South, President Nixon decided on a policy of slowing the country's desegregation efforts. In September of 1969, less than a year after being elected president, Nixon made clear his views on civil rights. "There are those who want instant integration and those who want segregation forever. I believe we need to have a middle course between those two extremes," he said.

Throughout his first term, President Nixon worked to reverse several civil rights policies. In 1969, he ordered the Department of Health, Education, and Welfare (HEW) to delay desegregation plans for school districts in South Carolina and Mississippi. Nixon's actions violated the Supreme Court's second *Brown* v. *Board of Education* ruling—which called for the desegregation of schools "with all deliberate speed." In response to an NAACP suit, the high court ordered Nixon to abide by the second Brown ruling. The president did so reluctantly, and by 1972, nearly 90 percent of children in the South attended desegregated schools—up from about 20 percent in 1969.

In a further attempt to chip away at civil rights advances, Nixon opposed the extension of the Voting Rights Act of 1965. The act had added nearly one million African Americans to the voting rolls. Despite the president's opposition, Congress voted to extend the act. D

MAIN IDEA

Analyzing Motives

D Why did President Nixon oppose the extension of the Voting Rights Act?

CONTROVERSY OVER BUSING President Nixon then attempted to stop yet another civil rights initiative—the integration of schools through busing. In 1971, the Supreme Court ruled in *Swann* v. *Charlotte-Mecklenburg Board of Education* that school districts may bus students to other schools to end the pattern of all-black or all-white educational institutions. White students and parents in cities such as Boston and Detroit angrily protested busing. One South Boston mother spoke for other white Northerners, many of whom still struggled with the integration process.

A Personal Voice

"**I'm not against any individual child. I am not a racist, no matter what those high-and-mighty suburban liberals with their picket signs say. I just won't have my children bused to some . . . slum school, and I don't want children from God knows where coming over here.**"

—A South Boston mother quoted in *The School Busing Controversy, 1970–75*

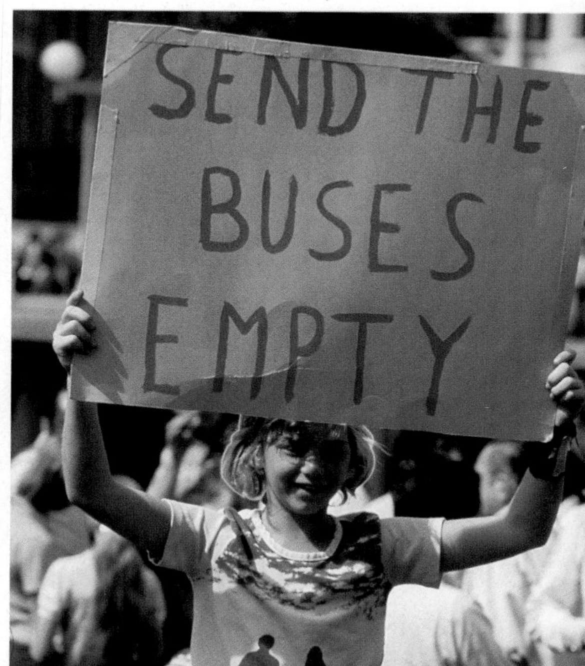

A demonstrator in Boston protests court-ordered school busing during the early 1970s.

HISTORICAL SPOTLIGHT

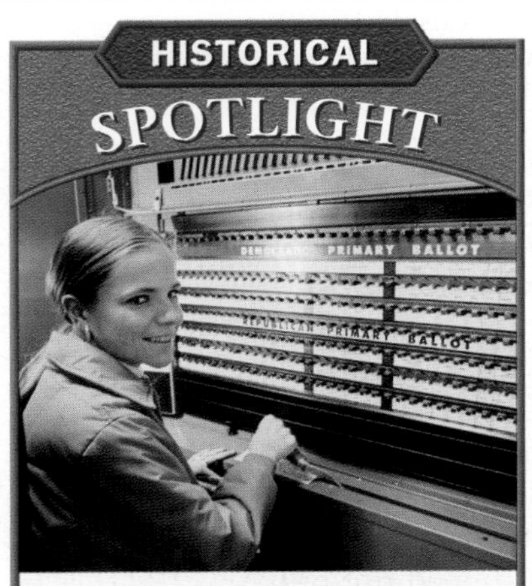

THE TWENTY-SIXTH AMENDMENT

During President Nixon's first term, the Twenty-sixth Amendment was ratified in 1971, extending voting rights to Americans 18 years or older. The amendment was one example of efforts in the 1960s and 1970s to expand opportunities to participate in government.

At the time, liberals supported the amendment because they believed that young people were more likely to be liberal. Conservatives opposed it because they didn't want to extend the vote to more liberals.

Opponents also argued that the amendment would be too expensive for states to administer and that 18-year-olds were not mature enough for the responsibility. Many Americans, however, considered it unfair to be asked to fight and die for their country in Vietnam without being allowed to vote.

Nixon also opposed integration through busing and went on national television to urge Congress to halt the practice. While busing continued in some cities, Nixon had made his position clear to the country—and to the South.

A BATTLE OVER THE SUPREME COURT During the 1968 campaign, Nixon had criticized the Warren Court for being too liberal. Once in the White House, Nixon suddenly found himself with an opportunity to change the direction of the court. During Nixon's first term, four justices, including chief justice Earl Warren, left the bench through retirement. President Nixon quickly moved to put a more conservative face on the Court. In 1969, the Senate approved Nixon's chief justice appointee, U.S. Court of Appeals judge Warren Burger.

Eventually, Nixon placed on the bench three more justices, who tilted the Court in a more conservative direction. However, the newly shaped Court did not always take the conservative route—for example, it handed down the 1971 ruling in favor of racially integrating schools through busing. E

MAIN IDEA

Summarizing
E What was Nixon's Southern strategy and how did he implement it?

Confronting a Stagnant Economy

One of the more pressing issues facing Richard Nixon was a troubled economy. Between 1967 and 1973, the United States faced high inflation and high unemployment—a situation economists called **stagflation.**

THE CAUSES OF STAGFLATION The economic problems of the late 1960s and early 1970s had several causes. Chief among them were high inflation—a result of Lyndon Johnson's policy to fund the war and social programs through deficit spending. Also, increased competition in international trade, and a flood of new workers, including women and baby boomers, led to stagflation. Another cause of the nation's economic woes was its heavy dependency on foreign oil. During the 1960s, America received much of its petroleum from the oil-producing countries of the

Dependent on foreign oil, Americans in 1979 wait in line for gas during the oil embargo. ▼

Vocabulary
cartel: a bloc of independent business organizations that controls a service or business

Background
See *embargo* on page R40 in the Economics Handbook.

Middle East. Many of these countries belonged to a cartel called **OPEC (Organization of Petroleum Exporting Countries).** During the 1960s, OPEC gradually raised oil prices. Then in 1973, the Yom Kippur War broke out, with Israel against Egypt and Syria. When the United States sent massive military aid to Israel, its longtime ally, the Arab OPEC nations responded by cutting off all oil sales to the United States. When OPEC resumed selling its oil to the United States in 1974, the price had quadrupled. This sharp rise in oil prices only worsened the problem of inflation.

NIXON BATTLES STAGFLATION President Nixon took several steps to combat stagflation, but none met with much success. To reverse deficit spending, Nixon attempted to raise taxes and cut the budget. Congress, however, refused to go along with this plan. In another effort to slow inflation, Nixon tried to reduce the amount of money in circulation by urging that interest rates be raised. This measure did little except drive the country into a mild recession, or an overall slowdown of the economy. (F)

MAIN IDEA
Analyzing Causes
(F) What factors brought on the country's economic problems in the late 1960s and early 1970s?

In August 1971, the president turned to price and wage controls to stop inflation. He froze workers' wages as well as businesses' prices and fees for 90 days. Inflation eased for a short time, but the recession continued.

WORLD STAGE

THE YOM KIPPUR WAR

On October 6, 1973, Syria and Egypt invaded Israel on Yom Kippur, the most sacred Jewish holiday. The war—the climax of years of intense border disputes—was short but brutal. Even though fighting lasted only three weeks, as many as 7,700 Egyptians, 7,700 Syrians, and 4,500 Israelis were killed or wounded.

Although the United States supplied massive amounts of military aid to Israel, U.S. officials also worked to broker a cease-fire between the warring nations. In what became known as "shuttle diplomacy," Secretary of State Henry Kissinger traveled back and forth between Middle Eastern countries in an attempt to forge a peace agreement. Kissinger's diplomatic efforts finally paid off. Israel signed an official peace accord with Egypt in January 1974. Four months later in May, Israel signed a cease-fire with Syria.

Nixon's Foreign Policy Triumphs

Richard Nixon admittedly preferred world affairs to domestic policy. "I've always thought this country could run itself domestically without a president," he said in 1968. Throughout his presidency, Nixon's top priority was gaining an honorable peace in Vietnam. At the same time, he also made significant advances in America's relationships with China and the Soviet Union.

KISSINGER AND REALPOLITIK The architect of Nixon's foreign policy was his adviser for national security affairs, Henry Kissinger. Kissinger, who would later become Nixon's secretary of state, promoted a philosophy known as **realpolitik,** from a German term meaning "political realism." According to realpolitik, foreign policy should be based solely on consideration of power, not ideals or moral principles. Kissinger believed in evaluating a nation's power, not its philosophy or beliefs. If a country was weak, Kissinger argued, it was often more practical to ignore that country, even if it was Communist.

Realpolitik marked a departure from the former confrontational policy of containment, which refused to recognize the major Communist countries. On the other hand, Kissinger's philosophy called for the United States to fully confront the powerful nations of the globe. In the world of realpolitik, however, confrontation largely meant negotiation as well as military engagement.

Nixon shared Kissinger's belief in realpolitik, and together the two men adopted a more flexible approach in dealing with Communist nations. They called their policy **détente—**a policy aimed at easing Cold War tensions. One of the most startling applications of détente came in early 1972 when President Nixon—who had risen in politics as a strong anti-Communist—visited Communist China. (G)

MAIN IDEA
Summarizing
(G) What was the philosophy of realpolitik?

President Nixon tours the Great Wall as part of his visit to China in 1972.

KEY PLAYER

RICHARD M. NIXON
1913–1994

The hurdles that Richard Nixon overcame to win the presidency in 1968 included his loss in the 1960 presidential race and a 1962 defeat in the race for governor of California.

Nixon faced many obstacles from the start. As a boy, he rose every day at 4 A.M. to help in his father's grocery store. Nixon also worked as a janitor, a bean picker, and a barker at an amusement park.

The Nixon family suffered great tragedy when one of Nixon's brothers died from meningitis and another from tuberculosis.

None of these traumatic experiences, however, dulled the future president's ambition. Nixon finished third in his law class at Duke University, and after serving in World War II, he launched his political career.

After winning a seat in Congress in 1946, Nixon announced, "I had to win. That's the thing you don't understand. The important thing is to win."

NIXON VISITS CHINA Since the takeover of mainland China by the Communists in 1949, the United States had not formally recognized the Chinese Communist government. In late 1971, Nixon reversed that policy by announcing to the nation that he would visit China "to seek the normalization of relations between the two countries."

By going to China, Nixon was trying, in part, to take advantage of the decade-long rift between China and the Soviet Union. China had long criticized the Soviet Union as being too "soft" in its policies against the West. The two Communist superpowers officially broke ties in 1960. Nixon had thought about exploiting the fractured relationship for several years. "We want to have the Chinese with us when we sit down and negotiate with the Russians," he told a reporter in 1968. Upon his arrival at the Beijing Airport in February, 1972, Nixon recalls his meeting with Chinese premier Zhou En-lai.

A PERSONAL VOICE RICHARD M. NIXON

"I knew that Zhou had been deeply insulted by Foster Dulles's refusal to shake hands with him at the Geneva Conference in 1954. When I reached the bottom step, therefore, I made a point of extending my hand as I walked toward him. When our hands met, one era ended and another began."

—*The Memoirs of Richard Nixon*

Besides its enormous symbolic value, Nixon's visit also was a huge success with the American public. Observers noted that it opened up diplomatic and economic relations with the Chinese and resulted in important agreements between China and the United States. The two nations agreed that neither would try to dominate the Pacific and that both would cooperate in settling disputes peacefully. They also agreed to participate in scientific and cultural exchanges as well as to eventually reunite Taiwan with the mainland. **H**

MAIN IDEA

Analyzing Effects

H How did Nixon's trip change the United States' relationship with China?

NIXON TRAVELS TO MOSCOW In May 1972, three months after visiting Beijing, President Nixon headed to Moscow—the first U.S. president ever to visit the

◀ A 1973 military parade in Moscow displays the Soviet Union's arsenal, components of which were frozen at 1972 levels as a result of the Salt I Treaty.

Soviet capital. Like his visit to China, Nixon's trip to the Soviet Union received wide acclaim. After a series of meetings called the Strategic Arms Limitation Talks (SALT), Nixon and Brezhnev signed the **SALT I Treaty.** This five-year agreement limited the number of intercontinental ballistic missiles (ICBMs) and submarine-launched missiles to 1972 levels.

Background
Prior to Nixon's visit, FDR was the only other President to travel to the U.S.S.R. He attended the Yalta conference in 1945.

The foreign policy triumphs with China and the Soviet Union and the administration's announcement that peace "is at hand" in Vietnam helped reelect Nixon as president in 1972.

But peace in Vietnam proved elusive. The Nixon administration grappled with the war for nearly six more months before withdrawing troops and ending America's involvement in Vietnam. By that time, another issue was about to dominate the Nixon administration—one that would eventually lead to the downfall of the president.

ASSESSMENT

1. **TERMS & NAMES** For each term or name, write a sentence explaining its significance.
   - **Richard M. Nixon**
   - **New Federalism**
   - **revenue sharing**
   - **Family Assistance Plan**
   - **Southern strategy**
   - **stagflation**
   - **OPEC (Organization of Petroleum Exporting Countries)**
   - **realpolitik**
   - **détente**
   - **SALT I Treaty**

MAIN IDEA

2. **TAKING NOTES**
   In a two-column chart similar to the one shown, list the policies of Richard Nixon that promoted change and those that slowed it down.

Promoted Change	Slowed Change
Policies:	Policies:

   In what ways do you think Nixon was most conservative? In what ways was he least conservative? Explain.

CRITICAL THINKING

3. **ANALYZING EFFECTS**
   What were the effects of the Arab OPEC oil embargo on the United States?

4. **DRAWING CONCLUSIONS**
   Why was the timing of Nixon's foreign policy achievements particularly important? Relate his achievements to other events.

5. **EVALUATING DECISIONS**
   In your opinion, did Nixon's policy of détente help solve the country's major foreign policy problems? Support your answer with evidence from the text. **Think About:**
   - the definition and origin of détente
   - the effect of détente on U.S. dealings with Communist countries
   - the effect of détente on the American public

Watergate: Nixon's Downfall

MAIN IDEA

President Richard Nixon's involvement in the Watergate scandal forced him to resign from office.

WHY IT MATTERS NOW

The Watergate scandal raised questions of public trust that still affect how the public and media skeptically view politicians.

Terms & Names

- impeachment
- Watergate
- H. R. Haldeman
- John Ehrlichman
- John Mitchell
- Committee to Reelect the President
- John Sirica
- Saturday Night Massacre

One American's Story

On July 25, 1974, Representative Barbara Jordan of Texas, a member of the House Judiciary Committee, along with the other committee members, considered whether to recommend that President Nixon be impeached for "high crimes and misdemeanors." Addressing the room, Jordan cited the Constitution in urging her fellow committee members to investigate whether impeachment was appropriate.

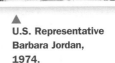

▲ U.S. Representative Barbara Jordan, 1974.

A PERSONAL VOICE BARBARA JORDAN

> "'We the people'—it is a very eloquent beginning. But when the Constitution of the United States was completed . . . I was not included in that 'We the people'. . . . But through the process of amendment, interpretation, and court decision, I have finally been included in 'We the people'. . . . Today . . . [my] faith in the Constitution is whole. It is complete. It is total. I am not going to sit here and be an idle spectator in the diminution, the subversion, the destruction of the Constitution. . . . Has the President committed offenses . . . which the Constitution will not tolerate?"
>
> —quoted in *Notable Black American Women*

The committee eventually voted to recommend the **impeachment** of Richard Nixon for his role in the Watergate scandal. However, before Congress could take further action against him, the president resigned. Nixon's resignation, the first by a U.S. president, was the climax of a scandal that led to the imprisonment of 25 government officials and caused the most serious constitutional crisis in the United States since the impeachment of Andrew Johnson in 1868.

President Nixon and His White House

The **Watergate** scandal centered on the Nixon administration's attempt to cover up a burglary of the Democratic National Committee (DNC) headquarters at the Watergate office and apartment complex in Washington, D.C. However, the

Watergate story began long before the actual burglary. Many historians believe that Watergate truly began with the personalities of Richard Nixon and those of his advisers, as well as with the changing role of the presidency.

AN IMPERIAL PRESIDENCY When Richard Nixon took office, the executive branch—as a result of the Great Depression, World War II, and the Cold War—had become the most powerful branch of government. In his book *The Imperial Presidency*, the historian Arthur Schlesinger, Jr., argued that by the time Richard Nixon became president, the executive branch had taken on an air of imperial, or supreme, authority.

President Nixon settled into this imperial role with ease. Nixon believed, as he told a reporter in 1980, that "a president must not be one of the crowd. . . . People . . . don't want him to be down there saying, 'Look, I'm the same as you.'" Nixon expanded the power of the presidency with little thought to constitutional checks, as when he impounded funds for federal programs that he opposed, or when he ordered troops to invade Cambodia without congressional approval. A

MAIN IDEA

Summarizing
A What is meant by "imperial presidency"?

THE PRESIDENT'S MEN As he distanced himself from Congress, Nixon confided in a small and fiercely loyal group of advisers. They included **H. R. Haldeman,** White House chief of staff; **John Ehrlichman,** chief domestic adviser; and **John Mitchell,** Nixon's former attorney general. These men had played key roles in Nixon's 1968 election victory and now helped the president direct White House policy.

These men also shared President Nixon's desire for secrecy and the consolidation of power. Critics charged that these men, through their personalities and their attitude toward the presidency, developed a sense that they were somehow above the law. This sense would, in turn, prompt President Nixon and his advisers to cover up their role in Watergate, and fuel the coming scandal.

The Drive Toward Reelection

Throughout his political career, Richard Nixon lived with the overwhelming fear of losing elections. By the end of the 1972 reelection campaign, Nixon's campaign team sought advantages by any means possible, including an attempt to steal information from the DNC headquarters.

A BUNGLED BURGLARY At 2:30 A.M., June 17, 1972, a guard at the Watergate complex in Washington, D.C., caught five men breaking into the campaign headquarters of the DNC. The burglars planned to photograph documents outlining Democratic Party strategy and to place wiretaps, or "bugs," on the office telephones. The press soon discovered that the group's leader, James McCord, was a former CIA agent. He was also a security coordinator for a group known as the **Committee to Reelect the President** (CRP). John Mitchell, who had resigned as attorney general to run Nixon's reelection campaign, was the CRP's director. B

MAIN IDEA

Analyzing Motives
B Why would the Nixon campaign team take such a risky action as breaking into the opposition's headquarters?

Just three days after the burglary, H. R. Haldeman noted in his diary Nixon's near obsession with how to respond to the break-in.

A PERSONAL VOICE H. R. HALDEMAN

"**The P[resident] was concerned about what our counterattack is. . . . He raised it again several times during the day, and it obviously is bothering him. . . . He called at home tonight, saying that he wanted to change the plan for his press conference and have it on Thursday instead of tomorrow, so that it won't look like he's reacting to the Democratic break-in thing.**"

—*The Haldeman Diaries*

HISTORICAL SPOTLIGHT

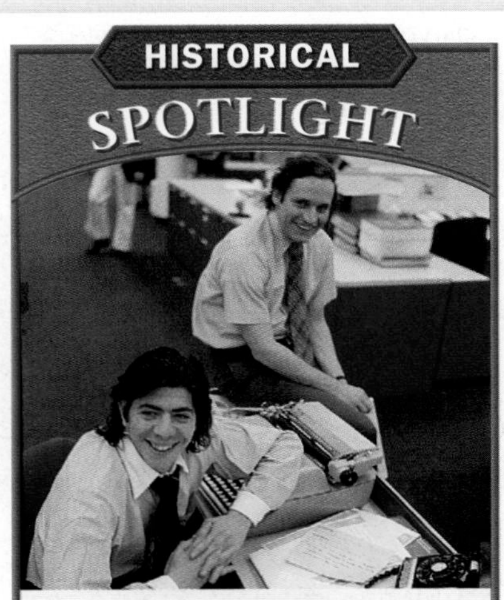

WOODWARD AND BERNSTEIN

Bob Woodward and Carl Bernstein of the *Washington Post* seemed an unlikely team. Woodward, 29 (at right in the photo above), had graduated from Yale, while the 28-year-old Bernstein was a college dropout.

As the two men dug deeper into the Watergate break-in, a mysterious inside source helped them to uncover the scandal. For more than 30 years the reporters refused to identify their source. Then in June 2005, W. Mark Felt, the No. 2 man at the FBI at the time of Watergate, stepped forward and identified himself as the inside source of the reporters' information.

While people lauded the two reporters for their dogged determination, some Nixon officials remain bitter toward them.

Woodward defended the reporters' work, saying, "We tried to do our job and, in fact, if you look at it, our coverage was pretty conservative."

The cover-up quickly began. Workers shredded all incriminating documents in Haldeman's office. The White House, with President Nixon's consent, asked the CIA to urge the FBI to stop its investigations into the burglary on the grounds of national security. In addition, the CRP passed out nearly $450,000 to the Watergate burglars to buy their silence after they were indicted in September of 1972. **C**

MAIN IDEA

Chronological Order

C What steps did the White House take to cover up its involvement in the Watergate break-in?

Throughout the 1972 campaign, the Watergate burglary generated little interest among the American public and media. Only the *Washington Post* and two of its reporters, Bob Woodward and Carl Bernstein, kept on the story. In a series of articles, the reporters uncovered information that linked numerous members of the administration to the burglary. The White House denied each new *Post* allegation. Upon learning of an upcoming story that tied him to the burglars, John Mitchell told Bernstein, "That's the most sickening thing I ever heard."

The firm White House response to the charges, and its promises of imminent peace in Vietnam, proved effective in the short term. In November, Nixon was reelected by a landslide over liberal Democrat George S. McGovern. But Nixon's popular support was soon to unravel.

The Cover-Up Unravels

In January 1973, the trial of the Watergate burglars began. The trial's presiding judge, **John Sirica,** made clear his belief that the men had not acted alone. On March 20, a few days before the burglars were scheduled to be sentenced, James McCord sent a letter to Sirica, in which he indicated that he had lied under oath. He also hinted that powerful members of the Nixon administration had been involved in the break-in.

THE SENATE INVESTIGATES WATERGATE McCord's revelation of possible White House involvement in the burglary aroused public interest in Watergate. President Nixon moved quickly to stem the growing concern. On April 30, 1973, Nixon dismissed White House counsel John Dean and announced the resignations of Haldeman, Ehrlichman, and Attorney General Richard Kleindienst, who had recently replaced John Mitchell following Mitchell's resignation. The president then went on television and denied any attempt at a cover-up. He announced that he was appointing a new attorney general, Elliot Richardson, and was authorizing him to appoint a special prosecutor to investigate Watergate. "There can be no whitewash at the White House," Nixon said.

The president's reassurances, however, came too late. In May 1973, the Senate began its own investigation of Watergate. A special committee, chaired by Senator Samuel James Ervin of North Carolina, began to call administration officials to give testimony. Throughout the summer millions of Americans sat by their televisions as the "president's men" testified one after another.

> ***"Divine right went out with the American Revolution and doesn't belong to White House aides."***
>
> **SENATOR SAM ERVIN**

STARTLING TESTIMONY John Dean delivered the first bomb. In late June, during more than 30 hours of testimony, Dean provided a startling answer to Senator Howard Baker's repeated question, "What did the president know and when did he know it?" The former White House counsel declared that President Nixon had been deeply involved in the cover-up. Dean referred to one meeting in which he and the president, along with several advisers, discussed strategies for continuing the deceit.

The White House strongly denied Dean's charges. The hearings had suddenly reached an impasse as the committee attempted to sort out who was telling the truth. The answer came in July from an unlikely source: presidential aide Alexander Butterfield. Butterfield stunned the committee when he revealed that Nixon had taped virtually all of his presidential conversations. Butterfield later claimed that the taping system was installed "to help Nixon write his memoirs." However, for the Senate committee, the tapes were the key to revealing what Nixon knew and when he knew it. **D**

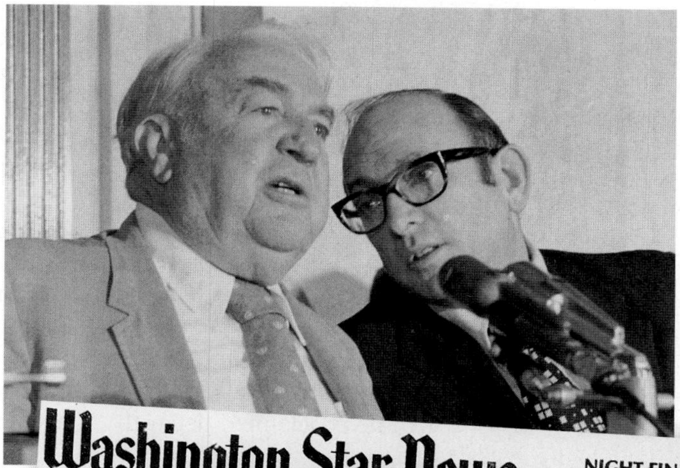

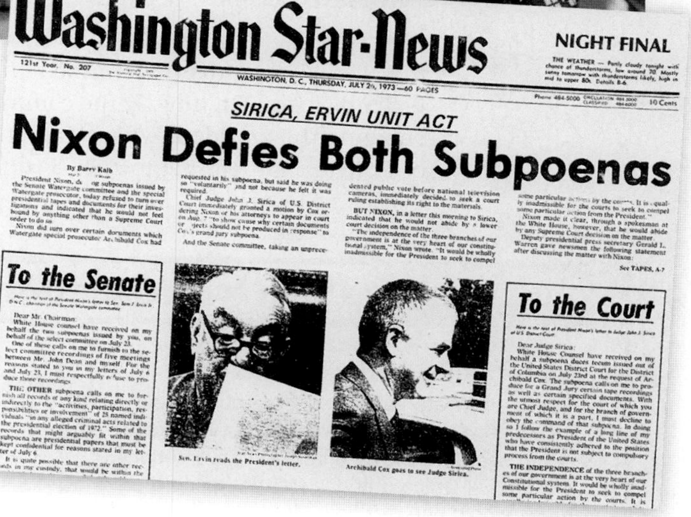

Washington Star-News

NIGHT FINAL

121st Year. No. 207

WASHINGTON, D. C., THURSDAY, JULY 2[illegible], 1973—60 PAGES

10 Cents

SIRICA, ERVIN UNIT ACT

Nixon Defies Both Subpoenas

By Barry Kalb

See TAPES, A-7

To the Senate

Dear Mr. Chairman:

White House counsel have received on my behalf the two subpoenas issued by you, on behalf of the select committee on July 23.

Sen. Ervin reads the President's letter.

Archibald Cox goes to see Judge Sirica.

To the Court

Dear Judge Sirica:

White House Counsel have received on my behalf a subpoena duces tecum issued out of the United States District Court for the District of Columbia on July 23rd at the request of Archibald Cox.

▲ **The Watergate hearings, chaired by Senator Sam Ervin, shown *(top left)* with Sam Dash, chief counsel to the Senate Watergate Committee, made headlines throughout the summer of 1973.**

MAIN IDEA

Drawing Conclusions

D What was significant about the revelation that Nixon taped his conversations?

THE SATURDAY NIGHT MASSACRE

A year-long battle for the "Nixon tapes" followed. Archibald Cox, the special prosecutor whom Elliot Richardson had appointed to investigate the case, took the president to court in October 1973 to obtain the tapes. Nixon refused and ordered Attorney General Richardson to fire Cox. In what became known as the **Saturday Night Massacre,** Richardson refused the order and resigned. The deputy attorney general also refused the order, and he was fired. Solicitor General Robert Bork finally fired Cox. However, Cox's replacement, Leon Jaworski, proved equally determined to get the tapes. Several months after the "massacre," the House Judiciary Committee began examining the possibility of an impeachment hearing. **E**

MAIN IDEA

Summarizing

E What events led to the Saturday Night Massacre?

The entire White House appeared to be under siege. Just days before the Saturday Night Massacre, Vice President Spiro Agnew had resigned after it was revealed that he had accepted bribes from engineering firms while governor of Maryland. Agnew pleaded *nolo contendere* (no contest) to the charge. Acting under the Twenty-fifth

Amendment, Nixon nominated the House minority leader, Gerald R. Ford, as his new vice-president. Congress quickly confirmed the nomination.

The Fall of a President

In March 1974, a grand jury indicted seven presidential aides on charges of conspiracy, obstruction of justice, and perjury. The investigation was closing in on the president of the United States.

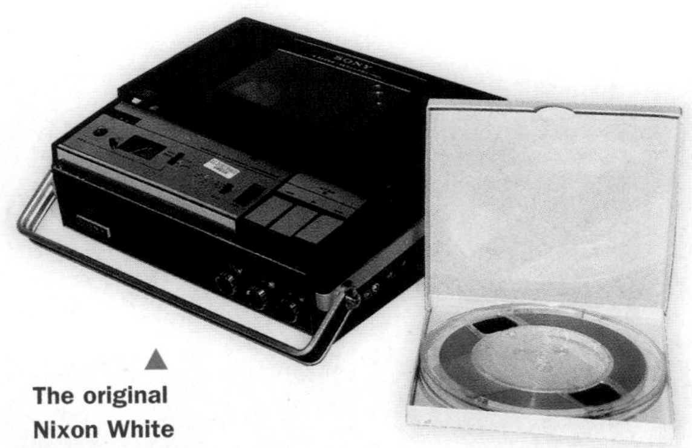

▲ The original Nixon White House tape recorder and tape from the 1970s.

NIXON RELEASES THE TAPES In the spring of 1974, President Nixon told a television audience that he was releasing 1,254 pages of edited transcripts of White House conversations about Watergate. Nixon's offering failed to satisfy investigators, who demanded the unedited tapes. Nixon refused, and the case went before the Supreme Court. On July 24, 1974, the high court ruled unanimously that the president must surrender the tapes. The Court rejected Nixon's argument that doing so would violate national security. Evidence involving possible criminal activity could not be withheld, even by a president. President Nixon maintained that he had done nothing wrong. At a press conference in November 1973, he proclaimed defiantly, "I am not a crook."

Background
Although historians sued for access to thousands of hours of tapes, it was not until some 21 years later, in 1996, that an agreement was made for over 3,700 hours of tape to be made public.

THE PRESIDENT RESIGNS Even without holding the original tapes, the House Judiciary Committee determined that there was enough evidence to impeach Richard Nixon. On July 27, the committee approved three articles of impeachment, charging the president with obstruction of justice, abuse of power, and contempt of Congress for refusing to obey a congressional subpoena to release the tapes.

Analyzing *Political Cartoons*

THE WHITE HOUSE TAPES

During the Watergate hearings a bombshell exploded when it was revealed that President Nixon secretly tape-recorded all conversations in the Oval Office. Although Nixon hoped the tapes would one day help historians document the triumphs of his presidency, they were used to confirm his guilt.

SKILLBUILDER
Analyzing Political Cartoons

1. What does this cartoon imply about privacy during President Nixon's term in office?
2. What building has been transformed into a giant tape recorder?

SEE SKILLBUILDER HANDBOOK, PAGE R24.

On August 5, Nixon released the tapes. They contained many gaps, and one tape revealed a disturbing 18½-minute gap. According to the White House, Rose Mary Woods, President Nixon's secretary, accidentally erased part of a conversation between H. R. Haldeman and Nixon. More importantly, a tape dated June 23, 1972—six days after the Watergate break-in—that contained a conversation between Nixon and Haldeman, disclosed the evidence investigators needed. Not only had the president known about the role of members of his administration in the burglary, he had agreed to the plan to obstruct the FBI's investigation.

The evidence now seemed overwhelming. On August 8, 1974, before the full House vote on the articles of impeachment began, President Nixon announced his resignation from office. Defiant as always, Nixon admitted no guilt. He merely said that some of his judgments "were wrong." The next day, Nixon and his wife, Pat, returned home to California. A short time later, Gerald Ford was sworn in as the 38th president of the United States.

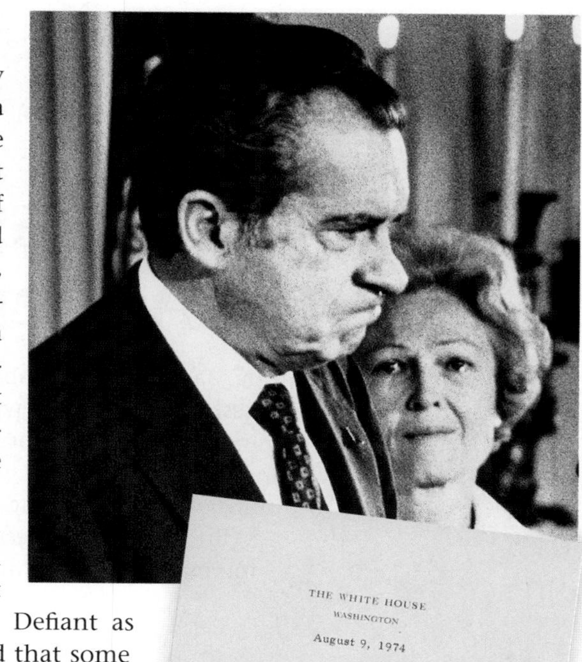

THE WHITE HOUSE
WASHINGTON

August 9, 1974

Dear Mr. Secretary:

I hereby resign the Office of President of the United States.

Sincerely,

Richard Nixon

The Honorable Henry A. Kissinger
The Secretary of State
Washington, D.C. 20520

11:35 AM
HK

▲ **With wife Pat looking on, Richard Nixon bids farewell to his staff on his final day as president. Nixon's resignation letter is shown above.**

THE EFFECTS OF WATERGATE The effects of Watergate have endured long after Nixon's resignation. Eventually, 25 members of the Nixon Administration were convicted and served prison terms for crimes connected to Watergate. Along with the divisive war in Vietnam, Watergate produced a deep disillusionment with the "imperial" presidency. In the years following Vietnam and Watergate, the American public and the media developed a general cynicism about public officials that still exists today. Watergate remains the scandal and investigative story against which all others are measured.

ASSESSMENT

1. **TERMS & NAMES** For each term or name, write a sentence explaining its significance.
   - **impeachment**
   - **Watergate**
   - **H. R. Haldeman**
   - **John Ehrlichman**
   - **John Mitchell**
   - **Committee to Reelect the President**
   - **John Sirica**
   - **Saturday Night Massacre**

MAIN IDEA

2. **TAKING NOTES**
   Use a time line like the one below to trace the events of the Watergate scandal.

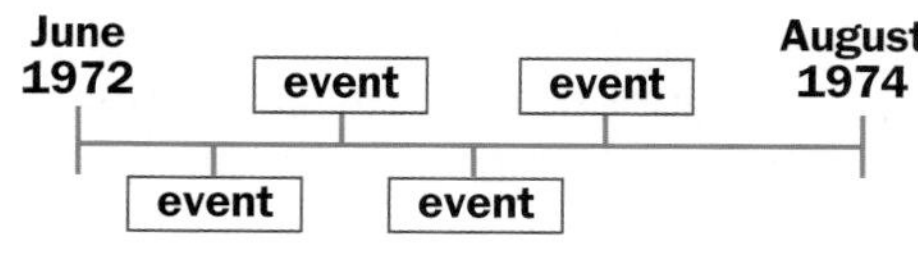

   Which event made Nixon's downfall certain?

CRITICAL THINKING

3. **HYPOTHESIZING**
   If Nixon had admitted to and apologized for the Watergate break-in, how might subsequent events have been different? Explain.
   Think About:
   - the extent of the cover-up
   - the impact of the cover-up
   - Nixon's public image

4. **ANALYZING EVENTS**
   How did the Watergate scandal create a constitutional crisis?

5. **EVALUATING**
   Do you think that Nixon would have been forced to resign if the tapes had not existed? Explain your answer.

DAILY LIFE 1968–1980

Television Reflects American Life

From May until November 1973, the Senate Watergate hearings were the biggest daytime TV viewing event of the year. Meanwhile, television programming began to more closely reflect the realities of American life. Shows more often addressed relevant issues, more African-American characters appeared, and working women as well as homemakers were portrayed. In addition, the newly established Public Broadcasting System began showing many issue-oriented programs.

▲ EDUCATIONAL PROGRAMMING

Public television devoted much of its programming to quality children's television. Shows such as *Sesame Street* and *Zoom!* made it fun for children to learn. They were deliberately fast-paced to appeal to the new generation of "television babies."

▼ DIVERSITY

Chico and the Man was the first series set in a Mexican-American barrio, East Los Angeles. The program centered on the relationship between Ed Brown, a cranky garage owner, and Chico Rodriguez, an optimistic young mechanic Brown reluctantly hired.

◀ SOCIAL VALUES

All in the Family was the most popular series of the 1970s. It told the story of a working-class family, headed by the bigoted Archie Bunker and his long-suffering wife, Edith. Through the barbs Bunker traded with his son-in-law and his African-American neighbor, George Jefferson, the show dealt openly with the divisions in American society.

◀ INDEPENDENT WOMEN

The Mary Tyler Moore Show depicted Mary Richards, a single woman living in Minneapolis and working as an assistant manager in a local TV news department. Mary symbolized the young career woman of the 1970s.

▼ CULTURAL IDENTITY

The miniseries *Roots*, based on a book by Alex Haley, told the saga of several generations of an African-American family. The eight-part story began with Kunta Kinte, who was captured outside his West African village and taken to America as a slave. It ended with his great-grandson's setting off for a new life as a free man. The groundbreaking series, broadcast in January 1977, was one of the most-watched television events in history.

DATA FILE

TV EVENTS OF THE 1970s

- A congressional ban on TV cigarette commercials took effect in 1971.
- ABC negotiated an $8-million-a-year contract to televise *Monday Night Football*, first broadcast in September 1970.
- In 1972, President Nixon, accompanied by TV cameras and reporters from the major networks, made a groundbreaking visit to China.
- *Saturday Night Live*—a show that would launch the careers of Dan Aykroyd, Jane Curtin, Eddie Murphy, and many other comic actors—premiered in October 1975.
- WTCG-TV (later WTBS) in Atlanta, owned by Ted Turner, became the basis of the first true satellite-delivered "superstation" in 1976.
- In November 1979, ABC began broadcasting late-night updates on the hostage crisis in Iran. These reports evolved into the program *Nightline* with Ted Koppel.

Average Weekly Hours of TV Viewing

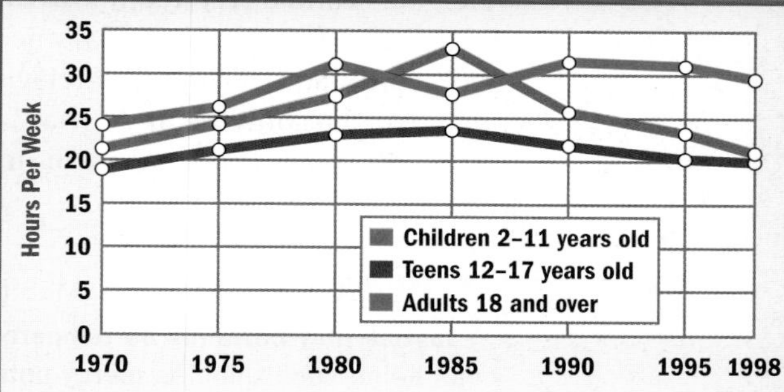

Source: Nielson Media Research

THINKING CRITICALLY

CONNECT TO HISTORY

1. **Analyzing Causes** In what ways did television change to reflect American society in the 1970s? What factors might have influenced these changes?

 **SEE SKILLBUILDER HANDBOOK, PAGE R7.**

CONNECT TO TODAY

2. **Creating a Graph** Use the Internet or an almanac to find data on the number of televisions owned in the United States and the number of hours of TV watched every day. Make a graph that displays the data.

 **RESEARCH LINKS** **CLASSZONE.COM**

The Ford and Carter Years

MAIN IDEA	WHY IT MATTERS NOW	Terms & Names
The Ford and Carter administrations attempted to remedy the nation's worst economic crisis in decades.	**Maintaining a stable national economy has remained a top priority for every president since Ford and Carter.**	**•Gerald R. Ford •Jimmy Carter •National Energy Act •human rights •Camp David Accords •Ayatollah Ruhollah Khomeini**

One American's Story

James D. Denney couldn't believe what he was hearing. Barely a month after Richard Nixon had resigned amid the Watergate scandal, President **Gerald R. Ford** had granted Nixon a full pardon. "[S]omeone must write, 'The End,'" Ford had declared in a televised statement. "I have concluded that only I can do that." Denney wrote a letter to the editors of *Time* magazine, in which he voiced his anger at Ford's decision.

A PERSONAL VOICE JAMES D. DENNEY

"Justice may certainly be tempered by mercy, but there can be no such thing as mercy until justice has been accomplished by the courts. Since it circumvented justice, Mr. Ford's act was merely indulgent favoritism, a bland and unworthy substitute for mercy."

—*Time*, September 23, 1974

Two women protest President Ford's pardon of Richard Nixon.

James Denney's feelings were typical of the anger and the disillusionment with the presidency that many Americans felt in the aftermath of the Watergate scandal. During the 1970s, Presidents Gerald Ford and Jimmy Carter sought to restore America's faith in its leaders. At the same time, both men had to focus much of their attention on battling the nation's worsening economic situation.

Ford Travels a Rough Road

Upon taking office, Gerald R. Ford urged Americans to put the Watergate scandal behind them. "Our long national nightmare is over," he declared. The nation's nightmarish economy persisted, however, and Ford's policies offered little relief.

"A FORD, NOT A LINCOLN" Gerald Ford seemed to many to be a likable and honest man. Upon becoming vice president after Spiro Agnew's resignation, Ford candidly admitted his limitations. "I'm a Ford, not a Lincoln," he remarked. On September 8, 1974, President Ford pardoned Richard Nixon in an attempt to move the country beyond Watergate. The move cost Ford a good deal of public support.

FORD TRIES TO "WHIP" INFLATION By the time Ford took office, America's economy had gone from bad to worse. Both inflation and unemployment continued to rise. After the massive OPEC oil-price increases in 1973, gasoline and heating oil costs had soared, pushing inflation from 6 percent to over 10 percent by the end of 1974. Ford responded with a program of massive citizen action, called "Whip Inflation Now" or WIN. The president called on Americans to cut back on their use of oil and gas and to take other energy-saving measures.

In the absence of incentives, though, the plan fell flat. Ford then tried to curb inflation through a "tight money" policy. He cut government spending and encouraged the Federal Reserve Board to restrict credit through higher interest rates. These actions triggered the worst economic recession in 40 years. As Ford implemented his economic programs, he continually battled a Democratic Congress intent on pushing its own economic agenda. During his two years as president, Ford vetoed more than 50 pieces of legislation. A

MAIN IDEA

Making Inferences

A Why was Ford's call for voluntary actions to help the economy unsuccessful?

Ford's Foreign Policy

Ford fared slightly better in the international arena. He relied heavily on Henry Kissinger, who continued to hold the key position of secretary of state.

CARRYING OUT NIXON'S FOREIGN POLICIES Following Kissinger's advice, Ford pushed ahead with Nixon's policy of negotiation with China and the Soviet Union. In November 1974, he met with Soviet premier Leonid Brezhnev. Less than a year later, he traveled to Helsinki, Finland, where 35 nations, including the Soviet Union, signed the Helsinki Accords—a series of agreements that promised greater cooperation between the nations of Eastern and Western Europe. The Helsinki Accords would be Ford's greatest presidential accomplishment.

ONGOING TURMOIL IN SOUTHEAST ASIA Like presidents before him, Ford encountered trouble in Southeast Asia. The 1973 cease-fire in Vietnam had broken down. Heavy fighting resumed and Ford asked Congress for over $722 million to help South Vietnam. Congress refused. Without American financial help, South Vietnam surrendered to the North in 1975. In the same year, the Communist government of Cambodia seized the U.S. merchant ship *Mayagüez* in the Gulf of Siam. President Ford responded with a massive show of military force to rescue 39 crew members aboard the ship. The operation cost the lives of 41 U.S. troops. Critics argued that the mission had cost more lives than it had saved.

DIFFICULT DECISIONS

PARDONING PRESIDENT NIXON

President Ford's pardon of Richard Nixon outraged many Americans. But President Ford argued that the pardon of Richard Nixon was in the country's best interest. In the event of a Watergate trial, Ford argued, "ugly passions would again be aroused. . . . And the credibility of our free institutions . . . would again be challenged at home and abroad." Ford called the pardon decision "the most difficult of my life, by far."

In 2001, after more than 25 years, Ford received the John F. Kennedy Profiles in Courage Award for his courageous decision in the face of public opposition.

1. How might the country have been affected if a former United States president had gone on trial for possible criminal wrongdoing?
2. If you had been in President Ford's position, would you have pardoned Richard Nixon? Why or why not?

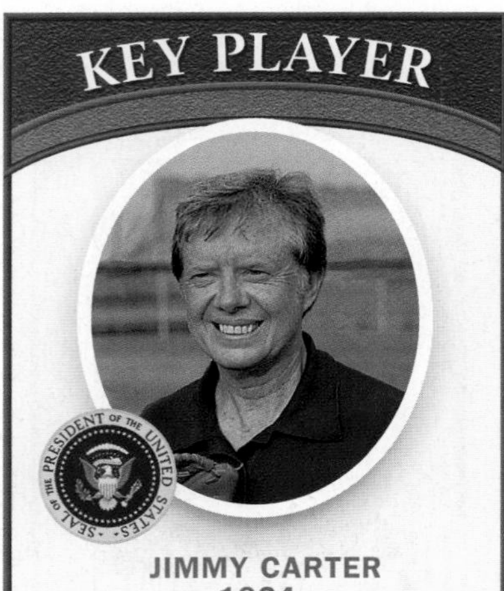

JIMMY CARTER
1924–

James Earl Carter, Jr., was born into relative prosperity. His father, Earl Carter, was a disciplinarian who tried to instill a sense of hard work and responsibility in his son.

To earn money for himself, Carter undertook a variety of jobs selling peanuts, running a hamburger and hot dog stand, collecting newspapers and selling them to fish markets, and selling scrap iron.

Before entering politics, Carter joined the navy, where he excelled in electronics and naval tactics. In 1952, he joined a select group of officers who helped develop the world's first nuclear submarines. The group's commander was Captain Hyman G. Rickover. Carter later wrote that Rickover "had a profound effect on my life—perhaps more than anyone except my own parents. . . . He expected the maximum from us, but he always contributed more."

This 1976 ▶ campaign toy exaggerates Jimmy Carter's well-known smile and parodies his occupation as a peanut farmer.

Carter Enters the White House

Gerald Ford won the Republican nomination for president in 1976 after fending off a powerful conservative challenge from former California governor Ronald Reagan. Because the Republicans seemed divided over Ford's leadership, the Democrats confidently eyed the White House. "We could run an aardvark this year and win," predicted one Democratic leader. The Democratic nominee was indeed a surprise: a nationally unknown peanut farmer and former governor of Georgia, **Jimmy Carter.**

MR. CARTER GOES TO WASHINGTON During the post-Watergate era, cynicism toward the Washington establishment ran high. The soft-spoken, personable man from Plains, Georgia, promised to restore integrity to the nation's highest office, "I will never tell a lie to the American people."

Throughout the presidential campaign, Carter and Ford squared off over the key issues of inflation, energy, and unemployment. On Election Day, Jimmy Carter won by a narrow margin, claiming 40.8 million popular votes to Ford's 39.1 million. (B)

MAIN IDEA

Analyzing Causes

(B) What factors played a significant role in Carter's election?

From the very beginning, the new first family brought a down-to-earth style to Washington. After settling into office, Carter stayed in touch with the people by holding Roosevelt-like "fireside chats" on radio and television.

Carter failed to reach out to Congress in a similar way, refusing to play the "insider" game of deal making. Relying mainly on a team of advisers from Georgia, Carter even alienated congressional Democrats. Both parties on Capitol Hill often joined to sink the president's budget proposals, as well as his major policy reforms of tax and welfare programs.

Carter's Domestic Agenda

Like Gerald Ford, President Carter focused much of his attention on battling the country's energy and economic crises but was unable to bring the United States out of its economic slump.

CONFRONTING THE ENERGY CRISIS Carter considered the energy crisis the most important issue facing the nation. A large part of the problem, the president believed, was America's reliance on imported oil. On April 18, 1977, during a fireside chat, Carter urged his fellow Americans to cut their consumption of oil and gas.

A PERSONAL VOICE JIMMY CARTER

"The energy crisis . . . is a problem . . . likely to get progressively worse through the rest of this century. . . . Our decision about energy will test the character of the American people. . . . This difficult effort will be the 'moral equivalent of war,' except that we will be uniting our efforts to build and not to destroy."

—quoted in *Keeping Faith*

In addition, Carter presented Congress with more than 100 proposals on energy conservation and development. Representatives from oil- and gas-producing states fiercely resisted some of the proposals. Automobile manufacturers also lobbied against gas-rationing provisions. "It was impossible for me to imagine the bloody legislative battles we would have to win," Carter later wrote.

Vocabulary
lobby: a special-interest group that tries to influence the legislature

Out of the battle came the **National Energy Act**. The act placed a tax on gas-guzzling cars, removed price controls on oil and natural gas produced in the United States, and extended tax credits for the development of alternative energy. With the help of the act, as well as voluntary conservation measures, U.S. dependence on foreign oil had eased slightly by 1979. C

MAIN IDEA
Summarizing
C How did the National Energy Act help ease America's energy crisis?

THE ECONOMIC CRISIS WORSENS Unfortunately, these energy-saving measures could do little to combat a sudden new economic crisis. In the summer of 1979, renewed violence in the Middle East produced a second major fuel shortage in the United States. To make matters worse, OPEC announced another major price hike. In 1979 inflation soared from 7.6 percent to 11.3 percent.

Faced with increasing pressure to act, Carter attempted an array of measures, none of which worked. Carter's scattershot approach convinced many people that he had no economic policy at all. Carter fueled this feeling of uncertainty by delivering his now-famous "malaise" speech, in which he complained of a "crisis of spirit" that had struck "at the very heart and soul of our national will." Carter's address made many Americans feel that their president had given up.

By 1980, inflation had climbed to nearly 14 percent, the highest rate since 1947. The standard of living in the United States slipped from first place to fifth place in the world. Carter's popularity slipped along with it. This economic downswing—and Carter's inability to solve it during an election year—was one key factor in sending Ronald Reagan to the White House.

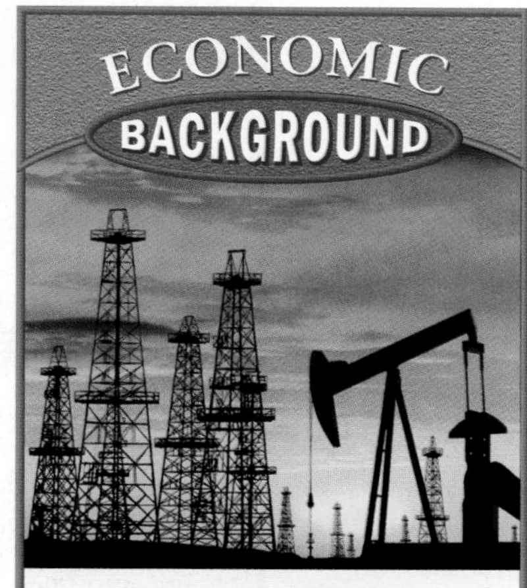

THE EARLY 1980s TEXAS OIL BOOM

The economic crisis that gripped the country in the late 1970s was largely caused by the increased cost of oil. The OPEC cartel raised the price of oil by agreeing to restrict oil production. The resulting decrease in the supply of oil in the market caused the price to go up.

Most Americans were hurt by the high energy prices. However, in areas that produced oil, such as Texas, the rise in prices led to a booming economy in the early 1980s. Real-estate values—for land on which to drill for oil, as well as for office space in cities like Houston and Dallas—increased greatly. (See *supply and demand* on page R46 in the Economics Handbook.)

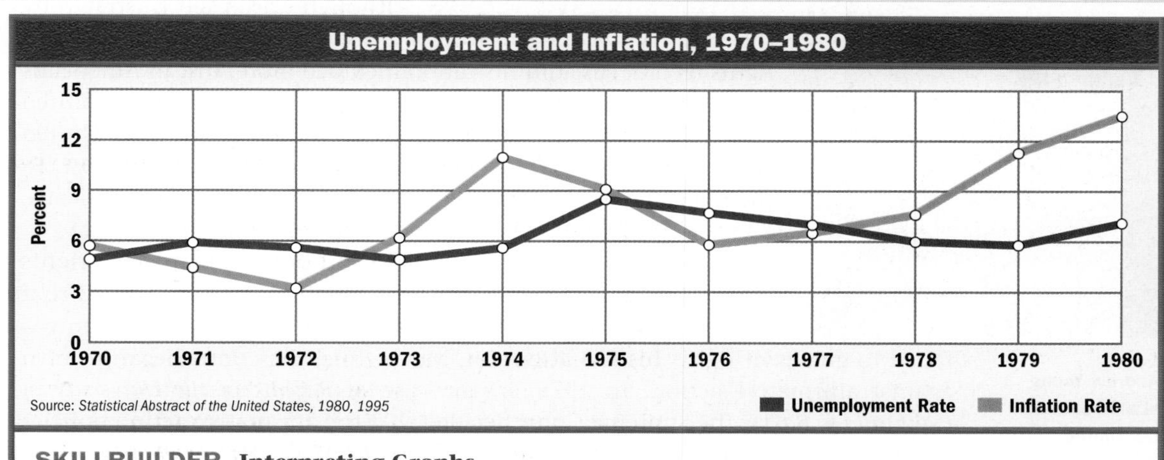

Source: *Statistical Abstract of the United States, 1980, 1995*

SKILLBUILDER Interpreting Graphs
1. What trends did the economy experience during the Carter years?
2. Which year of the Carter administration saw the greatest stagflation (inflation plus unemployment)?

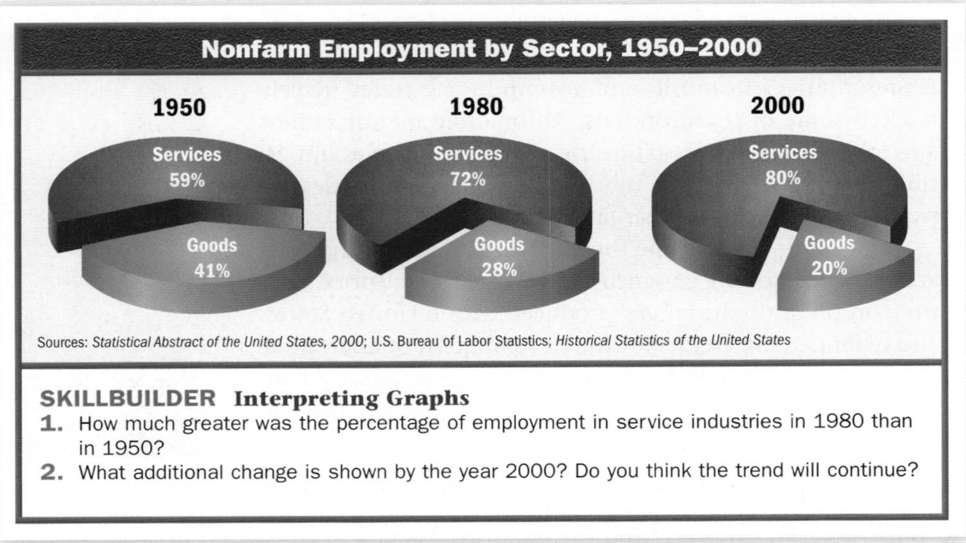

SKILLBUILDER Interpreting Graphs

1. How much greater was the percentage of employment in service industries in 1980 than in 1950?
2. What additional change is shown by the year 2000? Do you think the trend will continue?

A CHANGING ECONOMY Many of the economic problems Jimmy Carter struggled with resulted from long-term trends in the economy. Since the 1950s, the rise of automation and foreign competition had reduced the number of manufacturing jobs. At the same time, the service sector of the economy expanded rapidly. This sector includes industries such as communications, transportation, and retail trade.

The rise of the service sector and the decline of manufacturing jobs meant big changes for some American workers. Workers left out of manufacturing jobs faced an increasingly complex job market. Many of the higher-paying service jobs required more education or specialized skills than did manufacturing jobs. The lower-skilled service jobs usually did not pay well.

Growing overseas competition during the 1970s caused further change in America's economy. The booming economies of West Germany and countries on the Pacific Rim (such as Japan, Taiwan, and Korea) cut into many U.S. markets. Many of the nation's primary industries—iron and steel, rubber, clothing, automobiles—had to cut back production, lay off workers, and even close plants. Especially hard-hit were the automotive industries of the Northeast. There, high energy costs, foreign competition, and computerized production led companies to eliminate tens of thousands of jobs. D

MAIN IDEA

Analyzing Causes

D What factors played a role in America's economic stagnation?

CARTER AND CIVIL RIGHTS Although Carter felt frustrated by the country's economic woes, he took special pride in his civil rights record. His administration included more African Americans and women than any before it. In 1977, the president appointed civil rights leader Andrew Young as U.S. ambassador to the United Nations. Young was the first African American to hold that post. To the judicial branch alone, Carter appointed 28 African Americans, 29 women (including 6 African Americans), and 14 Latinos.

▲ **Andrew Young stands outside the United Nations in New York City, in 1997.**

However, President Carter fell short of what many civil rights groups had expected in terms of legislation. Critics claimed that Carter—preoccupied with battles over energy and the economy—failed to give civil rights his full attention. Meanwhile, the courts began to turn against affirmative action. In 1978, in the case of *Regents of the University of California* v. *Bakke,* the Supreme Court decided that the affirmative action policies of the university's medical school were unconstitutional. The decision made it more difficult for organizations to establish effective affirmative action programs. (See *Regents of the University of California* v. *Bakke,* page 818.)

A Human Rights Foreign Policy

Jimmy Carter rejected the philosophy of realpolitik—the pragmatic policy of negotiating with powerful nations despite their behavior—and strived for a foreign policy committed to human rights.

ADVANCING HUMAN RIGHTS Jimmy Carter, like Woodrow Wilson, sought to use moral principles as a guide for U.S. foreign policy. He believed that the United States needed to commit itself to promoting **human rights**—such as the freedoms and liberties listed in the Declaration of Independence and the Bill of Rights—throughout the world.

Putting his principles into practice, President Carter cut off military aid to Argentina and Brazil, countries that had good relations with the United States but had imprisoned or tortured thousands of their own citizens. Carter followed up this action by establishing a Bureau of Human Rights in the State Department.

Carter's philosophy was not without its critics. Supporters of the containment policy felt that the president's policy undercut allies such as Nicaragua, a dictatorial but anti-Communist country. Others argued that by supporting dictators in South Korea and the Philippines, Carter was acting inconsistently. In 1977, Carter's policies drew further criticism when his administration announced that it planned to give up ownership of the Panama Canal. (E)

MAIN IDEA

Identifying Problems

(E) What criticisms were made of Carter's foreign-policy philosophy?

YIELDING THE PANAMA CANAL Since 1914, when the United States obtained full ownership over the Panama Canal, Panamanians had resented having their nation split in half by a foreign power. In 1977, the two nations agreed to two treaties, one of which turned over control of the Panama Canal to Panama on December 31, 1999.

In 1978, the U.S. Senate, which had to ratify each treaty, approved the agreements by a vote of 68 to 32—one more vote than the required two-thirds. Public opinion was also divided. In the end, the treaties did improve relationships between the United States and Latin America.

THE COLLAPSE OF DÉTENTE When Jimmy Carter took office, détente—the relaxation of tensions between the world's superpowers—had reached a high point. Beginning with President Nixon and continuing with President Ford, U.S. officials had worked to ease relations with the Communist superpowers of China and the Soviet Union.

However, Carter's firm insistence on human rights led to a breakdown in relations with the Soviet Union. President Carter's dismay over the Soviet Union's treatment of dissidents, or opponents of the government's policies, delayed a second round of SALT negotiations. President Carter and Soviet premier Leonid Brezhnev finally met in June of 1979 in Vienna, Austria, where they signed an agreement known as SALT II. Although the agreement did not reduce armaments, it did provide for limits on the number of strategic weapons and nuclear-missile launchers that each side could produce.

The SALT II agreement, however, met sharp opposition in the Senate. Critics argued that it would put the United States at a military disadvantage. Then, in December 1979, the Soviets invaded the neighboring country of Afghanistan. Angered over the invasion, President Carter refused to fight for the SALT II agreement, and the treaty died. (F)

MAIN IDEA

Analyzing Causes

(F) What led to the collapse of détente with the Soviet Union?

WORLD STAGE

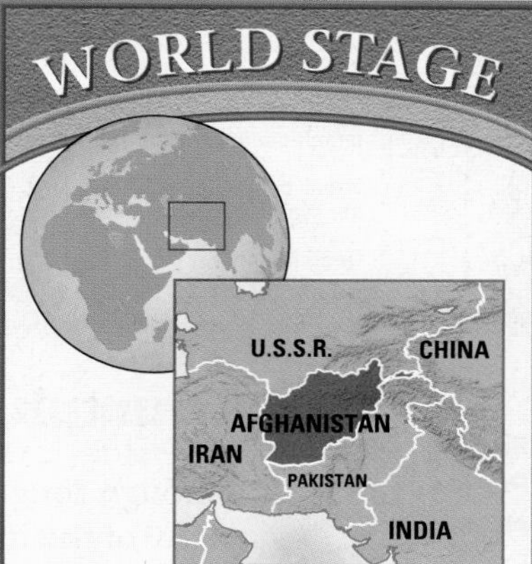

SOVIET–AFGHANISTAN WAR

Afghanistan, an Islamic country along the southern border of the Soviet Union, had been run by a pro-Soviet government for a number of years. However, a strong Muslim rebel group was intent on overthrowing the Afghan government. Fearing a rebel victory in Afghanistan, the Soviet Union sent troops to Afghanistan in late 1979.

While the Soviets had superior weaponry, the rebels fought the Soviets to a stalemate by using guerrilla tactics and knowledge of the country's mountainous terrain.

After suffering thousands of casualties, the last Soviet troops pulled out of Afghanistan in February 1989. Fighting between rival factions continued for years. The Taliban, a radical Muslim faction, eventually gained control of the country and imposed harsh rule based on its version of Islamic fundamentalism.

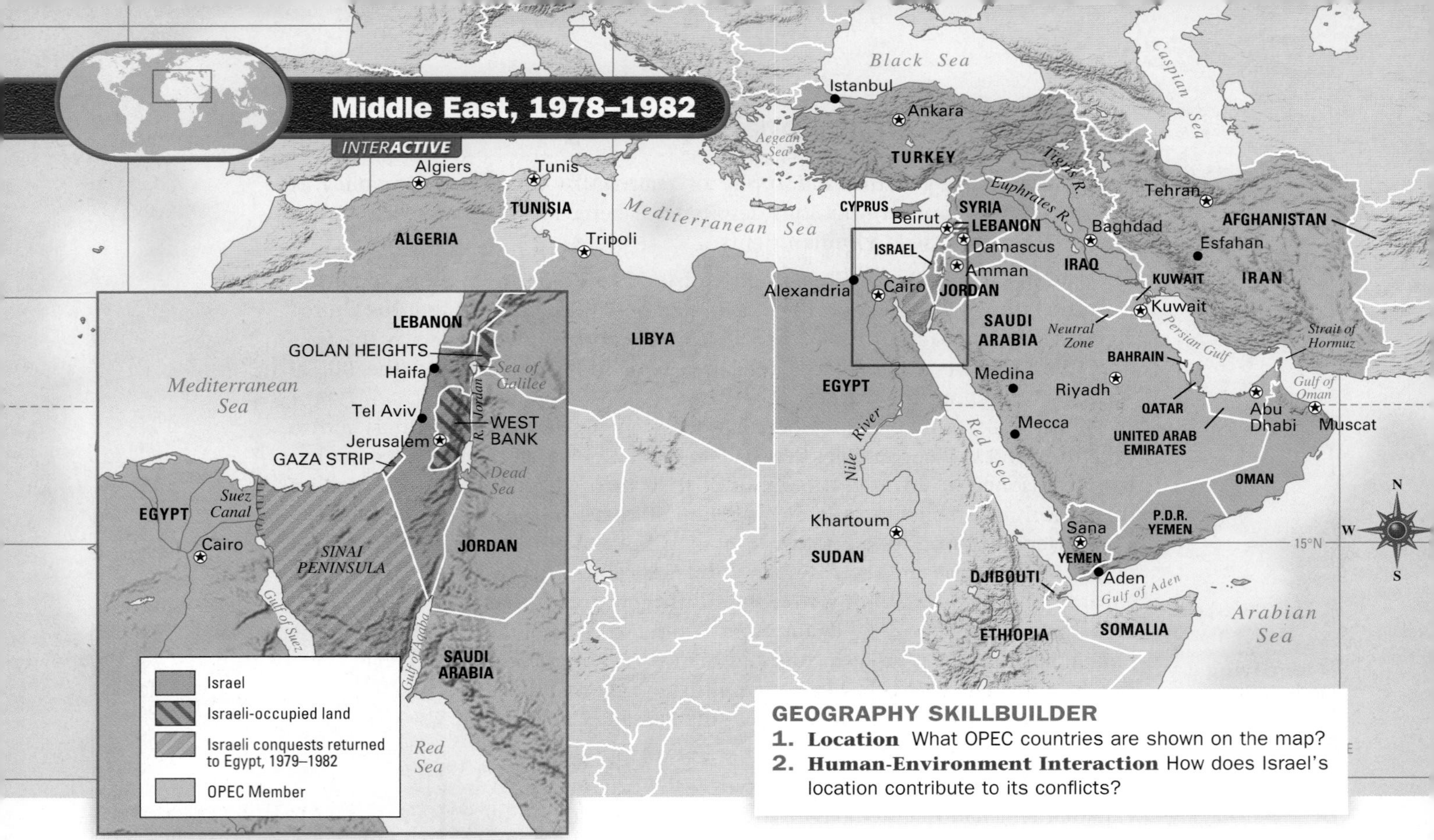

Middle East, 1978–1982

INTERACTIVE

Israel

Israeli-occupied land

Israeli conquests returned to Egypt, 1979–1982

OPEC Member

GEOGRAPHY SKILLBUILDER

1. **Location** What OPEC countries are shown on the map?
2. **Human-Environment Interaction** How does Israel's location contribute to its conflicts?

Triumph and Crisis in the Middle East

Through long gasoline lines and high energy costs, Americans became all too aware of the troubles in the Middle East. In that area of ethnic, religious, and economic conflict, Jimmy Carter achieved one of his greatest diplomatic triumphs—and suffered his most tragic defeat.

THE CAMP DAVID ACCORDS Through negotiation and arm-twisting, Carter helped forge peace between long-time enemies Israel and Egypt. In 1977, Egyptian president Anwar el-Sadat and Israeli prime minister Menachem Begin met in Jerusalem to discuss an overall peace between the two nations. In the summer of 1978, Carter seized on the peace initiative. When the peace talks stalled, he invited Sadat and Begin to Camp David, the presidential retreat in Maryland.

After 12 days of intense negotiations, the three leaders reached an agreement that became known as the **Camp David Accords.** Under this first signed peace agreement with an Arab country, Israel agreed to withdraw from the Sinai Peninsula, which it had seized from Egypt during the Six-Day War in 1967. Egypt, in turn, formally recognized Israel's right to exist. Still, many issues were left unresolved. G

President Carter, President Anwar el-Sadat, and Prime Minister Menachem Begin reach a peace agreement in 1978. ▼

MAIN IDEA

Summarizing

G What was the significance of the Camp David Accords?

Joking at the hard work ahead, Carter wrote playfully in his diary, "I resolved to do everything possible to get out of the negotiating business!" Little did the president know that his next Middle East negotiation would be his most painful.

THE IRAN HOSTAGE CRISIS By 1979, the shah of Iran, an ally of the United States, was in deep trouble. Many Iranians resented his regime's widespread corruption and dictatorial tactics.

In January 1979, revolution broke out. The Muslim religious leader **Ayatollah Ruhollah Khomeini** (ī′yə-tō′lə ro͞o-hō′lə kō-mā′nē) led the rebels in overthrowing the shah and establishing a religious state based on strict obedience to the Qur'an, the sacred book of Islam. Carter had supported the shah until the very end. In October 1979, the president allowed the shah to enter the United States for cancer treatment, though he had already fled Iran in January 1979.

The act infuriated the revolutionaries of Iran. On November 4, 1979, armed students seized the U.S. embassy in Tehran and took 52 Americans hostage. The militants demanded that the United States send the shah back to Iran in return for the release of the hostages.

Carter refused, and a painful yearlong standoff followed, in which the United States continued quiet but intense efforts to free the hostages. The captives were finally released on January 20, 1981, shortly after the new president, Ronald Reagan, was sworn in as president. Despite the hostages' release after 444 days in captivity, the crisis in Iran seemed to underscore the limits that Americans faced during the 1970s. Americans also realized that there were limits to the nation's environmental resources. This realization prompted both citizens and the government to actively address environmental concerns.

▲ **U.S. hostages were blindfolded and paraded through the streets of Tehran.**

SECTION 3 ASSESSMENT

1. **TERMS & NAMES** For each term or name, write a sentence explaining its significance.
   - **Gerald R. Ford**
   - **Jimmy Carter**
   - **National Energy Act**
   - **human rights**
   - **Camp David Accords**
   - **Ayatollah Ruhollah Khomeini**

MAIN IDEA

2. **TAKING NOTES**
   Create a time line of the major events of the Ford and Carter administrations, using a form such as the one below.

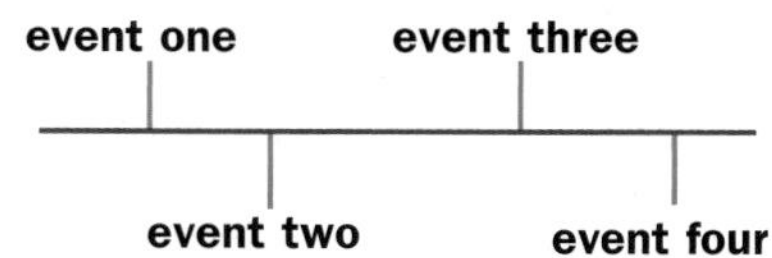

   Which two events do you think were the most important? Why?

CRITICAL THINKING

3. **EVALUATING DECISIONS**
   Do you think that Ford made a good decision in pardoning Nixon? Explain why or why not.

4. **COMPARING**
   How were the actions taken by Presidents Ford and Carter to address the country's economic downturn similar? How did they differ?

5. **ANALYZING ISSUES**
   Do you agree with President Carter that human rights concerns should steer U.S. foreign policy? Why or why not? **Think About:**
   - the responsibility of promoting human rights
   - the loss of good relations with certain countries
   - the collapse of détente with the Soviet Union

REGENTS OF THE UNIVERSITY OF CALIFORNIA v. *BAKKE* (1978)

ORIGINS OF THE CASE In 1973, Allan Bakke applied to the University of California at Davis medical school. The school had a quota-based affirmative-action plan that reserved 16 out of 100 spots for racial minorities. Bakke, a white male, was not admitted to the school despite his competitive test scores and grades. Bakke sued for admission, arguing that he had been discriminated against on the basis of race. The California Supreme Court agreed with Bakke, but the school appealed the case.

THE RULING **The Court ruled that racial quotas were unconstitutional, but that schools could still consider race as a factor in admissions.**

LEGAL REASONING

The Court was closely divided on whether affirmative-action plans were constitutional. Two different sets of justices formed 5-to-4 majorities on two different issues in *Bakke.*

Five justices agreed the quota was unfair to Bakke. They based their argument on the equal protection clause of the Fourteenth Amendment. Justice Lewis Powell, writing for the majority, explained their reasoning.

"The guarantee of equal protection cannot mean one thing when applied to one individual and something else when applied to a person of another color. If both are not accorded the same protection, then it is not equal."

▲ **Allan Bakke receives his degree in medicine from the medical school at U.C. Davis on June 4, 1982.**

The four justices that joined Powell in this part of the decision said race should *never* play a part in admissions decisions. Powell and the other four justices disagreed. These five justices formed a separate majority, arguing that "the attainment of a diverse student body . . . is a constitutionally permissible goal for an institution of higher education." In other words, schools could have affirmative-action plans that consider race as *one* factor in admission decisions in order to achieve a diverse student body.

LEGAL SOURCES

LEGISLATION

U.S. CONSTITUTION, FOURTEENTH AMENDMENT (1868)

"No state shall . . . deprive any person of life, liberty, or property, without due process of law; nor deny to any person within its jurisdiction the equal protection of the laws."

RELATED CASES

***UNITED STEELWORKERS OF AMERICA* v. *WEBER* (1979)**

The Court said a business could have a short-term program for training minority workers as a way of fixing the results of past discrimination.

***ADARAND CONSTRUCTORS* v. *PENA* (1995)**

The Court struck a federal law to set aside 10 percent of highway construction funds for minority-owned businesses. The Court also said that affirmative-action programs must be focused to achieve a compelling government interest.

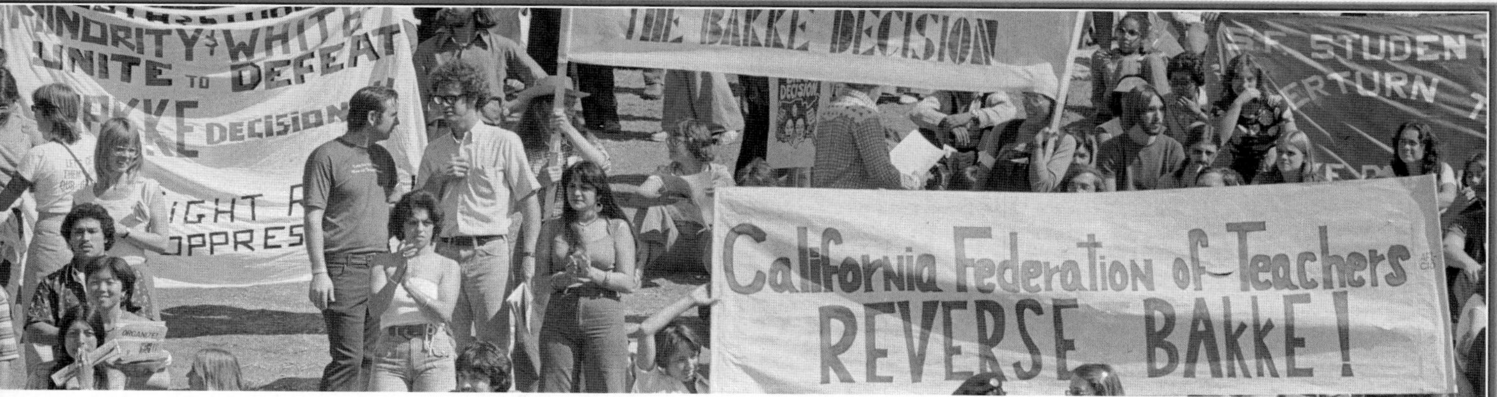

▲ On October 8, 1977, protestors march in suppport of affirmative action at a park in Oakland, California.

WHY IT MATTERED

Many people have faced discrimination in America. The struggle of African Americans for civil rights in the 1950s and 1960s succeeded in overturning Jim Crow segregation. Even so, social inequality persisted for African Americans, as well as women and other minority groups. In 1965, President Lyndon Johnson explained why more proactive measures needed to be taken to end inequality.

> **"You do not take a person who for years has been hobbled by chains and . . . bring him up to the starting line of a race and then say, 'you are free to compete with all the others' and still justly believe that you have been completely fair."**

As a result, Johnson urged companies to begin to take "affirmative action" to hire and promote African Americans, helping them to overcome generations of inequality. Critics quickly opposed affirmative action plans as unfair to white people and merely a replacement of one form of racial discrimination with another.

University admissions policies became a focus of the debate over affirmative action. The Court's ruling in *Bakke* allowed race to be used as one factor in admissions decisions. Schools could consider a prospective student's race, but they could not use quotas or use race as the *only* factor for admission.

HISTORICAL IMPACT

Since *Bakke,* the Court has ruled on affirmative action several times, usually limiting affirmative-action plans. For example, in *Adarand Constructors* v. *Pena* (1995), the Court struck a federal law to set aside "not less than 10 percent" of highway construction funds for businesses owned by "socially and economically disadvantaged individuals." The Court said that affirmative-action programs must be narrowly focused to achieve a "compelling government interest."

On cases regarding school affirmative-action plans, the Supreme Court has chosen not to act. The Court refused to hear a case challenging a California law banning the consideration of race or gender for admission to the state's universities. Similarly, the Court refused to hear an appeal of a 1996 lower court ruling that outlawed any consideration of race for admission to the University of Texas law school. In December of 2000, however, supporters of affirmative action won a victory in the federal court. A federal judge ruled that a University of Michigan affirmative action plan was constitutional. He noted that *Bakke*—not the Texas case—was the law of the land, and schools still had the right to consider race in admissions decisions.

In recent years, some states have found new ways of helping minority students enter state universities. For instance, California, Florida, and Texas have enacted plans guaranteeing admittance to state universities for top students from each high school graduating class.

THINKING CRITICALLY

CONNECT TO HISTORY

1. **Evaluating** Research articles about *Bakke* in the library or on the Internet. Read the articles and write a paragraph for each one explaining the writer's point of view on the case. Conclude by telling which article gives the best discussion of the case. Cite examples to support your choice.

 **SEE SKILLBUILDER HANDBOOK, PAGE R16.**

CONNECT TO TODAY

2.  **INTERNET ACTIVITY** **CLASSZONE.COM**

Visit the links for Historic Decisions of the Supreme Court to research and read about Proposition 209, California's 1996 law banning affirmative action at state universities. Prepare arguments for an in-class debate about whether the law will have a positive or negative long-term effect.

Environmental Activism

MAIN IDEA

During the 1970s, Americans strengthened their efforts to address the nation's environmental problems.

WHY IT MATTERS NOW

The nation today continues to struggle to balance environmental concerns with industrial growth.

Terms & Names

- **Rachel Carson**
- **Earth Day**
- **environmentalist**
- **Environmental Protection Agency (EPA)**
- **Three Mile Island**

One American's Story

In 1972, Lois Gibbs and her family moved to Niagara Falls, New York. Underneath this quiet town, however, was a disaster in the making. In the 1890s, the Love Canal had been built to provide hydroelectric power for the Niagara Falls area. Chemical companies were dumping hazardous waste into the canal. In 1953, bulldozers filled in the canal. Shortly thereafter, a school and rows of homes were built nearby.

In 1977, when Lois Gibbs's son fell sick, she decided to investigate. She eventually uncovered the existence of the toxic waste and mobilized the community to demand government action. In 1980, President Carter authorized funds for many Niagara Falls families to move to safety. Years later, Lois Gibbs wrote a book detailing her efforts.

A PERSONAL VOICE LOIS GIBBS

> **"I want to tell you our story—my story—because I believe that ordinary citizens—using the tools of dignity, self-respect, common sense, and perseverance—can influence solutions to important problems in our society. . . . In solving any difficult problem, you have to be prepared to fight long and hard, sometimes at great personal cost; but it can be done. It must be done if we are to survive . . . at all."**
>
> —*Love Canal: My Story*

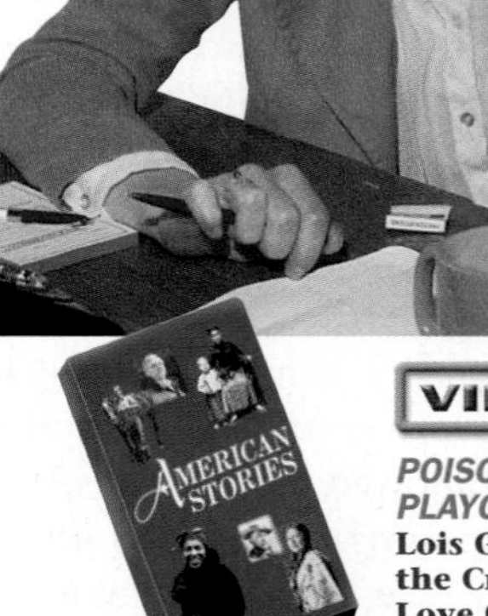

VIDEO

POISONED PLAYGROUND
Lois Gibbs and the Crisis at Love Canal

Lois Gibbs's concerns about environmental hazards were shared by many Americans in the 1970s. Through the energy crisis, Americans learned that their natural resources were limited; they could no longer take the environment for granted. Americans—from grassroots organizations to the government—began to focus on conservation of the environment and new forms of energy.

The Roots of Environmentalism

The widespread realization that pollution and overconsumption were damaging the environment began in the 1960s. One book in particular had awakened

America's concerns about the environment and helped lay the groundwork for the activism of the early seventies.

RACHEL CARSON AND SILENT SPRING In 1962, **Rachel Carson**, a marine biologist, published a book entitled *Silent Spring*. In it, she warned against the growing use of pesticides—chemicals used to kill insects and rodents. Carson argued that pesticides poisoned the very food they were intended to protect and as a result killed many birds and fish.

Carson cautioned that America faced a "silent spring," in which birds killed off by pesticides would no longer fill the air with song. She added that of all the weapons used in "man's war against nature," pesticides were some of the most harmful.

KEY PLAYER

RACHEL CARSON 1907–1964

The marine biologist Rachel Carson was born far from the sea, in the small town of Springdale, Pennsylvania.

Carson was a sickly child who often had to remain at home, where her mother tutored her. Throughout her youth and into her college years, Carson was a studious, but quiet and aloof, person.

Carson entered college intent on becoming a writer. During her sophomore year, she took a biology class to fulfill her science requirement and quickly fell in love with the study of nature. By the next year Carson switched her major from English to zoology—the study of animals.

A PERSONAL VOICE RACHEL CARSON

"These sprays, dusts, and aerosols . . . have the power to kill every insect, the 'good' and the 'bad,' to still the song of birds and the leaping of fish in the streams, to coat the leaves with a deadly film, and to linger on in soil—all this though the intended target may be only a few weeds or insects. Can anyone believe it is possible to lay down such a barrage of poisons on the surface of the earth without making it unfit for all life?"

—*Silent Spring*

Within six months of its publication, *Silent Spring* sold nearly half a million copies. Many chemical companies called the book inaccurate and threatened legal action. However, for a majority of Americans, Carson's book was an early warning about the danger that human activity posed to the environment. Shortly after the book's publication, President Kennedy established an advisory committee to investigate the situation.

With Rachel Carson's prodding, the nation slowly began to focus more on environmental issues. Although Carson would not live to see the U.S. government outlaw DDT in 1972, her work helped many Americans realize that their everyday behavior, as well as the nation's industrial growth, had a damaging effect on the environment. (A)

MAIN IDEA

Analyzing Effects

(A) What effects did Rachel Carson's book have on the nation as a whole?

Environmental Concerns in the 1970s

During the 1970s, the administrations of Richard Nixon and Jimmy Carter confronted such environmental issues as conservation, pollution, and the growth of nuclear energy.

THE FIRST EARTH DAY The United States ushered in the 1970s—a decade in which it would actively address its environmental issues—fittingly enough with the first **Earth Day** celebration. On that day, April 22, 1970, nearly every community

A flag celebrating the first Earth Day in 1970.

in the nation and more than 10,000 schools and 2,000 colleges hosted some type of environmental-awareness activity and spotlighted such problems as pollution, the growth of toxic waste, and the earth's dwindling resources. The Earth Day celebration continues today. Each year on April 22, millions of people around the world gather to heighten public awareness of environmental problems.

Vocabulary
toxic: capable of causing injury or death, especially by chemical means; poisonous

THE GOVERNMENT TAKES ACTION Although President Nixon was not considered an **environmentalist,** or someone who takes an active role in the protection of the environment, he recognized the nation's growing concern about the environment. In an effort to "make our peace with nature," President Nixon set out on a course that led to the passage of several landmark measures. In 1970, he consolidated 15 existing federal pollution programs into the **Environmental Protection Agency (EPA).** The new agency was given the power to set and enforce pollution standards, to conduct environmental research, and to assist state and local governments in pollution control. Today, the EPA remains the federal government's main instrument for dealing with environmental issues.

In 1970 Nixon signed a new Clean Air Act that added several amendments to the Clean Air Act of 1963. The new act gave the government the authority to set air standards. Following the 1970 Clean Air Act, Congress also passed the Endangered Species Act, in addition to laws that limited pesticide use and curbed strip mining—the practice of mining for ore and coal by digging gaping holes in the land. Some 35 environmental laws took effect during the decade, addressing every aspect of conservation and clean-up, from protecting endangered animals to regulating auto emissions. B

MAIN IDEA

Summarizing
B What were the environmental actions taken during the Nixon administration?

BALANCING PROGRESS AND CONSERVATION IN ALASKA During the 1970s, the federal government took steps to ensure the continued well-being of Alaska, the largest state in the nation and one of its most ecologically sensitive.

The discovery of oil there in 1968, and the subsequent construction of a massive pipeline to transport it, created many new jobs and greatly increased state revenues. However, the influx of new development also raised concerns about Alaska's wildlife, as well as the rights of its native peoples. In 1971, Nixon signed the Alaska Native Claims Settlement Act, which turned over millions of acres of land to the state's native tribes for conservation and tribal use. In 1978, President Carter enhanced this conservation effort by setting aside an additional 56 million acres in Alaska as national monuments. In 1980, Congress added another 104 million acres as protected areas.

The Trans-Alaska Pipeline, stretching across hundreds of miles of tundra, was completed in 1977. ▼

THE DEBATE OVER NUCLEAR ENERGY As the 1970s came to a close, Americans became acutely aware of the dangers that nuclear power plants posed to both humans and the environment. During the 1970s, as America realized the drawbacks to its heavy dependence on foreign oil for energy, nuclear power seemed to many to be an attractive alternative.

Opponents of nuclear energy warned the public against the industry's growth. They contended that nuclear plants, and the wastes they produced, were potentially dangerous to humans and their environment.

THREE MILE ISLAND In the early hours of March 28, 1979, the concerns of nuclear energy opponents were validated. That morning, one of the nuclear reactors at a plant on **Three Mile Island** near Harrisburg, Pennsylvania, malfunctioned. The reactor overheated after its cooling system failed, and fear quickly arose that radiation might escape and spread over the region. Two days later,

Science & Technology

THE ACCIDENT AT THREE MILE ISLAND

A series of human and mechanical errors that caused the partial meltdown of the reactor core brought the Three Mile Island nuclear power plant to the brink of disaster. The accident at Three Mile Island caused widespread concern about nuclear power throughout the American public.

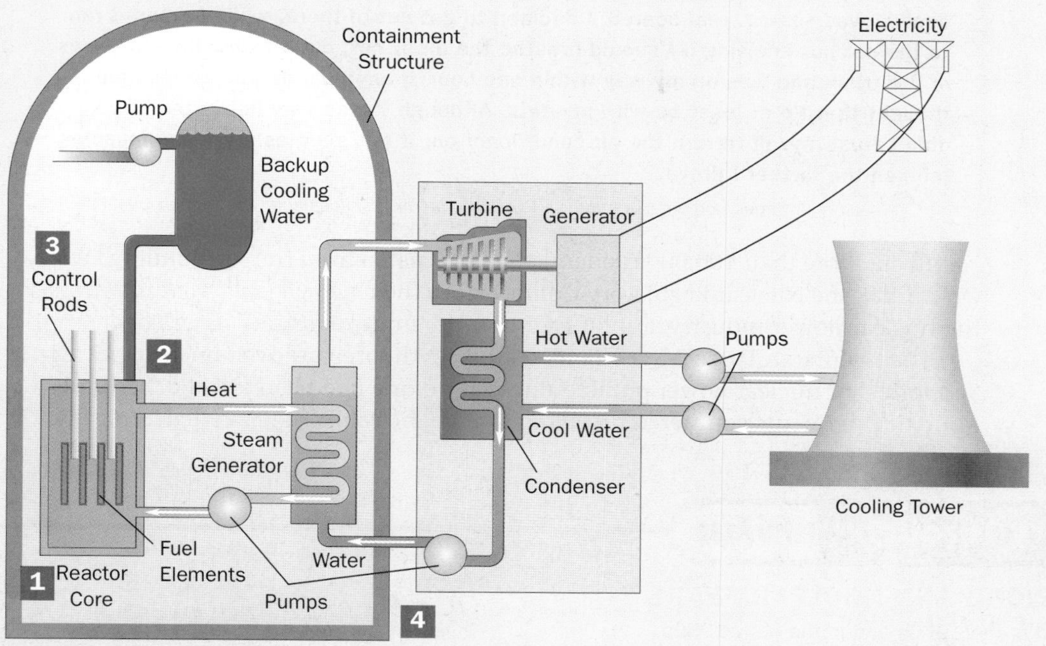

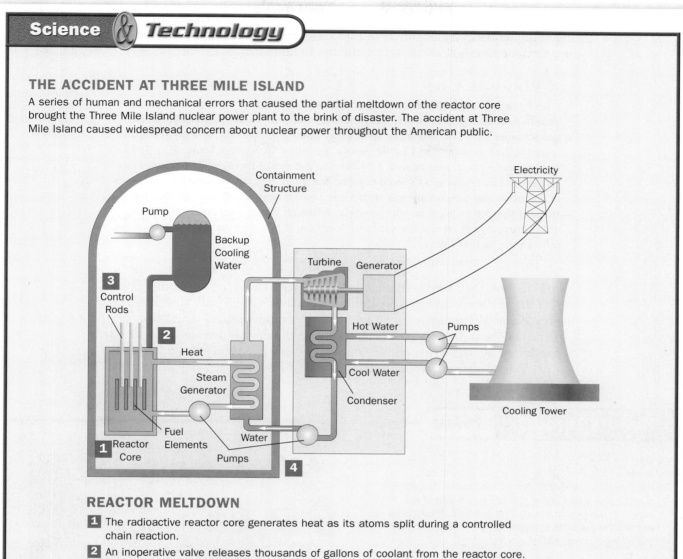

REACTOR MELTDOWN

1. The radioactive reactor core generates heat as its atoms split during a controlled chain reaction.
2. An inoperative valve releases thousands of gallons of coolant from the reactor core.
3. Half of the 36,816 exposed fuel rods melt in temperatures above five thousand degrees.
4. The melted material burns through the lining of the reactor chamber and spills to the floor of the containment structure.

More than 20 years after the accident, clean-up at Three Mile Island continues. The final 'clean-up bill' could soar to more than $3 billion. The TMI-2 reactor was dangerously contaminated and could not be entered for two years. All the materials in the containment structure, along with anything used in the clean-up, had to be decontaminated. Because the reactor will never be completely free of radioactivity, it will one day be entombed in cement.

low-level radiation actually did escape from the crippled reactor. Officials evacuated some residents, while others fled on their own. One homemaker who lived near the plant recalled her desperate attempt to find safety.

Background
The U.S. government does not expect to have a permanent burial site for nuclear waste until 2010. A proposed site is beneath the Yucca Mountains in southern Nevada about 100 miles northwest of Las Vegas.

A Personal Voice

"**On Friday, a very frightening thing occurred in our area. A state policeman went door-to-door telling residents to stay indoors, close all windows, and turn all air conditioners off. I was alone, as were many other homemakers, and my thoughts were focused on how long I would remain a prisoner in my own home. . . . Suddenly, I was scared, real scared. I decided to get out of there, while I could. I ran to the car not knowing if I should breathe the air or not, and I threw the suitcases in the trunk and was on my way within one hour. If anything dreadful happened, I thought that I'd at least be with my girls. Although it was very hot in the car, I didn't trust myself to turn the air conditioner on. It felt good as my tense muscles relaxed the farther I drove.**"

—an anonymous homemaker quoted in *Accident at Three Mile Island: The Human Dimensions*

In all, more than 100,000 residents were evacuated from the surrounding area. On April 9, the Nuclear Regulatory Commission, the federal agency that monitors the nuclear power industry, announced that the immediate danger was over.

The events at Three Mile Island rekindled the debate over nuclear power. Supporters of nuclear power pointed out that no one had been killed or seriously injured. Opponents countered by saying that chance alone had averted a tragedy.

History Through *Film*

HOLLYWOOD AND NUCLEAR FEARS

At the end of the 1970s and in the early 1980s, Hollywood responded to Americans' concerns over nuclear power by making pointed social-awareness films exposing dangers in the nuclear industry. These films alerted the public to the importance of regulations in the relatively new field of atomic energy.

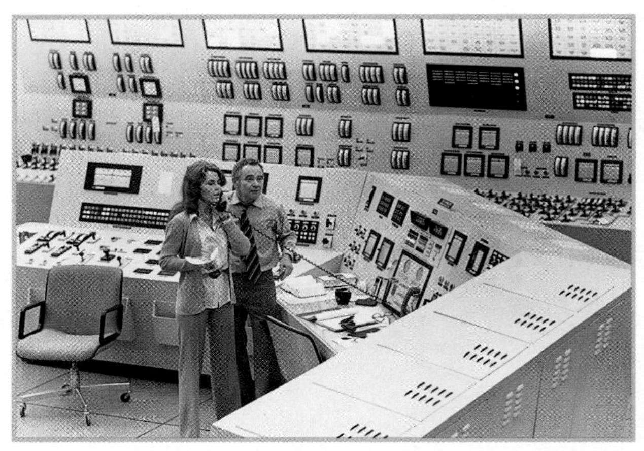

In 1979, *The China Syndrome,* starring Jane Fonda and Jack Lemmon, became the movie everyone was talking about. Only 12 days after the film's release, a serious accident similar to the one portrayed in the movie occurred at the Three Mile Island nuclear power plant. ▶

◀ **In 1983, on her way to meet with a reporter from the *New York Times,* Karen Silkwood, a worker at a nuclear power facility, was hit and died in a car crash. In the film dramatization, *Silkwood* (1983), Meryl Streep played Karen, and Kurt Russell and Cher, her co-workers.**

SKILLBUILDER Interpreting Visual Sources

1. Why do you think movies based on real events are popular with the general public?
2. How do you think these films influenced present-day nuclear energy policy?

SEE SKILLBUILDER HANDBOOK, PAGE R23.

They demanded that the government call a halt to the construction of new power plants and gradually shut down existing nuclear facilities.

MAIN IDEA

Analyzing Effects

C How did the Three Mile Island incident affect the use of nuclear power in America?

While the government did not do away with nuclear power, federal officials did recognize nuclear energy's potential danger to both humans and the environment. As a result of the accident at Three Mile Island, the Nuclear Regulatory Commission strengthened its safety standards and improved its inspection procedures. **C**

A Continuing Movement

Although the environmental movement of the 1970s gained popular support, opponents of the movement also made their voices heard. In Tennessee, for example, where a federal dam project was halted because it threatened a species of fish, local developers took out ads asking residents to "tell the government that the size of your wallet is more important than some two-inch-long minnow." When confronted with environmental concerns, one unemployed steelworker spoke for others when he remarked, "Why worry about the long run, when you're out of work right now?"

The environmental movement that blossomed in the 1970s became in the 1980s and 1990s a struggle to balance environmental concerns with jobs and progress. In the years since the first Earth Day, however, environmental issues have gained increasing attention and support.

HISTORICAL SPOTLIGHT

PRIVATE CONSERVATION GROUPS

As concerns about pollution and the depletion of nonrenewable resources grew, so did membership in private, nonprofit organizations dedicated to the preservation of wilderness and endangered species. Many of these groups lobbied government for protective legislation. Some filed lawsuits to block projects such as road or dam construction or logging that would threaten habitats. The Environmental Defense Fund (today Environmental Defense) brought lawsuits that led to the bans on DDT and on leaded gasoline.

Radical groups also emerged. Members of Greenpeace risked their lives at sea to escort whales and protect them from commercial hunters.

ASSESSMENT

1. **TERMS & NAMES** For each term or name, write a sentence explaining its significance.
   - **Rachel Carson**
   - **Earth Day**
   - **environmentalist**
   - **Environmental Protection Agency (EPA)**
   - **Three Mile Island**

MAIN IDEA

2. **TAKING NOTES**
   Re-create the web below on your paper and fill in events that illustrate the main idea in the center.

CRITICAL THINKING

3. **ANALYZING CAUSES**
   How much should the United States rely on nuclear power as a source of energy? Explain your view.
   Think About:
   - the safety of nuclear power
   - the alternatives to nuclear power
   - U.S. energy demands

4. **ANALYZING VISUAL SOURCES**
   What message does this 1969 poster from the Environmental Protection Agency give about the government's role in pollution?

Clean air
is a product of the
United States Environmental
Protection Agency.

CHAPTER 24 ASSESSMENT

TERMS & NAMES

For each term or name below, write a sentence explaining its significance to the Nixon, Ford, or Carter administrations.

1. Richard M. Nixon
2. stagflation
3. OPEC (Organization of Petroleum Exporting Countries)
4. SALT I Treaty
5. Watergate
6. Saturday Night Massacre
7. Camp David Accords
8. Ayatollah Ruhollah Khomeini
9. Rachel Carson
10. Environmental Protection Agency (EPA)

MAIN IDEAS

Use your notes and the information in the chapter to answer the following questions.

The Nixon Administration *(pages 794–801)*

1. In what ways did President Nixon attempt to reform the federal government?
2. How did Nixon try to combat stagflation?

Watergate: Nixon's Downfall *(pages 802–807)*

3. In what ways did the participants in Watergate attempt to cover up the scandal?
4. What were the results of the Watergate scandal?

The Ford and Carter Years *(pages 810–817)*

5. What were Gerald Ford's greatest successes as president?
6. How did President Carter attempt to solve the energy crisis?

Environmental Activism *(pages 820–825)*

7. What factors increased Americans' concerns about environmental issues during the 1960s and 1970s?
8. What was the impact of the Three Mile Island incident?

CRITICAL THINKING

1. **USING YOUR NOTES** In a chart like the one shown, identify one major development for each issue listed that occurred between 1968 and 1980. Indicate whether you think the impact of the development was positive (+) or negative (–).

Issue	Development	Impact
Economic conditions		
Democratic government		
Efficient energy use		
Environmental protection		

2. **ANALYZING EVENTS** Between 1972 and 1974, Americans were absorbed by the fall of President Nixon in the Watergate scandal. What might Americans have learned about the role of the executive office? Explain.

3. **INTERPRETING GRAPHS** Study the graph on page 813. Describe the changes in unemployment as compared to inflation from 1970 to 1980.

VISUAL SUMMARY AN AGE OF LIMITS

THE NIXON ADMINISTRATION

- Revenue sharing
- Law-and-order politics
- Integration delays
- Inflation, recession, and unemployment
- Opening to China
- Détente with the Soviet Union
- Watergate scandal
- Nixon resignation

THE FORD ADMINISTRATION

- Unelected president
- Nixon pardon
- Whip Inflation Now program
- Economic recession
- Mayagüez incident
- Helsinki Accords

TIME
Special Issue
THE HEALING BEGINS

THE CARTER ADMINISTRATION

- Energy crisis
- Worsening inflation
- Panama Canal Treaties
- Camp David Accords
- Nuclear power
- Iran hostage crisis

Standardized Test Practice

Use the two graphs below and your knowledge of U.S. history to answer question 1.

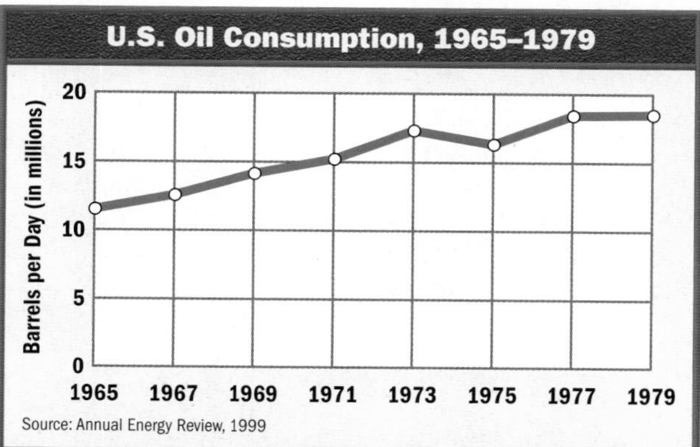

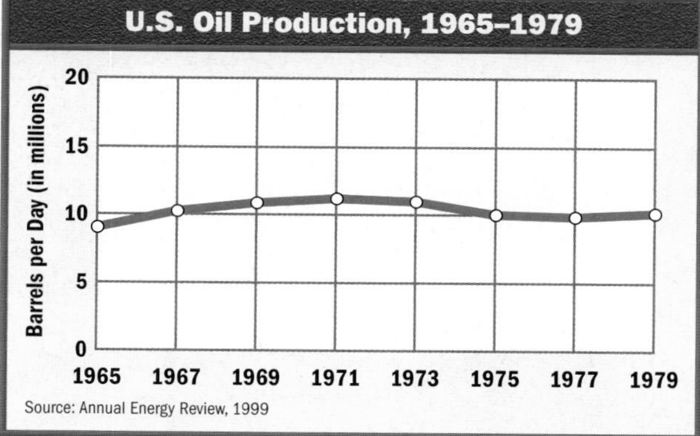

1. The OPEC oil embargo hit the United States so hard in 1973 because —
   - **A** domestic oil consumption decreased as production decreased
   - **B** domestic oil consumption remained steady as production decreased
   - **C** domestic oil consumption increased while production decreased slightly
   - **D** domestic production increased, although consumption increased faster

2. How did Watergate affect the presidents who followed after Richard Nixon?
   - **F** It caused them to be less trusted and less powerful.
   - **G** It made them reluctant to oppose Congress.
   - **H** It made them more popular with the media.
   - **J** It caused them to rely less on the counsel of cabinet members.

3. Which of the following is a contribution made by Rachel Carson to the American environmental movement?
   - **A** Carson researched "cleaner" sources of energy.
   - **B** Carson lobbied for the passage of the National Energy Act.
   - **C** Carson lobbied for making April 22, 1970, the first Earth Day.
   - **D** Carson published a book on the hazards of pesticide use.

ADDITIONAL TEST PRACTICE, pages S1–S33.

TEST PRACTICE CLASSZONE.COM

ALTERNATIVE ASSESSMENT

1. INTERACT WITH HISTORY Recall your discussion of the question on page 793:

   ### *In what ways can a president misuse power?*

   Now that you've learned how your country's highest office holder, President Nixon, lost the nation's trust after the Watergate scandal, would you change your response? Discuss your suggestions with a small group. Then create a list, ranking the misuses from least to most severe.

2.  **LEARNING FROM MEDIA** View the *American Stories* video "Poisoned Playground." Discuss the following questions in a group; then do the activity.
   - How did Lois Gibbs's struggle affect her personal life?
   - What finally prompted the government to evacuate the residents of Love Canal?

   Cooperative Learning Activity In a small group, discuss possible environmental problems in each group member's neighborhood, listing them on a sheet of paper. Compare lists with other groups to determine the most common problems. List possible solutions for each problem.

CHAPTER 25 THE CONSERVATIVE TIDE

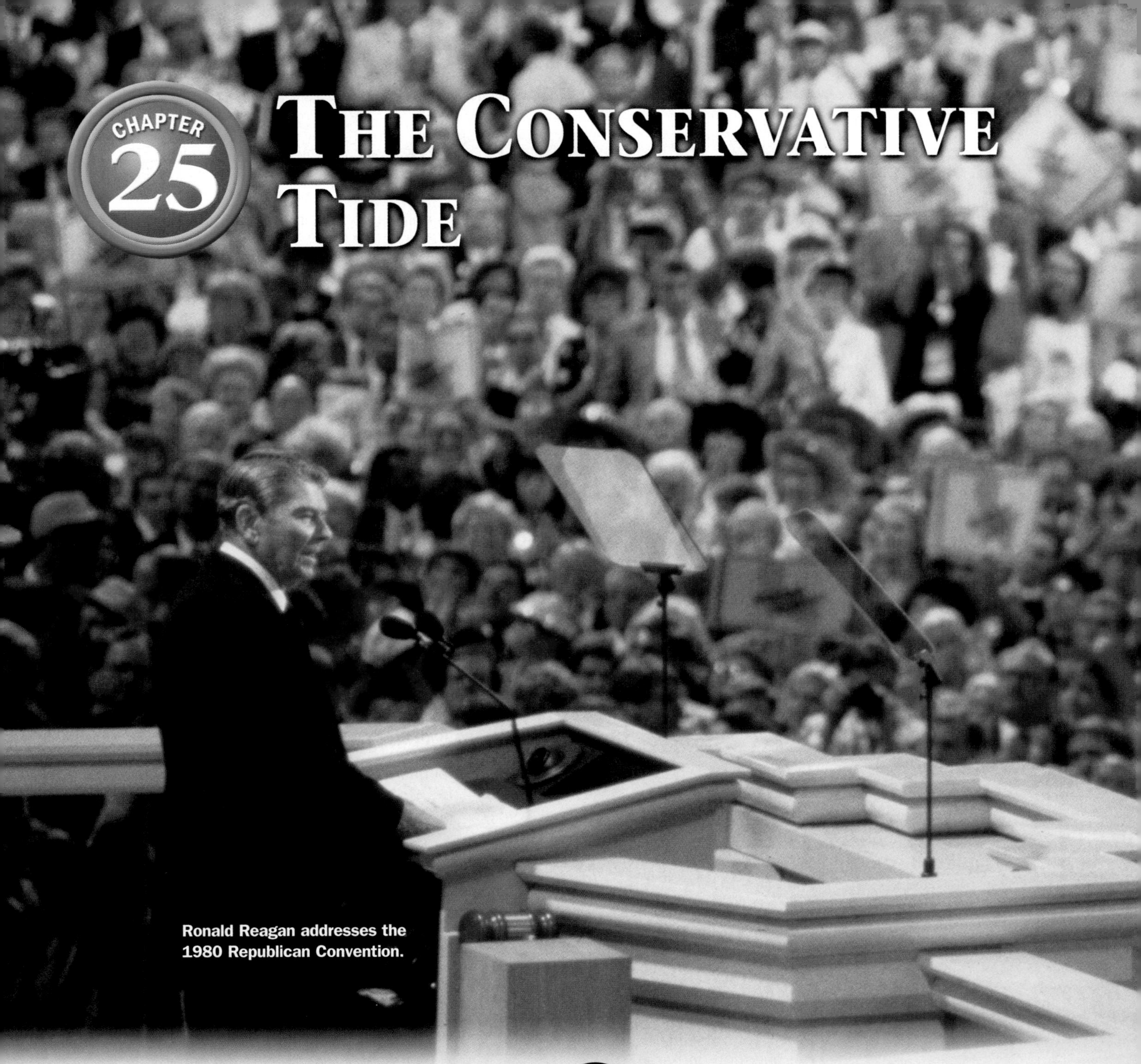

Ronald Reagan addresses the 1980 Republican Convention.

1980 Ronald Reagan is elected president.

1981 Sandra Day O'Connor becomes the first woman appointed to the Supreme Court.

1982 Equal Rights Amendment fails to win ratification.

1984 President Reagan is reelected.

USA
WORLD

1980 | 1982 | 1984

1980 Zimbabwe claims independence.

1982 Great Britain and Argentina go to war over the Falkland Islands.

1984 South African Bishop Desmond Tutu receives the Nobel Peace Prize.

INTERACT
WITH HISTORY

It is the autumn of 1980. You are a campaign manager for Republican presidential candidate, Ronald Reagan, former film star and past governor of California. Reagan must defeat President Jimmy Carter, who has lost support. Carter has failed to bring home the hostages in Iran and to revive the economy. Reagan, an optimist, pledges to do both. He also plans to cut taxes and cut back on government programs.

What campaign slogan will you create?

Examine the Issues

- What qualities in your candidate will win support?
- What issues are important?
- How can you present Reagan as a winner?

RESEARCH LINKS **CLASSZONE.COM**

Visit the Chapter 25 links for more information about The Conservative Tide.

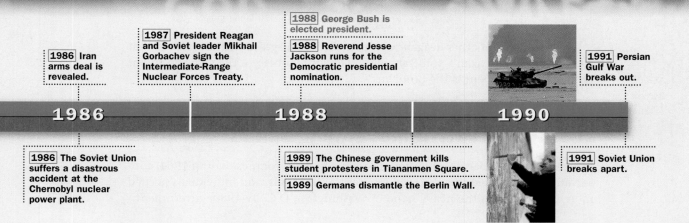

1986 Iran arms deal is revealed.

1987 President Reagan and Soviet leader Mikhail Gorbachev sign the Intermediate-Range Nuclear Forces Treaty.

1988 George Bush is elected president.

1988 Reverend Jesse Jackson runs for the Democratic presidential nomination.

1991 Persian Gulf War breaks out.

1986 | 1988 | 1990

1986 The Soviet Union suffers a disastrous accident at the Chernobyl nuclear power plant.

1989 The Chinese government kills student protesters in Tiananmen Square.

1989 Germans dismantle the Berlin Wall.

1991 Soviet Union breaks apart.

A Conservative Movement Emerges

MAIN IDEA

Conservatism reached a high point with the election in 1980 of President Ronald Reagan and Vice-President George Bush.

WHY IT MATTERS NOW

In the early 21st century, conservative views strongly influenced both major political parties.

Terms & Names

- **entitlement program**
- **New Right**
- **affirmative action**
- **reverse discrimination**
- **conservative coalition**
- **Moral Majority**
- **Ronald Reagan**

One American's Story

Peggy Noonan grew up with a strong sense of social and political justice. As a child, she idolized the liberal Kennedys; as a teenager, she devoured articles on social and political issues. After college, Noonan went to work for CBS.

Over the years, Noonan's political views became increasingly conservative. She eventually won a job as a speechwriter for Ronald Reagan, whose commitment to his conservative values moved her deeply. Noonan recalled that her response to Reagan was not unusual.

A PERSONAL VOICE PEGGY NOONAN

"The young people who came to Washington for the Reagan revolution came to make things better. . . . They looked at where freedom was and . . . where freedom wasn't and what that did, and they wanted to help the guerrilla fighters who were trying to overthrow the Communist regimes that had been imposed on them. . . . The thing the young conservatives were always talking about, . . . was freedom, freedom:

we'll free up more of your money,
we'll free up more of the world,
freedom freedom freedom—

It was the drumbeat that held a disparate group together, the rhythm that kept a fractious, not-made-in-heaven alliance in one piece."

—*What I Saw at the Revolution: A Political Life in the Reagan Era*

Peggy Noonan

Like millions of other Reagan supporters, Noonan agreed with the slogan that was the heart of Reagan's political creed: "Government is not the solution to our problem. Government is the problem."

The Conservative Movement Builds

Ever since Senator Barry Goldwater of Arizona had run for president in 1964, conservatives had argued that state governments, businesses, and individuals needed more freedom from the heavy hand of Washington, D.C. By 1980, government spending on **entitlement programs**—programs that provide guaranteed benefits to particular groups—was nearly $300 billion annually. The costs together with stories of fraudulent benefits caused resentment among many taxpayers.

In addition, some people had become frustrated with the government's civil rights policies. Congress had passed the Civil Rights Act of 1964 in an effort to eliminate racial discrimination. Over the years, however, judicial decisions and government regulations had broadened the reach of the act. A growing number of Americans viewed with skepticism what had begun as a movement toward equal opportunity. Although many people had rejected separate schools for blacks and whites as unfair and unequal, few wanted to bus their children long distances to achieve a fixed ratio of black and white students.

THE NEW RIGHT As the 1970s progressed, right-wing grass-roots groups across the country emerged to support and promote single issues that reflected their key interests. These people became known as the **New Right.** The New Right focused its energy on controversial social issues, such as opposing abortion, blocking the Equal Rights Amendment, and evading court-ordered busing. It also called for a return to school prayer, which had been outlawed by the Supreme Court in 1962.

▲ **Several high school students in New York hold a prayer meeting in 1973.**

Many in the New Right criticized the policy of **affirmative action.** Affirmative action required employers and educational institutions to give special consideration to women, African Americans, and other minority groups, even though these people were not necessarily better qualified. Many conservatives saw affirmative action as a form of **reverse discrimination,** favoring one group over another on the basis of race or gender. To members of the New Right, liberal positions on affirmative action and other issues represented an assault on traditional values. (A)

MAIN IDEA

Analyzing Issues

(A) What was the agenda of the New Right?

THE CONSERVATIVE COALITION Beginning in the mid-1960s, the conservative movement in the United States grew in strength. Eventually, conservative groups formed the **conservative coalition**—an alliance of business leaders, middle-class voters, disaffected Democrats, and fundamentalist Christian groups.

Conservative intellectuals argued the cause of the conservative coalition in newspapers such as *The Wall Street Journal* and magazines such as the *National Review,* founded in 1955 by conservative William F. Buckley, Jr. Conservative think tanks, such as the American Enterprise Institute and The Heritage Foundation, were founded to develop conservative policies and principles that would appeal to the majority of voters.

THE MORAL MAJORITY Religion, especially evangelical Christianity, played a key role in the growing strength of the conservative coalition. The 1970s had brought a huge religious revival, especially among fundamentalist sects. Each week, millions of Americans watched evangelist preachers on television or listened to them on the radio. Two of the most influential televangelists were Jerry Falwell and Pat Robertson. Falwell formed an organization called the **Moral Majority.** The Moral Majority consisted mostly of evangelical and fundamentalist Christians who interpreted

Goals of the Conservative Movement
• Shrink the size of the federal government and reduce spending
• Promote family values and patriotic ideals
• Stimulate business by reducing government regulations and lowering taxes
• Strengthen the national defense

the Bible literally and believed in absolute standards of right and wrong. They condemned liberal attitudes and behaviors and argued for a restoration of traditional moral values. They worked toward their political goals by using direct-mail campaigns and by raising money to support candidates. Jerry Falwell became the spokesperson for the Moral Majority. **B**

MAIN IDEA

Summarizing
B What were the main concerns of the Moral Majority?

A PERSONAL VOICE REVEREND JERRY FALWELL

> **"Our nation's internal problems are the direct result of her spiritual condition. . . . Right living must be reestablished as an American way of life. . . . Now is the time to begin calling America back to God, back to the Bible, back to morality."**

As individual conservative groups formed networks, they created a movement dedicated to bringing back what they saw as traditional "family values." They hoped their ideas would help to reduce the nation's high divorce rate, lower the number of out-of-wedlock births, encourage individual responsibility, and generally revive bygone prosperity and patriotic times.

KEY PLAYER

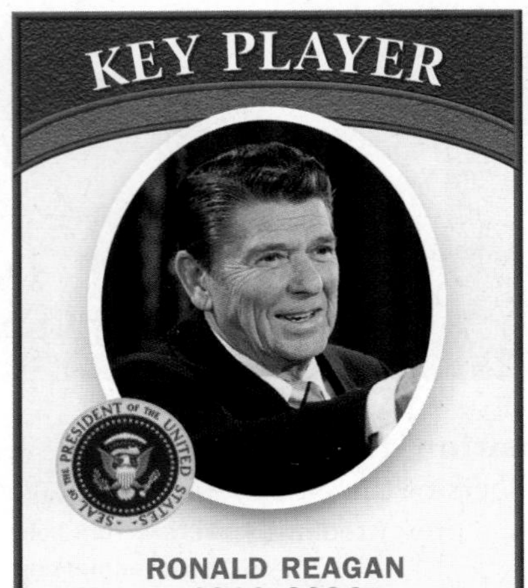

RONALD REAGAN
1911–2004

Ronald Wilson Reagan was born in 1911 in Tampico, Illinois. He grew up in Dixon, Illinois, graduated from nearby Eureka College, and then worked as a sports announcer in Iowa. In 1937, Reagan moved to Hollywood and became a movie actor, eventually making more than 50 films. As president of the Screen Actors Guild, he worked actively to remove alleged Communist influences from the movie industry.

Reagan had the ability to express his ideas in simple and clear language that the average voter could understand. When he proposed a 10 percent cut in government spending on social programs, he stated, "We can lecture our children about extravagance until we run out of voice and breath. Or we can cure their extravagance by simply reducing their allowance."

Conservatives Win Political Power

In 1976, **Ronald Reagan** lost the Republican nomination to the incumbent, Gerald Ford, in a very closely contested race. Four years later in a series of hard-fought primaries, Reagan won the 1980 nomination and chose George H. W. Bush as his running mate. Reagan and Bush ran against the incumbent president and vice-president, Jimmy Carter and Walter Mondale, who were nominated again by the Democrats despite their low standing in the polls.

REAGAN'S QUALIFICATIONS Originally a New Deal Democrat, Ronald Reagan had become a conservative Republican during the 1950s. He claimed that he had not left the Democratic Party but rather that the party had left him. As a spokesman for General Electric, he toured the country making speeches in favor of free enterprise and against big government. In 1964, he campaigned hard for Barry Goldwater, the Republican candidate for president. His speech supporting Goldwater in October 1964 made Reagan a serious candidate for public office. In 1966, Reagan was elected governor of California, and in 1970, he was reelected.

Background
See *free enterprise* on page R41 in the Economics Handbook.

THE 1980 PRESIDENTIAL ELECTION In 1980, Reagan ran on a number of key issues. Supreme Court decisions on abortion, pornography, the teaching of evolution, and prayer in public schools all concerned conservative voters, and they rallied to Reagan. The prolonged Iranian hostage crisis and the weak economy under Carter, particularly the high rate of inflation, also helped Reagan.

Thanks in part to his acting career and his long experience in the public eye, Reagan was an extremely effective candidate. In contrast to Carter, who often seemed stiff and nervous, Reagan was relaxed, charming, and affable. He loved making quips: "A recession is when your neighbor loses his job. A depression is when you lose yours. And recovery is when Jimmy Carter loses his." Reagan's long-standing skill at simplifying issues and presenting clear-cut answers led his supporters to call him the Great Communicator. Also, his commitment to military and economic strength appealed to many Americans.

Only 52.6 percent of American voters went to the polls in 1980. Reagan won the election by a narrow majority; he got 44 million votes, or 51 percent of the total. His support, however, was spread throughout the country, so that he carried 44 states and won 489 electoral votes. Republicans also gained control of the Senate for the first time since 1954. As Reagan assumed the presidency, many people were buoyed by his genial smile and his assertion that it was "morning again in America." C

MAIN IDEA

Analyzing Causes

C What factors led to Reagan's victory in 1980?

Now, conservatives had elected one of their own—a true believer in less government, lower taxes, and traditional values. Once elected, Reagan worked to translate the conservative agenda into public policy.

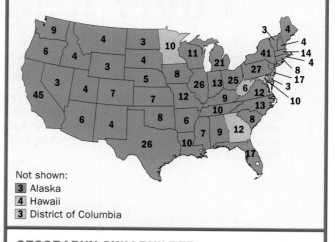

Presidential Election of 1980

Party	Candidate	Electoral Votes	Popular Votes
Republican	Ronald Reagan	489	43,904,153
Democratic	Jimmy Carter	49	35,483,883
Independent	John Anderson		5,720,060

Not shown:
3 Alaska
4 Hawaii
3 District of Columbia

GEOGRAPHY SKILLBUILDER

1. **Location** Which states and/or district voted for Jimmy Carter in 1980?
2. **Region** Which region of the country—North, South, East, or West—voted exclusively for Ronald Reagan?

ASSESSMENT

1. **TERMS & NAMES** For each term or name below, write a sentence explaining its significance.
   - **entitlement program**
   - **New Right**
   - **affirmative action**
   - **reverse discrimination**
   - **conservative coalition**
   - **Moral Majority**
   - **Ronald Reagan**

MAIN IDEA

2. **TAKING NOTES**
   Use a cluster diagram to record the issues that conservatives strongly endorsed.

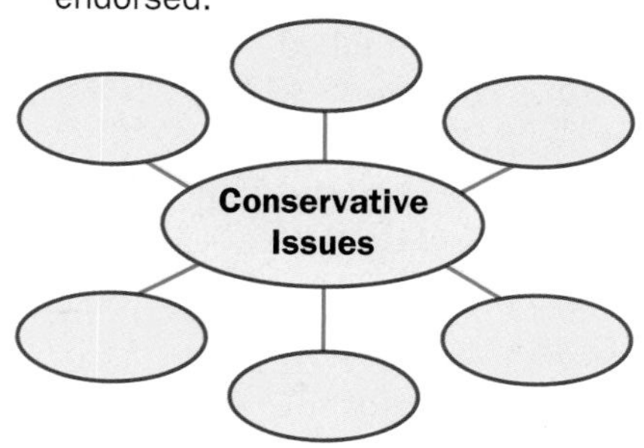

Choose one issue and explain in a paragraph the conservative position on that issue.

CRITICAL THINKING

3. **ANALYZING MOTIVES**
   How did the leaders of the conservative movement of the 1980s want to change government?
   Think About:
   - the difference between the conservative view of government and the liberal view
   - the groups that made up the conservative coalition
   - conservatives' attitudes toward existing government programs

4. **ANALYZING EFFECTS**
   What role did the Moral Majority play in the conservative movement of the 1970s and early 1980s?

5. **EVALUATING LEADERSHIP**
   What personal qualities in Ronald Reagan helped him to win election as president in 1980?

Conservative Policies Under Reagan and Bush

MAIN IDEA

Presidents Reagan and Bush pursued a conservative agenda that included tax cuts, budget cuts, and increased defense spending.

WHY IT MATTERS NOW

The conservative views of Reagan and Bush created policies and priorities that affect government spending and budgeting today.

Terms & Names

- **Reaganomics**
- **supply-side economics**
- **Strategic Defense Initiative**
- **Sandra Day O'Connor**
- **deregulation**
- **Environmental Protection Agency (EPA)**
- **Geraldine Ferraro**
- **George Bush**

One American's Story

Throughout the 1980 presidential campaign and in the early days of his administration, President Reagan emphasized the perilous state of the economy during the Carter administration. In a speech to the nation on February 5, 1981—his first televised speech from the White House—Reagan announced his new economic program. He called for a reduction in income tax rates for individuals and a big reduction in government spending.

President Ronald Reagan

A PERSONAL VOICE RONALD REAGAN

"I'm speaking to you tonight to give you a report on the state of our nation's economy. I regret to say that we're in the worst economic mess since the Great Depression. . . . It's time to recognize that we've come to a turning point. We're threatened with an economic calamity of tremendous proportions, and the old business-as-usual treatment can't save us. Together, we must chart a different course."

—televised speech to the nation, February 5, 1981

President Reagan would deal with these problems by consistently stressing a sweeping package of new economic policies. These economic policies, dubbed "**Reaganomics,**" consisted of three parts: (1) budget cuts, (2) tax cuts, and (3) increased defense spending.

"Reaganomics" Takes Over

As soon as Reagan took office, he worked to reduce the size and influence of the federal government, which, he thought, would encourage private investment. Because people were anxious about the economy in 1980, their concern opened the door for new approaches to taxes and the federal budget.

BUDGET CUTS Reagan's strategy for downsizing the federal government included deep cuts in government spending on social programs. Yet his cuts did not affect all segments of the population equally. Entitlement programs that benefited the middle class, such as Social Security, Medicare, and veterans' pensions, remained intact. On the other hand, Congress slashed by 10 percent the budget for programs that benefited other groups: urban mass transit, food stamps, welfare benefits, job training, Medicaid, school lunches, and student loans.

Background
See *supply-side economics* on page R46 in the Economics Handbook.

TAX CUTS "Reaganomics" rested heavily upon **supply-side economics.** This theory held that if people paid fewer taxes, they would save more money. Banks could then loan that money to businesses, which could invest the money in resources to improve productivity. The supply of goods then would increase, driving down prices. At Reagan's urging, Congress lowered income taxes by about 25 percent over a three-year period. Reagan based his ideas for supply-side economics on the work of economists such as George Gilder and Arthur Laffer. (A)

MAIN IDEA

Summarizing
(A) What are the main ideas of supply-side economics?

A PERSONAL VOICE ARTHUR LAFFER

"The most debilitating act a government can perpetrate on its citizens is to adopt policies that destroy the economy's production base, for it is the production base that generates any prosperity to be found in the society. U.S. tax policies over the last decade have had the effect of damaging this base by removing many of the incentives to economic advancement. It is necessary to restore those incentives if we are to cure our economic palsy."

—*The Economics of the Tax Revolt: A Reader*

INCREASED DEFENSE SPENDING At the same time, Reagan authorized increases in military spending that more than offset cuts in social programs. Between 1981 and 1984, the Defense Department budget almost doubled. Indeed, the president revived two controversial weapons systems—the MX missile and the B-1 bomber. In 1983, Reagan asked the country's scientists to develop a defense system that would keep Americans safe from enemy missiles. Officially called the **Strategic Defense Initiative,** or SDI, the system quickly became known as Star Wars, after the title of a popular movie. The Defense Department estimated that the system would cost trillions of dollars.

Background
See *recession* on page R44 in the Economics Handbook.

RECESSION AND RECOVERY While Reagan was charting a new course for the American economy, the economy itself was sinking into recession. Lasting from July 1981 until November 1982, it was the most severe recession since the Great Depression. However, early in 1983, an economic upturn began as consumers went on a spending spree. Their confidence in the economy was bolstered by tax cuts, a decline in interest rates, and lower inflation. The stock market surged, unemployment declined, and the gross national product went up by almost 10 percent. The stock market boom lasted until 1987, when the market crashed, losing 508 points in one day. This fall was due in large part to automated and computerized buying and selling systems. However, the market recovered and then continued its upward climb.

Background
See *national debt* on page R43 in the Economics Handbook.

THE NATIONAL DEBT CLIMBS Beneath the surface of recovery lay problems that continued to plague the economy. Tax cuts had helped the rich, while social welfare cuts had hurt the poor. Despite large reductions in parts of the

ECONOMIC BACKGROUND

THE "TRICKLE-DOWN" THEORY

Ronald Reagan's budget director, David Stockman, used supply-side economics to draft the Economic Recovery Tax Act of 1981. His tax package cut income taxes and business taxes by an average of 25 percent; the largest tax cuts went to those with the highest incomes. Administration officials defended the plan by claiming that as prosperity returned, the profits at the top would trickle down to the middle class and even the poor.

Despite Reagan's "trickle-down" theory, the wealthy gained the most from these tax cuts. In the 1980s, the rich got richer as poverty deepened for many others.

Analyzing *Political Cartoons*

"THE INFLATION STAGECOACH"

During Reagan's first term, federal spending far outstripped federal revenue and created a huge budget deficit. In this cartoon, Reagan (with budget director David Stockman sitting beside him on the inflation stagecoach) sees something that "shouldn't be there."

SKILLBUILDER

Analyzing Political Cartoons

1. What is the meaning of the wheel flying off the stagecoach?
2. Whom do the passengers inside the stagecoach represent?

SEE SKILLBUILDER HANDBOOK, PAGE R24.

budget, federal spending still outstripped federal revenue. Budget deficits were growing. Even though Reagan backed away from supply-side economics in 1982 and imposed new taxes, they were not enough to balance the budget. By the end of his first term, the national debt had almost doubled. (B)

MAIN IDEA

Analyzing Effects

(B) What were some of the effects of "Reaganomics"?

Judicial Power Shifts to the Right

One of the most important ways in which Reagan accomplished his conservative goals was through his appointments to the Supreme Court. Reagan nominated **Sandra Day O'Connor,** Antonin Scalia, and Anthony M. Kennedy to fill seats left by retiring judges. O'Connor was the first woman to be appointed to the Court. He also nominated Justice William Rehnquist, the most conservative justice on the court at the time, to the position of chief justice.

Anita Hill and Clarence Thomas testify before the Senate Judiciary Committee in October 1991.

President Bush later made the Court even more conservative when David H. Souter replaced retiring justice William Brennan. Bush also nominated Clarence Thomas to take the place of Thurgood Marshall. However, controversy exploded when law professor Anita Hill testified that Thomas had sexually harassed her when she worked for him in the 1980s. During several days of televised Senate hearings, committee members questioned Thomas, Hill, and witnesses for each side. Thomas eventually won approval by a final vote of 52 to 48.

The Reagan and Bush appointments to the Supreme Court ended the liberal control over the Court that had begun under Franklin Roosevelt. These appointments became increasingly significant as the Court revisited constitutional issues related to such topics as discrimination, abortion, and affirmative action. In 1989, the Court, in a series of rulings, restricted a woman's right to an abortion. The Court also imposed new restrictions on civil rights laws that had been designed to protect the rights of women and minorities. During the 1990–1991 session, the Court narrowed the rights of arrested persons.

Deregulating the Economy

Reagan achieved one of his most important objectives—reducing the size and power of the federal government—in part by cutting federal entitlement programs but also through **deregulation,** the cutting back of federal regulation of industry. As part of his campaign for smaller government, he removed price controls on oil and eliminated federal health and safety inspections for nursing homes. He deregulated the airline industry (allowing airlines to abandon unprofitable air routes) and the savings and loan industry. One of the positive results of this deregulation was that it increased competition and often resulted in lower prices for consumers.

In a further effort at deregulation, President Reagan cut the budget of the **Environmental Protection Agency (EPA),** which had been established in 1970 to fight pollution and conserve natural resources. He ignored pleas from Canada to reduce acid rain and appointed opponents of the regulations to enforce them. For example, James Watt, Reagan's secretary of the interior, sold millions of acres of public land to private developers—often at bargain prices. He opened the continental shelf to oil and gas drilling, which many people thought posed environmental risks. Watt also encouraged timber cutting in national forests and eased restrictions on coal mining.

HISTORICAL SPOTLIGHT

AN ASSASSINATION ATTEMPT

On March 30, 1981, President Reagan and other members of his staff were shot by a mentally unbalanced man named John Hinckley, Jr. While being wheeled into surgery to have a bullet removed, the president said to his wife, "Honey, I forgot to duck" (a line first used by boxer Jack Dempsey in the 1920s, after losing his heavyweight title). In the operating room, Reagan said to the team of surgeons, "I hope you fellas are Republicans." Reagan recovered speedily and his popularity grew.

Conservative Victories in 1984 and 1988

It was clear by 1984 that Reagan had forged a large coalition of conservative voters who highly approved of his policies. These voters included the following:

- *businesspeople*—who wanted to deregulate the economy
- *Southerners*—who welcomed the limits on federal power
- *Westerners*—who resented federal controls on mining and grazing
- *Reagan Democrats*—who agreed with Reagan on limiting federal government and thought that the Democratic Party had drifted too far to the left

THE 1984 PRESIDENTIAL ELECTION In 1984, Reagan and Bush won the Republican nominations for reelection without challenge. Walter Mondale, who had been vice-president under President Carter, won the Democratic Party's nomination and chose Representative **Geraldine Ferraro** of New York as his running mate. Ferraro became the first woman on a major party's presidential ticket.

In 1984 the economy was strong. Reagan and Bush won by a landslide, carrying every state but Mondale's home state of Minnesota and the District of Columbia.

▲ President Reagan is pushed into a presidential limousine after being shot by a deranged man.

◀ **George Bush announces his presidential candidacy at a rally in 1987.**

THE 1988 PRESIDENTIAL ELECTION

In 1988, a majority of Americans were economically comfortable, and they attributed their comfort to Reagan and Bush. When Michael Dukakis, the Democratic governor of Massachusetts, ran for the presidency in 1988 against **George Bush,** Reagan's vice-president, most voters saw little reason for change.

George Bush simply built on President Reagan's legacy by promising, "Read my lips: no new taxes" in his acceptance speech at the Republican Convention. He stressed his commitment to the conservative ideas of the Moral Majority. Though Bush asserted that he wanted a "kinder, gentler nation," his campaign sponsored a number of negative "attack ads" aimed at his opponents. He told audiences that Dukakis was an ultraliberal whose views were outside the mainstream of American values. In particular, Bush suggested that Dukakis was soft on crime and unpatriotic.

> *"Read my lips: no new taxes."*
> **GEORGE BUSH**

Some commentators believed that the negative ads contributed to the lowest voter turnout in 64 years. Only half of the eligible voters went to the polls in 1988. Fifty-three percent voted for George Bush, who won 426 electoral votes. Bush's electoral victory was viewed, as Reagan's had been, as a mandate for conservative social and political policies. **C**

MAIN IDEA

Analyzing Causes

C What factors contributed to Reagan's victory in 1984 and Bush's victory in 1988?

ASSESSMENT

1. **TERMS & NAMES** For each term or name below, write a sentence explaining its significance.
   - **Reaganomics**
   - **supply-side economics**
   - **Strategic Defense Initiative**
   - **Sandra Day O'Connor**
   - **deregulation**
   - **Environmental Protection Agency (EPA)**
   - **Geraldine Ferraro**
   - **George Bush**

MAIN IDEA

2. **TAKING NOTES**
   Use a diagram like the one below to explore the effects of "Reaganomics."

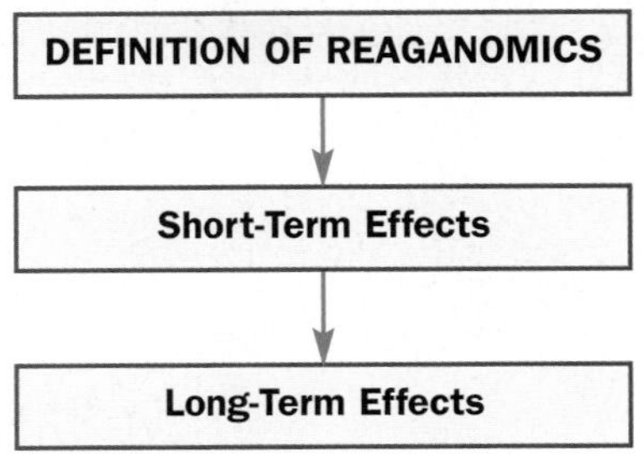

Explain in a paragraph whether you think "Reaganomics" was good or bad for the economy.

CRITICAL THINKING

3. **ANALYZING MOTIVES**
   Why did President Reagan and President Bush think it was important to appoint conservative justices to the Supreme Court?

4. **EVALUATING**
   In your opinion, was Reagan's first term a success? **Think About:**
   - how his tax cuts impacted the rich and the poor
   - the economy
   - the federal budget

5. **ANALYZING PRIMARY SOURCES**
   Read the following excerpt from Ronald Reagan's speech at the 1992 Republican Convention.

> **"We mustn't forget . . . the very different America that existed just 12 years ago; an America with 21 percent interest rates and . . . double-digit inflation; an America where mortgage payments doubled, paychecks plunged, and motorists sat in gas lines; an America whose leaders told us . . . that what we really needed was another good dose of government control and higher taxes."**

What picture did Reagan paint of the Carter administration?

Social Concerns in the 1980s

MAIN IDEA

Beneath the surge of prosperity that marked the conservative era of the 1980s lay serious social problems.

WHY IT MATTERS NOW

Issues involving health care, education, civil rights, and equal rights for women continue to challenge American society.

Terms & Names

- **AIDS (acquired immune deficiency syndrome)**
- **pay equity**
- **L. Douglas Wilder**
- **Jesse Jackson**
- **Lauro Cavazos**
- **Antonia Coello Novello**

One American's Story

Trevor Ferrell lived an ordinary life in Gladwyne, an affluent suburb 12 miles from downtown Philadelphia. Trevor had brothers and sisters, his own room, a favorite pillow, a fondness for video games, and a bike. In short, he seemed like a typical 11-year-old boy until he watched a television news report about homeless people.

Trevor was astonished. "Do people really live like that?" he asked his parents. "I thought they lived like that in India, but not here, I mean in America." Trevor convinced his parents to drive downtown that night, where he gave a pillow and a blanket to the first homeless man he saw. Soon he and his family were collecting food and clothes to give to the homeless.

A PERSONAL VOICE TREVOR FERRELL

"They have to live on the streets, and right after you see one of them, you see somebody in a limousine pull up to a huge, empty mansion. It's such a difference. Some people can get anything they want, and these other people couldn't get a penny if they needed one."

—quoted in *Trevor's Place*

Trevor Ferrell listens to a homeless person on the corner of 12th and Chestnut streets in Philadelphia.

As Trevor saw, the restored American economy of the 1980s did not mean renewed prosperity for everyone. As Presidents Reagan and Bush pursued conservative domestic policies, people disagreed about the impact of these policies.

Health, Education, and Cities in Crisis

In the 1980s, both in the cities and in rural and suburban areas, local governments strove to deal with crises in health, education, and safety. Americans directed their attention to issues such as AIDS, drug abuse, abortion, and education.

▲ The AIDS quilt was displayed on the National Mall in Washington, D.C., in 1987. Each panel honors a person who died of AIDS.

NOW & THEN

AIDS WORLDWIDE

In the year 2000, it was estimated that 5.3 million people worldwide became infected with HIV/AIDS. Impoverished countries that lie in sub-Saharan Africa remain hardest hit by the deadly pandemic, accounting for an estimated 3.8 million, or 72 percent, of new cases during the year. At the end of December 2000, the number of adults and children living with HIV/AIDS worldwide was estimated at 36.1 million people, of whom the proportions of males and females were almost equal.

HEALTH ISSUES One of the most troubling issues that concerned Americans in the 1980s was **AIDS (acquired immune deficiency syndrome).** Possibly beginning as early as the 1960s, AIDS spread rapidly throughout the world. Caused by a virus that destroys the immune system, AIDS weakens the body so that it is prone to infections and normally rare cancers.

AIDS is transmitted through bodily fluids, and most of the early victims of the disease were either homosexual men or intravenous drug users who shared needles. However, many people also contracted AIDS through contaminated blood transfusions, and children acquired it by being born to infected mothers. As the 1980s progressed, increasing numbers of heterosexuals began contracting AIDS. As the epidemic grew, so did concern over prevention and cure.

ABORTION Many Americans were concerned about abortion in the 1980s. Abortion had been legal in the United States since 1973, when the Supreme Court ruled in *Roe* v. *Wade* that first-trimester abortions were protected by a woman's right to privacy. Opponents of legalized abortion quickly organized under the pro-life banner. They argued that human life begins at conception and that no woman has the right to terminate a human life by her individual decision. Proponents of legalized abortion described themselves as pro-choice. They argued that reproductive choices were personal health-care matters and noted that many women had died from abortions performed by unskilled people in unsterile settings before the procedure was legalized.

In July 1989, the Supreme Court ruled in *Webster* v. *Reproductive Health Care Services* that states had the right to impose new restrictions on abortion. As a result, abortion restrictions varied from state to state. (A)

MAIN IDEA

Contrasting
(A) What are the two viewpoints on legalized abortion?

DRUG ABUSE Battles over abortion rights sometimes competed for public attention with concerns about rising drug abuse. A few people argued that drugs should be legalized to reduce the power of gangs who made a living selling illegal drugs. Others called for treatment facilities to treat addictions. The Reagan administration launched a war on drugs and supported moves to prosecute users as well as dealers. First Lady Nancy Reagan toured the country with an antidrug campaign that admonished students to "Just say no!" to drugs.

"Just say no!"

NANCY REAGAN, SLOGAN IN THE WAR ON DRUGS

EDUCATION Education became another issue that stirred people's concerns. In 1983, a federal commission issued a report on education titled *A Nation at Risk*. The report revealed that American students lagged behind students in most other industrialized nations. In addition, the report stated that 23 million Americans were unable to follow an instruction manual or fill out a job application form.

The commission's findings touched off a debate about the quality of education. The commission recommended more homework, longer school days, and an extended school year. It also promoted increased pay and merit raises for teachers, as well as a greater emphasis on basic subjects such as English, math, science, social studies, and computer science.

In April 1991, President Bush announced an education initiative, "America 2000." He argued that choice was the salvation of American schools and recommended allowing parents to use public funds to send their children to schools of their choice—public, private, or religious. First Lady Barbara Bush toured the country to promote reading and writing skills. B

Identifying Problems

B What problems in education emerged during the 1980s?

THE URBAN CRISIS The crisis in education was closely connected to the crisis in the cities. Many undereducated students lived in cities such as Baltimore, Chicago, Detroit, Philadelphia, and Washington, D.C. During the 1970s, the United States had become increasingly suburbanized as more and more white families responded to the lure of new homes, big lawns, shopping malls, and well-equipped schools outside the cities. Businesses moved, too, taking jobs and tax revenue with them.

Poor people and racial minorities were often left in cities burdened by high unemployment rates, crumbling infrastructures, inadequate funds for sanitation and health services, deteriorating schools, and growing social problems. By 1992, thousands of people were homeless, including many families with children. Cities were increasingly divided into wealthy neighborhoods and poverty-stricken areas.

One poverty-stricken area, south-central Los Angeles (which had erupted in violence in 1965 and 1968) erupted again in 1992. Four white police officers had been videotaped beating an African-American man named Rodney King, who had been fleeing from the officers in a speeding car. An all-white jury found the officers not guilty on charges of brutality. This verdict resulted in riots that lasted five days and caused the deaths of 53 people.

DIFFICULT DECISIONS

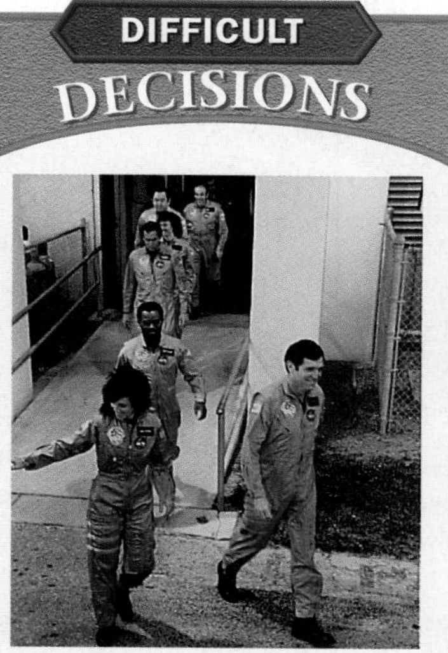

SENDING MONEY INTO SPACE

Under the Reagan administration, the government shifted the emphasis of the space program from scientific to military and commercial applications.

Beginning in 1981, NASA directed a series of space shuttle flights. The agency hoped to establish a space station and have the shuttle ferry workers and materials to it.

The explosion of the space shuttle *Challenger* in 1986 in which the crew was killed *(crew shown above)* caused a reexamination of ventures into space. Many people thought the money spent on space should be spent on social needs.

1. Should the federal government spend money on space exploration when so many American citizens require basic assistance?
2. If you were a legislator being asked to vote in favor of funding space exploration today, how would you vote? Why?

The Equal Rights Struggle

Within this environment of dwindling resources and social struggle, women worked to achieve economic and social gains.

Geraldine Ferraro speaks at the 1984 Democratic Convention.

POLITICAL LOSSES AND GAINS During the early 1980s, women's rights activists worked to obtain ratification of the Equal Rights Amendment (ERA). Although Congress had passed the amendment in 1972, it had not yet been ratified, or approved, by three-fourths of the states. Supporters of the amendment had until June 30, 1982, to gain ratification from 38 states. They obtained only 35 of the 38 ratifications they needed, and the ERA did not become law. With the failure of the Equal Rights Amendment, women's organizations began to concentrate on electing women to public office. More women candidates began to run for office, and in 1984 the Democrats chose Geraldine Ferraro as their vice-presidential candidate. She had spoken of the necessity for women to continue working for equal opportunities in American society.

A PERSONAL VOICE GERALDINE FERRARO

"It is not just those of us who have reached the top who are fighting this daily battle. It is a fight in which all of us—rich and poor, career and home oriented, young and old—participate, simply because we are women."

—quoted in *Vital Speeches of the Day*

In the November 1992 election, the number of women in the House of Representatives increased from 23 to 47, and the number of women senators tripled—from two to six. President Reagan also had earlier named two women to his cabinet: In 1983, Elizabeth Dole became secretary of transportation, and Margaret Heckler became secretary of health and human services. Nevertheless, women remained under-represented in political affairs. C

MAIN IDEA

Summarizing

C What steps did women take to help them move forward after the ERA failed to pass?

INEQUALITY Several factors contributed to what some called the "feminization of poverty." By 1992, 57.8 percent of the nation's women were part of the work force, and a growing percentage of women worked as professionals and managers. However, in that year women earned only about 75 cents for every dollar men earned. Female college graduates earned only slightly more than male high-school graduates. Also, about 31 percent of female heads of households lived in poverty, and among African-American women, the poverty rate was even higher. New trends in divorce settlements aggravated the situation. Because of no-fault divorce, fewer women won alimony payments, and the courts rarely enforced the meager child support payments they awarded.

To close the income gap that left so many women poor, women's organizations and unions proposed a system of **pay equity.** Jobs would

Women's and Men's Average Yearly Earnings in Selected Careers, 1982

Career	Women	Men
Accountant	$19,916	$25,272
Advertising Manager	19,396	32,292
Computer Operator	13,728	17,992
Cook	8,476	9,880
Engineer	26,052	31,460
Financial Manager	19,136	30,004
High School Teacher	18,980	21,424
Insurance Salesperson	15,236	22,152
Lawyer	30,264	34,008
Personnel Specialist	17,836	26,832
Physician	21,944	26,884
Police/ Detective	15,548	20,072
Real Estate Salesperson	16,432	24,076
Registered Nurse	20,592	20,696
Retail Sales Worker	8,736	13,728
Social Worker	15,600	20,436
University Professor	20,748	26,832

Source: Bureau of Labor Statistics, Current Population Survey, 1983–1989.

SKILLBUILDER Interpreting Charts

1. Name one career that paid men and women almost equally.
2. What conclusion can you draw from this chart?

be rated on the basis of the amount of education they required, the amount of physical strength needed to perform them, and the number of people that an employee supervised. Instead of relying on traditional pay scales, employers would establish pay rates that reflected each job's requirements. By 1989, 20 states had begun adjusting government jobs to offer pay equity for jobs of comparable worth.

MAIN IDEA

Analyzing Issues
D What gains did women make during the 1980s and early 1990s?

Women also fought for improvements in the workplace. Since many working women headed single-parent households or had children under the age of six, they pressed for family benefits. Government and corporate benefit packages began to include maternity leaves, flexible hours and workweeks, job sharing, and work-at-home arrangements. Some of these changes were launched by individual firms, while others required government intervention. Yet the Reagan administration sharply cut the budget for daycare and other similar programs. D

The Fight for Rights Continues

Cuts in government programs and the backlash against civil rights initiatives, such as affirmative action, affected other groups as well.

AFRICAN AMERICANS African Americans made striking political gains during the 1980s, even though their economic progress suffered. By the mid-1980s, African-American mayors governed many cities, including Los Angeles, Detroit, Chicago, Atlanta, New Orleans, Philadelphia, and Washington, D.C. Hundreds of communities in both the North and the South had elected African Americans to serve as sheriffs, school board members, state legislators, and members of Congress. In 1990, **L. Douglas Wilder** of Virginia became the nation's first African-American governor. The Reverend **Jesse Jackson** ran for the Democratic presidential nomination in 1984 and 1988.

▲ Jesse Jackson campaigns for the Democratic presidential nomination in 1984.

Middle-class African Americans often held professional and managerial positions. But the poor faced an uncertain future of diminishing opportunities. In 1989, the newly conservative Supreme Court handed down a series of decisions that continued to change the nation's course on civil rights. In the case of *Richmond* v. *J. A. Croson Company*, for example, the Court further limited the scope of affirmative action, policies that were designed to correct the effects of discrimination in the employment or education of minority groups or women. Other decisions by the Court outlawed contracts set aside for minority businesses. Sylvester Monroe, an African-American correspondent for *Newsweek* magazine, commented on the way in which some African Americans saw the backlash against affirmative action. E

MAIN IDEA

Analyzing Issues
E What political gains did African Americans make during the 1980s?

A PERSONAL VOICE SYLVESTER MONROE

"There's a finite pie and everybody wants his piece. Everybody is afraid of losing his piece of the pie. That's what the fight against affirmative action is all about. People feel threatened. As for blacks, they're passé. They're not in anymore. Nobody wants to talk about race."

—quoted in *The Great Divide*

▲ Dr. Antonia Coello Novello served as surgeon general under President Bush.

GAINS FOR LATINOS Latinos became the fastest growing minority during the 1980s. By 1990, they constituted almost nine percent of the population, and demographers estimated that Latinos would soon outnumber African Americans as the nation's largest minority group. About two out of three Latinos were Mexican Americans, who lived mostly in the Southwest. A Puerto Rican community thrived in the Northeast, and a Cuban population was concentrated in Florida. Like African Americans, Latinos gained political power during the 1980s. Toney Anaya became governor of New Mexico, while Robert Martinez became governor of Florida. In August 1988, President Reagan appointed **Lauro Cavazos** as secretary of education. In 1990, President Bush named Dr. **Antonia Coello Novello** to the post of surgeon general.

Vocabulary
demographer: a person who studies the characteristics of human population, such as growth, density, and distribution

Many Latinos supported bilingual education. They feared that abandoning Spanish would weaken their distinctive culture. In the words of Daniel Villanueva, a television executive, "We want to be here, but without losing our language and our culture. They are a richness, a treasure that we don't care to lose." The Bilingual Education Act of 1968 and the 1975 amendent to the Voting Rights Act enabled Spanish speakers to attend school and vote in their own language, but by the mid-1980s opposition to bilingualism was rising. Critics argued that it slowed the rate at which Spanish-speaking people entered mainstream American life. They also feared that the nation would become split between English speakers and Spanish speakers.

NOW & THEN

AFFIRMATIVE ACTION

Affirmative action refers to the effort to provide education and employment opportunities for historically disadvantaged groups, such as women and racial and ethnic minorities. The federal government first instituted affirmative action policies under the Civil Rights Act of 1964.

Presidents Reagan and Bush actively opposed affirmative action and racial quotas. In the 1990s, President Clinton supported affirmative action. Despite his support, in 1996, voters in California approved a referendum that did away with state affirmative action programs.

In 2001, the future of affirmative action was uncertain. President Bush expressed support for equal opportunity, but his Attorney General, John Ashcroft, was denounced by civil rights groups, in part because of his anti-affirmative action record.

NATIVE AMERICANS SPEAK OUT Native Americans also became more self-conscious of their dignity and more demanding of their rights. In the 1970s, they organized schools to teach young Native Americans about their past. They also began to fight for the return of ancestral lands wrongfully taken from them.

During the 1980s, the Reagan administration slashed aid to Native Americans for health, education, and other services. Driven to find new sources of revenue, Native Americans campaigned for gambling casinos on their land as a way to bring in money. After the Supreme Court ruled in favor of Native Americans, many tribes opened Las Vegas-style casinos, which provided additional funding for the tribes that operated them. Nonetheless, the long-term problems faced by Native Americans have not been solved by gambling casinos, although the new wealth has helped to some extent. F

MAIN IDEA

Identifying Problems
F What problems did Native Americans face in the 1980s?

AN EXPANDING ASIAN-AMERICAN POPULATION Asian Americans were the second-fastest growing minority in the United States during the 1980s. By 1992, the U.S. population included about 8.3 million Asian Americans and Pacific Islanders. Asian Americans constituted 3.25 percent of the population.

Some have cited Asian Americans as an example of how minorities can succeed in the U.S. Yet while Asian Americans have low crime rates, low school dropout rates, and low divorce rates, Asian-American unemployment and poverty have been higher than the national figures.

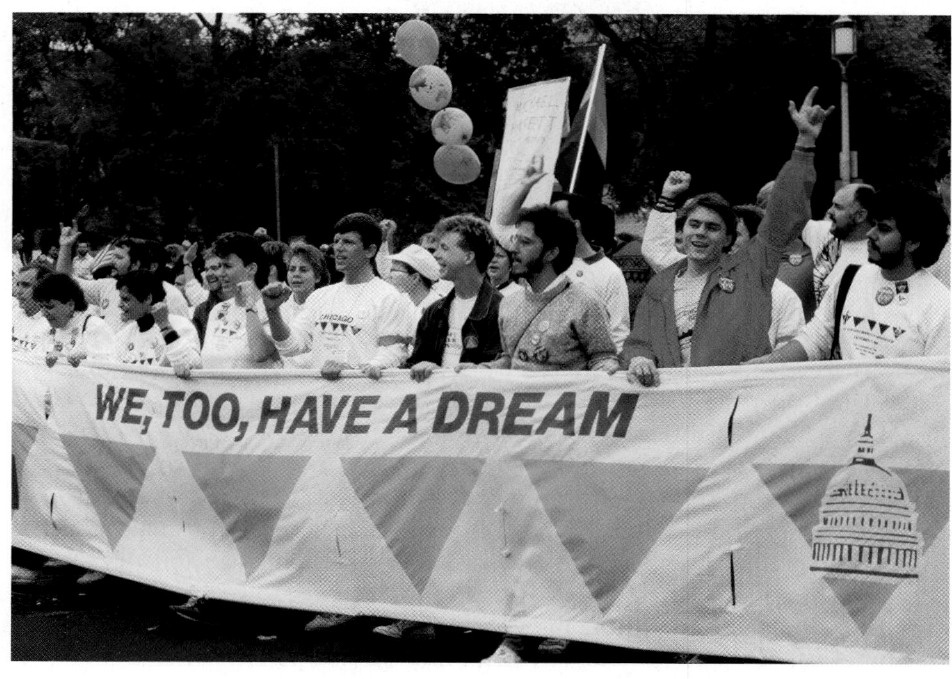

◀ A gay rights march in Washington, D.C., October 1987

THE GAY RIGHTS MOVEMENT ADVANCES During the 1970s and 1980s, gay men and lesbians began to fight openly for civil rights. While the gay rights movement suffered a setback during the early 1980s in the face of conservative opposition and the AIDS crisis, by the late 1980s and early 1990s a new surge of gay activism was under way in the country. Direct action groups sprang up throughout the country, calling for an end to anti-gay discrimination. Although several speakers at the 1992 Republican National Convention condemned gay activism, these speakers were unable to slow the pace of change. By the year 1993, seven states and 110 communities had outlawed such discrimination.

ASSESSMENT

1. **TERMS & NAMES** For each term or name below, write a sentence explaining its significance.
   - **AIDS (acquired immune deficiency syndrome)**
   - **pay equity**
   - **L. Douglas Wilder**
   - **Jesse Jackson**
   - **Lauro Cavazos**
   - **Antonia Coello Novello**

MAIN IDEA

2. **TAKING NOTES**
   Use a chart like the one below to list some of the social problems of the Reagan and Bush years and how the government responded to them.

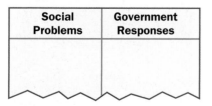

Social Problems	Government Responses

Choose one issue and write other responses the government might have made.

CRITICAL THINKING

3. **PREDICTING EFFECTS**
   How might improvements in the educational system help solve other social problems? **Think About:**
   - the impact education might have on health-related problems
   - the impact that education might have on urban problems
   - the impact that education might have on unemployment

4. **COMPARING**
   Compare the political gains and losses experienced by various groups during the Reagan and Bush administrations.

5. **FORMING GENERALIZATIONS**
   Why might a widening gap between the richest and poorest citizens of a country be a cause for concern about that country's future?

GEOGRAPHY SPOTLIGHT

Sunbelt, Rustbelt, Ecotopia

In the 1970s, people on the move created new names for areas to which they moved. The West was sometimes called ***Ecotopia*** because of its varied scenery and ecological attractions. The South and Southwest were called the ***Sunbelt*** because of their warm climate. The North Central and Northeast regions were called the ***Rustbelt*** because many of their aging factories had been closed.

As a geographical term, *region* is used to designate an area with common features or characteristics that set it apart from its surroundings. For example, the Mississippi Valley is a large physical region; Warren Woods is a small physical region. The term is often used for groups of states that share an area and certain characteristics.

As people move from state to state, and from region to region, they gradually transform the balance of political and economic power in the nation. Each census in recent times has recorded how certain states have gained population and others have lost population. If the gains or losses are large enough, a state's representation in the U.S. House of Representatives will increase or decrease commensurately.

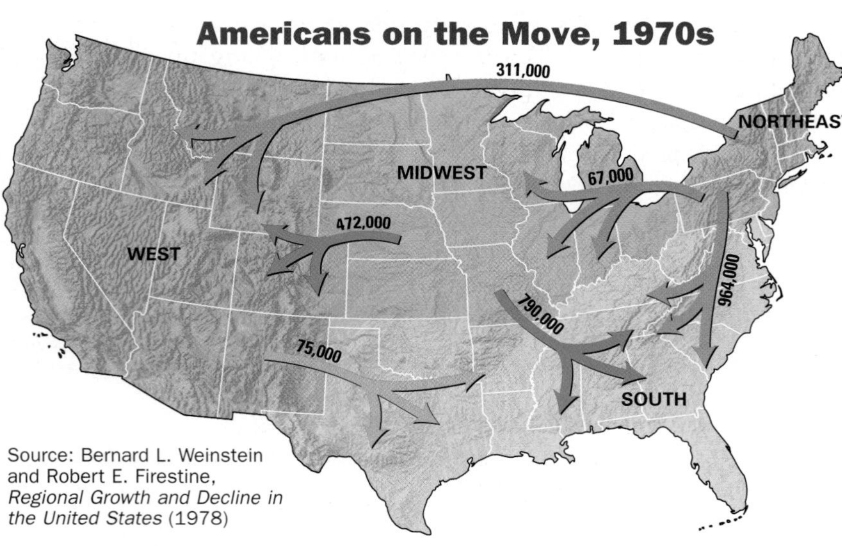

Source: Bernard L. Weinstein and Robert E. Firestine, *Regional Growth and Decline in the United States* (1978)

REGIONAL EXCHANGES

Between 1970 and 1975, the population center of the United States, which had generally moved westward for 17 decades, suddenly moved southward as well. The arrows show the net number of Americans who migrated and their patterns of migration in the early 1970s. The West gained 311,000 from the Northeast plus 472,000 from the North Central region, for a total of 783,000 people. However, it also lost 75,000 people to the South. During the 1980s and 1990s the southward and westward shift continued.

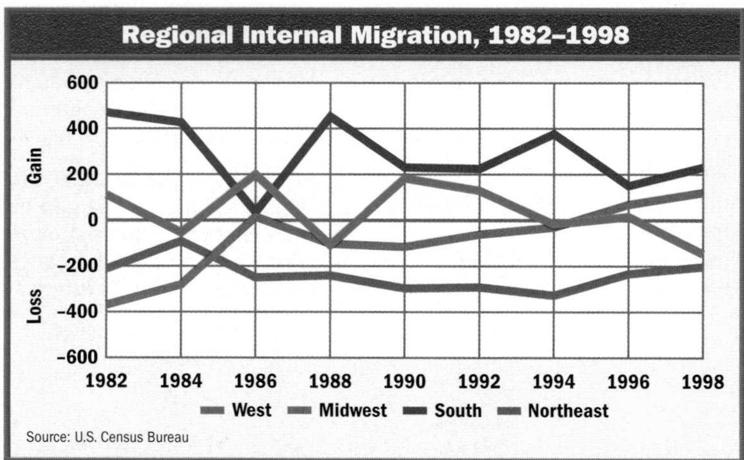

Source: U.S. Census Bureau

Americans on the Move, 1990–2000

Between 1990 and 2000, our country's population grew by a record 32.7 million people to 281.4 million. For the first time in the 20th century, all 50 states gained people between census years. But because of internal migration (see graph on page 846) and other factors, 10 states lost and 8 states gained seats in the 2000 Congressional apportionment.

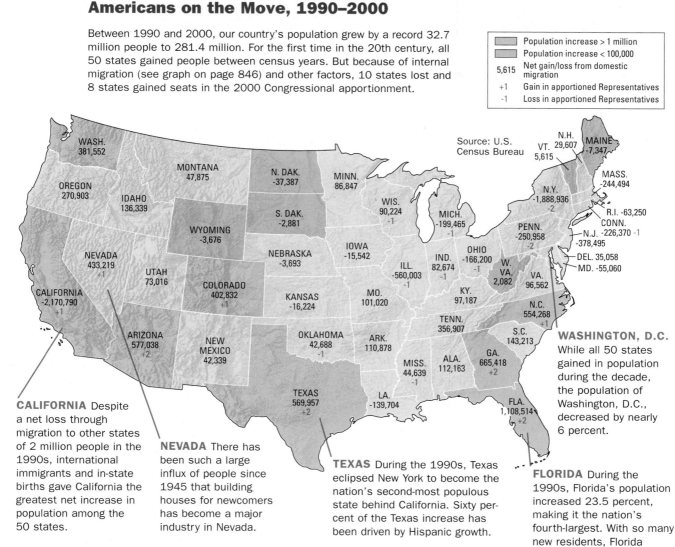

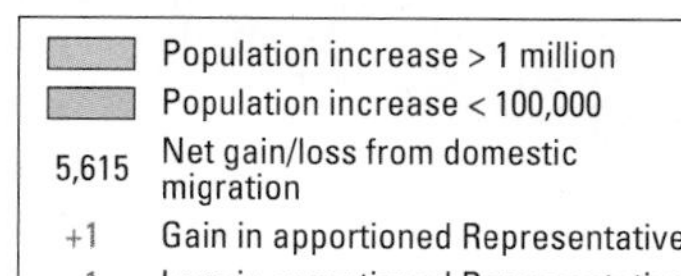

CALIFORNIA Despite a net loss through migration to other states of 2 million people in the 1990s, international immigrants and in-state births gave California the greatest net increase in population among the 50 states.

NEVADA There has been such a large influx of people since 1945 that building houses for newcomers has become a major industry in Nevada.

TEXAS During the 1990s, Texas eclipsed New York to become the nation's second-most populous state behind California. Sixty percent of the Texas increase has been driven by Hispanic growth.

FLORIDA During the 1990s, Florida's population increased 23.5 percent, making it the nation's fourth-largest. With so many new residents, Florida gained two additional House seats, bringing its congressional delegation to 25.

WASHINGTON, D.C. While all 50 states gained in population during the decade, the population of Washington, D.C., decreased by nearly 6 percent.

***(below)* Housing development near Danville, California, 1990**

THINKING CRITICALLY

1. **Analyzing Distributions** Which states lost the most people between 1990 and 2000? Which states gained the most people?
2. **Creating a Graph** Choose one of the most populous states and then pose a historical question about population in that state. Create a graph or graphs that show various aspects of population for the state you have chosen. Be sure that the graph(s) help to answer the question you posed. Then display the graph(s) and the question in the classroom.

SEE SKILLBUILDER HANDBOOK, PAGE R28.

CLASSZONE.COM

Foreign Policy After the Cold War

MAIN IDEA	WHY IT MATTERS NOW	Terms & Names
The end of the Cold War, marked by the breakup of the Soviet Union in 1991, led to a redirection of many U.S. goals and policies.	**After the Cold War, the United States provided and continues to provide substantial economic support to the new capitalistic and democratic nations.**	• **Mikhail Gorbachev** • ***glasnost*** • ***perestroika*** • **INF Treaty** • **Tiananmen Square** • ***Sandinistas*** • ***Contras*** • **Operation Desert Storm**

One American's Story

Colin Powell did not start out in life with any special privileges. He was born in Harlem and raised in the Bronx, where he enjoyed street games and tolerated school. Then, while attending the City College of New York, he joined the Reserve Officer Training Corps (ROTC). He got straight A's in ROTC, and so he decided to make the army his career.

Powell served first in Vietnam and then in Korea and West Germany. He rose in rank to become a general; then President Reagan made him national security adviser. In this post, Powell noted that the Soviet Union was a factor in all the administration's foreign policy decisions.

General Colin Powell

A Personal Voice COLIN POWELL

"Our choosing sides in conflicts around the world was almost always decided on the basis of East-West competition. The new Soviet leader, Mikhail Gorbachev, however, was turning the old Cold War formulas on their head. . . . Ronald Reagan . . . had the vision and flexibility, lacking in many knee-jerk Cold Warriors [participants in the Cold War between the U.S. and the USSR], to recognize that Gorbachev was a new man in a new age offering new opportunities for peace."

—*My American Journey*

Though U.S. foreign policy in the early 1980s was marked by intense hostility toward the Soviet Union, drastic economic problems in the Soviet Union destroyed its ability to continue the Cold War standoff.

The Cold War Ends

In March of 1985, **Mikhail Gorbachev** became the general secretary of the Communist Party in the Soviet Union. His rise to power marked the beginning of a new era in the Soviet Union.

GORBACHEV INITIATES REFORM Gorbachev had inherited a host of problems in the Soviet Union. Many of them revolved around the Soviet economy, which was under a great amount of stress. Reagan added pressure by increasing U.S. defense spending. When the Soviets attempted to keep up, their economy was pushed to the brink of collapse.

A skilled diplomat and political leader, Gorbachev advocated a policy known as ***glasnost*** (Russian for "openness"). He allowed open criticism of the Soviet government and took steps toward freedom of the press. In 1985, he outlined his plans for ***perestroika,*** a restructuring of Soviet society. He called for less government control of the economy, the introduction of some private enterprise, and steps toward establishing a democratic government.

Gorbachev recognized that better relations with the United States would allow the Soviets to reduce their military spending and reform their economy. As a result, he initiated a series of arms-control meetings that led to the **INF Treaty (Intermediate-Range Nuclear Forces Treaty)** signed on December 8, 1987. The treaty eliminated two classes of weapons systems in Europe and allowed each nation to make on-site inspections of the other's military installations. (A)

MAIN IDEA

Evaluating Leadership

(A) Which evidence in the text supports the viewpoint that Gorbachev was a skilled politician and diplomat?

THE SOVIET UNION DECLINES Gorbachev's introduction of democratic ideals led to a dramatic increase in nationalism on the part of the Soviet Union's non-Russian republics. In December 1991, 14 non-Russian republics declared their independence from the Soviet Union. Muscled aside by Russian reformers who thought he was working too slowly toward democracy, Gorbachev resigned as Soviet president. After 74 years, the Soviet Union dissolved.

A loose federation known as the Commonwealth of Independent States (CIS) took the place of the Soviet Union. In February 1992, President George Bush and Russian president Boris Yeltsin issued a formal statement declaring an end to the Cold War that had plagued the two nations and divided the world since 1945. In January 1993, Yeltsin and Bush signed the START II pact, designed to cut both nations' nuclear arsenals by two-thirds.

WORLD STAGE

DEMOCRATIC ELECTIONS IN RUSSIA

After the Soviet Union dissolved in 1991, Boris Yeltsin continued as president of Russia. Yeltsin ended price controls and increased private business ownership. The Russian parliament opposed Yeltsin's policies, even though a majority of voters supported them.

In December 1993, Russian voters installed a new parliament and approved a new constitution, parts of which resembled the U.S. Constitution. In 1996, Yeltsin won reelection as president of Russia. He was succeeded in 2000 by Vladimir Putin.

THE COLLAPSE OF COMMUNIST REGIMES Before his resignation, Gorbachev had encouraged the people of East Germany and Eastern Europe to go their own ways. In 1988, when the Soviet Union was still intact, he reduced the number of Soviet troops in Eastern Europe and allowed non-Communist parties to organize in satellite nations, such as East Germany and Poland. He encouraged the satellite nations to move toward democracy.

During a speech given at the Berlin Wall in 1987, President Reagan challenged Gorbachev to back up his reforms with decisive action.

A PERSONAL VOICE RONALD REAGAN

"General Secretary Gorbachev, if you seek peace, if you seek prosperity for the Soviet Union and Eastern Europe, if you seek liberalization: Come here to this gate! Mr. Gorbachev, open this gate! Mr. Gorbachev, tear down this wall!"

—speech, June 12, 1987

▲ A demonstrator pounds away on the Berlin Wall as East German border guards look on from above at the Brandenberg Gate, on November 11, 1989.

In October 1989, East Germans startled the world by repudiating their Communist government. On November 9, 1989, East Germany opened the Berlin Wall, allowing free passage between the two parts of the city for the first time in 28 years. East German border guards stood by and watched as Berliners pounded away with hammers and other tools at the despised wall. In early 1990, East Germany held its first free elections, and on October 3 of that year, the two German nations were united. **B**

MAIN IDEA

Analyzing Events

B What signs signaled that the Cold War had come to an end?

Other European nations also adopted democratic reforms. Czechoslovakia withdrew from the Soviet bloc. The Baltic states of Latvia, Estonia, and Lithuania declared their independence from the Soviet Union. Hungary, Bulgaria, and Romania made successful transitions from communism.

Yugoslavia, however, collapsed. Four of its six republics seceded. Ethnic rivalries deteriorated into a brutal war among Muslims, Orthodox Serbs, and Roman Catholic Croats, who were dividing Yugoslavia, each claiming parts of it. Serbia backed Serb minorities that were stirring up civil unrest in Croatia and Bosnia.

COMMUNISM CONTINUES IN CHINA Even before perestroika unfolded in the Soviet Union, economic reform had begun in China. Early in the 1980s, the Chinese Communist government loosened its grip on business and eliminated some price controls. Students in China began to demand freedom of speech and a greater voice in government.

In April 1989, university students in China held marches that quickly grew into large demonstrations in Beijing's **Tiananmen** (tyän′än′mĕn′) **Square** and on the streets of other cities. In Tiananmen Square, Chinese students constructed a version of the Statue of Liberty to symbolize their struggle for democracy.

China's premier, Li Peng, eventually ordered the military to crush the protesters. China's armed forces stormed into Tiananmen Square, slaughtering unarmed students. The world's democratic countries watched these events in horror on television. The collapse of the pro-democracy movement left the future in China uncertain. As one student leader said, "The government has won the battle here today. But they have lost the people's hearts."

A Chinese protester defies the tanks in Tiananmen Square in 1989. ▶

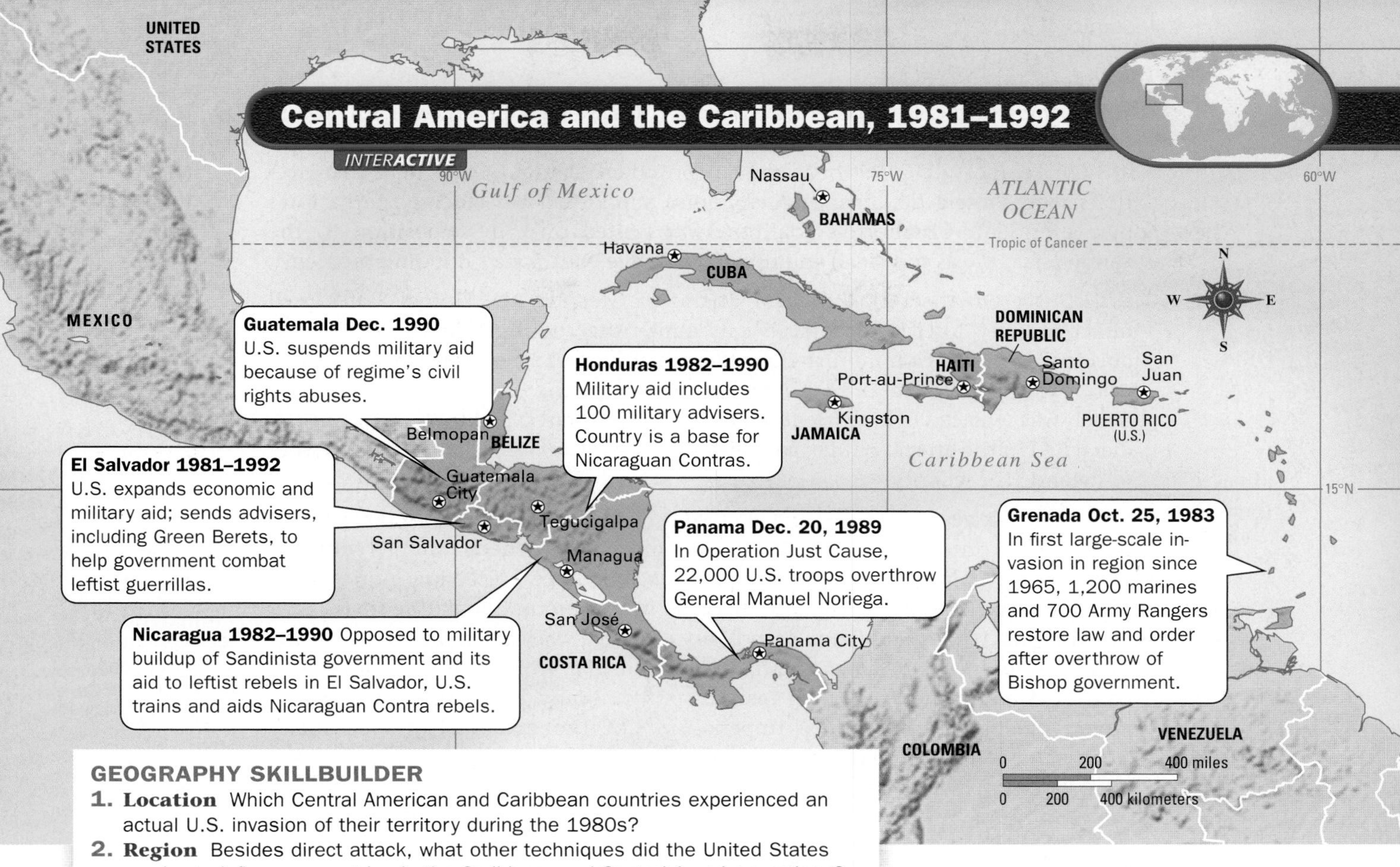

GEOGRAPHY SKILLBUILDER

1. **Location** Which Central American and Caribbean countries experienced an actual U.S. invasion of their territory during the 1980s?
2. **Region** Besides direct attack, what other techniques did the United States employ to influence countries in the Caribbean and Central American regions?

Central American and Caribbean Policy

Cold War considerations during the Reagan and Bush administrations continued to influence affairs in Central America and the Caribbean. In these places, the United States still opposed left-leaning and socialist governments in favor of governments friendly to the United States.

NICARAGUA The United States had had a presence in Nicaragua ever since 1912, when President Taft sent U.S. Marines to protect American investments there. The marines left in 1933, but only after helping the dictator Anastasio Somoza come to power.

The Somoza family ruled Nicaragua for 42 years. To keep control of its business empire, the family rigged elections and assassinated political rivals. Many people believed that only a revolution would end the Somoza dictatorship.

Between 1977 and 1979, Nicaragua was engulfed in a civil war between Somoza's national guard and the ***Sandinistas,*** rebels who took their name from a rebel leader named Sandino who had been killed in 1934. When Sandinista rebels toppled the dictatorship of Somoza's son in 1979, President Carter recognized the new regime and sent it $83 million in economic aid. The Soviet Union and Cuba sent aid as well.

In 1981, however, President Reagan charged that Nicaragua was a Soviet outpost that was exporting revolution to other Central American countries. Reagan cut all aid to the Sandinista government and threw his support to guerrilla forces known as the ***Contras*** because they were against the Sandinistas. By 1983, the Contra army had grown to nearly 10,000 men, and American officials from the CIA had stationed themselves to direct operations—without congressional approval. In response, Congress passed the Boland Amendment, banning military aid to the Contras for two years. However, Reagan's administration still found ways to negotiate aid to the Contras.

On February 25, 1990, Nicaraguan president Daniel Ortega held free elections, and Violeta de Chamorro, a Contra supporter, was elected the nation's new president. Chamorro's coalition was united only in opposition to the Sandinistas; it was too weak and divided to solve Nicaragua's ongoing problems.

GRENADA On the tiny Caribbean island of Grenada, the United States used direct military force to accomplish its aims. After noting that the island was developing ties to Communist Cuba, President Reagan sent approximately 2,000 troops to the island in 1983. There they overthrew the pro-Cuban government, which was replaced by one friendlier to the United States. Eighteen American soldiers died in the attack, but Reagan declared that the invasion had been necessary to defend U.S. security.

PANAMA Six years later, in 1989, President Bush sent more than 20,000 soldiers and marines into Panama to overthrow and arrest General Manuel Antonio Noriega on charges of drug trafficking. Noriega had been receiving money since 1960 from the CIA, but he was also involved in the international drug trade. After he was indicted by a Miami grand jury, Noriega was taken by force by the American military and flown to Miami to stand trial. In April 1992, Noriega was convicted and sentenced to 40 years in prison. Many Latin American governments deplored the "Yankee imperialism" of the action. However, many Americans—and Panamanians—were pleased by the removal of a military dictator who supported drug smuggling. C

MAIN IDEA

Comparing
C Between 1980 and 1992, how did U.S. policies regarding Central America differ from those regarding Europe?

Middle East Trouble Spots

Results favorable to U.S. interests were more difficult to obtain in the Middle East. Negotiating conflicts between ever-shifting governments drew the United States into scandal and its first major war since Vietnam.

THE IRAN-CONTRA SCANDAL In 1983, terrorist groups loyal to Iran took a number of Americans hostage in Lebanon. Reagan denounced Iran and urged U.S. allies not to sell arms to Iran for its war against Iraq. In 1985, he declared that "America will never make concessions to terrorists." Therefore, Americans were shocked to learn in 1986 that President Reagan had approved the sale of arms to Iran. In exchange for those sales, Iran promised to win the release of seven American hostages held in Lebanon by pro-Iranian terrorists. What's more, members of Reagan's staff sent part of the

President Reagan's message to television audiences about selling arms to Iran differed greatly from what was going on behind the scenes.

profits from those illegal arms sales to the Contras in Nicaragua—in direct violation of the Boland Amendment. President Reagan held a press conference to explain what had happened.

A PERSONAL VOICE RONALD REAGAN

"I am deeply troubled that the implementation of a policy aimed at resolving a truly tragic situation in the Middle East has resulted in such controversy. As I've stated previously, I believe our policy goals toward Iran were well founded."

—presidential press conference, November 25, 1986

In the summer of 1987, special committees of both houses of Congress conducted a dramatic inquiry into the Iran-Contra affair during a month of joint televised hearings. Among those testifying was Lieutenant Colonel Oliver North, a member of the National Security Council staff who played a key role in providing aid to the Contras. North appeared in military uniform adorned with service ribbons and badges. In defending his actions, North talked about patriotism and love of country. He asserted that he thought he was carrying out the president's wishes and that the end of helping the Contras justified almost any means.

After a congressional investigation, Special Prosecutor Lawrence E. Walsh, early in 1988, indicted various members of the Reagan administration who were involved in the scandal. Oliver North was found guilty of aiding the cover-up. He was fined and sentenced to perform community service. (His conviction was later overturned because he testified under a grant of limited immunity.). On Christmas Eve of 1992, President Bush pardoned a number of Reagan officials.

THE PERSIAN GULF WAR Regardless of the scandal surrounding the Iran-Contra affair, conflict with Iraq (which was Iran's long-standing enemy) and its leader, Saddam Hussein, soon eclipsed U.S. problems with Iran. During the 1980s, Iran and Iraq had fought a prolonged war, and Hussein found himself with enormous war debts to pay. Several times, Hussein had claimed that the oil-rich nation of Kuwait was really part of Iraq. On August 2, 1990, Iraqi troops invaded Kuwait. The Iraqi invaders looted Kuwait; then they headed toward Saudi Arabia and

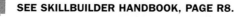

POINT

"The United States must occasionally intervene militarily in regional conflicts."

Proponents of U.S. military intervention abroad agreed with General Norman Schwarzkopf that "as the only remaining superpower, we have an awesome responsibility . . . to the rest of the world."

"The United States must take the lead in promoting democracy," urged Morton H. Halperin, former director of the ACLU (American Civil Liberties Union). "To say 'Let the UN do it' is a cop-out," stated adviser Robert G. Neumann.

Political scientist Jane Sharp expressed a similar sentiment. She asked, "Can any nation that has taken no action [in Bosnia] to stop the Serbian practice of ethnic cleansing continue to call itself civilized?"

COUNTERPOINT

"The United States should not intervene militarily in regional conflicts."

A foreign-policy analyst at the Cato Institute, Barbara Conry, stated that "intervention in regional wars is a distraction and a drain on resources." What's more, she argued, "it does not work." Recalling the presence of American troops in Lebanon, Conry argued that intervention not only jeopardized American soldiers, it often obstructed what it sought to achieve.

"The internal freedom of a political community can be achieved only by members of that community," agreed Professor Stephen R. Shalom. He added that "using [military action] encourages quick fix solutions that ignore the underlying sources of conflict."

THINKING CRITICALLY

1. **CONNECT TO TODAY** **Comparing and Contrasting** What do you think are the strongest arguments for and against military intervention in regional conflicts?

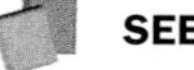

SEE SKILLBUILDER HANDBOOK, PAGE R8.

2. **CONNECT TO HISTORY** **Hypothesizing** With at least one partner, research the events leading up to U.S. involvement in one of these countries: Lebanon, Grenada, Panama, or Kuwait. Then negotiate to resolve the conflict.

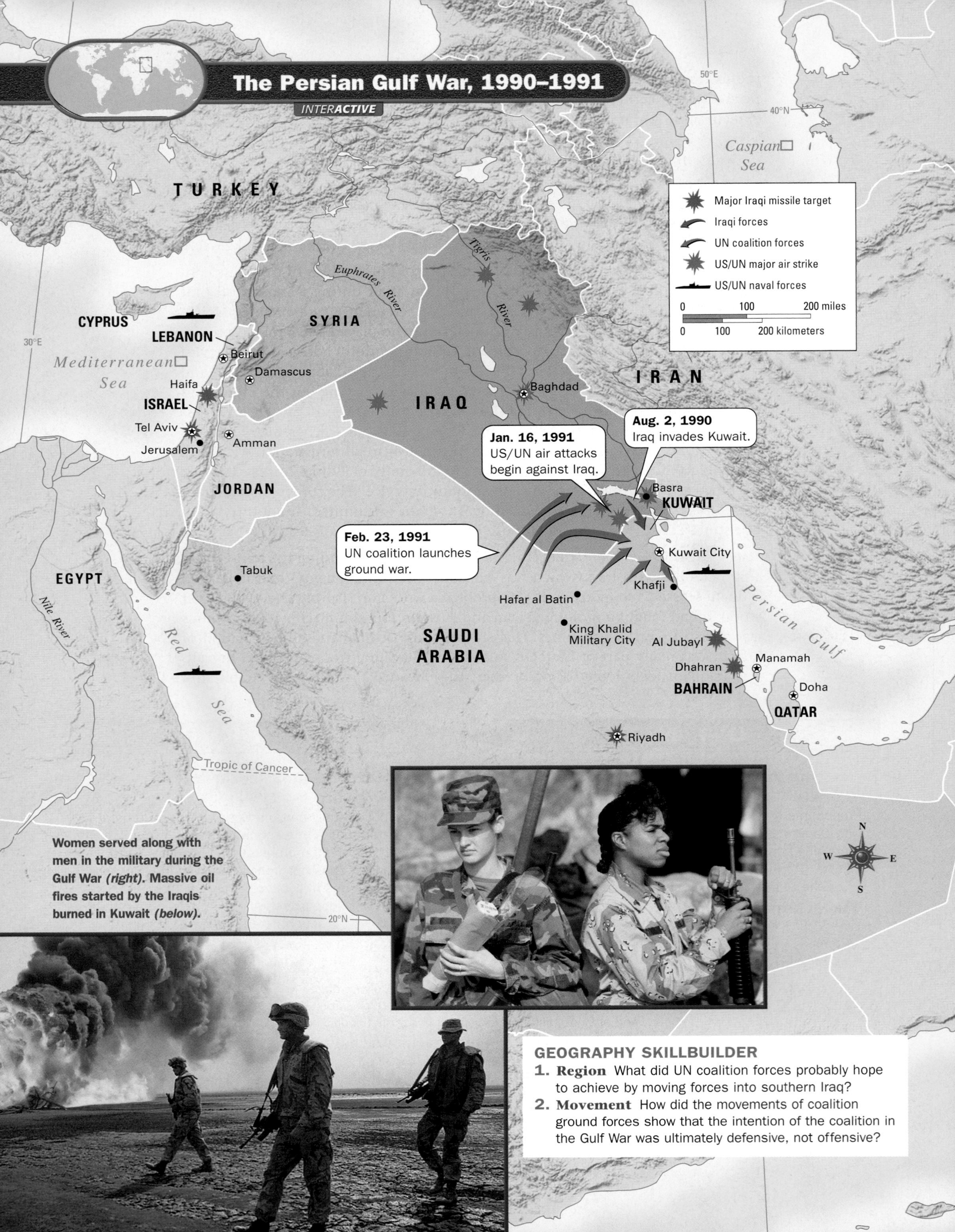

Women served along with men in the military during the Gulf War *(right)*. Massive oil fires started by the Iraqis burned in Kuwait *(below)*.

GEOGRAPHY SKILLBUILDER

1. **Region** What did UN coalition forces probably hope to achieve by moving forces into southern Iraq?
2. **Movement** How did the movements of coalition ground forces show that the intention of the coalition in the Gulf War was ultimately defensive, not offensive?

MAIN IDEA

Drawing Conclusions
D What issue led to the conflict in the Middle East?

one-half of the world's known oil reserves, which would severely threaten U.S. oil supplies. **D**

For several months, President Bush and Secretary of State James Baker organized an international coalition against Iraqi aggression. With the support of Congress and the UN, President Bush launched **Operation Desert Storm** to liberate Kuwait from Iraqi control. On January 16, 1991, the United States and its allies staged a massive air assault against Iraq. On February 23, they launched a successful ground offensive from Saudi Arabia. On February 28, 1991, President Bush announced a cease-fire. Operation Desert Storm was over. Kuwait was liberated.

Millions of Americans turned out for the victory parades that greeted returning soldiers. After the debacle in Vietnam, they were thrilled the war was over, with fewer than 400 casualties among UN coalition forces. (However, there were subsequent reports that Gulf veterans were suffering from disabilities caused by chemicals used in the war.) By contrast, Iraq had suffered an estimated 100,000 military and civilian deaths. During the embargo that followed, many Iraqi children died from outbreaks of cholera, typhoid, enteritis, and other diseases.

BUSH'S DOMESTIC POLICIES Despite his great achievement in the Persian Gulf War, President Bush was not as successful on the domestic front. He was hurt by rising deficits and a recession that began in 1990 and lasted through most of 1992. Bush was forced to raise taxes despite his campaign pledge. His approval rating had dropped to 49 percent by 1992. The weak economy and the tax hike doomed Bush's reelection campaign, and 12 years of Republican leadership came to an end.

KEY PLAYER

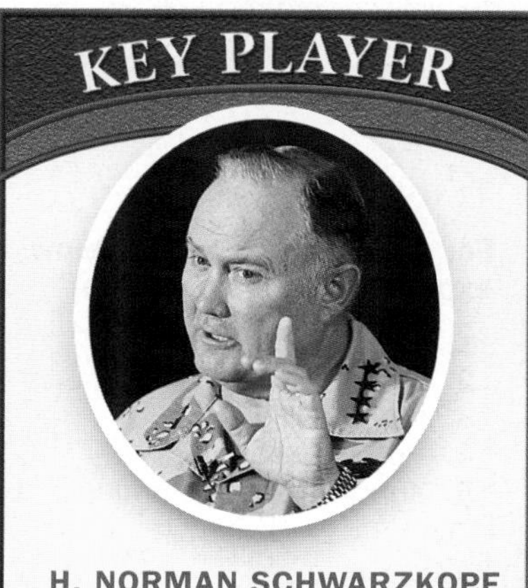

H. NORMAN SCHWARZKOPF
1934–

In 1988, Norman Schwarzkopf, shown above, became commander in chief of forces in Asia and Africa. During the Persian Gulf War, more than 540,000 men and women served under the command of "Stormin' Norman." Schwarzkopf said of Saddam Hussein that he was "neither a strategist, nor is he schooled in the operational art, nor is he a tactician, nor is he a general, nor is he a soldier. Other than that, he is a great military man."

SECTION 4 ASSESSMENT

1. **TERMS & NAMES** For each term or name, write a sentence explaining its meaning.
   - **Mikhail Gorbachev**
   - ***glasnost***
   - ***perestroika***
   - **INF Treaty**
   - **Tiananmen Square**
   - ***Sandinistas***
   - ***Contras***
   - **Operation Desert Storm**

MAIN IDEA

2. **TAKING NOTES**
   Use a chart like the one below to explain U.S. foreign policy toward world regions.

U.S. Foreign Policy
Europe
Central America and Caribbean
Middle East

Now write a paragraph in which you describe a trouble spot in one of these regions.

CRITICAL THINKING

3. **ANALYZING CAUSES**
   What factors caused the end of the Cold War? **Think About:**
   - events in the Soviet Union
   - events in Germany and Eastern Europe
   - how U.S. leaders responded to those events

4. **FORMING GENERALIZATIONS**
   What factors do you think determined whether or not the United States intervened militarily in other nations?

5. **HYPOTHESIZING**
   Is it possible for an authoritarian government to make economic reforms without also making political reforms? Support your answer with details from the text.

CHAPTER 25 ASSESSMENT

TERMS & NAMES

For each term or name below, write a sentence explaining its significance.

1. entitlement program
2. affirmative action
3. Moral Majority
4. Ronald Reagan
5. supply-side economics
6. Geraldine Ferraro
7. AIDS
8. Mikhail Gorbachev
9. *Contras*
10. Operation Desert Storm

MAIN IDEAS

Use your notes and the information in the chapter to answer the following questions.

A Conservative Movement Emerges
(pages 830–833)

1. What caused the conservative revolution of the early 1980s?
2. What factors led to Ronald Reagan's victory in 1980?

Conservative Policies Under Reagan and Bush *(pages 834–838)*

3. What principles formed the basis of "Reaganomics"?
4. What is deregulation, and how did it affect certain industries in the 1980s?

Social Concerns in the 1980s *(pages 839–845)*

5. What progress and obstacles did different minority groups experience in the 1980s?
6. What were some gains that women achieved in the 1980s?

Foreign Policy After the Cold War
(pages 848–855)

7. What caused the downfall of the Soviet Union and the founding of the Commonwealth of Independent States?
8. Summarize the U.S. response to Iraq's invasion of Kuwait.

CRITICAL THINKING

1. **USING YOUR NOTES** Choose two events from each of the sections of the chapter and place them in chronological order on a timeline like the one below.

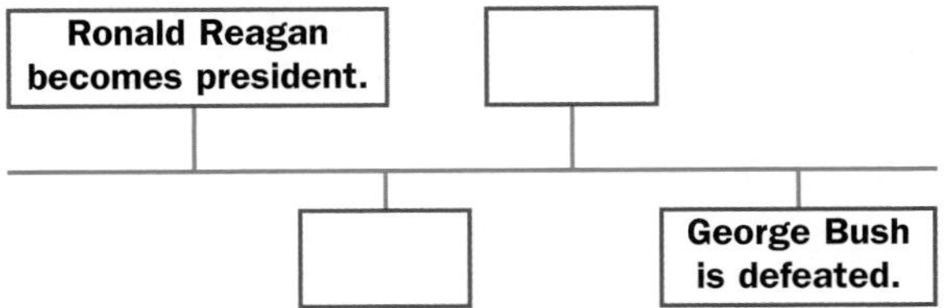

2. **EVALUATING** Review the goals of the conservative movement and the actions of the government under Reagan and Bush. Evaluate how well the goals had been achieved by the end of Bush's term.

3. **INTERPRETING MAPS** Look at the map on page 851. Between 1982 and 1992, the United States intervened in Latin America many times. How might the presence of a Communist government on the island of Cuba have influenced U.S. actions?

VISUAL SUMMARY THE CONSERVATIVE TIDE

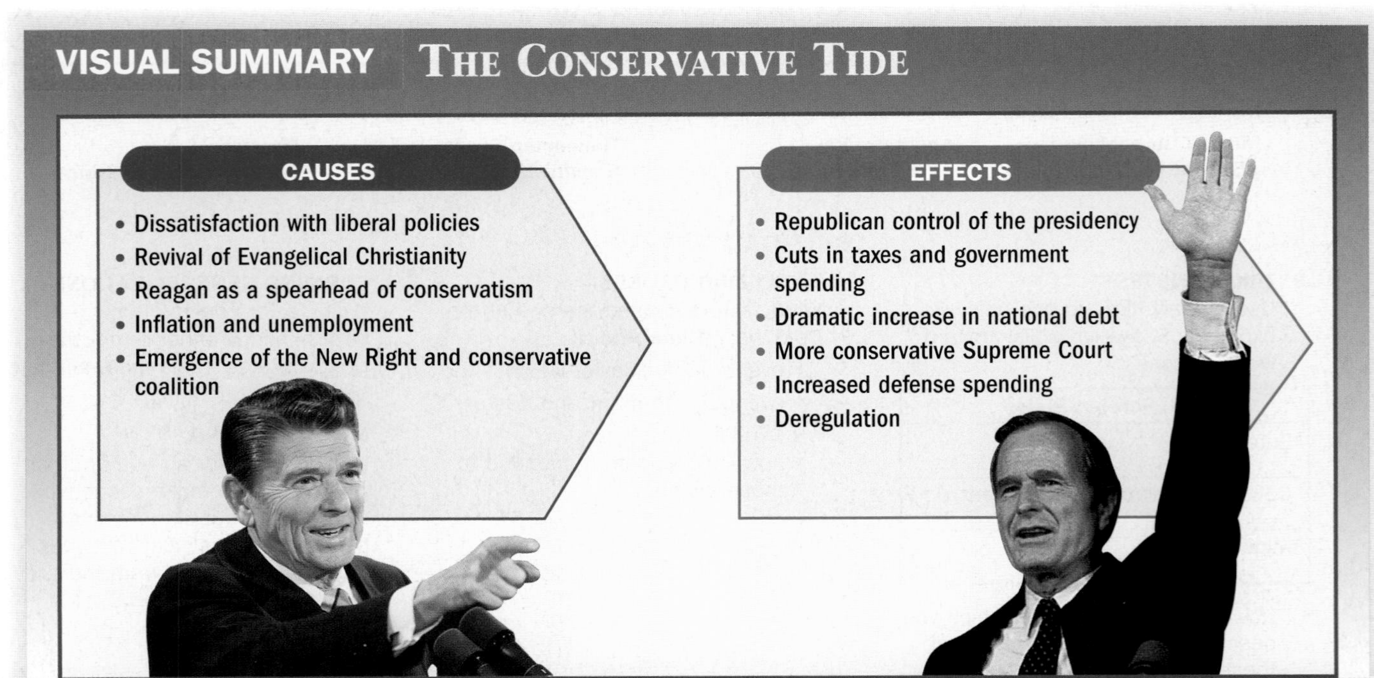

CAUSES
• Dissatisfaction with liberal policies
• Revival of Evangelical Christianity
• Reagan as a spearhead of conservatism
• Inflation and unemployment
• Emergence of the New Right and conservative coalition
EFFECTS
• Republican control of the presidency
• Cuts in taxes and government spending
• Dramatic increase in national debt
• More conservative Supreme Court
• Increased defense spending
• Deregulation

Standardized Test Practice

Use the passage and your knowledge of U.S. history to answer question 1.

> **"That system [of republican government] has never failed us, but, for a time, we failed the system. We asked things of government that government was not equipped to give. We yielded authority to the national government that properly belonged to states or to local governments or to the people themselves. We allowed taxes and inflation to rob us of our earnings and savings and watched the great industrial machine that had made us the most productive people on Earth slow down and the number of unemployed increase."**
>
> —Ronald Reagan, Second Inaugural Address, 1985

1. The passage suggests that President Ronald Reagan supported which point of view?
   - **A** There should be an end to all social welfare programs.
   - **B** The role of the federal government should be reduced.
   - **C** The role of the federal government should be increased.
   - **D** The federal government should raise taxes.

2. Which of the following events signaled the end of the Cold War?
   - **F** Operation Desert Storm
   - **G** Iran-Contra Scandal
   - **H** collapse of the Soviet Union
   - **J** protests at Tiananmen Square

Use the graph and your knowledge of U.S. history to answer question 3.

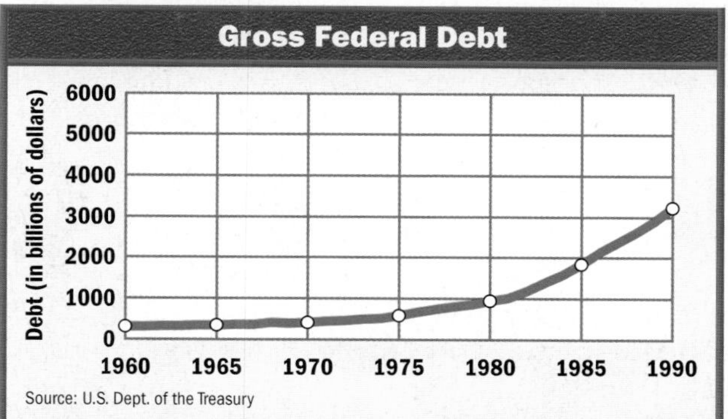

3. The graph shows that the gross federal debt —
   - **A** stayed the same during the Reagan and Bush years.
   - **B** greatly increased during the Reagan and Bush years.
   - **C** greatly decreased during the Reagan and Bush years.
   - **D** did not exist during the Reagan and Bush years.

4. Which of the following was *not* a goal of the conservative movement of the 1980s?
   - **F** strengthen the national defense
   - **G** reduce government regulations
   - **H** promote family values and patriotic ideals
   - **J** increase taxes

ADDITIONAL TEST PRACTICE, pages S1–S33.

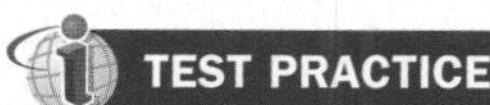

CLASSZONE.COM

ALTERNATIVE ASSESSMENT

1. **INTERACT WITH HISTORY** Recall your discussion of the question on page 829:

   ### *What campaign slogan will you create?*

   As a speechwriter for Ronald Reagan in 1980, write an effective speech that contains your campaign slogan and presents reasons why people should vote for Reagan. Present your speech to the class.

2. **INTERNET ACTIVITY CLASSZONE.COM**
   Visit the links for Chapter Assessment to find out more about Saddam Hussein's rise to power in Iraq. Write a short (3 to 5 paragraphs) biography. What tactics did he use to become dictator? Why is he often compared to Germany's Adolf Hitler? How do his policies affect the people of Iraq? Describe his present relationship with the United States.

THE UNITED STATES IN TODAY'S WORLD

Participants at the Walk For Hunger, held annually in Massachusetts, help to support local and emergency food programs.

USA

1992 Twenty-seventh Amendment prohibits midterm congressional pay raises.

1992 William Jefferson Clinton is elected president.

1994 Republicans gain control of both houses of Congress.

1995 "Million Man March" held in Washington, D.C.

1996 President Clinton is reelected.

1992 | 1994 | 1996

WORLD

1993 Russia and United States sign START-II treaty reducing warheads and ICBMs.

1994 In South Africa's first all-race election, Nelson Mandela is elected president.

1995 Israeli prime minister Yitzhak Rabin is assassinated.

INTERACT WITH HISTORY

You are a high school senior who is active in student government and community service. You have been chosen from among thousands of students nationwide to address an international youth symposium on global issues and reforms. As a U.S. delegate to the event, you address the crowd, confident that young people will be able to change the future.

What are the most important issues that affect the world today?

Examine the Issues

- What makes nations increasingly dependent on one another?
- How does technology affect society worldwide?
- What are the ways to foster cooperation among nations?

RESEARCH LINKS **CLASSZONE.COM**

Visit the Chapter 26 links for more information about The United States in Today's World.

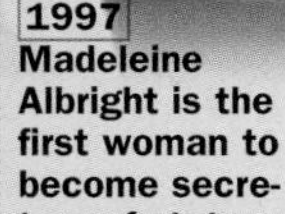

1997 Madeleine Albright is the first woman to become secretary of state.

1998 President Clinton is impeached.

1999 Senate acquits President Clinton.

2000 George W. Bush is elected 43rd president.

2001 On September 11, terrorists attack New York's World Trade Center and the Pentagon with hijacked jets.

1998 — **2000** — **2002**

1997 Scottish scientist clones "Dolly" the sheep.

1998 Northern Ireland, the Irish Republic, and the United Kingdom sign peace agreements.

2000 The dreaded "Y2K" bug proves harmless to computer systems globally.

2001 Serbian president Slobodan Milosevic is brought before the UN war crimes tribunal.

The 1990s and the New Millennium

MAIN IDEA	WHY IT MATTERS NOW	Terms & Names
The nation became divided as the Democrats gained control of the White House in the 1990s, and the Republicans came to power at the beginning of the new millennium.	Democrats and Republicans need to find a way to work together and unite a divided nation.	•William Jefferson Clinton •H. Ross Perot •Hillary Rodham Clinton •NAFTA •Newt Gingrich •Contract with America •Al Gore •George W. Bush

One American's Story

On January 20, 1993, poet Maya Angelou was honored as the first woman and the first African American to read her work at a presidential inauguration. Bill Clinton asked Angelou to compose and deliver a poem. Angelou expressed the optimism of the day, recalling the dream of Martin Luther King, Jr., as she recited her poem "On the Pulse of Morning."

A Personal Voice MAYA ANGELOU

"Lift up your faces, you have a piercing need
For this bright morning dawning for you.
History, despite its wrenching pain,
Cannot be unlived, but if faced
With courage, need not be lived again.

Lift up your eyes
Upon this day breaking for you.
Give birth again
To the dream."

—"On the Pulse of Morning"

Maya Angelou

Moments later, William Jefferson Clinton was inaugurated as the 42nd president of the United States. Clinton entered the presidency at a time when America was at a turning point. A severe economic recession had made many Americans uneasy about the future. They looked to Clinton to lead a government that would be more responsive to the people.

Clinton Wins the Presidency

Governor **William Jefferson Clinton** of Arkansas became the first member of the baby-boom generation to win the presidency. He captured the White House, at the age of 46, by vowing to strengthen the nation's weak economy and to lead the Democratic Party in a more moderate direction.

THE ELECTION OF 1992 After the U.S. victory in the Persian Gulf War in 1991, Republican president George Bush's popularity had climbed to an 89 percent approval rating. Shortly after the war ended, however, the nation found itself in the grips of a recession. In early 1992, Bush's approval rating nose-dived to 40 percent. In his run for reelection, President Bush could not convince the public that he had a clear strategy for ending the recession and creating jobs. (A)

MAIN IDEA

Analyzing Causes

(A) What factors accounted for Bush's decline in popularity?

Throughout the presidential race, Bill Clinton campaigned as the candidate to lead the nation out of its economic crisis. So did a third-party candidate—Texas billionaire **H. Ross Perot.** Perot targeted the soaring federal budget deficit as the nation's number one problem. A budget deficit occurs when the federal government borrows money to meet all its spending commitments. "It's time," Perot declared in his usual blunt style, "to take out the trash and clean up the barn."

Election Day results, however, demonstrated that Clinton's center-of-the-road strategy had the widest appeal. Though Clinton won, he captured only 43 percent of the popular vote. Bush received 38 percent, while Perot managed an impressive 19 percent.

A "NEW" DEMOCRAT Bill Clinton won the presidency in part by promising to move away from traditional Democratic policies. He also emphasized the need to move people off welfare and called for growth in private business as a means to economic progress.

In office, Clinton worked to move the Democratic Party toward the political center by embracing both liberal and conservative programs. According to an ally, Clinton hoped "to modernize liberalism so it could sell again." By doing so, he sought to create a "new" and more inclusive Democratic Party.

KEY PLAYER

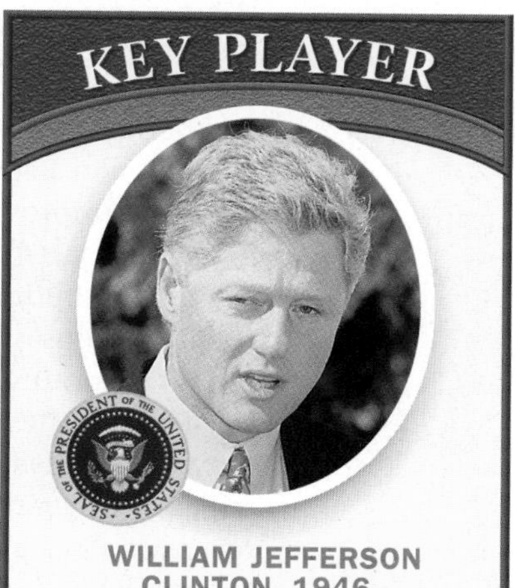

WILLIAM JEFFERSON CLINTON, 1946–

Born in Hope, Arkansas, at the beginning of the baby boom, Bill Clinton had wanted to be president most of his life. As a college student in the 1960s, he had opposed the Vietnam War and pulled strings to avoid being drafted.

After studying in England as a Rhodes scholar and graduating from Yale Law School, Clinton returned to Arkansas. He taught at the University of Arkansas School of Law and dived into politics, becoming governor in 1979 at the age of thirty-two.

Moderate Reform and Economic Boom

President Clinton demonstated his willingness to pursue both liberal and conservative policies on health care, the budget deficit, crime, and welfare.

HEALTH CARE REFORM Clinton had pledged to create a plan to guarantee affordable health care for all Americans, especially for the millions of Americans who lacked medical insurance. Once in office, Clinton appointed First Lady **Hillary Rodham Clinton,** a skilled lawyer and child-welfare advocate, to head the team creating the plan. The president presented the health care reform bill to Congress in September 1993.

MAIN IDEA

Analyzing Causes

(B) What factors led to the defeat of Clinton's health care plan?

Congress debated the plan for a year. Intense lobbying and Republican attacks on the plan for promoting "big government" sealed its doom. In the end, Congress never even voted on the bill. (B)

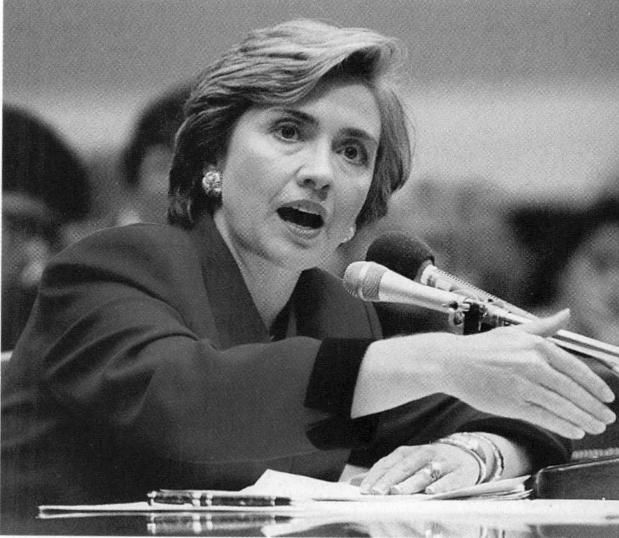

▲ **Hillary Rodham Clinton explains the health care reform plan to a Senate subcommittee.**

BALANCED BUDGET AND AN ECONOMIC BOOM President Clinton was more successful in his efforts to reduce the federal budget deficit. Clinton and the Republican-controlled Congress agreed in 1997 on legislation to balance the federal budget by the year 2002. The bill cut spending by billions of dollars, lowered taxes to win Republican support, and included programs aimed at helping children and improving health care.

A year later, Clinton announced that—for the first time in nearly 30 years—the federal budget had a surplus. That is, the government took in more than it spent. Surpluses were used, in part, to pay down the nation's debt, which had soared to around $5.5 trillion.

Background
See *national debt* on page R43 in the Economics Handbook.

Perhaps the most effective tool in generating a surplus was the booming economy. About the time Clinton took office, the economy rebounded. Unemployment fell and the stock market soared to new heights. As a result, the government's tax revenues rose, and fewer people received public aid. These factors helped slash the federal debt.

REFORMING WELFARE Clinton and the congressional Republicans cooperated to reform the welfare system. In 1996, a bill was proposed to place limits on how long people could receive benefits. It also put an end to a 61-year federal guarantee of welfare, and instead gave states "block grants"—set amounts of federal money they could spend on welfare or for other social concerns.

Although liberal Democrats feared the effects of eliminating the federal safety net for the poor, the president backed the bill. Over the next few years, states moved millions of people from welfare to jobs. Because of the strong economy, the transition was more successful than some had been predicting.

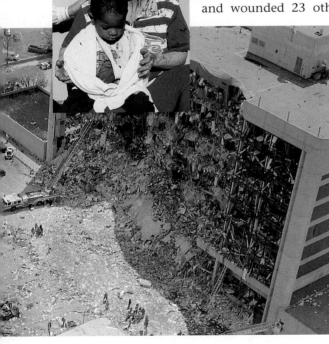

Injured victims after the April 1995 bombing of the Alfred P. Murrah Federal Building in Oklahoma City, Oklahoma. ▼

Crime and Terrorism

The improved economy—along with enlargement of police forces—combined to lower crime rates in the 1990s. However, fears were raised among Americans by acts of violence and terrorism around the country.

A shocking crime occurred April 1999 when two students at Columbine High School, in Colorado, killed 12 students and a teacher and wounded 23 others, and then shot themselves. Americans were appalled at copycat crimes that began to occur. Some called for tougher gun control, while others argued that exposure to violent imagery should be curtailed. Violence had pervaded television news throughout the decade.

In 1993, terrorists had exploded bombs in the World Trade Center in New York City. This was closely followed by a 1995 blast that destroyed a nine-story federal office building in Oklahoma City, killing 168 children, women, and men. Timothy McVeigh, an American veteran of the Gulf War, was found guilty in the Oklahoma bombing. He was executed in 2001, the first use of the federal death penalty in 38 years. Although American embassies and military targets abroad were subject to sporadic and deadly terrorist attacks during the decade, the U.S. was in no way prepared for a devastating attack that took place on its own soil on the morning of September 11, 2001. Ⓒ

MAIN IDEA

Summarizing
Ⓒ What acts of terrorism targeted Americans in the decade preceding 2001?

In a coordinated effort, two hijacked commercial jets struck the twin towers of the World Trade Center in New York City, one crashing just minutes after the other. The jets exploded on impact and subsequently leveled the tallest buildings of New York's skyline, the symbolic center of American finance. About an hour later, a third plane tore into the Pentagon building, the U.S. military headquarters outside Washington, D.C. Air travel ceased almost immediately; across the nation planes in the air were ordered to land. During the evacuation of the White House and the New York financial district, a fourth hijacked plane crashed near Pittsburgh, Pennsylvania.

About 3,000 people were killed in the attacks. These included all the passengers on all four planes, workers and visitors in the World Trade Center and the Pentagon, and hundreds of rescue workers. (See the first issue in "Issues for the 21st Century," on page 894.)

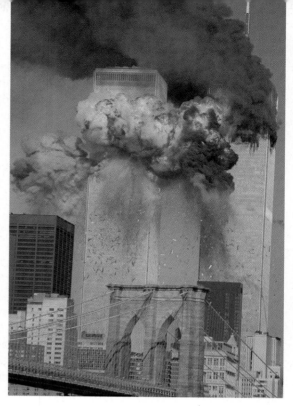

▲ **A view across the Brooklyn Bridge shows the devastating impact of two jets used by terrorists as missiles to destroy the World Trade Center.**

New Foreign Policy Challenges

Vocabulary
globalization: to make worldwide in scope or application

Conflicts and confused alliances grew in the wake of the Cold War. The question of U.S. intervention overseas, and the globalization of the economy presented the United States with a host of new challenges.

RELATIONS WITH FORMER COLD WAR FOES Maintaining strong relations with Russia and China became major goals for the Clinton administration. Throughout the 1990s, the U.S. and Russia cooperated on economic and arms-control issues. Still, Russia criticized U.S. intervention in Yugoslavia, where a bloody civil war raged. Meanwhile, U.S. officials protested against Russian attacks on rebels in the Russian region of Chechnya.

U.S. relations with China were strained as well. Clinton had stressed that he would lean on China to grant its citizens more democratic rights. As president, however, he put greater emphasis on increasing trade with China. Despite concerns that Chinese spies had stolen U.S. defense secrets, Clinton supported a bill—passed in 2000—granting China permanent trade rights.

TROOPS ABROAD With the Cold War over, the United States turned more of its attention to regional conflicts. President Clinton proved willing to use troops to end conflicts overseas. In 1991, military leaders in Haiti forced the elected president from office. Thousands of refugees fled the military leaders' harsh rule. In 1994, President Clinton dispatched American troops to Haiti, and the military rulers were forced to step down.

Other interventions occurred in Yugoslavia. In 1991, Yugoslavia broke apart into five nations. In Bosnia, one of the new states, some Serb militias under Slobodon Milosevic (mee • LOH • sheh • vihch) began "ethnic cleansing," killing or expelling from their homes people of certain ethnic groups. In 1995, the United States helped negotiate a peace in Bosnia. Clinton sent U.S. troops to join NATO troops to help ensure the deal. About three years later, Serb forces attacked ethnic Albanians in the Serb province of Kosovo. The U.S. and its NATO allies launched air strikes against Serbian targets in 1999, forcing the Serbs to back down. American troops followed up by participating in an international

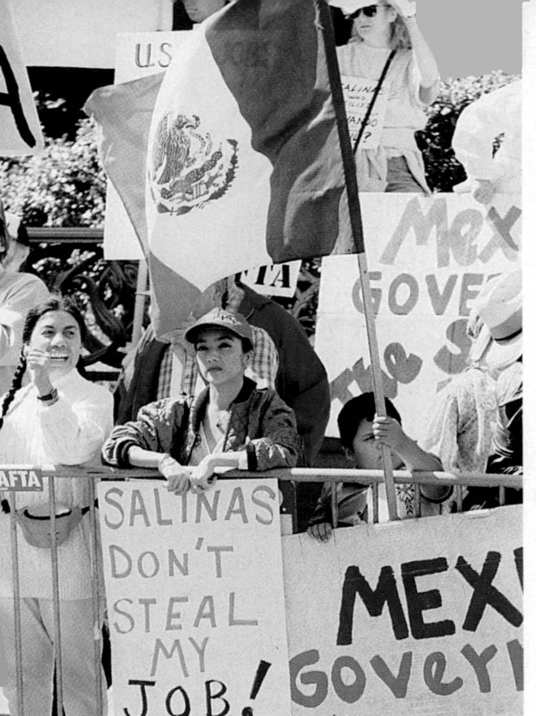

▲ **American workers protest against the North American Free Trade Agreement (NAFTA).**

peace-keeping force. In both Bosnia and Kosovo, the administration promised early withdrawal. However, the U.S. troops stayed longer than had been intended, drawing criticism of Clinton's policies. **D**

> **MAIN IDEA**
> **Analyzing Causes**
> **D** Why did the United States send troops to Yugoslavia and Kosovo?

TRADE AND THE GLOBAL ECONOMY Seeing flourishing trade as essential to U.S. prosperity and to world economic and political stability, President Clinton championed the **North American Free Trade Agreement (NAFTA).** This legislation would bring Mexico into the free-trade zone that the United States and Canada already had formed. Supporters said NAFTA would strengthen all three economies and create more American jobs. Opponents insisted that NAFTA would transfer American jobs to Mexico, where wages were lower, and harm the environment because of Mexico's weaker antipollution laws. Congress rejected these arguments, and the treaty was ratified by all three countries' legislatures in 1993. Once the treaty took effect, on January 1, 1994, trade with Mexico increased.

Critics of free trade and the global economy remained vocal, however. In late 1999, the World Trade Organization (WTO), an organization that promotes trade and economic development, met in Seattle. Demonstrators protested that the WTO made decisions with little public input and that these decisions harmed poorer countries, the environment, and American manufacturing workers.

Subsequent anti-globalization protests have been held worldwide. Violent clashes erupted between police and demonstrators at the April 2001 third Summit of the Americas, held in Quebec City, Canada. Nevertheless, the activists failed to halt plans to launch, by 2006, the Free Trade Area of the Americas (FTAA)—an enlarged version of NAFTA covering the 34 countries in the Western Hemisphere, except Cuba.

Partisan Politics and Impeachment

While Clinton and Congress worked together on deficit reduction and NAFTA, relations in Washington became increasingly partisan. In the midst of political wrangling, a scandal rocked the White House, and Bill Clinton became the second president in U.S. history to be impeached.

> **Vocabulary**
> **partisan:** devoted to or biased in support of a party, group, or cause

REPUBLICANS TAKE CONTROL OF CONGRESS In mid-1994, after the failure of President Clinton's health care plan and recurring questions regarding his leadership, Republican congressman **Newt Gingrich** began to turn voters' dissatisfaction with Clinton into support for Republicans. He drafted a document called the **Contract with America**—ten items Republicans promised to enact if they won control of Congress. They included congressional term limits, a balanced-budget amendment, tax cuts, tougher crime laws, and welfare reform. **E**

> **MAIN IDEA**
> **Summarizing**
> **E** What were some of the provisions of the Contract of America?

In the November 1994 election, the Republicans handed the Democrats a humiliating defeat. Voters gave Republicans control of both houses of Congress for the first time since 1954. Chosen as the new Speaker of the House, Newt Gingrich was jubilant.

A PERSONAL VOICE NEWT GINGRICH

> **"I will never forget mounting the rostrum . . . for the first time. . . . The whole scene gave me a wonderful sense of the romance of America and the magic by which Americans share power and accept changes in government."**
>
> —*To Renew America*

President Clinton and the Republican-controlled Congress clashed. Clinton opposed Republican budgets that slowed entitlements—federal programs which provide for basic human needs—such as Social Security and Medicaid. Clinton and Congress refused to compromise, and the Republicans refused to pass the larger budgets he wanted. As a result, the federal government shut down for almost a week in November 1995, and again for several weeks in the next two months.

THE 1996 REELECTION The budget standoff helped Clinton, as did the strong economy and passage of the welfare reform law of 1996, which suggested an improved working relationship with Congress. As a result, voters reelected Clinton in November 1996. With 49 percent of the popular vote, he outpolled the Republican nominee, U.S. Senator Bob Dole, and the Reform Party candidate, H. Ross Perot. Still, the Republicans maintained control of the House and Senate. Both President Clinton and Republican leaders pledged to work more cooperatively. Soon however, the president faced his most severe problems yet. (F)

MAIN IDEA

Analyzing Causes

(F) What factors contributed most to Clinton's reelection?

CLINTON IMPEACHED President Clinton was accused of improperly using money from a land deal with the Whitewater Development Company to fund his 1984 gubernatorial reelection campaign. In addition, Clinton allegedly had lied under oath about having an improper relationship with a young White House intern. In 1998, Clinton admitted that he had had an improper relationship with the young woman, but he denied lying about the incident under oath or attempting to obstruct the investigation.

In December 1998, the House of Representatives approved two articles of impeachment, charging the president with perjury and obstruction of justice. Clinton became only the second president—and the first in 130 years—to face a trial in the Senate. At the trial a month later, the Senate fell short of the 67 votes—a two-thirds majority—required to convict him. Clinton remained in office and apologized for his actions.

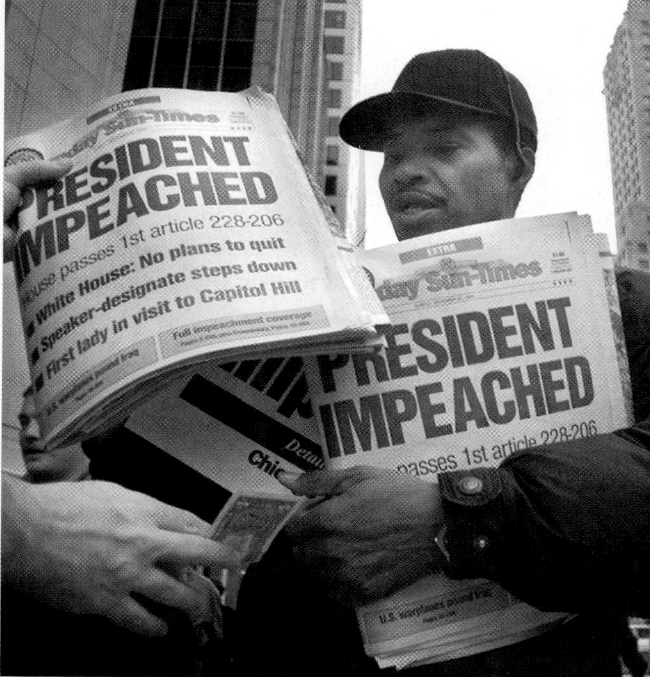

Chicago newspaper headlines leave no doubt about President Clinton's impeachment.

The Race for the White House

In the 2000 presidential race, the Democrats chose Vice President **Al Gore** to succeed Bill Clinton. The Republicans nominated **George W. Bush,** governor of Texas and the son of the former president. Ralph Nader, a long-time consumer advocate, ran for the Green Party, which championed environmental causes and promoted an overall liberal agenda. On the eve of the election, polls showed that the race would be tight. In fact, the election proved one of the closest in U.S. history. Determining a winner would take over a month.

ELECTION NIGHT CONFUSION As election night unfolded, Al Gore appeared to take the lead. The television networks projected that he would win Florida, Pennsylvania, and Michigan—states rich in electoral votes that would ultimately decide the winner of the race. Then, in a stunning turn of events, the TV networks recanted their original projection about Gore's victory in Florida and proclaimed the state "too close to call."

As midnight passed, it became clear that whoever won Florida would gain the 270 electoral votes needed to win the election. About 2 A.M., the networks predicted Bush the winner of Florida—and thus the presidency. However, as the final votes in Florida rolled in, Bush's lead shrank considerably and the state again became too close to call. By the next day, Al Gore had won the popular vote by more than 500,000 votes out of 105 million cast across the nation. Meanwhile, George Bush's razor-thin victory in Florida triggered an automatic recount.

DISPUTE RAGES IN FLORIDA In the weeks following the election, lawyers and spokespersons went to Florida to try to secure victory. The recount of the state's ballots gave Bush a win by just over 500 votes—but the battle for the presidency did not end there. The Gore campaign requested manual recounts in four mostly Democratic counties. Bush representatives opposed the manual recounts. James A. Baker III, former secretary of state and leader of the Bush team in Florida, argued that such recounts would raise the possibility of political mischief.

▶ More than a month after the votes were cast, Al Gore concedes the 2000 presidential election.

MAIN IDEA

Analyzing Issues

G How did the election of 2000 highlight both the weaknesses and the strengths of America's election process?

THE BATTLE MOVES TO THE COURTS As the manual recounting began on November 12, the Republicans sued to stop the recounts; a month-long court fight followed. The battle ultimately reached the Supreme Court. On December 12, the court voted 5 to 4 to stop the recounts, thus awarding the Florida electoral votes and the presidency to Bush. The justices argued that manual recounts lacked uniform standards and, therefore, violated equal protection for voters. G

The Bush Administration

After the protests and legal actions subsided, George W. Bush was inaugurated as the 43rd president of the United States on January 20, 2001. Bush inherited several challenges, including a weakening national economy and an energy problem in California.

During his first months as president, Bush began to advance his political agenda. He declared plans to reform the federal role in education and to privatize Social Security. Bush also proposed a $1.35 trillion tax cut, which became law in June 2001.

ANTITERRORIST MEASURES The political landscape changed dramatically after the September 11 terrorist attacks. The Bush administration, now with the overwhelming support of Congress and the American people, shifted its energy and attention to combating terrorism.

In October 2001, Bush signed an antiterrorism bill into law. The law allowed the government to detain foreigners suspected of terrorism for seven days without charging them with a crime. By the following month, Bush had created the Department of Homeland Security, a government body set up to coordinate national efforts to combat terrorism. In addition, the federal government increased its involvement in aviation security.

KEY PLAYER

GEORGE W. BUSH, 1946–

George W. Bush was born into a family steeped in politics. His father, George H. W. Bush, was the 41st president of the United States (1989–1993). However, George W. Bush did not immediately follow in his father's political footsteps. In 1975, he started an oil company in Midland, Texas. For a time, he also was part owner of the Texas Rangers baseball team.

Eventually, Bush was elected governor of Texas in 1994. Six years later, he became the 43rd president of the United States. He won reelection in 2004.

The Bush Administration also began waging a war against terrorism. In October 2001, coalition forces led by the United States began bombing Afghanistan. The Afghan government was harboring Osama bin Laden and his al-Qaeda terrorist network believed responsible for the September 11 attacks. In 2002, the coalition successfully broke up the al-Qaeda network in Afghanistan. Osama bin Laden, however, remained at large. (See the first issue in "Issues for the 21st Century," on page 894.) Nonetheless, the Bush administration gained widespread public approval for the decisive steps taken. H

MAIN IDEA

Evaluating Leadership

H How do you think the American people responded to Bush's antiterrorist measures?

Bush also scored a major success when direct elections were held for the first time in Afghanistan in October 2004. The Afghan people elected interim president Hamid Karzai as their first democratically elected president. Although Afghanistan still faced many problems, the elections were considered a positive move toward resolving them.

▲ **Hamid Karzai is victorious in Afghanistan's first direct presidential election.**

WAR AGAINST IRAQ In 2003, Bush expanded the war on terrorism to Iraq. Following the Persian Gulf War, Iraq had agreed to UN demands to stop the production of biological, chemical, and nuclear weapons. However, throughout the 1990s, the leader of Iraq, Saddam Hussein, refused to cooperate with UN arms inspectors and eventually barred them from entering his country.

After the September 11 attacks, Bush feared that Hussein was supplying terrorists with weapons of mass destruction (WMD) and called for renewed arms inspections in Iraq. But Hussein refused to cooperate fully with the renewed inspection process. The United States and Great Britain then ended diplomacy with Iraq and ordered Hussein to leave the country.

When Hussein refused to give up control, U.S. and British forces invaded Iraq in March 2003. Within a month, Iraq's forces were defeated and Hussein had gone into hiding. U.S. forces then began an intensive search for WMD in Iraq. No trace of chemical or biological weaponry were found. However, in December 2003, U.S. forces captured Saddam Hussein after they found him hiding in a hole in the ground. The former dictator was handed over to the Iraqis to stand trial for crimes against humanity. (See the second issue in "Issues for the 21st Century," on page 898.)

DOMESTIC AGENDA Meanwhile, on the home front, President Bush concentrated on education and the economy. He signed into law an education reform plan entitled No Child Left Behind. This plan called for more accountability by states for students' success, mandatory achievement testing, and more school options available for parents.

The economy posed a greater challenge, as corporate scandals, such as those related to such highly successful companies as Enron and WorldCom, rocked the nation. Congress responded to these corporate scandals by passing the Sarbanes-Oxley Act. This act established a regulatory board to oversee the accounting industry and its involvement with corporations. The scandals caused investors to lose faith in corporations, which had a negative effect on an already sluggish U.S. economy.

In 2003, Congress passed and Bush signed into law a $350 billion tax cut. Bush claimed that the tax cut would help the sagging economy and create jobs. Democrats opposed the cuts, saying they would mostly benefit the rich. The Democrats were overruled, however, because the Republican Party had gained control of Congress in the 2002 election. Now the Republicans held 51 of 100 seats in the Senate and 229 of 435 seats in the House of Representatives.

Republicans Gain More Power

▲ This family is among the thousands left homeless by Hurricane Katrina, which devastated the New Orleans region in August 2005.

Two more elections garnered even more power for the Republicans. The party expanded its influence at the state level in a rare recall election in California in 2003. The Republicans then consolidated their control of the White House with the reelection of George W. Bush in 2004.

CALIFORNIA RECALL The economic problems that had rocked the country were especially acute in California. These problems, as well as a statewide electricity crisis, caused many Californians to lose confidence in Democratic governor Gray Davis. Nonetheless, he was reelected in 2002 by a slim margin.

Early the next year, however, Davis opponents began petitioning for a recall vote under state law to remove the governor from office. Eventually, they gathered more than 1.3 million signatures—enough to force a recall election. On October 7, 2003, more than 55 percent of voters chose to recall Davis. In the highly publicized gubernatorial election that followed, the well-known actor Arnold Schwarzenegger defeated 134 other candidates, capturing over 48 percent of the vote.

BUSH REELECTED IN 2004 Although President Bush had received much initial support for the war on terrorism that he began waging after the September 11 attacks, many Americans had come to question his decision to invade Iraq. They were dismayed by the daily reports of violence and chaos in the country and the failure to find weapons of mass destruction there. In 2004, the Democrats chose Massachusetts senator John Kerry to challenge Bush. Once again, Bush found himself in a presidential race that deeply divided the nation. However, this time, Bush won a majority of the popular vote. After taking the lead in Ohio, he also won the electoral vote, which ensured him reelection.

ASSESSMENT

1. **TERMS & NAMES** For each term or name, write a sentence explaining its significance.
   - **William Jefferson Clinton**
   - **H. Ross Perot**
   - **Hillary Rodham Clinton**
   - **North American Free Trade Agreement (NAFTA)**
   - **Newt Gingrich**
   - **Contract with America**
   - **Al Gore**
   - **George W. Bush**

MAIN IDEA

2. **TAKING NOTES**
   Create a time line of President Clinton's major actions during his two terms. Use a form such as the one below.

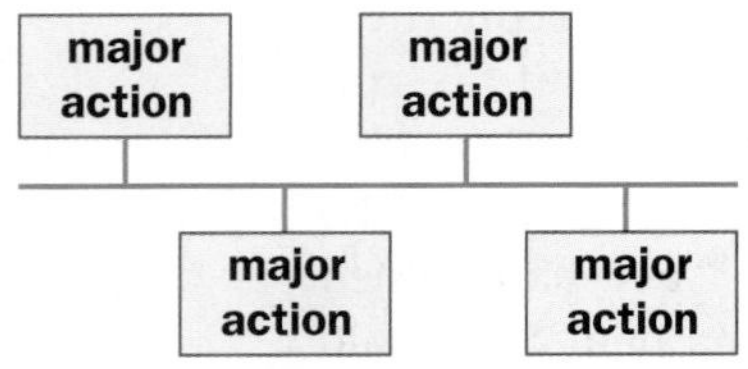

Explain whether each action was a success or a failure for Clinton.

CRITICAL THINKING

3. **EVALUATING**
   What event or trend during the Clinton administration do you think will have the most lasting impact on the United States? Why?

4. **ANALYZING MOTIVES**
   Why did the Gore campaign support manual recounts in Florida and the Bush campaign oppose them?

5. **EVALUATING DECISIONS**
   Do you think President Bush's decision to invade Iraq was justified? Explain why or why not.
   Think About:
   - arms inspections in Iraq
   - fear created by the September 11 attacks
   - the search for WMD

The New Global Economy

MAIN IDEA

Because of technological advances and new trade laws, the U.S. economy underwent a boom during the late 20th century.

WHY IT MATTERS NOW

New types of business have meant new work environments and new challenges for American workers.

Terms & Names

- **service sector**
- **downsize**
- **Bill Gates**
- **NASDAQ**
- **dotcom**
- **General Agreement on Tariffs and Trade (GATT)**

One American's Story

As Bill Clinton took office in 1993, some regions of the nation, particularly the Northeast, were still in an economic recession. Near Kennebunkport, Maine, the John Roberts clothing factory faced bankruptcy. With help from their union, the factory workers were able to turn their factory into an employee-owned company.

Ethel Beaudoin, who worked for the company for more than 30 years, was relieved that the plant would not be closing.

▲ **Workers at the John Roberts clothing factory**

A PERSONAL VOICE ETHEL BEAUDOIN

"It's a nice feeling to be part of the process . . . of deciding what this company buys for machinery and to know the customers more intimately. They're our customers, and it's a nicer feeling when the customers know that the coat that we put out is made by owners."

—quoted in *Divided We Fall*

Beaudoin's experience offered one example of the economic possibilities in America. A new global economy—brought about by new technologies, increased international competition, and the end of the Cold War—changed the nation's economic prospects.

The Shifting Economy

Americans heard a great deal of good news about the economy. Millions of new jobs were created between 1993 and 1999. By the fall of 2000, the unemployment rate had fallen to the lowest it had been since 1970.

ECONOMIC BACKGROUND

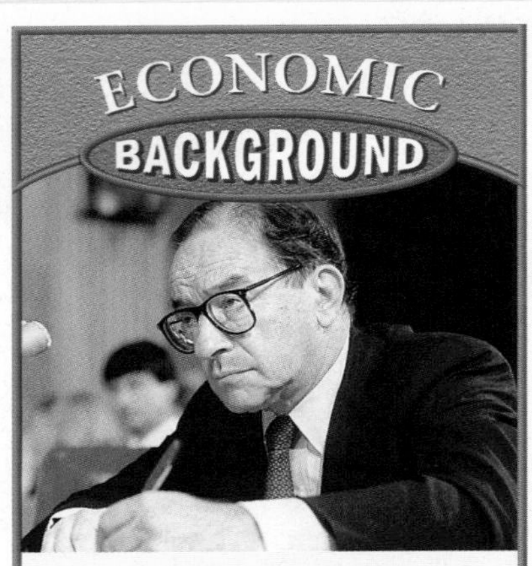

GREENSPAN AND THE FED

Alan Greenspan has been chairman of the Federal Reserve System (the Fed) since 1987, when he was appointed by President Ronald Reagan. The Fed has been described as the economic pacemaker of the United States because it helps determine how much money there will be in the American economy.

Before being elected president in 2000, George W. Bush made it a point to meet with Alan Greenspan before meeting with anyone else in Washington. (See *interest rate* in the Economics Handbook, page R42.)

But there was alarming news as well. Wage inequality between upper- and lower-income Americans—the income gap—widened. Median household income began to drop. Although economists disagreed about the reasons for the economy's instability, most everyone agreed it was undergoing significant changes.

MORE SERVICE, LESS SECURITY Chief among the far-reaching changes in the workplace of the 1990s was the explosive growth of jobs in the **service sector,** the part of the economy that provides services to consumers. By 2000, nearly 80 percent of American workers were teachers, medical professionals, lawyers, engineers, store clerks, waitstaff, and other service workers.

Low-paying jobs, such as sales and fast-food, grew fastest. These positions, often part-time or temporary, offered limited benefits. Many corporations, rather than invest in salaries and benefits for full-time staff, instead hired temporary workers, or temps, and began to **downsize**—trim payrolls to streamline operations and increase profits. Manpower, Inc., a temporary services agency, became the largest U.S. employer, earning $2 billion in 1993 when fully 640,000 Americans cashed its paychecks. In 1998, over one-fourth of the nation's work force worked in temporary or part-time positions. (A)

MAIN IDEA

Summarizing

(A) How did the change from an industrial economy to a service economy affect Americans' economic security?

Of those cut in downsizing, younger workers suffered higher rates of unemployment. In 1999, an average 11 percent of workers aged 16 to 24 were unemployed—more than double the national rate. Three out of four young Americans expected to earn less money as adults than their parents did.

FARMS AND FACTORIES The nation's shift to a service economy came at the expense of America's traditional workplaces. Manufacturing, which surpassed farming midcentury as the largest job sector, experienced a sharp decline in the 1980s and 1990s. In 1992, for example, 140,000 steelworkers did the same work that 240,000 had accomplished ten years earlier. Larry Pugh talked about the downsizing of a farm equipment factory in his hometown of Waterloo, Iowa.

A PERSONAL VOICE LARRY PUGH

"There used to be 17,500 people working here. . . . Now there are 6000. Those people spent their money. They bought the cars. They bought the houses. They were replaced by people that are at the minimum wage—seven or eight dollars an hour, not 15 or 20 dollars an hour. These people can hardly eke out a living at today's wages."

—quoted in *Divided We Fall*

The decline in industrial jobs contributed to a drop in union membership. In 1945, 35 percent of American workers belonged to unions; by 1998, only 14 percent were union members. In the 1990s, unions had trouble organizing. High-tech and professional workers felt no need for unions, while low-wage service employees feared losing their jobs in a strike. Some workers saw their incomes decline. The increased use of computer-driven robots to make manufactured goods eliminated many jobs, but it also spurred a vibrant high-tech economy. Those with advanced training and specialized technical skills or a sense of entrepreneurial risk-taking saw their salaries rise and their economic security expand. (B)

MAIN IDEA

Analyzing Effects

(B) How did downsizing affect people?

Persons Employed in Three Economic Sectors*			
Year	Farming	Manufacturing	Service Producing
1900	11,050	7,252	6,832
1950	6,001	18,475	20,721
2006 (projected)	3,618	24,451	111,867

*numbers in millions

Sources: *Historical Statistics of the United States, Colonial Times to 1970; Statistical Abstracts of the United States, 1953, 1954, 1999*

SKILLBUILDER Interpreting Charts

1. What sector of the U.S. economy has seen the greatest decline in workers over the past century?
2. In terms of employee participation, by roughly what percent is the service sector expected to grow between 1950 and 2006?

HIGH-TECH INDUSTRIES In the late 1990s, entrepreneurs turned innovative ideas about computer technology into huge personal fortunes, hoping to follow in the footsteps of **Bill Gates,** the decade's most celebrated entrepreneur. Gates founded the software company Microsoft. In 2000, it had made him the wealthiest individual in the world, with assets estimated at about $60 billion.

A rapid outcropping of new businesses accompanied the explosive growth of the Internet late in the decade. The **NASDAQ** (National Association of Securities Dealers Automated Quotation System), a technology-dominated stock index on Wall Street, rose dramatically as enthusiasm grew for high-tech businesses. These businesses were known as **dotcoms,** a nickname derived from their identities, or addresses, on the World Wide Web, which often ended in ".com." The dotcoms expanded rapidly and attracted young talent and at times excessive investment funding for such untested fledgling companies.

Background
See *e-commerce* on page R40 in the Economics Handbook.

Thousands of smaller businesses were quick to anticipate the changes that the Internet would bring. Suddenly companies could work directly with consumers or with other companies. Many predicted that the price of doing business would fall dramatically and that overall worldwide productivity would jump dramatically. The boom of new business was termed "The New Economy."

However, the positive economic outlook fueled by "The New Economy" was short lived. In 2000, only 38 percent of online retailing made a profit. As a result, many dotcoms went out of business. This decline had many causes. Entrepreneurs often provided inadequate advertising for their e-companies. Also, many dotcoms had hard-to-use Web sites that confused customers. The unsuccessful dotcoms caused many investors to stop putting money in Internet businesses.

In 2002, the U.S. economy was also hard hit by corporate scandals, when Enron was charged with using illegal accounting practices and WorldCom filed the largest bankruptcy claim in U.S. history. These and other corporate scandals caused investors to lose faith in corporations. In addition, after the September 11 attacks, the continued threat of terrorism had a negative effect on the economy. All of these factors caused the NASDAQ index to decline for three straight years (2000–2002). The Dow Jones Industrial Average fell 16.8 percent in 2002.

At 18 years old, Shawn Fanning started a free music downloading service on the Internet called Napster. He became a multimillionaire after forming an alliance with a German media company. ▼

World Trading Blocs, 2000

GEOGRAPHY SKILLBUILDER

1. **Location** What is the only G-8 country located outside Europe and North America?
2. **Location** To which world trade organizations does the United States belong?

Change and the Global Economy

In 1900, airplanes hadn't yet flown and telephone service was barely 20 years old. U.S. trade with the rest of the world was worth about $2.2 billion (roughly 12 percent of the economy). Nearly a century later, New Yorkers could hop a supersonic jet and arrive in London within three hours, information traveled instantly by fax machines and computers, and U.S. trade with other countries approached $2 trillion (more than 25 percent of the economy). As American companies competed for international and domestic markets, American workers felt the sting of competing with workers in other countries.

INTERNATIONAL TRADE The expansion of U.S. trade abroad was an important goal of President Clinton's foreign policy, as his support of NAFTA had shown. In 1994, in response to increasing international economic competition among trading blocs, the United States joined many other nations in adopting a new version of the **General Agreement on Tariffs and Trade (GATT)**. The new treaty lowered trade barriers, such as tariffs, and established the World Trade Organization (WTO) to resolve trade disputes. As President Clinton announced at the 1994 meeting of the Group of Seven, (the world's seven leading economic powers, which later became the Group of Eight when Russia joined in 1996), "[T]rade as much as troops will increasingly define the ties that bind nations in the twenty-first century."

Background
"Job flight" had occurred in the 1970s, when cheap but quality auto imports from Japan and Germany forced many U.S. workers out of high-paying jobs.

INTERNATIONAL COMPETITION International trade agreements caused some American workers to worry about massive job flight to countries that produced the same goods as the United States but at a lower cost.

In the 1990s, U.S. businesses frequently moved their operations to less economically advanced countries, such as Mexico, where wages were lower. After the passage of NAFTA, more than 100,000 low-wage jobs were lost in U.S. manufacturing industries such as apparel, auto parts, and electronics. Also, competition with foreign companies caused many U.S. companies to maintain low wages. C

MAIN IDEA
Analyzing Effects
C What were some of the effects of NAFTA and GATT?

In Montreal, Canada, on March 29, 2001, protesters demonstrate at a summit on globalization and the Free Trade Area of the Americas (FTAA).

INTERNATIONAL SLOWDOWN Around the turn of the 21st century, the global economy began to slow down. Between 1997 and 2002, the gross domestic product in Japan declined by 6 percent. In 2001, the economies of more than a dozen countries were in recession, and many other countries reported lower growth rates than they had the previous year.

The flow of foreign direct investment (FDI) to developing countries declined dramatically. As a result, the economies of these countries were particularly hard hit. For example, the overall growth of Africa's economies slowed to 2.7 percent in 2002.

The U.S. economy also suffered. During April 2002, factory orders declined 2.9 percent, the largest drop in 17 months. Because of the size of the U.S. economy, many financial analysts believed that an economic resurgence in the United States would be vital to the recovery of the global economy.

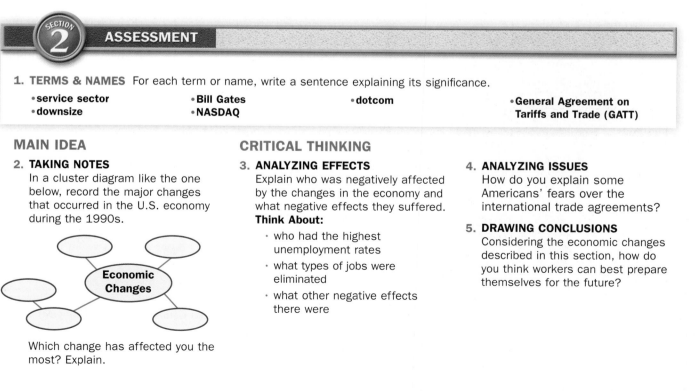

SECTION 2 ASSESSMENT

1. **TERMS & NAMES** For each term or name, write a sentence explaining its significance.
   - **service sector**
   - **downsize**
   - **Bill Gates**
   - **NASDAQ**
   - **dotcom**
   - **General Agreement on Tariffs and Trade (GATT)**

MAIN IDEA

2. **TAKING NOTES**
In a cluster diagram like the one below, record the major changes that occurred in the U.S. economy during the 1990s.

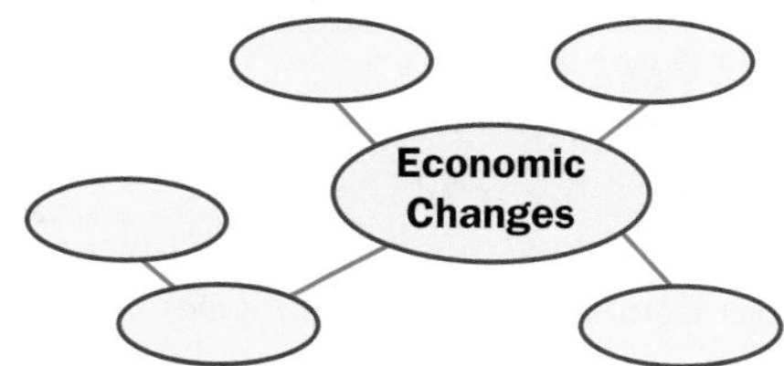

Which change has affected you the most? Explain.

CRITICAL THINKING

3. **ANALYZING EFFECTS**
Explain who was negatively affected by the changes in the economy and what negative effects they suffered.
Think About:
   - who had the highest unemployment rates
   - what types of jobs were eliminated
   - what other negative effects there were

4. **ANALYZING ISSUES**
How do you explain some Americans' fears over the international trade agreements?

5. **DRAWING CONCLUSIONS**
Considering the economic changes described in this section, how do you think workers can best prepare themselves for the future?

Women Writers Reflect American Diversity

1978–2000 The broadening of opportunities for American women that began in the 1970s is as evident in literature as it is in other fields. Toni Morrison, Mary Oliver, Nikki Giovanni, Amy Tan, Anne Tyler, Alice Walker, Marge Piercy, Sandra Cisneros—these are just a few of the talented women novelists and poets who reflect the multicultural nature of the American identity. These women's writing shares a common characteristic—that of conveying the American experience through the exploration of personal memories, nature, childhood, and family.

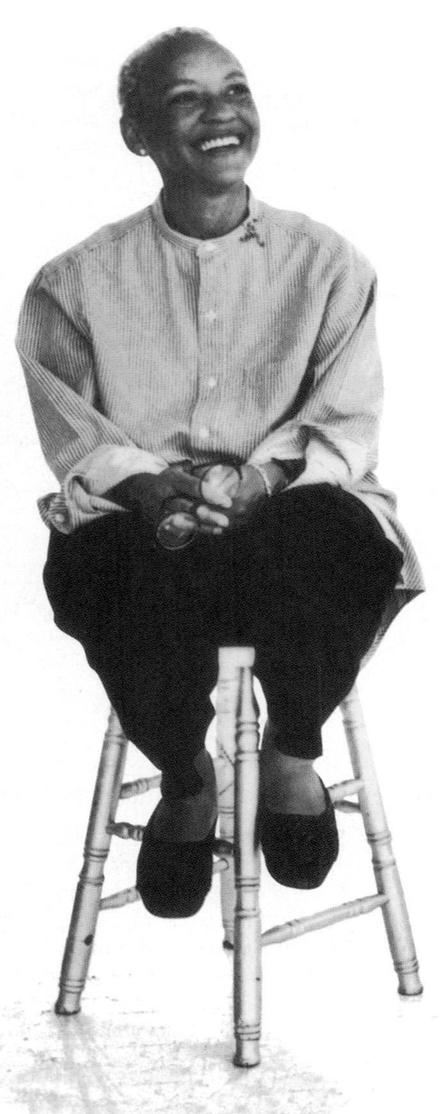

◄ **NIKKI GIOVANNI**
In the late 1960s, Nikki Giovanni won instant attention as an African American poet writing about the Black Power movement. Since then her poetry has often focused on childhood, family ties, and other personal concerns. In the following poem, Giovanni deals with individual empowerment—even under less than ideal circumstances.

Choices

if i can't do
what i want to do
then my job is to not
do what i don't want
to do

it's not the same thing
but it's the best i can
do

if i can't have
what i want then
my job is to want
what i've got
and be satisfied
that at least there
is something more
to want

since i can't go
where i need
to go then i must go
where the signs point
though always understanding
parallel movement
isn't lateral

when i can't express
what i really feel
i practice feeling
what i can express
and none of it is equal
i know
but that's why mankind
alone among the mammals
learns to cry

—Nikki Giovanni,
"Choices," from *Cotton Candy on a Rainy Day* (1978)

AMY TAN

A native of Oakland, California, Amy Tan draws on personal experiences in *The Joy Luck Club*, a series of interconnected stories about four Chinese-American daughters and their immigrant mothers. The four mothers establish a club for socializing and playing the game of mahjong.

My mother started the San Francisco version of the Joy Luck Club in 1949, two years before I was born. This was the year my mother and father left China with one stiff leather trunk filled only with fancy silk dresses. There was no time to pack anything else, my mother had explained to my father after they boarded the boat. Still his hands swam frantically between the slippery silks, looking for his cotton shirts and wool pants.

When they arrived in San Francisco, my father made her hide those shiny clothes. She wore the same brown-checked Chinese dress until the Refugee Welcome Society gave her two hand-me-down dresses, all too large in sizes for American women. The society was composed of a group of white-haired American missionary ladies from the First Chinese Baptist Church. And because of their gifts, my parents could not refuse their invitation to join the church. Nor could they ignore the old ladies' practical advice to improve their English through Bible study class on Wednesday nights and, later, through choir practice on Saturday mornings. This was how my parents met the Hsus, the Jongs, and the St. Clairs. My mother could sense that the women of these families also had unspeakable tragedies they had left behind in China and hopes they couldn't begin to express in their fragile English. Or at least, my mother recognized the numbness in these women's faces. And she saw how quickly their eyes moved when she told them her idea for the Joy Luck Club.

—Amy Tan, *The Joy Luck Club* (1989)

SANDRA CISNEROS ▶

Sandra Cisneros is one of many Chicana writers to win fame in recent years. In *The House on Mango Street*, she traces the experiences of a poor Hispanic girl named Esperanza (Spanish for *hope*) and her warm-hearted family. Nenny is her sister.

Four Skinny Trees

They are the only ones who understand me. I am the only one who understands them. Four skinny trees with skinny necks and pointy elbows like mine. Four who do not belong here but are here. Four raggedy excuses planted by the city. From our room we can hear them, but Nenny just sleeps and doesn't appreciate these things.

Their strength is secret. They send ferocious roots beneath the ground. They grow up and they grow down and grab the earth between their hairy toes and bite the sky with violent teeth and never quit their anger. This is how they keep.

Let one forget his reason for being, they'd all droop like tulips in a glass, each with their arms around the other. Keep, keep, keep, trees say when I sleep. They teach.

When I am too sad and too skinny to keep keeping, when I am a tiny thing against so many bricks, then it is I look at trees. When there is nothing left to look at on this street. Four who grew despite concrete. Four who reach and do not forget to reach. Four whose only reason is to be and be.

—Sandra Cisneros
The House on Mango Street (1989)

THINKING CRITICALLY

1. **Comparing** From these selections, what can you infer about women's experiences in American life today? Cite passages to support your response.

SEE SKILLBUILDER HANDBOOK, PAGE R8.

2. **INTERNET ACTIVITY** **CLASSZONE.COM**
Visit the links for American Literature to find and choose selections for an anthology of writing by three contemporary American women. Write a "capsule biography" summarizing each writer's background and achievements.

Technology and Modern Life

MAIN IDEA

Advances in technology have increased the pace but also the comfort of many Americans' daily lives.

WHY IT MATTERS NOW

Providing access to the new technology and regulating its use are two current challenges facing 21st-century America.

Terms & Names

- **information superhighway**
- **Internet**
- **telecommute**
- **Telecommunications Act Of 1996**
- **genetic engineering**

One American's Story

The crowds stand four-deep cheering for 12-year-old Rudy Garcia-Tolson as he captures a new national record for his age group at the San Diego half-marathon. Despite the loss of his legs, Rudy competes in sports and is headed for the 2004 paralympics.

For years, Rudy was confined to a wheelchair. After undergoing a double amputation he was fitted with carbon fiber prostheses—artificial replacements for missing body parts. These lightweight, strong, and durable new legs now make many things possible for Rudy.

A PERSONAL VOICE RUDY GARCIA-TOLSON

"I told them to cut my legs off. I saw pictures of people running with prosthetic legs. I didn't want to stay in a wheelchair. . . . My legs won't stop me. Nothing stops me. . . . I like to show kids that there's no limitations—kids or challenged people or adults, there's no limitations to what a person can do. . . . My motto is, if you have a brave heart, that's a powerful weapon."

—quoted in *Press-Enterprise*, January 1, 2000

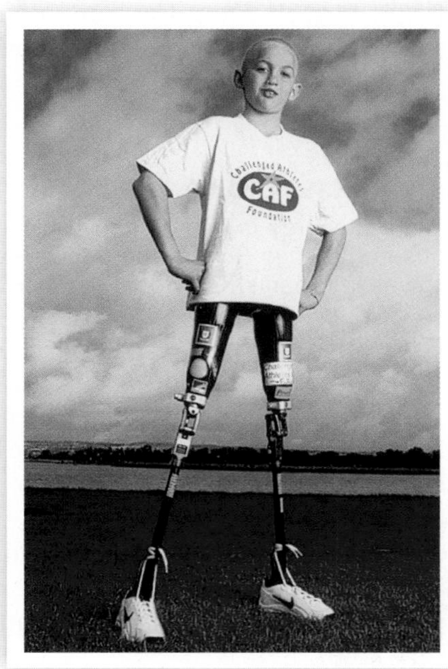

Rudy Garcia-Tolson, 2001

Advances in medical technology have permitted Rudy to live a more fully active life. Throughout the 20th century and into the 21st, technological developments helped Americans become more active in many ways.

The Communications Revolution

The computer industry transformed the 1980s. Instead of giant mainframes and minicomputers, desktop workstations now ruled business. Home computers became widely available, and many thousands of people joined online subscription services that provided electronic mail and magazine-style information.

Analyzing *Political Cartoons*

"VACATION, 2000"

By the end of the 20th century, millions of Americans owned any number of personal communication devices. People were able to speak to or correspond with each other instantaneously almost anytime, almost anywhere. The cartoon suggests that Americans are dependent on their communication devices, and that the once relaxing and peaceful family vacation has given way to the hustle and bustle of constant access.

SKILLBUILDER
Analyzing Political Cartoons

1. What modern-day communication devices are being used in this cartoon?
2. In what ways do the characters in this cartoon seem trapped by modern-day communications technology?

SEE SKILLBUILDER HANDBOOK, PAGE R24.

ENTERING THE INFORMATION AGE The **information superhighway**—a network of communication devices linking people and institutions across the nation and the world—promised to advance the revolution that had begun with the personal computer. In 1994, Vice President Al Gore began to oversee the government's participation in developing this superhighway. Even though private industries would build the superhighway, the government would keep access democratic, ensure affordable service for everyone, protect privacy and property rights, and develop incentives for investors.

The 1990s enjoyed explosive growth of the **Internet,** an international network linking computers and allowing almost instant transmittal of text, images, and sound. Originally developed in the late 1960s by the U.S. Department of Defense for defense research, the Internet drew early popularity at universities. By the mid-1990s *Internet* became a household word. Use of the network was further popularized by the World Wide Web, which provided a simple visual interface for words and pictures to be seen by an unlimited audience. As businesses, schools, and organizations began to use the Web as a primary form of communication, new forms of social interaction emerged. Users developed "electronic presence" in virtual worlds, fantasy environments created with electronics.

Vocabulary
interface: the point of communication between a computer and any other entity, such as a printer or human operator

NEW TOOLS, NEW MEDIA Through an electronic connection, such as a TV cable or phone line, users accessed an array of media, from streaming video to research archives, from on-line shopping catalogs to customized news broadcasts. Users could interact with each other across the world. By 2003, as many as 131 million Americans used the Internet regularly to send e-mail (electronic notes and messages), to share music, or to browse or search through "pages" on the Web. During the 1990s, classrooms across the nation increasingly used computer networking. By 2002, 92 percent of public-school classrooms offered Internet access. Long-distance video and audio transmissions also linked American students. Some content was delivered not on networks but stored on a CD-ROM (Compact Disc Read-Only Memory), which evolved from music CDs that contained code for sound waves. CD-ROMs also carry digital code for pictures, text, and animation to be played on a computer.

The late-20th-century advances in computers and communications have had an impact on American society and business comparable to the industrial developments of the late 1800s. Americans now have more entertainment options, as cable service has multiplied the number of television channels available and greater bandwidth offers the possibility for high-definition television. Because of cellular phones, fax machines, the Internet, and overnight shipping, people can more readily **telecommute,** or work out of their homes instead of going to an office every day. (A)

MAIN IDEA

Summarizing

(A) Explain the revolutionary nature of communicating via the Internet.

LEGISLATING TECHNOLOGY In the 1980s, the government was slow to recognize the implications of the new communications technology. In 1994, however, the Federal Communications Commission (FCC) began to auction the valuable rights to airwaves and collected over $9 billion. Then, with the rapid growth in the communications industry, the federal government took several steps to ensure that consumers received the best service. Congress passed the **Telecommunications Act of 1996,** removing barriers that had previously prevented one type of communications company from starting up or buying another related one. While it increased competition in the industry, the law also paved the way for major media mergers. When Capital Cities/ABC Inc. joined the Walt Disney Company, industry watchdogs noted that this reflected the trend toward concentrating media influence in the hands of a few powerful conglomerates.

The passage of the Telecommunications Act won applause from the communications industry but only mixed reviews from the public. Consumer activists worried that the law would fail to ensure equal access to new technologies for rural residents and poor people. Civil rights advocates contended that the Communications Decency Act (part of the Telecommunications Act) restricted free speech because it barred the transmission of "indecent" materials to minors via the Internet. In addition, Congress also called for a "V-chip" in television sets—a computer chip that would enable parents to block TV programs that they deemed inappropriate for their children. Parts of these laws were later struck down in court. (B)

MAIN IDEA

Predicting Effects

(B) How might the Telecommunications Act affect consumers?

Scientific Advances Enrich Lives

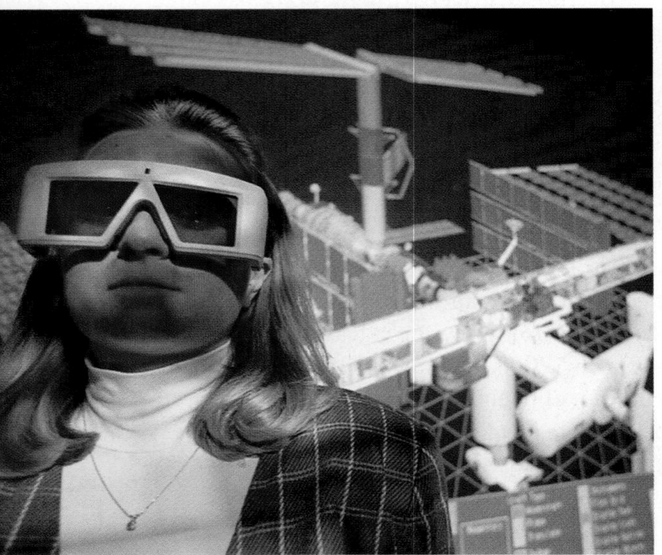

▲ **At NASA Langley Research Center in Virginia, an aerospace engineer wearing stereo glasses sees a 3-D view of a space station simulation, as shown in the background.**

The exciting growth in the telecommunications industry in the 1990s was matched by insights that revolutionized robotics, space exploration, and medicine. The world witnessed marvels that for many of the "baby boom generation," people born in the late 1940s and the 1950s, echoed science fiction.

SIMULATION, ROBOTICS, AND MACHINE INTELLIGENCE Visual imaging and artificial intelligence (a computer's ability to perform activities that require intelligence) were combined to provide applications in industry, medicine, and education. For example, virtual reality began with the flight simulators used to train military and commercial pilots. Today, with a headset that holds tiny video screens and earphones, and with a data glove that translates hand movements to a computer screen, a user can navigate a "virtual landscape." Doctors have used virtual reality to take a computerized tour of a patient's throat and lungs to check for medical problems. Surgeons have performed long-distance surgery through telepresence systems—gloves, computers, and robotic elements specially wired so that a doctor can operate on a patient hundreds of miles away. Architects and engineers have used virtual reality to create visual, rather than physical, models of their buildings, cars, and other designs. Modeling also affected the nightly newscast. Using supercomputers and improved satellite data, meteorologists could offer three-day weather forecasts that reached the accuracy of one-day forecasts of 1980.

As technology became more sophisticated, computers increased in capability. IBM's Deep Blue defeated chess champion Garry Kasparov in 1997. Computational linguists steadily improved natural language understanding in computers, thus fine-tuning the accuracy of voice recognition systems.

Robots grew more humanlike as engineers equipped them with high-capacity chips simulating brain function. By the year 2000, robots had the ability to walk on two legs, interact with people, learn taught behaviors, and express artificial feelings with facial gestures.

SPACE EXPLORATION In the 1990s, astronomy expanded our view of the universe. In 1997, NASA's *Pathfinder* and its rover *Sojourner* transmitted live pictures of the surface of Mars to millions of Internet users.

Shuttle missions, meanwhile, concentrated on scientific research and assembly, transport, and repair of orbiting objects, paving the way to possible human missions to Mars and other space travel in the coming century. NASA concentrated on working with other nations to build the *International Space Station (ISS)*. The *ISS* promised to offer scientists a zero-gravity laboratory for research in medicine, space mechanics and architecture, and long-term living in space. Ellen Ochoa, part of the first shuttle crew to dock to the *ISS,* hoped to inspire young students:

Background
The *International Space Station* was established by joining and expanding upon the Russian station, *Mir,* and the American *Spacelab.*

Dr. Ellen Ochoa

A Personal Voice ELLEN OCHOA

"I'm not trying to make everyone an astronaut, but I want students to think about a career and the preparation they'll need. . . . I tell students that the opportunities I had were a result of having a good educational background. Education is what allows you to stand out."

—quoted in *Stanford University School of Engineering Annual Report,* 1997–98.

Another shuttle crew in 1993 aboard the *Endeavour* repaired the Hubble Space Telescope, which returns dazzling intergalactic views. In late 1995, astronomers using observatories discovered a planet orbiting the fourth closest star to Earth, the first planet to be detected outside our own solar system. Since then dozens more have been detected. Astronomers back on Earth have also spent considerable effort tracking asteroids and comets whose paths might collide with our planet. Astrobiologists hailed the discovery on Antarctica of a small meteorite that traveled to Earth from Mars about 15 million years ago.

BIOTECHNOLOGY The most profound insight into the book of life came from the field of biotechnology. The Human Genome Project, an international effort to map the genes of the human body, and Celera, a private company in molecular biology, simultaneously announced in 2000 that they had sequenced nearly all of the human genome only a decade after the research began. Cooperation via the Internet and access to computerized databases by multiple research groups vastly accelerated the scientists' ability to identify and order over three billion chemical

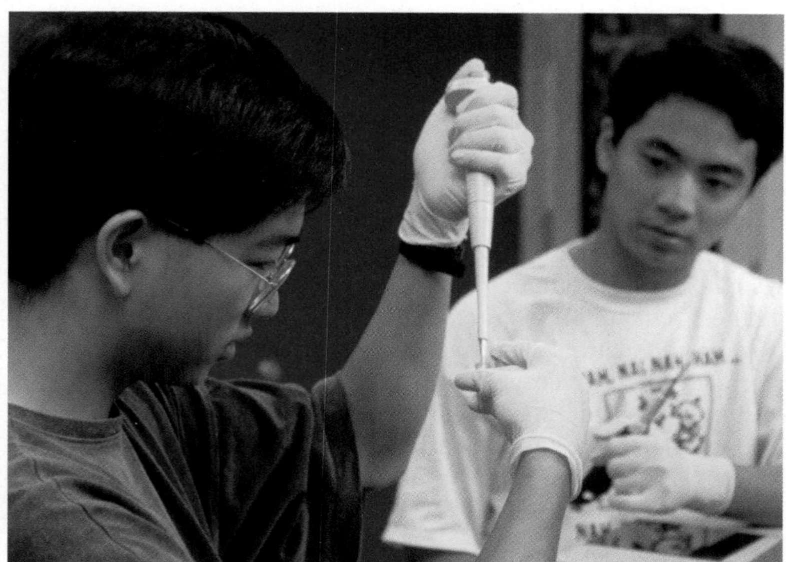

▲ **High school students Li-Ho *(left)* and Yu-Fong Hong *(right)*, among the youngest scientists to have worked on the Human Genome Project, are shown at a San Ramon, California, laboratory.**

"letters" of the genetic code of DNA. Molecular biologists hoped that this genetic map would offer the key to treating many inherited diseases and diagnosing congenital disabilities, and that drug makers could one day design pharmaceuticals for each patient's particular profile.

DNA had been in the spotlight before the breakthrough announcement. In well-publicized legal proceedings, prosecutors relied on DNA evidence to help prove the guilt of defendants who may have left behind a single hair at a crime scene. Others, wrongly imprisoned, were released when genetic analysis proved their innocence.

But different opinions arose over some of the new "biotechnology." Some speculated that technological progress outpaced social evolution and society's ability to grapple with the consequences. In 1997, Scottish researchers cloned Dolly the sheep from one cell of an adult sheep. Shortly thereafter, two Rhesus monkeys were cloned in Oregon, and many wondered whether human cloning was next. Firms sought to patent genes used for medical and research applications, using the principle of invention and property. Advances such as these, as well as gene therapy, artificial human chromosomes, and testing embryos for genetic defects all sparked heated debates among scientists, ethicists, religious leaders, and politicians.

The use of **genetic engineering**—the artificial changing of the molecular biology of organisms' cells to alter an organism—also aroused public concern. However, the Federal Department of Agriculture (FDA) holds that genetically engineered foods are safe and that they require no extra labeling. Scientists in the late 1990s modified corn and rice to provide resistance to pests and increase nutritional value. In 1996, the European Union limited the importation of such products in response to consumer pressure, allowing only those clearly labeled as having been genetically modified.

MEDICAL PROGRESS People suffering from some diseases benefited from advances in medicine in the 1990s. Cancer survival rates improved drastically as clinicians explored the use of gene therapy, genetically engineered antibodies, and immune system modulation. Improvements in tracking the spread of HIV—the virus that causes AIDS (acquired immune deficiency syndrome)—through the body made researchers better prepared to find a cure. AIDS patients were treated with combination therapies, and public health officials advocated abstinence and "safer sex" practices to control the spread of HIV.

Background
In 1998, fewer than 13,500 Americans died from AIDS, roughly one-third the 1992 number.

Improved technology for making medical diagnoses offered new hope as well. Magnetic resonance imaging (MRI), for example, was used to produce cross-sectional images of any part of the body. Advances that will make the MRI procedure ten times faster will also make MRI more widely available and cheaper to use. Medical researchers look ahead to using fleets of tiny "nanosensors" one-thousandth the width of a human hair to find tumors and to deploying "nanobots" to repair tissues and even genes. C

MAIN IDEA

Summarizing
C Describe how technology affected health care.

ALTERNATIVE CARS

In an effort to reduce the nation's dependence on fossil fuels, researchers have been working to develop a "cleaner" car, or one that runs on something other than gasoline. Such alternative models include an electric car, which uses a rechargable battery and gas power, and a vehicle that runs on compressed natural gas.

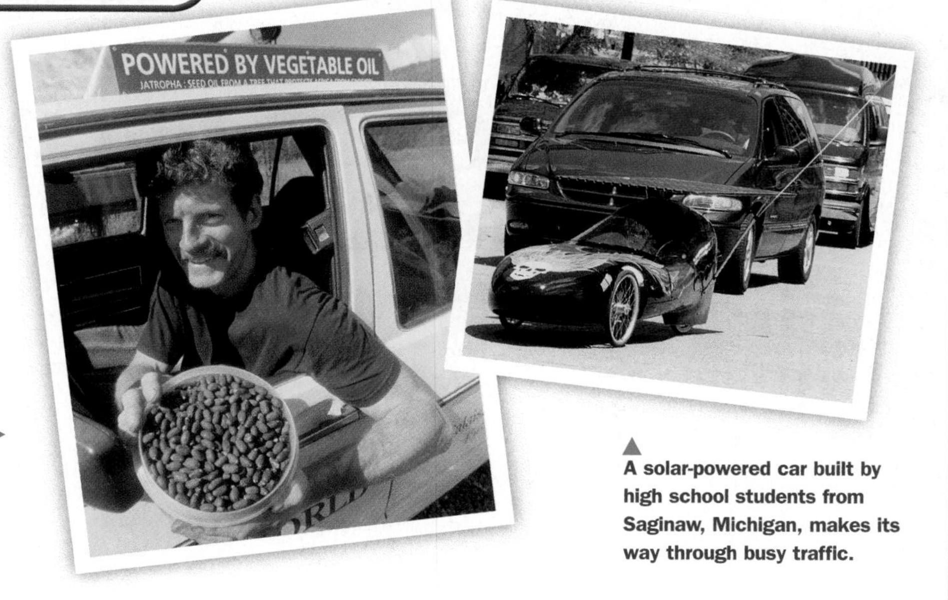

Carl Bielenberg of Calais, Vermont, holds a container of seeds of the jatropha plant. He runs his compact car on vegetable oil that is made from the seed.

A solar-powered car built by high school students from Saginaw, Michigan, makes its way through busy traffic.

ENVIRONMENTAL MEASURES With the spreading use of technology came greater concern about the impact of human activities on the natural environment. Scientists have continued examining ways to reduce American dependence on pollution-producing fossil fuels. Fossil fuels such as oil provided 85 percent of the energy in the United States in the 1990s but also contributed to poor air quality, acid rain, and global warming. Many individuals have tried to help by reducing consumption of raw materials. By the early 1990s, residents set out glass bottles and jars, plastic bottles, newspapers, phone books, cardboard, and aluminum cans for recycling at curbsides, and consumers purchased new products synthesized from recycled materials.

SECTION 3 ASSESSMENT

1. **TERMS & NAMES** For each term or name, write a sentence explaining its significance.
   - **information superhighway**
   - **Internet**
   - **telecommute**
   - **Telecommunications Act of 1996**
   - **genetic engineering**

MAIN IDEA

2. **TAKING NOTES**
   On a chart like the one shown, list four of the technological changes described in this section and explain how each change has affected your life.

Technological Change	Effect on Me
1.	
2.	
3.	
4.	

CRITICAL THINKING

3. **MAKING INFERENCES**
   Explain how government, business, and individuals are important to the existence of the information superhighway. **Think About:**
   - the costs of developing the superhighway
   - the equipment and personnel needed to maintain it
   - who uses the superhighway and why they use it

4. **ANALYZING ISSUES**
   Why is genetic engineering a source of controversy?

5. **EVALUATING**
   Which area of technological change described in this section do you think was the most important one for the country? Explain.

The Changing Face of America

MAIN IDEA	WHY IT MATTERS NOW	Terms & Names
At the end of the 20th century, the U.S. population grew more diverse both in ethnic background and in age.	**Americans of all backgrounds share common goals: the desire for equal rights and economic opportunity.**	**•urban flight •gentrification •Proposition 187**

One American's Story

Every ten years the United States conducts a census, or head count of its population. The results of the census determine, among other things, how billions of federal dollars are spent for housing, health care, and education over the coming decade. The Census Bureau estimates that the 1990 census undercounted Latinos by more than five percent. This undercount resulted in a loss of millions of dollars of aid to municipalities with large Latino populations, as well as denying Latinos political representation in all levels of government.

During the latest census conducted in 2000, Antonia Hernandez, President and General Counsel of the Mexican American Legal Defense and Education Fund (MALDEF), spearheaded the national *¡Hágase Contar!* Make Yourself Count! campaign. MALDEF workers canvassed neighborhoods urging residents to complete the census. They stressed that all information was confidential and discussed the high stakes of being counted.

Antonia Hernandez, MALDEF's president

A PERSONAL VOICE ANTONIA HERNANDEZ

"**The census not only measures our growth and marks our place in the community, but it is the first and indispensable step toward fair political representation, equal distribution of resources, and enforcement of our civil rights.**"

—Public statement for *¡Hágase Contar!* campaign, 2000

Data from the 2000 census revealed that the Hispanic population had grown by close to 58 percent since 1990, reaching 35.3 million. The 2000 census also confirmed a vast increase in what were once ethnic minorities.

Urban Flight

One of the most significant socio-cultural changes in American history has been the movement of Americans from the cities to the suburbs. The years after World War II through the 1980s saw a widespread pattern of **urban flight,** the process in which Americans left the cities and moved to the suburbs. At mid-century, the population of cities exceeded that of suburbs. By 1970, the ratio became even.

In the year 2000, after decades of decline, some major cities across the country had increased their populations while others slowed or halted declines. The transformation of the United States into a nation of suburbs had intensified the problems of the cities.

CAUSES OF URBAN CHANGE Several factors contributed to the movement of Americans out of the cities. Because of the continued movement of job-seeking Americans into urban areas in the 1950s and 1960s, many urban American neighborhoods became overcrowded. Overcrowding in turn contributed to such urban problems as increasing crime rates and decaying housing.

During the 1970s and early 1980s, city dwellers who could afford to do so moved to the suburbs for more space, privacy, and security. Often, families left the cities because suburbs offered newer, less crowded schools. As many middle-class Americans left cities for the suburbs, the economic base of many urban neighborhoods declined, and suburbs grew wealthy. Following the well-educated labor force, more industries relocated to suburban areas in the 1990s. The economic base that provided tax money and supported city services in large cities such as New York, Detroit, and Philadelphia continued to shrink as people and jobs moved outward.

MAIN IDEA

Analyzing Causes

A List the factors that influenced middle-class residents to leave cities for suburbs.

In addition, many downtown districts fell into disrepair as suburban shoppers abandoned city stores for suburban shopping malls. According to the 1990 census, the 31 most impoverished communities in the United States were in cities. **A**

By the mid-1990s, however, as the property values in the nation's inner cities declined, many people returned to live there. In a process known as **gentrification,** they purchased and rehabilitated deteriorating urban property, oftentimes displacing lower income people. Old industrial sites and neighborhoods in locations convenient to downtown became popular, especially among young, single adults who preferred the excitement of city life and the uniqueness of urban neighborhoods to the often more uniform environment of the suburbs.

History Through *Architecture*

REBUILDING THE RIVERFRONTS

As part of the effort to revitalize cities, a number of architects, landscape architects, and urban planners have focused on enhancing what for many urban centers had become a neglected eyesore—their waterfronts. In Pittsburgh, landscape architects turned a dreary strip of concrete and parking lot into Allegheny Riverfront Park, an inviting stretch of natural walkways and recreation areas.

SKILLBUILDER

Interpreting Visual Sources

1. Why might landscape architects consider improving riverfronts to be a key part of revitalizing cities?
2. In what other ways could architects and urban designers make city living more attractive?

SEE SKILLBUILDER HANDBOOK, PAGE R23.

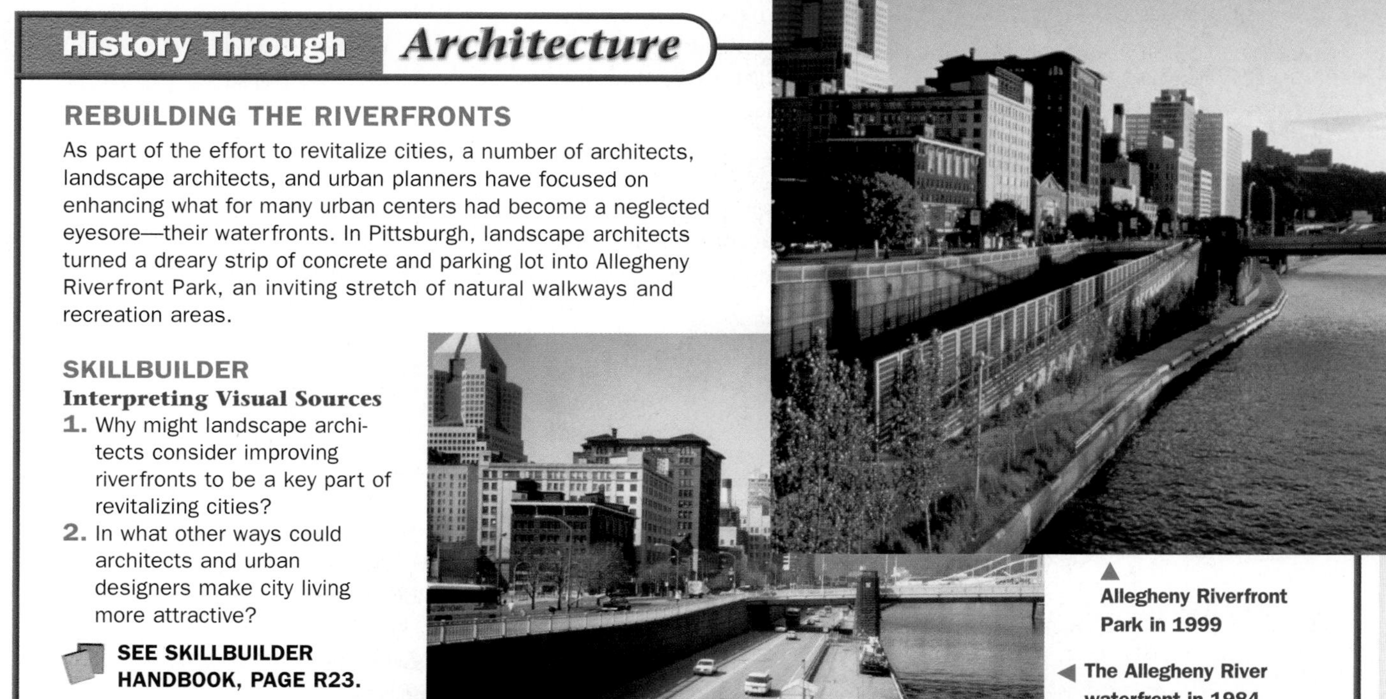

▲ Allegheny Riverfront Park in 1999

◀ The Allegheny River waterfront in 1984

SUBURBAN LIVING While many suburbanites continued to commute to city jobs during the 1990s, increasing numbers of workers began to telecommute, or use new communications technology, such as computers, modems, and fax machines, to work from their homes. Another notable trend was the movement of minority populations to the suburbs. Nationwide, by the early 1990s, about 43 percent of the Latino population and more than half of the Asian-American population lived in suburbs.

Suburban growth led to intense competition between suburbs and cities, and among the suburbs themselves, for business and industry. Since low-rise suburban homes yielded low tax revenues, tax-hungry suburbs offered tax incentives for companies to locate within their borders. These incentives resulted in lower tax revenues for local governments—meaning that less funds were available for schools, libraries, and police departments. Consequently, taxes were often increased to fund these community services as well as to build the additional roads and other infrastructure necessary to support the new businesses.

Vocabulary
infrastructure: the basic facilities, services, and installations needed for the functioning of a community or society

The shift of populations from cities to suburbs was not the only significant change in American life in the 1990s. The American public was also growing older, and its aging raised complex issues for American policymakers.

The Aging of America

The 2000 census documents that Americans were older than ever before, with a median age of 35.3—two years older than a decade prior. Increased longevity and the aging of the baby boom generation were the primary reasons for the rising median age.

Behind the rising median age lie several broad trends. The country's birthrate has slowed slightly, and the number of seniors has increased as Americans live longer because of advances in medical care and living healthier lifestyles. The number of people over 85 has increased at a faster rate than any other segment of the population, to 4.3 million in the year 2000.

The graying of America has placed new demands on the country's programs that provide care for the elderly. These programs accounted for only 6 percent of the national budget in 1955. It was projected that the programs would consume about 39 percent of the budget by 2005.

The major programs that provide care for elderly and disabled people are Medicare and Social Security. Medicare, which pays medical expenses for senior citizens, began in 1965, when most Americans had lower life expectancies. By 2000, the costs of this program exceeded $200 billion.

The Graying of America, 1990–2030

Year	Number of Americans 65 and older*	Percent of U.S. population
1990	31,081	12.4
2000	34,837	12.7
2010	37,385**	13.2**
2020	53,733**	16.5**
2030	70,319**	20**

*numbers in thousands
**projected totals

Source: U.S. Census Bureau; *Statistical Abstract of the United States 2000*

SKILLBUILDER Interpreting Charts
1. Between what years is America's elderly population expected to grow the most?
2. By roughly what percentage is America's elderly population expected to increase between 1990 and 2030?

Senior athletes compete at the first U.S. National Senior Olympics held in St. Louis, Missouri, in 2000.

Social Security, which pays benefits to retired Americans, was designed to rely on continued funding from a vast number of younger workers who would contribute taxes to support a small number of retired workers. That system worked well when younger workers far outnumbered retirees and when most workers didn't live long after retirement.

In 1996, it took Social Security contributions from three workers to support every retiree. By 2030, however, with an increase in the number of elderly persons and an expected decline in the birthrate, there will be only two workers' contributions available to support each senior citizen. Few issues loomed as large in the 2000 presidential election as what to do about Social Security. If President Bush and Congress do not restructure the system, Social Security will eventually pay out more money than it will take in. Some people suggest that the system be reformed by raising deductions for workers, taxing the benefits paid to wealthier Americans, and raising the age at which retirees can collect benefits. **B**

> **MAIN IDEA**
>
> **Predicting Effects**
>
> **B** What are the factors that will force an eventual restructuring of Social Security?

The Shifting Population

In addition to becoming increasingly suburban and elderly, the population of the United States has also been transformed by immigration. Between 1970 and 2000, the country's population swelled from 204 million to more than 284 million. Immigration accounted for much of that growth. As the nation's newest residents yearned for U.S. citizenship, however, other Americans debated the effects of immigration on American life.

A CHANGING IMMIGRANT POPULATION The most recent immigrants to the United States differ from immigrants of earlier years. The large numbers of immigrants who entered the country before and just after 1900 came from Europe.

Change in U.S. Immigration, 2000

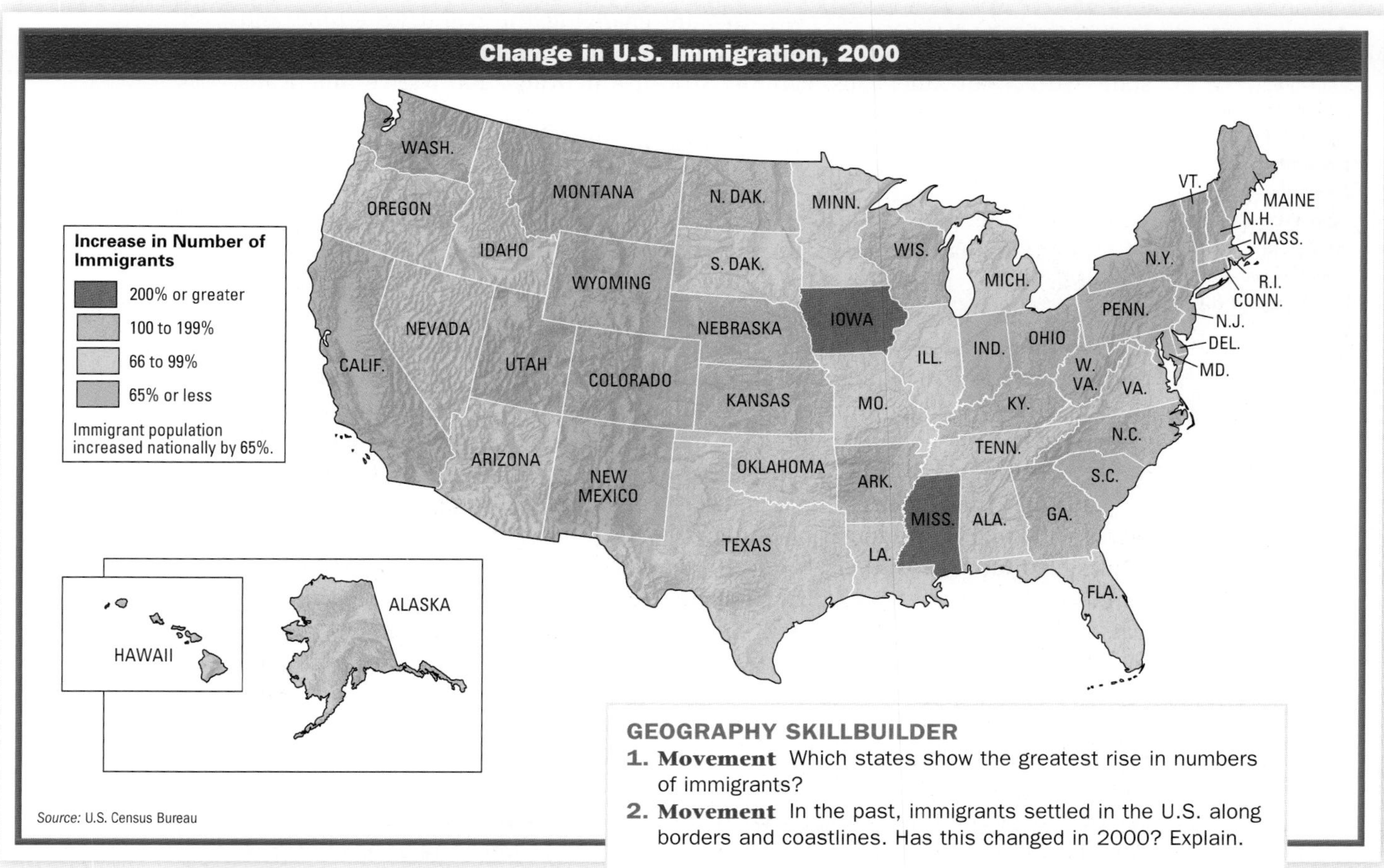

GEOGRAPHY SKILLBUILDER

1. **Movement** Which states show the greatest rise in numbers of immigrants?
2. **Movement** In the past, immigrants settled in the U.S. along borders and coastlines. Has this changed in 2000? Explain.

▲ **Lowe Shee Miu, of Oakland, California, stands in front of a monument commemorating Chinese immigrants at Angel Island—the Ellis Island of the West.**

In contrast, about 45 percent of immigrants since the 1960s have come from the Western Hemisphere, primarily Mexico, and 30 percent from Asia.

In Mexico, for example, during three months in 1994–1995, the Mexican peso was devalued by 73 percent. The devaluation made the Mexican economy decline. As a result, almost a million Mexicans lost their jobs. Many of the unemployed headed north in search of jobs in the United States.

This search for a better opportunity continues today as thousands of immigrants and refugees—more than 2,000 legal and 4,000–10,000 illegal—arrive each day. About 4,000 of those who enter illegally are deported to Mexico shortly after crossing the U.S.-Mexico border. To help those seeking more opportunity in America, in July 2001, President Bush's administration proposed a temporary guest worker program for the 3 million Mexicans residing illegally in the United States.

Based on the 2000 census, it was reported that patterns of immigration are changing the country's ethnic and racial makeup. By 2001, for example, California had become a majority minority state, with Asian Americans, Latinos, African Americans, and Native Americans making up more than half its population. The 2000 census indicated that if current trends continue, by the year 2050 Latinos will become the nation's largest minority community overall.

Background
The U.S. Census has asked a race question on every census since the first survey in 1790. Since 1890, the categories and definitions have changed with nearly every census.

DEBATES OVER IMMIGRATION POLICY The presence of such a large number of immigrants has also added to the continuing debate over U.S. immigration policies. Many Americans believe that their country can't absorb more immigrants. By the early 1990s, an estimated 3.2 million illegal immigrants from Mexico, El Salvador, Guatemala, and Haiti had made their way to the United States. Many illegal immigrants also arrived from Canada, Poland, China, and Ireland. They took jobs many Americans turned down, as farm workers and domestic servants—often receiving the minimum wage or less and no benefits. By 2003, an estimated 8.7 million illegal immigrants resided in the United States.

Hostility toward illegal immigration peaked in California and Florida, two states with high percentages of immigrants. In 1994, Florida Governor Lawton Chiles filed suit against the U.S. government for "its continuing failure to enforce or rationally administer its own immigration laws." That same year, California passed **Proposition 187,** which cut all education and nonemergency health benefits to illegal immigrants. By March 1998, Proposition 187 was ruled unconstitutional. Although never implemented, the law inspired political participation among Hispanic voters, who saw themselves as targets.

As more immigrants make their way to the U.S. and the nation's ethnic composition changes, debates about immigration will continue. Those who favor tighter restrictions argue that immigrants take desired jobs. Others, however, point to America's historical diversity and the new ideas and energy immigrants bring. C

MAIN IDEA

Comparing
C How are current arguments against immigration similar to those used in the past?

NATIVE AMERICANS CONTINUE LEGAL BATTLES As the nation debated its immigrant policies, the ancestors of America's original inhabitants continued to struggle. The end of the 20th century found most members of this minority enduring extremely difficult lives. In 2001, about 32 percent of Native Americans lived below the poverty line, more than three times the poverty rate for white Americans. Furthermore, Native Americans endured a suicide rate that was 72 percent higher than that of the general population and an alcoholism rate seven times greater.

In the face of such hardships, Native Americans strived to improve their lives. Throughout the 1990s, dozens of tribes attained greater economic independence by establishing thriving gaming resorts. Although controversial for promoting gambling, reservation gaming—a nearly $10 billion a year industry by 2000—provided Native Americans with much-needed money for jobs, education, social services, and infrastructure. Over the past decades, Native Americans have used the courts to attain greater recognition of their tribal ancestry and land rights. In 1999, for example, the U.S. Supreme Court ruled that the Chippewa Indians of Minnesota retained fishing and hunting rights on some 13 million acres of land that were guaranteed to them in an 1837 treaty. Across the nation, a number of other tribes have had similar land rights affirmed.

America in a New Millennium

As the 21st century begins, Americans face both new problems and old ones. Environmental concerns have become a global issue and have moved to center stage. Furthermore, poverty remains a problem for many Americans in the late 20th century, as does the increasing threat that terrorist acts pose to Americans at home and abroad.

It is clear that the new century America faces will bring changes, but those changes need not deepen divisions among Americans. With effort and cooperation, the change could foster growth and tolerance. The 20th century brought new ways of both destroying and enriching lives. What will the 21st bring? Much will depend on you—the dreamers, the decision makers, and the voters of the future.

ASSESSMENT

1. **TERMS & NAMES** For each term or name, write a sentence explaining its significance.
   - **urban flight**
   - **gentrification**
   - **Proposition 187**

MAIN IDEA

2. **TAKING NOTES**
   Demography is the study of statistics about human populations. Use a table like the one below to summarize the demographic changes occurring in the United States.

Demographic Changes	
Urban distribution	
Age	
Ethnic and racial makeup	

CRITICAL THINKING

3. **HYPOTHESIZING**
   As urban problems become more common in the suburbs, how might the residents of suburbs respond? Base your answer on existing behavior patterns. **Think About:**
   - the spread of suburbs farther and farther from the city
   - the new ability to telecommute
   - the tax problems that suburbs face

4. **COMPARING AND CONTRASTING**
   How was the immigration that occurred in the years 1990–2000 similar to and different from earlier waves of immigration?

5. **DRAWING CONCLUSIONS**
   How do disagreements over immigration policy reflect the benefits and challenges of a diverse population?

Immigration and Migration

Immigrants to the United States have been part of a worldwide movement pushing people away from traditional means of support and pulling them toward better opportunities. Most immigrants have left their homelands because of economic problems, though some have fled oppressive governments or political turmoil.

War has often been the deciding factor for people to immigrate to the United States or to migrate within the country. Others have migrated to escape poverty, religious persecution, and racial violence. But the chief lure in coming to the United States or migrating within its borders continues to be the opportunity to earn a living.

1840s

MIGRATING TO THE WEST ▶

Throughout the 19th century, Americans continued their movement westward to the Pacific Ocean. Victory in the War with Mexico in 1848 greatly increased the amount of land under American control, and thousands of Americans moved out West to take advantage of it.

Two important consequences emerged from this movement. First, following the discovery of gold in California, hundreds of thousands of people from around the world rushed in to strike it rich. Within a year, there were enough residents in California to qualify it for statehood. Second, Americans disagreed over whether the new lands should be open to slavery. That disagreement fueled the fires that led to the Civil War.

1910–1920

◀ ADAPTING TO AMERICAN WAYS

With hope and apprehension, millions of foreign immigrants poured into America's pulsing cities during the early 20th century. Bringing with them values, habits, and attire from the Old World, they faced a multitude of new experiences, expectations, and products in the New World.

Many native-born Americans feared that the new immigrants posed a threat to American culture. Instead of the immigrants being allowed to negotiate their existence by combining the old with the new, they were pressured to forget their old cultures, languages, and customs for more "American" ways.

1940s

MIGRATING FOR JOBS ▶

Throughout the 20th century, African Americans migrated across the United States. In the Great Migration of the early 20th century, they left their homes in the rural South. Of the millions of African Americans who left, most moved to cities, usually in the North.

The Second Migration, sparked by World War II, allowed African Americans to take industrial jobs—many formerly held by whites—to support the war effort. This migration had lasting consequences for the civil rights movement. Many African Americans who remained in the South moved to cities, where they developed organizations that helped them fight segregation.

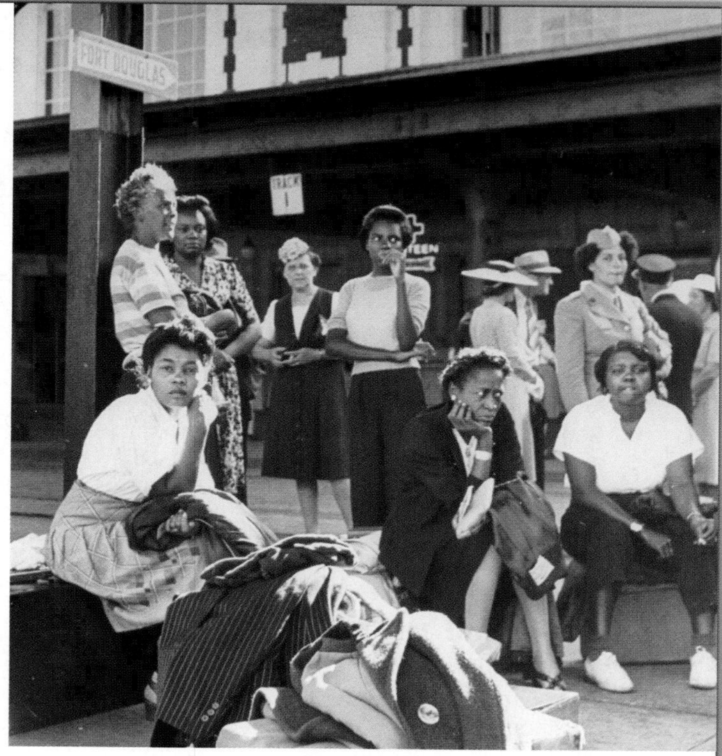

1970–2000

▼ IN SEARCH OF A NEW LIFE

In 1964, 603 Vietnamese lived in the United States. A decade later, as the Vietnam War ended, hundreds of thousands of Vietnamese refugees fled their homeland for other nations, including the United States. Vietnamese immigration to America continued, and by 1998 there were nearly 1 million Vietnamese-born persons living in the United States.

The men and women who made this long and arduous journey from Vietnam are part of the changing face of U.S. immigration. Beginning in the 1970s, Asians and Latin Americans replaced Europeans as the two largest immigrant groups in the United States. Between 1970 and 1990, about 1.5 million Europeans journeyed to America's shores. During that same period, roughly 5.6 million Latin Americans and 3.5 million Asians arrived. This trend continued into the 1990s, as the largest immigrant groups in the United States in 1995 hailed from Mexico, the Philippines, Vietnam, and China. These most recent arrivals to America have come for largely the same reasons—greater freedom and economic opportunity and the chance to begin a new life.

THINKING CRITICALLY

CONNECT TO HISTORY

1. **Forming Generalizations** Based on what you have read about immigration, what generalizations can you make about the causes that led to a rise in the number of immigrants to the United States? How have wars affected the flow of immigration? How does this affect economic change?

 **SEE SKILLBUILDER HANDBOOK, PAGE R21.**

CONNECT TO TODAY

2. **Research** Interview family members and people in your community to find out how immigration and migration have shaped your current surroundings. Try to record specific stories and events that compare a recent immigration with one in the more distant past.

CLASSZONE.COM

CHAPTER 26 ASSESSMENT

TERMS & NAMES

For each term or name below, write a sentence explaining its significance.

1. William Jefferson Clinton
2. NAFTA
3. Contract with America
4. George W. Bush
5. service sector
6. General Agreement on Tariffs and Trade (GATT)
7. Telecommunications Act of 1996
8. genetic engineering
9. urban flight
10. Proposition 187

MAIN IDEAS

Use your notes and the information in the chapter to answer the following questions.

The 1990s and The New Millennium *(pages 860–868)*

1. What happened following the investigation of President Clinton?
2. What factors led George W. Bush to victory in 2000?

The New Global Economy *(pages 869–873)*

3. Summarize which parts of the economy grew during the 1990s and which declined.
4. Why was the World Trade Organization founded?

Technology and Modern Life *(pages 876–881)*

5. What resources did the Internet make available?
6. What were the positive and negative influences that technology had on American lives in the 1990s?

The Changing Face of America *(pages 882–887)*

7. How has urban flight changed both cities and suburbs?
8. What challenges do experts think the United States will face in the future?

CRITICAL THINKING

1. **USING YOUR NOTES** Create a time line of important events from the 2000 election, using a form like the one below.

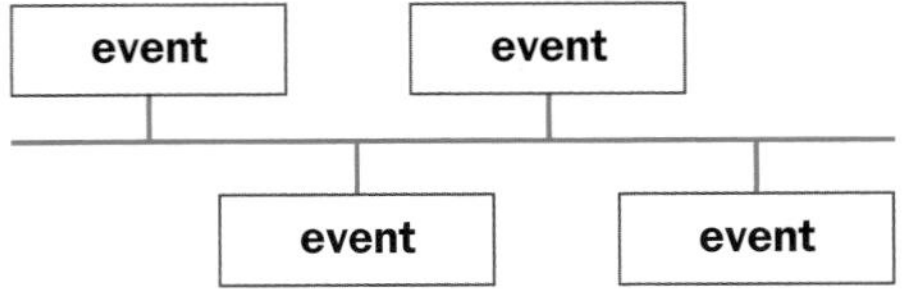

Which event do you think was the turning point? Explain.

2. **PREDICTING EFFECTS** Compile a list of technological innovations of the late 20th century described in the chapter. Then predict what kinds of technological advancements might change American life during the 21st century.

3. **INTERPRETING MAPS** Look carefully at the map on page 885. What might account for the high percentage change in numbers of immigrants in Iowa and Mississippi, compared with more traditional destinations—such as California and New York?

VISUAL SUMMARY THE UNITED STATES IN TODAY'S WORLD

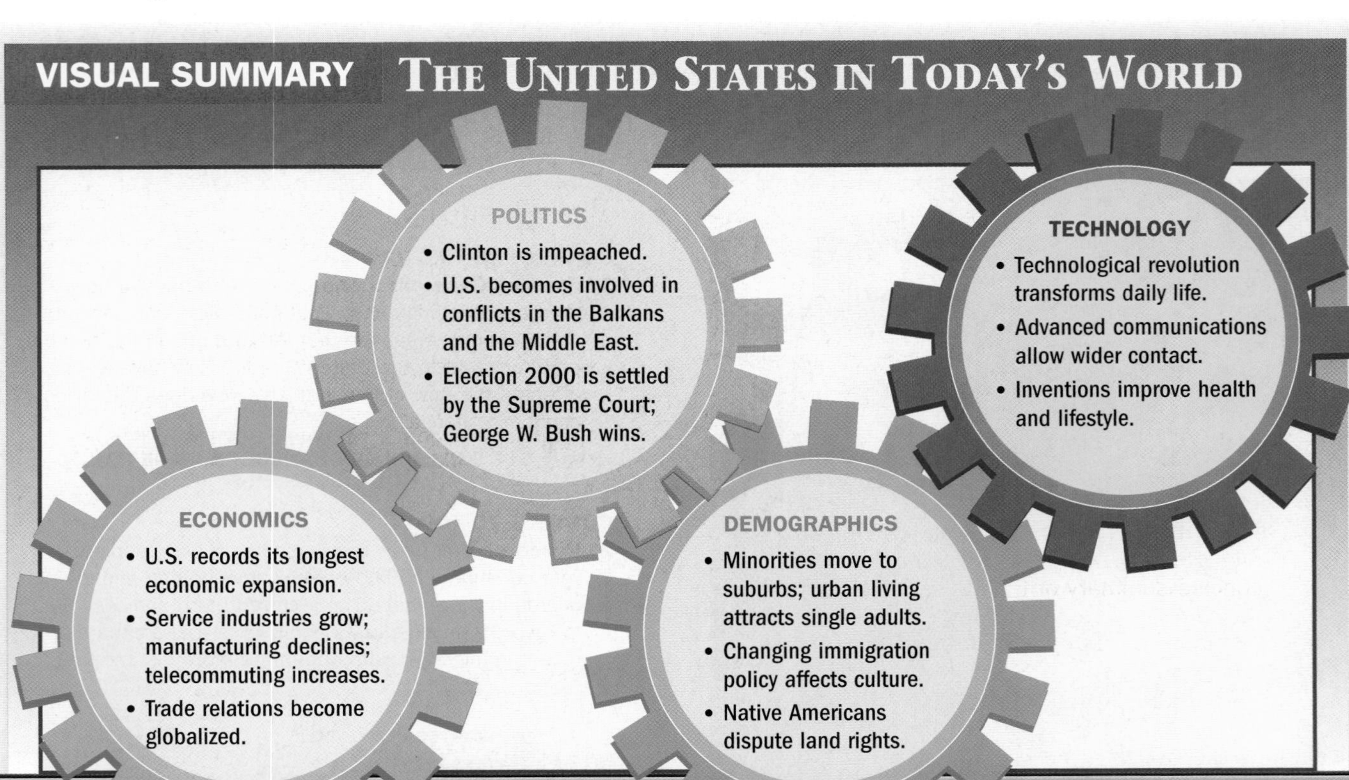

POLITICS
• Clinton is impeached.
• U.S. becomes involved in conflicts in the Balkans and the Middle East.
• Election 2000 is settled by the Supreme Court; George W. Bush wins.
TECHNOLOGY
• Technological revolution transforms daily life.
• Advanced communications allow wider contact.
• Inventions improve health and lifestyle.
ECONOMICS
• U.S. records its longest economic expansion.
• Service industries grow; manufacturing declines; telecommuting increases.
• Trade relations become globalized.
DEMOGRAPHICS
• Minorities move to suburbs; urban living attracts single adults.
• Changing immigration policy affects culture.
• Native Americans dispute land rights.

Standardized Test Practice

Use the graphs below and your knowledge of U.S. history to answer questions 1 and 2.

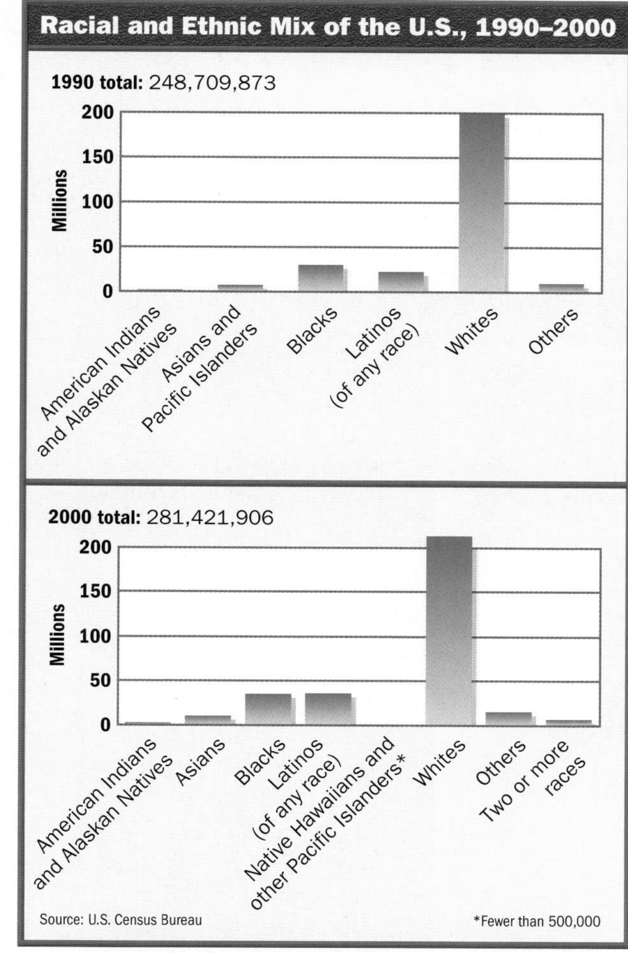

1. Which U.S. population increased the most between 1990 and 2000?
   - **A** Latinos
   - **B** Native Americans
   - **C** whites
   - **D** blacks

2. What conclusion can be drawn from the 2000 census data, compared with the data from 1990?
   - **F** There were more immigrants in the Midwest.
   - **G** The population of non-Latino whites declined.
   - **H** The 2000 census reflects a broader range of categories.
   - **J** Immigration slowed in the 1990s.

3. Which country was not a member of the G8 in 2000?
   - **A** China
   - **B** Japan
   - **C** Italy
   - **D** United States

ADDITIONAL TEST PRACTICE, pages S1–S33.

TEST PRACTICE CLASSZONE.COM

ALTERNATIVE ASSESSMENT

1. **INTERACT WITH HISTORY** Recall your discussion of the question on page 859:

What are the most important issues that affect the world today?

As a "think tank" director who researches and analyzes future issues, you are asked to write a concise summary of the five most important issues facing Americans in the 21st century. Present and distribute your summary to the class.

2. 

CLASSZONE.COM

Visit the links for Chapter Assessment to research the results of the 2000 census. What are some important facts and trends? Consider the following:

- What significant changes took place in the United States during the 1990s?
- What states increased the most in population? the least?
- What changes took place in your state?

Present your findings in an organized poster.

EPILOGUE

ISSUES FOR THE 21ST CENTURY

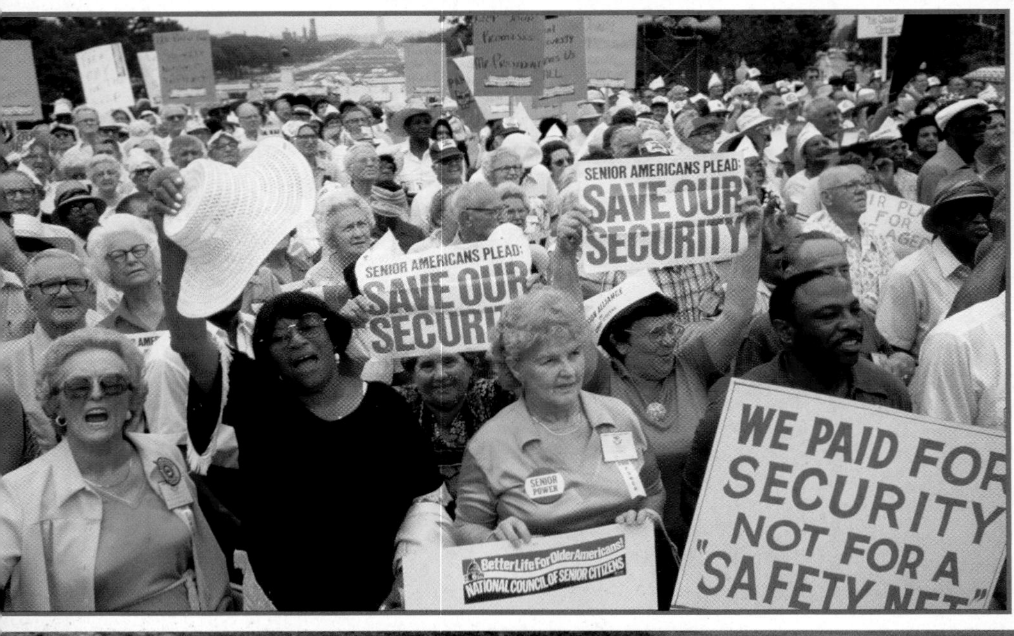

The War on Terrorism 894

Iraq: Confronting a Dictatorship 898

The Debate over Immigration 900

Crime and Public Safety 902

Issues in Education 904

The Communications Revolution 906

Curing the Health Care System 908

Breaking the Cycle of Poverty 910

Tough Choices About Social Security 912

Women in the Work Force 914

The Conservation Controversy 916

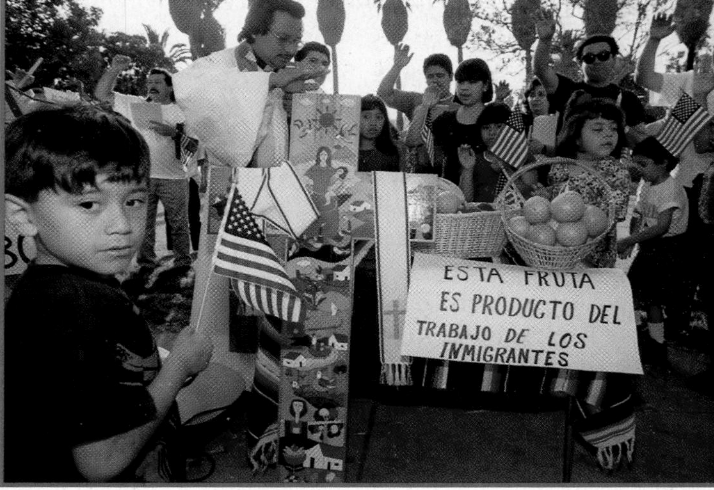

ESTA FRUTA
ES PRODUCTO DEL
TRABAJO DE LOS
INMIGRANTES

The War on Terrorism

How can the United States combat terrorism?

On the morning of September 11, 2001, two airliners crashed into the twin towers of the World Trade Center in New York City and a third smashed into a section of the Pentagon near Washington, D.C. A fourth airliner crashed in a field in the Pennsylvania countryside. Nineteen Arab terrorists had hijacked the four planes and used them as missiles in an attempt to destroy predetermined targets. The first three planes hit their targets. In the fourth plane, passengers fought the hijackers and the plane went down short of its target.

Explosions and raging fire severely weakened the twin towers. Within two hours after the attacks, both skyscrapers had crumbled to the ground. One wing of the Pentagon was extensively damaged. About 3,000 people were killed in the attacks—the most destructive acts of terrorism in modern history.

The twin towers of the World Trade Center in New York burn after the September 11 attacks.

HISTORICAL PERSPECTIVE

Terrorism is the use of violence against people or property to try to force changes in societies or governments. Acts of terrorism are not new. Throughout history, individuals and groups have used terror tactics to achieve political or social goals. In recent decades, however, terrorist groups have carried out increasingly destructive attacks. And terrorist attacks are on the rise. More than 14,000 terrorist attacks have occurred throughout the world since the late 1960s.

The problem of modern international terrorism first gained world attention during the 1972 Summer Olympic Games in Munich, Germany. Members of a Palestinian terrorist group killed two Israeli athletes and took nine others hostage. Five of the terrorists, all the hostages, and a police officer were later killed in a bloody gun battle.

Since then, terrorist activities have occurred across the globe. In Europe, the Irish Republican Army (IRA) used terrorist tactics for decades against Britain. The IRA has long opposed British control of Northern Ireland. Since 1998, the two sides have been working toward a peaceful solution to their conflict. In South America, a group known as the Shining Path terrorized the residents of Peru throughout the late 20th century. The group sought to overthrow the government and establish a Communist state.

Africa, too, has seen its share of terrorism. Groups belonging to the al-Qaeda terrorist organization operated in many African countries. Indeed, officials have linked several major attacks against U.S. facilities in Africa to al-Qaeda, including bombings at the U.S. embassies in Kenya and Tanzania.

TACTICS AND MOTIVES

Most terrorists target high-profile events or crowded places such as subway stations, restaurants, or shopping malls. Terrorists choose these spots carefully to gain the most attention and to achieve the highest level of intimidation.

Terrorists use bullets and bombs as their main weapons. In recent years, however, some terrorist groups have used biological and chemical agents in their attacks. These actions involve the release of bacteria or poisonous gas into the air. Gas was the weapon of choice for a radical Japanese religious cult, Aum Shinrikyo. In 1995, cult members released sarin, a deadly nerve gas, in subway stations in Tokyo. Twelve people were killed and more than 5,700 injured. The possibility of this type of terrorism is particularly worrying, because biochemical agents are relatively easy to acquire.

The reasons for terrorist attacks vary. Traditional motives include gaining independence, expelling foreigners, or changing society. These reasons often give rise to domestic terrorism—violence used by people to change the policies of their own government or to overthrow their government.

In the late 20th century, another type of terrorism began to emerge. Terrorists wanted to achieve political ends or destroy what they considered to be forces of evil. They attacked targets not just in their own country, but anywhere in the world. These terrorists were even willing to die to ensure the success of their attacks.

RESCUE AND REBUILDING

On September 11, the weapons the terrorists used were planes loaded with fuel. The planes became destructive missiles when they crashed into their targets.

Amidst the brutal destruction at the World Trade Center, the courage, selflessness, and noble actions of New York City's firefighters, police officers, and rescue workers stood as a testament. Many of the first firefighters at the scene disappeared into the burning buildings to help those inside and never came out again. Entire squads were lost.

The attacks of September 11 dramatically altered the way Americans looked at life.

Firefighters worked around the clock trying to find survivors in the wreckage. They had to contend with shifting rubble and smoky, ash-filled air. Medical workers from the area rushed to staff the city's trauma centers. But after the first wave of injured, there were few survivors to treat.

A flood of volunteers assisted rescue workers. From around the country, people sent donations of blood, food, and money to New York City.

After the first few days, the work at "ground zero," the World Trade Center disaster site, shifted to recovering bodies and removing the massive amount of debris. The destroyed twin towers accounted for an estimated 2 billion pounds of rubble.

Once the area was cleared, plans to rebuild the site were proposed. In February 2003, a development committee chose a design for a new building complex that would rise taller than the World Trade Center towers. The complex, which officials estimated would take about 10 years to build, would include a memorial, a cultural center, and a 1,776-foot spire.

IMPACT OF 9/11

The attacks of September 11 dramatically altered the way Americans looked at life. For the first time, many Americans became afraid that terrorism could happen in their own country at any time.

This sense of vulnerability was intensified when another wave of terrorist attacks hit the United States a few days after September 11. Letters containing anthrax spores were sent to peo-

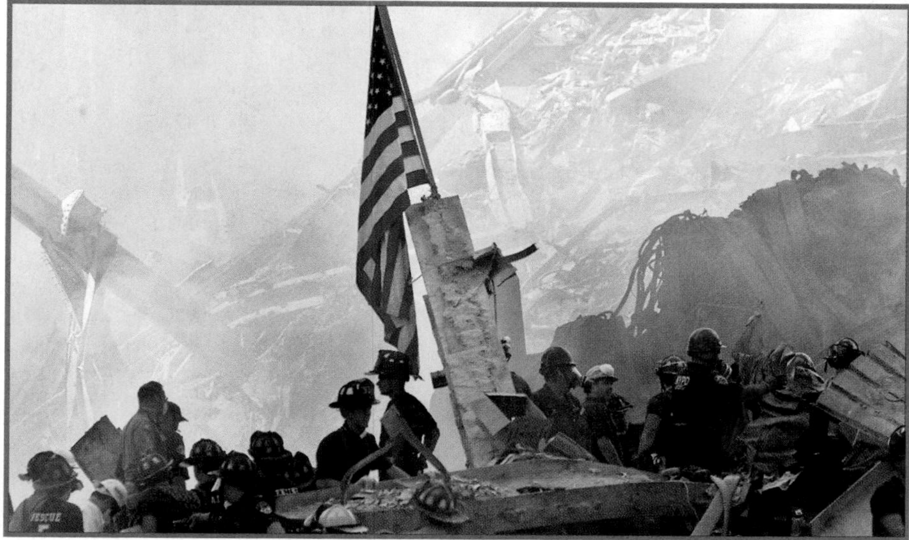

A flag flies over the rubble of the World Trade Center while firefighters and rescue workers search for survivors.

ple in the news media and to members of Congress in Washington, D.C. When inhaled, these spores could damage the lungs and cause death. Five people died after inhaling the spores in tainted letters. Two were postal workers.

Some investigators believed that the letters were sent by a lone terrorist and not by a terrorist group. No link between the letters and the September 11 attacks was ever found. The anthrax letters increased Americans' fear of terrorism.

THE UNITED STATES RESPONDS

After conducting a massive investigation, the U.S. government determined that Osama bin Laden, a Saudi Arabian millionaire, had directed the terrorists responsible for the September 11 attacks. The terrorists were part of the al-Qaeda network. The home base for al-Qaeda was Afghanistan, ruled by a strict Islamic regime called the Taliban. The Taliban supported the terrorist group. In return, bin Laden provided fighters to the Taliban.

The United States, led by President George W. Bush, built an international coalition, or alliance, to fight terrorism and the al-Qaeda network. Great Britain played a prominent role in this coalition. After the Taliban refused to turn over bin Laden, coalition forces led by the United States began military action in Afghanistan.

In October 2001, the United States launched Operation Enduring Freedom. The military began bombing Taliban air defenses, airfields, and command centers, as well as al-Qaeda training camps. Within two months, U.S. special forces and marines and fighters from the Northern Alliance, a coalition of anti-Taliban Afghan troops, drove the Taliban from power. However, the fight to destroy al-Qaeda continued. Bin Laden was not captured, and his fate remained unknown. Meanwhile, the United Nations worked with the Northern Alliance and other Afghan groups to establish an interim government to replace the Taliban. Later, in 2003, Afghan leaders adopted a constitution, and in 2004, Hamid Karzai was elected president of Afghanistan. Peace, however, was elusive. In 2005, insurgent attacks by Taliban and al-Qaeda militants posed a continuing threat.

ANTITERRORIST ACTIONS

To combat terrorism on the home front, the Bush administration created the Department of Homeland Security in 2002, initially headed by former Pennsylvania governor Tom Ridge. This executive department was designed to analyze threats, guard the nation's borders and airports, and coordinate the country's response to attacks. To help share information about the risk of terrorist attacks with the American people, the department created the Homeland Security Advisory System. This system used a set of "Threat Conditions" to advise the public about the level of terrorist threats and provided guidelines for response during a period of heightened alert.

The Department of Homeland Security also searched for terrorists in the United States. The government soon discovered that the al-Qaeda network had used "sleepers" to carry out its terrorist attacks. Sleepers are agents who enter a country, blend into a community, and when called upon, secretly prepare for and commit terrorist acts. An intensive search began for any al-Qaeda terrorists, including sleepers, that remained in the United

Tom Ridge, the first to hold the position of Secretary of Department of Homeland Security, introduces the color-coded threat advisory system.

History of Terrorist Attacks Against the United States

1978 Theodore Kaczynski, the Unabomber, uses mail bombs to kill 3 people over 17 years.

1983 Shi'ites explode a truck near U.S. military barracks in Beirut, Lebanon, killing 241 Marines.

1988 Libyan terrorists explode a bomb in an airplane, causing it to crash in Lockerbie, Scotland, killing 270 people.

1993 Suspected al-Qaeda terrorists explode bombs in the World Trade Center in New York City, killing 6 and injuring at least 1,040 (page 862).

1995 Timothy McVeigh uses a truck to destroy the Murrah Federal Building in Oklahoma City, Oklahoma, killing 168 people.

States. U.S. officials detained and questioned Arabs and other Muslims who behaved suspiciously or who violated immigration regulations. Most suspects were held in a prison camp at Guantanamo Bay, Cuba. The United States faced mounting criticism both at home and abroad regarding its treatment of detainees. Critics claimed that detaining these people violated their civil rights. The government argued that limiting civil liberties in wartime to protect national security was not unusual. U.S. officials used the same argument to try some terrorist suspects in military tribunals rather than in criminal courts.

In 2002, President Bush called for a commission to investigate whether the September attacks could have been prevented and how to prevent future attacks. In 2004, the 9/11 Commission issued a report that stressed the need for greater cooperation and coordination within the government. It also recommended the creation of a new Cabinet post—that of national intelligence director. On April 21, 2005, the U.S. Senate confirmed John Negroponte's appointment to that position.

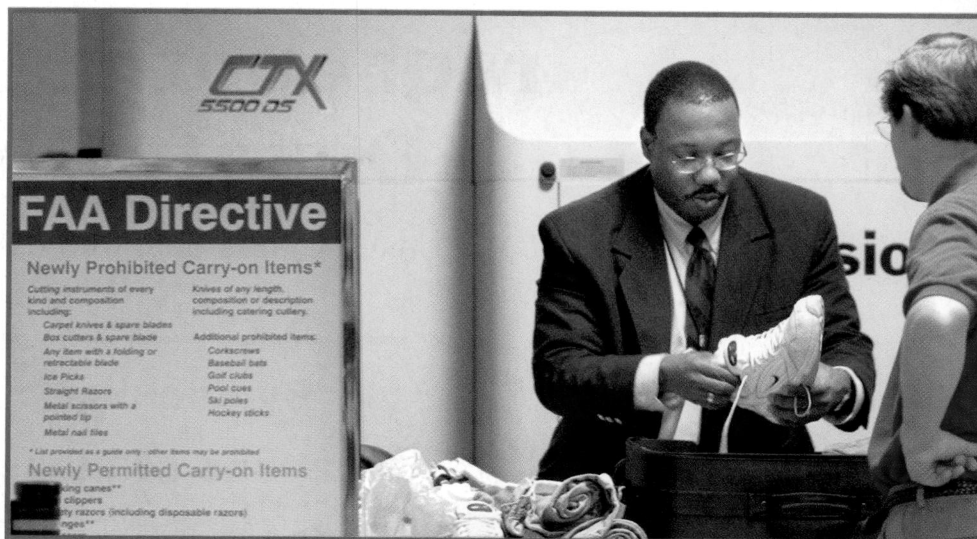

An airport security official inspects a traveler's shoe at a security checkpoint.

USA PATRIOT ACT

To give the government the power to conduct search and surveillance of suspected terrorists, the USA Patriot Act was signed into law on October 26, 2001. This law allowed the government to:

- detain foreigners suspected of terrorism for seven days without charging them with a crime. In some cases, prisoners were held indefinitely.
- tap all phones used by suspects and monitor their e-mail and Internet use.
- make search warrants valid across states.
- order U.S. banks to investigate sources of large foreign accounts.
- prosecute terrorist crimes without any time restrictions or limitations.

People who opposed the law feared that it would allow the government to invade the privacy of ordinary citizens and threaten their basic rights. Although provisions of the Patriot Act were set to expire in 2005, President Bush urged that they be permanently enacted.

AVIATION SECURITY

The federal government's role in aviation security also increased. National Guard troops began patrolling airports, and sky marshals were assigned to airplanes. In addition, the Federal Aviation Administration (FAA) had bars installed on cockpit doors to prevent hijackers from entering cockpits.

In November 2001, President Bush signed into law the Aviation and Transportation Security Act, which made airport security the responsibility of the federal government. Previously, individual airports had been responsible for their own security. Because of this law, a federal security force was assigned to inspect airline passengers and carry-on bags. The law also required checked baggage to be screened.

These measures created several major concerns, including long delays at airports and possible invasion of passengers' privacy. In addition, growing concerns about Department of Homeland Security shortcomings led Secretary Michael Chertoff to announce in June 2005 that major agency changes would soon be forthcoming. As the United States fought terrorism and tried to balance national security with civil rights, the public debate over security measures continued.

PREDICTING EFFECTS

How effective do you think the antiterrorist measures taken by the Bush administration will be in preventing or dealing with future terrorist attacks?

RESEARCH LINKS

CLASSZONE.COM Visit the links for the Epilogue to find out more about War on Terrorism.

1996 The Islamic militant group Hezbollah explodes a truck bomb in Dhahran, Saudi Arabia, killing 19 American servicemen.

1998 Al-Qaeda explodes bombs near two U.S. embassies in Nairobi, Kenya, and Dar es Salaam, Tanzania, killing 224.

2000 The bombing of the USS *Cole* in Aden, Yemen, is linked to Osama bin Laden and kills 17 American sailors.

2001 Arab terrorists crash planes into the World Trade Center, the Pentagon, and a Pennsylvania field, killing about 3,000.

Iraq: Confronting a Dictatorship

How should the United States deal with dangerous dictators?

Since 1979, Saddam Hussein's regime in Iraq had brutally repressed opposition. The Iraqi dictator had ruled without regard for the welfare of his people or for world opinion. During his State of the Union address in January 2003, President George W. Bush declared Hussein too great a threat to ignore in an age of increased terrorism. He promised to do everything possible to prevent Iraq from launching a terrorist attack on the United States.

HISTORICAL PERSPECTIVE

In August 1990, the Iraqi army had invaded Kuwait, a small country that shares Iraq's southwestern border. Saddam Hussein wanted Kuwait's huge oil reserves. The United Nations (UN) condemned the occupation and approved the use of force to end it.

On January 16, 1991, the Persian Gulf War began. Coalition forces led by the United States drove Iraq's army out of Kuwait within six weeks. A cease-fire agreement with the UN prohibited Iraq from producing chemical, biological, and nuclear weapons.

The United Nations periodically sent arms inspectors to Iraq to make sure Hussein was complying with the cease-fire agreement. However, the Iraqi dictator refused to cooperate fully with the inspectors. Because of this, the United States and Great Britain declared in 1998 that they supported the removal of Hussein from his office and the ending of his regime. In response, Hussein barred arms inspectors from entering his country.

> **"By seeking weapons of mass destruction, these regimes pose a grave and growing danger."**
>
> PRESIDENT GEORGE W. BUSH

STEPS TOWARD WAR

After the attacks on September 11, 2001, the United States called for a renewal of the arms inspections in Iraq. In November 2002, the UN Security Council passed a resolution designed to force Iraq to give up all weapons of mass destruction (WMD). Arms inspections resumed, but Hussein again refused to cooperate fully. As a result, the United States and Great Britain cut off diplomatic relations with Iraq.

In early February 2003, U.S. Secretary of State Colin Powell gave a presentation to the UN Security Council, maintaining that Iraq was hiding WMD. Soon thereafter, the United States and Great Britain pressed the UN to pass a resolution that authorized the use of military force against Iraq. As an alternative, France, Germany, and Russia presented a plan that called for intensifying the inspections.

The United States and Great Britain countered by claiming that a new UN resolution was not necessary since Iraq was in violation of the old agreement and that Iraq's violation justified the use of military force to overturn Hussein's regime.

Meanwhile, protests against a possible war in Iraq increased at home and abroad. Antiwar protesters participated in more than 600 rallies around the globe on a single day in February. An estimated 750,000 protesters turned out in London—the largest demonstration ever in the British capital. Most demonstrations were peaceful.

WAR IN IRAQ

On March 17, 2003, President Bush gave Hussein 48 hours to leave Iraq. After the dictator refused, the United States and Great Britain launched Operation Iraqi Freedom.

History of Saddam Hussein's Regime

1979	1980	1988	1990
Saddam Hussein seizes power in Iraq.	Iraq invades Iran's oil fields, triggering the Iran-Iraq War, which continues until 1988.	The Iraqi Air Force releases poisonous gases over the Kurdish town of Halabja, Iraq, killing about 5,000 people.	Iraq invades Kuwait in an attempt to seize that nation's oil revenues.

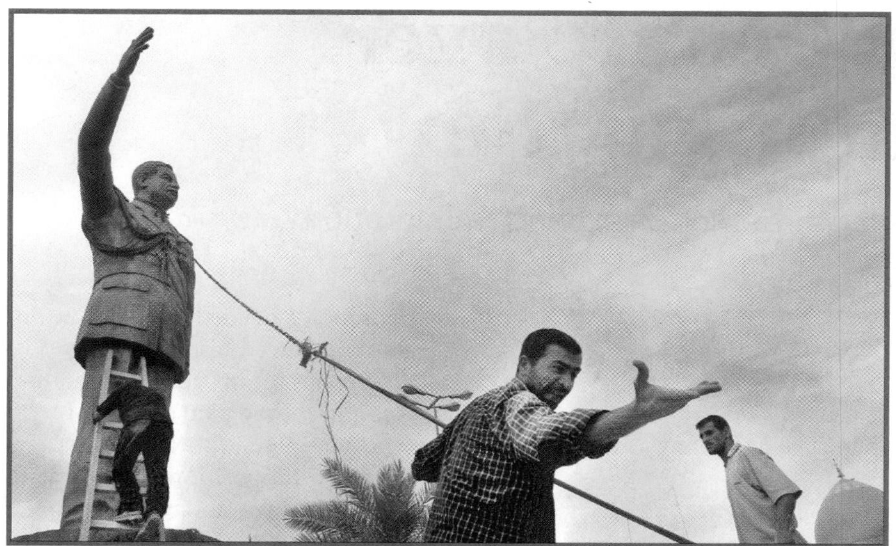

In Baghdad, Iraqis pull down a statue of Saddam Hussein after the dictator's regime is overthrown.

The war began with massive air raids; sections of Baghdad were the primary targets. U.S. ground troops then raced toward the Iraqi capital. By April 2, U.S. forces had reached the outskirts of the city. Within a week, Baghdad had fallen to the U.S. military. Meanwhile, British troops seized the city of Basra. Coalition troops had taken control of most of Iraq by April 14. Hussein survived the attack and was finally captured on December 13, 2003. In 2004, reports about U.S. treatment of detainees in Iraq's Abu Ghraib prison generated widespread criticism.

After the fall of Hussein's regime, the United States led in the establishment of the Coalition Provisional Authority (CPA) to temporarily govern Iraq and oversee its reconstruction. On June 28, 2004, the CPA was replaced by a temporary government made up of Iraqis. And on January 30, 2005, Shiite Muslim parties won a majority of seats in Iraq's election for a transitional National Assembly that would draft Iraq's constitution. Shiites eventually agreed to allow members of the Sunni Muslim minority to participate in shaping the constitution.

Despite the war's end, violence continued. Objecting to the CPA—and later, to the Shiite government—insurgents, or rebels, engaged in acts of violence that killed thousands, including many Americans.

SEARCH FOR WMD

Much of the case for going to war against Iraq was based on assertions by the U.S. and British governments that Saddam Hussein had WMD. Once major combat ended on May 1, U.S. forces began an extensive search for these weapons. Movable biological laboratories containing sophisticated equipment were located, but by mid-2005, no WMD had been found. This led many in the United States and Great Britain to question the necessity for the war. Bush and British Prime Minister Tony Blair responded by claiming that they had based their decision on intelligence later proved to have been faulty. In May 2005, a top-secret memo known as the Downing Street memo became public. It suggested that the Bush administration had planned to invade Iraq as early as July 2002. As a result, 560,000 Americans signed a letter by U.S, Representative Conyers to President Bush asking for the truth about the decision to invade Iraq. In June, as U.S. casualties continued to rise, a majority of polled Americans supported withdrawal from Iraq.

NORTH KOREA AND IRAN

According to the U.S. government, Iraq was not the only country attempting to develop nuclear, chemical, and biological weapons. In his State of the Union address in 2002, President Bush named three countries that constituted a dangerous "axis of evil": Iraq, North Korea, and Iran. He stated: "By seeking weapons of mass destruction, these regimes pose a grave and growing danger."

North Korea, led by Kim Jong Il, clashed with the United States over nuclear weapons development. In 1985, North Korea had signed the Nuclear Nonproliferation Treaty. In 2003, North Korea pulled out of the agreement and reactivated its nuclear power facilities. Iran also started to pursue a nuclear program.

PREDICTING EFFECTS

Do you think the U.S.-led strike against Iraq will result in similar wars against other dangerous regimes?

RESEARCH LINKS

CLASSZONE.COM Visit the links for the Epilogue to find out more about Iraq: Confronting a Dictatorship.

1991
The Persian Gulf War begins in January and ends six weeks later. The UN prohibits Iraq from producing WMD.

1998
Iraq's refusal to cooperate with UN arms inspectors leads to a four-day strike by the United States and Great Britain.

2003
In March, the United States and Great Britain launch Operation Iraqi Freedom. Major combat ends in May, and Hussein is overthrown.

The Debate over Immigration

Should new laws restrict or expand immigration?

For hundreds of years, immigrants working for their dreams have shaped the United States. Latino ranchers developed many of the tools and skills of the American cowboy. Chinese laborers laid the tracks of the transcontinental railroad. African Americans, though not voluntary immigrants, labored to develop the agriculture of the South and the industry of the North. Farmers and workers of every origin built the nation we know today.

HISTORICAL PERSPECTIVE

But immigration has been argued throughout American history. In the 1700s, Benjamin Franklin worried about the number of Germans immigrating to Pennsylvania. Sharp anti-immigration sentiment spurred the nativist movement that developed in the 1830s and the "America First" campaign of the 1920s.

Americans today are divided on the issue. Some agree with former New York City mayor Rudolph Giuliani that immigrants "challenge us with new ideas and new perspectives." Others side with Dan Stein of the Federation for American Immigration Reform, who has said that "large-scale immigration is not serving the needs and interests of the country."

RISING NUMBERS

From 1900 into the 1940s, economic troubles and rapid population growth spurred more than 16 million Europeans to move to the United States. The same pressures have recently hit Asia and Latin America, with the same effect on the United States. Between 1989 and 2004, more than 15 million new immigrants came to the United States.

> **"America's immigration system is . . . unsuited to the needs of our economy and the values of our country."**
>
> PRESIDENT GEORGE W. BUSH

ILLEGAL ENTRY

Complicating the debate has been the issue of illegal immigrants. By 2005, the number of illegal immigrants living in the United States was estimated at about 10 million. A 2004 report by the Center for Immigration Studies stated that households headed by illegal immigrants received approximately $10 billion more in government services than they paid in taxes.

In 1994, California's voters approved Proposition 187, denying illegal immigrants access to public education and state-funded health care. A federal court later ruled that law unconstitutional. In 1996, Congress passed a law that toughened measures to bar illegal entry into the United States.

In February 2005, President Bush proposed a new immigration policy. Stating that "America's immigration system is . . . unsuited to the needs of our economy and the values of our country," the president endorsed a guest worker program. The program would allow foreigners to work in the United States for up to six years, after which they would be required to return to their own countries. Alternate programs also were being considered.

ECONOMIC DEBATE

Those who favor limits claim that immigrants take jobs from Americans. However, data suggest that immigration has not hurt the economy and may have helped fuel its growth. At the same time that millions of immigrant workers—including some undocumented workers—were joining the work

History of Immigration in the United States

1751	1853	1882	1896	1921
Benjamin Franklin denounces German immigrants.	Nativists form Know-Nothing Party to protest increase in immigration (page 297).	Chinese Exclusion Act severely restricts immigration from China (page 254).	President Cleveland vetoes bill requiring immigrants to pass literacy test.	Emergency Quota Act begins era of limits on immigration (page 415).

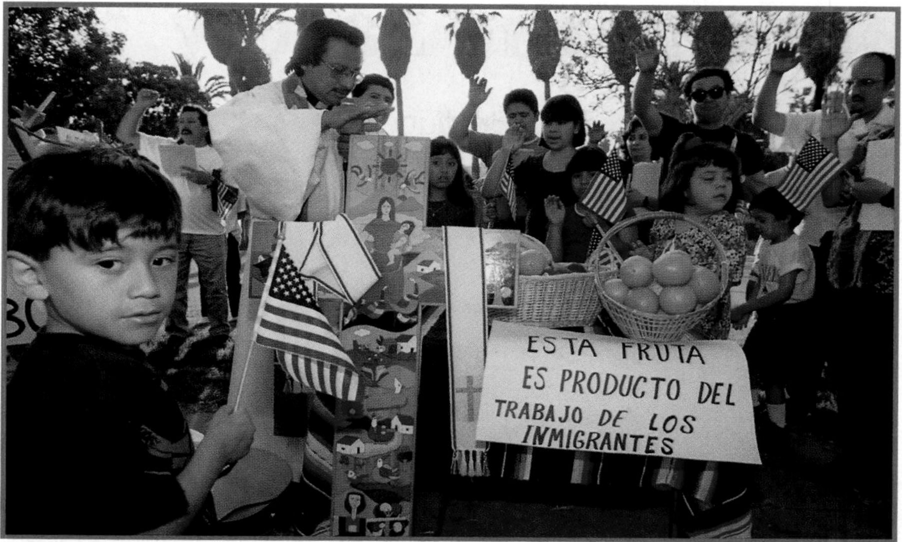
ESTA FRUTA
ES PRODUCTO DEL
TRABAJO DE LOS
INMIGRANTES

Members of the Latin American community in Los Angeles raise their hands to bless fruit baskets as a sign of immigrants' daily work in California's fields. The sign reads "This fruit is the product of immigrants' labor."

force, unemployment fell from 7.1 percent in 1980 to 4.3 percent in March 2001, the lowest rate in 30 years. Although the rate had risen to 5.1 percent by May 2005, it was still relatively low.

Another argument focuses on wages. Economists agree that immigrants tend to work for lower wages than native-born workers. Harvard University economists estimated that one-third of the gap between low-paid and high-paid workers results from higher numbers of immigrants. But they also reported that other factors—foreign trade, declining union membership, and new technology—play a greater role in lowering wages.

Immigrants fill skilled, high-paying jobs as well. Current law limits the number of immigrants who may enter the United States within specific employment categories, or preferences. The 2004 limit was set at 204,422. However, only 155,330 immigrants entered under these categories during 2004.

CITIZENSHIP RESPONSIBILITY

Some people are concerned that many immigrants never become citizens and so fail to completely participate in U.S. life. Statistics show that the percentage of immigrants gaining citizenship declined from 64 percent in 1970 to 38 percent in 2005, one of the lowest rates in a century. Experts attribute the drop to a variety of factors, including rising numbers of illegal immigrants, a backlog of applications, and a presumed lack of interest among many immigrants. The oath of U.S. citizenship carries with it such responsibilities as voting, serving on juries, and, in some cases, military service.

CULTURAL CONCERNS

The diversity of the U.S. population has raised concerns that America has no common culture. Some say that at 12 percent of the population, foreigners are too numerous in America. Historian David Kennedy points out that in 1910 the percentage was even higher—14.7 percent.

Those who favor limits claim that new immigrants do not mix with other groups, forming ethnic neighborhoods that divide society. Others believe that immigrants enrich American cultural life.

MORAL ISSUES

The issue of asylum—providing a safe place for people fleeing oppresson—has been the toughest of all. While immigration is allowed for political asylum, those who flee famine or poverty are turned away. Are such choices fair?

Some rules allow relatives of immigrants to enter the country. Representative Lamar Smith of Texas believes that these rules admit immigrants who "have no marketable skills and end up on welfare." Yet, social scientist Nathan Glazer says that concern about the number of immigrants conflicts with sympathy for those "trying to bring in wives, children, parents, brothers, and sisters."

Alan Simpson, a former U.S. senator, believes that there are simply too many immigrants. Slow immigration for five years, he proposed. But in Gallup polls taken at the turn of this century, 43 percent of those polled favored Simpson's idea, while 54 percent agreed that immigration should either be kept at its present level or increased.

1965
Immigration Act loosens restrictions in place since 1924 (page 691).

1994
California passes Proposition 187, excluding benefits to illegal immigrants (page 886).

1996
Congress passes laws that limit benefits to illegal immigrants.

2005
Census Bureau estimates nation's foreign-born at 34.8 million, or 1 in 10 residents (page 886).

PREDICTING EFFECTS

How might the measures restricting illegal immigrants affect future laws that regulate legal immigration?

 **RESEARCH LINKS**

CLASSZONE.COM Visit the links for the Epilogue to find out more about The Debate over Immigration.

Crime and Public Safety

Will tougher gun control laws reduce the incidence of crime?

On an early March day in 2001, Alicia Zimmer, a student at Santana High School outside San Diego, found herself in the middle of gunfire in the hallways. A 15-year-old boy had brought a gun to school and had begun firing at his fellow students. "I was probably about 10 feet away from some of the victims," Zimmer said, adding that she saw "a boy laying on the floor with his face down," and a girl with "blood all over her arm." Before the shooter was apprehended, two people were killed and 13 were injured. School shootings have become more common in the United States and are just one reason why, despite an overall decrease in crime during the 1990s and into the 21st century, Americans continue to express concerns over public safety.

School students at John Bartram High School in Philadelphia go through metal detectors as they enter the school one day after a school shooting.

HISTORICAL PERSPECTIVE

In 1968, opinion polls reported that for the first time, Americans called crime the nation's single worst problem. Since then, crime has remained high on the list of national problems.

Crime rates generally increased during the 1970s, due in part to rising unemployment and inflation, increased drug use, civil unrest, and protests against the Vietnam War. But in the 1980s, the spread of crack cocaine abuse fueled a major jump in crime. From 1986 to the early 1990s, the rates of violent crimes and car thefts increased by more than 20 percent.

Beginning in 1992, however, these rates began to drop and continued declining throughout the decade. The FBI announced that in 2003 violent crime rate had dipped to a 20-year low and was a third lower than in 1994. In 2000 the murder rate also had reached a 20-year low but then showed a slight rise over the next three years.

RECENT SUCCESS

Experts have identified a few causes for falling crime rates:

- The trade in crack cocaine slowed.
- The unemployment rate gradually decreased throughout the 1990s. Generally, when more people have jobs, crime rates fall.

Perhaps the biggest factor has been new policing efforts. Police departments have taken officers out of patrol cars and put them back on the streets. Police have also taken a more active role in their neighborhoods. Crime prevention methods now focus on an intense effort to intervene with troubled youth before they commit a crime.

History of Crime and Public Safety in the United States

1791	1844	1920s	1966	1980s	1993
Second Amendment, protecting right to bear arms, is ratified (page 70).	New York City organizes first full-time, salaried police force (page 265).	Organized crime thrives during Prohibition (page 437).	*Miranda* v. *Arizona:* police must inform suspects of their legal rights (pages 690, 694).	Increased drug abuse contributes to rising crime.	Brady Act aims to reduce the spread of handguns.

CONTINUING EFFORTS

Despite what appears to be a safer nation, however, many Americans continue to worry about crime. For one thing, gun violence is extremely high. According to the FBI, guns were used in nearly 67 percent of all homicides in 2003. In addition, some social scientists contend that with a slumping economy a new crime wave is just over the horizon. Even though the overall murder rate has declined since 1990, crime continues to command public attention. Experts are split over two issues related to reducing crime further: gun control and tougher sentencing.

As the 21st century begins, Americans find themselves grappling with new forms of violent crime.

GUN CONTROL

In 1993, President Bill Clinton signed the Brady Act, which called for states to place a five-day waiting period on the sale of handguns. During that period, police check the potential buyer's background. If they find a criminal record, a gun permit is denied. However, four years later, in June 1997, the Brady Act was substantially weakened when the Supreme Court ruled that the federal government could not force state or local officials to run background checks on potential buyers of handguns.

At the center of the gun-control issue lies a long-standing constitutional debate. The Second Amendment to the Constitution states this: "A well-regulated militia, being necessary to the security of a free state, the right of the people to keep and bear arms shall not be infringed." The National Rifle Association (NRA), which is opposed to tougher gun-control laws, argues that gun-control laws violate this right to bear arms. Others contend that the amendment was not intended to guarantee a right to personal weapons. Rather, its purpose is to protect the state's right to maintain military units.

TOUGHER SENTENCES

In addition to looking at hand gun laws, Americans have sought to battle crime by putting more people in prison. The federal government and many states recently passed "three strikes" laws. Under these laws, any person found guilty of two previous crimes receives a stiff sentence of twenty to thirty years after conviction for a third.

While many applaud this get-tough policy, others claim that it suffers from a serious problem: racial bias. Blacks represent just 12 percent of the U.S. population and about 13 percent of those who reported using illegal drugs on a monthly basis. Yet three-quarters of all prison sentences for possession of drugs involve African Americans. Many civil rights groups say that such differential treatment must end.

NEW CHALLENGES

As the 21st century begins, Americans face a number of new challenges. Deadly school shootings have brought attention to the issue of youth violence, and violent crime in America's cities remains a national concern. But the greatest challenge to public safety may be the renewed threat of terrorism. During the mid-1990s, a series of bombings signaled a disturbing new era of terrorism in America. The bombing of the World Trade Center in 1993, the 1995 Oklahoma City bombing, and the bombing at Atlanta's Centennial Park in 1996 all contributed to a growing sense of public vulnerability.

Following the events of September 11, 2001, in October President Bush signed into law new anti-terrorism measures. These laws greatly increased the authority of local, state, and federal law enforcement agencies to obtain and to share information about anyone living in the United States, but drew severe criticism for intruding on personal privacy.

It now appears that Americans will be struggling to balance the need for domestic security against its costs—in terms of privacy, convenience, and dollars—well into the 21st century.

PREDICTING EFFECTS

What methods do you think the nation will employ to more effectively prevent terrorist attacks?

CLASSZONE.COM Visit the links for the Epilogue to find out more about Crime and Public Safety.

1994 Republicans include tougher crime laws in their Contract with America (page 864).

1997 Supreme Court rules that certain provisions of the Brady Act are unconstitutional.

1999 2 students kill 13 and then themselves at Columbine High School in Colorado (page 862).

2001 On September 11, terrorist attacks in New York and at the Pentagon kill thousands.

Issues in Education

How can a country guarantee equal education for all?

In the winter of 2001, Paul Vallas, former head of the Chicago public school system, received some discouraging news. A three-year study found "little significant change" in the city's ailing public high schools—despite six years of intense reform efforts. "The issue is that the problem is tougher than we thought it was," the study reported, "and we have to find more intense ways of improving what we've been doing." In response to the study, Vallas echoed those sentiments. "We still have a long way to go," he said. The plight of Chicago's public schools highlights the nation's ongoing struggle to improve education.

HISTORICAL PERSPECTIVE

From the earliest days of the nation, American leaders have stressed the importance of education. In the 19th century, reformers helped establish a system of government-supported public schools. By 1900, almost three-quarters of all eight- to fourteen-year-olds attended school. Even with these advances, some groups suffered. Public secondary education failed to reach most African Americans in the early 20th century. Not until 1954, with the Supreme Court decision *Brown* v. *Board of Education of Topeka*, did federal court decisions call for an end to separate—and usually inferior—schools for African Americans.

By the 1960s, the nation's schools wrestled with the problem of a rising discrepancy between suburban schools and inner-city schools. Many students in inner cities attended schools that were housed in decaying buildings and that had dated instructional materials. On the other hand, students in the suburbs enjoyed new facilities and equipment. In both the inner city and the suburbs, violence and drugs have raised issues of safety.

KEY ISSUES

The debate over public education has focused on three key issues. First is the question of how to change schools to improve the quality of education. Second is the issue of school financing. Should different school systems in a state receive equal funding? The third issue has to do with affirmative action—programs intended to remedy past discrimination.

From the earliest days of the nation, American leaders have stressed the importance of education.

IMPROVING QUALITY

People have offered many ideas on how to improve schools. Some critics say that lack of discipline is a major problem. Others point to the disparity in technology between wealthy and poor schools. During his presidency, Bill Clinton called for all schools in the country to be connected to the Internet and its vast supply of information.

Another reform receiving support is the creation of charter schools. In this plan, certain schools receive a charter, or contract, from a local school district, a state education department, or a university. Charter schools promise innovations in education. In return for freedom to operate as they choose, charter schools promise to increase students' achievement levels. By April 2005, about 3,400 such schools were in place in approximately 40 states.

Some school reformers favor the voucher system, in which states issue a certificate to parents, who then use it to pay for their child's education at a school of their choice. The school exchanges the voucher for payment from the government. Supporters of the voucher system believe that parents will seek schools that provide higher-quality education. Public schools will then be forced to compete with private and parochial schools, and with one another. The competition should increase the overall quality of education, supporters argue.

History of Education in the United States

1821	1837	1865	1954	1965
Emma Willard opens Troy Female Seminary, an academic school for girls (page 148).	Horace Mann begins the push to spread public education (page 282).	African Americans who had been slaves begin to create and attend schools (pages 187, 284-285).	*Brown* v. *Board of Education* finds segregated schools unconstitutional (pages 702, 708).	Federal government begins providing aid to public schools (page 689).

During his run for office in 2000, President George W. Bush voiced support for vouchers. "I don't know whether or not the voucher system is a panacea," he said, "but I'm willing to give it a shot to determine whether it makes sense."

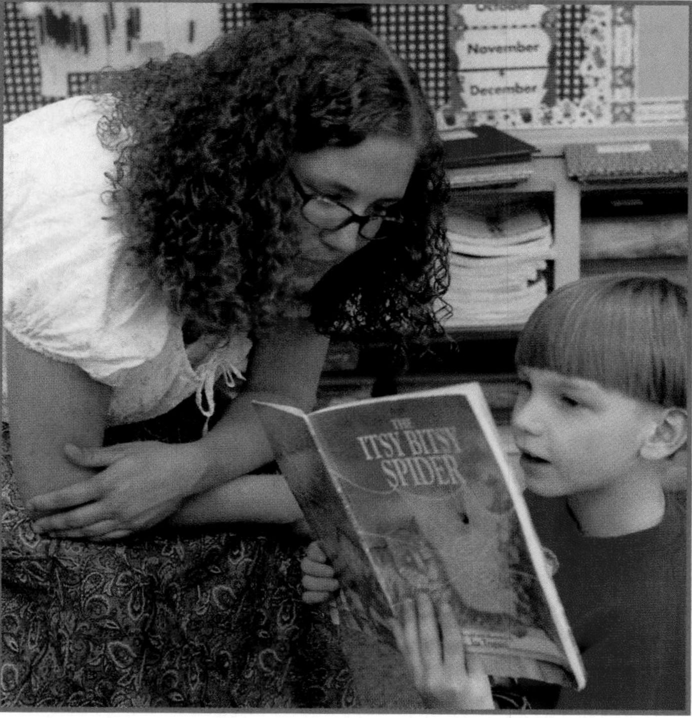

Jessica Riley, a hearing-impaired volunteer teacher, helps a hearing-impaired second grader with his reading.

FINANCING EDUCATION

In most states, school funding relies on local property taxes—taxes paid on the value of real estate in a town or city. When schools are funded primarily by property taxes, however, schools in poorer areas receive less money than those in wealthier communities. According to the magazine *Washington Monthly*, one New Jersey town spends $13,394 per pupil on schooling. Another town just five miles away spends only $7,889. Court cases have raised legal challenges to unequal school funding in more than 20 states.

In 1993, Michigan voters approved a plan that abandoned reliance on local property taxes as the basis of school funding. Now schools get their money from a smaller state-controlled property tax, an increased sales tax on consumer purchases, and increased taxes on purchases of such items as cigarettes and alcohol. Because the state sets property tax rates and monitors its school systems' budgets, it can even out inequalities.

AFFIRMATIVE ACTION

Many Americans support the idea of programs that give women and minorities greater educational and workplace opportunities. At the same time, a large majority disapprove of quotas, the setting aside of a certain number of jobs or college admissions for members of these groups.

This point became the focus of a court case challenging affirmative action. In the 1970s, Allan Bakke had twice been rejected by the medical school at the University of California, Davis, which instead admitted a number of minority students who had lower grades and test scores. Bakke argued that his rights had been denied. The Supreme Court, in *Regents of the University of California* v. *Bakke* (1978), ruled that the school had to admit Bakke—but also said that institutions could use race as one factor among others in determining admission to a college. In 1996, voters in California passed an initiative that banned race or gender preferences in college admissions.

On January 3, 2001, a lower federal court issued a new ruling that expanded upon the *Bakke* decision. In *Hopwood* v. *Texas*, a federal judge ruled that a university could not legally have separate admissions tracks for white and minority candidates. The court said that such a plan discriminates against nonminority students.

On January 8, 2002, President Bush signed into law his education program, No Child Left Behind. A cornerstone of the program is accountability for student performance with national annual reading and math assessments in grades 3 through 8. Clearly the issue of how to reform public education will continue to be the subject of debate.

PREDICTING EFFECTS

What do you think will be the most important education issue the country will face in the coming years? Why?

 **RESEARCH LINKS**

CLASSZONE.COM Visit the links for the Epilogue to find out more about Issues in Education.

1983 A federal commission report *A Nation at Risk* severely criticizes public education (page 841).

1989 Education summit issues Goals 2000.

1996 California voters ban affirmative action in education and other areas.

2005 Number of charter schools in America reaches roughly 3,400.

The Communications Revolution

Can information on the Internet be both reliable and accessible?

On a spring day in 1997, 12-year-old Sean Redden had just logged onto the Internet in his home in Denton, Texas, when he encountered a startling message: "Would someone help me?" The plea turned out to be a distress call from an Internet user nearly 7,000 miles away in Finland. The person had suffered an asthmatic attack that left her barely able to breathe. After obtaining more information from the women, Redden contacted his local police. They in turn alerted Finnish authorities, who located the women and rushed her to medical care at a nearby hospital. This digital rescue is just one example of the power and reach of the Internet, which has dramatically changed American society like nothing else in recent history.

Many observers credit computer technology with driving the nation's astonishing economic growth during the 1990s.

HISTORICAL PERSPECTIVE

In the 1940s, when computers first came into use, they took up huge rooms and required fans or elaborate air-conditioning systems to cool the parts that provided them with power. In the years since, the parts that power computers have become miniaturized and have been made much more powerful. Today, not only can personal computers perform more operations more quickly than the first giant computers did, but they are also affordable for many people. The development of inexpensive personal computers has made it possible for ordinary families to use the latest technology.

THE INTERNET

A very important component of computer use today is the Internet, a worldwide computer network. In the 1960s, the Department of Defense began to network its computers in order to protect its ability to launch nuclear missiles following a feared Soviet attack. Then in the late 1980s, the National Science Foundation created its own network, NSFNET, and allowed anyone to access it. However, only a small group of computer-science graduates and professors used the system.

At about this time a digital revolution arose as thousands of industries across the country began using computers to run their businesses, and millions of Americans bought personal computers for their homes. With so many computers suddenly in use, NSFNET steadily grew into the large and crowded Internet, which includes the World Wide Web.

THE COMPUTER REVOLUTION

The numbers alone demonstrate the influence of computer technology on modern life. By fall 2003, more than 131 million Americans were logging onto the Internet either at home or at work. In 2003, close to 62 percent of U.S. households owned at least one personal computer. What's more, nearly every business in the nation, from hospitals to accounting firms and airports, has implemented computer systems to handle many of its daily operations.

Many observers credit computer technology with driving the nation's astonishing economic growth during the 1990s. With computers allowing employees in nearly every field to perform their jobs more quickly and easily, worker productivity and output increased—a major reason for the decade-long boom.

History of the Communications Revolution

1969
U.S. Department of Defense creates ARPANET.

1991
First browser, or software for accessing the World Wide Web, developed.

1994
Three million people worldwide use the Internet.

EVERYDAY USES

Computer technology not only has improved how Americans work, but also has dramatically altered how they live. Millions of citizens now buy everything from flowers to books to stock online. In 2002, the nation spent nearly $32 billion in electronic transactions, also known as e-commerce, and analysts predict that amount will soar to more than $122 billion by 2004.

While Americans once communicated strictly by phone or letter, they now talk to each other more and more through their computers. Computers have also affected the way Americans learn. In 2002, 92 percent of public school classrooms had Internet access, up 15 percent from 2000. A growing number of universities offer classes and even complete degree programs wholly over the Internet.

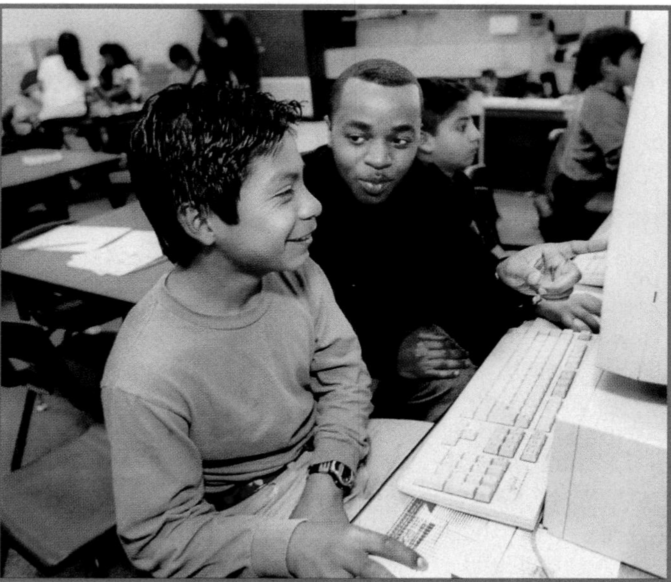

College senior Demetress Roberts uses a computer program to teach Latino Outreach student Angel Leonardo about fractions.

HIGH-TECH CHALLENGES

For all the benefits and opportunities it has brought, computer technology also has created its own set of challenges. There are few laws and regulations governing the Internet. Thus, while it is a treasure trove of useful information, the World Wide Web also has become a center for the dissemination of pornographic and hate material.

The growth of computers also has led to the growth of "cybercrime." Computer vandals, known commonly as hackers, engage in everything from the theft of social security numbers and other vital personal information to the disabling of entire computer systems. The Federal Bureau of Investigation estimates that cybercrime costs Americans more than $10 billion a year. What concerns officials even more is the growing possibility of "cyberterrorism"—hackers stealing or altering vital military information such as nuclear missile codes.

Meanwhile, a large number of Americans worry about the growing "digital divide," the notion that computer technology remains out of reach for many of the nation's poor. According to recent statistics, nearly 92 percent of households earning $75,000 or more owned a computer, compared with only about 42 percent of households earning between $15,000 and $25,000. Many fear that poor families unable to purchase computers are falling even further behind in a country where computer skills are fast becoming a necessity.

CLOSING THE GAP

Actually, the nation is working to close the gap. In San José, California, for example, officials were able to invest $90,000 in a program to teach computer skills to welfare recipients and homeless people. In LaGrange, Georgia, the mayor helped the local cable company by endorsing a deal to give free Internet access for one year to all the town's residents who sign up for basic cable. Meanwhile, libraries, schools, and senior centers provide free access. A number of proposals to provide people with greater access to computers and training are working their way through the federal and various state governments.

THE FUTURE

As the 21st century begins, the computer revolution shows no sign of slowing. The digital technology that has so transformed the nation continues to improve. As the computer age rolls on, Americans and the rest of the world most likely will face exciting new opportunities.

PREDICTING EFFECTS

What do you think will be a new breakthrough and a new challenge for Americans in the next decade of the Computer Age?

RESEARCH LINKS

CLASSZONE.COM Visit the links for the Epilogue to find out more about The Communications Revolution.

1996

Congress passes Telecommunications Act, allowing companies to engage in a variety of communications endeavors (page 878).

2001

Over 200 million people around the world use the Internet.

Curing the Health Care System

How should medical coverage for the uninsured be funded?

To pay for the medicine she needs, 79-year-old Winifred Skinner walks the streets of Des Moines every day collecting cans. "I don't want to ask for handouts. I want to earn it," she insists. The soaring cost of prescription drugs—especially among the elderly—is just one of the key issues facing American health care today.

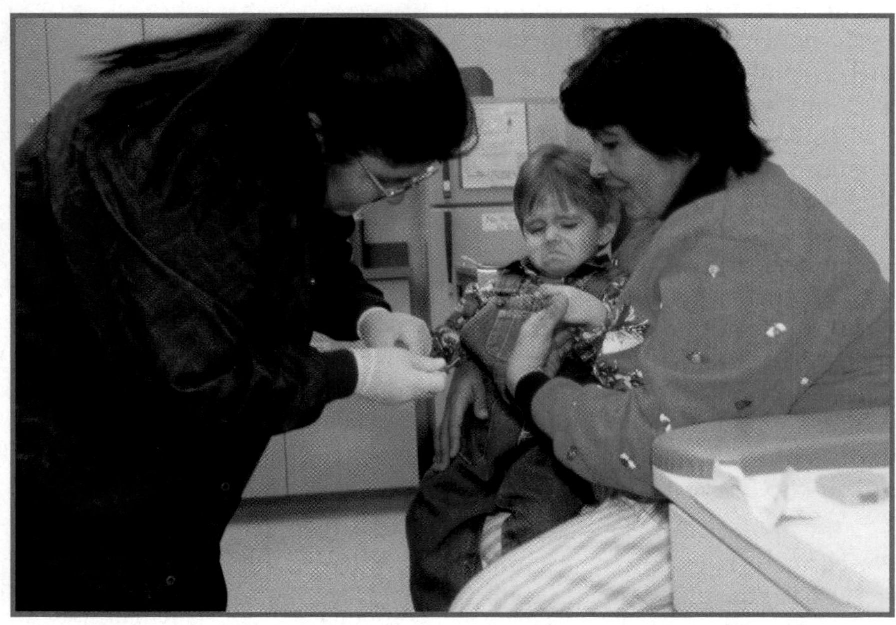

Irene Holmes holds her son while technician Roberta Montoya takes a blood sample at the Sandia Health Center.

HISTORICAL PERSPECTIVE

National health insurance for Americans was first proposed by President Harry S. Truman in 1949, but Congress failed to approve it. It took the legislative skill of President Lyndon B. Johnson to enact Medicare in 1965. The program covered most of the cost of medical care for people age 65 and above.

By the 1990s, Medicare was taking an increasing share of federal spending. In hopes of controlling costs and providing universal coverage, President Clinton proposed a complex plan. However, lobbying by doctors and private insurers and the public's mistrust of big government caused Congress to defeat Clinton's plan in 1994.

Meanwhile, many Americans were afraid they would be denied health insurance because of preexisting conditions—medical conditions that are present when a person applies for coverage. The Health Insurance Portability and Accountability Act, passed in 1996, removed that concern. It required insurers to provide coverage to all new employees who had had health insurance before changing jobs.

HEALTH CARE REFORM

Health care continued to be a hot topic during the 2000 presidential campaign and beyond. One of the issues up for debate was the need for prescription-drug coverage for the elderly, a reform many thought should be addressed as part of an overhaul of the Medicare system. Also high on the agenda were the need to protect patients' rights and the need to expand health coverage to the ranks of the uninsured.

SOARING DRUG COSTS

When Medicare began in 1965, the cost of prescription drugs was small compared with that of hospital stays and doctors' visits. But with the development of new medicines and treatments for heart disease, arthritis, and other chronic conditions, drugs became the fastest-growing component of health-care spending. About 40 percent of people on Medicare were without

History of Health Care in the United States

1949	1953	1965	1970s	1981
Truman introduces a bill for national health insurance that is ultimately rejected by Congress (page 639).	Department of Health, Education, and Welfare is established.	President Johnson and Congress enact Medicare and Medicaid into law (page 690).	President Nixon increases funding for Medicare and Medicaid (pages 795–796).	AIDS (Acquired Immune Deficiency Syndrome) is first identified (page 840).

prescription-drug coverage. Many elderly citizens were paying well over $1,000 a year out of pocket for medicine—or else did without.

During the 2000 campaign, the Democrats proposed a drug benefit through Medicare, while Republicans wanted to give seniors the option to choose their own insurance plans, subsidized by the federal government. Following President George W. Bush's election, Congress passed the Medicare Prescription Drug, Improvement, and Modernization Act of 2003 (MMA). The law provided access to drug coverage for elderly and disabled people on Medicare, beginning in 2006.

Meanwhile, looming large on the horizon was one of the toughest questions facing policymakers in the early 21st century: whether the government should reform Medicare as a whole.

THE FATE OF MEDICARE

If nothing changes, Medicare will start running out of money by 2010 and is expected to go bankrupt in 2025. The reasons are rising costs and demographic changes.

Americans are living longer now than they were in 1965—about seven years longer on average. As a result, seniors form a greater proportion of the population than before. While rising numbers of elderly drive up the cost of Medicare, the revenues targeted to pay for it are expected to go down. As the population ages, fewer people will work and pay the taxes that fund Medicare.

Today, four workers pay taxes for every person who receives Medicare, while in 2035, only two workers will be available to do the job. Workers' taxes will go up—especially if health costs rise.

> **"Health care is too important for any modern society to permit many of its citizens to go without it."**
>
> HENRY J. AARON, FORMER DIRECTOR, BROOKINGS ECONOMIC STUDIES PROGRAM

What is to be done? Among the approaches that have been proposed are placing more restrictions on Medicare benefits, raising the age of eligibility, or increasing the share to be paid by the elderly. Michael Tanner of the Cato Institute favors raising the age rather than the premium: "premiums already represent a significant burden for many elderly Americans. . . . Any major increase . . . risk[s] pushing many of the elderly into poverty."

PROTECTING PATIENTS' RIGHTS

Still unresolved at the time of the 2004 presidential campaign were the need to protect patients' rights and the need to expand health coverage to the nation's uninsured. And, once again, Bush proposed tax credits for individuals purchasing insurance and association health plans for small businesses.

In 2005, Congress continued to consider solutions to the nation's health care needs. In May, the Patient Protection Act of 2005 was introduced in the House. The bill outlined standards for medical care and included a provision allowing patients access to clinical trials. In June, hearings were held for the Health Care Choice Act, a House bill designed to make health care insurance more affordable by expanding the range of insurance options.

THE UNINSURED MILLIONS

The number of people without health insurance continues to be extensive, totaling 15.2 percent of Americans in 2002.

Some 8 million of the uninsured are children. In 1997, the federal government developed the State Children's Health Insurance Program (SCHIP) to provide funding to states so that they could offer health coverage to children of low-income people who earn too much to qualify for Medicaid (which covers the cost of medical care for the poor). By the end of 2003, more than 4 million children had benefited from the program. However, financial stress led a number of states to restrict Medicaid and SCHIP enrollment.

In 2003, Congress established Health Savings Accounts (HSAs) as part of the MMA legislation. HSAs were created to help Americans save for medical expenses. To be eligible, individuals were required to have a high-deductible health insurance plan.

PREDICTING EFFECTS

Do you think that more or fewer Americans will receive health care coverage ten years from now? Explain why you think so.

CLASSZONE.COM Visit the links for the Epilogue to find out more about Curing the Health Care System.

1996 Congress passes Health Insurance Portability and Accountability Act (HIPAA).

1997 The State Children's Health Insurance Program (SCHIP) is enacted.

2001 Congress extends the Medical Savings Accounts pilot program through 2002 as "Archer MSAs."

Breaking the Cycle of Poverty

Who has the responsibility for helping the poor?

Jim, a 55-year-old painter by trade, retreats each night to a Boston homeless shelter. He spends his days engaging in any work he can find—but it's never enough to provide him with a roof over his head. Too many of the jobs available, he says, "pay only the minimum wage or a bit higher, and they cannot cover the rent and other bills." Jim, who says his dream is to "get a steady job, find an apartment, and settle down," insists that he never imagined he would find himself homeless. "I never thought it could happen to me," he says. Jim is just one of more than 32 million citizens considered poor in a nation that continues to cope with the challenge of eradicating poverty.

HISTORICAL PERSPECTIVE

Some part of the American population has faced poverty since the "starving time" at Jamestown during the winter of 1609–1610. In the 20th century, poverty was most widespread during the Great Depression of the 1930s. That economic disaster led to several new government programs such as the 1935 Social Security Act, which created a pension fund for retired people over age 65 and offered government aid to poor people for the first time.

Though the Depression ended with World War II, postwar prosperity did not last. In the 1960s, President Lyndon B. Johnson declared "unconditional war on poverty" as his administration expanded education, training, and financial aid for the poor. The proportion of people living below the poverty level—the minimum income necessary to provide basic living standards—fell from 20 percent in 1962 to only 11 percent in 1973. However, economic hard times reappeared in the early 1980s and the poverty rate began to rise. In 2003, 35.9 million Americans lived below the poverty line—which that year was marked by an annual income of $18,810 or less for a family of four.

Many of those Americans who live in poverty are employed.

AMERICANS IN POVERTY

Many Americans who live in poverty are employed. Known as the working poor, they hold low-wage jobs with few benefits and almost never any health insurance. Children also account for a major share of the poor, and their numbers are growing rapidly for many ethnic groups. The poverty rate among children in the United States is higher than that in any other Western industrialized nation.

Like Jim in Boston, many of the poor are homeless. During the 1980s, cuts in welfare and food stamp benefits brought the problem of homelessness to national attention. According to the National Alliance to End Homelessness (NAEH), about 750,000 Americans are without shelter on any given night.

Many experts on the homeless believe that the lack of housing is simply a symptom of larger problems. These include unemployment, low-wage jobs, and high housing costs, and in some cases, personal problems such as substance abuse or mental illness.

SOME CAUSES OF POVERTY

Experts agree that there are numerous causes of poverty. Lack of skills keeps many welfare recipients from finding or keeping jobs. They need more than job training, many observers insist, they also need training in work habits.

Another factor that holds back increased employment is limited access to child care. Economist David Gordon related the results of a study of mothers who received

History of the Cycle of Poverty in the United States

1894 High unemployment in the wake of the panic of 1893 leaves thousands homeless (pages 221–222).

1935 Social Security Act is passed; government gives aid to poor for first time (pages 492, 501).

1962 Michael Harrington's *The Other America* shocks the nation by revealing extent of poverty (page 682).

1964 President Johnson announces War on Poverty (page 688).

Amherst College freshmen in Massachusetts hoe a field for a farm run by a local food bank in a school outreach community-service project.

welfare. They could eke out a living, he found, by combining paid work and some outside support with welfare payments and food stamps. But, Gordon asked, suppose one of these mothers left welfare and took a full-time minimum-wage job. "[If] she cannot find free child care and has to pay the going rate, her standard of living . . . would decline by 20 percent." To help meet the need for child care, a 1996 federal welfare law included $3.5 billion in funding for day care.

For millions of Americans, the U.S. public education system has failed to provide the tools necessary for climbing out of poverty. Anne Lewis, an education writer, points out that "three-fourths of all welfare/food stamp recipients perform at the lowest levels of literacy." In turn, she notes, low levels of literacy generally lead to low employment rates and lower wages.

Another factor contributing to poverty has been discrimination against racial minorities. Current statistics highlight how much more prevalent poverty is among minorities. In 2003, the poverty rate among whites was 8.2 percent, while among Hispanics and African Americans it was 22.5 percent and 24.4 percent, respectively.

FEDERAL WELFARE REFORM

As the nation continued to struggle with poverty and homelessness, the cry for welfare reform grew louder. Critics of the system argued that providing financial aid to the poor gave them little incentive to better their lives and thus helped to create a culture of poverty. In 1996, the Republican Congress and President Clinton signed a bill—the Personal Responsibility and Work Opportunity Reconciliation Act—that cut more than $55 billion in welfare spending over six years and put a five-year limit on how long people could receive welfare payments. In addition, the bill cut benefits to recipients who had not found a job within two years.

Supporters cheered the reforms, claiming that they transformed a system from one that fosters dependence to one that encourages self-reliance. Opponents of the law accused the federal government of turning its back on the poor—especially children.

Both proponents and critics of the bill agreed on one thing: the law's success depended on putting welfare recipients to work. The federal government offered three incentives to encourage businesses to hire people from the welfare rolls: tax credits for employers who hire welfare recipients, wage subsidies, and establishment of enterprise zones, which provide tax breaks to companies that locate in economically depressed areas.

Throughout 2001, President George W. Bush called for $8 billion to help religious and other volunteer organizations to assume more responsibility for the needy. He supported time limits on welfare benefits and called for able-bodied welfare recipients to get jobs, attend school, or train for work. It may be years before anyone can say whether or not the president's or other proposed welfare reforms break the cycle of poverty.

PREDICTING EFFECTS

What can be done to provide affordable child care to help the working poor?

RESEARCH LINKS

CLASSZONE.COM Visit the links for the Epilogue to find out more about Breaking the Cycle of Poverty.

1970	1980s	1996	2001
Nixon's welfare reform bill—the Family Assistance Plan—dies in the Senate (page 795).	Welfare benefits and food stamps are cut under President Reagan (page 835).	Congress passes Personal Responsibility and Work Opportunity Reconciliation Act (page 862).	President Bush pushes for Charitable Choice Act, passed in the House in July.

Tough Choices About Social Security

How can Social Security be reformed so that it will have enough money to pay retirees?

Economist Lester Thurow gives new meaning to the term *generation gap.* "In the years ahead, class warfare is apt to be redefined as the young against the old, rather than the poor against the rich," he warns. Economics may become a major issue dividing generations, as young workers shoulder the costs of Social Security, Medicare, and Medicaid—the three major entitlement programs funded by the federal government.

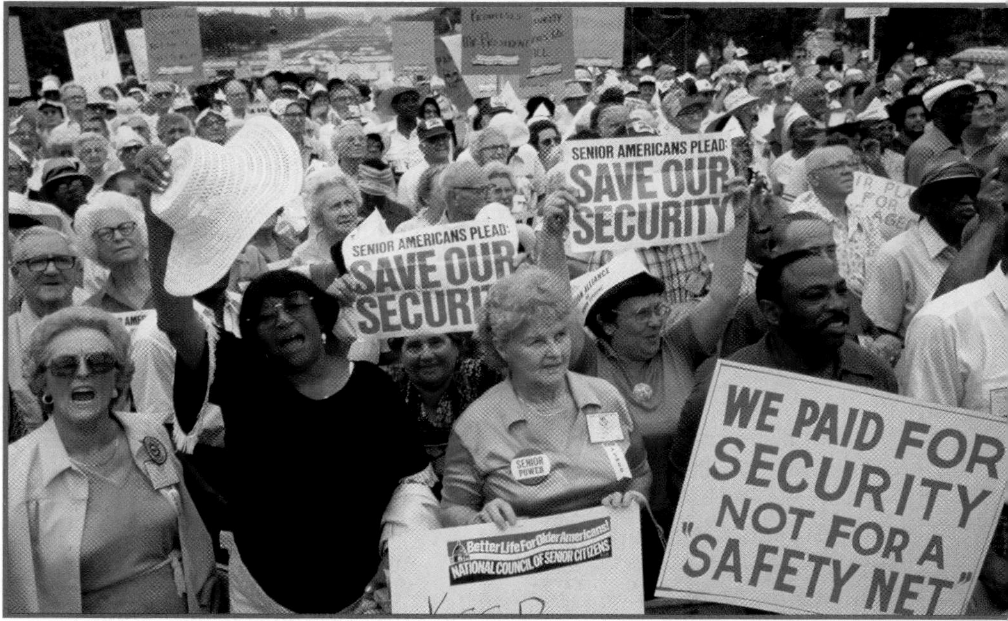

Citizens in favor of protecting Social Security rally on the U.S. Capitol grounds.

HISTORICAL PERSPECTIVE

In the 1935 Social Security Act, the government promised to pay a pension to older Americans, funded by a tax on workers and employers. At that time, President Franklin D. Roosevelt said that Social Security was not intended to provide all of an individual's retirement income, but it was a base on which workers would be able to build with private pension funds.

In 1965, new laws extended Social Security support. In addition, the government assumed most health care costs for the elderly through the Medicare program and for the poor through Medicaid. These programs are called entitlements because the recipients are entitled by law to the benefits.

Social Security, Medicare, and Medicaid have received a lot of attention because the United States population is aging. This aging population will put a severe financial strain on these programs.

SOCIAL SECURITY FUNDING

Social Security's problem can be attributed to a few important factors. First, when the baby boomers (those born between 1946 and 1964) retire, their huge numbers—about 70 million by the year 2020—may overburden the entitlement programs. Second, Americans now live longer, so an individual's share of benefits from the program is greater than in the past. Third, the number of workers paying into Social Security per beneficiary will drop when the boomers start retiring.

Currently, Social Security collects more in taxes than it pays in benefits. The extra goes into a "trust fund" that is invested. Around the year 2018 the program will begin paying out more to beneficiaries than it takes in from the payroll tax. The program will begin to rely on the Social Security trust fund to pay retirees. If that trend continues, after about the year 2052, the fund will

History of Entitlements in the United States

1935	1961	1965	1970s	1975
President Roosevelt signs Social Security Act (page 501).	**Changes to Social Security allow reduced benefits at early retirement—age 62.**	**President Johnson signs Medicare and Medicaid into law (page 690).**	**President Nixon increases Social Security payments (pages 795-796).**	**Congress includes cost-of-living adjustments for Social Security benefits.**

pay retirees only 75 percent of the benefits due to them.

Most experts recommend reform, and Americans have listened. One poll found that 81 percent of Americans under 40 believe that the Social Security program needs to be changed to guarantee its financial stability.

OPTIONS FOR CHANGE

A number of plans for reforming Social Security have been proposed. These different views have become the main options being debated in Congress and around the country.

- **Raise Social Security Taxes** Some people have suggested small tax hikes, arguing that since people's incomes are expected to rise, they will be able to afford an increase.
- **Cut Benefits** Some argue that benefits should be reduced by ending automatic cost-of-living adjustments or lowering payments made to retirees who earn over a certain amount of money each year. These wealthier people, they say, do not need to receive higher payments.
- **Raise the Retirement Age** Because people can now work productively later in life than they used to, some propose raising the retirement age. That will reduce the payments made and increase tax receipts.
- **Invest Funds in the Stock Market** Some people suggest that the government should invest some of Social Security money in the stock market. They assume that stocks will rise, making the system healthier.
- **Allow Individual Investing** Others agree with allowing the funds to be invested but want individuals to control where their own funds are invested.

Social Security, Medicare, and Medicaid have received much attention because the U.S. population is aging.

THE FUTURE OF THE FUNDS

During the 2000 presidential election, exit polls found that some 57 percent of Americans supported the "privatization" approach outlined by President Bush during his campaign: allow workers to divert a portion of their Social Security taxes into individual stock-market accounts. During the 2004 election campaign, President Bush continued to maintain that privatization of social security would "keep the system solvent." His opponent, Senator John Kerry, opposed privatization, claiming that "personal retirement accounts are an invitation to disaster." Following the election, President Bush continued his attempts to persuade Americans to support his privatization plan.

Meanwhile, the proposal drew its share of critics. Among them were advocates for disabled workers and their families—a group that in 2003 made up 12 percent of all Social Security beneficiaries. According to a report from the General Accounting Office, under President Bush's plan a worker who becomes disabled and retires at age 45, for example, would receive 4 percent to 18 percent less in benefits.

Some women's groups also opposed privatization. They said that it would jeopardize the guarantee of lifetime, inflation-adjusted benefits that the current Social Security system provides. Because women earn less than men, they would have less to invest, and their returns would be lower.

Still others were concerned about the risk involved in relying on a volatile stock market. They questioned whether the funds in which people would invest their Social Security taxes would be secure.

Leaders of both parties recognize the importance of keeping Social Security funds safe. Republicans and Democrats pledged during the 2000 elections not to touch the Social Security surplus (funds paid each year toward future pensions), but the 2001 federal budget fell short of expectations. The Congressional Budget Office announced that the government would likely tap Social Security funds in 2003. However, such a measure was intended to be a loan, not a permanent loss of funds.

PREDICTING EFFECTS

How would the economy be both helped and hurt if Social Security benefits were cut?

RESEARCH LINKS

CLASSZONE.COM Visit the links for the Epilogue to find out more about Tough Choices About Social Security.

1983
Social Security is reformed to provide financial stability for many years.

1994
President Clinton appoints Advisory Council on Social Security to report on system's financial health.

2000
President-Elect Bush proposes a plan to divert a portion of Social Security tax into individual stock-market accounts.

Women in the Work Force

Will the American workplace grant men and women equal opportunities?

Thirty-two years after entering a management training program at Boston's Federal Reserve Bank, Cathy Minehan—now the bank's president—is one of a select group of female executives who hold 3.3 percent of the nation's highest-paying jobs. "A critical element in making it to the top is being in the pipeline to do so, . . ." says Minehan. "Aside from . . . [that,] they have to believe they can make it. . . . It is hard for women or minorities to believe they can progress if they cannot look up and see faces like their own at the top."

HISTORICAL PERSPECTIVE

In 1961, President John F. Kennedy named a commission to study the status of women in the workplace. Its report revealed that employers paid women less than men for equal work. The report also said that women were rarely promoted to top positions in their fields.

Almost 40 years later, the U.S. Census Bureau found that more women than ever before worked outside the home—about 60 percent. Women made up 47 percent of the American work force. Yet they held only 12.5 percent of the most senior jobs in a sampling of the Fortune 500, the nation's 500 largest companies.

Women are still making less than their male counterparts—averaging only 80 cents for every dollar.

Some women who choose to pursue careers in business, government, or other organizations feel that a glass ceiling limits their career progress. It is said to be glass because it is an invisible barrier that keeps women and minorities from attaining promotion above a certain level. Its invisibility makes it difficult to combat.

POSITIVE TRENDS

Women have made great strides in recent decades. In 2002, they filled half of all jobs in managerial and professional specialty areas. Women have also been entering new fields, including construction work and blue-collar jobs such as equipment repair.

In the academic world, women are better represented than ever before. In 2000–2001, women received a record number—nearly 45 percent—of all doctorate degrees issued by universities. Women earned an even higher percentage—46.2—of first professional degrees.

For many women, job success involved getting the right credentials and targeting a growth industry. A 2000 survey by the women's advocacy group Catalyst found that 91 percent of women with MBA degrees working in information technology reported high satisfaction with their current jobs, compared with only 82 percent of their male counterparts. "This translates into opportunity for women in this growing industry," said Sheila Wellington, president of Catalyst. "They're essentially telling us, 'This is the place to be.'"

MONEY AND UPWARD MOBILITY

Despite these positive signs, the key issues of unequal pay and unequal representation remain. Women are still making less than their male counterparts—averaging only 80 cents for every dollar earned by men. According to the National Committee on Pay Equity, there are

History of Women at Work in the United States

1834	1860	1899	1900	1920s
Women working in Lowell, Massachusetts, textile mills strike (pages 142, 244-245).	1 out of 10 single white women works outside the home, earning half the pay of men (pages 244).	Average pay for women workers is $269 a year, compared with $498 for men.	One out of five women works outside the home (pages 313-314).	Women enter new professions but battle unequal wages (page 442).

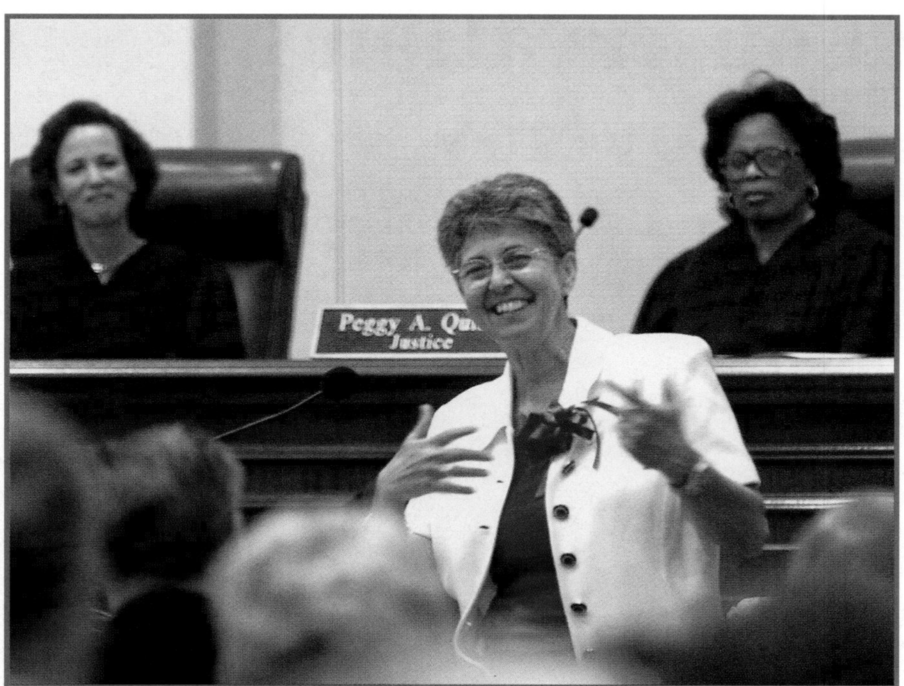

U.S. Appeals Court judge Rosemary Barkett (*center*) delivers the keynote address during a special session of Florida's high court honoring the state's first 150 female lawyers on June 15, 2000, in Tallahassee, Florida.

a variety of reasons for this discrepancy: women are often socialized to aim toward lower-paying jobs, often have limited expectations about their leadership potential, and may have conflicts between the demands of work and family life.

In the nation's most top-level jobs, women continue to be vastly outnumbered by men. As of 2002, women headed only eight Fortune 500 corporations. Women held 15.7 percent of corporate officer positions in Fortune 500 companies, an increase of 7 percent since 1995. Of all line officers—positions with profit-and-loss responsibility—9.9 percent were held by women, while men held an overwhelming 90.1 percent of these positions.

Why are women underrepresented in the top jobs? In one Catalyst poll of women executives, blame was placed on three factors: male stereotyping and preconceptions of women, women's exclusion from informal networks of communication, and women's lack of significant management experience.

On the other hand, the respondents suggested some approaches that had helped them succeed in the corporate world: consistently exceed expectations, develop a style with which managers are comfortable, seek out difficult assignments, and have an influential mentor.

STRIKING OUT ON THEIR OWN

Many women who are frustrated by the corporate environment at their existing companies are choosing to start their own business. According to the center for Women's Business Research, in 2004 10.6 million firms were at least 50 percent owned by women—and constituted the fastest-growing sector of all U.S. firms. Notes Dixie Junk, owner of Junk Architects in Kansas City, "It's more than having a business—you get to create the culture you want."

IT PAYS TO BE FLEXIBLE

Another area of change affecting women in the work force has been an increasing number of options for flexible work arrangements, such as part-time work and telecommuting opportunities. In 2004, 71 percent of companies surveyed had formal policies or guidelines for some type of flexible work arrangement.

One Catalyst study tracking 24 women who first used flexible work arrangements more than a decade ago found that all of the women now held mid- and senior-level positions, and more than half had earned promotions in the last 10 years. Says Marcia Brumit Kropf, vice-president of research and information services, "Findings from this report suggest that even though working mothers may reduce career involvement for a period of time—with the support of the right company—career advancement does not have to get sidelined."

PREDICTING EFFECTS

What can be done to afford women the same opportunities as men?

RESEARCH LINKS

CLASSZONE.COM Visit the links for the Epilogue to find out more about Women in the Work Force.

1961	1989	1998	2005
Presidential Commission on the Status of Women reports: women are paid less than men (page 777).	**20 states begin adjusting pay scales to equalize pay (page 843).**	**Women earn 76 cents for every dollar a man earns.**	**Women-owned businesses are the fastest-growing sector of the U.S. economy.**

The Conservation Controversy

Can the nation balance conservation with economic progress?

In 1990, Oregon logger Bill Haire hung a new ornament on the mirror of his truck: a tiny owl with an arrow through its head. The trinket represented the spotted owl as well as Haire's feelings about the federal government's decision to declare millions of acres of forest off limits to the logging industry in order to protect this endangered species of bird.

"If it comes down to my family or that bird," said Haire, "that bird's going to suffer." The battle between loggers and environmentalists over the fate of the spotted owl is just one example of the nation's ongoing struggle to balance conservation with industrial progress.

HISTORICAL PERSPECTIVE Conservation, the management and protection of the earth's resources, began as a national movement in the United States during the early 1900s. In the wake of the country's industrial revolution, the federal government enacted numerous measures to protect the nation's natural surroundings. President Theodore Roosevelt expressed a particular interest in preserving America's forestlands. "Like other men who had thought about the national future at all," he once remarked, "I had been growing more and more concerned over the destruction of the forests." Roosevelt established the first wildlife refuge in Florida and added more than 150 million acres to the nation's forest preserves.

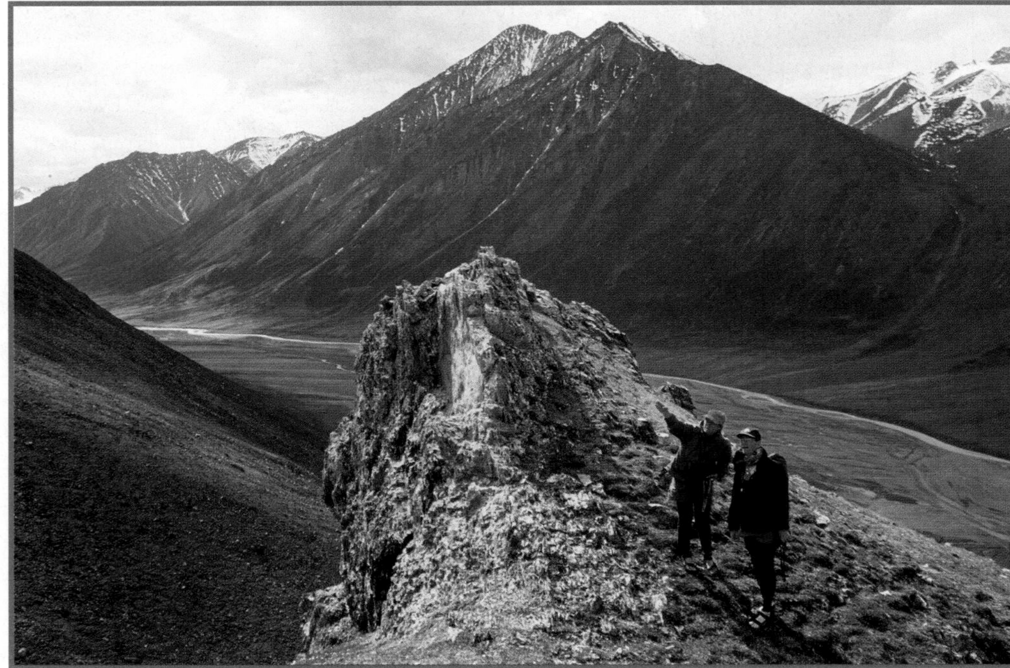

Hikers stand on a rock outcropping above the Jago River at the Arctic National Wildlife Refuge in the Brooks Range of Alaska.

The 1960s and 1970s witnessed a resurgence of the conservation movement. In 1962, marine biologist Rachel Carson published *Silent Spring*, which warned of the destructive effects of pesticides. The book awakened Americans to the damage they were inflicting on the environment. In the two decades that followed, Congress created the Environmental Protection Agency (EPA) and enacted such measures as the Clean Air Act, the Clean Water Act, and the Endangered Species Act—all in an effort to restore the health of the country's natural resources. And, since 1970, the country nearly tripled the size of its national park space.

History of Conservation in the United States

1903	1933	1962	1970	1973
President Theodore Roosevelt establishes the first federal wildlife refuge (page 323).	President Franklin Roosevelt creates the Civilian Conservation Corps (page 491).	Rachel Carson publishes *Silent Spring* (page 691).	Congress establishes the Environmental Protection Agency; Congress passes Clean Air Act (page 822).	Congress passes the Endangered Species Act (page 822).

THE MOVEMENT CONTINUES

By the 1990s, Americans had done much to improve the environment. Between 1970 and 2000, for example, the nation's yearly production of carbon monoxide emissions into the air dropped from 197.3 million tons to 102.4 million.

A number of states have made independent efforts. California, for instance, has some of the nation's strictest air-pollution control laws, and these have helped to provide the Golden State with much cleaner air. Other states are playing their part as well in the nation's ongoing conservation effort.

However, there is still much to be done, especially about water pollution. One indicator is data collected by the Environmental Protection Agency for the year 2003, which showed that beach closings—mostly due to unsafe levels of water pollution—were on the rise.

Not all action has been through government. Private groups such as the Nature Conservancy and numerous local land trusts have raised money to purchase forest and watershed lands and keep them pristine. In Texas several entrepreneurs created the Fossil Rim Wildlife Center, a 2,700-acre wildlife sanctuary for more than 30 animal species.

ONGOING DEBATES

Despite the strides Americans have made in protecting their natural resources over the past half century, environmental problems still exist, and the nation still struggles to strike a balance between conservation and economic growth. Such a struggle is clearly visible in the greenhouse effect. The greenhouse effect is the rise in temperature that Earth experiences because certain gases in the atmosphere trap energy from the sun. Without these gases, heat would escape back into space and Earth's average temperature would be about 60°F colder.

As the 21st century begins, the nation faces the challenge of balancing energy needs with environmental concerns.

Some greenhouse gases, such as carbon dioxide, methane, and nitrous oxide, occur naturally in the air. But the burning of fossil fuels and other human activities add to the levels of these gases, causing global warming. Many scientists and public officials believe that global warming could prompt a range of environmental calamities, from severe flooding in some parts of the world to drought in others.

Despite such dire warnings, the United States—the world's largest producer of greenhouse gas emissions—has done little to scale back its output of such gases. Many of the nation's business leaders insist that measures to "cool down" the atmosphere are too costly and thus would hurt the nation's economy.

An issue of greater concern to Americans today—and one that also is stirring debate between environmentalists and industrialists—is the nation's growing appetite for energy. The United States consumes 25 percent of the world's energy, nearly all of it in the form of fossil fuels such as oil, coal, and natural gas. Much of the fuel America uses comes from overseas—in places such as the oil-rich Middle East. The reliance on foreign sources has left the United States vulnerable to price increases and fuel shortages.

In May 2001, President George W. Bush revealed his energy plan. In the plan, he proposed loosening regulations on oil and gas exploration, a review of gas mileage standards, and a $4 billion tax credit for the use of "hybrid" cars that use a combination of gas and battery power. The plan also stressed the president's commitment to drill for oil in the Arctic National Wildlife Refuge (ANWR). Environmentalists strongly oppose this plan, claiming that such drilling will destroy a fragile ecosystem. However in April 2005, the House of Representatives passed an energy bill that would allow drilling in ANWR. A Senate vote was still to come.

As the 21st century begins, the nation faces the challenge of balancing energy needs with environmental concerns. It is an issue that Americans will grapple with for years.

PREDICTING EFFECTS

Do you think the United States eventually will engage in greater domestic exploration of its natural resources to solve its growing energy needs? Why or why not?

RESEARCH LINKS

CLASSZONE.COM Visit the links for the Epilogue to find out more about The Conservation Controversy.

1977 Congress passes Clean Water Act.

1990 Congress amends Clean Air Act to address new environmental problems, including acid rain and ozone depletion.

2001 Nations agree to a revised Kyoto Protocol, which requires industrial nations to preserve "environnmental integrity."

RAND McNALLY

World Atlas

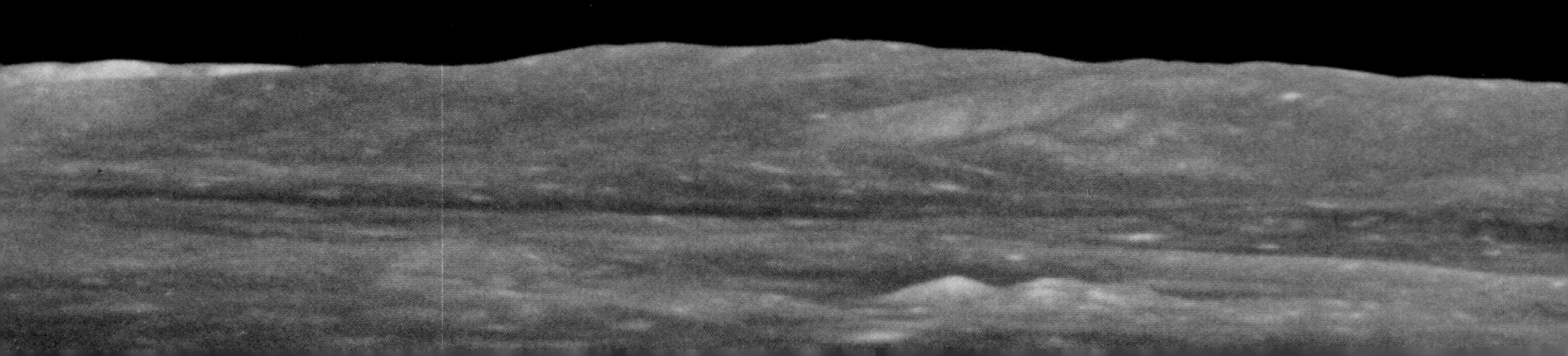

CONTENTS

Human Emergence on Earth . A2
World: Political A4
World: Physical A6
North America: Physical A8
South America: Physical A9
Africa: Physical A10
Australia and Oceania A11
Europe: Physical A12
Asia: Physical A14
Mexico, Central America, and the Caribbean: Political A16
Native America A18
United States: Political A20
United States: Physical A22
U.S. Outlying Areas A24
North America 1783 . . . . A26
United States 1775–1799 . . . . A27
U.S. Territorial Expansion . . . A28
Slavery in the United States 1820–1860 . . . . A30
Secession 1860–1861 . . . . A31
Western Frontiers 1860–1890 . . . . A32
The Civil War A33
U.S. Industries 1920 . . . . A34
The Great Depression 1929–1939 . . . . A35
Major Sources of Immigration A36
Immigration's Impact 1910 . . A37
African-American Migration 1940–1970 . . . . A38
U.S. Population Density A39

Complete Legend for Physical and Political Maps

Symbols

Lake

Salt Lake

Seasonal Lake

River

Waterfall

Canal

Mountain Peak

Highest Mountain Peak

Cities

■ Los Angeles	City over 1,000,000 population
▣ Calgary	City of 250,000 to 1,000,000 population
• Haifa	City under 250,000 population
⊛ *Paris*	National Capital
★ Vancouver	Secondary Capital (State, Province, or Territory)

Type Styles Used to Name Features

CHINA	Country
O N T A R I O	State, Province, or Territory
PUERTO RICO (U.S.)	Possession
A T L A N T I C O C E A N	Ocean or Sea
A l p s	Physical Feature
Borneo	Island

Boundaries

International Boundary

Secondary Boundary

Land Elevation and Water Depths

Land Elevation

Meters	Feet
3,000 and over	9,840 and over
2,000 - 3,000	6,560 - 9,840
500 - 2,000	1,640 - 6,560
200 - 500	656 - 1,640
0 - 200	0 - 656

Water Depth

Meters	Feet
Less than 200	Less than 656
200 - 2,000	656 - 6,560
Over 2,000	Over 6,560

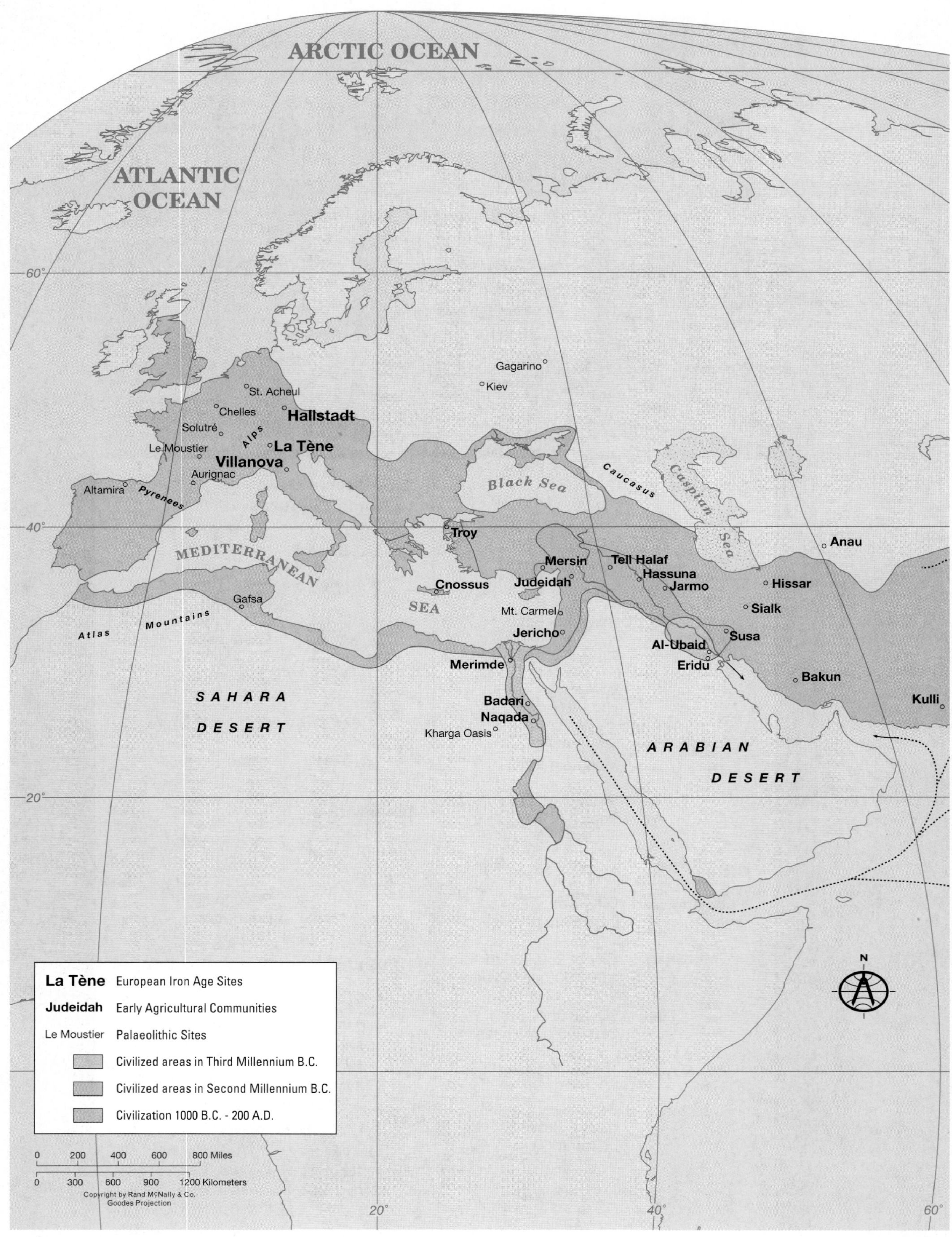
ARCTIC OCEAN
ATLANTIC OCEAN
60°
Gagarino
Kiev
St. Acheul
Chelles
Hallstadt
Solutré
Alps
La Tène
Le Moustier
Villanova
Aurignac
Altamira
Pyrenees
Black Sea
Caucasus
Caspian Sea
40°
Troy
Anau
MEDITERRANEAN
Mersin
Tell Halaf
Hassuna
Jarmo
Cnossus
Judeidah
Hissar
Gafsa
SEA
Mt. Carmel
Sialk
Atlas
Mountains
Jericho
Susa
Al-Ubaid
Eridu
Merimde
Bakun
SAHARA
DESERT
Kulli
Badari
Naqada
Kharga Oasis
ARABIAN
DESERT
20°
La Tène European Iron Age Sites
Judeidah Early Agricultural Communities
Le Moustier Palaeolithic Sites
Civilized areas in Third Millennium B.C.
Civilized areas in Second Millennium B.C.
Civilization 1000 B.C. - 200 A.D.
N
0 200 400 600 800 Miles
0 300 600 900 1200 Kilometers
Goodes Projection
20°
40°
60°

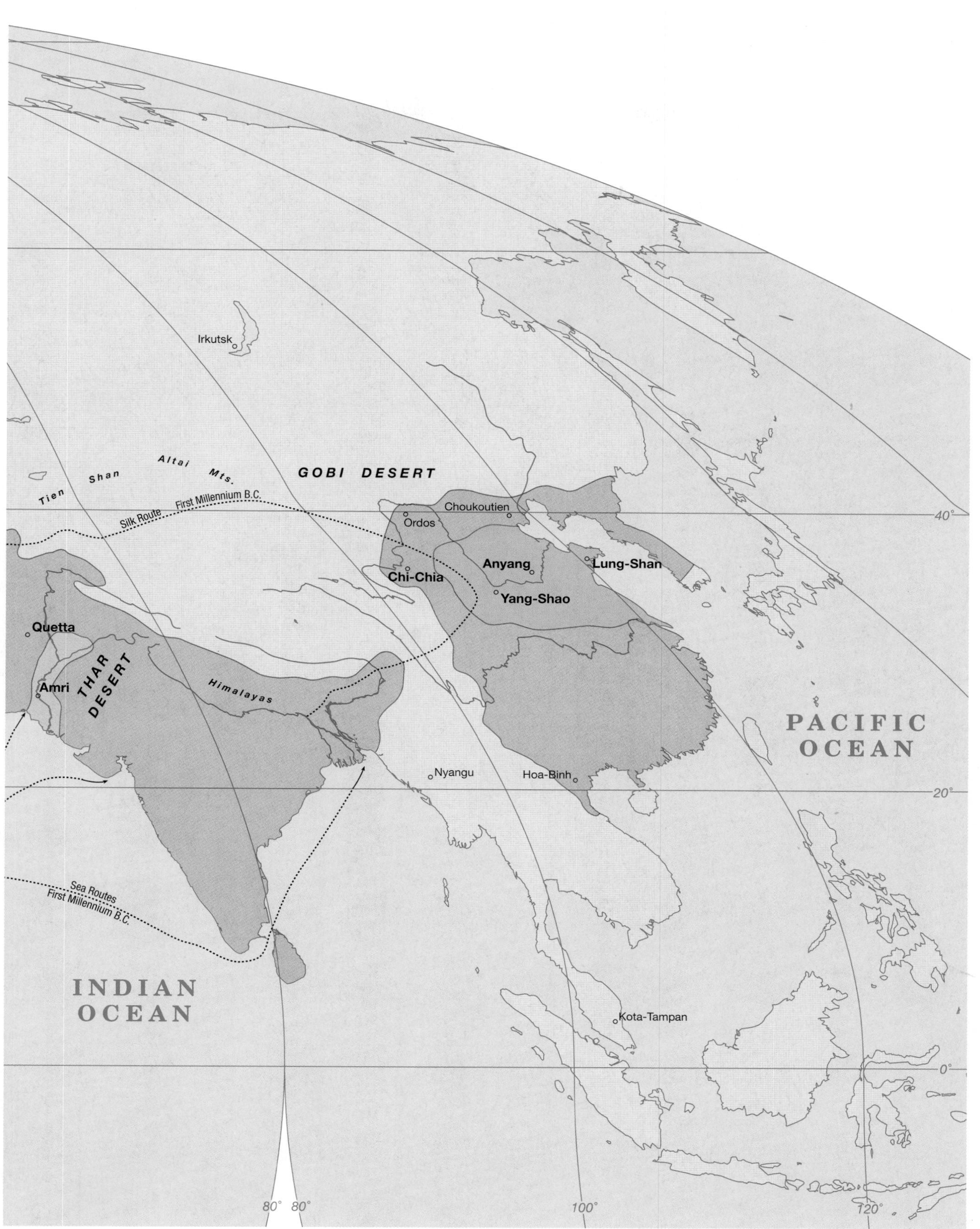
Irkutsk
Tien Shan
Altai Mts.
GOBI DESERT
Silk Route First Millennium B.C.
Choukoutien
Ordos
Anyang
Lung-Shan
Chi-Chia
Yang-Shao
Quetta
THAR DESERT
Amri
Himalayas
PACIFIC OCEAN
Nyangu
Hoa-Binh
Sea Routes First Millennium B.C.
INDIAN OCEAN
Kota-Tampan
40°
20°
0°
80°
80°
100°
120°

ARCTIC OCEAN
GREENLAND (Den.)
Baffin Bay
Arctic Circle
ICELAND
FAROE IS. (Den.)
ALASKA
RUSSIA
Yukon (U.S.)
Anchorage
Hudson Bay
CANADA
UNITED KINGDOM
IRELAND
London
Aleutian Islands
Vancouver
Newfoundland
Missouri
Montréal
Ottawa
FRANCE
Chicago
New York
Washington D.C.
Madrid
PORTUGAL
SPAIN
Azores (Port.)
UNITED STATES
Colorado
Mississippi
Los Angeles
Casablanca
MOROCCO
Houston
ATLANTIC
MIDWAY IS. (U.S.)
Canary Islands (Sp.)
Gulf of Mexico
MEXICO
BAHAMAS
Tropic of Cancer
Hawaiian Islands (U.S)
CUBA
HAITI
DOM. REP.
PUERTO RICO (U.S.)
Mexico City
BELIZE
JAMAICA
Caribbean Sea
CAPE VERDE
MAURITANIA
MALI
GUAT.
HOND.
SENEGAL
EL. SAL.
NIC.
GAMBIA
GUINEA-BISSAU
GUINEA
BURK. FASO
PACIFIC
Caracas
TRINIDAD AND TOBAGO
COSTA RICA
PANAMA
VENEZUELA
GUYANA
SIERRA LEONE
COTE D'IVOIRE
GHANA
LIBERIA
SURINAME
FRENCH GUIANA
COLOMBIA
Equator
KIRIBATI
Galapagos Islands (Ecuador)
ECUADOR
Amazon
BRAZIL
PERU
Lima
OCEAN
OCEAN
SAMOA
AMERICAN SAMOA
COOK ISLANDS (N.Z.)
TONGA
BOLIVIA
ST. HELENA (U.K.)
FRENCH POLYNESIA
Tropic of Capricorn
PARAGUAY
Rio de Janeiro
Easter Island (Chile)
ARGENTINA
URUGUAY
Santiago
Buenos Aires
CHILE
N
0 1000 2000 Miles
0 1000 2000 3000 Kilometers
Copyright by Rand McNally & Co.
Robinson Projection
FALKLAND IS. (U.K.)
South Georgia (U.K.)
South Orkney Is. (U.K.)
South Shetland Is. (U.K.)
Antarctic Circle
Weddell Sea
180° 165° 150° 135° 120° 105° 90° 75° 60° 45° 30° 15°
75° 60° 45° 30° 15° 0° 15° 30° 45° 60° 75°

- National Capital
- Major Cities

ARCTIC OCEAN
Greenland
Jan Mayen
Baffin Island
Baffin Bay
Arctic Circle
Iceland
Faroe Is.
British Isles
London
Yukon
Mackenzie
Mt. McKinley
20,320 Ft.
6,194m
Hudson Bay
Canadian Shield
NORTH AMERICA
Rocky Mountains
Great Plains
Aleutian Islands
Vancouver
Newfoundland
St. Lawrence
Appalachian Mts.
Mississippi
Colorado
Washington D.C.
Cape Hatteras
Los Angeles
Azores
Iberian Peninsula
Atlas Mts.
Midway Is.
Baja California
Gulf of Mexico
ATLANTIC
Canary Islands
Tropic of Cancer
Hawaiian Islands
Yucatan Peninsula
Cuba
Hispaniola
Puerto Rico
Jamaica
Caribbean Sea
Cape Verde Islands
Cape Verde
Niger
PACIFIC
Trinidad
Orinoco
OCEAN
Palmyra
Equator
Galapagos Islands
Amazon
Amazon Basin
SOUTH AMERICA
Kiribati
OCEAN
Andes
Marquesas Is.
Samoa Islands
Mato Grosso Plateau
St. Helena
Cook Islands
Tonga Is.
Tahiti
Tropic of Capricorn
Rio de Janeiro
Easter Island
Paraná
Mt. Aconcagua
22,831 Ft.
6,959m
Buenos Aires
Archipiélago Juan Fernández
Chatham Is.
Patagonia
0 1000 2000 Miles
0 1000 2000 3000 Kilometers
Copyright by Rand McNally & Co.
Robinson Projection
Falkland Is.
South Georgia
Tierra del Fuego
Cape Horn
South Sandwich Is.
South Orkney Is.
South Shetland Is.
Antarctic Circle
Antarctic Peninsula
Weddell Sea
Ross Sea
Marie Byrd Land
Vinson Massif
16,066 Ft.
4,897m

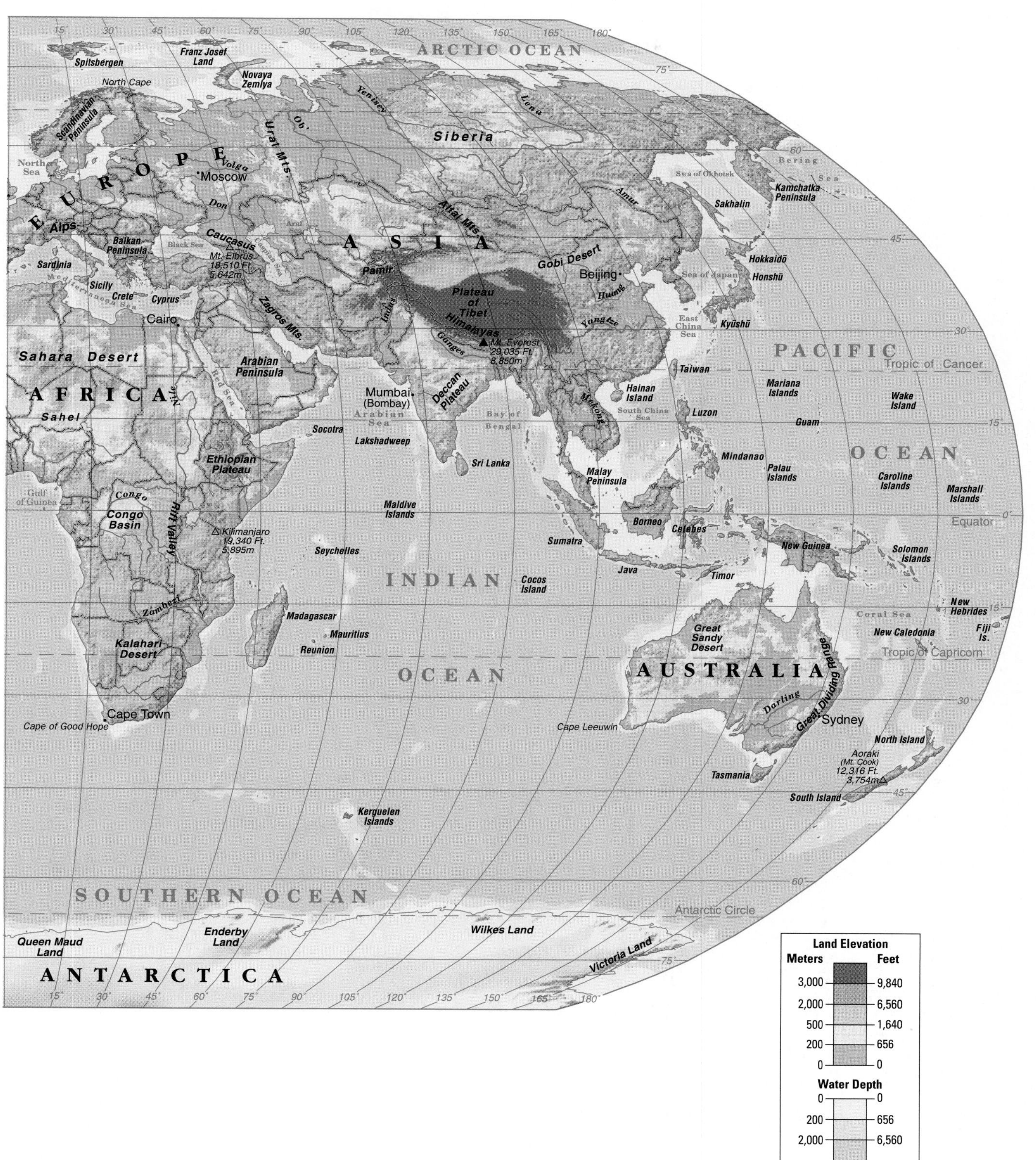

ARCTIC OCEAN
Spitsbergen
Franz Josef Land
North Cape
Novaya Zemlya
Scandinavian Peninsula
North Sea
EUROPE
Moscow
Volga
Don
Alps
Balkan Peninsula
Black Sea
Caucasus
Mt. Elbrus 18,510 Ft. 5,642m
Caspian Sea
Aral Sea
Sardinia
Sicily
Crete
Cyprus
Mediterranean Sea
Cairo
Ural Mts.
Ob'
Yenisey
Lena
Siberia
Altai Mts.
ASIA
Pamir
Plateau of Tibet
Himalayas
Mt. Everest 29,035 Ft. 8,850m
Indus
Ganges
Zagros Mts.
Arabian Peninsula
Red Sea
Gobi Desert
Beijing
Huang
Yangtze
Amur
Sea of Okhotsk
Bering Sea
Kamchatka Peninsula
Sakhalin
Hokkaidō
Honshū
Sea of Japan
Kyūshū
East China Sea
Taiwan
Hainan Island
South China Sea
Mekong
Luzon
Mindanao
Mumbai (Bombay)
Deccan Plateau
Arabian Sea
Bay of Bengal
Socotra
Lakshadweep
Sri Lanka
Maldive Islands
Malay Peninsula
Borneo
Celebes
Sumatra
Java
Timor
New Guinea
Sahara Desert
AFRICA
Nile
Sahel
Ethiopian Plateau
Gulf of Guinea
Congo
Congo Basin
Rift Valley
Kilimanjaro 19,340 Ft. 5,895m
Seychelles
Zambezi
Madagascar
Mauritius
Reunion
Kalahari Desert
Cape Town
Cape of Good Hope
INDIAN OCEAN
Cocos Island
PACIFIC OCEAN
Tropic of Cancer
Mariana Islands
Wake Island
Guam
Palau Islands
Caroline Islands
Marshall Islands
Equator
Solomon Islands
Coral Sea
New Hebrides
New Caledonia
Fiji Is.
Tropic of Capricorn
Great Sandy Desert
AUSTRALIA
Great Dividing Range
Darling
Sydney
Cape Leeuwin
Tasmania
North Island
Aoraki (Mt. Cook) 12,316 Ft. 3,754m
South Island
Kerguelen Islands
SOUTHERN OCEAN
Antarctic Circle
Queen Maud Land
Enderby Land
Wilkes Land
Victoria Land
ANTARCTICA
15° 30° 45° 60° 75° 90° 105° 120° 135° 150° 165° 180°
75° 60° 45° 30° 15° 0° 15° 30° 45° 60° 75°
Land Elevation
Meters Feet
3,000 9,840
2,000 6,560
500 1,640
200 656
0 0
Water Depth
0 0
200 656
2,000 6,560

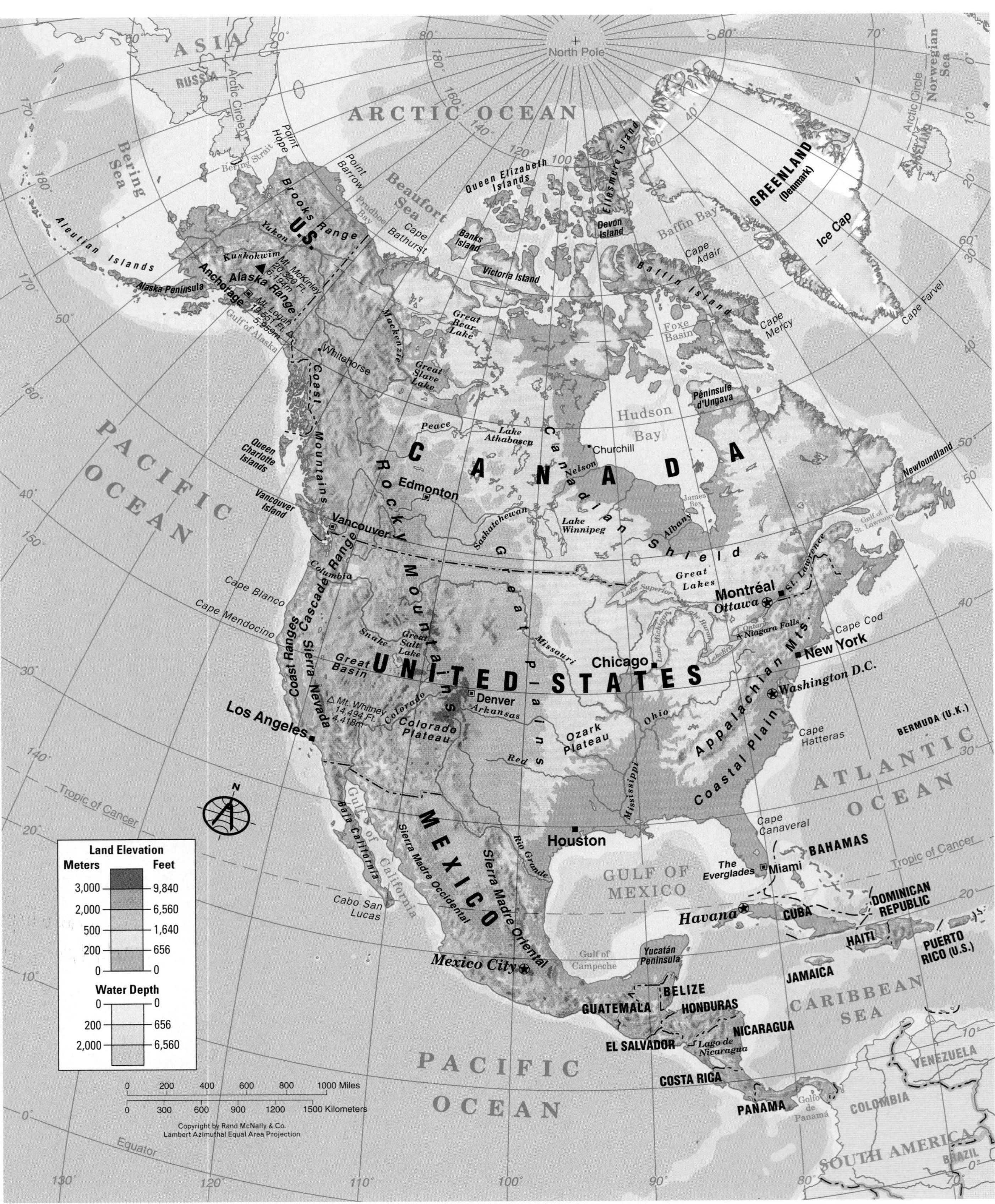
North Pole
ARCTIC OCEAN
ASIA
RUSSIA
Arctic Circle
Bering Sea
Bering Strait
Point Hope
Point Barrow
Prudhoe Bay
Beaufort Sea
Cape Bathurst
Queen Elizabeth Islands
Ellesmere Island
Devon Island
Banks Island
Victoria Island
GREENLAND (Denmark)
Ice Cap
Baffin Bay
Cape Adair
Baffin Island
Cape Mercy
Cape Farvel
Norwegian Sea
ICELAND
Aleutian Islands
Alaska Peninsula
U.S.
Brooks Range
Yukon
Kuskokwim
Mt. McKinley 20,320 Ft. 6,194m
Alaska Range
Anchorage
Mt. Logan 19,551 Ft. 5,959m
Gulf of Alaska
Whitehorse
Mackenzie
Great Bear Lake
Great Slave Lake
Foxe Basin
Péninsule d'Ungava
Hudson Bay
Churchill
Peace
Lake Athabasca
Canadian Shield
CANADA
Nelson
James Bay
Newfoundland
Gulf of St. Lawrence
Queen Charlotte Islands
Coast Mountains
Rocky Mountains
Edmonton
Saskatchewan
Lake Winnipeg
Albany
Vancouver Island
Vancouver
PACIFIC OCEAN
Columbia
Cascade Range
Great Plains
Great Lakes
Lake Superior
Lake Michigan
Lake Huron
Lake Erie
Lake Ontario
Niagara Falls
St. Lawrence
Montréal
Ottawa
Cape Cod
New York
Cape Blanco
Cape Mendocino
Snake
Great Salt Lake
Great Basin
Missouri
Chicago
UNITED STATES
Coast Ranges
Sierra Nevada
Mt. Whitney 14,494 Ft. 4,418m
Colorado
Denver
Arkansas
Colorado Plateau
Los Angeles
Ozark Plateau
Ohio
Washington D.C.
Appalachian Mts.
Coastal Plain
Cape Hatteras
BERMUDA (U.K.)
ATLANTIC OCEAN
Red
Mississippi
Tropic of Cancer
Baja California
Gulf of California
Sierra Madre Occidental
MEXICO
Sierra Madre Oriental
Rio Grande
Houston
Cape Canaveral
BAHAMAS
The Everglades
Miami
GULF OF MEXICO
Cabo San Lucas
Havana
CUBA
DOMINICAN REPUBLIC
HAITI
PUERTO RICO (U.S.)
JAMAICA
Gulf of Campeche
Yucatán Peninsula
Mexico City
BELIZE
GUATEMALA
HONDURAS
CARIBBEAN SEA
NICARAGUA
EL SALVADOR
Lago de Nicaragua
COSTA RICA
PANAMA
Golfo de Panamá
VENEZUELA
COLOMBIA
SOUTH AMERICA
BRAZIL
Equator
Land Elevation
Meters
Feet
3,000
9,840
2,000
6,560
500
1,640
200
656
0
0
Water Depth
0
0
200
656
2,000
6,560
0 200 400 600 800 1000 Miles
0 300 600 900 1200 1500 Kilometers
Copyright by Rand McNally & Co.
Lambert Azimuthal Equal Area Projection

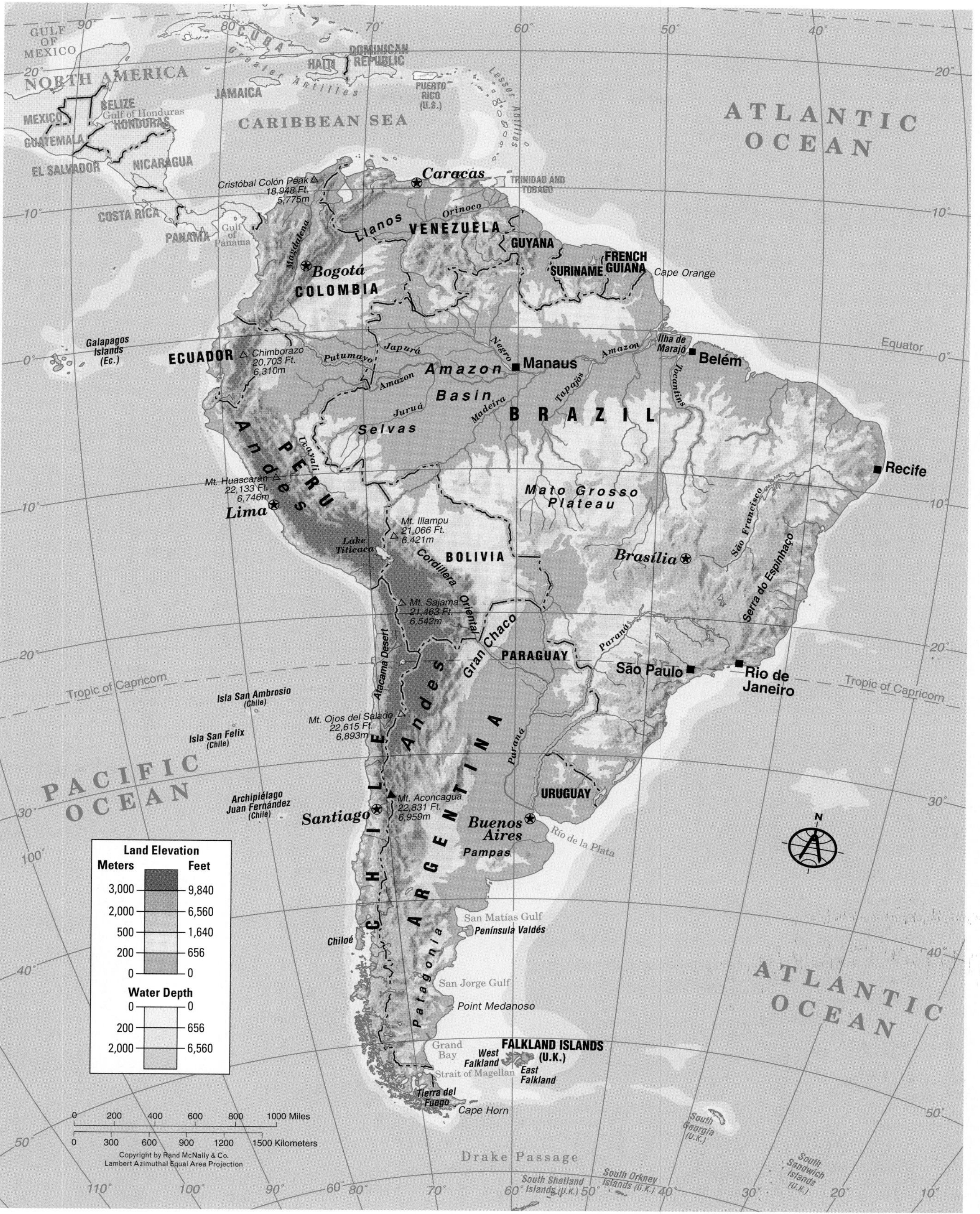

GULF OF MEXICO
NORTH AMERICA
CUBA
Greater Antilles
HAITI
DOMINICAN REPUBLIC
JAMAICA
PUERTO RICO (U.S.)
Lesser Antilles
BELIZE
MEXICO
Gulf of Honduras
HONDURAS
GUATEMALA
CARIBBEAN SEA
EL SALVADOR
NICARAGUA
ATLANTIC OCEAN
Cristóbal Colón Peak 18,948 Ft. 5,775m
Caracas
TRINIDAD AND TOBAGO
COSTA RICA
PANAMA
Gulf of Panama
Llanos
Orinoco
VENEZUELA
GUYANA
Magdalena
Bogotá
COLOMBIA
SURINAME
FRENCH GUIANA
Cape Orange
Galapagos Islands (Ec.)
ECUADOR
Chimborazo 20,703 Ft. 6,310m
Putumayo
Japurá
Negro
Manaus
Amazon
Ilha de Marajó
Belém
Equator
Amazon Basin
Tapajós
Tocantins
Juruá
Madeira
BRAZIL
Selvas
Ucayali
PERU
Andes
Mt. Huascarán 22,133 Ft. 6,746m
Lima
Recife
Mato Grosso Plateau
Mt. Illampu 21,066 Ft. 6,421m
Lake Titicaca
BOLIVIA
São Francisco
Brasília
Cordillera Oriental
Serra do Espinhaço
Mt. Sajama 21,463 Ft. 6,542m
Paraná
Gran Chaco
Atacama Desert
PARAGUAY
São Paulo
Rio de Janeiro
Tropic of Capricorn
Isla San Ambrosio (Chile)
Mt. Ojos del Salado 22,615 Ft. 6,893m
Isla San Felix (Chile)
PACIFIC OCEAN
ARGENTINA
URUGUAY
Archipiélago Juan Fernández (Chile)
Mt. Aconcagua 22,831 Ft. 6,959m
Santiago
Buenos Aires
Río de la Plata
Pampas
CHILE
N
Land Elevation
Meters
Feet
3,000
9,840
2,000
6,560
500
1,640
200
656
0
0
Water Depth
0
0
200
656
2,000
6,560
San Matías Gulf
Península Valdés
Chiloé
Patagonia
San Jorge Gulf
Point Medanoso
Grand Bay
West Falkland
FALKLAND ISLANDS (U.K.)
East Falkland
Strait of Magellan
Tierra del Fuego
Cape Horn
South Georgia (U.K.)
0 200 400 600 800 1000 Miles
0 300 600 900 1200 1500 Kilometers
Copyright by Rand McNally & Co.
Lambert Azimuthal Equal Area Projection
Drake Passage
South Shetland Islands (U.K.)
South Orkney Islands (U.K.)
South Sandwich Islands (U.K.)

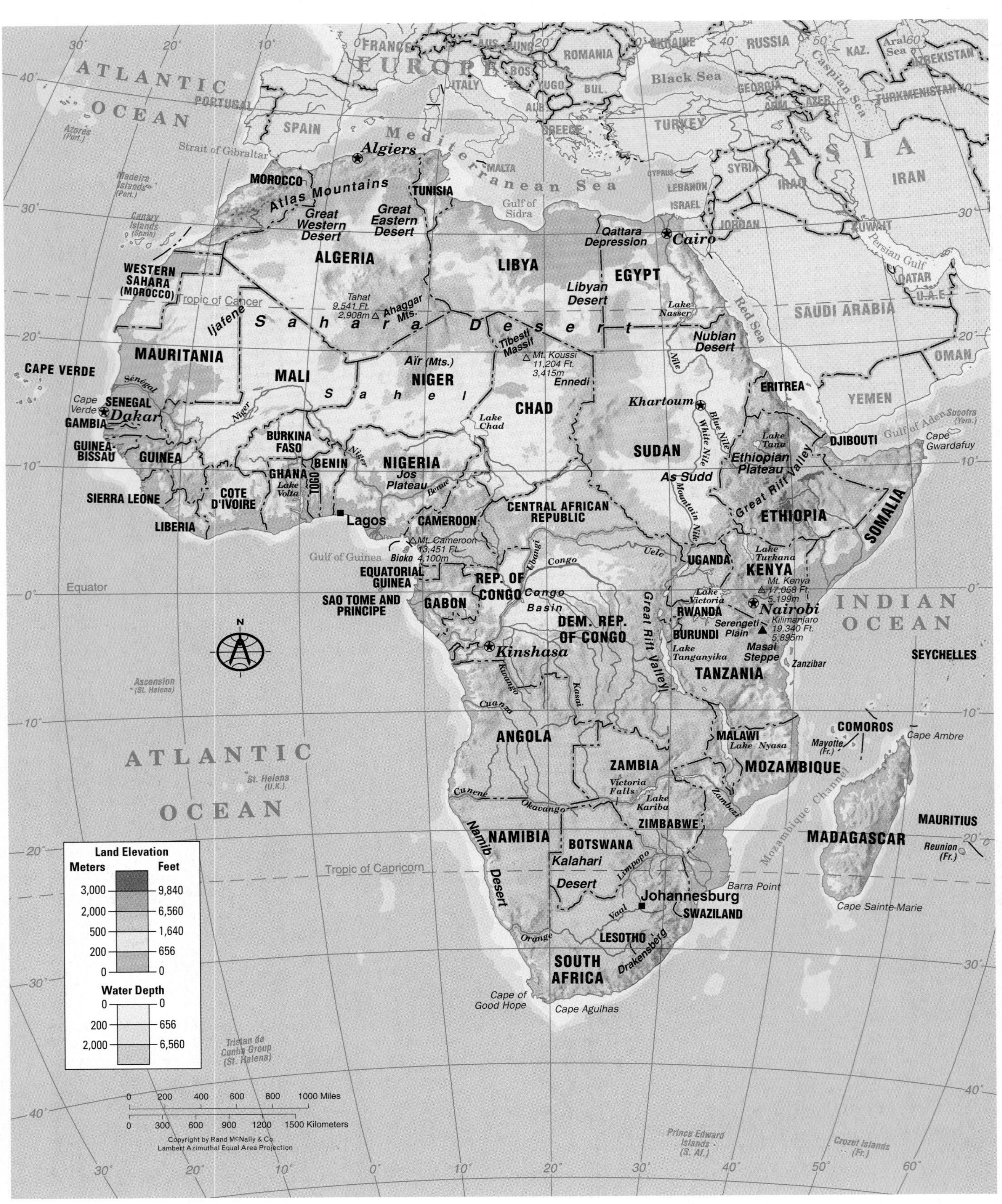
ATLANTIC OCEAN
EUROPE
Mediterranean Sea
Algiers
Atlas Mountains
Great Western Desert
Great Eastern Desert
ALGERIA
LIBYA
EGYPT
Cairo
Qattara Depression
Libyan Desert
Sahara Desert
Tahat 9,541 Ft. 2,908m
Ahaggar Mts.
Tibesti Massif
Mt. Koussi 11,204 Ft. 3,415m
MAURITANIA
MALI
NIGER
CHAD
SUDAN
Khartoum
Sahel
Aïr (Mts.)
Dakar
NIGERIA
Lagos
Lake Chad
Gulf of Guinea
Equator
CENTRAL AFRICAN REPUBLIC
Congo Basin
DEM. REP. OF CONGO
Kinshasa
ETHIOPIA
Ethiopian Plateau
Great Rift Valley
KENYA
Nairobi
Mt. Kenya 17,058 Ft. 5,199m
Kilimanjaro 19,340 Ft. 5,895m
TANZANIA
INDIAN OCEAN
ANGOLA
ZAMBIA
MOZAMBIQUE
MADAGASCAR
NAMIBIA
BOTSWANA
Kalahari Desert
Namib Desert
SOUTH AFRICA
Johannesburg
Cape of Good Hope
Cape Agulhas
Tropic of Cancer
Tropic of Capricorn
Land Elevation
Meters Feet
3,000 9,840
2,000 6,560
500 1,640
200 656
0 0
Water Depth
0 0
200 656
2,000 6,560
0 200 400 600 800 1000 Miles
0 300 600 900 1200 1500 Kilometers
Copyright by Rand McNally & Co.
Lambert Azimuthal Equal Area Projection

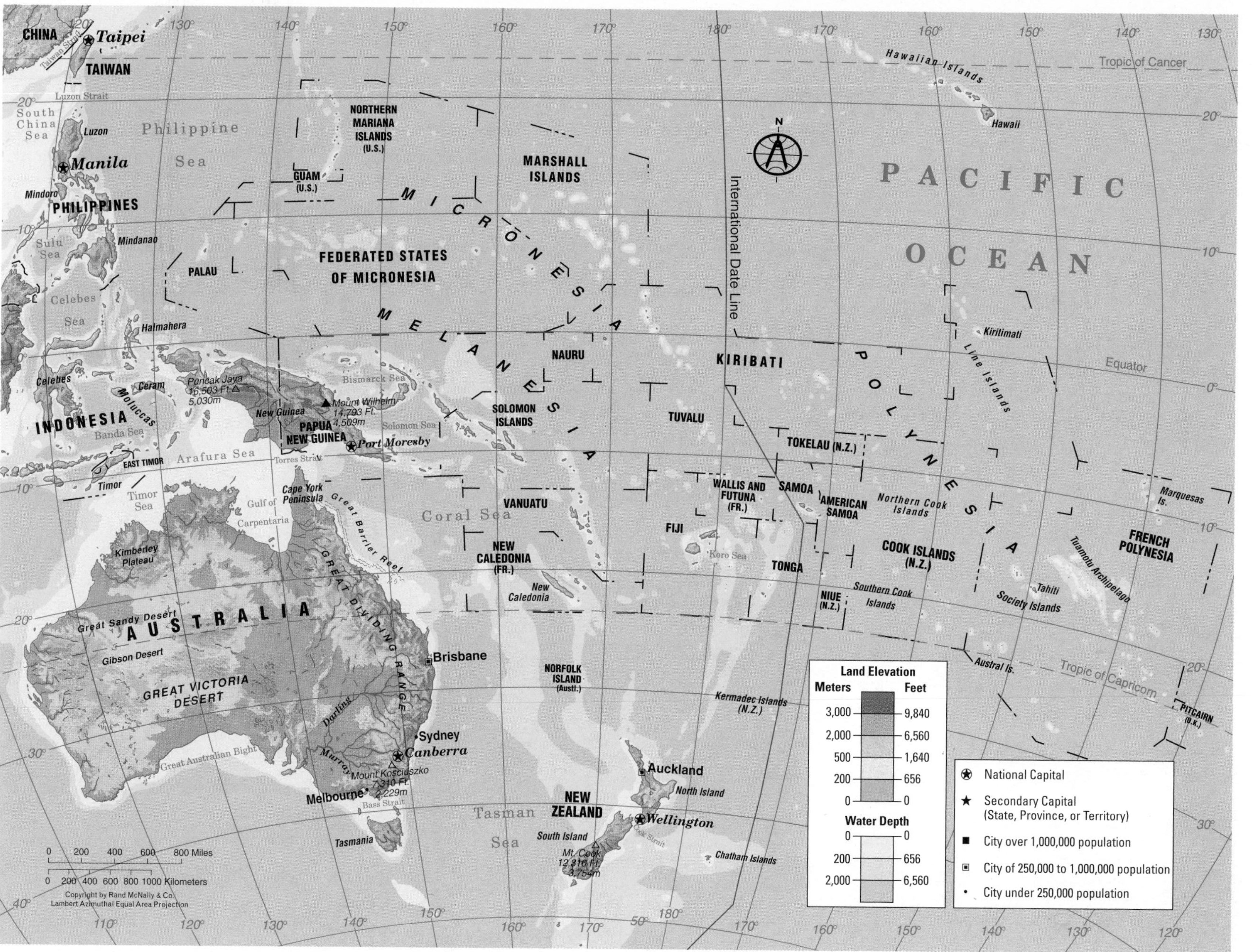
CHINA
Taipei
TAIWAN
Taiwan Strait
Luzon Strait
South China Sea
Luzon
Philippine Sea
Manila
Mindoro
PHILIPPINES
Mindanao
Sulu Sea
Celebes Sea
Halmahera
Celebes
Ceram
Moluccas
INDONESIA
Banda Sea
EAST TIMOR
Timor
Timor Sea
Arafura Sea
Puncak Jaya 16,503 Ft. 5,030m
New Guinea
PAPUA NEW GUINEA
Mount Wilhelm 14,793 Ft. 4,509m
Bismarck Sea
Solomon Sea
Port Moresby
Torres Strait
Cape York Peninsula
Gulf of Carpentaria
Great Barrier Reef
Kimberley Plateau
Great Sandy Desert
AUSTRALIA
Gibson Desert
GREAT VICTORIA DESERT
GREAT DIVIDING RANGE
Darling
Murray
Brisbane
Sydney
Canberra
Mount Kosciuszko 7,310 Ft. 2,229m
Melbourne
Bass Strait
Great Australian Bight
Tasmania
Tasman Sea
NORTHERN MARIANA ISLANDS (U.S.)
GUAM (U.S.)
PALAU
FEDERATED STATES OF MICRONESIA
MICRONESIA
MARSHALL ISLANDS
MELANESIA
NAURU
SOLOMON ISLANDS
VANUATU
Coral Sea
NEW CALEDONIA (FR.)
New Caledonia
NORFOLK ISLAND (Austl.)
NEW ZEALAND
North Island
South Island
Auckland
Wellington
Cook Strait
Mt. Cook 12,316 Ft. 3,754m
Chatham Islands
Kermadec Islands (N.Z.)
International Date Line
KIRIBATI
TUVALU
FIJI
Koro Sea
WALLIS AND FUTUNA (FR.)
SAMOA
AMERICAN SAMOA
TOKELAU (N.Z.)
TONGA
NIUE (N.Z.)
POLYNESIA
Northern Cook Islands
COOK ISLANDS (N.Z.)
Southern Cook Islands
Hawaiian Islands
Hawaii
PACIFIC OCEAN
Kiritimati
Line Islands
Equator
Marquesas Is.
FRENCH POLYNESIA
Tuamotu Archipelago
Tahiti
Society Islands
Austral Is.
PITCAIRN (U.K.)
Tropic of Cancer
Tropic of Capricorn
Land Elevation
Meters Feet
3,000 9,840
2,000 6,560
500 1,640
200 656
0 0
Water Depth
0 0
200 656
2,000 6,560
National Capital
Secondary Capital (State, Province, or Territory)
City over 1,000,000 population
City of 250,000 to 1,000,000 population
City under 250,000 population
0 200 400 600 800 Miles
0 200 400 600 800 1000 Kilometers
Copyright by Rand McNally & Co.
Lambert Azimuthal Equal Area Projection

ICELAND
Horn
Fontur
Surtsey
Arctic Circle
NORWEGIAN SEA
Lofoten Islands
Kebnekaise 6,926 Ft. 2,111m
Torneälven
Lap
Luleälven
Umeälven
Scandinavian Peninsula
Gulf of Bothnia
ATLANTIC OCEAN
FAROE ISLANDS (Den.)
NORWAY
SWEDEN
Galdhøpiggen 8,100 Ft. 2,469m
Glama
Klarälven
Dalälven
Hebrides
Orkney Islands
Stockholm
Grampian Mts.
Land Elevation
Meters
Feet
3,000
9,840
2,000
6,560
500
1,640
200
656
0
0
Water Depth
0
0
200
656
2,000
6,560
UNITED KINGDOM
Skagerrak
Vänern
Vättern
NORTH SEA
Cheviot Hills
DENMARK
Öland
BALTIC SEA
IRELAND
Irish Sea
Great Britain
St. George's Channel
Bornholm (Den.)
RUSSIA
Thames
London
NETHERLANDS
Elbe
Berlin
Northern Euro
Oder
POLAND
Wisła
English Channel
Strait of Dover
BELGIUM
GERMANY
Rhine
0
100
200
300
400 Miles
0
200
400
600 Kilometers
Copyright by Rand McNally & Co.
Lambert Conformal Conic Projection
LUX.
Paris
Paris Basin
Seine
Loire
Bohemian Forest
CZECH REPUBLIC
Black Forest
SLOVAKIA
Danube
FRANCE
Bay of Biscay
Saône
Jura
SWITZERLAND
LIECH.
AUSTRIA
HUNGARY
Great Hungarian Plain
Mt. Blanc 15,771 Ft. 4,808m
Alps
Dordogne
Massif Central
Rhône
SLOVENIA
Drava
Cantabrian Mts.
CROATIA
Po
Douro
Duero
Iberian Mts.
Ebro
Pyrenees
ANDORRA
Apennines
SAN MARINO
Dinaric Alps
BOSNIA AND HERZEGOVINA
MONACO
Balkan
SERBIA AND MONTENEGRO
Lisbon
PORTUGAL
Iberian Peninsula
Tagus
SPAIN
Corsica (Fr.)
ADRIATIC SEA
Rome
ITALY
Sierra Morena
Balearic Islands
Minorca
Majorca
Ibiza
Sardinia (It.)
Vesuvius 4,190 Ft. 1,277m
ALBANIA
MACEDONIA
Pindus Mts.
Strait of Gibraltar
GIBRALTAR (U.K.)
TYRRHENIAN SEA
Mt. Etna 10,902 Ft. 3,323m
Sicily
IONIAN SEA
Algiers
MEDITERRANEAN
AFRICA
ALGERIA
MOROCCO
TUNISIA
MALTA

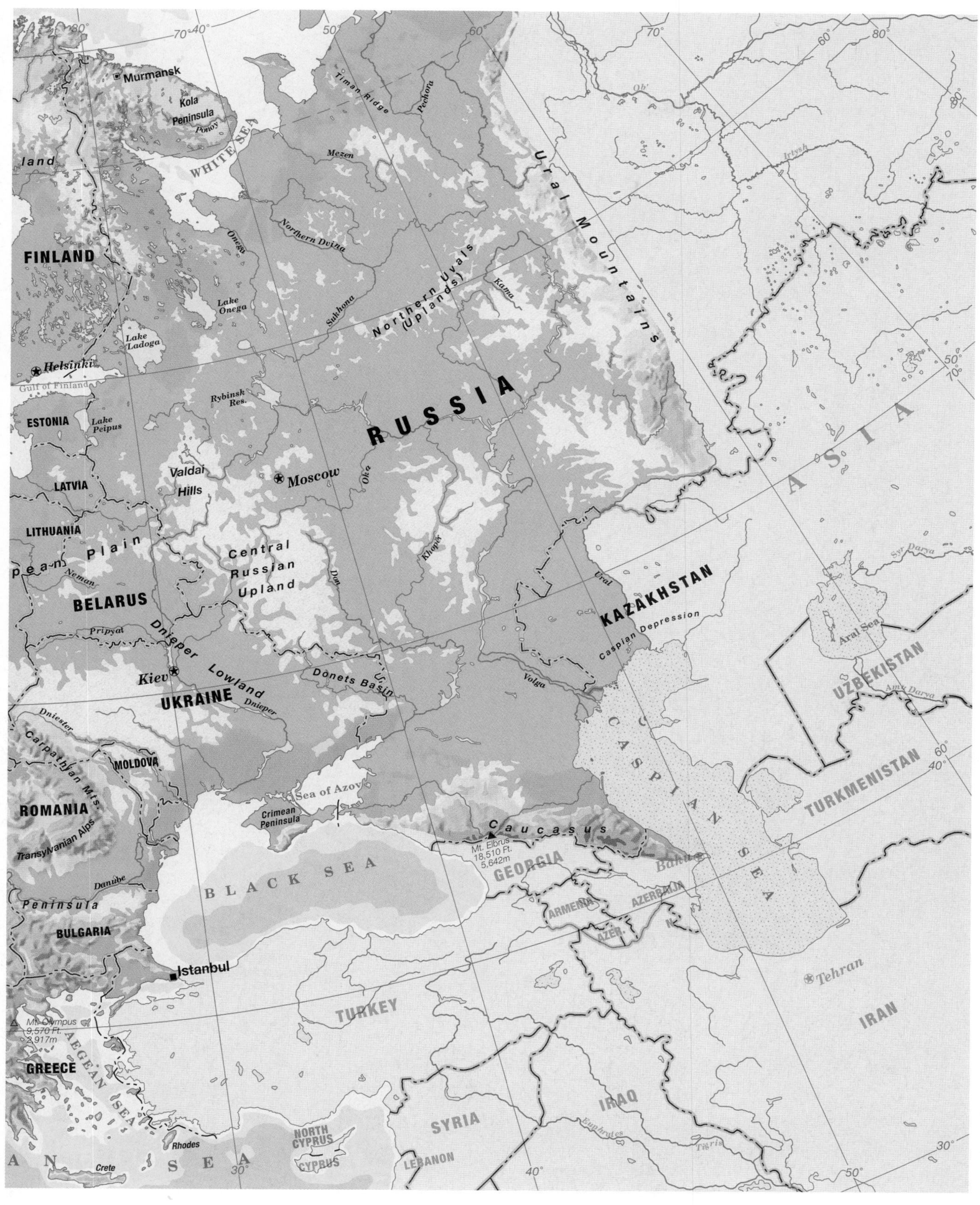
Murmansk
Kola Peninsula
WHITE SEA
Timan Ridge
Pechora
Mezen
Northern Dvina
Onega
FINLAND
Lake Onega
Lake Ladoga
Helsinki
Gulf of Finland
Sukhona
Northern Uvals (Uplands)
Kama
Ural Mountains
Ob'
Irtysh
ESTONIA
Lake Peipus
Rybinsk Res.
RUSSIA
Moscow
Valdai Hills
Oka
LATVIA
LITHUANIA
Plain
Central Russian Upland
Don
Khoper
Neman
BELARUS
Pripyat
Dnieper Lowland
Kiev
UKRAINE
Dnieper
Donets Basin
Volga
Ural
KAZAKHSTAN
Caspian Depression
ASIA
Syr Darya
Aral Sea
UZBEKISTAN
Amu Darya
TURKMENISTAN
Dniester
Carpathian Mts.
MOLDOVA
ROMANIA
Transylvanian Alps
Sea of Azov
Crimean Peninsula
Caucasus
Mt. Elbrus 18,510 Ft. 5,642m
GEORGIA
CASPIAN SEA
Baku
ARMENIA
AZERBAIJAN
AZER.
Danube
BLACK SEA
Peninsula
BULGARIA
Istanbul
Tehran
TURKEY
IRAN
Mt. Olympus 9,570 Ft. 2,917m
AEGEAN SEA
GREECE
IRAQ
SYRIA
Euphrates
Tigris
NORTH CYPRUS
CYPRUS
LEBANON
Rhodes
Crete
SEA

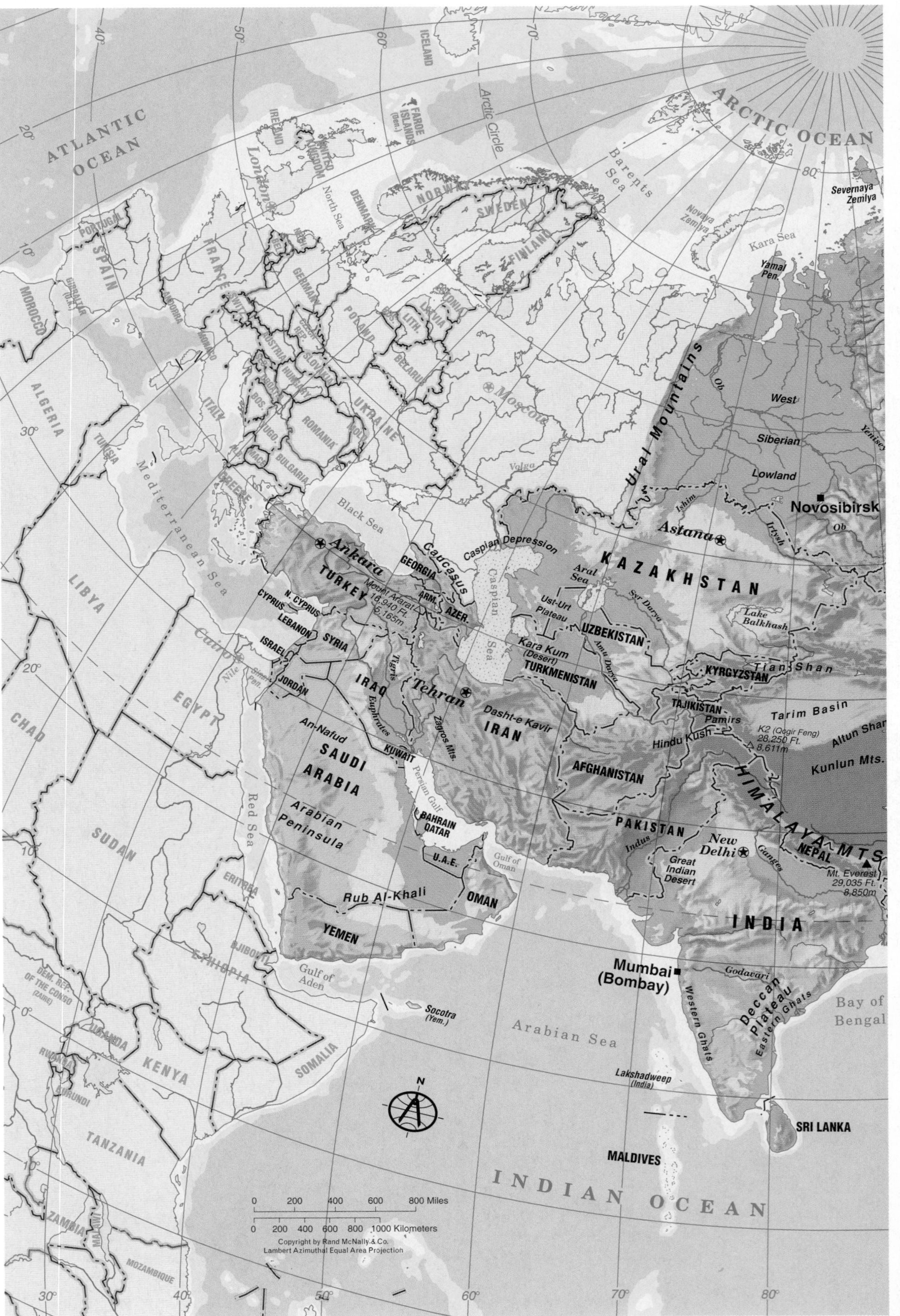

ATLANTIC OCEAN
ARCTIC OCEAN
Arctic Circle
Barents Sea
Kara Sea
Novaya Zemlya
Severnaya Zemlya
Yamal Pen.
ICELAND
FAROE ISLANDS (Den.)
IRELAND
UNITED KINGDOM
London
North Sea
DENMARK
NORWAY
SWEDEN
FINLAND
ESTONIA
LATVIA
LITH.
BELARUS
POLAND
GERMANY
FRANCE
PORTUGAL
SPAIN
GIBRALTAR (U.K.)
ANDORRA
MONACO
MOROCCO
ALGERIA
TUNISIA
LIBYA
EGYPT
CHAD
SUDAN
ERITREA
DJIBOUTI
ETHIOPIA
SOMALIA
KENYA
UGANDA
RWANDA
BURUNDI
TANZANIA
DEM. REP. OF THE CONGO (ZAIRE)
ZAMBIA
MOZAMBIQUE
ITALY
AUSTRIA
SLOVAKIA
HUNGARY
ROMANIA
MOLD.
UKRAINE
BULGARIA
GREECE
YUGO.
BOS.
MAC.
Mediterranean Sea
Black Sea
Moscow
Volga
Ural Mountains
Ob
West Siberian Lowland
Yenisey
Novosibirsk
Ishim
Irtysh
Astana
Caspian Depression
Caucasus
Caspian Sea
KAZAKHSTAN
Aral Sea
Syr Darya
Ust-Urt Plateau
UZBEKISTAN
Amu Darya
Kara Kum (Desert)
TURKMENISTAN
Lake Balkhash
KYRGYZSTAN
Tian Shan
TAJIKISTAN
Pamirs
Tarim Basin
K2 (Qogir Feng) 28,250 Ft. 8,611m
Altun Shan
Kunlun Mts.
Hindu Kush
HIMALAYA MTS.
NEPAL
Mt. Everest 29,035 Ft. 8,850m
Ankara
TURKEY
GEORGIA
ARM.
AZER.
Mount Ararat 16,940 Ft. 5,165m
N. CYPRUS
CYPRUS
LEBANON
SYRIA
ISRAEL
JORDAN
Cairo
Nile
Sinai Pen.
IRAQ
Tigris
Euphrates
Tehran
Zagros Mts.
Dasht-e Kavir
IRAN
AFGHANISTAN
PAKISTAN
Indus
New Delhi
Ganges
Great Indian Desert
INDIA
An-Nafud
SAUDI ARABIA
KUWAIT
Persian Gulf
BAHRAIN
QATAR
U.A.E.
Gulf of Oman
OMAN
Arabian Peninsula
Rub Al-Khali
YEMEN
Red Sea
Gulf of Aden
Socotra (Yem.)
Arabian Sea
Mumbai (Bombay)
Godavari
Western Ghats
Deccan Plateau
Eastern Ghats
Bay of Bengal
Lakshadweep (India)
MALDIVES
SRI LANKA
INDIAN OCEAN
N
0 200 400 600 800 Miles
0 200 400 600 800 1000 Kilometers
Copyright by Rand McNally & Co.
Lambert Azimuthal Equal Area Projection

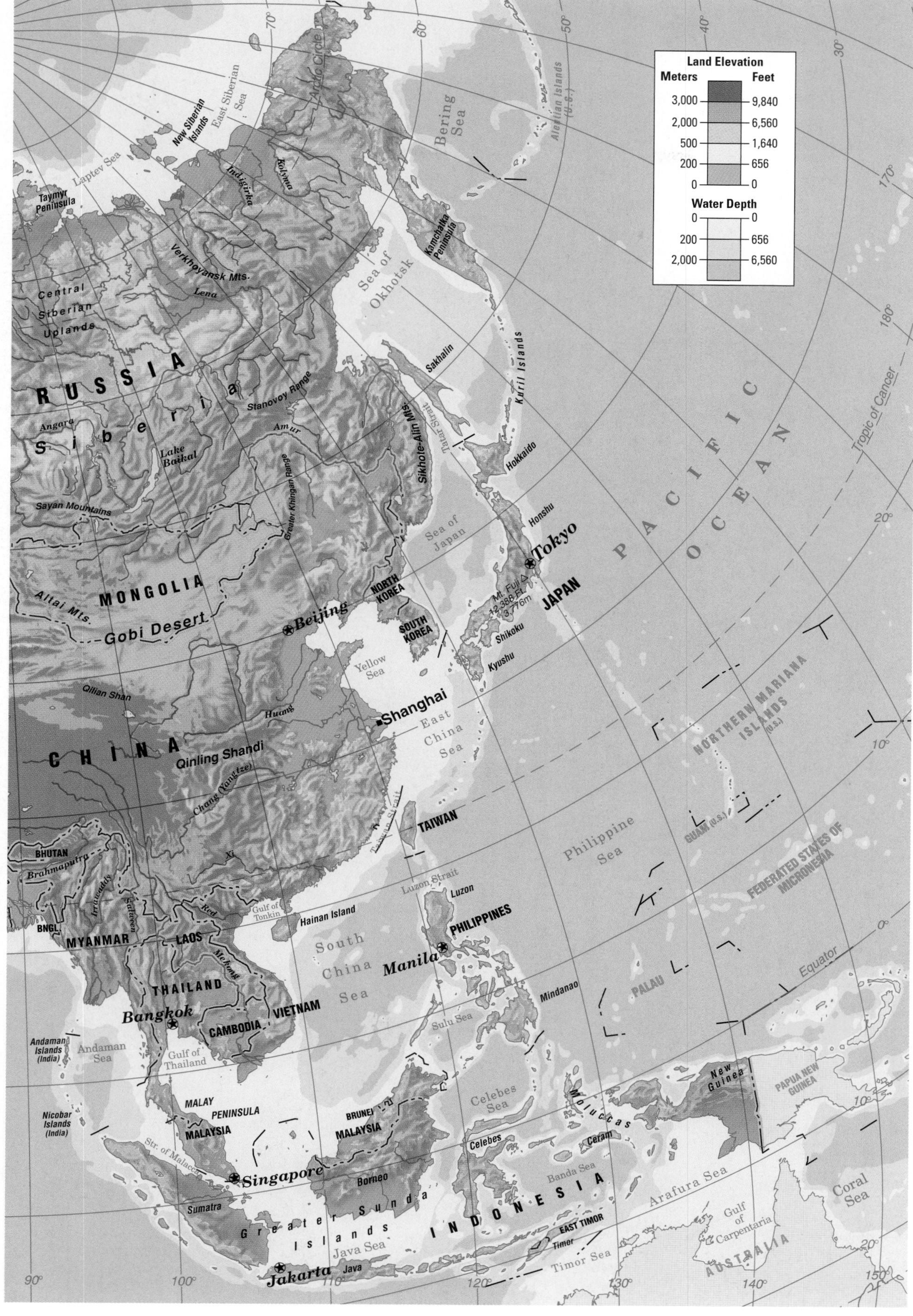
Land Elevation
Meters
Feet
3,000
9,840
2,000
6,560
500
1,640
200
656
0
0
Water Depth
0
0
200
656
2,000
6,560
Arctic Circle
East Siberian Sea
New Siberian Islands
Laptev Sea
Taymyr Peninsula
Indigirka
Kolyma
Bering Sea
Aleutian Islands (U.S.)
Kamchatka Peninsula
Sea of Okhotsk
Verkhoyansk Mts.
Lena
Central Siberian Uplands
RUSSIA
Siberia
Stanovoy Range
Angara
Amur
Lake Baikal
Sakhalin
Kuril Islands
Tatar Strait
Sikhote-Alin Mts.
Hokkaido
Greater Khingan Range
Sayan Mountains
Honshu
Sea of Japan
Tokyo
PACIFIC OCEAN
Tropic of Cancer
MONGOLIA
Altai Mts.
Gobi Desert
Beijing
NORTH KOREA
SOUTH KOREA
Mt. Fuji 12,388 ft. 3,776m
JAPAN
Shikoku
Kyushu
Yellow Sea
Qilian Shan
Huang
Shanghai
East China Sea
NORTHERN MARIANA ISLANDS (U.S.)
CHINA
Qinling Shandi
Chang (Yangtze)
Taiwan Strait
TAIWAN
GUAM (U.S.)
Philippine Sea
FEDERATED STATES OF MICRONESIA
BHUTAN
Brahmaputra
Irrawaddy
Salween
Xi
Luzon Strait
Luzon
Gulf of Tonkin
Red
Hainan Island
PHILIPPINES
BNGL.
MYANMAR
LAOS
Mekong
South China Sea
Manila
THAILAND
PALAU
Equator
Mindanao
Bangkok
VIETNAM
CAMBODIA
Sulu Sea
Andaman Islands (India)
Andaman Sea
Gulf of Thailand
New Guinea
PAPUA NEW GUINEA
Celebes Sea
MALAY PENINSULA
BRUNEI
Moluccas
Nicobar Islands (India)
MALAYSIA
MALAYSIA
Celebes
Ceram
Str. of Malacca
Singapore
Borneo
Banda Sea
Arafura Sea
Coral Sea
Sumatra
Greater Sunda Islands
INDONESIA
Gulf of Carpentaria
EAST TIMOR
Timor
Java Sea
Timor Sea
AUSTRALIA
Jakarta
Java
90°
100°
110°
120°
130°
140°
150°
70°
60°
50°
40°
30°
20°
10°
0°
170°
180°

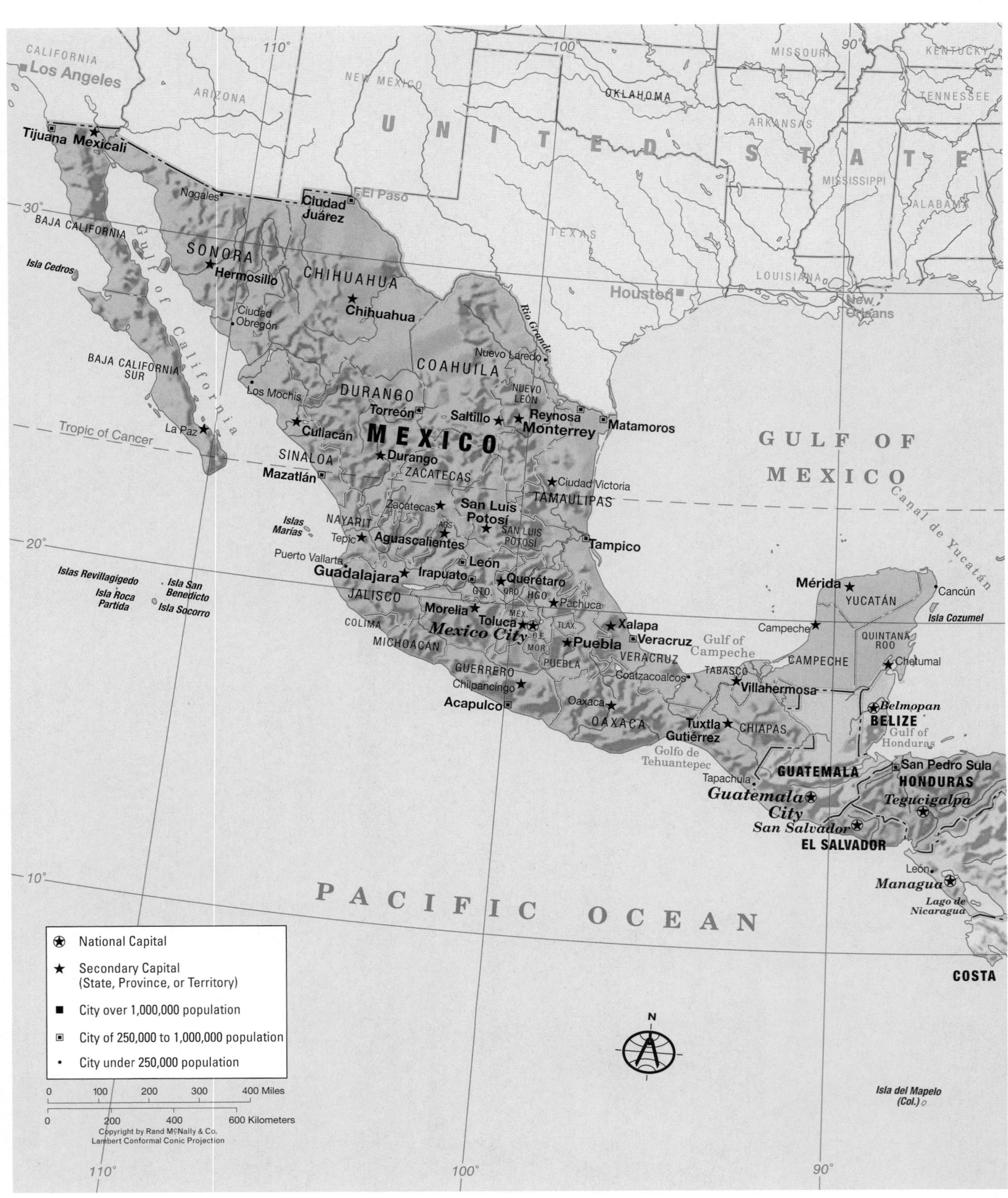
CALIFORNIA
Los Angeles
ARIZONA
NEW MEXICO
OKLAHOMA
MISSOURI
KENTUCKY
TENNESSEE
ARKANSAS
UNITED STATES
MISSISSIPPI
ALABAMA
TEXAS
LOUISIANA
Houston
New Orleans
El Paso
Tijuana
Mexicali
Nogales
Ciudad Juárez
BAJA CALIFORNIA
SONORA
Hermosillo
Isla Cedros
Gulf of California
CHIHUAHUA
Chihuahua
Ciudad Obregón
Rio Grande
Nuevo Laredo
COAHUILA
BAJA CALIFORNIA SUR
Los Mochis
DURANGO
NUEVO LEÓN
Torreón
Saltillo
Reynosa
Monterrey
Matamoros
La Paz
Tropic of Cancer
Culiacán
MEXICO
GULF OF MEXICO
SINALOA
Durango
Mazatlán
ZACATECAS
Ciudad Victoria
TAMAULIPAS
Zacatecas
San Luis Potosí
Islas Marías
NAYARIT
AGS.
SAN LUIS POTOSÍ
Tepic
Aguascalientes
Tampico
Canal de Yucatán
Puerto Vallarta
León
Islas Revillagigedo
Isla San Benedicto
Isla Roca Partida
Isla Socorro
Guadalajara
Irapuato
Querétaro
Mérida
Cancún
JALISCO
GTO.
QRO.
HGO.
YUCATÁN
Pachuca
Isla Cozumel
Morelia
MÉX.
COLIMA
Toluca
Xalapa
Campeche
Mexico City
TLAX.
Veracruz
Gulf of Campeche
QUINTANA ROO
D.F.
MICHOACÁN
MOR.
Puebla
VERACRUZ
PUEBLA
CAMPECHE
Chetumal
TABASCO
GUERRERO
Coatzacoalcos
Chilpancingo
Villahermosa
Acapulco
Oaxaca
Belmopan
OAXACA
Tuxtla Gutiérrez
CHIAPAS
BELIZE
Gulf of Honduras
Golfo de Tehuantepec
San Pedro Sula
Tapachula
GUATEMALA
HONDURAS
Guatemala City
Tegucigalpa
San Salvador
EL SALVADOR
León
Managua
Lago de Nicaragua
PACIFIC OCEAN
COSTA
Isla del Mapelo (Col.)
30°
20°
10°
110°
100°
90°
National Capital
Secondary Capital (State, Province, or Territory)
City over 1,000,000 population
City of 250,000 to 1,000,000 population
City under 250,000 population
0 100 200 300 400 Miles
0 200 400 600 Kilometers
Copyright by Rand McNally & Co.
Lambert Conformal Conic Projection
N

RAND McNALLY

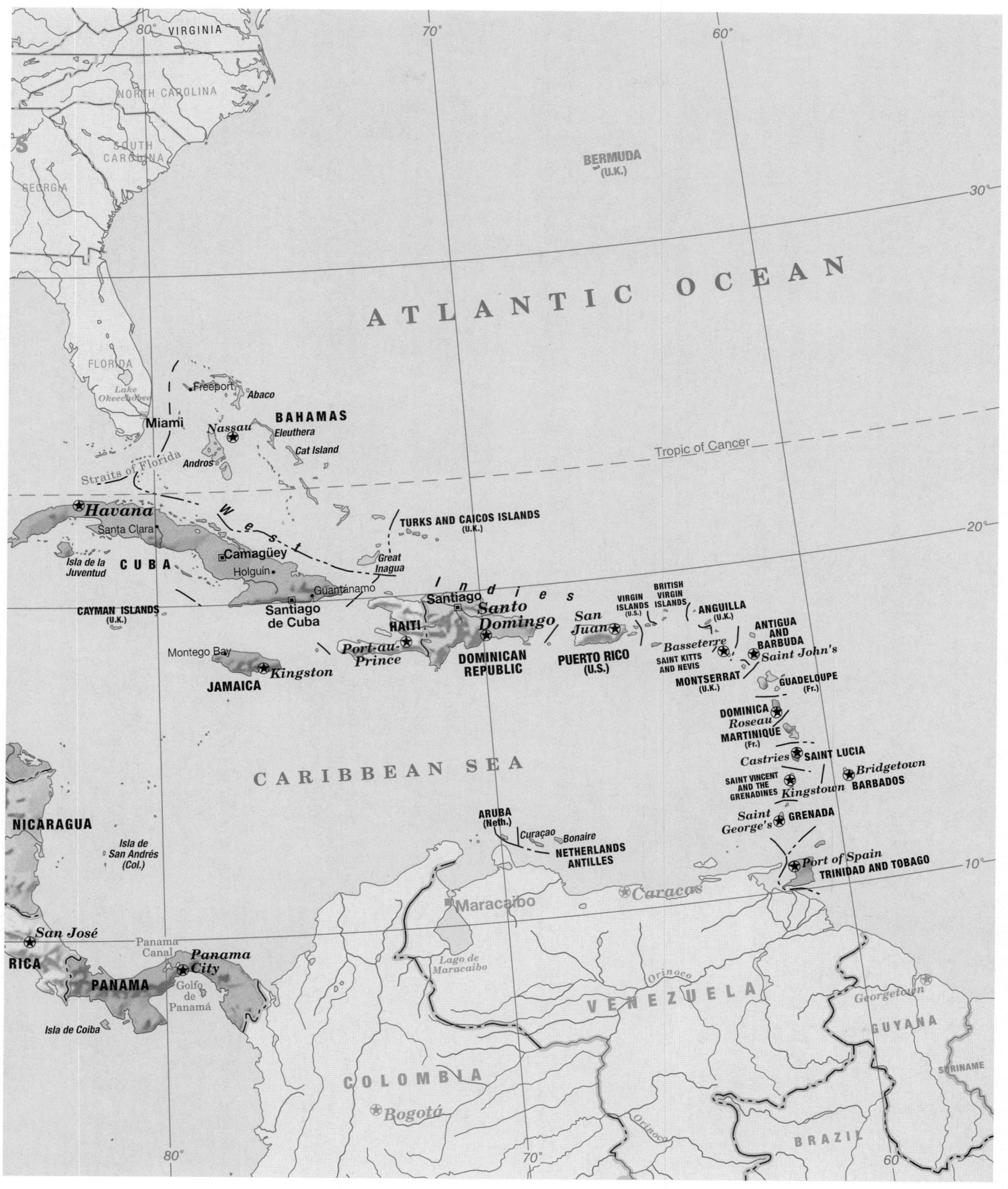
VIRGINIA
NORTH CAROLINA
SOUTH CAROLINA
GEORGIA
FLORIDA
Lake Okeechobee
Miami
Freeport
Abaco
Nassau
BAHAMAS
Eleuthera
Cat Island
Andros
Straits of Florida
BERMUDA (U.K.)
ATLANTIC OCEAN
Tropic of Cancer
West Indies
Havana
Santa Clara
Camagüey
Holguín
CUBA
Isla de la Juventud
Guantánamo
Santiago de Cuba
Great Inagua
TURKS AND CAICOS ISLANDS (U.K.)
CAYMAN ISLANDS (U.K.)
Montego Bay
JAMAICA
Kingston
HAITI
Port-au-Prince
Santiago
Santo Domingo
DOMINICAN REPUBLIC
San Juan
PUERTO RICO (U.S.)
VIRGIN ISLANDS (U.S.)
BRITISH VIRGIN ISLANDS
ANGUILLA (U.K.)
ANTIGUA AND BARBUDA
Saint John's
Basseterre
SAINT KITTS AND NEVIS
MONTSERRAT (U.K.)
GUADELOUPE (Fr.)
DOMINICA
Roseau
MARTINIQUE (Fr.)
Castries
SAINT LUCIA
SAINT VINCENT AND THE GRENADINES
Kingstown
Bridgetown
BARBADOS
Saint George's
GRENADA
Port of Spain
TRINIDAD AND TOBAGO
CARIBBEAN SEA
ARUBA (Neth.)
Curaçao
Bonaire
NETHERLANDS ANTILLES
NICARAGUA
Isla de San Andrés (Col.)
San José
RICA
Panama Canal
Panama City
PANAMA
Golfo de Panamá
Isla de Coiba
Maracaibo
Lago de Maracaibo
Caracas
Orinoco
VENEZUELA
Georgetown
GUYANA
SURINAME
COLOMBIA
Bogotá
BRAZIL
80°
70°
60°
30°
20°
10°

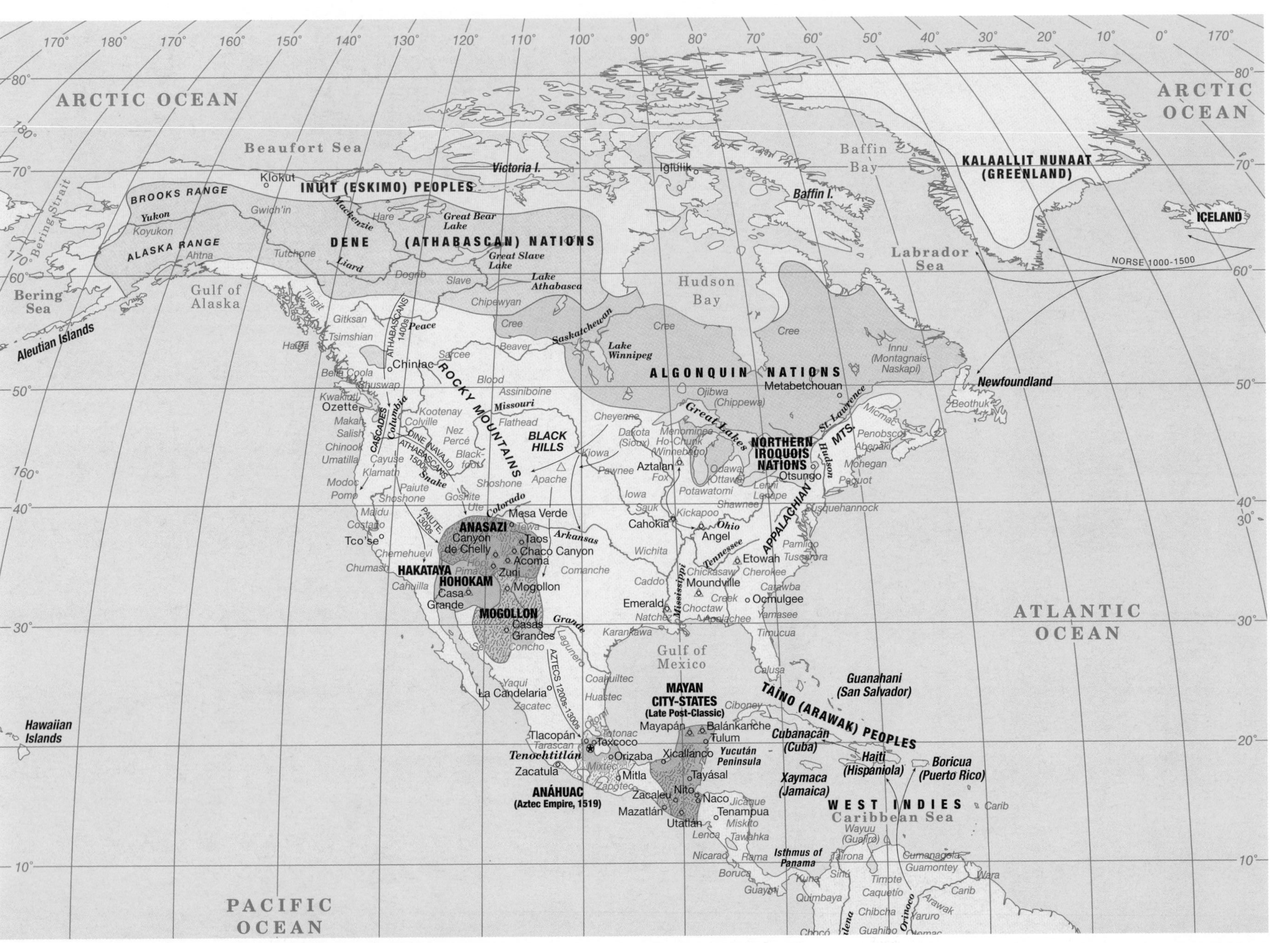
ARCTIC OCEAN
Beaufort Sea
Bering Strait
Bering Sea
Aleutian Islands
Gulf of Alaska
BROOKS RANGE
ALASKA RANGE
Yukon
Koyukon
Ahtna
Gwich'in
Tutchone
Klokut
INUIT (ESKIMO) PEOPLES
DENE (ATHABASCAN) NATIONS
Mackenzie
Hare
Liard
Dogrib
Slave
Great Bear Lake
Great Slave Lake
Lake Athabasca
Chipewyan
Victoria I.
Iglulik
Baffin I.
Baffin Bay
Hudson Bay
Labrador Sea
KALAALLIT NUNAAT (GREENLAND)
ICELAND
NORSE 1000-1500
ARCTIC OCEAN
Tlingit
Gitksan
Tsimshian
Haida
Bella Coola
Kwakiutl
Ozette
Makah
Salish
Chinook
Umatilla
Cayuse
Klamath
Modoc
Pomo
Maidu
Costano
Tco'se
Chumash
Chemehuevi
Cahuilla
Shuswap
Chinlac
ATHABASCANS 1400s
Peace
Sarcee
Beaver
Cree
Blood
Assiniboine
Kootenay
Colville
Nez Percé
Blackfoot
DINE (NAVAJO)
ATHABASCANS 1500s
Snake
Paiute
Shoshone
PAIUTE 1300s
Goshute
Ute
CASCADES
Columbia
ROCKY MOUNTAINS
Missouri
Flathead
BLACK HILLS
Apache
Colorado
Mesa Verde
Taos
Chaco Canyon
Acoma
Zuni
Mogollon
Tewa
Hopi
Pima
ANASAZI
Canyon de Chelly
HAKATAYA
HOHOKAM
Casa Grande
MOGOLLON
Casas Grandes
Concho
Seri
Yaqui
La Candelaria
Zacatec
Lagunero
AZTECS 1200s-1300s
Grande
Arkansas
Comanche
Saskatchewan
Lake Winnipeg
Cheyenne
Dakota (Sioux)
Kiowa
Pawnee
Iowa
Aztalan
Fox
Sauk
Cahokia
Wichita
Caddo
Emerald
Natchez
Karankawa
Mississippi
ALGONQUIN NATIONS
Metabetchouan
Ojibwa (Chippewa)
Great Lakes
Menominee
Ho-Chunk (Winnebago)
Odawa (Ottawa)
Potawatomi
Kickapoo
Shawnee
Ohio
Angel
Tennessee
Etowah
Chickasaw
Moundville
Creek
Choctaw
Ocmulgee
Apalachee
Cherokee
Catawba
Yamasee
Timucua
Calusa
Tuscarora
Pamlico
APPALACHIAN MTS.
NORTHERN IROQUOIS NATIONS
Otsungo
Lenni Lenape
Susquehannock
Hudson
St. Lawrence
Mohegan
Pequot
Abenaki
Penobscot
Micmac
Innu (Montagnais-Naskapi)
Beothuk
Newfoundland
ATLANTIC OCEAN
Gulf of Mexico
Coahuiltec
Huastec
Totonac
Tlacopán
Texcoco
Tarascan
Tenochtitlán
Zacatula
Orizaba
Mixtec
Mitla
Zapotec
ANÁHUAC (Aztec Empire, 1519)
MAYAN CITY-STATES (Late Post-Classic)
Mayapán
Balánkanche
Tulum
Xicallanco
Yucatán Peninsula
Tayásal
Nito
Naco
Zacaleu
Mazatlán
Utatlán
Jicaque
Tenampua
Miskito
Lenca
Tawahka
Nicarao
Rama
Boruca
Guaymi
Isthmus of Panama
Kuna
Sinú
Quimbaya
Chocó
Ciboney
TAÍNO (ARAWAK) PEOPLES
Guanahani (San Salvador)
Cubanacán (Cuba)
Xaymaca (Jamaica)
Haiti (Hispaniola)
Boricua (Puerto Rico)
WEST INDIES
Caribbean Sea
Carib
Wayuu (Guajiro)
Tairona
Cumanagota
Guamontey
Timote
Caquetío
Chibcha
Guahibo
Yaruro
Arawak
Orinoco
Warao
Hawaiian Islands
PACIFIC OCEAN

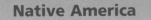

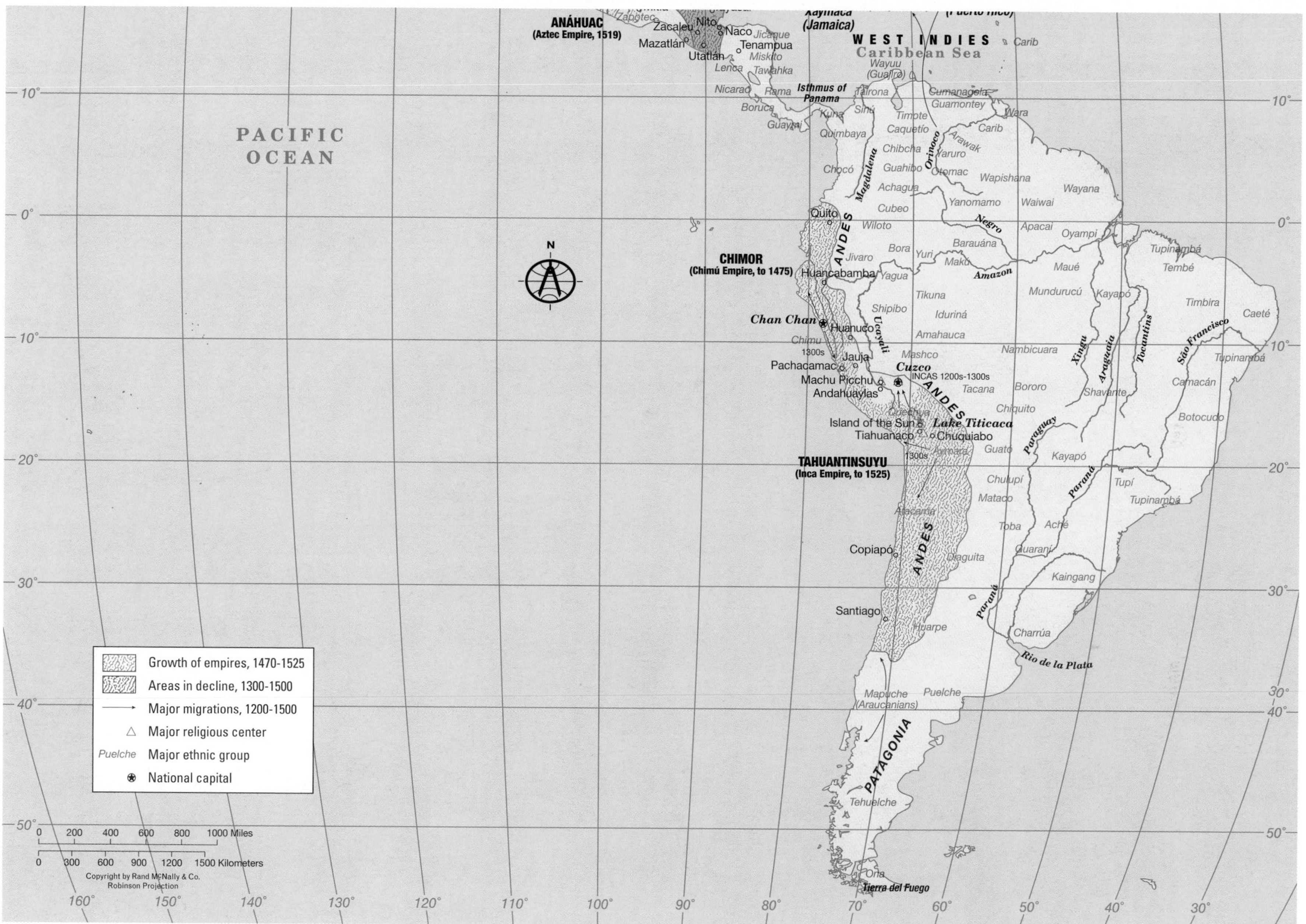

PACIFIC OCEAN
ANÁHUAC
(Aztec Empire, 1519)
Zapotec
Zacaleu
Nito
Naco
Jicaque
Mazatlán
Tenampua
Utatlán
Miskito
Lenca
Tawahka
Nicarao
Rama
Boruca
Guaymí
Xaymaca
(Jamaica)
WEST INDIES
Caribbean Sea
Carib
Wayuu
(Guajiro)
Isthmus of Panama
Tairona
Sinú
Kuna
Quimbaya
Cumanagota
Guamontey
Warao
Timote
Caquetío
Carib
Chibcha
Arawak
Yaruro
Guahibo
Otomac
Wapishana
Wayana
Chocó
Achagua
Magdalena
Orinoco
Cubeo
Yanomamo
Waiwai
Quito
Wiloto
Negro
Apacai
Oyampi
Tupinambá
Tembé
CHIMOR
(Chimú Empire, to 1475)
ANDES
Jivaro
Bora
Yuri
Barauána
Makú
Maué
Amazon
Huancabamba
Yagua
Tikuna
Mundurucú
Kayapó
Timbira
Caeté
Chan Chan
Shipibo
Iduriná
Huanuco
Ucayali
Amahauca
Chimu
1300s
Jauja
Mashco
Nambicuara
Xingu
Araguaia
Tocantins
São Francisco
Tupinambá
Pachacamac
Cuzco
INCAS 1200s-1300s
Machu Picchu
Tacana
Bororo
Shavante
Camacán
Andahuaylas
ANDES
Quechua
Chiquito
Botocudo
Island of the Sun
Lake Titicaca
Tiahuanaco
Chuquiabo
Aymara
1300s
Guató
Paraguay
Kayapó
TAHUANTINSUYU
(Inca Empire, to 1525)
Chulupí
Paraná
Tupí
Mataco
Tupinambá
Atacama
Toba
Aché
ANDES
Copiapó
Guaraní
Diaguita
Kaingang
Paraná
Santiago
Huarpe
Charrúa
Río de la Plata
Mapuche
(Araucanians)
Puelche
PATAGONIA
Tehuelche
Ona
Tierra del Fuego
N
Growth of empires, 1470-1525
Areas in decline, 1300-1500
Major migrations, 1200-1500
Major religious center
Puelche Major ethnic group
National capital
0 200 400 600 800 1000 Miles
0 300 600 900 1200 1500 Kilometers
Copyright by Rand McNally & Co.
Robinson Projection
10°
0°
10°
20°
30°
40°
50°
160°
150°
140°
130°
120°
110°
100°
90°
80°
70°
60°
50°
40°
30°

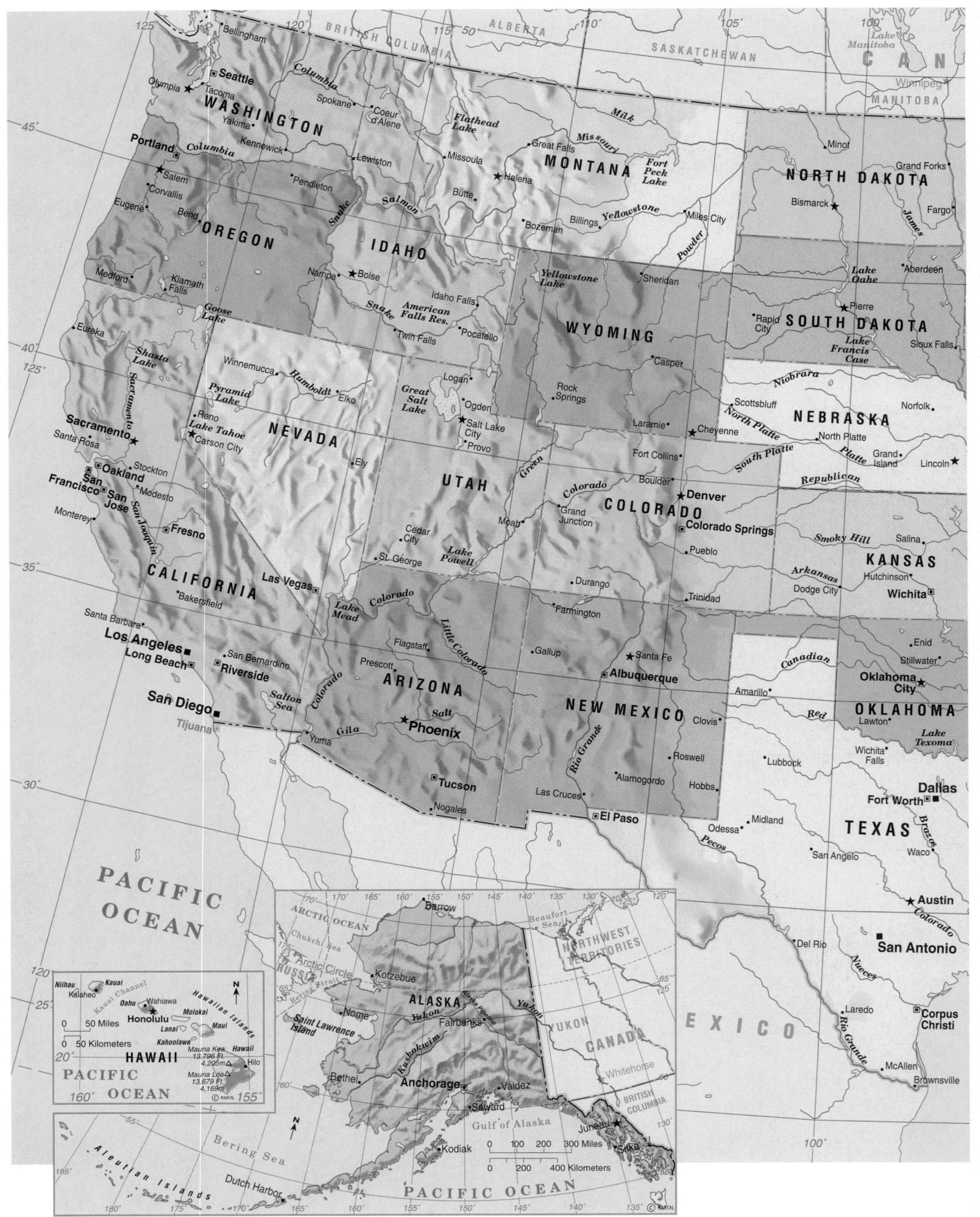
BRITISH COLUMBIA
ALBERTA
SASKATCHEWAN
MANITOBA
CANADA
Lake Manitoba
Winnipeg
WASHINGTON
Bellingham
Seattle
Olympia
Tacoma
Spokane
Coeur d'Alene
Yakima
Kennewick
Columbia
Portland
Salem
Corvallis
Eugene
Bend
Pendleton
OREGON
Medford
Klamath Falls
Goose Lake
Snake
Lewiston
Salmon
IDAHO
Nampa
Boise
Idaho Falls
American Falls Res.
Pocatello
Twin Falls
Flathead Lake
Missoula
Butte
Helena
Great Falls
Milk
Missouri
MONTANA
Fort Peck Lake
Billings
Yellowstone
Bozeman
Miles City
Powder
Minot
Grand Forks
NORTH DAKOTA
Bismarck
Fargo
James
Lake Oahe
Aberdeen
Pierre
Rapid City
SOUTH DAKOTA
Lake Francis Case
Sioux Falls
Yellowstone Lake
Sheridan
WYOMING
Casper
Rock Springs
Laramie
Cheyenne
Niobrara
Scottsbluff
North Platte
NEBRASKA
Norfolk
Platte
Grand Island
Lincoln
South Platte
Republican
Eureka
Shasta Lake
Sacramento
Winnemucca
Humboldt
Elko
Pyramid Lake
Reno
Lake Tahoe
Carson City
NEVADA
Ely
Santa Rosa
Oakland
Stockton
San Francisco
San Jose
Modesto
Monterey
San Joaquin
Fresno
CALIFORNIA
Las Vegas
Bakersfield
Santa Barbara
Los Angeles
Long Beach
San Bernardino
Riverside
Salton Sea
San Diego
Tijuana
Logan
Great Salt Lake
Ogden
Salt Lake City
Provo
Green
UTAH
Cedar City
St. George
Lake Powell
Moab
Colorado
Grand Junction
Fort Collins
Boulder
Denver
COLORADO
Colorado Springs
Pueblo
Durango
Trinidad
Smoky Hill
Salina
KANSAS
Arkansas
Hutchinson
Dodge City
Wichita
Lake Mead
Flagstaff
Little Colorado
Prescott
ARIZONA
Gila
Salt
Phoenix
Yuma
Tucson
Nogales
Farmington
Gallup
Santa Fe
Albuquerque
NEW MEXICO
Rio Grande
Roswell
Alamogordo
Las Cruces
Clovis
Hobbs
El Paso
Enid
Stillwater
Canadian
Oklahoma City
OKLAHOMA
Amarillo
Red
Lawton
Lake Texoma
Wichita Falls
Lubbock
Dallas
Fort Worth
Midland
Odessa
Pecos
TEXAS
Brazos
San Angelo
Waco
Austin
Colorado
Del Rio
San Antonio
Nueces
Laredo
Corpus Christi
Rio Grande
McAllen
Brownsville
MEXICO
PACIFIC OCEAN
Niihau
Kauai
Kalaheo
Kauai Channel
Oahu
Wahiawa
Honolulu
Molokai
Lanai
Maui
Kahoolawe
Hawaiian Islands
HAWAII
Hawaii
Mauna Kea 13,796 Ft. 4,205m
Mauna Loa 13,679 Ft. 4,169m
Hilo
0 50 Miles
0 50 Kilometers
PACIFIC OCEAN
ARCTIC OCEAN
Barrow
Beaufort Sea
NORTHWEST TERRITORIES
Chukchi Sea
Arctic Circle
RUSSIA
Bering Strait
Kotzebue
ALASKA
Alaska Pipeline
Yukon
Nome
Saint Lawrence Island
Fairbanks
Kuskokwim
YUKON
CANADA
Whitehorse
BRITISH COLUMBIA
Bethel
Anchorage
Valdez
Seward
Gulf of Alaska
Juneau
Sitka
Kodiak
Bering Sea
Aleutian Islands
Dutch Harbor
PACIFIC OCEAN
0 100 200 300 Miles
0 200 400 Kilometers
© RMCN.

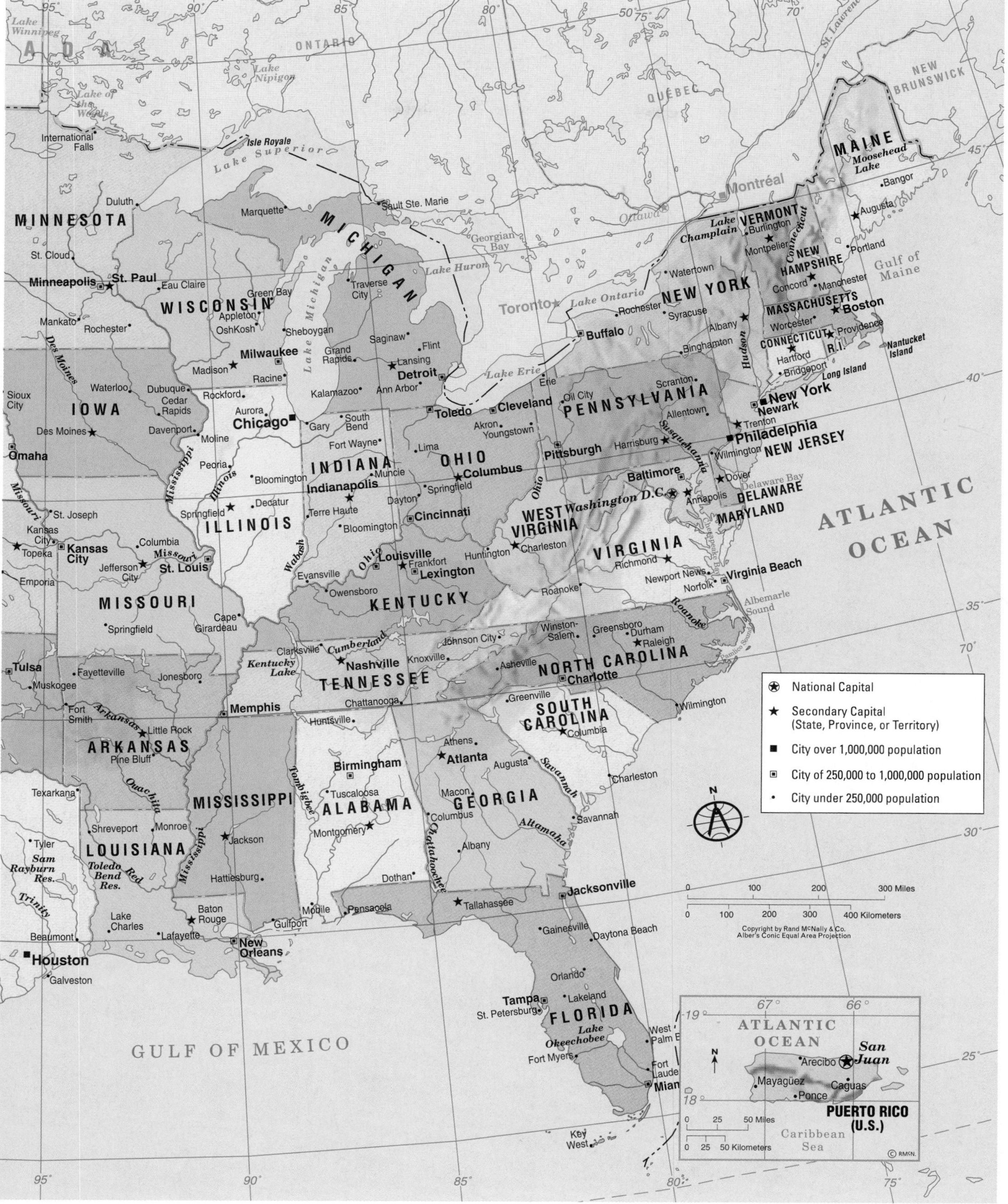

ATLANTIC OCEAN
GULF OF MEXICO
ONTARIO
QUÉBEC
NEW BRUNSWICK
Gulf of Maine
Lake Superior
Lake Michigan
Lake Huron
Lake Erie
Lake Ontario
Georgian Bay
Lake Nipigon
Lake of the Woods
Lake Winnipeg
Isle Royale
Lake Champlain
Long Island
Nantucket Island
Delaware Bay
Albemarle Sound
Pamlico Sound
Lake Okeechobee
Kentucky Lake
Toledo Bend Res.
Sam Rayburn Res.
MINNESOTA
WISCONSIN
MICHIGAN
IOWA
ILLINOIS
INDIANA
OHIO
PENNSYLVANIA
NEW YORK
VERMONT
NEW HAMPSHIRE
MAINE
MASSACHUSETTS
CONNECTICUT
R.I.
NEW JERSEY
DELAWARE
MARYLAND
WEST VIRGINIA
VIRGINIA
KENTUCKY
TENNESSEE
NORTH CAROLINA
SOUTH CAROLINA
GEORGIA
FLORIDA
ALABAMA
MISSISSIPPI
LOUISIANA
ARKANSAS
MISSOURI
Washington D.C.
Chicago
New York
Philadelphia
Detroit
Houston
Boston
Atlanta
Miami
Montréal
Toronto
National Capital
Secondary Capital (State, Province, or Territory)
City over 1,000,000 population
City of 250,000 to 1,000,000 population
City under 250,000 population
0 100 200 300 Miles
0 100 200 300 400 Kilometers
Copyright by Rand McNally & Co.
Alber's Conic Equal Area Projection
PUERTO RICO (U.S.)
San Juan
Arecibo
Mayagüez
Ponce
Caguas
Caribbean Sea
0 25 50 Miles
0 25 50 Kilometers
© RMcN.

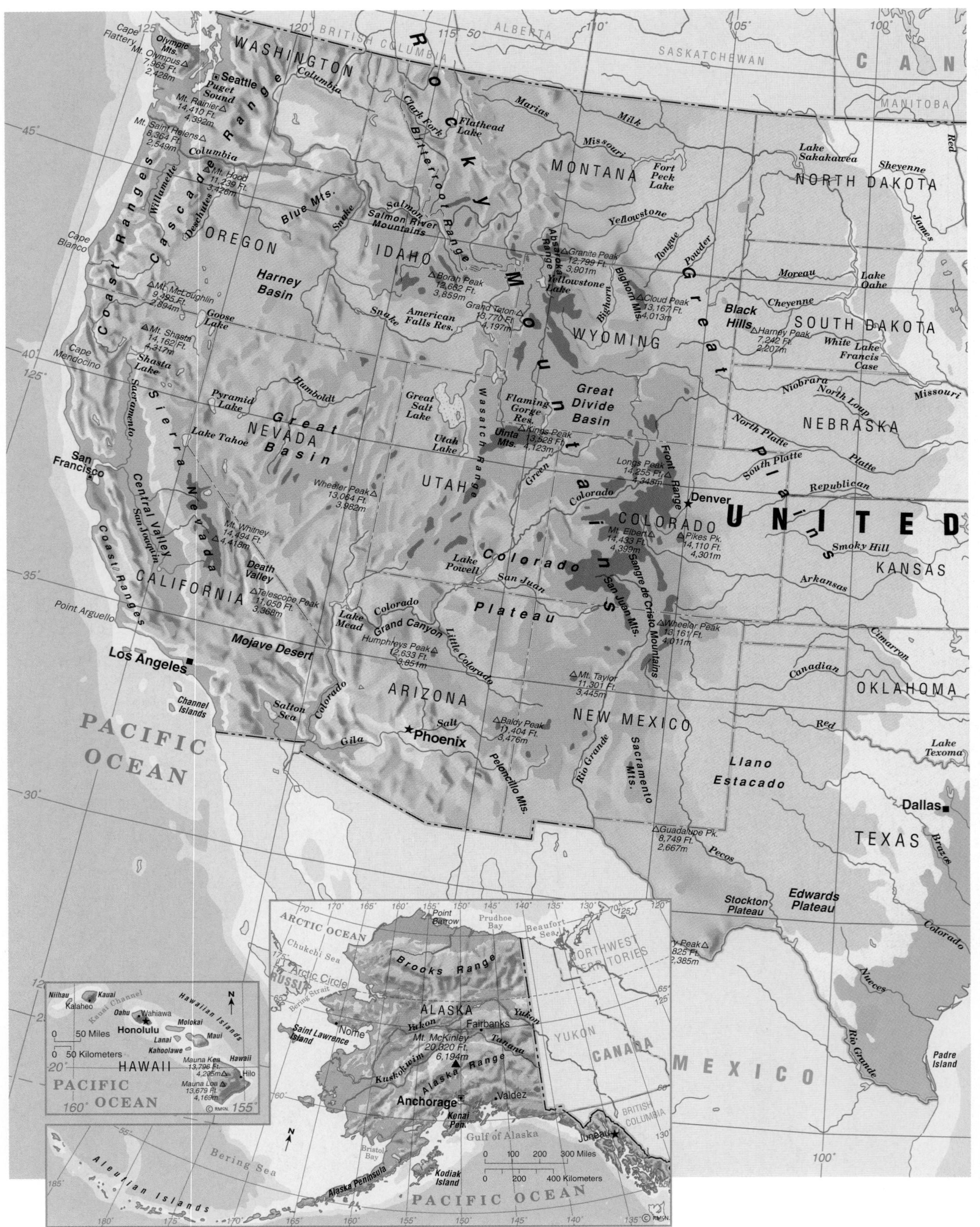
PACIFIC OCEAN
WASHINGTON
OREGON
IDAHO
MONTANA
WYOMING
NORTH DAKOTA
SOUTH DAKOTA
NEBRASKA
KANSAS
OKLAHOMA
TEXAS
NEW MEXICO
COLORADO
UTAH
NEVADA
ARIZONA
CALIFORNIA
UNITED
MEXICO
BRITISH COLUMBIA
ALBERTA
SASKATCHEWAN
MANITOBA
CAN
Rocky Mountains
Great Plains
Cape Flattery
Olympic Mts.
Mt. Olympus 7,965 Ft. 2,428m
Seattle
Puget Sound
Mt. Rainier 14,410 Ft. 4,392m
Mt. Saint Helens 8,364 Ft. 2,549m
Mt. Hood 11,239 Ft. 3,426m
Cascade Range
Coast Ranges
Willamette
Deschutes
Columbia
Clark Fork
Flathead Lake
Bitterroot Range
Marias
Milk
Missouri
Fort Peck Lake
Lake Sakakawea
Sheyenne
James
Red
Blue Mts.
Snake
Salmon
Salmon River Mountains
Yellowstone
Absaroka Range
Granite Peak 12,799 Ft. 3,901m
Tongue
Powder
Bighorn
Bighorn Mts.
Cloud Peak 13,167 Ft. 4,013m
Yellowstone Lake
Borah Peak 12,662 Ft. 3,859m
Grand Teton 13,770 Ft. 4,197m
American Falls Res.
Cape Blanco
Harney Basin
Mt. McLoughlin 9,495 Ft. 2,894m
Goose Lake
Mt. Shasta 14,162 Ft. 4,317m
Shasta Lake
Cape Mendocino
Sacramento
Sierra Nevada
Pyramid Lake
Humboldt
Lake Tahoe
Great Basin
Great Salt Lake
Wasatch Range
Utah Lake
Flaming Gorge Res.
Uinta Mts.
Kings Peak 13,528 Ft. 4,123m
Great Divide Basin
Green
Moreau
Lake Oahe
Cheyenne
Black Hills
Harney Peak 7,242 Ft. 2,207m
White
Lake Francis Case
Niobrara
North Loup
North Platte
South Platte
Platte
Republican
Front Range
Longs Peak 14,255 Ft. 4,345m
Denver
Colorado
Mt. Elbert 14,433 Ft. 4,399m
Pikes Pk. 14,110 Ft. 4,301m
Smoky Hill
Arkansas
San Juan Mts.
Sangre de Cristo Mountains
Wheeler Peak 13,161 Ft. 4,011m
Cimarron
Canadian
San Francisco
Central Valley
San Joaquin
Wheeler Peak 13,064 Ft. 3,982m
Mt. Whitney 14,494 Ft. 4,418m
Death Valley
Telescope Peak 11,050 Ft. 3,368m
Lake Powell
San Juan
Colorado Plateau
Point Arguello
Lake Mead
Grand Canyon
Little Colorado
Humphreys Peak 12,633 Ft. 3,851m
Mojave Desert
Los Angeles
Channel Islands
Salton Sea
Gila
Salt
Phoenix
Baldy Peak 11,404 Ft. 3,476m
Mt. Taylor 11,301 Ft. 3,445m
Rio Grande
Sacramento Mts.
Peloncillo Mts.
Llano Estacado
Red
Lake Texoma
Dallas
Brazos
Guadalupe Pk. 8,749 Ft. 2,667m
Pecos
Stockton Plateau
Edwards Plateau
Colorado
Nueces
Rio Grande
Padre Island
ARCTIC OCEAN
Point Barrow
Prudhoe Bay
Beaufort Sea
Chukchi Sea
RUSSIA
Arctic Circle
Bering Strait
Brooks Range
NORTHWEST TERRITORIES
ALASKA
Yukon
Saint Lawrence Island
Nome
Fairbanks
Mt. McKinley 20,320 Ft. 6,194m
Tanana
Kuskokwim
Alaska Range
YUKON
CANADA
Anchorage
Valdez
Kenai Pen.
BRITISH COLUMBIA
Juneau
Gulf of Alaska
Bristol Bay
Bering Sea
Aleutian Islands
Alaska Peninsula
Kodiak Island
PACIFIC OCEAN
0 100 200 300 Miles
0 200 400 Kilometers
Niihau
Kauai
Kalaheo
Kauai Channel
Hawaiian Islands
Oahu
Wahiawa
Honolulu
Molokai
Lanai
Maui
Kahoolawe
Hawaii
Mauna Kea 13,796 Ft. 4,205m
Hilo
Mauna Loa 13,679 Ft. 4,169m
HAWAII
0 50 Miles
0 50 Kilometers
PACIFIC OCEAN
© RMSN.

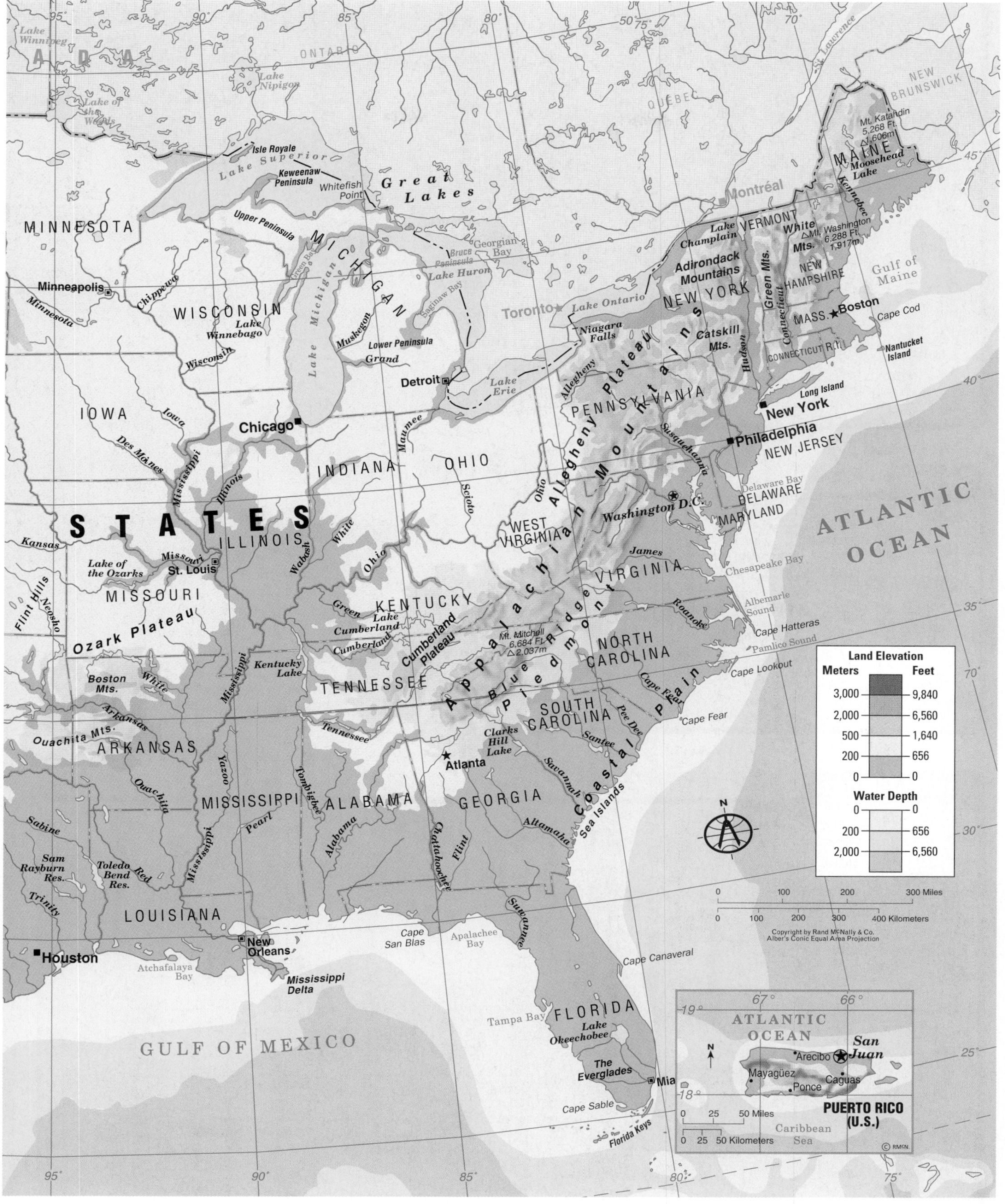
Great Lakes
Lake Superior
Lake Michigan
Lake Huron
Lake Erie
Lake Ontario
MINNESOTA
WISCONSIN
MICHIGAN
IOWA
ILLINOIS
INDIANA
OHIO
MISSOURI
KENTUCKY
TENNESSEE
ARKANSAS
MISSISSIPPI
ALABAMA
GEORGIA
LOUISIANA
FLORIDA
SOUTH CAROLINA
NORTH CAROLINA
VIRGINIA
WEST VIRGINIA
MARYLAND
DELAWARE
NEW JERSEY
PENNSYLVANIA
NEW YORK
CONNECTICUT
R.I.
MASS.
VERMONT
NEW HAMPSHIRE
MAINE
STATES
Appalachian Mountains
Allegheny Plateau
Allegheny Mountains
Blue Ridge
Piedmont
Coastal Plain
Cumberland Plateau
Ozark Plateau
Ouachita Mts.
Boston Mts.
Adirondack Mountains
Catskill Mts.
Green Mts.
White Mts.
Mt. Washington 6,288 Ft. 1,917m
Mt. Katahdin 5,268 Ft. 1,606m
Mt. Mitchell 6,684 Ft. 2,037m
Chicago
St. Louis
Minneapolis
Detroit
Atlanta
New Orleans
Houston
Washington D.C.
Philadelphia
New York
Boston
Toronto
Montréal
ATLANTIC OCEAN
GULF OF MEXICO
Land Elevation
Meters Feet
3,000 9,840
2,000 6,560
500 1,640
200 656
0 0
Water Depth
0 0
200 656
2,000 6,560
0 100 200 300 Miles
0 100 200 300 400 Kilometers
Copyright by Rand McNally & Co.
Alber's Conic Equal Area Projection
PUERTO RICO (U.S.)
San Juan
Arecibo
Mayagüez
Ponce
Caguas
Caribbean Sea
0 25 50 Miles
0 25 50 Kilometers
© RMcN.

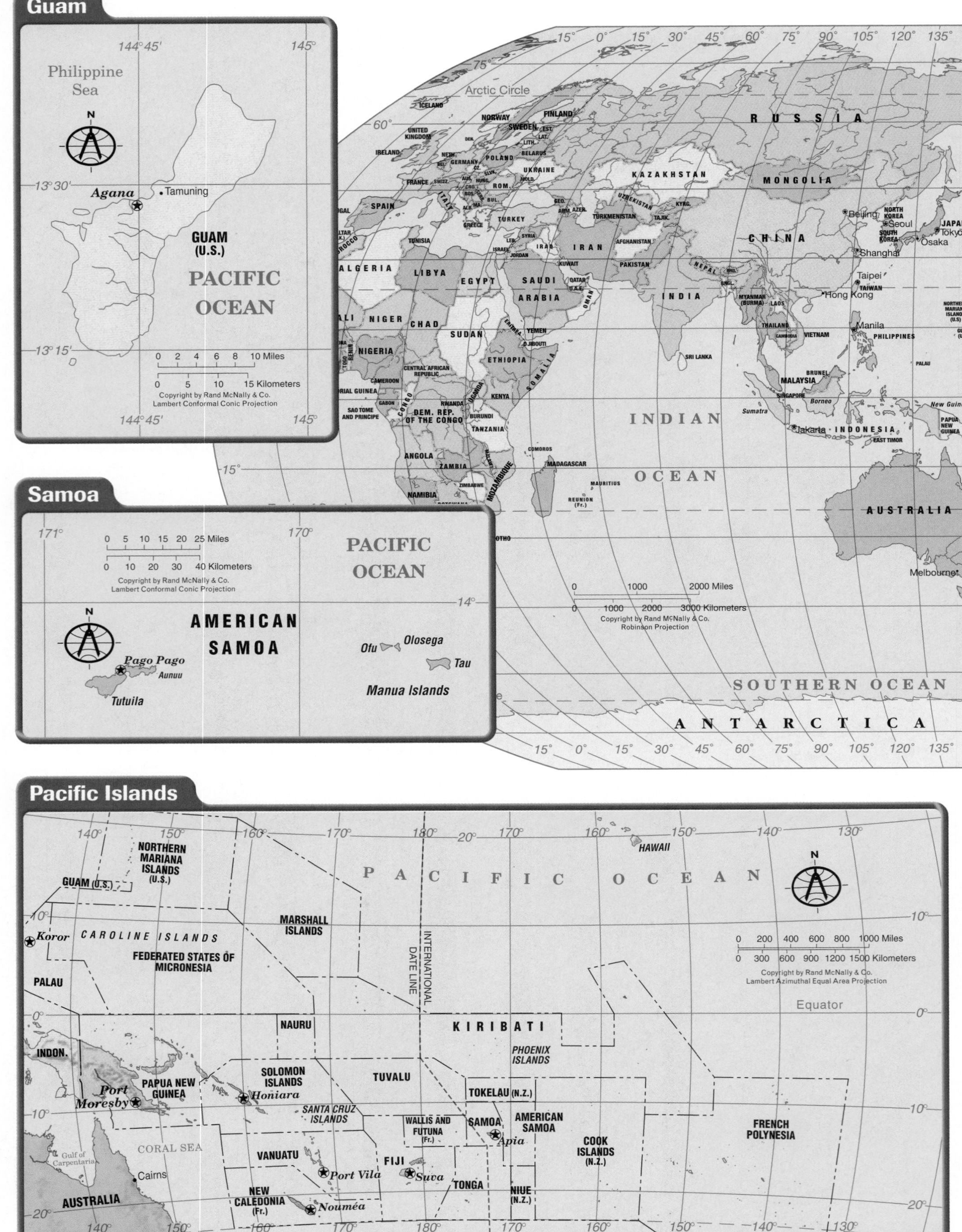
Guam
144°45'
145°
Philippine Sea
N
13°30'
Agana
Tamuning
GUAM (U.S.)
PACIFIC OCEAN
13°15'
0 2 4 6 8 10 Miles
0 5 10 15 Kilometers
Copyright by Rand McNally & Co.
Lambert Conformal Conic Projection
Samoa
171°
170°
0 5 10 15 20 25 Miles
0 10 20 30 40 Kilometers
Copyright by Rand McNally & Co.
Lambert Conformal Conic Projection
PACIFIC OCEAN
14°
AMERICAN SAMOA
Pago Pago
Aunuu
Tutuila
Ofu
Olosega
Tau
Manua Islands
Arctic Circle
ICELAND
NORWAY
SWEDEN
FINLAND
UNITED KINGDOM
IRELAND
POLAND
BELARUS
UKRAINE
FRANCE
SPAIN
ITALY
GREECE
TURKEY
RUSSIA
KAZAKHSTAN
MONGOLIA
TURKMENISTAN
AFGHANISTAN
IRAN
IRAQ
SYRIA
ISRAEL
JORDAN
KUWAIT
PAKISTAN
NEPAL
CHINA
NORTH KOREA
SOUTH KOREA
JAPAN
Beijing
Seoul
Tokyo
Osaka
Shanghai
Taipei
TAIWAN
Hong Kong
INDIA
ALGERIA
LIBYA
EGYPT
SAUDI ARABIA
OMAN
YEMEN
NIGER
CHAD
SUDAN
ERITREA
DJIBOUTI
ETHIOPIA
SOMALIA
NIGERIA
CENTRAL AFRICAN REPUBLIC
CAMEROON
GABON
CONGO
DEM. REP. OF THE CONGO
SAO TOME AND PRINCIPE
RWANDA
BURUNDI
UGANDA
KENYA
TANZANIA
ANGOLA
ZAMBIA
MALAWI
MOZAMBIQUE
ZIMBABWE
NAMIBIA
COMOROS
MADAGASCAR
MAURITIUS
REUNION (Fr.)
MYANMAR (BURMA)
LAOS
THAILAND
CAMBODIA
VIETNAM
Manila
PHILIPPINES
NORTHERN MARIANA ISLANDS (U.S.)
GUAM (U.S.)
PALAU
SRI LANKA
BRUNEI
MALAYSIA
SINGAPORE
Borneo
Sumatra
Jakarta
INDONESIA
EAST TIMOR
New Guinea
PAPUA NEW GUINEA
INDIAN OCEAN
AUSTRALIA
Melbourne
0 1000 2000 Miles
0 1000 2000 3000 Kilometers
Copyright by Rand McNally & Co.
Robinson Projection
SOUTHERN OCEAN
ANTARCTICA
15° 0° 15° 30° 45° 60° 75° 90° 105° 120° 135°
Pacific Islands
140° 150° 160° 170° 180° 170° 160° 150° 140° 130°
NORTHERN MARIANA ISLANDS (U.S.)
GUAM (U.S.)
HAWAII
PACIFIC OCEAN
N
MARSHALL ISLANDS
Koror
CAROLINE ISLANDS
FEDERATED STATES OF MICRONESIA
PALAU
INTERNATIONAL DATE LINE
0 200 400 600 800 1000 Miles
0 300 600 900 1200 1500 Kilometers
Copyright by Rand McNally & Co.
Lambert Azimuthal Equal Area Projection
Equator
NAURU
KIRIBATI
PHOENIX ISLANDS
INDON.
SOLOMON ISLANDS
TUVALU
PAPUA NEW GUINEA
Port Moresby
Honiara
TOKELAU (N.Z.)
SANTA CRUZ ISLANDS
WALLIS AND FUTUNA (Fr.)
SAMOA
AMERICAN SAMOA
Apia
FRENCH POLYNESIA
Gulf of Carpentaria
CORAL SEA
VANUATU
COOK ISLANDS (N.Z.)
FIJI
Port Vila
Suva
Cairns
TONGA
NIUE (N.Z.)
AUSTRALIA
NEW CALEDONIA (Fr.)
Nouméa

ARCTIC OCEAN
GREENLAND (Den.)
Arctic Circle
ALASKA (U.S.)
Anchorage
CANADA
Aleutian Islands
Vancouver
Seattle
Newfoundland
San Francisco
UNITED STATES
Los Angeles
ATLANTIC OCEAN
BERMUDA (U.K.)
MIDWAY ISLANDS (U.S.)
Tropic of Cancer
MEXICO
BAHAMAS
WAKE ISLAND (U.S.)
INTERNATIONAL DATE LINE
Hawai'ian Islands (U.S.)
Mexico City
CUBA
DOM. REP.
HAITI
PUERTO RICO (U.S.)
JAMAICA
BELIZE
Johnston Atoll (U.S.)
Micronesia
MARSHALL ISLANDS
PACIFIC OCEAN
HOND.
GUAT.
EL SAL.
NIC.
COSTA RICA
TRINIDAD AND TOBAGO
VENEZUELA
GUYANA
SURINAME
FRENCH GUIANA
FED. STATES OF MICRONESIA
Polynesia
PANAMA
COLOMBIA
Palmyra (U.S.)
Equator
Galapagos Islands (Ecua.)
ECUADOR
NAURU
KIRIBATI
Phoenix Islands
Line Islands
Melanesia
SOLOMON ISLANDS
TUVALU
TOKELAU (N.Z.)
Marquesas Islands (Fr.)
BRAZIL
PERU
SAMOA
Lima
VANUATU
AMERICAN SAMOA
Tuamotu Islands (Fr.)
Society Islands
Tahiti
FRENCH POLYNESIA
NEW CALEDONIA (Fr.)
FIJI
NIUE (N.Z.)
COOK ISLANDS (N.Z.)
BOLIVIA
TONGA
Tropic of Capricorn
PARAGUAY
Easter Island (Chile)
NORFOLK ISLAND (Austl.)
ARGENTINA
Sydney
Santiago
URUGUAY
CHILE
NEW ZEALAND
Wellington
Auckland Islands (N.Z.)
FALKLAND ISLANDS (U.K.)
Macquaire Island (Austl.)
Antarctic Circle
165° 180° 165° 150° 135° 120° 105° 90° 75° 60° 45°
75° 60° 45° 30° 15° 0° 15° 30° 45° 60° 75°

National Capital
Major Cities

Puerto Rico and the U.S. Virgin Islands

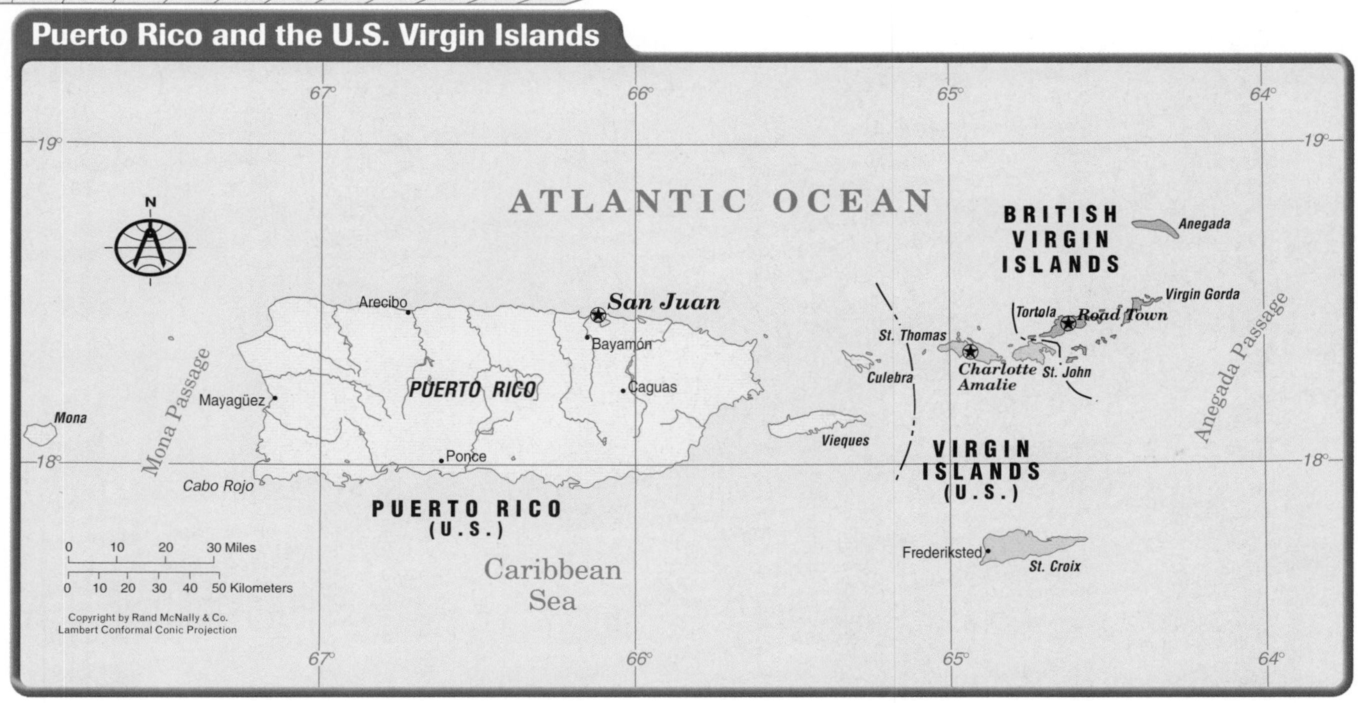

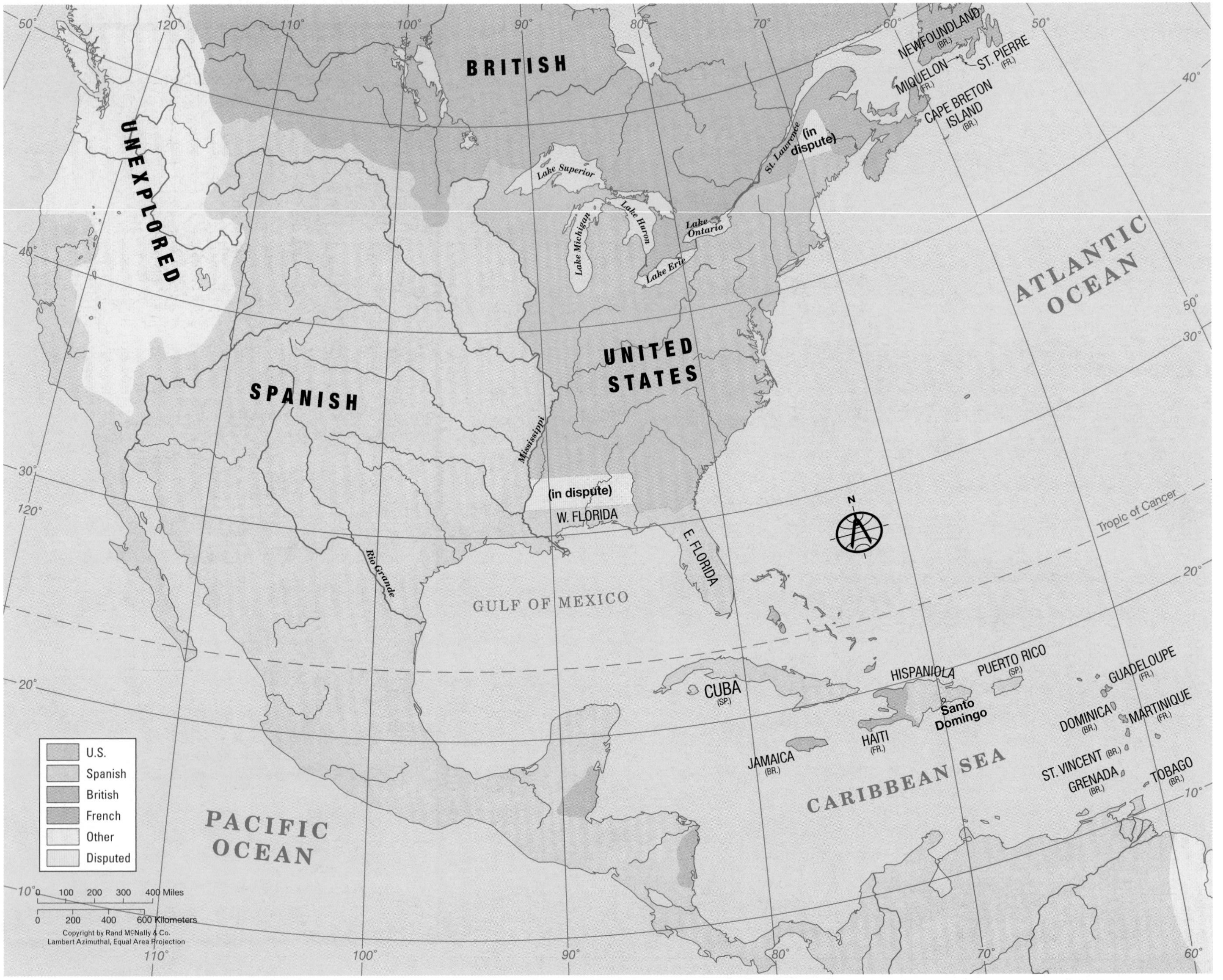
BRITISH
UNEXPLORED
SPANISH
UNITED STATES
NEWFOUNDLAND (BR.)
MIQUELON (FR.)
ST. PIERRE (FR.)
CAPE BRETON ISLAND (BR.)
(in dispute)
St. Lawrence
Lake Superior
Lake Michigan
Lake Huron
Lake Ontario
Lake Erie
ATLANTIC OCEAN
Mississippi
(in dispute)
W. FLORIDA
E. FLORIDA
Rio Grande
GULF OF MEXICO
Tropic of Cancer
N
CUBA (SP.)
HISPANIOLA
PUERTO RICO (SP.)
Santo Domingo
HAITI (FR.)
JAMAICA (BR.)
GUADELOUPE (FR.)
DOMINICA (BR.)
MARTINIQUE (FR.)
ST. VINCENT (BR.)
GRENADA (BR.)
TOBAGO (BR.)
CARIBBEAN SEA
PACIFIC OCEAN
U.S.
Spanish
British
French
Other
Disputed
0 100 200 300 400 Miles
0 200 400 600 Kilometers
Copyright by Rand McNally & Co.
Lambert Azimuthal, Equal Area Projection

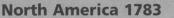

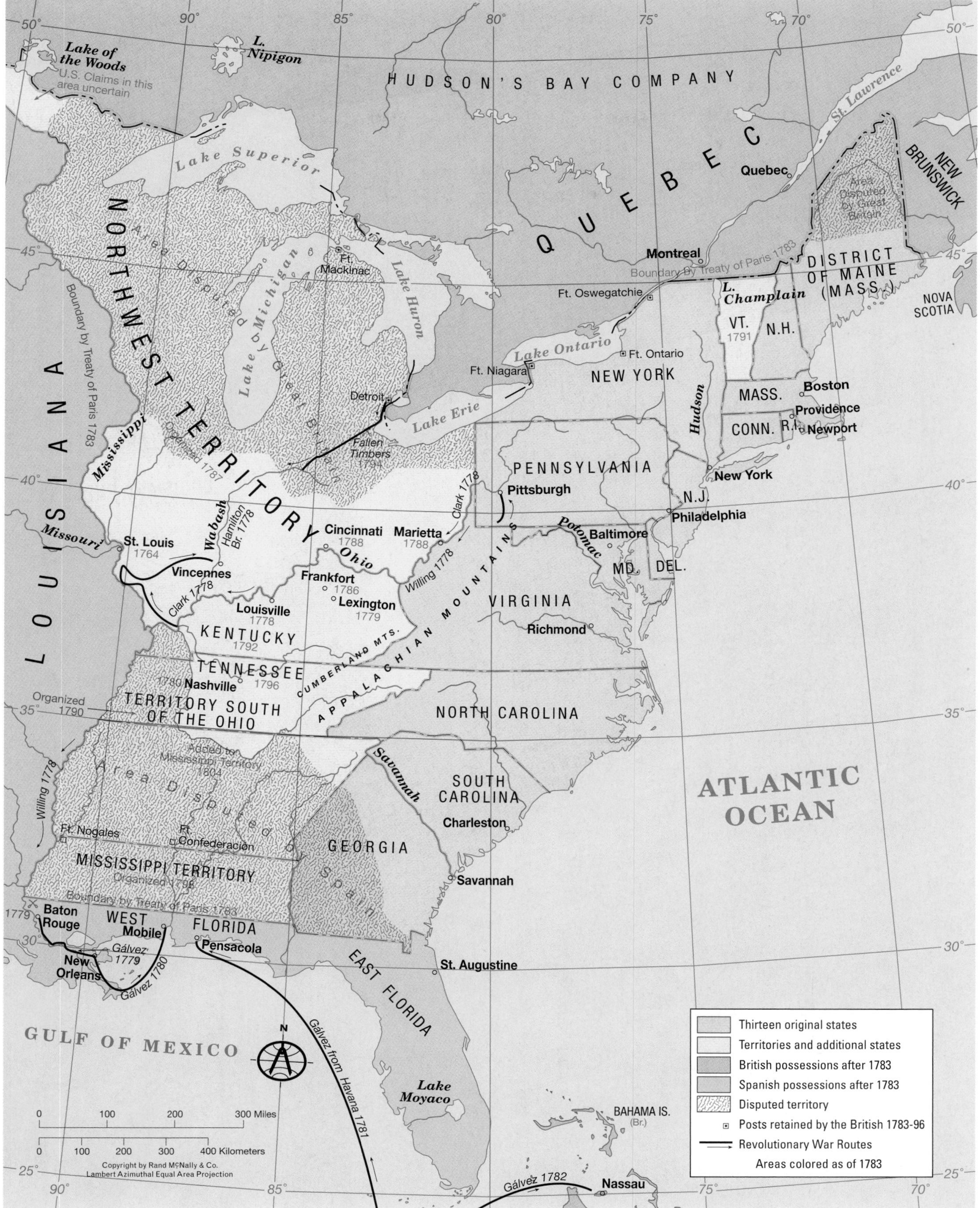
Lake of the Woods
U.S. Claims in this area uncertain
L. Nipigon
HUDSON'S BAY COMPANY
St. Lawrence
QUEBEC
Quebec
NEW BRUNSWICK
Area Disputed by Great Britain
Lake Superior
NORTHWEST TERRITORY
Organized 1787
Area Disputed by Great Britain
Ft. Mackinac
Lake Michigan
Lake Huron
Montreal
Boundary by Treaty of Paris 1783
DISTRICT OF MAINE (MASS.)
Ft. Oswegatchie
L. Champlain
NOVA SCOTIA
VT. 1791
N.H.
Lake Ontario
Ft. Ontario
Ft. Niagara
NEW YORK
Hudson
MASS.
Boston
Providence
CONN.
R.I.
Newport
Detroit
Lake Erie
Fallen Timbers 1794
PENNSYLVANIA
New York
Pittsburgh
N.J.
Philadelphia
Clark 1778
LOUISIANA
Boundary by Treaty of Paris 1783
Mississippi
Missouri
St. Louis 1764
Wabash
Hamilton Br. 1778
Cincinnati 1788
Marietta 1788
Ohio
Potomac
Baltimore
MD.
DEL.
Vincennes
Frankfort 1786
Lexington 1779
Willing 1778
APPALACHIAN MOUNTAINS
VIRGINIA
Clark 1778
Louisville 1778
Richmond
KENTUCKY 1792
CUMBERLAND MTS.
TENNESSEE 1796
1780 Nashville
Organized 1790
TERRITORY SOUTH OF THE OHIO
NORTH CAROLINA
Added to Mississippi Territory 1804
Area Disputed by Spain
Savannah
SOUTH CAROLINA
Charleston
ATLANTIC OCEAN
Willing 1778
Ft. Nogales
Ft. Confederación
GEORGIA
MISSISSIPPI TERRITORY
Organized 1798
Savannah
Boundary by Treaty of Paris 1783
1779 Baton Rouge
WEST FLORIDA
Mobile
Pensacola
Gálvez 1779
Gálvez 1780
New Orleans
St. Augustine
EAST FLORIDA
Gálvez from Havana 1781
GULF OF MEXICO
N
Lake Moyaco
BAHAMA IS. (Br.)
Gálvez 1782
Nassau
0 100 200 300 Miles
0 100 200 300 400 Kilometers
Copyright by Rand McNally & Co.
Lambert Azimuthal Equal Area Projection
Thirteen original states
Territories and additional states
British possessions after 1783
Spanish possessions after 1783
Disputed territory
Posts retained by the British 1783-96
Revolutionary War Routes
Areas colored as of 1783
50° 45° 40° 35° 30° 25°
90° 85° 80° 75° 70°

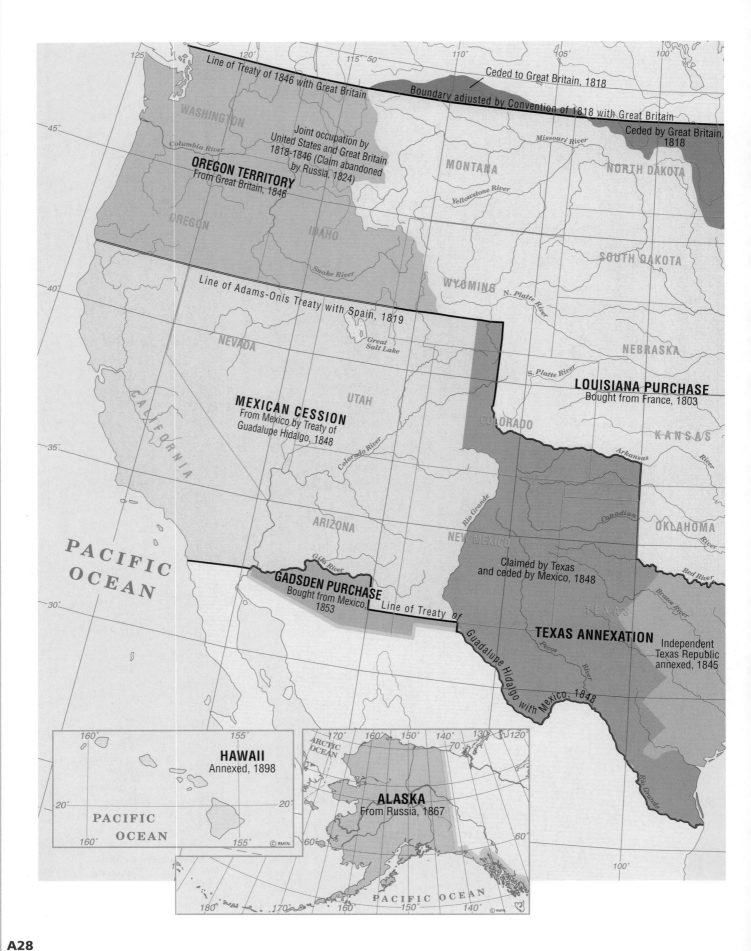

Line of Treaty of 1846 with Great Britain

Ceded to Great Britain, 1818

Boundary adjusted by Convention of 1818 with Great Britain

Ceded by Great Britain, 1818

WASHINGTON

Joint occupation by United States and Great Britain 1818-1846 (Claim abandoned by Russia, 1824)

Columbia River

OREGON TERRITORY
From Great Britain, 1846

MONTANA

Missouri River

NORTH DAKOTA

Yellowstone River

OREGON

IDAHO

SOUTH DAKOTA

Snake River

WYOMING

N. Platte River

Line of Adams-Onís Treaty with Spain, 1819

Great Salt Lake

NEVADA

NEBRASKA

S. Platte River

LOUISIANA PURCHASE
Bought from France, 1803

CALIFORNIA

MEXICAN CESSION
From Mexico by Treaty of Guadalupe Hidalgo, 1848

UTAH

COLORADO

KANSAS

Arkansas River

Colorado River

Rio Grande

Canadian River

ARIZONA

NEW MEXICO

OKLAHOMA

PACIFIC OCEAN

Gila River

Claimed by Texas and ceded by Mexico, 1848

Red River

GADSDEN PURCHASE
Bought from Mexico, 1853

Line of Treaty of Guadalupe Hidalgo with Mexico, 1848

Brazos River

TEXAS

TEXAS ANNEXATION

Independent Texas Republic annexed, 1845

Pecos River

Rio Grande

HAWAII
Annexed, 1898

PACIFIC OCEAN

© RMcN.

ARCTIC OCEAN

ALASKA
From Russia, 1867

PACIFIC OCEAN

© RMcN.

THE UNITED STATES IN 1783
ORIGINAL 13 COLONIES
From Great Britain by Treaty of Paris, 1783
Boundary adjusted by Webster-Ashburton Treaty with Great Britain, 1842
From Great Britain, 1842
Boundary adjusted by Webster-Ashburton Treaty with Great Britain, 1842
From Great Britain, 1842
From Spain, 1795
Boundary adjusted by Pinckney's Treaty with Spain, 1795
Ceded by Spain, 1818
1810
1813
Annexed by the United States
FLORIDA CESSION
From Spain by Adams-Onís Treaty, 1819
Lake of the Woods
Lake Superior
Lake Michigan
Lake Huron
Lake Ontario
Lake Erie
Mississippi River
Missouri River
Ohio River
Cumberland River
Tennessee River
Savannah River
Hudson River
Connecticut River
MINNESOTA
WISCONSIN
MICHIGAN
IOWA
ILLINOIS
INDIANA
OHIO
MISSOURI
KENTUCKY
TENNESSEE
ARKANSAS
MISSISSIPPI
ALABAMA
GEORGIA
LOUISIANA
FLORIDA
SOUTH CAROLINA
NORTH CAROLINA
VIRGINIA
WEST VIRGINIA
MARYLAND
DEL.
NEW JERSEY
PENNSYLVANIA
NEW YORK
CONN.
R.I.
MASS.
VT.
N.H.
MAINE
ATLANTIC OCEAN
GULF OF MEXICO
N
0 100 200 300 Miles
0 100 200 300 400 Kilometers
Copyright by Rand McNally & Co.
Alber's Conic Equal Area Projection
95°
90°
85°
80°
75°
70°
50°
45°
40°
35°
30°
25°

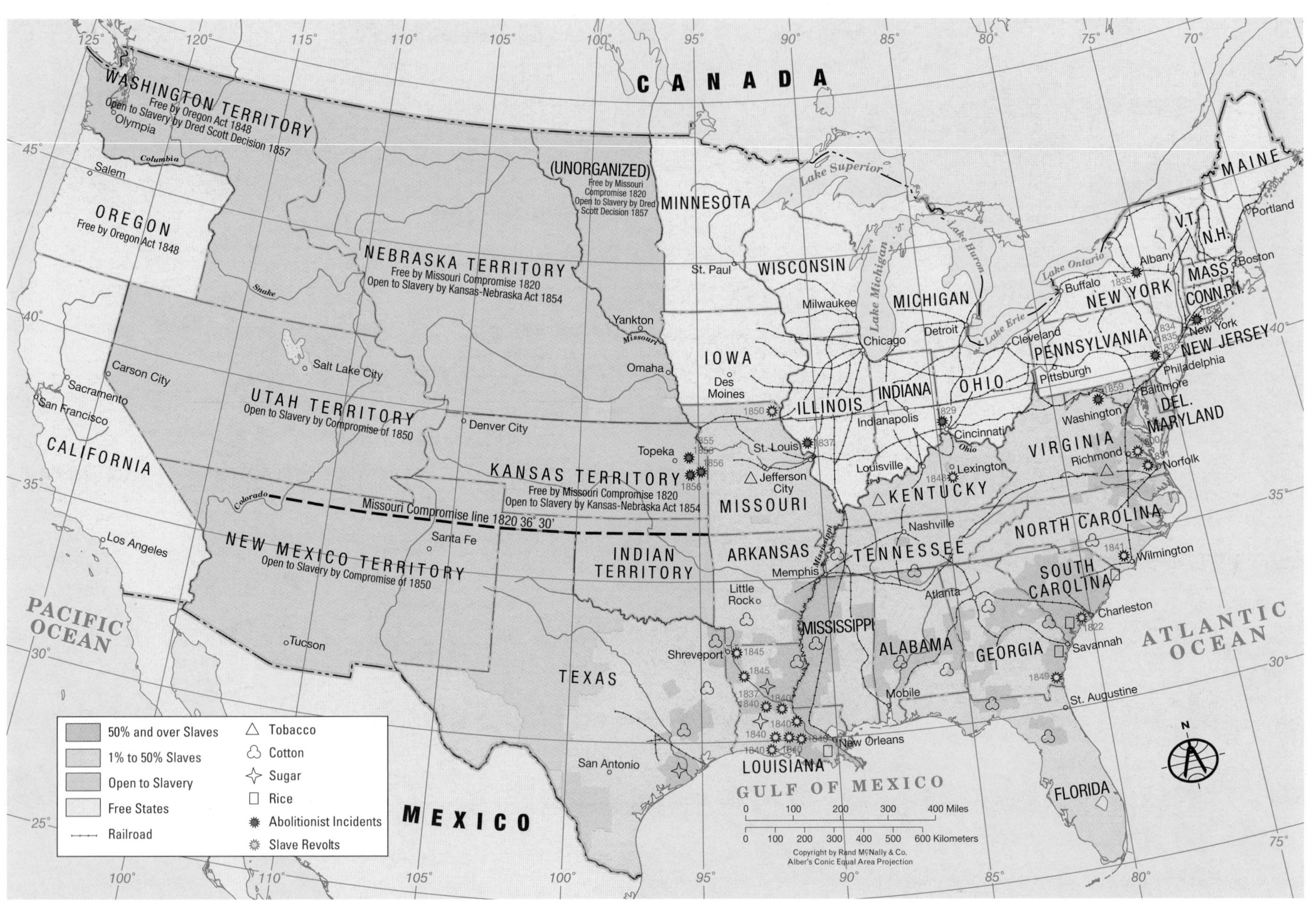
CANADA
WASHINGTON TERRITORY
Free by Oregon Act 1848
Open to Slavery by Dred Scott Decision 1857
Olympia
Salem
OREGON
Free by Oregon Act 1848
(UNORGANIZED)
Free by Missouri Compromise 1820
Open to Slavery by Dred Scott Decision 1857
MINNESOTA
NEBRASKA TERRITORY
Free by Missouri Compromise 1820
Open to Slavery by Kansas-Nebraska Act 1854
UTAH TERRITORY
Open to Slavery by Compromise of 1850
KANSAS TERRITORY
Free by Missouri Compromise 1820
Open to Slavery by Kansas-Nebraska Act 1854
Missouri Compromise line 1820 36° 30'
NEW MEXICO TERRITORY
Open to Slavery by Compromise of 1850
CALIFORNIA
INDIAN TERRITORY
TEXAS
MEXICO
PACIFIC OCEAN
ATLANTIC OCEAN
GULF OF MEXICO
WISCONSIN
MICHIGAN
IOWA
ILLINOIS
INDIANA
OHIO
PENNSYLVANIA
NEW YORK
MAINE
V.T.
N.H.
MASS.
CONN.
R.I.
NEW JERSEY
DEL.
MARYLAND
VIRGINIA
KENTUCKY
MISSOURI
ARKANSAS
TENNESSEE
NORTH CAROLINA
SOUTH CAROLINA
GEORGIA
ALABAMA
MISSISSIPPI
LOUISIANA
FLORIDA
Lake Superior
Lake Michigan
Lake Huron
Lake Erie
Lake Ontario
Columbia
Snake
Missouri
Colorado
Mississippi
Ohio
Carson City
Sacramento
San Francisco
Los Angeles
Salt Lake City
Tucson
Denver City
Santa Fe
Yankton
Omaha
St. Paul
Des Moines
Topeka
San Antonio
Little Rock
Shreveport
Milwaukee
Chicago
Detroit
St. Louis
Jefferson City
Indianapolis
Louisville
Cincinnati
Lexington
Nashville
Memphis
Atlanta
Mobile
New Orleans
Cleveland
Pittsburgh
Buffalo
Albany
Portland
Boston
New York
Philadelphia
Baltimore
Washington
Richmond
Norfolk
Wilmington
Charleston
Savannah
St. Augustine
1835
1834
1836
1859
1800
1831
1829
1848
1837
1850
1855
1856
1841
1822
1849
1845
1840
125°
120°
115°
110°
105°
100°
95°
90°
85°
80°
75°
70°
45°
40°
35°
30°
25°
50% and over Slaves
1% to 50% Slaves
Open to Slavery
Free States
Railroad
Tobacco
Cotton
Sugar
Rice
Abolitionist Incidents
Slave Revolts
0 100 200 300 400 Miles
0 100 200 300 400 500 600 Kilometers
Copyright by Rand McNally & Co.
Alber's Conic Equal Area Projection
N

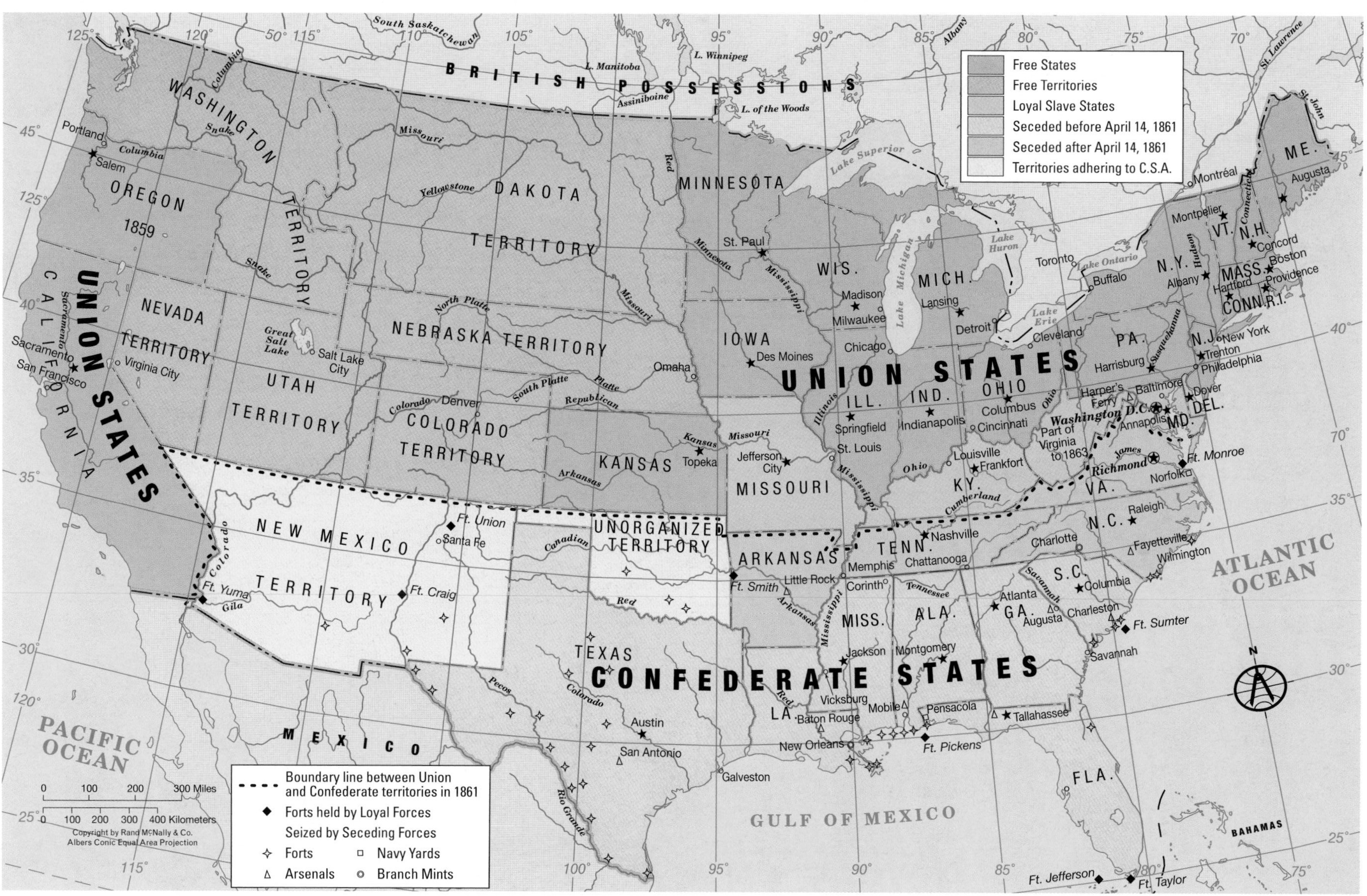
Free States
Free Territories
Loyal Slave States
Seceded before April 14, 1861
Seceded after April 14, 1861
Territories adhering to C.S.A.
Boundary line between Union and Confederate territories in 1861
Forts held by Loyal Forces
Seized by Seceding Forces
Forts
Navy Yards
Arsenals
Branch Mints
0 100 200 300 Miles
0 100 200 300 400 Kilometers
Copyright by Rand McNally & Co.
Albers Conic Equal Area Projection
BRITISH POSSESSIONS
UNION STATES
CONFEDERATE STATES
WASHINGTON TERRITORY
OREGON 1859
CALIFORNIA
NEVADA TERRITORY
UTAH TERRITORY
DAKOTA TERRITORY
NEBRASKA TERRITORY
COLORADO TERRITORY
KANSAS
NEW MEXICO TERRITORY
UNORGANIZED TERRITORY
TEXAS
MINNESOTA
IOWA
MISSOURI
ARKANSAS
LA.
WIS.
ILL.
MICH.
IND.
OHIO
KY.
TENN.
MISS.
ALA.
GA.
FLA.
S.C.
N.C.
VA.
PA.
N.Y.
N.J.
DEL.
MD.
VT.
N.H.
ME.
MASS.
CONN.
R.I.
Part of Virginia to 1863
MEXICO
PACIFIC OCEAN
ATLANTIC OCEAN
GULF OF MEXICO
BAHAMAS
Portland
Salem
Sacramento
San Francisco
Virginia City
Salt Lake City
Great Salt Lake
Denver
Omaha
Topeka
Ft. Union
Santa Fe
Ft. Craig
Ft. Yuma
Ft. Smith
St. Paul
Des Moines
Madison
Milwaukee
Chicago
Springfield
St. Louis
Jefferson City
Lansing
Detroit
Indianapolis
Columbus
Cincinnati
Louisville
Frankfort
Nashville
Memphis
Chattanooga
Little Rock
Corinth
Jackson
Vicksburg
Baton Rouge
New Orleans
Mobile
Montgomery
Pensacola
Ft. Pickens
Tallahassee
Atlanta
Augusta
Columbia
Charleston
Ft. Sumter
Savannah
Charlotte
Raleigh
Fayetteville
Wilmington
Richmond
Norfolk
Ft. Monroe
Washington D.C.
Annapolis
Harper's Ferry
Baltimore
Dover
Harrisburg
Philadelphia
Trenton
New York
Hartford
Providence
Boston
Concord
Montpelier
Albany
Augusta
Montréal
Toronto
Buffalo
Cleveland
Austin
San Antonio
Galveston
Ft. Jefferson
Ft. Taylor
Lake Superior
Lake Michigan
Lake Huron
Lake Erie
Lake Ontario
L. Winnipeg
L. Manitoba
L. of the Woods
Mississippi
Missouri
Ohio
Red
Arkansas
Rio Grande
Colorado
Pecos
Platte
Snake
Columbia

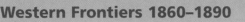

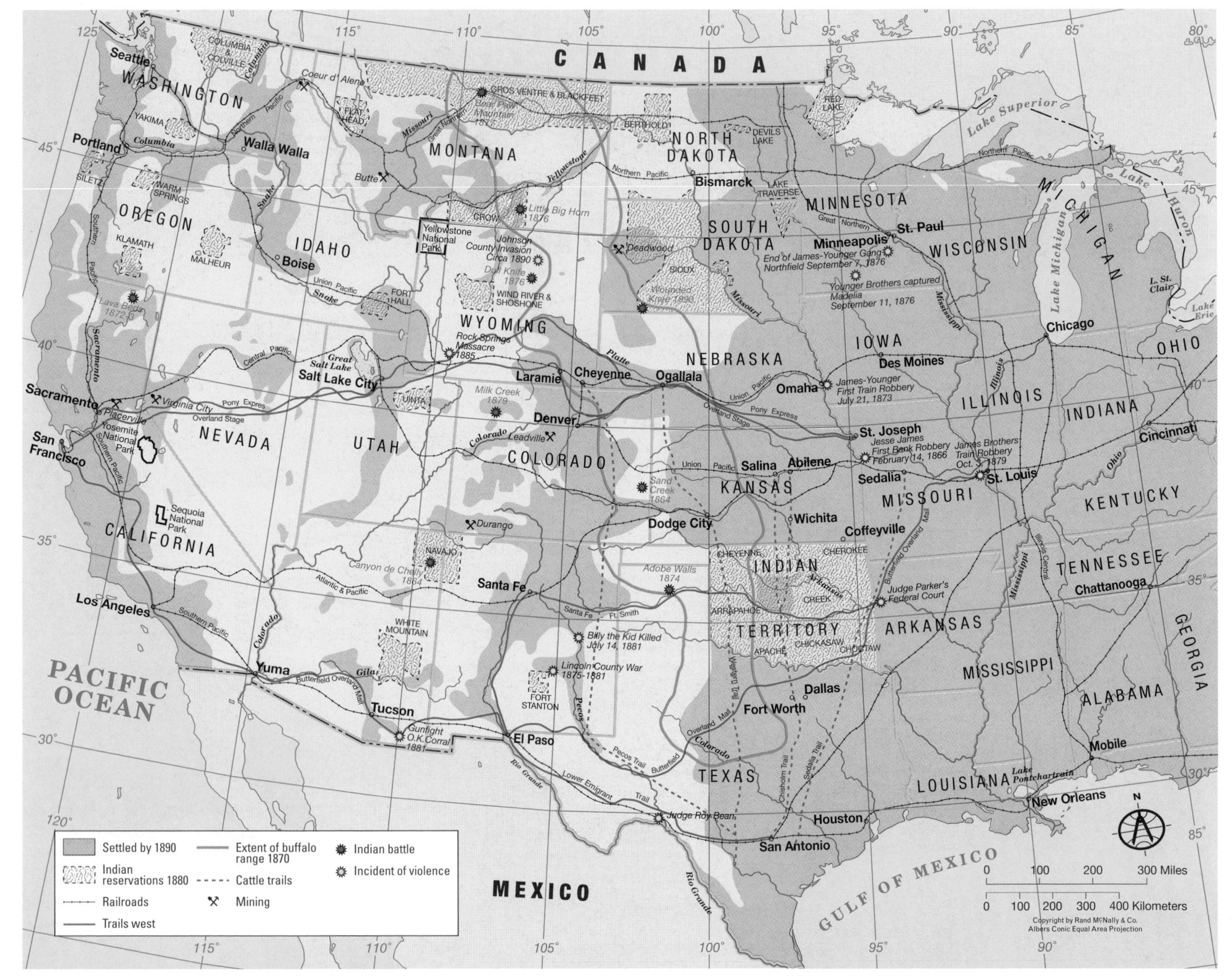
CANADA
MEXICO
PACIFIC OCEAN
GULF OF MEXICO
WASHINGTON
OREGON
CALIFORNIA
NEVADA
IDAHO
MONTANA
WYOMING
UTAH
COLORADO
NORTH DAKOTA
SOUTH DAKOTA
NEBRASKA
KANSAS
INDIAN TERRITORY
TEXAS
MINNESOTA
IOWA
MISSOURI
ARKANSAS
LOUISIANA
WISCONSIN
ILLINOIS
MICHIGAN
INDIANA
OHIO
KENTUCKY
TENNESSEE
MISSISSIPPI
ALABAMA
GEORGIA
Seattle
Portland
Walla Walla
Coeur d' Alene
Butte
Boise
Sacramento
Placerville
Virginia City
San Francisco
Yosemite National Park
Sequoia National Park
Los Angeles
Yuma
Tucson
Salt Lake City
Great Salt Lake
Yellowstone National Park
Laramie
Cheyenne
Denver
Leadville
Durango
Santa Fe
El Paso
Ogallala
Bismarck
Deadwood
Wounded Knee 1890
Omaha
Salina
Abilene
Wichita
Dodge City
Coffeyville
Dallas
Fort Worth
San Antonio
Houston
St. Joseph
Sedalia
St. Louis
Des Moines
Minneapolis
St. Paul
Chicago
Cincinnati
Chattanooga
Mobile
New Orleans
COLUMBIA & COLVILLE
YAKIMA
WARM SPRINGS
SILETZ
KLAMATH
MALHEUR
FLAT HEAD
FORT HALL
GROS VENTRE & BLACKFEET
CROW
WIND RIVER & SHOSHONE
UINTA
NAVAJO
WHITE MOUNTAIN
FORT STANTON
BERTHOLD
DEVILS LAKE
LAKE TRAVERSE
RED LAKE
SIOUX
CHEYENNE
CHEROKEE
CREEK
ARRAPAHOE
APACHE
CHICKASAW
CHOCTAW
Lava Beds 1872-3
Bear Paw Mountain 1877
Little Big Horn 1876
Johnson County Invasion Circa 1890
Dull Knife 1876
Rock Springs Massacre 1885
Milk Creek 1879
Sand Creek 1864
Canyon de Chelly 1864
Adobe Walls 1874
Billy the Kid Killed July 14, 1881
Lincoln County War 1875-1881
Gunfight O.K. Corral 1881
Judge Roy Bean
Judge Parker's Federal Court
End of James-Younger Gang Northfield September 7, 1876
Younger Brothers captured Madelia September 11, 1876
James-Younger First Train Robbery July 21, 1873
Jesse James First Bank Robbery February 14, 1866
James Brothers Train Robbery Oct. 3, 1879
Columbia
Snake
Missouri
Yellowstone
Platte
Sacramento
Colorado
Gila
Rio Grande
Pecos
Arkansas
Mississippi
Illinois
Ohio
Lake Superior
Lake Michigan
Lake Huron
Lake Erie
L. St. Clair
Lake Pontchartrain
Northern Pacific
Great Northern
Union Pacific
Central Pacific
Southern Pacific
Atlantic & Pacific
Illinois Central
Santa Fe
Pony Express
Overland Stage
Butterfield Overland Mail
Overland Mail
Butterfield
Ft. Smith
Pecos Trail
Lower Emigrant Trail
Western Trail
Chisholm Trail
Sedalia Trail
Settled by 1890
Indian reservations 1880
Railroads
Trails west
Extent of buffalo range 1870
Cattle trails
Mining
Indian battle
Incident of violence
0 100 200 300 Miles
0 100 200 300 400 Kilometers
Copyright by Rand McNally & Co.
Albers Conic Equal Area Projection

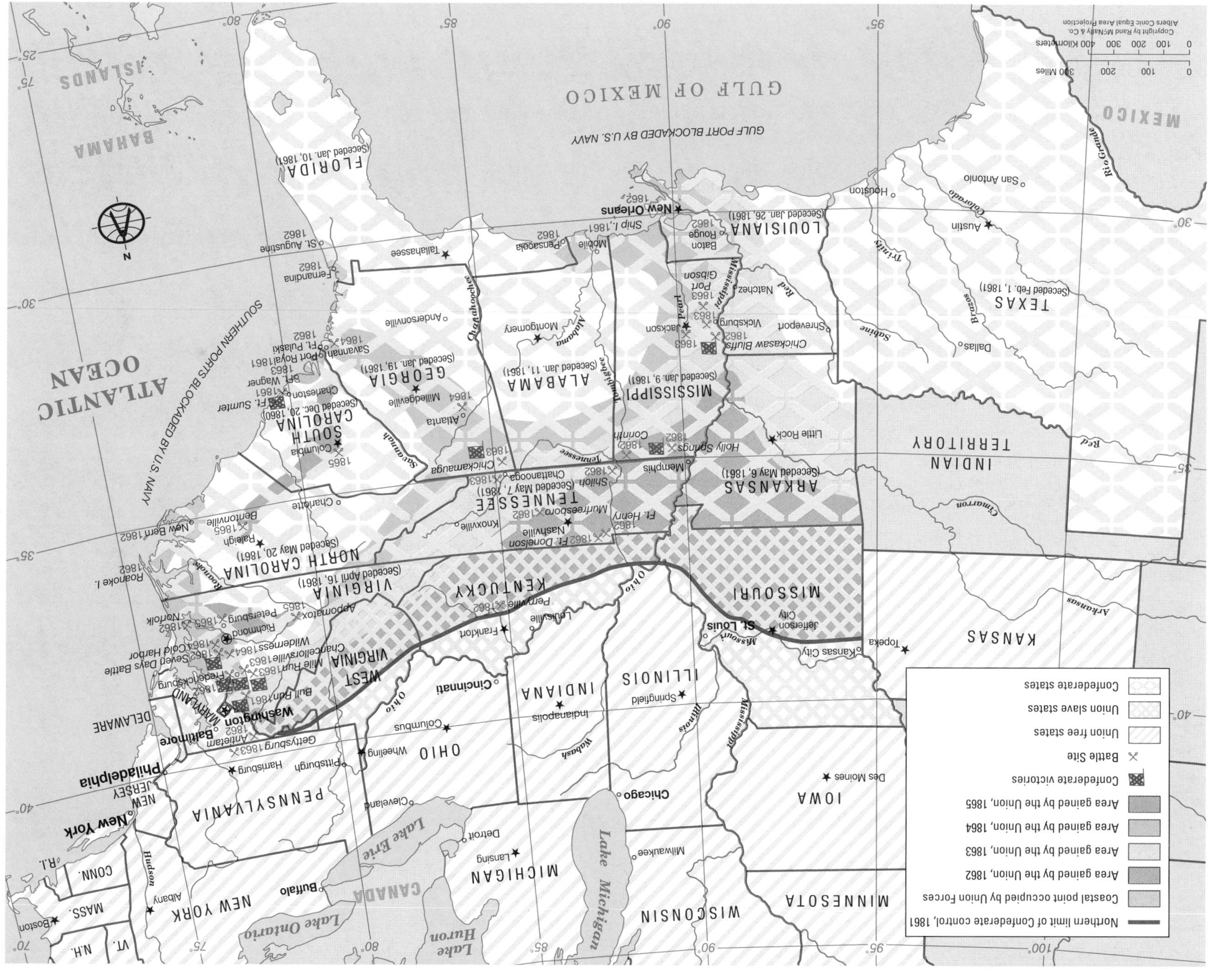
Northern limit of Confederate control, 1861
Coastal point occupied by Union Forces
Area gained by the Union, 1862
Area gained by the Union, 1863
Area gained by the Union, 1864
Area gained by the Union, 1865
Confederate victories
Battle Site
Union free states
Union slave states
Confederate states
ATLANTIC OCEAN
GULF OF MEXICO
SOUTHERN PORTS BLOCKADED BY U.S. NAVY
GULF PORT BLOCKADED BY U.S. NAVY
CANADA
MEXICO
BAHAMA ISLANDS
FLORIDA (Seceded Jan. 10, 1861)
GEORGIA (Seceded Jan. 19, 1861)
SOUTH CAROLINA (Seceded Dec. 20, 1860)
NORTH CAROLINA (Seceded May 20, 1861)
VIRGINIA (Seceded April 16, 1861)
TENNESSEE (Seceded May 7, 1861)
ALABAMA (Seceded Jan. 11, 1861)
MISSISSIPPI (Seceded Jan. 9, 1861)
LOUISIANA (Seceded Jan. 26, 1861)
ARKANSAS (Seceded May 6, 1861)
TEXAS (Seceded Feb. 1, 1861)
INDIAN TERRITORY
KANSAS
MISSOURI
KENTUCKY
WEST VIRGINIA
MARYLAND
DELAWARE
NEW JERSEY
PENNSYLVANIA
NEW YORK
OHIO
INDIANA
ILLINOIS
IOWA
MINNESOTA
WISCONSIN
MICHIGAN
VT.
N.H.
MASS.
CONN.
R.I.
Lake Ontario
Lake Erie
Lake Huron
Lake Michigan
Washington
New York
Philadelphia
Baltimore
Boston
Albany
Buffalo
Harrisburg
Pittsburgh
Cleveland
Wheeling
Columbus
Cincinnati
Detroit
Lansing
Chicago
Milwaukee
Springfield
Indianapolis
Frankfort
Louisville
St. Louis
Jefferson City
Kansas City
Topeka
Des Moines
Richmond
Norfolk
Petersburg
Raleigh
Charlotte
Columbia
Charleston
Savannah
Milledgeville
Atlanta
Andersonville
Tallahassee
Montgomery
Mobile
Pensacola
Jackson
Vicksburg
Natchez
Baton Rouge
New Orleans
Shreveport
Little Rock
Memphis
Nashville
Knoxville
Chattanooga
Dallas
Austin
San Antonio
Houston
Gettysburg 1863
Antietam 1862
Bull Run 1861 1862
Fredericksburg 1862
Chancellorsville 1863
Mine Run 1863
Wilderness 1864
Seven Days Battle 1862
Cold Harbor 1864
Appomattox 1865
Petersburg 1865
Bentonville 1865
New Bern 1862
Roanoke I. 1862
Ft. Sumter 1861
Ft. Wagner 1863
Port Royal 1861
Ft. Pulaski 1862
Fernandina 1862
St. Augustine 1862
Ft. Donelson 1862
Ft. Henry 1862
Murfreesboro 1862
Shiloh 1862
Chickamauga 1863
Chattanooga 1863
Perryville 1862
Corinth 1862
Holly Springs 1862
Chickasaw Bluffs 1862
Port Gibson 1863
Ship I. 1861
Savannah 1864
Columbia 1865
Atlanta 1864
Hudson
Ohio
Wabash
Illinois
Mississippi
Missouri
Tennessee
Tombigbee
Alabama
Chattahoochee
Savannah
Roanoke
Pearl
Red
Sabine
Trinity
Brazos
Colorado
Rio Grande
Arkansas
Cimarron
0 100 200 300 Miles
0 100 200 300 400 Kilometers
Copyright by Rand McNally & Co.
Albers Conic Equal Area Projection

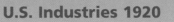

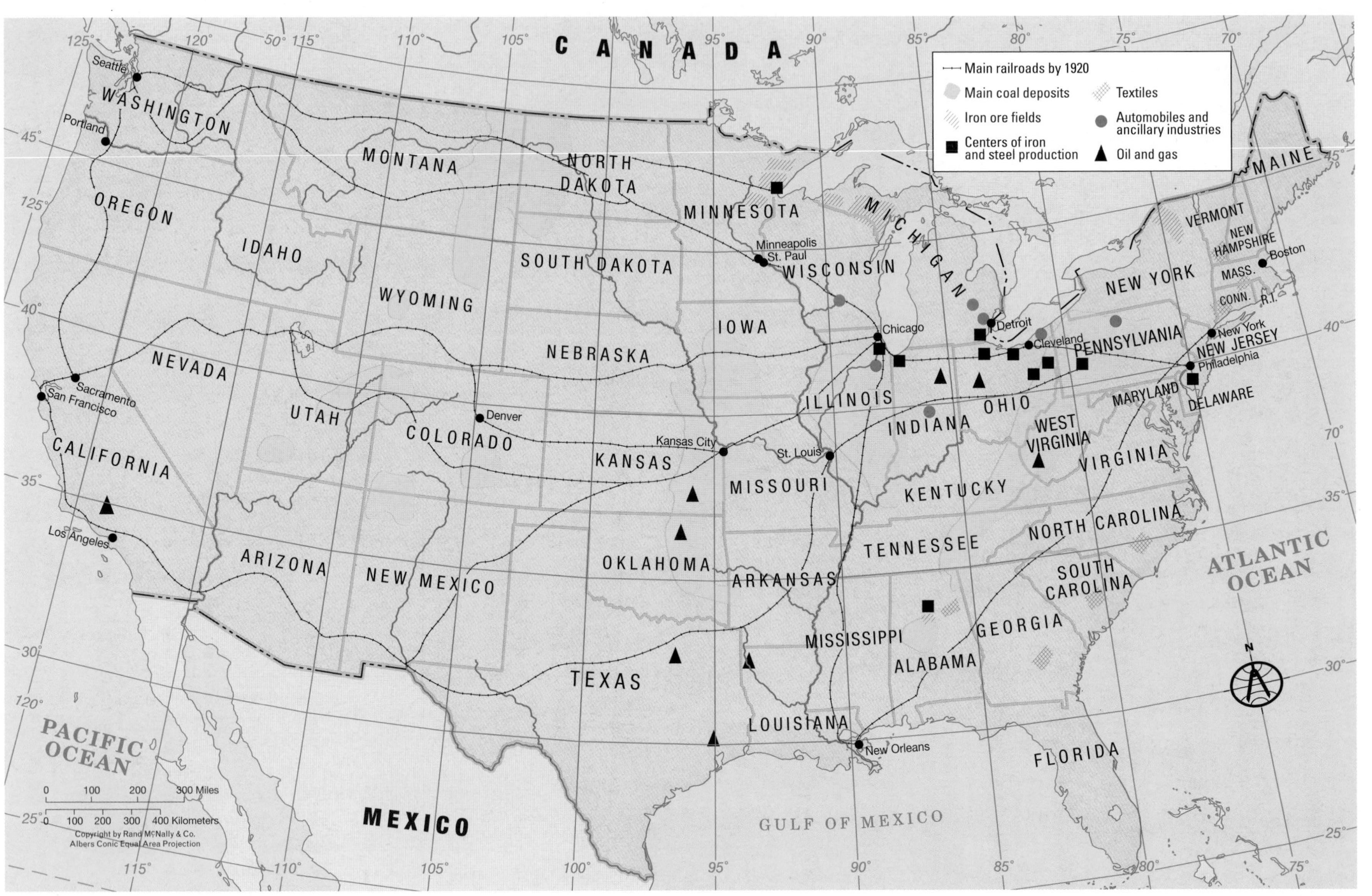
CANADA
MEXICO
PACIFIC OCEAN
ATLANTIC OCEAN
GULF OF MEXICO
Main railroads by 1920
Main coal deposits
Iron ore fields
Centers of iron and steel production
Textiles
Automobiles and ancillary industries
Oil and gas
WASHINGTON
OREGON
CALIFORNIA
NEVADA
IDAHO
MONTANA
WYOMING
UTAH
ARIZONA
COLORADO
NEW MEXICO
NORTH DAKOTA
SOUTH DAKOTA
NEBRASKA
KANSAS
OKLAHOMA
TEXAS
MINNESOTA
IOWA
MISSOURI
ARKANSAS
LOUISIANA
WISCONSIN
ILLINOIS
MICHIGAN
INDIANA
OHIO
KENTUCKY
TENNESSEE
MISSISSIPPI
ALABAMA
GEORGIA
FLORIDA
SOUTH CAROLINA
NORTH CAROLINA
VIRGINIA
WEST VIRGINIA
MARYLAND
DELAWARE
PENNSYLVANIA
NEW JERSEY
NEW YORK
CONN.
R.I.
MASS.
VERMONT
NEW HAMPSHIRE
MAINE
Seattle
Portland
Sacramento
San Francisco
Los Angeles
Denver
Kansas City
St. Louis
Minneapolis
St. Paul
Chicago
Detroit
Cleveland
New Orleans
New York
Philadelphia
Boston
0 100 200 300 Miles
0 100 200 300 400 Kilometers
Copyright by Rand McNally & Co.
Albers Conic Equal Area Projection

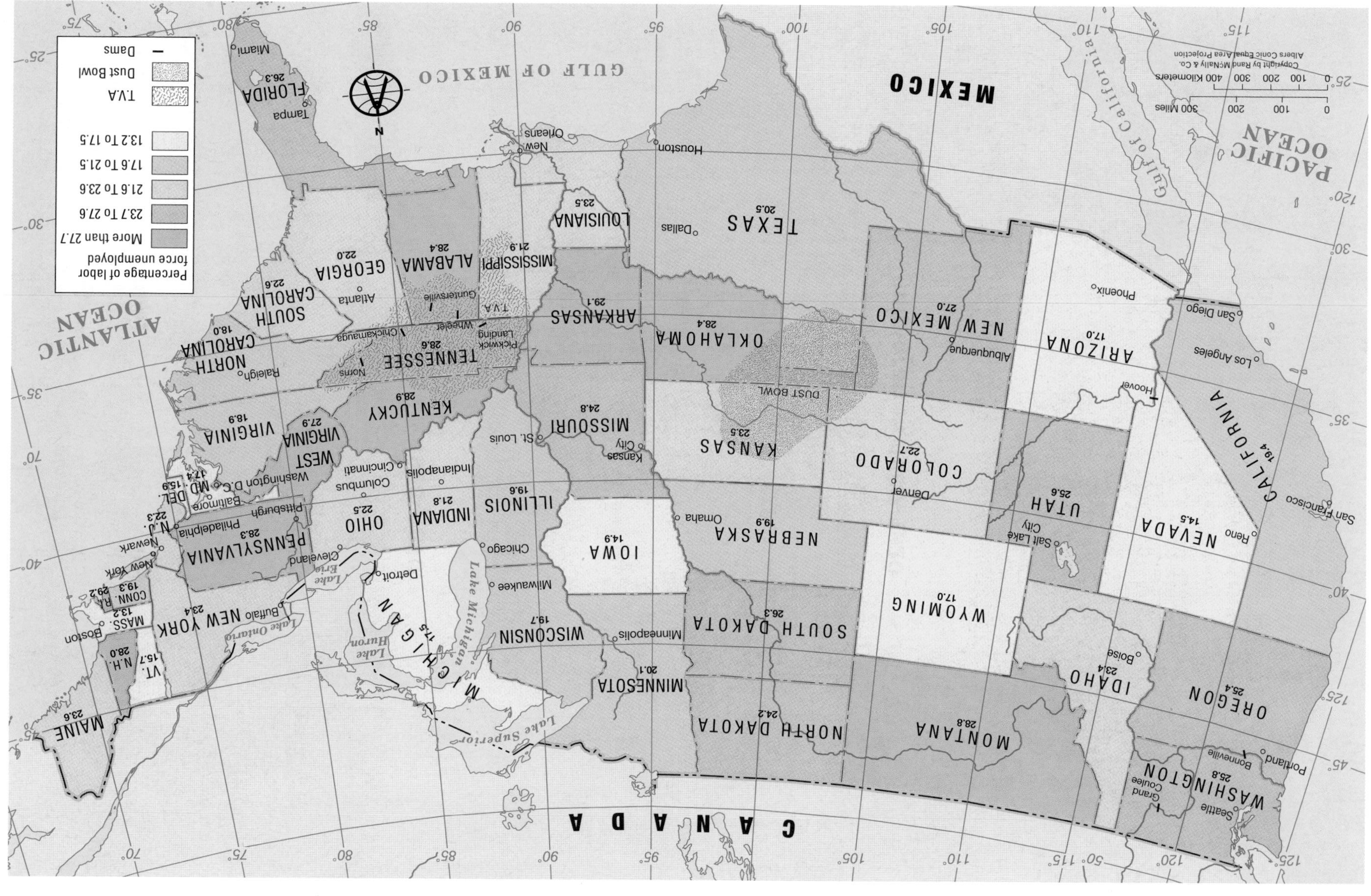
Percentage of labor force unemployed
More than 27.7
23.7 To 27.6
21.6 To 23.6
17.6 To 21.5
13.2 To 17.5
T.V.A
Dust Bowl
Dams
CANADA
MEXICO
ATLANTIC OCEAN
PACIFIC OCEAN
GULF OF MEXICO
Gulf of California
Lake Superior
Lake Michigan
Lake Huron
Lake Erie
Lake Ontario
WASHINGTON 25.8
OREGON 25.4
CALIFORNIA 19.4
NEVADA 14.5
IDAHO 23.4
MONTANA 28.8
WYOMING 17.0
UTAH 25.6
ARIZONA 17.0
COLORADO 22.7
NEW MEXICO 27.0
NORTH DAKOTA 24.2
SOUTH DAKOTA 26.3
NEBRASKA 19.9
KANSAS 23.5
OKLAHOMA 28.4
TEXAS 20.5
MINNESOTA 20.1
IOWA 14.9
MISSOURI 24.8
ARKANSAS 29.1
LOUISIANA 23.5
WISCONSIN 19.7
ILLINOIS 19.6
MICHIGAN 17.5
INDIANA 21.8
OHIO 22.5
KENTUCKY 28.9
TENNESSEE 28.6
MISSISSIPPI 21.9
ALABAMA 28.4
GEORGIA 22.0
FLORIDA 26.3
SOUTH CAROLINA 22.6
NORTH CAROLINA 18.0
VIRGINIA 18.9
WEST VIRGINIA 27.9
PENNSYLVANIA 28.3
NEW YORK 23.4
VT. 15.7
N.H. 28.0
MAINE 23.6
MASS. 13.2
CONN. 19.3
R.I. 29.2
N.J. 22.3
DEL. 15.9
MD. 17.4
DUST BOWL
T.V.A.
Seattle
Portland
Bonneville
Grand Coulee
Boise
San Francisco
Reno
Los Angeles
San Diego
Hoover
Phoenix
Salt Lake City
Denver
Albuquerque
Dallas
Houston
New Orleans
Omaha
Kansas City
Minneapolis
St. Louis
Milwaukee
Chicago
Indianapolis
Detroit
Cincinnati
Columbus
Cleveland
Pittsburgh
Buffalo
Philadelphia
Baltimore
Washington D.C.
Newark
New York
Boston
Raleigh
Atlanta
Tampa
Miami
Norris
Chickamauga
Wheeler
Guntersville
Pickwick Landing
0 100 200 300 Miles
0 100 200 300 400 Kilometers
Copyright by Rand McNally & Co.
Albers Conic Equal Area Projection

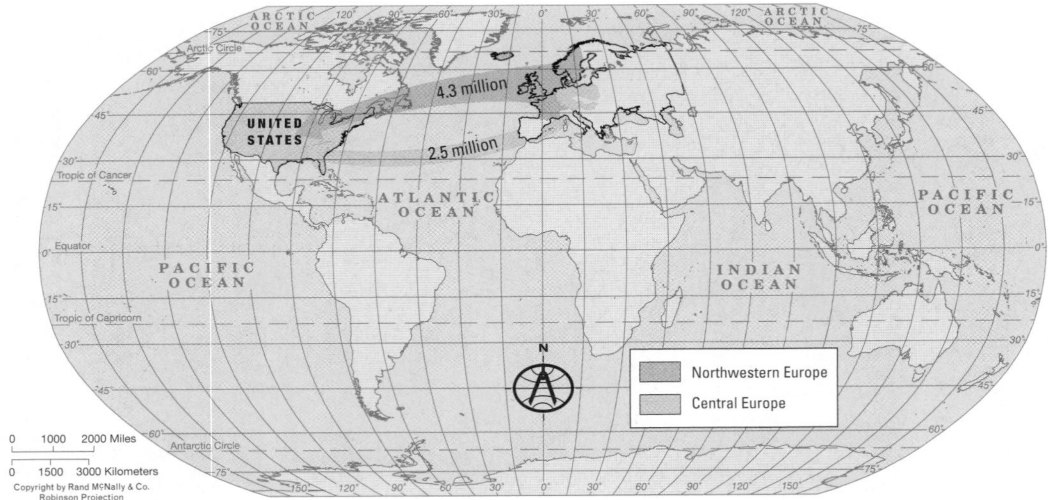

Immigration 1820–1870

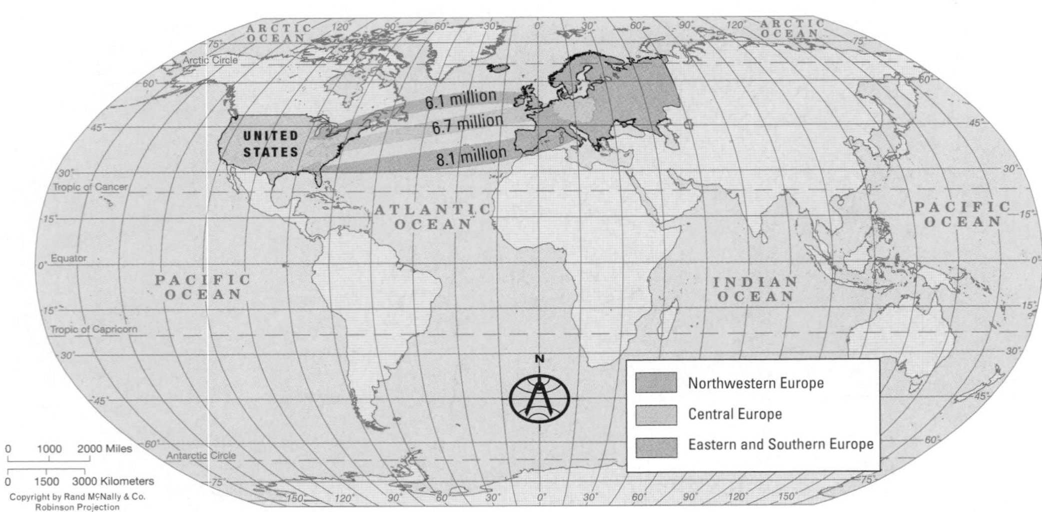

Immigration 1880–1920

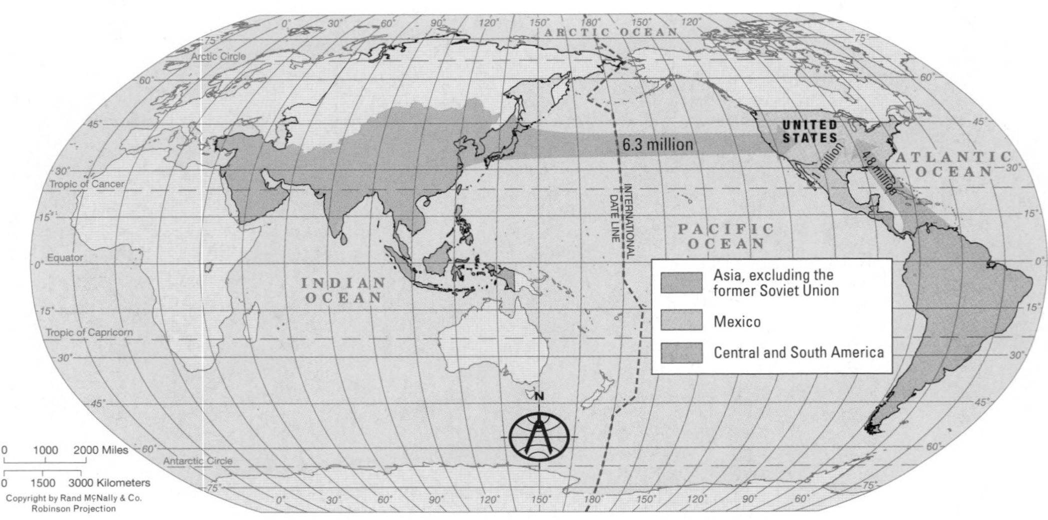

Immigration 1960s–1990s

Immigration's Impact 1910

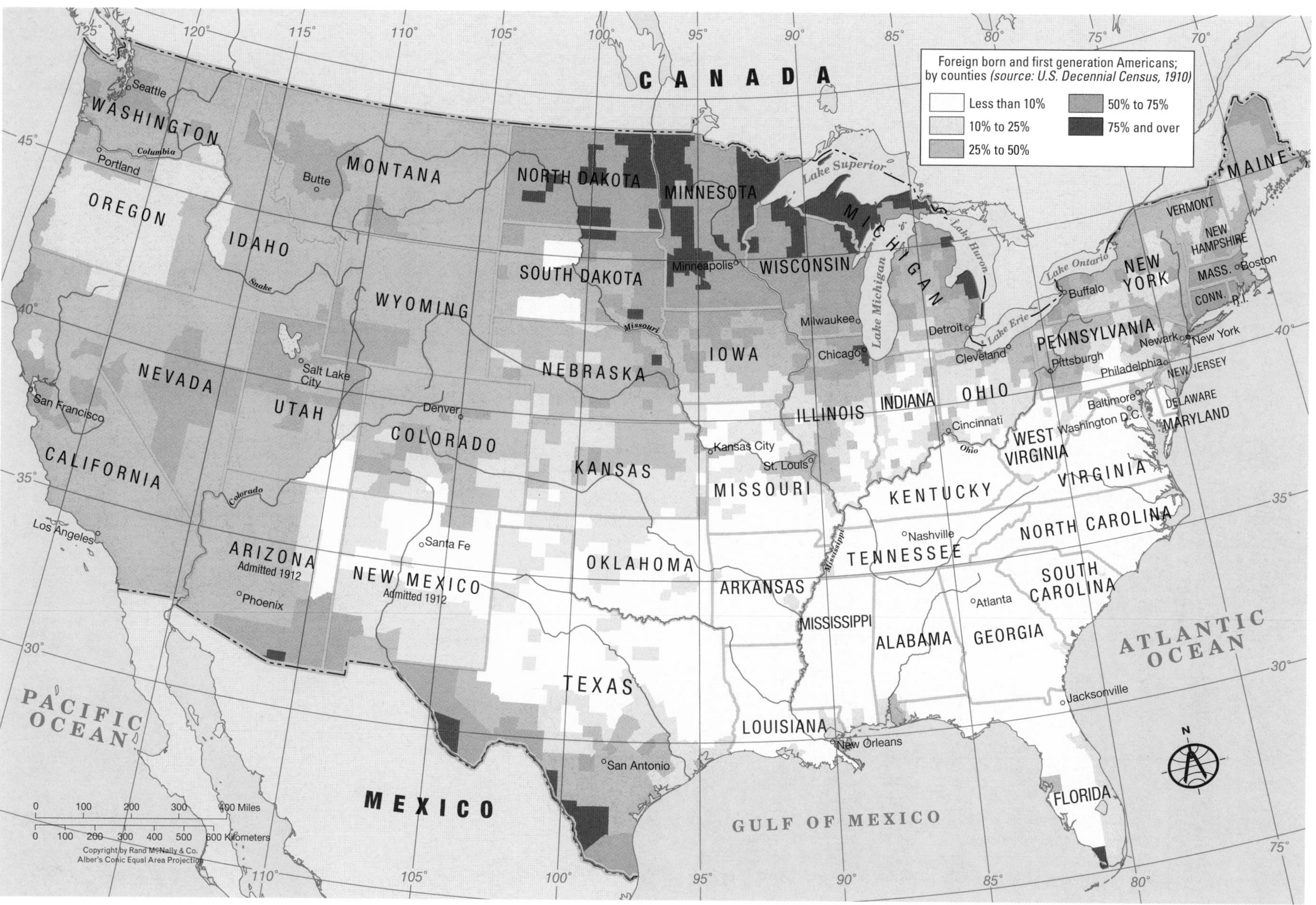

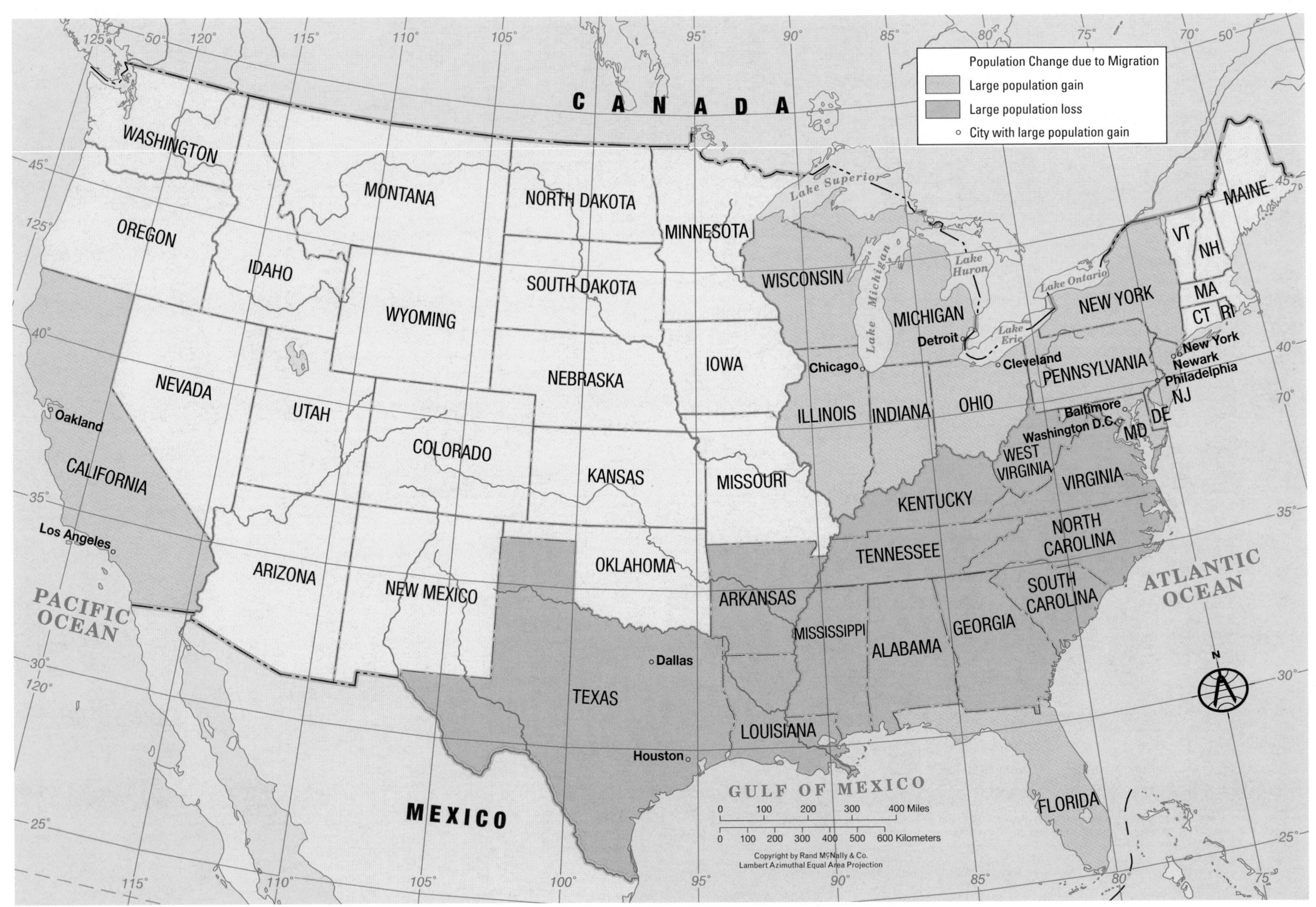
Population Change due to Migration
Large population gain
Large population loss
City with large population gain
CANADA
MEXICO
PACIFIC OCEAN
ATLANTIC OCEAN
GULF OF MEXICO
Lake Superior
Lake Michigan
Lake Huron
Lake Erie
Lake Ontario
WASHINGTON
OREGON
CALIFORNIA
NEVADA
IDAHO
MONTANA
WYOMING
UTAH
ARIZONA
COLORADO
NEW MEXICO
NORTH DAKOTA
SOUTH DAKOTA
NEBRASKA
KANSAS
OKLAHOMA
TEXAS
MINNESOTA
IOWA
MISSOURI
ARKANSAS
LOUISIANA
WISCONSIN
ILLINOIS
MICHIGAN
INDIANA
OHIO
KENTUCKY
TENNESSEE
MISSISSIPPI
ALABAMA
GEORGIA
FLORIDA
SOUTH CAROLINA
NORTH CAROLINA
VIRGINIA
WEST VIRGINIA
PENNSYLVANIA
NEW YORK
MD
DE
NJ
CT
RI
MA
VT
NH
MAINE
Oakland
Los Angeles
Dallas
Houston
Chicago
Detroit
Cleveland
Baltimore
Washington D.C.
Philadelphia
Newark
New York
N
0 100 200 300 400 Miles
0 100 200 300 400 500 600 Kilometers
Copyright by Rand McNally & Co.
Lambert Azimuthal Equal Area Projection

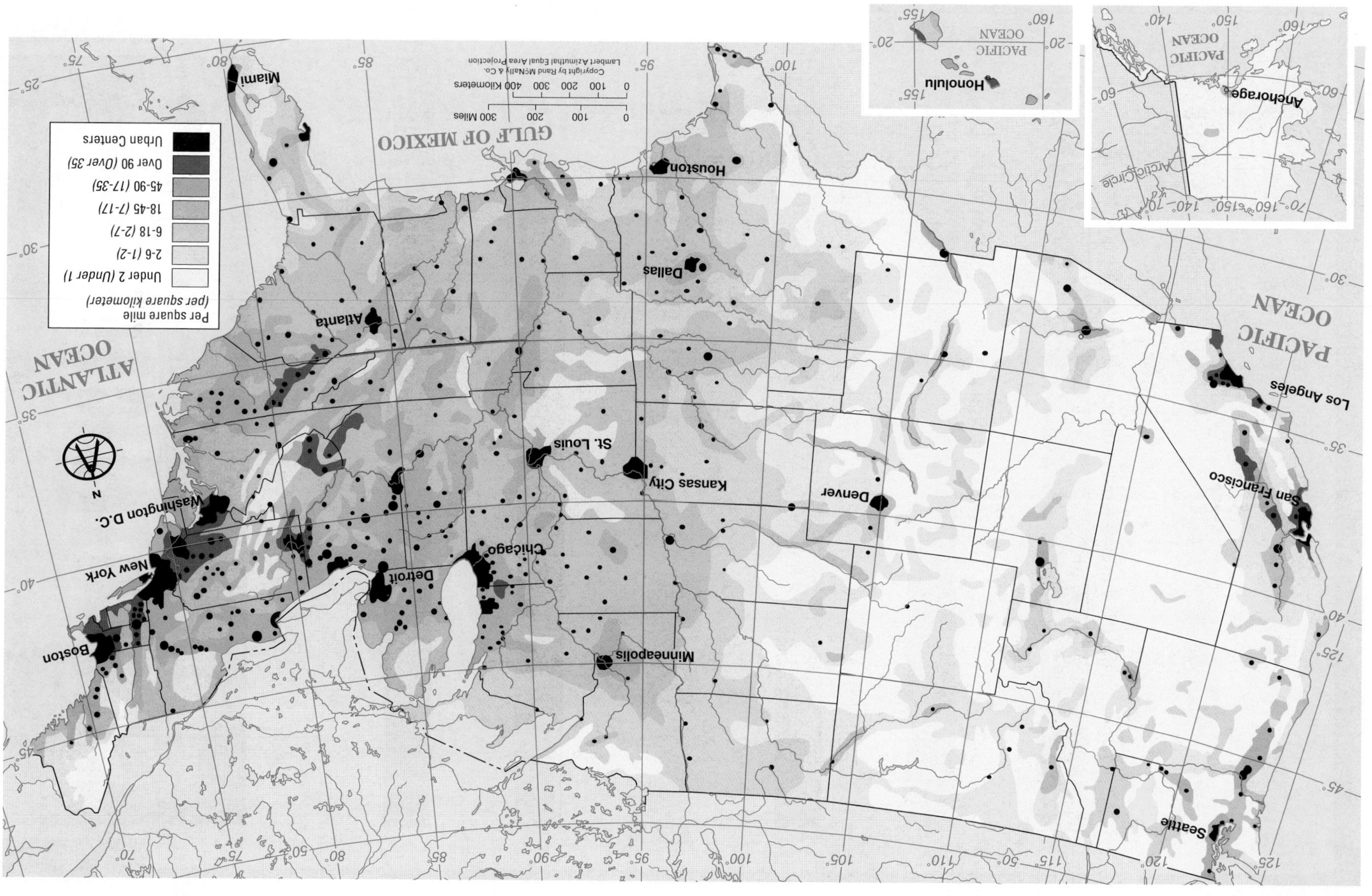
ATLANTIC OCEAN
GULF OF MEXICO
PACIFIC OCEAN
N
Per square mile
(per square kilometer)
Under 2 (Under 1)
2-6 (1-2)
6-18 (2-7)
18-45 (7-17)
45-90 (17-35)
Over 90 (Over 35)
Urban Centers
0 100 200 300 Miles
0 100 200 300 400 Kilometers
Copyright by Rand McNally & Co.
Lambert Azimuthal Equal Area Projection
Boston
New York
Washington D.C.
Detroit
Chicago
Atlanta
Miami
St. Louis
Minneapolis
Kansas City
Dallas
Houston
Denver
Seattle
San Francisco
Los Angeles
Honolulu
Anchorage
Arctic Circle

REFERENCE SECTION

SKILLBUILDER HANDBOOK

Skills for reading, thinking, and researching R1

ECONOMICS HANDBOOK

Glossary of economic terms R38

FACTS ABOUT THE STATES

Information about individual states R48

PRESIDENTS OF THE UNITED STATES

Information about all 43 presidents R50

GLOSSARY

Important terms and definitions R53

SPANISH GLOSSARY

Important terms and definitions translated into Spanish R67

INDEX

Listing of all topics in this textbook R82

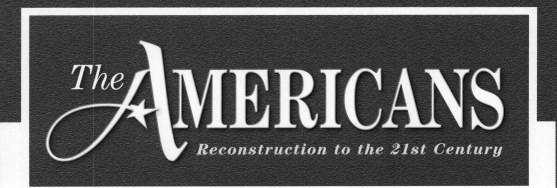

Skillbuilder Handbook

1. Understanding Historical Readings

1.1 Finding Main Ideas R2
1.2 Following Chronological Order R3
1.3 Clarifying; Summarizing R4
1.4 Identifying Problems R5
1.5 Analyzing Motives R6
1.6 Analyzing Causes and Effects R7
1.7 Comparing; Contrasting R8
1.8 Distinguishing Fact from Opinion R9
1.9 Making Inferences R10

2. Using Critical Thinking

2.1 Developing Historical Perspective R11
2.2 Formulating Historical Questions R12
2.3 Hypothesizing R13
2.4 Analyzing Issues R14
2.5 Analyzing Assumptions and Biases R15
2.6 Evaluating Decisions and Courses of Action R16
2.7 Forming Opinions (Evaluating) R17
2.8 Drawing Conclusions R18
2.9 Synthesizing R19
2.10 Making Predictions R20
2.11 Forming Generalizations R21

3. Print, Visual, and Technological Sources

3.1 Primary and Secondary Sources R22
3.2 Visual, Audio, Multimedia Sources R23
3.3 Analyzing Political Cartoons R24
3.4 Interpreting Maps R25
3.5 Interpreting Charts R27
3.6 Interpreting Graphs R28
3.7 Using the Internet R29

4. Presenting Information

4.1 Creating Charts and Graphs R30
4.2 Creating Models R31
4.3 Creating Maps R32
4.4 Creating Databases R33
4.5 Creating Written Presentations R34
4.6 Creating Oral Presentations R36
4.7 Creating Visual Presentations R37

1.1 Finding Main Ideas

DEFINING THE SKILL

Finding main ideas means identifying words that sum up the single most important thought in an entire paragraph or section. To find the main idea of a passage, identify the topic. Then, as you read, ask, What central idea do the many details explain or support?

APPLYING THE SKILL

This excerpt from President Richard M. Nixon's memoirs is about wiretapping, or bugging—planting a concealed microphone to get information. The diagram that follows identifies and organizes information in the passage.

HOW TO FIND MAIN IDEAS

Strategy ❶ Identify the topic by looking at the title, or by looking for key words. This passage repeats the words *bugged*, *bugging*, *tapped*, and *wiretap*.

Strategy ❷ Look for a topic sentence. Ask whether any one sentence sums up the point of the whole passage. In this passage, the second sentence states Nixon's attitude toward bugging.

Strategy ❸ Look for details or examples. The many examples support the attitude that wiretapping was a common practice.

NIXON ON WIRETAPPING ❶

I had been in politics too long, and seen everything from dirty tricks to vote fraud. ❷ I could not muster much moral outrage over a political ❶ bugging.

Larry O'Brien [director of the Democratic National Committee] might affect astonishment and horror, but he knew as well as I did that political bugging had been around nearly since the invention of the wiretap. ❸ As recently as 1970 a former member of Adlai Stevenson's [Democratic candidate for president in 1952 and 1956] campaign staff had publicly stated that he had tapped the [John F.] Kennedy organization's phone lines at the 1960 Democratic convention. ❸ Lyndon Johnson felt that the Kennedys had had him tapped; ❸ Barry Goldwater said that his 1964 campaign had been bugged; ❸ and Edgar Hoover [director of the FBI, 1924–1972] told me that in 1968 Johnson had ordered my campaign plane bugged.

Source: Richard Nixon, *The Memoirs of Richard Nixon* (New York: Grosset & Dunlap, 1978), pp. 628–629.

Make a Diagram

State the topic and list the supporting details in a chart. Use the information you record to help you state the main idea.

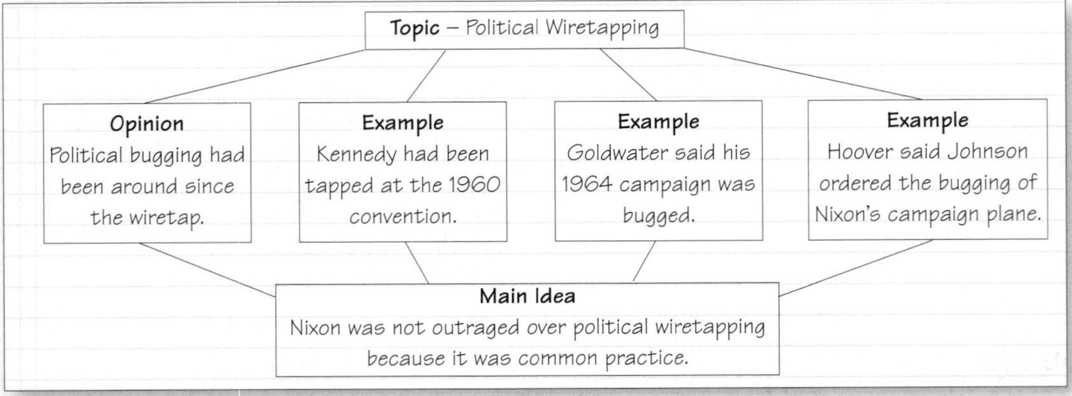

PRACTICING THE SKILL

Turn to Chapter 26, Section 3, p. 879 and read the passage headed "Space Exploration." Make a diagram, like the one above, to identify the topic, the most important details, and the main idea of the passage.

1.2 Following Chronological Order

DEFINING THE SKILL

Chronological order is "time order"—the sequence of events in time. Chronology may be either relative or absolute. Relative chronology relates one event to another. This helps historians to see causes, effects, and other relationships between events. Absolute chronology ties events to an exact time or date, pinpointing dates in one universal framework—the passage of time.

APPLYING THE SKILL

The following paragraph is about several events leading up to the Watergate scandal that brought down the Nixon administration. The time line that follows puts the events of the passage in chronological order.

HOW TO FOLLOW CHRONOLOGICAL ORDER

Strategy 1 Look for clue words about time. These are words like *initial, first, next, then, before, after, finally,* and *by that time.*

Strategy 2 Use specific dates provided in the text.

Strategy 3 Watch for references to previous historical events that are included in the background. Usually a change in verb tense will indicate a previous event.

The Pentagon Papers

The (1) initial event that many historians believe led to Watergate took place on (2) June 13, 1971, when the *New York Times* began publishing articles called the Pentagon Papers, which divulged government secrets about the U.S. involvement in Vietnam. The information had been leaked by a former Defense Department official, Daniel Ellsberg. The Justice Department asked the courts to suppress publication of the articles, but on (2) July 30, 1971, the Supreme Court ruled that the information could be published. (1) Two months later, in September, a group of special White House agents known as the plumbers burglarized the office of Ellsberg's psychiatrist in a vain attempt to find evidence against Ellsberg. President Nixon (3) had authorized the creation of the plumbers in 1971, after the Pentagon Papers were published, to keep government secrets from leaking to the media and to help ensure his reelection in November 1972.

Make a Time Line

If the events in a passage are numerous and complex, make a time line to represent them. The time line here lists the events from the passage above in time order.

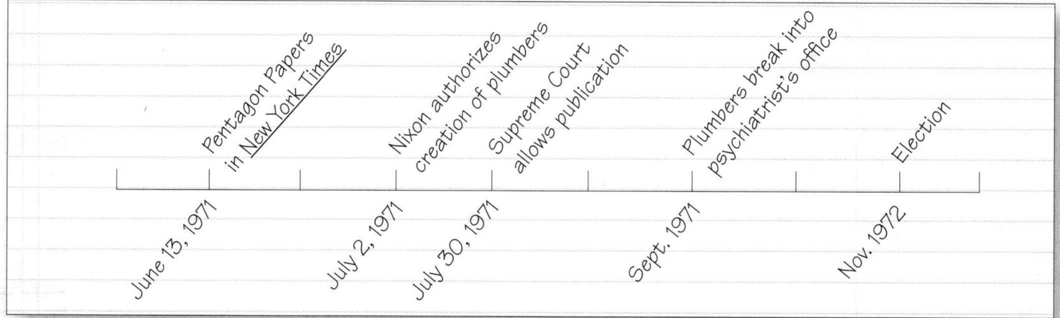

PRACTICING THE SKILL

Skim, Chapter 21, Section 2, p. 710 "The Triumphs of a Crusade," to find out how the civil rights movement helped end segregation in the South. Make a list of the important dates you find, starting with the freedom ride in May 1961 and ending with the passage of the Voting Rights Act of 1965. Use the model above to help you create your own time line, showing what happened on each date.

1.3 Clarifying; Summarizing

DEFINING THE SKILL

Clarifying means checking to be sure you clearly understand what you have read. One way to do this is by asking yourself questions. In your answers, you might restate in your own words what you have read.

When you **summarize,** you condense what you have read into fewer words, stating only the main idea and the most important supporting details. It is important to use your own words in a summary.

APPLYING THE SKILL

The excerpt below describes a major oil spill. Following the excerpt is a summary that condenses the key information in the passage into a few sentences.

HOW TO SUMMARIZE

Strategy ❶ Look for topic sentences stating the main ideas. These are often at the beginning of a section or paragraph. In a summary, rewrite the main ideas in your own words.

Strategy ❷ Include only the most important facts and statistics. Pay attention to numbers, dates, quantities, and other data.

Strategy ❸ Clarify understanding by asking questions. Also, look up any words you do not recognize.

THE *EXXON VALDEZ* OIL SPILL

❶ In March 1989, the oil tanker *Exxon Valdez* ran aground in Prince William Sound along the coast of Alaska, dumping about ❷ 11 million gallons of crude oil into the sea. Within days, 1,800 miles of coastline were fouled with thick black oil that coated rocks and beaches. At least 10 percent of the area's birds, sea otters, and other animals were killed, and commercial fisheries estimated that they would lose at least 50 percent of the season's catch.

The captain of the *Exxon Valdez* was found guilty of ❸ negligence, and attempts were made to clean up the spill. ❷ Ten years later, however, scientists found that pools of oil buried in coves were still poisoning shellfish, otters, and ducks, while several bird species failed to reproduce.

❷ Between 1989 and 1994, Exxon spent about $2.1 billion in efforts to clean up Prince William Sound. In the meantime, some 34,000 commercial fishers and other Alaskans sued the company for damages, claiming that the oil spill had ruined their livelihoods.

Write a Summary

You can write your summary in a paragraph. The paragraph below summarizes the passage about the *Exxon Valdez* oil spill. After writing your summary, review it to see that you have included only the most important details.

In 1989, the *Exxon Valdez* ran aground off the Alaskan coast, spilling 11 million gallons of oil. The water and coastline for hundreds of miles were badly polluted, and many animals died. Alaskans sued the oil company for lost income. Exxon spent $2.1 billion for a cleanup effort and was subject to litigation from people who lost their livelihoods because of the spill.

PRACTICING THE SKILLS

Turn to Chapter 14, Section 1, p. 464 and read the passage headed "Economic Troubles on the Horizon." Make notes of the main ideas. Look up any words you don't recognize. Then write a summary of the passage, using the model above as your guide.

1.4 Identifying Problems

DEFINING THE SKILL

Identifying problems means recognizing and understanding difficulties faced by particular people or groups at particular times. Being able to focus on specific problems helps historians understand the motives for actions and the forces underlying historical events.

APPLYING THE SKILL

The following passage tells about the experience of newcomers to Northern cities, like Boston and Philadelphia, in the late 1800s. Below the passage is a chart that organizes the information the passage contains.

HOW TO IDENTIFY PROBLEMS

Strategy 1 Look for problems that are implied but not stated. Problems are sometimes stated indirectly. This sentence implies that many immigrants settled in the cities because of limited opportunities elsewhere.

Strategy 2 Look for difficulties people faced.

Strategy 3 Evaluate solutions to problems.

Strategy 4 Recognize that sometimes the solution to one problem may cause another problem.

IMMIGRANT LIFE IN THE CITIES

1 The lure that drew many immigrants to America and its cities often was the same one that had attracted settlers to the West—opportunity. In the nation's industrialized centers people saw a chance to 2 escape poverty, find work, and carve out a better life.

Cities offered unskilled laborers steady jobs in mills and factories and provided the social support of neighborhoods of people with the same ethnic background. 3 Living among people who shared their background enabled the newcomers to speak their own language while learning about their new home. 4 Overcrowding soon became a problem, however—one that was intensified by the migration of people from America's rural areas.

Make a Chart

The chart below summarizes the problems and solutions in the passage. The chart details what the problems were, what steps people took to solve the problems, and how those solutions affected them.

Problems	Solutions	Outcomes
poverty	coming to U.S. cities	jobs available
lack of opportunity	coming to U.S. cities	jobs, housing, communities
lack of work skills	factory and mill jobs requiring low level of training	enough jobs for the time being
unfamiliarity with language	living in ethnic communities	community but overcrowding

PRACTICING THE SKILL

Turn to Chapter 23, Section 2, p. 776 and read the passage headed "Women Fight for Equality." Note the social and economic problems many women faced in the 1960s and 1970s. Then make a chart, like the one above, in which you summarize the information you found in the passage. Be sure to read to the end of the section so that you can evaluate the solutions attempted and their outcomes.

1.5 Analyzing Motives

DEFINING THE SKILL

Analyzing motives in history means examining the reasons why a person, group, or government took a particular action. These reasons often go back to the needs, emotions, and prior experiences of the person or group, as well as their plans, circumstances, and objectives.

APPLYING THE SKILL

The following paragraphs tell how the early Mormons were treated and why they moved west in the mid-1800s. The diagram below the passage summarizes the Mormons' motives for that journey.

HOW TO ANALYZE MOTIVES

Strategy 1 Look for different kinds of motives. Some motives are negative, and others are positive.

Strategy 2 Look for the influence of important individuals or leaders in motivating others.

Strategy 3 Look for basic needs and human emotions as powerful motivators. Such needs and emotions include food and shelter, greed, ambition, compassion, and fear.

The Mormon Migration

Some of the Mormons' beliefs alarmed and angered other Americans. 1 Plagued by persecution and violence and seeking to convert Native Americans, Mormon church founder Joseph Smith led his followers west to a small community in Illinois. Conflict soon developed again when Smith allowed male members to have more than one wife. This idea infuriated many of Smith's neighbors, and he was eventually murdered by a mob.

2 The Mormons rallied around a new leader, Brigham Young, who urged them to move farther west. There they encountered a desert area near a salt lake, just beyond the moutains of what was then part of Mexico. The salty water was useless for crops and animals. Because the land was not desirable to others, 3 Young realized that his people might be safe there. The Mormons began to build Salt Lake City.

Make a Diagram

In the center of the diagram, list the important actions from the passage. Around it, list motives in different categories.

PRACTICING THE SKILL

Turn to Chapter 17, Section 3, p. 583 and read the passage headed "The Atomic Bomb Ends the War." Take notes about President Truman's motives in dropping atomic bombs on Japan. Then create a diagram similar to the one shown here.

1.6 Analyzing Causes and Effects

DEFINING THE SKILL

A **cause** is an action in history that prompts something to happen. An **effect** is a historical event or condition that is the result of the cause. A single event may have several causes. It is also possible for one cause to result in several effects. Historians identify cause-and-effect relationships to help them understand why historical events took place.

APPLYING THE SKILL

The following paragraphs describe the early events leading to the Battle of Little Bighorn. The diagram that follows the passage summarizes the chain of causes and effects.

HOW TO IDENTIFY CAUSES AND EFFECTS

Strategy 1 Look for reasons behind the events. Here the discovery of gold motivated white Americans to move into Sioux territory.

Strategy 2 Look for clue words indicating cause. These include *because, due to, since,* and *therefore.*

Strategy 3 Look for clue words indicating consequences. These include *brought about, led to, as a result, thus, consequently,* and *responded.* Remember that a cause may have several effects.

Broken Treaties

The Treaty of Fort Laramie (1868) had promised the Sioux that they could live forever in Paha Sapa, the Black Hills area of what is now South Dakota and Wyoming. The area was sacred to the Sioux. It was the center of their land and the place where warriors went to await visions from their guardian spirits.

Unfortunately for the Sioux, the Black Hills contained large deposits of gold. (1) As soon as white Americans learned that gold had been discovered, they poured into the Native Americans' territory and began staking claims.

(2) Because the Sioux valued their land so highly, they appealed to the government to enforce the treaty terms and remove the miners. The government (3) responded by offering to purchase the land from the Sioux. When the Sioux refused, the government sent in the Seventh Cavalry to remove the Native Americans.

Make a Cause-and-Effect Diagram

Starting with the first cause in a series, fill in the boxes until you reach the end result.

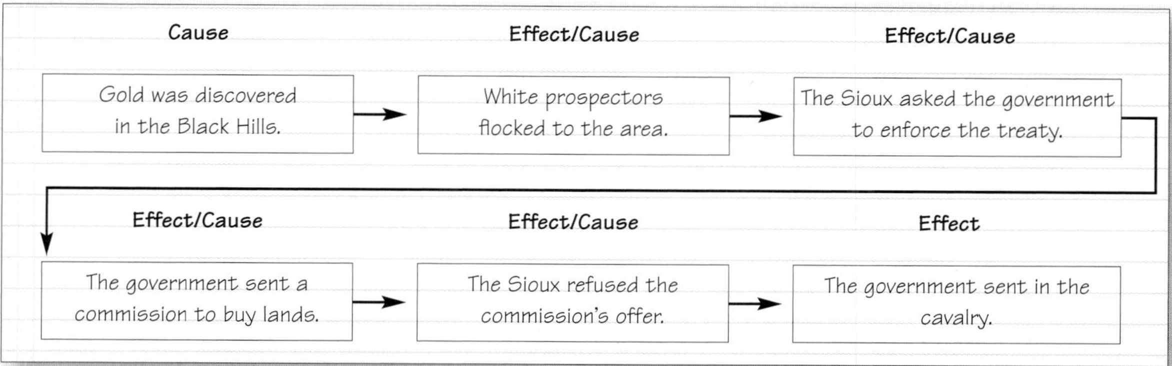
Cause
Gold was discovered in the Black Hills.
Effect/Cause
White prospectors flocked to the area.
Effect/Cause
The Sioux asked the government to enforce the treaty.
Effect/Cause
The government sent a commission to buy lands.
Effect/Cause
The Sioux refused the commission's offer.
Effect
The government sent in the cavalry.

PRACTICING THE SKILL

Turn to Chapter 11, Section 3, p. 392 and read the passage headed "African Americans and the War." Take notes about the causes and effects of African-American migration. Make a diagram, like the one shown above, to organize the information you find.

1.7 Comparing; Contrasting

DEFINING THE SKILL

Comparing involves looking at the similarities and differences between two or more things. **Contrasting** means examining only the differences between them. Historians might compare and contrast events, personalities, beliefs, institutions, works of art, or many other types of things in order to give them a context for the period of history they are studying.

APPLYING THE SKILL

The following passage describes life in colonial America during the last half of the 1600s. The Venn diagram below shows the similarities and differences between the Northern and Southern colonies.

HOW TO COMPARE AND CONTRAST

Strategy 1 Look for clue words that show how two things differ. Clue words include *different, differ, unlike, by contrast, however,* and *on the other hand.*

Strategy 2 Look for clue words indicating that two things are alike. Clue words include *both, all, like, as, likewise,* and *similarly.*

Strategy 3 Look for features that two things have in common.

Life in the Early American Colonies

Not long after the English colonies were established, it became apparent that two very (1) different ways of life were developing in the Northern and Southern colonies. In the South, both (2) rich plantation owners and poorer frontier farmers sought land. Virginia and Maryland became known as the tobacco colonies. (3) Large farms, but few towns, appeared there.

Slavery existed in (3) all the colonies, but it became a vital source of labor in the South. (1) By contrast, the New England and middle colonies did not rely on slave labor or single staple crops, such as tobacco or rice. Most people were farmers, but they grew a wide variety of crops. The New England colonies traded actively with the islands of the West Indies. In addition to foods, they exported all kinds of other items, ranging from barrels to horses. In return, they imported sugar and molasses. (3) All this trade resulted in the growth of small towns and larger port cities.

Make a Venn Diagram

Use the two ovals to contrast the Northern and Southern colonies and the overlapping area to show what the two regions have in common.

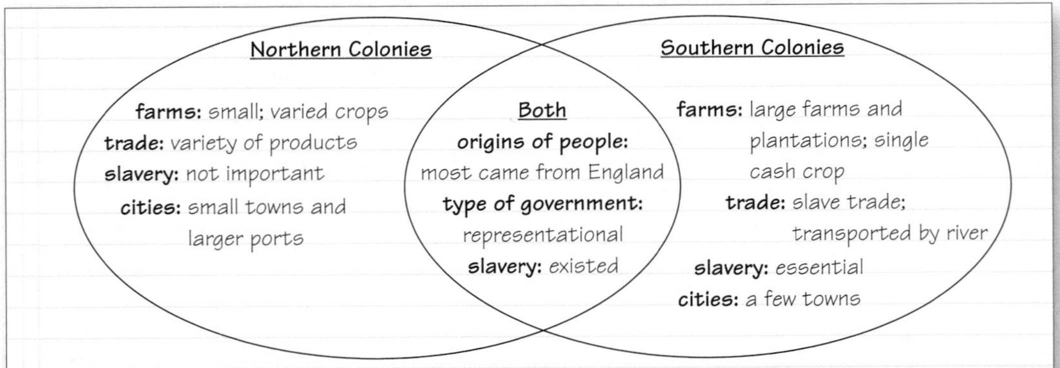

PRACTICING THE SKILL

Turn to Chapter 5, Section 1, pp. 202, 203 and read the passages headed "The Culture of the Plains Indians" and "Settlers Push Westward." Pay special attention to descriptions of the American settlers and Native Americans on the Great Plains. Make a Venn diagram showing what the two groups had in common and what made them different.

1.8 Distinguishing Fact from Opinion

DEFINING THE SKILL

Facts are dates, statistics, and accounts of events, or they are statements that are generally known to be true. Facts can be checked for accuracy.
Opinions are the judgments, beliefs, and feelings of a writer or speaker.

APPLYING THE SKILL

The following excerpt describes the 1886 Haymarket affair in Chicago. The chart summarizes the facts and opinions.

HOW TO DISTINGUISH FACT FROM OPINION

Strategy 1 Look for specific events, dates, and statistics that can be verified.

Strategy 2 Look for assertions, claims, hypotheses, and judgments. Here a speaker at the event is expressing an opinion.

Strategy 3 Look for judgments the historian makes about events. Here the writer states the opinion that the event was a disaster and then backs up this opinion by explaining the negative consequences of the event.

The Haymarket Affair

1 At ten o'clock another speaker stepped forward, the main burden of his address being that 2 there was no hope of improving the condition of workingmen through legislation; it must be through their own efforts. . . .

The speaker hurried to a conclusion, but at that point 180 police officers entered the square and headed for the wagon body that had served as a speakers' platform. The captain in charge called on the meeting to disperse. . . .

1 At that moment someone threw a bomb into the ranks of the policemen gathered about the speakers. After the initial shock and horror, the police opened fire on the 300 or 400 people who remained. One policeman had been killed by the bomb, and more than 60 injured. One member of the crowd was killed by police fire, and at least 12 were wounded. . . .

3 In almost every . . . way Haymarket was a disaster. It vastly augmented [increased] the already considerable paranoia of most Americans in regard to anarchists, socialists, communists, and radicals in general. It increased hostility toward . . . foreigners. . . . It caused a serious impairment of freedom of speech in every part of the country.

Source: Page Smith, *The Rise of Industrial America* (New York: Penguin, 1990), pp. 244–256.

Make a Chart

List the facts you learn in a passage as well as the opinions that are expressed.

Facts	Opinions
Just after 10:00, as a speaker was finishing up, someone threw a bomb into the group of 180 policemen surrounding the speakers. More than 60 police were injured, and about 13 civilians were injured or killed when police fired into the crowd.	speaker: Workers must improve their own situations since legislation can't do it for them. historian: Nothing good came of the Haymarket affair; and in fact it had many negative consequences: • increased paranoia about radicals • increased hostility toward foreigners • impaired freedom of speech

PRACTICING THE SKILL

Read Chapter 7, Section 3, p. 267, "The Emergence of Political Machines." Make a chart in which you list some facts about political machines and some opinions on graft expressed in the passage.

1.9 Making Inferences

DEFINING THE SKILL

Making inferences from a piece of historical writing means drawing conclusions based on facts, examples, opinions, and the author's use of language. To make inferences, use clues in the text and your own personal experience, historical knowledge, and common sense.

APPLYING THE SKILL

The following passage is from a speech by President Ronald Reagan promoting his economic program. The chart below lists some inferences that can be drawn from the first paragraph.

HOW TO MAKE INFERENCES

Strategy ❶ From the facts in the text and historical knowledge, you can infer that Reagan is blaming the Democrats for the poor economy.

Strategy ❷ Look for clues about the writer's opinion. From Reagan's language and the goals of his program, you can infer that he sees government spending and taxation as a major cause of the economic crisis.

Strategy ❸ Note opinionated language. You can infer from words such as *exaggerated* and *inaccurate* that Reagan disagrees with criticism of his plan.

On the Program for Economic Recovery

❶ All of us are aware of the punishing inflation which has for the first time in 60 years held to double-digit figures for 2 years in a row. Interest rates have reached absurd levels of more than 20 percent and over 15 percent for those who would borrow to buy a home. . . . Almost 8 million Americans are out of work. . . .

❷ I am proposing a comprehensive four-point program . . . aimed at reducing the growth in government spending and taxing, reforming and eliminating regulations which are unnecessary and unproductive or counterproductive, and encouraging a consistent monetary policy aimed at maintaining the value of the currency.

Now, I know that ❸ exaggerated and inaccurate stories about these cuts have disturbed many people. . . . Those who, through no fault of their own, must depend on the rest of us—the poverty stricken, the disabled, the elderly, all those with true need—can rest assured that the social safety net of programs they depend on are exempt from any cuts.

Make a Chart

Record clues in the text as well as what you know about the topic on the basis of your own experience, knowledge, and common sense.

Clues in the Text: Facts, Examples, Language	Personal Experience, Historical Knowledge, Common Sense	Inference
• inflation in double digits • Interest rates over 20% • 8 milion unemployed • Inflation is "punishing" • Interest rates "absurd"	• Reagan defeated Democratic incumbent Jimmy Carter in the 1980 election.	Reagan blames the Democrats for the current economic problems.

PRACTICING THE SKILL

Turn to Chapter 10, Section 3, p. 358 and read the passage headed "The Impact of U.S. Territorial Gains." Create a chart like the one above, making inferences based on clues in the text and on your own personal experience, historical knowledge, and common sense.

2.1 Developing Historical Perspective

DEFINING THE SKILL

Historical perspective is an understanding of events and people in the context of their times. Using historical perspective can help you avoid judging the past solely in terms of present-day norms and values.

APPLYING THE SKILL

The following passage is the opening portion of an address by President Theodore Roosevelt. Below it is a chart that summarizes the information from a historical perspective.

HOW TO DEVELOP HISTORICAL PERSPECTIVE

Strategy 1 Identify any historical figures, occasions, events, and dates.

Strategy 2 Notice words, phrases, and settings that reflect the period. Here the language used by the president reflects the optimism of the Progressive Era.

Strategy 3 Explain how people's actions and words reflect attitudes, values, and passions of the era. Here Roosevelt equates a strong nation with "manly virtues."

1 INAUGURAL ADDRESS, 1905
President Theodore Roosevelt

My fellow-citizens, no people on earth have more cause to be thankful than ours, and this is said . . . with gratitude to the Giver of Good who has blessed us with the conditions which have enabled us to achieve so large a measure of well-being and happiness. To us as a people it has been granted to lay the foundations of our national life in a **2** new continent. We are the **2** heirs of the ages, and yet we have had to pay few of the penalties which in old countries are exacted by the dead hand of a bygone civilization. We have not been obliged to fight for our existence against any alien race; and yet our life has called for the **3** vigor and effort without which the manlier and hardier virtues wither away. . . . [The] success which we confidently believe the future will bring, should cause in us no feeling of vainglory, but rather a deep and abiding realization of all which life has offered us; a full acknowledgment of the responsibility which is ours; and a fixed determination to show that under a free government a mighty people can thrive best, alike as regards the things of the body and the things of the soul.

Write a Summary

In a chart, list key words, phrases, and details from the passage, and then write a short paragraph summarizing the basic values and attitudes it conveys.

Key Phrases	Attitudes	Roosevelt's Inaugural Address
• Giver of Good • blessed us • heirs of the ages • bygone civilization • manlier and hardier virtues • mighty people • things of the body and things of the soul	• belief in God • optimistic about the future • grateful for the past	Theodore Roosevelt reveals a strong and resilient optimism about the American nation. His confidence is grounded in deep religious faith in God (the "Giver of Good") and God's plan for the nation. Roosevelt clearly believes in the ability of the American people to solve whatever problems they face as they move into a bright future. Roosevelt's faith and appeal to the manly virtues reflects typical attitudes and values of the 19th- and early 20th-century Americans.

PRACTICING THE SKILL

Turn to Chapter 8, Section 2, p. 282 and read the One American's Story feature, which discusses ideas about educational reform in the late 19th century. Use historical perspective to summarize those ideas in a chart like the one above.

2.2 Formulating Historical Questions

DEFINING THE SKILL

Formulating historical questions entails asking questions about events and trends—what caused them, what made them important, and so forth. The ability to formulate historical questions is an important step in doing research. Formulating questions will help you to guide and focus your research as well as to understand maps, graphs, and other historical sources.

APPLYING THE SKILL

At a women's rights convention in the mid-1800s, the delegates adopted a "Declaration of Sentiments" that set forth a number of grievances. The following passage is a description of that event. Below is a web diagram that organizes historical questions about the event.

HOW TO FORMULATE HISTORICAL QUESTIONS

Strategy 1 Ask about the basic facts of the event. Who were the leaders? What did they do? Where and when did the event take place?

Strategy 2 Ask about the cause of an event. Why did an event take place?

Strategy 3 Ask about historical influences on a speaker or event. What other historical events was it similar to? How was it different?

Strategy 4 Ask about the results produced by various causes. What were the results of the event?

Seneca Falls, 1848

1 Elizabeth Cady Stanton and Lucretia Mott decided to act on their resolution to hold a women's rights convention. In 1848, more than 300 women and men convened at Seneca Falls, New York, the small town that gave the convention its name. Before the convention, Stanton and Mott spent a day composing an agenda and a 2 detailed statement of grievances. Stanton carefully modeled this "Declaration of Sentiments" on the 3 Declaration of Independence. 4 The participants approved all measures unanimously, except for one: women's right to vote. This measure passed by a narow margin due to Stanton's insistence. The franchise for women, though it passed, remained a controversial topic.

Make a Web Diagram

Using a web diagram, ask a broad question about the event described above. Then ask specific questions to help you explore the first.

PRACTICING THE SKILL

Turn to Chapter 22, Section 1, p. 734 and read the passage headed "The Tonkin Gulf Resolution." Use a web diagram to write a historical question about the passage, as well as more specific questions that could guide your research into the topic.

2.3 Hypothesizing

DEFINING THE SKILL

Hypothesizing means developing a possible explanation for historical events. A hypothesis is a tentative assumption about what happened in the past or what might happen in the future. A hypothesis takes available information, links it to previous experience and knowledge, and comes up with a possible explanation, conclusion, or prediction.

APPLYING THE SKILL

As the Cold War came to an end, people offered various hypotheses to explain why the Soviet Union broke up and to predict what would replace it. Read this passage and form your own hypothesis. Below the passage is a chart that presents a hypothesis and the facts used to support it.

HOW TO FORM A HYPOTHESIS

Strategy ❶ Identify the events, pattern, or trend you want to explain. Develop a hypothesis that might explain the event. You might hypothesize that Gorbachev's new policies would deeply affect politics in the Soviet Union and Eastern Europe.

Strategy ❷ Determine what facts you have about the situation. These facts support various hypotheses about how Gorbachev's policies affected politics both inside and outside the Soviet Union.

The Cold War Ends

In March 1985, Mikhail Gorbachev became the general secretary of the Communist Party in the Soviet Union. ❶ He initiated a new policy of openness and reform within the USSR, putting an end to the collective ownership of resources, most government censorship, and controlled elections. ❷ A dramatic increase in nationalism on the part of the non-Russian republics followed the open elections, and in December 1991, all republics except Russia declared independence. ❷ The USSR was replaced by a loose federation of 12 republics called the Commonwealth of Independent States. ❷ Gorbachev's new policies led to massive changes in Eastern Europe, as the satellite states, with his encouragement, moved toward democracy.

Make a Chart

Use a chart to summarize your hypothesis about Gorbachev's reforms and the facts that support it. Then you can see what additional information you need to help prove or disprove it.

Hypothesis	Facts that support the hypothesis	Additional information needed
Gorbachev's new policies would help lead to Western victory in the Cold War.	• increase in nationalism in non-Russian republics • USSR replaced by a loose federation • Satellite states moved towards democracy	• Were democratic reforms put into effect? • Did free elections result in greater stability? • Did the end of collective ownership advance private enterprise?

PRACTICING THE SKILL

Turn to Chapter 24, Section 2, p. 803 and read the passage headed "A Bungled Burglary." Make a chart in which you hypothesize about the consequences of the burglary at the Democratic National Committee headquarters. Then list facts and indicate whether they support your hypothesis.

2.4 Analyzing Issues

DEFINING THE SKILL

Analyzing issues in history means taking apart complicated issues to identify the different points of view in economic, social, political, or moral debates.

APPLYING THE SKILL

The following passage describes working conditions in U.S. factories in the late 1800s and early 1900s. Notice how the cluster diagram below it helps you to analyze the issue of child labor.

HOW TO ANALYZE ISSUES

Strategy 1 Identify the central point of view and how it is defended.

Strategy 2 Look for facts and statistics. The numbers supplied by facts and statistics can help you decide on a position.

Strategy 3 Look for the other side to an issue. You need to look at all sides of an issue before deciding what you think.

Children at Work

1 Wages for most factory workers were so low that many families could not survive unless all their members, including children, worked. 2 Between 1890 and 1910, 20 percent of boys and 10 percent of girls under age 15—some as young as five years old—held full-time jobs. 2 A typical work week was 12 hours a day, six days a week. Many of these children worked from dawn to dusk, wasted by hunger and exhaustion that made them prone to crippling accidents. With little time or energy left for school, child laborers gave up their futures to help their families make ends meet.

3 Nonetheless, factory owners and some parents praised child labor for keeping children out of mischief. They believed that idleness for children was bad and that work provided healthy occupation. Meanwhile, the reformer Jacob Riis and others worked for decent conditions, better wages, and laws that restricted child labor.

Make a Cluster Diagram

In order to better analyze an issue, make a diagram and distinguish the facts as well as the different points of view.

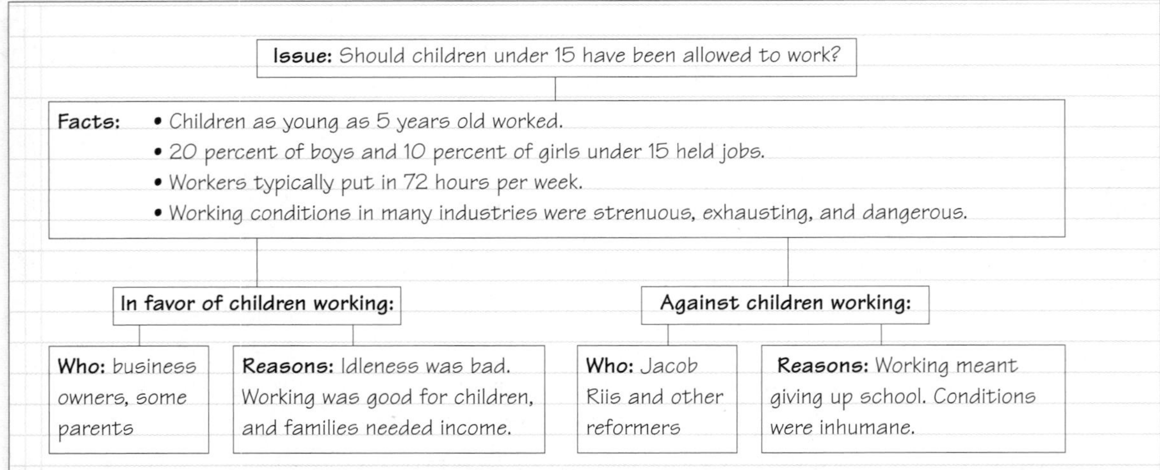

Issue: Should children under 15 have been allowed to work?
Facts:
• Children as young as 5 years old worked.
• 20 percent of boys and 10 percent of girls under 15 held jobs.
• Workers typically put in 72 hours per week.
• Working conditions in many industries were strenuous, exhausting, and dangerous.
In favor of children working:
Who: business owners, some parents
Reasons: Idleness was bad. Working was good for children, and families needed income.
Against children working:
Who: Jacob Riis and other reformers
Reasons: Working meant giving up school. Conditions were inhumane.

PRACTICING THE SKILL

Read the passages headed "The Equal Rights Amendment (ERA)" and "The New Right Emerges" in Chapter 23, Section 2, p. 779. Make a cluster diagram to analyze the central issue and the positions of the people involved.

2.5 Analyzing Assumptions and Biases

DEFINING THE SKILL

An **assumption** is a belief or an idea that is taken for granted. Some assumptions are based on evidence; some are based on feelings. A **bias** is a prejudiced point of view. Historical accounts that are biased reflect the personal prejudices of the author or historian and tend to be one-sided.

APPLYING THE SKILL

The following passage is from *The Americans at Home* by the Scottish minister David Macrae, who wrote the book after visiting the United States in the 1860s. The chart below the excerpt helps to summarize information about the writer's assumptions and biases.

HOW TO ANALYZE ASSUMPTIONS AND BIASES

Strategy ❶ Identify the author and information about him or her. Does the author belong to a special-interest group, religious organization, political party, or social movement that might promote a one-sided or slanted viewpoint on the subject?

Strategy ❷ Examine the evidence. Is what the author relates consistent with other accounts or supported by factual data?

Strategy ❸ Look for words, phrases, statements, or images that might convey a positive or negative slant, and thus reveal the author's bias.

The Americans at Home

❶ by David Macrae

[T]he American girls are very delightful. ❷ And in one point they fairly surpass the majority of English girls—they are all educated and well informed. . . . The admirable educational system . . . covering the whole area of society, has given them education whether they are rich or poor, has furnished them with a great deal of information, and has quickened their desire for more. . . . ❸ Their tendency is perhaps to talk too much, and . . . it seemed to me sometimes to make no perceptible difference whether they knew anything of the subject they talked about or not. But they usually know a little of everything; and their general intelligence and vivacity make them very delightful companions.

Make a Chart

For each of the heads listed on the left-hand side of the chart, summarize what information you can find in the passage.

David Macrae's Impression of American Girls	
speaker	David Macrae
date	1860s
occasion	Macrae's visit to the United States
tone	humorous, light-hearted
assumptions	The author assumes that girls are to be measured by companionship abilities.
bias	The author seems to have a prejudice that girls are inferior to boys or men.

PRACTICING THE SKILL

Look at the opinions expressed by A. Mitchell Palmer in the feature A Personal Voice in Chapter 12, Section 1, p. 413. Summarize his underlying assumptions and biases in a chart like the one shown above.

2.6 Evaluating Decisions and Courses of Action

DEFINING THE SKILL

Evaluating decisions means making judgments about the decisions that historical figures made. Historians evaluate decisions on the basis of their moral implications and their costs and benefits from different points of view. **Evaluating alternative courses** of action means carefully judging the choices that historical figures had in order to better understand why they made the decisions they did.

APPLYING THE SKILL

The following passage describes the decisions President John F. Kennedy had to make when he learned of Soviet missile bases in Cuba. Below the passage is a chart in which one possible alternative decision is analyzed.

HOW TO EVALUATE DECISIONS

Strategy 1 Look at decisions made by individuals or by groups. Notice the decisions Kennedy made in response to Soviet actions.

Strategy 2 Look at the outcome of the decisions.

Strategy 3 Analyze a decision in terms of the alternatives that were possible. Both Kennedy and Khrushchev faced the alternatives of either escalating or defusing the crisis.

Make a Chart

Make a chart evaluating an alternative course of action regarding the Cuban missile crisis based on its possible pros and cons.

The Cuban Missile Crisis

During the summer of 1962, the flow of Soviet weapons into Cuba—including nuclear missiles—greatly increased. (1) President Kennedy responded cautiously at first, issuing a warning that the United States would not tolerate the presence of offensive nuclear weapons in Cuba.

(1) On the evening of October 22, after the president learned that the Soviets were building missile bases in Cuba, he delivered a public ultimatum: any missile attack from Cuba would trigger an all-out attack on the Soviet Union. Soviet ships continued to head toward the island, while the U.S. military prepared to invade Cuba. To avoid confrontation, (2) the Soviet premier, Khrushchev, offered to remove the missiles from Cuba in exchange for a pledge not to invade the island. Kennedy agreed, and the crisis ended.

(3) Some people criticized Kennedy for practicing brinkmanship when private talks might have resolved the crisis without the threat of nuclear war. Others believed he had been too soft and had passed up an ideal chance to invade Cuba and to oust its communist leader, Fidel Castro.

alternative	pros	cons	evaluation
Negotiate a settlement quietly without threatening nuclear war.	1. Avoid the threat of nuclear war 2. Avoid frightening U.S. citizens	1. The U.S. would not look like a strong world leader. 2. The government would lose favor with Cuban exiles living in the U.S.	your answer: Would this have been a good choice? Why or why not?

PRACTICING THE SKILL

Turn to Chapter 17, Section 3, p. 583 and read the passage headed "The Atomic Bomb Ends the War." Evaluate the U.S. decision to drop the bomb. Make a chart like the one shown to summarize the pros and cons of an alternative decision, and then write an evaluation of that decision.

2.7 Forming Opinions (Evaluating)

DEFINING THE SKILL

Forming opinions, or evaluating, means deciding what your own thoughts or feelings are and making judgments about events and people in history. Opinions should be supported with facts and examples.

APPLYING THE SKILL

The following passage includes comments on the French Revolution by Gouverneur Morris, one of the participants in the Constitutional Convention, and by Thomas Jefferson.

HOW TO FORM AN OPINION AND SUPPORT IT WITH FACTS

Strategy 1 Decide what you think about a subject after reading all the information available to you. After reading this description, you might decide that political causes either do or do not sometimes justify violence.

Strategy 2 Support your opinion with facts, quotations, and examples, including references to similar events in other historical eras.

Strategy 3 Look for the opinions of historians and other experts. Consider their opinions when forming your own.

A Scene of Mob Violence

Gouverneur Morris was a visitor to Paris during the early days of the French Revolution. In the following journal entry he describes a scene of revolutionary mob violence: 1 "The head and body of Mr. de Foulon are introduced in triumph. . . . His crime [was] to have accepted a place in the Ministry. This mutilated form of an old man of seventy-five is shown to Bertier, his son-in-law, the intend't. [another official] of Paris, and afterwards 2 he also is put to death and cut to pieces. . . ." Such violence was common during the French Revolution and shocked a good many Americans. 3 However, Thomas Jefferson was a supporter of the Revolution, saying, "The liberty of the whole earth was depending on the issue of the contest, and . . . rather than it should have failed, I would have seen half the earth desolated."

Make a Chart

Summarize your opinion and supporting information in a chart. List facts, quotations, and examples.

Opinion: The French Revolution was especially violent and cruel.		
facts:	**quotations:**	**examples:**
• Violence escalated. • Jacobins launched Reign of Terror. • Moderates sent to guillotine. • Jacobins declared war on other countries.	"he also is put to death and cut to pieces"	Jacobins beheaded Louis XVI

PRACTICING THE SKILL

Read the Point/Counterpoint feature in Chapter 15, Section 5, p. 516. Form your own opinion about the success or failure of the New Deal. Record your opinion in a chart like the one shown, and provide supporting information to back it up.

2.8 Drawing Conclusions

DEFINING THE SKILL

Drawing conclusions involves considering the implications of what you have read and forming a final statement about its meaning or consequences. To draw conclusions, you need to look closely at facts and then use your own experience and common sense to decide what those facts mean.

APPLYING THE SKILL

The following passage tells about employment trends in the 1990s. The highlighted text indicates information from which conclusions can be drawn. In the diagram below, the information and conclusions are organized in a clear way.

HOW TO DRAW CONCLUSIONS

Strategy 1 Use the facts to draw a conclusion. Conclusion: In general, the economy was good in the mid-1990s.

Strategy 2 Read carefully to understand all the facts. Conclusion: Income expectations were lower.

Strategy 3 Ask questions of the material. How did the use of temporary workers affect job security? (It reduced it.) What did employment statistics for young people indicate? (Jobs were harder for young people to find.)

Job Outlook in the Mid-1990s

Several trends emerged in the workplace of the 1990s. **1** Inflation was at its lowest level since the 1960s, and 10 million new jobs created between 1993 and 1996 helped lower the unemployment rate to 5.1 percent in 1996. **2** Median household income adjusted for inflation, however, declined from $33,585 to $31,241, even though there were many households in which both parents worked.

In addition, **3** many jobs once done by permanent employees of a company were done by temporary workers, who were paid only for the time they were needed and who typically received no benefits. Three out of four young Americans thought they would earn less in their lifetimes than their parents did. Unemployment in their age group continued at the same rate, while the unemployment rate for other adults had fallen. **3** In 1993, about one in seven workers between the ages of 16 and 25 was out of work, double the national average.

Make a Diagram

Summarize the data and your conclusion about the above passage in a diagram.

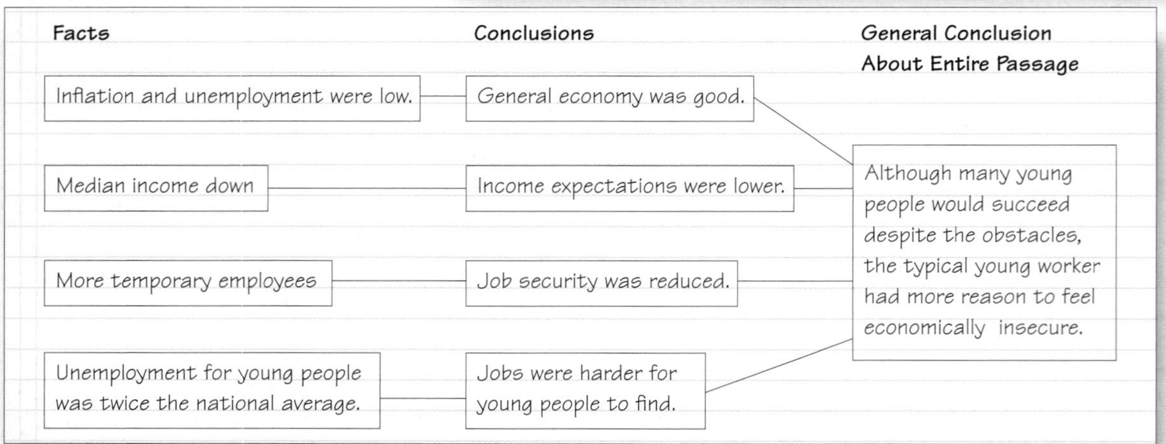

Facts
Conclusions
General Conclusion About Entire Passage
Inflation and unemployment were low.
General economy was good.
Median income down
Income expectations were lower.
More temporary employees
Job security was reduced.
Unemployment for young people was twice the national average.
Jobs were harder for young people to find.
Although many young people would succeed despite the obstacles, the typical young worker had more reason to feel economically insecure.

PRACTICING THE SKILL

Turn to Chapter 26, Section 4, p. 884 and read the passage headed "The Aging of America." Draw conclusions based on the facts in the passage. Using the model as a guide, create your own diagram, showing the facts and conclusions you have used to arrive at a general conclusion.

2.9 Synthesizing

DEFINING THE SKILL

Synthesizing is the skill historians use in developing interpretations of the past. Like detective work, synthesizing involves putting together clues, information, and ideas to form an overall picture of a historical event.

APPLYING THE SKILL

The following passage describes the earliest inhabitants of the Americas. The highlighted text indicates how some information leads toward a synthesis—an overall picture.

HOW TO SYNTHESIZE

Strategy 1 Read carefully to understand the facts.

Strategy 2 Look for explanations that link the facts together. This assertion is based on the evidence provided in the next couple of sentences.

Strategy 3 Consider what you already know in order to accept statements as reasonable.

Strategy 4 Bring together the information you have gathered to arrive at a new understanding of the subject.

The First Americans

From the 1 discovery of chiseled arrowheads and charred bones at ancient sites, it appears that the earliest Americans lived as big-game hunters. 2 People gradually shifted to hunting smaller game and gathering available plants. They collected nuts and wild rice. They invented snares, as well as bows and arrows, to hunt small animals, and they wove nets to catch fish.

Between 10,000 and 15,000 years ago, a revolution took place in what is now central Mexico. 3 People began to raise plants as food. Maize may have been the first domesticated plant. Agriculture eventually spread to other regions.

The rise of agriculture brought tremendous changes to the Americas. Agriculture made it possible for people to remain in one place. It also enabled them to accumulate and store surplus food. As their surplus increased, people had the time to develop skills and more complex ideas about the world. 4 From this agricultural base rose larger, more stable, and increasingly complex societies.

Make a Cluster Diagram

Use a cluster diagram to organize the facts, opinions, examples, and interpretations that you have brought together to form a synthesis.

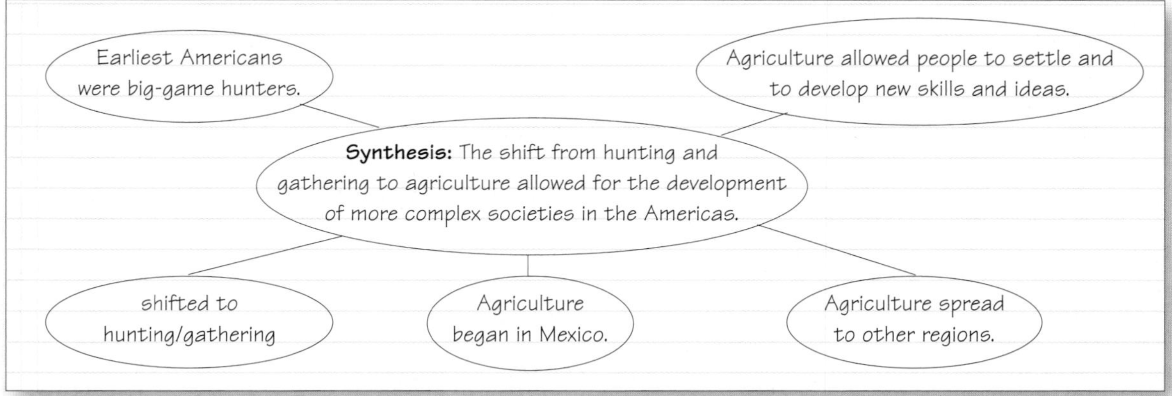

PRACTICING THE SKILL

Turn to Chapter 13, Section 2, p. 441 and read "Women Shed Old Roles at Home and at Work." Look for information to support a synthesis about the fundamental changes in the family brought about by women's new opportunities.

2.10 Making Predictions

DEFINING THE SKILL

Making predictions entails identifying situations that leaders or groups face or have faced in the past, and then suggesting what course of action they might take as well as what might happen as a result of that action. Making predictions about the effects of past events helps you to understand how events in the past shape the future. Making predictions about the effects of proposed actions, such as proposed legislation, helps you to evaluate possible courses of action.

APPLYING THE SKILL

The following passage discusses the central weaknesses of the Treaty of Versailles, which ended World War I. Below the passage is a chart that lists decisions made by those who framed the treaty, along with alternative decisions and predictions of possible outcomes.

HOW TO MAKE PREDICTIONS

Strategy ❶ Identify the decisions.

Strategy ❷ Decide what other decisions might have been made.

Strategy ❸ Predict the outcomes of the alternative decisions.

Weaknesses of the Treaty of Versailles

❶ First, the treaty humiliated Germany. The war-guilt clause, which forced Germany to accept blame for the war and pay financial reparations, caused Germans of all political viewpoints to detest the treaty.

❷ Second, Russia, which had fought with the Allies, was excluded from the peace conference. Russia had suffered almost the same number of casualties as Germany—the two countries had by far the highest casualty rates of the war. Russia lost more territory than Germany did. The Union of Soviet Socialist Republics, as Russia was called after 1922, grew determined to regain its lost territory.

❸ Third, the treaty ignored the claims of colonized people for self-determination. For example, the Allies dismissed the claims of the Vietnamese, who wanted freedom from French colonial rule.

Make a Chart

Record decisions made as well as alternative decisions and possible outcomes.

Decision: The treaty included a war-guilt clause.	**Decision:** Russia was excluded from the peace conference.	**Decision:** Treaty ignored the claims of colonized peoples.
Alternative decision: The treaty had no war-guilt clause.	**Alternative decision:** Russia was included in the peace negotiations.	**Alternative decision:** The treaty respected the claims of colonized peoples.
Possible outcome: Germany rebuilds. World War II does not occur.	**Possible outcome:** Tension between the Soviet Union and the West decreases.	**Possible outcome:** Tensions are reduced world-wide; Vietnam War is averted.

PRACTICING THE SKILL

Turn to Chapter 26, Section 1, p. 862 and read the passage "Reforming Welfare." Make a chart like the one above in which you identify provisions of the welfare reform law, alternative provisions that might have been included, and their possible outcomes. Consider how the effects of each law might change depending on the health of the nation's economy.

2.11 Forming Generalizations

DEFINING THE SKILL

Forming generalizations means making broad judgments based on the information in texts. When you form generalizations, you need to be sure they are valid. They must be based on sufficient evidence, and they must be consistent with the information given.

APPLYING THE SKILL

The following three excerpts deal with Herbert Hoover and his relation to the Great Depression. Notice how the information in the web diagram below supports the generalization drawn.

HOW TO FORM GENERALIZATIONS

Strategy 1 Determine what information the sources have in common. All the sources suggest that people blamed Hoover for the Great Depression.

Strategy 2 State your generalization in sentence form. A generalization often needs a qualifying word, such as *most*, *many*, or *some*, to make it valid.

On President Hoover and the Great Depression

1 "By 1930, people were calling the shantytowns in American cities Hoovervilles. . . . Homeless people called the newspapers in which they wrapped themselves 'Hoover blankets.' Empty pockets turned inside out were 'Hoover flags.'"

—*The Americans*

"[My aunt] told me . . . . 1 People were starving because of Herbert Hoover. My mother was out of work because of Herbert Hoover. Men were killing themselves because of Herbert Hoover."

—Russell Baker

1 "If someone bit an apple and found a worm in it, Hoover would get the blame."

—Will Rogers

Make a Web Diagram

Use a web diagram to record relevant information and make a valid generalization.

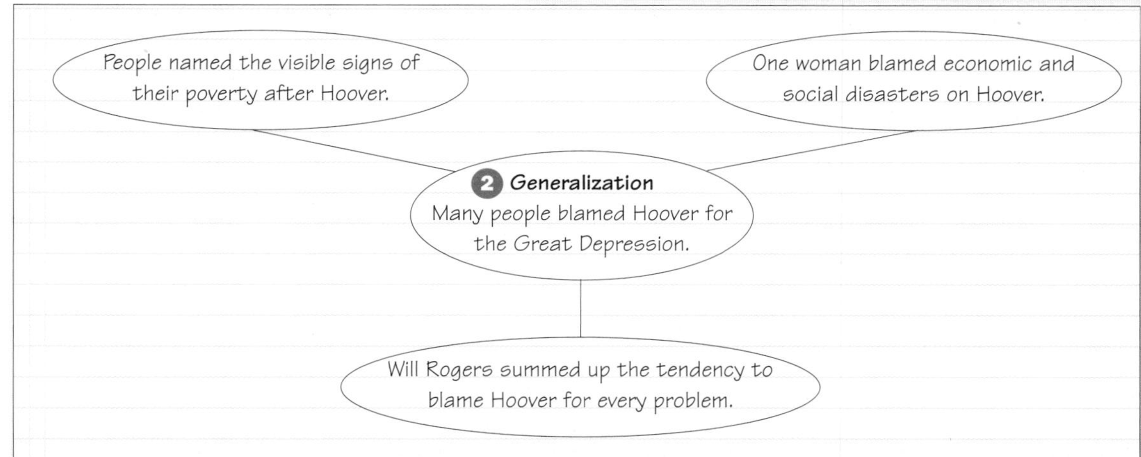
People named the visible signs of their poverty after Hoover.
One woman blamed economic and social disasters on Hoover.
2 Generalization
Many people blamed Hoover for the Great Depression.
Will Rogers summed up the tendency to blame Hoover for every problem.

PRACTICING THE SKILL

Study the Daily Life feature "Signs of the Sixties" in Chapter 23, p. 786. Create a diagram like the one above to make a generalization about teenagers during the 1960s. Use information from textual and visual sources to support your generalization.

3.1 Primary and Secondary Sources

DEFINING THE SKILL

Primary sources are accounts written or created by people who were present at historical events, either as participants or as observers. These include letters, diaries, journals, speeches, some news articles, eyewitness accounts, government data, statutes, court opinions, and autobiographies.

Secondary sources are based on primary sources and are produced by people who were not present at the original events. They often combine information from a number of different accounts. Secondary sources include history books, historical essays, some news articles, and biographies.

APPLYING THE SKILL

The following passage describes the explosion of the first atomic bomb in 1945. It is mainly a secondary source, but it quotes an eyewitness account that is a primary source.

(1)
The First Atomic Bomb

As the time to test the bomb drew near, the air around Los Alamos crackled with rumors and fears. (2) At one end of the scale were fears that the bomb wouldn't work at all. At the other end was the prediction that the explosion would set fire to the atmosphere, which would mean the end of the earth.

On July 16, 1945, the first atomic bomb was detonated in the desert near Alamogordo, New Mexico. (3) In his book *What Little I Remember,* Otto Frisch, a Manhattan Project scientist, described what happened next:

"[T]hat object on the horizon which looked like a small sun was still too bright to look at. . . . After another ten seconds or so it had grown and . . . was slowly rising into the sky from the ground, with which it remained connected by a lengthening grey stem of swirling dust. . . ."

(4) That blinding flash was followed by a deafening roar as a tremendous shock wave rolled across the trembling desert. The bomb not only worked, but it was more powerful than most had dared hope.

HOW TO LOCATE AND IDENTIFY PRIMARY AND SECONDARY SOURCES

Strategy (1) Locating sources: The catalog in your school library or a local public library lists resources alphabetically by subject, title, and author. Most of these are secondary sources but may contain copies or excerpts of primary sources. Articles in a general encyclopedia such as *World Book* or *Encyclopedia Americana* can give you an overview of a topic and usually provide references to additional sources.

Strategy (2) Secondary source: Look for information collected from several sources.

Strategy (3) Primary source: Identify the title and author and evaluate his or her credentials. What qualifies the writer to report on the event? Here the writer actually worked on developing the bomb.

Strategy (4) Secondary source: Look for information collected after the event. A secondary source provides a perspective that is missing in a primary source.

Make a Chart

Summarize information from primary and secondary sources in a chart.

Primary Source	Secondary Source
Author: Otto Frisch	Author: unknown
Qualifications: scientist working on Manhattan Project	Qualifications; had access to multiple accounts of the time leading up to and following event
Information: detailed description, sensory observations, feeling of awe	Information: description of range of points of view and of information available only after event

PRACTICING THE SKILLS

Turn to Chapter 25, Section 1, p. 830, and read the One American's Story feature, which includes a quotation. Use a chart like the one above to summarize information from the primary and secondary sources.

3.2 Visual, Audio, Multimedia Sources

DEFINING THE SKILL

Visual sources can be paintings, illustrations, photographs, political cartoons, and advertisements. **Audio sources** include recorded speeches, interviews, press conferences, and radio programs. Movies, CD-ROMs, television, and computer software are the newest kind of historical sources, called **multimedia sources.** These sources are rich with historical details and sometimes convey the feelings and points of view of an era better than words do.

APPLYING THE SKILL

The following photograph shows a group of college students and civil rights activists joined in song as they protest unfair voting laws in 1964.

1 In the summer of 1964, college students volunteered to go to Mississippi to help register that state's African-American voters.

HOW TO INTERPRET VISUAL SOURCES

Strategy 1 Identify the subject and the source. A title or caption often gives a description of a photo or other visual source. This photograph shows volunteers who worked in the 1964 voting rights drive in Mississippi.

Strategy 2 Identify important visual details. In this photograph, white and black college students are holding hands and singing. Behind them is a bus.

Strategy 3 Make inferences from the visual details. Holding hands and singing together suggest fellowship and unity—the students are showing solidarity in the fight for civil rights.

Make a Chart

Summarize your interpretation of the photograph in a simple chart.

Subject	A diverse group of college students.
Details	Bus, joined hands, white and black Americans side by side, singing
Inferences	The subjects share a belief in racial equality, freedom, and solidarity. Some or all of the group may have traveled to Mississippi together on the bus.

PRACTICING THE SKILL

Turn to the photograph in Chapter 21, Section 2, p. 712, showing police dogs in Birmingham, Alabama, attacking African Americans. Use a chart like the one at the right to analyze and interpret the photograph.

3.3 Analyzing Political Cartoons

DEFINING THE SKILL

Political cartoons use humor to make a serious point. Political cartoons often express a point of view on an issue better than words do. Understanding signs and symbols will help you to interpret political cartoons.

Like many text sources that express a point of view, cartoons are often **biased,** or unfairly weighted toward one point of view. To identify a cartoon's bias, look for exaggerations and caricature. Try to restate the message of the cartoon in words, then identify overgeneralizations and opinions stated as facts.

APPLYING THE SKILL

The following political cartoon shows President Calvin Coolidge playing the saxophone while big business dances. The chart below it summarizes historical information gained from interpreting the visual source.

HOW TO INTERPRET VISUAL SOURCES

Strategy 1 Identify the subject. This cartoon deals with President Calvin Coolidge's relationship with big business.

Strategy 2 Identify important symbols and details. Big business is shown as a carefree flapper of the 1920s. The president's saxophone is labeled "Praise," suggesting his positive attitude toward the fun-loving flapper.

Strategy 3 Interpret the message. The image implies that serving big business interests is important to the president.

Strategy 4 Analyze the point of view. The cartoonist suggests that the relationship between the president and big business is too cozy.

Strategy 5 Identify bias. The president is caricatured by being depicted engaging in frivolity and at the service of big business. The cartoon charges that the president does not take his responsibilities seriously.

Make a Chart

Summarize your interpretation of the cartoon in a simple chart.

Subject: Coolidge's Relationship with big business		
Point of View	Symbols/Details	Message
Satirical of the Coolidge administration and of big business	Flapper: big business, carefree and overgrown President: playing a tune for business	Big business and the president are too close. Business is having too good a time—with the president's help.

PRACTICING THE SKILL

Turn to the political cartoon on p. 426, which presents an opinion about Franklin D. Roosevelt's New Deal programs. Use a chart like the one above to analyze and interpret the cartoon.

3.4 Interpreting Maps

DEFINING THE SKILL

Maps are representations of features on the earth's surface. Historians use maps to locate historical events, to demonstrate how geography has influenced history, and to illustrate patterns and distributions of human activity and its environmental effects.

Political maps show political units, from countries, states, and provinces to counties, districts, and towns. **Physical maps** show mountains, hills, plains, rivers, lakes, and oceans. They may include elevations of land and depths of water. **Historical maps** illustrate such things as economic activity, political alliances, migrations, battles, and population density. While reading maps, historians pose questions and use the following features to find answers:

A **compass rose** indicates the map's orientation on the globe. It may show all four cardinal directions (N, S, E, W) or just one, north.

Lines indicate boundaries between political areas, roads and highways, routes of exploration or migration, and rivers and other waterways. Lines may vary in width and color.

Symbols or icons represent real objects or events. Cities, towns, and villages often appear as dots. A capital city is often shown as a star within a circle. An area's products or resources may be indicated by symbols. Battles are often shown by starbursts, troop movements by arrows.

Labels designate key places, such as cities, states, bodies of water, and events.

Lines of longitude and latitude appear on maps to indicate the absolute location of the area shown. Lines of latitude show distance north or south of the equator, measured in degrees. Lines of longitude show distance in degrees east or west of the prime meridian, which runs through Greenwich, England.

A **legend or key** is a small table in which the symbols, types of lines, and special colors that appear in the map are listed and explained.

Sometimes **colors** are used to indicate areas under different political or cultural influence. Colors and **shading** are also used to show distributions, patterns, and such features as altitudes.

A **map's scale** shows the ratio between a unit of length on the map and a unit of distance on the earth. A typical scale shows a one-inch segment and indicates the number of miles that length represents on the map. A map on which an inch represents 500 miles has a scale of 1:31,680,000.

Continued on page R26.

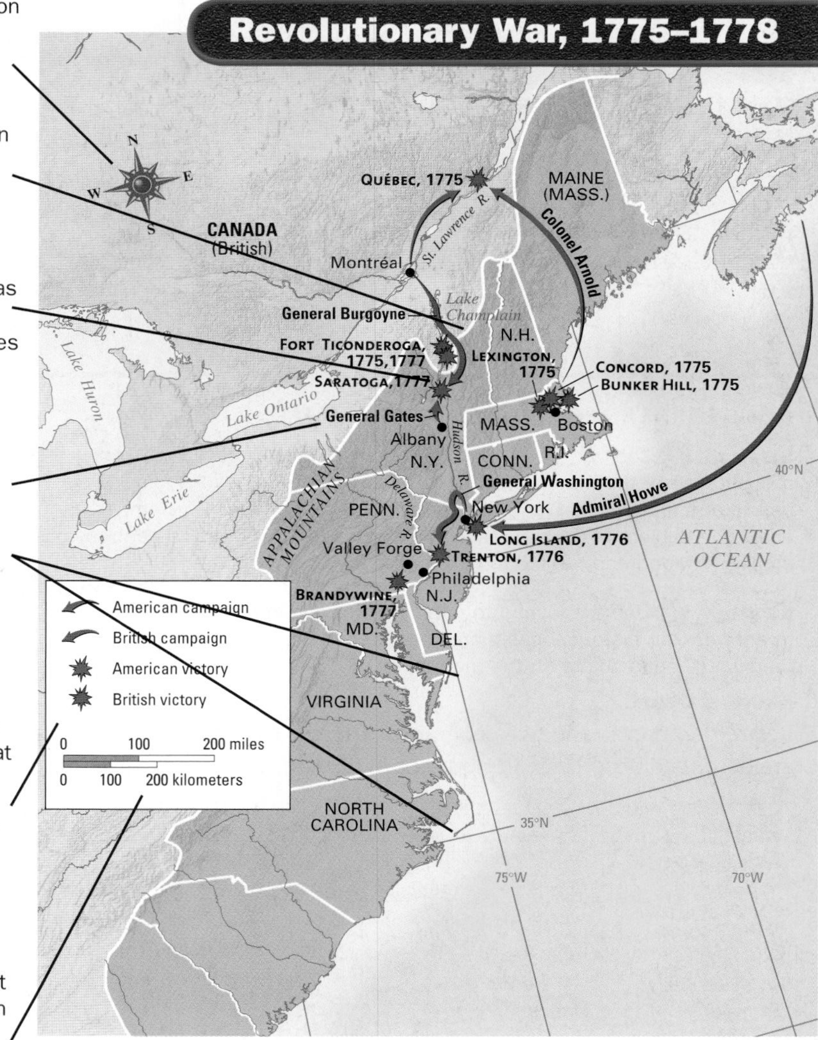

Distributions on a map are where certain symbols, such as those for cities, fall. Sometimes distributions show patterns, such as a cluster, a line, or a wide circle. On this map, for example, the battle symbols show a pattern of being fought near rivers or ports.

APPLYING THE SKILL

The historical maps below show land claims in Europe in 1915 and after 1919. Together they show the political effects of World War I.

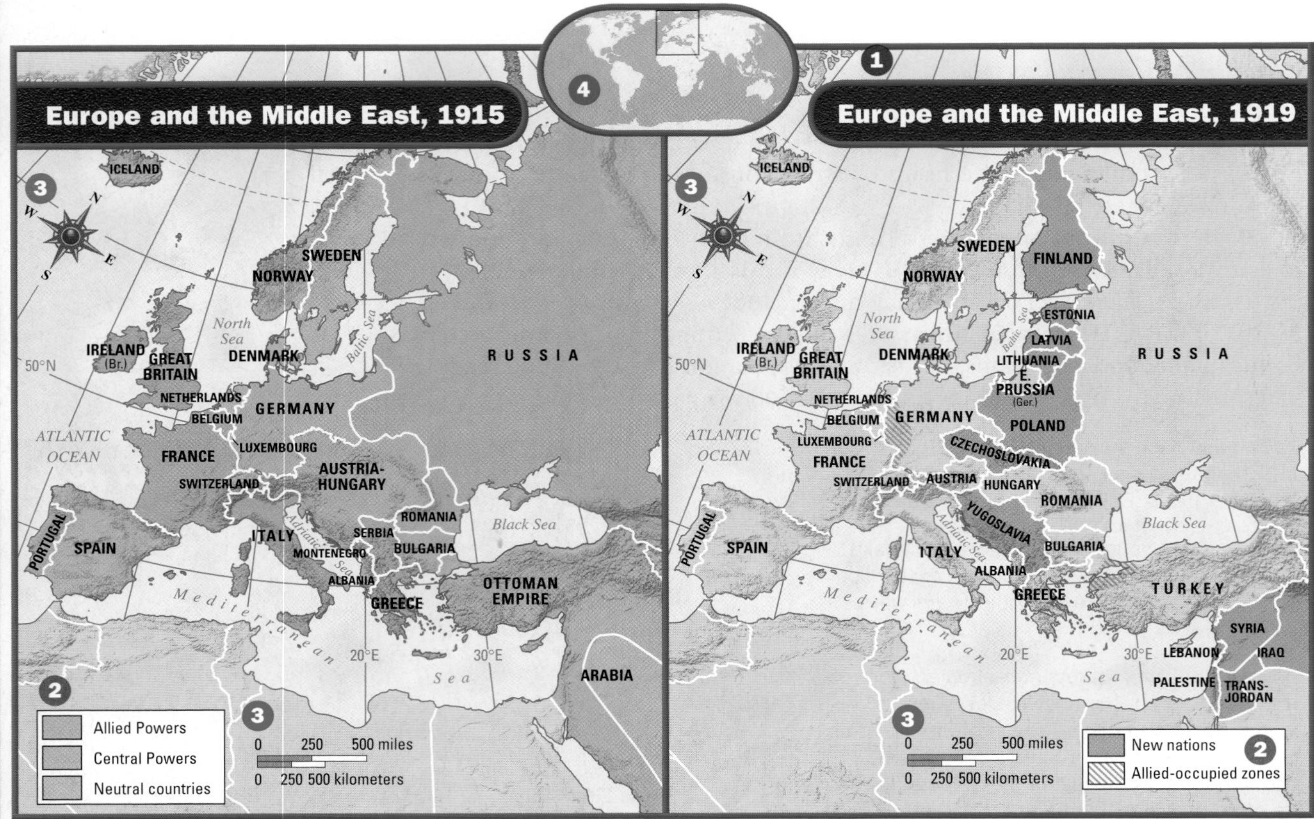

HOW TO INTERPRET A HISTORICAL MAP

Strategy 1 Look at the map's title to learn the subject and purpose of the map. Here the maps show Europe before and after World War I. Pose a historical question about the subject of the map, such as "How were old empires divided and new countries formed?"

Strategy 2 Use the legend to interpret the map in order to answer your historical question. The legend tells you what the symbols and colors on the map mean.

Strategy 3 Look at the scale and compass rose. The scale shows you what distances are represented. On these maps, 1.4 cm represents 500 miles. The compass rose shows you which direction on the map is north.

Strategy 4 Find where the map area is located on the earth. These maps span a large area from the Arctic Circle to below latitude 30° N, and from 10° W to 40° E.

Make a Chart

Relate the map to the five geographic themes by making a chart. The five themes are described on p. xxx. In your chart, also analyze distributions and find patterns.

Location:	Place:	Region:	Movement:	Human-Environment Interaction:
Europe and the Middle East; from the Arctic Circle to below 30° North and from 10° West to 40° East	A continent that is a peninsula surrounded by the Mediterranean Sea, the Atlantic Ocean, the North Sea, as well as western-most Asia	The old empires of the Central Powers are distributed within Central Europe and the Middle East. The new nations are in Eastern Europe and the Middle East.	Political boundaries shifted after the war. The Treaty of Versailles established nine new nations.	The new boundaries fall along rivers, bodies of water, and mountain ranges. There is a pattern. The pattern shows that the new countries form a narrow strip from North to South.

PRACTICING THE SKILL

Study the maps titled "D-Day, June 6, 1944" on p. 575. Make a chart like the one shown above, in which you summarize what the maps show.

3.5 Interpreting Charts

DEFINING THE SKILL

Charts are visual presentations of material. Historians use charts to organize, simplify, and summarize information in a way that makes it more meaningful or memorable.

Simple charts are used to consolidate or compare information. **Tables** are used to organize numbers, percentages, or other information into columns and rows for easy reference. Diagrams provide visual clues to the meaning of the information they contain. Illustrated diagrams are sometimes called **infographics.**

APPLYING THE SKILL

The following diagram gives a visual representation of how the economy functions. The paragraph below summarizes the information contained in the diagram.

HOW TO INTERPRET CHARTS

Strategy 1 Identify the symbols. Here the symbols represent individuals, producers, government, and the product market.

Strategy 2 Look for the main idea. The arrows show the cycle of supply and demand in a free enterprise system of economy. Here individuals are at the top of the chart, indicating that they begin the cycle by creating a demand for goods and services.

Strategy 3 Follow the arrows to study the chart. Read the description of each image in the diagram. Together, the images show the flow of economic activity from producers to individuals and back. The government affects the cycle by regulating and stabilizing economic activity.

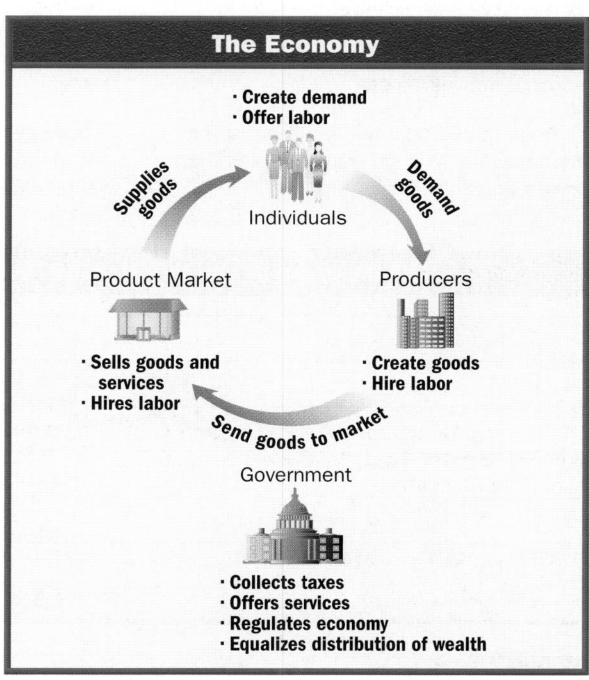

Write a Summary

Write a paragraph to summarize what you learned from the diagram.

Individuals want or need products or services. Producers try to fulfill that demand by hiring workers (labor) to produce the good or service. Producers then make the goods and services available for sale on the market. During this process, the government regulates economic activity and equalizes the distribution of wealth, among other functions. Once goods are sent to stores or other distribution centers, people must be hired (labor) to sell the goods.

PRACTICING THE SKILL

Turn to Chapter 6, Section 3, p. 242, and study the chart titled "Vertical and Horizontal Integration." Write a paragraph in which you summarize what you learned from the chart. Tell how the process of vertical integration works, and describe how it is different from horizontal integration.

3.6 Interpreting Graphs

DEFINING THE SKILL

Graphs show statistical information in a visual manner. Historians use graphs to visualize and compare amounts, ratios, economic trends, and changes over time.

Line graphs typically show quantities on the vertical axis (up the left side) and time in various units on the horizontal axis (across the bottom). **Pie graphs** are useful for showing relative proportions. The circle represents the whole and the slices represent the parts belonging to various subgroups. **Bar graphs** are commonly used to display information about quantities.

PRACTICING THE SKILL

The image below shows a double line graph. The lines show the rate of inflation as compared with the rate of unemployment from 1970 to 1980.

HOW TO INTERPRET A GRAPH

Strategy 1 Read the title to identify the main idea of the graph. When two subjects are shown, such as unemployment and inflation, the graph will probably show a relationship between them.

Strategy 2 Read the vertical and horizontal axes of the graph. The horizontal axis shows years, and the vertical axis gives percents.

Strategy 3 Look at the legend. Find out what each symbol in the graph represents. In this graph the gold line represents the inflation rate and the purple line represents the unemployment rate.

Strategy 4 Summarize the information shown in each part of the graph. What trends do you see in the line graph over certain years? When did unemployment rise and fall? What about inflation? What can you infer from the patterns?

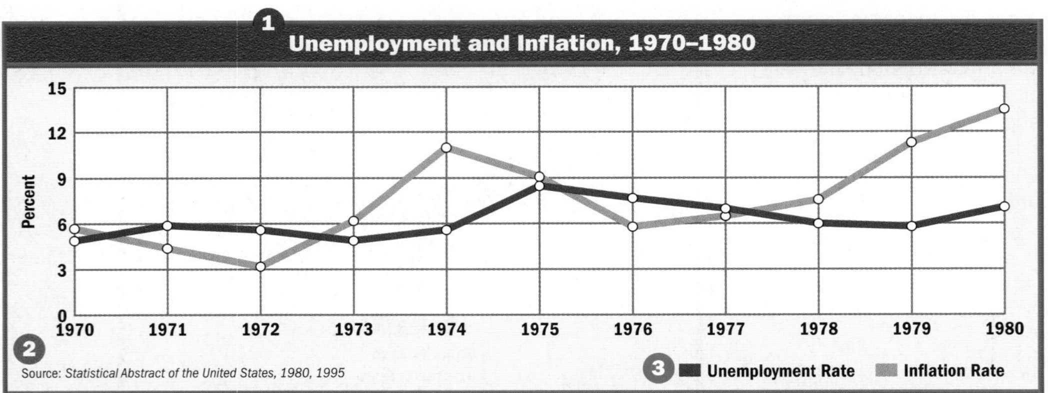

Write a Summary

Write a paragraph to summarize what you learned from the graph.

Unemployment declined between 1976 and 1979 but rose between 1974 and 1975, while inflation declined between 1975 and 1976 and rose in the periods 1973–1974 and 1977–1980. From the graph it appears that unemployment rises or falls following inflation rate changes, but less dramatically.

PRACTICING THE SKILL

Turn to Chapter 19, Section 3, p. 653, and look at the two graphs titled "Glued to the Set." Study the graphs and write a paragraph in which you summarize what you learned from them. Explain how the two line graphs work together.

3.7 Using the Internet

DEFINING THE SKILL

The **Internet** is a network of computers associated with universities, libraries, news organizations, government agencies, businesses, and private individuals worldwide. Every page of information on the Internet has its own address, or **URL.**

The international collection of sites known as the **World Wide Web** is a source of information about current events as well as research on historical subjects. This textbook contains many suggestions for using the World Wide Web. You can begin by entering the URL for McDougal Littell's site: www.classzone.com.

APPLYING THE SKILL

The computer screen below shows the home page of the Library of Congress.

HOW TO USE THE INTERNET

Strategy 1 Go directly to a Web page. If you know the address of a particular Web page, type the address in the strip at the top of the screen and press RETURN. After a few seconds, that page will appear on your screen.

If you want to research the Web for information on a topic, visit a general search site such as www.google.com or www.yahoo.com. The following sites have information that may be useful in your research:

Library of Congress—www.loc.gov

National Archives and Records Administration—www.nara.gov

Smithsonian Institution—www.si.org

PBS—www.pbs.org

National Geographic—www.nationalgeographic.com

Strategy 2 Learn about the page. Click on one of the topics across the top of the page to learn more about the Library of Congress and how to use its Web site.

Strategy 3 Explore the features of the page. Click on any one of the images or topics to find out more about a specific subject.

PRACTICING THE SKILL

Turn to Chapter 21, Section 2, p. 710, "The Triumphs of a Crusade." Read the section, making a list of topics you would like to research. If you have a computer with Internet access, go to the McDougal Littell site, www.classzone.com. There you will be able to search the Chapter 21 Research Links and other features to explore a variety of historical topics.

4.1 Creating Charts and Graphs

DEFINING THE SKILL

Charts and **graphs** are visual representations of information. (See Skillbuilders 3.5 and 3.6.) Three types of graphs are **bar graphs, line graphs,** and **pie graphs.** Use a bar graph to display information about quantities and to compare related quantities. Use a line graph to show a change in a single quantity over time. Use a pie graph to show relative proportions among parts of a single thing. Charts can be used to condense and organize written information or lists.

APPLYING THE SKILL

The following passage includes data about American commuting choices between 1960 and 1990. The bar graph below shows how the information in the passage might be represented.

HOW TO CREATE A BAR GRAPH

Strategy 1 Use a title that sums up the information; include a time span.

Strategy 2 Note dates and the percentages. Dates will form the horizontal axis of your graph; percentages will form the vertical axis.

Strategy 3 Organize the data. Group numbers that provide information about the same year.

Strategy 4 Decide how best to represent the information. Sketch a graph and a legend, denoting the meanings of any colors and symbols.

American Commuting Choices, 1960–1990

In 1960, 64% of the population traveled to work by car, truck, or van; 12% took public transportation; 7% worked at home; and 17% got to work by other means. In 1990, 87% traveled to work by car, truck, or van; 5% took public transportation; 3% worked at home; and 5% went to work by other means.

Create a Bar Graph

Clearly label vertical and horizontal axes. Draw bars accurately. Include a legend.

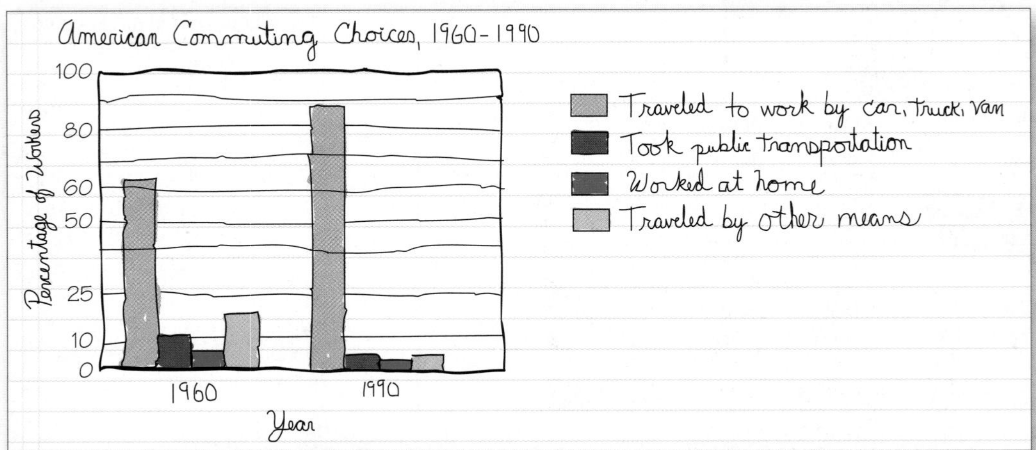

PRACTICING THE SKILL

Turn to Chapter 26, Section 4, p. 885, and read the passage headed "A Changing Immigrant Population." Use a pie graph to show percentages of ethnic distribution of the American population in 1990.

4.2 Creating Models

DEFINING THE SKILL

Models, like maps, are visual representations of information. Historians make models of geographical areas, villages, cities, inventions, buildings, and other physical objects of historical importance. A model can be a two-dimensional representation, such as a poster or a diagram that explains how something happened. It also can be a three-dimensional representation or even a computer-created image.

APPLYING THE SKILL

The following image is a two-dimensional model of the tunnel system used by the Vietcong during the Vietnam War. Examine the strategies used in making this model to learn how to create your own.

HOW TO CREATE A MODEL

Strategy 1 Gather the information you need to understand the situation or event. Here the creator has gathered information about the tunnel system from various reference sources.

Strategy 2 Think about symbols you may want to use. Since the model should give information in a visual way, think about ways you can use color, pictures, or other visuals to tell the story.

Strategy 3 Gather the supplies you will need to create the model. For this model, the creator might have used computer software or colored markers or pencils.

Strategy 4 Visualize and sketch an idea for your model. Once you have created a picture in your mind from either written text or other images, make an actual sketch to plan how your model might look.

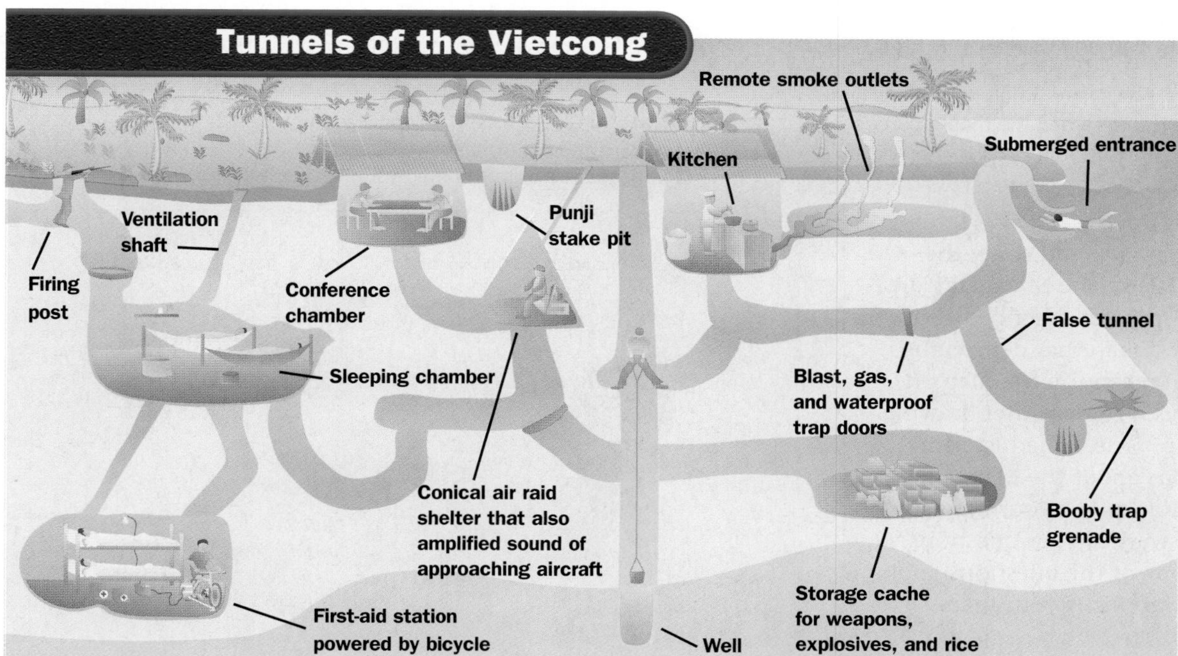

PRACTICING THE SKILL

Turn to Chapter 6, Section 3, p. 244, and read the text under the heading "Labor Unions Emerge." Use the information to create a model of a "sweatshop" factory during the turn of the century. Use the process described above as a guide.

4.3 Creating Maps

DEFINING THE SKILL

Maps are scale representations, usually of land surfaces. (See Skillbuilder 3.4.) Creating a map involves representing geographical data visually. When you draw a map, it is easiest to use an existing map as a guide. You can include data on climate and population and on patterns or distributions of human activity.

APPLYING THE SKILL

The following chart shows the numbers of 1995 immigrants who planned to settle in the southwestern states of the United States. The map below depicts the data given in the chart.

Immigrants, by State of Intended Residence, 1995					
Arizona	7,700	Nevada	4,306	Texas	49,963
California	166,482	New Mexico	2,758	Utah	2,831
Colorado	7,713				

HOW TO CREATE A MAP

Strategy 1 Determine what map you should use as a guide. Find a map of the Southwest that you can re-create.

Strategy 2 Decide how best to show the data. These data can be grouped in three broad categories of numbers: more than 100,000; 10,000 to 100,000; and less than 10,000.

Strategy 3 Select a title that identifies the geographical area and the map's purpose. Include a date or time span.

Strategy 4 Draw and label the lines of latitude and longitude. Use the guide map's scale and a ruler to help you correctly space the lines of latitude and longitude.

Strategy 5 Draw the subject of your map, following your guide map carefully. Color or mark the map to show its purpose. Use each color or symbol to represent similar information.

Strategy 6 Include a key or legend explaining colors, symbols, or shading. Reproduce the scale and compass rose from the map you used as a guide.

PRACTICING THE SKILL

Turn to p. 606 and study the graph titled "The Marshall Plan." Use the process described above to draw a map that depicts the data. (You can use the map on p. 605 as a guide.) After drawing the map, pose some historical questions about the Marshall Plan. How might your map convey answers to your questions? Write one of the questions and its answer below your map.

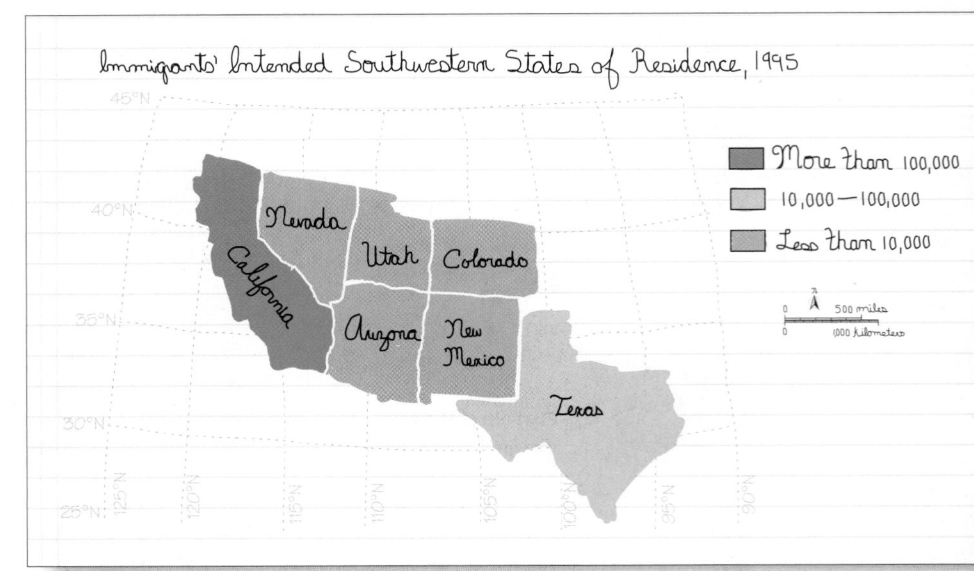

4.4 Creating Databases

DEFINING THE SKILL

A **database** is a collection of data, or information, that is organized so that you can find and retrieve information on a specific topic quickly and easily. Once a computerized database is set up, you can search it to find specific information without going through the entire database. The database will provide a list of all stored information related to your topic. Learning how to use a database will help you learn how to create one.

APPLYING THE SKILL

The chart below is a database for some of the significant legislation passed during President Johnson's Great Society program.

1 Significant Great Society Legislation

2 Legislation	Date	Significance
3 Economic Opportunity Act	1964	4 created Job Corps and other programs to help the poor
Civil Rights Act	1964	outlawed discrimination in public accomodations
Medical Care Act	1965	4 established Medicare and Medicaid programs to help the elderly and the poor
Higher Education Act	1965	provided low-interest loans for college students
Truth in Packaging Act	1966	set standards for labeling consumer products
Highway Safety Act	1966	required states to set up highway safety programs
Demonstration Cities and Metropolitan Area Redevelopment Act	1966	4 provided funds to rebuild poor neighborhoods
Air Quality Act	1967	set federal air pollution guidelines

HOW TO CREATE A DATABASE

Strategy 1 Identify the topic of the database. The keywords, or most important words, in the title are "Great Society" and "Legislation." These words were used to begin the research for this database.

Strategy 2 Identify the kind of data you need to enter in your database. These will be the column headings—or categories—of your database. The keywords "Legislation," "Date," and "Significance," were chosen to categorize this research.

Strategy 3 Once you find the data you want to include, identify the entries under each heading.

Strategy 4 Use the database to help you find the information quickly. For example, in this database you could search by the word "poor" for programs related to anti-poverty measures.

PRACTICING THE SKILL

Turn to Chapter 11, "The First World War," and create a database of key battles of World War I. Use a format like the one above for your database and include the following column headings: "Battle," "Date," "Location," and "Signficance." You can create your database using computer software or by setting up a 4-column chart on paper.

4.5 Creating Written Presentations

DEFINING THE SKILL

Written presentations are in-depth reports on a topic in history. Often, written presentations take a stand on an issue or try to support a specific conclusion. To successfully report on an event or make a point, your writing needs to be clear, concise, and supported by factual details.

APPLYING THE SKILL

The following is a written presentation about the main goals of progressivism. Use the strategies listed below to help you learn to create a written presentation.

HOW TO CREATE A WRITTEN PRESENTATION

Strategy ❶ Identify a topic that you wish to research, focusing on one or more questions that you hope to answer about the topic. Then research the topic using library resources and the Internet.

Strategy ❷ Formulate a hypothesis. This will serve as the main idea, or thesis, of your presentation. Analyze the information in your sources and develop a hypothesis that answers your questions about the topic.

Strategy ❸ Organize the facts and supporting details around your main idea. These facts and examples should be presented in a way that helps you build a logical case to prove your point.

Strategy ❹ To express your ideas clearly, use standard grammar, spelling, sentence structure, and punctuation. Proofread your work to make sure it is well-organized and grammatically correct.

For more on how to create a historical research paper and other written presentations, see the ***Writing for Social Studies*** handbook.

Make an Outline

Creating an outline like the one shown here will help you organize your ideas and produce an effective written presentation.

❶ The Goals of Progressivism

I. ❷ All progressive reforms had one of four goals.
   A. Protecting Social Welfare
      ❸ 1. Social Gospel movement sought to help the poor.
      2. Settlement houses provided aid to poor city dwellers.
   B. Promoting Moral Improvement
      1. Reformers sought to improve Americans' personal behavior.
      2. WCTU worked for prohibition.
   C. Creating Economic Reform
      1. Writers criticized capitalism.
      2. American Socialist Party formed.
      3. Muckrakers exposed corruption in business and government.
   D. Fostering Efficiency
      1. Emergence of scientific management in the workplace
      2. Development of the assembly line

Write a Draft

The Goals of Progressivism

As America approached the 20th century a number of citizens tried to reform society. Their efforts formed what became known as the progressive movement. Progressive reformers had the following four goals; social welfare, moral improvement, economic reform, and efficiency.

Many reformers sought to promote social welfare—especially in the crowded, run-down, and unhealthy areas of the cities. The Social Gospel movement inspired followers to erect churches in poor communities. It also persuaded business leaders to treat workers more fair. Other reformers established settlement house in slum neighborhoods which provided educational, cultural, and social services to people—especially to immigrants.

Another group of reformers felt that the lives of poor people could be improved through moral instruction. These reformers offer programs to improve personal behavior. The Women's Christian Temperence Union, for instance, promoted prohibition. It believed that alcohol was the root of many of society's problems.

Other progressives, such as Henry George and Edward Bellamy, blamed the competitive nature of capitalism for creating a large underclass. Some Americans, especially workers, embraced socialism. In 1898, Eugene Debs helped organize the american socialist party. Advocated communal living and a classless society. During the early 20th century, journalists exposed the corrupt side of business and politics known as muckrakers.

Meanwhile, some tried to make American society more efficient. Frederick Winslow Taylor popularized scientific management, the effort to improve efficiency in the workplace by applying scientific principles. Out of this concept emerged the assembly line, which required workers to perform the same task over and over, and thus sped up production.

Through their hard work, the progressives reformed many levels of society and helped Americans live better lives.

4 Edit and Revise

Use punctuation marks for their correct purposes. A colon precedes a list.

Use the correct parts of speech. An adverb modifies a verb.

Check for common agreement errors. Subjects and verbs must agree in person and number.

Use consistent verb tense. Use past tense for events in the past.

Check spelling with both an electronic spell checker and a dictionary.

Capitalize all proper nouns, including names of political parties.

Use correct sentence structure. Every sentence needs a subject and a verb.

Be sure sentence structure leads clearly from one phrase to the next. Correct misplaced modifiers.

PRACTICING THE SKILL

Create a two-page written presentation on a topic of historical importance that interests you. Use the strategies and sample outline and draft to help you create your presentation.

4.6 Creating Oral Presentations

DEFINING THE SKILL

An **oral presentation** is a speech or talk given before an audience. Oral presentations can be given to inform an audience about a certain topic or persuade an audience to think or act in a certain way. You can learn how to give effective oral presentations by examining some of the more famous ones in history.

APPLYING THE SKILL

The following is an excerpt from a student's speech supporting Southern secession. Use the strategies listed below to help you learn to create an oral presentation.

HOW TO CREATE AN ORAL PRESENTATION

Strategy 1 Choose one central idea or theme and organize your presentation to support it. Here, the writer calls for the United States government to allow the Southern states to secede.

Strategy 2 Use words or images to persuade your audience. In this speech, the writer has used a metaphor of family conflict to express the antagonism between North and South.

Strategy 3 Make sure your arguments support your central idea or theme. In this speech, the writer's arguments all support the main theme.

(1) The Southern states should be allowed to secede. (3) Since it was the states that helped create the national government, surely the states have the right to declare their independence from that government.

The industrial North will never understand the needs of the farmers and plantation owners of the South. (2) The South and the North are like two brothers whose lives and attitudes have become so different that they can no longer live under the same roof. Why should they be forced to remain together?

Giving an Oral Presentation

When you give an oral presentation, make sure to

- maintain eye contact with your audience.
- use gestures and body language to emphasize your main points and to help express your ideas.
- pace yourself. Do not rush to finish your presentation.
- vary your tone of voice to help bring out the meaning of your words.

PRACTICING THE SKILL

Turn to Chapter 16, Section 4, p. 552, and study the Point/Counterpoint feature about U.S. involvement in WWII. Choose a side and create an outline for a speech that supports that side. Use the strategies to help you make an oral presentation.

4.7 Creating Visual Presentations

DEFINING THE SKILL

A **visual presentation** of history uses visual sources to explain a particular historical event. Such sources could include paintings, maps, charts and graphs, costume drawings, photographs, political cartoons, and advertisements. Movies, CD-ROMs, television, and computer software are the newest kind of visual sources, called multimedia sources because they also include sound. (See Skillbuilder 3.2.) Visual sources can provide much insight into various eras and events of the past. Creating a visual presentation will help you to become more familiar with the many different sources of historical information available.

APPLYING THE SKILL

The image below shows a student using a computer to create a visual presentation. Use the strategies listed below to help you plan out the steps needed to compile a clear, engaging, and informative presentation.

HOW TO CREATE A VISUAL PRESENTATION

Strategy 1 Identify the topic of your presentation and decide which types of visuals will most effectively convey your information. For example, you might want to use slides and posters along with a map. If you want to include multimedia sources, you could use documentary film or television footage of an event.

Strategy 2 Conduct research to determine what visual sources are available. Some topics, such as wars, may have more visual source material than others. You can create your own visual sources, such as a graph or chart, to accompany what you find.

Strategy 3 Write a script for the presentation. A narration of events to accompany the visuals will tie the various sources together and aid you in telling the story.

Strategy 4 Videotape the presentation. Videotaping the presentation will preserve it for future viewing and allow you to show it to different groups of people.

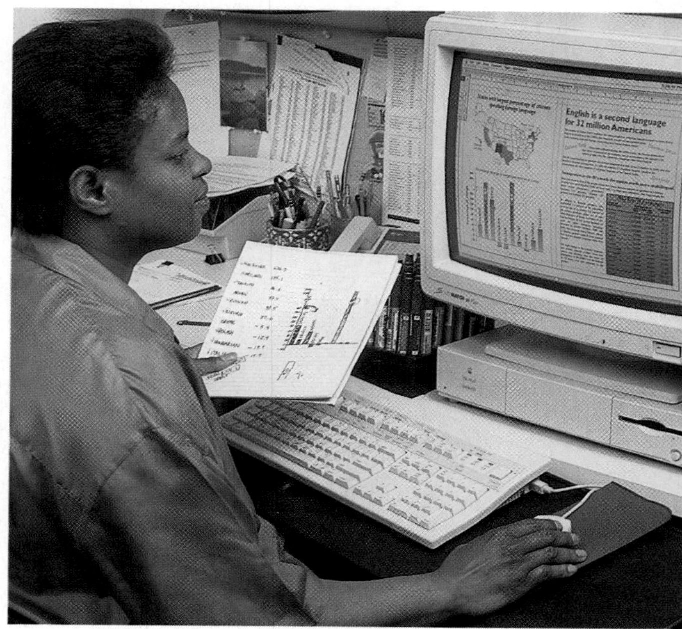

PRACTICING THE SKILL

Turn to Chapter 5, Section 1, p. 210, and read "A Day in the Life of a Cowboy," or choose another section in the chapter. Use the strategies above to create a visual presentation of the topic.

ECONOMICS HANDBOOK

NOTE: *Boldfaced words are terms that appear in this handbook.*

BOYCOTT *A refusal to have economic dealings with a person, a business, an organization, or a country.* The purpose of a boycott is to show disapproval of particular actions or to force changes in those actions. A boycott often involves an economic act, such as refusing to buy a company's goods or services.

African Americans in Montgomery, Alabama (shown below), organized a bus boycott in 1955 to fight segregation on city buses. The boycotters kept many buses nearly empty for 381 days. The boycott ended when the Supreme Court outlawed bus segregation.

American labor unions have sometimes used boycotts to win concessions for their members. Consumer groups, too, have organized boycotts to win changes in business practices.

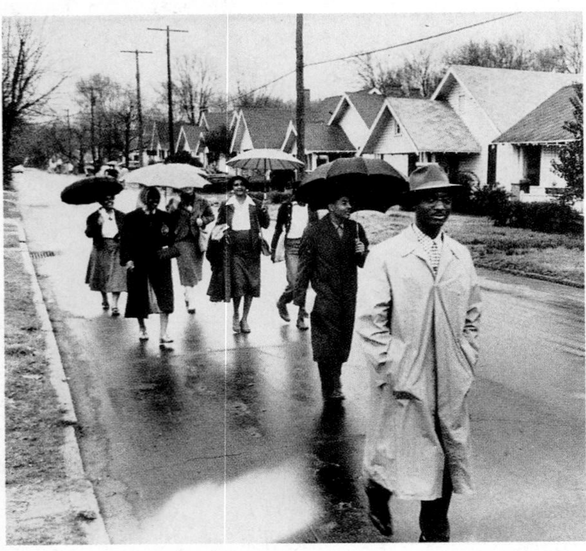

BUSINESS CYCLE *A pattern of increases and decreases in economic activity.* A business cycle generally consists of four distinct phases—expansion, peak, contraction, and trough, as shown in the graph in the next column.

An expansion is marked by increased business activity. The **unemployment rate** falls, businesses produce more, and consumers buy more goods and services. A peak is a transition period in which expansion slows. A contraction, or **recession,** occurs when business activity decreases. The unemployment rate rises, while both production and consumer spending fall. A deep and long-lasting contraction is called a **depression.** Business activity reaches its lowest point during a trough. After time, business activity starts to increase and a new cycle begins.

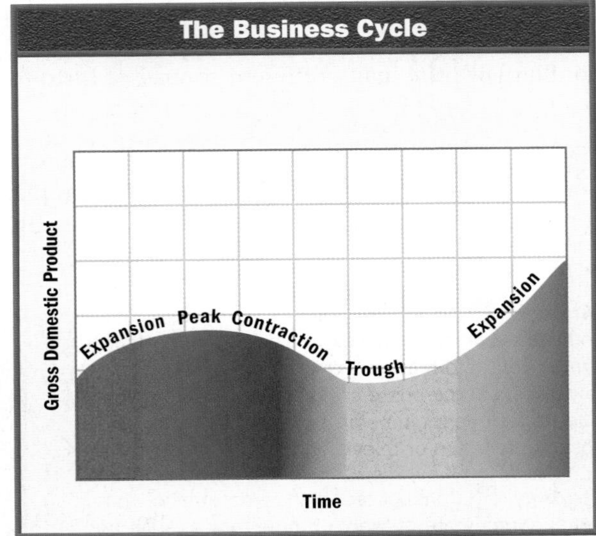

CAPITALISM *An economic system in which there is private ownership of natural resources and capital goods.* The basic idea of capitalism is that producers are driven by the desire to make a profit—the money left over after costs have been subtracted from revenues. This desire for profit motivates producers to provide consumers with the goods and services they desire. Prices and wages are determined by **supply and demand.**

Along with the opportunity to earn a profit there is a risk. Businesses tend to fail if they don't produce goods people want at prices they are willing to pay. Because anyone is free to start a business or enterprise, a capitalist system is also known as a **free enterprise** system.

Capitalism contrasts with **socialism,** an economic system in which the government owns and controls capital and sets prices and production levels. Critics of capitalism argue that it allows decisions that ought to be made democratically to be made instead by powerful business owners and that it allows too-great disparities in wealth and well-being between the poor and the rich.

COMMUNISM *An economic system based on one-party rule, government ownership of the means of production, and decision making by centralized authorities.* Under communism there is little or no private ownership of property and little or no political freedom. Government planners make economic decisions, such as which and how many goods and services should be produced. Individuals have little say in a communist economy. Such a system, communists believe, would end inequality. For more information on the ideas on which communism is based, read the Economic Background on page 413.

During the 20th century, most communist economies failed to achieve their goals. Economic decisions frequently were made to benefit only Communist Party officials. Also, government economic planning was inefficient, often creating shortages of goods. Those goods that were available were often of poor quality.

People became discontented with the lack of prosperity and political freedom and began to call for change. These demands led in the late 1980s and early 1990s to the collapse of communist governments in the Soviet Union and Eastern Europe.

Even governments that clung to communism introduced elements of **free enterprise.** Some communist countries—such as China—have experienced economic growth but have not granted more political freedom to their citizens.

CONSUMER PRICE INDEX (CPI) *A measure of the change in cost of the goods and services most commonly bought by consumers.* The CPI notes the prices of over 200 goods and services bought by average urban consumers on a regular basis. Items on which consumers spend a good deal of their income—such as food and housing—are given more weight in the CPI than items on which consumers spend less.

Price changes are calculated by comparing current prices with prices at a set time in the past. In 2001, for example, the CPI used the period from 1982 to 1984 as this base. Prices for this period are given a base value of 100. The prices for subsequent years are expressed as percentages of the base. Therefore, a CPI of 160 means that prices have risen by 60 percent since 1982–1984. The graph below illustrates changes in the CPI from 1960 to 2000.

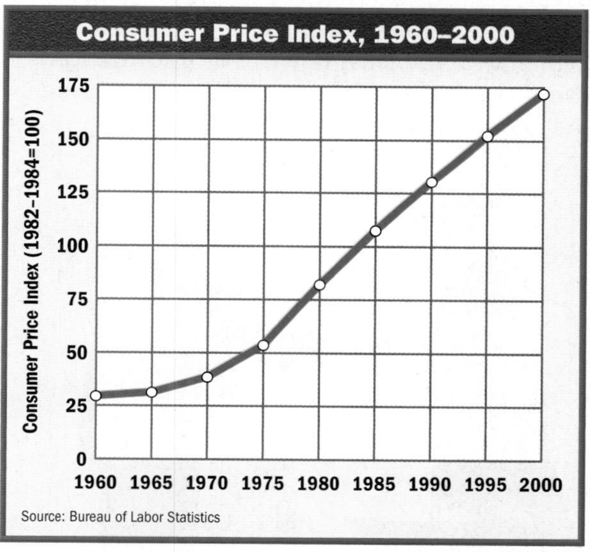

DEFICIT SPENDING *A situation in which a government spends more money than it receives in revenues.* For the most part, the government engages in deficit spending when the economy is in a contraction phase of the **business cycle.** The government borrows or issues money to finance deficit spending.

In theory, the extra funds should stimulate business activity, pushing the economy into an expansion phase. As the economy recovers, revenues should increase, providing the government with a budget surplus. The government then can use the surplus to pay back the money it borrowed. For more information on deficit spending, read the Economic Background on page 492.

DEPRESSION *A very severe and prolonged contraction in economic activity.* During a depression, consumer spending, production levels, wages, prices, and profits fall sharply. Many businesses fail, and many workers lose their jobs.

The United States has experienced several economic depressions in its history. The worst was the Great Depression, which started in 1929 and lasted throughout the 1930s. Between 1929 and 1932, business activity in the United States decreased by an average of 10 percent each year. During the same period, some 40 percent of the country's banks failed, and prices for farm products dropped more than 50 percent. By 1933, the worst year of the Great Depression, 25 percent of American workers were unemployed—some, like the man shown below, were reduced to selling apples on the street.

For a personal account of life during the Great Depression, view the *American Stories* video "Broke, but Not Broken: Ann Marie Low Remembers the Dust Bowl." For information about the effects of war on a depression, read the Economic Background on page 557.

E-COMMERCE *All forms of buying and selling goods and services electronically.* Short for "electronic commerce," e-commerce refers to business activity on the Internet and on private computer networks. There are two main types of e-commerce: business-to-consumer and business-to-business.

Consumer-related e-commerce includes sales to the public over the computer, usually through a seller's Web site. Many business transactions can be completed wholly electronically, such as sales of computer software, which can be paid for with a credit card number and delivered over the Internet directly to the buyer's computer. A growing proportion of financial transactions are also moving online, such as electronic banking and **stock market** trading, or e-trading. The convenience of online shopping has turned it into a booming enterprise. Between 1998 and 1999, for instance, U.S. consumer spending online grew from about $7.7 billion to more than $17 billion.

Business-to-business e-commerce is growing at an even greater rate, reaching nearly $177 billion in 1999. Much of that business includes Web site design and servicing and online advertising. Businesses also use networked computers to purchase supplies and merchandise and to access information from subscription services.

For many businesses, e-commerce is not only convenient but also cost-effective. On average, corporations spend $100 on paperwork alone each time they make a purchase. Moving those transactions online could save companies millions of dollars annually.

EMBARGO *A government ban on trade with another nation, commonly backed by military force.* In a civil embargo the nation imposing an embargo prevents exports to or imports from the country against which it has declared the embargo. A hostile embargo involves seizing the goods of another nation.

The major purpose of an embargo is to show disapproval of a nation's actions. For example, in 1980 the United States imposed a civil embargo on grain sales to the Soviet Union to protest the December 1979 Soviet invasion of Afghanistan.

FREE ENTERPRISE *An economic system based on the private ownership of the means of production, free markets, and the right of individuals to make most economic decisions.* The free enterprise system is also called the free market system or **capitalism.** The United States has a free enterprise economic system.

In a free enterprise system, producers and consumers are motivated by self-interest. To maximize their profits, producers try to make goods and services that consumers want. Producers also engage in competition—through lowering prices, advertising their products, and improving product quality—to encourage consumers to buy their goods. Consumers serve their self-interest by purchasing the best goods and services for the lowest price.

Government plays a limited, but important, role in most free-enterprise economies:

- It regulates economic activity to ensure there is fair competition, such as by preventing and prosecuting fraud and barring **monopolies.**
- It produces certain necessary goods and services that private producers consider unprofitable, such as roadways.
- It protects the public health and safety, such as through building codes, environmental protection laws, and labor laws.
- It provides economic stability, such as by regulating banks, coining money, and supervising unemployment insurance programs.

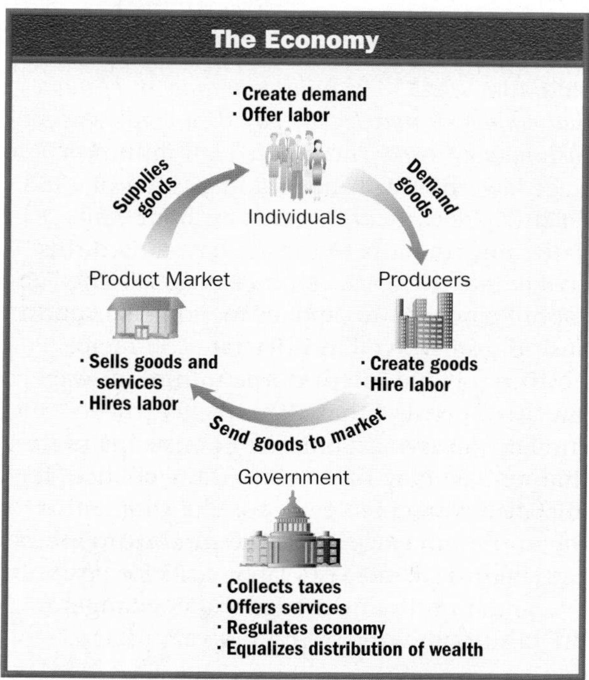

GOLD STANDARD *A monetary system in which a country's basic unit of currency is valued at, and can be exchanged for, a fixed amount of gold.* The gold standard tends to curb **inflation,** since a government cannot put more currency into circulation than it can back with its gold supplies. This gives people confidence in the currency.

This advantage is also a weakness of the gold standard. During times of **recession,** a government may want to increase the amount of money in circulation to encourage economic growth. Economic disruption during the Great Depression of the 1930s caused most nations to abandon the gold standard. The United States moved to a modified gold standard in 1934 and abandoned the gold standard completely in 1971.

GROSS DOMESTIC PRODUCT (GDP) *The market value of all the goods and services produced in a nation within a specific time period, such as a quarter (three months) or a year.* It is the standard measure of how a nation's economy is performing. If GDP is growing, the economy is probably in an expansion phase. If GDP is not increasing or is declining, the economy is probably in a contraction phase.

GDP is calculated by adding four components: spending by individual consumers on goods and services; investment in such items as new factories, new factory machinery, and houses; government spending on goods and services; and net exports—the value of exports less the value of imports. GDP figures are presented in two ways. Nominal GDP is reported in current dollars. Real GDP is reported in constant dollars, or dollars adjusted for **inflation.**

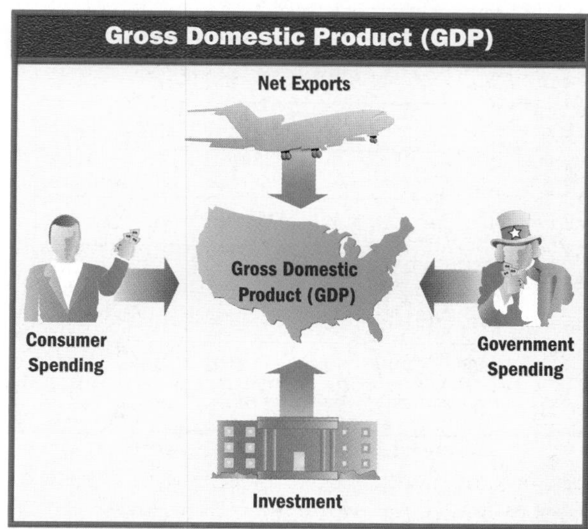

INFLATION *A sustained rise in the average level of prices.* Since more money is required to make purchases when prices rise, inflation is sometimes defined as a decrease in the purchasing value of money. Economists measure price changes with indexes. The most widely used index in the United States is the **consumer price index (CPI).**

Inflation may result if the demand for goods increases without an increase in the production of goods. Inflation may also take place if the cost of producing goods increases. Producers pass on increased costs, such as higher wages and more expensive raw materials, by charging consumers higher prices.

INTEREST RATE *The cost of borrowing money.* Interest is calculated as a yearly percentage, or rate, of the money borrowed. A 10 percent interest rate, therefore, would require a borrower to pay $10 per year for every $100 borrowed.

When interest rates are low, people will borrow more, because the cost of borrowing is lower. However, they will save and invest less, because the return on their savings or investment is lower. With high interest rates, people save and invest more but borrow less. Because interest rates affect the economy, the government takes steps to control them through the Federal Reserve System, the nation's central banking system. The graph below shows the relationship between the rate of **inflation** and interest rates over time.

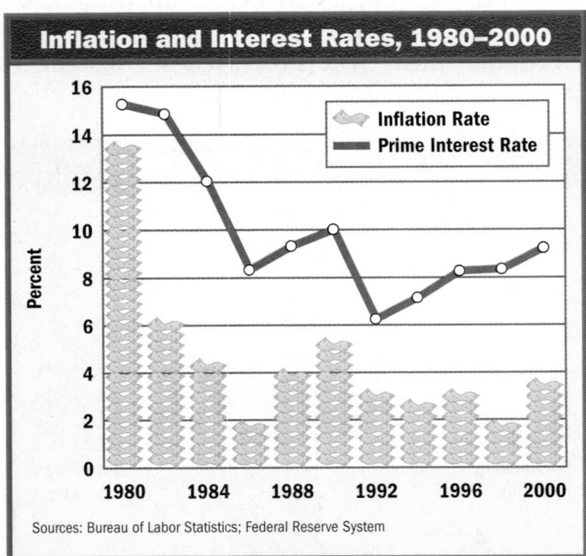

KEYNESIAN ECONOMICS *The use of government spending to encourage economic activity by increasing the demand for goods.* This approach is based on the ideas of British economist John Maynard Keynes (shown below). In a 1936 study, Keynes pointed out that during economic downturns, more people are unemployed and have less income to spend. As a result, businesses cut production and lay off more workers.

Keynes's answer to this problem was for government to increase spending and reduce **taxes.** This would stimulate demand for goods and services by replacing the decline in consumer demand. Government would want goods and services for its new programs. More people would be working and earning an income and, therefore, would want to buy more goods and services. Businesses would increase production to meet this new demand. As a result, the economy would soon recover.

Critics maintain, however, that Keynesian economics has led to the growth of government and to high taxes, inflation, high unemployment, and low economic growth. For an example of Keynesian economics at work, read the Economic Background on page 557.

MINIMUM WAGE *The minimum amount of money that employers may legally pay their employees for each hour of work.* The first federal minimum wage law, the Fair Labor Standards Act of 1938, set the base wage at 25 cents an hour. Since then, amendments to the act have raised this hourly rate to $5.15, effective in 1997. The Fair Labor Standards Act applies to workers in most businesses involved in interstate commerce.

The original intent of the minimum wage law was to ensure that all workers earned enough to survive. Some economists maintain that the law may have reduced the chances for unskilled workers to get jobs. They argue that the minimum wage raises the **unemployment rate** because it increases labor costs for business. The graph on the next page shows changes in the minimum wage over a ten-year period.

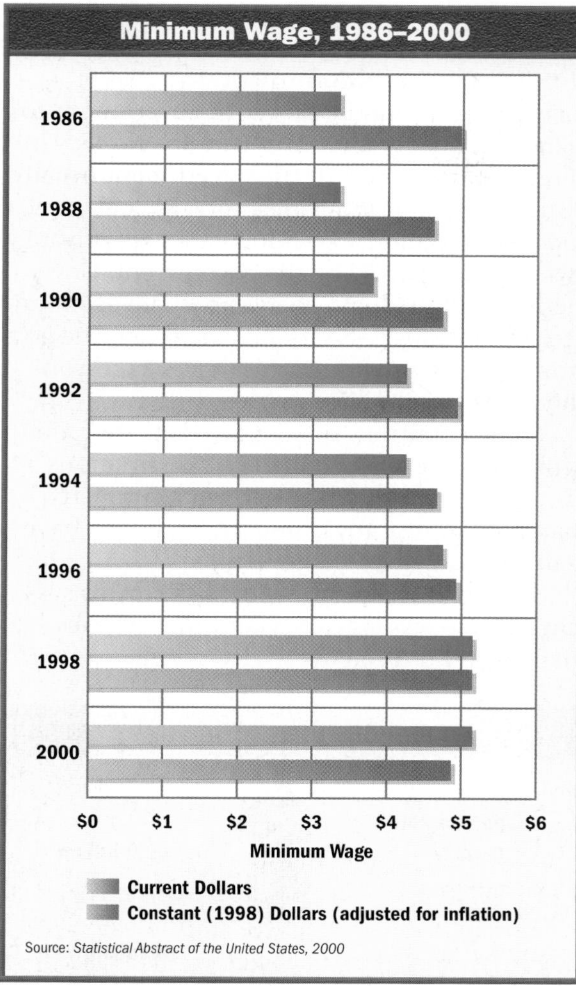

Source: *Statistical Abstract of the United States, 2000*

MONOPOLY *A situation in which only one seller controls the production, supply, or pricing of a product for which there are no close substitutes.* In the United States, basic public services such as electrical power distributors and cable television suppliers operate as local monopolies. This way of providing utilities is economically more efficient than having several competing companies running electricity or cable lines in the same area.

Monopolies, however, can be harmful to the economy. Since it has no competition, a monopoly does not need to respond to the wants of consumers by improving product quality or by charging fair prices. The government counters the threat of monopoly either by breaking up or regulating the monopoly.

NATIONAL DEBT *The money owed by a national government.* During wartime, during economic recession, or at other times, the government may employ **deficit spending.** However, the government may not pay back all the money it has borrowed to fund this policy. Each year's federal budget deficit adds to the national debt. By 2000, the national debt of the United States stood at $5.67 trillion, or about $20,000 for each citizen.

The rapid growth of the U.S. national debt since 1980 has prompted many Americans to call for changes in government economic policies. Some suggest that the government raise taxes and cut spending to reduce the debt. Others recommend a constitutional amendment that would require the government to have a balanced budget, spending only as much as it takes in.

POVERTY *The lack of adequate income to maintain a minimum* ***standard of living.*** In the United States, this adequate income is referred to as the poverty line. In 1999, the poverty threshold for a family of four was $17,029. That year, the poverty rate dropped to 11.8 percent—the lowest rate since 1979, and more than 32 million Americans lived in poverty.

While poverty rates have remained relatively steady over the last 30 or so years, inequality in the distribution of income has grown. Between 1970 and 2000, the share of income received by the wealthiest 20 percent of families increased from 43.3 percent to 56.7 percent. In the same period, the poorest 20 percent of families' share of income fell from 4.1 percent to 2.7 percent.

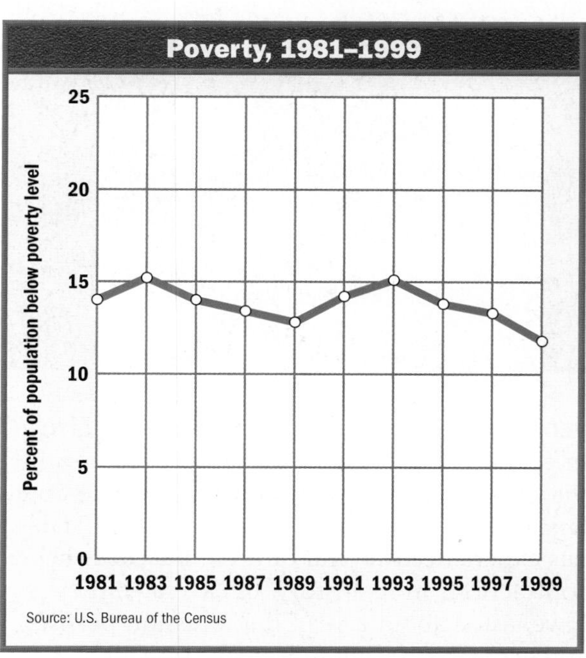

Source: U.S. Bureau of the Census

PRODUCTIVITY *The relationship between the output of goods and services and the input of resources.* Productivity is the amount of goods or services that a person can produce at a given time. It is closely linked to economic growth, which is defined as an increase in a nation's real **gross domestic product (GDP)** from one year to the next. A substantial rise in productivity means the average worker is producing more, a key factor in spurring economic expansion. Between 1995 and 2000, for example, worker productivity in the United States increased about 3 percent each year. This increase, along with other economic factors, helped the nation's real GDP grow an average of about 4 percent during those years.

A number of elements affect productivity, including available supplies of labor and raw materials, education and training, attitudes toward work, and technological innovations. Computer technology, for instance, is believed to have played a significant role in bolstering productivity during the 1990s by allowing workers to do their jobs more quickly and efficiently. Conversely, a lack of adequate training and fewer innovations were thought to be behind the meager productivity growth rates of the 1970s and 1980s—when productivity rose at an annual rate of less than 1 percent.

RECESSION *A period of declining economic activity.* In economic terms, a recession takes place when the **gross domestic product** falls for two quarters, or six months, in a row. The United States has experienced several of these **business-cycle** contractions in its history. On average, they have lasted about a year. If a recession persists and economic activity plunges, it is called a **depression.** For more information on recessions, read the Economic Background on page 680.

SOCIALISM *An economic system in which the government owns most of the means of production and distribution.* Like **communism,** the goal of socialism is to use the power of government to reduce inequality and meet people's needs. Under socialism, however, the government usually owns only major industries, such as coal, steel, and transportation. Other industries are privately owned but regulated by the government. Government and individuals, therefore, share economic decision-making. Also, under socialism, the government may provide such services as reasonably priced health care.

Some countries, such as Sweden, are called democratic socialist countries. These nations have less government ownership of property than communist governments. They also have democratically elected governments.

Critics of socialism maintain that this system leads to less efficiency and higher taxes than does the **free enterprise** system.

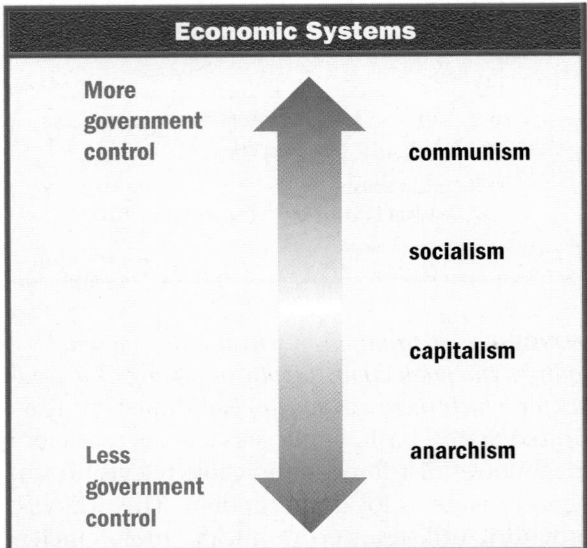

STANDARD OF LIVING *The overall economic situation in which people live.* Economists differ on how best to measure the standard of living. Some suggest average personal income, while others propose per capita **gross domestic product**—the GDP divided by the population. Another possible measure is the value of the goods and services bought by consumers during a year. In general terms, the nation's standard of living rises as these measures rise. Some people argue that measuring the quality of life also requires consideration of noneconomic factors such as pollution, health, work hours, and even political freedom.

STOCK MARKET *or* STOCK EXCHANGE *A place where stocks and bonds are bought and sold.* Since stocks and bonds together are known as securities, a stock market is sometimes called a securities market.

Large companies often need extra money to fund expansion and to help cover operating costs. To raise money, they sell stocks, or shares of ownership, in their companies or borrow by issuing bonds, or certificates of debt, promising to repay the money borrowed, plus interest.

Individuals invest in securities to make a profit. Most stockholders receive dividends, or a share of the company's profits. Bondholders receive interest. Investors may also make a profit by selling their securities. This sale of securities takes place in the stock exchange.

Stocks and bonds are traded on exchanges. The largest and most important exchange in the United States is the New York Stock Exchange (pictured below; for more information on the New York Stock Exchange, read the Now & Then on page 468). Activity on this and other exchanges often signals how well the economy is doing. A bull market—when stock prices rise—usually indicates economic expansion. A bear market—when stock prices fall—usually indicates economic contraction.

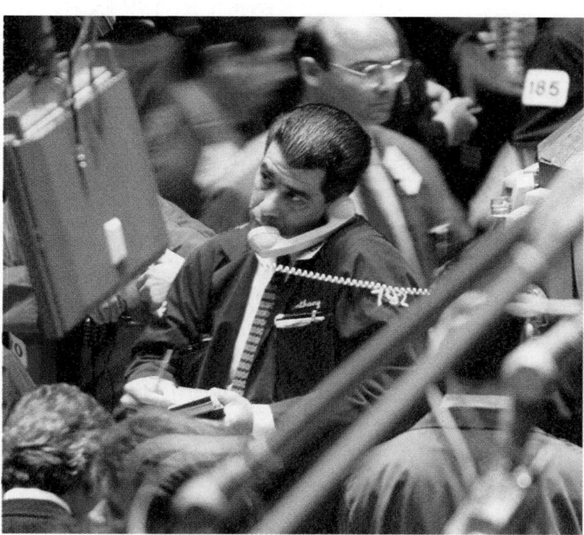

A rapid fall in stock prices is called a crash. The worst stock market crash in the United States came in October 1929. To help protect against another drastic stock market crash, the federal government set up the Securities and Exchange Commission (SEC), which regulates the trading of securities.

Selected World Stock Exchanges

Exchange	Products
New York Stock Exchange (NYSE)	stocks, bonds
American Stock Exchange (AMEX) (New York)	stocks, bonds
National Association of Securities Dealers Automated Quotations (NASDAQ)	over-the-counter stocks
London Stock Exchange	stocks
Tokyo Stock Exchange	stocks, bonds, futures, options
Stock Exchange of Hong Kong	stocks, bonds, commodity futures
German Stock Exchange (Frankfurt)	stocks

STRIKE *A work stoppage by employees to gain higher wages, better working conditions, or other benefits.* Strikes are also sometimes used as political protests. A strike is usually preceded by a failure in collective bargaining—the negotiation of contracts between labor unions and employers. Union members may decide to call a strike if they believe negotiations with the employer are deadlocked. Collective bargaining and strikes are regulated by the NLRA, or Wagner Act, of 1935, administered by the National Labor Relations Board (NLRB). There are also wildcat strikes, which do not involve unions.

When strikes do occur, union representatives and employers try to negotiate a settlement. An outside party is sometimes asked to help work out an agreement.

For a personal account of a strike, view the *American Stories* video, "A Child on Strike: The Testimony of Camella Teoli, Mill Girl.

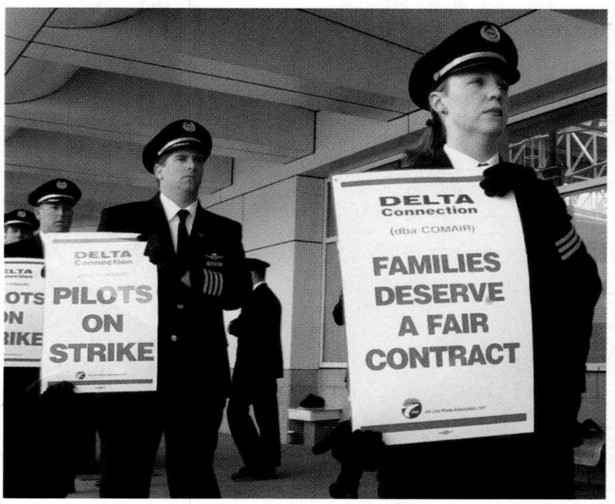

SUPPLY AND DEMAND *The forces that determine prices of goods and services in a market economy.* Supply is the amount of a good or service that producers are willing and able to produce at a given price. Demand is the amount of a good or service consumers are willing and able to buy at a given price. In general, producers are willing to produce more of a good or service when prices are high; conversely, consumers are willing to buy more of a good or service when prices are low.

The table and graph below show supply and demand for a certain product. The line *S* shows the amount of the good that producers would be willing to make at various prices. The line *D* shows the amount that consumers would be willing to buy at various prices. Point *E*, where the two lines intersect, is called the equilibrium price. It is the price at which the amount produced and the amount demanded would be the same.

When the equilibrium price is the market price, the market operates efficiently. At prices above the equilibrium price, consumers will demand less than producers supply. Producers, therefore, will have to lower their prices to sell the surplus, or excess, products. At prices below equilibrium, consumers will demand more. Producers will be able to raise their prices because the product is scarce, or in short supply.

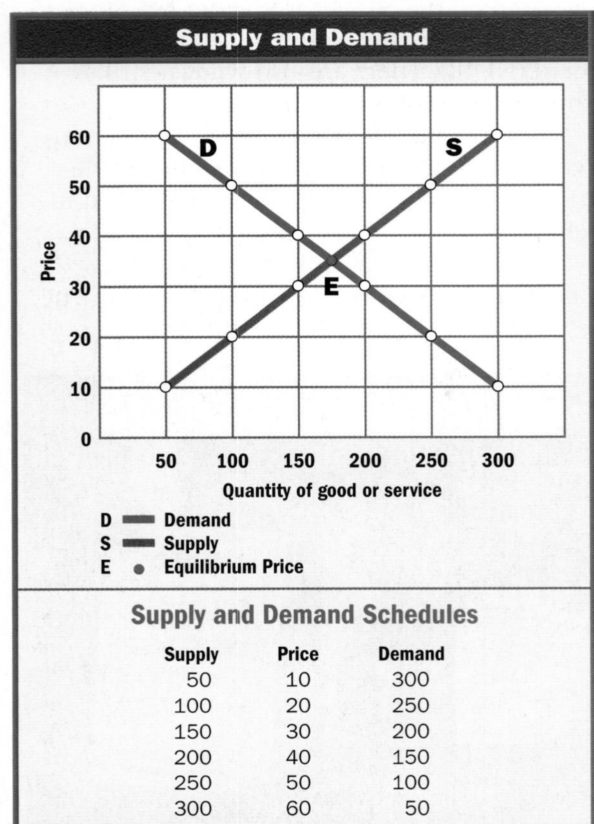

Supply and Demand Schedules

Supply	Price	Demand
50	10	300
100	20	250
150	30	200
200	40	150
250	50	100
300	60	50

SUPPLY-SIDE ECONOMICS *Government policies designed to stimulate the production of goods and services, or the supply side of the economy.* Supply-side economists developed these policies in opposition to **Keynesian economics.**

Supply-side policies call for low tax rates particularly in income from investments. Lower taxes mean that people keep more of each dollar they earn. Therefore, supply-side economists argue, people will work harder in order to earn more. They will then use their extra income to save and invest. This investment will fund the development of new businesses and, as a result, create more jobs. For more information on supply-side economics, read the Economic Background on page 835.

TARIFF *A fee charged for goods brought into a state or country from another state or country.* Beginning in 1789, Congress created tariffs to raise revenue and to protect American products from foreign competition. Soon, however, special interest groups used tariffs to protect specific industries and increase profits.

Trade without tariffs is called free trade. In recent decades, a growing number of U.S. economists have favored free trade policies because they believe that such policies will help increase U.S. exports to other countries. In 1994, the North American Free Trade Agreement (NAFTA) established a free-trade zone among the United States, Canada, and Mexico.

TAXATION *The practice of requiring persons, groups, or businesses to contribute funds to the government under which they reside or transact business.* All levels of government—federal, state, and local—collect many kinds of taxes. Income taxes are the chief source of revenue for the federal government and an important revenue source for many states. Both corporations and individuals pay income tax, or taxes on earnings. Since its inception in 1913, the federal income tax has been a progressive tax, one that is graduated, or scaled, such that those with greater incomes are taxed at a greater rate.

Sales taxes are another important source of income for state governments.

Property taxes are the main source of funds for local governments. Property tax is calculated as a percentage of the assessed value of real estate—land and improvements such as buildings.

TRADE *The exchange of goods and services between countries.* Almost all nations produce goods that other countries need, and they sell (export) those goods to buyers in other countries. At the same time, they buy (import) goods from other countries as well. For example, Americans sell goods such as wheat to people in Japan and buy Japanese goods such as automobiles in return.

Nations that trade with one another often become dependent on one another's products. Sometimes this brings nations closer together, as it did the United States, Great Britain, and France before World War I. Other times it causes tension among nations, such as that between the United States and Arab oil-producing countries in the 1970s. For an example of how trade influences foreign policy, read the Economic Background on page 377.

TRUST *A form of business merger in which the major stockholders in several corporations turn over their stock to a group of trustees.* The trustees then run the separate corporations as one large company, or trust. In return for their stock, the stockholders of the separate corporations receive a share of the trust's profits.

American business leaders of the late 1800s used trusts to stifle competition and take control of entire industries, as in a **monopoly.** Trusts were outlawed by the Sherman Antitrust Act of 1890. However, business leaders eventually found other ways to merge corporations in an industry.

UNEMPLOYMENT RATE *The percentage of the labor force that is unemployed but actively looking for work.* The labor force consists of all civilians 16 years of age and older who are employed or who are unemployed but actively looking and available for work. The size of the labor force and the unemployment rate are determined by surveys conducted by the U.S. Bureau of the Census.

The unemployment rate provides an indicator of economic health. Rising unemployment rates signal a contraction in the economy, while falling rates indicate an economic expansion. The graphs below show two different methods of portraying unemployment in the United States.

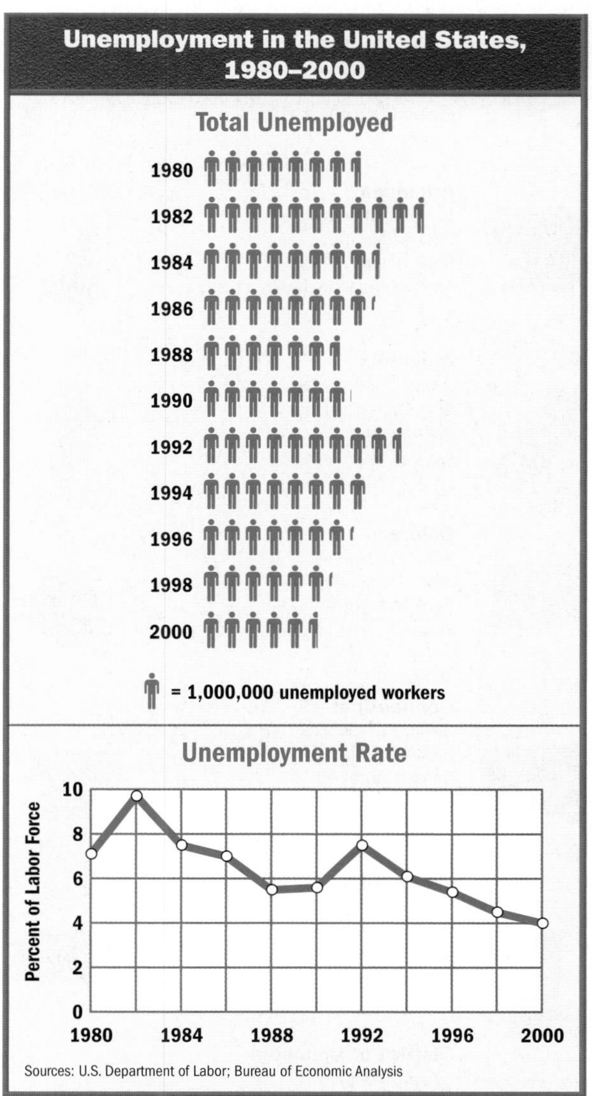

Facts About the States

Alabama
4,447,100 people
52,237 sq. mi.
Rank in area: 30
Entered Union in 1819

Alaska
626,932 people
615,230 sq. mi.
Rank in area: 1
Entered Union in 1959

Arizona
5,130,632 people
114,006 sq. mi.
Rank in area: 6
Entered Union in 1912

Arkansas
2,673,400 people
53,182 sq. mi.
Rank in area: 28
Entered Union in 1836

California
33,871,648 people
158,869 sq. mi.
Rank in area: 3
Entered Union in 1850

Colorado
4,301,261 people
104,100 sq. mi.
Rank in area: 8
Entered Union in 1876

Connecticut
3,405,565 people
5,544 sq. mi.
Rank in area: 48
Entered Union in 1788

Delaware
783,600 people
2,396 sq. mi.
Rank in area: 49
Entered Union in 1787

District of Columbia
572,059 people
68 sq. mi.

Florida
15,982,378 people
59,928 sq. mi.
Rank in area: 23
Entered Union in 1845

Georgia
8,186,453 people
58,977 sq. mi.
Rank in area: 24
Entered Union in 1788

Hawaii
1,211,537 people
6,459 sq. mi.
Rank in area: 47
Entered Union in 1959

Idaho
1,293,953 people
83,574 sq. mi.
Rank in area: 14
Entered Union in 1890

Illinois
12,419,293 people
57,918 sq. mi.
Rank in area: 25
Entered Union in 1818

Indiana
6,080,485 people
36,420 sq. mi.
Rank in area: 38
Entered Union in 1816

Iowa
2,926,324 people
56,276 sq. mi.
Rank in area: 26
Entered Union in 1846

Kansas
2,688,418 people
82,282 sq. mi.
Rank in area: 15
Entered Union in 1861

Kentucky
4,041,769 people
40,411 sq. mi.
Rank in area: 37
Entered Union in 1792

Louisiana
4,468,976 people
49,651 sq. mi.
Rank in area: 31
Entered Union in 1812

Maine
1,274,923 people
33,741 sq. mi.
Rank in area: 39
Entered Union in 1820

Maryland
5,296,486 people
12,297 sq. mi.
Rank in area: 42
Entered Union in 1788

Massachusetts
6,349,097 people
9,241 sq. mi.
Rank in area: 45
Entered Union in 1788

Michigan
9,938,444 people
96,705 sq. mi.
Rank in area: 11
Entered Union in 1837

Minnesota
4,919,479 people
86,943 sq. mi.
Rank in area: 12
Entered Union in 1858

Mississippi
2,844,658 people
48,286 sq. mi.
Rank in area: 32
Entered Union in 1817

Missouri
5,595,211 people
69,709 sq. mi.
Rank in area: 21
Entered Union in 1821

Montana
902,195 people
147,046 sq. mi.
Rank in area: 4
Entered Union in 1889

Population figures are according to the Census 2000.

Nebraska
1,711,263 people
77,538 sq. mi.
Rank in area: 16
Entered Union in 1867

Nevada
1,998,257 people
110,567 sq. mi.
Rank in area: 7
Entered Union in 1864

New Hampshire
1,235,786 people
9,283 sq. mi.
Rank in area: 44
Entered Union in 1788

New Jersey
8,414,350 people
8,215 sq. mi.
Rank in area: 46
Entered Union in 1787

New Mexico
1,819,046 people
121,598 sq. mi.
Rank in area: 5
Entered Union in 1912

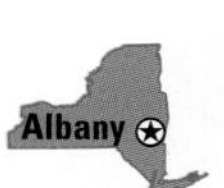

New York
18,976,457 people
53,989 sq. mi.
Rank in area: 27
Entered Union in 1788

North Carolina
8,049,313 people
52,672 sq. mi.
Rank in area: 29
Entered Union in 1789

North Dakota
642,200 people
70,704 sq. mi.
Rank in area: 18
Entered Union in 1889

Ohio
11,353,140 people
44,828 sq. mi.
Rank in area: 34
Entered Union in 1803

Oklahoma
3,450,654 people
69,903 sq. mi.
Rank in area: 20
Entered Union in 1907

Oregon
3,421,399 people
97,132 sq. mi.
Rank in area: 10
Entered Union in 1859

Pennsylvania
12,281,054 people
46,058 sq. mi.
Rank in area: 33
Entered Union in 1787

Rhode Island
1,048,319 people
1,231 sq. mi.
Rank in area: 50
Entered Union in 1790

South Carolina
4,012,012 people
31,189 sq. mi.
Rank in area: 40
Entered Union in 1788

South Dakota
754,844 people
77,121 sq. mi.
Rank in area: 17
Entered Union in 1889

Tennessee
5,689,283 people
42,146 sq. mi.
Rank in area: 36
Entered Union in 1796

Texas
20,851,820 people
267,277 sq. mi.
Rank in area: 2
Entered Union in 1845

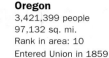

Utah
2,233,169 people
84,904 sq. mi.
Rank in area: 13
Entered Union in 1896

Vermont
608,827 people
9,615 sq. mi.
Rank in area: 43
Entered Union in 1791

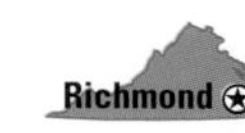

Virginia
7,078,515 people
42,326 sq. mi.
Rank in area: 35
Entered Union in 1788

Washington
5,894,121 people
70,637 sq. mi.
Rank in area: 19
Entered Union in 1889

West Virginia
1,808,344 people
24,231 sq. mi.
Rank in area: 41
Entered Union in 1863

Wisconsin
5,363,675 people
64,599 sq. mi.
Rank in area: 22
Entered Union in 1848

Wyoming
493,782 people
97,818 sq. mi.
Rank in area: 9
Entered Union in 1890

United States: Major Dependencies (as of 1999)

American Samoa 63,781 people; 90 sq. mi.

Guam 151,968 people; 217 sq. mi.

Commonwealth of Puerto Rico 3,889,507 people; 3,508 sq. mi.

Virgin Islands of the United States 119,615 people; 171 sq. mi.

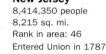

Presidents of the United States

Dates given are for term in office.

Here are some little-known facts about the presidents of the United States:

- First president born in the new United States: **Martin Van Buren** (8th president)
- Only president who was a bachelor: **James Buchanan**
- First left-handed president: **James A. Garfield**
- Largest president: **William Howard Taft** (6 feet, 2 inches; 332 pounds)
- Youngest president: **Theodore Roosevelt** (42 years old)
- Oldest president: **Ronald Reagan** (77 years old when he left office in 1989)
- First president born west of the Mississippi River: **Herbert Hoover** (born in West Branch, Iowa)
- First president born in the 20th century: **John F. Kennedy** (born May 29, 1917)

1 **George Washington**
1789–1797
No Political Party
Birthplace: Virginia
Born: February 22, 1732
Died: December 14, 1799

2 **John Adams**
1797–1801
Federalist
Birthplace: Massachusetts
Born: October 30, 1735
Died: July 4, 1826

3 **Thomas Jefferson**
1801–1809
Democratic-Republican
Birthplace: Virginia
Born: April 13, 1743
Died: July 4, 1826

4 **James Madison**
1809–1817
Democratic-Republican
Birthplace: Virginia
Born: March 16, 1751
Died: June 28, 1836

5 **James Monroe**
1817–1825
Democratic-Republican
Birthplace: Virginia
Born: April 28, 1758
Died: July 4, 1831

6 **John Quincy Adams**
1825–1829
Republican
Birthplace: Massachusetts
Born: July 11, 1767
Died: February 23, 1848

7 **Andrew Jackson**
1829–1837
Democrat
Birthplace: South Carolina
Born: March 15, 1767
Died: June 8, 1845

8 **Martin Van Buren**
1837–1841
Democrat
Birthplace: New York
Born: December 5, 1782
Died: July 24, 1862

9 **William H. Harrison**
1841
Whig
Birthplace: Virginia
Born: February 9, 1773
Died: April 4, 1841

10 **John Tyler**
1841–1845
Whig
Birthplace: Virginia
Born: March 29, 1790
Died: January 18, 1862

11 **James K. Polk**
1845–1849
Democrat
Birthplace: North Carolina
Born: November 2, 1795
Died: June 15, 1849

12 **Zachary Taylor**
1849–1850
Whig
Birthplace: Virginia
Born: November 24, 1784
Died: July 9, 1850

13 Millard Fillmore
1850–1853
Whig
Birthplace: New York
Born: January 7, 1800
Died: March 8, 1874

14 Franklin Pierce
1853–1857
Democrat
Birthplace: New Hampshire
Born: November 23, 1804
Died: October 8, 1869

15 James Buchanan
1857–1861
Democrat
Birthplace: Pennsylvania
Born: April 23, 1791
Died: June 1, 1868

16 Abraham Lincoln
1861–1865
Republican
Birthplace: Kentucky
Born: February 12, 1809
Died: April 15, 1865

17 Andrew Johnson
1865–1869
Democrat
Birthplace: North Carolina
Born: December 29, 1808
Died: July 31, 1875

18 Ulysses S. Grant
1869–1877
Republican
Birthplace: Ohio
Born: April 27, 1822
Died: July 23, 1885

19 Rutherford B. Hayes
1877–1881
Republican
Birthplace: Ohio
Born: October 4, 1822
Died: January 17, 1893

20 James A. Garfield
1881
Republican
Birthplace: Ohio
Born: November 19, 1831
Died: September 19, 1881

21 Chester A. Arthur
1881–1885
Republican
Birthplace: Vermont
Born: October 5, 1829
Died: November 18, 1886

22 24 Grover Cleveland
1885–1889, 1893–1897
Democrat
Birthplace: New Jersey
Born: March 18, 1837
Died: June 24, 1908

23 Benjamin Harrison
1889–1893
Republican
Birthplace: Ohio
Born: August 20, 1833
Died: March 13, 1901

25 William McKinley
1897–1901
Republican
Birthplace: Ohio
Born: January 29, 1843
Died: September 14, 1901

26 Theodore Roosevelt
1901–1909
Republican
Birthplace: New York
Born: October 27, 1858
Died: January 6, 1919

27 William H. Taft
1909–1913
Republican
Birthplace: Ohio
Born: September 15, 1857
Died: March 8, 1930

28 Woodrow Wilson
1913–1921
Democrat
Birthplace: Virginia
Born: December 29, 1856
Died: February 3, 1924

29 Warren G. Harding
1921–1923
Republican
Birthplace: Ohio
Born: November 2, 1865
Died: August 2, 1923

30 Calvin Coolidge
1923–1929
Republican
Birthplace: Vermont
Born: July 4, 1872
Died: January 5, 1933

31 Herbert C. Hoover
1929–1933
Republican
Birthplace: Iowa
Born: August 10, 1874
Died: October 20, 1964

32 Franklin D. Roosevelt
1933–1945
Democrat
Birthplace: New York
Born: January 30, 1882
Died: April 12, 1945

33 Harry S. Truman
1945–1953
Democrat
Birthplace: Missouri
Born: May 8, 1884
Died: December 26, 1972

34 Dwight D. Eisenhower
1953–1961
Republican
Birthplace: Texas
Born: October 14, 1890
Died: March 28, 1969

35 John F. Kennedy
1961–1963
Democrat
Birthplace: Massachusetts
Born: May 29, 1917
Died: November 22, 1963

36 Lyndon B. Johnson
1963–1969
Democrat
Birthplace: Texas
Born: August 27, 1908
Died: January 22, 1973

37 Richard M. Nixon
1969–1974
Republican
Birthplace: California
Born: January 9, 1913
Died: April 22, 1994

38 Gerald R. Ford
1974–1977
Republican
Birthplace: Nebraska
Born: July, 14, 1913

39 James E. Carter, Jr.
1977–1981
Democrat
Birthplace: Georgia
Born: October 1, 1924

40 Ronald W. Reagan
1981–1989
Republican
Birthplace: Illinois
Born: February 6, 1911
Died: June 5, 2004

41 George H. W. Bush
1989–1993
Republican
Birthplace: Massachusetts
Born: June 12, 1924

42 William J. Clinton
1993–2001
Democrat
Birthplace: Arkansas
Born: August 19, 1946

43 George W. Bush
2001–
Republican
Birthplace: Connecticut
Born: July 6, 1946

GLOSSARY

The Glossary is an alphabetical listing of many of the key terms from the chapters, along with their meanings. The definitions listed in the Glossary are the ones that apply to the way the words are used in this textbook. The Glossary gives the part of speech of each word. The following abbreviations are used:

adj. **= adjective** ***n.*** **= noun** ***v.*** **= verb**

PRONUNCIATION KEY

Symbol	Examples	Symbol	Examples	Symbol	Examples
ă	**a**t, g**a**s	m	**m**an, see**m**	v	**v**an, sa**v**e
ā	**a**pe, d**ay**	n	**n**ight, mitte**n**	w	**w**eb, t**w**ice
ä	f**a**ther, b**a**rn	ng	si**ng**, a**n**ger	y	**y**ard, law**y**er
âr	f**air**, d**are**	ŏ	**o**dd, n**o**t	z	**z**oo, rea**s**on
b	**b**ell, ta**b**le	ō	**o**pen, r**oa**d, gr**ow**	zh	trea**s**ure, gara**g**e
ch	**ch**in, lun**ch**	ô	**aw**ful, b**ough**t, h**o**rse	ə	**a**wake, ev**e**n, penc**i**l, pil**o**t, foc**u**s
d	**d**ig, bore**d**	oi	c**oi**n, b**oy**		
ĕ	**e**gg, t**e**n	o͝o	l**oo**k, f**u**ll	ər	p**er**form, lett**er**
ē	**e**vil, s**ee**, m**ea**l	o͞o	r**oo**t, gl**ue**, thr**ough**		
f	**f**all, lau**gh**, **ph**rase	ou	**ou**t, c**ow**	**Sounds in Foreign Words**	
g	**g**old, bi**g**	p	**p**ig, ca**p**	KH	*German* i**ch**, au**ch**; *Scottish* lo**ch**
h	**h**it, in**h**ale	r	**r**ose, sta**r**		
hw	**wh**ite, every**wh**ere	s	**s**it, fa**ce**	N	*French* e**n**tre, bo**n**, fi**n**
ĭ	**i**nch, f**i**t	sh	**sh**e, ma**sh**	œ	*French* f**eu**, c**oeu**r; *German* sch**ö**n
ī	**i**dle, m**y**, tr**ie**d	t	**t**ap, hopp**ed**		
îr	d**ear**, h**ere**	th	**th**ing, wi**th**	ü	*French* **u**tile, r**u**e; *German* gr**ü**n
j	**j**ar, **g**em, ba**dge**	*th*	**th**en, o**th**er		
k	**k**eep, **c**at, lu**ck**	ŭ	**u**p, n**u**t		
l	**l**oad, ratt**le**	ûr	f**ur**, **ear**n, b**ir**d, w**or**m		

STRESS MARKS

′ This mark indicates that the preceding syllable receives the primary stress. For example, in the word *lineage,* the first syllable is stressed: [lĭn′ē-ĭj].

′ This mark is used only in words in which more than one syllable is stressed. It indicates that the preceding syllable is stressed, but somewhat more weakly than the syllable receiving the primary stress. In the word *consumerism,* for example, the second syllable receives the primary stress, and the fourth syllable receives a weaker stress: [kən-so͞o′mə-rĭz′əm].

A

abolition *n.* movement to end slavery. (p. 144)

affirmative [ə-fûr′mə-tĭv] **action** *n.* a policy that seeks to correct the effects of past discrimination by favoring the groups who were previously disadvantaged. (pp. 723, 831)

Agent Orange *n.* a toxic leaf-killing chemical sprayed by U.S. planes in Vietnam to expose Vietcong hideouts. (p. 739)

Agricultural Adjustment Act (AAA) *n.* a law enacted in 1933 to raise crop prices by paying farmers to leave a certain amount of their land unplanted, thus lowering production. (p. 491)

AIDS [ādz] **(acquired immune deficiency syndrome)** *n.* a disease caused by a virus that weakens the immune system, making the body prone to infections and otherwise rare forms of cancer. (p. 840)

Alamo, the [ăl′ə-mō′] *n.* a mission and fort in San Antonio, Texas, where Mexican forces massacred rebellious Texans in 1836. (p. 134)

Alien and Sedition [ā′lē-ən] [sĭ-dĭsh′ən] **Acts** *n.* a series of four laws enacted in 1798 to reduce the political power of recent immigrants to the United States. (p. 78)

Alliance [ə-lī′əns] **for Progress** *n.* a U.S. foreign-aid program of the 1960s, providing economic and technical assistance to Latin American countries. (p. 680)

Allies [ăl′īz] *n.* **1.** in World War I, the group of nations—originally consisting of Great Britain, France, and Russia and later joined by the United States, Italy, and others—that opposed the Central Powers (p. 373). **2.** in World War II, the group of nations—including Great Britain, the Soviet Union, and the United States—that opposed the Axis powers. (p. 554)

American Expeditionary [ĕk′spĭ-dĭsh′ə-nĕr′ē] **Force (AEF)** *n.* the U.S. forces, led by General John Pershing, who fought with the Allies in Europe during World War I. (p. 384)

American Federation of Labor (AFL) *n.* an alliance of trade and craft unions, formed in 1886. (p. 245)

American Indian Movement (AIM) *n.* a frequently militant organization that was formed in 1968 to work for Native American rights. (p. 771)

Americanization [ə-mĕr′ĭ-kə-nĭ-zā′shən] **movement** *n.* education program designed to help immigrants assimilate to American culture. (p. 263)

American System *n.* a pre-Civil War set of measures designed to unify the nation and strengthen its economy by means of protective tariffs, a national bank, and such internal improvements as the development of a transportation system. (p. 122)

anarchist [ăn′ər-kĭst] *n.* a person who opposes all forms of government. (p. 413)

Anasazi [ä′nə-sä′zē] *n.* a Native American group that lived on the mesa tops, cliff sides, and canyon bottoms of the Four Corners region (where the present-day states of Arizona, New Mexico, Colorado, and Utah meet) from about A.D. 100 to 1300. (p. 5)

Antifederalist [ăn′tē-fĕd′ər-ə-lĭst] *n.* an opponent of a strong central government. (p. 69)

appeasement [ə-pēz′mənt] *n.* the granting of concessions to a hostile power in order to keep the peace. (p. 538)

Appomattox [ăp′ə-măt′əks] **Court House** *n.* town near Appomatox, Virginia, where Lee surrendered to Grant on April 9, 1865. (37°N 79°W) (p. 181)

arbitration *n.* a method of settling disputes in which both sides submit their differences to a mutually approved judge. (p. 245)

armistice [är′mĭ-stĭs] *n.* a truce, or agreement to end an armed conflict. (p. 387)

Army of the Republic of Vietnam (ARVN) *n.* the southern Vietnamese soldiers with whom U.S. troops fought against communism and forces in the North during the Vietnam War. (p. 737)

Articles of Confederation [kən-fĕd′ə-rā′shən] *n.* a document, adopted by the Second Continental Congress in 1777 and finally approved by the states in 1781, that outlined the form of government of the new United States. (p. 67)

Ashcan school *n.* a group of early 20th-century American artists who often painted realistic pictures of city life—such as tenements and homeless people—thus earning them their name. (p. 295)

assimilation [ə-sĭm′ə-lā′shən] *n.* a minority group's adoption of the beliefs and way of life of the dominant culture. (p. 206)

Atlantic Charter *n.* a 1941 declaration of principles in which the United States and Great Britain set forth their goals in opposing the Axis powers. (p. 554)

Axis [ăk′sĭs] **powers** *n.* the group of nations—including Germany, Italy, and Japan—that opposed the Allies in World War II. (p. 551)

Aztec [ăz′tĕk′] *n.* a Native American people that settled in the Valley of Mexico in the 1200s A.D. and later developed a powerful empire. (p. 5)

B

baby boom *n.* the sharp increase in the U.S. birthrate following World War II. (p. 643)

Battle of the Bulge *n.* a month-long battle of World War II, in which the Allies succeeded in turning back the last major German offensive of the war. (p. 576)

Battle of Midway *n.* a World War II battle that took place in early June 1942. The Allies decimated the Japanese fleet at Midway, an island lying northwest of Hawaii. The Allies then took the offensive in the Pacific and began to move closer to Japan. (p. 579)

Battle of Wounded Knee [wo͞on′dĭd nē′] *n.* the massacre by U.S. soldiers of 300 unarmed Native Americans at Wounded Knee Creek, South Dakota, in 1890. (pp. 207–208)

Beatles, the [bēt′lz] *n.* a British band that had an enormous influence on popular music in the 1960s. (p. 783)

beat movement *n.* a social and artistic movement of the 1950s, stressing unrestrained literary self-expression and nonconformity with the mainstream culture. (p. 655)

Benin [bə-nĭn′] *n.* a West African kingdom that flourished in the Niger Delta region (in what is now Nigeria) from the 14th to the 17th century. (p. 9)

Berlin airlift [bûr-lĭn′ âr′lĭft′] *n.* a 327-day operation in which U.S. and British planes flew food and supplies into West Berlin after the Soviets blockaded the city in 1948. (p. 607)

Berlin Wall *n.* a concrete wall that separated East Berlin and West Berlin from 1961 to 1989, built by the Communist East German government to prevent its citizens from fleeing to the West. (p. 677)

Bessemer [bĕs′ə-mər] **process** *n.* a cheap and efficient process for making steel, developed around 1850. (p. 231)

Bill of Rights *n.* the first ten amendments to the U.S. Constitution, added in 1791 and consisting of a formal list of citizens' rights and freedoms. (p. 70)

bimetallism [bī-mĕt′l-ĭz′əm] *n.* the use of both gold and silver as a basis for a national monetary system. (p. 222)

blacklist [blăk′lĭst′] *n.* a list of about 500 actors, writers, producers, and directors who were not allowed to work on Hollywood films because of their alleged Communist connections. (p. 618)

Black Panthers *n.* a militant African-American political organization formed in 1966 by Huey Newton and Bobby Seale to fight police brutality and to provide services in the ghetto. (p. 720)

Black Power *n.* a slogan used by Stokely Carmichael in the 1960s that encouraged African-American pride and political and social leadership. (p. 720)

Black Tuesday *n.* a name given to October 29, 1929, when stock prices fell sharply. (p. 468)

blitzkrieg [blĭts′krēg′] *n.* from the German word meaning "lightning war," a sudden, massive attack with combined air and ground forces, intended to achieve a quick victory. (p. 539)

bonanza [bə-năn′zə] **farm** *n.* an enormous farm on which a single crop is grown. (p. 218)

Bonus [bō′nəs] **Army** *n.* a group of World War I veterans and their families who marched on Washington, D.C., in 1932 to demand the immediate payment of a bonus they had been promised for military service. (p. 482)

bootlegger [bo͞ot′lĕg′ər] *n.* a person who smuggled alcoholic beverages into the United States during Prohibition. (p. 437)

Boston Massacre [bô′stən măs′ə-kər] *n.* a clash between British soldiers and Boston colonists in 1770, in which five of the colonists were killed. (p. 48)

Boston Tea Party *n.* the dumping of 18,000 pounds of tea into Boston Harbor by colonists in 1773 to protest the Tea Act. (p. 49)

Boulder [bōl′dər] **Dam** *n.* a dam on the Colorado River—now called Hoover Dam—that was built during the Great Depression as part of a public-works program intended to stimulate business and provide jobs. (p. 480)

Boxer Rebellion *n.* a 1900 rebellion in which members of a Chinese secret society sought to free their country from Western influence. (p. 357)

bracero [brə-sâr′ō] *n.* a Mexican laborer allowed to enter the United States to work for a limited period of time during World War II. (p. 662)

bread line *n.* a line of people waiting for free food. (p. 473)

brinkmanship [brĭngk′mən-shĭp′] *n.* the practice of threatening an enemy with massive military retaliation for any aggression. (p. 623)

Brown* v. *Board of Education of Topeka *n.* a 1954 case in which the Supreme Court ruled that "separate but equal" education for black and white students was unconstitutional. (p. 702)

Bull Moose Party *n.* a name given to the Progressive Party, formed to support Theodore Roosevelt's candidacy for the presidency in 1912. (p. 330)

buying on margin [mär′jĭn] *n.* the purchasing of stocks by paying only a small percentage of the price and borrowing the rest. (p. 467)

C

cabinet [kăb′ə-nĭt] *n.* the group of department heads who serve as the president's chief advisers. (p. 75)

Camp David Accords [ə-kôrdz′] *n.* historic agreements between Israel and Egypt, reached in negotiations at Camp David in 1978. (p. 816)

carpetbagger [kär′pĭt-băg′ər] *n.* a Northerner who moved to the South after the Civil War. (p. 186)

Central Powers *n.* the group of nations—led by Germany, Austria-Hungary, and the Ottoman Empire—that opposed the Allies in World War I. (p. 374)

checks and balances *n.* the provisions in the U.S. Constitution that prevent any branch of the U.S. government from dominating the other two branches. (p. 69)

Chinese Exclusion Act *n.* a law, enacted in 1882, that prohibited all Chinese except students, teachers, merchants, tourists, and government officials from entering the United States. (p. 259)

Chisholm [chĭz′əm] **Trail** *n.* the major cattle route from San Antonio, Texas, through Oklahoma to Kansas. (p. 209)

chlorination *n.* a method of purifying water by mixing it with chemical chlorine. (p. 264)

Christianity [krĭs′chē-ăn′ĭ-tē] *n.* a religion based on the life and teachings of Jesus Christ. (p. 10)

CIA *n.* the Central Intelligence Agency—a U.S. agency created to gather secret information about foreign governments. (p. 623)

Civilian Conservation Corps [kôr] **(CCC)** *n.* an agency, established as part of the New Deal, that put young unemployed men to work building roads, developing parks, planting trees, and helping in erosion-control and flood-control projects. (p. 491)

Civil Rights Act of 1964 *n.* a law that banned discrimination on the basis of race, sex, national origin, or religion in public places and most workplaces. (p. 714)

Civil Rights Act of 1968 *n.* a law that banned discrimination in housing. (p. 722)

civil service *n.* the nonmilitary branches of government administration. (p. 270)

Clayton Antitrust [klāt′n ăn′tē-trŭst′] **Act** *n.* a law, enacted in 1914, that made certain monopolistic business practices illegal and protected the rights of labor unions and farm organizations. (p. 333)

Cold War *n.* the state of hostility, without direct military conflict, that developed between the United States and the Soviet Union after World War II. (p. 606)

Columbian Exchange [kə-lŭm′bē-ən ĭks-chānj′] *n.* the transfer—beginning with Columbus's first voyage—of plants, animals, and diseases between the Western Hemisphere and the Eastern Hemisphere. (p. 15)

Committee to Reelect the President *n.* an organization formed to run President Nixon's 1972 reelection campaign, which was linked to the break-in at the Democratic National Committee headquarters that set off the Watergate scandal. (p. 803)

Common Sense *n.* a pamphlet by Thomas Paine, published in 1776, that called for separation of the colonies from Britain. (p. 52)

Commonwealth [kŏm′ən-wĕlth′] **v. *Hunt*** *n.* an 1842 case in which the Massachusetts Supreme Court upheld workers' right to strike. (p. 143)

communism [kŏm′yə-nĭz′əm] *n.* an economic and political system based on one-party government and state ownership of property. (p. 413)

concentration [kŏn′sən-trā′shən] **camp** *n.* a prison camp operated by Nazi Germany in which Jews and other groups considered to be enemies of Adolf Hitler were starved while doing slave labor or were murdered. (p. 546)

Confederacy [kən-fĕd′ər-ə-sē] *n.* the Confederate States of America, a confederation formed in 1861 by the Southern states after their secession from the Union. (p. 165)

conglomerate [kən-glŏm′ər-ĭt] *n.* a major corporation that owns a number of smaller companies in unrelated businesses. (p. 642)

Congress of Industrial Organizations (CIO) *n.* a labor organization composed of industrial unions founded in 1938, it merged with the AFL in 1955. (p. 508)

Congress of Racial Equality [rā′shəl ĭ-kwŏl′ĭ-tē] **(CORE)** *n.* an interracial group founded in 1942 by James Farmer to work against segregation in Northern cities. (p. 593)

conquistador [kŏng-kē′stə-dôr′] *n.* one of the Spaniards who traveled to the Americas as an explorer and conqueror in the 16th century. (p. 16)

conscientious objector [kŏn′shē-ĕn′shəs ŏb-jĕk′tər] *n.* a person who refuses, on moral grounds, to participate in warfare. (p. 386)

conscription [kən-skrĭp′shən] *n.* the drafting of citizens for military service. (p. 173)

conservation [kŏn′sûr-vā′shən] *n.* the planned management of natural resources, involving the protection of some wilderness areas and the development of others for the common good. (p. 323)

conservative coalition [kən-sûr′və-tĭv kō′ə-lĭsh′ən] *n.* an alliance formed in the mid-1960s of right-wing groups opposed to big government. (p. 831)

consolidation (kən-sŏl′ĭ-dā′shən) *n.* the act of uniting or combining. (p. 240)

consumerism [kən-sōō′mə-rĭz′əm] *n.* a preoccupation with the purchasing of material goods. (p. 648)

containment [kən-tān′mənt] *n.* the blocking of another nation's attempts to spread its influence—especially the efforts of the United States to block the spread of Soviet influence during the late 1940s and early 1950s. (p. 605)

Contract [kŏn′trăkt′] **with America** *n.* a document that was drafted by Representative Newt Gingrich and signed by more than 300 Republican candidates in 1994, setting forth the Republicans' conservative legislative agenda. (p. 864)

Contras [kŏn′trəz] *n.* Nicaraguan rebels who received assistance from the Reagan administration in their efforts to overthrow the Sandinista government in the 1980s. (p. 851)

convoy [kŏn′voi′] **system** *n.* the protection of merchant ships from U-boat—German submrine—attacks by having the ships travel in large groups escorted by warships. (p. 383)

counterculture [koun′tər-kŭl′chər] *n.* the culture of the young people who rejected mainstream American society in the 1960s, seeking to create an alternative society based on peace, love, and individual freedom. (p. 781)

credibility [krĕd′ə-bĭl′ĭ-tē] **gap** *n.* a public distrust of statements made by the government. (p. 741)

credit [krĕd′ĭt] *n.* an arrangement in which a buyer pays later for a purchase, often on an installment plan with interest charges. (p. 466)

Crédit Mobilier [krĕd′ĭt mō-bēl′yər] *n.* a construction company formed in 1864 by owners of the Union Pacific Railroad, who used it to fraudulently skim off railroad profits for themselves. (p. 238)

D

Dawes [dôz] **Act** *n.* a law, enacted in 1887, that was intended to "Americanize" Native Americans by distributing reservation land to individual owners. (p. 206)

D-Day *n.* a name given to June 6, 1944—the day on which the Allies launched an invasion of the European mainland during World War II. (p. 574)

debt peonage [dĕt′ pē′ə-nĭj] *n.* a system in which workers are bound in servitude until their debts are paid. (p. 289)

Declaration [dĕk′lə-rā′shən] **of Independence** *n.* the document, written by Thomas Jefferson in 1776, in which the delegates of the Continental Congress declared the colonies' independence from Britain. (p. 53)

de facto segregation [dĭ făk′tō sĕg′rĭ-gā′shən] *n.* racial separation established by practice and custom, not by law. (p. 718)

deficit [dĕf′ĭ-sĭt] **spending** *n.* a government's spending of more money than it receives in revenue. (p. 492)

de jure segregation [dē jŏŏr′ē sĕg′rĭ-gā′shən] *n.* racial separation established by law. (p. 718)

Democratic-Republican *n.* political party known for its support of strong state governments, founded by Thomas Jefferson in 1792 in opposition to the Federalist Party. (pp. 76, 112)

deregulation *n.* the cutting back of federal regulation of industry. (p. 837)

détente [dā-tänt′] *n.* the flexible policy, involving a willingness to negotiate and an easing of tensions, that was adopted by President Richard Nixon and his adviser Henry Kissinger in their dealings with communist nations. (p. 799)

direct relief [rĭ-lēf′] *n.* the giving of money or food by the government directly to needy people. (p. 475)

Dixiecrat [dĭk′sē-krăt′] *n.* one of the Southern delegates who, to protest President Truman's civil rights policy, walked out of the 1948 Democratic National Convention and formed the States' Rights Democratic Party. (p. 638)

dollar diplomacy [dĭ-plō′mə-sē] *n.* the U.S. policy of using the nation's economic power to exert influence over other countries. (p. 363)

domino theory [dŏm′ə-nō′ thē′ə-rē] *n.* the idea that if a nation falls under communist control, nearby nations will also fall under communist control. (p. 731)

dotcom *n.* a business related to or conducted on the Internet. (p. 871)

double standard *n.* a set of principles granting greater sexual freedom to men than to women. (p. 441)

dove [dŭv] *n.* a person who opposed the Vietnam War and believed that the United States should withdraw from it. (p. 746)

Dow Jones [dou′ jōnz′] **Industrial Average** *n.* a measure based on the prices of the stocks of 30 large companies, widely used as a barometer of the stock market's health. (p. 467)

downsize [doun′sīz′] *v.* to dismiss numbers of permanent employees in an attempt to make operations more efficient and save money. (p. 870)

draft *n.* required enrollment in the armed services. (p. 742)

Dust Bowl *n.* the region, including Texas, Oklahoma, Kansas, Colorado, and New Mexico, that was made worthless for farming by drought and dust storms during the 1930s. (p. 474)

E

Earth Day *n.* a day set aside for environmental education, celebrated annually on April 22. (p. 821)

Economic Opportunity Act *n.* a law, enacted in 1964, that provided funds for youth programs, antipoverty measures, small-business loans, and job training. (p. 688)

egalitarianism [ĭ-găl′ĭ-târ′ē-ə-nĭz′əm] *n.* the belief that all people should have equal political, economic, social, and civil rights. (p. 63)

Eisenhower Doctrine [ī′zən-hou′ər dŏk′trĭn] *n.* a U.S. commitment to defend the Middle East against attack by any communist country, announced by President Dwight D. Eisenhower in 1957. (p. 625)

Emancipation Proclamation [prŏk′lə-mā′shən] *n.* an executive order issued by Abraham Lincoln on January 1, 1863, freeing the slaves in all regions behind Confederate lines. (p. 172)

encomienda [ĕng-kô-myĕn′dä] *n.* a system in which Spanish authorities granted colonial landlords the service of Native Americans as forced laborers. (p. 16)

Enlightenment [ĕn-līt′n-mənt] *n.* an 18th-century intellectual movement that emphasized the use of reason and the scientific method as means of obtaining knowledge. (p. 35)

entitlement [ĕn-tīt′l-mənt] **program** *n.* a government program—such as Social Security, Medicare, or Medicaid—that guarantees and provides benefits to a specific group. (p. 831)

entrepreneur [ŏn′trə-prə-nûr′] *n.* a person who organizes, operates, and assumes the risk for a business venture. (p. 140)

environmentalist [ĕn-vī′rən-mĕn′tl-ĭst] *n.* a person who works to protect the environment from destruction and pollution. (p. 822)

Environmental Protection Agency (EPA) *n.* a federal agency established in 1970 for the regulation of water and air pollution, toxic waste, pesticides, and radiation. (p. 837)

Equal Rights Amendment (ERA) *n.* a proposed and failed amendment to the U.S. Constitution that would have prohibited any government discrimination on the basis of sex. (p. 779)

Espionage and Sedition [ĕs′pē-ə-näzh′ ənd sĭ-dĭsh′ən] **Acts** *n.* two laws, enacted in 1917 and 1918, that imposed harsh penalties on anyone interfering with or speaking against U.S. participation in World War I. (p. 392)

exoduster [ĕk′sə-dŭs′tər] *n.* an African American who migrated from the South to Kansas in the post-Reconstruction years. (p. 215)

extortion *n.* illegal use of one's official position to obtain property or funds. (p. 269)

F

Fair Deal *n.* President Harry S. Truman's economic program—an extension of Franklin Roosevelt's New Deal—which included measures to increase the minimum wage, to extend social security coverage, and to provide housing for low-income families. (p. 639)

Family Assistance Plan *n.* a welfare-reform proposal, approved by the House of Representatives in 1970 but defeated in the Senate, that would have guaranteed an income to welfare recipients who agreed to undergo job training and to accept work. (p. 795)

Farmers' Alliances *n.* groups of farmers, or those in sympathy with farming issues, who sent lecturers from town to town to educate people about agricultural and rural issues. (p. 221)

fascism [făsh′ĭz′əm] *n.* a political philosophy that advocates a strong, centralized, nationalistic government headed by a powerful dictator. (p. 530)

Federal Communications Commission (FCC) *n.* an agency that regulates U.S. communications industries, including radio and television broadcasting. (p. 653)

Federal Deposit Insurance Corporation (FDIC) *n.* an agency created in 1933 to insure individuals' bank accounts, protecting people against losses due to bank failures. (p. 517)

Federal Home Loan Bank Act *n.* a law, enacted in 1931, that lowered home mortgage rates and allowed farmers to refinance their loans and avoid foreclosure. (p. 481)

federalism *n.* a political system in which a national government and constituent units, such as state governments, share power. (p. 68)

Federalist [fĕd′ər-ə-lĭst] *n.* a supporter of the Constitution and of a strong national government. (p. 69)

Federal Reserve System *n.* a national banking system, established in 1913, that controls the U.S. money supply and the availability of credit in the country. (p. 334)

Federal Securities [sĭ-kyŏŏr′ĭ-tēz] **Act** *n.* a law, enacted in 1933, that required corporations to provide complete, accurate information on all stock offerings. (p. 490)

Federal Trade Commission (FTC) *n.* a federal agency established in 1914 to investigate and stop unfair business practices. (p. 333)

feminism [fĕm′ə-nĭz′əm] *n.* the belief that women should have economic, political, and social equality with men. (p. 776)

Fifteenth Amendment *n.* an amendment to the U.S. Constitution, adopted in 1870, that prohibits the denial of voting rights to people because of their race or color or because they have previously been slaves. (p. 186)

flapper *n.* one of the free-thinking young women who embraced the new fashions and urban attitudes of the 1920s. (p. 441)

flexible response [flĕk′sə-bəl rĭ-spŏns′] *n.* a policy, developed during the Kennedy administration, that involved preparing for a variety of military responses to international crises rather than focusing on the use of nuclear weapons. (p. 673)

Foraker [fôr′ə-kər] **Act** *n.* legislation passed by Congress in 1900, in which the U.S. ended military rule in Puerto Rico and set up a civil government. (p. 353)

Fordney-McCumber Tariff [fôrd′nē mə-kŭm′bər tăr′ĭf] *n.* a set of regulations, enacted by Congress in 1922, that raised taxes on imports to record levels in order to protect American businesses against foreign competition. (p. 420)

Fourteen Points *n.* the principles making up President Woodrow Wilson's plan for world peace following World War I. (p. 399)

Fourteenth Amendment *n.* an amendment to the U.S. Constitution, adopted in 1868, that makes all persons born or naturalized in the United States—including former slaves—citizens of the country and guarantees equal protection of the laws. (p. 185)

franchise [frăn′chīz′] *n.* a business that has bought the right to use a parent company's name and methods, thus becoming one of a number of similar businesses in various locations. (p. 642)

Freedmen's Bureau [frēd-mĕnz byŏŏr′ō] *n.* a federal agency set up to help former slaves after the Civil War. (p. 184)

freedom rider *n.* one of the civil rights activists who rode buses through the South in the early 1960s to challenge segregation. (p. 710)

Freedom Summer *n.* a 1964 project to register African-American voters in Mississippi. (p. 715)

free enterprise [ĕn′tər-prīz′] *n.* the economic system in which private businesses and individuals control the means of production. (p. 140)

Free Speech Movement *n.* an antiestablishment New Left organization that originated in a 1964 clash between students and administrators at the University of California at Berkeley. (p. 744)

French and Indian War *n.* a conflict in North America, lasting from 1754 to 1763, that was a part of a worldwide struggle between France and Britain and that ended with the defeat of France and the transfer of French Canada to Britain. (p. 37)

Fundamentalism [fŭn′də-mĕn′tl-ĭz′əm] *n.* a Protestant religious movement grounded in the belief that all the stories and details in the Bible are literally true. (p. 438)

G

General Agreement on Tariffs and Trade (GATT) [găt] *n.* an international agreement first signed in 1947. In 1994, the U.S. and other countries adopted a new version of GATT. This treaty lowered trade barriers, such as tariffs, and created the World Trade Organization, which resolves trade disputes. (p. 872)

genetic engineering [jə-nĕt′ĭk ĕn′jə-nîr′ĭng] *n.* the alteration of the molecular biology of organisms' cells in order to create new varieties of bacteria, plants, and animals. (p. 880)

Geneva Accords [jə-nē′və ə-kôrdz′] *n.* a 1954 peace agreement that divided Vietnam into Communist-controlled North Vietnam and non-Communist South Vietnam until unification elections could be held in 1956. (p. 732)

genocide [jĕn′ə-sīd′] *n.* the deliberate and systematic extermination of a particular racial, national, or religious group. (p. 544)

Gentlemen's Agreement *n.* a 1907–1908 agreement by the government of Japan to limit Japanese emigration to the United States. (p. 259)

gentrification [jĕn′trə-fĭ-kā′shən] *n.* the process of restoring deteriorated urban property by middle-class people, which often results in the displacement of lower-income residents. (p. 883)

Gettysburg Address [gĕt′ēz-bûrg′ ə-drĕs′] *n.* a famous speech delivered by Abraham Lincoln in November 1863, at the dedication of a national cemetery on the site of the Battle of Gettysburg. (p. 177)

ghetto [gĕt′ō] *n.* a city neighborhood in which a certain minority group is pressured or forced to live. (p. 545)

GI Bill of Rights *n.* a name given to the Servicemen's Readjustment Act, a 1944 law that provided financial and educational benefits for World War II veterans. (pp. 592, 635)

glasnost [gläs′nəst] *n.* the open discussion of social problems that was permitted in the Soviet Union in the 1980s. (p. 849)

Glass-Steagall [glăs′ stē′gəl] **Act** *n.* the 1933 law that established the Federal Deposit Insurance Corporation to protect individuals' bank accounts. (p. 490)

gold standard *n.* a monetary system in which the basic unit of currency is defined in terms of a set amount of gold. (p. 222)

Gone with the Wind *n.* a 1939 movie dealing with the life of Southern plantation owners during the Civil War—one of the most popular films of all time. (p. 511)

graft *n.* the illegal use of political influence for personal gain. (p. 269)

grandfather clause *n.* a provision that exempts certain people from a law on the basis of previously existing circumstances—especially a clause formerly in some Southern states' constitutions that exempted whites from the strict voting requirements used to keep African Americans from the polls. (p. 287)

Grange [grānj] *n.* the Patrons of Husbandry—a social and educational organization through which farmers attempted to combat the power of the railroads in the late 19th century. (p. 221)

Grapes of Wrath, The *n.* a novel by John Steinbeck, published in 1939, that deals with a family of Oklahomans who leave the Dust Bowl for California. (p. 514)

Great Awakening *n.* a revival of religious feeling in the American colonies during the 1730s and 1750s. (p. 35)

Great Depression *n.* a period, lasting from 1929 to 1940, in which the U.S. economy was in severe decline and millions of Americans were unemployed. (p. 469)

Great Migration [mī-grā′shən] *n.* the large-scale movement of African Americans from the South to Northern cities in the early 20th century. (p. 393)

Great Plains *n.* the vast grassland that extends through the central portion North America, from Texas northward to Canada, east of the Rocky Mountains. (p. 202)

Great Society *n.* President Lyndon B. Johnson's program to reduce poverty and racial injustice and to promote a better quality of life in the United States. (p. 689)

H

Haight-Ashbury [hāt′ ăsh′bĕr-ē] *n.* a San Francisco district that became the "capital" of the hippie counterculture during the 1960s. (p. 782)

Harlem Renaissance [här′ləm rĕn′ĭ-säns′] *n.* a flowering of African-American artistic creativity during the 1920s, centered in the Harlem community of New York City. (p. 454)

hawk *n.* a person who supported U.S. involvement in the Vietnam War and believed that the United States should use increased military force to win it. (p. 746)

Hawley-Smoot Tariff [hô′lē smo͞ot′ tăr′ĭf] **Act** *n.* a law, enacted in 1930, that established the highest protective tariff in U.S. history, worsening the depression in America and abroad. (p. 471)

H-bomb *n.* the hydrogen bomb—a thermonuclear weapon much more powerful than the atomic bomb. (p. 623)

Ho Chi Minh [hō′ chē′ mĭn′] **Trail** *n.* a network of paths used by North Vietnam to transport supplies to the Vietcong in South Vietnam. (p. 732)

Hollywood Ten *n.* ten witnesses from the film industry who refused to cooperate with the HUAC's investigation of Communist influence in Hollywood. (p. 617)

Holocaust [hŏl′ə-kôst′] *n.* the systematic murder—or genocide—of Jews and other groups in Europe by the Nazis before and during World War II. (p. 542)

Homestead [hōm′stĕd′] **Act** *n.* a U.S. law enacted in 1862, that provided 160 acres in the West to any citizen or intended citizen who was head of household and would cultivate the land for five years; a law whose passage led to record numbers of U.S. settlers claiming private property which previously had been reserved by treaty and by tradition for Native American nomadic dwelling and use; the same law strengthened in 1889 to encourage individuals to exercise their private property rights and develop homesteads out of the vast government lands. (p. 215)

horizontal integration [hôr′ĭ-zŏn′tl ĭn′tĭ-grā′shən] *n.* the merging of companies that make similar products. (p. 242)

hot line *n.* a communication link established in 1963 to allow the leaders of the United States and the Soviet Union to contact each other in times of crisis. (p. 678)

House Un-American Activities Committee (HUAC) [hyo͞o′ăk′] *n.* a congressional committee that investigated Communist influence inside and outside the U.S. government in the years following World War II. (p. 617)

human rights *n.* the rights and freedoms, such as those named in the Declaration of Independence and the Bill of Rights, to which all people are entitled. (p. 815)

I

immigration [ĭm′ĭ-grā′shən] *n.* coming to and settling in a country of which one is not a native. (p. 142)

Immigration Act of 1965 *n.* a law that increased the number of immigrants allowed to settle in the United States. (p. 691)

impeachment *n.* the process of accusing a public official of wrongdoing. (p. 802)

imperialism [ĭm-pîr′ē-ə-lĭz′əm] *n.* the policy of extending a nation's authority over other countries by economic, political, or military means. (p. 342)

impressment [ĭm-prĕs′mənt] *n.* the forcible seizure of men for military service. (p. 114)

incandescent [ĭn′kən-dĕs′ənt] *adj.* giving off visible light as a result of being heated. (p. 232)

income tax *n.* a tax on earnings. (p. 174)

indentured [ĭn-dĕn′chərd] **servant** *n.* a person who has contracted to work for another for a limited period, often in return for travel expenses, shelter, and sustenance. (p. 23)

Industrial Workers of the World (IWW) *n.* a labor organization for unskilled workers, formed by a group of radical unionists and socialists in 1905. (p. 246)

inflation [ĭn-flā′shən] *n.* an increase in prices or decline in purchasing power caused by an increase in the supply of money. (p. 60)

information superhighway [so͞o′pər-hī′wā] *n.* a computer communications network linking people and institutions throughout the world, providing individuals with services such as libraries, shopping, movies, and news. (p. 877)

INF Treaty *n.* the Intermediate-Range Nuclear Forces Treaty—a 1987 agreement between the United States and the Soviet Union that eliminated some weapons systems and allowed for on-site inspection of military installations. (p. 849)

initiative [ĭ-nĭsh′ə-tĭv] *n.* a procedure by which a legislative measure can be originated by the people rather than by lawmakers. (p. 312)

installment [ĭn-stôl′mənt] **plan** *n.* an arrangement in which a purchaser pays over an extended time, without having to put down much money at the time of purchase. (p. 426)

Internet [ĭn′tər-nĕt′] *n.* a worldwide network, originally developed by the U.S. Department of Defense, that links computers and allows almost immediate communication of texts, pictures, and sounds. (p. 877)

internment *n.* confinement or a restriction in movement, especially under wartime conditions. (p. 594)

Interstate [ĭn′tər-stāt′] **Commerce Act** *n.* a law, enacted in 1887, that established the federal government's right to supervise railroad activities and created a five-member Interstate Commerce Commission to do so. (p. 239)

iron curtain [ī′ərn kûr′tn] *n.* a phrase used by Winston Churchill in 1946 to describe an imaginary line that separated Communist countries in the Soviet bloc of Eastern Europe from countries in Western Europe. (p. 605)

Iroquois [ĭr′ə-kwoi′] *n.* a group of Native American peoples inhabiting the woodlands of the Northeast. (p. 6)

Islam [ĭs-läm′] *n.* a religion founded in Arabia in A.D. 622 by the prophet Muhammad; its believers are called Muslims. (p. 9)

isolationism [ī′sə-lā′shə-nĭzm] *n.* opposition to political and economic entanglements with other countries. (p. 412)

J

Jacksonian democracy [jăk-sō′nē-an dĭ-mŏk′rə-sē] *n.* Jackson's political philosophy, based on his belief that common people were the source of American strength. (p. 123)

Japanese American Citizens League (JACL) *n.* an organization that pushed the U.S. government to compensate Japanese Americans for property they had lost when they were interned during World War II. (p. 595)

jazz *n.* a style of music characterized by the use of improvisation. (p. 657)

Jeffersonian republicanism [jĕf′ər-sō′nē-ən rĭ-pŭb′lĭ-kə-nĭz′əm] *n.* Jefferson's theory of government, which held that a simple government best suited the needs of the people. (p. 113)

Jim Crow laws *n.* laws enacted by Southern state and local governments to separate white and black people in public and private facilities. (p. 287)

joint-stock companies *n.* businesses in which investors pool their wealth for a common purpose. (p. 21)

judicial review *n.* the Supreme Court's power to declare an act of Congress unconstitutional. (p. 113)

Judiciary [jo͞o-dĭsh′ ē-ĕr′ē] **Act of 1789** *n.* a law that established the federal court system and the number of Supreme Court justices and that provided for the appeal of certain state court decisions to the federal courts. (p. 74)

Jungle, The *n.* a novel by Upton Sinclair, published in 1906, that portrays the dangerous and unhealthy conditions prevalent in the meatpacking industry at that time. (p. 317)

K

kamikaze [kä′mĭ-kä′zē] *adj.* involving or engaging in the deliberate crashing of a bomb-filled airplane into a military target. (p. 581)

Kent State University *n.* an Ohio university where National Guardsmen opened fire on students protesting the Vietnam War on May 4, 1970, wounding nine and killing four. (p. 756)

Kerner [kûr′nər] **Commission** *n.* a group that was appointed by President Johnson to study the causes of urban violence and that recommended the elimination of de facto segregation in American society. (p. 722)

King Philip's War *n.* a conflict, in the years 1675–1676, between New England colonists and Native American groups allied under the leadership of the Wampanoag chief Metacom. (p. 25)

Kongo [kŏng′gō] *n.* a group of small kingdoms along the Zaire River in West-Central Africa, united under a single leader in the late 1400s. (p. 9)

Korean [kə-rē′ən] **War** *n.* a conflict between North Korea and South Korea, lasting from 1950 to 1953, in which the United States, along with other UN countries, fought on the side of the South Koreans and China fought on the side of the North Koreans. (p. 611)

Kristallnacht [krĭ-stäl′näKHt′] *n.* "night of broken glass," a name given to the night of November 9, 1938, when gangs of Nazi storm troopers attacked Jewish homes, businesses, and synagogues in Germany. (p. 543)

Ku Klux Klan [ko͞o′ klŭks klăn′] **(KKK)** *n.* a secret organization that used terrorist tactics in an attempt to restore white supremacy in Southern states after the Civil War. (p. 188)

L

La Raza Unida [lä rä′sä o͞o-nē′dä] *n.* a Latino political organization founded in 1970 by José Angel Gutiérrez. (p. 770)

League of Nations *n.* an association of nations established in 1920 to promote international cooperation and peace. (p. 399)

Lend-Lease Act *n.* a law, passed in 1941, that allowed the United States to ship arms and other supplies, without immediate payment, to nations fighting the Axis powers. (p. 552)

Limited Test Ban Treaty *n.* the 1963 treaty in which the United States and the Soviet Union agreed not to conduct nuclear-weapons tests in the atmosphere. (p. 678)

long drive *n.* the moving of cattle over trails to a shipping center. (p. 210)

longhorn [lông′hôrn′] *n.* a breed of sturdy, long-horned cattle brought by the Spanish to Mexico and suited to the dry conditions of the Southwest. (p. 208)

Louisiana Purchase *n.* the 1803 purchase by the United States of France's Louisiana Territory—extending from the Mississippi River to the Rocky Mountains—for $15 million. (p. 114)

Lowell textile [lō′əl tĕks′tīl′] **mills** *n.* 19th-century mills for the manufacture of cloth, located in Lowell, Massachusetts, that mainly employed young women. (p. 142)

Loyalist [loi′ə-lĭst] *n.* a colonist who supported the British government during the American Revolution. (p. 59)

Lusitania [lo͞o′sĭ-tā′nē-ə] *n.* a British passenger ship that was sunk by a German U-boat in 1915. (p. 378)

M

mandate [măn′dāt′] *n.* the authority to act that an elected official receives from the voters who elected him or her. (p. 680)

Manhattan Project [măn-hăt′n prŏj′ĕkt′] *n.* the U.S. program to develop an atomic bomb for use in World War II. (p. 567)

manifest destiny [măn′ə-fĕst′ dĕs′tə-nē] *n.* the 19th-century belief that the United States would inevitably expand westward to the Pacific Ocean and into Mexican territory. (p. 131)

Marbury* v. *Madison [mär′bûr-ē vûr′səs măd′ĭ-sən] *n.* an 1803 case in which the Supreme Court ruled that it had the power to abolish legislative acts by declaring them unconstitutional; this power came to be known as judicial review. (p. 113)

market revolution *n.* the major change in the U.S. economy produced by people's beginning to buy and sell goods rather than make them for themselves. (p. 139)

Marshall [mär′shəl] **Plan** *n.* the program, proposed by Secretary of State George Marshall in 1947, under which the United States supplied economic aid to European nations to help them rebuild after World War II. (p. 606)

mass media [mē′dē-ə] *n.* the means of communication—such as television, newspapers, and radio—that reach large audiences. (p. 652)

mass transit *n.* transportation systems designed to move large numbers of people along fixed routes. (p. 264)

McCarthyism [mə-kär′thē-ĭz′əm] *n.* the attacks, often unsubstantiated, by Senator Joseph McCarthy and others on people suspected of being Communists in the early 1950s. (p.620)

Meat Inspection Act *n.* a law, enacted in 1906, that established strict cleanliness requirements for meatpackers and created a federal meat-inspection program. (p. 320)

Medicaid [mĕd′ĭ-kād′] *n.* a program, established in 1965, that provides health insurance for people on welfare. (p. 690)

Medicare [mĕd′ĭ-kâr′] *n.* a federal program, established in 1965, that provides hospital insurance and low-cost medical insurance to Americans aged 65 and over. (p. 690)

melting pot *n.* a mixture of people from different cultures and races who blend together by abandoning their native languages and cultures. (p. 258)

mercantilism [mûr′kən-tē-lĭz′əm] *n.* an economic system in which nations seek to increase their wealth and power by obtaining large amounts of gold and silver and by establishing a favorable balance of trade. (p. 28)

mestizo [mĕs-tē′zō] *adj.* of mixed Spanish and Native American ancestry. (p. 16)

middle passage *n.* the voyage that brought enslaved Africans to the West Indies and later to North America. (p. 32)

militarism [mĭl′ĭ-tə-rĭz′əm] *n.* the policy of building up armed forces in aggressive preparedness for war and their use as a tool of diplomacy. (p. 373)

Missouri Compromise [kŏm′prə-mīz′] *n.* a series of agreements passed by Congress in 1820–1821 to maintain the balance of power between slave states and free states. (p. 122)

Monroe Doctrine [mən-rō′ dŏk′trĭn] *n.* a policy of U.S. opposition to any European interference in the affairs of the Western Hemisphere, announced by President Monroe in 1823. (p. 117)

Moral Majority [môr′əl mə-jôr′ĭ-tē] *n.* a political alliance of religious groups, consisting mainly of evangelical and fundamentalist Christians, that was active in the 1970s and 1980s, condemning liberal attitudes and behavior and raising money for conservative candidates. (p. 831)

Morrill [môr′əl] **Acts** *n.* laws enacted in 1862 and 1890 to help create agricultural colleges by giving federal land to states. (p. 217)

muckraker [mŭk′rā′kər] *n.* one of the magazine journalists who exposed the corrupt side of business and public life in the early 1900s. (p. 308)

Munn* v. *Illinois [mŭn′ vûr′səs ĭl′ə-noi′] *n.* an 1877 case in which the Supreme Court upheld states' regulation of railroads for the benefit of farmers and consumers, thus establishing the right of government to regulate private industry to serve the public interest. (p. 239)

My Lai [mē′ lī′] *n.* a village in northern South Vietnam where more than 200 unarmed civilians, including women and children, were massacred by U.S. troops in May 1968. (p. 756)

N

NAACP [ĕn′ dŭb′əl ā′ sē′ pē′] *n.* the National Association for the Advancement of Colored People—an organization founded in 1909 to promote full racial equality. (p. 325)

NACW *n.* the National Association of Colored Women—a social service organization founded in 1896. (p. 315)

NAFTA [năf′tə] *n.* the North American Free Trade Agreement—a 1993 treaty that lowered tariffs and brought Mexico into the free-trade zone established by the United States and Canada. (p. 864)

napalm [nā′päm′] *n.* a gasoline-based substance used in bombs that U.S. planes dropped in Vietnam in order to burn away jungle and expose Vietcong hideouts. (p. 739)

NASDAQ [năz′dăk′] *n.* the National Association of Securities Dealers Automated Quotation System—a stock exchange for over-the-counter sales, comprised largely of technology companies. (p. 871)

National Energy Act *n.* a law, enacted during the Carter administration, that established a tax on "gas-guzzling" automobiles, removed price controls on U.S. oil and natural gas, and provided tax credits for the development of alternative energy sources. (p. 813)

National Industrial Recovery Act (NIRA) *n.* a law enacted in 1933 to establish codes of fair practice for industries and to promote industrial growth. (p. 491)

nationalism *n.* a devotion to the interests and culture of one's nation. (p. 373)

National Labor Relations Board (NLRB) *n.* an agency created in 1935 to prevent unfair labor practices and to mediate disputes between workers and management. (p. 518)

National Organization for Women (NOW) *n.* an organization founded in 1966 to pursue feminist goals, such as better child-care facilities, improved educational opportunities, and an end to job discrimination. (p. 778)

National Trades' Union *n.* the first national association of trade unions, formed in 1834. (p. 143)

National Youth Administration *n.* an agency that provided young Americans with aid and employment during the Great Depression. (p. 499)

Nation of Islam [ĭs-läm′] *n.* a religious group, popularly known as the Black Muslims, founded by Elijah Muhammad to promote black separatism and the Islamic religion. (p. 719)

nativism [nā′tĭ-vĭz′əm] *n.* favoring the interests of native-born people over foreign-born people. (pp. 258, 412)

Navigation [năv′ĭ-gā′shən] **Acts** *n.* a series of laws enacted by Parliament, beginning in 1651, to tighten England's control of trade in its American colonies. (p. 28)

NAWSA *n.* the National American Woman Suffrage Association—an organization founded in 1890 to gain voting rights for women. (p. 316)

Nazism [nät′sĭz′əm] *n.* the political philosophy—based on extreme nationalism, racism, and militaristic expansionism—that Adolf Hitler put into practice in Germany from 1933 to 1945. (p. 531)

Neutrality Acts *n.* a series of laws enacted in 1935 and 1936 to prevent U.S. arms sales and loans to nations at war. (p. 535)

New Deal *n.* President Franklin Roosevelt's program to alleviate the problems of the Great Depression, focusing on relief for the needy, economic recovery, and financial reform. (p. 489)

New Deal Coalition [kō′ə-lĭsh′ən] *n.* an alliance of diverse groups—including Southern whites, African Americans, and unionized workers—who supported the policies of the Democratic Party in the 1930s and 1940s. (p. 507)

New Federalism [fĕd′ər-ə-lĭz′əm] *n.* President Richard Nixon's program to turn over part of the federal government's power to state and local governments. (p. 795)

New Frontier *n.* President John F. Kennedy's legislative program, which included proposals to provide medical care for the elderly, to rebuild blighted urban areas, to aid education, to bolster the national defense, to increase international aid, and to expand the space program. (p. 677)

New Left *n.* a youth-dominated political movement of the 1960s, embodied in such organizations as Students for a Democratic Society and the Free Speech Movement. (p. 744)

New Right *n.* a late-20th-century alliance of conservative special-interest groups concerned with cultural, social, and moral issues. (p. 831)

Niagara Movement *n.* founded by W. E. B. Du Bois in 1905 to promote the education of African Americans in the liberal arts. (p. 285)

Nineteenth Amendment *n.* an amendment to the U.S. Constitution, adopted in 1920, that gives women the right to vote. (p. 335)

nomadic *adj.* having no fixed home, moving from place to place according to seasons and availability of food and water. (p. 5)

"no man's land" *n.* an unoccupied region between opposing armies. (p. 376)

nonaggression [nŏn′ə-grĕsh′ən] **pact** *n.* an agreement in which two nations promise not to go to war with each other. (p. 539)

North Atlantic Treaty Organization (NATO) *n.* a defensive military alliance formed in 1949 by ten Western European countries, the United States, and Canada. (p. 608)

Northwest Ordinance [ôr′dn-əns] **of 1787** *n.* a law that established a procedure for the admission of new states to the Union. (p. 67)

nullification [nŭl′ə-fĭ-kā′shən] *n.* a state's refusal to recognize an act of Congress that it considers unconstitutional. (p. 79)

Nuremberg [no͝or′əm-bûrg′] **trials** *n.* the court proceedings held in Nuremberg, Germany, after World War II, in which Nazi leaders were tried for war crimes. (p. 586)

O

Office of Price Administration (OPA) *n.* an agency established by Congress to control inflation during World War II. (p. 567)

Ohio gang *n.* a group of close friends and political supporters whom President Warren G. Harding appointed to his cabinet. (p. 420)

OPEC [ō′pĕk′] *n.* the Organization of Petroleum Exporting Countries—an economic association of oil-producing nations that is able to set oil prices. (p. 799)

Open Door notes *n.* messages sent by Secretary of State John Hay in 1899 to Germany, Russia, Great Britain, France, Italy, and Japan, asking the countries not to interfere with U.S. trading rights in China. (p. 356)

Operation Desert Storm [dĕz′ərt stôrm′] *n.* a 1991 military operation in which UN forces, led by the United States, drove Iraqi invaders from Kuwait. (p. 855)

Oregon Trail *n.* a route from Independence, Missouri, to Oregon City, Oregon, used by pioneers traveling to the Oregon Territory. (p. 131)

P

Panama Canal [păn′ə-mä′ kə-năl′] *n.* an artificial waterway cut through the Isthmus of Panama to provide a shortcut between the Atlantic and Pacific oceans, opened in 1914. (p. 360)

parity [păr′ĭ-tē] *n.* a government-supported level for the prices of agricultural products, intended to keep farmers' incomes steady. (p. 518)

Patriot [pā′trē-ət] *n.* a colonist who supported American independence from Britain. (p. 59)

patronage [pā′trə-nĭj] *n.* an officeholder's power to appoint people—usually those who have helped him or her get elected—to positions in government. (p. 270)

pay equity [ĕk′wĭ-tē] *n.* the basing of an employee's salary on the requirements of his or her job rather than on the traditional pay scales that have frequently provided women with smaller incomes than men. (p. 842)

Payne-Aldrich Tariff [pān′ ôl′drĭch tăr′ĭf] *n.* a set of tax regulations, enacted by Congress in 1909, that failed to significantly reduce tariffs on manufactured goods. (p. 329)

Peace Corps *n.* an agency established in 1961 to provide volunteer assistance to developing nations in Asia, Africa, and Latin America. (p. 680)

Pendleton [pĕn′dl-tən] **Civil Service Act** *n.* a law, enacted in 1883, that established a bipartisan civil service commission to make appointments to government jobs by means of the merit system. (p. 270)

Pentagon [pĕn′tə-gŏn′] **Papers** *n.* a 7,000-page document—leaked to the press in 1971 by the former Defense Department worker Daniel Ellsberg—revealing that the U.S. government had not been honest about its intentions in the Vietnam War. (p. 757)

perestroika [pĕr′ĭ-stroi′kə] *n.* the restructuring of the economy and the government instituted in the Soviet Union in the 1980s. (p. 849)

planned obsolescence [ŏb′sə-lĕs′əns] *n.* the designing of products to wear out or to become outdated quickly, so that people will feel a need to replace their possessions frequently. (p. 648)

Platt [plăt] **Amendment** *n.* a series of provisions that, in 1901, the United States insisted Cuba add to its new constitution, commanding Cuba to stay out of debt and giving the United States the right to intervene in the country and the right to buy or lease Cuban land for naval and fueling stations. (p. 354)

Plessy* v. *Ferguson [plĕs′ē vûr′səs fûr′gə-sən] *n.* an 1896 case in which the Supreme Court ruled that separation of the races in public accommodations was legal, thus establishing the "separate but equal" doctrine. (p. 287)

political machine *n.* an organized group that controls a political party in a city and offers services to voters and businesses in exchange for political and financial support. (p. 268)

poll [pōl] **tax** *n.* an annual tax that formerly had to be paid in some Southern states by anyone wishing to vote. (p. 287)

popular sovereignty [sŏv′ər-ĭn-tē] *n.* a system in which the residents vote to decide an issue. (p. 157)

Populism [pŏp′yə-lĭz′əm] *n.* a late-19th-century political movement demanding that people have a greater voice in government and seeking to advance the interests of farmers and laborers. (p. 221)

price support *n.* the maintenance of a price at a certain level through government intervention. (p. 465)

Proclamation [prŏk′lə-mā′shən] **of 1763** *n.* an order in which Britain prohibited its American colonists from settling west of the Appalachian Mountains. (p. 39)

progressive [prə-grĕs′ĭv] **movement** *n.* an early-20th-century reform movement seeking to return control of the government to the people, to restore economic opportunities, and to correct injustices in American life. (p. 307)

prohibition [prō′ə-bĭsh′ən] *n.* the banning of the manufacture, sale, and possession of alcoholic beverages. (p. 307)

Prohibition [prō′ə-bĭsh′ən] *n.* The period from 1920–1933 during which the Eighteenth Amendment forbidding the manufacture and sale of alcohol was in force in the United States. (p. 436)

propaganda [prŏp′ə-găn′də] *n.* a kind of biased communication designed to influence people's thoughts and actions. (p. 390)

Proposition 187 *n.* a bill passed in California in 1994 that ended all education and nonemergency health benefits to illegal immigrants. (p. 886)

protective tariff [prə-tĕk′tĭv tăr′ĭf] *n.* a tax on imported goods that is intended to protect a nation's businesses from foreign competition. (p. 76)

protectorate [prə-tĕk′tə-rĭt] *n.* a country whose affairs are partially controlled by a stronger power. (p. 354)

Pueblo [pwĕb′lō] *n.* a group of Native American peoples—descendants of the Anasazi—inhabiting the deserts of the Southwest. (p. 6)

Pure Food and Drug Act *n.* a law enacted in 1906 to halt the sale of contaminated foods and drugs and to ensure truth in labeling. (p. 322)

Puritan [pyo͝or′ĭ-tn] *n.* a member of a group that wanted to eliminate all traces of Roman Catholic ritual and traditions in the Church of England. (p. 24)

Q

Quaker [kwā′kər] *n.* a member of the Society of Friends, a religious group persecuted for its beliefs in 17th-century England. (p. 26)

quota [kwō′tə] **system** *n.* a system that sets limits on how many immigrants from various countries a nation will admit each year. (p. 415)

R

ratification [răt′ə-fĭ-kā′shən] *n.* the official approval of the Constitution, or of an amendment, by the states. (p. 69)

rationing [răsh′ə-nĭng] *n.* a restriction of people's right to buy unlimited amounts of particular foods and other goods, often implemented during wartime to ensure adequate supplies for the military. (p. 568)

Reaganomics [rā′gə-nŏm′ĭks] *n.* the economic policies of President Ronald Reagan, which were focused on budget cuts and the granting of large tax cuts in order to increase private investment. (p. 834)

realpolitik [rā-äl′pō′lĭ-tēk′] *n.* a foreign policy advocated by Henry Kissinger in the Nixon administration based on consideration of a nation's power rather than its ideals or moral principles. (p. 799)

reapportionment [rē′ə-pôr′shən-mənt] *n.* the redrawing of election districts to reflect changes in population. (p. 691)

recall [rĭ-kôl′] *n.* a procedure for removing a public official from office by a vote of the people. (p. 312)

Reconstruction [rē′kən-strŭk′shən] *n.* the period of rebuilding that followed the Civil War, during which the defeated Confederate states were readmitted to the Union. (p. 184)

Reconstruction Finance [fə-năns′] **Corporation (RFC)** *n.* an agency established in 1932 to provide emergency financing to banks, life-insurance companies, railroads, and other large businesses. (p. 481)

referendum [rĕf′ə-rĕn′dəm] *n.* a procedure by which a proposed legislative measure can be submitted to a vote of the people. (p. 312)

Reformation [rĕf′ər-mā′shən] *n.* a religious movement in 16th-century Europe, growing out of a desire for reform in the Roman Catholic Church and leading to the establishment of various Protestant churches. (p. 10)

Renaissance [rĕn′ĭ-säns′] *n.* a period of European history, lasting from about 1400 to 1600, during which renewed interest in classical culture led to far-reaching changes in art, learning, and views of the world. (p. 11)

reparations [rĕp′ə-rā′shənz] *n.* the compensation paid by a defeated nation for the damage or injury it inflicted during a war. (p. 400)

republic [rĭ-pŭb′lĭk] *n.* a government in which the citizens rule through elected representatives. (p. 67)

Republic of California *n.* the nation proclaimed by American settlers in California when they declared their independence from Mexico in 1846. (p. 136)

revenue [rĕv′ə-nōō] **sharing** *n.* the distribution of federal money to state and local governments with few or no restrictions on how it is spent. (p. 795)

reverse discrimination [dĭ-skrĭm′ə-nā′shən] *n.* an unfair treatment of members of a majority group—for example, white men—resulting from efforts to correct discrimination against members of other groups. (p. 831)

rock 'n' roll [rŏk′ən-rōl′] *n.* a form of American popular music that evolved in the 1950s out of rhythm and blues, country, jazz, gospel, and pop; the American musical form characterized by heavy rhythms and simple melodies which has spread worldwide having significant impacts on social dancing, clothing fashions, and expressions of protest. (p. 655)

Roosevelt Corollary [rō′zə-vĕlt′ kôr′ə-lĕr-ē] *n.* an extension of the Monroe Doctrine, announced by President Theodore Roosevelt in 1904, under which the United States claimed the right to protect its economic interests by means of military intervention in the affairs of Western Hemisphere nations. (p. 362)

Rough Riders *n.* a volunteer cavalry regiment, commanded by Leonard Wood and Theodore Roosevelt, that served in the Spanish-American War. (p. 350)

rural free delivery (RFD) *n.* the free government delivery of mail and packages to homes in rural areas, begun in 1896. (p. 297)

S

SALT I [sôlt′ wŭn′] **Treaty** *n.* a five-year agreement between the United States and the Soviet Union, signed in 1972, that limited the nations' numbers of intercontinental ballistic missiles and submarine-launched missiles. (p. 801)

Sandinista [săn′dĭ-nēs′tə] *adj.* belonging to a leftist rebel group that overthrew the Nicaraguan government in 1979. (p. 851)

Santa Fe [săn′tə fā′] **Trail** *n.* a route from Independence, Missouri, to Santa Fe, New Mexico, used by traders in the early and mid-1800s. (p. 131)

satellite [săt′l-īt′] **nation** *n.* a country that is dominated politically and economically by another nation. (p. 605)

Saturday Night Massacre [măs′ə-kər] *n.* a name given to the resignation of the U.S. attorney general and the firing of his deputy in October 1973, after they refused to carry out President Nixon's order to fire the special prosecutor investigating the Watergate affair. (p. 805)

scalawag [skăl′ə-wăg′] *n.* a white Southerner who joined the Republican Party after the Civil War. (p. 186)

scientific management *n.* the application of scientific principles to increase efficiency in the workplace. (p. 308)

Scopes [skōps] **trial** *n.* a sensational 1925 court case in which the biology teacher John T. Scopes was tried for challenging a Tennessee law that outlawed the teaching of evolution. (p. 438)

search-and-destroy mission [sûrch′ ənd′ dĭ-stroi′ mĭsh′ən] *n.* a U.S. military raid on a South Vietnamese village, intended to root out villagers with ties to the Vietcong but often resulting in the destruction of the village and the displacement of its inhabitants. (p. 739)

secession [sĭ-sĕsh′ən] *n.* the formal withdrawal of a state from the Union. (p. 157)

Securities and Exchange [sĭ-kyŏŏr′ĭ-tēz ənd ĭks-chānj′] **Commission (SEC)** *n.* an agency, created in 1934, that monitors the stock market and enforces laws regulating the sale of stocks and bonds. (p. 517)

segregation [sĕg′rĭ-gā′shən] *n.* the separation of people on the basis of race. (p. 287)

Selective [sĭ-lĕk′tĭv] **Service Act** *n.* a law, enacted in 1917, that required men to register for military service. (p. 382)

Seneca Falls [sĕn′ĭ-kə fôlz′] **Convention** *n.* a women's rights convention held in Seneca Falls, New York, in 1848. (p. 149)

service sector [sĕk′tər] *n.* the part of the economy that provides consumers with services rather than goods. (p. 870)

settlement house *n.* a community center providing assistance to residents—particularly immigrants—in a slum neighborhood. (p. 266)

Seventeenth Amendment *n.* an amendment to the U.S. Constitution, adopted in 1913, that provides for the election of U.S. senators by the people rather than by state legislatures. (p. 312)

shantytown [shăn′tē-toun′] *n.* a neighborhood in which people live in makeshift shacks. (p. 473)

sharecropping [shâr′krŏp′ĭng] *n.* a system in which landowners give farm workers land, seed, and tools in return for a part of the crops they raise. (p. 188)

Shays's [shā′zəz] **Rebellion** *n.* an uprising of debt-ridden Massachusetts farmers protesting increased state taxes in 1787. (p. 67)

Sherman Antitrust [shûr′mən ăn′tē-trŭst′] **Act** *n.* a law, enacted in 1890, that was intended to prevent the creation of monopolies by making it illegal to establish trusts that interfered with free trade. (p. 244)

silent majority [mə-jôr′ĭ-tē] *n.* a name given by President Richard Nixon to the moderate, mainstream Americans who quietly supported his Vietnam War policies. (p. 756)

sit-in *n.* a form of demonstration used by African Americans to protest discrimination, in which the protesters sit down in a segregated business and refuse to leave until they are served. (p. 706)

Social Darwinism [sō′shəl där′wĭ-nĭz′əm] *n.* an economic and social philosophy—supposedly based on the biologist Charles Darwin's theory of evolution by natural selection—holding that a system of unrestrained competition will ensure the survival of the fittest. (p. 242)

Social Gospel [gŏs′pəl] **movement** *n.* a 19th-century reform movement based on the belief that Christians have a responsibility to help improve working conditions and alleviate poverty. (p. 266)

Social Security Act *n.* a law enacted in 1935 to provide aid to retirees, the unemployed, people with disabilities, and families with dependent children. (p. 501)

soddy [sŏd′ē] *n.* a home built of blocks of turf. (p. 216)

soup kitchen *n.* a place where free or low cost food is served to the needy. (p. 473)

Southern Christian Leadership Conference (SCLC) *n.* an organization formed in 1957 by Dr. Martin Luther King, Jr., and other leaders to work for civil rights through nonviolent means. (p. 706)

Southern strategy *n.* President Nixon's attempt to attract the support of Southern conservative Democrats who were unhappy with federal desegregation policies and the liberal Supreme Court. (p. 797)

speakeasy [spēk′ē′zē] *n.* a place where alcoholic drinks were sold and consumed illegally during Prohibition. (p. 436)

speculation [spĕk′yə-lā′shən] *n.* an involvement in risky business transactions in an effort to make a quick or large profit. (p. 467)

Square Deal *n.* President Theodore Roosevelt's program of progressive reforms designed to protect the common people against big business. (p. 319)

stagflation [stăg-flā′shən] *n.* an economic condition marked by both inflation and high unemployment. (p. 798)

Stamp Act *n.* a 1765 law in which Parliament established the first direct taxation of goods and services within the British colonies in North America. (p. 47)

Strategic Defense Initiative [strə-tē′jĭk dĭ-fĕns′ ĭ-nĭsh′ə-tĭv] **(SDI)** *n.* a proposed defense system—popularly known as Star Wars—intended to protect the United States against missile attacks. (p. 835)

strike *n.* a work stoppage intended to force an employer to respond to demands. (p. 142)

Student Nonviolent Coordinating [nŏn-vī′ə-lənt kō-ôr′dn-ā′tĭng] **Committee (SNCC)** [snĭk] *n.* an organization formed in 1960 to coordinate sit-ins and other protests and to give young blacks a larger role in the civil rights movement. (p. 706)

Students for a Democratic Society (SDS) *n.* an antiestablishment New Left group, founded in 1960, that called for greater individual freedom and responsibility. (p. 744)

suburb [sŭb′ûrb′] *n.* a residential town or community near a city. (p. 635)

suffrage [sŭf′rĭj] *n.* the right to vote. (p. 315)

Sugar Act *n.* a trade law enacted by Parliament in 1764 in an attempt to reduce smuggling in the British colonies in North America. (p. 47)

supply-side economics *n.* the idea that a reduction of tax rates will lead to increases in jobs, savings, and investments, and therefore to an increase in government revenue. (p. 835)

T

Taino [tī′nō] *n.* a Native American people of the Caribbean islands—the first group encountered by Columbus and his men when they reached the Americas. (p. 14)

Teapot Dome scandal [skăn′dl] *n.* Secretary of the Interior Albert B. Fall's secret leasing of oil-rich public land to private companies in return for money and land. (p. 421)

Telecommunications [tĕl′ĭ-kə-myo͞o′nĭ-kā′shənz] **Act of 1996** *n.* a law enacted in 1996 to remove barriers that had previously prevented communications companies from engaging in more than one type of communications business. (p. 878)

telecommute [tĕl′ĭ-kə-myo͞ot′] *v.* to work at home for a company located elsewhere, by using such communications technologies as computers, the Internet, and fax machines. (p. 878)

tenement [tĕn′ə-mənt] *n.* a multifamily urban dwelling, usually overcrowded and unsanitary. (p. 264)

Tennessee Valley Authority (TVA) *n.* a federal corporation established in 1933 to construct dams and power plants in the Tennessee Valley region to generate electricity as well as to prevent floods. (p. 519)

termination [tûr′mə-nā′shən] **policy** *n.* the U.S. government's plan, announced in 1953, to give up responsibility for Native American tribes by eliminating federal economic support, discontinuing the reservation system, and redistributing tribal lands. (p. 663)

Tet offensive [tĕt′ ə-fĕn′sĭv] *n.* a massive surprise attack by the Vietcong on South Vietnamese towns and cities early in 1968. (p. 749)

Texas Revolution *n.* the 1836 rebellion in which Texas gained its independence from Mexico. (p. 134)

Thirteenth Amendment *n.* an amendment to the U.S. Constitution, adopted in 1865, that has abolished slavery and involuntary servitude. (p. 183)

Tiananmen [tyän′än′mĕn′] **Square** *n.* the site of 1989 demonstrations in Beijing, China, in which Chinese students demanded freedom of speech and a greater voice in government. (p. 850)

Tonkin Gulf [tŏn′kĭn′ gŭlf′] **Resolution** *n.* a resolution adopted by Congress in 1964, giving the president broad powers to wage war in Vietnam. (p. 735)

totalitarian [tō-tăl′ĭ-târ′ē-ən] *adj.* characteristic of a political system in which the government exercises complete control over its citizens' lives. (p. 529)

Trail of Tears [tîrz] *n.* the marches in which the Cherokee people were forcibly removed from Georgia to the Indian Territory in 1838–1840, with thousands of the Cherokee dying on the way. (p. 124)

transcendentalism [trăn′sĕn-dĕn′tl-ĭz′əm] *n.* a philosophical and literary movement of the 1800s that emphasized living a simple life and celebrated the truth found in nature and in personal emotion and imagination. (p. 145)

transcontinental [trăns′kŏn-tə-nĕn′tl] **railroad** *n.* a railroad line linking the Atlantic and Pacific coasts of the United States, completed in 1869. (p. 237)

Treaty of Fort Laramie *n.* the treaty requiring the Sioux to live on a reservation along the Missouri River. (p. 204)

Treaty of Guadalupe Hidalgo [gwäd′l-o͞op′ hĭ-däl′gō] *n.* the 1848 treaty ending the U.S. war with Mexico, in which Mexico ceded California and New Mexico to the United States. (p. 136)

Treaty of Paris (1783) *n.* the treaty that ended the Revolutionary War, confirming the independence of the United States and setting the boundaries of the new nation. (p. 62)

Treaty of Paris (1898) *n.* the treaty ending the Spanish-American War, in which Spain freed Cuba, turned over the islands of Guam and Puerto Rico to the United States, and sold the Philippines to the United States for $20 million. (p. 350)

Treaty of Tordesillas [tôr′də-sē′əs] *n.* the 1494 treaty in which Spain and Portugal agreed to divide the lands of the Western Hemisphere between them. (p. 15)

Treaty of Versailles [vər-sī′] *n.* the 1919 peace treaty at the end of World War I which established new nations, borders, and war reparations. (p. 400)

trench warfare *n.* military operations in which the opposing forces attack and counterattack from systems of fortified ditches rather than on an open battlefield. (p. 376)

triangular [trī-ăng′gyə-lər] **trade** *n.* the transatlantic system of trade in which goods and people, including slaves, were exchanged between Africa, England, Europe, the West Indies, and the colonies in North America. (p. 32)

Truman Doctrine [tro͞o′mən dŏk′trĭn] *n.* a U.S. policy, announced by President Harry S. Truman in 1947, of providing economic and military aid to free nations threatened by internal or external opponents. (p. 606)

Tuskegee [tŭs-kē′gē] **Normal and Industrial Institute** *n.* founded in 1881, and led by Booker T. Washington, to equip African Americans with teaching diplomas and useful skills in the trades and agriculture. (p. 285)

two-party system *n.* a political system dominated by two major parties. (p. 76)

U

Underground Railroad *n.* a system of routes along which runaway slaves were helped to escape to Canada or to safe areas in the free states. (p. 158)

Unitarian [yo͞o′nĭ-târ′ē-ən] *n.* member of a religious group that emphasizes reason and faith in the individual. (p. 145)

United Farm Workers Organizing Committee (UFWOC) *n.* a labor union formed in 1966 to seek higher wages and better working conditions for Mexican-American farm workers in California. (p. 770)

United Nations (UN) *n.* an international peacekeeping organization to which most nations in the world belong, founded in 1945 to promote world peace, security, and economic development. (p. 603)

urban [ûr′bən] **flight** *n.* a migration of people from cities to the surrounding suburbs. (p. 882)

urbanization [ûr′bə-nĭ-zā′shən] *n.* the growth of cities. (p. 262)

urban renewal [rĭ-no͞o′əl] *n.* the tearing down and replacing of buildings in rundown inner-city neighborhoods. (p. 661)

urban sprawl [sprôl′] *n.* the unplanned and uncontrolled spreading of cities into surrounding regions. (p. 424)

USS *Maine* *n.* a U.S. warship that mysteriously exploded and sank in the harbor of Havana, Cuba, on February 15, 1898. (p. 348)

U-2 incident *n.* the downing of a U.S. spy plane and capture of its pilot by the Soviet Union in 1960. (p. 627)

V

V-E Day *n.* a name given to May 8, 1945, "Victory in Europe Day" on which General Eisenhower's acceptance of the unconditional surrender of Nazi Germany marked the end of World War II in Europe. (p. 577)

vertical integration [vûr′tĭ-kəl ĭn′tĭ-grā′shən] *n.* a company's taking over its suppliers and distributors and transportation systems to gain total control over the quality and cost of its product. (p. 242)

Vietcong [vē-ĕt′kŏng′] *n.* the South Vietnamese Communists who, with North Vietnamese support, fought against the government of South Vietnam in the Vietnam War. (p. 732)

Vietminh [vē-ĕt′mĭn′] *n.* an organization of Vietnamese Communists and other nationalist groups that between 1946 and 1954 fought for Vietnamese independence from the French. (p. 731)

Vietnamization [vē-ĕt′nə-mĭ-zā′shən] *n.* President Nixon's strategy for ending U.S. involvement in the Vietnam War, involving the gradual withdrawal of U.S. troops and their replacement with South Vietnamese forces. (p. 755)

Voting Rights Act of 1965 *n.* a law that made it easier for African Americans to register to vote by eliminating discriminatory literacy tests and authorizing federal examiners to enroll voters denied at the local level. (p. 716)

W

Wagner [wăg′nər] **Act** *n.* a law—also known as the National Labor Relations Act—enacted in 1935 to protect workers' rights after the Supreme Court declared the National Industrial Recovery Act unconstitutional. (p. 499)

war-guilt [wôr′ gĭlt′] **clause** *n.* a provision in the Treaty of Versailles by which Germany acknowledged that it alone was responsible for World War I. (p. 400)

War Industries Board (WIB) *n.* an agency established during World War I to increase efficiency and discourage waste in war-related industries. (p. 389)

War Powers Act (WPA) *n.* a law enacted in 1973, limiting a president's right to send troops into battle without consulting Congress. (p. 761)

War Production Board (WPB) *n.* an agency established during World War II to coordinate the production of military supplies by U.S. industries. (p. 568)

Warren [wôr′ən] **Commission** *n.* a group, headed by Chief Justice Earl Warren, that investigated the assassination of President Kennedy and concluded that Lee Harvey Oswald was alone responsible for it. (p. 683)

Warren Court *n.* the Supreme Court during the period when Earl Warren was chief justice, noted for its activism in the areas of civil rights and free speech. (p. 691)

Warsaw [wôr′sô′] **Pact** *n.* a military alliance formed in 1955 by the Soviet Union and its Eastern European satellites. (p. 624)

Watergate [wô′tər-gāt′] *n.* a scandal arising from the Nixon administration's attempt to cover up its involvement in the 1972 break-in at the Democratic National Committee headquarters in the Watergate apartment complex. (p. 802)

Women's Auxiliary [ôg-zĭl′yə-rē] **Army Corps (WAAC)** *n.* U.S. army unit created during World War II to enable women to serve in noncombat positions. (p. 563)

Woodstock [wo͝od′stŏk′] *n.* a free music festival that attracted more than 400,000 young people to a farm in upstate New York in August 1969. (p. 783)

Works Progress Administration (WPA) *n.* an agency, established as part of the Second New Deal, that provided the unemployed with jobs in construction, garment making, teaching, the arts, and other fields. (p. 498)

X

XYZ Affair *n.* a 1797 incident in which French officials demanded a bribe from U.S. diplomats. (p. 78)

Y

yellow journalism [jûr′nə-lĭz′əm] *n.* the use of sensationalized and exaggerated reporting by newspapers or magazines to attract readers. (p. 347)

Z

Zimmermann [zĭm′ər-mən] **note** *n.* a message sent in 1917 by the German foreign minister to the German ambassador in Mexico, proposing a German-Mexican alliance and promising to help Mexico regain Texas, New Mexico, and Arizona if the United States entered World War I. (p. 379)

Spanish Glossary

A

abolition [abolición] *s.* movimiento para acabar con la esclavitud. (p. 144)

affirmative action [acción afirmativa] *s.* medidas para corregir los efectos de la discriminación anterior; favorecen a grupos que estaban en desventaja. (pp. 723, 831)

Agent Orange [Agente Naranja] *s.* químico tóxico exfoliante que fumigaron las tropas estadounidenses en Vietnam para poner al descubierto refugios del Vietcong. (p. 739)

Agricultural Adjustment Act [Ley de Ajustes Agrícolas] *s.* ley de 1933 que elevó el precio de las cosechas al pagarle a los granjeros para que no cultivaran cierta porción de sus tierras, reduciendo así la producción. (p. 491)

AIDS (acquired immune deficiency syndrome) [SIDA, síndrome de inmunodeficiencia adquirida] *s.* enfermedad causada por un virus que debilita el sistema inmunológico y hace que el cuerpo sea vulnerable a infecciones y formas poco comunes de cáncer. (p. 840)

Alamo, the [El Álamo] *s.* misión y fuerte situado en San Antonio, Texas, en donde fuerzas mexicanas masacraron a rebeldes texanos en 1836. (p. 134)

Alien and Sedition Acts [Leyes de Extranjeros y de Sedición] *s.* cuatro leyes aprobadas en 1798 para reducir el poder político de los nuevos inmigrantes a EE.UU. (p. 78)

Alliance for Progress [Alianza para el Progreso] *s.* programa de los sesenta para ofrecer ayuda económica a los países latinoamericanos. (p. 680)

Allies [Aliados] *s.* 1. en la I Guerra Mundial, naciones aliadas en un tratado contra Alemania y las otras Potencias Centrales; originalmente Gran Bretaña, Francia y Rusia; más adelante se unieron Estados Unidos, Japón, Italia y otros. (p. 396) 2. en la II Guerra Mundial, naciones asociadas contra el Eje, en particular Gran Bretaña, la Unión Soviética y Estados Unidos. (p. 554)

American Expeditionary Force (AEF) [Fuerza Americana de Expediciones] *s.* fuerzas dirigidas por el general John Pershing, quien lucho con los aliados en Europa durante la Primera Guerra Mundial. (p. 384)

American Federation of Labor (AFL) [Federación Norteamericana del Trabajo] *s.* sindicato de trabajadores calificados creado en 1886 y dirigido por Samuel Gompers. (p. 245)

American Indian Movement (AIM) [Movimiento Indígena Americano] *s.* organización con frecuencia militante creada en 1968 con el fin de luchar por los derechos de los amerindios. (p. 771)

Americanization movement [movimiento de americanización] *s.* programa educativo ideado para facilitar la asimilación de los inmigrantes a la cultura estadounidense. (p. 263)

American System [Sistema Americano] *s.* programa económico previo a la Guerra Civil diseñado para fortalecer y unificar a Estados Unidos por medio de aranceles proteccionistas, un banco nacional y un sistema de transporte eficiente. (p. 122)

anarchist [anarquista] *s.* persona que se opone a toda forma de gobierno. (p. 413)

Anasazi *s.* grupo amerindio que vivió cerca de la región de Four Corners —donde Arizona, New Mexico, Colorado y Utah se unen— de los años 100 a 1400 d.C., aproximadamente. (p. 5)

Antifederalist [antifederalista] *s.* oponente de la Constitución y de un gobierno central fuerte. (p. 69)

appeasement [apaciguamiento] *s.* política de ceder a las demandas de una potencia hostil con el fin de mantener la paz. (p. 538)

Appomattox Court House *s.* pueblo cerca de Appomatox, Virginia, donde Lee se rindió a Grant el 9 de abril de 1865. (37°N 79°O) (p. 181)

arbitration [arbitraje] *s.* método de resolver disputas en el cual ambos lados someten sus diferencias a un juez elegido por las dos partes. (p. 245)

armistice [armisticio] *s.* tregua o acuerdo para terminar un conflicto armado. (p. 387)

Army of the Republic of Vietnam (ARVN) [Ejército de la República de Vietnam] *s.* soldados del sur de Vietnam que lucharon junto a soldados estadounidenses contra el comunismo y las fuerzas del norte de Vietnam durante la Guerra de Vietnam. (p. 737)

Articles of Confederation [Artículos de la Confederación] *s.* documento aprobado por el Segundo Congreso Continental en 1777 y ratificado por los estados finalmente en 1781. Detallaba la forma del gobierno de los nuevos Estados Unidos. (p. 67)

Ashcan school *s.* grupo de artistas estadounidenses de principios del siglo XX que a menudo pintaban escenas realistas de la vida urbana —como arrabales y gente sin hogar— ganándose así el nombre de la escuela del basurero. (p. 295)

assimilation [asimilación] *s.* adopción, por parte de un grupo minoritario, de las creencias y estilo de vida de la cultura dominante. (p. 206)

Atlantic Charter [Carta del Atlántico] *s.* declaración de principios de 1941 en que Estados Unidos y Gran Bretaña establecieron sus objetivos contra las Potencias del Eje. (p. 554)

Axis powers [Potencias del Eje] *s.* países unidos contra los Aliados en la II Guerra Mundial, que incluyeron a Alemania, Italia y Japón. (p. 551)

Aztec [azteca] *s.* pueblo amerindio que colonizó el Valle de México en 1200 A.C. y desarrolló un gran imperio. (p. 5)

B

baby boom *s.* marcado aumento en el índice de natalidad en Estados Unidos después de la II Guerra Mundial. (p. 643)

Battle of the Bulge [Batalla del Bolsón] *s.* batalla de un mes de duración en la II Guerra Mundial durante la cual los Aliados rompieron la última gran ofensiva alemana de la guerra. (p. 576)

Battle of Midway [Batalla de Midway] *s.* batalla de la Segunda Guerra Mundial que ocurrió a principios de junio en 1942. Los aliados redujeron la flotilla japonesa en Midway, una isla al Noreste de Hawai. A partir de esta batalla los aliados tomaron la ofensiva y comenzaron a moverse a Japón. (p. 579)

Battle of Wounded Knee [Batalla de Wounded Knee] *s.* masacre de 300 indígenas desarmados en Wounded Knee Creek, South Dakota, en 1890. (p. 208)

Beatles, the *s.* conjuntó inglés que tuvo gran influencia en la música popular en los años 60. (p. 783)

beat movement [movimiento beat] *s.* movimiento social y literario de los años 50 que enfatizó la expresión literaria sin reglas y la disconformidad. (p. 655)

Benin *s.* reino de África occidental que existió en la actual Nigeria; floreció en los bosques del delta del Níger del siglo 14 al 17. (p. 9)

Berlin airlift [puente aéreo de Berlín] *s.* operación de 327 días de duración, en la que aviones estadounidenses y británicos llevaron alimentos y provisiones a Berlín Occidental después de que la Unión Soviética bloqueó la ciudad en 1948. (p. 607)

Berlin Wall [Muro de Berlín] *s.* muro de concreto que separó Berlín Oriental y Occidental de 1961 a 1989; construido por Alemania Oriental para impedir que sus ciudadanos se escaparan al occidente. (p. 677)

Bessemer process [método Bessemer] *s.* técnica más eficiente y barata de fabricar acero, desarrollada hacia 1850. (p. 231)

Bill of Rights [Carta de Derechos] *s.* primeras diez enmiendas a la Constitución que identifican los derechos de los ciudadanos; se adoptaron en 1791. (p. 70)

bimetallism [bimetalismo] *s.* sistema monetario nacional que utiliza el oro y la plata para respaldar la moneda. (p. 222)

blacklist [lista negra] *s.* lista de unos 500 actores, escritores, productores y directores a quienes no se permitía trabajar en películas de Hollywood debido a sus supuestos vínculos comunistas. (p. 618)

Black Panthers [Panteras Negras] *s.* organización política afroamericana militante formada por Huey Newton y Bobby Seale en 1966 para luchar contra la violencia de la policía y suministrar servicios en el ghetto. (p. 720)

Black Power [Poder Negro] *s.* consigna usada por Stokely Carmichael en los años 60, que pedía poder político y social para los afroamericanos. (p. 720)

Black Tuesday [Martes Negro] *s.* octubre 29 de 1929, día en que los precios de las acciones bajaron drásticamente. (p. 468)

blitzkrieg *s.* proveniente de la palabra alemana que significa "guerra relámpago". Repentina ofensiva de fuerzas aéreas y terrestres a gran escala con el fin de obtener una victoria rápida. (p. 539)

bonanza farm [granja de bonanza] *s.* extensa granja dedicada a un solo cultivo. (p. 218)

Bonus Army *s.* grupo de veteranos de la I Guerra Mundial que marcharon en Washington, D.C., en 1932 para exigir bonos prometidos a cambio de su servicio militar. (p. 482)

bootlegger *s.* persona que contrabandeaba bebidas alcohólicas durante la época de Prohibición. (p. 437)

Boston Massacre [Masacre de Boston] *s.* choque entre soldados británicos y colonos en Boston en 1770, durante el cual cinco colonos fueron asesinados. (p. 48)

Boston Tea Party [Motín del Té de Boston] *s.* protesta en 1773 contra el impuesto británico sobre el té; los colonos arrojaron 18,000 libras de té al puerto de Boston. (p. 49)

Boulder Dam [Presa de Boulder] *s.* presa del río Colorado construida durante la Depresión con fondos federales para estimular la economía; ahora llamada Presa Hoover. (p. 480)

Boxer Rebellion [Rebelión de los Boxer] *s.* rebelión encabezada en 1900 por los Boxer, sociedad secreta de China, para detener la difusión de la influencia occidental. (p. 357)

bracero *s.* trabajador mexicano que laboró temporalmente en Estados Unidos durante la Segunda Guerra Mundial. (p. 662)

bread line [cola para comer] *s.* fila de personas que esperan comida gratis. (p. 473)

brinkmanship *s.* práctica de amenazar al enemigo con represalias militares extremas ante cualquier agresión. (p. 623)

Brown* v. *Board of Education of Topeka *s.* decisión de la Suprema Corte en 1954 que declaró que la segregación de estudiantes negros y blancos era inconstitucional. (p. 702)

Bull Moose Party [Partido Bull Moose] *s.* apodo del Partido Progresista, bajo el que Theodore Roosevelt aspiró, sin éxito, a la presidencia en 1912. (p. 330)

buying on margin [compra con margen] *s.* compra de acciones en la que se paga sólo una porción del valor de la acción al vendedor o corredor de bolsa, y se presta el resto. (p. 467)

C

cabinet [gabinete] *s.* jefes de departamentos que son asesores directos del presidente. (p. 75)

Camp David Accords [Acuerdos de Camp David] *s.* acuerdos de paz históricos entre Israel y Egipto, negociados en Camp David, Maryland, en 1978. (p. 816)

carpetbagger *s.* norteños que se trasladaron al Sur después de la Guerra Civil. (p. 186)

Central Powers [Potencias Centrales] *s.* en la I Guerra Mundial, el grupo de naciones —Alemania, Austro-Hungría y el imperio otomano— que se opuso a los Aliados. (p. 374)

checks and balances [control y compensación de poderes] *s.* sistema en el cual cada rama del gobierno controla o restringe a las demás ramas. (p. 69)

Chinese Exclusion Act [Ley de Exclusión de Chinos] *s.* ley de 1882 que prohibía la inmigración de ciudadanos chinos, con la excepción de estudiantes, maestros, comerciantes, turistas y funcionarios gubernamentales. (p. 259)

Chisholm Trail [Sendero Chisholm] *s.* la ruta principal de ganado que iba desde San Antonio, Texas, por Oklahoma hasta Kansas. (p. 209)

chlorination [cloración] *s.* purificación del agua al mezclarla químicamente con cloro. (p. 264)

Christianity [cristianismo] *s.* religión basada en la vida y las enseñanzas de Jesucristo. (p. 10)

CIA *s.* Central Intelligence Agency (Agencia Central de Inteligencia), agencia gubernamental establecida para espiar y realizar operaciones secretas en países extranjeros. (p. 623)

Civilian Conservation Corps (CCC) [Cuerpo Civil de Conservación] *s.* agencia establecida como parte del New Deal con el fin de ocupar a jóvenes desempleados en trabajos como la construcción de carreteras y el cuidado de parques nacionales y ayudar en situaciones de emergencia. (p. 491)

Civil Rights Act of 1964 [Ley de Derechos Civiles de 1964] *s.* ley que prohíbe la discriminación en lugares públicos, en la educación y en los empleos por cuestión de raza, color, sexo, nacionalidad o religión. (p. 714)

Civil Rights Act of 1968 [Ley de Derechos Civiles de 1968] *s.* ley que prohíbe la discriminación en la vivienda. (p. 722)

civil service [servicio civil] *s.* cualquier servicio gubernamental en el que se obtiene un cargo mediante exámenes públicos. (p. 270)

Clayton Antitrust Act [Ley Antitrust Clayton] *s.* ley de 1914 que declaraba ilegales ciertas prácticas empresariales injustas y protegía el derecho de los sindicatos y organizaciones agrícolas. (p. 333)

Cold War [Guerra Fría] *s.* estado de hostilidad, sin llegar a conflictos armados, entre Estados Unidos y la Unión Soviética tras la II Guerra Mundial. (p. 606)

Columbian Exchange [Transferencia Colombina] *s.* transferencia —iniciada con el primer viaje de Colón a las Américas— de plantas, alimentos, animales y enfermedades entre el Hemisferio Occidental y el Hemisferio Oriental. (p. 15)

Committee to Reelect the President [Comité de Reelección del Presidente] *s.* grupo que dirigió la campaña para la reelección del presidente Nixon en 1972, cuya conexión con el allanamiento de la Sede Nacional del Partido Demócrata hizo estallar el escándalo Watergate. (p. 803)

Common Sense [Sentido común] *s.* folleto escrito en 1776 por Thomas Paine que exhortaba la separación de las colonias británicas. (p. 52)

Commonwealth* v. *Hunt *s.* caso judicial de 1842 en el cual la Suprema Corte de Massachusetts ratificó el derecho de los obreros a la huelga. (p. 143)

communism [comunismo] *s.* sistema económico y político basado en un gobierno de un solo partido y en la propiedad estatal. (p. 413)

concentration camp [campo de concentración] *s.* campamento de presos operado por la Alemania nazi para judíos y otros grupos que consideraba enemigos de Adolfo Hitler; a los presos los mataban o los hacían morir de hambre y a causa de trabajos forzados. (p. 546)

Confederacy [Estados Confederados de América] *s.* confederación formada en 1861 por los estados del Sur después de que se separaron de la unión. (p. 165)

conglomerate [conglomerado] *s.* corporación grande que posee compañías más pequeñas dedicadas a negocios diversos. (p. 642)

Congress of Industrial Organizations [Congreso de Organizaciones Industriales] *s.* organización sindical expulsada de la Federación Norteamericana del Trabajo en 1938. (p. 508)

Congress of Racial Equality (CORE) [Congreso de Igualdad Racial] *s.* grupo interracial, fundado por James Farmer en 1942, que luchaba contra la segregación en ciudades del Norte. (p. 593)

conquistador *s.* explorador y colonizador español de las Américas en el siglo 16. (p. 16)

conscientious objector [objetor de conciencia] *s.* persona que se opone a toda guerra por principio de conciencia. (p. 386)

conscription [conscripción] *s.* servicio militar obligatorio de ciertos miembros de la población. (p. 173)

conservation [conservación] *s.* práctica de preservar algunas zonas naturales y desarrollar otras por el bien común. (p. 323)

conservative coalition [coalición conservadora] *s.* alianza de grupos de ultraderecha opuestos a la ingerencia del gobierno formada a mediados de los años sesenta. (p. 831)

consolidation [consolidación] *s.* acto de unir o combinar. (p. 240)

consumerism [consumismo] *s.* gran interés en la compra de bienes materiales. (p. 648)

containment [contención] *s.* política estadounidense de formar alianzas con países más pequeños y débiles con el fin de bloquear la expansión de la infuencia soviética tras la II Guerra Mundial. (p. 605)

Contract with America [Contrato con América] *s.* documento elaborado por el representante Newt Gingrich y firmado por 300 candidatos republicanos el 27 de septiembre de 1994, que presentaba sus planes legislativos conservadores. (p. 864)

Contras [la contra] *s.* fuerzas anticomunistas nicaragüenses que recibieron asistencia de la administración Reagan para derrocar al gobierno sandinista de Nicaragua. (p. 851)

convoy system [flotilla de escolta] *s.* medio de proteger los buques mercantes del ataque de submarinos alemanes al hacer que viajaran con una escorta de destructores. (p. 383)

counterculture [contracultura] *s.* cultura de la juventud de los años 60 que rechazaba la sociedad tradicional y buscaba paz, amor y libertad individual. (p. 781)

credibility gap [falta de credibilidad] *s.* desconfianza del público en las declaraciones oficiales del gobierno. (p. 741)

credit [crédito] *s.* acuerdo en el que se compran artículos en el presente para ser pagados en el futuro mediante un plan de cuotas con intereses. (p. 466)

Crédit Mobilier *s.* compañía constructora formada en 1864 por los dueños de la Union Pacific Railroad; quienes la usaron ilegalmente para obtener ganancias. (p. 238)

D

Dawes Act [Ley Dawes] *s.* ley aprobada por el Congreso en 1887 para "americanizar" a los indígenas distribuyendo a individuos la tierra de las reservaciones. (p. 206)

D-Day [Día D] *s.* junio 6 de 1944, día en que los Aliados emprendieron una invasión por tierra, mar y aire contra el Eje. (p. 574)

debt peonage [deuda por peonaje] *s.* sistema de servidumbre en el que una persona es obligada a trabajar para pagar una deuda. (p. 289)

Declaration of Independence [Declaración de Independencia] *s.* documento escrito por Thomas Jefferson en 1776 en el cual los delegados del Congreso Continental declaron la independencia de las colonias de Gran Bretaña. (p. 53)

de facto segregation [segregación *de facto*] *s.* segregación racial impuesta por la práctica y la costumbre más que por las leyes. (p. 718)

deficit spending [gasto deficitario] *s.* práctica por parte de un gobierno de gastar más de lo que recibe por concepto de rentas públicas. (p. 492)

de jure segregation [segregación *de jure*] *s.* segregación racial impuesta por la ley. (p. 718)

Democratic-Republican [Demócrata-Republicano] *s.* partido político conocido por su apoyo a un fuerte gobierno estatal. Fue fundado por Thomas Jefferson en 1792 en oposición al Federalist Party [Partido Federalista]. (p. 76, 112)

deregulation [liberalización] *s.* acción de limitar el alcance de la regulación federal sobre la industria. (p. 837)

détente [distensión] *s.* política flexible con la intención de negociar y disminuir tensiones; fue adoptada por Richard Nixon y su consejero Henry Kissinger para tratar con países comunistas. (p. 799)

direct relief [ayuda directa] *s.* alimentos o dinero que el gobierno da directamente a los necesitados. (p. 475)

Dixiecrat *s.* delegado sureño que se retiró de la convención del Partido Demócrata en 1948 para protestar la plataforma del Presidente Truman sobre derechos civiles y formó un grupo denominado States' Rights Democratic Party. (p. 638)

dollar diplomacy [diplomacia del dólar] *s.* política de usar el poder económico o la influencia económica de Estados Unidos para alcanzar sus objetivos de política exterior en otros países. (p. 363)

domino theory [teoría del dominó] *s.* teoría que supone que si una nación se vuelve comunista, las naciones vecinas inevitablemente se volverán comunistas también. (p. 731)

dotcom [puntocom] *s.* negocio relacionado con el Internet o conducido a través de éste. (p. 871)

double standard [doble moral] *s.* conjunto de principios que permite mayor libertad sexual al hombre que a la mujer. (p. 441)

dove [paloma] *s.* persona que se oponía a la Guerra de Vietnam y creía que Estados Unidos debía retirarse. (p. 746)

Dow Jones Industrial Average [Promedio Industrial Dow Jones] *s.* medida que computa el valor de las acciones de 30 compañías grandes; se usa como barómetro de los mercados bursátiles. (p. 467)

downsize [recortar] *v.* despedir trabajadores de una organización con el fin de hacer las operaciones más eficientes y ahorrar dinero. (p. 870)

draft [reclutamiento] *s.* requisito de matrícula en las fuerzas armadas. (p. 742)

Dust Bowl *s.* región que incluye Texas, Oklahoma, Kansas, Colorado, y New Mexico que quedó inservible para la agricultura debido a la sequía y a las tormentas de arena durante los años 30. (p. 474)

E

Earth Day [Día de la Tierra] *s.* día dedicado a la educación ambiental que desde 1970 se celebra el 22 de abril de cada año. (p. 821)

Economic Opportunity Act [Ley de Oportunidades Económicas] *s.* ley promulgada en 1964, que adjudicó fondos a programas para la juventud, medidas para combatir la pobreza, préstamos para pequeños negocios y capacitación laboral. (p. 688)

egalitarianism [igualitarismo] *s.* creencia de que todas las personas deben tener igualdad de derechos políticos, económicos, sociales y civiles. (p. 63)

Eisenhower Doctrine [Doctrina Eisenhower] *s.* advertencia del presidente Eisenhower en 1957 de que Estados Unidos defendería el Oriente Medio contra el ataque de cualquier país comunista. (p. 625)

Emancipation Proclamation [Proclama de Emancipación] *s.* orden ejecutiva de Abraham Lincoln el 1º de enero de 1863 que abolía la esclavitud en los estados confederados. (p. 172)

encomienda *s.* institución colonial de España en las Américas que repartía indígenas a los conquistadores para hacer trabajos forzados. (p. 16)

Enlightenment [Ilustración] *s.* movimiento intelectual del siglo 18 que enfatizaba la razón y los métodos científicos para obtener conocimientos. (p. 35)

entitlement program [programa de subvención] *s.* programa gubernamental, como Social Security, Medicare y Medicaid, que brinda beneficios a grupos específicos. (p. 831)

entrepreneur [empresario] *s.* persona que organiza, opera y asume todo el riesgo de una ventura de negocios. (p. 140)

environmentalist [ambientalista] *s.* persona que procura proteger el medio ambiente de la destrucción y de la contaminación. (p. 822)

Environmental Protection Agency (EPA) [Agencia de Protección Ambiental] *s.* agencia federal establecida en 1970 para la regulación de la contaminación del agua y el aire, los desperdicios tóxicos, los pesticidas y la radiación. (p. 837)

Equal Rights Amendment (ERA) [Enmienda de Igualdad de Derechos] *s.* enmienda propuesta pero rechazada que hubiese prohibido la discriminación del gobierno en razón del sexo de una persona. (p. 779)

Espionage and Sedition Acts [Leyes de Espionaje y Sedición] *s.* dos leyes aprobadas en 1917 y 1918, que castigaban fuertemente a quienes criticaran o bloquearan la participación de Estados Unidos en la II Guerra Mundial. (p. 392)

exoduster *s.* afroamericano que emigró del Sur a Kansas después de la Reconstrucción. (p. 215)

extortion [extorsión] *s.* uso ilegal de un cargo público para obtener dinero o propiedad. (p. 269)

F

Fair Deal *s.* plan económico del presidente Truman que expandió el New Deal de Roosevelt; aumentó el salario mínimo, amplió el seguro social y le dio vivienda a familias de bajos recursos, entre otras medidas. (p. 639)

Family Assistance Plan [Plan de Asistencia Familiar] *s.* propuesta de reforma a los programas de beneficencia, aprobada por la Cámara de Representantes en 1970 pero rechazada por el Senado, que garantizaba un ingreso a los beneficiarios de ayuda pública que aceptaran capacitarse y emplearse en un oficio. (p. 795)

Farmers' Alliances [Alianzas de granjeros] *s.* grupos de granjeros o simpatizantes de éstos, que enviaban a oradores a viajar de pueblo a pueblo para educar a la gente sobre cuestiones agrarias y rurales. (p. 221)

fascism [fascismo] *s.* filosofía política que propone un gobierno fuerte, centralizado, nacionalista, caracterizado por una rígida dictadura unipartidista. (p. 530)

Federal Communications Commission (FCC) [Comisión Federal de Comunicaciones] *s.* agencia del gobierno que regula la industria de comunicaciones en EE.UU., incluso la transmisión de radio y televisión. (p. 653)

Federal Deposit Insurance Corporation (FDIC) [Corporación Federal de Seguros de Depósitos] *s.* agencia creada en 1933 para garantizar depósitos bancarios individuales cuando un banco quiebra. (p. 517)

Federal Home Loan Bank Act [Ley Federal para Préstamos de Vivienda] *s.* ley aprobada en 1931 que redujo las cuotas hipotecarias y permitió a los agricultores refinanciar sus préstamos para prevenir juicios hipotecarios. (p. 481)

federalism [federalismo] *s.* sistema político gubernamental en el cual el poder se comparte entre un gobierno nacional y las entidades que lo constituyen, como los gobiernos estatales. (p. 68)

Federalist [federalista] *s.* partidario de la Constitución y de un gobierno nacional fuerte. (p. 69)

Federal Reserve System [Sistema de la Reserva Federal] *s.* sistema bancario nacional establecido por Woodrow Wilson en 1913 que controla el dinero circulante del país. (p. 334)

Federal Securities Act [Ley Federal de Valores] *s.* ley de 1933 que obliga a las corporaciones a suministrar información completa y fidedigna sobre sus ofertas de acciones. (p. 490)

Federal Trade Commission (FTC) [Comisión Federal de Comercio] *s.* agencia federal establecida en 1914 para investigar y parar prácticas empresariales injustas. (p. 333)

feminism [feminismo] *s.* creencia de que la mujer debe tener igualdad económica, política y social con respecto al hombre. (p. 776)

Fifteenth Amendment [Enmienda 15] *s.* enmienda a la Constitución, adoptada en 1870, que establece que a nadie puede negársele el derecho al voto por motivos de raza, color o por haber sido esclavo. (p. 186)

flapper *s.* jovencita típica de los años 20 que actuaba y se vestía de manera atrevida y nada convencional. (p. 441)

flexible response [respuesta flexible] *s.* doctrina, desarrollada durante la administración Kennedy, de prepararse para una variedad de respuestas militares, en vez de concentrarse en las armas nuclerares. (p. 673)

Foraker Act [Ley Foraker] *s.* legislación que el Congreso aprobó en 1900 para acabar con el gobierno militar en Puerto Rico y autorizar un gobierno civil. (p. 353)

Fordney-McCumber Tariff [Arancel Fordney-McCumber] *s.* serie de reglas, aprobada por el Congreso en 1922, que elevó a niveles sin precedentes los impuestos a las importaciones en 1922 para proteger las compañías estadounidenses de la competencia extranjera. (p. 420)

Fourteen Points [los catorce puntos] *s.* plan del presidente Wilson en pro de la paz mundial tras la I Guerra Mundial. (p. 399)

Fourteenth Amendment [Enmienda 14] *s.* enmienda a la constitución adoptada en 1868 que hace ciudadano a toda persona nacida o naturalizada en Estados Unidos, incluso a antiguos esclavos, y garantiza igualdad de protección bajo la ley. (p. 185)

franchise [franquicia] *s.* forma de negocio en la que individuos compran el derecho a usar el nombre y los métodos de una compañía matriz, con lo que la compañía se multiplica. (p. 642)

Freedmen's Bureau [Oficina de libertos] *s.* agencia federal formada después de la Guerra Civil para ayudar a personas que habían sido esclavos antes. (p. 184)

freedom rider *s.* activista de derechos civiles que viajó en autobús a través del Sur a comienzos de los años 60 para protestar contra la segregación. (p. 710)

Freedom Summer *s.* campaña de registro de votantes afroamericanos en el verano de 1964 en Mississippi. (p. 715)

free enterprise [libre empresa] *s.* sistema económico en el que compañías privadas e individuos controlan los medios de producción. (p. 140)

Free Speech Movement [Movimiento de Libre Expresión] *s.* movimiento activista de los años 60 que surgió a raíz de un enfrentamiento entre los estudiantes y la administración de la Universidad de California en Berkeley en 1964. (p. 744)

French and Indian War [Guerra contra Franceses e Indígenas] *s.* guerra librada en Norteamérica (1757-1763) como parte de un conflicto mundial entre Francia y Gran Bretaña; finalizó con la derrota de Francia y el traspaso del Canadá francés a Gran Bretaña. (p. 37)

Fundamentalism [fundamentalismo] *s.* movimiento religioso protestante basado en la interpretación textual, o palabra por palabra, de las escrituras. (p. 438)

G

General Agreement on Tariffs and Trade (GATT) [Acuerdo General de Aranceles y Comercio] *s.* acuerdo internacional firmado inicialmente en 1947. En 1994, EE.UU. y otros países del mundo adoptaron una nueva versión de GATT. Este tratado redujo las barreras de comercio y los aranceles, como las tarifas, y creó la Organización Mundial de Comercio. (p. 872)

genetic engineering [ingeniería genética] *s.* alteración de la biología molecular de las células de un organismo para crear nuevas variedades de bacterias, plantas o animales. (p. 880)

Geneva Accords [Acuerdos de Ginebra] *s.* plan de paz de Indochina en 1954 en el que Vietnam fue dividido temporalmente en Vietnam del Norte y Vietnam del Sur, mientras se celebraban las elecciones de 1956. (p. 732)

genocide [genocidio] *s.* exterminio deliberado y sistemático de un grupo de personas por su raza, nacionalidad o religión. (p. 544)

Gentlemen's Agreement [Acuerdo de Caballeros] *s.* acuerdo concertado durante 1907 y 1908, mediante el cual el gobierno de Japón limitó la emigración a Estados Unidos. (p. 259)

gentrification [aburguesamiento] *s.* restauración de propiedades urbanas por personas de la clase media que a menudo resulta en la pérdida de vivienda para personas de medios escasos. (p. 883)

Gettysburg Address [Discurso de Gettysburg] *s.* famoso discurso de Abraham Lincoln durante la Guerra Civil al inaugurar un cementerio nacional en el campo de batalla de Gettysburg, Pennsylvania, el 19 de noviembre de 1863. (p. 177)

ghetto [gueto] *s.* tipo de vecindario urbano donde cierto grupo minoritario es obligado o forzado a vivir. (p. 545)

GI Bill of Rights [Carta de Derechos de los Veteranos] *s.* nombre dado a la Ley de Reajuste de Militares de 1944, que ofrecía beneficios financieros y educativos a los veteranos de la II Guerra Mundial. (pp. 592, 635)

glasnost *s.* la discusión abierta de problemas sociales que se dio en la Unión Soviética durante los años 80. (p. 849)

Glass-Steagall Banking Act [Ley Bancaria Glass-Steagall] *s.* ley de 1933 que aseguró los depósitos bancarios mediante la Corporación Federal de Seguros de Depósitos. (p. 490)

gold standard [patrón de oro] *s.* sistema monetario en el cual la unidad básica de moneda se define en relación a una cantidad fija de oro. (p. 222)

Gone with the Wind *[Lo que el viento se llevó]* *s.* película de 1939 sobre la vida de los dueños de plantaciones del Sur durante la Guerra Civil; una de las más populares de todos los tiempos. (p. 511)

graft [corrupción] *s.* uso ilegal de un cargo político con el fin de ganacia personal. (p. 269)

grandfather clause [cláusula del abuelo] *s.* estipulación que exime de cumplir una ley a ciertas personas por circunstancias previas; específicamente, cláusula de la constitución de algunos estados sureños que eximía a los blancos de los estrictos requisitos que impedían que los afroamericanos votaran. (p. 287)

Grange [la Granja] *s.* *The Patrons of Husbandry*—organización de granjeros que intentaron, a partir de la década de 1870, combatir el poder de los ferrocarriles. (p. 221)

Grapes of Wrath, The *[Las uvas de la ira]* *s.* novela de John Steinbeck, publicada en 1939, sobre una familia de Oklahoma que se va de la región del Dust Bowl a California. (p. 514)

Great Awakening [Gran Despertar] *s.* serie de grandes asambleas religiosas en las décadas de 1730 y 1750. (p. 35)

Great Depression [Gran Depresión] *s.* período de 1929 a 1940 en el que la economía estadounidense quebró y millones quedaron sin empleo. (p. 469)

Great Migration [Gran Migración] *s.* movimiento de cientos de miles de afroamericanos sureños a ciudades del Norte a principios del siglo 20. (p. 393)

Great Plains [Grandes Praderas] *s.* vasta pradera que se extiende a través de Norteamérica, de Texas a Canadá en dirección Norte y hacia el este de las Montañas Rocosas. (p. 202)

Great Society [Gran Sociedad] *s.* ambicioso programa legislativo del presidente Lyndon B. Johnson para reducir la pobreza y la injusticia racial, y mejorar el nivel de vida. (p. 689)

H

Haight-Ashbury *s.* distrito de San Francisco, "capital" de la contracultura hippie durante los años 60. (p. 782)

Harlem Renaissance [Renacimiento de Harlem] *s.* período de sobresaliente creatividad afroamericana durante los años 20 y 30, en la zona de Harlem en New York City. (p. 454)

hawk [halcón] *s.* persona que respaldaba la Guerra de Vietnam y creía que Estados Unidos debía incrementar su fuerza militar para ganarla. (p. 746)

Hawley–Smoot Tariff Act [Ley de Aranceles Hawley-Smoot] *s.* ley de 1930 que estableció los más altos aranceles proteccionistas en la historia estadounidense, afectando negativamente el comercio internacional y empeorando le depresión mundial y doméstica. (p. 471)

H-bomb [bomba de hidrógeno] *s.* bomba de hidrógeno, o termonuclear, mucho más poderosa que la bomba atómica. (p. 623)

Ho Chi Minh Trail [Sendero de Ho Chi Minh] *s.* red de caminos por la que Vietnam del Norte abastecía al Vietcong en Vietnam del Sur. (p. 732)

Hollywood Ten [los Diez de Hollywood] *s.* diez testigos de la industria cinematográfica que se negaron a cooperar con la investigación de influencia comunista en Hollywood. (p. 617)

Holocaust [Holocausto] *s.* asesinato sistemático o genocidio de judíos y de otros grupos en Europa por los nazis antes y durante la II Guerra Mundial. (p. 542)

Homestead Act [Ley de la Heredad] *s.* ley aprobada en 1862 que otorgaba 160 acres de tierra en el Oeste a cualquier ciudadano or ciudadano futuro que fuera cabeza de familia y que cultivara la tierra por cinco años; ley cuya aprobación llevó a un gran número de colonos estadounidenses a reclamar como propiedad privada tierra que había sido reservada por tratados y tradiciones para la vivienda de indígenas americanos; la misma ley, reforzada en 1889, dio incentivas para que los individuos ejercieran su derecho de propiedad privada y desarrollaran viviendas. (p. 215)

horizontal integration [integración horizontal] *s.* proceso mediante el cual compañías que fabrican productos similares se unen y reducen la competencia. (p. 242)

hot line [línea de emergencia] *s.* línea directa de comunicación establecida en 1963 para que los líderes de Estados Unidos y la Unión Soviética pudieran hablarse durante una crisis. (p. 678)

House Un-American Activities Committee (HUAC) [Comité de la Cámara de Representantes sobre Actividades Antiamericanas] *s.* comité del Congreso creado en 1938 que investigó la influencia comunista dentro y fuera del gobierno durante los años que siguieron la II Guerra Mundial. (p. 617)

human rights [derechos humanos] *s.* derechos y libertades considerados básicos, como los que establece la Declaración de Independencia y la Carta de Derechos. (p. 815)

I

immigration [inmigración] *s.* llegada a un país distinto al país natal para vivir en él. (p. 142)

Immigration Act of 1965 [Ley de Inmigración de 1965] *s.* ley que abrió las puertas a más inmigrantes. (p. 691)

impeachment [acusación] *s.* proceso por el cual se acusa a un funcionario público de delitos. (p. 802)

imperialism [imperialismo] *s.* política de controlar países por medios económicos, políticos o militares. (p. 342)

impressment [leva] *s.* práctica de reclutar hombres a la fuerza para prestar servicio militar. (p. 114)

incandescent [incandescente] *adj.* que emite luz visible como resultado de haber sido calentado (p. 232)

income tax [impuesto sobre la renta] *s.* impuesto que retiene un porcentaje específico de ingresos. (p. 174)

indentured servant [sirviente por contrato] *s.* inmigrante que, a cambio de un pasaje para las Américas, era contratado a trabajar por un periodo limite. (p. 23)

Industrial Workers of the World (IWW) *s.* sindicato de trabajadores de mano de obra no calificada creado en 1905. (p. 246)

inflation [inflación] *s.* fenómeno económico en el que hay un aumento constante en los precios por el incremento del dinero circulante; reduce el poder adquisitivo. (p. 60)

information superhighway [supercarretera de información] *s.* red de comunicación por computadoras para unir a personas e instituciones por todo el mundo y suministrar a individuos servicios de bibliotecas, compras, cines y noticias. (p. 877)

INF Treaty [Tratado sobre Fuerzas Nucleares Intermedias] *s.* tratado entre Estados Unidos y la Unión Soviética firmado en 1987, que eliminó algunas armas y permitió la inspección directa de emplazamientos de misiles. (p. 849)

initiative [iniciativa] *s.* reforma gubernamental que permite a los ciudadanos presentar proyectos de ley en el Congreso o en cuerpos legislativos estatales. (p. 312)

installment plan [pago a plazos] *s.* práctica de comprar a crédito mediante pagos regulares durante determinado período de tiempo. (p. 426)

Internet *s.* red mundial, originalmente diseñada por el Departamento de Defensa, que une computadores y permite una comunicación casi instantánea de textos, ilustraciones y sonidos. (p. 877)

internment [confinamiento] *s.* restricción de movimiento, en especial durante condiciones de guerra. (p. 594)

Interstate Commerce Act [Ley de Comercio Interestatal] *s.* ley de 1887 que restablecía el derecho del gobierno federal a supervisar los ferrocarriles; creó una Comisión de Comercio Interestatal de cinco miembros. (p. 239)

iron curtain [cortina de hierro] *s.* frase usada por Winston Churchill en 1946 para describir una línea imaginaria que separaba los países comunistas que estaban en la parte soviética al este de Europa de los países en Europa occidental. (p. 605)

Iroquois [iroqueses] *s.* grupo de pueblos amerindios que vivían en los bosques del Noreste. (p. 6)

Islam [islamismo] *s.* religión fundada en Arabia por el profeta Mahoma en el año 622; a sus seguidores se les llama musulmanes. (p. 9)

isolationism [aislacionismo] *s.* política que se opone a participar en conflictos políticos y económicos con otros países. (p. 412)

J

Jacksonian democracy [democracia Jacksoniana] *s.* filosofía política de Jackson, basada en su creencia de que la gente común y corriente era la fuente de la fortaleza nacional. (p. 123)

Japanese Americans Citizens League (JACL) [Sociedad de Ciudadanos Americano-Japoneses] *s.* organización que presionó al gobierno a compensar a los estadounidenses de origen japonés por las propiedades que perdieron al ser internados durante la II Guerra Mundial. (p. 595)

jazz *s.* estilo de música caracterizado por la improvisación. (p. 657)

Jeffersonian republicanism [republicanismo Jeffersoniano] *s.* teoría de gobierno de Jefferson; sostenía que un gobierno sencillo correspondía a las necesidades del pueblo. (p. 113)

Jim Crow laws [leyes Jim Crow] *s.* leyes impuestas por los gobiernos estatales y municipales del Sur con el fin de separar a blancos y afroamericanos en instalaciones públicas y privadas. (p. 287)

joint-stock company [sociedad de capitales] *s.* institución empresarial tipo corporación en la que inversionistas unen riquezas con un fin común; se usaron para financiar la exploración de las Américas. (p. 21)

judicial review [revisión judicial] *s.* poder de la Suprema Corte de declarar inconstitucional una ley del Congreso. (p. 113)

Judiciary Act of 1789 [Ley Judicial de 1789] *s.* ley que estableció el sistema de tribunales federales y la Suprema Corte que permitió la apelación a cortes federales de ciertas decisiones tomadas por cortes estatales. (p. 74)

Jungle, The *[La jungla] s.* novela publicada en 1906 por el periodista Upton Sinclair que denunciaba la insalubridad de la industria de carne en aquella época; llevó a reformas nacionales. (p. 317)

K

kamikaze *adj.* que estrellaba deliberadamente un avión bombardero contra un blanco militar. (p. 581)

Kent State University [Universidad Estatal de Kent] *s.* universidad de Ohio donde guardias militares abrieron fuego contra estudiantes durante una protesta contra la Guerra de Vietnam el 4 de mayo de 1970, hiriendo a nueve de ellos y matando a cuatro. (p. 756)

Kerner Commission [Comisión Kerner] *s.* grupo designado por el presidente Lyndon B. Johnson para estudiar las causas de la violencia urbana; recomendó eliminar la segregación de facto en la sociedad estadounidense. (p. 722)

King Philip's War [Guerra del Rey Felipe] *s.* conflicto, en los años 1675 y 1676, entre los colonos de Nueva Inglaterra y grupos amerindios aliados bajo la dirección del cacique Metacom de los wampanoagas. (p. 25)

Kongo *s.* serie de pequeños reinos unidos bajo un líder a finales del siglo 15 en las selvas tropicales a lo largo del río Zaire (Congo) en África Central-Occidental. (p. 9)

Korean War [Guerra de Corea] *s.* guerra de 1950 a 1953 entre Corea del Norte y Corea del Sur; China respaldó a Corea del Norte y las tropas de las Naciones Unidas, integradas en su mayoría por soldados estadounidenses, apoyaron a Corea del Sur. (p. 611)

Kristallnacht *s.* "noche del cristal quebrado", noviembre 9 de 1938, noche en que milicianos nazis atacaron viviendas, negocios y sinagogas judías en Alemania. (p. 543)

Ku Klux Klan *s.* sociedad secreta de hombres blancos en los estados sureños después de la Guerra Civil que desató terror para restaurar la supremacía blanca. (p. 188)

L

La Raza Unida *s.* organización política latina establecida en 1969 por José Ángel Gutiérrez. (p. 770)

League of Nations [Liga de las Naciones] *s.* organización internacional establecida en 1920 para promover la cooperación y la paz internacional. (p. 399)

Lend-Lease Act [Ley de Préstamo y Alquiler] *s.* ley aprobada en 1941, que autorizó al gobierno a mandar armas y otros productos, sin pago inmediato, a las naciones que luchaban contra el Eje. (p. 552)

Limited Test Ban Treaty [Tratado de Limitación de Pruebas Nucleares] *s.* tratado de 1963 en que Estados Unidos y la Unión Soviética acordaron no realizar pruebas de armas nucleares en la atmósfera. (p. 678)

long drive [arreo de ganado] *s.* proceso mediante el cual los vaqueros llevaban por tierra ganado hacia el mercado. (p. 210)

longhorn *s.* resistente raza de ganado vacuno de cuernos largos llevada por los españoles a México, muy apta para las condiciones de esa región. (p. 208)

Louisiana Purchase [Compra de Louisiana] *s.* compra de terrenos a Francia por 15 millones de dólares en 1803 de las tierras desde el río Mississippi hasta las montañas Rocosas. (p. 114)

Lowell textile mills [fábrica de textiles de Lowell] *s.* talleres para la fabricación de tela de Lowell, Massachusetts, del siglo 19; empleaban principalmente a trabajadoras jóvenes. (p. 142)

Loyalist [realista] *s.* colono que apoyaba al gobierno británico durante la Revolución Norteamericana. (p. 59)

Lusitania *s.* barco británico de pasajeros que se hundió cerca de costas irlandesas el 7 de mayo de 1915, tras ser atacado por un submarino alemán. (p. 378)

M

mandate [mandato] *s.* conquista de una porción suficientemente grande del voto, que indica que un líder elegido tiene apoyo popular para sus programas. (p. 680)

Manhattan Project [Proyecto Manhattan] *s.* programa estadounidense que se inició en 1942 con el fin de diseñar una bomba atómica para la II Guerra Mundial. La primera detonación atómica completa ocurrió en Alamogordo, New Mexico, el 16 de julio de 1945. (p. 567)

manifest destiny [destino manifiesto] *s.* término usado en la década de 1840 para describir la creencia de que Estados Unidos estaba inexorablemente destinado a adquirir más territorio, especialmente mediante su expansión hacia el oeste. (p. 131)

Marbury* v. *Madison *s.* caso de 1803 en que la Suprema Corte decidió que tenía el poder de abolir decretos legislativos declarándolos inconstitucionales; ese poder se conoce como revisión judicial. (p. 113)

market revolution [revolución mercantil] *s.* gran cambio económico que llevó a comprar y vender productos en lugar de hacerlos en el hogar. (p. 139)

Marshall Plan [Plan Marshall] *s.* plan formulado por el Secretario de Estado George Marshall en 1947, mediante el que se ofreció ayuda a países europeos con el fin de reparar los daños de la II Guerra Mundial. (p. 606)

mass media [medios informativos] *s.* medios de comunicación —tales como televisión, prensa y radio— que llegan a grandes audiencias. (p. 652)

mass transit [transporte público] *s.* sistemas de transporte diseñados para llevar grandes números de personas por rutas fijas. (p. 264)

McCarthyism [macartismo] *s.* ataques, a menudo sin respaldo, del senador Joseph McCarthy y otros contra presuntos comunistas en los años 50. (p. 620)

Meat Inspection Act [Ley de Inspección de la Carne] *s.* ley de 1906 que establecía estrictos requisitos sanitarios en las empacadoras de carne, así como un programa federal de inspección de carnes. (p. 320)

Medicaid *s.* programa federal que se inició en 1965 para brindar atención médica a las personas que reciben ayuda pública. (p. 690)

Medicare *s.* programa federal que se inició en 1965 para brindar seguros médicos y de hospitalización a bajo costo a los mayores de 65 años. (p. 690)

melting pot [crisol de culturas] *s.* mezcla de personas de diferentes culturas y razas que se amalgaman y abandonan su idioma y cultura natal. (p. 258)

mercantilism [mercantilismo] *s.* sistema económico en que un país aumenta su riqueza y poder al incrementar su posesión de oro y plata, y al exportar más productos de los que importa. (p. 28)

mestizo *adj.* con mezcla de español e indígena. (p. 16)

middle passage [travesía intermedia] *s.* tramo de África a las Antillas; parte del triángulo comercial de esclavos. (p. 32)

militarism [militarismo] *s.* política de mantener una sólida organización militar como preparación agresiva para la guerra y su empleo como herramienta diplomática. (p. 373)

Missouri Compromise [Acuerdo de Missouri] *s.* serie de acuerdos aprobados por el Congreso en 1820–1821 para mantener un equilibrio seccional entre los estados esclavistas y los estados libres. (p. 122)

Monroe Doctrine [Doctrina Monroe] *s.* declaración del presidente Monroe en 1823 que establecía que Estados Unidos no permitiría la interferencia europea en los asuntos del Hemisferio Occidental. (p. 117)

Moral Majority [Mayoría Moral] *s.* coalición política de organizaciones religiosas conservadoras en los años 70 y 80 que recaudó dinero para respaldar agendas y candidatos conservadores, y condenó actitudes y comportamientos liberales. (p. 831)

Morrill Acts [Leyes Morrill] *s.* leyes aprobadas en 1862 y 1890 que otorgaban tierras federales a los estados para financiar universidades agrícolas. (p. 217)

muckraker *s.* uno de los reporteros de revistas que desenmascaraban el lado corrupto de las empresas y de la vida pública a principios del siglo 20. (p. 308)

Munn* v. *Illinois *s.* caso de la Suprema Corte en 1877; estableció el derecho del gobierno federal a regular la industria privada en beneficio del interés público. (p. 239)

My Lai *s.* pueblo del norte de Vietnam del Sur, donde más de 200 civiles desarmados, incluso mujeres y niños, fueron masacrados por las tropas de EE.UU. en mayo de 1968. (p. 756)

N

NAACP *s.* National Association for the Advancement of Colored People (Asociación Nacional para el Avance de la Gente de Color), organización fundada en 1909 y dedicada a la igualdad racial. (p. 325)

NACW *s.* National Association of Colored Women (Asociación Nacional de Mujeres de Color), organización de servicio social fundada en 1896. (p. 315)

NAFTA *s.* North American Free Trade Agreement (Tratado de Libre Comercio, TLC), tratado de 1993 que redujo aranceles e incorporó a México en la zona de libre comercio ya vigente entre Estados Unidos y Canadá. (p. 864)

napalm *s.* sustancia incendiaria de gasolina que lanzaban los aviones estadounidenses en Vietnam, con el fin de incendiar la selva y revelar los escondites del Vietcong. (p. 739)

NASDAQ *s.* sigla de National Association of Securities Dealers Automated Quotation System, una bolsa de valores de venta directa dominada por companías tecnológicas. (p. 871)

National Energy Act [Ley Nacional de Energía] *s.* ley promulgada durante la administración Carter para aliviar la crisis energética; aplicó impuestos a los autos que usan gasolina de manera ineficiente y suspendió el control de precios del petróleo y el gas natural estadounidenses. (p. 813)

National Industrial Recovery Act (NIRA) [Ley Nacional de Recuperación Industrial] *s.* ley aprobada en 1933 que establecía agencias para supervisar industrias y suministrar empleos. (p. 491)

nationalism [nacionalismo] *s.* devoción a los intereses y la cultura de la nación propia. (p. 373)

National Labor Relations Board (NLRB) [Junta Nacional de Relaciones Laborales] *s.* agencia creada en 1935 con el fin de prevenir prácticas laborales injustas y mediar en disputas laborales. (p. 518)

National Organization for Women (NOW) [Organización Nacional de la Mujer] *s.* organización fundada en 1966 con el fin de impulsar metas feministas, tales como mejores guarderías, mayores oportunidades educativas y el fin de la discriminación laboral. (p. 778)

National Trades' Union [Unión Nacional de Sindicatos] *s.* primera asociación nacional de sindicatos, creada en 1834. (p. 143)

National Youth Administration [Administración Nacional de Recursos para la Juventud] *s.* programa que suministraba ayuda y empleos a jóvenes durante la Depresión. (p. 499)

Nation of Islam [Nación del Islam] *s.* grupo religioso, popularmente conocido como musulmanes negros, fundado por Elijah Muhammad para promover el separatismo negro y la religión islámica. (p. 719)

nativism [patriotería] *s.* favoritismo de los intereses de las personas nacidas en un lugar sobre los de las personas extranjeras. (pp. 258, 412)

Navigation Acts [Leyes de Navegación] *s.* serie de leyes aprobadas a partir de 1651 que imponían un control más rígido del comercio en las colonias inglesas. (p. 28)

NAWSA *s.* National American Woman Suffrage Association (Asociación Nacional Americana del Sufragio Femenino), creada en 1890 para obtener derechos electorales para la mujer. (p. 316)

Nazism [nazismo] *s.* movimiento político basado en un extremo nacionalismo, racismo y expansionismo militar; instituido en Alemania como sistema de gobierno por Adolfo Hitler en 1933. (p. 531)

Neutrality Acts [Leyes de Neutralidad] *s.* serie de leyes aprobadas por el Congreso en 1935 y 1936 que prohibieron la venta y el alquiler de armas a naciones en guerra. (p. 535)

New Deal *s.* medidas económicas y políticas adoptadas por el presidente Franklin Roosevelt en los años 30 para promover recuperación económica, ayuda a los necesitados y reforma financiera. (p. 489)

New Deal Coalition [Coalición del New Deal] *s.* alianza temporal de distintos grupos, tales como blancos sureños, afroamericanos y sindicalistas, que apoyaban al Partido Demócrata en los años 30 y 40. (p. 507)

New Federalism [Nuevo Federalismo] *s.* programa del presidente Richard Nixon para distribuir una porción del poder del gobierno federal a gobiernos estatales y locales. (p. 795)

New Frontier [Nueva Frontera] *s.* agenda legislativa del presidente John F. Kennedy; tenía medidas de atención médica para ancianos, renovación urbana y apoyo a la educación, que fueron rechazadas por el Congreso, así como medidas que sí se aprobaron de defensa nacional, ayuda internacional y programas espaciales. (p. 677)

New Left [Nueva Izquierda] *s.* movimiento político juvenil de los años 60 con organizaciones como Students for a Democratic Society (Estudiantes por una Sociedad Democrática) y el Free Speech Movement (Movimiento de Libre Expresión). (p. 744)

New Right [Nueva Derecha] *s.* alianza política de grupos conservadores de fines del siglo 20, con énfasis en asuntos culturales, sociales y morales. (p. 831)

Niagara Movement [Movimiento Niágara] *s.* fundado en 1905 por W. E. B. Du Bois para promover la enseñanza de humanidades entre los afroamericanos. (p. 285)

Nineteenth Amendment [Enmienda 19] *s.* enmienda a la Constitución adoptada en 1920 que le otorga a la mujer el derecho de votar. (p. 335)

"no man's land" [tierra de nadie] *s.* en la I Guerra Mundial, extensión baldía de tierra entre trincheras de ejércitos enemigos. (p. 376)

nomadic [nómade] *adj.* que no tiene hogar fijo, que se muda de un lugar a otro según las estaciones y la disponibilidad de comida y agua. (p. 5)

nonaggression pact [pacto de no agresión] *s.* acuerdo entre dos naciones de no luchar entre sí. (p. 539)

North Atlantic Treaty Organization (NATO) [Organización del Tratado del Atlántico Norte] *s.* alianza militar defensiva formada en 1949 por diez países de Europa del oeste, Estados Unidos y Canadá. (p. 608)

Northwest Ordinance of 1787 [Ordenanza del Noroeste de 1787] *s.* procedimiento para la admisión de nuevos estados a la Unión. (p. 67)

nullification [anulación] *s.* rechazo de un estado a reconocer cualquier ley del Congreso que considere inconstitucional. (p. 79)

Nuremberg trials [juicios de Nuremberg] *s.* juicios llevados a cabo en Nuremberg, Alemania, inmediatamente después de la II Guerra Mundial, a líderes nazis por sus crímenes de guerra. (p. 586)

O

Office of Price Administration (OPA) [Oficina de Administración de Precios] *s.* agencia establecida por el Congreso durante la II Guerra Mundial con facultad para combatir la inflación al congelar los precios de la mayoría de los artículos. (p. 567)

Ohio gang [pandilla de Ohio] *s.* amigos y partidarios políticos del presidente Warren G. Harding, a quienes éste nombró a su gabinete. (p. 420)

OPEC *s.* Organization of Petroleum Exporting Countries (Organización de Países Exportadores de Petróleo, OPEP), alianza económica para ejercer influencia sobre los precios del petróleo. (p. 799)

Open Door notes [notas de Puertas Abiertas] *s.* notas que el Secretario de Estado John Hay envió a Gran Bretaña, Francia, Alemania, Italia, Japón y Rusia, instándolos a no interponerse entre el comercio de Estados Unidos y China. (p. 356)

Operation Desert Storm [Operación Tormenta del Desierto] *s.* operación militar en la que fuerzas de las Naciones Unidas, encabezadas por Estados Unidos, liberaron a Kuwait y derrotaron al ejército iraquí. (p. 855)

Oregon Trail [Sendero de Oregon] *s.* camino que va de Independence, Missouri, a la ciudad de Oregon, Oregon. (p. 131)

P

Panama Canal [canal de Panamá] *s.* canal artificial construido a través del istmo de Panamá para abrir paso entre los océanos Atlántico y Pacífico; se abrió en 1914. (p. 360)

parity [paridad] *s.* regulación de precios de ciertos productos agrícolas, apoyada por el gobierno, con el fin de mantener estables los ingresos agrícolas. (p. 518)

Patriot [patriota] *s.* colono que apoyaba la independencia norteamericana de Gran Bretaña. (p. 59)

patronage [clientelismo] *s.* sistema de otorgar empleos a personas que ayudan a la elección de un candidato. (p. 270)

pay equity [equidad salarial] *s.* sistema que basa el salario de un empleado en los requisitos del trabajo y no en escalas salariales tradicionales, que normalmente pagan menos a la mujer. (p. 842)

Payne-Aldrich Tariff [Arancel Payne-Aldrich] *s.* serie de reglamentos de impuestos, aprobados por el Congreso en 1909, que no logró reducir mucho los aranceles de productos manufacturados. (p. 329)

Peace Corps [Cuerpo de Paz] *s.* programa fundado en 1965 bajo iniciativa del presidente Kennedy, que envía voluntarios a las naciones en desarrollo de Asia, África y Latinoamérica para ayudar en escuelas, clínicas y otros proyectos. (p. 680)

Pendleton Act [Ley Pendleton] *s.* ley de 1883 que autorizaba nombrar empleados del servicio civil por mérito. (p. 270)

Pentagon Papers [Documentos del Pentágono] *s.* documento de 7,000 páginas que dejó filtrar a la prensa en 1971 el antiguo funcionario del Departamento de Defensa Daniel Ellsberg, donde se revela que el gobierno mintió sobre sus planes en la Guerra de Vietnam. (p. 757)

perestroika *s.* palabra rusa para designar la reestructuración económica y burocrática de la Unión Soviética que ocurrió en los años 80. (p. 849)

planned obsolescence [obsolencia planeada] *s.* diseño de artículos que se desgastan o pasan de moda muy pronto, para crear la necesidad de remplazarlos con frecuencia. (p. 648)

Platt Amendment [Enmienda Platt] *s.* serie de medidas implantadas por Estados Unidos en 1901, las cuales debieron ser incluidas por Cuba en su nueva constitución para quedar libre de su deuda y por las que Estados Unidos obtenía el derecho a intervenir el país y a comprar o alquilar el territorio cubano para establecer estaciones navales y de combustible. (p. 354)

Plessy* v. *Ferguson *s.* caso de 1896 en que la Suprema Corte declaró legal la separación de razas en instalaciones públicas y estableció la doctrina de "separados aunque iguales". (p. 287)

political machine [maquinaria política] *s.* grupo organizado que controla un partido político en una ciudad y ofrece servicios a los votantes y negocios a cambio de apoyo político y financiero. (p. 268)

poll tax [impuesto para votar] *s.* impuesto anual que los ciudadanos debían pagar en algunos estados sureños para poder votar. (p. 287)

popular sovereignty [soberanía popular] *s.* sistema en el cual los ciudadanos votan para decidir sobre un tema. (p. 157)

Populism [populismo] *s.* movimiento político de finales del siglo 19 que exigía la voz popular en el gobierno y que representaba los intereses de los granjeros y promovía una reforma del sistema monetario. (p. 221)

price support [apoyo de precios] *s.* apoyo de los precios de ciertos artículos al valor del mercado o por encima, algunas veces mediante la compra de excedentes por parte del gobierno. (p. 465)

Proclamation of 1763 [Proclama de 1763] *s.* decreto británico que prohibía que los colonos se instalaran al oeste de los montes Apalaches. (p. 39)

progressive [progresista] *s.* que favorece el avance hacia mejores condiciones o nuevas ideas. (p. 258)

progressive movement [movimiento progresista] *s.* movimiento reformista de comienzos del siglo 20 cuyos objetivos eran mejorar el bienestar social, promover la moralidad, incrementar la justicia económica y devolver a la ciudadanía el control del gobierno. (p. 307)

prohibition [prohibición] *s.* prohibición de bebidas alcohólicas. (p. 307)

Prohibition [Ley Seca] *s.* período entre 1920 y 1933 durante el cual, por medio de la decimoctava enmienda, se prohibió la producción y la venta de alcohol en Estados Unidos. (p. 436)

propaganda *s.* comunicación prejuiciada diseñada para influir los pensamientos y actos de la gente. (p. 390)

Proposition 187 [Propuesta 187] *s.* proyecto de ley aprobado en California en 1994, el cual canceló todos los beneficios educativos y de salud que no fueran emergencias a los inmigrantes ilegales. (p. 886)

protective tariff [arancel proteccionista] *s.* impuesto aplicado a productos importados para proteger las empresas nacionales de la competencia extranjera. (p. 76)

protectorate [protectorado] *s.* nación cuyo gobierno y asuntos son controlados por una potencia más fuerte. (p. 354)

Pueblo *s.* amerindios descendientes de los anasazi; viven en los desiertos del Suroeste. (p. 6)

Pure Food and Drug Act [Ley de Pureza de Alimentos y Drogas] *s.* ley de 1906 que paró la venta de alimentos y drogas contaminadas y demandó etiquetas fidedignas. (p. 322)

Puritan [puritano] *s.* miembro de la Iglesia Anglicana que deseaba eliminar las tradiciones católicas y simplificar los servicios religiosos. (p. 24)

Q

Quaker [cuáquero] *s.* miembro de una secta religiosa considerada radical en el siglo 17, también conocida como Sociedad de Amigos. (p. 26)

quota system [sistema de cuotas] *s.* sistema que limita el número de inmigrantes de varios países que pueden ser admitidos a Estados Unidos cada año. (p. 415)

R

ratification [ratificación] *s.* aprobación oficial de la Constitución, o de una enmienda, por parte de los estados. (p. 69)

rationing [racionamiento] *s.* medida tomada durante tiempos de guerra para limitar la cantidad de ciertos alimentos y otros productos que cada persona puede comprar. (p. 568)

Reaganomics [reaganomía] *s.* nombre dado a la política económica del presidente Reagan, que abogaba por recortes presupuestarios y por una gran reducción en los impuestos con el fin de incrementar la inversión privada y por consiguiente expandir el suministro de productos y servicios. (p. 834)

realpolitik *s.* enfoque de política exterior, identificado con Henry Kissinger y Richard Nixon, que propone hacer lo que resulte realista y práctico en lugar de seguir una política al pie de la letra. (p. 799)

reapportionment [nueva repartición] *s.* redistribución de distritos electorales cuando cambia el número de personas en un distrito. (p. 691)

recall [destitución] *s.* reforma gubernamental que permite a los votantes deponer a funcionarios públicos elegidos. (p. 312)

Reconstruction [Reconstrucción] *s.* período de reconstrucción después de la Guerra Civil y readmisión a la Unión de los estados de la Confederación que habían sido derrotados; de 1865 a 1877. (p. 184)

Reconstruction Finance Corporation (RFC) [Corporación Financiera de la Reconstrucción] *s.* organización establecida en 1932 para dar financiación de emergencia a bancos, aseguradoras de vida, compañías ferroviarias y otras empresas grandes. (p. 481)

referendum [referendo] *s.* procedimiento que permite someter al voto popular propuestas legislativas. (p. 312)

Reformation [Reforma] *s.* movimiento religioso en la Europa de comienzos del siglo 16, encaminado a reformar la Iglesia Católica Romana; condujo a la formación del protestantismo. (p. 10)

Renaissance [Renacimiento] *s.* período de la historia europea, que se extendió aproximadamente desde 1400 a 1600, durante el cual un renovado interés en la cultura clásica originó cambios trascendentales en las artes, el aprendizaje y la visión del mundo. (p. 11)

reparations [reparación] *s.* compensación que paga una nación derrotada en una guerra por las pérdidas económicas del vencedor o por crímenes cometidos contra individuos. (p. 400)

republic [república] *s.* gobierno en el que los ciudadanos mandan por medio de sus representantes elegidos. (p. 67)

Republic of California [República de California] *s.* nación proclamada por los colonos estadounidenses en California, al declarar éstos su independencia de México en 1846. (p. 136)

revenue sharing [distribución de rentas] *s.* plan puesto en práctica en 1972 que faculta a los gobiernos estatales y locales a invertir el dinero federal a su conveniencia. (p. 795)

reverse discrimination [discriminación a la inversa] *s.* tratamiento injusto de los miembros de un grupo mayoritario, típicamente hombres blancos, como resultado de los esfuerzos por remediar la discriminación contra otros grupos. (p. 831)

rock 'n' roll *s.* forma de música popular estadounidense que evolucionó a finales de los 40 y durante los 50, a partir del rhythm and blues, el country, el jazz, el gospel y el pop; forma musical estadounidense caracterizada por ritmos fuertes y melodías simples, la cual se ha expandido por todo el mundo y ha tenido impactos significantes en el baile social, la moda de la vestimenta y las expresiones de protesta. (p. 655)

Roosevelt Corollary [Corolario de Roosevelt] *s.* declaración de 1904 del presidente Theodore Roosevelt en que advertía que Estados Unidos intervendría militarmente en los asuntos de cualquier nación del Hemisferio Occidental para proteger sus intereses económicos si fuera necesario. (p. 362)

Rough Riders *s.* regimiento de caballería voluntario comandado por Leonard Wood y Theodore Roosevelt en la Guerra Española-Norteamericana-Cubana. (p. 350)

rural free delivery (RFD) [correo rural gratuito] *s.* entrega gubernamental gratis de correo y paquetes a zonas rurales; se inició en 1896. (p. 321)

S

SALT I Treaty [Tratado Salt I] *s.* acuerdo de cinco años entre Estados Unidos y la Unión Soviética que surgió de las Conversaciones sobre Limitación de Armas Estratégicas de 1972; limitó el número de misiles balísticos intercontinentales y de misiles de submarinos. (p. 801)

Sandinista *adj.* relativo a las fuerzas izquierdistas rebeldes que derrocaron al gobierno nicaragüense en 1979; el presidente Reagan, quien respaldaba a la contra anticomunista, se les opuso. (p. 851)

Santa Fe Trail [Sendero de Santa Fe] *s.* camino que va de Independence, Missouri, a Santa Fe, New Mexico. (p. 131)

satellite nation [nación satélite] *s.* país dominado política y económicamente por otro. (p. 605)

Saturday Night Massacre [Masacre de Sábado en la Noche] *s.* nombre dado a la renuncia del procurador general y al despido de su comisionado el 20 de octubre de 1973, después de haberse negado a acatar la orden del presidente Nixon de despedir al fiscal especial en el caso Watergate. (p. 805)

scalawag *s.* término despectivo para referirse a los sureños blancos que se unieron al Partido Republicano y apoyaron la Reconstrucción después de la Guerra Civil. (p. 186)

scientific management [administración científica] *s.* aplicación de principios científicos para simplificar y facilitar las tareas laborales. (p. 308)

Scopes trial [juicio de Scopes] *s.* sensacional juicio de 1925 en el que el maestro de biología John T. Scopes fue juzgado por desafiar una ley de Tennessee que prohibía la enseñanza de la evolución. (p. 438)

search-and-destroy mission [misión de búsqueda y destrucción] *s.* ataque militar estadounidense a aldeas de Vietnam del Sur con el fin de erradicar al Vietcong, que solía resultar en la destrucción de la aldea y el desplazamiento de sus habitantes. (p. 739)

secession [secesión] *s.* retiro formal de un estado de la Unión federal. (p. 157)

Securities and Exchange Commission (SEC) [Comisión de Valores y Cambios] *s.* agencia creada en 1934 para controlar el mercado bursátil y hacer cumplir las leyes que rigen la venta de acciones y bonos. (p. 517)

segregation [segregación] *s.* separación de la gente según su raza. (p. 287)

Selective Service Act [Ley de Servicio Selectivo] *s.* ley aprobada por el Congreso en mayo de 1917 que ordena que todos los hombres se inscriban para el servicio militar obligatorio. (p. 382)

Seneca Falls Convention [convención de Seneca Falls] *s.* convención de derechos femeninos celebrada en 1848 en Seneca Falls, New York. (p. 149)

service sector [sector de servicios] *s.* renglón de la economía que ofrece servicios en vez de productos. (p. 870)

settlement house [casa de beneficencia] *s.* centro comunitario en un barrio pobre que ayudaba a los residentes, particularmente a los inmigrantes. (p. 266)

Seventeenth Amendment [Enmienda 17] *s.* enmienda a la Constitución adoptada en 1913; dispone que los senadores federales sean elegidos por los votantes y no por cuerpos legislativos estatales. (p. 312)

shantytown [tugurio] *s.* vecindario en donde la gente vivía en chozas temporales. (p. 473)

sharecropping [aparcería] *s.* sistema en el cual se da a los agricultores tierra, semillas, herramientas y alimentos para vivir, así como una parte de la cosecha, por cultivar la tierra. (p. 188)

Shays's Rebellion [Rebelión de Shays] *s.* sublevación de granjeros endeudados de Massachusetts en 1787, en protesta por los impuestos estatales. (p. 67)

Sherman Antitrust Act [Ley Antitrust Sherman] *s.* ley contra los monopolios de 1890 que declaró ilegal la formación de consorcios que obstruyeran el libre comercio. (p. 244)

silent majority [mayoría silenciosa] *s.* nombre dado por el presidente Richard Nixon a los estadounidenses moderados que apoyaban silenciosamente su involucramiento en la Guerra de Vietnam. (p. 756)

sit-in *s.* forma de protesta —iniciada por el Congreso de Igualdad Racial en los años 40 y empleada con frecuencia en los años 60— en la que afroamericanos ingresaban a un lugar segregado, tal como el mostrador de un restaurante, y se negaban a salir hasta que se les sirviera. (p. 706)

Social Darwinism [darvinismo social] *s.* conjunto de creencias políticas y económicas basadas en la teoría del biólogo Charles Darwin sobre la selección natural o supervivencia del más apto; favorecía una competencia libre, no regulada, y creía que los individuos o grupos triunfaban porque eran genéticamente superiores. (p. 242)

Social Gospel movement [movimiento del Evangelio Social] *s.* movimiento de reforma del siglo 19 basado en la noción de que los cristianos tenían la responsabilidad social de mejorar las condiciones laborales y aliviar la pobreza urbana. (p. 266)

Social Security Act [Ley de Seguro Social] *s.* ley aprobada en 1935 para ayudar a los jubilados, desempleados, incapacitados y familias con niños dependientes. (p. 501)

soddy [choza de tepe] *s.* casa provisional hecha de césped, muy común en las llanuras, donde la madera era escasa. (p. 216)

soup kitchen [comedor de beneficencia] *s.* lugar donde se sirven alimentos gratis o a bajo costo a los necesitados, muy común durante la Depresión. (p. 473)

Southern Christian Leadership Conference (SCLC) [Conferencia de Líderes Cristianos del Sur] *s.* organización formada en 1957 por el doctor Martin Luther King, Jr., y otros líderes para promover los derechos civiles sin violencia. (p. 706)

Southern strategy [estrategia sureña] *s.* estrategia del presidente Nixon de apelar a los demócratas conservadores sureños que estaban descontentos con la integración y con una Suprema Corte liberal. (p. 797)

speakeasy *s.* lugar donde se vendían bebidas alcohólicas ilegalmente, como ocurrió durante la Prohibición. (p. 436)

speculation [especulación] *s.* transacciones de alto riesgo con el fin de obtener ganancias rápidas o grandes. (p. 467)

Square Deal *s.* programa de reformas progresistas del presidente Theodore Roosevelt para proteger a la gente común y corriente de las grandes empresas. (p. 319)

stagflation [estanflación] *s.* situación económica en la que hay niveles altos de inflación y desempleo simultáneamente. (p. 798)

Stalwart *s.* republicano seguidor del "jefe" de New York City, Roscoe Conkling, quien favorecía el sistema de prebendas y se oponía a la reforma al servicio civil. (p. 292)

Stamp Act [Ley del Timbre] *s.* primer impuesto directo aplicado en 1765 por Gran Bretaña a una variedad de artículos y servicios, tales como documentos legales y periódicos. (p. 47)

Strategic Defense Initiative (SDI) [Iniciativa para la Defensa Estratégica] *s.* sistema de defensa propuesto en los años 80, popularmente conocido como la Guerra de las Galaxias, cuyo fin era proteger a Estados Unidos de ataques de misiles. (p. 835)

strike [huelga] *s.* interrupción del trabajo para presionar a un patrono a responder a ciertas demandas. (p. 142)

Student Nonviolent Coordinating Committee (SNCC) [Comité Coordinador de Estudiantes no Violentos] *s.* organización fundada en 1961, conocida como SNCC, para coordinar sit-ins y otras protestas, y para darles a los jóvenes negros mayor participación en el movimiento de derechos civiles. (p. 706)

Students for a Democratic Society (SDS) [Estudiantes por una Sociedad Democrática] *s.* grupo activista de los años 60, conocido como SDS, que urgía una mayor libertad y responsabilidad individual. (p. 744)

suburb [suburbio] *s.* pueblo o comunidad residencial cerca de una ciudad. (p. 635)

suffrage [sufragio] *s.* derecho a votar. (p. 315)

Sugar Act [Ley del Azúcar] *s.* ley británica de 1764 que aplicó un impuesto comercial a la melaza, el azúcar y otras importaciones para reducir el contrabando en las colonias. (p. 44)

supply-side economics [economía de oferta] *s.* teoría económica, practicada por el presidente Ronald Reagan, que sostiene que recortar los impuestos de los ricos beneficia a todos pues aumenta empleos, ahorros e inversiones. (p. 835)

T

Taino [taíno] *s.* pueblo amerindio que Colón y su tripulación vieron al arribar a la isla hoy conocida como San Salvador, el 12 de octubre de 1492. (p. 14)

Teapot Dome scandal [escándalo de Teapot Dome] *s.* escándalo generado cuando Albert Fall, Secretario del Interior del presidente Warren G. Harding, concedió en secreto valiosas reservas de petróleo en Wyoming y California a compañías privadas a cambio de dinero y tierras. (p. 421)

Telecommunications Act of 1996 [Ley de Telecomunicaciones] *s.* ley de 1996 que retiró las barreras que impedían que un tipo de compañía de comunicaciones ingresara a otro tipo de negocio en el mismo campo. (p. 878)

telecommute *v.* trabajar desde la casa para una compañía ubicada en otra parte, mediante la nueva tecnología de comunicaciones, como computadoras, Internet y máquinas de fax. (p. 878)

tenement [casa de pisos] *s.* vivienda urbana de varias familias, usualmente sobrepoblada y poco sanitaria. (p. 264)

Tennessee Valley Authority (TVA) [Autoridad del Valle de Tennessee] *s.* corporación federal creada en 1933 para construir presas y centrales eléctricas en la región del valle de Tennessee con el objeto de generar electricidad así como prevenir inundaciones. (p. 519)

termination policy [política de terminación] *s.* programa del gobierno federal en 1953 de cesar su responsabilidad hacia las naciones amerindias y eliminar el apoyo económico federal, suspender el sistema de reservaciones y redistribuir las tierras tribales. (p. 663)

Tet offensive [ofensiva de Tet] *s.* sorpresivo ataque masivo del Vietcong a pueblos y ciudades de Vietnam del Sur a comienzos de 1968; la batalla, de un mes de duración, convenció a muchos estadounidenses de que no era posible ganar la guerra. (p. 749)

Texas Revolution [Revolución de Texas] *s.* rebelión de 1836 con la que Texas se independizó de México. (p. 134)

Thirteenth Amendment [Enmienda 13] *s.* enmienda a la Constitución, ratificada en 1865, que ha abolido la esclavitud y la servidumbre involuntaria. (p. 183)

Tiananmen Square [plaza Tianamen] *s.* lugar de protestas estudiantiles en 1989 en Beijing, China, por la falta de libertades democráticas, donde el gobierno atacó a los estudiantes. (p. 850)

Tonkin Gulf Resolution [Resolución del Golfo de Tonkin] *s.* resolución aprobada por el Congreso en 1964 que le otorgaba al presidente Johnson amplios poderes para la Guerra de Vietnam. (p. 735)

totalitarian [totalitario] adj. característico de un sistema político en que el gobierno ejerce completo control sobre la vida de los ciudadanos. (p. 529)

Trail of Tears [Sendero de las Lágrimas] *s.* marcha obligada del pueblo cherokee desde Georgia hasta el Territorio Indio entre 1838 y 1840, durante la cual murieron miles de ellos. (p. 124)

transcendentalism [trascendentalismo] *s.* movimiento filosófico y literario que proponía llevar una vida sencilla y celebrar la verdad implícita de la naturaleza, la emoción personal y la imaginación. (p. 145)

transcontinental railroad [ferrocarril transcontinental] *s.* línea férrea finalizada en 1869 que unía la costa Atlántica y la costa Pacífica. (p. 237)

Treaty of Fort Laramie [Tratado del Fuerte Laramie] *s.* tratado que requería que los sioux vivieran en una reservación a lo largo del río Missouri. (p. 204)

Treaty of Guadalupe Hidalgo [Tratado de Guadalupe Hidalgo] *s.* tratado de 1848 que puso fin a la guerra entre Estados Unidos y México, mediante el cual Estados Unidos obtuvo enormes tierras en el Oeste y el Suroeste. (p. 136)

Treaty of Paris (1783) [Tratado de París] *s.* tratado que puso fin a la Guerra Revolucionaria Norteamericana y estableció las fronteras de la nueva nación. (p. 62)

Treaty of Paris (1898) [Tratado de París] *s.* tratado el cual puso fin a la guerra entre España y Estados Unidos. Por medio de este tratado España liberó a Cuba, cedió las islas de Guam y Puerto Rico a Estados Unidos y vendió las Filipinas a este país por 20 millones de dólares. (p. 350)

Treaty of Tordesillas [Tratado de Tordesillas] *s.* tratado de 1494 que dividió las Américas entre España y Portugal mediante una línea vertical imaginaria en el Atlántico; cada país tenía poder sobre un lado de la línea. (p. 15)

Treaty of Versailles [Tratado de Versalles] *s.* tratado de paz firmado en 1919 al finalizar la I Guerra Mundial, el cual establecía nuevas naciones, fronteras y reparaciones de guerra. (p. 400)

trench warfare [guerra de trincheras] *s.* guerra en que los combatientes atacan desde un sistema de zanjas fortificadas y no en un campo abierto de batalla. (p. 376)

triangular trade [triángulo comercial de esclavos] *s.* sistema transatlántico de comercio en el cual la mercancía, incluidos los esclavos, se intercambiaba entre África, Inglaterra, Europa, las Indias Occidentales y las colonias de Norteamérica. (p. 32)

Truman Doctrine [Doctrina Truman] *s.* declaración del presidente Truman en 1947, que establecía que Estados Unidos debía dar apoyo económico y militar para liberar a naciones amenazadas por fuerzas internas o externas. (p. 606)

Tuskegee Normal and Industrial Institute [Instituto Normal e Industrial Tuskegee] *s.* fundado en 1881 y dirigido por Booker T. Washington para otorgar diplomas de magisterio y enseñar destrezas comerciales y agrícolas a los afroamericanos. (p. 285)

two-party system [bipartidismo] *s.* sistema político dominado por dos partidos. (p. 76)

U

Underground Railroad [Ferrocarril Subterráneo] *s.* red secreta de personas que ayudaban a los esclavos fugitivos a escapar a lo largo de diversas rutas hacia Canadá o hacia zonas seguras en los estados libres. (p. 158)

Unitarian [unitario] *s.* miembro de un grupo religioso que destaca la razón y la fe en el individuo. (p. 145)

United Farm Workers Organizing Committee (UFWOC) [Comité Organizador de Trabajadores Agrícolas Unidos] *s.* sindicato establecido en 1966 por César Chávez para mejorar los salarios y las condiciones laborales de los trabajadores agrícolas. (p. 770)

United Nations (UN) [Naciones Unidas] *s.* organización internacional promotora de la paz a la que pertenecen la mayoría de naciones, fundada en 1945 para fomentar la paz, la seguridad y el desarrollo económico del mundo. (p. 603)

urban flight [huida urbana] *s.* migración de las ciudades a los suburbios aledaños. (p. 882)

urbanization [urbanización] *s.* movimiento de personas a una ciudad. (p. 262)

urban renewal [renovación urbana] *s.* práctica que se inició con la Ley Nacional de Vivienda de 1949, de remplazar vecindarios urbanos decaídos por viviendas nuevas para gente de bajos recursos. (p. 661)

urban sprawl [explosión urbana] *s.* expansión desordenada y desmedida de las ciudades a las áreas contiguas. (p. 424)

USS *Maine* *s.* buque de guerra estadounidense que explotó y naufragó misteriosamente el 15 de febrero de 1898 en el puerto de La Habana, Cuba. (p. 348)

U-2 incident [incidente del U-2] *s.* derribo en 1960 de un avión espía estadounidense U-2 en suelo soviético; complicó las conversaciones de paz entre Estados Unidos y la Unión Soviética. (p. 627)

V

V-E Day [Día V-E] *s.* mayo 8 de 1945, día de la victoria europea, cuando el general Eisenhower aceptó la rendición incondicional de Alemania; puso fin a la II Guerra Mundial en Europa. (p. 585)

vertical integration [integración vertical] *s.* proceso mediante el cual una compañía se adueña de sus proveedores y distribuidores así como de los sistemas de transporte, con lo que obtiene control total sobre la calidad y el costo de su producción. (p. 242)

Vietcong *s.* rebeldes comunistas de Vietnam del Sur apoyados por Vietnam del Norte a partir de 1959. (p. 73)

Vietminh [Vietmin] *s.* organización de comunistas vietmanitas y otros grupos nacionalistas que luchó contra los franceses por la independencia de Vietnam de 1946 a 1954. (p. 731)

Vietnamization [vietnamización] *s.* plan del presidente Nixon de retiro gradual de las tropas estadounidenses de Vietnam y su remplazo por el ejército vietnamita. (p. 755)

Voting Rights Act of 1965 [Ley de Derechos Electorales de 1965] *s.* ley para facilitarles a los afroamericanos inscribirse para votar; eliminó las pruebas discriminatorias de lectura y escritura, y autorizó a los examinadores federales inscribir votantes rechazados a nivel local. (p. 716)

W

Wagner Act [Ley Wagner] *s.* ley—también conocida como Ley Nacional de Relaciones Laborales—promulgada en 1935 para proteger los derechos de los trabajadores después de que la Corte Suprema consideró que la Ley Nacional de Recuperación Industrial (NIRA) era inconstitucional. (p. 499)

war-guilt clause [cláusula de culpabilidad] *s.* cláusula del Tratado de Versalles que obligaba a Alemania a reconocer que había sido totalmente responsable por la I Guerra Mundial. (p. 400)

War Industries Board (WIB) [Junta de Industrias Bélicas] *s.* junta establecida en 1917 que animaba a las compañías a usar técnicas de producción en masa para mejorar la eficiencia durante la I Guerra Mundial. (p. 389)

War Powers Act (WPA) [Ley de Poderes de Guerra] *s.* ley aprobada en 1973 tras la Guerra de Vietnam que limitaba el derecho de un presidente a enviar tropas a combatir sin consultar con el Congreso. (p. 761)

War Production Board (WPB) [Junta de Producción Bélica] *s.* agencia establecida durante la II Guerra Mundial para coordinar la producción de suministros militares por la industria nacional. (p. 578)

Warren Commission [Comisión Warren] *s.* grupo encabezado por Earl Warren, presidente de la Suprema Corte, que realizó la investigación oficial del asesinato del presidente Kennedy y concluyó que Lee Harvey Oswald había actuado por su cuenta. (p. 683)

Warren Court [la Corte Warren] *s.* la Suprema Corte de la que fue presidente Earl Warren, que se destacó por sus actividades en torno a los derechos civiles y la libre expresión. (p. 691)

Warsaw Pact [Pacto de Varsovia] *s.* alianza militar formada en 1955 por la Unión Soviética y las naciones satélite de Europa del este. (p. 624)

Watergate *s.* serie de escándalos en que el presidente Nixon trató de encubrir la participación de su comité de relección en el allanamiento de la sede del Partido Demócrata en los apartamentos Watergate en 1972. (p. 802)

Women's Auxiliary Army Corps (WAAC) [Unidad Auxiliar de Mujeres (WAAC)] *s.* unidad del Ejército de EE.UU. creada durante la Segunda Guerra Mundial para permitir que las mujeres colaboraran en puestos que no fueran de combate. (p. 563)

Woodstock *s.* festival gratuito de música que atrajo a más de 400,000 jóvenes a una granja del estado de New York en agosto de 1969. (p. 782)

Works Progress Administration (WPA) [Administración para el Progreso de Obras] *s.* agencia gubernamental del New Deal que empleó a personal desocupado en construcción de escuelas y hospitales, reparación de carreteras, enseñanza, escritura y artes. (p. 498)

X

XYZ Affair [Asunto XYZ] *s.* incidente diplomático de 1797 en el que funcionarios franceses trataron de sobornar a funcionarios estadounidenses para entrevistarse con un alto ministro francés. (p. 78)

Y

yellow journalism [prensa amarillista] *s.* uso de métodos sensacionalistas en periódicos o revistas para atraer o influenciar lectores. (p. 347)

Z

Zimmermann note [nota Zimmermann] *s.* mensaje enviado por el canciller alemán en 1917 al canciller mexicano en el que prometía a México los estados de Texas, New Mexico y Arizona si se aliaba a Alemania en contra de Estados Unidos en la I Guerra Mundial. (p. 379)

INDEX

An *i* preceding a page number in italics refers to an illustration on the page. An *m* or a *c* preceding a page number in italics refers to a map or chart on the page.

A

AAA. *See* Agricultural Adjustment Act.
Abilene, Kansas, 209–210, 238
***Ableman* v. *Booth*,** 166
abolitionists. *See* antislavery movement.
abortion rights, 97, 779, 840
***Abrams* v. *United States*,** 396–397
ACLU. *See* American Civil Liberties Union.
acquired immune deficiency syndrome (AIDS), 840, 880, R53
Adams, Abigail, 56, *i* 56
Adams, John, 56, 62, 77–78, *i* 77, 79, 86, 112–113, 118–119, R50
Adams, John Quincy, 116, 123, R50
Adams, Samuel, 47
Adams-Onís Treaty, 116, *m* 116
***Adarand Constructors* v. *Pena*,** 818, 819
Addams, Jane, 266, *i* 266, 337, 358, 394
Adena culture, 6
***Adventures of Huckleberry Finn, The* (Twain),** 296
advertising, 297, 425–426, 648–649
AEF. *See* American Expeditionary Force.
affirmative action, 429, 818–819, 843, 844, 905, R53
  reverse discrimination and, 831, R63
Afghanistan, 815, R40
  elections in, 867
  Muslim terrorists and, 867, 896
  U.S. military action in, 867, 896
AFL. *See* American Federation of Labor.
Africa, 13, 144, 343. *See also* North Africa; West Africa.
  slave trade and, 10, 15, 32–33
***Africana*,** 456
African Americans, *c* 147, 182–183, 260, 324–325, 452–454, 473, 505–506, 843. *See also* antislavery movement; civil rights; exodusters; segregation; slavery; slaves; *names of specific individuals.*
  in business, 187–188
  churches of, 145, 187–188
  in cities, 187, 263, 266, 288, 393–394, 435, 452–453, 454, 455, *i* 455, 718
  in Civil War, 173
  in Congress, 188, 722
  as cowboys, 210
  discrimination against, 71, 173, 286–288, 564, 565–566, 903, 911
  education of, 148, 184, 187, 188, 283, 284–285, *i* 285, 701, *c* 701, 702–703, 722, 723, *c* 723, 904
  Farmers' Alliances and, 220–221
  female, 148, 149, 314, 315
  Harlem Renaissance and, 454, 455, *i* 455, 456
  in labor force, 215, 314, 565–566
  in labor movement, 245, 418, 565–566
  migrations of, 204, 215, *i* 215, 393–394, 452–453, 591, *m* 591, 701, 889
  music of, 298, 299, 655–657, 786
  in Philippine-American War, 355
  popular culture and, 655–656, *i* 656
  race riots and, 288, 394, 453, 841
  Reconstruction and, 184, 185–188, 189
  in Revolutionary War, 59, 61
  in Spanish-American War, 350, *i* 350
  as U.S. citizens, 166–167
  in Vietnam War, 743
  voting rights of, 71, 102, 104, 185–186, 187, 286–287, 315, 637, 715–716
  in World War I, 382, 392–394
  in World War II, 563, *i* 563, 564, 573, *i* 573, 702, 889
Africans, in American colonies, 15, 23, 32–33
Afrika Korps, 572
Agee, James, 514
Agent Orange, 739
***Age of Innocence, The* (Wharton),** 451
Agnew, Spiro T., 796, 805, 811
Agricultural Adjustment Act (AAA), 491, 496
agriculture. *See also* farmers.
  education in, 217
  in English colonies, 23, 31–32, 34
  farm worker movement and, 770
  inventions for, 121, 141, 217, *c* 217, 232, 263
  in Midwest, 141
  migrant workers and, 684–685, *i* 684, *i* 685, *m* 685
  of Native Americans, 5, 6, 25
  New Deal and, 518
  plantation, 15, 31–32, 146, *i* 147
  in South, 121–122, 141, 182, 187–188
  in Soviet Union, 529
  water projects and, 256, 289, 324
Aguinaldo, Emilio, 349, 355
AIDS. *See* acquired immune deficiency syndrome.
AIM. *See* American Indian Movement.
airlines, deregulation of, 837
airline industry. *See* industry, airline.
airplane(s)
  airmail and, 280, *i* 280, 281
  commercial use of, 424, *i* 424, 588, *i* 588
  famous flights of, 449, *m* 449
  first flight of, 279, 280, *i* 280
  hijacking of, 863, 894
  security on, 897
  as terrorist weapons, 894, 895
  in World War I, 381, 384–385, *i* 384, 588
  in World War II, 539, 540–541
airports, security at, 897, *i* 897
Alabama, 165, 704–705, 716, 774
  facts about, R48
Alamo, 134–135, *i* 134, R53
Alaska, 5, 6, 116, 117, 212, 773, *c* 773, 822
  1857, *m* 45
  facts about, R48
  U.S. purchase of, 344
Alaska Native Claims Settlement Act, 773, 822
Alaskan Pipeline, 822, *i* 822
Albany, New York, 60, 120, 139, 140
Alcott, Louisa May, 174
Alexander II (czar of Russia), 116–117
Alexander, Harold, 572
Alien and Sedition Acts, 78–79, 392
Allen, Frederick Lewis, 469, 475
Allen, Gracie, 511, *i* 512
Alliance for Progress, 680–681, R54
Allies, R54
  in World War I, 373–374, 376, 377, 378, *i* 386
  in World War II, 554
al-Qaeda, 867, 894–895, 896
Álvarez de Piñeda, Alonso, 18
Amendments to Constitution. *See specific number.*
American Civil Liberties Union (ACLU), 438
American Colonization Society, 145
American Expeditionary Force (AEF), 384, R54
American Federation of Labor (AFL), 245–246, 333, 417, 508, R54
***American Gothic* (Wood),** 513, *i* 513
American Independent Party, 753
American Indian Movement (AIM), 771–772
American Indians. *See* Native Americans.
Americanization movement, 263, R54
American Liberty League, 493
American Protective Association, 258
American Railway Union (ARU), 246, 248
American Revolution. *See* Revolutionary War.
American Socialist Party, 309
American System, 122, R54
America Online (AOL), 871
Ameringer, Oscar, 478
Amnesty Act, 189
amusement parks, 292–293
analyzing causes, 11, 13, 23, 39, 121, 127, 208, 211, 215, 220, 222, 247, 256, 270, 271, 277, 296, 310, 314, 356, 373, 439, 451, 457, 475, 512, 530, 534, 535, 554, 570, 591, 593, 603, 604, 610, 612, 618, 619, 623, 636, 646, 648, 655, 703, 715, 716, 719, 740, 778, 799, 809, 812, 814, 815, 825, 809, 833, 838, 855, 861, 864, 865, 883, R7

analyzing distributions, 73, 521, 847, R25, R32
analyzing effects, 5, 13, 20, 30, 35, 36, 53, 63, 138, 161, 174, 177, 182, 186, 196, 197, 206, 215, 233, 237, 259, 265, 266, 271, 287, 315, 320, 337, 343, 351, 360, 374, 379, 385, 392, 394, 421, 423, 424, 437, 442, 448, 453, 469, 476, 477, 491, 508, 514, 519, 544, 551, 573, 576, 592, 595, 607, 625, 643, 644, 646, 649, 653, 657, 661, 674, 677, 681, 691, 693, 701, 741, 761, 770, 777, 800, 801, 821, 825, 833, 836, 862, 870, 873, 878, R7
analyzing events, 15, 26, 79, 81, 124, 160, 335, 345, 349, 414, 467, 568, 611, 615, 621, 630, 702, 714, 723, 753, 807, 817, 826, 850, R13
analyzing issues, 23, 24, 25, 39, 47, 68, 71, 79, 134, 136, 138, 143, 147, 149, 183, 196, 204, 220, 223, 239, 245, 316, 325, 329, 353, 358, 380, 415, 418, 427, 439, 483, 499, 514, 543, 555, 598, 662, 663, 692, 703, 704, 711, 723, 725, 749, 751, 757, 796, 817, 831, 843, 866, 873, 881, R14
analyzing motives, 18, 49, 78, 106, 122, 126, 133, 173, 176, 179, 226, 240, 261, 263, 266, 268, 307, 337, 347, 363, 377, 405, 413, 532, 538, 540, 541, 549, 585, 595, 605, 608, 621, 678, 683, 687, 720, 732, 750, 771, 779, 797, 803, 833, 838, 868, R6
analyzing patterns, 151, 235, 367, 416, *c* 416, 651, 685, R25, R32
analyzing political cartoons, 43, 71, 78, 81, 97, 107, 126, 161, 187, 220, 223, 240, 243, 269, 273, 312, 319, 351, 354, 362, 369, 391, 421, 426, 431, 439, 467, 481, 493, 519, 534, 551, 559, 608, 620, 621, 631, 678, 693, 765, 795, 806, 836, 877, R24
analyzing primary sources. *See* primary sources, analyzing.
analyzing relationships, 235, *m* 349, *m* 356, 358, 426, *c* 517, 685, 696, 753, 800, 857, R28
analyzing visual sources. *See* visual sources, analyzing.
anarchists, 392, 413, 415, *c* R44, R54
Anasazi, 5, 6, R54
Anaya, Toney, 844
Anderson, Marian, 506, *i* 506, 672
Anderson, Robert, 168
Angel Island, 257, *i* 258, *i* 886
Angelou, Maya, 590, 860, *i* 860
Anglican Church. *See* Church of England.
Anthony, Susan B., 105, 315, 316, *i* 316, 335
anthrax, 896
  effects of, 896
  September 11 terrorist attack and, 896
Antietam, Battle of, 171
Antifederalists, 69–70, R54
Anti-Imperialist League, 358
Anti-Saloon League, 308, 436
antislavery movement, 145–147, 148, 157–158, 162, 172
antiterrorism bill, 866
antiterrorism coalition, 867, 896
  Great Britain and, 896, 899
AOL. *See* America Online.
Apache, 19
apartheid, 701
Appomattox Court House, Virginia, 181, *i* 181, 183, R54
Arapaho, 206
architecture, *i* 27, *i* 278, *i* 336, *i* 883
Arizona, 18, 137, 688, 847
  facts about, R48
Arkansas, 169, 185, 703, 709, 716, 860, 861
  facts about, R48
Armstrong, Louis, *i* 455, 456, *i* 456, 457
Armstrong, Neil, 796
art, *i* 11, *i* 48, *i* 164, *i* 210, *i* 295, *i* 364, *i* 393, *i* 414, *i* 435, *i* 450, *i* 512–513, *i* 645. *See also specific works, artists, and movements.*
Arthur, Chester A., 270, *i* 270, R51
Articles of Confederation, 67, *c* 67, 68, 84, 104
artificial intelligence, 878–879
ARU. *See* American Railway Union.
Asbury, Herbert, 437
Ashcan school of American art, 295
Asian Americans, 844, 884, 886, 889. *See also* Chinese immigrants; Japanese Americans; Japanese immigrants.
  in World War II, 564
assembly line, 309, *i* 309
assimilation, 205, 206–207, 284, 662–663, 771, R54
assumptions and biases, analyzing, R15
Atlanta, Georgia, 181, 843
Atlantic, Battle of the, 570
Atlantic Charter, 554
Atlee, Clement, 604
atomic bomb, 567, 583–584, 585, 589, *i* 589, 622. *See also* nuclear weapons.
attainder, bill of, 89
Attucks, Crispus, 46, *i* 46, 48
Austin, Stephen F., 130, *i* 130, 133, 134
Australian ballot, 312
Austria, German annexation of, 536–537
Austria-Hungary, 255, 373–374, 391
automobile, 231, 422–424, *i* 422, 426
  industry, 423–424, 465, 814
  in 1950s, 646, 647, *i* 647
  pollution and, 822, 881
  safety and, 691
  urban sprawl and, 423–424, 643
Aviation and Transportation Security Act, 897
Axis powers, 551, *i* 551, 554, R54
Aycock, Charles B., 310
Aztecs, 5, 16, R54

B

Babbitt **(Lewis),** 450
baby boom, 643–644, *c* 643, *i* 643, 884, 912, R54
Bacon, Nathaniel, 23
Bacon's Rebellion, 23
Bahamas, 14
Baker, Ella, 706
Baker, Howard, 805
Baker, James A., 866
Baker, Josephine, 456
Baker, Newton, 388
***Baker* v. *Carr*,** 692, 774–775
Bakke, Allan Paul, 818, *i* 818, 905
Baldwin, James, 660, *i* 660
Balkan Peninsula, in World War I, 373, 374
Ball, George, 737
Ballinger, Richard A., 329
Baltimore, Maryland, 268
Baltimore and Ohio Railroad, 247
Bank of the United States, 75, 88, 113. *See also* Second Bank of the United States.
Banks, Dennis, 772, *i* 772
banks and banking, 75, 122, 126, 127, 221, 425–426
  Federal Reserve System and, 334, R42
  Great Depression and, 469, *c* 470, 481
  New Deal and, 490, 518
Baptists, 36
barbed wire, 211, 217, *c* 217, 232
Barkett, Rosemary, *i* 915
Barnett, Ross, 711
Barnum, P. T., 298
Barrett, Janie Porter, 266
Barton, Clara, 174, *i* 174
Baruch, Bernard M., 389
baseball, 294, *i* 294, 448
Batista, Fulgencio, 673
Battle of . . . *See distinctive part of battle's name.*
Baumfree, Isabella. *See* Truth, Sojourner.
Bay of Pigs, 674
Beach Boys, 786
beat movement, 655, R54
Beaudoin, Ethel, 869
Beaumont, Texas, 230
Beckwourth, Jim, 131, *i* 131
Begin, Menachem, 816, *i* 816
Belgium, 374, 375, 376, 377, 540, 574
Bell, Alexander Graham, 140, 233
Bell, John, 164
Benin, 9
Benny, Jack, 511
Benton, Thomas Hart, 513
Beringia, 5
Bering Strait, 5
Berkeley, William, 23
Berlin, Germany
  airlift to, *i* 605, *i* 606, R54
  division of, 607, 677–678, *m* 677
Berlin Wall, 677–678, *i* 677, 849–850, *i* 850, R54
Bernstein, Carl, 804, *i* 804
Berry, Chuck, 656, *i* 656
Bessemer, Henry, 231–232
Bessemer process, 231–232, 241
Bethune, Mary McLeod, 505, *i* 505
bias, identifying, 108, 250, 339, R15
bicameral legislature, 68
bicycles, 293, *i* 293
Big Four, 399, 400
Bilingual Education Act, 844
Bill of Rights
  in U.S. Constitution, 70–71, 89, 96–97, 99, 103, 724, R54

bimetallism, 222, R54
bin Laden, Osama, 867, 896
  as head of al-Qaeda, 867, 896
biological weapons. *See* weapons of mass destruction.
biotechnology, 879–880
Birmingham riots, 712, *i* 712, 725
Bishop, Joseph Bucklin, 359
Black Americans. *See* African Americans.
black codes, 185, 291
Black Hills, 206, 212
blacklist, 618, R54
Black Panthers, 720–721, R54
Black Power, 720, R54
Black Tuesday, 468, R54
Bland-Allison Act, 220
Blatch, Harriet Stanton, 388, *i* 388
blitzkrieg, 539, R54
***Body Snatchers, The* (Finney),** 628
Boland Amendment, 853
Bolsheviks, 413
bonanza farms, 218, *i* 218, R54
Bonaparte, Napoleon, 114, 116
Bonus Army, 482–483, *i* 483, R55
Booth, John Wilkes, 183
bootleggers, 437
Bork, Robert, 805
Bosnia, 374, 850, 863–864
Boston, Massachusetts, 264, 268, 278, 417, 509, 797
  colonial, 24, 46, 47, 48–49, 50, 51
Boston Massacre, 48, *i* 48, R55
Boston Port Act, 55
Boston Tea Party, 49, *i* 49, 55, R55
Boulder Dam, 480, *i* 480, 481, R55
boundary settlements
  with France, 114
  with Great Britain, 116, *m* 116, 133
  with Mexico, *m* 136, 137
  with Spain, 77, 116, *m* 116, 117
  after World War I, 399, 400–401, *m* 400
  after World War II, 585–586
Boxer Protocol, 357
Boxer Rebellion, 357, *i* 357, R55
boxing, 294
boycott, 47, 64, 700, 704–705, *i* R38
Bozeman Trail, 204, *m* 205
braceros, 662, R55
Braddock, Edward, 37, *i* 37
Bradley, Omar, 574
Brady, Mathew, 178
Brady Act, 903
Brandeis, Louis D., 311
brand names, 293
Breckinridge, John C., 164
Breed's Hill, 51
Brennan, William, 836
Breyer, Stephen, *i* 93
Brezhnev, Leonid, 800, 811, 815
brinkmanship, 622–623, R55
Britain, Battle of, 540–541, *i* 540
British East India Company, 49
Brooklyn Bridge, 232, 276, *i* 276, 277
Brooks, Preston S., 161, *i* 161
Brotherhood of Sleeping Car Porters, 411, 566
Brown, John, 163–164, *i* 164
Brown, Linda, 702, 708, *i* 708
***Brown* v. *Board of Education of Topeka*,** 99, *i* 99, 129, 291, 640, 691, 702–703, 708–709, 797, 904, R55
Bryan, William Jennings, 222, *i* 222, *i* 223, 328, 358, 377, 438–439, *i* 439
Buchanan, James, 162, R51
Buckley, William F., Jr., 831
Buddhism, 732
Budget, Bureau of the, 420
buffalo, *i* 207, 208
  Native Americans and, 203, 207
  whites' hunting of, 207
Buford, John, 176
Bulge, Battle of the, 576, R55
Bullard, Florence, 385
Bull Moose Party, 330, R55
Bull Run, First Battle of, 169
Bunau-Varilla, Philippe, 360
Bunker Hill, Battle of, 51, *i* 51
***Bunting* v. *Oregon*,** 311
Burger, Warren, 798
Burgoyne, John, 60
Burnham, Daniel H., 277, 278–279
Burns, George, 511, *i* 512
Burns, Lucy, 332, 335
Burr, Aaron, 98, 113
Bush, George, H. W., 595, 832, 837, 838, *i* 838, 844, 855, 861, R52
  education and, 841
  end of Cold War and, 849
  Iran-Contra scandal and, 853
  Supreme Court and, 836
Bush, George W., 619, 859, 865–868, *i* 866, R52
  antiterrorism bill and, 866
  economy and, 867
  education and, 867, 905
  social security and, 913
  Supreme Court and, 866
  tax cuts and, 866, 867
  war against terrorism and, 866–867, 896–897, 898, 899
  welfare reform and, 911
business. *See also* corporations; economy; entrepreneurs; free enterprise; industry; trade.
  African Americans in, 187–188
  Andrew Carnegie and, 241–242
  conglomerates, 642, R55
  consolidation of, 243–244
  Cuba and, 354–355
  downsizing and, 870
  franchises and, *i* 642, 643, R57
  Great Depression and, 469, *c* 470, 492
  growth of, in 1920s, 422–423
  horizontal integration and, 242, *c* 242
  on the Internet, 871, R40
  regulation of, 239–240, 244
  scientific management and, 308
  Social Darwinism and, 242–243
  in South, 244
  temporary workers in, 870
  vertical integration and, 242, *c* 242
business cycle, *c* R38, R40
  Cold War and, 604, 606, 611
busing, 723, 797–798, *i* 797, 831
Butler, Andrew P., 161
Butterfield, Alexander, 805

C

cabinet, 75, R55
  Bush's (George H. W.), 844, 855
  FDR's, 505
  Harding's, 420–421
  Kennedy's, 672
  Nixon's, 803
  Reagan's, 836, 837
  Washington's, 75, 76
Cabrillo, Juan Rodriguez, *m* 17, 19
Cagney, James, 511
Calamity Jane. *See* Cannary, Martha Jane.
Calhoun, John C., 122, 124, 128, *i* 128, 156, *i* 156, *i* 157
California, 47, 116, 127, 135, 136–137, 157, 424
  admission to Union of, 157
  air pollution in, 824
  economy of, 138
  facts about, R48
  farm workers in, 770
  gold rush in, 137–138, 157, 209, 224, 255
  immigration and migration and, 137, 258–259, 474, 847, *c* 847, 888
  Native Americans in, 4, 6, *m* 7
  recall election, 868
  Republic of, 137
  Spanish missions in, 19–20, *i* 19, 33
Calloway, Cab, 457
Cambodia, 756, 757, 760, 811
Camino Real, 18
Campbell, Ben Nighthorse, 771, *i* 771
Camp David Accords, 816–817, R55
Canada, 38, 60, 62, 114, 133, 158, 864
canals, 139, 141
***Cane* (Toomer),** 454
Cannary, Martha Jane (Calamity Jane), 211, *i* 211
Cannon, Joseph, 329
***Canticle for Leibowitz, A* (Miller),** 629
Cantwell, Maria, 65
capitalism, 246, 283, R41. *See also* free enterprise.
Capitol, 116
Capone, Al, 437, *i* 437
Capra, Frank, 511
Caputo, Philip, 763
caravel, *i* 12
Caribbean region, 14, 18, 146, 851–852, *m* 851. *See also* Cuba; Dominican Republic; Puerto Rico; West Indies.
Carmichael, Stokely, 720, *i* 720
Carnegie, Andrew, 241–242, *i* 241, 244, 283, 355, 358
  philanthropy of, 244
Carnegie Steel Company, 241–242, 243, 247
carpetbaggers, 186–187, *i* 187, R55
Carranza, Venustiano, 363, 364–365
Carson, Rachel, 691, 821
Carter, Jimmy, 812, *i* 812, 832–833, 851, R52
  Camp David Accords and, 816–817
  civil rights and, 814
  domestic agenda of, 812–813
  energy crisis and, 812–813
  human rights and, 725, 815
  inflation under, 813, *c* 813
  Iran hostage crisis and, 817, 832
  unemployment under, *c* 813

Carter, Robert, III, 31
Carter, Rosalyn, 725
Cartier, Jacques, *m* 17
Casablanca conference, 573
Castro, Fidel, 673–674, *i* 674, 677, 683, 769
categorizing, R6
Cather, Willa, 296, 451
Catholic Church. *See* Roman Catholicism and Roman Catholics.
Catt, Carrie Chapman, 332, *i* 332, 334–335
cattle drive, 209–211, *m* 209
cattle ranching, 208–211, 323
causes, analyzing. *See* analyzing causes.
Cavazos, Lauro, 844
CCC. *See* Civilian Conservation Corps.
CD-ROMs, 877
"Celebrated Jumping Frog of Calaveras County, The" (Twain), 224
Celera
human genome research and, 879
Cemetery Ridge, 177
census, 882
Central America, 18, 360, 851–852, *m* 851. *See also* Guatemala; Nicaragua; Panama; Panama Canal.
Central Intelligence Agency (CIA), 623–624, 626, 674, 796, 803, 804, R55
Central Pacific Railroad, 215, 237
Central Park, 277–278
Central Powers, 374, 377, 378, 386, R55
***Century of Dishonor, A* (Jackson),** 206
chain stores, 296–297
Challenger, 841
Chamberlain, Neville, 537
Chambers, Whittaker, 618
Chamorro, Violeta de, 852
Chancellorsville, Battle of, 175
Charles I (king of England), 26, 28
Charles II (king of England), 26, 28
Charleston or Charles Town, South Carolina, 33, 62, 168
Charleston (dance), *i* 426, *i* 444–445, 445
charter schools, 904
charts
creating, 73, 81, 106, 129, 138, 152, 174, 300, 301, 331, 407, 429, 501, 631, 657, 709, 741, R5, R9, R10, R13, R15, R16, R17, R20, R22, R23, R24, R26, R30
interpreting, 49, 69, 76, 87, 105, 226, 447, 545, 604, 621, 681, 690, 714, 753, 842, 871, 884, R27
using, 30, 42, 63, 79, 80, 117, 127, 183, 189, 190, 211, 222, 227, 233, 240, 242, 250, 271, 280, 281, 285, 316, 331, 365, 380, 395, 406, 418, 494, 558, 587, 595, 598, 608, 649, 665, 693, 735, 801, 826, 845, 846, 855, 881, 887, R11, R23, R24, R32, R33
Chávez, César, 768, 770, *i* 770
Chechnya, 863
checks and balances, 69, 106, 119, R55
chemical weapons. *See* weapons of mass destruction.
Cherokee, 125, *i* 125, *m* 125, 135
Chesapeake Bay, 21, 28, 62
Chesnut, Mary, 175, *i* 175
Cheyenne, 203, 204, 206
Chiang Kai-shek, 609–610, *i* 610, 611
Chicago, Illinois, 209, 232, 247, 263, 296, 317, 435, 437, 508, 509, 722, 841, 843
Great Fire in, *c* 265, *i* 265
1968 Democratic convention in, 751–752, *i* 752
railroads and, 238
urban planning and, 278–279, *m* 278
Chicago, University of, 243
Chicanos(as). *See* Mexican Americans.
child labor, 245, 248, 306, 310–311, *i* 311, 321, *i* 321
Chiles, Lawton, 886
China, 12
Boxer Protocol and, 357
Boxer Rebellion in, 357, *i* 357
civil war in, 610
Clinton administration and, 863
communism in, 609–610, *c* 610, 616, 799–800, 850
human rights abuses in, 863
Japan and, 532, 535
Korean War and, 612
Nationalist government in, 609–610, *c* 610, 611
Open Door policy and, 356
Soviet Union and, 800
Tiananmen Square demonstrations, 850, *i* 850
trade with, 117, 356
Chinese Exclusion Act, 259
Chinese immigrants, 246, 254, 255, 257, 258–259, *i* 258, *i* 259, 260, *i* 886
exclusion of, 258–259, *i* 259
as railroad workers, 215, 229, 237, *i* 237, 255
Chippewa, 887
Chisholm, Shirley, 722, *i* 722
Chisholm Trail, 209–210, *m* 209, R55
Chivington, John M., 204
Choctaw, *m* 125
Christianity, 10–11, 18, 19–20, 438–439, R55. *See also* Great Awakening; Second Great Awakening; *names of specific denominations.*
chronological order, 299, 758, 804, R3
absolute, 856, R3. *See also* time lines.
relative, R3
Churchill, Winston, 538, 541, *i* 541, 551, 554, *i* 605
"Iron Curtain" speech of, 605
in World War II, 560, 561, 570, 572, 583, 585–586
Church of England, 24, 27, 36
Church of Jesus Christ of Latter Day Saints. *See* Mormons.
CIA. *See* Central Intelligence Agency.
Cigar Makers' International Union, 245
CIO. *See* Congress of Industrial Organizations.
circus, 298
CIS. *See* Commonwealth of Independent States.
Cisneros, Sandra, 875
cities. *See also* suburbs.
African Americans in, 187, 263, 266, 288, 393–394, 435, 452–453, 454, 455, *i* 455, 718
automobile and, 423–424
colonial, 33, 34, *i* 34
governments of, 309–310
housing in, 262, 264, 883
immigrants in, 142, *i* 143, 262–263, 266, 435
industry and, 234
merchants in, 296–297
migration to, 187, 263, 393–394, 434, 452–453, 454, 455, 718
in 1920s, 434–436
in 1950s, 660–661
opportunities in, 262–263
political machines and, 267–268
poverty in, 266, 660–661, 841, 883
problems in, 264–265, 883
railroads and, 238
reformers and, 266, 307, 309–310
settlement houses in, 266
transportation in, 264, 277
urban planning and, 277–278, 883
urban renewal and, 661
"white flight" from, 660–661, 718, 723, 841
***City of Boerne* v. *Flores*,** 119
civil disobedience, 705
Civilian Conservation Corps (CCC), *i* 486–487, 491, *i* 491, *c* 500, 505, 519, R55
civil rights, 843–845. *See also* domestic policy; slavery; Thirteenth Amendment; Fourteenth Amendment; Fifteenth Amendment; Twenty-fourth Amendment; Voting Rights Act; *names of specific rights.*
Birmingham march and, 712, *i* 712
Black Muslims and, 719–720
Black Power movement, 720
Carter (Jimmy) and, 814
Eisenhower and, 640
election of 1960 and, 671
freedom riders and, 710–711, *i* 711
Freedom Summer and, 715
homosexuals and, 845
Jim Crow laws and, 287, 291, 701, 708–709
Johnson (Lyndon) and, 687–688
Malcolm X and, 719, *i* 719, 720
march on Washington and, 714
Montgomery bus boycott and, 700, 704–705, R38
movement in 18th century, 24–25, *i* 44–45, 47, 52–53, 69–71, 145–149, 157–158, 159, *m* 159, 162–165, 172, 173, 724
movement in 19th century, 185, 286–288, 290–291, 700–701, 724
movement in 20th century, 99, 291, 324–325, 506, 637–638, 640, 671, 682, 687–688, 698–727, 797, 814, 831, 843–845
NAACP and, 291, 702
in 1970s, 722–723
Nixon and, 796–797
Reconstruction and, 185, 286
Roosevelt (Franklin) and, 506
Roosevelt (Theodore) and, 324–325

Selma campaign and, 716
"separate but equal" doctrine and, 287, 291
sit-ins and, 706–707, *i* 707, R64
Supreme Court and, 290–291, 596–597, 691–692, 708–709
Truman and, 637–638
Wilson and, 335–336
Civil Rights Act
of 1866, 185, 724
of 1875, 700
of 1957, 687, *c* 714
of 1964, 429, 688, *c* 714, 831, R55
of 1968, 714, *c* 714, 722, R55
civil service, 270–271, R55
Civil War, 94, 168–174, *m* 170–171, *i* 173, 175–181, 184, 888
effects of, 181–183, 186–187, 244
photographs of, 178, *i* 178
resources of North and South, *c* 169
Civil Works Administration (CWA), 488, *i* 488, 491, *c* 500
clarifying, R4. *See also* summarizing.
Clark, William, 114
Clay, Henry, 122, 123, 126, 157–158, *i* 157
Clayton Antitrust Act, 333, R55
Clean Air Act, 822
Clemenceau, Georges, 399, *i* 399
Clemens, Samuel (Mark Twain), 224, 267, 294, 296, 358, *i* 358
***Clermont*,** 120, 140
Cleveland, Grover, 248, 258, 271, 330, 345, 358, R51
Cleveland, Ohio, 231, 234–235, 264, 307, 310
Clifford, Clark, 749
Clinton, Bill, 85, *i* 597, 844, 860–868, *i* 861, 904, 911, R52
Bosnia and, 863–864
Congress and, 862, 864–865
foreign policy of, 863–864
GATT and, 872
health-care reform and, 861, 908
impeachment and, 865
NAFTA and, 864, 872
Russia and, 863
welfare reform and, 862
Clinton, Henry, 62
Clinton, Hillary Rodham, 861, *i* 861
cloning, 880
CNLU. *See* Colored National Labor Union.
coal, 231, *m* 231, 237, 465
mining of, *i* 321
Coca-Cola, 293
Cody, William F. "Buffalo Bill"
Wild West Show of, 206, 211
***Cohens* v. *Virginia*,** 118
Coit, Stanton, 266
Cold War, 405, 589, 606, R55. *See also* Soviet Union.
arms race and, 622–623, 670, 849
Berlin and, 677–678
communism in China and, 609–610
communism in U.S. and, 616–621
covert actions in, 623–624
Cuba and, 673–674, 676
defense spending in, *c* 626
development of, 602–605
effects of end of, 848–850
end of, 848–849
in Europe, 606
flexible response in, 673, R57
Geneva summit and, 624
hot line in, 678, R58
impact on business cycle, 604, 606, 611
Kennedy and, 671–674, 676–678
Korean War and, 611–612, 614–615
McCarthyism and, 620–621
Nixon and, 799–800
reasons for Western victory in, 849–850
science fiction and, 628–629
Truman Doctrine and, 606
U-2 incident in, 626, *i* 627, 670
U.S. foreign policy and, 622–623
Colfax, Schuyler, 238
collective bargaining, 246
Collier, John, 507, *i* 507
Colombia, 360
colonial America, *m* 25, *m* 29. *See also* Revolutionary War; Spain, American colonies of; *names of specific colonies.*
courtship in, 40–41, *i* 40, *i* 41
governments in, 30
life in, 32, 33–36
meetinghouses, *i* 27
relations with Britain in, 28, 30, 39, 46–53, *c* 48, *c* 49, 55, 56, 58, 59, 64
relations with Native Americans in, 23, 25–26, 37, 39, 53
settlement of, 21, 23–30
slaves in, 23, 28, 32–33, 34, 53
women in, 32, 34, 41, 53, 64
Colorado, 137, 204, 204
facts about, R48
Colored Farmers' National Alliance, 221
Colored National Labor Union (CNLU), 245
Colton, Walter, 137
Columbian Exchange, 15, *m* 15, R55
Columbian Exposition, *i* 274–275, 279
Columbus, Christopher, 10, 12, 13, 14–16, *i* 14, *m* 17
Comanche, 206
Committee on Public Information, 390
committees of correspondence, 49
Committee to Reelect the President (CRP), 803–804
***Common Sense* (Paine),** 52, *i* 52
Commonwealth of Independent States (CIS), 849
***Commonwealth* v. *Hunt*,** 143
communications, advances in, 140, *c* 140–141, 141, 279, 589, 876–878, 906–907. *See also* telegraph; telephone; television.
Communications Decency Act, 878
communism, 246, 412, 413, R39, *c* R44, R55. *See also* Cold War.
in China, 609–610, *c* 610, 616, 799–800, 850, R39
in Eastern Europe, 605, 677–678, 849–850, R39
Hollywood and, 616, 617–618, *i* 617
roots of, 413
in Soviet Union, 413, 529, 603, 800, 848–849, R39
in United States, 412, 413, 417, 456, 616–621
in Vietnam, 688, 730, 731, 732
***Communist Manifesto* (Marx and Engels),** 413
Community Action Program, 688
comparing, 9, 42, 119, 163, 182, 211, 272, 285, 289, 322, 358, 397, 417, 426, 445, 459, 468, 558, 579, 595, 614, 626, 642, 690, 716, 763, 817, 827, 845, 852, 875, 886, 889, R8. *See also* contrasting.
comparing and contrasting, 27, 41, 42, 178, 195, 225, 327, 365, 441, 477, 516, 657, 659, 723, 853, 887, R8
Compromise of 1850, 157–158, 160, *m* 160
computers, 140, 141, 429, 871, 872, 876–878, 906–907
using, 3, 43, 108, 369, 697, R29, R33, R37. *See also* Internet, using for research
concentration camps, *i* 548, R55
in Cuba, 347
in World War II, 546–549, *i* 546–547, 576
conclusions, drawing. *See* drawing conclusions.
Concord, Battle of, *c* 49, 50, 52
Coney Island, 292–293, *i* 292
Confederate States of America, or Confederacy, R55. *See also* Civil War.
formation of, 165, 168–169
life in, 174, 180
Conflict in Korea. *See* Korean War.
Conflict in Vietnam. *See* Vietnam War.
Congdon, Don, 510
Congress, 74–75, 84–90, *c* 87, 353, 691, 862, 864–865, 867. *See also* House of Representatives; Senate; *names of specific acts.*
African Americans in, 188, 722
under Articles of Confederation, 67, 69
plans for, in Constitutional Convention, 68, 69, *c* 69
powers of, 71, 88–90, 116–117, 166–167, 502–503
role of, in New Deal, 489–490, 492, 493, 496, 497, 498–499, 502, 503
role of, in Reconstruction, 185–186, 189
women in, 65, 372, 722
Congress of Industrial Organizations (CIO), 508
Congress of Racial Equality (CORE), 593, 706, 710–711, 715, R55
Conkling, Roscoe, 268, 270
Connally, John, 682
Connecticut
facts about, R48
settlement of, 25
Connor, Bull, 712
conquistadors, 16, R55
conscientious objector, 386, R56
conscription. *See* draft.
consequences. *See* analyzing effects; evaluating effects.

conservation. *See* environment, protection of.
Conservative Coalition, 831, R56
conservatives, 794, 830–833, 838. *See also* Contract with America; Reagan, Ronald.
Constitution, 74, 75, 77, 82–83, 104, 113, 124, 128
amendments to, 69–70, 94–95, 96–103. *See also specific amendments by number.*
Bill of Rights in, 70–71, 89, 96–97, 724
drafting of, 68–69
ratification of, 69–70, 95
relevance of, 71
text of, 84–103
Constitutional Convention, 68–69, *c* 69, 82–83, *i* 83, 95, 128, 724, *i* 724
Constitutional Union Party, 164
consumer price index, *c* 389, *c* R39, R42
consumers, 233, 648–649, R38, R40, R41, R46, R56
protection of, 691
containment, 605, 737, R56
Continental Army, 51, 60, 61. *See also* Revolutionary War.
Continental Congress. *See* First Continental Congress; Second Continental Congress.
Continentals (currency), 60
Contract with America, 864, R56
Contras, 851–852. *See also* Iran-Contra scandal.
contrasting, 28, 37, 67, 75, 76, 78, 135, 162, 174, 185, 187, 246, 288, 289, 309, 330, 336, 355, 435, 477, 493, 564, 640, 645, 683, 692, 707, 718, 720, 737, 741, 761, 840, R8. *See also* comparing and contrasting.
Convention of 1818, 116, *m* 116
convoy system, 383, *i* 383, 570, *i* 570, R56
Coolidge, Calvin, 417, 421, 422–423, 424, 426, R52
Copernicus, Nicolaus, 34–35
Coral Sea, Battle of the, 579
CORE. *See* Congress of Racial Equality.
Cornwallis, Charles, 62
Coronado, Francisco Vásquez de, *m* 17, 18
corporations, 307, 642, 867. *See also* business.
scandals involving, 867
corridos, 225
Cortés, Hernándo, 16, *i* 16, *m* 17
Cortez, Gregorio, 225
cotton, 121–122, 124, 141, 169, 171
Cotton Club, *i* 455, 457
cotton gin, 121, *i* 121
Coughlin, Charles, 493, 494
counterculture, 786, R56
courts, 47, 74–75, 143, 249, 438–439. *See also* judicial branch; Supreme Court.
cowboys, 208–211, *i* 210, 260
Cox, Archibald, 805
craft unions, 245
Crane, Stephen, 296
Crandall, Prudence, 148
Crazy Horse, 204, 206
creating charts. *See* charts, creating.
creating databases. *See* databases, creating
creating diagrams, *See* diagrams, creating.
creating graphs, *See* graphs, creating.
creating maps, *See* maps, creating.
creating models, *See* models, creating.
creating presentations. *See* presentations, creating.
creating time lines. *See* time lines, creating.
Crédit Mobilier scandal, 238, R56
Creek, *m* 125
Creel, George, 390–391
Creelman, James, 346, 347
crime, 265, 883, 902–903, *c* 902–903
Cripple Creek, Colorado, 212, 213
critical thinking, xxviii–xxix, xxx, 13, 20, 30, 39, 41, 42, 53, 63, 73, 79, 80, 84, 85, 86, 88, 89, 90, 91, 92, 93, 94, 95, 96, 97, 98, 99, 100, 101, 102, 103, 105, 106, 117, 119, 127, 138, 143, 149, 152, 165, 167, 174, 183, 189, 190, 211, 213, 218, 223, 225, 226, 233, 235, 240, 249, 250, 259, 261, 266, 271, 272, 281, 285, 289, 291, 297, 300, 312, 316, 325, 327, 331, 337, 338, 345, 351, 358, 365, 380, 387, 395, 397, 401, 402, 405, 406, 418, 421, 427, 429, 430, 439, 443, 445, 451, 457, 459, 471, 477, 483, 494, 501, 503, 509, 514, 516, 519, 521, 522, 535, 541, 549, 552, 557, 558, 568, 577, 585, 587, 589, 595, 598, 608, 615, 621, 627, 630, 640, 649, 651, 657, 663, 664, 678, 683, 693, 695, 696, 707, 709, 716, 723, 725, 735, 741, 747, 753, 761, 763, 764, 773, 775, 780, 787, 801, 807, 809, 817, 819, 825, 826, 833, 838, 847, 853, 855, 856, 868, 873, 875, 881, 887, 889, 890
Croatia, 850
Cromwell, Oliver and Richard, 26
Cronkite, Walter, 749–750
"Cross of Gold" speech, 222–223
CRP. *See* Committee to Reelect the President.
Crusades, 10
Cuba, 14, 16, 256, 454, 768, 769
aid to Nicaragua by, 851
American interest in, 346–347, 351, 354–355, *i* 369
Bay of Pigs invasion and, 674
communism in, 673
de Lôme letter and, 347–348
first war for independence of, 347
missile crisis and, 674, *m* 675, 676
second war for independence of, *i* 346, 347–348
Soviet Union and, 670
Spain and, 347–348
in Spanish-American War, 347, 348–350
as U.S. protectorate, 351, 353–354
Cubans, 769, 844
Cumming* v. *Board of Education of Richmond County, 290
Curtis, S. R., 204
Custer, George Armstrong, 206, *i* 206, 211
CWA. *See* Civil Works Administration.
Czechoslovakia, 400
World War II and, 536–538, *m* 538

D

Daladier, Edouard, 537
Daley, Richard J., 752
dams, 480, 519
dance marathons, *i* 444–445, 445
Daniels, Josephus, 336
Darrow, Clarence, 438–439, *i* 439
Darwin, Charles, 242–243, 438
data
interpreting, 41, 105, 299, 659, 775
databases
creating, 651, 685, R33
using, 108, R33
da Vinci, Leonardo, 12
Davis, Gray, 868
Davis, Jefferson, 165, 172, *i* 172, 173, 188
Davis, Richard Harding, 374
Davis, Thulani, 657
Dawes, Charles G., 420
Dawes, William, 50
Dawes Act, 206–207, 313, 507, 662, R56
Dawes Plan, 420
Dayton, Ohio, 309
D-Day, 574, *m* 575
DDT, 821
Dean, James, 654, *i* 654
Dean, John, *i* 803, 804, 805
debates
Kennedy-Nixon, 618, *i* 618, 671, *i* 671
Lincoln-Douglas, 163
Debs, Eugene V., 246, 248, *i* 248, 308, 330–331, 396, *i* 397
Debs* v. *United States, 396
debt peonage, 289, R56
decisions and courses of action, evaluating, R16
decisions, making. *See* making decisions.
Declaration of Independence, 53, 66, 75, 260, 351, 724, R56
text of, 54–57
Declaration of Sentiments, 64
Declaratory Act, 47
Deere, John, 141, 217, 232
de facto segregation, 718, R56
deficit spending, 492, 515, *c* 517, R39, R43, R56
de Gaulle, Charles, 540
de jure segregation, 718, R56
De La Beckwith, Byron, 714
Delaware (Native American people), 39
Delaware (state), 26, 34, 104, 165, 169, 709
facts about, R48
Delaware River, 26, 60
de Lôme, Enrique Dupuy, 348
Deloria, Vine, Jr., 771
democracy, 24, 67
Democratic National Committee (DNC), 802, 803
Democratic Party, 123, 126, 161, 162, 163, 164, 189, 221, 222–223, 328, 480, 507, 638, 751–752. *See also* election, presidential.

Democratic-Republican Party, 76, 77, 78, 79, 112–113, 119, 123
Dempsey, Jack, 446
Denmark, 545
Denney, James D., 810
Department of Homeland Security, 866, 896–897
department stores, 296
depression, 222, 240, R38, *i* R40, R44. *See also* Great Depression.
deregulation, 333, 837, R56
Deseret, 133
Desert Storm, Operation. *See* Persian Gulf War.
détente, 799, R56
collapse of, 815
Detroit, Michigan, 263, 423, 424, 841, 843
developing historical perspective. *See* historical perspective, developing.
Dewey, A. Peter, 730, *i* 730
Dewey, George, 349
Dewey, Thomas E., 638
diagrams, creating, 39, 53, 71, 226, 259, 297, 325, 338, 369, 403, 427, 430, 439, 460, 514, 568, 621, 630, 683, 696, 726, 747, 764, 773, 788, 825, R2, R6, R7, R8, R12, R14, R18, R19, R21
diagrams, using, 13, 149, 312, 345, 351, 387, 443, 457, 471, 477, 483, 509, 519, 522, 535, 649, 663, 664, 678, 696, 707, 716, 747, 761, 833, 838, 873, R27
Dias, Bartolomeu, 13
Díaz, Adolfo, 362–363
Díaz, Porfirio, 363
Dickinson, John, 66, *i* 66
dictatorships
Hitler, 403, 516, *i* 527, 531, *i* 531, 536, *i* 537, 603
Hussein, Saddam, 867, 898–899, *i* 899
Mao, 610, *i* 610, 721
Mussolini, 530, 531, *i* 531, 573
Stalin, 529, *i* 531, 539, 540, 585–586, 603, *i* 603, 604
Diem, Ngo Dinh, 732, 734
Dien Bien Phu, 731
Dietrich, Marlene, 511
Dillon, C. Douglas, 676
diplomacy. *See* foreign affairs and foreign policy.
direct primary, 312
direct relief, 475, 492, R56
diseases. *See also* health care.
AIDS, 840, 845
influenza epidemic of 1918, 395
in Jamestown settlement, 23
Native Americans and, 15, 26, 39
polio, 644
slaves and, 32–33
smallpox, 39
trench foot and trench mouth, 385
tuberculosis, 256
yellow fever, 353
Disney, Walt, 450
distinguishing fact from opinion, R9, R14
distributions, analyzing. *See* analyzing distributions.
distributions, geographic. *See* geographic distributions.
District of Columbia, 102, 709. *See also* Washington, D.C.
facts about, R48
Dixiecrats, 638, R56
DNA, 879–880
DNC. *See* Democratic National Committee.
Dobbin, George, 515
Doenitz, Karl, 570
Dole, Elizabeth, 842
Dole, Robert, 865
Dole, Sanford B., 345
dollar diplomacy, 362–363, R56
domestic policy, 75, 122, 127, 157–158, 163, 172, 185, 194–195, 322–323, 335–337, 429, 436–437, 479, 481–482, 489, 496, 498–499, 501, 506, 637–640, 671, 680, 681, 682, 693, 712, 714–716, 796–799, 811, 812–814, 834–836, 837, 841, 861–862, 867. *See also* antislavery movement; civil rights; crime; economy; education; environment, protection of; health care; housing; inflation; poverty; Prohibition; unemployment.
Dominican Republic, 768
domino theory, 731, R56
Donne, John, 35
Doolittle, James, 579
Dos Passos, John, 451
dotcom, 871, R56
Douglas, Stephen A., 158, 160, 163, *i* 163
Douglass, Frederick, 146, *i* 146
Dowd, C. F., 237
Dow Jones Industrial Average, 467, 871
draft, R56
in Civil War, 173
in Vietnam War, 742–743, 745–746
in World War I, 382–383, *i* 382
in World War II, 554, 563
Drake, Edwin L., 231
drawing conclusions, 20, 33, 71, 117, 171, 183, 189, 192, 194, 209, 211, 218, 249, 283, 294, 295, 300, 345, 351, 376, 386, 387, 395, 418, 457, 471, 477, 483, 501, 514, 535, 541, 553, 581, 583, 587, 617, 640, 663, 678, 695, 707, 739, 741, 787, 801, 805, 842, 855, 873, 887, R18. *See also* making inferences.
drawing inferences. *See* making inferences.
***Dred Scott* v. *Sandford*,** 166–167
Dreiser, Theodore, 296
drug abuse, 841
Dubinsky, David, 508
Du Bois, W. E. B., 285, 288, 325, *i* 325, 392–393, *i* 392, 453, 454
Dukakis, Michael, 838
Dulles, John Foster, 623, 800
Dust Bowl, 474, *i* 474, *m* 474, R56
Dutch, 26, 34. *See also* Netherlands, the.
Dutch West India Company, 26

E

Eakins, Thomas, 295, *i* 295
Earhart, Amelia, 424, 449, *i* 449
Earth Day, 821, *i* 821, 822, 825, R56
Eastern woodlands, Native Americans of, *m* 7
East Germany, 608, 677–678, 849–850
Eastman, George, 281, *i* 281
Easy Rider, 787
e-commerce, 429, 871, R40
Economic Opportunity Act (EOA), 688, R56
economics, R39–R47
Keynesian, 492, R42, R46
laissez-faire, 242
mercantilist, 28, 30
supply-side, 835, R46
trickle-down theory of, 835
economy, 139–140. *See also* depression; domestic policy; economics; tariffs; trade.
Bush (George W.) and, 867
of California, 138
Carter and, 813–814
Civil War and, 174, 186, 244
Clinton and, 861–862, 864
cycles in, R38, R44
in early 1800s, 120–121
effect of corporate scandals on, 867
effect of entertainment industry on, 140, 294, 448, 645
effect of science and technology on, 196, 870, 871, 906
in English colonies, 28, *c* 29, 30, 31–32, 33–34
farmers and, 218, 222, 471
Ford and, 810–811
free enterprise and, 140, R41, R44
global, 872–873
Great Depression and, 469, 470, *c* 470, *i* 470
Hamilton and, 75
of Hawaii, 344
Hoover and, 478–480, 481–482
Kennedy and, 680
Madison and, 122
in mid-1990s, 869–871
in 1920s, 425, 464–465
Nixon and, 798–799
poverty and, 910–911
Reagan and, 834–836
Roosevelt (Franklin) and, 489–490, 499
reform and, 308–309
service sector in, 870, R63
Van Buren and, 127
in World War I, 388–390, *c* 389
in World War II, 567–568, *c* 567, 591
after World War II, 635–636, *c* 636
See also September 11 terrorist attack, effect on economy of.
Ecotopia, 846
Ederle, Gertrude, 448, *i* 448
Edison, Thomas Alva, 232
education, 446–447, *c* 447, 841, 904–905, *c* 904–905
of African Americans, 148, 184, 187, 283, 284–285, *i* 285, 701, *m* 701, 702–703, 711, 722, 723, *c* 723, 904
agricultural, 217
bilingual, 844
culture and, 446–447
expansion of, 282–285, *c* 283

Great Society programs and, 689–691, *i* 689, *c* 690
of immigrants, 284, 447
of Native Americans, 772–773
and poverty, 905, 911
technology and, 284
of women, 148, 314–315
Edwards, Jonathan, 36, *i* 36
EEOC. *See* Equal Employment Opportunity Commission.
effects, analyzing. *See* analyzing effects.
effects, predicting. *See* predicting effects.
egalitarianism, 63, R56
Egypt, 625, 799, 816
Ehrlichman, John, 803, *i* 803, 804
1868, Treaty of, 204, 206
Eighteenth Amendment, 100, 434, 436, 437
Eighth Amendment, 97
Einstein, Albert, 567
Eisenhower, Dwight D., 585, 615, *i* 638, 639–640, 670, R52
Bonus Army and, 483
civil rights and, 640
Cold War and, 623–624, 626–627
farewell address of, 673
at Geneva summit, 624
U-2 incident and, 626–627
Vietnam and, 688, 731
as World War II general, 572, 574, *i* 574
Eisenhower Doctrine, 625, R56
election, presidential
of 1796, 77
of 1800, 98, 112–113
of 1824, 123
of 1828, 123
of 1836, 127
of 1840, 127
of 1852, 161
of 1856, 162
of 1860, 163
of 1864, 181
of 1868, 186
of 1876, 189
of 1880, 270
of 1884, 271
of 1888, 271
of 1892, 271, 330
of 1896, 222
of 1908, 328
of 1912, 330–331, *c* 331
of 1916, 379
of 1920, 419
of 1928, 466
of 1932, 488–489
of 1936, 496
of 1940, 551
of 1948, 638, *c* 638
of 1952, 640
of 1960, 670–671
of 1964, 688
of 1968, 751–752, *c* 753
of 1972, 804
of 1976, 812
of 1980, 832–833, *c* 833
of 1984, 837
of 1988, 838
of 1992, 861
of 1996, 865
of 2000, 619, *i* 619, 865–866
of 2004, 868
Electoral College, 69, 90, 113, 866
electricity, 35, 232–233
conveniences and, 425, *c* 425, *i* 425
transportation and, 277
electronic commerce. *See* e-commerce.
Elementary and Secondary Education Act, 689
Eleventh Amendment, 98
Elijah Muhammad, 719–720
Eliot, T. S., 451
Elkins Act, 320
Ellington, Edward Kennedy "Duke," 457, *i* 457
Ellis Island, 256–257
Ellsberg, Daniel, 757
e-mail, 141, 877
emancipation, 122, 145–146, 172–173, 260
Emancipation Proclamation, 172–173, 183, 260, *i* 260, R57
embargo, 555, R40
Emergency Banking Relief Act, 490, *c* 500
Emergency Quota Act, 415, 416
Emerson, Ralph Waldo, 145
encomienda, 16, R57
energy, alternative sources of, 881, *i* 881
Enforcement Acts, 188–189
Engels, Friedrich, 413
England, 11, 13, 20. *See also* Great Britain.
American colonies of, 20, 21, 23–28, *c* 29, *m* 29, 30
civil war and Restoration in, 26
Enlightenment, 34–35, 36, 52, R57
Enola Gay, 584
Enron, 867, 871
entertainment. *See* leisure activities; motion pictures; music; radio; sports; television.
entitlement programs, 831, 865, 912–913, *c* 912–913, R57
entrepreneurs, 140, 243, 244, 429, R57
environment, protection of, 216, 322–324, 328, 329, 519, 691, 820–822, 824, 837, 881, 912–913. *See also* pollution.
Environmental Protection Agency (EPA), 822, 837
EOA. *See* Economic Opportunity Act.
EPA. *See* Environmental Protection Agency.
Equal Employment Opportunity Commission (EEOC), 778, 779
Equal Rights Amendment (ERA), 65, 779, 780, 842, R57
Equiano, Olaudah, 33, *i* 33
ERA. *See* Equal Rights Amendment.
eras
Cold War, 405, 606
Colonial Era, 21, 23–26, *m* 25, 28, *m* 29, 30, 31–39, *i* 34, 40–41, *i* 40–41
globalization, 872–873
Great Depression, *i* 462–463, 464–469, *c* 470, 471, 472–477, 478–483, *i* 478, 488
Great Society, 689–691, *c* 690, 719, 741
Industrial Age, 120–121, 141, 230–233, 234–235, 236–238, 241–243
New Deal, 488–494, 506–507
post–Cold War, 848–852
Progressive Era, 306–312, 313–316, 317–320, 322–325, 326–327, 328–331, 332–337, 419
Roaring Twenties, 434–439, 440–443, 444–445, *i* 444–445, 446–451, 452–454, 455–457
Vietnam War era, 91, 103, 619, *i* 619, 730–732, *m* 733, 734–741, *i* 736, 742–747, *c* 743, *i* 744, 748–753, *m* 749, *i* 750, 754–755, 801
Watergate era, 619, *i* 619, 758, 802–807, *i* 805, *i* 807
World War I, 374, 375–380, *m* 375, 381–387, 388–391, 588, *i* 588
World War II, 536–541, *m* 538, 542–549, 550–555, *m* 556, 557, 562–568, 569–574, *m* 572, *m* 575, 576–577, 578–579, *m* 580, 581, 583–585, 590–595, *i* 602
Erie, Lake, 139, 234
Erie Canal, 139, *i* 139, 141
Erie Railroad, 221
Ervin, Sam J., Jr., 805, *i* 805
***Escobedo* v. *Illinois*,** 692, 694
Espionage and Sedition Acts, 392, 396, 397, R57
Ethiopia, 533
ethnic groups. *See* specific groups.
European societies of 1400s, 10–11
evaluating, 30, 50, 53, 62, 63, 71, 80, 106, 117, 127, 138, 145, 149, 152, 181, 218, 223, 244, 259, 266, 272, 281, 308, 325, 331, 334, 345, 358, 395, 418, 429, 439, 441, 443, 451, 460, 492, 494, 499, 506, 509, 516, 539, 574, 589, 627, 649, 654, 657, 663, 681, 692, 706, 722, 735, 746, 747, 773, 807, 819, 838, 856, 868, 881, R17, R20
decisions, 113, 365, 482, 501, 541, 549, 557, 577, 585, 587, 615, 678, 759, 801, 817, 868, R16
effects, 53, 125, 190, 223, 238, 269, 358, 421, 497, 509, 519, 592, 621, 640, 704, 761, 838, 881, 889. *See also* analyzing effects.
leadership, 79, 117, 165, 249, 271, 420, 490, 494, 519, 608, 639, 640, 683, 693, 833, 849, 867
Evans, Walker, 514
events, analyzing. *See* analyzing events.
Evers, Medgar, 714
Ewuare, 9
examining issues. *See* issues, examining.
executive branch, 69, 75, 90–92, 803
Executive Order 9066, 596–597
exodusters, 215, *i* 215, R57
expansionism, 343–344, 346–347, 350–351, 353, *i* 354, *m* 356
exploration by Europeans
of Africa, 12–13
of Americas, 14–15, 16, *m* 17, 18–19, 26
ex post facto law, 89

F

fact from opinion, distinguishing. *See* distinguishing fact from opinion.
factories, 121, 142, 870
  conditions in, 142, 233, 244–245, 248–249, 306, 309
Fair Deal, 639, 680, R57
Fair Labor Standards Act, 499, *c* 500, 518, R42
Fajans, Irving, 412, *i* 412
Fall, Albert B., 421
***Fallen Angels* (Myers),** 763
Fallen Timbers, Battle of, 77
Fall of New Orleans, 170, *m* 170
Falwell, Jerry, 831–832
families
  early-20th-century, 313
  Great Depression and, 474–475
  Native American, 8, 203
  in 1920s, 442–443
  poverty among, 661, *c* 723, 769
  Puritan, 24–25
  Stop-ERA movement and, 779
  in West Africa, 9
  after World War II, 634, 635, 641, 643–644, 658
Family Assistance Plan, 795, R57
***Farewell to Arms, A* (Hemingway),** 451
Farmer, James, 593, 711
farmers, 31–32, 75, 121, 870. *See also* agriculture.
  African-American, 221
  alliances of, 220–221
  financial problems of, 67, 218, 219, 220, *i* 220, 222, 263, 465, *i* 465
  Great Depression and, 469, 480, 481
  on Great Plains, 217, 219
  New Deal and, 491, 496, 498, 518
  Populism and, 221
  railroads and, 218, 219, 220, 238–240
  women and, 214, 217, 219, 313
  World War I and, 465
  World War II and, 591
Farmers' Alliances, 220–221, R57
Farm Security Administration, 498
Farragut, David G., 170
Farrell, James T., 514
fascism, 530, R57
Faubus, Orval, 703
FBI. *See* Federal Bureau of Investigation.
FCC. *See* Federal Communications Commission.
FDA. *See* U.S. Food and Drug Administration.
FDIC. *See* Federal Deposit Insurance Corporation.
Federal Art Project, 512
Federal Aviation Administration (FAA), 897
Federal Bureau of Investigation (FBI), 796, 807, 903, 907
Federal Communications Commission (FCC), 653, 878, R57
Federal Conservation Lands, 1872–1996, *m* 323
Federal Deposit Insurance Corporation (FDIC), 490, *c* 500, 517, 518, R57
Federal Emergency Relief Administration (FERA), 492, 498, *c* 500
Federal Farm Board, 481
federal government, powers of, 68–70, 82–83, 118–119, 126, 128–129, 493, 503, 692, 774, 819
  aviation security and, 897
  changes in, 75–76, 113, 118–119, 122, 489–490, 493, 502–503, 689–691, *i* 689, *c* 690, 795–796, 834–837
  checks and balances, 69, *c* 87, 119
  in Constitution, 69–70, 74–75, 82–83, 128
  and New Deal, 489–490, 492, 493, 495, 499, 503
  separation of, 69
  and Supreme Court, 74–75, 118–119, 124, 128–129, 290, 503, 692, 774, 819
Federal Home Loan Bank Act, 481, R57
Federal Housing Administration (FHA), 492, *c* 500
federalism, 68, R57
Federalist Papers, 70–71
Federalist Party, 76, 77, 78, 112–113, 114
Federalists, 69–70, 119, R57
Federal Reserve Act, 334
Federal Reserve Board, 811
Federal Reserve System, 334, 870, R42, R57
Federal Securities Act, 490, R57
Federal Theater Project, 513
Federal Trade Commission (FTC), 333, R57
Federal Writers' Project (FWP), 514
Felt, W. Mark, 804
***Feminine Mystique, The* (Friedan),** 644, 776, 778
feminism, 779, R57
FERA. *See* Federal Emergency Relief Administration.
Ferdinand (king of Spain), 10
Ferraro, Geraldine, 837, 842, *i* 842
Ferrell, Trevor, 839
Fetterman, William J., 204
Fetterman Massacre, 204, *m* 205
FHA. *See* Federal Housing Administration.
Field, Cyrus W., *i* 240
Field, Marshall, 296
Fifteenth Amendment, 100, 104, 186, 187, 189, 315, 725, R57
Fifth Amendment, 96, 99, 162, 166, 596, 694
Fillmore, Millard, 158, R51
finding main ideas. *See* main ideas, finding.
fine arts, 295. *See also* art; literature; music.
fireside chats, 490
First Amendment, 70, 79, 96, 119, 392, 396–397
First Continental Congress, 49, 50
Fithian, Philip Vickers, 31
Fitzgerald, F. Scott, 440, 449, 450, 451, *i* 451, 458
Fitzgerald, Robert G., 184, *i* 184
Fitzgerald, Zelda Sayre, 440, *i* 440, 451
flagpole sitting, 444, *i* 444
flappers, 441, *i* 441, R57
Flatiron Building (New York), 277, *i* 277
***Fletcher.* v. *Peck*,** 118
Florida, 18, 33, 38, 77, 116, 165, 844, 847, 865, 866
  facts about, R48
Foch, Ferdinand, 386
Fong See, 254, *i* 254, 255
Food Administration, 389–390
Foraker Act, 353, R57
Forbes, Charles R., 421
Force Bill, 126
Ford, Gerald, 597, 758–759, 806, 807, 810–811, *i* 811, 815, R52
Ford, Henry, 393, 424
Ford Motor Company, 422
Fordney-McCumber Tariff, 420, R57
Ford's Theatre, 183
foreign affairs and foreign policy, *i* 351, 725. *See also* Cold War; imperialism, U.S.; Vietnam War; World War I; World War II.
  under Adams (John), 78
  under Carter, 815
  under Clinton, 863–864
  under Ford, 811
  under Harding, 419–420
  under Madison, 114
  under Monroe, 116–117
  under Nixon, 799–801, 815
  under Polk, 135
  under Reagan and Bush, 848–853
  under Roosevelt (Theodore), 358, 359–360, 362, 534–535
  under Washington, 76–77
  under Wilson, 363–365, 379–380
foreign trade. *See* trade.
forming generalizations, 24, 59, 152, 177, 188, 193, 312, 325, 384, 425, 457, 466, 535, 565, 627, 734, 741, 797, 845, 855, 889, R21.
forming opinions, 71, 79, 81, 108, 191, 240, 331, 345, 365, 368, 421, 509, 514, 615, 707, 838, 421, 421, 427, 523, 615, 696, 707, 723, 761, R17
Formosa. *See* Taiwan.
formulating questions. *See* questions, formulating.
Fort Boisée or Fort Boise, 131, *i* 151
Fort Donelson, 170
Fort Duquesne, 37
Forten, James, 144, *i* 144
Fort Henry, 170
Fort Laramie, Treaty of, 204, R65
Fort Sumter, 168, *i* 168, 169
forty-niners, 137–138
Foster, Andrew "Rube," 448, *i* 448
Fourteen Points, 399, R57
Fourteenth Amendment, 99, 167, 185–186, 189, 287, 290–291, 315–316, 701, 708, 724, 725, 774, 818, R57
Fourth Amendment, 70, 96
frames of reference. *See* developing historical perspective.
France, 11, 13, 76–77, 373
  American colonies of, 37
  British relations with, 37, 38, 60, 62, 76–77, 78, 114, 373
  forces of, in Revolutionary War, 61, 62
  Louisiana Purchase and, 114
  North American claims of, *m* 29, *m* 38
  U.S. relations with, 60, 76–77, 78
  Vietnam and, 730, 731
  war debts and, 419, 420, 469

in World War I, 373, 374, 376, 377, 382
in World War II, 537, 538, 539, 540, 550, 551, 574
Franciscans, 19
Franco, Francisco, 533
Frankfurter, Felix, 483
Franklin, Benjamin, 35, 36, *i* 36, 57, 58, 62, *i* 88
Franklin, William, 58, *i* 58
Franz Ferdinand, Archduke, 374
Fredericksburg, Battle of, 175
Freedmen's Bureau, 184, 185, 187, 189, 284, R57
freedom riders, 710–711, *i* 711, R57
Freedom Summer, 715, R57
free enterprise, 140, *c* R41, R44, R57
Free-Soil Party, 162, 163
Free Speech Movement (FSM), 744, R57
Free Trade Area of the Americas (FTAA), 864, *i* 873
Frémont, John C., 136, 150–151, 162
French and Indian War, 37–38, 46, 47, 55, 63, 114, R57
French Revolution, 76–77, *i* 76
Frick, Henry Clay, 247–248
Friedan, Betty, 644, 776, *i* 776, 778
Frisch, Otto, 583
***Frohwerk* v. *United States*,** 396
FSM. *See* Free Speech Movement.
FTAA. *See* Free Trade Area of the Americas.
FTC. *See* Federal Trade Commission.
Fugitive Slave Act, 158
Fulbright, J. William, 741
Fulton, Robert, 120, 140
Fundamentalism, 438, R58
Fundamental Orders of Connecticut, 23
fur trade, 26, 28, 37
FWP. *See* Federal Writers' Project.

G

Gable, Clark, 511, *i* 511
Gadsden, James, 137
Gadsden Purchase, *m* 136, 137
Gagarin, Yuri A., 681
Gage, Thomas, 49, 50, 51
Galbraith, John Kenneth, 636
Galilei, Galileo, 34–35
Galveston, Texas, 309
Gama, Vasco da, 13
Gandhi, Mohandas K., 463, 705
Garcia-Tolson, Rudy, 876, *i* 876
Garfield, James, 238, 270, *i* 270, R51
garment workers, 248–249
Garrison, William Lloyd, 145–146
Garvey, Marcus, 453–454, *i* 454
gasoline, 231. *See also* oil.
Gass, Patrick, 112, *i* 112
Gates, Bill, 871
GATT. *See* General Agreements on Tariffs and Trade.
Gaye, Marvin, 786
gays and lesbians, 845, *i* 845
Gellhorn, Martha, 528, *i* 528, 533
General Agreement on Tariffs and Trade (GATT), 872, R58
generalizations, forming. *See* forming generalizations.
genetic engineering, 880, R58
Geneva Accords, 732, R58
Geneva summit, 624
genocide, 544, R58
Gentlemen's Agreement, 259, 415, R58
gentrification, 883, R58
geographic distributions, xxx, *m* 7, *m* 25, *m* 38, *m* 72 *m* 73, *m* 116, *m* 125, *m* 160, *m* 205, *m* 323, *m* 345, *m* 349, *m* 356, *m* 400, *m* 474, *m* 521, *m* 532, *m* 605, *m* 624, c 665, *m* 816, *m* 833, *m* 847
geographic factors
human, *m* 115, *m* 125, *m* 132, *m* 136, 138, *m* 159, *m* 160, *m* 176, *m* 205, *m* 255, *m* 263, *m* 416, *m* 474, *m* 591, *m* 594, *m* 638, *m* 833, *m* 885, R25. *See also* human-environment interactions.
physical, xxx, *m* 134, *m* 176, *m* 278, *m* 349, *m* 375, *m* 386, *m* 530, *m* 538, *m* 556, *m* 580, *m* 594, *m* 613, *m* 733, *m* 854, R25
geographic patterns, xxx, *m* 136, *m* 209, *m* 235, *m* 239, *m* 255, *m* 263, *m* 366–367, *m* 416, *m* 591, *m* 685, *m* 885, 887
George II (king of Great Britain), 28, 38
George III (king of Great Britain), 46, 49, 51, 52, 54, 58
George, Walter L., 435
Georgia, 28, 32, 53, 104, 124, 165, 180, 812
facts about, R48
German immigrants, 32, 34, 204, *c* 255
World War I and, 391–392
Germany. *See also* East Germany; West Germany.
colonies of, 400
Holocaust and, 542–549
inflation in, *i* 420
Nazism and, 531
Nuremberg trials and, 586
occupation of, 585, 607–608
postwar division of, *m* 605, 607
reparations and, 400, 420, 469
reunification of, 850
Treaty of Versailles and, 400
war debts and, *i* 529
World War I and, 373–374, 376, 378–379, 383
World War II and, 536–541, *i* 539, 551–554, 571, 572
Gershwin, George, 450
Gesner, Abraham, 231
Gettysburg, Battle of, 176–177, *m* 176
Gettysburg Address, 177, R58
Ghana, 8
Ghent, Treaty of, 114
ghetto, 545, 720, R58
Ghost Dance, 207
***Gibbons* v. *Ogden*,** 118, 122
Gibbs, Lois, 820, *i* 820
GI Bill of Rights, 592, 635, R58
***Gideon* v. *Wainwright*,** 692, 694
***Gilded Age, The* (Twain and Warner),** 267
Gilder, George, 835
Gingrich, Newt, 864
Ginsberg, Allen, 655
Ginsburg, Ruth Bader, *i* 93
Giovanni, Nikki, 874
***glasnost*,** 849, R58
Glass-Steagall Act of 1933, 490, R58
Glidden, Joseph, 211, 232
***Going After Cacciato* (O'Brien),** 763
gold, 13, 60, 212–213, 222
in Black Hills, 206, 212
in California, 137–138, *i* 137, 224, 255, 888
in Colorado, 204, 212, 213
in Spanish colonies, 16, 18
in West Africa, 9
gold bugs, 222, *c* 222, 223
Goldman, Emma, 392
Goldmark, Josephine, 311
gold rush. *See* gold.
gold standard, 222, R41, R58
Goldwater, Barry, 688, 832
Goliad, Battle of, 134–135
Gompers, Samuel, 245–246, 333, 351
***Gone with the Wind* (Mitchell),** 324, 511, R58
González, Pedro J., 504, *i* 504
Good Neighbor policy, 534
Gorbachev, Mikhail, 848–849
Gore, Albert, 619, 865–866, *i* 866, 877
Gould, Jay, *i* 240
grandfather clause, 287, R58
Grange, 220–221, 238–239, R58
Granger laws, 239
Grant, Madison, 415
Grant, Ulysses S., 180, *i* 180, *i* 181, R51
as Civil War general, 170, 179, 180, 181, 183
presidency of, 186
***Grapes of Wrath* (Steinbeck),** *i* 496, 514, R58
graphs
bar, 169, 182, 301, 407, 416, 606, 891, R28, R30
circle, 147, 169, 255, 442, 466, 626, 681, 723, 814, R28, R30
creating, 213, 431, 787, 809, 847, R30. *See also* charts, creating.
interpreting, 147, 169, 182, 247, 283, 300, 301, 331, 334, 344, 377, 389, 416, 427, 470, 517, 564, 606, 626, 636, 643, 653, 659, 661, 681, 697, 723, 743, 755, 777, 809, 813, 814, 826, R28
line, 247, 334, 344, 377, 389, 427, 470, 508, 517, 564, 636, 643, 653, 659, 661, 681, 697, 743, 809, 813, 827, 846, 857, R28, R30
using, 255, 407, 442, 466, 508, 697, 809, 827, 846, 857, 891, R30
graphs, interpreting, R28
***Gray* v. *Sanders*,** 774–775
Great Awakening, 35, 36, R58
Great Britain, 121. *See also* England; Revolutionary War.
American colonies' relations with, 28, 30, 39, 46–53, *c* 48, *c* 49, 58, 59, 64
antiterrorism coalition and, 896, 899

French relations with, 37, 38, 60, 62, 76–77, 78, 114, 373
North American claims of, *m* 29, *m* 38, 133
U.S. relations with, 76, 77, 114, 133, 171
war debts and, 419, 420, 469
in World War I, 373, 374, 377, 378–379, 383, 384
in World War II, 537, 538, 539, 540, 550, 551–554, 570, 573, 574
Great Compromise, 68
Great Depression, *i* 462–463, 464, *c* 470, *i* 478, 803, 910, R40, R41, R58. *See also* New Deal; stock market.
bread line and, R55
causes of, 471
cities and, 472–473, *i* 473
Dust Bowl and, 474
end of, 517
families and, 474–477
as global event, 469, *i* 469, 471
Nazis and, 531
New Deal and, 488–494
psychological impact of, 477
in rural areas, 473, 474, *i* 477, 478
shantytown, 473, R63
social impact of, 477
soup kitchen, 473, R64
stock market crash and, 467, *i* 467, 468–469
women and, 475–476
work projects and, 491–492
worldwide trade and, 471
Great Gatsby, The **(Fitzgerald),** 450, 458
Great Migration (of African Americans), 393–394, *i* 393, 452–453, 889, R58
Great Plains, 202, *m* 205, 209, 323, R58
Dust Bowl in, 475
farming on, 217
Native Americans of, 202–203, 204, 206–207
white settlers on, 203–204, 206, 207, 214
Great Potato Famine, 142
Great Salt Lake, 131
Great Society, 689–691, *c* 690, 719, 741, 795, R58
impact of, 693
Great Strike of 1877, 247, 248
"Great White Fleet" (U.S. Navy), *i* 343
Greenspan, Alan, 870, *i* 870
Grenada, 852
Grenville, George, 46, 47, 48
Grimké, Sarah, 148
***Griswold* v. *Connecticut*,** 97
"ground zero," 895, *i 895*. *See also* September 11 terrorist attack; war on terrorism.
group, working with a. *See* working with a group.
gross domestic product, *c* R41, R44
Guadalcanal, Battle of, 581
Guadalupe Hidalgo, Treaty of, *m* 136, 137, R65
Guam, 346, 350
facts about, R48
Guatemala, 5, 18, 624
Gubar, Stephan, 742, *i* 742
Guiteau, Charles, 270
Gulf of Tonkin Resolution. *See* Tonkin Gulf Resolution.
Gulf War. *See* Persian Gulf War.
gun control, 903
Gutenberg, Johann, 12
Gwathmey, Robert, 513

H

habeas corpus, writ of, 89, 173
Haber, Al, 744
Haida, 6
Haight-Ashbury, 782, R58
Haile Selassie, 533, *i* 533
Haiti
U.S. troops in, 863
Haldeman, H. R., 803, *i* 803, 804, 807
Hamer, Fanny Lou, 715–716
Hamilton, Alexander, 70, 75–76, *i* 75, *c* 76, 98, 113
Hancock, John, 57, *i* 57
Harding, Warren G., 417, 419, *i* 419, R51
death of, 421
foreign policy of, 419–420
scandals and, 420–421
Harlan, John Marshall, 290, *i* 290
Harlem Renaissance, 454, 455, *i* 455, 456, 458, 459, R58
Harpers Ferry, Virginia, 163–164
Harrington, Michael, 682
Harris, William Torrey, 282, 283
Harrison, Benjamin, 271, R51
Harrison, William Henry, 91, 127, 271, R50
Harte, Bret, 224
Hastie, William H., 505
Hatch Act, 217
Hawaii, 255, 342, *c* 344, 345–346
1898, *m* 345
facts about, R48
Hawley-Smoot Tariff Act, 471, R58
Hay, John, 350, 356, 357
Hayden, Tom, 744, 751
Hayes, Roland, 456
Hayes, Rutherford B., 189, 247, 270, *i* 270, R51
Haymarket affair, 247
Hayne, Robert, 124
Hay-Pauncefote Treaty, 360
Hays, Mary Ludwig (Molly Pitcher), 61, *i* 61
Haywood, William "Big Bill," 246, 392
H-bomb, 623, R58
headright system, 23
health care, *c* 908–909. *See also* diseases.
in Civil War, 173–174
Medicare and Medicaid and, 690, 796, 865, 884, 908–909, 912
reform of, 861, 908
vaccinations, 644
in World War I, 385
Health, Education, and Welfare, Department of (HEW), 797
Health Insurance Portability and Accountability Act, 908
health maintenance organization (HMO), 909
Hearst, William Randolph, 295, 347
Heckler, Margaret, 842
Helena, Montana, 204
Helsinki Accords, 811
Hemingway, Ernest, 451
Henri, Robert, 295
Henry VIII (king of England), 24
Henry, Patrick, 70
Henry the Navigator, Prince, 13
Hepburn Act, 320
Hernandez, Antonia, 882
Hessians, 59, 60
HEW. *See* Health, Education, and Welfare, Department of.
Hickock, James Butler "Wild Bill," 211
Higgins, Pattillo, 230, *i* 230
Higher Education Act, 779
hijacking. See airplanes, hijacking of.
Hill, A. P., 176
Hill, Anita, 836, *i* 836
Hill, Esther Clark, 214
Hindenburg **disaster,** 512
Hine, Lewis, 311
***Hirabayashi* v. *United States*,** 596
Hirohito (emperor of Japan), 584
Hiroshima, Japan, 584, *i* 584
Hispanic Americans. *See* Latinos; Mexican Americans; Puerto Ricans.
Hispaniola, 14, 15
Hiss, Alger, 618
historical context. *See* developing historical perspective.
historical perspective, developing, 12, 42, 51, 60, 77, 80, 106, 133, 138, 157, 165, 167, 183, 190, 195, 338, 344, 391, 399, 403, 406, 417, 430, 437, 503, 511, 518, 522, 549, 587, 595, 656, 672, 726, 735, 747, 764, 788, R11
historical questions, formulating, R12
history, interacting with, 3, 43, 45, 81, 107, 111, 153, 191, 201, 227, 229, 251, 253, 273, 275, 301, 305, 339, 341, 369, 371, 407, 411, 433, 461, 463, 487, 523, 527, 559, 561, 599, 601, 631, 633, 665, 669, 697, 699, 727, 729, 765, 767, 789, 793, 827, 829, 857, 859, 891
History of the Standard Oil Company, The **(Tarbell),** 308, 326
history through architecture, 27, 278, 336, 883
history through art, 11, 48, 164, 210, 295, 364, 393, 414, 435, 513, 645
history through film, 402, 566 , 824
history through music, 656
history through photojournalism, 178, 311, 497, 582, 713, 757
Hitler, Adolf, 403, 516, 531, *i* 531, 536, 537, *i* 537, 603
death of, 577
Final Solution, the, 544–546
rise to power of, 531–533
in World War II, 538, 539, 540, 543, 550, 553, 570, 571, 572, 573, 574, 576
HMO. *See* health maintenance organization.
Hobby, Oveta Culp, 563
Ho Chi Minh, 731, *i* 731, 732
Ho Chi Minh Trail, 732, R58

Hogg, James S., 310, *i* 310
Hohokam, 5, 6
HOLC. *See* Home Owners Loan Corporation.
holding company, 243
Holland Tunnel, 423
Hollywood Ten, 617, R58
Holmes, Oliver Wendell, 96, 396–397, *i* 396
Holocaust, 542–549, *c* 545, *i* 546–547, R58
Home Insurance Building (Chicago), 232
Homeland Security Advisory System, 896–897, *i* 896
homelessness, 910
Home Owners Loan Corporation (HOLC), 492, *c* 500
Homestead Act, 215, 428, R58
homesteaders, 215, 428
Homestead strike, 247–248
Hoover, Herbert, 422, 466, *i* 466, 478–480, *i* 478, 481, 489, R52
  Bonus Army and, 482–483
  Food Administration and, 389–390
  Great Depression and, 471, 478–480
  philosophy of government of, 479
  as secretary of commerce, 420
Hoover Dam. *See* Boulder Dam.
Hope, Bob, 511
Hopewell culture, 5
Hopkins, Harry, 492, 498, 512
Hopper, Edward, 450
***Hopwood* v. *Texas*,** 905
horizontal integration, 242, R58
horses
  Native Americans and, 203
  Spanish and, 203, 208
House, Edward M., 398, *i* 398
House Judiciary Committee, 802, 805, 806
House of Burgesses, 23
House of Representatives, 68, 84–85, 86, 186, 330, 846, 847, 865. *See also* Congress.
  election of 1800 and, 98, 113
House Un-American Activities Committee (HUAC), 617, R58
housing, 465
  in cities, 264, 883
  Great Society and, 690
  New Deal and, 492
  after World War II, 635
Housing and Urban Development, Department of (HUD), 690
Houston, Sam, 134–135, *i* 135
Howard, Ebenezer, 279
Howe, Julia Ward, 316
HUAC. *See* House Un-American Activities Committee.
Hubble Space Telescope, 879
HUD. *See* Housing and Urban Development, Department of.
Hudson, Henry, *m* 17, 26
Hudson River, 26, 120
Huerta, Dolores, 770
Huerta, Victoriano, 363
Hughes, Charles Evans, 379, 419
Hughes, Langston, 454, 456, 459, *i* 459
Hull, Cordell, 552
Hull House, 266
human-environment interaction, xxx, 231, 239, 323, 345, 356, 575, 580, 605, 675, 816. *See also* geographic factors, human.
Human Genome Project, 879
human rights, 725, 815
  in China, 863, R59
Humphrey, Hubert, 751–752, 753
Humphrey, R. M., 221
Hundred Days, 489, 495
Hungary, 625–626
hunting and gathering, 5, 6
Hupa, 6
Hurston, Zora Neale, 452, *i* 452, 453, 456, 514
Hussein, Saddam, 853, 867, 898–899, *i*899
  capture of, 867
  history of regime of, *c* 898–899
Hutchinson, Anne, 25
hypothesizing, 165, 233, 249, 271, 281, 285, 331, 368, 403, 468, 494, 514, 589, 597, 615, 621, 627, 664, 773, 807, 853, 855, 887, R13, R34

I

ICC. *See* Interstate Commerce Commission.
Ice Age, 4–5
Idaho, 316
  facts about, R48
identifying bias. *See* bias, identifying.
identifying problems. *See* problems, identifying.
ILGWU. *See* International Ladies' Garment Workers' Union.
Illinois, 131, 162, 163, 166, 231
  facts about, R48
***I Love Lucy*,** 653, *i* 654
immigrants, 78, *i* 143, 885–886, 888, 900–901, *i* 901. *See also* immigration.
  at Angel Island, 257, *i* 258
  Chinese, 204, 215, *i* 237, 254, 255, *c* 255, 257, 258–259, *i* 258, *i* 259, 289
  in cities, 262–263, 266, 435
  Cuban, 844
  difficulties of, 256–258
  education of, 284
  at Ellis Island, 256–257
  European, 32, 34, 142, *i* 143, 255, 415, *i* 416, 428
  female, 314
  German, 32, 34, 204, *c* 255, 391–392
  illegal, 769, 886, 901
  Irish, 142, 215, 237, *c* 255, 263
  Italian, *c* 255, 415
  Japanese, 255, *c* 255, 259, 415
  Jewish, 34, 255, 258, 284
  Mexican, 256, *c* 256, *i* 416, 769, 886
  nativism and, 258–259, 414–415, 900
  origins of, 255–256, *c* 255, *c* 416, 885–886
  political machines and, 268
  Scandinavian, 34, *c* 255
  Scottish and Scots-Irish, 32, 34
  Vietnamese, 889, *i* 889
  West Indian, 256
  World War I and, 391–392, 393
immigration, 142, 254–259, 260, *i* 260, 428, 691, 885–886, *m* 885, 900–901, *c* 900–901. *See also* immigrants.
  economic implications, 900–901
  patterns of, *c* 255, *c* 416
  restrictions on, 258–259, 414–415, 417, 900–901
  U.S. citizenship and, 901
  westward expansion and, 204, 215, 138, 888, *i* 888
Immigration Acts of 1924 and 1965, 691, R59
Immigration Restriction League, 258
impeachment, 85, 92, 186, 806, 807, 865, R59
imperialism, R59
  Asian, 343
  European, 342, 343, 373
  U.S., 342, 343, 346–347, 350–351, 353, *i* 354, *m* 356
imperial presidency, 803
***Imperial Presidency, The* (Schlesinger),** 803
impressment, 114, R59
Inca, 5, 18
income
  difference between men's and women's, *c* 842
  uneven distribution of, *c* 466, 471, *c* 661
income tax, 100, 174, 182, 221, 390, 334, *c* 334, 423, 567, R59
inferences, making. *See* making inferences.
indentured servants, 23, 34, R59
Independence, Missouri, 131
Indian, 15. *See also* Native Americans; Plains Indians.
Indiana, 231
  facts about, R48
Indian Affairs, Bureau of, 772
Indian Education Act, 772
Indian Removal Act, 124, *m* 125
Indian Reorganization Act, 662–663
Indian Self-Determination and Education Assistance Act, 772–773
Indian Territory, 124
Indochina, 579, 731, *m* 733. *See also* Cambodia; Laos; Vietnam.
Industrial Revolution, 121
Industrial Workers of the World (IWW), 246, *i* 246, 392, *i* 392, 413, R59
industry, 28, 33, 120–121, 141, 244, *c* 814, 870–871. *See also* business; factories; inventions; railroads; steel industry; textile industry.
  effect on, of September 11 terrorist attack, 871
  electricity and, 232–233
  expansion of, in late 19th century, 231–232, 241–244
  natural resources and, 230–232, *m* 231
  in 1920s, 464, 465
  pollution and, 234–235, 820
  railroads and, 237–238
  in World War II, 564–565, *c* 564
inferences, making, R10
inflation, 60, 567–568, 798, 811, 813, *c* 813, R41, R42, R59

***Influence of Sea Power upon History, 1660–1783, The* (Mahan)**, 344
information superhighway, 877, R59
INF Treaty. *See* Intermediate-Range Nuclear Forces Treaty.
Ingram, David, 8
initiative, 312, R59
installment plan, 425–426, R59
interacting with history. *See* history, interacting with.
interest rate, 811, *c* R42
Interior, Department of the, 216, 421
Intermediate-Range Nuclear Forces Treaty (INF Treaty), 849, R59
Internal Revenue Service, 796
International Ladies' Garment Workers' Union (ILGWU), 248–249, 508
international relations. *See* foreign affairs and foreign policy.
International Space Station (ISS), 879
Internet, 140, 141, 429, 877, 906, R59. *See also* computers, using; researching.
using for research, 3, 45, 107, 108, 111, 119, 155, 167, 201, 225, 230, 253, 275, 291, 301, 302, 305, 327, 341, 371, 397, 405, 411, 431, 433, 459, 463, 487, 503, 527, 561, 597, 599, 601, 633, 665, 669, 695, 699, 709, 729, 763, 767, 775, 789, 793, 809, 819, 829, 857, 875, 891, 897, 899, 901, 903, 905, 907, 909, 911, 913, 915, 917, R29, R34
internment, 594–597, R59
interpreting charts. *See* charts, interpreting.
interpreting data. *See* interpreting data.
interpreting graphs. *See* graphs, interpreting.
interpreting maps. *See* maps, interpreting.
interpreting time lines. *See* time lines, interpreting.
interstate commerce, 239, 249, 310–311, 502–503
Interstate Commerce Act, 239, 320, R59
Interstate Commerce Commission (ICC), 239–240, 320, 711
Intolerable Acts, 49, 55
Invasion of the Body Snatchers, 628, *i* 628
inventions, 121, 140, 141–142, 217, *c* 217, 232–233, *c* 232, 277, 279–280, *i* 280, *i* 281, 878–881, *i* 881. *See also* technology.
Iowa (Native American people), 203
Iowa (state), 215
facts about, R48
Iran, 623–624, 899. *See also* Iran-Contra scandal.
revolution in, 817
U.S. hostages in, 817, 832
war with Iraq, 853
Iran-Contra scandal, 852–853
Iraq
Persian Gulf War and, 853, *m* 854, 855, 861, 867, 898
U.S.-led war against, 867, 898–899
war with Iran, 853
Irish immigrants, 78, 142, *c* 255, 263
as railroad workers, 215, 237
iron, 33, 231, *m* 231, 237
ironclad ship, 182
Iron Curtain, 605, *m* 605, R59
Iroquois, 6, R59
Isabella (queen of Spain), 10, *i* 10
Islam, 9, 10, 817, 896, R59. *See also* Muslims.
isolationism, 362, *i* 362, 404, *i* 404, 412, 534–535, *i* 534, 552, R59
Israel, 625, 816
Camp David Accords, 816
Yom Kippur War and, 799
ISS. *See* International Space Station.
issues, analyzing. *See* analyzing issues.
Italy, 11, 255
Ethiopia and, 533, *m* 532
fascism in, 530
World War I and, 373
World War II and, 551, 573
Iwo Jima, 582, *i* 582, 583
IWW. *See* Industrial Workers of the World.

J

Jackson, Andrew, 40, *i* 40, 114, 122–123, *i* 123, *i* 126, 127, 128, *i* 128, R50
Jackson, Helen Hunt, 206
Jackson, Jesse, 722, 843, *i* 843
Jackson, Robert, 586
Jackson State, 756
Jackson, Thomas J. "Stonewall," 169, 171, 176
Jacksonian democracy, 123, 145, R59
JACL. *See* Japanese American Citizens League.
Jamaica, 256
James, Henry, 296
James River, 62
Jamestown, Virginia, 21, *i* 22, *m* 22, 23
Japan, 343, 532, 814
in Russo-Japanese War, 359–360
in World War II, 551, 554–557, 562, 570, 578, 579, 581, 582, 583–586, 587, *m* 580
Japanese American Citizens League (JACL), 595, R59
Japanese Americans, 246
internment of, during World War II, 594–595, *i* 594, *i* 595, *m* 595, 596–597
as soldiers in World War II, 564, 573, 595
Japanese immigrants, 255, *c* 255, 259, 415
Jaworski, Leon, 805
Jay, John, 62, 70, 77
Jay's Treaty, 77
jazz, 456–457, 458, 657, *i* 657, R59
Jazz Singer, The, 450
Jefferson, Thomas, 35, 53, *i* 54, 55, 56, 75–76, *i* 75, *c* 76, 77, 79, 98, 112–113, 119, 724, R50
Jeffersonian republicanism, 113, R59
Jeffords, Jim, 868
Jenney, William LeBaron, 232
Jewett, Sarah Orne, 296
Jews, 61, 509, 531
in American colonies, 34
in Holocaust, 542, 543, 544–549, *c* 545, *i* 548
as immigrants, 255, 258, 284
in pre–World War II Germany, 542–544, *i* 543, *i* 544
Jim Crow laws, 287, 291, 701, 708–709, R59
Job Corps, 688, 796
Johnson, Andrew, 85, *i* 92, 184, 185–186, *i* 185, R51
Johnson, Henry, 382
Johnson, James Weldon, 453, *i* 453, 454
Johnson, Lyndon B., 681, 683, R52
affirmative action and, 429, 819
civil rights and, 687–688, 714, 715, 716
containment policy and, 737
Great Society and, 689–693, 719
tax reduction and, 687–688
Tet offensive and, 750
Tonkin Gulf Resolution and, 735
Vietnam and, 734–735, 736–737, 740–741, 745, 747
War on Poverty of, 688, 693, 719
Johnson, Tom, 310
Jones, John Paul, 61
Jones, Len, 541
Jones, Mary Harris "Mother," 248, *i* 248
Jordan, Barbara, 802, *i* 802
Jordan, Vernon, 722
journalism. *See* magazines; newspapers; photography.
***Joy Luck Club, The* (Tan)**, 875
judicial branch, 69, 92, 119. *See also* courts; Supreme Court; Supreme Court cases.
judicial review, 93, 113, 119, R59
Judiciary Act of 1789, 74, 113, R59
***Jungle, The* (Sinclair)**, 317, 320, 327, R59

K

Kahn, Gordon, 616
Kahn, Tony, 616, *i* 616
Kaiser, Henry J., 565
Kalakaua, 345
kamikaze pilots, 581, *i* 581, R59
Kansas, 18, 160, 208, 215, 708–709, R48
Kansas City, Missouri, 268
Kansas-Nebraska Act, 160, *m* 160, 161, 162
Karzai, Hamid, 867, *i* 867
Kashaya Pomo, 4, 6
Katrina, *i 868*
Kearney, Denis, 259
Kearny, Stephen, 136
Keating-Owen Act, 311
Kelley, Florence, 307, *i* 307, 311
Kelley, Oliver Hudson, 220–221
Kellogg-Briand Pact, 419–420, 534
Kelly, William, 231
Kennan, George F., 605
Kennedy, Anthony M., *i* 93, 836
Kennedy, Jacqueline, 672, *i* 672, *i* 682
Kennedy, John F., 469, 670–671, *i* 670, 674, 676–678, 777, 914, R52
Alliance for Progress and, 680–681
arms race and, 673
assassination of, 682–683, *i* 682, 714
Bay of Pigs invasion and, 674
Berlin crisis and, 677–678

civil rights and, 671, 682, 711, 712, 714
Cuban missile crisis and, 674, 676
economy and, 680
election of, 670–671
environment and, 821
New Frontier program of, 679–680
Peace Corps and, 680
space exploration and, 681
Kennedy, Joseph P., 469
Kennedy, Robert F., 672, 682, 711, 721, *i* 721, 722, 750–751, *i* 751, 770
Kent State University, 756–757, *i* 757, R59
Kentucky, 79, 94, 165, 169, 231
facts about, R48
Kentucky Resolutions, 79
Kerner Commission, 722, R59
kerosene, 231
Kerouac, Jack, 655, *i* 655
Kerry, John, 868
Keynes, John Maynard, 492, *i* 492, R42
Khmer Rouge, 760
Khomeini, Ayatollah Ruhollah, 817, *i* 817
Khrushchev, Nikita, 674, 676, *i* 676
Kim Il Sung, 611
Kim Jong Il, 899
King, Martin Luther, Jr., 671, *i* 698–699, 705–706, *i* 706, 712, 714, 716, 719, 720, 721, 722, 743, 750
King, Rodney, 841
King Philip. *See* Metacom.
King Philip's War, 25–26, R59
Kiowa, 206, 225
Kissinger, Henry, 758, *i* 758, 794, *i* 794, 799, 811
Klein, Gerda Weissmann, 542, *i* 542, 549
Knights of Labor, 245, 246
Know-Nothing Party, 161–162
Knox, Henry, 75
Kodak camera, 281, *i* 281
Kongo, 9, R59
Kopecki, Lilli, 548
Koran. *See* Qur'an.
Korea, 360, 611. *See also* Korean War.
Korean War, 91, 609, *i* 609, 611–615, *m* 613, 731, R59
domestic effects of, 611, 615
international effects of, 612, 615
***Korematsu* v. *United States*,** 595, 596–597
Kramer, Alyce Mano, 565
***Kristallnacht*,** 543, *i* 543, R60
Ku Klux Klan, 188, 415, *i* 415, R60
Kuwait, 853, *i* 854, 855
Kwakiutl, 6

L

labor force, 246, 642–643, *c* 814, 842–843, 869–871, *c* 871. *See also* economy; industry; labor movement; unions; working conditions.
children in, *i* 244, 245, 248, 306, 310–311, *i* 311, 321, *i* 321
in factories, 142, 233, 244–245, 306, 309
New Deal and, 499, 503, 518
unemployment and, 127, 222, 240, 469, *c* 470, *c* 517, *c* 813, R40, R47
women in, 142, *i* 142, 233, 244–245, 307, 311, 313–314, 388, 441–442, *c* 442, *i* 442, 565, *i* 565, 591, *i* 591, 777, *c* 777, 869, *i* 869, 914–915, *c* 914–915
in World War II, 565–566
labor movement, 142–143, 244–249, 389, 412, 417, 418. *See also* labor force; strikes; unions.
African Americans in, 245, 418, 565–566
agricultural workers and, 246, 768, 770
women in, 248–249, *i* 417, 777, 842–843
labor unions. *See* unions.
Lafayette, Marquis de, 61, 62
Laffer, Arthur, 835
La Flesche, Susette, 313, *i* 313
La Follette, Robert M., 310
laissez faire doctrine, 242
land mines, 182, 739
Landon, Alfred, 496
Land Ordinance of 1785, 67, 72, *m* 72
Lange, Dorothea, 495, *i* 496, 497
Laos, 732, *m* 733, 755
La Raza Unida, 770, R60
La Salle, Sieur de (Robert Cavelier), *m* 17
Latin America, 362, 680–681, 768–769. *See also* Panama Canal; *names of specific nations*.
and Alliance for Progress, 680–681
Good Neighbor Policy in, 534
Latinos, 473, 768–771, 844, 882, 884, 886. *See also* Mexican Americans; Puerto Ricans.
Lawrence, Joseph D., 383, *i* 383
Lazarus, Emma, 261
League of Nations, 398, 399, 401, 402, 412, 531–533, R60
learning new vocabulary. *See* vocabulary, learning new.
Lease, Mary Elizabeth, 219, *i* 219, 221
Le Duc Tho, 758
Lee, Richard Henry, 52, 70
Lee, Robert E., 170–171, 175–177, 180, *i* 180, 181, *i* 181, 183
legislative branch, 69, 84–90. *See also* Congress.
Leigh, Vivian, *i* 511
leisure activities, 293–294, 298–299, 645. *See also* entertainment; sports.
Lend-Lease Act, 552, 553, R60
Lenin, Vladimir I., *i* 405, 411, 413, 529
"Letter from a Birmingham Jail" (King), 712
***Letters from the Federal Farmer* (Lee),** 70
***Letters on the Equality of the Sexes and the Condition of Woman* (Grimké),** 148
***Let Us Now Praise Famous Men* (Agee and Evans),** 514, *i* 514
Lewis, John, 748, *i* 748
Lewis, John L., 418, *i* 418, 508
Lewis, Meriwether, 114
Lewis, Sinclair, 450
Lewis and Clark expedition, 112, 114, *m* 115
Lexington, Battle of, *c* 49, 50, *i* 50, 52
Leyte Gulf, Battle of, 581
***Liberator, The*,** 145–146, *i* 145
Liberty League. *See* American Liberty League.
Liberty Party, 162
light bulb, 232, 233
Liliuokalani, 342, *i* 342, 345
Limited Test Ban Treaty, 678
Lin, Maya, 760, *i* 760
Lincoln, Abraham, 163, *i* 163, 164, 168, 172, *i* 172, *i* 183, R51
assassination of, 91, 183, *i* 183
in Civil War, 169, 172, 173, 177, 180, 181, 260
Reconstruction and, 184–185, 186
Lindbergh, Charles, 424, 449, *i* 449, 552
Li Peng, 850
literacy test, 258, 287
literature
beat movement and, 655
Harlem Renaissance and, 454, 456, 458, 459
in 1920s, 450–451, 458–459
in 1930s, 514
science fiction, 628–629
at turn of century, 296
of Vietnam War, 762–763
of West, 224–225
women and, 459, 874–875
Little Bighorn, Battle of, 204, *m* 205, 206
Little Rock, Arkansas, 703–704, *i* 703
Livingston, Robert, 114
Lloyd George, David, 399, *i* 399
lobbying, 109, 666
location, xxx, 7, 25, 59, 136, 159, 176, 179, 205, 345, 349, 356, 375, 386, 400, 530, 532, 538, 594, 605, 733, 749, 816, 833, 851, 872
Locke, Alain, 454, 457
Locke, John, 52, 53, 54
Locust Street Social Settlement, 266
Lodge, Henry Cabot, Sr., 401
London, Jack, 265, 296
Long, Huey, 494, *i* 494
long drive. *See* cattle drive. R60
longhorn cattle, 208, 210, R60
longhouse, *i* 7
Longoria, Felix, 662
Looking Glass, Chief, *i* 150
Lopez de la Cruz, Jessie, 768
Los Angeles, California, 719, 841, 843
Lost Generation, 451
Louis XIV (king of France)
Louisiana, 165, 185, 494, 701
facts about, R48
French, Spanish, and U.S. territory of, 114, 122
Louisiana Purchase, 114, *i* 115, 157, R60
Love Canal, 820
Low, Ann Marie, 472, *i* 472
Lowell, Massachusetts, 142, R60
Loyalists, in Revolutionary War, 59, R60
Loyalty Review Board, 617
Lucas, Anthony F., 230
Luftwaffe, 539, 540–541
***Lusitania*,** *m* 375, 378, *i* 378, R60
Lyon, Mary, 148

M

MacArthur, Douglas, 483, 579, 581, 583, *i* 583, 587, 612, 614–615, *i* 614
Madero, Francisco, 363
Madison, James, 68, *i* 68, 70, *i* 70, 75, 113, 114, 116, 118–119, 122, R50
magazines, 279, 441, 447
Maginot Line, 540, *i* 540
magnetic resonance imaging (MRI), 880
Mahan, Alfred T., 343, *i* 343
mahjong, 448
Mahpiua Luta. *See* Red Cloud.
mail-order catalogs, 297, *i* 297
Maine, 94, 122, 133, 681, *c* 773
  facts about, R48
***Maine*, USS,** 340, 348, *i* 348, 404
main ideas, finding, 327, 829, 835, R2, R27
making decisions, 109, 129, 329, 586
***Making Do* (Westin),** 475
making inferences, 8, 10, 13, 33, 39, 52, 67, 69, 113, 142, 146, 149, 169, 170, 179, 186, 211, 223, 233, 240, 293, 316, 351, 379, 389, 393, 395, 402, 421, 450, 471, 481, 552, 608, 656, 682, 683, 704, 721, 735, 739, 744, 753, 761, 779, 780, 811, 875, 881, R10, R23. *See also* drawing conclusions.
making predictions. *See* predicting effects.
Malcolm X, 719, *i* 719, 720
MALDEF. *See* Mexican American Legal Defense and Education Fund.
Mali, 8
Manchester, William, 578, 583
Manchuria, 360, 532, *m* 532, 554
mandate, 680, R60
Mandela, Nelson, 701
Manhattan Project, 567, 583–584, R60
manifest destiny, 130
***manikongo*,** 9
manufacturing. *See* industry; factories.
Mao Zedong, 610, *i* 610, 721
MAPA. *See* Mexican American Political Association.
***Mapp* v. *Ohio*,** 692, 694
maps
  creating, 151, 235, 266, R32
  interpreting, 42, 190, 368, 406, 430, 558, 598, 630, 726, 775, 856, 890, R25–26
  using, 7, 15, 17, 22, 25, 29, 38, 59, 62, 72, 73, 115, 116, 125, 132, 134, 136, 159, 160, 170, 171, 176, 179, 205, 209, 231, 239, 255, 263, 278, 323, 331, 345, 349, 356, 367, 369, 374, 386, 400, 407, 416, 423, 449, 474, 520–521, 530, 532, 538, 556, 572, 575, 580, 591, 594, 599, 605, 613, 624, 638, 675, 677, 685, 701, 733, 749, 753, 816, 833, 846, 847, 851, 854, 872, 885
Marbury, William, 118–119
***Marbury* v. *Madison*,** 113, 118–119, R60
Marconi, Guglielmo, 140
Marines, U.S., 582, 583
Marquette, Jacques, *m* 17
Marshall, George, 563, 574, 606
Marshall, John, 113, *i* 113, 124, 118–119
Marshall, Thurgood, *i* 99, 669, 702, *i* 702, 708, 836
Marshall Plan, 606, *c* 606, 636, R60
Martí, José, 347, *i* 347, 353
***Martian Chronicles, The* (Bradbury),** 629
Marx, Karl, 246, 413
Maryland, 28, 32, 165, 169, 171, 176, 311
  facts about, R48
Massachusetts, 35, 49, 50, 67
  facts about, R48
Massachusetts Bay Colony, 24
Massachusetts Bay Company, 24
Massasoit, 25
mass media. *See* communications; journalism; radio; television. R60
Maya, 5
***Mayagüez* incident,** 811
Mayflower Compact, 23, 24
Mayhew, Jonathan, 52
McCarran Internal Security Act, 618
McCarthy, Eugene, 750
McCarthy, Joseph, 618, *i* 618, 620–621
McCarthyism, 620–621, *c* 621
McClellan, George, 169, 170–171
McCord, James, 803
McCormick, Cyrus, 141, 217, 232
McCoy, Joseph, 209
***McCulloch* v. *Maryland*,** 122
McGrath, John Patrick, 569
***McLaurin* v. *Oklahoma State* (1950),** 708
McKay, Claude, 454
McKinley, William, 222, 223, 317–316, 345, 347–348, 350–351, 358, 359, R51
McKinley Tariff Act, 271, 344
McNamara, Robert, 672, 673, 737, 739, 741, 747, 749
McNary-Haugen bill, 465
McPherson, Aimee Semple, 438, *i* 438
McVeigh, Timothy, 862
Meade, George, 176
Means, Gardiner C., 492
Means, Russell, 772
Meat Inspection Act, 320, 322, *i* 322, 327, R60
Medicaid, 690, 796, 865, 908, R60
Medicare, 690, 691, 796, 865, 884, 908–909, 912, R60
medicine. *See* health care.
***Mein Kampf* (Hitler),** 531
Mellon, Andrew, 420
Melville, Herman, 238
melting pot, 258, R60
Mencken, H. L., 437
mercantilism, 28, 30, R60
Mercer, Mabel, 456
merchandising, 296–297
  advertising and, 297, 425–426, 648–649
Meredith, James, 711
merit system, 270, 271
***Merrimack*,** 182
Mesabi Range, 231
***mestizo*,** 16, R60
Metacom, 25
Methodists, 36
Mexica. *See* Aztecs.
Mexican American Legal Defense and Education Fund (MALDEF), 882
Mexican American Political Association (MAPA), 770
Mexican Americans, 246, 769, 844
  as cowboys, 210
  discrimination against, 288–289
  deportation of, 506
  Longoria incident and, 662
  New Deal and, 504, 506–507
  in 1950s, 662
  as railroad workers, 215, 288–289, *i* 289
  World War II and, 564, 573, *i* 593
Mexican War. *See* Mexico, U.S. war with.
Mexico, 8, 16, 18, 133–134, 365, 379, 768, 769. *See also* Latinos; Mexican Americans.
  ancient cultures of, 5
  immigrants from, 256, 260, 886
  NAFTA and, 864, 873
  revolution in, 363–365
  Texas and, 130, 133–135
  U.S. war with, 130, 135–137, *m* 136, 180
Mexico City, 18, 133, 363
Meyers, Isaac, 245
MFDP. *See* Mississippi Freedom Democratic Party.
Michigan, 424, 865
  facts about, R48
Michigan, Lake 279
middle colonies, *m* 25, 26, 28, *c* 29, *m* 29, 34. *See also* colonial America.
Middle East, 9, 10, 799, 816–817, *m* 816, 852–853. *See also* Organization of Petroleum Exporting Countries.
middle passage, 32–33, R60
Midway, Battle of, 579
Mifflin, Sarah and Thomas, 64
migrant workers, 497, *i* 497, 684–685, *i* 684, *i* 685, *m* 685
migration, 137, 193, 204, 215, 263, 393–394, 434, 452–453, 474, 591, *m* 591, 701, 718, 846–847, 888–889
Miles, Nelson A., 353
militarism, R60
  in European nations, 373
  in Japan, 532
military technology. *See* technology, warfare and.
Millay, Edna St. Vincent, 451, 459, *i* 459
Miller, Thomas W., 421
Mills, Florence, 456
minimum wage, 499, R42, *c* R43
mining, 321, 465. *See also* coal; gold; iron; silver.
  labor movement and, 246, 248, 418, 637
  in West, 204, 212–213
Minneapolis, Minnesota, 238
Minnesota, 133, 215, 231, 837, 887
  facts about, R48
minorities. *See* African Americans; Asian Americans; Latinos; Jews; Native Americans.
minstrel shows, 298
minutemen, 50
Miranda, Ernesto, 694
Miranda rights, 97, 695, *i* 695

Miranda v. Arizona, 97, 692, 694–695
missionary diplomacy, 363
Mission San José y San Miguel de Aguayo, 19
Mississippi, 165, 179, 711, 715, 720, 797
facts about, R48
Mississippian culture, 6
Mississippi Freedom Democratic Party (MFDP), 715–716
Mississippi River, 77, 140, 170, 171, 179
Missouri, 122, 160, 162, 165, 166, 169
facts about, R48
Missouri Compromise, 122, 157, 160, *m* 160, 162, R60
Missouri River, 203, 204
Missouri v. Holland, 95
Mitchell, John, 803, *i* 803, 804
Mitchell, Margaret, 324
modeling, 879
models
creating, 367, 521, R31
using, R18
Mondale, Walter, 832, 837
money supply, 221–222
Monitor, 183
Monmouth, Battle of, 61, *i* 61
monopoly, 243, 330–331, 333, 356, R43
Monroe, James, 114, 116–117, *i* 117, 363, R50
Monroe, Sylvester, 843
Monroe Doctrine, 116–117, *i* 351, 362, 363, 404, R60
Montana
facts about, R48
Montezuma, 16
Montgomery, Alabama, 165
bus boycott in, 700, 704–705, *i* 705, R38
Montgomery Ward, 297
moon landing, 796, *i* 796
Moral Majority, 831–832, 838, R60
Morgan, J. P., 240, 243
Morgan v. Virginia, 702
Mormons, 131, 133
Morrill Act, 217, R60
Morris, Robert, 61
Morse Code, 140
Morse, Samuel F. B., 140
motion pictures, 294, 299, *i* 299, 402, 450, 510–511, *i* 510, 566, *i* 566, 654–655, 787, 824
motives, analyzing. *See* analyzing motives.
Mott, Lucretia, 64, 148
Mount Holyoke Female Seminary, 148
movement (geographic theme), xxx, 17, 62, 115, 125, 132, 159, 176, 179, 205, 239, 255, 263, 423, 474, 532, 556, 572, 580, 591, 613, 675, 733, 854, 885
movies. *See* motion pictures.
MRI. *See* magnetic resonance imaging.
muckrakers, 308, 326–327, R60
Muhammad, 9
Muir, John, 323, 329
Muller v. Oregon, 311
Muncie, Indiana, 209
Munn v. Illinois, 239, R60
Muñoz Rivera, Luis, 352, *i* 352
Murphy, Audie, 576, *i* 576
Murray, Patty, 65
Murrow, Edward R., 653
music
jazz, 456–457, 657
popular, 652
ragtime, 299
rock 'n' roll, 655–656, *i* 656, 786, R63
soul, 786
surf, 786
Muslims, 9, 10, 850, 896, 897. *See also* Islam.
Mussolini, Benito, 530, *m* 530, 531, *i* 531, 573
My Ántonia (Cather), 451
Myers, Deb, 563
Myers, Walter Dean, 763
My Lai massacre, 756, R60

N

NAACP. *See* National Association for the Advancement of Colored People.
NACW. *See* National Association of Colored Women.
Nader, Ralph, 691
Green Party and, 865
NAFTA. *See* North American Free Trade Agreement.
Nagasaki, Japan, 584
napalm, 739, R61
Napoleon. *See* Bonaparte, Napoleon.
NASA. *See* National Aeronautics and Space Administration.
NASDAQ. *See* National Association of Securities Dealers Automated Quotation System.
Nasser, Gamal Abdel, 625
Nast, Thomas, 269
Nation, Carry, *i* 307
National Aeronautics and Space Administration (NASA), 681, 879
National American Woman Suffrage Association (NAWSA), 316, 332, 335 , R61
National Association for the Advancement of Colored People (NAACP), 288, 291, 325, 335–336, 453, R61
National Association of Colored Women (NACW), 315, R61
National Association of Securities Dealers Automated Quotation System (NASDAQ), 871, R61
national bank. *See* Bank of the United States; Second Bank of the United States.
National Child Labor Committee, 310
National Council of Indian Opportunity, 771
national debt, 75, *c* 76, 835–836, 862, R43
National Energy Act, 813, R61
National Farm Workers Association, 770
National Housing Act, 492
National Industrial Recovery Act (NIRA), 491–492, 499, R61
nationalism, 116, 373, 528, *m* 530, R61
National Labor Relations Act (Wagner Act), 499, *c* 500, 502–503, 507, R65
National Labor Relations Board (NLRB), 499, 500, 502, 517, R61
National Labor Union (NLU), 245
National Organization for Women (NOW), 778, R61
National Origins Act, 691
National Park System. *See also* Yellowstone National Park; Yosemite National Park.
establishment of, 323
National Reclamation Act, 256, 289, 323–324
National Recovery Administration (NRA), 492, *c* 500
National Republican Party, 123
National Rifle Association, 903
National Security Council, 853
National Trades' Union, 143, R61
National War Labor Board, 389
National Youth Administration (NYA), 499, *i* 499, *c* 500, 505, R61
Nation at Risk, A, 841
Nation of Islam, 719–720, R61
Native Americans, 4–5, 6, 71, 114, 216, 224, 231, 260, 288, 313, 844, 886–887. *See also names of specific individuals and peoples.*
ancient cultures of, 4–5, *i* 6, 260
assimilation of, 206–207, 662–663, 771
buffalo and, 203, 207
colonial Americans and, 23, 25–26, 37, 38, 39, 53, 428
diseases and, 15, 26, 39
education of, 772–773, 887
in 1400s, *i* 2–3, 6, *m* 7, 8–9
French and, 37, 39
horses and, 203
land claims of, 67, 77, *m* 204, 507, 772–773, 887
land use of, 8, 25, 203, 428
New Deal and, 507
religious beliefs of, 7, 8, 203
removal of, 124, 428
in Revolutionary War, 59, 61, 63
social organization of, 8
Spanish and, 14–15, 16, 18–20
struggle for rights of, 105, 662–663, 771–773, 886–887
trading networks of, *m* 7, 8
westward expansion and, 39, 77, 131, 203–204, 428
white settlers and, *i* 200–201
World War II and, 564, 579, *i* 579
nativism, 161, 258–259, 412, 414–415, R61
NATO. *See* North Atlantic Treaty Organization.
Navajo, *i* 132, 579, *i* 579
Navigation Acts, 28, 30, R61
Navy, U.S., 113, 169, 343, 348, 383, 570, 579, 735
NAWSA. *See* National American Woman Suffrage Association.
Nazism and Nazis, *i* 526–527, 530, 543, 545, R61. *See also* Germany; Nuremberg trials; World War II.
Nebraska, 160, 215
facts about, R49
Nehru, Jawaharlal, 614, *i* 614

Netherlands, the, 540
Neutrality Acts, 535, 550, R61
Nevada, 137, 847
facts about, R49
New Amsterdam, 26
New Deal, 488–494, 506–507, R61. *See also* Great Depression.
agencies of, *c* 500
banking relief, 490
Civilian Conservation Corps in, 491, *i* 491, 505, 519
Civil Works Administration in, 488, *i* 488, 491
effects of, 488–493, 495–496, 498–499, *c* 500, 501, 503, 504–509, 518
effects on state governments, 491, 492, 493, 499, 502–503, 518
Fair Labor Standards Act and, 499, 518
farmers under, 491, 496, 498, 518
Federal Deposit Insurance Corporation, 490, 517, 518
Hundred Days, 489
labor unions and, 502–503, 507–509
National Labor Relations Act and, 499, 518
National Recovery Administration and, 492, 499
opposition to, 493–494, 516
Public Utilities Holding Company Act and, 501
Public Works Administration and, 491
Second, 495–501
Securities and Exchange Commission, 490, 518, R45
Social Security system and, 501, 518
Supreme Court and, 493, 496, 499
Tennessee Valley Authority and, 519, *m* 520–521
women and, 504–505
Works Progress Administration and, 498–499, 512–513
New Deal coalition, 507, R61
"New Democrats," 861
New England, 59, 60, 121
colonies in, 24–26, *m* 25, *c* 29, *m* 29, 34, 35, 50
New Federalism, 795, R61
New France, 37
New Frontier, 679, R61
New Hampshire, 25
facts about, R49
New Jersey, 26, 101, 423
facts about, R49
New Jersey Plan, 68
Newlands Act. *See* National Reclamation Act.
New Left, 744, R61
Newman, Pauline, 248–249
New Mexico, 18, 136, 137, 157, 160
facts about, R49
Mexican province of, 131, 135, 136
Spanish settlement of, 18, 20, 203
***New Negro, The* (Locke),** 454
New Netherland, 26
New Orleans, Louisiana, 38, 77, 170
New Orleans, Battle of, 114
New Right, 779, 780, 831, R61
New South, 797
New Spain, 18, 20
newspapers, 279, 294–295, 346, 347, 447
New Sweden, 26
Newton, Huey, 720
Newton, Isaac, 34–35
New York, 26, 34, 60, 95, 249, 847
New York City, 120, 140, 141, 209, 232, 249, 264, 265, 276, 277, 288, 318, 435, 509. *See also* September 11 terrorist attack.
colonial, 26, 33, 47
draft riot in, 173
facts about, R49
immigrants in, *i* 143, 262, 263, *m* 263
political machines and, 268, 269
in Revolutionary War, 59, 60, 62
tenements in, 262, 264
terrorism in, 862, 863, 894, *i* 894
urban planning and, 277–278
New York Stock Exchange, 467, 468, *i* 468, R45
Nez Perce, 150, 208
Ngo Dinh Diem, 732, 734
Niagara Falls Conference, *i* 324, 325
Niagara Movement, 285, R61
Nicaragua, 360, 362–363, 851–852
Nicholas II (czar of Russia), 360
Nimitz, Chester, 579
***Niña*,** 14
9-11 terrorist attack. *See* September 11 terrorist attack.
Nineteenth Amendment, 64, 101, 105, 335, R61
Ninth Amendment, 70, 97
NIRA. *See* National Industrial Recovery Act.
Nixon, Richard M., 91, 639–640, *i* 640, 746, 753, *i* 792–793, *i* 794, 800, 803–804, R52
"Checkers speech" of, 639–640
civil rights and, 796–797
détente and, 799, 815
environment and, 821–822
foreign policy of, 799–801, 815
impeachment and, 806, 807
New Federalism and, 795
pardon of, 810, 811
resignation of, 806–807, *i* 807
SALT I Treaty and, 800–801
Saturday Night Massacre and, 805–806
Southern strategy of, 796–797, R64
stagflation and, 798–799
Vietnam War and, 754–758, 794, 796
visit to China of, 800–801, *i* 800
Watergate scandal and, 623, *i* 623, 802–807
welfare reform and, 795
NLRB. *See* National Labor Relations Board.
***NLRB* v. *Jones and Laughlin Steel Corp.*,** 502–503
NLU. *See* National Labor Union.
Nobel Peace Prize, 360
No Child Left Behind, 867
nonaggression pact, 539, R61
Noonan, Peggy, 830, *i* 830
Nootka, 6
Noriega, Manuel, 852
Normandy invasion, 574
North, Frederick, 48, 49
North, Oliver, 853
North Africa, 9
in World War II, 572, *m* 572
North American Free Trade Agreement (NAFTA), 864, *i* 864, 873, R61
North Atlantic Treaty Organization (NATO), 608, *i* 608, 624, *m* 624, 863, R46, R61
North Carolina, 28, 32, 52, 104, 169, 706
facts about, R49
North Dakota, 474
facts about, R49
Northern Alliance, 896
Northern colonies, 30, 33–34. *See also* middle colonies; New England, colonies in.
Northern Pacific Railroad, 221
Northern Securities Company, 319
North Korea, 899
***North Star, The*,** 146
Northwest Coast, Native Americans of, 6, *m* 7
Northwest Ordinance of 1787, 67, 72, 167, R61
Northwest Territory, 67, *m* 72, 77, 130
notes, using, 42, 80, 152, 190, 226, 250, 272, 300, 338, 369, 406, 430, 460, 522, 558, 598, 630, 664, 696, 726, 764, 788, 826, 856, 890
note-taking. *See* taking notes.
Novello, Antonia Coello, 844, *i* 844
NOW. *See* National Organization for Women.
NRA. *See* National Recovery Administration.
nuclear energy, 822, 824–825
Nuclear Nonproliferation Treaty, 899
Nuclear Regulatory Commission, 824
nuclear weapons, 622, 623–624, 670, 678, 849
Limited Test Ban Treaty and, 678, R60
nullification, 79, 124, 125, 128, R61
Nuremberg Laws, 543
Nuremberg trials, 586–587, *i* 586, R61
NYA. *See* National Youth Administration.
Nye, Gerald, 534

O

Oakley, Annie, 211
oba, 9
Obregón, Alvaro, 365
O'Brien, Tim, 736, 763
Ochoa, Ellen, 879
O'Connor, Sandra Day, *i* 93, 836
Oettinger, Hank, 488
Office of Alien Property, 421
Office of Economic Opportunity, 796
Office of Price Administration (OPA), 567, 635, R61
Office of Scientific Research and Development (OSRD), 567
Oglethorpe, James, 28
Ohio, 73, 77, 131, 231
facts about, R49
Ohio gang, 420, R61
Ohio River, 37, 165

oil, 231, *m* 231, 243
in Alaska, 822
energy crisis and, 812–813
Organization of Petroleum Exporting Countries and, 799, 811
Persian Gulf War and, 853–854, 898
in Texas, 230, 231, 813
O'Keeffe, Georgia, 450
Okinawa, 583
Oklahoma, 18, 215
facts about, R49
Olmec culture, 5
Olive Branch Petition, 51, 52
Oliver, Joe "King," 456
Olmsted, Frederick Law, 277
Omaha, Nebraska, 215, 221
Omaha Beach, 574, 575
Onís, Luis de, 116
***On the Road* (Kerouac),** 655
OPA. *See* Office of Price Administration.
OPEC. *See* Organization of Petroleum Exporting Countries.
Open Door notes, 356, 357, 359, R61
Open Door policy, 356, 357
open-hearth process, 231
Operation Desert Storm, 855, R61
Operation Enduring Freedom, 896
Operation Iraqi Freedom, 899
Operation Overlord, 574
Operation Rolling Thunder, 735
Operation Torch, 572
opinions, forming. *See* forming opinions.
Oppenheimer, J. Robert, 583
oral presentations, creating, R36
Oregon, 11, 208
facts about, R49
Oregon Territory, 116, *m* 116, 133
Oregon Trail, 131, *m* 132, 150
m 150–151, R62
***Organization Man, The* (Whyte),** 643
Organization of Petroleum Exporting Countries (OPEC), 799, 811, 813, R62
***Origin of Species, On The* (Darwin),** 242
Orlando, Vittorio, 399
Ortega, Daniel, 852
Oswald, Lee Harvey, 683
Osage, 203
Osama bin Laden. *See* bin Laden, Osama.
OSRD. *See* Office of Scientific Research and Development.
***Other America, The* (Harrington),** 661
Ottoman Empire, 374, *m* 375
outline, creating a, R35, R36

P

Paine, Thomas, 52
painting. *See* art.
Palmer, A. Mitchell, 413
Palmer raids, 413
Panama, 360–361, 367, 815, 852
Panama Canal, 353, 359, *i* 359, 360–361, *i* 361, 366–367, *i* 366–367, 815, R62
panic of 1837, 127, 137
panic of 1873, 189
panic of 1893, 221–222, 240, 248
Pankhurst, Emmeline, 335, *i* 335
Paris, Treaty of, R65
of 1763, 38
of 1783, 62, 63
of 1898, 350–351, 353, 355
parity, 518, R62
Parker, Dorothy, 450
Parks, Gordon, 464, *i* 464
Parks, Rosa, 291, *i* 291, 704, *i* 704
Parliament (British), 26, 28, 47, 49, 51, 55
Parrish, Essie, 4, *i* 4
participation, political, 744–746, 756–757. *See also* lobbying; Vietnam War, protests against; voting rights.
of minorities, 64–65,105, 148–149, 286–288, 314–316, 332, 334–335, 637, 715–716
Supreme Court and, 775, 844
Paterson, William, 68
***Pathfinder*,** 879
Patman, Wright, 482
Patman Bill, 482
Patriots
in Revolutionary War, 59, 60, R62
patronage, 270, R62
Patrons of Husbandry. *See* Grange.
patterns, analyzing. *See* analyzing patterns.
patterns, geographic. *See* geographic patterns.
Patton, George S., 574
Paul, Alice, 332, 335
Payne-Aldrich Tariff, 329, 330, R62
Peace Corps, 680, *i* 680, R62
Pearl Harbor, 344, 555–557, *i* 555, *i* 556, *m* 556, *i* 560–561, 562, 578, 579
Peck, James, 710, *i* 710
Pendergast, James "Big Jim," 268
Pendleton Civil Service Act, 270–271, R62
Penn, William, 26, 28
Pennsylvania, 26, 28, 60, 104, 176, 822, 865
facts about, R49
Pentagon
September 11 terrorist attack on, 863, 894
Pentagon Papers, 757, R62
People's Party. *See* Populist Party.
Peralta, Pedro de, 18
***perestroika*,** 849, R62
Perkins, Frances, 501, 504–505, *i* 505
Perot, H. Ross, 861, 865
Pershing, John J., 364–365, 384, *i* 384, 386
Persian Gulf War, 853, *m* 854, 855, 861, 867, 898
Personal Responsibility and Work Opportunity Act, 911
perspective, developing historical. *See* historical perspective, developing.
Pétain, Philippe, 540
petroleum-based product, 231. *See also* oil; gasoline.
Philadelphia, Pennsylvania, 60, 61, 435, 509, 839, 843
colonial, 33, 34, 47, 49
Philadelphia and Reading Railroad, 221
Philippine-American War, 355, *i* 355
Philippines
independence of, 355
rebellion in, 355
in Spanish-American War, 349
as Spanish colony, 346, 349
U.S. annexation of, 350–351, 355
war with U.S., 355, *i* 355
World War II and, *i* 578, 579, 581
photography
inventions in, 281
journalism and, 178, 311, 497, 582, 713, 757
Pierce, Franklin, 137, 161, R51
Pilgrims, 24
Pinchot, Gifford, 323, 328, *i* 328, 329
Pinckney, Thomas, 77
Pinckney Treaty, 77
Pingree, Hazen, 310
Pinkerton Detective Agency, 247–248
***Pinta*,** 14
Pitt, William, 38
Pitcher, Molly. *See* Hays, Mary Ludwig.
Pittsburgh, Pennsylvania, 231, *m* 231
Pizarro, Francisco, 17, 18
place, xxx, 17, 38, 59, 62, 116, 125, 134, 159, 160, 170, 209, 263, 375, 386, 423, 572, 575, 594, 613
Plains Indians, *m* 7
battles with, 204, *m* 205, 206, 207–208
culture of, 202–203
restriction of, 204, 207–208
Plains of Abraham, 38
planned obsolescence, 648, R62
plantation. *See* agriculture.
Platt Amendment, 354, R62
Plessy, Homer A., 290
***Plessy* v. *Ferguson*,** 287, 290–291, 701, 702–703, 708–709, R62
points of view. *See* developing historical perspective.
Poland, 604–605, 849
in World War II, 538, 539, *i* 539, 542, 551, 576
political cartoons, analyzing. *See* analyzing political cartoons.
political machines, 267–268, R62
Polk, James K., 135–136, R50
poll tax, 102, 287, 637, 716, R62
pollution
of air, 824
automobiles and, 881
DDT and, 821
industrial, 234–235, 820
Love Canal and, 820
Polo, Marco, 12
Ponca, 313
Ponce de León, Juan, *m* 17, 18
Pontiac, 39
Popé, 20
popular American culture, 298–299, 444–445, 658–659, 786–787, 808–809. *See also* art, literature, motion pictures, music, radio, television.
impact on world culture, 299, R63
popular sovereignty, 157, 160, 163, R62
population. *See also* migration.
changes, effects of, 591, 846–847, 434
growth, 591

shifts in, 591, 846–847
Populism, 221, R62
Populist Party, 221, 222, 223
Port Hudson, Louisiana, 170, 179
Portsmouth, Treaty of, 360
Portugal, 10, 11, 13, 15, 116–117
posing questions. *See* questions, posing.
Post Office, U.S., 297
Potomac, Army of the, 175, *i* 178, 179
Potomac River, 171, 176
Potsdam conference, 604
Pound, Ezra, 451
poverty, 266, 660–661, 681, 688, *c* 723, 842, 910–911, *c* 910–911, *c* R43
Powell, Colin, 848, *i* 848
Powers, Francis Gary, 626–627, *i* 627
Powhatan, 23
pow wow, *i* 6
predicting effects, 124, 26, 30, 117, 131, 261, 331, 427, 557, 671, 845, 885, 890, 897, 899, 901, 903, 905, 907, 909, 911, 913, 915, 917, R20
predictions, making, R20
Prescott, Samuel, 50
presentations, creating, 43, 153, 213, 273, 339, 397, 408, 523, 552, 665, 727, 857, 891
oral, 108, 109, 167, 198, 369, 709, 857, R36
visual, 225, R37
written, 108, 109, 725, R34–35
president, 69, 78, 85, 87, 90–92. *See also names of specific presidents.*
Presidential Commission on the Status of Women, 777
Presley, Elvis, 656, *i* 656
Preuss, Charles, 150
price controls
under New Deal, 492
under Nixon, 799
price supports, 465
primary sources, 54–57, 129
analyzing, 39, 143, 174, 189, 291, 337, 345, 387, 397, 443, 557, 577, 664, 693, 709, 716, 773, 780, 788, 838, R21. *See also* sources, primary.
Princip, Gavrilo, 374
printing, 12, 279
private property. *See* property, private.
problems, identifying, 194, 218, 250, 257, 259, 264, 289, 361, 401, 429, 465, 507, 529, 568, 635, 680, 688, 693, 769, 815, 841, 844
problem solving, 325, 494, 557
Proclamation of Amnesty and Reconstruction, 185
Proclamation of 1763, 39, 46, R62
productivity, R44
progressive movement or progressivism, 306–312, 335–337, 419, R62. *See also* Roosevelt, Theodore; Taft, William Howard; Wilson, Woodrow.
architecture and, 336
women and, 314–316
Progressive Party, 330
Prohibition, 100, 101–102, 307–308, 436–437, R62
Project Head Start, 688
Promontory, Utah, 237
propaganda, 377, *i* 378, 390–391, *i* 391
in motion pictures, 566, *i* 566, R62
property
private, 215, 216, 428
Proposition Thirteen, 47
Proposition 187, 886, 900, R62
prosperity, economic
in 1920s, 425–427, 464–465
in 1950s, 641, 643, 644, 645, 648
protective tariff, R62. *See also* tariffs.
protectorate, 354, R62
Providence, Rhode Island, 25
Ptolemy, 12–13
Public Utilities Holding Company Act, 501
Public Works Administration (PWA), 491, *c* 500
pueblo (housing), *i* 7
Pueblo (Native Americans), 6, 20, R62
Puerto Ricans, 769, 844
Puerto Rico, 256, 346, 350, 352, 353, 454, 768, 769
facts about, R49
Pulitzer, Joseph, 294–295, 347
Pullman, George M., 236, 238
Pullman, Illinois, 236, *i* 236, 238
Pullman cars, *i* 238
Pullman strike, 238, 248
Pure Food and Drug Act, 322, R62
Puritans, 24–25, 26, 27, 35, 40, 41, R62
PWA. *See* Public Works Administration.
Pyle, Ernie, 572, *i* 572

Q

Quakers, 26, 27, 28, 41, 61, R62
Quartering Act, 49, 55
Quebec, 38
Quebec Act, 55
questions
formulating, R4, R12
posing, 73, 83, 235, 651, 685, 847
quota, 415, R62
Qur'an, 9, 817

R

race riots, 288, 394, 453, 718–719, 841
racial groups. *See specific groups.*
Radical Republicans, 185, 186, 189
radicals, 413
radio, 140, 447–448, *i* 447, 511–512, 654
ragtime, 299, *i* 299
railroads, 169, 221, 231, *m* 239, 244, 465
cattle ranching and, 209, *m* 209
consolidation of, 240, *i* 240
farmers and, 218, 219, 220, 238–240
growth of, 141, *i* 228–229, 236–238
industry and, 237–238
land grants to, 214–215, 216
regulation of, 239–240, 310, 320
time zones and, 237
transcontinental, 237
in West, 209, 214–215
workers on, 215, *i* 228–229, *i* 237, *i* 289
urban growth and, 237–238
Rainey, Gertrude "Ma," *i* 432–433
Randolph, A. Philip, 418, 566, *i* 566, 705, 714
Rankin, Jeannette, 372, *i* 372
rationing, 568, R62
ratification, 69, R62
Ray, James Earl, 721
REA. *See* Rural Electrification Administration.
Reagan, Nancy, 841
Reagan, Ronald, 595, 812, 832–833, *i* 832, 834, 835, *i* 828–829, *i* 836, 842, 844, 848, 849, 851–852, R52
assassination attempt on, 837, *i* 837
deregulation and, 83
drug abuse and, 841
economic policy and, 834–836, 837
Grenada and, 852
Iran-Contra affair nd, 852–853
national debt and 835–836
Panama and, 852
space exploratio 841
Strategic Defens Initiative and, 835
Supreme Court nd, 836
Reaganomics, 834–35, R62
realpolitik, 799, R6
reaper, 141, 217, 217, 263
reapportionment, 91, R63
recall, 312, 868, 63
recession, 680, 8, R41, R43, R4
Reciprocal TradeAgreement Act, 534
recognizing effets. *See* effects, recognizng.
Reconstructior 184–189, 286, R3
ReconstructioAct of 1867, 186
Reconstructio Finance Corporaton (RFC), 481–42, R63
Red Cloud (Mhpiua Luta), 204, 06
Red Cross, 35, 394, 744
Reder, Rudoh, 546, 548
Red River W, 206
Red Scare, 13
referendum 312, R63
Reformatio 10–11, R63
reform movments, 144–148, 3–312, 31-316
***Regents* c*the University of Caornia* v. *Bake*,** 818, 905
region, xx, 7, 25, 29, 38, 116 32, 134, 13, 160, 170, 209, 23 323, 400, 41, 530, 538, 556, 62 638, 701, 83, 851, 854
Rehnquit, Willian H., *i* 93, 83
relationnips, andyzing. *See* aryzing rlationshps.
Remingon, Fredeic, 347
Renaisance, 11-12, 34, R63
reparatons, 400, R63
republc, 67, R63
republcanism, 13
Repulican Party 161, 162, 1, 222, 238, 329–30, 480, 86 864–865, 867–868. *e also* elecn, presidentl.
Reconstructi and, 185 36, 187, 188–189
researching, 3, 4 43, 45, 65 1, 83, 105, 107, 108, 11, 119, 1 155, 167, 201, 213, 25, 229, 2 253, 261, 275, 291, 99, 302, 3 325, 341, 369, 371, 97, 405, 4 429, 431,

433, 445, 459, 463, 487, 516, 527, 552, 561, 597, 599, 601, 633, 665, 669, 685, 695, 699, 709, 725, 729, 763, 765, 767, 775, 787, 793, 819, 829, 853, 859, 889, 891, 897, 899, 901, 903, 905, 907, 909, 911, 913, 915, 917, R12, R29, R34. *See also* Internet, using for research; primary sources; sources, secondary.
Reserve Officer Training Corps (ROTC), 744–745
Resettlement Administration, 498
Revels, Hiram, 188, *i* 188
revenue sharing, 795, R63
Revere, Paul, 48, 50
revivalism, 145
Revolutionary War, 36, 58–63, *m* 59, *m* 62, 67
***Reynolds* v. *Sims*,** 692, 774–775
RFC. *See* Reconstruction Finance Corporation.
RFD. *See* rural free delivery.
Rhee, Syngman, 611
Rhode Island, 25, 49, 95
  facts about, R49
Richardson, Elliot, 805
Richmond, Virginia, 169, 170, 181, 277
***Richmond* v. *J. A. Croson Company*,** 843
Richthofen, Manfred von, 381
Rickenbacker, Eddie, 381, *i* 381, 384
Ridge, Tom, 896, *i* 896
Riis, Jacob, 245, 262, 264
Rio Grande, 18, 135, 136
Rivera, Diego, 512
Roaring Twenties, 444–445, *i* 444–445
robber barons, 243–244
Roberts, Needham, 382
Robertson, Pat, 831
Robeson, Paul, 456, 617
Robinson, Bill "Bojangles," *i* 298
Robinson, Jackie, 637, *i* 637
Robinson, Jo Ann Gibson, 700, *i* 700
robotics, 878–879
Rockefeller, John D., 243, *i* 243, 308, 326
Rockefeller Foundation, 243
rock 'n' roll, 655–656, *i* 656, 786, R63
***Roe* v. *Wade*,** 97, 779, 840
Rogers, Will, 424
Roman Catholicism and Roman Catholics, 11, 18, 24, 284
  prejudice against, 142, 258
Rome-Berlin Axis Pact, 533
Rommel, Erwin, 572
Roosevelt, Eleanor, 489, *i* 489, 496, *i* 496, 505–506, 557, 568, 636
Roosevelt, Franklin Delano, 483, 488–490, *i* 489, *i* 490, 496, 515–516, 550, *i* 550, 593, R52
  Atlantic Charter and, 554
  "Day of Infamy" speech of, 557
  death of, 577, 636
  fireside chats of, 490, 511, 552
  Good Neighbor policy of, 534
  lend-lease and, 552, 553
  New Deal and, 488–494, 495–501, 505–509, 515–516, 596
  physical problems of, 489, 644
  Supreme Court and, 493
  wartime conferences and, 569–570, 585–586
  World War II and, 550–555, 557, 566, 567, 569, 570, 573, 586–586
Roosevelt, Theodore, 240, 248, 316, 317–318, *i* 318, 326, 328, 330–331, 358, 360, *i* 360, *i* 362, R51
  civil rights and, 324–325
  coal strike of 1902 and, 320
  conservation and, 322–324
  Gentlemen's Agreement and, 259, 415
  health protection and, 320, 322
  Japan and, 360
  Latin America and, 362
  Panama Canal and, 360–361
  railroads and, 320
  Rough Riders and, 318, 350
  Treaty of Portsmouth and, 360, 360
  trusts and, 319
Roosevelt Corollary, 362, 363, R63
***Roots*,** 809, *i* 809
Rosenberg, Ethel and Julius, 619–620, *i* 619
ROTC. *See* Reserve Officers Training Corps.
Rough Riders, 318, 350, R63
Route 66, 423, *m* 423, 474
row house, 264
***Rumor of War, A* (Caputo),** 763
Rural Electrification Administration (REA), *c* 500, 501
rural free delivery (RFD), 297, R63
Rusk, Dean, 672, 676, 737
Russia, 255, 401, 849, 863. *See also* Soviet Union.
  revolution in, 380, 413
  war with Japan, 359–360
  World War I and, 373, 374, 386
Russo-Japanese War, 359–360
Rustbelt, 846
Ruth, Babe, 448, *i* 448

S

Sacajawea, *i* 115, *m* 115
Sacco and Vanzetti, 413–414, *i* 414
Sacco, Nicola, 413–414, *i* 414
Sacramento, California, 215, 137
Sadat, Anwar, 816, *i* 816
Sahara, 8, 9, 10
St. Augustine, Florida, 18
St. Louis, Missouri, 112, 278
Sakhalin Island, 360
Salk, Jonas, 644, *i* 644
Salomon, Haym, 61
SALT. *See* Strategic Arms Limitation Talks.
Salt Lake City, Utah, 133
Salvation Army, 307
Sampson, William T., 349
San Antonio, Texas, 19, 134, 209
Sand Creek Massacre, 204, *m* 205
***Sandinistas*,** 851, 852, R63
San Francisco, California, 137, 138, *i* 138, 257, 259, 264, 268
  earthquake in, 265, *c* 265, *i* 265
San Jacinto, Battle of, 135
San Juan Hill, Battle of, 318, 350
San Salvador, 14
Santa Anna, Antonio López de, 134–135, *i* 135
Santa Fe, New Mexico, 18, 20, 131, 136
Santa Fe Railroad, 221
Santa Fe Trail, 131, *m* 132, R63
***Santa María*,** 14
Sarajevo, 374, *m* 375
Saratoga, Battle of, 60, 62
Sarbanes-Oxley Act, 867
Satanta, Chief, 225, *i* 225
Saturday Night Massacre, 805–806, R63
Saudi Arabia, 853, 855
Savannah, Georgia, 62
savings and loan industry, 837
scabs, 248, 508
scalawags, 186–187, R63
Scalia, Antonin, *i* 93, 836
***Schechter Poultry Corp.* v. *United States*,** 502
Schenck, Charles, 396, 397
***Schenck* v. *United States*,** 96, 396–397
Schlafly, Phyllis, 779, *i* 779
Schlesinger, Arthur M., Jr., 803
Schlieffen Plan, 374
Schurz, Carl, *i* 187
Schwarzenegger, Arnold, 868
Schwarzkopf, Norman, 855, *i* 855
schools. *See* education.
scientific management, 308–309, R63
SCLC. *See* Southern Christian Leadership Conference.
Scopes, John T., 438, 439
Scopes trial, 222, 438–439, *i* 439, R63
Scott, Bev, 612, *i* 612
Scott, Dred, 162, *i* 162, 166, *i* 167
Scott, Winfield, 136
Scottish and Scots-Irish immigrants, 32, 34
SDI. *See* Strategic Defense Initiative.
SDS. *See* Students for a Democratic Society.
Sears Roebuck, 297
SEC. *See* Securities and Exchange Commission.
secession, 126, 129, 157, 164–165, 183, R63
Second Amendment, 70, 96, 899
Second Bank of the United States (BUS), 88, 122, 126
Second Continental Congress, 51, 52, 56, 57, 60, 61, 63, 66, 67, 260
Second Great Awakening, 145, 147
Second Hundred Days, 495–496
Securities and Exchange Commission (SEC), 490, *c* 500, 518, R45, R63
Sedalia, Missouri, 209
Sedition Act
  of 1798, 78–79
  of 1918, 392, 397
See, Fong, 254, *i* 254, 255
segregation, R63
  Birmingham march and, 712, *i* 712
  de facto and de jure, 718
  freedom riders and, 710–711, *i* 711
  Freedom Summer and, 715
  Jim Crow laws and, 287, *i* 287, 291, 701, 708–709
  laws against, 129
  legalized, 291, 700–701, *m* 701
  march on Washington and, 714
  Montgomery bus boycott and, 700, 704–705, R38

National Association for the Advancement of Colored People and, 291, 702
Nixon and, 797–798
in North, 718
Selma campaign and, *i* 698–699, 716
"separate but equal" doctrine and, 287
sit-ins against, 706–707, *i* 707, R64
in Washington, D.C., 335
Selective Service Act, 382, R63
Selective Service System, 563, 565. *See also* draft.
Selma, Alabama, 716
Senate, 68, 85, 86, 87, 160–161, 186, 804–805. *See also* Congress.
control of, 868
direct election of, 100, 312
Seneca Falls convention, 64, 148–149, 315, 335, R63
separation of powers, 68–69
Separatists, 24
September 11 terrorist attack, 863, 866, 894, *i* 894, 895, *i* 895
effect on air travel of, 897, *i* 897
anthrax and, 896
effect on economy of, 871
impact of, 863, 896
rescue and rebuilding efforts, and, 895–896
sequencing. *See* chronological order.
Serbia and Serbs, 373, 374, 863
Serra, Junípero, 19
Servicemen's Readjustment Act. *See* GI Bill of Rights.
service organizations, 425–426
settlement-house movement, 266, 307, R63
Seventeenth Amendment, 85, 100, 312, R63
Seventh Amendment, 97
Seventh Cavalry, 206, 208
Sewall, Arthur, 223
Seward, William H., 344
sex discrimination, 777
sexual harassment, 836
***Shame of the Cities, The* (Steffens),** 327
sharecropping, 188, R63
Shays, Daniel, 67
Shays's Rebellion, 67, R63
Shepard, Alan, 679, *i* 679
Sheridan, Philip, 206, 207
Sherman, Roger, 68
Sherman, William Tecumseh, 164–165, 180
Sherman Antitrust Act, 244, 249, 319, 333, R47, R63
Shiloh, Battle of, 170, 180
shipbuilding
in English colonies, 30, 33
in World War I, 382–383
in World War II, 565, 570
Shirer, William, 536, *i* 536, 540
Sholes, Christopher, 233
***Shuffle Along*,** 456
Shumlin, Herman, 473
silent majority, 756
***Silent Spring* (Carson),** 691, 821
silver, 13, 60, 204, 220, 222, 223
silverites, 222, *c* 222
***Since Yesterday* (Allen),** 475
Sinclair, Upton, 317, *i* 317, 320, 326, 327
Sioux, 202, *i* 203, 204, 206–207
Sirica, John, 804
sit-down strike, 508, *i* 508
Sitting Bull (Tatanka Yotanka), 204, *i* 204, 206, 207
Sixteenth Amendment, 100, 334
Sixth Amendment, 97
skyscrapers, 232, 277
slavery. *See also* antislavery movement; civil rights; slaves.
abolition of, by Thirteenth Amendment, 98–99, 167, 183
in Africa, 10
in American colonies, 15, 23, 28, 32–33, 34
Cuban abolition of, 347
in North, 122
opposition to, 63, 145–147, 148, 158, 162, 163, 166–167
in South, 116, 122, 135, 182–183
in Texas, 133, 135
in U.S. territories, 122, 135, 156–157, 160, 162, 163, 164, 166–167
slaves, 53, 71, 145–146, 157. *See also* slavery.
in Civil War, 172, 260
emancipation of, 122, 145–147, 166–167, 172–173, 260
fugitive, 61, 158
lives of, 33, 41, *i* 41, 146
rebellions of, 33, 146–147
Three-Fifths Compromise and, 68
trade in, 10, 15, 32–33, *i* 33, 53, 89
Slidell, John, 135
Smith, Alfred E., 466
Smith, Bessie, 444, *i* 444, 457
Smith, John, 21, *i* 21, 23
Smith, Joseph, 131
Smith, Margaret Chase, 620
Smith, Sophia, 316
snack foods, 293
SNCC. *See* Student Nonviolent Coordinating Committee.
Social Darwinism, 242–243, 344, R64
Social Gospel movement, 266, 307, R64
socialism, 246, 308, *c* R44
Socialist Party of America, 248, 330
Social Security, 501, 518, *i* 518, 690, 795–796, 865, 884–885, 912–913
Social Security Act, 501, 518, 910, 912, R64
Society of Friends. *See* Quakers.
soddy, 216–217, *i* 216, R64
Soil Conservation and Domestic Allotment Act, 496
Soil Conservation Service, 519
Solomon Islands, 581
Sojourner, 879
Somme, Battle of the, 384
Somoza, Anastasio, 851
Songhai, 8–9
Sons of Liberty, *i* 44–45, 47
***Souls of Black Folk, The* (Du Bois),** 325
sources. *See also* political cartoons, analyzing.
audio, R23
databases, 108
evaluating, 108, R21, R22, R23
locating, 108, 167, 405, 407, 809, 819, R22
multimedia, 43, 58, 81, 107, 153, 191, 227, 251, 273, 339, 369, 407, 408, 523, 559, 631, 697, 727, 765, 827, R23, R37
primary, 54–57, 82–103, 129, 143, 174, 189, 337, 503, R22. *See also* primary sources.
secondary, 129, R22
visual, 11, 27, 48, 164, 178, 210, 278, 295, 311, 312, 336, 364, 393, 402, 414, 435, 497, 501, 513, 519, 566, 568, 582, 640, 649, 713, 824, 883, R23
Souter, David H., *i* 93, 836
South, 122, 124, 141, 157, 161, 164. *See also* Confederate States of America or Confederacy; Southern colonies.
agriculture in, 121–122, 182, 186
effects of Civil War on, 182–183, 186–187, 244
plantations, *i* 147
Reconstruction and, 185–186, 186–187, 188–189
Revolutionary War in, 62
South Africa, 701
South America, 5, 18
South Carolina, 28, 32, 53, 62, 124, 125, 129, *i* 129, 164–165, 797
facts about, R49
South Dakota, 207, *c* 773, 804
facts about, R49
Southeast Asia, 401. *See also* Vietnam; Vietnam War.
Southern Alliance, 221
Southern Christian Leadership Conference (SCLC), 706, 720, R64
Southern colonies, *c* 29, *m* 29, 30, 31–33, 41
Southwest, 20, 133, 662
agriculture in, 289
corridos of, 225
Mexican workers in, 288–289, 662
Native Americans of, 5, 6, *m* 7
Spanish settlement of, 18–20
Soviet Union, 401, 413, *i* 801. *See also* Cold War.
aid to Nicaragua, 851
arms race and, 622–623, 849
Carter and, 815
China and, 800
Cuban missile crisis and, 674, 676
development of Cold War and, 602–605
dissolution of, 849, R39
division of Germany and, 607–608
domination of Eastern Europe by, 604–605, 625
Five-Year Plans and, 529
industrialization of, 529
installation of hot line, 678
invasion of Afghanistan, 815, R40
Nixon and, 800–801
nuclear testing and, 678
reforms of Gorbachev in, 849
space exploration and, 589, *i* 589, 626
Stalin and, 529
U.S. containment policy and, 605

Warsaw Pact and, 624
in World War II, 539, 553, 571, 572, 576, 585
space exploration, *i* 668–669, 679–680, *i* 679, 681, *c* 681
Challenger disaster and, 841
communications satellites and, 589, 681
Kennedy and, 681, *c* 681
of moon, 681, 796
Reagan and, 841
Soviet Union and, 589, *i* 589, 626, 670, 681
technology and, 879
Spain, 10, 11, 13, 14, 16, 18, 38, 114, 116–117, 133, 208, 224, 346–347
American colonies of, 15, 16, 18–20, 346
civil war in, 533, *i* 533
North American claims of, 15, *m* 29, *m* 38
in Revolutionary War, 61
in Spanish-American-Cuban War, 348–349, 404
U.S. relations with, 77, 117, 346–347, 350, 404
Spanish
cattle ranching, 208
explorations, 14–15, 16, 18–20
missions, 18–20, *i* 19, 133, 260, *i* 260
Spanish-American War, 348–349, *m* 349. *See also* Cuba.
Spanish Armada, 20
Spanish Civil War, 533, *i* 533
speakeasies, 436, R64
Spencer, Herbert, 242
Spindletop, 230
Spock, Benjamin, 644
spoils system, 123, 270
sports, 293, 294, 446, 448, 637
Spotted Tail, 206
Sputnik I, 589, *i* 589, 626, 670
Square Deal, 319, R64
stagflation, 798–799, R64
Stalin, Joseph, 529, *i* 531, 539, 540, 585–586, 603, *i* 603, 604
Stalingrad, Battle of, 571, 572
Stalwarts, 270
Stamp Act, 47, *c* 48, R64
standard of living, R43, R45
Standard Oil Company, 234, 243, 244, 319, 326
Stanton, Edwin, 186
Stanton, Elizabeth Cady, 64, *i* 64, 148, *i* 148, 315
Starr, Ellen Gates, 266
START II pact, 849
State, Department of, 75
states' rights, 69, 70, 122, 124, 126, 128–129, 163, 194
statistics. *See* data, interpreting.
Statue of Liberty, 261
steamboat, 120, *i* 120, 140
Steamboat Willie, 450
steel industry, 174, 232, 237, 243, 244, 426, 465
Andrew Carnegie and, 241–242
decline of, 814
strikes in, 247–248, 417, 637
Steffens, Lincoln, 327, *i* 327
Stein, Gertrude, 451
Steinbeck, John, 496, 514, 645
Steinem, Gloria, 778, *i* 778
Stephens, Uriah, 245
Steuben, Friedrich von, 61
Stevens, John L., 345
Stevens, John Paul, *i* 93
Stevens, Thaddeus, 185
Stevenson, Adlai, 639
Stimson, Henry, 585
stock market, 221, 871. *See also* September 11 terrorist attack, effect on economy of.
buying on margin and, 490, *i,* R45, *c* R45
crash, 466–467, *i* 467, 468–469
speculation and, 467, R64
Stone, Lucy, 316
Stono Rebellion, 33
Stover, Charles, 266
Stowe, Harriet Beecher, 158, *i* 158
Strategic Arms Limitation Talks (SALT), 800, 815
SALT I Treaty, 800–801, R63
SALT II agreement, 815
Strategic Defense Initiative (SDI), 835, R64
strikes, 142–143, 245, 246, 249, *i* R45, R64. *See also* labor movement.
federal arbitration and, 320
by garment workers, 248–249
at Homestead, Pennsylvania, 247–248
at Lawrence, Massachusetts, 306, *i* 306
at Lowell, Massachusetts, 142
by mill workers, *i* 410–411
in mining industry, 246, 248, 320, 418, 637
by police, 417
at Pullman Company, 238, 248
railroad, 246, 247, 637
sit-down, 508, *i* 508
in steel industry, 247–248, 417, 637
violence and, 247–248, 508–509
Student Nonviolent Coordinating Committee (SNCC), 706–707, 711, 715–716, 720, R64
Students for a Democratic Society (SDS), 744, 745, R64
submarines, 378–379, 383, 553, *i* 553, 554, 570
suburbs, 882–884, R64
automobile and, 423–424, 643, 646
commuters and, 277
growth of, after World War II, 635, *i* 635
lifestyle in, 643–644
in 1970s, 841
urban flight and, 882–883
Sudetenland, 537
Suez Canal, 625
suffrage, *i* 304–305, 315–316, R64. *See also* voting rights.
sugar, 32, 344, 347
Sugar Act, 47, R64
Sugar Beet and Farm Laborers' Union of Oxnard, 246
Sullivan, Louis, 277
summarizing, 6, 13, 16, 32, 39, 47, 53, 61, 70, 73, 114, 119, 116, 122, 129, 141, 142, 148, 158, 164, 167, 183, 189, 203, 209, 216, 217, 221, 232, 238, 242, 243, 249, 258, 268, 277, 279, 281, 284, 288, 297, 299, 310, 312, 324, 327, 333, 348, 350, 351, 380, 382, 383, 390, 400, 401, 403, 420, 429, 438, 443, 447, 451, 454, 457, 471, 473, 479, 482, 489, 496, 503, 507, 509, 513, 516, 529, 531, 533, 537, 547, 549, 554, 567, 572, 585, 586, 597, 624, 627, 637, 638, 655, 657, 673, 693, 705, 745, 752, 758, 772, 795, 798, 799, 803, 805, 813, 816, 822, 832, 835, 842, 864, 870, 875, 878, 880, 887, 891, R4, R11, R13, R15, R16, R17, R18, R22, R23, R24, R27, R28. *See also* clarifying.
summary, writing a, R4, R11, R27, R28
Sumner, Charles, 160–161, 185
Sumner, William Graham, 242
Sun Also Rises, The **(Hemingway),** 451
Sunbelt, 846
Sunday, Billy, 434, *i* 434, 438
supply and demand, *c* R46
supply-side economics, 835, R46, R64
Supreme Court, 74–75, 92–93, 94, 96, 102, 189, 311. *See also* Supreme Court cases.
civil rights and, 596–597, 637–638, 640, 700–701, 702–703
Dred Scott decision of, 162–163, 166–167, 186
gun control and, 903
interstate commerce and, 239–240, 502–503
judicial review and, 93, 113
landmark cases, 118–119, 166–167, 290–291, 396–397, 502–503, 596–597, 694–695, 708–709, 774–775, 818–819
New Deal and, 493, 496, 499
Nixon and, 797–798
presidential election of 2000 and, 866
Reagan and, 836
social issues and, 836
trusts and, 244, 319
voting rights and, 287, 316
Supreme Court cases
Ableman v. *Booth* (1858), 166
Adarand Constructors v. *Pena* (1995), 818, 819
Baker v. *Carr* (1962), 692, 774–775
Brown v. *Board of Education of Topeka* (1954), 99, *i* 99, 129, 291, 640, 691, 702–703, 708–709, 797, 904
Bunting v. *Oregon* (1917), 311
City of Boerne v. *Flores* (1997), 119
Cohens v. *Virginia* (1821), 118
Cumming v. *Board of Education of Richmond County* (1899), 290
Dred Scott v. *Sanford* (1857), 166–167
Escobedo v. *Illinois* (1964), 692, 694

Fletcher v. *Peck* (1810), 118
Gibbons v. *Ogden* (1824), 118, 122
Gideon v. *Wainwright* (1963), 692, 694
Gray v. *Sanders* (1963), 774–775
Griswold v. *Connecticut* (1965), 97
Hirabayashi v. *United States* (1943), 596
Korematsu v. *United States* (1944), 595, 596–597
Mapp v. *Ohio* (1961), 692, 694
Marbury v. *Madison* (1803), 113, 118–119
McCulloch v. *Maryland* (1819), 122
McLaurin v. *Oklahoma State* (1950), 708
Miranda v. *Arizona* (1966), 97, 692, 694–695
Missouri v. *Holland* (1920), 95
Morgan v. *Virginia* (1946), 702
Muller v. *Oregon* (1908), 311
Munn v. *Illinois* (1877), 239
NLRB v. *Jones and Laughlin Steel Corp.* (1937), 502–503
Plessy v. *Ferguson* (1896), 287, 290–291, 701, 702, 708–709
Regents of the University of California v. *Bakke* (1978), 818, 905
Reynolds v. *Sims* (1964), 692, 774–775
Richmond v. *J. A. Croson Company* (1989), 843
Roe v. *Wade* (1973), 97, 779, 840
Schechter Poultry Corp. v. *United States* (1935), 502
Schenck v. *United States* (1919), 96, 396–397
Swann v. *Charlotte-Mecklenburg Board of Education* (1971), 797
Sweatt v. *Painter* (1950), 702, 708–709
Tinker v. *Des Moines* (1969), 397
United Steelworkers of America v. *Weber* (1979), 818
Webster v. *Reproductive Health Care Services* (1989), 840
Wesberry v. *Sanders* (1964), 774–775
Williams v. *Mississippi* (1898), 290
Worcester v. *Georgia* (1832), 124
Supremes, 786, *i* 786
Sutter's Mill, 137
***Swann* v. *Charlotte-Mecklenburg Board of Education*,** 797
Swanson, Mrs. Charles, 562, *i* 562
***Sweatt* v. *Painter*,** 702, 708–709
Sylvis, William H., 245
synthesizing, 41, 65, 140, 240, 244, 285, 316, 319, 380, 451, 456, 505, 571, 716, 731, 735, 743, 755, 761, R11, R19
Szilard, Leo, 585

T

Taft, William Howard, 328–329, *i* 329, 362–363, R51
Taft-Hartley Act, 637
Taino, 14, 15, R64
Taiwan (Formosa), 610, 611
taking notes, 13, 20, 30, 39, 53, 63, 71, 79, 106, 117, 127, 138, 143, 149, 165, 174, 183, 189, 211, 218, 223, 233, 240, 249, 259, 266, 271, 281, 285, 289, 297, 312, 316, 325, 331, 337, 345, 351, 358, 365, 380, 387, 395, 402, 418, 421, 427, 439, 443, 451, 457, 471, 477, 483, 494, 501, 509, 514, 519, 535, 541, 549, 557, 568, 577, 587, 595, 608, 615, 621, 627, 640, 649, 657, 663, 678, 683, 707, 716, 723, 735, 741, 747, 753, 761, 773, 780, 801, 807, 817, 825, 833, 838, 845, 855, 868, 873, 881, 887, R4, R6, R7
Taliban, 867, 896
Talleyrand-Périgord, Charles Maurice de, 78
Tammany Hall, 269, *i* 269
Tan, Amy, 874, 875
Taney, Chief Justice Roger, 166–167, *i* 166
Tarbell, Ida M., 308, 326, *i* 326
Tariff of Abominations, 124
Tariff of 1816, 122, 124
tariffs, 76, 116, 122, 124, 125, 128, 271, 329, 333–334, 344, 420, 422–423, 471, R46, R62. *See also* taxation.
Tatanka Yotanka. *See* Sitting Bull.
taxation, 10, 11, 49, 67, 76, 688, R46. *See also* tariffs.
of colonies by Britain, 47–49
of income, 100, 174, 221, 390, 334, *c* 334, 567
under Woodrow Wilson, 333–334
World War I and, 390
Taylor, Frederick Winslow, 309
Taylor, Zachary, 136, 158, R50
Taylor Grazing Act, 519
Tea Act, 49
Teapot Dome scandal, 421, *i* 421, R64
technology. *See also* inventions.
communications and, 140–141, *c* 140–141, 279, 876–878, 906–907, *c* 906–907. *See also* radio; telegraph; telephone; television.
economy and, 871, 906
education and, 284
entertainment and. *See also* motion pictures; radio; television.
genetic engineering and, 880
health care and, 880
of sailing, 13
space exploration and, 879
transportation and, 276, 277, 281, 881. *See also* airplanes, automobile; canals; railroads; steamboat.
warfare and, 13, 182, 384–385, *c* 384–385, 567, 588–589, *c* 589
telecommunications. *See* communications, advances in.
Telecommunications Act of 1996, 878, R64
telecommuting, 878, 884, R64
telegraph, 140, *c* 140
telephone, 140, 233, 314, *i* 314
televangelists, 831–832
television
elections and, 671, *i* 671
news and, 618–619
in 1950s, 644, 652–654, *c* 653, *i* 653
in 1970s, 808–809
Vietnam War and, 619, *i* 619, 741, 749
Teller Amendment, 353
temperance movement, 147, 307–308
tenements, 262, 264, R64
Tennessee, 94, 169, 170, 185, 438–439
facts about, R49
Tennessee Valley Authority (TVA), *c* 500, 519, 520–521, *i* 520, *m* 520–521, R64
Tenochtitlán, *i* 5, 16
Ten-Percent Plan, 184
Tenth Amendment, 70, 97
Tenure of Office Act, 186
Teoli, Camella, 306
tepee, *i* 7
termination policy, 663, R64
terrorism,
against United States, 862–863, 866, 894, *i* 894, 895, *i* 895, *c* 896–897, 903
antiterrorism and, 896–897
coalition against. *See* antiterrorism coalition.
definition of, 894
domestic, 862, 903
effects of, 894, 895
reasons for, 895
tactics of, 894–895
war on, 867, 894–897
weapons of, 895
terrorist attacks. *See also* September 11 terrorist attack.
casualties of, 863, 894
in Oklahoma City, 863, 903
in United States, 862–863, 866, 894, *i* 894, 895, *i* 895, *c* 896–897, 903
terrorist groups
in Africa, 894–895
in Asia, 895, 896
Aum Shinrikyo, 895
in Europe, 894
in Latin America, 894
Shining Path, 894
in United States, 894, 897
Tet offensive, 748–749, *m* 749, R64
Texas, 18–19, 135, 136, 157, 165, 682, 709, 716, 847, 865
American settlers in, 127, 130, 133–134
facts about, R49
Mexican policies in, 133–134
oil in, 230, 231, 424, 813
slavery in, 133, 135
Spanish missions in, 18–20, *i* 19, 133
U.S. annexation of, 135
war for independence of, 134–135, *m* 134
Texas Revolution, 133–134, R64
***Texas* v. *Johnson* (1989),** 297
textile industry, 121, 142, 244, 306, 426, 465
theater, 298, 456, 513
***Their Eyes Were Watching God* (Hurston),** 514
themes
in history, xxviii–xxix. *See also* thematic review, 192–197.
of geography, xxx. *See also* location, movement, place.
Third Amendment, 70, 96
Third Reich, 531, 538

third parties, impact on elections, 223
Thirteenth Amendment, 98–99, 167, 183, 189, 289, R64
***This Side of Paradise* (Fitzgerald),** 450, 451
Thomas, Clarence, *i* 93, 836, *i* 836
Thoreau, Henry David, 705
Three-Fifths Compromise, 68
Three Mile Island, 822–825, *i* 823
***Three Soldiers* (Dos Passos),** 451
Thurmond, J. Strom, 638
Tiananmen Square, 850, *i* 850, R64
Tilden, Samuel J., 189
Timbuktu, *i* 8, 9
time lines. *See also* chronological order, absolute.
  creating, 20, 143, 165, 218, 249, 337,358, 451, 557, 577, 640, 709, 723, 753, 780, 817, 868, 890, R3
  interpreting, 2–3, 44–45, 110–111, 154–155, 200–201, 228–229, 232, 252–253, 274–275, 304–305, 340–341, 370–371, 410–411, 432–433, 462–463, 486–487, 526–527, 560–561, 600–601, 632–633, 668–669, 698–699, 728–729, 766–767, 792–793, 828–829, 858–859, 896–897, 898–899, 900–901, 902–903, 904–905, 906–907, 908–909, 910–911, 912–913, 914–915, 916–917
  using, 289, 299, 523, 541, 580–581, 615, 675, 726, 764, 787, 807, 856
time zones, 237, *m* 239
***Tinker* v. *Des Moines School District* (1969),** 397
Titusville, Pennsylvania, 231
tobacco, 15, 23, 28, 32, 34, 141, 244
Tojo, Hideki, 554, *i* 554, 555, 587
Tompkins, Sally, 174
Tonkin, Gulf of, 734
Tonkin Gulf Resolution, 734–735, 737, R64
Toomer, Jean, 454
Tordesillas, Treaty of, 15, R65
totalitarianism, 529, R64
Townsend, Francis, 493, 494
Townshend, Charles, 47
Townshend Acts, 47, 48, *c* 48, 49
trade, 120, 124, 333, 377, 872–873, *c* 872, *m* 872, *c* R47
  with China, 117, 356
  in colonial America, 23, 26, 28, 30, 32, 33, 37, 47–48, 49
  Crusades and, 10
  depression and, 469, R38, R40
  North American Free Trade Agreement and, 864
  among Native Americans, *m* 7, 8
  Panama Canal and, 366–367
  in slaves, 10, 15, 32–33, *i* 33, 53, 89
  between states, 239–240, 249, 311
  transportation and, 140–141
  triangular, 32
  in West Africa, 9, 10
Trail of Tears, 124, *i* 124, *m* 125, R64
transcendentalism, 145, R65
transcontinental railroad, 237, R65
transportation. *See also* automobile; canals; railroads; steamboat.
  bridges and, 276, 277
  in cities, 264, 277
  mass transit for, 264, R60
Travis, William, 134
Treasury, Department of the, 75, 436, 490
Treaty of . . . *See distinctive part of treaty's name.*
Trenton, Battle of, 60
Triangle Shirtwaist Factory fire, 248, *i* 248, 314
triangular trade, 32, R65
trickle-down theory, 835
Tripartite Pact, 551
Triple Entente, 374
Trotter, William Monroe, 337
Troy Female Seminary, 148
Truman, Harry S., 574, 577, 583–585, 603–604, 636–639, 731, 908, R52
  atomic bomb and, 584, 585
  civil rights and, 637–638
  communism and, 617
  Fair Deal and, 639, 680
  Korean War and, 611, 614
  at Potsdam conference, 604
Truman Doctrine, 606, R65
trusts, 243, 244, 319, 329, 333, R47
Truth, Sojourner, 149, *i* 149
Tubman, Harriet, 158, *i* 158
Tunney, Gene, 446, *i* 446
Turner, Frederick Jackson, 216
Turner, Nat, 146
Tuskegee Airmen, 573, *i* 573
Tuskegee Normal and Industrial Institute, 285, R65
Tutankhamen, tomb of, 448
TVA. *See* Tennessee Valley Authority.
Twain, Mark. *See* Clemens, Samuel.
Tweed, William M. "Boss," 269, *i* 269
Tweed Ring, 269
Twelfth Amendment, 98, 113
Twentieth Amendment, 101, 489
Twenty-fifth Amendment, 91, 102–103, 805–806
Twenty-first Amendment, 101–102, 437, 490
Twenty-fourth Amendment, 102, 104, *c* 690, 716
Twenty-second Amendment, 102
Twenty-seventh Amendment, 103
Twenty-sixth Amendment, 103, 105, 798
Twenty-third Amendment, 102
two-party system, 76, R65
***2001: A Space Odyssey*,** 787
Tyler, John, 91, 127, R50
typewriter, 233, *i* 233

U

U-boats, 378–379, *i* 378, 383, 553, *i* 553, 570
UFWOC. *See* United Farm Workers Organizing Committee.
UMW. *See* United Mine Workers of America.
UN. *See* United Nations.
***Uncle Tom's Cabin* (Stowe),** 158, 160
Underground Railroad, 158, *i* 159, *m* 159, R65
Underwood Act, 333
unemployment, 127, 222, 240, 469, *c* 470, *c* 517, *c* 813, 910–911, R40, *c* R47
UNIA. *See* Universal Negro Improvement Association.
Union Pacific Railroad, 215, 221, 237, 238
unions, 143, 244–249, *c* 247, 412, 499, 502–503, 507–509, *c* 508, R38. *See also* strikes; *names of specific unions.*
Union Stock Yards, 209
Unitarians, 145, R65
United Farm Workers Organizing Committee (UFWOC), 770, R65
United Mine Workers of America (UMW), 248, 508
United Nations (UN), 603, 625, R65
  arms inspections in Iraq and, 867, 898–899
  founding of, 586
  Korean War and, 611, 612
  Persian Gulf War and, 898
  U.S.-led war against Iraq and, 898–899
United Services Organization (USO), 744
U.S. Chamber of Commerce, 383
U.S. Food and Drug Administration (FDA), 880
U.S. Forest Bureau, 322
U.S. Forest Service, 323, 329
United States history, themes of. *See also* foreign affairs and foreign policy.
  America in world affairs, 404–405.
  civil rights, 194–195, 724–725. *See also* civil rights.
  constitutional concerns. *See also* Constitution; Supreme Court decisions.
  cultural diversity, 193–194. *See also* African Americans; Asian Americans; immigrants; Latinos.
  diversity and the national identity, 260–261
  economic opportunity, 196. *See also* economy; labor force.
  immigration and migration, 192–193, 888–889. *See also* African Americans, migrations of; immigration; westward expansion.
  science and technology, 196, 588–589. *See also* communications; inventions; technology.
  states' rights, 128–129.
  voting rights, 104–105.
  women and political power, 195–196, 64–65. *See also* women.
United States Steel, 243, 417
***United Steelworkers of America* v. *Weber*,** 818
Universal Negro Improvement Association (UNIA), 453–454
unrestricted submarine warfare, 379
***Unsafe at Any Speed* (Nader),** 691
urbanization. *See* cities. R65
U'Ren, William S., 312
USA Patriot Act, 897
using charts. *See* charts, using.
using computers. *See* computers, using.
using databases. *See* databases, using.
using diagrams. *See* diagrams, using.

using graphs. *See* graphs, using.
using the Internet for research. *See* Internet, using for research.
using maps. *See* maps, using.
using models. *See* models, using.
using notes. *See* notes, using.
using time lines. *See* time lines, using.
USO. United Services Organization.
USS *Maine*, 348, R65
Utah, 137, 157, 160, 316. *See also* Deseret.
  facts about, R49
utilities
  as monopolies, R43
  public ownership of, 310
  regulation of, 501
U-2 incident, 626–627, R65

V

vaccinations, 644
Valley Forge, Pennsylvania, 60, 61
Van Buren, Martin, 127, R50
Vanderbilt, William, *i* 240
Vanzetti, Bartolomeo, 413–414, *i* 414
vaqueros, 208–209, *i* 208, *i* 225
vaudeville, 298, *i* 298
Vaux, Calvert, 277
V-E Day, 577, *i* 577, R65
Velasco, Treaty of, 135
Velázquez, Diego, 16
Vermont, 94, 104
  facts about, R49
Versailles, Treaty of, 400–401, 529, R65
vertical integration, 242, R65
Veterans Bureau, 421
Vicksburg, Mississippi, 170, 179, *m* 179
victory garden, 390, *i* 390
Vietcong, 732, 734, 735, 736, 738–739, 741, 748–749, 755, 756, R65
Vietminh, 731, 732, R65
Vietnam. *See also* Vietnam War.
  France and, 730, 731
  U.S. recognition of, 761
Vietnamization, 755, R65
Vietnam Veterans Memorial, 760, *i* 760
Vietnam War, 91, 103, 688, 719, 801, 889
  costs of, 741
  draft and, 742–743, 745–746
  Johnson (Lyndon) and, 734–735, 736–738, 740–741, 745, 747
  Kennedy and, 732, 734
  literature of, 762–763
  My Lai massacre in, 756
  Nixon and, 754–759
  Pentagon Papers and, 757
  protests against, 744–746, 756–757
  search and destroy missions, 739, R63
  television and, 619, *i* 619, 741, 749
  Tet offensive in, 748–749, *m* 749
  Tonkin Gulf Resolution and, 735, 737, 757
  U.S. containment policy and, 737
  U.S. involvement in, 730, 732, 734, 736–741
  veterans of, 759–760
Villa, Francisco "Pancho," 364–365, *i* 365
Villard, Oswald Garrison, 336
Virginia, 62, 79, 95, 113, 169, 177, 180, 716
  colonial, 23, 28, 31, 32, 37, 41, 49
  facts about, R49
Virginia City, Nevada, 204
Virginia Company, 21, 23
Virginia Plan, 68
Virginia Resolutions, 79
virtual reality, 878
VISTA. *See* Volunteers in Service to America.
visual sources
  analyzing, 71, 297, 387, 435, 621, 678, 747, 757, 825, 868
Volstead Act, 436
Volunteers in Service to America (VISTA), 686, *i* 686, 688
voting rights. *See also* participation, political. 100, 104–105, 123, 195
  of African Americans, 71, 102, 104, 185–186, 187, 286–288, 637, 715–716
  extension of, to 18-year-olds, 103, 105, 798
  of Native Americans, 105
  of women, 32, 63, 101, 105, 149, 315–316, 332, 334–335
Voting Rights Act
  of 1965, 104, *c* 714, 716, 775
  of 1975, 844, R65

W

WAAC. *See* Women's Auxiliary Army Corps.
wage and price controls. *See* price controls.
Wagner, Robert F., 499, *i* 508
Wagner Act. *See* National Labor Relations Act.
Wainwright Building (St. Louis), 277
Walker, Alice, 717, *i* 717
Wallace, George, 712, 753, 797
Wallace, Henry A., 638
Wampanoag, 26
War, Department of, 75
War Industries Board (WIB), 389, R65
War of 1812, 114, 131
***War of the Worlds, The*,** 511
War on Poverty, 686, 688, 693, 719
War on Terrorism, 867, 894–897
War Powers Act, 91, 761, R65
War Production Board (WPB), 568, *i* 568, R65
Warren, Earl, 691, *i* 691, 694–695, 774, 797
Warren Commission, 683, R66
Warren Court, 691–692, 695, 775, R66
Warsaw Pact, 624, *m* 624, R66
Washburn, Henry D., 216
Washington (state)
  facts about, R49
Washington, Booker T., 285, 288, 324–325, 351
Washington, George, *i* 44–45, 51, *i* 60, 69, *i* 74, R50
  in French and Indian War, 37–38
  as president, 74–75, 76, 77
  in Revolutionary War, 60, 61, 62
Washington, D.C., 88, 102, 114, 165, 169, 278, 841, 843
  civil rights march on, 714
  facts about, R48
Washington Naval Conference, 419
***Waste Land, The* (Eliot),** 451
Watergate scandal, 619, 758, 802–807, R66
Water Quality Act, 691
Waters, Ethel, 456
Watson, Thomas E., 223
Watt, James, 837
Watts riots, *i* 718, 719
WCTU. *See* Women's Christian Temperance Union.
weapons of mass destruction (WMD), 867, 868, 898, 899
Weaver, Robert C., 505, 690
web-perfecting press, 279
Webster, Daniel, 124, 157–158, *i* 157
Webster-Ashburton Treaty, 133
***Webster* v. *Reproductive Health Care Services*,** 840
welfare reform, 795, 862, 911
Welles, Orson, 511, *i* 511
Wells, Ida B., 286, *i* 286, 288, 453
***Wesberry* v. *Sanders*,** 774–775
West, literature of, 224–225
West Africa, 8–10, 15, 32. *See also* Africa.
West Germany, 608, 814
West Indies, 32, 33, 38, 454
Westinghouse, George, 232
Westin, Jeane, 475
Westmoreland, William, 737, *i* 737, 739, 741, 749
West Virginia, 94, 169
  facts about, R49
westward expansion, 112, 888
  British attempt to slow, 39
  on Great Plains, 203–204, 214–215
  Louisiana Purchase and, 114
  in mid-19th century, 130–131, 133, 137–138, 150–151
  Native Americans and, 39, 77, 131, 203–204, 206–207, 428
  after Revolutionary War, 63, 67, 72, 77
Weyler, Valeriano, 347
Wharton, Edith, 296, 451
Wheeler, Burton, 557
Wheeler, Edward, 296
Whig Party, 126, 127, 161, 162
Whiskey Rebellion, 76
White, Walter, 506
Whitefield, George, *i* 35
Whitewater Development Company, 865
Whitman, Marcus and Narcissa, 131, 150
Whitney, Eli, 121
Wholesome Meat Act, 691
***Why We Fight* (Capra),** 566, *i* 566
WIB. *See* War Industries Board.
Wiesel, Elie, 549, *i* 549
Wilder, L. Douglas, 843
Wiley, Harvey Washington, 322
Wilhelm II (kaiser of Germany), 373, *i* 373
Willard, Emma, 148
Willard, Frances, 307
Williams, Roger, 24–25
***William* v. *Mississippi*,** 290
Willkie, Wendell, 551
Wills, Helen, 448, *i* 448
Wilson, Woodrow, 92, 222, 330–331, 358, 363, 379, *i* 379, 380, 398–399, *i* 399, 417, 418, R51
  banking system under, 334

civil rights and, 335–336
foreign policy of, 363–365, 379–380
Fourteen Points of, 399
League of Nations and, 399, 401, 402
Mexican revolution and, 363–365
presidency of, 333–334, 388–389
propaganda campaign of, 390–391
tariffs and, 333–334
taxation and, 334
war economy and, 388–389
woman suffrage and, 334–335
World War I and, 379–380, 391, 394
Wilson-Gorman Tariff, 271
Winthrop, John, 24
Wisconsin, 162, 215
facts about, R49
Withers, Ernest, 713, *i* 713
Wobblies. *See* Industrial Workers of the World.
Womack, Bob, 213
woman suffrage. *See* women, voting rights of.
Woman Suffrage Party, 335
women. *See also* progressive movement; women's rights movement; names of individual women.
African American, 148, 149, 314, 316
bicycling and, 293
in Civil War, 174, 175
in colonial America, 32, 34, 41, 53, 64
in Congress, 65, 372, 722
education of, 148, 314–315
on farms, 214, 217, 219, 313
Great Depression and, 475–476
in labor force, 142, *i* 142, 233, 244–245, 307, 311, 313–314, 388, 441, 442, *c* 442, *i* 442, 565, 591, *i* 591, 777, *c* 777, 869, *i* 869, 914–915, *c* 914–915
in labor movement, 248–249, *i* 417, 777, 842–843
literature by, 451, 459, 874–875
in mining camps, 204
New Deal and, 504–505
in 1920s, 440–443
in 1950s, 644–645
pay equity and, 842, 914, 915, R62
political power and, 63, 71, 64–65, 195–196, 842
as reformers, 147–149, 314–316, 777
in Revolutionary War, 61
in Vietnam War, 744
voting rights of, 32, 64, 101, 105, 149, 315–316, 332, 334–335
in World War I, 382, 388, 394, *i* 394
in World War II, 563, *i* 563, 591, *i* 591
Women's Auxiliary Army Corps (WAAC), 563, R66
Women's Christian Temperance Union (WCTU), 307–308, 436
Women's Peace Party, 394
women's rights movement, 65, 148–149, 776–780
Wonder, Stevie, 786
Woodbridge, Cloverleaf, 423
Wood, Grant, 513
Woodstock, 783, R66
Woodward, Bob, 804, *i* 804
Woolworth, F. W., 296–297
***Worcester* v. *Georgia*,** 124
workers' compensation, 311
work force. *See* labor force.
working conditions, 245, 310–311, 321, *i* 321. *See also* labor force; labor movement.
in factories, 142, 233, 244–245, 248, 249, 306, 309
on railroads, 237
Workingmen's Party, 259
working with a group, 43, 107, 109, 153, 191, 227, 273, 301, 339, 397, 445, 461, 524, 589, 631, 665, 727, 765, 787, 827
Works Progress Administration (WPA), 498–499, *c* 500, 512–513, R66
WorldCom, 867, 871
World Trade Center (New York), 862–863, 894, *i* 894, 895, *i* 895. *See also* September 11 terrorist attack; terrorism.
World Trade Organization (WTO), 864, 872
World War I, *m* 375, *m* 386
African Americans in, 382
alliances in, 373–374
Allies in, 373–374
American neutrality in, 377
battles of, *i* 370–371, 374, 376, 383–385
blockade and, 378–379
causes of, 372–374
Central Powers in, 374
civil liberties and, 391–392
debts from, 419
draft in, 382–383, *i* 382
economy and, 388–390, *c* 389
end of, 386–387
Europe after, *m* 400
financing of, 390–391
home front in, 388–390
legacy of, 403
medical care in, 385
naval arms race and, 373
"no man's land" in, 376, R61
peace settlement for, 400, 529
selling of, 390–391
social changes and, 392–393
trench warfare in, 376, *i* 376, R65
U-boats in, 378–379, 383
U.S. involvement in, 378–379, 588
war guilt clause and, 400, R65
war resolution and, 380
weapons in, 384–385, *i* 384–385, 589
woman suffrage and, 335
women in, 382, 388, 394, *i* 394
World War II, *m* 572, *c* 580–581, 803
African Americans in, 563, *i* 563, 564, 573, *i* 573, 702, 889
Allied plans for, 569, 570
blitzkrieg tactics in, 539, *i* 539
bombing of Hiroshima and Nagasaki, 584, *i* 584, 585, 586
conferences during, 573, 585–586
D-Day and, 574–575
economy and, 567–568, *c* 567, 591
end of, *i* 602
end of Great Depression and, 557, 590–591
events leading to, 529–535, 536–537
German advances in, *m* 538
horrors of, 571, *i* 571
industry in, 564–565
internment of Japanese Americans in, 594–595, *i* 594, *m* 594, 596–597
lend-lease plan and, 552, 553
Normandy invasions in, 574, *m* 575
in North Africa, 572, *m* 572
in Pacific, 578–579, *m* 580, 581, 582, 583, 584
phony war in, 540
population shifts and, 591
Potsdam conference after, 604
rationing in, 568
scientists in, 567, 583, 585
social adjustments and, 592
submarines in, 553, *i* 553, 554, 570
surrender of Japan in, 584
technological developments and, *i* 539, 588–589, *c* 589
two-front war, 557
U.S. involvement in, 552–557, 562–563
women in, 563, *i* 563, 591, *i* 591
Wounded Knee, South Dakota, *m* 205, 207, 772
battle of, 207, R53
WPA. *See* Works Progress Administration.
WPB. *See* War Production Board.
Wright, Frank Lloyd, 277, 336
Wright, Orville and Wilbur, 279, *i* 279, 280, 281
Wright, Richard, 514
written presentations, creating, R34–35
WTO. *See* World Trade Organization.
Wyoming, 216, 316
facts about, R49

X

XYZ Affair, 78, *i* 78, R66

Y

Yalta Conference, 585–586
yellow fever, 243, 353
yellow journalism, 347, R66
Yellowstone National Park, 207
Yeltsin, Boris, 849
YMCA. *See* Young Men's Christian Association.
Yom Kippur War, 799
York, Alvin, 386, *i* 386
Yorktown, Battle of, 62
Yosemite National Park, 324, *i* 324
Young, Andrew, 722, 814, *i* 814
Young, Brigham, 131, 133
Young Men's Christian Association (YMCA), 307
Yucatán Peninsula, 5
Yugoslavia, 374, 400, 850, 863
Yurok, 6

Z

Zapata, Emiliano, 364
Zapatistas, *i* 364
Zhou Enlai, 612
Zimmermann note, 379, R66
Zitkala-Ša, 202, *i* 202

Acknowledgments

TEXT ACKNOWLEDGMENTS

CHAPTER 5, page 225: Excerpt from "El Corrido de Gregorio Cortez," from *With His Pistol in His Hands: A Border Ballad and Its Hero* by Américo Paredes. Copyright © 1958, renewed 1986. Reprinted by permission of the author and the University of Texas Press.

CHAPTER 7, page 257: Excerpt from "The Reminiscences of Edward Ferro," from *I Was Dreaming to Come to America: Memories from the Ellis Island Oral History Project*, page 24. Selected and illustrated by Veronica Lawlor; forward by Rudolph W. Giuliani. Copyright © 1995 by Viking.

CHAPTER 13, page 459: "First Fig," from *Collected Poems* by Edna St. Vincent Millay, published by HarperCollins. Copyright © 1922, 1950 by Edna St. Vincent Millay. Reprinted by permission of Elizabeth Barnett, literary executor.

"Dream Variations," from *The Collected Poems of Langston Hughes* by Langston Hughes. Copyright © 1994 by the Estate of Langston Hughes. Used by permission of Alfred A. Knopf, a division of Random House, Inc.

CHAPTER 14, pages 473, 483: Excerpts from "A. Everette McIntyre" and "Herman Shumlin," from *Hard Times* by Studs Terkel. Copyright © 1970. Reprinted by permission of Donadio & Olson, Inc.

CHAPTER 15, page 513: Excerpt from "Dust Bowl Refugee," words and music by Woody Guthrie. Copyright © 1960 (renewed) and 1963 (renewed) by Ludlow Music, Inc., New York, New York. Used by permission.

CHAPTER 16, page 542: Excerpt from Gerda Weissmann Klein's interview in the film *One Survivor Remembers*, a production of Home Box Office and the United States Holocaust Museum. By permission of Gary Greenberg for Gerda Weissmann Klein.

CHAPTER 17, page 562: Excerpts from "Wife's Recorded Message Made Many Long for Home," from *We Pulled Together . . . and Won!* by Charles Swanson (Reminisce Books). Reprinted by permission of the Estate of Charles Swanson.

CHAPTER 18, page 628: Excerpt from *The Body Snatchers* by Jack Finney. Copyright © 1955 by Jack Finney. Copyright © renewed 1983 by Jack Finney. Reprinted by permission of Don Congdon Associates.

page 629: Excerpt from *The Martian Chronicles* by Ray Bradbury. Copyright © 1945 by Street and Smith. Copyright © renewed 1972 by Ray Bradbury. Reprinted by permission of Don Congdon Associates.

CHAPTER 22, page 739: Excerpt from *Dear America: Letters Home from Vietnam*, edited by Bernard Edelman for the New York Vietnam Veterans Memorial Commission. Published in 1985 by W. W. Norton & Company. Copyright © 1985 by the New York Vietnam Veterans Memorial Commission. Reprinted by permission of Bernard Edelman.

page 745: Excerpt from "Eve of Destruction," words and music by P. F. Sloan. Copyright © 1965 by Duchess Music Corporation. Sole selling agent MCA Music Publishing, a division of MCA Inc. International copyright secured. All rights reserved.

Excerpt from "Ballad of the Green Berets" by Barry Sadler. Reprinted by permission of Estaboga Music.

page 762: Excerpt from *Going After Cacciato* by Tim O'Brien. Copyright © 1978 by Tim O'Brien. Reprinted by permission of Dell Publishing, a division of Random House, Inc.

page 763: Excerpt from *A Rumor of War* by Philip Caputo. Copyright © 1977 by Philip Caputo. Reprinted by permission of Henry Holt and Company, L.L.C.

Excerpt from *Fallen Angels* by Walter Dean Myers. Copyright © 1988 by Walter Dean Myers. Used by permission of Scholastic. Hardcover, a trademark of Scholastic, Inc.

CHAPTER 25, page 846: "Americans on the Move, 1970s" from *Regional Growth and Decline in the United States*. Copyright © 1978 by Bernard L. Weinstein, Harold T. Gross, and John Rees. Reprinted by permission of Bernard L. Weinstein, University of North Texas, Denton, Texas.

CHAPTER 26, page 860: Excerpt from "On the Pulse of the Morning" by Maya Angelou. Copyright © 1993 by Maya Angelou. Used by permission of Random House, Inc.

page 874: "Choices," from *Cotton Candy on a Rainy Day* by Nikki Giovanni. Copyright © 1978 by Nikki Giovanni. Used by permission of HarperCollins Publishers, Inc.

page 875: Excerpt from *The Joy Luck Club* by Amy Tan. Copyright © 1989 by Amy Tan. Used by permission of G. P. Putnam's Sons, a division of Penguin Putnam, Inc.

"Four Skinny Trees," from *The House on Mango Street* by Sandra Cisneros. Copyright © 1984 by Sandra Cisneros. Published by Vintage Books, a division of Random House, Inc., and in hardcover by Alfred A. Knopf. Reprinted by permission of Susan Bergholz Literary Services, New York. All rights reserved.

McDougal Littell Inc. has made every effort to locate the copyright holders for selections used in this book and to make full acknowledgment for their use. Omissions brought to our attention will be corrected in a subsequent edition.

ART CREDITS

COVER AND FRONTISPIECE

Jane Addams: Copyright © Bettmann/Corbis
Ben Nighthorse Campbell: AP/Wide World Photos
César Chávez: Copyright © 1990 Lisa Quinones/Black Star/PNI
Lyndon B. Johnson: Copyright © Corbis
Barbara Jordan: AP/Wide World Photos
Martin Luther King, Jr.: Copyright © Flip Schulke/Black Star
Gerda Weissman Klein: Photograph by Scott Wachter, courtesy of Gerda Weissman Klein/HBO
Queen Liliuokalani: The Granger Collection, New York
Maya Lin: Copyright © 1993 Richard Howard/Black Star/PNI

Sandra Day O'Connor: Copyright © Roger Ressmeyer/Corbis
Ronald Reagan: Copyright © Bettmann/Corbis
Franklin Delano Roosevelt: Hulton Archive by Getty Images

Maps: MapQuest.com, Inc.
7, 17, 22, 25, 29, 38, 59, 62, 72, 73, 115, 116, 125, 132, 134, 136, 150, 159, 160, 170, 176, 179, 205, 209, 231, 234, 239, 255, 263, 278, 323, 331, 345, 349, 356, 366, 375, 386, 400, 416, 423, 449, 455, 474, 521, 530, 532, 538, 556, 572, 575, 580, 591, 594, 605, 611, 613, 624, 625, 638, 650, 675, 677, 685, 688, 701, 733, 749, 753, 775, 815, 816, 833, 846, 847, 851, 854, 866, 872, 885, R25, R26

The presidential seal is used throughout by permission of The Office of the Counsel to the President, The White House, Washington, D.C. Photo provided by The Granger Collection, New York.

vi *top to bottom* The Granger Collection, New York; *Battle of Lexington* (c. 1850), Alonzo Chappel. Photograph Copyright © Bettmann/Corbis; Photograph by Richard Strauss, 1994. Collection of the Supreme Court Historical Society; **vii** *top to bottom* National Museum of American History, Smithsonian Institution [75-2348]; Matthew Brady Studio (1864), Hulton Archive by Getty Images; The Granger Collection, New York; **viii** *top to bottom, Portrait of a Sioux Man and Woman* (date unknown), Gertrude Käsebier. Photographic History Collection, National Museum of American History, Smithsonian Institution; Culver Pictures; **ix** *all* Copyright © Bettmann/Corbis; **x** *top to bottom* Culver Pictures; Beinecke Rare Book and Manuscript Library, Yale University; Underwood Photo Archives; **xi** *top to bottom* Courtesy of Gerda Weissman Klein; Copyright © Bettmann/Corbis; Courtesy of Republic Entertainment, Inc.; **xii** *top to bottom* Hulton Archive by Getty Images; Courtesy of Arthur L. Freeman; Copyright © 1995 Paul Fusco/Magnum Photos; **xiii** *top* Reprinted by permission of Tribune Media Services; *bottom* Getty Images; **xiv** *top* Copyright © Bettmann/Corbis; *bottom* National Archives; **xvi** *top* Illustration by Matthew Pippin; *center* Panel no. 1: *During the World War There Was a Great Migration North by Southern Negroes*, from the Migration of the Negro mural series (1940–1941), Jacob Lawrence. Tempera on masonite, 12″ × 18″. Acquired through Downtown Gallery, 1942. The Phillips Collection, Washington, D.C.; *bottom* Joe Rosenthal AP/Wide World Photos; **xvii** *top* Copyright © Stock Montage; *bottom* Copyright © Seny Norasingh/Light Sensitive; **xviii** Dale Atkins AP/Wide World Photos; **xix** The Granger Collection, New York; **xx** *top* from *Puerto Rico: A Political and Cultural History*, Arturo Morales Carrion; *bottom* Copyright © The Dorothea Lange Collection, Oakland Museum of California, City of Oakland. Gift of Paul S. Taylor; **xxi** *top* Hulton Archive by Getty Images; *bottom* Copyright © Flip Schulke/Black Star; **xxii** *top* Copyright © Donald J. Weber; *bottom* Copyright © 1993 Jim Stratford/Black Star; **xxiv** Copyright © UPI/Corbis-Bettmann; **xxv** National Archives; **xxviii** *top* National Aeronautics and Space Administration; *bottom* Copyright © Reuters NewMedia Inc./CORBIS; **xxix** *top* The Granger Collection, New York; *center* H. Armstrong Roberts; *bottom* Photo by Howard Sochurek/*Life* Magazine. Copyright © Time, Inc.; **xxx** Copyright © 1991 Woodward Payne.

Chapter 1
1 *across Signing of the Constitution*, Howard Chandler Christy. Art Resource, New York; **2–3** *across* The Granger Collection, New York; **2** *bottom left* Copyright © Nik Wheeler/Corbis; *bottom right* Museo del Templo Mayor, Mexico City, D.F., Mexico, Michel Zabé/Art Resource, New York; **3** *bottom left, The Mayflower in Plymouth Harbor* (late 19th century) William Halsall. Copyright © Burstein Collection/Corbis; *bottom right* Copyright © Bettmann/Corbis; **4** *top right* Copyright © Library of Congress/Corbis; *center right* Phoebe A. Hearst Museum of Anthropology, University of California at Berkeley; **5** *top* Courtesy Arizona State Museum, University of Arizona, Tucson, Arizona. Photograph Copyright © 1996 Jerry Jacka; *bottom* Reconstruction of the Valley of Mexico, Lake Texcoco, and Great Tenochtitlan. Museum of Mexico City. Copyright © C. Lenars/Photo Researchers; **6** Copyright © Mike Zens/Corbis; **7** *top* Hulton Getty/Getty News Services; *center left* Edward S. Curtis, 1900. Copyright © Corbis; *center right* Copyright © Nathan Benn-Corbis; **8** Copyright © Stock Montage; **10** The Granger Collection, New York; **11** *June* from *Les Tres Riches Hueres du Duc de Berry* (early 15th century), Limbourg Brothers. Musée Conde, Chantilly, France. Giraudon/Art Resource, New York; **12** Matthew Pippin; **14** *top right* Copyright © Library of Congress/Corbis; *center right, Portrait of a Man Called Christopher Columbus* (1519), Sebastiano del Piombo. Oil on canvas, 42″ × $34\frac{3}{4}$″. The Metropolitan Museum of Art, New York. Gift of J. Pierpont Morgan, 1900. Copyright © 1979 The Metropolitan Museum of Art; **16, 17** *inset* Copyright © The Granger Collection, New York; **19** *bottom left* Copyright © Ted Streshinsky/Corbis; *bottom right* Illustration by Lawrence Ormsby. Reprinted by permission from *Spanish Colonial Missions* by Gloria Giffords. Published by Southwest Parks and Monuments Association. Copyright © 1988; **21** *top right* Copyright © Library of Congress/Corbis; *center left* The Granger Collection, New York; **22** *top right, top inset* Courtesy of the Association for the Preservation of Virginia Antiquities; *bottom* Hulton Getty/Getty News Services; **24** Pilgrim Society, Plymouth, Massachusetts; **27** Matthew Pippin **31** *top right* Copyright © Library of Congress/Corbis; *center right* Copyright © Taylor Lewis. Courtesy Catherine Fallin, Kerhonkson, New York; **32** Library of Congress, Prints and Photographs Division [LC-USZ62-44000]; **33** The Granger Collection, New York; **34** *left* Photograph by John Chew. Courtesy of Cliveden of the National Trust; *right* Copyright © Lee Snider/Corbis; **35** The Granger Collection, New York; **36** *left, Benjamin Franklin* (c. 1785), Joseph Siffred Duplessis. Oil on canvas, $28\frac{1}{2}$″ × $23\frac{1}{2}$″. National Portrait Gallery, Smithsonian Institution, gift of the Morris and Gwendolyn Cafritz Foundation/Art Resource, New York; **36** *right*, **37** The Granger Collection, New York; **40** *bottom left, Celebrating Couple: General Jackson and His Lady* (date unknown), Reverend H. Young. Pen and watercolor, $10\frac{1}{4}$″ × $7\frac{5}{8}$″. Courtesy, Museum of Fine Arts, Boston, gift of Maxim Karolik; **40–41** *across*, **41** *top* Abby Aldrich Rockefeller Folk Art Center, Williamsburg, Virginia; **41** *bottom* Library of Congress, Prints and Photographs Division [LC-USZ62-33939]; **43** Copyright © Corbis.

Chapter 2
44–45 *across* The Granger Collection, New York; **44** *bottom left* Copyright © Leonard de Selva/Corbis; *bottom right* Copyright © Leif Skoogfors/Corbis; **45** *bottom center* Engraving after Gilbert Stewart, 1789. Copyright © Corbis; *bottom* Copyright © Paul Almasy/Corbis; **46** *top right* Detail of *Washington Crossing The Delaware* (1851), Emanuel Gottlieb Leutze. Photograph Copyright © Bettmann/Corbis; *center right* Copyright © Stock Montage; **48** *top* Rare Books and Manuscripts Division, The New York Public Library, Astor, Lenox and Tilden Foundations; *bottom, The Boston Massacre (The Bloody Massacre)* (1770), Paul Revere. Hand-colored engraving, $10\frac{1}{4}$″ × $9\frac{1}{8}$″. The Metropolitan Museum of Art, New York. Gift of Mrs. Russell Sage, 1909. Copyright © 1979 The Metropolitan Museum of Art, New York; **49** American Antiquarian Society; **50** *Battle of Lexington* (c. 1850), Alonzo Chappel. Photograph Copyright © Bettmann/Corbis; **51** *Attack on Bunker's Hill, with the Burning of Charles Town* (c. 1783), unknown artist. Oil on canvas, $23\frac{7}{8}$″ × $30\frac{1}{2}$″ × $1\frac{1}{2}$″ framed. Copyright © 1996 Board of Trustees, National Gallery of Art, Washington, D.C. Gift of Edgar William and Bernice Chrysler Garbisch; **52** Library of Congress, Prints and Photographs Division [LC-USZ62-10658]; **54** *signature* National Archives; *portrait* The Granger Collection, New York; **55** Photograph by Sharon Hoogstraten; **56** Massachusetts Historical Society; **57** *top* Photograph by Sharon Hoogstraten; *signature, top* The Granger Collection, New York; *other signatures* National Archives; *center right* Copyright © Bettmann/Corbis; **58** *top right* Detail of *Washington Crossing The Delaware* (1851),

Emanuel Gottlieb Leutze. Photograph Copyright © Bettmann/Corbis; *center right* Collection of Mrs. Jackson C. Boswell, Arlington, Virginia. Courtesy of the Frick Art Reference Library; **59** *top, bottom* David Kamerman; **60** The Granger Collection, New York; **61** *Molly Pitcher at the Battle of Monmouth,* (1854) Dennis Malone Carter. Oil on canvas, 42″ × 56″. Gift of Herbert P. Whitlock, 1913. Courtesy of Fraunces Tavern Museum, New York City; **63** Image by courtesy of the Trustees of the Wedgwood Museum, Barlaston, Staffordshire, England **64** *top, Governor and Mrs. Mifflin,* J.S. Copley. The Historical Society of Pennsylvania; *center left* Courtesy of Seneca Falls (New York) Historical Society; **64–65** *across* The Granger Collection, New York; **65** *top* Photograph by Sharon Hoogstraten; *top right* Copyright © Reuters NewMedia Inc./Corbis; **66** *top right* Detail of *Washington Crossing The Delaware* (1851), Emanuel Gottlieb Leutze. Photograph Copyright © Bettmann/Corbis; *center right* Detail of *John Dickinson* (c. 1835), James Barton Longacre, after Charles Wilson Peale. Sepia watercolor on artist board, 11⅝″ × 8⅞″. National Portrait Gallery, Smithsonian Institution/Art Resource, New York; **68, 70, 71** The Granger Collection, New York; **72** Copyright © Stone; **73** *Township VII, Range XIV, Ohio Company* (1787), Rufus Putnam. Clements Library, University of Michigan; **74** *top right* Detail of *Washington Crossing The Delaware* (1851), Emanuel Gottlieb Leutze. Photograph Copyright © Bettmann/Corbis; *center right* The Granger Collection, New York; **75** *left, Alexander Hamilton* (c. 1796), James Sharples, the elder. Pastel on paper. National Portrait Gallery, Smithsonian Institution/Art Resource, New York; *right* Copyright © Bettmann/Corbis; **76** *Taking of the Bastille, 14 July 1789* (late 1700s), unknown artist, Chateau Versailles, France. Giraudon/Art Resource, New York; **77** Copyright © Bettmann/Corbis; **78** The Granger Collection, New York; **80** *top, bottom* David Kamerman; **81** Library of Congress, Prints and Photographs Division [LC-USZ62-9487] **82** The Granger Collection, New York; **83** Bettmann/Corbis; **92** *top* Joe Marquette/AP/Wide World Photos; *bottom* The Granger Collection, New York; **93** Photograph by Richard Strauss, 1994. Collection of the Supreme Court Historical Society; **97** *The Federal Edifice: On the Erection of the Eleventh Pillar,* cartoon from *The Massachusetts Centinel,* August 2, 1788. Courtesy of the New-York Historical Society, New York City; **99** HWG/AP/Wide World Photos; **100** Copyright © Bettmann/Corbis; **103** AP/Wide World Photos; **104** *left* Copyright © Bettmann/Corbis; *right* Detail of *Daniel Boardman* (1789), Ralph Earl. Oil on canvas, 81⅝″ × 55¼″. Copyright © 1996, Board of Trustees, National Gallery of Art, Washington, D.C. Gift of Mrs. W. Murray Crane; **105** *top* FPG International; *bottom* AP/Wide World Photos; **106** The Granger Collection, New York; **107** From *The Herblock Gallery*. Simon & Schuster, 1968. Copyright © Herblock; **108** *top* Photograph by Sharon Hoogstraten; *bottom* Copyright © David Young-Wolff/PhotoEdit; **109** Copyright © Photo Edit.

Chapter 3

110–111 *across,* **110** *bottom left, bottom center* Copyright © Bettmann/Corbis; *bottom right* Library of Congress, Prints and Photographs Division [LC-USZ62-116232]; **111** *bottom left* Copyright © Bettmann/Corbis; *bottom center* Copyright © Corbis; *bottom right* The Granger Collection, New York; **112** *top right* Undated colored woodcut by F. O. C. Darley. Copyright © Bettmann/Corbis; *center right* Courtesy of Mrs. V. James Taranik; **113** Detail of *John Marshall, Chief Justice of the United States* (c. 1832), William James Hubard, National Portrait Gallery, Smithsonian Institution/Art Resource, New York; **115** *top left* US Mint/AP/Wide World Photos; *top right, Mandan Village* (c. 1834), Karl Bodmer. From *Travels in the Interior of North America* by Maximilian Prince zu Wied. Yale Collection of Western Americana, Beinecke Rare Book and Manuscript Library, Yale University; *bottom left* American Philosophical Society Library; *bottom right* National Museum of American History, Smithsonian Institution [75-2348]; **117** Copyright © Bettmann/Corbis; **118** *Portrait of Chief Justice John Marshall,* Rembrandt Peale. Courtesy of the Supreme Court of the United States; **119** *Portrait of Chief Justice William Marbury* (c. 1820–1830), Rembrandt Peale. Photographer: Vic Boswell, National Geographic Society. Courtesy of the Supreme Court of the United States; **120** *top right* Undated colored woodcut by F.O.C. Darley. Copyright © Bettmann/Corbis; *center right, Telegraph,* James Bard, The Mariners' Museum; **121** National Museum of American History, Smithsonian Institution, [73-11287]; **123** *top, Portrait of Andrew Jackson, 1767–1845, Seventh President of the United States* (1820), James Barton Longacre. Hand-colored stipple engraving, 37.2 cm × 30 cm. National Portrait Gallery, Smithsonian Institution/Art Resource, New York; *bottom* The Granger Collection, New York; **124** *The Trail of Tears,* Troy Anderson/Sun Valley Photography; **125** *top left* Smithsonian Institution; *top right* The Granger Collection, New York; *bottom* Detail of *Trail of Tears* (date unknown), Robert Lindneux, Woolaroc Museum, Bartlesville, Oklahoma; **126** Library of Congress, Prints and Photographs Division [LC-USZ62-1562]; **128** *bottom left* The Granger Collection, New York; *center* The Library Company of Philadelphia; **128–129** *top across* Copyright © Bettmann/Corbis; **129** Copyright © 1957 Burt Glinn/Magnum Photos; **130** *top right* Undated colored woodcut by F. O. C. Darley. Copyright © Bettmann/Corbis; **131** Courtesy, Colorado Historical Society; **132** *top* National Archives; *bottom left* Edward S. Curtis (c. 1904), Library of Congress, Prints and Photographs Division [LC-USZ62-97089]; *bottom right* Edward S. Curtis (c. 1904)/Library of Congress, Prints and Photographs Division [LC-USZ62-103498]; **134** *inset* The Granger Collection, New York; **135** *top left* Copyright © Bettmann/Corbis; *top right* The Granger Collection, New York; **137** California State Library; **138** The Bancroft Library, University of California, Berkeley; **139** *top right* Undated colored woodcut by F. O. C. Darley. Copyright © Bettmann/Corbis; *center right* The Granger Collection, New York; **140** *bottom left* Courtesy of the Smithsonian Institution, Washington, D.C.; *bottom center* Copyright © H. Armstrong Roberts; **140** *bottom right,* **141** *bottom left* Copyright © UPI/Bettmann/Corbis; **141** *bottom center* Copyright © Charles E. Rotkin/Corbis; *bottom right* School Division, Houghton Mifflin Company; *bottom right, screen image* Martha Granger/EDGE Productions; **142** Jack Naylor Collection/PRC Archive; **143** The Granger Collection, New York; **144** *top right* Undated colored woodcut by F. O. C. Darley. Copyright © Bettmann/Corbis; *center right* Historical Society of Pennsylvania, Leon Gardiner Collection; **145** North Wind Picture Archives; **146** The Granger Collection, New York; **147** *top* Matthew Pippin; *inset* Collection of the New-York Historical Society, neg. 48169; **148, 149** The Granger Collection, New York; **150** *bottom left* Courtesy of the Smithsonian Institution; **150–151** *center across* National Archives; **151** *top* Idaho State Historical Society. Photograph number 1254-D-1; *bottom* Copyright © Ric Ergenbright Photography; **152** *bottom left* Courtesy of the Smithsonian Institution, Washington, D.C.; *bottom center* National Museum of American History, Smithsonian Institution [75-2348]; **152** *bottom right,* **153** The Granger Collection, New York.

Chapter 4

154–155 *across* Engraving, 1859. Copyright © Corbis; **154** *bottom left, above time line* From the Collection of Edith Hariton/Antique Textile Resource. Picture Research Consultants and Archives; *bottom left, below time line* Copyright © Hulton-Deutsch Collection/Corbis; *bottom right* Copyright © Tria Giovan/Corbis; **155** *bottom* Copyright © Corbis; **156** *top right, Battle of Gettysburg* (1884). Color illustration. Copyright © Hulton Archive by Getty Images; *center right* Daguerreotype, Mathew Brady Studio, 1848–1849/The Granger Collection, New York; **157** The Granger Collection, New York; **159** C.T. Weber, 1893. Copyright © Bettmann/Corbis; **161, 162** The Granger Collection, New York; **163** *bottom left, Stephen Douglas* (c. 1860), Mathew Brady Studio. Photograph, albumen silver print, 3⅛″ × 2⅛″. National Portrait Gallery, Smithsonian Instiitution/Art Resource, New York; *bottom right* The Granger Collection, New York; **164** *John Brown Going to His Hanging* (1942), Horace Pippin. Oil on canvas, 24⅛″ × 30¼″. Courtesy of the Museum of American Art of the Pennsylvania Academy of the Fine Arts, Philadelphia, Pennsylvania. John Lambert Fund; **166** Copyright © Bettmann/Corbis; **167** Library of Congress, Prints and Photographs Division [US-0989-46]; **168** *top right, Battle of Gettysburg* (1884). Color illustration. Copyright © Hulton Archive by Getty Images; *center right* Beverley R. Robinson Collection, United States Naval Academy Museum, Annapolis,

Maryland. Accession number 51.7.667; **169** *top left* George Eastman House; *top right* Library of Congress, Prints and Photographs Division [LC-B8184-10374]; **171** The Granger Collection, New York; **172** *top left, Portrait of Abraham Lincoln,* (1864), William Willard, National Portrait Gallery, Smithsonian Institution/Art Resource, New York; *top right* Copyright © Bettmann/Corbis; **173** Mathew Brady Studio (1864). The Granger Collection, New York; **174** *top* The Granger Collection, New York; *bottom* Copyright © Tria Giovan/Corbis; **175** *top right, Battle of Gettysburg* (1884). Color illustration. Copyright © Hulton Archive by Getty Images; *center right, Mary Boykin Chesnut* (1854), Samuel Osgood. On loan from Serena Willliams Miles Van Rensselaer. National Portrait Gallery, Smithsonian Institution/Art Resource, New York; **178** *top* Mathew Brady Studio (1864). Copyright © Hulton Archive by Getty Images; *bottom* Mathew Brady Studio/Library of Congress, Prints and Photographs Division [LC-B8171-1214]; **180** *top left* Library of Congress, Prints and Photographs Division [LC-USZ62-115549]; *top right* Library of Congress, Prints and Photographs Division [504790 LC U5260-20244]; **181** Copyright © Tom Lovell/NGS Image Collection; **182** The Granger Collection, New York; **183** Illinois State Historical Library; **184** *top right, Battle of Gettysburg* (1884). Color illustration. Copyright © Hulton Archive by Getty Images; *center right* Copyright © 1956, 1978 by Pauli Murray. Reprinted by permission of Frances Collin, literary agent; **185** *A Burial Party: Civil War, Cold Harbor, Virginia* (1865), Alexander Gardner. Photograph. Chicago Historical Society; **186, 187** *top* The Granger Collection, New York; **187** *bottom* Indianapolis Children's Museum; **188** The Granger Collection, New York; **189** Copyright © Bettmann/Corbis; **192** Copyright © Sylvain Grandadam/Photo Researchers, Inc.; **193** The Granger Collection, New York; **194** *top, Taking of the Bastille, 14 July 1789* (late 1700's), unknown artist, Chateau Versailles, France. Giraudon/Art Resource, New York; **195** *top* Beverley R. Robinson Collection, United States Naval Academy Museum, Annapolis, Maryland. Accession number 51.7.667; *bottom* The Granger Collection, New York; **196** *top* The Granger Collection, New York; bottom Copyright © Bettmann/Corbis; **197** California State Library.

Chapter 5

198–199, *Champions of the Mississippi,* The Currier & Ives, lithograph. Scala/Art Resource, New York; **200** *bottom left to right* Copyright © Bettmann/Corbis; The Granger Collection, New York; Hulton Archive by Getty Images; **200–201** National Anthropological Archives, National Museum of Natural History, Smithsonian Institution; **201** *bottom left to right* Copyright © Bettmann/Corbis; Hulton Archive by Getty Images; **202** *top right, And So, Unemotionally, There Begun One of the Wildest and Strangest Journeys Ever Made in Any Land* (date unknown), William Henry David Koerner. Oil on canvas, $22\frac{1}{4}'' \times 72\frac{1}{4}''$. Buffalo Bill Historical Center, Cody Wyoming; *center right* Courtesy of Brigham Young University; **203** *top right, Portrait of a Sioux Man and Woman* (date unknown), Gertrude Käsebier. Photographic History Collection, National Museum of American History, Smithsonian Institution; *bottom* Copyright © The Detroit Institute of Arts, Founders Society Purchase with funds from Flint Ink Corporation; **204** The Granger Collection, New York; **205** The Granger Collection, New York; **206** *top right* Buffalo Bill Historical Center, Cody Wyoming. Gift Olin Corporation, Winchester Arms Collection; *center left* The Granger Collection, New York; *bottom right* American Museum of Natural History, New York. Photograph by Lee Boltin; **207** *bottom left to right* T. Ulrich/H. Armstrong Roberts; Copyright © Steven Fuller/Animals, Animals; Copyright © Marilyn "Angel" Wynn/Native Stock; **208** *top* Marilyn "Angel" Wynn/Native Stock; *bottom, Vaqueros in a Horse Coral* (1887), James Walker. Oil on canvas, $24\frac{1}{4}'' \times 40''$. Gilcrease Museum.; **210** *top, The Stampede* (date unknown), Frederic Remington. Oil on canvas, $27'' \times 40''$. Gilcrease Museum; **211** The Granger Collection, New York; **212** *bottom left* Photograph by E.A. Hegg. Special collections division, University of Washington Libraries, Seattle. Negative number 1312; **212** *top* The Granger Collection, New York; **213** *top left, Miners Underground* (1897), unknown photographer. Glass plate negative. Amon Carter Museum, Fort Worth, Texas, Mazzulla Collection; **213** *bottom* Photograph by J.G. Wilson. Denver Public Library, Western History Department Collection; *top right* Chuck Lawliss; **214** *top right, And So, Unemotionally, There Begun One of the Wildest and Strangest Journeys Ever Made in Any Land* (date unknown), William Henry David Koerner. Oil on canvas, $22\frac{1}{4}'' \times 72\frac{1}{4}''$. Buffalo Bill Historical Center, Cody Wyoming; *center right, Pioneer Woman* (date unknown), Harvey Dunn. Hazel L. Meyer Memorial Library, De Smet, South Dakota; **215** *top* Kansas State Historical Society, Topeka; *bottom* Library of Congress; **216** The Granger Collection, New York; **217** *left to right* The Granger Collection, New York; 1999, North Wind Pictures; The Granger Collection, New York; North Wind Pictures; *background* James Schuebel/ Panoramic Images; **218** State Historical Society of North Dakota; **219** *top right, And So, Unemotionally, There Begun One of the Wildest and Strangest Journeys Ever Made in Any Land* (date unknown), William Henry David Koerner. Oil on canvas, $22\frac{1}{4}'' \times 72\frac{1}{4}''$. Buffalo Bill Historical Center, Cody Wyoming; *center* Kansas State Historical Society, Topeka; **220** Culver Pictures; **222** Courtesy of Chicago Tribune/Chicago American Photo File, Copyright © KMTV; **223** The Granger Collection, New York; **224** The Granger Collection, New York; **225** *top right* Detail of *Vaquero* (modeled 1980/cast 1990), Luis Jimenez. Cast fiber glass and epoxy. Courtesy of the National Museum of Art, Smithsonian Institution, Washington D.C./Art Resource, New York. Gift of Judith and Wilbur L. Ross, Jr.; *left* Photograph by William Stinson Soule, Archives & Manuscripts Division of the Oklahoma Historical Society. Courtesy of the Oklahoma Historical Society (neg. no. 3969); **226** *clockwise from top left* American Museum of Natural History, New York. Photograph by Lee Boltin; The Granger Collection, New York; Northwind Pictures; The Granger Collection, New York; Copyright © Steve Fuller/Animals/Animals.

Chapter 6

228 *bottom left to right* Underwood Photo Archives, San Francisco; National Museum of American History/Smithsonian Institution; **228–229** California State Railroad Museum; **229** *bottom left and right* The Granger Collection, New York; **230** *top right* The Granger Collection, New York; Reproduced from *Prospectus: The True History of the Beaumont Oil Fields* by Pattillo Higgins. 1902 Pattillo Higgins. Courtesy of the estate of Pattillo Higgins; **232** The Granger Collection, New York; **233** Copyright © Corbis; **234** *top left* From the *Atlas of Cuyahoga County, Ohio,* Titus, Simmons and Titus; *bottom* Western Reserve Historical Society, Cleveland; **234–235** From the *Atlas of Cuyahoga County, Ohio,* Titus, Simmons and Titus; **235** *top right* Copyright © Cleveland Public Library/Bettmann/Corbis; **236** *top right* The Granger Collection, New York; *center* Historic Pullman Foundation Archives, Chicago; **237** *right* Copyright © Jake Lee; **238** The Granger Collection, New York; **240** The Granger Collection, New York; **241** *both,* The Granger Collection, New York; **242** The Granger Collection, New York; **243** *top, bottom* Library of Congress; **244** Courtesy of George Eastman House; **246** Copyright © Bettmann/Corbis; **248** *left* Eugene Debs Collection/Tamiment Institute Library, New York University; *right* The Granger Collection, New York; **249** Copyright © Bettmann/Corbis; **250** Western Reserve Historical Society, Cleveland, Ohio.

Chapter 7

252 *bottom left* Copyright © Bettmann/Corbis; *bottom center, right* The Granger Collection, New York; **252–253** The Granger Collection, New York; **253** The Granger Collection, New York; **254** *top right* Copyright © Corbis; *center* Courtesy of the Fong See Family; **256** National Park Service/Statue of Liberty National Monument; **257** *top left* Culver Pictures; top right New York Academy of Medicine Library; **258** The Granger Collection, New York; **259** Copyright © Bettmann/Corbis; **260** *left to right, Mission Francisco Solano de Sonoma* (date unknown), Oriana Day.

Fine Arts Museum of San Francisco (California), gift of Eleanor Martin, 37573; Culver Pictures, Inc.; From *An Illustrated History of the Civil War* by Miller and Pohankas, *Time-Life*; **261** *top right* The Granger Collection, New York; *bottom left* Copyright © Bettmann/Corbis; **262** *top right* Copyright © Corbis; *center* The Granger Collection, New York; **264** Library of Congress; **265** *bottom left* The Granger Collection, New York; *bottom right* Copyright © Bettman/Corbis; **266** University of Illinois at Chicago Library, the Jane Addams Memorial Collection; **267** *top right* Copyright © Bettmann/Corbis; *center right* The Granger Collection, New York; **268** Copyright © Bettmann/Corbis; **269** *center, bottom* The Granger Collection, New York; **270** *all* The Granger Collection, New York; **273** *top* Harper's Weekly, August 19, 1871.

Chapter 8

274 *bottom left* The Granger Collection, New York; **274–275** Stock Montage; **275** *bottom left to right* Copyright © Bettmann/Corbis Copyright © Charles & Josette Lenars/Corbis; Hulton Archive by Getty Images; **276** *top right* The Granger Collection, New York; *center right* Library of Congress; **277** Library of Congress; **278** *top, Plan of the Center of the City, Showing the Present Street and Boulevard System*, plate 111 from *Plan of Chicago* (1909), Daniel H. Burnham and Edward H. Bennett, Chicago partnership 1903–1912. Ink and watercolor on paper, 131.1 cm × 102.4 cm. On permanent loan to the Art Institute of Chicago, 19.148.1966. Photograph, The Art Institute of Chicago. All rights reserved; *bottom* The Granger Collection, New York; **279** Copyright © Bettmann/Corbis; **280** *top* Copyright © John Batchelor/World Wide Publishing Solutions; *center* Copyright © Smithsonian Institution; *bottom* National Archives and Records Administration; **281** *top* Copyright © Bettmann/Corbis; *bottom* Copyright © Eastman Kodak Company; **282** *top right* The Granger Collection, New York; *center* Culver Pictures; **284** Copyright © 1991 Stephen Frisch/Stock Boston; **285** *top right* Moorland-Spingarn Research Center, Howard University Archives; **286** *top right, center* The Granger Collection, New York; **287** Hulton Archive by Getty Images; **289** Sacramento Archives and Museum Collection Center; **290** The Granger Collection, New York; **291** *top* Copyright © 1965 Danny Lyon/Magnum Photos; *bottom* Copyright © Reuters NewMedia, Inc./Corbis; **292** *top right* The Granger Collection, New York; *center* Culver Pictures; **294** National Baseball Hall of Fame; **295** *bottom, The Champion Single Sculls (Max Schmitt in a Single Scull)* (1871), Thomas Eakins. Oil on canvas, 32¼″ × 46¼″. The Metropolitan Museum of Art, purchase, The Alfred N. Punnett Endowment Fund George D. Pratt Gift, 1934 (34.92); **296** The Granger Collection, New York; **297** *both* Courtesy Sears, Roebuck and Co.; **298** *left* Archive Photos; *right* The Granger Collection, New York; **299** *top right* Hulton Archive by Getty Images; *bottom right* The Granger Collection, New York; **300** *bottom* The Granger Collection, New York.

Chapter 9

302–303 *The Statue of Liberty* (date unknown), Francis Hopkinson Smith. Oil on canvas. 11″ × 15″ (27.9 cm × 38.1 cm). Courtesy of Christie's Images; **304–305** *across* Copyright © Bettmann/Corbis; *bottom left* Copyright © Michael Maslin Historic Photographs/Corbis; *bottom right* Copyright © Bettmann/Corbis; **305** *bottom left* Copyright © Bettmann/Corbis; *bottom center* Peter Ruhe/Hulton Archive by Getty Images; *bottom right* The Granger Collection, New York; **306** *top right, center right* Copyright © Bettmann/Corbis; **307** *top* Copyright © UPI/Bettmann/Corbis; *bottom* Hulton Archive by Getty Images; **309** Copyright © Bettmann/Corbis; **310** Archives & Information Services Division, Texas State Library, Austin; **311** *center left* Lewis W. Hine (1912), Courtesy George Eastman House; *top right* Lewis W. Hine (1908), Copyright © Bettmann/Corbis **312** Hulton Archive by Getty Images; **313** *top right* Copyright © Bettmann/Corbis; *center right* The Granger Collection, New York **314** Copyright © Bettmann/Corbis; **315** Copyright © Corbis; **316, 317** *top right, center right* Copyright © Bettmann/Corbis; **318** *top left* National Museum of American History, Smithsonian Institution; **318** *bottom,* **319** Copyright © Bettmann/Corbis; **321** *illustration* Matthew Pippin; *inset, top right* Lewis W. Hine (1909), Copyright © George Eastman House/Hulton Archive by Getty Images; *inset, center* Hulton Archive by Getty Images; **322** *top* Copyright © UPI/Bettmann/Corbis; *bottom left* The Granger Collection, New York; **324** *top left* Copyright © Bill Ross/Corbis; *bottom* The Granger Collection, New York; **325** Hulton Getty/Getty News Services; **326, 327** *top right* The Granger Collection, New York; **327** *bottom left* Jacket from *The Jungle*. Used by permission of University of Illinois Press. Cover art from the Chicago Historical Society; **328** *top right* Copyright © Bettmann/Corbis; *center right* The Granger Collection, New York; **329** Copyright © Bettmann/Corbis **330** The Granger Collection, New York; **332** *top right, center right,* **335** Copyright © Bettmann/Corbis; **336** *center left* Ezra Stoller, Copyright © Esto; *top right* Copyright © Michael T. Sedam/Corbis.

Chapter 10

340 *bottom, left to right* Copyright © Bettmann/Corbis; Hulton Archive by Getty Images; **340–341** Copyright © Corbis; **341** *bottom, left to right* Panama Canal Company; Copyright © Corbis; **342** *top right* Library of Congress, Prints and Photographs Division (LC-USZC4-5232); *center* Copyright © Bettmann/Corbis; **343** *top* Culver Pictures; *bottom* The Granger Collection, New York; **346** *top right* Library of Congress, Prints and Photographs Division (LC-USZC4-5232); *center* Copyright © Bettmann/Corbis; **347** The Granger Collection, New York; **348** Copyright © Bettmann/Corbis; **350** Copyright © Corbis; **351** Copyright © Bettmann/Corbis; **352** *top right* Library of Congress, Prints and Photographs Division (LC-USZC4-5232); *center, From Puerto Rico: A Political and Cultural History*, Arturo Morales Carrion; **353** Copyright © AFP/Corgis; **354** The Granger Collection, New York; **355** Keystone-Mast Collection (24039), UCR/California Museum of Photography, University of California, Riverside; **357** Copyright © The British Museum; **358** Copyright © Bettmann/Corbis; **359** *top right* Library of Congress, Prints and Photographs Division (LC-USZC4-5232); *center* UPI/Corbis-Bettmann; **360** The Granger Collection, New York; **361** Copyright © Corbis; **362** *top* The Granger Collection, New York; *bottom* Theodore Roosevelt Collection, Harvard College Library; **364** *Zapatistas Marching*, Jose Clemente Orozco. Private Collection/Index/Bridgeman Art Library, Copyright © Estate of Jose Clemente Orozco/Licensed by Vaga, New York, NY; **365** The Granger Collection, New York; **366** *top* Panama Canal Company; *bottom* Copyright © Will and Deni McIntyre/Stone; **367** *top* Copyright © The Mariner's Museum/Corbis; *bottom* Courtesy of The Historic New Orleans Collection, New Orleans, LA; **368** Copyright © Corbis; **369** *left* Culver Pictures; *right* Michelle Hlubinka.

Chapter 11

370 *bottom, left to right* Copyright © Bettmann/Corbis; Copyright © Dorling Kindersley; Copyright © Underwood & Underwood/Corbis; **370–371** Copyright © Bettmann/Corbis; **371** *bottom, left to right* San Francisco Chronicle; The Granger Collection, New York; **372** *top* Copyright © PhotoDisc, Inc; Photograph by Michael Vines, from the collection of the Old Rhinebeck Aerodrome; *center* Copyright © Corbis; **373** Copyright © Corbis; **374** AP Photo/Rikard Larma; **376** Illustrations by Chris Costello, *inset* Copyright © Corbis; **378** *top* Hulton Archive by Getty Images; *right* The Granger Collection, New York; **379** Culver Pictures; **381** *top* Copyright © PhotoDisc, Inc; Photograph by Michael Vines, from the collection of the Old Rhinebeck Aerodrome; *center* Copyright © Bettmann/Corbis; **382** *top* Copyright © Corbis; *left* The Granger Collection, New York; **384** *top* The Granger Collection, New York; *bottom center* Photograph by Michael Vines, from the collection of the Old Rhinebeck Aerodrome; **384–385** Hulton Archive by Getty Images; **385** *bottom center* Copyright © Dorling Kindersley; *bottom right* Hulton Archive by Getty Images; **386** Copyright © Bettmann/Corbis; **387** Library of Congress, Prints and Photographs Division; **388** *top* Copyright © PhotoDisc, Inc; Photograph by Michael Vines, from the collection of the Old Rhinebeck Aerodrome; *center* Brown Brothers; **390** *top* Copyright © Bettmann/Corbis; *left* The Granger Collection, New York; **390** *top left* Copyright © Bettmann/Corbis; **391** Copyright © Corbis; **392** *left* Courtesy of The Industrial Workers of the World; *bottom* Copyright © Bettmann/Corbis; **393** Panel no. 1: *During the World War There Was a Great Migration North by Southern Negroes*, from the Migration of the Negro mural series (1940–1941), Jacob

Lawrence. Tempera on masonite, 12″ × 18″. Acquired through Downtown Gallery, 1942. The Phillips Collection, Washington, D.C.; **394** Copyright © UPI/Corbis-Bettmann; **395** Copyright © Bettmann/Corbis; **396** *top* Copyright © PhotoDisc, Inc; *bottom* Copyright © Bettmann/Corbis; **397** *both* Copyright © Bettmann/Corbis; **398** *top* Copyright © PhotoDisc, Inc; Photograph by Michael Vines, from the collection of the Old Rhinebeck Aerodrome; *center left* Hulton Archive by Getty Images; **399** *top* The Granger Collection, New York; *bottom* Copyright © Corbis; **402** *top right* Photofest; *top center* Photofest; *top left* Photofest; *bottom left* From *Frankenstein* (1931), Universal, Courtesy of The Kobal Collection; **404** *both* The Granger Collection, New York; **405** *top left* Copyright © Reuters/Corbis-Bettmann; *top right* Copyright © 1968 Philip Jones Griffiths/Magnum Photos; *bottom* Photograph by George Rodger/*Life* Magazine; **407** Michelle Hlubinka.

Chapter 12

408–409 *Drouth Stricken Area* (1934), Alexandre Hogue. Oil on canvas, 30″ × 42¼″. Dallas Museum of Art, Dallas Art Association Purchase; **410** *bottom, left to right* Copyright © David J. & Janice L. Frent Collection/Corbis; Photograph by Martin Plomer, Copyright © Dorling Kindersley; **410–411** Copyright © Bettmann/Corbis; **411** *bottom, left to right* Hulton Archive by Getty Images; Copyright © UPI/Corbis-Bettmann; Copyright © Bettmann/Corbis; **412** *top right* Copyright © Bettmann/Corbis; *center* From *The Jewish Americans*, Copyright © 1982 by Milton Meltzer. Thomas Y. Crowell Junior Books/Harper Collins Childrens' Books; **414** *Sacco and Vanzetti* (1932), Ben Shahn. Tempera 21″ × 48″. Private Collection. Photograph courtesy of Kennedy Galleries, New York. Copyright © Estate of Ben Shahn/Licensed by VAGA, New York, NY; **415** Copyright © UPI/Corbis-Bettmann; **416** Library of Congress, Prints and Photographs Division (LC-USZ4-5584); **417** Library of Congress, Prints and Photographs Division; **418** Copyright © UPI/Corbis-Bettmann; **419** *top right* Copyright © Bettmann/Corbis; *center* Detail of *Warren Gamaliel Harding* (about 1923), Margaret Lindsay William. National Portrait Gallery, Smithsonian Institution/Art Resource, New York; **420** Hulton Archive by Getty Images; **421** Stock Montage; **422** *top right* Copyright © Bettmann/Corbis; *center* H. Armstrong Roberts; **423** *both* Brown Brothers; **424** *bottom*, courtesy of United Airlines; **425** Copyright © Camerique Stock Photos; **426** Culver Pictures; **428** *top* Library of Congress, Prints and Photographs Division (LC-USZC4-2635); *bottom* Library of Congress, Prints and Photographs Division (LC-B2-3982); **429** *top* Pittsburgh Courier Archives/Hulton Archive by Getty Images; *bottom* FPG Internatonal; **430** *top* Copyright © American Stock/Hulton Archive by Getty Images; *bottom* Copyright © Dan McCoy/Rainbow; **431** Daniel Fitzpatrick, courtesy of the State Historical Society of Missouri, Columbia, Missouri.

Chapter 13

432–433 *across* Frank Driggs Collection/Hulton Archive by Getty Images; *bottom left, above time line* Hulton Archive by Getty Images; *bottom left, below time line* Copyright © Bettmann/Corbis; *bottom right* TimePix; *bottom left* Copyright © Bettmann/Corbis; *bottom center* Copyright © UPI/Bettmann/Corbis; **434** *top right, center right* Copyright © Bettmann/Corbis; **435** Aaron Douglas, *Aspects of Negro Life: Song of the Towers* (1934). Oil on canvas, 9′ × 9′. Schomburg Center for Research in Black Culture, Art & Artifacts division, the New York Public Library, Astor, Lenox and Tilden Foundations; **436** *bottom, left and right* Copyright © Underwood and Underwood/Bettmann/Corbis; **437** Copyright © Underwood and Underwood/Corbis; **438** Copyright © UPI/Bettmann/Corbis; **439** The Granger Collection, New York; **440** *top right* Copyright © Bettmann/Corbis; **440** *center right,* **441** Hulton Archive by Getty Images; **442** Lewis W. Hine/Courtesy George Eastman House; **444** *bottom left* Brown Brothers; *bottom right* Frank Driggs Collection/Hulton Archive by Getty Images **444–445** *center across* Copyright © Minnesota Historical Society/Corbis; **445** *top* National Archives; *bottom* Copyright © Bettmann/Corbis; **446** *top right* Copyright © Bettmann/Corbis; *center right* Copyright © UPI/Bettmann/Corbis; **447** *bottom left, bottom center* Copyright © Underwood and Underwood/Corbis; *bottom right* Copyright © Hulton-Deutsch Collection/Corbis; **448** *bottom left* National Baseball Hall of Fame, Cooperstown, NY; *center* Copyright © UPI/Bettmann/Corbis; *top right* New York Times Co./Hulton Archive by Getty Images; *bottom right* Hulton Archive by Getty Images; **449** *top, center left* Copyright © UPI/Bettmann/Corbis; *center right* Copyright © Bettmann/Corbis; **450** *Radiator Building—Night, New York* (1927), Georgia O'Keeffe. Oil on canvas. The Alfred Stieglitz Collection, Fisk University Art Galleries, Nashville, Tennessee. Photograph by Vando Rogers; **451** Hulton Archive by Getty Images; **452** *top right* Copyright © Bettmann/Corbis; *center right* Brown Brothers; **453** Fisk University, Nashville, Tennessee; **454** Copyright © UPI/ Bettmann/Corbis; **455** *map* Karen Minot; *inset, top left* Frank Driggs Collection/Hulton Archive by Getty Images; *inset, center right* Copyright © Hulton-Deutsch Collection/Corbis; **455** *bottom,* **456, 457** Frank Driggs Collection/Hulton Archive by Getty Images; **458** Book cover from first edition, *The Great Gatsby* by F. Scott Fitzgerald (New York, Charles Scribner's Sons, 1925). Used by permission of Scribner, a division of Simon and Schuster; **459** *top left, Edna St. Vincent Millay* (1930), unknown photographer, National Portrait Gallery, Smithsonian Institution/Art Resource; *center right Langston Hughes* (c. 1920), Winold Reiss. National Portrait Gallery, Smithsonian Institution/ Art Resource **460** *top* Photofest; *2nd from top* Frank Driggs Collection/Hulton Archive by Getty Images; *3rd from top* Copyright © Underwood and Underwood/Corbis; *bottom* Copyright © UPI/Bettmann/Corbis; **461** Culver Pictures.

Chapter 14

462 *bottom, left to right* Copyright © 1933 Condé Nast Publications, Inc. Courtesy of Vanity Fair; Copyright © Bettmann/Corbis; Copyright © UPI/Corbis-Bettmann; **462–463** Hulton Archive by Getty Images; **463** *bottom, left to right* Copyright © Bettmann/Corbis; Courtesy of The Chicago Historical Society; **464** *top right* Hulton Archive by Getty Images; *center* AP/Wide World Photos; **465** Copyright © Arthur Rothstein/Corbis; **466** Hulton Archive by Getty Images; **467** *Dies Irae* (October 29, 1929), James Naumburg Rosenberg. National Museum of American Art, Washington, D.C./Art Resource, New York; **468** *top* Copyright © Bettmann/Corbis; *bottom* Copyright © Reuters NewMedia Inc./Corbis; **469** Conservative Research Department, Conservative Party, London; **470** *background* Library of Congress, Prints and Photographs Division (LC-USF34-028362-D); *inset, both* Copyright © Underwood Photo Archives; **472** *top right* Hulton Archive by Getty Images; *center* Reproduced from *Dust Bowl Diary* by Ann Marie Low, by permission of the University of Nebraska Press. Copyright © 1984 by the University of Nebraska Press; **473** Franklin D. Roosevelt Library and UPI/Corbis-Bettmann; **474** Library of Congress, Prints and Photographs Division (LC-USZCA-4840, LC-USZ62-11491); **476** National Archives (119-CAL-11); **477** Farm Security Administration; **478** *top right* Hulton Archive by Getty Images; *center* Library of Congress, Prints and Photographs Division; **479** Detail of *Herbert Clark Hoover* (1931), Douglas Chandor. Oil on Canvas. National Portrait Gallery, Smithsonian Institution/Art Resource, New York; **480** Copyright © Lake County Museum/Corbis; **481** Reprinted from The Albany Evening News, June 7, 1931, with permission of the Times Union, Albany, New York; **483** Copyright © Bettmann/Corbis.

Chapter 15

486–487 *across* Franklin D. Roosevelt Library/National Archives; **486** *bottom left* Copyright © Corbis; *bottom center* Copyright © Bettmann/Corbis; *bottom right, Vanity Fair* cover (February 1934) by Leon Carlin. Copyright © 1934 (renewed 1962) by the Condé Nast Publications, Inc.; **487** *bottom center* The Granger Collection, New York; *bottom right* MGM/The Kobal Collection; **488** *top right, Construction of the Dam* (1937), by William Gropper. Mural study done for the Department of the Interior,

Washington D.C. National Museum of American Art, Washington, D.C./Art Resource, New York; *center right* Copyright © 1984 John Gutmann; **489** *center left, Franklin Delano Roosevelt* (1935), Henry Salem Hubbell, National Portrait Gallery, Smithsonian Institution/ Art Resource, New York; *center right* Detail of *Anna Eleanor Roosevelt* (1949), Douglas Chandor. Oil on canvas. 49½″ × 38¼″. White House Historical Association;
490 *Franklin D. Roosevelt at Hilltop Cottage with Ruthie Bie and Fala* (1941), Margaret Suckley. Photograph, Franklin D. Roosevelt Library; **491** National Archives; **492** AP/Wide World Photos; **493** *top right* Jay N. "Ding" Darling. Copyright © 1937 by the Des Moines Register and Tribune Company. Reprinted with permission/Stock Montage; **493** *bottom right,* **494** Copyright © Bettmann/Corbis; **495** *top right, Construction of the Dam* (1937), by William Gropper. Mural study done for the Department of the Interior, Washington D.C. National Museum of American Art, Washington, D.C./Art Resource, New York; *center right* Copyright © The Dorothea Lange Collection, Oakland Museum of California, City of Oakland. Gift of Paul S. Taylor; **496** *top left* Copyright © Underwood and Underwood/Corbis; *bottom left* Photofest; **497** *top, Migrant Mother, Nipomo, California* (1936), Dorothea Lange/Library of Congress [LC-USZ62- 95653]; *bottom* Dorothea Lange/Library of Congress [LC-USZ62-58355]; **498** Margaret Bourke-White/ TimePix; **499** Copyright © UPI/Bettmann/Corbis; **500** *center left* Copyright © Bettmann/Corbis; *top right* The Granger Collection, New York; *center right* National Archives; **501** Lester Beall/Library of Congress, Prints and Photographs Division [U.S. B415.3]; **502, 503** Copyright © Bettmann/Corbis; **504** *top right, Construction of the Dam* (1937), by William Gropper. Mural study done for the Department of the Interior, Washington D.C. National Museum of American Art, Washington, D.C./Art Resource, New York; **505** *top right* Copyright © UPI/Bettmann/Corbis; *bottom right* Detail of *Mary McLeod Bethune (1875–1955), Educator* (1943–1944), Betsy Graves Reyneau. National Portrait Gallery, Smithsonian Institution/Art Resource, New York; **506** Pictorial Parade/Hulton Archive by Getty Images; **507** Copyright © UPI/Bettmann/Corbis; **508** *top left* AP/Wide World Photos; *top inset* The Granger Collection, New York; *top right* Copyright © UPI Bettmann/Corbis; **509** Carl Linde/Courtesy of the Illinois Labor History Society; **510** *top right, Construction of the Dam* (1937), by William Gropper. Mural study done for the Department of the Interior, Washington D.C. National Museum of American Art, Washington, D.C./Art Resource, New York; *center right* Russell Lee (1941)/Library of Congress, Prints and Photographs Division [USF34-38814-D]; **511** *top right, bottom right,* **512** *top left* Photofest; **512** *bottom, Industries of California* (1934), Ralph Stackpole. Photograph courtesy of the San Francisco (California) Art Commission. Photograph by Malcolm Kimberlin; **513** *top right American Gothic* (1930), Grant Wood. Oil on beaver board. 74.3 cm × 62.4 cm. All rights reserved. The Art Institute of Chicago, Friends of American Art Collection. 1930.934/VAGA. New York, NY; *bottom right* Courtesy of the Woody Guthrie Foundation and Archives; **514** Walker Evans (1935)/Library of Congress, Prints and Photographs Division [LC-USF342-008138-A]; **515** *top right, Construction of the Dam* (1937), by William Gropper. Mural study done for the Department of the Interior, Washington D.C. National Museum of American Art, Washington, D.C./Art Resource, New York; *center right* Franklin D. Roosevelt Library and AP/Wide World Photos; **517** Dorothea Lange (1936)/Library of Congress, Prints and Photographs Division [LC-USF34- 009669-E]; **518** Library of Congress, Prints and Photographs Division [LC-USZC4-4890]; **519** Courtesy of the Franklin D. Roosevelt Library; **520** Chris Costello; **521** *bottom left* Lewis W. Hine (1933)/Courtesy of the Tennessee Valley Authority; *top right* Courtesy of the Tennessee Valley Authority.

Chapter 16

524–525 *Dawn Patrol of Launching* (1942), Paul Sample. Army Art Collection, Washington D.C.; **526** *bottom, left to right* Copyright © M. Howell/Camerique/H. Armstrong Roberts; Library of Congress, Prints and Photographs Division; **526–527** Copyright © Corbis; **527** *bottom, left to right* Library of Congress, Prints and Photographs Division (LC-USZ62-45002); Hulton Archive by Getty Images; **528** *top right* Hulton Archive by Getty Images; *center* Copyright © Bettmann/Corbis; **529** *left* Hulton Archive by Getty Images; *right* Copyright © Archivo Iconografico, S.A./Corbis; **531** *left to right* Copyright © Bettmann/Corbis; Copyright © Hulton-Deutsch Collection/Corbis; Hulton Archive by Getty Images; **533** *both* Hulton Archive by Getty Images; **534** Copyright © The Washington Post. Reprinted with permission; **536** *top right* Hulton Archive by Getty Images; *center* Copyright © Bettmann/ Corbis; **537** Hulton Archive by Getty Images, J.D. Hackett; **539** *top* Hulton Archive by Getty Images; *bottom* AP/Wide World Photos; **540** *top* March of Time/*Life* Magazine. Copyright © TIME, Inc.; *bottom* Copyright © John Topham/Black Star; **541** Woodfin Camp; **542** *top right* Hulton Archive by Getty Images; *center* Courtesy of Gerda Weissmann Klein; **543** *left* Hulton Archive by Getty Images; *right* Yad Vashem Archives; **544** *Albert Einstein Among Other Immigrants* (date unknown), Ben Shahn. Scala/Art Resource, New York/licensed by VAGA, New York, NY; **546** *bottom* Copyright © UPI/Corbis-Bettmann; **546–547** U.S. Army Military History Institute; **547** KZ Gedenkstaette Dachau, courtesy of USHMM Photo Archives; **548** Main Commission for the Prosecution of the Crimes against the Polish Nation, courtesy of USHMM Photo Archives; **549** Magnum Photos; **550** *both* Hulton Archive by Getty Images; **551** National Archives; **553** National Archives (NWDNS-080-G-43376); **554** AP/WideWorld Photos; **555** *left* Library of Congress, Prints and Photographs Division (LC-USF34-71206-D); *right* Reprinted by permission of the Honolulu Star Bulletin; **556** Copyright © UPI/Corbis-Bettmann; **559** Library of Congress, Prints and Photographs Division (CD1 Shoemaker, no. 2 (B size).

Chapter 17

560 *bottom* Copyright © Corbis; **560–561** Copyright © Corbis; **561** *bottom, second from left* Martha Swope/TimePix; *all others* Hulton Archive by Getty Images; **562** *top right* Copyright © PhotoDisc, Inc.; *center* Courtesy of Charles Swanson; **563** *top* Copyright © Bettmann/Corbis; *bottom* Al Aumuller/Library of Congress, Prints and Photographs Division (LC-USZ62-118263); **565** Library of Congress, Prints and Photographs Division (LC-USW361-295); **566** *top* Library of Congress, Prints and Photographs Division (LC-USW3-11696-C); *bottom left, right* Photofest; **568** *top* AP/Wide World Photos; **569** *top right* Copyright © PhotoDisc, Inc.; *center (both),* Courtesy of Adrienne McGrath; **570** Copyright © Corbis; **571** Copyright © UPI/Corbis-Bettmann; **572** Copyright © Bettmann/Corbis; **573** *top* Copyright © Bettmann/Corbis; *bottom* Alan B. Taylor Collection; **574** AP/Wide World Photos; **575** Robert F. Sargent/Library of Congress, Prints and Photographs Division (LC-USZC4-4731); **576** Copyright © UPI/Corbis-Bettmann; **577** New York Daily News Photo; **578** *top right* Copyright © PhotoDisc, Inc. *center* Copyright © UPI/Corbis-Bettmann; **579** Copyright © Corbis; **581** Courtesy of the U.S. Navy/PhotoAssist, Inc./Woodfin Camp; **582** *top* AP/Wide World Photos; *bottom* AP/Wide World Photos; **583** Copyright © Bettmann/Corbis; **584** *top* Courtesy of the Air Force Administration/PhotoAssist, Inc./Woodfin Camp; *bottom* Copyright © Bernard Hoffman/TimePix; **586** National Archives; **588** *top* Copyright © Dan McCoy/Rainbow; *bottom* Copyright © 1999 Russell Munson/The Stock Market; **588–589** Copyright © Hank Morgan/Rainbow; **589** *top* AP/Wide World Photos; *center* Sovfoto/Eastfoto; *bottom* Copyright © 1993 Larry Mulvehill/ Rainbow; **590** *top right* Copyright © PhotoDisc, Inc.; *center, Twice a Patriot* (1943), unknown artist. Lithograph. Amistad Foundation Collection at the Wadsworth Atheneum, Hartford, Connecticut; **591** Photograph courtesy of the Franklin D. Roosevelt Library; **592** Copyright © Bettmann/Corbis; **593** Library of Congress, Prints and Photographs Division (LC-USZ62-48275); **594** Copyright © Seattle Post-Intelligencer Collection; Museum of History and Industry/Corbis; **597** *top* Copyright © Eliot Elisofon/TimePix; *right* Dennis Cook/ AP/Wide World Photos; **598** AP/Wide World Photos; **599** Michelle Hlubinka.

Chapter 18

600 *bottom, left to right* Copyright © PhotoDisc, Inc.; Copyright © Bettmann/Corbis; **600–601** AP/Wide World Photos; **601** *bottom, left to right* Copyright © Aereo Graphics, Inc./Corbis; Sovfoto/ Eastfoto; **602** *top right* Hulton Archive by Getty Images; *center top*

Copyright © Bettmann/Corbis; *center bottom* Copyright © United States Postal Service; **603** *both* Hulton Archive by Getty Images; **605** Hulton Archive by Getty Images; **606** Copyright © UPI/ Corbis-Bettmann; **607** AP/Wide World Photos; **608** Library of Congress, Prints and Photographs Division (LC-USZ62-53089); **609** *both* Hulton Archive by Getty Images; **610** *left* AP/Wide World Photos; *right* Hsinhua News Agency/AP/Wide World Photos; **612** Courtesy of Beverly Scott; **613** AP/Wide World Photos; **614** *both* Copyright © Bettmann/Corbis; **615** Yonhap/ POOL/AP/Wide World Photos; **616** *top right* Hulton Archive by Getty Images; *center* Courtesy of Tony Kahn; **617** *top* Library of Congress, Prints and Photographs Division (LC-USF34-013363-C); *bottom* Photofest; **618** *left* Copyright © Bettmann/Corbis; *right* Photofest; **619** *top* Photofest; *bottom, left to right* AP/Wide World Photos; Copyright © AFP/Corbis; AP/Wide World Photos; **620** from *Herblock Special Report* (W.W. Norton and Company, 1974); **621** from *Herblock's Here & Now* (Simon & Schuster, 1955); **622** *top right* Hulton Archive by Getty Images; *center* AP/Wide World Photos; **623** The American Civil Defense Association, photograph courtesy of Eric Green; **625** Copyright © Bettmann/Corbis; **627** *top* Sovfoto/Eastfoto; *bottom* Hulton Archive by Getty Images; **628** Courtesy of Republic Entertainment, Inc.; **629** *left* Courtesy of Bantam Books; *right* Courtesy of Bantam Doubleday Books; **631** Copyright © Corbis.

Chapter 19

632 *bottom, left to right* Copyright © Bettmann/Corbis; Copyright © Dorling Kindersley; Copyright © George Lepp/ Corbis; **632–633** Copyright © 1957 SEPS: The Curtis Publishing Company, Agent; **633** *bottom, left to right* National Aeronautics and Space Administration; Copyright © SuperStock, Inc.; **634** *top right* Copyright © 2001 Ken Whitmore/Stone; *center* Harold M. Lambert/Hulton Archive by Getty Images; **635** Copyright © J.R. Eyerman/TimePix; **637** Culver Pictures; **638** *top, Wipe Out Discrimination* (1949), Milton Ackoff. Offset lithograph, printed in color, 43⅞" × 32¾". The Museum of Modern Art, New York. Gift of the Congress of Industrial Organizations. Photography Copyright 1999 the Museum of Modern Art, New York; *bottom* Copyright © UPI/Corbis-Bettmann; **639** *top to bottom* Cousley Historical Collections. Photograph by Stephen Mays, New York; Cousley Historical Collections. Photograph by Stephen Mays, New York; Blank Archives/Hulton Archive by Getty Images; **640** Copyright © George Silk/TimePix; **641** *top right* Copyright © 2001 Ken Whitmore/Stone; *center* Copyright © SuperStock, Inc.; **642** Copyright © Bettmann/Corbis; **643** *top* Copyright © Harold M. Lambert/Hulton Archive by Getty Images; *bottom* The Image bank; **644** Copyright © Bettmann/Corbis; **645** *top, After the Prom* (September 1957). Printed by permission of the Norman Rockwell Family Trust. Copyright © 1957 the Norman Rockwell Family trust. Photograph courtesy of The Norman Rockwell Museum at Stockbridge; *bottom* Copyright © UPI/ Corbis-Bettmann; **646** Copyright © Aldo Torelli/Stone; **647** *background* Copyright © PhotoDisc, Inc.; *clockwise from top right* Copyright © Alfred Eisenstaedt/TimePix; The Granger Collection, New York; Copyright © Carl Iwasaki/TimePix; Copyright © Francis Miller/TimePix; **648** *both* The Granger Collection, New York; **649** Hulton Archive by Getty Images/ Michael Barson Collection; **650** *both* Courtesy of The Park Forest Historical Society; **650–651** Courtesy of The Park Forest Historical Society; **651** *center* Courtesy of The Park Forest Historical Society; *top right* Copyright © Dab Weiner, courtesy Sandra Weiner; **652** *top right* Copyright © 2001 Ken Whitmore/ Stone; *center* Michael Ochs Archives; **653** Copyright © TimePix; **654** *top left* Robert Vose/Library of Congress Prints and Photographs Division (LC-USZ4-4889); *bottom* Photofest; **655** Hulton Archive by Getty Images; **656** *top left* Frank Driggs Collection/Hulton Archive by Getty Images; *bottom left* Hulton Archive by Getty Images; *bottom right* Copyright © Bettmann/ Corbis; **657** Hulton Archive by Getty Images; **658** *center left* Copyright © 2001 Archie Comic Publications. Reprinted by permission of the Copyright holder, Archie Comic Publications; *center right* Equinox Archives; *bottom left* Blank Archives/Hulton Archive by Getty Images. Photograph by Sharon Hoogstraten; **658–659** Copyright © Paul Schutzer/TimePix; **659** *top left* Photofest; **659** *center* Copyright © Paul Schutzer/TimePix; **660** *top right* Copyright © 2001 Ken Whitmore/Stone; *center* The Granger Collection, New York; **662** Copyright © William Shrout/TimePix; **663** *Milwaukee (Wisconsin) Journal/Milwaukee Sentinel.*

Chapter 20

666–667 *Civil Rights March, May 1965*, Copyright © James H. Karales. **668** *bottom, left to right* Blank Archive/Hulton Archive by Getty Images; Hulton Archive by Getty Images; **668–669** National Aeronautics and Space Administration; **669** *bottom, left to right* Copyright © Marilyn Silverstone/ Magnum Photos; Copyright © Bettmann/Corbis; **670** Copyright © 1961 Black Star; **671** Copyright © Bettmann/Corbis; **672** Courtesy of John F. Kennedy Library; **674** *top left* Burt Glinn/Magnum Photos; *bottom, Kennedy and Exploding Cuban Cigar*. Leslie Illingsworth, Apr. 21, 1961. Courtesy of National Library of Wales; **675** *left* Copyright © Bettmann/Corbis; *bottom* Hulton Archive by Getty Images; **676** *both* Copyright © Bettmann/Corbis; **677** *background* Copyright © 1976 Leonard Freed/Magnum Photos; *inset* Kreusch/AP/Wide World Photos; **678** *top* John F. Kennedy Library, Boston; *bottom* Library of Congress; **679** *both* National Aeronautics and Space Administration; **680** Copyright © Bettmann/Corbis; **682** *left* Copyright © 1963, 1964 by The New York Times Company. Reprinted by permission; *right, New York Daily News* photograph; **684** *left* Copyright © T Resource/Stone; *right* Copyright © Bruce Forster/Stone; Copyright © Richard Elliot/Stone; **686** AP/Wide World Photos; **687** Hulton Archive by Getty Images; *inset* Copyright © Bettmann/Corbis; **688** Museum of American Political Life, University of Hartford, West Hartford, Connecticut. Photograph by Sally Anderson-Bruce; **689** Copyright © Paul Conklin/Photo Edit; **691** Copyright © Bettmann/Corbis; **693** LBJ Library; **694** Copyright © Bettmann/ Corbis; **695** *left* Photograph by Sharon Hoogstraten, *right* Copyright © Bob Daemmrich/Stock Boston; **696** *clockwise from top left* Copyright © 1961 Black Star; Hulton Archive by Getty Images; Copyright © Paul Conklin/PhotoEdit; Hulton Archive by Getty Images.

Chapter 21

698 *bottom, left to right* Copyright © Archive Photos/Express Newspaper by Getty Images; Copyright © Hulton Deutsch/ Bettmann/Corbis; Copyright © Bettmann/Corbis; **698–699** Copyright © Ivan Massar/Black Star; **699** *left to right* Hulton Archive by Getty Images; AP/Wide World Photos; **700** *top right* Francis Miller/TimePix; *center* Courtesy of Arthur L. Freeman; **701** *both* Library of Congress; **702** Copyright © Archive Photos/Consolidated News by Getty Images; **703** Copyright © UPI/Bettmann/Corbis; **704** AP/Wide World Photos; **705** Dan Weiner/Courtesy of Sandra Weiner; **706** Copyright © Flip Schulke/Bettmann/Corbis; **707** AP/Wide World Photos; **708** Carl Iwasaki/TimePix; **709** *left* Copyright © Bettmann/Corbis; *right* The Granger Collection, New York; **710** *top right* Francis Miller/TimePix; *center* Copyright © UPI/Corbis-Bettmann; **711** Copyright © UPI/Corbis-Bettmann; **712** *top* AP/Wide World Photos; **713** *All* Photographs by Ernest C. Withers. Courtesy of Panopticon Gallery; **715** *top* Copyright © 1964 Steve Shapiro/ Black Star; **717** *top right* Francis Miller/TimePix; *center* Copyright © UPI/Corbis-Bettmann; **718** *left* Photograph by J.R. Eyerman/ *Life* Magazine; *right* Copyright © UPI/Corbis-Bettmann; **719** Copyright © 1964 John Launois/Black Star; **720** *left* Photograph by Sharon Hoogstraten; *right* Ken Regan/Camera 5; **721** *top* Black Star; *bottom* Copyright © Bettmann/Corbis; **722** Copyright © Leif Skoogfors/Bettmann/Corbis; **724** *both* The Granger Collection, New York; **725** *top right* Copyright © 1963 Charles Moore/Black Star; *center* UPI/Corbis-Bettmann; **726** *top left* Carl Iwasaki/TimePix; *top right* Dan Weiner/Courtesy of Sandra Weiner; *center* Copyright © 1964 Steve Shapiro/Black Star; *bottom* AP/Wide World Photos.

Chapter 22

728 *bottom left* Copyright © Corbis; *bottom right* Copyright © SuperStock, Inc.; **728–729** Copyright © Tim Page/Corbis; **729** *bottom left* Photograph by V. Merritt. Copyright © Time, Inc.; **730** *top right* Copyright © PhotoDisc, Inc.; **731** AP/Wide World Photos; **733** *top* Hulton Archive by Getty Images; *bottom left* Copyright © Corbis; *bottom right* Scott Swanson Collection, Hulton Archive by Getty Images; **734** AP/Wide World Photos; **735** Copyright © 1963, 1964, by The New York Times Company. Reprinted by permission; **736** *top right* Copyright © PhotoDisc, Inc.; *center* U.S. Army/Hulton Archive by Getty Images; **737** Copyright © Bettmann/Corbis; **740** The Granger Collection, New York; **741** Photograph by Sharon Hoogstraten; **742** *top right* Copyright © PhotoDisc, Inc.; *center* Courtesy of Stephan Gubar; **743** *top* Photograph by Mark Kauffman/*Life* Magazine. Copyright © 1965 Time, Inc.; *bottom* Copyright © 1967 James Pickerell/Black Star; **744** AP/Wide World Photos; **746** Copyright © 1995 Burt Glinn/Magnum Photos; **747** Peter Newark's Pictures; **748** *top right* Copyright © PhotoDisc, Inc.; *center* Copyright © 1996 Danny Lyon/Magnum Photos; **749** Copyright © Time, Inc.; **750** Courtesy of Jack Kightlinger; **751** Photogaph by Bill Eppridge/*Life* Magazine. Copyright © Time, Inc.; **752** Copyright © Jeffrey Blankfort/Jereboam; **754** *top right* Copyright © PhotoDisc, Inc.; *center* Copyright © Donald J. Weber; **756** Copyright © Bettmann/Corbis; **757** Copyright © John Paul Filo; **758** Copyright © UPI/Corbis-Bettmann; **759** AP/Wide World Photos; **760** *top left* Copyright © Seny Norasingh/Light Sensitive; *top right* Copyright © Wolfgang Kaehler/Corbis; *center left* Copyright © 1993 Richard Howard/Black Star/PNI; **762** *left* From *Going After Cacciato* (jacket cover) by Tim O'Brien. Used by permission of Delacorte Press/Seymour Lawrence, a division of Bantam Doubleday Dell Publishing Group Inc.; **762–763** *background* Copyright © UPI/Corbis-Bettmann; **763** *top* From the cover of *A Rumor of War* by Philip Caputo, copyright 1977, 1996 by Philip Caputo. All rights reserved. Reproduced by permission of Henry Holt and Company, New York. Cover photograph copyright © Don McCullin/Magnum Photos; *bottom* Cover illustration by Jim Dietz from *Fallen Angels* by Walter Dean Myers. Illustration Copyright © 1988 by Jim Dietz. Reprinted with permission of Scholastic, Inc.; **764** *top* Photo by Mark Kauffman/*Life* Magazine. Copyright © 1965 Time, Inc.; *center* Copyright © UPI/Corbis-Bettmann; *bottom* Peter Newark's Pictures; **765** Copyright © by Karl Hubenthal - All Rights Reserved.

Chapter 23

766 *bottom left to right* Copyright © UPI/Bettmann/Corbis; Liaison by Getty Images; Copyright © 1980 Arnold Zann/Black Star; **766–767** Lisa Law/The Image Works; **767** *bottom left to right* Sahm Doherty/TimePix; Jon Hammer/Archive Photos by Getty Images; UPI/Corbis-Bettmann; **768** Copyright © Paul Fusco/Magnum Photos; **769** Copyright © Underwood Photo Archives; **770** photograph by Arthur Schatz/*Life* Magazine. Copyright © TIME, Inc.; **771** Copyright © Liaison by Getty Images; **772** Copyright © Rick Smolan; **774** Photograph by Harris and Ewing, collection of the Supreme Court of the United States; **775** Data courtesy of Alabama State Archives; **776** Copyright © UPI/Bettmann/Corbis; **778** Copyright © Mark Klamkin/Black Star; **779** *top* Copyright © Werner Wolf/Black Star; *bottom* Copyright © Lynda Gordon/Liaison by Getty Images; **780** *left* Library of Congress; *right* Courtesy MS. Magazine; **781** *center* Copyright © Bob Fitch/Black Star; **782** *top* Photograph by Sharon Hoogstraten; *bottom* Copyright © Bettmann/Corbis; **783** Courtesy of Apple Records/EMI Records Ltd.; **784** *center left* Copyright © Danny Lyon/Magnum Photos; *center right* Copyright © Bettmann/Corbis; *bottom left* Agence France Presse/Archive Photos by Getty Images; **785** *top* Copyright © UPI/Bettmann/Corbis; **786** *clockwise, top left* Photofest Copyright © Coni Kaufman/Southern Stock/PNI; Copyright © Joel Axelrod/Michael Ochs Archives; Poster #75 Bonnie Maclean; **787** *top* Photofest; *Marilyn Monroe* (1967), Andy Warhol. Screenprint on white paper, 36″ × 36″. The Andy Warhol Foundation, Inc./Art Resource, New York;

Chapter 24

790–791 Statue of Liberty National Monument/National Park Service/photograph copyright © Norman McGrath, all rights reserved; **792** *bottom, left to right* Photograph by Sharon Hoogstraten; Copyright © Bettmann/Corbis; **792–793** AP/Wide World Photos; **793** *bottom, left to right* Courtesy of the Jimmy Carter Library; Copyright © Charles E. Rotkin/Corbis; Copyright © Bettmann/ Corbis; **794** *top right* Copyright © PhotoDisc, Inc.; *center* Copyright © UPI/ Corbis-Bettmann; **795** Courtesy of Paul Szep; **796** National Aeronautics and Space Administraton; **797** Copyright © Ira Wyman/Sygma; **798** *both* Copyright © Bettmann/Corbis; **799** AP/Wide World Photos; **800** Copyright © Bettmann/Corbis; **801** AP/Wide World Photos; **802** *top right* Copyright © PhotoDisc, Inc.; *center* AP/Wide World Photos; **803** *background* H. Armstrong Roberts; *top left, top right* J.P. Laffront/Sygma; *bottom left, bottom right* AP/Wide World Photos; **804** Copyright © 1973 Dennis Brack/ Black Star; **805** *top* Copyright © Wally McNamee/Corbis; **806** *top* National Archives/AP/Wide World Photos; *bottom* reprinted by permission of Tribune Media Services; **807** *top* Copyright © 1974 Harry Benson; *bottom* National Archives; **808** *top left* Courtesy of TV Guide; *center, bottom* PhotoFest; **809** *top* Photofest; *center* Copyright © 1977 ABC/Warner TV/MPTV; **810** *top right* Copyright © PhotoDisc, Inc.; *center* Bill Pierce/Time Magazine.; **811** Copyright © 1974 Time, Inc. Reprinted by permission; **812** *top* Copyright © Owen Franken/Sygma; *bottom* Museum of American Political Life, University of Hartford, West Hartford, Connecticut. Photograph by Sally Anderson-Bruce; **813** Copyright © Bill Ross/Corbis; **814** Copyright © 1977 Alex Webb/Magnum Photos; **816** Courtesy of the Jimmy Carter Library; **817** Copyright © Alain Mingam/ Liaison Agency, Inc.; **818** AP/Wide World Photos; **819** Copyright © Bettmann/Corbis; **820** *top right* Copyright © PhotoDisc, Inc.; *center* Copyright © UPI/Corbis-Bettmann; **821** *top* Copyright © 1962 Eric Hartmann/Magnum Photos; *bottom* Hulton Archive by Getty Images; **822** Copyright © Leonard Lee Rue III/Stock Boston; **823** Copyright © 1994 John McGrail; **824** *left* 20th Century Fox (courtesy The Kobal Collection); *right* COLUMBIA (courtesy The Kobal Collection); **825** Library of Congress, Prints and Photographs Division (LC-USZ62-102359). Source: U.S. EPA; **826** *left to right* Copyright © Bettmann/Corbis; Copyright © 1974 Time, Inc. Reprinted by permission; Museum of American Political Life, University of Hartford, West Hartford, Connecticut. Photograph by Sally Anderson-Bruce.

Chapter 25

828 *bottom, left to right* Hulton Archive by Getty Images; Copyright © Wally McNamee/Corbis; Hulton Archive by Getty Images; **828–829** Copyright © Robert Maass/Corbis; **829** *bottom, left to right* Copyright © Giles Bassignac/Liaison Agency, Inc.; Copyright © Owen Franken/Corbis; **830** *top right* Copyright © Corbis; *center* Copyright © 1988 Dennis Brack/Black Star; **831** Copyright © Bettmann/Corbis; **832** Copyright © 1991 Dennis Brack/Black Star; **834** *top right* Copyright © Corbis; *center* Copyright © Wally McNamee/Corbis; **836** *top* Cartoon by Pat Oliphant. Copyright © Universal Press Syndicate; *bottom, both* Copyright © 1991 Dennis Brack/Black Star; **837** AP/WideWorld Photos; **838** Copyright © 1987 Dennis Brack/Black Star; **839** *top right* Copyright © Corbis; *center* From *Trevor's Place: The Story of the Boy Who Brings Hope to the Homeless*. Copyright © 1985 by Frank and Janet Ferrell; **840** Copyright © Brad Markel/Liaison Agency, Inc.; **841** National Aeronautics and Space Administration; **842** Copyright © Wally McNamee/Corbis; **843** Copyright © 1994 P.F. Bentley/Black Star; **844** Copyright © 1991 Dennis Brack/Black Star; **845** Copyright © Lee Snider/Corbis; **847** *left* Copyright © Bob Rowan/Progressive Images/Corbis; *right* Copyright © Dewitt Jones/Corbis; **848** *top right* Copyright © Corbis; *center* Reuters/ Stephen Jaffe/Hulton Archive by Getty Images; **849** Copyright © 1989 by National Review, Inc.; 150 East 35th St. New York, NY 10016. Reprinted by Permission; **850** *top* Reuters/David Brauchli/ Hulton Archive by Getty Images; *bottom* AP/Wide World Photos; **852** Library of Congress, Prints and Photographs Division (LC-USZ62-126881); **854** *left* AP/Wide World Photos; *right* Copyright © David & Peter Turnley/Corbis; **855** AP/Wide World Photos; **856** *left* Copyright © 1991 Dennis Brack/Black Star; *right* Copyright © 1987 Dennis Brack/Black Star.

Chapter 26

858 *bottom left* Copyright © US Air Force/TimePix; *bottom right* Steve Helber/AP/Wide World Photos; **858–859** Copyright © Nancy Sheehan/PhotoEdit; **859** *bottom, left to right* Copyright © Robert Maass/CORBIS; John Chadwick/AP/Wide World Photos; Copyright © Kevin Lamarque/Reuters/TimePix; **860** *top right* Copyright © PhotoDisc, Inc.; *center* Copyright © 1993 Jim Stratford/Black Star; **861** *top* Copyright © Reuters/Corbis-Bettmann; *bottom* John Duricka/AP/Wide World Photos; **862** *top* Copyright © 1995 David Longstreath/AP/Wide World Photos; *bottom* AP/Wide World Photos; **863** Steve Ludlum/The New York Times; **864** Copyright © Reuters/Corbis-Bettmann; **865** Michael S. Green/AP/Wide World Photos; **867** *top* AP/Wide World Photos; *bottom* © Corbis Sygma; **868** © Michael Ainsworth/Dallas Morning News/Corbis; **869** *top right* Copyright © PhotoDisc, Inc.; *center* Courtesy of Mike Cavanaugh/UNITE; **870** Copyright © UPI/ Corbis-Bettmann; **871** Copyright © Lou Dematteis/Reuters/ TimePix; **873** Copyright © Shaun Best/Reuters/TimePix; **874** Copyright © Barron Claiborne/Outline; **875** *top* Jacket from *The Joy Luck Club*. Used by permission of G.P. Putnam Sons. Cover illustration Copyright © Gretchen Shields; *bottom* Copyright © Greg Smith/SABA; **876** *top right* Copyright © PhotoDisc, Inc.; *center* Courtesy of Challenged Athletes Foundation, photograph by Tim Mantoani; **877** Courtesy of Gary Brookins/Richmond Times-Dispatch; **878** Adrin Snider/ Daily Press/AP/Wide World Photos; **879** Copyright © Corbis; **880** Copyright © James A. Sugar/Corbis; **881** *left* Toby Talbot/AP/ Wide World Photos; *right* Dale Atkins/AP Wide World Photos; **882** *top right* Copyright © PhotoDisc, Inc.; *center* Courtesy of MALDEF; **883** *both* Courtesy of Michael Van Valkenburgh Associates, Inc., and Ann Hamilton. Photograph by Ed Massery; **884** Copyright © Joseph Sohm; Chromosohm, Inc./Corbis; **886** Paul Sakuma/AP/Wide World Photos; **888** *left* Hulton Archive by Getty Images; *right* Library of Congress, Prints and Photographs Division (LC-USZC4-4580, LC-USZ62-20359); **889** *top* Copyright © Sam Shere/TimePix; *bottom* National Archives (WDNS -428-K-108890).

Epilogue

892 *left* Copyright © Wally McNamee/Corbis; **892–893** Copyright © Tom Bean/Corbis; **893** *top* Stephen Morton/AP/Wide World Photos; *bottom* Damian Dovarganes/ AP/Wide World Photos; **894** AP/Wide World Photos; **895** AP/Wide World Photos; **896** © AFP/Corbis; **897** AP/Wide World Photos; **899** Getty Images; **901** Damian Dovarganes/AP/Wide World Photos; **902** Dan Loh/Pool/AP/Wide World Photos; **905** Jack Sauer, File/ The Day/AP/Wide World Photos; **907** Stephen Morton/AP/Wide World Photos; **908** Copyright © Miguel Gandert/Corbis; **911** Copyright © Steve Liss/TimePix; **912** Copyright © Wally McNamee/Corbis; **915** Mark Foley/AP/Wide World Photos; **916** Copyright © Tom Bean/Corbis

Reference Section

R23 Copyright © Steve Schapiro/Black Star; **R24** Culver Pictures; **R37** Kindra Clineff; **R38** *Life* Magazine. Copyright © 1956 Time, Inc.; **R39** Copyright © 1989 by National Review, Inc.; 150 East 35th St., New York, NY 10016. Reprinted by Permission; **R40** *left* Copyright © UPI/Corbis-Bettmann; *right* Copyright © Luc Beziat/Stone; **R42** AP/WideWorld Photos; **R44** Copyright © H. David Seawell/CORBIS; **R45** *left* Copyright © Reuters NewMedia, Inc./CORBIS; *right* Copyright © Reuters/John Sommers II/ TimePix.

REVIEWERS (*continued*)

Manuscript Reviewers

(*continued from page v*)

Marci Smith Deal
Hurst-Euless-Bedford
Independent School District
Bedford, Texas

Eric DeMeulanaere
Burton Academic High School
San Francisco, California

Gail Dent
Lincoln High School
San Francisco, California

Dr. Simone Dorman
Burton Academic High School
San Francisco, California

Kenward Goode
Robert E. Lee High School
Tyler, Texas

Gary Gregus
Shakopee High School
Shakopee, Minnesota

Patti Harrlod
Edmond Memorial
High School
Edmond, Oklahoma

Terry Holt
South Rowan High School
China Grove, North Carolina

Al Juengling
Lamar High School
Chicago, Illinois

James Lee
Lamar High School
Arlington, Texas

Judith Mahnke
Wallenberg High School
San Francisco, California

Gary Marksbury
Lakewood High School
Lakewood, California

Terry McRae
Robert E. Lee High School
Tyler, Texas

Peyton Mullins
Robert E. Lee High School
Tyler, Texas

Brenda Sims Palmer
Lehigh High School
Lehigh Acres, Florida

David Pasternak
Edison Technical High School
Rochester, New York

Dean Pedersen
North Fayette High School
West Union, Iowa

Lindy Poling
Millbrook High School
Raleigh, North Carolina

Kent Rettig
Pensacola High School
Pensacola, Florida

Diane Ring
St. Charles High School
St. Charles, Illinois

Susan Roe
C. E. Jordan High School
Durham, North Carolina

Tom Sewell
Inglemoor High School
Bothell, Washington

Mary Smith
Secondary Social Studies
Coordinator
Cypress-Fairbanks
Independent School District
Houston, Texas

Clara Spence
Millikan High School
Long Beach, California

Wayne Sylvester
Pentucket High School
Westbury, Massachusetts

Bill Von Vihl
Conifer High School
Conifer, Colorado

Pattie Willbanks
Robert E. Lee High School
Tyler, Texas

Nancy Williams
Jersey Village High School
Houston, Texas

Student Board

(*continued from page v*)

Tonya Gieseking
Broad Ripple High School
Indianapolis, Indiana

Yolande Godfrey
Ocean Township High School
Ocean Township, New Jersey

Norma Jaquez
Odessa High School
Ector County, Texas

Mary McCarthy
Penfield High School
Penfield, New York

Dan McKinley
Bulkeley High School
Hartford, Connecticut

Kris Miller
Midland High School
Cabell County, West Virginia

Brandi Nicholas
Meadowdale High School
Dayton, Ohio

Michael Pancherz
Clark Lake High School
Houston, Texas

Elizabeth Porter
Burnsville High School
Burnsville, Minnesota

Edwin Reyes
Miami Palmetto High School
Dade County, Florida

Misty Sisk
Jackson High School
Jacksonville, Florida

Christopher Sizemore
Community High School
Ann Arbor, Michigan

Jennifer Vasquez
Gilbert High School
Gilbert, Arizona

Everett Wheeler-Bell
East High School
Denver, Colorado

LuKisha Williams
Mackenzie High School
Detroit, Michigan